OFFICIAL OVERSTREET® No. 32 Comic Book PRICE GUIDE

32ND EDITION

COMICS FROM 1828-PRESENT INCLUDED
FULLY ILLUSTRATED CATALOGUE & EVALUATION GUIDE

BY ROBERT M. OVERSTREET

GEMSTONE PUBLISHING

J. C. Vaughn, **Executive Editor**
Arnold T. Blumberg, **Editor** • Brenda Busick, **Creative Director**
Mark Huesman, **Pricing Coordinator**
Kimberly Grover, **Administrative Assistant**

SPECIAL CONTRIBUTORS TO THIS EDITION

Robert L. Beerbohm • Arnold T. Blumberg • M. Thomas Inge
Matt Nelson • Richard D. Olson, Ph.D. • J. C. Vaughn • Doug Wheeler

SENIOR ADVISORS FOR OVER 25 YEARS

Dave Alexander • Landon Chesney • Bruce Hamilton • Paul Levitz • Michelle Nolan
Terry Stroud • Harry B. Thomas •Doug Sulipa • Raymond S. True

SENIOR ADVISORS FOR OVER 20 YEARS

Gary M. Carter • Bill Cole • Gene Seger • Steve Geppi • Stan Gold
M. Thomas Inge • Phil Levine • Richard Olson • Ron Pussell
David R. Smith • John K. Snyder

SPECIAL ADVISORS TO THIS EDITION

Dave Anderson • David J. Anderson, D.D.S. • Robert L. Beerbohm • Jon Berk • Steve Borock
Michael Browning • John Chruscinski • Michael Carbonaro • Gary Colabuono • Larry Curcio • Gary Dolgoff
Joe Dungan • Bruce Ellsworth • Conrad Eschenberg •Richard Evans • Stephen Fishler • Philip J. Gaudino
Steve Gentner • Michael Goldman • Tom Gordon • Jamie Graham • Daniel Greenhalgh • Eric Groves • Gary Guzzo
John Grasse • Mark Haspel • John Hauser • Jef Hinds • John Hone • George Huang • Bill Hughes • Rob Hughes
Ed Jaster • Joe Mannarino • Rick Manzella • Jon McClure • Michael McKenzie • Matt Nelson • Michael Naiman
Josh Nathanson • James Payette •Yolanda Ramirez • Todd Reznik • "Doc" Robinson • Robert Rogovin • Rory Root
Robert Roter • Chuck Rozanski • Matt Schiffman • Dave Smith • Laura Sperber • Tony Starks • Michael Tierney
Joe Vereneault • Frank Verzyl • John Verzyl • Rose Verzyl • Jerry Weist • Doug Wheeler • Harley Yee • Vincent Zurzolo, Jr.

The Crown Publishing Group
New York

GEMSTONE PUBLISHING

Gemstone Publishing

THE OVERSTREET COMIC BOOK PRICE GUIDE. Copyright © 1992, 1993, 1994, 1995, 1996, 1997, 1998, 1999, 2000, 2001, 2002 by Gemstone Publishing, Inc. All rights reserved. Printed in the United States of America. No part of this book may be used or reproduced in any manner whatsoever without written permission except in the case of brief quotations embodied in critical articles and reviews. For information, write to: Gemstone Publishing, 1966 Greenspring Drive, Suite LL3, Timonium, Maryland 21093.

Front cover/spine art: Superman is a trademark of DC Comics and is used with permission. ©2002 DC Comics. All rights reserved. Superman created by Jerry Siegel and Joe Shuster. Amazing Spider-Man and logo style ©2002 Marvel Characters, Inc. and used with permission. Archie characters and logo style ©2002 Archie comics. All rights reserved.

Cover illustrations: Superman #1 re-created by Murphy Anderson; Archie illustration by Rex Lindsey; Random House edition — Spider-Man and the Green Goblin by Alex Ross; used with permission.

THE OFFICIAL OVERSTREET COMIC BOOK PRICE GUIDE (32nd Edition) is an original publication of Gemstone Publishing, Inc. and House of Collectibles. Distributed by The Crown Publishing Group, a division of Random House, Inc., New York and simultaneously in Canada by Random House of Canada Limited, Toronto. This edition has never before appeared in book form.

House of Collectibles
The Crown Publishing Group
299 Park Ave.
New York, New York 10171

www.randomhouse.com

Overstreet is a registered trademark of Gemstone Publishing, Inc.

 House of Collectibles is a registered trademark and the H colophon is a trademark of Random House, Inc.

Published by arrangement with Gemstone Publishing.

ISBN: 0-609-80821-4
ISSN: 0891-8872

Printed in the United States of America

10 9 8 7 6 5 4 3 2 1

Thirty-Second Edition: May 2002

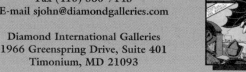

TABLE OF CONTENTS

ACKNOWLEDGEMENTS 14

FEATURE ARTICLES
SUPERMAN: PATRIOTIC
COVERS THROUGH THE
YEARS
  by Arnold T. Blumberg 40
SPIDEY GOES HOLLYWOOD:
  by Arnold T. Blumberg 44
ARCHIE AT 60:
  by J. C. Vaughn 47

MARKET REPORT 2001
  by Robert M. Overstreet
  & Overstreet Advisors 50
KEY SALES 2000 86
TOP 100 GOLDEN AGE 91
TOP 10 PLATINUM AGE 93
TOP 10 SILVER AGE 93
TOP 10 BRONZE AGE 93
TOP 10 CRIME 93
TOP 10 HORROR 94
TOP 10 ROMANCE 94
TOP 10 SCI-FI 94
TOP 10 WESTERN 94

FIRST AD SECTION 95

ABOUT THIS BOOK 213
How To Use This Book 213
New Comic Books 213
Comic Book Values 213
How Comics Are Listed 214
What Comics Are Listed 214
New Comic Listings 214

GRADING 214
How To Grade 215
Grading Definitions 215
Dust Jackets 217
Restored Comics 217
Scarcity Of Comics 218
COLLECTING COMICS 219

Back Issues 220
PRESERVATION
& STORAGE 220
BUYING & SELLING 221
Selling Your Comics 221
Where To Buy And Sell 222
Comic Conventions 222
COMIC BOOK FANDOM 223
RELATED COLLECTIBLES 224
Foreign Edition Comics 224
Newspaper Strips 224
Original Art 224
Toys and More 224
COVER BAR CODES 225
MARVEL REPRINTS 225
PUBLISHERS' CODES 225
Timely/Marvel/Atlas 226
COMIC BOOK ARTISTS 226
Artists' First Work 227

PRICE GUIDE LISTINGS
THE AMERICAN COMIC
  BOOK: 1842-2001
  Yours "Free:"
  Promotional Comics
  by Arnold T. Blumberg 228
PROMOTIONAL COMICS
  GUIDE 232
THE AMERICAN COMIC
  BOOK: 1828-1899
  THE VICTORIAN AGE
  Before the Yellow Kid: American
  Comics of the 19th Century by Doug
  Wheeler, Robert L. Beerbohm
  & Richard D. Olson, PhD 260
VICTORIAN AGE GUIDE 271
THE AMERICAN COMIC
  BOOK: 1900-1938
  THE PLATINUM AGE
  In the Beginning: Knowledge
  Continues to Expand! by Robert L.
  Beerbohm, Doug Wheeler
  & Richard D. Olson, PhD 281

PLATINUM AGE GUIDE 288
THE AMERICAN COMIC
BOOK: 1938-PRESENT
  THE MODERN AGE
  A Concise Origin of the Modern
  Comic Book by Robert L. Beerbohm
  & Richard D. Olson, PhD 303
MAIN GUIDE 312
CLASSIC COMICS/
CLASSICS ILLUSTRATED
  Understanding Classics
  Illustrated by Dan Malan
  (See Classic Comics) 407

SECOND AD SECTION 871

BUSINESS CARD ADS 914
CLASSIFIED ADS 917
SHOP DIRECTORY 919
GLOSSARY 926
A CHRONOLOGY OF THE
  DEVELOPMENT OF THE
  AMERICAN COMIC BOOK
  by M. Thomas Inge 929
HISTORIC FIRSTS 935
COVER GALLERY 936
HALL OF FAME 972
PRICE GUIDE
  BACK ISSUES 976
PRICE GUIDE BACK ISSUE
  ARTICLE INDEX 978
OVERSTREET ADVISORS 980
ADVERTISERS' INDEX 982

Mark Arnold (Harvey data); Larry Bigman (Frazetta-Williamson data); Glenn Bray (Kurtzman data); Gary Carter (DC data); J. B. Clifford Jr. (EC data); Gary Coddington (Superman data); Wilt Conine (Fawcett data); Dr. S. M. Davidson (Cupples & Leon data); Al Dellinges (Kubert data); David Gerstein (Walt Disney Comics data); Kevin Hancer (Tarzan data); Charles Heffelfinger and Jim Ivey (March of Comics listing); R. C. Holland and Ron Pussell (Seduction and Parade of Pleasure data); Grant Irwin (Quality data); Richard Kravitz (Kelly data); Phil Levine (giveaway data); Dan Malan & Charles Heffelfinger (Classic Comics data); Fred Nardelli (Frazetta data); Michelle Nolan (love comics); Mike Nolan (MLJ, Timely, Nedor data); George Olshevsky (Timely data); Chris Pedrin (DC War data); Scott Pell ('50s data); Greg Robertson (National data); Don Rosa (Late 1940s to 1950s data); Matt Schiffman (Bronze Age data); Frank Scigliano (Little Lulu data); Gene Seger (Buck Rogers data); Rick Sloane (Archie data); David R. Smith, Archivist, Walt Disney Productions (Disney data); Tony Starks (Silver and Bronze Age data); Don and Maggie Thompson (Four Color listing); Mike Tiefenbacher & Jerry Sinkovec (Atlas and National data); Raymond True & Philip J. Gaudino (Classic Comics data); Jim Vadeboncoeur Jr. (Williamson and Atlas data); Kim Weston (Disney and Barks data); Cat Yronwode (Spirit data); Andrew Zerbe and Gary Behymer (M. E. data).

Celebrating the 40th anniversary of the Amazing Spider-Man, we thank Alex Ross for his inspiring book store alternate cover. I would also like to thank Murphy Anderson for his re-creation of Superman #1, and to Rex Lindsey for his "malt shop" Archie alternate cover. Appreciation is also given Stephen Fishler for inspiring and helping develop the new 10 point grading system adopted in the 30th Edition.

Credit is due my two grading advisors, Steve Borock and Mark Haspel of Comics Guaranty Corp., for reviewing the new grading changes in this edition. Tribute is also given to Chuck Rozanski for his voluminous contribution of pricing data for this edition, which included Internet sales.

Special recognition is due Jon McClure for his brilliant research and contribution of dates for the final Whitman books published in the 1980s and to Bruce Ellsworth for researching the exact issue when Superman began to fly.

Thanks again to Doug Sulipa, Jon McClure and Tony Starks for continuing to provide detailed Bronze Age data. To Dave Alexander, Lauren Becker, Bruce Ellsworth, Richard Evans, Tom Gordon, Jamie Graham, Jef Hinds, Bill Hughes, Rob Hughes, Ed Jaster, Josh Nathanson, Jim Payette, Ron Pussell, Rob Rogovin, Terry Stroud, Harry Thomas, John Verzyl, Frank Verzyl and Vincent Zurzolo Jr., who supplied detailed pricing data, market reviews or other material in this edition.

My gratitude is given to Chris Pedrin for his advice on DC war comics data and to Stephen Fishler and Marc Patten for "How to Sell Your Comic Collection;" to Dr. Richard Olson for grading and Yellow Kid information; to Tom Inge for his "Chronology of the American Comic Book;" to Matt Nelson for his rewriting of the restored comics section; to Arnold T. Blumberg for his introduction to the Promotional Comics section; to Bill Blackbeard of the San Francisco Academy of Comic Art for his Platinum Age cover photos; to Bill Spicer and Zetta DeVoe (Western Publishing Co.) for their contribution of data; and especially to Bill for his kind permission to reprint portions of his and Jerry Bails' America's Four Color Pastime.

Special Recognition is due Bob Beerbohm and Doug Wheeler who spent months researching the Platinum and Victorian Sections in this edition. Bob organized a team of experts from around the world who sent him detailed data for updating this section. My hat is off to Bob and his colleagues for a job well done.

Acknowledgement is also due to the following people who generously contributed much needed data for this edition: Mark Arnold, Stephen Baer, Jonathan Bennett, Jeff Birkel, Chris Boyko, Mike Bromberg, Ed Buchman, Douglas Chambers, Howard Leroy Davis, Marty Hay, Jerry Howell, David Kell, Joseph Latino, Rob Ledford, Paul Levitz, Roy Massengill, Howard E. Michaels Jr., John Mlachnik, Stan Molson, Danny Owens, Dennis Petilli, Robert Quesinberry, Ben Samuels, Eugene Seger, Robert J. Simpson, Tom Sodano, Jim Stangas, T.L. Steed, West Stephan, Kirk Ticknor, Jeff Tignor, Jeff Walker, Bob Wayne, Richard Samuel West, M. Wayne Williams, Doug Wheeler, Larry Yasgar.

Finally, special credit is due our talented production staff for their assistance with this edition; to Arnold T. Blumberg (Editor), Brenda Busick (Creative Director), Mark Huesman (Pricing Coordinator), and Kimberley Grover (Advertising), as well as to our Executive Editor, J.C. Vaughn, for their valuable contributions to this edition. Thanks to my wife, Caroline, for her encouragement and support on such a tremendous project, and to all who placed ads in this edition.

Comprehensive Set of Comic Book Hobby

CGC Presents the CGC Census Report

The CGC Census Report is the only tool of its kind, and allows CGC customers to visit our website www.CGCcomics.com, click on "Census", and search through the many thousands of comic books CGC has certified to date.

This revolutionary and invaluable tool enables buyers and sellers to better understand the rarity of the grade of each comic book they are buying and selling, so they have all the data at their fingertips to make informed decisions.

The census will be updated no less than every quarter and is completely free.

CGC Holds the Most Respected Endorsements

For information on submitting your comic books call us or visit our website at CGCcomics.com!

Auctioning your comics?

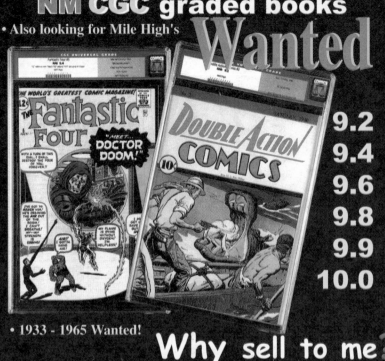

For All Your Collecting Supplies Visit:
WWW.BCEMYLAR.COM

✓ **Secure Shopping 24 Hours A Day**

✓ **Full Product Descriptions and Info**

✓ **Easy to Navigate**

✓ **Latest Product Info**

✓ **100% Product Satisfaction Guarantee**

✓ **Product In Stock & Ready For Immediate Shipment**

✓ **Plus Many More Reasons That We Haven't Even Thought Of Yet!**

Join Our Email Mailing List On-Line and receive a $5.00 Coupon Good On Your First Order

Bill Cole Enterprises, Inc.
P.O. Box 60, Dept. PG02
Randolph, MA 02368-0060
(781)986-2653 Fax: (781)986-2656
Email: bcemylar@cwbusiness.com

34

www.classiccomicinvestments.com

For the Investment Minded

The **Golden Age** of comics coincided with an era of patriotism and optimism in America.

The **Silver Age** was marked with stark contrast in established values and the new American youth.

A wave of change swept the country during the **Bronze Age**.

www.classiccomicinvestments.com
was founded for the comic book lover.

The site is an emporium for the serious investor.
The investor who appreciates a good book and can spot a great value.

Joseph Serpico, proprietor of Classic Comic Investments, has dedicated over 35 years to the business. He offers much more than a site to buy books, it is a dedication to quality comics that mark the era and weather the test of time.

Optimal ROI's are found in books of rarity, condition and demand.

For the Nostalgic

www.classiccomicinvestments.com

37

WE WANT THE ACTION

The Rarest and The Finest

Jay Parrino's
The MINT L.L.C.

Post Office Drawer 9326
Kansas City, MO 64133
Toll Free (866) 355-4591
(816) 373-7744 Fax
www.JayParrino.com

SUPERMAN: PA
THROUGH

Recently, in the wake of the terrorist attacks on the United States on September 11, DC Comics released a special poster intended to express sympathy for the families of those who lost their lives and to celebrate our love of and trust in the superiority of our nation. The poster featured a Golden Age Superman standing before a red, white and blue shield with an eagle perched on one arm. The grinning Man of Steel was drawn from the cover of the classic *Superman* #14. But although this was a special commemorative release, it was hardly the first time that Superman served as a patriotic figure meant to instill confidence and respect, as the original date of the poster's artwork will attest (see at right). Since his introduction in 1938, a few short years before America's entry into World War II, the strange being from another planet has made our country his

home, adopting our devotion t truth, justice and the American way

Over the years, the ideals t which Superman has pledged hi abilities and Kryptonian heart hav been captured in a series of cove images that reflect the Man o Tomorrow's American spirit. As cre ated by Jerry Siegel and Joe Shuste Superman has often been seen as a immigrant in superhero clothing – man who came to Earth with th desire to better himself and th world. As a surrogate for all thos men and women who came to ou shores a century ago with little mor than the hope of a good life Superman is the very embodiment o the American dream. On the ne few pages, we present a gallery o some of those striking covers fror the past and present that best exem plify Superman's status as a symbc of all that is strong and suprem about America.

RIOTIC COVERS
THE YEARS

Clockwise from top left: Action Comics #37 (Jun. '41), #43 (Dec. '41), #44 (Jan. '42), Superman #14 (Jan./Feb. '42), Superman #150 (Vol. 2) (Nov. '99)

Clockwise
from top left:
Superman #17 (July/Aug. '42),
#18 (Sept./Oct. '42),
Vol. 2 #69 (Jul. '92),
Vol. 2 #53 (Mar. '91)

SPIDEY GOES

The Wall-Crawler's First Silver Screen Sojourns.................

For years, Spider-Man fans have eagerly awaited the day when their favorite red-and-blue garbed hero would finally take his place alongside DC icons like Superman and Batman as one of the premiere superstars of the silver screen. But for all of his popularity and status as Marvel Comics' most recognizable hero, Spidey has seen cinematic fame elude him time and time again.

by

Arnold T. Blumberg

Spidey the prima donna!

There have been animated TV shows, even a short-lived live-action television series, but never a full-blown big screen romp. But now, at long last, the wait is over. May 2002 sees the release of **Spider-Man**, a Sam (**Evil Dead**) Raimi film starring Tobey Maguire as Peter Parker and Willem Dafoe as the arachnid's arch-foe, the Green Goblin.

With all the hype surrounding the movie, you might be forgiven for thinking

THE PLOT SOUNDS KINDA *CORNY* TO ME--

Y--LET'S THINGS OLLIN'!

VHERE'S THE TORCH?

BUT I SHOULD WORRY!

--JUST SO LONG AS THEY *PAY* ME!

I DON'T BELIEVE IN WASTING WORDS! I'LL GIVE YOU FIFTY THOUSAND DOLLARS TO STAR IN *"THE SPIDER-MAN STORY!"* WE'LL WRITE AN ORIGINAL SCRIPT IN WHICH YOU FIGHT THE *ENFORCERS* AND THE *GREEN GOBLIN!*

IF I ACCEPT-- I DON'T WANT ANY INTERVIEWS -- NO PUBLICITY-- NO SIGHTSEERS ON THE SET!! AND NO PHONY ROMANCE BUILD-UPS WITH STARLETS!

OKAY, OKAY! BUT YOU'LL BREAK A MILLION HOLLYWOOD HEARTS!

HOLLYWOOD

this is Spider-Man's first brush with cinematic greatness...but you'd be wrong! Decades ago, when Parker's career as a crime-fighter was just beginning in the 1960s, he had already made the pilgrimage to Hollywood in a number of now classic comic book adventures that introduced Spidey to the prospect of movie stardom. So as we prepare to witness the debut of the new Spider-Man film, it behooves us to take a look back at how Spidey's quest for fame began in the pages of those early issues of **The Amazing Spider-Man**.

Spider-Man's first success as a superstar came early enough, in the pages of **Amazing Fantasy**

#15 (August 1962). In Spidey's now legendary origin story, Peter Parker first employs his powers not for protecting the innocent or meting out justice, but to make a few bucks. He quickly becomes a major star, appearing on television shows, winning awards, and even planning to headline his own series. Later variations on the theme would indeed suggest that for a time, Spider-Man was a Hollywood fixture with an extensive career ahead of him. Alas, fate decreed that this was not the web-slinger's time to be a matinee idol (the mask got in the way anyway), and his performances ceased when Uncle Ben died and that familiar lesson in great power and great responsibility set him on a very different path.

Of all of the villains to match wits with the wall-crawler in those early years, none was as perplexing as the mist-enshrouded Mysterio. A master of illusion – if a bit of a fashion victim – the fishbowl-festooned criminal could conjure any image and envelop our hero in countless phantasmic perils. In their first encounter in **Amazing Spider-Man #13** (June 1964), Mysterio masqueraded as Spider-Man and began a crime wave intended to sully the spider's already shaky reputation. Ah, but beneath the fancy green robes and chemical fog was nothing more than a special effects guru with a black heart. That's right, one of Spider-Man's earliest foes was a refugee from a soundstage, and their first major battle spilled over onto the set of an unnamed star-faring space epic! Spidey even quipped that "I'm not a member of Actors' Equity, but I don't have time to get a union card right now!" Presumably he's taken care of that detail in the intervening years.

The very next issue (**Amazing Spider-Man #14**, July 1964) would be a fateful adventure for the wall crawler in more ways than one. First, it would introduce him to his greatest arch-enemy and future film co-star, the Green Goblin. Second, it would presage their 2002 big screen romp by pitting them both against each other on a motion picture set! Producer B.J. Cosmos is casting about for a follow-up to his Oscar-winning "The Nameless Thing From the Black Lagoon in the Murky Swamp" when the Goblin flies through his window and proposes a film featuring Spider-Man, the Enforcers and himself in pitched battle. Dubbed "The Spider-Man Story," the film will gross Spidey $50,000 (do you think Tobey Maguire worked for that little?), but it's all a trap of course. As the webbed one signs on the dotted line, the Goblin muses that Spider-Man's "trip to Hollywood will be a one-way journey—with no return!!" The eager fans lining up for this summer's opus might have something to say about that.

Filming in New Mexico, Spidey quickly learns that he's in big trouble, and not from rabid film critics. The Enforcers and the Goblin turn on him, and their fight leads them to a series of caverns frequented by none other than the Incredible Hulk! While Spidey mops up the bad guys and returns to B.J., he finds the fickle producer now has his sights set on the Green Goliath instead. Parker gets bus fare home, and so ends his first shot at stardom on the silver screen. But he would be on a movie set again even sooner than he

thought, and although the circumstances would be slightly different, the outcome would be virtually identical. Just the old Parker luck running true to form.

As many fans will recall, Spidey had quite a long-running rivalry with the Fantastic Four's Human Torch, alias Johhny Storm. Ever the hot-rodding hothead, Johnny was exactly the kind of swingin' teen that might ridicule the bookish Parker, so when the two heroes converged, they were more than likely to clash rather than cooperate. Eventually their sparring matches settled into a warm friendship, but not before they headed off for Tinseltown and the promise of stardom...yes, again. It seems superheroes never quite lose that starry-eyed optimism when it comes to film fame.

Amazing Spider-Man Annual #4 (November 1967) tells the tale of Spidey's next big journey to La La Land in "The Web and the Flame." When Spidey and the Torch are both asked to star in a film, the wall-crawler suggests they call a truce and shake hands on the deal. Ah, but in the world of superheroes, even that exciting movie contract carries with it an air of menace. As it turns out, the film is a trap concocted by the Wizard and Mysterio (what, him again?!), and the two heroes still wind up fighting due to one of those patented Marvel misunderstandings. While the two adventurers share a reward for nabbing the bad guys, they don't become big movie stars. Fame – what a fickle mistress. By now, you'd think Spidey would expect that any Hollywood offer was automatically hiding a secret supervillain agenda, and he certainly wouldn't hear any arguments from the Fantastic Four either, who faced similar movie mendacity with the Sub-Mariner masquerading as a producer! One wonders how Sam Raimi ever managed to direct the hero in the first place. You know, once or twice or twelve times burned...

So when you witness the silver screen debut of our favorite wall-crawler this summer, remember that although this is the first feature film to chronicle the exploits of the one and only Amazing Spider-Man, the webhead was an old hand at the Hollywood game since the very beginning of his spandex-swathed career. There were a few more star-studded sojourns throughout the '60s as well, including a memorable stint on the *Tonight Show* with Johnny Carson, so once you're done thrilling to the webbed one's exploits in theaters, hop on over to the local comic shop and hunt down some of these early Hollywood adventures. Tell 'em Overstreet sent ya, bunky!

ARCHIE AT 60

America's oldest teenager, barring Dick Clark, is Archie Andrews

by J.C. Vaughn

With all the time spent looking for it throughout history, who would have thought the secret of eternal youth would be found in Riverdale? That's where it is, though, and Archie Andrews and his friends seem happy enough to keep that secret to themselves while sharing their trials, tribulations and milkshakes with generations of readers.

Founded in November 1939, the fledgling MLJ Magazines was named for its three founding partners, Maurice Coyne, Louis Silberkleit and John Goldwater. After testing the waters of competition with their own superheroes in

titles such as *Blue Ribbon Comics*, *Top-Notch Comics* and, in 1940, *Pep Comics*, they turned from supermen to an everyman.

In *Pep Comics #22*, surrounded by standard (albeit enjoyable) super-hero fare, there was a six-page story featuring Archie Andrews and his friends. Not too long after that, in 1942, Archie made the leap to his own title. By May 1946, the company changed its name to Archie Publications. Archie was, one might correctly surmise, a hit. In the 60 years since, Archie has been featured in more than 30 different titles, on radio, and in cartoons, movies and TV shows. He's appeared in model kits, fan club kits, on cereal boxes, pinbacks, magazines, calendars, and other character collectibles. The comics even inspired the creation of The Archies, a pop group that scored a couple of hit records (like "Sugar, Sugar," originally intended for the Monkees!) and in turn inspired another cartoon interpretation of the characters.

Archie has spawned spin-offs like *Josie & The Pussycats* and *Sabrina The Teenage Witch*, and he's even met The Punisher and lived to talk about it. What makes Archie particularly interesting, though, is that he really hasn't changed that much. Situations have been updated, but Archie remained basically untouched by the counter culture of the '60s, the "Me Generation" of the '70s or its better-dressed sequel, the '90s. In each case there were nods to the prevailing mores, but they were mainly of appearance in nature and not in substance. Archie was, and is, still what he was created to be – family entertainment.

The birth of the

comic book specialty market, or direct market, precipitated a major decrease in the number of comics aimed at kids. Many publishers severely scaled back or flat out abandoned their efforts to cultivate the next generation of comics readers. Archie Publications, however, did not. They achieved the kind of cool you only get to be when you're not worried about whether you're cool or not. They produce family entertainment, they're good at it, and they stick with what works (or, more precisely, what their readers want).

"It's what we do best," said Archie's Victor Gorelick. "What's out there for young readers today? Not much in comics. We produce a product that parents are comfortable giving to their children. Archie Comics has entertained six generations of readers and hopefully will for another six."

Recent years have lead to some small but key successes for family fare such as *Bone* (from Cartoon Books), *Akiko* (from Sirius Entertainment), *Amelia Rules!* (from Renaissance Press) and a few other titles. These have been roundly celebrated for their all-ages accessibility, but even now few others seem to be willing to commit to Archie's level. The familiar characters—obnoxious Reggie, perpetually hungry Jughead, girl-next-door Betty, socialite

Veronica and, of course, Archie—exist in the Rockwellian paradise of Riverdale, where the main concerns range from where to go on a big date to Betty & Veronica's perpetual rivalry over Archie.

A recent example of how the characters are frequently tweaked slightly can be found in the series *Archie's Weird Mysteries*, itself based on yet another cartoon incarnation of the gang. In this particular instance, it was sort of a *Scooby Doo meets The X-Files* take. Not surprisingly, the situations changed more than the characters.

Gorelick predicts his sixtieth anniversary as a headliner will be a big one for the not-so-young Mr. Andrews, and it's probably more than just another dodge to get out of doing his homework.

"We're developing live action Archie and Josie & the Pussycats singing groups, Archie and Betty and Veronica live action and/or animated movies, and Archie live or animated TV shows." There is also, he said, a possible theatrical musical production. But it's safe to predict that whether these particular ventures rise or fall, Archie will be Archie, and not much will change that.

WILL 2002

SEE A CONTINUED HOT MARKET?

BY ROBERT M. OVERSTREET

With uncertainty caused by bad economic projections, layoffs and a downward spiraling stock market, it became anyone's guess as to how our collectible markets in general would react to the worsening resession.

And then the whole world changed after the events of September 11th. But in spite of all the bad news, strangely enough, the comic book market rebounded!

2001 ended as one of the most volatile years on record, with the sale of the high grade pay copy of **Marvel Comics** #1 bringing a staggering $350,000 (the most ever paid for a comic book). This was a cash deal with no trade involved; John Snyder of Diamond International Galleries sold the book to Bill Hughes, who was representing Jay Parrino.

This record price was set in November, shattering the previous record set a month earlier in the Mastronet Auction sale of a CGC certified 8.0 copy of **Detective** #27 at $278,190!

With the dramatic back-to-back price increases for the higher grades reported in this and the 2001 guides, the current year is poised to be one of our most volatile to date.

Collector demand

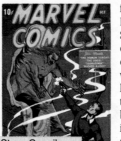

Steve Geppi's
Marvel Comics #1
pay copy goes for
record $350,000!

for many books from Platinum to Bronze continued to increase. Sales activity at the major comic cons last year was brisk, but not quite on the level of 2000. There were more individual sales, but less expensive books were sold at the shows. However, record sales began to occur late in the year, indicating a strong pick-up in the market.

Certified Comics: Professionally graded comic books by Comics Guaranty Corp. entered their second year and continued to set the pace for record sales as more and more collectors added these issues to their collections. Certified Gaines file copies were bringing four to ten times Guide for copies graded from 9.0 to 9.8. Demand for certified books continued to rise throughout the year. A **Sensation** #1 in CGC NM 9.4 sold for $100,000! A certified **Fantastic Four** #2 in NM 9.4 brought $27,457, a #5 in NM 9.4 got $17,046 and the White Mountain copy of **Amazing Spider-Man** #1 in 9.4 sold for a record $67,305 at auction. Other sales included: **Double Action Comics** #2, CGC 9.2 $35,187; **Haunt of Fear** #17/3 in CGC 8.5 $1,730;

Superman Comics
#1 ashcan copy goes
for record $36,099
at Mastro auction!

Detective Comics
#27 in CGC 8.0
sells for $278,190
at Mastro auction!!

Amazing Spider-Man #1 in CGC 9.2, **$67,305!!**

Fantastic Four #1 in CGC 8.0, **$16,002!!**

Fantastic Four #2 in CGC 9.4, **$27,457!!**

Fantastic Four #5 in CGC 9.4, **$17,046!!**

Planet Comics #1, CGC 9.2 $25,558.

Comics Guaranty Corp. released their first population report in the Summer of 2001, which had an immediate impact on certain books. It was interesting to note that **Spawn** #1 had the honor of having the most certified copies of all Modern Age comics. It is still too early to place much credence on the population report, but these data will play an increasingly important role in understanding comic book rarity and values in the years ahead.

Double Action Comics #2 in CGC 9.2 fetches $35,187!

Professional Auctions: Two new auction houses entered our market last year, attracted primarily by the ease and confidence of selling certified comics. Both of these auction houses knew the certification company, Comics Guaranty Corp., and had experience selling their certified coins and cards in other markets. Mastronet, Inc. had their first Americana auction last October, and it was a resounding success, with many record prices realized. The second auction house was Heritage Comics, famous for their auctions in the coin market, who had their first signature auction last November. At the same time, Greg Manning auctions, who entered the comics market in 2000, dropped out in 2001. The new auction houses exposed our market to thousands of potential new collectors.

Changes in this Guide: Since most books graded over VF have continued to sell for multiples of Guide, it became imperative to insert a VF price column to more accurately report the VF to NM prices. Space for the column was accomplished by dropping the decimal and cents from all prices above $6. In the past, all increases in the NM column would automatically pull up the value of every grade between FN and NM. It had always been assumed that the VF price was half-way between FN and NM; this is not the case. VF prices have not been increasing at the same rate as NM prices, and in today's market, this grade is somewhere below center between FN and NM. As NM prices continue to escalate in the future, with the VF column it will be easier to anchor a FN, VF and NM price as the market dictates; increasing NM will not by itself increase the VF price.

Another important change in this edition is the addition of a new section, "The Victorian Age," which will contain all the books from the 1800s–the earliest period of comic books. Special thanks is due Doug Wheeler, Bob Beerbohm and Richard Olson for spearheading this new section.

Haunt of Fear #17/3 in CGC 8.5 goes for $1,730!

Important: The following market reports were submitted by some of our many advisors and are published here for your information only. The opinions in these reports belong to each contributor and do not necessarily reflect the views of the publisher.

DAVID ALEXANDER (CULTUREANDTHRILLS.COM)

Average older material is declining in value due to over-availability caused by the Internet. Spectacular, rare, one-of-a-kind items are increasing. You must find the right buyer to realize outstanding prices.

Original owner collections that recently surfaced: 300 Golden Age comics, 155 pulps, Spider (pulp) ring; and one with 2000 comics from the early '40s to mid '70s. This collection also included Platinum Age comics and hundreds of '30s-'40s magazines. The majority of material that changed hands in 2001 was already in the hobby. **Terror Tales**, **Witches Tales** and similar titles from Eerie Pub. are selling at four to five times Guide in Good to Fine. These comics reprint '50s pre-Code horror comics, and some issues of the reprints are selling for more than the originals.

Prices realized have declined as the year wore on. People are chasing bargains more than a specific title or issue.

CGC: Older comics, 1950s and earlier, do not sell for a premium in a slab unless they are keys or pedigree.

Going Up: EC science fiction, Frazetta art, Archies with cover price of 20¢ and lower (selling at three to five times Guide, lower grades sell at higher percentages of Guide), **Katy Keene** 1983 series ($10 each in VG-), **Wonder Woman** Golden Age issues (VG and lower sell at three times Guide), and 1970s romance titles (all publishers sell at two to five times Guide).

Going Down: 1980s titles generally move below Guide. Centaur Publications titles have slowed – non-key issues sell at 15%-25% below Guide. Non-key Marvels in less than NM usually need to be discounted to move. Dell comics are available beyond demand.

DAVE ANDERSON

Although the comic book market remains strong and healthy, things have stabilized somewhat this year. Last year saw extreme volatility in the market due to the Internet, CGC, and an influx of pure investors. New collectors are now realizing they don't have to pay over Guide (or even Guide) for VG Marvels or Dells because they're always readily available. Dealers are finding that collectors and investors are becoming more educated and adjust their selling prices (and buying prices as well) downward and closer to Guide. This is

especially true for books in the Good to Fine range. Thus, lower grade books are pretty stable sellers at and below Guide.

On the other hand, higher grade books are still selling over Guide. Just as CGC and the Internet have shown us that lower grade books are generally always available, they have also shown that higher grade

© FH

Planet Comics #1 in CGC 9.2 goes for $25,558!

books are not. With the CGC population report, we are starting to get a feel for what's out there, and true NM and better books have proven to be scarce. For this reason, prices on these books have continued their upward climb, with record sales for multiples of Guide.

CGC: I have not seen a distinct difference in prices realized for slabbed comics vs. unslabbed comics when the grade is VF- or less. Books in VF to VF+ bring about 10-20% more; books in VF/NM (9.0) and NM- (9.2) bring about 20% more; and in 9.4 and higher, you may actually get 2-3 or more times NM Guide. Books with a restored label are difficult to sell anywhere near their apparent grade.

Internet Sales: Due to higher confidence in encapsulated books, sales are closer to Guide on the Internet than with non-encapsulated books. Most books will sell below Guide on the Internet – Internet buyers are becoming more savvy!

STEPHEN BARRINGTON

The 2001 comic book market was one of ups and downs. The first quarter showed continued strong sales in our sector, with all issues from the 1940s to the present selling well. The second quarter softened with sales plunging over 30 percent. The third quarter improved with strong sales in new and back issues, with Silver Age comics priced at Guide or below selling quickly. **Superman**, **Batman** and **Amazing Spider-Man** (Vol. 1) were particularly hot in all grades. Mid grade Silver Age **X-Men** were slow, as there seems to be a glut on the market. The only Bronze Age **X-Men** selling quickly in all grades are **Giant-Size #1** and **X-Men** #94. Prices on **Giant-Size** range from $100 in very good to $300 in Fine, with #94 going for slightly less. High grade copies of **X-Men**

#95-140 sell well on eBay but at Guide. Copies of **Hulk** #181 also sell in all grades from $100 to $1000.

Current issues of DC and Marvel are hit-and-miss. Superman titles sell well while Batman titles are in a slump. The Ultimate titles by Marvel have cooled, with **Ultimate Spider-Man** and **Ultimate X-Men** still selling well. DC's **JLA** and **JSA** titles sell well, while **Amazing Spider-Man** (Vol. 2) and **Peter Parker: Spider-Man** (Vol. 2) have seen increases. All Spider-Man titles from the '70s through the '90s are enjoying brisk sales, perhaps in anticipation of the big-screen debut in May.

At the San Diego ComicCon, CGC graded issues were in abundance but it was hard to tell if they were selling. Two exceptions I noted were **Action** #7 (CGC 1.5) going for $4,500 and a Near Mint CGC **Amazing Spider-Man** #6 (Vol. 1) going for an astonishing $7,500, almost five times Guide. There was a lot of high grade Silver Age at the show but not CGC graded. A VF **Amazing Spider-Man** #14 (Vol. 1) netted $3000.

EC comics continue to reign supreme with issues in all grades selling. High grade copies are scarce. EC reprints continue to move quickly. The low print runs on these issues will eventually dry up, causing prices to rise.

Bargain bin comics (five for a dollar) continue to show incredible growth, particularly with a lot of comics produced from the 1980s to present.

© MAR

Comic fans are eagerly waiting for Spider-Man to hit the big screen in May.

MICHAEL BROWNING

CGC: Certain issues will bring very high prices, while others barely bring enough to make up for the cost of having the books slabbed. I bought a **Miracleman** #1 (NM 9.6) for a mere $26 online. A **Spawn** #1 (NM 9.6) has been hanging on one dealer's wall for nearly a year and has had no buyers, but several **Spawn** #1s have sold for high prices even though there's a ton of them out there. The CGC census report should help to calm the market, letting people know exactly what books are tough to find. Slabbed Mile Highs seem to bring a lot more than unslabbed Mile Highs.

Internet Sales: The Internet market appeared to be filled with speculators trying to find the 'hot'

books, with a lot of toy and card collectors entering the market on a daily basis. Any and all issues of **Miracleman** are going for way over Guide, as are **Transformers**, **Rom**, **G.I. Joe**, and several other 1980s books that many believe will be hot items. The last issues of these books, which could still be found in dollar and quarter boxes for most of last year, are going for astronomical prices.

Prices on the **G.I. Joe Special** #1 (released after the last issue of the regular series) is going for upwards of $70. This book was still in quarter boxes only a couple of months ago, until someone said it was 'rare' and 'hot.' Those two words are bandied around too frequently. Books like the **Miracleman** keys are not rare by any means. If these books are so rare, how can there be three to four copies of each at any given time for sale online? Will the title stay hot after all the controversy dies down?

Golden Age: Lots of Golden Age books have been moving online for over Guide prices. If a book is listed in the Guide as rare, then it makes it all the more desirable online. Either people are looking to complete collections, or 'rare' and 'scarce' mean future profits, so they grab it even if it's higher than Guide. Collectors and investors both know that rare and scarce will lead to another buyer willing to pay a premium.

Bronze Age: Giant-Size X-Men #1 is the single most important book of the Bronze Age, along with **Incredible Hulk** #181. Both have been selling for higher than Guide due to the slabbing of high-grade copies. They are both easily $1,000 books. On the low end, I've seen copies of **Incredible Hulk** #181 in VG sell for as low as $12 and I bought a fair copy of **X-Men** #94 recently for only $20, so the lower grade copies aren't selling for much. That may have to do with availability.

House of Secrets #92 is easily a $1,000 book in Near Mint. The **Star Wars** 35-cent variant is the scarcest of the **Star Wars** books and very seldom comes up for sale. When one does, if it's in grade, it sells for nearly $1,000. **DC 100 Page Super Spectacular** #5, **All-Star Western** #10 and **Vampirella** #113 are fine where they are and **Cerebus** #1 is a prime candidate for an increase to $500 in Near Mint. Low grade copies of this book also sell for high prices.

Valiant: Valiant books are picking up steam. A copy of **Harbinger** #0 (pink covered edition, not the blue-covered trade paperback copy) went for $77. Copies of **Magnus** #0, **Harbinger** #1-5, **Rai** #1-4 and early **Solars** are still as tough to get as they were several years ago when they boomed, and the stories are still as good. Collectors are realizing this and snatching these up. Gold Valiants still bring a premium when they pop up online and are still very popular when found in lots. The Gold books still don't sell for the hundreds they were going for during Valiant's boom. One book that's still tough to get is Valiant's **Chaos Effect Omega Gold**, which has sold online for upwards of $26. The book is reportedly the rarest Valiant ever produced, with only 1,000 printed.

Truly scarce books, like the **Elseworlds 80-page Giant**, are still continuing to rise. One sold online for $218.37 in NM. If it's true that only about 2,000 of these exist, this may be a good book to buy and keep, especially with the **Bizarro Comics** hardcover reprinting of the controversial "Letitia Lerner: Superman's Babysitter." Controversy controls pricing!

Last issues are still very hot. From Golden Age endings to the Bronze Age toy book finales, last issues are in most cases tough to find at Guide. Leading the way is **Flash** #104, which climbs in price with every sale. Other DC last issues and Timely endings are in great demand and usually bring above Guide, even for Poor and incomplete copies. Try finding a **Rom** #75 in good shape for Guide! These books stayed too long in the quarter bins and nice copies are very hard to find.

Binky #82 has to be the rarest 1970s comic of any publisher. One sold on eBay for more than $50 in Fine. It is also the oddest of the 1970s books – it contained a Green Lantern/Green Arrow letters page, an election cover (in 1978) and was a one-shot which continued the numbering of its previous incarnations. The hottest books of the year were last issues. **Transformers** #80, **G.I. Joe** #155, **Rom** #75, **Miracleman** #24, **Akira** #38 and several others have become high-priced items, due to low print runs. Copies are selling for multiples of Guide. I believe **Rom** #75 to be as low-printed as **G.I. Joe** #155 and

Transformers #80 and maybe even harder to find in high grade. It contained Steve Ditko and P. Craig Russell artwork and had a beautiful Russell cover.

Religious-themed comics are also hot, with the Spire/Barbour line getting the highest prices. **Hansi, the Girl Who Loved the Swastika** is always a good seller, as is **Tom Landry and the Dallas Cowboys**. High-grade copies of **Hansi** have sold for more than $50 each. Obscure comics are always in demand. Comics from the Rural/Enwil Production line of books are always going for over Guide. The **Blazing Comics**, **Red Circle**, **Red Band** and **Blue Circle** books are highly sought after. These books are mysteries for collectors of oddball books, because a person could buy a **Blazing** #5 and get a **Marvel Tales** issue inside, or as I found, the missing **Feature Stories Magazine** #4 that is not supposed to exist! The same goes for **Blazing** #6, **Red Circle** #4 and **Blue Circle** #6, all of which contain remaindered copies of comics inside their covers. Only **Blazing** #5 has been found to have an original interior, which is very rare. The 'true' **Blazing** #5 could very well be listed as rare in the Guide. I've only ever seen two of them for sale or otherwise and I own both. Also, very rare variant covers of **Blue Circle** #6 and **Red Circle** #4 exist, with writing on the covers detailing the interiors of the books, most likely printed later onto the covers by whatever company bought the cover stock and stapled them onto remaindered books.

Charlton: The Charltons from the 1970s to the company's end in 1986-87 are in very high demand, especially in grade. Issues of **Atomic Mouse** have sold for more than $50 in high grade. Issues with certain artists' work tend to bring more online, but the horror books keep on climbing, as do books like **E-Man**, **Emergency**, **Space: 1999** and the **Six Million Dollar Man** and **The Bionic Woman**. These are easier to find than some of the more eclectic books, such as **Thane of Bagarth**, **The Lonely War of Willie Schultz**, **Iron Corporal**, **Timmy the Timid Ghost** and others. The Charlton **Bullseye Specials** are also very rare and I have never seen any pop up online or in shops.

Some of the Charltons that have been much maligned over the years are now being sought

© Hasbro

Final issues like **Transformers #80** have optimally prime appeal.

after by collectors who are trying (almost in vain) to complete collections with mid to high grade copies. High grade collectors beware – there's not an abundance of high-grade Charltons to be found, so get them while you can.

Charlton magazines are also climbing in popularity. The black and whites are tough to find in high grade and are almost always a hot online item. Also, when **Scary Tales** started running new material, the issues apparently did not take off too well and appear to be low-printed. These books are very scarce and are rarely found for sale, especially the issues with new material. The Mitch O'Connell cover on #36 is an all-new cover and those last ten issues are very tough to find, especially in grade. The Charlton **Bullseye Special** from 1987 is very rare. The publisher has said in printed interviews that even he has never seen a copy, but knows a few were printed. The **Doomsday+1** series reprints used interior panels for the cover art following #7. John Byrne painted the covers for the first six issues. Also, Fantagraphics' **Doomsday Squad** #7, reprinting the Charlton Bullseye **Doomsday+1** stories, is a tough book to find. The first six issues are common, but #7 is hard to locate.

Charlton's last comic, reportedly, was **Professor Coffin** #21, published in February 1986. This information is found in Steve Duin and Mike Richardson's book, **Comics: Between the Panels**. At the end, **Prof. Coffin** was a reprint comic containing 1970s Wayne Howard stories and art. Those last issues from Charlton were low-printed and very tough to find in any condition.

Books which are low printed are selling for higher than Guide prices in all cases. Low distributed comics, variants and last issues have all been booming. Next-to-last issues are sometimes rarer than the final issues and sometimes as hard to find. Whitman comics from the early 1980s (the final years of the company) are all hard to find. High grade copies of any and all of these "last gasp" titles are also selling for higher than Guide prices on the net.

A copy of **3-D Exotic Beauties** from The 3-D Zone, with reprints of 1950s jungle girl comics, sold on eBay for more than $20. The comic has an L.B. Cole cover of naked women and was pub-

© DC

The Hunger Dogs from Jack Kirby and DC is tough to find in high grade.

lished in 1990, making it one of the last covers he drew. The book is also very tough to find. Copies without the 3-D glasses are available occasionally online, also selling above Guide.

The Babes of Broadway, published by Broadway Comics, is a tough book to find and may be the last comic published by the company. It contains art by J.G. Jones, Dick Giordano, Michael Kaluta and several others. It may be the shortest printed Broadway comic next to the **Fatale** trade paperback that was released in limited quantities but nearly impossible to find.

The **Manhunter** special from 1984 that reprinted the 1970s backup saga from **Detective Comics** is very tough to find. I believe it to be as tough as the **New Gods** #6 which reprinted part of the **New Gods** series from the 1970s. That book had an original Jack Kirby story that led into **The Hunger Dogs** graphic novel, which is another tough DC book to find in high grade. Copies of **The Hunger Dogs** sell for upwards of $50 in VF.

Try finding the **Rainbow Brite** comic from DC in the mid-1980s and the **Bill and Ted's Excellent Adventures** giveaway comic. Another very tough DC is the **Superfriends Special** (giveaway). In 22 years of collecting, I've only found one copy. I've only ever seen two copies of the **Bill and Ted** book anywhere.

A tough book to find, and it may have been short-printed, was **Skrull Kill Crew**, which was Grant Morrison's and Mark Millar's first work for Marvel. It was a four-issue limited series during the mid-1990s and did not go over very well. First issues are fairly easy to locate, while #2-4 are tough.

Every single copy of **All-Negro** #1 has sold for much more than Guide. It's probably rarer than Green Giant #1 and is more historical, as it tied with **Negro Heroes** as the first black comic book.

Miracleman: The first issue also had a gold edition that was signed and numbered, and limited to only 500. It was listed in a back issues ad in Eclipse comics and was, at one time, very expensive ($50 when it came out). There is also a blue edition that was signed by the publisher, limited and very expensive even in the mid-1980s ($20 when it was released). MM #23 and 24 are probably as rare as #15. The last issue of the title advertised the next issue (#25), but Eclipse closed up shop before it was released. Also, **X-Men Archives** featuring **Captain Britain** #4 may be the sleeper hit of the year with its appearance of Miracleman getting blown away. It even says the name Miracleman in it, making it an authentic MM appearance. This book is nearly non-existent on eBay and can usually be found in rough shape in quarter boxes. The series reprints the Alan Moore-Alan Davis Captain Britain stories from the Marvel UK magazine, **Daredevils**. The MM appearance is a reprint of **Daredevils** #7. Try finding that one, MM collectors!

MICHAEL CARBONARO (COMIC BOX PRODUCTIONS)

Comics can't lose! If the stock market goes up, people have more money to spend on things they want. If the market goes down, people look for a safer place to put their money. The Internet has yet to achieve full market penetration, especially in the international markets. Once this occurs (and it will!), there will be an unprecedented demand for quality material such as CGC high grade copies. Silver Age, diverse and unusual books have been snapped up quickly, whether 'raw' or certified. Collectors are coming back to the hobby. There was an incredible demand for CGC graded books at San Diego. I have never sold so many quality books in one place at one time.

CGC: CGC books have been in high demand. CGC has dramatically altered the comic landscape just as it did in both the coin and collectible card worlds. Consumer confidence is incredibly high in the product now. The presence of a trusted independent third party grading system has opened up the marketplace to collectors and/or investors who might otherwise have stayed away. Result: more buyers. Sales are brisk at shows once people get over the 'sticker shock' of the highest graded copies. Transactions go far more smoothly – grade is never a point of contention, only price. Mail order and Internet sales are booming. With CGC books online, our business has quadrupled. With no give and take over grading, returns are virtually nonexistent.

Internet Sales: The introduction of CGC material has produced a quadrupling of our sales, primar-

© MAR

Incredible Hulk #102 in CGC 9.8 sold on eBay for $1,800.

ily over the Internet. The Internet provides the ideal selling environment for product in which the buyer can place absolute faith. Everyone benefits.

Going Up: Lower grade, unrestored Golden Age books should rise, especially the earlier Marvel (Timely) #1s. They are undervalued, especially given that the CGC population report has not shown the presence of the quantities found in issues of later vintage. The key Golden Age books should go up by a substantial amount. Restored copies are stagnating, with collectors scrambling to pay top dollar for choice unrestored keys.

Going Down: Many of the newer books are being driven up by either speculation or the presence of super high grade CGC graded issues (9.8-10.0). Is a comic issued after 1985 really worth the money currently being realized? Many topical issues, such as those associated with **SOTI** and **POP**, are overrated and overpriced. Many ultra high grade Bronze and Modern Age books are going for many multiples of Guide and drive the price up on books that are not truly worth it. The prices should drop on some of these.

GARY DOLGOFF

2001 has been a very solid year for our hobby. With the vast gulf between Good and Near Mint prices, two types of buyers have become more prominent–those who want reading copies, and investors, many of whom will pay well for true NM or Mint comics, especially if they're CGC graded!

I am selling a goodly amount of comics on eBay this year (including a 9.8 **Hulk** #102 for $1,800, and a 9.6 **Avengers** #24 for $200). Also selling are inexpensive '60s-'90s. I put up about 20-50 lots per week, and sell about 25%-50% of what I list - a lot better than your average convention.

Golden Age: They continue to move on out! These seem to be the tried and true perennial sellers in comicdom. Other genres may get hot then cool off, but these stay simmering, the true essence of comics. Timely leads the pick, and it's tough to get them.

1940s DC: A strong seller all around. **All-Star, Detective, Wonder Woman, Flash** and any of the other JLA characters – I consider these pre-sold books by their nature, whether in high, low or mid grade. Pre-hero 'New Comics' are somewhat slow but solid. I am deluged by requests for the early books, i.e. **Action #1-20**, **Detective #1-50** (the 'big logo' issues) early **All-Stars**, **Supermans**, **Flashs**, etc.

Fawcett: Higher grade mid-'40s **Capt. Marvels** are meeting some sales resistance. I've had to sell some a bit below Guide. Cheap, late Fawcett move briskly. **Capt.** in high grade seem pretty slow, as are **Don Winslows**. I have not had any **Spy Smashers** in a while, but I'm sure they would sell well!

Quality: Anything 1943 and earlier sell briskly at around Guide. Late '40s sell OK but not thrilling.

MLJ: These seem to be tougher to attain lately. I'd imagine they still move well as the characters and covers are pretty interesting.

Fiction House: Again, early '40s always seems to sell quickly. Late '40s move at variable rates - **Planets** sell faster it seems. **Rangers** may be a little slower; **Jumbo**, **Jungle** and **Wings** are OK sellers.

Fox: Those late '40s **Blue Beetles** are a good bet. Early **Mystery Men** and **Wonderworld** with those wondrous Lou Fine covers are smart movers.

Archie: '40s **Archies** sell well - they are fun to own!

Disney/Dell: Donald Duck Four **Colors** #4, 9, 62 sell quite well. In general, early '40s **Four Colors** sell well, though not as well as early '40s DCs. Late '40s Dells can be moderate (like westerns) to slow (like **WDC&S**).

1950s DC: Always requested and bought. If they're early '50s superhero, they're sold in all grades. Late '50s don't sell as fast as early '50s, but still quite well. **Showcase #1-22** sell well, as do **Viking Prince Brave and Bolds #1-24**. The only '50s DC that moves real slow is **Mutt and Jeff**. Other non-superhero '50s DCs are slow to moderate sellers.

Dell/Disneys: Westerns have picked up in sales over years ago. TV/movie sell just OK. **Little Lulus** are pretty solid sellers and good reading! **I Love Lucy** comics are very good sellers!

Horror: Though cooled down somewhat from their previous fiendish frenzy of selling, they are still brisk sellers. ECs, long ignored, are moving out quite well, whether in tattered shape or sharp.

© DC

The Legion in **Adventure Comics** is a solid seller.

I had several batches of ECs this year, and they're almost all gone!

Crime Comics: Solid but not super sellers. If covers are by S&K, then they move well.

Sci-Fi: Good sellers. ECs are finally moving well, although horror ECs seem to move a bit faster.

Classics: People like **Classics** if they are priced at $3-$5. I noticed collectors buying small stacks of them at last year's San Diego Convention.

1960s DC: **Batman** and **Wonder Woman** are the best '60s sellers. Superman family titles (**Action**, **Superman**, **Lois Lane**, etc.) are solid sellers, as well as **Adventure** with Legion of Superheroes. **Flash**, **GL** and **JLA** move decently. **Aquaman**, **Atom**, **Hawkman**, **Metal Men** are somewhat slow. The worst sellers of '60s DC seems to be the superhero **House of Mystery** and **House of Secrets**.

Marvel: Yes! 1964 and earlier Marvels are great sellers! Especially brisk are **FF #1-12**, **ASM #1-14**, **Avengers #1-9**, **DD #1**, **JIM #83-112**, **Amaz. Fantasy #15**, **X-Men #1-9**, **TTA #27**, **Sgt. Fury #1**, and **Strange Tales Annual #1** and 2. Also, any pre-superhero Marvels sell despite price rises in recent years.

1965-1971: Spidey and **X-Men** are great sellers. **FF** sells well. I can't keep **Avengers #57-100** in stock as they are still priced low to moderate in the Guide (#12-56 sell OK). **Daredevil** also sells OK. Later '60s **Strange Tales**, **Sub-Mariner**, **Tales of Suspense**, **Tales to Astonish** are a bit slow, unless priced at $5 or less. **Sgt. Furys** are pretty slow despite being a good read. The exception to all that is extremely high grade (VF/NM or better) '60s Marvels; they sell really well for Guide and above.

Dell/Gold Key: TV sells decently, with Westerns doing quite well. Movies sell OK, funny animals sell slow.

Archie: Sells OK, especially at $3 or so.

Warrens: **Creepy** and **Eerie** move well if one is willing to sell them at $3 (for low grade) to $5 or so (for nicer copies). **Famous Monsters** sell solidly; #1-30 seem increasingly hard to get. Although meeting some price resistance, **Vampirellas** sell solidly, especially the $5 issues.

1970s: Yes, the Bronze Age is alive and well!

DC: 100 Pagers move briskly despite those price increases of late. **Batman** sells great in all grades.

Although many Kirby DCs have found their way to my warehouse, they still move decently if not terrifically. Folks enjoy any DC Giant in general. Early '70s DCs seem to be more popular than later '70s, except my 75¢-$1 mid/late '70s; they like them at that price!

Marvel: Can't keep **Avengers** #101-140 in stock; I have a line of buyers for many of them! **Spider-Man** #140 and earlier move quite well, as do **Defenders** and **Team-Up** #1-10. **Tomb of Dracula** sells and is a great read. Mainline '70s Marvels sell well, with 20 cent cover '70s doing much better than later '70s. Later '70s are also a lot more available. **X-Men** #142 and earlier continue to sell quite decently, including those reprint issues. Of course, **X-Men** #94, **GS #1**, and **Hulk #181** (1st Wolverine) continue to be in demand in all grades, Fair/Poor to Near Mint. Many of the discontinued titles (**Ms. Marvel, Nova, Omega,** etc.) are slow sellers; the only way to sell them is to mark them at 75¢-$1, and even then they are pretty slow. Some of those titles are light, fun, cheap reading; maybe someday... Non-superhero '70s Marvels have slowed somewhat, but still sell OK.

1980s and 1990s: Move OK at 1/3 of Guide or less. One exception - **Wolverine** #1 (regular series) moves well at 1/3 to 1/2 Guide. One important note: late '90s seem pretty popular as a kind of genre, with low print runs. I will sometimes sell them by the box at 1/3 to 40% of Guide.

CONRAD ESCHENBERG

CGC: High grade books, specifically 9.0 or better, sell briskly at multiples of Guide. 9.4 or better are very rare and prices at four times Guide and more are realized. High grade early Silver Age Marvels, 1961-1965, sell the best and at higher multiples of Guide. It seems there is no end to what people will pay for these books. **Internet Sales:** The Internet is changing the way we do business. Dealers will have to pay more for product as the public can easily sell their comics and art over the Internet. Prices will go higher on good items and lower on common items.

High grade early Silver Age Marvels are up 20%; pre-hero Marvels, 15%; **X-Men** #94, **GS#1**, **Hulk** #180-182, **Spider-Man** #96-100, 121, 122, 129, 20%; DC comics 1955-1965, 20%; all '40s and

'50s books with Schomburg, Ditko, Frazetta and L.B. Cole art, 20%; DC and Timely Golden Age, 10%, all '50s crime, horror, and good girl, 10%. Classics, Dells, Disneys, and Gold Keys are down 15%.

RICHARD EVANS (BEDROCK CITY)

The market is due for a correction. Golden Age prices have escalated at such a rate that there are fewer collectors putting together runs. Also-ran issues of expensive runs are stagnating as collectors look for specific examples. The Silver Age market is healthier, with more people buying low grade and finishing runs. It is still too soon to get an accurate picture of the CGC high grade market for Silver Age. Most high grade Silver and Golden Age is selling above Guide. Early '90s across the board should come down, as well as Dell Giants and **True Comics**.

DAN FOGEL & JIM PITTS (HIPPY COMIX, INC.)

The one-two combination of Internet trading and CGC grading has led to the healthiest back issue market in over a decade. Between auctions both private and on eBay, and the growing number of comics retailing web sites, a broader investing/collecting base has come into the market. In the graded sports cards market, we observed this phenomenon of ridiculously large initial sales temporarily inflating prices followed by a big slump. Now that the **Comics Buyer's Guide** publishes a CGC population report, telling how many books in each grade have been charted, we expect to see a drop in people paying 100 times or more over Guide for recent books that number in the hundreds of thousands in high grade. However, truly high grade Golden and Silver Age keys will always command multiples of Guide.

The supply of Golden Age books on the market is gradually dwindling, as there are fewer new books coming into the market and more collectors are stashing away their personal runs. Most high grade pedigree books sell well at auctions, while collectors who can only afford low to mid grade are getting less picky about condition.

The Silver and Bronze Age market is extremely

© MAR

The Avengers from #101-140 are hard to keep in stock. (#103 shown)

robust, as most of the new Internet blood appreciate these from their childhood. Truly high grade Marvel keys are both more plentiful and highly sought after than DCs. There are more collectors interested in western, romance, and war books these days, which are considerably undervalued compared to the superhero titles. **X-Men** and **Spider-Man** books sell well in mid to high grade, followed by **Fantastic Four** and **Avengers**. Most low to mid grade DC superhero titles sell extremely slowly.

The Modern Age back issue market is over-saturated with books from the early '80s to the mid-'90s. There is far more supply than demand and prices are very soft. More recent mainstream back issues have smaller print runs, and ongoing titles are in strong demand and are better long-term investments than the books from the early '90s speculator boom and bust. The cover prices on a lot of new comics are so high that most collectors are only interested in ongoing titles they can complete. Many fans follow creators from company to company, instead of the "Marvel zombie" phenomenon we used to see. The hottest of the current crop of mainstream comics creators include: Alan Moore, Neil Gaiman, Frank Miller, Garth Ennis, Warren Ellis, Ed McGuinness, Frank Quitely, Tim Sale, George Perez, Brian Michael Bendis, Jeph Loeb, Grant Morrison, and J. Michael Straczynski.

The past year's recent back issue market has been shaped by competing philosophies at Marvel and DC. Incoming Marvel president Bill Jemas and editor-in-chief Joe Quesada have combined a brash in-your-face WWF style bad-boy image that has excited fans while insulting retailers, especially with their no-reprint policy for hot new books like the Ultimate line. This creates a manipulated collecting frenzy at the expense of broadening the initial readership. Retailers don't like being unable to reorder hot books because many of these potential new customers will not return if the book is not on the shelves. DC, in contrast, has an immediate reprint policy for unexpected big hits like Kevin Smith's **Green Arrow** series, and will go back to press several times until reader demand is met. Marvel is following DC's lead in

© ABC

Reader loyalty to creators like Alan Moore are a boost to such titles as **Promethea**.

releasing and re-releasing trade paperbacks and collected editions, which is the largest growing segment of the modern market and the one most likely to grow a new readership.

By far, our fastest growing genre of comics sold are underground and adult titles from the '60s to the present. Top sellers remain **Zap Comix**, **Fabulous Furry Freak Brothers**, **Cherry**, and any title with work by Robert Crumb or Vaughn Bode. **The Hippy Comix Underground Price Guide** is due out in 2002 and should greatly stimulate collecting and investment interest.

STEPHEN H. GENTNER

The revelations of this year's market can be summed up in two words: CGC and eBay. The accepted grading of CGC material to the hobby and the public has been dramatically demonstrated on eBay, and eBay itself has opened up areas of the world to comics both for sale and to purchase. Being stung by unscrupulous people has been minimized. This has opened the market as hoped to showcase comic books in a new, safer light. Consequently, good things have happened to the appreciation of many areas, i.e. Silver Age Marvel and DC, and Golden Age to a lesser extent.

All the way through, my experience with CGC has been positive. There are some questionable instances where tougher books seem to get the benefit of the doubt grade-wise over more commonly found issues. There will always be small glitches in something as subjective as comic book grading, but as long as the playing field remains level, we should be OK.

For icon material in both Marvel and DC in high grade, the sky seems to be the limit. Multiples increase as you go from 9.0 to 9.2 to 9.4 etc. I have seen up to 17 times NM pricing for plum books in several titles, such as **TOS, TTA, Strange Tales, Spider-Man, FF**, and **Journey into Mystery**. The extremely high multiples occur on books perceived as underpriced in the Guide, so dollars dictate more so than multiples.

For example, an **FF** #73 white-covered "battle" issue selling for close to $1,000 in 9.6 is 22 times Guide, but a book like **TOS** #44 selling for $2,000 in 9.2-9.4 is only six times Guide. The dollars involved are driving the prices, not necessarily the multiples 'carved in stone.' Some **Flash** issues came up on eBay that brought several thousands of dollars.

The bottom line is that motivated collectors with discretionary income are making substantial commitments to high grade Silver Age material, and in many instances competing for the privilege. This holds true for Marvel and DC. Dells, Charlton and off-brand stuff is not nearly so sought after.

With so much focus on Silver Age right now, buyers of Golden Age material may have some quiet opportunities to purchase great stuff at favorable prices. That isn't to say **Seven Seas** #6 or **Startling** #49 are now bargains, but non-icon, non-war covered issues can be bought more readily. Tougher runs like most Timelys (**Cap** in particular) will always be dear, as will cool Schomburg, Baker, Kamen, and Raboy covers. But as hot spots occur in some areas, you can score that off-beat run you've been jonesing for (i.e. **Fighting American**).

© MAR

DANIEL GREENHALGH (SHOWCASE NEW ENGLAND)

CGC: It remains to be seen whether CGC has a viable business model for comics. Their cases crack easily. We send less and less books to them because they tend to be inconsistent, slow and expensive.

Internet Sales: The Internet will and has changed collectibles forever. The playing field has been leveled so that dealers have to pay more for books and those having collections can generally get more money. Buying and selling has become much more competitive.

Golden Age: Timelys are heating up again; it is more difficult to keep these books in stock. Prices are climbing and inventories are generally small. Unrestored early Golden Age, like **Action**s, **More Fun**s, and **Adventure**s are in high demand and sell for premiums if they are CGC Fine or better. Unrestored high grade **Batman**s and **Superman**s are soft, whether CGC graded or not, for most issues. Restored Golden Age books are soft regardless of title.

Silver Age: Marvels rule! The premiums on NM, CGC graded books are staggering for 9.4s and

Silver Age Marvels in CGC 9.4 and above fetch many multiples of Guide prices.

above, fetching 10 to 20 times Guide for books priced under $100 by Guide; and 5 to 10 times Guide for books price over $100, sometimes more. Prices on DC books are about right; some exceptions are CGC graded 10/12¢ DCs from mainstream titles, which get 5 to 10 times NM Guide.

ERIC J. GROVES (THE COMIC ART FOUNDATION)

CGC: Everyone is aroused by news of modern comics slabbed and graded at 9.5 or better selling at astonishing multiples of Guide. We remain convinced that in most instances, this is a departure from reality that will eventually correct itself. The key to understanding these transactions is information. The recent release of the comic book population graded by CGC tells the tale. For example, there are 750 slabbed copies of **Spider-Man** #1, of which 5 are graded 10.0. How many more are out there, awaiting encapsulation? Thousands. Of greater significance is the population of genuinely scarcer comics graded by CGC and then sold on eBay, particularly Golden Age issues. This data will help inform the hobby of the number of extant high grade issues and provide an additional indication of market value. One other factor is CGC itself. In order for this process to continue, CGC must be able to conduct it profitably. Whether this is possible remains to be seen. Finally, we are wary of speculators who invest in slabbed books with no knowledge, experience or interest in comic art. This has been a recipe for trouble in the past.

Internet Sales: Internet buying and selling continued at an accelerated pace in 2001. Of principal importance is the auction process, chiefly on eBay, which in many cases allows collectors to obtain mid grade or lower grade books at Guide or below. It also permits serious collectors or investors to purchase CGC graded books, frequently at premium prices. The excitement of bidding adds to the attraction. Equally significant is the opportunity for collectors to sell directly to other collectors, eliminating the dealer/middleman and his mark-up. Even so, Internet trading is not risk-free, with instances of over-grading and fraud being reported. However, to the best of our knowledge, only CGC sales on eBay are being tracked. Thousands of other transactions are not followed in any systematic way, and when they are observed or reported, remarkable inconsistencies emerge. Clearly, this medium of exchange is here to stay. Good or bad? On balance, more good than bad, because it enables dealers and collectors to trade in a broader context. Drawing legitimate fans into the hobby is always desirable and benefits fandom as a whole.

Archie's not the only one interested in **Betty and Veronica**. (#13 shown)

© AP

Golden Age: All Timely titles continue to sell quickly in all grades, led by **Capt. America, Human Torch** and **Marvel Mystery**. DC titles likewise sold well, but are clearly preferred in Fine or better. We note increased interest in **All-American, Sensation** and **Boy Commandos**. **Detective** and **Batman** were not as hot as last year, perhaps due to increased prices. Early Quality titles featuring the work of Fine or Eisner are continually sought.

Fox titles like **Weird** and **Science** sell steadily in all grades, but demand has lessened. Fawcetts will move in most grades, particularly **Capt. Marvel, Master, Whiz,** and **Capt. Marvel Jr.** Titles like **Don Winslow** and **Spy Smasher** are a bit slower. Fiction House comics are reliable sellers, led by **Planet** and **Jumbo**. Collectors are seeking early issues of **Wing**. Quality titles also trade. MLJ comics will sell as usual, and appear to be in short supply. Early Dell comics – the **Four Color** series – are of only moderate interest, and tend to sell to specialized collectors, such as Walt Kelly fans or Barks completists. They are often beautiful books in high grade, and those who like them prefer them that way.

Very few Golden Age titles are dead. Historical comics – **True Comics, It Really Happened, Real Life** and the like – are of limited interest. We have also observed a lull in Street and Smith titles; the **Shadow** is lagging.

Atom Age: Post-war Timelys are sought after, and some first issues are scarce, i.e. **Nellie the Nurse** and **Millie the Model**. Likewise, the Atlas titles are still hot across most genres, particularly horror or suspense. War titles are a bit slower, even though collector curiosity is aroused about some of the artists in them, such as Maneely. Atomic Age DCs like **Strange Adventures** sell well, as do other science

fiction comics from this era.

EC comics, which have been slow perhaps because of reprints, are picking up, particularly Pre-Trends. DCs from this period still move, but not as quickly as in the past, such as **Alan Ladd, Bob Hope, Real Screen** and **Fox and Crow**. There is increased interest in **Archie** and **Betty and Veronica**. Ziff Davis titles sell steadily, except for **G.I. Joe**, which lags despite gorgeous Norman Saunders covers. Avon comics plod along, and even some of the traditionally slower western and war titles move. The same may be said of M.E. comics, particularly with Powell collectors. Certain crime comics do better than others, such as the Atlas titles and Lev Gleason; **Crime Does Not Pay** and **Daredevil** are plodders; collectors prefer the Golden Age issues.

Some Dell titles are slower than they should be, particularly westerns such as **Roy Roger, Gene Autry** and **Lone Ranger**. Too many copies exist apparently. We are offered collections quite frequently, but only take them when the books are in high grade.

Silver Age: Marvel leads the way. Interest is up in **Amazing Spider-Man, Fantastic Four, Capt. America** and **X-Men**. Collectors still prefer copies in higher grade, but we sell them in Fine; below that is tougher. **Hulk** follows behind the others; early issues are very desirable. Pre-superhero issues are sought, but not as often as in previous years.

DC comics are steady sellers, but the intense interest in **Brave and Bold** and **Showcase** has diminished. Likewise, **Batman** and **Detective** are a bit slower, as are **Action, Adventure** and **Superman**. Early issues – under #20 – of **Lois Lane, Jimmy Olsen** and **Superboy** still move briskly. DC war comics sell, but are not as hot as they once were.

With a few exceptions, most Dell and Gold Key comics from this time period are slow sellers, even in higher grades. This is probably cyclical. The same is true of ACG books, with the exception of **Herbie**, which sells well for us. Most Charlton comics have slowed, with the exception of those featuring Ditko artwork.

Auctions: We were pleased that several original owner comic collections from the Golden and

Atom Ages turned up this year in live estate auctions around the mid-west. Often, only a very few books were offered, or they were in deplorable condition. However, in September, we appeared at a live estate auction in Missouri where 2,000 books were offered. Of these, perhaps 350 were Golden or Atom Age comics; the remainder were Silver or Bronze. Notably, collectors and dealers bid very competitively against and among each other for these books, which generally averaged VG in condition. Very few lots went for less than 50% of Guide; most sold for 60-65%, and in a few instances, the winning bid was full retail. Anyone present at this auction could not help but be impressed with the confidence these bidders expressed in the current comic book market. In some recent instances, we understand that prices allegedly paid in auctions were illusory, so future auctions may be worth watching.

JEF HINDS

The market for high grade certified books has remained red-hot all year, but with the publication of the CGC census it is becoming more selective. No more are we seeing blind multiples paid for any high grade CGC book unless it is now a "Finest Known" or "Highest Graded." The frenzy we have seen on **Giant-Size X-Men** #1, **Hulk** #181, and **Fantastic Four** #48 has cooled considerably. It seems likely that this will become more important than pedigrees in determining value, since ultimately condition is more important than provenance. Historically, before certification the main reason one would pay three to six times Guide for a pedigree book is that it was very likely you were buying the finest known or highest graded copy.

CGC: Over the past year it has become apparent that if a book is VF or less or restored, it does not pay to have it certified. It seems like the worst defect a book can have is to be restored. There should be three categories: unrestored, repaired and restored. If what you see is all original except for a micro color touch or glue spot or small tear seal or centerfold reattachment, then the book is repaired and it should be noted in the grade or on the blue label. If a number of those things have been done and the book's cover has been washed

© STAR

The L.B. Cole cover helps boost the appeal of **Startling Terror Tales #11.**

and/or had missing pieces re-created in a comprehensive attempt to cosmetically raise the apparent grade and eye appeal, then that is restored and, if certified, should get a purple label and be further subdivided as to extent and quality of work.

I've had and sold several hundred CGC books and I'm very pleased with the prices they realized. It has become apparent that they've adopted a coin grading approach moreso than the traditional comic grading standards. What is paramount to them is physical wear: stress marks, blunted corners, tears, wrinkles and creases, but not aging and deterioration defects such as paper color and loss of gloss or suppleness. Eye appeal and white pages don't get factored in very much. CGC also needs more consistency in their page quality designations. I've sent them books with snow white pages that came back labeled "off-white." Then I've sent books with noticeable edge tan that came back as "white pages."

Internet Sales: I am an eBay Gold Powerseller with over 6,000 positive feedbacks and no neutrals or negatives. We do 500 to 700 lots per week. eBay is great for selling low and high grades, keys and CGC books above VF+, and for selling $10 to $50 more common Silver Age books at roughly 70% to 75% of Guide. It is not so good at selling mid-grade books worth $100 or more at Guide. Those do better at a convention or in a print ad. One interesting aspect of eBay is the number of books we sell to people that are not even comic collectors.

Going Up: Archie #1, very rare book, high demand; **Strange Tales Annual** #2; **Startling Terror Tales** #11 (L.B. Cole Spider cover); all DC war books, crime, horror, sci-fi, and romance.

Going Down: Non-original **Classics**, **Treasure Chests**, **MAD Magazines**, **Looney Tunes and Merry Melodies**, **Walt Disney's Comics & Stories.**

ED JASTER (JASTER COLLECTIBLES)

Sales were very strong almost all year. Convention sales were very good, although down from last year's dizzying totals. The one exception has been mid grade Golden Age. This area is getting too expensive for the average collector. The other trend is the chasm developing between traditional (ungraded) and certified (CGC) markets. While the product is ostensibly the same, they are virtually two different hobbies.

Among the key books, **FF #1**, **AF #15** and **Wonder Woman** #1 seem relatively inexpensive. These books sell repeatedly at 1.25 to 1.5 times Guide in all grades. In DC, **Wonder Woman** tends to sell well above Guide in all grades and eras. Pre-1955 Dell is very cheap. How can a **Four Color** from 1942 and a **Four Color** from 1960 be worth about the same? Pre-hero DC is too pricey as well. Some DC second tier keys are still very high, specifically **World's Fair** 1939 and 1940 **Big All-American**.

CGC: There are two types of comic books – CGC 9.4 or better, and everything else. It has become clear that 9.4 (unrestored) is the standard. Pricing 9.4 or better books is almost folly. There is little or no value to slabbing books under 9.4. Some books might gain marginally in value when slabbed, but these gains are negligible when compared to traditional pricing. Non-key books in 8.5 or less actually sell at a discount to non-certified books.

Internet Sales: I have sold over 4,000 lots on eBay in the last two years. Generally, I use eBay for three types of books: items I don't want to carry in inventory; items that will do better on eBay; and CGC graded Marvels. The first category includes westerns, Dells, Gold Keys, Charltons, damaged/incomplete Golden Age, low and mid grade Silver Age sold in groups, and funny animals. Typically I will only buy this material very cheaply. It is astounding to me that someone always wants it.

Titles in the second category include **Richie Rich**, **Little Dot**, and **Katy Keene**, which usually do very well. There is strong demand for this material, but that demand is coming from people who are not in the hobby mainstream. These people have little idea of what a price guide is, and certainly don't travel to conventions or buy CBGs or CBMs. In the final category are Marvels in 9.0 or better and certified keys in any grade. Any Marvel key will sell on eBay when it is in a Universal Holder at or above traditional sticker prices in any grade. Marvels (non-keys) in 9.0 or better will fetch sticker price or better 90%

© DC

Wonder Woman sells above Guide in all grades and eras. (#200 shown)

of the time. In 9.4 or better, amazing prices are always achieved.

JOE AND NADIA MANNARINO (ALL STAR AUCTIONS)

The popular culture phenomenon has grown by leaps and bounds over the past year. We saw the trend develop over the past decade or so, and it is our belief that it will continue to mount. In our opinion, an auction forum is the most accurate reflection of current market cash transactions. We saw enough record prices shattered this year to know this is true.

The Internet (particularly eBay, basically a convention everyday) and CGC graded books continue to add fuel to the market. Courtesy of CGC, we saw the elimination of two major stumbling blocks – fear of restoration and inaccurate grading. This coupled with the availability of non-conventional market pricing and information, through eBay, has boosted consumer confidence, and in turn has translated into record prices.

This enthusiasm must be tempered with a dose of reality. There are outside forces exerting power on our hobby. The economic downturn has taken its toll on summer conventions and sales. The old precept of supply and demand will stabilize prices and things will level off, possibly to higher planes than prior to this feeding frenzy. Meanwhile, enjoy this burgeoning market as a buyer and seller, because there are still bargains to be had out there.

PATRICK MARCHBANKS (GOLDEN AGE COMICS AND GAMES)

New collectors and investors have been swarming our hobby and the results have been mind-boggling. Prices realized for high grade Golden and Silver Age keys have been higher than ever. Any Golden or Silver Age book in VF or better quickly sells and most of the time at multiples of Guide. Low to mid grade books continue to sell consistently and even restored books have seen an increase in realized prices, most likely due to the fact that the average collector cannot keep up with the astronomical prices being paid for high grade unrestored material.

CGC: To date I have had nothing but positive experiences with encapsulated comics. They have raised sales both online and off. Encapsulated books give buyers enormous confidence in the book they are purchasing. It allows them to focus more on a book and not worry about the possibility of restoration, a missing page or some small detail that they could have overlooked. CGC simply eliminates guess work and makes for fast, easy transactions.

Internet Sales: eBay continues to head the list. Most Golden and Silver Age books will sell for around Guide. Prices continue to be higher for CGC books on the Internet, simply because they give the buyer a sense of security that promotes high bids. Unrestored books that grade VF or better and are graded by CGC almost always bring multiples of Guide online.

MICHAEL R. MCKENZIE (ALTERNATE WORLDS)

Last year, certification was a license to print money as the supply of certified books remained restricted due to growing pains by CGC. There is growing evidence that as the supply of certified books grows, and the data regarding the numbers and conditions of certified copies is made public via the CGC population report, the buying public will become more selective. This is turn has begun a slow but definite shakeout of the speculative frenzy of CGC certified books and a more stable and predictable pricing environment. It is always important to reiterate that eBay auction prices represent the maximum value that is supported at that time in the market, whereas the Guide tends to reflect a more aggregate price level. It should be noted that for two identical condition high-grade comics, one certified and the other not, the certified copy will almost always command the premium. This creates the illusion that a certified book is somehow a different product than its identical, non-certified counterpart.

We have been selling Silver, Bronze and Modern books primarily through the collectors at our retail store this year with a few periods of regular Internet sales on eBay. Most of our new comic buyers are not interested in buying old comics (although I know that many of them have been collecting and reading regularly for 20-40 years

and probably already have fairly complete collections of the books they like). That leaves a small but active and dedicated group of buyers for the older material.

Key issues in all grades seem to be the order of the day. Major and minor keys, and even un-discovered ones in Silver and Bronze, are regular purchases. This includes first issues, first appearances (of major and minor characters), origins, anniversary specials and any other issues of particular note. There seem to be very few completists filling out runs of titles, except for **The Amazing Spider-Man**, which outsells every other title. Interest in Spider-Man is further fueled by the anticipated summer 2002 movie release, and could well bring a public recognition of comics not seen since 1989 with the release of the first Batman film. There continues to be increasing numbers of Bronze Age collectors re-entering the market as that age group enters their period of greatest earnings, just as the kids of the '60s did before them.

© MAR

Amazing Spider-Man outsells every other title for many dealers.

The quality and strength of the new comic market has a direct bearing on the sales of back issues. If new comics are well written and exciting, it draws in new readers and re-invigorates the existing base, and that leads to greater interest in the previous history of those characters (i.e. back issues). We are in the midst of a comic renaissance the likes of which have not been seen before, and Marvel Comics once again is the leading publisher of quality new comics. It is also well documented that the Marvel characters tend to be the most popular in general among fans, and that Marvel back issues far outsell the nearest competitors in Silver and Bronze sales. Although the back issue market has been brisk and growing these past several years, a renewed and sustained resurgence of Marvel characters in the new comics market could be an early sign that the best is yet to come. It is also a possibility that a sustained slowdown in the national economy could derail these rosy forecasts or some other unforeseen event such as (gasp, choke!) the final bankruptcy and death of Marvel, but that doesn't appear as likely as it did one year ago.

The 'no reprint' and 'no overprint' policy of Marvel's new comic line, combined with the quality of these books, has helped to fuel a new wave of speculator frenzy that is only just beginning. We have regularly sold the under-printed **Ultimate Spider-Man** #1 (white variant cover) for around $100 on eBay (now bringing an average of $150), and the #2 variant easily brings $30. The more available **Ultimate X-Men** #1 can easily be found in the $10 range. The newly released **Origin** #1 (featuring the never-before-told origin of Wolverine) was closing on eBay for an average price of $12 - $15 the day it was released. Look for more of this activity in the near future.

Like no time in the past, the word "restored" carries a very negative connotation regarding price and collectibility. Of course, the unrestored example will always command a premium over the restored copy, but the mere presence of restoration should not be such an automatic disqualifier of desirability. Hopefully, there will soon be a more serious examination of this subject. There needs to be a designation that notes the difference between professional archival quality (and reversible) restoration and the non-professional and irreversible type.

© DC

DC 100 Page Super Spectacular #5 is a favorite rare comic of the Bronze Age

DALE MOORE, JASON MCKIBBEN (CLARENCE ROAD)

CGC: We have enjoyed great success with buying and selling CGC books. Clients we refer to CGC are always happy to receive their books. What many people find is that their own grading skills are seriously in need of fine-tuning. Shying away from CGC books are those content in their own ignorance. We have enjoyed the hunt for high grade material, as it has become a cannonball run/scavenger hunt/holy grail type of situation. Those who grade honestly and accurately will have the future of our industry well in hand.

Internet Sales: We have enjoyed great success on the Internet. We have also found generous response to our non-profit efforts, like Comics 4 Kids. We give Code-approved comics to children so they can appreciate literacy and perhaps become future collectors.

Going Up: Prices for Bronze Age in high grade should be rising as CGC kicks into gear. The percentage of these books that remain unslabbed will be comparable to unrestored Golden Age keys.

Some of the rarest comics of the Bronze Age include **Cerebus** #1, **DC 100 Page Super Spectacular** #5, **Marvel Spotlight** #2, **Chilling Adventures in Sorcery** #1, **Hot Wheels** #1-6, **Batman** #232.

Going Down: Modern comics – artificially high print runs and variant cover madness really don't lend themselves to a rare state of existence. Low print and underground titles like **TMNT** #1 command a premium as they are rarely found in any grade. Pacific and Atlas in high grade are moving up, not down. Most issues and titles from the last ten years sell well at cover or less.

RICHARD OLSON

The market for Victorian and Platinum Age books is stronger than ever! With the Guide listing these books, collectors are better informed about their historical significance. Unlike modern comics, which may be found in grades of NM and even MT, these books usually exist in grades from Poor to Fine, and sometimes VF. Books in higher grades are extremely rare.

Most buyers are true collectors. Because demand greatly exceeds supply, these books are typically purchased as fast as they are found. Dealers can't maintain stocks, and eBay auctions always do well.

In addition to the books themselves, most collectors also collect related materials, like art, sheet music, games, etc. In the past year for example, original Yellow Kid art brought record prices, with "The Toastmaster" breaking the six figure mark. Yellow Kid posters routinely sold for $3,500 to $7,500.

TERRY O'NEILL (TERRY'S COMICS)

2001 has been a slower market for comic sales. There was still a high demand for high-grade Bronze and Silver Age comics. This was true mostly for Marvel titles. Fortunately, I was able to locate enough of the nicer books to keep up with this demand, and most of the better books were from original owners.

Golden Age: Timely comics have slowed down at conventions and even on the Internet. Since most dealers have paid high prices to have a few in stock, the amount that collectors shell out to get one in any grade has become formidable. Nonetheless, they still seem to sell. Most Golden Age superhero books were selling fast at, or slightly below, Guide. Mid-forties to mid-fifties DC titles have been really slow. These books are still scarce, so most of the collectors looking for these books have their collection near complete. On the other hand, I bought some Nedors and MLJ superhero books and found that almost all of these sold fast at, or slightly above, Guide. Most Golden Age comics are moving within two to three months of purchase when priced according to market. Even with strong sales, it still takes a long time to recover your initial investment. I have been paying higher percentages of Guide to get certain titles.

Atom Age: This group is as scarce as ever and demand is still strong. Pre-code horror has been the slowest group because of asking prices and not lack of desire. Crime titles are showing up on more want lists. The prices are still affordable and you usually get some good artwork and stories. Westerns have slowed down a bit, but they continue to move. Certain titles like **John Wayne, White Indian** and the **Durango Kid** always sell fast. Atlas/Marvel western titles such as **Two-Gun Kid, Rawhide Kid** and **Kid Colt** are in very high demand. DC war and sci-fi titles are being requested but mostly in lower grade.

Atlas titles are my specialty; most have great stories and art while being still quite affordable. It is becoming harder to find them in large collections. **Strange Tales** and **Journey Into Mystery** precode titles sell the best, followed by **Adventure into Weird Worlds** and **Menace**. Romance and teen comics continue to be in high demand. Even the higher priced books are starting to move. Matt Baker art is almost always a quick sell, while the L.B. Cole covers have cooled down. Early **Archie** titles are always good movers. Funny animal comics are selling better, but still at sizable discounts. **Tarzan, Lulu, Gene Autry, Dick Tracy** and other popular long

Journey Into Mystery pre-code titles sell the best. (#1 shown)

© MAR

running titles continue to be good sellers. Over all, the Atom Age is the most diverse era; there always seem to be customers for them.

Silver Age: This era continues to be the mainstay for most dealers, with Marvel being the king. **Amazing Spider-Man** and **X-Men** are still the best sellers, but early **Thor** and **Avengers** have also been selling fast and often over Guide. **Fantastic Four** below #30 are hard to find in any grade and usually sell fast. The star titles of DC are **Batman** and **Detective** from the late Silver Age. Most of the second-string titles, such as **Tales to Astonish, Strange Tales** and **Blackhawk**, are still selling. My nomination for the most underrated book from the later Silver Age would be **Sub-Mariner** #1. I sell it almost immediately every time I get one, and I don't get them very often. Tower comics are always sought after but are rarely in stock. Charlton, Dell and Gold Key continue to sell, but seldom at full Guide. There are a few exceptions, such as titles with Steve Ditko and covers with popular celebrities such as Lucy, the Beatles and the Monkees.

Bronze Age: A strong runner-up to Silver Age in sales. It is certainly much easier to get books from this vintage in high grade. The crazy high prices for earlier age books does not apply here yet. There are a few titles, such as **Night Nurse** and DC's love giants, that are truly hard to find in high grade. There will undoubtedly be many more titles that prove hard to find. But will any of these be the next **Hulk** #181? Some books that I have a lot of requests for but seldom stock are: **X-Men** #94, **X-Men** #100, **Iron Fist** #14 and **Marvel Spotlight** #5. The aforementioned **Hulk** #181 always sells fast in any grade if a copy can be found. Some popular DC titles are **Phantom Stranger, Witching Hour, Shazam!** and **Ghosts**. Marvel titles include **Conan, Chamber of Chills, Dr. Strange, The Defenders** and, back from the dead, **Howard the Duck**. Of the few other Bronze Age publishers, only Charlton's Ditko issues and high number **Twilight Zones** are in demand.

Magazines and Independents: The magazine market seems to have turned into a fanzine market. This seems to be the best-selling genre of my magazine inventory. Also of note are the higher number **Epic Illustrated** and **Savage Sword of Conan** titles. All the Epic magazines have good artwork and stories. The same thing goes for **Savage Sword of Conan**, which has to be the longest running single character magazine. Those few magazines that feature love and romance are also very sought after.

Modern Age: The only modern comics I stock in quantity are independents and **X-Men**. **X-Men #266** is by far the most requested modern book, followed by **Daredevil #158** and **Wolverine** V1#1. **Miracleman** is the most requested independent title.

RON PUSSELL (REDBEARD'S BOOK DEN)

Golden Age: The cornerstone of the hobby. Collections are very difficult to obtain. Demand far outstrips supply. CGC certified books have driven the high grade copies to record heights. Most of the mainline titles in less than Fine sell for 75%-145% of Guide. Sales were solid throughout the year at these prices.

1930s Titles: Although this is not a large area of collecting, supply limitations still govern prices. DC titles were still the most requested. One can only expect the existence of between 0-2 copies of an issue that could be certified in 9.4 or better with at least off-white to white pages.

1940s Titles: Superhero titles still lead the way. DC is the hottest area followed by Timely. Early years from this time period may have between 0-3 copies of a book that would possibly certify in 9.4. The war period books would number usually between 5-25 copies of a book capable of a 9.4. DCs and Fawcetts would be the easiest to find due to their popularity when originally published. Fox would be much scarcer due to poorer paper quality. Some of DCs most popular characters from this time period may have up to 50 copies or more of a book that may certify in 9.4.

DC: Mainline superhero titles in higher grade sell at 125%-400% of Guide; in lesser grade the books were selling for 80% -150%. Key scarcer issues sell at even higher percentages. Best-selling are **Batman, Superman, Flash**, and **Green Lantern**.

Timely: Steady demand and sales. High grade copies for most titles sell for 125%-400% of Guide, lesser conditions sell for 80%-150%. **Captain America** titles are still the most popular. Solid demand for **Human Torch, Sub-Mariner** and their related titles. Good sales for all superhero titles.

Fawcett: Still led by **Captain Marvel** and his

Daredevil Comics #3 is one of the Lev Gleason best-sellers.

© LEV

related titles, sales at 70%-140% of Guide in lesser condition, and 115%-300% of Guide for higher grade. Good sales for **Spy Smasher** and **Captain Midnight**.

Centaur: Further gains are still linked to Timely values. Books are selling at 75%-145% of Guide in lesser condition, and 120%-325% in higher grade.

Fox: Superhero titles sold at 75%-145% above Guide in lesser grade, and 125%-325% in higher grade. Continued strong demand for early Lou Fine covers.

Gleason: 70%-140% above Guide in lesser condition, and 115%-275% in higher grade. Best-sellers are still **Silver Streak**, **Daredevil Comics** and early issues of **Boy**.

Fiction House: Good Girl art continues to lead to above average sales. **Planet** is still the most popular, followed by **Jumbo, Jungle, Fight, Rangers** and **Wings**. These sell for 70%-140% over Guide in lesser condition, and 125%-285% in higher grade.

Quality: Lou Fine titles still lead the way. 70%-140% in lesser condition and 120%-280% in higher grade. Sales of **Blackhawk** and all related titles at 70%-135% over Guide in lesser grade, and 120%-250% in higher grade.

MLJ: 75%-145% of Guide in lesser condition, 125%-325% in higher grade.

Classic Comics: Moderate sales for #1-50 1st editions in most grades. Slow sales on #51 up with a few exceptions.

Funny Animal: Most requested publishers are still Timely and DC. Very small gains for all publishers. Sales at 55%-125% of Guide in lesser condition, and 110%-200% in higher grade.

Atom Age: Continues to be a hot area. Demand still exceeds current supply. Fox is still the most popular publisher. Demand is very strong in all grades due to their relative scarcity. Print runs were much lower during this time period for many publishers. Possibly between 5-25 copies in existence of each book that will certify 9.4 or better. Since Fox had resorted to using remaindered paper when publishing their books, page quality can vary enormously for this publisher. How brown are the pages when the book has been published using pink, blue or green paper?

Dell/GK: Good sales on lesser condition titles. Most collections of older books have large amounts of lesser condition Dell/GK titles. Carl Barks Duck One-Shot and early **Comics & Stories** are currently unavailable in high grade at current prices. Where are all those high grade copies of prior years? The fact that these remain in private collections still says a lot about the collectiblity and desirability of Barks books.

Atlas: This publisher is still very popular. Horror/science fiction titles still lead the way at 90%-145% of Guide in lesser condition, and 125%-295% in higher grade. Crime titles are selling well at 75%-135% in lesser condition, and 120%-275% in higher grade.

Key **Showcase** issues like #45 lead DC Silver Age.

© DC

EC: Horror and SF titles are still very popular with sales at 70%-135% of Guide in lesser condition, and 135%-325% in higher grade. **MAD** comics still lead the way at 75%-140% of Guide in lesser condition, and 145-335% in higher grade. Gaines file copies continue to sell for record prices. ·

Westerns: Average sales led yet again by the photo cover issues. Gene Autry titles sell well.

Giants: If reasonable, annuals sell well in lower grade. Sales in higher grades at 100%-225% of Guide. Most collections of older books have large amounts of lesser condition Dell Giants that sell OK at 65%-90% of Gide.

Romance: Large demand. Sales at 80%-135% of Guide in lesser condition, and 125%-300% in higher grade. Fox romance titles are still very hot. Sales in lesser condition at 105%-195%, and 135%-350% in higher grade.

Good Girl Art: Solid demand. Phantom Lady remains the most popular. Atlas titles have above average sales. Large demand for the recognized cover classics. Sales at 80%-150% of Guide in lesser condition, and 135%-325% in higher grade

Avon: Good sales for horror/science fiction titles and crime titles. Sales at 75%-150% of Guide in lesser condition, and 125%-315% in higher grade. Western and war titles are still a bit slower. Sales in lesser condition at 65%-135%, and 115%-245% in higher grade.

Horror/Science Fiction: Still the hottest area of the Atom Age. Very good sales and demand at 90%-175% over Guide, and 150%-395% in higher grade. DC horror/science fiction titles still have a solid following, but higher prices have tem-

porarily slowed sales.

Sports: Good demand at 70%-150% in lower grade, and 125%-300% in higher grade.

Art Titles: Baker is still selling very well at 90%-180% of in lesser condition, and 145%-400% in higher grade. LB Cole sells at 75%-165% in lesser grade, and 135%-385% in higher grade. Good demand for Wolverton horror/science fiction titles with sales at 85%-175% in lesser condition, and 140%-395% in higher grade. Ditko and Kirby books still selling well at 80%-170% in lesser condition, and 135%-385% in higher grade. Above average sales for Kubert books, with sales at 70%-155% in lesser condition and 125%-360% in higher grade. Very strong sales for Frazetta work with sales for lesser condition at 90%-180% and 145%-400% in higher grade. Krigstein, Toth and Williamson requested at a slower rate then those previously mentioned with prices at around 65%-150% in lesser condition, and 120%-350% in higher grade. Katz and Torres demand slight in comparison to others. Prices at around 60%-145% in lesser condition, and 115%-340% in higher grade.

Silver Age: Highly impacted area from Internet trading. Good sales of lesser condition books via the Internet. These same books continue to sell slowly from mail order catalogues or at conventions. Most sales over Guide are still in the high grade area. Hottest Marvel title is still **Spider-Man**, followed by **Fantastic Four**. DC is led by key **Showcase** and **Brave And The Bold** in high grade. With the advent of full scale comic book dealing in the early 1960s, high grade scarcity became greatly reduced. One may expect between 15-100 copies of each pre-1965 book to exist in a certifiable 9.4 or better. The period of 1965-1970 would probably produce between 50-250 copies of each book capable of a 9.4 or better.

Bronze Age: Record prices are still being realized for very high-grade copies of mid-'70s books. Sales of better condition books from this period sell very well at both conventions and the Internet. Due to wide spread collecting, this time period will have between 100-1,000 copies of each book capable of a 9.4.

MARNIN ROSENBERG
(COMICCOLLECTORS.NET/ COLLECTORSASSEMBLE.COM)

Amid all the positive feedback from dealers about how healthy the comic book genre has become over the past few years, there are a few things that I find increasingly troubling.

The greedy misuse of CGC certified books by dealers and obsessive collectors/investors has caused prices to escalate to a unrealistic level that has left the majority of collectors clamoring for the good old days, unable to ever afford the books they desire in ultra high grades. To this date, ComicCollectors.net has mostly avoided the certification of approximately 80% of its inventory. Fortunately, there are still many collectors who trust the non-certified grading of a company which has offered consistent grading for 35 years.

CGC has caused the many loose graders in our hobby to tighten up their grading skills considerably. In cases where certain dealers simply could not grade, and/or could not stop themselves from restoring and/or selling restored books, CGC has either thankfully forced them out of the hobby, or forced them to certify every book in their inventory in order to make a sale. Initially, CGC graded loosely. Then, when faced with criticism, went in the opposite direction, undergrading NM 9.4s as NM 9.2s and sometimes as VF/NM 9.0s.

© MAR

Competitive bidding for lower grade Timelys sends prices into the VG range.
(Young Allies Comics #4 shown)

For quite some time, I refused to allow CGC to turn books I had graded and easily sold as uncertified NM 9.4s into undergraded 9.2s and 9.0s, because the disparity between a 9.4 and everything else below it is becoming an ever widening monetary gap, translating to tens of thousands of dollars.

I intentionally submitted six books I had Susan Cicconi restore for me. All six came back in unrestored holders! I don't claim to be a expert when it comes to identifying restoration, but CGC makes that claim and blew six for six with me. Conversely, both myself and other collectors and dealers have gotten books back from CGC denoting restoration

that when sent to Susan for a second opinion were found to be restoration free.

CGC is a wonderful tool for our hobby for many more positive than negative reasons. Those have been well publicized; the dangers of CGC have not. These dangers occur when an all-too-trusting collector base places too much trust in only one certification company that has no competition. As more and more collectors support CGC, the higher the prices will be for those self-same collectors who will realize they can no longer afford those books. In addition, the more dependent today's collectors and dealers become on certified books, the more they will find the art of holding, smelling and grading a comic book will become obsolete. Face front! 'Nuff said!

MATT SCHIFFMAN

Low Grade Books: Golden and Atom Age books in lower grade (GD+ and lower), surprisingly brought well over Guide prices, especially key books and Timelys. Double and triple Guide seems to be the norm for these books, bringing close to Guide in the higher grades. Timely in lower grade came very close to bringing VG prices through competition of bidding. Those in VG brought only close to Guide. Barring keys, the FN Timelys did not bring FN prices and were closer to VG. A grouping of grades from GD to FN- seem to all bring the same prices, with only grade leaps made in the VF or better books.

Mid Grade Books: Golden Age and Atom Age books, especially DC, Standard Nedor, and Dells, were lucky to bring anywhere close to Guide. When a mid-range DC hero book is on eBay, it is very lucky to get even close to VG prices. Even mid-grade **Detectives** and **Actions** are lucky to bring 50% of Guide on eBay, and many dealers are stock-heavy and unable to move them. This is a trend that has been developing over the past three years and does not seem to be able to reverse itself.

Disney books are extremely overrated and are lucky to bring even close to Guide in any grade. This trend continues in Bronze Age, with VF/NM and down selling for much the same prices; that is usually around the VG level. Even GD books bring a bit more than Guide, but FN and VG are lucky to achieve Guide levels.

CGC: The main difficulty over the past year is trying to reconcile the CGC prices on high grade material and their identically graded counterparts that have yet to be slabbed It would be a mistake to assume that these prices apply across the board, as they seem to only apply to those in holders (Marvel Silver being an anomaly of that) unless purchased from a reputable dealer. Of course, it is extremely evident that the standard ratios of the past have broken down even further with the advent of CGC.

Golden Age: Timely continues to lead the way quietly behind the scenes of the Marvel Silver Age hype. **Sub-Mariner, All Select** and **Captain America** sell for well over Guide in all instances except in VG to FN, and those are lucky to bring Guide. DC books, unless they are true keys, are very lucky to bring Guide. Those books in high grade are asking such high multiples of Guide that many have not been moving, leading to market apathy when one does come up for sale. Standard Nedor key issues do very well in all grades, especially the Schomburg war or 'Good Girl.' Otherwise, they do not do well at all. In lower than VF, without a war cover, the book tends to bring only about 35% of Guide. New icon covers are breaking out and even replacing the old ones. Centaur, Fox and Fiction House continue to have very strong followings.

Atom Age: Growth in this area was also the largest again this year, outside of high grade Marvel Silver. Westerns were up as they easily crossed over outside our hobby and made gains in huge increments, especially in the lower grade issues, with **Red Ryder** leading the way. As a percentage, the pre-Code crime books gained the most over the last year, followed very closely by the romance titles. DC is still the most popular, but the smaller publishers continue to make inroads and with larger leaps in price. Fox romance continues to be the sleeper and most sought after this past summer. 'Good Girl' as always leads the way, but without the largest jumps in pricing. Since these books are so difficult to find in grade, the lower grade books have made the most gains.

Collectors have discovered the Seven Seas titles and have pushed those prices upward in all grades. GD books – Fox, Standard Nedor, Star, and more – all had huge gains in the lower grade

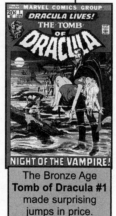

©MAR

NIGHT OF THE VAMPIRE!

The Bronze Age **Tomb of Dracula #1** made surprising jumps in price.

copies and have broken down the traditional ratios, with GD at 20-35% of NM. Pre-code horror continues to be very popular but difficult to find, tempering demand. Lower grade books can be found, and do sell for a bit over Guide. Keys and rare issues continue to astound, but not as heavily as last year. Also, the war titles have made huge jumps, often selling in any grade to collectors outside of the hobby and to war buffs. Atlas and Harvey are quietly gaining in popularity and tough to find for even the most ardent collectors. Prices have been pushing higher over the past eight months and show no signs of slowing down.

Silver Age: The high grade market drove the entire genre, and for most of 2001, Marvel superheroes drove the market, brining upwards of 10 times Guide in the CGC holder or not. If the grading could be trusted, **Spider-Man, FF, TOS** and **X-Men** brought the same multiples throughout the year. It was rare to see any high grade Marvel for sale by any dealers out of a CGC holder, on eBay, on their site, or at a convention. DC was only slightly behind. Price ratios really fall out of historical relevance in the Silver arena. VF- and below (excluding keys) are even lower this past year than ever before. Good will bring up to around $10 to $15 and not much more than that, while Fine is lucky to bring even 30% of Guide and VF- is lucky to bring 40%. My opinion is that the Silver Age needs another shot in the arm.

Bronze Age: Bronze books in high grade have made some of the most astounding gains over the past year. With the triumvirate leading the way – **X-Men #94** and **GS #1**, and **Hulk #181** – records continued to be set. **Tomb of Dracula** #1 and **Tarzan** #207 surprised many with their huge jumps. Another pleasant surprise is the monumental jumps in high grade DC war titles. Unfortunately, with collectors focused on the ultra high grade books and the stiff affordability of them, the prices for VF/NM or lower are well below Guide ratios. Non-key GD books are lucky to bring 5% of Guide and even VF- or lower can be lumped into one price, usually around 20% of Guide. No one wants these books and no one is paying for them. The Bronze Age books have pushed out in interest to around 1980, and those in high grade seem to be doing very well into the 1980s. DC Horror reprints and 52/48 page books are extremely popular and bring huge multiples in high grade, with **Secret House of Sinister Love, Dark Mansion,** and **Werewolf by Night** leading the way.

DAVID H. SINCERE & JEFF McMANUS (SINCERE COMICS)

The market seems to be in an upswing, with new comic sales up 20-25%. Anything that doesn't sell directly off the newsstand can be guaranteed to quickly move as a trade paperback. We feel more like a bookstore everyday. There is a genuine interest in comics from 1960-1975, which are being bought by all customers both young and old.

Silver Age: Books from the early 1960s are really taking off. Key issues, especially low grades, and popular titles are in extremely high demand. The biggest sales are not at conventions but on the Internet and in the store. **Amazing Spider-Man** is generally selling for approximately 35% over the prices listed in the Guide. **Spider-Man, X-Men, Wonder Woman, Green Lantern,** and **Batman** are this period's hot sellers.

Most books in the late 1960s are slow movers unless they are in high grades. Hot titles include **X-Men, Wonder Woman,** Popular TV Comics, **Amazing Spider-Man, Batman, Green Lantern, Archie** Comics, Disney Comics, and Harvey Comics. Interest in **Silver Surfer** has increased greatly due to eBay.

We have a reputation of having the largest Silver Age collection in Alabama, Southern Georgia, and the Florida Panhandle. We've bought more Silver Age comics in the last year than we've bought in the last five years combined.

Bronze Age: The interest in books from the 1970s continues to increase. Sales in this area have not been as strong as they could be due to the limited collections offered. Hot books from this period are **Wonder Woman, X-Men** (especially #94), Bernie Wrightson Horror covers, **Weird Western Tales** (Jonah Hex appearances), and **Amazing Adventures** (Beast appearances). Warren Magazines (particularly **Vampirella**) are also becoming popular again.

Marvel: Marvel finally has strong editorial direc-

© AP

Many Archie fans are coming to conventions with long want lists.

tion; it's very unfortunate that the business side is run so poorly, with a bad fill ratio on trades, especially the **Essentials** line. Also, with print overages at 1-2%, we are unable to reorder sufficient amounts of popular titles. We think Marvel is looking at this the wrong way. It's not how much money they are making, but how much money is potentially lost due to short print runs, the retailer's inability to reorder new comics, and the nearly nonexistent stock of trade paperbacks. Marvel's sales should be up 20-25%, if not 35-45%. The only good side to Marvel's printing flaws is that although initial sales are hurt tremendously, the resale market will benefit greatly. Other companies plagued with short print runs include TokyoPop and Viz Communications.

Archie: There has been a strong demand for **Archie**; we have doubled our sales in the last year. 80% of books sold are generally graded from Good to Fine. Generally, **Archie**s are able to sell from $1-3 in any condition. We were amazed to see people at conventions with long want lists. Last year, we sold over ten long boxes of **Archie Comics** from $1-5.

New Comics: New comic sales have increased substantially since last year, averaging approximately 25% increases for all titles. 50-100% increases in titles which were selling poorly in previous years is not uncommon. Generally, the people entering the market are ages 15-20. 80% are buying newsstand comics, on a monthly to bi-monthly basis. The other 20% are buying trade paperbacks. Trades that are selling are primarily manga and DC, although Marvel is making a strong showing with their **Essentials** line.

Back Issues: There is very little demand for comics from the '80s and '90s. Most popular titles can be easily found at $1 each. Most movement in these books comes from mainstream Marvel titles and hot DC titles, such as the **Justice League of America** and **Wonder Woman**.

We feel that in the next year, there will be a 15-20% growth increase in our store. We are all but giving up conventions due to the decreasing sales, and major costs incurred from travelling, not to mention the shows themselves. The only positive note is that cons provide a great buying ground.

We feel that the Internet is our largest growth potential. Through eBay and Yahoo! Auctions, and our ever-growing storefront on Auctionworks.com, we are gaining customers from all over the United States, Canada, and the United Kingdom, not to mention the rest of Europe, Australia, Japan, and continental Asia. The potential for us to sell $15-20,000 a year is not far-fetched. It's become relatively easy for small businesses such as ours to become a medium-level player in the market today.

DOUG SULIPA (COMIC WORLD)

CGC: CGC graded comics are now a permanent part of our market. Only about 1 in 100 vintage comics is worthy of slabbing due to the high costs of encapsulation. Record prices have already subsided and are now becoming more predictable and stable. Requests for high grade copies and unslabbed books is near an all-time high as buyers try to save a few dollars.

Most CGC activity is with traditional well-known key issues and mainstream titles, especially Marvel, followed by DC. Buyers of slabbed comics see the best known titles as the safest buys. Oddball titles do not seem to fare as well. Many new "investors" and returning collectors are buying certified comics. Those who bought too early in the CGC market now find they cannot recover initial high prices paid. These buyers should consult knowledgeable dealers before paying high multiples. Especially down in value are the multiples paid for 9.6 to 10.0 comics post-1985. Many 1970s comics are scarce in strict high grades, but especially those from 1970-1974. This has stopped slabbing of many pre-1975 Bronze books and has skewed the view of rarity by condition. Many long-time high grade collectors are resisting paying the "new" multiples for slabbed copies and instead lowering their expectations to VF unslabbed copies.

The CGC Population Report is already an important reference for the market. Prices have already turned downward on all over-slabbed books. Many do not even recover the cost of slabbing. New **X-Men** and related titles have suffered the biggest downturn. Buyers have now decided they want the best existing copies, so the great scavenger hunt has begun. Most of the best

© MAR

CGC-savvy buyers only want the best existing copies of newer X-Men titles. **(X-Men #1 shown)**

copies, especially in Silver Age, are in permanent collections – thus we may never know what the best existing copies are.

Most Silver Age graded less than 9.0 now bring below Guide, as buyers are spoiled by all the high grade copies in the current market. Issues judged to have minor restoration go at fire sale prices. These two groups are perhaps the biggest bargains in CGC collectibles.

Restoration: Professional grading has all but destroyed the market for restored books. Dealers cry the blues when a CGC book comes back with the dreaded purple label. Silver Age comics in apparent VF or better now bring only GD to VG range prices. Golden Age does better, but still below Guide in general. The pro restoration experts report most of their traditional business is all but gone. This is insanity, as perhaps 25-50% of all comics over $1000 have some amount of restoration. A formula needs to be made to relate the amount, type and mode (pro or amateur) of restoration to price. In most other collectibles, preservation is a positive feature and can increase value, but this is not dealt with in our hobby. Preservation should be encouraged, not shunned. Some of the best deals in our hobby are now beautiful, restored books which are currently avoided like the plague due to lack of knowledge and firm hobby guidelines. Unpreserved comics may continue their current deterioration and desperately need to be treated by professionals. This needs to be addressed immediately, before we lose all the restoration experts in our hobby.

Theme and Completionist Collecting: This has been perhaps our strongest year ever for theme collecting. Huge libraries and potential museum collections are being built daily through eBay and accommodating dealers. The Internet has made this type of collecting blossom. This is one of the most challenging and exciting areas in our hobby today, yet it remains affordable to most.

The strongest theme markets and items we sold heavily this year include one panel cameos or larger (parodies included), appearances in anything of; vampires/Dracula, Spider-Man, Sherlock Holmes, girl spanking panels, Archie swimsuit covers, and golf covers.

Other themes include: Amazon women, author

adaptations (Poe, etc.), Black people, Black heroes, Bondage, Cheerleaders, Chess, Christmas, Crossovers, Devil/Satan, Dinosaurs, Errors, Female Heroes, Halloween, Last issues, Lingerie panels, Monsters, #100s, Nudity panels, Out of Character, Paper Dolls, Politically incorrect panels, Religion, Robots, Rock/Music star, Slavery/Slaves, Space/SF/Rockets, TV character parody, UFO/Flying Saucers, Time Machine/Travel, Titanic, Torture panel(s), various Wars (WW-II, Civil War, etc.), Werewolf, Witches/ Witchcraft, and Zombies. In addition, many collectors are now competing to get one copy of each and every appearance of their favorite character or artist. Character favorites include: Capt. Marvel/Shazam, Edgar Rice Burroughs characters, Flash Gordon, Hanna-Barbera, Howard the Duck, Hulk, JLA, JSA, Phantom, Pulp heroes, Robert E. Howard characters, Silver Surfer, Spider-Man, Wolverine, and Wonder Woman.

Captain Marvel remains a character favorite.
(**Shazam! #1** shown)

© DC

Platinum Age: The revised section in the Guide has more collectors looking at this market. While not a hot market, it is rather steady and has its serious collectors. The Internet has made more new finds possible. Many items sell below Guide on eBay as buyers do not think to search for the item on the week offered. Many items in this category are historically important, but lost and unknown to current collectors. Surprisingly, when compared to Golden Age prices, almost everything seems a bargain, especially when scarcity is considered. We had several requests for Yellow Kid, but had none.

Our bestsellers included: **Bringing Up Father, Buster Brown, Disney, Little Orphan Annie**, and **Mutt and Jeff**. Much is still unknown, as these museum-bound relics continue to age. Perhaps more prudent buyers should look again at these historical gems. They started it all and need to be preserved, studied and appreciated.

Silver Age: For perhaps the first time, all grades seem to be selling well. The lowest and highest grades are still the most popular, but attractive mid-grade copies have really begun to move. This is likely due to the new record prices on high grade. We have noticed that almost everything under $20 sells, especially low grade readers under $10. Perhaps the only Silver Age that are

around in surplus quantities are Marvel superhero comics from 1965-1968. Most issues from 1963 and older, as well as 1969-70, move out fast.

We do very well with war, teen, cartoon, love and western titles because we have monster selections with little competition. Customers no longer expect to find these in high grade and usually choose between reading copies and highest available grades. The shortage of most 1969-1973 superhero comics grows bigger as most are still undervalued in the Guide. Many 1962 Dells and 1963 Gold Keys remain elusive and continue to enjoy high demand. All comics published by Tower are again up in demand. Good artist comics are still in big demand. Early Adams and Wrightson are particularly hot. More buyers are discovering Alex Toth, and we expect future price rises. Pre-1965 Ditko and Wood has always been hot, but recently the demand is notable for 1965 through Bronze Age issues.

Most long-time proven series, especially those that still publish today, were very strong sellers. Demand for all Silver Age giants was relentless with little supply, especially on non-hero genres. Oddball comics and giants are not around in high grades, save for file copies and pedigree collections. Buyers should either lower expectations or prepare to pay high market values.

Bronze Age: Because they are still affordable and findable, the Bronze Age comics are perhaps the most widely collected category. Just as most buyers used to begin with Silver Age a decade ago, now they strive for Bronze keys and sets. SA has priced many casual and new buyers out of the market. Once they have dabbled a while in Bronze and begin to become advanced collectors, many will choose to move into SA or GA titles, but many will instead become Bronze completionists. This era is hot.

Buying patterns suggest that the Bronze era ends with **Secret Wars** and **Crisis**. There are currently more completionists in this era than any other, causing anything uncommon to scarce to continue elevating in price. Any grade sells, but most popular are still highest grade investment copies and lowest grade reading copies. There are just not enough high grade copies, especially of 1969-

1973 era comics, to meet demand.

There is still a shortage of almost all traditionally non-collected titles and it grows each year as more disappear into collections. Shortages of high numbered issues from many cancelled titles continue. In general for comics post-1974, the #1 issues are the most common and the final issues the least common.

All non-regular format items continue to sell well and at over Guide, including: magazines, fanzines, digests, treasuries, paperbacks, promo items, giveaways and all types of memorabilia. Superhero comics have made a big comeback, followed by strong demand for everything horror, and finally by relentless demand for traditionally non-collected titles. Atlas-Seaboard, Archie's Red Circle and Warren are very high on many collection completion agendas. All giants were in big demand, as are treasuries and digests, all scarce in true NM. Many buyers find reprint titles an affordable way to collect SA and older titles.

Modern Age: The slowest comics on the market are mostly from the 1987-1993 era of mainstream Marvel and DC titles. This is where the most overprinted and over-hoarded comics of all time exist. If you are a reader on a low budget, this is where you should go. Before you write off this era, you should look again, as many future collectibles abound.

The new comic market and back issue market now survive independent of each other. The back issue market is growing; the new comic market has slowed its shrinkage and slump. New comics now have very small print runs, with almost no one stocking recent back issues. Thus, if you miss a recent title, it can be very hard to find. Most new comic shops have dropped back issues from their valuable floor space because their market is not buying. Post-1994 comics one day may actually gain respectable value by virtue of their tight print runs. The spillover Bronze titles of 1980-86 remain in high and growing demand, especially high numbers of titles cancelled in the period. All publishers and genres that died in this era had low final print runs, and as collectors try to fill in runs, many remain elusive.

Most newer comics are too volatile to firmly

© ATARI

Mini-comics like **Atari Force #1** are among the most popular promotional comics.

report. Many of the best selling post-'80s comics are alternates, especially: Popular artists and writers, TV/Movie, character and cartoon, manga, comic strip reprints, horror, 3-D, sports/personality/rock titles, and most items known in other media. Modern Age comics graded by CGC have slowed dramatically in price, many not even selling for the cost of slabbing, as the Census shows how common they are in high grade. Modern books may begin to disappear from the CGC market until they become proven long-term investments rather than fads.

Promotional Comics and Giveaways: Promotional comics continue to intrigue and mystify collectors. They are difficult to collect due to low supply, condition and lack of knowledge. eBay has brought many onto the market, with 100s still unlisted in the Guide. If one includes the many variants, there are about 100 Spider-Man titles alone not yet in the Guide. Anything with a popular character, artist or theme sells with little resistance to price or condition. Literally 1000s of regional giveaways, non-character titles, and especially post-1980 titles, many of very little interest, remain unlisted.

Supergear Comics and **Boston Pops' Biff Bam Pops with Spider-Man** would easily bring $500-$1000 in high grades if you could find them. The most requested promo comics this year were: **The He-Man/Masters of the Universe** and **She-Ra/Princess of Power** mini-comics that came with the action figures, including variants, plus the DC mini-comics from Atari games like **Swordquest** and **Atari Force**. All promo comics based on long-standing, proven characters showed more demand than supply. Completionists pay the highest prices for these items.

Limited Editions and Variants: We get many requests for virtually unfindable variant editions, like Gold, Platinum, signed and numbered, polybagged specials, cover variants, etc. On any popular character, we can get well over Guide. These were made to be scarce and are. They can be very frustrating to collect, as it takes too much legwork to find them. This, plus the fact that there are too many, holds down values. There is something inherently wrong with new items made to be scarce, because if they catch on, endless quantities of small editions can be easily made, as was done in the sports card market. This leads to diluted prices and slow sales. Only completionists stay long in this market, thus strong characters and artists are the safest bet.

The slowest segment of this market is the signed and numbered editions that come with a Certificate of Authenticity. Vintage variants, on the other hand, are in big demand. Demand is directly related to character popularity. Marvel 30-cent price variants sell from five to twenty times the regular issue price for a character like Spider-Man. Marvel 35-cent price variants sell for two to three times the multiples as compared to 30-cent variants. One of the most common variants is **Star Wars** #1, but it brings the highest multiples only because it has been documented for 20 years and has reached mythical status as a collectible.

Artist Issues: Most Silver Age era and older artists remain steady in demand, but many Bronze and newer era artists have gained huge followings. One segment of the market wants anything ever printed in any format on their favorite artists. The most sought artists are: Byrne, Kirby, Jones, Miller, Perez, Steranko, Starlin, Toth and Wrightson. Other hot artists include: Neal Adams, Baker, Boris Vallejo, Corben, Ditko, Eisner, Glanzman, Golden, Heath, Newton, Wendy Pini, Alex Ross, Don Rosa, Dave Sim, Barry Smith, Sutton, Wood, and Wolverton. Many will buy reprints when available. Many 1968-1975 issues by the above artists are in very high demand and are due for increases, especially Neal Adams, Charlton-era Byrne, Don Newton, most pre-1980 Perez, everything with Steranko, and all Wrightson.

British Editions: We had another great year selling UK Reprints of USA comics. Great selling was the Alan Class Pub. 1960s-'80s B&W squarebound giant reprints of USA horror and SF titles, with some superhero from Atlas, ACG, Charlton, Archie and others, in the $5-$15 range. As fast as we find them, we sell the 1960s featured all-new UK-only material digests from World Adventure library, including: **Batman, Superman, Phantom, Flash Gordon, Man from Uncle,** and others, selling in the $10-$25 each range. We sold 100s of the UK weekly comics by Marvel from the 1967-

© Lucasfilms

The 35¢ cover variant of **Star Wars #1** has reached mythical status as a collectible.

1982 era for $3-$15 each. We imported and sold many of the 1980 era British Marvel "pocketbook" Comics Digests in the $5-$12 range. The hot UK Marvel Digest output includes: **Chiller** #1-27 (Dracula, Man-Thing, etc), **Conan** #1-13 (Smith-r), **Fantastic Four** #1-24 (Kirby-r), **Hulk** #1-13 (Kirby and TTA-r), **Marvel Classics** #1-12, **Spider-Man** #1-22, **Star Heroes** #1-11 (**Micronauts** and **Battlestar**; becomes **X-Men** #12-up), **Titans** #1-13, **X-Men** #12-28, and **Young Romance** #1-10.

We also sold 100s of the superb UK-only '50s-'80s war comic digests like **Commando, War Picture Library,** etc., in the $3-$20 range. British hardcover annual collecting is fast growing in demand. These annuals are still a bargain and sell in the $10 to $50 range. The rare to scarce '50s and '60s **Superman** and **Batman** annuals bring prices in the $50-$200 range. Most requested are annuals which had no US equivalent, or all-new UK stories and art. Also hot are the dozen or so original UK **Classic Illustrated** titles that have no US equivalent, averaging around $100+ in VF. The most famous of these is **Dr. No**, which was reprinted as DC's **Showcase** #43. The uncensored and racist-implied UK **Classic** #158A version of **Dr. No** sells in the $300-500 range for higher grades. Blazing Hot were the '70s UK full color **Vampirella** mags #1-4 in the $50-$100 range.

Canadian Editions: Many new record prices are being set lately, with four books recently breaking the $1000 barrier. The EC title **Weird Suspense** #1 and the vintage **Super Comic** that is the Canadian Edition of **Pep** #22 and an FR copy of the Canadian Timely **Capt. America Annual** sold for about $1500 at a UK auction. Last year, the **Roy Rogers Annual** brought $1500 in VG/FN. The Canadian editions that are vintage variants of US comics attract the most attention and best prices. They survive in quantities of 1-20 copies on most of the GA Canadian variant issues of Archie, Atlas, Avon, Classics, DC, Dell, EC, Fawcett, Fiction House, Lev Gleason, Quality, Timely, Toby, and others. The EC reprints still bring 25%-35% less than US edition due to poor printing quality. The Western titles by Dell and Fawcett bring about 75% of the US editions. EC and westerns had the highest survival rate.

The other GA variants' selling price is related to Guide value. Highly desirable characters and artist issues bring 100-300% value of US equivalent for books that Guide in the $10-$100 range by condition. Most surviving copies are FR to VG. Titles that Guide in the $101-$500 range by condition sell for 75-150% of US equivalent. Titles that guide in the $501-$2000+ range by condition vary widely from 25-75% of US equivalent. Many generic Giant Annuals exist with leftover copies rebound in new covers, often mixing contents. Depending on contents, VG copies bring $50 to $200 each or more. Everything published by Superior remains scarce and in demand, at 25-50% over Guide, as love and horror collectors continue to seek these gems.

The rare all-new material GA "Canadian Whites" are in high demand with no supply, in the $35-$100 range for GD-VG average copies. The Fawcett hero titles, with US comics re-drawn by Canadian artists, are hot, especially issues with Captain Marvel that sell for $50-$150 in the GD-VG range.

Due to growing awareness, Canadian cover price newsstand edition variants are rising in price and demand. May to August 1968 Canadian 15-cent cover price variants of all Gold Key titles now bring 150-200% guide values. Completionists and variant collectors are paying 200%-300% guide for the Canadian newsstand variant editions of the 1980s Marvel (10/82-8/86) and DC (10/82-9/88). It is now known that most 1981-1984 Whitmans also had a Canadian cover price. Canada also had a fairly big French language edition industry from the '70s thru the '90s. DC and Marvel French titles in VG average sell for: 1960s ($10-$25), 1970s ($6-$15), 1980s ($3-$9).

Many large softcover Giants exist, with rebound leftover French comics bound with a new outer cover, and sell for $10-$30 in VG depending on contents and age. '70s and '80s French language Archie digests and comics from Quebec sell for $3-$10. The fastest sellers were issues with Betty and Veronica, Josie and Sabrina.

Foreign Language: We imported a great collection of French digests, which typically consist of horror titles. Loaded with great Marvel and DC Bronze Age reprints and artists, many of these sold fast. These French digests also contained reprints

of Italian sex and gore comics, plus similar all-new material horror comics. These vintage digests dated from 1975-1985 and contain graphic covers and rampant bondage, nudity, and violence, art that would never be allowed in the USA market yet were normal items in their market. Jaded US horror collectors love them.

We also imported and sold many European Disney digests, many with new European stories and art, some reprinted in Gladstone, plus vintage Barks reprints. Finally we imported a collection of **Spider-Man** digests from Brazil and sold most of them as soon as we received them. Most of the Foreign digests moved from steady to fast in the $4-$12 range. Foreign language editions of any popular US characters and artists are in demand. Value is determined by content and formats, which include comics (color and B&W), magazines, digests, graphic novels and others, typically in the $4-$12 range.

Comic Digests: These little gems are like mini trade paperbacks and are loaded with great reprints of o/w expensive vintage classics, artists and characters. Low supply and scarcity in high grade makes them great collectibles. Many are trying to complete the DC digests set, with Best of DC #41-up still elusive. Some have new material, notably **Adventure** with new Shazam stories and **Best of DC** #10, with the first-ever origin of Penguin. Some stories are only otherwise seen in the legendary **Cancelled Comic Cavalcade**.

DC Special Blue Ribbon Digest #20 has been known to sell as high as $125, with #21-24 also being scarce. The **Jonah Hex** digest was hot. All the Gold Key digests remain in high demand, but especially **Mystery Comic Digest**. We sold several Whitman variants of the GK digests in the same price range. **Golden Comics Digest** #2, 7, and 11, the Hanna-Barbera issues, are our most requested of all digests, with the **Tarzan**, **Turok** and **Lone Ranger** issues also enjoying high demand. We bought these at over Guide and sold even higher.

Fiction Illustrated #3 (Steranko) was hot, with the large TBK version being scarce and selling instantly in the $75+ range. Many people have begun the big task of finishing **Archie Digest** sets. All '70s issues and keys brought over Guide.

© DC

Rare in high grade, DC's digests are a great collectible. **(Best of DC #24 shown)**

Shocking Tales #1, and **Archie Superhero** #1-2 and all other Archies with Neal Adams or other artists are always top sellers. '70s Harvey digest are finite sets and thus easier to collect, so more buyers are asking. Marvel digests are in steady demand, including **G.I. Joe, Spider-Man, Star** and **Transformers**. The Skylark digests of **Doc Savage** and **Twilight Zone** remain rare. We discovered and sold '70s Charlton digests of **Space-1999** and **Flintstones**; these are quite rare in any grade.

Fanzines: Fanzines have become a very popular collectible. They are loaded with early and obscure works of now famous artists and writers (many never reprinted), plus have in-depth articles, pinups, covers and art on all the popular characters. Many items are very hard to find and therefore sell for top dollar in any condition. 1960s 'zines had print runs in the 100-500 copy range; untold quantities of historical info are in their pages. A good fanzine/prozine collection can be like gold. In very high demand were: **Squa Tront, Spa Fon, Foom, Amazing World of DC, Marvelmania, Comics Journal, Comics Interview**, art of titles (Byrne, Adams, etc), **Witzend**, etc.

Horror: Next to superheroes, horror was the strongest seller for post-1960 comics. In magazines, it was the best seller. Warren had a banner year, in part due to the **Warren Companion** and recent attention in fan media. All scarcer Warren items brought 50-100% over Guide. Marvel mags are strong sellers and still diminishing in supply. All Marvel horror sold well, but best-selling was the '70s Atlas reprint titles, with NM #1s bringing up to double Guide. Eerie the publisher later became Modern Day Pub., with its final titles **Terrors of Dracula** and **Weird Vampire Tales** being the most elusive. Stanley Publications were hot because of finite titles and pre-Code reprints. All Skywald titles were in very high demand (**Psycho, Nightmare** and **Scream**) with high numbers bringing 50-100% over Guide due to almost no supply. Even at the higher price levels, **Web of Horror** is hard to find and sells instantly. **Famous Monsters, Charlton's Mad Monsters, Horror Monsters, Fangoria** and all photo horror mags sold well. **Movie Monsters** #1-4 from

Atlas/Seaboard were in high demand in the $15-$20 range for FN copies. Every DC horror title from 1968 through the'80s was hot, with all issues in any grade selling. Even the assorted 1980s horror alternates sold well, especially Quality titles from Pacific, Eclipse, etc.

Humor and Parodies: The four main parody mags are **Mad, Crazy, Sick** and **Cracked**. Now over half the issues we sell are based on the satires they contain as opposed to people who collect the entire title. Thus prices can vary widely, especially at auction. It is common to get from $5-$15 for VG '70s and '80s issues, regardless of Guide value by condition. **MAD**s from #86-150 are scarce in high grade, as they are early fold-in issues. **Cracked** before #120 are in short supply. **Crazy** #81-94 had smaller print runs and are scarcer. All **Sick** mags had lower print runs, but especially #1-50 and 120-up. **Help** from Warren has had a large increase in demand. **Help** mags are scarce in high grades, especially #11-20, which all have spines that split easily. **Help** mags bring in the $15-$35 range for VG copies. All parody titles seem to be moving better, whether color or B&W.

Other great sellers include: **Humbug, Trump, Eh, Go-Go, International Insanity, Inferior Five, Not Brand Echh, Plop,** and **National Lampoon**. Those who love obscure and oddball are seeking: **Brother Billy the Pain From Plains, Wacko, Parody, Goose, Great Society, Bat Fink, Ape, 1001 Jokes, Apple Pie,** and others. **National Lampoon** in particular has Bronze Age issues loaded with great artists like Jones, Wrightson, Barry Smith, Adams, Frazetta and many more. Most 1973-1980 issues in VG with this caliber of artists bring in the $10-$15 range in VG.

Miscellaneous: Oddball comics remain very popular, but have lost some momentum to CGC and the return of superhero demand. Collectors seem to be sampling most affordable obscure titles from 1945 right through to 1990. We have dusted off and are now often looking at titles not asked for in years, even vintage obscure funny animal. Up in demand are the very early appearances of **Peanuts** in United Feature titles of 1952-54, including: **Fritzi Ritz, United Comics, Sparkle,**

© MAR

A good prozine collection can be like gold.
(FOOM #17 shown)**

Sparkler, etc. At ACG, all artist issues are up in demand, along with **Herbie** and superhero issues. **Gasp, Midnight Mystery** and **Magic Agent** sold fastest as smaller and easy to complete sets. All small output publishers are in demand as they fascinate buyers. Many have asked for **Mod Love** by Western, but none have turned up at any price, which makes us wonder if this 36-page, high-priced 50-cent cover comic from 1967 exists. Tower comics have risen sharply in demand, with everything selling, but strict VF or better copies are very elusive, as all their titles were squarebound giants. Still hot are: **Fatman, Capt. Marvel** (MF Ent.), **Henry Brewster, True Comics and Adv.** (1965 Parents), **Fast Willie Jackson, All-Star Story of Dodgers, Golden Legacy, Wham-O Giant Comics**.

Religion: Religious comics, especially Christian comics, were again very strong sellers this year. We had customers trying to complete their Spire titles, and with most, condition did not matter. The single printing 1980s titles are getting harder to find and bring highest prices at about $7-$15 for FN or better copies. **Hansi, The Girl Who Loved The Swastika** sold instantly when located at $15 range in FN. **Archie** Spires are the best-selling of all Christian comics. The **Barney Bear** Spire activity books remained scarce and sold out at $20 each.

The Marvel titles are fast sellers and getting harder to find. The scarcest issues are **Illuminator** #3, #4 ($7-10) and the **Pilgrims**

© MAR

Issues of **Our Love Story** are climbing in demand. (#1 shown)

Progress TPBK ($15-$20). The DC Bible treasury was hot in the $15-$25 range. The Cosmics Pub and United Bible Society Pub titles all had low print runs and poor distribution, with VG copies bringing $5-8 each.

Red hot again was the 1977 classic **Marx, Lenin, Mao and Christ** by Open Door Pub at $25 for VF. Low grade reading copies of **Treasure Chest** sold well, but there was resistance to high grades. Crusaders, with great art and over-the-top themes, sold well at $5-$10 each, but #15-17 remained scarce. **Dennis the Menace** and the **Bible Kids** were hot at $6 each in VG, but #7-10 had only regional distribution and were unfindable. They could easily bring triple Guide. All the Catechetical Guild one-shots are in very high

demand, and sold in VG/FN at $10-20 or more.

Romance: Love comics now sell well from all eras. This still remained one of the most unexplored areas of collecting. Most of the major name artists in GA, SA and Bronze Age history tried their hand at love comics; much of these artists' scarcest work lies here. Strict high grade copies remain almost nonexistent. Kirby art issues brought 20% to 50% over Guide. All key, first and last issues, good artist, good cover, and neat theme issues bring premiums of 25-100% over Guide.

Atom Age and Silver Age issues are typically low grade and thus cheerfully cheap, so we sold many in the $7-$20 range. Painted covers sold best, followed by photo covers, with lesser demand for line drawn covers. Atlas Marvel titles sold twice as fast as any other publisher. The Classic Steranko Mod story in **Our Love Story** #5 is easily the most requested and sells instantly in all grades. A CGC 9.4 copy is estimated to be worth in the $500 range.

The reprints in **My Love** #23, **Capt. America Special** #2 and **Young Romance UK comic Digest** #3 all bring double Guide. **My Love** and **Our Love Story** are by far the most requested, and will continue to climb in value due to big demand. The Kirby, #1, and giant issues all bring 50-100% over Guide. **My Love** #20 was red-hot for the Starlin art. DC titles sold well, especially anything with a name artist and all Giants. Toth and Adams cover issues were the most requested.

We helped fill many Charlton runs for buyers this year, all being equally scarce from 1965-1979. **Soap Opera Love** and **Soap Opera Romance** both appeared on many want lists and remain in low supply. We sold many issues of the scarce **Teen Love Stories** mag from Warren for $25-$35 each. Atlas/Seaboard's **Gothic Romance** #1 and Marvel's **Gothic Tales of Love** #1-2 are all scarce and in huge demand, with VF+ copies bringing $150-200+ with ease. IW and Super reprints titles are now about forty years old and sell for about $10 each for a nice FN copy.

Teenage (non-Archie) Comics: Beyond Archie, most people would be hard-pressed to name five teen comic titles, yet there are dozens. These comics have suddenly become extremely collectible in all eras, but especially in post-1960 titles. The main appeal is scarcity, but people soon realize many of these comics are quite enjoyable. This is one of the most forgotten and overlooked genres.

The single hottest title is **Vicki** from Atlas/Seaboard, with #1-2 being elusive, hot and fast-selling. **Vicki** #3-4 are scarce due to endless demand and no supply, with VF or better copies bringing $50-$75 each on eBay. The second hottest series this year is **Millie the Model**, with the "Blonde Bombshell" issues from the early '60s being most requested and #192, 200-206 and Annual #1-5 being elusive. Annual #1 is perhaps the scarcest Marvel annual, and a NM copy would easily bring triple Guide. **Chili, Patsy Walker**, and **Mad about Millie** all sold well at 25-50% over Guide. **Tippy Teen** was the third most requested, with many trying to complete runs. Issue #26 and #27 likely do not exist, as 100% of want lists have them on it. Teen-In remains more elusive. **Bunny** by Harvey is highly sought, low in supply and contains great art requested in this genre.

On Pre-1960 titles, the Marvel Atlas sell two to three times as fast as any other publisher. All issues that have paper dolls, if identified, bring premiums. But one has to be careful, as these comics are notorious for having pages missing, especially in squarebound annuals, where they are hard to detect. Most Pre-1960 series are too scarce to try and complete, so buyers buy what they can find, or buy samples of each titles, or buy by condition/price range. All grades are selling.

Vintage **Katy Keene** had slowed for a while due to high prices, but has begun to heat up online. Many grew up with these and many want them for the paper dolls. The more affordable 1980s series is actually hot, with higher numbers having low print runs and bringing $10-$25 each on eBay, often even in mid grades! The **Katy Keene** digests are now scarce too and bring $7-$15 each. Charlton's **Ponytail** has gained momentum and are already hard to find.

TV/Movie, Toy, Cartoon: TV and cartoon titles continue to have strong demand. Hanna-Barbera was perhaps the hottest. '50s and '60s TV photo covers have leveled a bit, mostly in favor of lower priced and affordable '70s-'80s titles. Movie comics without popular themes have slowed, but those with good actors, horror and Disney titles still move. TV titles and TV cartoons of the 1975-1985 period were hot with titles like **Happy Days, A-Team, Masters of the Universe, Strawberry Shortcake, Space**

1999, Battle of the Planets, Smurfs, Transformers, G.I. Joe, Care Bears, Ewoks, Droids, Scooby Doo, Rock Comics, Kiss, Madonna, Blip, parody mags and others.

War Comics: Most buyers actually read all these comics rather than just invest. DC was still the most requested, with **Sgt. Rock** easily the fastest selling. There was a big shortage of copies on **Our Army at War** #83-120, and #190-220 in all grades, and they sold as fast as we got them at 25% over Guide. All **OAAW** #83-280 sold well, and high Grade copies brought premiums up to 50% over Guide. **Unknown Soldier, Enemy Ace** and **Haunted Tank** were all in very high demand, double-hot for all key and minor key issues. **Weird War** remained very hot, especially #1-10, with CGC copies bringing high premiums.

The pre-series '50s issues in the $100-up range were slower but moved occasionally. DC keys from 1958-1970 all sold very fast. We sold endless copies of every war comic from any company that was priced at $5 and under, with condition not being important. Atlas titles are very much requested and sold as fast as we found them. All Marvel war sold well, except for **Sgt. Fury** #14-80. **War is Hell** #9-15 was hot and are still undervalued. Many buyers tried to build high grade Marvel sets and happily bought our pedigree "SOO" (Sault Ste Marie) original owner collection copies at 50% over Guide.

G.I. Joe was by far the hottest title, especially the scarce high numbers from #141-155. We could easily sell a CGC 9.4 copy of #155 at around $100. Also hot were issues #1-27 and #93-120 at 25-50% over Guide. The digest brought double Guide in condition. All Charlton war sold very well, especially '60s and lower print '80s issues. All artist, series-within-series, and key issues were much requested and brought 25-50% over Guide. We got in four big collections of the classic UK **Weekly War** comic digests from '50s-'80s and had a banner year with them. The '60s Dell titles – **Combat, Jungle War,** etc. – are much in

AYYY**Y!**
What gives?
The Fonz a thief?

© Paramont Pictures

Happy Days (#3 shown) is one of the hot TV titles from 1975-1985.

demand. All '50s obscure titles sold well if in the $5-$20 range.

Westerns: Dell and Fawcett sold steady, with nothing being hot. There is still resistance to all graded above FN, but no problems selling GD and VG copies. Best known characters outsold shorter TV titles. Alex Toth art issues sold extra well due to double demand. Most difficult to keep in stock were **Western Roundup, Lone Ranger** #1-40, #131-145, **Red Ryder** #51-100, all **Sgt. Preston**, and all **King of The Royal Mounted**. Charlton westerns that finished Fawcett titles outsold the latter by 3-to-1 and even brought premiums. The Gold Key titles sold faster and were in smaller supply than most Dell titles. Charlton westerns again moved well, especially series-within-series issues, any key or minor key issue, giants and artist issues. Westerns continue to sell well for specialists, but slow for dealers with low selections.

All Marvel western titles sold well in all grades. Many collectors bought our pedigree "SOO" collection copies at 50% over Guide, with all giants selling instantly. Vintage and reprint Kirby art issues were all top sellers. **All Star/Weird Western** #1-38 were top selling at DC, with CGC copies of #10 bringing record prices. **Jonah Hex** comics and digests, **Johnny Thunder, Trigger Twins** and most '50s DC titles sold steadily. We picked up a 300+ issue Atlas collection of westerns, and best-selling were **Rawhide Kid, Kid Colt, Two Gun, Western Gunfighters**, and all with art by Kirby, Heath, Severin and Maneely. We also sold many popular and obscure '50s westerns by lesser publishers, with most in the $5-$20 range moving fastest.

Skywald: The B&W mags **Nightmare, Psycho** and **Scream** are red-hot. Demand is consistently twice that off supply, and we sell all fast at 150-200% Guide. **Psycho** #22 does not exist and is likely a special they forgot to double number. All better artist issues sell twice as fast. **Nightmare** #20 with the first Byrne is in huge demand and commands up to $100 in high grades. Fans have discovered that all issues written by Al Hewetson are among the best-written comics in horror history and influenced the likes of Stephen King. All are scarce to rare in strict 9.0 VF/NM or better. All

There's a feeding frenzy for later **Vampirella** issues. (#113 shown)

the squarebound color comic titles are again up in demand. **Tender Love Stories** are scarce and easily brought 200% Guide. Next in demand were **Heap** and **Jungle Adventures** at about 150% Guide.

Walt Disney: All Disneys that have been over-reprinted, mostly the Mickey and Duck titles, are still slow in originals. When they do sell, they are usually lower grade cheaper copies. There is resistance to high grade prices on most of the $100 and up classics. But most under $50 and especially under $20 titles still sell steady, with many buyers filling in runs of the more affordable eras. We now suspect that the rare Whitman **Uncle Scrooge** #179, **Donald Duck** #222 and **WDC&S** #480 were released only in Canada, as this is where they are usually found. Most non-reprinted titles sold well, with animation titles selling best. Best-selling Disneys included **Animation Movie Classics, Aristokittens**, all Annette, **Beagle Boys**, Dell and GK giant issues, Don Rosa art issues, Dynabrite titles, foreign editions, many **Four Colors**, Gladstone digests, '70s variant issues with posters, **Jungle Book** treasury, **Moby Duck, Scarecrow, Super Goof, Walt Disney Comics Digest** (GK), **WD Paint Books, WD Presents, WD Showcase**, pre-1980 Whitman variant issues, **Winnie the Pooh** and **Zorro**.

Warren: Warren mags have come of age, as many are now attempting to get a complete set. **Creepy** and **Eerie** middle numbers were still in low supply. High numbers of **Creepy, Eerie** and **Vampirella** were scarcer due to low final print runs and difficult to re-stock. **Creepy, Eerie** and **Vampirella** roundbound mid-series issues were printed with spines that split easily and thus many are scarcer in high grades. This year, demand for high grade copies tripled and they now outsell low grade readers that sold best in previous years.

All issues with color sections sold faster, and top artist issues are bringing decent premiums. **Vampirella** has several issues among the most valuable Bronze Age comics and thus is an important title not to be overlooked.

Whitman: Five years ago all comics by this publisher were shunned, but now that knowledge is growing, they are gaining hot status. This compa-

© WB

Does **The Searchers Four Color #709** have the best John Wayne photo cover?

ny had perhaps the most varied and wildest of printing schedules by any newsstand publisher ever. The Scarce Whitman pre-packs are in high demand on almost all titles, with almost no supply. It is estimated that about 20-25 copies of **Uncle Scrooge** #179 are known and the high prices have peaked and leveled at about $200-300 for VG and $700-1000 for VF. **Donald Duck** #222 and **WDC&S** #480 remain rare and VF copies bring $100-$200. **Battle of the Planets** #7-9 are next in demand, at $50+ in VF. The 11/71-2/80 Whitmans are variants of Gold Keys and sell to completionists for 200-300% of GK issue values. All Whitmans from 8-12/1980 are confirmed scarce, all with poor distribution Next is the un-dated, no Code issues from 1983-84. The 127 known Whitman variants of DCs in 14 titles have a growing number of completionists, and variant collectors seeking them out, with most bringing $5-$10 for VG to VF.

HARRY B. THOMAS

The collectors' market is the best it has ever been. Most of my dealing over the last four years has been via eBay. I was one of the first convention dealers to go in that direction. One big-time dealer recently remarked that eBay was a "wholesale business" – not so! Almost every major dealer and thousands of collectors are now online and buying on eBay. Some mail order dealers can still raid listings and sell at multiples of Guide to their regular customers. eBay has proven a few things: every comic book will sell if the opening bid at least gives the buyers a chance at a bargain, and a high reserve or opening bid gets lesser results.

Books from Good to Fine will generally bring Guide or better, especially the more collectible books. F+ and up seem to struggle to reach Guide and dealers risk a lot listing very high grade and pedigree books without a protective reserve.

I still detest, from a collector's standpoint, the whole idea of slabbing. I like what's inside, art/storywise, and not just a cover. I do see some problems coming with CGC and pedigree books. With CGC grading, will there be an effect on pedigrees? For example, the Mile High collection has long been perceived by collectors as the best. So far I have seen or heard of very few Mile Highs being graded by CGC. For years, Mile Highs have brought from double to 10 times Guide. Now, if CGC grades these books at say 8.2, 7.7, are they now worth a multiple of Guide? I maintain that with a CGC graded non-pedigree book at 9.2, and the same book with a pedigree at 8.8, the pedigree now means nothing! Is this why the pedigree books are not being sent in any great quantity to CGC?

Late '40s and early '50s books are super hot on eBay - any company from minor lines like Ajax to popular lines like Atlas, Dell, and DC. Dells from this period sell well in any grade; these are probably the most popular listings at present. **Little Lulu, Roy Rogers, Gene Autry, Tarzan** and the entire **Four Color** run bring good returns when listed. All the later photo cover Dell **Four Colors** based on TV shows are now starting to really move.

Restored comics are alive and well; collectors still love them. I have sold many from my own collection and most have brought very decent prices – many All Stars, for instance, approached the price of the condition to which they had been restored! Too much press is being given to the high end, high grade investors over the backbone of the hobby, the collectors who spend millions each year. The folks buying the high end books have the money to do so and the air at that level is thin. Investors buy the book for its value or to say they own it, but collectors buy the book for its aesthetic value and enjoy it for what it is. Very few people in the hobby can afford the high grade books and really pay little attention to that end of the market.

Going Up: Key Dell **Four Colors**, **Little Lulu** issues, the two **Four Color Tarzans**, all the **Lone Rangers**, **Roy Rogers**, Barks ducks, regular **Roy Rogers** #1. **The Searchers** is one of the most undervalued comics out there. It has the best John Wayne photo cover ever, it has a classic movie adaptation, and it is scarce in high grade. Sought by movie memorabilia fans, John Wayne fans, western fans, John Ford fans, etc. Very high demand. A NM copy would bring multiples of Guide.

Going Down: Except for #1, all **Looney Tunes**. Later issues of **Daredevil** and **Boy Comics**, Lev

Gleason crime titles, and maybe mid-run to later issues of Fawcett westerns.

MICHAEL TIERNEY (COLLECTOR'S EDITION)

This year's 'Diamond in the Gravel' was the Holy Grail of comics for historian Bill Jones, author of the upcoming **Classics Illustrated: A Cultural History, with Illustrations**. A collection of early **Classics Illustrated** yielded a rare Giant edition of **An illustrated Library of Great Indian Stories**, containing four stories by James Fenimore Cooper. Despite a lifetime devoted to researching the **Classics**, it was the first copy of one of these scarce Giants that Bill had ever seen.

No one knows for certain what future key investments are being printed today, because the marketplace is always in flux. The recent influx of women readers has changed Japanese manga from a curiosity to a growth leader in my stores, with Viz leading the way.

Another publisher that has been growing steadily is CrossGen. They made a wise decision to overprint their early issues and the market has since absorbed them. Watch the first issues of these series closely in the near future.

DC Comics continues to be the stable leader in the new comics industry, and that has been reflected in the sales of collectible back issues. Where Marvel was once a juggernaut and DC slow, these positions have been steadily reversing over the last decade. In the last year, I bought several Marvel and DC Silver Age collections, and it's strange to see **World's Finest** and **Blackhawk** comics selling faster than similarly priced **Amazing Spider-Man** and **X-Men**.

Marvel's aggressive push to improve the editorial content of their books, exemplified by the hiring of J. Michael Straczynski of **Babylon 5** fame to take over the writing chores of **Amazing Spider-Man**, has not yet boosted the consumer confidence that has been falling for years. I purchased a nearly complete run of lower grade **Amazing Spider-Man** issues #1-104, with duplicates of many key Green Goblin appearances, and have sold only a few books, like the #1 issue in GD for $325. Marvel's latest relaunch of the **X-Men** comics led to the most repeated customer comment: "Don't they relaunch every other year?"

The exception for back issue Marvel sales are their black and white magazines. While even color comics of **Conan the Barbarian** by Barry Windsor Smith gather dust, the black and white **Savage Sword of Conan** magazine is a steady seller.

Internet Sales: The Internet continues to be a new factor in the hobby. It serves as an additional source of sales and purchasing material. Doing research to determine what items I wanted to auction has led to many acquisitions of gems at ludicrous prices, like a **Savage Tales** #1 in Fine Plus for only $10.

Further evidence of the inaccuracy of Internet auction values as opposed to averaged nationwide sales are the illogical patterns of bidding that occur on graded comics. Books with CGC grades lower than 9.0 sometimes sell for less than if they were not graded at all, while grades approaching 10.0 go for auction prices that could get a traditional retailer lynched.

TROPIC COMICS

Over the past year, the economic changes that American society has undergone have significantly impacted the comic collecting market. We have seen the stock market rise and fall so drastically that many investors have begun to re-evaluate the investment potential of collectible ephemera. With the rebirth of this mindset, we have seen Internet retailers and Internet auction sites receive noticeable spikes in their sales as the public more readily accesses such items on a global scale.

This type of shopping behavior has been enhanced by the renewed sense of safety and awareness that was sparked by the September 11, 2001 World Trade Center attack. Americans are finding shopping from home to be a much safer option. In the past, this would have created a great many difficulties for the more grade-conscious collector who needs to be able to see the condition of the book before purchasing it, since it is not uncommon for there to be slight differences in the grading habits of one collector to another. Fortunately, the timely arrival of CGC last year has provided shoppers

© DC

Silver Age **World's Finest**s are selling better than similarly priced **Amazing Spider-Man** and **X-Men**.

with an efficient system of evaluation that has taken the possibility of discrepancies out of grading and instituted a standard that has restored confidence in the comic collecting market as a nostalgic hobby and a stable financial investment.

We are confident that this trend will continue, because this past year provided us with the rare opportunity to have our company's president, John Chruscinski, asked to join the grading team of CGC. Although the staff and working environment meshed seamlessly with John's personality traits, he nonetheless found that he longed to be home and in control of his own company. He resigned with the company's blessings and he looks forward to their continued success. John's belief is that CGC will continue to lead and direct the establishment of greater confidence between collectors and retailers and will aid in promoting the market's overall growth.

On the global and local sales fronts, the past year saw the closing of the physical storefront of our last retail location and the solidification of our Internet site. The market dictated to us that there was a great lull in the foot traffic that has been historically associated with the back issue collector. Our inquiries and research found that eBay, Internet shops, and the increased production and promotion of trade paperbacks significantly contributed to this trend. In response to this market shift, we found that by selling our back issues from the '70s to the present at 50% off, we were able to increase our back issue sales from 10% of our overall sales to 40%.

Golden Age: Timely and DC Comics are continuing to be strong sellers in the Golden Age market, with prices helped by the entrance of higher grade issues into the market graded by CGC. Books that feature 'Good Girl' covers and classic horror books have maintained their popularity from last year and are selling for prices that are three to four times that of Guide.

Silver Age: Silver Age books continue to be unchanged except for the spike in Silver Age keys that receive high grades from CGC. These books are commanding prices that are four and five times Guide.

Bronze Age: 1970s horror comics are receiving

© DC

Batman related titles have been seeing a consistent sell-through. **(Batman: No Man's Land** one-shot shown)

a great deal of interest from collectors and are becoming harder to find as many back issue bins are being emptied of their stock. DC war comics, specifically **Our Army at War** (the Sgt. Rock issues), are selling out with a similar regularity.

Modern Age: CGC graded Modern Age books that receive grades of 9.8 to 10 are commanding prices that are 10 to 20 times guide. This has caused the search for the perfect book to become a new hobby among some collectors, and for some on the Internet, a new business.

The Modern Age market has seen a shift this year from an artist-driven market to a writer-driven market. There has been a renewed interest in any books written by Grant Morrison, with back issues of titles like **Animal Man, JLA, Invisibles, Swamp Thing**, and **Aztec** selling out. This year also saw Alan Moore's fan base increase, with collectors picking up issues of **Miracle Man, V For Vendetta, Swamp Thing, Watchmen** and **From Hell**. The Batman "No Man's Land" stories introduced readers to a more detective-oriented writing style as DC introduced novelists into their writing stable. This has been well received, with the Batman-related titles all seeing a consistent sell-through. Marvel introduced the Ultimate universe and has found great success with its **Ultimate Spider-Man** and **Ultimate X-Men** titles. These titles are also writer-driven in their appeal, with fans flocking to Brian Michael Bendis' work on **Ultimate Spider-Man** and **Powers** (another consistent seller) and Mark Millar on **Ultimate X-Men**. The back issues for these titles are consistently sold out and with Marvel's new 'print to order' policy, they will continue to be tough to find, with **Ultimate X-Men** #1 and **Ultimate Spider-Man** #1 selling for $12.

Other titles that have been selling well are early issues of the **Authority, Planetary**, and **Rising Stars**, but the introduction of trade paperbacks of these issues have damaged the value. The recent increase in the production of trade paperbacks and collected editions of story arcs are damaging the back issue market and will continue to devalue Modern Age books as a collectible genre in the foreseeable future.

Artists who are still producing consistently collectible books are George Perez on **CrossGen Chronicles**, Joe Maduriera on **Battle Chasers**, and Alex Ross on his oversized book **Shazam: The Power of Hope**. Ross comics continue to command prices slightly over Guide, but the oversized books are falling prey to the plight of the treasury editions of the '70s in that they are difficult to store.

The books to watch over the next year will be those Golden Age books that have light restoration that can be removed and then sent to CGC. CGC graded restored books are great for the collector who just wants to complete a run because they are inexpensive in comparison to their unrestored counterparts. The investor, on the other hand, is looking for unrestored books, and although this will probably continue to be the norm for some time, this does not exclude the potential creation of a new market. As population reports from CGC continue to reveal the scarcity of some books, we will begin to see the restored book market grow into a far more volatile field. Due to their current lower prices, these books will probably prove to be the wise move for the long-term collector.

HARLEY YEE

2001 has been very strong with record sales. As with the general state of the economy, sales slowed down in the second half but still at a record pace. Internet sales through eBay have continued to become more important in the market. Some bargains can be had from established dealers, but I still hear of problems with grading on many auctions. High grade books are selling at record prices that this old-time dealer would never have thought possible.

CGC: Golden Age books graded 8.0 to 8.5 and Silver Age books at 8.5 to 9.0 are selling very well at over Guide with higher grades selling at 200-300% Guide. The 9.4 or better books are selling at amazing prices, 300-1000% are commonplace. On these grades, the trend should continue in 2002.

Internet Sales: I only started to sell on eBay earlier in 2001, and I have been amazed at how many non-collectors buy through eBay. These buyers go for less mainstream titles like **Little Lulu, Archie**s, westerns, TV/movie. These collectors have never seen a price guide and just want the books. Non-CGC

© MAR

Captain America Comics leads the way in Timely sales. (#2 shown)

books, Marvel, DC, Silver Age, and Golden Age sell at 50-70% Guide, but if CGC, they sell closer to Guide. CGC books 8.5 to 9.0 sell at over Guide but when you have 9.4 or better you never know how high these books will go.

Golden Age: This area has shown steady strength with high grade books selling at 200-300% of Guide. Low to mid-grades are selling at 110-200% of Guide. Leading the way are **Wonder Woman, Sensation, Action, Superman** and **Flash**.

Misc. Golden Age: In the other groups, Fiction House and Centaurs are leading the way with buyers feeling that they are undervalues with room to grow. Prices range from 150-200% of Guide. Fawcetts, Fox, MLJ, Quality, Nedors are all selling at a steady pace with Lou Fine covers, **Pep**s and **Master** selling particularly well.

Timely: Although the supply has improved in the last year, the supply is still tight with **Captain America** and related titles leading the way. It's hard to keep any in stock even at 200% of Guide. The other titles sell well at 150% in general.

Atom Age: These books are selling very well, with Good Girl and horror leading the way. Collectors are concentrating more on key issues from each title, which are selling for 200-400% Guide. Finding these books in high grade is still a problem, illustrated by the fact that I recently purchased about 100 high grade Fox Jungle and Fiction House and even at over 200% Guide I sold them all.

DC Silver Age: Pre-1964 books in VF or better are truly scarce and generally sell for 150-250% of Guide. Books in Fine or better are also selling well over Guide. Post-1964 books are selling well and high grade at 150-250%, but in lower grades the demand is slower.

Bronze Age: These books are now 25 to 30 years old and are still scarce in NM condition and will sell for 200-400% of Guide in that grade. Lower grade still sell very well but at nearer Guide prices.

Marvel: By far the strongest area. With the Spider-Man movie out next year, many new and old collectors are rushing to complete their runs. Also strong are **Fantastic Four** and **X-Men**. High grade books are selling for 200-400% and remain the strongest area, but these prices may be pricing out many collectors, so earlier issues in solid Fine of better are selling very well at over Guide prices.

Romance: This is another area that has seen large increases in demand over the last few years. Recent trends are to concentrate on Baker books and other key issues with these books selling for 200-400% Guide.

Archie: Sales have been very strong in all grades and even running in the 1960s books. **Archie #1-20** are rarely seen in any grade and command over 200% of Guide.

Dell/Gold Key/Disney: In general, these books are slow with large supplies. The exceptions are **Little Lulu**, early **Comics and Stories**, and TV/movie comics which are selling steady at Guide.

Going Up: Fiction House, **Archies**, Centaurs, DC war books, Atlas war/romance, Marvel Bronze Age, **Cerebus #1-20**, EC.

Going Down: Non-TV/movie Dells, non-early **FC** Disneys and **C&S** #1-50 Disneys, most later **FC** #400 and up, Dell Giants.

VINCENT ZURZOLO (METROPOLIS)

2001 has been a very challenging year. After completing initial annual financial reviews of our company and speaking with several members of the comic book community, I have come to the following conclusions: The comic book collecting and investing market is healthy. Prices on comics are either stable or increasing throughout almost every genre and time period from Platinum Age to current comics. I have seen an increase in demand for investment grade books as well as reader copies. While nobody is surprised by the first, the latter is of great comfort to us all; it means people are actually reading their comics.

The only areas in which I have seen a continued lack of interest are **Dell Giants**, movie adaptation comics and funny animal comics. **Archie** and **Pep** have had a steady increase in demand over the last two years. They are both hard to find and very undervalued. Crime comics are also seeing a resurgence with collectors.

CGC: High-grade CGC comics continue to set records. The only area I have seen a decrease in prices on CGC books is late Silver Age, Bronze Age keys and Modern Age comics where the population reports have revealed many high grade copies have been slabbed.

Internet Sales: For the first time since I started using ebay in 1999, there seems to be a slowdown in sales. Exceptions include CGC graded comics in 9.4 or better condition. I believe this is due to unfair changes in policies toward sellers, increased fees, increased fraud, poor customer service and more people opening up their own e-stores.

Pedigrees: Mile High, Gaines File Copy, the Rockford Collection and the Northland Collection have all been high in demand. Collectors and investors love these books for their incredible condition and provenance. I can't recommend Pedigree comics enough. They do sell for multiples of Guide but are well worth it.

Restored Comics: The demand for professionally restored comics has increased. With the rising prices of high-grade comics over the last two years, collectors are looking for nice books that they don't have to take out a second mortgage on their home to own. Sales on everything from key Golden and Silver to early and mid issue Silver Age have risen in demand.

Golden Age: Timely Comics have been strong sellers, with Captain America once again leading the pack. DC Golden Age has also been strong, with **Batman**, **Superman** and **Wonder Woman** among the strongest. Demand for key issues like **Action** #1, **Detective** #27, **Captain America** #1 and **Batman** #1 are very high. **Marvel Comics** #1 is also very highly sought after but not as available. Strip reprint comics like **Ace**, **King** and **Crackajack Funnies** continue to sell well. Disney comics have slowed down a bit over the last year, though early **Four Colors** and **Walt Disney Comics and Stories** do well.

Silver Age: Marvels continue to outsell all of the other Silver Age publishers. DC comics have been doing better than usual with increased interest in high-grade mid-1960s comics.

Bronze Age: This era has the largest potential for growth due to low prices and continued demand. Many of these books, while not rare, are in high demand. If you haven't started collecting Bronze Age books yet, don't worry, and at the same time don't wait.

In closing I would like to offer some advice. The most important aspects of collecting or investing in comics are learning how to grade, understanding the market, and enjoying what you are buying. Make sure to protect and preserve your collection. Collectors should enjoy the hunt as much as they do reading the comics. Investors should learn to be patient and allow time for their investments to appreciate. Until next year may your lives be filled with peace, love and comic books.

The following lists of sales were reported to Gemstone during the year and represent only a small portion of the total amount of important books that have sold.

GOLDEN-ATOM AGE SALES

Action Comics #33 VF $650
All-Select Comics #1 VG $2000
All Star Comics #29 VF- $392
All Star Comics #31 FN- $291
All Top Comics #8 VF+ $3,600
Amazing Comics #1 (Mile High)NM $16,000
Archie Comics #1 VG+ $7,000
Archie Comics #1 G+ $3,200
Batman #1 (Overstreet) VF+ $150,000
Batman #1 (Denver) NM $70,000
Batman #10 G $400
Blackhawk #27 VG+ $100
Bugs Bunny FC #187 VF $80
Captain America Comics #1 NM+ (Allentown) $265,000
Captain America Comics #1 VF/NM (Denver) $166,750
Detective Comics #120 NM $2,035
Famous Funnies -Carnival VF/NM $10,500
Famous Funnies #211 VG+ $213
Flash Comics #9 VG $435
Green Giant #1 VF $16,500
Hit Comics #5 (Mile High) F+ $3,000
Humbug #1 G/VG $50
Jumbo Comics #88 NM $200

Marvel Comics #1 G $19,000
Marvel Mystery Comics #10 FN- $2,000
Marvel Mystery Comics #37 (San Francisco) NM $8,000
Mad #24 (Gaines) NM/M $6,346
Master Comics #25 (Mile High) NM- $4,700
Master Comics #27 (Mile High) NM- $5,600
Master Comics #40 (Mile High) NM+ $3,200
Namora #2 VG- $400
Phantom Lady #17 FN/VF $3,900
Planet Comics #32 VG+ $165
Police Comics #42 NM $1,782
Police Comics #44 NM $2,002
Punch Comics #12 FN/VF $2,400
Sensation Comics #1 NM $100,000
Star Spangled Comics #67 VG+ $150
Sun Girl #1 VG $270
Superman #4 G $418
Wambi, Jungle Boy #2 (Mile High) NM $2,100
Weird Fantasy #15 (Gaines File) NM $1,175
Weird Science #12(#1) (Gaines File) NM- $7,590
Weird Science #13(Gaines File) NM $3,322
Wonderworld #7 (Allentown) NM $16,000
World's Best Comics #1 G $1,700
Wow Comics #33 (Mile HIgh) NM $950

SILVER-BRONZE-MODERN AGE SALES

Silver Age Sales:
Adventure Comics #300 G/VG $52
Amazing Fantasy #15 VG- $1,650
Amazing Spider-Man #1 VG+ $1,900
Amazing Spider-Man #10 VG $150
Amazing Spider-Man #17 VG $250
Amazing Spider-Man #19 NM+ $3,421
Amazing Spider-Man #40 VF/NM $315
Amazing Spider-Man #50 FN+ $175
Aquaman #1 FN- $127
Atom #7 VF/NM $104
Avengers #1 VF/NM $4,860
Avengers #1 VG- $325
Avengers #4 VG $300
Batman #181 NM+ $350
Brave and the Bold #1 FN $425
Brave and the Bold #28 VG+ $480
Brave and the Bold #45 NM $100
Captain America #100 FN/VF $85

Captain America #105 NM $50
Daredevil #1 NM $7,000
Daredevil #1 FN $700
Daredevil #1 G $125
Daredevil #158 NM- $54
Daredevil #1 NM $700
Detective Comics #359 FN/VF $100
Fantastic Four #1 FN $1,800
Fantastic Four #1 GD $600
Fantastic Four #4 GD/VG $300
Fantastic Four #5 GD/VG $225
Fantastic Four #25 VF/NM $500
Fantastic Four #48 NM $1,650
Fantastic Four #48 NM- $1,750
Fantastic Four #48 VF $850
Flash #105 VG $750
Flash #123 FN+ $370
Green Lantern #1 FN $519
Hawkman #1 (White Mountain) VF/NM $810

Incredible Hulk #6 NM- $4,536
Incredible Hulk #6 FN/VF $600
Incredible Hulk #6 VG+ $153
Iron Man #1 FN+ $76
Iron Man & Submariner #1 NM $88
Justice League of America #1 VG/FN $400
Justice League of America #9 FN+ $275
Metal Men #1 VG+ $51
Our Army at War #200 FN $14
Our Fighting Forces #31 FN $178
Showcase #22 G+ $145
Silver Surfer #1 VF $200
Star Spangled War #55 FN+ $203
Strange Tales #23 VF+ $250
Strange Tales #115 FN $150
Strange Tales Annual #2 VF- $178
Tales of Suspense #37 VF $80
Tales To Astonish #52 NM- $114
Tales To Astonish #100 NM $50
X-Men #1 G $600
X-Men #1 G $450
X-Men #3 FN $165
X-Men #3 FN $145

Bronze Age Sales:
All Star Western #10 VF/NM $198
Amazing Spider-Man #100 NM $200
Amazing Spider-Man #101 NM $185

Amazing Spider-Man #122 NM $200
Amazing Spider-Man #129 VF+ $185
Amazing Spider-Man #238 NM+ $80
Avengers #100 NM $125
Cerebus #1 FN+ $600
Conan the Barbarian #1 VF/NM $180
Defenders #1 NM- $85
Fear, Adventure Into.. #10 NM $40
Green Lantern #77 NM- $134
Green Lantern #85 NM+ $274
House of Secrets #92 VF/NM $500
Incredible Hulk #180 NM $160
Incredible Hulk #181 VF $450
Iron Fist #15 NM $50
Machine Man #1 NM+ $26
Marvel Two-In-One #1 VF $31
Micronauts #1 NM+ $39
Tomb of Dracula #1 VF- $63
X-Men #94 NM $1,900
X-Men #99 NM- 90
X-Men #141 NM- $45

Modern Age Sales:
Akira #38 NM $50
Elseworlds 80-Page Giant #1 NM $218
G.I. Joe Special #1 VF/NM $46
Miracleman #15 NM $118
Miracleman #24 NM $32

SALES OF CGC GRADED COMICS

Golden Age Sales:
Action Comics #1 VF/NM w/moderate rest.(9.0) $58,139
Action Comics #1 VF-(7.5) $52,000
Action Comics #1 G(2.0) $60,000
Action Comics #55 (Rockford) NM-(9.2) $1,300
Action Comics #58 NM(9.4) $6,612
Action Comics #76 NM+(9.6) $7,900
Action Comics #76 (Mile High) NM+(9.6) $5,200
Adventure Comics #51 VF+(8.5) $3,289
All-American Comics #89 VF(8.0) $650
All-Flash Comics #1 (Denver) NM(9.4) $35,000
All-Star Comics #22 VF/NM(9.0) $2,000
All-Star Comics #31 VG+(4.5) $235
All-Star Comics #57 VF-(7.5) $1,500
All Winners Comics #1 FN+(6.5) $1,375
All Winners Comics #5 F/VF(7.0) $892
Batman #1 FN-(5.5) $6,225
Batman #1 VG+(4.5) $17,500
Batman #3 F/VF(7.0) $3,750
Batman #5 VF-(7.5) $2,900
Batman #6 NM-(9.2) $8,500
Batman #14 NM-(9.2) $4,900
Batman #40 VF/NM(9.0) $1,120
Big All-American Comic #1 VG(4.0) $1,800

Blue Beetle #32 NM(9.4) $2,677
Blue Beetle #54 VG+(4.5) $977
Brenda Starr #14(#2) (Mile High) NM(9.4) $10,062
Captain America Comics #1 (Windy City) VF+(8.5) $95,000
Captain America Comics #1 VF(8.0) $42,981
Captain America Comics #1 FN+(6.5) $25,000
Captain America Comics #2 F/VF(7.0) $4,180
Captain America #28 (Denver) VF/NM(9.0) $166,750
Captain America #32 VF+(8.5) $2,645
Captain Midnight #20 VF+(8.5) $238
Crimes By Women #3 FN+(6.5) $305
Crime SuspenStories #20 (Gaines) NM-(9.2) $2,300
Crime SuspenStories #22 (Gaines) VF/NM(9.0) $2,300
Daredevil Comics #3 NM(9.4) $5,500
Detective Comics #27 VF(8.0) $278,190
Detective Comics #27 G/VG(3.0) $45,000
Detective Comics #38 VG/F(5.0) $6,800
Detective Comics #121 NM+(9.6) $4,025
Detective Comics #174 NM(9.4) $2,600
Donald Duck Four Color #108 FN(6.0) $325
Donald Duck Four Color #147 VF-(7.5) $281
Donald Duck #27 VF+(8.5) $295
Double Action #2 NM-(9.2) $35,187
Exciting Comics #26 (Mile High) NM+(9.6) $4,370

Famous Funnies #209 NM+(9.6) $5,175
Famous Funnies #209 NM+(9.6) $4,125
Famous Funnies #210 NM+(9.6) $5,250
Felix the Cat #1 F(6.0) $228
Fighting Yank #13 (Mile High) NM(9.4) $3,450
Four Color #375: John Carter VF/NM(9.0) $290
Haunted Thrills #1 VF/NM(9.0) $600
Haunt of Fear #15 (Gaines) NM/M(9.8) $19,176
Haunt of Fear #16 VF(8.0) $200
Haunt of Fear #17 VF+(8.5) $1,730
Haunt of Fear #22 VF/NM(9.0) $350
House of Mystery #1 VF/NM(9.0) $3,450
Human Torch #9 (San Francisco) NM+(9.6) $16,531
Human Torch #21 NM-(9.2) $2,800
Journey Into the Unknown #24 NM-(9.2) $385
Lassie #1 NM-(9.2) $400
Leading Comics #6 FN+(6.5) $227
Mad #1 (Gaines) NM+(9.6) $25,300
Mad #2 (Gaines) NM+(9.6) $5,750
Mad #3 (Gaines) NM+(9.6) $6,325
Mad #3 VF(8.0) $430
Mad #4 (Gaines) NM/M(9.8) $5,750
Mad #5 (Gaines) NM(9.4) $5,750
Mad #6 (Gaines) NM-(9.2) $3,220
Mad #7 (Gaines) NM-(9.2) $2,990
Mad #8 (Gaines) NM(9.4) $3,680
Mad #9 (Gaines) VF/NM(9.0) $2,415
Mad #10 (Gaines) NM(9.4) $4,140
Mad #16 VF/NM(9.0) $4,125
Marvel Comics #1 (Pay Copy) VF/NM(9.0) $350,000
Marvel Comics #1 VG(4.0) $45,000
Marvel Mystery Comics #2 VF(8.0) $21,000
Marvel Mystery Comics #5 VG+(4.5) $6,000
Marvel Mystery Comics #19 VF-(7.5) $515
Marvel Mystery Comics #92 VF/NM(9.0) $21,000
Mary Marvel #1 VF+(8.5) $1,696
Master Comics #25 (Mile High) NM-(9.2) $5,000
Master Comics #26 (Mile High) NM+(9.6) $3,000
Master Comics #32 (Mile High) NM(9.4) $3,500
Master Comics #34 (Mile High) NM+(9.6) $5,463
Master Comics #38 (Mile High) VF/NM(9.0) $2,700
More Fun Comics #10 FN+(6.5) $3,500
More Fun Comics #38 NM(9.4) $5,718
More Fun Comics #51 (Mile High) VF/NM(9.0) $19,176
More Fun Comics #52 (Mile High) NM-(9.2) $207,000
More Fun Comics #54 VF(8.0) $13,225
More Fun Comics #56 (Mile High) NM-(9.2) $40,000
More Fun Comics #56 VF(8.0) $11,000
More Fun Comics #61 (Mile High) NM+(9.6) $27,000
More Fun Comics #67 G-(1.8) $585
More Fun Comics #102 VG(4.0) $239
National Comics #23 VF-(7.5) $204

National Comics #26 (Mile High) NM+(9.6) $2,300
New Adventure Comics #24 VF(8.0) $1,400
Pep Comics #7 (Larson) VF(8.0) $1,188
Personal Love #32 VF-(7.5) $455
Planet Comics #1 NM-(9.2) $25,558
Pogo Possum #1 NM-(9.2) $768
Police Comics #11 VF(8.0) $1,800
Popular Comics #62 NM+(9.6) $800
Rangers Comics #4 NM-(9.2) $1,100
Rocket to the Moon #1 VF-(7.5) $900
Sensation Comics #1 NM(9.4) $100,000
Sensation Comics #55 NM(9.4) $735
Shadow Comics #1 (Mile High) VF(8.0) $11,641
Shock Suspenstories #8 NM-(9.2) $500
Smash Comics #17 VF(8.0) $510
Space Patrol #2 VF+(8.5) $950
Special Edition Comics #1 (Denver) NM(9.4) $25,450
Spy Smasher #8 NM+(9.6) $5,500
Strange Adventures #10 (White Mt.) NM+(9.6) $5,750
Strange Worlds #3 NM-(9.2) $3,479
Sub-Mariner Comics #1 VG(4.0) $3,220
Superboy #1 VF+(8.5) $8,447
Superman #1 VG+(4.5) $6,140
Superman #2 FN+(6.5) $6,325
Superman #4 FN+(6.5) $1,525
Superman #14 VF/NM(9.0) $4,830
Superman #20 FN(6.0) $462
Superman Ashcan VF/NM(9.0) $36,099
Thing! #16 NM-(9.2) $325
3-D Tales From the Crypt #2 VF+(8.5) $1,229
Thun'da #1 VF+(8.5) $1,124
Tomahawk #1 (Mile High) NM+(9.6) $6,325
Torchy #1 VF/NM(9.0) $450
Uncle Scrooge Four Color #386 FN+(6.5) $255
USA Comics #1 VF/NM(9.0) $14,547
USA Comics #1 VG+(4.5) $1,725
Vault of Horror #20 NM-(9.2) $550
Vault of Horror #39 (Gaines) NM/M(9.8) $2,530
War Against Crime #10 (Gaines) NM(9.4) $8,050
Weird Comics #1 VG(4.0) $899
Weird Science #22 F/VF(7.0) $342
Weird Tales of the Future #6 VF-(7.5) $750
Wings #1 (Mile High) NM/M(9.8) $16,531
Wings #1 NM(9.4) $7,000
Wonder Woman #1 VF(8.0) $15,000
Wonder Woman #1 F/VF(7.0) $8,625
Wonder Woman #1 G/VG(3.0) $2,500
Wonder Woman #73 F/VF(7.0) $610
World's Best Comics #1 F/VF(7.0) $6,350
World's Finest Comics #4 VF/NM(9.0) $2,600
World's Finest Comics #5 FN(6.0) $700
World's Finest Comics #58 NM(9.4) $1,350

Silver Age Sales:

Amazing Fantasy #15 NM(9.4) $95,000
Amazing Fantasy #15 VF+(8.5) $4,000
Amazing Fantasy #15 F/VF(7.0) $8,050
Amazing Fantasy #15 F/VF(7.0) $3,900
Amazing Fantasy #15 FN+(6.5) $6,500
Amazing Spider-Man #1 NM(9.4) $67,305
Amazing Spider-Man #1 NM-(9.2) $40,250
Amazing Spider-Man #1 VF(8.0) $9,000
Amazing Spider-Man #1 G/VG(3.0) $1,050
Amazing Spider-Man #5 NM(9.4) $9,500
Amazing Spider-Man #5 VG/F(5.0) $425
Amazing Spider-Man #6 NM(9.4) $8,450
Amazing Spider-Man #6 NM-(9.2) $3,350
Amazing Spider-Man #6 VF/NM(9.0) $1,350
Amazing Spider-Man #8 NM+(9.6) $5,975
Amazing Spider-Man #8 NM(9.4) $2,700
Amazing Spider-Man #9 NM-(9.2) $1,785
Amazing Spider-Man #14 NM(9.4) $8,200
Amazing Spider-Man #14 NM-(9.2) $3,200
Amazing Spider-Man #14 NM-(9.2) $3,000
Amazing Spider-Man #14 VF/NM(9.0) $2,550
Amazing Spider-Man #14 VF/NM(9.0) $2,200
Amazing Spider-Man #17 VF/NM(9.0) $850
Amazing Spider-Man #25 NM-(9.2) $650
Amazing Spider-Man #29 NM(9.4) $1,200
Amazing Spider-Man #33 NM+(9.6) $1,250
Amazing Spider-Man #39 NM-(9.2) $680
Amazing Spider-Man #40 NM(9.4) $1,800
Amazing Spider-Man #42 NM+(9.6) $945
Amazing Spider-Man #43 NM-(9.2) $250
Amazing Spider-Man #45 NM+(9.6) $1,500
Amazing Spider-Man #47 NM(9.4) $500
Amazing Spider-Man #49 NM-(9.2) $285
Amazing Spider-Man #57 VF/NM(9.0) $100
Amazing Spider-Man Annual #2 VF/NM(9.0) $375
Amazing Spider-Man Special #3 NM(9.4) $800
Amazing Spider-Man #1 (Golden Record reprint)
NM(9.4) $305
Aquaman #1 NM-(9.2) $1,500
Atom #4 NM+(9.6) $1,009
Avengers #3 F/VF(7.0) $195
Avengers #4 NM(9.4) $5,900
Avengers #4 NM-(9.2) $2,875
Avengers #4 VF-(7.5) $695
Avengers #5 VF/NM(9.0) $350
Avengers #10 NM-(9.2) $380
Avengers #11 NM(9.4) $775
Batman #181 VF/NM(9.0) $325
Batman #191 NM+(9.6) $200
Brave and the Bold #34 (Slabodian) NM(9.4) $10,000
Brave and the Bold #34 FN(6.0) $311

Captain America #100 NM+(9.6) $1,100
Captain Marvel #1 NM/M(9.8) $1,500
Daredevil #1 NM-(9.2) $4,500
Daredevil #1 VF(8.0) $900
Daredevil #1 VF-(7.5) $750
Daredevil #2 VF/NM(9.0) $700
Daredevil #3 VF/NM(9.0) $365
Doctor Strange #169 NM(9.4) $345
Eighty-Page Giant #8 VF/NM(9.0) $232
Fantastic Four #1 NM+(9.6) $6,311
Fantastic Four #1 (White Mountain) NM-(9.2) $37,500
Fantastic Four #1 VF(8.0) $16,002
Fantastic Four #1 VF-(7.5) $7,000
Fantastic Four #2 NM(9.4) $27,457
Fantastic Four #3 VF/NM(9.0) $4,600
Fantastic Four #4 VF/NM(9.0) $4,100
Fantastic Four #4 VF+(8.5) $1,975
Fantastic Four #5 NM(9.4) $17,046
Fantastic Four #5 FN+(6.5) $650
Fantastic Four #6 NM-(9.2) $4,500
Fantastic Four #12 NM-(9.2) $3,400
Fantastic Four #14 NM(9.4) $1,800
Fantastic Four #17 NM(9.4) $2,000
Fantastic Four #25 NM-(9.2) $1,000
Fantastic Four #28 NM-(9.2) $750
Fantastic Four #30 NM-(9.2) $275
Fantastic Four #48 NM+(9.6) $3,400
Fantastic Four #48 NM(9.4) $1,700
Fantastic Four #52 NM-(9.2) $300
Fantastic Four Annual #1 NM-(9.2) $1,775
Fantastic Four Annual #1 VF/NM(9.0) $1,201
Flash #106 VF/NM(9.0) $5,510
Flash #110 VF(8.0) $1,430
Flash #123 NM-(9.2) $3,350
Flash #129 VF/NM(9.0) $500
Flash #187 NM+(9.6) $350
Four Color #907: Sugar Foot NM+(9.6) $456
Four Color #1089: Restless Gun NM+(9.6) $341
Four Color #1252: Andy Griffith NM(9.4) $850
Hawkman #6 NM(9.4) $395
Hawkman #15 NM+(9.6) $325
Incredible Hulk #1 VF-(7.5) $4,500
Incredible Hulk #2 NM-(9.2) $6,900
Incredible Hulk #3 NM-(9.2) $3,500
Incredible Hulk #3 VF+(8.5) $1,600
Incredible Hulk #4 NM-(9.2) $3,900
Incredible Hulk #5 NM(9.4) $6,500
Incredible Hulk #102 NM+(9.6) $795
Incredible Hulk #102 VF/NM(9.0) $150
Iron Man #1 NM/M(9.8) $2,550
Iron Man #1 NM+(9.6) $1,200
Iron Man #6 NM+(9.6) $200

Iron Man & Submariner #1 NM-(9.2) $175
Journey Into Mystery #83 VF/NM(9.0) $7,500
Journey Into Mystery #85 NM-(9.2) $2,550
Journey Into Mystery #86 NM-(9.2) $1200
Journey Into Mystery #99 VF/NM(9.0) $380
Journey Into Mystery #112 VF(8.0) $200
Journey Into Mystery #118 VF+(8.5) $110
Justice League of America #1 VG/F(5.0) $410
Justice League of America #3 VF(8.0) $505
Nick Fury #1 NM+(9.6) $335
Nick Fury #1 NM+(9.6) $291
Showcase #4 NM-(9.2) $52,000
Showcase #4 VF(8.0) $2,762
Showcase #14 G/VG(3.0) $300
Showcase #22 VG(4.0) $650
Showcase #27 VF-(7.5) $305
Showcase #55 NM(9.4) $808
Showcase #60 VF/NM(9.0) $282
Silver Surfer #6 NM+(9.6) $695
Silver Surfer #14 NM+(9.6) $1,100
Star Trek #1 NM-(9.2) $975
Strange Tales #110 FN-(5.5) $375
Submariner #1 NM+(9.6) $350
Submariner #1 NM(9.4) $300
Superboy #81 NM(9.4) $265
Tales Of Suspense #42 NM-(9.2) $800
Tales Of Suspense #46 VF+(8.5) $250
Tales Of Suspense #73 NM(9.4) $300
Tales Of Suspense #82 NM(9.4) $300
Tales Of Suspense #89 NM(9.4) $200
Tales Of Suspense #99 NM(9.4) $220
Tales To Astonish #35 VF/NM(9.0) $1,400
Tales To Astonish #39 NM(9.4) $1,500
Tales To Astonish #44 NM(9.4) $2,100
X-Men #1 NM-(9.2) $16,000
X-Men #1 NM-(9.2) $15,000
X-Men #1 VF(8.0) $5,000
X-Men #4 VF-(7.5) $350
X-Men #6 NM(9.4) $1,800
X-Men #6 VF/NM(9.0) $600
X-Men #9 VF+(8.5) $375
X-Men #10 VF/NM(9.0) $350
X-Men #12 VF/NM(9.0) $475
X-Men #14 NM(9.4) $1,125
X-Men #15 NM(9.4) $1,150
X-Men #15 NM(9.4) $800
X-Men #27 NM-(9.2) $225
X-Men #48 NM+(9.6) $650
X-Men #58 NM(9.4) $405
X-Men #59 NM-(9.2) $180
X-Men #63 NM-(9.2) $113
X-Men #64 NM(9.4) $325

Bronze Age Sales:

All Star Western #10 NM+(9.6) $2,415
Amazing Spider-Man #98 NM(9.4) $400
Amazing Spider-Man #121 NM/M(9.8) $2,138
Amazing Spider-Man #121 NM+(9.6) $1,950
Amazing Spider-Man #121 NM+(9.6) $1,495
Amazing Spider-Man #121 NM-(9.2) $350
Amazing Spider-Man #122 NM(9.4) $750
Amazing Spider-Man #122 NM(9.4) $560
Aquaman #52 VF/NM(9.0) $125
Avengers #100 NM(9.4) $260
Batman #227 NM(9.4) $330
Batman #237 NM(9.4) $233
Conan #1 NM/M(9.8) $1,525
Conan #1 NM(9.4) $570
Conan #1 NM(9.4) $500
Conan #1 NM-(9.2) $350
Conan #7 NM/M(9.8) $360
DC 100-Page Super Spectacular #5 NM-(9.2) $1000
Defenders #2 NM(9.4) $150
Detective Comics #400 NM(9.4) $350
Fantastic Four #100 NM(9.4) $900
Fantastic Four #112 NM(9.4) $625
Giant-Size X-Men #1 NM+(9.6) $1,750
Giant-Size X-Men #1 NM-(9.2) $700
Giant-Size X-Men #1 VF(8.0) $300
House of Secrets #92 NM(9.4) $2,000
House of Secrets #92 VF/NM(9.0) $400
Incredible Hulk #181 NM(9.4) $1,800
Incredible Hulk #181 NM(9.4) $1,525
Incredible Hulk #181 NM(9.4) $1,400
Incredible Hulk #181 NM-(9.2) $800
Iron Fist #14 NM+(9.6) $400
Marvel Feature #1 NM-(9.2) $375
New Gods #1 NM(9.4) $229
Richie Rich Jackpots #1 NM+(9.6) $198
Shadow #1 NM-(9.2) $37
X-Men #94 NM-(9.2) $625
X-Men #95 NM+(9.6) $500
X-Men #99 NM/M(9.8) $450

Modern Age Sales:

Batman: Dark Knight #1 NM/M(9.8) $265
Miracleman #1 NM+(9.6) $27
Miracleman #15 NM+(9.6) $152
Miracleman #16 NM(9.4) $52
Spectacular Spider-Man #1 NM/M(9.8) $381
Spider-Man # (Gold cover w/UPC code, 2nd printing) NM/M(9.8) $320
Ultimate Spider-Man #1 (Red-c) NM/M(9.8) $660
Ultimate Spider-Man #1 (White-c) NM/M(9.8) $655
Web of Spider-Man #100 M(10.0) $355

The following tables denote the rate of appreciation of the top Golden Age, Platinum Age, Silver Age and Bronze Age books, as well as selected genres over the past year. The retail value for a Near Mint copy of each book (or VF where a Near Mint copy is not known to exist) in 2002 is compared to its value in 2001. The rate of return for 2002 over 2001 is given. The place in rank is given for each comic by year, with its corresponding value in highest known grade. These tables can be very useful in forecasting trends in the market place. For instance, the investor might want to know which book is yielding the best dividend from one year to the next, or one might just be interested in seeing how the popularity of books changes from year to year. For instance, *Wonder Woman* #1 was in 34th place in 2001 and has increased to 31st place in 2002. Premium books are also included in these tables and are denoted with an asterisk(*).

The following tables are meant as a guide to the investor. However, it should be pointed out that trends may change at anytime and that some books can meet market resistance with a slowdown in price increases, while others can develop into real comers from a presently dormant state. In the long run, if the investor sticks to the books that are appreciating steadily each year, he shouldn't go very far wrong.

TOP GOLDEN AGE BOOKS

2002 OVER 2001 GUIDE VALUES

ISSUE NO.	2002 RANK	2002 NM PRICE	2001 RANK	2001 NM PRICE	$ INCR.	% INCR.
Action Comics #1	1	$350,000	1	$285,000	$65,000	23%
Detective Comics #27	2	$300,000	2	$240,000	$60,000	25%
Marvel Comics #1	3	$250,000	3	$175,000	$75,000	43%
Superman #1	4	$210,000	4	$175,000	$35,000	20%
All-American Comics #16	5	$115,000	5	$100,000	$15,000	15%
Batman #1	6	$100,000	6	$85,000	$15,000	18%
Captain America Comics #1	6	$100,000	7	$80,000	$20,000	25%
Flash Comics #1	8	$85,000	8	$75,000	$10,000	13%
Whiz Comics #2 (#1)	9	$77,000	9	$72,000	$5,000	7%
More Fun Comics #52	10	$72,000	10	$62,000	$10,000	16%
Detective Comics #1	11	VF $55,000	11	VF $55,000	$0	0%
Adventure Comics #40	12	$52,000	12	$44,000	$8,000	18%
Detective Comics #33	13	$50,000	13	$44,000	$6,000	14%
All Star Comics #3	14	$45,000	15	$40,000	$5,000	13%
Detective Comics #38	14	$45,000	16	$38,000	$7,000	18%
Green Lantern #1	16	$42,000	17	$35,000	$7,000	20%
New Fun Comics #1	16	VF $42,000	14	VF $42,000	$0	0%
Action Comics #2	18	$37,000	23	$30,000	$7,000	23%
Detective Comics #29	18	$37,000	21	$32,000	$5,000	16%
Detective Comics #31	18	$37,000	22	$32,000	$5,000	16%
All Star Comics #8	21	$36,000	19	$32,000	$4,000	13%
Captain Marvel Adventures #1	21	$36,000	20	$32,000	$4,000	13%
More Fun Comics #53	21	$36,000	18	$33,000	$3,000	9%
Human Torch #2 (#1)	24	$35,000	24	$28,000	$7,000	25%
Sub-Mariner Comics #1	25	$33,000	26	$27,000	$6,000	22%
Sensation Comics #1	26	$32,000	25	$27,000	$5,000	19%
Marvel Mystery Comics #2	27	$29,500	30	$25,000	$4,500	18%
New York World's Fair 1939	28	$29,400	27	$26,000	$3,400	13%
Adventure Comics #48	29	$29,000	28	$25,000	$4,000	16%
Marvel Mystery Comics #9	30	$28,000	31	$23,000	$5,000	22%
Wonder Woman #1	31	$27,000	34	$22,000	$5,000	23%
Action Comics #7	32	$25,000	36	$20,000	$5,000	25%
Daring Mystery Comics #1	32	$25,000	35	$21,000	$4,000	19%
Famous Funnies-Series 1 #1	32	$25,000	29	$25,000	$0	0%
All Winners Comics #1	35	$24,000	37	$20,000	$4,000	20%
* Motion Picture Funnies Weekly #1	35	$24,000	33	$22,000	$2,000	9%
Marvel Mystery Comics #5	37	$23,800	39	$19,500	$4,300	22%
Action Comics #3	38	$23,000	40	$19,000	$4,000	21%
Detective Comics #28	39	$22,500	41	$19,000	$3,500	18%
* Century Of Comics nn	40	VF $22,000	32	VF $22,000	$0	0%

ISSUE NO.	2002 RANK	2002 NM PRICE	2001 RANK	2001 NM PRICE	$ INCR.	% INCR.
Marvel Mystery Comics 132 pg.	41	VF $20,000	46	VF $18,000	$2,000	11%
New Fun Comics #6	41	VF $20,000	38	VF $20,000	$0	0%
Walt Disney's Comics & Stories #1	43	$19,750	43	$19,000	$750	4%
Jumbo Comics #1	44	VF $19,500	42	VF $19,000	$500	3%
All-American Comics #19	45	$19,000	50	$16,000	$3,000	19%
Amazing Man Comics #5	45	$19,000	48	$17,000	$2,000	12%
World's Best Comics #1	45	$19,000	49	$17,000	$2,000	12%
New Comics #1	48	VF $18,500	44	VF $18,500	$0	0%
All Flash #1	49	$18,000	51	$16,000	$2,000	13%
Captain America Comics 132 pg.	49	$18,000	52	$16,000	$2,000	13%
Famous Funnies #1	49	$18,000	45	$18,000	$0	0%
New Fun Comics #2	49	VF $18,000	47	VF $18,000	$0	0%
Wonder Comics #1	49	$18,000	53	$16,000	$2,000	13%
Action Comics #10	54	$17,500	62	$14,000	$3,500	25%
All-American Comics #17	54	$17,500	55	$15,000	$2,500	17%
Mystic Comics #1	54	$17,500	56	$15,000	$2,500	17%
Archie Comics #1	57	$17,000	59	$14,500	$2,500	17%
Pep Comics #22	57	$17,000	66	$14,000	$3,000	21%
Wow Comics #1	57	$17,000	57	$15,000	$2,000	13%
All Star Comics #1	60	$16,500	58	$14,500	$2,000	14%
Batman #2	60	$16,500	63	$14,000	$2,500	18%
Silver Streak #6	60	$16,500	61	$14,500	$2,000	14%
Double Action Comics #2	63	$16,000	69	$13,000	$3,000	23%
More Fun Comics #55	63	$16,000	64	$14,000	$2,000	14%
Suspense Comics #3	63	$16,000	67	$14,000	$2,000	14%
New York World's Fair 1940	66	$15,800	65	$14,000	$1,800	13%
Detective Comics #2	67	VF $15,500	54	VF $15,500	$0	0%
Captain America Comics #2	68	$15,000	74	$12,500	$2,500	20%
Marvel Mystery Comics #3	68	$15,000	86	$11,500	$3,500	30%
USA Comics #1	68	$15,000	78	$12,500	$2,500	20%
Young Allies Comics #1	68	$15,000	79	$12,500	$2,500	20%
Adventure Comics #61	72	$14,500	72	$12,500	$2,000	16%
Adventure Comics #73	72	$14,500	73	$12,500	$2,000	16%
Daredevil Comics #1	72	$14,500	75	$12,500	$2,000	16%
* Funnies on Parade nn	72	$14,500	60	$14,500	$0	0%
Mickey Mouse Magazine #1	72	$14,500	94	$11,000	$3,500	32%
Superman #2	72	$14,500	71	$12,750	$1,750	14%
Action Comics #4	78	$14,000	88	$11,000	$3,000	27%
Action Comics #5	78	$14,000	89	$11,000	$3,000	27%
Action Comics #6	78	$14,000	90	$11,000	$3,000	27%
Adventure Comics #72	78	$14,000	80	$12,000	$2,000	17%
More Fun Comics #73	78	$14,000	76	$12,500	$1,500	12%
Big Book of Fun Comics #1	83	VF $13,500	68	VF $13,500	$0	0%
Looney Tunes and Merrie Melodies #1	83	$13,500	82	$12,000	$1,500	13%
Planet Comics #1	83	$13,500	87	$11,500	$2,000	17%
Red Raven Comics #1	83	$13,500	84	$12,000	$1,500	13%
Silver Streak #1	83	$13,500	77	$12,500	$1,000	8%
All-Select Comics #1	88	$13,000	-	$11,000	$2,000	18%
Four Color Ser. 1 (Donald Duck) #4	88	$13,000	81	$12,000	$1,000	8%
Green Giant Comics #1	88	$13,000	93	$11,000	$2,000	18%
Marvel Mystery Comics #4	88	$13,000	-	$9,000	$4,000	44%
More Fun Comics #54	88	$13,000	95	$11,000	$2,000	18%
New Book of Comics #1	88	VF $13,000	70	VF $13,000	$0	0%
Mystery Men Comics #1	94	$12,500	96	$11,000	$1,500	14%
More Fun Comics #14	95	VF $12,200	83	VF $12,000	$200	2%
Big All-American #1	96	$12,000	85	$11,500	$500	4%
Captain America Comics #3	96	$12,000	99	$10,000	$2,000	20%
Detective Comics #35	96	$12,000	100	$10,000	$2,000	20%
Four Color Ser. 1 (Mickey Mouse) #16	96	VF $12,000	92	VF $11,000	$1,000	9%
Tough Kid Squad Comics #1	96	$12,000	-	$10,000	$2,000	20%

TOP 10 PLATINUM AGE BOOKS

2002 OVER 2001 GUIDE VALUES

TITLE/ISSUE#	2002 RANK	2002 VF PRICE	2001 RANK	2001 VF PRICE	$ INCR.	% INCR.
Mickey Mouse Book (2nd printing)-variant....1		FN $12,000	1	FN $12,000	$0	0%
Mickey Mouse Book (1st printing)................2		VF $11,000	2	VF $11,000	$0	0%
Mickey Mouse Book (2nd printing)..............3		VF $10,000	3	VF $10,000	$0	0%
Yellow Kid in McFadden Flats......................4		FN $8,500	4	FN $8,500	$0	0%
Pore Li'l Mose 5		FN $5,000	5	FN $5,000	$0	0%
Buster Brown and His Resolutions 1903.......6		FN $4,500	6	FN $4,500	$0	0%
* Buster Brown's Blue Ribbon #1 1904.........7		VF $3,600	7	VF $3,600	$0	0%
Little Sammy Sneeze 8		FN $3,400	8	FN $3,400	$0	0%
Little Nemo 1906 9		FN $3,000	9	FN $3,000	$0	0%
Yellow Kid...9		FN $3,000	9	FN $3,000	$0	0%

TOP 10 SILVER AGE BOOKS

2002 OVER 2001 GUIDE VALUES

TITLE/ISSUE#	2002 RANK	2002 NM PRICE	2001 RANK	2001 NM PRICE	$ INCR.	% INCR.
Amazing Fantasy #15.....................................1		$42,000	1	$35,000	$7,000	20%
Showcase #4 (The Flash).................................2		$35,000	2	$32,000	$3,000	9%
Amazing Spider-Man #1 3		$28,000	3	$25,000	$3,000	12%
Fantastic Four #1 4		$27,000	4	$24,000	$3,000	13%
Incredible Hulk #1 5		$17,000	5	$15,000	$2,000	13%
Showcase #8 (The Flash).................................6		$15,200	6	$14,000	$1,200	9%
X-Men #1 7		$10,000	7	$9,500	$500	5%
Showcase #9 (Lois Lane) 8		$9,000	8	$8,400	$600	7%
Brave and the Bold #28 9		$7,000	9	$6,000	$1,000	17%
The Flash #105 9		$7,000	-	$6,000	$1,000	17%

TOP 10 BRONZE AGE BOOKS

2002 OVER 2001 GUIDE VALUES

TITLE/ISSUE#	2002 RANK	2002 NM PRICE	2001 RANK	2001 NM PRICE	$ INCR.	% INCR.
Giant-Size X-Men #1 1		$1,100	1	$900	$200	22%
Incredible Hulk #181 1		$1,100	2	$900	$200	22%
X-Men #94 3		$900	3	$750	$150	20%
House of Secrets #92 4		$700	4	$600	$100	17%
Star Wars #1 (35¢ cover price variant) 4		$700	5	$600	$100	17%
DC 100 Page Super Spectacular #5 6		$600	6	$475	$125	26%
All-Star Western #10 7		$450	8	$350	$100	29%
Vampirella Special HC 7		$450	7	$400	$50	13%
Cerebus #1 9		$350	9	$350	$0	0%
Vampirella #113...9		$350	10	$300	$50	17%

TOP 10 CRIME BOOKS

2002 OVER 2001 GUIDE VALUES

TITLE/ISSUE#	2002 RANK	2002 NM PRICE	2001 RANK	2001 NM PRICE	$ INCR.	% INCR.
Crime Does Not Pay #22.................................1		$2,600	1	$2,200	$400	18%
True Crime Comics #2 2		$1,550	2	$1,300	$250	19%
Crime Does Not Pay #23.................................3		$1,400	3	$1,200	$200	17%
Crimes By Women #1.......................................3		$1,400	4	$1,190	$210	18%
The Killers #1...5		$1,150	7	$950	$200	21%
True Crime Comics #3 5		$1,150	5	$975	$175	18%
Crime Does Not Pay #24.................................7		$1,125	6	$950	$175	18%
True Crime Comics #4 8		$1,025	8	$875	$150	17%
The Killers #2...9		$950	9	$800	$150	19%
True Crime Comics Vol. 2 #1.........................10		$925	10	$775	$150	19%

TOP 10 HORROR BOOKS

TITLE/ISSUE#	2002 RANK	2002 NM PRICE	2001 RANK	2001 NM PRICE	$ INCR.	% INCR.
Vault of Horror #12	1	$5,300	1	$4,600	$700	15%
Eerie #1	2	$4,000	3	$3,200	$800	25%
Tales of Terror Annual #1	2	VF $4,000	2	VF $3,400	$600	18%
Journey into Mystery #1	4	$3,500	4	$3,100	$400	13%
Strange Tales #1	4	$3,500	5	$3,100	$400	13%
Crypt of Terror #17	6	$3,300	6	$2,800	$500	18%
Haunt of Fear #15	6	$3,300	7	$2,800	$500	18%
Crime Patrol #15	8	$3,000	8	$2,600	$400	15%
House of Mystery #1	9	$2,400	9	$2,000	$400	20%
Tales to Astonish #1	10	$2,100	10	$1,800	$300	17%

TOP 10 ROMANCE BOOKS

TITLE/ISSUE#	2002 RANK	2002 NM PRICE	2001 RANK	2001 NM PRICE	$ INCR.	% INCR.
Giant Comics Edition #12	1	$1,100	1	$975	$125	13%
Intimate Confessions #1	2	$825	2	$700	$125	18%
Romance Trail #1	3	$650	4	$550	$100	18%
Young Lovers #18	3	$650	5	$550	$100	18%
DC 100 Page Super Spectacular #5	5	$600	7	$475	$125	26%
Giant Comics Edition #15	5	$600	3	$550	$50	9%
Giant Comics Edition #9	7	$585	6	$535	$50	9%
Secret Hearts #1	8	$575	8	$475	$100	21%
Personal Love #32	9	$550	-	$450	$100	22%
Women in Love - 1952	9	$550	10	$465	$85	18%

TOP 10 SCI-FI BOOKS

TITLE/ISSUE#	2002 RANK	2002 NM PRICE	2001 RANK	2001 NM PRICE	$ INCR.	% INCR.
Strange Adventures #1	1	$4,000	1	$3,500	$500	14%
Mystery In Space #1	2	$3,700	2	$3,200	$500	16%
Showcase #17 (Adam Strange)	3	$3,000	3	$2,600	$400	15%
Journey Into Unknown Worlds #36	4	$2,500	5	$2,100	$400	19%
Strange Adventures #9	5	$2,450	4	$2,200	$250	11%
Fawcett Movie #15 (Man From Planet X)	6	$2,400	7	$2,000	$400	20%
Showcase #15 (Space Ranger)	6	$2,400	6	$2,100	$300	14%
Weird Fantasy #13 (#1)	8	$2,300	8	$2,000	$300	15%
Weird Science #12 (#1)	8	$2,300	9	$2,000	$300	15%
Weird Science-Fantasy Annual 1952	10	$2,250	10	$1,800	$450	25%

TOP 10 WESTERN BOOKS

TITLE/ISSUE#	2002 RANK	2002 NM PRICE	2001 RANK	2001 NM PRICE	$ INCR.	% INCR.
Gene Autry Comics #1	1	$9,500	1	$8,400	$1,100	13%
*Lone Ranger Ice Cream 1939 2nd	2	VF $6,500	2	VF $6,000	$500	8%
Hopalong Cassidy #1	3	$6,000	4	$5,200	$800	15%
*Lone Ranger Ice Cream 1939	3	VF $6,000	3	VF $5,500	$500	9%
*Red Ryder Victory Patrol '42	5	$4,600	5	$4,400	$200	5%
*Red Ryder Victory Patrol '43	6	$4,200	6	$4,000	$200	5%
*Red Ryder Victory Patrol '44	6	$4,200	7	$3,800	$400	11%
*Tom Mix Ralston #1	8	$3,600	8	$3,500	$100	3%
Red Ryder Comics #1	9	$3,300	9	$3,000	$300	10%
Roy Rogers Four Color #38	10	$2,850	10	$2,600	$250	10%

**When you sell Golden and Silver Age comics,
there is one clear choice.**

***Metropolis is the largest dealer
of comic books in the world.**

873 Broadway, Suite 201, New York, NY 10003
Toll-Free (800) 229-6387 or call (212) 260-4147
Fax (212) 260-4304
buying@metropoliscomics.com
www.metropoliscomics.com

Prince Namor, the Sub-Mariner from Young Men Comics #26 (Atlas, 1954). Artwork by Namor's legendary creator Bill Everett. © Atlas/ Marvel.

Silver-Age Hawkman of Thanagar
by Joe Kubert.

Where Super-Heroes Dwell

JUST THE FACTS.

Fact 1: ABSOLUTELY NO OTHER COMIC DEALER BUYS MORE GOLDEN AND SILVER AGE COMICS THAN METROPOLIS.

Although the pages of the price guide are filled with other dealers offering to pay "top dollar," the simple truth is that Metropolis spends more money on more quality comic book collections year in and year out than any other dealers in the country. We have the funds and the expertise to back up our word. The fact is that we have spent nearly 4 million dollars on rare comic books and movie posters over the last year. If you have comic books to sell please call us at **1-800-229-6387**. A generous finder's fee will be given if you know of any comic book or movie poster collections that we purchase. All calls will be strictly confidential.

Fact 2: ABSOLUTELY NO OTHER COMIC DEALER SELLS MORE GOLDEN AND SILVER AGE COMICS THAN METROPOLIS.

We simply have the best stock of Golden and Silver Age comic books in the country. The thousands of collectors familiar with our strict grading standards and excellent service can attest to this. Chances are, if you want it, we have it !

METROPOLIS
COLLECTIBLES

873 Broadway, Suite 201 New York, NY 10003
Tel: (212) 260-4147 Fax: (212) 260-4304
Toll Free: 1-800-229-6387
email: buying@metropoliscomics.com Web: www.metropoliscomics.com

COMIC BOOKS WANTED

The following prices represent a small sample of the prices that we will pay for your comic books. Other dealers say that they will pay top dollar, but when it really comes down to it, they simply do not. If you have comics to sell, we invite you to contact every comic dealer in the country to get their offers. Then come to us to get your best offer. We can afford to pay the highest price for your Golden and Silver Age comics because that is all we sell. If you wish to sell us your comic books, please either ship us the books securely via Registered U.S. Mail or UPS. However, if your collection is too large to ship, kindly send us a detailed list of what you have and we will travel directly to you. The prices below are for NM copies, but we are interested in all grades. Thank You.

Action #1	$500,000
Action #242	$4,000
Adventure #40	$60,000
Adventure #48	$28,000
Adventure #210	$6,000
All-American #16	$80,000
All-American #19	$18,000
All-Star #3	$75,000
Amazing Fantasy #15	$65,000
Amaz.Spiderman #1	$35,000
Arrow #1	$3,600
Batman #1	$90,000
Brave & the Bold #28	$6,200
Captain America #1	$78,000
Detective #1	$88,000
Detective #27	$390,000
Detective #38	$45,000
Detective #168	$5,000
Detective #225	$5,000
Detec. Picture Stories#1	$4,000
Donald Duck #9	$6,0000
Fantastic Comics #3	$17,000
Fantastic Four #1	$60,000
Fantastic Four #5	$5,000
Flash Comics #1	$88,000
Green Hornet #1	$3,800
Green Lantern #1 (GA)	$38,000
Green Lantern #1 (SA)	$4,200
Human Torch #2(#1)	$24,000
Incredible Hulk #1	$17,000
Journey into Myst. #83	$7,000
Justice League #1	$5,000
Jumbo Comics #1	$20,000
Marvel Comics #1	$125,000
More Fun #52	$80,000
More Fun #54	$14,500
More Fun #55	$22,000
More Fun #73	$18,000
More Fun #101	$10,000
New Fun #6	$26,000
Pep Comics #22	$20,000
Showcase #4	$40,000
Showcase #8	$9,000
Superboy #1	$9,000
Superman #1	$225,000
Superman #2	$5,000
Suspense Comics #3	$25,000
Tales of Suspense #1	$2,900
Tales of Suspense #39	$7,000
Tales to Astonish #27	$5,500
Target Comics V1#7	$5,500
Walt Disney C&S #1	$17,000
Whiz #2 (#1)	$55,000
Wonder Woman #1	$18,500
Wow #1 (1936)	$8,500
Young Allies #1	$8,500
X-Men #1	$15,000

The following is a sample of the books we are purchasing:

Action Comics	#1-400
Adventure Comics	#32-400
Advs. Into Weird Worlds	all
All-American Comics	#1-102
All-Flash Quarterly	#1-32
All-Select	#1-11
All-Star Comics	#1-57
All-Winners	#1-21
Amazing Spiderman	#1-150
Amazing Man	#5-26
Amaz. Mystery Funnies	#1
Avengers	#1-100
Batman	#1-300
Blackhawk	#9-130
Boy Commandos	#1-32
Brave & the Bold	#1-100
Captain America	#1-78
Captain Marvel Advs.	#1-150
Challengers	#1-25
Classic Comics	#1-169
Comic Cavalcade	#1-63
Daredevil Comics	#1-60
Daredevil (MCG)	#1-50

COLLECTIBLES
873 BROADWAY, SUITE 201
NEW YORK, NY 10003
Toll Free: 1-800-229-6387
Tel: 212-260-4147 Fax: 212-260-4304
Email: buying@metropoliscomics.com
Web: www.metropoliscomics.com

Daring Mystery	#1-8
Detective Comics	#1-450
Donald Duck 4-Colors	#4-up
Fantastic Four	#1-100
Fight Comics	#1-86
Flash	#105-150
Flash Comics	#1-104
Funny Pages	#6-42
Green Lantern (GA)	#1-38
Green Lantern (SA)	#1-90
Hit Comics	#1-65
Human Torch	#2(#1)-38
Incredible Hulk	#1-6
Jimmy Olsen	#1-150
Journey Into Mystery	#1-125
Jumbo Comics	#1-167
Jungle Comics	#1-163
Justice League	#1-110
Mad	#1-50
Marvel Mystery	#1-92
Military Comics	#1-43
More Fun Comics	#7-127
Mystery in Space	#1-75
Mystic Comics	#1-up
National Comics	#1-75
New Adventure	#12-31
New Comics	#1-11
New Fun Comics	#1-6
Our Army at War	#1-200
Our Fighting Forces	#1-180
Planet Comics	#1-73
Rangers Comics	#1-69
Reform School Girl	all
Sensation Comics	#1-116
Shadow Comics	all
Showcase	#1-100
Star-Spangled Comics	#1-130
Strange Tales	#1-145
Sub-Mariner	#1-42
Superboy	#1-110
Superman	#1-250
Tales From The Crypt	#20-46
Tales of Suspense	#1-80
Tales to Astonish	#1-80
Terrific Comics	all
Thing	#1-17
USA Comics	#1-17
Weird Comics	#1-20
Weird Mysteries	#1-11
Weird Tales From The Future	all
Wings Comics	#1-124
Whiz Comics	#1-155
Wonder Comics	#1-20
Wonder Woman	#1-200
Wonderworld	#3-33
World's Finest	#1-200
X-Men	#1-30

109

The REDISTRIBUTOR

Jef Hinds COMICS

WHY?

This is what I ask myself every time I hear of a significant collection being sold for less money than I would pay, and I wasn't contacted. You have nothing to lose and everything to gain by contacting me. I have purchased many of the major collections over the years. We are serious about buying your comics and paying you the most for them.

If you have comics or related items for sale, please call or send a list for my quote. Remember, no collection is too large or small, even if it's $200,000 or more.

These are some of the high prices I will pay for comics. Percentages stated will be paid for any grade unless otherwise noted, and are based on the Overstreet Guide.

—JAMES F. PAYETTE

Action #2–20	85%	Detective #28–100	60%
Action #21–200	65%	Detective #27 (Mint)	125%
Action #1 (Mint)	125%	Green Lantern #1 (Mint)	150%
Adventure #247	75%	Jackie Gleason #1–12	70%
All American #16 (Mint)	150%	Keen Detective Funnies	70%
All Star #8	70%	Ken Maynard	70%
Amazing Man	70%	More Fun #7–51	75%
Amazing Mystery Funnies	70%	New Adventure #12–31	80%
The Arrow	70%	New Comics #1–11	70%
Batman #2–100	60%	New Fun #1–6	70%
Batman #1 (Mint)	150%	Sunset Carson	70%
Bob Steele	70%	Superman #1 (Mint)	150%
Detective #1–26	85%	Whip Wilson	70%

We are also paying 70% of Guide for the following:

All Winners	Detective Picture Stories	Mystery Men
Andy Devine	Funny Pages	Marvel Mystery
Captain America (1st)	Funny Picture Stories	Tim McCoy
Congo Bill	Hangman	Wonder Comics
Detective Eye	Jumbo 1–10	(Fox 1 & 2)

BUYING & SELLING GOLDEN AND SILVER AGE COMICS SINCE 1975

129

131

TAKE TWO!
GET BOTH COVERS!

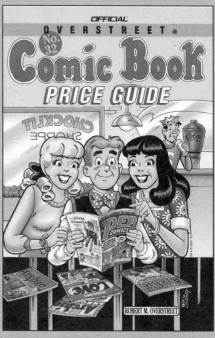

THE OVERSTREET® COMIC BOOK PRICE GUIDE
THIRTY-SECOND EDITION

SPIDER-MAN IN THE MOVIES • SUPERMAN GETS PATRIOTIC
ARCHIE AT SIXTY
MARKET REPORTS, KEY SALES & MUCH MORE!
The MOST COMPLETE LISTING of COMICS from the 1800s to Present!

These covers available at your local comic book shop
or call (888) 375-9800 ext. 249 to order

138

HEROES CONVENTION
CHARLOTTE

America's Favorite Comic Convention!

June 14·16
2002

Early Confirmations

Dan Brereton
Nick Cardy
Ron Garney
Butch Guice
Tony Harris
Adam Hughes
Terry Moore
Kevin Nowlan
Carlos Pacheco
George Perez
Brian Stelfreeze
Roy Thomas
Tim Townsend
Charles Vess
Mike Wieringo
plus many more!

Professionals·Publishers·Exhibitors
For more info and to sign-up...
Contact:

Heroes Aren't Hard To Find
P.O. Box 9181 · Charlotte, NC 28299 · 704-375-7463
Visit our new store location...
1957 East 7th Street·Charlotte
www.heroesonline.com

144

'nuff said

150

From Collector to Collector...

At Heritage Comics Auctions, we know what collectors want because we ARE collectors. We know what's important to fans, because we ARE fans.

NAME:

John Petty

COLLECTS:
Silver Age Marvel, Golden Age Timely, Original Art featuring Mister Miracle, or virtually anything by Jack Kirby, George Tuska, Winsor McKay, or Graham Ingels.

John Petty, the Director of HCA, and Jim Halperin, Co-Chairman of Heritage Capital Corporation, have been fans and collectors for years. Jim published comics and fanzines in the early 1960s before he was a teenager. Part of John's collection was shown in a museum exhibition when he was in junior high school. John and Jim have each bought, sold, collected and traded comics, comic art, animation and illustration art, and related collectibles for longer than either would care to remember!

From Fan to Fan...

hat's why HCA's first and foremost goal
outstanding customer service. Ever
een ripped off by dealers who overgrade
heir books? No kidding, so have we.
ver been frustrated by sales listings
rith inadequate descriptions? Small
rorld: Us, too. Ever been surprised to
pen up a package and have the mer-
handise not be what you expected?
een there, done that.

o if you have comics and collectibles
ou'd like to sell outright or consign to
uction call John Petty at 214-252-4392,
r e-mail him at
'etty@HeritageComics.com. You won't be
alking to some anonymous businessman
rho doesn't know the difference
etween IRON MAN and THE IRON
IANT, you'll be talking to a fan and a
ollector. Just like you.

nd be sure to join our free online com-
nunity at www.HeritageComics.com to
ceive lots of benefits and stay up-to-date

NAME:
Jim Halperin
COLLECTS:
High-grade
EC comics and
original art,
American
illustration art,
MAD magazines,
MAD and
EC collectibles.
(will gladly buy entire
collections just to
obtain needed items).

Heritage COMICS Auctions

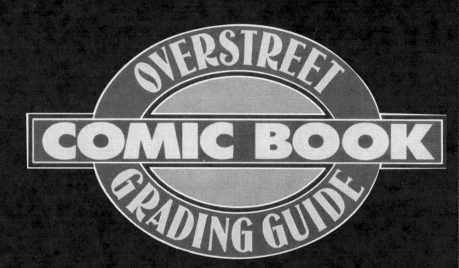

THE SECOND EDITION

Will you make the grade?

COMING IN 2002

170

171

©MARVEL

J.A.HARPER

Buying Old Comics and related items made between 1930-1975.
LHCOMICS@LYCOS.COM
Leroy Harper
P.O. Box 63
Clinton, KY 42031
270-653-5118

195

Advertise!

GEMSTONE PUBLISHING is your ticket to the comics and collectibles market!

To advertise in any of our publications including
Hake's Price Guide To Character Toys,
The Overstreet® Comic Book Price Guide, and
The Overstreet® Indian Arrowheads Price Guide
call Toll Free (888) 375-9800 ext. 402

Visit us on the web at www.gemstonepub.com

199

www.comiclink.com

208

JOHN VERZYL AND DAUGHTER ROSE, "HARD AT WORK."

John Verzyl started collecting comic books in 1965, and within ten years he had amassed thousands of Golden and Silver Age comic books. In 1979, with his wife Nanette, he opened "COMIC HEAVEN," a retail store devoted entirely to the buying and selling of comic books.

Over the years, John Verzyl has come to be recognized as an authority in the field of comic books. He has served as a special advisor to the "Overstreet Comic Book Price Guide" for the last ten years. Thousands of his "mint" comics were photographed for Ernst Gerber's newly-released "Photo-Journal Guide To Comic Books." His tables and displays at the annual San Diego Comic Convention and the Chicago Comic Convention draw customers from all over the country.

The first COMIC HEAVEN AUCTION was held in 1987, and today his Auction Catalogs are mailed out to more than ten thousand interested collectors and dealers.

Comic Heaven
John and Nanette Verzyl
P.O. Box 900
Big Sandy, TX 75755
1-903-636-5555

Congratulations! We at Gemstone welcome you to the hobby of comic books. This book is the most comprehensive reference work available on comics. It is also respected and used by dealers and collectors everywhere. The Overstreet price is the accepted price around the world, and we have not earned this privilege easily. Through hard work, diligence and constant contact with the market for decades, Overstreet has become the most trusted name in comics.

HOW TO USE THIS BOOK

This volume is an accurate, detailed alphabetical list of comic books and their retail values. Comic books are listed by title, regardless of company. Prices listed are shown in Good, Fine and Near Mint condition with many key books priced in an additional Very Fine grade. Comic books that fall in between the grades listed can be priced simply with the following procedure: Very Good is half way between Good and Fine; Very Fine is half way between Fine and Near Mint (unless a VF price is already shown). The older true Mint books usually bring a premium over the Near Mint price. Books in Fair bring 50 to 70% of the Good price. Some books only show a Very Fine price as the highest grade. The author has not been able to determine if these particular books exist in better than Very Fine condition, thus the omission of a Near Mint price. Most comic books are listed in groups, i.e., 11-20, 21-30, 31-50, etc.

The prices listed opposite these groupings represent the value of each issue in that group. More detailed information is given for individual comic books. If you are looking for a particular character, consult the first appearance indexes which will help you locate the correct title and issue. This book also contains hundreds of ads covering all aspects of this hobby. Whether you are buying or selling, the advertising sections can be of tremendous benefit to you.

NEW COMIC BOOKS

This book lists all new comic books at cover price, regardless of their performance in the secondary market. In many cases, new comics are not worth their cover price in the secondary market, and collectors may pay pennies on the dollar for copies of these issues. Nevertheless, since these comics have yet to establish themselves as collectors' items, they are listed at full cover price.

It should also be noted that regarding polybagged comics, it is the official policy of **The Overstreet Comic Book Price Guide** to grade comics regardless of whether they are still sealed in their polybag or not. If opened, the polybag and its contents should be preserved separately so that all components of the original package remain together.

COMIC BOOK VALUES

All values listed in this book are in U.S. currency and are retail prices based on (but not limited to) reports from our extensive network of experienced advisors which include convention sales, mail order, auctions, unpublished personal sales and stores. Overstreet, with several decades of market experience, has developed a unique and comprehensive system for gathering, documenting, averaging and pricing data on comic books. The end result is a true fair market value for your use. We have earned the reputation for our cautious, conservative approach to pricing comic books. You, the collector, can be assured that the prices listed in this volume are the most accurate and useful in print.

IMPORTANT NOTE: This book is not a dealer's price list, although some dealers may base their prices on the values listed. The true value of any comic book is what you are willing to pay. Prices listed herein are an indication of what collectors (not dealers) would probably pay. For one reason or another, these collectors might want certain books badly, or else need specific issues to complete their runs and so are willing to pay more.

DEALERS' POSITION: Dealers are not in a position to pay the full prices listed, but work on a percentage depending largely on the amount of investment required and the quality of material offered. Usually they will pay from 20 to 70% of the list price depending on how long it will take them to sell the collection after making the investment; the higher the demand and better the condition, the more the percentage. Most dealers are faced with expenses such as advertising, travel, telephone and mailing, rent, employee salaries, plus convention costs. These costs must all be factored in before the books are sold. The high demand books usually sell right away but there are many other titles that are difficult to sell due to low demand. Sometimes a dealer will have costs tied up in this types of books for several years before finally moving them. Remember, his position is that of handling, demand, and overhead. Most dealers are victims of these economics.

Comic books are listed alphabetically by title. The true title of a comic book can usually be found listed with the publisher's information, or indicia, often found at the bottom of the first page. Titles that appear on the front cover can vary from the official title listed inside.

Comic book titles, sequence of issues, dates of first and last issues, publishing companies, origin and special issues are listed when known. Prominent and collectible artists are also pointed out (usually in footnotes). Page counts will always include covers. Most comic books began with a #1, but occasionally many titles began with an odd number. There is a reason for this. Publishers had to register new titles with the post office for 2nd class permits. The registration fee was expensive. To avoid this expense, many publishers would continue the numbering of new titles from old defunct titles. For instance, **Weird Science** #12 (1st issue) was continued from the defunct **Saddle Romances** #11 (the last issue). In doing this, the publishers hoped to avoid having to register new titles. However, the post office would soon discover the new title and force the publisher to pay the registration fee as well as to list the correct number. For instance, the previous title mentioned began with #12 (1st issue). Then #13 through #15 were published. The next issue became #5 after the Post Office correction. Now the sequence of published issues (see the listings)

is #12-15, 5-on. This created a problem in early fandom for the collector because the numbers 12-15 in this title were duplicated.

The Guide lists primarily American comic books due to space limitations. The earliest comic books date back to 1897 and are included in their own section under The Platinum Age. These books basically reprinted newspaper strips and were published in varying sizes, usually with cardboard covers, but sometimes as hardbacks. The format of **Funnies On Parade**, published in 1933 (saddle-stitched), soon became the standard for the modern comic book, although squarebound versions were also published. Most of these formats that appeared on newsstands will be included.

The 1980s and '90s have experienced an explosion of publishers with hundreds of new titles appearing in black & white and color. Many of these comics are listed in this book, but not all due to space limitation. We will attempt to list complete information only on those titles that show some collector interest. The selection of titles to include is constantly being monitored by our board of advisors. Please do not contact us to list your new comic books. Listings are determined by the marketplace. However, we are interested in receiving review copies of all new comic books published.

GRADING

Comic book grading has evolved over the past several decades from a much looser interpretation of standards in the beginning to the very tight professional scrutiny in use by the market today. In recent years, grading criteria have become even tighter, especially in Silver and Bronze Age books, due to their higher survival rate.

Several events have impacted grading over the years. The first has to be the arrival of comic book conventions. Here, collectors could easily compare and discuss grading with dealers. The second major event was the discovery of the Mile High collection in 1977, which showed fandom true NM/MT Golden Age books.

Probably the most important event to date, however, was the arrival of comic book certification with Comics Guaranty Corp. (CGC). After two years

in our market, over 100,000 books have now been certified. The technical grading applied to each comic book has now become the standard used by almost everyone for buying and selling comics.

However, there are a group of special books, known as "pedigrees," that have high cover gloss, brilliant cover inks and white, fresh, supple pages that place them far above other books that might receive the same technical grade. Books from these pedigree collections actually transcend their technical grade. Of these, many collectors and dealers agree that the most important collections are the Mile High (Edgar Church) collection, the San Francisco (Reilly) collection, and the Gaines file copies. They are the most sought after and generally the most well-documented, making it easier to ascertain identity or provenance. Books from these collections all exhibit the extra qualities mentioned above.

This striking difference becomes apparent when comparing two comic books of the same grade, one pedigree and one generic. In most cases, the pedigree book will far outshine the generic one. This is the reason why Mile Highs, San Franciscos and Gaines file copies bring multiples of Guide. Many also agree that a book from one of these collections could very well be one of, if not the, best surviving copies.

To the beginner, it may seem odd that a 9.2 Mile High will bring a higher price than a non-pedigree 9.4, but to the seasoned collector with a good understanding of the hobby and its historical backgroun, it makes perfect sense. The novice collector should understand these facts and acquire as much knowledge as possible about all the other pedigree collections and their place in the market before paying large multiples of Guide for books that are not of pedigree quality.

For complete, detailed information on grading and restoration, consult the **Overstreet Comic Book Grading Guide**. Copies are available through all normal distribution channels or can be ordered direct from the publisher by sending $12 plus $2 postage and handling. You can also call Gemstone toll free at 1-888-375-9800.

The Overstreet Comic Book Grading Card, known as the **ONE** and **OWL Card** is also available. This card has two functions. The **ONE Card** (**O**verstreet's **N**umerical **E**quivalent) is used to convert grading condition terms to the new numerical grading system. The **OWL Card** (**O**verstreet's **W**hiteness **L**evel) is used for grading the whiteness of paper. The color scale on the **OWL Card** is simply placed over the interior comic book paper. The paper color is matched with the color on the card to get the **OWL** number. The **ONE/OWL Card** may be ordered direct from the publisher by sending $1.30 per card.

HOW TO GRADE

Before a comic book's true value can be assessed, its condition or state of preservation must be determined. In all comic books, the better the condition the more desirable and valuable the book. Comic books in **MINT** condition will bring several times the price of the same book in **POOR** condition. Therefore it is very important to be able to properly grade your books. Comics should be graded from the inside out, so the following comic book areas should be examined before assigning a final grade.

Check inside pages, inside spine and covers and outside spine and covers for any tears, markings, brittleness, tape, soiling, chunks out or other defects that would affect the grade. After all the above steps have been taken, then the reader can begin to consider an overall grade for his or her book. The grading of a comic book is done by simply looking at the book and describing its condition, which may range from absolutely perfect newsstand condition **MINT** to extremely worn, dirty, and torn **POOR**.

Numerous variables influence the evaluation of a comic book's condition and all must be considered in the final evaluation. Although the grade of a comic book is based upon an accumulation of defects, some defects may be more extreme for a particular grade as long as other acceptable listed defects are almost non-existent. As grading is the most subjective aspect of determining a comic's value, it is very important that the grader be careful not to allow wishful thinking to influence what the eyes see. It is also very important to realize that older comics in **MINT** condition are extremely scarce and are rarely advertised for sale; most of the higher grade comics advertised range from **VERY FINE** to **NEAR MINT**.

GRADING DEFINITIONS

Note: This edition uses both the traditional grade abbreviations and the **ONE** number throughout the listings. The **O**verstreet **N**umerical **E**quivalent (**ONE**) spread range is given with each grade.

MINT (MT) (ONE 9.9-10.0): Near perfect in every way. Only the most subtle bindery or printing defects are allowed. Cover is flat with no surface wear. Cover inks are bright with high reflectivity and minimal fading. Corners are cut square and sharp. Staples are generally centered, clean with no rust. Cover is generally well centered and firmly secured to interior pages. Paper is supple and fresh. Spine is tight and flat.

NEAR MINT/MINT (NM/MT) (ONE 9.8): A comic book that has enough positive qualities to make it better than a NM+, but has enough detracting qualities to keep it from being a MT 9.9. In most cases the comic book has a better appearance than a NM+.

NEAR MINT (NM) (ONE 9.2-9.7): Nearly perfect with only minor imperfections allowed. This grade should have no corner or impact creases, stress marks should be almost invisible, and bindery tears must be less than 1/16 inch. A couple of very tiny color flecks, or a combination of the above that keeps the book from being perfect, where the overall eye appeal is less than Mint drops the book into this grade. Only the most subtle binding and/or printing defects allowed. Cover is flat with no surface wear. Cover inks are bright with high reflectivity and minimum of fading. Corners are cut square and sharp with ever so slight blunting permitted. Staples are generally centered, clean with no rust. Cover is well centered and firmly secured to interior pages. Paper is supple and like new. Spine is tight and flat.

VERY FINE/NEAR MINT (VF/NM) (ONE 9.0): A comic book that has enough positive qualities to make it better than a VF+, but has enough detracting qualities to keep it from being a NM-. In most cases the comic book has a better appearance than a VF+.

VERY FINE (VF) (ONE 7.5-8.5): An excellent copy with outstanding eye appeal. Sharp, bright and clean with supple pages. Cover is relatively flat with almost no surface wear. Cover inks are generally bright with moderate to high reflectivity. Staples may show some discoloration. Spine may have a couple of almost insignificant transverse stress lines and is almost completely flat. A barely unnoticeable 1/4 inch crease is acceptable, if color is not broken. Pages and covers can be yellowish/tannish (at the least, but not brown and will usually be off-white to white).

FINE/VERY FINE (FN/VF) (ONE 7.0): A comic book that has enough positive qualities to make it better than a FN+, but has enough detracting qualities to keep it from being a VF-. In most cases the comic book has a better appearance than a FN+.

FINE (FN) (ONE 5.5-6.5): An above-average copy that shows minor wear but is still relatively flat and clean with no significant creasing or other serious defects. Eye appeal is somewhat reduced because of slight surface wear and possibly a small defect such as a few slight cross stress marks on spine or a very slight spine split (1/4"). A Fine condition comic book appears to have been read a few times and has been handled with moderate care. Compared to a VF, cover inks are beginning to show a significant reduction in reflectivity but it is still a highly collectible and desirable book.Pages and interior covers may be tan, but pages must still be fairly supple with no signs of brittleness.

VERY GOOD/FINE (VG/FN) (ONE 5.0): A comic book that has enough positive qualities to make it better than a VG+, but has enough detracting qualities to keep it from being a FN-. In most cases the comic book has a better appearance than a VG+.

VERY GOOD (VG) (ONE 3.5-4.5): The average used comic book. A comic in this grade shows some wear, can have a reading or center crease or a moderately rolled spine, but has not accumulated enough total defects to reduce eye appeal to the point that it is not a desirable copy. Some discoloration, fading and even minor soiling is allowed. As much as a 1/4" triangle can be missing out of the corner or edge. A missing square piece (1/8" by 1/8") is also acceptable. Store stamps, name stamps, arrival dates, initials, etc. have no effect on this grade. Cover and interior pages can have some minor tears and folds and the centerfold may be detached at one staple. The cover may also be loose, but not completely detached. Common bindery and printing defects do not affect grade. Pages and inside covers may be brown but not brittle. Tape should never be used for comic book repair; however many VG condition comics have minor tape repair.

GOOD/VERY GOOD (GD/VG) (ONE 3.0): A comic book that has enough positive qualities to keep it better than a GD+, but has enough detracting qualities to keep it from being a VG-. In most cases the comic book has a better appearance than a GD+.

GOOD (GD) (ONE 1.8-2.5): A copy in this grade has all pages and covers, although there may be small pieces missing inside; the largest piece allowed from front or back cover is a 1/2" triangle or a square 1/4" by 1/4". Books in this grade are commonly creased, scuffed, abraded, soiled and may have as much as a 2" spine split, but are still completely readable. Often paper quality is low but not brittle. Cover reflectivity is low and in some cases completely absent. This grade can have a moderate accumulation of defects but still maintains its basic structural integrity.

FAIR/GOOD (FR/GD) (ONE 1.5): A comic book

that has enough positive qualities to keep it better than a FR+, but has enough detracting qualities to keep it from being a GD-. In most cases the comic book has a better appearance than a FR+.

FAIR (FR) (ONE 1.0): A copy in this grade is usually soiled, ragged and possibly unattactive. Creases, tears and/or folds are prevalent. Spine may be split up to 2/3rds its entire length. Staples may be gone. Up to 1/10th of the front cover may be missing. These books are readable although soiling, staining, tears, markings or chunks missing may moderately interfere with reading the complete story. Some collectors consider this the lowest collectible grade because comic books in lesser condition are usually defaced and/or brittle. Very often paper quality is low and may have slight brittleness around the edges but not in the central portions of the pages. Comic books in this grade may have a clipped coupon so long as it is noted along side of the nomenclature; ie: "Fair (1.0) Coupon Clipped." Valued at 50-70% of good.

POOR (PR) (ONE 0.5): Most comic books in this grade have been sufficiently degraded to the point that copies may have extremely severe stains, missing staples, brittleness, mildew or moderate to heavy cover abrasion to the point that some cover inks are indistinct/absent. Comic books in this grade can have small chunks missing and pieces out of pages. They may have been defaced with paints, varnishes, glues, oil, indelible markers or dyes. Covers may be split the entire length of the book, but both halves must be present and basically still there with some chunks missing. A page(s) may be missing as long as it is noted along side of the nomenclature; ie: " POOR (0.5) 2nd Page Missing." Value depends on extent of defects but would average about 1/3 of GOOD.

DUST JACKETS

Many of the early strip reprint comics were printed in hardback with dust jackets. Books with dust jackets are worth more. The value can increase from 20 to 50 percent depending on the rarity of book. Usually, the earlier the book, the greater the percentage. Unless noted, prices listed are without dust jackets. The condition of the dust jacket should be graded independently of the book itself.

RESTORED COMICS

When restoration of comics first began, it was a collection of crude, damaging attempts to preserve or fix comics exhibiting defects like tears or missing pieces. At first using tape, glue and color pens, restoration soon evolved, utilizing more advanced techniques like chemical baths and deacidification. Today, professional restorers work in a quickly maturing field using methods that have stood the test of time. There is still a stigma attached to restoration, however, often due to a lack of knowledge about how restored comics relate to the market.

Many restored comics are unnecessarily put through the process, begging the question, 'when should I restore my comics?' If a comic is in VG or better, do not restore it. Restoration is meant to preserve deteriorating comics, taking an ugly pile of loose pages and restoring them to an attractive form that can be handled and enjoyed. In the case of comics in VG or higher grades, the book is already an attractive item and restoration would be excessive.

The value of the comic should also be high enough to justify restoration. With prices of $30-$75 an hour to restore a comic, only very valuable books should be candidates. It's recommended to avoid restoring Silver Age comics, apart from key issues, due to their relative availability. Restored Silver Age comics also do not rise in value as much as a restored Golden Age comic.

Bindery chips, a common defect in Golden Age comics, are considered printing defects and are relatively acceptable in the market. Restoration on such a defect by itself would usually be considered excessive. Books with brown or brittle pages are usually not good candidates either. Even though the comic will look better, its page quality will still rate a lower grade. Bleaching and other treatments can be used, but are expensive, frowned upon and not very effective. Only the most expensive books should ever be considered for page treatment. Similarly, books missing covers and interior pages are poor candidates for restoration. A comic must be relatively complete to be successfully restored.

Preventative restoration, widely used and accepted by collectors, consists of "non-additive" restoration on a book with one or two major defects. A prime example would be a $2,000 book in Fine that has a 2" piece of tape on the cover. Removal of the tape improves the value and appearance of the book. The process is cheap and quick, and nothing is "added" to the comic, such as Japan paper or color touch (see the glossary for definitions). Although it's always imperative to disclose any and all restoration work on a book, some collectors don't even view these simple repairs as restoration. Other defects fixable by "preventative" techniques are water stains, warping, dirt or writing, rusty staples, and spine rolls. These minor fixes work best with books above VG, the one exception to the rule noted earlier.

Once restored, a comic's value depends upon several factors:

The amount of restoration: In general, the more restoration has been performed, the less the comic is worth compared to its apparent grade value. A lightly restored book will be valued higher than a book with heavy restoration in the same apparent grade.

The "before" and "restored" grades: As a rule of thumb, consider these formulae:

Golden Age key issues:
(guide value of comic before restoration)
+(guide value of comic's apparent grade)/2.5

Golden Age common issues:
(guide value of comic before restoration)
+(guide value of comic's apparent grade)/2.0

Silver Age issues:
(guide value of comic before restoration)
+(guide value of comic's apparent grade)/3.0

These formulae serve only as a benchmark. Each book is unique and may vary in pricing.

The market demand: This is highly subjective, but the higher the demand, the likelier your restored book will fetch its apparent grade price. Consequently, if the comic is slow on the market, a restored copy may be less than the value derived from the above formulae.

The market value: The market fluctuates widely on restored copies of expensive books. A small variance in perception of what a restored copy is worth can mean a difference of thousands of dollars on high end comics (see formulae above). Values tend to be more stable on common books.

Age of the comic: The younger a comic, the less likely the book will increase in value significantly from restoration. This applies mainly to Silver Age comics, as noted earlier.

Armed with this knowledge and a good understanding of the market, you should be able to make an informed decision about restoration. When in doubt, contact a reputable dealer or collector who is familiar with restored comics in the marketplace.

SCARCITY OF COMICS

1897-1933 Comics: Most of these books are bound with thick cardboard covers and are very rare to non-existent in VF or better condition. Due to their extreme age, paper browning is very common. Brittleness could be a problem.

1933-1940 Comics: There are many issues from this period that are very scarce in any condition, especially from the early to mid-1930s. Surviving copies of any particular issue range from a handful to several hundred. Near Mint to Mint copies are virtually non-existent with known examples of any particular issue limited to five or fewer copies. Most surviving copies are in FN-VF or less condition. Brittleness or browning of paper is fairly common and could be a problem.

1941-1952 Comics: Surviving comic books would number from less than 100 to several thousand copies of each issue. Near Mint to Mint copies are a little more common but are still relatively scarce with only a dozen or so copies in this grade existing of any particular issue. Exceptions would be recent warehouse finds of most Dell comics (6-100 copies, but usually 30 or less), and Harvey comics (1950s-1970s) surfacing. Due to low paper quality of the late 1940s and 1950s, many comics from this period are rare in Near Mint to Mint condition. Most remaining copies are VF or less. Browning of paper could be a problem.

1953-1959 Comics: As comic book sales continued to drop during the 1950s, production values were lowered resulting in cheaply printed comics. For this reason, high grade copies are extremely rare. Many Atlas and Marvel comics have chipping along the trimmed edges (Marvel chipping) which reduces even more the number of surviving high grade copies.

1960-1979 Comics: Early '60s comics are rare in Near Mint to Mint condition. Most copies of early '60s Marvels and DCs grade no higher than VF. Many early keys in NM or MT exist in numbers less than 10-20 of each. Mid-'60s to late-'70s books in high grade are more common due to the hoarding of comics that began in the mid-'60s.

1980-Present: Comics of today are common in high grade. VF to NM is the standard rather than the exception.

When you consider how few Golden and Silver Age books exist compared to the current market, you will begin to appreciate the true rarity of these early books. In many cases less than 5-10 copies exist of a particular issue in Near Mint to Mint condition, while most of the 1930s books do not exist in this grade at all.

New comic books are available in many different kinds of stores. Grocery stores, drug stores, Wal-Mart, K-Mart, book stores, comic book stores and card and comics specialty shops are a few examples. Local flea markets and, of course, comic book conventions in your area are excellent sources for new and old comic books.

Most collectors begin by buying new issues in Mint condition directly off the newsstand or from their local comic store. (Subscription copies are available from several mail-order services, and often the publishers themselves.) Each week new comics appear on the stands that are destined to become true collectors' items. The trick is to locate a store that carries a complete line of comics. In several localities this may be difficult. Most collectors frequent several magazine stands in order not to miss something they want. Even then, it pays to keep in close contact with collectors in other areas. Sooner or later, nearly every collector has to rely upon a friend in Fandom or a dealer to obtain for him an item that is unavailable locally (see ads in this book).

Before you buy any comic to add to your collection, you should carefully inspect its condition. Unlike stamps and coins, defective comics are generally not highly prized. The cover should be properly cut and printed. Remember that every blemish or sign of wear depreciates the beauty and value of your comics.

The serious collector usually buys extra copies of popular titles. He may trade these multiples for items unavailable locally (for example, foreign comics), or he may store the multiples for resale at some future date. Such speculation is, of course, a gamble. Selecting the right investment books is tricky business that requires special knowledge. With experience, the beginner will improve his buying skills. Remember, if you play the new comics market, be prepared to buy and sell fast as values rise and fall rapidly.

Today's comic books offer a wide variety of subjects, art styles and writers to satisfy even the most discriminating fan. Whether it's the latest new hot title or company, or one of many popular titles that have been around for a long time, the comic book fan has a broad range from which to pick. Print runs of many popular titles have dropped over the past few years, creating the possibility of a true rarity occurring when demand outstrips supply. Less "gimmicky" covers are seen these days, but occasionally an eye-catching specialty cover will appear, such as the Superman new costume issue (#123) that glows-in-the-dark. Some cover variants continue to appear as well. "Bad Girl" and horror titles have been popular along with the standard superhero fare. The collector should always stay informed about the new trends developing in this fast-moving market. Since the market fluctuates greatly, and there is a vast array of comics to choose from, it's recommended first and foremost that you collect what you enjoy reading; that way, despite any value changes, you will always maintain a sense of personal satisfaction with your collection.

POLYBAGGED COMICS: It is the official policy of this Guide to grade comics regardless of whether they are still sealed in their polybag or not. Sealed comics in bags are not always in MINT condition and could even be damaged. The value should not suffer as long as the bag (opened) and all of its original manufactured contents are preserved and kept together.

COLLECTING ON A BUDGET: Collectors check out their local newsstand or comic specialty store for the latest arrivals. Hundreds of brand new comic books are displayed each week for the collector, much more than anyone can afford to purchase. Today's reader must be careful and budget his money wisely in choosing what to buy.

COLLECTING ARTISTS: Many collectors enjoy favorite artists and follow their work from issue to issue, title to title, company to company. In recent years, some artists have achieved "star" status. Autograph signings occur at all major comic conventions as well as special promotions with local stores. Fans line up by the hundreds at such events to meet these superstars. Some of the current top artists of new comics are: Todd McFarlane, Alex Ross, Jim Lee, Michael Turner, Marc Silvestri, Rob Liefeld, Chris Bachalo, J. Scott Campbell, Humberto Ramos, and Adam and Andy Kubert. Original artwork from these artists have been bringing record prices at auctions and from dealers' lists.

COLLECTING BY COMPANIES: Some collectors become loyal to a particular company and only collect its titles. It's another way to specialize and collect in a market that expands faster than your pocket book.

COLLECTING #1 ISSUES: For decades, comic enthusiasts have always collected first (#1) issues. This is yet another way to control spending and build an interesting collection for the future. #1 issues have everything going for them--some introduce new characters, while others are underprinted, creating a rarity factor. #1 issues cross many subjects as well as companies, and make for an intriguing collection.

BACK ISSUES

A back issue is any comic currently not available on the stands. Collectors of current titles often want to find the earlier issues in order to complete the run. Thus a back issue collector is born. Comic books have been published and collected for over 100 years. However, the earliest known comic book dealers didn't appear until the late 1930s. But today, there are hundreds of dealers that sell old comic books (See ads in this book).

LOCATING BACK ISSUES: The first place to begin, of course, is with your collector friends who may have unwanted back issues or duplicates for sale. Look in the yellow pages, or call the Comic Shop Locator Service at 1-888-COMIC-BOOK, to see if you have a comic book store available. If you do, they would know of other collectors in your area. Advertising in local papers could get good results. Go to regional markets and look for comic book dealers. There are many trade publications in the hobby that would put you in touch with out-of-town dealers. This Annual Guide has ads buying and selling old comic books. Some dealers publish regular price lists of old comic books for sale. Get on their mailing list.

Putting a quality collection of old comics together takes a lot of time, effort and money. Many old comics are not easy to find. Persistence and luck play a big part in acquiring needed issues. Most quality collections are put together over a long period of time by placing mail orders with dealers and other collectors.

Comics of early vintage are extremely expensive if they are purchased through a regular dealer or collector. Unless you have unlimited funds to invest in your hobby, you will find it necessary to restrict your collecting in certain ways. However you define your collection, you should be careful to set your goals well within affordable limits.

PRESERVATION & STORAGE

Comic books are fragile and easy to damage. Most dealers and collectors hesitate to let anyone personally handle their rare comics. It is common courtesy to ask permission before handling another person's comic book. Most dealers would prefer to remove the comic from its bag and show it to the customer themselves. In this way, if the book is damaged, it would be the dealer's responsibility–not the customer's. Remember, the slightest crease or chip could render an otherwise Mint book to Near Mint or even Very Fine.

Consult the **Overstreet Comic Book Grading Guide** and learn the proper way to hold a comic book. The following steps are provided to aid the novice in the proper handling of comic books: 1. Remove the comic from its protective sleeve or bag very carefully. 2. Gently lay the comic (unopened) in the palm of your hand so that it will stay relatively flat and secure. 3. You can now leaf through the book by carefully rolling or flipping the pages with the thumb and forefinger of your other hand. Caution: Be sure the book always remains relatively flat or slightly rolled. Avoid creating stress points on the covers with your fingers and be particularly cautious in bending covers back too far on Mint books. 4. After examining the book, carefully insert it back into the bag or protective sleeve. Watch corners and edges for folds or tears as you replace the book. Always keep tape completely away while inserting a comic in a bag.

Comic books should also be protected from the elements as well as the dangers of light, heat, and humidity. This can easily be achieved with proper storage. Improper storage methods will be detrimental to the "health" of your collection, and may even quicken its deterioration.

Store comic books away from direct light sources, especially florescent which contains high levels of ultraviolet (UV) radiation. UV lights are like sunlight, and will quickly fade the cover inks. Tungsten filament lighting is safer than florescent but should still be used at brief intervals. Remember, exposure to light accumulates damage, so store your collection in a cool, dark place away from windows.

Temperatures must also be carefully regulated. Fungus and mold thrives in higher temperatures, so the lower the temperature, the longer the life of your collection.

Atmospheric pollution is another problem associated with long term storage of paper. Sulfuric dioxide which can occur from automobile exhaust will cause paper to turn yellow over a period of time. For this reason, it is best not to store your valuable comics close to a garage. Some of the best preserved comic books known were protected from exposure to the air such as the Gaines EC collection. These books were carefully wrapped in paper at time of publication, and completely sealed from the air. Each package was then sealed in a box and stored in a closet in New York. After over 40 years of storage when the packages were opened, you could instantly catch the odor of fresh newsprint; the paper was snow white and supple, and the cover inks were as brilliant as the day they were printed. This illustrates how important it is to protect your comics from the atmosphere.

Like UV, high relative humidity (rh) can also be damaging to paper. Maintaining a low and stable relative humidity, around 50%, is crucial; varying humidity will only damage your collection.

Care must be taken when choosing materials for storing your comics. Many common items such as plastic bags, boards, and boxes may not be as safe as they seem. Some contain chemicals that will actually help to destroy your collection rather than save it. Always purchase materials designed for long-term storage, such as Mylar type "D" sleeves and acid-free boards and boxes. Polypropylene and polyethylene bags, while safe for temporary storage, should be changed every three to five years.

Comics are best stored vertically in boxes. For shelving, make sure that comics do not come into direct contact with the shelving surface. Use acid-free boards as a buffer between shelves comics. Also, never store comics directly on the floor; elevate them 6-10 inches to allow for flooding. Similarly, never store your collection directly against a wall, particularly an outside wall. Condensation and poor air circulation will encourage mold and fungus growth.

When handling your high grade comics, wash your hands first, eliminating harmful oils from the skin before coming into contact with the books. Lay the comic on a flat surface and slowly turn the pages. This will minimize the stress to the staples and spine. With these guidelines, your collection should enjoy a long life and maintain a reasonable condition and value.

BUYING & SELLING

Whether you're a new collector just starting to acquire comics or a long-time collector now interested in selling a collection, by purchasing this Guide, you have begun the long process necessary to successfully buy and sell comics.

SELLING YOUR COMICS

If you are planning to sell a collection, you must first decide what category listed below best describes your collection. As a rule of thumb, the lower categories will need less detail provided in your inventory list. A collection of key late '30s DCs will require you to list exact titles, numbers, and grades, as well as possible restoration information. If, however, you have 20,000 miscellaneous '80s and '90s comics for sale, a rough list of the number of books and publishers should be enough. The categories are:

1. PLATINUM AGE (1897-1932): The supply is very scarce. More people are becoming interested in these early books due to comics passing their 100th birthday. Moderate interest among average dealers, but high interest with dealers that specialize in this material. A detailed list will be necessary paying attention to brittleness, damage and pages missing. Dealers will pay up to a high percentage of Guide list for key titles.

2. GOLDEN AGE, All Grades (1933 - pre-1956): The most desirable. A detailed inventory will be necessary. Key higher grade books are easier to sell, but lower grades in most titles show the best selling potential, due to the fact that many collectors cannot afford a $20,000 VF book but may be able to afford a GD for only $2,000. Highest demand is for the superhero titles such as **Batman**, **Superman**, **Human Torch**, etc. The percentage of Guide that dealers will pay for your collection will vary depending on condition and contents. A collection of low demand titles will not bring the same percentage as a collection of prime titles.

3. High Grade SILVER AGE (1956-mid 1960s): A detailed inventory will be necessary. There are always investors looking for VF or better books from this period. Dealers will usually pay a high percentage of Guide list for these high grade books. Silver Age below VF will fall into category #4.

4. Low Grade SILVER AGE: Spanning books lower than VF from the late '50s to 1970, this category exhibits the average grade of most collections. Consequently, the supply of this material is much more common than category #2. This means that you could be competing with many other similar collections being offered at the same time. You will have to shop this type of collection to get the best price, and be prepared to sell at a significant discount if you find a willing buyer with good references.

5. MODERN AGE (post-1970): Certain titles from the early 1970s in high grade are showing increasing demand. However, many books from the 1980s to the 1990s are in low demand with the supply for the most part always being of high grade books. These collections are typified by long runs of certain titles and/or publishers. A detailed inventory will not be necessary. Contact local comic stores or buyers first to gauge their level of interest. Dealing with buyers outside your area should be avoided if possible.

IMPORTANT: Many of the 1980s and 1990s books are listed at cover price. This indicates that these books have not established a collector's value. When selling books of this type, the true market value could be 20-50% of cover price or less.

6. BULK (post-1980 in quantities greater than 5,000): These collections usually contain multiple copies of the same issues. It is advisable to price on a per-book basis (2¢ and 20¢ each). Do NOT attempt an inventory list, and only contact buyers who advertise buying in bulk quantity.

You should never deal with a buyer without fully checking their references. For additional verification, consult The Better Business Bureau; the local BBB may be able to help you in establishing a buyer's credibility, as well as assisting in resolving any disputes. **The Overstreet Comic Book Price Guide** and **Comic Book Marketplace** are also recognized authorities. Advertised dealers will likely have a more established reputation.

Potential buyers will be most concerned with the retail value of your entire collection, which may be more or less than Guide depending what you have and their current demand. Some rare early books in VF or NM may bring a price over Guide list while other titles in lower grade may sell for a price under Guide list. Most vintage books, however, will sell for around the Guide price. However, 1980s or 1990s books that list at cover price may only be worth a percentage of that price. You must then decide on what percentage you would be willing to accept for your collection, taking into account how the collection breaks down into fast, moderate and slow moving books. To expect someone to pay full retail is unrealistic. You will have to be flexible in order to close a deal.

Many buyers may want to purchase only certain key or high grade books from your collection, almost always favoring the buyer. While you may be paid a high percentage of retail, you will find that "cherry-picked" collections are much more difficult to sell. Furthermore, the percentage of retail that you will receive for a "cherry-picked" collection will be much lower than if the collection had been left intact. Remember, key issues and/or high grade issues make or break a collection. Selling on consignment, another popular option in today's market, could become a breeding ground for cherry-pickers, so again, always check a dealer's references thoroughly.

Some collectors may choose to sell their comic books on a piecemeal basis, requiring much greater care and detail in preparing an inventory list and grading comics for sale. You will be able to realize a higher percentage of retail by selling your collection this way, but the key books will certainly sell first, leaving a significant portion of the collection unsold. You will need to keep repricing and discounting your books to encourage buyers.

You can advertise your collection in trade publications or through mass mailings. If you sell books through the mail, you must also establish a reasonable return policy, as some books will unquestionably be returned. Check the local post office and/or UPS regarding the various rates and services available for shipping your books. Marketing your books at conventions is another option. As a dealer, you will also incur overhead expenses such as postage, mailing and display supplies, advertising costs, etc.

In all cases, be willing to establish trust with a prospective buyer. By following the procedures outlined here, you will be able to sell your collection successfully, for a fair price, with both parties walking away satisfied. After all, collecting comic books is supposed to be fun; it only becomes a chore if you let it.

WHERE TO BUY AND SELL

Throughout this book you will find the advertisements of many reputable dealers who sell back-issue comics magazines. If you are an inexperienced collector, be sure to compare prices before you buy. When a dealer is selected (ask for references), send him a small order (under $100) first to check out his grading accuracy, promptness in delivery, guarantees of condition advertised, and whether he will accept returns when dissatisfied. Never send cash through the mail. Send money orders or checks for your personal protection. Beware of bargains, as the items advertised sometimes do not exist but are only a fraud to get your money.

The Price Guide is indebted to everyone who placed ads in this volume. Your mentioning this book when dealing with the advertisers would be greatly appreciated.

COMIC CONVENTIONS

The first comic book conventions, or cons, were originally conceived as the comic book counterpart to science fiction fandom conventions. There were many attempts to form successful national cons, but they were all stillborn. It is interesting that after only three relatively organized years of existence, the first comic con was held. Of course, its magnitude was nowhere near as large as most established cons held today.

What is a comic con? Dealers, collectors, fans, publishers, distributors, manufacturers, whatever they call themselves can be found trading, selling, and buying the adventures of their favorite characters for hours on end. Additionally most cons have guests of honor, usually professionals in the field of comic art, either writers, artists, or editors. The committees put together panels for the con attendees in which the assembled pros talk about certain areas of comics, most of the time fielding questions from the assembled audience. At cons one can usually find displays of various and sundry things, usually toys, thousands of comic books, original art, and more. There can be the showing of movies or videos. Of course there is always the chance to get together with friends at cons and just talk about comics. One also has a good opportunity to make new friends who have similar interests and with whom one can correspond after the convention is over.

It is difficult to describe accurately what goes on at a con. The best way to find out is to go to one and see for yourself. The largest cons are WonderCon (April), Pittsburgh (April), San Diego (July), Chicago (July), and Atlanta (July). For accurate dates and addresses, consult ads in this edition as well as some of the adzines. Please remember when writing for convention information to include a self addressed, stamped envelope for reply.

COMIC BOOK FANDOM

It's possible to discern two distinct and largely unrelated movements in the history of Comics Fandom. The first began around 1953 as a response to the the trend-setting EC lines of comics. The first true comics fanzines of this movement were short-lived. Bob Stewart's **EC FAN BULLETIN** was a hectographed newsletter that ran two issues about six months apart; Jimmy Taurasi's **FANTASY COMICS**, a newsletter devoted to all science-fiction comics of the period, was a monthly that ran for about six months. These were followed by other newsletters such as Mike May's **EC FAN JOURNAL**, and George Jennings' **EC WORLD PRESS**. EC fanzines of a wider and more critical scope appeared somewhat later. Two of the finest were **POTRZEBIE**, from a number of fans, and Ron Parker's **HOOHAH**. Gauging from the response that **POTRZEBIE** received from an EC letter column plug, Ted White estimated the average age of EC fans at 9 to 13, while many were actually in their mid-teens. This was discouraging to many fanzine editors hoping to reach an older audience. Consequently, many gave up their efforts on behalf of Comics Fandom, especially with the demise of the EC groups, and turned to SF (science fiction) fandom with its longer tradition and older membership. While the flourish of fan activity in response to the EC comics was certainly noteworthy, it never developed into a full-fledged, independent, and self-sustaining movement.

The second movement began in 1960, largely as a response to (and later stimulus for) the reappearance of the costumed hero and the Second Heroic Age of Comics. Most historians date the Second Heroic Age from **Flash** #105, February 1959. The letter departments of Julius Schwartz (editor at National Periodicals), and later those of Stan Lee (Marvel Group) and Bill Harris (Gold Key) were influential in bringing comics readers into Fandom. Sparks were lit among SF fans first, when experienced fan writers, who were part of an established tradition, produced the first in a series of articles on '40s comics–ALL IN COLOR FOR A DIME. The series was introduced in **XERO** #1 (September 1960), a general SF fanzine edited and published by Dick Lupoff.

Meanwhile, outside SF fandom, Jerry Bails and Roy Thomas, two comics fans of long-standing, conceived the first true comics fanzine in response to the Second Heroic Age, **ALTER EGO**, appearing in March 1961. The first issues were widely circulated, and profoundly influenced the comics fan movement, attracting many fans in their twenties and thirties, unlike the earlier EC fan following. Many of these older fans had been collectors for years but were largely unknown to each other. Joined by scores of new, younger fans, this group formed the nucleus of a self-sustaining and still growing movement. Although it has borrowed a few appropriate SF terms, Comics Fandom of the '60s was an independent movement without the advantages and disadvantages of a longer tradition. What Comics Fandom did derive from SF fans was largely thanks to fanzines produced by so-called double fans, the most notable being **COMIC ART**, edited and published by Don and Maggie Thompson.

The **ROCKET'S BLAST COMIC COLLECTOR** by G.B. Love was the first suceesful adzine in the early 1960s and was instrumental in the development of the comics market. G.B. remembers beginning his fanzine **THE ROCKET'S BLAST** in late 1961. Only six copies of the first 4 page issue were printed. Soon after Mr. Love had a letter published in **MYSTERY IN SPACE**, telling all about his new fanzine. His circulation began to grow. Buddy Saunders, a well known comic book store owner, designed the first **ROCKET'S BLAST** logo and was an artist on the publication for many years thereafter. With issue #29 he took over **THE COMICOLLECTOR** fanzine from Biljo White and combined it with **ROCKET'S BLAST** to form the **RBCC**. He remembers that the **RBCC** hit its highest circulation of 2,500 around 1971. Many people who wrote, drew or otherwise contributed to the **RBCC** went on to become well known writers, artists, dealers and store-owners in the comics field.

RELATED COLLECTIBLES

FOREIGN EDITION COMICS

One interesting and relatively inexpensive source of early vintage comics is the foreign market. Many American newspaper and magazine strips are reprinted abroad (in English and other languages) months and even years after they appear in the States. By arranging trades with foreign collectors, one can obtain substantial runs of American comic book reprints and newspaper strips dating back years. These reprints are often in black and white, and sometimes the reproduction is poor. Once interest in foreign-published comics has been piqued, a collector might become interested in original strips from these countries.

NEWSPAPER STRIPS

Collecting newspaper comic strips is somewhat different than collecting comic books, although it can be equally satisfying. Most strip collectors begin by clipping strips from their local paper, but soon branch out to out-of-town papers. Naturally this can become more expensive and more frustrating, as it is easy to miss out-of-town editions. Consequently, most strip collectors work out trade agreements with collectors in other cities. This usually means saving local strips for trade only.

Back issues of some newspaper comic strips are also occasionally available from dealers. Prices vary greatly depending on age, condition, and demand.

ORIGINAL ART

Some enthusiasts collect original comic book and strip art. These mostly black and white, inked drawings are usually done on illustration paper at about 30 percent larger than the original printed panels.

Because original art is a one-of-a-kind article, it is highly prized and can be difficult to obtain.

Interest in original comic art has increased tremendously in the past few years because more current art is available now that companies return originals to the artists, who then either sell the work themselves at cons, or through agents and dealers. The best way to find the piece you want is to scour cons and get on as many art dealers' mailing lists as possible. Although the masters' works from the Golden and Silver Ages bring fine art prices, most current work is available at moderate prices, with something for everyone at various costs, from Kirby to McFarlane, Ditko to Bachalo.

TOYS AND MORE

In the past ten years or so, interest in collecting comic-related merchandise has soared. Comic book and toy shows are often dominated by toys and related products.

Action figures and limited edition statues based on comic characters are currently the most popular. Highly successful toy action figure lines based on Batman, Spawn, Spider-Man, and many others cram toy store shelves. Statues and figurines, either painted or in kit form, are very popular higher-end collectibles. Statues of characters like Witchblade, Sandman, Shi, and many more draw collector attention through print, web, and convention advertising.

Numerous other tie-in products based on comic characters are released every year and seem to represent a large percentage of the collectible market today. Books like **Hake's Price Guide to Character Toys**, and periodicals like **Collecting Figures** and **Toyfare** track the collectibility of these items.

COVER BAR CODES

Today's comic books are cover-coded for the direct sales (comic shop, newsstand, and foreign markets). They are all first printings, with the special coding being the only difference. The comics sold to the comic shops have to be coded differently, as they are sold on a no-return basis while newsstand comics are not. The Price Guide has not detected any price difference between these versions. Currently, the difference is easily detected by looking at the front cover bar code (a box located at the lower left). The bar code used to be filled in for newsstand sales and left blank or contain a character for comic shop sales. Now, as you can see above, direct sale editions are clearly marked, both versions containing the bar code.

Newsstand

Direct Sales (DC)

Direct Edition (Marvel)

MARVEL REPRINTS

In recent years Marvel has reprinted some of their comics. There has been confusion in identifying the reprints from the originals, but in 99% of the cases, the reprints have listed "reprint," or "2nd printing," etc. in the indicia, along with a later copyright date in some cases. Some Marvel 2nd printings have a gold logo. The only known exceptions are a few of the movie books such as **Star Wars**, the **Marvel Treasury Editions**, and tie-ins such as **G.I. Joe**. These books were reprinted and not identified as reprints. The **Star**

Wars reprints have a large diamond with no date and a blank UPC symbol on the cover. Others had cover variations such as a date missing or different colors. Beginning in mid-1990, all Marvel 2nd printings have a gold logo.

Gold Key and other comics were also sold with a Whitman label. Even though collectors may prefer one label over the other, the Price Guide does not differentiate in the price. Beginning in 1980, all comics produced by Western carried the Whitman label.

PUBLISHERS' CODES

The following abbreviations are used with cover reproductions throughout the book for copyright purposes:

AC-AC Comics	**DH**-Dark Horse	**HILL**-Hillman Periodicals	**STD**-Standard Comics
ACE-Ace Periodicals	**DMP**-David McKay Publishing	**HOKE**-Holyoke Publishing Co.	**STJ**-St. John Publishing Co.
ACG-American Comics Group	**DS**-D. S. Publishing Co.	**IM**-Image Comics	**SUPR**-Superior Comics
AJAX-Ajax-Farrell	**EAS**-Eastern Color Printing Co.	**KING**-King Features Syndicate	**TC**-Tower Comics
AP-Archie Publications	**EC**-E. C. Comics	**LEV**-Lev Gleason Publications	**TM**-Trojan Magazines
ATLAS-Atlas Comics (see below)	**ECL**-Eclipse Comics	**MAL**-Malibu Comics	**TOBY**-Toby Press
AVON-Avon Periodicals	**ENWIL**-Enwil Associates	**MAR**-Marvel Characters, Inc.	**TOPS**-Tops Comics
BP-Better Publications	**EP**-Elliott Publications	**ME**-Magazine Enterprises	**UFS**-United Features Syndicate
C & L-Cupples & Leon	**ERB**-Edgar Rice Burroughs	**MLJ**-MLJ Magazines	**VAL**-Valiant
CC-Charlton Comics	**FAW**-Fawcett Publications	**MS**-Mirage Studios	**VITL**-Vital Publications
CEN-Centaur Publications	**FC**-First Comics	**NOVP**-Novelty Press	**WDC**-The Walt Disney Company
CCG-Columbia Comics Group	**FF**-Famous Funnies	**PG**-Premier Group	**WEST**-Western Publishing Co.
CG-Catechetical Guild	**FH**-Fiction House Magazines	**PINE**-Pines	**WHIT**-Whitman Publishing Co.
CHES-Harry 'A' Chesler	**FOX**-Fox Features Syndicate	**PMI**-Parents' Magazine Institute	**WHW**-William H. Wise
CLDS-Classic Det. Stories	**GIL**-Gilberton	**PRIZE**-Prize Publications	**WMG**-William M. Gaines (E. C.)
CM-Comics Magazine	**GK**-Gold Key	**QUA**-Quality Comics Group	**WP**-Warren Publishing Co.
DC-DC Comics, Inc.	**GP**-Great Publications	**REAL**-Realistic Comics	**YM**-Youthful Magazines
DEF-Defiant Comics	**HARV**-Harvey Publications	**RH**-Rural Home	**Z-D**-Ziff-Davis Publishing Co.
DELL-Dell Publishing Co.	**H-B**-Hanna-Barbera	**S & S**-Street and Smith Publishers	
		SKY-Skywald Publications	
		STAR-Star Publications	

"A Marvel Magazine" and "Marvel Group" were the designations used between December 1946 and May 1947 for the Timely/Marvel/Atlas group of comics during that period, although these taglines were not used on all of the titles/issues during that time. The Timely Comics symbol was used between July 1942 and September 1942, although again not on all titles/issues during the period. The round "Marvel Comic" symbol was used between February 1949 and June 1950. An early Comics Code symbol (star and bar) was used between April 1952 and February 1955. The Atlas globe symbol was used between December 1951 and September 1957. The M over C symbol (signifying the beginning of Marvel Comics as we know it today) was introduced in July 1961 and remained until the price increased to 12 cents in February 1962. We present here the publishers' codes for the Timely/Marvel/Atlas group of comics:

ACI-Animirth Comics, Inc.
AMI-Atlas Magazines, Inc.
ANC-Atlas News Co., Inc.
BPC-Bard Publishing Corp.
BFP-Broadcast Features Pubs.
CBS-Crime Bureau Stories
CLDS-Classic Detective Stories
CCC-Comic Combine Corp.
CDS-Current Detective Stories
CFI-Crime Files, Inc.
CmPI-Comedy Publications, Inc.
CmPS-Complete Photo Story
CnPC-Cornell Publishing Corp.
CPC-Chipiden Publishing Corp.
CPI-Crime Publications, Inc.
CPS-Canam Publishing Sales Corp.
CSI-Classics Syndicate, Inc.
DCI-Daring Comics, Inc.
EPC-Euclid Publishing Co.
EPI-Emgee Publications, Inc.
FCI-Fantasy Comics, Inc.
FPI-Foto Parade, Inc.
GPI-Gem Publishing, Inc.
HPC-Hercules Publishing Corp.
IPS-Interstate Publishing Corp.
JPI-Jaygee Publications, Inc.
LBI-Lion Books, Inc.
LCC-Leading Comic Corp.
LMC-Leading Magazine Corp.
MALE-Male Publishing Corp.
MAP-Miss America Publishing Corp.

MCI-Marvel Comics, Inc.
MgPC-Margood Publishing Corp.
MjMC-Marjean Magazine Corp.
MMC-Mutual Magazine Corp.
MPC-Medalion Publishing Corp.
MPI-Manvis Publications, Inc.
NPI-Newsstand Publications, Inc.
NPP-Non-Pareil Publishing Corp.
OCI-Official Comics, Inc.
OMC-Official Magazine Corp.
OPI-Olympia Publications, Inc.
PPI-Postal Publications, Inc.
PrPI-Prime Publications, Inc.
RCM-Red Circle Magazines, Inc.
SAI-Sports Actions, Inc.
SePI-Select Publications, Inc.
SnPC-Snap Publishing Co.
SPC-Select Publishing Co.
SPI-Sphere Publications, Inc.
TCI-Timely Comics, Inc.
TP-Timely Publications
20 CC-20th Century Comics Corp.
USA-U.S.A. Publications, Inc.
VPI-Vista Publications, Inc.
WFP-Western Fiction Publishing
WPI-Warwick Publications, Inc.
YAI-Young Allies, Inc.
ZPC-Zenith Publishing Co., Inc.

COMIC BOOK ARTISTS

Many of the more popular artists in the business are specially noted in the listings. When more than one artist worked on a story, their names are separated by a (/). The first name did the pencil drawings and the second the inks. When two or more artists work on a story, only the most prominent will be noted in some cases. We wish all good artists could be listed, but due to space limitation, only the most popular can. The following list of artists are considered to be either the most collected in the comic field or are historically significant. Artists designated below with an (*) indicate that only their most noted work will be listed. The rest will eventually have all their work shown as the information becomes available. This list could change from year to year as new artists come into prominence:

Adams, Arthur
Adams, Neal
Aparo, Jim
Bachalo, Chris
Bagley, Mark
Baker, Matt
Barks, Carl
Beck, C. C.
*Brunner, Frank
*Buscema, John
Byrne, John
Campbell, J. Scott
Capullo, Greg
*Check, Sid
Colan, Gene
Cole, Jack
Cole, L. B.
Craig, Johnny
Crandall, Reed
Darrow, Geof
Davis, Jack

Disbrow, Jayson
*Ditko, Steve
Eisner, Will
*Elder, Bill
Evans, George
Everett, Bill
Feldstein, Al
Fine, Lou
Foster, Harold
Fox, Matt
Frazetta, Frank
Gibbons, Dave
*Giffen, Keith
Golden, Michael
Gottfredson, Floyd
*Guardineer, Fred
Gustavson, Paul
*Heath, Russ
Howard, Wayne
*Infantino, Carmine
Ingels, Graham
Jones, Jeff
Kamen, Jack
Kane, Bob
*Kane, Gil
Kelly, Walt
Kieth, Sam
Kinstler, E. R.
Kirby, Jack
Krenkel, Roy
Krigstein, Bernie

Kubert, Adam
Kubert, Andy
*Kubert, Joe
Kurtzman, Harvey
Lapham, Dave
Larsen, Erik
Lee, Jae
Lee, Jim
Liefeld, Rob
Madureira, Joe
Manning, Russ
McFarlane, Todd
McWilliams, Al
Meskin, Mort
Mignola, Mike
Miller, Frank
Moreira, Ruben
*Morisi, Pete
*Newton, Don
Nostrand, Howard
Orlando, Joe
Pakula, Mac
*Palais, Rudy
*Perez, George
Portacio, Whilce
Powell, Bob
Quesada, Joe
Raboy, Mac
Ramos, Humberto
Raymond, Alex
Ravielli, Louis

*Redondo, Nestor
Rogers, Marshall
Ross, Alex
Schomburg, Alex
Sears, Bart
Siegel & Shuster
Silvestri, Marc
Simon & Kirby (S&K)
*Simonson, Walt
Smith, Paul
Stanley, John
*Starlin, Jim
Steranko, Jim
Stevens, Dave
Texeira, Mark
Thibert, Art
Torres, Angelo
Toth, Alex
Turner, Michael
Tuska, George
Ward, Bill
Williamson, Al
Windsor-Smith, Barry
Woggon, Bill
Wolverton, Basil
Wood, Wallace
Wrightson, Bernie
Zeck, Mike

Adams, Neal - (1 pg.) **Archie's Jokebook Mag.** #41, 9/59; (1st on Batman, cvr only) **Detective Comics** #370, 12/67; (1st Warren art) **Creepy** #14

Aparo, Jim - **Go-Go** #1, 6/66

Balent, Jim - **Sgt. Rock** #393, 10/84

Barks, Carl - (art only) **Donald Duck Four Color** #9, 8/42; (scripts only) **Large Feature Comic** #7, ca. Spring 1942

Broderick, Pat - (cover & art) **Planet of Vampires** #1, 2/75

Brunner, Frank - (fan club sketch) **Creepy** #10, 1965

Buckler, Rich - **Flash Gordon** #10, 11/67

Burnley, Jack - (cover & art) **NY World's Fair** nn, '40

Buscema, John - (1st at Marvel) **Strange Tales** #150, 11/66

Byrne, John - **Nightmare** #20, 8/74; (1st at DC) **Untold Legend of the Batman** #1, 7/80; (1st at Marvel) **Giant-Size Dracula** #5, 6/75

Capullo, Greg - (1st on X-Force) **X-Force Annual** #1, '92

Colan, Gene - **Wings Comics** #53, 1/45

Cole, Jack - (1 pg.) **Star Comics** #11, 4/38

Crandall, Reed - **Hit Comics** #10, 4/41

Davis, Jack - (cartoon) **Tip Top Comics** #32, 12/38

Ditko, Steve - (1st publ.) **Black Magic** V4#3, 11-12/53 (1st drawn story), **Fantastic Fears** #5, 1-2/54

Everett, Bill - **Amazing Mystery Funnies** V1#2, 9/38

Fine, Lou - (1st cvr) **Wonder Comics** #2, 6/39; **Jumbo Comics** #4, 12/38

Frazetta, Frank - **Tally-Ho Comics** nn, 12/44

Garney, Ron - **G. I. Joe, A Real American Hero** #110, 3/91

Giffen, Keith - (1 pg.) **Deadly Hands of Kung-Fu** #17, 11/75; (1st story) **Deadly Hands of Kung-Fu** #22, 4?/76; (tied w/Deadly Hands) **Amazing Adventures** #35, 3/76

Golden, Michael - **Marvel Classics Comics** #28, '77

Grell, Mike - **Adventure Comics** #435, 9-10/74

Hamner, Cully - **Green Lantern: Mosaic** #1, 6/92

Hughes, Adam - **Blood of Dracula** #1, 11/87

Ingels, Graham art at E.C. - **Saddle Justice** #4, Sum '48

Jurgens, Dan - **Warlord** #53, 1/82

Kaluta, Michael - **Teen Confessions** #59, 12/69

Kelly, Walt - **New Comics** #1, 12/35

Keown, Dale - **Samurai** #13, 1987; **Nth Man the Ultimate Ninja** #8, 1/90; (1st at Marvel); (1st on Hulk) **Incredible Hulk** #367, 3/90

Kieth, Sam - **Primer** #5, 11?/83

Kirby, Jack - **Jumbo Comics** #1, 9/38;

Kubert, Adam/Andy/Joe art - **Sgt. Rock** #422, 7/88

Kurtzman, Harvey - **Tip Top Comics** #36, 4/39; (1st at E.C.) **Lucky Fights It Through** nn, 1949

Larsen, Erik - **Megaton** #1, 11/83

Lee, Jae - **Marvel Comics Presents** #85, '91

Lee, Jim - (1st at Marvel) **Alpha Flight** #51, 10/87; (1st on X-Men)

X-Men #248?, ?/89; (art on Punisher) **Punisher War Journal** #1, 11/88

Liefeld, Rob - (1st at DC) **Warlord** #131, 9/88; (1st at Marvel) **X-Factor** #40, 4?/89; (1st full story) **Megaton** #8, 8/87; (inside front cover only) **Megaton** #5, 6/86

Lim, Ron - (art on Silver Surfer) **Silver Surfer Ann.** #1, '88

Matsuda, Jeff - **Brigade** #0, 9/93

Mayer, Sheldon - **New Comics** #1, 12/35

McFarlane, Todd - **Coyote** #11, ?/85; (1st full story) **All Star Squadron** #47, 7/85; (1st on Hulk) **Incredible Hulk** #330, 4/87

Medina, Angel - (pin-up only) **Megaton** #3, 2/86

Mignola, Mike - **Marvel Fanfare** #15, 5/83

Miller, Frank - (1st on Batman) **DC Special Series** #21, Spr '80; (1st on Daredevil) **Spectacular Spider-Man** #27, 2/79

Newton, Don - **Many Ghosts of Dr. Graves** #45, 5/74

Perez, George - (1st at DC) **Flash** #289, 9/80; (2 pgs.) **Astonishing Tales** #25, 8/74

Portacio, Whilce - (1st on X-Men) **X-Men** #201, 1/86

Pulido, Brian - **Evil Ernie** #1, 12/91

Quesada, Joe - (1st on X-Factor) **X-Factor Ann.** #7, '92

Raboy, Mac - (1st cover for Fawcett) **Master Comics** #21, 12/41

Ramos, Humberto - (1st U.S. work) **Hardwire** #15, 6/94

Romita, John - **Strange Tales** #4, 12/51; (1st at Marvel) **Daredevil** #12, 1/66

Romita, John Jr. - (1st complete story) **Iron Man** #115, 10/78

Ross, Alex - **The Terminator: The Burning Earth** V2#1, 3/90

Shuster, Joe - (cover) **New Adv. Comics** #16, 6/37

Siegel & Shuster - **New Fun Comics** #6, 10/35

Simon & Kirby - **Blue Bolt** #2, 7/40

Simonson, Walter - **Magnus, Robot Fighter** #10, 5/65

Smith, Paul - (1 pg. pin-up) **King Conan** #7, 9/81; (1st full story) **Marvel Fanfare** #1, 3/82

Steranko, Jim - **Spyman** #1, Sep '66; (1st at Marvel) **Strange Tales** #151, 12/66

Swan, Curt - **Dick Cole** #1, 12-1/48-49

Talbot, Bryan - (1st U.S. work) **Hellblazer Annual** #1, Summer '89

Thomas, Roy - (scripts) **Son of Vulcan** #50, 1/66

Torres, Angelo - **Crime Mysteries** #13, 5/54

Turner, Mike - **Cyberforce Origins-Stryker**, 2/95

Weeks, Lee - **Tales of Terror** #5, 11/85

Weiss, Alan - (illo) **Blue Beetle** #5, 3-4/65

Williamson, Al - (1st at E.C.) **Tales From the Crypt** #31, 9/52; (text illos) **Famous Funnies** #169, 8/48

Windsor-Smith, Barry - **X-Men** #53, 2/69

Wood, Wally - (1st at E.C.) **Saddle Romances** #10, 1-2/50

Wrightson, Bernie - **House of Mystery** #179, 4/68; (1st at Marvel) **Chamber of Darkness** #7, 10/70; (1st cover) **Web of Horror** #3, 4/70; (fan club sketch) **Creepy** #9

Zeck, Mike - (illos) **Barney and Betty Rubble** #11, 2/75

The American Comic Book: 1842-2001
THE MARKETING OF A MEDIUM

by Arnold T. Blumberg

A very rare piece indeed, this represents one of the few existing examples of Palmer Cox's signature, as Cox always printed his name on his art. The character depicted in the upper left, "The Dude," represents a typical New Yorker and was Cox's favorite.

*Starting with the 30th edition of **The Overstreet Comic Book Price Guide**, we now list premium and giveaway comics (now collectively referred to as "promotional comics" in this edition) in their own section. This article first appeared in the 30th edition and provides a brief introduction to this often overlooked corner of the comic book collecting universe. We hope that by setting promotional comics apart, we can draw attention to this fertile but as yet poorly represented area of comic book history.*

Everyone wants something for free. It's in our nature to look for the quick fix, the good deal, the complimentary gift. We long to hit the lottery and quit our job, to win the trip around the world, or find that pot of gold at then end of the proverbial rainbow. Collectors in particular are certainly built to appreciate the notion of the "free gift," since it not only means a new item to collect and enjoy, but no risk or obligation in order to acquire it.

Ah, but there's the rub. Because things are not always what they seem, and "free gifts" usually come with a price. As the saying goes, "there's no such thing as a free lunch," so if it seems too good to be true, it probably is. This is the case even in the world of comics, where premiums and giveaways have a familiar agenda hidden behind the bright colors and fanciful stories. But where did it all begin?

One of the best examples of the Brownies' proliferation into all kinds of merchandise. This rare Luden's Cough Drop ad (1890s) is the earliest known character die-cut sign.

EXTRA EXTRA

As we learn more about the early history of the comic book industry through continual investigation and the publishing of articles like those regularly featured in this book, we gain a much greater understanding of the financial and creative forces at work in shaping the medium, but perhaps one of the most intriguing and least recognized factors that influenced the dawn of comics is the concept of the premium or giveaway. (Note: Some of the historical information referenced in this article is derived from material also presented in Robert L. Beerbohm's introductory articles to the Platinum Age and Modern Age sections.)

The birth of the comic book as we know it today is intimately connected with the development of the comic strip in American newspapers and their use as an advertising and marketing tool for staple products such as bread, milk, and cereal. From the very beginning, comic characters have played several roles in pop culture, entertaining the youth of the country while also (sometimes none too subtly) acting as hucksters for whatever corpora-

tion foots the bill. From important staples to frivolous material produced simply to make a buck, these products have utilized the comics medium to sell, sell, sell. And what better way to hook a prospective customer than to give them "something for nothing?"

Although comic characters were already being aggressively merchandised all around the world by the mid-1890s--as with, for example, Palmer Cox's **The Brownies**--the real starting point for the success of comics as a giveaway marketing mechanism can be traced to the introduction of **The Yellow Kid**, Richard Outcault's now legendary newspaper strip.

Newspaper publishers had already recognized that comic strips could boost circulation as well as please sponsors and advertisers by drawing more eyes to the page, so Sunday "supplements" were introduced to entice fans. Outcault's creation cemented the theory with proof of comic characters' marketing and merchandising power.

Soon after, Outcault (who had most likely been inspired by Cox's merchandising success with **The Brownies** in the first place) caught lightning in a bottle once more with **Buster Brown**, who has the distinction of being America's first nationally licensed comic strip character. Soon, comic strips proliferated throughout the nation's newspapers, offering companies the chance to license recognizable personas as their own personal pitchmen (or women or animals...). Comic character merchandise wasn't far behind, resulting in a boom of future collectibles now catalogued in volumes like **Hake's Price Guide to Character Toys**.

Comic books themselves were at the heart of this movement, and giveaway and premium collections of comic strips not only appealed to children and adults alike, but provided the impetus for the birth of the modern comic book format itself. It could be said that without the concept of the giveaway comic or the marketing push behind it, there would be no comic book industry as we have it today.

Thanks to men like Harry I. Wildenberg of Eastern Printing and companies like Gulf Oil (who liked Wildenberg's idea of an advertising-driven comics tabloid and produced **Gulf Comic Weekly**), the modern comic came into being around 1932-33.

What most people agree was the first modern format comic, **Funnies on Parade**, was released as a result of this growing merchandising movement, and sparked by the success of Wildenberg's and Gulf Oil's grand experiment. Through the auspices of Proctor & Gamble, **Funnies on Parade** was printed and given away in the Spring of 1933. A medium was born, and a marketing tool had completed its first step in the long road to maturity.

The impact of this new approach to advertising was not lost on the business world. Contrary to modern belief, comic books were hardly discounted by the adults of the time, at least, not those who had the marketing savvy to recognize an opportunity--or a threat--when they saw one.

READ ALL ABOUT IT

In the April 1933 issue of **Fortune** magazine, an article titled "The Funny Papers" trumpeted the arrival of comics as a force to be reckoned with in the world of advertising and business, and what's more, a force to fear as well. At first providing a brief survey of the newspaper comic strip business (which for many of the magazine's readers must have seemed a foreign topic for serious discussion), the article goes on to examine the incredible financial draw of comics and their characters:

"Between 70 and 75 per cent {sic} of the readers of any newspaper follow its comic sections regularly...Even the advertiser has succumbed to the comic, and in 1932 spent well over $1,000,000 for comic-paper space."

"Comic Weekly is the comic section of seventeen Hearst Sunday papers...Advertisers who market their wares through balloon-speaking manikins {sic} may enjoy the proximity of Jiggs, Maggie, Barney Google, and other funny Hearst headliners."

Although the article continues to cast the notion of relying on comic strip material to sell product in a negative light, actually suggesting that advertisers who utilize comics are violating unspoken rules of "advertising decorum" and bringing themselves "down to the level" of comics (and since when have advertisers been stalwart preservers of good taste and high moral standards), there is no doubt that they are viewing comics in a new light. The comic characters have arrived by 1933...and they're ready to help sell your merchandise too.

THE MARCH OF WAR AND BEYOND

Through the relentless currents of time, comic strips, books, and the characters that starred in them became more and more an intrinsic part of American culture. During the turmoil of the Great Depression and World War II, comic characters in print and celluloid form entertained while inform-

One of the earliest examples of the business world acknowledging and investigating the influence of the comic book on modern pop culture and American enterprise.
FORTUNE Magazine, April 1933.

ing and selling at the same time, and premium and giveaway comics came well and truly into their own, pushing everything from loaves of bread to war bonds.

In the 1950s and '60s, there was a shift in focus as the power of giveaway and premium comics was applied to more altruistic endeavors than simply selling something. Comic book format pamphlets, fully illustrated and often inventively written, taught children about banking, money, the dangers of poison and other household products, and even chronicled moments in American history. The comic book as giveaway was now not only a marketing gimmick--it was a tool for educating as well.

The 1970s and '80s saw another boom in premium and giveaway comics. Every product imaginable seemed to have a licensing deal with a comic book character, usually one of the prominent flag bearers of the Big Two, Marvel or DC. Spider-Man fought bravely against the Beetle for the benefit of All Detergent; Captain America allied himself with the Campbell Kids; and Superman helped a class of computer students beat a disaster-conjuring foe at his own game with the help of Radio Shack Tandy computers.

Newspapers rediscovered the power of comics, not just with enlarged strip supplements but with actual comic books. Spider-Man, the Hulk, and others turned up as giveaway comic extras in various American newspapers (including Chicago and Dallas publications), while a whole series of public information comics like those produced decades earlier used superheroes to caution children about the dangers of smoking, drugs, and child abuse.

Comics also turned up in a plethora of other toy products as the 1980s introduced kids to the joy of electronic games and action figures. Supplementary comics provided "free" with action figure and video game packages told the backstory about the product, adding depth to the play experience while pro-

This 1998 U.S. Postal Service premium is one of the most recent examples of the continuing popularity of promotional comics.

viding an extra incentive to buy. Comics became an intrinsic part of the Atari line of video cartridges, for example, eventually spawning its own full-blown newsstand series as well.

Today, premium comics continue to thrive and are still utilized as a valuable marketing and promotional tool. "Free" comics are still packaged with action figures and video games, and offered as mail-away premiums from a variety of product manufacturers. The comic industry itself has expanded its use of giveaway comics to self-promote as well, with "ashcan" and other giveaway editions turning up at conventions and comic shops to advertise upcoming series and special events. Many of these function as old-fashioned premiums, with a coupon or other response required from the reader to receive the comic.

As for the supplements and giveaways printed all those years ago, they have spawned a collectible fervor all their own, thanks to their atypical distribution and frequent rarity. For that and the desire to delve deeper into comics history, we hope that by focusing more directly on this genre, we can enhance our understanding of this vital component in the development and history of the modern comic book.

Whether you're a collector or not, we're all motivated by that desire to get something for nothing. For as long as consumers are enticed by the notion of the "free gift," promotional comics will remain a vital marketing component in many business models, but they will also continue to fight the stigma that has long been associated with the industry as a whole. "Respectable" sources like **Fortune** may have taken notice of the power of comic-related advertising 67 years ago, but after all this time comics still fight an uphill battle to establish some measure of dignity for the medium. Perhaps the higher visibility of promotional comics will eventually prove to be a deciding factor in that intellectual war.

See ya in the funny papers.

Adventures of Big Boy #266 © Shoney's

Adventures of Kool-Aid Man #2 © General Foods

Amazing Spider-Man and the Incredible Hulk © MAR

	GD2.0	FN6.0	VF8.0	NM9.4

ACTION COMICS
DC Comics: 1947 - 1998 (Giveaway)

1 (1976, 1983) paper cover w/10¢ price, 16 pgs. in color; reprints complete Superman story from #1 ('38)	2	6	13	20
1 (1976) Safeguard Giveaway; paper cover w/"free", 16 pgs. in color; reprints complete Superman story from #1 ('38)	2	6	15	22
1 (1987 Nestle Quik; 1988, 50¢)	1	3	6	8
1 (1993)-Came w/Reign of Superman packs				1.50
1 (1998 U.S. Postal Service, $7.95) Reprints entire issue; extra outer half-cover contains First Day Issuance of 32¢ Superman stamp with Sept. 10, 1998 Cleveland, OH postmark	1	3	6	8
Theater (1947, 32 pgs., 6-1/2 x 8-1/4", nn)-Vigilante story based on Columbia Vigilante serial; no Superman-c or story	66	198	412	650

ADVENTURE COMICS
IGA: No date (early 1940s) (Paper-c, 32 pgs.)

Two diff. issues; Super-Mystery-r from 1941	25	75	143	225

ADVENTURE IN DISNEYLAND
Walt Disney Productions (Dist. by Richfield Oil): May, 1955 (Giveaway, soft-c., 16 pgs.)

nn	10	30	55	85

ADVENTURES @ EBAY
eBay: 2000 (6 3/4" x 4 1/2", 16 pgs.)

1 - Judd Winick-a/Rucka & Van Meter-s; intro to eBay comic buying				2.25

ADVENTURES OF BIG BOY
Timely Comics Adv. Corp./Illus. Features: 1956 - Present (Giveaway) (East & West editions of early issues)

1-Everett-a	150	425	675	950
2-Everett-a	50	125	165	325
3-5: 4-Robot-c	25	75	100	150
6-10: 6-Sci/fic issue	10	30	70	120
11-20	5	15	38	60
21-30	3	10	23	35
31-50	2	6	13	20
51-100	1	4	7	10
101-150	1	3	6	8
151-240				6.00
241-265,267-269,271-300:				4.00
266-Superman x-over	3	9	20	30
270-TV's Buck Rogers-c/s	3	9	17	25
301-400				3.00
401-500				2.50
1-(2nd series - '76-'84,Paragon Prod.) (...Shoney's Big Boy)	1	3	6	8
2-20				4.00
21-50				2.50
Summer, 1959 issue, large size	11	33	56	95

ADVENTURES OF G. I. JOE
1969 (3-1/4x7") (20 & 16 pgs.)

First Series: 1-Danger of the Depths. 2-Perilous Rescue. 3-Secret Mission to Spy Island. 4-Mysterious Explosion. 5-Fantastic Free Fall. 6-Eight Ropes of Danger. 7-Mouth of Doom. 8-Hidden Missile Discovery. 9-Space Walk Mystery. 10-Fight for Survival. 11-The Shark's Surprise.
Second Series: 2-Flying Space Adventure. 4-White Tiger Hunt. 7-Capture of the Pygmy Gorilla. 12-Secret of the Mummy's Tomb.
Third Series: Reprinted surviving titles of First Series. Fourth Series: 13-Adventure Team Headquarters. 14-Search For the Stolen Idol.

each....	2	6	12	18

ADVENTURES OF KOOL-AID MAN
Marvel Comics: 1983; 1984 (Mail order giveaway)

1,2				5.00

ADVENTURES OF MARGARET O'BRIEN, THE
Bambury Fashions (Clothes): 1947 (20 pgs. in color, slick-c, regular size) (Premium)

In "The Big City" movie adaptation (scarce)	20	60	110	175

ADVENTURES OF QUIK BUNNY
Nestle's Quik: 1984 (Giveaway, 32 pgs.)

nn-Spider-Man app.	2	6	9	12

ADVENTURES OF STUBBY, SANTA'S SMALLEST REINDEER, THE
W. T. Grant Co.: nd (early 1940s) (Giveaway, 12 pgs.)

nn	5	15	25	35

ADVENTURES OF VOTEMAN, THE
Foundation For Citizen Education Inc.: 1968

nn	5	15	38	60

ADVENTURES WITH SANTA CLAUS
Promotional Publ. Co. (Murphy's Store): No date (early 50's) (9-3/4x 6-3/4", 24 pgs., giveaway, paper-c)

nn-Contains 8 pgs. ads	5	15	23	30
16 pg. version	5	15	25	35

AIR POWER (CBS TV & the U.S. Air Force Presents)
Prudential Insurance Co.: 1956 (5-1/4x7-1/4", 32 pgs., giveaway, soft-c)

nn-Toth-a? Based on 'You Are There' TV program by Walter Cronkite	11	33	56	80

ALICE IN BLUNDERLAND
Industrial Services: 1952 (Paper cover, 16 pgs. in color)

nn-Facts about big government waste and inefficiency	14	43	70	110

ALICE IN WONDERLAND
Western Printing Company/Whitman Publ. Co.: 1965; 1969; 1982

Meets Santa Claus(1950s), nd, 16 pgs.	5	15	25	35
Rexall Giveaway(1965, 16 pgs., 5x7-1/4) Western Printing (TV, Hanna-Barbera)	3	9	20	30
Wonder Bakery Giveaway(1969, 16 pgs, color, nn, nd) (Continental Baking Company)	3	9	19	28

ALICE IN WONDERLAND MEETS SANTA
No publisher: nd (6-5/8x9-11/16", 16 pgs., giveaway, paper-c)

nn	11	33	56	80

ALL ABOARD, MR. LINCOLN
Assoc. of American Railroads: Jan, 1959 (16 pgs.)

nn-Abraham Lincoln and the Railroads	6	18	32	45

ALL NEW COMICS
Harvey Comics: Oct, 1993 (Giveaway, no cover price, 16 pgs.)(Hanna-Barbera)

1-Flintstones, Scooby Doo, Jetsons, Yogi Bear & Wacky Races previews for upcoming Harvey's new Hanna-Barbera line-up				5.00

NOTE: Material previewed in Harvey giveaway was eventually published by Archie.

AMAZING SPIDER-MAN, THE
Marvel Comics Group

Aim Toothpaste Giveaway (36 pgs., reg. size)-1 pg. origin recap; Green Goblin-c/story	2	6	10	14
Aim Toothpaste Giveaway (16 pgs., reg. size)-Dr. Octopus app.	2	6	10	14
All Detergent Giveaway (1979, 36 pgs.), nn-Origin-r	2	6	11	16
Giveaway-Acme & Dingo Children's Boots (1980)-Spider-Woman app.	2	6	11	16
Amazing Spider-Man nn (1990, 6-1/8x9", 28 pgs.)-Shan-Lon giveaway; r/ Amazing Spider-Man #303 w/McFarlane-c/a	1	3	6	9
...& Power Pack (1984, nn)(Nat'l Committee for Prevention of Child Abuse (two versions, mail offer & store giveaway)-Mooney-a; Byrne-c				
Mail offer	1	4	7	10
Store giveaway				3.00
...& The Hulk (Special Edition)(6/8/80; 20 pgs.)-Supplement to Chicago Tribune (giveaway)	2	6	11	16
...& The Incredible Hulk (1981, 1982; 36 pgs.)-Sanger Harris or May D&F supplement to Dallas Times, Dallas Herald, Denver Post, Kansas City Star, Tulsa World; Foley's supplement to Houston Chronicle (1982, 16 pgs.)- "Great Rodeo Robbery"; The Jones Store-giveaway (1983, 16 pgs.)	2	6	12	18
...and the New Mutants Featuring Skids nn (National Committee for				

Archie Comics - Fairmont Potato Chip © AP

Atari Force #2 © Atari

Aurora Comic Scene Instruction Booklet Superboy © DC

	GD2.0	FN6.0	VF8.0	NM9.4		GD2.0	FN6.0	VF8.0	NM9.4
Prevention of Child Abuse/K-Mart giveaway)-Williams-c(i)				5.00	(1944-47)-issues	14	42	72	120
..Captain America, The Incredible Hulk, & Spider-Woman (1981)					2/48-Peggy Lee photo-c	13	39	66	110
(7-11 Stores giveaway; 36 pgs.)	2	6	10	14	3/48-Marylee Robb photo-c	12	36	61	100
.: Danger in Dallas (1983) (Supplement to Dallas Times Herald)					4/48-Gloria De Haven photo-c	13	39	66	110
giveaway	2	6	10	14	5/48,6/48,7/48	12	36	61	100
.: Danger in Denver (1983) (Supplement to Denver Post)					8/48-Story on Shirley Temple	14	42	72	120
giveaway for May D&F stores	2	6	10	14	10/48-Archie as Wolf on cover	13	39	66	110
., Fire-Star, And Ice-Man at the Dallas Ballet Nutcracker (1983; supplement to					5/49-Kathleen Hughes photo-c	10	30	55	80
Dallas Times Herald)-Mooney-p	2	6	10	14	7/49	9	27	51	75
iiveaway-Esquire Magazine (2/69)-Miniature-Still attached					8/49-Archie photo-c from radio show	16	48	83	140
	10	30	73	125	10/49-Gloria Mann photo-c from radio show	13	39	66	110
iiveaway-Eye Magazine (2/69)-Miniature-Still attached					11/49,12/49	9	27	51	75
	10	30	73	125					

ARCHIE'S JOKE BOOK MAGAZINE (See Joke Book ...)
Archie Publications

						GD2.0	FN6.0	VF8.0	NM9.4
., Storm & Powerman (1982; 20 pgs.)(American Cancer Society)					Drug Store Giveaway (No. 39 w/new-c)	5	15	25	35
giveaway	1	3	6	8					
.Vs. The Hulk (Special Edition; 1979, 20 pgs.)(Supplement to Columbus					**ARCHIE'S TEN ISSUE COLLECTOR'S SET** (Title inside of cover only)				
Dispatch)-Giveaway	2	6	12	18	**Archie Publications:** June, 1997 - No. 10, June, 1997 ($1.50, 20 pgs.)				
.Vs. The Prodigy (Giveaway, 16 pgs. in color (1976, 5x6-1/2")-Sex					1-10: 1,7-Archie. 2,8-Betty & Veronica. 3,9-Veronica. 4-Betty. 5-World of Archie.				
education; (1 million printed; 35-50¢)	2	6	15	22	6-Jughead. 10-Archie and Friends				3.00

MERICA MENACED!
ital Publications: 1950 (Paper-c)

ASTRO COMICS
American Airlines (Harvey): 1968 - 1979 (Giveaway)

						GD2.0	FN6.0	VF8.0	NM9.4
n-Anti-communism	40	120	180	280	Reprints of Harvey comics. 1968-Hot Stuff. 1969-Casper, Spooky, Hot Stuff,				

MERICAN COMICS
Theatre Giveaways (Liberty Theatre, Grand Rapids, Mich. known): 1940's

Many possible combinations. "Golden Age" superhero comics with new cover added and given way at theaters. Following known: Superman #59, Capt. Marvel #20, Capt. Marvel Jr. #5, Action 33, Classics Comics #8, Whiz #39. Value would vary with book and should be 70-80 percent of the original.

					Stumbo the Giant, Little Audrey, Little Lotta, & Richie Rich reprints.				
					1970-r/Richie Rich #97 (all scarce)	2	6	15	22
					1973-r/Richie Rich #122. 1975-Wendy. 1975-Richie Rich & Casper.				
					1977-r/Richie Rich & Casper #20. 1978-r/Richie Rich #25.				
					1979-r/Richie Rich & Casper #30 (scarce)	2	6	13	20

ANDY HARDY COMICS
Western Printing Co.:

ATARI FORCE
DC Comics: 1982 - No. 5, 1983

						GD2.0	FN6.0	VF8.0	NM9.4
..& the New Automatic Gas Clothes Dryer (1952, 5x7-1/4", 16 pgs.)					1-3 (1982, 5X7", 52 pgs.)-Given away with Atari games				5.00
Bendix Giveaway (soft-c)	7	22	32	45	4,5 (1982-1983, 52 pgs.)-Given away with Atari games (scarcer)				
						1	3	6	8

ANIMANIACS EMERGENCY WORLD
DC Comics: 1995

AURORA COMIC SCENES INSTRUCTION BOOKLET
Aurora Plastics Co.: 1974 (6-1/4x9-3/4", 8 pgs., slick paper)

					(Included with superhero model kits)				
n-American Red Cross				3.00	181-140-Tarzan; Neal Adams-a	3	9	19	28

APACHE HUNTER
Creative Pictorials: 1954 (18 pgs. in color) (promo copy) (saddle stitched)

					182-140-Spider-Man.	4	12	25	38
n-Severin, Heath stories	17	51	90	140	183-140-Tonto(Gil Kane art). 184-140-Hulk. 185-140-Superman. 186-140-				
					Superboy. 187-140-Batman. 188-140-The Lone Ranger(1974-by Gil Kane).				
					192-140-Captain America(1975). 193-140-Robin	3	9	17	24

AQUATEERS MEET THE SUPER FRIENDS
DC Comics: 1979

BACK TO THE FUTURE
Harvey Comics

nn				5.00	Special nn (1991, 20 pgs.)-Brunner-c; given away at Universal Studios in				
					Florida				3.00

ARCHIE AND HIS GANG (Zeta Beta Tau Presents...)
Archie Publications: Dec. 1950 (St. Louis National Convention giveaway)

BALTIMORE COLTS
American Visuals Corp.: 1950 (Giveaway)

						GD2.0	FN6.0	VF8.0	NM9.4
nn-Contains new cover stapled over Archie Comics #47 (11-12/50) on inside;					nn-Eisner-c	47	141	260	420
produced for Zeta Beta Tau	15	45	77	130					

BAMBI (Disney)
K. K. Publications (Giveaways): 1941, 1942

ARCHIE COMICS
Archie Publications

						GD2.0	FN6.0	VF8.0	NM9.4
.. And Friends - A Timely Tale (10/01, 8 1/2"x 5 1/2") Diamond Comic Dist.				1.00	1941-Horlick's Malted Milk & various toy stores; text & pictures; most copies				
...And His Friends Help Raise Literacy Awareness In Mississippi nn (3/94)-					mailed out with store stickers on-c	50	125	200	300
Giveaway				5.00	1942-Same as 4-Color #12, but no price (Same as '41 issue?) (Scarce)				
..And the History of Electronics nn (5/90, 36 pgs.)-Radio Shack giveaway;						75	200	300	450
Howard Bender-c/a				5.00					

BATMAN
DC Comics: 1966 - Present

-Fairmont Potato Chips Giveaway-Mini comics 1970 (8 issues-nn's., 8 pgs. each)					Act II Popcorn mini-comic(1998)				2.25
	2	7	15	22	Batman #121 Toys R Us edition (1997) r/1st Mr. Freeze				2.25
-Fairmont Potato Chips Giveaway-Mini comics 1970 (6 issues-nn's.,6 7/8" x 2 1/4"					Batman #362 Mervyn's edition (1989)				2.25
8 pgs. each)	2	7	15	22	Batman Adventures #25 Best Western edition (1997)				2.25
-Fairmont Potato Chips Giveaway-Mini comics 1971 (4 issues-nn's.,6 7/8" x 5",					Batman and Other DC Classics 1 (1989, giveaway)-DC Comics/Diamond				
8 pgs. each)	2	7	15	22	Comic Distributors; Batman origin-r/Batman #47, Camelot 3000-r by Bolland,				
-Official Boy Scout Outfitter (1946, 9-1/2x6-1/2, 16 pgs.)-B. R. Baker Co.					Justice League-r('87), New Teen Titans-r by Perez.				2.25
(Scarce)	47	141	270	450	Batman Beyond Six Flags edition				5.00
-Shoe Store giveaway (1948, Feb?)	17	51	85	140	Batman: Canadian Multiculturalism Custom (1992)				2.25
..'s Weird Mysteries (9/99, 8 1/2"x 5 1/2") Diamond Comic Dist.				2.25					

ARCHIE SHOE-STORE GIVEAWAY
Archie Publications: 1944-49 (12-15 pgs. of games, puzzles, stories like
Superman-Tim books, No nos. - came out monthly)

Blind Justice nn © DC

Blood is the Harvest
© Catechetical Guild

Buck Rogers 370A © KING

	GD2.0	FN6.0	VF8.0	NM9.4		GD2.0	FN6.0	VF8.0	NM

Batman Claritan edition (1999) 2.25

Kellogg's Poptarts comics (1966, Set of 6, 16 pgs.); All were folded and placed in Poptarts boxes. Infantino art on Catwoman and Joker issues.

"The Man in the Iron Mask", "The Penguin's Fowl Play", "The Joker's Happy Victims", "The Catwoman's Catnapping Caper", "The Mad Hatter's Hat Crimes", "The Case of the Batman II"
each.... 4 12 26 40

Mask of the Phantasm (1993) Mini-comic released w/video 5.00

Pizza Hut giveaway (12/77)-exact-r of #122,123; Joker-c/story
1 3 6 8

Prell Shampoo giveaway (1966, 16 pgs.)- "The Joker's Practical Jokes"
(6-7/8x3-3/8") 4 12 26 40

Revell in pack (1995) 2.25

BATMAN RECORD COMIC
National Periodical Publications: 1966 (one-shot)

1-With record (still sealed) 13 40 94 160
Comic only 7 21 50 80

BEETLE BAILEY
Charlton Comics: 1969-1970 (Giveaways)

Armed Forces ('69)-same as regular issue (#68) 1 4 7 10
Bold Detergent ('69)-same as regular issue (#67) 1 4 7 10
Cerebral Palsy Assn. V2#71('69) - V2#73(#1,1/70) 1 4 7 10
Red Cross (1969, 5x7", 16 pgs., paper-c) 1 4 7 10

BEST WESTERN GIVEAWAY
DC Comics: 1999

nn-Best Western hotels 2.25

BIG BOY (see Adventures of...)

BIG JIM'S P.A.C.K.
Mattel, Inc. (Marvel Comics): No date (1975) (16 pgs.)

nn-Giveaway with Big Jim doll; Buscema/Sinnott-c/a 3 9 19 28

"BILL AND TED'S EXCELLENT ADVENTURE" MOVIE ADAPTATION
DC Comics: 1989 (No cover price)

nn-Torres-a 2.50

BLACK GOLD
Esso Service Station (Giveaway): 1945? (8 pgs. in color)

nn-Reprints from True Comics 6 18 28 38

BLAZING FOREST, THE (See Forest Fire and Smokey Bear)
Western Printing: 1962 (20 pgs., 5x7", slick-c)

nn-Smokey The Bear fire prevention 2 6 10 14

BLESSED PIUS X
Catechetical Guild (Giveaway): No date (Text/comics, 32 pgs., paper-c)

nn 5 14 21 28

BLIND JUSTICE (Also see Batman: Blind Justice)
DC Comics/Diamond Comic Distributors: 1989 (Giveaway, squarebound)

nn-Contains Detective #598-600 by Batman movie writer Sam Hamm, w/covers; published same time as originals? 6.00

BLONDIE COMICS
Harvey Publications: 1950-1964

1950 Giveaway 6 18 29 40
1962,1964 Giveaway 2 6 12 18
N. Y. State Dept. of Mental Hygiene Giveaway-(1950) Regular size;
16 pgs.; no # 3 9 20 30
N. Y. State Dept. of Mental Hygiene Giveaway-(1956) Regular size;
16 pgs.; no # 2 6 13 20
N. Y. State Dept. of Mental Hygiene Giveaway-(1961) Regular size;
16 pgs.; no # 2 6 11 16

BLOOD IS THE HARVEST
Catechetical Guild: 1950 (32 pgs., paper-c)

(Scarce)-Anti-communism (13 known copies) 106 320 625 950
Black & white version (5 known copies), saddle stitched
40 120 220 360

Untrimmed version (only one known copy); estimated value-$600
NOTE: In 1979 nine copies of the color version surfaced from the old Guild's files plus the five

black & white copies.

BLUE BIRD CHILDREN'S MAGAZINE, THE
Graphic Information Service: V1#2, 1957 - No. 10 1958 (16 pgs., soft-c, regular size)

V1#2-10: Pat, Pete & Blue Bird app. 1 3 6

BLUE BIRD COMICS
Various Shoe Stores/Charlton Comics: Late 1940's - 1964 (Giveaway)

nn(1947-50)(36 pgs.)-Several issues; Human Torch, Sub-Mariner app. in some
20 60 100 150
1959-Li'l Genius, Timmy the Timid Ghost, Wild Bill Hickok (All #1)
3 9 17 2(
1959-(6 titles; all #2) Black Fury #1,4,5, Freddy #4, Li'l Genius, Timmy the
Timid Ghost #4, Masked Raider #4, Wild Bill Hickok (Charlton)
3 9 17 2(
1959-(#5) Masked Raider #21 3 9 17 2(
1960-(6 titles)(All #4) Black Fury #8,9, Masked Raider, Freddy #8,9, Timmy
the Timid Ghost #9, Li'l Genius #7,9 (Charlt.) 2 6 13 2(
1961,1962-(All #10's) Atomic Mouse #12,13,16, Black Fury #11,12, Freddy,
Li'l Genius, Masked Raider, Six Gun Heroes, Texas Rangers in Action,
Timmy the Ghost, Wild Bill Hickok, Wyatt Earp #3,11-13,16-18 (Charlton)
2 6 13 2(
1963-Texas Rangers #17 (Charlton) 2 6 10 1(
1964-Mysteries of Unexplored Worlds #18, Teenage Hotrodders #18, War
Heroes #18 (Charlton) 2 6 10 1(
1965-War Heroes #18 1 4 7 1(
NOTE: More than one issue of each character could have been published each year. Numbering is sporadic.

BOB & BETTY & SANTA'S WISHING WHISTLE
Sears Roebuck & Co.: 1941 (Christmas giveaway, 12 pgs.)

nn 11 33 55 9(

BOBBY BENSON'S B-BAR-B RIDERS (Radio)
Magazine Enterprises/AC Comics

...in the Tunnel of Gold-(1936, 5-1/4x8"; 100 pgs.) Radio giveaway by
Hecker-H.O. Company(H.O. Oats); contains 22 color pgs. of comics,
rest in novel form 10 30 55 8(
...And The Lost Herd-same as above 10 30 55 8(

BOBBY SHELBY COMICS
Shelby Cycle Co./Harvey Publications: 1949

nn 4 12 18 2(

BOY SCOUT ADVENTURE
Boy Scouts of America: 1954 (16 pgs., paper cover)

nn 4 11 17 22

BOYS' RANCH
Harvey Publications: 1951

Shoe Store Giveaway #5,6 (Identical to regular issues except Simon & Kirby
centerfold replaced with ad) 25 75 110 16(

BOZO THE CLOWN (TV)
Dell Publishing Co.: 1961

Giveaway-1961, 16 pgs., 3-1/2x7-1/4", Apsco Products
4 12 30 5(

BRER RABBIT IN "ICE CREAM FOR THE PARTY"
American Dairy Association: 1955 (5x7-1/4", 16 pgs., soft-c) (Walt Disney) (Premium)

nn-(Scarce) 50 150 250 375

BUCK ROGERS (In the 25th Century)
Kelloggs Corn Flakes Giveaway: 1933 (6x8", 36 pgs)

370A-By Phil Nowlan & Dick Calkins; 1st Buck Rogers radio premium & 1st app.
in comics (tells origin) (Reissued in 1995) 100 350 600 9(
with envelope 175 450 700 9(

BUGS BUNNY (Puffed Rice Giveaway)
Quaker Cereals: 1949 (32 pgs. each, 3-1/8x6-7/8")

A1-Traps the Counterfeiters, A2-Aboard Mystery Submarine, A3- Rocket to the Moon, A4-Lion Tamer, A5-Rescues the Beautiful Princess, B1-Buried Treasure, B2-Outwits the Smugglers, B3-

Bulletman - Well Known Comics © FAW

Captain America Goes to War Against Drugs © MAR

Captain Marvel and the Lts. of Safety #2 © FAW

	GD2.0	FN6.0	VF8.0	NM9.4

Joins the Marines, B4-Meets the Dwarf Ghost, B5-Finds Aladdin's Lamp, C1-Lost in the Frozen North, C2-Secret Agent, C3-Captured by Cannibals, C4-Fights the Man from Mars, C5-And the Haunted Cave

each....	8	25	42	60
Mailing Envelope (has illo of Bugs on front)(Each envelope designates what set it contains, A,B or C on front)	8	25	42	60

BUGS BUNNY (3-D)
Cheerios Giveaway: 1953 (Pocket size) (15 titles)

each....	10	30	50	70
Mailing Envelope (has Bugs drawn on front)	10	30	50	70

BUGS BUNNY
DC Comics: May, 1997 ($4.95, 24 pgs., comic-sized)
1-Numbered ed. of 100,000; "1st Day of Issue" stamp cancellation on-c   5.00

BUGS BUNNY POSTAL COMIC
DC Comics: 1997 (64 pgs., 7.5" x 5")
nn -Mail Fan; Daffy Duck app.   4.00

BULLETMAN
Fawcett Publications
Well Known Comics (1942)-Paper-c; glued binding; printed in red

(Bestmaid/Samuel Lowe giveaway)	20	65	100	150

BULLS-EYE (Cody of The Pony Express No. 8 on)
Charlton: 1955
Great Scott Shoe Store giveaway-Reprints #2 with new cover

	20	75	115	170

BUSTER BROWN COMICS (Radio)(Also see My Dog Tige in Promotional sec.)
Brown Shoe Co: 1945 - No. 43, 1959 (No. 5: paper-c)
nn, nd (#1,scarce)-Featuring Smilin' Ed McConnell & the Buster Brown gang "Midnight" the cat, "Squeaky" the mouse & "Froggy" the Gremlin; covers mention dift. shoe stores. Contains adventure stories

	62	187	380	600
2	19	58	100	170
3,5-10	11	33	55	90
4 (Rare)-Low print run due to paper shortage	16	48	83	140
11-20	8	23	42	55
21-24,26-28	6	18	28	38
25,33-37,40,41-Crandall-a in all	10	30	55	80
29-32-"Interplanetary Police Vs. the Space Siren" by Crandall (pencils only #29)				
	10	30	55	80
38,39,42,43	6	18	28	38

BUSTER BROWN COMICS (Radio)
Brown Shoe Co: 1950s
...Goes to Mars (2/58-Western Printing), slick-c, 20 pgs., reg. size

	11	33	55	90
...In "Buster Makes the Team!" (1959-Custom Comics)				
	8	23	42	55
...In The Jet Age (`50s), slick-c, 20 pgs., 5x7-1/4"	10	30	55	85
...Of the Safety Patrol (`60-Custom Comics)	3	10	23	35
...Out of This World ('59-Custom Comics)	7	21	36	50
...Safety Coloring Book ('58, 16 pgs.)-Slick paper	7	21	36	50

CALL FROM CHRIST
Catechetical Educational Society: 1952 (Giveaway, 36 pgs.)

nn	4	12	18	24

CANCELLED COMIC CAVALCADE
DC Comics, Inc.: Summer, 1978 - No. 2, Fall, 1978 (8-1/2x11", B&W)
(Xeroxed pgs. on one side only w/blue cover and taped spine)

1-(412 pgs.) Contains xeroxed copies of art for: Black Lightning #12, cover to #13; Claw #13, 14; The Deserter #1; Doorway to Nightmare #6; Firestorm #6; The Green Team #2,3.
2-(532 pgs.) Contains xeroxed copies of art for: Kamandi #60 (including Omac), #61; Prez #5; Shade #9 (including The Odd Man); Showcase #105 (Deadman), 106 (The Creeper); Secret Society of Super Villains #16 & 17; The Vixen #1; and more to Army at War #2, Battle Classics #3, Demand Classics #1 & 2, Dynamic Classics #3, Mr. Miracle #26, Ragman #6, Weird Mystery #25 & 26, & Western Classics #1 & 2. (Rare)
              (Number 2 set sold in 2001 for $800.00)

NOTE: In June, 1978, DC cancelled several of their titles. For copyright purposes, the unpublished original art for these titles was xeroxed, bound in the above books, published and distributed. Only 35 copies were made.

CAP'N CRUNCH COMICS (See Quaker Oats)
Quaker Oats Co.: 1963; 1965 (16 pgs.; miniature giveaways; 2-1/2x6-1/2")
(1963 titles)- "The Picture Pirates", "The Fountain of Youth", "I'm Dreaming of a Wide Isthmus". (1965 titles)- "Bewitched, Betwitched, & Betweaked", "Seadog Meets the Witch Doctor", "A Witch in Time"

	9	27	40	60

CAPTAIN ACTION (Toy)
National Periodical Publications
...& Action Boy('67)-Ideal Toy Co. giveaway (1st app. Captain Action)

	20	60	100	160

CAPTAIN AMERICA
Marvel Comics Group
...& The Campbell Kids (1980, 36pg. giveaway, Campbell's Soup/U.S. Dept.

of Energy)	1	4	7	10
...Goes To War Against Drugs(1990, no #, giveaway)-Distributed to direct sales shops; 2nd printing exists				5.00
...Meets The Asthma Monster (1987, no #, giveaway, Your Physician and Glaxo, Inc.)				6.00
...Vs. Asthma Monster (1990, no #, giveaway, Your Physician & Allen & Hanbury's)				5.00

CAPTAIN AMERICA COMICS
Timely/Marvel Comics: 1954

Shoestore Giveaway #77	56	170	340	550

CAPTAIN ATOM
Nationwide Publishers
...- Secret of the Columbian Jungle (16 pgs. in color, paper-c, 3-3/4x5-1/8")-Fireside Marshmallow giveaway

	5	14	21	28

CAPTAIN BEN DIX
Bendix Aviation Corporation: 1943 (Small size)

nn	8	24	42	60

CAPTAIN BEN DIX IN ACTION WITH THE INVISIBLE CREW
Bendix Aviation Corp.: 1940s (nd), 20 pgs, 8-1/4"x11", heavy paper
nn-WWII bomber-c; Jap app.

	5	15	25	35

CAPTAIN FORTUNE PRESENTS
Vital Publications: 1955 - 1959 (Giveaway, 3-1/4x6-7/8", 16 pgs.)
"Davy Crockett in Episodes of the Creek War", "Davy Crockett at the Alamo", "In Sherwood Forest Tells Strange Tales of Robin Hood" ('57), "Meets Bolivar the Liberator" ('59), "Tells How Buffalo Bill Fights the Dog Soldiers" ('57), "Young Davy Crockett"

	3	7	11	14

CAPTAIN GALLANT (...of the Foreign Legion) (TV)
Charlton Comics
Heinz Foods Premium (#1?)(1955; regular size)-U.S. Pictorial; contains Buster Crabbe photos; Don Heck-a

	1	3	6	8

CAPTAIN MARVEL ADVENTURES
Fawcett Publications
Bond Bread Giveaways-(24 pgs.; pocket size-7-1/4x3-1/2"; paper cover): "...& the Stolen City" ('48), "The Boy Who Never Heard of Capt. Marvel", "Meets the Weatherman" -(1950)(reprint)

each....	37	110	165	240
...Well Known Comics (1944; 12 pgs.; 8-1/2x10-1/2")-printed in red & in blue; soft-c; glued binding-Bestmaid/Samuel Lowe Co. giveaway				
	25	75	115	175

CAPTAIN MARVEL ADVENTURES
Fawcett Publications (Wheaties Giveaway): 1945 (6x8", full color, paper-c)
nn- "Captain Marvel & the Threads of Life" plus 2 other stories (32 pgs.)

	79	300	400	575

NOTE: All copies were taped at each corner to a box of Wheaties and are never found in Fine or Mint condition. Prices listed for each grade include tape.

CAPTAIN MARVEL AND THE LTS. OF SAFETY
Ebasco Services/Fawcett Publications: 1950 - 1951 (3 issues - no No.'s)

nn (#1)"Danger Flies a Kite" ('50, scarce)	233	700	1400	-
nn (#2)"Danger Takes to Climbing" ('50)	183	550	1000	-
nn (#3)"Danger Smashes Street Lights" ('51)	183	550	1000	-

Carvel Comics #1 © Carvel

Century of Comics nn © EAS

Cheerios Premiums Y1 © WDC

	GD2.0	FN6.0	VF8.0	NM9.4

CAPTAIN MARVEL, JR.
Fawcett Publications: (1944; 12 pgs.; 8-1/2x10-1/2")

...Well Known Comics (Printed in blue; paper-c, glued binding)-Bestmaid/Samuel Lowe Co. giveaway	14	42	72	120

CARDINAL MINDSZENTY (The Truth Behind the Trial of...)
Catechetical Guild Education Society: 1949 (24 pgs., paper cover)

nn-Anti-communism	7	21	36	50
Press Proof-(Very Rare)-(Full color, 7-1/2x11-3/4", untrimmed) Only two known copies				150.00
Preview Copy (B&W, stapled), 18 pgs.; contains first 13 pgs. of Cardinal Mindszenty and was sent out as an advance promotion. Only one known copy			150.00 - 200.00	

NOTE: Regular edition also printed in French. There was also a movie released in 1949 called "Guilty of Treason" which is a fact-based account of the trial and imprisonment of Cardinal Mindszenty by the Communist regime in Hungary.

CARNIVAL OF COMICS
Fleet-Air Shoes: 1954 (Giveaway)

nn-Contains a comic bound with new cover; several combinations possible; Charlton's Eh! known	4	10	15	20

CARTOON NETWORK
DC Comics: 1997 (Giveaway)

nn-reprints Cow and Chicken, Scooby-Doo, & Flintstones stories				2.25

CARVEL COMICS (Amazing Advs. of Capt. Carvel)
Carvel Corp. (Ice Cream): 1975 - No. 5, 1976 (25¢; #3-5: 35¢) (#4,5: 3-1/4x5")

1-3	1	3	6	8
4,5(1976)-Baseball theme	2	6	9	12

CASE OF THE WASTED WATER, THE
Rheem Water Heating: 1972? (Giveaway)

nn-Neal Adams-a	4	12	29	45

CASPER SPECIAL
Target Stores (Harvey): nd (Dec, 1990) (Giveaway with $1.00 cover)

Three issues-Given away with Casper video				4.00

CASPER, THE FRIENDLY GHOST (Paramount Picture Star...)(2nd Series)
Harvey Publications

American Dental Association (Giveaways):

...'s Dental Health Activity Book-1977	1	3	6	8
...Presents Space Age Dentistry-1972	1	4	7	10
..., His Den, & Their Dentist Fight the Tooth Demons-1974				
	1	4	7	10

CELEBRATE THE CENTURY SUPERHEROES STAMP ALBUM
DC Comics: 1998 - No. 5, 2000 (32 pgs.)

1-5: Historical stories hosted by DC heroes				3.00

CENTIPEDE
DC Comics: 1983

1-Based on Atari video game				3.00

CENTURY OF COMICS
Eastern Color Printing Co.: 1933 (100 pgs.) (Probably the 3rd comic book) Bought by Wheatena, Milk-O-Malt, John Wanamaker, Kinney Shoe Stores, & others to be used as premiums and radio giveaways. No publisher listed.

nn-Mutt & Jeff, Joe Palooka, etc. reprints	3670	11,000	22,000	-

CHEERIOS PREMIUMS (Disney)
Walt Disney Productions: 1947 (16 titles, pocket size, 32 pgs.)

Mailing Envelope for each set "W,X,Y & Z" (has Mickey illo on front)(each envelope designates the set it contains on the front)	10	30	50	75
Set "W"				
W1-Donald Duck & the Pirates	10	30	50	75
W2-Bucky Bug & the Cannibal King	5	15	25	35
W3-Pluto Joins the F.B.I.	5	15	25	35
W4-Mickey Mouse & the Haunted House	6	18	32	45
Set "X"				
X1-Donald Duck, Counter Spy	10	30	50	70
X2-Goofy Lost in the Desert	5	15	25	35
X3-Br'er Rabbit Outwits Br'er Fox	5	15	25	35

X4-Mickey Mouse at the Rodeo

X4-Mickey Mouse at the Rodeo	6	18	32	45
Set "Y"				
Y1-Donald Duck's Atom Bomb by Carl Barks. Disney has banned reprinting this book	90	270	560	900
Y2-Br'er Rabbit's Secret	5	15	25	35
Y3-Dumbo & the Circus Mystery	6	18	28	38
Y4-Mickey Mouse Meets the Wizard	6	18	28	38
Set "Z"				
Z1-Donald Duck Pilots a Jet Plane (not by Barks)	10	30	50	75
Z2-Pluto Turns Sleuth Hound	5	15	25	35
Z3-The Seven Dwarfs & the Enchanted Mtn.	6	18	32	45
Z4-Mickey Mouse's Secret Room	6	18	32	45

CHEERIOS 3-D GIVEAWAYS (Disney)
Walt Disney Productions: 1954 (24 titles, pocket size) (Glasses came in envelopes)

Glasses only...	7	21	36	50
Mailing Envelope (no art on front)	10	30	45	65
(Set 1)				
1-Donald Duck & Uncle Scrooge, the Firefighters	10	30	50	75
2-Mickey Mouse & Goofy, Pirate Plunder	10	30	48	70
3-Donald Duck's Nephews, the Fabulous Inventors	10	30	50	75
4-Mickey Mouse, Secret of the Ming Vase	10	30	48	70
5-Donald Duck with Huey, Dewey, & Louie; ...the Seafarers (title on 2nd page)	10	30	50	75
6-Mickey Mouse, Moaning Mountain	10	30	48	70
7-Donald Duck, Apache Gold	10	30	50	75
8-Mickey Mouse, Flight to Nowhere	10	30	48	70
(Set 2)				
1-Donald Duck, Treasure of Timbuktu	10	30	50	75
2-Mickey Mouse & Pluto, Operation China	10	30	48	70
3-Donald Duck in the Magic Cows	10	30	50	75
4-Mickey Mouse & Goofy, Kid Kokonut	10	30	48	70
5-Donald Duck, Mystery Ship	10	30	50	75
6-Mickey Mouse, Phantom Sheriff	10	30	48	70
7-Donald Duck, Circus Adventures	10	30	50	75
8-Mickey Mouse, Arctic Explorers	10	30	48	70
(Set 3)				
1-Donald Duck & Witch Hazel	10	30	50	75
2-Mickey Mouse in Darkest Africa	10	30	48	70
3-Donald Duck & Uncle Scrooge, Timber Trouble	10	30	50	75
4-Mickey Mouse, Rajah's Rescue	10	30	48	70
5-Donald Duck in Robot Reporter	10	30	50	75
6-Mickey Mouse, Slumbering Sleuth	10	30	48	70
7-Donald Duck in the Foreign Legion	10	30	50	75
8-Mickey Mouse, Airwalking Wonder	10	30	48	70

CHESTY AND COPTIE (Disney)
Los Angeles Community Chest: 1946 (Giveaway, 4pgs.)

nn-(One known copy) by Floyd Gottfredson	95	285	590	950

CHESTY AND HIS HELPERS (Disney)
Los Angeles War Chest: 1943 (Giveaway, 12 pgs., 5-1/2x7-1/4")

nn-Chesty & Coptie	62	185	390	625

CHRISTMAS ADVENTURE, THE
S. Rose (H. L. Green Giveaway): 1963 (16 pgs.)

nn	2	6	9	12

CHRISTMAS AT THE ROTUNDA (Titled Ford Rotunda Christmas Book 1957 on) (Regular size)
Ford Motor Co. (Western Printing): 1954 - 1961 (Given away every Christmas at one location)

1954-56 issues (nn's)	5	15	24	32
1957-61 issues (nn's)	4	12	19	25

CHRISTMAS CAROL, A
Sears Roebuck & Co.: No date (1942-43) (Giveaway, 32 pgs., 8-1/4x10-3/4", paper cover)

nn-Comics & coloring book	18	54	94	160

CHRISTMAS CAROL, A
Sears Roebuck & Co.: 1940s ? (Christmas giveaway, 20 pgs.)

Christmas is Coming

Cinema Comics Herald - Bedtime Story
© Columbia Pictures

Classics Giveaways - Saks 34th St.

CL

P R O M O T I O N A L   C O M I C S

	GD2.0	FN6.0	VF8.0	NM9.4
nn-Comic book & animated coloring book	16	48	83	140

CHRISTMAS CAROLS
Hot Shoppes Giveaway: 1959? (16 pgs.)

nn	4	11	17	22

CHRISTMAS COLORING FUN
H. Burnside: 1964 (20 pgs., slick-c, B&W)

nn	2	6	11	15

CHRISTMAS DREAM, A
Promotional Publishing Co.: 1950 (Kinney Shoe Store Giveaway, 16 pgs.)

nn	5	14	21	28

CHRISTMAS DREAM, A
J. J. Newberry Co.: 1952? (Giveaway, paper cover, 16 pgs.)

nn	4	12	19	25

CHRISTMAS DREAM, A
Promotional Publ. Co.: 1952 (Giveaway, 16 pgs., paper cover)

nn	4	12	19	25

CHRISTMAS FUN AROUND THE WORLD
No publisher: No date (early 50's) (16 pgs., paper cover)

nn	5	14	21	28

CHRISTMAS IS COMING!
No publisher: No date (early 50's?) (Store giveaway, 16 pgs.)

nn	4	12	18	24

CHRISTMAS JOURNEY THROUGH SPACE
Promotional Publishing Co.: 1960

nn-Reprints 1954 issue Jolly Christmas Book with new slick cover

	3	9	20	30

CHRISTMAS ON THE MOON
W. T. Grant Co.: 1958 (Giveaway, 20 pgs., slick cover)

nn	8	24	42	60

CHRISTMAS PLAY BOOK
Gould-Stoner Co.: 1946 (Giveaway, 16 pgs., paper cover)

nn	8	24	42	60

CHRISTMAS ROUNDUP
Promotional Publishing Co.: 1960

nn-Marv Levy-c/a

	2	6	11	15

CHRISTMAS STORY CUT-OUT BOOK, THE
Catechetical Guild: No. 393, 1951 (15¢, 36 pgs.)

393-Half text & half comics

	6	18	32	45

CHRISTMAS USA (Through 300 Years) (Also see Uncle Sam's...)
Promotional Publ. Co.: 1956 (Giveaway)

nn-Marv Levy-c/a

	3	8	12	15

CHRISTMAS WITH SNOW WHITE AND THE SEVEN DWARFS
Kobackers Giftstore of Buffalo, N.Y.: 1953 (16 pgs., paper-c)

nn	7	21	36	50

CHRISTOPHERS, THE
Catechetical Guild: 1951 (Giveaway, 36 pgs.) (Some copies have 15¢ sticker)

nn-Stalin as Satan in Hell

	25	75	135	210

CINDERELLA IN "FAIREST OF THE FAIR"
American Dairy Association (Premium): 1955 (5x7-1/4", 16 pgs., soft-c)
(Walt Disney)

nn	10	30	55	80

CINEMA COMICS HERALD
Paramount Pictures/Universal/RKO/20th Century Fox/Republic:
1941 - 1943 (4-pg. movie "trailers", paper-c, 7-1/2x10-1/2")(Giveaway)

"Mr. Bug Goes to Town" (1941)	11	33	55	90
"Bedtime Story"	8	24	42	60
"Lady For A Night", John Wayne, Joan Blondell ('42)	14	42	72	120
"Reap The Wild Wind" (1942)	8	24	45	65
"Thunder Birds" (1942)	8	24	42	60

	GD2.0	FN6.0	VF8.0	NM9.4
"They All Kissed the Bride"	8	24	42	60
"Arabian Nights" (nd)	8	24	45	65
"Bombardie" (1943)	8	24	42	60
"Crash Dive" (1943)-Tyrone Power	8	24	45	65

NOTE: The 1941-42 issues contain line art with color photos. 1943 issues are line art.

CLASSICS GIVEAWAYS (Classic Comics reprints)
12/41–Walter Theatre Enterprises (Huntington, WV) giveaway containing #2
(orig.) w/new generic-c (only 1 known copy) 113 339 650 1000
1942–Double Comics containing CC#1 (orig.) (diff. cover) (not actually a
giveaway) (very rare) (also see Double Comics) (only one known copy)
218 654 1250 1950
12/42–Saks 34th St. Giveaway containing CC#7 (orig.) (diff. cover)
(very rare; only 6 known copies) 714 2142 3300 5000
2/43–American Comics containing CC#8 (orig.) (Liberty Theatre giveaway)
(different cover) (only one known copy) (see American Comics)
163 490 900 1400
12/44–Robin Hood Flour Co. Giveaway - #7-CC(R) (diff. cover) (rare)
(edition probably 5 [22]) 300 900 1500 2400
NOTE: How are above editions determined without CC covers? 1942 is dated 1942, and CC#1-first
reprint did not come out until 5/43. 12/42 and 2/43 are determined by blue note at bottom of first text
page only in original edition. 12/44 is estimated from page width each reprint edition had progres-
sively smaller page width.

1951–Shelter Thru the Ages (C.I. Educational Series) (actually Giveaway by
the Ruberoid Co.) (16 pgs.) (contains original artwork by H. C. Kiefer) (there
are 5 diff. back cover ad variations: "Ranch" house ad, "Igloo" ad, "Doll
House" ad, "Tree House" ad & blank)(scarce) 88 264 480 750
1952–George Daynor Biography Giveaway (CC logo) (partly comic book/
pictures/newspaper articles) (story of man who built Palace Depression
out of junkyard swamp in NJ) (64 pgs.)(very rare; only 3 known copies,
one missing-bc) 857 2571 4200 6300
1953–Westinghouse/Dreams of a Man (C.I. Educational Series) (Westinghouse
bio./Westinghouse Co. giveaway) (contains original artwork by H. C. Kiefer)
(16 pgs.) (also French/Spanish/Italian versions)
(scarce) 84 252 455 700
NOTE: Reproductions of 1951, 1952, and 1953 exist with color photocopy covers and black & white
photocopy interior ("W.C.N. Reprint") 2 5 8 10
1951-53–Coward Shoe Giveaways (all editions very rare); 2 variations of
back-c ad exist:
With back-c photo ad: 5 (87), 12 (89), 22 (85), 32 (85),49 (85), 69 (87), 72
(no HRN), 80 (0), 91 (0), 92 (0), 96 (0), 98 (0), 100 (0), 101 (0), 103-105
(all Os) 42 126 240 365
With back-c cartoon ad: 106-109 (all 0s), 110 (111), 112 (0)
47 141 260 400
1956–Ben Franklin 5-10 Store Giveaway (#65-PC with back cover ad)
(scarce) 39 117 200 315
1956–Ben Franklin Insurance Co. Giveaway (#65-PC with diff. back cover ad)
(very rare) 74 221 450 700
11/56–Sealtest Co. Edition - #4 (135) (identical to regular edition except for
Sealtest logo printed, not stamped, on front cover) (only two copies known
to exist) 43 129 245 375
1958–Get-Well Giveaway containing #15-CI (new cartoon-type cover)
(Pressman Pharmacy) (only one copy known to exist)
40 120 210 325
1967-68–Twin Circle Giveaway Editions - all HRN 166, with back cover ad
for National Catholic Press.
2(R68), 4(R67), 10(R68), 13(R68) 3 9 21 32
48(R67), 128(R68), 535(576-R68) 4 12 25 38
16(R68), 68(R67) 4 12 30 50
12/69–Christmas Giveaway ("A Christmas Adventure") (reprints Picture
Parade #4-1953, new cover) (4 ad variations)
Stacy's Dept. Store 3 9 19 28
Anne & Hope Store 5 15 34 55
Gibson's Dept. Store (rare) 5 15 34 55
"Merry Christmas" & blank ad space 3 9 19 28

CLIFF MERRITT SETS THE RECORD STRAIGHT
Brotherhood of Railroad Trainsmen: Giveaway (2 different issues)
...and the Very Candid Candidate by Al Williamson 1 3 6 8
...Sets the Record Straight by Al Williamson (2 different-c: one by
Williamson, the other by McWilliams) 1 3 6 8

237

C-M-O Comics #2 © CEN

Crackajack Funnies nn © DELL

Dan Curtis Giveaways - Dark Shadows © WEST

	GD2.0	FN6.0	VF8.0	NM9.4

CLYDE BEATTY COMICS (Also see Crackajack Funnies)
Commodore Productions & Artists, Inc.
...African Jungle Book('56)-Richfield Oil Co. 16 pg. giveaway, soft-c

	11	33	59	85

C-M-O COMICS
Chicago Mail Order Co.(Centaur): 1942 - No. 2, 1942 (68 pgs., full color)

1-Invisible Terror, Super Ann, & Plymo the Rubber Man app. (all Centaur costume heroes)	84	253	540	850
2-Invisible Terror, Super Ann app.	55	165	325	525

COCOMALT BIG BOOK OF COMICS
Harry 'A' Chesler (Cocomalt Premium): 1938 (Reg. size, full color, 52 pgs.)

1-(Scarce)-Biro-c/a; Little Nemo by Winsor McCay Jr., Dan Hastings; Jack Cole, Guardineer, Gustavson, Bob Wood-a	225	675	1400	2200

COMIC BOOK (Also see Comics From Weatherbird)
American Juniors Shoe: 1954 (Giveaway)
Contains a comic rebound with new cover. Several combinations possible. Contents determine price.

COMIC BOOK MAGAZINE
Chicago Tribune & other newspapers: 1940 - 1943 (Similar to Spirit Sections) (7-3/4x10-3/4"; full color; 16-24 pgs. ea.)

1940 issues	8	24	39	55
1941, 1942 issues	6	18	29	40
1943 issues	5	15	25	35

NOTE: Published weekly. Texas Slim, Kit Carson, Spooky, Josie, Nuts & Jolts, Lew Loyal, Brenda Starr, Daniel Boone, Captain Storm, Rocky, Smokey Stover, Tiny Tim, Little Joe, Fu Manchu appear among others. Early issues had photo stories with pictures from the movies; later issues had comic art.

COMIC BOOKS (Series 1)
Metropolitan Printing Co. (Giveaway): 1950 (16 pgs.; 5-1/4x8-1/2"; full color; bound at top; paper cover)

1-Boots and Saddles; intro The Masked Marshal	6	18	28	38
1-The Green Jet; Green Lama by Raboy	30	90	160	250
1-My Pal Dizzy	4	10	15	20
1-New World; origin Atomaster (costumed hero)	10	30	50	75
1-Talullah (Teen-age)	4	10	15	20

COMIC CAVALCADE
All-American/National Periodical Publications

Giveaway (1944, 8 pgs., paper-c, in color)-One Hundred Years of Co-operation-r/Comic Cavalcade #9	75	225	460	725
Giveaway (1945, 16 pgs., paper-c, in color)-Movie "Tomorrow The World" (Nazi theme); r/Comic Cavalcade #10	100	300	600	950
Giveaway (c. 1944-45; 8 pgs., paper-c, in color)-The Twain Shall Meet-r/Comic Cavalcade #8	75	225	460	725

COMIC SELECTIONS (Shoe store giveaway)
Parents' Magazine Press: 1944-46 (Reprints from Calling All Girls, True Comics, True Aviation, & Real Heroes)

1	5	15	23	30
2-5	4	10	15	20

COMICS FROM WEATHER BIRD (Also see Comic Book, Edward's Shoes, Free Comics to You & Weather Bird)
Weather Bird Shoes: 1954 - 1957 (Giveaway)
Contains a comic bound with new cover. Many combinations possible. Contents would determine price. Some issues do not contain complete comics, but only parts of comics.Value equals 40 to 60 percent of contents.

COMICS READING LIBRARIES (Educational Series)
King Features (Charlton Publ.): 1973, 1977, 1979 (36 pgs. in color) (Giveaways)

R-01-Tiger, Quincy	1	3	6	8
R-02-Beetle Bailey, Blondie & Popeye	2	6	9	12
R-03-Blondie, Beetle Bailey	1	3	6	8
R-04-Tim Tyler's Luck, Felix the Cat	2	6	13	20
R-05-Quincy, Henry	1	3	6	8
R-06-The Phantom, Mandrake	2	6	13	20
1977 reprint(R-04)	1	4	7	10
R-07-Popeye, Little King	2	6	11	15

R-08-Prince Valiant(Foster), Flash Gordon	3	9	17	25
1977 reprint	2	6	10	14
R-09-Hagar the Horrible, Boner's Ark	2	6	9	12
R-10-Redeye, Tiger	1	3	6	8
R-11-Blondie, Hi & Lois	1	3	6	8
R-12-Popeye-Swee'pea, Brutus	2	6	11	15
R-13-Beetle Bailey, Little King	1	3	6	8
R-14-Quincy-Hamlet	1	3	6	8
R-15-The Phantom, The Genius	2	6	11	15
R-16-Flash Gordon, Mandrake	3	9	17	25
1977 reprint	2	6	9	12
Other 1977 editions....				6.00
1979 editions (68 pgs.)				6.00

NOTE: Above giveaways available with purchase of $45.00 in merchandise. Used as a reading skill aid for small children.

COMMANDMENTS OF GOD
Catechetical Guild: 1954, 1958

300-Same contents in both editions; diff-c	4	11	17	22

COMPLIMENTARY COMICS
Sales Promotion Publ.: No date (1950's) (Giveaway)

1-Strongman by Powell, 3 stories	7	21	36	50

CRACKAJACK FUNNIES (Giveaway)
Malto-Meal: 1937 (Full size, soft-c, full color, 32 pgs.)(Before No. 1?)

nn-Features Dan Dunn, G-Man, Speed Bolton, Buck Jones, The Nebbs, Clyde Beatty, Freckles, Major Hoople, Wash Tubbs	100	300	625	1000

CROSLEY'S HOUSE OF FUN (Also see Tee and Vee Crosley...)
Crosley Div. AVCO Mfg. Corp.: 1950 (Giveaway, paper cover, 32 pgs.)

nn-Strips revolve around Crosley appliances	4	13	19	26

DAGWOOD SPLITS THE ATOM (Also see Topix V8#4)
King Features Syndicate: 1949 (Science comic with King Features characters) (Giveaway)

nn-Half comic, half text; Popeye, Olive Oyl, Henry, Mandrake, Little King, Katzenjammer Kids app.	7	21	38	55

DAISY COMICS (Daisy Air Rifles)
Eastern Color Printing Co.: Dec, 1936 (5-1/4x7-1/2")

nn-Joe Palooka, Buck Rogers (2 pgs. from Famous Funnies No. 18, 1st full cover app.), Napoleon Flying to Fame, Butty & Fally	34	103	180	280

DAISY LOW OF THE GIRL SCOUTS
Girl Scouts of America: 1954, 1965 (16 pgs., paper-c)

1954-Story of Juliette Gordon Low	4	12	19	25
1965	2	6	9	12

DAN CURTIS GIVEAWAYS
Western Publishing Co.:1974 (3x6", 24 pgs., reprints)

1-Dark Shadows	2	6	11	15
2,6-Star Trek	2	6	13	20
3,4,7-9: Twilight Zone. 4-Ripley's Believe it or Not! 7-The Occult Files of Dr. Spektor. 8-Dagar the Invincible. 9-Grimm's Ghost Stories	1	4	7	10
5-Turok, Son of Stone (partial-r/Turok #78)	2	6	11	15

DANNY KAYE'S BAND FUN BOOK
H & A Selmer: 1959 (Giveaway)

nn	6	18	32	45

DAREDEVIL
Marvel Comics Group: 1993
...Vs. Vapora 1 (Engineering Show Giveaway, 16 pg.)–Intro Vapora 4.00

DAVY CROCKETT (TV)
Dell Publishing Co.

...Christmas Book (no date, 16 pgs., paper-c)-Sears giveaway	6	18	30	42
...Safety Trails (1955, 16pgs, 3-1/4x7")-Cities Service giveaway	7	21	38	55

DAVY CROCKETT
Charlton Comics

Dick Tracy Original © KING

Double Talk © Feature Pub.

Dumbo 1941 © WDC

	GD2.0	FN6.0	VF8.0	NM9.4

Hunting With… nn ('55, 16 pgs.)-Ben Franklin Store giveaway (Publ.-S. Rose)

| | | 5 | 15 | 24 | 32 |

DAVY CROCKETT
Walt Disney Prod.: (1955, 16 pgs., 5x7-1/4", slick, photo-c)
…In the Raid at Piney Creek-American Motors giveaway

| | | 7 | 21 | 38 | 55 |

DC SAMPLER
DC Comics : nn (#1) 1983 - No. 3, 1984 (36 pgs.; 6 1/2" x 10", giveaway)
nn(#1) -3: nn-Wraparound-c, previews upcoming issues. 3-Kirby-a ... 5.00

DC SPOTLIGHT
DC Comics : 1985 (50th anniversary special) (giveaway)
1-Includes profiles on Batman:The Dark Knight & Watchmen ... 4.00

DENNIS THE MENACE
Hallden (Fawcett)
…& Dirt ('59)-Soil Conservation giveaway; r-# 36; Wiseman-c/a

| | | 2 | 6 | 9 | 12 |

…& Dirt ('68)-reprints '59 edition

| | | 1 | 3 | 6 | 8 |

…Away We Go('70)-Caladryl giveaway ... 6.00
…Coping with Family Stress-giveaway ... 5.00
…Takes a Poke at Poison('61)-Food & Drug Admin. giveaway; Wiseman-c/a

| | | 1 | 3 | 6 | 8 |

…Takes a Poke at Poison-Revised 1/66, 11/70 ... 4.00
…Takes a Poke at Poison-Revised 1972, 1974, 1977, 1981 ... 4.00

DETECTIVE COMICS (Also see other Batman titles)
National Periodical Publications/DC Comics
27 (1984)-Oreo Cookies giveaway (32 pgs., paper-c) r-/Det. 27, 38 & Batman No. 1 (1st Joker)

| | | 4 | 12 | 30 | 50 |

38 (1995) Blockbuster Video edition; reprints 1st Robin app. ... 3.00
38 (1997) Toys R Us edition ... 3.00
359 (1997) Toys R Us edition; reprints 1st Batgirl app. ... 3.00

DICK TRACY GIVEAWAYS
1939 - 1958; 1990
Buster Brown Shoes Giveaway (1940s?, 36 pgs. in color); 1938-39-r by Gould

| | | 36 | 107 | 200 | 320 |

Gillmore Giveaway (See Superbook)
…Hatful of Fun (No date, 1950-52, 32pgs.; 8-1/2x10")-Dick Tracy hat promotion; Dick Tracy games, magic tricks. Miller Bros. premium

| | | 18 | 54 | 95 | 150 |

Motorola Giveaway (1953)-Reprints Harvey Comics Library #2; "The Case of the Sparkle Plenty TV Mystery"

| | | 5 | 15 | 26 | 40 |

Original Dick Tracy by Chester Gould, The (Aug, 1990, 16 pgs., 5-1/2x8-1/2")- Gladstone Publ.; Bread Giveaway

| | | 3 | 9 | 20 | 30 |

Popped Wheat Giveaway (1947, 16 pgs. in color)-1940-r; Sig Feuchtwanger Publ.; Gould-a

| | | 3 | 8 | 12 | 16 |

…Presents the Family Fun Book; Tip Top Bread Giveaway, no date or number (1940, Fawcett Publ., 16 pgs. in color)-Spy Smasher, Ibis, Lance O'Casey app.

| | | 56 | 170 | 340 | 550 |

Same as above but without app. of heroes & Dick Tracy on cover only

| | | 14 | 42 | 72 | 120 |

Service Station Giveaway (1958, 16 pgs. in color)(regular size, slick cover)- Harvey Info. Press

| | | 4 | 10 | 15 | 20 |

Shoe Store Giveaway (Weatherbird)(1939, 16 pgs.)-Gould-a

| | | 14 | 42 | 72 | 120 |

DICK TRACY SHEDS LIGHT ON THE MOLE
Western Printing Co.: 1949 (16 pgs.) (Ray-O-Vac Flashlights giveaway)
nn-Not by Gould

| | | 7 | 21 | 38 | 55 |

DICK WINGATE OF THE U.S. NAVY
Superior Publ./Toby Press: 1951; 1953 (no month)
nn-U.S. Navy giveaway

| | | 4 | 12 | 19 | 25 |

1(1953, Toby)-Reprints nn issue? (same-c)

| | | 4 | 11 | 17 | 22 |

DIG 'EM
Kellogg's Sugar Smacks Giveaway: 1973 (2-3/8x6", 16 pgs.)
nn-4 different issues

| | | 1 | 3 | 6 | 8 |

DOC CARTER VD COMICS

	GD2.0	FN6.0	VF8.0	NM9.4

Health Publications Institute, Raleigh, N. C. (Giveaway): 1949 (16 pgs. in color) (Paper-c)
nn

| | | 18 | 54 | 94 | 160 |

DONALD AND MICKEY MERRY CHRISTMAS (Formerly Famous Gang Book Of Comics)
K. K. Publ./Firestone Tire & Rubber Co.: 1943 - 1949 (Giveaway, 20 pgs.)
Put out each Christmas; 1943 issue titled "Firestone Presents Comics" (Disney)
1943-Donald Duck-r/WDC&S #32 by Carl Barks

| | | 75 | 225 | 469 | 825 |

1944-Donald Duck-r/WDC&S #35 by Barks

| | | 70 | 210 | 437 | 775 |

1945- "Donald Duck's Best Christmas", 8 pgs. Carl Barks; intro. & 1st app. Grandma Duck in comic books

| | | 105 | 315 | 653 | 1150 |

1946-Donald Duck in "Santa's Stormy Visit", 8 pgs. Carl Barks

| | | 73 | 219 | 455 | 800 |

1947-Donald Duck in "Three Good Little Ducks", 8 pgs. Carl Barks

| | | 73 | 219 | 455 | 800 |

1948-Donald Duck in "Toyland", 8 pgs. Carl Barks

| | | 73 | 219 | 455 | 800 |

1949-Donald Duck in "New Toys", 8 pgs. Barks

| | | 66 | 198 | 412 | 725 |

DONALD DUCK
K. K. Publications: 1944 (Christmas giveaway, paper-c, 16 pgs.)(2 versions)
nn-Kelly cover reprint

| | | 82 | 246 | 515 | 825 |

DONALD DUCK AND THE RED FEATHER
Red Feather Giveaway: 1948 (8-1/2x11", 4 pgs., B&W)
nn

| | | 17 | 51 | 99 | 170 |

DONALD DUCK IN "THE LITTERBUG"
Keep America Beautiful: 1963 (5x7-1/4", 16 pgs., soft-c) (Disney giveaway)
nn

| | | 4 | 12 | 26 | 40 |

DONALD DUCK "PLOTTING PICNICKERS" (See Frito-Lay Giveaway)

DONALD DUCK'S SURPRISE PARTY
Walt Disney Productions: 1948 (16 pgs.) (Giveaway for Icy Frost Twins Ice Cream Bars)
nn-(Rare)-Kelly-c/a

| | | 314 | 943 | 1600 | 2500 |

DOT AND DASH AND THE LUCKY JINGLE PIGGIE
Sears Roebuck Co.: 1942 (Giveaway, 12 pgs.)
nn-Contains a war stamp album and a punch out Jingle Piggie bank

| | | 10 | 30 | 55 | 80 |

DOUBLE TALK (Also see Two-Faces)
Feature Publications: No date (1962?) (32 pgs., full color, slick-c) Christian Anti-Communism Crusade (Giveaway)
nn-Sickle with blood-c

| | | 8 | 24 | 60 | 100 |

DUMBO (Walt Disney's…, The Flying Elephant)
Weatherbird Shoes/Ernest Kern Co.(Detroit)/ Wieboldt's (Chicago): 1941 (K.K. Publ. Giveaway)
nn-16 pgs., 9x10" (Rare)

| | | 47 | 141 | 286 | 500 |

nn-52 pgs., 8-1/2x8-1/2", slick cover in color; B&W interior; half text, half reprints 4-Color No. 17 (Dept. store)

| | | 27 | 81 | 145 | 250 |

DUMBO WEEKLY
Walt Disney Prod.: 1942 (Premium supplied by Diamond D-X Gas Stations)
1

| | | 75 | 225 | 460 | 750 |

2-16

| | | 23 | 69 | 121 | 210 |

Binder only ... 450
NOTE: A cover and binder came separate at gas stations. Came with membership card.

EAT RIGHT TO WORK AND WIN
Swift & Company: 1942 (Giveaway)
Blondie, Henry, Flash Gordon by Alex Raymond, Toots & Casper, Thimble Theatre(Popeye), Tillie the Toiler, The Phantom, The Little King, & Bringing up Father - original strips just for this book -(in daily strip form which shows what foods we should eat and win)

| | | 50 | 150 | 260 | 400 |

EDWARD'S SHOES GIVEAWAY
Edward's Shoe Store: 1954 (Has clown on cover)
Contains comic with new cover. Many combinations possible. Contents determines price, 50-60 percent of original. (Similar to Comics From Weatherbird & Free Comics to You)

ELSIE THE COW

Escape From Fear 1962
© Planned Parenthood

Fearless Fosdick © Capp Ent. Inc.

Flash Gordon - Gordon Bread #2
© KING

	GD2.0	FN6.0	VF8.0	NM9.4

D. S. Publishing Co.
Borden's cheese comic picture bk ("40, giveaway)   20   60   105   175
Borden Milk Giveaway-(16 pgs., nn) (3 ishs, 1957)   14   42   72   125
Elsie's Fun Book(1950; Borden Milk)   14   42   72   125
Everyday Birthday Fun With… (1957; 20 pgs.)(100th Anniversary); Kubert-a
   14   42   72   125

ESCAPE FROM FEAR
Planned Parenthood of America: 1956, 1962, 1969 (Giveaway, 8 pgs. full color)
(On birth control)
1956 edition   10   30   55   80
1962 edition   4   12   30   50
1969 edition   3   9   17   25

EVEL KNIEVEL
Marvel Comics Group (Ideal Toy Corp.): 1974 (Giveaway, 20 pgs.)
nn-Contains photo on inside back-c   3   9   21   32

FAMOUS COMICS (Also see Favorite Comics)
Zain-Eppy/United Features Syndicate: No date; Mid 1930's (24 pgs., paper-c)
nn-Reprinted from 1933 & 1934 newspaper strips in color; Joe Palooka,
  Hairbreadth Harry, Napoleon, The Nebbs, etc. (Many different versions
  known)   50   150   300   475

FAMOUS FAIRY TALES
K. K. Publ. Co.: 1942; 1943 (32 pgs.); 1944 (16 pgs.) (Giveaway, soft-c)
1942-Kelly-a   40   120   232   400
1943-r/Fairy Tale Parade No. 2,3; Kelly-a   30   90   162   280
1944-Kelly-a   27   81   145   250

FAMOUS FUNNIES -A CARNIVAL OF COMICS
Eastern Color: 1933
(Probably the second comic book), 36 pgs., no date given, no publisher, no number; contains strip reprints of The Bungle Family, Dixie Dugan, Hairbreadth Harry, Joe Palooka, Keeping Up With the Jones, Mutt & Jeff, Reg'lar Fellers, S'Matter Pop, Strange As It Seems, and others. This book was sold by M. C. Gaines to Wheatena, Milk-O-Malt, John Wanamaker, Kinney Shoe Stores, & others to be given away as premiums and radio giveaways (1933). Originally came with a mailing envelope.   913   2740   5480   10,500

FAMOUS GANG BOOK OF COMICS (Becomes Donald & Mickey Merry
Christmas 1943 on)
Firestone Tire & Rubber Co.: Dec, 1942 (Christmas giveaway, 32 pgs., paper-c)
nn-(Rare)-Porky Pig, Bugs Bunny, Mary Jane & Sniffles, Elmer Fudd;
  r/Looney Tunes   64   192   398   700

FANTASTIC FOUR
Marvel Comics: 1981(32 pgs., Young Model Builders Club)
nn   6.00

FATHER OF CHARITY
Catechetical Guild Giveaway: No date (32 pgs.; paper cover)
nn   3   8   12   15

FAVORITE COMICS (Also see Famous Comics)
Grocery Store Giveaway (Diff. Corp.) (detergent): 1934 (36 pgs.)
Book 1-The Nebbs, Strange As It Seems, Napoleon, Joe Palooka, Dixie Dugan,
  S'Matter Pop, Hairbreadth Harry, etc. reprints   79   237   485   850
Book 2,3   55   165   316   550

FAWCETT MINIATURES (See Mighty Midget)
Fawcett Publications: 1946 (3-3/4x5", 12-24 pgs.) (Wheaties giveaways)
Captain Marvel "And the Horn of Plenty"; Bulletman story
   18   54   94   160
Captain Marvel "& the Raiders From Space"; Golden Arrow story
   18   54   94   160
Captain Marvel Jr. "The Case of the Poison Press!" Bulletman story
   18   54   94   160
Delecta of the Planets; C. C. Beck art; B&W inside; 12 pgs.; 3 printing
  variations (coloring) exist   25   75   130   225

FEARLESS FOSDICK
Capp Enterprises Inc.: 1951
…& The Case of The Red Feather   5   15   23   30

FIGHT FOR FREEDOM

National Assoc. of Mfgrs./General Comics: 1949, 1951 (Giveaway, 16 pgs.)
nn-Dan Barry-c/a; used in POP, pg. 102   6   18   30   42

FIRE AND BLAST
National Fire Protection Assoc.: 1952 (Giveaway, 16 pgs., paper-c)
nn-Mart Baily A-Bomb-c; about fire prevention   15   45   77   130

FIRE CHIEF AND THE SAFE OL' FIREFLY, THE
National Board of Fire Underwriters: 1952 (16 pgs.) (Safety brochure given
away at schools) (produced by American Visuals Corp.)(Eisner)
nn-(Rare) Eisner-c/a   50   150   300   475

FLASH
DC Comics: 1990
nn-Brochure for CBS TV series   3.00

FLASH COMICS
National Periodical Publications: 1946 (6-1/2x8-1/4", 32 pgs.)
(Wheaties Giveaway)
nn-Johnny Thunder, Ghost Patrol, The Flash & Kubert Hawkman app.; Irwin
  Hasen-c/a   325   1400   -   -
NOTE: All known copies were taped to Wheaties boxes and are never found in mint condition. Copies with light tape residue bring the listed prices in all grades.

FLASH FORCE 2000
DC Comics: 1984
1-5   3.00

FLASH GORDON
Dell Publishing Co.: 1943 (20 pgs.)
Macy's Giveaway-(Rare); not by Raymond   59   176   360   600

FLASH GORDON
Harvey Comics: 1951 (16 pgs. in color, regular size, paper-c)
(Gordon Bread giveaway)
1,2: 1-r/strips 10/24/37 - 2/6/38. 2-r/strips 7/14/40 - 10/6/40; Reprints by
  Raymond   each….   2   5   8   10
NOTE: Most copies have brittle edges.

FOREST FIRE (Also see The Blazing Forest and Smokey Bear)
American Forestry Assn.(Commerical Comics): 1949 (dated-1950) (16 pgs.,
paper-c)
nn-Intro/1st app. Smokey The Forest Fire Preventing Bear; created by Rudy
  Wendelein; Wendelein/Sparling-a; 'Carter Oil Co' on back-c of original
   17   51   88   150

FOREST RANGER HANDBOOK
Wrather Corp.: 1967 (5x7", 20 pgs., slick-c)
nn-With Corey Stuart & Lassie photo-c   2   6   15   22

FORGOTTEN STORY BEHIND NORTH BEACH, THE
Catechetical Guild: No date (8 pgs., paper-c)
nn   4   9   14   18

48 FAMOUS AMERICANS
J. C. Penney Co. (Cpr. Edwin H. Stroh): 1947 (Giveaway) (Half-size in color)
nn-Simon & Kirby-a   12   36   61   100

FRANKIE LUER'S SPACE ADVENTURES
Luer Packing Co.: 1955 (5x7", 36 pgs., slick-c)
nn- With Davey Rocket   4   10   15   20

FREDDY
Charlton Comics
Schiff's Shoes Presents… #1 (1959)-Giveaway   2   6   10   14

FREE COMICS TO YOU FROM… (name of shoe store) (Has clown on cover
& another with a rabbit) (Like comics from Weather Bird & Edward's Shoes)
Shoe Store Giveaway: Circa 1956, 1960-61
Contains a comic bound with new cover - several combinations possible; some
Harvey titles known. Contents determine price.

FREEDOM TRAIN
Street & Smith Publications: 1948 (Giveaway)
nn-Powell-c w/mailer   20   60   105   175

Freihofer's Comic Book © DC

Funnies on Parade © EAS

Gene Autry Adventure Comics and Play-Fun Book © Gene Autry

	GD2.0	FN6.0	VF8.0	NM9.4

FREIHOFER'S COMIC BOOK
All-American Comics: 1940s (7 1/2 x 10 1/4")

2nd edition-(Scarce) Cover features All-American Comics characters Ultra-Man, Hop Harrigan, Red, White and Blue and others	59	176	360	600

FRIENDLY GHOST, CASPER, THE (Becomes Casper... #254 on)
Harvey Publications

American Dental Assoc. giveaway-Small size (1967, 16 pgs.)	3	9	17	25

FRITO-LAY GIVEAWAY
Frito-Lay: 1962 (3-1/4x7", soft-c, 16 pgs.) (Disney)

nn-Donald Duck "Plotting Picnickers"	5	15	38	60
nn-Ludwig Von Drake "Fish Stampede"	4	12	25	38
nn- Mickey Mouse & Goofy "Bicep Bungle"	4	12	27	42

FRONTIER DAYS
Robin Hood Shoe Store (Brown Shoe): 1956 (Giveaway)

1	4	9	14	18

FUNNIES ON PARADE (Premium)(See Toy World Funnies)
Eastern Color Printing Co.: 1933 (Probably the 1st comic book)
(36 pgs., slick cover) No date or publisher listed

nn-Contains Sunday page reprints of Mutt & Jeff, Joe Palooka, Hairbreadth Harry, Reg'lar Fellers, Skippy, & others (10,000 print run). This book was printed for Proctor & Gamble to be given away & came out before Famous Funnies or Century of Comics.	1160	3480	6960	14,500

FUNNY PICTURE STORIES (Comic Pages V3#4 on)
Comics Magazine Co./Centaur Publications

Laundry giveaway (16-20 pgs., 1930s)-slick-c	30	100	160	250

FUNNY STUFF
National Periodical Publications (Wheaties Giveaway): 1946 (6-1/2x8-1/4")

nn-(Scarce)-Dodo & the Frog, Three Mouseketeers, etc.; came taped to Wheaties box; never found in better than fine	170	475	–	–

FUTURE COP: L.A.P.D. (Electronic Arts video game)
DC Comics (WildStorm): 1998

nn-Ron Lim-a/Dave Johnson-c				2.25

GABBY HAYES WESTERN (Movie star)
Fawcett Publications
Quaker Oats Giveaway nn's(#1-5, 1951, 2-1/2x7") (Kagran Corp.)-...In Tracks of Guilt, ...In the Fence Post Mystery, ...In the Accidental Sherlock, ... In the Frame-Up, ...In the Double Cross Brand known

	10	30	55	85
Mailing Envelope (has illo of Gabby on front)	10	30	55	85

GARY GIBSON COMICS (Donut club membership)
National Dunking Association: 1950 (Included in donut box with pin and card)

1-Western soft-c, 16 pgs.; folded into the box	4	12	19	25

GENE AUTRY COMICS
Dell Publishing Co.
...Adventure Comics And Play-Fun Book ('47)-32 pgs., 8x6-1/2"; games, comics, magic (Pillsbury premium)

comics, magic (Pillsbury premium)	40	120	210	360

Quaker Oats Giveaway(1950)-2-1/2x6-3/4"; 5 different versions; "Death Card Gang", "Phantoms of the Cave", "Riddle of Laughing Mtn.", "Secret of Lost Valley", "Bond of the Broken Arrow" (came in wrapper)

each...	15	45	77	130
Mailing Envelope (has illo. of Gene on front)	15	45	77	130
3-D Giveaway(1953)-Pocket-size; 5 different	15	45	77	130
Mailing Envelope (no art on front)	12	36	61	100

GENE AUTRY TIM (Formerly Tim) (Becomes Tim in Space)
Tim Stores: 1950 (Half-size) (B&W Giveaway)

nn-Several issues (All Scarce)	17	51	88	150

GENERAL FOODS SUPER-HEROES
DC Comics: 1979, 1980

1-4 (1979), 1-4 (1980)				3.00

G. I. COMICS (Also see Jeep & Overseas Comics)
Giveaways: 1945 - No. 73?, 1946 (Distributed to U. S. Armed Forces)

1-73-Contains Prince Valiant by Foster, Blondie, Smilin' Jack, Mickey Finn, Terry & the Pirates, Donald Duck, Alley Oop, Moon Mullins & Capt. Easy strip reprints (at least 73 issues known to exist)

	8	24	42	60

GOLDEN ARROW
Fawcett Publications
...Well Known Comics (1944; 12 pgs.; 8-1/2x10-1/2"; paper-c; glued binding)-Bestmaid/Samuel Lowe giveaway; printed in green

	9	27	51	75

GOLDILOCKS & THE THREE BEARS
K. K. Publications: 1943 (Giveaway)

nn	10	30	55	85

GREAT PEOPLE OF GENESIS, THE
David C. Cook Publ. Co.: No date (Religious giveaway, 64 pgs.)

nn-Reprint/Sunday Pix Weekly	4	10	15	20

GREAT SACRAMENT, THE
Catechetical Guild: 1953 (Giveaway, 36 pgs.)

nn	4	11	17	22

GRIT (YOU'VE GOT TO HAVE...)
GRIT Publishing Co.: 1959
nn-GRIT newspaper sales recruitment comic;Schaffenberger-a. Later version has altered artwork

has altered artwork	4	12	19	25

GULF FUNNY WEEKLY (Gulf Comic Weekly No. 1-4)(See Standard Oil Comics)
Gulf Oil Company (Giveaway): 1933 - No. 422, 5/23/41 (in full color; 4 pgs.; tabloid size to 2/3/39; 2/10/39 on, regular comic book size)(early issues undated)

1	75	300	475	750
2-5	30	90	165	260
6-30	19	56	96	160
31-100	13	39	66	110
101-196	8	24	45	65
197-Wings Winfair begins(1/29/37); by Fred Meagher beginning in 1938				
	28	83	140	240
198-300 (Last tabloid size)	14	42	72	120
301-350 (Regular size)	8	24	42	60
351-422	6	18	32	45

GULLIVER'S TRAVELS
Macy's Department Store: 1939, small size

nn-Christmas giveaway	14	42	72	120

GUN THAT WON THE WEST, THE
Winchester-Western Division & Olin Mathieson Chemical Corp.: 1956 (Giveaway, 24 pgs.)

nn-Painted-c	5	15	25	35

HAPPINESS AND HEALING FOR YOU (Also see Oral Roberts'...)
Commercial Comics: 1955 (36 pgs., slick cover) (Oral Roberts Giveaway)

nn	9	27	49	70

NOTE: The success of this book prompted Oral Roberts to go into the publishing business himself to produce his own material.

HAPPY TOOTH
DC Comics: 1996

1				2.50

HAWTHORN-MELODY FARMS DAIRY COMICS
Everybody's Publishing Co.: No date (1950's) (Giveaway)

nn-Cheerie Chick, Tuffy Turtle, Robin Koo Koo, Donald & Longhorn Legends	2	6	9	12

HENRY ALDRICH COMICS (TV)
Dell Publishing Co.

Giveaway (16 pgs., soft-c, 1951)-Capehart radio	3	9	17	25

HERE IS SANTA CLAUS
Goldsmith Publishing Co. (Kann's in Washington, D.C.): 1930s (16 pgs., 8 in color) (stiff paper covers)

nn	10	30	55	85

HERE'S HOW AMERICA'S CARTOONISTS HELP TO SELL U.S. SAVINGS

	GD2.0	FN6.0	VF8.0	NM9.4		GD2.0	FN6.0	VF8.0	NM9.4

BONDS
Harvey Comics: 1950? (16 pgs., giveaway, paper cover)
Contains: Joe Palooka, Donald Duck, Archie, Kerry Drake, Red Ryder, Blondie
& Steve Canyon   18   54   94   160

HISTORY OF GAS
American Gas Assoc.: Mar, 1947 (Giveaway, 16 pgs.)
nn-Miss Flame narrates   6   18   28   38

HONEYBEE BIRDWHISTLE AND HER PET PEPI (Introducing…)
Newspaper Enterprise Assoc.: 1969 (Giveaway, 24 pgs., B&W, slick cover)
nn-Contains Freckles newspaper strips with a short biography of Henry
Fornhals (artist) & Fred Fox (writer) of the strip   5   15   34   55

HOPALONG CASSIDY
Fawcett Publications
Grape Nuts Flakes giveaway (1950,9x6")   15   45   77   130
…& the Mad Barber (1951 Bond Bread giveaway)-7x5"; used in **SOTI**, pgs.
308,309   25   75   130   225
…Meets the Brend Brothers Bandits (1951 Bond Bread giveaway, color,
paper-c, 16pgs. 3-1/2x7")-Fawcett Publ.   12   36   61   105
…Strange Legacy (1951 Bond Bread giveaway)   12   36   61   105
White Tower Giveaway (1946, 16pgs., paper-c)   12   36   61   105

HOPPY THE MARVEL BUNNY (WELL KNOWN COMICS)
Fawcett Publications: 1944 (8-1/2x10-1/2", paper-c)
Bestmaid/Samuel Lowe (printed in red or blue)   10   30   55   80

HOT STUFF, THE LITTLE DEVIL
Harvey Publications (Illustrated Humor):1963
Shoestore Giveaway   2   6   13   20

HOW STALIN HOPES WE WILL DESTROY AMERICA
Joe Lowe Co. (Pictorial Media): 1951 (Giveaway, 16 pgs.)
nn   50   150   300   475

HURRICANE KIDS, THE (Also See Magic Morro, The Owl, Popular Comics #45)
R.S. Callender: 1941 (Giveaway, 7-1/2x5-1/4", soft-c)
nn-Will Ely-a.   10   30   52   75

IF THE DEVIL WOULD TALK
Roman Catholic Catechetical Guild/Impact Publ.: 1950; 1958 (32 pgs.; paper cover; in full color)
nn-(Scarce)-About secularism (20-30 copies known to exist); very low
distribution   81   245   500   800
1958 Edition-(Impact Publ.); art & script changed to meet church criticism of
earlier edition; 80 plus copies known to exist   25   75   130   210
Black & White version of nn edition; small size; only 4 known copies exist
    30   90   150   260
NOTE: *The original edition of this book was printed and killed by the Guild's board of directors. It is believed that a very limited number of copies were distributed. The 1958 version was a complete bomb with very limited, if any, circulation. In 1979, 11 original, 4 1958 reprints, and 4 B&W's surfaced from the Guild's old files in St. Paul, Minnesota.*

IN LOVE WITH JESUS
Catechetical Educational Society: 1952 (Giveaway, 36 pgs.)
nn   5   15   23   30

INTERSTATE THEATRES' FUN CLUB COMICS
Interstate Theatres: Mid 1940's (10¢ on cover) (B&W cover) (Premium)
Cover features MLJ characters looking at a copy of Top-Notch Comics, but contains an early
Detective Comic on inside; many combinations possible   9   27   49   70

IN THE GOOD HANDS OF THE ROCKEFELLER TEAM
Country Art Studios: No date (paper cover, 8 pgs.)
nn-Joe Simon-a.   7   21   36   50

IRON GIANT
DC Comics: 1999 (4 pages, theater giveaway)
1-Previews movie   2.50

IRON HORSE GOES TO WAR, THE
Association of American Railroads: 1960 (Giveaway, 16 pgs.)
nn-Civil War & railroads   3   9   20   30

IS THIS TOMORROW?
Catechetical Guild: 1947 (One Shot) (3 editions) (52 pgs.)
1-Theme of communists taking over the USA; (no price on cover) Used in
POP, pg. 102   16   48   83   140
1-(10¢ on cover)   21   63   110   190
1-Has blank circle with no price on cover   22   66   116   200
Black & White advance copy titled "Confidential" (52 pgs.)-Contains script and
art edited out of the color edition, including one page of extreme violence
showing mob nailing a Cardinal to a door; (only two known copies)
    50   150   300   475
NOTE: *The original color version first sold for 10 cents. Since sales were good, it was later printed as a giveaway. Approximately four million in total were printed. The two black and white copies listed plus two other versions as well as a full color untrimmed version surfaced in 1979 from the Guild's old files in St. Paul, Minnesota.*

IT'S FUN TO STAY ALIVE
National Automobile Dealers Association: 1948 (Giveaway, 16 pgs., heavy stock paper)
Featuring: Bugs Bunny, The Berrys, Dixie Dugan, Elmer, Henry, Tim Tyler, Bruce Gentry, Abbie
& Slats, Joe Jinks, The Toodles, & Cokey; all art copyright 1946-48 drawn especially for this
book.   17   51   88   150

JACK & JILL VISIT TOYTOWN WITH ELMER THE ELF
Butler Brothers (Toytown Stores): 1949 (Giveaway, 16 pgs., paper cover)
nn   5   14   21   28

JACK ARMSTRONG (Radio)(See True Comics)
Parents' Institute: 1949
12-Premium version(distr. in Chicago only); Free printed on upper right-c;
no price (Rare)   21   64   100   170

JACKIE JOYNER KERSEE IN HIGH HURDLES (Kellogg's Tony's Sports Comics)
DC Comics: 1992 (Sports Illustrated)
nn   2.50

JACKPOT OF FUN COMIC BOOK
DCA Food Ind.: 1957, giveaway
nn-Features Howdy Doody   11   33   55   90

JEEP COMICS
R. B. Leffingwell & Co.: 1945 - 1946
1-46 (Giveaways)-Strip reprints in all; Tarzan, Flash Gordon, Blondie, The
Nebbs, Little Iodine, Red Ryder, Don Winslow, The Phantom, Johnny
Hazard, Katzenjammer Kids; distr. to U.S. Armed Forces from 1945-1946
    6   18   29   40

JINGLE BELLS CHRISTMAS BOOK
Montgomery Ward (Giveaway): 1971 (20 pgs., B&W inside, slick-c)
nn   5.00

JOAN OF ARC
Catechetical Guild (Topix) (Giveaway): No date (28 pgs.)
nn   9   27   51   75
NOTE: *Unpublished version exists which came from the Guild's files.*

JOE PALOOKA (2nd Series)
Harvey Publications
…Body Building Instruction Book (1958 B&M Sports Toy giveaway, 16pgs.,
5-1/4x7")-Origin   9   27   49   70
…Fights His Way Back (1945 Giveaway, 24 pgs.) Family Comics
    16   48   83   140
…in Hi There! (1949 Red Cross giveaway, 12 pgs., 4-3/4x6")
    8   24   45   65
…in It's All in the Family (1945 Red Cross giveaway, 16 pgs., regular size)
    10   30   55   80

JOE THE GENIE OF STEEL
U.S. Steel Corp., Pittsburgh, PA: 1950 (16 pgs.)
nn   4   12   19   25

JOHNNY JINGLE'S LUCKY DAY
American Dairy Assoc.: 1956 (16 pgs.; 7-1/4x5-1/8") (Giveaway) (Disney)
nn   5   15   23   30

JO-JOY (The Adventures of…)

Joe the Genie of Steel

Kirby's Shoes Comics © Kirby's Shoes

KIRBY'S SHOES
COMICS
Featuring Kirby, the GOLDEN BEAR
"PICNIC PROBLEMS"

Kite Fun Book 1961 Huckleberry Hound © H-B

Huckleberry Hound's
Kite Fun Book

	GD2.0	FN6.0	VF8.0	NM9.4

W. T. Grant Dept. Stores: 1945 - 1953 (Christmas gift comic, 16 pgs., 7-1/16x10-1/4")

1945-53 issues	5	15	25	35

JOLLY CHRISTMAS BOOK (See Christmas Journey Through Space)
Promotional Publ. Co.: 1951; 1954; 1955 (36 pgs.; 24 pgs.)

1951-(Woolworth giveaway)-slightly oversized; no slick cover; Marv Levy-c/a				
	7	21	36	50
1954-(Hot Shoppes giveaway)-regular size-reprints 1951 issue; slick cover added; 24 pgs.; no ads	6	18	32	45
1955-(J. M. McDonald Co. giveaway)-reg. size	6	18	29	40

JOURNEY OF DISCOVERY WITH MARK STEEL (See Mark Steel)
JUMPING JACKS PRESENTS THE WHIZ KIDS
Jumping Jacks Stores giveaway: 1978 (In 3-D) with glasses (4 pgs.)

nn				5.00

JUNGLE BOOK FUN BOOK, THE (Disney)
Baskin Robbins: 1978

nn-Ice Cream giveaway	2	6	11	15

JUSTICE LEAGUE OF AMERICA
DC Comics: 1999 (included in Justice League of America Monopoly game)

nn-Reprints 1st app. in Brave and the Bold #28				2.50

KASCO KOMICS
Kasko Grainfeed (Giveaway): 1945; No. 2, 1949 (Regular size, paper-c)

1(1945)-Similar to Katy Keene; Bill Woggon-a; 28 pgs.; 6-7/8x9-7/8"				
	17	51	88	150
2(1949)-Woggon-c/a	13	39	66	110

KATY AND KEN VISIT SANTA WITH MISTER WISH
S. S. Kresge Co. : 1948 (Giveaway, 16 pgs., paper-c)

nn	5	15	25	35

KELLOGG'S CINNAMON MINI-BUNS SUPER-HEROES
DC Comics: 1993 (4 1/4" x 2 3/4")

4 editions: Flash, Justice League America, Superman, Wonder Woman and the Star Riders each.....				2.50

KERRY DRAKE DETECTIVE CASES
Publisher's Syndicate

...in the Case of the Sleeping City-(1951)-16 pg. giveaway for armed forces; paper cover	5	15	25	35

KEY COMICS
Key Clothing Co./Peterson Clothing: 1951 - 1956 (32 pgs.) (Giveaway)
Contains a comic from different publishers bound with new cover. Cover changed each year. Many combinations possible. Distributed in Nebraska, Iowa, & Kansas. Contents would determine price, 40-60 percent of original.

KIRBY'S SHOES COMICS
Kirby's Shoes: 1959 (8 pgs., soft-c)

nn-Features Kirby the Golden Bear	2	6	9	12

KITE FUN BOOK
Pacific, Gas & Electric/Sou. California Edison/Florida Power & Light/ Missouri Public Service Co.: 1953 - 1981 (16pgs, 5x7-1/4", soft-c)

1953-Pinocchio Learns About Kites (Disney)	47	141	260	450
1954-Donald Duck Tells About Kites-Fla. Power, S.C.E. & version with label issues-Barks pencils-8 pgs.; inks-7 pgs. (Rare)	400	1200	2000	3200
1954-Donald Duck Tells About Kites-P.G.&E. issue -7th page redrawn changing middle 3 panels to show P.G.&E. in story line; (All Barks; last page Barks pencils only) Scarce	247	741	1470	2400
1955-Brer Rabbit in "A Kite Tail" (Disney)	34	103	165	280
1956-Woody Woodpecker (Lantz)	14	42	72	120
1957-?				
1958-Tom And Jerry (M.G.M.)	10	30	50	70
1960-Porky Pig (Warner Bros.)	5	15	34	55
1960-Bugs Bunny (Warner Bros.)	5	15	34	55
1961-Huckleberry Hound (Hanna-Barbera)	6	18	40	65
1962-Yogi Bear (Hanna-Barbera)	4	12	29	45
1963-Rocky and Bullwinkle (TV)(Jay Ward)	10	30	70	120
1963-Top Cat (TV)(Hanna-Barbera)	5	15	34	55

	GD2.0	FN6.0	VF8.0	NM9.4
1964-Magilla Gorilla (TV)(Hanna-Barbera)	4	12	30	50
1965-Jinks, Pixie and Dixie (TV)(Hanna-Barbera)	3	10	23	35
1965-Tweety and Sylvester (Warner); S.C.E. version with Reddy Kilowatt app.				
	2	6	13	20
1966-Secret Squirrel (Hanna-Barbera); S.C.E. version with Reddy Kilowatt app.				
	7	21	50	80
1967-Beep! Beep! The Road Runner (TV)(Warner)	3	9	17	25
1968-Bugs Bunny (Warner Bros.)	3	9	19	28
1969-Dastardly and Muttley (TV)(Hanna-Barbera)	4	12	30	50
1970-Rocky and Bullwinkle (TV)(Jay Ward)	7	21	50	80
1971-Beep! Beep! The Road Runner (TV)(Warner)	2	6	15	22
1972-The Pink Panther (TV)	2	6	13	20
1973-Lassie (TV)	3	10	23	35
1974-Underdog (TV)	3	9	17	25
1975-Ben Franklin	2	6	9	12
1976-The Brady Bunch (TV)	3	10	23	35
1977-Ben Franklin	2	6	9	12
1977-Popeye	2	6	15	22
1978-Happy Days (TV)	3	9	17	25
1979-Eight is Enough (TV)	2	6	15	22
1980-The Waltons (TV, released in 1981)	2	6	15	22

KNOW YOUR MASS
Catechetical Guild: No. 303, 1958 (35¢, 100 Pg. Giant) (Square binding)

303-In color	5	15	25	35

KOLYNOS PRESENTS THE WHITE GUARD
Whitehall Pharmacal Co.: 1949 (paper cover, 8 pgs.)

nn	5	15	25	35

K. O. PUNCH, THE (Also see Lucky Fights It Through)
E. C. Comics: 1948 (Educational giveaway)

nn-Feldstein-splash; Kamen-a	94	282	540	850

KOREA MY HOME (Also see Yalta to Korea)
Johnstone and Cushing: nd (1950s)

nn-Anti-communist; Korean War	24	73	118	200

KRIM-KO KOMICS
Krim-ko Chocolate Drink: 5/18/35 - No. 6, 6/22/35; 1936 - 1939 (weekly)

1-(16 pgs., soft-c, Dairy giveaways)-Tom, Mary & Sparky Advs. by Russell Keaton, Jim Hawkins by Dick Moores, Mystery Island! by Rick Yager begin				
	14	42	72	120
2-6 (6/22/35)	10	30	55	80
Lola, Secret Agent; 184 issues, 4 pg. giveaways - all original stories each....	7	21	36	50

LABOR IS A PARTNER
Catechetical Guild Educational Society: 1949 (32 pgs., paper-c)

nn-Anti-communism	18	54	94	160
Confidential Preview-(8-1/2x11", B&W, saddle stitched)-only one known copy; text varies from color version, advertises next book on secularism (If the Devil Would Talk)	21	63	110	185

LADY AND THE TRAMP IN "BUTTER LATE THAN NEVER"
American Dairy Assoc. (Premium): 1955 (16 pgs., 5x7-1/4", soft-c) (Disney)

nn	10	30	55	85

LASSIE (TV)
Dell Publ. Co

The Adventures of... nn-(Red Heart Dog Food giveaway, 1949)-16 pgs, soft-c; 1st app. Lassie in comics	33	99	174	300

LIFE OF THE BLESSED VIRGIN
Catechetical Guild (Giveaway): 1950 (68pgs.) (square binding)

nn-Contains "The Woman of the Promise" & "Mother of Us All" rebound	5	15	25	35

LIGHTNING RACERS
DC Comics: 1989

1				3.00

LI'L ABNER (Al Capp's) (Also see Natural Disasters!)
Harvey Publ./Toby Press

Little Miss Sunbeam 1957 © ME

Little Tree That Wasn't Wanted © W.T. Grant Co.

Lone Ranger Comics Ice Cream Book 1 © Lone Ranger Inc.

	GD2.0	FN6.0	VF8.0	NM9.4

...& the Creatures from Drop-Outer Space-nn (Job Corps giveaway; 36 pgs.,
in color)(entire book by Frank Frazetta)   29   88   135   230
...Joins the Navy (1950) (Toby Press Premium)   15   45   65   95
...by Al Capp Giveaway (Circa 1955, nd)   15   45   65   95

LITTLE ALONZO
Macy's Dept. Store: 1938 (B&W, 5-1/2x8-1/2")(Christmas giveaway)
nn-By Ferdinand the Bull's Munro Leaf   8   24   45   65

LITTLE DOT
Harvey Publications
Shoe store giveaway 2   4   12   27   42

LITTLE FIR TREE, THE
W. T. Grant Co.: nd (1942) (8-1/2x11") (12 pgs. with cover, color & B&W, heavy paper) (Christmas giveaway)
nn-Story by Hans Christian Anderson; 8 pg. Kelly-r/Santa Claus Funnies (not signed); X-Mas-c
(One copy in Mint sold for $1750.00 in 1986 & another copy in VF sold for $1000.00 in 1991)

LITTLE KLINKER
Little Klinker Ventures: Nov, 1960 (20 pgs.) (slick cover) (Montgomery Ward Giveaway)
nn   2   6   11   15

LITTLE MISS SUNBEAM COMICS
Magazine Enterprises/Quality Bakers of America
Bread Giveaway 1-4(Quality Bakers, 1949-50)-14 pgs. each
                                                              6   18   29   40
Bread Giveaway (1957,61; 16pgs, reg. size)   5   15   25   35

LITTLE ORPHAN ANNIE
David McKay Publ./Dell Publishing Co.
Junior Commandos Giveaway (same-c as 4-Color #18, K.K. Publ.)(Big Shoe Store); same back cover as '47 Popped Wheat giveaway; 16 pgs; flag-c; r/strips 9/7/42-10/10/42   34   102   185   285
Popped Wheat Giveaway ('47)-16 pgs. full color; reprints strips from 5/3/40 to 6/20/40   4   10   15   20
Quaker Sparkies Giveaway (1940)   21   64   108   175
Quaker Sparkies Giveaway (1941, full color, 20 pgs.); "LOA and the Rescue"; r/strips 4/13/39-6/21/39 & 7/6/39-7/17/39. "LOA and the Kidnappers"; r/strips 11/28/38-1/28/39   19   58   96   160
Quaker Sparkies Giveaway (1942, full color, 20 pgs.); "LOA and Mr. Gudge"; r/strips 2/13/38-3/21/38 & 4/18/37-5/30/37. "LOA and the Great Am"
                                                             17   51   88   150

LITTLE TREE THAT WASN'T WANTED, THE
W. T. Grant Co. Giveaway: 1960, (Color, 28 pgs.)
nn-Christmas story, puzzles and games   3   9   20   30

LOADED (Also see Re-Loaded)
DC Comics: 1995 (Interplay Productions)
1-Garth Ennis-s; promotes video game   3.00

LONE RANGER, THE
Dell Publishing Co.
Cheerios Giveaways (1954, 16 pgs., 2-1/2x7", soft-c) #1- "The Lone Ranger, His Mask & How He Met Tonto". #2- "The Lone Ranger & the Story of Silver"   each....   20   60   95   140
Doll Giveaways (Gabriel Ind.)(1973, 3-1/4x4'5")- "The Story of The Lone Ranger," "The Carson City Bank Robbery" & "The Apache Buffalo Hunt"
                                                              2   6   11   16
How the Lone Ranger Captured Silver Book(1936)-Silvercup Bread giveaway
                                                             90   270   400   600
...In Milk for Big Mike (1955, Dairy Association giveaway), soft-c; 5x7-1/4", 16 pgs.   20   60   100   150
Legend of The Lone Ranger (1969, 16 pgs., giveaway)-Origin The Lone Ranger
                                                              3   10   23   35
Merita Bread giveaway (1954, 16 pgs., 5x7-1/4")- "How To Be a Lone Ranger Health & Safety Scout"   25   75   120   175

LONE RANGER COMICS, THE
Lone Ranger, Inc.: Book 1, 1939(inside) (shows 1938 on-c) (52 pgs. in color;

regular size) (Ice cream mail order)
Book 1-(Scarce)-The first western comic devoted to a single character; not by Vallely   923   3000   6000   -
2nd version w/large full color promo poster pasted over centerfold & a smaller poster pasted over back cover; includes new additional premiums not originally offered (Rare)   1040   3200   6500   -

LOONEY TUNES
DC Comics: 1991, 1998
Claritan promotional issue (1998)   2.25
Colgate mini-comic (1998)   2.25
Tyson's 1-10 (1991)   3.00

LUCKY FIGHTS IT THROUGH (Also see The K. O. Punch)
Educational Comics: 1949 (Giveaway, 16 pgs. in color, paper-c)
nn-(Very Rare)-1st Kurtzman work for E. C.; V.D. prevention
                                                            125   375   700   1050
nn-Reprint in color (1977)   6.00
NOTE: Subtitled "The Story of That Ignorant, Ignorant Cowboy". Prepared for Communications Materials Center, Columbia University.

LUDWIG VON DRAKE (See Frito-Lay Giveaway)

MACO TOYS COMIC
Maco Toys/Charlton Comics: 1959 (Giveaway, 36 pgs.)
1-All military stories featuring Maco Toys   2   6   10   14

MAD MAGAZINE
DC Comics: 1997, 1999
Special Edition (1997, Tang giveaway)   2.25
Stocking Stuffer (1999)   2.25

MAGAZINELAND
DC Comics: 1977
nn   3.00

MAGIC MORRO (Also see Super Comics #21, The Owl, & The Hurricane Kids)
K. K. Publications: 1941 (7-1/2x5-1/4, giveaway, soft-c)
nn-Ken Ernst-a.   13   39   66   110

MAGIC OF CHRISTMAS AT NEWBERRYS, THE
E. S. London: 1967 (Giveaway) (B&W, slick-c, 20 pgs.)
nn   1   3   6   9

MAJOR INAPAK THE SPACE ACE
Magazine Enterprises (Inapac Foods): 1951 (20 pgs.) (Giveaway)
1-Bob Powell-c/a   5.00
NOTE: Many warehouse copies surfaced in 1973.

MAMMY YOKUM & THE GREAT DOGPATCH MYSTERY
Toby Press: 1951 (Giveaway)
nn-Li'l Abner   17   51   88   150
nn-Reprint (1956)   5   15   23   30

MAN NAMED STEVENSON, A
Democratic National Committee: 1952 (20 pgs., 5 1/4 x 7")
nn   9   27   49   70

MAN OF PEACE, POPE PIUS XII
Catechetical Guild: 1950 (See Pope Pius XII... To V2#8)
nn-All Powell-a   5   15   25   35

MAN OF STEEL BEST WESTERN
DC Comics: 1997
nn-Best Western hotels   2.50

MAN WHO WOULDN'T QUIT, THE
Harvey Publications Inc.: 1952 (16 pgs., paper cover)
nn-The value of voting   4   11   17   22

MARCH OF COMICS (Boys' and Girls'...#3-353)
K. K. Publications/Western Publishing Co.: 1946 - No. 488, April, 1982 (#1-4 are not numbered) (K.K. Giveaway) (Founded by Sig Feuchtwanger)
Early issues were full size, 32 pages, and were printed with and without an extra cover of slick stock, just for the advertiser. The binding was stapled the slick cover was added; otherwise, the pages were glued together at the spine. Most 1948 - 1951 issues were full size,24 pages, pulp covers.

March of Comics #19 © Howard Garis

March of Comics #104 © Gene Autry

March of Comics #112 © UFS

PROMOTIONAL COMICS

	GD2.0	FN6.0	VF8.0	NM9.4

Starting in 1952 they were half-size (with a few exceptions) and 32 pages with slick covers. 1959 and later issues had only 16 pages plus covers. 1952 -1959 issues read oblong; 1960 and later issues read upright. All have new stories except where noted.

	GD2.0	FN6.0	VF8.0	NM9.4
nn (#1, 1946)-Goldilocks; Kelly back-c (16 pgs., stapled)				
	31	93	171	260
nn (#2, 1946)-How Santa Got His Red Suit; Kelly-a (11 pgs., r/4-Color #61				
from 1944) (16pgs., stapled)	29	87	160	250
nn (#3, 1947)-Our Gang (Walt Kelly)	40	120	220	340
nn (#4)-Donald Duck by Carl Barks, "Maharajah Donald", 28 pgs.; Kelly-c?				
(Disney)	825	2475	4538	7000
5-Andy Panda (Walter Lantz)	18	54	99	150
6-Popular Fairy Tales; Kelly-c; Noonan-a(2)	21	63	115	175
7-Oswald the Rabbit	19	57	105	165
8-Mickey Mouse, 32 pgs. (Disney)	59	177	325	500
9(nn)-The Story of the Gloomy Bunny	11	33	60	90
10-Out of Santa's Bag	10	30	55	80
11-Fun With Santa Claus	8	24	45	65
12-Santa's Toys	8	24	45	65
13-Santa's Surprise	8	24	45	65
14-Santa's Candy Kitchen	8	24	45	65
15-Hip-It-Ty Hop & the Big Bass Viol	8	24	42	60
16-Woody Woodpecker (1947)(Walter Lantz)	13	39	72	110
17-Roy Rogers (1948)	28	84	154	235
18-Popular Fairy Tales	11	33	60	90
19-Uncle Wiggily	17	51	93	75
20-Donald Duck by Carl Barks, "Darkest Africa", 22 pgs.; Kelly-c (Disney)				
	470	1410	2585	4000
21-Tom and Jerry	11	33	60	90
22-Andy Panda (Lantz)	10	30	55	80
23-Raggedy Ann & Andy; Kerr-a	14	42	77	115
24-Felix the Cat, 1932 daily strip reprints by Otto Messmer				
	25	75	138	210
25-Gene Autry	25	75	138	210
26-Our Gang; Walt Kelly	22	66	121	185
27-Mickey Mouse; r/in M. M. #240 (Disney)	41	123	225	350
28-Gene Autry	24	72	132	200
29-Easter Bonnet Shop	6	18	29	40
30-Here Comes Santa	6	18	28	38
31-Santa's Busy Corner	6	18	28	38
32-No book produced				
33-A Christmas Carol (12/48)	6	18	32	45
34-Woody Woodpecker	10	30	55	80
35-Roy Rogers (1948)	26	78	143	225
36-Felix the Cat(1949); by Messmer; '34 strip-r	21	63	115	175
37-Popeye	15	45	83	125
38-Oswald the Rabbit	8	24	42	60
39-Gene Autry	24	72	132	200
40-Andy and Woody	8	24	42	60
41-Donald Duck by Carl Barks, "Race to the South Seas", 22 pgs.; Kelly-c				
	412	1236	2265	3500
42-Porky Pig	8	24	45	65
43-Henry	7	21	38	55
44-Bugs Bunny	9	27	51	75
45-Mickey Mouse (Disney)	32	96	176	270
46-Tom and Jerry	9	27	51	75
47-Roy Rogers	23	69	127	195
48-Greetings from Santa	5	15	23	30
49-Santa is Here	5	15	23	30
50-Santa Claus' Workshop (1949)	5	15	23	30
51-Felix the Cat (1950) by Messmer	18	54	99	150
52-Popeye	12	36	66	105
53-Oswald the Rabbit	8	24	42	60
54-Gene Autry	21	63	115	175
55-Andy and Woody	7	21	38	55
56-Donald Duck; not by Barks; Barks art on back-c (Disney)				
	30	90	165	255
57-Porky Pig	8	24	42	60
58-Henry	6	18	29	40
59-Bugs Bunny	8	24	45	65
60-Mickey Mouse (Disney)	29	87	160	245

	GD2.0	FN6.0	VF8.0	NM9.4
61-Tom and Jerry	7	21	38	55
62-Roy Rogers	22	66	121	185
63-Welcome Santa (1/2-size, oblong)	5	15	23	30
64(nn)-Santa's Helpers (1/2-size, oblong)	5	15	23	30
65(nn)-Jingle Bells (1950) (1/2-size, oblong)	5	15	23	30
66-Popeye (1951)	11	33	60	90
67-Oswald the Rabbit	7	21	38	55
68-Roy Rogers	22	66	121	180
69-Donald Duck; Barks-a on back-c (Disney)	26	78	143	220
70-Tom and Jerry	7	21	36	50
71-Porky Pig	7	21	38	55
72-Krazy Kat	8	24	45	65
73-Roy Rogers	19	57	105	160
74-Mickey Mouse (1951)(Disney)	24	72	132	200
75-Bugs Bunny	7	21	38	55
76-Andy and Woody	7	21	38	50
77-Roy Rogers	18	54	99	150
78-Gene Autry (1951); last regular size issue	17	51	94	140
Note: All pre #79 issues came with or without a slick protective wrap-around cover over the regular cover which advertised Poll Parrott Shoes, Sears, etc. This outer cover protects the inside pages making them in nicer condition. Issues with the outer cover are worth 15-25% more				
79-Andy Panda (1952, 5x7" size)	5	15	25	35
80-Popeye	10	30	55	80
81-Oswald the Rabbit	5	15	23	30
82-Tarzan; Lex Barker photo-c	19	57	105	160
83-Bugs Bunny	6	18	29	40
84-Henry	5	15	23	30
85-Woody Woodpecker	5	15	23	30
86-Roy Rogers	14	41	77	120
87-Krazy Kat	7	21	38	55
88-Tom and Jerry	5	15	25	35
89-Porky Pig	5	15	23	30
90-Gene Autry	12	36	66	105
91-Roy Rogers & Santa	13	39	66	115
92-Christmas with Santa	4	12	19	25
93-Woody Woodpecker (1953)	4	12	18	24
94-Indian Chief	9	27	49	70
95-Oswald the Rabbit	4	12	18	24
96-Popeye	9	27	49	70
97-Bugs Bunny	5	15	25	35
98-Tarzan; Lex Barker photo-c	18	54	99	150
99-Porky Pig	4	12	18	24
100-Roy Rogers	11	33	60	90
101-Henry	4	11	17	22
102-Tom Corbett (TV)('53, early app.); painted-c	14	42	77	115
103-Tom and Jerry	4	12	18	24
104-Gene Autry	10	30	55	85
105-Roy Rogers	10	30	55	85
106-Santa's Helpers	4	12	19	25
107-Santa's Christmas Book - not published				
108-Fun with Santa (1953)	4	12	19	25
109-Woody Woodpecker (1954)	4	12	19	25
110-Indian Chief	5	15	25	35
111-Oswald the Rabbit	4	11	17	22
112-Henry	4	10	15	20
113-Porky Pig	4	11	17	22
114-Tarzan; Russ Manning-a	18	54	99	150
115-Bugs Bunny	5	14	21	28
116-Roy Rogers	10	30	55	85
117-Popeye	9	27	49	70
118-Flash Gordon; painted-c	12	36	67	100
119-Tom and Jerry	4	11	17	22
120-Gene Autry	10	30	55	85
121-Roy Rogers	10	30	55	85
122-Santa's Surprise (1954)	4	11	17	22
123-Santa's Christmas Book	4	11	17	22
124-Woody Woodpecker (1955)	4	10	15	20
125-Tarzan; Lex Barker photo-c	17	51	94	140
126-Oswald the Rabbit	4	10	15	20

	GD2.0	FN6.0	VF8.0	NM9.4
127-Indian Chief	6	18	29	40
128-Tom and Jerry	4	10	15	20
129-Henry	3	9	14	17
130-Porky Pig	4	10	15	20
131-Roy Rogers	10	30	55	85
132-Bugs Bunny	4	12	18	24
133-Flash Gordon; painted-c	10	30	55	85
134-Popeye	7	21	36	50
135-Gene Autry	9	27	51	75
136-Roy Rogers	9	27	51	75
137-Gifts from Santa	3	7	11	14
138-Fun at Christmas (1955)	3	7	11	14
139-Woody Woodpecker (1956)	4	10	15	20
140-Indian Chief	6	18	29	40
141-Oswald the Rabbit	4	10	15	20
142-Flash Gordon	10	30	55	85
143-Porky Pig	4	10	15	20
144-Tarzan; Russ Manning-a; painted-c	15	45	83	130
145-Tom and Jerry	4	10	15	20
146-Roy Rogers; photo-c	9	27	51	75
147-Henry	3	8	12	15
148-Popeye	7	21	36	50
149-Bugs Bunny	4	11	17	22
150-Gene Autry	9	27	51	75
151-Roy Rogers	9	27	51	75
152-The Night Before Christmas	3	8	12	16
153-Merry Christmas (1956)	3	8	15	20
154-Tom and Jerry (1957)	4	10	15	20
155-Tarzan; photo-c	15	45	83	125
156-Oswald the Rabbit	4	10	15	20
157-Popeye	6	18	29	40
158-Woody Woodpecker	4	10	15	20
159-Indian Chief	6	18	29	40
160-Bugs Bunny	4	11	17	22
161-Roy Rogers	8	24	45	65
162-Henry	3	8	12	15
163-Rin Tin Tin (TV)	7	21	36	50
164-Porky Pig	4	10	15	20
165-The Lone Ranger	9	27	49	70
166-Santa and His Reindeer	3	7	11	14
167-Roy Rogers and Santa	8	24	45	65
168-Santa Claus' Workshop (1957, full size)	3	8	12	16
169-Popeye (1958)	6	18	29	40
170-Indian Chief	6	18	29	40
171-Oswald the Rabbit	4	9	14	18
172-Tarzan	11	33	55	95
173-Tom and Jerry	4	9	14	18
174-The Lone Ranger	9	27	49	70
175-Porky Pig	4	9	14	18
176-Roy Rogers	8	24	42	60
177-Woody Woodpecker	4	9	14	18
178-Henry	3	8	12	15
179-Bugs Bunny	4	9	14	18
180-Rin Tin Tin (TV)	6	18	32	45
181-Happy Holiday	2	6	9	12
182-Happi Tim	3	8	12	16
183-Welcome Santa (1958, full size)	2	6	9	12
184-Woody Woodpecker (1959)	3	8	12	16
185-Tarzan; photo-c	11	33	55	90
186-Oswald the Rabbit	3	8	12	16
187-Indian Chief	5	15	24	32
188-Bugs Bunny	3	8	12	16
189-Henry	2	7	11	14
190-Tom and Jerry	3	8	12	16
191-Roy Rogers	7	21	35	55
192-Porky Pig	3	8	12	16
193-The Lone Ranger	8	24	45	65
194-Popeye	5	15	25	35
195-Rin Tin Tin (TV)	6	18	29	40
196-Sears Special - not published				
197-Santa Is Coming	2	7	11	14
198-Santa's Helpers (1959)	2	7	11	14
199-Huckleberry Hound (TV)(1960, early app.)	7	21	36	50
200-Fury (TV)	5	15	24	32
201-Bugs Bunny	3	8	12	16
202-Space Explorer	7	21	38	55
203-Woody Woodpecker	2	7	11	14
204-Tarzan	9	27	49	70
205-Mighty Mouse	6	18	28	38
206-Roy Rogers; photo-c	7	21	38	55
207-Tom and Jerry	2	7	11	14
208-The Lone Ranger; Clayton Moore photo-c	11	33	55	90
209-Porky Pig	2	7	11	14
210-Lassie (TV)	6	18	28	38
211-Sears Special - not published				
212-Christmas Eve	2	7	11	14
213-Here Comes Santa (1960)	2	7	11	14
214-Huckleberry Hound (TV)(1961)	6	18	29	40
215-Hi Yo Silver	6	18	32	45
216-Rocky & His Friends (TV)(1961); predates Rocky and His Fiendish Friends #1 (see Four Color #1128)	9	27	51	75
217-Lassie (TV)	5	15	25	35
218-Porky Pig	2	7	11	14
219-Journey to the Sun	5	15	24	32
220-Bugs Bunny	3	8	12	16
221-Roy and Dale; photo-c	7	21	36	50
222-Woody Woodpecker	2	7	11	14
223-Tarzan	9	27	49	70
224-Tom and Jerry	2	7	11	14
225-The Lone Ranger	7	21	36	50
226-Christmas Treasury (1961)	2	7	11	14
227-Letters to Santa (1961)	2	7	11	14
228-Sears Special - not published?				
229-The Flintstones (TV)(1962); early app.; predates 1st Flintstones Gold Key issue (#7)	10	30	55	85
230-Lassie (TV)	5	15	23	30
231-Bugs Bunny	3	8	12	16
232-The Three Stooges	9	27	49	70
233-Bullwinkle (TV) (1962, very early app.)	10	30	55	80
234-Smokey the Bear	4	12	18	24
235-Huckleberry Hound (TV)	6	18	29	40
236-Roy and Dale	6	18	29	40
237-Mighty Mouse	5	15	23	30
238-The Lone Ranger	7	21	36	50
239-Woody Woodpecker	2	7	11	14
240-Tarzan	8	24	42	60
241-Santa Claus Around the World	2	6	9	12
242-Santa's Toyland (1962)	2	6	9	12
243-The Flintstones (TV)(1963)	8	24	42	60
244-Mister Ed (TV); early app.; photo-c	6	18	29	40
245-Bugs Bunny	3	8	12	16
246-Popeye	5	14	21	28
247-Mighty Mouse	5	14	21	28
248-The Three Stooges	9	27	49	70
249-Woody Woodpecker	2	7	11	14
250-Roy and Dale	6	18	29	40
251-Little Lulu & Witch Hazel	12	36	66	100
252-Tarzan; painted-c	7	21	38	55
253-Yogi Bear	7	21	36	50
254-Lassie (TV)	5	15	24	32
255-Santa's Christmas List	2	7	11	14
256-Christmas Party (1963)	2	7	11	14
257-Mighty Mouse	5	14	21	28
258-The Sword in the Stone (Disney)	7	21	38	55
259-Bugs Bunny	3	8	12	16
260-Mister Ed (TV)	5	15	25	35
261-Woody Woodpecker	2	7	11	14
262-Tarzan	7	21	36	50
263-Donald Duck; not by Barks (Disney)	8	24	45	65
264-Popeye	5	14	21	28

March of Comics #287 © WB
March of Comics #334 © MGM

March of Comics #362 © Smokey Bear

	GD2.0	FN6.0	VF8.0	NM9.4
265-Yogi Bear (TV)	5	15	25	35
266-Lassie (TV)	4	12	19	25
267-Little Lulu; Irving Tripp-a	10	30	55	80
268-The Three Stooges	8	24	42	60
269-A Jolly Christmas	2	5	8	10
270-Santa's Little Helpers	2	5	8	10
271-The Flintstones (TV)(1965)	8	24	45	65
272-Tarzan	7	21	36	50
273-Bugs Bunny	3	8	12	16
274-Popeye	5	14	21	28
275-Little Lulu; Irving Tripp-a	8	24	45	65
276-The Jetsons (TV)	14	42	77	120
277-Daffy Duck	3	8	12	16
278-Lassie (TV)	4	12	19	25
279-Yogi Bear (TV)	5	15	25	35
280-The Three Stooges; photo-c	8	24	42	60
281-Tom and Jerry	2	6	9	12
282-Mister Ed (TV)	5	15	25	35
283-Santa's Visit	2	7	11	14
284-Christmas Parade (1965)	2	7	11	14
285-Astro Boy (TV); 2nd app. Astro Boy	35	105	193	300
286-Tarzan	6	18	32	45
287-Bugs Bunny	3	8	12	16
288-Daffy Duck	2	7	11	14
289-The Flintstones (TV)	8	24	45	65
290-Mister Ed (TV); photo-c	5	14	21	28
291-Yogi Bear (TV)	5	15	23	30
292-The Three Stooges; photo-c	8	24	42	60
293-Little Lulu; Irving Tripp-a	7	21	38	55
294-Popeye	5	14	21	28
295-Tom and Jerry	2	6	9	12
296-Lassie (TV); photo-c	4	11	17	22
297-Christmas Bells	2	6	9	12
298-Santa's Sleigh (1966)	2	6	9	12
299-The Flintstones (TV)(1967)	8	24	45	65
300-Tarzan	6	18	32	45
301-Bugs Bunny	2	7	11	14
302-Laurel and Hardy (TV); photo-c	5	15	24	32
303-Daffy Duck	2	5	8	10
304-The Three Stooges; photo-c	7	21	38	55
305-Tom and Jerry	2	5	8	10
306-Daniel Boone (TV); Fess Parker photo-c	6	18	29	40
307-Little Lulu; Irving Tripp-a	6	18	32	45
308-Lassie (TV); photo-c	4	11	17	22
309-Yogi Bear (TV)	5	14	21	28
310-The Lone Ranger; Clayton Moore photo-c	11	33	55	90
311-Santa's Show	2	7	11	14
312-Christmas Album (1967)	2	7	11	14
313-Daffy Duck (1968)	2	5	8	10
314-Laurel and Hardy (TV)	5	15	23	30
315-Bugs Bunny	2	7	11	14
316-The Three Stooges	6	18	32	45
317-The Flintstones (TV)	7	21	38	55
318-Tarzan	6	18	29	40
319-Yogi Bear (TV)	5	14	21	28
320-Space Family Robinson (TV); Spiegle-a	13	39	71	110
321-Tom and Jerry	2	5	8	10
322-The Lone Ranger	6	18	32	45
323-Little Lulu; not by Stanley	5	14	21	28
324-Lassie (TV); photo-c	4	11	17	22
325-Fun with Santa	3	7	11	14
326-Christmas Story (1968)	3	7	11	14
327-The Flintstones (TV)(1969)	7	21	38	55
328-Space Family Robinson (TV); Spiegle-a	13	39	66	110
329-Bugs Bunny	3	7	11	14
330-The Jetsons (TV)	10	30	55	80
331-Daffy Duck	2	5	8	10
332-Tarzan	5	15	24	32
333-Tom and Jerry	2	5	8	10
334-Lassie (TV)	4	10	15	20

	GD2.0	FN6.0	VF8.0	NM9.4
335-Little Lulu	5	14	21	28
336-The Three Stooges	6	18	32	45
337-Yogi Bear (TV)	5	14	21	28
338-The Lone Ranger	6	18	32	45
339-(Was not published)				
340-Here Comes Santa (1969)	2	6	9	12
341-The Flintstones (TV)	7	21	38	55
342-Tarzan	3	9	21	32
343-Bugs Bunny	2	6	9	12
344-Yogi Bear (TV)	3	9	17	25
345-Tom and Jerry	1	4	7	10
346-Lassie (TV)	2	6	13	20
347-Daffy Duck	1	4	7	10
348-The Jetsons (TV)	6	18	42	70
349-Little Lulu; not by Stanley	2	6	15	22
350-The Lone Ranger	3	9	20	30
351-Beep-Beep, the Road Runner (TV)	2	6	10	14
352-Space Family Robinson (TV); Spiegle-a	9	27	65	110
353-Beep-Beep, the Road Runner (1971) (TV)	2	6	10	14
354-Tarzan (1971)	3	9	19	28
355-Little Lulu; not by Stanley	2	6	15	22
356-Scooby Doo, Where Are You? (TV)	5	15	35	60
357-Daffy Duck & Porky Pig	1	4	7	10
358-Lassie (TV)	2	6	13	20
359-Baby Snoots	2	6	10	14
360-H. R. Pufnstuf (TV); photo-c	5	15	35	60
361-Tom and Jerry	1	4	7	10
362-Smokey Bear (TV)	1	4	7	10
363-Bugs Bunny & Yosemite Sam	2	6	9	12
364-The Banana Splits (TV); photo-c	4	12	30	50
365-Tom and Jerry (1972)	1	4	7	10
366-Tarzan	3	9	19	28
367-Bugs Bunny & Porky Pig	2	6	9	12
368-Scooby Doo (TV)(4/72)	4	12	30	50
369-Little Lulu; not by Stanley	2	6	12	18
370-Lassie (TV); photo-c	2	6	13	20
371-Baby Snoots	2	6	9	12
372-Smokey the Bear (TV)	1	4	7	10
373-The Three Stooges	4	12	26	40
374-Wacky Witch	1	4	7	10
375-Beep-Beep & Daffy Duck (TV)	1	4	7	10
376-The Pink Panther (1972) (TV)	2	6	10	14
377-Baby Snoots (1973)	2	6	9	12
378-Turok, Son of Stone; new-a	10	30	68	115
379-Heckle & Jeckle New Terrytoons (TV)	1	4	7	10
380-Bugs Bunny & Yosemite Sam	1	4	7	10
381-Lassie (TV)	2	6	11	16
382-Scooby Doo, Where Are You? (TV)	4	12	26	40
383-Smokey the Bear (TV)	1	4	7	10
384-Pink Panther (TV)	1	4	7	10
385-Little Lulu	2	6	11	15
386-Wacky Witch	1	4	7	10
387-Beep-Beep & Daffy Duck (TV)	1	4	7	10
388-Tom and Jerry (1973)	1	4	7	10
389-Little Lulu; not by Stanley	2	6	11	15
390-Pink Panther (TV)	1	4	7	10
391-Scooby Doo (TV)	3	9	20	30
392-Bugs Bunny & Yosemite Sam	1	3	6	8
393-New Terrytoons (Heckle & Jeckle) (TV)	1	3	6	8
394-Lassie (TV)	2	6	9	12
395-Woodsy Owl	1	3	6	8
396-Baby Snoots	1	4	7	10
397-Beep-Beep & Daffy Duck (TV)	1	3	6	8
398-Wacky Witch	1	3	6	8
399-Turok, Son of Stone; new-a	8	24	60	100
400-Tom and Jerry	1	3	6	8
401-Baby Snoots (1975) (r/#371)	1	4	7	10
402-Daffy Duck (r/#313)	1	3	5	7
403-Bugs Bunny (r/#343)	1	3	6	8
404-Space Family Robinson (TV)(r/#328)	6	18	45	75

March of Comics #435 © Terrytoons

Marvel Comics Presents Care Bears © MAR

The Matrix © WB

	GD2.0	FN6.0	VF8.0	NM9.4
405-Cracky	1	3	5	7
406-Little Lulu (r/#355)	2	6	10	14
407-Smokey the Bear (TV)(r/#362)	1	3	6	8
408-Turok, Son of Stone; c-r/Turok #20 w/changes; new-a	6	18	42	70
409-Pink Panther (TV)	1	3	5	7
410-Wacky Witch				6.00
411-Lassie (TV)(r/#324)	2	6	9	12
412-New Terrytoons (1975) (TV)				6.00
413-Daffy Duck (1976)(r/#331)				6.00
414-Space Family Robinson (r/#328)	6	18	42	70
415-Bugs Bunny (r/#329)				6.00
416-Beep-Beep, the Road Runner (r/#353)(TV)				6.00
417-Little Lulu (r/#323)	2	6	10	14
418-Pink Panther (r/#384) (TV)				6.00
419-Baby Snoots (r/#377)	1	3	5	7
420-Woody Woodpecker				6.00
421-Tweety & Sylvester				6.00
422-Wacky Witch (r/#386)				6.00
423-Little Monsters	1	3	5	7
424-Cracky (12/76)				6.00
425-Daffy Duck				6.00
426-Underdog (TV)	3	10	23	35
427-Little Lulu (r/#335)	1	4	7	10
428-Bugs Bunny				5.00
429-The Pink Panther (TV)				5.00
430-Beep-Beep, the Road Runner (TV)				5.00
431-Baby Snoots				6.00
432-Lassie (TV)	1	3	6	8
433-437: 433-Tweety & Sylvester. 434-Wacky Witch. 435-New Terrytoons. 436-Wacky Advs. of Cracky. 437-Daffy Duck				5.00
438-Underdog (TV)	3	9	20	30
439-Little Lulu (r/#349)	1	4	7	10
440-442,444-446: 440-Bugs Bunny. 441-The Pink Panther (TV). 442-Beep-Beep, the Road Runner (TV). 444-Tom and Jerry. 445-Tweety and Sylvester. 446-Wacky Witch				6.00
443-Baby Snoots				6.00
447-Mighty Mouse	1	3	6	8
448-455,457,458: 448-Cracky. 449-Pink Panther (TV). 450-Baby Snoots 451-Tom and Jerry. 452-Bugs Bunny. 453-Popeye. 454-Woody Woodpecker. 455-Beep-Beep, the Road Runner (TV). 457-Tweety & Sylvester. 458-Wacky Witch				6.00
456-Little Lulu (r/#369)	1	3	6	8
459-Mighty Mouse	1	3	6	8
460-466: 460-Daffy Duck. 461-The Pink Panther (TV). 462-Baby Snoots. 463-Tom and Jerry. 464-Bugs Bunny. 465-Popeye. 466-Woody Woodpecker				6.00
467-Underdog (TV)	3	9	17	25
468-Little Lulu (r/#385)				6.00
469-Tweety & Sylvester				6.00
470-Wacky Witch				6.00
471-Mighty Mouse	1	3	5	7
472-474,476-478: 472-Heckle & Jeckle(12/80). 473-Pink Panther(1/81)(TV). 474-Baby Snoots. 476-Bugs Bunny. 477-Popeye. 478-Woody Woodpecker				6.00
475-Little Lulu (r/#323)	1	3	5	7
479-Underdog (TV)	2	6	13	20
480-482: 480-Tom and Jerry. 481-Tweety and Sylvester. 482-Wacky Witch				6.00
483-Mighty Mouse	1	3	5	7
484-487: 484-Heckle & Jeckle. 485-Baby Snoots. 486-The Pink Panther (TV). 487-Bugs Bunny				6.00
488-Little Lulu (4/82) (r/#335) (Last issue)	1	4	7	10

MARGARET O'BRIEN (See The Adventures of...)

MARK STEEL
American Iron & Steel Institute: 1967, 1968, 1972 (Giveaway) (24 pgs.)

	GD2.0	FN6.0	VF8.0	NM9.4
1967,1968- "Journey of Discovery with..."; Neal Adams art	3	9	20	30
1972- "...Fights Pollution"; N. Adams-a	2	6	12	18

MARVEL COLLECTOR'S EDITION: X-MEN
Marvel Comics: 1993 (3-3/4x6-1/2")

	GD2.0	FN6.0	VF8.0	NM9.4
1-4-Pizza Hut giveaways				3.00

MARVEL COMICS PRESENTS
Marvel Comics: 1987, 1988 (4 1/4 x 6 1/4, 20 pgs.)
...Mini Comic Giveaway

	GD2.0	FN6.0	VF8.0	NM9.4
nn-(1988) Alf	1	3	6	8
nn-(1987) Captain America r/ #250	1	3	5	7
nn-(1987) Care Bears (Star Comics...)	1	3	5	7
nn-(1988) Flintstone Kids	1	3	6	8
nn-(1987) Heathcliffe (Star Comics...)	1	3	5	7
nn-(1987) Spider-Man-r/Spect. Spider-Man #21	1	3	5	7
nn-(1988) Spider-Man-r/Amazing Spider-Man #1	1	3	5	7
nn-(1988) X-Men-reprints X-Men #53; B. Smith-a	1	3	5	7

MARVEL MINI-BOOKS
Marvel Comics Group: 1966 (50 pgs., B&W; 5/8x7/8") (6 different issues)
(Smallest comics ever published) (Marvel Mania Giveaways)

	GD2.0	FN6.0	VF8.0	NM9.4
Captain America, Millie the Model, Spider-Man, Sgt. Fury, Hulk, Thor each...	8	24	56	90

NOTE: *Each came in six different color covers, usually one color: Pink, yellow, green, etc.*

MARY'S GREATEST APOSTLE (St. Louis Grignion de Montfort)
Catechetical Guild (Topix) (Giveaway): No date (16 pgs.; paper cover)

	GD2.0	FN6.0	VF8.0	NM9.4
nn	4	10	15	20

MASK
DC Comics: 1985

	GD2.0	FN6.0	VF8.0	NM9.4
1-3				3.00

MASKED PILOT, THE (See Popular Comics #43)
R.S. Callender: 1939 (7-1/2x5-1/4", 16 pgs., premium, non-slick-c)

	GD2.0	FN6.0	VF8.0	NM9.4
nn-Bob Jenney-a	10	30	55	80

MASTERS OF THE UNIVERSE (He-Man)
DC Comics: 1982

	GD2.0	FN6.0	VF8.0	NM9.4
1-7				3.00

MATRIX, THE (1999 movie)
Warner Brothers: 1999 (Recalled by Warner Bros. over questionable content)

	GD2.0	FN6.0	VF8.0	NM9.4
nn-Paul Chadwick-s/a (16 pgs.); Geof Darrow-c				5.00

McCRORY'S CHRISTMAS BOOK
Western Printing Co: 1955 (36 pgs., slick-c) (McCrory Stores Corp. giveaway)

	GD2.0	FN6.0	VF8.0	NM9.4
nn-Painted-c	4	12	18	24

McCRORY'S TOYLAND BRINGS YOU SANTA'S PRIVATE EYES
Promotional Publ. Co.: 1956 (16 pgs.) (Giveaway)

	GD2.0	FN6.0	VF8.0	NM9.4
nn-Has 9 pg. story plus 7 pgs. toy ads	4	10	15	20

McCRORY'S WONDERFUL CHRISTMAS
Promotional Publ. Co.: 1954 (20 pgs., slick-c) (Giveaway)

	GD2.0	FN6.0	VF8.0	NM9.4
nn	4	12	18	24

McDONALDS COMMANDRONS
DC Comics: 1985

	GD2.0	FN6.0	VF8.0	NM9.4
nn-Four editions				3.00

MEET HIYA A FRIEND OF SANTA CLAUS
Julian J. Proskauer/Sundial Shoe Stores, etc.: 1949 (18 pgs.?, paper-c)-(Giveaway)

	GD2.0	FN6.0	VF8.0	NM9.4
nn	6	18	30	42

MEET THE NEW POST GAZETTE SUNDAY FUNNIES
Pittsburgh Post Gazette: 3/12/49 (7-1/4x10-1/4", 16 pgs., paper-c)
Commercial Comics (insert in newspaper) (Rare)
Dick Tracy by Gould, Gasoline Alley, Terry & the Pirates, Brenda Starr, Buck Rogers by Yager, The Gumps, Peter Rabbit by Fago, Superman, Funnyman by Siegel & Shuster, The Saint, Archie, & others done especially for this book. A fine copy sold at auction in 1985 for $276.00.

	GD2.0	FN6.0	VF8.0	NM9.4
	500	1500	4000	

MEN OF COURAGE
Catechetical Guild: 1949

	GD2.0	FN6.0	VF8.0	NM9.4
Bound Topix comics-V7#2,4,6,8,10,16,18,20	5	15	25	35

Mickey Mouse Magazine V2 #4 © WDC

Motion Picture Funnies Weekly #2 © First Funnies Inc.

New Teen Titans nn © DC

	GD2.0	FN6.0	VF8.0	NM9.4

MEN WHO MOVE THE NATION
Publisher unknown: (Giveaway) (B&W)

nn-Neal Adams-a	5	15	25	35

MERRY CHRISTMAS, A
K. K. Publications (Child Life Shoes): 1948 (Giveaway)

nn	6	18	29	40

MERRY CHRISTMAS
K. K. Publications (Blue Bird Shoes Giveaway): 1956 (7-1/4x5-1/4")

nn	4	12	18	24

MERRY CHRISTMAS FROM MICKEY MOUSE
K. K. Publications: 1939 (16 pgs.) (Color & B&W) (Shoe store giveaway)

nn-Donald Duck & Pluto app.; text with art (Rare); c-reprint/Mickey Mouse Mag. V3#3 (12/37)(Rare)

	315	1260	1800	2800

MERRY CHRISTMAS FROM SEARS TOYLAND (See Santa's Christmas Comic)
Sears Roebuck Giveaway: 1939 (16 pgs.) (Color)

nn-Dick Tracy, Little Orphan Annie, The Gumps, Terry & the Pirates

	109	436	682	1200

MICKEY MOUSE (Also see Frito-Lay Giveaway)
Dell Publ. Co

...& Goofy Explore Business(1978)	1	3	6	8
...& Goofy Explore Energy(1976-1978, 36 pgs.); Exxon giveaway in color; regular size	1	3	6	8
...& Goofy Explore Energy Conservation(1976-1978)-Exxon	1	3	6	8
...& Goofy Explore The Universe of Energy(1985, 20 pgs.); Exxon giveaway in color; regular size				6.00
The Perils of Mickey nn (1993, 5-1/4x7-1/4", 16 pgs.)-Nabisco giveaway w/ games, Nabisco coupons & 6 pgs. of stories; Phantom Blot app.				4.00

MICKEY MOUSE MAGAZINE
Walt Disney Productions: V1#1, Jan, 1933 - V1#9, Sept, 1933 (5-1/4x7-1/4")
No. 1-3 published by Kamen-Blair (Kay Kamen, Inc.)

(Scarce)-Distributed by dairies and leading stores through their local theatres. First nine issues had 5¢ listed on cover, later ones had no price.

V1#1	533	2132	5000	-
2-9	218	545	1250	-

MICKEY MOUSE MAGAZINE
Walt Disney Productions: V1#1, 11/33 - V2#12, 10/35 (Mills giveaways issued by different dairies)

V1#1	240	960	1300	1900
2-12: 2-X-Mas issue	80	320	450	650
V2#1-12: 2-X-Mas issue. 4-St. Valentine-c	55	192	290	425
V4#1 (Giveaway)	55	192	290	425

MIGHTY ATOM, THE
Whitman

Giveaway (1959, '63, Whitman)-Evans-a	2	6	13	20
Giveaway ('64r, '65r, '66r, '67r, '68r)-Evans-r?	1	4	7	10
Giveaway ('73r, '76r)				6.00

MILITARY COURTESY
U.S. Army : (16 pgs.)

nn-Regulations and saluting instructions	4	12	19	25

MINUTE MAN
Sovereign Service Station giveaway: No date (16 pgs., B&W, paper-c blue & red)

nn-American history	3	8	12	15

MINUTE MAN ANSWERS THE CALL, THE
By M. C. Gaines: 1942 (4 pgs.) (Giveaway inserted in Jr. JSA Membership Kit)

nn-Sheldon Moldoff-a	22	66	116	200

MIRACLE ON BROADWAY
Broadway Comics: Dec, 1995 (Giveaway)

1-Ernie Colon-c/a; Jim Shooter & Co. story; 1st known digitally printed comic book; 1st app. Spire & Knights on Broadway (1150 print run)				20.00

NOTE: *Miracle on Broadway was a limited edition comic given to 1100 VIPs in the entertainment industry for the 1995 Holiday Season.*

	GD2.0	FN6.0	VF8.0	NM9.4

MISS SUNBEAM (See Little Miss Sunbeam Comics)
MR. BUG GOES TO TOWN (See Cinema Comics Herald)
K.K. Publications: 1941 (Giveaway, 52 pgs.)

nn-Cartoon movie (scarce)	75	300	500	750

MOTHER OF US ALL
Catechetical Guild Giveaway: 1950? (32 pgs.)

nn	4	10	15	20

MOTION PICTURE FUNNIES WEEKLY (Amazing Man #5 on?)
First Funnies, Inc.: 1939 (Giveaway)(B&W, 36 pgs.)
No month given; last panel in Sub-Mariner story dated 4/39
(Also see Colossus, Green Giant & Invaders No. 20)

1-Origin & 1st printed app. Sub-Mariner by Bill Everett (8 pgs.); Fred Schwab-c; reprinted in Marvel Mystery #1 with color added over the craft tint which was used to shade the black & white version; Spy Ring, American Ace (reprinted in Marvel Mystery #3) app. (Rare)-only eight (8) known copies, one near mint with white pages, rest with brown pages.

	4400	11,000	16,500	24,000
Covers only to #2-4 (set)				900

NOTE: *The only eight known copies (with a ninth suspected) were discovered in 1974 in the estate of the deceased publisher. Covers only to issues No. 2-4 were also found which evidently were printed in advance along with #1. #1 was to be distributed only through motion picture movie houses. However, it is believed that only advanced copies were sent out and the motion picture houses not going for the idea. Possible distribution at local theaters in Boston suspected. The last panel of Sub-Mariner contains a rectangular box with "Continued Next Week" printed in it. When reprinted in Marvel Mystery, the box was left in with lettering omitted.*

MY DOG TIGE (Buster Brown's Dog)
Buster Brown Shoes: 1957 (Giveaway)

nn	5	15	25	35

MY GREATEST THRILLS IN BASEBALL
Mission of California: Date? (16 pg. Giveaway)

nn-By Mickey Mantle	79	212	390	600

NATURAL DISASTERS!
Graphic Information Service/ Civil Defense: 1956 (16 pgs., soft-c)

nn-Al Capp Li'l Abner-c; Li'l Abner cameo (1 panel); narrated by Mr. Civil Defense

	10	30	55	85

NAVY: HISTORY & TRADITION
Stokes Walesby Co./Dept. of Navy: 1958 - 1961 (nn) (Giveaway)

1772-1778, 1778-1782, 1782-1817, 1817-1865, 1865-1936, 1940-1945:

1772-1778: in color	5	15	23	30
1861: Naval Actions of the Civil War: 1865-36 pg. in color; flag-c	5	15	23	30

NEW ADVENTURE OF WALT DISNEY'S SNOW WHITE AND THE SEVEN DWARFS, A (See Snow White Bendix Giveaway)
NEW ADVENTURES OF PETER PAN (Disney)
Western Publishing Co.: 1953 (5x7-1/4", 36 pgs.) (Admiral giveaway)

nn	14	42	72	120

NEW TEEN TITANS, THE
DC Comics: Nov. 1983

nn(11/83-Keebler Co. Giveaway)-In cooperation with "The President's Drug Awareness Campaign"; came in Presidential envelope w/letter from White House (Nancy Reagan)

				5.00

nn-(re-issue of above on Mando paper for direct sales market); American Soft Drink Ind. version; I.B.M. Corp. version

				4.00

NOLAN RYAN IN THE WINNING PITCH (Kellogg's Tony's Sports Comics)
DC Comics: 1992 (Sports Illustrated)

nn				2.50

OLD GLORY COMICS
Chesapeake & Ohio Railway: 1944 (Giveaway)

nn-Capt. Fearless reprint	6	18	32	45

ON THE AIR
NBC Network Comic: 1947 (Giveaway, paper-c)

nn-(Rare)	27	80	140	210

	GD2.0	FN6.0	VF8.0	NM9.4

OUT OF THE PAST A CLUE TO THE FUTURE
E. C. Comics (Public Affairs Comm.): 1946? (16 pgs.) (paper cover)

nn-Based on public affairs pamphlet "What Foreign Trade Means to You"				
	24	71	118	195

OUTSTANDING AMERICAN WAR HEROES
The Parents' Institute: 1944 (16 pgs., paper-c)

nn-Reprints from True Comics	4	12	19	25

OVERSEAS COMICS (Also see G.I. Comics & Jeep Comics)
Giveaway (Distributed to U.S. Armed Forces): 1944 - No. 105?, 1946
(7-1/4x10-1/4"; 16 pgs. in color)

23-105-Bringing Up Father (by McManus), Popeye, Joe Palooka, Dick Tracy, Superman, Gasoline Alley, Buz Sawyer, Li'l Abner, Blondie, Terry & the Pirates, Out Our Way	6	18	32	45

OWL, THE (See Crackajack Funnies #25 & Popular Comics #72)(Also see The Hurricane Kids & Magic Morro)
Western Pub. Co./R.S. Callender: 1940 (Giveaway)(7-1/2x5-1/4")(Soft-c, color)

nn-Frank Thomas-a	22	66	108	180

OXYDOL-DREFT
Oxydol-Dreft:1950 (Set of 6 pocket-size giveaways; distributed through the mail as a set) (Scarce)

1-3: 1-Li'l Abner. 2-Daisy Mae. 3-Shmoo	13	40	66	110
4-John Wayne; Williamson/Frazetta-c from John Wayne #3				
	17	51	88	150
5-Archie	16	48	83	140
6-Terrytoons Mighty Mouse	13	40	66	110
Mailing Envelope (has All Capp's Shmoo on front)	15	45	72	125

OZZIE SMITH IN THE KID WHO COULD (Kellogg's Tony's Sports Comics)
DC Comics: 1992 (Sports Illustrated)

nn-Ozzie Smith app.				2.50

PADRE OF THE POOR
Catechetical Guild: nd (Giveaway) (16 pgs., paper-c)

nn	4	11	17	22

PAUL TERRY'S HOW TO DRAW FUNNY CARTOONS
Terrytoons, Inc. (Giveaway): 1940's (14 pgs.) (Black & White)

nn-Heckle & Jeckle, Mighty Mouse, etc.	12	36	61	100

PETER PAN (See New Adventures of Peter Pan)

PETER PENNY AND HIS MAGIC DOLLAR
American Bankers Association, N.Y. (Giveaway): 1947 (16 pgs., paper-c; regular size)

nn-(Scarce)-Used in SOTI, pg. 310, 311	17	51	88	150
Diff. version (7-1/4x11")-redrawn, 16 pgs., paper-c	10	30	53	75

PETER WHEAT (The Adventures of...)
Bakers Associates Giveaway: 1948 - 1956? (16 pgs in color) (paper covers)

nn(No.1)-States on last page, end of 1st Adventure of...; Kelly-a				
	33	130	200	280
nn(4 issues)-Kelly-a	20	80	120	165
6-10-All Kelly-a	15	45	75	125
11-20-All Kelly-a	13	40	66	110
21-35-All Kelly-a	11	33	55	95
36-66	8	24	45	65
...Artist's Workbook ('54, digest size)	8	24	45	65
...Four-In-One Fun Pack (Vol. 2, '54), oblong, comics w/puzzles				
	10	30	53	75
...Fun Book ('52, 32 pgs., paper-c, B&W & color, 8-1/2x10-3/4")-Contains cutouts, puzzles, games, magic & pages to color	12	36	61	100

NOTE: Al Hubbard art #36 on; written by Del Connell.

PETER WHEAT NEWS
Bakers Associates: 1948 - No. 30, 1950 (4 pgs. in color)

Vol. 1-All have 2 pgs. Peter Wheat by Kelly	27	110	160	240
2-10	18	54	90	150
11-20	11	33	55	95
21-30	8	24	45	65

NOTE: Early issues have no date and Kelly art.

	GD2.0	FN6.0	VF8.0	NM9.

PINOCCHIO
Cocomalt/Montgomery Ward Co.: 1940 (10 pgs.; giveaway, linen-like paper)

nn-Cocomalt edition	40	120	232	400
nn-store edition	33	99	174	300

PIUS XII MAN OF PEACE
Catechetical Guild: No date (12 pgs.; 5-1/2x8-1/2") (B&W)

nn-Catechetical Guild Giveaway	5	15	23	30

PLOT TO STEAL THE WORLD, THE
Work & Unity Group: 1948, 16pgs., paper-c

nn-Anti communism	18	54	94	160

POCAHONTAS
Pocahontas Fuel Company (Coal): 1941 - No. 2, 1942

nn(#1), 2-Feat. life story of Indian princess Pocahontas & facts about Pocahontas coal, Pocahontas, VA.	16	48	83	140

POLL PARROT
Poll Parrot Shoe Store/International Shoe
K. K. Publications (Giveaway): 1950 - No. 4, 1951; No. 2, 1959 - No. 16, 1962

1 ('50)-Howdy Doody; small size	27	82	110	175
2-4('51)-Howdy Doody	22	66	95	140
2('59)-16('62): 2-The Secret of Crumbley Castle. 5-Bandit Busters. 7-The Make-Believe Mummy. 8-Mixed Up Mission('60). 10-The Frightful Flight. 11-Showdown at Sunup. 12-Maniac at Mubu Island. 13-...and the Runaway Genie. 14-Bully for You. 15-Trapped In Tall Timber. 16-...& the Rajah's Ruby('62)	2	6	15	22

POPEYE
Whitman

Bold Detergent giveaway (Same as regular issue #94) 1	3	6		9
Quaker Cereal premium (1989, 16pp, small size,4 diff.)(Popeye & the Time Machine,--On Safari, -& Big Foot, --vs. Bluto)	2	6	11	16

POPEYE
Charlton (King Features) (Giveaway): 1972 - 1974 (36 pgs. in color)

E-1 to E-15 (Educational comics)	1	3	6	9
nn-Popeye Gettin' Better Grades-4 pgs. used as intro. to above giveaways (in color)	1	3	6	9

POPSICLE PETE FUN BOOK (See All-American Comics #6)
Joe Lowe Corp.: 1947, 1948

nn-36 pgs. in color; Sammy 'n' Claras, The King Who Couldn't Sleep & Popsicle Pete stories, games, cut-outs	11	33	55	90
Adventure Book ('48)-Has Classics ad with checklist to HRN #343 (Great Expectations #43)	10	30	55	80

PORKY'S BOOK OF TRICKS
K. K. Publications: 1942 (8-1/2x5-1/2", 48 pgs.)

nn-7 pg. comic story, text stories, plus games & puzzles				
	50	200	340	500

POST GAZETTE (See Meet the New...)

POWER RECORD COMICS
Marvel Comics/Power Records: 1974 - 1978 ($1.49, 7x10" comics, 20 pgs. with 45 R.P.M. record)

PR10-Spider-Man-r/from #124,125; Man-Wolf app. PR18-Planet of the Apes-r. PR19-Escape From the Planet of the Apes-r. PR20-Beneath the Planet of the Apes-r. PR21-Battle for the Planet of the Apes-r. PR24-Spider-Man II-New-a begins. PR27-Batman "Stacked Cards"; N. Adams-a(p). PR30-Batman; N. Adams-r/Det.(7 pgs.)				
With record; each...	4	12	26	40
PR11-Hulk-r. PR12-Captain America-r/#168. PR13-Fantastic Four-r/#126. PR14-Frankenstein-Ploog-r/#1. PR15-Tomb of Dracula-Colan-r/#2. PR16-Man-Thing-Ploog-r/#5. PR17-Werewolf By Night-Ploog-r/Marvel Spotlight #2. PR28-Superman "Alien Creatures". PR29-Space: 1999 "Breakaway". PR31-Conan-N. Adams-a; reprinted in Conan #116. PR32-Space: 1999 "Return to the Beginning". PR33-Superman-G.A. origin, Buckler-a(p). PR34-Superman. PR35-Wonder Woman-Buckler-a(p)				
With record; each...	3	10	23	35
PR25-Star Trek "Passage to Moauv". PR26-Star Trek "Crier in Emptiness". PR36-Holo-Man. PR37-Robin Hood. PR39-Huckleberry Finn. PR40-Davy Crockett. PR41-Robinson Crusoe. PR42-20,000 Leagues Under the Sea. PR46-Star Trek "The Robot Masters". PR47-Little Women				
With record; each...	3	9	20	30

The Red Iceberg © Impact Pub.

The Red Iceberg © Impact Pub.

Red Ryder Victory Patrol 1943 © DELL

Richie Rich, Casper & Wendy National League © HARV

	GD2.0	FN6.0	VF8.0	NM9.4

PURE OIL COMICS (Also see Salerno Carnival of Comics, 24 Pages of Comics, & Vicks Comics)
Pure Oil Giveaway: Late 1930's (24 pgs., regular size, paper-c)

nn-Contains 1-2 pg. strips; i.e., Hairbreadth Harry, Skyroads, Buck Rogers by Calkins & Yager, Olly of the Movies, Napoleon, S'Matter Pop, etc.				
Also a 16 pg. 1938 giveaway w/Buck Rogers	50	150	240	350

QUAKER OATS (Also see Cap'n Crunch)
Quaker Oats Co.: 1965 (Giveaway) (2-1/2x5-1/2") (16 pgs.)

"Plenty of Glutton", starring Quake & Quisp	2	6	15	22
"Lava Come-Back", "Kite Tale"	1	3	6	8

RAILROADS DELIVER THE GOODS!
Assoc. of American Railroads: Dec, 1954; Sept, 1957 (16 pgs.)

nn-The story of railway freight	6	18	32	45

RAILS ACROSS AMERICA!
Assoc. of American Railroads: nd (16 pgs.)

nn	6	18	32	45

REAL FUN OF DRIVING!!, THE
Chrysler Corp.: 1965, 1966, 1967 (Regular size, 16 pgs.)

nn-Schaffenberger-a (12 pgs.)				6.00

REAL HIT
Fox Features Publications: 1944 (Savings Bond premium)

1-Blue Beetle-r	18	54	94	160

NOTE: *Two versions exist, with and without covers. The coverless version has the title, No. 1 and price printed at top of splash page.*

RED BALL COMIC BOOK
Parents' Magazine Institute: 1947 (Red Ball Shoes giveaway)

nn-Reprints from True Comics	3	8	12	16

REDDY GOOSE
International Shoe Co. (Western Printing): No #, 1958?; No. 2, Jan, 1959 - No. 16, July, 1962 (Giveaway)

nn (#1)	5	15	38	60
2-16	3	10	23	35

REDDY KILOWATT (5¢) (Also see Story of Edison)
Educational Comics (E. C.): 1946 - No. 2, 1947; 1956 - 1960 (no month) (16 pgs., paper-c)

nn-Reddy Made Magic (1946, 5¢)	12	36	61	105
nn-Reddy Made Magic (1958)	8	24	45	65
2-Edison, the Man Who Changed the World (3/4" smaller than #1) (1947, 5¢)	12	36	61	105
…Comic Book 2 (1954)- "Light's Diamond Jubilee"	9	27	49	70
…Comic Book 2 (1958, 16 pgs.)- "Wizard of Light"	8	24	45	65
…Comic Book 3 (1956, 8 pgs.)- "The Space Kite"; Orlando story; regular size	8	24	45	65
…Comic Book 3 (1960, 8 pgs.)- "The Space Kite"; Orlando story; regular size	5	15	34	55

NOTE: *Several copies surfaced in 1979.*

REDDY MADE MAGIC
Educational Comics (E. C.): 1956, 1958 (16 pgs., paper-c)

1-Reddy Kilowatt-r (splash panel changed)	11	33	55	90
1 (1958 edition)	6	18	32	45

RED ICEBERG, THE
Impact Publ. (Catechetical Guild): 1960 (10¢, 16 pgs., Communist propaganda)

nn-(Rare)- 'We The People' back-c	31	93	205	360
2nd version- 'Impact Press' back-c	31	93	205	360
3rd version-"Explains comic" back-c	31	93	205	360
4th version-"Impact Press w/World Wide Secret Heart Program ad"	31	93	205	360

NOTE: *This book was the Guild's last anti-communist propaganda book and had very limited circulation. 3 - 4 copies surfaced in 1979 from the defunct publisher's files. Other copies do turn up.*

RED RYDER COMICS
Dell Publ. Co.

Buster Brown Shoes Giveaway (1941, color, soft-c, 32 pgs.)

Red Ryder Super Book of Comics (1944, paper-c, 32 pgs.; blank back-c) Magic Morro app.	27	81	142	240
	29	86	150	250
Red Ryder Victory Patrol-nn(1942, 32 pgs.)(Langendorf bread; includes cut-out membership card and certificate, order blank and "Slide-Up" decoder, and a Super Book of Comics in color (same content as Super Book #4 w/diff. cover (Pan-Am)) (Rare)	463	1621	3000	4600
Red Ryder Victory Patrol-nn(1943, 32 pgs.)(Langendorf bread; includes cut-out "Rodeomatic" radio decoder, order coupon for "Magic V-Badge", cut-out membership card and certificate and a full color Super Book of comics comic book) (Rare)	421	1475	2700	4200
Red Ryder Victory Patrol-nn(1944, 32 pgs.)-r-/#43,44; comic has a paper-c & is stapled inside a triple cardboard fold-out-c; contains membership card, decoder, map of R.R. home range, etc. Herky app. (Langendorf Bread giveaway; sub-titled 'Super Book of Comics')(Rare)	400	1400	2700	4200
Wells Lamont Corp. giveaway (1950)-16 pgs. in color; regular size; paper-c; 1941-r	25	75	125	210

RE-LOADED (Also see Loaded)
DC Comics: 1996 (Interplay Productions)

1-Promotes video game				3.00

RICHIE RICH, CASPER & WENDY NATIONAL LEAGUE
Harvey Publications: June, 1976 (52 pgs.)

1 (Released-3/76 with 6/76 date)	2	6	11	16
1 (6/76)-2nd version w/San Francisco Giants & KTVU 2 logos; has "Compliments of Giants and Straw Hat Pizza" on-c	2	6	11	16
1-Variants for other 11 NL teams, similar to Giants version but with different ad on inside front-c	2	6	11	16

RIDE THE HIGH IRON!
Assoc. of American Railroads: Jan, 1957 (16 pgs.)

nn-The Story of modern passenger trains	6	18	32	45

RIPLEY'S BELIEVE IT OR NOT!
Harvey Publications

J. C. Penney giveaway (1948)	8	24	45	65

ROBIN HOOD (New Adventures of…)
Walt Disney Productions: 1952 (Flour giveaways, 5x7-1/4", 36 pgs.)

"New Adventures of Robin Hood", "Ghosts of Waylea Castle", & "The Miller's Ransom" each….	5	14	21	28

ROBIN HOOD'S FRONTIER DAYS (…Western Tales, Adventures of… #1)
Shoe Store Giveaway (Robin Hood Stores): 1956 (20 pgs., slick-c)(7 issues?)

nn	5	15	24	32
nn-Issues with Crandall-a	7	21	38	55

ROCKETS AND RANGE RIDERS
Richfield Oil Corp.: May, 1957 (Giveaway, 16 pgs., soft-c)

nn-Toth-a	17	51	85	140

ROUND THE WORLD GIFT
National War Fund (Giveaway): No date (mid 1940's) (4 pgs.)

nn	12	36	61	100

ROY ROGERS COMICS
Dell Publishing Co.

…& the Man From Dodge City (Dodge giveaway, 16 pgs., 1954)-Frontier, Inc. (5x7-1/4")	14	43	72	125
Official Roy Rogers Riders Club Comics (1952; 16 pgs., reg. size, paper-c)	40	160	205	350

RUDOLPH, THE RED-NOSED REINDEER
Montgomery Ward: 1939 (2,400,000 copies printed); Dec, 1951 (Giveaway)

Paper cover-1st app. in print; written by Robert May; ill. by Denver Gillen	14	42	72	125
Hardcover version	20	60	105	175
1951 Edition (Has 1939 date)-36 pgs., slick-c printed in red & brown; pulp interior printed in four mixed-ink colors: red, green, blue & brown	9	27	51	75

1951 Edition with red-spiral promotional booklet printed on high quality stock, 8-1/2"x11", in red & brown, 25 pages composed of 4 fold outs, single sheets

Rudolph the Red-Nosed Reindeer © Montgomery Ward

Sergeant Preston - How He Became a Mountie © Quaker

	GD2.0	FN6.0	VF8.0	NM9.4
and the Rudolph comic book inserted (rare)	50	150	290	500

SAD CASE OF WAITING ROOM WILLIE, THE
American Visuals Corp. (For Baltimore Medical Society): (nd, 1950?)
(14 pgs. in color; paper covers; regular size)

	GD2.0	FN6.0	VF8.0	NM9.4
nn-By Will Eisner (Rare)	48	144	280	450

SAD SACK COMICS
Harvey Publications: 1957-1962
Armed Forces Complimentary copies, HD #1-40 (1957-1962)

	2	6	10	14

SALERNO CARNIVAL OF COMICS (Also see Pure Oil Comics, 24 Pages of Comics, & Vicks Comics)
Salerno Cookie Co.: Late 1930s (Giveaway, 16 pgs, paper-c)

nn-Color reprints of Calkins' Buck Rogers & Skyroads, plus other strips from Famous Funnies	50	150	290	475

SALUTE TO THE BOY SCOUTS
Association of American Railroads: 1960 (16 pgs.)

nn-History of scouting and the railroad	2	6	15	22

SANTA AND POLLYANNA PLAY THE GLAD GAME
Sales Promotion: Aug, 1960 (16 pgs.) (Disney giveaway)

nn	2	6	13	20

SANTA & THE BUCCANEERS
Promotional Publ. Co.: 1959 (Giveaway)

nn-Reprints 1952 Santa & the Pirates	2	6	12	18

SANTA & THE CHRISTMAS CHICKADEE
Murphy's: 1974 (Giveaway, 20 pgs.)

nn	1	3	6	9

SANTA & THE PIRATES
Promotional Publ. Co.: 1952 (Giveaway)

nn-Marv Levy-c/a	4	10	15	20

SANTA CLAUS FUNNIES (Also see The Little Fir Tree)
W. T. Grant Co./Whitman Publishing: nd; 1940 (Giveaway, 8x10"; 12 pgs., color & B&W, heavy paper)

nn-(2 versions- no date and 1940)	14	42	72	120

SANTA ON THE JOLLY ROGER
Promotional Publ. Co. (Giveaway): 1965

nn-Marv Levy-c/a	1	4	7	10

SANTA! SANTA!
R. Jackson: 1974 (20 pgs.) (Montgomery Ward giveaway)

nn	1	3	6	8

SANTA'S BUNDLE OF FUN
Gimbels: 1969 (Giveaway, B&W, 20 pgs.)

nn-Coloring book & games	1	4	7	10

SANTA'S CHRISTMAS COMIC VARIETY SHOW (See Merry Christmas From Sears Toyland)
Sears Roebuck Co.: 1943 (24 pgs.)
Contains puzzles & new comics of Dick Tracy, Little Orphan Annie, Moon Mullins, Terry & the Pirates, etc.

	81	325	480	675

SANTA'S CHRISTMAS TIME STORIES
Premium Sales, Inc.: nd (Late 1940s) (16 pgs., paper-c) (Giveaway)

nn	6	18	29	40

SANTA'S CIRCUS
Promotional Publ. Co.: 1964 (Giveaway, half-size)

nn-Marv Levy-c/a	2	6	9	12

SANTA'S FUN BOOK
Promotional Publ. Co.: 1951, 1952 (Regular size, 16 pgs., paper-c) (Murphy's giveaway)

nn	5	14	21	28

SANTA'S GIFT BOOK
No Publisher: No date (16 pgs.)

	GD2.0	FN6.0	VF8.0	NM9.4
nn-Puzzles, games only	4	10	15	20

SANTA'S NEW STORY BOOK
Wallace Hamilton Campbell: 1949 (16 pgs., paper-c) (Giveaway)

nn	6	18	29	40

SANTA'S REAL STORY BOOK
Wallace Hamilton Campbell/W. W. Orris: 1948, 1952 (Giveaway, 16 pgs.)

nn	6	18	29	40

SANTA'S RIDE
W. T. Grant Co.: 1959 (Giveaway)

nn	2	6	15	22

SANTA'S RODEO
Promotional Publ. Co.: 1964 (Giveaway, half-size)

nn-Marv Levy-a	2	6	9	12

SANTA'S SECRET CAVE
W. T. Grant Co.: 1960 (Giveaway, half-size)

nn	2	6	12	18

SANTA'S SECRETS
Sam B. Anson Christmas giveaway: 1951, 1952? (16 pgs., paper-c)

nn-Has games, stories & pictures to color	4	11	17	22

SANTA'S STORIES
K. K. Publications (Klines Dept. Store): 1953 (Regular size, paper-c)

nn-Kelly-a	17	51	88	150
nn-Another version (1953, glossy-c, half-size, 7-1/4x5-1/4")-Kelly-a	11	33	55	95

SANTA'S SURPRISE
K. K. Publications: 1947 (Giveaway, 36 pgs., slick-c)

nn	7	21	36	50

SANTA'S TOYTOWN FUN BOOK
Promotional Publ. Co.: 1953 (Giveaway)

nn-Marv Levy-c	4	10	15	20

SANTA TAKES A TRIP TO MARS
Bradshaw-Diehl Co., Huntington, W.VA.: 1950s (nd) (Giveaway, 16 pgs.)

nn	4	10	15	20

SERGEANT PRESTON OF THE YUKON
Quaker Cereals: 1956 (4 comic booklets) (Soft-c, 16 pgs., 7x2-1/2" & 5x2-1/2") Giveaways
"How He Found Yukon King", "The Case That Made Him A Sergeant", "How Yukon King Saved Him From The Wolves", "How He Became A Mountie" each...

	10	30	55	85

SHAZAM! (Visits Portland Oregon in 1943)
DC Comics: 1989 (69¢ cover)

nn-Promotes Super-Heroes exhibit at Oregon Museum of Science and Industry; reprints Golden Age Captain Marvel story	1	3	5	7

SHERIFF OF COCHISE, THE (TV)
Mobil: 1957 (16 pgs.) Giveaway

nn-Schaffenberger-a	4	10	15	20

SILLY PUTTY MAN
DC Comics: 1978

1				5.00

SKATING SKILLS
Custom Comics, Inc./Chicago Roller Skates: 1957 (36 & 12 pgs.; 5x7", two versions) (10¢)

nn-Resembles old ACG cover plus interior art	4	9	14	18

SKIPPY'S OWN BOOK OF COMICS (See Popular Comics)
No publisher listed: 1934 (Giveaway, 52 pgs., strip reprints)

nn-(Scarce)-By Percy Crosby	450	1350	2900	5200

Published by Max C. Gaines for Phillip's Dental Magnesia to be advertised on the Skippy Radio Show and given away with the purchase of a tube of Phillip's Tooth Paste. This is the first four-color comic book of reprints about one character.

Smokey Bear, True Story of... © DELL

Snow White - Mystery of the Missing Magic © WDC

Special Agent
© Assoc. of American Railroads

	GD2.0	FN6.0	VF8.0	NM9.4			GD2.0	FN6.0	VF8.0	NM9.4

SKY KING "RUNAWAY TRAIN" (TV)
National Biscuit Co.: 1964 (Regular size, 16 pgs.)

nn	20	50	65	85

SLAM BANG COMICS
Post Cereal Giveaway: No. 9, No date

9-Dynamic Man, Echo, Mr. E, Yankee Boy app.	9	27	49	70

SMILIN' JACK
Dell Publishing Co.
Popped Wheat Giveaway (1947)-1938 strip reprints; 16 pgs. in full color

	2	5	8	10
Shoe Store Giveaway-1938 strip reprints; 16 pgs.	5	15	25	35
Sparked Wheat Giveaway (1942)-16 pgs. in full color	5	15	25	35

SMOKEY BEAR (See Forest Fire for 1st app.)
Dell Publ. Co.: 1959,1960
True Story of..., The -U.S. Forest Service giveaway-Publ. by Western Printing Co.; reprints 1st 16 pgs. of Four Color #932. Inside front-c differs slightly in 1959 & 1960 editions

	4	12	18	24
1964,1969 reprints	4	9	14	18

SMOKEY STOVER
Dell Publishing Co.

General Motors giveaway (1953)	7	21	36	50
National Fire Protection giveaway(1953 & 1954)-16 pgs., paper-c	7	21	36	50

SNOW FOR CHRISTMAS
W. T. Grant Co.: 1957 (16 pgs.) (Giveaway)

nn	4	12	18	24

SNOW WHITE AND THE SEVEN DWARFS
Bendix Washing Machines: 1952 (32 pgs., 5x7-1/4", soft-c) (Disney)

nn	11	33	55	95

SNOW WHITE AND THE SEVEN DWARFS
Promotional Publ. Co.: 1957 (Small size)

nn	5	15	23	30

SNOW WHITE AND THE SEVEN DWARFS
Western Printing Co.: 1958 (16 pgs, 5x7-1/4", soft-c) (Disney premium)

nn- "Mystery of the Missing Magic"	7	21	38	55

SNOW WHITE AND THE 7 DWARFS IN "MILKY WAY"
American Dairy Assoc.: 1955 (16 pgs., soft-c, 5x7-1/4") (Disney premium)

nn	11	33	55	95

SPACE GHOST COAST TO COAST
Cartoon Network: Apr, 1994 (giveaway to Turner Broadcasting employees)

1-(8 pgs.); origin of Space Ghost				5.00

SPACE PATROL (TV)
Ziff-Davis Publishing Co. (Approved Comics)

...'s Special Mission (8 pgs.), B&W, Giveaway)	78	275	400	560

SPECIAL AGENT
Assoc. of American Railroads: Oct, 1959 (16 pgs.)

nn-The Story of the railroad police	8	24	42	60

SPECIAL DELIVERY
Post Hall Synd.: 1951 (32 pgs.; B&W) (Giveaway)
nn-Origin of Pogo, Swamp, etc.; 2 pg. biog. on Walt Kelly
(One copy sold in 1980 for $150.00)

SPECIAL EDITION (U. S. Navy Giveaways)
National Periodical Publications: 1944 - 1945 (Regular comic format with wording simplified, 52 pgs.)

1-Action (1944)-Reprints Action #80	59	177	365	600
2-Action (1944)-Reprints Action #81	59	177	365	600
3-Superman (1944)-Reprints Superman #33	59	177	365	600
4-Detective (1944)-Reprints Detective #97	59	177	365	600
5-Superman (1945)-Reprints Superman #34	59	177	365	600
6-Action (1945)-Reprints Action #84	59	177	365	600

NOTE: **Wayne Boring** c-1, 2, 6. **Dick Sprang** c-4.

SPIDER-MAN (See Amazing Spider-Man, The)

SPIRIT, THE (Weekly Comic Book)
Will Eisner: 6/2/40 - 10/5/52 (16 pgs.; 8 pgs.) (no cover) (in color)
(Distributed through various newspapers and other sources)
NOTE: **Eisner** script, pencils/inks for the most part from 6/2/40-4/26/42; a few stories assisted by Jack Cole, Fine, Powell and Kotsky.

6/2/40(#1)-Origin/1st app. The Spirit; reprinted in Police #11; Lady Luck (Brenda Banks)(1st app.) by Chuck Mazoujian & Mr. Mystic (1st. app.) by S. R. (Bob) Powell begin	55	165	341	600
6/9/40(#2)	27	81	145	250
6/16/40(#3)-Black Queen app. in Spirit	17	51	88	150
6/23/40(#4)-Mr. Mystic receives magical necklace	14	42	72	125.
6/30/40(#5)	14	42	72	125
7/7/40(#6)-1st app.: Spirit carplane; Black Queen app. in Spirit	14	42	72	125
7/14/40(#7)-8/4/40(#10): 7/21/40-Spirit becomes fugitive wanted for murder	12	36	61	100
8/11/40-9/22/40	11	33	55	90
9/29/40-Ellen drops engagement with Homer Creep	10	30	55	80
10/6/40-11/3/40	10	30	55	80
11/10/40-The Black Queen app.	10	30	55	80
11/17/40, 11/24/40	10	30	55	80
12/1/40-Ellen spanking by Spirit on cover & inside; Eisner-1st 3 pgs., J. Cole rest	14	42	72	120
12/8/40-3/9/41	8	24	45	65
3/16/41-Intro. & 1st app. Silk Satin	12	36	61	105
3/23/41-6/1/41: 5/11/41-Last Lady Luck by Mazoujian; 5/18/41-Lady Luck by Nick Viscardi begins, ends 2/22/42	8	24	45	65
6/8/41-2nd app. Satin; Spirit learns Satin is also a British agent	10	30	55	85
6/15/41-1st app. Twilight	9	27	51	75
6/22/41-Hitler app. in Spirit	9	27	51	75
6/29/41-1/25/42,2/8/42	7	21	38	55
2/1/42-1st app. Duchess	9	27	51	75
2/15/42-4/26/42-Lady Luck by Klaus Nordling begins 3/1/42	8	24	42	60
5/3/42-8/16/42-Eisner/Fine/Quality staff assists on Spirit	6	18	29	40
8/23/42-Satin cover splash; Spirit by Eisner/Fine although signed by Fine	10	30	55	80
8/30/42,9/27/42-10/11/42,10/25/42-11/8/42-Eisner/Fine/Quality staff assists on Spirit	6	18	29	40
9/6/42-9/20/42,10/18/42-Fine/Belfi art on Spirit; scripts by Manly Wade Wellman	5	14	21	28
11/15/42-12/6/42,12/20/42,12/27/42,1/17/43-4/18/43,5/9/43-8/8/43-Wellman/ Woolfolk scripts, Fine pencils, Quality staff inks	5	14	21	28
12/13/42,1/3/43,1/10/43,4/25/43,5/2/43-Eisner scripts/layouts; Fine pencils, Quality staff inks	5	15	25	35
8/15/43-Eisner script/layout; pencils/inks by Quality staff; Jack Cole-a	4	12	18	24
8/22/43-12/12/43-Wellman/Woolfolk scripts, Fine pencils, Quality staff inks; Mr. Mystic by Guardineer-10/10/43-10/24/43	4	12	18	24
12/19/43-8/13/44-Wellman/Woolfolk/Jack Cole scripts; Cole, Fine & Robin King-a; Last Mr. Mystic-5/14/44	4	11	17	22
8/20/44-12/16/45-Wellman/Woolfolk scripts; Fine art with unknown staff assists	4	11	17	22

NOTE: Scripts/layouts by Eisner, or Eisner/Nordling, Eisner/Mercer or Spranger/Eisner; inks by Eisner or Eisner/Spranger in issues 12/23/45-2/2/47.

12/23/45-1/6/46: 12/23/45-Christmas-c	5	15	25	35
1/13/46-Origin Spirit retold	7	21	38	55
1/20/46-1st postwar Satin app.	6	18	32	45
1/27/46-3/10/46: 3/3/46-Last Lady Luck by Nordling	5	15	25	35
3/17/46-Intro. & 1st app. Nylon	6	18	32	45
3/24/46,3/31/46,4/14/46	5	15	25	35
4/7/46-2nd app. Nylon	6	18	29	40
4/21/46-Intro. & 1st app. Mr. Carrion & His Pet Buzzard Julia	7	21	38	55
4/28/46-5/12/46,5/26/46-6/30/46: Lady Luck by Fred Schwab in issues 5/5/46-11/3/46	5	15	25	35

The Spirit 6/2/40 © Will Eisner

The Spirit 7/28/40 © Will Eisner

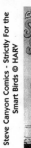
Steve Canyon Comics - Strictly For the Smart Birds © HARV

	GD2.0	FN6.0	VF8.0	NM9.4
5/19/46-2nd app. Mr. Carrion	6	18	29	40
7/7/46-Intro. & 1st app. Dulcet Tone & Skinny	6	18	32	45
7/14/46-9/29/46	5	15	25	35
10/6/46-Intro. & 1st app. P'Gell	7	21	38	55
10/13/46-11/3/46,11/16/46-11/24/46	5	15	25	35
11/10/46-2nd app. P'Gell	6	18	29	40
12/1/46-3rd app. P'Gell	6	18	28	38
12/8/46-2/2/47	5	15	23	30
NOTE: Scripts, pencils/inks by Eisner except where noted in issues 2/9/47-12/19/48.				
2/9/47-7/6/47: 6/8/47-Eisner self satire	5	15	23	30
7/13/47- "Hansel & Gretel" fairy tales	6	18	32	45
7/20/47-Li'L Abner, Daddy Warbucks, Dick Tracy, Fearless Fosdick parody; A-Bomb blast-c	7	21	36	50
7/27/47-9/14/47	5	15	23	35
9/21/47-Pearl Harbor flashback	5	15	25	35
9/28/47-1st mention of Flying Saucers in comics-3 months after 1st sighting in Idaho on 6/25/47	10	30	55	80
10/5/47- "Cinderella" fairy tales	6	18	32	45
10/12/47-11/30/47	5	15	23	30
12/7/47-Intro. & 1st app. Powder Pouf	7	21	38	55
12/14/47-12/28/47	5	15	23	30
1/4/48-2nd app. Powder Pouf	6	18	29	40
1/11/48-1st app. Sparrow Fallon; Powder Pouf app.	6	18	29	40
1/18/48-He-Man ad cover; satire issue	6	18	29	40
1/25/48-Intro. & 1st app. Castanet	7	21	36	50
2/1/48-2nd app. Castanet	5	15	25	35
2/8/48-3/7/48	5	15	23	30
3/14/48-Only app. Kretchma	5	15	25	35
3/21/48,3/28/48,4/11/48-4/25/48	5	15	23	30
4/4/48-Only app. Wild Rice	5	15	23	30
5/2/48-2nd app. Sparrow	5	15	23	30
5/9/48-6/27/48,7/11/48,7/18/48: 6/13/48-TV issue	5	15	23	30
7/4/48-Spirit by Andre Le Blanc	4	12	18	24
7/25/48-Ambrose Bierce's "The Thing" adaptation classic by Eisner/ Grandenetti	10	30	55	80
8/1/48-8/15/48,8/29/48-9/12/48	5	15	23	30
8/22/48-Poe's "Fall of the House of Usher" classic by Eisner/Grandenetti	10	30	55	80
9/19/48-Only app. Lorelei	6	18	29	40
9/26/48-10/31/48	5	15	23	30
11/7/48-Only app. Plaster of Paris	6	18	32	45
11/14/48-12/19/48	5	15	23	30
NOTE: Scripts by Eisner or Feiffer or Eisner/Feiffer or Nordling. Art by Eisner with backgrounds by Eisner, Grandenetti, Le Blanc, Stallman, Nordling, Dixon and/or others in issues 12/26/48-4/1/51 except where noted.				
12/26/48-Reprints some covers of 1948 with flashbacks	5	15	23	30
1/2/49-1/16/49	5	15	23	30
1/23/49,1/30/49-1st & 2nd app. Thorne	6	18	29	40
2/6/49-8/14/49	5	15	23	30
8/21/49,8/28/49-1st & 2nd app. Monica Veto	6	18	29	40
9/4/49,9/11/49	5	15	23	30
9/18/49-Love comic cover; has gag love comic ads on inside	6	18	29	40
9/25/49-Only app. Ice	5	15	25	35
10/2/49,10/9/49-Autumn News appears & dies in 10/9 issue				
	5	15	25	35
10/16/49-11/27/49,12/18/49,12/25/49	5	15	23	30
12/4/49,12/11/49-1st & 2nd app. Flaxen	5	15	23	30
1/1/50-Flashbacks to all of the Spirit girls-Thorne, Ellen, Satin, & Monica	8	24	42	60
1/8/50-Intro. & 1st app. Sand Saref	9	27	51	75
1/15/50-2nd app. Saref	7	21	38	55
1/22/50-2/5/50	5	15	23	30
2/12/50-Roller Derby issue	6	18	29	40
2/19/50-Half Dead Mr. Lox - Classic horror	6	18	32	45
2/26/50-4/23/50,5/14/50,5/28/50,7/23/50-9/3/50	5	15	23	30
4/30/50-Script/art by Eisner with framing	4	10	15	20
5/7/50,6/4/50-7/16/50-Abe Kanegson-a	4	10	15	20
5/21/50-Script by Feiffer/Eisner, art by Blaisdell, Eisner framing				
	4	10	15	20

	GD2.0	FN6.0	VF8.0	NM9.4
9/10/50-P'Gell returns	6	18	29	40
9/17/50-1/7/51	5	15	23	30
1/14/51-Life Magazine cover; brief biography of Comm. Dolan, Sand Saref, Silk Satin, P'Gell, Sammy & Willum, Darling O'Shea, & Mr. Carrion & His Pet Buzzard Julia, with pin-ups by Eisner	6	18	32	45
1/21/51,2/4/51-4/1/51	5	15	23	30
1/28/51- "The Meanest Man in the World" classic by Eisner				
	6	18	32	45
4/8/51-7/29/51,8/12/51-Last Eisner issue	5	15	23	30
8/5/51,8/19/51-7/20/52-Not Eisner	4	9	14	18
7/27/52-(Rare)-Denny Colt in Outer Space by Wally Wood; 7 pg. S/F story of E.C. vintage	32	95	160	260
8/3/52-(Rare)- "Mission...The Moon" by Wood	32	95	160	260
8/10/52-(Rare)- "A DP On The Moon" by Wood	32	95	160	260
8/17/52-(Rare)- "Heart" by Wood/Eisner	27	81	135	220
8/24/52-(Rare)- "Rescue" by Wood	32	95	160	260
8/31/52-(Rare)- "The Last Man" by Wood	32	95	160	260
9/7/52-(Rare)- "The Man in The Moon" by Wood	32	95	160	260
9/14/52-(Rare)-Eisner/Wenzel-a	10	30	55	80
9/21/52-(Rare)- "Denny Colt, Alias The Spirit/Space Report" by Eisner/Wenzel				
	11	33	55	95
9/28/52-(Rare)- "Return From The Moon" by Wood	32	95	160	260
10/5/52-(Rare)- "The Last Story" by Eisner	12	36	61	100
Large Tabloid pages from 1946 on (Eisner) - Price 200 percent over listed prices.				
NOTE: Spirit sections came out in both large and small format. Some newspapers went to the 8-pg. format months before others. Some printed the pages so they cannot be folded into a small comic book section; these are worth less. (Also see Three Comics & Spiritman).				

SPY SMASHER
Fawcett Publications
Well Known Comics (1944, 12 pgs., 8-1/2x10-1/2), paper-c, glued binding, printed in green; Bestmaid/Samuel Lowe giveaway

	GD2.0	FN6.0	VF8.0	NM9.4
	16	48	83	140

STANDARD OIL COMICS (Also see Gulf Funny Weekly)
Standard Oil Co.: 1933 (Giveaway, tabloid size, 4 pgs. in color)

	GD2.0	FN6.0	VF8.0	NM9.4
1-Series has original art	55	165	315	525
2-5	25	75	126	210
6-14: 14-Fred Opper strip, 1 pg.	13	39	66	110

STAR TEAM
Marvel Comics Group: 1977 (6-1/2x5", 20 pgs.) (Ideal Toy Giveaway)

	GD2.0	FN6.0	VF8.0	NM9.4
nn	2	6	9	12

STEVE CANYON COMICS
Harvey Publications

	GD2.0	FN6.0	VF8.0	NM9.4
Dept. Store giveaway #3(6/48, 36pp)	10	30	55	80
...'s Secret Mission (1951, 16 pgs., Armed Forces giveaway); Caniff-a	9	27	51	75
Strictly for the Smart Birds (1951, 16 pgs.)-Information Comics Div. (Harvey) Premium	9	27	49	70

STORIES OF CHRISTMAS
K. K. Publications: 1942 (Giveaway, 32 pgs., paper cover)

	GD2.0	FN6.0	VF8.0	NM9.4
nn-Adaptation of "A Christmas Carol"; Kelly story "The Fir Tree"; Infinity-c	38	113	195	320

STORY HOUR SERIES (Disney)
Whitman Publ. Co.: 1948, 1949; 1951-1953 (36 pgs., paper-c) (4-3/4x6-1/2")
Given away with subscription to Walt Disney's Comics & Stories

	GD2.0	FN6.0	VF8.0	NM9.4
nn(1948)-Mickey Mouse and the Boy Thursday	12	36	61	100
nn(1948)-Mickey Mouse the Miracle Master	12	36	61	100
nn(1948)-Minnie Mouse and Antique Chair	12	36	61	100
nn(1949)-The Three Orphan Kittens(B&W & color)	7	21	38	55
nn(1949)-Danny-The Little Black Lamb	7	21	38	55
800(1948)-Donald Duck in "Bringing Up the Boys"	17	51	88	150
1953 edition	11	33	55	95
801(1948)-Mickey Mouse's Summer Vacation	9	27	51	75
1951, 1952 editions	5	15	25	35
802(1948)-Bugs Bunny's Adventures	8	24	42	60
803(1948)-Bongo	6	18	32	45
804(1948)-Mickey and the Beanstalk	8	24	42	60

Story of Harry S. Truman © DNC

Super-Book of Comics #1 ('44) © KING

Super-Book of Comics #2 ('44) © KING

	GD2.0	FN6.0	VF8.0	NM9.4
805-15(1949)-Andy Panda and His Friends	7	21	36	50
806-15(1949)-Tom and Jerry	7	21	38	55
808-15(1949)-Johnny Appleseed	6	18	32	45
1948, 1949 Hard Cover Edition of each….30% - 40% more.				

STORY OF EDISON, THE
Educational Comics: 1956 (16 pgs.) (Reddy Killowatt)

nn-Reprint of Reddy Kilowatt #2(1947)	7	21	36	50

STORY OF HARRY S. TRUMAN, THE
Democratic National Committee: 1948 (Giveaway, regular size, soft-c, 16 pg.)

nn-Gives biography on career of Truman; used in SOTI, pg. 311				
	14	42	72	120

STORY OF THE BALLET, THE
Selva and Sons, Inc.: 1954 (16 pgs., paper cover)

nn	4	10	15	20

STRANGE AS IT SEEMS
McNaught Syndicate: 1936 (B&W, 5x7", 24 pgs.)

nn-Ex-Lax giveaway	7	21	38	55

SUGAR BEAR
Post Cereal Giveaway: No date, circa 1975? (2-1/2x4-1/2", 16 pgs.)

"The Almost Take Over of the Post Office", "The Race Across the Atlantic",				
"The Zoo Goes Wild" each…	1	3	6	8

SUNDAY WORLD'S EASTER EGG FULL OF EASTER MEAT FOR LITTLE PEOPLE
Supplement to the New York World: 3/27/1898 (soft-c, 16pg, 4"x8" approx., opens at top, color & B&W)(Giveaway)(shaped like an Easter egg)

nn-By R.F. Outcault	17	51	88	150

SUPER BOOK OF COMICS
Western Publishing Co.: nd (1942-1943?) (Soft-c, 32 pgs.) (Pan-Am/Gilmore Oil/Kelloggs premiums)

nn-Dick Tracy (Gilmore)-Magic Morro app.	40	120	232	400
1-Dick Tracy & The Smuggling Ring; Stratosphere Jim app. (Rare) (Pan-Am)				
	40	120	232	400
1-Smilin' Jack, Magic Morro (Pan-Am)	15	45	77	135
2-Smilin' Jack, Stratosphere Jim (Pan-Am)	15	45	77	135
2-Smitty, Magic Morro (Pan-Am)	15	45	77	135
3-Captain Midnight, Magic Morro (Pan-Am)	31	93	168	290
3-Moon Mullins?	15	45	77	135
4-Red Ryder, Magic Morro (Pan-Am). Same content as Red Ryder Victory				
Patrol comic w/diff. cover	19	57	99	165
4-Smitty, Stratosphere Jim (Pan-Am)	15	45	77	135
5-Don Winslow, Magic Morro (Gilmore)	19	57	99	165
5-Don Winslow, Stratosphere Jim (Pan-Am)	19	57	99	165
5-Terry & the Pirates	22	66	116	200
6-Don Winslow, Stratosphere Jim (Pan-Am)-McWilliams-a				
	19	57	99	165
6-King of the Royal Mounted, Magic Morro (Pan-Am)				
	19	57	99	165
7-Dick Tracy, Magic Morro (Pan-Am)	25	75	133	230
7-Little Orphan Annie	13	39	66	115
8-Dick Tracy, Stratosphere Jim (Pan-Am)	22	66	116	200
8-Dan Dunn, Magic Morro (Pan-Am)	13	39	66	115
9-Terry & the Pirates, Magic Morro (Pan-Am)	22	66	116	200
10-Red Ryder, Magic Morro (Pan-Am)	19	57	99	165

SUPER-BOOK OF COMICS
Western Publishing Co.: (Omar Bread & Hancock Oil Co. giveaways) 1944 - No. 30, 1947 (Omar); 1947 - 1948 (Hancock) (16 pgs.)

Note: The Hancock issues are all exact reprints of the earlier Omar issues. The issue numbers were removed in some of the reprints.

1-Dick Tracy (Omar, 1944)	22	66	116	195
1-Dick Tracy (Hancock, 1947)	16	48	83	145
2-Bugs Bunny (Omar, 1944)	8	24	42	60
2-Bugs Bunny (Hancock, 1947)	6	18	32	46
3-Terry & the Pirates (Omar, 1944)	12	36	61	105
3-Terry & the Pirates (Hancock, 1947)	11	33	55	90

	GD2.0	FN6.0	VF8.0	NM9.4
4-Andy Panda (Omar, 1944)	8	24	42	60
4-Andy Panda (Hancock, 1947)	6	18	32	46
5-Smokey Stover (Omar, 1945)	6	18	32	46
5-Smokey Stover (Hancock, 1947)	5	15	25	35
6-Porky Pig (Omar, 1945)	8	24	42	60
6-Porky Pig (Hancock, 1947)	6	18	32	46
7-Smilin' Jack (Omar, 1945)	8	24	42	60
7-Smilin' Jack (Hancock, 1947)	6	18	32	46
8-Oswald the Rabbit (Omar, 1945)	6	18	32	46
8-Oswald the Rabbit (Hancock, 1947)	5	15	25	35
9-Alley Oop (Omar, 1945)	13	39	66	115
9-Alley Oop (Hancock, 1947)	12	36	61	105
10-Elmer Fudd (Omar, 1945)	6	18	32	46
10-Elmer Fudd (Hancock, 1947)	5	15	25	35
11-Little Orphan Annie (Omar, 1945)	8	24	44	64
11-Little Orphan Annie (Hancock, 1947)	7	21	37	54
12-Woody Woodpecker (Omar, 1945)	6	18	32	46
12-Woody Woodpecker (Hancock, 1947)	5	15	25	35
13-Dick Tracy (Omar, 1945)	13	39	66	115
13-Dick Tracy (Hancock, 1947)	12	36	61	105
14-Bugs Bunny (Omar, 1945)	6	18	32	46
14-Bugs Bunny (Hancock, 1947)	5	15	25	35
15-Andy Panda (Omar, 1945)	6	18	29	40
15-Andy Panda (Hancock, 1947)	5	15	25	35
16-Terry & the Pirates (Omar, 1945)	12	36	61	105
16-Terry & the Pirates (Hancock, 1947)	9	27	51	75
17-Smokey Stover (Omar, 1946)	6	18	32	46
17-Smokey Stover (Hancock, 1948?)	5	15	25	35
18-Porky Pig (Omar, 1946)	6	18	29	40
18-Porky Pig (Hancock, 1948?)	5	15	25	35
19-Smilin' Jack (Omar, 1946)	6	18	32	46
nn-Smilin' Jack (Hancock, 1948)	5	15	25	35
20-Oswald the Rabbit (Omar, 1946)	6	18	29	40
nn-Oswald the Rabbit (Hancock, 1948)	5	15	25	35
21-Gasoline Alley (Omar, 1946)	8	24	44	64
nn-Gasoline Alley (Hancock, 1948)	7	21	37	54
22-Elmer Fudd (Omar, 1946)	6	18	29	40
nn-Elmer Fudd (Hancock, 1948)	5	15	25	35
23-Little Orphan Annie (Omar, 1946)	8	24	42	60
nn-Little Orphan Annie (Hancock, 1948)	6	18	32	46
24-Woody Woodpecker (Omar, 1946)	6	18	29	40
nn-Woody Woodpecker (Hancock, 1948)	5	15	25	35
25-Dick Tracy (Omar, 1946)	12	36	61	105
nn-Dick Tracy (Hancock, 1948)	10	30	55	80
26-Bugs Bunny (Omar, 1946))	6	18	29	40
nn-Bugs Bunny (Hancock, 1948)	5	15	25	35
27-Andy Panda (Omar, 1946)	6	18	29	40
27-Andy Panda (Hancock, 1948)	5	15	25	35
28-Terry & the Pirates (Omar, 1946)	12	36	61	105
28-Terry & the Pirates (Hancock, 1948)	10	30	55	75
29-Smokey Stover (Omar, 1947)	6	18	29	40
29-Smokey Stover (Hancock, 1948)	5	15	25	35
30-Porky Pig (Omar, 1947)	6	18	29	40
30-Porky Pig (Hancock, 1948)	5	15	25	35
nn-Bugs Bunny (Hancock, 1948)-Does not match any Omar book				
	6	18	29	40

SUPER CIRCUS (TV)
Cross Publishing Co.

1-(1951, Weather Bird Shoes giveaway)	7	21	36	50

SUPER FRIENDS
DC Comics: 1981 (Giveaway, no ads, no code or price)

…Special 1 -r/Super Friends #19 & 36				5.00

SUPERGEAR COMICS
Jacobs Corp.: 1976 (Giveaway, 4 pgs. in color, slick paper)

nn-(Rare)-Superman, Lois Lane; Steve Lombard app. (500 copies printed,				
over half destroyed?)	7	21	50	80

SUPERGIRL
DC Comics: 1984, 1986 (Giveaway, Baxter paper)

Super Friends Special #1 © DC

Superman Radio Shack Giveaway © DC

Superman-Tim 7/43 © DC

	GD2.0	FN6.0	VF8.0	NM9.4

nn-(American Honda/U.S. Dept. Transportation) Torres-c/a 3.00

SUPER HEROES PUZZLES AND GAMES
General Mills Giveaway (Marvel Comics Group): 1979 (32 pgs., regular size)

nn-Four 2-pg. origin stories of Spider-Man, Captain America, The Hulk, & Spider-Woman	2	6	13	20

SUPERMAN
National Periodical Publ./DC Comics

	GD2.0	FN6.0	VF8.0	NM9.4
72-Giveaway(9-10/51)-(Rare)-Price blackened out; came with banner wrapped around book; without banner	74	221	450	750
72-Giveaway with banner	103	308	625	1050
Bradman birthday custom (1988)				3.00
… For the Animals (2000, Doris Day Animal Foundation, 30 pgs.) polybagged with Gotham Adventures #22, Hourman #12, Impulse #58, Looney Tunes #62, Stars and S.T.R.I.P.E. #8 and Superman Adventures #41				2.50
Kelloggs Giveaway-(2/3 normal size, 1954)-r-two stories/Superman #55		34	103	165	280
Kenner: Man of Steel (Doomsday is Coming) (1995, 16 pgs.) packaged with set of Superman and Doomsday action figures				2.50
…Meets the Quik Bunny (1987, Nestles Quik premium, 36 pgs.)				5.00
Pizza Hut Premiums (12/77)-Exact reprints of 1950s comics except for paid ads (set of 6 exist?); Vol. 1-r#97 (#113-r also known)				6.00
Radio Shack Giveaway-36 pgs. (7/80) "The Computers That Saved Metropolis", Starlin/Giordano-a; advertising insert in Action #509, New Advs. of Superboy #7, Legion of Super-Heroes #265, & House of Mystery #282. (All comics were 68 pgs.) Cover of inserts printed on newsprint. Giveaway contains 4 extra pgs. of Radio Shack advertising that inserts do not have				4.00
Radio Shack Giveaway-(7/81) "Victory by Computer"				4.00
Radio Shack Giveaway-(7/82) "Computer Masters of Metropolis"				4.00

SUPERMAN ADVENTURES, THE (TV)
DC Comics: 1996 (Based on animated series)

1-(1996) Preview issue distributed at Warner Bros. stores				3.00
Titus Game Edition (1998)				2.25

SUPERMAN AND THE GREAT CLEVELAND FIRE
National Periodical Publ.: 1948 (Giveaway, 4 pgs., no cover) (Hospital Fund)

nn-In full color	90	300	450	650

SUPERMAN (Miniature)
National Periodical Publ.: 1942; 1955 - 1956 (3 issues, no #'s, 32 pgs.)
The pages are numbered in the 1st issue: 1-32; 2nd: 1A-32A and 3rd: 1B-32B

	GD2.0	FN6.0	VF8.0	NM9.4
No date-Py-Co-Pay Tooth Powder giveaway (8 pgs.; circa 1942)	74	221	450	750
1-The Superman Time Capsule (Kellogg's Sugar Smacks)(1955)	48	144	300	480
1A-Duel in Space (1955)	45	135	270	425
1B-The Super Show of Metropolis (also #1-32, no B)(1955)	45	135	270	425

NOTE: Numbering variations exist. Each title could have any combination-#1, 1A, or 1B.

SUPERMAN RECORD COMIC
National Periodical Publications: 1966 (Golden Records)

	GD2.0	FN6.0	VF8.0	NM9.4
(With record)-Comic reads origin of Superman from comic; came with iron-on patch, decoder, membership card & button; comic-r/Superman #125,146				
	22	66	116	200
Comic only	13	39	66	110

SUPERMAN'S BUDDY (Costume Comic)
National Periodical Publications: 1954 (4 pgs., slick paper-c; one-shot)
(Came in box w/costume)

	GD2.0	FN6.0	VF8.0	NM9.4
1-w/box & costume	131	395	830	1400
Comic only	63	189	390	650
1-(1958 edition)-Printed in 2 colors	20	60	105	175

SUPERMAN'S CHRISTMAS ADVENTURE
National Periodical Publications: 1940, 1944 (Giveaway, 16 pgs.)
Distributed by Nehi drinks, Bailey Store, Ivey-Keith Co., Kennedy's Boys Shop, Macy's Store, Boston Store

	GD2.0	FN6.0	VF8.0	NM9.4
1(1940)-Burnley-a; F. Ray-c/r from Superman #6 (Scarce)-Superman saves Santa Claus. Santa makes real Superman Toys offered in 1940. 1st merchandising story	625	2500	3600	5200

	GD2.0	FN6.0	VF8.0	NM9.4
nn(1944) w/Santa Claus & X-mas tree-c	128	511	790	1200
nn(1944) w/Candy cane & Superman-c	117	467	725	1100

SUPERMAN-TIM (Becomes Tim)
Superman-Tim Stores/National Periodical Publ.: Aug, 1942 - May, 1950
(Half size) (B&W Giveaway w/2 color covers) (Publ. monthly 2/43 on)

	GD2.0	FN6.0	VF8.0	NM9.4
8/42 (#1)-All have Superman illos.	150	600	900	1250
1/43 (#2)	44	133	260	425
2/43 (#3)	42	125	245	400
3/43 (#4)	42	125	245	400
4/43, 5/43, 6/43, 7/43, 8/43	40	120	206	350
9/43, 10/43, 11/43, 12/43	35	105	178	300
1/44-12/44	28	83	140	240
1/45-5/45, 10-12/45, 1/46-8/46	25	75	128	220
6/45-Classic Superman-c	28	84	140	240
7/45-Classic Superman flag-c	28	84	140	240
9/45-1st stamp album issue	60	180	370	600
9/46-2nd stamp album issue	48	144	290	475
10/46-1st Superman story	35	105	180	300
11/46, 12/46, 1/47-8/47 issues-Superman story in each; 2/47-Infinity-c. All 36 pgs.	35	105	180	300
9/47-Stamp album issue & Superman story	45	135	265	450
10/47, 11/47, 12/47-Superman stories (24 pgs.)	35	105	180	300
1/48-7/48,10/48, 11/48, 2/49, 4/49-11/49	28	84	140	240
8/48-Contains full page ad for Superman-Tim watch giveaway	28	83	140	240
9/48-Stamp album issue	36	108	190	325
1/49-Full page Superman bank cut-out	28	83	147	250
3/49-Full page Superman boxing game cut-out	28	83	147	250
4/49-3/50, 5/50-Superman stories	31	94	160	275
4/50-Superman story, baseball stories; photo-c without Superman	33	99	174	300

NOTE: All issues have Superman illustrations throughout. The page count varies depending on whether a Superman-Tim comic story is inserted. If it is, the page count is either 36 or 24 pages. Otherwise all issues are 16 pages. Each issue has a special place for inserting a full color Superman stamp. The stamp album issues had spaces for the stamps given away the past year. The books were mailed as a subscription premium. The stamps were given away free (or when you made a purchase) when you physically came into the store.

SUPER SEAMAN SLOPPY
Allied Pristine Union Council, Buffalo, NY: 1940s, 8pg., reg. size (Soft-c)

	GD2.0	FN6.0	VF8.0	NM9.4
nn	4	11	17	22

SWAMP FOX, THE
Walt Disney Productions: 1960 (14 pgs, small size) (Canada Dry Premiums)
Titles: (A)-Tory Masquerade, (B)-Turnabout Tactics, (C)-Rindau Rampage; each came in paper sleeve, books 1,2 & 3;

	GD2.0	FN6.0	VF8.0	NM9.4
Set with sleeves	5	15	38	60
Comic only	2	6	12	18

SWORDQUEST
DC Comics/Atari Pub.: 1982, 52pg., 5"x7" (Giveaway with video games)

	GD2.0	FN6.0	VF8.0	NM9.4
1,2-Roy Thomas & Gerry Conway-s; George Pérez & Dick Giordano-c/a in all	2	6	9	12
3-Low print	2	6	11	15

SYNDICATE FEATURES (Sci/fi)
Harry A. Chesler Syndicate: V1#3, 11/15/37 (Tabloid size, 3 colors, 4 pgs.) (Editors premium)(Came folded)

	GD2.0	FN6.0	VF8.0	NM9.4
V1#3-Dan Hastings daily strips-Guardineer-a	560	1680	2200	3000

TASTEE-FREEZ COMICS
Harvey Comics: 1957 (10¢, 36 pgs.)(6 different issues given away)

	GD2.0	FN6.0	VF8.0	NM9.4
1,3: 1-Little Dot. 3-Casper	4	12	30	50
2,4,5: 2-Rags Rabbit. 4-Sad Sack. 5-Mazie	3	10	23	35
6-Dick Tracy	4	12	30	50

TAYLOR'S CHRISTMAS TABLOID
Dept. Store Giveaway: Mid 1930s, Cleveland, Ohio (Tabloid size; in color)

nn-(Very Rare)-Among the earliest pro work of Siegel & Shuster; one full color page called "The Battle in the Stratosphere", with a pre-Superman look; Shuster art throughout. (Only 1 known copy) Estimated value…				4000.00

	GD2.0	FN6.0	VF8.0	NM9.4

TAZ'S 40TH BIRTHDAY BLOWOUT
DC Comics: 1994 (K-Mart giveaway, 16 pgs.)

nn-Six pg. story, games and puzzles				2.25

TEE AND VEE CROSLEY IN TELEVISION LAND COMICS
(Also see Crosley's House of Fun)
Crosley Division, Avco Mfg. Corp. : 1951 (52 pgs.; 8x11"; paper cover; in color) (Giveaway)

Many stories, puzzles, cut-outs, games, etc.	6	18	29	40

TENNESSEE JED (Radio)
Fox Syndicate? (Wm. C. Popper & Co.): nd (1945) (16 pgs.; paper cover; regular size; giveaway)

nn	25	75	130	225

TENNIS (...For Speed, Stamina, Strength, Skill)
Tennis Educational Foundation: 1956 (16 pgs.; soft cover; 10¢)

Book 1-Endorsed by Gene Tunney, Ralph Kiner, etc. showing how tennis has helped them	5	15	25	35

TERRY AND THE PIRATES
Dell Publishing Co.: 1939 - 1953 (By Milton Caniff)

Buster Brown Shoes giveaway(1938)-32 pgs.; in color	25	75	130	225
Canada Dry Premiums-Books #1-3(1953, 36 pgs.; 2x5")-Harvey; #1-Hot Shot Charlie Flies Again; 2-In Forced Landing; 3-Dragon Lady in Distress)	16	48	83	140
Gambles Giveaway (1938, 16 pgs.)	9	27	51	75
Gillmore Giveaway (1938, 24 pgs.)	10	30	55	80
Popped Wheat Giveaway(1938)-Strip reprints in full color; Caniff-a	2	5	8	10
Shoe Store giveaway (Weatherbird)(1938, 16 pgs., soft-c)(2-diff.)	10	30	55	80
Sparked Wheat Giveaway(1942, 16 pgs.)-In color	10	30	55	80

TERRY AND THE PIRATES
Libby's Radio Premium: 1941 (16 pgs.; reg. size)(shipped folded in the mail)

"Adventure of the Ruby of Genghis Khan" - Each pg. is a puzzle that must be completed to read the story	400	1320	2500	-

THAT THE WORLD MAY BELIEVE
Catechetical Guild Giveaway: No date (16 pgs.) (Graymoor Friars distr.)

nn	3	7	11	14

3-D COLOR CLASSICS (Wendy's Kid's Club)
Wendy's Int'l Inc.: 1995 (5 1/2" x 8", comes with 3-D glasses)

The Elephant's Child, Gulliver's Travels, Peter Pan, The Time Machine, 20,000 Leagues Under the Sea: Neal Adams-a in all each....			3.00

350 YEARS OF AMERICAN DAIRY FOODS
American Dairy Assoc.: 1957 (5x7", 16 pgs.)

nn-History of milk	3	8	12	15

THUMPER (Disney)
Grosset & Dunlap: 1942 (50¢, 32pgs., hardcover book, 7"x8-1/2" w/dust jacket)

nn-Given away (along with a copy of Bambi) for a $2.00, 2-year subscription to WDC&S in 1942. (Xmas offer). Book only	17	51	88	150
Dust jacket only	9	27	51	75

TILLY AND TED-TINKERTOTLAND
W. T. Grant Co.: 1945 (Giveaway, 20 pgs.)

nn-Christmas comic	7	21	36	50

TIM (Formerly Superman-Tim; becomes Gene Autry-Tim)
Tim Stores: June, 1950 - Oct, 1950 (B&W, half-size)

4 issues; 6/50, 9/50, 10/50 known	17	51	88	150

TIM AND SALLY'S ADVENTURES AT MARINELAND
Marineland Restaurant & Bar, Marineland, CA: 1957 (5x7", 16 pgs., soft-c)

nn-copyright Oceanarium, Inc.	2	6	9	12

TIME OF DECISION
Harvey Publications Inc.: (16 pgs., paper cover)

nn-ROTC recruitment	4	10	15	20

	GD2.0	FN6.0	VF8.0	NM9.4

TIM IN SPACE (Formerly Gene Autry Tim; becomes Tim Tomorrow)
Tim Stores: 1950 (1/2 size giveaway) (B&W)

nn	12	36	61	100

TIM TOMORROW (Formerly Tim In Space)
Tim Stores: 8/51, 9/51, 10/51, Christmas, 1951 (5x7-3/4")

nn-Prof. Fumble & Captain Kit Comet in all	12	36	61	100

TITANS BEAT (Teen Titans)
DC Comics: Aug, 1996 (16 pgs., paper-c)

1-Intro./preview new Teen Titans members; Pérez-a				2.25

TOM MIX (...Commandos Comics #10-12)
Ralston-Purina Co.: Sept, 1940 - No. 12, Nov, 1942 (36 pgs.); 1983 (one-shot)
Given away for two Ralston box-tops; 1983 came in cereal box

1-Origin (life) Tom Mix; Fred Meagher-a	350	1750	2500	3600
2	106	319	650	1000
3-9	66	197	400	650
10-12: 10-Origin Tom Mix Commando Unit; Speed O'Dare begins; Japanese sub-c. 12-Sci/fi-c	55	165	325	550
1983- "Taking of Grizzly Grebb", Toth-a; 16 pg. miniature	2	6	11	15

TOM SAWYER COMICS
Giveaway: 1951? (Paper cover)

nn-Contains a coverless Hopalong Cassidy from 1951; other combinations known	3	9	17	25

TOPPS COMICS PRESENTS
Topps Comics: No. 0, 1993 (Giveaway, B&W, 36 pgs.)

0-Dracula vs. Zorro, Teenagents, Silver Star, & Bill the Galactic Hero				2.50

TOWN THAT FORGOT SANTA, THE
W. T. Grant Co.: 1961 (Giveaway, 24 pgs.)

nn	3	9	17	25

TOY LAND FUNNIES (See Funnies On Parade)
Eastern Color Printing Co.: 1934 (32 pgs., Hecht Co. store giveaway)

nn-Reprints Buck Rogers Sunday pages #199-201 from Famous Funnies #5. A rare variation of Funnies On Parade; same format, similar contents, same cover except for large Santa placed in center (value will be based on sale)				

TOY WORLD FUNNIES (See Funnies On Parade)
Eastern Color Printing Co.: 1933 (36 pgs., slick cover, Golden Eagle and Wanamaker giveaway)

nn-Contains contents from Funnies On Parade/Century Of Comics. A rare variation of Funnies On Parade; same format, similar contents, same cover except for large Santa placed in center (value will be based on sale)				

TRAPPED
Harvey Publications (Columbia Univ. Press): 1951 (Giveaway, soft-c, 16 pgs)

nn-Drug education comic (30,000 printed?) distributed to schools.; mentioned in SOTI, pgs. 256,350	2	5	8	10

NOTE: Many copies surfaced in 1979 causing a setback in price; beware of trimmed edges, because many copies have a brittle edge.

TRIP TO OUTER SPACE WITH SANTA
Sales Promotions, Inc/Peoria Dry Goods: 1950s (paper-c)

nn-Comics, games & puzzles	4	12	19	25

TRIP WITH SANTA ON CHRISTMAS EVE, A
Rockford Dry Goods Co.: No date (Early 1950s) (Giveaway, 16 pgs., paper-c)

nn	4	12	19	25

TRUTH BEHIND THE TRIAL OF CARDINAL MINDSZENTY, THE (See Cardinal Mindszenty)

24 PAGES OF COMICS (No title) (Also see Pure Oil Comics, Salerno Carnival of Comics, & Vicks Comics)
Giveaway by various outlets including Sears: Late 1930s

nn-Contains strip reprints-Buck Rogers, Napoleon, Sky Roads, War on Crime	50	150	250	350

TWISTED METAL (Video game)
DC Comics: 1996

	GD2.0	FN6.0	VF8.0	NM9.4

	GD2.0	FN6.0	VF8.0	NM9.

nn   2.25

TWO FACES OF COMMUNISM (Also see Double Talk)
Christian Anti-Communism Crusade, Houston, Texas: 1961 (Giveaway, paper-c, 36 pgs.)

nn	13	39	66	110

2001, A SPACE ODYSSEY (Movie)
Marvel Comics Group
Howard Johnson giveaway (1968, 8pp); 6 pg. movie adaptation, 2 pg. games, puzzles; McWilliams-a

	1	3	6	9

UNCLE SAM'S CHRISTMAS STORY
Promotional Publ. Co.: 1958 (Giveaway)
nn-Reprints 1956 Christmas USA   2   6   11   15

UNKEPT PROMISE
Legion of Truth: 1949 (Giveaway, 24 pgs.)
nn-Anti-alcohol   9   27   49   70

UNTOLD LEGEND OF THE BATMAN, THE
DC Comics: 1989 (28 pgs., 6X9", limited series)
1-3: Batman cereal premiums; 1st & 2nd printings known   6.00

UNTOUCHABLES, THE (TV)
Leaf Brands, Inc.
Topps Bubblegum premiums produced by Leaf Brands, Inc.-2-1/2x4-1/2", 8 pgs. (3 diff. issues) "The Organization, Jamaica Ginger, The Otto Frick Story (drug), 3000 Suspects, The Antidote, Mexican Stakeout, Little Egypt, Purple Gang, Bugs Moran Story, & Lily Dallas Story"   3   9   20   30

VICKS COMICS (See Pure Oil Comics, Salerno Carnival of Comics & 24 Pages of Comics)
Eastern Color Printing Co. (Vicks Chemical Co.): nd (circa 1938) (Giveaway, 68 pgs. in color)
nn-Famous Funnies-r (before #40); contains 5 pgs. Buck Rogers (4 pgs. from F.F. #15, & 1 pg. from #16) Joe Palooka, Napoleon, etc. app.   69   206   420   675
nn-16 loose, untrimmed page giveaway; paper-c; r/Famous Funnies #14; Buck Rogers, Joe Palooka app. Has either "Vicks Comics" printed on cover or only a local store name as the logo.   26   79   130   220

WALT DISNEY'S COMICS & STORIES
K.K. Publications: 1942-1963 known (7-1/3"x10-1/4", 4 pgs. in color, slick paper) (folded horizontally once or twice as mailers) (Xmas subscription offer)
1942 mailer-r/Kelly cover to WDC&S 25; 2-year subscription + two Grosset & Dunlap hardcover books (32-pages each), of Bambi and of Thumper, offered for $2.00; came in an illustrated C&S envelope with an enclosed postage paid envelope (Rare)   Mailer only   25   75   156   275
     with envelopes   32   96   200   350
1947,1948 mailer   18   54   113   200
1949 mailer-A rare Barks item: Same WDC&S cover as 1942 mailer, but with art changed so that nephew is handing teacher Donald a comic book rather than an apple, as originally drawn by Kelly. The tiny, 7/8"x1-1/4" cover shown was a rejected cover by Barks that was intended for C&S 110, but was redrawn by Kelly for C&S 111. The original art has been lost and this is its only app. (Rare)   45   135   285   500
1950 mailer-P.1 r/Kelly cover to Dell Xmas Parade 1 (without title); p.2 r/Kelly cover to C&S 101 (w/o title), but with the art altered to show Donald reading C&S 122 (by Kelly); hardcover book, "Donald Duck in Bringing Up the Boys" given with a $1.00 one-year subscription; P.4 r/full Kelly Xmas cover to C&S 99 (Rare)   18   54   113   200
1953 mailer-P.1 r/cover Dell Xmas Parade 4 (w/o title); insides offer "Donald Duck Full Speed Ahead," a 28-page, color, 5-5/8"x6-5/8" book, not of the Story Hour series; P.4 r/full Barks C&S 148 cover (Rare)   13   39   81   140
1963 mailer-Pgs. 1,2 & 4 r/GK Xmas art; P.3 r/a 1963 C&S cover (Scarce)   9   27   56   95
NOTE: *It is assumed a different mailer was printed each Xmas for at least twenty years. A 1952 mailer is known.*

WALT DISNEY'S COMICS & STORIES
Walt Disney Productions: 1943 (36 pgs.) (Dept. store Xmas giveaway)

---

nn-X-Mas-c with Donald & the Boys; Donald Duck by Jack Hannah; Thumper by Ken Hultgren   49   147   306   540

WATCH OUT FOR BIG TALK
Giveaway: 1950
nn-Dan Barry-a; about crooked politicians   6   18   29   40

WEATHER-BIRD (See Comics From..., Dick Tracy, Free Comics to You... Super Circus & Terry and the Pirates)
International Shoe Co./Western Printing Co.: 1958 - No. 16, July, 1962 (Shoe store giveaway)

	GD	FN	VF	NM
1	4	12	26	40
2-16	2	6	13	20

NOTE: *The numbers are located in the lower bottom panel, pg. 1. All feature a character called Weather-Bird.*

WEATHER BIRD COMICS (See Comics From Weather Bird)
Weather Bird Shoes: 1957 (Giveaway)
nn-Contains a comic bound with new cover. Several combinations possible; contents determines price (40 - 60 percent of contents).

WEEKLY COMIC MAGAZINE
Fox Publications: May 12, 1940 (16 pgs.) (Others exist w/o super-heroes)
(1st Version)-8 pg. Blue Beetle story, 7 pg. Patty O'Day story; two copies known to exist. Estimated value... $600
(2nd Version)-7 two-pg. adventures of Blue Beetle, Patty O'Day, Yarko, Dr. Fung, Green Mask, Spark Stevens, & Rex Dexter; one copy known to exist. Estimated value...   500
(3rd version)-Captain Valor (only one known copy)   300
Discovered with business papers, letters and exploitation material promoting **Weekly Comic Magazine** for use by newspapers in the same manner of **The Spirit** weeklies. Interesting note: these are dated three weeks before the first Spirit comic. Letters indicate that samples may have been sent to a few newspapers. These sections were actually 15-1/2x22" pages which would fold down to an approximate 8x10" comic booklet. Other various comic sections were found with the above but were more like the Sunday comic sections in format.

WHAT DO YOU KNOW ABOUT THIS COMICS SEAL OF APPROVAL?
No publisher listed (DC Comics Giveaway): nd (1955) (4 pgs., slick paper-c)
nn-(Rare)   68   205   426   750

WHAT'S BEHIND THESE HEADLINES
William C. Popper Co.: 1948 (16 pgs.)
nn-Comic insert "The Plot to Steal the World"   6   18   29   40

WHAT'S IN IT FOR YOU?
Harvey Publications Inc.: (16 pgs., paper cover)
nn-National Guard recruitment   4   10   15   20

WHEATIES (Premiums)
Walt Disney Productions: 1950 & 1951 (32 titles, pocket-size, 32 pgs.)

Mailing Envelope (no art on front)(Designates sets A,B,C or D on front)
     8   24   42   60
(Set A-1 to A-8, 1950)
A-1-Mickey Mouse & the Disappearing Island, A-5-Mickey Mouse, Roving Reporter each...   6   18   29   40
A-2-Grandma Duck, Homespun Detective, A-6-Li'l Bad Wolf, Forest Ranger, A-7-Goofy, Tightrope Acrobat, A-8-Pluto & the Bogus Money each...   5   15   25   35
A-3-Donald Duck & the Haunted Jewels, A-4-Donald Duck & the Giant Ape each...   9   27   49   70
(Set B-1 to B-8, 1950)
B-1-Mickey Mouse & the Pharoah's Curse, B-4-Mickey Mouse & the Mystery Sea Monster each...   6   18   29   40
B-2-Pluto, Canine Cowpoke, B-5-Li'l Bad Wolf in the Hollow Tree Hideout, B-7-Goofy & the Gangsters each...   5   15   25   35
B-3-Donald Duck & the Buccaneers, B-6-Donald Duck, Trail Blazer, B-8 Donald Duck, Klondike Kid each...   9   27   49   70
(Set C-1 to C-8, 1951)
C-1-Donald Duck & the Inca Idol, C-5-Donald Duck in the Lost Lakes, C-8-Donald Duck Deep-Sea Diver each...   9   27   49   70
C-2-Mickey Mouse & the Magic Mountain, C-6-Mickey Mouse & the Stagecoach Bandits each...   6   18   29   40

	GD2.0	FN6.0	VF8.0	NM9.4

C-3-Li'l Bad Wolf, Fire Fighter, C-4-Gus & Jaq Save the Ship, C-7-Goofy, Big Game Hunter   each…   5   15   25   35

(Set D-1 to D-8, 1951)

D-1-Donald Duck in Indian Country, D-5-Donald Duck, Mighty Mystic each…   9   27   49   70

D-2-Mickey Mouse and the Abandoned Mine, D-6-Mickey Mouse & the Medicine Man   each…   6   18   29   40

D-3-Pluto & the Mysterious Package, D-4-Bre'r Rabbit's Sunken Treasure, D-7-Li'l Bad Wolf and the Secret of the Woods, D-8-Minnie Mouse, Girl Explorer   each…   5   15   25   35

NOTE: Some copies lack the Wheaties ad.

WHIZ COMICS (Formerly Flash Comics & Thrill Comics #1)
Fawcett Publications

Wheaties Giveaway(1946, Miniature, 6-1/2x8-1/4", 32 pgs.); all copies were taped at each corner to a box of Wheaties and are never found in very fine or mint condition; "Capt. Marvel & the Water Thieves", plus Golden Arrow, Ibis, Crime Smasher stories   150   600   —   —

WILD KINGDOM (TV) (Mutual of Omaha's…)
Western Printing Co.: 1965 (Giveaway, regular size, slick-c, 16 pgs.)

nn-Front & back-c are different on 1966 edition   2   6   11   15

WISCO/KLARER COMIC BOOK (Miniature)
Marvel Comics/Vital Publ./Fawcett Publ.: 1948 - 1964 (3-1/2x6-3/4", 24 pgs.)

Given away by Wisco "99" Service Stations, Carnation Malted Milk, Klarer Health Wieners, Fleers Dubble Bubble Gum, Rodeo All-Meat Wieners, Perfect Potato Chips, & others; see ad in Tom Mix #21

Blackstone & the Gold Medal Mystery (1948)   8   24   42   60

Blackstone "Solves the Sealed Vault Mystery" (1950)   8   24   42   60

Blaze Carson in "The Sheriff Shoots It Out" (1950)   8   24   42   60

Captain Marvel & Billy's Big Game (r/Capt. Marvel Adv. #76)   31   93   165   285

(Prices vary widely on this book)

China Boy in "A Trip to the Zoo" #10 (1948)   5   15   25   35

Indoors-Outdoors Game Book   4   10   15   20

Jim Solar Space Sheriff in "Battle for Mars", "Between Two Worlds", "Conquers Outer Space", "The Creatures on the Comet", "Defeats the Moon Missile Men", "Encounter Creatures on Comet", "Meet the Jupiter Jumpers", "Meets the Man From Mars", "On Traffic Duty", "Outlaws of the Spaceways", "Pirates of the Planet X", "Protects Space Lanes", "Raiders From the Sun", "Ring Around Saturn", "Robots of Rhea", "The Sky Ruby", "Spacetts of the Sky", "Spidermen of Venus", "Trouble on Mercury"   7   21   36   50

Johnny Starboard & the Underseas Pirates (1948)   5   15   23   30

Kid Colt in "He Lived by His Guns" (1950)   9   27   49   70

Little Aspirin as "Crook Catcher" #2 (1950)   4   10   15   20

Little Aspirin in "Naughty But Nice" #6 (1950)   4   10   15   20

Return of the Black Phantom (not M.E. character)(Roy Dare)(1948)   6   18   29   40

Secrets of Magic   4   11   17   22

Slim Morgan "Brings Justice to Mesa City" #3   4   11   17   22

Super Rabbit(1950)-Cuts Red Tape, Stops Crime Wave!   10   30   55   85

Tex Farnum, Frontiersman (1948)   4   12   19   25

Tex Taylor in "Draw or Die, Cowpoke!" (1950)   6   18   32   45

Tex Taylor in "An Exciting Adventure at the Gold Mine" (1950)   6   18   29   40

Wacky Quacky in "All-Aboard"   3   8   12   15

When School Is Out   3   8   12   15

Willie in a "Comic-Comic Book Fall" #1   5   15   25   20

Wonder Duck "An Adventure at the Rodeo of the Fearless Quacker!" (1950)   9   27   49   70

Rare uncut version of three; includes Capt. Marvel, Tex Farnum, Black Phantom   Estimated value…   400.00

Rare uncut version of three; includes China Boy, Blackstone, Johnny Starboard & the Underseas Pirates   Estimated value…   125.00

WOLVERINE
Marvel Comics: 1999 (Nabisco mail-in offer)

145-Variant cover by Sienkiewicz   10   30   70   120

WOMAN OF THE PROMISE, THE
Catechetical Guild: 1950 (General Distr.) (Paper cover, 32 pgs.)

nn   5   15   23   30

WONDERFUL WORLD OF DUCKS (See Golden Picture Story Book)
Colgate Palmolive Co.: 1975

1-Mostly-r   6.00

WONDER WOMAN
DC Comics: 1977

Pizza Hut Giveaways (12/77)-Reprints #60,62   6.00

WONDER WORKER OF PERU
Catechetical Guild: No date (5x7", 16 pgs., B&W, giveaway)

nn   5   14   21   28

WOODY WOODPECKER
Dell Publishing Co.

Clover Stamp-Newspaper Boy Contest('56)-9 pg. story-(Giveaway)   6   18   29   40

In Chevrolet Wonderland(1954-Giveaway)(Western Publ.)-20 pgs., full story line; Chilly Willy app.   20   60   105   175

…Meets Scotty MacTape(1953-Scotch Tape giveaway)-16 pgs., full size   20   60   105   175

WOOLWORTH'S CHRISTMAS STORY BOOK
Promotional Publ. Co.(Western Printing Co.): 1952 - 1954 (16 pgs., paper-c) (See Jolly Christmas Book)

nn   6   18   29   40

NOTE: 1952 issue-Marv Levy c/a.

WOOLWORTH'S HAPPY TIME CHRISTMAS BOOK
F. W. Woolworth Co.(Western Printing Co.): 1952 (Christmas giveaway)

nn-36 pgs.   6   18   29   40

WORLD'S FINEST COMICS
National Periodical Publ./DC Comics

Giveaway (c. 1944-45, 8 pgs., in color, paper-c)-Johnny Everyman-r/World's Finest   25   75   130   225

Giveaway (c. 1949, 8 pgs., in color, paper-c)- "Make Way For Youth" r/World's Finest; based on film of same name   22   66   116   200

#176, #179- Best Western reprint edition (1997)   2.50

WORLD'S GREATEST SUPER HEROES
DC Comics (Nutra Comics) (Child Vitamins, Inc.): 1977 (Giveaway, 3-3/4x3-3/4", 24 pgs.)

nn-Batman & Robin app.; health tips   1   4   7   10

XMAS FUNNIES
Kinney Shoes: No date (Giveaway, paper cover, 36 pgs.?)

Contains 1933 color strip-r; Mutt & Jeff, etc.   50   200   260   340

X-MEN THE MOVIE
Marvel Comics/Toys R' Us: 2000

Special Movie Prequel Edition   5.00

YALTA TO KOREA (Also see Korea My Home)
M. Phillip Corp. (Republican National Committee): 1952 (Giveaway; paper-c)

nn-(8 pgs.)-Anti-communist propaganda book   19   57   99   170

YOGI BEAR (TV)
Dell Publishing Co.

Giveaway ('84, '86)-City of Los Angeles, "Creative First Aid" & "Earthquake Preparedness for Children"   5.00

YOUR TRIP TO NEWSPAPERLAND
Philadelphia Evening Bulletin (Printed by Harvey Press): June, 1955 (14x11-1/2", 12 pgs.)

nn-Joe Palooka takes kids on newspaper tour   5   15   24   32

YOUR VOTE IS VITAL!
Harvey Publications Inc.: 1952 (5" x 7", 16 pgs., paper cover)

nn-The importance of voting   4   11   17   22

The American Comic Book: 1828-1899

THE VICTORIAN AGE
BEFORE THE YELLOW KID:
AMERICAN COMICS OF
THE 19TH CENTURY

by Doug Wheeler, Robert L. Beerbohm
& Richard D. Olson, PhD ©2002

With special thanks to Richard Samuel West

Title page to the earliest known sequential
comic book published in America,
"The Adventures of Mr. Obadiah Oldbuck"
by Rodolphe Töpffer,
Sept. 1842, Wilson & Co. New York.

Adventures of Mr. Obadiah Oldbuck.
Page 8 of a 40 page 1842 graphic novel
by Rodolphe Töpffer...the history
books are being rewritten right here.

With this edition of **The Overstreet Comic Book Price Guide** we debut a section devoted to comic books published during the years the United States expanded across the North American continent, fought a Civil War, shifted from an agrarian to an industrial society, "welcomed" waves of immigrants, and struggled over race, class, religion, temperance, and suffrage - and all of it depicted and satirized by cartoonists. The social attitudes, beliefs, and conventions of 19th century America, the good as well as the bad, are to be found in abundance. That warning given, we can imagine the first question to pop into most readers' minds will be, "What, beyond the happenstance of publication date, are Victorian Age comics?"

The feature which most distinguishes Victorian comics from those of later eras is the extremely rare use of word balloons within sequential (multi-picture) comic stories. When word balloons are used, it is nearly always within single panel cartoons. On the occasions when they appear inside a strip, with very few exceptions the ballooned dialogue is non-essential to understanding the story. Nineteenth Century comics tended to place both narration and dialogue beneath comic panels rather than within the panel's borders. These comics are to the word balloon-strewn post-**Yellow Kid** comics of the 20th Century as silent movies are to the later "talkies." Just as sound changed how stories were structured on film, so too did comics change when the words were moved from beneath panels to inside

them, and dialogue rather than narration was made to forward a story in conjunction with the pictures.

The Victorian Age of comic books began on different dates in different nations, depending on when the first publication of a sequential comic book on their soil is known to have occurred. For the U.S., this happened on September 14, 1842. On that date, the American humor periodical **Brother Jonathan** printed the 40-page, 195-panel graphic novel **The Adventures of Mr. Obadiah Oldbuck**. Almost six decades later, America's Victorian comics came to their end, replaced by the onslaught of Platinum Age books reprinting newspaper strips from Bennett, Hearst & Pulitzer Sunday comic sections, among others.

Apart from the newspaper-derived **Yellow Kid in McFadden's Flats** and **Yellow Kid Magazine**, both published in 1897 and found in the Platinum Age, little overlap exists between the Victorian and Platinum Ages. Those publications which continued from one century into the next, such as **Puck**, **Judge**, and **Life**, have their pre-1900 issues listed within the Victorian Age section, while their post-1899 issues can be found inside the Platinum Age. Some non-sequential (i.e., single panel) American comic items existing prior to 1842 are also listed herein, going back at present to 1828. These belong to what could tentatively be called the **Age of Caricature** (1770s through 1830s), during which Gillray, Rowlandson, Cruikshank, and Heath were England's top cartoonists.

The earliest known cartoon printed on paper in North America was in a Puritan children's book first published in 1646 (see #29, pg. 212). Titled simply "The Burning of Mr. John Rogers," it showed in flaming graphic detail what happens to those who stray from the flock and have to be burned at the stake. Wertham would have had a field day with that one!

Cartoon broadsheets and other single panel images, often using word balloons, appeared from Pre-Revolution days through the end of the 19th Century. The first cartoon published in an American newspaper is generally credited as the Benjamin Franklin designed "God Helps Those Who Help Themselves," which appeared in his periodical **Plain Truth** in 1747.

The most popularly remembered 18th Century American cartoons likely are Franklin's "Join or Die" in 1753, representing the American Colonies as severed snake parts, and "The Bloody Massacre Perpetrated in King Street" - Paul Revere's 1770 depiction of the Boston Massacre, whose design he likely pirated from the Henry Pelham broadsheet cartoon "The Fruits of Arbitrary Power."

The first American famous for his cartoons was David Claypool Johnston (1798-1865). Johnston

Political parody Before & After A Locofoco Christmas Present, self published in 1837 by David Claypool Johnston.

provided illustrations for various almanacs, books, and periodicals, including the masthead for **Brother Jonathan**. This same masthead appears on the top half of the cover of the **Brother Jonathan** edition of **Obadiah Oldbuck**. Most notable of Johnston's comics work was his nine-issue series **Scraps**, which he self-published from 1828 to 1849. Johnston was widely known in his day as "the American Cruikshank." His **Scraps** series was highly influenced by George Cruikshank's series **Scraps and Sketches**, which first appeared in 1827. Each issue of Johnston's **Scraps** consists of four large folio-sized pages, printed on one side, with 9 to 12 single panel cartoons per page, and each page often organized around a theme.

After Johnston's **Scraps**, the next step forward in the development of comics in America - a leap forward, really - occurred on September 14, 1842. The weekly humor periodical **Brother Jonathan** also published a parallel "Extra" series which reprinted prose European novels. Becoming adventurous, the editors chose Rodolphe Töpffer's graphic novel, **The Adventures of Mr. Obadiah Oldbuck** for **Extra**, NO. IX, reformatting it from its original small oblong strip shape to the side-stitched magazine shape in which the earlier Extras were published. This had the inadvertent prophetic effect of making this edition (alone) of **Obadiah Oldbuck** resemble a modern 21st Century comic book. The arrival of this comic on the shores of the New World would directly inspire a wave of American imitators, as happened earlier in European nations where Töpffer's comics had appeared. You can view most of the first Wilson printing of **Oldbuck** from 1842 online at www.reuben.org/evry/obadiah.html

According to **The New York Times** (Sept. 3, 1904), the first American comic book was issued as a supplement to **Brother Jonathan** (New York, Sept. 14, 1842). Even so, by the beginning of the 20th century, this comics pioneer was largely forgotten. It is high time he received credit long overdue as the person who invented the modern comic strip, laying previously held myths to rest.

Töpffer (1799-1846) was a playwright, novelist, artist, and teacher from Geneva, Switzerland, who in 1827 had begun producing what he called "picture novels," sharing them with his friends and students. These first full blown sequential comic books, scripted in Töpffer's native French language, found their way to Paris and became an instant hit. The demand for his comic books soon outstripped the supply, and pirated editions, redrawn and re-engraved by others, were created by Parisian publisher Aubert to capitalize on this. In a world where international copyright conventions did not exist, this was perfectly legal, if morally questionable. Aubert's agents in London struck a deal with British publisher Tilt & Bogue, resulting in the 1841 translated-into-English version of Aubert's piracy of **Les Amours de M. Vieux Bois**.

This English translation was co-financed by George Cruikshank, and sported a new cover page by George's brother Robert, based on a montage of Töpffer's scenes. An unknown deal led to America's Wilson and Company reprinting this translation. Tilt & Bogue followed up their success by translating into English two additional stories of Töpffer's eight graphic novels: **Beau Ogleby**, circa 1843 (originally **Histoire de M. Jabot**), and **Bachelor Butterfly** two years later (from **Histoire de M. Cryptogame**). Wilson & Company picked up the latter, reprinting **Bachelor Butterfly** in the States in 1846. In 1849, Wilson & Company reformatted **Obadiah Oldbuck** back into its original British shape, dropping a handful of comic panels and altering the text to hide these deletions.

Perhaps inspired by his involvement with Töpffer's **Obadiah Oldbuck**, George Cruikshank soon created several sequential comic books of his own. These too found their way to America. **The Bachelor's Own Book**, published first in Britain in 1844, became the second known U.S. published sequential comic book when reprinted by Burgess, Stringer & Company the following year.

Next was Cruikshank's masterpiece **The Bottle**, the Hogarthian-style tale of a man whose addiction to alcohol brings himself and his family to ruin. After debuting in London in 1847, it was reprinted the same year in a British-American co-publication between David Bogue and Americans Wiley and Putnam. Both printings were in huge folio form, available in either black & white or professionally hand-tinted versions. In 1848, the story saw American print again, this time in smaller form, placed at the front of the otherwise prose volume **Temperance Tales; Or, Six Nights with the Washingtonians**. It continued to be reprinted by a variety of publishers into the early 20th Century. **The Bottle** was popular in Revival and Temperance circles, made moreso by its use in lectures, where the story was reproduced onto painted glass slides then projected for audiences by a magic lantern. **The Drunkard's Children**, Cruikshank's sequel to **The Bottle**, was issued on July 1, 1848 as a British-American-Australian co-publishing venture, but was less successful, and so had not nearly as many reprints.

The most clearly sequential, and fun, of George Cruikshank's comic books was **The Toothache**, issued in London in 1849, and reprinted in the U.S. that same year by Philadelphia map maker J.L. Smith.

When closed, this booklet appears an unassuming 5-1/4 inches tall by 3-1/4 inches wide. Its striking feature is that the book folds open accordian style, stretching the entire 43-panel story along one single strip of paper, which when fully extended is seven feet, three inches long! **The Toothache** was issued in both black & white and professionally hand-colored editions. Abridged editions of the story, printed in black & white and with a "normal" page-turning rather than fold-out presentation, appeared inside promotional giveaway comics issued by American companies in the 1880s.

Between Töpffer and Cruikshank, 1842-1849

1849's "Journey to the Gold Diggins By Jeremiah Saddlebags", the earliest known sequential comic book by American creators, was recently rediscovered.

had seen six sequential European comic books reprinted in the U.S., not to mention additional comics imported directly without American reproduction. At that decade's end, this combined influence met with a national mania screaming for a satirization - California's Gold Rush. The result was the earliest known American created sequential comic book.

Journey to the Gold Diggins by Jeremiah Saddlebags, by brothers James and Donald Read, was published in 1849, first in New York City by Stringer & Townsend, then soon after re-published in Cincinnati, Ohio, by U.P. James. This Töpffer-influenced comic book chronicles the adventures of its hero **Jeremiah Saddlebags** in his get-rich-quick quest for gold in California and is highly sought by collectors of Western Americana. Interestingly, the back cover of the Stringer & Townsend edition carries an advertisement for **Rose and Gertrude-a Genevese Story**, one of Rodolphe Töpffer's non-comics prose novels.

Stringer was one of the 1845 participants in the American publication of **The Bachelor's Own**

The Tooth-Ache, by George Cruikshank, opens up accordion-like into a single strip seven feet, three inches long!

Jerimiah Saddlebags by Read Bros. Sample panels, 1849.

Panel details from George Cruikshank's The Tooth-Ache, 1849.

Book. One might speculate that his earlier involvement with Cruikshank's comic could have made Stringer more receptive to the Read brothers' **Jeremiah Saddlebags**.

Still other contemporary Gold Rush comics appeared. **The Adventures of Mr. Tom Plump** (a fat man who nearly starves to death in his failed attempt at California Gold riches) saw print in 1850. **The Adventures of Jeremiah Oldpot** was serialized across all twelve monthly issues of **Yankee Notions** in 1852. Gold Rush cartoons are found in the 1849 edition of David Claypool Johnston's **Scraps**, in comic almanacs, and in broadsheets from Currier & Ives. The circa 1850-51 booklet **The Clown, Or The Banquet Of Wit**, includes a 13-page comic story "Moses

Richard Doyles Foreign Tour, as it first appeared in America within The Clown, or The Banquet of Wit, 1850-51, pirated from Punch

Keyser the Bowery Bully's Trip to the California Gold Mines."

The Clown, Or The Banquet Of Wit is also notable as the earliest known anthology of sequential comics, with the bonus that each multi-panel story is by a different artist. Many of the artists are as yet unidentified, and how much of it is original American material versus that reprinted from Europe is presently unknown. But verified are cartoons by George Cruikshank, Elton (American), the Read brothers, Grandville (French), and Richard Doyle (British). The Doyle contribution reprints the comics story "Brown, Jones and Robinson and How They Went to a Ball," which originally saw print in the August 24,

1850 issue of **Punch**. This is the first known American appearance of these Doyle characters, and was almost certainly pirated.

Richard Doyle's **The Foreign Tour of Messrs. Brown, Jones, and Robinson** is basically a travelogue in illustrated form, told via humorous episodes, part sequential cartoon sequences, and part snapshots of moments jumping forward in time. This halfway sequential format was ideal for most 19th century cartoonists, who, with rare exception, had not quite grasped how to maintain a single sequential story for much longer than two dozen successive panels.

Doyle had simplified Töpffer's formula in a manner most artists could attempt to emulate. Episodes of "Brown, Jones, and Robinson" originally appeared in **Punch** in 1850, until a dispute between the Roman Catholic Doyle and **Punch's** editors over anti-Papal jokes ended with Doyle quitting. Doyle redrew and expanded the story into a single album, which first saw print in 1854 from British publisher Bradbury & Evans.

New York publisher D. Appleton brought the album to America, where he reprinted it in 1860, 1871, and 1877. Next, Dick & Fitzgerald (NY) pirated Doyle's story some time in the early 1870s. Doyle's format from **Foreign Tour** was emulated again and again. Examples include: the 1857 **Mr. Hardy Lee, His Yacht**, by Charles Stedman; the 1860s to 1870s Carleton published **Our Artist In...** series, set in various Latin American countries; the Augustus Hoppin 1870s sketch novels **On The Nile, Crossing the Atlantic**, and **Ups and Downs on Land and Water**; and **Life** founder John Ames Mitchell's 1881 (pre-**Life**) **The Summer School of Philosophy at Mt. Desert**. D. Appleton, the official, authorized American publisher of **Foreign Tour**, even commissioned an American artist - Toby - to create a sequel comic album involving Doyle's characters visiting the U.S. and Canada, published in 1872 as **The American Tour of Messrs Brown, Jones and Robinson**. In terms of influencing the development of mid-19th Century American comics, Doyle's **Foreign Tour** ranks with the works of Töpffer, Cruikshank, and Busch.

Doyle additionally produced a second, earlier cartoon series for **Punch**, the popularity of which likewise exerted influence decades beyond its publication. In **Manners and Customs of Ye Englyshe. Mr. Pips Hys Diary**, gathered from **Punch** and reprinted in 1849, Doyle told his story using a deliberately primitive almost stick-figure art style, combined with the Hogarthian structure of large single panel cartoons leaping forward in time with each picture.

Manners and Customs of Ye Harvard Studente, which ran in the **Harvard Lampoon**, shows the clearest influence. The series by then student Francis Gilbert Attwood was collected in

1877 by Houghton Mifflin. Attwood followed it up with **Manners and Customs of Ye Bostonians**, again in the pages of the **Harvard Lampoon**, but it is unknown whether that series was ever reprinted in book form. Attwood later became one of the regular artists in **Life**.

The British humor periodical **Punch** additionally influenced American comics beyond Richard Doyle's series. Consisting of humorous text interspersed with (mostly) single panel cartoons, it began its weekly run in July 1841, and continued uninterrupted well into the 20th Century. A large subset of **Punch**'s subscriber base was located in the U.S., to which thousands of copies were exported on an ongoing basis. The result was that when American humor periodicals emerged, they invariably imitated Punch's format and style.

The earliest known of these American imitators, **Yankee Doodle**, debuted on October 10, 1846, and lasted one year. **Punch in Canada** likewise appeared in the late 1840s, kicking off a smaller parallel comics evolution just north of the U.S. (The earliest known "illustrated" American humor periodical, **The Humourist**, was published monthly in Baltimore from January 1829 to at least December of that same year, sans input from **Punch**. This monthly contained but one cartoon per issue, albeit hand-colored.)

Collections reprinting cartoons from **Punch** saw print in the U.S., such as **Merry Pictures by the Comic Hands**, imported for the 1859 Christmas Season, plus various John Leech, George Du Maurier, and Phil May books which appeared from the 1850s through 1910s. Finally, many American illustrated newspapers and periodicals, humorous and non, carried reprints of **Punch** cartoons. Such inclusions often became a prelude to switching to original material by American artists, should that publication's cartoon section become popular. Such was the case with **Harper's Monthly**. In the early 1850s, near the rear of each issue, it began to carry a few pages of single panel cartoons reprinted from **Punch**. This evolved into reprinting sequential comic pages from the British periodical **Town Talk**, and then, starting December 1853, original sequential comics by American artist Frank Bellew.

Bellew (1828-1888) could be regarded as the father of American sequential comics. His earliest work shows an influence from Doyle, but he rapidly developed his own unique art style. Bellew's comics, both sequential and single panel, graced numerous periodicals from the 1850s through 1870s.

In the year prior to his **Harper's Monthly** appearances, in **The Lantern** Volume One, Bellew had presented the 18-panel story "Mr.

Blobb in Search of a Physician," serialized across six weekly issues. This was followed soon after by the 16-panel, three issue story "Mr. Bulbear's Dream", which concluded with the main character awakened from his dream by falling out of bed, in the exact same manner as would **Little Nemo** five decades later.

According to a 1923 article on famous cartoonists written by Charles Dana Gibson, it was Bellew's conception of **Uncle Sam** which "became the popular figure emblematic of the United States" starting with **The Lantern** issue published March 13, 1852. This was in a cartoon titled "Collins and Cunard - Raising the Wind; Or Both Sides of the Story." Gibson went on, "Thomas Nast (later) added whiskers and put stars on the vest, retaining Bellew's hat, high collar, and striped trousers."

Frank Bellew's son, Frank Bellew Jr., also

Frank Bellew Sr's "The Flying Machine; And Professor High's Adventure therein in a Trip accros the Ocean," Merrymans Monthly v3#5, May 1865; sample panels.

became a cartoonist of note, which has caused confusion amongst those trying to identify the work of 19th Century cartoonists. The senior Bellew often signed his work by placing his name or initials within a triangle, while the junior Bellew most frequently signed his work using the nickname "Chips."

While Bellew stood out for his sequential comics, Thomas Nast (1840-1902) brought a new style to American political cartoons, of which he is regarded the father. Nast made his name in the pages of the national news periodical **Harper's Weekly**, whose staff he joined a year into the Civil War. As Nast grew in prominence and success, American cartoonists increasingly emulated him. U.S. humor publications evolved towards an amalgamation of Nast and **Punch**, rather than sheer imitation of the latter.

While the northern **Vanity Fair** (December 31, 1859 - July 4, 1863) and the Confederate **Southern Punch** (August 15, 1863 - September 1864) were both modeled after **Punch**, other Civil War era humor periodicals such as J.C. Haney's **Comic Monthly** and Frank Leslie's **Budget of Fun** were clearly absorbing lessons from Nast. These latter two were issued in the same large folio size as **Harper's Weekly**, with a large front page cartoon, often a larger double-page cartoon centerfold, and still more cartoons located on the back cover - a format approaching what eventually emerged in **Puck**.

After the War, with Nast's style of cartoons more entrenched in American readers' minds, efforts to launch **Punch**-like American periodicals floundered quickly. **Mrs. Grundy**, ironically most famous for its cover design by Nast, died after a mere twelve issues (running July 8 to September 23, 1865). **Punchinello** (April 2 to December 24, 1870) struggled nine months before its backers gave up. **Punchinello** had been financed by Tammany Hall politicians Tweed and Sweeney, as counter-propaganda against Nast's ongoing assault upon their corruption. They attempted to buy and threaten Nast into silence, to no avail.

American comics were also being pulled away from their initial Anglo-Franco imitation by the infusion of a third major source of European influence. Numerous European humor periodicals besides **Punch** found significant subscriber bases in America. The large German immigrant population imported their favorite humor periodicals into the U.S., including the popular **Fliegende Blätter** ("Flying Leaves") and **Münchener Bilderbogen**. As high in quality as these were, one German comic artist in particular excelled beyond the rest, his stories breaking out and crossing over into English language translations, the demand for which resulted in numerous printings. This artist, of course, was Wilhelm Busch (1832-1908).

Busch's work appeared in English in the 1860s in both British and American periodicals, often uncredited. For example, four of Busch's strips appeared in English in the pages of **Merryman's Monthly** in 1864, while in 1879 his graphic story "Fipps der Affe" was serialized across a 10-issue

Wilhelm Busch Trade Cards in the Fritz Spindle Shanks series to advertise Raven Gloss Shoe Polish; early 1880's.

run of **Puck** as "Troddledums the Simian." The earliest known English language appearance of Busch in book form was **The Fly-ing Dutchman, or The Wrath of Herr von Stoppelnoze**, in 1862, from New York publisher Carleton. Carleton not only pirated Busch's strip, but went so far as to credit the story to American poet John G. Saxe, with Busch's cartoons mere illustrations accompanying Saxe's prose!

The next known English language Busch book was **A Bushel of Merry Thoughts**, an 1868 London-published anthology collecting various Busch strips. Some of these same stories appeared in the U.S.-published **The Mischief Book** (1880), newly translated and with a few more Busch tales added. One of these additions was "Hans Huckebein." The tale of a mischievous pet raven who in the end gets drunk and accidentally hangs himself, it became, at least in the States, Busch's second most popular sequential comic story. The unrepentant bird was promoted to title character in two later collections: **Jack Huckaback, the Scapegrace Raven**, circa 1888, and the rarer **Hookeybeak the Raven and Other Tales** in 1878. There were also at least three trade card series in the 1870s and 1880s which reprinted the ending sequence, titled as **Fritz Spindle-Shanks - The Raven Black**.

The most popular Busch tale, though, was easily **Max und Moritz**, which in the U.S. saw print as **Max and Maurice - A Juvenile History in Seven Tricks**. Published in Boston in 1871, this English language version saw at minimum 60 reprintings by the century's end, plus countless more printings later. A separate British translation debuted in 1874, under the title **Max & Mortiz**. It is well known that the later Rudolph Dirks comic strip series, **Katzenjammer Kids** (1897), was based on **Max und Moritz**.

According to documents found by Alfredo Castelli, **Katzenjammer Kids** was not yet another rip-off of Busch. Rather, William R. Hearst licensed the characters. Hearst's paper was published in different language editions for New York City's immigrant communities. In the German edition, the strip was published under its original name, **Max und Moritz**. Numerous other translations of Busch were published in America - too many to name in this article. Many can be found in the listings of Victorian Age comics.

The seemingly disparate influences of Thomas Nast and German comics came together in Austrian immigrant Joseph Keppler (1838-1894). Like many cartoonists in America, Keppler's desire was to rival Nast. Unlike most, he possessed the talent and drive to accomplish it. Keppler had settled in St. Louis, Missouri, where he took his first stab at starting a comic weekly, the German language **Die Vehme** (August 28, 1869 - August 20, 1870). Seven months later, still in St. Louis, he tried again, launching another German language humor periodical, titled **Puck**. This German **Puck** began on March 18, 1871, and was joined by an English language version one year later, but both soon folded, ending together on August 24, 1872.

Keppler moved to New York City, doing cartoons primarily for Frank Leslie publications (including a one-shot, English language publication - **Centennial Fun** - which capitalized on the July 1876 Centennial Exposition in Philadelphia). Four years after the first **Puck** died, Keppler was ready to try again. He re-launched the German language edition of **Puck** in New York City on September 27, 1876.

It was a Presidential Election year, with Republican candidate Hayes versus the Democrat Tilden. Keppler lucked out with material to satirize, when the election ended so close that each candidate needed only the electoral college votes of a few states in question - most notably Florida and Louisiana - and both parties were claiming to have won. Keppler depicted the two candidates as two trains on the same track, steaming towards each other, with the stability of the nation in the balance. After months of dispute, the victory was handed to the loser of the popular vote, the Republican Hayes. (Much later, scholars showed that Tilden, in truth, was the electoral as well as popular winner).

With his second **Puck** series, Keppler introduced a new element to American humor periodicals - color lithography. The color was initially limited, but it appeared, ambitiously, every week, and set **Puck** apart from anything else on American stands. The parallel English language edition of **Puck** launched six months after the German version, on March 14, 1877. The English edition of **Puck** was a money-loser for several years, kept afloat by the German edition's profits and the determination of the English edition's literary editor, H.C. Bunner, not to give up. **Puck** became the new model for American humor publications. Keppler brought in other artists over time, most notably Opper, Zim and Howarth, and added black & white sequential comics and cartoons in the pages between the color front cover,

Back cover from Puck Illustrirtes Humoristisches Wochenblatt # 11, NY, December 1876, by Joseph Keppler, concerning controversial 1876 Presidential Election results.

back cover, and center-spread.

Puck was the model which William Randolph Hearst followed in 1895 when he added a color comics section to his Sunday newspaper. He basically wanted to offer a "free" **Puck**-like supplement within his newspaper. Further, **Puck** artist F.M. Howarth pointed the direction of those future newspaper comics pages, by creating full page sequential color comic strips on most **Puck** back covers starting in the early 1890s.

With the first issue dated Oct. 29, 1881, **Puck's** chief rival, **Judge**, was born. Founded by **Puck** artist James A. Wales, **Judge** made several forays into **Puck's** talent pool over the years. Their best capture was Eugene Zimmerman (known popularly as "Zim"), who became for **Judge** the star artist that Frederick Burr Opper was for **Puck**.

Wales had at one point been the most prominent artist in the earlier, largely forgotten 1870s humor periodicals, **Wild Oats** and **Schnedered -deng** (a German language companion publication to **Wild Oats**). In terms of the quality of their cartoons and comics, these two New York City publications were in 1875 at a level **Puck** would not achieve until 1880. **Schnedereddeng** and **Wild Oats** carried a crossroads of old and next generation comic artists, containing both Bellew, Woolf, and Worth (known for his Currier & Ives cartoon sheets), and up-and-comers such as Livingston Hopkins, Opper, and Wales. When Wales broke away to form **Judge**, it was from amongst these pre-**Puck** associates that he first recruited. One can speculate that being the star artist in these earlier magazines may have driven Wales' desire to have more control of his cartoons rather than remain subordinate to Keppler.

Judge struggled financially for several years, and likely would have ceased publication if not for the Presidential Election of 1884, in which Republicans blamed Keppler and **Puck** for their loss. In response, Republican backers bought and poured money into **Judge** as a counterweight against **Puck's** influence. Numerous other **Puck** imitators emerged in the 1880s but quickly died. Note should be made of the **Puck**-like San Francisco **Wasp**, which debuted October 14, 1876 (too early for it to have been a mere **Puck** knockoff), and the black & white **Texas Siftings**, which debuted on May 9, 1881. Though neither approached **Puck** or **Judge** in circulation, both cut their own editorial paths, managing to survive as cartoon humor publications into the '90s.

Another magazine which blazed its own trail was **Life**. Founded on January 4, 1883 by J.A. Mitchell, and modeled after the **Harvard Lampoon**, **Life** became the third pillar of late 1800s American humor periodicals. Smaller in size, black & white, and priced the same as **Puck** and **Judge**, it nevertheless succeeded by appealing to the more genteel, romantic and apolitical notions of the white upper class. Its earliest artists included Kemble and Palmer Cox, but its foremost artist would be Charles Dana Gibson, who became world reknowned as the hand behind the aristocratic "Gibson Girls."

Unlike **Judge**, which had to change format to survive in the next century, and **Puck**, which faded to a shadow of its former self, **Life** transitioned into the 20th Century virtually unaltered, and thrived. By the mid-1880s, with **Puck**, **Judge**, and **Life** all solidly in place, American comics and cartoon humor had become very much their own, no longer looking first at Europe to take their cues.

Also very American in character were its promotional comics, which flourished throughout the latter half of the 19th Century, starting first with comic almanacs in the mid 1850s. These free almanacs, usually created by medicine and farm product companies, initially killed off the more elaborate illustrated almanacs of the 1830s to early 1850s, which readers paid for. Competition amongst companies, whose goal was to get customers to read the almanacs and the advertisements contained therein again and again, meant that attention-getting humorous cartoons soon found their way back into these giveaway pamphlets. Initially their cartoons were done cheap, either poorly drawn or pirated from elsewhere, such as those found in the **Hostetter's** and **Wright's** almanac series. More elaborate

Judge #791, Dec 12, 1896, depicting Tammany Hall politicians as Yellow Kid & Brownies. Art by Hamilton.

promotional almanacs eventually did evolve, though, and amongst the best of these was **Barker's Illustrated Almanac**, first produced for the year 1878, and annually into the 1930s. Each **Barker's Almanac** contained ten to twelve full page cartoons, wonderful and bizarre in design, frequently racist, but also comically manic and crammed with details in a manner similar to Outcault's much later **Yellow Kid** pages. The cartoons in **Barker's Almanac** were so popular that in 1892, The Barker, Moore, and Mein Medicine Company published their first edition of **Barker's Komic Picture Souvenir**, reprinting nearly 150 pages of cartoons from their almanacs.

This first Barker's souvenir features a wraparound color cover depicting people headed towards the Columbian World's Fair Exposition, which was to be held in Chicago the next year. It is the earliest confirmed "premium" comic book, sent to customers who mailed in a box label and outside wrapper from two different Barker's products. The **Souvenir** album was Barker's most in-demand premium, and was reprinted as a thick unnumbered booklet three more times in the 1890s, with the contents reorganized each time. Later, between 1901 and 1903, Barker's broke the album into three separate "Parts," each of which required still more box labels and wrappers to obtain. The three part series of reprint albums expanded to four parts circa 1906 or

Sample cartoon from inside the 1889 Barker's Illustrated Almanac, depicting Buffalo Bill performance before Queen Victoria in England. Art by R.A. Williams.

1907. Both the three and four part album series had multiple printings.

The first promotional comics which did not double as almanacs began to appear in the 1870s. They included the aforementioned reprints of Cruikshank and Busch strips, reprints of strips lifted from American sources (A.B. Frost's strip "The Bull Calf" was a particular favorite), and original material placing the product being promoted as the focus of the story. These original short cartoon dramas were in many ways similar in storyline to that found in modern television advertisements, except that the clothing is Victorian, and the claims, pre-F.D.A. and F.C.C., were unabashedly wild, over-the-top, and blunt. Chewing tobacco and snuff which saved romances, calmed crying babies, and made the sick well. Stove polish that propelled you to wealth and power. The objective of course, in an era before television or radio, was to make each comic handout so entertaining that customers would want to keep and read the advertisement again and again.

The more wonderful graphics and outrageous claims tended to come from tobacco companies, who were using comic books and strips to sell their products more than a century before cries against "Joe Camel." The most elaborate of these were printed full color, and unfolded into a single long strip, just like Cruikshank's **The Toothache** from the 1840s, though usually limited to just the cover plus seven panels.

Examples are the Jackson Chewing Tobacco comics **How Adolphus Slim-Jim Used Jackson's Best** and **Ye Veracious Chronicle of Gruff & Pompey**, and Durham Smoking Tobacco's **Home Made Happy A Romance for Married Men**. The artists of these comics are mostly unidentified, but their level of skill was equal to anything in **Puck** and **Judge**. The **Home Made Happy** comic, in fact, was produced for Durham by The Graphic Company -- the publisher of **The Daily Graphic**, an 1870s illustrated newspaper which included cartoon work.

In addition to the debut of **Puck** and the spread of non-almanac promotional comics, the 1870s saw a third major development. It was at this time that an unusually high number of full-length sequential comic book stories, or graphic novels, began to appear. A sort of mini-boom had occurred in the U.S. following the 1840s appearances of Töpffer's and Cruikshank's comic books, but then largely died down for an approximately twenty year span. With the 1870s, graphic novels were back in even greater numbers.

A large part of this revival was brought about by New York City publisher Dick & Fitzgerald, infamous for their piracies, who issued seven such comic books. These included Doyle's

Foreign Tour and reprints of the two Wilson and Company-printed Töpffer booklets, but also four others of American origin, most likely lifted from earlier editions whose original source is yet unknown. Amongst the four are: the **Bachelor Butterfly**-inspired **The Wonderful Doings by Sea & Land of Oscar Shanghai**; artist John McLenan's parody of a nationally scandalized 1840s-50s romance between European dancer/actress Fanny Elssler and American aristocrat Henry Wikoff, titled **Sad Tale of the Courtship of Chevalier Slyfox-Wikof**; and the Yale-derived **College Experiences of Ichabod Academicus**. (Ichabod Academicus' original publication was in New Haven, CT in 1850, placing it right after **Jeremiah Saddlebags**).

Another highly desirable American graphic novel, sought especially by collectors of Western Americana, is **Quiddities of an Alaskan Trip** by William H. Bell. Bell was Timothy O'Sullivan's assistant photographer on the 1871-74 expedi-

From Quiddities of an Alaskan Trip.

tions of Lieutenant George Wheeler, surveying and mapping the western territories for the U.S. government. The story panels are laid out within ornate frames like those of stereograph cards, such as Bell was involved in creating on the expedition. It involves a parody of a trip from Washington, D.C. to survey the newly purchased territory of Alaska, which at the time was derisively referred to as "Seward's Folly." Bell published **Quiddities** in Portland, Oregon in 1873, a date which would have required that he drew it during the time he was on just such an expedition.

Other graphic novels also appeared during this period which have been mentioned earlier. The earliest known anthology devoted to collecting the comic strips of a single American artist was A.B. Frost's **Stuff and Nonsense** in 1884. The next known American collection came in 1888 - the very rare Frederick Burr Opper anthology, **Puck's Opper Book**. Both proved popular, so more Frost and Opper collections followed, to be joined within a few years by reprints collecting the cartoons and strips of American artists Kemble, Zim, Keppler, Gibson, Mayer, Taylor, "Chips," Howarth, Woolf, etc

Puck, **Judge**, and **Texas Siftings** all began monthly **Library** series - smaller 8-1/2" x 11" magazines, mostly black & white, which organized previously published material around one theme or one artist. For example, the first **Puck's Library**, published July 1887, was titled "The National Game," and gathered beneath one cover material from **Puck** poking fun at the game of baseball.

Life tended more towards hardcover collections, such as its annual ten-issue series **The Good Things of Life** (1884-1893), which included cartoons and strips by Palmer Cox, T.S. Sullivant, Hy Mayer, and others.

The Good Things of Life was published initially by the firm of White, Stokes, and Allen, but by the fourth book, the reprint series was published by Frederick A. Stokes alone. Stokes published a number of other cartoon books in the 1880s and 1890s, the majority of them reprint collections. The experience he gained at this time with these reprint albums placed Stokes in the perfect position to pick up the wealth of material about to be created for the comics supplements of William R. Hearst's newspapers, making Frederick A. Stokes the first major publisher of the coming Platinum Age.

In 1892, Charles Scribner's Sons published A. B. Frost's **Bull Calf and Other Tales**. It contains sequential comic strip art on quite a few pages as well as single panel cartoons. By 1898, Charles Scribner's Sons also issued Kemble's **The Billy Goat and Other Comicalities** as a 112 page hardcover, which also has sequential comic strips.

In the early 1890s, the slum children cartoons of artist Michael Woolf (many of which were reprinted in the 1899 collection **Sketches of Lowly Life in a Great City**) were popular. **Truth** magazine, which followed **Puck**'s format of color front cover, back cover and center-spread cartoons, but in style was more akin to the aristocratic **Life**, was initially unable to secure Woolf's services, creating an opportunity for the young cartoonist Richard F. Outcault, who desired to break into one of the weekly comic periodicals.

It was in his Woolf-inspired slum children cartoons for **Truth** that Outcault's prototype of the **Yellow Kid** first emerged. The bald, sack-clothed youngster made four appearances in **Truth**, starting with #372 on June 2, 1894, prior to his newspaper debut.

Later, after the rise of **Yellow Kid**'s popularity, he re-appeared in American comic magazines in parodies drawn by others, with politicians, even Hearst and Pulitzer, dressed up as the **Yellow Kid**. Such cartoons are known to have appeared in **Judge**, **Life**, and **Vim** plus various newspapers across the country. The reprinting of Yellow Kid comic strips within the 1897 book **The Yellow Kid in McFadden's Flats** - the first known collection of comics reprinting newspaper strips - signalled the arrival of the Platinum Age.

While comics have their roots in Europe, and the earliest American comic books either reprinted or emulated those of Europe, the direction of influence was by no means one way. By at least the 1870s, American cartoons were being seen in the Old World, as evidenced by the arrest in Spain of the on-the-lamb corrupt Tammany Hall politician Boss Tweed by Spanish police who recognized Tweed from a Thomas Nast cartoon.

European piracy of American cartoons was just as lucrative as the American piracy of Europeans. In the 1880s and '90s, the comics of Zim, Chips Bellew, and Charles Dana Gibson all saw reprint in Europe. F.M. Howarth's domestic comedies from **Puck** were favorites in France. American Hy Mayer was commissioned to create original comics work for **Black and White** (Britain), **Le Rire** (France), and **Fliegende Blätter**. Michael Woolf's slum children cartoons saw print in the British periodical **Pick-Me-Up**, during the same years that top British artist Phil May's first published work debuted in that publication. May later became famous for his Woolf-inspired street children cartoons as well as his influence on the development of comics in Australia.

As the 19th Century ended, American comics were coming to the fore worldwide, soon to explode into a position of dominance with the Platinum Age revolution brought about by the emergence of the color comic supplement in America's newspapers and the arrival of Richard F. Outcault's **Yellow Kid.**

*Doug Wheeler has scripted various comics stories, including a two-year run on **Swamp Thing**, the Volume 2 run of **Primortals**, the parody series **Classics Desecrated**, and the Eisner-nominated graphic novel **Fairy Tales of the Brothers Grimm**. For the past several years, he has been engaged in the study of 19th and early 20th Century American comics - or, in other words, goofing off. He can be reached at MidgetEyeball @aol.com.*

Robert Beerbohm set up at his first comicon in 1967, helped found the Comics & Comix chain stores in August 1972, and is now working on a detailed comics business history book. You can contact him at this e-mail address: beerbohm@teknetwork.com.

Richard Olson is an Emeritus Research Professor at the University of New Orleans and may be reached directly at olson32@attglobal.net.

All three are life-long collectors and students of all forms of the comics. We welcome any and all corrections and additions to this compilation of our earliest comics heritage.

Happy Hunting!

**The Strange and Wonderful Adventures
of Bachelor Butterfly by Rodolphe Töpffer
1870s © Dick & Fitzgerald, New York**

**Bachelor's Own Book by Cruickshank
1845 © Burgess, Stringer & Co., NY**

**Barker's Illustrated Almanac
1889 © Barker, Moore & Mein Medicine Co.**

FR1.0 **GD**2.0 **FN**6.0   **FR**1.0 **GD**2.0 **FN**6.0

COLLECTOR'S NOTE: Some of books listed in this section were published well over a century before organized comics fandom began archiving and helping to preserve these fragile popular culture artifacts. Consequently, copies of most all of these comics almost never surface in Fine+ or better shape. Most are in the Poor to VG range. If you want to collect these only in high grade, your collection will be extremely small.

The prices given for Fair, Good and Fine categories are for strictly graded editions. If you need help grading your item, we refer you to the grading section in this book or contact the authors of this essay. Items marked rare are trying to ascertain how many copies might still be in existence. Your help is welcome.

For ease of ascertaining the contents of each item of this listing, we offer the following revised list of categories found immediately following each title:

E - REPRINT OF EUROPEAN COMICS MATERIAL
G - GRAPHIC NOVEL (LONGER FORMAT COMIC TELLING A SINGLE STORY)
H - "HOW TO DRAW CARTOONS" BOOKS
I - ILLUSTRATED BOOKS NOTABLE FOR THE ARTIST, BUT NOT A COMIC.
M - REPRINT OF MAGAZINE / PERIODICAL COMICS MATERIAL
N - REPRINT OF NEWSPAPER COMICS MATERIAL
O - ORIGINAL COMIC MATERIAL NOT REPRINTED FROM ANOTHER SOURCE
P - PROMOTIONAL COMIC, EITHER GIVEN AWAY FOR FREE, OR A PREMIUM GIVEN IN CONJUNCTION WITH THE PURCHASE OF A PRODUCT.
S - SINGLE PANEL / NON-SEQUENTIAL CARTOONS (ENTIRELY OR PREDOMINANTLY)

Measurements are in inches. The first dimension given is Height and the second is Width. Some original British editions are included in the section, so as to better explain and differentiate their American counter-parts. This section revised, revised, and expanded by Robert Beerbohm, Doug Wheeler & Richard Olson with acknowledgment to Bill Blackbeard, Alfredo Castelli, Darrell Coons, Leonardo De Sá, Scott Deschaine, Joe Evans, Tom Gordon, Michel Kempeneers, Andy Konkykru, Don Kurtz, Gabriel Laderman, Robert Quesinberry, Steve Rowe, Randy Scott, John Snyder, Art Spiegelman, Steve Thompson, Richard Samuel West.

ACROBATIC ANIMALS
R.H. Russell: 1899 (9x11-7/8", 72 pgs, B&W, hard-c)
nn-   40.00   80.00 160.00
NOTE: Animal strips by Gustave Verbeck, presented 1 panel per page.

ADVENTURES OF TEASING TOM AND NAUGHTY NED
F. B. Patterson: 1879 (3-1/8x4-3/8, 12 pgs, B&W)
nn - By H. Blashfield   17.50   35.00   70.00
NOTE: Promotional comic for Clark's ONT (Originally Necessary To) Spool Cotton Thread in a complete single story.

ALMY'S SANTA CLAUS (P,E)
Edward C. Almy & Co., Providence, R.I.: nd (1880's) (5-3/4x4-5/8", 20 pgs, B&W, paper cover)
nn- (Rare)   12.50   40.00   80.00
NOTE: Department store Christmas giveaway containing an abbreviated 28-panel reprinting of George Cruikshank's The Tooth-ache. Santa Claus cover.

AMERICANS (see GIBSON'S PUBLISHED DRAWINGS)

AMERICAN TOUR OF MESSRS BROWN JONES AND ROBINSON, THE (O,G)
D. Appleton & Co., New York: 1872 (11-5/8x9-1/2", 158 pgs, printed one side only, B&W, green gilted hard-c)
nn- By Toby   70.00 140.00 300.00
NOTE: Original American graphic novel sequel to Richard Doyle's Foreign Tour of Brown, Jones, and Robinson, with the same characters visiting New York, Canada, and Cuba. Protective sheets between each page (not part of page count).

ATTWOOD'S PICTURES - AN ARTIST'S HISTORY OF THE LAST TEN YEARS OF THE NINETEENTH CENTURY (M,S)
Life Publishing Company, New York: 1900 (11-1/4x9-1/8", 156 pgs, B&W, gilted blue hard-c)
nn - By Attwood   40.00   80.00 160.00
NOTE: Reprints monthly calendar cartoons which appeared in LIFE, for 1887 through 1899.

BACHELOR BUTTERFLY, THE VERITABLE HISTORY OF MR. (E,G)
D. Bogue, London: 1845 (5-1/2x10-1/4", 74 pgs, B&W, gilted hardcover)
nn- By Rodolphe Töpffer (Scarce)   ???   ???   ???
nn- Hand colored edition (Very Rare)   ???   ???   ???

NOTE: This is the British Edition, translated from the re-engraved by Cham serialization found in L'Illustration - a periodical from Paris publisher Dubochet. Predates the first French collected edition. Third Töpffer comic book published in English. The first story page is numbered Page 3. Page 17 shows Bachelor Butterfly being swallowed by a whale.

BACHELOR BUTTERFLY, THE STRANGE ADVENTURES OF (E,G)
Wilson & Co., New York: 1846 (5-3/8x10-1/8", 68 pgs, B&W, hardcover)
nn- By Rodolphe Töpffer (Very Rare)   ???   ???   ???
nn- At least one hand colored copy exists (Very Rare) ??? ??? ???
NOTE: 2nd Töpffer comic book printed in the U.S., 3rd earliest known sequential comic book in the USA. Reprinted from the British D. Bogue 1845 edition, itself from the earlier French language Histoire de Mr. Cryptogame. Released the same year as the French Dubochet edition. Two variations known, the earlier printing with Page number 17 placed on the inside (left) bottom corner in error, with slightly later printings corrected to place page number 17 on the outside (right) bottom corner of that page. For both printings: the first story page is numbered 2. Page 17 shows Bachelor Butterfly already in the whale. In most panels with 3 lines of text, the third line is indented further than the second, which is in turn indented further than the first.

BACHELOR BUTTERFLY, THE STRANGE & WONDERFUL ADVENTURES OF
Dick & Fitzgerald, New York: nd (various printings; est. late 1860's to 1877+) (30 Cents, 68 pgs, B&W, paper cover) (all versions Rare) (E,G)
nn- Black print on blue cover (5-1/2x10-1/2"); string bound   ???   ???
nn- Black print on green cover(5-1/2x10-1/2"); string bound   ???   ???
NOTE: reprints the earlier Wilson & Co. edition. Page 2 is the first story page. Page 17 shows Bachelor Butterfly already in the whale. In most panels with 3 lines of text, the second and third lines are equally indented in from the first. Unknown which cover (blue or green) is earlier.

BACHELOR'S OWN BOOK. BEING THE PROGRESS OF MR. LAMBKIN, (GENT.) IN THE PURSUIT OF PLEASURE AND AMUSEMENT (E,O,G)
(See also PROGRESS OF MR. LAMBKIN)
D. Bogue, London: August 1, 1844 (5x8-1/4", 28 pgs printed one side only, cardboard cover & interior) (all versions Rare)
nn- First printing hand colored   ???   ???   ???
nn- First printing black and white   ???   ???   ???
NOTE: First printing has misspellings in the title. "PURSUIT" is spelled "PERSUIT", and "AMUSEMENT" is spelled "AMUSEMEMT".
nn- Second printing hand colored   ???   ???   ???
nn- Second printing black & white   ???   ???   ???
NOTE: Second printing. The misspelling of "PURSUIT" has been corrected, but "AMUSEMEMT" error is still present.
nn- Third printing hand colored   No misspellings   ???   ???   ???
nn- Third printing black & white   ???   ???   ???
NOTE: By George Cruikshank. This is the British Edition. Issued both in black & white, and professionally hand-colored editions. Hand-colored editions have survived in higher quantities than uncolored.

BACHELOR'S OWN BOOK. BEING TWENTY-FOUR PASSAGES IN THE LIFE OF MR. LAMBKIN, GENT. (E,G)
Burgess, Stringer & Co., New York on cover; Carey & Hart, Philadelphia on title page: 1845 (31-1/4 cents, 7-1/2x4-5/8", 52 pgs, B&W, paper cover)
nn- By George Cruikshank (Very Rare)   ???   ???   ???
NOTE: This is the second known sequential comic book story published in America. Reprints the earlier British edition. Pages printed on one side only. New cover art by an unknown artist.

BAD BOY'S FIRST READER (O,S)
G.W. Carleton & Co.: 1881 (5-3/4 x 4-1/8", 44 pgs, B&W, paper cover)
nn- By Frank Bellew (Senior)   50.00 100.00 200.00
NOTE: parody of a children's ABC primer, one cartoon illustration plus text per page. Includes one panel of Boss Tweed. Frank Bellew is considered the "Father of the American Sequential Comics"

BARKER'S ILLUSTRATED ALMANAC (O,P,S)
Barker, Moore & Mein Medicine Co: 1878-1932+ (36 pgs, B&W, color paper-cr)
1878-1880 (Rare)   40.00   80.00 160.00
1881-1884 (Scarce, 7-3/4x6-1/8")   30.00   60.00 120.00
NOTE: c-art shows 4 mast ships & lighthouse
1885-1889 (8x6-1/4")   20.00   40.00   80.00
NOTE: new c-art shows horse & rider jumping picket fence
1890-1897 (8-1/8x6-1/4")   20.00   40.00   80.00
1898-1899 (7-3/8x5-7/8")   20.00   40.00   80.00
1900+: see the Platinum Age Comics section (7x5-7/8")
NOTE: Barker's Almanacs were actually issued in November of the year preceding the year which appears on the almanac. For example, the 1878 dated almanac was issued November 1877. They were given away to retailers of Barker's farm animal medicinal products, to in turn be given away to customers. Each Barker's almanac contains 10 full page cartoons. These frequently included racist stereotypes of blacks. Each cartoon contained advertisements for Barker's products. It is unknown whether the cartoons appeared only in the almanacs, or if they also ran as newspaper ads or flyers. Originally issued with a metal hook attached in the upper right hand corner, which could be used to hang the almanac.

Barker's "Komic" Picture Souvenir,
Third Edition
1894 © Barker. Moore & Klein Medicine Co.

The Bottle by George Cruickshank
1871 © Geo.Gebbie, Philadelphia

The Story of The Man of Humanity
and The Bull Calf by A. B. Frost
1890 © C.H. Fargo & Co.

BARKER'S "KOMIC" PICTURE SOUVENIR (P,S)
Barker, Moore & Mein Medicine Co: nd (1892-94) (color cardboard cover, B&W interior)(all unnumbered editions Very Rare)

nn- (1892) (1st edition, 150 pgs) wraparound cover showing people headed
  towards Chicago for the 1893 World's Fair   80.00   160.00   320.00
nn- (1893) (2nd edition, ??? pgs) same cover as 1st edition
                                                   80.00   160.00   320.00
nn- (1894) (3rd edition, 180 pgs, 6-3/4x10-3/8") 25.00   50.00   100.00
NOTE: new cover art showing crowd of people laughing with a copy of Barker's Almanac
nn- (1894) (4th edition, 124 pgs, 6-3/8x9-3/8") same-c as 3rd edition
                                                   20.00   40.00   80.00
NOTE: The 2nd through 4th editions state their printing on the first interior page, in the paragraph beneath the picture of the Barker's Building. These have been confirmed as premium comic books, predating the Buster Brown premiums. They reprint advertising cartoons from Barker's Illustrated Almanac. For the 50 page booklets by this same name, numbered as "Part"s, see the PLATINUM AGE SECTION. All "Editions in Parts", without exception, were published after 1900.

BEAU OGLEBY, THE COMICAL ADVENTURES OF (E,G)
Tilt & Bogue: nd (c1843) (5-7/8x9-1/8", 72 pgs, printed one side only, green gilted hard-c, B&W)

nn- By Rodolphe Töpffer (Rare)   ???   ???   ???
nn- Hand coloured edition (Very Rare) ???   ???   ???
NOTE: British Edition; no known American Edition. Second Töpffer comic book published in English. Translated from Paris publisher Aubert's unauthorized redrawn 1839 bootleg edition of Töpffer's *Histoire de Mr. Jabot*. The backmost interior page is an advertisement for **Obadiah Oldbuck**, showing the cover for that comic book.

BEFORE AND AFTER. A LOCOFOCO CHRISTMAS PRESENT. (O)
D.C. Johnston, Boston: 1837 (4-3/4x3", 1 page, hand colored cardboard)

nn- (Very Rare) by David Claypool Johnston (sold at auction for $400 in GD)
NOTE: Pull-tab cartoon envelope, parodying the 1836 New York City mayoral election, picturing the candidate of the Locofoco Party smiling "Before the N.York election", then, when the tab is pulled, picturing him with an angry sneer "After the N.York election".

BILLY GOAT AND OTHER COMICALITIES, THE (M)
Charles Scribner's Sons: 1898 (6-3/4x8-1/2", 116 pgs., B&W, Hardcover)

nn- By E. W. Kemble   67.50   133.00   400.00

BLACKBERRIES, THE
R. H. Russell: 1897 (9"x12", 76 pgs, hard-c, every other page in color, every other page in one color sepia tone)

nn-By E. W. Kemble   139.50   279.00   975.00
NOTE: Tasefully done comics about Black Americana during the USA's Jim Crow days.

BOOK OF DRAWINGS BY FRED RICHARDSON (N,S)
Lakeside Press, Chicago: 1899 (13-5/8x10-1/2", 116 pgs, B&W, hard-c)

nn- (Scarce)   80.00   160.00   320.00
NOTE: Reprinted from the Chicago Daily News. Mostly single panel. Includes one Yellow Kid parody, some Spanish-American War cartoons.

BOTTLE, THE (E,O) (see also **THE DRUNKARD'S CHILDREN**, and **TEA GARDEN TO TEA POT**, and **TEMPERANCE TALES; OR, SIX NIGHTS WITH THE WASHINGTONIANS**)
D. Bogue, London, with others in later editions: nd (1846) (11-1/2x16-1/2", 16 pgs, printed one side only, paper cover)

D. Bogue, London (nd; 1846): first edition:
nn- Black & white (Scarce)   ???   ???   ???
nn- Hand colored (Rare)   ???   ???   ???
D. Bogue, London, and Wiley and Putnam, New York (nd; 1847) : second edition, misspells American publisher "Putnam" as "Putman":
nn- Black & white (Scarce)   ???   ???   ???
nn- Hand colored (Rare)   ???   ???   ???
D. Bogue, London, and Wiley and Putnam, New York (nd; 1847) : third edition (1847), has "Putnam" spelled correctly.
nn- Black & white (Scarce)   ???   ???   ???
nn- Hand colored (Rare)   ???   ???   ???
D. Bogue, London, Wiley and Putnam, New York, and J. Sands, Sydney, New South Wales: (nd; 1847) : fourth edition with no misspellings
nn- Black & white (Scarce)   ???   ???   ???
nn- Hand colored (Rare)   ???   ???   ???
NOTE: By George Cruikshank. Temperance/anti-alcohol story. All editions are in precisely identical format. The only difference to be found on the cover, where it lists who published it. Cover is text only - no cover art.

BOTTLE, THE (E)

W. Tweedie, London: nd (1862) (11-1/2x17-1/3", 16 pgs, printed one side only, paper cover)

nn- Black & white; By George Cruikshank (Scarce)   ???   ???   ???
nn- Hand colored (Scarce)   ???   ???   ???

BOTTLE, THE (E)
Geo. Gebbie, Philadelphia: nd (c.1871) (11-3/8x17-1/8", 42 pgs, tinted interior, hard-c)

nn- By George Cruikshank   ???   ???   ???
NOTE: new cover art (cover not by Cruikshak).

BOTTLE, THE (E)
National Temperance, London: nd (1881) (11-1/2x16-1/2", 16 pgs, printed one side only, paper-c, color)

nn- By George Cruikshank   ???   ???   ???
NOTE: See Platinum Age section for 1900s printings

BOTTLE, THE (E) (for the later Gowans & Gray, and the Frederick A. Stokes printings, see PLATINUM AGE SECTION).

BULL CALF, THE (P,M)
Creme Oatmeal Toilet Soap: nd (c1890's) (3-7/8x4-1/8", 16 pgs, B&W, paper-c)

nn- By A.B. Frost   25.00   50.00   100.0
NOTE: Reprints the popular strip story by Frost, with the art modified to place a sign for Creme Oatmeal Soap within each panel. The back cover advertises the specific merchant who gave this booklet away - multiple variations exist.

BULL CALF AND OTHER TALES, THE (M)
Charles Scribner's Sons: 1892 (120 pgs., 6-3/4x8-7/8", B&W, illus. hard cover)

nn- By Arthur Burdett Frost   50.00   100.00   450.0
NOTE: Blue, grey, tan hard covers known to exist

BULL CALF, THE STORY OF THE MAN OF HUMANITY AND THE (P,M)
C.H. Fargo & Co.: 1890 (5-1/4x6-1/4", 24 pgs, B&W, color paper-c)

nn- by A.B. Frost   42.50   85.00   185.0
NOTE: Fargo shoe company giveaway; pages alternate between shoe advertisements and the strip story.

BUSHEL OF MERRY THOUGHTS, A (see Mischief Book, The) (E)
Samson Low Son & Marsten: 1868 (68 pgs, handcolored hardcover, B&W)

nn- (6-1/4 x 9-7/8", 138 pgs) red binding, publisher's name on title page
  only.   200.00   400.00   800.0
nn- (6-1/2 x 10", 134 pgs) green binding, publisher's name on cover & title
  page.   200.00   400.00   800.0
NOTE: Cover plus story title pages designed by Leighton Brothers, based on Busch art. Translated by Harry Rogers (who is credited instead of Busch). This is a British publication, notable as the earliest known English language anthology collection of Wilhelm Busch comic strips. Page 13 of second story missing from all editions (panel dropped). Unknown which of these two editions was published first. Had a modern reprint, by Dover in 1971.

BUZZ A BUZZ OR THE BEES (E)
Griffith & Farran, London: September 1872 (8-1/2x5-1/2", 168 pgs, printed on side only, orange, black & white hardcover, B&W interior)

nn- By Wilhelm Busch (Scarce)   ???   ???   ???

BUZZ A BUZZ OR THE BEES (E)
Henry Holt & Company, New York: 1873 (9x6", 96 pgs, gilted hardcover, hand colored)

nn- By Wilhelm Busch (Scarce)   ???   ???   ???
NOTE: Completely different translation than the Griffith & Farran version. Also, contains 28 additional illustrations by Park Benjamin. The lower page count is because the Henry Holt edition prints on both sides of each page, and the Griffith & Farran edition is printed one side only.

CALENDAR FOR THE MONTH; YE PICTORIAL LYSTE OF YE MATTERS OF INTEREST FOR SUMMER READING (P,M)
S.E. Bridgman & Company, Northampton, Mass: nd (c late 1880's-1890's) (5-5/8x7-1/4", 64 pgs, paper-c, B&W)

nn- (Very Rare) by T.S. Sullivant-c/a   ???   ???   ???
NOTE: Book seller's catalog, with every other page reprinting cartoons and strips (from Life??). Art by: Chips Bellew, Gibson, Howarth, Kemble, Sullivant, Townsend, Woolf.

CARICATURE AND OTHER COMIC ART
Harper & Brothers, NY: 1877 (9-5/16x7-1/8", 360 pgs, B&W, green hard-c)

nn - By James Parton (over 200 illustrations)   25.00   75.00   150.0
NOTE: This is the earliest known serious history of comics & related genre from around the wor produced by an American. Parton was a cousin of Thomas Nast's wife Sarah. A large portion of this book was first serialized in **Harper's Monthly** in 1875.

A Bushel of Merry Thoughts by Wilhelm Busch
1868 © Samuel Low Son & Marston

Buzz A Buzz Or The Bees by Wilhelm Busch
1872 © Griffith & Farran, London

Centennial Fun
1876 © Frank Leslie, Philadelphia

	FR1.0	GD2.0	FN6.0		FR1.0	GD2.0	FN6.0

ARICATURE HISTORY OF CANADIAN POLITICS (M,S)
rip, Toronto: 1886; 1886 (12-3/4x10-3/8", 440 pgs, hard-c, B&W)

1 (Vol. 1) - (blue gilted-c) cartoon-r from 1849-1878   67.50 125.00 250.00
ote: the pages of Volume 1 are heavily interlaced with advertising sheets for Toronto businesses
ese are not part of the page count), including a smaller sized 96-pg machinery catalog, all
-bound into the volume.

ol. 2 - (brown gilted-c) cartoon-r from 1879-1884   67.50 125.00 250.00
OTE: Chronologically organized reprinting of single panel Canadian political cartoons, taken
om a variety of Canadian publications. Each right-hand page is a full page cartoon, while each
t-hand page is text describing the political situation which was being satirized.

ARTOONS BY HOMER C. DAVENPORT (M,N,S)
e Witt Publishing House: 1898 (16-1/8x12", 102 pgs, hard-c, B&W)

1   70.00 140.00 280.00
OTE: Reprinted from Harper's Weekly and the New York Journal. Includes cartoons about the
panish-American War. Title page reads "Davenport's Cartoons".

ARTOONS BY WILL E. CHAPIN (P,N,S)
he Times-Mirror Printing and Binding House, Los Angeles: 1899 (15-
x12", 98 pgs, hard-c, B&W)

1-   70.00 140.00 280.00
OTE: Premium item for subscribing to the Los Angeles Times-Mirror newspaper, from which
ese cartoons were reprinted. Includes cartoons about the Spanish-American War.

ARTOONS OF OUR WAR WITH SPAIN (N,S)
rederick A. Stokes Company: 1898 (11-1/2x10", 72 pgs, hardcover, B&W)
1- By Charles Nelan (r-New York Herald)   40.00 80.00 160.00
1- 2nd printing noted on copy right page   30.00 60.00 120.00

ARTOONS OF THE WAR OF 1898 (E,M,N,S)
elford, Middlebrook & Co., Chicago: 1898 (7x10-3/8",190 pgs, B&W, hard-c)
1-   50.00 100.00 200.00
OTE: Reprints single panel editorial cartoons on the Spanish-American War, from American,
panish, Latino, and European newspapers and magazines, at rate of 2 to 6 cartoons per page.
rt by Bart, Berryman, Bowman, Bradley, Chapin, Gillam, Nelan, Tenniel, others.

ENTENNIAL FUN (O,S) (Very Rare)
rank Leslie, Philadelphia: (July) 1876 (25¢, 11x8", 32 pgs, paper cover, B&W)
1- by Joseph Keppler-c;Thomas Worth-a   ??? ??? ???
OTE: Issued for the 1876 Centennial Exposition in Philadelphia.

CHILDREN'S CHRISTMAS BOOK, THE
he New York Sunday World: 1897 (10-1/4x8-3/4", 16 pgs, full color)
ec 12, 1897 - By George Luks, G.H. Grant, Will Crawford, others) (Rare)
  50.00 100.0 280.00

HIP'S DOGS (M)
R.H. Russell and Son Publishers: 1895 hardcover, B&W

1- By Frank P. W. "Chip" Bellew   25.00 50.00 100.00
early printing 80 pgs, 8-7/8x11-7/8"; dark green border of hardcover surrounds all four sides
pasted on cover image; pages arranged in error -- see NOTE below. (more scarce)
1- By Frank P. W. "Chip" Bellew   12.50 25.00 50.00
later printing 72 pgs, 8-7/8x11-3/4";green border only on the binding side (one side) of the
ver image.
OTE: Both are strip reprints from **LIFE** . The difference in page count is due to more blank
ages in the first printing – all printings have the same comics contents, but with the pages in
rst printing arranged differently. This is noticeable particularly in the 2-page strip "Getting a
ointer", which appears on the 2nd & 3rd to last pages of the later printings, but in the early print-
g last story page.

HIP'S OLD WOOD CUTS (M,S)
R.H. Russell & Son: 1895 (8-7/8x11-3/4", 72 pgs, hardcover, B&W)
1n- By Frank P. W. ("Chip") Bellew   25.00 50.00 100.00

HIP'S UN-NATURAL HISTORY (O,S)
rederick A. Stokes & Brother: 1888 (7x5-1/4", 64 pgs, hardcover, B&W)
1n- By Frank P. W. ("Chip") Bellew   12.50 25.00 50.00
OTE: Title page lists publisher as "Successors to White, Stokes & Allen."

CLOWN, OR THE BANQUET OF WIT, THE (E,M,O)
Fisher & Brother, Philadelphia, Baltimore, New York, Boston: nd (c.1851)
7-3/8x4-1/2", 88 pgs, paper cover, B&W)
1- (Very Rare; 1 copy known)   ??? ??? ???
IOTE: Earliest known multi-artist anthology of sequential comics; contains multiple sequential
comics, plus numerous single panel cartoons. A mixture of reprinted and original material, involv-
ng both European and American artists. "Jones, Smith, and Robinson Goes to a Ball" by Richard
Doyle (1st app. of Doyle's "Foreign Tour") in America, reprinted from PUNCH, August 24, 1850);

"Moses Keyser The Bowery Bully's Trip to the Californian Gold Mines", by JHM; "The Adventures
of Mr. Gulp" (by the Read brothers?); more comics by artists unknown; cartoons by George
Cruikshank, Grandville, Elton.

COLD CUTS AND PICKLED EELS' FEET; DONE BROWN BY JOHN BROWN
P.J. Cozans, New York: nd (c1855-60) (B&W)
nn-   ??? ??? ???
NOTE: Mostly a children's book. But, pages 87 to 110, and 111 to 122, both contain narrative
sequential stories.

COLLEGE SCENES (O,G)
N. Hayward, Boston: 1850 (14 x 18 cm, 68 pgs, printed one side only, B&W)
nn- (Rare) by Nathan Hayward   ??? ??? ???

COMICAL COONS (M)
R.H. Russell: 1898 (8-7/8 x 11-7/8", 68 pgs, hardcover, B&W)
nn- By E. W. Kemble   ??? ??? ???
NOTE: Black Americana collection of 2-panel stories

COMICAL PEEP SHOW, THE (E) (see also THE FOOLS PARADISE)
McLoughlin Bros., New York: 1902 (9-5/8x7-3/8", 36 pgs, glossy color
cardboard cover, B&W)   60.00 120.00 240.00
nn- By Wilhelm Busch
NOTE: Two variations in the coloring of the cover are known. All comics herein are reprinted from
the Hotten edition of **The Fools Paradise**.

COMIC ANNUAL, AMERICAN (O,I)
Richardson, Lord, & Holbrook, Boston: 1831 (6-7/8x4-3/8", 268 pgs, B&W,
hard-c)
nn- (Very Rare)   ??? ??? ???
NOTE: mostly text; front & back cover illustrations, 13 full page, and scattered smaller illustrations
by David Claypool Johnston; edited by Henry J. Finn

COMIC HISTORY OF THE UNITED STATES, (A)
Cassell, Petter, Galpin & Co.: 1880 (6-7/8x5-1/8", 336 pgs, hardcover, B&W)
nn-By Livingston Hopkins   12.50 25.00 50.00
NOTE: Text with many B&W illustrations; some are multi-panel comics. Not to beconfused with
Bill Nye's Comic History Of The U.S. which contains Frederick Opper illustrations.

COMICS FROM SCRIBNER'S MAGAZINE (M)
Scribner's: nd (1891) (10 cents, 9-1/2x6-5/8", 24 pgs, paper cover, side
stapled, B&W)
nn- (Rare) F.M.Howarth C&A   ??? ??? ???
NOTE: Advertised in SCRIBNER'S MAGAZINE in the June 1891 issue, page 793, as available
by mail order for 10 cents. Collects together comics material which ran in the back pages of
Scribner's Magazine. Art by Attwood, "Chip" Bellew, Dões, Frost, Gibson, Zim.

CROSSING THE ATLANTIC (O,G)
James R. Osgood & Co., Boston: 1872 ; Houghton, Osgood & Co., Boston:
1880 (68 pgs, hardcover, B&W)
1st printing (1872; 11x16") - by Augustus Hoppin   45.00 90.00 180.00
2nd printing (1880; 8-1/8x11-1/8")   32.50 65.00 150.00

CUBAN PICTURES (see OUR ARTIST IN CUBA) (O)

DAVENPORT'S CARTOONS (see CARTOONS BY HOMER C. DAVENPORT)

DIE VEHME, ILLUSTRIRTES WOCHENBLATT FUR SCHERZ UND
ERNEST (M,O) (see also PUCK)
Heinrich Binder, St.Louis: No.1 Aug 28, 1869 - No.?? Aug 20, 1870 (10 cents,
8 pgs, B&W, paper-c)
1-?? (Very Rare) by Joseph Keppler   ??? ??? ???
NOTE: Joseph Keppler's first attempt at a weekly American humor periodical. Entirely in German.
The title translates into: "The Star Chamber: An Illustrated Weekly Paper in Fun and Ernest".

DRAWINGS BY C.D. GIBSON (M,S) (see GIBSON'S PUBLISHED DRAWINGS)

DRUNKARD'S CHILDREN, THE (see also THE BOTTLE) (E,O)
David Bogue, London; John Wiley and G.P. Putnam, New York; J. Sands,
Sydney, New South Wales: July 1, 1848 (11x16", 16 pgs, printed on one side
only, paper-c)
nn- Black & white edition (Rare)   ??? ??? ???
nn- Hand colored edition (Rare)   ??? ??? ???
NOTE: Sequel story to THE BOTTLE, by George Cruikshank. Temperance/anti-alcohol story.
British-American-Australian co-publication. Cover is text only - no cover art.

EDUCATION OF MR. PIPP, THE (M) (see GIBSON'S PUBLISHED DRAWINGS)

ENTER: THE COMICS (E,G)
University of Nebraska Press: 1965

The Clown, or The Banquet of Wit
1851 © Fisher & Brother,

Crossing the Atlantic by Augustus Heppin
1880 © Houghton, Osgood & Co., Boston

The Evolution of A Democrat
A Darwinian Tale
1888 © Paquet & Co., New York

	FR1.0	GD2.0	FN6.0

nn- By E. Weisse   25.00   50.00   100.00
NOTE: Contains overview of Töpffer's life and career plus only published English translation of Töpffer's Monsieur Crepin (1837).

EVOLUTION OF A DEMOCRAT - A DARWINIAN TALE, THE (O,G)
Paquet & Co., New York: 1888 (25 cents, 7-7/8x5-1/2", 100 pgs, printed one side only, orange paper cover, B&W) (Very Rare)

nn- Written by Henry Liddell, art by G. Roberty   ???   ???   ???
NOTE: Political parody about the rise of an Irishman through Tammany Hall. Grover Cleveland appears as linked with Tammany. Ireland becomes the next state in the USA.

50 GREAT CARTOONS (M,P,S)
Ram's Horn Press: 1899

nn- By Frank Beard   30.00   60.00   120.00
NOTE: Premium in return for a subscription to **The Ram's Horn** magazine.

F**** A*** K*****, OUTLINES ILLUSTRATIVE OF THE JOURNAL OF** (O,S)
D.C. Johnston, Boston: 1835 (9-5/16 x 6", 12 pgs, printed one side only, blue paper cover, B&W interior) (see also **SCRAPS**)

nn - (Rare) by David Claypool Johnston   ???   ???   ???
NOTE: This is a series of 8 plates parodying passages from the Journal of Fanny (Frances) A. Kemble, a British woman who wrote a highly negative book about American Culture after returning from the U.S. Though remembered now for her campaign against slavery, she was prejudiced against most everything American culture, thus inspiring Johnston's satire. Contains 4 protective sheets (not part of page count)

FLY-ING DUTCHMAN; OR, THE WRATH OF HERR VON STOPPELNOZE, THE (E)
Carleton Publishing, New York: 1862 (7-5/8x5-1/4", 84 pgs, printed on one side only, gilted hardcover, B&W)

nn- By Wilhelm Busch (Scarce)   35.00   70.00   140.00
NOTE: This is the earliest known English language book publication of a Wilhelm Busch book. The story is plagiarized by American poet John G. Saxe, who is credited with the text, while the uncredited Busch cartoons are described merely as accompanying illustrations.

FOOLS PARADISE WITH THE MANY ADVENTURES THERE AS SEEN IN THE STRANGE SURPRISING PEEP SHOW OF PROFESSOR WOLLEY COB-BLE, THE (E) (see also THE COMICAL PEEP SHOW)
John Camden Hotten, London: Nov 1871 (1 crown, 9-7/8x7-3/8", 172 pgs, printed one side only, gilted green hardcover, hand colored interior)

nn- By Wilhelm Busch (Rare)   400.00   800.00   1600.00
NOTE: Title on cover is: WALK IN! WALK IN!! JUST ABOUT TO BEGIN!!! the FOOLS PARADISE; below the above title page. Anthology of Wilhelm Busch comics, translated into English.

FOOLS PARADISE WITH THE MANY WONDERFUL SIGHTS AS SEEN IN THE STRANGE SURPRISING PEEP SHOW OF PROFESSOR WOLLEY COB-BLE, FURTHER ADVENTURES IN (E)
Chatto & Windus, London: 1873 (10x7-3/8", 128 pgs, printed one side only, brown hardcover, hand colored interior)

nn- By Wilhelm Busch (Rare)   300.00   600.00   1200.00
NOTE: Sequel to the 1871 FOOLS PARADISE, containing a completely different set of Busch stories, translated from English.

FOOLS PARADISE MIRTH AND FUN FOR OLD & YOUNG (E)
Griffith & Farran, London: May 1883 (9-3/4x7-5/8", 78 pgs, color cover, color interior)

nn- By Wilhelm Busch (Rare)   100.00   200.00   400.00
NOTE: Collection of selected stories reprinted from both the 1871 & 1873 FOOLS PARADISE

FOREIGN TOUR OF MESSRS. BROWN, JONES, AND ROBINSON, THE
(see also THE CLOWN, OR THE BANQUET OF WIT) (E,M,O,G)
Bradbury & Evans, London: 1854 (11-5/8x9-1/2", 196 pgs, gilted hard-c, B&W)

nn- By Richard Doyle   35.00   70.00   140.00
nn- Bradbury & Evans 1900 reprint   20.00   40.00   80.00
NOTE: Protective sheets between each page (not part of page count). Expanded and redrawn sequential comics story from the serialized episodes originally published in PUNCH. Also comes in a 174 pg 8-3/4x11" version

FOREIGN TOUR OF MESSRS. BROWN, JONES, AND ROBINSON, THE (see also THE AMERICAN TOUR OF MESSRS BROWN JONES AND ROBINSON) (E,M,G)
D. Appleton & Co., New York: 1860 & 1877 (11-5/8x9-1/2", 196 pgs, gilted hard-c, B&W)

nn- (1860 printing) by Richard Doyle   30.00   60.00   120.00
nn- (1871 printing) by Richard Doyle   30.00   60.00   120.00
nn- (1877 printing) by Richard Doyle   30.00   60.00   120.00
NOTE: Protective sheets between each page (not part of page count).

	FR1.0	GD2.0	FN

FOREIGN TOUR OF MESSRS. BROWN, JONES, AND ROBINSON, THE (E,M,G)
Dick & Fitzgerald: nd (late 1860's - 1870's) (5-3/4x9-1/4", 100 pgs, printed one side only, green paper-c, B&W)

nn- (Scarce) by Richard Doyle   60.00   120.00   240.

FUNNY FOLK (M)
E. P. Dutton: 1899 (12x16-1/2", 90 pgs,14 strips in color-rest in b&w, hard-c) (Reprints many sequential strips & sngle panel cartoons from **Puck**)

nn - By Franklin Morris Howarth   162.50   325.00   1300.
NOTE: This might be considered a "missing link" between Victorian & Platinum Age comic boo

GIBSON BOOK, THE (M,S)
Charles Scribner's Sons & R.H. Russell, New York: 1906 (11-3/8x17-5/8", gilted red hard-c, B&W)

Book I -   50.00   100.00   200.
NOTE: reprints in whole the books: Drawings, People, London,Sketches and Cartoons, Education of Mr. Pipp, Americans. 414 pgs. 1907 2nd editions exist same value
Book II -   50.00   100.00   200.
NOTE: reprints in whole the books: A Widow and Her Friends, The Weaker Sex, Everyday People, Our Neighbors. 314 pgs 1907 second edition for both also exists. Same value.

GIBSON'S PUBLISHED DRAWINGS, MR. (M,S)
R.H. Russell, New York: No.1 1894 - ??? (11x17-3/4", hard-c, B&W)

nn (No.1; 1894) Drawings   96 pgs   30.00   60.00   120.
nn (No.2; 1896) Pictures of People   92 pgs   30.00   60.00   120.
nn (No.3; 1898) Sketches and Cartoons   94 pgs   30.00   60.00   120.
nn (No.4; 1899) The Education of Mr. Pipp   88 pgs   30.00   60.00   120.
nn (No.5; 1900) Americans   30.00   60.00   120.
nn (No.6; 1901) A Widow and her Friends   90 pgs   30.00   60.00   120.
nn (No.7; 1902) The Social Ladder   88 pgs   30.00   60.00   120.
NOTE: by Charles Dana Gibson cartoons, reprinted from magazines, primarily LIFE. The Education of Mr. Pipp tells a story. Series continues how long after 1902?

GIRL WHO WOULDN'T MIND GETTING MARRIED, THE (O)
Frederick Warne & Co., London & New York: nd (c1870's) (9-1/2x11-1/2", 2 pgs, printed 1 side, paper-c, B&W)

nn- By Harry Parkes   62.50   125.00   250.
NOTE: Published simultaneously with its companion volume, **The Man Who Would Like to Marry.**

GOBLIN SNOB, THE (O)
DeWitt & Davenport, New York: nd (c1853-56) (24 x 17 cm, 96 pgs, B&W, c hard-c)

nn- (Rare) by H.L. Stephens   ???   ???   ???

GOOD THINGS OF LIFE, THE (see LIFE, THE GOOD THINGS OF)

GREAT LOCOFOCO JUGGERNAUT, THE (S)
Imprint Society: 1971

nn- By David Claypool Johnston   -   12.00   25.

HAIL COLUMBIA! HISTORICAL, COMICAL, AND CENTENNIAL (O,S)
The Graphic Co., New York & Walter F. Brown, Providence, RI: 1876 (10x11-3/8", 60 pgs, red gilted hard-c, B&W)

nn- (Rare) by Walter F. Brown   100.00   200.00   400.

HEALTH GUYED
Frederick A. Stokes Company: 1890 (5-3/8 x 8-3/8, 56 pgs, hardcover, B&W)

nn- By Frank P.W. ("Chip") Bellew (Junior)   25.00   50.00   175.
NOTE: Text & cartoon illustration parody of a health guide.

HOME MADE HAPPY. A ROMANCE FOR MARRIED MEN IN SEVEN CHAPTERS (O,P)
Genuine Durham Smoking Tobacco & The Graphic Co.: nd (c1870's) (5-1/ tall x 3-3/8" wide folded, 27" wide unfolded, color cardboard)

nn- With all 8 panels attached (Scarce)   60.00   120.00   300.
nn- Individual panels/cards   5.00   10.00   25.
NOTE: Consists of 8 attached cards, printed on one side, which unfold into a strip story of title card & 7 panels. Scrapbook hobbyists in the 19th Century tended to pull the panels apart and paste into their scrapbooks, making copies with all panels still attached scarce.

HOME PICTURE BOOK FOR LITTLE CHILDREN (E,P)
Home Insurance Company, New York: July 1887 (8x6-1/8", 36 pgs, b&w, co paper cover)

nn-   40.00   80.00   160.
NOTE: Contains an abbreviated 32-panel reprinting of "THE TOOTHACHE" by George

The Fools Paradise Mirth
and Fun for Old & Young
1883 © Griffith & Farran, London

Imagerie d'Epinal sample page #44
1888 © Humoristic Publishing Co, Kansas City

Jack Huckabuck, The Scapegrace Raven
1888 © Stroefer & Kirchner, New York

	FR1.0	GD2.0	FN6.0
	FR1.0	**GD2.0**	**FN6.0**

uikshank. Remainder of booklet does not contain comics.

OOD'S COMICALITIES. COMICAL PICTURES FROM HIS WORKS (E,S)
rter & Coates: nd (8-1/2x10-3/8", 104 pgs, printed one side, hard-c, B&W)

| | 20.00 | 40.00 | 80.00 |

TE: Reprints 4 cartoon illustrations per page from the British *Hood's Comic Annuals*, which re poetry books by Thomas Hood.

OOKEYBEAK THE RAVEN, AND OTHER TALES (see also **JACK ICKABACK, THE SCAPEGRACE RAVEN**) (E)
eorge Routledge and Sons, London & New York: nd (1878) (7-1/4x5-5/8", 4 pgs, hardcover, B&W)

| - By Wilhelm Busch (Very Rare) | ??? | ??? | ??? |

W ADOLPHUS SLIM-JIM USED JACKSON'S BEST, AND WAS HAPPY. LENGTHY TALE IN 7 ACTS. (O,P)
ckson's Best Chewing Tobacco & Donaldson Brothers: nd(c1870's) (5-1/8 I x 3-3/8" wide folded, 27" wide unfolded, color cardboard)

| - With all 8 panels attached (Scarce) | 60.00 | 120.00 | 300.00 |
| - Individual panels/cards | 5.00 | 10.00 | 25.00 |

TE: consists of 8 attached cards, printed on one side, which unfold into a strip story of title d & 7 panels. Scrapbook hobbyists in the 19th Century tended to pull the panels apart and ste into their scrapbooks, making copies with all panels still attached scarce.

JGGINIANA; OR, HUGGINS' FANTASY, BEING A COLLECTION OF IE MOST ESTEEEMED MODERN LITERARY PRODUCTIONS (S,P)
C. Southwick, New York: 1808 (18 pgs, printed one side, B&W)

| - (Very Rare) | ??? | ??? | ??? |

TE: The earliest known surviving collected promotional cartoons in America. This is a booklet lecting 7 folded plus 1 full page flyer advertisements for barber John Richard Desborus ising the hired American artists Elkanah Tisdale and William S. Leney to modify previously blished illustrations into cartoons referring to his barber shop.

JMOROUS MASTERPIECES - PICTURES BY JOHN LEECH (E,M)
ederick A. Stokes: nd (late 1900's - early 1910's) No.1-2 (5-5/8x3-7/8", 68 js, cardboard covers, B&W)

| - John Leech (single panel cartoon-r from **Punch**) | 17.50 | 35.00 | 70.00 |
| - John Leech (single panel cartoon-r from **Punch**) | 17.50 | 35.00 | 70.00 |

UMORIST, THE (E,I,S)
V. Nickerson and Lucas and Deaver, Baltimore: No.1 Jan 1829 - No.12 Dec 29 (5-3/4x3-1/2", B&W text w/hand colored cartoon pg.)

| ound volume No.1-12 (Very Rare; 1 copy known; 270 pgs) | ??? | ??? |

TE: Earliest known American published periodical to contain a cartoon every issue. Surviving issues currently unknown – all information comes from 1 surviving bound volume. Each sue is mostly text, with one full page hand-colored cartoon. Bound volume contains an additional hand-colored cartoons at front of each six month set (total of 14 cartoons in volume). Cartoons pear to be of British origin, possibly by George Cruikshank.

USBAND AND WIFE, OR THE STORY OF A HAIR. (O,P)
arland Stoves and Ranges, Michigan Stove Co.: 1883 (4-3/16 tall x 2-11/16" de folded, 16" wide unfolded, color cardboard)

| h- With all 6 panels attached (Scarce) | 50.00 | 100.00 | 250.00 |
| - Individual panels/cards | 5.00 | 10.00 | 25.00 |

TE: Consists of 6 attached cards, printed on one side, which unfold into a strip story of title d & 5 panels. Scrapbook hobbyists in the 19th Century tended to pull the panels apart and ste into their scrapbooks, making copies with all panels still attached scarce.

HABOD ACADEMICUS, THE COLLEGE EXPERIENCES OF (O,G)
illiam T. Peters, New Haven, CT: 1850 (5-1/2x9-3/4",108 pgs, B&W)

| - By William T. Peters (Very Rare) | ??? | ??? | ??? |

TE: Pages are not uniform in size

HABOD ACADEMICUS, THE COLLEGE EXPERIENCES OF (O,G)
ck & Fitzgerald, New York: nd (late 1860's-1877+) (paper-c, B&W)

| - By William T. Peters (Very Rare) | ??? | ??? | ??? |

TE: Pages are uniform in size

LUSTRATED SCRAP-BOOK OF HUMOR AND INTELLIGENCE (M)
ohn J. Dyer & Co.: nd (c1859-1860)

| - Very Rare | ??? | ??? | ??? |

TE: A "printed scrapbook" of images culled from some unidentified periodical. About half of it illustrations that would have accompanied prose pieces. There are pages of single panel cartoons (multiple per page). And there are roughly 8 to 12 pages of sequential comics (all different ories, but appears to all be by the same presently unidentified artist). -

MAGERIE d'EPINAL (untrimmed individual sheets) (E)
ellerin for Humoristic Publishing Co, Kansas City, Mo.: nd (1888) No.1-60

(15-7/8x11-3/4",single sheets, hand colored) (All are Rare)

| 1-14, 21, 22, 25-46, 49-60 - in the Album d'Images | 25.00 | 50.00 | 100.00 |
| 15-20, 23,24, 47, 48 - not in the Album d'Images | 40.00 | 80.00 | 160.00 |

NOTE: Printed and hand colored in France expressly for the Humoristic Publishing Company . Printed on one side only. These are single sheets, sold separately. Reprints and translates the sheets from their original French.

IMAGERIE d'EPINAL ALBUM d'IMAGES (E)
Pellerin for Humoristic Publishing Co., Kansas City. Mo: nd (1888)
(15-1/2x11-1/2",108 pgs plus full color hard-c, hand colored interior)

| nn - Various French artists (Rare) | 200.00 | 400.00 | 1600.00 |

NOTE: Printed and hand colored in France expressly for the Humoristic Publishing Company . Printed on one side only. This is supposedly a collection of sixty broadsheets, originally sold separately. All copies known only have fifty of the sixty known of these broadsheets (slightly bigger, before binding, trimming the margins in the process, down to 15-1/4x11-3/8".). Three slightly different covers known to exist, with or without the indication in French "Textes en Anglais" ("Texts in English), with or without the general title "Contes de FEes" ("Fairy Tales"). All known copies were collected with sheets 15-20, 23,24, 47, and 48 missing.

IN THE "400" AND OUT (M,S) (see also **THE TAILOR-MADE GIRL**)
Keppler & Schwarzmann, New York: 1888 (8-1/4x12", 64 pgs, hardc, B&W)

| nn- By C.J. Taylor | 42.50 | 85.00 | 170.00 |

NOTE: Cartoons reprinted from Puck. The "400" is a reference to New York City's aristocratic elite.

IN VANITY FAIR (M,S)
R.H.Russell & Son, New York: 1896 (11-7/8x17-7/8", 80 pgs, hard-c, B&W)

| nn- by A.B.Wenzell, r-LIFE and HARPER'S | 45.00 | 90.00 | 180.00 |

JACK HUCKABUCK, THE SCAPEGRACE RAVEN (see also **HOOKEYBEAK THE RAVEN**) (E)
Stroefer & Kirchner, New York: nd (c1888) (9-3/8x6-3/8", 56 pgs, printed one side only, hand colored hardcover, B&W interior)

| nn- By Wilhelm Busch (Rare) | ??? | ??? | ??? |

NOTE: The 1888 date is derived from a gift signature on one known copy. The publication date might in truth be earlier.

JACK THE GIANT KILLER
David S. Brown Co., NY: 1898 (8x12-1/4", 16 pgs, B&Red)

| nn - | ??? | ??? | ??? |

JOURNEY TO THE GOLD DIGGINS BY JEREMIAH SADDLEBAGS (O,G)
Various publishers: 1849 (25 cents, 5-5/8 x 8-3/4", 68 pgs, green & black paper cover, B&W interior)

nn -- New York edition, Stringer & Townsend, Publishers			
(Very Rare)	???	???	???
nn -- Cincinnati, Ohio edition, published by U.P. James			
(Very Rare)	???	???	???
nn -- 1950 reprint, with introduction, published by William P. Wreden, Burlingame, California: 1950 (5-7/8 x 9", 92 pgs, hardcover, color interior)			
(390 copies printed)	25.00	50.00	100.00

NOTE: By J.A. and D.F. Read. Earliest known sequential comic book by an American creator; directly inspired by Töpffer's comic book. The New York and Cincinnati editions were both published in 1849, one soon after the other. Antiquarian Book sources have traditionally cited the Cincinnati edition preceded the New York, but without referencing their evidence. Conflicting with this, the Cincinnati edition lists the New York publishers' 1849 copyright, while the New York edition makes no reference to the Cincinnati publishers. Such would indicate that the New York edition was first. Both are very rare, and until resolved both might be regarded as published simultaneously. A New York copy with missing back c, detached front c, and G/VG condition sold for $2000 in 2000.

JUDGE (M,O)
Judge Publishing, New York: No.1 Oct 29, 1881 - No. 950, Dec ??, 1899
(10 cents, color front/back c and centerspread, remainder B&W, paper-c)

1 (Scarce)	???	???	???
2-26 (Volume 1; Scarce)	20.00	40.00	80.00
27-790,792-950	12.50	25.00	50.00
791 (12/12/1896; Vol.31) - satirical-c depicting Tammany Hall politicians as the Yellow Kid & Brownies	25.00	50.00	100.00
Bound Volumes (six month, 26 issue run each):			
Vol.1 (Scarce)	???	???	???
Vol.2-30,32-37	140.00	280.00	560.00
Vol.31 - includes issue 791 **YK/Brownies** parody	165.00	230.00	660.00

NOTE: Rival publication to Puck, owned by Republican Party backers.

JUDGE'S LIBRARY (M)
Judge Publishing, New York: No.1, April 1890 - No. 141, Dec 1899 (10 cents, 11x8-1/8", 36 pgs, color paper c, B&W)

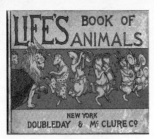

Life's Book of Animals
1888 © Doubleday & McLure Co.

Life's Picture Gallery
1898 © Life Publishing Company, New York

Max and Maurice by Wilhelm Busch
1871 © Roberts Brothers, Boston

	FR1.0	GD2.0	FN6.0
1	7.50	15.00	30.00
2-141	7.50	15.00	30.00
151-??? (post-1900 issues; see Plat section)			

NOTE: **Judge's Library** was a monthly magazine reprinting cartoons & prose from **Judge**, with each issue's material organized around the same subject. The cover art was often original. All issues were kept in print for the duration of the series, so, later issues are more scarce than earlier ones.

JUDGE'S QUARTERLY (M)
Judge Publishing Company/Arkell Publishing Company, New York: No.1 April 1892 - 31 Oct 1899 (25¢, 13-3/4x10-1/4", 64 pgs, color paper-c, B&W)

1-31	15.00	30.00	60.00

NOTE: Similar to **Judge's Library**, except larger in size, and issued quarterly. All reprint material, except for the cover art.

JUVENILE GEM, THE (see also THE ADVENTURES OF MR. TOM PLUMP, and OLD MOTHER MITTEN)
Huestis & Cozans: nd (1850-1852) (6x3-7/8", 64 pgs, hand colored paper-c, B&W) (all versions Very Rare)

nn- First printing(s) publisher's address is 104 Nassau Street (1850-1851)???
nn- 2nd printing(s) publisher's address is 116 Nassau Street (1851-1852) ???
nn- 3rd printing(s) publisher's address is 107 Nassau Street (1852+) ???
NOTE: The JUVENILE GEM is a gathering of multiple booklets under a single, hand colored cover (none of the individual booklets have the covers which they were given when sold separately). The publisher appears to have gathered whichever printings of each booklet were available when copies of THE JUVENILE GEM was assembled, so that the booklets within, and the conglomerate cover, may be from a mixture of printings. Contains two sequential comic booklets: THE ADVENTURES OF MR. TOM PLUMP, and OLD MOTHER MITTEN AND HER FUNNY KITTEN, plus five heavily illustrated children's booklets - **The Pretty Primer, The Funny Book, The Picture Book, The Two Sisters,** and **Story Of The Little Drummer.** Six of these -- including the two comic books -- were reprinted in the 1960's by Americana Review as a set of individual booklets, and included in a folder collectively titled "Six Children's Books of the 1850's".

LATER PENCILLINGS FROM PUNCH (see also PICTURES OF LIFE AND CHARACTER) (M,S,E)
Bradbury and Evans, London: nd (13-1/4x11",272 pgs, red gilted hard-c, B&W)

nn- By John Leech; reprints from Punch | 25.00 | 50.00 | 100.00 |

LIFE (miniature reprint of issue No.1) (M,P)
Mutual Life Insurance Company: falsely dated Jan 4, 1883 (actually published 1933) (3x2-1/2", 16 pgs, B&W, paper-c)

1	.25	2.00	5.00

NOTE: Fiftieth Anniversary miniaturized reprint of **Life** No. 1, given away by the Mutual Life Insurance Company. This item is frequently misrepresented by sellers, knowingly or unknowingly, as the actual **Life** Number 1. It is an extremely common and near worthless item, listed here only to prevent further misrepresentation.

LIFE (M,O) (continues with Vol.35 No. 894+ in the Platinum Age section)
J.A.Mitchell: Vol.1 No.1 Jan. 4, 1883 - Vol.1 No.26 June 29, 1883 (10-1/4x8", 16 pgs, b&w, paper cover); J.A.Mitchell: Vol.2 No.27 July 5, 1883 - Vol.6 No.148 Oct 29, 1885 (10-1/4x8-1/4", 16 pgs, b&w, paper cover) Mitchell & Miller: Vol.6 No.149, Nov. 5, 1885 - Vol.31, No.796, March 17, 1898 (10-3/8x8-3/8", 16 pgs, B&W, paper cover); Life Publishing Company: Vol. 31 No.797 March 24, 1898 - Vol.34 No.893 Dec 28, 1899 (10-3/8 x 8-1/2", 20 pgs, b&w, paper cover)

1-26 (Scarce)	???	???	???
27-799	5.00	10.00	20.00
800 (4/7/1898) parody Yellow Kid / Spanish-American War cover (not by Outcault)	25.00	50.00	100.00
801-893	5.00	10.00	20.00

NOTE: All covers for issues 1 - 26 are identical, apart from issue number & date.
Hard bound collected volumes:

V. 1 (No.1-26) (Scarce)	???	???	???
V. 2-34	45.00	90.00	180.00
V. 31 YK #800 parody-c not by RFO	70.00	140.00	280.00

NOTE: Because the covers of all issues in Volume 1 are identical, it was common practice to remove the covers before binding the issues together. This is not true of later volumes, though, in all volumes it was common to drop the advertising pages which appeared at the rear of each issue. Information on many more individual volumes will expand future Guide.

LIFE'S BOOK OF ANIMALS (M,S)
Doubleday & McClure Co.: 1898 (7-1/4x10-1/8", 88 pgs,color hardcover, B&W)

nn	???	???	???

NOTE: Reprints funny animal single panel and strip cartoons reprinted from LIFE. art by Blaisdell, Chip Bellew, Kemble, Hy Mayer, Sullivant, Woolf

LIFE'S COMEDY (M,S)
Charles Scribner's Sons: Series 1 1897 - Series 3 1898 (12x9-3/8", 138 pgs, hardcover, B&W)

1-3	60.00	120.00	240.

NOTE: Gibson a-1-3; c-3. Hy Mayer a-1-3. Rose O'Neill a-2-3. Stanlaws a-2-3. Sullivant a-1-2 Verbeek a-2. Wenzell a-1-3; c(painted)-2

LIFE, THE GOOD THINGS OF (M,S)
White, Stokes, & Allen, NY: 1884 - No.3 1886 ; Frederick A. Stokes, NY: No 1887; Frederick Stokes & Brother, NY: No.5 1888 - No.6 1889; Frederick A. Stokes Company, NY: No.7 1890 - No.10 1893(8-3/8x10-1/2", 74 pgs, gilted hardcover, B&W)

nn - 1884 (most common issue)	32.50	65.00	130.
2 - 1885	32.50	65.00	130.
3 - 1886	32.50	65.00	130.
4 - 1887	32.50	65.00	130.
5 - 1888	32.50	65.00	130.
6 - 1889	32.50	65.00	130.
7 - 1890	32.50	65.00	130.
8 - 1891	32.50	65.00	130.
9 - 1892	32.50	65.00	130.
10 - 1893	32.50	65.00	130.

NOTE: Contains mostly single panel, and some sequential, comics reprinted from LIFE. Attwo a-1-4,10. Roswell Bacon a-5. Chip Bellew a-4-6. Frank Bellew a-4,6. Palmer Cox a-1. H. E. C a-5. C. D. Gibson a-4-10. F.M. Howarth a-5-6. Kemble a-1-3. Klapp a-5. Walt McDougall a-1-2 McVickar a-5; J. A. Mitchell a-5. Peter Newell a-2-3. Gray Parker a-4-5,7. J. Smith a-5. Albert Steiner a-5; T. S. Sullivant a-7-9. Wenzell a-8-10. Wilder a-3. Woolf a-3-6.

LIFE, MINIATURE (see also LIFE (miniature reprint of issue No. 1) (M,P,S)
Life Publishing Co.: No. 1 ??? - No.2 1913 (5-3/4x4-5/8", 20 pgs, color paper cover, mostly B&W interior)

1- Exist?	???	???	???
2- (Rare)	???	???	???

NOTE: Giveaway item from Life, to promote subscriptions. All reprint material. No.2: James Montgomery Flagg-c; a-Chip Bellew, Gus Dirks, Gibson, F.M.Howarth, Art Young.

LIFE, THE SPICE OF (M,S)
White and Allen: 1888 NY & London: 1888 (8-3/8x10-1/2",76 pgs, hard-c, B&W)

nn	50.00	100.00	200.

NOTE: Resembles THE GOOD THINGS OF LIFE in layout and format, and appears to be an attempt to compete with their former partner Frederick A. Stokes. However, the material is not from LIFE, but rather is reprinted and translated German sequential and single panel comics.

LIFE'S PICTURE GALLERY (becomes LIFE'S PRINTS) (M,S,P)
Life Publishing Company, New York: nd (1898-1899) (paper cover, B&W) (are Scarce)

nn- (nd; 1898, 100 pgs, 5-1/4x8-1/2") Gibson-c of a woman with closed umbrella; 1st interior page announcing that after January 1, 1899 Gibson w draw exclusively for LIFE; the word "SPECIMEN" is printed in red, diagonal across every print; a-Gibson, Rose O'Neill, Sullivant ??? ??? ???

nn- (nd; 1899, 128 pgs, 4-7/8x7-3/8") Gibson-c of a woman golfer; 1st interior page announcing that Gibson & Hanna, Jr. draw exclusively for LIF the word "SPECIMEN" is printed in red, horizontally, across every print. Includes prints from Gibson's THE EDUCATION OF MR. PIPP; a-Gibson, Sullivant ??? ??? ???

NOTE: Catalog of prints reprinted from LIFE covers & centerspreads. The first catalog was giv away free to anyone requesting it, but after many people got the catalog without ordering any-thing, subsequent catalogs were sold at 10 cents.

MANNERS AND CUSTOMS OF YE HARVARD STUDENTE (M,S)
Houghton Mifflin & Co., Boston & Moses King, Cambridge: 1877 (7-7/8x1 72 pgs, printed one side, hardc, B&W)

nn- by F.G. Attwood | 175.00 | 350.00 | 700. |
NOTE: Collection of cartoons originally serialized in the **Harvard Lampoon**. Attwood later became a major cartoonist for **Life**.

MAN WHO WOULD LIKE TO MARRY, THE (O)
Frederick Warne & Co., London & New York: nd (c 1880's) (9-1/2x11-1/2", pgs, printed 1 side, paper-c, B&W)

nn- By Harry Parkes | 62.50 | 125.00 | 250 |
NOTE: Published simultaneously with its companion volume, **The Girl Who Wouldn't Mind Getting Married.**

MAX AND MAURICE: A Juvenile History in Seven Tricks (E)
(see also Teasing Tom and Naughty Ned)
Roberts Brothers, Boston: 1871 first edition (8-1/8 x 5-5/8", 74 pgs, hardcov B&W)

nn- By Wilhelm Busch	150.00	300.00	600
nn- 1882 reprint (76 pgs, hand colored- c/a, 75¢)	100.00	200.00	400

The Mischief Book by Wilhelm Busch
color cover art variation
1880 © R. Worthington, New York

Merryman's Monthly v3#5 with Bellew strip
May 1865 © J. C. Haney & Co., New York

Museum of Wonders by Opper
1894 © Routledge & Sons

	FR1.0	GD2.0	FN6.0

	FR1.0	GD2.0	FN6.0

TE: Each of the above contains 56 pages of art and text in a transitional format between a
ular children's book and a comic book (the page count difference is ad pages in back).
ninal inspiration for William Randolph Hearst to acquire as a "new comic" (following the wild
cess of Outcault's Yellow Kid) to license M&M from Busch and hire Rudolph Dirks in late 1897
eate a New York American newspaper incarnation. In Hearst's English language newspa-
s it was called The Katzenjammer Kids and in his German language NYC newspaper it was
d Max & Moritz, Busch's original title. An unknown number of other reprints exist. Translated
n the 1865 German original.

X AND MAURICE: A Juvenile History in Seven Tricks (E) (see also
asing Tom and Naughty Ned)

tle, Brown, and Company, Boston: 1899 first edition(?) (8-1/8 x 5-5/8", 72
s, hardcover, black ink on orange paper)

1899 By Wilhelm Busch	50.00	100.00	200.00
1902 (64 pages, B&W)	10.00	30.00	90.00

RRYMAN'S MONTHLY A COMIC MAGAZINE FOR THE FAMILY
. Haney & Co, NY: 1863-1877 (10-7/8x7-13/16", 30 pgs average, B&W)

rtain issues with short sequential comics	25.00	50.00	150.00

TE: Sequential strips by Frank Bellew Sr, Wilhelm Busch found so far; others?

NNEAPOLIS JOURNAL WAR CARTOONS (N,S)
nneapolis Journal: Jan 1899 (9x8", 160 pgs, paperback, punched & string
und)

By Charles L. Bartholomew	24.00	96.00	170.00

SCHIEF BOOK, THE (E)
Worthington, New York: 1880 (7-1/8 x 10-3/4", 176 pgs, hard-c, B&W)

green cloth binding; green on brown cover; cover art by R. Lewis based on
Busch art by Wilhelm Busch

	175.00	350.00	700.00

blue cloth binding; hand colored cover; completely different cover art
based on Busch by Wilhelm Busch

	175.00	350.00	700.00

TE: Translated by Rudolph Langdon Alger. American published anthology collection of Wilhelm
ch comic strips. Includes two of the strips found in the British "Bushel of Merry-Thoughts" col-
ion, translated better, and with the dropped panel restored. Unknown which cover version was

SEUM OF WONDERS, A (O,S)
utledge & Sons: 1894 (13x10", 64 pgs, color-c, color thru out)

By Frederick Opper	100.00	200.00	400.00

ADIAH OLDBUCK, THE ADVENTURES OF MR. (E,G)
& Bogue, London: nd (1840-41) (5-15/16x9-3/16", 176 pgs,B&W, gilted
rd-c)

By Rodolphe Töpffer (Scarce)	???	???	???
Hand coloured edition (Very Rare)	???	???	???

TE: This is the British edition, translating the unauthorized redrawn 1839 edition from Parisian
lisher Aubert, adapted from Töpffer's "Les Amours de Mr. Vieux Bois" (aka "Histoire de Mr.
ux Bois"), originally published in French in Switzerland, in 1837 (2nd ed. 1839). Early 19th
tury books are often found rebound, with original cover and/or title page gone. To distinguish
tions having no cover or title page: the British oblong editions (published by Tilt & Bogue) use
man Numerals to number pages. American oblong shaped editions use Arabic Numerals.
ish are printed on one side only. This is the earliest known English language sequential comic
k. Has a new title page with art by Robert Cruikshank.

ADIAH OLDBUCK, THE ADVENTURES OF MR. (E,G)
lson and Company, New York: September 14, 1842 (11-3/4x9", 44 pgs,
W, yellow paper-c, hemp paper interior)

other Jonathan Extra, No. IX - by Rodolphe Töpffer (Very Rare) ??? ??? ???
TE: Earliest known sequential American comic book, reprinting the 1841 British edition. Pages
numbered via Roman numerals. States "BROTHER JONATHAN EXTRA - ADVENTURES OF
OBADIAH OLDBUCK." at the top of each page. Prints 2 to 3 tiers of panels on both sides of
ch page. Copies could be had for ten cents according to adverts in Brother Jonathan. By
dolphe Töpffer, with new masthead design by David Claypool Johnston, and cover art
eath the masthead reprinting Robert Cruikshank's title page art from the Tilt & Bogue edition.
ly 1 known copy possesses (partially) the outer yellow cover.

ADIAH OLDBUCK, THE ADVENTURES OF MR. (E,G)
lson & Co, New York: nd (1849) (5-11/16x8-3/8", 92 pgs, B&W, hard-c)

by Rodolphe Töpffer; title page by Robert Cruikshank (Very Rare)
??? ??? ???
TE: 2nd Wilson & Co printing, reformatted into a small oblong format, with nine panels edited
, and text modified to smooth out this removal. Results in four less printed tiers/strips. Pages
numbered via Arabic numerals. Every panel on Pages 11, 14, 19, 21, 24, 34, 35 has one line
ext. Reformatted to conform with British first edition.

ADIAH OLDBUCK, THE ADVENTURES OF MR. (E,G)
ck & Fitzgerald, New York: nd (various printings; est. late 1860's to
76+) (Thirty Cents, 84 pgs, b&w, paper-c) (all versions Rare)

nn- Black print on green cover(5-11/16x8-15/16"); string bound ??? ???
nn- Black print on blue cover suspected to exist, same format as green-c ???
nn- Black print on white cover(5-13/16x9-3/16"); staple bound beneath
cover); this is a later printing than the blue or green-c??? ??? ???
NOTE: Reprints the abbreviated 1849 Wilson & Co. 2nd printing. Pages are numbered via Arabic
numerals. Many of the panels on Pages 11, 14, 19, 21, 24, 34, 35 take two lines to print the same
words found in the Wilson & Co version, which used only one text line for the same panels.
Unknown whether the blue or green cover is earlier. White cover version has "thirty cents" line
blackened out on the two copies known to exist. Robert Cruikshank's title page has been made
the cover in the D&F editions.

OLD MOTHER MITTEN AND HER FUNNY KITTEN (see also **The Juvenile
Gem**) (O)
Huestis & Cozans: nd(1850-1852) (6x3-7/8"12pgs, hand colored paper-c, B&W)

nn- first printing(s) publisher's address is 104 Nassau Street (1850-1851)
(Very Rare) ??? ??? ???
NOTE: A hand colored outer cover is highly rare, with only 1 recorded copy possessing it. Front
cover image and text is repeated precisely on page 3 (albeit b&w), and only interior pages are
numbered, together leading owners of coverless copies to believe they have the cover. The true
back cover has ads for the publisher. Cover was issued only with copies which were sold separately - books which were bound together as part of THE JUVENILE GEM never had such covers.

OLD MOTHER MITTEN AND HER FUNNY KITTEN (see **JUVENILE GEM**) (O)
Philip J. Cozans: nd (1850-1852) (6x3-7/8",12 pgs, hand colored paper-c, B&W)

nn- Second printing(s) publisher's address is 116 Nassau Street (1851-1852)
(Very Rare) ??? ??? ???
nn- Third printing(s) publisher's address is 107 Nassau Street (1852+) (Very
Rare)

OLD MOTHER MITTEN AND HER FUNNY KITTEN (O)
Americana Review, Scotia, NY: nd (1960's) (6-1/4x4-1/8", 8 pgs, side-stapled,
cardboard, B&W)

nn- Modern reprint	2.50	5.00	10.00

NOTE: Issued within a folder titled SIX CHILDREN'S BOOKS OF THE 1850'S. States "Reprinted
by American Review" at bottom of front cover. Reprints the 104 Nassau Street address.

ON THE NILE (O,G)
James R. Osgood & Company: Boston: 1874 ; Houghton, Osgood & Co., Boston:
1880 (112 pgs, gilted green hardcover, B&W)

1st printing (1874; 10-3/4x16") - by Augustus Hoppin	45.00	90.00	180.00
2nd printing (1880; smaller sized)	32.50	65.00	130.00

**OSCAR SHANGHAI, THE WONDERFUL AND AMUSING DOINGS BY
SEA AND LAND OF** (O,G)
Dick & Fitzgerald: nd (c late 1860s to late 1870's) (25 ¢, 5-3/4x9-1/4", 100
pgs, printed one side only, green paper c, B&W)

nn- Cover by Avery; interior by ALC (Rare) ??? ??? ???

OUR ARTIST IN CUBA (O)
Carleton, New York: 1865 (6-5/8x4-3/8", 120 pgs, printed one side only,
gilted hardcover, B&W)

nn- By Geo. W. Carleton	37.50	75.00	150.00

OUR ARTIST IN CUBA, PERU, SPAIN, AND ALGIERS (O)
Carleton: 1877 (6-1/2x5-1/8", 156 pgs, hardcover, B&W)

nn- By Geo. W. Carleton	32.50	65.00	130.00

NOTE: Reprints OUR ARTIST IN CUBA and OUR ARTIST IN PERU, then adds new section on
Spain and Algiers.

OUR ARTIST IN PERU (O)
Carleton, New York: 1866 (7-3/4x5-7/8", 68 pgs, gilted hardcover, B&W)

nn- By Geo. W. Carleton	37.50	75.00	150.00

NOTE: Contains advertisement for the upcoming books OUR ARTIST IN ITALY and OUR
ARTIST IN FRANCE, but no such publications have been found to date.

PHIL MAY'S SKETCH BOOK (E,S,M)
Chatto & Windus, London: 1897 (14-1/2x9-3/4", 64 pgs, red hard-c, B&W)

nn- by Phil May	42.50	85.00	170.00

PHIL MAY'S SKETCH BOOK (E,S,M)
R.H. Russell, New York: 1899 (14-5/8x10", 64 pgs, brown hard-c, B&W)

nn- by Phil May	32.50	65.00	130.00

NOTE: American reprint of the British edition

PICTURES OF ENGLISH SOCIETY (Parchment-Paper Series, No.4) (M,S,E)
D. Appleton & Co., New York: 1884 (5-5/8x4-3/8", 108 pgs, paper-c, B&W)

4- by George du Maurier; Punch-r	15.00	30.00	60.00

The Wonderful and Amusing Doings by
Sea & Land of Oscar Shanghai
1870s © Dick & Fitzgerald, New York

PUCK, #502, Oct. 20, Frederick Opper cover
1886 © Keppler & Schwarzman, NY

Rays of Light
1886 © Morse Bros., Canton, Mass.

NOTE: Every other page is a full page cartoon, with the opposite page containing the cartoon's caption.

PICTURES OF LIFE AND CHARACTER (M,S,E)
Bradbury and Evans, London: No.1 1855 - No.5 c1864 (12-1/2x18", 100 pgs, illustrated hard-c, B&W)

nn(No.1) (1855)	32.50	65.00	130.00
2 (1858), 3 (1860)	32.50	65.00	130.00
4 (nd; c1862) 5 (nd; c1864)	32.50	65.00	130.00
nn (nd (late 1860's)	32.50	65.00	130.00

NOTE: 2-1/2x18-1/4", 494 pgs, green gilted-c) reprints 1-5 in one book

1-3 John Leech's... (nd; 12-3/8x10", ? pgs, red gilted-c)25.00 50.00 100.00
NOTE: reprints John Leech cartoons from PUNCH. note that the Volume Number is mentioned only on the last page of these versions.

PICTURES OF LIFE AND CHARACTER (E,M,S)
G.P. Putnam's Sons: 1880's (8-5/8x6-1/4", 218 pgs, hardcover, color-cr, B&W)

nn- John Leech (single panel **Punch** cartoon-r)   20.00 40.00 160.00
NOTE: Leech reprints which extend back to the 1850s

PICTURES OF LIFE AND CHARACTER (Parchment-Paper Series) (E,M,S)
(see also HUMOROUS MASTERPIECES)
D. Appleton & Co., NY: 1884 (30¢, 5-3/4 x 4-1/2", 104 pgs, paper-c, B&W)

nn - John Leech (single panel **Punch** cartoon-r)   20.00 40.00 160.00
NOTE: an advertisement in the back refers to a cloth-bound edition for 50 cents

PICTURES OF PEOPLE (see GIBSON'S PUBLISHED DRAWINGS)

PLISH AND PLUM (E,G)
Roberts Brothers, Boston: 1883 (8-1/8x5-3/4", 80 pgs, hardcover, B&W)

nn- by Wilhelm Busch (Scarce)	40.00	80.00	160.00
nn- reprint (1899)	40.00	80.00	160.00

NOTE: The adventures of two dogs.

PROGRESS OF MR. LAMBKIN, (GENT) (E,G) (see also **Bachelor's Own Book**)
David Bryce and Son, Glasgow: 1884 (1 shilling, 7-7/8x5-3/4", 60 pgs, printed one side only, cardboard cover, B&W)

nn-   17.50 35.00 70.00
NOTE: Reprint of George Cruikshank's **Bachelor's Own Book**.

PUCK (German language edition, St. Louis) (M,O) (see also **DIE VEHME**)
Publisher unknown, St.Louis: No.1 March 18, 1871 - No.?? Aug. 24, 1872 (B&W, paper-c)

1-?? (Very Rare) by Joseph Keppler   ??? ??? ???
NOTE: Joseph Keppler's second attempt at a weekly humor periodical, following **Die Vehme** one year earlier. This was his first attempt to launch using the title **Puck**. This German language version ran for a full year before being joined by an English language version.

PUCK (English language edition, St. Louis) (M,O)
Publisher unknown, St. Louis: No.1 March ?? 1872 - No.?? Aug 24, 1872 (B&W, paper c)

1-?? (Very Rare) by Joseph Keppler   ??? ??? ???
NOTE: Same material as in the German language edition, but in English.

PUCK, ILLUSTRIRTES HUMORISTISCHES WOCHENBLATT (German language edition, NYC) (M,O)
Keppler & Schwarzmann, New York: No.1 Sept (27) 1876 - 1164 Dec ?? 1899 (10 cents, color front/back-c and centerspread, remainder B&W, paper-c)

1-26 (Volume 1; Rare) by Joseph Keppler - these issues precede the English language version, and contain cartoons not found in them. Includes cartoons on the controversial Tilden-Hayes 1876 Presidential Election debacle.   ???
27-52 (Volume 2; Rare) by Joseph Keppler - contains some cartoon material not found in the English language editions. Particularly in the earlier issues.   ???
53-1164   7.50 15.00 30.00
Bound Volumes (six month, 26 issue run each):

Vol.1 (Rare)	???	???	???
Vol.2-4 (Rare)	???	???	???
Vol.5-47	62.50	125.00	250.00

NOTE: Joseph Keppler's second, and successful, attempt to launch **Puck**. The first six months precede the launch of the English language edition. Soon after (but not immediately after) the launch of the English edition, both editions began sharing the same cartoons, but, their prose material always remained different. The German language edition ceased publication at the end of 1899, while the English language edition continued into the early 20th Century. First American periodical to feature printed color every issue.

PUCK (English language edition, NYC) (M,O)
Keppler & Schwarzmann, New York: No.1 March (14) 1877 - 1190 Dec ??

1899 (10 cents, color front/back-c and centerspread, remainder B&W, paper-‹

1 (Rare) by Joseph Keppler	???	???	???
2-26 (Rare) by Joseph Keppler	???	???	???
27-1190	12.50	25.00	5(

(see Platinum Age section for year 1900+ issues)
Bound volumes (six month, 26 issue run each):

Vol.1 (Rare)	???	???	???
Vol.2 (Scarce)	???	???	???
Vol.3-6 (pre-1880 issues)	175.00	350.00	70(
Vol.7-46	140.00	280.00	56(

NOTE: The English language editions began six months after the German editions, and so th English edition numbering is always one volume number, and 26 issue numbers, behind its p lel German language edition. Pre-1880 & post-1900 issues are more scarce than 1880's & 18

PUCK (miniature) (M,P,I)
Keppler & Schwarzmann, New York: nd (c1895) (7x5-1/8", 12 pgs, color fro back paper-c, B&W interior)

nn- Scarce   ??? ??? ???
NOTE: C.J.Taylor-c; F.M.Howarth-a; F.Opper-a; giveaway item promoting **Puck's** various pu cations. Mostly text, with art reprinted from **Puck**.

PUCK, CARTOONS FROM (M,S)
Keppler & Schwarzmann, New York: 1893 (14-1/4x11-1/2", 244 pgs, hard-c, mostly B&W)

nn- (Scarce) by Joseph Keppler (S/N)   ??? ??? ???
NOTE: Reprints **Puck** cartoons from 1877 to 1893, mostly in B&W, though a few in color, a text opposite each cartoon explaining the situation then being satirized. Issued only in an e of 300 numbered issues, signed by Keppler. Only 1/4 of the pages are cartoons.

PUCK'S LIBRARY (M)
Keppler & Schwarzmann, New York: No.1, July, 1887 - No. 174, Dec, 1899 (10 cents, 11-1/2x8-1/4", 36 pgs, color paper-c, B&W)

1- "The National Game" (Baseball)   ??? ??? ???
2-149   7.50 15.00 30
NOTE: **Puck's Library** was a monthly magazine reprinting cartoons & prose from **Puck**, each issue's material organized around the same subject. The cover art was often original. A issues were kept in print for the duration of the series, so, later issues are more scarce than earlier ones.

PUCK'S OPPER BOOK (M)
Keppler & Schwarzmann, New York: 1888 (30 cents, color paper-c, B&W)

nn- (Very Rare) by F. Opper   ??? ??? ???
NOTE: Solidly strip and cartoon material by Opper, all of it reprinted from **Puck**.

PUCK, PICKINGS FROM (M)
Keppler & Schwarzmann, New York: No.1, Sept, 1891 - No. 34, Dec, 1899 (25 cents, 13-1/4x10-1/4", 68 pgs, color paper-c, B&W)

1-34   15.00 30.00 60
NOTE: Similar to **Puck's Library**, except larger in size, and issued quarterly. All reprint mate except for the cover art. There also exist variations with "RAILROAD EDITION 30 CENTS" p ed on the cover in place of the standard 25 cent price.

PUCK PROOFS (M,P,S)
Keppler & Schwarzmann, New York: nd (1906-1909) (76 pgs, paper cover; B&W) (all are Scarce)

nn- (c.1906, no price, 4-1/8x5-1/4") B&W painted -c of couple kissing over a chess board; 1905 & 1906-r   ??? ??? ???
nn- (c.1909, 10 cents, 4-3/8x5-3/8") plain green paper-c; 1905-1909-r   ???
NOTE: Catalog of prints available from **Puck**, reprinting mostly cover & centerspread art fron **Puck**. There likely exist more as yet unreported Puck Proofs catalogs. Art by Rose O'Neill.

PUCK, THE TARIFF ?, CARTOONS AND COMMENTS FROM (M,S)
Keppler & Schwarzmann, New York: 1888 (10 cents, 6-7/8x10-3/8", 36 p§ paper-c, B&W)

nn (Scarce)   ??? ??? ???
NOTE: Reprints both cartoons and commentary from **Puck**, concerning the issue of tariffs wl were then being debated in Congress. Art by Gillam, Keppler, Opper, Taylor.

PUCK, WORLD'S FAIR
Keppler & Schwarzmann, PUCK BUILDING, World's Fair Grounds, Chica
No.1 May 1, 1893 - No.26 Oct 30, 1893 (10 cents, 11-1/4x8-3/4, 14 pgs, pape color front/back/center pages, rest B&W)(All issues Scarce to Rare)

1-26   30.00 60.00 120
1-26 bound edition   500.00 1000.00 2000
NOTE: Art by Joseph Keppler, F. Opper, F.M. Howarth, C.J. Taylor, W.A. Rogers. This was a separate, parallel run of **Puck**, published during the 1893 Chicago World's Fair from within th

Scraps, New Series #1 by D.C. Johnston
1849 © D. C. Johnston, Boston

Shakespeare Would Ride the Bicycle If Alive
Today. "The Reasons Why" by Opper
1896 © H. A. Lozier & Co.

Stuff and Nonsense by A.B. Frost
1884 © Charles Scribner's Sons

	FR1.0	GD2.0	FN6.0

grounds, and containing all new and different material than the regular weekly **Puck**. Smaller
-d and priced the same, this originally sold poorly, and had not as wide distribution as **Puck**,
so consequently prices are much more rare than regular **Puck** issues from the same period.
to be confused with the larger sized regular **Puck** issues from 1893 which sometimes also
tained World's Fair related material, and sometimes had the words "World's Fair" appear on
cover. Can also be distinguished by the fact that **Puck's** issue numbering was in the 800's in
3, while these issues number 1 through 26.

IDDITIES OF AN ALASKAN TRIP (O,G)
A. Steel & Co., Portland, OR: 1873 (6-3/4x10-1/2", 80 pgs, gilted blue hard-c,
W)

By William H. Bell (Very Rare)	???	???	???

TE: highly sought by collectors of Western Americana - parady on "Sewards
lly" of a trip from Washington DC to Alaska by a member of the survey trek

RE CARTOONS OF CANADIAN HISTORY (see **CARICATURE HISTORY
CANADIAN POLITICS**)

YS OF LIGHT (O,P)
rse Bros., Canton, Mass.: No.1 1886 (7-1/8x5-1/8", 8 pgs, color paper-c,
W)

'Rare)	???	???	???

TE: Giveaway pamphlet in guise of an educational publication, consisting entirely of a sequen-
story in which a teacher instructs her classroom of young girls in the use of Rising Sun Stove
sh. Color front & back covers

:RAPS (O,S) (see also **F****** A*** K*****)**
C. Johnston, Boston: 1828 - No.8 1840; New Series No.1 1849 (12 pgs,
-ited one side only, paper-c, B&W)

1828 (9-1/4 x 11-3/4") (Very Rare)	???	???	???
1830 (9-3/4 x 12-3/4") (Very Rare)	???	???	???
1832 (10-7/8 x 13-1/8") (Very Rare)	???	???	???
1833 (11 x 13-5/8") (Very Rare)	???	???	???
1834 (10-3/8 x 13-1/4") (Very Rare)	???	???	???
1835 (10-3/8 x 13-1/4") red lettering in title SCRAPS (Very Rare)			
	200.00	400.00	800.00
1835 (10-3/8 x 13-1/4") no red lettering in title (Very Rare)			
	200.00	400.00	800.00
1837 (10-3/4 x 13-7/8") 1st Edition (Very Rare)	200.00	400.00	800.00
1837 (10-3/4 x 13-3/4") 2nd Edition (so stated) (Scarce)			
	75.00	125.00	250.00
1840 (10-1/2 x 13-7/8") (Very Rare)	200.00	400.00	800.00
w Series 1 - 1849 (10-7/8 x 13-3/4") (Scarce)	75.00	125.00	250.00

TE: By David Claypool Johnston. All issues consist of four one-sided sheets with 9 to 12 sin-
panel cartoons per sheet. The other pages are blank or text. Contains 4 protective sheets (not
t of page count) Only the 1849 New Series Number 1 has cover art. New Number 1, and the
cond printing of issue 7, have survived in higher numbers due to a 1940s warehouse discovery

**IAKESPEARE WOULD RIDE THE BICYCLE IF ALIVE TODAY. "THE
:ASON "WHY"** (O,P,S)
eveland Bicycles H.A. Lozier & Co., Toledo, OH: 1896 (5-1/2x4", 16 pgs,
per-c, color)

By F. Opper (Rare)	70.00	140.00	280.00

TE: Original cartoons of Shakespearian characters riding bicycles; also popular amongst col-
tors of bicycle ephemera

:ETCHES AND CARTOONS (see **GIBSON'S PUBLISHED DRAWINGS**)

:ETCHES OF LOWLY LIFE IN A GREAT CITY (M,S)
P. Puntam's Sons: 1899 (8-5/8x11-1/4", 200 pgs, hard-c, B&W)
prints from Life and Judge of Woolf's cartoons of NYC slum children)

By Michael Angelo Woolf	75.00	150.00	300.00

TE: Woolf's cartoons are regarded as a primary influence on R.F. Outcault in the later devel-
ment of The Yellow Kid newspaper strip.

**OVELY PETER; or, Cheerful Stories and Funny Pictures, For Good
:tle People.** (E,I)
rter & Coates, Philadelphia: 1880 (4to, 100 pgs, handcolored hard-c)

By Heinrich Hoffman	50.00	100.00	400.00

te: The John C. Winston Co. did a number of reprints from at least 1901-1940 which range in
ce from $95 to $350 plus The Limited Editions Club, New York, published 1500 copies of a
muel ("Mark Twain") Clemons translated version done in 1891 in Berlin but not reprinted until
35, range in price from $285 to $450

OCIAL LADDER, THE (see **GIBSON'S PUBLISHED DRAWINGS**)

OCIETY PICTURES (M,S,E)
harles H. Sergel Company, Chicago: 1895 (5-1/4x7-3/4", 168 pgs,
inted 1 side, paper-c, B&W)

nn- by George du Maurier; reprints from **Punch**.	12.50	25.00	50.00

**SOUVENIR OF SOHMER CARTOONS FROM PUCK, JUDGE, AND
FRANK LESLIE'S** (M,S,P)
Sohmer Piano Co.: nd(c.1893) (6x4-3/4", 16 pgs, paper-c, B&W)

nn-	20.00	40.00	80.00

NOTE: Reprints painted "cartoon" Sohmer Piano advertisements which appeared in the above
publications. Artists include Keppler, Gillam, others.

STORY OF THE MAN OF HUMANITY AND THE BULL CALF, THE
(see **BULL CALF, THE STORY OF THE MAN OF HUMANITY AND THE**)
NOTE: reprints of two of A. B. Frost's mostfamous sequential comic strips

STUFF AND NONSENSE (Harper's Monthly strip-r) (M)
Charles Scribner's Sons: 1884 (10-1/4x7-3/4", 100 pgs, hardcover, B&W)

nn - By Arthur Burdett Frost	60.00	120.00	240.00
nn - By A.B. Frost (1888 reprint, 104 pgs)	40.00	80.00	160.00

NOTE: earliest known anthology devoted to collecting the comic strips of a single American artist

SUMMER SCHOOL OF PHILOSOPHY AT MT. DESERT, THE
Henry Holt & Co.: 1881 (10-3/8x8-5/8", 60 pgs, illus. gilt hard-c, B&W)

nn - By J. A. Mitchell	60.00	120.00	240.00

NOTE: J.A.Mitchell went on to found LIFE two years later in 1883. Also, the long-running mascot
for LIFE was Cupid - which saw multitudes of Cupids flying around in this story.

**TAILOR-MADE GIRL, HER FRIENDS, HER FASHIONS, AND HER FOLLIES,
THE** (see also **IN THE "400" AND OUT**) (O,I)
Charles Scribner's Sons, New York: 1888 (8-3/8x10-1/2", 68 pgs, hardc, B&W)

nn- Art by C.J. Taylor	17.50	35.00	70.00

NOTE: Format is a full page cartoon on every other page, with a script style vignette, written by
Philip H. Welch, on every page opposite the art.

TALL STUDENT, THE
Roberts Brothers, Boston: 1873 (7x5", 48 pgs, printed one side only, gilted
hard-c, B&W)

nn- By Wilhelm Busch (Scarce)	30.00	60.00	120.00

TARIFF ?, CARTOONS AND COMMENTS FROM PUCK, THE (see also
PUCK, THE TARIFF ?, CARTOONS AND COMMENTS FROM)

**TEASING TOM AND NAUGHTY NED WITH A SPOOL OF CLARK'S COTTON,
THE ADVENTURES OF** (O,P)
Clark's O.N.T. Spool Cotton: nd (c1879-1880) (4-1/4x3", 12 pgs, B&W, paper-c)

nn-	17.50	35.00	70.00

NOTE: Knock-off of the "First Trick" in Wilhelm Busch's **Max and Maurice**, modified to involve
Clark's Spool Cotton in the story, with similar but new art by an artist identified as "HB". The back
cover advertises the specific merchant who gave this booklet away -- multiple variations of back
cover suspected

**TEMPERANCE TALES; OR, SIX NIGHTS WITH THE WASHINGTONIANS,
VOL I & II**
W.A.Leary & Co., Philadelphia: 1848 (50¢, 6-1/8x4", 328 pgs, B&W, hard-c)

nn-	???	???	???

NOTE: Mostly text. This edition gathers Volume I & II together. The first 8 pages reprints George
Cruikshank's **THE BOTTLE**, re-drawn & re-engraved by Phil A. Pilliner. Later editions of this book
do not include **THE BOTTLE** reprint and are therefore of little interest to comics collectors.

TOM PLUMP, THE ADVENTURES OF MR. (see also **THE JUVENILE GEM**) (O)
Huestis & Cozans, New York: nd (c1850-1851) (6x3-7/8", 12 pgs, hand colored
paper-c, B&W)

nn- First printing(s) publisher's address is 104 Nassau Street (1850-1851)			
(Very Rare)	???	???	???

NOTE: California Gold Rush story. The hand colored outer cover is highly rare, with only 1
recorded copy possessing it. The front cover image and text is repeated precisely on page 3
(albeit b&w), and only interior pages are numbered, together leading owners of coverless copies
to believe they have the cover. The true back cover contains ads for the publisher. The cover was
issued only with copies which were sold separately - booklets which were bound together as part
of **THE JUVENILE GEM** never had such covers.

TOM PLUMP, THE ADVENTURES OF MR. (see also **THE JUVENILE GEM**) (O)
Philip J. Cozans: nd (1851-1852) (6x3-7/8", 12 pgs, hand colored paper-c, B&W)

nn- Second printing(s) publisher's address is 116 Nassau Street (1851-1852)			
(Very Rare)	???	???	???
nn- Third printing(s) publisher's address is 107 Nassau Street (1852+) (Very			
Rare)	???	???	???

TOM PLUMP, THE ADVENTURES OF MR.
Americana Review, Scotia, NY: nd(1960's) (6-1/4x4-1/8", 8 pgs, side-stapled,

The Adventures of Mr. Tom Plump
1851 © Philip J. Cozans, New York

The Tooth Ache by George Cruickshank
1849 © J. L. Smith, Philadelphia, PA

Truth #372 (first app The Yellow Kid)
June 2 1894 © Truth Company, NY

	FR1.0	GD2.0	FN6.0

cardboard-c, B&W

nn- Modern reprint — 12.00 24.00
NOTE: Issued within a folder titled SIX CHILDREN'S BOOKS OF THE 1850'S. States "Reprinted by American Review" at bottom of front cover. Reprints the 104 Nassau Street address.

TOM PLUMP, THE ADVENTURES OF MR.
unknown: nd (1980's) (5-1/2x4-1/4", 8 pgs, side-stapled, black ink on colored paper)

nn- Modern reprint (Scarce) — 5.00 10.00
NOTE: photocopy reprint by a comix zine publisher, from an Americana Review copy, and available by mail order only.

TOOTH-ACHE, THE (E,O)
D. Bogue, London: 1849 (???) --

nn- by Cruikshank, B&W (Very Rare) ??? ??? ???
nn- by Cruikshank, hand colored (Rare) ??? ??? ???
NOTE: Scripted by Horace Mayhew, art by George Cruikshank. This is the British edition. Price 1/6 b&w, 3 hand colored. In British editions, the panels are not numbered. Publisher's name appears on cover. Booklet's "pages" unfold into a single, long, strip.

TOOTH-ACHE, THE (E) (see also ALMY'S SANTA CLAUS, and HOME PICTURE BOOK FOR LITTLE CHILDREN)
J.L. Smith, Philadelphia, PA: nd (1849) (15 cents, 5-1/8"x 3-3/4" folded, 86-7/8" wide unfolded, 26 pgs, cardboard-c, color)

nn- By Cruikshank, hand colored (Very Rare) ??? ??? ???
NOTE: Reprints the D. Bogue edition. In American editions, the panels are numbered (43 panels, not counting front & back cover). Publisher's name stamped on inside front cover, plus printed along left-hand side of first interior page. Page 1 is pasted to inside back cover, and unfolds from there. Front cover not attached to back cover by design. Booklet's "pages" unfold into a single, long, strip (made from four individual strips pasted together on the blank back side).

TOOTH-ACHE, THE (E)
Arts Council of Great Britain: nd (1974) (5-1/2x3-5/8", 28 pgs, B&W, cardboard-c, color interior)

nn- By Cruikshank, printed color — 15.00 30.00
NOTE: Modern reprint of D. Bogue edition. 5000 copies printed, included in a catalogue issued with a show at the Victoria and Albert Museum, in London, 28 February-28 April 1974. Also included in the catalogue was a modern reprint of the Cruikshank booklet "A Comic Alphabet".

TRUTH (See Plat sectionfor 1900-1906 issues)
Truth Company, NY: 1886-1906? (13-11/16x10-5/16", 16 pgs, process color-c & centerfolds, rest B&W)

1886-1887 issues	20.00	40.00	90.00
1888-1893 issues	15.00	30.00	70.00
1894-1895 non Outcault issues	10.00	20.00	50.00
Mar 10 1894 - precursor YK RFO	50.00	150.00	300.00
#372 June 2 1894 - first app Yellow Kid RFO	150.00	450.00	900.00
June 23 1894 - precursor YK R. F. Outcault	50.00	150.00	300.00
July 14 1894 -2nd app Yellow Kid RFO	100.00	300.00	600.00
Sept 15 1894 - (2) 3rd app YK RFO plus YK precursor	100.00	300.00	600.00
Feb 9 1895 - 4th app Yellow Kid RFO	100.00	300.00	600.00
1896-1899 issues	10.00	20.00	50.00

NOTE: this magazine contains the earliest known appearances of The Yellow Kid by Richard Felton Outcault. Feb 9 1895 issue's YK cartoon was reprinted one week later in the New York World Feb 17 1895 edition. We are still sorting out further Outcault appearances. Truth also contained full color sequential strips by Hy Mayer on the back plus Woolf, Verbeek, etc.

TRUTH, 99 WOOLF CARTOONS FROM (M,S) Very rare - little is known ???

TWO HUNDRED SKETCHES, HUMOROUS AND GROTESQUE, BY GUSTAVE DORE
Frederick Warne & Co, London: 1867 (13-3/4x11-3/8, 94 pgs, hard-c, B&W)

nn-(1867) by Gustave Dore ??? ??? ???
nn-(Second Edition; 1871)- by Gustave Dore ??? ??? ???
nn-(Third Edition; 1870's)- by Gustave Dore ??? ??? ???
nn-(Fourth Edition; 1870's- by Gustave Dore ??? ??? ???
NOTE: Contains sequential comics stories, single panel cartoons, and sketches. Reprints and translates material which originally appeared in the French publications "Le Journal pour Rire", circa 1848-49. Although dated 1867, it was likely published & available for the 1866 Christmas Season, as has been confirmed for the American edition. Printed by Dalziel. The American & first British editions were printed simultaneously, the American edition is not a reprint of the British.

TWO HUNDRED SKETCHES, HUMOROUS AND GROTESQUE, BY GUSTAVE DORE (E)
Roberts Brothers, Boston: 1867 (13-3/4x11-3/8", 94 pgs, hardc, B&W)

nn- By Gustave Dore ??? ??? ???
NOTE: Although dated 1867, it was published & available for the 1866 Christmas Season. Printed

---

by Dalziel, in England, and imported to the USA for a USA publisher

UNCLE BANTAM'S FUNNY BOOKS, FOR THE AMUSEMENT OF HIS LIT NEPHEWS AND NIECES. WITH SEVENTY-FIVE ILLUSTRATIONS. (I)2
Philadelphia: Davis Porter & Co.: 1865 (Quarto, 54 pgs, col. ill. ; pictorial paper covered boards) (See also Slovenly Peter)

nn-By Heinrich Hoffman 250.00 500.00 1000
NOTE: Translation of "Der Struwwelpeter", first published in Germany in 1844. Hand-colored trations with lines of verse. This is a complete collection of six of the "Uncle Bantam's Funny Books" in one volume, each with 8 pgs.

UNTIDY TOM & OTHER STORIES. (I)
Davis Porter & Co., Philadelphia: 1865 (8 pgs.,col. ill. ; 24 cm.)

nn - By Henrich Hoffman ??? ??? ???
NOTE: Uncle Bantam's funny books for the amusement of his little nephews and nieces. Pu lisher's advertisement on back cover.(Contents: Untidy Tom -- Story of Johnny Look-in-the-A Story of Augustus who would not have any soup -- Story of Little Suck-a-Thumb -- Story of Fi Robert.

UPS AND DOWNS ON LAND AND WATER)O,G)
James R. Osgood & Co., Boston: 1871 ; Houghton, Osgood & Co., Bosto 1880 (108 pgs, gilted blue hard-c, B&W)

1st printing (1871; 10-3/4x16") - by Augustus Hoppin	45.00	90.00	180
2nd printing (1880; smaller sized)	32.50	65.00	130

VERY VERY FUNNY (M,S)
Dick & Fitzgerald, New York: nd(c1880's) (10¢, 7-1/2x5", 68 pgs, paper-c, E

nn 22.50 45.00 90
NOTE: unauthorized reprints of prose and cartoons extracted from Puck, Texas Siftings, and other publications. Includes work by Chips Bellew, Bisbee, Graetz, Opper, Wales, Zim.

WIDOW AND HER FRIENDS, A (see GIBSON'S PUBLISHED DRAWINGS)

WORLD OVER, THE (I)
G. W. Dillingham Company, New York: 1897 (192 pgs, hardbound)

nn - By Joe Kerr; 80 illus by R.F. Outcault 30.00 90.00

YE VERACIOUS CHRONICLE OF GRUFF & POMPEY IN 7 TABLEAUX. (C
Jackson's Best Chewing Tobacco & Donaldson Brothers: nd (c1870's) (5 tall x 3-3/8" wide folded, 27" wide unfolded, color cardboard)

nn- With all 8 panels attached (Scarce) 80.00 160.00 320
nn- Individual panels/cards 6.00 12.00 24
NOTE: Black Americana interest. Consists of 8 attached cards, printed on one side, which ur into a strip story of title card & 7 panels. Scrapbook hobbyists in the 19th Century tended to pi the panels apart and paste into their scrapbooks, making copies with all panels attached sca

A VERY SHORT LIST OF RECOMMENDED REFERENCE TOOLS:

A HISTORY OF AMERICAN GRAPHIC HUMOR by William Murrell
Vol. 1: 1747-1865 (Whitney Museum of Art, New York) 1933)
Vol 2: 1865-1938 (Whitney Museum of Art, New York) 1938)
CARTOON CAVALCADE By Thomas Craven (Simon & Schuster, 1943)
FROM CAVE PAINTING TO COMIC STRIPS By L. Hogben (Chanticleer, 194
THE HISTORY OF THE COMIC STRIP by David Kunzle
Vol 1: THE EARLY COMIC STRIP c1450-1825 (Univ of Calif Press, 1973)
Vol 2: THE NINETEENTH CENTURY (Univ of Calif. Press, 1991)
SATIRE ON STONE By Richard Samuel West (Univ of Illinois Press, 1988)
Biography of Joseph Keppler & history of Puck with Opper, Howarth, etc.
A REJECTION OF ORDER, THE DEVELOPMENT OF THE NEWSPAPER
COMIC STRIP IN AMERICA, 1830-1920 By Elsa Ann Nystrom (UMI, 1989)
THE AMERICAN COMIC BOOK CATALOGUE THE EVOLUTIONARY ERA
1884-1939 By Denis Gifford (Mansell Publishing, London: 1990)
FORGING A NEW MEDIUM edited by Dierick & Lefevre(VUB University, 199
For on-line discussons, go to PlatinumAgeComics@Yahoogroups.com

END NOTE: Victorian Age comics come in many relatively obscure formats compared to wh most of us are used to today. This brand new section can only grow as there are many more heretofore unrediscovered comics from the 1800s which have fallen off the radar of history.
Some many wonder why many of the items listed contain as of yet no prices. The reason simple. These books are part of a relatively "new" market which has yet to establish itself.
High grade copies are almost unheard of. Some books may truly have only a handful left existence. We are sure there are some known to have been published which no as of yet kn copies have survived the ravages of time and neglect. Next year expect another quantum le our ever expanding knowledge of the fascinating earliest origins of the comics as they relate North America. Your input in helping this section of the Guide grow is most welcome.

The American Comic Book: 1900-1938

IN THE BEGINNING: THE PLATINUM AGE KNOWLEDGE CONTINUES TO EXPAND!

Opper-McDougall-Outcault-Fenderson Swinnerton- Dirks-Howarth-Taylor-Condo-More! by Robert L. Beerbohm, Doug Wheeler and Richard D. Olson, PhD ©2002

This year this earliest comics section has been split in two with yet again many more new listings. The story of the success of the comic strip as we know it today is tied closely to the companies who sponsored them and paid licenses to the copyright holder for the purpose of advertising products. What mainly keeps the Platinum Age from being collected as much as later era comics is simply a general lack of awareness as well as the extreme rarity of many of these volumes, especially in any type of high grade. Many Platinum Age books are much rarer than so-called Golden Age comic books, yet despite this rarity, **Mutt & Jeff**, **Bringing Up Father**, **The Katzenjammer Kids**, and many more were as popular, if not more so, than **Superman** and **Batman** when they were introduced. Recent research has come up with some more amazing rediscoveries. There is much that can be learned and applied to today's comics market by a simple historical examination of the medium's evolution.

Palmer Cox's **The Brownies** were the first North American comics-type characters to be internationally merchan-dised. For over a quarter of a century, Cox deftly combined the popular advertising motifs of animals and fairies into a wonderful, whimsical world of society at its best and worst. Cox's (1840-1924) first work in **St. Nicholas**, a magazine for children, was in the March 1879 issue, titled "The Wasp and the Bee." He began his famous creation with his trademark verse and art with a creation entitled **The Brownies' Ride** in the February 1883 issue. Note illustration on this page.

The Brownies' first book was issued by 1887, titled **The Brownies: Their Book**; many more followed. Cox also added a run of his hugely popular characters in **Ladies Home Journal** from October 1891 through February 1895, as well as a special on December 1910. With the 1892-93 World's Fair, the merchandising exploded with a host of products, including pianos, paper dolls and other figurines, chairs, stoves, puzzles, cough drops, coffee, soap, boots, candy, and many more. **Brownies** material was being produced in Europe as well as the United States of America.

Cox ran **The Brownies** as a newspaper strip in

THE BROWNIES' RIDE.

BY PALMER COX.

One night a cunning brownie band
Was roaming through a farmer's land,
And while the rogues went prying round,
The farmer's mare at rest they found;

And peeping through the stable-door,
They saw the harness that they wore:
The whip was hanging on the wall,
Old Mag was grinding in the stall;

The Brownies by Palmer Cox, 1883, were the earliest known recurring comic characters merchandised in North America, inspiring Outcault on YK & BB.

Walt McDougall & Mark Fenderson, the 2nd American newspaper sequential comic strip, NY World, Feb 4, 1894, predates Yellow Kid.

the **San Francisco Examiner** during 1898 and in the **New York World** in 1900. It was syndicated from 1903 through 1907. He seems to have retired from regularly drawing **The Brownies** with the January 1914 issue of **St. Nicholas** when he was 74. A wealthy man, he lived to the ripe old age of 84.

By the mid-1890s, while keeping careful track of quickly rising circulations of magazines with graphic humor such as **Harper's**, **Puck**, **St. Nicholas**, **Judge**, **Life** and **Truth**, New York based newspaper publishers began to recognize that illustrated humor would sell extra papers. Thus was born the Sunday "comic supplement." Most of the regular favorites were under contract with these magazines. However, there was an artist working for **Truth** who wasn't. Roy L McCardell, then a staffer at **Puck**, informed Morrill Goddard, Sunday editor of **The New York World**, that he knew someone who could fit what was needed at the then largest newspaper in America.

Richard F. Outcault (1863-1928) first introduced his street children strip in **Truth** #372, June 2, 1894, somewhat inspired by Michael Angelo Woolf's slum kids single panel cartoons in **Life** which had begun in the mid 1880s. The interested collector should seek out a copy of Woolf's **Sketches of Lowly Life In A Great City** (1899) listed in the Guide. It's also possible that Outcault's **Hogan's Alley** cast, including the Yellow Kid, was inspired by

Charles W. Saalburg's **The Ting Ling Kids,** which began in the **Chicago Inter-Ocean** by May 1894. By 1895, Saalburg was Art Director in charge of coloring for the new color printing press at the **New York World**. Edward Harrigan's play "O'Reilly and the Four Hundred,' which had a song beginning with the words "Down in Hogan's Alley..." likely provided direct inspiration.

By the November 18, 1894 issue of the **World**, Outcault was working for Goddard and Saalburg. Outcault produced a successful Sunday newspaper sequential comic strip in color with "The Origin of a New Species" on the back page in the World's first colored Sunday supplement. Long time pro Walt McDougall, a famous cartoonist reputed to have turned the 1884 Presidential race with a single cartoon that ran in the **World**, handled the cartoon art on the front page. Earlier, **The World** began running full page color single panels on May 21, 1893. McDougall did various other page panels during 1893, but it was January 28, 1894 when the first sequence of comic pictures in a newspaper appeared in panels in the same format as our comic strips today. It was a full page cut up into nine panels. This historic sequence was drawn entirely in pantomime, with no words, by Mark Fenderson.

The second page to appear in panels was an eight panel strip from February 4, 1894, also lacking words except for the title. This page was a collaboration between Walt McDougall and Mark Fenderson titled "The Unfortunate Fate of a Well-Intentioned Dog." From then on, many full page color strips by McDougall and Fenderson appeared; they were the first cartoonists to draw for the Sunday newspaper

"Fourth Ward Brownies," artwork by Richard F. Outcault, Feb. 17, 1895. First appearance in Pulitzer's NY World. Note the Yellow Kid, second from left.

comic section. It was Outcault, however, who soon became the most famous cartoonist featured. After first appearing in black and white in Pulitzer's **The New York World** on February 17, 1895, and again on March 10, 1895, **The Yellow Kid** was introduced to the public in color on May 5, 1895.

Some have erroneously reported in scholarly journals that perhaps it was Frank Ladendorf's "Uncle Reuben," first introduced May 26, 1895, which became the first regularly recurring comics character in newspapers. This is wrong, as even Outcault's "Yellow Kid" began in Pulitzer's paper a good three months before **Uncle Reuben.** Until firm evidence to the contrary comes to light, that honor will forever be enshrined with Jimmy Swinnerton's **Little Bears** cartoon characters, found all over inside Hearst's **San Francisco Examiner** as early as 1892. Though never actually a comic strip, they nonetheless were the earliest presently known recurring comics characters in American newspapers. There never was a strip titled **Little Bears and Tigers**, as the Tigers portion was strictly for New York consumption when Hearst ordered Swinnerton to move to the Big Apple to compete better in the brewing comic strip wars.

The Yellow Kid is widely recognized today as the first newspaper comic strip to demonstrate without a doubt that the general public was ready for full color comics. **The Yellow Kid** was the first in the USA to show that (1), comics could increase newspaper sales, and that (2), comic characters could be merchandised. **The Yellow Kid** was the headlining spark of what was soon dubbed by Hearst as "eight pages of polychromatic effulgence that makes the rainbow look like a lead pipe."

Ongoing research suggests that Palmer Cox's fabulous success with **The Brownies** was a direct inspiration for Richard Outcault's future merchandising work. The ultimate proof lies in the fourth Yellow Kid cartoon, which appeared in the February 9, 1895 issue of **Truth**. It was reprinted in the **New York World** eight days later on February 17, 1895, becoming the first Yellow Kid cartoon in the newspapers. The caption read "FOURTH WARD BROWNIES. MICKEY, THE ARTIST (adding a finishing touch) Dere, Chimmy! If Palmer Cox wuz t' see yer, he'd git yer copyrighted in a minute." The Yellow Kid was widely licensed in the greater New York area for all kinds of products, including gum and cigarette cards, toys, pin backs, cookies, post cards, tobacco products, and appliances. There was also a short-lived humor magazine from Street & Smith named **The Yellow Kid**, featuring exquisite Outcault covers, plus a 196-page comic book from Dillingham & Co. known as **The Yellow Kid**

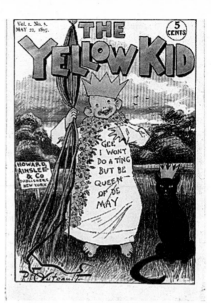

Yellow Kid #5, May 22, 1897, Street & Smith as Howard Ainslee, NY cover by Richard F. Outcault.

in McFadden's Flats, dated to early 1897. In addition, there were several Yellow Kid plays produced, spawning other collectibles like show posters, programs and illustrated sheet music. (For those interested in more information regarding the Yellow Kid, it is available on the Internet at www.neponset.com/yellowkid.)

Mickey Dugan burned brightly for a few years as Outcault secured a copyright on the character with the United States Government by Sept. 1896. By the time he completed the necessary paper work, however, hundreds of business people nationwide had pirated the image of The Yellow Kid and plastered it all over every product imaginable; mothers were even dressing their newborns to look like Dugan. (Outcault, however, kept regularly utilizing images of **The Yellow Kid** in his comics style advertising work confirmed as late as 1915.) Outcault soon found himself in a maelstrom not of his choosing, which probably pushed him to eventually drop the character. Outcault's creation went back and forth between newspaper giants Pulitzer and Hearst until Bennett's New York Herald mercifully snatched the cartoonist away in 1900 to do what amounted to a few relatively short-run strips. Later, he did one particular strip for a year—a satire of rural Black America titled **Pore Li'l Mose**, and then his newer creation, **Buster Brown**, debuted May 4, 1902. Mose had a very rare comic book collection published in 1902 by Cupples & Leon, now highly sought after by today's savvy collectors.

Outcault continued drawing him in the background of occasional **Buster Brown** strips for many years to come.

William Randolph Hearst loved the comic strip medium ever since he was a little boy growing up on **Max & Moritz** by Wilhelm Busch in American collected book editions translated from the original German (these collections were first published in book form in 1871, serving as the influence for **The Katzenjammer Kids**). One of the ways Hearst responded to losing Outcault in 1900 was by purchasing the highly successful 23 year old humor magazine **Puck** from the heirs of founder Joseph Keppler. With **Puck** and its exclusive cartoonist contracts, he acquired, among others, the very popular F. M. Howarth and Frederick Burr Opper's undivided attention. Opper had first burst upon the comics scene in America back in 1880. Within a year Hearst had transformed this **National Lampoon** of its day into the colored Sunday comics section, **Puck-The Comic Weekly**. At first featuring Rudolph Dirk's **The Katzenjammer Kids** (1897), **Happy Hooligan** and other fine strips by the wildly popular Opper and a few others including Rudolph's brother Gus Dirks, the Hearst comic section steadily added more strips. For decades to come, there wasn't anything else that could compete with **Puck**. Hearst hired the best of the best and transformed **Puck** into the most popular comics section anywhere.

Outcault, meanwhile, followed in Palmer Cox's footprints a decade later by using the nexus of a World's Fair as a jumping off venue. **Buster Brown** was an instant sensation when he debuted as the new merchandising mascot of the Brown Shoe Company at the 1904 St. Louis World's Fair in a special Buster Brown Shoes pavilion. The character has the honor of being the first nationally licensed comic strip character in America. Many hundreds of different **Buster Brown** premiums have been issued. Comic books by Frederick A. Stokes

Company featuring **Buster Brown & His Dog Tige** began as early as 1903 with **Buster Brown and His Resolutions**, simultaneously published in several different languages throughout the world.

After a few years, Buster and Outcault returned to Hearst in late 1905, joining what soon became the flagship of the comics world. Buster's popularity quickly spread all over the United States and then the world as he single-handedly spawned the first great comics licensing dynasty. For years, there were little people traveling from town to town performing as **Buster Brown** and selling shoes while accompanied by small dogs named Tige. Many other highly competitive licensed strips would soon follow. We suggest checking out **Hake's Price Guide to Character Toys** for information on several hundred **Buster Brown** competitors, as well as several pages of the more fascinating **Buster Brown** material.

Soon there were many comic strip syndicates not only offering hundreds of various comic strips but also offering to license the characters for any company interested in paying the fee. The history of the comic strips with wide popularity since **The Yellow Kid** has been intertwined with giveaway premiums and character-based, store-bought merchandise of all kinds. Since its infancy as a profitable art form unto itself with **The Yellow Kid**, the comic strip world has profited from selling all sorts of "stuff" to the public featuring their favorite character or strip as its motif. American business gladly responded to the desire for comic character memorabilia with thousands of fun items to enjoy and collect. Most of the early comics were not aimed specifically at kids, though children understandably enjoyed them as well.

The comic book has generally been associated with almost all of the licensed merchandise in this century. In the Platinum Age section beginning right after this essay, you will find a great many comic books in varied formats and sizes published before the advent of the first successful monthly newsstand comic book, **Famous Funnies**. What drove each of these evolutionary format changes was the need by their producers to make money.

A very significant format was F. M. Howarth's **Funny Folks**, published in 1899 by E. P. Dutton and drawn from color as well as black and white pages of **Puck**. This rather large hardcover volume measured 16 1/2 wide by 12 tall. It contains numerous sequential comic strip pages as well as single gag illustrations. Howarth's art was a joy to behold and deserves wider recognition.

By Oct. 1900, Hearst had already caused

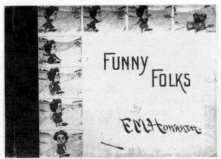

Funny Folks, F. M. Howarth, 1899, collected many early sequential comics; bridges the Victorian & Platinum Ages.

Vaudvilles And Other Things, 1900, first printing. Carl Schultze soon went on to create FoxyGrandpa.

Opper's **Folks In Funny ville** to be collected by publisher R. H. Russell, NY in a 12x9 hard cover format from his **New York Journal American Humorist** section. At the end of 1900, Carl Shultze had a first edition of **Vaudevilles and Other Things** published by Isaac H. Blanchard Co., NY. It measures 10 1/2 wide by 13 tall with 22 pages including covers. Each interior page is a 2 to 7 panel comic strip with lots of color.

There were also recently unearthed format variation second and third printings of **Vaudevilles** with the inscription "From the Originator of the 'Foxy Grandpa' Series" at the bottom of its front cover of the third printing. This note is lacking on the earlier first two editions, and it also switches format size to 11 tall by 13 inches wide.

E. W. Kemble's **The Blackberries** had a color collection by

Happy Hooligan Book #1, 1902, by Frederick Opper, was wildly popular.

They both measure 15 5/16 wide by 10 inches tall and contain 88 pages including covers. Confirmed also the fact that there are two separate editions with different covers for the pictured 1902 first edition and a 1903 Frederick Stokes edition of **Katzenjammer Kids** and **Happy Hooligan** with differing contents. They both are two different books entirely, and what confuses many collectors is that they have identical indicia title pages, as does an entirely different **KK** from 1905.

The 2nd Happy Hooligan comic book, 1903, by Frederick Opper.

1901, also published by R. H. Russell, NY, as well as a few other comic-related volumes by Kemble still to be unearthed and properly identified. If you have information you wish to share, please send it to the authors of this essay for future updates.

Confirmed is the exact format of Hearst's 1902 **The Katzenjammer Kids** and **Happy Hooligan And His Brother Gloomy Gus.**

Settling on a popular size of 17 wide by 11 tall, comic books were soon available that featured Charles "Bunny" Shultze's **Foxy Grandpa**, Rudolph Dirk's **The Katzenjammer Kids**, Winsor McCay's **Little Sammy Sneeze**, **Rarebit Fiend** and **Little Nemo**, and Fred Opper's **Happy Hooligan** and **Maud**, in addition to dozens of **Buster Brown** comic books. For well over a decade, these large-size, full-color volumes were the norm, retailing for 60 cents. These collections offered Sunday comics at full-size with the back side blank per page.

The very rare **Brainy Bowers and Drowsy Dugan** by R. W. Taylor is now crowned the first collection of daily newspaper strip reprints

The first Katzenjammer Kids comic book, 1902, by Rudolph Dirks.

Little Sammy Sneeze, 1905, by Winsor McCay is his best looking.

This is the 2nd daily strip collection published, 1907.

published in America. **The Outbursts of Everett True** by A. D. Condo and J. W. Raper was first published by Saalfield in 1907 in a 88 page hardcover collection. It qualifies as the second daily comic strip collection as it predates first **Mutt & Jeff** collection by three years. Condo & Raper's creation began its regular run several times a week in 1905 daily newspapers and lasted until 1927, when Condo became too sick to continue. This same **Everett True** collection was later truncated a bit by Saalfield in 1921 to 56 strips in just 32 pages measuring the 10x10 Cupples & Leon size.

By 1908 Stokes had a large backlist of full color comic books for sale at 60 cents each. Some of these titles date back to 1903 and were reprinted over and over as demanded warranted. Note the number of titles in the advertisement pulled from the back of **The Three Fun Makers** shown above.

With the ever-increasing popularity of Bud Fisher's new daily strip sensation, **Mutt & Jeff**, a new format was created for reprinting daily strips in black and white, a hardcover

Above, The Three FunMakers, 1908, first anthology Plat comic book. Below, Mutt & Jeff #5 by Bud Fisher, 1916, is one the rarest Plats out there.

book about 15 wide by 5 tall, published by Ball starting in 1910 for five volumes. In 1912, Ball also branched out to at least the recently unearthed **Doings of the Van Loons** by Fred. I. Leipziger, a rare comic book in the same format as the Ball **Mutt & Jeff** books.

Cartoons Magazine also began in 1912 and ran thru 1921 before undergoing a radical format change. It is notable as a wonderful source for information on early comics and their creators. See Plat index for listings.

The next significant evolutionary change

Earliest known display ad for comic books found in The Three Fun Makers, with 27 titles then in print. Note 1908 cover prices are 60 cents!

STOKES' COMIC JUVENILES

Foxy Grandpa and the Boys
Foxy Grandpa's Triumphs
Foxy Grandpa's Frolics
Foxy Grandpa's Surprises
Foxy Grandpa Up-to-date
Jimmy and His Scrapes
Little Sammy Sneeze
The Trials of Lulu and Leander
Sam and His Laugh
Handy Happy Hooligan
Happy Hooligan Home Again
Happy Hooligan's Travels
Maud the Mirthful Mule
Maud the Matchless
Maud

Outcault's Buster, Mary Jane and Tige
Outcault's Buster Brown and Company
Buster Brown's Antics
Buster Brown's Pranks
Buster Brown, His Dog Tige and Their Troubles
Buster Brown and His Resolutions
Willie Westinghouse Edison Smith
The Komical Katzenjammers
The Cruise of the Katzenjammer Kids
The Tricks of the Katzenjammer Kids
The Three Funmakers: (Hooligan, Maud and the Katzenjammer Kids)

Each, oblong 4to, boards in colors, pictures in colors, 60 cents

286

Regular Fellers by Gene Byrne, 1921, one of the very last oblong comics.

occurred in 1919, when Cupples & Leon began issuing their black and white daily strip reprint books in a new aforementioned format, about 10 wide by 10 tall, with four panels reprinted per page in a two by two matrix. These books were 52 pages for 25 cents. The first ones featured **Bringing Up Father** and **Mutt & Jeff**; there were about 100 others.

A 1921 example of C&L revolutionary format.

By 1921, the last of the oblong (11x15 approx. size) color comic books were issued, with Cupples & Leon's **Jimmie Dugan And The Reg'lar Fellers** by Gene Byrne and EmBee's **The Trouble Of Bringing Up Father** by self publisher George McManus. Of special historical interest, Embee issued the first 10 cent monthly comic book, **Comic Monthly**, with a first issue dated January 1922. A dozen 8-1/2x9 issues were published, each featuring solo adventures of popular King Features strips. The monthly 10 cent comic book concept had finally arrived, though it would be more than a decade before it became successful.

In 1926, Cupples & Leon added a new 7 wide by 9 tall format with **Little Orphan Annie**, **Smitty**, and others. These books were issued in both soft cover and hardcover editions with dust jackets, and became extremely popular at 60 cents per copy. Dell began publishing all original material in **The Funnies** in late 1929 in a larger tabloid

Comic Monthly #11, 1922; the first 10¢ monthly newsstand comic book

format. At least three dozen issues were published before Delacorte threw in the towel. Even the extremely popular **Big Little Book**, introduced in 1932, can be viewed as a smaller version of the existing formats. The competition amongst publishers now included Dell, McKay, Sonnet. Saalfield and Whitman. The 1930s saw a definite shift in merchandising comic strip material from adults to children. This was the decade when Kellogg's placed **Buck Rogers** on the map, and when Ovaltine issued tons of **Little Orphan Annie** material. Merchandising pioneers Sam Gold and Kay Kamen spearheaded this next re-transformation of the comics biz.

Upwards of a thousand of these **Funnies On Parade** precursors, in all formats, were published through 1935 and were very popular. Toward the end of this era, beautiful collections of **Popeye**, **Mickey Mouse**, **Dick Tracy**, and many others were published which today command ever higher prices on the open market as they are rediscovered by the advanced collector.

1935: David McKay published the last of the 10x10 comic books.

END NOTE: We are also beginning to add in many of the late 1930s variant formats such as the **Little Lulu** series by Marjorie Henderson Buell reprinted from her Saturday Evening Post 1935-1944 run. Each year, this Platinum Age section grows as advanced collectors continue to report in with new finds. We encourage readers to help with this section of the book, as each new data entry is very important.

For further information on this earlier fascinating era of American comic books, check out Robert L. Beerbohm's "The American Comic Book 1897-1932," originally printed in the 27th edition of **The Overstreet Comic Book Price Guide** - also available on Gemstone Publishing's website at www.gemstonepub. com plus see Price Guides #29, #30, and #31.

Robert may be contacted for corrections and additions to the articles & indexes for next year's guide at this e-mail address: beerbohm@teknetwork.com

Alphonse and Gaston by Opper
1902 © Hearst's NY American & Journal

American-Journal-Examiner Joke Book
Special Supplement #2 - M&J by Bud Fisher
1911 © New York American

At the Bottom of the Ladder by Kessler
1926 © J. P. Lippincott Company

	GD2.0	FN6.0	VF8.0		GD2.0	FN6.0	VF

COLLECTOR'S NOTE: The books listed in this section were published many decades before organized comics fandom began archiving and helping to preserve these fragile popular culture artifacts. Consequently, copies of most all of these comics almost never surface in Fine+ or better shape. Most Platinum Age comic books are in the Fair to VG range. If you want to collect these only in high grade, your collection will be extremely small. The prices given for Good, Fine and Very Fine categories are for strictly graded editions. If you need help grading your item, we refer you to the grading section in this book or contact the authors of this essay. Items marked rare we are trying to ascertain how many copies might still be in existence. Your help is welcome.

For ease of ascertaining the contents of each item of this listing, we offer the following revised list of categories found immediately following each title:

E - REPRINT OF EUROPEAN COMICS MATERIAL
G - GRAPHIC NOVEL (LONGER FORMAT COMIC TELLING A SINGLE STORY)
H - "HOW TO DRAW CARTOONS" BOOKS
I - ILLUSTRATED BOOKS NOTABLE FOR THE ARTIST, BUT NOT A COMIC.
M - REPRINT OF MAGAZINE / PERIODICAL COMICS MATERIAL
N - REPRINT OF NEWSPAPER COMICS MATERIAL
O - ORIGINAL COMIC MATERIAL NOT REPRINTED FROM ANOTHER SOURCE
P - PROMOTIONAL COMIC, EITHER GIVEN AWAY FOR FREE, OR A PREMIUM GIVEN IN CONJUNCTION WITH THE PURCHASE OF A PRODUCT.
S - SINGLE PANEL / NON-SEQUENTIAL CARTOONS (ENTIRELY OR PRE DOMINANTLY)

Measurements are in inches. The first dimension given is Height and the second is Width. Most measurements are in inches, a few in centimetres.

This section created, revised, and expanded by Robert Beerbohm, Doug Wheeler and Richard Olson with able assistance from Bill Blackbeard, Ray Bottorff Jr., Alfredo Castelli, Darrell Coons, Leonardo De Sa, Scott Deschaine, Mitchell Duval, Joe Evans, Tom Gordon, Bruce Hamilton, Andy Konkykru, Don Kurtz, Gabriel Laderman, Robert Quesinberry, Steve Rowe, Randy Scott, John Snyder, Art Spiegelman, Steve Thompson, Richard Samuel West, Craig Yoe

ADVENTURES OF EVA, PORA AND TED (M)
Evaporated Milk Association: 1932 (5x15", 16 pgs, B&W)
nn-By Steve   10.00   30.00   60.00
NOTE: Appears to have had green, blue or white paper cover versions.

ADVENTURES OF HAWKSHAW (N) (See Hawkshaw The Detective)
The Saalfield Publishing Co.: 1917 (9-3/4x13-1/2", 48 pgs., color & two-tone)
nn-By Gus Mager (only 24 pgs. of strips, reverse of each pg. is blank)
        50.00   175.00   300.00
nn-1927 Reprints 1917 issue   43.00   152.00   260.00

ADVENTURES OF SLIM AND SPUD, THE (M)
Prairie Farmer Publ. Co.: 1924 (3-3/4x 9-3/4", 104 pgs., B&W strip reprints)
nn   21.00   84.00   150.00
NOTE: Illustrated mailing envelope exists postmarked out of Chicago, add 50%.

ADVENTURES OF WILLIE WINTERS, THE
Kelloggs Toasted Corn Flake Co.: 1912 (6-7/8x9-1/2", 20 pgs, full color)
nn-By Byron Williams & Dearborn Melvill 42.00 146.00 250.00

ADVENTURES OF WILLIE GREEN, THE (N)
Frank M. Acton Co.: 1915 (50¢, 52 pgs, 8-1/2X16", B&W, soft-c)
Book 1-By Harris Brown; strip-r 54.00 189.00 325.00

A. E. F. IN CARTOONS BY WALLY, THE (N)
Don Sowers & Co.: 1933 (12x10-1/8", 88 pgs, hardcover B&W)
nn-By Wally Wallgren (WW One Stars & Stripes-r) 20.00 60.00 120.00

AFTER THE TOWN GOES DRY (I)
The Howell Publishing Co, Chicago: 1919 (48 pgs, hardbound two color cover)
nn-By Henry C. Taylor; illus by Frank King 20.00 70.00 140.00

AIN'T IT A GRAND & GLORIOUS FEELING? (S) (Also see Mr. & Mrs.)

Whitman Publishing Co.: 1922 (9x9-3/4", 52 pgs., stiff cardboard-c)
nn-1921 daily strip-r; B&W, color-c; Briggs-a 43.00 172.00 300
nn-(9x9-1/2", 28pgs., stiff cardboard-c)-Sunday strip-r in color (inside front-c
says "More of the Married Life of Mr. & Mrs".) 36.00 143.00 250
NOTE: This is the 2nd Whitman comic book, after Brigg's MR. & MRS.

ALL THE FUNNY FOLKS (I)
World Press Today, Inc.: 1926 (11-1/2x8-1/2", 112 pgs., color, hard-c)
nn-Barney Google, Spark Plug, Jiggs & Maggie, Tillie The Toiler, Happy
Hooligan, Hans & Fritz, Toots & Casper, etc. 100.00 400.00 700
With Dust Jacket By Louis Biedermann 143.00 571.00 1000
NOTE: booklength race horse story masterfully enveloping all major King Features characte

ALPHONSE AND GASTON AND THEIR FRIEND LEON (N)
Hearst's New York American & Journal: 1902,1903 (10x15-1/4", Sunday st
reprints in color)
nn-(1902) - By Frederick Opper 371.00 1300.00 -
nn-(1903) - By Frederick Opper 279.00 975.00 -

ALWAYS BELITTLIN' (I)
Percy Crosby, Publisher: 1933 (14-1/4x11", 72 pgs, hard-c, B&W)
nn - By Percy Crosby 45.00 157.50 300

AMERICAN-JOURNAL-EXAMINER JOKE BOOK SPECIAL SUPPLEMENT
New York American: 1911-12 (12x9 3/4", 16 pgs) (known issues) (Very Rar
1 Tom Powers Joke Book(12/10/11) 80.00 280.00 -
2 Mutt & Jeff Joke Book (Bud Fisher 12/17/11) 100.00 350.00 -
3 TAD's Joke Book (Thomas Dorgan 12/24/11) 80.00 280.00 -
4 F. Opper's Joke Book (Frederick Burr Opper 12/31/11)
  (contains Happy Hooligan) 100.00 350.00 -
5 ??? (01/07/12) exist? ??? ??? ???
6 Swinnerton's Joke Book (Jimmy Swinnerton 01/14/12)
  (contains Mr. Jack) 100.00 350.00 -
7 The Monkey's Joke Book (Gus Mager 01/21/12)
  (contains Sherlocko the Monk) 100.00 350.00 -
8 Joys And Glooms Joke Book (T. E. Powers 01/28/12)
  80.00 280.00 -
9 The Dingbat Family's Joke Book (George Herriman 02/04/12)
  (contains early Krazy Kat & Ignatz) 200.00 700.00 -
10 Valentine Joke Book, A (Opper,Howarth,Mager, T. E. Powers 02/11/12)
  80.00 280.00 -
11 Little Hatchet Joke Book (T. E. Powers 02/18/12)
  80.00 280.00 -
12 Jungle Joke Book (Rudolph Dirks 02/25/12) 100.00 350.00 -
13 The Hayseeds Joke Book (03/03/12) 80.00 280.00 -
14 Married Life Joke Book (T.E. Powers 03/10/12) 80.00 280.00 -
NOTE: These were insert newspaper supplements similar to Eisner's later Spirit sections. A
Valentine Joke Book recently surfaced from Hearst's Boston Sunday American proving that
cities besides New York City had these special supplements. Each issue also contains work
other cartoonists besides the cover featured creator and those already listed above such as
Sidney Smith, Winsor McCay, Hy Mayer, Grace Wederseim (later Drayton), others.

AMERICA'S BLACK & WHITE BOOK (S)
100 Pictured Reasons Why We Are At War
Cupples & Leon: 1917 (10-3/4x8", 216 pgs)
nn-W. A. Rogers (New York Herald-r) 32.00 114.00 195

ANGELIC ANGELINA (N)
Cupples & Leon Company: 1909 (11-1/2x17", 30 pgs., 2 colors)
nn-By Munson Paddock 67.00 233.00 400

ANDY GUMP, HIS LIFE STORY (I)
The Reilly & Lee Co, Chicago: 1924 (192 pgs, hardbound)
nn-By Sidney Smith (over 100 illustrations) 20.00 80.00 140

ANIMAL SERIALS
T. Y. Crowell: 1906 (9x6-7/8", 214 pgs, hard-c, B&W)
nn - By E Warde Balisdell 20.00 80.00 140
NOTE: multi-page comic strip stories

ney Google & Spark Plug #1 by Billy DeBeck
1923 © Cupples & Leon

Bill the Boy Artist's Book by Ed Payne
1910 © C.M. Clark Publishing Co

Brainy Bowers and Drowsy Duggan by R.W. Taylor
1905 © Star Publishing Co. - the first daily reprints

	GD2.0	FN6.0	VF8.0		GD2.0	FN6.0	VF8.0

THE BOTTOM OF THE LADDER (M)
Lippincott Company: 1926 (11x8-1/4", 296 pgs, hardcover, B&W)

By Camillus Kessler	32.00	128.00	225.00

E: Hilarious single panel cartoons showing first jobs of then important "captains of industry."

NANA OIL (N)
Publ. Co.: 1924 (9-7/8x10", 52 pgs., B&W)

Milt Gross-a; not reprints	61.00	244.00	425.00

RKER'S ILLUSTRATED ALMANAC (O,P,S) (See Barkers in Victorian)
rker, Moore & Mein Medicine Co: 1900-1932+ (36 pgs, B&W, color paper-c)

0-1932+ (7x5-7/8")	10.00	30.00	60.00

RKER'S "KOMIC" PICTURE SOUVENIR (P,S) (see Barkers in Victorian)
rker, Moore & Mein Medicine Co: nd (1900s) (color cardboard-c, B&W
rior)(all are numbered editions, 50 pages)

00-???	10.00	30.00	60.00

TE: These have been confirmed as premium comic books, predating the Buster Brown premi-
s. They reprint advertising cartoons from Barker's Illustrated Almanac. For the 50 page book-
by this same name, numbered as "Part's, without exception, were published after 1900.

RNEY GOOGLE AND SPARK PLUG (N) (See Comic Monthly)
pples & Leon Co.: 1923 - No. 6, 1928 (52 pgs., B&W, daily strip-r)

(nn)-By Billy DeBeck	57.00	229.00	400.00
4 (#5 & #6 do not exist)	46.00	186.00	325.00

TE: Started June 17, 1919 as newspaper strip; Spark Plug introduced July 17, 1922.

RT'S CARTOONS FOR 1902 FROM THE MINNEAPOLIS JOURNAL
NNEAPOLIS JOURNAL: 1903 (11x9", 102 pgs, paperback, B&W)

By Charles L. Bartholomew	28.00	99.00	170.00

LIEVE IT OR NOT! by Ripley (S)
mon & Schuster: 1929 (8x 5-1/4", 68 pgs, red, B&W cover, B&W interior)

By Robert Ripley (strip-r text & art)	40.00	120.00	240.00

TE: There are many reprintings of this, 1929 was the first print.

N WEBSTER (N)
andard Printing Company: 1928-1931 (13-3/4x4-7/16", 768 pgs, soft-c)

"Bound to Win"	40.00	120.00	240.00
"...in old Mexico"	40.00	120.00	240.00
"...At Wilderness Lake"	40.00	120.00	240.00
"...in the Oil Fields"	40.00	120.00	240.00

TE: Self Published by Edwin Alger, also contains fan's letter pages.

LLY BOUNCE (I)
onahue & Co.: 1906 (288 pgs, hardbound)

By W.W. Denslow & Dudley Bragdon	100.00	350.00	600.00

TE: Billy Bounce was created in 1901 as a comic strip by W. W. Denslow (strip ran from
1 NOV 11 to 1905 DEC 3), but the series is best remembered in the C. W. Kahles version
om 1902 SEP 28). Denslow resumed his character in the above illustrated book.

LLY HON'S FAMOUS CARTOON BOOK (H)
asley Publishing Co.: 1927 (7-1/2x10", 68 pgs, softbound wraparound)

By Billy Hon	12.00	48.00	80.00

LLY THE BOY ARTIST'S BOOK OF FUNNY PICTURES (N)
M.Clark Publishing Co.: 1910 (9x12", hardcover-c, Boston Globe strip-r)

By Ed Payne	79.00	316.00	550.00

TE: This long lived strip ran in The Boston Globe from Nov 5 1899-Jan 7 1955.

RD CENTER CARTOONS: A Chronicle of Social Happenings
C. McClurg & Co.: 1904 (12-3/8x9-1/2", 216 pgs, hardcover, B&W)

By John McCutcheon	40.00	140.00	240.00

TE: Satirical cartoons and text concerning a mythical town.

OBBY THATCHER & TREASURE CAVE (N)
temus Co.: 1932 (9x7", 86 pgs., B&W, hard-c)

Reprints; Storm-a	43.00	172.00	300.00

OBBY THATCHER'S ROMANCE (N)
he Bell Syndicate/Henry Altemus Co.: 1931 (8-3/4x7", color cover, B&W)

By Storm	43.00	172.00	300.00

BOOK OF CARTOONS, A (S)
Edward T. Miller: 1903 (12-1/4x9-1/4", 120 pgs, hardcover, B&W)

nn-By Harry J. Westerman (Ohio State Journal-r)	20.00	70.00	120.00

BOTTLE, THE (E) (see Victorian Age section for earlier printings)
Gowans & Gray, London & Glasgow: June 1905 (3-3/4x6", 72 pgs, printed one
side only, paper cover, B&W)

nn- 1st printing (June 1905)	17.50	35.00	70.00
nn- 2nd printing (March 1906)	17.50	35.00	70.00
nn- 3rd printing (January 1911)	17.50	35.00	70.00

NOTE: By George Cruikshank. Reprints both THE BOTTLE and THE DRUNKARD'S CHILDREN.
Cover is text only - no cover art.

BOTTLE, THE (E)
Frederick A. Stokes: nd (c1906) (3-3/4x6", 72 pgs, printed one side only, paper
cover, B&W)

nn- by George Cruikshank	17.50	35.00	70.00

NOTE: reprint of the Gowans & Gray edition. Reprints both THE BOTTLE and THE
DRUNKARD'S CHILDREN. Cover is text only - no cover art.

BOY'S & GIRLS' BIG PAINTING BOOK OF INTERESTING COMIC PICTURES
M. A. Donohue & Co.: 1914-16 (9x15, 70 pgs)

nn-By Carl "Bunny" Schultze (Foxy Grandpa-r)	81.00	284.00	-
#2 (1914)	81.00	284.00	-
#337 (1914) (sez "Big Painting & Drawing Book")	81.00	284.00	-
nn-(1916) (sez "Big Painting Book")(9-1/4x15")	81.00	284.00	-

NOTE: These are all Foxy Grandpa items.

BRAIN LEAKS: Dialogues of Mutt & Flea (N)
O. K. Printing Co. (Rochester Evening Times): 1911 (76 pgs, 6-5/8x4-5/8,
hardcover, B&W)

nn-By Leo Edward O'Melia; newspaper strip-r	29.00	100.00	171.00

BRAINY BOWERS AND DROWSY DUGGAN (N)
Star Publishing: 1905 (7-1/4 x 4-9/16", 98 pgs, blue, brown & white color cover,
B&W interior, 25¢) (daily strip-r 1902-04 Chicago Daily News)

nn- By R. W. Taylor (Very Rare)	200.00	700.00	-

**BRAINY BOWERS AND DROWSY DUGGAN GETTING ON IN THE WORLD
WITH NO VISIBLE MEANS OF SUPPORT (STORIES TOLD IN PICTURES TO
MAKE THEIR TELLING SHORT)** (N)
Max Stein/Star Publishing: 1905 (7-3/8x5 1/8", 164 pgs, slick black, red & tan
color cover, interior newsprint) (daily strip-r 1902-04 Chicago Daily News)

nn-By R. W. Taylor (Very Rare)	200.00	700.00	-
nn-possible hard cover edition also?	???	???	???

NOTE: Brainy Bowers is the earliest known daily strip reprint book.

BRINGING UP FATHER (King Features): 1917 (5-1/2x16-1/2", 100 pgs., B&W, cardboard-c)

nn-(Rare)-Daily strip- by George McManus	158.00	553.00	950.00

BRINGING UP FATHER (N)
Cupples & Leon Co.: 1919 - No. 26, 1934 (10x10", 52 pgs., B&W,
stiff cardboard-c) (No. 22 is 9-1/4x9-1/2")

1-Daily strip-r by George McManus in all	32.00	128.00	225.00
2-10	32.00	128.00	225.00
11-20 (Scarcer)	50.00	200.00	350.00
21-26 (Rare)	100.00	300.00	500.00
The Big Book 1 (1926)-Thick book (hardcover; 10-1/4x10-1/4", 142 pgs.)	121.00	484.00	850.00
w/dust jacket (rare)	183.00	732.00	1275.00
The Big Book 2 (1929)	96.00	384.00	675.00
w/dust jacket (rare)	183.00	732.00	1275.00

NOTE: The Big Books contain 3 regular issues rebound.

BRINGING UP FATHER, THE TROUBLE OF (N)
Embee Publ. Co.: 1921 (9x15", 46 pgs, Sunday-r in color)

nn-(Rare)	75.00	300.00	525.00

NOTE: Ties in with Mutt & Jeff (EmBee) and Jimmie Dugan And The Reg'lar Fellers (C&L) as the
last of the oblong size era. This was self published by George Mcmanus

Bringing Up Father #12 by George McManus
1927 © Cupples & Leon

Brownie Clown of Brownie Town by Palmer Cox
1908 © The Century Co.

Buster Brown - The Busy Body
1909 © Cupples & Leon

	GD2.0	FN6.0	VF8.0

BROWNIE CLOWN OF BROWNIE TOWN (N)
The Century Co.: 1908 (6-7/8 x 9-3/8", 112 pgs, color hardcover & interior)
nn-By Palmer Cox (rare; 1907 newspaper strip-r) 200.00 700.00 1200.00

BUDDY TUCKER & HIS FRIENDS (N) (Also see Buster Brown Nuggets)
Cupples & Leon Co.: 1906 (11 1/4 x17 1/2", color)
nn-1905 Sunday strip-r by R. F. Outcault 271.00 950.00 -

BUFFALO BILL'S PICTURE STORIES
Street & Smith Publications: 1909 (Soft cardboard cover)
nn-Very rare 67.00 233.00 400.00

BUGHOUSE FABLES (N) (see also Comic Monthly)
Embee Distributing Co. (King Features): 1921 (10¢, 4x4-1/2", 48 pgs.)
1-By Barney Google (Billy DeBeck) 43.00 172.00 300.00

BUG MOVIES (O) (Also see Clancy The Cop & Deadwood Gulch)
Dell Publishing Co.: 1931 (9-13/16x9-7/8", 52 pgs., B&W)
nn-Original material; Stookie Allen-a 43.00 172.00 300.00

BULL
Bull Publishing Company, New York: No.1 March 1916 - No.12 Feb 1917
(10 cents, 10-3/4x8-3/4", 24 pgs, color paper-c, B&W)
1-12 (Very Rare) ??? ??? ???
NOTE: Pro-German, Anti-British cartoon/humor monthly, whose goal was to keep the U.S. neutral
and out of World War I.

BUNNY'S BLUE BOOK (see also Foxy Grandpa) (N)
Frederick A. Stokes Co.: 1911 (10x15, 60¢)
nn-By Carl "Bunny" Shultze strip-r 100.00 350.00 -

BUNNY'S RED BOOK (see also Foxy Grandpa) (N)
Frederick A. Stokes Co.: 1912 (10x15)
nn-By Carl "Bunny" Schultze strip-r 100.00 350.00 -

BUNNY'S GREEN BOOK (see also Foxy Grandpa) (N)
Frederick A. Stokes Co.: 1913 (10x15")
nn-By Carl "Bunny" Schultze 100.00 350.00 -

BUSTER BROWN (C) (Also see Brown's Blue Ribbon Book of Jokes
and Jingles & Buddy Tucker & His Friends)
Frederick A. Stokes Co.: 1903 - 1916 (Daily strip-r in color)
1903...& His Resolutions (11-1/4x16", 66 pgs.) by R. F. Outcault (Rare)-1st
nationally distributed comic. Distr. through Sears & Roebuck(Rare)
1285.00 4500.00 -
1904...His Dog Tige & Their Troubles (11-1/4x16-1/4", 66 pgs.)(Rare)
429.00 1500.00 -
1905...Pranks (11-1/4x16-3/8", 66 pgs.) 371.00 1300.00 -
1906...Antics (11-1/4x16-3/8", 66 pgs.) 371.00 1300.00 -
1906...And Company (11x16-1/2", 66 pgs.) 271.00 950.00 -
1906...Mary Jane & Tige (11-1/4x16, 66 pgs.) 271.00 950.00 -
1908 Collection of Buster Brown Comics 214.00 750.00 -
1909 Outcault's Real Buster and The Only Mary Jane (11x16, 66 pgs, Stokes)
208.00 729.00 -
1910...Up to Date (10-1/8x15-3/4", 66 pgs.) 208.00 729.00 1250.00
1911...Fun And Nonsense (10-1/8x15-3/4", 66 pgs.) 183.00 642.00 1100.00
1912...The Fun Maker (10-1/8x15-3/4", 66 pgs.) -Yellow Kid (4 pgs.)
183.00 642.00 1100.00
1913...At Home (10-1/8x15-3/4", 56 pgs.) 167.00 583.00 1000.00
1914...And Tige Here Again (10x16, 62 pgs, Stokes)
150.00 525.00 900.00
1915...And His Chum Tige (10x16, Stokes) 150.00 525.00 900.00
1916...The Little Rogue (10-1/8x15-3/4", 62 pgs.) 162.00 567.00 975.00
1917...And the Cat (5-1/2x 6-1/2, 26 pgs, Stokes) 112.00 392.00 675.00
1917...Disturbs the Family (5-1/2x 6 1/2, 26 pgs, Stokes
112.00 392.00 675.00
NOTE: Story featuring statue of the "Chinese Yellow Kid"
1917...The Real Buster Brown (5-1/2x 6 -/2, 26 pgs, Stokes
112.00 392.00 675.00
Frederick A. Stokes Co. Hard Cover Series (I)

...Abroad (1904, 10-1/4x8", 86 pgs., B&W, hard-c)-R. F. Outcault-a (Rare)
200.00 700.00 1200.
...Abroad (1904, B&W, 67 pgs.)-R. F. Outcault-a 200.00 700.00 1200.
..."Tige" His Story 1905 (10x8", 63 pgs., B&W) (63 illos.)
nn-By RF Outcault 143.00 500.00 -
...My Resolutions 1906 (10x8", B&W, 68 pgs.)-R.F. Outcault-a (Rare)
233.00 817.00 1400.
...Autobiography 1907 (10x8", B&W, 71 pgs.) (16 color plates & 36 B&W illos
67.00 233.00 400.
...And Mary Jane's Painting Book 1907 (10x13-1/4", 60 pgs, both card &
hardcover versions exist
nn-RFO (first printing blank on top of cover) 67.00 233.00 400.
First Series- this is a reprint if it says First Series 67.00 233.00 400.
Volume Two - By RFO 67.00 233.00 400.
... My Resolutions by Buster Brown (1907, 68 pgs, small size, cardboard cover)
scarce 43.00 150.00 260.
NOTE: Not actual comic book per se, but is a compilation of the Resolutions found at the end o
Outcault's Buster Brown newspaper strips.

BUSTER BROWN (N)
Cupples & Leon Co./N. Y. Herald Co.: 1906 - 1917 (11x17", color, strip-r)
NOTE: Early issues by R. F. Outcault; most C&L editions are not by Outcault.
1906...His Dog Tige And Their Jolly Times (11-3/8x16-5/8", 68 pgs.)
283.00 992.00 1700.
1906...His Dog Tige & Their Jolly Times (11x16, 46 pgs.)
158.00 554.00 950.
1907...Latest Frolics (11-3/8x16-5/8", 66 pgs., reprints 1905-06 strips)
158.00 554.00 950.
1908...Amusing Capers (58 pgs.) 125.00 438.00 750.
1909...The Busy Body (11-3/8x16-5/8", 62 pgs.) 125.00 438.00 750.
1910...On His Travels (11x16", 58 pgs.) 112.00 392.00 675.
1911...Happy Days (11-3/8x16-5/8", 58 pgs.) 112.00 392.00 675.
1912...In Foreign Lands (10x16", 58 pgs.) 112.00 392.00 675.
1913...And His Pets (11x16", 58 pgs.) 112.00 392.00 675.
1914...Funny Tricks (11-3/8x16-5/8", 58 pgs.) 112.00 392.00 675.
1916...At Play (10x16, 58 pgs) 112.00 392.00 675.

BUSTER BROWN NUGGETS (N)
Cupples & Leon Co./N.Y.Herald Co.: 1907 (1905, 7-1/2x6-1/2", 36 pgs., col
strip-r, hard-c)(By R. F. Outcault) (NOTE: books are all unnumbered)
Buster Brown Goes Fishing 39.00 137.00 235.
Buster Brown Goes Swimming 39.00 137.00 235.
Buster Brown Plays Indian 39.00 137.00 235.
Buster Brown Goes Shooting 39.00 137.00 235.
Buster Brown Plays Cowboy 39.00 137.00 235.
Buster Brown On Uncle Jack's Farm 39.00 137.00 235.
Buster Brown Tige And The Bull 39.00 137.00 235.
Buster Brown and Uncle Buster 39.00 137.00 235.
Buddy Tucker Meets Alice in Wonderland 50.00 175.00 300.
Buddy Tucker Visits The House That Jack Built 39.00 137.00 235.

BUSTER BROWN MUSLIN SERIES (N)
Saalfield: 1907 (also contain copyright Cupples & Leon)
...Goes Fishing (1907, 6-7/8x6-1/8", 24 pgs., color)-r/1905 Sunday
comics page by Outcault(Rare) 50.00 175.00 300.
...Plays Indian (1907, 6-7/8x6-1/8", 24 pgs., color)-r/1905 Sunday comics
page by Outcault(Rare) 42.00 146.00 250.
...Plays Cowboy (1907, 6-3/4x6", 10 pgs., color)-r/1905 Sunday comics
page by Outcault (Rare) 42.00 146.00 250.
...And The Donkey (1907, 6-7/8x6-1/8", 24 pgs., color)-r/1905 Sunday comics
page by Outcault (Rare) 42.00 146.00 250.
NOTE: Muslin books are all cloth books, made to be washable so as not easily stained/destro
by very young children. The muslin books contain one strip each (the title strip), to the more c
mon NUGGET's three strips.

BUSTER BROWN PREMIUMS (Advertising premium booklets)
Various Publishers: 1904 - 1912 (3x5" to 5x7"; sizes vary)

Buster Brown Nuggets - Goes Swimming
1907 © Cupples & Leon

Buster Brown Drawing Book
1904 © Buster Brown Stocking Co

Cartoons Magazine - Sept
1917 © H. H. Windsor

	GD2.0	FN6.0	VF8.0

American Fruit Product Company, Rochester, NY
ster Brown Duffy's 1842 Cider (1904, 7x5". 12 pgs, C.E. Sherin Co, NYC)
- By R. F. Outcault (scarce)   100.00   350.00   600.00
The Brown Shoe Company, St. Louis, USA
Set of five books (5x7", 16 pgs., color)
wn's Blue Ribbon Book of Jokes and Jingles Book 1 (nn, 1904)-By R. F.
Outcault; Buster Brown & Tige, Little Tommy Tucker, Jack & Jill, Little Boy
Blue, Dainty Jane; The Yellow Kid app. on back-c
(1st BB comic book premium)   600.00   2100.00   3600.00
ster Brown's Blue Ribbon Book of Jokes and Jingles Book 2 (1905)-
Original color art by Outcault   267.00   933.00   1600.00
ster's Book of Jokes & Jingles Book 3 (1909)
not signed by R.F. Outcault   267.00   933.00   1600.00
TE: Reprinted from the Blue Ribbon post cards with advert jingles added.
ster's Book of Instructive Jokes and Jingles Book 4 (1910)-Original color art
not signed by R.F. Outcault   267.00   933.00   1600.00
Book of Travels nn (1912, 3x5")-Original color art not signed by Outcault
   117.00   408.00   700.00
TE: Estimated 5 or 6 known copies exist of books #1-4.
The Buster Brown Bread Company
uster Brown" Bread Book of Rhymes, The (1904, 4x6", 12 pgs., half color,
B&W)- Original color art not signed by RFO   158.00   553.00   950.00
Buster Brown's Hosiery Mills
ow Buster Brown Got The Pie" nn (nd, 7x5-1/4". 16 pgs, color paper cover and
color interior By R.F. Outcault   83.00   292.00   500.00
he Autobiography of Buster Brown" nn (nd,9x6-1/8", 36 pgs, text story & art by
R.F. Outcault   83.00   292.00   500.00
TE: Similar to, but a distinctly different item than "Buster Brown's Autobiography."
The Buster Brown Stocking Company
ster Brown Drawing Book, The nn (nd, 5x6", 20 pgs.)-B&W reproductions
of 1903 R.F. Outcault art to trace   100.00   350.00   600.00
TE: Reprints a comic strip from Burr McIntosh Magazine, which includes Buster, Yellow Kid,
d Pore Li'l Mose (only known story involving all three.)
Collins Baking Company
ster Brown Drawing Book nn (1904, 5x3", 12 pgs.)-Original B&W art to
trace not signed by R.F. Outcault   100.00   350.00   600.00
C. H. Morton, St. Albans, VT
erry Antics of Buster Brown, Buddy Tucker & Tige nn (nd, 3-1/2x5-1/2",
16 pgs.)-Original B&W art by R.F. Outcault   83.00   292.00   500.00
Ivan Frank & Company
ster Brown nn (1904, 3x5", 12 pgs.)-B&W repros of R. F. Outcault Sunday
pages (First premium to actually reproduce Sunday comic pages – may be
first premium comic strip-r book?)   125.00   438.00   750.00
ster Brown's Pranks (1904, 3-1/2x5-1/8", 12 pgs.)-reprints intro of Buddy
Tucker into the BB newspaper strip before he was spun off into his own short
lived newspaper strip   125.00   438.00   750.00
Pond's Extract
ster Brown's Experiences With Pond's Extract nn (1904, 6-3/4x4-1/2",
28 pgs.)-Original color art by R.F. Outcault (may be the first BB premium
comic book with original art)   200.00   700.00   1200.00
Ringen Stove Company
uick Meal Steel Ranges nn (nd, 5x3", 16 pgs.)-Original B&W art not signed
by R.F. Outcault   83.00   292.00   500.00
Steinwender Stoffregen Coffee Co.
uster Brown Coffee" (1905, 4-7/8x3", color paper cover, B&W interior, 12 print
ed pages, plus 1 tracing paper page above each interior image (total of 8
sheets) (Very Rare)   83.00   292.00   500.00
OTE: Part of a BB drawing contest. If instructions had been followed, most copies would have
ded up destroyed.
U. S. Playing Card Company
ster Brown - My Own Playing Cards (1906, 2-1/2x1-3/4", full color
n - By R. F. Outcault
OTE: series of full color panels tell stories, average about 5 cards per story
No Publisher Listed
he Drawing Book nn (1906, 3-9/16x5", 8 pgs.)-Original B&W art to trace not
signed by R.F. Outcault   83.00   292.00   500.00

BUTLER BOOK A Series of Clever Cartoons of Yale Undergraduate Life
Yale Record: June 16, 1913 (10-3/4 x 17", 34 pgs, paper cover B&W)
nn-By Alban Bernard Butler   20.00   70.00   120.00
NOTE: Cartoons and strips reprinted from The Yale Record student newspaper.
BUTTONS & FATTY IN THE FUNNIES
Whitman Publishing Co.: nd 1927 (10-1/4x15-1/2", 28pg., color)
W936-Signed "M.E.B.", probably Merrill Blosser; strips in color copyright The
Brooklyn Daily Eagle; (very rare)   61.00   244.00   425.00
CAMION CARTOONS
Marshall Jones Company: 1919 (7-1/2x5", 136 pgs, B&W)
nn-By Kirkland H. Day (W.W.One occupation)   20.00   70.00   120.00
CANYON KIDDIES (M)
Doubleday, Page & Co: 1923 (8x10-1/4", 88 pgs, hard-c, B&W)
nn - By James Swinnerton   39.00   137.00   235.00
CARLO (H)
Doubleday, Page & Co.: 1913 (8 x 9-5/8, 120 pgs, hardcover, B&W)
nn - by A.B. Frost   40.00   140.00   240.00
NOTE: Original sequential strips about a dog. Became short lived newspaper comic strip in 1914.
CARTOON BOOK, THE
Bureau of Publicity, War Loan Organization, Treasury Department,
Washington, D.C. : 1918 (6-1/2x4-7/8", 48 pgs, paper cover, B&W)
nn-By various artists   31.00   108.00   185.00
NOTE: U.S. government issued booklet of WW I propaganda cartoons by 46 artists promoting the
third sale of Liberty Loan bonds. The artists include: Berryman, Clare Briggs, Cesare, J. N.
"Ding" Darling, Rube Goldberg, Kemble, McCutcheon, George McManus, F. Opper, T. E. Powers,
Ripley, Satterfield, H. T. Webster, Gaar Williams.
CARTOON CATALOGUE (S)
The Lockwood Art School, Kalamazoo, Mich.: 1919 (11-5/8x9, 52 pgs, B&W)
nn - edited by Mr. Lockwood   20.00   60.00   100.00
NOTE: Jammed with 100s of single panel cartoons and some sequential comics; Mr Lockwood
ebgan the very first cartoonist school back in 1892. Clare Briggs was one of his students.
CARTOON HUMOR
Collegian Press: 1938 (102 pgs, squarebound, B&W)
nn -   20.00   70.00   120.00
NOTE: contains cartoons & strips by Otto Soglow, Syd Hoff, Peter Arno, Abner Dean, others
CARTOONS BY BRADLEY: CARTOONIST OF THE CHICAGO DAILY NEWS
Rand McNally & Company: 1917 (11-1/4x8-3/4", 112 pgs, hardcover, B&W)
nn-By Luther D. Bradley (editorial)   20.00   70.00   120.00
CARTOONS BY FONTAINE FOX (Tooneville Trolley) (S)
Harper & Brothers Publishers: nd early '20s (9x7-7/8",102 pgs.,hardcover,B&W)
Second Book- By Fontaine Fox (Tooneville-r)   54.00   189.00   325.00
CARTOONS BY HALLADAY (N,S)
Providence Journal Co., Rhode Island: Dec 1914 (116 pgs, 10-1/2 x 7-3/4",
hard-c, B&W)
nn- (Scarce)   50.00   125.00   250.00
NOTE: cartoons on Rhode Island politics, plus some Teddy Roosevelt & WW I cartoons.
CARTOONS BY McCUTCHEON (S)
A. C. McClurg & Co.: 1903 (12-3/8x9-3/4", 212 pgs, hardcover, B&W)
nn-By John McCutcheon   20.00   70.00   120.00
CARTOONS BY W. A. IRELAND (S)
The Columbus-Evening Dispatch: 1907 (13-3/4 x 10-1/2", 66 pgs, hardcover)
nn-By W. A. Ireland (strip-r)   20.00   70.00   120.00
CARTOONS MAGAZINE (I,N,S)
H. H. Windsor, Publisher: Jan 1912-June 1921 (1912-June 1913 issues 12x9-
1/4", 68-76 pgs; 1913-1921 issues 10x7", average 112 to 188 pgs, color covers)
1912-Jan-Dec   15.00   51.00   90.00
1913-1915   15.00   51.00   90.00
1916-1917   15.00   51.00   90.00
1917-(Apr) "How Comickers Regard Their Characters"   30.00   105.00   150.00

CH

PLATINUM AGE

Charlie Chaplin in the Army by Segar
1917 © Essaney

Comic Monthly #7 by James Swinnerton
1922 © Embee Dist. Co.

How Dick Tracy and Dick Tracy, Jr.
Caught the Racketeers by Chester Goul
1933 © Cupples & Leon

	GD2.0	FN6.0	VF8.0		GD2.0	FN6.0	VF

1917-(June) "A Genius of the Comic Page" - long article on George Herriman, Krazy Kat, etc with lots of Herriman art; "Cartoonists and Their Cars"

	58.00	204.00	350.00
1918-1919	20.00	70.00	120.00
1920-1921	15.00	53.00	90.00

NOTE: Many issues contain a wealth of historical background on then current cartoonists of the day with an international slant; each issue profusely illustrated with many cartoons.

CARTOON BY J. N. DARLING (S,N - some sequantial strips)
The Register & Tribune Co., Des Moines, Iowa: 1909?-1920 (12x8-7/8",B&W)

Book 1	15.00	51.00	90.00
Book 2 Education of Alonzo Applegate (1910)	15.00	51.00	90.00
2nd printing	10.00	30.00	90.00
Book 3 Cartoons From The Files (1911)	15.00	51.00	90.00
Book 4	15.00	51.00	90.00
Book 5 In Peace And War (1916)	15.00	51.00	90.00
Book 6 Aces & Kings War Cartoons (Dec 1, 1918)	15.00	51.00	90.00
Book 7 The Jazz Era (Dec 1920)	15.00	51.00	90.00

NOTE: Some of the most inspired hard hitting cartoons ever printed. Are there more?

CHARLIE CHAPLIN (N)
Essanay/M. A. Donohue & Co.: 1917 (9x16", B&W, large size soft-c)

Series 1, #315-Comic Capers (9-3/4x15-3/4")-18 pgs. by Segar; Series 1,			
#316-In the Movies	233.00	817.00	1400.00
Series 1, #317-Up in the Air, #318-In the Army	233.00	817.00	1400.00
Funny Stunts-(12-1/2x16-3/8", color)	233.00	817.00	1400.00

NOTE: All contain pre-Thimble Theatre Segar art.

CHASING THE BLUES
Doubleday Page: 1912 (7-1/2x10", 52 pgs., B&W, hard-c)

nn-By Rube Goldberg	150.00	525.00	900.00

CLANCY THE COP (O))
Dell Publishing Co.: 1930 - No. 2, 1931 (10x10", 52 pgs., B&W, cardboard-c) (Also see Bug Movies & Deadwood Gulch)

1, 2- By Vep (original material; not reprints)	50.00	200.00	350.00

CLIFFORD MCBRIDE'S IMMORTAL NAPOLEON & UNCLE ELBY (N)
The Castle Press: 1932 (12x17"; soft-c cartoon book)

nn-Intro. by Don Herod	36.00	144.00	250.00

COLLECTED DRAWINGS OF BRUCE BAIRNSFATHER, THE
W. Colston Leigh: 1931 (11-1/4x8-1/4 ", 168 pages, hardcover, B&W)

nn-By Bruce Bairnsfather	24.00	96.00	165.00

COMICAL PEEP SHOW
McLoughlin Bros.: 1902 (36 pgs, B&W)

nn	24.00	96.00	165.00

NOTE: Comic stories of Wilhelm Busch redrawn; two versions with green or gold front cover logos; back covers different.

COMIC ANIMALS (I)
Charles E. Graham & Co.: 1903 (9-3/4x7-1/4", 90 pgs, color cover)

nn-By Walt McDougall (not comic strips)	43.00	150.00	260.00

COMIC CUTS (O)
H. L. Baker Co., Inc.: 5/19/34-7/28/34 (Tabloid size 10-1/2x15-1/2", 24 pgs., 5¢) (full color, not reprints; published weekly; created for news stand sales)

V1#1 - V1#7(6/30/34), V1#8(7/14/34), V1#9(7/28/34)-Idle Jack strips			
	50.00	150.00	300.00

NOTE: According to a 1958 Lloyd Jacquet interview, this short-lived comics mag was the direct inspiration for Major Malcolm Wheeler-Nicholson's New Fun Comics, not Famous Funnies.

COMIC MONTHLY (O)
Embee Dist. Co.: Jan, 1922 - No. 12, Dec, 1922 (10¢, 8-1/2"x9", 28 pgs., 2-color covers) (1st monthly newsstand comic publication) (Reprints 1921 B&W dailies)

1-Polly & Her Pals by Cliff Sterrett	193.00	772.00	1350.00
2-Mike & Ike by Rube Goldberg	114.00	456.00	800.00
3-S'Matter, Pop?	114.00	456.00	800.00
4-Barney Google by Billy DeBeck	114.00	456.00	800.00
5-Tillie the Toiler by Russ Westover	114.00	456.00	800.00
6-Indoor Sports by Tad Dorgan	114.00	456.00	800.00

NOTE: #6 contains more Judge Rummy than Indoor Sports

7-Little Jimmy by James Swinnerton	114.00	456.00	800
8-Toots and Casper by Jimmy Murphy	114.00	456.00	800
9-New Bughouse Fables by Barney Google	114.00	456.00	800
10-Foolish Questions by Rube Goldberg	114.00	456.00	800
11-Barney Google & Spark Plug by Billy DeBeck	114.00	456.00	800
12-Polly & Her Pals by Cliff Sterrett	193.00	772.00	1350

NOTE: This series was published by George McManus (Bringing Up Father) as Em & Rudolp Block, Jr., son of Hearst's cartoon editor for many years, as "Bee." One would have thought th series would have done very well considering the tremendous amount of talent assembled. Al issues are extremely hard to find these days and rarely show up in any type of higher grade.

COMIC PAINTING AND CRAYONING BOOK (H)
Saalfield Publ. Co.: 1917 (13-1/2x10", 32 pgs.) (No price on-c)

nn-Tidy Teddy by F. M. Follett, Clarence the Cop, Mr. & Mrs. Butt-In; regular comic stories to read or color	50.00	175.00	300.

COMPLETE TRIBUNE PRIMER, THE (I)
Mutual Book Company: 1901 (7 1/4 x 5", 152 pgs, red hard-c)

nn-By Frederick Opper; has 75 Opper cartoons	25.00	88.00	150.

COURTSHIP OF TAGS, THE (N)
McCormick Press: pre-1910 (9x4", 88 pgs, red & B&W-c, B&W interior)

nn-By O. E. Wertz (strip-r Wichita Daily Beacon)	25.00	88.00	150.

DAFFYDILS (N)
Cupples & Leon Co.: 1911 (6x8", 52 pgs., B&W, hard-c)

nn-By "Tad" Dorgan	58.00	204.00	350.

DAN DUNN SECRET OPERATIVE 48 (Also See Detective Dan) (N)
Whitman Publishing: 1937 ((5 1/2 x 7 1/4", 68pgs., xolor cardbaord-c, B&V)

1010 And The Gansters' Frame-Up	36.00	144.00	250.

NOTE: There are two versions of the book the later printing has a 5 cent cover price.Dick Tra look-alike character by Norman Marsh.

DANGERS OF DOLLY DIMPLE, THE (N)
Penn Tobacco Co.: nd (1930's) (9-3/8x7-7/8", 28 pgs, red cardboard-c, B&W,

nn- (Rare) by Walter Enright	???	???	???

NOTE: Reprints newspaper comic strip advertisements, in which in every episode, Dolly Dimpl life is saved by Penn's Smoking Tobacco.

DEADWOOD GULCH (O) (See The Funnies 1929)(also see Bug Movies & Clancy The Cop)
Dell Publishing Co.: 1931 (10x10", 52 pgs., B&W, color covers, B&W interior)

nn-By Charles "Boody" Rogers (original material)	50.00	200.00	350.

DESTINY A Novel In Pictures (O)
Farrar & Rinehart: 1930 (8x7", 424 pgs., B&W hard-c, dust jacket?)

nn-By Otto Nuckel (original graphic novel)	25.00	100.00	175.

DICK TRACY & DICK TRACY JR. CAUGHT THE RACKETEERS, HOW
Cupples & Leon Co.: 1933 (8-1/2x7", 88 pgs., hard-c) (See Treasure Box of Famous Comics) (N)

2-(Numbered on pg. 84)-Continuation of Stooge Viller book (daily strip reprin from 8/3/33 thru 11/8/33)(Rarer than #1)	86.00	344.00	600.
With dust jacket…	118.00	472.00	825.

DICK TRACY & DICK TRACY JR. AND HOW THEY CAPTURED "STOOGE VILLER (N)
Cupples & Leon Co.: 1933 (8-1/2x7", 100 pgs., hard-c, one-shot)
Reprints 1932 & 1933 Dick Tracy daily strips

nn(No.1)-1st app. of "Stooge" Viller	86.00	344.00	600.
with dust jacket…	118.00	472.00	825.

DIMPLES By Grace Drayton (N) (See Dolly Dimples)
Hearst's International Library Co.: 1915 (6 1/4 x 5 1/4, 12 pgs) (5 known)

nn-Puppy and Pussy; nn-She Goes For a Walk; nn-She Had A Sneeze; nn-She Has a Naughty Play Husband; nn-Wait Till Fido Comes Home	20.00	70.00	140.

DOINGS OF THE DOO DADS, THE (N) (see Mutt & Jeff #1-#5)
Detroit News (Universal Feat. & Specialty Co.): 1922 (50¢, 7-3/4x7-3/4", 34

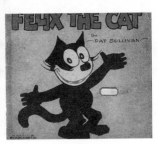

Felix the Cat Book 260 by Otto Messmer
1931 © McLoughlin Bros.

F. Fox's Funny Folk by Fontaine Fox
1917 © George H. Doran Company

Foolish Questions by Rube Goldberg
1921 © EmBee Distributing Co., NY.

	GD2.0	FN6.0	VF8.0

s, B&W, red & white-c, square binding)
-Reprints 1921 newspaper strip "Text & Pictures" given away as prize in the
 Detroit News Doo Dads contest; by Arch Dale 43.00 173.00 300.00

)INGS OF THE VAN-LOONS (N)
ll Publications: 1912 (5-3/4X15-1/2", 68pg., B&W, hard-c)
-By Fred I. Leipziger 88.00 306.00 525.00

)LLY DIMPLES & BOBBY BOUNCE (See Dimples)
upples & Leon Co.: 1933 (8-3/4x7")
-Grace Drayton-a 24.00 96.00 165.00

REAMS OF THE RAREBIT FIEND (N)
ederick A. Stokes Co.:1905 (10-1/4x7-1/2", 68 pgs, thin paper cover all B&W)
wspaper reprints from the New York Evening Telegram
-By Winsor "Silas" McCay (Very Rare) (Four copies known to exist)
 Estimated value.... 571.00 2000.00 -

RISCOLL'S BOOK OF PIRATES (O)
avid McKay Publ.: 1934 (9x7", 124 pgs, B&W hardcover)
-By Montford Amory (original material) 21.00 64.00 150.00

UCKY DADDLES
ederick A. Stokes Co: July 1911 (15x10")
-by Grace Weiderseim (later Drayton) strip-r 50.00 175.00 300.00

UMBUNNIES AND THEIR FRIENDS IN RABBITBORO, THE (O)
lbertine Randall Wheelan: 1931 (8-3/4x7-7/8", 82 pgs, color hardcover, B&W)
a-By Albertine Randall Wheelan (self-pub) 100.00 240.00

DISON - INSPIRATION TO YOUTH (N)(Also see Life of Thomas---)
homas A. Edison, Incorporated: 1939 (9-1/2 x 6-1/2, paper cover, B&W)
n - photo-c 46.00 138.00 275.00
DTE: Reprints strip material found in the 1928 Life of Thomas A. Edison in Word and Picture.

RBIE AND 'IS PLAYMATES
emocratic National Committe: 1932 (8x9-1/2, 16 pgs, B&W)
n - By Frederick Opper (Rare) 34.00 103.00 240.00
DTE: Anti-Hoover/Pro-Roosevelt politic comics

XPANSION BEING BART'S BEST CARTOONS FOR 1899
inneapolis Journal: 1900 10-1/4x8-1/2", 124 pgs, paperback, B&W)
2#1 - By Charles L. Bartholomew 24.00 84.00 145.00

AMOUS COMICS (N)
ing Features Synd. (Whitman Pub. Co.): 1934 (100 pgs., daily newspaper-r)
-1/2x8-1/2"; paper cover)(came in an illustrated box)
34 (#1) - Little Jimmy, Katz Kids & Barney Google 34.00 103.00 240.00
34 (#2) - Polly, Little Jimmy, Katzenjammer Kids 34.00 103.00 240.00
84 (#3) - Little Annie Rooney, Polly and Her Pals, Katzenjammer Kids
 34.00 103.00 240.00
ox price... 32.00 96.00 225.00

AMOUS COMICS CARTOON BOOKS (N)
Vhitman Publishing Co.: 1934 (8x7-1/4", 72 pgs, B&W hard-c, daily strip-r)
200-The Captain & the Kids; Dirks reprints credited to Bernard
 Dibble 29.00 86.00 200.00
202-Captain Easy & Wash Tubbs by Roy Crane; 2 slightly different
 versions of cover exist 34.00 103.00 240.00
203-Ella Cinders By Conselman & Plumb 28.00 84.00 195.00
204-Freckles & His Friends 25.00 75.00 175.00
NOTE: Called Famous Funnies Cartoon Books inside back area sales advertisement.

ANTASIES IN HA-HA (M)
leyer Bros & Co.: 1900 (14 x 11-7/8", 64 pgs, color cover hardcover, B&W)
n-By Hy Mayer 40.00 140.00 240.00

ELIX (N)
lenry Altemus Company: 1931 (6-1/2"x8-1/4", 52 pgs., color, hard-c w/dust
 acket)
1-3-Sunday strip reprints of Felix the Cat by Otto Messmer. Book No. 2 r/1931

Sunday panels mostly two to a page in a continuity format oddly arranged so
 each tier of panels reads across two pages, then drops to the next tier.
 (Books 1 & 3 have not been documented.)(year)
Each 104.00 416.00 725.00
With dust jacket 150.00 600.00 1050.00

FELIX THE CAT BOOK (N)
McLoughlin Bros.: 1927 (8"x15-3/4", 52 pgs, half in color-half in B&W)
nn-Reprints 23 Sunday strips by Otto Messmer from 1926 & 1927, every other
 one in color, two pages per strip. (Rare) 200.00 800.00 1400.00
260-Reissued (1931), reformatted to 9-1/2"x10-1/4" (same color plates, but one
 strip per every three pages), retitled ("Book" dropped from title) and abridged
 (only eight strips repeated from first issue, 28 pgs.).(Rare)
 79.00 316.00 550.00

F. FOX'S FUNNY FOLK (see Toonerville Trolley; Cartoons by Fontaine Fox) (C)
George H. Doran Company: 1917 (10-1/4x8-1/4", 228 pgs, red, B&W cover,
 B&W interior, hardcover; dust jacket?)
nn-By Fontaine Fox (Toonerville Trolley strip-r) 50.00 200.00 350.00

52 LETTERS TO SALESMEN
Steven-Davis Company: 1927 (???)
nn - rare ??? ??? ???
NOTE: 52 motivational letters to salesmen, with page of comics foreach week, bound into
 embossed leather binder

FOLKS IN FUNNYVILLE (S)
R.H. Russell: 1900 (12"Tx9"w)(cardboard-c)
nn-By Frederick Opper 271.00 950.00
NOTE: Reprinted from Hearst's NY Journal American Humorist supplements.

FOOLISH QUESTIONS (S)
Small, Maynard & Co.: 1909 (6-7/8 x 5-1/2", 174 pgs, hardcover, B&W)
nn-By Rube Goldberg (first Goldberg item) 75.00 263.00 450.00

FOOLISH QUESTIONS THAT ARE ASKED BY ALL
Levi Strauss & Co./Small, Maynard & Co.: 1909 (5-1/2x5-3/4", 24 pgs, paper-c,
 B&W)
nn- (Rare) by Rube Goldberg 46.00 160.00 275.00

FOOLISH QUESTIONS (Boxed card set) (S)
Wallie Dorr Co., N.Y.: 1919 (5-1/4x3-3/4")(box & card backs are red)
nn-Boxed set w/52 B&W comics on cards; each a single panel gag
 complete set w/box 75.00 263.00 450.00

FOOLISH QUESTIONS (S)
EmBee Distributing Co.: 1921 (10¢, 4x5 1/2", 52 pgs, 3 color covers; B&W)
1-By Rube Goldberg 46.00 160.00 275.00

FOXY GRANDPA (Also see The Funnies, 1st series) (N)
N. Y. Herald/Frederick A. Stokes Co./M. A. Donahue & Co./Bunny Publ.
(L. R. Hammersly Co.): 1901 - 1916 (Strip-r in color, hard-c)
1901-9x15" in color-N. Y. Herald 271.00 950.00 -
1902- "Latest Advs of...", 32 pgs., 9-1/2x15-1/2" 164.00 575.00 -
1902- The Many Advs. of...", 9x12", 148 pgs., Hammersly Co.
 179.00 625.00 -
1903- "Latest Advs", 9x15", 24 pgs., Hammersly Co.
 164.00 575.00 -
1903- "...'s New Advs.", 11x15", 66 pgs., Stokes 164.00 575.00 -
1904- "Up to Date", 10x15", 66 pgs., Stokes 146.00 510.00 875.00
1904- "The Many Adventures of...", 9x15, 144pgs, Donahue
 146.00 510.00 875.00
1905- "& Flip Flaps, 9-1/2x15-1/2", 52 pgs. 146.00 510.00 875.00
1905- "The Latest Advs. of...", 9x15", 28, 52, & 66 pgs, M.A. Donahue
 Co.; re-issue of 1902 issue 104.00 365.00 625.00
1905- "Latest Larks of...", 9-1/2x15-1/2", 52 pgs, Donahue; re-issue
 of 1902 issue 104.00 365.00 625.00
1905- "Latest Larks of...", 9-1/2x15-1/2", 24 pgs. edition, Donahue;
 re-issue of 1902 issue 104.00 365.00 625.00
1905- "Merry Pranks of...", 9-1/2x15-1/2", 28, 52 & 62 pgs., Donahue

The Latest Adventures of Foxy Grandpa by Schultze
1905 © Bunny Publ.

Giggles #6 by Walt McDougall
1908-09? © Pratt Food Co.

Harold Teen #2 by Carl Ed
1931 © Cupples & Leon

	GD2.0	FN6.0	VF8.0
		104.00	365.00	625.00

	GD2.0	FN6.0	VF

	GD2.0	FN6.0	VF8.0
		104.00	365.00	625.00
1905-"...Surprises",10x15", color, 64 pg,Stokes, 60¢	104.00	365.00	625.00
1906- "Frolics", 10x15", 30 pgs., Stokes	104.00	365.00	625.00
1907?-"...& His Boys",10x15", 64 color pgs, Stokes	104.00	365.00	625.00
1907- "Triumphs", 10x15", 62 pgs, Stokes	104.00	365.00	625.00
1908-"...Mother Goose", Stokes	104.00	365.00	625.00
1909- "...& Little Brother", 10x15, 58 pgs, Stokes	104.00	365.00	625.00
1911- "Latest Tricks", r-1910,1911 Sundays-Stokes Co.			
	104.00	365.00	625.00
1914-(9-1/2x15-1/2", 24 pgs.)-6 color cartoons/page, Bunny Publ. Co.			
	88.00	306.00	525.00
1915 - ...Always Jolly (10x16, Stokes)	88.00	306.00	525.00
1916- "Merry Book", (10x15", 64 pgs, Stokes)	88.00	306.00	525.00
1917-"...Adventures (5 1/2 x 6 1/2, 26 pgs, Stokes)	52.00	184.00	315.00
1917-"...Frolics (5 1/2 x 6 1/2, 26 pgs, Stokes)	52.00	184.00	315.00
1917-"...Triumphs (5 1/2 x 6 1/2, 26 pgs, Stokes)	52.00	184.00	315.00

FOXY GRANDPA SPARKLETS SERIES (N)
M. A. Donahue & Co.: 1908 (7-3/4x6-1/2"; 24 pgs.; color)

"... Rides the Goat", "...& His Boys", "...Playing Ball", "...Fun on the Farm", "...Fancy Shooting", "...Show His Boys Up-To-Date Sports", "...Plays Santa Claus"

each	88.00	306.00	525.00
900- "Playing Ball"; Bunny illos; 8 pgs.; linen like pgs., no date			
	73.00	254.00	435.00

FRAGMENTS FROM FRANCE (S)
G. P. Putnam & Sons: 1917 (9x6-1/4", 168 pgs, hardcover, $1.75)

nn- By Bruce Bairnsfather	25.00	88.00	150.00

NOTE: WW 1 trench warfare cartoons; color dust jacket.

FUNNIES, THE (H) (See Clancy the Cop, Deadwood Gulch, Bug Movies)
Dell Publishing Co.: 1929 - No. 36, 10/18/30 (10¢; No. 22 on) (16 pgs.)
Full tabloid size in color; not reprints; published every Saturday

1-My Big Brudder, Jonathan, Jazzbo & Jim, Foxy Grandpa, Sniffy, Jimmy Jams & other strips begin; first four-color comic newsstand publication; also contains magic, puzzles & stories	186.00	684.00	1300.00
2-21 (1930, 10¢	54.00	214.00	375.00
22(nn-7/12/30-5¢)	43.00	171.00	300.00
23(nn-7/19/30-5¢), 24(nn-7/26/30-5¢), 25(nn-8/2/30), 26(nn-8/9/30), 27(nn-8/16/30), 28(nn-8/23/30), 29(nn-8/30/30), 30(nn-9/6/30), 31(nn-9/13/30), 32(nn-9/20/30), 33(nn-9/27/30), 34(nn-10/4/30), 35(nn-10/11/30), 36(nn, no date-10/18/30) each....	43.00	171.00	300.00

GASOLINE ALLEY (Also see Popular Comics & Super Comics) (N)
Reilly & Lee Publishers: 1929 (8-3/4x7", B&W daily strip-r, hard-c)

nn-By King (96 pgs.)	57.00	228.00	400.00
Dust Wrapper-add 50% more
NOTE: Of all the Frank King reprint books, this is the only one to reprint actual complete newspaper strips - all others are illustrated prose text stories.

GIGGLES
Pratt Food Co.: 1908-09? (12x9", 8 pgs, color)

1-6 By Walt McDougall (#6 dated Jan 1909)	40.00	140.00	

GOD'S MAN (H)
Jonathan cape and Harrison Smith Inc.: 1929 (8-1/4x6", 298 pgs, B&W hardcover w/dust jacket) (original graphic novel in wood cuts)

nn-By Lynd Ward	-	-	-

GOLD DUST TWINS
N. K. Fairbank Co.: 1904 (4-5/8x6-3/4", 18 pgs, color and B&W)

nn - By E. W. Kemble (Rare)			
NOTE: Promo comic for Gold DustWashing Powder; includes page of watercolor paints

GUMPS, THE (N)
Landfield-Kupfer/Cupples & Leon No. 2: No. 1, 1918 - No. 6, 1921;

Book No. 1(1918)(Rare)-cardboard-c, 5-1/4x13-1/3", 64 pgs., daily strip-r by Sidney Smith	67.00	233.00	400.00
Book No.2(1918)-(Rare); 5-1/4x13-1/3"; paper cover; 36 pgs. daily strip			

	GD2.0	FN6.0	VF
reprints by Sidney Smith	67.00	233.00	400.
Book No. 3-6 (Rare)	121.00	423.00	725.

GUMPS, ANDY AND MIN, THE (N)
Landfield-Kupfer Printing Co., Chicago/Morrison Hotel: nd (1920s)
(Giveaway, 5-1/2"x14", 20 pgs., B&W, soft-c)

nn-Strip-r by Sidney Smith; art & logo embossed on cover w/hotel restaurant menu on back-c or a hotel promo ad; 4 different contents of issues known	50.00	175.00	300.

GUMPS, THE (N)
Cupples & Leon: 1924-1930 (10x10, 52 pgs, B&W)

nn(1924)-By Sidney Smith	61.00	244.00	425.
2,3	39.00	154.00	270.
4-7	33.00	131.00	230.

GUMP'S CARTOON BOOK, THE (N)
The National Arts Company: 1931 (13-7/8x10", 36 pgs, color covers, B&W)

nn-By Sidney Smith	57.00	228.00	400.

GUMPS PAINTING BOOK, THE (N)
The National Arts Company: 1931 (11 x 15 1/4", 20 pgs, half in full color)

nn-By Sidney Smith	57.00	228.00	400.

HALT FRIENDS! (see also HELLO BUDDY)
???: 1918? (4-3/8x5-3/4", 36 pgs, color-c, B&W, no cover price listed)

nn - unknown	25.00	75.00	175.
NOTE: says on front cover: "Comics of War Facts of Service Sold on its merits by Unemploy or Disabled Ex-Service Men. Credentials Shown On Request. Price - Pay What You Please"

HAMBONE'S MEDITATIONS (N)
Jahl & Co.: no date 1920 (6-1/8 x 7-1/2, 108 pgs, paper cover, B&W)

nn - By J. P. Alley	33.00	132.00	230.
NOTE: Reprint of racist single panel newspaper series, 2 cartoons per page.

HAN OLA OG PER (N)
Anundsen Publishing Co, Decorah, Iowa: 1927
(10-3/8 x 15-3/4", 54 pgs, paper cover, B&W)

nn-American origin Norwegian language strips-r	33.00	131.00	230.
NOTE: 1940s and modern reprints exist.

HANS UND FRITZ (N)
The Saalfield Publishing Co.: 1917, 1927-29 (10x13-1/2", 28 pgs., B&W)

nn-By R. Dirks (1917, r-1916 strips)	96.00	335.00	575.
nn - By R. Dirks (1923 edition- reprint of reprints?)	58.00	204.00	350.
The Funny Larks Of... By R. Dirks (©1917 outside cover; ©1916 inside indica)	96.00	335.00	575.
The Funny Larks Of... (1927) reprints 1917 edition of 1916 strips Halloween-c	58.00	204.00	350.
The Funny Larks of... 2 (1929)	58.00	204.00	350.
193 - By R. Dirks; contains 1916 Sunday strip reprints of Katzenjammer Kids & Hawkshaw the Detective - reprint of 1917 nn edition (1929) this edition is not rare	58.00	204.00	350.

HAPPY DAYS (S)
Coward-McCann Inc.: 1929 (12-1/2x9-5/8", 110 pgs, hardcover B&W)

nn-By Alban Butler (WW 1 cartoons)	20.00	60.00	120.

HAPPY HOOLIGAN (See Alphonse...) (N)
Hearst's New York American & Journal: 1902,1903

Book 1-(1902)-"And His Brother Gloomy Gus", By Fred Opper; has 1901-02-r; (yellow & black)(86 pgs.)(10x15-1/4")	371.00	1300.00	-
New Edition, 1903 -10x15" 82 pgs. in color	279.00	975.00	-

HAPPY HOOLIGAN (N)
Frederick A. Stokes Co.: 1906-08 (10x15", cardboard color-c)

1906-;Travels of...), 32 pgs,10-1/4x15-3/4", 1905-r	200.00	700.00	-
1908-"Handy-", 68 pgs, color	200.00	700.00	-
1908?-"--Home Again", 68 pgs, 60¢; by F. Opper; full color-c			
	200.00	700.00	-

Hawkshaw the Detective by Gus Mager
1917 © Saalfield Publishing Co.

Highlights of History by J. Mansfield
The Winning of the Old West
1934 © World Syndicate Publishing Co.

Joys & Glooms By T.E. Powers
1912 © Reilly & Britton Co.

	GD2.0	FN6.0	VF8.0

HAPPY HOOLIGAN (Story of...) (G)
McLoughlin Bros.: No. 281, 1932 (12x9-1/2", 16 pgs., soft-c)
81-Three-color text, pictures on heavy paper | 57.00 | 228.00 | 400.00

HAROLD TEEN (N)
Cupples & Leon Co.: 1929 (9-7/8x9-7/8", 52 pgs, cardboard covers)
nn-By Carl Ed | 41.00 | 164.00 | 290.00
nn-(1931, 8-11/16x6-7/8", 96 pgs, hardcover w/dj) | 41.00 | 164.00 | 290.00
NOTE: Title 2nd book: HAROLD TEEN AND HIS OLD SIDE-KICK-- POP JENKINS, (Adv. of...)

HAROLD HARDHIKE'S REJUVENATION
O'Sullivan Rubber: 1917 (6-1/4x3-1/2, 16 pgs, B&W)
nn- | 25.00 | 100.00 | 175.00
NOTE: comic book to promote rubber shoe heels

HAROLD TEEN PAINT AND COLOR BOOK (N)
McLoughlin Bros Inc.: 1932 (13x9-3/4, 28 pgs, B&W and color)
#2054 | 25.00 | 100.00 | 175.00

HAWKSHAW THE DETECTIVE (See Advs. of..., Hans Und Fritz & Okay) (N)
The Saalfield Publishing Co.: 1917 (10-1/2x13-1/2", 24 pgs., B&W)
nn-By Gus Mager (Sunday strip-r) | 54.00 | 190.00 | 325.00
nn-By Gus Mager (1926 edition) | 25.00 | 100.00 | 175.00

HE DONE HER WRONG (O)
Doubleday, Doran & Company: 1930 (8-1/4x 7-1/4", 276pgs, hardcover with dust jacket, B&W interiors)
nn-By Milt Gross | 50.00 | 200.00 | 350.00
NOTE: A seminal original material wordless graphic novel, not reprints. Several modern reprints.

HELLO BUDDY (see also **HALT FRIENDS**)
???: 1919? (4-3/8x5-3/4", 36 pgs, color-c, B&W, 15¢)
nn - unknown | 25.00 | 100.00 | 175.00
NOTE: Says on front cover: "Comics of War Facts of Service Sold on its merits by Unemployed or Disabled Ex-Service Men."

HENRY (N)
David McKay Co.: 1935 (25¢, soft-c)
Book 1-By Carl Anderson | 50.00 | 200.00 | 350.00
NOTE: Ties with Popeye (David McKay) and Little Annie Rooney (David McKay) as the last of the 10x10" Platinum Age comic books.

HENRY (N)
Greenberg Publishers Inc.: 1935 (11-1/4x 8-5/8", 72 pgs, red & blue color hard-cover,dust jacket, B&W interiors) (strip-r from Saturday Evening Post)
nn-By Carl Anderson | 50.00 | 200.00 | 350.00

HIGH KICKING KELLYS, THE (M)
Vaudeville News Corporation, NY: 1926 (5x11", B&W, two color soft-c)
nn-By Jack A. Ward (scarce) | 40.00 | 160.00 | 280.00

HIGHLIGHTS OF HISTORY (N)
World Syndicate Publishing Co.: 1933-34 (4-1/2x4", 288 pgs)
nn-5 different unnumbered issues; daily strip-r | 10.00 | 40.00 | 70.00
NOTE: Titles include Buffalo Bill, Daniel Boone, Kit Carson, Pioneers of the Old West, Winning of the Old Northwest. There are line drawing color covers and embossed hardcover versions. It is unknown which came out first.

HOMER HOLCOMB AND MAY (N)
no publisher listed: 1920s (4 x 9-1/2", 40 pgs, paper cover, B&W)
nn-By Doc Bird Finch (strip-r) | 10.00 | 40.00 | 70.00

HOME, SWEET HOME (N)
M.S. Publishing Co.: 1925 (10-1/4x10")
nn-By Tuthill | 33.00 | 134.00 | 235.00

HOW THEY DRAW PROHIBITION (S)
Association Against Prohibition: 1930 (10x9", 100 pgs.)
nn-Single panel and multi-panel comics (rare) | 71.00 | 285.00 | 500.00
NOTE: Contains art by J.N. "Ding" Darling, James Flagg, Rollin Kirby, Winsor McCay, T.E. Powers, H.T. Webster, others. Also comes with a loose sheet listing all the newspapers where the cartoons originally appeared.

HOW TO BE A CARTOONIST (H)
Saalfield Pub. Co: 1936 (10-3/8x12-1/2", 16 pgs, color-c, B&W)
nn - By Chas. H. Kuhn | 10.00 | 40.00 | 70.00

HOW TO DRAW: A PRACTICAL BOOK OF INSTRUCTION (H)
Harper & Brothers: 1904 (9-1/4x12-3/8", 128 pgs, hardcover, B&W)
nn-Edited By Leon Barritt | 57.00 | 228.00 | 400.00
NOTE: Strips reprinted include: "Buster Brown" by Outcault, "Foxy Grandpa" by Bunny, "Happy Hooligan" by Opper, "Katzenjammer Kids" by Dirks, "Lady Bountiful" by Gene Carr, "Mr. Jack" by Swinnerton, "Panhandle Pete" by George McManus, "Mr E.Z. Mark" by F.M. Howarth; non-character strips by Hy Mayer, Winsor McCay, T.E. Powers, others; single panel cartoons by Davenport, Frost, McDougall, Nast, W.A. Rogers, Sullivant, others.

HOW TO DRAW CARTOONS (H)
Garden City Publishing Co.: 1926, 1937 (10 1/4 x 7 1/2, 150 pgs)
1926 first edition By Clare Briggs | 25.00 | 75.00 | 150.00
1937 2nd edition By Clare Briggs | 20.00 | 60.00 | 120.00
NOTE: Seminal "how to" break into the comics syndicates with art by Briggs, Fisher, Goldberg, King, Webster, Opper, Tad, Hershfield, McCay, Ding, others. Came with Dust Jacket -add 50%.

HOW TO DRAW FUNNY PICTURES: A Complete Course in Cartooning (H)
Frederick J. Drake & Co.: 1936 (10-1/4x6-3/4", 168 pgs, hardcover, B&W)
nn-By E.C. Matthews (200 illus by Zimmerman) | 20.00 | 60.00 | 120.00

HY MAYER (M)
Puck Publishing: 1915 (13-1/2 x 20-3/4", 52 pgs, hardcover, color & B&W interiors) (reprints from Puck)
nn-By Hy Mayer | 40.00 | 140.00 | 240.00

HYSTERICAL HISTORY OF THE CIVILIAN CONSERVATION CORPS
Peerless Engraving: 1934 (10-3/4x7-1/2", 104 pgs, soft-c, B&W)
nn - various | 20.00 | 60.00 | 120.00
NOTE: Comics about CCC life, includes two color insert postcards in back.

IT HAPPENS IN THE BEST FAMILIES (N)
Powers Photo Engraving Co.: 1920 (52 pgs.)(9-1/2x10-3/4")
nn-By Briggs; B&W Sunday strips-r | 29.00 | 114.00 | 200.00
Special Railroad Edition (30¢)-r/strips from 1914-1920 | 26.00 | 103.00 | 180.00

JIMMIE DUGAN AND THE REG'LAR FELLERS (N)
Cupples & Leon: 1921, 46 pgs. (11"x16")
nn-By Gene Byrne | 71.00 | 284.00 | 500.00
NOTE: Ties with EmBee's Mutt & Jeff and Trouble of Bringing Up Father as the last of this size.

JIMMY (N)
N. Y. American & Journal: 1905 (10x15", 40 pgs., color)
nn-By Jimmy Swinnerton | 179.00 | 625.00 | 1075.00
NOTE: James Swinnerton was one of the original first pioneers of the American newspaper comic strip

JIMMY AND HIS SCRAPES (N)
Frederick A. Stokes: 1906, (10-1/4x15-1/4", 66 pgs, cardboard-c, color)
nn-By Jimmy Swinnerton | 64.00 | 256.00 | 450.00

JIMMY, STORY OF (I)
McLoughlin Bros.:1932 (9-1/2"X12", 16 pgs., soft cover)
nn-By Jimmy Swinnerton and Mary Kinnaird | 5700 | 228.00 | 400.00

JOE PALOOKA (N)
Cupples & Leon Co.: 1933 (9-13/16x10", 52 pgs., B&W daily strip-r)
nn-by Ham Fisher (scarce) | 114.00 | 456.00 | 800.00

JOLLY POLLY'S BOOK OF ENGLISH AND ETIQUETTE (S)
Jos. J. Frisch: 1931 (60 cents, 8 x 5-1/8, 88 pgs, paper cover, B&W)
nn-By Jos. J. Frisch | 20.00 | 60.00 | 120.00
NOTE: Reprint of single panel newspaper series, 4 per page, of English and etiquette lessons taught by a flapper.

JOYS AND GLOOMS (N)
Reilly & Britton Co.: 1912 (11x8", 68 pgs, hardcover, B&W interior)
nn-By T. E. Powers (newspaper strip-r) | 3900 | 156.00 | 275.00

The Katzenjammer Kids Magic Drawing & Coloring Book
1931 © San L. Gabriel Sons & Company

The Katzenjammer Kids by Rudolph Dirks
1921 © EmBee Distributing Co.

Little Orphan Annie by Harold Gr
1926 © Cupples & Leon

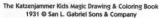

	GD2.0	FN6.0	VF8.0

JUDGE - to be indexed in next year's Guide

JUST KIDS, THE STORY OF (I)
McLoughlin Bros.: No. 283, 1932 (12x9-1/2", 16 pgs., paper-c)

283-Three-color text, pictures on heavy paper	39.00	156.00	275.00

KAPTAIN KIDDO AND PUPPO (N)
Frederick A. Stokes Co.: 1910-1913 (11x16-1/2", 62 pgs)

1910-By Grace Wiederseim (later Drayton)	40.00	140.00	240.00
1910-Turr-ble Tales of... By Grace Wiederseim.	40.00	140.00	240.00
Edward Stern & Co.: 1910 (11x16-1/2", 64 pgs)			
1913- ...'Speriences By Grace Drayton	40.00	140.00	240.00

KATZENJAMMER KIDS, THE (Also see Hans Und Fritz) (N)
New York American & Journal: 1902,1903 (10x15-1/4", 86 pgs., color)
(By Rudolph Dirks; strip first appeared in 1897) © W.R. Hearst
NOTE: All KK books 1902-1905 all have the same exact title page with a 1902 copyright by W.R. Hearst; almost always look instead on the front cover.

1902 (Rare) (red & black); has 1901-02 strips	457.00	1600.00	-
1903- A New Edition (Rare), 86 pgs	400.00	1400.00	-
1904- 10x15", 84 pgs	214.00	750.00	-
1905?-The Cruise of the, 10x15", 60¢, in color	214.00	750.00	-
1905-A Series of Comic Pictures, 10x15", 84 pgs. in color, possible reprint of 1904 edition	214.00	750.00	-
1905-Tricks of... (10x15", 66 pgs, Stokes)	214.00	750.00	-
1906-Stokes (10x16", 32 pgs. in color	186.00	650.00	-
1907- The Cruise of the, 10x15", 62 pgs 1905-r?	186.00	650.00	-
1910-The Komical...(10x15)	108.00	379.00	650.00
1921-Embee Dist. Co., 10x16", 20 pgs. in color	100.00	350.00	600.00

KATZENJAMMER KIDS MAGIC DRAWING AND COLORING BOOK (N)
Sam L Gabriel Sons And Company: 1931 (8 1/2 x 12", 36 pages, stiff-c)

838 By Knerr	50.00	200.00	350.00
NOTE:			

KEEPING UP WITH THE JONESES (N)
Cupples & Leon Co.: 1920 - No. 2, 1921 (9-1/4x9-1/4",52 pgs.,B&W daily strip-r)

1,2-By Pop Momand	39.00	154.00	270.00

KID KARTOONS (N,S)
The Century Co.: 1922 (232 pgs, printed 1 side, 9-3/4 x 7-3/4", hard-c, B&W)

nn- by Gene Carr	60.00	240.00	

LADY BOUNTIFUL (N)
Saalfield Publ. Co./Press Publ. Co.: 1917 (13-13/8x10", 36 pgs, color cardboard-c, B&W interiors)

nn-By Gene Carr; 2 panels per page	50.00	175.00	300.00
193S - 2nd printing (13-1/8x10",28 pgs color-c,B&W)33.00	117.00	200.00	

LAUGHS YOU MIGHT HAVE HAD From The Comic Pages of Six Week Day Issues of the Post-Dispatch (N)
St. Louis Post-Dispatch: 1921 (9 x 10 1/2", 28 pgs, B&W, red ink cover)

nn-Various comic strips	39.00	154.00	270.00

LIFE, DOGS FROM (M)
Doubleday, Page & Company: nn 1920 - No.2 1926 (130 pgs, 11-1/4 x 9", color painted-c, hard-c, B&W)

nn (No.1)	120.00	360.00	-
Second Litter	80.00	320.00	-

NOTE: reprints strips & cartoons featuring dogs from Life Magazine. Edited by Thomas L. Masson. Highly sought by collectors of dog ephemera. Art in both books is mostly by Robert L. Dickey. Other art: Carl Anderson-1,2; Barbes-1; Chip Bellew-1; Lang Campbell-1,2; Percy Crosby-1,2; Edwina-2; Frueh-2; R.B. Fuller-1; Gibson-1,2; Don Herold-2; Gus Mager-2; Orr-1; J.R. Shaver-1,2; T.S. Sullivant-2; Russ Westover-1,2; Crawford Young-1

LIFE OF DAVY CROCKETT IN PICTURE AND STORY, THE
Cupples & Leon: 1935 (8-3/4x7", 64 pgs, B&W hardcover, dust jacket?)

nn-By C. Richard Schaare	28.00	112.00	195.00

LIFE OF THOMAS A. EDISON IN WORD AND PICTURE, THE (N)(Also see Edison---)

	GD2.0	FN6.0	VF8.(

Thomas A. Edison Industries: 1928 (10x8", 52 pgs, paper cover, B&W)

nn-Photo-c	50.00	200.00	350.0(

NOTE: Reprints newspaper strip which ran August to November 1927.

LIFE'S LITTLE JOKES (S)
M.S. Publ. Co.: No date (1924)(10-1/16x10", 52 pgs., B&W)

nn-By Rube Goldberg	64.00	257.00	450.0(

LIFE'S PRINTS (was LIFE'S PICTURE GALLERY - See Vict. Section) (M,S,P)
Life Publishing Company, New York: nd (c1907) (7x4-1/2", 132 pgs, paper cover, B&W) (all are Scarce)

nn- (nd; c1907) unillustrated black construction paper cover; reprints art from 1895-1907; a-J.M.Flagg, A.B.Frost, Gibson	-	-	-
nn- (nd; c1908) b&w cardboard painted cover by Gibson, showing angel raising a champagne glass; reprints art from 1901-1908; a-J.M.Flagg, A.B.Frost, Gibson, Walt Kuhn, Art Young	-	-	-

NOTE: Catalog of prints reprinted from LIFE covers & centerspreads. There are likely more as y unreported catalogs.

LILY OF THE ALLEY IN THE FUNNIES
Whitman Publishing Co.: No date (1927) (10-1/4x15-1/2"; 28 pgs., color)

W936-By T. Burke (Rare)	57.00	228.00	400.0(

LITTLE ANNIE ROONEY (N)
David McKay Co.: 1935 (25¢, soft-c)

Book 1	43.00	172.00	300.0(

NOTE: Ties with Henry & Popeye (David McKay) as the last of the 10x10" size Plat comic books

LITTLE BIRD TOLD ME, A (E)
Life Publishing Co.: 1905? (96 pgs, hardbound)

nn-By Walt Kuhn (Life-r)	38.00	134.00	230.0(

LITTLE FOLKS PAINTING BOOK (N)
The National Arts Company: 1931 (10-7/8 x 15-1/4", 20 pgs, half in full color)

nn-By "Tack" Knight (strip-r)	33.00	132.00	230.0(

LITTLE JOHNNY & THE TEDDY BEARS (reprints from Judge) (M)
Reilly & Britton Co.: 1907 (10x14", 32 pgs.; green, red, black interior color)

nn-By J. R. Bray-a/Robert D. Towne-s	67.00	233.00	400.0(

LITTLE JOURNEY TO THE HOME OF BRIGGS THE SKY-ROCKET, THE
Lockhart Art School: 1917 (10-3/4x7-7/8", 20 pgs, B&W) (I)

nn-About Clare Briggs (bio & lots of early art)	38.00	134.00	230.0(

LITTLE KING, THE (see New Yorker Cartoon Albums for 1st appearance) (M)
Farrar & Reinhart, Inc: 1933 (10 1/4 x 8 3/4, 80 pgs, hardcover w/dust jacket)

nn- By Otto Soglow (strip-r The New Yorker)	43.00	129.00	300.0(

NOTE: Copies with dust jacket are worth 50% more.

LITTLE NEMO (...in Slumberland) (N)
Doffield & Co.(1906)/Cupples & Leon Co.(1909): 1906, 1909 (Sunday strip-r in color, cardboard covers)

1906-11x16-1/2" by Winsor McCay; 30 pgs. (Rare)	857.00	3000.00	-
1909-10x14" by Winsor McCay (Rare)	714.00	2500.00	-

LITTLE ORPHAN ANNIE (See Treasure Box of Famous Comics) (N)
Cupples & Leon Co.: 1926 - 1934 (8-3/4x7", 100 pgs., B&W daily strip-r, hard-c)

1(1926)-Little Orphan Annie	50.00	200.00	350.00
1(1926)-softback (see Treasure Box...)			
2('27)-In the Circus	36.00	144.00	250.00
3('28)-The Haunted House	36.00	144.00	250.00
4('29)-Bucking the World	36.00	144.00	250.00
5('30)-Never Say Die	30.00	120.00	210.00
6('31)-Shipwrecked	30.00	120.00	210.00
7('32)-A Willing Helper	24.00	96.00	170.00
8('33)-In Cosmic City	24.00	96.00	170.00
9('34)-Uncle Dan Army	43.00	172.00	300.00

NOTE: Each book reprints dailies from the previous year. Each hardcover came with a dust jacket. Books with dust jackets are worth 50% more.

LITTLE SAMMY SNEEZE (N)

The Trials of Lulu and Leander by Howarth
1906 © NY American & Journal

Maud the Mirthful Mule by Opper
1908 © Frederick A. Stokes

Mickey Mouse Book
1930 © Bibo & Lang

	GD2.0	FN6.0	VF8.0

w York Herald Co.: Dec 1905 (11x16-1/2", 72 pgs., color)

-By Winsor McCay (Very Rare) 971.00 3400.00 -
TE: Rarely found in fine to mint condition.

TLE SKEEZIX BOOKS (Also see Skeezix) (G)
illy & Lee Co.: No date (1927-28?) Boxed set of three Skeezix books)

-Box with 3 issues of Skeezix (possibly remainders). Skeezix & Pal, Skeezix
at the Circus, Skeezix & Uncle Walt known. Set... 80.00 320.00 550.00

VE AND LET LIVE
avelers Insurance Co.:** 1936 (5-3/4x7/3/4", 16 pgs. color and B&W)

- Bill Holman, Carl Anderson, etc 20.00 60.00 120.00

TTLE LULU BY MARGE (M)
nd McNally & Company, Chicago: 1936 (6-9/16x6", 68 pgs, yellow hard-c,
&W)

- By Marjorie Henderson Buell 25.00 100.00 200.00
TE: Begins reprinting single panel Little Lulu cartoons which began with Saturday Evening
st Feb. 23, 1935. This book was reprinted several times as late as 1940.

LU AND LEANDER (N)
avelers Insurance Co.:** ew York American & Journal: 1904 (76 pgs); William A Stokes & Co: 1906

-By F.M. Howarth 143.00 500.00 860.00
-The Trials of...(1906, 10x16", 68 pgs. in color) 143.00 500.00 860.00
TE: F. M. Howarth helped pioneer the American comic strip in the pages of PUCK magazine
the early 1890s before the Yellow Kid

ADMAN'S DRUM (O)
nathan Cape and Harrison Smith Inc.: 1930 (8-1/4x6", 274 pgs, B&W hard-
ver w/dust jacket) (original graphic novel in wood cuts)

-By Lynd Ward - - -

AMA'S ANGEL CHILD IN TOYLAND (I)
nd McNally & Company, Chicago: 1915 (128 pgs, hardbound)

-By M.T. "Penny" Ross & Marie C, Sadler 40.00 140.00 240.00
TE: Mamma's Angel Child published as a comic strip by the "Chicago Tribune" 1908 Mar 1 to
20 Oct 17.This novel dedicated to Esther Starring Richartz, "the original Mamma's Angel Kid."

AUD (I)
ederick A. Stokes Co.: 1906 - 1908? (10x15-1/2", cardboard-c)

906-By Fred Opper (Scarce), 66 pgs. color 257.00 900.00 -
907-The Matchless, 10x15" 70 pgs in color 200.00 700.00 -
908-The Mirthful Mule, 10x15", 64 pgs in color 200.00 700.00 -

EMORIAL EDITION The Drawings of Clare Briggs (S)
m H. Wise & Company: 1930 (7-1/2x8-3/4", 284 pgs, pebbled false black
ather, B&W) posthumous boxed set of 7 books by Clare Briggs

-The Days of Real Sport; nn-Golf; nn-Real Folks at Home; nn-Ain't it a Grand
and Glorious Feeling?; nn-That Guiltiest Feeling; nn-Somebody's Always
Taking the Joy Out of Life; nn-When a Feller Needs a Friend
Each book 30.00 120.00 210.00
TE: Also exists in a whitish cream colored paper back edition; first edition unknown presently.

ENACE CARTOONS (M, S)
enace Publishing Company, Aurora, Missouri: 1914 (10-3/8x8", 80 pgs,
ardboard-c, B&W)

n- (Rare) 50.00 150.00 450.00
TE: reprints anti-Catholic cartoons from K.K.K. related publication **The Menace.**

EN OF DARING (N)
upples & Leon Co.: 1933 (8-3/4x7", 100 pgs)

n-By Stookie Allen, intro by Lowell Thomas 30.00 90.00 180.00

ICKEY MOUSE BOOK
ibo & Lang: 1930-1931 (12x9", stapled-c, 20 pgs., 4 printings)

n-First Disney licensed publication (a magazine, not a book–see first book,
dventures of Mickey Mouse). Contains story of how Mickey met Walt and got
is name; games, cartoons & song "Mickey Mouse (You Cute Little Feller)," writ-
en by Irving Bibo; Minnie, Clarabelle Cow, Horace Horsecollar & caricature of
Valt shaking hands with Mickey. The changes made with the 2nd printing have
een verified by billing affidavits in the Walt Disney Archives and include:Two

	GD2.0	FN6.0	VF8.0

Win Smith Mickey strips from 4/15/30 and 4/17/30 added to page 8 & back-c;
"Printed in U.S.A." added to front cover; Bobette Bibo's age of 11 years added to
title page; faulty type on the word "tail" corrected top of page 3; the word "start"
added to bottom of page 7, removing the words "start 1 2 3 4" from the top of
page 7; music and lyrics were rewritten on pages 12-14. A green ink border was
added beginning with 2nd printing and some covers have inking variations. Art by
Albert Barbelle, drawn in an Ub Iwerks style. Total circulation : 97,938 copies
varying from 21,000 to 26,000 per printing.

1st printing. Contains the song lyrics censored in later printings, "When little
Minnie's pursued by a big bad villain we feel so bad then we're glad when you
up and kill him." Attached to the Nov. 15, 1930 issue of the Official Bulletin of
the Mickey Mouse Club notes: "Attached to this Bulletin is a new Mickey
Mouse Book that has just been published." This is thought to be the reason
why a slightly disproportionate larger number of copies of the first printing still
exist 1200.00 5400.00 11,000.00
2nd printing with a theater/advertising. Christmas greeting added to inside front
cover (1 copy known with Dec. 27, 1930 date) ---- 12,000.00 ----
2nd-4th printings 1100.00 5000.00 10,000.00
NOTE: Theater/advertising copies do not qualify as separate printings. Most copies are missing
pages 9 & 10 which have a puzzle to be cut out. Puzzle (pages 9 and 10) cut out or missing, sub-
tract 60% to 75%.

MICKEY MOUSE COLORING BOOK (S)
Saalfield Publishing Company:1931 (15-1/4x10-3/4", 32 pgs, color soft cover,
half printed in full color interior, rest B&W, only Saalfield MM item known)

871 - By Ub Iwerks & Floyd Gottfredson (rare) 400.00 1200.00 2400.00
NOTE: Contains reprints of first MM daily strip ever, including the "missing" speck the chicken is
after found only on the original daily strip art by Iwerks plus other very early MM art.

MICKEY MOUSE, THE ADVENTURES OF (I)
David McKay Co.: Book I, 1931 - Book II, 1932 (5-1/2"x8-1/2", 32 pgs.)

Book I-First Disney book, by strict definition (1st printing-50,000 copies)(see
Mickey Mouse Book by Bibo & Lang). Illustrated text refers to Clarabelle Cow
as "Carolyn" and Horace Horsecollar as "Henry". The name "Donald Duck"
appears with a non-costumed generic duck on back cover & inside, not in the
context of the character that later debuted in the Wise Little Hen.
Hardback w/characters on back-c 75.00 300.00 525.00
Softcover w/characters on back-c 38.00 151.00 265.00
Version without characters on back-c 45.00 180.00 315.00
Book II-Less common than Book I. Character development brought into confor-
mity with the Mickey Mouse cartoon shorts and syndicated strips. Captain
Church Mouse, Tanglefoot, Peg-Leg Pete and Pluto appear with Mickey &
Minnie 46.00 186.00 325.00

MICKEY MOUSE COMIC (N)
David McKay Co.: 1931 - No. 4, 1934 (10"x9-3/4", 52 pgs., cardboard-c)
(Later reprints exist)

1 (1931)-Reprints Floyd Gottfredson daily strips in black & white from 1930 &
1931, including the famous two week sequence in which Mickey tries to
commit suicide 229.00 914.00 1600.00
2 (1932)-1st app. of Pluto reprinted from 7/8/31 daily. All pgs. from 1931
164.00 656.00 1150.00
3 (1933)-Reprints 1932 & 1933 Sunday pages in color, one strip per page,
including the "Lair of Wolf Barker" continuity pencilled by Gottfredson and
inked by Al Taliaferro & Ted Thwaites. First app. Mickey's nephews, Morty &
Ferdie, one identified by name of Mortimer Fieldmouse, not to be confused
with Uncle Mortimer Mouse who is introduced in the Wolf Barker story
214.00 856.00 1500.00
4 (1934)-1931 dailies, include the only known reprint of the infamous strip
of 2/4/31 where the villainous Kat Nipp snips off the end of Mickey's tail with a
pair of scissors 129.00 514.00 900.00

MICKEY MOUSE (N)
Whitman Publishing Co.: 1933-34 (10x8-3/4", 34 pgs, cardboard-c)

948-1932 & 1933 Sunday strips in color, printed from the same plates as Mickey
Mouse Book #3 by David McKay, but only pages 5-17 & 32-48 (including all
of the "Wolf Barker" continuity) 157.00 629.00 1100.00
NOTE: Some copies bound with back cover upside down. Variance doesn't affect value. Same

Moon Mullins #5 by Frank Willard
1931 @ Cupples & Leon

Mutt & Jeff #17 by Bud Fisher
1932 © Cupples & Leon

The Newlyweds by George McManus
1907 © Saalfield Publishing Co.

art appears on front and back covers of all copies. Height of Whitman reissue trimmed 1/2 inch.

MILITARY WILLIE
J. I. Austen Co.: 1907 (7x9-1/2", 12 pgs., every other page in color, stapled)

nn-By F. R. Morgan	70.00	245.00	400.00

MINNEAPOLIS TRIBUNE CARTOON BOOK (S)
Minneapolis Tribune: 1899-1903 (11-3/8x9-3/8", B&W, paper cover)

nn (#1) (1899)	28.00	99.00	170.00
nn (#2) (1900)	28.00	99.00	170.00
nn (#3) (1901) (published Jan 01, 1901)	28.00	99.00	170.00
nn (#4) (1902) (114 pgs)	28.00	99.00	170.00
nn (#5) (1903 (9x10-3/4",110 pgs, B&W; color-c)	28.00	99.00	170.00

NOTE: All by Roland C. Bowman (editorial-r)

MINUTE BIOGRAPHIES: INTIMATE GLIMPSES INTO THE LIVES OF 150 FAMOUS MEN AND WOMEN
Grossett & Dunlap: 1931, 1933 (10-1/4x7-3/4", 168 pgs, hardcover, B&W)

nn-By Nisenson (art) & Parker(text)	20.00	60.00	120.00
More.... (1933)	20.00	60.00	120.00

MISCHIEVOUS MONKS OF CROCODILE ISLE, THE (N)
J. I. Austen Co., Chicago: 1908 (8-1/2x11-1/2", 12 pgs., 4 pgs. in color)

nn-By F. R. Morgan; reads longwise	96.00	335.00	575.00

MR. & MRS. (Also see Ain't It A Grand and Glorious Feeling?) (N)
Whitman Publishing Co.: 1922 (9x9-1/2", 52 & 28 pgs., cardboard-c)

nn-By Briggs (B&W, 52 pgs.)	37.00	149.00	260.00
nn-28 pgs.-(9x9-1/2")-Sunday strips-r in color	41.00	163.00	285.00

NOTE: The earliest presently known Whitman comic books were published in 1922.

MR. BLOCK (N)
Industrial Workers of the World (IWW): 1913, 1919

nn-By Ernest Riebe (C)	50.00	150.00	-
...And The Profiteers (original material) (H)	50.00	150.00	-

NOTE: Mr Block was a daily strip published from 1912 NOV 7 to 1913 SEP ? by the socialist newspaper "Industrial Worker"; Mr Block was a "square" guy (his head was in fact a block) who enthusiastically supported the same system that exploited him. The noted Joe Hill wrote a song about him (Mr Block,1913, on the air of "It loooks like a big time tonight") in the "Industrial Worker Songbook".

MR. TWEE-DEEDLE (N)
Cupples & Leon: 1913, 1917 (10 x 16, color strips-r from NY Herald)

nn-By John B. Gruelle (later of Raggedy Ann fame)	143.00	500.00	-
nn-"Further Adventures of..." by Gruelle	143.00	500.00	-

MONKEY SHINES OF MARSELEEN AND SOME OF HIS ADVENTURES (C)
McLaughlin Bros. New York: 1906 (10 x 12-3/8", 36 pgs, full color hardcover)

nn-By Norman E. Jennett strip-r NY Evening Telegram	67.00	233.00	400.00

MONKEY SHINES OF MARSELEEN (N)
Cupples & Leon Co.: 1909 (11-1/2 x 17", 28 pgs. in two colors)

nn-By Norman E. Jennett	63.00	219.00	375.00

MOON MULLINS (N)
Cupples & Leon Co.: 1927 - 1933 (52 pgs., B&W daily strip-r)

Series 1('27)-By Willard	57.00	228.00	400.00
Series 2('28), Series 3('29), Series 4('30)	39.00	156.00	275.00
Series 5('31), 6('32), 7('33)	36.00	144.00	250.00
Big Book 1('30)-B&W (scarce)	100.00	400.00	700.00
w/dust jacket (rare)	183.00	732.00	1275.00

MUTT & JEFF (...Cartoon, The) (N)
Ball Publications: 1911 - No. 5, 1916 (5-3/4 x 15-1/2", 68 pgs, B&W, hard-c)

1(1910)(50¢) very common	71.00	286.00	500.00
2,3: 2 (1911)-Opium den panels; Jeff smokes opium (pipe dreams).			
3 (1911) both very common	71.00	286.00	500.00
2 -Reprint of 1913 edition with black ink cover	50.00	175.00	300.00
4 (1915) (50¢) (Scarce)	111.00	443.00	775.00
5 (1916) (Rare) -Photos of Fisher, 1st pg.	171.00	685.00	1200.00

NOTE: Mutt & Jeff first appeared in newspapers in 1907. Cover variations exist showing Mutt & Jeff reading various newspapers; i.e., The Oregon Journal, The American, and The Detroit News. Reprinting of each issue began soon after publication. No. 4 and 5 may not have been reprinted. Values listed include the reprints. Mutt & Jeff was the first successful American daily newspaper comic strip and as such remains one of the seminal strips of all time.

MUTT & JEFF (N)
Cupples & Leon Co.: No. 6, 1919 - No. 22, 1934? (9-1/2x9-1/2", 52 pgs., B&W dailies, stiff-c)

6, 7 - By Bud Fisher (very common)	32.00	128.00	225.
8-10	46.00	186.00	325.
11-18 (Somewhat Scarcer)	60.00	240.00	420.
19-22 (Rare) (do these #s even exist?)	71.00	286.00	500.
nn (1920)-(Advs. of...) 11x16"; 44 pgs.; full color reprints of 1919 Sunday strip	93.00	372.00	650.
Big Book nn (1926, 144 pgs., hardcovers)	114.00	456.00	800.
w/dust jacket	193.00	772.00	1350.
Big Book 1 (1928) - Thick book (hardcovers)	114.00	456.00	800.
w/dust jacket (rare)	182.00	729.00	1275.
Big Book 2 (1929) - Thick book (hardcovers)	114.00	456.00	800.
w/dust jacket (rare)	182.00	729.00	1275.

NOTE: The Big Books contain three previous issues rebound.

MUTT & JEFF (N)
Embee Publ. Co.: 1921 (9x15", color cardboard-c & interior)

nn-Sunday strips in color (Rare)- BY Bud Fisher	143.00	572.00	1000.

NOTE: Ties with The Trouble of Bringing Up Father (EmBee) and Jimmie Dugan & The Reg'la Fellers (C&L) as the last of this size.

MYSTERIOUS STRANGER AND OTHER CARTOONS, THE
McClure, Phillips & Co.: 1905 (12-3/8x9-3/4", 338 pgs, hardcover, B&W)

nn-By John McCutcheon	32.00	128.00	225.

NEBBS, THE (N)
Cupples & Leon Co.: 1928 (52 pgs., B&W daily strip-r)

nn-By Sol Hess; Carlson-a	40.00	160.00	280.

NERVY NAT'S ADVENTURES (E)
Leslie-Judge Co.: 1911 (90 pgs, 85¢, 1903 strip reprints from *Judge*)

nn-By James Montgomery Flagg	75.00	263.00	450.

THE NEWLYWEDS AND THEIR BABY (N)
Saalfield Publ. Co.: 1907 (13x10, 52 pg hardcover)

...& Their Baby' by McManus; daily strips 50% color	200.00	700.00	-

THE NEWLYWEDS AND THEIR BABY'S COMIC PICTURES FOR PAINTING AND CRAYONING (N)
Saalfield Publishign Company: 1916 (10-1/4x14-3/4", 52 pg. Cardboard-c)

nn 44 B&W pages, covers, and one color wrap glued to B&W title page.			
Color wrap: color title pg & 3 pgs of color strips	82.00	286.00	490.
nn (1917, 10x14", 20 pgs, oblong, cardboard-c) partial reprint of 1916 edition	30.00	120.00	240.

THE NEWLYWEDS AND THEIR BABY (N)
Saalfield Publishing Company: 1917 (10-1/8x13-9/16 ", 52 pgs, full color cardstock-c, some pages full color, others two color (orange, blue)\

nn	82.00	286.00	490.

NEW YORKER CARTOON ALBUM, THE (M)
Doubleday, Doran& Company Inc.: (1928-1931); **Harper & Brothers.:** (1931-1933) **Random House** (1935-1937), various pg counts, hardcovers w/dust jackets)

1928: nn-114 pgs Arno, Held, Soglow, Williams, etc	20.00	60.00	120.
1928: SECOND-114 pgs Arno, Bairnsfather, Gross, Held, Soglow, Williams	10.00	30.00	60.
1930: THIRD-172 pgs Arno, Bairnsfather, Held, Soglow, Art Young	10.00	30.00	60.
1931: FOURTH-154 pgs Arno, Held, Soglow, Steig, Thurber, Williams, Art Young, "Little King" by Soglow begins	10.00	30.00	60.
1932: FIFTH-156 pgs Arno, Bairnsfather, Held, Hoff, Soglow, Steig, Thurber, Williams	10.00	30.00	60.
1933: SIXTH-156 pgs same as above	10.00	30.00	60.

Oh Skin-nay! by Claire Briggs
1913 © P.F. Volland

The Adventures of Peck's Bad Boy With
the Teddy Bear Show by McDougall
1907 © Charles C. Thompson, Co.

Pore Li'l Mose by R. F. Outcault
1902 © New York Herald Co.

	GD2.0	FN6.0	VF8.0
...35: SEVENTH-164 pgs	10.00	30.00	60.00
...37: 168 pgs; Charles Addams plus same as above but no Little King, two page			
"Gone With The Wind" parody strip	10.00	30.00	60.00

NOTE: Some sequential strips but mostly single panel cartoons.

...PPY'S POP (N)
...ne Saalfield Publishing Co.: 1917 (10-1/2x13-1/2", B&W, Sunday strip-r)

| ...-32 pgs. | 43.00 | 152.00 | 260.00 |

...H, MAN (A Bully Collection of Those Inimitable Humor Cartoons) (S)
...F. Volland & Co.: 1919 (8-1/2x13")

| ...-By Briggs | 43.00 | 152.00 | 260.00 |

NOTE: Originally came in illustrated box with Briggs art (box is Rare - worth 50% more with box).

...H SKIN-NAY! (S)
...F. Volland & Co.: 1913 (8-1/2x13", 125 pgs)

| ...-The Days Of Real Sport by Briggs | 43.00 | 152.00 | 260.00 |

NOTE: Originally came in illustrated box with Briggs art (box is Rare - worth 50% more with box).

...N AND OFF MOUNT ARARAT (also see Tigers) (N)
...earst's New York American & Journal: 1902, 86pgs. 10x15-1/4"

| ...-Noah's Ark satire by Jimmy Swinnerton (rare) | 286.00 | 1000.00 | - |

...N THE LINKS (N)
...associated Feature Service: Dec, 1926 (9x10", 48 pgs.)

| ...-Daily strip-r | 25.00 | 100.00 | 175.00 |

...NE HUNDRED WAR CARTOONS (S)
...aho Daily Statesman: 1918 (7-3/4x10", 102 pgs, paperback, B&W)

| ...-By Villeneuve (WW I cartoons) | 20.00 | 60.00 | 120.00 |

...UTBURSTS OF EVERETT TRUE, THE (N)
...aalfield Publ. Co.(Werner Co.): 1907 (92 pgs, 9-7/16x5-1/4")

...907 (2-4 panel strips-r)-By Condo & Raper	75.00	300.00	525.00
...921-Full color-c; reprints 56 of 88 cartoons from1907 ed. (10x10", 32 pgs B&W)			
	37.00	148.00	260.00

...VER THERE COMEDY FROM FRANCE
...bserver House Printing: nd (WW 1 era) (6x14", 60 pgs, paper cover)

| ...-artist(s) unknown | 15.00 | 53.00 | 90.00 |

...ECKS BAD BOY (N)
...harles C. Thompson Co, Chicago (by Walt McDougal): 1906-1908 (strip-r)

...& His Country Cousin Cynthia (1907)-12x16-1/2", 34 pgs In color			
	100.00	400.00	700.00
...dvs. of...And His Country Cousins (1907) 5-1/2x10 1/2", 18 pgs In color			
	50.00	175.00	300.00
...& Their Advs With The Teddy Bear (1907) 5-1/2x10-1/2", 18 pgs in color			
	50.00	175.00	300.00
...& Their Balloon Trip To the Country (1907) 5-1/2x 10-1/2, 18 pgs in color			
	50.00	175.00	300.00
...With the Teddy Bear Show (1907) 5-1/2x 10-1/2	50.00	175.00	300.00
...With The Billy Whiskers Goats (1907) 5-1/2 x 10-1/2, 18 pgs in color			
	50.00	175.00	300.00
...& His Chums (1908) - 11x16-1/4, 34 pgs Stanton & Van Vliet Co			
	100.00	400.00	700.00
...& His Chums (1908)-Hardcover; full color;16 pgs.	100.00	350.00	600.00
...dvs. of...in Pictures (1908) (11x17, 36 pgs)-In color; Stanton & Van V. Liet Co.			
	100.00	400.00	700.00

...ERCY & FERDIE (N)
...upples & Leon Co.: 1921 (10x10", 52 pgs., B&W dailies, cardboard-c)

| ...-By H. A. MacGill (Rare) | 61.00 | 244.00 | 425.00 |

...ETER RABBIT (N)
...ohn H. Eggers Co. The House of Little Books Publishers: 1922 - 1923

...-B4-(Rare)-(Set of 4 books which came in a cardboard box)-Each book
reprints half of a Sunday page per page and contains 8 B&W and 2 color
pages; by Harrison Cady (9-1/4x6-1/4", paper-c)

| ...each.... | 43.00 | 172.00 | 300.00 |

	GD2.0	FN6.0	VF8.0
Box only	57.00	228.00	400.00

**PICTORIAL HISTORY OF THE DEPARTMENT OF COMMERCE UNDER
HERBERT HOOVER (see Picture Life of a Great American) (O)**
Hoover-Curtis Campaign Committee of New York State: no date, 1928 (3-1/4
x 5-1/4, 32 pgs, paper cover, B&W)

| nn - by Satterfield (scarce) | 40.00 | 120.00 | 240.00 |

NOTE: 1928 Presidential Campaign giveaway. Original material, contents completely different
from Picture Life of a Great American.

**PICTURE LIFE OF A GREAT AMERICAN (see Pictorial History of the
Department of Commerce under Herbert Hoover) (O)**
Hoover-Curtis Campaign Committee of New York State: no date, 1928
paper cover, B&W)

nn- (8-3/4 x 7, 20 pgs) Text cover, 2 page text introduction,			
18 pgs of comics (scarcer first print)	40.00	120.00	240.00
nn- (9 x 6-3/4,24 pgs) Illustrated cover,5 page text introduction,			
18 pgs of comics (scarce)	40.00	120.00	240.00

NOTE: 1928 Presidential Campaign giveaway. Unknown which above version was published first.
Both contain the same original comics material by Satterfield.

PINK LAFFIN (I)
Whitman Publishing Co.: 1922 (9x12")(Strip-r)

| ...the Lighter Side of Life, ...He Tells 'Em, ...and His Family, ...Knockouts; | | | |
| Ray Gleason-a (All rare) each... | 26.00 | 104.00 | 185.00 |

POLLY (AND HER PALS) - THERE IS A LIMIT TO PA'S PATIENCE (N)
Newspaper Feature Service: 1916 (3x2-1/2", full color single sheet unfolds into
12 panel story

| nn - By Cliff Sterrett | 20.00 | 60.00 | 120.00 |

POPEYE PAINT BOOK (N)
McLaughlin Bros, Inc., Springfield, Mass.: 1932 (9-7/8x13", 28 pgs, color-c)

| 2052 - By E. C. Segar | 64.00 | 256.00 | 450.00 |

NOTE: contains a full color panel above and the exact same art in below panel n B&W which one
was to color in; strip-r panels

POPEYE CARTOON BOOK (N)
The Saalfield Co.: 1934 (8-1/2x13", 40 pgs, cardboard-c)

2095-(Rare)-1933 strip reprints in color by Segar. Each page contains a vertical
half of a Sunday strip, so the continuity reads row by row completely across
each double page spread. If each page is read by itself, the continuity makes
no sense. Each double page spread reprints one complete Sunday page

| from 1933 | 300.00 | 900.00 | 2400.00 |
| 12 Page Version | 100.00 | 300.00 | 800.00 |

POPEYE (See Thimble Theatre for earlier Popeye) (N)
David McKay Publications: 1935 (25¢; 52 pgs, B&W) (By Segar)

| 1-Daily strip reprints- "The Gold Mine Thieves" | 107.00 | 321.00 | 750.00 |
| 2-Daily strip-r (scarce) | 100.00 | 300.00 | 700.00 |

NOTE: Ties with Henry & Little Annie Rooney (David McKay) as the last of the 10x10" size books.

PORE LI'L MOSE (N)
New York Herald Publ. by Grand Union Tea
Cupples & Leon Co.: 1902 (10-1/2x15", 78 pgs., color)

| nn-By R. F. Outcault; Earliest known C&L comic book | | | |
| (Rare in high grade- very high demand) | 1429.00 | 5000.00 | - |

NOTE: Black Americana one page newspaper strips; falls inbetween Yellow Kid & Buster Brown

PRETTY PICTURES (M)
Farrar & Rinehart: 1931 (12 x 8-7/8", 104 pgs, color hardcover w/dust jacket,
B&W; reprints from New Yorker, Judge, Life, Collier's Weekly)

| nn-By Otto Soglow (contains "The Little King") | 33.00 | 134.00 | 235.00 |

PUCK - to be indexed in next year's Guide

QUAINT OLD NEW ENGLAND (M)
Triton Syndicate: 1936 (5-1/4x6-1/4", 100 pgs, soft-c squarebound, B&W)

| nn - By Jack Withycomb | 36.00 | 144.00 | 250.00 |

NOTE: Comics about weird doings in Old New England

RAMBILICUS BOOK, THE (I)

Sam And His Laugh by Swinnerton
1906 © Frederick A. Stokes

Seaman Si by Pierce Pearce
1916 © Pierce Publ. Co.

Smitty #1 By Walter Berndt
1928 © Cupples & Leon

	GD2.0	FN6.0	VF8.0
Jacobs & Co.: 1903 (10x7", 240 pgs, hardcover)			
nn-By Walt McDougall (not a true comic book)	34.00	120.00	-
RED CARTOONS (S)			
Daily Worker Publishing Company:1926 (12 x 9,68 pgs,cardboard cover,B&W)			
nn-By Various (scarce)	40.00	160.00	280.00

NOTE: Reprint of American Communist Party editorial cartoons, from The Daily Worker, The Workers Monthly, and the Liberator. Art by Fred Ellis, William Gropper, Clive Weed, Art Young.

REG'LAR FELLERS (See All-American Comics, Jimmie Dugan & The..., Popular Comics & Treasure Box of Famous Comics) (N)
Cupples & Leon Co./MS Publishing Co.: 1921-1929

	GD2.0	FN6.0	VF8.0
1(1921)-52 pgs. B&W dailies (Cupples & Leon, 10x10")	43.00	171.00	300.00
1925, 48 pgs. B&W dailies (MS Publ.)	39.00	157.00	275.00
Hardcover (1929, 96 pgs.)-B&W reprints	54.00	214.00	375.00

RIPLEY (See Believe It Or Not)

ROGER BEAN, R. G. (Regular Guy) (N)
The Indiana News Co, Distributers.: 1915 - No. 2, 1915 (5-3/8x17", 68 pgs., B&W,hardcovers); #3-#5 published by **Chas. B. Jackson:** 1916-1919
(No. 1 2 4 & 5 bound on side, No. 3 bound at top)

	GD2.0	FN6.0	VF8.0
1-By Chas B. Jackson (68pgs.)(Scarce)	60.00	210.00	360.00
2- 5-5/8x17-1/8", 66 pgs (says 1913 inside - an obvious printing error) (red or green binding)	60.00	210.00	360.00
3-Along the Firing Line... (1916 62 pgs, 6x17")	60.00	210.00	360.00
4-Into the Trenches and Out Again with... (68 pgs)	60.00	210.00	360.00
5 ...And The Reconstruction Period (5-3/8x15-1/2", 84 pgs) (Scarce) (has $1 printed on cover)	60.00	210.00	360.00
Baby Grand Editions 1-5 (10x10", cardboard-c)	60.00	210.00	360.00

RUBAIYKT OF THE EGG
The John C Winston Co, Philadelphia: 1905 (7x5/12", 64 pgs, purple-c, B&W)

	GD2.0	FN6.0	VF8.0
nn- By Clare Victor Dwiggins	20.00	60.00	120.00

NOTE: book is printed & cut into the shape of an egg

RULING CLAWSS, THE (N,S)
The Daily Worker: 1935 (192 pgs, 10-1/4 x 7-3/8", hard-c, B&W)

	GD2.0	FN6.0	VF8.0
nn- by Redfield	60.00	240.00	-

NOTE: reprints cartoons from the American Communist Party newspaper The Daily Worker.

SAM AND HIS LAUGH (N)
Frederick A. Stokes: 1906 (10x15", cardboard-c, Sunday strip-r in color)

	GD2.0	FN6.0	VF8.0
nn-By Jimmy Swinnerton (Very Rare)	200.00	700.00	1200.00

SCHOOL DAYS (N)
Harper & Bros.: 1919 (9x8", 104 pgs.)

	GD2.0	FN6.0	VF8.0
nn-By Clare Victor Dwiggins	42.00	144.00	250.00

SEAMAN SI - A Book of Cartoons About the Funniest "Gob" in the Navy (N)
Pierce Publishing Co.: 1916 (4 x 8 1/2, 200 pgs, hardcover, B&W)

	GD2.0	FN6.0	VF8.0
nn-By Perce Pearce (The American Sailor strip-r)	43.00	150.00	260.00
nn- 1918 reprint (4-1/8x8-1/4")(Reilly & Britton Co.)	26.00	90.00	156.00

SECRET AGENT X-9 (N)
David McKay Pbll.: 1934 (Book 1: 84 pgs; Book 2: 124 pgs.) (8x7-1/2")

	GD2.0	FN6.0	VF8.0
Book 1-Contains reprints of the first 13 weeks of the strip by Dashiell Hammett & Alex Raymond, complete except for 2 dailies	83.00	250.00	575.00
Book 2-Contains reprints immediately following contents of Book 1, for 20 weeks by Dashiell Hammett & Alex Raymond; complete except for two dailies.	83.00	250.00	575.00

NOTE: Raymond misdated the last 5 strips from 6/34, and while the dating sequence is confusing, the continuity is correct.

SILK HAT HARRY'S DIVORCE SUIT (N)
M. A. Donoghue & Co.: 1912 (5-3/4x15-1/2", B&W)

	GD2.0	FN6.0	VF8.0
nn-Newspaper-r by Tad (Thomas A. Dorgan)	33.00	117.00	200.00

SIS HOPKINS OWN BOOK AND MAGAZINE OF FUN
Leslie-Judge Co.: 1910 (36 pgs, color-c, B&W)

	GD2.0	FN6.0	VF8.0
119 - various	33.00	117.00	200.00

NOTE: Zim, Flagg, Young, Newell, Adams, etc

SKEEZIX (Also see Gasoline Alley & Little Skeezix Books) (I)
Reilly & Lee Co.: 1925 - 1928 (Strip-r, soft covers) (pictures & text)

	GD2.0	FN6.0	VF8.0
...and Uncle Walt (1924)-Origin	26.00	104.00	180.00
...and Pal (1925)	21.00	84.00	150.00
...at the Circus (1926)	21.00	84.00	150.00
...& Uncle Walt (1927)	21.00	84.00	150.00
...Out West (1928)	21.00	84.00	150.00
Hardback Editions...	34.00	136.00	235.00

SKEEZIX COLOR BOOK (N)
McLaughlin Bros. Inc, Springfield, Mass: 1929 (9-1/2x10-1/4", 28 pgs, one third in full color, rest in B&W)

	GD2.0	FN6.0	VF8.0
2023 By Frank King; strip-r to color	20.00	75.00	135.00

SKIPPY
No publisher listed: Circa 1920s (10x8", 16 pgs., color/B&W cartoons)

	GD2.0	FN6.0	VF8.0
nn-By Percy Crosby	81.00	322.00	565.00

SKIPPY (I)
Grossett & Dunlap: 1929 (7-3/8x6, 370 pgs, hardcover text with some art)

	GD2.0	FN6.0	VF8.0
nn-By Percy Crosby (issued with a dust jacket)	21.00	84.00	150.00

S'MATTER POP? (N)
Saalfield Publ. Co.: 1917 (10x14", 44 pgs., B&W, cardboard-c)

	GD2.0	FN6.0	VF8.0
nn-By Charlie Payne; in full color; pages printed on one side	48.00	169.00	290.00

SMITTY (See Treasure Box of Famous Comics) (N)
Cupples & Leon Co.: 1928 - 1933 (9x7", 96 pgs., B&W strip-r, hardcover)

	GD2.0	FN6.0	VF8.0
1928-(96 pgs. 7x8-3/4") By Walter Berndt	41.00	166.00	290.00
1929-At the Ball Game (Babe Ruth on cover)	57.00	229.00	400.00
1930-The Flying Office Boy, 1931-The Jockey, 1932-In the North Woods each	31.00	126.00	220.00
1933-At Military School	31.00	126.00	220.00

NOTE: Each hardbound was published with a dust jacket; worth 50% more with dust jacket. Th 1923 edition is very popular with baseball collectors. Strip debuted Nov 27, 1922.

SOCIAL HELL, THE (O)
Rich Hill: 1902

	GD2.0	FN6.0	VF8.0
nn-By Ryan Walker	20.00	70.00	120.00

NOTE: "The conditions of workers and the corruption of a political system beholden to corporate interests have been a major focus of human rights concerns since the 19th century. This early graphic novel depicts the social evils of unreformed capitalism. Ryan Walker was a syndicate cartoonist for many mainstream newspapers as well as for the communist Daily Worker." This description comes from <http://www.lib.uconn.edu/DoddCenter/ascexh3.html>, where you can find also a reproduction of the cover. I add that Ryan Walker was the editor of "The Saint Louis Republic" comic section since its inception in 1897; the supplement published "Alma and Oliver" George Macmanus's first series.

SPORT AND THE KID (See The Umbrella Man) (N)
Lowman & Hanford Co.: 1913 (6-1/4x6-5/8",114 pgs, hardcover, B&W&orange

	GD2.0	FN6.0	VF8.0
nn-By J.R. "Dok" Hager	20.00	70.00	120.00

STRANGE AS IT SEEMS (S)
Blue-Star Publishing Co.: 1932 (64 pgs., B&W, square binding)

	GD2.0	FN6.0	VF8.0
1-Newspaper-r	32.00	128.00	225.00

NOTE: Published with and without No. 1 and price on cover.

	GD2.0	FN6.0	VF8.0
Ex-Lax giveaway(1936, B&W, 24 pgs., 5x7")-McNaught Synd.	13.00	52.00	90.00

TAILSPIN TOMMY STORY & PICTURE BOOK (N)
McLoughlin Bros.: No. 266, 1931? (nd) (10x10-1/2", color strip-r)

	GD2.0	FN6.0	VF8.0
266-By Forrest	43.00	172.00	300.00

TAILSPIN TOMMY (Also see Famous Feature Stories & The Funnies)(N)
Cupples & Leon Co.: 1932 (100 pgs., hard-c)

	GD2.0	FN6.0	VF8.0
nn-(Scarce)-B&W strip reprints from 1930 by Hal Forrest & Glenn Claffin	200.00	600.00	-

Thimble Theater #1 by E.C. Segar
1931 © Sonnet Publishing Co.

Tillie the Toiler #7 by Russ Westover
1932 © Cupples & Leon

Tim McCoy, Police Car 17
1934 © Whitman Publ. Co.

	GD2.0	FN6.0	VF8.0

TALES OF DEMON DICK AND BUNKER BILL (O)
Whitman Publishing Co.: 1934 (5-1/4x10-1/2", 80 pgs, color hardcover, B&W)
'93 - By Spencer   33.00   100.00   225.00

TARZAN BOOK (The Illustrated...) (N)
Grosset & Dunlap: 1929 (9x7", 80 pgs.)
1(Rare)-Contains 1st B&W Tarzan newspaper comics from 1929. By Hal Foster
  Cloth reinforced spine & dust jacket (50¢); Foster-c
  With dust jacket...   86.00   344.00   600.00
  Without dust jacket...   43.00   172.00   300.00
2nd Printing(1934, 25¢, 76 pgs.)-4 Foster pgs. dropped; paper spine, circle in
  lower right cover with 25¢ price. The 25¢ is barely visible on some copies
     34.00   136.00   240.00
1967-House of Greystoke reprint-7x10", using the complete 300 illustrations/
  text from the 1929 edition minus the original indicia, foreword, etc. Initial
  version bound in gold paper & sold for $5.00. Officially titled **Burroughs
  Bibliophile #2**. A very few additional copies were bound in heavier blue
  paper. Gold binding...   2.25   6.75   18.00
    Blue binding...   2.50   7.50   24.00

TARZAN OF THE APES TO COLOR (N)
Saalfield Publishing Co.: No. 988, 1933 (15-1/4x10-3/4", 24 pgs)
Coloring book)
988-(Very Rare)-Contains 1929 daily reprints with some new art by Hal Foster.
  Two panels blown up large on each page with one at the top of opposing
  pages on every other double-page spread. Believed to be the only time these
  panels appeared in color. Most color panels are reproduced a second time in
  B&W to be colored   257.00   1028.00   1800.00

TARZAN OF THE APES The Big Little Cartoon Book (N)
Whitman Publishing Company: 1933 (4-1/2x3 5/8", 320 pgs, color-c, B&W)
744 - By Hal Foster (comics on every page)   36.00   144.00   250.00

TECK HASKINS AT OHIO STATE (S)
Lea-Mar Press: 1908 (7-1/4x5-3/8", 84 pgs, B&W hardcover)
nn-By W.A. Ireland; football cartoons-r from Columbus Ohio Evening Dispatch
    28.00   99.00   170.00
NOTE: Small blue & white patch of cover art pasted atop a color cloth quilt patter; pasted patch
can easily peel off some copies.

TECK 1909 (S)
Lea-Mar Press: 1909 (8-5/8 x 8-1/8", 124 pgs., B&W hardcover, 25¢)
nn-By W.A. Ireland; Ohio State University baseball cartoons-r
  from Columbus Evening Dispatch   28.00   99.00   170.00

TEXAS HISTORY MOVIES (N)
various editions, 1928 to 1986 (B&W)
Book I -1928 Southwest Press (7-1/4 x 5-3/8, 56 pgs, cardboard cover)
  for the Magnolia Petroleum Company   30.00   90.00   180.00
nn-1928 Southwest Press (12-3/8 x 9-1/4, 232 pgs, hardcover)
    50.00   150.00   300.00
nn-1935 Magnolia Petroleum Company (6 x 9, 132 pgs, paper cover)
    20.00   60.00   120.00
NOTE: Exists with either Wagon Train or Texas Flag & Lafitte/pirate covers.
nn-1943 Magnolia Petroleum Company (132 pgs, paper cover)
    15.00   45.00   90.00
nn-1963 Graphic Ideas Inc (11 x 8-1/2, softcover)   10.00   30.00   60.00
NOTE: Reprints daily newspaper strips from the Dallas News, on Texas history. 1935 editions
onward distributed within the Texas Public School System. Prior to that they appear to be giveaway comic books for the Magnolia Petroleum Company. There are many more editions than
the ones pointed out above.

THAT ROOKIE FROM THE 13TH SQUAD (N)
Harper & Brothers Publishers: Feb 1918 (8x9-1/4", 72 pgs, hardcover, B&W)
nn-By Lieut. L. (Percy) L. Crosby   58.00   204.00   350.00

THIMBLE THEATRE STARRING POPEYE (See also Popeye) (N)
Sonnet Publishing Co.: 1931 - No. 2, 1932 (25¢, B&W, 52 pgs.)(Rare)
1-Daily strip serial-r in both by Segar   157.00   628.00   1100.00

---

2   136.00   544.00   950.00
NOTE: The very first Popeye reprint book. Popeye first entered Thimble Theatre in 1929.

THREE FUN MAKERS, THE (N)
Stokes and Company: 1908 (10x15", 64 pgs., color) (1904-06 Sunday strip-r)
nn-Maud, Katzenjammer Kids, Happy Hooligan   314.00   1100.00
NOTE: This is the first comic book to compile more than one newspaper strip together.

TIGERS (Also see On and Off Mount Ararat) (N)
Hearst's New York American & Journal: 1902, 86pgs. 10x15-1/4"
nn-Funny animal strip-r by Jimmy Swinnerton   286.00   1000.00

TILLIE THE TOILER (N)
Cupples & Leon Co.: 1925 - No. 8, 1933 (52 pgs., B&W, daily strip-r)
nn (#1) By Russ Westover   54.00   216.00   375.00
2-8   39.00   156.00   275.00
NOTE: First strip appearance was January, 1921.

TIMID SOUL, THE (N)
Simon & Schuster: 1931 (12-1/4x9", 136 pgs, B&W hardcover, dust jacket?)
nn- By H. T. Webster (newspaper strip-r)   40.00   120.00   240.00

TIM McCOY, POLICE CAR 17 (O)
Whitman Publishing Co.: 1934 (14-3/4x11", 32 pgs, stiff color covers)
674-1933 movie illustrated; first movie adaptation in comic book
  original material?   46.00   186.00   325.00

TOAST BOOK (N)
John C. Winston Co: 1905 (7-1/4 x 6,104 pgs,skull-shaped book, feltcover, B&W)
nn-by Clare Dwiggins   50.00   175.00   300.00
NOTE: Cartoon illustrations accompanying toasts/poems, most involving alcohol.

TOM SAWYER & HUCK FINN (N)
Stoll & Edwards Co.: 1925 (10x10-3/4", 52 pgs, stiff covers)
nn-By Dwiggins; 1923, 1924-r color Sunday strips   39.00   156.00   275.00

TOONERVILLE TROLLEY AND OTHER CARTOONS (N) (See Cartoons by
Fontaine Fox)
Cupples & Leon Co.: 1921 (10 x10", 52 pgs., B&W, daily strip-r)
1-By Fontaine Fox   68.00   272.00   475.00

TREASURE BOX OF FAMOUS COMICS (N)
Cupples & Leon Co.: 1934 8-1/2x(6-7/8", 36 pgs, soft covers)
(Boxed set of 5 books)
Little Orphan Annie (1926)   21.00   84.00   150.00
Reg'lar Fellers (1928)   19.00   76.00   130.00
Smitty (1928)   19.00   76.00   130.00
Harold Teen (1931)   19.00   76.00   130.00
How Dick Tracy & Dick Tracy Jr. Caught The Racketeers (1933)
    26.00   104.00   185.00
  Softcover set of five books in box   160.00   640.00   1125.00
  Box only   57.00   228.00   400.00
NOTE: Dates shown are copyright dates; all books actually came out in 1934 or later. The soft-
covers are abbreviated versions of the hardcover editions listed under each character.

TRUTH (See Victorian section for earlier issues)
Truth Company, NY: 1886-1906? (13-11/16x10-5/16", 16 pgs, process color-c
& centerfolds, rest B&W)
1900-1906 issues   10.00   20.00   25.00

**TRUTH SAVE IT FROM ABUSE & OVERWORK BEING THE EPISODE OF
THE HIRED HAND & MRS. STIX PLASTER, CONCERTIST** (N)
Radio Truth Society of WBAP: no date, 1924 (6-3/8 x 4-7/8, 40 pgs, paper
cover, B&W)
nn - by V.T. Hamlin (Very Rare)   100.00   400.00   700.00
NOTE: Radio station WBAP giveaway reprints strips from the Ft. Worth Texas Star-Telegram set
at local radio station. 1st collected work by V.T. Hamlin, pre-Alley Oop.

TWENTY FIVE YEARS AGO (See At The Bottom Of The Ladder) (M,S)
Coward-McCann: 1931 (5-3/4x8-1/4, 328 pgs, hardcover, B&W)
nn - By Camillus Kessler   32.00   128.00   225.00
NOTE: Multi-image panel cartoons showing historical events for dates during the year

When a Feller Needs a Friend by Briggs
1914 © P.F. Volland & Co.

Willie and His Papa & the Rest of the Family by Opper
1901 © Grossett & Dunlap

The Yellow Kid #4 cover by Outcault
1897 © Howard Ainslee & Co.

	GD2.0	FN6.0	VF8.0

UMBRELLA MAN, THE (N) (See Sport And The Kid)
Lowman & Hanford Co.: 1911 (8-7/8x5-1/8",112 pgs, paperback, B&W&orange)
nn - By J.R. "Dok" Hager (Seattle Times-r)   20.00   70.00   120.00

UNCLE REMUS AND BRER RABBIT (N)
Frederick A. Stokes Co.: 1907 (64 pgs, hardbound, color)
nn- By Joel C Harris & J.M. Conde   50.00   175.00   300.00

UPSIDE DOWNS OF LITTLE LADY LOVEKINS AND OLD MAN MUFFAROO
New York Herald: 1905 (?) (N)
nn- By Gustav Verbeck   100.00   350.00   650.00

VAUDEVILLES AND OTHER THINGS (N)
Isaac H. Blandiard Co.: 1900 (13x10-1/2", 22 pgs., color) plus two reprints
nn-By Bunny (Scarce)   229.00   800.00   -
nn-2nd print "By the Creator of Foxy Grapda" on-c but only has copyright info of
  1900 (10-1/2x15 1/2, 28 pgs, color)   171.00   600.00   -
nn-3rd print. "By the creator of Foxy Grapda" on-c; has both 1900 and 1901
  copyright info (11x13")   171.00   600.00   -

VIGNETTES OF LIFE
The Reilly & Lee Co.: 1930 (9x12-1/4", 104 pgs, hardcover w/dust jacket, B&W)
nn-By Norman J. Lynd (intro by C.D. Gibson)   20.00   60.00   90.00

WALLY - HIS CARTOONS OF THE A.E.F. (N)
Stars & Stripes: 1917 (7x18; 96 pgs, B&W)
nn-By Wally Wallgeen   20.00   70.00   120.00
NOTE: World War One cartoons reprints from Stars & Stripes; sold to U.S. servicemen with profits to go to French War Orphans Fund.

WAR CARTOONS (S)
Dallas News: 1918 (11x9", 112 pgs, hardcover, B&W)
nn-By John Knott (WWOne cartoons)   20.00   70.00   120.00

WAR CARTOONS FROM THE CHICAGO DAILY NEWS (N,S)
Chicago Daily News: 1914 (10 cents, 7-3/4x10-3/4", 68 pgs, paper-c, B&W)
nn- by L.D. Bradley   20.00   70.00   120.00

WEBER & FIELD'S FUNNYISMS (S,M,O)
Arkell Comoany, NY: 1904 (10-7/8x8", 112 pgs, color-c, B&W)
1 - By various (later issues?)   20.00   70.00   120.00
NOTE: includes some sequential & many single panel strips by Outcault, George Luks, CA
David, Houston, L Smith, Hy Mayer, Verbeck, Woolf, Sydney Adams, Frank "Chip" Bellew,
Eugene "ZIM" Zimmerman, Phil May, FT Richards, Billy Marriner, Grosvenor and many others.

WHEN A FELLER NEEDS A FRIEND (S)
P. F. Volland & Co.: 1914 (11-11/16x8-7/8)
nn-By Clare Briggs   37.00   131.00   225.00
NOTE: Originally came in box with Briggs art (box is Rare - worth more with box. There are also
numerous more modern reprints)

WILD PILGRIMAGE (O)
Harrison Smith & Robert Haas: 1932 (9-7/8x7", 210 pgs, B&W hardcover
w/dust jacket) (original wordless graphic novel in woodcuts)
nn-By Lynd Ward

WILLIE AND HIS PAPA AND THE REST OF THE FAMILY (I)
Grossett & Dunlap: 1901 (9-1/2x8", 200 pgs, hardcover from N.Y. Evening
Journal by Permission of W. R. Hearst) (pictures & text)
nn-By Frederick Opper   50.00   200.00   340.00
NOTE: Political satire series of single panel cartoons, involving whiny child Willie (President
William McKinley), his rambunctious and uncontrollable cousin Teddy (Vice President Roosevelt),
and Willie's Papa (trusts/monopolies) and their Maid (Senator) Hanna.

WILLIE GREEN COMICS, THE (I)
Frank M. Acton Co./Harris Brown: 1915 (8x15, 36 pgs); 1921 (6x10-1/8", 52
pgs, color paper cover, B&W interior, 25¢)
Book No. 1 By Harris Brown   45.00   158.00   270.00
Book 2 (#2 sold via mail order directly from the artist)(rare) 45.00 158.00 270.00
NOTE: Book No. 1 possible reprint of Adv. of Willie Green.

WILLIE WESTINGHOUSE EDISON SMITH THE BOY INVENTOR (N)
William A. Stokes Co.: 1906 (10x16", 36 pgs. in color)

nn-By Frank Crane (Scarce)   214.00   750.00   -

WINNIE WINKLE (N)
Cupples & Leon Co.: 1930 - No. 4, 1933 (52 pgs., B&W daily strip-r)
1   43.00   172.00   300.00
2-4   29.00   116.00   200.00

WISDOM OF CHING CHOW, THE (see also The Gumps)
R. J. Jefferson Printing Co.: 1928 (4x3", 100 pgs, red & B&W cardboard cover)
(newspaper strip-r The Chicago Tribune)
nn-By Sidney Smith (scarce)   20.00   80.00   120.00

WORLD OF TROUBLE, A (S)
Minneapolis Journal: 1901 (10x8-3/4", 100 pgs, 40 pgs full color)
v3#1 - By Charles L. Bartholomew (editorial-r)   28.00   99.00   170.00

WORLD OVER, THE (I)
G. W. Dillingham Company, New York: 1897 (192 pgs, hardbound)
nn-By Joe Kerr; 80 illus by R.F. Outcault   200.00   700.00   -

WRIGLEY'S "SPEARMEN"
Wm. Wrigley Jr Company: ???? (4x6", 24 pgs, B&W?)
nn - unknown   ???   ???   ???
NOTE: promo comic book for Wrigley's Spearmint and Doublemint gums

YELLOW KID, THE (Magazine)(I) (becomes **The Yellow Book #10** on)
Howard Ainslee & Co., N.Y.: Mar. 20, 1897 - #9, July 17, 1897
(5¢, B&W w/color covers, 52p., stapled) (not a comic book)
1-R.F. Outcault Yellow kid on-c only #1-6. The same Yellow Kid color ad app. o
  back-c #1-6 (advertising the New York Sunday Journal)
    857.00   3000.00   -
2-6 (#2 4/3/97, #5 5/22/97, #6, 6/5/97)   743.00   2600.00   -
7-9 (Yellow Kid not on-c)   121.00   425.00   -
NOTE: Richard Outcault's Yellow Kid from the Hearst New York American represents the very
first successful newspaper comic strip in America. Listed here due to historical importance.

YELLOW KID IN MCFADDEN'S FLATS, THE (N)
G. W. Dillingham Company, New York: 1897 (50¢, 7-1/2x5-1/2", 196 pgs.,
B&W, squarebound)
nn-The first "comic" book featuring The Yellow Kid; E. W. Townsend narrative
w/R. F. Outcault Sunday comic page art-r & some original drawings
    5000.00   8500.00   -

A VERY SHORT LIST OF RECOMMENDED REFERENCE TOOLS:

THE COMICS By Coulton Waugh (Macmillian, 1947)
COMIC ART IN AMERICA By Stephen Becker (Simon & Schuster, 1959)
THE COMICS By Jerry Robinson (G. Putnam's Sons, 1974)
NEMO MAGAZINE edited by Richard Marschall (FBI, 1983-1991)
THE INTERNATIONAL BOOK OF COMICS By Denis Gifford (Crescent, 1984)
HISTORY OF THE COMIC BOOK:1899-1936 By Charles Wooley (Wooley,1986
AMERICA'S GREAT COMIC-STRIP ARTISTS By Richard Marschall (Abbeville, 1989, 97)
THE AMERICAN COMIC BOOK CATALOGUE: THE EVOLUTIONARY ERA,
1884-1939 By Denis Gifford (Mansell Publishing, London: 1990)
THE ART OF THE FUNNIES By RC Harvey (Univ of Mississippi Press, 1994)
INKS CARTOON & COMIC ART STUDIES ed. by Lucy Caswell (OSU, 1994-97
THE COMIC STRIP CENTURY By Bill Blackbeard Two volume set (KSP, 1995)
THE FUNNIES:100 Years of American Comic Strips By Ron Goulart(Adams,1995
THE YELLOW KID edited by Bill Blackbeard (KSP, 1995)
COMIC STRIPS & CONSUMER CULTURE By Ian Gordon (Smithsonian, 1998)
WEIRD BUT TRUE TOON FACTOIDS By Craig Yoe (Random House, 1999)

For a free, lively e-mail discussion group of Platinum Age comics collectors, fans
enthusiasts, dealers, and scholars you can join to look, listen, learn, and share b
going to PlatinumAgeComics@Yahoogroups.com as well as The Grand Comics
Database at www.comics.org. Also go www.bugpowder.com/andy/early and
www.geocities.com/~quesinberry/comics/comlist for more great resources.
Any additions or corrections to this section are always welcome.

The American Comic Book: 1933-PRESENT

CONCISE ORIGINS
OF THE
MODERN COMIC BOOK

by Robert L. Beerbohm & Richard D. Olson, PhD
©2002

The formats that comic publishing pioneer Cupples & Leon popularized in 1919, although similar in appearance to comics of the Golden Age, are quite different in appearance from today's comics. Even so, the books and those formats were consistently successful until 1929, when they had to compete against The Great Depression; the Depression eventually won. One major reason for a format change was that at a cost of 25¢ per book for the 10" x 10" cardboard style and 60¢ for the 7" x 8 1/2" dustjacketed hardcovers, the price became increasingly prohibitive for most consumers already stifled by the crushed economy. As a result, all Cupples & Leon style books published between 1929-1935 are much rarer than their earlier counterparts because most Americans had little money to spend after paying for necessities like food and shelter.

By the early 1930s, the era of the Prestige Format black & white reprint comic book was over. In 1932-33 a lot of format variations arose, collecting such newspaper strips as **Bobby Thatcher, Bringing Up Father, Buck Rogers, Dick Tracy, Happy Hooligan, Joe Palooka, The Little King, Little Orphan Annie, Mickey Mouse, Moon Mullins, Mutt & Jeff,**

THE FUNNIES #1, early 1929, Dell Publishing Company, NY This was the very first original material newsstand comic book!

Smitty, Tailspin Tommy, Tarzan, Thimble Theater starring Popeye, Tillie the Toiler, Winnie Winkle, and the **Highlights of History** series. With the 1933 newsstand appearance of Humor's Detective Dan, **Adventures of Detective Ace King, Bob Scully, Two Fisted Hick Detective**, and possibly **Happy Mulligan**, these little understood original material comic books were the direct inspiration for Jerry Siegel and Joe Shuster to transform their fanzine character The Superman from **Science Fiction #3** (January 1933) into a comic strip that would stand as a watershed mark in American pop culture. The stage was set for a new frontier.

Prior to Humor's very rare output, there was Embee's **Comic Monthly**'s dozen issues in 1922, and several dozen of Dell's **The Funnies** tabloid in 1929-30. All except **Comic Monthly** contained only original material and still failed. With another format change, however, including four colors, double page counts and a hefty price reduction (starting for free as promotional premiums due to the nationwide numbing effects of worldwide deflation), the birthing pangs of the modern American comic book occurred in late 1932. Created

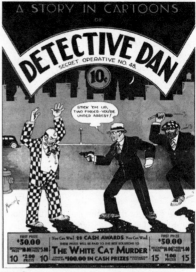

Bob Scully The Two Fisted Hick Detective & Detective Dan Secret Op 48, early 1933, Humor Publishing Co. Very Rare from the 2nd original newsstand comic book publisher & direct inspiration for Jerry Siegel & Joe Shuster in 1933 to convert The Superman into a comic book.

out of desperation, to keep the printing presses rolling, the modern American comic book was born when a 45-year-old sales manager for Eastern Color Printing Company of New York reinvented the format.

Harry I. Wildenberg's job was to come up with ideas that would sell color printing for Eastern, a company which also printed the comic sections for a score of newspapers, including the **Boston Globe**, the **Brooklyn Times**, the **Providence Journal**, and the **Newark Ledger**. Down-time meant less take-home pay, so Wildenberg was always racking his brains for something to fit the color presses. He was fascinated by the miles of funny sheets which rolled off Eastern's presses each week, and he constantly sought new ways to exploit their commercial possibilities. If the funny papers were this popular, he reasoned, they should prove a good advertising medium. He decided to suggest a comics tabloid

Gulf Funny Weekly #5, early 1933, Wildenberg's very first successful comics experiment.

to a client.

Gulf Oil Company liked the idea and hired a few artists to create an original comic called **Gulf Comic Weekly**. The comic was dated April 1933 and was 10 1/2" x 15". It was the first comic to be advertised nationally on the radio beginning April 30th. Its first artists were Stan Schendel doing **The Uncovered Wagon**, Victor doing **Curly and the Kids**, and Svess on a strip named **Smileage**. All were full page, full color comic strips. Wildenberg promptly had Eastern print this four page comic, making it probably the first tabloid newsprint comic published for American distribution outside of a newspaper in the 20th Century. Wildenberg and Gulf were astonished when the tabloids were grabbed up as fast as Gulf service stations could offer them. Distribution shot up to 3,000,000 copies a week after Gulf changed the name to **Gulf Funny Weekly** with its 5th issue. The series remained a tabloid until early 1939 & ran for 422 issues until May 23, 1941.

Recent research has also turned up "new" rediscovered comics material from other oil companies from this same time span of 1933-34. Perhaps spurred by the runaway success of **Gulf Funny Weekly**, these other oil companies found they had to compete with licensed comic strip material of their own in order to remain profitable. The authors of this essay are actively soliciting help in uncovering more information regarding the following: There are at least 14 issues (and possibly many more) of a four page tabloid-size full color comics giveaway titled **Standard Oil Comics**, dating from 1933. The issues seen so far contain

Standard Oil Comics Weekly #14, 1933. Newly discovered comics tabloid, same size as Gulf Funny Weekly. The oil companies recognized the power of comics early on!

Fred Opper's **Si & Mirandi**, an older couple who interact with perennial favorites, **Happy Hooligan** & **Maud the Mule**.

Other strips include **Pesty And His Pop** & **Smiling Slim** by Sid Hicks. Considering the concept of **Gulf Funny Weekly** has been well known for decades while **Standard Oil Comics** remains virtually unknown, our guess is **Gulf Comic Weekly** began first and ran many years longer than Rockefeller's version.

Beginning with the March-April 1934 issue of **Shell Globe** (V4 #2), characters from Bud Fisher (**Mutt & Jeff**) and Fontaine Fox (**Toonerville Folks**) were licensed to sell gas & oil for this company. 52,000 eight foot standees were made for Fisher's **Mutt and Jeff** and Fox's **Powerful Katrinka** and **The Skipper** for placement around 13,000 Shell gas stations. Augmenting them was an army of 250,000 miniature figures of the same characters. In addition, more than 1,000,000 play masks were given away to children along with more than 285,000 window stickers. If that wasn't

Not to be outdone, Shell Oil began a huge comics promotion in March 1934 to compete with Gulf and Standard Oil.

enough, hundreds of thousands of 3x5 foot posters featuring these characters were released in conjunction with twenty-four sheet outdoor billboards. Radio announcements of this promotion began running April 7th, 1934. It is presently unknown if Shell had a comics tabloid created to give away to customers.

The idea for creating an actual comic book, however, did not occur to Wildenberg until later in 1933, when he was idly folding a newspaper in halves then in quarters. As he looked at the twice-folded paper, it occurred to him that it was a convenient book size (actually it was late stage "Dime Novel" size, which companies like Street & Smith were pumping out). The format had its heyday from the 1880s through the 1910s, having been invented by the firm of Beadle and Adam in 1860 in more of a digest format. According to a 1942 article by Max Gaines, another contributing factor in the development of the format was an inspection of a promotional folder published by the Ledger Syndicate, in which four-color Sunday comic pages were printed in 7" x 9".

According to a 1949 interview with Wildenberg, he thought "why not a comic book? It would have 32 or 64 pages and make a fine item for concerns which distribute premiums." Wildenberg obtained publishing rights to certain Associated, Bell, Fisher, McNaught and Public Ledger Syndicate comics, had an artist make up a few dummies by hand, and then had his sales staff walk them around to his biggest advertisers. Wildenberg received a telegram from Proctor & Gamble for an order of a million copies for a 32-page color comic magazine called **Funnies on Parade**. The entire print run was given away in just a few weeks in the Spring of 1933.

Also working for Eastern Color at this same time were quite a few fu-ture legends of the comics business, such as Max Gaines, Lev Gleason and a fellow named Harold Moore (all sales staff directly underneath the supervision of Wildenberg), Sol Harrison as a color separator, and George Dougherty Sr. as a printer. All of them worked on the **Funnies on Parade** project. Morris Margolis was brought in from Charlton Publications in Derby, Connecticut to solve binding problems centered on getting the pages in proper numerical sequence on that last fold to "modern" comic book size. All were infected with the comics bug for most of the rest of their lives.

The success of **Funnies on Parade** quickly led to Eastern publishing additional giveaway books in the same format by late 1933, including the 32 page **Famous Funnies A Carnival of Comics**, the 100 page **A Century of Comics** and **Skippy's Own Book of Comics**; the latter became the first "new" format comic book about a single character. These thicker issues had press runs of up to 500,000 per title. The idea that anyone would pay for them seemed fantastic to Wildenberg, so Max Gaines stickered ten cents on several dozen of the latest premium, **Famous Funnies A Carnival of Comics**, as a test, and talked a couple newsstands into participating in this experiment. The copies sold out over the weekend and newsies asked for more.

Eastern sales staffers then approached Woolworth's. The late Oscar Fitz-Alan Douglas, sales brains of Woolworth, showed some interest, but after several months of deliberation decided the book would not give enough value for ten cents. Kress, Kresge,

Funnies On Parade, 1933, what we recognize today as the first "modern" comic book.

The issue Gaines stickered to 10¢ a copy one weekend.

Famous Funnies Series One is the rare one as only 40,000 copies were printed.

McCrory, and several other dime stores turned them down even more abruptly. Wildenberg next went to George Hecht, editor of **Parents Magazine**, and tried to persuade him to run a comic supplement or publish a "higher level" comic magazine. Hecht also frowned on the idea.

In Wildenberg's 1949 interview, he noted that "even the comic syndicates couldn't see it. 'Who's going to read old comics?' they asked." With the failures of EmBee's **Comic Monthly** (1922) and Dell's **The Funnies** (1929) still fresh in some minds, no one could see why children would pay ten cents for a comic magazine when they could get all they want for free in a Sunday newspaper. But Wildenberg had become convinced that children as well as grown-ups were not getting all the comics they wanted in the Sunday papers; otherwise, the **Gulf Comic Weekly** and the premium comics would not have met with such success. Wildenberg said, "I decided that if boys and girls were willing to work for premium coupons to obtain comic books, they might be willing to pay ten cents on the newsstands." This conviction was also strengthened by Max Gaines' ten cent sticker experiment.

George Janosik, the president of Eastern Color, then called on George Delacorte to form a 50-50 joint venture to publish and market a comic book "magazine" for retail sales, but American News turned them down cold. The magazine monopoly also remembered Delacorte's abortive **The Funnies** from just a few years before. After much discussion on how to proceed, Delacorte finally agreed to publish it and a partnership was formed. They printed 40,000 copies for distribution to a few chain

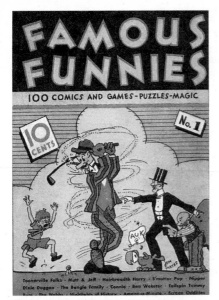

Famous Funnies #1, July 1934, was the first successful newsstand comic book, and it ran until 1955.

stores. Known today as **Famous Funnies Series One**, half of its pages came from reprints of the reprints in **Funnies on Parade** and **Famous Funnies A Carnival of Comics**. It is the scarcest issue.

With 68 full-color pages at only ten cents a piece, it sold out in thirty days with not a single returned copy. Delacorte refused to print a second edition. "Advertisers won't use it," he complained. "They say it's not dignified enough." The profit, however, was approximately $2,000. This particular edition is the rarest of all these early Eastern comic book experiments.

In early 1934, while riding the train, another Eastern Color employee named Harold A. Moore read an account from a prominent New York newspaper that indicated they owed much of their circulation success to their comics section. Mr. Moore went back to Harry Gold, President of American News, with the article in hand. He succeeded in acquiring a print order for 250,000 copies for a proposed monthly comics magazine. In May 1934, **Famous Funnies** #1 (with a July cover date) hit the newsstands with Steven O. Douglass as its only editor (even though Harold Moore was listed as such in #1) until it ceased publication some twenty years later. It was a 64-page ver-

New Fun #1, Feb 1935, and Major Malcolm Wheeler-Nicholson is busily establishing the industry standard of $5 per new page for finished art - cheaper than buying strip reprints!

sion of the 32-page giveaways, and more importantly, it still sold for a dime! The first issue lost $4,150.60. Ninety percent of the copies sold out and a second issue dated September debuted in July. From then on, the comic book was published monthly. **Famous Funnies** also began carrying original material, apparently as early as the second issue. With #3, Buck Rogers took center stage and stayed there for the next twenty years, with covers by Frank Frazetta towards the end of the run–some of his best comics work ever.

Delacorte got cold feet and sold back his interest to Eastern, even though the seventh issue cleared a profit of $2,664.25. Wildenberg emphasized that Eastern could make a manufacturer's profit by printing its own books as well as the publishing profits once it was distributed. Every issue showed greater sales than the preceding one, until within a year, close to a million 64-page books were being sold monthly at ten cents apiece; Eastern received the lion's share of the receipts, and soon found it was netting $30,000 per issue. The comic syndicates received $640 ($10 a page) for publishing rights. Original material could be obtained from budding professionals for just $5 a page. According to Will Eisner in R. C. Harvey's **The Art of the Comic Book**, the prices then paid for original material had a long range effect of keeping creator wages low for years.

Initially, Eastern's experiment was eyed with skepticism by the publishing world, but within a year or so after **Famous Funnies** was nonchalantly placed on sale alongside slicker magazines like **Atlantic Monthly** or **Harper's**, at least five other competitors entered this brand new format.

In late 1934, pulp writer turned publisher Major Wheeler-Nicholson introduced **New Fun #1** at almost tabloid-size containing all original material. Lloyd Jacquet wrote in 1957, "When Major Malcolm Wheeler-Nicholson set up his card table and chair in an eleventh-floor office of the Hathaway Building in New York that Fall of 1934, these most modest beginnings sparked off what can rightly be called the 'comic book era.' When he came back to the U.S. after his last stay abroad, he looked over the American newsstand, and thought that the European juvenile weekly papers, with their picture-story continu-ities, their colorful illustrations, and their low price would appeal to the American boys and girls in the same way. He knew that those European publications were made up of new material, specially drawn and produced for each little magazine. He also knew that the American presentation of such material would have to be different, and merely importing, or translating European produced features for republication here was not the answer. This

Tim McCoy Police Car 17, Whitman's first 1930s comic book (1934), & also the first movie adaptation comic book. This has been a sleeper far too long.

was about the time I joined with him in his project. It was still embryonic, but beginning to take form under Nicholson's direction. We were in the depression then, and it was not too difficult to secure writers and artists - but it was a task to instruct them as to exactly what

New Comics #1 12/35 was the Major's 2nd entry into comic books - re-emphasizing the concept of "New!"

was wanted. We finally rounded up a small but gift-ed group of creative people, and we produced our first issue of a monthly magazine composed of original fea-tures and material, and which was called, simply, "FUN."

Around this same time, long-time comics publisher Whitman brought out the first original material movie adaptation, **Tim McCoy Police Car 17**, in the tabloid **New Fun** format with stiff card covers. A few years before, they had intro-duced the new comics for-mats known as the **Big Little Book** and the **Big Big Book**. The BLB and BBB formats would go toe-to-toe with Eastern's cre-ation through out the 1930s, but Eastern would win out with their new comics maga-zine format.

The very last 10" x 10" comic books pioneered by Cupples & Leon were published by the David McKay Publishing Company around mid-1935. Around this same time the Major published his 2nd comic book in which the editorial men-tions amongst other exciting stories they were going to be showcasing the adventures of "hero supermen of the days to come"

By late 1935, Max Gaines (with his youthful assistant Sheldon Mayer) reached a business agreement with George Delacorte (who was re-entering the comic book business a third time) and **Charlie Gaines & Sheldon Mayer packaged Popular Comics #1, 2/36 for George Delecorte in late '35 after leaving Eastern Color.**

McClure Syndicate (a growing newspaper comic strip enterprise) to be come edi-tor of reprint newspaper comic strips in **Popular Comics**. Also by late 1935, Lev Gleason, another pio-neer who participated in **Funnies on Parade**,

King Comics #1, April 1936, marked King Features Syndicate's entry into the new 64 page color comic market with their heavyweights of Flash Gordon & Popeye. By this point Hearst has been publishing comic books for close to 40 years.

The Comics Magazine#2, June 1936 was Centaur's first comics title; very soon had a name change and soon made history.

had become the first editor of United Feature's own **Tip Top Comics**. In 1939 he would begin publishing his own titles, creating the crime comic book as a separate popular genre by 1942 with **Crime Does Not Pay** which had a long run until early 1955.

Industry giant King Features introduced **King Comics #1** (April 1936) thru publisher David McKay, with Ruth Plumly Thompson as editor. McKay had already been issuing various format comic books with King Feature characters for a few years, including Mickey Mouse, Henry, Popeye and Secret Agent X-9, wherein Dashiell Hammett received cover billing and Alex Raymond was listed inside simply as "illustrator." McKay readily adapted to this format. Soon most young comic book illustrators were copying Raymond's style. The following month, William Cook & John Mahon, former disgruntled employees of Major Wheeler Nicholson, brought out their first issue of **The Comics Magazine**#1 dated 5/36.

Lev Gleason left Eastern & Wildenberg about the same time as Gaines to edit Tip Top Comics #1 4/36 for United Features.

This was followed by Henle Publishing issuing **Wow What A Magazine**, which contained the earliest comic work of Will Eisner Bob Kane, Dick Briefer & others. By the end of 1936, Cook and Mahon pioneered the first single theme comic books: **Funny Picture Stories** (adven-

ture), **Detective Picture Stories** (crime), as well as **Western Picture Stories** (the Western). The company would eventually be known historically as Centaur Comics, and serve as the subject of endless debate among fan historians regarding their earliest origins as to who the owners were.

Almost forty years after the first newspaper strip comic book compilations were issued at the dawn of international popularity for American comic strips, the race was on to get titles out of the starting block. In late 1937 Major Wheeler-Nicholson began stumbling when he couldn't pay his printing bill to Harry Donenfeld. In a recent intervew, Harry's son, Irwin, who as a 12 year old read the original art to the first issue of **Action Comics #1** and **Detective Comics** #27 said "in 1932 my father & Paul Sampliner started Independent News with Jack Liebowitz as the accountant. The company was begun with Paul Sampliner's mother's money. If it hadn't been for her investments into building the distribution as well as purchasing color printing presses, there might never have been a DC Comics."

Soon after the Major lost control of his company, **Action Comics #1** was published with a cover date of June 1938, and the Golden Age of superhero comics had begun. Early in 1938 at McClure Syndicate, Max Gaines and Shelly Mayer

Wow What a Magazine ran for 4 issues beginning June 1936 with Briefer, Eisner, Kane

showed editor Vin Sullivan a many times rejected sample strip. Sullivan then talked Harry Donenfeld, Paul Sampliner and Jack Liebowitz into publishing Jerry Siegel and Joe Shuster's creation of "The Last Son of Krypton." This was followed in 1939 by a lucrative partnership for Gaines beginning with Harry Donenfeld as the All-American Comics Group.

While there's a great deal of controversy surrounding such labeling, the Golden Age is viewed these days as beginning with **Action Comics** #1 and continuing through the end of World War II. There was a time not that long ago that the newspaper reprint comic book was collected with more fervor than the heroic comics of the '40s. **Prince Valiant Feature Book** #26, **Flash Gordon Four Color** #10 and **Tarzan Single Series** #20 were some of the highest holy grails of collecting.

The Atom Age began in early 1946, revamping the industry once again as circulations soon hit their all-time highs with over a billion issues sold a year. By the early 1950s one in three periodicals sold in the USA was a comic book. This continued until the advent of the self-censoring, industry-stifling Comics Code, created in response to a public outcry spearheaded by Dr. Frederic Wertham's tirade against the American comics industry, published as a book titled **Seduction of the Innocent.**

It took a year or two to recover from that moralistic assault, with many historians speculating the Silver Age of Superheroes began with the publication of **Showcase** #4 in 1956, continuing through those turbulent times until Jack Kirby left Marvel for DC in 1969. Others point to the 1952 successful releases of Kurtzman's **MAD** #1 and Bark's **Uncle Scrooge** Four Color #386 (#1) as true Silver,

Action Comics #1, June, 1938, revolutionized the fledgling comics industry when Superman by Siegel & Shuster was released.

since those titles soon broke the "million sold per issue" mark when the rest of the comic book industry was reeling from the effects of the public uproar fueled by Wertham.

The term Bronze Age has been stated to begin when the Code approved newsstand comic book industry raised its standard cover price from 12 to 15 cents. As circulations plummeted after the Batman TV craze wore off by 1968 and the ensuing superhero glut withered on the stands, out in the Bay Area cartoonist Robert Crumb's creator-owned **Zap Comics** #1 appeared, printed by Charles Plymell and Don Donahue. Soon thereafter, Jay Lynch and Skip Williamson brought out Bijou Funnies, Gilbert Shelton self-published Feds N Heads and Crumb let S. Clay Wilson, Victor Moscoso and Rick Griffin into Zap. As originally published by the Print Mint beginning with #2 in 1968, **Zap Comics** almost single-handedly spawned an industry with tremendous growth in alternative comix running through the 1970s. During this decade the San Francisco Bay Area was an intense hotbed of comix being issued without a comics code "seal of approval" from companies such as Rip Off Press, Last Gasp, San

In the early 1950s, Carl Barks increased the circulation of WDCS to over 4 million per issue, and in 1952 his creation, Uncle Scrooge, got his own comic book, selling over a million an issue while the superhero slumbered.

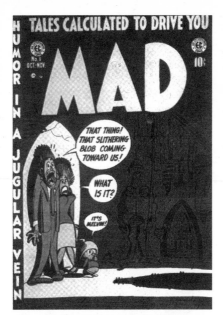

Harvey Kurtzman created Mad Comics #1, 1952, and soon sent the comics industry in an entirely "New" Direction and directly inspired countless comics creators.

Zap Comics #1, Feb. 1968, was the "direct" inspiration for the earliest successful origins of the Direct Market and has sold over a million copies, most issues have been continuously in print for over 30 years.

Francisco Comic Book Company, Company & Sons, Weirdom Publications, Star*Reach, and Comics & Comix and Kitchen Sink prospered for many years in Wisconsin and many small press comix publishers scattered across the USA and Canada which created the Direct Sales Market. Phil Seuling introduced DC and Marvel to this San Francisco Bay Area based comix business as a "new" way of selling comics in 1973, acknowledged in his interview in Will Eisner's Quarterly #3, Summer, 1984. After DC and Marvel joined the DM in 1979 in a serious way, the last 20 years have generally been called "The Modern Age", although there are hints of a new age emerging since the mid-1990s. In each of the above Ages, however, the secret for consumers and collectors has remained the same: buy what you enjoy.

We did, and we are still collectors today!

Portions are excerpted from **Comics Archeology 101**, *a detailed book in progress on the history of the comics business, which are ©2002 Robert L. Beerbohm. His E-mail is: beerbohm@teknetwork.com*

Last Gasp's first comic book was Slow Death #1 (1970), below left, with a great cover by Greg Irons. Bijou Funnies #8 (1973) is in color & sports a cover by Kurtzman!

Accelerate #1 © Kadrey & Panders Bros.

Ace Comics #55 © DMP

SEE BATTLE OF THE ATLANTIC

ACE COMICS

10¢

Acme Novelty Library #10 © Chris Ware

The correct title listing for each comic book can be determined by consulting the indicia (publication data) on the beginning interior pages of the comic. The official title is determined by those words of the title in capital letters only, and not by what is on the cover.

Titles are listed in this book as if they were one word, ignoring spaces, hyphens, and apostrophes, to make finding titles easier. Comic books listed should be assumed to be in color unless noted "B&W".

Comic publishers are invited to send us sample copies for possible inclusion in future guides.

PRICING IN THIS GUIDE: Prices for **GD** (good), **FN** (fine), **VF** (very fine), and **NM** (near mint) are listed in whole U.S. dollars except for prices below $7 which show dollars and cents. **The minimum price listed is $2.25,** the cover price for current new comics. Most books listed at this price can be found in 25¢ boxes at conventions and dealers stores.

Near Mint is the highest value listed in this price guide. True mint books from the 1970s through the present do exist, so the Near Mint value listed should be interpreted as a Mint value for those books.

A-1 (See A-One)

AARON STRIPS
Image Comics: Apr, 1997 - No. 4, Oct, 1997;
Amazing Aaron Prod.: No. 5, Jan, 1999 - Present ($2.95, B&W)

1-6-Reprints Adventures of Aaron newspaper strips				3.00

ABBIE AN' SLATS (...With Becky No. 1-4) (See Comics On Parade, Fight for Love, Giant Comics Edition 2, Giant Comics Editions #1, Sparkler Comics, Tip Topper, Treasury of Comics, & United Comics)
United Features Syndicate: 1940; March, 1948 - No. 4, Aug, 1948 (Reprints)

Single Series 25 ('40)	39	117	208	360
Single Series 28	33	99	174	300
1 (1948)	18	54	94	160
2-4: 3-r/Sparkler #68-72	10	30	55	80

ABBOTT AND COSTELLO (...Comics)(See Giant Comics Editions #1 & Treasury of Comics)
St. John Publishing Co.: Feb, 1948 - No. 40, Sept, 1956 (Mort Drucker-a in most issues)

1	55	165	341	600
2	31	93	165	285
3-9 (#8, 8/49; #9, 2/50)	19	57	99	170
10-Son of Sinbad story by Kubert (new)	23	69	121	210
11,13-20 (#11, 10/50; #13, 8/51; #15, 12/52)	14	42	72	125
12-Movie issue	15	45	77	130
21-30: 28-r/#8. 30-Painted-c	10	30	55	85
31-40: 33,38-Reprints	8	24	45	65
3-D #1 (11/53, 25¢)-Infinity-c	36	108	191	330

ABBOTT AND COSTELLO (TV)
Charlton Comics: Feb, 1968 - No. 22, Aug, 1971 (Hanna-Barbera)

1	8	24	56	90
2	4	12	27	42
3-10	3	10	23	35
11-22	3	9	18	27

ABC (See America's Best TV Comics)

ABE SAPIEN: DRUMS OF THE DEAD
Dark Horse Comics: Mar, 1998 ($2.95, one-shot)

1-McDonald-s/Thompson-a. Hellboy back-up; Mignola-s/a/c				3.00

A. BIZARRO
DC Comics: Jul, 1999 - No. 4, Oct, 1999 (2.50, limited series)

1-4-Gerber-s/Bright-a				2.50

ABOMINATIONS (See Hulk)
Marvel Comics: Dec, 1996 - No. 3, Feb, 1997 (1.50, limited series)

1-3-Future Hulk storyline				2.25

ABRAHAM LINCOLN LIFE STORY (See Dell Giants)

ABRAHAM STONE

Marvel Comics (Epic): July, 1995 - No. 2, Aug, 1995 ($6.95, limited series)

1,2-Joe Kubert-s/a				7.00

ABSENT-MINDED PROFESSOR, THE
Dell Publishing Co.: Apr, 1961 (Disney)

Four Color #1199-Movie, photo-c	8	24	56	100

ABSOLUTE VERTIGO
DC Comics (Vertigo): Winter, 1995 (99¢, mature)

nn-1st app. Preacher. Previews upcoming titles including Jonah Hex: Riders of the Worm, The Invisibles (King Mob), The Eaters, Ghostdancing & Preacher	1	3	6	8

ABYSS, THE (Movie)
Dark Horse Comics: June, 1989 - No. 2, July, 1989 ($2.25, limited series)

1,2-Adaptation of film; Kaluta & Moebius-a				3.00

ACCELERATE
DC Comics (Vertigo): Aug, 2000 - No. 4, Nov, 2000 ($2.95, limited series)

1-4-Pander Bros.-a/Kadrey-s				3.00

ACCLAIM ADVENTURE ZONE
Acclaim Books: 1997 ($4.50, digest size)

1-Short stories of Turok, Troublemakers, Ninjak and others				4.50

ACE COMICS
David McKay Publications: Apr, 1937 - No. 151, Oct-Nov, 1949 (All contain some newspaper strip reprints)

1-Jungle Jim by Alex Raymond, Blondie, Ripley's Believe It Or Not, Krazy Kat begin (1st app. of each)	317	951	1979	3800
2	95	285	597	1050
3-5	64	192	398	700
6-10	47	141	286	500
11-The Phantom begins (1st app., 2/38) (in brown costume)	77	231	483	850
12-20	40	120	220	380
21-25,27-30	36	108	191	330
26-Origin & 1st app. Prince Valiant (5/39); begins series?	100	300	625	1100
31-40: 37-Krazy Kat ends	26	78	136	235
41-60	19	57	99	170
61-64,66-76-(7/43; last 68 pgs.)	17	51	88	150
65-(8/42)-Flag-c	19	57	99	165
77-84 (3/44; all 60 pgs.)	14	42	72	120
85-99 (52 pgs.)	12	36	61	100
100 (7/45; last 52 pgs.)	14	42	72	120
101-134: 128-(11/47)-Brick Bradford begins. 134-Last Prince Valiant (all 36 pgs.)	10	30	55	80
135-151: 135-(6/48)-Lone Ranger begins	9	27	49	70

ACE KELLY (See Tops Comics & Tops In Humor)

ACE KING (See Adventures of Detective...)

ACES
Acme Press (Eclipse): Apr, 1988 - No. 5, Dec, 1988 ($2.95, B&W, magazine)

1-5				3.00

ACES HIGH
E.C. Comics: Mar-Apr, 1955 - No. 5, Nov-Dec, 1955

1-Not approved by code	19	57	134	240
2	11	33	77	135
3-5	10	30	70	125

NOTE: *All have stories by Davis, Evans, Krigstein, and Wood. Evans c-1-5.*

ACES HIGH
Gemstone Publishing: Apr, 1999 - No. 5, Aug, 1999 ($2.50)

1-5-Reprints E.C. issues				2.50
Annual 1 ($13.50) r/#1-5				13.50

ACME NOVELTY LIBRARY, THE
Fantagraphics Books: Winter 1993-94 - Present (quarterly, various sizes)

1-Introduces Jimmy Corrigan; Chris Ware-s/a in all				7.00
1-2nd and later printings				4.00
2,3: 2-Quimby				5.00

Action Comics #17 © DC

Action Comics #50 © DC

Action Comics #262 © DC

AC

	GD2.0	FN6.0	VF8.0	NM9.4

	GD2.0	FN6.0	VF8.0	NM9.4

4-Sparky's Best Comics & Stories				6.00
5-12: Jimmy Corrigan in all				5.00
13,15-($10.95-c)				11.00
14-($12.95-c) Concludes Jimmy Corrigan saga				13.00

Jimmy Corrigan, The Smartest Kid on Earth (2000, Pantheon Books, Hardcover, $27.50, 380 pgs.) Collects Jimmy Corrigan stories; folded dust jacket 27.50
NOTE: Multiple printings exist for most issues.

ACTION ADVENTURE (War) (Formerly Real Adventure)
Gillmor Magazines: V1#2, June, 1955 - No. 4, Oct, 1955

V1#2-4	5	15	24	32

ACTION COMICS (...Weekly #601-642) (Also see The Comics Magazine #1, More Fun #14-17 & Special Edition) (Also see Promotional Comics section)
National Periodical Publ./Detective Comics/DC Comics: 6/38 - No. 583, 9/86; No. 584, 1/87 - Present

	GD2.0	FN6.0	VF8.0	NM9.4
1-Origin & 1st app. Superman by Siegel & Shuster, Marco Polo, Tex Thompson, Pep Morgan, Chuck Dawson & Scoop Scanlon; 1st app. Zatara & Lois Lane; Superman story missing 4 pgs. which were included when reprinted in Superman #1; Clark Kent works for Daily Star; story continued in #2	38,000	105,000	185,000	350,000
1-Reprint, Oversize 13-1/2x10". WARNING: This comic is an exact reprint of the original except for its size. DC published it in 1974 with a second cover titling it as a Famous First Edition. There have been many reported cases of the outer cover being removed and the interior sold as the original edition. The reprint with the new outer cover removed is practically worthless.				
See Famous First Edition for value.				
2-O'Mealia non-Superman covers thru #6	3217	9650	21,700	37,000
3 (Scarce)-Superman apps. in costume in only one panel	2000	6000	13,500	23,000
4-6: 6-1st Jimmy Olsen (called office boy)	1217	3650	8200	14,000
7-2nd Superman cover	2175	6525	14,700	25,000
8,9	825	2475	5570	9500
10-3rd Superman cover by Siegel & Shuster	1520	4560	10,250	17,500
11,14: 14-Clip Carson begins, ends #41; Zatara-c	417	1250	2604	5000
12-Has 1 pg. Batman ad for Det. #27 (5/39); Zatara sci-fi cover	442	1326	2762	5300
13-Shuster Superman-c; last Scoop Scanlon	692	2076	4500	9000
15-Guardineer Superman-c; Detective Comics ad	554	1662	3600	7200
16	300	900	1875	3500
17-Superman cover; last Marco Polo	430	1290	2795	5600
18-Origin 3 Aces; 1st X-Ray Vision?	300	900	1875	3500
19-Superman story begins; has full pg. ad for New York World's Fair 1939	442	1326	2762	5300
20-The 'S' left off Superman's chest; Clark Kent works at 'Daily Star'	417	1250	2604	5000
21-Has 2 ads for More Fun #52 (1st Spectre)	282	846	1763	3100
22,24,25: 24-Kent at Daily Planet. 25-Last app. Gargantua T. Potts, Tex Thompson's sidekick	273	819	1705	3000
23-1st app. Luthor (w/red hair) & Black Pirate; Black Pirate by Moldoff; 1st mention of The Daily Planet (4/40)-Has 1 panel ad for Spectre in More Fun #41	631	1893	4100	8200
26-28,30	227	681	1420	2500
29-1st Lois Lane-c (10/40)	273	819	1705	3000
31,32: 32-Intro/1st app. Krypto Ray Gun in Superman story by Burnley	145	435	909	1600
33-Origin Mr. America; Superman by Burnley has half page ad for All Star Comics #3	168	505	1050	1850
34,35,38,39	136	408	852	1500
36,37: 36-Classic robot-c. 37-Origin Congo Bill	145	435	909	1600
40-(9/41)-Intro/1st app. Star Spangled Kid & Stripesy; Jerry Siegel photo	150	450	938	1650
41	118	354	738	1300
42-1st app./origin Vigilante; Bob Daley becomes Fat Man; origin Mr. America's magic flying carpet; The Queen Bee & Luthor app; Black Pirate ends; not in #41	168	505	1050	1850
43-46,48-50: 44-Fat Man's i.d. revealed to Mr. America. 45-1st app. Stuff (Vigilante's oriental sidekick)	118	354	738	1300
47-1st Luthor cover in comics (4/42)	182	546	1136	2000
51-1st app. The Prankster	127	381	795	1400
52-Fat Man & Mr. America become the Ameri-commandos; origin Vigilante retold; classic Superman and back-ups-c	136	408	852	1500

	GD2.0	FN6.0	VF8.0	NM9.4
53-57,59,60: 56-Last Fat Man. 57-2nd Lois Lane-c in Action (3rd anywhere, 2/43. 59-Kubert Vigilante begins?, ends #70. 60-First app. Lois Lane a Super-woman	95	285	597	1050
58-"Slap a Jap-c"	109	327	682	1200
61-Historic Atomic Radiation-c (6/43)	100	300	625	1100
62,63-Japan war-c: 63-Last 3 Aces	95	285	597	1050
64-Intro Toyman	100	300	625	1100
65-70	80	240	500	875
71-79: 74-Last Mr. America	73	219	455	800
80-2nd app. & 1st Mr. Mxyztplk-c (1/45)	100	300	625	1100
81-88,90: 83-Intro Hocus & Pocus	70	210	438	775
89-Classic rainbow cover	75	225	469	825
91-99: 93-X-Mas-c. 99-1st small logo (8/46)	68	204	426	750
100	68	204	426	750
101-Nuclear explosion-c (10/46)	127	381	795	1400
102-107,109-120: 102-Mxyztplk-c. 105,117-X-Mas-c	61	183	381	675
108-Classic molten metal-c	68	204	426	750
121,122,124-126,128-140: 135,136,138-Zatara by Kubert	55	165	341	600
123-(8/48) 1st time Superman flies rather than leaps	55	165	341	600
127-Vigilante by Kubert; Tommy Tomorrow begins (12/48, see Real Fact #6)	61	183	381	675
141-157,159-161: 151-Luthor/Mr. Mxyztplk/Prankster team-up. 156-Lois Lane as Super Woman. 160- Last 52 pgs.	53	159	318	550
158-Origin Superman retold	118	354	738	1300
162-180: 168,176-Used in POP, pg. 90. 173-Robot-c	45	135	281	475
181-201: 191-Intro. Janu in Congo Bill. 198-Last Vigilante. 201-Last pre-code issue	43	129	257	450
202-220,232: 212-(1/56)-Includes 1956 Superman calendar that is part of story. 232-1st Curt Swan-c in Action	40	120	232	400
221-231,233-240: 221-1st S.A. issue. 224-1st Golden Gorilla story. 228-(5/57)-Kongorilla in DC Silver Age story (Congorilla try-out) 36	108	191	330	
241,243-251: 241-Batman x-over. 248-Origin/1st app. Congorilla; Congo Bill renamed Congorilla. 251-Last Tommy Tomorrow	29	87	156	270
242-Origin & 1st app. Brainiac (7/58); 1st mention of Shrunken City of Kandor	131	393	1114	2100
252-Origin & 1st app. Supergirl (5/59); intro new Metallo	131	393	1114	2100
253-2nd app. Supergirl	47	142	286	500
254-1st meeting of Bizarro & Superman-c/story	38	114	203	350
255-1st Bizarro Lois Lane-c/story & both Bizarros leave Earth to make Bizarro World	30	90	159	275
256-260: 259-Red Kryptonite used	20	60	105	175
261-1st X-Kryptonite which gave Streaky his powers; last Congorilla in Action; origin & 1st app. Streaky The Super Cat	21	63	110	185
262,264,266,268-270	17	51	88	150
263-Origin Bizarro World	22	66	116	200
267(8/60)-3rd Legion app; 1st app. Chameleon Boy, Colossal Boy, & Invisible Kid; 1st app. of Supergirl as Superwoman.	45	135	270	475
271-275,277-282: 274-Lois Lane as Superwoman; 282-Last 10¢ issue	14	42	72	120
276(5/61)-6th Legion app; 1st app. Brainiac 5, Phantom Girl, Triplicate Girl, Bouncing Boy, Sun Boy, & Shrinking Violet; Supergirl joins Legion	24	72	133	230
283(12/61)-Legion of Super-Villains app. 1st 12¢	11	33	77	130
284(1/62)-Mon-el app.	11	33	77	130
285(2/62)-12th Legion app; Brainiac 5 cameo; Supergirl's existence revealed to world; JFK & Jackie cameos	12	36	88	150
286-292,294-299: 286(3/62)-Legion of Super Villains app. 287(4/62)-15th Legion app.(cameo). 288-Mon-el app.; r-origin Supergirl. 289(6/62)-16th Legion app. (Adult); Lightning Man & Saturn Woman's marriage 1st revealed. 290(7/62)-17th Legion app. (cameo); Phantom Girl app. 1st Supergirl emergency squad				
291,292,294-299: 291-1st meeting Supergirl & Mr. Mxyzptlk. 292-2nd app. Superhorse (see Adv. #293). 297-Mon-el app. 298-Legion cameo				
293-Origin Comet (Superhorse)	8	24	58	95
300-(5/63)	11	33	77	130
301-308,310-313,315-320: 304-Origin/1st app. Black Flame (9/63). 306-Brainiac 5, Mon-el app. 307-Saturn Girl app. 313-Batman app. 317-Death of Nor-Kan of Kandor. 319-Shrinking Violet app.	4	12	30	50

Action Comics #485 © DC

Action Comics #770 © DC

Action Girl #18 © SLG

	GD2.0	FN6.0	VF8.0	NM9.4

309-(2/64)-Legion app.;Batman & Robin-c & cameo; JFK app. (he died 11/22/63;
on stands same time as death) — 5 15 34 55
314-Retells origin Supergirl; J.L.A. x-over — 4 12 30 50
321-333,335-339: 336-Origin Akvar (Flamebird) — 4 12 26 40
334-Giant G-20; origin Supergirl, Streaky, Superhorse & Legion (all-r)
— 8 24 56 90
340-Origin, 1st app. of the Parasite — 4 12 29 45
341-346,348-359: 341-Batman app. in Supergirl back-up story. 342-UFO story.
344-Batman x-over. 345-Allen Funt/Candid Camera story. 350-Batman, Green
Arrow & Green Lantern app. in Supergirl back-up story. 358-Superboy meets
Supergirl — 3 9 20 33
347,360-Giant Supergirl G-33,G-45; 347-Origin Comet-r plus Bizarro story.
360-Legion-r; r/origin Supergirl — 5 15 38 60
361-364,367-372,374-378: 361-2nd app. Parasite. 363-366-Leper/Death story.
370-New facts about Superman's origin. 376-Last Supergirl in Action.
377-Legion begins (thru #392). 378-Last 12¢ issue
— 3 9 17 25
365,366: 365-JLA & Legion app. 366-JLA app. — 3 9 17 25
373-Giant Supergirl G-57; Legion-r — 5 15 34 55
379-399,401: 388-Sgt. Rock app. 392-Batman-c/app.; last Legion in Action;
Saturn Girl gets new costume. 393-401-All Superman story
— 2 6 13 20
400 — 3 9 19 28
402-Last 15¢ issue; Superman vs. Supergirl duel — 3 9 17 25
403-413: All 52 pg. issues. 411-Origin Eclipso-(r). 413-Metamorpho begins,
ends #418 — 3 9 19 28
414-424: 419-Intro. Human Target. 421-Intro Capt. Strong; Green Arrow
begins. 422,423-Origin Human Target — 2 6 9 12
425-Neal Adams-a(p); The Atom begins — 2 6 13 20
426-431,433-436,438,439 — 1 4 7 10
432-1st S.A. Toyman app. (2/74). — 2 6 13 20
437,443-(100 pg. Giants) — 3 10 23 35
440-1st Grell-a on Green Arrow — 2 6 10 14
441,442,444-448: 441-Grell-a on Green Arrow continues
— 1 3 6 8
449-(68 pgs.) — 2 6 10 14
450-483,485-499: 454-Last Atom. 456-Grell Jaws-c. 458-Last Green Arrow.
466-Batman, Flash app. 485-Adams-c. 487,488-(44 pgs.). 487-Origin & 1st
app. Microwave Man; origin Atom retold — 6.00
482,485-492,496,498,504,505,507,508-Whitman variants (low print run; all have
no # on cover) — 6.00
484-Earth II Superman & Lois Lane wed; 40th anniversary issue(6/78)
— 1 3 6 8
484-Variant includes 3-D Superman punchout doll in cello. pack; 4 different
inserts; Canadian promo?) — 2 6 9 12
500-($1.00, 68 pgs.)-Infinity-c; Superman life story; shows Legion statues in
museum — 3.00
501-543,545-551,554-582: 511-514-Airwave II solo stories. 513-The Atom
begins. 517-Aquaman begins; ends #541. 521-1st app. The Vixen. 532,536-
New Teen Titans cameo. 535,536-Omega Men app. 546-J.L.A., New Teen
Titans app. 551-Starfire becomes Red-Star — 3.00
504,505,507,508-Whitman variants (no cover price) — 3.00
544-(6/83, Mando paper, 68 pgs.)-45th Anniversary issue; origins new Luthor &
Brainiac; Omega Men app.; Shuster-a (pin-up); article by Siegel — 6.00
552,553-Animal Man-c & app. (2/84 & 3/84) — 4.50
583-Alan Moore scripts; last Earth 1 Superman story (cont'd from Superman
#423) — 1 2 5 7
584-Byrne-a begins; New Teen Titans app. — 5.00
585-599: 586-Legends x-over. 596-Millennium x-over; Spectre app. 598-1st app.
Checkmate — 3.00
600-($2.50, 84 pgs., 5/88) — 6.00
601-642-Weekly issues ($1.50, 52 pgs.): 601-Re-intro The Secret Six. 611-614-:
Catwoman stories (new costume in #611). 613-618-Nightwing stories — 3.00
643-Superman & monthly issues begin again; Perez-c/a/scripts begin; swipes
cover to Superman #1 — 4.00
644-649,651-661,663-673,675-683: 645-1st app. Maxima. 654-Part 3 of
Batman storyline. 655-Free extra 8 pgs. 660-Death of Lex Luthor. 661-Begin
$1.00-c. 675-($1.75, 52 pgs.). 675-Deathstroke cameo. 679-Last $1.00 issue.
683-Doomsday cameo — 2.50
650-($1.50, 52 pgs.)-Lobo cameo (last panel) — 3.00

	GD2.0	FN6.0	VF8.0	NM9.

662-Clark Kent reveals i.d. to Lois Lane; story cont'd in Superman #53 — 4.00
674-Supergirl logo & c/story (reintro) — 5.00
683,685-2nd & 3rd printings — 2.25
684-Doomsday battle issue — 3.00
685,686-Funeral for a Friend issues; Supergirl app. — 2.50
687-($1.95)-Collector's Ed.w/die-cut-c — 2.50
687-($1.50)-Newsstand Edition with mini-poster — 2.25
688-699,701-703-($1.50): 688-Guy Gardner-c/story. 697-Bizarro-c/story.
703-(9/94)-Zero Hour — 2.25
695-($2.50)-Collector's Edition w/embossed foil-c — 2.50
700-($2.95, 68 pgs.)-Fall of Metropolis Pt 1; Pete Ross marries Lana Lang;
Curt Swan & Murphy Anderson inks — 3.00
700-Platinum — 15.00
700-Gold — 18.00
0(10/94), 704(11/94)-710-719,721-731: 710-Begin $1.95-c. 714-Joker app.
719-Batman-c/app. 721-Mr. Mxyzptlk app. 723-Brainiac as Superman;
Dave Johnson-c. 727-Final Night x-over. — 2.25
720-Lois breaks off engagement w/Clark — 3.00
720-2nd print. — 2.25
732-749,751-767: 732-New powers. 733-New costume, Ray app. 738-Immonen-
s/a(p) begins. 741-Legion app. 744-Millennium Giants x-over. 745-747-70's-
style Superman vs. Prankster. 753-JLA-c/app. 757-Hawkman-c. 760-1st
Encantadora. 761-Wonder Woman app. 765-Joker & Harley-c/app.
766-Batman-c/app. — 2.25
750-($2.95) — 3.00
768,769,771-774: 768-Begin $2.25-c; Marvel Family-c/app. 771-Nightwing-c/app.
772,773-Ra's al Ghul app. 774-Martian Manhunter-c/app. — 2.25
770-($3.50) Conclusion of Emperor Joker x-over — 3.50
775-($3.75) Bradstreet-c; intro. The Elite — 3.75
776-786: 776-Farewell to Krypton; Rivoche-c. 780-782-Our Worlds at War x-over.
781-Hippolyta and Maj. Lane killed. 782-War ends. 784-Joker: Last Laugh;
Batman & Green Lantern app. — 2.25
#1,000,000 (11/98) Gene Ha-c; 853rd Century x-over — 2.25
Annual 1-6('87-'94, $2.95)-1-Art Adams-c/a(p); Batman app. 2-Perez-c/a(i)
3-Armageddon 2001. 4-Eclipso vs. Shazam. 5-Bloodlines; 1st app. Loose
Cannon. 6-Elseworlds story — 3.00
Annual 7,9 ('95, '97, $3.95)-7-Year One story. 9-Pulp Heroes sty — 4.00
Annual 8 (1996, $2.95)-Legends of the Dead Earth story — 3.00

NOTE: *Supergirl's* origin in 262, 280, 285, 291, 305, 309. N. Adams-c-356, 358, 359, 361-364, 367, 370-374, 377-379, 398-400, 402, 404,405, 419b, 466, 468, 469, 473, 485. Aparo a-64? Austin a-682l. Baily a-24, 25. Boring a-164, 194, 211, 223, 233, 241, 250, 261, 266-268, 34 348, 352, 356, 357. Burnley a-28-33; c-487, 53-55, 58, 59?, 60-63, 65, 66p, 67p, 70p, 71p, 7? 82p, 84-86p, 90-92p, 93p?, 94p, 107p, 108p. Byrne a-584-598p, 599l, 600p; c-584-591, 596-60? Ditko a-642. Giffen a-560, 563, 565, 577, 579; c-539, 560, 563, 565, 577, 579. Grell a-440-44? 444-446, 450-452, 456-458; c-456. Guardineer a-24, 25; c-8, 11, 12, 14-16, 18, 25. Guice a(p)-67? 681, 683-698, 700; c-683, 685, 686, 687(direct), 688-693, 694-696, 697, 698-700. Infantino a-54? Kaluta c-613. Bob Kane's Clip Carson-14-41. Gil Kane a-193?, 493r, 539-541, 544-546, 551-55? 601-605, 642; c-535p, 540, 541, 544p, 545-549, 551-554, 580, 627. Kirby c-638. Meskin a-? 121(most). Mignola a-600, Annual 2; c-c-614. Moldoff a-23-25, 443r. Mooney a-667p. Mortimer? 153, 154, 159-172, 174, 178-181, 184, 186-189, 191-193, 196, 200, 206. Orlando a-617p; c-62? Perez a-600l, 643-652p, Annual 2p; c-529p, 602, 643-651, Annual 2p. Quesada c-Annual 4p. Fre? Ray c-34, 36-46, 50-52. Siegel & Shuster a-1-27. Paul Smith c-608. Starlin a-509; c-631. Leona? Starr a-597(part), Staton a-525p, 526p, 531p, 535p, 536p. Swan/Moldoff c-281, 286, 287, 25? 298, 334. Thibert c-676, 677p, 678-681, 684. Toth a-406, 407, 413, 431; c-616. Tuska a-486p, 55? Williamson a-568l. Zeck c-Annual 5

ACTION FORCE (Also see G.I. Joe European Missions)
Marvel Comics Ltd. (British): Mar, 1987 - No. 50, 1988 ($1.00, weekly,
magazine)
1,3: British G.I. Joe series. 3-w/poster insert — 6.00
2,4 — 4.00
5-10 — 3.00
11-50 — 2.50
...Special 1 (7/87) Summer holiday special; Snake Eyes-c/app. — 6.00
...Special 2 (10/87) Winter special; — 4.00

ACTION GIRL
Slave Labor Graphics: Oct, 1994 - Present ($2.50/$2.75, B&W)
1-19: 4-Begin $2.75-c. 19-Begin $2.95-c — 3.00
1-6 (2nd and 3rd printings): All read 2nd Print in indicia. 1-(2/96). 2-(10/95).
3-(2/96). 4-(7/96). 5-(2/97). 6-(9/97) — 2.75
1-4 ($2.75, 3rd printings): All read 3rd Print in indicia. — 2.75

ACTION PLANET COMICS
Action Planet: 1996 - No. 3, Sept, 1997 ($3.95, B&W, 44 pgs.)

Adventure Comics #48 © DC

Adventure Comics #165 © DC

Adam-12 #9 © GK

	GD2.0	FN6.0	VF8.0	NM9.4

1-3: 1-Intro Monster Man by Mike Manley & other stories — 4.00
Giant Size Action Planet Halloween Special (1998, $5.95, oversized) — 6.00

ACTUAL CONFESSIONS (Formerly Love Adventures)
Atlas Comics (MPI): No. 13, Oct, 1952 - No. 14, Dec, 1952

	GD2.0	FN6.0	VF8.0	NM9.4
13,14	6	18	32	45

ACTUAL ROMANCES (Becomes True Secrets #3 on?)
Marvel Comics (IPS): Oct, 1949 - No. 2, Jan, 1950 (52 pgs.)

	GD2.0	FN6.0	VF8.0	NM9.4
1	11	33	55	90
2-Photo-c	7	21	38	55

ADAM AND EVE
Spire Christian Comics (Fleming H. Revell Co.): 1975,1978 (35¢/49¢)

nn-By Al Hartley	1	3	6	8

ADAM STRANGE (Also see Green Lantern #132, Mystery In Space #53 & Showcase #17)
DC Comics: 1990 - No. 3, 1990 ($3.95, 52 pgs, limited series, squarebound)
Book One - Three: Andy & Adam Kubert-c/a — 4.00

ADAM-12 (TV)
Gold Key: Dec, 1973 - No. 10, Feb, 1976 (Photo-c)

1	6	18	42	80
2-10	3	9	21	35

ADDAM OMEGA
Antarctic Press: Feb, 1997 - No. 4, Aug, 1997 ($2.95, B&W)
1-4 — 3.00

ADDAMS FAMILY (TV cartoon)
Gold Key: Oct, 1974 - No. 3, Apr, 1975 (Hanna-Barbera)

1	9	27	63	110
2,3	5	15	35	70

ADLAI STEVENSON
Dell Publishing Co.: Dec, 1966

12-007-612-Life story; photo-c	3	10	23	35

ADOLESCENT RADIOACTIVE BLACK BELT HAMSTERS (See Clint)
Comic Castle/Eclipse Comics: 1986 - No. 9, Jan, 1988 ($1.50, B&W)
1-9: 1st & 2nd printings exist — 2.25
1-Limited Edition — 3.00
1-In 3-D (7/86) — 2.50
2-4 ($2.50) — 2.50
Massacre The Japanese Invasion #1 (8/89, $2.00) — 2.25

ADRENALYNN (See The Tenth)
Image Comics: Aug, 1999 - No. 4, Feb, 2000 ($2.50)
1-4-Tony Daniel-s/Marty Egeland-a; origin of Adrenalynn — 2.50

ADULT TALES OF TERROR ILLUSTRATED (See Terror Illustrated)

ADVANCED DUNGEONS & DRAGONS (Also see TSR Worlds)
DC Comics: Dec, 1988 - No. 36, Dec, 1991 (Newsstand #1 is Holiday, 1988-89)
($1.25/$1.50/$1.75?)
1-Based on TSR role playing game — 4.00
2-36: 25-$1.75-c begins — 2.25
Annual 1 (1990, $3.95, 68 pgs.) — 4.00

ADVENTURE BOUND
Dell Publishing Co.: Aug, 1949

Four Color 239	5	15	35	60

ADVENTURE COMICS (Formerly New Adventure)(...Presents Dial H For Hero #479-490)
National Periodical Publications/DC Comics: No. 32, 11/38 - No. 490, 2/82; No. 491, 9/82 - No. 503, 9/83

32-Anchors Aweigh (ends #52), Barry O'Neil (ends #60, not in #33), Captain Desmo (ends #47), Dale Daring (ends #47), Federal Men (ends #70), The Golden Dragon (ends #36), Rusty & His Pals (ends #52) by Bob Kane, Todd Hunter (ends #38) and Tom Brent (ends #39)

	466	1400	2400	3600
33-38: 37-Cover used on Double Action #2	216	650	1125	1700

39(6/39)-Jack Wood begins, ends #42; 1st mention of Marijuana in comics

	216	650	1125	1700

	GD2.0	FN6.0	VF8.0	NM9.4

40-(Rare, 7/39, on stands 6/10/39)-The Sandman begins by Bert Christman (who died in WWII); believed to be 1st conceived story (see N.Y. World's Fair for 1st published app.); Socko Strong begins, ends #54

	4000	12,000	26,000	52,000
41-O'Mealia shark-c	492	1476	3200	6400
42,44-Sandman-c by Flessel. 44-Opium story	631	1893	4100	8200
43,45	300	900	1875	3500
46,47-Sandman covers by Flessel. 47-Steve Conrad Adventurer begins, ends #76	438	1314	2850	5700
48-Intro & 1st app. The Hourman by Bernard Baily; Baily-c (Hourman c-48,50,52-59)	2070	6210	14,500	29,000

49,50: 50-Cotton Carver by Jack Lehti begins, ends #64

	236	708	1477	2600
51,60-Sandman-c: 51-Sandman-c by Flessel.	308	924	1927	3700

52-59: 53-1st app. Jimmy "Minuteman" Martin & the Minutemen of America in Hourman; ends #78. 58-Paul Kirk Manhunter begins (1st app.), ends #72

	214	642	1338	2350
61-1st app. Starman by Jack Burnley (4/41); Starman c-61-72; Starman by Burnley in #61-80	1033	3100	7250	14,500

62-65,67,68,70: 67-Origin & 1st app. The Mist; classic Burnley-c
70-Last Federal Men

	182	546	1136	2000
66-Origin/1st app. Shining Knight (9/41)	223	669	1394	2450
69-1st app. Sandy the Golden Boy (Sandman's sidekick) by Paul Norris (in a Bob Kane style); Sandman dons new costume	191	573	1194	2100
71-Jimmy Martin becomes costumed aide to the Hourman; 1st app. Hourman's Miracle Ray machine	173	519	1080	1900

72-1st Simon & Kirby Sandman (3/42, 1st DC work)

	1000	3000	7000	14,000

73-Origin Manhunter by Simon & Kirby; begin new series; Manhunter-c

	1033	3100	7250	14,500

74-78,80: 74-Thorndyke replaces Jimmy, Hourman's assistant; new Sandman-c begin by S&K. 75-Thor app. by Kirby; 1st Kirby Thor (see Tales of the Unexpected #16). 77-Origin Genius Jones; Mist story.

80-Last S&K Manhunter by Burnley Starman	182	546	1136	2000
79-Classic Manhunter-c	218	654	1364	2400

81-90: 83-Last Hourman. 84-Mike Gibbs begins, ends #102

	118	354	738	1300
91-Last Simon & Kirby Sandman	105	315	656	1150
92-99,101,102: 92-Last Manhunter. 101-Shining Knight origin retold. 102-Last Starman, Sandman, & Genius Jones; most-S&K-c (Genius Jones cont'd in More Fun #108)	95	285	597	1050
100-S&K-c	127	381	795	1400
103-Aquaman, Green Arrow, Johnny Quick & Superboy all move over from More Fun Comics #107; 8th app. Superboy; Superboy-c begins with that small logo (4/46)	300	900	1875	3300
104	105	315	656	1150
105-110	73	219	455	800
111-120: 113-X-mas-c	66	198	412	725

121,122-126,128-130: 128-1st meeting Superboy & Lois Lane

	57	171	356	625
127-Brief origin Shining Knight retold	59	177	369	650
131-141,143-149: 132-Shining Knight 1st return to King Arthur time; origin aide Sir Butch	50	150	300	525
142-Origin Shining Knight & Johnny Quick retold	55	165	330	575
150,151,153,155,157,159,161,163-All have 6 pg. Shining Knight stories by Frank Frazetta. 159-Origin Johnny Quick	64	192	398	700
152,154,156,158,160,162,164-169: 166-Last Shining Knight. 168-Last 52 pg. issue	43	129	257	450
170-180	40	120	240	420
181-199: 189-B&W and color illo in POP	40	120	232	400
200 (5/54)	55	165	330	575
201-208: 207-Last Johnny Quick (not in 205)	37	111	203	350
209-Last pre-code issue; origin Speedy	39	117	217	375

210-1st app. Krypto (Superdog)-c/story (3/55)

	263	790	2100	4200
211-213,215-219	35	105	188	325
214-2nd app. Krypto	52	157	314	550
220-Krypto-c/sty	39	117	208	360

221-246: 229-1st S.A. issue. 237-1st Intergalactic Vigilante Squadron (6/57)

	30	90	162	280

Adventure Comics #325 © DC

Adventure Comics #430 © DC

Adventure Comics #475 © DC

	GD2.0	FN6.0	VF8.0	NM9.4			GD2.0	FN6.0	VF8.0	NM9.4

247(4/58)-1st Legion of Super Heroes app.; 1st app. Cosmic Boy, Lightning Boy (later Lightning Lad in #267), & Saturn Girl (origin)
333 1000 3000 6300

248-252,254,255-Green Arrow in all: 255-Intro. Red Kryptonite in Superboy (used in #252 but with no effect) 24 72 127 220

253-1st meeting of Superboy & Robin; Green Arrow by Kirby in #250-255 (also see World's Finest #96-99) 30 90 162 280

256-Origin Green Arrow by Kirby 64 192 398 700

257-259: 258-Green Arrow x-over in Superboy 20 60 105 180

260-1st Silver-Age origin Aquaman (5/59) 73 219 455 800

261-265,268,270: 262-Origin Speedy in Green Arrow. 270-Congorilla begins, ends #281,283 16 48 83 140

266-(11/59)-Origin & 1st app. Aquagirl (tryout, not same as later character)
17 51 88 150

267(12/59)-2nd Legion of Super Heroes; Lightning Boy now called Lightning Lad; new costumes for Legion 86 258 540 950

269-Intro. Aqualad (2/60); last Green Arrow (not in #206)
29 87 156 270

271-Origin Luthor retold 33 99 174 300

272-274,277-280: 279-Intro White Kryptonite in Superboy. 280-1st meeting Superboy-Lori Lemaris 14 42 72 125

275-Origin Superman-Batman team retold (see World's Finest #94)
25 75 130 225

276-(9/60)-Re-intro Metallo (3rd app?); story similar to Superboy #49
15 45 77 135

281,284,287-289: 281-Last Congorilla. 284-Last Aquaman in Adv. 287,288-Intro Dev-Em, the Knave from Krypton. 287-1st Bizarro Perry White & J. Olsen. 288-Bizarro cameo (statues) 13 39 66 115

282(3/61)-5th Legion app; intro/origin Star Boy 25 75 130 225

283-Intro. The Phantom Zone 23 69 121 210

285-1st Tales of the Bizarro World-c/story (ends #299) in Adv. (see Action #255) 20 60 105 175

286-1st Bizarro Mxyzptlk; Bizarro-c 18 54 94 160

290(11/61)-9th Legion app; origin Sunboy in Legion (last 10¢ issue)
23 69 121 210

291,292,295-298: 291-1st 12¢ ish, (12/61). 292-1st Bizarro Lana Lang & Lucy Lane. 295-Bizarro-c; 1st Bizarro Titano 9 27 63 105

293(2/62)-13th Legion app; Mon-el & Legion Super Pets (1st app./origin) app. (1st Superhorse). 1st Bizarro Luthor & Kandor 14 42 102 175

294-1st Bizarro Marilyn Monroe, Pres. Kennedy. 11 33 77 130

299-1st Gold Kryptonite (8/62) 9 27 65 110

300-Tales of the Legion of Super-Heroes series begins (9/62); Mon-el leaves Phantom Zone (temporarily), joins Legion 35 105 263 475

301-Origin Bouncing Boy 14 42 100 170

302-305: 303-1st app. Matter-Eater Lad. 304-Death of Lightning Lad in Legion 10 30 68 115

306-310: 306-Intro. Legion of Substitute Heroes. 307-1st app. Element Lad in Legion. 308-1st app. Lightning Lass in Legion 9 27 63 105

311-320: 312-Lightning Lad back in Legion. 315-Last new Superboy story; Colossal Boy app. 316-Origins & powers of Legion given. 317-Intro. Dream Girl in Legion (1st app.); Lightning Lass becomes Light Lass; Hall of Fame series begins. 320-Dev-Em 2nd app. 8 24 56 90

321-Intro Time Trapper 6 18 45 75

322-330: 327-Intro/1st app. Lone Wolf in Legion. 329-Intro The Bizarro Legionnaires; intro Legion flight rings 6 18 40 65

331-340: 337-Chlorophyll Kid & Night Girl app. 340-Intro Computo in Legion 5 15 34 55

341-Triplicate Girl becomes Duo Damsel 5 15 29 45

342-345,347-351: 345-Last Hall of Fame; returns in 356,371. 348-Origin Sunboy; intro Dr. Regulus in Legion. 349-Intro Universo & Rond Vidar. 351-1st app. White Witch. 4 12 26 40

346-1st app. Karate Kid, Princess Projectra, Ferro Lad, & Nemesis Kid.
5 15 34 55

352,354-360: 354,355-Superman meets the Adult Legion (4/67). 355-Insect Queen joins Legion 4 12 25 38

353-Death of Ferro Lad in Legion 4 12 30 50

361-364,366,368-370: 369-Intro Mordru in Legion 3 10 23 35

365(367: 365-Intro Shadow Lass (memorial to Shadow Woman app. in #354's Adult Legion-s); lists powers of L.S.H. 367-New Legion headquarters 4 12 25 38

371,372: 371-Intro. Chemical King (mentioned in #354's Adult Legion-s).
372-Timber Wolf & Chemical King join 4 12 25 38

373,374,376-380: 373-Intro. Tornado Twins (Flash descendants). 374-Article on comics fandom. 380-Last Legion in Adventure; last 12¢-c
3 10 23 35

375-Intro Quantum Queen & The Wanderers 4 12 25 38

381-Supergirl begins; 1st full length Supergirl story & her 1st solo book (6/69)
8 24 56 90

382-389 3 9 20 30

391-396,398 3 9 17 25

390-Giant Supergirl G-69 4 12 30 50

397-1st app. new Supergirl 3 9 20 30

399-Unpubbed G.A. Black Canary story 3 9 20 30

400-New costume for Supergirl (12/70) 3 10 23 35

401,402: 402-Last 15¢-c 2 6 13 20

403-68 pg. Giant G-81; Legion-r/#304,305,308,312 4 12 30 50

404-408-(20¢-c) 2 6 11 15

409-411,413-415,417-420-(52 pgs.): 413-Hawkman by Kubert r/B&B #44; G.A. Robotman-r/Det. #178; Zatanna by Morrow. 414-r-2nd Animal Man/Str. Advs. #184. 415-Animal Man-r/Str. Adv.#190 (origin recap). 417-Morrow Vigilante; Frazetta Shining Knight-r/Adv. #161; origin The Enchantress; no Zatanna. 418-Prev. unpub. Dr. Mid-Nite story from 1948; no Zatanna. 420-Animal Man-r/Str. Adv. #195 3 9 17 25

412-(52 pgs.) Reprints origin & 1st app. of Animal Man from Strange Adventures #180 3 9 17 25

416-Also listed as DC 100 Pg. Super Spectacular #10; Golden Age-r; r/1st app. Black Canary from Flash #86; no Zatanna (see DC 100 Pg. Super Spectacular #10 for price)

421-424,427: Last Legion in Adventure. 427-Last Vigilante
2 6 9 12

425-New look, content change to adventure; Kaluta; Toth-a, origin Capt. Fear
3 9 17 25

426-1st Adventurers Club. 2 6 9 12

428-Origin/1st app. Black Orchid (c/story, 6-7/73) 4 12 30 50

429,430-Black Orchid-c/stories 3 9 17 25

431-Spectre by Aparo begins, ends #440. 5 15 34 55

432-439-Spectre app. 433-437-Cover title is Weird Adv. Comics. 436-Last 20¢ issue. 3 9 19 28

440-New Spectre origin. 4 12 26 40

441-458: 441-452-Aquaman app. 443-Fisherman app. 445-447-The Creeper app. 446-Flag-c. 449-451-Martian Manhunter app. 450-Weather Wizard app. in Aquaman story. 453-458-Superboy app. 453-Intro. Mighty Girl.
457,458-Eclipso app. 1 3 6 8

459(460 (68 pgs.): 459-New Gods/Darkseid storyline concludes from New Gods #19 (#459 is dated 9-10/78) without missing a month. 459-Flash (ends #466), Deadman (ends #466), Wonder Woman (ends #464), Green Lantern (ends #460), 460-Aquaman (ends #478) 2 6 12 18

461,462 ($1.00, 68 pgs.): 461-Justice Society begins; ends 466.
461,462-Death Earth II Batman 3 9 17 25

463-466 ($1.00 size, 68 pgs.) 2 6 9 12

467-Starman by Ditko & Plastic Man begins; 1st app. Prince Gavyn (Starman).
2 6 9 12

468-490: 470-Origin Starman. 479-Dial 'H' For Hero begins, ends #490.
478-Last Starman & Plastic Man. 480-490: Dial 'H' For Hero 5.00

491-503: 491-100pg. Digest size begins; r/Legion of Super-Heroes/Adv. #247, 267; Spectre, Aquaman, Superboy, S&K Sandman, Black Canary-r app; new Shazam by Newton begin. 492,495,496,499-S&K Sandman-r/Adventure in all. 493-Challengers of the Unknown begins by Tuska w/brief origin. 493-495, 497-499-G.A. Captain Marvel-r. 494-499-Spectre-r/Spectre 1-3, 5-7. 496-Capt. Marvel Jr. new-s; Cockrum-a. 498-Mary Marvel new-s; Plastic Man-r begin; origin Bouncing Boy-r/#301. 500-Legion-r (Digest size, 148 pgs.).
501-503: G.A.-r 2 6 11 15

... 80 Page Giant (10/98, $4.95) Wonder Woman, Shazam, Supergirl, Green Arrow, Legion, Bizarro World stories 5.00

NOTE: Bizarro covers-285, 286, 288, 294, 295, 329. Vigilante app.-420, 426, 427. N. Adams a(r)-495i-498i; c-365-369, 371-373, 375-379, 381-383. Aparo a-431-433, 434i, 435, 436, 437i, 438i, 439-452, 503i; c-431-440. Bernard Baily c-48, 50, 52-59. Bolland c-478. Austin a-449i 451i. Burnley c-61-72, 116-120p. Chaykin a-438. Ditko a-467-478p; c-467p. Creig Flessel c-32, 33, 40, 42, 44, 46, 47, 51, 60. Giffen c-491p-494p, 500p. Grell a-435-437, 440. Guardineer c-34, 35, 37. Infantino a-416r. Kaluta c-425. Bob Kane a-38. G. Kane a-414r; 425; c-496-499, 537. Kirby a-250-256. Kubert a-413. Meskin a-81,127. Moldoff a-494i; c-49. Morrow a-413-415, 417, 422, 502r, 503r. Netzer/Nasser a-449-451. Newton a-459-461, 464-466, 491p, 492p. Paul Norris a-...

	GD2.0	FN6.0	VF8.0	NM9.4

*Orlando a-457p, 458p. **Perez** c-484-486, 490p. **Simon/Kirby** a-503r; c-73-97, 100-102. **Starlin** c-471. **Staton** a-445-447i, 456-458p, 459, 460, 461p-465p, 466,467p-478p, 502p(r); c-458, 461(back). **Toth** a-418, 419, 425, 431, 495p-497p. **Tuska** a-494p.*

ADVENTURE COMICS (Also see All Star Comics 1999 crossover titles)
DC Comics: May, 1999 ($1.99, one-shot)

1-Golden Age Starman and the Atom; Snejbjerg-a ... 2.25

ADVENTURE INTO MYSTERY
Atlas Comics (BFP No. 1/OPI No. 2-8): May, 1956 - No. 8, July, 1957

1-Powell s/f-a; Forte; Everett-c	38	114	203	350
2-Flying Saucer story	21	63	110	190
3,6-Everett-c/a	18	54	94	160
4-7: 4-Williamson-a, 4 pgs; Powell-a. 5-Everett-c/a, Orlando-a. 7-Torres-a; Everett-c	20	60	105	180
8-Moriera, Sale, Torres, Woodbridge-a; Severin-c	18	54	94	160

ADVENTURE IS MY CAREER
U.S. Coast Guard Academy/Street & Smith: 1945 (44 pgs.)

nn-Simon, Milt Gross-a	20	60	105	175

ADVENTURERS, THE
Aircel Comics/Adventure Publ.: Aug, 1986 - No. 10, 1987? ($1.50, B&W)
V2#1, 1987 - V2#9, 1988; V3#1, Oct, 1989 - V3#6, 1990

1-Peter Hsu-a		3.00
1-Cover variant, limited ed.		5.00
1-2nd print (1986); 1st app. Elf Warrior		2.25
2,3, 0 (#4, 12/86)-Origin, 5-10, Book II, reg. & Limited Ed. #1		2.25
Book II, #2,3,0,4-7		2.25
Book III, #1 (10/89, $2.25)-Reg. & limited-c, Book III, #2-6		2.25

ADVENTURES (No. 2 Spectacular… on cover)
St. John Publishing Co.: Nov, 1949 - No. 2, Feb, 1950 (No. 1 …in Romance on cover) (Slightly larger size)

1(Scarce); Bolle, Starr-a(2)	27	81	145	250
2(Scarce)-Slave Girl; China Bombshell app.; Bolle, L. Starr-a	40	120	232	400

ADVENTURES FOR BOYS
Bailey Enterprises: Dec, 1954

nn-Comics, text, & photos	6	18	32	45

ADVENTURES IN PARADISE (TV)
Dell Publishing Co.: Feb-Apr, 1962

Four Color#1301	5	15	35	65

ADVENTURES IN ROMANCE (See Adventures)

ADVENTURES IN SCIENCE (See Classics Illustrated Special Issue)

ADVENTURES IN THE DC UNIVERSE
DC Comics: Apr, 1997 - No. 19, Oct, 1998 ($1.75/$1.95/$1.99)

1-Animated style in all: JLA-c/app	4.00
2-11,13-17,19: 2-Flash app. 3-Wonder Woman. 4-Green Lantern. 6-Aquaman. 7-Shazam Family. 8-Blue Beetle & Booster Gold. 9-Flash. 10-Legion. 14-Superboy/Flash race	3.00
12,18-JLA-c/app	3.00
Annual 1(1997, $3.95)-Dr. Fate, Impulse, Rose & Thorn, Superboy, Mister Miracle app.	4.00

ADVENTURES IN THE RIFLE BRIGADE
DC Comics (Vertigo): Oct, 2000 - No. 3, Dec, 2000 ($2.50, limited series)

1-3-Ennis-s/Ezquerra-a/Bolland-c	2.50

ADVENTURES IN THE RIFLE BRIGADE: OPERATION BOLLOCK
DC Comics (Vertigo): Oct, 2001 - No. 3, Jan, 2002 ($2.50, limited series)

1-3-Ennis-s/Ezquerra-a/Fabry-c	2.50

ADVENTURES IN 3-D (With glasses)
Harvey Publications: Nov, 1953 - No. 2, Jan, 1954 (25¢)

1-Nostrand, Powell-a, 2-Powell-a	19	57	99	165

ADVENTURES INTO DARKNESS (See Seduction of the Innocent 3-D)
Better-Standard Publications/Visual Editions: No. 5, Aug, 1952- No. 14, 1954

5-Katz-c/a; Toth-a(p)	39	117	208	360

	GD2.0	FN6.0	VF8.0	NM9.4

6-Tuska, Katz-a	25	75	130	225
7-9: 7-Katz-c/a. 8,9-Toth-a(p)	25	75	130	225
10-12: 10,11-Jack Katz-a. 12-Toth-a; lingerie panel	22	66	116	200
13-Toth-a(p); Cannibalism story cited by T. E. Murphy articles				
	26	78	139	240
14	17	51	88	150

NOTE: *Fawcette a-13. Moriera a-5. Sekowsky a-10, 11, 13(2).*

ADVENTURES INTO TERROR (Formerly Joker Comics)
Marvel/Atlas Comics (CDS): No. 43, Nov, 1950 - No. 31, May, 1954

43(#1)	64	192	398	700
44(#2, 2/51)-Sol Brodsky-c	43	129	257	450
3(4/51), 4	29	87	156	270
5-Wolverton-c panel/Mystic #6; Rico-c panel also; Atom Bomb story				
	34	102	179	310
6,8: 8-Wolverton text illo r-/Marvel Tales #104	27	81	145	250
7-Wolverton-a "Where Monsters Dwell", 6 pgs.; Tuska-c; Maneely-c panels				
	55	165	341	600
9,10,12-Krigstein-a. 9-Decapitation panels	24	72	127	215
11,13-20	21	63	110	190
21-24,26-31	19	57	99	165
25-Matt Fox-a	24	72	127	220

NOTE: *Ayers a-21. Colan a-3, 5, 14, 21, 24, 25, 28, 29; c-27. Colletta a-30. Everett c-13, 21, 25. Fass a-28, 29. Forte a-28. Heath a-43, 44, 4-6, 22, 24, 26; c-43, 9, 11. Lazarus a-7. Maneely a-7(3 pg.), 10, 11, 21., 22 c-15, 29. Don Rico a-4, 5(3 pg.). Sekowsky a-43, 3, 4. Sinnott a-8, 9, 11, 28. Tuska a-14; c-7.*

ADVENTURES INTO THE UNKNOWN
American Comics Group: Fall, 1948 - No. 174, Aug, 1967 (No. 1-33: 52 pgs.)
(1st continuous series Supernatural comic; see Eerie #1)

1-Guardineer-a; adapt. of 'Castle of Otranto' by Horace Walpole				
	200	600	1250	2200
2,3-Feldstein-a (9 pgs)	75	225	470	825
4,5: 5-'Spirit Of Frankenstein' series begins, ends #12 (except #11)				
	40	120	232	400
6-10	34	102	179	310
11-16,18-20: 13-Starr-a	27	81	145	250
17-Story similar to movie 'The Thing'	33	99	174	300
21-26,28-30	23	69	121	210
27-Williamson/Krenkel-a (8 pgs)	30	90	162	280
31-50: 38-Atom bomb panels	18	54	94	160
51-(1/54)-(3-D effect-c/story)-Only white cover	36	108	191	330
52-58: (3-D effect-c/stories with black covers). 52-E.C. swipe/Haunt Of Fear #14				
	34	102	179	310
59-3-D effect story only; new logo	27	81	145	250
60-Woodesque-a by Landau	13	39	66	110
61-Last pre-code issue (1-2/55)	13	39	66	110
62-70	7	21	50	80
71-90	6	18	40	65
91,96(#95 on inside),107,116-All have Williamson-a	7	21	50	80
92-95,97-99,101-106,108-115,117-128: 109-113,118-Whitney painted-c.				
128-Williamson/Krenkel-a(r)/Forbidden Worlds #63; last 10¢ issue				
	4	12	30	50
100	5	15	34	55
129-153,157: 153,157-Magic Agent app.	4	12	26	40
154-Nemesis series begins (origin), ends #170	4	12	30	50
155,156,158-167,170-174	4	12	25	38
168-Ditko-a(p)	4	12	29	45
169-Nemesis battles Hitler	4	12	29	45

NOTE: *"Spirit of Frankenstein" series in 5, 6, 8-10, 12, 16. Buscema a-100, 106, 108-110, 158r, 165r. Cameron a-34. Craig a-152, 160. Goode a-45, 47, 60. Landau a-51, 65-69, 59-63. Lazarus a-34, 48, 51, 52, 56, 58, 79, 87; c-31-56, 58. Reinman a-102, 111, 112, 115-118, 124, 130, 137, 141, 145, 164. Whitney c-12-30, 57, 59-on (most.) Torres/Williamson a-116.*

ADVENTURES INTO WEIRD WORLDS
Marvel/Atlas Comics (ACI): Jan, 1952 - No. 30, June, 1954

1-Atom bomb panels	57	171	356	625
2-Sci/fic stories (2); one by Maneely	39	117	208	360
3-10: 7-Tongue ripped out. 10-Krigstein, Everett-a	27	81	145	250
11-20	22	66	116	200
21-Hitler in Hell story	24	72	127	220
22-26: 24-Man holds hypo & splits in two	20	60	105	175

Adventures of Barry Ween, Boy Genius
3: Monkey Tales #1 © Judd Winick

Adventures of Cyclops & Phoenix #3
© MAR

Adventures of Dean Martin and
Jerry Lewis #7 © DC

	GD2.0	FN6.0	VF8.0	NM9.4
27-Matt Fox end of world story-a; severed head-c	37	111	197	340
28-Atom bomb story; decapitation panels	22	66	116	200
29,30	16	48	83	140

NOTE: *Ayers* a-8, 26. *Everett* a-4, 5; c-6, 8, 10-13, 18, 19, 22, 24, 25; a-4, 25. *Fass* a-7. *Forte* a-21, 24. *Al Hartley* a-2. *Heath* a-1, 4, 17, 22; c-7, 9, 20. *Maneely* a-2, 3, 11, 20, 22, 23, 25; c-1, 3, 22, 25-27, 29. *Reinman* a-24. 28. *Rico* a-13. *Robinson* a-13. *Sinnott* a-25, 30. *Tuska* a-1, 2, 15. *Whitney* a-7. *Wildey* a-28. *Bondage* c-22.

ADVENTURES IN WONDERLAND
Lev Gleason Publications: April, 1955 - No. 5, Feb, 1956 (Jr. Readers Guild)

1-Maurer-a	10	30	55	85
2-4	6	18	32	45
5-Christmas issue	7	21	36	50

ADVENTURES OF AARON
Image Comics: Mar, 1997 - No. 3, Sept, 1997 (2.95, B&W)

1,2,100(#3),3(#4)				3.00

ADVENTURES OF ALAN LADD, THE
National Periodical Publ.: Oct-Nov, 1949 - No. 9, Feb-Mar, 1951 (All 52 pgs.)

1-Photo-c	95	285	597	1050
2-Photo-c	50	150	300	525
3-6: Last photo-c	40	120	220	380
7-9	34	102	179	310

NOTE: *Dan Barry* a-1. *Moreira* a-3, 7.

ADVENTURES OF ALICE (Also see Alice in Wonderland & ...at Monkey Island)
Civil Service Publ./Pentagon Publishing Co.: 1945

1	12	36	61	105
2-Through the Magic Looking Glass	10	30	55	80

ADVENTURES OF BARON MUNCHAUSEN, THE
Now Comics: July, 1989 - No. 4, Oct, 1989 ($1.75, limited series)

1-4: Movie adaptation				2.25

ADVENTURES OF BARRY WEEN, BOY GENIUS, THE
Image Comics: Mar, 1999 - No. 3, May, 1999 ($2.95, B&W, limited series)

1-3-Judd Winick-s/a				3.00
TPB (Oni Press, 11/99, $8.95)				9.00

ADVENTURES OF BARRY WEEN, BOY GENIUS 2.0, THE
Oni Press: Feb, 2000 - No. 3, Apr, 2000 ($2.95, B&W, limited series)

1-3-Judd Winick-s/a				3.00
TPB (2000, $8.95)				9.00

ADVENTURES OF BARRY WEEN, BOY GENIUS 3, THE : MONKEY TALES
Oni Press: Feb, 2001 - No. 6 ($2.95, B&W, limited series)

1-5-Judd Winick-s/a				3.00
TPB (2001, $8.95) r/#1-3; intro. by Peter David				9.00

ADVENTURES OF BAYOU BILLY, THE
Archie Comics: Sept, 1989 - No. 5, June, 1990 ($1.00)

1-5: Esposito-c/a(i). 5-Kelley Jones-c				2.50

ADVENTURES OF BOB HOPE, THE (Also see True Comics #59)
National Per. Publ.: Feb-Mar, 1950 - No. 109, Feb-Mar, 1968 (#1-10: 52pgs.)

1-Photo-c	173	519	1080	1900
2-Photo-c	77	231	483	850
3,4-Photo-c	47	141	286	500
5-10	40	120	232	400
11-20	25	75	130	225
21-31 (2-3/55; last precode)	17	51	88	150
32-40	9	27	65	110
41-50	8	24	56	90
51-70	5	15	38	60
71-93	4	12	26	40
94-Aquaman cameo	4	12	29	45
95-1st app. Super-Hip & 1st monster issue (11/65)	5	15	38	60
96-105: Super-Hip and monster stories in all. 103-Batman, Robin, Ringo Starr cameos	4	12	26	40
106-109-All monster-c/stories by N. Adams-c/a	6	18	40	65

NOTE: *Buzzy* in #34. *Kitty Karr of Hollywood* in #15, 17-20, 23, 28. *Liz* in #26, 109. *Miss Beverly Hills of Hollywood* in #7, 8, 10, 13, 14. *Miss Melody Lane of Broadway* in #15. *Rusty* in #23, 25. *Tommy* in #24. No 2nd feature in #2-4, 6, 8, 11, 12, 28-108.

ADVENTURES OF CAPTAIN AMERICA

Marvel Comics: Sept, 1991 - No. 4, Jan, 1992 ($4.95, 52 pgs., squarebound, limited series)

1-4: 1-Origin in WW2; embossed-c; Nicieza scripts; Maguire-c/a(p) begins, ends #3. 2-4-Austin-c/a(i). 3,4-Red Skull app.				5.00

ADVENTURES OF CYCLOPS AND PHOENIX (Also see Askani'son & The Further Adventures of Cyclops And Phoenix)
Marvel Comics: May, 1994 - No. 4, Aug, 1994 ($2.95, limited series)

1-4-Characters from X-Men; origin of Cable				4.00
Trade paperback ($14.95)-reprints #1-4				15.00

ADVENTURES OF DEAN MARTIN AND JERRY LEWIS, THE
(The Adventures of Jerry Lewis #41 on) (See Movie Love #12)
National Periodical Publications: July-Aug, 1952 - No. 40, Oct, 1957

1	91	273	568	1000
2-3 pg origin on how they became a team	45	135	270	475
3-10: 3- I Love Lucy text featurette	26	78	139	240
11-19: Last precode (2/55)	17	51	88	150
20-30	14	42	72	120
31-40	11	33	55	90

ADVENTURES OF DETECTIVE ACE KING, THE (Also see Bob Scully-- & Detective Dan)
Humor Publ. Corp.: No date (1933) (36 pgs., 9-1/2x12") (10¢, B&W, one-shot) (paper-c)

Book 1-Along with Bob Scully & Detective Dan, the first comic w/original art & the first of a single theme.; Not reprints; Ace King by Martin Nadle (The American Sherlock Holmes). A Dick Tracy look-alike	320	960	2400	-

ADVENTURES OF EVIL AND MALICE, THE
Image Comics: June, 1999 - No. 3, Nov, 1999 ($3.50/$3.95, limited series)

1,2-Jimmie Robinson-s/a				3.50
3-($3.95)				4.00

ADVENTURES OF FELIX THE CAT, THE
Harvey Comics: May, 1992 ($1.25)

1-Messmer-r				3.00

ADVENTURES OF FORD FAIRLANE, THE
DC Comics: May, 1990 - No. 4, Aug, 1990 ($1.50, limited series, mature)

1-4: Andrew Dice Clay movie tie-in; Don Heck inks				2.25

ADVENTURES OF HOMER COBB, THE
Say/Bart Prod. : Sept, 1947 (Oversized)
(Published in the U.S., but printed in Canada)

1-(Scarce)-Feldstein-c/a	29	87	156	270

ADVENTURES OF HOMER GHOST (See Homer The Happy Ghost)
Atlas Comics: June, 1957 - No. 2, Aug, 1957

V1#1,2: 2-Robot-c	8	24	45	65

ADVENTURES OF JERRY LEWIS, THE (Adventures of Dean Martin & Jerry Lewis No. 1-40)(See Super DC Giant)
National Periodical Publ.: No. 41, Nov, 1957 - No. 124, May-June, 1971

41	8	24	56	90
42-60	6	18	42	70
61-67,69-73,75-80	5	15	34	55
68,74-Photo-c (movie)	6	18	40	65
81,82,85-87,90,91,94,96,98,99	4	12	26	40
83,84,88: 83-1st Monsters-c/s. 84-Jerry as a Super-hero-c/s. 88-1st Witch, Miss Kraft	4	12	29	45
89-Bob Hope app.; Wizard of Oz & Alfred E. Neuman in MAD parody	4	12	30	50
92-Superman cameo	5	15	34	55
93-Beatles parody as babies	4	12	26	40
95-1st Uncle Hal Wack-A-Buy Camp-c/s	4	12	29	45
97-Batman/Robin/Joker-c/story; Riddler & Penguin app; Dick Sprang-c	7	21	53	85
100	5	15	29	45
101,103,104-Neal Adams-c/a	6	18	40	65
102-Beatles app.; Neal Adams c/a	8	24	56	90
105-Superman x-over	5	15	34	55
106-111,113-116	3	9	20	30

	GD2.0	FN6.0	VF8.0	NM9.4

112,117: 112-Flash x-over. 117-W. Woman x-over

	5	15	34	55
118-124	3	9	17	25

NOTE: *Monster-c/s-90,93,96,98,101. Wack-A-Buy Camp-c/s-96,99,102,107,108.*

ADVENTURES OF JO-JOY, THE (See Jo-Joy)

ADVENTURES OF LASSIE, THE (See Lassie)

ADVENTURES OF LUTHER ARKWRIGHT, THE
Valkyrie Press/Dark Horse Comics: Oct, 1987 - No. 9, Jan, 1989 ($2.00, B&W)
V2, #1, Mar, 1990 - V2#9, 1990 ($1.95, B&W)

1-9: 1-Alan Moore intro., V2#1-9 (Dark Horse): r-1st series; new-c				4.00
TPB (1997, $14.95) r/#1-9 w/Michael Moorcock intro.				15.00

ADVENTURES OF MIGHTY MOUSE (Mighty Mouse Adventures No. 1)
St. John Publishing Co.: No. 2, Jan, 1952 - No. 18, May, 1955

2	25	75	130	225
3-5	14	42	72	120
6-18	10	30	55	80

ADVENTURES OF MIGHTY MOUSE (2nd Series)
(Two No. 144's; formerly Paul Terry's Comics; No. 129-137 have nn's)
(Becomes Mighty Mouse No. 161 on)
St. John/Pines/Dell/Gold Key: No. 126, Aug, 1955 - No. 160, Oct, 1963

126(8/55), 127(10/55), 128(11/55)-St. John	9	27	49	70
nn(129, 4/56)-144(8/59)-Pines	5	15	34	55
144(10-12/59)-155(7-9/62) Dell	4	12	29	45
156(10/62)-160(10/63) Gold Key	4	12	29	45

NOTE: *Early issues titled "Paul Terry's Adventures of ...."*

ADVENTURES OF MIGHTY MOUSE (Formerly Mighty Mouse)
Gold Key: No. 166, Mar, 1979 - No. 172, Jan, 1980

166-172				6.00

ADVS. OF MR. FROG & MISS MOUSE (See Dell Junior Treasury No. 4)

ADVENTURES OF OZZIE & HARRIET, THE (See Ozzie & Harriet)

ADVENTURES OF PATORUZU
Green Publishing Co.: Aug, 1946 - Winter, 1946

nn's-Contains Animal Crackers reprints	5	15	25	35

ADVENTURES OF PINKY LEE, THE (TV)
Atlas Comics: July, 1955 - No. 5, Dec, 1955

1	27	81	145	250
2-5	17	51	88	150

ADVENTURES OF PIPSQUEAK, THE (Formerly Pat the Brat)
Archie Publications (Radio Comics): No. 34, Sept, 1959 - No. 39, July, 1960

34	4	12	25	38
35-39	3	9	19	28

ADVENTURES OF QUAKE & QUISP, THE (See Quaker Oats "Plenty of Glutton")

ADVENTURES OF REX THE WONDER DOG, THE (Rex…No. 1)
National Periodical Publications: Jan-Feb, 1952 - No. 45, May-June, 1959; No. 46, Nov-Dec, 1959

1-(Scarce)-Toth-c/a	114	342	713	1250
2-(Scarce)-Toth-c/a	55	165	341	600
3-(Scarce)-Toth-a	45	135	270	475
4,5	39	117	208	360
6-10	29	87	156	270
11-Atom bomb-c/story; dinosaur-c/sty	34	102	179	310
12-19: 19-Last precode (1-2/55)	17	51	88	150
20-46	13	39	66	110

NOTE: *Infantino, Gil Kane art in 5-19 (most)*

ADVENTURES OF RHEUMY PEEPERS AND CHUNKY HIGHLIGHTS, THE
Oni Press: Feb, 1999 ($2.95, B&W, one-shot)

nn-Penn Jillette-s/Renée French-a				3.00

ADVENTURES OF ROBIN HOOD, THE (Formerly Robin Hood)
Magazine Enterprises (Sussex Publ. Co.): No. 7, 9/57 - No. 8, 11/57
(Based on Richard Greene TV Show)

7,8-Richard Greene photo-c. 7-Powell-a	16	48	83	140

ADVENTURES OF ROBIN HOOD, THE
Gold Key: Mar, 1974 - No. 7, Jan, 1975 (Disney cartoon) (36 pgs.)

1(90291-403)-Part-r of $1.50 editions	2	6	11	15
2-7: 1-7 are part-r	1	3	6	8

ADVENTURES OF SNAKE PLISSKEN
Marvel Comics: Jan, 1997 ($2.50, one-shot)

1-Based on Escape From L.A. movie; Brereton-c				2.50

ADVENTURES OF SPIDER-MAN, THE (Based on animated TV series)
Marvel Comics: Apr, 1996 - No. 12, Mar, 1997 (99¢)

1-12: 1-Punisher app. 2-Venom app. 3-X-Men. 6-Fantastic Four				2.25

ADVENTURES OF SUPERBOY, THE (See Superboy, 2nd Series)

ADVENTURES OF SUPERMAN (Formerly Superman)
DC Comics: No. 424, Jan, 1987 - No. 499, Feb, 1993;
No. 500, Early June, 1993 - Present

424-Ordway-c/a/Wolfman-s begin following Byrne's Superman revamp				3.00

425-435,437-462: 426-Legends x-over. 432-1st app. Jose Delgado who becomes Gangbuster in #434. 437-Millennium x-over. 438-New Brainiac app.

440-Batman app. 449-Invasion				3.00
436-Byrne scripts begin; Millennium x-over				3.50
463-Superman/Flash race; cover swipe/Superman #199				5.00
464-Lobo-c & app. (pre-dates Lobo #1)				4.00

465-495: 467-Part 2 of Batman story. 473-Hal Jordan, Guy Gardner x-over.

477-Legion app. 491-Last $1.00-c. 480-($1.75, 52 pgs.). 495-Forever People.-c/story; Darkseid app.				2.50
496-Doomsday cameo. 497-Doomsday battle issue				3.00
496,497-2nd printings				2.25
498,499-Funeral for a Friend; Supergirl app.				2.50
498-2nd & 3rd printings				2.25
500-($2.95, 68 pgs.)-Collector's edition w/card				3.50
500-($2.50, 68 pgs.)-Regular edition w/different-c				2.25
500-Platinum edition				20.00
501-($1.95)-Collector's edition w/die-cut-c				2.25
501-($1.50)-Regular edition w/mini-poster & diff.-c				2.25

502-516: 502-Supergirl-c/story. 508-Challengers of the Unknown app.

510-Bizarro-c/story. 516-9(9/94)-Zero Hour				2.25
505-($2.50)-Holo-grafx foil-c edition				2.50
0,517-523: 0-(10/94). 517-(11/94)				2.25

524-549,551-580: 524-Begin $1.95-c. 527-Return of Alpha Centurion (Zero Hour) 533-Impulse c/app. 535-Luthor-c/app. 536-Brainiac app. 537-Parasite app. 540-Final Night x-over. 541 Superboy c/app.; Lois & Clark honeymoon. 545-New powers. 546-New costume. 551-Cyborg app. 555-Red & Blue Supermen battle. 557-Millennium Giants x-over, 558-560: Superman Silver Age-style story; Krypto app. 561-Begin $1.99-c. 565-JLA app.

				2.25
550-($3.50)-Double sized				3.50

581-588: 581-Begin $2.25-c. 583-Emperor Joker. 588-Casey-s

				2.25

589-595: 589-Return to Krypton; Rivoche-c. 591-Wolfman-s. 593-595-Our Worlds at War x-over. 593-New Suicide Squad formed. 594-Doomsday-c/app.

596-Aftermath of "War" x-over has panel showing damaged World Trade Center buildings; issue went on sale the day after the Sept. 11 attack

				5.00
597-599: 597-Joker: Last Laugh				2.25
600-($3.95) Wieringo-a; painted-c by Adel; pin-ups by various				4.00
#1,000,000 (11/98) Gene Ha-c; 853rd Century x-over				3.00
Annual 1 (1987, $1.25, 52 pgs.)-Starlin-c & scripts				3.00

Annual 2,3 (1990, 1991, $2.00, 68 pgs.): 2-Byrne-c/a(i); Legion '90 (Lobo) app. 3-Armageddon 2001 x-over

				3.00

Annual 4-6 ('92-'94, $2.50, 68 pgs.): 4-Guy Gardner/Lobo-c/story; Eclipso storyline; Quesada-c(p). 5-Bloodlines storyline. 6-Elseworlds sty.

				3.00
Annual 7,9('95, '97, $3.95)-7-Year One story. 9-Pulp Heroes sty				4.00
Annual 8 (1996, $2.95)-Legends of the Dead Earth story				3.00

NOTE: *Erik Larsen a-431.*

ADVENTURES OF THE DOVER BOYS
Archie Comics (Close-up): September, 1950 - No. 2, 1950 (No month given)

1,2	9	27	49	70

ADVENTURES OF THE FLY (The Fly #1-6; Fly Man No. 32-39; See The Double Life of Private Strong, The Fly, Laugh Comics & Mighty Crusaders)
Archie Publications/Radio Comics: Aug, 1959 - No. 30, Oct, 1964; No. 31, May, 1965

1-Shield app.; origin The Fly; S&K-c/a	48	144	386	700
2-Williamson, S&K-a	28	85	196	350

Adventures of the Jaguar #3 © AP

The Agency #1 © TCOW

Age of Bronze #10 © Eric Shanower

	GD2.0	FN6.0	VF8.0	NM9.4

	GD2.0	FN6.0	VF8.0	NM9.4
3-Origin retold; Davis, Powell-a	23	69	160	285
4-Neal Adams-a(p)(1 panel); S&K-c; Powell-a; 2 pg. Shield story				
	13	39	94	160
5,6,9,10: 9-Shield app. 9-1st app. Cat Girl. 10-Black Hood app.				
	9	27	63	105
7,8: 7-1st S.A. app. Black Hood (7/60). 8-1st S.A. app. Shield (9/60)				
	10	30	73	125
11-13,15-20: 13-1st app. Fly Girl w/o costume. 16-Last 10¢ issue. 20-Origin Fly Girl retold	6	18	40	65
14-Origin & 1st app. Fly Girl in costume	7	21	53	85
21-30: 23-Jaguar cameo. 27-29-Black Hood 1 pg. strips. 30-Comet x-over (1st S.A. app.) in Fly Girl	4	12	26	40
31-Black Hood, Shield, Comet app.	4	12	29	45

NOTE: *Simon* c-2-4. *Tuska* a-1. Cover title to #31 is Flyman; Advs. of the Fly inside.

ADVENTURES OF THE JAGUAR, THE (See Blue Ribbon Comics, Laugh Comics & Mighty Crusaders)
Archie Publications (Radio Comics): Sept, 1961 - No. 15, Nov, 1963

	GD2.0	FN6.0	VF8.0	NM9.4
1-Origin Jaguar (1st app?) by J. Rosenberger	18	54	123	225
2,3: 3-Last 10¢ issue	9	27	65	110
4-6-Catgirl app. (#4's-c is same as splash pg.)	7	21	53	85
7-10	5	15	38	60
11-15:13,14-Catgirl,Black Hood app. in both	4	12	30	50

ADVENTURES OF THE MASK (TV cartoon)
Dark Horse Comics: Jan, 1996 - No. 12, Dec, 1996 ($2.50)

1-12: Based on animated series				2.50

ADVENTURES OF THE NEW MEN (Formerly Newmen #1-21)
Maximum Press: No. 22, Nov, 1996; No. 23, March, 1997 ($2.50)

22,23-Sprouse-c/a				2.50

ADVENTURES OF THE OUTSIDERS, THE (Formerly Batman & The Outsiders; also see The Outsiders)
DC Comics: No. 33, May, 1986 - No. 46, June, 1987

33-46: 39-45-r/Outsiders #1-7 by Aparo				2.00

ADVENTURES OF THE SUPER MARIO BROTHERS (See Super Mario Bros.)
Valiant: 1990 - No. 9, Oct, 1991 ($1.50)

V2#1-9				4.00

ADVENTURES OF THE THING, THE (Also see The Thing)
Marvel Comics: Apr, 1992 - No. 4, July, 1992, ($1.25, limited series)

1-4: 1-r/Marvel Two-In-One #50 by Byrne; Kieth-c. 2-4-r/Marvel Two-In-One #80,51 & 77; 2-Ghost Rider-c/story; Quesada-a. 3-Miller-r/Quesada-c; new Perez-a (4 pgs.)				2.25

ADVENTURES OF THE X-MEN, THE (Based on animated TV series)
Marvel Comics: Apr, 1996 - No. 12, Mar, 1997 (99¢)

1-12: 1-Wolverine/Hulk battle. 3-Spider-Man-c. 5,6-Magneto-c/app.				3.00

ADVENTURES OF TINKER BELL (See Tinker Bell, 4-Color Nos. 896 & 982)

ADVENTURES OF TOM SAWYER (See Dell Junior Treasury No. 10)

ADVENTURES OF YOUNG DR. MASTERS, THE
Archie Comics (Radio Comics): Aug, 1964 - No. 2, Nov, 1964

		GD2.0	FN6.0	VF8.0	NM9.4
1		3	9	17	25
2		2	6	12	18

ADVENTURES ON OTHER WORLDS (See Showcase #17 & 18)

ADVENTURES ON THE PLANET OF THE APES (Also see Planet of the Apes)
Marvel Comics Group: Oct, 1975 - No. 11, Dec, 1976

		GD2.0	FN6.0	VF8.0	NM9.4
1-Planet of the Apes magazine-r in color; Starlin-c; adapts movie thru #6		2	6	15	22
2-5: 5-(25¢-c edition)		1	4	7	10
5-7-(30¢-c variants, limited distribution)		2	6	13	20
6-10: 6,7-(25¢-c edition). 7-Adapts 2nd movie (thru #11)		2	6	9	12
11-Last issue; concludes 2nd movie adaptation		2	6	11	15

NOTE: *Alcala* a-6-11r. *Buckler* c-2p. *Nasser* c-7. *Ploog* a-1-9. *Starlin* c-6. *Tuska* a-1-5r.

AFRICA
Magazine Enterprises: 1955

		GD2.0	FN6.0	VF8.0	NM9.4
1(A-1 #137)-Cave Girl, Thun'da;Powell-c/a(4)		25	75	130	225

AFRICAN LION (Disney movie)
Dell Publishing Co.: Nov, 1955

		GD2.0	FN6.0	VF8.0	NM9.4
Four Color #665		5	15	35	65

AFTER DARK
Sterling Comics: No. 6, May, 1955 - No. 8, Sept, 1955

		GD2.0	FN6.0	VF8.0	NM9.4
6-8-Sekowsky-a in all		9	27	49	70

AFTERMATH (Leads into Lady Death: Dark Millennium)
Chaos! Comics: Feb, 2000 ($2.95, one-shot)

1-Pulido & Kaminski-s/Luke Ross-a; Reis-c				3.00
1-($6.95) DF Edition; Brereton painted-c				7.00

AGAINST BLACKSHARD 3-D (Also see SoulQuest)
Sirius Comics: August, 1986 ($2.25)

1				3.00

AGENCY, THE
Image Comics (Top Cow): August, 2001 - Present ($2.50)

1,2: 1-Jenkins-s/Hotz-a; three covers by Hotz, Turner, Silvestri				2.50
3-5 ($2.95)				3.00
Preview (2001, 16 pgs.) B&W pages, cover previews, sketch pages				1.00

AGENT LIBERTY SPECIAL (See Superman, 2nd Series)
DC Comics: 1992 ($2.00, 52 pgs, one-shot)

1-1st solo adventure; Guice-c/a(i)				2.25

AGENTS OF LAW (Also see Comic's Greatest World)
Dark Horse Comics: Mar, 1995 - No.6, Sept, 1995 ($2.50)

1-6: 5-Predator app. 6-Predator app.; death of Law				2.50

AGE OF APOCALYPSE: THE CHOSEN
Marvel Comics: Apr, 1995 ($2.50, one-shot)

1-Wraparound-c				3.00

AGE OF BRONZE
Image Comics: Nov, 1998 - Present ($2.95/$3.50, B&W, limited series)

1-6-Eric Shanower-c/s/a				3.00
7-12-($3.50)				3.50
...Special (6/99, $2.95) Story of Agamemnon and Menelaus				3.00
A Thousand Ships (7/01, $19.95, TPB) r/#1-9				20.00

AGE OF HEROES, THE
Halloween Comics/Image Comics #3 on: 1996 - Present ($2.95, B&W)

1-5: James Hudnall scripts; John Ridgway-c/a				3.00
...Special ($4.95) r/#1,2				5.00
...Special 2 ($6.95) r/#3,4				7.00
...Wex 1 ('98, $2.95) Hudnall-s/Angel Fernandez-a				3.00

AGE OF INNOCENCE: THE REBIRTH OF IRON MAN
Marvel Comics: Feb, 1996 ($2.50, one-shot)

1-New origin of Tony Stark				3.00

AGE OF REPTILES
Dark Horse Comics: Nov, 1993 - No. 4, Feb, 1994 ($2.50, limited series)

1-4: Delgado-c/a/scripts in all				3.00

AGE OF REPTILES: THE HUNT
Dark Horse Comics: May, 1996 - No. 5, Sept, 1996 ($2.95, limited series)

1-5: Delgado-c/a/scripts in all; wraparound-c				3.00

AGGIE MACK
Four Star Comics Corp./Superior Comics Ltd.: Jan, 1948 - No. 8, Aug, 1949

	GD2.0	FN6.0	VF8.0	NM9.4
1-Feldstein-a, "Johnny Prep"	35	105	185	320
2,3-Kamen-c	18	54	94	160
4-Feldstein "Johnny Prep"; Kamen-c	25	75	130	225
5-8-Kamen-c/a	19	57	99	165

AGGIE MACK
Dell Publishing Co.: Apr - Jun, 1962

	GD2.0	FN6.0	VF8.0	NM9.4
Four Color #1335	3	9	21	40

AIR ACE (Formerly Bill Barnes No. 1-12)
Street & Smith Publications: V2#1, Jan, 1944 - V3#8(No. 20), Feb-Mar, 1947

	GD2.0	FN6.0	VF8.0	NM9.4
V2#1	31	93	168	290

Air Ace V3 #3 © Condé Nast

Air Fighters Comics V2 #6 © HILL

Akiko #1 © Mark Crilley

	GD2.0	FN6.0	VF8.0	NM9.4
²2#2-Classic-c	30	90	159	275
²2#3-12: 7-Powell-a	15	45	77	130
³3#1-6	12	36	61	105
³3#7-Powell bondage-c/a; all atomic issue	23	69	121	210
³3#8 (V5#8 on-c)-Powell-c/a	13	39	66	115

AIRBOY (Also see Airmaidens, Skywolf, Target: Airboy & Valkyrie)
Eclipse Comics: July, 1986 - No. 50, Oct, 1989 (#1-8, 50¢, 20 pgs., bi-weekly; 9-on, 36pgs.; #34-on monthly)

1-4: 2-1st Marisa; Skywolf gets new costume. 3-The Heap begins				4.00
5-Valkyrie returns; Dave Stevens-c				6.00
6-49: 9-Begin $1.25-c; Skywolf begins. 11-Origin of G.A. Airboy & his plane Birdie. 28-Mr. Monster vs. The Heap. 33-Begin $1.75-c. 38-40-The Heap by Infantino. 41-r/1st app. Valkyrie from Air Fighters. 42-Begin $1.95-c. 46,47-part-r/Air Fighters. 48-Black Angel-r/A.F				3.00
50 ($4.95, 52 pgs.)-Kubert-c				5.00

NOTE: *Evans* c-21. *Gulacy* c-7, 20. *Spiegle* a-34, 35, 37. *Ken Steacy* painted c-17, 33.

AIRBOY COMICS (Air Fighters Comics No. 1-22)
Hillman Periodicals: V2#11, Dec, 1945 - V10#4, May, 1953 (No V3#3)

V2#11	70	210	438	775
12-Valkyrie-c/app.	47	141	286	500
V3#1,2(no #3)	39	117	208	360
4-The Heap app. in Skywolf	35	105	188	325
5,7,8,10,11	30	90	159	275
6-Valkyrie-c/app.	33	99	174	300
9-Origin The Heap	35	105	188	325
12-Skywolf & Airboy x-over; Valkyrie-c/app.	39	117	208	360
V4#1-Iron Lady app.	34	102	179	310
2,3,12: 2-Rackman begins	24	72	127	215
4-Simon & Kirby-c	27	81	142	245
5-9,11-All S&K-a	26	78	136	235
10-Valkyrie-c/app.	27	81	145	250
V5#1-4,6-11: 4-Infantino Heap. 10-Origin The Heap	18	54	94	160
5-Skull-c	20	60	105	180
12-Krigstein-a(p)	20	60	105	175
V6#1-3,5-12: 6,8-Origin The Heap	17	51	88	150
4-Origin retold	22	66	116	195
V7#1-12: 7,8,10-Origin The Heap	17	51	88	150
V8#1,3,5-12	16	48	83	140
4-Krigstein-a	17	51	88	150
V9#1,3,4,6-12: 7-One pg. Frazetta ad	13	39	66	115
2-Valkyrie app.	14	42	72	125
5(#100)	14	42	72	125
V10#1-4	12	36	61	105

NOTE: *Barry* a-V2#3, 7. *Bolle* a-V4#12. *McWilliams* a-V3#7, 9. *Powell* a-V7#2, 3, V8#1, 6. *Starr* a-V5#1, 12. *Dick Wood* a-V4#12. Bondage-c V5#8.

AIRBOY MEETS THE PROWLER
Eclipse Comics: Aug, 1987 ($1.95, one-shot)

1-John Snyder, III-c/a				3.00

AIRBOY-MR. MONSTER SPECIAL
Eclipse Comics: July, 1987 ($1.75, one-shot)

1				3.00

AIRBOY VERSUS THE AIR MAIDENS
Eclipse Comics: July, 1988 ($1.95)

1				3.00

AIR FIGHTERS CLASSICS
Eclipse Comics: Nov, 1987 - No. 6, May, 1989 ($3.95, 68 pgs., B&W)

1-6: Reprints G.A. Air Fighters #2-7. 1-Origin Airboy				4.00

AIR FIGHTERS COMICS (Airboy Comics #23 (V2#11) on)
Hillman Periodicals: Nov, 1941; No. 2, Nov, 1942 - V2#10, Fall, 1945

V1#1-(Produced by Funnies, Inc.); Black Commander only app.	218	654	1364	2400
2(11/42)-(Produced by Quality artists & Biro for Hillman); Origin & 1st app. Airboy & Iron Ace; Black Angel (1st app.), Flying Dutchman & Skywolf (1st app.) begin; Fuje-a; Biro-c/a	1100	2083		4000
3-Origin/1st app. The Heap; origin Skywolf; 2nd Airboy app./c	173	519	1080	1900

4-Japan war-c	114	342	713	1250
5-Japanese octopus War-c	95	285	597	1050
6-Japanese soldiers as rats-c	105	315	656	1150
7-Classic Nazi swastika-c	100	300	625	1100
8-12: 8,10,11-War covers	77	231	483	850
V2#1-Classic Nazi War-c	80	240	500	875
2-Skywolf by Giunta; Flying Dutchman by Fuje; 1st meeting Valkyrie & Airboy (she worked for the Nazis in beginning); 1st app. Valkyrie (11/43); Valkyrie-c	105	315	656	1150
3,4,6,8,9	64	192	398	700
5,7: 5-Flag-c; Fuje-a. 7-Valkyrie app.	68	204	426	750
10-Origin The Heap & Skywolf	73	219	455	800

NOTE: *Fuje* a-V1#2, 5, 7, V2#2, 3, 5, 7-9. *Giunta* a-V2#2, 3, 7, 9.

AIRFIGHTERS MEET SGT. STRIKE SPECIAL, THE
Eclipse Comics: Jan, 1988 ($1.95, one-shot, stiff-c)

1-Airboy, Valkyrie, Skywolf app.				3.00

AIR FORCES (See American Air Forces)

AIRMAIDENS SPECIAL
Eclipse Comics: August, 1987 ($1.75, one-shot, Baxter paper)

1-Marisa becomes La Lupina (origin)				3.00

AIR RAIDERS
Marvel Comics (Star Comics)/Marvel #3 on: Nov, 1987- No. 5, Mar, 1988 ($1.00)

1,5: Kelley Jones-a in all				3.50
2-4: 2-Thunderhammer app.				2.50

AIRTIGHT GARAGE, THE (Also see Elsewhere Prince)
Marvel Comics (Epic Comics): July, 1993 - No. 4, Oct, 1993 ($2.50, limited series, Baxter paper)

1-4: Moebius-c/a/scripts				2.50

AIR WAR STORIES
Dell Publishing Co.: Sept-Nov, 1964 - No. 8, Aug, 1966

1-Painted-c; Glanzman-c/a begins	4	12	26	40
2-8: 2-Painted-c (all painted?)	3	9	17	25

A.K.A. GOLDFISH
Caliber Comics: 1994 - 1995 (B&W, $3.50/$3.95)

...:Ace; ...:Jack; ...:Queen; ...:Joker; ...:King -Brian Michael Bendis-s/a				4.00
TPB (1996, $17.95)				20.00
Goldfish: The Definitive Collection (Image, 2001, $19.95) r/series plus promo art and new prose story; intro. by Matt Wagner				20.00

AKIKO
Sirius: Mar, 1996 - Present ($2.50/$2.95, B&W)

1-Crilley-c/a/scripts in all				5.00
2				4.00
3-39: 25-($2.95, 32 pgs.)-w/Asala back-up pages				3.00
40-46: 40-Begin $2.95-c				3.00
TPB Volume 1,4 ('97, 2/00, $14.95) 1-r/1-7. 4-r/#19-25				15.00
TPB Volume 2,3 ('98, '99, $11.95) 2-r/#8-13. 3- r/#14-18				12.00

AKIKO ON THE PLANET SMOO
Sirius: Dec, 1995 ($3.95, B&W)

V1#1-($3.95)-Crilley-c/a/scripts; gatefold-c	1	3	5	7
Ashcan ('95, mail offer)				3.00
Hardcover V1#1 (12/95, $19.95, B&W, 40 pgs.)				20.00
The Color Edition(2/00,$4.95)				5.00

AKIRA
Marvel Comics (Epic Comics): Sept, 1988 - No. 38, Dec, 1995 ($3.50/$3.95/$6.95, deluxe, 68 pgs.)

1-Manga by Katsuhiro Otomo	3	9	17	25
1,2-2nd printings (1989, $3.95)				5.00
2	2	6	9	12
3-5	1	3	6	9
6-16	1	3	5	7
17-33: 17-$3.95-c begins				6.00
34-38: 34-(1994)-$6.95-c begins. 35-37: 35-(1995). 37-Texeira back-up, Gibbons, Williams pin-ups. 38-Moebius, Allred, Pratt, Toth, Romita, Van Fleet, O'Neill, Madureira pin-ups.	1	3	6	9

Alarming Tales #3 © HARV

Alias #1 © MAR

Alien Legion #16 © Carl Potts

	GD2.0	FN6.0	VF8.0	NM9.4

ALADDIN & HIS WONDERFUL LAMP (See Dell Jr Treasury #2)

ALAN LADD (See The Adventures of...)

ALAN MOORE'S AWESOME UNIVERSE HANDBOOK
Awesome Entertainment: Apr, 1999 - Present ($2.95, B&W)

1-Alan Moore-text/ Alex Ross-sketch pages and 2 covers ... 3.00

ALAN MOORE'S SONGBOOK
Caliber Comics: 1998 ($5.95, B&W)

1-Alan Moore song lyrics w/illust. by various ... 6.00

ALARMING ADVENTURES
Harvey Publications: Oct, 1962 - No. 3, Feb, 1963

1-Crandall/Williamson-a	8	24	60	100
2-Williamson/Crandall-a	5	15	38	60
3	4	12	30	50

NOTE: *Bailey* a-1, 3. *Crandall* a-1p, 2i. *Powell* a-2(2). *Severin* c-1-3. *Torres* a-2? *Tuska* a-1. *Williamson* a-1i, 2p.

ALARMING TALES
Harvey Publications (Western Tales): Sept, 1957 - No. 6, Nov, 1958

1-Kirby-a(4); Kamandi prototype story by Kirby	25	75	130	225
2-Kirby-a(4)	19	57	99	165
3,4-Kirby-a. 4-Powell, Wildey-a	14	42	72	120
5-Kirby/Williamson-a; Wildey-a; Severin-a	15	45	77	130
6-Williamson-a?; Severin-c	12	36	61	100

ALBEDO
Thoughts And Images: Apr, 1985 - No. 14, Spring, 1989 (B&W)
Antarctic Press: (Vol. 2) Jun, 1991 - No. 10 ($2.50)

0-Yellow cover; 50 copies	6	18	42	70
0-White cover, 450 copies	3	9	17	24
0-Blue, 1st printing, 500 copies	3	9	17	24
0-Blue, 2nd printing, 1000 copies	2	6	10	14
0-3rd & 4th printing				5.00
1-Dark red	2	6	10	14
1-Bright red	1	3	5	7
2-1st app. Usagi Yojimbo by Stan Sakai; 2000 copies - no 2nd printing				
	2	6	10	14
3				5.00
4-Usagi Yojimbo-c				6.00
5-14				3.00
(Vol. 2) 1-10, Color Special				3.00

ALBEDO ANTHROPOMORPHICS
Antarctic Press: (Vol. 3) Spring, 1994 - No. 4, Jan, 1996 ($2.95, color); (Vol. 4) Dec, 1999 - No. 2, Jan, 1999 ($2.95/$2.99, B&W)

V3#1-4-Steve Gallacci-c/a. V4#1,2 ... 3.00

ALBERTO (See The Crusaders)

ALBERT THE ALLIGATOR & POGO POSSUM (See Pogo Possum)

ALBUM OF CRIME (See Fox Giants)

ALBUM OF LOVE (See Fox Giants)

AL CAPP'S DOGPATCH (Also see Mammy Yokum)
Toby Press: No. 71, June, 1949 - No. 4, Dec, 1949

71(#1)-Reprints from Tip Top #112-114	25	75	130	225
2-4: 4-Reprints from Li'l Abner #73	17	51	88	150

AL CAPP'S SHMOO (Also see Oxydol-Dreft & Washable Jones & Shmoo)
Toby Press: July, 1949 - No. 5, Apr, 1950 (None by Al Capp)

1	40	120	220	380
2-5: 3-Sci-fi trip to moon. 4-X-mas cover; origin/1st app. Super-Shmoo				
	29	87	153	265

AL CAPP'S WOLF GAL
Toby Press: 1951 - No. 2, 1952

1,2-Edited-r from Li'l Abner #63,64	35	105	185	320

ALEXANDER THE GREAT (Movie)
Dell Publishing Co.: No. 688, May, 1956

Four Color 688-Buscema-a; photo-c	7	21	49	85

ALF (TV) (See Star Comics Digest)

	GD2.0	FN6.0	VF8.0	NM9.4

Marvel Comics: Mar, 1988 - No. 50, Feb, 1992 ($1.00)

1-Photo-c				4.00
1-2nd printing				2.50
2-19: 6-Photo-c				2.50
20-22: 20-Conan parody. 21-Marx Brothers. 22-X-Men parody				3.00
23-30: 24-Rhonda-c/app. 29-3-D cover				2.50
31-43,46-49				3.00
44,45: 44-X-Men parody. 45-Wolverine, Punisher, Capt. America-c				4.00
50-($1.75, 52 pgs.)-Final issue; photo-c				4.00
Annual 1-3: 1-Rocky & Bullwinkle app. 2-Sienkiewicz-c. 3-TMNT parody				3.00
...Comics Digest 1,2: 1-(1988)-Reprints Alf #1,2	1	3	6	8
Holiday Special 1,2 ('88, Wint. '89, 68 pgs.): 2-X-Men parody-c				3.00
Spring Special 1 (Spr/89, $1.75, 68 pgs.) Invisible Man parody				3.00
TPB (68 pgs.) r/#1-3; photo-c				5.00

ALFRED HARVEY'S BLACK CAT
Lorne-Harvey Productions: 1995 ($3.50, B&W/color)

1-Origin by Mark Evanier & Murphy Anderson; contains history of Alfred Harvey
  & Harvey Publications; 5 pg. B&W Sad Sack story; Hildebrandts-c ... 4.00

ALGIE
Timor Publ. Co.: Dec, 1953 - No. 3, 1954

1-Teenage	6	18	29	40
1-Misprint exists w/Secret Mysteries #19 inside	8	24	42	60
2,3	4	12	19	25
Accepted Reprint #2(2nd)	3	8	12	15
Super Reprint #15	2	6	9	12

ALIAS:
Now Comics: July, 1990 - No. 5, Nov, 1990 ($1.75)

1-5: 1-Sienkiewicz-c ... 2.25

ALIAS
Marvel Comics (MAX Comics): Nov, 2001 - Present ($2.99)

1-Bendis-s/Gaydos-a/Mack-c; intro Jessica Jones; Luke Cage app.				5.00
2-5				3.00

ALICE (New Adventures in Wonderland)
Ziff-Davis Publ. Co.: No. 10, 7-8/51 - No. 11(#2), 11-12/51

10-Painted-c; Berg-a	23	69	121	210
11-(#2 on inside) Dave Berg-a	13	39	66	115

ALICE AT MONKEY ISLAND (See The Adventures of Alice)
Pentagon Publ. Co. (Civil Service): No. 3, 1946

3	9	27	49	70

ALICE IN WONDERLAND (Disney; see Advs. of Alice, Dell Jr. Treasury #1, The Dreamery, Movie Comics, Walt Disney Showcase #22, and World's Greatest Stories)
Dell Publishing Co.: No. 24, 1940; No. 331, 1951; No. 341, July, 1951

Single Series 24 (#1)(1940)	42	125	252	440
Four Color 331, 341-"Unbirthday Party w/..."	14	42	98	185
1-(Whitman; 3/84)-r/4-Color #331				5.00

ALIEN ENCOUNTERS (Replaces Alien Worlds)
Eclipse Comics: June, 1985 - No. 14, April, 1987 ($1.75, Baxter paper, mature)

1-14: Nudity, strong language in all. 9-Snyder-a ... 3.00

ALIEN LEGION (See Epic & Marvel Graphic Novel #25)
Marvel Comics (Epic Comics): Apr, 1984 - No. 20, Sept, 1987

nn-With bound-in trading card; Austin-i				4.00
2-20: 2-$1.50-c. 7,8-Portacio-i				3.00

ALIEN LEGION (2nd Series)
Marvel Comics (Epic): Aug, 1987(indicia)(10/87 on-c) - No. 18, Aug, 1990

V2#1-18-Stroman-a in all. 7-18-Farmer-i ... 2.25

ALIEN LEGION: (Series of titles; all Marvel/Epic Comics)
--BINARY DEEP, 1993 ($3.50, one-shot, 52 pgs.), nn-With bound-in trading card ... 3.50

--JUGGER GRIMROD, 8/92 ($5.95, one-shot, 52 pgs.) Book 1 ... 6.00

--ONE PLANET AT A TIME, 5/93 - Book 3, 7/93 ($4.95, squarebound, 52 pgs.)
  Book 1-3: Hoang Nguyen-a ... 5.00

Aliens: Labyrinth #3 © 20th Century Fox

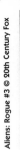

Aliens: Rogue #3 © 20th Century Fox

All-American Comics #4 © DC

--ON THE EDGE (The... #2 & 3), 11/90 - No. 3, 1/91 ($4.50, 52 pgs.)
1-3-Stroman & Farmer-a ... 4.50

--TENANTS OF HELL, '91 - No. 2, '1 ($4.50, squarebound, 52 pgs.)
Book 1,2-Stroman-c/a(p) ... 4.50

ALIEN NATION (Movie)
DC Comics: Dec, 1988 ($2.50; 68 pgs.)
1-Adaptation of film; painted-c ... 4.00

ALIEN RESURRECTION (Movie)
Dark Horse Comics: Oct, 1997 - No. 2, Nov, 1997 ($2.50; limited series)
1,2-Adaptation of film; Dave McKean-c ... 3.00

ALIENS, THE (Captain Johner and...)(Also see Magnus Robot Fighter...)
Gold Key: Sept-Dec, 1967; No. 2, May, 1982
1-Reprints from Magnus #1,3,4,6-10; Russ Manning-a in all
       3   9   20   30
2-(Whitman) Same contents as #1 ... 6.00

ALIENS (Movie) (See Alien: The Illustrated..., Dark Horse Comics & Dark Horse Presents #24)
Dark Horse Comics: May, 1988 - No. 6, July, 1989 ($1.95, B&W, limited series)
1-Based on movie sequel;1st app. Aliens in comics 2   6   11   15
1-2nd - 6th printings; 4th w/new inside front-c ... 3.00
2   1   3   5   7
2-2nd & 3rd printing, 3-6-2nd printings ... 3.00
3 ... 5.00
4-6 ... 4.00
Mini Comic 1 (2/89, 4x6")-Was included with Aliens Portfolio ... 4.00
Collection 1 ($10.95,)-r/#1-6 plus Dark Horse Presents #24 plus new-a ... 12.00
Collection 1-2nd printing (1991, $11.95)-On higher quality paper than 1st print;
    Dorman painted-a ... 12.00
Hardcover ('90, $24.95, B&W)-r/1-6, DHP #24 ... 25.00
Platinum Edition - (See Dark Horse Presents: Aliens Platinum Edition) ... -

ALIENS
Dark Horse Comics: V2#1, Aug, 1989 - No. 4, 1990 ($2.25, limited series)
V2#1-Painted art by Denis Beauvais ... 5.00
1-2nd printing (1990), 2-4 ... 3.00

ALIENS (Series of titles, all Dark Horse)
--ALCHEMY, 10/97 - No. 3, 11/97 ($2.95), 1-3-Corben-c/a, Arcudi-s ... 3.00
--APOCALYPSE - THE DESTROYING ANGELS, 1/99 - No. 4, 4/99 ($2.95)
1-4-Doug Wheatly-a/Schultz-s ... 3.00
--BERSERKERS, 1/95 - No. 4, 4/95 ($2.50) 1-4 ... 3.00
--COLONIAL MARINES, 1/93 - No. 10, 7/94 ($2.50) 1-10 ... 3.00
--EARTH ANGEL, 8/94 ($2.95) 1-Byrne-s/story; wraparound-c ... 3.00
--EARTH WAR, 6/90 - No. 4, 10/90 ($2.50) 1-All have Sam Kieth & Bolton
    painted-c ... 5.00
1-2nd printing, 3,4 ... 3.00
2 ... 4.00
--GENOCIDE, 11/91 - No. 4, 2/92 ($2.50) 1-4-Arthur Suydam painted-c. 4-
    Wraparound-c, poster ... 3.00
--GLASS CORRIDOR, 6/98 ($2.95) 1-David Lloyd-s/a
--HARVEST (See Aliens: Hive)
--HAVOC, 6/97 - No. 2, 7/97 ($2.95) 1,2: Schultz-s, Kent Williams-c, 40 artists
    including Art Adams, Kelley Jones, Duncan Fegredo, Kevin Nowlan ... 3.00
--HIVE, 2/92 - No. 4,5/92 ($2.50) 1-4: Kelley Jones-c/a in all ... 3.00
...Harvest TPB ('98, $16.95) r/series; Bolton-c ... 17.00
--KIDNAPPED, 12/97 - No. 3, 2/98 ($2.50) 1-3 ... 3.00
--LABYRINTH, 9/93 - No. 4, 1/94 ($2.50)1-4: 1-Painted-c ... 3.00
--LOVESICK, 12/96 ($2.95) 1 ... 3.00
--MONDO HEAT, 2/96 ($2.50) nn-Sequel to Mondo Pest ... 3.00
--MONDO PEST, 4/95 ($2.95, 44 pgs.)nn-r/Dark Horse Comics #22-24 ... 3.00
--MUSIC OF THE SPEARS, 1/94 - No. 4, 4/94 ($2.50) 1-4 ... 3.00
--NEWT'S TALE, 6/92 - No. 2, 7/92 ($4.95) 1,2-Bolton-a ... 5.00

--PIG, 3/97 ($2.95)1 ... 3.00
--PREDATOR: THE DEADLIEST OF SPECIES, 7/93 - No. 12,8/95 ($2.50)
1-Bolton painted-c; Guice-a(p) ... 5.00
1-Embossed foil platinum edition ... 10.00
2-12: Bolton painted-c. 2,3-Guice-a(p) ... 3.00
--PURGE, 8/97 ($2.95) nn-Hester-a ... 3.00
--ROGUE, 4/993 - No. 4, 7/93 ($2.50)1-4: Painted-c ... 3.00
--SACRIFICE, 5/93 ($4.95, 52 pgs.) nn-P. Milligan scripts; painted-c/a ... 5.00
--SALVATION, 11/93 ($4.95, 52 pgs.)nn-Mignola-c/a(p); Gibbons script ... 5.00
--SPECIAL, 6/97 ($2.50) 1 ... 3.00
--STALKER, 6/98 ($2.50)1-David Wenzel-s/a ... 3.00
--STRONGHOLD, 5/94 - No. 4, 9/94 ($2.50) 1-4 ... 3.00
--SURVIVAL, 2/98 - No. 3, 4/98 ($2.95)1-3-Tony Harris-c ... 3.00
ALIENS VS. PREDATOR (See Dark Horse Presents #36)
Dark Horse Comics: June, 1990 - No. 4, Dec, 1990 ($2.50; limited series)
1-Painted-c   1   3   6   8
1-2nd printing ... 3.00
0-(7/90, $1.95, B&W)-r/Dark Horse Pres.#34-36 1   3   6   9
2,3 ... 5.00
4-Dave Dorman painted-c ... 4.00
Annual (7/99, $4.95) Jae Lee-c ... 5.00
--VS. PREDATOR: BOOTY, 1/96 ($2.50) nn-painted-c ... 3.00
--VS. PREDATOR: DUEL, 3/95 - No. 2, 4/95 ($2.50) 1,2 ... 3.00
--VS. PREDATOR: ETERNAL, 6/98 - No. 4, 9/98 ($2.50)1-4: Edginton-s/Maleev-
    a; Fabry-c ... 3.00
--VS. PREDATOR VS. THE TERMINATOR, 4/00 - No. 4, 7/00 ($2.95)
1-4: Ripley app.; Dwayne Turner-c ... 3.00
--VS. PREDATOR: WAR, 0, 5/95 - No. 4, 8/95 ($2.50) 0-4: Corben painted-c ... 3.00
--VS. PREDATOR: XENOGENESIS, 12/99 - No. 4, 3/00 ($2.95) 1-4: Watson-s/
    Mel Rubi-a ... 3.00
--WRAITH, 7/98 ($2.95)1-Jay Stephens-s ... 3.00
--XENOGENESIS, 8/99 - No. 4, 11/99 ($2.95) 1-4: T&M Bierbaum-s ... 3.00
ALIEN TERROR (See 3-D Alien Terror)
ALIEN: THE ILLUSTRATED STORY (Also see Aliens)
Heavy Metal Books: 1980 ($3.95, soft-c, 8x11")
nn-Movie adaptation; Simonson-a   2   6   13   20
ALIEN³ (Movie)
Dark Horse Comics: June, 1992 - No. 3, July, 1992 ($2.50, limited series)
1-3: Adapts 3rd movie; Suydam painted-c ... 3.00
ALIEN WORLDS (Also see Eclipse Graphic Album #22)
Pacific Comics/Eclipse: Dec, 1982 - No. 9, Jan, 1985
1,2,4: 2,4-Dave Stevens-c/a ... 6.00
3,5-9: ... 3.00
3-D No. 1-Art Adams 1st published art ... 6.00
ALISON DARE, LITTLE MISS ADVENTURES (Also see Return of ...)
Oni Press: Sept, 2000 ($4.50, B&W, one-shot)
1-J. Torres-s/J.Bone-c/a ... 4.50
ALISTER THE SLAYER
Midnight Press: Oct, 1995 ($2.50)
1-Boris-c ... 2.50
ALL-AMERICAN COMICS (...Western #103-126, ...Men of War #127 on; also
see The Big All-American Comic Book)
All-American/National Periodical Publ.: April, 1939 - No. 102, Oct, 1948
1-Hop Harrigan (1st app.), Scribbly by Mayer (1st DC app.), Toonerville Folks,
    Ben Webster, Spot Savage, Mutt & Jeff, Red White & Blue (1st app.), Adv. in
    the Unknown, Tippie, Reg'lar Fellers, Skippy, Bobby Thatcher, Mystery Men of
    Mars, Daiseybelle, Wiley of West Point begin 700 2100 4200 6800
2-Ripley's Believe it or Not begins, ends #24 200 600 1100 1900
3-5: 5-The American Way begins, ends #10 155 465 880 1400

All-American Comics #99 © DC

All-American Men of War #7 © DC

All-American Western #104 © DC

	GD2.0	FN6.0	VF8.0	NM9.4

	GD2.0	FN6.0	VF8.0	NM9.4
6,7: 6-Last Spot Savage; Popsicle Pete begins, ends #26, 28. 7-Last Bobby Thatcher	130	390	700	1150
8-The Ultra Man begins & 1st-c app.	200	600	1250	2200
9,10: 10-X-Mas-c	120	360	680	1100
11,15: 11-Ultra Man-c. 15-Last Tippie & Reg'lar Fellars; Ultra Man-c	130	390	700	1150
12-14: 12-Last Toonerville Folks	105	315	630	1050
16-(Rare)-Origin/1st app. Green Lantern by Sheldon Moldoff (c/a)(7/40) & begin series; appears in costume on-c & one panel inside; created by Martin Nodell. Inspired in 1940 by a switchman's green lantern that would give trains the go ahead to proceed.	8214	24,640	57,500	115,000
17-2nd Green Lantern	1250	3750	8750	17,500
18-N.Y. World's Fair-c/story	846	2538	5500	11,000
19-Origin/1st app. The Atom (10/40); last Ultra Man	1357	4071	9500	19,000
20-Atom dons costume; Ma Hunkle becomes Red Tornado (c/a)(1st DC costumed heroine, before Wonder Woman, 11/40); Rescue on Mars begins, ends #25; 1 pg. origin Green Lantern	430	1290	2795	5600
21-23: 21-Last Wiley of West Point & Skippy. 23-Last Daiseybelle; 3 Idiots begin, end #82	273	819	1705	3000
24-Sisty & Dinky become the Cyclone Kids; Ben Webster ends; origin Dr. Mid-Nite & Sargon, The Sorcerer in text with app.	300	900	1875	3500
25-Origin & 1st story app. Dr. Mid-Nite by Stan Asch; Hop Harrigan becomes Guardian Angel; last Adventure in the Unknown	833	2500	5200	10,000
26-Origin/1st story app. Sargon, the Sorcerer	350	1050	2188	4200
27: #27-32 are misnumbered in indicia with correct No. appearing on-c. Intro. Doiby Dickles, Green Lantern's sidekick	367	1100	2292	4400
28-Hop Harrigan gives up costumed i.d.	173	519	1080	1900
29,30	173	519	1080	1900
31-40: 35-Doiby learns Green Lantern's i.d.	127	381	795	1400
41-50: 50-Solomon Grundy	105	315	656	1150
51-60: 59-Scribbly & the Red Tornado ends	89	237	556	975
61-Origin/1st app. Solomon Grundy (11/44)	462	1380	3000	6000
62-70: 70-Kubert Sargon; intro Sargon's helper, Maximillian O'Leary	82	246	511	900
71-88: 71-Last Red White & Blue. 72-Black Pirate begins (not in #74-82); last Atom. 73-Winky, Blinky & Noddy begins, ends #82. 79,83-Mutt & Jeff-c.	68	205	426	750
89-Origin & 1st app. Harlequin	105	315	656	1150
90-99: 90-Origin/1st app. Icicle. 99-Last Hop Harrigan (Scarce)	100	300	625	1100
100-1st app. Johnny Thunder by Alex Toth (8/48); western theme begins (Scarce)	190	570	1187	2100
101-Last Mutt & Jeff (Scarce)	127	381	795	1400
102-Last Green Lantern, Black Pirate & Dr. Mid-Nite (Scarce)	273	819	1705	3000

NOTE: No Atom in 47, 62-69. **Kinstler** Black Pirate-89. **Stan Aschmeier** a (Dr. Mid-Nite) 25-84; c-7. **Mayer** c-1, 2(part), 6, 10. **Moldoff** c-16-23. **Nodell** c-31. **Paul Reinman** a (Green Lantern)-53-55p, 56-64, 87; (Black Pirate)-83-88, 90; c-52, 55-76, 78, 80, 81, 87. **Toth** a-88, 92, 96, 98-102; c(p)-92, 96-102. Scribbly by **Mayer** in 1-59. Ultra Man by **Mayer** in 8-19.

ALL-AMERICAN COMICS (Also see All Star Comics 1999 crossover titles)
DC Comics: May, 1999 ($1.99, one-shot)

1-Golden Age Green Lantern and Johnny Thunder; Barreto-a				2.25

ALL-AMERICAN MEN OF WAR (Previously All-American Western)
National Periodical Publ.: No. 127, Aug-Sept, 1952 - No. 117, Sept-Oct, 1966

127 (#1, 1952)	78	234	663	1250
128 (1952)	50	150	400	725
2(12-1/52-53)-5	43	129	344	625
6-Devil Dog story; Ghost Squadron story	34	102	255	460
7-10: 8-Sgt. Storm Cloud-s	34	102	255	460
11-16,18: 18-Last precode (2/55)	31	93	211	380
17-1st Frogman-s in this title	31	93	222	400
19,20,22-27	22	66	151	270
21-Easy Co. prototype	24	72	165	295
28 (12/55)-1st Sgt. Rock prototype; Kubert-a	30	90	210	375
29,30,32-Wood-a	23	69	160	260
31,33-38,40: 39-Gunner prototype-s. 35-Greytone-c. 36-Little Sure Shot prototype-s. 38-1st S.A. issue	18	54	123	220
39 (11/56)-2nd Sgt Rock prototype; 1st Easy Co.?	26	78	182	325

41,43-47,49,50: 46-Tankbusters-c/s	15	45	105	180
42-Pre-Sgt. Rock Easy Co.-c/s	16	48	112	200
48-Easy Co.-c/s; Nick app.; Kubert-a	16	48	112	200
51-56,58-62,65,66: 61-Gunner-c/s	11	33	80	135
57(5/58),63,64 -Pre-Sgt. Rock Easy Co.-c/s	16	48	110	190
67-1st Gunner & Sarge by Andru & Esposito	31	93	222	400
68,69: 68-2nd app. Gunner & Sarge. 69-1st Tank Killer-c/s	14	42	100	170
70	11	33	77	130
71-80: 71,72,76-Tank Killer-c/s. 74-Minute Commandos-c/s	8	24	56	90
81,84-88: 88-Last 10¢ issue	7	21	53	85
82-Johnny Cloud begins(1st app.), ends #117	13	39	91	155
83-2nd Johnny Cloud	8	24	56	90
89-100: 89-Battle Aces of 3 Wars begins, ends #98	5	15	34	55
101-111,113-117: 111,114,115-Johnny Cloud. 117-Johnny Cloud-c & 3-part story	4	12	26	40
112-Balloon Buster series begins, ends #114,116	4	12	29	45

NOTE: Frogman stories in 17, 38, 44, 45, 50, 51, 53, 55-58, 63, 65, 66, 72, 76, 77. **Colan** a-112. **Drucker** a-47, 58, 61, 63, 65, 69, 71, 74, 77. **Grandenetti** c(p)-127, 128, 2-17(most). **Heath** a-14, 27, 32, 38, 41, 45, 47, 50, 51, 55-58, 62, 64, 71, 75, 76, 78, 95, 111-117; c-85, 91, 94-96, 100, 101, 110-112, others? **Infantino** a-8. **Kirby** a-128('52), 2, 3, 5. **Kubert** a-22, 24, 28, 29, 33, 34, 36, 38, 39, 41-43, 47-50, 52, 53, 55, 56, 59, 60, 63-65, 69, 71-73, 76, 102, 103, 105, 106, 108, 114; c-41, 44, 52, 54, 55, 58, 64, 69, 76, 77, 79, 102-106, 108, 113-117, others? Tank Killer in 69, 71, 76 by **Kubert**. **P. Reinman** c-55, 57, 61, 62, 71, 72, 74-76, 80. **J. Severin** a-58.

ALL-AMERICAN SPORTS
Charlton Comics: Oct, 1967

1	3	9	19	28

ALL-AMERICAN WESTERN (Formerly All-American Comics; Becomes All-American Men of War)
National Periodical Publications: No. 103, Nov, 1948 - No. 126, June-July, 1952 (103-121: 52 pgs.)

103-Johnny Thunder & his horse Black Lightning continues by Toth, ends #126; Foley of The Fighting 5th, Minstrel Maverick, & Overland Coach begin; Captain Tootsie by Beck; mentioned in Love and Death	52	157	314	550
104-Kubert-a	40	120	214	370
105,107-Kubert-a	34	102	179	310
106,108-110,112: 112-Kurtzman's "Pot-Shot Pete" (1 pg.)	27	81	145	250
111,114-116-Kubert-a	29	87	153	265
113-Intro. Swift Deer, J. Thunder's new sidekick (4-5/50); classic Toth-c; Kubert-a	31	93	165	285
117-126: 121-Kubert-a; bondage-c	20	60	105	175

NOTE: **G. Kane** c(p)-119, 120, 123. **Kubert** a-103-105, 107, 111, 121(1 pg.), 113-116, 121. **Toth** a-103-126; c(p)-103-116, 121, 122, 124-126. Some copies of #125 had #12 on-c.

ALL COMICS
Chicago Nite Life News: 1945

1	14	42	72	120

ALLEGRA
Image Comics (WildStorm): Aug, 1996 - No. 4, Dec, 1996 ($2.50)

1-4				2.50

ALLEY CAT (Alley Baggett)
Image Comics: July, 1999 - Present ($2.50)

Preview Edition				6.00
Prelude				5.00
Prelude w/variant-c				6.00
1-Photo-c				2.50
1-Painted-c by Dorian				3.50
1-Another Universe Edition, 1-Wizard World Edition				7.00
2-6				2.50
Lingerie Edition (10/99, $4.95) Photos, pin-ups, cover gallery				5.00
...Vs. Lady Pendragon ('99, $3.00) Stinsman-c				3.00

ALLEY OOP (See The Comics, The Funnies, Red Ryder and Super Book #9)
Dell Publishing Co.: No. 3, 1942

Four Color 3 (#1)	50	150	350	650

ALLEY OOP
Argo Publ.: Nov, 1955 - No. 3, Mar, 1956 (Newspaper reprints)

Alley Oop Adventures #1 © Newspaper Ent. Assoc.

All-Flash #10 © DC

All Humor Comics #10 © QUA

	GD2.0	FN6.0	VF8.0	NM9.4
1	17	51	88	150
2,3	12	36	61	100

ALLEY OOP
Dell Publishing Co.: 12-2/62-63 - No. 2, 9-11/63

1	6	18	42	75
2	5	15	35	60

ALLEY OOP
Standard Comics: No. 10, Sept, 1947 - No. 18, Oct, 1949

10	24	72	127	215
11-18: 17,18-Schomburg-c	19	57	99	165

ALLEY OOP ADVENTURES
Antarctic Press: Aug, 1998 - No. 3, Dec, 1998 ($2.95)

1-3-Jack Bender-s/a				3.00

ALLEY OOP ADVENTURES (Alley Oop Quarterly in indicia)
Antarctic Press: Sept, 1999 - No. 3, Mar, 2000 ($2.50/$2.99, B&W)

1-3-Jack Bender-s/a				3.00

ALL-FAMOUS CRIME (Formerly Law Against Crime #1-3; becomes All-Famous Police Cases #6 on)
Star Publications: No. 4, 2/50 - No. 5, 5/50; No. 8, 5/51 - No. 10, 11/51

4 (#1-1st series)-Formerly Law-Crime	29	87	153	265
5 (#2)	19	57	99	170
8 (#3-2nd series)	18	54	94	160
9 (#4)-Used in **SOTI**, illo- "The wish to hurt or kill couples in lovers' lanes is a not uncommon perversion;" L.B. Cole-c/a(r)/Law-Crime #3	35	105	185	320
10 (#5)-Becomes All-Famous Police Cases #6	17	51	88	150

NOTE: All have **L.B. Cole** covers.

ALL FAMOUS CRIME STORIES (See Fox Giants)

ALL-FAMOUS POLICE CASES (Formerly All Famous Crime #10 [#5])
Star Publications: No. 6, Feb, 1952 - No. 16, Sept, 1954

6	18	54	94	160
7,8: 7-Baker story; 8-Marijuana story	17	51	88	150
9-16	15	45	77	130

NOTE: L. B. Cole c-all; a-15, 1pg. Hollingsworth a-15.

ALL-FLASH (...Quarterly No. 1-5)
National Per. Publ./All-American: Summer, 1941 - No. 32, Dec-Jan, 1947-48

1-Origin The Flash retold by E. E. Hibbard; Hibbard c-1-10,12-14,16,31p.	1286	3858	9000	18,000
2-Origin recap	317	951	1979	3800
3,4	173	519	1080	1900
5-Winky, Blinky & Noddy begins (1st app.), ends #32	127	381	795	1400
6-10	105	315	656	1150
11-13: 12-Origin/1st The Thinker. 13-The King app.	91	273	568	1000
14-Green Lantern cameo	105	315	656	1150
15-20: 18-Mutt & Jeff begins, ends #22	75	225	469	825
21-31	59	177	369	650
32-Origin/1st app. The Fiddler; 1st Star Sapphire	109	327	682	1200

NOTE: Book length stories in 2-13, 16. Bondage c-31, 32. **Martin Nodell** c-15, 17-28.

ALL FOR LOVE (Young Love V3#5-on)
Prize Publications: Apr-May, 1957 - V3#4, Dec-Jan, 1959-60

V1#1	7	21	50	80
2-6: 5-Orlando-c	4	12	29	45
V2#1-5(1/59), 5(3/59)	3	9	21	32
V3#1(5/59), 1(7/59)-4: 2-Powell-a	2	6	15	22

ALL FUNNY COMICS
Tilsam Publ./National Periodical Publications (Detective): Winter, 1943-44 - No. 23, May-June, 1948

1-Genius Jones (1st app.), Buzzy (1st app., ends #4), Dover & Clover (see More Fun #93) begin; Bailey-a	50	150	300	525
2	24	72	127	220
3-10	15	45	77	130
11-13,15,18,19-Genius Jones app.	14	42	72	125
14,17,20-23	10	30	55	90

	GD2.0	FN6.0	VF8.0	NM9.4
16-DC Super Heroes app.	33	99	174	300

ALL GOOD
St. John Publishing Co.: Oct, 1949 (50¢, 260 pgs.)

nn-(8 St. John comics bound together)	64	192	398	700

NOTE: Also see Li'l Audrey Yearbook & Treasury of Comics.

ALL GOOD COMICS (See Fox Giants)
Fox Features Syndicate: No.1, Spring, 1946 (36 pgs.)

1-Joy Family, Dick Transom, Rick Evans, One Round Hogan	25	75	133	230

ALL GREAT (See Fox Giants)
Fox Feature Syndicate: 1946 (36 pgs.)

1-Crazy House, Bertie Benson Boy Detective, Gussie the Gob	25	75	133	230

ALL GREAT
William H. Wise & Co.: nd (1945?) (132 pgs.)

nn-Capt. Jack Terry, Joan Mason, Girl Reporter, Baron Doomsday; Torture scenes	40	120	232	400

ALL GREAT COMICS (Formerly Phantom Lady #13? Dagar, Desert Hawk No. 14 on)
Fox Features Syndicate: No. 14, Oct, 1947 - No. 13, Dec, 1947 (Newspaper strip reprints)

14(#12)-Brenda Starr & Texas Slim-r (Scarce)	55	165	341	600
13-Origin Dagar, Desert Hawk; Brenda Starr (all-r); Kamen-c; Dagar covers begin	59	177	369	650

ALL-GREAT CONFESSIONS (See Fox Giants)
ALL GREAT CRIME STORIES (See Fox Giants)
ALL GREAT JUNGLE ADVENTURES (See Fox Giants)

ALL HALLOW'S EVE
Innovation Publishing: 1991 ($4.95, 52 pgs.)

1-Painted-c/a				5.00

ALL HERO COMICS
Fawcett Publications: Mar, 1943 (100 pgs., cardboard-c)

1-Capt. Marvel Jr., Capt. Midnight, Golden Arrow, Ibis the Invincible, Spy Smasher, Lance O'Casey, 1st Banshee O'Brien; Raboy-c	164	492	1023	1800

ALL HUMOR COMICS
Quality Comics Group: Spring, 1946 - No. 17, December, 1949

1	20	60	105	180
2-Atomic Tot story; Gustavson-a	11	33	55	90
3-9: 3-Intro Kelly Poole who is cover feature #3 on. 5-1st app. Hickory?	6	18	33	48
8-Gustavson-a				
10-17	5	15	25	35

ALLIANCE, THE
Image Comics (Shadowline Ink): Aug, 1995 - No. 3, Nov, 1995 ($2.50)

1-3: (9/95)				2.50

ALL LOVE (...Romances No. 26)(Formerly Ernie Comics)
Ace Periodicals (Current Books): No. 26, May, 1949 - No. 32, May, 1950

26 (No. 1)-Ernie, Lily Belle app.	9	27	49	70
27-L.B. Cole-a	13	39	66	110
28-32	6	18	29	40

ALL-NEGRO COMICS
All-Negro Comics: June, 1947 (15¢)

1 (Rare)	625	1875	3438	5000

NOTE: Seldom found in fine or mint condition; many copies have brown pages.

ALL-NEW COLLECTORS' EDITION (Formerly Limited ...)
DC Comics, Inc.: Jan, 1978 - Vol. 8, No. C-62, 1979 (No. 54-58: 76 pgs.)

C-53-Rudolph the Red-Nosed Reindeer	4	16	29	45
C-54-Superman Vs. Wonder Woman	3	12	23	35
C-55-Superboy & the Legion of Super-Heroes; Wedding of Lightning Lad & Saturn Girl; Grell-c/a	3	12	23	35
C-56-Superman Vs. Muhammad Ali: story & wraparound N. Adams-c/a	5	20	34	55
C-56-Superman Vs. Muhammad Ali (Whitman variant)-low print				

All Picture All True Love Story #2 © STJ

All-Select Comics #9 © MAR

All Star Comics #22 © DC

	GD2.0	FN6.0	VF8.0	NM9.4
C-58-Superman Vs. Shazam	6	24	46	70
C-60-Rudolph's Summer Fun(8/78)	3	12	21	32
C-61-(See Famous First Edition-Superman #1)	4	16	26	40
C-62-Superman the Movie (68 pgs.; 1979)-Photo-c from movie plus photos inside (also see DC Special Series #25)	2	8	13	20

NOTE: **Buckler** a-C-58; c-C-58

ALL-NEW COMICS (…Short Story Comics No. 1-3)
Family Comics (Harvey Publications): Jan, 1943 - No. 14, Nov, 1946; No. 15, Mar-Apr, 1947 (10 x 13-1/2")

1-Steve Case, Crime Rover, Johnny Rebel, Kayo Kane, The Echo, Night Hawk, Ray O'Light, Detective Shane begin (all 1st app.?); Red Blazer on cover only; Sultan-a	291	873	1818	3200
2-Origin Scarlet Phantom by Kubert	105	315	656	1150
3	75	225	469	825
4	61	182	381	675
5-11: 5-Schomburg-c thru #11. 6-The Boy Heroes & Red Blazer (text story) begin, end #12; Black Cat app.; intro. Sparky in Red Blazer. 7-Kubert, Powell-a; Black Cat & Zebra app. 8,9: 8-Shock Gibson app.; Kubert, Powell-a; Schomburg-c. 9-Black Cat app.; Kubert-a. 10-The Zebra app. (from Green Hornet Comics); Kubert-a(3). 11-Girl Commandos, Man In Black app.	73	219	455	800
12,13: 12-Kubert-a. 13-Stuntman by Simon & Kirby; Green Hornet, Joe Palooka, Flying Fool app.; Green Hornet-c	59	177	369	650
14-The Green Hornet & The Man in Black Called Fate by Powell, Joe Palooka app.; J. Palooka-c by Ham Fisher	55	165	331	580
15-(Rare)-Small size (5-1/2x8-1/2"; B&W; 32 pgs.). Distributed to mail subscribers only. Black Cat and Joe Palooka app.	86	258	540	950

NOTE: Also see Boy Explorers No. 2, Flash Gordon No. 5, and Stuntman No. 3. **Powell** a-11. **Schomburg** c-5-11. Captain Red Blazer & Spark on c-5-11 (w/Boy Heroes #12).

ALL-OUT WAR
DC Comics: Sept-Oct, 1979 - No. 6, Aug, 1980 ($1.00, 68 pgs.)

1-The Viking Commando(origin), Force Three(origin), & Black Eagle Squadron begin	1	4	7	10
2-6				6.00

NOTE: **Ayers** a(p)-1-6. **Elias** r-2. **Evans** a-1-6. **Kubert** c-16.

ALL PICTURE ADVENTURE MAGAZINE
St. John Publishing Co.: Oct, 1952 - No. 2, Nov, 1952 (100 pg. Giants, 25¢, squarebound)

1-War comics	29	87	156	270
2-Horror-crime comics	43	129	257	450

NOTE: Above books contain three St. John comics rebound; variations possible. **Baker** art known in both.

ALL PICTURE ALL TRUE LOVE STORY
St. John Publishing Co.: Oct, 1952 - No. 2, Nov., 1952 (100 pgs., 25¢)

1-Canteen Kate by Matt Baker	47	141	286	500
2-Baker-c/a	32	96	171	295

ALL-PICTURE COMEDY CARNIVAL
St. John Publishing Co.: October, 1952 (100 pgs., 25¢)(Contains 4 rebound comics)

1-Contents can vary; Baker-a	40	120	232	400

ALL REAL CONFESSION MAGAZINE (See Fox Giants)

ALL ROMANCES (Mr. Risk No. 7 on)
A. A. Wyn (Ace Periodicals): Aug, 1949 - No. 6, June, 1950

1	10	30	55	80
2	5	15	25	35
3-6	5	15	23	30

ALL-SELECT COMICS (Blonde Phantom No. 12 on)
Timely Comics (Daring Comics): Fall, 1943 - No. 11, Fall, 1946

1-Capt. America (by Rico #1), Human Torch, Sub-Mariner begin; Black Widow story (4 pgs.); Classic Schomburg-c	1000	3000	6500	13,000
2-Red Skull app.	333	1000	2083	4000
3-The Whizzer app.	218	654	1364	2400
4,5-Last Sub-Mariner	155	465	966	1700
6-9: 6-The Destroyer app. 8-No Whizzer	123	369	769	1350
10-The Destroyer & Sub-Mariner app.; last Capt. America & Human Torch				

issue	123	369	769	1350
11-1st app. Blonde Phantom; Miss America app.; all Blonde Phantom-c by Shores	255	765	1591	2800

NOTE: **Schomburg** c-1-10. **Sekowsky** a-7. #7 & 8 show 1944 in indicia, but should be 1945.

ALL SPORTS COMICS (Formerly Real Sports Comics; becomes All Time Sports Comics No. 4 on)
Hillman Periodicals: No. 2, Dec-Jan, 1948-49; No. 3, Feb-Mar, 1949

2-Krigstein-a(p), Powell, Starr-a	36	108	191	330
3-Mort Lawrence-a	25	75	130	225

ALL STAR COMICS (All Star Western No. 58 on)
National Periodical Publ./All-American/DC Comics: Sum, '40 - No. 57, Feb-Mar, '51; No. 58, Jan-Feb, '76 -No. 74, Sept-Oct, '76

1-The Flash (#1 by E.E. Hibbard), Hawkman(by Shelly), Hourman(by Bernard Baily), The Sandman(by Creig Flessel), The Spectre(by Baily), Biff Bronson, Red White & Blue(ends #2) begin; Ultra Man's only app. (#1-3 are quarterly; #4 begins bi-monthly issues)	1180	3540	8250	16,500
2-Green Lantern (by Martin Nodell), Johnny Thunder begin; Green Lantern figure swipe from the cover of All-American Comics #16; Flash figure swipe from the cover of Flash Comics #8; Moldoff/Bailey-c (cut & paste-c.)	3215	9645	22,500	45,000
3-Origin & 1st app. The Justice Society of America (Win/40); Dr. Fate & The Atom begin	2571	7713	18,000	36,000
3-Reprint, Oversize 13-1/2x10". WARNING: This comic is an exact reprint of the original except for its size. DC published it in 1974 with a cover titling it as a Famous First Edition. There have been many reported cases of the outer cover being removed and the interior sold as the original edition. The reprint with the new outer cover removed is practically worthless. See Famous First Edition for value.				
4-1st adventure for J.S.A.	507	1521	3295	6600
5-1st app. Shiera Sanders as Hawkgirl (1st costumed super-heroine, 6-7/41)	438	1314	2847	5700
6-Johnny Thunder joins JSA	300	900	1875	3500
7-Batman, Superman, Flash cameo; last Hourman; Doiby Dickles app.	333	1000	2083	4000
8-Origin & 1st app. Wonder Woman (12-1/41-42)(added as 9 pgs. making book 76 pgs.; origin cont'd in Sensation #1; see W.W. #1 for more detailed origin); Dr. Fate debuts new helmet; Hop Harrigan text stories & Starman begin; Shiera app.; Hop Harrigan JSA guest; Starman & Dr. Mid-Nite become members	2571	7713	18,000	36,000
9-11: 9-JSA's girlfriends cameo; Shiera app.; J. Edgar Hoover of FBI made associate member of JSA. 10-Flash, Green Lantern cameo; Sandman new costume. 11-Wonder Woman begins; Spectre cameo; Shiera app.; Moldoff Hawkman-c	300	900	1875	3300
12-Wonder Woman becomes JSA Secretary	264	792	1648	2900
13,15: Sandman w/Sandy in #14 & 15. 15-Origin & 1st app. Brain Wave; Shiera app.	245	735	1534	2700
14-(12/42) Junior JSA Club begins; w/membership offer & premiums	250	750	1562	2750
16-20: 19-Sandman w/Sandy. 20-Dr. Fate & Sandman cameo	182	546	1136	2000
21-23: 21-Spectre & Atom cameo; Dr. Fate by Kubert; Dr. Fate, Sandman end. 22-Last Hop Harrigan; Flag-c. 23-Origin/1st app. Psycho Pirate; last Spectre & Starman	159	477	994	1750
24-Flash & Green Lantern cameo; Mr. Terrific only app.; Wildcat, JSA guest; Kubert Hawkman begins; Hitler-c	159	477	994	1750
25-27: 25-Flash & Green Lantern start again. 26-Robot-c. 27-Wildcat, JSA guest (#24-26: only All-American imprint)	136	408	852	1500
28-32	123	369	769	1350
33-Solomon Grundy & Doiby Dickles app.; classic Solomon Grundy cover. Last Solomon Grundy G.A. app.	317	951	1976	3800
34,35-Johnny Thunder cameo in both	118	354	738	1300
36-Batman & Superman JSA guests	282	846	1763	3100
37-Johnny Thunder cameo; origin & 1st app. Injustice Society; last Kubert Hawkman	155	465	966	1700
38-Black Canary begins; JSA Death issue	182	546	1136	2000
39,40: 39-Last Johnny Thunder	114	342	712	1250
41-Black Canary joins JSA; Injustice Society app. (2nd app.?)	114	342	712	1250
42-Atom & the Hawkman don new costumes	114	342	712	1250
43-49,51-56: 43-New logo; Robot-c. 55-Sci/Fi story. 56-Robot-c	114	342	712	1250

All Star Comics #74 © DC

All-Star Squadron #13 © DC

All Top Comics #12 © FOX

	GD2.0	FN6.0	VF8.0	NM9.4
50-Frazetta art, 3 pgs.	123	369	769	1350
57-Kubert-a, 6 pgs. (Scarce); last app. G.A. Green Lantern, Flash & Dr. Mid-Nite	164	492	1023	1800
V12 #58-(1976) JSA (Flash, Hawkman, Dr. Mid-Nite, Wildcat, Dr. Fate, Green Lantern, Star Spangled Kid, & Robin) app.; intro Power Girl.	3	9	17	25
V12 #59-68,70-74(1976-78)	2	6	9	12
V12 #69-1st Earth-2 Huntress (Helena Wayne)	2	6	15	22

NOTE: No Atom-27, 36; no Dr. Fate-13; no Flash-8, 9, 11-23; no Green Lantern-8, 9,11-23; Hawkman in 1-57 (only one to app. in all 57 issues); no Johnny Thunder-5, 36; no Wonder Woman-9, 10, 23. Book length stories in 4-9, 11-14, 18-22, 25, 26, 29, 30, 32-36, 42, 43. Johnny Peril in #42-46, 48, 49, 51, 52,54-57. **Baily** a-1-10, 12, 13, 14i, 15-20. **Burnley** Starman-8-13; c-12, 13. **Grell** c-58. **E.E. Hibbard** c-3, 4, 6-10. **Infantino** c-40. **Kubert** Hawkman-24-30, 33-37. **Lampert/Baily/Flessel** c-1, 2. **Moldoff** Hawkman-3-23; c-11. **Mart Nodell** c-25i, 26i, 27-32. **Purcell** c-5. **Simon & Kirby** Sandman 14-17, 19. **Staton** a-66-74p. c-74p. **Toth** a-37(2), 38(2), 40, 41; c-38, 41. **Wood** a-58i-63i, 64, 65; c-63i, 64, 65. Issues 1-7, 9-16 are 68 pgs.; #8 is 76 pgs.; #17-19 are 60 pgs.; #20-57 are 52 pgs.

ALL STAR COMICS (Also see crossover 1999 editions of Adventure, All-American, National, Sensation, Smash, Star Spangled and Thrilling Comics)
DC Comics: May, 1999 - No. 2, May, 1999 ($2.95, bookends for JSA x-over)

1,2-Justice Society in World War 2; Robinson-s/Johnson-c				3.00
...80-Page Giant (9/99, $4.95) Phantom Lady app.				5.00

ALL STAR INDEX, THE
Independent Comics Group (Eclipse): Feb, 1987 ($2.00, Baxter paper)

1				6.00

ALL-STAR SQUADRON (See Justice League of America #193)
DC Comics: Sept, 1981 - No. 67, Mar, 1987

1-Original Atom, Hawkman, Dr. Mid-Nite, Robotman (origin), Plastic Man, Johnny Quick, Liberty Belle, Shining Knight begin				5.00
2-46,48,49: 4, 7-Spectre app. 5-Danette Reilly becomes new Firebrand. 8-Re-intro Steel, the Indestructible Man. 12-Origin G.A. Hawkman retold. 23-Origin/1st app. The Amazing Man. 24-Batman app. 25-1st app. Infinity, Inc. (9/83), 26-Origin Infinity, Inc. (2nd app.). Robin app. 27-Dr. Fate vs. the Spectre. 30-35-Sspectre app. 33-Origin Freedom Fighters of Earth-X. 36,37-Superman vs. Capt. Marvel; Ordway-c. 47-Origin Starman				3.50
47-Origin Dr. Fate; McFarlane-a (1st small story)/part-c (7/85)	1	3	5	7
50-Double size; Crisis x-over				5.00
51-67: 51-56-Crisis x-over. 61-Origin Liberty Belle. 62-Origin The Shining Knight. 63-Origin Robotman. 65-Origin Johnny Quick. 66-Origin Tarantula				4.00
Annual 1-3: 1(11/82)-Retells origin of G.A. Atom, Guardian & Wildcat; Jerry Ordway's first pencils for DC.(1st work was inking artist Carmine Infantino in House of Mystery #94) 2(11/83)-Infinity, Inc. app. 3(9/84)				4.00

NOTE: **Buckler** a-1-5; c-1, 3-5, 51. **Kubert** c-2, 7-18. JLA app. in 14, 15. JSA app. in 4, 15, 19, 27, 28.

ALL-STAR STORY OF THE DODGERS, THE
Stadium Communications: Apr, 1979 ($1.00)

1	2	6	9	12

ALL STAR WESTERN (Formerly All Star Comics No. 1-57)
National Periodical Publ.: No. 58, Apr-May, 1951 - No. 119, June-July, 1961

58-Trigger Twins (ends #116), Strong Bow, The Roving Ranger & Don Caballero begin	44	132	264	460
59,60: Last 52 pgs.	25	75	133	230
61-66: 61-64-Toth-a	21	63	110	185
67-Johnny Thunder begins; Gil Kane-a	25	75	133	230
68-81: Last precode (2-3/55)	12	36	61	100
82-98: 97-1st S.A. issue	11	33	55	90
99-Frazetta-r/Jimmy Wakely #4	11	33	55	95
100	11	33	55	95
101-107,109-116,118,119	9	27	51	75
108-Origin J. Thunder; J. Thunder logo begins	21	63	110	190
117-Origin Super Chief	13	39	66	110

NOTE: **Gil Kane** c(p)-58, 59, 61, 63, 64, 68, 69, 70-95(most), 97-109(most). **Infantino** art in most issues. Madame .44 app.-#117-119.

ALL-STAR WESTERN (Weird Western Tales No. 12 on)
National Periodical Publications: Aug-Sept, 1970 - No. 11, Apr-May, 1972

1-Pow-Wow Smith-r; Infantino-a	4	12	26	40
2-Outlaw begins; El Diablo by Morrow begins; has cameos by Williamson,				

	GD2.0	FN6.0	VF8.0	NM9.4
Torres, Kane, Giordano & Phil Seuling	3	10	23	35
3-Origin El Diablo	3	9	20	30
4-6: 5-Last Outlaw issue. 6-Billy the Kid begins, ends #8	3	9	17	25
7-9-(52 pgs.) 9-Frazetta-a, 3pgs.(r)	3	9	20	30
10-(52 pgs.) Jonah Hex begins (1st app., 2-3/72)	33	99	250	450
11-(52 pgs.) 2nd app. Jonah Hex	15	45	105	180

NOTE: **Neal Adams** c-2-5; **Aparo** a-5. **G. Kane** a-3, 4, 6, 8. **Kubert** a-4r, 7-9r. **Morrow** a-2-4, 10, 11. No. 7-11 have 52 pgs..

ALL SURPRISE (Becomes Jeanie #13 on) (Funny animal)
Timely/Marvel (CPC): Fall, 1943 - No. 12, Winter, 1946-47

1-Super Rabbit, Gandy & Sourpuss begin	33	99	174	300
2	15	45	77	135
3-10,12	12	36	61	100
11-Kurtzman "Pigtales" art	13	39	66	110

ALL TEEN (Formerly All Winners; All Winners & Teen Comics No. 21 on)
Marvel Comics (WFP): No. 20, January, 1947

20-Georgie, Mitzi, Patsy Walker, Willie app.; Syd Shores-c	11	33	55	95

ALL-TIME SPORTS COMICS (Formerly All Sports Comics)
Hillman Per.: V2No. 4, Apr-May, 1949 - V2No. 7, Oct-Nov, 1949 (All 52 pgs.)

V2#4	23	69	121	210
5-7: 5-(V1#5 inside)-Powell-a; Ty Cobb sty. 7-Krigstein-p; Walter Johnson & Knute Rockne sty	17	51	88	150

ALL TOP
William H. Wise Co.: 1944 (132 pgs.)

Capt. V, Merciless the Sorceress, Red Robbins, One Round Hogan, Mike the M.P., Snooky, Pussy Katnip app.	30	90	162	280

ALL TOP COMICS (My Experience No. 19 on)
Fox Features Synd./Green Publ./Norlen Mag.: 1945; No. 2, Sum, 1946 - No. 18, Mar, 1949; 1957 - 1959

1-Cosmo Cat & Flash Rabbit begin (1st app.)	24	72	127	220
2 (#1-7 are funny animal)	11	33	55	95
3-7	9	27	49	70
8-Blue Beetle, Phantom Lady, & Rulah, Jungle Goddess begin (11/47); Kamen-c	245	735	1534	2700
9-Kamen-c	127	381	795	1400
10-Kamen bondage-c	136	408	852	1500
11-13,15-17: 15-Rulah-c. 15-No Blue Beetle	109	327	682	1200
14-No Blue Beetle; used in SOTI, illo- "Corpses of colored people strung up by their wrists"	141	423	881	1550
18-Dagar, Jo-Jo, Blue Beetle app.	68	205	426	750
6(1957-Green Publ.)-Patoruzu the Indian; Cosmo Cat on cover only. 6(1958-Literary Ent.)-Muggy Doo; Cosmo Cat on cover only. 6(1959-Norlen)-Atomic Mouse; Cosmo Cat on cover only. 6(1959)-Little Eva. 6(Cornell)-Supermouse on-c	5	15	23	30

NOTE: Jo-Jo by **Kamen**-12,18.

ALL TRUE ALL PICTURE POLICE CASES
St. John Publishing Co.: Oct, 1952 - No. 2, Nov, 1952 (100 pgs.)

1-Three rebound St. John crime comics	40	120	232	400
2-Three comics rebound	31	93	165	285

NOTE: Contents may vary.

ALL-TRUE CRIME (...Cases No. 26-35; formerly Official True Crime Cases)
Marvel/Atlas Comics: No. 26, Feb, 1948 - No. 52, Sept, 1952
(OFI #26,27/CFI #28,29/LCC #30-46/LMC #47-52)

26(#1)-Syd Shores-c	34	102	179	310
27(4/48)-Electric chair-c	25	75	133	230
28-41,43,48,50-52: 35-Photo-c	11	33	55	90
42,49-Krigstein-a. 49-Used in POP, pg 79	12	36	61	100

NOTE: **Robinson** a-47, 50. **Shores** c-26. **Tuska** a-48(3).

ALL-TRUE DETECTIVE CASES (Kit Carson No. 5 on)
Avon Periodicals: #2, Apr-May, 1954 - No. 4, Aug-Sept, 1954

2(#1)-Wood-a	22	66	116	200
3-Kinstler-c	12	36	61	100
4-r/Gangsters And Gun Molls #2; Kamen-a	19	57	99	165

All True Romance #3 © Artful Pub.

Alpha Flight #95 © MAR

Alpha Flight V2 #12 © MAR

	GD2.0	FN6.0	VF8.0	NM9.4
nn(100 pgs.)-7 pg. Kubert-a, Kinstler back-c	39	117	208	360

ALL TRUE ROMANCE (...Illustrated No. 3)
Artful Publ. #1-3/Harwell(Comic Media) #4-20?/Ajax-Farrell(Excellent Publ.)
No. 22 on/Four Star Comic Corp.: 3/51 - No. 20, 12/54; No. 22, 3/55 - No. 30?,
7/57; No. 3(#31), 9/57; No. 4 (#32), 11/57; No. 33, 2/58 - No. 34, 6/58

1 (3/51)	16	48	83	140
2 (10/51; 11/51 on-c)	8	24	45	65
3(12/51) - #5(5/52)	7	21	36	50
6-Wood-a, 9 pgs. (exceptional)	16	48	83	140
7-10 (2-#7s: #7(11/52, 9/52 inside, #7(11/52, 11/52 inside))				
	6	18	29	40
11-13,16-19(9/54),20(12/54) (no #21)	5	15	24	32
14-Marijuana story	5	15	25	35
22: Last precode issue (1st Ajax, 3/55)	5	15	24	32
23-27,29,30(7/57)	4	12	18	24
28 (9/56)-L. B. Cole, Disbrow-a	10	30	55	80
3(#31, 9/57),4(#32, 11/57),33,34 (Farrell, '57 - '58)	4	11	17	22

ALL WESTERN WINNERS (Formerly All Winners; becomes Western Winners
with No. 5; see Two-Gun Kid No. 5)
Marvel Comics(CDS): No. 2, Winter, 1948-49 - No. 4, April, 1949

2-Black Rider (origin & 1st app.) & his horse Satan, Kid Colt & his horse Steel, & Two-Gun Kid & his horse Cyclone begin; Shores c-2-4				
	80	240	500	875
3-Anti-Wertham editorial	40	120	220	380
4-Black Rider i.d. revealed; Heath, Shores-a	40	120	220	380

ALL WINNERS COMICS (All Teen #20) (Also see Timely Presents: ...)
USA No. 1-7/WFP No. 10-19/YAI No. 21: Summer, 1941 - No. 19, Fall, 1946; No.
21, Winter, 1946-47; (No #20) (No. 21 continued from Young Allies No. 20)

1-The Angel & Black Marvel only app.; Capt. America by Simon & Kirby, Human Torch & Sub-Mariner begin (#1 was advertised as All Aces); 1st app. All-Winners Squad in text story by Stan Lee				
	1714	5142	12,000	24,000
2-The Destroyer & The Whizzer begin; Simon & Kirby Captain America				
	446	1338	2900	5800
3	300	900	1875	3500
4-Classic War-c by Al Avison	317	951	1919	3800
5	205	615	1281	2250
6-The Black Avenger only app.; no Whizzer story; Hitler, Hirohito & Mussolini-c	240	720	1500	2650
7-10	173	519	1080	1900
11,13-18: 11-1st Atlas globe on-c (Winter, 1943-44; also see Human Torch #14). 14-16-No Human Torch	127	381	795	1400
12-Red Skull story; last Destroyer; no Whizzer story				
	155	465	966	1700
19-(Scarce) 1st story app. & origin All Winners Squad (Capt. America & Bucky, Human Torch & Toro, Sub-Mariner, Whizzer, & Miss America; r-in Fantasy Masterpieces #10	417	1250	2604	5000
21-(Scarce)-All Winners Squad; bondage-c	350	1050	2188	4200

NOTE: *Everett* Sub-Mariner-1, 3, 4; *Burgos* Torch-1, 3, 4. *Schomburg* c-1, 7-18. *Shores* c-19p, 21.
(2nd series - August, 1948, Marvel Comics (CDS))
(Becomes All Western Winners with No. 2)

1-The Blonde Phantom, Capt. America, Human Torch & Sub-Mariner app.				
	282	846	1763	3100

ALL YOUR COMICS (See Fox Giants)
Fox Feature Syndicate (R. W. Voight): Spring, 1946 (36 pgs.)

1-Red Robbins, Merciless the Sorceress app.	20	60	105	175

ALMANAC OF CRIME (See Fox Giants)

AL OF FBI (See Little Al of the FBI)

ALPHA AND OMEGA
Spire Christian Comics (Fleming H. Revell): 1978 (49¢)

nn	1	3	5	7

ALPHA CENTURION (See Superman, 2nd Series & Zero Hour)
DC Comics: 1996 ($2.95, one-shot)

1				3.00

ALPHA FLIGHT (See X-Men #120,121 & X-Men/Alpha Flight)
Marvel Comics: Aug, 1983 - No. 130, Mar, 1994 (#52-on are direct sales only)

	GD2.0	FN6.0	VF8.0	NM9.4
1-Byrne-a begins (52pgs.)-Wolverine & Nightcrawler cameo				4.00
2-12,14-16,18-32,35-50: 2-Vindicator becomes Guardian; origin Marrina & Alpha Flight. 3-Concludes origin Alpha Flight. 6-Origin Shaman. 7-Origin Snowbird. 10,11-Origin Sasquatch. 12-(52 pgs.)-Death of Guardian. 16-Wolverine cameo. 20-New headquarters. 25-Return of Guardian. 28-Last Byrne issue. 39-47,49-Portacio-a(i). 50-Double size; Portacio-a(i)				2.50
13,17,33,34: 13-Wolverine app. 17-X-Men x-over (70% r-/X-Men #109); Wolverine cameo. 33-X-Men (Wolverine) app. 34-Origin Wolverine				3.00
51-Jim Lee's 1st work at Marvel (10/87); Wolverine cameo; 1st Jim Lee Wolverine; Portacio-a(i)				5.00
52,53-Wolverine app.; Lee-a on Wolverine; Portacio-a(i); 53-Lee/Portacio-a				3.00
54-73,76,86,91-99,101-105: 54,63,64-No Jim Lee art. 54-Portacio-a(i). 55-62-Jim Lee-a(p). 71-Intro The Sorcerer (villain). 91-Dr. Doom app. 94-F.F. x-over. 99-Galactus, Avengers app. 102-Intro Weapon Omega				2.25
74,75,87-90,100: 74-Wolverine, Spider-Man & The Avengers app. 75-Double size ($1.95, 52 pgs.). 87-90-Wolverine. 4 part story w/Jim Lee-c. 89-Original Guardian returns. 100-($2.00, 52 pgs.)-Avengers & Galactus app.				3.00
106-Northstar revelation issue				2.50
106-2nd printing (direct sale only)				2.25
107-119,121-129: 107-X-Factor x-over. 110-112-Infinity War x-overs. 110, 111-Wolverine app. (brief). 111-Thanos cameo				2.00
120-($2.25)-Polybagged w/Paranormal Registration Act poster				2.25
130-($2.25, 52 pgs.)				2.50
Annual 1,2 (9/86, 12/87)				2.25
Special V2#1(6/92, $2.50, 52 pgs.)-Wolverine-c/story				2.50

NOTE: *Austin* c-1i, 2i, 53. *Byrne* c-81, 82. *Guice* c-85, 91-99. *Jim Lee* a(p)-51, 53, 55-62, 64; c-53, 87-90. *Mignola* a-29-31p. *Whilce Portacio* a(i)-39-47, 49-54.

ALPHA FLIGHT (2nd Series)
Marvel Comics: Aug, 1997 - No. 20, Mar, 1999 ($2.99/$1.99)

1-($2.99)-Wraparound cover				6.00
2,3: 2-Variant-c				4.00
4-11,13-20: 8,9-Wolverine-c/app.				3.00
12-($2.99) Death of Sasquatch; wraparound-c				4.00
.../Inhumans '98 Annual ($3.50) Raney-a				3.50

ALPHA FLIGHT: IN THE BEGINNING
Marvel Comics: July, 1997 ($1.95, one-shot)

(-1)-Flashback w/Wolverine				2.25

ALPHA FLIGHT SPECIAL
Marvel Comics: July, 1991 - No. 4, Oct, 1991 ($1.50, limited series)

1-4: 1-3-r-A.Flight #97-99 w/covers. 4-r-A.Flight #100				2.25

ALPHA KORPS
Diversity Comics: Sept, 1996 ($2.50)

1-Origin/1st app. Alpha Korps				2.50

ALPHA WAVE
Darkline Comics: Mar, 1987 ($1.75, 36 pgs.)

1				2.25

ALTERED IMAGE
Image Comics: Apr, 1998 - No. 3, Sept, 1998 ($2.50, limited series)

1-3-Spawn, Witchblade, Savage Dragon; Valentino-s/a				3.00

ALTER EGO
First Comics: May, 1986 - No. 4, Nov, 1986 (Mini-series)

1-4				2.25

ALVIN (TV) (See Four Color Comics No. 1042)
Dell Publishing Co.: Oct-Dec, 1962 - No. 28, Oct, 1973

12-021-212 (#1)	9	27	63	110
2	5	15	38	60
3-10	4	12	30	50
11-28	4	12	26	40
Alvin For President (10/64)	4	12	29	45
...& His Pals in Merry Christmas with Clyde Crashcup & Leonardo 1 (02-120-402)-12-2/64)	8	24	58	95
Reprinted in 1966 (12-023-604)	5	15	38	60

ALVIN & THE CHIPMUNKS
Harvey Comics: July, 1992 - No. 5, May, 1994

Amazing Adult Fantasy #12 © MAR

Amazing Adventures #28 © MAR

Amazing Detective Cases #9 © MAR

AM

| | GD2.0 | FN6.0 | VF8.0 | NM9.4 | | | GD2.0 | FN6.0 | VF8.0 | NM9.4 |

1-5   2.50

AMALGAM AGE OF COMICS, THE: THE DC COMICS COLLECTION
DC Comics: 1996 ($12.95, trade paperback)
nn-r/Amazon, Assassins, Doctor Strangefate, JLX, Legends of the Dark Claw,
& Super Soldier   13.00

AMANDA AND GUNN
Image Comics: Apr, 1997 - No. 4, Oct, 1997 ($2.95, B&W, limited series)
1-4   3.00

AMAZING ADULT FANTASY (Formerly Amazing Adventures #1-6; becomes
Amazing Fantasy #15)
Marvel Comics Group (AMI): No. 7, Dec, 1961 - No. 14, July, 1962

7-Ditko-c/a begins, ends #14	50	150	400	725
8-Last 10¢ issue	41	123	306	550
9-13: 12-1st app. Mailbag. 13-Anti-communist sty	39	118	292	525
14-Prototype issue (Professor X)	42	126	315	575

AMAZING ADVENTURE FUNNIES (Fantoman No. 2 on)
Centaur Publications: June, 1940 - No. 2, Sept. 1940

1-The Fantom of the Fair by Gustavson (r/Amaz. Mystery Funnies V2#7,V2#8), The Arrow, Skyrocket Steele From the Year X by Everett (r/AMF #2); Burgos-a	182	546	1136	2000
2-Reprints; Published after Fantoman #2	116	348	725	1275

NOTE: *Burgos a-1(2). Everett a-1(3). Gustavson a-1(5), 2(3). Pinajian a-2.*

AMAZING ADVENTURES (Also see Boy Cowboy & Science Comics)
Ziff-Davis Publ. Co.: 1950; No. 1, Nov, 1950 - No. 6, Fall, 1952 (Painted covers)
1950 (no month given) (8-1/2x11) (8 pgs.) Has the front & back cover plus
Schomburg story used in Amazing Advs. #1 (Sent to subscribers of Z-D s/f
magazines & ordered from mail for 10¢. Used to test market)

	47	141	286	500
1-Wood, Schomburg, Anderson, Whitney-a	73	219	455	800
2-5: 2-Schomburg-a. 2,4,5-Anderson-a. 3,5-Starr-a	38	114	203	350
6-Krigstein-a	39	117	208	360

AMAZING ADVENTURES (Becomes Amazing Adult Fantasy #7 on)
Atlas Comics (AMI)/Marvel Comics No. 3 on: June, 1961 - No. 6, Nov, 1961

1-Origin Dr. Droom (1st Marvel-Age Superhero) by Kirby; Kirby/Ditko-a (5 pgs.) Ditko & Kirby-a in all; Kirby throughout	109	327	926	1750
2	48	144	386	700
3-6: 6-Last Dr. Droom	42	126	315	575

AMAZING ADVENTURES
Marvel Comics Group: Aug, 1970 - No. 39, Nov, 1976

1-Inhumans by Kirby(p) & Black Widow (1st app. in Tales of Suspense #52) double feature begins	4	12	30	50
2-4: F.F. later app. 4-Last Inhumans by Kirby	2	6	15	22
5-8: Adams-a(p); 8-Last Black Widow; last 15¢-sz	3	9	21	32
9,10: Magneto app. 10-Last Inhumans (origin-r by Kirby)				
	2	6	13	20
11-New Beast begins(1st app. in mutated form; origin in flashback); X-Men cameo in flashback (#11-17 are X-Men tie-ins)	10	30	73	125
12-17: 12-Beast battles Iron Man. 13-Brotherhood of Evil Mutants x-over from X-Men. 15-X-Men app. 16-Rutland Vermont - Bald Mountain Halloween x-over; Juggernaut app. 17-Last Beast (origin); X-Men app.				
	3	10	23	35
18-War of the Worlds begins (5/73); 1st app. Killraven; Neal Adams-a(p)				
	2	6	13	20
19-35,38,39: 19-Chaykin-a. 25-Buckler-a. 35-Giffen's first published story (art), along with Deadly Hands of Kung-Fu #22 (3/76)	1	3	6	8
36,37-(Regular 25¢ edition)(7-8/76)	1	3	6	8
36,37-(30¢-c variants, limited distribution)	2	6	11	16

NOTE: *N. Adams c-6-8. Buscema a-1p, 2p. Colan a-3-5p, 26p. Ditko a-24r. Everett a(i)3-5, 7-9. Giffen a-35i, 38p. G. Kane c-11, 25p, 29p. Ploog a-12i. Russell a-27-32, 34-37, 39r; c-28, 30-32, 33i, 34, 35, 37, 39i. Starling a-17. Starlin c-15p, 16, 17, 27. Sutton a-11-15p.*

AMAZING ADVENTURES
Marvel Comics Group: Dec, 1979 - No. 14, Jan, 1981

V2#1-Reprints story/X-Men #1 & 38 (origins)				6.00
2-14: 2-6-Early X-Men-r. 7,8-Origin Iceman				5.00

NOTE: *Byrne c-6p, 9p. Kirby a-1-14r; c-7, 9. Steranko a-12r. Tuska a-7-9.*

AMAZING ADVENTURES

Marvel Comics: July, 1988 ($4.95, squarebound, one-shot, 80 pgs.)
1-Anthology; Austin, Golden-a   5.00

AMAZING ADVENTURES OF CAPTAIN CARVEL AND HIS CARVEL CRUSADERS, THE, (See Carvel Comics)

AMAZING CHAN & THE CHAN CLAN, THE (TV)
Gold Key: May, 1973 - No. 4, Feb, 1974 (Hanna-Barbera)

1-Warren Tufts-a in all	3	9	20	30
2-4	2	6	13	20

AMAZING COMICS (Complete Comics No. 2)
Timely Comics: Fall, 1944

1-The Destroyer, The Whizzer, The Young Allies (by Sekowsky), Sergeant Dix; Schomburg-c	200	600	1250	2200

AMAZING DETECTIVE CASES (Formerly Suspense No. 2?)
Marvel/Atlas Comics (CCC): No. 3, Nov, 1950 - No. 14, Sept, 1952

3	27	81	145	250
4-6	16	48	83	140
7-10	14	42	72	125
11,12,14: 11-(3/52)-Change to horror. 12-Krigstein-a	26	78	139	240
13-(Scarce)-Everett-a; electrocution-c/story	30	90	162	280

NOTE: *Colan a-9. Maneely c-13. Sekowsky a-12. Sinnott a-13. Tuska a-10.*

AMAZING FANTASY (Formerly Amazing Adult Fantasy #7-14)
Atlas Magazines/Marvel: #15, Aug, 1962 (Sept, 1962 shown in indicia); #16,
Dec, 1995 - #18, Feb, 1996

15-Origin/1st app. of Spider-Man by Ditko (11 pgs.); 1st app. Aunt May & Uncle Ben; Kirby/Ditko-c	1200	3600	13,200	42,000
16-18 ('95-'96, $3.95)-Kurt Busiek scripts; painted-c/a by Paul Lee				4.00

AMAZING GHOST STORIES (Formerly Nightmare)
St. John Publishing Co.: No. 14, Oct, 1954 - No. 16, Feb, 1955

14-Pit & the Pendulum story by Kinstler; Baker-c	33	99	174	300
15-r/Weird Thrillers #5; Baker-c, Powell-a	23	69	121	210
16-Kubert reprints of Weird Thrillers #4; Baker-c; Roussos, Tuska-a; Kinstler-a (1 pg.)	24	72	127	215

AMAZING HIGH ADVENTURE
Marvel Comics: 8/84; No. 2, 10/85; No. 3, 10/86 - No. 5, 1986 ($2.00)

1-5: Painted-c on all. 3,4-Baxter paper. 4-Bolton-c/a. 5-Bolton-a				3.00

NOTE: *Bissette a-4. Severin a-1, 3. Sienkiewicz a-1,2. Paul Smith a-2. Williamson a-2i.*

AMAZING-MAN COMICS (Formerly Motion Picture Funnies Weekly?)
(Also see Stars And Stripes Comics)
Centaur Publications: No. 5, Sept, 1939 - No. 26, Jan, 1942

5(#1)(Rare)-Origin/1st app. A-Man the Amazing Man by Bill Everett; The Cat-Man by Tarpe Mills (also #8), Mighty Man by Filchock, Minimidget & sidekick Ritty, & The Iron Skull by Burgos begins				
	1360	4080	9500	19,000
6-Origin The Amazing Man retold; The Shark begins; Ivy Menace by Tarpe Mills app.	300	900	1875	3500
7-Magician From Mars begins; ends #11	218	654	1364	2400
8-Cat-Man dresses as woman	155	465	966	1700
9-Magician From Mars battles the 'Elemental Monster', swiped into The Spectre in More Fun #54 & 55. Ties w/Marvel Mystery #4 for 1st Nazi War-c on a comic (2/40)	164	492	1023	1800
10,11: 11-Zardi, the Eternal Man begins; ends #16; Amazing Man dons costume; last Everett issue	127	381	795	1400
12,13	109	327	682	1200
14-Reef Kinkaid, Rocke Wayburn (ends #20) & Dr. Hypno (ends #21) begin; no Zardi or Chuck Hardy	91	273	568	1000
15,17-20: 15-Zardi returns; no Rocke Wayburn. 17-Dr. Hypno returns; no Zardi	79	237	494	875
16-Mighty Man's powers of super strength & ability to shrink & grow explained; Rocke Wayburn returns; no Dr. Hypno; Al Avison (a character) begins, ends #18 (a tribute to the famed artist)	84	252	525	925
21-Origin Dash Dartwell (drug-use story); origin & app. T.N.T.				
	84	252	525	925
22-Dash Dartwell, the Human Meteor & The Voice app; last Iron Skull & The Shark; Silver Streak app. (classic-c)	109	327	682	1200
23-Two Amazing Man stories; intro/origin Tommy the Amazing Kid; The				

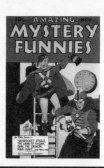

Amazing Mystery Funnies #3 © CEN

Amazing Spider-Man #3 © MAR

Amazing Spider-Man #59 © MAR

	GD2.0	FN6.0	VF8.0	NM9.4
Marksman only app.	75	225	469	825
24-King of Darkness, Nightshade, & Blue Lady begin; end #26; 1st app.				
Super-Ann	75	225	469	825
25,26 (Scarce): Meteor Martin by Wolverton in both; 26-Electric Ray app.				
	114	342	712	1250

NOTE: *Everett* a-5-11; c-5-11. *Gilman* a-14-20. *Giunta/Mirando* a-7-10. *Sam Glanzman* a-14-16, 18-21, 23. *Louis Glanzman* a-6, 9-11, 14-21; c-13-19, 21. *Robert Golden* a-9. *Gustavson* a-6; c-22, 23. *Lubbers* a-14-21. *Simon* a-10. *Frank Thomas* a-6, 9-11, 14, 15, 17-21.

AMAZING MYSTERIES (Formerly Sub-Mariner Comics No. 31)
Marvel Comics (CCC): No. 32, May, 1949 - No. 35, Jan, 1950 (1st Marvel Horror Comic)

32-The Witness app.	79	237	494	875
33-Horror format	39	117	208	360
34,35: Changes to Crime. 34,35-Photo-c	20	60	105	175

AMAZING MYSTERY FUNNIES
Centaur Publications: Aug, 1938 - No. 24, Sept, 1940 (All 52 pgs.)

V1#1-Everett-c(1st); Dick Kent Adv. story; Skyrocket Steele in the Year X on cover only	342	1026	2138	4100
2-Everett 1st-a (Skyrocket Steele)	182	546	1136	2000
3	91	273	568	1000
3(#4, 12/38)-nn on cover, #3 on inside; bondage-c				
	82	246	511	900
V2#1-4,6: 2-Drug use story. 3-Air-Sub DX begins by Burgos. 4-Dan Hastings, Hastings, Sand Hog begins (ends #5). 6-Last Skyrocket Steele				
	75	225	469	825
5-Classic Everett-c	109	327	682	1200
7 (Scarce)-Intro. The Fantom of the Fair & begins; Everett, Gustavson, Burgos-a	333	1000	2083	4000
8-Origin & 1st app. Speed Centaur	127	381	791	1400
9-11: 11-Self portrait and biog. of Everett; Jon Linton begins; early Robot cover (11/39)	75	225	469	825
12 (Scarce)-1st Space Patrol; Wolverton-a (12/39); new costume Phantom of the Fair	191	573	1194	2100
V3#1(#17, 1/40)-Intro. Bullet; Tippy Taylor serial begins, ends #24 (continued in The Arrow #2)	75	225	469	825
18,20: 18-Fantom of the Fair by Gustavson	73	219	455	800
19,21-24: Space Patrol by Wolverton in all	91	273	568	1000

NOTE: *Burgos* a-V2#3-9. *Eisner* a-V1#2, 3(2). *Everett* a-V1#2-4, V2#1, 3-6; c-V1#1-4, V2#3, 5, 18. *Filchock* a-V2#9. *Flessel* a-V2#4. *Guardineer* a-V1#4, V2#4-6. *Gustavson* a-V1#4, 5, 9-12, V3#1, 18, 19; c-V2#7, 9, 12, V3#1, 21, 22. *McWilliams* a-V2#9, 10. *TarpeMills* a-V2#2, 4-6, 9-12, V3#1. *Leo Morey*(Pulp artist) c-V2#10; text illo-V2#11. *FrankThomas* a-6-V2#4. *Webster* a-V2#4.

AMAZING SAINTS
Logos International: 1974 (39¢)

nn-True story of Phil Saint	1	3	5	7

AMAZING SCARLET SPIDER
Marvel Comics: Nov, 1995 - No. 2, Dec, 1995 ($1.95, limited series)

1,2: Replaces "Amazing Spider-Man" for two issues. 1-Venom/Carnage cameos. 2-Green Goblin & Joystick-c/app.   2.25

AMAZING SPIDER-MAN, THE (See All Detergent Comics, Amazing Fantasy, America's Best TV Comics, Aurora, Deadly Foes of Spider-Man, Fireside Book Series, Giant-Size Spider-Man, Giant Size Super-Heroes Featuring..., Marvel Collectors Item Classics, Marvel Fanfare, Marvel Graphic Novel, Marvel Spec. Ed., Marvel Tales, Marvel Team-Up, Marvel Treasury Ed., Nothing Can Stop the Juggernaut, Official Marvel Index To..., Peter Parker..., Power Record Comics, Spectacular..., Spider-Man, Spider-Man Digest, Spider-Man Saga, Spider-Man 2099, Spider-Man Vs. Wolverine, Spidey Super Stories, Strange Tales Annual #2, Superman Vs. ..., Try-Out Winner Book, Web of Spider- Man & Within Our Reach)

AMAZING SPIDER-MAN, THE
Marvel Comics Group: March, 1963 - No. 441, Nov, 1998

1-Retells origin by Steve Ditko (ties w/F.F. #12 as first Marvel x-over); intro. John Jameson & The Chameleon; Spider-Man's 2nd app.; Kirby/Ditko; Ditko-c/a #1-38	800	2400	8800	28,000
1-Reprint from the Golden Record Comic set	12	36	88	150
With record (1966)	18	54	126	225
2-1st app. The Vulture & The Terrible Tinkerer	250	750	2250	4500
3-1st full-length story; Human Torch cameo; intro. & 1st app. Doc Octopus; Spider-Man pin-up by Ditko	188	564	1600	3200
4-Origin & 1st app. The Sandman (see Strange Tales #115 for its origin); Intro. Betty Brant & Liz Allen	156	468	1325	2650
5-Dr. Doom app.	138	414	1169	2200

	GD2.0	FN6.0	VF8.0	NM9.4
6-1st app. Lizard	125	375	1062	2000
7,8,10: 7-Vs. The Vulture; 1st monthly issue. 8-Fantastic Four app. in back-up story by Kirby/Ditko. 10-1st app. Big Man & The Enforcers				
	81	244	690	1300
9-Origin & 1st app. Electro (2/64)	88	264	744	1400
11,12: 11-1st app. Bennett Brant. 12-Doc Octopus unmasks Spider-Man-c/story				
	48	144	386	700
13-1st app. Mysterio	63	189	531	1000
14-(7/64)-1st app. The Green Goblin (c/story)(Norman Osborn); Hulk x-over				
	153	459	1300	2500
15-1st app. Kraven the Hunter; 1st mention of Mary Jane Watson (not shown)	56	169	478	900
16-Spider-Man battles Daredevil (1st x-over 9/64); still in old yellow costume				
	41	123	331	600
17-2nd app. Green Goblin (c/story); Human Torch x-over (also in #18 & #21)				
	55	164	468	875
18-1st app. Ned Leeds who later becomes Hobgoblin; Fantastic Four cameo; 3rd app. Sandman	41	123	306	550
19-Sandman app.	33	100	250	450
20-Origin & 1st app. The Scorpion	43	129	344	625
21-2nd app. The Beetle (see Strange Tales #123)	31	93	222	400
22-1st app. Princess Python	29	87	202	360
23-3rd app. The Green Goblin-c/story; Norman Osborn app.				
	39	117	293	525
24	32	72	168	300
25-(6/65)-1st app. Mary Jane Watson (cameo; face not shown); 1st app. Spencer Smythe; Norman Osborn app.	30	90	210	375
26-4th app. The Green Goblin-c/story; 1st app. Crime Master; dies in #27				
	32	96	240	425
27-5th app. The Green Goblin-c/story; Norman Osborn app.				
	31	93	222	400
28-Origin & 1st app. Molten Man (9/65, scarcer in high grade)				
	43	129	344	625
29,30	20	60	140	250
31-38: 31-1st app. Harry Osborn who later becomes 2nd Green Goblin; Gwen Stacy & Prof. Warren. 34-4th app. Kraven the Hunter. 36-1st app. Looter. 37-Intro. Norman Osborn. 38-(7/66)-2nd app. Mary Jane Watson (face not shown); last Ditko issue	20	60	140	250
39-The Green Goblin-c/story; Green Goblin's i.d. revealed as Norman Osborn; Romita-a begins (8/66; see Daredevil #16 for 1st Romita-a on Spider-Man)				
	26	78	182	325
40-1st told origin The Green Goblin-c/story	33	100	250	450
41-1st app. Rhino	24	72	168	300
42-(11/66)-3rd app. Mary Jane Watson (cameo in last 2 panels); 1st time face is shown	17	51	118	210
43-49: 44,45-2nd & 3rd app. The Lizard. 46-Intro. Shocker. 47-M. J. Watson & Peter Parker 1st date. 47-Green Goblin cameo; Harry & Norman Osborn app. 47,49-5th & 6th app. Kraven the Hunter	12	36	88	150
50-1st app. Kingpin (7/67)	41	123	318	575
51-2nd app. Kingpin	18	54	129	230
52-60: 52-1st app. Joe Robertson & 3rd app. Kingpin. 56-1st app. Capt. George Stacy. 57,58-Ka-Zar app. 59-1st app. Brainwasher (alias Kingpin; 1st-c app. M. J. Watson	9	27	65	110
61-74: 67-1st app. Randy Robertson. 69-Kingpin-c. 69,70-Kingpin app. 73-1st app. Silvermane. 74-Last 12¢ issue	7	21	50	80
75-89,91-93,95,99: 78,79-1st app. The Prowler. 83-1st app. Schemer & Vanessa (Kingpin's wife). 84,85-Kingpin-c/story. 86-Re-intro & origin Black Widow in new costume. 93-1st app. Arthur Stacy	5	15	38	60
90-Death of Capt. Stacy	7	21	53	85
94-Origin retold	9	27	63	105
96-98-Green Goblin app. (97,98-Green Goblin-c); drug books not approved by CCA	11	33	77	130
100-Anniversary issue (9/71); Green Goblin cameo (2 pgs.)				
101-1st app. Morbius the Living Vampire; Wizard cameo; last 12¢ issue (10/71)				
	14	42	102	175
101-Silver ink 2nd printing (9/92, $1.75)				2.25
102-Origin & 2nd app. Morbius (25¢, 52 pgs.)	10	30	70	120
103-118: 104,111-Kraven the Hunter-c/stories. 108-1st app. Sha-Shan. 109-Dr. Strange-c/story (6/72). 110-1st app. Gibbon. 113-1st app.				

330

Amazing Spider-Man #194 © MAR

Amazing Spider-Man #246 © MAR

Amazing Spider-Man #352 © MAR

	GD2.0	FN6.0	VF8.0	NM9.4		GD2.0	FN6.0	VF8.0	NM9.4

Hammerhead. 116-118-reprints story from Spectacular Spider-Man Mag. in color with some changes — 4 12 29 45

119,120-Spider-Man vs. Hulk (4 & 5/73) — 6 18 42 70

121-Death of Gwen Stacy (6/73) (killed by Green Goblin) (reprinted in Marvel Tales #98 & 192) — 15 45 107 185

122-Death of The Green Goblin-c/story (7/73) (reprinted in Marvel Tales #99 & 192) — 16 48 112 200

123,125-128: 123-Cage app. 125-Man-Wolf origin. 127-1st mention of Harry Osborn becoming Green Goblin — 3 10 23 35

124-1st app. Man-Wolf (9/73) — 5 15 34 55

129-1st app. Jackal & The Punisher (2/74) — 18 54 129 230

130-133: 131-Last 20¢ issue — 3 9 20 30

134-(7/74); 1st app. Tarantula; Harry Osborn discovers Spider-Man's ID; Punisher cameo — 4 12 26 40

135-2nd full Punisher app. (8/74) — 6 18 40 65

136-Reappearance of The Green Goblin (Harry Osborn; Norman Osborn's son) — 5 15 38 60

137-Green Goblin-c/story (2nd Harry Osborn) — 5 15 34 55

138-141: 139-1st app Grizzly. 140-1st app. Glory Grant — 2 6 15 22

142,143-Gwen Stacy clone cameos: 143-1st app. Cyclone — 3 9 20 30

144-147: 144-Full app. of Gwen Stacy clone. 145,146-Gwen Stacy clone story line continues. 147-Spider-Man learns Gwen Stacy is clone — 3 9 17 25

148-Jackal revealed — 3 9 21 32

149-Spider-Man clone story begins; clone dies (?); origin of Jackal — 5 15 34 55

150-Spider-Man decides he is not the clone — 3 9 17 25

151-Spider-Man disposes of clone body — 3 9 17 25

152-160-(Regular 25¢ editions). 159-Last 25¢ issue(8/76) — 2 6 12 18

155-159-(30¢-c variants, limited distribution) — 3 10 23 36

161-Nightcrawler app. from X-Men; Punisher cameo; Wolverine & Colossus app. — 3 9 17 25

162-Punisher, Nightcrawler app.; 1st Jigsaw — 3 9 17 25

163-168,181-188: 167-1st app. Will O' The Wisp. 181-Origin retold; gives life history of Spidey; Punisher cameo in flashback (1 panel). 182-(7/78)-Peter's first proposal to Mary Jane, but she refuses — 2 6 9 12

169-173-(Regular 30¢ edition). 169-Clone story recapped. 171-Nova app. — 2 6 9 12

169-173-(35¢-c variants, limited dist.)(6-10/77) — 2 6 11 15

174,175-Punisher app. — 2 6 11 15

176-180-Green Goblin app. — 2 6 15 22

189,190-Byrne-a — 2 6 11 15

191-193,195-199,203-205,207,208,210-219: 193-Peter & Mary Jane break up. 196-Faked death of Aunt May. 203-3rd app. Dazzler. 210-1st app. Madame Web. 212-1st app. Hydro-Man; origin Sandman — 2 6 9 12

194-1st app. Black Cat — 2 6 12 18

200-Giant origin issue (1/80) — 3 9 20 30

201,202-Punisher app. — 2 6 9 12

206-Byrne-a — 2 6 9 12

209-Origin & 1st app. Calypso (10/80) — 2 6 10 14

220-241: 225-(2/82)-Foolkiller-c/story. 226,227-Black Cat returns. 236-Tarantula dies. 234-Free 16 pg. insert "Marvel Guide to Collecting Comics". 235-Origin Will-'O-The-Wisp — 1 3 6 8

238-(3/83)-1st app. Hobgoblin (Ned Leeds); came with skin "Tattooz" decal.

Note: The same decal appears in the more common Fantastic Four #252 which is being removed & placed in this issue as incentive to increase value (Value listed is with or without tattoos) — 6 18 42 70

239-2nd app. Hobgoblin & 1st battle w/Spidey — 4 12 26 40

240-243,246-248: 241-Origin The Vulture. 243-Reintro Mary Jane Watson after 4 year absence — 6.00

244-3rd app. Hobgoblin (cameo) — 2 6 9 12

245-(10/83)-4th app. Hobgoblin (cameo); Lefty Donovan gains powers of Hobgoblin & battles Spider-Man — 2 6 9 12

249-251: 3 part Hobgoblin/Spider-Man battle. 249-Retells origin & death of 1st Green Goblin. 251-Last old costume — 2 6 9 12

252-Spider-Man dons new black costume (5/84); ties with Marvel Team-Up #141 & Spectacular Spider-Man #90 for 1st new costume (See Marvel S-H Secret Wars #8) — 3 9 20 30

253-1st app. The Rose — 1 3 5 7

254-258: 256-1st app. Puma. 257-Hobgoblin cameo; 2nd app. Puma; M. J. Watson reveals she knows Spidey's i.d. 258-Hobgoblin (minor) — 6.00

259-Full Hobgoblin app.; Spidey back to old costume; origin Mary Jane Watson — 1 4 7 10

260-Hobgoblin app. — 1 3 6 8

261-Hobgoblin-c/story; painted-c by Vess — 1 3 6 9

262-Spider-Man unmasked; photo-c — 6.00

263,264,266-274,277-280,282,283: 274-Zarathos (The Spirit of Vengeance) app. 277-Vess back-up art. 279-Jack O'Lantern-c/story. 282-X-Factor x-over — 5.00

265-1st app. Silver Sable (6/85) — 1 4 7 10

265-Silver ink 2nd printing ($1.25) — 2.25

275-($1.25, 52 pgs.)-Hobgoblin-c/story; origin-r by Ditko — 2 6 10 14

276-Hobgoblin app. — 1 3 6 8

281-Hobgoblin battles Jack O'Lantern — 1 3 6 8

284,285: 284-Punisher cameo; Gang War story begins; Hobgoblin-c/story. 285-Punisher app.; minor Hobgoblin app. — 1 3 6 8

286-288: 286-Hobgoblin-c & app. (minor). 287-Hobgoblin app. (minor). 288-Full Hobgoblin app.; last Gang War — 1 3 6 8

289-(6/87, $1.25, 52 pgs.)-Hobgoblin's i.d. revealed as Ned Leeds; death of Ned Leeds; Macendale (Jack O'Lantern) becomes new Hobgoblin app. — 2 6 13 20

290-292,295-297: 290-Peter proposes to Mary Jane. 292-She accepts; leads into Amazing Spider-Man Annual #21 — 5.00

293,294-Part 2 & 5 of Kraven story from Web of Spider-Man. 294-Death of Kraven — 1 3 5 7

298-Todd McFarlane-c/a begins (3/88); 1st app. Eddie Brock who becomes Venom; (McFarlane on last pg.) — 3 10 23 35

299-1st app. Venom with costume (cameo) — 2 6 15 22

300 ($1.50, 52 pgs.; 25th Anniversary)-1st full Venom app.; last black costume (5/88) — 6 18 45 75

301-305: 301 ($1.00 issues begin). 304-1st bi-weekly issue — 2 6 9 12

306-311,313,314: 306-Swipes-c from Action #1. 315-317-Venom app. — 1 3 6 8

312-Hobgoblin battles Green Goblin — 2 6 10 14

315-317-Venom app. — 2 6 10 14

318-323,325: 319-Bi-weekly begins again — 1 3 5 7

324-Sabretooth app.; McFarlane cover only — 1 3 5 7

326,327,329: 327-Cosmic Spidey continues from Spectacular Spider-Man (no McFarlane-c/a) — 4.00

328-Hulk x-over; last McFarlane issue — 1 3 6 8

330,331-Punisher app. 331-Minor Venom app. — 3.00

332,333-Venom-c/story — 6.00

334-336,338-343: 341-Tarantula app. — 3.00

337-Hobgoblin app. — 4.00

344-1st app. Cletus Kasady (Carnage) — 1 4 7 10

345-1st full app. Cletus Kasady; Venom cameo on last pg. — 6.00

346,347-Venom app. — 6.00

348,349,351-359: 348-Avengers x-over. 351,352-Nova of New Warriors app. 353-Darkhawk app.; brief Punisher app. 354-Punisher cameo & Nova, Night Thrasher (New Warriors), Darkhawk & Moon Knight app. 357,358-Punisher, Darkhawk, Moon Knight, Night Thrasher, Nova x-over. 358-3 part gatefold-c; last $1.00-c — 2.50

350-($1.50, 52pgs.)-Origin retold; Spidey vs. Dr. Doom; pin-ups; Uncle Ben app. — 4.00

360-Carnage cameo — 3.00

361-Intro Carnage (the Spawn of Venom); begin 3 part story; recap of how Spidey's alien costume became Venom — 1 4 7 10

361-($1.25)-2nd printing; silver-c — 2.50

362,363-Carnage & Venom-c/story — 6.00

362-2nd printing — 2.25

364,366-374,376-387: 364-The Shocker app. (old villain). 366-Peter's parents-c/story. 369-Harry Osborn back-up (Gr. Goblin II). 373-Venom back-up. 374-Venom-c/story. 376-Cardiac app. 378-Maximum Carnage part 3. 381,382-Hulk app. 383-The Jury app. 384-Venom/carnage app. — 2.50

387-New costume Vulture

365-($3.95, 84 pgs.)-30th anniversary issue w/silver hologram on-c; Spidey/

Amazing Spider-Man #386 © MAR

Amazing Spider-Man #411 © MAR

Amazing Spider-Man V2 #20 © MAR

	GD2.0	FN6.0	VF8.0	NM9.4

Venom/Carnage pull-out poster; contains 5 pg. preview of Spider-Man 2099 (1st app.); Spidey's origin retold; Lizard app.; reintro Peter's parents in Stan Lee 3 pg. text w/illo (story continues thru #370). ... 5.00
365-Second printing; gold hologram on-c ... 4.00
375-($3.95, 68 pgs.)-Holo-grafx foil-c; vs. Venom story; ties into Venom: Lethal Protector #1; Pat Olliffe-a. ... 5.00
388-($2.25, 68 pgs.)-Newsstand edition; Venom back-up & Cardiac & chance back-up ... 2.25
388-($2.95, 68 pgs.)-Collector's edition w/foil-c ... 3.00
389-396,398,399,401-420: 389-$1.50-c begins; bound-in trading card sheet; Green Goblin app. 394-Power & Responsibility Pt. 2. 396-Daredevil-c & app. 403-Carnage app. 406-1st New Doc Octopus. 407-Human Torch, Silver Sable, Sandman app. 409-Kaine, Rhino app. 410-Carnage app. 414-The Rose app. 415-Onslaught story; Spidey vs. Sentinels. 416-Epilogue to Onslaught; Garney-a(p); Williamson-a(i) ... 2.25
390-($2.95)-Collector's edition polybagged w/16 pg. insert of new animated Spidey TV show plus animation cel ... 3.00
394-($2.95, 48 pgs.)-Deluxe edition; flip book w/Birth of a Spider-Man Pt. 2; silver foil both-c ... 3.00
397-($2.25)-Flip book w/Ultimate Spider-Man ... 2.25
400-($2.95)-Death of Aunt May ... 3.00
400-($3.95)-Death of Aunt May; embossed double-c ... 5.00
400-Collector's Edition; white-c ... 1 3 6 9
408-($2.95) Polybagged version with TV theme song cassette ... 8.00
421-424-($1.95-c) ... 2.25
425-($2.99)-48 pgs., wraparound-c ... 3.00
426,428-433: 426-Begin $1.99-c. 432-Spiderhunt pt. 2 ... 2.25
427-($2.25) Return of Dr. Octopus; double gatefold-c ... 2.25
434-440: 434-Double cover with "Amazing Ricochet #1". 438-Daredevil app. 439-Avengers-c(p). 440-Byrne-s ... 2.25
441-Final issue; Byrne-s ... 4.00
#(-1) Flashback issue (7/97, $1.95-c) ... 2.25
Annual 1 (1964, 72 pg.)-Origin Spider-Man; 1st app. Sinister Six (Dr. Octopus, Electro, Kraven the Hunter, Mysterio, Sandman, Vulture) (new 41 pg. story); plus gallery of Spidey foes; early X-Men app. ... 69 207 584 1100
Annual 2 (1965, 25¢, 72 pgs.)-Reprints from #1,2,5 plus new Doctor Strange story ... 30 90 210 375
Special 3 (11/66, 25¢, 72 pgs.)-New Avengers story & Hulk x-over; Doctor Octopus-r from #11,12; Romita-a ... 12 36 88 150
Special 4 (11/67, 25¢, 68 pgs.)-Spidey battles Human Torch (new 41 pg. story) ... 11 33 77 130
Special 5 (11/68, 25¢, 68 pgs.)-New 40 pg. Red Skull story; 1st app. Peter Parker's parents; last annual with new-a ... 10 30 73 125
Special 6 (11/69, 25¢, 68 pgs.)-Reprints 41 pg. Sinister Six story from annual #1 plus 2 Kirby/Ditko stories (r) ... 4 12 29 45
Special 7 (12/70, 25¢, 68 pgs.)-All-r(#1,2) new Vulture-c ... 4 12 29 45
Special 8 (12/71)-All-r ... 4 12 29 45
King Size 9 ('73)-Reprints Spectacular Spider-Man (mag.) #2; 40 pg. Green Goblin-c/story (re-edited from 58 pgs.) ... 4 12 29 45
Annual 10 (1976)-Origin Human Fly (vs. Spidey); new-a begins ... 2 6 13 20
Annual 11-13 ('77-'79)-12-Spidey vs. Hulk-r/#119,120. 13-New Byrne/Austin-a; Dr. Octopus x-over w/Spectacular S-M Ann. #1 ... 2 6 9 12
Annual 14 (1980)-Miller-a(p); Dr. Strange app. ... 2 6 11 15
Annual 15 (1981)-Miller-a(p); Punisher app. ... 2 6 11 15
Annual 16-20: 16 ('82)-Origin app. new Capt. Marvel (female heroine). 17 ('83)-Kingpin app. 18 ('84)-Scorpion app.; JJJ weds. 19 ('85). 20 ('86)-Origin Iron Man of 2020 ... 6.00
Annual 21 (1987)-Special wedding issue; newsstand & direct sale versions exist & are worth same ... 1 4 7 10
Annual 22 (1988, $1.75, 68 pgs.)-1st app. Speedball; Evolutionary War x-over; Daredevil app. ... 6.00
Annual 23 (1989, $2.00, 68 pgs.)-Atlantis Attacks; origin Spider-Man retold; She-Hulk app.; Byrne-c; Liefeld-a(p), 23 pgs. ... 4.00
Annual 24 (1990, $2.00, 68 pgs.)-Ant-Man app. ... 3.00
Annual 25 (1991, $2.00, 68 pgs.)-3 pg. origin recap; Iron Man app.; 1st Venom solo story; Ditko-a (6 pgs.) ... 5.00
Annual 26 (1992, $2.25, 68 pgs.)-New Warriors-c/story; Venom solo story cont'd in Spectacular Spider-Man Annual #12 ... 4.00

Annual 27,28 ('93, '94, $2.95, 68 pgs.)-27-Bagged w/card; 1st app. Annex. 28-Carnage-c/story; Cloak and Dagger back-ups ... 3.00
'96 Special-($2.95, 64 pgs.)-"Blast From The Past" ... 3.00
'97 Special-($2.99)-Wraparound-c,Sundown app. ... 3.00
Marvel Graphic Novel - Parallel Lives (3/89, $8.95) ... 1 4 7 10
Marvel Graphic Novel - Spirits of the Earth (1990, $18.95, HC) ... 3 9 17 25
Super Special 1 (4/95, $3.95)-Flip Book ... 4.00
...: Skating on Thin Ice 1(1990, $1.25, Canadian)-McFarlane-c; anti-drug issue; Electro app. ... 1 3 6 9
...: Skating on Thin Ice 1 (2/93, $1.50, American) ... 4.00
...: Double Trouble 2 (1990, $1.25, Canadian) ... 6.00
...: Double Trouble 2 (2/93, $1.50, American) ... 3.00
...: Hit and Run 3 (1990, $1.25, Canadian)-Ghost Rider-c/story ... 1 3 6 9
...: Hit and Run 3 (2/93. $1.50, American) ... 3.00
...: Carnage (6/93, $6.95)-r/ASM #344,345,359-363 ... 1 3 5 7
...: Chaos in Calgary 4 (Canadian; part of 5 part series)-Turbine,Night Rider, Frightful app. ... 2 6 10 14
...: Chaos in Calgary 4 (2/93, $1.50, American) ... 3.00
...: Deadball 5 (1993, $1.60, Canadian)-Green Goblin-c/story; features Montreal Expos ... 2 6 12 18
Note: Prices listed above are for English Canadian editions. French editions are worth double.
...: Soul of the Hunter nn (8/92, $5.95, 52 pgs.)-Zeck-c/a(p) ... 6.00
Artists: Austin a(i)-248, 335, 337, Annual 13; c(i)-188, 241, 242, 248, 331, 334, 343, Annual 25. J. Buscema a(i)-73, 76-81, 84, 85. Byrne a-189p, 190p, 206p, Annual 3r, 6r, 7r; 13p; c-189p, 268, 296, Annual 12. Ditko a-1-38, Annual 1, Special 3(r), 2, 24(2); c-1i, 2-38. Guice c/a-Annual 18i. Gil Kane a(p)-89-105, 120-124, 150, Annual 10, 12; c/a-90p, 96, 98, 99, 101-105p, 129p, 131p, 132p, 137-140p, 143p, 148p, 149p, 151p, 153p, 160p, 161p, Annual 10p, 24. Kirby a-8. Erik Larsen a-324, 327, 329-350; c-327, 329-350, 354i, Annual 25. McFarlane a-298p, 299p, 300-303, 304-323p, 325p, 328; c-298-325, 328. Miller c-218, 219. Mooney a-65i, 67-82i, 84-88i, 173i, 178i, 189i, 190i, 192i, 193i, 196-202i, 207i, 211-219i, 221i, 222i, 226i, 227i, 229-233i, Annual 11i, 17i. Nasser c-228p. Nebres a-Annual 24i. Russell c-357i. Simonson c-222, 337i. Starlin a-113i, 114i, 187p. Williamson a-365i.

AMAZING SPIDER-MAN (Volume 2)
Marvel Comics: Jan, 1999 - Present ($2.99/$1.99/$2.25)
1-($2.99)-Byrne-a ... 4.00
1-($6.95) Dynamic Forces variant-c by the Romitas ... 1 4 7 10
2-($1.99) Two covers -by John Byrne and Andy Kubert ... 3.00
3-11: 4-Fantastic Four app. 5-Spider-Woman-c ... 2.25
12-($2.99) Sinister Six return (cont. in Peter Parker #12) ... 3.00
13-17: 13-Mary Jane's plane explodes ... 2.25
18,19,21-24,26-28: 18-Begin $2.25-c. 19-Venom-c. 24-Maximum Security ... 2.25
20-($2.99, 100 pgs.) Super-Slayer issue; new story and reprints ... 3.00
25-($2.99) Regular cover; Peter Parker becomes the Green Goblin ... 3.00
25-($3.99) Holo-foil enhanced cover ... 4.00
29-Peter is reunited with Mary Jane ... 2.25
30-Straczynski-s/Campbell-c begin; intro. Ezekiel ... 3.00
31-35: Battles Morlun ... 2.25
36-Black cover; aftermath of the Sept. 11 tragedy in New York ... 3.00
1999, 2000 Annual (6/99, '00, $3.50) 1999-Buscema-a ... 3.50
2001 Annual ($2.99) Follows Peter Parker: S-M #29; last Mackie-s ... 3.00
Collected Edition #30-32 ($3.95) reprints #30-32 w/cover of #30 ... 3.00

AMAZING WILLIE MAYS, THE
Famous Funnies Publ.: No date (Sept, 1954)
nn ... 73 219 455 800

AMAZING WORLD OF DC COMICS
DC Comics: Jul, 1974 - No. 17, 1978 ($1.50, B&W, mail-order DC Pro-zine)
1-Kubert interview; unpublished Kirby-a; Infantino-c ... 5 15 38 60
2-4: 3-Julie Schwartz profile. 4-Batman; Robinson-c ... 4 12 29 45
5-Sheldon Mayer ... 3 10 23 35
6,8,13: 6-Joe Orlando; EC-r; Wrightson pin-up. 8-Infantino; Batman-r from Pop Tart giveaway. 13-Humor; Aragonés-i; Wood/Ditko-a; photos from serials of Superman, Batman, Captain Marvel ... 2 6 15 22
7,10-12: 7-Superman; r/1955 Pep comic giveaway. 10-Behind the scenes at DC; Showcase article. 11-Super-Villains; unpubl. Secret Society of S.V. story. 12-Legion; Grell-c/interview ... 3 9 18 26
9-Legion of Super-Heroes; lengthy bios and history; Cockrum-c ... 7 21 50 80

Amazing World of DC Comics #15 © DC

American Century #1
© Howard Chaykin & DC

America's Best Comics #10 © STD

	GD2.0	FN6.0	VF8.0	NM9.4
14-Justice League	3	9	20	30
15-Wonder Woman; Nasser-c	4	12	26	40
16-Golden Age heroes	3	10	23	35
17-Shazam; G.A., 70s, TV and Fawcett heroes	3	9	20	30
Special 1 (Digest size)	3	9	17	25

AMAZING WORLD OF SUPERMAN (See Superman)

AMAZING X-MEN
Marvel Comics: Mar, 1995 - No. 4, July, 1995 ($1.95, limited series)
1-Age of Apocalypse; Andy Kubert-c/a				3.50
2-4				2.50

AMAZON
Comico: Mar, 1989 - No. 3, May, 1989 ($1.95, limited series)
1-3: Ecological theme				2.25

AMAZON (Also see Marvel Versus DC #3 & DC Versus Marvel #4)
DC Comics (Amalgam): Apr, 1996 ($1.95, one-shot)
1-John Byrne-c/a/scripts				2.25

AMAZON ATTACK 3-D
The 3-D Zone: Sept, 1990 ($3.95, 28 pgs.)
1-Chaykin-a				5.00

AMAZON WOMAN (1st Series)
FantaCo: Summer, 1994 - No. 2, Fall, 1994 ($2.95, B&W, limited series, mature)
1,2: Tom Simonton-c/a/scripts				3.00

AMAZON WOMAN (2nd Series)
FantaCo: Feb, 1996 - No. 4, May, 1996 ($2.95, B&W, limited series, mature)
1-4: Tom Simonton-a/scripts				3.00
...: Invaders of Terror ('96, $5.95) Simonton-a/s				6.00

AMBUSH (See Zane Grey, Four Color 314)

AMBUSH BUG (Also see Son of...)
DC Comics: June, 1985 - No. 4, Sept, 1985 (75¢, limited series)
1-4: Giffen-c/a in all				3.00
Nothing Special 1 (9/92, $2.50, 68pg.)-Giffen-c/a				3.00
Stocking Stuffer (2/86, $1.25)-Giffen-c/a				3.00

AMERICA AT WAR - THE BEST OF DC WAR COMICS (See Fireside Book Series)

AMERICA IN ACTION
Dell(Imp. Publ. Co.)/Mayflower House Publ.: 1942; Winter, 1945 (36 pgs.)
1942-Dell-(68 pgs.)	17	51	88	150
1-(1945)-Has 3 adaptations from American history; Kiefer, Schrotter & Webb-a	12	36	61	105

AMERICAN, THE
Dark Horse Comics: July, 1987 - No. 8, 1989 ($1.50/$1.75, B&W)
1-8: ($1.50)				2.25
Collection ($5.95, B&W)-Reprints				6.00
Special 1 (1990, $2.25, B&W)				2.25

AMERICAN AIR FORCES, THE (See A-1 Comics)
William H. Wise(Flying Cadet Publ. Co./Hasan(No.1)/Life's Romances/
Magazine Ent. No. 5 on): Sept-Oct, 1944-No. 4, 1945; No. 5, 1951-No. 12, 1954
1-Article by Zack Mosley, creator of Smilin' Jack; Jap war-c	17	51	88	150
2-Classic-Jap war-c	22	66	116	200
3,4-Jap war-c	10	30	55	80
NOTE: All part comic, part magazine. Art by Whitney, Chas. Quinlan, H. C. Kiefer, and Tony Dipreta.
5(A-1 45)(Formerly Jet Powers), 6(A-1 54), 7(A-1 58), 8(A-1 65), 9(A-1 67), 10(A-1 74), 11(A-1 79), 12(A-1 91)	7	21	36	50
NOTE: Powell c/a-5-12.

AMERICAN CENTURY
DC Comics (Vertigo): May, 2001 - Present ($2.50)
1-Chaykin-s/painted-c; Tischman-a				4.00
2-10-New story arc begins. 10-Orbik-c				2.50
Scars & Stripes (2001, $8.95, TPB) r/#1-4; Tischman intro.				9.00

AMERICAN FLAGG! (See First Comics Graphic Novel 3,9,12,21 & Howard Chaykin's..)

First Comics: Oct, 1983 - No. 50, Mar, 1988
1,21-27,50: 1-Chaykin-c/a begins. 21-27-Alan Moore scripts				4.00
2-20,28-49: 31-Origin Bob Violence				3.00
Special 1 (11/86)-Introduces Chaykin's Time²				4.00

AMERICAN FREAK: A TALE OF THE UN-MEN
DC Comics (Vertigo): Feb, 1994 - No. 5, Jun, 1994 ($1.95, mini-series, mature)
1-5				2.25

AMERICAN GRAPHICS
Henry Stewart: No. 1, 1954; No. 2, 1957 (25¢)
1-The Maid of the Mist, The Last of the Eries (Indian Legends of Niagara) (sold at Niagara Falls)	10	30	55	85
2-Victory at Niagara & Laura Secord (Heroine of the War of 1812)	7	21	36	50

AMERICAN INDIAN, THE (See Picture Progress)

AMERICAN LIBRARY
David McKay Publ.: 1943 - No. 6, 1944 (15¢, 68 pgs., B&W, text & pictures)
nn (#1)-Thirty Seconds Over Tokyo (movie)	37	111	197	340
nn (#2)-Guadalcanal Diary; painted-c (only 10¢)	27	81	145	250
3-6: 3-Look to the Mountain. 4-Case of the Crooked Candle (Perry Mason). 5-Duel in the Sun. 6-Wingate's Raiders	13	39	66	110

AMERICAN: LOST IN AMERICA, THE
Dark Horse Comics: July, 1992 - No. 4, Oct, 1992 ($2.50, limited series)
1-4: 1-Dorman painted-c. 2-Phillips painted-c. 3-Mignola-c. 4-Jim Lee-c				2.50

AMERICAN SPLENDOR: (Series of titles)
Dark Horse Comics: 1998 - Present (B&W, all one-shots)
--COMIC-CON COMICS (8/96) 1-H. Pekar script. --MUSIC COMICS (11/97) nn-H. Pekar-s/Sacco-a; r/Village Voice jazz strips. --ODDS AND ENDS (12/97) 1-Pekar-s. --ON THE JOB (5/97) 1-Pekar-s. --A STEP OUT OF THE NEST (8/94) 1-Pekar-s. --TERMINAL (9/99) 1-Pekar-s. --TRANSATLANTIC (7/98) 1 "American Splendour" on cover; Pekar-s.				3.00
--A PORTRAIT OF THE AUTHOR IN HIS DECLINING YEARS (4/01, $3.99) 1-Photo-c. --BEDTIME STORIES (6/00, $3.95)				4.00

AMERICAN SPLENDOR: WINDFALL
Dark Horse Comics: Sept, 1995 - No. 2, Oct,1995 ($3.95, B&W, limited series)
1,2-Pekar script				4.00

AMERICAN TAIL: FIEVEL GOES WEST, AN
Marvel Comics: Early Jan, 1992 - No. 3, Early Feb, 1992 ($1.00, limited series)
1-3-Adapts Universal animated movie; Wildman-a				2.50
1-($2.95-c, 69 pgs.) Deluxe squarebound edition				4.00

AMERICAN WOMAN
Antarctic Press (Barrage Studios): Jun, 1998 - No. 2 ($2.95)
1,2: 1-Denham-s/a. 2-Stockton-s				3.00

AMERICA'S BEST COMICS
Nedor/Better/Standard Publications: Feb, 1942; No. 2, Sept, 1942 - No. 31, July, 1949 (New logo with #9)
1-The Woman in Red, Black Terror, Captain Future, Doc Strange, The Liberator, & Don Davis, Secret Ace begin	245	735	1531	2700
2-Origin The American Eagle; The Woman in Red ends	100	300	625	1100
3-Pyroman begins (11/42, 1st app.); also see Startling Comics #18, (12/42)	73	219	455	800
4-6: 5-Last Capt. Future (not in #4); Lone Eagle app. 6-American Crusader app.	55	165	341	600
7-Hitler, Mussolini & Hirohito-c	86	258	540	950
8-Last Liberator	55	165	330	575
9-The Fighting Yank begins; The Ghost app.	61	183	381	675
10,12-17,19-21: 10-Flag-c. 14-American Eagle ends. 21-Infinity-c.	50	150	300	525
11-Hirohito & Tojo-c. (10/44)	57	171	356	625
18-Classic-c	55	165	341	600
22-Capt. Future app.	45	135	270	475
23-Miss Masque begins; last Doc Strange	55	165	330	575
24-Miss Masque bondage-c	52	157	314	550
25-Last Fighting Yank; Sea Eagle app.	40	120	232	400

America's Greatest Comics #4 © FAW

Amethyst, Princess of Gemworld #1 © DC

A-Next #1 © MAR

	GD2.0	FN6.0	VF8.0	NM9.4

26-31: 26-The Phantom Detective & The Silver Knight app.; Frazetta text illo & some panels in Miss Masque. 27,28-Commando Cubs. 27-Doc Strange.

| 28-Tuska Black Terror. 29-Last Pyroman | 40 | 120 | 220 | 380 |

NOTE: *American Eagle* not in 3, 8, 9, 13. *Fighting Yank* not in 10, 12. *Liberator* not in 2, 6, 7. *Pyroman* not in 9, 11, 14-16, 23, 25-27. *Schomburg (Xela)* c-5, 7-31. Bondage c-18, 24.

AMERICA'S BEST COMICS PREVIEW
Wizard: 1999 (Magazine supplement)

| 1-Previews Tom Strong, Top Ten, Promethea, Tomorrow Stories | | | | 2.25 |

AMERICA'S BEST COMICS SKETCHBOOK
America's Best: 2002 ($5.95, square-bound)

| 1-Design sketches by Sprouse, Ross, Adams, Nowlan, Ha and others | | | | 6.00 |

AMERICA'S BEST COMICS SPECIAL
America's Best: Feb, 2001 ($6.95, square-bound)

| 1-Short stories of Alan Moore's characters; art by various; Ross-c | | | | 7.00 |

AMERICA'S BEST TV COMICS (TV)
American Broadcasting Co. (Prod. by Marvel Comics): 1967 (25¢, 68 pgs.)

| 1-Spider-Man, Fantastic Four (by Kirby/Ayers), Casper, King Kong of the Jungle, Journey to the Center of the Earth stories (promotes new TV cartoon show) | 14 | 42 | 102 | 175 |

AMERICA'S BIGGEST COMICS BOOK
William H. Wise: 1944 (196 pgs., one-shot)

| 1-The Grim Reaper, The Silver Knight, Zudo, the Jungle Boy, Commando Cubs, Thunderhoof app. | 40 | 120 | 232 | 400 |

AMERICA'S FUNNIEST COMICS
William H. Wise: 1944 - No. 2, 1944 (15¢, 80 pgs.)

| nn(#1), 2 | 29 | 87 | 156 | 270 |

AMERICA'S GREATEST COMICS
Fawcett Publications: May?, 1941 - No. 8, Summer, 1943 (15¢, 100 pgs., soft cardboard-c)

1-Bulletman, Spy Smasher, Capt. Marvel, Minute Man & Mr. Scarlet begin; Classic Mac Raboy-c. 1st time that Fawcett's major super-heroes appear together as a group on a cover. Fawcett's 1st squarebound book.				
	291	873	1818	3200
2	137	411	852	1500
3	100	300	625	1100
4,5: 4-Commando Yank begins; Golden Arrow, Ibis the Invincible & Spy Smasher cameo in Captain Marvel	75	225	469	825
6,7: 7-Balbo the Boy Magician app.; Captain Marvel, Bulletman cameo in Mr. Scarlet	68	205	426	750
8-Capt. Marvel Jr. & Golden Arrow app.; Spy Smasher x-over in Capt. Midnight; no Minute Man or Commando Yank	68	205	426	750

AMERICA'S SWEETHEART SUNNY (See Sunny, …)

AMERICA VS. THE JUSTICE SOCIETY
DC Comics: Jan, 1985 - No. 4, Apr, 1985 ($1.00, limited series)

| 1-Double size; Alcala-a(i) in all | | | | 6.00 |
| 2-4: 3,4-Spectre cameo | | | | 5.00 |

AMERICOMICS
Americomics: April, 1983 - No. 6, Mar, 1984 ($2.00, Baxter paper/slick paper)

1-Intro/origin The Shade; Intro. The Slayer, Captain Freedom and The Liberty Corps; Perez-c				5.00
1,2-2nd printings ($2.00)				2.25
2-6: 2-Messenger app. & 1st app. Tara on Jungle Island. 3-New & old Blue Beetle battle. 4-Origin Dragonfly & Shade. 5-Origin Commando D. 6-Origin the Scarlet Scorpion				3.00
Special 1 (8/83, $2.00)-Sentinels of Justice (Blue Beetle, Captain Atom, Nightshade & The Question)				4.00

AMETHYST
DC Comics: Jan, 1985 - No. 16, Aug, 1986 (75¢)

| 1-16: 8-Fire Jade's i.d. revealed | | | | 2.25 |
| Special 1 (10/86, $1.25), 1-4 (11/87 - 2/88)(Limited series) | | | | 2.25 |

AMETHYST, PRINCESS OF GEMWORLD (See Legion of Super-Heroes #298)
DC Comics: May, 1983 - No. 12, Apr, 1984 (Maxi-series)

| 1-(60¢) | | | | 2.25 |

	GD2.0	FN6.0	VF8.0	NM9.4

| 1,2-(35¢): tested in Austin & Kansas City | 2 | 6 | 13 | 20 |
| 2-12: Perez-c(p) #6-11, Annual 1(9/84) | | | | 2.25 |

NOTE: *Perez* c-4i, 5-11p.

AMY RACECAR COLOR SPECIAL (See Stray Bullets)
El Capitán Books: July, 1997; Oct, 1999 ($2.95/$3.50)

| 1,2-David Laphan-a/scripts. 2-($3.50) | | | | 3.50 |

ANARCHO DICTATOR OF DEATH (See Comics Novel)

ANARKY (See Batman titles)
DC Comics: May, 1997 - No. 4, Aug, 1997 ($2.50, limited series)

| 1 | | | | 3.50 |
| 2-4 | | | | 2.50 |

ANARKY (See Batman titles)
DC Comics: May, 1999 - No. 8, Dec, 1999 ($2.50)

| 1-8: 1-JLA app.; Grant-s/Breyfogle-a. 3-Green Lantern app. 7-Day of Judgment; Haunted Tank app. 8-Joker-c/app. | | | | 2.50 |

ANCHORS ANDREWS (The Saltwater Daffy)
St. John Publishing Co.: Jan, 1953 - No. 4, July, 1953
(Anchors the Saltwater… No. 4)

| 1-Canteen Kate by Matt Baker (9 pgs.) | 20 | 60 | 105 | 175 |
| 2-4 | 7 | 21 | 36 | 50 |

ANCIENT JOE
Dark Horse Comics: Oct, 2001 - No. 3 ($3.50, B&W, limited series)

| 1-C. Scott Morse-s/a | | | | 3.50 |

ANDY & WOODY (See March of Comics No. 40, 55, 76)

ANDY BURNETT (TV, Disney)
Dell Publishing Co.: Dec, 1957

| Four Color 865-Photo-c | 9 | 27 | 63 | 120 |

ANDY COMICS (Formerly Scream Comics; becomes Ernie Comics)
Current Publications (Ace Magazines): No. 20, June, 1948-No. 21, Aug, 1948

| 20,21-Archie-type comic | 7 | 21 | 36 | 50 |

ANDY DEVINE WESTERN
Fawcett Publications: Dec, 1950 - No. 2, 1951

| 1 | 57 | 171 | 356 | 625 |
| 2 | 41 | 123 | 246 | 425 |

ANDY GRIFFITH SHOW, THE (TV)(1st show aired 10/3/60)
Dell Publishing Co.: #1252, Jan-Mar, 1962; #1341, Apr-Jun, 1962

| Four Color 1252(#1), Four Color 1341-Photo-c | 35 | 105 | 245 | 450 |

ANDY HARDY COMICS (See Movie Comics #3 by Fiction House)
Dell Publishing Co.: April, 1952 - No. 6, Sept-Nov, 1954

| Four Color 389(#1) | 4 | 12 | 29 | 45 |
| Four Color 447,480,515, #5,#6 | 3 | 9 | 21 | 32 |

ANDY PANDA (Also see Crackajack Funnies #39, The Funnies, New Funnies & Walter Lantz…)
Dell Publishing Co.: 1943 - No. 56, Nov-Jan, 1961-62 (Walter Lantz)

Four Color 25(#1, 1943)	54	162	378	700
Four Color 54(1944)	30	90	210	400
Four Color 85(1945)	16	48	112	210
Four Color 130(1946),154,198	10	30	70	130
Four Color 216,240,258,280,297	7	21	49	85
Four Color 326,345,358	5	15	34	55
Four Color 383,409	3	9	21	40
16(11-1/52-53) - 30	2	6	14	24
31-56	2	6	12	18

(See March of Comics #5, 22, 79, & Super Book #14, 15, 27.)

A-NEXT (See Avengers)
Marvel Comics: Oct, 1998 - No. 12, Sept, 1999 ($1.99)

| 1-Next generation of Avengers; Frenz-a | | | | 3.00 |
| 2-12: 2-Two covers. 3-Defenders app. | | | | 2.25 |

ANGEL
Dell Publishing Co.: Aug, 1954 - No. 16, Nov-Jan, 1958-59

| Four Color 576(#1, 8/54) | 3 | 9 | 19 | 28 |

Angel and the Ape #1 © DC

Animal Man #6 © DC

TRUE FUN

Animaniacs #26 © WB

	GD2.0	FN6.0	VF8.0	NM9.4
2(5-7/55) - 16	2	6	12	18

ANGEL (TV) (Also see Buffy the Vampire Slayer)
Dark Horse Comics: Nov, 1999 - No. 17, Apr, 2001 ($2.95/$2.99)

1-17: 1-3,5-7,10-14-Zanier-a. 1-4,7,10-Matsuda & photo-c. 16-Buffy-c/app.				3.00

ANGEL (Buffy the Vampire Slayer)
Dark Horse Comics: Sept, 2001 - No. 4 ($2.99, limited series)

1,2-Joss Whedon & Greenwalt-s/Rubi-a; photo-c				3.00

ANGELA
Image Comics (Todd McFarlane Productions): Dec, 1994 - No. 3, Feb, 1995 ($2.95, limited series)

1-Gaiman scripts & Capullo-c/a in all; Spawn app.	1	3	6	8
2				6.00
3				5.00
Special Edition (1995)-Pirate Spawn-c	3	9	17	25
Special Edition (1995)-Angela-c	3	9	17	25
TPB ($9.95, 1995) reprints #1-3 & Special Ed. w/additional pin-ups				10.00

ANGELA/GLORY: RAGE OF ANGELS (See Glory/Angela: Rage of Angels)
Image Comics (Todd McFarlane Productions): Mar, 1996 ($2.50, one-shot)

1-Liefeld-c/Cruz-a(p); Darkchylde preview flip book				4.00
1-Variant-c				4.00

ANGEL AND THE APE (Meet Angel No. 7) (See Limited Collector's Edition C-34 & Showcase No. 77)
National Periodical Publications: Nov-Dec, 1968 - No. 6, Sept-Oct, 1969

1-(11-12/68)-Not Wood-a	4	12	29	45
2-6-Wood inks in all. 4-Last 12¢ issue	3	9	20	30

ANGEL AND THE APE (2nd Series)
DC Comics: Mar, 1991 - No. 4, June, 1991 ($1.00, limited series)

1-4				2.50

ANGEL AND THE APE (3rd Series)
DC Comics(Vertigo): Oct, 2001 - No. 4, Jan 2002 ($2.95, limited series)

1-4-Chaykin & Tischman-s/Bond-a/Art Adams-c				3.00

ANGEL FIRE
Crusade Comics: June, 1997 - No. 3, Oct, 1997 ($2.95, limited series)

1-3: 1-(3 variant covers). 3-B&W				3.00

ANGEL LOVE
DC Comics: Aug, 1986 - No. 8, Mar, 1987 (75¢, limited series)

1-8, Special 1 (1987, $1.25, 52 pgs.)				2.25

ANGEL OF LIGHT, THE (See The Crusaders)

ANIMA
DC Comics: Mar, 1994 - No. 15, July, 1995 ($1.75/$1.95/$2.25)

1-7,0,8-15: 7-(9/94)-Begin $1.95-c; Zero Hour x-over				2.50

ANIMAL ADVENTURES
Timor Publications/Accepted Publ. (reprints): Dec, 1953 - No. 3, May?, 1954

1-Funny animal	6	18	32	45
2,3: 2-Featuring Soopermutt (2/54)	5	14	21	28
1-3 (reprints, nd)	3	7	11	14

ANIMAL ANTICS (Movietown... No. 24 on)
National Periodical Publ: Mar-Apr, 1946 - No. 23, Nov-Dec, 1949 (All 52 pgs.?)

1-Raccoon Kids begins by Otto Feur; some-c by Grossman; Seaman Sy Wheeler by Kelly in some issues	45	135	270	475
2	26	78	136	235
3-10: 10-Post-c/a	16	48	83	140
11-23: 14,15,18,19-Post-a	11	33	55	90

ANIMAL COMICS
Dell Publishing Co.: Dec-Jan, 1941-42 - No. 30, Dec-Jan, 1947-48

1-1st Pogo app. by Walt Kelly (Dan Noonan art in most issues)	95	285	618	1100
2-Uncle Wiggily begins	48	144	312	550
3,5	35	105	228	400
4,6,7-No Pogo	20	60	130	230
8-10	24	72	156	285

	GD2.0	FN6.0	VF8.0	NM9.4
11-15	15	45	98	170
16-20	10	30	65	115
21-30: 24-30- "Jigger" by John Stanley	8	24	49	90

NOTE: *Dan Noonan* a-18-30. *Gollub* art in most later issues; c-29, 30. *Kelly* c-7-26, part #27-30.

ANIMAL CRACKERS (Also see Adventures of Patoruzu)
Green Publ. Co./Norlen/Fox Feat.(Hero Books): 1946; No. 31, July, 1950; No. 9, 1959

1-Super Cat begins (1st app.)	18	54	94	160
2	10	30	55	80
31(Fox)-Formerly My Love Secret	6	18	32	45
9(1959-Norlen)-Infinity-c	4	12	18	24
nn, nd ('50s), no publ.; infinity-c	4	12	18	24

ANIMAL FABLES
E. C. Comics (Fables Publ. Co.): July-Aug, 1946 - No. 7, Nov-Dec, 1947

1-Freddy Firefly (clone of Human Torch), Korky Kangaroo, Petey Pig, Danny Demon begin	43	129	257	450
2-Aesop Fables begin	27	81	145	250
3-6	22	66	116	200
7-Origin Moon Girl	59	177	369	650

ANIMAL FAIR (Fawcett's...)
Fawcett Publications: Mar, 1946 - No. 11, Feb, 1947

1	26	78	139	240
2	13	39	66	110
3-6	10	30	50	80
7-11	8	24	42	60

ANIMAL FUN
Premier Magazines: 1953 (25¢, came w/glasses)

1-(3-D)-Ziggy Pig, Silly Seal, Billy & Buggy Bear	37	111	197	340

ANIMAL MAN (See Action Comics #552, 553, DC Comics Presents #77, 78, Secret Origins #39, Strange Adventures #180 & Wonder Woman #267, 268)
DC Comics (Vertigo imprint #57 on): Sept, 1988 - No. 89, Nov, 1995 ($1.25/$1.50/$1.75/$1.95/$2.25)

1-Grant Morrison scripts begin, ends #26				6.00
2-10: 2-Superman cameo. 6-Invasion tie-in. 9-Manhunter-c/story				3.00
11-49,51-55,57-89: 24-Arkham Asylum story; Bizarro Superman app. 25-Inferior Five app. 26-Morrison apps. in story; part photo-c (of Morrison)				2.50
50-($2.95, 52 pgs.)-Last issue w/Veitch scripts				4.00
56-($3.50, 68 pgs.)				4.00
Annual 1 (1993, $3.95, 68 pgs.)-Bolland-c; Children's Crusade Pt. 3				5.00

NOTE: *Bolland* c-1-63. 71-*Sutton*-a(i)

ANIMAL MYSTIC (See Dark One...)
Cry For Dawn/Sirius: 1993 - No. 4, 1995 ($2.95?/$3.50, B&W)

1	2	6	13	20
1-Alternate	4	12	26	40
1-2nd printing				4.00
2	2	6	11	15
2,3-2nd prints (Sirius)				3.00
3 ,4: 4-Color poster insert, Linsner-s	1	3	6	8
TPB ($14.95) r/				15.00

ANIMAL MYSTIC WATER WARS
Sirius: 1996 - Present ($2.95, limited series)

1-6-Dark One-c/a/scripts				5.00

ANIMAL WORLD, THE (Movie)
Dell Publishing Co.: No. 713, Aug, 1956

Four Color 713	3	9	21	38

ANIMANIACS (TV)
DC Comics: May, 1995 - No. 59, Apr, 2000 ($1.50/$1.75/$1.95/$1.99)

1				6.00
2-20: 13-Manga issue. 19-X-Files parody; Miran Kim-c; Adlard-a (4 pgs.)				4.00
21-59: 26-E.C. parody-c. 34-Xena parody. 43-Pinky & the Brain take over				2.50
A Christmas Special (12/94, $1.50, "1" on-c)				3.00

ANIMATED COMICS
E. C. Comics: No date given (Summer, 1947?)

1 (Rare)	70	210	438	770

Ant-Man's Big Christmas #1 © MAR

A-1 #7 © ME

A-1 #82 © ME

	GD2.0	FN6.0	VF8.0	NM9.4

ANIMATED FUNNY COMIC TUNES (See Funny Tunes)

ANIMATED MOVIE-TUNES (Movie Tunes No. 3)
Margood Publishing Corp. (Timely): Fall, 1945 - No. 2, Sum, 1946

1,2-Super Rabbit, Ziggy Pig & Silly Seal	25	75	130	225

ANIMAX
Marvel Comics (Star Comics): Dec, 1986 - No. 4, June, 1987

1-4: Based on toys; Simonson-a				3.00

ANNE RICE'S INTERVIEW WITH THE VAMPIRE
Innovation Books: 1991 - No. 12, Jan, 1994 ($2.50, limited series)

1-12: Adapts novel; Moeller-a 3.00

ANNE RICE'S THE MASTER OF RAMPLING GATE
Innovation Books: 1991 ($6.95, one-shot)

1-Bolton painted-c; Colleen Doran painted-a 7.00

ANNE RICE'S THE MUMMY OR RAMSES THE DAMNED
Millennium Publications: Oct, 1990 - No. 12, Feb, 1992 ($2.50, limited series)

1-12: Adapts novel; Mooney-p in all 3.00

ANNE RICE'S THE WITCHING HOUR
Millennium Publ./Comico: 1992 - No. 13, Jan, 1993 ($2.50, limited series)

1-13 .... 3.00

ANNETTE (Disney, TV)
Dell Publishing Co.: No. 905, May, 1958; No. 1100, May, 1960
(Mickey Mouse Club)

Four Color 905-Annette Funicello photo-c	28	84	196	365
Four Color 1100-...'s Life Story (Movie); A. Funicello photo-c				
	23	69	161	300

ANNEX (See Amazing Spider-Man Annual #27 for 1st app.)
Marvel Comics: Aug, 1994 - No. 4, Nov, 1994 ($1.75)

1-4: 1,4-Spider-Man app. 2.25

ANNIE
Marvel Comics Group: Oct, 1982 - No. 2, Nov, 1982 (60¢)

1,2-Movie adaptation				3.00
Treasury Edition ($2.00, tabloid size)	2	6	15	22

ANNIE OAKLEY (See Tessie The Typist #19, Two-Gun Kid & Wild Western)
Marvel/Atlas Comics(MPI No. 1-4/CDS No. 5 on): Spring, 1948 - No. 4, 11/48;
No. 5, 6/55 - No. 11, 6/56

1 (1st Series, 1948)-Hedy Devine app.	43	129	257	450
2 (7/48, 52 pgs.)-Kurtzman-a, "Hey Look", 1 pg; Intro. Lana; Hedy Devine app; Captain Tootsie by Beck	27	81	145	250
3,4	23	69	121	210
5 (2nd Series, 1955)-Reinman-a ; Maneely-c	17	51	88	150
6-9; 6,8-Woodbridge-a. 9-Williamson-a (4 pgs.)	13	39	66	110
10,11: 11-Severin-c	12	36	61	100

ANNIE OAKLEY AND TAGG (TV)
Dell Publishing Co./Gold Key: 1953 - No. 18, Jan-Mar, 1959; July, 1965
(Gail Davis photo-c #3 on)

Four Color 438 (#1)	15	45	105	190
Four Color 481,575 (#2,3)	9	27	63	115
4(7-9/55)-10	8	24	56	100
11-18(1-3/59)	6	18	42	80
1(7/65-Gold Key)-Photo-c (c-r/#6)	5	15	35	60
NOTE: *Manning* a-13. Photo back c-4, 9, 11.

ANOTHER WORLD (See Strange Stories From...)

ANTHRO
National Periodical Publications: July-Aug, 1968 - No. 6, July-Aug, 1969

1-(7-8/68)-Howie Post-a in all	5	15	38	60
2-6: 5-Last 12¢ issue. 6-Wood-c/a (inks)	3	10	23	35

ANTI-HITLER COMICS
New England Comics Press: Summer, 1992 ($2.75, B&W, one-shot)

1-Reprints Hitler as Devil stories from wartime comics 3.00

ANT-MAN'S BIG CHRISTMAS
Marvel Comics: Feb, 2000 ($5.95, square-bound, one-shot)

1-Bob Gale-s/Phil Winslade-a; Avengers app. 6.00

ANTONY AND CLEOPATRA (See Ideal, a Classical Comic)

ANYTHING GOES
Fantagraphics Books: Oct, 1986 - No. 6, 1987 ($2.00, #1-5 color & B&W/#6 B&W, limited series)

1-6: 1-Flaming Carrot app. (1st in color?); G. Kane-c. 2-6: 2-Miller-c(p); Alan Moore scripts; Kirby-a; early Sam Kieth-a (2 pgs.). 3-Capt. Jack, Cerebus app.; Cerebus-c by N. Adams. 4-Perez-c. 5-3rd color Teenage Mutant Ninja Turtles app. 3.50

A-1
Marvel Comics (Epic Comics): 1992 - No. 4, 1993 ($5.95, limited ser., mature)

1-4: 1-Fabry-c/a, Russell-a, S. Hampton-a. 3-Bisley-c; Kent Williams-a. 4-McKean-a; Dorman-a/s. 6.00

A-1 COMICS (A-1 appears on covers No. 1-17 only)(See individual title listings for #11-139) (1st two issues not numbered.)
Life's Romances Publ.-No. 1/Compix/Magazine Ent.: 1944 - No. 139, Sept-Oct, 1955 (No #2)

nn-(1944) (See Kerry Drake Detective Cases)

1-Dotty Dripple (1 pg.), Mr. Ex, Bush Berry, Rocky, Lew Loyal (20 pgs.)				
	10	30	55	80
3-8,10: Texas Slim & Dirty Dalton, The Corsair, Teddy Rich, Dotty Dripple, Inca Dinca, Tommy Tinker, Little Mexico & Tugboat Tim, The Masquerader & others. 7-Corsair-c/s. 8-Intro Rodeo Ryan	7	21	38	55
9-All Texas Slim	8	24	42	60

(See Individual Alphabetical listings for prices)

11-Teena; Ogden Whitney-c	12,15-Teena
13-Guns of Fact & Fiction (1948). Used in SOTI, pg. 19; Ingels & Johnny Craig-a	14-Tim Holt Western Adventures #1
	16-Vacation Comics; The Pixies, Tom Tom, Flying Fredd, & Koko & Kola
17-Tim Holt #2; photo-c; last issue to carry A-1 on cover (9-10/48)	18,20-Jimmy Durante; photo covers on both
19-Tim Holt #3; photo-c	21-Joan of Arc (1949)-Movie adaptation; Ingrid Bergman photo-covers & interior photos; Whitney-a
22-Dick Powell (1949)-Photo-c	
23-Cowboys and Indians #6; Doc Holiday-c/story	24-Trail Colt #1-Frazetta-r in-Manhunt #13; Ingels-c; L. B. Cole-a
25-Fibber McGee & Molly (1949) (Radio)	27-Ghost Rider #1(1950)-Origin
26-Trail Colt #2-Ingels-c	29-Ghost Rider #2-Frazetta-c (1950)
28-Christmas-(Koko & Kola #6) ("50)	31-Ghost Rider #3-Frazetta-c & origin ('51)
30-Jet Powers #1-Powell-a	
32-Jet Powers #2	34-Ghost Rider #4-Frazetta-c (1951)
33-Muggsy Mouse #1('51)	36-Muggsy Mouse #2; Racist-c
35-Jet Powers #3-Williamson/Evans-a	38-Jet Powers #4-Williamson/Wood-a
37-Ghost Rider #5-Frazetta-c (1951)	40-Dogface Dooley #1('51)
39-Muggsy Mouse #3	42-Best of the West #1-Powell-a
41-Cowboys 'N' Indians #7 (1951)	44-Ghost Rider #6
43-Dogface Dooley #2	46-Best of the West #2
45-American Air Forces #5-Powell-a	48-Cowboys 'N' Indians #8
47-Thun'da, King of the Congo #1-Frazetta-c/a(1952)	49-Dogface Dooley #3
50-Danger Is Their Business #11 ('52)-Powell-a	51-Ghost Rider #7 ('52)
	52-Best of the West #3
53-Dogface Dooley #4	54-American Air Forces #6(8/52)-Powell-a
55-U.S. Marines #5-Powell-a	
56-Thun'da #2-Powell-c/a	57-Ghost Rider #8
58-American Air Forces #7-Powell-a	59-Best of the West #4
60-Thu'da, U.S. Marines #6-Powell-a	61-Space Ace #5('53)-Guardineer-a
62-Starr Flagg, Undercover Girl #5 (#1) reprinted from A-1 #24	63-Manhunt #13-Frazetta
	64-Dogface Dooley #5
65-American Air Forces #8-Powell-a	66-Best of the West #5
67-American Air Forces #9-Powell-a	68-U.S. Marines #7-Powell-a
69-Ghost Rider #9(10/52)	70-Best of the West #6
71-Ghost Rider #10(12/52)-Vs. Frankenstein	72-U.S. Marines #8-Powell-a(3)
74-American Air Forces #10-Powell-a	73-Thun'da #3-Powell-c/a
76-Best of the West #7	75-Ghost Rider #11(3/52)
78-Thun'da #4-Powell-c/a	77-Manhunt #14
80-Ghost Rider #12(6/52)-One-eyed Devil-c	79-American Air Forces #11-Powell-a
	81-Best of the West #8
	82-Cave Girl #11(1953)-Powell-c/a;

Aphrodite IX #2 © TCOW

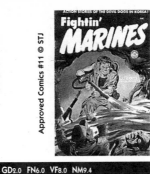

Approved Comics #11 © STJ

Aquaman #29 © DC

	GD2.0	FN6.0	VF8.0	NM9.4

83-Thun'da #5-Powell-c/a
84-Ghost Rider #13(7-8/53)
86-Thun'da #6-Powell-c/a
88-Bobby Benson's B-Bar-B Riders #20
90-Red Hawk #11(1953)-Powell-c/a
91-American Air Forces #12-Powell-a
93-Great Western #8('54)-Origin
   The Ghost Rider; Powell-a
95-Muggsy Mouse #4
96-Cave Girl #12, with Thun'da;
   Powell-c/a
99-Muggsy Mouse #5
101-White Indian #12-Frazetta-a(r)
101-Dream Book of Romance #6
   (4-6/54); Marlon Brando photo-c;
   Powell, Bolle, Guardineer-a
105-Great Western #9-Ghost Rider
   app.; Powell-a, 6 pgs.; Bolle-a
107-Hot Dog #1
108-Red Fox #15 (1954)-L.B. Cole
   c/a; Powell-a
110-Dream Book of Romance #8
   (10/54)-Movie photo-c
112-Ghost Rider #14 ('54)
114-Dream Book of Love #2-
   Guardineer, Bolle-a; Piper Laurie,
   Victor Mature photo-c
118-Undercover Girl #7-Powell-c
120-Badmen of the West #2
121-Mysteries of Scotland Yard #1;
   reprinted from Manhunt (5 stories)
124-Dream Book of Romance #8
   (10-11/54)
126-I'm a Cop #2-Powell-a
128-I'm a Cop #3-Powell-a
130-Strongman #1-Powell-a (2-3/55)
132-Strongman #2
134-Strongman #3
136-Hot Dog #4
138-The Avenger #4-Powell-c/a

origin (#1)
85-Best of the West #9
87-Best of the West #10(9-10/53)
89-Home Run #3-Powell-a;
   Stan Musial photo-c
92-Dream Book of Romance #5-
   Photo-c; Guardineer-a
94-White Indian #11-Frazetta-a(r);
   Powell-a
97-Best of the West #11
98-Undercover Girl #6-Powell-c
100-Badmen of the West #1-
   Meskin-a(?)
103-Best of the West #12-Powell-a
104-White Indian #13-Frazetta-a(r)
   ('54)
106-Dream Book of Love #1 (6-7/54)
   -Powell, Bolle-a; Montgomery Clift,
   Donna Reed photo-c
109-Dream Book of Romance #7
   (7-8/54). Powell-a; movie photo-c
111-I'm a Cop #1 ('54); drug
   mention story; Powell-a
113-Great Western #10; Powell-a
115-Hot Dog #3
116-Cave Girl #13-Powell-c/a
117-White Indian #14
119-Straight Arrow's Fury #1 (origin);
   Fred Meagher-c/a
122-Black Phantom #1 (11/54)
123-Dream Book of Love #3
   (10-11/54)-Movie photo-c
125-Cave Girl #14-Powell-a
127-Great Western #11('54)-Powell-a
129-The Avenger #1('55)-Powell-c
131-The Avenger #2('55)-Powell-c/a
133-The Avenger #3-Powell-a
135-White Indian #15
137-Africa #1-Powell-c/a(4)
139-Strongman #4-Powell-a

NOTE: *Bolle*-a-110. Photo-c-17-22, 89, 92, 101, 106, 109, 110, 114, 123, 124.

APACHE
Fiction House Magazines: 1951

1	22	66	116	200
I.W. Reprint No. 1-r/#1 above	3	9	20	30

APACHE KID (Formerly Reno Browne; Western Gunfighters #20 on)
(Also see Two-Gun Western & Wild Western)
Marvel/Atlas Comics(MPC No. 53-10/CPS No. 11 on): No. 53, 12/50 - No. 10, 1/52; No. 11, 12/54 - No. 19, 4/56

53(#1)-Apache Kid & his horse Nightwind (origin), Red Hawkins by Syd				
Shores begins	35	105	188	325
2(2/51)	17	51	88	150
3-5	12	36	61	100
6-10 (1951-52): 7-Russ Heath-a	10	30	55	85
11-19 (1954-56)	8	24	45	65

NOTE: *Heath*-a-7. c-11, 13. *Maneely*-a-53; c-53(#1), 12, 14-16. *Powell*-a-14. *Severin*-c-17.

APACHE MASSACRE (See Chief Victorio's...)

APACHE TRAIL
Steinway/America's Best: Sept, 1957 - No. 4, June, 1958

1	11	33	55	90
2-4: 2-Tuska-a	7	21	36	50

APE (Magazine)
Dell Publishing Co.: 1961 (52 pgs., B&W)

1-Comics and humor	3	10	23	35

APHRODITE IX
Image Comics (Top Cow): Sept, 2000 - Present ($2.50)

1-3: 1-Four covers by Finch, Turner, Silvestri, Benitez				2.50

1-Tower Record Ed.; Finch-c				2.50
1-DF Chrome ($14.99)				15.00
Convention Preview				10.00
Wizard #0 (4/00, bagged w/Tomb Raider magazine) Preview & sketchbook				5.00
#0-(6/01, $2.95) r/Wizard #0 with cover gallery				3.00

APOLLO SMILE
Eagle Wing Press: July, 1998 - No. 2 ($2.95)

1,2-Manga				3.00

APPARITION
Caliber Comics: 1995 ($3.95, 52 pgs., B&W)

1 ($3.95)				4.00
V2#1-6 ($2.95)				3.00
Visitations				4.00

APPLESEED
Eclipse Comics: Sept, 1988 - Book 4, Vol. 4, Aug, 1991 ($2.50/$2.75/$3.50, 52/68 pgs, B&W)

Book One, Vol. 1-5: 5-(1/89), Book Two, Vol. 1(2/89) -5(7/89): Art Adams-c,
   Book Three, Vol. 1(8/89) -4 ($2.75), Book Three, Vol. 5 ($3.50), Book Four,
| Vol. 1 (1/91) - 4 (8/91) ($3.50, 68 pgs.) | | | | 4.00 |

APPLESEED DATABOOK
Dark Horse Comics: Apr, 1994 - No. 2, May, 1994 ($3.50, B&W, limited series)

1,2: 1-Flip book format				3.50

APPROVED COMICS (Also see Blue Ribbon Comics)
St. John Publishing Co. (Most have no c-price): March, 1954 - No. 12, Aug, 1954 (Painted-c on #1-5,7,8,10)

1-The Hawk #5-r	10	30	55	85
2-Invisible Boy (3/54)-Origin; Saunders-c	17	51	88	150
3-Wild Boy of the Congo #11-r (4/54)	10	30	55	85
4,5: 4-Kid Cowboy-r. 5-Fly Boy-r	10	30	55	85
6-Daring Adv.-r (5/54); Krigstein-a(2); Baker-c	13	39	66	110
7-The Hawk #6-r	10	30	55	85
8-Crime on the Run (6/54); Powell-a; Saunders-c	10	30	55	85
9-Western Bandit Trails #3-r, with new-c; Baker-c/a	13	39	66	115
10-Dinky Duck (Terrytoons)	5	15	23	30
11-Fightin' Marines #3-r (8/54); Canteen Kate app; Baker-c/a				
	14	42	72	120
12-Northwest Mounties #4-r(8/54); new Baker-c	14	42	72	120

AQUAMAN (See Adventure #260, Brave & the Bold, DC Comics Presents #5, DC Special #28, DC Special Series #1, DC Super Stars #7, Detective, JLA, Justice League of America, More Fun #73, Showcase #30-33, Super DC Giant, Super Friends, and World's Finest Comics)

AQUAMAN (1st Series)
National Periodical Publications/DC Comics: Jan-Feb, 1962 - #56, Mar-Apr, 1971; #57, Aug-Sept,1977 - #63, Aug-Sept, 1978

1-(1-2/62)-Intro. Quisp	63	189	531	1000
2	30	90	210	375
3-5	17	51	118	210
6-10	12	36	84	140
11-20: 11-1st app. Mera. 18-Aquaman weds Mera; JLA cameo				
	9	27	63	105
21-32: 23-Birth of Aquababy. 26-Huntress app.(3-4/66). 29-1st app.				
Ocean Master, Aquaman's step-brother. 30-Batman & Superman-c &				
cameo	6	18	40	65
33-1st app. Aqua-Girl (see Adventure #266)	6	18	45	75
34-40: 40-Jim Aparo's 1st DC work (8/68)	4	12	29	45
41-46,47,49: 45-Last 12¢-c	4	12	10	35
48-Origin reprinted	4	12	26	40
50-52-Deadman by Neal Adams	6	18	40	65
53-56('71): 56-1st app. Crusader; last 15¢-c	2	6	10	14
57('77)-63: 58-Origin retold	1	3	6	8

NOTE: *Aparo*-a-40-45, 46p, 47-59; c-58-63. *Nick Cardy* c-1-39. *Newton* a-60-63.

AQUAMAN (1st limited series)
DC Comics: Feb, 1986 - No. 4, May, 1986 (75¢, limited series)

1-New costume; 1st app. Nuada of Thierna Na Oge.				5.00
2-4: 3-Retelling of Aquaman & Ocean Master's origins.				3.50
Special 1 (1988, $1.50, 52 pgs.)				3.50

NOTE: *Craig Hamilton* c/a-1-4p. *Russell* c-2-4i.

Aquaman (3rd series) #63 © DC

Archer and Armstrong #3 © VAL

Archie & Friends #47 © AP

	GD2.0	FN6.0	VF8.0	NM9.4

AQUAMAN (2nd limited series)
DC Comics: June, 1989 - No. 5, Oct, 1989 ($1.00, limited series)

1-5: Giffen plots/breakdowns; Swan-a(p).		2.50
Special 1 (Legend of..., $2.00, 1989, 52 pgs.)-Giffen plots/breakdowns; Swan-a(p).		2.50

AQUAMAN (2nd Series)
DC Comics: Dec, 1991 - No. 13, Dec, 1992 ($1.00/$1.25)

1-5	2.50
6-13: 6-Begin $1.25-c. 9-Sea Devils app.	2.50

AQUAMAN (3rd Series)(Also see Atlantis Chronicles)
DC Comics: Aug, 1994 - No. 75, Jan, 2001 ($1.50/$1.75/$1.95/$1.99/$2.50)

1-(8/94)-Peter David scripts begin; reintro Dolphin	5.00
2-(9/94)-Aquaman loses hand	6.00
0-(10/94)-Aquaman replaces lost hand w/hook.	6.00
3-8: 3-(11/94)-Superboy-c/app. 4-Lobo app. 6-Deep Six app.	3.00
9-42,44-69: 9-Begin $1.75-c. 10-Green Lantern app. 11-Reintro Mera. 15-Reintro Kordax. 16-vs. JLA. 18-Reintro Ocean Master & Atlan (Aquaman's father). 19-Reintro Garth (Aqualad). 23-1st app. Deep Blue (Neptune Perkins & Tsunami's daughter). 23,24-Neptune Perkins, Nuada, Tsunami, Arion, Power Girl, & The Sea Devils app. 26-Final Night. 28-Martian Manhunter-c/app. 29-Black Manta-c/app. 32-Swamp Thing-c/app. 37-Genesis x-over 41-Thanagar-c/app. 44-G.A. Flash & Sentinel app. 50-Larsen-s begins. 53-Superman app. 60-Tempest marries Dolphin; Teen Titans app. 63-Kaluta covers begin. 66-JLA app.	2.50
43-Millennium Giants x-over; Superman-c/app.	3.00
70-75: 70-Begin $2.50-c. 71-73-Warlord-c/app. 75-Final issue	2.50
#1,000,000 (11/98) 853rd Century x-over	3.00
Annual 1 (1995, $3.50)-Year One story	3.50
Annual 2 (1996, $2.95)-Legends of the Dead Earth story	3.00
Annual 3 (1997, $3.95)-Pulp Heroes story	4.00
Annual 4,5 ('98, '99, $2.95)-4-Ghosts; Wrightson-c. 5-JLApe	3.00
...Secret Files 1 (12/98, $4.95) Origin-s and pin-ups	5.00

NOTE: *Art Adams*-c, Annual 5. *Mignola* c-6. *Simonson* c-15.

AQUAMAN: TIME & TIDE (3rd limited series) (Also see Atlantis Chronicles)
DC Comics: Dec, 1993 - No. 4, Mar, 1994 ($1.50, limited series)

1-4: Peter David scripts; origin retold.	3.00
Trade paperback ($9.95)	10.00

AQUANAUTS (TV)
Dell Publishing Co.: May - July, 1961

Four Color 1197-Photo-c	7	21	49	90

ARABIAN NIGHTS (See Cinema Comics Herald)

ARACHNOPHOBIA (Movie)
Hollywood Comics (Disney Comics): 1990 ($5.95, 68 pg. graphic novel)

nn-Adaptation of film; Spiegle-a	6.00
Comic edition ($2.95, 68 pgs.)	3.00

ARAK/SON OF THUNDER (See Warlord #48)
DC Comics: Sept, 1981 - No. 50, Nov, 1985

1,24,50: 1-1st app. Angelica, Princess of White Cathay. 24,50-(52 pgs.)	3.00
2-23,25-49: 3-Intro Valda. 12-Origin Valda. 20-Origin Angelica	2.25
Annual 1(10/84)	3.00

ARCANA (Also see Books of Magic limited & ongoing series and Mister E)
DC Comics (Vertigo): 1994 ($3.95, 68 pgs., annual)

1-Bolton painted-c; Children's Crusade/Tim Hunter story	4.00

ARCANUM
Image Comics (Top Cow Productions): Apr, 1997 - No. 8, Feb, 1998 ($2.50)

1/2 Gold Edition	12.00
1-Brandon Peterson-s/a(p), 1-Variant-c, 4-American Ent. Ed.	3.00
2-8	2.50
3-Variant-c	4.00

ARCHANGEL (See Uncanny X-Men, X-Factor & X-Men)
Marvel Comics: Feb, 1996 ($2.50, B&W, one-shot)

1-Milligan story	2.50

ARCHER & ARMSTRONG
Valiant: July (June inside), 1992 - No. 26, Oct, 1994 ($2.50)

0-(7/92)-B. Smith-c/a; Reese-i assists	3.00
0-(Gold Logo)	6.00
1-7,9-26: 1-(8/92)-Origin & 1st app. Archer; Miller-c; B. Smith/Layton-a. 2-2nd app Turok(c/story); Smith/Layton-a; Simonson-c. 3,4-Smith-c&a(p) & scripts. 10-2nd app. Ivar. 10,11-B. Smith-c. 21,22-Shadowman app. 22-w/bound-in trading card. 25-Eternal Warrior app. 26-Flip book w/Eternal Warrior #26	2.50
8-($4.50, 52 pgs.)-Combined with Eternal Warrior #8; B. Smith-c/a & scripts; 1st app. Ivar the Time Walker	4.50

ARCHIE (See Archie Comics) (Also see Christmas & Archie, Everything's..., Explorers of the Unknown, Jackpot, Little..., Oxydol-Dreft, Pep, Riverdale High, Teenage Mutant Ninja Turtles Adventures & To Riverdale and Back Again)

ARCHIE AMERICANA SERIES, BEST OF THE FORTIES
Archie Publications: 1991 ($10.95, trade paperback)

V1-r/early strips from 1940's; intro. by Steven King.	2	6	11	15

ARCHIE AMERICANA SERIES, BEST OF THE FIFTIES
Archie Publications: 1991 ($8.95, trade paperback)

V2-r/strips from 1950's;	2	6	10	14
2nd printing (1998, $9.95)				10.00

ARCHIE AMERICANA SERIES, BEST OF THE SIXTIES
Archie Publications: 1995 ($9.95, trade paperback)

V3-r/strips from 1960's; intro. by Frankie Avalon.	12.00

ARCHIE AMERICANA SERIES, BEST OF THE SEVENTIES
Archie Publications: 1997 ($9.95, trade paperback)

V4-r/strips from 1970's	12.00

ARCHIE AMERICANA SERIES, BEST OF THE EIGHTIES
Archie Publications: 2001 ($10.95, trade paperback)

V5-r/strips from 1980's; forward by Steve Geppi	11.00

ARCHIE AND BIG ETHEL
Spire Christian Comics (Fleming H. Revell Co.): 1982 (69¢)

nn -(Low print run)	2	6	9	12

ARCHIE & FRIENDS
Archie Comics: Dec, 1992 - Present ($1.25/$1.50/$1.75/$1.79/$1.99, bi-monthly)

1	5.00
2,4,10-14,17,18,20-Sabrina app. 20-Archie's Band-c	4.00
3,5-9,16	2.50
15-Babewatch w/Sabrina app.	6.00
19-Josie and the Pussycats app.; E.T. parody-c/s	5.00
21-46	2.25
47-All Josie and the Pussycats issue; movie and actress profiles/photos	2.25
48-53-Josie and the Pussycats-c/s	2.25

ARCHIE AND ME (See Archie Giant Series Mag. #578, 591, 603, 616, 626)
Archie Publications: Oct, 1964 - No. 161, Feb, 1987

1	16	48	110	190
2	8	24	58	95
3-5	5	15	34	55
6-10	3	9	20	32
11-20	3	6	15	22
21(6/68)-26,28-30: 21-UFO story. 26-X-Mas-c	2	6	12	18
27-Groovyman & Knowman superhero-s; UFO-sty	3	9	17	24
31-42: 37-Japan Expo '70-c/s	2	6	9	12
43-48,50-63-(All Giants): 43-(8/71) Mummy-s. 44-Mermaid-s. 62-Elvis cameo-c. 63-(2/74)	2	6	12	18
49-(Giant) Josie & the Pussycats-c/app.	3	9	17	24
64-66,68-99-(Regular size): 85-Bicentennial-s. 98-Collectors Comics	1	3	6	9
67-Sabrina app.(8/74)	2	6	10	14
100-(4/78)	2	6	9	12
101-120: 107-UFO-s				6.00
121(8/80)-159: 134-Riverdale 2001				5.00
160,161: 160-Origin Mr. Weatherbee. 161-Last issue				6.00

ARCHIE AND MR. WEATHERBEE
Spire Christian Comics (Fleming H. Revell Co.): 1980 (59¢)

nn -(Low print run)	1	3	6	9

Archie at Riverdale High #3 © AP   Archie Comics #57 © AP   Archie Comics #378 © AP   **AR**

	GD2.0	FN6.0	VF8.0	NM9.4

ARCHIE...ARCHIE ANDREWS, WHERE ARE YOU? (...Comics Digest #9, 10; ...Comics Digest Mag. No. 11 on)
Archie Publications: Feb, 1977 - Present (Digest size, 160-128 pgs., quarterly)

	GD2.0	FN6.0	VF8.0	NM9.4
1	3	9	17	25
2,3,5,7-9-N. Adams-a; 8-r-/origin The Fly by S&K. 9-Steel Sterling-r	2	6	11	15
4,6,10 ($1.00/$1.50)	2	6	9	12
11-20: 17-Katy Keene story	1	3	6	9
21-50,100	1	3	5	7
51-70				4.00
71-117: 113-Begin $1.95-c				3.00

ARCHIE AS PUREHEART THE POWERFUL (Also see Archie Giant Series #142, Jughead as Captain Hero, Life With Archie & Little Archie)
Archie Publications (Radio Comics): Sept, 1966 - No. 6, Nov, 1967

	GD2.0	FN6.0	VF8.0	NM9.4
1-Super hero parody	9	27	63	105
2	5	15	38	60
3-6	4	12	29	45

NOTE: Evilheart cameos in all. Title: Archie As Pureheart the Powerful #1-3; ...As Capt. Pureheart-#4-6.

ARCHIE AT RIVERDALE HIGH (See Archie Giant Series Magazine #573, 586, 604 & Riverdale High)
Archie Publications: Aug, 1972 - No. 113, Feb, 1987

	GD2.0	FN6.0	VF8.0	NM9.4
1	6	18	40	65
2	3	9	21	32
3-5	3	9	17	24
6-10	2	6	12	18
11-30	2	6	12	18
31(12/75)-46,48-50(12/77)	1	3	6	9
47-Archie in drag-s; Betty mud wrestling-s	2	6	9	12
51-80,100 (12/84)				6.00
81(8/81)-88, 91,93-95,97,98: 96-Anti-smoking issue				5.00
89,90-Early Cheryl Blossom app. 90-Archies Band app.	2	6	10	14
92,96,99-Cheryl Blossom app.	1	4	7	10
101,102,104-109,111,112: 102-Ghost-c				4.00
103-Archie dates Cheryl Blossom-s	1	4	7	10
110,113: 110-Godzilla-s. 113-Last issue				6.00

ARCHIE COMICS (Archie #114 on; 1st Teen-age comic; Radio show aired 6/2/45 by NBC)
MLJ Magazines No. 1-19/Archie Publ.No. 20 on: Winter, 1942-43 - No. 19, 3-4/46; No. 20, 5-6/46 - Present

	GD2.0	FN6.0	VF8.0	NM9.4
1 (Scarce)-Jughead, Veronica app.; 1st app. Mrs. Andrews	1214	3642	8500	17,000
2	300	900	1875	3300
3 (60 pgs.)(scarce)	236	708	1477	2600
4,5: 4-Article about Archie radio series	127	381	795	1400
6,8-10: 6-X-Mas-c.	89	267	556	975
7-1st definitive love triangle story	93	279	581	1025
11-20: 15,17,18-Dotty & Ditto by Woggon. 16-Woggon-a	59	177	369	650
21-30: 23-Betty & Veronica by Woggon. 25-Woggon-a. 30-Coach Piffle app., a Coach Kleets prototype. 34-Pre-Dilton try-out (named Dilbert)	40	120	232	400
31-40	26	78	139	240
41-50	18	54	94	160
51-60: (1954) 51-Katy Keene app.	9	27	65	110
61-70 (1954): 65-70, Katy Keene app.	7	21	53	85
71-80: 72-74-Katy Keene app.	6	18	40	65
81-99: 94-1st Coach Kleets	4	12	30	50
100	6	18	40	65
101-122,124-130 (1962)	3	10	23	35
123-UFO-c/s; Vampire-s	4	12	26	40
131-157,159,160	2	6	15	22
158-Archie in drag story	3	9	17	25
161(2/66)-182,184,186-195,197-199: 168-Superhero gag-c. 176,178-Twiggy-s	1	4	11	15
183-1st Caveman Archie gang story	2	6	12	18
185-1st "The Archies" Band story	3	9	17	25

	GD2.0	FN6.0	VF8.0	NM9.4
196 (12/69)-1st Cricket O'Dell	3	9	19	28
200 (6/70)	2	6	12	18
201-230(11/73): 213-Sabrina/Josie-c cameos. 229-Lost Child issue	1	4	7	10
231-260(3/77): 253-Tarzan parody	1	3	6	8
261-282, 284-299	1	3	5	7
283(8/79)-Cover/story plugs "International Children's Appeal" which was a fraudulent charity, according to TV's 20/20 news program broadcast July 20, 1979	1	3	6	8
300(1/81)-Anniversary issue	1	3	6	8
301-321,323-325,327-335,337-350: 323-Cheryl Blossom pin-up				5.00
322-E.T. story				6.00
326-Early Cheryl Blossom story	2	6	11	16
336-Michael Jackson/Boy George parody				6.00
351-399: 356-Calgary Olympics Special. 393-Infinity-c; 1st comic book printed on recycled paper				4.00
400 (6/92)-Shows 1st meeting of Little Archie and Veronica				3.00
401-428				2.25
429-Love Showdown part 1				5.00
430-517: 467- "A Storm Over Uniforms" x-over parts 3,4				2.25
Annual 1 ('50)-116 pgs. (Scarce)	164	492	1023	1800
Annual 2 ('51)	82	246	511	900
Annual 3 ('52)	50	150	300	525
Annual 4,5 (1953-54)	39	117	208	360
Annual 6-10 (1955-59): 8-(100 pgs.). 10-(84 pgs.) Elvis record on-c	14	42	102	175
Annual 11-15 (1960-65): 12,13-(84 pgs.) 14,15-(68 pgs.)	7	21	53	85
Annual 16-20 (1966-70)(all 68 pgs.): 20-Archie's band-c	4	12	26	40
Annual 21,22,24-26 (1971-75): 21,22-(68 pgs.). 22-Archie's band-s. 24-26-(52 pgs.). 25-Cavemen-c	2	6	13	20
Annual 23-Archie's band-c/s; Josie/Sabrina-c	3	9	17	25
Annual Digest 27 ('75)	3	10	23	35
...28-30	2	6	13	20
...31-34	2	6	11	15
...35-40 (...Magazine #35 on)	1	4	7	10
...41-65 ('94)				4.50
...66-69				3.00
...All-Star Specials(Winter '75, $1.25)-6 remaindered Archie comics rebound in each; titles: "The World of Giant Comics", "Giant Grab Bag of Comics", "Triple Giant Comics" & "Giant Spec. Comics	3	10	23	35
Special Edition-Christmas With Archie 1(1/75)-Treasury (rare)	4	12	30	50

NOTE: Archies Band-s-185, 188-192, 197, 198, 201, 204, 205, 208, 209, 215, 329, 330; Band-c-191, 330. Caveman Archie Gang-s-183, 192, 197, 208, 210, 220, 223, 282, 333, 335, 338, 340. Al Fagly c-17-35. Bob Montana c-38, 41-50, 58, Annual 1-4. Bill Woggon c-53, 54.

ARCHIE COMICS DIGEST (...Magazine No. 37-95)
Archie Publications: Aug, 1973 - Present (Small size, 160-128 pgs.)

	GD2.0	FN6.0	VF8.0	NM9.4
1-(1st Archie digest?)	9	27	63	105
2	4	12	30	50
3-5	4	12	25	38
6-10	2	6	15	22
11-33: 32,33-The Fly-r by S&K	2	6	10	14
34-60	1	4	7	10
61-80,100	1	3	6	9
81-99				5.00
101-140: 36-Katy Keene story				4.00
141-165				3.00
166-185				2.25

NOTE: Neal Adams a-1, 2, 4, 5, 19-21, 24, 25, 27, 29, 31, 33. X-mas c-88, 94, 100, 106.

ARCHIE COMICS PRESENTS: THE LOVE SHOWDOWN COLLECTION
Archie Publications: 1994 ($4.95, squarebound)

	GD2.0	FN6.0	VF8.0	NM9.4
nn-r/Archie #429, Betty #19, Betty & Veronica #82, & Veronica #39				6.00

ARCHIE GETS A JOB
Spire Christian Comics (Fleming H. Revell Co.): 1977

	GD2.0	FN6.0	VF8.0	NM9.4
nn	1	3	6	8

ARCHIE GIANT SERIES MAGAZINE
Archie Publications: 1954 - No. 632, July, 1992 (No #36-135, no #252-451)

Archie Giant Series #19 © AP

Archie Giant Series #139 © AP

Archie Giant Series #226 © AP

	GD2.0	FN6.0	VF8.0	NM9.4

(#1 not code approved) (#1-233 are Giants; #12-184 are 68 pgs.;#185-194,197-233 are 52 pgs.; #195,196 are 84 pgs.; #234-up are 36 pgs.)

	GD2.0	FN6.0	VF8.0	NM9.4
1-Archie's Christmas Stocking	118	354	738	1300
2-Archie's Christmas Stocking('55)	68	205	426	750
3-6-Archie's Christmas Stocking('56-'59)	47	141	286	500

7-10: 7-Katy Keene Holiday Fun(9/60); Bill Woggon-c. 8-Betty & Veronica Summer Fun(10/60); baseball story w/Babe Ruth & Lou Gehrig. 9-The World of Jughead (12/60). 10-Archie's Christmas Stocking(1/61)

| | | 37 | 111 | 197 | 340 |

11,13,16,18: 11-Betty & Veronica Spectacular (6/61). 13-Betty & Veronica Summer Fun (10/61). 16-Betty & Veronica Spectacular (6/62). 18-Betty & Veronica Summer Fun (10/62) 24 72 127 215

12,14,15,17,19,20: 12-Katy Keene Holiday Fun (9/61). 14-The World of Jughead (12/61); Vampire-s. 15-Archie's Christmas Stocking (1/62). 17-Archie's Jokes (9/62); Katy Keene app. 19-The World of Jughead (12/62). 20-Archie's Christmas Stocking (1/63) 16 48 88 150

21,23,26,28: 21-Betty & Veronica Spectacular (6/63). 23-Betty & Veronica Summer Fun (10/63). 26-Betty & Veronica Spectacular (6/64). 28-Betty & Veronica Summer Fun (9/64) 9 27 65 110

22,24,25,27,29,30: 22-Archie's Jokes (9/63). 24-The World of Jughead (12/63). 25-Archie's Christmas Stocking (1/64). 27-Archie's Jokes (8/64). 29-Around the World with Archie (10/64); Doris Day-s. 30-The World of Jughead (12/64) 8 24 56 90

31-35,136-141: 31-Betty & Veronica Christmas Stocking (1/65). 32-Betty & Veronica Summer Fun (9/65). 33-Archie's Jokes (8/65). 34-Betty & Veronica Summer Fun (9/65). 35-Around the World with Archie (10/65). 136-The World of Jughead (12/65). 137-Archie's Christmas Stocking (1/66). 138-Betty & Veronica Spectacular (6/66). 139-Archie's Jokes (6/66). 140-Betty & Veronica Summer Fun (8/66). 141-Around the World with Archie (9/66) 6 18 45 75

36-135-Do not exist

142-Archie's Super-Hero Special (10/66)-Origin Capt. Pureheart, Capt. Hero, and Evilheart 7 21 50 80

143-The World of Jughead(12/66); Capt. Hero-c/s; Man From R.I.V.E.R.D.A.L.E., Pureheart, Superteen app. 5 15 38 60

144-160: 144-Archie's Christmas Stocking (1/67). 145-Betty & Veronica Summer Fun (8/67). 146-Archie's Jokes (6/67). 147-Betty & Veronica Summer Fun (8/67) 148-World of Jughead (9/67). 150-Archie's Christmas Stocking (1/68). 151-World of Jughead (2/68). 152-World of Jughead (2/68). 153-Betty & Veronica Spectacular (6/68). 154-Archie Jokes (6/68). 155-Betty & Veronica Summer Fun (8/68). 156-Archie's Jokes (10/68). 157-World of Jughead (12/68). 158-Archie's Christmas Stocking (1/69). 159-Betty & Veronica Christmas Spectacular (1/69). 160-World of Archie (2/69); Frankenstein-s each... 3 10 23 35

161-World of Jughead (2/69); Super-Jughead-s; 11 pg.early Cricket O'Dell-s 4 12 25 38

162-183: 162-Betty & Veronica Spectacular (6/69). 163-Archie's Jokes(8/69). 164-Betty & Veronica Summer Fun (9/69). 165-World of Jughead (9/69). 166-World of Jughead (9/69). 167-Archie's Christmas Stocking (1/70). 168-Betty & Veronica Christmas Spect. (1/70). 169-Archie's Christmas Love-In (1/70). 170-Jughead's Eat-Out Comic Book Mag. (12/69). 171-World of Archie (2/70). 172-World of Jughead (2/70). 173-Betty & Veronica Spectacular (6/70). 174-Archie's Jokes (8/70). 175-Betty & Veronica Summer Fun (9/70). 176-Li'l Jinx Giant Laugh-Out (8/70). 177-World of Archie (9/70). 178-World of Jughead (9/70). 179-Archie's Christmas Stocking (1/71). 180-Betty & Veronica Christmas Spect. (1/71). 181-Archie's Christmas Love-In (1/71). 182-World of Archie (2/71). 183-World of Jughead (2/71)-Last squarebound each... 3 9 17 24

184-189,193,194,197-199 (52 pgs.): 184-Betty & Veronica Spectacular (6/71). 185-Li'l Jinx Giant Laugh-Out (6/71). 186-Archie's Jokes (8/71). 187-Betty & Veronica Summer Fun (9/71). 188-World of Archie (9/71). 189-World of Jughead (9/71). 193-Archie (3/72). 194-World of Jughead (4/72). 197-Betty & Veronica Spectacular (6/72). 198-Archie's Jokes (8/72). 199-Betty & Veronica Summer Fun (9/72) each... 2 6 15 22

190-192: 190-Archie's Christmas Stocking (12/71). 191-Betty & Veronica Christmas Spect.(2/72); Sabrina app.. 192-Archie's Christmas Love-In (1/72); Archie Band-c/s 3 9 20 30

195-(84 pgs.)-Li'l Jinx Christmas Bag (1/72). 3 10 23 35

196-(84 pgs.)-Sabrina's Christmas Magic (1/72) 5 15 34 55

200-(52 pgs.)-World of Archie (10/72) 3 9 20 30

201-206,208-219,221-230,232,233 (All 52 pgs.): 201-Betty & Veronica Spectacular (10/72). 202-World of Jughead (11/72). 203-Archie's Christmas Stocking (12/72). 204-Betty & Veronica Christmas Spectacular (2/73). 205-Archie's Christmas Love-In (1/73). 206-Li'l Jinx Christmas Bag (12/72). 208-World of Archie (3/73). 209-World of Jughead (4/73). 210-Betty & Veronica Spectacular (6/73). 211-Archie's Jokes (8/73). 212-Betty & Veronica Summer Fun (9/73). 213-World of Archie (10/73). 214-Betty & Veronica Christmas Stocking (12/73). 215-World of Jughead (11/73). 216-Archie's Christmas Spectacular (2/74). 218-Archie's Christmas Love-In (1/74). 219-Li'l Jinx Christmas Bag (12/73). 221-Betty & Veronica Spectacular (Advertised as World of Archie) (6/74). 222-Archie's Jokes (advertised as World of Jughead) (8/74). 223-Li'l Jinx (8/74). 224-Betty & Veronica Summer Fun (9/74). 225-World of Archie (9/74). 226-Betty & Veronica Spectacular (10/74). 227-World of Jughead (10/74). 228-Archie's Christmas Stocking (12/74). 229-Betty & Veronica Christmas Spectacular (12/73). 230-Archie's Christmas Love-In (1/75). 232-World of Archie (3/75). 233-World of Jughead (4/75) each... 2 6 9 12

207,220,231,243: Sabrina's Christmas Magic. 207-(12/72). 220-(12/73). 231-(1/75). 243-(1/76) each... 2 6 13 20

234-242,244-251 (36 pgs.): 234-Betty & Veronica Spectacular (6/75). 235-Archie's Jokes (8/75). 236-Betty & Veronica Summer Fun (9/75). 237-World of Jughead (9/75) 238-Betty & Veronica Spectacular (10/75). 239-World of Jughead (10/75). 240-Betty & Veronica Christmas Spectacular (12/75). 241-Betty & Veronica Christmas Love-In (1/76). 244-World of Archie (3/76). 245-World of Jughead (4/76). 246-Betty & Veronica Spectacular (6/76). 247-Archie's Jokes (8/76). 248-Betty & Veronica Summer Fun (9/76). 249-World of Archie (9/76). 250-Betty & Veronica Spectacular (10/76). 251-World of Jughead each.... 1 4 7 10

252-451-Do not exist

452-454,456-466,468-478, 480-490,492-499: 452-Archie's Christmas Stocking (12/76). 453-Betty & Veronica Spectacular (12/76). 454-Archie's Christmas Love-In (1/77). 456-World of Archie (3/77). 457-World of Jughead (4/77). 458-Betty & Veronica Spectacular (6/77). 459-Archie's Jokes (8/77)-Shows 8/76 in error. 460-Betty & Veronica Summer Fun (9/77). 461-World of Archie (9/77). 462-Betty & Veronica Spectacular (10/77). 463-World of Jughead (10/77). 464-Archie's Christmas Stocking (12/77). 465-Betty & Veronica Christmas Spectacular (12/77). 466-Archie's Christmas Love-In (1/78). 468-World of Archie (2/78). 469-World of Jughead (2/78). 470-Betty & Veronica Spectacular(6/78). 471-Archie's Jokes (8/78). 472-Betty & Veronica Summer Fun (9/78). 473-World of Archie (9/78). 474-Betty & Veronica Spectacular (10/78). 476-World of Jughead (10/78). 477-Betty & Veronica Christmas Spectacular (12/78). 478-Archie's Christmas Love-In (1/79). 480-The World of Archie (3/79). 481-World of Jughead (4/79). 482-Betty & Veronica Spectacular (6/79). 483-Archie's Jokes (8/79). 484-Betty & Veronica Summer Fun(9/79). 485-The World of Jughead (9/79). 486-Betty & Veronica Spectacular(10/79). 487-The World of Jughead (10/79). 488-Archie's Christmas Stocking (12/79). 489-Betty & Veronica Christmas Love-in (1/80). 492-The World of Archie (2/80). 493-World of Jughead (4/80). 494-Betty & Veronica Spectacular (6/80). 495-Archie's Jokes (8/80). 496-Betty & Veronica Summer Fun (9/80). 497-The World of Archie (9/80). 498-Betty & Veronica Spectacular (10/80). 499-The World of Jughead (10/80). each... 1 3 6 9

455,467,479,491,503-Sabrina's Christmas Magic: 455-(1/77). 467-(1/78). 479-(1/79) 491-(1/80), 503(1/81) 2 6 11 16

491(1/79) Dracula/Werewolf-s. 491-(1/80), 503(1/81) 2 6 12

500-Archie's Christmas Stocking (12/80) 2 6 12

501-514,516-527,529-532,534-539,541-543,545-550: 501-Betty & Veronica Christmas Spectacular (12/80). 502-Archie's Christmas Love-in (1/81). 504-The World of Archie (3/81). 505-The World of Jughead (4/81). 506-Betty & Veronica Summer Fun (6/81). 507-Archie's Jokes (8/81). 508-Betty & Veronica Summer Fun (9/81). 509-The World of Archie (9/81). 510-Betty & Veronica Spectacular (9/81). 511-The World of Jughead (10/81). 512-Archie's Christmas Stocking (12/81). 513-Betty & Veronica Christmas Spectacular (12/81). 514-Archie's Christmas Love-In (1/82). 516-The World of Archie (3/82). 517-The World of Jughead (4/82). 518-Betty & Veronica Spectacular

Archie Giant Series #611 © AP

Archie Double Digest #192 © AP

Archie's Girls, Betty and Veronica #8 © AP

	GD2.0	FN6.0	VF8.0	NM9.4		GD2.0	FN6.0	VF8.0	NM9.4

(6/82). 519-Archie's Jokes (8/82). 520-Betty & Veronica Summer Fun (9/82). 521-The World of Archie (9/82). 522-Betty & Veronica Spectacular (10/82). 523-The World of Jughead (10/82).524-Archie's Christmas Stocking (1/83). 525-Betty and Veronica Christmas Spectacular (1/83). 526-Betty and Veronica Spectacular (5/83). 527-Little Archie (8/83). 529-Betty and Veronica Summer Fun (8/83). 530-Betty and Veronica Spectacular (9/83). 531-The World of Jughead (9/83). 532-The World of Archie (10/83). 534-Little Archie (1/84). 535-Archie's Christmas Stocking (1/84). 536-Betty and Veronica Christmas Spectacular (1/84). 537-Betty and Veronica Spectacular (6/84). 538-Little Archie (8/84). 539-Betty and Veronica Summer Fun (8/84). 541-Betty and Veronica Spectacular (9/84). 542-The World of Jughead (9/84). 543-The World of Archie (10/84). 545-Little Archie (12/84). 546-Archie's Christmas Stocking (12/84). 547-Betty and Veronica Christmas Spectacular (12/84). 548-?. 549-Little Archie. 550-Betty and Veronica Summer Fun

each...	1	3	5	7

515,528,533,540,544: 515-Sabrina's Christmas Magic (1/82). 528-Josie and the Pussycats (8/83). 533-Sabrina; Space Pirates by Frank Bolling (10/83). 540-Josie and the Pussycats (8/84). 544-Sabrina the Teen-Age Witch (10/84).

each...	2	6	10	14
551,562,571,584,597-Josie and the Pussycats	1	3	6	9

552-561,563-570,572-583,585-596,598-600: 552-Betty & Veronica Spectacular. 553-The World of Jughead. 554-The World of Archie. 555-Betty's Diary. 556-Little Archie (1/86). 557-Archie's Christmas Stocking (1/86). 558-Betty & Veronica Christmas Spectacular (1/86). 559-Betty & Veronica Spectacular. 560-Little Archie. 561-Betty & Veronica Summer Fun. 563-Betty & Veronica Spectacular. 564-World of Jughead. 565-World of Archie. 566-Little Archie. 567-Archie's Christmas Stocking. 568-Betty & Veronica Spectacular. 569-Betty & Veronica Spring Spectacular. 570-Little Archie. 571-Dracula-c/s. 572-Betty & Veronica Summer Fun. 573-Archie At Riverdale High. 574-World of Archie. 575-Betty & Veronica Spectacular. 576-Pep. 577-World of Jughead. 578-Archie And Me. 579-Archie's Christmas Stocking. 580-Betty and Veronica Christmas Spectacular. 581-Little Archie Christmas Special. 582-Betty & Veronica Spring Spectacular. 583-Little Archie. 585-Betty & Veronica Summer Fun. 586-Archie At Riverdale High. 587-The World of Archie (10/88); 1st app. Explorers of the Unknown. 588-Betty & Veronica Spectacular. 589-Pep (10/88). 590-The World of Jughead. 591-Archie & Me. 592-Archie's Christmas Stocking. 593-Betty & Veronica Christmas Spectacular. 594-Little Archie. 595-Betty & Veronica Spring Spectacular. 596-Little Archie. 598-Betty & Veronica Summer Fun. 599-The World of Archie (10/89); 2nd app. Explorers of the Unknown. 600-Betty and Veronica Spectacular   each...   5.00
601,602,604-609,611-629: 601-Pep. 602-The World of Jughead. 604-Archie at Riverdale High. 605-Archie's Christmas Stocking. 606-Betty and Veronica Spectacular. 607-Little Archie. 608-Betty and Veronica Spectacular. 609-Little Archie. 611-Betty and Veronica Summer Fun. 612-The World of Archie. 613-Betty and Veronica Spectacular. 614-Pep (10/90). 615-Veronica's Summer Special. 616-Archie and Me. 617-Archie's Christmas Stocking. 618-Betty & Veronica Christmas Spectacular. 619-Little Archie. 620-Betty and Veronica Spectacular. 621-Betty and Veronica Summer Fun. 622-Josie & the Pussycats; not published. 623-Betty and Veronica Spectacular. 624-Pep Comics. 625-Veronica's Summer Special. 626-Archie and Me. 627-World of Archie. 628-Archie's Pals 'n' Gals Holiday Special. 629-Betty & Veronica Christmas Spectacular.

each....				3.00
603-Archie and Me; Titanic app.				4.00
610-Josie and the Pussycats				6.00

630-632: 630-Archie's Christmas Stocking. 631-Archie's Pals 'n' Gals. 632-Betty & Veronica Spectacular   3.00
NOTE: Archies Band-c-173,180,192; s-189,192. Archie Cavemen-165,225,232,244,249. Little Sabrina-527,533,538,545,556,566. UFO-s-178,487,594.

ARCHIE MEETS THE PUNISHER (Same contents as The Punisher Meets Archie)
Marvel Comics & Archie Comics Publ.: Aug, 1994 ($2.95, 52 pgs., one-shot)

1-Batton Lash story, J. Buscema-a on Punisher, S. Goldberg-a on Archie				4.00

ARCHIE'S ACTIVITY COMICS DIGEST MAGAZINE
Archie Enterprises: 1985 - No. 4? (Annual, 128 pgs., digest size)

1	1	4	7	10
2-4				6.00

ARCHIE'S CAR

Spire Christian Comics (Fleming H. Revell co.): 1979 (49¢)

nn	1	3	5	7

ARCHIE'S CHRISTMAS LOVE-IN (See Archie Giant Series Mag. No. 169, 181,192, 205, 218, 230, 242, 454, 466, 478, 490, 502, 514)

ARCHIE'S CHRISTMAS STOCKING (See Archie Giant Series Mag. No. 1-6,10, 15, 20, 25, 31, 137, 144, 150, 158, 167, 179, 190, 203, 216, 228, 240, 452, 464, 476, 488, 500, 512, 524, 535, 546, 557, 567, 579, 592, 605, 617, 630)

ARCHIE'S CHRISTMAS STOCKING
Archie Comics: 1993 -Present ($2.00, 52 pgs.)(Bound-in calendar poster in all)

1-Dan DeCarlo-c/a				5.00
2-5				4.00
6,7: 6-(1998, $2.25). 7-(1999, $2.29)				3.00

ARCHIE'S CLEAN SLATE
Spire Christian Comics (Fleming H. Revell Co.): 1973 (35/49¢)

1-(35¢-c edition)(Some issues have nn)	1	4	7	10
1-(49¢-c edition)	1	3	6	8

ARCHIE'S DATE BOOK
Spire Christian comics (Fleming H. Revell Co.): 1981

nn	1	3	6	8

ARCHIE'S DOUBLE DIGEST QUARTERLY MAGAZINE
Archie Comics: 1981 - Present ($1.95/$2.75/$2.95/$3.19, 256 pgs.) (A.D.D. Magazine No. 10 on)

1	3	9	17	24
2-10: 6-Katy Keene story.	2	6	10	14
11-30: 29-Pureheart story	1	4	7	10
31-50	1	3	5	7
51-70,100				5.00
71-99,101-130: 115-Begin $3.19-c. 123-Begin $3.29-c				3.50

ARCHIE'S FAMILY ALBUM
Spire Christian Comics (Fleming H. Revell Co.): 1978 (39¢, 36 pgs.)

nn	1	3	5	7

ARCHIE'S FESTIVAL
Spire Christian Comics (Fleming H. Revell Co.): 1980 (49¢)

nn	1	3	6	9

ARCHIE'S GIRLS, BETTY AND VERONICA (Becomes Betty & Veronica)(Also see Veronica)
Archie Publications (Close-Up): 1950 - No. 347, Apr, 1987

1	164	492	1023	1800
2	75	225	469	825
3-5	45	135	270	475
6-10: 6-Dan DeCarlo's 1st Archie work; Betty's 1st ponytail. 10-Katy Keene app. (2 pgs.)	40	120	220	380
11-20: 11,13,14,17-19-Katy Keene app. 17-Last pre-code issue (3/55).				
20-Debbie's Diary (2 pgs.)	29	87	156	270
21-30: 27,30-Katy Keene app. 29-Tarzan	21	63	116	190
31-43,45-50: 41-Marilyn Monroe and Brigitte Bardot mentioned. 45-Fabian 1 pg.				
photo & bio. 46-Bobby Darin 1 pg. photo & bio	14	42	72	120
44-Elvis Presley 1 pg. photo & bio	16	48	83	140
51-55,57-74: 73-Sci-fi-c	7	21	50	80
56-Elvis and Bobby Darin records parody	8	24	58	95
75-Betty & Veronica sell souls to Devil	14	42	102	175
76-99: 82-Bobby Rydell 1 pg. illustrated bio; Elvis mentioned on-c.				
84-Connie Francis 1 pg. illustrated bio	4	12	30	50
100	5	15	38	60
101-117,120 (12/65): 113-Monsters-c	3	9	21	32
118-(10/65) 1st app./origin Superteen (also see Betty & Me #3)				
	5	15	34	55
119-2nd app./last Superteen story	3	10	23	35
121,122,124-126,128-140 (8/67): 135,140-Mod-c. 136-Slave Girl-s				
123-"Jingo"-Ringo parody-c	6	15	22	
127-Beatles Fan Club-s	2	6	15	22
141-156,158-163,165-180 (12/70)	3	10	23	35
157,164-Archies Band	2	6	11	16
181-193,195-199	3	9	17	24
	2	6	9	12

Archie's Joke Book #27 © AP

Archie's Madhouse #64 © AP

Archie's Pal, Jughead #110 © AP

	GD2.0	FN6.0	VF8.0	NM9.4
194-Sabrina-c/s	2	6	15	22
200-(8/72)	2	6	11	15
201-205,207,209,211-215,217-240	1	4	7	10
206,208,216-Sabrina c/app. 206-Josie-c. 210-Sabrina app.	2	6	12	18
241 (1/76)-270 (6/78)	1	3	6	8
271-299: 281-UFO-s	1	3	5	7
300 (12/80)-Anniversary issue	1	3	6	8
301-309,311-319				5.00
310-John Travolta parody story	1	3	5	7
320 (10/82)-Intro. of Cheryl Blossom on cover and inside story (she also appears, but not on the cover, in Jughead #325 with same 10/82 publication date)	3	10	23	35
321,322-Cheryl Blossom app.	2	6	11	16
323,326,327,330,331,333-347: 333-Monsters-s				4.00
324,325-Crickett O'Dell app.				5.00
328-Cheryl Blossom app.	1	4	7	10
329,332: 329-Betty dressed as Madonna. 332-Superhero costume party				6.00
Annual 1 (1953)	84	253	525	925
Annual 2(1954)	40	120	232	400
Annual 3-5 (1955-1957)	35	105	185	320
Annual 6-8 (1958-1960)	23	69	121	210

ARCHIE'S HOLIDAY FUN DIGEST
Archie Comics: 1997 - Present ($1.75/$1.95/$1.99/$2.19, annual)

1-6-Christmas stories				2.50

ARCHIE'S JOKEBOOK COMICS DIGEST ANNUAL (See Jokebook...)

ARCHIE'S JOKE BOOK MAGAZINE (See Joke Book ...)
Archie Publ: 1953 - No. 3, Sum, 1954; No. 15, Fall, 1954 - No. 288, 11/82 (subtitled...Laugh-In #127-140; ...Laugh-Out #141-194)

	GD2.0	FN6.0	VF8.0	NM9.4
1953-One Shot (#1)	86	258	540	950
2	45	135	270	475
3 (no #4-14)	39	117	208	360
15-20: 15-Formerly Archie's Rival Reggie #14; last pre-code issue (Fall/54).				
15-17-Katy Keene app.	23	69	121	210
21-30	14	42	72	120
31-40,42,43: 42-Bio of Ed "Kookie" Byrnes. 43-story about guitarist Duane Eddy	10	30	55	80
41-1st professional comic work by Neal Adams (9/59), 1 pg.	23	69	121	210
44-47-N. Adams-a in all, 1-3 pgs.	13	39	66	110
48-Four pgs. N. Adams-a	14	42	72	120
49,50	4	12	30	50
51-56,58-60 (1962)	3	10	23	35
57-Elvis mentioned; Marilyn Monroe cameo	4	12	29	45
61-80 (8/64): 66-(12¢ cover)	2	6	15	22
66-(15¢ cover variant)	3	9	19	28
81-89,91,92,94-99	2	6	11	16
90,93: 90-Beatles gag. 93-Beatles cameo	2	6	15	22
100 (5/66)	2	6	13	20
101,103-117,119-123,127,129,131-140 (9/69): 105-Superhero gag-c. 108-110-Archies Archers Band-s. 116-Beatles/Monkees/Bob Dylan cameos (posters)	2	6	10	14
102 (7/66) Archie Band prototype-c; Elvis parody panel, Rolling Stones mention	3	9	17	24
118,124,125,126,128,130: 118-ArchieBand-c. 121-Veronica & Groovers band-s. 124-Archies Band c/app. 125-Beatles cameo (poster). 126,130-Monkees cameo. 128-Veronica/Archies Band app.	2	6	15	22
141-173,175-181,183-199	1	4	7	10
174-Sabrina-c. 182-Sabrina cameo	2	6	10	14
200 (9/74)	2	6	10	14
201-230 (3/77)	1	3	5	7
231-239,241-288				5.00
240-Elvis record-c	1	3	5	7

NOTE: Archies Band-c-118,124,147,172; 1 pg.-s-127,128,138,140,143,147,167; 2 pg.-s-124,131, 155. Sabrina app.-247,248,252-259,261,262,264,266-270,274,277,284-286.

ARCHIE'S JOKES (See Archie Giant Series Mag. No. 17, 22, 27, 33, 139, 146, 154, 163, 174, 186, 198, 211, 222, 235, 247, 459, 471, 483, 495, 519)

ARCHIE'S LOVE SCENE
Spire Christian Comics (Fleming H. Revell Co.): 1973 (35¢/49¢/no price)

	GD2.0	FN6.0	VF8.0	NM9.4
1-(35¢ Edition)	2	6	9	12
1-(49¢ Edition/no price) (Some copies have nn)	1	3	6	8

ARCHIE'S MADHOUSE (Madhouse Ma-ad on No. 67 on)
Archie Publications: Sept, 1959 - No. 66, Feb, 1969

	GD2.0	FN6.0	VF8.0	NM9.4
1-Archie begins	23	68	160	285
2	12	36	84	140
3-5	8	24	58	95
6-10	6	18	40	65
11-17 (Last w/regular characters)	4	12	30	50
18-21,29: 18-New format begins	3	10	23	35
22-1st app. Sabrina, the Teen-age Witch (10/62)	22	66	154	275
23-Sabrina app.	10	30	70	120
24-Sabrina app.	8	24	56	90
25,26,28-Sabrina app. 25-1st app. Captain Sprocket (4/63)	6	18	42	70
27-Sabrina-c; no story	5	15	34	55
30,34,38-40: No Sabrina. 34-Bordered-c begin.	2	6	13	20
31,32-Sabrina app.?	2	6	13	20
33,37-Sabrina app.	4	12	30	50
35-Beatles cameo. No Sabrina	3	9	19	28
36-1st Salem the Cat w/Sabrina story	6	18	42	70
41-48,51-57,60-62,64-66: No Sabrina 43-Mighty Crusaders cameo. 44-Swipes Mad #4 (Super-Duperman) in "Bird Monsters From Outer Space"	2	6	12	18
49,50,58,59,63-Sabrina stories	3	10	23	35
Annual 1 (1962-63) no Sabrina	7	21	53	85
Annual 2 (1964) no Sabrina	4	12	30	50
Annual 3 (1965)-Origin Sabrina the Teen-age Witch	8	24	60	100
Annual 4,5('66-68)(Becomes Madhouse Ma-ad Annual #7 on); no Sabrina	3	9	17	25
Annual 6 (1969)-Sabrina the Teen-age Witch-sty	5	15	34	55

NOTE: Cover title to #61-65 is "Madhouse" and to #66 is "Madhouse Ma-ad Jokes".

ARCHIE'S MECHANICS
Archie Publications: Sept, 1954 - No. 3, 1955

	GD2.0	FN6.0	VF8.0	NM9.4
1-(15¢, 52 pgs.)	77	231	483	850
2-(10¢)-Last pre-code issue	47	141	286	500
3-(10¢)	40	120	232	400

ARCHIE'S ONE WAY
Spire Christian Comics (Fleming H. Revell Co.): 1972 (35¢/39¢/49¢, 36 pgs.)

	GD2.0	FN6.0	VF8.0	NM9.4
nn-(35¢ Edition)	1	4	7	10
nn-(39¢, 49¢, no price editions)	1	3	6	8

ARCHIE'S PAL, JUGHEAD (Jughead No. 127 on)
Archie Publications: 1949 - No. 126, Nov, 1965

	GD2.0	FN6.0	VF8.0	NM9.4
1 (1949)-1st app. Moose (see Pep #33)	127	381	795	1400
2 (1950)	61	182	381	675
3-5	40	120	232	400
6-10: 7-Suzie app.	29	87	156	270
11-20: 20-Jughead as Sherlock Holmes parody	19	57	99	165
21-30: 23-25,28,30-Katy Keene app. 23-Early Dilton-s. 28-Debbie's Diary app.	13	39	66	110
31-50: 49-Archies Rock 'N' Rollers band-c	6	18	40	65
51-70: 59-Bio of Will Hutchins of TV's Sugarfoot. 67-Betty seducing Jughead-c. 68-Early Archie Gang Cavemen-s	4	12	26	40
71-76,81-84,89-99: 72-Jughead dates Betty & Veronica	3	9	17	25
77,78,80,85,86,88-Horror/Sci-Fi-c	3	9	20	30
79-Creature from the Black Lagoon-c	4	12	29	45
87-Early Big Ethel app.; UGAJ (United Girls Against Jughead)-s	3	10	23	35
100	3	9	20	30
101-Return of Big Ethyl	3	9	20	30
102-126	2	6	15	22
Annual 1 (1953, 25¢)	54	162	324	575
Annual 2 (1954, 25¢)-Last pre-code issue	39	117	208	360
Annual 3-5 (1955-57, 25¢)	27	81	145	250
Annual 6-8 (1958-60, 25¢)	17	51	88	150

ARCHIE'S PAL JUGHEAD COMICS (Formerly Jughead #1-45)
Archie Comic Publ.: No. 46, June, 1993 - Present ($1.25/$1.50/$1.75/$1.79/$1.99)

Archie's Pals 'N' Gals #4 © AP

Archie's Rival Reggie #9 © AP

Archie's TV Laugh-Out #11 © AP

	GD2.0	FN6.0	VF8.0	NM9.4		GD2.0	FN6.0	VF8.0	NM9.4

46-60 — 3.00
61-141: 100-"A Storm Over Uniforms" x-over part 1,2 — 2.25

ARCHIE'S PALS 'N' GALS (Also see Archie Giant Series Magazine #628)
Archie Publ: 1952-53 - No. 6, 1957-58; No. 7, 1958 - No. 224, Sept, 1991
(...All News Stories on-c #49-59)

1-(116 pgs., 25¢)	73	219	455	800
2(Annual)('54, 25¢)	40	120	232	400
3-5(Annual, '55-57, 25¢): 3-Last pre-code issue	30	90	159	275
6-10('58-'60)	18	54	94	160
11-18,20 (84 pgs.): 12-Harry Belafonte 2 pg. photos & bio				
17-B&W paper dolls	10	30	55	85
19-Marilyn Monroe app.	12	36	61	105
21,22,24-28,30 (68 pgs.)	5	15	34	55
23-(Wint./62) 6 pg. Josie-s with Pepper and Melody (1st app.?);				
Betty in towel pin-up	9	27	63	100
29-Beatles satire (68 pgs.)	7	21	53	85
31(Wint. 64/65)-39 -(68 pgs.)	4	12	29	45
40-Early Superteen-s; with Pureheart	5	15	38	60
41(8/67)-43,45-50(2/69) (68 pgs.)	3	9	20	30
44-Archies Band-s; WEB cameo	4	12	25	38
51(4/69),52,55-64(6/71): 62-Last squarebound	3	9	17	24
53-Archies Band-c/s	3	9	20	30
54-Satan meets Veronica-s	4	12	25	38
65(8/70),67-70,73-81,83(6/74) (52 pgs.)	2	6	12	18
66,82-Sabrina-c	3	9	19	28
71,72-Two part drug story (8/72,9/72)	3	9	17	24
75-Archies Band-s	3	9	17	24
84-99	1	4	7	10
100 (12/75)	2	6	10	14
101-130(3/79): 125,126-Riverdale 2001-s	1	3	6	8
131-160,162-170 (7/84)				6.00
161 (11/82) 3rd app./1st solo Cheryl Blossom-s and pin-up; 2nd Jason Blossom				
	3	9	19	28
171-173,175,177-197,199: 197-G. Colan-a				4.00
174,176,198: 174-New Archies Band-s. 176-Cyndi Lauper-c. 198-Archie gang				
on strike at Archie Ent. offices				6.00
200(9/88)-Illiteracy-s				6.00
201,203-224: Later issues $1.00 cover				3.00
202-Explains end of Archie's jalopy; Dezerland-c/s; James Dean cameo				6.00

NOTE: *Archies Band-c-45,47,49,53,56; s-44,53,75,174. UFO-s-50,63,209,220.*

ARCHIE'S PALS 'N' GALS DOUBLE DIGEST MAGAZINE
Archie Comic Publications: Nov, 1992 - Present ($2.50-$3.29)

1-Capt. Hero story; Pureheart app.	1	4	7	10
2,3: 2-Superduck story; Little Jinx in all				6.00
4-29: 4-Begin $2.75-c.				4.00
30-63: 40-Begin $2.99-c. 48-Begin $3.19-c. 56-Begin $3.29-c				3.50

ARCHIE'S PARABLES
Spire Christian Comics (Fleming H. Revell Co.): 1973,1975 (39/49¢, 36 pgs.)

nn-By Al Hartley,39¢ Edition	1	4	7	10
49¢, no price editions	1	3	6	8

ARCHIE'S R/C RACERS (Radio controlled cars)
Archie Comics: Sept, 1989 - No. 10, Mar, 1991 (95¢/$1)

1				6.00
2,5-7,10: 5-Elvis parody. 7-Supervillain-c/s. 10-UFO-c/s				4.00
3,4,8,9				3.00

ARCHIE'S RIVAL REGGIE (Reggie & Archie's Joke Book #15 on)
Archie Publications: 1950 - No. 14, Aug, 1954

1-Reggie 1st app. in Jackpot Comics #5	75	225	469	825
2	40	120	220	380
3-5	29	87	156	270
6-10	21	63	110	185
11-14: Katy Keene in No. 10-14, 1-2 pgs.	15	45	77	130

ARCHIE'S RIVERDALE HIGH (See Riverdale High)

ARCHIE'S ROLLER COASTER
Spire Christian Comics (Fleming H. Revell Co.): 1981 (69¢)

nn	1	4	7	10

ARCHIE'S SOMETHING ELSE
Spire Christian Comics (Fleming H. Revell Co.): 1975 (39/49¢, 36 pgs.)

nn -(39¢-c) Hell's Angels Biker on motorcycle-c	2	6	9	12
nn-(49¢-c)	1	3	6	8
Barbour Christian Comics Edition ('86, no price listed) 1	3	5	7

ARCHIE'S SONSHINE
Spire Christian Comics (Fleming H. Revell Co.): 1973, 1974 (39/49¢, 36 pgs.)

39¢ Edition	1	4	7	10
49¢, no price editions	1	3	6	8

ARCHIE'S SPORTS SCENE
Spire Christian Comics (Fleming H. Revell Co.): 1983 (no cover price)

nn	1	4	7	10

ARCHIE'S SPRING BREAK
Archie Comics: 1996 - Present ($2.00, 48 pgs., annual)

1-Dan DeCarlo-c				3.00
2-4: 2-Dan DeCarlo-c				2.50

ARCHIE'S STORY & GAME COMICS DIGEST MAGAZINE
Archie Enterprises: Nov, 1986 - Present ($1.25/1.35/$1.50/$1.95, 128 pgs., digest-size)

1: Many copies were marked-up in print run	2	6	11	16
2-10	1	4	7	10
11-20				6.00
21-38				3.00
39-42-($1.95)				2.50

ARCHIE'S SUPER HERO SPECIAL (See Archie Giant Series Mag. No. 142)

ARCHIE'S SUPER HERO SPECIAL (...Comics Digest Mag. 2)
Archie Comics (Red Circle): Jan, 1979 - No. 2, Aug, 1979(95¢, 148 pgs.)

1-Simon & Kirby r/Double Life of Pvt. Strong #1,2; Black Hood, The Fly,				
Jaguar, The Web app.	2	6	12	18
2-Contains contents to the never published Black Hood #1; origin Black				
Hood; N. Adams, Wood, McWilliams, Morrow, S&K-a(r); N. Adams-c. The				
Shield, The Fly, Jaguar, Hangman, Steel Sterling, The Web, The Fox-r				
	2	6	13	20

ARCHIE'S SUPER TEENS
Archie Comic Publications, Inc.: 1994 - No. 4, 1996 ($2.00, 52 pgs.)

1-Staton/Esposito-c/a; pull-out poster				3.00
2-4: 2-Fred Hembeck script; Bret Blevins/Terry Austin-a				2.50

ARCHIE'S TV LAUGH-OUT ("...Starring Sabrina" on-c #1-50)
Archie Publications: Dec, 1969 - No. 106, Apr, 1986 (#1-7: 68 pgs.)

1-Sabrina begins, thru #106	9	27	65	110
2 (68 pgs.)	5	15	34	55
3-6 (68 pgs.)	3	10	23	35
7-Josie begins, thru #105; Archie's & Josie's Bands cover logos begin				
	6	18	42	70
8-23 (52 pgs.): 10-1st Josie on-c. 12-1st Josie and Pussycats on-c. 14-Beatles				
cameo on poster	3	9	20	30
24-40: 37,39,40-Bicentennial-c	2	6	12	18
41,47,56: 41-Alexandra rejoins J&P band. 47-Fonz cameo; voodoo-s. 56-Fonz				
parody; B&V with Farrah hair-c	2	6	13	20
42-46,48-55,57-60	2	6	9	12
61-68,70-80: 63-UFO-s. 79-Mummy-s	1	3	6	9
69-Sherlock Holmes parody	1	3	6	8
81-90,94,95,97-99: 84 Voodoo-s	1	3	5	7
91-Early Cheryl Blossom-s; Sabrina/Archies Band-c	2	6	12	18
92-A-Team parody	1	3	6	9
93-(2/84) Archie in drag-s; Hill Street Blues-s; Groucho Marx parody; cameo				
parody app. of Batman, Spider-Man, Wonder Woman and others				
	2	6	9	12
96-MASH parody-s; Jughead in drag; Archies Band-c 1	3	6	9
100-(4/85) Michael Jackson parody-c/s; J&P band and Archie band on-c				
	2	6	10	14
101-104-Lower print run. 104-Miami Vice parody-c 1	3	6	9
105-Wrestling/Hulk Hogan parody-c; J&P band-s	2	6	9	12
106-Last issue; low print run	2	6	9	12

NOTE: *Dan DeCarlo-c 78-up(most). c-89-up(most). Archies Band-s 2,7,9-11,15,20,25,*

Archie 3000 #1 © AP

Area 52 #1 © Brian Haberlin

Aristokittens #9 © W/DC

37,64,65,67,68,70,73,76,78,79,83,84,86,90,96,100,101; **Archies Band-c** 2,17,20,91,94,96,99-103. **Josie-s** 12,21,26,35,52,78,80,90. **Josie-c** 10,91,94. **Josie and the Pussycats (as a band in costume)-s** 7,9,10,37,38,41,42,66,84,99-101,105. **Josie w/Pussycats member Valerie &/or Melody-s** 17,20,22,25,27-29,31,33,36,39,40,43-51,53-65,67-77,79,81-83,85-89,92-94,102-104. **Josie w/Pussycats band-c** 12,14,17,18,22,24. **Sabrina-s** 1-9,11-86,88-106. **Sabrina-c** 1-18,21,23,27,49,91,94.

ARCHIE'S VACATION SPECIAL
Archie Publications: Winter, 1994 - Present ($2.00/$2.25/$2.29/$2.49, annual)

1			3.00
2-8: 8-(2000, $2.49)			2.50

ARCHIE'S WEIRD MYSTERIES (TV)
Archie Comics: Feb, 2000 - Present ($1.79/$1.99)

1-18: 3,14-Mighty Crusaders app. 14-Super Teens-c/app.			2.25

ARCHIE'S WORLD
Spire Christian Comics (Fleming H. Revell Co.): 1973, 1976 (39/49¢)

39¢ Edition	1	4	7	10
49¢ Edition, no price editions	1	3	6	8

ARCHIE 3000
Archie Comics: May, 1989 - No. 16, July, 1991 (75¢/95¢/$1.00)

1,16: 16-Aliens-c/s			4.00
2-15: 6-Begin $1.00-c; X-Mas-c			3.00

ARCOMICS PREMIERE
Arcomics: July, 1993 ($2.95)

1-1st lenticular-c on a comic (flicker-c)			3.00

AREA 52
Image Comics: Jan, 2001 - No. 4, June, 2001 ($2.95)

1-4-Haberlin-s/Henry-a			3.00

AREA 88
Eclipse Comics/VIZ Comics #37 on: May 26, 1987 - No. 42, 1989 ($1.50/$1.75, B&W)

1-42: 1,2-2nd printings exist			2.25

AREALA: ANGEL OF WAR (See Warrior Nun titles)
Antarctic Press: Sept, 1998 - No. 4, June, 1999 ($2.95/$2.99, color/B&W)

1-4: 3,4-B&W. 4-($2.99-c)			3.00

ARENA
Alchemy Studios: Jan, 1990 ($1.50, 7x10-1/8", 20 pgs.)

1-Science fiction			2.25
1-Signed & numbered ed. (500 copies)			3.00

ARGUS (See Flash, 2nd Series) (Also see Showcase '95 #1,2)
DC Comics: Apr, 1995 - No. 6, Oct, 1995 (1.50, limited series)

1-6: 4-Begin $1.75-c			2.25

ARIA
Image Comics (Avalon Studios): Jan, 1999 - Present ($2.50)

Preview (11/98, $2.95)				5.00
1-Anacleto-c/a	1	3	5	8
1-Variant-c by Michael Turner	1	3	5	8
1-($10.00) Alternate-c by Turner	1	4	7	10
1,2-(Blanc & Noir) Black and white printing of pencil art				3.00
1-(Blanc & Noir) DF Edition				5.00
2-4: 2,4-Anacleto-c/a. 3-Martinez-a				3.00
4-($6.95) Glow in the Dark-c	1	4	7	10
Aria Angela 1 (2/00, $2.95) Anacleto-a; 4 covers by Anacleto, JG Jones, Portacio and Quesada				3.00
Aria Angela Blanc & Noir 1 (4/00, $2.95) Anacleto-a				3.00
Aria Angela European Ashcan				10.00
Aria Angela 2 (10/00, $2.95) Anacleto-a/c				3.00

ARIA: THE SOUL MARKET
Image Comics (Avalon Studios): Mar, 2001 - No. 6, Dec, 2001 ($2.95)

1-6-Anacleto-c/Holguin-s			3.00

ARIANE AND BLUEBEARD (See Night Music #8)

ARIEL & SEBASTIAN (See Cartoon Tales & The Little Mermaid)

ARION, LORD OF ATLANTIS (Also see Warlord #55)

DC Comics: Nov, 1982 - No. 35, Sept, 1985

1-Story cont'd from Warlord #62			3.00
2-35, Special #1 (11/85)			2.25

ARION THE IMMORTAL (Also see Showcase '95 #7)
DC Comics: July, 1992 - No. 6, Dec, 1992 ($1.50, limited series)

1			3.00
2-6: 4-Gustovich-a(i)			2.25

ARISTOCATS (See Movie Comics & Walt Disney Showcase No. 16)

ARISTOKITTENS, THE (...Meet Jiminy Cricket No. 1)(Disney)
Gold Key: Oct, 1971 - No. 9, Oct, 1975

1	3	9	19	28
2-5,7-9	2	6	12	18
6-(52 pgs.)	2	6	13	20

ARIZONA KID, THE (Also see The Comics & Wild Western)
Marvel/Atlas Comics(CSI): Mar, 1951 - No. 6, Jan, 1952

1	24	72	127	220
2-4: 2-Heath-a(3)	12	36	61	100
5,6	10	30	55	85

NOTE: **Heath** a-1-3; c-1-3. **Maneely** c-4-6. **Morisi** a-4-6. **Sinnott** a-6.

ARK, THE (See The Crusaders)

ARKAGA
Image Comics: Sept, 1997 ($2.95, one-shot)

1-Jorgensen-s/a			3.00

ARMAGEDDON
Chaos! Comics: Oct, 1999 - No. 4, Jan, 2000 ($2.95, limited series)

Preview			5.00
1-4-Lady Death, Evil Ernie, Purgatori app.			3.00

ARMAGEDDON: ALIEN AGENDA
DC Comics: Nov, 1991 - No. 4, Feb, 1992 ($1.00, limited series)

1-4			2.25

ARMAGEDDON FACTOR, THE
AC Comics: 1987 - No. 2, 1987; No. 3, 1990 ($1.95)

1,2: Sentinels of Justice, Dragonfly, Femforce			2.25
3-($3.95, color)-Almost all AC characters app.			4.00

ARMAGEDDON: INFERNO
DC Comics: Apr, 1992 - No. 4, July, 1992 ($1.00, limited series)

1-4: Many DC heroes app. 3-A. Adams/Austin-a			2.50

ARMAGEDDON 2001
DC Comics: May, 1991 - No. 2, Oct, 1991 ($2.00, squarebound, 68 pgs.)

1-Features many DC heroes; intro Waverider			4.00
1-2nd & 3rd printings; 3rd has silver ink-c			2.25
2			3.00

ARMATURE
Olyoptics: Nov, 1996 - No. 2, ($2.95, limited series)

1,2-Steve Oliff-c/s/a; Maxx app.			3.00

ARMED & DANGEROUS
Acclaim Comics (Armada): Apr, 1996 - No.4, July, 1996 ($2.95, B&W)

1-4-Bob Hall-c/a & scripts			3.00
Special 1 (8/96, $2.95, B&W)-Hall-c/a & scripts.			3.00

ARMED & DANGEROUS HELL'S SLAUGHTERHOUSE
Acclaim Comics (Armada): Oct, 1996 - No. 4, Jan, 1997 ($2.95, B&W)

1-4: Hall-c/a/scripts.			3.00

ARMOR (AND THE SILVER STREAK) (Revengers Featuring... in indicia for #1-3)
Continuity Comics: Sept, 1985 - No.13, Apr, 1992 ($2.00)

1-13: 1-Intro/origin Armor & the Silver Streak; Neal Adams-c/a. 7-Origin Armor; Nebres-i			3.00

ARMOR (DEATHWATCH 2000)
Continuity Comics: Apr, 1993 - No.6, Nov, 1993 ($2.50)

1-6: 1-3-Deathwatch 2000 x-over			2.50

ARMORED TROOPER VOTOMS (Manga)

Army of Darkness #3 © Sam Raimi & Renaissance Pictures

The Arrow #2 © CEN

Ascension #13 © TCOW

	GD2.0	FN6.0	VF8.0	NM9.4

CPM Comics: July, 1996 ($2.95)

1				3.00

ARMORINES (See X-O Manowar #25)
Valiant: June, 1994 - No. 12, June, 1995 ($2.25)

| 1-12: 7-Wraparound-c. 12-Byrne-c/swipe (X-Men, 1st Series #138) | | | | 2.50 |

ARMORINES (Volume 2)
Acclaim Comics: Oct, 1999 - No. 4 ($3.95/$2.50, limited series)

| 1-($3.95) Calafiore & P. Palmiotti-a | | | | 4.00 |
| 2,3-($2.50) | | | | 2.50 |

ARMY AND NAVY COMICS (Supersnipe No. 6 on)
Street & Smith Publications: May, 1941 - No. 5, July, 1942

1-Cap Fury & Nick Carter	52	157	300	550
2-Cap Fury & Nick Carter	31	93	165	285
3,4-Jack Farr-c/a	22	66	116	200
5-Supersnipe app.; see Shadow V2#3 for 1st app.; Story of Douglas				
MacArthur; George Marcoux-c/a	52	157	300	550

ARMY ATTACK
Charlton Comics: July, 1964 - No. 4, Feb, 1965; V2#3, July, 1965 - No. 47, Feb, 1967

V1#1	4	12	26	40
2-4(2/65)	3	9	17	24
V2#38(7/65)-47 (formerly U.S. Air Force #1-37)	2	6	13	20
NOTE: Glanzman a-1-3. Montes/Bache a-44.

ARMY AT WAR (Also see Our Army at War & Cancelled Comic Cavalcade)
DC Comics: Oct-Nov, 1978

| 1-Kubert-c; all new story and art | 1 | 4 | 7 | 10 |

ARMY OF DARKNESS (Movie)
Dark Horse Comics: Nov, 1992 - No. 2, Dec, 1992; No. 3, Oct, 1993 ($2.50, limited series)

| 1-3-Bolton painted-c/a | | | | 4.00 |

ARMY SURPLUS KOMIKZ FEATURING CUTEY BUNNY
Army Surplus Komikz/Eclipse Comics: 1982 - No. 5, 1985 ($1.50, B&W)

| 1-Cutey Bunny begins | 1 | 3 | 5 | 7 |
| 2-5: 5-(Eclipse)-JLA/X-Men/Batman parody | | | | 4.00 |

ARMY WAR HEROES (Also see Iron Corporal)
Charlton Comics: Dec, 1963 - No. 38, June, 1970

1	4	12	29	45
2-10	3	9	19	28
11-21,23-30: 24-Intro. Archer & Corp. Jack series	2	6	13	20
22-Origin/1st app. Iron Corporal series by Glanzman	3	9	20	30
31-38	2	6	10	14
Modern Comics Reprint 36 ('78)				4.00
NOTE: Montes/Bache a-1, 16, 17, 21, 23-25, 27-30.

AROUND THE BLOCK WITH DUNC & LOO (See Dunc and Loo)

AROUND THE WORLD IN 80 DAYS (Movie) (See A Golden Picture Classic)
Dell Publishing Co.: Feb, 1957

| Four Color 784-Photo-c | 6 | 18 | 42 | 80 |

AROUND THE WORLD UNDER THE SEA (See Movie Classics)

AROUND THE WORLD WITH ARCHIE (See Archie Giant Series Mag. #29, 35, 141)

AROUND THE WORLD WITH HUCKLEBERRY & HIS FRIENDS (See Dell Giant No. 44)

ARRGH! (Satire)
Marvel Comics Group: Dec, 1974 - No. 5, Sept, 1975 (25¢)

1-Dracula story; Sekowsky-a(p)	2	6	15	22
2-5: 2-Frankenstein. 3-Mummy. 4-Nightstalker(TV); Dracula-c/app., Hunchback.				
5-Invisible Man, Dracula	2	6	11	15
NOTE: Alcala a-1, 16, 17, 21, 23-25, 27-30. Everett a-1r, 2r. Grandenetti a-4. Maneely a-4r. Sutton a-1-3.

ARROW (See Protectors)
Malibu Comics: Oct, 1992 ($1.95, one-shot)

| 1-Moder-a(p) | | | | 2.25 |

ARROW, THE (See Funny Pages)
Centaur Publications: Oct, 1940 - No. 2, Nov, 1940; No. 3, Oct, 1941

	GD2.0	FN6.0	VF8.0	NM9.4

1-The Arrow begins(r/Funny Pages)	300	900	1875	3300
2,3: 2-Tippy Taylor serial continues from Amazing Mystery Funnies #24. 3-				
Origin Dash Dartwell, the Human Meteor; origin The Rainbow-r; bondage-c	127	381	795	1400
NOTE: Gustavson a-1, 2; c-3.

ARROWHEAD (See Black Rider and Wild Western)
Atlas Comics (CPS): April, 1954 - No. 4, Nov, 1954

| 1-Arrowhead & his horse Eagle begin | 17 | 51 | 88 | 150 |
| 2-4: 4-Forte-a | 10 | 30 | 55 | 80 |
NOTE: Heath c-3. Jack Katz a-3. Maneely c-2. Pakula a-2. Sinnott a-1-4; c-1.

ARSENAL (Teen Titans' Speedy)
DC Comics: Oct, 1998 - No. 4, Jan, 1999 ($2.50, limited series)

| 1-4: Grayson-s. 1-Black Canary app. 2-Green Arrow app. | | | | 2.50 |

ARSENAL SPECIAL (See New Titans, Showcase '94 #7 & Showcase '95 #8)
DC Comics: 1996 ($2.95, one-shot)

| 1 | | | | 3.00 |

ARTBABE
Fantagraphics Books: May, 1996 - Apr, 1999 ($2.50/$2.95/$3.50, B&W)

| V1 #5, V2 1-3 | | | | 3.00 |
| #4-($3.50) | | | | 3.50 |

ARTEMIS: REQUIEM (Also see Wonder Woman, 2nd Series #90)
DC Comics: June, 1996 - No. 6, Nov, 1996 ($1.75, limited series)

| 1-6: Messner-Loebs scripts & Benes-c/a in all. 1,2-Wonder Woman app. | | | | 3.00 |

ARTESIA
Sirius Entertainment: Jan, 1999 - No. 6, June, 1999 ($2.95, limited series)

1-6-Mark Smylie-s/a				3.00
Annual 1 (1999, $3.50)				3.50
Annual 2 (2001, $3.95) Crilley back-c				3.95

ARTESIA AFIELD
Sirius Entertainment: Jul, 2000 - No. 6, Feb, 2001 ($2.95, limited series)

| 1-6-Mark Smylie-s/a | | | | 3.00 |

ART OF ZEN INTERGALACTIC NINJA, THE
Entity Comics: 1994 - No. 2, 1994 ($2.95)

| 1,2 | | | | 3.00 |

ARZACH (See Moebius...)
Dark Horse Comics: 1996 ($6.95, one-shot)

| nn-Moebius-c/a/scripts | 1 | 3 | 5 | 7 |

ASCENSION
Image Comics (Top Cow Productions): Oct, 1997 - No. 22, Mar, 2000 ($2.50)

Preview				5.00
Preview Gold Edition				8.00
Preview San Diego Edition	2	6	9	12
0				4.00
1/2				6.00
1-David Finch-s/a(p)/Batt-s/a(i)				4.00
1-Variant-c w/Image logo at lower right				6.00
2-6				3.00
7-22				2.50
Fan Club Edition				5.00

...COLLECTED EDITION
1998 - No. 2 ($4.95, squarebound) 1,2: 1-r/#1,2. 2-r/#3,4

| | | | | 5.00 |

ASH
Event Comics: Nov, 1994 - No. 6, Dec, 1995; No. 0, May, 1996 ($2.50/$3.00)

0-Present & Future (Both 5/96, $3.00, foil logo-c)-w/pin-ups				3.00
0-Blue Foil logo-c (Present and Future) (1000 each)				4.00
0-Silver Prism logo-c (Present and Future) (500 each)				10.00
0-Red Prism logo-c (Present and Future) (250 each)				20.00
0-Gold Hologram logo-c (Present and Future) (1000 each)				8.00
1-Quesada-p/story; Palmiotti-i/story: Barry Windsor-Smith pin-up				
	2	6	9	12
2-Mignola Hellboy pin-up	1	3	5	7
3,4: 3-Big Guy pin-up by Geoff Darrow. 4-Jim Lee pin-up				4.00
4-Fahrenheit Gold				7.00

	GD2.0	FN6.0	VF8.0	NM9.4

4-6-Fahrenheit Red (5,6-1000) — 8.00
4-6-Fahrenheit White — 12.00
5, 6-Double-c w/Hildebrandt Bros.-a, Quesada & Palmiotti. 6-Texeira-c — 3.00
5,6-Fahrenheit Gold (2000) — 4.00
6-Fahrenheit White (500)-Texeira-c — 12.00
Volume 1 (1996, $14.95, TPB)-r/#1-5, intro by James Robinson — 12.00
Wizard Mini-Comic (1996, magazine supplement) — 2.25
Wizard #1/2 (1997, mail order) — 4.00

ASH: CINDER & SMOKE
Event Comics: May, 1997 - No. 6, Oct, 1997 ($2.95, limited series)

1-6: Ramos-a/Waid, Augustyn-s in all. 2-6-variant covers by Ramos and Quesada — 3.00

ASH: FILES
Event Comics: Mar, 1997 ($2.95, one-shot)

1-Comics w/text — 3.00

ASH: FIRE AND CROSSFIRE
Event Comics: Jan, 1999 - No. 5 ($2.95, limited series)

1,2-Robinson-s/Quesada & Palmiotti-c/a — 3.00

ASH: FIRE WITHIN, THE
Event Comics: Sept, 1996 - No. 2, Jan, 1997 ($2.95, unfinished limited series)

1,2-Quesada & Palmiotti-c/s/a — 3.00

ASH/ 22 BRIDES
Event Comics: Dec, 1996 - No. 2, Apr, 1997 ($2.95, limited series)

1,2-Nicieza-s/Ramos-c/a — 3.00

ASKANI'SON (See Adventures of Cyclops & Phoenix limited series)
Marvel Comics: Jan, 1996 - No. 4, May, 1996 ($2.95, limited series)

1-4: Story cont'd from Advs. of Cyclops & Phoenix; Lobdell/Loeb story; Gene Ha-c/a(p) — 3.00
TPB (1997, $12.99) r/#1-4; Gene Ha painted-c — 13.00

ASSASSINETTE
Pocket Change Comics: 1994 - No.7, 1995? ($2.50, B&W)

1-7: 1-Silver foil-c — 2.50

ASSASSINETTE HARDCORE
Pocket Change Comics: No.2, 1995 ($2.50, B&W, limited series)

1,2 — 2.50

ASSASSINS
DC Comics (Amalgam): Apr, 1996 ($1.95)

1 — 2.25

ASSASSINS, INC.
Silverline Comics: 1987 - No. 2, 1987 ($1.95)

1,2 — 2.25

ASTER
Entity Comics: Oct, 1994 - No. 4, 1995 ($2.95)

0-4: 1,3,4-Foil Logo. 2-Foil-c. 3-Variant-c exists. — 3.00

ASTER: THE LAST CELESTIAL KNIGHT
Entity Comics: 1995 - No. 3, 1996 ($2.50)

1-3 — 2.50

ASTONISHING (Formerly Marvel Boy No. 1, 2)
Marvel/Atlas Comics(20CC): No. 3, Apr, 1951 - No. 63, Aug, 1957

3-Marvel Boy continues; 3-5-Marvel Boy-c	91	273	568	1000
4-6-Last Marvel Boy; 4-Stan Lee app.	64	192	398	700
7-10: 7-Maneely s/f story. 10-Sinnott s/f story	33	99	174	300
11,12,15,17,20	29	87	153	265
13,14,16,18,19-Krigstein-a. 18-Jack The Ripper sty				
	29	87	153	270
21,22,24	25	75	130	225
23-E.C. swipe "The Hole In The Wall" from Vault Of Horror #16				
	25	75	133	230
25,29: 25-Crandall-a. 29-Decapitation-c	23	69	121	210
26-28	21	63	110	190
30-Tentacled eyeball-c/story; classic-c	30	90	159	275
31-37-Last pre-code issue	19	57	99	165

	GD2.0	FN6.0	VF8.0	NM9.4

38-43,46,48-52,56,58,59,61	14	42	72	120
44,45,47,53-55,57,60: 44-Crandall swipe/Weird Fantasy #22. 45,47-Krigstein-a. 53-Ditko-a. 54-Torres-a, 55-Crandall, Torres-a. 57-Williamson/Krenkel-a (4 pgs.). 60-Williamson/Mayo-a (4 pgs.)	15	45	77	135
62,63: 62-Torres, Powell-a. 63-Woodbridge-a	15	45	77	130

NOTE: Ayers a-16. Berg a-36, 53, 56. Cameron a-50. Gene Colan a-12, 20, 29, 56. Ditko a-53. Drucker a-41, 62. Everett a-3-6(3), 6, 10, 12, 37, 47, 48, 58; c-3-5, 13,15, 16, 18, 29, 47, 49, 51, 53-55, 57, 59-63. Fass a-11, 34. Forte a-53, 58, 60. Fuje a-11. Heath a-8, 29; c-8, 9, 19, 22, 25, 26. Kirby a-56. Lawrence a-28, 37, 38, 42. Maneely a-7(2); c-7, 31, 33, 34, 56. Moldoff a-33. Morisi a-10, 60. Morrow a-52, 61. Orlando a-47, 58, 61. Pakula a-10. Powell a-43, 44, 48. Ravielli a-28. Reinman a-32, 34. Robinson a-20. J. Romita a-7, 18, 24, 43, 57,61. Roussos a-55. Sale a-28, 38, 59; c-32. Sekowsky a-13. Severin c-46. Shores a-16, 60. Sinnott a-11, 30. Whitney a-13. Ed Win a-20. Canadian reprints exist.

ASTONISHING TALES (See Ka-Zar)
Marvel Comics Group: Aug, 1970 - No. 36, July, 1976 (#1-7: 15¢; #8: 25¢)

1-Ka-Zar (by Kirby(p) #1,2; by B. Smith #3-6) & Dr. Doom (by Wood #1-4; by Tuska #5,6; by Colan #7,8; 1st Marvel villain solo series) double feature begins; Kraven the Hunter-c/story; Nixon cameo	4	12	30	50
2-Kraven the Hunter-c/story; Kirby, Wood-a	3	9	17	25
3-6: B. Smith-p; Wood-a/#3,4. 5,6-Red Skull 2-part story				
	3	9	21	32
7-Last 15¢ issue; Black Panther app.	3	9	18	28
8-(25¢, 52 pgs.)-Last Dr. Doom of series	3	9	19	28
9-All Ka-Zar issues begin; Lorna-r/Lorna #14	2	6	11	15
10-B. Smith/Sal Buscema-a.	2	6	13	20
11-Origin Ka-Zar & Zabu; death of Ka-Zar's father	2	6	11	16
12-2nd app.Man-Thing; by Neal Adams (see Savage Tales #1 for 1st app.)				
	3	9	19	28
13-3rd app.Man-Thing	2	6	15	22
14-20: 14-Jann of the Jungle-r (1950s); reprints censored Ka-Zar-s from Savage Tales #1. 17-S.H.I.E.L.D. begins. 19-Starlin-a(p). 20-Last Ka-Zar (continues into 1974 Ka-Zar)	1	3	6	9
21-(12/73)-It! the Living Colossus begins, ends #24 (see Supernatural Thrillers #1)	3	9	17	25
22-24: 23,24-IT vs. Fin Fang Foom	2	6	11	16
25-1st app. Deathlok the Demolisher; full length stories begin, end #36; Perez's 1st work, 2 pgs. (8/74)	4	12	26	40
26-28,30	2	6	9	12
29-r/origin/1st app. Guardians of the Galaxy from Marvel Super-Heroes #18 plus-c w/4 pgs. omitted; no Deathlok story	1	3	6	8
31-34: 31-Watcher-c/Silver Surfer #3	1	4	7	10
35,36-(Regular 25¢ edition)(5,7/76)	1	4	7	10
35,36-(30¢-c, low distribution)	2	6	10	14

NOTE: Buckler a-13i, 16p, 25, 26p, 27p, 28, 29p-36p; c-13, 25p, 26-30, 32-35p, 36. John Buscema a-9, 12p-14p, 16p; c-4-6p, 12p. Colan a-7p, 8p. Ditko a-21r. Everett a-6i. G. Kane a-11p, 15p; c-9, 10p, 11p, 14, 15p, 21p. McWilliams a-30i. Starlin a-19p; c-16p. Sutton & Trimpe a-8. Tuska a-5p, 6p, 8p. Wood a-1-4. Wrightson c-31i.

ASTONISHING X-MEN
Marvel Comics: Mar, 1995 - No.4, July, 1995 ($1.95, limited series)

1-Age of Apocalypse; Magneto-c				4.00
2-4				3.00

ASTONISHING X-MEN
Marvel Comics: Sept, 1999 - No.3, Nov, 1999 ($2.50, limited series)

1-3-New team, Cable & X-Man app.; Peterson-a — 2.50
TPB (11/00, $15.95) r/#1-3, X-Men #92 & #95, Uncanny X-Men #375 — 16.00

ASTOUNDING SPACE THRILLS: THE COMIC BOOK
Image Comics: Apr, 2000 - No. 4, Dec, 2000 ($2.95, limited series)

1-4-Steve Conley-s/a. 2,3-Flip book w/Crater Kid — 3.00
Galaxy-Sized Astounding Space Thrills 1 (10/01, $4.95) — 5.00

ASTRA
CPM Manga: 2001 - No. 8 ($2.95, B&W, limited series)

1-4: Created by Jerry Robinson; Tanaka-a. 1-Balent variant-c — 3.00

ASTRO BOY (TV) (See March of Comics #285 & The Original…)
Gold Key: August, 1965 (12¢)

1(10151-508)-Scarce;1st app. Astro Boy in comics — 44, 132, 308, 575

ASTRO CITY (See Kurt Busiek's Astro City)

ASYLUM
Millennium Publications: 1993 ($2.50)

Atari Force #4 © Atari

The Atom #1 © DC

Atom-Age Combat #5 © STJ

	GD2.0	FN6.0	VF8.0	NM9.4

1-3: 1-Bolton-c/a; Russell 2-pg. illos — 2.50

ASYLUM
Maximum Press: Dec, 1995 - No. 11, Jan, 1997 ($2.95/$2.99, anthology) (#1-6 are flip books)
1-10: 1-Warchild by Art Adams, Beanworld, Avengelyne, Battlestar Galactica. 2-Intro Mike Deodato's Deathkiss; Cybrid story begins, ends #5. 4-1st app.Christian; painted Battlestar Galactica story begins. 5-Intro Black Seed (formerly Black Flag) by Dan Fraga; B&W Christian story. 6-Intro Bionix (Six Million Dollar Man & the Bionic Woman). 7-Begin $2.99-c; Don Simpson's Megaton Man; Black Seed pinup. 8-B&W-a. 9- Foot Soldiers & Kid Supreme. 10-Lady Supreme by Terry Moore-c/app. — 4.00

ATARI FORCE (Also see Promotional comics section)
DC Comics: Jan, 1984 - No. 20, Aug, 1985 (Mando paper)
1-(1/84)-Intro Tempest, Packrat, Babe, Morphea, & Dart — 4.00
2-20 — 3.00
Special 1 (4/86) — 3.00
NOTE: Byrne c-Special 1i. Giffen a-12p, 13i. Rogers a-18p, Special 1p.

A-TEAM, THE (TV) (Also see Marvel Graphic Novel)
Marvel Comics Group: Mar, 1984 - No. 3, May, 1984

1-3				4.00
1,2-(Whitman bagged set) w/75¢-c	1	3	6	8
3-(Whitman, no bag) w/75¢-c	1	3	5	7

ATHENA INC. THE BEGINNING
Image Comics: Dec, 2001 ($5.95)
1-Anacleto-c/a; Haberlin-s — 6.00

ATLANTIS CHRONICLES, THE (Also see Aquaman, 3rd Series & Aquaman: Time & Tide)
DC Comics: Mar, 1990 - No. 7, Sept, 1990 ($2.95, limited series, 52 pgs.)
1-7: 1-Peter David scripts. 7-True origin of Aquaman; nudity panels — 3.25

ATLANTIS, THE LOST CONTINENT
Dell Publishing Co.: May, 1961

Four Color #1188-Movie, photo-c	11	33	77	140

ATLAS (See 1st Issue Special)

ATLAS
Dark Horse Comics: Feb, 1994 - No. 4, 1994 ($2.50, limited series)
1-4 — 2.50

ATOM, THE (See Action #425, All-American #19, Brave & the Bold, D.C. Special Series #1, Detective, Flash Comics #80, Power Of The Atom, Showcase #34 -36 , Super Friends, Sword of The Atom, Teen Titans & World's Finest)
ATOM, THE (...& the Hawkman No. 39 on)
National Periodical Publ.: June-July, 1962 - No. 38, Aug-Sept, 1968

1-(6-7/62)-Intro Plant-Master; 1st app. Maya	69	207	584	1100
2	31	93	222	400
3-1st Time Pool story; 1st app. Chronos (origin)	21	63	146	260
4,5: 4-Snapper Carr x-over	16	48	112	200
6,9,10	12	36	84	140
7-Hawkman x-over (6-7/63); 1st Atom & Hawkman team-up); 1st app. Hawkman since Brave & the Bold tryouts	28	84	196	350
8-Justice League, Dr. Light app.	12	36	55	150
11-15: 13-Chronos-c/story	8	24	58	95
16-20: 19-Zatanna x-over	6	18	45	75
21-28,30: 28-Chronos-c/story	5	15	38	60
29-1st solo Golden Age Atom x-over in S.A.	15	45	105	180
31-35,37,38: 31-Hawkman x-over. 37-Intro. Major Mynah; Hawkman cameo	5	15	34	55
36-G.A. Atom x-over	6	18	42	70

NOTE: Anderson a-1-11i, 13i; c-inks-1-25, 31-35, 37. Sid Greene a-8i-37i. Gil Kane c-1-1p-28p, 29, 33p, 34. George Roussos 38i Mike Sekowsky 38p Time Pool stories also in 6, 9,12, 17, 21, 27, 35.

ATOM, THE (See Tangent Comics/ The Atom)
ATOM AGE (See Classics Illustrated Special Issue)
ATOM-AGE COMBAT
St. John Publishing Co.: June, 1952 - No. 5, Apr, 1953; Feb, 1958

1-Buck Vinson in all	45	135	270	475
2-Flying saucer story	29	87	153	265
3,5: 3-Mayo-a (6 pgs.). 5-Flying saucer-c/story	24	72	127	220
4 (Scarce)	29	87	153	265
1(2/58-St. John)	20	60	105	175

ATOM-AGE COMBAT
Fago Magazines: No. 2, Jan, 1959 - No. 3, Mar, 1959

2-A-Bomb explosion-c;	26	78	139	240
3	20	60	105	175

ATOMAN
Spark Publications: Feb, 1946 - No. 2, April, 1946

1-Origin & 1st app. Atoman; Robinson/Meskin-a; Kidcrusaders, Wild Bill Hickok, Marvin the Great app.	64	192	398	700
2-Robinson/Meskin-a; Robinson c-1,2	43	129	257	450

ATOM & HAWKMAN, THE (Formerly The Atom)
National Periodical Publ.: No. 39, Oct-Nov, 1968 - No. 45, Oct-Nov, 1969

39-43: 40-41-Kubert/Anderson-a. 43-(7/69)-Last 12¢ issue; 1st app. Gentleman Ghost	4	12	30	48
44,45: 44-(9/69)-1st 15¢-c; origin Gentleman Ghost	4	12	30	48

NOTE: M. Anderson a-39, 40i, 41i, 43, 44. Sid Greene a-40i-45i. Kubert a-40p, 41p; c-39-45.

ATOM ANT (TV) (See Golden Comics Digest #2) (Hanna-Barbera)
Gold Key: January, 1966 (12¢)

1(10170-601)-1st app. Atom Ant, Precious Pup, and Hillbilly Bears	31	93	217	400

ATOM ANT & SECRET SQUIRREL (See Hanna-Barbera Presents)

ATOMIC AGE
Marvel Comics (Epic Comics): Nov, 1990 - No. 4, Feb, 1991 ($4.50, limited series, squarebound, 52 pgs.)
1-4: Williamson-a(i); sci-fi story set in 1957 — 4.50

ATOMIC ATTACK (True War Stories; formerly Attack, first series)
Youthful Magazines: No. 5, Jan, 1953 - No. 8, Oct, 1953 (1st story is sci/fi in all issues)

5-Atomic bomb-c; science fiction stories in all	40	120	220	380
6-8	26	78	136	235

ATOMIC BOMB
Jay Burtis Publications: 1945 (36 pgs.)

1-Airmale & Stampy (scarce)	64	192	398	700

ATOMIC BUNNY (Formerly Atomic Rabbit)
Charlton Comics: No. 12, Aug, 1958 - No. 19, Dec, 1959

12	12	36	61	100
13-19	7	21	38	55

ATOMIC COMICS
Daniels Publications (Canadian): Jan, 1946 (Reprints, one-shot)

1-Rocketman, Yankee Boy, Master Key app.	38	114	203	350

ATOMIC COMICS
Green Publishing Co.: Jan, 1946 - No. 4, July-Aug, 1946 (#1-4 were printed w/o cover gloss)

1-Radio Squad by Siegel & Shuster; Barry O'Neal cover-r/ Detective Comics (Classic-c)	134	400	838	1475
2-Inspector Dayton; Kid Kane by Matt Baker; Lucky Wings, Congo King, Prop Powers (only app.) begin	63	189	394	690
3,4: 3-Zero Ghost Detective app. Baker-a(2) each; 4-Baker-c	43	129	257	450

ATOMIC KNIGHTS (See Strange Adventures #117)

ATOMIC MOUSE (TV, Movies) (See Blue Bird, Funny Animals, Giant Comics Edition & Wotalife Comics)
Capitol Stories/Charlton Comics: 3/53 - No. 54, 6/63; No. 1, 12/84; V2#10, 19/85 - No. 12, 1/86

1-Origin & 1st app.; Al Fago-c/a in all?	33	99	174	300
2	13	39	66	115
3-10: 5-Timmy The Timid Ghost app.; see Zoo Funnies	10	30	55	85
11-13,16-25	6	18	32	45
14,15-Hoppy The Marvel Bunny app.	8	24	45	65

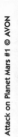

The Atomics #3 © Mike Allred

Attack on Planet Mars #1 © AVON

The Authority #16 © WSP

	GD2.0	FN6.0	VF8.0	NM9.4
26-(68 pgs.)	11	33	55	90
27-40: 36,37-Atom The Cat app.	5	15	25	35
41-54	4	11	17	22
1 (1984)-Low print run	2	6	9	12
V2#10 (9/85) -12(1/86)-Low print run	1	4	7	10

ATOMIC RABBIT (Atomic Bunny #12 on; see Giant Comics #3 & Wotalife)
Charlton Comics: Aug, 1955 - No. 11, Mar, 1958

1-Origin & 1st app.; Al Fago-c/a in all?	29	87	153	265
2	12	36	61	105
3-10	8	24	45	65
11-(68 pgs.)	12	36	61	105

ATOMICS, THE
AAA Pop Comics: Jan, 2000 - No. 15, Nov, 2001 ($2.95)

1-11-Mike Allred-s/a; 1-Madman-c/app.				3.00
12-15-($3.50): 13-15-Savage Dragon-c/app. 15-Afterword by Alex Ross; colored reprint of 1st Frank Einstein story				3.50
...King-Size Giant Spectacular: Jigsaw (2000, $10.00) r/#1-4				10.00
...King-Size Giant Spectacular: Lessons in Light, Lava, & Lasers (2000, $8.95) r/#5-8				9.00
...King-Size Giant Spectacular: Worlds Within Worlds ('01, $8.95) r/#9-12				9.00

ATOMIC SPY CASES
Avon Periodicals: Mar-Apr, 1950 (Painted-c)

1-No Wood-a; A-bomb blast panels; Fass-a	33	99	174	300

ATOMIC THUNDERBOLT, THE
Regor Company: Feb, 1946 (one-shot) (scarce)

1-Intro. Atomic Thunderbolt & Mr. Murdo	64	192	398	700

ATOMIC TOYBOX
Image Comics: Dec, 1999 ($2.95)

1- Aaron Lopresti-c/s-a				3.00

ATOMIC WAR!
Ace Periodicals (Junior Books): Nov, 1952 - No. 4, Apr, 1953

1-Atomic bomb-c	89	267	556	975
2,3: 3-Atomic bomb-c	57	171	356	625
4-Used in POP, pg. 96 & illo.	57	171	356	625

ATOMIK ANGELS
Crusade Comics: May, 1996 - No. 4, Nov. 1996 ($2.50)

1-4: 1-Freefall from Gen 13 app.				3.00
1-Variant-c				4.00
Intrep-Edition (2/96, B&W, giveaway at launch party)-Previews Atomik Angels #1; includes Billy Tucci interview.				4.00

ATOM SPECIAL (See Atom & Justice League of America)
DC Comics: 1993/1995 ($2.50/$2.95)(68pgs.)

1,2: 1-Dillon-c/a. 2-McDonnell-a/Bolland-c/Peyer-s				3.00

ATOM THE CAT (Formerly Tom Cat; see Giant Comics #3)
Charlton Comics: No. 9, Oct, 1957 - No. 17, Aug, 1959

9	9	27	49	70
10,13-17	6	18	29	40
11,12: 11(64 pgs)-Atomic Mouse app. 12(100 pgs.)	10	30	55	90

ATTACK
Youthful Mag./Trojan No. 5 on: May, 1952 - No. 4, Nov, 1952; No. 5, Jan, 1953 - No. 5, Sept, 1953

1-(1st series)-Extreme violence	31	93	165	285
2,3-Both Harrison-c/a; bondage, whipping	16	48	83	140
4-Krenkel-a (7 pgs.); Harrison-a (becomes Atomic Attack #5 on)	16	48	83	140
5-(#1, Trojan, 2nd series)	13	39	66	110
6-8 (#2-4), 5	10	30	55	80

ATTACK
Charlton Comics: No. 54, 1958 - No. 60, Nov, 1959

54 (25¢, 100 pgs.)	11	33	55	90
55-60	5	15	24	32

ATTACK!
Charlton Comics: 1962 - No. 15, 3/75; No. 16, 8/79 - No. 48, 10/84

nn(#1)-('62) Special Edition	4	12	27	42
2('63), 3(Fall, '64)	3	9	19	28
V4#3(10/66), 4(10/67)-(Formerly Special War Series #2; becomes Attack At Sea V4#5)	2	6	15	22
1(9/71)	2	6	15	22
2-5: 4-American Eagle app.	2	6	9	12
6-15(3/75)	1	3	6	9
16(8/79) - 40				4.00
41-47 Low print run				5.00
48(10/84)-Wood-r; S&K-c (low print)	1	3	6	8
Modern Comics 13('78)-r				3.00
NOTE: *Sutton* a-9,10,13.				

ATTACK!
Spire Christian Comics (Fleming H. Revell Co.): 1975 (39¢/49¢, 36 pgs.)

nn	1	3	5	7

ATTACK AT SEA (Formerly Attack!, 1967)
Charlton Comics: V4#5, Oct, 1968

V4#5	2	6	15	22

ATTACK ON PLANET MARS (See Strange Worlds #18)
Avon Periodicals: 1951

nn-Infantino, Fawcette, Kubert & Wood-a; adaptation of Tarrano the Conqueror by Ray Cummings	75	225	469	825

ATTITUDE LAD
Slave Labor Graphics: Apr, 1994 - No. 3, Nov, 1994 ($2.95, B&W)

1-3				3.00

AUDREY & MELVIN (Formerly Little...)(See Little Audrey & Melvin)
Harvey Publications: No. 62, Sept, 1974

62	2	6	9	12

AUGIE DOGGIE (TV) (See Hanna-Barbera Band Wagon, Quick-Draw McGraw, Spotlight #2, Top Cat & Whitman Comic Books)
Gold Key: October, 1963 (12¢)

1-Hanna-Barbera character	18	54	126	230

AUTHENTIC POLICE CASES
St. John Publishing Co.: 2/48 - No. 6, 11/48; No. 7, 5/50 - No. 38, 3/55

1-Hale the Magician by Tuska begins	43	129	257	450
2-Lady Satan, Johnny Rebel app.	27	81	145	250
3-Veiled Avenger app.; blood drainage story plus 2 Lucky Coyne stories; used in SOTI, illo. from Red Seal #16	45	135	270	475
4,5: 4-Masked Black Jack app. 5-Late 1930s Jack Cole-a(r); transvestism story	27	81	145	250
6-Matt Baker-c; used in SOTI, illo- "An invitation to learning", r-in Fugitives From Justice #3; Jack Cole-a; also used by the N.Y. Legis. Comm.	47	141	286	500
7,8,10-14: 7-Jack Cole-a; Matt Baker-a begins #8, ends #?; Vic Flint in #10-14. 10-12-Baker-a(2 each)	23	69	121	210
9-No Vic Flint	19	57	99	165
15-Drug-c/story; Vic Flint app.; Baker-c	23	69	121	210
16,18,20,21,23: Baker-a(i)	14	42	72	120
17,19,22-Baker-c	16	48	83	140
24-28 (All 100 pgs): 26-Transvestism	30	90	162	280
29,31,32-Baker-c	11	33	55	90
30	9	27	51	75
33-38: 33-Transvestism; Baker-c. 34-Baker-c; r/#9. 35-Baker-c/a(2); r/#10 36-r/#11; Vic Flint strip-r; Baker-c/a(2) unsigned. 37-Baker-c; r/#17. 38-Baker-c/a; r/#18	13	39	66	110
NOTE: *Matt Baker* c-6-16, 17, 19, 22, 27, 29, 31-38; a-13, 16. Bondage c-1, 3.				

AUTHORITY, THE (See Stormwatch and Jenny Sparks: The Secret History of...)
DC Comics (WildStorm): May, 1999 - Present ($2.50)

1-Wraparound-c; Warren Ellis-s/Bryan Hitch and Paul Neary-a				10.00
2-4				7.00
5-12: 12-Death of Jenny Sparks; last Ellis-s				5.00
13-Mark Millar-s/Frank Quitely & Trevor Scott-a begins				8.00
14-16-Authority vs. Marvel-esque villains				5.00
17-22: 17,18-Weston-a. 19,20,22-Quitely-a. 21-McCrea-a				2.50
23-27: 23-26-Peyer-s/Nguyen-a; new Authority. 24-Preview of "The				

Automation #1 © Flypaper Press

Avengelyne/Glory: Godyssey #1 © Rob Liefeld

The Avengers #7 © MAR

AV

	GD2.0	FN6.0	VF8.0	NM9.4

Establishment." 25,26-Jenny Sparks app. 27-Millar-s/Adams-a/c   2.50
Annual 2000 ($3.50) Devil's Night x-over; Hamner-a/Bermejo-c   3.50
... :Relentless TPB (2000, $17.95) r/#1-8   18.00
... :Under New Management TPB (2000, $17.95) r/#9-16; new Quitely-c   18.00

AUTOMATON
Image Comics (Flypaper Press): Sept, 1998 - No. 3, 1998 ($2.95, lim. series)
   1-3-R.A. Jones-s/Peter Vale-a   3.00

AUTUMN
Caliber Comics: 1995 - No. 3, 1995 ($2.95, B&W)
   1-3   3.00

AUTUMN ADVENTURES (Walt Disney's...)
Disney Comics: Autumn, 1990; No. 2, Autumn, 1991 ($2.95, 68 pgs.)
   1-Donald Duck-r(2) by Barks, Pluto-r, & new-a   4.00
   2-D. Duck-r by Barks; new Super Goof story   4.00

AVATAARS: COVENANT OF THE SHIELD
Marvel Comics: Sept, 2000 - No. 3, Nov, 2000 ($2.99, limited series)
   1-3-Kaminski-s/Oscar Jimenez-a   3.00

AVATAR
DC Comics: Feb, 1991 - No. 3, Apr, 1991 ($5.95, limited series, 100 pgs.)
   1-3: Based on TSR's Forgotten Realms   6.00

AVENGEBLADE
Maximum Press: July, 1996 - No. 2, Aug, 1996 ($2.99, limited series)
   1,2: Bad Girls parody   3.00

AVENGELYNE
Maximum Press: May, 1995 - No. 3, July, 1995 ($2.50/$3.50, limited series)

1/2		2	6	9	12
1/2 Platinum				15.00
1-Newstand ($2.50)-Photo-c; poster insert				6.00
1-Direct Market ($3.50)-Chromium-c; poster	1	3	5	7
1-Glossy edition	2	6	13	20
1-Gold				12.00
2-3: Polybagged w/card				3.00
3-Variant-c; Deodato pin-up				5.00
.../Glory Swimsuit Special (9/96, $2.95) photo and illos. covers				4.00

...Swimsuit (8/95, $2.95)-Pin-ups/photos. 3-Variant-c exist (2 photo, 1 Liefeld-a)   4.00
...Swimsuit (1/96, $3.50, 2nd printing)-photo-c   4.00
Trade paperback (12/95, $9.95)   10.00

AVENGELYNE
Maximum Press: V2#1, Apr, 1996 - No. 14, Apr, 1997 ($2.95/$2.50)

V2#1-Four covers exist (2 photo-c).				4.00
V2#2-Three covers exist (1 photo-c); flip book w/Darkchylde		2	6	11	15

V2#0, 3-14: 0-(10/96).3-Flip book w/Priest preview. 4-Cybrid app;
   w/Darkchylde/Avengelyne poster. 5-Flip book w/Blindside   3.00
...Bible (10/96, $3.50)   4.00

AVENGELYNE (Volume 3)
Awesome Comics: Mar, 1999 ($2.50)
   1-Fraga & Liefeld-a   3.00

AVENGELYNE: ARMAGEDDON
Maximum Press: Dec, 1996 - No. 3, Feb, 1997 ($2.95, limited series)
   1-3-Scott Clark-a(p)   3.00

AVENGELYNE: DEADLY SINS
Maximum Press: Feb, 1996 - No. 2, Mar, 1996 ($2.95, limited series)
   1,2: 1-Two-c exist (1 photo, 1 Liefeld-a). 2-Liefeld-c; Pop Mhan-a(p).   3.00

AVENGELYNE/GLORY
Maximum Press: Sept, 1995 ($3.95, one-shot)
   1-Chromium-c   4.00
   1-Variant-c   5.00

AVENGELYNE/GLORY: GODYSSEY, THE (See Glory/...)
Maximum Press: Sept, 1996 ($2.99, one-shot)
   1-Two covers (1 photo)   3.00

AVENGELYNE/POWER
Maximum Press: Nov, 1995 - No.3, Jan, 1996 ($2.95, limited series)
   1-3: 1,2-Liefeld-c. 3-Three variant-c. exist (1 photo-c)   3.00
   1-Variant-c   3.50

AVENGELYNE • PROPHET
Maximum Press: May, 1996; No. 2, Feb. 1997 ($2.95, unfinished lim. series)
   1,2-Liefeld-c/a(p)   3.00

AVENGELYNE: REVELATION ONE
Avatar Press: Jan, 2001 ($3.50, one-shot)
   1-Three regular covers by Haley, Rio, Shaw; Shaw-a   3.50

AVENGELYNE/SHI
Avatar Press: Nov, 2001 ($3.50, one-shot)
   1-Eight covers; Waller-a   3.50

AVENGELYNE/ WARRIOR NUN AREALA (See Warrior Nun/...)
Maximum Press: Nov, 1996 ($2.99, one-shot)
   1   4.00

AVENGER, THE (See A-1 Comics)
Magazine Enterprises: Feb-Mar, 1955 - No. 4, Aug-Sept, 1955

1(A-1 #129)-Origin	40	120	220	380
2(A-1 #131), 3(A-1 #133) Robot-c, 4(A-1 #138)	27	81	145	250
IW Reprint #9('64)-Reprints #1 (new cover)	3	9	21	32

NOTE: *Powell a-2-4; c-1-4.*

AVENGERS, THE (TV)(Also see Steed and Mrs. Peel)
Gold Key: Nov, 1968 ("John Steed & Emma Peel" cover title) (15¢)

1-Photo-c	23	68	161	300
1-(Variant with photo back-c)	28	85	196	375

AVENGERS, THE (See Essential..., Giant-Size..., Kree/Skrull War Starring..., Marvel Graphic Novel #27, Marvel Super Action, Marvel Super Heroes('66), Marvel Treasury Ed., Marvel Triple Action, Solo Avengers, Tales Of Suspense #49, West Coast Avengers & X-Men Vs....)

AVENGERS, THE (The Mighty Avengers on cover only #63-69)
Marvel Comics Group: Sept, 1963 - No. 402, Sept, 1996

1-Origin & 1st app. The Avengers (Thor, Iron Man, Hulk, Ant-Man, Wasp); Loki app.	218	654	1853	3700
2-Hulk leaves Avengers	55	165	468	875
3-1st Sub-Mariner x-over (outside the F.F.); Hulk & Sub-Mariner team-up & battle Avengers; Spider-Man cameo (1/64)	39	117	293	525
4-Revival of Captain America who joins the Avengers; 1st Silver Age app. of Captain America & Bucky (3/64)	144	432	1222	2300
4-Reprint from the Golden Record Comic set With Record (1966)	10	30	70	120
	15	45	105	180
5-Hulk app.	26	78	182	325
6-8: 6-Intro/1st app. original Zemo & his Masters of Evil. 8-Intro Kang	20	60	140	250
9-Intro Wonder Man who dies in same story	21	63	146	260
10-Intro/1st app. Immortus; early Hercules app. (11/64)	18	54	129	230
11-Spider-Man-c & x-over (12/64)	22	66	154	275
12-15: Death of original Zemo	13	39	94	160
16-New Avengers line-up (Hawkeye, Quicksilver, Scarlet Witch join; Thor, Iron Man, Giant-Man, Wasp leave)	14	42	98	165
17,18	10	30	68	115
19-1st app. Swordsman; origin Hawkeye (8/65)	10	30	73	125
20-22: Wood inks	7	21	50	80
23-30: 23-Romita Sr. inks (1st Silver Age Marvel work). 25-Dr. Doom-c/story. 28-Giant-Man becomes Goliath (5/66)	5	15	38	60
31-40	4	12	29	45

41-46,49-52,54-56: 43,44-1st app. Red Guardian. 46-Ant-Man returns (re-intro,
11/67). 52-Black Panther joins; 1st app. The Grim Reaper. 54-1st app. new
Masters of Evil. 56-Zemo app; story explains how Capt. America became
imprisoned in ice during WWII, only to be rescued in Avengers #4

	3	10	23	35
47-Magneto-c/story	4	12	26	40
48-Origin/1st app. new Black Knight (1/68)	4	12	26	40
53-X-Men app.	4	12	30	50
57-1st app. S.A. Vision (10/68)	8	24	60	100
58-Origin The Vision	5	15	38	60

The Avengers #161 © MAR

The Avengers #186 © MAR

The Avengers #374 © MAR

	GD2.0	FN6.0	VF8.0	NM9.4

59-65: 59-Intro. Yellowjacket. 60-Wasp & Yellowjacket wed. 63-Goliath becomes Yellowjacket; Hawkeye becomes the new Goliath. 65-Last 12¢ issue | 3 | 9 | 20 | 30
66,67-B. Smith-a | 3 | 10 | 23 | 35
68-70: 70-Nighthawk on cover | 3 | 9 | 18 | 28
71-1st app. The Invaders (12/69); 1st app. Nighthawk; Black Knight joins | 4 | 12 | 30 | 50
72-79,81,82,84-86,89-91: 82-Daredevil app | 3 | 9 | 17 | 25
80-Intro. Red Wolf (9/70) | 3 | 9 | 20 | 30
83-Intro. The Liberators (Wasp, Valkyrie, Scarlet Witch, Medusa & the Black Widow) | 3 | 9 | 21 | 32
87-Origin The Black Panther | 3 | 10 | 23 | 35
88-Written by Harlan Ellison | 3 | 9 | 19 | 28
92-Last 15¢ issue; Neal Adams-c | 3 | 9 | 20 | 30
93-(52 pgs.)-Neal Adams-c/a | 7 | 21 | 50 | 80
94-96-Neal Adams-c/a | 4 | 12 | 29 | 45
97-G.A. Capt. America, Sub-Mariner, Human Torch, Patriot, Vision, Blazing Skull, Fin, Angel, & new Capt. Marvel x-over | 3 | 9 | 20 | 30
98,99: 98-Goliath becomes Hawkeye; Smith c/a(i). 99-Smith-c, Smith/Sutton-a | 3 | 9 | 20 | 30
100-(6/72)-Smith-c/a; featuring everyone who was an Avenger | 8 | 24 | 58 | 95
101-Harlan Ellison scripts | 2 | 6 | 13 | 20
102-106,108,109 | 2 | 6 | 12 | 18
107-Starlin-a(p) | 2 | 6 | 13 | 20
110,111-X-Men app. | 2 | 6 | 13 | 20
112-1st app. Mantis | 2 | 6 | 15 | 22
113-115,119-124,126-130: 123-Origin Mantis | 2 | 6 | 11 | 15
116-118-Defenders/Silver Surfer app. | 3 | 9 | 17 | 24
125-Thanos-c & brief app. | 2 | 6 | 13 | 20
131-133,136-140: 136-Ploog-r/Amazing Advs. #12 | 1 | 4 | 7 | 10
134,135-True origin Vision | 2 | 6 | 11 | 15
141-143,145,152-163 | 1 | 3 | 6 | 8
144-Origin & 1st app. Hellcat | 1 | 4 | 7 | 15
146-149-(Reg.25¢ editions)(4-7/76) | 1 | 3 | 6 | 8
146-149-(30¢-c variants, limited distribution) | 2 | 6 | 11 | 16
150-Kirby-a(r); new line-up: Capt. America, Scarlet Witch, Iron Man, Wasp, Yellowjacket, Vision & The Beast | 1 | 4 | 7 | 10
150-(30¢-c variant, limited distribution) | 2 | 6 | 12 | 18
151-Wonder Man returns w/new costume | 1 | 4 | 7 | 10
160-164-(35¢-c variants, limited dist.)(6-10/77) | 2 | 6 | 10 | 14
164-166: Byrne-a | 1 | 3 | 6 | 9
167-180: 168-Guardians of the Galaxy app. 174-Thanos cameo. 176-Starhawk app. | | | | 6.00
181-191-Byrne-a: 181-New line-up: Capt. America, Scarlet Witch, Iron Man, Wasp, Vision, Beast & The Falcon. 183-Ms. Marvel joins. 185-Origin Quicksilver & Scarlet Witch | 1 | 3 | 5 | 7
192-199: 195-1st Taskmaster | | | | 5.00
200-(1/80, 52 pgs.)-Ms. Marvel leaves. | | | | 6.00
201-213,217-238,241-249, 251-262: 211-New line-up: Capt. America, Iron Man, Tigra, Thor, Wasp & Yellowjacket. 217-Yellowjacket & Wasp return. 221-Hawkeye & She-Hulk join. 227-Capt. Marvel (female) joins; origins of Ant-Man, Wasp, Giant-Man, Goliath, Yellowjacket, & Avengers. 230-Yellowjacket quits. 231-Iron Man leaves. 232-Starfox (Eros) joins. 234-Origin Quicksilver, Scarlet Witch. 236-New logo. 238-Origin Blackout | | | | 3.50
214-Ghost Rider-c/story | | | | 6.00
215,216,239,240,250: 215,216-Silver Surfer app. 216-Tigra leaves. 239-(1/84) Avengers app. on David Letterman show. 240-Spider-Woman revived. 250-($1.00, 52 pgs.) | | | | 4.00
263-1st app. X-Factor (1/86)(story continues in Fant. Four #286) | | | | 6.00
264-299: 272-Alpha Flight app. 291-$1.00 issues begin. 297-Black Knight, She-Hulk & Thor resign. 298-Inferno tie-in | | | | 3.00
300 (2/89, $1.75, 68 pgs.)-Thor joins; Simonson-a | | | | 4.00
301-304,306-313,319-325,327,329-343: 302-Re-intro Quasar. 320-324-Alpha Flight app. (320-cameo). 327-2nd app. Rage. 341,342-New Warriors app. 343-Last $1.00-c | | | | 3.00
305,314-318: 305-Byrne scripts begin. 314-318-Spider-Man x-over | | | | 3.50
326-1st app. Rage (11/90) | | | | 4.00
328,344-349,351-359,361,362,364,365,367: 328-Origin Rage. 365-Contains coupon for Hunt for Magneto contest | | | | 3.00
350-($2.50, 68 pgs.)-Double gatefold-c showing-c to #1; r/#53 w/cover in flip book format; vs. The Starjammers | | | | 3.50
360-($2.95, 52 pgs.)-Embossed all-foil-c; 30th ann. | | | | 4.00
363-($2.95, 52 pgs.)-All silver foil-c | | | | 4.00
366-($3.95, 68 pgs.)-Embossed all gold foil-c | | | | 4.00
368,370-374,376-399: 368-Bloodties part 1; Avengers/X-Men x-over. 374-bound-in trading card sheet. 380-Deodato-a. 390,391-"The Crossing." 395-Death of "old" Tony Stark; wraparound-c. | | | | 3.00
369-($2.95)-Foil embossed-c; Bloodties part 5 | | | | 4.00
375-($2.00, 52 pgs.)-Regular ed.; Thunderstrike returns; leads into Malibu Comics' Black September. | | | | 3.00
375-($2.50, 52 pgs.)-Collector's ed. w/bound-in poster; leads into Malibu Comics' Black September. | | | | 3.50
400-402: Waid-s; 402-Deodato breakdowns; cont'd in X-Men #56 & Onslaught: Marvel Universe. | | | | 4.00
Special 1 (9/67, 25¢, 68 pgs.)-New-a; original & new Avengers team-up | 8 | 24 | 56 | 90
Special 8 (9/68, 25¢, 68 pgs.)-New-a; original vs. new Avengers | 4 | 12 | 29 | 45
Special 3 (9/69, 25¢, 68 pgs.)-r/Avengers #4 plus 3 Capt. America stories by Kirby (art); origin Red Skull | 3 | 9 | 20 | 30
Special 4 (1/71, 25¢, 68 pgs.)-Kirby-r/Avengers #5,6 | 2 | 6 | 13 | 20
Special 5 (1/72, 52 pgs.)-Spider-Man x-over | 2 | 6 | 13 | 20
Annual 6 (11/76) | 2 | 6 | 9 | 12
Annual 7 (11/77)-Starlin-c/a; Warlock dies; Thanos app. | 3 | 9 | 20 | 30
Annual 8 (1978)-Dr. Strange, Ms. Marvel app. | 1 | 3 | 6 | 9
Annual 9 (1979)-Newton-a(p) | | | | 6.00
Annual 10 (1981)-Golden-p; X-Men cameo; 1st app. Rogue & Madelyne Pryor | 3 | 9 | 20 | 30
Annual 11-18 (1982)-Vs. The Defenders. 12('83), 13('84), 14('85),15('86), 16('87), 17 ('88)-Atlantis Attacks | | | | 4.00
Annual 19-23 (90-'94, 68 pgs.). 22-Bagged/card | | | | 3.00
...Kree-Skrull War ('00, $24.95, TPB) new Neal Adams-c | | | | 25.00
Marvel Double Feature...Avengers/Giant-Man #379 ($2.50, 52 pgs.)-Same as Avengers #379 w/Giant-Man flip book | | | | 2.50
Marvel Graphic Novel - Deathtrap The Vault (1991, $9.95) Venom-c/app. | 2 | 6 | 9 | 12
The Yesterday Quest ($6.95)-r/#181,182,185-187 | 1 | 3 | 5 | 7
Under Siege ('98, $16.95, TPB) r/#270,271,273-277 | | | | 17.00
.... Visionaries ('99, $16.95)-r/early George Perez art | | | | 17.00
NOTE: *Austin* a(i)-157, 167, 168, 170-177, 181, 183-188, 198-201, Annual 8. *John Buscema* a-41-44p, 46p, 47p, 49,50, 51-62p, 74-77, 79-85, 87-91, 97, 105p, 121p, 124p,125p, 152, 153p, 255-279p, 281-302p; c-41-66, 68-71, 73-91, 97-99, 178, 256-259p, 261-279p, 281-302p. *Byrne* a-164-166p, 181-191p, 233p, Annual 13, 14p; c-186-190p, 233p, 260, 305p; scripts-305-312. *Colan* a(p)-63-65, 111, 206-208, 210, 211; c(p)-65, 206-208, 210, 211. *Ditko* a-Annual 13. *Guice* a-Annual 12. *Don Heck* a-9-15, 17-40, 157. *Kane* c-37p, 159p. *Kane/Everett* c-97. *Kirby* a-1-8p, Special 3, 4r(p); c-1-30, 148, 151-158; layouts-14-16. *Ron Lim* c(p)-335-341. *Miller* c-193p. *Mooney* a-86i, 179p, 180p. *Nebres* a-178i; c-179i. *Newton* a-204p, Annual 9p. *Perez* a(p)-141, 143, 144, 148, 150, 154, 155, 160, 161, 162, 167,168, 170, 171, 194-196, 198-202, Annual 6, 8; c(p)-160-162, 164-166, 170-174, 181,183-185, 191, 192, 194-201, 379-382, Annual 8. *Starlin* c-121, 135. *Staton* a-127-134i. *Tuska* a-47,48i, 51i, 53i, 54i, 106p, 107p, 135p, 137-140p, 163p. Guardians of the Galaxy app. in #167, 168, 170, 173, 175, 181.

AVENGERS, THE (Volume Two)
Marvel Comics: V2#1, Nov, 1996 - No. 13, Nov, 1997 ($2.95/$1.95/$1.99) (Produced by Extreme Studios)

1-($2.95)-Heroes Reborn begins; intro new team (Captain America, Swordsman, Scarlet Witch, Vision, Thor, Hellcat & Hawkeye); 1st app. Avengers Island; Loki & Enchantress app.; Rob Liefeld-p & plot; Chap Yaep-p; Jim Valentino scripts; variant-c exists | | | | 5.00
1-($1.95)-Variant-c | | | | 6.00
2-13: 2,3-Jeph Loeb scripts begin, Kang app. 4-Hulk-c/app. 5-Thor/Hulk battle; 2 covers. 10,11,13-"World War 3"-pt. 2, x-over w/Image characters. 12-($2.99) "Heroes Reunited"-pt. 2 | | | | 4.00

AVENGERS, THE (Volume Three)
Marvel Comics: Feb, 1998 - Present ($2.99/$1.99)

1-($2.99, 48 pgs.)-Busiek-s/Perez-a/wraparound-c; Avengers reassemble after Heroes Return | | | | 5.00
1-Variant Heroes Return cover | 1 | 3 | 5 | 7
1-Rough Cut-Features original script and pencil pages | | | | 3.00

The Avengers V3 #4 © MAR

Avengers Forever #2 © MAR

Avengers United They Stand #4 © MAR

	GD2.0	FN6.0	VF8.0	NM9.4

2-($1.99)Perez-c, 2-Lago painted-c	4.00
3,4: 3-Wonder Man-c/app. 4-Final roster chosen; Perez poster	3.00
5-11: 5,6-Squadron Supreme-c/app. 8-Triathlon-c/app.	2.50
12-($2.99) Thunderbolts app.	3.00
12-Alternate-c of Avengers w/white background; no logo	15.00
13-24,26,28: 13-New Warriors app. 16-18-Ordway-s/a. 19-Ultron returns.	
26-Immonen-a	2.25
16-Variant-c with purple background	5.00
25,27-($2.99) 25-vs. the Exemplars; Spider-Man app. 27-100 pgs.	3.00
29-33,35-47: 29-Begin $2.25-c. 35-Maximum Security x-over; Romita Jr.-a.	
36-Epting-a; poster by Alan Davis. 38-Davis-a begins ($1.99-c)	2.25
34-($2.99) Last Pérez-a; Thunderbirds app.	3.00
48-($3.50, 100 pgs.) new story w/Dwyer-a & r/#98-100	3.50
49-'Nuff Said story	2.25
#11/2 (12/99, $2.50) Timm-c/a/Stern-s; 1963-style issue	2.50
.../ Squadron Supreme '98 Annual ($2.99)	3.00
1999, 2000 Annual (7/99, '00, $3.50) 1999-Manco-a. 2000-Breyfogle-a.	3.50
2001 Annual ($2.99) Reis-a; back-up's art by Churchill	3.00
The Morgan Conquest TPB ('00, $14.95) r/#1-4	15.00
...: Clear and Present Dangers TPB ('01, $19.95) r/#8-15	20.00
...Supreme Justice TPB (4/01, $17.95) r/Squadron Supreme appearances in	
Avengers #5-7, '98 Annual, Iron Man #7, Capt. America #8, Quicksilver #10;	
Pérez-c	18.00
The Morgan Conquest TPB ('00, $14.95) r/#1-4	15.00
Ultron Unleashed TPB (8/99, $3.50) reprints early app.	3.50
Ultron Unlimited TPB (4/01, $14.95) r/#19-22 & #0 prelude	15.00
Wizard #0-Ultron Unlimited prelude	2.50

AVENGERS: CELESTIAL QUEST
Marvel Comics: Nov, 2001 - No. 8 ($2.50, limited series)

1-4-Englehart-s/Santamaría-a; Thanos app.	2.50

AVENGERS COLLECTOR'S EDITION, THE
Marvel Comics: 1993 (Ordered through mail w/candy wrapper, 20 pgs.)

1-Contains 4 bound-in trading cards	5.00

AVENGERS FOREVER
Marvel Comics: Dec, 1998 - No. 12, Feb, 2000 ($2.99)

1-Busiek-s/Pacheco-a in all	4.00
2-12:-Four covers. 6-Two covers. 12-Rick Jones becomes Capt. Marvel	3.00
TPB (1/01, $24.95) r/#1-12; Busiek intro.; new Pacheco-c	25.00

AVENGERS INFINITY
Marvel Comics: Sept, 2000 - No. 4, Dec, 2000 ($2.99, limited series)

1-4-Stern-s/Chen-a	3.00

AVENGERS LOG, THE
Marvel Comics: Feb, 1994 ($1.95)

1-Gives history of all members; Perez-c	2.25

AVENGERS SPOTLIGHT (Formerly Solo Avengers #1-20)
Marvel Comics: No. 21, Aug, 1989 - No. 40, Jan, 1991 (75¢/$1.00)

21-Byrne-c/a	3.00
22-40: 26-Acts of Vengeance story. 31-34-U.S. Agent series. 36-Heck-i.	
37-Mortimer-i. 40-The Black Knight app.	2.25

AVENGERS STRIKEFILE
Marvel Comics: Jan, 1994 ($1.75, one-shot)

1	2.25

AVENGERS: THE CROSSING
Marvel Comics: July, 1995 ($4.95, one-shot)

1-Deodato-c/a; 1st app. Thor's new costume	5.00

AVENGERS: THE TERMINATRIX OBJECTIVE
Marvel Comics: Sept, 1993 - No. 4, Dec, 1993 ($1.25, limited series)

1 ($2.50)-Holo-grafx foil-c	3.00
2-4-Old vs. current Avengers	2.25

AVENGERS: THE ULTRON IMPERATIVE
Marvel Comics: Nov, 2001 ($5.99, one-shot)

1-Follow-up to the Ultron Unlimited ending in Avengers #42; BWS-c	6.00

AVENGERS: TIMESLIDE

Marvel Comics: Feb, 1996 ($4.95, one-shot)

1-Foil-c	5.00

AVENGERS TWO: WONDER MAN & BEAST
Marvel Comics: May, 2000 - No. 3, July, 2000 ($2.99, limited series)

1-3: Stern-s/Bagley-c/a	3.00

AVENGERS/ULTRAFORCE (See Ultraforce/Avengers)
Marvel Comics: Oct, 1995 ($3.95, one-shot)

1-Wraparound foil-c by Perez	4.00

AVENGERS UNITED THEY STAND
Marvel Comics: Nov, 1999 - No. 7, June, 2000 ($2.99/$1.99)

1-Based on the animated series	3.00
2-6-($1.99) 2-Avengers battle Hydra	2.25
7-($2.99) Devil Dinosaur-c/app.; reprints Avengers Action Figure Comic	3.00

AVENGERS UNIVERSE
Marvel Comics: Jun, 2000 - Present ($3.99)

1-3-Reprints recent stories	4.00

AVENGERS UNPLUGGED
Marvel Comics: Oct, 1995 - No. 6, Aug, 1996 (99¢, bi-monthly)

1-6	2.25

AVENGERS WEST COAST (Formerly West Coast Avengers)
Marvel Comics: No. 48, Sept, 1989 - No. 102, Jan, 1994 ($1.00/$1.25)

48,49: 48-Byrne-c/a & scripts continue thru #57	3.00
50-Re-intro original Human Torch	4.00
51-69,71-74,76-83,85,86,89-99: 54-Cover swipe/F.F. #1. 78-Last $1.00-c.	
79-Dr. Strange x-over. 93-95-Darkhawk app.	2.25
70,75,84,87,88: 70-Spider-Woman app. 75 (52 pgs.)-Fantastic Four x-over.	
84-Origin Spider-Woman retold; Spider-Man app. (also in #85,86).	
87,88-Wolverine-c/story	3.00
100-($3.95, 68 pgs.)-Embossed all red foil-c	4.00
101,102: 100-X-Men x-over	4.00
Annual 5-8 ('90- '93, 68 pgs.)-5,6-West Coast Avengers in indicia. 7-Darkhawk	
app. 8-Polybagged w/card	3.00

AVIATION ADVENTURES AND MODEL BUILDING
Parents' Magazine Institute: No. 16, Dec, 1946 - No. 17, Feb, 1947
(True Aviation Advs. ...No. 15)

16,17-Half comics and half pictures	7	21	38	55

AVIATION CADETS
Street & Smith Publications: 1943

nn	18	54	94	160

A-V IN 3-D
Aardvark-Vanaheim: Dec, 1984 ($2.00, 28 pgs. w/glasses)

1-Cerebus, Flaming Carrot, Normalman & Ms. Tree	3.00

AWAKENING, THE
Image Comics: Oct, 1997 - No. 4, Apr, 1998 ($2.95, B&W, limited series)

1-4-Stephen Blue-s/c/a	3.00

AWESOME ADVENTURES
Awesome Entertainment: Aug, 1999 ($2.50)

1-Alan Moore-s/ Steve Skroce-a; Youngblood story	2.50

AWESOME HOLIDAY SPECIAL
Awesome Entertainment: Dec, 1997 ($2.50, one-shot)

1-Flip book w/covers of Fighting American & Coven. Holiday stories also	
featuring Kaboom and Shaft by regular creators.	3.00
1-Gold Edition	5.00

AWFUL OSCAR (Formerly & becomes Oscar Comics with No. 13)
Marvel Comics: No. 11, June, 1949 - No. 12, Aug, 1949

11,12	11	33	55	90

AWKWARD UNIVERSE
Slave Labor Graphics: 12/95 ($9.95, graphic novel)

nn	10.00

AXA

Azrael #73 © DC

Babe #6 © PRIZE

Babylon 5 #5 © WB

	GD2.0	FN6.0	VF8.0	NM9.4

Eclipse Comics: Apr, 1987 - No. 2, Aug, 1987 ($1.75)

1,2				2.25

AXEL PRESSBUTTON (Pressbutton No. 5; see Laser Eraser &...)
Eclipse Comics: Nov, 1984 - No. 6, July, 1985 ($1.50/$1.75, Baxter paper)

1-6: Reprints Warrior (British mag.). 1-Bolland-c; origin Laser Eraser & Pressbutton				3.00

AXIS ALPHA
Axis Comics: Feb, 1994 ($2.50, one-shot)

V1-Previews Axis titles including, Tribe, Dethgrip, B.E.A.S.T.I.E.S. & more; Pitt app. in Tribe story.				3.00

AZRAEL (...Agent of the Bat #47 on)(Also see Batman: Sword of Azrael)
DC Comics: Feb, 1995 - Present ($1.95/$2.25/$2.50)

1-Dennis O'Neil scripts begin				5.00
2,3				3.00
4-46,48-62: 5,6-Ras Al Ghul app. 13-Nightwing-c/app. 15-Contagion Pt. 5 (Pt. 4 on)-c. 16-Contagion Pt. 10. 22-Batman-c/app. 23, 27-Batman app. 27,28-Joker app. 35-Hitman app. 36-39-Batman, Bane app. 50-New costume. 53-Joker-c/app. 56,57,60-New Batgirl app.				2.50
47-($3.95) Flip book with Batman: Shadow of the Bat #80				4.00
63-66: 63-Huntress-c/app.; returns to old costume				2.50
67-74,76-86: 67-Begin $2.50-c. 70-79-Harris-c. 83-Joker app.				2.50
75-($3.95) New costume; Harris-c				4.00
#1,000,000 (11/98) Giarrano-a				2.50
Annual 1 (1995, $3.95)-Year One story				4.00
Annual 2 (1996, $2.95)-Legends of the Dead Earth story				3.00
Annual 3 (1997, $3.95)-Pulp Heroes story; Orbik-c				4.00
Plus (12/96, $2.95)-Question-c/app.				3.00

AZRAEL/ ASH
DC Comics: 1997 ($4.95, one-shot)

1-O'Neil-s/Quesada, Palmiotti-a				5.00

AZTEC ACE
Eclipse Comics: Mar, 1984 - No. 15, Sept, 1985 ($2.25/$1.50/$1.75, Baxter paper)

1-$2.25-c (52 pgs.)				3.00
2-15: 2-Begin 36 pgs.				2.25

NOTE: *N. Redondo* a-1/-8i, 10i. c-6-8i.

AZTEK: THE ULTIMATE MAN
DC Comics: Aug, 1996 - No. 10, May 1997 ($1.75)

1-1st app. Aztek & Synth; Grant Morrison & Mark Millar scripts in all				4.00
2-9: 2-Green Lantern app. 3-1st app. Death-Doll. 4-Intro The Lizard King. 5-Origin. 6-Joker app.; Batman cameo. 7-Batman app. 8-Luthor app. 9-vs. Parasite-c/app.				
10-JLA-c/app.	1	4	7	10

NOTE: *Breyfogle* c-5p. *N. Steven Harris* a-1-5p. *Porter* c-1p. *Wieringo* c-2p.

BABE (...Darling of the Hills, later issues)(See Big Shot and Sparky Watts)
Prize/Headline/Feature: June-July, 1948 - No. 11, Apr-May, 1950

1-Boody Rogers-a	23	69	121	210
2-Boody Rogers-a	14	42	72	120
3-11-All by Boody Rogers	12	36	61	100

BABE
Dark Horse Comics (Legend): July, 1994 - No. 4, Jan, 1994 ($2.50, lim. series)

1-4: John Byrne-c/a/scripts; ProtoTykes back-up story				2.50

BABE RUTH SPORTS COMICS (Becomes Rags Rabbit #11 on?)
Harvey Publications: April, 1949 - No. 11, Feb, 1951

1-Powell-a	40	120	232	400
2-Powell-a	28	84	151	260
3-11: Powell-a in most	23	69	121	210

NOTE: *Baseball c-2-4, 9. Basketball c-1, 6. Football c-5. Yogi Berra c/story-8. Joe DiMaggio c/story-3. Bob Feller c/story-4. Stan Musial c-9.*

BABES IN TOYLAND (Disney, Movie) (See Golden Pix Story Book ST-3)
Dell Publishing Co.: No. 1282, Feb-Apr, 1962

Four Color 1282-Annette Funicello photo-c	13	39	91	170

BABES OF BROADWAY
Broadway Comics: May, 1996 ($2.95, one-shot)

1-Pin-ups of Broadway Comics' female characters; Alan Davis, Michael Kaluta, J. G. Jones, Alan Weiss, Guy Davis & others-a; Giordano-c.				3.00

BABE 2
Dark Horse Comics (Legend): Mar, 1995 - No. 2, May, 1995 ($2.50, lim. series)

1,2: John Byrne-c/a/scripts				2.50

BABY HUEY
Harvey Comics: No. 100, Oct, 1990 - No. 101, Nov, 1990; No. 1, Oct, 1991 - No. 9, June, 1994 ($1.00/$1.25/$1.50, quarterly)

100,101,1 ($1.00): 1-Cover says "Big Baby Huey"				5.00
2-9 ($1.25-$1.50)				3.00

BABY HUEY AND PAPA (See Paramount Animated...)
Harvey Publications: May, 1962 - No. 33, Jan, 1968 (Also see Casper The Friendly Ghost)

1	17	51	118	210
2	8	24	60	100
3-5	5	15	38	60
6-10	3	9	20	30
11-20	2	6	15	22
21-33	2	6	12	18

BABY HUEY DIGEST
Harvey Publications: June, 1992 (Digest-size, one-shot)

1-Reprints	1	3	5	7

BABY HUEY DUCKLAND
Harvey Publications: Nov, 1962 - No. 15, Nov, 1966 (25¢ Giants, 68 pgs.)

1	13	39	91	155
2-5	5	15	38	60
6-15	3	9	20	30

BABY HUEY, THE BABY GIANT (Also see Big Baby Huey, Casper, Harvey Hits #22, Harvey Comics Hits #60, & Paramount Animated Comics)
Harvey Publ: 9/56 - #97, 10/71; #98, 10/72; #99, 10/80; #100, 10/90 - #102?

1-Infinity-c	41	123	306	550
2	20	60	140	250
3-Baby Huey takes anti-pep pills	13	39	94	160
4,5	9	27	65	110
6-10	5	15	38	60
11-20	4	12	29	45
21-40	3	9	21	32
41-60	2	6	15	22
61-79 (12/67)	2	6	12	18
80(12/68) - 95-All 68 pg. Giants	3	9	19	28
96,97-Both 52 pg. Giants	2	6	13	20
98-Regular size	2	6	9	12
99-Regular size	1	3	5	7
100-102 ($1.00)				4.00

BABYLON 5 (TV)
DC Comics: Jan, 1995 - No. 11, Dec, 1995 ($1.95/$2.50)

1	2	6	9	12
2-5	1	3	6	8
6-11: 7-Begin $2.50-c				6.00
... The Price of Peace (1998, $9.95, TPB) r/#1-4,11				10.00

BABYLON 5: IN VALEN'S NAME
DC Comics: Mar, 1998 - No. 3, May, 1998 ($2.50, limited series)

1-3				4.00

BABY SNOOTS (Also see March of Comics #359, 371, 396, 401, 419, 431,443, 450, 462, 474, 485)
Gold Key: Aug, 1970 - No. 22, Nov, 1975

1	3	9	19	28
2-11	2	6	10	14
12-22: 22-Titled Snoots, the Forgetful Elefink	1	3	5	8

BACCHUS (Also see Eddie Campbell's ...)
Harrier Comics (New Wave): 1988 - No. 2, Aug, 1988 ($1.95, B&W)

1,2: Eddie Campbell-c/a/scripts.				2.25

BACHELOR FATHER (TV)

BA

	GD2.0	FN6.0	VF8.0	NM9.4
	GD2.0	FN6.0	VF8.0	NM9.4

Dell Publishing Co.: No. 1332, 4-6/62 - No. 2, 1962

Four Color 1332 (#1), 2-Written by Stanley	8	24	56	100

BACHELOR'S DIARY
Avon Periodicals: 1949 (15¢)

1(Scarce)-King Features panel cartoons & text-r; pin-up, girl wrestling photos; similar to Sideshow	40	120	232	400

BACKPACK MARVELS (B&W backpack-sized reprint collections)
Marvel Comics: Nov, 2000 - Present ($6.95, B&W, digest-size)

Avengers 1 -r/Avengers #181-189; profile pages	7.00
Spider-Man 1 -r/ASM #234-240	7.00
X-Men 1 -r/Uncanny X-Men #167-173	7.00
X-Men 2-r/Uncanny X-Men #174-179; new painted-c by Greg Horn	7.00

BACKLASH (Also see The Kindred)
Image Comics (WildStorm Prod.): Nov,1994 - No. 32, May, 1997 ($1.95/$2.50)

1-Double-c; variant-double-c	3.00
2-7,9-32: 5-Intro Mindscape; 2 pinups. 19-Fire From Heaven Pt 2. 20-Fire From Heaven Pt 10. 31-WildC.A.T.S app.	2.50
8-($1.95, newsstand)-Wildstorm Rising Pt. 8	2.50
8-($2.50, direct market)-Wildstorm Rising Pt. 8	2.50
25-($3.95)-Double-size	4.00
..& Taboo's African Holiday (9/99, $5.95) Booth-s/a(p)	6.00

BACKLASH/SPIDER-MAN
Image Comics (WildStorm Productions): Aug, 1996 - No. 2, Sept, 1996 ($2.50, limited series)

1,2: Pike (villain from WildC.A.T.S) & Venom app.	3.00

BACK TO THE FUTURE (Movie, TV cartoon)
Harvey Comics: Nov, 1991 - No. 4, June, 1992 ($1.25)

1-4; 1,2-Gil Kane-c; based on animated cartoon	3.00

BACK TO THE FUTURE: FORWARD TO THE FUTURE
Harvey Comics: Oct, 1992 - No. 3, Feb, 1993 ($1.50, limited series)

1-3	3.00

BAD BOY
Oni Press: Dec, 1997 ($4.95, one-shot)

1-Frank Miller-s/Simon Bisley-a/painted-c	5.00

BAD COMPANY
Quality Comics/Fleetway Quality #15 on: Aug, 1988 - No. 19?, 1990 ($1.50/$1.75, high quality paper)

1-19; 5,6-Guice-c	2.25

BAD EGGS, THE
Acclaim Comics (Armada): June, 1995 - No. 8, Jan, 1997 ($2.95)

1-8: Layton scripts; Perlin-a. 5-8-"That Dirty Yellow Mustard." 5-William Shatner app.	3.00

BADGE OF JUSTICE (Formerly Crime And Justice #21)
Charlton Comics: No. 22, 1/55 - No. 2, 4/55 - No. 4, 10/55

22(#1)(1/55)	10	30	55	85
2-4	6	18	29	40

BADGER, THE
Capital Comics(#1-4)/First Comics: Dec, 1983 - No. 70, Apr, 1991; V2#1, Spring, 1991

1	5.00
2-70: 52-54-Tim Vigil-c/a	3.00
50-($3.95, 52 pgs.)	4.00
V2#1 (Spring, 1991, $4.95)	5.00

BADGER, THE
Image Comics: V3#78, May, 1997 - V3#88 ($2.95, B&W)

78-Cover lists #1, Baron-s	3.00
79/#2, 80/#3, 81(indicia lists #80)/#4,82-88/#5-11	3.00

BADGER GOES BERSERK
First Comics: Sept, 1989 - No. 4, Dec, 1989 ($1.95, lim. series, Baxter paper)

1-4: 2-Paul Chadwick-c/a(2pgs.)	3.00

BADGER: SHATTERED MIRROR
Dark Horse Comics: July, 1994 - No. Oct, 1994 ($2.50, limited series)

1-4	3.00

BADGER: ZEN POP FUNNY-ANIMAL VERSION
Dark Horse Comics: July, 1994 - No. 2, Aug, 1994 ($2.50, limited series)

1,2	3.00

BAD KITTY
Chaos! Comics: Feb, 2001 - No. 3, Apr, 2001 ($2.99, limited series)

1-3-Pulido-s/Batista-a	3.00
1-Premium Edition ($9.99) Scott Lewis-c	10.00
...Mischief Night 1 (11/01, one-shot) Mota-a	3.00
...Reloaded 1-3 (10/01- No. 4) Batista-a; Chastity app.	3.00

BADLANDS
Vortex Comics: May, 1990 ($3.00, glossy stock, mature)

1-Chaykin-c	3.00

BADLANDS
Dark Horse Comics: July, 1991 - No. 6, Dec, 1991 ($2.25, B&W, limited series)

1-6: 1-John F. Kennedy-c; reprints Vortex Comics issue	2.25

BADMEN OF THE WEST
Avon Periodicals: 1951 (Giant) (132 pgs., painted-c)

1-Contains rebound copies of Jesse James, King of the Bad Men of Deadwood, Badmen of Tombstone; other combinations possible. Issues with Kubert-a...	40	120	220	380

BADMEN OF THE WEST! (See A-1 Comics)
Magazine Enterprises: 1953 - No. 3, 1954

1(A-1 100)-Meskin-a?	25	75	130	225
2(A-1 120), 3: 2-Larsen-a	16	48	83	140

BADMEN OF TOMBSTONE
Avon Periodicals: 1950

nn	16	48	83	140

BADROCK (Also see Youngblood)
Image Comics (Extreme Studios): Mar, 1995 - No. 2, Jan, 1996 ($1.75/$2.50)

1-Variant-c (3)	3.00
2-Liefeld-c/a & story; Savage Dragon app. flipbook w/Grifter/Badrock #2; variant-c exist	2.50
Annual 1(1995,$2.95)-Arthur Adams-c	3.00
Annual 1 Commemorative ($9.95)-3,000 printed	10.00
.../Wolverine (6/96, $4.95, squarebound)-Sauron app; pin-ups; variant-c exists	5.00
.../Wolverine (6/96)-Special Comicon Edition	5.00

BADROCK AND COMPANY (Also see Youngblood)
Image Comics (Extreme Studios): Sept, 1994 - No.6, Feb, 1995 ($2.50)

1-6 : 6-Indicia reads "October 1994"; story cont'd in Shadowhawk #17	2.50

BAFFLING MYSTERIES (Formerly Indian Braves No. 1-4; Heroes of the Wild Frontier No. 26-on)
Periodical House (Ace Magazines): No. 5, Nov, 1951 - No. 26, Oct, 1955

5	38	114	203	350
6-19,21-24: 8-Woodish-a by Cameron. 10-E.C. Crypt Keeper swipe on-c. 24-Last pre-code issue	23	69	121	210
20-Classic-c	30	90	159	275
25-Reprints; surrealistic-c	19	57	99	165
26-Reprints	16	48	83	140

NOTE: **Cameron** a-8, 10, 16-18, 20-22. **Colan** a-5, 11, 25r/5. **Sekowsky** a-5, 6, 22. Bondage c-20, 23. Reprints in 19(1), 19(1), 24(3).

BALBO (See Master Comics #33 & Mighty Midget Comics)

BALDER THE BRAVE
Marvel Comics Group: Nov, 1985 - No. 4, 1986 (Limited series)

1-4: Simonson-c/a; character from Thor	3.00

Banana Splits #1 © H-B

Barbie #9 © Mattel

Barb Wire: Ace of Spades #1 © DH

BALLAD OF HALO JONES, THE
Quality Comics: Sept, 1987 - No. 12, Aug, 1988 ($1.25/$1.50)
1-12: Alan Moore scripts in all			2.25

BALL AND CHAIN
DC Comics (Homage): Nov, 1999 - No. 4, Feb, 2000 ($2.50, limited series)
1-4-Lobdell-s/Garza-a			2.50

BALLISTIC (Also See Cyberforce)
Image Comics (Top Cow Productions): Sept, 1995 - No. 3, Dec, 1995 ($2.50, limited series)
1-3: Wetworks app, Turner-c/a			3.00

BALLISTIC ACTION
Image Comics (Top Cow Productions): May, 1996 ($2.95, one-shot)
1-Pin-ups of Top Cow characters participating in outdoor sports			3.00

BALLISTIC IMAGERY
Image Comics (Top Cow Productions): Jan, 1996 ($2.50, anthology, one-shot)
1-Cyberforce app.			2.50

BALLISTIC/ WOLVERINE
Image Comics (Top Cow Productions): Feb, 1997 ($2.95, one-shot)
1-Devil's Reign pt. 4; Witchblade cameo (1 page)			4.00

BALOO & LITTLE BRITCHES (Disney)
Gold Key: Apr, 1968
1-From the Jungle Book	3	10	23	35

BAMBI (Disney) (See Movie Classics, Movie Comics, and Walt Disney Showcase No. 31)
Dell Publishing Co.: No. 12, 1942; No. 30, 1943; No. 186, Apr, 1948; 1984
Four Color 12-Walt Disney's...	59	177	413	775
Four Color 30-Bambi's Children (1943)	56	168	392	725
Four Color 186-Walt Disney's...; reprinted as Movie Classic Bambi #3 (1956)	17	51	119	215
1-(Whitman, 1984; 60¢)-r/Four Color #186 (3-pack)	1	3	5	7

BAMBI (Disney)
Grosset & Dunlap: 1942 (50¢, 7"x8-1/2", 32pg, hard-c w/dust jacket)
nn-Given away w/a copy of Thumper for a $2.00, 2-yr. subscription to WDC&S in 1942 (Xmas offer).	Book only	20	60	105	175
	w/dust jacket	35	105	188	325

BAMM BAMM & PEBBLES FLINTSTONE (TV)
Gold Key: Oct, 1964 (Hanna-Barbera)
1		9	27	63	110

BANANA SPLITS, THE (TV) (See Golden Comics Digest & March of Comics No. 364)
Gold Key: June, 1969 - No. 8, Oct, 1971 (Hanna-Barbera)
1-Photo-c on all	11	33	77	140
2-8	7	21	49	85

BAND WAGON (See Hanna-Barbera Band Wagon)

BANDY MAN, THE
Caliber: 1996 - No. 3, ($2.95, B&W, limited series)
1-3-Stephan Petrucha scripts; 1-Jill Thompson-a; Miran Kim-c			3.00

BANG-UP COMICS
Progressive Publishers: Dec, 1941 - No. 3, June, 1942
1-Cosmo Mann & Lady Fairplay begin; Buzz Balmer by Rick Yager in all (origin #1)	100	300	625	1100
2,3	50	150	300	525

BANISHED KNIGHTS (See Warlands)
Image Comics: Dec, 2001 - Present ($2.95)
1-Two covers (Alvin Lee, Pat Lee)			3.00

BANNER COMICS (Becomes Captain Courageous No. 6)
Ace Magazines: No. 3, Sept, 1941 - No. 5, Jan, 1942
3-Captain Courageous (1st app.) & Lone Warrior & Sidekick Dicky begin; Jim Mooney-c	105	315	656	1150
4,5: 4-Flag-c	64	192	398	700

BARABBAS
Slave Labor Graphics: Aug, 1986 - No. 2, Nov, 1986 ($1.50, B&W, lim. series)
1,2			2.25

BARBARIANS, THE
Atlas Comics/Seaboard Periodicals: June, 1975
1-Origin, only app. Andrax; Iron Jaw app.; Marcos-a			6.00

BARBIE
Marvel Comics: Jan, 1991 - No. 66, Apr, 1996 ($1.00/$1.25/$1.50)
1-Polybagged w/Barbie Pink Card; Romita-c	2	6	9	12
2-49,51-66	1	3	6	8
50-(Giant)	1	4	7	10

BARBIE & KEN
Dell Publishing Co.: May-July, 1962 - No. 5, Nov-Jan, 1963-64
01-053-207(#1)-Based on Mattel toy dolls	38	114	266	500
2-4	30	90	210	390
5 (Rare)	33	99	235	430

BARBIE FASHION
Marvel Comics: Jan, 1991 - No. 63, Jan, 1996 ($1.00/$1.25/$1.50)
1-Polybagged w/doorknob hanger	2	6	9	12
2-49,51-63: 4-Contains preview to Sweet XVI. 14-Begin $1.25-c	1	3	6	8
50-(Giant)	1	4	7	10

BARBI TWINS, THE
Topps Comics: 1995 ($2.50/$5.00)
1-Razor app.			2.50
Swimsuit Art Calendar ($5.00)-art by Linsner, Bradstreet, Hughes; Julie Bell-c			5.00

BARB WIRE (See Comics' Greatest World)
Dark Horse Comics: Apr, 1994 - No. 9, Feb, 1995 ($2.00/$2.50)
1-9: 1-Foil logo			3.00
Trade paperback (1996, $8.95)-r/#2,3,5,6 w/Pamela Anderson bio			9.00

BARB WIRE: ACE OF SPADES
Dark Horse Comics: May, 1996 - No. 4, Sept, 1996 ($2.95, limited series)
1-4: Chris Warner-c/a(p)/scripts; Tim Bradstreet-c/a(i) in all			3.00

BARB WIRE COMICS MAGAZINE SPECIAL
Dark Horse Comics: May, 1996 ($3.50, B&W, magazine, one-shot)
nn-Adaptation of film; photo-c; poster insert.			3.50

BARB WIRE MOVIE SPECIAL
Dark Horse Comics: May, 1996 ($3.95, one-shot)
nn-Adaptation of film; photo-c; 1st app. new look			4.00

BARKER, THE (Also see National Comics #42)
Quality Comics Group/Comic Magazine: Autumn, 1946 - No. 15, Dec, 1949
1	21	63	110	190
2	11	33	55	95
3-10	8	24	45	65
11-14	6	18	29	40
15-Jack Cole-a(p)	6	18	32	45
NOTE: *Jack Cole art in some issues.*

BARNABY
Civil Service Publications Inc.: 1945 (25¢, 102 pgs., digest size)
V1#1-r/Crocket Johnson strips from 1942	4	11	17	22

BARNEY AND BETTY RUBBLE (TV) (Flintstones' Neighbors)
Charlton Comics: Jan, 1973 - No. 23, Dec, 1976 (Hanna-Barbera)
1	4	12	26	40
2-11: 11(2/75)-1st Mike Zeck-a (illos)	2	6	13	20
12-23	2	6	10	14

BARNEY BAXTER (Also see Magic Comics)
David McKay/Dell Publishing Co./Argo: 1938 - No. 2, 1956
Feature Books 15(McKay-1938)	40	120	217	375
Four Color 20(1942)	27	80	189	350
1,2 (1956-Argo)	9	27	49	70

Barnyard Comics #18 © Nedor

Batgirl #14 © DC

Bat Lash #3 © DC

	GD2.0	FN6.0	VF8.0	NM9.4		GD2.0	FN6.0	VF8.0	NM9.4

BARNEY BEAR ...
Spire Christian Comics (Fleming H. Revell Co.): 1977-1981

...Home Plate nn-(1979, 49¢), ...Lost and Found nn-(1979, 49¢), Out of The
Woods nn-(1980, 49¢), Sunday School Picnic nn-(1981, 69¢, The Swamp
Gang!-(1977, 39¢)

	1	3	5	7

BARNEY GOOGLE & SNUFFY SMITH
Dell Publishing Co./Gold Key: 1942 - 1943; April, 1964

Four Color 19(1942)	38	115	266	500
Four Color 40(1944)	22	66	154	290
Large Feature Comic 11(1943)	35	105	188	325
1(10113-404)-Gold Key (4/64)	4	12	29	45

BARNEY GOOGLE & SNUFFY SMITH
Toby Press: June, 1951 - No. 4, Feb, 1952 (Reprints)

1	13	39	66	110
2,3	8	24	42	60
4-Kurtzman-a "Pot Shot Pete", 5 pgs.; reprints John Wayne #5				
	13	39	66	110

BARNEY GOOGLE AND SNUFFY SMITH
Charlton Comics: Mar, 1970 - No. 6, Jan, 1971

1	3	9	19	28
2-6	2	6	11	16

BARNYARD COMICS (Dizzy Duck No. 32 on)
Nedor/Polo Mag./Standard(Animated Cartoons): June, 1944 - No. 31, Sept,
1950; No. 10, 1957

1 (nn, 52 pgs.)-Funny animal	20	60	105	175
2 (52 pgs.)	10	30	55	85
3-5	7	21	38	55
6-12,16	6	18	32	45
13-15,17,21,23,26,27,29-All contain Frazetta text illos				
	8	24	45	65
18-20,22,24,25-All contain Frazetta-a & text illos	11	33	55	90
28,30,31	5	15	23	30
10 (1957)(Exist?)	3	8	12	15

BARRY M. GOLDWATER
Dell Publishing Co.: Mar, 1965 (Complete life story)

12-055-503-Photo-c	3	9	21	40

BARRY WINDSOR-SMITH: STORYTELLER
Dark Horse Comics: Oct, 1996 - No. 9, July, 1997 ($4.95, oversize)

1-9: 1-Intro Young Gods, Paradox Man & the Freebooters; Barry				
Smith-c/a/scripts				5.00
Preview				4.00

BAR SINISTER (Also see Shaman's Tears)
Acclaim Comics (Windjammer): Jun, 1995 - No. 4, Sept, 1995 ($2.50, lim. series)

1-4: Mike Grell-c/a/scripts				2.50

BARTMAN (Also see Simpson's Comics & Radioactive Man)
Bongo Comics: 1993 - No. 6, 1994 ($1.95/$2.25)

1-($2.95)-Foil-c; bound-in jumbo Bartman poster				5.00
2-6: 3-w/trading card				3.00

BART SIMPSON (See Simpsons Comics Presents Bart Simpson)

BASEBALL COMICS
Will Eisner Productions: Spring, 1949 (Reprinted later as a Spirit section)

1-Will Eisner-c/a	68	205	426	750

BASEBALL COMICS
Kitchen Sink Press: 1991 ($3.95, coated stock)

1-r/1949 ish. by Eisner; contains trading cards				6.00

BASEBALL HEROES
Fawcett Publications: 1952 (one-shot)

nn (Scarce)-Babe Ruth photo-c; baseball's Hall of Fame biographies				
	80	205	426	750

BASEBALL'S GREATEST HEROES
Magnum Comics: Dec, 1991 - No. 2, May, 1992 ($1.75)

1-Mickey Mantle #1; photo-c; Sinnott-a(p)				5.00

2-Brooks Robinson #1; photo-c; Sinnott-a(i)				4.00

BASEBALL THRILLS
Ziff-Davis Publ. Co.: No. 10, Sum, 1951 - No. 3, Sum, 1952
(Saunders painted-c No.1,2)

10(#1)-Bob Feller, Musial, Newcombe & Boudreau stories				
	40	120	240	420
2-Powell-a(2)(Late Sum, '51); Feller, Berra & Mathewson stories				
	31	93	165	285
3-Kinstler-c/a; Joe DiMaggio story	31	93	165	285

BASEBALL THRILLS 3-D
The 3-D Zone: May, 1990 ($2.95, w/glasses)

1-New L.B. Cole-c; life stories of Ty Cobb & Ted Williams				6.00

BASICALLY STRANGE (Magazine)
John C. Comics (Archie Comics Group): Dec, 1982 ($1.95, B&W)

1-(21,000 printed; all but 1,000 destroyed; pgs. out of sequence)				
	2	6	12	18
1-Wood, Toth-a; Corben-c; reprints & new art	2	6	10	14

BASIC HISTORY OF AMERICA ILLUSTRATED
Pendulum Press: 1976 (B&W) (Soft-c $1.50; Hard-c $4.50)

07-1999-America Becomes a World Power 1890-1920. 07-2251-The Industrial Era 1865-1915.
07-226x-Before the Civil War 1830-1860. 07-2278-Americans Move Westward 1800-1850.
07-2286-The Civil War 1850-1876; Redondo-a. 07-2294-The Fight for Freedom 1750-1783.
07-2308-The New World 1500-1750. 07-2316-Problems of the New Nation 1800-1830.
07-2324-Roaring Twenties and the Great Depression 1920-1940. 07-2332-The United States
Emerges 1783-1800. 07-2340-America Today 1945-1976. 07-2359-World War II 1940-1945

Softcover editions each				5.00
Hardcover editions each				10.00

BASIL (...the Royal Cat)
St. John Publishing Co.: Jan, 1953 - No. 4, Sept, 1953

1-Funny animal	6	18	32	45
2-4	4	12	19	25
I.W. Reprint 1	2	6	9	12

BASIL WOLVERTON'S FANTASTIC FABLES
Dark Horse Comics: Oct, 1993 - No. 2, Dec, 1993 ($2.50, B&W, limited series)

1,2-Wolverton-c/a(r)				5.00

BASIL WOLVERTON'S GATEWAY TO HORROR
Dark Horse Comics: June, 1988 ($1.75, B&W, one-shot)

1-Wolverton-r				5.00

BASIL WOLVERTON'S PLANET OF TERROR
Dark Horse Comics: Oct, 1987 ($1.75, B&W, one-shot)

1-Wolverton-r; Alan Moore-c				5.00

BATGIRL (See Batman: No Man's Land stories)
DC Comics: Apr, 2000 - Present ($2.50)

1-Scott & Campanella-a				4.00
1-(2nd printing)				2.50
2-24: 12-"Officer Down" x-over. 15-Joker-c/app.				2.50
Annual 1 ('00, $3.50) Planet DC; intro. Aruna				3.50
...: A Knight Alone (2001, $12.95, TPB) r/#7-11,13,14				12.95
...: Silent Running (2001, $12.95, TPB) r/#1-6				12.95

BATGIRL ADVENTURES (See Batman Adventures, The)
DC Comics: Feb, 1998 ($2.95, one-shot) (Based on animated series)

1-Harley Quinn and Poison Ivy app.; Timm-c				5.00

BATGIRL SPECIAL
DC Comics: 1988 ($1.50, one-shot, 52 pgs)

1-Kitson-a/Mignola-c		1	3	6	8

BAT LASH (See DC Special Series #16, Showcase #76, Weird Western Tales)
National Periodical Publications: Oct-Nov, 1968 - No. 7, Oct-Nov, 1969
(All 12¢ issues)

1-(10-11/68)-2nd app. Bat Lash	4	12	29	45
2-7	3	9	19	28

BATMAN (See Anarky, Aurora, Azrael, The Best of DC #2, Blind Justice, The Brave &
the Bold, Cosmic Odyssey, DC 100-Page Super Spec. #14,20, DC Special, DC Special Series,
Detective, Dynamic Classics, 80-Page Giants, Gotham By Gaslight, Gotham Nights, Greatest

Batman #4 © DC

Batman #44 © DC

Batman #255 © DC

	GD2.0	FN6.0	VF8.0	NM9.4

Batman Stories Ever Told, Greatest Joker Stories Ever Told, Heroes Against Hunger, JLA,The Joker, Justice League of America, Justice League Int., Legends of the Dark Knight, Limited Coll. Ed., Man-Bat, Nightwing, Power Record Comics, Real Fact #5, Robin, Saga of Ra's Al Ghul, Shadow of the..., Star Spangled, Super Friends, 3-D Batman, Untold Legend of..., Wanted... & World's Finest Comics)

BATMAN
National Per. Publ./Detective Comics/DC Comics: Spring, 1940 - Present (#1-5 were quarterly)

1-Origin The Batman reprinted (2 pgs.) from Det. #33 w/splash from #34 by Bob Kane; see Detective #33 for 1st origin; 1st app. Joker (2 stories intended for 2 separate issues of Det. Comics which would have been 1st & 2nd app.); splash pg. to 2nd Joker story is similar to cover of Det. #40 (story intended for #40); 1st app. The Cat (Catwoman)(1st villainess in comics); has Batman story (w/Hugo Strange) without Robin originally planned for Det. #38; mentions location (Manhattan) where Batman lives (see Det. #31). This book was created entirely from the inventory of Det. Comics; 1st Batman/Robin pin-up on back-c; has text piece & photo of Bob Kane

6450 19,350 45,150 100,000

1-Reprint, oversize 13-1/2x10". **WARNING:** This comic is an exact duplicate reprint of the original except for its size. DC published it in 1974 with a second cover titling it as a Famous First Edition. There have been many reported cases of the outer cover being removed and the interior sold as the original edition. The reprint with the new outer cover removed is practically worthless. See Famous First Edition for value.

2-2nd app. The Joker; 2nd app. Catwoman (out of costume) in Joker story; 1st time called Catwoman

NOTE: A 15¢-c exists for Canadian distr. exists.

1178 3534 8245 16,500

3-3rd app Catwoman (1st in costume & 1st costumed villainess); 1st Puppet Master app.; classic Kane & Moldoff-c. 807 2421 5245 10,500

4-3rd app. The Joker app. The Joker (5th for 4th); 1st mention of Gotham City in a Batman comic (on newspaper)(Win/40) 630 1890 4095 8200

5-1st app. the Batmobile with its bat-head front 462 1386 3000 6000

6,7: 7-Bullseye-c. 423 1269 2708 5200

8-Infinity-c. 350 1050 2188 4200

9-10:9-1st Batman x-mas story; Burnley-c. 10-Catwoman story (gets new costume) 333 1000 2083 4000

11-Classic Joker-c by Ray/Robinson (3rd Joker-c, 6-7/42); Joker & Penguin app. 615 1845 4000 8000

12,15: 15-New costume Catwoman 291 873 1818 3200

13-Jerry Siegel (Superman's co-creator) appears in a Batman story. 300 900 1875 3300

14-2nd Penguin-c; Penguin app. (12-1/42-43) 300 900 1875 3400

16-Intro/origin Alfred (4-5/43); cover is a reverse of #9 cover by Burnley; 1st small logo 485 1455 3150 6300

17,20: 17-Classic war-c; Penguin app. 20-1st Batmobile-c (12-1/43-44); Joker app. 200 600 1250 2200

18-Hitler, Hirohito, Mussolini-c. 273 819 1705 3000

19-Joker app. 190 570 1187 2100

21,22,24,26,28-30: 21-1st skinny Alfred in Batman (2-3/44). 21,30-Penguin app. 22-1st Alfred solo-c/story (Alfred solo stories in 22-32,36); Catwoman & The Cavalier app. 28-Joker story 150 450 938 1650

23-Joker-c/story 213 639 1331 2350

25-Only Joker/Penguin team-up; 1st team-up between two major villains 218 654 1364 2400

27-Classic Burnley Christmas-c; Penguin app. 195 584 1218 2150

31,32,34-36,39: 32-Robin retold. 35-Catwoman story (in new costume w/o cat head mask). 36-Penguin app. 111 332 694 1225

33-Christmas-c 118 355 738 1300

37,40,44-Joker-c/stories 150 450 938 1650

38-Penguin-c/story 127 381 795 1400

41,45,46: 41-1st Sci-fi cover/story in Batman; Penguin app.(6-7/47). 45-Christmas-c/story; Catwoman story 79 237 494 875

42-2nd Catwoman app (1st in costume)(8-9/47); Catwoman story also. 123 369 769 1350

43-Penguin-c/story 107 321 669 1175

47-1st detailed origin The Batman (6-7/48); 1st bat-signal-c this title (see Detective #108); Batman tracks down his parent's killer and reveals i.d. to him 308 924 1927 3700

48-1000 Secrets of the Batcave; r-in #203; Penguin story 107 321 669 1175

49-Joker-c/story; 1st app. Mad Hatter; 1st app. Vicki Vale

50-Two-Face impostor app. 91 273 568 1000

51,53,54,56,57,59,60: 57-Centerfold is a 1950 calendar. 59-1st app. Deadshot; Batman in the future-c/story 77 231 483 850

52,55-Joker-c/stories 100 300 625 1100

58,61: 58-Penguin-c. 61-Origin Batman Plane II 84 253 525 925

62-Origin Catwoman; Catwoman-c 118 354 738 1300

63,80-Joker stories. 63-Flying saucer story(2-3/51) 73 219 455 800

64,67,70-72,74-77,79: 67-Joker story. 70-Robot-c. 72-Last 52 pg. issue. 74-Used in POP, pg. 90. 76-Penguin story. 79-Vicki Vale in "The Bride of Batman" 61 183 381 675

65,69,84-Catwoman-c/stories. 84-Two-Face story. 73 219 455 800

66,73-Joker-c/stories. 66-Pre-2nd Batman & Robin team-up. 73-Vicki Vale story 82 245 511 900

68,81-Two-Face-c/stories 64 192 398 700

78-(8-9/53)-Roh Kar, The Man Hunter from Mars story-the 1st lawman of Mars to come to Earth (green skinned) 76 229 475 840

82,83,85-89: 86-Intro Batmarine (Batman's submarine). 87-Joker story. 89-Last pre-code issue 57 171 356 625

90,91,93-99: 97-2nd app. Bat-Hound-c/story; Joker story. 99-(4/56)-Last G.A. Penguin app. 50 150 300 525

92-1st app. Bat-Hound-c/story 64 192 398 700

100-(6/56) 250 750 1562 2750

101-(8/56)-Clark Kent x-over who protects Batman's i.d. (3rd story) 51 153 306 540

102-104,106-109: 103-1st S.A. issue; 3rd Bat-Hound-c/story 43 129 257 450

105-1st Batwoman in Batman (2nd anywhere) 55 165 341 600

110-Joker story 44 132 264 460

111-120: 112-1st app. Signalman (super villain). 113-1st app. Fatman; Batman meets his counterpart on Planet X w/a chest plate similar to S.A. Batman's design (yellow oval w/black design inside). 39 117 208 360

121- Origin/1st app. of Mr. Zero (Mr. Freeze). 45 135 270 475

122,124-126,128,130: 124-2nd app. Signal Man. 126-Batwoman-c/story. 128-Batwoman returns-c/story. 130-Lex Luthor app. 27 81 145 250

123,127: 123-Joker story; Bat-Hound app. 127-(10/59)-Batman vs. Thor the Thunder God-c/story; Joker story; Superman cameo 30 90 159 275

129-Origin Robin retold; bondage-c; Batwoman-c/story (reprinted in Batman Family #8) 31 93 168 290

131-135,137-139,141-143: 131-Intro 2nd Batman & Robin series (see #66; also in #135,145,154,159,163). 133-1st Bat-Mite in Batman (3rd app. anywhere). 134-Origin The Dummy (not Vigilante's villain). 139-Intro 1st original Bat-Girl; only app. Batwoman as the Blue Bowman. 141-2nd app. original Bat-Girl. 21 63 110 185

136-Joker-c/story 25 75 130 225

140,144-Batman stories. 140-Batwoman-c/story; Superman cameo. 144-(12/61)-1st 12¢ issue 16 48 110 195

145,148-Joker-c/stories 18 54 123 210

146,147,149,150 12 36 84 140

151-154,156-158,160-162,164-168,170: 152-Joker story. 156-Ant-Man/Robin team-up(6/63). 164-New Batmobile(6/64) new look & Mystery Analysts series begins 9 27 65 110

155-1st S.A. app. The Penguin (5/63) 31 93 211 380

159,163-Joker stories. 159-Bat-Girl app. 12 36 84 140

169-2nd SA Penguin app. 13 39 91 155

171-1st Riddler app.(5/65) since Dec. 1948 37 112 278 500

172,175,177,178,180,184 7 21 50 80

176-(80-Pg. Giant G-17); Joker-c/story; Penguin app. in strip-r; Catwoman reprint 9 27 63 105

179-2nd app. Silver Age Riddler 14 42 102 175

181-Batman & Robin poster insert; intro. Poison Ivy 16 48 112 200

182,187-(80 Pg. Giants G-24, G-30); Joker-c/stories 8 24 56 90

183-2nd app. Poison Ivy 9 27 65 110

185-(80 Pg. Giant G-27) 7 21 53 85

186-Joker-c/story 7 21 53 85

188,191,192,194-196,199 4 12 29 45

189-1st S.A. app. Scarecrow; retells origin of G.A. Scarecrow from World's Finest #3(1st app.) 9 27 63 105

190-Penguin-c/app. 5 15 34 55

Batman #342 © DC

Batman #389 © DC

Batman #494 © DC

BA

	GD2.0	FN6.0	VF8.0	NM9.4

193-(80-Pg. Giant G-37) — 6 18 45 75

197-4th S.A. Catwoman app. cont'd from Det. #369; 1st new Batgirl app. in Batman (5th anywhere) — 6 18 45 75

198-(80-Pg. Giant G-43); Joker-c/story-r/World's Finest #61; Catwoman-r/ Det. #211; Penguin-r; origin-r/#47 — 7 21 53 85

200-(3/68)-Joker cameo; retells origin of Batman & Robin; 1st Neal Adams work this title (cover only) — 13 39 91 155

201-Joker story — 4 12 29 45

202,204-207,209-212,: 212-Last 12¢ issue — 3 10 23 35

203-(80 Pg. Giant G-49); r/#48, 61, & Det. 185; Batcave Blueprints — 5 15 38 60

208-(80 Pg. Giant G-55); New origin Batman by Gil Kane plus 3 G.A. Batman reprints w/Catwoman, Vicki Vale & Batwoman — 5 15 38 60

213-(80-Pg. Giant G-61); 30th anniversary issue (7-8/69); origin Alfred (r/Batman #16), Joker(r/Det. #168), Clayface; new origin Batman with new facts — 8 24 56 90

214-217: 214-Alfred given a new last name- "Pennyworth" (see Detective #96) — 3 9 20 30

218-(80-Pg. Giant G-67) — 5 15 34 55

219-Neal Adams-a — 4 12 30 50

220,221,224-226,229-231 — 3 9 19 28

222-Beatles take-off; art lesson by Joe Kubert — 4 12 29 45

223,228,233-(80-Pg. Giants G-73,G-79,G-85) — 5 15 38 60

227-Neal Adams cover swipe of Detective #31 — 4 12 25 38

232-N. Adams-a. Intro/1st app. Ras Al Ghul; origin Batman & Robin retold; last 15¢ issue — 10 30 73 125

234-(4/71)-1st modern app. of Harvey Dent/Two-Face; (see World's Finest #173 for Batman as Two-Face; only S.A. mention of character); N. Adams-a; 52 pg. issues begin, end #242 — 13 39 94 160

235,236,239-242: 239-XMas-c. 241-Reprint/#5 — 3 10 23 35

237-N. Adams-a. 1st Rutland Vermont - Bald Mountain Halloween x-over. G.A. Batman-r/Det. #37; 1st app. The Reaper; Wrightson/Ellison plots — 6 18 45 75

238-Also listed as DC 100 Page Super Spectacular #8; Batman, Legion, Aquaman-r; G.A. Atom, Sargon (r/Sensation #57), Plastic Man (r/Police #14) stories; Doom Patrol origin-r; N. Adams wraparound-c (see DC 100 Pg. Super Spectacular #8 for price) — 4 12 30 50

243-245-Neal Adams-a — 4 12 30 50

246-250,252,253: 246-Scarecrow app. 253-Shadow-c & app. — 3 9 19 28

251-(9/73)-N. Adams-c/a; Joker-c/story — 6 18 45 75

254,256-259,261-All 100 pg. editions; part-r: 254-(2/74)-Man-Bat-c & app. 256-Catwoman app. 257-Joker & Penguin app. 258-The Cavalier-r. 259-Shadow-c/app. — 4 12 29 45

255-(100 pgs.)-N. Adams-c/a; tells of Bruce Wayne's father who wore bat cos- tume & fought crime (r/Det. #235); r/story Batman #22 — 5 15 38 60

260-Joker-c/story (100 pgs.) — 5 15 38 60

262 (68pgs.) — 3 9 21 32

263,264,266-285,287-290,292,293,295-299: 266-Catwoman back to old costume — 2 6 11 15

265-Wrightson-a(i) — 2 6 12 17

286,291,294: 294-Joker-c/stories — 2 6 13 20

300-Double-size — 2 6 15 22

301-(7/78)-310,312-315,317-320,325-331,333-352: 304-(44 pgs.). 306-3rd app. Black Spider. 308-Mr. Freeze app. 310-1st modern app. The Gentleman Ghost in Batman; Kubert-c. 312,314,346-Two-Face appss. 313-2nd app. Calendar Man. 318-Intro Firebug. 319-2nd modern age app. The Gentleman Ghost; Kubert-a. 344-Poison Ivy app. 345-app. new Dr. Death. 345,346,351-7 pg. Catwoman back-ups — 2 6 9 12

306,307,312-315,320,323,324,326-(Whitman variants; low print run; none have #000 on cover) — 2 6 10 14

311,316,322-324: 311-Batgirl-c/story; Batgirl reteams w/Batman. 316-Robin returns. 322-324-Catwoman (Selina Kyle) app. 322,323-Cat-Man cameos (1st in Batman, 1 panel each). 323-31st meeting Catwoman & Cat-Man. 324-1st full app. Cat-Man this title — 2 6 10 14

321,353,359-Joker-c/stories. — 2 6 11 15

332-Catwoman's 1st solo. — 2 6 11 15

354-356,358,360-365,369,370: 361-1st app Harvey Bullock — 1 3 6 9

357-1st app. Jason Todd (3/83); see Det. #524; 1st app. Croc (cameo) — 2 6 9 12

366-Jason Todd 1st in Robin costume; Joker-c/story — 2 6 11 15

367-Jason in red & green costume (not as Robin) — 1 4 7 10

368-1st new Robin in costume (Jason Todd) — 2 6 9 12

371-399,401-403: 371-Cat-Man-c/story; brief origin Cat-Man (cont'd in Det. #538). 386,387-Intro Black Mask (villain). 380-391-Catwoman app. 398-Catwoman & Two-Face app. 401-2nd app. Magpie (see Man of Steel #3 for 1st). 403-Joker cameo — 6.00

NOTE: Most issues between 397 & 432 were reprinted in 1989 and sold in multi-packs. Some are not identified as reprints but have newer ads copyrighted after cover dates. 2nd and 3rd print- ings exist.

400 ($1.50, 68pgs.)-Dark Knight special; intro by Stephen King; Art Adams/ Austin-a — 2 6 15 22

404-Miller scripts begin (end 407); Year 1; 1st modern app. Catwoman (2/87) — 2 6 9 12

405-407: 407-Year 1 ends (See Det. Comics for Year 2) — 1 3 6 9

408-410: New Origin Jason Todd (Robin) — 6.00

411-416,421-425: 411-Two-face app. 412-Origin/1st app. Mime. 414-Starlin scripts begin, end #429. 416-Nightwing-c/story. 423-McFarlane-c — 5.00

417-420: "Ten Nights of the Beast" storyline — 1 3 6 8

426-($1.50, 52 pg.)- "A Death In The Family" storyline begins, ends #429 — 2 6 11 15

427- "A Death In The Family" part 2. — 2 6 9 12

428-Death of Robin (Jason Todd) — 2 6 9 12

429-Joker-c/story; Superman app. — 1 3 6 8

430-432 — 3.00

433-Many Deaths of the Batman story by John Byrne-c/scripts — 3.00

436-Year 3 begins (ends #439); origin original Robin retold by Nightwing (Dick Grayson); 1st app. Timothy Drake (8/89) — 4.00

436-441: 436-2nd printing. 437-Origin Robin cont. 440,441: "A Lonely Place of Dying" Parts 1 & 3 — 3.00

442-1st app. Timothy Drake in Robin costume — 4.00

443-456,458,459,462-464: 445-447-Batman goes to Russia. 448,449-The Penguin Affair Pts 1 & 3. 450-Joker app. 450,451-Joker-c/stories. 452-454-Dark Knight Dark City storyline; Riddler app. 455-Alan Grant scripts begin, ends #466, 470. 464-Last solo Batman story; free 16 pg. preview of Impact Comics line — 3.00

457-Timothy Drake officially becomes Robin & dons new costume — 5.00

457-Direct sale edition (has #000 in indicia) — 5.00

460,461,465-487: 460,461-Two part Catwoman story. 465-Robin returns to action with Batman. 470-War of the Gods x-over. 475,476-Return of Scarface- c/story. 476-Last $1.00-c.477,478-Photo-c — 3.00

488-Cont'd from Batman: Sword of Azrael #4; Azrael-c & app. — 1 3 6 8

489-Bane-c/story; 1st app. Azrael in Bat-costume — 5.00

490-Riddler-c/story; Azrael & Bane app. — 6.00

491,492: 491-Knightfall lead-in; Joker-c/story; Azrael & Bane app.; Kelley Jones-c begins. 492-Knightfall part 1; Bane app. — 4.00

492-Platinum edition (promo copy) — 10.00

493-496: 493-Knightfall Pt. 3. 494-Knightfall Pt. 5; Joker-c & app. 495-Knightfall Pt. 7; brief Bane & Joker apps. 496-Knightfall Pt. 9, Joker-c/story; Bane cameo. — 3.00

497-(Late 7/93)-Knightfall Pt. 11; Bane breaks Batman's back; B&W outer-c; Aparo-a(p); Giordano-a(i) — 5.00

497-499: 497-2nd printing. 497-Newsstand edition w/o outer cover. 498-Knightfall part 15; Bane & Catwoman-c & app. (see Showcase 93 #7 & 8) 499-Knightfall Pt. 17; Bane app. — 3.00

500-($2.50, 68 pg.)- Pt. 19; Azrael in new Bat-costume; Bane-c/ story — 3.00

500-($3.95, 68 pgs.)-Collector's Edition w/die-cut double-c w/foil by Joe Quesada & 2 bound-in post cards — 5.00

501-508,510,511: 500-Begin. Pt.-c. 501-508-Knightquest. 503,504-Catwoman app. 507-Ballistic app.; Jim Balent-a(p). 510-KnightsEnd Pt. 7. 511-(9/94)- Zero Hour; Batgirl-c/story — 2.50

509-($2.50, 52 pgs.)-KnightsEnd Pt. 1 — 3.00

512-514,516-518: 512-(11/94)-Dick Grayson assumes Batman role — 2.50

515-Special Ed.($2.50)-Kelley Jones-a begins; all black embossed-c; Troika Pt. 1 — 3.00

Batman #575 © DC

Batman Annual #16 © DC

Batman: Fortunate Son HC © DC

	GD2.0	FN6.0	VF8.0	NM9.4

515-Regular Edition 2.50
519-534,536-549: 519-Begin $1.95-c. 521-Return of Alfred, 522-Swamp Thing
   app. 525-Mr. Freeze app. 527,528-Two Face app. 529-Contagion Pt. 6.
   530-532-Deadman app. 533-Legacy prelude. 534-Legacy Pt. 5. 536-Final
   Night x-over; Man-Bat-c/app. 540,541-Spectre-c app. 544-546-Joker
   & The Demon. 548,549-Penguin-c/app. 2.50
530-532 ($2.50)-Enhanced edition; glow-in-the-dark-c. 3.00
535-(10/96, $2.95)-1st app. The Ogre 3.00
535-(10/96, $3.95)-1st app. The Ogre; variant, cardboard, foldout-c 4.00
550-($3.50)-Collector's Ed., includes 4 collector cards; intro. Chase, return
   of Clayface; Kelley Jones-c 3.50
550-($2.95)-Standard Ed.; Williams & Gray-c 3.00
551,552,554-560: 551,552-Ragman c/app. 554-Cataclysm pt. 12. 2.50
553-Cataclysm pt.3 4.00
563-No Man's Land; Joker-c by Campbell; Bob Gale-s 5.00
564-574: 569-New Batgirl-c/app. 572-Joker and Harley app. 2.50
575-579: 575-New look Batman begins; McDaniel-s 2.50
580-598: 580-Begin $2.25-c. 587-Gordon shot. 591,592-Deadshot-c/app. 2.50
#0 (10/94)-Zero Hour issue released between #511 & #512; Origin retold 2.50
#1,000,000 (11/98) 853rd Century x-over 2.50

Annual 1 (8-10/61)-Swan-c	56	169	478	900
Annual 2	29	87	202	360
Annual 3 (Summer, '62)-Joker-c/story	30	90	210	375
Annual 4,5	13	39	94	160
Annual 6,7 (7/64, 25¢, 80 pgs.)	10	30	73	125
Annual V5#8 (1982)-Painted-c	1	3	6	8

Annual 9,10,12: V9#10(1986). 12(1988, $1.50) 6.00

Annual 11 (1987, $1.25)-Penguin-c/story; Moore-s	1	3	6	8

Annual 13 (1989, $1.75, 68 pgs.)-Gives history of Bruce Wayne, Dick Grayson,
   Jason Todd, Alfred, Comm. Gordon, Barbara Gordon (Batgirl) & Vicki Vale;
   Morrow-i 5.00
Annual 14-17 ('90-'93, 68 pgs.)-14-Origin Two-Face. 15-Armageddon 2001 x-
   over; Joker app. 15 (2nd printing). 16-Joker-c/s; Kieth-c.

17 (1993, $2.50, 68 pgs.)-Azrael in Bat-costume; intro Ballistic				4.00

Annual 18 (1994, $2.95) 3.00
Annual 19 (1995, $3.95)-Year One story; retells Scarecrow's origin 4.00
Annual 20 (1996, $2.95)-Legends of the Dead Earth story; Giarrano-a 3.00
Annual 21 (1997, $3.95)-Pulp Heroes story 4.00
Annual 22,23 ('98, '99, $2.95)-22-Ghosts; Wrightson-c. 23-JLApe; Art Adams-c.
    3.00
Annual 24 ('00, $3.50) Planet DC; intro. The Boggart; Aparo-a 3.00

Special 1 (4/84)-Mike W. Barr story; Golden-c	1	3	5	7

NOTE: Art Adams a-400p. Neal Adams a-200; 203, 210, 217, 219-222, 224-227, 229, 230, 232,
234, 236-241, 243-246, 251, 255, Annual c-200; 251-253, 255, Annual 17. Aparo a-414-420, 426-435, 440-448, 450, 451, 480-
483, 486-491, 494-500; c-414-416, 481, 482, 463, 486, 487i. Bolland a-400; c-445-447. Burnley
a-10, 12-18, 20, 22, 25, 27; c-9, 15, 16, 27, 28p, 40p, 42p. Byrne c-401, 433-435, 533-535, Annual
11. Travis Charest c-488-490p. Colan a-340p, 343-345p, 348-351p, 373p, 383p; c-343p, 345p,
350p. J. Cole a-238r. Cowan a-Annual 10p. Golden a-295p, 303p, 484, 485. Alan Grant scripts-
455-466, 470, 474-476, 479, 480, 484, 485-490, 494, 495, 500, Annual 16(part). Gordon c-287-290.
Infantino/Anderson a-167, 173, 175, 181, 186, 191, 192, 194, 195, 198, 199. Kelley Jones a-513-
519, 521-525, 527; c-491-499, 500(newsstand), 501-510, 513. Kaluta c-242, 248, 253, Annual 12.
G. Kane/Anderson a-178-180. Bob Kane a-1, 2, 5; c-1-5, 7, 17, G. Kane a-(r)-254, 255, 259, 261,
353i. Kubert a-238; 400; c-310, 319p, 327, 328, 344. McFarlane c-423. Mignola c-406. Moldoff a-242-
454, Annual 18. Moldoff a-101-160. Moldoff/Giella a-164-175, 177-181, 183, 184, 186.
Moldoff/Greene a-169, 172-174, 177-179, 181, 184. Mooney a-255r. Morrow a-Annual 13i.
Newton a-305, 306, 328p, 331p, 332p, 337p, 338p, 346p, 352-357p, 360-372p, 374-378p; c-374p,
378p. Nino a-Annual 9. Irv Novick c-201, 202. Perez a-401; 400. Fred Ray c-8, 10;
w/Robinson-11. Robinson/Roussos a-12-17, 20, 22, 24, 25, 27, 28, 31, 33, 37. Robinson a-2,
14, 18, 22-32,34, 36, 37, 255r, 260r, 261r; c-6, 8, 10-12, 15, 18, 21, 24, 26, 30, 34, 36p. Simonson
a-300p, 312p, 321p; c-300p, 312p, 366, 431i. P. Smith a-Annual 3. Dick Sprang c-19, 20, 22, 23,
25, 29, 31-36, 38, 51, 55, 66, 73, 76. Starlin c/a-402. Staton a-400. Sutton a-400. Wrightson a-
265i, 400; c-320r. Bat-Hound app. in 92, 97, 103, 125, 133, 156, 158. Bat-Mite app. in 133, 136,
144, 146, 158, 161. Batwoman app. in 105, 116, 122, 125, 128, 129, 131, 133, 139, 141, 144,
145, 150, 151, 153, 154, 157, 159, 162, 163. Black Canary back-ups in 332, 345,
346, 348-351. Joker app. in 1, 2, 4, 5, 7, 9, 11-13, 19, 20, 23, 25, 28, 32 & many more. Robin solo
back-up stories in 337-339, 341-347.

BATMAN (Hardcover books and trade paperbacks)
.... A LONELY PLACE OF DYING (1990, $3.95, 132 pgs.)-r/Batman #440-442
   & New Titans #60,61; Perez-c 4.00
...: ANARKY TPB (1999, $12.95) r/early appearances 13.00
...AND DRACULA: RED RAIN nn (1991, $24.95)-Hard-c.; Elseworlds storyline
    32.00
....AND DRACULA: Red Rain nn (1992, $9.95)-SC 12.00
ARKHAM ASYLUM Hard-c (1989, $24.95) 30.00

ARKHAM ASYLUM Soft-c ($14.95) 15.00
BIRTH OF THE DEMON Hard-c (1992, $24.95)-Origin of Ras al Ghul 25.00
BIRTH OF THE DEMON Soft-c (1993, $12.95) 13.00
BLIND JUSTICE nn (1992, $7.50)-r/Det. #598-600 7.50
BLOODSTORM (1994, $24.95,HC) Kelley Jones-c/a 28.00
BRIDE OF THE DEMON Hard-c (1990, $19.95) 20.00
BRIDE OF THE DEMON Soft-c ($12.95) 13.00
... CASTLE OF THE BAT ($5.95)-Elseworlds story 6.00
... CATACLYSM ('99, $17.95)-r/ story arc 18.00
... COLLECTED LEGENDS OF THE DARK KNIGHT nn
   (1994, $12.95)-r/Legends of the Dark Knight #32-34,38,42,43 13.00
... CRIMSON MIST (1999, $24.95,HC)-Vampire Batman Elseworlds story
   Doug Moench-s/Kelley Jones-c/a 25.00
... CRIMSON MIST (2001, $14.95,SC) 25.00
... DARK JOKER-THE WILD (1993, $24.95,HC)-Elseworlds story
   Doug Moench-s/Kelley Jones-c/a 25.00
... DARK JOKER-THE WILD (1993, $9.95,SC) 10.00
...DARK KNIGHT DYNASTY nn (1997, $24.95)-Hard-c.; 3 Elseworlds stories;
   Barr-s/ S. Hampton painted-a, Gary Frank, McDaniel-a(p) 25.00
...DARK KNIGHT DYNASTY Softcover (2000, $14.95) Hampton-c 15.00
...DEADMAN: DEATH AND GLORY nn (1996, $24.95)-Hard-c.;
   Robinson-s/ Estes-c/a 25.00
...DEADMAN: DEATH AND GLORY ($12.95)-SC 15.00
DEATH IN THE FAMILY (1988, $3.95, trade paperback)-r/Batman #426-429 by
   Aparo 5.00
DEATH IN THE FAMILY: (2nd - 5th printings) 4.00
DIGITAL JUSTICE nn (1990, $24.95, Hard-c.)-Computer generated art 25.00
... :EVOLUTION (2001, $12.95, SC)-r/Detective Comics #743-750 13.00
... FACES (1995, $9.95, TPB) 10.00
... FORTUNATE SON HC (1999, $24.95) Gene Ha-a 25.00
... FORTUNATE SON SC (2000, $14.95) Gene Ha-a 15.00
FOUR OF A KIND TPB (1998, $14.95)-r/1995 Year One Annuals featuring
   Poison Ivy, Riddler, Scarecrow, & Man-Bat 15.00
...GOTHIC (1992, $12.95, TPB)-r/Legends of the Dark Knight #6-10 13.00
...: HARVEST BREED-(2000, $24.95) George Pratt-s/painted-a 25.00
...: HAUNTED KNIGHT-(1997, $12.95) r/ Halloween specials 13.00
... IN THE SEVENTIES TPB ($19.95) Intro. by Dennis O'Neil 20.00
... IN THE SIXTIES TPB ($19.95) Intro. by Adam West 20.00
... LEGACY-(1996,17.95) reprints Legacy 18.00
....THE MANY DEATHS OF THE BATMAN (1992, $3.95, 84 pgs.)-r/Batman
   #433-435 w/new Byrne-c 4.00
...: THE MOVIES (1997, $19.95)-r/movie adaptions of Batman, Batman Returns,
   Batman Forever, Batman and Robin 20.00
... OFFICER DOWN (2001, $12.95)-r/Commissioner shot x-over; Talon-c 13.00
...: PREY (1992, $12.95)-Gulacy/Austin-a 13.00
...: PRODIGAL (1997, $14.95)-Gulacy/Austin-a 15.00
SHAMAN (1993, $12.95)-r/Legends/D.K. #1-5 13.00
...: SON OF THE DEMON Hard-c (9/87, $14.95) 30.00
...: SON OF THE DEMON limited signed & numbered Hard-c (1,700) 45.00
...: SON OF THE DEMON Soft-c w/new-c ($8.95) 10.00
...: SON OF THE DEMON Soft-c (1989, $9.95, 2nd printing - 4th printing)
    10.00
...: STRANGE APPARITIONS ($12.95) r/'77-'78 Englehart/Rogers stories from
   Detective #469-479; also Simonson-a 13.00
...: TALES OF THE DEMON (1991, $17.95, 212 pgs.)-Intro by Sam Hamm;
   reprints by N. Adams(3) & Golden; contains Saga of Ra's Al Ghul #1
    18.00
...: TEN NIGHTS OF THE BEAST (1994, $5.95)-r/Batman #417-420 6.00
...: THE CHALICE (HC, '99) $24.95) Van Fleet painted-a 25.00
...: THE CHALICE (SC, '00, $14.95) Van Fleet painted-a 15.00
...: THE LAST ANGEL (1994, $12.95, TPB) 13.00
...: THRILLKILLER (1998, $12.95, TPB)-r/series & Thrillkiller '62 13.00
...: VENOM (1993, $12.95, TPB)-r/Legends of the Dark Knight #16-20;
   embossed-c 10.00
YEAR ONE Hard-c (1988, $24.95) 18.00
YEAR ONE (1988, $9.95, TPB)-r/Batman #404-407 by Miller; intro by Miller
    10.00
YEAR ONE (TPB, 2nd & 3rd printings) 10.00
YEAR TWO (1990, $9.95, TPB)-r/Det. 575-578 by McFarlane; wraparound-c
    10.00

Batman Year One TPB © DC

Batman Adventures #18 © DC

Batman and Robin Adventures #11 © DC

	GD2.0	FN6.0	VF8.0	NM9.4

BATMAN (one-shots)
...: ABDUCTION, THE (1998, $5.95)		6.00
... & ROBIN (1997, $5.95)-Movie adaption		6.00
...: ARKHAM ASYLUM - TALES OF MADNESS (5/98, $2.95)		
Cataclysm x-over pt. 16; Grant-s/Taylor-a		3.00
...: BANE (1997, $4.95)-Dixon-s/Burchett-a; Stelfreeze-c;		
cover interlocks w/Batman:(Batgirl, Mr. Freeze, Poison Ivy)		5.00
...: BATGIRL (1997, $4.95)-Puckett-s/Haley,Kesel-a; Stelfreeze-c;		
cover interlocks w/Batman:(Bane, Mr. Freeze, Poison Ivy)		5.00
...: BATGIRL (6/98, $1.95)-Girlfrenzy; Balent-a		2.50
...: BLACKGATE (1/97, $3.95) Dixon-s		4.00
...: BLACKGATE - ISLE OF MEN (4/98, $2.95) Cataclysm x-over pt. 8;		
Moench-s/Aparo-a		3.00
... BOOK OF SHADOWS, THE (1999, $5.95)		6.00
... BROTHERHOOD OF THE BAT (1995, $5.95)-Elseworlds-s		6.00
... BULLOCK'S LAW (8/99, $4.95) Dixon-s		5.00
.../CAPTAIN AMERICA (1996, $5.95, DC/Marvel) Elseworlds story;		
Byrne-c/s/a		6.00
... : CATWOMAN DEFIANT nn (1992, $4.95, prestige format)-Milligan scripts;		
cover interlocks w/Batman: Penguin Triumphant; special foil logo.		5.00
.../DAREDEVIL (2000, $5.95)-Barreto-a		6.00
...: DARK ALLEGIANCES (1996, $5.95)-Elseworlds story, Chaykin-c/a.		
		6.00
...: DARK KNIGHT GALLERY (1/96, $3.50)-Pin-ups by Pratt, Balent, & others.		
		3.50
...:DAY OF JUDGMENT (11/99, $3.95)		4.00
...:DEATH OF INNOCENTS (12/96, $3.95)-O'Neil-s/ Staton-a(p)		4.00
.../DEMON (1996, $4.95)-Alan Grant scripts		5.00
.../DEMON: A TRAGEDY (2000, $5.95)-Grant-s/Murray painted-a		6.00
...: D.O.A. (1999, $6.95)-Bob Hall-s/a		7.00
...:DREAMLAND (2000, $5.95)-Grant-s/Breyfogle-a		6.00
... : EGO (2000, $6.95)-Darwyn Cooke-s/a		7.00
... 80-PAGE GIANT (8/98, $4.95) Stelfreeze-c		6.00
... 80-PAGE GIANT 2 (10/99, $4.95) Luck of the Draw		6.00
... 80-PAGE GIANT 3 (5/00, $4.95) Calendar Man		6.00
... FOREVER (1995, $5.95, direct market)		6.00
... FOREVER (1995, $3.95, newsstand)		4.00
... FULL CIRCLE nn (1991, $5.95, 68 pgs.)-Sequel to Batman: Year Two		6.00
...GALLERY, The 1 (1992, $2.95)-Pin-ups by Miller, N. Adams & others		3.00
...GOTHAM BY GASLIGHT (1989, $3.95)		4.00
...GOTHAM CITY SECRET FILES 1 (4/00, $4.95) Batgirl app.		5.00
...GOTHAM NOIR (2001, $6.95)-Elseworlds; Brubaker-s/Phillips-c/a		7.00
.../GREEN ARROW: THE POISON TOMORROW nn (1992, $5.95, square-		
bound, 68 pgs.)-Elseworlds story		6.00
... HOLY TERROR nn (1991, $4.95, 52 pgs.)-Elseworlds story		5.00
...:HOUDINI: THE DEVIL'S WORKSHOP (1993, $5.95)		6.00
... :HUNTRESS/SPIOLER - BLUNT TRAUMA (5/98, $2.95) Cataclysm pt. 13		
Dixon-s/Barreto & Sienkiewicz-a		3.00
...: I, JOKER nn (1998, $4.95)-Elseworlds story; Bob Hall-s/a		5.00
...: IN DARKEST KNIGHT nn (1994, $4.95, 52 pgs.)-Elseworlds story; Batman		
w/Green Lantern's ring.		5.00
...JOKER'S APPRENTICE (5/99, $3.95) Von Eeden-a		4.00
...:JUDGE DREDD: JUDGEMENT ON GOTHAM nn (1991, $5.95, 68 pgs.)		
Grant/Wagner scripts; Simon Bisley-c/a		6.00
...:JUDGE DREDD: JUDGEMENT ON GOTHAM nn (2nd printing)		6.00
...JUDGE DREDD: THE ULTIMATE RIDDLE (1995, $5.95)		6.00
...:JUDGE DREDD: VENDETTA IN GOTHAM (1993, $5.95)		6.00
...KNIGHTGALLERY (1995, $3.50)-Elseworlds sketchbook.		3.50
... / LOBO (2000, $5.95)-Elseworlds; Joker app.; Bisley-a		6.00
... MASK OF THE PHANTASM (1994, $2.95)-Movie adapt.		3.00
... MASK OF THE PHANTASM (1994, $4.95)-Movie adapt.		5.00
...: MASQUE (1997, $6.95)-Elseworlds; Grell-c/s/a		7.00
... MASTER OF THE FUTURE nn (1991, $4.95, 68 pgs.)-Elseworlds storyline;		
sequel to Gotham By Gaslight; embossed-c		6.00
...MITEFALL (1995, $4.95)-Alan Grant script, Kevin O'Neill-a		5.00
...: MR. FREEZE (1997, $4.95)-Dini-s/Buckingham-a; Stelfreeze-c;		
cover interlocks w/Batman:(Bane, Batgirl, Poison Ivy)		5.00
...: NOSFERATU (1999, $5.95) McKeever-a		6.00
...: OF ARKHAM (2000, $5.95)-Elseworlds; Grant-s/Alcatena-a		6.00
...: OUR WORLDS AT WAR (8/01, $2.95)-Jae Lee-c		3.00

	GD2.0	FN6.0	VF8.0	NM9.4

...: PENGUIN TRIUMPHANT nn (1992, $4.95)-Staton-a(p); foil logo		5.00
•PHANTOM STRANGER nn (1997, $4.95) nn-Grant-s/Ransom-a		5.00
... : PLUS (2/97, $2.95) Arsenal-c/app.		3.00
...: POISON IVY (1997, $4.95)-J.F. Moore-s/Apthorp-a; Stelfreeze-c;		
cover interlocks w/Batman:(Bane, Batgirl, Mr. Freeze)		5.00
...:PUNISHER: LAKE OF FIRE (1994, $4.95, DC/Marvel)		5.00
...:REIGN OF TERROR ('99, $4.95) Elseworlds		5.00
...RETURNS MOVIE SPECIAL (1992, $3.95)		4.00
...RETURNS MOVIE PRESTIGE (1992, $5.95, squarebound)-Dorman		
painted-c		6.00
...RIDDLER-THE RIDDLE FACTORY (1995, $4.95)-Wagner script		5.00
...: SCARECROW 3-D (12/98, $3.95) w/glasses		4.00
.../ SCARFACE: A PSYCHODRAMA (2001, $5.95)-Adlard-a/Sienkiewicz-c		6.00
...: SCAR OF THE BAT nn (1996, $4.95)-Elseworlds story; Max Allan Collins		
script; Barreto-a.		5.00
...:SCOTTISH CONNECTION (1998, $5.95) Quitely-a		6.00
...: SEDUCTION OF THE GUN nn (1992, $2.50, 68 pgs.)		3.00
.../SPAWN: WAR DEVIL nn (1994, $4.95, 52 pgs.)		5.00
.../SPIDER-MAN (1997, $4.95) Dematteis-s/Nolan & Kesel-a		5.00
... : THE ABDUCTION ('98, $5.95)		6.00
...: THE BLUE, THE GREY, & THE BAT (1992, $5.95)-Weiss/Lopez-a		6.00
... :THE HILL (5/00, $2.95)-Priest-s/Martinbrough-a		3.00
...: THE KILLING JOKE (1988, deluxe 52 pgs., mature readers)-Bolland-c/a;		
Alan Moore scripts; Joker cripples Barbara Gordon	2	6	11	15
...: THE KILLING JOKE (2nd thru 8th printings)		4.00
... : THE OFFICIAL COMIC ADAPTATION OF THE WARNER BROS. MOTION		
PICTURE (1989, $2.50, regular format, 68 pgs.)-Ordway-c.		3.00
...: THE OFFICIAL COMIC ADAPTATION OF THE WARNER BROS. MOTION		
PICTURE (1989, $4.95, prestige format, 68 pgs.)-same interiors but		
different-c than regular format.		5.00
... : TWO-FACE-CRIME AND PUNISHMENT-(1995, $4.95)-Scott McDaniel-a		
		5.00
... : TWO FACES (11/98, $4.95) Elseworlds		5.00
...: VENGEANCE OF BANE SPECIAL 1 (1992, $2.50, 68 pgs.)-Origin & 1st app.		
Bane (see Batman #491)	2	6	9	12
...: VENGEANCE OF BANE SPECIAL 1 (2nd printing)		2.50
...:VENGEANCE OF BANE II nn (1995, $3.95)-sequel		4.00
...Vs. THE INCREDIBLE HULK (1995, $3.95)-r/DC Special Series #27		4.00
...: VILLAINS SECRET FILES (10/98, $4.95)-Origin-s		5.00

BATMAN ADVENTURES, THE (Based on animated series)
DC Comics: Oct, 1992 - No. 36, Oct, 1995 ($1.25/$1.50)
1-Penguin-c/story				4.00
1 ($1.95, Silver Edition)-2nd printing				2.25
2-6,8-19: 2,12-Catwoman-c/story. 3-Joker-c/story. 5-Scarecrow-c/story.				
10-Riddler-c/story. 11-Man-Bat-c/story. 12-Batgirl & Catwoman-c/story.				
16-Joker-c/story; begin 1.50-c. 18-Batgirl-c/story. 19-Scarecrow-c/story.				3.00
7-Special edition polybagged with Man-Bat trading card				5.00
20-24,26-32: 26-Batgirl app.				2.50
25-($2.50, 52 pgs.)-Superman app.				3.00
33-36: 33-Begin $1.75-c				2.25
Annual 1,2 ('94, '95): 2-Demon-c/story; Ra's al Ghul app.				3.50
Holiday Special 1 (1995, $2.95)				4.00
The Collected Adventures Vol. 1,2 ('93, '95, $5.95)				6.00
TPB ('98, $7.95) r/#1-6; painted wraparound-c				8.00

BATMAN ADVENTURES, THE: MAD LOVE
DC Comics: Feb, 1994 ($3.95/$4.95)
1-Origin of Harley Quinn; Dini-s/Timm-c/a	2	6	9	12
1-($4.95, Prestige format) new Timm painted-c	1	3	6	8

BATMAN ADVENTURES, THE: THE LOST YEARS (TV)
DC Comics: Jan, 1998 - No. 5, May, 1998 ($1.95) (Based on animated series)
1-5-Leads into Fall '97's new animated episodes. 4-Tim Drake becomes Robin.		
5-Dick becomes Nightwing		2.25
TPB-(1999, $9.95) r/series		10.00

BATMAN/ALIENS
DC Comics/Dark Horse: Mar, 1997 - No. 2, Apr, 1997 ($4.95, lim. series)
1,2: Wrightson-c/a.		5.00
TPB-(1997, $14.95) w/prequel from DHP #101,102		15.00

Batman and the Outsiders #10 © DC

Batman Beyond #21 © DC

Batman: Gotham Adventures #3 © DC

BATMAN AND ROBIN ADVENTURES (TV)
DC Comics: Nov, 1995 - No. 25, Dec, 1997 ($1.75) (Based on animated series)

1-Dini-s.	3.00
2-24: 2-4-Dini script. 4-Penguin-c/story. 5-Joker-c/story; Poison Ivy, Harley Quinn-c/app. 9-Batgirl & Talia-c/story. 10-Ra's Al Ghul-c/story	
11-Man-Bat app. 12-Bane-c/app. 13-Scarecrow-c/app. 15 Deadman-c/app. 16-Catwoman-c/app. 18-Joker-c/app. 24-Poison Ivy app.	2.25
25-($2.95, 48 pgs.)	3.00
Annual 1,2 (11/96, 11/97): 1-Phantasm-c/app. 2-Zatara & Zatanna-c/app.	4.00
...: Sub-Zero(1998, $3.95) Adaption of animated video	4.00

BATMAN AND SUPERMAN ADVENTURES: WORLD'S FINEST
DC Comics: 1997 ($6.95, square-bound, one-shot) (Based on animated series)

1-Adaption of animated crossover episode; Timm-c	7.00

BATMAN AND SUPERMAN: WORLD'S FINEST
DC Comics: Apr, 1999 - No. 10, Jan, 2000 ($4.95/$1.99, limited series)

1,10-($4.95, squarebound) Taylor-a	5.00
2-9-($1.99) 5-Batgirl app. 8-Catwoman-c/app.	2.25

BATMAN AND THE OUTSIDERS (The Adventures of the Outsiders #33 on) (Also see Brave & The Bold #200 & The Outsiders) (Replaces The Brave and the Bold)
DC Comics: Aug, 1983 - No. 32, Apr, 1986 (Mando paper #5 on)

1-Batman, Halo, Geo-Force, Katana, Metamorpho & Black Lightning begin	4.00
2-32: 5-New Teen Titans x-over. 9-Halo begins. 11,12-Origin Katana. 18-More info on Metamorpho's origin. 28-31-Lookers origin. 32-Team disbands	2.50
Annual 1,2 (9/84, 9/85): 2-Metamorpho & Sapphire Stagg wed	3.00

NOTE: *Aparo a-1-9, 11-13p, 16-20; c-1-4, 6-21, Annual 1, 2. B. Kane a-3r. Layton a-19i, 20i. Lopez a-3p. Miller c-Annual 1. Perez c-5p. B. Willingham a-14p.*

BATMAN: BANE OF THE DEMON
DC Comics: Mar, 1998 - No. 4, June, 1998 ($1.95, limited series)

1-4-Dixon-s/Nolan-a; prelude to Legacy x-over	2.50

BATMAN BEYOND (Based on animated series)(Mini-series)
DC Comics: Mar, 1999 - No. 6, May, 1999 ($1.99)

1-6: 1,2-Adaption of pilot episode, Timm-c	2.25
TPB (1999, $9.95) r/#1-6	10.00

BATMAN BEYOND (Based on animated series)(Continuing series)
DC Comics: Nov, 1999 - No. 24, Oct, 2001 ($1.99)

1-24: 1-Rousseau-a; Batman vs. Batman. 14-Demon-c/app. 21,22-Justice League Unlimited-c/app.	2.25
...: Return of the Joker (2/01, $2.95) adaption of video release	3.00

BATMAN: BLACK & WHITE
DC Comics: June, 1996 - No. 4, Sept, 1996 ($2.95, B&W, limited series)

1-Stories by McKeever, Timm, Kubert, Chaykin, Goodwin; Jim Lee-c; Allred inside front-c; Moebius inside back-c	4.00
2-4: 2-Stories by Simonson, Corben, Bisley & Gaiman; Miller-c. 3-Stories by M. Wagner, Janson, Sienkiewicz, O'Neil & Kristiansen; B. Smith-c. Russell inside front-c; Silvestri inside back-c. 4-Stories by Bolland, Goodwin & Gianni, Strnad & Nowlan, O'Neil & Stelfreeze; Toth-c; pin-ups by Neal Adams & Alex Ross	3.00
Hardcover ('97, $39.95) r/series w/new art & cover plate	40.00
Softcover ('00, $19.95) r/series	20.00

BATMAN: BOOK OF THE DEAD
DC Comics: Jun, 1999 - No. 2, July, 1999 ($4.95, limited series, prestige format)

1,2-Elseworlds; Kitson-a	5.00

BATMAN: CATWOMAN DEFIANT (See Batman one-shots)

BATMAN CHRONICLES, THE
DC Comics: Summer, 1995 - No. 23, Winter, 2001 ($2.95, quarterly)

1-3,5-19: 1-Dixon/Grant/Moench script. 3-Bolland-c. 5-Oracle Year One story, Richard Dragon app.;Chaykin-c. 6-Kaluta-c; Ra's Al Ghul story. 7-Superman-c /app.11-Hal Pope-s/a. 12-Cataclysm pt. 10. 18-No Man's Land	3.50
4-Hitman story by Ennis, Contagion tie-in; Balent-c	2	6	9	12
20-23: 20-Catwoman and Relative Heroes-c/app. 21-Pander Bros.-a	3.00
...Gallery (3/97, $3.50) Pin-up	3.50
...Gauntlet, The (1997, $4.95, one-shot)	5.00

BATMAN: DARK KNIGHT OF THE ROUND TABLE

BATMAN: DARK VICTORY

DC Comics: 1999 - No. 2, 1999 ($4.95, limited series, prestige format)

1,2-Elseworlds; Giordano-a	5.00

BATMAN: DARK VICTORY
DC Comics: 1999 - No. 13, 2000 ($4.95/$2.95, limited series)

Wizard #0 Preview	2.25
1-($4.95) Loeb-s/Sale-c/a	5.00
2-12-($2.95)	3.00
13-($4.95)	5.00
Hardcover (2001, $29.95) with dust jacket; r/#0,1-13	30.00

BATMAN FAMILY, THE
National Periodical Pub./DC Comics: Sept-Oct, 1975 - No. 20, Oct-Nov, 1978 (#1-4, 17-on: 68 pgs.) (Combined with Detective Comics with No. 481)

1-Origin/2nd app. Batgirl-Robin team-up (The Dynamite Duo); reprints plus one new story beginning; N. Adams(r); r/1st app. Man-Bat from Det. #400		3	9	17	25
2-5: 2-r/Det. #369. 3-Batgirl & Robin learn each's i.d.; r/Batwoman app. from Batman #105. 4-r/1st Fatman app. from Batman #113.				
5-r/1st Bat-Hound app. from Batman #92	2	6	11	15
6,9-Joker's daughter on cover (1st app?)	2	6	12	18
7,8,14-16: 8-r/Batwoman app.14-Batwoman app. 15-3rd app. Killer Moth. 16-Bat-Girl cameo (last app. in costume until New Teen Titans #47)				
	2	6	9	12
10-1st revival Batwoman; Cavalier app.; Killer Moth app.				
	2	6	13	20
11-20: 11-13-Rogers-a(p): 11-New stories begin; Man-Bat begins. 13-Batwoman cameo. 17-($1.00 size)-Batman, Huntress begin; Batwoman & Catwoman 1st meet. 18-20: Huntress by Staton in all. 20-Origin Ragman retold				
	2	6	12	18

NOTE: *Aparo a-17; c-11-16. Austin a-12i. Chaykin a-14p. Michael Golden a-15-17,18-20p. Grell a-1; c-1. Gil Kane a-2r. Kaluta c-17, 19. Newton a-13. Robinson a-1r, 3i(r), 9r. Russell a-18i, 19i. Starlin a-17; c-18, 20.*

BATMAN: GCPD
DC Comics: Aug, 1996 - No. 4, Nov, 1996 ($2.25, limited series)

1-4: Features Jim Gordon; Aparo/Sienkiewicz-a	2.50

BATMAN: GORDON OF GOTHAM
DC Comics: June, 1998 - No. 4, Sept, 1998 ($1.95, limited series)

1-4: Gordon's early days in Chicago	2.50

BATMAN: GORDON'S LAW
DC Comics: Dec, 1996 - No. 3, Feb, 1997 ($1.95, limited series)

1-3: Dixon-s/Janson-c/a	2.50

BATMAN: GOTHAM ADVENTURES (TV)
DC Comics: June, 1998 - Present ($2.95/$1.95/$1.99)

1-($2.95) Based on Kids WB Batman animated series	3.00
2-3-($1.95): 2-Two-Face-c/app.	2.50
4-22: 4-Begin $1.99-c. 5-Deadman-c. 13-MAD #1 cover swipe	2.50
23-45: 31-Joker-c/app.	2.25
TPB (2000, $9.95) r/#1-6	10.00

BATMAN: GOTHAM KNIGHTS
DC Comics: Mar, 2000 - Present ($2.50)

1-10-Grayson-s; B&W back-ups by artists	2.50
11-($3.25) Bolland-c; Kyle Baker back-up story	3.25
12-24: 13-Officer Down x-over; Ellison back-up-s. 15-Colan back-up. 20-Superman-c/app.	2.50

BATMAN: GOTHAM NIGHTS II (First series listed under Gotham Nights)
DC Comics: Mar, 1995 - No. 4, June, 1995 ($1.95, limited series)

1-4	2.50

BATMAN/GRENDEL (1st limited series)
DC Comics: 1993 - No. 2, 1993 ($4.95, limited series, squarebound; 52 pgs.)

1,2: Batman vs. Grendel; Matt Wagner-c/a/scripts. 2-Devil's Masque; Matt Wagner-c/a/scripts	6.00

BATMAN/GRENDEL (2nd limited series)
DC Comics: June, 1996 - No. 2, July, 1996 ($4.95, limited series, squarebound)

1,2: Batman vs. Grendel Prime. 1-Devil's Bones. 2-Devil's Dance; Wagner-c/a/s	5.00

Batman: Legends of the Dark Knight #47 © DC

Batman: Orpheus Rising #2 © DC

Batman: Shadow of the Bat #75 © DC

	GD2.0	FN6.0	VF8.0	NM9.4		GD2.0	FN6.0	VF8.0	NM9.4

BATMAN: HARLEY QUINN
DC Comics: 1999 ($5.95, prestige format)

1-Intro. of Harley Quinn into regular DC continuity; Dini-s/Alex Ross-c	9.00
1-(2nd printing)	6.00

BATMAN: HAUNTED GOTHAM
DC Comics: 2000 - No. 4, 2000 ($4.95, limited series, squarebound)

1-4-Moench-s/Kelley Jones-c/a	5.00

BATMAN: HELLBOY/STARMAN
DC Comics/Dark Horse: Jan, 1999 - No. 2, Feb, 1999 ($2.50, limited series)

1,2: Robinson-s/Mignola-a. 2-Harris-c	2.50

BATMAN: HOLLYWOOD KNIGHT
DC Comics: Apr, 2001 - No. 3, Jun, 2001 ($2.50, limited series)

1-3-Elseworlds Batman as a 1940's movie star; Giordano-a/Layton-s	2.50

BATMAN/ HUNTRESS: CRY FOR BLOOD
DC Comics: Jun, 2000 - No. 6, Nov, 2000 ($2.50, limited series)

1-6: Rucka-s/Burchett-a	2.50

BATMAN: JOKER TIME (...: It's Joker Time! on cover)
DC Comics: 2000 - No. 3 ($4.95, limited series, squarebound)

1-3-Bob Hall-s/a	5.00

BATMAN/ JUDGE DREDD "DIE LAUGHING"
DC Comics: 1998 - No. 2, 1999 ($4.95, limited series, squarebound)

1,2: 1-Fabry-c/a. 2-Jim Murray-c/a	5.00

BATMAN: KNIGHTGALLERY (See Batman one-shots)

BATMAN: LEAGUE OF BATMEN
DC Comics: 2001 - No. 2, 2001 ($5.95, limited series, squarebound)

1,2-Elseworlds; Moench-s/Bright & Tanghal-a/Van Fleet-c	6.00

BATMAN: LEGENDS OF THE DARK KNIGHT (Legends of the Dark...#1-36)
DC Comics: Nov, 1989 - Present ($1.50/$1.75/$1.99/$2.25)

1- "Shaman" begins, ends #5; outer cover has four different color variations, all worth same	4.00
2-10- "Gothic" by Grant Morrison (scripts)	3.00
11-15: 11-15-Gulacy/Austin-a. 13-Catwoman app.	3.00
16-Intro drug Bane uses; begin Venom story	5.00
17-20	4.00
21-49,51-63: 38-Bat-Mite-c/story. 46-49-Catwoman app. w/Heath-c/a. 51-Ragman app.; Joe Kubert-c/a. 59,60,61-Knightquest x-over. 62,63-KnightsEnd Pt. 4 & 10	3.00
50-($3.95, 68 pgs.)-Bolland embossed gold foil-c; Joker-c/story; pin-ups by Chaykin, Simonson, Williamson, Kaluta, Russell, others	5.00
64-99: 64-67-Gulacy-a. 68-Bright app. 71-73-James Robinson-s, J. Watkiss-c/a. 74,75-Ted McKeever-c/a/s. 76-78-Scott Hampton-c/a/s. 81-Card insert. 83,84-Ellis-s. 85-Robinson-s. 91-93-Ennis-s. 94-Michael T. Gilbert-s/a.	3.00
100-($3.95) Alex Ross painted-c; gallery by various	5.00
101-115: 101-Ezquerra-a. 102-104-Robinson-a	2.50
116-No Man's Land stories begin; Huntress-c	4.00
117-119,121-126: 122-Harris-c	2.50
120-ID of new Batgirl revealed	4.00
127-131: Return to Legends stories; Green Arrow app.	2.50
132-151: 132-136 ($2.25-c) Archie Goodwin-s/Rogers-a. 137-141-Gulacy-a. 142-145-Joker and Ra's al Ghul app. 146-148-Kitson-a	2.50
#0-(10/94)-Zero Hour; Quesada/Palmiotti-c; released between #64&65	3.00
Annual 1-7 ('91-'97, $3.50-$3.95, 68 pgs.): 1-Joker app. 2-Netzer-c/a. 3-New Batman (Azrael) app. 4-Elseworlds story. 5-Year One; Man-Bat app. 6-Legend of the Dead Earth story.-Pulp Heroes story	4.00
Halloween Special 1 (12/93, $6.95, 84 pgs.)-Embossed & foil stamped-c	

	1	3	5	7
Batman Madness-...Halloween Special (1994, $4.95)				5.00
Batman Ghosts-...Halloween Special (1995, $4.95)				5.00

NOTE: Aparo a-Annual 1. Chaykin scripts-24-26. Giffen a-Annual 1. Golden a-Annual 1. Alan Grant scripts-38, 52, 53. Gil Kane a-24-26. Mignola a-54; c-54, 62. Morrow a-Annual 3i. Quesada a-Annual 1. James Robinson scripts- 71-73. Russell c/a-42, 43. Sears a-21, 23; c-21, 23. Zeck a-69, 70; c-69, 70.

BATMAN-LEGENDS OF THE DARK KNIGHT: JAZZ
DC Comics: Apr, 1995 - No. 3, June, 1995 ($2.50, limited series)

1-3	2.50

BATMAN: MANBAT
DC Comics: Oct, 1995 - No. 3, Dec, 1995 ($4.95, limited series)

1-3-Elseworlds-Delano-script; Bolton-a.	5.00
TPB-(1997, $14.95) r/#1-3	15.00

BATMAN: MITEFALL (See Batman one-shots)

BATMAN MINIATURE (See Batman Kellogg's)

BATMAN: NO MAN'S LAND (Also see 1999 Batman titles)
DC Comics: (one shots)

nn (3/99, $2.95) Alex Ross-c; Bob Gale-s; begins year-long story arc	3.00
Collector's Ed. (3/99, $3.95) Ross lenticular-c	5.00
#0 (: Ground Zero on cover) (12/99, $4.95) Orbik-c	5.00
...: Gallery (7/99, $3.95) Jim Lee-c	4.00
...: Secret Files (12/99, $4.95) Maleev-c	5.00
TPB ('99, $12.95) r/early No Man's Land stories; new Batgirl early app.	13.00
No Law and a New Order TPB(1999, $5.95) Ross-c	6.00
Volume 2 ('00, $12.95) r/later No Man's Land stories; Batgirl(Huntress) app.; Deodato-c	13.00
Volume 3-5 ('00,'01 $12.95) 3-Intro. new Batgirl. 4-('00). 5-('01) Land-c	13.00

BATMAN: ORPHEUS RISING
DC Comics: Oct, 2001 - No. 5, Feb, 2002 ($2.50, limited series)

1-5-Intro. Orpheus; Simmons-s/Turner & Miki-a	2.50

BATMAN: OUTLAWS
DC Comics: 2000 - No. 3, 2000 ($4.95, limited series)

1-3-Moench-s/Gulacy-a	5.00

BATMAN: PENGUIN TRIUMPHANT (See Batman one-shots)

BATMAN/PREDATOR III: BLOOD TIES
DC Comics/Dark Horse Comics: Nov, 1997 - No. 4, Feb, 1998 ($1.95, lim. series)

1-4: Dixon-s/Damaggio-a	2.50
TPB-(1998, $7.95) r/#1-4	8.00

BATMAN RETURNS MOVIE SPECIAL (See Batman one-shots)

BATMAN: RIDDLER-THE RIDDLE FACTORY (See Batman one-shots)

BATMAN: RUN, RIDDLER, RUN
DC Comics: 1992 - Book 3, 1992 ($4.95, limited series)

Book 1-3: Mark Badger-a & plot	5.00

BATMAN: SECRET FILES
DC Comics: Oct, 1997 ($4.95)

1-New origin-s and profiles	5.00

BATMAN: SHADOW OF THE BAT
DC Comics: June, 1992 - No. 94, Feb, 2000 ($1.50/$1.75/$1.95/$1.99)

1-The Last Arkham-c/story begins; Alan Grant scripts in all	4.00
1-($2.50)-Deluxe edition polybagged w/poster, pop-up & book mark	5.00
2-7: 4-The Last Arkham ends. 7-Last $1.50-c	3.00
8-28: 14,15-Staton-a(p). 16-18-Knightfall tie-ins. 19-28-Knightquest tie-ins w/Azrael as Batman. 25-Silver ink-c; anniversary issue	2.50
29-($2.95, 52 pgs.)-KnightsEnd Pt. 2	4.00
30-72: 30-KnightsEnd Pt. 8. 31-(9/94)-Begin $1.95-c; Zero Hour. 32-(11/94). 33-Robin-c. 35-Troika-Pt.2. 43,44-Cat-Man & Catwoman-c. 48-Contagion Pt. 1; card insert. 49-Contagion Pt.7. 56,57,58-Poison Ivy-c/app. 62-Two-Face app. 69,70-Fate app.	2.50
35-($2.95)-Variant embossed-c	3.00
73,74,76-78: 73-Cataclysm x-over pts.1,9. 76-78-Orbik-c	3.00
75-($2.95) Mr. Freeze & Clayface app.; Orbik-c	3.00
79,81,82: 79-Begin $1.99-c; Orbik-c	2.50
80-($3.95) Flip book with Azrael #47	4.00
83-No Man's Land; intro. new Batgirl (Huntress)	12.00
84,85-No Man's Land	4.00
86-94: 87-Deodato-a. 90-Harris-c. 92-Superman app. 93-Joker and Harley app.	
94-No Man's Land ends	3.00
#0 (10/94) Zero Hour; released between #31&32	3.00
#1,000,000 (11/98) 853rd Century x-over; Orbik-c	2.50
Annual 1-5 ('93-'97 $2.95-$3.95, 68 pgs.): 3-Year One story; Poison Ivy app. 4-Legends of the Dead Earth story; Starman cameo. 5-Pulp Heroes story; Poison Ivy app.	4.00

Batman: The Long Halloween #13 © DC

Batman Vs. Predator #1 © DC / 20th Century Fox

Battle #9 © MAR

	GD2.0	FN6.0	VF8.0	NM9.4

BATMAN-SPAWN: WAR DEVIL (See Batman one-shots)

BATMAN SPECTACULAR (See DC Special Series No. 15)

BATMAN: SWORD OF AZRAEL (Also see Azrael & Batman #488,489)
DC Comics: Oct, 1992 - No. 4, Jan, 1993 ($1.75, limited series)

1-Wraparound gatefold-c; Quesada-c/a(p) in all; 1st app. Azrael	2	6	9	12
2-4: 4-Cont'd in Batman #488	1	3	6	8
Silver Edition 1-4 (1993, $1.95)-Reprints #1-4				2.25
Trade Paperback (1993, $9.95)-Reprints #1-4				10.00
Trade Paperback Gold Edition				15.00

BATMAN/ TARZAN: CLAWS OF THE CAT-WOMAN
Dark Horse Comics/DC Comics: Sept, 1999 - No. 4, Dec, 1999 ($2.95, limited series)

1-4: Marz-s/Kordey-a				3.00

BATMAN: THE CULT
DC Comics: 1988 - No. 4, Nov, 1988 ($3.50, deluxe limited series)

1-Wrightson-a/painted-c in all				6.00
2-4				5.00
Trade Paperback ('91, $14.95)-New Wrightson-c				15.00

BATMAN: THE DARK KNIGHT RETURNS (Also see Dark Knight Strikes Again)
DC Comics: Mar, 1986 - No. 4, 1986 ($2.95, squarebound, limited series)

1-Miller story 1-4 c/a(p); set in the future	4	12	26	40
1,2-2nd & 3rd printings, 3-2nd printing				6.00
2-Carrie Kelly becomes 1st female Robin	2	6	13	20
3-Death of Joker; Superman app.	2	6	11	15
4-Death of Alfred; Superman app.	2	6	9	12
Hard-c, signed & numbered edition ($40.00)(4000 copies)				250.00
Hard-c, trade edition				50.00
Soft-c, trade edition (1st printing only)	2	6	12	18
Soft-c, trade edition (2nd thru 8th printings)	1	3	6	9
10th Anniv. Slipcase set ('96, $100.00): Signed & numbered hard-c edition (10,000 copies), sketchbook, copy of script for #1, 2 color prints				100.00
10th Anniv. Hard-c ('96, $45.00)				45.00
10th Anniv. Soft-c ('97, $14.95)				15.00

NOTE: The #2 second printings can be identified by matching the grey background colors on the inside front cover and facing page. The inside front cover of the second printing has a dark grey background which does not match the lighter grey of the facing page. On the true 1st printings, the backgrounds are both light grey. All other issues are clearly marked.

BATMAN: THE DOOM THAT CAME TO GOTHAM
DC Comics: 2000 - No. 3, 2001 ($4.95, limited series)

1-3-Elseworlds; Mignola-c/s; Nixey-a; Etrigan app.				5.00

BATMAN: THE KILLING JOKE (See Batman one-shots)

BATMAN: THE LONG HALLOWEEN
DC Comics: Oct, 1996 - No. 4, Oct, 1997 ($2.95/$4.95, limited series)

1-($4.95)-Loeb/Sale-c/a in all	1	3	6	8
2-5-($2.95): 2-Solomon Grundy-c/app. 3-Joker-c/app., Catwoman, Poison Ivy app.				6.00
6-10: 6-Poison Ivy-c. 7-Riddler-c/app.				5.00
11,12				4.00
13-($4.95, 48 pgs.)-Killer revelations				5.00
HC-($29.95) r/series				30.00
SC-($19.95)				20.00

BATMAN: THE OFFICIAL COMIC ADAPTATION OF THE WARNER BROS. MOTION PICTURE (See Batman one-shots)

BATMAN: THE ULTIMATE EVIL
DC Comics: 1995 ($5.95, limited series, prestige format)

1,2-Barrett, Jr. adaptation of Vachss novel.				6.00

BATMAN 3-D (Also see 3-D Batman)
DC Comics: 1990 ($9.95, w/glasses, 8-1/8x10-3/4")

nn-Byrne-a/scripts; Riddler, Joker, Penguin & Two-Face app. plus r/1953 3-D Batman; pin-ups by many artists	2	6	9	12

BATMAN: TOYMAN
DC Comics: Nov, 1998 - No. 4, Feb, 1999 ($2.25, limited series)

1-4-Hama-s				2.50

BATMAN: TURNING POINTS
DC Comics: Jan, 2001 - No. 5, Jan, 2001 ($2.50, weekly limited series)

1-5: 2-Giella-a. 3-Kubert-c/ Giordano-a. 4-Chaykin-c. 5-Pope-c/a				2.50

BATMAN: TWO-FACE-CRIME AND PUNISHMENT (See Batman one-shots)

BATMAN: TWO-FACE STRIKES TWICE
DC Comics: 1993 ($4.95, 52 pgs.)

1,2-Flip book format w/Staton-a. (G.A. side)				5.00

BATMAN VERSUS PREDATOR
DC Comics/Dark Horse Comics: 1991 - No. 3, 1992 ($4.95/$1.95, limited series) (1st DC/Dark Horse x-over)

1 (Prestige format, $4.95)-1 & 3 contain 8 Batman/Predator trading cards; Andy & Adam Kubert-a; Suydam painted-c				6.00
1-3 (Regular format, $1.95)-No trading cards				3.00
2,3-(Prestige)-2-Extra pin-ups inside; Suydam-c				5.00
TPB (1993, $5.95, 132 pgs.)-r/#1-3 w/new introductions & forward plus new wraparound-c by Gibbons				6.00

BATMAN VERSUS PREDATOR II: BLOODMATCH
DC Comics: Late 1994 - No. 4, 1995 ($2.50, limited series)

1-4-Huntress app.; Moench scripts; Gulacy-a				3.00
TPB (1995, $6.95)-r/#1-4				7.00

BATMAN VS. THE INCREDIBLE HULK (See DC Special Series No. 27)

BATMAN: WAR ON CRIME
DC Comics: Nov, 1999 ($9.95, treasury size, one-shot)

nn-Painted art by Alex Ross; story by Alex Ross and Paul Dini				10.00

BATMAN/ WILDCAT
DC Comics: Apr, 1997 - No.3, June, 1997 ($2.25, mini-series)

1-3: Dixon/Smith-s: 1-Killer Croc app.				2.50

BAT MASTERSON (TV) (Also see Tim Holt #28)
Dell Publishing Co.: Aug-Oct, 1959; Feb-Apr, 1960 - No. 9, Nov-Jan, 1961-62

Four Color 1013 (#1) (8-10/59)	12	36	84	160
2-9: Gene Barry photo-c on all. 2-Two different back-c exist	6	18	42	80

BATS (See Tales Calculated to Drive You Bats)

BATS, CATS & CADILLACS
Now Comics: Oct, 1990 - No. 2, Nov, 1990 ($1.75)

1,2: 1-Gustovich-a(i); Snyder-c				2.25

BAT-THING
DC Comics (Amalgam): June, 1997 ($1.95, one-shot)

1-Hama-s/Damaggio & Sienkiewicz-a				2.25

BATTLE
Marvel/Atlas Comics(FPI #1-62/ Male #63 on): Mar, 1951 - No. 70, Jun, 1960

1	31	93	165	285
2	15	45	77	130
3-10: 4-1st Buck Pvt. O'Toole. 10-Pakula-a	11	33	55	70
11-20: 11-Check-a	9	27	49	70
21,23-Krigstein-a	10	30	55	80
22,24-36: 32-Tuska-a. 36-Everett-a	7	21	38	55
37-Kubert-a (Last precode, 2/55)	8	24	45	65
38-40,42-48	6	18	33	48
41,49: 41-Kubert/Moskowitz-a. 49-Davis-a	8	24	42	60
50-54,56-58	6	18	32	45
55-Williamson-a (5 pgs.)	8	24	42	60
59-Torres-a	6	18	33	48
60-62: 60,62-Combat Kelly app. 61-Combat Casey app.				
	6	18	32	45
63-Ditko-a	10	30	55	85
64-66-Kirby-a. 66-Davis-a; has story of Fidel Castro in pre-Communism days (an admiring profile)	12	36	61	105
67,68: 67-Williamson/Crandall-a (4 pgs.); Kirby, Davis-a. 68-Kirby/ Williamson-a (4 pgs.); Kirby/Ditko-a	13	39	66	110
69,70: 69-Kirby-a. 70-Kirby/Ditko-a	12	36	61	105

NOTE: Andru a-37. Berg a-38, 14, 60-62. Colan a-33, 55. Everett a-36, 50, 70; c-56, 57. Heath a-6, 9, 13, 31, 69; c-6, 9, 12, 26, 35, 37. Kirby c-64-69. Maneely a-4, 6, 31, 61; c-4, 33, 59, 61. Orlando a-47. Powell a-53, 55. Reinman a-8, 9, 26, 32. Robinson a-9, 39. Romita a-26. Severin

Battle Action #7 © ATL

Battle Chasers #1 © Joe Madureira

Battlefield #3 © ATL

	GD2.0	FN6.0	VF8.0	NM9.4

a-28, 32-34, 66-69; c-36. Sinnott a-33, 37. Woodbridge a-52, 55.

BATTLE ACTION
Atlas Comics (NPI): Feb, 1952 - No. 12, 5/53; No. 13, 11/54 - No. 30, 8/57

1-Pakula-a	25	75	130	225
2	13	39	66	110
3,4,6,7,9,10: 6-Robinson-c/a. 7-Partial nudity	8	24	42	60
5-Used in POP, pg. 93,94	8	24	45	65
8-Krigstein-a	9	27	49	70
11-15 (Last precode, 2/55)	8	24	42	60
16-30: 27,30-Torres-a	7	21	38	55

NOTE: *Battle Brady* her. 5-7, 10-12. *Berg* a-3. *Check* a-11. *Everett* a-7; c-13, 25. *Heath* a-3, 8, 18; c-3,15, 18, 21. *Maneely* a-1; c-5. *Reinman* a-1. *Robinson* a-6, 7; c-6. *Shores* a-7(2). *Sinnott* a-3. *Woodbridge* a-28, 30.

BATTLE ATTACK
Stanmor Publications: Oct, 1952 - No. 8, Dec, 1955

1	10	30	55	85
2	6	18	32	45
3-8: 3-Hollingsworth-a	5	15	25	35

BATTLEAXES
DC Comics (Vertigo): May, 2000 - No. 4, Aug, 2000 ($2.50, limited series)

1-4: Terry LaBan-s/Alex Horley-a				2.50

BATTLE BEASTS
Blackthorne Publishing: Feb, 1988 - No. 4, 1988 ($1.50/$1.75, B&W/color)

1-4: 1-3- (B&W)-Based on Hasbro toys. 4-Color				2.50

BATTLE BRADY (Formerly Men in Action No. 1-9; see 3-D Action)
Atlas Comics: No. 10, Jan, 1953 - No. 14, June, 1953

10: 10-12-Syd Shores-c	15	45	77	135
11-Used in POP, pg. 95 plus B&W & color illos	10	30	55	80
12-14	8	24	45	65

BATTLE CHASERS
Image Comics (Cliffhanger): Apr, 1998 - No. 4, Dec, 1998;
DC Comics (Cliffhanger): No. 5, May, 1999 - No. 8, May, 2001 ($2.50)
Image Comics: No. 9, Sept, 2001 - Present ($3.50)

Prelude (2/98)	1	4	7	10
Prelude Gold Ed.	1	4	7	10
1-Madureira & Sharrieff-s/Madureira-a(p)/Charest-c	1	3	6	9
1-American Ent. Ed. w/"racy" cover	1	4	7	10
1-Gold Edition				9.00
1-Chromium cover				40.00
1-2nd printing				3.00
2				5.00
2-Dynamic Forces BattleChrome cover	2	6	9	12
3-Red Monika cover by Madureira				4.00
4-8: 4-Four covers. 6-Back-up by Warren-s/a. 7-Three covers (Madureira, Ramos, Campbell)				3.00
9-($3.50, Image) Image cover/story by Adam Warren				3.50
...: A Gathering of Heroes HC ('99, $24.95) r/#1-5, Prelude, Frank Frazetta Fantasy III.; cover gallery				25.00
...: A Gathering of Heroes SC ('99, $14.95)				15.00
...Collected Edition 1,2 (11/98, 5/99, $5.95) 1-r/#1,2. 2-r/#3,4				6.00

BATTLE CLASSICS (See Cancelled Comic Cavalcade)
DC Comics: Sept-Oct, 1978 (44 pgs.)

1-Kubert-r; new Kubert-c	1	3	6	8

BATTLE CRY
Stanmor Publications: 1952 (May) - No. 20, Sept, 1955

1	13	39	66	110
2	7	21	38	55
3,5-10: 8-Pvt. Ike begins, ends #13,17	5	15	25	35
4-Classic E.C. swipe	7	21	36	50
11-20	5	15	23	30

NOTE: *Hollingsworth* a-9; c-20.

BATTLEFIELD (War Adventures on the...)
Atlas Comics (ACI): April, 1952 - No. 11, May, 1953

1-Pakula, Reinman-a	21	63	110	185
2-5: 2-Heath, Maneely, Pakula, Reinman-a	11	33	55	90

6-11	8	24	42	60

NOTE: *Colan* a-11. *Everett* a-8. *Heath* a-1, 2, 5p; c-2, 8, 9, 11. *Ravielli* a-11.

BATTLEFIELD ACTION (Formerly Foreign Intrigues)
Charlton Comics: No. 16, Nov, 1957 - No. 62, 2-3/66; No. 63, 7/80 - No. 89, 11/84

V2#16	6	18	32	45
17,20-30	4	12	19	25
18,19-Check-a (2 stories in #18)	3	9	20	30
31-62(1966)	2	6	12	18
63-80(1983-84)				5.00
81-83,85-89 (Low print run)				6.00
84-Kirby reprints; 3 stories	1	3	6	9

NOTE: *Montes/Bache* a-43, 55, 62. *Glanzman* a-87r.

BATTLE FIRE
Aragon Magazine/Stanmor Publications: Apr, 1955 - No. 7, 1955

1	10	30	50	80
2	6	18	29	40
3-7	5	14	21	28

BATTLE FOR A THREE DIMENSIONAL WORLD
3D Cosmic Publications: May, 1983 (20 pgs., slick paper w/stiff-c, $3.00)

nn-Kirby c/a in 3-D; shows history of 3-D	1	3	6	9

BATTLEFORCE
Blackthorne Publishing: Nov, 1987 - No. 2, 1988 ($1.75, color/B&W)

1,2: Based on game. 1-In color. 2-B&W				2.50

BATTLE FOR INDEPENDENTS, THE (Also See Cyblade/Shi & Shi/Cyblade:
The Battle For Independents)
Image Comics (Top Cow Productions)/Crusade Comics: 1995 ($29.95)

nn-boxed set of all editions of Shi/Cyblade & Cyblade/Shi plus new variant.				
	4	12	26	40

BATTLE FOR THE PLANET OF THE APES (See Power Record Comics)

BATTLEFRONT
Atlas Comics (PPI): June, 1952 - No. 48, Aug, 1957

1-Heath-c	29	87	153	265
2-Robinson-a(4)	14	42	72	125
3-5	12	36	61	100
6-10: Combat Kelly in No. 6-10	10	30	55	85
11-22,24-28: 14,16-Battle Brady app. 22-Teddy Roosevelt & His Rough Riders story. 28-Last pre-code (2/55)	8	24	42	60
23,43-Check-a	8	24	45	65
29-39,41,44-47	7	21	36	50
40,42-Williamson-a	9	27	49	70
48-Crandall-a	8	24	42	60

NOTE: *Ayers* a-19, 32. *Berg* a-44. *Colan* a-21, 22, 32, 33, 40. *Drucker* a-28, 29. *Everett* a-44. *Heath* c-23, 26, 27, 29, 32. *Maneely* a-22; c-23; c-2, 13, 22, 35. *Morisi* a-42. *Morrow* a-41.*Orlando* a-47. *Powell* a-19, 21, 25, 29, 32, 40, 47. *Robinson* a-1-4, 5(4); c-4, 5. *Robert Sale* a-19. *Severin* a-32; c-40. *Woodbridge* a-45, 46.

BATTLEFRONT
Standard Comics: No. 5, June, 1952

5-Toth-a	15	45	77	130

BATTLE GODS: WARRIORS OF THE CHAAK
Dark Horse Comics: Apr, 2000 - No. 4, July, 2000 ($2.95)

1-4-Francisco Ruiz Velasco-s/a				3.00

BATTLE GROUND
Atlas Comics (OMC): Sept, 1954 - No. 20, Aug, 1957

1	21	63	110	185
2-Jack Katz-a	11	33	55	90
3,4-Last precode (3/55)	8	24	45	65
5-8,10	8	24	42	60
9,11,13,18: 9-Krigstein-a. 11,13,18-Williamson-a in each	10	30	55	80
12,15-17,19,20	7	21	38	55
14-Kirby-a	11	33	55	90

NOTE: *Ayers* a-13. *Colan* a-11, 13. *Drucker* a-7, 12, 13, 20. *Heath* c-2, 15. *Maneely* a-19; c-1, 19. *Orlando* a-17.*Pakula* a-11. *Severin* a-5, 12, 19. c-20. *Tuska* a-11.

BATTLE HEROES

Battle of the Planets #7 © WHIT

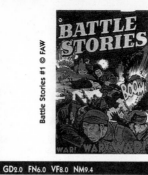

Battle Stories #1 © FAW

Beagle Boys #16 © WDC

	GD2.0	FN6.0	VF8.0	NM9.4

	GD2.0	FN6.0	VF8.0	NM9.4

Stanley Publications: Sept, 1966 - No. 2, Nov, 1966 (25¢)

1	3	9	20	30
2	2	6	13	20

BATTLE OF THE BULGE (See Movie Classics)

BATTLE OF THE PLANETS (TV)
Gold Key/Whitman No. 6 on: 6/79 - No. 10, 12/80
(Based on syndicated cartoon by Sandy Frank)

1: Mortimer a-1,4,7-10	2	6	13	20
2-6,10	2	6	9	12
7-9: All low print run. 8(11/80). 9-(3-pack only?)	2	6	15	22

BATTLE REPORT
Ajax/Farrell Publications: Aug, 1952 - No. 6, June, 1953

1	10	30	50	80
2-6	6	18	32	45

BATTLE SQUADRON
Stanmor Publications: April, 1955 - No. 5, Dec, 1955

1	9	27	49	70
2-5: 3-Iwo Jima & flag-c	5	15	25	35

BATTLESTAR GALACTICA (TV) (Also see Marvel Comics Super Special #8)
Marvel Comics Group: Mar, 1979 - No. 23, Jan, 1981

1: 1-5 adapt TV episodes	1	3	6	8
2-23: 1-3-Partial-r				6.00

NOTE: **Austin** c-9i, 10i. **Golden** c-18. **Simonson** a(p)-4, 5, 11-13, 15-20, 22, 23; c(p)-4, 5,11-17, 19, 20, 22, 23.

BATTLESTAR GALACTICA (TV) (Also see Asylum)
Maximum Press: July, 1995 - No.4, Nov, 1995 ($2.50, limited series)

1-4: Continuation of TV series		4.00
Trade paperback (12/95, $12.95)-reprints series		13.00

BATTLESTAR GALACTICA (TV)
Realm Press: Dec, 1997 - No. 5, July, 1998 ($2.99)

1-5-Chris Scalf-s/painted-a/c		3.00
...Search For Sanctuary (9/98, $2.99) Scalf & Kuhoric-s		3.00
...Search For Sanctuary Special (4/00, $3.99) Kuhoric-s/Scalf & Scott-a		4.00

BATTLESTAR GALACTICA: APOLLO'S JOURNEY (TV)
Maximum Press: Apr, 1996 - No. 3, June, 1996 ($2.95, limited series)

1-3: Richard Hatch scripts		4.00

BATTLESTAR GALACTICA: JOURNEY'S END (TV)
Maximum Press: Aug, 1996 - No. 4, Nov, 1996 ($2.99, limited series)

1-4-Continuation of the T.V. series		4.00

BATTLESTAR GALACTICA: SEASON III
Realm Press: June/July, 1999 - No. 3 ($2.99)

1-3: 1-Kuhoric-s/Scalf & Scott-a; Scalf-c. 2-Covers by Scalf and Stinsman.		
3-Two covers		3.00
1-Variant-c by Jae Lee		4.00
Gallery (4/00, $3.99) short story and pin-ups		4.00
1999 Tour Book (5/99, $2.99)		3.00
1999 Tour Book Convention Edition (6.99)		7.00
...Special: Centurion Prime (12/99, $3.99) Kuhoric-s		4.00

BATTLESTAR GALACTICA: SPECIAL EDITION (TV)
Maximum Press: Jan, 1997 ($2.99, one-shot)

1-Fully painted; Scalf-c/s/a; r/Asylum		3.00

BATTLESTAR GALACTICA: STARBUCK (TV)
Maximum Press: Dec, 1995 - No. 3, Mar, 1996 ($2.50, limited series)

1-3		4.00

BATTLESTAR GALACTICA: THE COMPENDIUM (TV)
Maximum Press: Feb, 1997 ($2.99, one-shot)

1		3.00

BATTLESTAR GALACTICA: THE ENEMY WITHIN (TV)
Maximum Press: Nov, 1995 - No. 3, Feb, 1996 ($2.50, limited series)

1-3: 3-Indicia reads Feb, 1995 in error.		4.00

BATTLESTONE (Also see Brigade & Youngblood)

Image Comics (Extreme): Nov, 1994 - No. 2, Dec, 1994 ($2.50, limited series)

1,2-Liefeld plots		2.50

BATTLE STORIES (See XMas Comics)
Fawcett Publications: Jan, 1952 - No. 11, Sept, 1953

1-Evans-a	15	45	77	130
2	8	24	45	65
3-11	7	21	36	50

BATTLE STORIES
Super Comics: 1963 - 1964

Reprints #10-12,15-18: 10-r/U.S Tank Commandos #? 11-r/? 11, 12,17-r/Monty Hall #?; 13-Kintsler-a (1pg).15-r/American Air Forces #7 by Powell; Bolle-r.

18-U.S. Fighting Air Force #?	2	6	10	14

BATTLETECH (See Blackthorne 3-D Series #41 for 3-D issue)
Blackthorne Publishing: Oct, 1987 - No. 6, 1988 ($1.75/$2.00)

1-6: Based on game. 1-Color. 2-Begin B&W		3.00
Annual 1 ($4.50, B&W)		5.00

BATTLETECH
Malibu Comics: Feb, 1995 ($2.95)

0		3.00

BATTLETECH FALLOUT
Malibu Comics: Dec, 1994 - No. 4, Mar, 1995 ($2.95)

1-4-Two edi. exist #1; normal logo		3.00
1-Gold version w/foil logo stamped "Gold Limited Edition		8.00
1-Full-c holographic limited edition		6.00

BATTLETIDE (Death's Head II & Killpower...)
Marvel Comics UK, Ltd.: Dec, 1992 - No. 4, Mar, 1993 ($1.75, mini-series)

1-4: Wolverine, Psylocke, Dark Angel app.		2.25

BATTLETIDE II (Death's Head II & Killpower...)
Marvel Comics UK, Ltd.: Aug, 1993 - No. 4, Nov, 1993 ($1.75, mini-series)

1-($2.95)-Foil embossed logo		3.00
2-4: 3-Hulk-c/story		2.25

BATTLEZONES: DREAM TEAM 2 (See Dream Team)
Malibu Comics (Ultraverse): Mar, 1996 ($3.95)

1-Pin-ups between Marvel & Malibu characters by Mike Wieringo, Phil Jimenez, Mike McKone, Cully Hamner, Gary Frank & others		4.00

BAY CITY JIVE
DC Comics (WildStorm): Jul, 2001 - No. 3, Sept, 2001 ($2.95, limited series)

1-3: Intro Sugah Rollins in 1970s S.F.; Layman-s/Johnson-a		3.00

BAYWATCH COMIC STORIES (TV) (Magazine)
Acclaim Comics (Armada): May, 1996 - No. 4, 1997 ($4.95) (Photo-c on all)

1-4: Photo comics based on TV show		5.00

BEACH BLANKET BINGO (See Movie Classics)

BEAGLE BOYS, THE (Walt Disney)(See The Phantom Blot)
Gold Key: 11/64; No. 2, 11/65; No. 3, 8/66 - No. 47, 2/79 (See WDC&S #134)

1	4	12	29	45
2-5	3	9	17	24
6-10	2	6	12	18
11-20: 11,14,19-r	2	6	10	14
21-30: 27-r	1	3	6	9
31-47	1	3	5	7

BEAGLE BOYS VERSUS UNCLE SCROOGE
Gold Key: Mar, 1979 - No. 12, Feb, 1980

1	2	6	10	14
2-12: 9-r	1	3	5	7

BEANBAGS
Ziff-Davis Publ. Co. (Approved Comics): Winter, 1951 - No. 2, Spring, 1952

1,2	11	33	55	90

BEANIE THE MEANIE
Fago Publications: No. 3, May, 1959

3	5	15	23	30

Beavis and Butthead #8 © MTV

Beep Beep, The Road Runner #12 © WB

Beetle Bailey #70 © CC

	GD2.0	FN6.0	VF8.0	NM9.4

BEANY AND CECIL (TV) (Bob Clampett's...)
Dell Publishing Co.: Jan, 1952 - 1955; July-Sept, 1962 - No. 5, July-Sept, 1963

Four Color 368	26	78	182	340
Four Color 414,448,477,530,570,635(1/55)	16	48	112	210
01-057-209 (#1)	15	45	105	200
2-5	10	30	70	130

BEAR COUNTRY (Disney)
Dell Publishing Co.: No. 758, Dec, 1956

Four Color 758-Movie	5	15	35	60

BEAST (See X-Men)
Marvel Comics: May, 1997 - No. 3, 1997 ($2.50, mini-series)

1-3-Giffen-s/Nocon-a	3.00

BEAST BOY (See Titans)
DC Comics: Jan, 2000 - No. 4, Apr, 2000 ($2.95, mini-series)

1-4-Justiano-c/a; Raab & Johns-s	3.00

B.E.A.S.T.I.E.S. (Also see Axis Alpha)
Axis Comics: Apr, 1994 ($1.95)

1-Javier Saltares-c/a/scripts	2.25

BEATLES, THE (See Girls' Romances #109, Go-Go, Heart Throbs #101, Herbie #5, Howard the Duck Mag. #4, Laugh #166, Marvel Comics Super Special #4, My LittleMargie #54, Not Brand Echh, Strange Tales #130, Summer Love, Superman's Pal Jimmy Olsen #79, Teen Confessions #37, Tippy's Friends & Tippy Teen)

BEATLES, THE (Life Story)
Dell Publishing Co.: Sept-Nov, 1964 (35¢)

1-(Scarce)-Stories with color photo pin-ups; Paul S. Newman-s				
	46	138	322	600

BEATLES EXPERIENCE, THE
Revolutionary Comics: Mar, 1991 - No. 8, 1991 ($2.50, B&W, limited series)

1-8: 1-Gold logo	5.00

BEATLES YELLOW SUBMARINE (See Movie Comics under Yellow...)

BEAUTIFUL PEOPLE
Slave Labor Graphics: Apr, 1994 ($4.95, 8-1/2x11", one-shot)

nn	5.00

BEAUTIFUL STORIES FOR UGLY CHILDREN
DC Comics (Piranha Press): 1989 - No. 30, 1991 ($2.00/$2.50, B&W, mature)

Vol. 1-30: 12-$2.50-c begins	3.00
A Cotton Candy Autopsy ($12.95, B&W)-Reprints 1st two volumes	13.00

BEAUTY AND THE BEAST, THE
Marvel Comics Group: Jan, 1985 - No. 4, Apr, 1985 (limited series)

1-4: Dazzler & the Beast from X-Men; Sienkiewicz-c on all	3.00

BEAUTY AND THE BEAST (Graphic novel)(Also see Cartoon Tales & Disney's New Adventures of...)
Disney Comics: 1992

nn-($4.95, prestige edition)-Adapts animated film	6.00
nn-($2.50, newsstand edition)	3.00

BEAUTY AND THE BEAST
Disney Comics: Sept., 1992 - No. 2, 1992 ($1.50, limited series)

1 ,2	3.00

BEAUTY AND THE BEAST: PORTRAIT OF LOVE (TV)
First Comics: May, 1989 - No. 2, Mar, 1990 ($5.95, 60 pgs., squarebound)

1,2: 1-Based on TV show, Wendy Pini-a/scripts. 2-...: Night of Beauty; by Wendy Pini	6.00

BEAVER VALLEY (Movie)(Disney)
Dell Publishing Co.: No. 625, Apr, 1955

Four Color 625	6	18	42	80

BEAVIS AND BUTTHEAD (MTV's...)(TV cartoon)
Marvel Comics: Mar, 1994 - No. 28, June, 1996 ($1.95)

1-Silver ink-c, 1, 2-Punisher & Devil Dinosaur app.	4.00
1-2nd printing	2.25
2,3: 2-Wolverine app. 3-Man-Thing, Spider-Man, Venom, Carnage, Mary Jane & Stan Lee cameos; John Romita, Sr. art (2 pgs.)	2.50

4-28: 5-War Machine, Thor, Loki, Hulk, Captain America & Rhino cameos.
6-Psylocke, Polaris, Daredevil & Bullseye app. 7-Ghost Rider & Sub-Mariner app. 8-Quasar & Eon app.9-Prowler & Nightwatch app. 11-Black Widow app. 12-Thunderstrike & Bloodaxe app. 13-Night Thrasher app. 14-Spider-Man 2099 app. 15-Warlock app. 16-X-Factor app. 25-Juggernaut app.   2.50

BECK & CAUL INVESTIGATIONS
Gauntlet Comics (Caliber): Jan, 1994 - No. 5, 1995? ($2.95, B&W)

1-5	3.00
Special 1 ($4.95)	5.00

BEDKNOBS AND BROOMSTICKS (See Walt Disney Showcase No. 6 & 50)

BEDLAM
Chaos! Comics: Sept, 2000 ($2.95, one-shot)

1-Steven Grant-s/David Brewer-a	3.00

BEDLAM!
Eclipse Comics: Sept, 1985 - No. 2, Sept, 1985 (B&W-r in color)

1,2: Bissette-a	3.00

BEDTIME STORY (See Cinema Comics Herald)

BEELZELVIS
Slave Labor Graphics: Feb, 1994 ($2.95, B&W, one-shot)

1	3.00

BEEP BEEP, THE ROAD RUNNER (TV)(See Daffy & Kite Fun Book)
Dell Publishing Co./Gold Key No. 1-88/Whitman No. 89 on: July, 1958 - No. 14, Oct-Dec, 1966 - No. 105, 1984

Four Color 918 (#1, 7/58)	9	27	63	120
Four Color 1008,1046 (11-1/59-60)	5	15	35	60
4(2-4/60)-14(Dell)	4	12	30	48
1(10/66, Gold Key)	5	15	34	55
2-5	3	10	23	35
6-14	3	9	17	25
15-18,20-40	2	6	12	18
19-With pull-out poster	3	10	23	35
41-50	2	6	10	14
51-70	1	3	6	9
71-88				6.00
89,90,94-100: 100(3/82), 101(4/82)	1	3	5	7
91(8/80), 92(9/80), 93 (3-pack?) (low printing)	2	6	11	16
102-105 (All #90189 on-c; nd or date code; pre-pack) 102(6/83), 103(7/83), 104(5/84), 105(6/84)	2	6	9	12

NOTE: See March of Comics #351, 353, 375, 387, 397, 416, 430, 442, 455. #5, 8-10, 35, 53, 59-62, 68-r; 96-102, 104 are 1/3-r.

BEETLE BAILEY (See Giant Comic Album, Sarge Snorkel; also Comics Reading Libraries in the Promotional Comics section)
Dell Publishing Co./Gold Key #39-53/King #54-66/Charlton #67-119/ Gold Key #120-131/Whitman #132: #459, 5/53 - #38, 5-7/62; #39, 11/62 - #53, 5/66; #54, 8/66 - #65, 12/67;#67, 2/69 - #119, 11/76; #120, 4/78 - #132, 4/80

Four Color 469 (#1) by Mort Walker	9	27	63	120
Four Color 521,552,622	5	15	35	60
5(2-4/56)-10(5-7/57)	4	12	30	50
11-20(4-5/59)	3	10	23	35
21-38(5-7/62)	3	9	17	25
39-53(5/66)	2	6	13	20
54-65 (No. 66 publ. overseas only?)	2	6	11	16
67-69: 69-Last 12¢ issue	2	6	11	15
70-99	2	6	9	12
100	2	6	11	16
101-119	1	3	6	9
120-132				6.00

BEETLE BAILEY
Harvey Comics: V2#1, Sept, 1992 - V2#9, Aug, 1994 ($1.25/$1.50)

V2#1	4.00
2-9-($1.50)	3.00
Big Book 1(11/92),2(5/93)(Both $1.95, 52 pgs.)	3.50
Giant Size V2#1(10/92),2(3/93)(Both $2.25,68 pgs.)	3.50

BEETLEJUICE (TV)
Harvey Comics: Oct, 1991 ($1.25)

Berlin #8 © Jason Lutes

Best Comics #2 © BP

The Best of DC #13 © DC

	GD2.0	FN6.0	VF8.0	NM9.4

1				3.00

BEETLEJUICE CRIMEBUSTERS ON THE HAUNT
Harvey Comics: Sept, 1992 - No. 3, Jan, 1993 ($1.50, limited series)

1-3				3.00

BEE 29, THE BOMBARDIER
Neal Publications: Feb, 1945

1-(Funny animal)	28	84	151	260

BEFORE THE FANTASTIC FOUR: BEN GRIMM AND LOGAN
Marvel Comics: July, 2000 - No. 3, Sept, 2000 ($2.99, limited series)

1-3-The Thing and Wolverine app.; Hama-s				3.00

BEFORE THE FANTASTIC FOUR: REED RICHARDS
Marvel Comics: Sept, 2000 - No. 3, Dec, 2000 ($2.99, limited series)

1-3-Peter David-s/Duncan Fegredo-c/a				3.00

BEFORE THE FANTASTIC FOUR: THE STORMS
Marvel Comics: Dec, 2000 - No. 3, Feb, 2001 ($2.99, limited series)

1-3-Adlard-a				3.00

BEHIND PRISON BARS
Realistic Comics (Avon): 1952

1-Kinstler-c	31	93	165	285

BEHOLD THE HANDMAID
George Pflaum: 1954 (Religious) (25¢ with a 20¢ sticker price)

nn		5	14	21	28

BELIEVE IT OR NOT (See Ripley's...)

BEN AND ME (Disney)
Dell Publishing Co.: No. 539, Mar, 1954

Four Color 539	4	12	26	40

BEN BOWIE AND HIS MOUNTAIN MEN
Dell Publishing Co.: 1952 - No. 17, Nov-Jan, 1958-59

Four Color 443 (#1)	6	18	42	80
Four Color 513,557,599,626,657	4	12	26	40
7(5-7/56)-11: 11-Intro/origin Yellow Hair	4	12	25	38
12-17	3	9	20	30

BEN CASEY (TV)
Dell Publishing Co.: June-July, 1962 - No. 10, June-Aug, 1965 (Photo-c)

12-063-207 (#1)	5	15	35	65
2(10/62),3,5-10	4	12	27	42
4-Marijuana & heroin use story	4	12	30	50

BEN CASEY FILM STORY (TV)
Gold Key: Nov, 1962 (25¢) (Photo-c)

30009-211-All photos	7	21	49	95

BENEATH THE PLANET OF THE APES (See Movie Comics & Power Record Comics)

BEN FRANKLIN (See Kite Fun Book)

BEN HUR
Dell Publishing Co.: No. 1052, Nov, 1959

Four Color 1052-Movie, Manning-a	10	30	70	130

BEN ISRAEL
Logos International: 1974 (39¢)

nn-Christian religious	1	3	6	9

BEOWULF (Also see First Comics Graphic Novel #1)
National Periodical Publications: Apr-May, 1975 - No. 6, Feb-Mar, 1976

1	1	4	7	10
2-6: 4-Dracula-c/s. 5-Flying saucer-c/story				6.00

BERLIN
Black Eye Productions: Apr, 1996 - Present ($2.50/$2.95, B&W)

1-8: Jason Lutes-c/a/scripts. 5-7-($2.95)				3.00
City of Stones TPB (2001, $15.95) r/#1-8				16.00

BERNI WRIGHTSON, MASTER OF THE MACABRE
Pacific Comics/Eclipse Comics No. 5: July, 1983 - No. 5, Nov, 1984 ($1.50, Baxter paper)

1-5: Wrightson-c/a(r). 4-Jeff Jones-r (11 pgs.)				5.00

BERRYS, THE (Also see Funny World)
Argo Publ.: May, 1956

1-Reprints daily & Sunday strips & daily Animal Antics by Ed Nofziger				
	6	18	29	40

BERZERKERS (See Youngblood V1#2)
Image Comics (Extreme Studios): Aug, 1995 - No. 3, Oct, 1995 ($2.50, limited series)

1-3: Beau Smith scripts, Fraga-a				2.50

BEST COMICS
Better Publications: Nov, 1939 - No. 4, Feb, 1940(Large size, reads sideways)

1-(Scarce)-Red Mask begins(1st app.) & c/s-all. Contains 6 pg. Boston Celtics photo story	82	246	511	900
2-4: 4-Cannibalism story	50	150	300	525

BEST FROM BOY'S LIFE, THE
Gilberton Company: Oct, 1957 - No. 5, Oct, 1958 (35¢)

1-Space Conquerors & Kam of the Ancient Ones begin, end #5; Bob Cousy photo/story	12	36	61	100
2,3,5	7	21	36	50
4-L.B. Cole-a	8	24	42	60

BEST LOVE (Formerly Sub-Mariner Comics No. 32)
Marvel Comics (MPI): No. 33, Aug, 1949 - No. 36, April, 1950 (Photo-c 33-36)

33-Kubert-a	12	36	61	100
34	7	21	36	50
35,36-Everett-a	9	27	49	70

BEST OF BUGS BUNNY, THE
Gold Key: Oct, 1966 - No. 2, Oct, 1968

1,2-Giants	5	15	34	55

BEST OF DC, THE (Blue Ribbon Digest) (See Limited Coll. Ed. C-52)
DC Comics: Sept-Oct, 1979 - No. 71, Apr, 1986 (100-148 pgs; mostly reprints)

1-Superman, w/"Death of Superman"-r	2	6	11	15
2,5-9: 2-Batman 40th Ann. Special. 5-Best of 1979. 6,8-Superman. 7-Superboy. 9-Batman, Creeper app.	1	4	7	10
3-Superfriends	2	6	9	12
4-Rudolph the Red Nosed Reindeer	2	6	11	15
10-Secret Origins of Super Villains; 1st ever Penguin origin-s	3	9	17	24
11-16,18-20: 11- The Year's Best Stories. 12-Superman Time and Space Stories. 13-Best of DC Comics Presents. 14-New origin stories of Batman villains. 15-Superboy. 16-Superman Anniv. 18-Teen Titans new-s., Adams, Kane-a; Perez-c. 19-Superman. 20-World's Finest	1	3	6	8
17-Supergirl	2	6	9	12
21,22: 21-Justice Society. 22-Christmas; unpublished Sandman story w/Kirby-a	2	6	11	16
23-27: 23-(148 pgs.)-Best of 1981. 24 Legion, new story and 16 pgs. new costumes. 25-Superman. 26-Brave & Bold. 27-Superman vs. Luthor	1	4	7	10
28,29: 28-Binky, Sugar & Spike app. 29-Sugar & Spike, 3 new stories; new Stanley & his Monster story	2	6	11	16
30,32-36,38,40: 30-Detective Comics. 32-Superman. 33-Secret origins of Legion Heroes and Villains. 34-Metal Men; has #497 on-c from Adv. Comics. 35-The Year's Best Comics Stories(148 pgs.). 36-Superman vs. Kryptonite. 38-Superman. 40-World of Krypton	2	6	9	12
31-JLA	2	6	11	16
37,39: 37-"Funny Stuff", Mayer-a. 39-Binky	2	6	11	16
41,43,45,47,49,53,55,58,60,63,65,68,70: 41-Sugar & Spike new stories with Mayer-a. 43,49,55-Funny Stuff. 45,53,70-Binky. 47,58,65,68-Sugar & Spike. 60-Plop!; Wood-c(r) & Aragonés-r (5/85). 63-Plop!; Wrightson-a(r)	2	6	12	18
42,44,48,50-52,54,56,57,59,61,62,64,66,67,69,71: 42,56-Superman vs. Aliens. 44,57,67-Superboy & LSH. 46-Jimmy Olsen. 48-Superman Team-ups 50-Year's best Superman. 51-Batman Family. 52 Best of 1984. 54,56,59-Superman. 61-(148 pgs.)Year's best. 62-Best of Batman 1985. 69-Year's best Team stories. 71-Year's best	2	6	10	14

NOTE: **N. Adams** a-2r, 14r, 18r, 26, 51. **Aparo** a-9, 14, 26, 30; c-9, 14, 26. **Austin** a-51i. **Buckler** a-40p; c-16, 22. **Giffen** a-50, 52; c-33p. **Grell** a-33p. **Grossman** a-37. **Heath** a-26. **Infantino** a-

The Best of Dennis the Menace #1 © FAW

Betty #100 © AP

Betty and Veronica #40 © AP

	GD2.0	FN6.0	VF8.0	NM9.4

10r, 18. **Kaluta** a-40. **G. Kane** a-10r, 18r; c-40, 44. **Kubert** a-10r, 21, 26. **Layton** a-21. **S. Mayer** c-29, 37, 41, 43, 47; a-28, 29, 37, 41, 43, 47, 58, 65, 68. **Moldoff** c-64p. **Morrow** a-40; c-40. **W. Mortimer** a-39p. **Newton** a-5, 51. **Perez** a-24, 50p; c-18, 21, 23. **Rogers** a-14, 51p. **Simonson** a-11r. **Spiegle** a-52. **Starlin** a-51. **Staton** a-5, 21. **Tuska** a-24. **Wolverton** a-60. **Wood** a-60, 63; c-60, 63. **Wrightson** a-60. New art in #14, 18, 24.

BEST OF DENNIS THE MENACE, THE
Hallden/Fawcett Publications: Summer, 1959 - No. 5, Spring, 1961 (100 pgs.)

1-All reprints; Wiseman-a	7	21	53	85
2-5	5	15	34	55

BEST OF DONALD DUCK, THE
Gold Key: Nov, 1965 (12¢, 36 pgs.)(Lists 2nd printing in indicia)

1-Reprints Four Color #223 by Barks	7	21	49	90

BEST OF DONALD DUCK & UNCLE SCROOGE, THE
Gold Key: Nov, 1964 - No. 2, Sept, 1967 (25¢ Giants)

1(30022-411)('64)-Reprints 4-Color #189 & 408 by Carl Barks; cover of F.C.				
#189 redrawn by Barks	8	24	56	100
2(30022-709)('67)-Reprints 4-Color #256 & "Seven Cities of Cibola"				
& U.S. #8 by Barks	7	21	49	90

BEST OF HORROR AND SCIENCE FICTION COMICS
Bruce Webster: 1987 ($2.00)

1-Wolverton, Frazetta, Powell, Ditko-r				5.00

BEST OF JOSIE AND THE PUSSYCATS
Archie Comics: 2001 ($10.95, TPB)

1-Reprints 1st app. and noteworthy stories				11.00

BEST OF MARMADUKE, THE
Charlton Comics: 1960

1-Brad Anderson's strip reprints	3	9	21	32

BEST OF MS. TREE, THE
Pyramid Comics: 1987 - No. 4, 1988 ($2.00, B&W, limited series)

1-4				2.50

BEST OF THE BRAVE AND THE BOLD, THE (See Super DC Giant)
DC Comics: Oct, 1988 - No. 6, Jan, 1989 ($2.50, limited series)

1-6: Neal Adams-r, Kubert-r & Heath-r in all				4.00

BEST OF THE WEST (See A-1 Comics)
Magazine Enterprises: 1951 - No. 12, April-June, 1954

1(A-1 42)-Ghost Rider, Durango Kid, Straight Arrow, Bobby Benson begin				
	40	120	240	420
2(A-1 46)	23	69	121	210
3(A-1 52), 4(A-1 59), 5(A-1 66)	19	57	99	165
6(A-1 70), 7(A-1 76), 8(A-1 81), 9(A-1 85), 10(A-1 87), 11(A-1 97),				
12(A-1 103)	14	42	72	120
NOTE: **Bolle** a-9. **Borth** a-12. **Guardineer** a-5, 12. **Powell** a-1, 12.

BEST OF UNCLE SCROOGE & DONALD DUCK, THE
Gold Key: Nov, 1966 (25¢)

1(30030-611)-Reprints part 4-Color #159 & 456 & Uncle Scrooge #6,7 by				
Carl Barks	7	21	49	90

BEST OF WALT DISNEY COMICS, THE
Western Publishing Co.: 1974 ($1.50, 52 pgs.) (Walt Disney)
(8-1/2x11" cardboard covers; 32,000 printed of each)

96170-Reprints 1st two stories less 1 pg. each from 4-Color #62				
	4	12	26	40
96171-Reprints Mickey Mouse and the Bat Bandit of Inferno Gulch from 1934				
(strips) by Gottfredson	4	12	26	40
96172-r/Uncle Scrooge #386 & two other stories	4	12	26	40
96173-Reprints "Ghost of the Grotto" (from 4-Color #159) & "Christmas on				
Bear Mountain" (from 4-Color #178)	4	12	26	40

BEST ROMANCE
Standard Comics (Visual Editions): No. 5, Feb-Mar, 1952 - No. 7, Aug, 1952

5-Toth-a; photo-c	13	39	66	110
6,7-Photo-c	6	18	29	40

BEST SELLER COMICS (See Tailspin Tommy)

BEST WESTERN (Formerly Terry Toons?) or Miss America Magazine
Marvel Comics (IPC): V7#24(#57)?; Western Outlaws & Sheriffs No. 60 on)

	GD2.0	FN6.0	VF8.0	NM9.4

No. 58, June, 1949 - No. 59, Aug, 1949

58,59-Black Rider, Kid Colt, Two-Gun Kid app.; both have Syd Shores-c				
	22	66	116	195

BETTIE PAGE COMICS
Dark Horse Comics: Mar, 1996 ($3.95)

1-Dave Stevens-c; Blevins & Heath-a; Jaime Hernandez pin-up				6.00

BETTIE PAGE COMICS: QUEEN OF THE NILE
Dark Horse Comics: Dec, 1999 - No. 3, Apr, 2000 ($2.95, limited series)

1-3-Silke-s/a; Stevens-c				3.00

BETTIE PAGE COMICS: SPICY ADVENTURE
Dark Horse Comics: Jan, 1997 ($2.95, one-shot, mature)

nn-Silke-c/s/a				4.00

BETTY (See Pep Comics #22 for 1st app.)
Archie Comics: Sept, 1992 - Present ($1.25/$1.50/$1.75/$1.79/$1.99)

1				5.00
2-18,20-24: 20-1st Super Sleuther-s				3.00
19-Love Showdown part 2				5.00
25-Pin-up page of Betty as Marilyn Monroe, Madonna, Lady Di				5.00
26-107: 57- "A Storm Over Uniforms" x-over part 5,6				2.25

BETTY AND HER STEADY (Going Steady with Betty No. 1)
Avon Periodicals: No. 2, Mar-Apr, 1950

2	10	30	55	80

BETTY AND ME
Archie Publications: Aug, 1965 - No. 200, Aug, 1992

1	9	27	65	110
2,3: 3-Origin Superteen	5	15	34	55
4-8: Superteen in new costume #4-7; dons new helmet in #5,				
ends #8.	4	12	25	38
9,10: Girl from R.I.V.E.R.D.A.L.E.	3	9	19	28
11-15,17-20(4/69): 9-UFO-s	2	6	15	22
16-Classic cover; w/risqué cover dialogue	3	9	20	30
21,24-35: 33-Paper doll page	2	6	11	15
22-Archies Band-c	2	6	12	18
23-I Dream of Jeannie parody	2	6	13	20
36(8/71),37,41-55 (52 pgs.): 42-Betty as vamp-c	2	6	12	18
38-Sabrina app.	3	9	20	30
39-Josie and Sabrina cover cameos	3	9	17	24
40-Betty & Veronica share a cabin	2	6	13	20
56(4/71)-80(12/76): 79 Betty Cooper mysteries thru #86. 79-81-Drago the				
Vampire-s	1	4	7	10
81-99: 83-Harem-c. 84-Jekyll & Hyde-c/s	1	3	6	8
100(3/79)	1	4	7	10
101,118: 101-Elvis mentioned. 118-Tarzan mentioned				6.00
102-117,119-130(9/82): 103,104-Space-s. 124-DeCarlo-c begins				5.00
131-138,140,142-147,149-154,156-158: 135,136-Jason Blossom app. 136-				
Cheryl Blossom cameo. 137-Space-s. 138-Tarzan parody				4.00
139,141,148: 139-Katy Keene collecting-s; Archie in drag-s. 141-Tarzan				
parody-s. 148-Cyndi Lauper parody-s.				5.00
155,159,160(8/87): 155-Archie in drag-s. 159-Superhero gag-c. 160-Wheel of				
Fortune parody				4.00
161-169,171-199				3.00
170-New Archie Superhero-s				4.00
200				5.00

BETTY AND VERONICA (Also see Archie's Girls…)
Archie Enterprises: June, 1987 - Present (75¢ /$1.25/$1.50/$1.75/$1.79/$1.99)

1				6.00
2-10				4.00
11-30				3.00
31-81,83-158				2.50
82-Love Showdown part 3				5.00
159-169				2.25
Summer Fun 1 (1994, $2.00, 52 pgs. plus poster)				5.00

BETTY & VERONICA ANNUAL DIGEST (…Digest Magazine #1-4, 44 on;
…Comics Digest Mag. #5-43)
Archie Publications: Nov, 1980 - Present ($1.00/$1.50/$1.75/$1.95/$1.99, digest

	GD2.0	FN6.0	VF8.0	NM9.4

	GD2.0	FN6.0	VF8.0	NM9.4
size)				
1	3	9	17	24
2-10: 2(11/81-Katy Keene story), 3(8/82)	2	6	10	14
11-30	1	3	6	9
31-50				6.00
51-70				3.50
71-126: 110-Begin $2.19-c				2.25

BETTY & VERONICA ANNUAL DIGEST MAGAZINE
Archie Comics: Sept, 1989 - Present ($1.50/$1.75/$1.79, 128 pgs.)

1	1	3	5	7
2-10: 9-Neon ink logo				5.00
11-17: 16-Begin $1.79-c				3.00

BETTY & VERONICA CHRISTMAS SPECTACULAR (See Archie Giant Series Magazine #159, 168, 180, 191, 204, 217, 229, 241, 453, 465, 477, 489, 501, 513, 525, 536, 547, 558, 568, 580, 593, 606, 618)

BETTY & VERONICA DOUBLE DIGEST MAGAZINE
Archie Enterprises: 1987 - Present ($2.25/$2.75/$1.50/$2.79/$2.95/$2.99, digest size, 256 pgs.)(...Digest #12 on)

1	1	4	7	10
2-10				6.00
11-25: 5,17-Xmas-c. 16-Capt. Hero story				4.00
26-102: 87-Begin $3.19-c. 95-Begin $3.29-c				3.30

BETTY & VERONICA SPECTACULAR (See Archie Giant Series Mag. #11, 16, 21, 26, 32, 138, 145, 153, 162, 173, 184, 197, 201, 210, 214, 221, 226, 234, 238, 246, 250, 458, 462, 470, 482, 486, 494, 498, 506, 510, 518, 522, 526, 530, 537, 552, 559, 563, 569, 575, 582, 588, 600, 608, 613, 620, 623, and Betty & Veronica)

BETTY AND VERONICA SPECTACULAR
Archie Comics: Oct, 1992 - Present ($1.25/$1.50/$1.75/$1.99)

1-Dan DeCarlo-c/a				5.00
2-20				3.00
21-51: 48-Cheryl Blossom leaves Riverdale				2.25

BETTY & VERONICA SPRING SPECTACULAR (See Archie Giant Series Magazine #569, 582, 595)

BETTY & VERONICA SUMMER FUN (See Archie Giant Series Mag. #8, 13, 18, 23, 28, 34, 140, 147, 155, 164, 175, 187, 199, 212, 224, 236, 248, 460, 484, 496, 508, 520, 529, 539, 550, 561, 572, 585, 598, 611, 621)
Archie Comics: 1994 - Present ($2.00/$2.25/$2.29)

1-6: 5 ($2.25-c). 6-($2.29-c)				2.50

BETTY BOOP'S BIG BREAK
First Publishing: 1990 ($5.95, 52 pgs.)

nn-By Joshua Quagmire; 60th anniversary ish.				6.00

BETTY PAGE 3-D COMICS
The 3-D Zone: 1991 ($3.95, "7-1/2x10-1/4", 28 pgs., no glasses)

1-Photo inside covers; back-c nudity	1	3	5	7

BETTY'S DIARY (See Archie Giant Series Magazine No. 555)
Archie Enterprises: April, 1986 - No. 40, Apr, 1991 (#1:65¢; 75¢/95¢)

1				6.00
2-10				4.00
11-40				2.50

BETTY'S DIGEST
Archie Enterprises: Nov, 1996 - Present ($1.75/$1.79)

1,2				3.00

BEVERLY HILLBILLIES (TV)
Dell Publishing Co.: 4-6/63 - No. 18, 8/67; No. 19, 10/69; No. 20, 10/70; No. 21, Oct, 1971

1-Photo-c	.17	51	119	220
2-Photo-c	9	27	63	110
3-9: All have photo covers	6	18	42	80
10: No photo cover	4	12	28	50
11-21: All have photo covers. 18-Last 12¢ issue. 19-21-Reprint #1-3 (covers and insides)	5	15	35	60
NOTE: #1-9, 11-21 are photo covers.

BEWARE (Formerly Fantastic; Chilling Tales No. 13 on)
Youthful Magazines: No. 10, June, 1952 - No. 12, Oct, 1952

10-E.A. Poe's Pit & the Pendulum adaptation by Wildey; Harrison/Bache-a; atom bomb and shrunken head-c	51	153	306	540
11-Harrison-a; Ambrose Bierce adapt.	35	105	188	325
12-Used in SOTI, pg. 388; Harrison-a	35	105	188	325

BEWARE
Trojan Magazines/Merit Publ. No. ?: No. 13, 1/53 - No. 16, 7/53; No. 5, 9/53 - No. 15, 5/55

13(#1)-Harrison-a	51	153	306	540
14(#2, 3/53)-Krenkel/Harrison-c; dismemberment, severed head panels	35	105	188	325
15,16(#3, 5/53; #4, 7/53)-Harrison-a	30	90	159	275
5,9,12,13	29	87	153	265
6-Ill. in SOTI: "Children are first shocked and then desensitized by all this brutality." Corpse on cover swipe/V.O.H. #26; girl on cover swipe/Advs. Into Darkness #10	55	165	330	575
7,8-Check-a	30	90	159	275
10-Frazetta/Check-c; Disbrow, Check-a	59	177	369	650
11-Disbrow-a; heart torn out, blood drainage	34	102	179	310
14,15: 14-Myron Fass-c. 15-Harrison-a	25	75	130	225
NOTE: Fass a-5, 6, 8; c-6, 11, 14. Forte a-8. Hollingsworth a-15(#3), 16(#4), 9; c-16(#4), 8, 9. Kiefer a-16(#4), 5, 6, 10.

BEWARE (Becomes Tomb of Darkness No. 9 on)
Marvel Comics Group: Mar, 1973 - No. 8, May, 1974 (All reprints)

1-Everett-c; Kirby & Sinnott-r ('54)	2	6	13	20
2-8: 2-Forte, Colan-r. 6-Tuska-a. 7-Torres-r/Mystical Tales #7	2	6	9	12
NOTE: Infantino a-4r. Gil Kane c-4. Wildey a-7r.

BEWARE TERROR TALES
Fawcett Publications: May, 1952 - No. 8, July, 1953

1-E.C. art swipe/Haunt of Fear #5 & Vault of Horror #26	45	135	270	475
2	36	93	165	285
3-7	25	75	130	225
8-Tothish-a; people being cooked-c	29	87	156	270
NOTE: Andru a-4r. Bernard Bailey a-1; c-1-5. Powell a-1, 2, 8. Sekowsky a-5.

BEWARE THE CREEPER (See Adventure, Best of the Brave & the Bold, Brave & the Bold, 1st Issue Special, Flash #318-323, Showcase #73, World's Finest #249)
National Periodical Publications: May-June, 1968 - No. 6, Mar-Apr, 1969 (All 12¢ issues)

1-(5-6/68)-Classic Ditko-c; Ditko-a in all	10	30	70	120
2-6: 2-5-Ditko-a. 2-Intro. Proteus. 6-Gil Kane-c	5	15	38	60

BEWITCHED (TV)
Dell Publishing Co.: 4-6/65 - No. 11, 10/67; No. 12, 10/68 - No. 13, 1/69; No. 14, 10/69

1-Photo-c	16	48	112	210
2-No photo-c	7	21	49	95
3-13-All have photo-c. 12-Repr. #1. 13-Last 12¢-c	5	15	35	70
14-No photo-c; reprints #2	4	12	28	45

BEYOND, THE
Ace Magazines: Nov, 1950 - No. 30, Jan, 1955

1-Bakerish-a(p)	40	120	232	400
2-Bakerish-a(p)	27	81	145	250
3-10: 10-Woodish-a by Cameron	18	54	94	160
11-20: 18-Used in POP, pgs. 81,82	15	45	77	130
21-26,28-30	14	42	72	125
27-Used in SOTI, pg. 111	15	45	77	130
NOTE: Cameron a-10, 11p, 12p, 15, 16, 21-27, 30; c-20. Colan a-6, 13, 17. Sekowsky a-2, 3, 5, 7, 11, 14, 27r. No. 1 was to appear as Challenge of the Unknown No. 1.

BEYOND THE GRAVE
Charlton Comics: July, 1975 - No. 6, June, 1976; No. 7, Jan, 1983 - No. 17, Oct, 1984

1-Ditko-a (6 pgs.); Sutton painted-c	3	9	17	25
2-6: 2-5-Ditko-a; Ditko c-2,3,6	2	6	11	15
7-17: ('83-'84) Reprints. 13-Aparo-c(r). 15-Sutton-c (low print run)				6.00
Modern Comics Reprint 2('78)				3.00
NOTE: Howard a-4. Kim a-1. Larson a-4, 6.

Big Bang Comics #28 © Gary Carlson
Big Chief Wahoo #1 © EAS

Big Shot Comics #7 © CCG

	GD2.0	FN6.0	VF8.0	NM9.4

BIBLE TALES FOR YOUNG FOLK (...Young People No. 3-5)
Atlas Comics (OMC): Aug, 1953 - No. 5, Mar, 1954

1	26	78	136	235
2-Everett, Krigstein-a	19	57	99	165
3-5: 4-Robinson-c	15	45	77	130

BIG (Movie)
Hit Comics (Dark Horse Comics): Mar, 1989 ($2.00)

1-Adaptation of film; Paul Chadwick-c				2.50

BIG ALL-AMERICAN COMIC BOOK, THE (See All-American Comics)
All-American/National Per. Publ.: 1944 (132 pgs., one-shot) (Early DC Annual)

1-Wonder Woman, Green Lantern, Flash, The Atom, Wildcat, Scribbly, The Whip, Ghost Patrol, Hawkman by Kubert (1st on Hawkman), Hop Harrigan, Johnny Thunder, Little Boy Blue, Mr. Terrific, Mutt & Jeff app.; Sargon on cover only; cover by Kubert/Hibbard/Mayer/others

	923	2769	6000	12,000

BIG BABY HUEY (Also see Baby Huey)
Harvey Comics: Oct, 1991 - No. 4, May, 1992 ($1.00, quarterly)

1-4				3.00

BIG BANG COMICS (Becomes Big Bang #4)
Caliber Press: Spring, 1994 - No. 4, Feb, 1995; No. 0, May, 1995 ($1.95, lim. series)

1-4-($1.95-c)				2.25
0-(5/95, $2.95) Alex Ross-c; color and B&W pages				3.00
Your Big Book of Big Bang Comics TPB ('98, $11.00) r/#0-2				11.00

BIG BANG COMICS (Volume 2)
Image Comics (Highbrow Entertainment): V2#1, May, 1996 - Present ($1.95/$2.50/$2.95/$3.95)

1-23,26: 1-Mighty Man app. 2-4-S.A. Shadowhawk app.5-Begin $2.95-c. 6-Curt Swan/Murphy Anderson-c.7-Begin B&W. 12-Savage Dragon-c/app. 15-Bissette-c. 16,17,21-Shadow Lady

				3.00

24,25,27-35-($3.95): 24,27-History of Big Bang Comics Vol. 1,2. 35-Big Bang vs. Alan Moore's "1963" characters

				4.00

BIG BLACK KISS
Vortex Comics: Sep, 1989 - No, 3, Nov, 1989 ($3.75, B&W, lim. series, mature)

1-3-Chaykin-s/a				4.00

BIG BLOWN BABY (Also see Dark Horse Presents)
Dark Horse Comics: Aug, 1996 - No. 4, Nov, 1996 ($2.95, lim. series, mature)

1-4: Bill Wray-c/a/scripts				3.00

BIG BOOK OF ...,THE
DC Comics (Paradox Press): 1994 - Present (B&W)($12.95 - $14.95)
nn-...BAD,1998 ($14.95),...CONSPIRACIES, 1995 ($12.95), ...DEATH,1994 ($12.95),...FREAKS, 1996 ($14.95),...GRIMM, 1999 ($14.95), ...HOAXES, 1996 ($14.95), ...LITTLE CRIMINALS, 1996 ($14.95),...LOSERS,1997 ($14.95),...MARTYRS, 1997 ($14.95),...SCANDAL,1997 ($14.95), ...THE WEIRD WILD WEST,1998 ($14.95), ...THUGS, 1997 ($14.95), ...UNEXPLAINED, 1997 (14.95),...URBAN LEGENDS, 1994 ($12.95), ...VICE, 1999 ($14.95), ...WEIRDOS, 1995 ($12.95)

				cover price

BIG BOOK OF FUN COMICS (See New Book of Comics)
National Periodical Publications: Spring, 1936 (Large size, 52 pgs.)
(1st comic book annual & DC annual)

1 (Very rare)-r/New Fun #1-5	2250	6750	13,500	-

BIG BOOK ROMANCES
Fawcett Publications: Feb, 1950 (no date given) (148 pgs.)

1-Contains remaindered Fawcett romance comics - several combinations possible

	39	117	208	360

BIG BRUISERS
Image Comics (WildStorm Productions): July, 1996 ($3.50, one-shot)

1-Features Maul from WildC.A.T.S, Impact from Cyberforce & Badrock from Youngblood; wraparound-c

				3.50

BIG CHIEF WAHOO
Eastern Color Printing/George Dougherty (distr. by Fawcett): July, 1942 - No. 7, Wint., 1943/44?(no year given)(Quarterly)

1-Newspaper-r (on sale 6/15/42)	40	120	232	400
2-Steve Roper app.	24	72	127	215
3-5: 4-Chief is holding a Katy Keene comic	18	54	94	155
6-7	13	39	66	110

NOTE: *Kerry Drake in some issues.*

BIG CIRCUS, THE (Movie)
Dell Publishing Co.: No. 1036, Sept-Nov, 1959

Four Color 1036-Photo-c	6	18	42	80

BIG COUNTRY, THE (Movie)
Dell Publishing Co.: No. 946, Oct, 1958

Four Color 946-Photo-c	7	21	49	90

BIG DADDY ROTH (Magazine)
Millar Publications: Oct-Nov, 1964 - No. 4, Apr-May, 1965 (35¢)

1-Toth-a	17	51	118	210
2-4-Toth-a	12	36	84	140

BIG GUY AND RUSTY THE BOY ROBOT, THE (Also See Madman Comics #6,7 & Martha Washington Stranded In Space)
Dark Horse (Legend): July, 1995 - No. 2, Aug, 1995 ($4.95, oversize, lim. series)

1,2-Frank Miller scripts & Geoff Darrow-c/a	1	3	5	7
Trade paperback (10/96, $14.95)-r/1,2 w/cover gallery				15.00

BIG HERO ADVENTURES (See Jigsaw)

BIG HAIR PRODUCTIONS
Image Comics: Feb, 2000 - Present ($3.50, B&W)

1,2				3.50

BIG JON & SPARKIE (Radio)(Formerly Sparkie, Radio Pixie)
Ziff-Davis Publ. Co.: No. 4, Sept-Oct, 1952 (Painted-c)

4-Based on children's radio program	20	60	105	175

BIG LAND, THE (Movie)
Dell Publishing Co.: No. 812, July, 1957

Four Color 812-Alan Ladd photo-c	9	27	63	120

BIG RED (See Movie Comics)

BIG SHOT COMICS
Columbia Comics Group: May, 1940 - No. 104, Aug, 1949

1-Intro. Skyman; The Face (1st app.) Tony Trent; The Cloak (Spy Master), Marvelo, Monarch of Magicians; Joe Palooka, Charlie Chan, Tom Kerry, Dixie Dugan, Rocky Ryan begin; Charlie Chan moves over from Feature Comics #31 (4/40).

	218	654	1364	2400
2	82	246	511	900
3-The Cloak called Spy Chief; Skyman-c	75	225	469	825
4,5	55	165	330	575
6-10: 8-Christmas-c	43	129	257	450
11-13	40	120	232	400
14-Origin & 1st app. Sparky Watts (6/41)	42	126	252	440
15-Origin The Cloak	43	129	257	450
16-20	34	102	179	310
21-23,26,27,29,30: 29-Intro. Capt. Yank; Bo (a dog) newspaper strip-r by Frank Beck begin, ends #104. 30-X-mas-c	27	81	145	250
24-Classic Tojo-c	40	120	217	375
25-Hitler-c	33	99	174	300
28-Hitler, Tojo & Mussolini-c	40	120	240	420
31,33-40	21	63	110	185
32-Vic Jordan newspaper strip reprints begin, ends #52; Hitler, Tojo & Mussolini-c	35	105	188	325
41,42,44,45,47-50: 42-No Skyman. 50-Origin The Face retold	17	51	88	150
43-Hitler-c	27	81	145	250
46-Hitler, Tojo-c (6/44)	24	72	127	215
51-56,58-60	15	45	77	130
57-Hitler, Tojo Halloween mask-c	20	60	105	175
61-70: 63 on-Tony Trent, the Face	12	36	61	100
71-80: 73-The Face cameo. 74-(2/47)-Mickey Finn begins. 74,80-The Face app. in Tony Trent. 78-Last Charlie Chan strip-r	11	33	55	90
81-90: 85-Tony Trent marries Babs Walsh. 86-Valentines-c	10	30	55	80
91-99,101-104: 69-94-Skyman in Outer Space. 96-Xmas-c				

Big-3 #6 © FOX

Big Town #3 © DC

Billy the Kid #7 © CC

	GD2.0	FN6.0	VF8.0	NM9.4

		GD2.0	FN6.0	VF8.0	NM9.4
		8	24	45	65
100		10	30	55	85

NOTE: **Mart Bailey** art on "The Face" No. 1-104. **Guardineer** a-5. Sparky Watts by **Boody Rogers**-No. 14-42, 77-104, (by others No. 43-76). Others than Tony Trent wear "The Face" mask in No. 46-63, 93. Skyman by Ogden Whitney-No. 1, 2, 4, 12-37, 49, 70-101. Skyman covers-No. 1, 3, 7-12, 14, 16, 20, 27, 89, 95, 100.

BIG TEX
Toby Press: June, 1953

	GD2.0	FN6.0	VF8.0	NM9.4
1-Contains (3) John Wayne stories-r with name changed to Big Tex				
	10	30	55	80

BIG-3
Fox Features Syndicate: Fall, 1940 - No. 7, Jan, 1942

	GD2.0	FN6.0	VF8.0	NM9.4
1-Blue Beetle, The Flame, & Samson begin	218	654	1364	2400
2	91	273	568	1000
3-5	64	192	398	700
6,7: 6-Last Samson. 7-V-Man app.	52	157	314	550

BIG TOP COMICS, THE (TV's Great Circus Show)
Toby Press: 1951 - No. 2, 1951 (No month)

	GD2.0	FN6.0	VF8.0	NM9.4
1,2	9	27	49	70

BIG TOWN (Radio/TV) (Also see Movie Comics, 1946)
National Periodical Publ: Jan, 1951 - No. 50, Mar-Apr, 1958 (No. 1-9: 52pgs.)

	GD2.0	FN6.0	VF8.0	NM9.4
1-Dan Barry-a begins	64	192	398	700
2	36	108	191	330
3-10	21	63	110	185
11-20	15	45	77	130
21-31: Last pre-code (1-2/55)	12	36	61	100
32-50	9	27	49	70

BIG VALLEY, THE (TV)
Dell Publishing Co.: June, 1966 - No. 5, Oct, 1967; No. 6, Oct, 1969

	GD2.0	FN6.0	VF8.0	NM9.4
1: Photo-c #1-5	5	15	35	60
2-6: 6-Reprints #1	3	10	23	35

BIKER MICE FROM MARS (TV)
Marvel Comics: Nov, 1993 - No. 3, Jan, 1994 ($1.50, limited series)

1-3: 1-Intro Vinnie, Modo & Throttle. 2-Origin				3.00

BILL & TED'S BOGUS JOURNEY
Marvel Comics: Sept, 1991 ($2.95, squarebound, 84 pgs.)

1-Adapts movie sequel				3.00

BILL & TED'S EXCELLENT COMIC BOOK (Movie)
Marvel Comics: Dec, 1991 - No. 12, 1992 ($1.00/$1.25)

1-12: 3-Begin $1.25-c				2.50

BILL BARNES COMICS (...America's Air Ace Comics No. 2 on)
(Becomes Air Ace Comics V2#1 on; also see Shadow Comics)
Street & Smith Publications: Oct, 1940(No. month given) - No. 12, Oct, 1943

	GD2.0	FN6.0	VF8.0	NM9.4
1-23-comics; Rocket Rooney begins	82	246	511	900
2-Barnes as The Phantom Flyer app.; Tuska-a	43	129	257	450
3-5	36	108	191	330
6-12	31	93	165	285

BILL BATTLE, THE ONE MAN ARMY (Also see Master Comics No. 133)
Fawcett Publications: Oct, 1952 - No. 4, Apr, 1953 (All photo-c)

	GD2.0	FN6.0	VF8.0	NM9.4
1	13	39	66	110
2	8	24	42	60
3,4	7	21	36	50

BILL BLACK'S FUN COMICS
Paragon #1-3/Americomics #4: Dec, 1982 - No. 4, Mar, 1983 ($1.75/$2.00, Baxter paper)(1st AC comic)

	GD2.0	FN6.0	VF8.0	NM9.4
1-(B&W fanzine; 7x8-1/2"; low print) Intro. Capt. Paragon & Commando D	2	6	11	15
2-4: 2,3-(B&W fanzines; 8-1/2x11"). 3-Kirby-a. 4-($2.00, color)-Origin Nightfall (formerly Phantom Lady); Nightveil app.; Kirby-a				6.00

BILL BOYD WESTERN (Movie star; see Hopalong Cassidy & Western Hero)
Fawcett Publ: Feb, 1950 - No. 23, June, 1952 (1-3,7,11,14-on: 36 pgs.)

	GD2.0	FN6.0	VF8.0	NM9.4
1-Bill Boyd & his horse Midnite begin; photo front/back-c				
	50	150	300	525

	GD2.0	FN6.0	VF8.0	NM9.4
2-Painted-c	29	87	153	265
3-Photo-c begin, end #23; last photo back-c	21	64	110	190
4-6(52 pgs.)	17	51	88	150
7,11(36 pgs.)	14	42	72	120
8-10,12,13(52 pgs.)	14	42	72	125
14-22	13	39	66	110
23-Last issue	14	42	72	120

BILL BUMLIN (See Treasury of Comics No. 3)
BILL ELLIOTT (See Wild Bill Elliott)

BILLI 99
Dark Horse Comics: Sept, 1991 - No. 4, 1991 ($3.50, B&W, lim. series, 52 pgs.)

1-4: Tim Sale-c/a				3.50

BILL STERN'S SPORTS BOOK
Ziff-Davis Publ. Co.(Approved Comics): Spring-Sum, 1951 - V2#2, Win, 1952

	GD2.0	FN6.0	VF8.0	NM9.4
V1#10-(1951)	21	63	110	185
2-(Sum/52; reg. size)	16	48	83	140
V2#2-(1952, 96 pgs.)-Krigstein, Kinstler-a	21	63	110	190

BILL THE BULL: ONE SHOT, ONE BOURBON, ONE BEER
Boneyard Press: Dec, 1994 ($2.95, B&W, mature)

1				3.00

BILL THE CLOWN
Slave Labor Graphics: Feb, 1992 ($2.50, one-shot)

1 ,1-(2nd printing, 4/93, $2.95)				3.00
Comedy Isn't Pretty 1 (11/92, $2.50)				3.00
Death & Clown White 1 (9/93, $2.95)				3.00

BILLY AND BUGGY BEAR (See Animal Fun)
I.W. Enterprises/Super: 1958; 1964

	GD2.0	FN6.0	VF8.0	NM9.4
I.W. Reprint #1, #7('58)-All Surprise Comics #?(Same issue-r for both)				
	2	6	11	15
Super Reprint #10(1964)	2	6	9	12

BILLY BUCKSKIN WESTERN (2-Gun Western No. 4)
Atlas Comics (IMC No. 1/MgPC No. 2,3): Nov, 1955 - No. 3, Mar, 1956

	GD2.0	FN6.0	VF8.0	NM9.4
1-Mort Drucker-a; Maneely-c/a	16	48	83	140
2-Mort Drucker-a	10	30	55	85
3-Williamson, Drucker-a	12	36	61	100

BILLY BUNNY (Black Cobra No. 6 on)
Excellent Publications: Feb-Mar, 1954 - No. 5, Oct-Nov, 1954

	GD2.0	FN6.0	VF8.0	NM9.4
1	8	24	42	60
2	5	15	23	30
3-5	4	12	19	25

BILLY BUNNY'S CHRISTMAS FROLICS
Farrell Publications: 1952 (25¢ Giant, 100 pgs.)

	GD2.0	FN6.0	VF8.0	NM9.4
1	20	60	105	175

BILLY COLE
Cult Press: May, 1994 - No. 4, Aug, 1994 ($2.75, B&W, limited series)

1-4				2.75

BILLY MAKE BELIEVE
United Features Syndicate: No. 14, 1939

	GD2.0	FN6.0	VF8.0	NM9.4
Single Series 14	31	93	165	285

BILLY NGUYEN, PRIVATE EYE
Caliber Press: V2#1, 1990 ($2.50)

V2#1				2.50

BILLY THE KID (Formerly The Masked Raider; also see Doc Savage Comics & Return of the Outlaw)
No. 9, Nov, 1957 - No. 121, Dec, 1976; No. 122, Sept, 1977 - No. 123,
Charlton Publ. Co.: Oct, 1977; No. 124, Feb, 1978 - No. 153, Mar, 1983

	GD2.0	FN6.0	VF8.0	NM9.4
9	10	30	55	80
10,12,14,17-19: 12-2 pg Check-sty	7	21	36	50
11-(68 pgs.)-Origin & 1st app. The Ghost Train	9	27	49	70
13-Williamson/Torres-a	8	24	42	60
15-Origin; 2 pgs. Williamson-a	8	24	42	60
16-Williamson-a, 2 pgs.	7	21	38	55

Billy West #6 © STD

Birds of Prey #23 © DC

Bishop The Last X-Man #13 © MAR

BI

	GD2.0	FN6.0	VF8.0	NM9.4

	GD2.0	FN6.0	VF8.0	NM9.4
20-26-Severin-a(3-4 each)	8	24	42	60
27-30: 30-Masked Rider app.	3	9	20	30
31-40	2	6	15	22
41-60	2	6	12	18
61-65	2	6	9	12
66-Bounty Hunter series begins.	2	6	11	15
67-80: Bounty Hunter series; not in #79,82,84-86	2	6	9	12
81-90: 87-Last Bounty Hunter	1	3	6	8

91-123: 110-Dr. Young of Boothill app. 111-Origin The Ghost Train.

117-Gunsmith & Co., The Cheyenne Kid app.				6.00
124(2/78)-153				4.00
Modern Comics 109 (1977 reprint)				3.00

NOTE: *Boyette* a-91-110. *Kim* a-73. *Morsi* a-12,14. *Sattler* a-118-123. *Severin* a(r)-121-129, 134; c-23, 25. *Sutton* a-111.

BILLY THE KID ADVENTURE MAGAZINE
Toby Press: Oct, 1950 - No. 29, 1955

1-Williamson/Frazetta-a (2 pgs) r/from John Wayne Adventure Comics #2;				
photo-c	31	93	165	285
2-Photo-c	10	30	55	85
3-Williamson/Frazetta "The Claws of Death", 4 pgs. plus Williamson art				
	35	105	185	320
4,5,7,8,10: 4,7-Photo-c	8	24	42	60
6-Frazetta assist on "Nightmare"; photo-c	15	45	77	130
9-Kurtzman Pot-Shot Pete; photo-c	12	36	61	100
11,12,15-20: 11-Photo-c	7	21	36	50
13-Kurtzman-r/John Wayne #12 (Genius)	8	24	42	60
14-Williamson/Frazetta: r-of #1 (2 pgs.)	10	30	55	80
21,23-29	6	18	29	40
22-Williamson/Frazetta-r(1pg.)/#1; photo-c	7	21	36	50

BILLY THE KID AND OSCAR (Also see Fawcett's Funny Animals)
Fawcett Publications: Winter, 1945 - No. 3, Summer, 1946 (Funny animal)

1	15	45	77	130
2,3	10	30	55	80

BILLY WEST (Bill West No. 9,10)
Standard Comics (Visual Editions): 1949-No. 9, Feb, 1951; No. 10, Feb, 1952

1	12	36	61	100
2	7	21	36	50
3-6,9,10	5	15	25	35
7,8-Schomburg-c	6	18	32	45

NOTE: *Celardo* a-1-6, 9; c-1-3. *Moreira* a-3. *Roussos* a-2.

BING CROSBY (See Feature Films)

BINGO (...Comics) (H. C. Blackerby)
Howard Publ.: 1945 (Reprints National material)

1-L. B. Cole opium-c	35	105	185	320

BINGO, THE MONKEY DOODLE BOY
St. John Publishing Co.: Aug, 1951; Oct, 1953

1(8/51)-By Eric Peters	6	18	32	45
1(10/53)	5	15	23	30

BINKY (Formerly Leave It to...)
National Periodical Publ./DC Comics: No. 72, 4-5/70 - No. 81, 10-11/71; No. 82, Summer/77

72-76	2	6	13	20

77-79: (68pgs.). 77-Bobby Sherman 1pg. story w/photo. 78-1 pg. sty on Barry

Williams of Brady Bunch. 79-Osmonds 1pg. story	4	12	26	40
80,81 (52pgs.)-Sweat Pain story	3	9	20	30
82 (1977, one-shot)	3	9	20	30

BINKY'S BUDDIES
National Periodical Publications: Jan-Feb, 1969 - No. 12, Nov-Dec, 1970

1	4	12	29	45
2-12: 3-Last 12¢ issue	2	6	13	20

BIONEERS
Mirage Publishing: Aug, 1994 ($2.75)

1-w/bound-in trading card				2.75

BIONIC WOMAN, THE (TV)
Charlton Publications: Oct, 1977 - No. 5, June, 1978

1	2	6	11	15
2-5	1	3	6	8

BIRDS OF PREY (Also see Black Canary/Oracle: Birds of Prey)
DC Comics: Jan, 1999 - Present ($1.99/$2.50)

1-Dixon-s/Land-c/a				4.00
2-38: 6-Nightwing-c/app. 15-Guice-a begins. 23-Grodd-c/app. 26-Bane				2.50
TPB (1999, $17.95) r/ previous series and one-shots				18.00

BIRDS OF PREY: BATGIRL
DC Comics: Feb, 1998 ($2.95, one-shot)

1-Dixon-s/Frank-c				4.00

BIRDS OF PREY: MANHUNT
DC Comics: Sept, 1996 - No. 4, Dec, 1996 ($1.95, limited series)

1-4: Features Black Canary, Oracle, Huntress, & Catwoman; Chuck Dixon				
scripts; Gary Frank-c on all. 1-Catwoman cameo only				5.00

NOTE: *Gary Frank* c-1-4. *Matt Haley* a-1-4p. *Wade Von Grawbadger* a-1i.

BIRDS OF PREY: REVOLUTION
DC Comics: 1997 ($2.95, one-shot)

1-Frank-c/Dixon-s				4.00

BIRDS OF PREY: THE RAVENS
DC Comics: June,1998 ($1.95, one-shot)

1-Dixon-s; Girlfrenzy issue				3.00

BIRDS OF PREY: WOLVES
DC Comics: Oct, 1997 ($2.95, one-shot)

1-Dixon-s/Giordano & Faucher-a				4.00

BIRTH CAUL, THE
Eddie Campbell Comics: 1999 ($5.95, B&W, one-shot)

1-Alan Moore-s/Eddie Campbell-a				6.00

BIRTH OF THE DEFIANT UNIVERSE, THE
Defiant Comics: May, 1993

nn-contains promotional artwork & text; limited print run of 1000 copies.

	1	4	7	10

BISHOP (See Uncanny X-Men & X-Men)
Marvel Comics: Dec, 1994 - No.4, Mar, 1995 ($2.95, limited series)

1-4: Foil-c; Shard & Mountjoy in all. 1-Storm app.				3.00

BISHOP THE LAST X-MAN
Marvel Comics: Oct, 1999 - No. 16, Jan, 2001 ($2.99/$1.99/$2.25)

1-($2.99)-Jeanty-a				3.50
2-8-($1.99): 2-Two covers				2.50
9-11,13-16: 9-Begin $2.25-c. 15-Maximum Security x-over; Xavier app.				2.50
12-($2.99)				3.00

BISHOP: XAVIER SECURITY ENFORCER
Marvel Comics: Jan, 1998 - No.3, Mar, 1998 ($2.50, limited series)

1-3: Ostrander-s				3.00

BIZARRE ADVENTURES (Formerly Marvel Preview)
Marvel Comics Group: No. 25, 3/81 - No. 34, 2/83 (#25-33: Magazine-$1.50)

25,26: 25-Lethal Ladies. 26-King Kull; Bolton-a	1	3	6	8
27,28: 27-Phoenix, Iceman & Nightcrawler app. 28-The Unlikely Heroes;				
Elektra by Miller; Neal Adams-a	1	4	7	10
29,30,32,33: 29-Stephen King's Lawnmower Man. 30-Tomorrow; 1st app.				
Silhouette. 32-Gods; Thor-c/s. 33-Horror; Dracula app.; photo-c	1	3	5	7
31-After The Violence Stops; new Hangman story; Miller-a				
	1	3	6	9
34 ($2.00, Baxter paper, comic size)-Son of Santa; Christmas special; Howard				
the Duck by Paul Smith				6.00

NOTE: *Alcala* a-27i. *Austin* a-25i, 28i. *Bolton* a-26, 32. *J. Buscema* a-27p, 29, 30p; c-26. *Byrne* a-31 (2 pg.). *Golden* a-25p, 28p. *Perez* a-27p. *Rogers* a-25p. *Simonson* a-29; c-29. *Paul Smith* a-34.

BIZARRO COMICS!
DC Comics: 2001 ($29.95, hardcover, one-shot)

nn-Short stories by various; includes "Superman's Babysitter" by Kyle Baker				
from Elseworlds 80-Page Giant recalled by DC; Groening-c				30.00

Black Cat Comics #1 © HARV

Black Cat Mystery #45 © HARV

Black Diamond Western #14 © LEV

	GD2.0	FN6.0	VF8.0	NM9.4

BLACK AND WHITE (See Large Feature Comic, Series I)
BLACK & WHITE (Also see Codename: Black & White)
Image Comics (Extreme): Oct,1994 - No. 3, Jan,1995 ($1.95, limited series)
1-3: Thibert-c/story 2.25
BLACK & WHITE MAGIC
Innovation Publishing: 1991 ($2.95, 98 pgs., B&W w/30 pgs. color, square-bound)
1-Contains rebound comics w/covers removed; contents may vary ... 3.00
BLACK AXE
Marvel Comics (UK): Apr, 1993 - No. 7, Oct, 1993 ($1.75)
1-4: 1-Romita Jr.-c. 2-Sunfire-c/s 3.00
5-7: 5-Janson-c; Black Panther app. 6,7-Black Panther-c/s 3.00
BLACKBALL COMICS
Blackball Comics: Mar, 1994 ($3.00)
1-Trencher-c/story by Giffen; John Pain by O'Neill 3.00
BLACKBEARD'S GHOST (See Movie Comics)
BLACK BEAUTY (See Son of Black Beauty)
Dell Publishing Co.: No. 440, Dec, 1952

Four Color 440	4	12	25	38

BLACK CANARY (See All Star Comics #38, Flash Comics #86, Justice League of America #75 & World's Finest #244)
DC Comics: Nov, 1991 - No. 4, Feb, 1992 ($1.75, limited series)
1-4 .... 2.50
BLACK CANARY
DC Comics: Jan, 1993 - No. 12, Dec, 1993 ($1.75)
1-7 .... 2.50
8-12: 8-The Ray-c/story. 9,10-Huntress-c/story 3.00
BLACK CANARY/ORACLE: BIRDS OF PREY (Also see Showcase '96 #3)
DC Comics: 1996 ($3.95, one-shot)

1-Chuck Dixon scripts & Gary Frank-c/a.	1	3	5	7

BLACK CAT COMICS (...Western #16-19; ...Mystery #30 on)
(See All-New #7,9, The Original Black Cat, Pocket & Speed Comics)
Harvey Publications (Home Comics): June-July, 1946 - No. 29, June, 1951

1-Kubert-a; Joe Simon c-1-3	68	204	426	750
2-Kubert-a	39	117	208	360
3,4: 4-The Red Demons begin (The Demon #4 & 5)				
	31	93	165	285
5,6,7: 5,6-The Scarlet Arrow app. in ea. by Powell; S&K-a in both. 6-Origin Red Demon. 7-Vagabond Prince by S&K plus 1 more story				
	39	117	208	360
8-S&K-a; Kerry Drake begins, ends #13	34	102	179	310
9-Origin Stuntman (#Stuntman #1)	39	117	208	360
10-20: 14,15,17-Mary Worth app. plus Invisible Scarlet O'Neil #15,20,24				
	26	78	136	235
21-26	21	63	110	185
27,28: 27-Used in SOTI, pg. 193; X-Mas-c; 2 pg. John Wayne story. 28-Intro. Kit, Black Cat's new sidekick	22	66	116	200
29-Black Cat bondage-c; Black Cat stories	22	66	116	195

BLACK CAT MYSTERY (Formerly Black Cat; ...Western #54;
...Western #55,56;...Mystery #57; ...Mystic #58-62; Black Cat #63-65)
Harvey Publications: No. 30, Aug, 1951 - No. 65, Apr, 1963

30-Black Cat on cover only	29	87	156	270
31,32,34,37,38,40	22	66	116	200
33-Used in POP, pg. 89; electrocution-c	24	72	127	220
35-Atomic disaster cover/story	26	78	139	240
36,39-Used in SOTI: #36-Pgs. 270,271; #39-Pgs. 386-388				
	27	81	145	250
41-43	22	66	116	200
44-Eyes, ears, tongue cut out; Nostrand-a	24	72	127	215
45-Classic "Colorama" by Powell; Nostrand-a	39	117	208	360
46-49,51-Nostrand-a in all	23	69	121	210
50-Check-a; classic Warren Kremer-c showing a man's face & hands burning away	64	192	398	700

52,53 (r/#34 & 35)	15	45	77	130
54-Two Black Cat stories (2/55, last pre-code)	19	57	99	165
55,56-Black Cat app.	15	45	77	130
57(7/56)-Kirby-c	14	42	72	125
58-60-Kirby-a(4). 58,59-Kirby-c. 60,61-Simon-c	19	57	99	170
61-Nostrand-a; "Colorama" r/#45	19	57	99	165
62 (3/58)-E.C. story swipe	14	42	72	120
63-65: Giants(10/62,1/63, 4/63); Reprints; Black Cat app. 63-origin Black Kitten.				
65-1 pg. Powell	18	54	94	160

NOTE: *Kremer* a-37, 39, 43; c-36, 37, 47. *Meskin* a-51. *Palais* a-30, 31(2), 32(2), 33-35, 37-40. *Powell* a-32-35, 36(2), 40, 41, 43-53, 57. *Simon* c-63-65. *Sparling* a-44. Bondage c-32, 34, 43.

BLACK COBRA (Bride's Diary No. 4 on) (See Captain Flight #8)
Ajax/Farrell Publications(Excellent Publ.): No. 1, 10-11/54; No. 6(No. 2), 12-1/54-55; No. 3, 2-3/55

1-Re-intro Black Cobra & The Cobra Kid (costumed heroes)				
	33	99	174	300
6(#2)-Formerly Billy Bunny	19	57	99	165
3-(Pre-code)-Torpedoman app.	17	51	88	150

BLACK CONDOR (Also see Crack Comics, Freedom Fighters & Showcase '94 #10,11)
DC Comics: June, 1992 - No. 12, May, 1993 ($1.25)
1-8-Heath-c 2.50
9-12: 9,10,12-Heath-c. 9,10-The Ray app. 12-Batman-c/app. 3.00
BLACK CROSS SPECIAL (See Dark Horse Presents)
Dark Horse Comics: Jan, 1988 ($1.75, B&W, one-shot)(Reprints & new-a)
1-1st printing 3.00
1-(2nd printing) has 2 pgs. new-a 2.50
BLACK CROSS: DIRTY WORK (See Dark Horse Presents)
Dark Horse Comics: Apr, 1997 ($2.95, one-shot)
1-Chris Warner-c/s/a 3.00
BLACK DIAMOND
Americomics: May, 1983 - No. 5, 1984 (no month)($2.00-$1.75, Baxter paper)
1-3-Movie adapt.; 1-Colt back-up begins 4.00
4,5 .... 3.00
NOTE: *Bill Black* a-1i; c-1. *Gulacy* c-2-5. *Sybil Danning* photo back-c-1.
BLACK DIAMOND WESTERN (Formerly Desperado No. 1-8)
Lev Gleason Publ.: No. 9, Mar, 1949 - No. 60, Feb, 1956 (No. 9-28: 52 pgs.)

9-Black Diamond & his horse Reliapon begin; origin & 1st app. Black Diamond	21	63	110	190
10	11	33	55	90
11-15	8	24	45	65
16-28(11/49-11/51)-Wolverton's Bing Bang Buster	11	33	55	95
29-40: 31-One pg. Frazetta anti-drug ad	6	18	32	45
41-50,53-59	5	15	25	35
51-3-D effect-c/story	14	42	72	120
52-3-D effect story	13	39	66	110
60-Last issue	6	18	32	45

NOTE: *Biro* c-9-35?. *Fass* a-58, c-54-56, 58. *Guardineer* a-9, 15, 18. *Kida* a-9. *Maurer* a-10. *Ed Moore* a-16. *Morisi* a-55. *Tuska* a-10, 48.

BLACK DRAGON, THE
Marvel Comics (Epic Comics): 5/85 - No. 6, 10/85 (Baxter paper, mature)
1-6: 1-Chris Claremont story & John Bolton painted-c/a in all ... 3.00
BLACK DRAGON, THE
Dark Horse Comics: Apr, 1996 ($17.95, B&W, trade paperback)
nn-Reprints Epic Comics limited series; intro by Anne McCaffrey .. 18.00
BLACK FLAG
Maximum Press: Jan, 1995 - No.4, 1995; No. 0, July, 1995 ($2.50, B&W)
(No. 0 in color)
Preview Edition (6/94, $1.95, B&W)-Fraga/McFarlane-c 3.00
0-4: 0-(7/95)-Liefeld/Fraga-c. 1-(1/95) 3.00
1-Variant cover 5.00
2,4-Variant covers 3.00
NOTE: *Fraga* a-0-4, Preview Edition; c-1-4. *Liefeld/Fraga* c-0. *McFarlane/Fraga* c-Preview Edition.
BLACK FURY (Becomes Wild West No. 58) (See Blue Bird)

Blackhawk #19 © QUA

Blackhawk #248 © DC

The Black Knight #2 © MAR

	GD2.0	FN6.0	VF8.0	NM9.4

Charlton Comics Group: May, 1955 - No. 57, Mar-Apr, 1966 (Horse stories)

	GD2.0	FN6.0	VF8.0	NM9.4
1	7	21	38	55
2	5	14	21	28
3-10	4	11	17	22
11-15,19,20	3	8	12	15
16-18-Ditko-a	7	21	38	55
21-30	2	6	9	12
31-57	1	3	6	9

BLACK GOLIATH (See Avengers #32-35,41,54)
Marvel Comics Group: Feb, 1976 - No. 5, Nov, 1976

1-Tuska-a(p) thru #3	1	4	7	10
2-5: 2-4-(Regular 25¢ editions). 4-Kirby-c/Buckler-a			6.00	
2-4-(30¢-c variants, limited distribution)(4,6,8/76)	1	3	6	8

BLACKHAWK (Formerly Uncle Sam 1-8; see Military & Modern Comics)
Comic Magazines(Quality)No. 9-107(12/56); **National Periodical Publications**No. 108(1/57)-250; **DC Comics** No. 251 = No. 9, Winter, 1944 - No. 243, 10-11/68; No. 244, 1-2/76 - No. 250, 1-2/77; No. 251, 10/82 - No. 273, 11/84

9 (1944)	333	1000	2083	4000
10 (1946)	116	348	725	1275
11-15: 14-Ward-a; 13,14-Fear app.	77	231	483	850
16-20: 20-Ward Blackhawk	61	183	381	675
21-30 (1950)	45	135	270	475
31-40: 31-Chop Chop by Jack Cole	39	117	208	360
41-49,51-60: 42-Robot-c	31	93	165	285
50-1st Killer Shark; origin in text	34	102	179	310
61,62: 61-Used in POP, pg. 91. 62-Used in POP, pg. 92 & color illo				
	27	81	142	245
63-70,72-80: 65-H-Bomb explosion panel. 66-B&W & color illos POP. 70-Return of Killer Shark; atomic explosion panel. 75-Intro. Blackie the Hawk				
	25	75	130	225
71-Origin retold; flying saucer-c; A-Bomb panels	29	87	153	265
81-86: Last precode (3/55)	23	69	121	210
87-92,94-99,101-107: 91-Robot-c. 105-1st S.A.	19	57	99	165
93-Origin in text	19	57	99	170
100	23	69	121	210
108-1st DC issue (1/57); re-intro. Blackie, the Hawk, their mascot; not in #115				
	41	123	306	550
109-117: 117-(10/57)-Mr. Freeze app.	16	48	112	200
118-(11/57)-Frazetta-r/Jimmy Wakely #4 (3 pgs.)	17	51	118	210
119-130 (11/58): 120-Robot-c	11	33	80	135
131-140 (9/59): 133-Intro. Lady Blackhawk	9	27	63	105
141-150,152-163,165,166: 141-Cat-Man returns-c/s. 143-Kurtzman-r/Jimmy Wakely #4. 150-(7/60)-King Condor returns. 166-Last 10¢ issue				
	6	18	45	75
151-Lady Blackhawk receives & loses super powers	7	21	50	80
164-Origin retold	7	21	53	85
167-180	4	12	29	45
181-190	3	9	21	32
191-196,199,201,202,204-210: 196-Combat Diary series begins.				
	3	9	17	25
197,198,200: 197-New look for Blackhawks. 198-Origin retold				
	3	9	21	32
203-Origin Chop Chop (12/64)	3	10	23	35
211,215,229-243(1968): 230-Blackhawks become superheroes; JLA cameo				
242-Return to old costumes	2	6	13	20
228-Batman, Green Lantern, Superman, The Flash cameos.				
	3	9	17	25
244 ('76) -250: 250-Chuck dies			6.00	
251-273: 251-Origin retold; Black Knights return. 252-Intro Domino. 253-Part origin Hendrickson. 258-Blackhawk's Island destroyed. 259-Part origin Chop Chop. 265-273 (75¢ cover price)			3.00	

NOTE: *Chaykin* a-260; c-257-260, 262. *Crandall* a-10, 11, 13, 16?, 18-20, 22-26, 30-33, 35p, 36(2), 37, 38?, 39-44, 46-50, 52-58, 60, 63, 64, 66, 67; c-14-20, 22-63(most except #28-33, 36, 37, 39). *Evans* a-244, 245,246i, 248-250. *G. Kane* c-263, 264. *Kubert* a-244, 245. *Newton* a-266p. *Severin* a-257. *Spiegle* a-261-267, 269-273; c-265-272. *Toth* a-260p. *Ward* a-16-27(Chop Chop, 8pgs. ea.); penciled stories-No. 17-63(approx.). *Wildey* a-268. Chop Chop solo stories in #10-95?

BLACKHAWK

DC Comics: Mar, 1988 - No. 3, May, 1988 ($2.95, limited series, mature)

1-3-Chaykin painted-c/a/scripts				4.00

BLACKHAWK (Also see Action Comics #601)
DC Comics: Mar, 1989 - No. 16, Aug, 1990 ($1.50, mature)

1				3.50
2-6,8-16: 16-Crandall-c swipe				2.50
7-($2.50, 52 pgs.)-Story-r/Military #1				3.00
Annual 1 (1989, $2.95, 68 pgs.)-Recaps origin of Blackhawk, Lady Blackhawk, and others				3.50
Special 1 (1992, $3.50, 68 pgs.)-Mature readers				3.50

BLACKHAWK INDIAN TOMAHAWK WAR, THE
Avon Periodicals: 1951 (Also see Fighting Indians of the Wild West)

nn-Kinstler-c; Kit West story	20	60	105	175

BLACK HEART ASSASSIN
Iguana Comics: Jan, 1994 ($2.95)

1				3.00

BLACK HOLE (See Walt Disney Showcase #54) (Disney, movie)
Whitman Publishing Co.: Mar, 1980 - No. 4, Sept, 1980

11295(#1) (1979, Golden, $1.50-c, 52 pgs., graphic novel; 8 1/2x11")				
Photo-c; Spiegle-a	2	6	13	20
1-4: 1,2-Movie adaptation. 2-4-Spiegle-a. 3-McWilliams-a; photo-c.				
3,4-New stories	1	3	6	9

BLACK HOOD, THE (See Blue Ribbon, Flyman & Mighty Comics)
Red Circle Comics (Archie): June, 1983 - No. 3, Oct, 1983 (Mandell paper)

1-Morrow, McWilliams, Wildey-a; Toth-c				6.00
2,3: The Fox by Toth-c/a; Boyette-a. 3-Morrow-a; Toth wraparound-c				4.00
(Also see Archie's Super-Hero Special Digest #2)				

BLACK HOOD
DC Comics (Impact Comics): Dec, 1991 - No. 12, Dec, 1992 ($1.00)

1				3.50
2-12: 11-Intro The Fox. 12-Origin Black Hood				2.50
Annual 1 (1992, $2.50, 68 pgs.)-w/Trading card				3.00

BLACK HOOD COMICS (Formerly Hangman #2-8; Laugh Comics #20 on; also see Black Swan, Jackpot, Roly Poly & Top-Notch #9)
MLJ Magazines: No. 9, Wint., 1943-44 - No. 19, Sum., 1946 (on radio in 1943)

9-The Hangman & The Boy Buddies cont'd	105	315	656	1150
10-Hangman & Dusty, the Boy Detective app.	60	180	375	660
11-Dusty app.; no Hangman	46	138	276	485
12-18: 15-Kinstler blood-c. 17-Hal Foster swipe from Prince Valiant; 1st issue with "An Archie Magazine" on-c	40	120	240	420
19-I.D. exposed; last issue	52	157	314	550

NOTE: *Hangman* by *Fuje* in 9, 10. *Kinstler* a-15, c-14-16.

BLACK JACK (Rocky Lane's...; formerly Jim Bowie)
Charlton Comics: No. 20, Nov, 1957 - No. 30, Nov, 1959

20	9	27	49	70
21,27,29,30	6	18	29	40
22,23: 22-(68 pgs.). 23-Williamson/Torres-a	8	24	42	60
24-26,28-Ditko-a	10	30	55	80

BLACK KNIGHT, THE
Toby Press: May, 1953; 1963

1-Bondage-c	25	75	130	225
Super Reprint No. 11 (1963)-Reprints 1953 issue	3	9	19	28

BLACK KNIGHT, THE (Also see The Avengers #48, Marvel Super Heroes & Tales To Astonish #52)
Atlas Comics (MgPC): May, 1955 - No. 5, April, 1956

1-Origin Crusader; Maneely-c/a	86	258	540	950
2-Maneely-c/a(4)	60	180	375	660
3-5: 4-Maneely-c. 5-Maneely-c, Shores-a	48	145	288	510

BLACK KNIGHT (Also see Avengers & Ultraforce)
Marvel Comics: June, 1990 - No. 4, Sept, 1990 ($1.50, limited series)

1-4: 1-Original Black Knight returns. 3,4-Dr. Strange app.				2.50

NOTE: *Buckler* c-1-4p

BLACK KNIGHT: EXODUS

Black Lightning #1 © DC

Black Magic #4 © Headline

Black Panther V2 #3 © MAR

GD2.0 FN6.0 VF8.0 NM9.4   GD2.0 FN6.0 VF8.0 NM9.

Marvel Comics: Dec, 1996 ($2.50, one-shot)

1-Raab-s; Apocalypse-c/app. 2.50

BLACK LAMB, THE
DC Comics (Helix): Nov, 1996 - No, 6, Apr, 1997 ($2.50, limited series)

1-6: Tim Truman-c/a/scripts 2.50

BLACK LIGHTNING (See The Brave & The Bold, Cancelled Comic Cavalcade, DC Comics Presents #16, Detective #490 and World's Finest #257)
National Periodical Publ./DC Comics: Apr, 1977 - No. 11, Sept-Oct, 1978

1-Origin Black Lightning	1	4	7	10
2,3,6-10				5.00
4,5-Superman-c/s. 4-Intro Cyclotronic Man				6.00
11-The Ray new solo story	1	3	6	8

NOTE: *Buckler* c-1-3p, 6-11p. #11 is 44 pgs.

BLACK LIGHTNING (2nd series)
DC Comics: Feb, 1995 - No. 13, Feb, 1996 ($1.95/$2.25)

1-5-Tony Isabella scripts, ends #8 .... 3.00
6-13: 6-Begin $2.25-c. 13-Batman-c/app. 3.00

BLACK MAGIC (...Magazine) (Becomes Cool Cat V8#6 on)
Crestwood Publ. V1#1-4, V6#1-V7#5/Headline V1#5-V5#3,V7#6-V8#5:
10-11/50 - V4#1, 6-7/53: V4#2, 9-10/53 - V5#3, 11-12/54: V6#1, 9-10/57 - V7#2, 11-12/58: V7#3, 7-8/60 - V8#5, 11-12/61
(V1#1-5, 52pgs.; V1#6-V3#3, 44pgs.)

V1#1-S&K-a, 10 pgs.; Meskin-a(2)	109	327	682	1200
2-S&K-a, 17 pgs.; Meskin-a	52	157	314	550
3-6(8-9/51)-S&K, Roussos, Meskin-a	45	135	270	475
V2#1(10-11/51),4,5,7(#13),9(#15),12(#18)-S&K-a	33	99	174	300
2,3,6,8,10,11(#17)	25	75	130	225
V3#1(#19, 12/52) - 6(#24, 5/53)-S&K-a	26	78	139	240
V4#1(#25, 6-7/53), 2(#26, 9-10/53)-S&K-a(3-4)	27	81	145	250
3(#27, 11-12/53)-S&K-a; Ditko-a (2nd published-a); also see Captain 3-D, Daring Love #1, Strange Fantasy #9, & Fantastic Fears (Fant. Fears was 1st drawn, but not 1st publ.)	43	129	257	450
4(#28)-Eyes ripped out/story-S&K, Ditko-a	38	114	203	350
5(#29, 3-4/54)-S&K, Ditko-a	28	84	151	260
6(#30, 5-6/54)-S&K, Powell?-a	22	66	116	200
V5#1(#31, 7-8/54 - 3(#33, 11-12/54)-S&K-a	17	51	88	150
V6#1(#34, 9-10/57), 2(#35, 11-12/57)	10	30	55	80
3(1-2/58) - 6(7-8/58)	10	30	55	80
V7#1(9-10/58) - 3(7-8/60)	10	30	55	80
4(9-10/60)	10	30	55	80
5(11-12/60)-Hitler-c; Torres-a	8	24	60	100
6(1-2/61)-Powell-a(2)	9	27	49	70
V8#1(3-4/61)-Powell-c/a	9	27	49	70
2(5-6/61)-E.C. story swipe/W.F. #22; Ditko, Powell-a				
	10	30	55	80
3(7-8/61)-E.C. story swipe/W.F. #22; Powell-a(2)	10	30	55	80
4(9-10/61)-Powell-a(5)	9	27	49	70
5-E.C. story swipe/W.S.F. #28; Powell-a(3)	10	30	55	80

NOTE: *Bernard Baily* a-V4#6?, V5#3(2), *Grandenetti* a-V2#3, 11. *Kirby* c-V1#1-6, V2#1-12, V3#1-6, V4#1, 2, 4-6, V5#1-3. *McWilliams* a-V3#2l. *Meskin* a-V1#1(2), 2, 3, 4(2), 5(2), 6, V2/1, 2, 3(2), 4(3), 5, 6(2), 7-9, 11, 12, V3#1-5, 6, V5#1(2), 2. *Orlando* a-V6#1, 4, V7#2(2)-c. *Powell* a-V5#1?, *Roussos* a-V1#3-5, 6(2), V2#3(2), 4, 5(2), 6, 8, 9, 10(2), 11, 12p, V3#1(2), 2i, 5, V5#2. *Simon* a-V2#12, V3#2, V7#5? c-V4#3?, V7#3?, 4, 5?, 6?, V8#1-5. *Simon & Kirby* a-V1#1, 2(2), 3-6, V2#1-5, 7, 9, 12, V3#1-6, V4#1(3), 2(4), 3(2), 4(2), 5, 6, V5#1-3; c-V2#1. *Leonard Starr* a-V1#5, 4. *Woodbridge* a-V6#3, 4. *Tuska* a-V6#3, 4.

BLACK MAGIC
National Periodical Publications: Oct-Nov, 1973 - No. 9, Apr-May, 1975

1-S&K reprints	3	9	19	28
2-8-S&K reprints	2	6	11	16
9-S&K reprints	2	6	12	18

BLACK MAGIC
Eclipse International: Apr, 1990 - No. 4, Oct, 1990 ($2.75, B&W, mini-series)

1-($3.50, 68pgs.)-Japanese manga 4.00
2-4 ($2.75, 52 pgs.) 3.00

BLACKMAIL TERROR (See Harvey Comics Library)

BLACK MASK
DC Comics: 1993 - No. 3, 1994 ($4.95, limited series, 52 pgs.)

BLACK OPS
Image Comics (WildStorm): Jan, 1996 - No. 5, May, 1996 ($2.50, lim. series)

1-5 .... 2.50

BLACK ORCHID (See Adventure Comics #428 & Phantom Stranger)
DC Comics: Holiday, 1988-89 - No. 3, 1989 ($3.50, lim. series, prestige format)

Book 1,3: Gaiman scripts & McKean painted-a in all			6.00
Book 2-Arkham Asylum story; Batman app.	1	3	6	8
TPB (1991, $19.95) r/#1-3; new McKean-c			20.00

BLACK ORCHID
DC Comics: Sept, 1993 - No. 22, June, 1995 ($1.95/$2.25)

1-22: Dave McKean-c all issues 2.50
1-Platinum Edition 12.00
Annual 1 (1993, $3.95, 68 pgs.)-Children's Crusade 4.00

BLACKOUTS (See Broadway Hollywood...)

BLACK PANTHER, THE (Also see Avengers #52, Fantastic Four #52, Jungle Action & Marvel Premiere #51-53)
Marvel Comics Group: Jan, 1977 - No. 15, May, 1979

1	2	6	15	22
2-13: 4,5-(Regular 30¢ editions). 8-Origin	1	4	7	10
4,5-(35¢-c variants, limited dist.)(7,9/77)	2	6	13	20
14,15-Avengers x-over. 14-Origin	2	6	9	12

NOTE: *J. Buscema* c-15p. *Kirby* c/a & scripts-1-12. *Layton* c-13i.

BLACK PANTHER
Marvel Comics Group: July, 1988 - No. 4, Oct, 1988 ($1.25)

1-4-Gillis-s/Cowan & Delarosa-a 2.50

BLACK PANTHER (Marvel Knights)
Marvel Comics: Nov. 1998 - Present ($2.50)

1-Texeira-a/c; Priest-s 5.00
1-($6.95) DF edition w/Quesada & Palmiotti-c 7.00
2-4: 2-Two covers by Texeira and Timm. 3-Fantastic Four app. ... 2.50
5-35,37-39: 5-Evans-a. 6-8-Jusko-a. 8-Avengers-c/app. 15-Hulk app. 22-Moon Knight app. 23-Avengers app. 25-Maximum Security x-over. 26-Storm-c/app. 28-Magneto & Sub-Mariner-c/app. 29-WWII flashback meeting w/Captain America. 35-Defenders-c/app. 37-Luke Cage and Falcon-c/app. ... 2.50
36-($3.50, 100 pgs.) 35th Anniversary issue incl. r/1st app. in FF #52 ... 3.50
...: The Client (6/01, $14.95, TPB) r/#1-5 .... 15.00

BLACK PANTHER: PANTHER'S PREY
Marvel Comics: May, 1991 - No. 4, Oct, 1991 ($4.95, squarebound, lim. series, 52 pgs.)

1-4: McGregor-s/Turner-a 5.00

BLACK PEARL, THE
Dark Horse Comics: Sept, 1996 - No. 5, Jan, 1997 ($2.95, limited series)

1-5: Mark Hamill scripts 3.00

BLACK PHANTOM (See Tim Holt #25, 38)
Magazine Enterprises: Nov, 1954 (one-shot) (Female outlaw)

1 (A-1 #122)-The Ghost Rider story plus 3 Black Phantom stories; Headlight-c/a	40	120	214	370

BLACK PHANTOM
AC Comics: 1989 - No. 3, 1990 ($2.50, B&W; #2 color)(Reprints & new-a)

1-3: 1-Ayers-r, Bolle-r/B.P. #1-3-Redmask-r 2.75

BLACK PHANTOM, RETURN OF THE (See Wisco)

BLACK RIDER (Western Winners #1-7; Western Tales of Black Rider #28-31; Gunsmoke Western #32 on)(See All Western Winners, Best Western, Kid Colt, Outlaw Kid, Rex Hart, Two-Gun Kid, Two-Gun Western, Western Gunfighters, Western Winners, & Wild Western)
Marvel/Atlas Comics(CDS No. 8-17/CPS No. 19 on): No. 8, 3/50 - No. 18, 1/52; No. 19, 11/53 - No. 27, 3/55

8 (#1)-Black Rider & his horse Satan begin; 36 pgs; Stan Lee photo-c as Black Rider)	43	129	257	450
9-12-Begin, end #14	24	72	127	220
10-Origin Black Rider	29	87	156	270
11-14: 14-Last 52pgs.	18	54	94	160

Blackstone, The Magician #2 © MAR

Black Terror #20 © BP

Blade: Sins of the Father © MAR

15-19: 19-Two-Gun Kid app. 15 45 77 135
20-Classic-c; Two-Gun Kid app. 17 51 88 150
21-27: 21-23-Two-Gun Kid app. 24,25-Arrowhead app. 26-Kid Colt app.
27-Last issue; last precode. Kid Colt app. The Spider (a villain) burns to
death 14 42 72 120
NOTE: Ayers c-22. Jack Keller a-15, 26, 27. Maneely a-14; c-16, 17, 25, 27. Syd Shores a-19,
21, 22, 23(3), 24(3), 25-27; c-19, 21, 23. Sinnott a-24, 25. Tuska a-12, 19-21.

BLACK RIDER RIDES AGAIN!, THE
Atlas Comics (CPS): Sept, 1957

1-Kirby-a(3); Powell-a; Severin-c 26 78 139 240

BLACK SEPTEMBER (Also see Avengers/Ultraforce, Ultraforce (1st series) #10
& Ultraforce/Avengers)
Malibu Comics (Ultraverse): 1995 ($1.50, one-shot)

Infinity-Intro to the newUltraverse; variant-c exists. 2.25

BLACKSTONE (See Super Magician Comics & Wisco Giveaways)

BLACKSTONE, MASTER MAGICIAN COMICS
Vital Publ./Street & Smith Publ.: Mar-Apr, 1946 - No. 3, July-Aug, 1946

1 30 90 159 275
2,3 20 60 105 175

BLACKSTONE, THE MAGICIAN (...Detective on cover only #3 & 4)
Marvel Comics (CnPC): No. 2, May, 1948 - No. 4, Sept, 1948 (No #1)
Cont'd from E.C. #1?)

2-The Blonde Phantom begins, ends #4 59 177 369 650
3,4: 3-Blonde Phantom by Sekowsky 40 120 220 380

BLACKSTONE, THE MAGICIAN DETECTIVE FIGHTS CRIME
E. C. Comics: Fall, 1947

1-1st app. Happy Houlihans 49 147 294 515

BLACK SUN (X-Men Black Sun on cover)
Marvel Comics: Nov. 2000 - No. 5, Nov, 2000 ($2.99, weekly limited series)

1-(...: X-Men), 2-(...: Storm), 3-(...: Banshee and Sunfire), 4-(...: Colossus and
Nightcrawler), 5-(...: Wolverine and Thunderbird); Claremont-s in all; Evans
interlocking painted covers; Magik returns 3.00

BLACK SWAN COMICS
MLJ Magazines (Pershing Square Publ. Co.): 1945

1-The Black Hood reprints from Black Hood No. 14; Bill Woggon-a;
Suzie app. 24 72 127 215

BLACK TARANTULA (See Feature Presentations No. 5)

BLACK TERROR (See America's Best Comics & Exciting Comics)
Better Publications/Standard: Winter, 1942-43 - No. 27, June, 1949

1-Black Terror, Crime Crusader begin 291 873 1818 3200
2 109 327 682 1200
3 75 225 469 825
4,5 64 192 398 700
6-10: 7-The Ghost app. 55 165 341 600
11-20: 16-The Scarab app. 47 141 286 500
21-Miss Masque app. 51 153 306 540
22-Part Frazetta-a on one Black Terror story 47 141 286 500
23,25-27 43 130 257 450
24-Frazetta-a (1/4 pg.) 44 130 264 460
NOTE: Schomburg (Xela) c-2-27; bondage c-2, 17, 24. Meskin a-27. Moreira a-27.
Robinson/Meskin a-23, 24(3), 25, 26. Roussos/Mayo a-24. Tuska a-26, 27.

BLACK TERROR, THE (Also see Total Eclipse)
Eclipse Comics: Oct, 1989 - No. 3, June, 1990 ($4.95, 52 pgs., squarebound,
limited series)

1-3: Beau Smith & Chuck Dixon scripts; Dan Brereton painted-c/a 5.00

BLACKTHORNE 3-D SERIES
Blackthorne Publishing Co.: May, 1985 - No. 80, 1989 ($2.25/$2.50)

1-Sheena in 3-D #1. D. Stevens-c/retouched-a 6.00
2-10: 2-MerlinRealm in 3-D #1. 3-3-D Heroes #1. Goldyn in 3-D #1. 5-Bizarre
3-D Zone #1. 6-Salimba in 3-D #1. 7-Twisted Tales in 3-D #1. 8-Dick Tracy in
3-D #1. 9-Salimba in 3-D #2. 10-Gumby in 3-D #1 5.00
11-19: 11-Betty Boop in 3-D #1. 12-Hamster Vice in 3-D #1. 13-Little Nemo in
3-D #1. 14-Gumby in 3-D #2. 15-Hamster Vice #6 in 3-D. 16-Laffin' Gas #6
in 3-D. 17-Gumby in 3-D #3. 18-Bullwinkle and Rocky in 3-D #1. 19-The

Flintstones in 3-D #1. 5.00
20,26,35,39,52,62-G.I. Joe in 3-D. 62-G.I. Joe Annual 1 3 6 8
21-24,27-28: 21-Gumby in 3-D #4. 22-The Flintstones in 3-D #2. 23-Laurel &
Hardy in 3-D #1. 24-Bozothe Clown in 3-D #1. 27-Bravestarr in 3-D #1.
28- Gumby in 3-D #5. 5.00
25,29,37-The Transformers in 3-D 1 3 6 8
30-Star Wars in 3-D #1 2 6 11 15
31-34,36,38,40: 31-The California Raisins in 3-D #1. 32-Richie Rich & Casper
in 3-D #1. 33-Gumby in 3-D #6. 34-Laurel & Hardy in 3-D #2. 36-The
Flintstones in 3-D #3. 38-Gumby in 3-D #7. 40-Bravestarr in 3-D #2 5.00
41-46,49,50: 41-Battletech in 3-D #1. 42-The Flintstones in 3-D #4.
43-Underdog in 3-D #1 44-The California Raisins in 3-D #2. 45-Red Heat
in 3-D #1 (movie adapt.). 46-The California Raisins in 3-D #3. 49-Rambo in
3-D #1. 49-Sad Sack in 3-D #1. 50-Bullwinkle For President in 3-D #1 5.00
47,48-Star Wars in 3-D #2,3 2 6 9 12
51,53-60: 51-Kull in 3-D #1. 53-Red Sonja in 3-D #1. 54-Bozo in 3-D #2.
55-Waxwork in 3-D #1 (movie adapt.). 56. 57-Casper in 3-D #1. 58-Baby
Huey in 3-D #1. 59-Little Dot in 3-D #1. 60-Solomon Kane in 3-D #1 5.00
61,63-80: 61-Werewolf in 3-D #1. 63-The California Raisins in 3-D #4.
64-To Die For in 3-D #1. 65-Capt. Holo in 3-D #1. 66-Playful Little Audrey
in 3-D #1. 67-Kull in 3-D #2. 68. 69-The California Raisins in 3-D #5.
70-Wendy in 3-D #1. 71. 72-Sports Hall of Shame #1. 73. 74-The Noid in 3-D
#1. 75-Moonwalker in 3-D #1 (Michael Jackson movie adapt.). 76-79. 80-The
Noid in 3-D #2 5.00

BLACK TIDE
Image Comics: Nov, 2001 - Present ($2.95)

1-Mike Miller-a; 3 covers by Miller, Park & Bachalo 3.00

BLACK WIDOW (Marvel Knights) (Also see Marvel Graphic Novel)
Marvel Comics: May, 1999 - No. 3, Aug, 1999 ($2.99, limited series)

1-(June on-c) Devin Grayson-s/J.G. Jones-c/a; Daredevil app. 5.00
1-Variant-c by J.G. Jones 6.00
2,3 4.00
...Web of Intrigue (6/99, $3.50) r/origin & early appearances 3.50
TPB (7/01, $15.95) r/Vol. 1 & 2; Jones-c 16.00

BLACK WIDOW (Marvel Knights) (Volume 2)
Marvel Comics: Jan, 2001 - No. 3, May, 2001 ($2.99, limited series)

1-3-Grayson & Rucka-s/Scott Hampton-c/a; Daredevil app. 3.00

BLACKWULF
Marvel Comics: June, 1994 - No. 10, Mar, 1995 ($1.50)

1-($2.50)-Embossed-c; Angel Medina-a 3.00
2-10 2.25

BLADE (The Vampire Hunter)
Marvel Comics: Mar, 1998 ($3.50, one-shot)

1-Colan-a(p)/Christopher Golden-s 3.50

BLADE (The Vampire Hunter)
Marvel Comics: Nov, 1998 - No. 3, Jan, 1999 ($3.50/$2.99)

1-($3.50) Contains Movie insider pages; McKean-a 3.50
2,3-($2.99): 2-Two covers 3.00
...Sins of the Father (10/98, $5.99) Sears-a; movie adaption 6.00

BLADE OF THE IMMORTAL (Manga)
Dark Horse Comics: June, 1996 - Present ($2.95/$3.95, B&W)

1 1 4 7 10
2-5: 2-#1 on cover in error 6.00
6-10 5.00
11,19,20,34-($3.95, 48 pgs.): 34-Food one-shot 4.00
12-18,21-33,35-41,43-62: 12-20- Dreamsong. 21-28-On Silent Wings.
29-33-Dark Shadow. 35-42-Heart of Darkness. 43-57-The Gathering 3.00
42-($3.50) Ends Heart of Darkness 3.50

BLADE RUNNER (Movie)
Marvel Comics Group: Oct, 1982 - No. 2, Nov, 1982

1,2-r/Marvel Super Special #22; 1-Williamson-c/a. 2-Williamson-a 3.00

BLADESMEN UNDERSEA
Blue Comet Press: 1994 ($3.50, B&W)

1-Polybagged w/trading card 3.50

Blaze #4 © MAR

Blazing Comics #2 © Enwil

Blazing West #7 © ACG

BLADE: THE VAMPIRE-HUNTER
Marvel Comics: July, 1994 - No. 10, Apr, 1995 ($1.95)

1-($2.95)-Foil-c; Dracula returns; Wheatley-c/a				3.50
2-10: 2,3,10-Dracula-c/app. 8-Morbius app.				2.50

BLADE: VAMPIRE-HUNTER
Marvel Comics: Dec, 1999 - No. 6, May, 2000 ($3.50/$2.50)

1-($3.50)-Bart Sears-s; Sears and Smith-a				3.50
2-6-($2.50): 2-Regular & Wesley Snipes photo-c				2.50

BLAIR WITCH CHRONICLES, THE
Oni Press: Mar, 2000 - No. 4, July, 2000 ($2.95, B&W, limited series)

1-4-Van Meter-s.1-Guy Davis-a. 2-Mireault-a				3.00
1-DF Alternate-c by John Estes				7.00
TPB (9/00, $15.95) r/#1-4 & Blair Witch Project one-shot				16.00

BLAIR WITCH: DARK TESTAMENTS
Image Comics: Oct, 2000 ($2.95, one-shot)

1-Edington-s/Adlard-a; story of murderer Rustin Parr				3.00

BLAIR WITCH PROJECT, THE (Movie companion, not adaption)
Oni Press: July, 1999 ($2.95, B&W, one-shot)

1-(1st printing) History of the Blair Witch, art by Edwards, Mireault, and Davis; Van Meter-s; only the stick figure is red on the cover				12.00
1-(2nd printing) Stick figure and title lettering are red on cover				4.00
1-(3rd printing) Stick figure, title, and creator credits are red on cover				3.00
DF Glow in the Dark variant-c ($10.00)				10.00

BLAST (Satire Magazine)
G & D Publications: Feb, 1971 - No. 2, May, 1971

1-Wrightson & Kaluta-a/Everette-c	6	18	42	70
2-Kaluta-c/a	4	12	30	50

BLAST CORPS
Dark Horse Comics: Oct, 1998 ($2.50, one-shot, based on Nintendo game)

1-Reprints from Nintendo Power magazine; Mahn-a				2.50

BLASTERS SPECIAL
DC Comics: 1989 ($2.00, one-shot)

1-Peter David scripts; Invasion spin-off				2.50

BLAST-OFF (Three Rocketeers)
Harvey Publications (Fun Day Funnies): Oct, 1965 (12¢)

1-Kirby/Williamson-a(2); Williamson/Crandall-a; Williamson/Torres/Krenkel-a; Kirby/Simon-c	5	15	38	60

BLAZE
Marvel Comics: Aug, 1994 - No. 12, July, 1995 ($1.95)

1-($2.95)-Foil embossed-c				3.50
2-12: 2-Man-Thing-c/story. 11,12-Punisher app.				2.50

BLAZE CARSON (Rex Hart #6 on)(See Kid Colt, Tex Taylor, Wild Western, Wisco)
Marvel Comics (USA): Sept, 1948 - No. 5, June, 1949

1: 1,2-Shores-c	27	81	145	250
2,4,5: 4-Two-Gun Kid app. 5-Tex Taylor app.	20	60	105	175
3-Used by N.Y. State Legis. Comm. (injury to eye splash); Tex Morgan app.	21	63	110	185

BLAZE: LEGACY OF BLOOD (See Ghost Rider & Ghost Rider/Blaze)
Marvel Comics (Midnight Sons imprint): Dec, 1993 - No. 4, Mar, 1994 ($1.75, limited series)

1-4				2.50

BLAZE OF GLORY
Marvel Comics: Feb, 2000 - No. 4, Mar, 2000 ($2.99, limited series)

1-4-Ostrander-s/Manco-a; Two-Gun Kid, Rawhide Kid, Red Wolf and Ghost Rider app.				3.00

BLAZE THE WONDER COLLIE (Formerly Molly Manton's Romances #1?)
Marvel Comics(Se Pl): No. 2, Oct, 1949 - No. 3, Feb, 1950 (Both have photo-c)

2(#1), 3-(Scarce)	24	72	127	215

BLAZING BATTLE TALES
Seaboard Periodicals (Atlas): July, 1975

1-Intro. Sgt. Hawk & the Sky Demon; Severin, McWilliams, Sparling-a; Nazi-c by Thorne	1	3	6	9

BLAZING COMBAT (Magazine)
Warren Publishing Co.: Oct, 1965 - No. 4, July, 1966 (35¢, B&W)

1-Frazetta painted-c on all	17	51	115	205
2	5	15	34	55
3,4: 4-Frazetta half pg. ad	4	12	29	45
nn-Anthology (reprints from No. 1-4) (low print)	5	15	34	55

NOTE: Adkins a-4. Colan a-3,4,nn. Crandall a-all. Evans a-1,4. Heath a-4,nn. Morrow a-1-3,nn. Orlando a-1-3,nn. J. Severin a-all. Torres a-1-4. Toth a-all. Williamson a-3,4,nn and Wood a-3,4,nn.

BLAZING COMBAT: WORLD WAR I AND WORLD WAR II
Apple Press: Mar, 1994 ($3.75, B&W)

1,2: 1-r/Colan, Toth, Goodwin, Severin, Wood-a. 2-r/Crandall, Evans, Severin, Torres, Williamson-a				4.00

BLAZING COMICS (Also see Blue Circle Comics and Red Circle Comics)
Enwil Associates/Rural Home: 6/44 - #3, 9/44; #4, 2/45; #5, 3/45; #5(V2#2), 3/55 - #6(V2#3), 1955?

1-The Green Turtle, Red Hawk, Black Buccaneer; origin Jun-Gal	52	157	314	550
2-5: 3-Briefer a. 5-(V2#2 inside)	35	105	188	325
5(3/55, V2#2-inside)-Black Buccaneer-c, 6(V2#3-inside, 1955)-Indian/Japanese-c; cover is from Apr. 1945	18	54	94	160

NOTE: No. 5 & 6 contain remaindered comics rebound and the contents can vary. Cloak & Daggar, Will Rogers, Superman 64, Star Spangled 130, Kaanga known. Value would be half of contents.

BLAZING SIXGUNS
Avon Periodicals: Dec, 1952

1-Kinstler-c/a; Larsen/Alascia-a(2), Tuska?-a; Jesse James, Kit Carson, Wild Bill Hickok app.	16	48	83	140

BLAZING SIXGUNS
I.W./Super Comics: 1964

1-I.W. Reprint #1,8,9: 1-r/Wild Bill Hickok #26, Western True Crime #? & Blazing Sixguns #1 by Avon; Blazing Western #?; Kinstler-c. 9-r/Blazing Western #1; Ditko?-r; Kintsler-c reprinted from Dalton Boys #1.				
1	3	6	11	16
Super Reprint #10,11,15,16: 10,11-r/The Rider #2,1. 15-r/Silver Kid Western #?. 16-r/Buffalo Bill #?; Wildey-r; Severin-a. 17(1964)-r/Western True Crime #?	2	6	11	16
12-Reprints Bullseye #1; S&K-a	3	10	23	35
18-r/Straight Arrow #? by Powell; Severin-c	2	6	11	16

BLAZING SIX-GUNS (Also see Sundance Kid)
Skywald Comics: Feb, 1971 - No. 2, Apr, 1971 (52 pgs.)

1-The Red Mask, Sundance Kid begin, Avon's Geronimo reprint by Kinstler; Wyatt Earp app.	2	6	12	18
2-Wild Bill Hickok, Jesse James, Kit Carson-r plus M.E. Red Mask-r	2	6	9	12

BLAZING WEST (The Hooded Horseman #21 on)
American Comics Group (B&I Publ./Michel Publ.): Fall, 1948 - No. 20, Nov-Dec, 1951

1-Origin & 1st app. Injun Jones, Tenderfoot & Buffalo Belle; Texas Tim & Ranger begins, ends #13	21	63	110	190
2,3 (1-2/49)	10	30	55	85
4-Origin & 1st app. Little Lobo; Starr-a (3-4/49)	9	27	49	70
5-10: 5-Starr-a	8	24	42	60
11-13	6	18	32	45
14(11-12/50)-Origin/1st app. The Hooded Horseman	12	36	61	100
15-20: 15,16,18,19-Starr-a	8	24	45	65

BLAZING WESTERN
Timor Publications: Jan, 1954 - No. 5, Sept, 1954

1-Ditko-a (1st Western-a?); text story by Bruce Hamilton	16	48	83	140
2-4	7	21	38	55
5-Disbrow-a	8	24	42	60

BLEAT
Slave Labor Graphics: Aug, 1995 ($2.95)

1				3.00

	GD2.0	FN6.0	VF8.0	NM9.4

BLINDSIDE
Image Comics (Extreme Studios): Aug, 1996 ($2.50)

1-Variant-c exists				2.50

BLINK (See X-Men Age of Apocalypse storyline)
Marvel Comics: March, 2001 - No. 4, June, 2001 ($2.99, limited series)

1-4-Adam Kubert-c/Lobdell-s/Winick-script; leads into Exiles #1				3.00

BLIP
Marvel Comics Group: 2/1983 - 1983 (Video game mag. in comic format)

1-1st app. Donkey Kong & Mario Bros. in comics, 6pgs.; photo-c	1	3	6	8
2-Spider-Man photo-c; 6pgs. Spider-Man comics w/Green Goblin	1	3	6	9
3,4,6				5.00
5-E.T., Indiana Jones; Rocky-c				6.00
7-6pgs. Hulk comics; Pac-Man & Donkey Kong Jr. Hints	1	3	5	7

BLISS ALLEY
Image Comics: July, 1997 - No. 2($2.95, B&W)

1,2-Messner-Loebs-s/a				3.00

BLITZKRIEG
National Periodical Publications: Jan-Feb, 1976 - No. 5, Sept-Oct, 1976

1-Kubert-c on all	4	12	26	40
2-5	2	6	15	22

BLONDE PHANTOM (Formerly All-Select #1-11; Lovers #23 on)(Also see Blackstone, Marvel Mystery, Millie The Model #2, Sub-Mariner Comics #25 & Sun Girl)
Marvel Comics (MPC): No. 12, Winter, 1946-47 - No. 22, Mar, 1949

12-Miss America begins, ends #14	155	465	966	1700
13-Sub-Mariner begins (not in #16)	95	285	597	1050
14,15: 15-Kurtzman's "Hey Look"	86	258	540	950
16-Captain America with Bucky story by Rico(p), 6 pgs.; Kurtzman's "Hey Look" (1 pg.)	118	354	738	1300
17-22: 22-Anti Wertham editorial	75	225	469	825
NOTE: Shores c-12-18.				

BLONDIE (See Ace Comics, Comics Reading Libraries (Promotional Comics section), Dagwood, Daisy & Her Pups, Eat Right to Work..., King & Magic Comics)
David McKay Publications: 1942 - 1946

Feature Books 12 (Rare)	77	231	483	850
Feature Books 27-29,31,34(1940)	21	63	110	190
Feature Books 36,38,40,42,43,45,47	20	60	105	175
...1944 (Hard-c, 1938, B&W, 128 pgs.)-1944 daily strip-r	16	48	83	140

BLONDIE & DAGWOOD FAMILY
Harvey Publ. (King Features Synd.): Oct, 1963 - No. 4, Dec, 1965 (68 pgs.)

1	3	10	23	35
2-4	2	6	15	22

BLONDIE COMICS (...Monthly No. 16-141)
David McKay #1-15/Harvey #16-163/King #164-175/Charlton #177 on: Spring, 1947 - No. 163, Nov, 1965; No. 164, Aug, 1966 - No. 175, Dec, 1967; No. 177, Feb, 1969 - No. 222, Nov, 1976

1	26	78	139	240
2	14	42	72	120
3-5	11	33	55	90
6-10	9	27	49	70
11-15	7	21	36	50
16-(3/50; 1st Harvey issue)	8	24	45	65
17-20: 20-(3/51)-Becomes Daisy & Her Pups #21 & Chamber of Chills #21	4	12	29	45
21-30	3	10	23	35
31-50	3	9	19	28
51-80	3	9	17	24
81-99	2	6	15	22
100	3	9	19	28
101-124,126-130	2	6	13	20
125 (80 pgs.)	4	12	25	38
131-136,138,139	2	6	11	16

	GD2.0	FN6.0	VF8.0	NM9.4
137,140-(80 pgs.)	3	10	23	35
141-147,149-154,156,160,164-167	2	6	12	18
148,155,157-159,161-163 are 68 pgs.	3	9	20	30
168-175	2	6	11	15
177-199 (no #176)	2	6	9	12
200	2	6	10	14
201-210,213-222	1	3	6	9
211,212-1st & 2nd app. Super Dagwood	2	6	9	12

BLOOD
Marvel Comics (Epic Comics): Feb, 1988 - No. 4, Apr, 1988 ($3.25, mature)

1-4: DeMatteis scripts & Kent Williams-c/a				3.50

BLOOD AND GLORY (Punisher & Captain America)
Marvel Comics: Oct, 1992 - No. 3, Dec, 1992 ($5.95, limited series)

1-3: 1-Embossed wraparound-c by Janson; Chichester & Clarke-s				6.00

BLOOD & ROSES: FUTURE PAST TENSE (Bob Hickey's...)
Sky Comics: Dec, 1993 ($2.25)

1-Silver ink logo				2.50

BLOOD & ROSES: SEARCH FOR THE TIME-STONE (Bob Hickey's...)
Sky Comics: Apr, 1994 ($2.50)

1				2.50

BLOOD AND SHADOWS
DC Comics (Vertigo): 1996 - Book 4, 1996 ($5.95, squarebound, mature)

Books 1-4: Joe R. Lansdale scripts; Mark A. Nelson-c/a.				6.00

BLOOD: A TALE
DC Comics (Vertigo): Nov, 1996 - No. 4, Feb, 1997 ($2.95, limited series)

1-4: Reprints Epic series w/new-c; DeMatteis scripts; Kent Williams-c/a				3.00

BLOODBATH
DC Comics: Early Dec, 1993 - No. 2, Late Dec, 1993 ($3.50, 68 pgs.)

1-Neon ink-c; Superman app.; new Batman-c /app.				3.50
2-Hitman 2nd app.	1	3	5	7

BLOODFIRE
Lightning Comics: June, 1993 - No. 12, May, 1994 ($2.95)

1-($3.50)-Foil-c; 1st app. Bloodfire				3.50
2-12: 2-Origin; contracts HIV virus via transfusion. 5-Polybagged w/card & collectors warning on bag. 12-(5/94)				3.00
0-(Indicia reads June 1994, May on-c, $3.50)				3.50
.../Hellina 1 (7/95, $3.00)				3.00
.../Hellina 1 (7/95, $9.95)-Nude edition; Deodato-c				10.00
.../Hellina (8/95, $9.95)-Commemorative edition				10.00

BLOOD LEGACY: THE STORY OF RYAN
Image Comics (Top Cow): May, 2000 - No. 4, Nov, 2000 ($2.50)

1-4-Kerri Hawkins-s. 1-Andy Park-a(p); 3 covers				2.50
Preview Special ('00, $4.95) B&W flip-book w/The Magdalena Preview				5.00

BLOODLINES: A TALE FROM THE HEART OF AFRICA (See Tales From the Heart of Africa)
Marvel Comics (Epic Comics): 1992 ($5.95, 52 pgs.)

1-Story cont'd from Tales From...				6.00

BLOOD OF DRACULA
Apple Comics: Nov, 1987 - No. 20?, 1990 ($1.75/$1.95, B&W)($2.25 #14,16 on)

1-3,5-14,20: 1-10-Chadwick-c				3.00
4,16-19-Lost Frankenstein pgs. by Wrightson				5.00
15-Contains stereo flexidisc ($3.75)				4.00

BLOOD OF THE INNOCENT (See Warp Graphics Annual)
WaRP Graphics: 1/7/86 - No. 4, 1/28/86 (Weekly mini-series, mature)

1-4				2.50

BLOODPACK
DC Comics: Mar, 1995 - No. 4, June,1995 ($1.50, limited series)

1-4				2.25

BLOODPOOL
Image Comics (Extreme): Aug, 1995 - No. 4, Nov, 1995 ($2.50, limited series)

1-4: Jo Duffy scripts in all				2.50

Bloodstone #1 © MAR

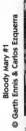
Bloody Mary #1
© Garth Ennis & Carlos Ezquerra

Blue Beetle #8 © FOX

	GD2.0	FN6.0	VF8.0	NM9.4

Special (3/96, $2.50)-Jo Duffy scripts — 2.50
Trade Paperback (1996, $12.95)-r/#1-4 — 13.00

BLOOD REIGN SAGA
London Night Studios: 1996 ($3.00, B&W, mature)

1-"Encore Edition" — 3.00

BLOODSCENT
Comico: Oct, 1988 ($2.00, one-shot, Baxter paper)

1-Colan-p — 2.50

BLOODSEED
Marvel Comics (Frontier Comics): Oct, 1993 - No. 2, Nov, 1993 ($1.95)

1,2: Sharp/Cam Smith-a — 3.00

BLOODSHOT (See Eternal Warrior #4 & Rai #0)
Valiant/Acclaim Comics (Valiant): Feb, 1993 - No. 51, Aug, 1996 ($2.25/$2.50)

1-($3.50)-Chromium embossed-c by B. Smith w/poster — 3.50
2-5,8-14: 3-$2.25-c begins; cont'd in Hard Corps #5. 4-Eternal Warrior-c/story.
5-Rai & Eternal Warrior app. 14-(3/94)-Reese-c(i) — 2.25
6,7-1st app. Ninjak (out of costume). 7-In costume — 2.25
0-(3/94, $3.50)-Wraparound chromium-c by Quesada(p); origin — 3.50
0-Gold variant — 5.00
15(4/94)-51: 16-w/bound-in trading card. 51-Bloodshot dies? — 2.25
Yearbook 1 (1994, $3.95) — 4.00
Special 1 (3/94, $5.95)-Zeck-c/a(p) — 6.00

BLOODSHOT (Volume Two)
Acclaim Comics (Valiant): July, 1997 - No. 16, Oct, 1998 ($2.50)

1-16: 1-Two covers. 5-Copycat-c. X-O Manowar-c/app — 2.50

BLOODSTONE
Marvel Comics: Dec, 2001 - Present ($2.99)

1-3-Intro. Elsa Bloodstone; Abnett & Lanning-s/Lopez-a — 3.00

BLOODSTRIKE (See Supreme V2#3)
Image Comics (Extreme Studios): 1993 - No. 22, May, 1995; No. 25, May, 1994 ($1.95/$2.50)

1-22, 25: Liefeld layouts in early issues. 1-Blood Brothers prelude. 2-1st app.
Lethal. 5-1st app. Noble. 9-Black and White part 6 by Art Thibert; Liefeld pin-
up. 9,10-Have coupon #3 & 7 for Extreme Prejudice #0. 10-(4/94). 11-(7/94).
16-Platt-c; Prophet app. 17-19-polybagged w/card . 25-(5/94)-Liefeld/Fraga-a — 3.00
NOTE: *Giffen* story/layouts-4-6. *Jae Lee* c-7, 8. *Rob Liefeld* layouts-1-3. *Art Thibert* c-6i.

BLOODSTRIKE ASSASSIN
Image Comics (Extreme Studios): June, 1995 - No. 3, Aug, 1995; No. 0, Oct, 1995 ($2.50, limited series)

0-3: 3-(8/95)-Quesada-a. 0-(10/95)-Battlestone app. — 3.00

BLOOD SWORD, THE
Jademan Comics: Aug, 1988 - No. 53, Dec, 1992 ($1.50/$1.95, 68 pgs.)

1-53: Kung Fu stories — 3.00

BLOOD SWORD DYNASTY
Jademan Comics: 1989 - No. 41, Jan, 1993 ($1.25, 36 pgs.)

1-41: Ties into Blood Sword — 2.50

BLOOD SYNDICATE
DC Comics (Milestone): Apr, 1993 - No. 35, Feb, 1996 ($1.50/-$3.50)

1-($2.95)-Collector's Edition; polybagged with poster, trading card, & acid-free
backing board (direct sale only) — 3.50
3,9,11-24,26,27,29,33-34: 8-Intro Kwai. 15-Byrne-c. 16-Worlds Collide Pt. 6;
Superman-c/app.17-Worlds Collide Pt. 13. 29-(99¢); Long Hot Summer
x-over — 2.25
10,28,30-32: 10-Simonson-c. 30-Long Hot Summer x-over — 2.50
25-($2.95, 52 pgs.) — 3.00
35-Kwai disappears; last issue — 3.50

BLOODWULF
Image Comics (Extreme): Feb, 1995 - No. 4, May, 1995 ($2.50, limited series)

1-4: 1-Liefeld-c w/4 diferent captions & alternate-c. — 2.50
Summer Special (8/95, $2.50)-Jeff Johnson-c/a; Supreme app; story takes place
between Legend of Supreme #3 & Supreme #23. — 2.50

BLOODY MARY
DC Comics (Helix): Oct, 1996 - No. 4, Jan, 1997 ($2.25, limited series)

1-4: Garth Ennis scripts; Ezquerra-c/a in all — 3.50

BLOODY MARY: LADY LIBERTY
DC Comics (Helix): Sept, 1997 - No. 4, Dec, 1997 ($2.50, limited series)

1-4: Garth Ennis scripts; Ezquerra-c/a in all — 3.00

BLUE
Image Comics (Action Toys): Aug, 1999 - Present ($2.50)

1,2-Aronowitz-s/Struzan-c — 2.50

BLUEBEARD
Slave Labor Graphics: Nov, 1993 - No. 3, Mar, 1994 ($2.95, B&W, lim. series)

1-3: James Robinson scripts. 2-(12/93) — 3.00
Trade paperback (6/94, $9.95) — 13.00
Trade paperback (2nd printing, 7/96, $12.95)-New-c — 13.00

BLUE BEETLE, THE (Also see All Top, Big-3, Mystery Men & Weekly Comic Magazine)
Fox Publ. No. 1-11, 31-60; Holyoke No. 12-30: Winter, 1939-40 - No. 57, 7/48; No. 58, 4/50 - No. 60, 8/50

	GD2.0	FN6.0	VF8.0	NM9.4
1-Reprints from Mystery Men #1-5; Blue Beetle origin; Yarko the Great-r/from Wonder/Wonderworld #2-5 all by Eisner; Master Magician app.; (Blue Beetle in 4 different costumes)	431	1293	2802	5600
2-K-51-r by Powell/Wonderworld #8,9	150	450	938	1650
3-Simon-c	109	327	682	1200
4-Marijuana drug mention story	73	219	455	800
5-Zanzibar The Magician by Tuska	64	192	398	700
6-Dynamite Thor begins (1st); origin Blue Beetle	59	177	369	650
7,8-Dynamo app. in both. 8-Last Thor	55	165	341	600
9-12: 9,10-The Blackbird & The Gorilla app. in both. 10-Bondage/hypo-c				
11(2/42)-The Gladiator app. 12(6/42)-The Black Fury app.	50	150	300	525
13-V-Man begins (1st app.), ends #18; Kubert-a; centerfold spread	59	177	369	650
14,15-Kubert-a in both. 14-Intro. side-kick (c/text only), Sparky (called Spunky #17-19)	52	157	314	550
16-18: 17-Brodsky-c	42	126	252	440
19-Kubert-a	43	129	257	450
20-Origin/1st app. Tiger Squadron; Arabian Nights begin	46	138	276	485
21-26: 24-Intro. & only app. The Halo. 26-General Patton story & photo	35	105	185	320
27-Tamaa, Jungle Prince app.	33	99	174	300
28-30(2/44)	29	87	153	265
31(6/44), 33,34,36-40: 34-38-"The Threat from Saturn" serial.	27	81	142	245
32-Hitler-c	40	120	232	400
35-Extreme violence	33	99	174	300
41-45 (#43 exist?)	25	75	130	225
46-The Puppeteer app.	28	84	151	260
47-Kamen & Baker begin	118	354	738	1300
48-50	95	285	597	1050
51,53	80	240	500	875
52-Kamen bondage-c; true crime stories begin	118	354	738	1300
54-Used in SOTI. Illo, "Children call these 'headlights' comics"	127	381	795	1400
55-57: 56-Used in SOTI, pg. 145. 57(7/48)-Last Kamen issue; becomes Western Killers?)	77	231	483	850
58(4/50)-60-No Kamen-a	17	51	88	150

NOTE: *Kamen* a-47-51, 53, 55-57; c-47, 49-52. *Powell* a-4(2). *Bondage-c* 9-12, 46, 52.

BLUE BEETLE (Formerly The Thing; becomes Mr. Muscles No. 22 on)
(See Charlton Bullseye & Space Adventures)
Charlton Comics: No. 18, Feb, 1955 - No. 21, Aug, 1955

	GD2.0	FN6.0	VF8.0	NM9.4
18,19-(Pre-1944-r). 18-Last pre-code issue. 19-Bouncer, Rocket Kelly-r	21	63	110	185
20-Joan Mason by Kamen	26	78	139	240
21-New material	19	57	99	170

BLUE BEETLE (Unusual Tales #1-49; Ghostly Tales #55 on)(See Captain Atom #83 & Charlton Bullseye)

Blue Beetle #10 © DC

Blue Circle Comics #6 © Enwil

Blue Monday: Absolute Beginners #4 © Chynna Clugston-Major

	GD2.0	FN6.0	VF8.0	NM9.4

Charlton Comics: V2#1, June, 1964 - V2#5, Mar-Apr, 1965; V3#50, July, 1965 - V3#54, Feb-Mar, 1966; #1, June, 1967 - #5, Nov, 1968

V2#1-Origin/1st S.A. app. Dan Garrett-Blue Beetle	8	24	60	100
2-5: 5-Weiss illo; 1st published-a?	5	15	38	60
V3#50-54-Formerly Unusual Tales	5	15	34	55
1(1967)-Question series begins by Ditko	10	30	73	125
2-Origin Ted Kord-Blue Beetle (see Capt. Atom #83 for 1st Ted Kord Blue Beetle); Dan Garrett x-over	5	15	38	60
3-5 (All Ditko-c/a in #1-5)	4	12	30	50
1,3(Modern Comics-1977)-Reprints	1	3	5	7

NOTE: #6 only appeared in the fanzine 'The Charlton Portfolio.'

BLUE BEETLE (Also see Americomics, Crisis On Infinite Earths, Justice League & Showcase '94 #2-4)
DC Comics: June, 1986 - No. 24, May, 1988

1-Origin retold; intro. Firefist				4.00
2-19,21-24: 2-Origin Firefist. 5-7-The Question app. 11-14-New Teen Titans x-over. 21-Millennium tie-in				2.00
20-Justice League app.; Millennium tie-in				3.00

BLUEBERRY (See Lt. Blueberry & Marshal Blueberry)
Marvel Comics (Epic Comics): 1989 - No. 5, 1990 ($12.95/$14.95, graphic novel)

1,3,4,5-($12.95)-Moebius-a in all				15.00
2-($14.95)				17.00

BLUE BOLT
Funnies, Inc. No. 1/Novelty Press/Premium Group of Comics: June, 1940 - No. 101 (V10#2), Sept-Oct, 1949

	GD	FN	VF	NM
V1#1-Origin Blue Bolt by Joe Simon, Sub-Zero Man, White Rider & Super Horse, Dick Cole, Wonder Boy & Sgt. Spook (1st app. of each)	3000	9000	1875	3500
2-Simon & Kirby's 1st art & 1st super-hero (Blue Bolt)	164	492	1023	1800
3-1 pg. Space Hawk by Wolverton; 2nd S&K-a on Blue Bolt (same cover date as Red Raven #1); 1st time S&K names app. in a comic; Simon-c	136	408	852	1500
4,5-S&K-a in each; 5-Everett-a begins on Sub-Zero	123	369	769	1350
6,8-10-S&K-a	114	342	712	1250
7-S&K-c/a	127	381	795	1400
11,12: 11-Robot-c	109	327	682	1200
V2#1-Origin Dick Cole & The Twister; Twister x-over in Dick Cole, Sub-Zero, & Blue Bolt; origin Simba Karno who battles Dick Cole thru V2#5 & becomes main supporting character V2#6 on; battle-c	39	117	208	360
2-Origin The Twister retold in text	31	93	165	285
3-5: 5-Intro. Freezum	28	84	151	260
6-Origin Sgt. Spook retold	23	69	121	210
7-12: 7-Lois Blake becomes Blue Bolt's costume aide; last Twister. 12-Text-sty by Mickey Spillaine	20	60	105	175
V3#1-3	16	48	83	140
4-12: 4-Blue Bolt abandons costume	12	36	61	105
V4#1-Hitler, Tojo, Mussolini-c	30	90	159	275
V4#2-12: 3-Shows V4#3 on-c, V4#4 inside (9-10/43). 5-Infinity-c. 8-Last Sub-Zero	11	33	55	90
V5#1-8, V6#1-3,5-10, V7#1-12	10	30	55	85
V6#4-Racist cover	13	39	66	110
V8#1-6,8-12, V9#1-4,7,8, V10#1(#100), V10#2(#101)-Last Dick Cole, Blue Bolt	10	30	55	80
V8#7,V9#6,9-L. B. Cole-c	20	60	105	175
V9#5-Classic fish in the face-c	14	42	72	120

Everett-c V1#4, 11, V2#1, 2. Gustavson a-V1#1-12, V2#1-7. Kiefer c-V3#1. Rico a-V6#10, V7#4. Blue Bolt not in V9#8.

BLUE BOLT (Becomes Ghostly Weird Stories #120 on; continuation of Novelty Blue Bolt) (...Weird Tales of Terror #111,112,...Weird Tales #113-119)
Star Publications: No. 102, Nov-Dec, 1949 - No. 119, May-June, 1953

102-The Chameleon, & Target app.	35	105	185	320
103,104-The Chameleon app. 104-Last Target	33	99	174	300
105-Origin Blue Bolt (from #1) retold by Simon; Chameleon & Target app.; opium den story	50	150	300	525
106-Blue Bolt by S&K begins; Spacehawk reprints from Target by Wolverton begin, ends #110; Sub-Zero begins; ends #109	47	142	286	500

107-110: 108-Last S&K Blue Bolt reprint. 109-Wolverton-c(r)/inside Spacehawk splash. 110-Target app.	45	135	270	475
111,112: 111-Red Rocket & The Mask-r; last Blue Bolt; 1pg. L. B. Cole-a				
112-Last Torpedo Man app.	42	126	252	440
113-Wolverton's Spacehawk-r/Target V3#7	44	132	264	460
114,116: 116-Jungle Jo-r	42	126	252	440
115-Sgt. Spook app.	44	132	264	460
117-Jo-Jo & Blue Bolt-r	43	129	257	450
118-"White Spirit" by Wood	44	132	264	460
119-Disbrow/Cole-c; Jungle Jo-r	43	129	257	450
Accepted Reprint #103(1957?, nd)	12	36	61	100

NOTE: L. B. Cole c-102-108, 110 on. Disbrow a-112(2), 113(3), 114(2), 115(2), 116-118. Hollingsworth a-117. Palais a-112r. Sci/Fi c-105-110. Horror c-111.

BLUE BULLETEER, THE (Also see Femforce Special)
AC Comics: 1989 ($2.25, B&W, one-shot)

1-Origin by Bill Black; Bill Ward-a				4.00

BLUE BULLETEER (Also see Femforce Special)
AC Comics: 1996 ($5.95, B&W, one-shot)

1-Photo-c				6.00

BLUE CIRCLE COMICS (Also see Red Circle Comics, Blazing Comics & Roly Poly Comic Book)
Enwil Associates/Rural Home: June, 1944 - No. 6, Apr, 1945

1-The Blue Circle begins (1st app.); origin & 1st app. Steel Fist	30	90	159	275
2	20	60	105	175
3-Hitler parody-c	25	75	130	225
4-6: 6-Last Steel Fist.	16	48	83	140
6-(Dated 4/45, Vol. 2#3 inside)-Leftover covers to #6 were later restapled over early 1950's coverless comics; variations of the coverless comics exist. Colossal Features known.	16	48	83	140

BLUE DEVIL (See Fury of Firestorm #24, Underworld Unleashed, Starman #38)
DC Comics: June, 1984 - No. 31, Dec, 1986 (75¢/$1.25)

1				4.00
2-16,19-31: 4-Origin Nebiros. 7-Gil Kane-a. 8-Giffen-a				2.50
17,18-Crisis x-over				3.00
Annual 1 (11/85)-Team-ups w/Black Orchid, Creeper, Demon, Madame Xanadu, Man-Bat & Phantom Stranger				3.00

BLUE MONDAY: ABSOLUTE BEGINNERS
Oni Press: Feb, 2001 - No. 4, Sept, 2001 ($2.95, B&W)

1-4-Chynna Clugston-Major-s/a/c				3.00
TPB (12/01, $11.95, 6" x 8") r/series				12.00

BLUE MONDAY: THE KIDS ARE ALRIGHT
Oni Press: Feb, 2000 - No. 3, May, 2000 ($2.95, B&W)

1-3-Chynna Clugston-Major-s/a/c. 1-Variant-c by Warren. 2-Dorkin-c				3.00
3-Variant cover by J. Scott Campbell				4.00
TPB (12/00, $10.95, digest-sized) r/#1-3 & earlier short stories				11.00

BLUE PHANTOM, THE
Dell Publishing Co.: June-Aug, 1962

1(01-066-208)-by Fred Fredericks	3	10	23	35

BLUE RIBBON COMICS (...Mystery Comics No. 9-18)
MLJ Magazines: Nov, 1939 - No. 22, Mar, 1942 (1st MLJ series)

1-Dan Hastings, Richy the Amazing Boy, Rang-A-Tang the Wonder Dog begin (1st app. of each); Little Nemo app. (not by W. McCay); Jack Cole-a(3) (1st MLJ comic)	333	1000	2083	4000
2-Bob Phantom, Silver Fox (both in #3), Rang-A-Tang Club & Cpl. Collins begin (1st app. of each); Jack Cole-a	136	408	852	1500
3-J. Cole-a	86	258	540	950
4-Doc Strong, The Green Falcon, & Hercules begin (1st app. each); origin & 1st app. The Fox & Ty-Gor, Son of the Tiger	95	285	597	1050
5-8: 8-Last Hercules; 6,7-Biro, Meskin-a. 7-Fox app. on-c	64	192	398	700
9-(Scarce)-Origin & 1st app. Mr. Justice (2/41)	291	873	1818	3200
10-13: 12-Last Doc Strong. 13-Inferno, the Flame Breather begins, ends #19; Devil-c	100	300	625	1100
14,15,17,18: 15-Last Green Falcon	84	254	525	925

Bobby Benson B-Bar-B #5 © ME

Bob Steele Western #7 © FAW

Body Count #3 © MS

	GD2.0	FN6.0	VF8.0	NM9.4

16-Origin & 1st app. Captain Flag (9/41) 164 492 1023 1800
19-22: 20-Last Ty-Gor. 22-Origin Mr. Justice retold 84 254 525 925
NOTE: Biro c-3-5; a-2 (Cpl. Collins & Scoop Smith). S. Cooper c-9-17. 20-22 contain "Tales From the Witch's Cauldron" (same strip as "Stories of the Black Witch" in Zip Comics). Mr. Justice c-9-18. Captain Flag c-16(w/Mr. Justice), 19-22.

BLUE RIBBON COMICS (Becomes Teen-Age Diary Secrets #4)
(Also see Approved Comics, Blue Ribbon Comics and Heckle &Jeckle)
Blue Ribbon (St. John): Feb, 1949 - No. 6, Aug, 1949

1,3-Heckle & Jeckle (Terrytoons) 10 30 55 80
2(4/49)-Diary Secrets; Baker-c 21 63 110 185
4(6/49)-Teen-Age Diary Secrets; Baker c/a(2) 21 63 110 185
5(8/49)-Teen-Age Diary Secrets; Oversize; photo-c; Baker-a(2)- Continues as Teen-Age Diary Secrets 27 81 142 245
6-Dinky Duck(8/49)(Terrytoons) 5 15 25 35

BLUE RIBBON COMICS
Red Circle Prod./Archie Ent. No. 5 on: Nov, 1983 - No. 14, Dec, 1984

1-S&K-r/Advs. of the Fly #1,2; Williamson/Torres-r/Fly #2; Ditko-c 6.00
2-7,9-11,13,14: 3-Origin Steel Sterling. 5-S&K Shield-r; new Kirby-c. 6,7-The Fox app. 11-Black Hood. 13-Thunder Bunny. 14-Web & Jaguar 5.00
8-Toth centerspread; Black Hood app.; Neal Adams-a(r) 6.00
12-Thunder Agents; Noman new Ditko-a 6.00
NOTE: N. Adams a(r)-8. Buckler a-4i. Nino a-8. McWilliams a-8. Morrow a-8.

BLUE STREAK (See Holyoke One-Shot No. 8)

BLYTHE (Marge's)
Dell Publishing Co.: No. 1072, Jan-Mar, 1960

Four Color 1072 5 15 35 60

B-MAN (See Double-Dare Adventures)

BO (Tom Cat #4 on) (Also see Big Shot #29 & Dixie Dugan)
Charlton Comics Group: June, 1955 - No. 3, Oct, 1955 (A dog)

1-3: Newspaper reprints by Frank Beck 8 24 42 60

BOATNIKS, THE (See Walt Disney Showcase No. 1)

BOB BURDEN'S ORIGINAL MYSTERYMEN PRESENTS
Dark Horse Comics: 1999 - No. 4 ($2.95/$3.50)

1-3-Bob Burden-s/Sadowski-a(p) 3.50
4-($3.50) All Villain issue 3.50

BOBBY BENSON'S B-BAR-B RIDERS (Radio) (See Best of The West, The Lemonade Kid & Model Fun)
Magazine Enterprises/AC Comics: May-June, 1950 - No. 20, May-June, 1953

1-The Lemonade Kid begins; Powell-a (Scarce) 43 130 257 450
2 18 54 94 155
3-5: 4,5-Lemonade Kid-c (#4-Spider-c) 14 42 72 120
6-8,10 13 39 66 110
9,11,13-Frazetta-c; Ghost Rider in #13-15 by Ayers-a. 13-Ghost Rider-c 35 105 185 320
12,17-20: 20-(A-1 #88) 12 36 61 100
14-Decapitation/Bondage-c & story; classic horror-c 26 78 136 235
15-Ghost Rider 20 60 105 180
16-Photo-c 14 42 72 120
1 (1990, $2.75, B&W)-Reprints; photo-c & inside covers 3.00
NOTE: Powell a-1-1(4 ea.), 13(3), 14-16(Red Hawk only); c-1-8,1 0, 12. Lemonade Kid in most 1-13.

BOBBY COMICS
Universal Phoenix Features: May, 1946

1-By S. M. Iger 8 24 42 60

BOBBY SHERMAN (TV)
Charlton Comics: Feb, 1972 - No. 7, Oct, 1972

1-Based on TV show "Getting Together" 4 12 29 45
2-7: 4-Photo-c 3 9 20 30

BOB COLT (Movie star)(See XMas Comics)
Fawcett Publications: Nov, 1950 - No. 10, May, 1952

1-Bob Colt, his horse Buckskin & sidekick Pablo begin; photo front/back-c begin 40 120 232 400
2 26 78 136 235
3-5 21 63 110 185

6-Flying Saucer story 18 54 94 155
7-10: 9-Last photo back-c 16 48 83 140

BOB HOPE (See Adventures of... & Calling All Boys #12)

BOB MARLEY, TALE OF THE TUFF GONG (Music star)
Marvel Comics: Aug, 1994 - No. 3, Nov, 1994 ($5.95, limited series)

1-3 6.00

BOB POWELL'S TIMELESS TALES
Eclipse Comics: March, 1989 ($2.00, B&W)

1-Powell-r/Black Cat #5 (Scarlet Arrow), 9 & Race for the Moon #1 3.00

BOB SCULLY, THE TWO-FISTED HICK DETECTIVE (Also see Advs. of Detective Ace King and Detective Dan)
Humor Publ. Co.: No date (1933) (36 pgs., 9-1/2x11", B&W, paper-c; 10¢-c)

nn-By Howard Dell; not reprints; along with Advs. of Det. Ace King and Detective Dan, the first comic w/original art & the first of a single theme; has a blue 2-tone cover 280 840 2100 –

BOB SON OF BATTLE
Dell Publishing Co.: No. 729, Nov, 1956

Four Color 729 4 12 26 40

BOB STEELE WESTERN (Movie star)
Fawcett Publications/AC Comics: Dec, 1950 - No. 10, June, 1952; 1990

1-Bob Steele & his horse Bullet begin; photo front/back-c begin 58 174 363 640
2 33 99 174 300
3-5: 4-Last photo back-c 24 72 127 220
6-10: 10-Last photo-c 19 57 99 170
1 (1990, $2.75, B&W)-Bob Steele & Rocky Lane reprints; photo-c & inside covers 3.00

BOB SWIFT (Boy Sportsman)
Fawcett Publications: May, 1951 - No. 5, Jan, 1952

1 10 30 55 80
2-5: Saunders painted-c #1-5 6 18 29 40

BOB, THE GALACTIC BUM
DC Comics: Feb, 1995 - No. 4, June, 1995 ($1.95, limited series)

1-4: 1-Lobo app. 2.50

BODY BAGS
Dark Horse Comics (Blanc Noir): Sept, 1996 - No. 4, Jan, 1997 ($2.95, mini-series, mature)(1st Blanc Noir series)

1-Jason Pearson-c/a/scripts in all. 1-Intro Clownface & Panda. 1 3 6 8
2 1 4 7 10
3,4 6.00

BODYCOUNT (Also see Casey Jones & Raphael)
Image Comics (Highbrow Entertainment): Mar, 1996 - No. 4, July, 1996 ($2.50, limited series)

1-4: Kevin Eastman-a(p)/scripts; Simon Bisley-c/a(i); Turtles app. 2.50

BODY DOUBLES (See Resurrection Man)
DC Comics: Oct, 1999 - No. 4, Jan, 2000 ($2.50, limited series)

1-4-Lanning & Abnett-s. 2-Black Canary app. 4-Wonder Woman app. 2.50
...(Villains) (2/98, $1.95, one-shot) 1-Pearson-c; Deadshot app. 2.50

BOFFO LAFFS
Paragraphics: 1986 - No. 5 ($2.50/$1.95)

1-($2.50) First comic cover with hologram 3.00
2-5 2.25

BOHOS
Image Comics (Flypaper Press): June, 1998 - No. 3 ($2.95)

1-3-Whorf-s/Penaranda-a 3.00

BOLD ADVENTURES
Pacific Comics: Oct, 1983 - No. 3, June, 1984 ($1.50)

1-Time Force, Anaconda, & The Weirdling begin 3.00
2,3: 2-Soldiers of Fortune begins. 3-Spitfire 3.00
NOTE: Kaluta c-3. Nebres a-1-3. Nino a-2, 3. Severin a-3.

Bone #12 © Jeff Smith

Book of the Dead #2 © MAR

The Books of Faerie: Molly's Story #4 © DC

	GD2.0	FN6.0	VF8.0	NM9.4

BOLD STORIES (Also see Candid Tales & It Rhymes With Lust)
Kirby Publishing Co.: Mar, 1950 - July, 1950 (Digest size, 144 pgs.)

March issue (Very Rare) - Contains "The Ogre of Paris" by Wood	127	381	795	1400
May issue (Very Rare) - Contains "The Cobra's Kiss" by Graham Ingels (21 pgs.)	109	327	682	1200
July issue (Very Rare) - Contains "The Ogre of Paris" by Wood	95	285	597	1050

BOLT AND STAR FORCE SIX
Americomics: 1984 ($1.75)

1-Origin Bolt & Star Force Six	3.00
Special 1 (1984, $2.00, 52pgs., B&W)	3.00

BOMBARDIER (See Bee 29, the Bombardier & Cinema Comics Herald)

BOMBAST
Topps Comics: 1993 ($2.95, one-shot) (Created by Jack Kirby)

1-Polybagged w/Kirbychrome trading card; Savage Dragon app.; Kirby-c; has coupon for Amberchrome Secret City Saga #0	3.00

BOMBA THE JUNGLE BOY (TV)
National Periodical Publ.: Sept-Oct, 1967 - No. 7, Sept-Oct, 1968 (12¢)

1-Intro. Bomba; Infantino/Anderson-c	3	10	23	35
2-7	2	6	15	22

BOMBER COMICS
Elliot Publ. Co./Melverne Herald/Farrell/Sunrise Times: Mar, 1944 - No. 4, Winter, 1944-45

1-Wonder Boy, & Kismet, Man of Fate begin	68	204	426	750
2-Hitler-c	47	141	286	500
3: 2-4-Have Classics Comics ad to HRN 20	40	120	232	400
4-Hitler, Tojo & Mussolini-c; Sensation Comics #13-c/swipe; has Classics Comics ad to HRN 20.	59	177	369	650

BONANZA (TV)
Dell/Gold Key: June-Aug, 1960 - No. 37, Aug, 1970 (All Photo-c)

Four Color 1110 (6-8/60)	37	111	259	480
Four Color 1221,1283, & #01070-207, 01070-210	18	54	126	234
1(12/62-Gold Key)	19	57	133	247
2	10	30	70	130
3-10	8	24	56	105
11-20	6	18	42	80
21-37: 29-Reprints	5	15	35	65

BONE
Cartoon Books #1-20, 28 on/Image Comics #21-27: July, 1991 - Present ($2.95, B&W)

1-Jeff Smith-c/a in all	8	24	56	90
1-2nd printing	2	6	9	12
1-3rd thru 5th printings				4.00
2-1st printing	4	12	29	45
2-2nd & 3rd printings				4.00
3-1st printing	3	10	23	35
3-2nd thru 4th printings				4.00
4,5	2	6	11	15
6-10	1	3	6	8
11-37: 21-1st Image issue				4.00
13 1/2 (1/95, Wizard)	1	4	7	10
13 1/2 (Gold)	2	6	9	12
38-($4.95) Three covers by Miller, Ross, Smith				5.00
39-45-($2.95)				3.00
1-27-($2.95): 1-Image reprints begin w/new-c. 2-Allred pin-up.				3.00
.. Holiday Special (1993, giveaway)				3.00
.. Reader -($9.95) Behind the scenes info				10.00
.. Sourcebook-San Diego Edition				3.00
...10th Anniversary Edition (8/01, $5.95) r/#1 in color; came with figure				6.00
Complete Bone Adventures Vol 1,2 ('93, '94, $12.95, r/#1-6 & #7-12)				13.00
Volume 1-($19.95, hard-c)-"Out From Boneville"				20.00
Volume 1-($12.95, soft-c)				13.00
Volume 2,5-($22.95, hard-c)-"The Great Cow Race" & "Rock Jaw"				23.00
Volume 2,5-($14.95, soft-c)				15.00
Volume 3,4-($24.95, hard-c)-"Eyes of the Storm" & "The Dragonslayer"				25.00

Volume 3,4,7-($16.95, soft-c)	17.00
Volume 6-($15.95, soft-c)-"Old Man's Cave"	16.00
Volume 7-($24.95, hard-c)-"Ghost Circles"	25.00
NOTE: Printings not listed sell for cover price.	

BONGO (See Story Hour Series)

BONGO & LUMPJAW (Disney, see Walt Disney Showcase #3)
Dell Publishing Co.: No. 706, June, 1956; No. 886, Mar, 1958

Four Color 706 (#1)	5	15	35	65
Four Color 886	4	12	28	50

BON VOYAGE (See Movie Classics)

BOOF
Image Comics (Todd McFarlane Prod.): July, 1994 - No. 6, Dec, 1994 ($1.95)

1-6	2.25

BOOF AND THE BRUISE CREW
Image Comics (Todd McFarlane Prod.): July, 1994 - No. 6, Dec, 1994 ($1.95)

1-6	2.25

BOOK AND RECORD SET (See Power Record Comics)

BOOK OF ALL COMICS
William H. Wise: 1945 (196 pgs.)(Inside f/c has Green Publ. blacked out)

nn-Green Mask, Puppeteer & The Bouncer	40	120	232	400

BOOK OF ANTS, THE
Artisan Entertainment: 1998 ($2.95, B&W)

1-Based on the movie Pi; Aronofsky-s	3.00

BOOK OF BALLADS AND SAGAS, THE
Green Man Press: Oct, 1995 - No. 4 ($2.95/$3.50/$3.25, B&W)

1-4: 1-Vess-c/a; Gaiman story.	3.50

BOOK OF COMICS, THE
William H. Wise: No date (1944) (25¢, 132 pgs.)

nn-Captain V app.	40	120	220	380

BOOK OF FATE, THE (See Fate)
DC Comics: Feb, 1997 - No. 12, Jan, 1998 ($2.25/$2.50)

1-12: 4-Two-Face-c/app. 6-Convergence. 11-Sentinel app.	3.00

BOOK OF LOVE (See Fox Giants)

BOOK OF NIGHT, THE
Dark Horse Comics: July, 1987 - No. 3, 1987 ($1.75, B&W)

1-3: Reprints from Epic Illustrated; Vess-a	2.25
TPB-r/#1-3	15.00
Hardcover-Black-c with red crest	100.00
Hardcover w/slipcase (1991) signed and numbered	50.00

BOOK OF THE DEAD
Marvel Comics: Dec, 1993 - No. 4, Mar, 1994 ($1.75, limited series, 52 pgs.)

1-4: 1-Ploog Frankenstein & Morrow Man-Thing-r begin; Wrightson-r/Chamber of Darkness #7. 2-Morrow new painted-c; Chaykin/Morrow Man-Thing; Krigstein-r/Uncanny Tales #54; r/Fear #10. 3-r/Astonishing Tales #10 & Starlin Man-Thing. 3,4-Painted-c	3.00

BOOKS OF FAERIE, THE
DC Comics (Vertigo): Mar, 1997 - No. 3, May,1997 ($2.50, limited series)

1-3-Gross-a	3.00
TPB (1998, $14.95) r/#1-3 & Arcana Annual #1	15.00

BOOKS OF FAERIE, THE : AUBERON'S TALE
DC Comics (Vertigo): Aug, 1998 - No. 3, Oct,1998 ($2.50, limited series)

1-3-Gross-a	3.00

BOOKS OF FAERIE, THE : MOLLY'S STORY
DC Comics (Vertigo): Sept, 1999 - No. 4, Dec,1999 ($2.50, limited series)

1-4-Ney Rieber-s/Mejia-a	3.00

BOOKS OF MAGIC
DC Comics: 1990 - No. 4, 1991 ($3.95, 52 pgs., limited series, mature)

1-Bolton painted-c/a; Phantom Stranger app.; Gaiman scripts in all	1	3	6	9

	GD2.0	FN6.0	VF8.0	NM9.4

2,3: 2-John Constantine, Dr. Fate, Spectre, Deadman app. 3-Dr. Occult app.; minor Sandman app. — 6.00
4-Early Death-c/app. (early 1991) — 1 — 3 — 5 — 7
Trade paperback-($19.95)-Reprints limited series — 20.00

BOOKS OF MAGIC (Also see Hunter: The Age of Magic and Names of Magic)
DC Comics (Vertigo): May, 1994 - No. 75, Aug, 2000 ($1.95/$2.50, mature)

1-Charles Vess-c	2	6	9	12
1-Platinum	2	6	13	20
2,3	1	3	5	7
4-Death app.	1	3	5	7

5-14; Charles Vess-c — 4.00
15-50: 15-$2.50-c begins. 22-Kaluta-c. 25-Death-c/app; Bachalo-c — 3.00
51-75: 51-Peter Gross-s/a begins. 55-Medley-a — 2.50
Annual 1,2 (2/97, 2/98, $3.95) — 4.00
Bindings (1995, $12.95, TPB)-r/#1-4 — 13.00
Death After Death (2001, $19.95, TPB)-r/#42-50 — 20.00
Girl in the Box (1999, $14.95, TPB)-r/#26-32 — 15.00
Reckonings (1997, $12.95, TPB)-r/#14-20 — 13.00
Summonings (1996, $17.50, TPB)-r/#5-13, Vertigo Rave #1 — 17.50
The Burning Girl (2000, $17.95, TPB)-r/#33-41 — 18.00
Transformations (1998, $12.95, TPB)-r/#21-25 — 13.00

BOONDOGGLE
Knight Press: Mar, 1995 - No. 4 ($2.95, B&W)
1-4: Stegelin-c/a/scripts — 3.00

BOONDOGGLE
Caliber Press: Jan, 1997 - No. 2 ($2.95, B&W)
1,2: Stegelin-c/a/scripts — 3.00

BOOSTER GOLD (See Justice League #4)
DC Comics: Feb, 1986 - No. 25, Feb, 1988 (75¢)
1 — 3.00
2-25: 4-Rose & Thorn app. 6-Origin. 6,7,23-Superman app. 8,9-LSH app. 22-JLI app. 24,25-Millennium tie-ins — 2.50
NOTE: *Austin* c-22i. *Byrne* c-23i.

BOOTS AND HER BUDDIES
Standard Comics/Visual Editions/Argo (NEA Service):
No. 5, 9/48 - No. 9, 9/49; 12/55 - No. 3, 1956

5-Strip-r	16	48	83	140
6,8	11	33	55	90
7-(Scarce)	13	39	66	110
9-(Scarce)-Frazetta-a (2 pgs.)	26	78	136	235
1-3(Argo-1955-56)-Reprints	6	18	29	40

BOOTS & SADDLES (TV)
Dell Publ. Co.: No. 919, July, 1958; No. 1029, Sept, 1959; No. 1116, Aug, 1960

Four Color 919 (#1)-Photo-c	8	24	56	100
Four Color 1029, 1116-Photo-c	5	15	35	60

BORDERLINE
Friction Press: June, 1992 ($2.25, B&W)
0-Ashcan edition; 1st app. of Cliff Broadway — 2.25
1-Painted-c — 3.00
1-Special Edition (bagged w/ photo, S&N) — 4.00

BORDER PATROL
P. L. Publishing Co.: May-June, 1951 - No. 3, Sept-Oct, 1951

1	12	36	61	105
2,3	9	27	49	70

BORDER WORLDS (Also see Megaton Man)
Kitchen Sink Press: 7/86 - No. 7, 1987; V2#1, 1990 - No. 4, 1990 ($1.95-$2.00, B&W, mature)
1-7, V2#1-4: Donald Simpson-c/a/scripts — 3.00

BORIS KARLOFF TALES OF MYSTERY (TV) (...Thriller No. 1,2)
Gold Key: No. 3, April, 1963 - No. 97, Feb, 1980

3-5-(Two #5's, 10/63,11/63): 5-(10/63)-11 pgs. Toth-a.	4	12	26	40
6-8,10: 10-Orlando-a	3	9	21	32
9-Wood-a	3	10	23	35

	GD2.0	FN6.0	VF8.0	NM9.
11-Williamson-a, 8 pgs.; Orlando-a, 5 pgs.	3	10	23	35
12-Torres, McWilliams-a; Orlando-a(2)	3	9	19	28
13,14,16-20	2	6	15	22
15-Crandall	3	9	17	25
21-Jeff Jones-a(3 pgs.) "The Screaming Skull"	3	9	17	25
22-Last 12¢ issue	2	6	12	18
23-30: 23-Reprint; photo-c	2	6	11	15
31-50: 36-Weiss-a	2	6	9	12
51-74: 74-Origin & 1st app. Taurus	1	4	7	10
75-79,87-97: 90-r/Torres, McWilliams-a/#12; Morrow-c	1	3	6	8
80-86-(52 pgs.)	1	4	7	10
Story Digest 1(7/70-Gold Key)-All text/illos.; 148pp.	4	12	26	40

(See Mystery Comics Digest No. 2, 5, 8, 11, 14, 17, 20, 23, 26)
NOTE: *Bolle* a-51-54, 56, 58, 59. *McWilliams* a-12, 14, 18, 19, 72, 80, 81, 93. *Orlando* a-11-15, 21. Reprints: 78, 81-86, 88, 90, 92, 95, 97.

BORIS KARLOFF THRILLER (TV) (Becomes Boris Karloff Tales...)
Gold Key: Oct, 1962 - No. 2, Jan, 1963 (84 pgs.)

1-Photo-c	8	24	56	100
2	5	15	35	60

BORIS THE BEAR
Dark Horse Comics/Nicotat Comics #13 on: Aug, 1986 - No. 34, 1990 ($1.50/$1.75/$1.95, B&W)
1, Annual 1 (1988, $2.50) — 3.00
1 (2nd printing),2,3,4A,4B,5-12, 14-34: 8-(44 pgs.) — 2.25
13-1st Nicotat Comics issue — 3.00

BORIS THE BEAR INSTANT COLOR CLASSICS
Dark Horse Comics: July, 1987 - No. 3, 1987 ($1.75/$1.95)
1-3 — 2.25

BORN AGAIN
Spire Christian Comics (Fleming H. Revell Co.): 1978 (39¢)
nn-Watergate, Nixon, etc. — 1 — 3 — 5 — 7

BOUNCER, THE (Formerly Green Mask #9)
Fox Features Syndicate: 1944 - No. 14, Jan, 1945

nn(1944, #10?)	30	90	159	275
11 (9/44)-Origin; Rocket Kelly, One Round Hogan app.	24	72	127	215
12-14: 14-Reprints no # issue	19	57	99	165

BOUNTY GUNS (See Luke Short's..., Four Color 739)

BOX OFFICE POISON
Antarctic Press: 1996 - No. 21, Sept, 2000 ($2.95, B&W)
1-Alex Robinson-s/a in all — 1 — 3 — 5 — 7
2-5 — 4.00
6-21, ...Kolor Karnival 1 (5/99, $2.99) — 3.00
...Super Special 0 (5/97, $4.95) — 5.00
Sherman's March: Collected BOP Vol. 1 (9/98, $14.95) r/#0-4 — 15.00

BOY AND HIS 'BOT, A
Now Comics: Jan, 1987 ($1.95)
1-A Holiday Special — 3.00

BOY AND THE PIRATES, THE (Movie)
Dell Publishing Co.: No. 1117, Aug, 1960
Four Color 1117-Photo-c — 6 — 18 — 42 — 80

BOY COMICS (Captain Battle No. 1 & 2; Boy Illustories No. 43-108)
(Stories by Charles Biro)(Also see Squeeks)
Lev Gleason Publ. (Comic House): No. 3, Apr, 1942 - No. 119, Mar, 1956

3(No.1)-Origin Crimebuster, Bombshell & Young Robin Hood; Yankee Longago, Case 1001-1008, Swoop Storm, & Boy Movies begin; 1st app. Iron Jaw; Crimebuster's pet monkey Squeeks begins	300	900	1875	3500
4-Hitler, Tojo, Mussolini-c	127	381	795	1400
5	91	273	568	1000
6-Origin Iron Jaw; origin & death of Iron Jaw's son; Little Dynamite begins, ends #39; 1st Iron Jaw-c	273	819	1705	3000
7-Flag & Hitler, Tojo, Mussolini-c	91	273	568	1000
8-Death of Iron Jaw; Iron Jaw-c	91	273	568	1000
9-Iron Jaw-c	80	240	556	87

Boy Comics #30 © LEV

Boy Commandos #3 © DC

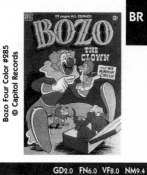

Bozo Four Color #285 © Capitol Records

BR

	GD2.0	FN6.0	VF8.0	NM9.4
10-Return of Iron Jaw; classic Biro-c; Iron Jaw-c	123	369	769	1350
11-Classic Iron Jaw-c	82	246	511	900
12,13	55	165	341	600
14-Iron Jaw-c	64	192	398	700
15-Death of Iron Jaw	73	219	455	800
16,18-20	40	120	217	375
17-Flag-c	40	120	232	400
21-29,31,32-(All 68 pgs.). 28-Yankee Longago ends. 32-Swoop Storm				
& Young Robin Hood end	26	78	139	240
30-(68 pgs.)-Origin Crimebuster retold	37	111	197	340
33-40: 34-Crimebuster story(2); suicide-c/story	20	60	105	180
41-50	17	51	88	150
51-59: 57-Dilly Duncan begins, ends #71	14	42	72	125
60-Iron Jaw returns	16	48	83	140
61-Origin Crimebuster & Iron Jaw retold	18	54	94	160
62-Death of Iron Jaw explained	17	51	88	150
63-73: 63-McWilliams-a. 73-Frazetta 1-pg. ad	12	36	61	100
74-88: 80-1st app. Rocky X of the Rocketeers; becomes "Rocky X" #101; Iron				
Jaw, Sniffer & the Deadly Dozen in 80-118	9	27	51	75
89-92-The Claw serial app. in all	10	30	55	80
93-Claw cameo; Rocky X by Sid Check	9	27	51	75
94-97,99	9	27	51	75
98,100: 98-Rocky X by Sid Check	9	27	49	70
101-107,109,111,119: 101-Rocky X becomes spy strip. 106-RobinHood app.				
119-Last Crimebuster. 111-Crimebuster becomes Chuck Chandler.	8	24	42	60
108,110,112-118-Kubert-a; 108-Ditko-a	9	27	49	70

NOTE: *Boy Movies in 3-5,40,41. Iron Jaw app.-3, 4, 6, 8, 10, 11, 13-15; returns-60-62, 68, 69, 72-79, 81-118. Biro c-all. Briefer a-5, 13, 14, 16-20 among others. Fuje a-55, 18 pgs. Palais a-14, 16, 17, 19, 20 among others.*

BOY COMMANDOS (See Detective #64 & World's Finest Comics #8)
National Periodical Publications: Winter, 1942-43 - No. 36, Nov-Dec, 1949

	500	1500	3250	6500
1-Origin Liberty Belle; The Sandman & The Newsboy Legion x-over in Boy Commandos; S&K-a, 48 pgs.; S&K cameo? (classic WWII-c)	500	1500	3250	6500
	182	546	1136	2000
2-Last Liberty Belle; Hitler!-c; S&K-a, 46 pgs.; WWII-c				
3-S&K-a, 45 pgs.; WWII-c	109	327	682	1200
4-6: All WWII-c. 6-S&K-a	77	231	483	850
7-10: All WWII-c	55	165	330	575
11-13: All WWII-c. 11-Infinity-c	40	120	220	380
14,16,18-19-All have S&K-a. 18-2nd Crazy Quilt-c	31	93	168	290
15-1st app. Crazy Quilt, their arch nemesis	40	120	232	400
17,20-Sci/fi-c/stories	35	105	185	320
21,22,25: 22-3rd Crazy Quilt-c; Judy Canova x-over	24	72	127	220
23-S&K-c/a(all)	33	99	174	300
24-1st costumed superhero satire-c (11-12/47).	29	87	156	270
26-Flying Saucer story (3-4/48)-4th of this theme; see The Spirit 9/28/47(1st),				
Shadow Comics V7#10 (2nd, 1/48) & Captain Midnight #60 (3rd, 2/48)				
	27	81	145	250
27,28,30: 30-Cleveland Indians story	23	69	121	210
29-S&K story (1)	25	75	133	230
31-35: 32-Dale Evans app. on-c & in story. 33-Last Crazy Quilt-c. 34-Intro. Wolf,				
their mascot	22	66	116	195
36-Intro The Atomobile c/sci-fi story (Scarce)	40	120	217	375

NOTE: *Most issues signed by Simon & Kirby are not by them. S&K c-1-9, 13, 14, 17, 21, 23, 24, 30-32. Feller c-30.*

BOY COMMANDOS
National Per. Publ.: Sept-Oct, 1973 - No. 2, Nov-Dec, 1973 (G.A. S&K reprints)

1,2: 1-Reprints from Boy Commandos #1 plus-c & Detective #66 by				
S&K. 2-Infantino/Orlando-a	2	6	9	12

BOY COWBOY (Also see Amazing Adventures & Science Comics)
Ziff-Davis Publ. Co.: 1950 (8 pgs. in color)

nn-Sent to subscribers of Ziff-Davis mags. & ordered through mail for 10¢;				
used to test market for Kid Cowboy	26	78	139	240

BOY DETECTIVE
Avon Periodicals: May-June, 1951 - No. 4, May, 1952

1	20	60	105	175

	GD2.0	FN6.0	VF8.0	NM9.4
2-4: 3,4-Kinstler-c	13	39	66	110

BOY EXPLORERS COMICS (Terry and The Pirates No. 3 on)
Family Comics (Harvey Publ.): May-June, 1946 - No. 2, Sept-Oct, 1946

1-Intro The Explorers, Duke of Broadway, Calamity Jane & Danny Dixon…				
Cadet; S&K-c/a, 24 pgs.	64	192	398	700
2-(Scarce)-Small size (5-1/2x8-1/2"; B&W; 32 pgs.). Distributed to mail				
subscribers only; S&K-a	86	258	540	950

(Also see All New No. 15, Flash Gordon No. 5, and Stuntman No. 3)

BOY ILLUSTORIES (See Boy Comics)

BOY LOVES GIRL (Boy Meets Girl No. 1-24)
Lev Gleason Publications: No. 25, July, 1952 - No. 57, June, 1956

25(#1)	7	21	36	50
26,27,29-33: 30-33-Serial, 'Loves of My Life'	5	15	23	30
34-42: 39-Lingerie panels	4	12	19	25
28-Drug propaganda story	5	15	25	35
43-Toth-a	6	18	32	45
44-50: 50-Last pre-code (2/55)	4	11	17	22
51-57: 57-Ann Brewster-a	4	9	14	18

BOY MEETS GIRL (Boy Loves Girl No. 25 on)
Lev Gleason Publications: Feb, 1950 - No. 24, June, 1952 (No. 1-17: 52 pgs.)

1-Guardineer-a	10	30	55	85
2	6	18	32	45
3-10	6	18	28	38
11-24	5	15	24	32

NOTE: *Briefer a-24. Fuje c-3,7. Painted-c 1-17. Photo-c 19-21, 23.*

BOYS' AND GIRLS' MARCH OF COMICS (See March of Comics)

BOYS' RANCH (Also see Western Tales & Witches' Western Tales)
Harvey Publ.: Oct, 1950 - No. 6, Aug, 1951 (No.1-3, 52 pgs.; No. 4-6, 36 pgs.)

1-S&K-c/a(3)	61	183	381	675
2-S&K-c/a(3)	43	129	257	450
3-S&K-c/a(2); Meskin-a	40	120	232	400
4-S&K-c/a, 5 pgs.	37	111	197	340
5,6-S&K-c, splashes & centerspread only; Meskin-a				
	21	63	110	185

BOZO (Larry Harmon's Bozo, the World's Most Famous Clown)
Innovation Publishing: 1992 ($6.95, 68 pgs.)

1-Reprints Four Color #285(#1)	1	3	5	7

BOZO THE CLOWN (TV) (Bozo No. 7 on)
Dell Publishing Co.: July, 1950 - No. 4, Oct-Dec, 1963

Four Color 285(#1)	19	57	133	250
2(7-9/51)-7(10-12/52)	11	33	77	140
Four Color 464,508,551,594(10/54)	9	27	63	110
1(nn, 5-7/62)	6	18	42	80
2 - 4(1963)	5	15	35	60

BOZZ CHRONICLES, THE
Marvel Comics (Epic Comics): Dec, 1985 - No. 6, 1986 (Lim. series, mature)

1-6-Logan/Wolverine look alike in 19th century. 1,3,5- Blevins-a				3.00

BRADLEYS, THE (Also see Hate)
Fantagraphics Books: Apr, 1999 - No. 6, Jan, 2000 ($2.95, B&W, limited series)

1-6-Reprints Peter Bagge's-s/a				3.00

BRADY BUNCH, THE (TV)(See Kite Fun Book and Binky #78)
Dell Publishing Co.: Feb, 1970 - No. 2, May, 1970

1	10	30	70	135
2	7	21	49	90

BRAIN, THE
Sussex Publ. Co./Magazine Enterprises: Sept, 1956 - No. 7, 1958

1-Dan DeCarlo-a in all including reprints	9	27	51	75
2,3	6	18	28	38
4-7	5	15	23	30
I.W. Reprints #1-4,8-10('63),14: 2-Reprints Sussex #2 with new cover				
added	2	6	10	14
Super Reprint #17,18(nd)	2	6	10	14

BRAINBANX

383

	GD2.0	FN6.0	VF8.0	NM9.4

DC Comics (Helix): Mar, 1997 - No. 6, Aug, 1997 ($2.50, limited series)

1-6: Elaine Lee-s/Temujin-a				2.50

BRAIN BOY
Dell Publishing Co.: Apr-June, 1962 - No. 6, Sept-Nov, 1963 (Painted c-#1-6)

Four Color 1330(#1)-Gil Kane-a; origin	13	39	91	170
2(7-9/62),3-6: 4-Origin retold	7	21	49	95

BRAM STOKER'S BURIAL OF THE RATS (Movie)
Roger Corman's Cosmic Comics: Apr, 1995 - No.3, June, 1995 ($2.50)

1-3: Adaptation of film; Jerry Prosser scripts				2.50

BRAM STOKER'S DRACULA (Movie)(Also see Dracula: Vlad the Impaler)
Topps Comics: Oct, 1992 - No. 4, Jan, 1993 ($2.95, limited series, polybagged)

1-(1st & 2nd printing)-Adaptation of film begins; Mignola-c/a in all; 4 trading cards & poster;photo scenes of movie				3.00
1-Crimson foil edition (limited to 500)				8.00
2-4: 2-Bound-in poster & cards. 4 trading cards in both. 3-Contains coupon to win 1 of 500 crimson foil-cedition of #1. 4-Contains coupon to win 1 of 500 uncut versions of all 16 trading cards				3.00

BRAND ECHH (See Not Brand Echh)

BRAND NEW YORK: WHAT JUSTICE
Comic Box Inc.: July, 1997 ($3.95, B&W&Red)

1-Zoltan-s/a, Peter Avanti-s				4.00

BRAND OF EMPIRE (See Luke Short's...Four Color 771)

BRASS
Image Comics (WildStorm Productions): Aug, 1996 - No. 3, May, 1997 ($2.50, limited series)

1-($4.50) Folio Ed.; oversized				4.50
1-3: Wiesenfeld-s/Bennett-a. 3-Grunge & Roxy(Gen 13) cameo				2.50

BRASS
DC Comics (WildStorm): Aug, 2000 - No. 6 ($2.50, limited series)

1-5-Arcudi-s				2.50

BRATPACK/MAXIMORTAL SUPER SPECIAL
King Hell Press: 1996 ($2.95, B&W, limited series)

1,2: Veitch-s/a				3.00

BRATS BIZARRE
Marvel Comics (Epic/Heavy Hitters): 1994 - No. 4, 1994 ($2.50, limited series)

1-4: All w/bound-in trading cards				2.50

BRAVADOS, THE (See Wild Western Action)
Skywald Publ. Corp.: Aug, 1971 (52 pgs., one-shot)

1-Red Mask, The Durango Kid, Billy Nevada-r; Bolle-a; 3-D effect story	2	6	11	16

BRAVE AND THE BOLD, THE (See Best Of... & Super DC Giant) (Replaced by Batman & The Outsiders)
National Periodical Publ./DC Comics: Aug-Sept, 1955 - No. 200, July, 1983

1-Viking Prince by Kubert, Silent Knight, Golden Gladiator begin; part Kubert-c	222	666	2000	4000
2		100	300	850	1600
3,4	55	165	468	875
5-Robin Hood begins (4-5/56, 1st DC app.), ends #15; see Robin Hood Tales #7	58	174	493	925
6-10: 6-Robin Hood by Kubert; last Golden Gladiator app.; Silent Knight; no Viking Prince. 8-1st S.A. issue	43	129	323	575
11-22,24: 12,14-Robin Hood-c. 18,21-23-Grey tone-c. 22-Last Silent Knight. 24-Last Viking Prince by Kubert (2nd solo book)	33	100	250	450
23-Viking Prince origin by Kubert; 1st B&B single theme issue & 1st Viking Prince solo book	43	129	323	575
25-1st app. Suicide Squad (8-9/59)	41	123	306	550
26,27-Suicide Squad	30	90	210	375
28-(2-3/60)-Justice League intro./1st app.; origin/1st app. Snapper Carr	368	1104	3316	7000
29-Justice League (4-5/60)-2nd app. battle the Weapons Master; robot-c	165	495	1400	2800
30-Justice League (6-7/60)-3rd app.; vs. Amazo	138	414	1169	2200
31-1st app. Cave Carson (8-9/60); scarce in high grade; 1st try-out series				

32,33-Cave Carson	37	111	278	475
34-Origin/1st app. Silver-Age Hawkman, Hawkgirl & Byth (2-3/61); Gardner Fox story, Kubert-c/a ; 1st S.A. Hawkman tryout series; 2nd in #42-44; both series predate Hawkman #1	22	66	154	275
	176	528	1500	3000
35-Hawkman by Kubert (4-5/61)-2nd app.	45	135	359	650
36-Hawkman by Kubert; origin & 1st app. Shadow Thief (6-7/61)-3rd app.	41	123	306	550
37-Suicide Squad (2nd tryout series)	23	69	160	285
38,39-Suicide Squad. 38-Last 10¢ issue	20	60	137	245
40,41-Cave Carson Inside Earth (2nd try-out series). 40-Kubert-a. 41-Meskin-a	15	45	105	180
42-Hawkman by Kubert (2nd tryout series); Hawkman earns helmet wings; Byth app.	29	88	202	360
43-Hawkman by Kubert; more detailed origin	33	100	250	450
44-Hawkman by Kubert; grey/tone-c	26	78	179	320
45-49-Strange Sports Stories by Infantino	8	24	56	90
50-The Green Arrow & Manhunter From Mars (10-11/63); 1st Manhunter x-over outside of Detective (pre-dates House of Mystery #143); team-ups begin	18	54	123	220
51-Aquaman & Hawkman (12-1/63-64); pre-dates Hawkman #1	23	69	160	285
52-(2-3/64)-3 Battle Stars; Sgt. Rock, Haunted Tank, Johnny Cloud, & Mlle. Marie team-up for 1st time by Kubert (c/a)	17	51	120	215
53-Atom & The Flash by Toth	8	24	56	90
54-Kid Flash, Robin & Aqualad; 1st app./origin Teen Titans (6-7/64)	28	84	196	350
55-Metal Men & The Atom	6	18	42	70
56-The Flash & Manhunter From Mars	6	18	42	70
57-Origin & 1st app. Metamorpho (12-1/64-65)	16	48	112	200
58-2nd app. Metamorpho by Fradon	8	24	60	100
59-Batman & Green Lantern; 1st Batman team-up in Brave and the Bold	10	30	73	125
60-Teen Titans (2nd app.)-1st app. new Wonder Girl (Donna Troy), who joins Titans (6-7/65)	10	30	70	120
61-Origin Starman & Black Canary by Anderson	13	39	91	155
62-Origin Starman & Black Canary cont'd. 62-1st S.A. app. Wildcat (10-11/65); 1st S.A. app. of G.A. Huntress (W.W. villain)	10	30	73	125
63-Supergirl & Wonder Woman	6	18	42	70
64-Wonder Versus Eclipso (see H.O.S. #61)	7	21	50	80
65-Flash & Doom Patrol (4-5/66)	4	12	29	45
66-Metamorpho & Metal Men (6-7/66)	4	12	29	45
67-Batman & The Flash by Infantino; Batman team-ups begin, end #200 (8-9/66)	8	24	56	90
68-Batman/Metamorpho/Joker/Riddler/Penguin-c/story; Batman as Bat-Hulk (Hulk parody)	8	24	56	90
69-Batman & Green Lantern	4	12	30	50
70-Batman & Hawkman; Craig-a(p)	4	12	30	50
71-Batman & Green Arrow	4	12	30	50
72-Spectre & Flash (6-7/67); 4th app. The Spectre; predates Spectre #1	5	15	34	45
73-Aquaman & The Atom	4	12	29	45
74-Batman & Metal Men	4	12	29	45
75-Batman & The Spectre (12-1/67-68); 6th app. Spectre; came out between Spectre #1 & #2	4	12	30	50
76-Batman & Plastic Man (2-3/68); came out between Plastic Man #8 & #9	4	12	29	45
77-Batman & The Atom	4	12	29	45
78-Batman, Wonder Woman & Batgirl	4	12	29	45
79-Batman & Deadman by Neal Adams (8-9/68); early Deadman app.	6	18	45	75
80-Batman & Creeper (10-11/68); N. Adams-a; early app. The Creeper; came out between Creeper #3 & #4	5	15	34	55
81-Batman & Flash; N. Adams-a	5	15	34	55
82-Batman & Aquaman; N. Adams-a; origin Ocean Master retold (2-3/69)	5	15	34	55
83-Batman & Teen Titans; N. Adams-a (4-5/69)	5	15	34	55
84-Batman (G.A., 1st S.A. app.) & Sgt. Rock; N. Adams-a; last 12¢ issue (6-7/69)	5	15	34	55
85-Batman & Green Arrow; 1st new costume for Green Arrow by Neal Adams				

The Brave and the Bold #184 © DC

The Brave and the Bold Annual #1 1969 Issue © DC

Brave Old World #1 © William Messner-Loebs & Guy Davis

	GD2.0	FN6.0	VF8.0	NM9.4

(8-9/69) — 5 15 38 60
86-Batman & Deadman (10-11/69); N. Adams-a; story concludes from Strange Adventures #216 (1-2/69) — 5 15 34 55
87-Batman & Wonder Woman — 3 10 23 35
88-Batman & Wildcat — 3 10 23 35
89-Batman & Phantom Stranger (4-5/70); early Phantom Stranger app. (came out between Phantom Stranger #6 & 7 — 3 9 21 32
90-Batman & Adam Strange — 3 9 21 32
91-Batman & Black Canary (8-9/70) — 3 9 21 32
92-Batman; intro the Bat Squad — 3 9 21 32
93-Batman-House of Mystery; N. Adams-a — 4 12 29 45
94-Batman-Teen Titans — 3 9 19 28
95-Batman & Plastic Man — 3 9 19 28
96-Batman & Sgt. Rock; last 15¢ issue — 3 9 20 30
97-Batman & Wildcat; 52 pg. issues begin, end #102; reprints origin & 1st app. Deadman from Strange Advs. #205 — 3 9 20 30
98-Batman & Phantom Stranger; 1st Jim Aparo Batman-a? — 3 9 20 30
99-Batman & Flash — 3 9 20 30
100-(2-3/72, 25¢, 52 pgs.)-Batman-Gr. Lantern-Gr. Arrow-Black Canary-Robin; Deadman-r by Adams/Str. Advs. #210 — 5 15 34 55
101-Batman & Metamorpho; Kubert Viking Prince — 3 9 19 28
102-Batman-Teen Titans; N. Adams-a(p) — 3 9 21 32
103-107,109,110: Batman team-ups: 103-Metal Men. 104-Deadman. 105-Wonder Woman. 106-Green Arrow. 107-Black Canary. 109-Demon. 110-Wildcat — 2 6 11 15
108-Sgt. Rock — 2 6 12 18
111-Batman/Joker-c/story — 2 6 13 20
112-117: All 100 pgs.; Batman team-ups: 112-Mr. Miracle. 113-Metal Men; reprints origin/1st Hawkman from Brave and the Bold #34; r/origin Multi-Man/Challengers #14. 114-Aquaman. 115-Atom; r/origin Viking Prince from #23; r/Dr. Fate/Hourman/Solomon Grundy/Green Lantern from Showcase #55. 116-Spectre. 117-Sgt. Rock; last 100 pg. issue — 3 10 23 35
118-Batman/Wildcat/Joker-c/story — 3 9 21 32
119,121-123,125-128,130-140: Batman team-ups: 119-Man-Bat. 121-Metal Men. 122-Swamp Thing. 123-Plastic Man/Metamorpho. 125-Flash. 126-Aquaman. 127-Wildcat. 128-Mr. Miracle. 132-Kung-Fu Fighter. 133-Deadman. 134-Green Lantern. 135-Metal Men. 136-Metal Men/Green Arrow. 137-Demon. 138-Mr. Miracle. 139-Hawkman. 140-Wonder Woman
1 4 7 10
120-Kamandi (68 pgs.) — 2 6 12 18
124-Sgt. Rock — 2 6 10 14
129,130-Batman/Green Arrow/Atom parts 1 & 2; Joker & Two Face-c/stories
2 6 11 16
131-Batman & Wonder Woman vs. Catwoman-c/sty — 2 6 9 12
141-160: Batman team-ups: 142-Aquaman. 143-Creeper; origin Human Target (44 pgs.) 144-Green Arrow; origin Human Target part 2 (44 pgs.). 145-Phantom Stranger. 146-G.A. Batman/Unknown Soldier. 147-Supergirl. 148-Plastic Man; X-Mas-c. 149-Teen Titans. 150-Anniversary issue; Superman. 151-Flash. 152-Atom. 153-Red Tornado. 154-Metamorpho. 155-Green Lantern. 156-Dr. Fate. 157-Batman vs. Kamandi (ties into Kamandi #59). 158-Wonder Woman. 159-Ra's Al Ghul. 160-Supergirl.
1 3 5 7
145(11/79),146,151-155,157,159,165(8/80)-(Whitman variants; low print run; none have issue # on cover) 1.10 3.30 9.00
161-181,183-190,192-195,198,199: Batman team-ups: 161-Adam Strange. 162-G.A. Batman/Sgt. Rock. 163-Black Lightning. 164-Hawkman. 165-Man-Bat. 166-Black Canary; Nemesis (intro) back-up story begins, ends #192; Penguin-c/story. 167-Batman/Blackhawk; origin Nemesis. 168-Green Arrow. 169-Zatanna. 170-Nemesis. 171-Scalphunter. 172-Firestorm. 173-Guardians of the Universe. 174-Green Lantern. 175-Lois Lane. 176-Swamp Thing. 177-Elongated Man. 178-Creeper. 179-Legion. 180-Spectre. 181-Hawk & Dove. 183-Riddler. 184-Huntress. 185-Green Arrow. 186-Hawkman. 187-Metal Men. 188,189-Rose & the Thorn. 190-Adam Strange. 192-Superboy vs. Mr. I.Q. 193-Nemesis. 194-Flash. 195-I....Vampire.
1 3 5 7
145-Karate Kid. 149-Teen Titans vs. The Spectre 5.00
182-G.A. Robin; G.A. Starman app.; 1st modern app. G.A. Batwoman 6.00
191-Batman/Joker-c/story; Nemesis app. 1 4 7 10
196-Ragman; origin Ragman retold. 1 3 5 7

197-Catwoman; Earth II Batman & Catwoman marry; 2nd modern app. of G.A. Batwoman 1 4 7 10
200-Double-sized (64 pgs.); printed on Mando paper; Earth One & Earth Two Batman app. in separate stories; intro/1st app. Batman & The Outsiders
1 4 7 10
NOTE: **Neal Adams** a-79-86, 93, 100r, 102; c-75, 76, 79-86, 88-90, 93, 95, 99, 100r. **M. Anderson** a-115r; c-72i, 96i. **Andru/Esposito** c-25-27. **Aparo** a-98, 100-102, 104-125, 126i, 127-136, 138-145, 147, 148i, 149-154, 155, 157-162, 165-170, 173-178, 180-182, 184, 186i-189i, 191i-193i, 195, 196, 200; c-105-109, 111-136, 137i, 138-175, 177, 180-184, 186-200. **Austin** a-166i. **Bernard Baily** c-32, 33, 58. **Buckler** a-185, 186p; c-137, 178p, 185p, 186p. **Giordano** a-143, 144. **Infantino** a-67p, 72p, 97i, 98i, 115r, 172p, 183p, 190p, 194p; c-45-49, 67p, 69p, 70p, 72p, 96p, 98r. **Kaluta** a-115r; c-59, 64. **Kubert &/or Heath** a-1-24; reprints-101, 113, 115, 117. **Kubert** a-99r; c-22-24, 34-36, 40, 42-44, 52. **Mooney** a-114r. **Mortimer** a-64, 69. **Newton** a-153p, 156p, 165p. **Irv Novick** c-1(part), 2-21. **Fred Ray** a-78r. **Roussos** a-50, 76i, 114r. **Staton** 148p. 52 pgs.-97, 100; 68 pgs.-120; 100 pgs.-112-117.

BRAVE AND THE BOLD, THE
DC Comics: Dec, 1991 - No. 6, June, 1992 ($1.75, limited series)
1-6: Green Arrow, The Butcher, The Question in all; Grell scripts in all 2.50
NOTE: Grell c-3, 4-6.

BRAVE AND THE BOLD ANNUAL NO. 1 1969 ISSUE, THE
DC Comics: 2001 ($5.95, one-shot)
1-Reprints silver age team-ups in 1960s-style 80 pg. Giant format 6.00

BRAVE AND THE BOLD SPECIAL, THE (See DC Special Series No. 8)

BRAVE EAGLE (TV)
Dell Publishing Co.: No. 705, June, 1956 - No. 929, July, 1958
Four Color 705 (#1)-Photo-c 6 18 42 80
Four Color 770, 816, 879 (2/58), 929-All photo-c 4 12 26 40

BRAVE OLD WORLD (V2K)
DC Comics (Vertigo): Feb, 2000 - No. 4, May, 2000 ($2.50, mini-series)
1-4-Messner-Loeb-s/Guy Davis & Phil Hester-a 2.50

BRAVE ONE, THE (Movie)
Dell Publishing Co.: No. 773, Mar, 1957
Four Color 773-Photo-c 5 15 35 60

BRAVURA
Malibu Comics (Bravura): 1995 (mail-in offer)
0-wraparound holographic-c; short stories and promo pin-ups of Chaykin's Power & Glory, Gil Kane's & Steven Grant's Edge, Starlin's Breed, & Simonson's Star Slammers. 5.00
1 1/2 7.00

BREAKFAST AFTER NOON
Oni Press: May, 2000 - No. 6, Jan, 2001($2.95, B&W, limited series)
1-6-Andi Watson-s/a 3.00
TPB (2001, $19.95) r/series 20.00

BREAKNECK BLVD.
MotioN Comics/Slave Labor Graphics Vol. 2: No. 0, Feb, 1994 - No. 2, Nov, 1994; Vol. 2#1, July, 1995 - #6, Dec., 1996 ($2.50/$2.95, B&W)
0-2, V2#1-6: 0-Perez/Giordano-c 3.00

BREAK-THRU (Also see Exiles V1#4)
Malibu Comics (Ultraverse): Dec, 1993 - No. 2, Jan, 1994 ($2.50, 44 pgs.)
1,2-Perez-a/c(p); has x-overs in Ultraverse titles 2.50

BREATHTAKER
DC Comics: 1990 - No. 4, 1990 ($4.95, 52 pgs., prestige format, mature)
Book 1-4: Mark Wheatley-painted-c/a & scripts; Marc Hempel-a 5.00
TPB (1994, $14.95) r/#1-4; intro by Neil Gaiman 15.00

'BREED
Malibu Comics (Bravura): Jan, 1994 - No. 6, 1994 ($2.50, limited series)
1-6: 1-(48 pgs.)-Origin & 1st app. 'Breed by Starlin; contains Bravura stamps; spot varnish-c. 3-contains Bravura stamps. 6-Death of Rachel 3.00
...:Book of Genesis (1994, $12.95)-reprints #1-6 13.00

'BREED II
Malibu Comics (Bravura): Nov, 1994 - No. 6, Apr, 1995 ($2.95, limited series)
1-6: Starlin-c/a/scripts in all. 1-Gold edition 3.00

BREEZE LAWSON, SKY SHERIFF (See Sky Sheriff)

Brenda Starr V1 #10 © SUPR

Brer Rabbit Four Color #129 © WDC

Brigade #6 © Rob Liefeld

	GD2.0	FN6.0	VF8.0	NM9.4

BRENDA LEE STORY, THE
Dell Publishing Co.: Sept, 1962

01-078-209	8	24	56	105

BRENDA STARR (Also see All Great)
Four Star Comics Corp./Superior Comics Ltd.: No. 13, 9/47; No. 14, 3/48;
V2#3, 6/48 - V2#12, 12/49

V1#13-By Dale Messick	80	240	500	875
14-Kamen bondage-c	82	246	511	900
V2#3-Baker-a?	67	201	419	740
4-Used in **SOTI**, pg. 21; Kamen bondage-c	80	240	500	875
5-10	65	195	406	715
11,12 (Scarce)	66	198	413	725

NOTE: *Newspaper reprints plus original material through #6. All original #7 on.*

BRENDA STARR (...Reporter)(Young Lovers No. 16 on?)
Charlton Comics: No. 13, June, 1955 - No. 15, Oct, 1955

13-15-Newspaper-r	39	117	208	360

BRENDA STARR REPORTER
Dell Publishing Co.: Oct, 1963

1	17	51	115	205

BRER RABBIT (See Kite Fun Book, Walt Disney Showcase #28 and Wheaties)
Dell Publishing Co.: No. 129, 1946; No. 208, Jan, 1949; No. 693, 1956 (Disney)

Four Color 129 (#1)-Adapted from Disney movie "Song of the South"				
	28	84	196	360
Four Color 208 (1/49)	12	36	84	150
Four Color 693-Part-r 129	9	27	63	110

BRIAN BOLLAND'S BLACK BOOK
Eclipse Comics: July, 1985 (one-shot)

1-British B&W-r in color				3.00

BRICK BRADFORD (Also see Ace Comics & King Comics)
King Features Syndicate/Standard: No. 5, July, 1948 - No. 8, July, 1949
(Ritt & Grey reprints)

5	20	60	105	175
6-Robot-c (by Schomburg?)	29	87	156	270
7-Schomburg-c. 8-Says #7 inside, #8 on-c	15	45	77	130

BRIDE'S DIARY (Formerly Black Cobra No. 3)
Ajax/Farrell Publ.: No. 4, May, 1955 - No. 10, Aug, 1956

4 (#1)	7	21	36	50
5-8	5	15	23	30
9,10-Disbrow-a	6	18	32	45

BRIDES IN LOVE (Hollywood Romances & Summer Love No. 46 on)
Charlton Comics: Aug, 1956 - No. 45, Feb, 1965

1	10	30	55	80
2	6	18	29	40
3-6,8-10	3	9	20	30
7-(68 pgs.)	4	12	26	40
11-20	2	6	13	20
21-45	2	6	9	12

BRIDES ROMANCES
Quality Comics Group: Nov, 1953 - No. 23, Dec, 1956

1	12	36	61	100
2	6	18	32	45
3-10: Last precode (3/55)	5	15	25	35
11-17,19-22: 15-Baker-a(p)?; Colan-a	5	14	21	28
18-Baker-a	6	18	29	40
23-Baker-c/a	9	27	49	70

BRIDE'S SECRETS
Ajax/Farrell(Excellent Publ.)/Four-Star: Apr-May, 1954 - No. 19, May, 1958

1	10	30	55	85
2	6	18	30	42
3-6: Last precode (3/55)	5	15	24	32
7-11,13-19: 18-Hollingsworth-a	5	14	21	28
12-Disbrow-a	5	15	25	35

BRIDE-TO-BE ROMANCES (See True...)

BRIGADE
Image Comics (Extreme Studios): Aug, 1992 - No. 4, 1993 ($1.95, lim. series)

1-Liefeld part plots/scripts in all, Liefeld-c(p); contains 2 Brigade trading cards; 1st app. Genocide				3.00
1-Gold foil stamped logo edition				8.00
2-Contains coupon for Image Comics #0 & 2 trading cards				3.00
2-With coupon missing				2.25
3-Contains 2 bound-in trading cards; 1st Birds of Prey				2.50
4-Flip book format featuring Youngblood #5				2.50

BRIGADE
Image Comics (Extreme): V2#1, May, 1993 - V2#22, July, 1995, V2#25, May, 1996 ($1.95/$2.50)

V2#1-22,25: 1-Gatefold-c; Liefeld co-plots; Blood Brothers part 1; Bloodstrike app.; 1st app. Boone & Hacker. 2-(6/93, V2#1 on inside)-Foil merricote-c (news stand ed. w/out foil-c exists). 3-1st app. Roman; Perez-c(i); Liefeld scripts. 6-1st app. Coral & Worlok. 6-8-Thibert-c(i). 8-Liefeld scripts; Black and White part 5 by Art Thibert. 8,9-Coupons #2 & 6 for Extreme Prejudice #0 bound-in. 11-(8/94, $2.50) WildC.A.T.S app. 16-Polybagged w/ trading card. 19-Glory app. 20 (Regular-c.)-Troll, Supreme, Shadowhawk, Glory,Vanguard, & Roman form new team. 22-"Supreme Apocalypse" Pt. 4; Marv Wolfman scripts; polybagged w/ trading card. 25-Images of Tomorrow				2.50
0-(9/93)-Liefeld scripts; 1st app. Warcry; Youngblood & Wildcats app.;				2.50
20-(Variant-c. by Quesada & Palmiotti)-Troll, Supreme, Shadowhawk, Glory, Vanguard, & Roman form new team.				2.50
Sourcebook 1 (8/94, $2.95)				3.00

BRIGADE
Awesome Entertainment: July, 2000 ($2.99)

1-Flip book w/Century preview				3.00

BRIGAND, THE (See Fawcett Movie Comics No. 18)

BRINGING UP FATHER
Dell Publishing Co.: No. 9, 1942 - No. 37, 1944

Large Feature Comic 9	28	84	151	260
Four Color 37	19	57	133	250

BRING BACK THE BAD GUYS
Marvel Comics: 1998($24.95, TPB)

1-Reprints stories of Marvel villains' secrets				25.00

BRING ON THE BAD GUYS (See Fireside Book Series)

BRINKE OF DESTRUCTION
High-Top and Brinke Stevens: Dec, 1995 - Jan, 1997($2.95)

1-3: 1-Boris-c. 2-Julie Bell-c. 3-Garris-c				3.00
Holiday Special ($6.99)-Comic w/audio tape	1	3	5	7

BRINKE OF DISASTER
Revenge Entertainment Group: 1996 ($2.25, B&W, one-shot)

nn-Photo-c				2.25

BRINKE OF ETERNITY
Chaos! Comics: Apr, 1994 ($2.75, one-shot)

1				3.00
1-Signed Edition				4.00

BROADWAY HOLLYWOOD BLACKOUTS
Stanhall: Mar-Apr, 1954 - No. 3, July-Aug, 1954

1	12	36	61	100
2,3	8	24	42	60

BROADWAY ROMANCES
Quality Comics Group: January, 1950 - No. 5, Sept, 1950

1-Ward-c/a (9 pgs.); Gustavson-a	35	105	188	325
2-Ward-a (9 pgs.); photo-c	25	75	130	225
3-5: All-Photo-c	13	36	61	100

BROKEN ARROW (TV)
Dell Publishing Co.: No. 855, Oct, 1957 - No. 947, Nov, 1958

Four Color 855 (#1)-Photo-c	5	15	35	65
Four Color 947-Photo-c	5	15	34	55

BROKEN CROSS, THE (See The Crusaders)

Broncho Bill #11 © STD

The Brotherhood #4 © MAR

Buccaneers #23 © QUA

	GD2.0	FN6.0	VF8.0	NM9.4

BRONCHO BILL (See Comics On Parade, Sparkler & Tip Top Comics)
United Features Syndicate/Standard(Visual Editions) No. 5-on: 1939 - 1940;
No. 5, 1?/48 - No. 16, 8?/50

Single Series 2 ('39)	50	150	300	525
Single Series 19 ('40)(#2 on cvr)	42	126	252	440
5	14	42	72	120
6(4/48)-10(4/49)	8	24	42	60
11(6/49)-16	6	18	32	45

NOTE: *Schomburg* c-6, 7, 9-13, 16.

BROOKLYN DREAMS
DC Comics (Paradox Press): 1994 ($4.95, B&W, limited series, mature)

1-4				5.00

BROOKS ROBINSON (See Baseball's Greatest Heroes #2)

BROTHER BILLY THE PAIN FROM PLAINS
Marvel Comics Group: 1979 (68pgs.)

1-B&W comics, satire, Jimmy Carter-c & x-over w/Brother Billy peanut jokes.

Joey Adams-a (scarce)	3	9	17	26

BROTHERHOOD, THE (Also see X-Men titles)
Marvel Comics: July, 2001 - Present ($2.25)

1-Intro. Orwell & the Brotherhood; Ribic-a/X-s/Sienkiewicz-c		2.25
2-7: 2-Two covers (JG Jones & Sienkiewicz). 4-6-Fabry-c. 7-Phillips-c/a		2.25

BROTHER POWER, THE GEEK (See Saga of Swamp Thing Annual & Vertigo Visions)
National Periodical Publications: Sept-Oct, 1968 - No. 2, Nov-Dec, 1968

1-Origin; Simon-c(i?)	5	15	38	60
2	3	9	20	30

BROTHERS, HANG IN THERE, THE
Spire Christian Comics (Fleming H. Revell Co.): 1979 (49¢)

nn	1	3	6	8

BROTHERS OF THE SPEAR (Also see Tarzan)
Gold Key/Whitman No. 18: June, 1972 - No. 17, Feb, 1976; No. 18, May, 1982

1	4	12	26	40
2-Painted-c begin, end #17	2	6	13	20
3-10	2	6	10	14
11-18: 12-Line drawn-c. 13-17-Spiegle-a. 18(5/82)-r/#2; Leopard Girl-r				
	1	4	7	10

BROTHERS, THE CULT ESCAPE, THE
Spire Christian Comics (Fleming H. Revell Co.): 1980 (49¢)

nn	1	3	5	7

BROWNIES (See New Funnies)
Dell Publishing Co.: No. 192, July, 1948 - No. 605, Dec, 1954

Four Color 192(#1)-Kelly-a	13	39	91	175
Four Color 244(9/49), 293 (9/50)-Last Kelly c/a	10	30	70	130
Four Color 337(7-8/51), 365(12-1/51-52), 398(5/52)	4	12	29	45
Four Color 436(11/52), 482(7/53), 522(12/53), 605	4	12	26	40

BRUCE GENTRY
Better/Standard/Four Star Publ./Superior No. 3: Jan, 1948 - No. 8, Jul, 1949

1-Ray Bailey strip reprints begin, end #3; E. C. emblem appears as a mono-
gram on stationery in story; negligee panels

	49	147	294	515
2,3	36	108	191	330
4-8	25	75	130	225

NOTE: *Kamen*ish a-2-7; c-1-8.

BRUCE LEE (Also see Deadly Hands of Kung Fu)
Malibu Comics: July, 1994 - No. 6, Dec, 1994 ($2.95, 36 pgs.)

1-6: 1-(44 pgs.)-Mortal Kombat prev., 1st app. in comics. 2,6-(36 pgs.)		5.00

BRUCE JONES' OUTER EDGE
Innovation: 1993 ($2.50, B&W, one-shot)

1-Bruce Jones-c/a/script		2.50

BRUCE WAYNE: AGENT OF S.H.I.E.L.D. (Also see Marvel Versus DC #3 & DC Versus Marvel #4)
Marvel Comics (Amalgam): Apr, 1996 ($1.95, one-shot)

1-Chuck Dixon scripts & Cary Nord-c/a.		2.50

	GD2.0	FN6.0	VF8.0	NM9.4

BRUISER
Anthem Publications: Feb, 1994 ($2.45)

1		2.50

BRUTE, THE
Seaboard Publ. (Atlas): Feb, 1975 - No. 3, July, 1975

1-Origin & 1st app; Sekowsky-a(p)	1	3	6	8
2-Sekowsky-a(p); Fleisher-s				6
3-Brunner/Starlin/Weiss-a(p)	1	3	5	7

BRUTE & BABE
Ominous Press: July, 1994 - No. 2, Aug, 1994

1-($3.95, 8 tablets plus-c)-"...It Begins..."; tablet format		4.00
2-($2.50, 36 pgs.)-"Mael's Rage", 2-(40 pgs.)-Stiff additional variant-c		2.50

BRUTE FORCE
Marvel Comics: Aug, 1990 - No. 4, Nov, 1990 ($1.00, limited series)

1-4: Animal super-heroes; Delbo & DeCarlo-a		2.50

BUBBLEGUM CRISIS: GRAND MAL
Dark Horse Comics: Mar, 1994 - No. 4, June, 1994 ($2.50, limited series)

1-4-Japanese manga		2.50

BUCCANEER
I. W. Enterprises: No date (1963)

I.W. Reprint #1(r-/Quality #20), #8(r-/#23): Crandall-a in each

	3	9	19	28

BUCCANEERS (Formerly Kid Eternity)
Quality Comics: No. 19, Jan, 1950 - No. 27, May, 1951 (No. 24-27: 52 pgs.)

19-Captain Daring, Black Roger, Eric Falcon & Spanish Main begin;

Crandall-a	52	157	314	550
20,23-Crandall-a	39	117	208	360
21-Crandall-c/a	40	120	240	420
22-Bondage-c	31	93	165	285
24-26: 24-Adam Peril, U.S.N. begins. 25-Origin & 1st app. Corsair Queen.				
26-last Spanish Main	27	81	145	250
27-Crandall-c/a	39	117	208	360
Super Reprint #12 (1964)-Crandall-r/#21	3	10	23	35

BUCCANEERS, THE (TV)
Dell Publishing Co.: No. 800, 1957

Four Color 800-Photo-c	7	21	49	90

BUCKAROO BANZAI (Movie)
Marvel Comics Group: Dec, 1984 - No. 2, Feb, 1985

1,2-Movie adaptation; r/Marvel Super Special #33; Texiera-c/a		2.50

BUCK DUCK
Atlas Comics (ANC): June, 1953 - No. 4, Dec, 1953

1-Funny animal stories in all	14	42	72	120
2-4: 2-Ed Win-a(5)	7	21	38	55

BUCK JONES (Also see Crackajack Funnies, Famous Feature Stories, Master Comics #7 & Wow Comics #1, 1936)
Dell Publishing Co.: No. 299, Oct, 1950 - No. 850, Oct, 1957 (All Painted-c)

Four Color 299(#1)-Buck Jones & his horse Silver-B begin; painted back-c

begins, ends #5	13	39	91	170
2(4-6/51)	7	21	49	85
3-8(10-12/52)	5	15	35	65
Four Color 460,500,546,589	5	15	35	60
Four Color 652,733,850	4	12	26	40

BUCK ROGERS (Also see Famous Funnies, Pure Oil Comics, Salerno Carnival of Comics, 24 Pages of Comics, & Vicks Comics)
Famous Funnies: Winter, 1940-41 - No. 6, Sept, 1943

NOTE: Buck Rogers first appeared in the pulp magazine Amazing Stories Vol. 3 #5 in Aug, 1928.

1-Sunday strip reprints by Rick Yager; begins with strip #190; Calkins-c

	300	900	1875	3500
2 (7/41)-Calkins-c	127	381	795	1400
3 (12/41), 4 (7/42)	109	327	682	1200
5,6: 5-Story continues with Famous Funnies No. 80; Buck Rogers, Sky Roads.				
6-Reprints of 1939 dailies; contains B.R. story "Crater of Doom" (2 pgs.)				
by Calkins not-r from Famous Funnies	95	285	597	1050

Bucky O'Hare #4 © Continuity

Buffy the Vampire Slayer #14 © 20th Century Fox

Buffy the Vampire Slayer: Willow & Tara © 20th Century Fox

	GD2.0	FN6.0	VF8.0	NM9.4

BUCK ROGERS
Toby Press: No. 100, Jan, 1951 - No. 9, May-June, 1951

100(#7)-All strip-r begin	29	87	156	270
101(#8), 9-All Anderson-a(1947-49-r/dailies)	23	69	121	210

BUCK ROGERS (...in the 25th Century No. 5 on) (TV)
Gold Key/Whitman No. 7 on: Oct, 1964; No. 2, July, 1979 - No. 16, May, 1982
(No #10; story was written but never released. #17 exists only as a press proof without covers and was never published)

1(10128-410, 12¢)-1st S.A. app. Buck Rogers & 1st new B. R. in comics since 1933 giveaway; painted-c; painted-c back-up pin-up	8	24	56	100
2(7/79)-6: 3,4,6-Movie adaptation; painted-c	1	3	6	9
7,11 (Whitman)	1	4	7	10
8,9 (prepack)(scarce)	2	6	13	20
12-16: 14(2/82), 15(3/82), 16(5/82)	1	3	5	7
Giant Movie Edition 11296(64pp, Whitman, $1.50); reprints GK #2-4 minus cover; tabloid size; photo-c (See Marvel Treasury)	26	15	22	
Giant Movie Edition 02489(Western/Marvel, $1.50), reprints GK #2-4 minus cover	2	6	13	20

NOTE: Bolle a-2p,3p, Movie Ed.(p). McWilliams a-2i,3i, 5-11, Movie Ed.(i). Painted c-1-9,11-13.

BUCK ROGERS (Comics Module)
TSR, Inc.: 1990 - No. 10, 1991 ($2.95, 44 pgs.)

1-10 (1990): 1-Begin origin in 3 parts. 2-Indicia says #1. 2,3-Black Barney back-up story. 4-All Black Barney issue; B. B.-c. 5-Indicia says #6; Black Barney-c & lead story; Buck Rogers back-up story. 10-Flip book (72pgs.) — 3.00

BUCKSKIN (TV)
Dell Publishing Co.: No. 1011, July, 1959 - No. 1107, June-Aug, 1960

Four Color 1011 (#1)-Photo-c	7	21	49	90
Four Color 1107-Photo-c	6	18	42	80

BUCKY O'HARE (Funny Animal)
Continuity Comics: 1988 ($5.95, graphic novel)

1-Michael Golden-c/a(r); r/serial-Echo of Futurepast #1-6				6.00
Deluxe Hardcover ($40, 52pg, 8x11")				40.00

BUCKY O'HARE
Continuity Comics: Jan, 1991 - No. 5, 1991 ($2.00)

1-6: 1-Michael Golden-c/a — 2.50

BUDDIES IN THE U.S. ARMY
Avon Periodicals: Nov, 1952 - No. 2, 1953

1-Lawrence-c	13	39	66	110
2-Mort Lawrence-c	9	27	49	70

BUFFALO BEE (TV)
Dell Publishing Co.: No. 957, Nov, 1958 - No. 1061, Dec-Feb, 1959-60

Four Color 957 (#1)	9	27	63	120
Four Color 1002 (8-10/59), 1061	7	21	49	85

BUFFALO BILL (See Frontier Fighters, Super Western Comics & Western Action Thrillers)
Youthful Magazines: No. 2, Oct, 1950 - No. 9, Dec, 1951

2-Annie Oakley story	13	39	66	110
3-9: 2-4-Walter Johnson-c/a. 9-Wildey-a	9	27	49	70

BUFFALO BILL CODY (See Cody of the Pony Express)

BUFFALO BILL, JR. (TV) (See Western Roundup)
Dell/Gold Key: Jan, 1956 - No. 13, Aug-Oct, 1959; 1965 (All photo-c)

Four Color 673 (#1)	7	21	49	85
Four Color 742,766,798,828,856(11/57)	5	15	34	55
7(2-4/58)-13	4	12	29	45
1(6/65, Gold Key)-Photo-c(r/F.C. #798); photo-b/c	4	12	29	45

BUFFALO BILL PICTURE STORIES
Street & Smith Publications: June-July, 1949 - No. 2, Aug-Sept, 1949

1,2-Wildey, Powell-a in each	14	42	72	120

BUFFY THE VAMPIRE SLAYER (Based on the TV series)
Dark Horse Comics: 1998 - Present ($2.95/$2.99)

1-Bennett-a/Watson-s; Art Adams-c				5.00
1-Variant photo-c				5.00
1-Gold foil logo Art Adams-c				15.00

	GD2.0	FN6.0	VF8.0	NM9.4
1-Gold foil logo photo-c				20.00
2-15-Regular and photo-c. 4-7-Gomez-a. 5,8-Green-c				4.00
16-38: 29,30-Angel x-over				3.00
Annual '99 ($4.95)-Two stories and pin-ups				5.00
...: Jonathan 1 (1/01, $2.99) two covers; Richards-a				3.00
... Lovers Walk (2/01, $2.99) short stories by various; Richards & photo-c				3.00
Wizard #1/2				12.00

BUFFY THE VAMPIRE SLAYER: ANGEL
Dark Horse Comics: May, 1999 - No. 3, July, 1999 ($2.95, limited series)

1-3-Gomez-a; Matsuda-c & photo-c for each — 3.00

BUFFY THE VAMPIRE SLAYER: GILES
Dark Horse Comics: Oct, 2000 ($2.95, one-shot)

1-Powell & photo-c — 3.00

BUFFY THE VAMPIRE SLAYER: OZ
Dark Horse Comics: July, 2001 - No. 3, Sept, 2001 ($2.99, limited series)

1-3-Totleben & photo-c; Golden-s — 3.00

BUFFY THE VAMPIRE SLAYER: SPIKE AND DRU
Dark Horse Comics: Apr, 1999; No. 2, Oct, 1999; No. 3, Dec, 2000 ($2.95)

1-3: 1,2-Photo-c. 3-Two covers (photo & Sook) — 3.00

BUFFY THE VAMPIRE SLAYER: THE ORIGIN (Adapts movie screenplay)
Dark Horse Comics: Jan, 1999 - No. 3, Mar, 1999 ($2.95, limited series)

1-3-Brereton-s/Bennett-a; reg & photo-c for each — 3.00

BUFFY THE VAMPIRE SLAYER: WILLOW & TARA
Dark Horse Comics: Apr, 2001 ($2.99, one-shot)

1-Terry Moore-a/Chris Golden & Amber Benson-s; Moore-c & photo-c — 3.00

BUG
Marvel Comics: Mar, 1997 ($2.99, one-shot)

1-Micronauts character — 3.00

BUGALOOS (TV)
Charlton Comics: Sept, 1971 - No. 4, Feb, 1972

1	4	12	26	40
2-4	3	9	17	25

NOTE: No. 3(1/72) went on sale late in 1972 (after No. 4) with the 1/73 issues.

BUGBOY
Image Comics: June, 1998 ($3.95, B&W, one-shot)

1-Mark Lewis-s/a — 4.00

BUGHOUSE (Satire)
Ajax/Farrell (Excellent Publ.): Mar-Apr, 1954 - No. 4, Sept-Oct, 1954

V1#1	20	60	105	175
2-4	12	36	61	100

BUGS BUNNY (See The Best of..., Camp Comics, Comic Album #2, 6, 10, 14, Dell Giant #28, 32, 46, Dynabrite, Golden Comics Digest #1, 3, 5, 6, 8, 10, 14, 15, 17, 21, 26, 30, 34, 39, 42, 47, Kite Fun Book, Large Feature Comic #8, Looney Tunes and Merry Melodies, March of Comics #44, 59, 75, 83, 97, 115, 132, 149, 160, 179, 188, 201, 220, 231, 245, 259, 273, 287, 301, 315, 329, 343, 363, 367, 380, 392, 403, 415, 428, 440, 452, 464, 476, 487, Porky Pig, Puffed Wheat, Story Hour Series #802, Super Book #14, 26 and Whitman Comic Books)

BUGS BUNNY (See Dell Giants for annuals)
Dell Publishing Co./Gold Key No. 86-218/Whitman No. 219 on: 1942 - No. 245, April, 1984
Large Feature Comic 8(1942)-(Rarely found in fine-mint condition)

	123	369	861	1600
Four Color 33 ('43)	115	345	805	1500
Four Color 51	36	108	252	475
Four Color 88	21	63	147	270
Four Color 123('46),142,164	16	48	112	205
Four Color 187,200,217,233	11	33	77	140
Four Color 250-Used in SOTI, pg. 309	12	36	84	150
Four Color 266,274,281,289,298('50)	9	27	63	110
Four Color 307,317(#1),327(#2),338,347,355,366,376,393	7	21	49	95
Four Color 407,420,432(10/52)	6	18	42	80
Four Color 498(9/53),585(9/54), 647(9/55)	5	15	35	60
Four Color 724(9/56),838(9/57),1064(12/59)	4	12	30	50
28(12-1/52-53)-30	4	12	30	50

Bugs Bunny #100 © WB

Bulletman #2 © FAW

Burke's Law #1 © DELL

	GD2.0	FN6.0	VF8.0	NM9.4
31-50	4	12	26	40
51-85(7-9/62)	3	9	20	30
86(10/62)-88-Bugs Bunny's Showtime-(25¢, 80pgs.)	6	18	42	75
89-99	2	6	15	22
100	3	9	17	25
101-118: 118-Last 12¢ issue	2	6	11	16
119-140	2	6	9	12
141-170	1	3	6	9
171-218	1	3	5	7
219,220,225-237(5/82): 229-Swipe of Barks story/WDC&S #223. 233(2/82)				
	1	3	6	8
221(9/80),222(11/80)-Pre-pack? (Scarce)	2	6	11	16
223 (1/81),224 (3/81)-Low distr.	2	6	9	12
238-245 (#90070 on-c, nd, nd code; pre-pack): 238(5/83), 239(6/83), 240(7/83),				
241(7/83), 242(8/83), 243(8/83), 244(3/84), 245(4/84)				
	2	6	10	14

NOTE: Reprints-100,102-104,110,115,123,143,144,147,167,173,175-177,179-185,187,190.

...Comic-Go-Round 11196-(224 pgs.)($1.95)(Golden Press, 1979)				
	3	9	21	32
...Winter Fun 1(12/67-Gold Key)-Giant	4	12	30	50

BUGS BUNNY
DC Comics: June, 1990 - No. 3, Aug, 1990 ($1.00, limited series)

1-3: Daffy Duck, Elmer Fudd, others app.				4.00

BUGS BUNNY (...Monthly on-c)
DC Comics: 1993 - No. 3, 1994? ($1.95)

1-3-Bugs, Porky Pig, Daffy, Road Runner				3.50

BUGS BUNNY & PORKY PIG
Gold Key: Sept, 1965 (Paper-c, giant, 100 pgs.)

1(30025-509)	8	24	56	100

BUGS BUNNY'S ALBUM (See Bugs Bunny, Four Color No. 498,585,647,724)

BUGS BUNNY LIFE STORY ALBUM (See Bugs Bunny, Four Color No. 838)

BUGS BUNNY MERRY CHRISTMAS (See Bugs Bunny, Four Color No. 1064)

BUILDING, THE
Kitchen Sink Press: 1987; 2000 (8 1/2" x 11" sepia toned graphic novel)

nn-Will Eisner-s/c-a				10.00
nn-(DC Comics, 9/00, $9.95) reprints 1987 edition				10.00

BULLET CROW, FOWL OF FORTUNE
Eclipse Comics: Mar, 1987 - No. 2, Apr, 1987 ($2.00, B&W, limited series)

1,2-The Comic Reader-r & new-a				2.50

BULLETMAN (See Fawcett Miniatures, Master Comics, Mighty Midget Comics, Nickel Comics & XMas Comics)
Fawcett Publications: Sum, 1941 - #12, 2/12/43; #14, Spr, 1946 - #16, Fall, 1946 (No #13)

1-Silver metallic-c	350	1050	2188	4200
2-Raboy-c	150	450	938	1650
3,5-Raboy-c each	107	321	669	1180
4	95	285	577	1020
6-10: 7-Ghost Stories told by night watchman of cemetery begins;				
hidden message "Chic Stone is a jerk"	77	231	483	850
11,12,14,16: 14(nn 13): 12-Robot-c	59	177	369	650

NOTE: Mac Raboy c-1-3, 5, 6, 10. "Bulletman the Flying Detective" on cover #8 on.

BULLETPROOF MONK
Image Comics (Flypaper Press): 1998 - No. 3, 1999 ($2.95, limited series)

1-3-Oeming-a				3.00

BULLETS AND BRACELETS (Also see Marvel Versus DC #3 & DC Versus Marvel #4)
Marvel Comics (Amalgam): Apr, 1996 ($1.95)

1-John Ostrander script & Gary Frank-c/a				2.50

BULLS-EYE (Cody of The Pony Express No. 8 on)
Mainline No. 1-5/Charlton No. 6,7: 7-8/54-No. 5, 3-4/55; No. 6, 6/55; No. 7, 8/55

1-S&K-c, 2 pgs.-a	55	165	330	575
2-S&K-c/a	45	135	270	475
3-5-S&K-c/a(2 each). 4-Last pre-code issue (1-2/55). 5-Censored issue with				
tomahawks removed in battle scene	40	120	217	375

	GD2.0	FN6.0	VF8.0	NM9.4
6-S&K-c/a	33	99	174	300
7-S&K-c/a(3)	40	120	217	375

BULLS-EYE COMICS (Formerly Komik Pages #10; becomes Kayo #12)
Harry 'A' Chesler: No. 11, 1944

11-Origin K-9, Green Knight's sidekick, Lance; The Green Knight, Lady Satan,				
Yankee Doodle Jones app.	40	120	240	420

BULLWHIP GRIFFIN (See Movie Comics)

BULLWINKLE (...and Rocky No. 20 on; See March of Comics #233 and Rocky & Bullwinkle)(TV) (Jay Ward)
Dell/Gold Key: 3-5/62 - #11, 4/74; #12, 6/76 - #19, 3/78; #20, 4/79 - #25, 2/80

Four Color 1270 (3-5/62)	20	60	140	260
01-090-209 (Dell, 7-9/62)	16	48	112	205
1(11/62, Gold Key)	14	42	98	180
2(2/63)	9	27	63	115
3(4/72)-11(4/74-Gold Key)	5	15	34	55
12-14: 12(6/76)-Reprints. 13(5/76), 14-New stories	2	6	15	22
15-25	2	6	10	14
Mother Moose Nursery Pomes 01-530-207 (5-7/62, Dell)				
	19	57	130	240

NOTE: Reprints: 6, 7, 20-24.

BULLWINKLE (...& Rocky No. 2 on)(TV)
Charlton Comics: July, 1970 - No. 7, July, 1971

1	6	18	40	65
2-7	4	12	30	50

BULLWINKLE AND ROCKY
Star Comics/Marvel Comics No. 3 on: Nov, 1987 - No. 9, Mar, 1989

1-9: Boris & Natasha in all. 3,5,8-Dudley Do-Right app. 4-Reagan-c				4.00
Marvel Moosterworks (1/92, $4.95)	1	4	7	10

BUMMER
Fantagraphics Books: June, 1995 ($3.50, B&W, mature)

1				3.50

BUNNY (Also see Harvey Pop Comics)
Harvey Publications: Dec, 1966 - No. 20, Dec, 1971; No. 21, Nov, 1976

1-68 pg. Giants begin	6	18	42	70
2-10	4	12	26	40
11-18: 18-Last 68 pg. Giant	3	10	23	35
19-21-52 pg. Giants: 21-Fruitman app.	3	9	20	30

BURKE'S LAW (TV)
Dell Publ.: 1-3/64; No. 2, 5-7/64; No. 3, 3-5/65 (All have Gene Barry photo-c)

1-Photo-c	5	15	34	55
2,3-Photo-c	4	12	27	42

BURNING ROMANCES (See Fox Giants)

BUSTER BEAR
Quality Comics Group (Arnold Publ.): Dec, 1953 - No. 10, June, 1955

1-Funny animal	10	30	55	80
2	6	18	29	40
3-10	5	15	23	30
I.W. Reprint #9,10 (Super on inside)	2	6	10	14

BUSTER BROWN COMICS (See Promotional Comics section)

BUSTER BUNNY
Standard Comics(Animated Cartoons)/Pines: Nov, 1949 - No. 16, Oct, 1953

1-Frazetta 1 pg. text illo.	10	30	55	80
2	6	18	29	40
3-16: 15-Racist-c	5	14	21	28

BUSTER CRABBE (TV)
Famous Funnies Publ.: Nov, 1951 - No. 12, 1953

1-1st app.(?) Frazetta anti-drug ad; text story about Buster Crabbe & Billy the				
Kid	40	120	220	380
2-Williamson/Evans-c; text story about Wild Bill Hickok & Pecos Bill				
	39	117	208	360
3-Williamson/Evans-c/a	40	120	220	380
4-Frazetta-c/a, 1pg.; bondage-c	47	141	286	500
5-Frazetta-c; Williamson/Krenkel/Orlando-a, 11pgs. (per Mr. Williamson)				

Buster Crabbe #12 © FF

Cable #55 © MAR

Cage #11 © MAR

	GD2.0	FN6.0	VF8.0	NM9.4

	118	354	738	1300
6,8	20	60	105	175
7-Frazetta one pg. ad	20	60	105	180
9-One pg. Frazetta Boy Scouts ad (1st?)	17	51	88	150
10-12	12	36	61	100

NOTE: Eastern Color sold 3 dozen each NM file copies of #s 9-12 a few years ago.

BUSTER CRABBE (The Amazing Adventures of…)(Movie star)
Lev Gleason Publications: Dec, 1953 - No. 4, June, 1954

1,4: 1-Photo-c. 4-Flash Gordon-c	22	66	116	200
2,3-Toth-a	21	63	110	185

BUTCH CASSIDY
Skywald Comics: June, 1971 - No. 3, Oct, 1971 (52 pgs.)

1-Red Mask reprint, retitled Maverick; Bolle-a; Sutton-a				
	2	6	13	20
2,3: 2-Whip Wilson-r. 3-Dead Canyon Days reprint/Crack Western No. 63;				
Sundance Kid app.; Crandall-a	2	6	10	14

BUTCH CASSIDY (…& the Wild Bunch)
Avon Periodicals: 1951

1-Kinstler-c/a	19	57	99	165

NOTE: *Reinman* story; Issue number on inside spine.

BUTCH CASSIDY (See Fun-In No. 11 & Western Adventure Comics)

BUTCHER, THE (Also see Brave and the Bold, 2nd Series))
DC Comics: May, 1990 - No. 5, Sept, 1990 ($1.50, mature)

1-5: 1-No indicia inside				2.50

BUTCHER KNIGHT
Image Comics (Top Cow): Jan, 2001 - No. 4, June, 2001 ($2.95, limited series)

Preview (B&W, 16 pgs.) Dwayne Turner-c/a				2.25
1-4-Dwayne Turner-c/a				3.00

BUZ SAWYER (Sweeney No. 4 on)
Standard Comics: June, 1948 - No. 3, 1949

1-Roy Crane-a	23	69	121	210
2-Intro his pal Sweeney	14	42	72	120
3	11	33	55	90

BUZ SAWYER'S PAL, ROSCOE SWEENEY (See Sweeney)

BUZZ, THE (Also see Spider-Girl)
Marvel Comics: July, 2000 - No. 3, Sept, 2000 ($2.99, limited series)

1-3-Buscema-a/DeFalco & Frenz-s				3.00

BUZZ BUZZ COMICS MAGAZINE
Horse Comics: May, 1996 ($4.95, B&W, over-sized magazine)

1-Paul Pope-c/a/scripts; Moebius-a				5.00

BUZZY (See All Funny Comics)
National Periodical Publications/Detective Comics: Winter, 1944-45 - No. 75, 1-2/57; No. 76, 10/57; No. 77, 10/58

1 (52 pgs. begin); "America's favorite teenster"	30	90	159	275
2 (Spr, 1945)	14	42	72	125
3-5	10	30	55	85
6-10	7	21	38	55
11-20	6	18	32	45
21-30	5	15	25	35
31,35-38	5	15	23	30
32-34,39-Last 52 pgs. Scribbly story by Mayer in each (these four stories were done for Scribbly #14 which was delayed for a year)				
	6	18	29	40
40-77: 62-Last precode (2/55)	5	14	21	28

BUZZY THE CROW (See Harvey Comics Hits #60 & 62, Harvey Hits #18 & Paramount Animated Comics #1)

BY BIZARRE HANDS
Dark Horse Comics: Apr, 1994 - No. 3, June, 1994 ($2.50, B&W, mature)

1-3: Lansdale stories				2.50

CABBOT: BLOODHUNTER (Also see Bloodstrike & Bloodstrike: Assassin)
Maximum Press: Jan, 1997 ($2.50, one-shot)

1-Rick Veitch-a/script; Platt-c; Thor, Chapel & Prophet cameos				2.50

	GD2.0	FN6.0	VF8.0	NM9.4

CABLE (See Ghost Rider &…, & New Mutants #87)
Marvel Comics: May, 1993 - Present ($3.50/$1.95/$1.50/$1.99/$2.25)

1-($3.50, 52 pgs.)-Gold foil & embossed-c; Thibert a-1-4p; c-1-3				5.00
2-15: 3-Extra 16 pg. X-Men/Avengers ann. preview. 4-Liefeld-a assist; last Thibert-a(p). 6-8-Reveals that Baby Nathan is Cable; gives background on Stryfe. 9-Omega Red-c/story. 11-Bound-in trading card sheet				3.50
16-Newsstand edition				2.50
16-Enhanced edition				5.00
17-20-($1.95)-Deluxe edition, 20-w/bound in '95 Fleer Ultra cards				3.00
17-20-($1.50)-Standard edition				2.50
21-24, 26-44, -1(7/97): 21-Begin $1.95-c; return from Age of Apocalypse. 24-Grizzly dies. 28-vs. Sugarman; Mr. Sinister app. 30-X-Man-c/app.; Exodus app. 31-vs. X-Man. 32-Post app. 33-Post-c/app; Mandarin app (flashback); includes "Onslaught Update". 34-Onslaught x-over; Hulk-c/app.; Apocalypse app (cont'd in Hulk #444). 35-Onslaught x-over; Apocalypse vs. Cable. 36-w/card insert. 38-Weapon X-c/app; Psycho Man & Micronauts app. 40-Scott Clark-a(p). 41-Bishop-c/app.				3.00
25 ($3.95)-Foil gatefold-c				4.00
45-49,51-74: 45-Operation Zero Tolerance. 51-1st Casey-s. 54-Black Panther. 55-Domino-c/app. 62-Nick Fury-c/app.63-Stryfe-c/app. 67,68-Avengers-c/app. 71,73-Liefeld-a				2.50
50-($2.99) Double sized w/wraparound-c				3.00
75 -($2.99) Liefeld-c/a; Apocalypse: The Twelve x-over				3.00
76-79: 76-Apocalypse: The Twelve x-over				2.25
80-96: 80-Begin $2.25-c. 87-Mystique-c/app.				2.50
97-99: 97-Tischman-s/Kordey-a/c begin				2.25
100($3.99) Dialogue-free 'Nuff Said back-up story				4.00
…/Machine Man '98 Annual ($2.99) Wraparound-c				3.00
…/X-Force '96 Annual ($2.95) Wraparound-c				3.00
…'99 Annual ($3.50) vs. Sinister; computer photo-c				3.50
…Second Genesis 1 (9/99, $3.99) r/New Mutants #99, 100 and X-Force #1; Liefeld-c				4.00

CABLE - BLOOD AND METAL (Also see New Mutants #87 & X-Force #8)
Marvel Comics: Oct, 1992 - No. 2, Nov, 1992 ($2.50, limited series, 52 pgs.)

1-Fabian Nicieza scripts; John Romita, Jr.-c/a in both; Cable vs. Stryfe; 2nd app. of The Wild Pack (becomes The Six Pack); wraparound-c.				4.00
2-Prelude to X-Cutioner's Song				3.00

CADET GRAY OF WEST POINT (See Dell Giants)

CADILLACS & DINOSAURS (TV)
Marvel Comics (Epic Comics): Nov, 1990 - No. 6, Apr, 1991 ($2.50, limited series, coated paper)

1-6: r/Xenozoic Tales in color w/new-c				3.00
…In 3-D #1 (7/92, $3.95, Kitchen Sink)-With glasses				6.00

CADILLACS AND DINOSAURS (TV)
Topps Comics: V2#1, Feb, 1994 - V2#9, 1995 ($2.50, limited series)

V2#1-($2.95)-Collector's edition w/Stout-c & bound-in poster; Buckler-a; foil stamped logo; Giordano-a in all				6.00
V2#1-9: 1-Newsstand ed. w/Giordano-c. 2,3-Collector's editions w/Stout-c & posters. 2,3-Newsstand ed. w/Giordano-c; w/o posters. 4-6-Collectors & Newsstand editions; Kieth-c. 7-9-Linsner-c				3.00

CAFFEINE
Slave Labor Graphics: Jan, 1996 - No. 10, 1999 ($2.95/$3.95, B&W)

1-9				3.00
10-($3.95)				4.00

CAGE (Also see Hero for Hire, Power Man & Punisher)
Marvel Comics: Apr, 1992 - No. 20, Nov, 1993 ($1.25)

1,3,10,12: 3-Punisher-c & minor app. 10-Rhino & Hulk-c/story. 12-(52 pgs.)-Iron Fist app.				3.00
2,4-9,11,13-20: 9-Rhino-c/story; Hulk cameo				2.50

CAGED HEAT 3000 (Movie)
Roger Corman's Cosmic Comics: Nov, 1995 - No. 3, Jan, 1996 ($2.50)

1-3: Adaptation of film				2.50

CAGES
Tundra Publ.: 1991 - No. 10, May, 1996 ($3.50/$3.95/$4.95, limited series)

1-Dave McKean-c/a in all	2	6	9	12

Calling All Boys #3 © PMI

Camera Comics #2 © USCPC

Candy #46 © QUA

CA

	GD2.0	FN6.0	VF8.0	NM9.4

	GD2.0	FN6.0	VF8.0	NM9.4

2-Misprint exists — 1, 3, 6, 8
3-9: 5-$3.95-c begins — 4.00
10-($4.95) — 5.00

CAIN'S HUNDRED (TV)
Dell Publishing Co.: May-July, 1962 - No. 2, Sept-Nov, 1962

nn(01-094-207)	3	9	20	30
2	2	6	13	20

CAIN/VAMPIRELLA FLIP BOOK
Harris Comics: Oct, 1994 ($6.95, one-shot, squarebound)

nn-contains Cain #3 & #4; flip book is r/Vampirella story from 1993 Creepy
Fearbook. — 1, 3, 6, 9

CALIBER PRESENTS
Caliber Press: Jan, 1989 - No. 24, 1991 ($1.95/$2.50, B&W, 52 pgs.)

1-Anthology; 1st app. The Crow; Tim Vigil-c/a — 5, 15, 38, 60
2-Deadworld story; Tim Vigil-a — 1, 3, 6, 8
3-24: 15-24 ($3.50, 68 pgs.) — 3.50

CALIBER PRESENTS: CINDERELLA ON FIRE
Caliber Press: 1994 ($2.95, B&W, mature)

1 — 3.00

CALIBER SPOTLIGHT
Caliber Press: May, 1995 ($2.95, B&W)

1-Kabuki app — 3.50

CALIBRATIONS
Caliber: 1996 - No. 5 (99¢, anthology)

1-5: 1-Jill Thompson-c/a. 1,2-Atmospherics by Warren Ellis — 2.50

CALIFORNIA GIRLS
Eclipse Comics: June, 1987 - No. 8, May, 1988 ($2.00, 40 pgs, B&W)

1-8: All contain color paper dolls — 3.00

CALLING ALL BOYS (Tex Granger No. 18 on)
Parents' Magazine Institute: Jan, 1946 - No. 17, May, 1948 (Photo c-1-5,7,8)

1	12	36	61	100
2-Contains Roy Rogers article	6	18	32	45

3-7,9,11,14-17: 6-Painted-c. 11-Rin Tin Tin photo on-c; Tex Granger begins.
14-J. Edgar Hoover photo on-c. 15-Tex Granger-c begins

	5	15	24	32
8-Milton Caniff story	7	21	38	55
10-Gary Cooper photo on-c	7	21	36	50
12-Bob Hope photo on-c	11	33	55	95
13-Bing Crosby photo on-c	10	30	55	80

CALLING ALL GIRLS
Parents' Magazine Institute: Sept, 1941 - No. 89, Sept, 1949 (Part magazine, part comic)

1	15	45	77	135
2-Photo-c	8	24	45	65
3-Shirley Temple photo-c	11	33	55	90
4-10: 4,5,7,9-Photo-c. 9-Flag-c	8	18	29	40
11-Tina Thayer photo-c; Mickey Rooney photo-b/c; B&W photo inside of Gary Cooper as Lou Gehrig in "Pride of Yankees"	7	21	36	50
12-20	5	15	25	35
21-39,41-43(10-11/45)-Last issue with comics	5	14	21	28
40-Liz Taylor photo-c	14	42	72	125
44-51(7/46)-Last comic book size issue	4	12	18	24
52-89	4	11	17	22

NOTE: *Jack Sparling* art in many issues; becomes a girls' magazine "Senior Prom" with #90.

CALLING ALL KIDS (Also see True Comics)
Parents' Magazine Institute: Dec-Jan, 1945-46 - No. 26, Aug, 1949

1-Funny animal	12	36	61	100
2	6	18	32	45
3-10	5	15	23	30
11-26	4	12	19	25

CALVIN (See Li'l Kids)

CALVIN & THE COLONEL (TV)
Dell Publishing Co.: No. 1354, Apr-June, 1962 - No. 2, July-Sept, 1962

Four Color 1354(#1)	9	27	63	115
2	5	15	35	70

CAMBION
Slave Labor Graphics: Dec, 1995 - No. 2, Feb, 1996 ($2.95, B&W)

1,2 — 3.00

CAMELOT 3000
DC Comics: Dec, 1982 - No. 11, July, 1984; No. 12, Apr, 1985 (Direct sales, maxi series, Mando paper)

1-12: 1-Mike Barr scripts & Brian Bolland-c/a begin. 5-Intro Knights of New
Camelot — 3.00
TPB (1988, $12.95) r/#1-12 — 15.00
NOTE: *Austin* a-7i-12i. *Bolland* a-1-12p; c-1-12.

CAMERA COMICS
U.S. Camera Publishing Corp./ME: July, 1944 - No. 9, Summer, 1946

nn (7/44)	25	75	130	225
nn (9/44)	20	60	105	175
1(10/44)-The Grey Comet	20	60	105	175
2	14	42	72	120
3-Nazi WW II-c; photos	13	39	66	110
4-9: All half photos	12	36	61	100

CAMP CANDY (TV)
Marvel Comics: May, 1990 - No. 6, Oct, 1990 ($1.00, limited series)

1-6: Post-c/a(p); featuring John Candy — 4.00

CAMP COMICS
Dell Publishing Co.: Feb, 1942 - No. 3, April, 1942 (All have photo-c)

1- "Seaman Sy Wheeler" by Kelly, 7 pgs.; Bugs Bunny app.; Mark Twain adaptation	66	198	413	725
2-Kelly-a, 12 pgs.; Bugs Bunny app.; classic-c	64	192	398	700
3-(Scarce)-Dave Berg & Walt Kelly-a	55	165	341	600

CAMP RUNAMUCK (TV)
Dell Publishing Co.: Apr, 1966

1-Photo-c — 3, 10, 23, 35

CAMPUS LOVES
Quality Comics Group (Comic Magazines): Dec, 1949 - No. 5, Aug, 1950

1-Ward-c/a (9 pgs.)	33	99	174	300
2-Ward-c/a	25	75	130	225
3-5	13	39	66	110

NOTE: *Gustavson* a-1-5. Photo c-3-5.

CAMPUS ROMANCE (...Romances on cover)
Avon Periodicals/Realistic: Sept-Oct, 1949 - No. 3, Feb-Mar, 1950

1-Walter Johnson-a; c-/Avon paperback #348	23	69	121	210
2-Grandenetti-a; c-/Avon paperback #151	17	51	88	150
3-c-/Avon paperback #201	17	51	88	150
Realistic reprint	8	24	42	60

CANADA DRY PREMIUMS (See Swamp Fox, The & Terry & The Pirates in the Promotional Comics section)

CANCELLED COMIC CAVALCADE (See the Promotional Comics section)

CANDID TALES (Also see Bold Stories & It Rhymes With Lust)
Kirby Publ. Co.: April, 1950; June, 1950 (Digest size) (144 pgs.) (Full color)

nn-(Scarce) Contains Wood female pirate story, 15 pgs., and 14 pgs. in June
issue; Powell-a — 95, 285, 597, 1050
NOTE: *Another version exists with Dr. Kilmore by Wood; no female pirate story.*

CANDY
William H. Wise & Co.: Fall, 1944 - No. 3, Spring, 1945

1-Two Scoop Scuttle stories by Wolverton	40	120	217	375
2,3-Scoop Scuttle by Wolverton, 2-4 pgs.	29	87	156	270

CANDY (Teen-age)(Also see Police Comics #37)
Quality Comics Group (Comic Magazines): Autumn, 1947 - No. 64, Jul, 1956

1-Gustavson-a	23	69	121	210
2-Gustavson-a	12	36	61	105
3-10	8	24	45	65
11-30	6	18	29	40
31-64: 64-Ward-c(p)?	5	15	25	35

Captain Action #1 © DC

Captain Aero Comics V2 #1 © HOKE

Captain America #202 © MAR

	GD2.0	FN6.0	VF8.0	NM9.4

Super Reprint No. 2,10,12,16,17,18('63- '64):17-Candy #12

| | 2 | 6 | 11 | 16 |

NOTE: *Jack Cole* 1-2 pg. art in many issues.

CANNON (See Heroes, Inc. Presents Cannon)

CANNONBALL COMICS
Rural Home Publishing Co.: Feb, 1945 - No. 2, Mar, 1945

1-The Crash Kid, Thunderbrand, The Captive Prince & Crime Crusader begin; skull-c	82	246	511	900
2-Devil-c	64	192	398	700

CANTEEN KATE (See All Picture All True Love Story & Fightin' Marines)
St. John Publishing Co.: June, 1952 - No. 3, Nov, 1952

1-Matt Baker-c/a	61	183	381	675
2-Matt Baker-c/a	43	129	257	450
3-(Rare)-Used in POP, pg. 75; Baker-c/a	52	157	314	550

CAP'N QUICK & A FOOZLE (Also see Eclipse Mag. & Monthly)
Eclipse Comics: July, 1984 - No. 3, Nov, 1985 ($1.50, color, Baxter paper)

1-3-Rogers-c/a				3.00

CAPTAIN ACTION (Toy)
National Periodical Publications: Oct-Nov, 1968 - No. 5, June-July, 1969
(Based on Ideal toy)

1-Origin; Wood-a; Superman-c app.	12	36	84	140
2,3,5-Kane/Wood-a	7	21	50	80
4	5	15	38	60

CAPTAIN AERO COMICS (Samson No. 1-6; also see Veri Best Sure Fire
& Veri Best Sure Shot Comics)
Holyoke Publishing Co.:V1#7(#1), Dec, 1941 - V2#4(#10), Jan, 1943;
V3#9(#11), Sept, 1943 -V4#3(#17), Oct, 1944; #21, Dec, 1944 - #26, Aug, 1946
(No #18-20)

V1#7(#1)-Flag-Man & Solar, Master of Magic, Captain Aero, Cap Stone, Adventurer begin	164	492	1023	1800
8-10: 8(#2)-Pals of Freedom app. 9(#3)-Alias X begins; Pals of Freedom app. 10(#4)-Origin The Gargoyle; Kubert-a	77	231	483	850
11,12(#5,6)-Kubert-a; Miss Victory in #6	64	192	398	700
V2#1,2(#7,8): 8-Origin The Red Cross; Miss Victory app.; Brodsky-c(i)	40	120	232	400
3(#9)-Miss Victory app.	37	111	197	340
4(#10)-Miss Victory app.	29	87	156	270
V3#9 - V3#13(#11-15): 11,15-Miss Victory app.	24	72	127	220
V4#2(#16)	23	69	121	210
V4#3(#17), 21-25-L. B. Cole covers. 22-Intro/origin Mighty Mite.	43	129	257	450
26-L. B. Cole S/F-c; Palais-a(2) (scarce)	86	258	540	950

NOTE: *L.B. Cole c-17. Hollingsworth a-23. Infantino a-23, 26. Schomburg c-15, 16.*

CAPTAIN AMERICA (See Adventures of..., All-Select, All Winners, Aurora, Avengers #4,
Blood and Glory, Captain Britain 16-20, Giant-Size..., The Invaders, Marvel Double Feature,
Marvel Fanfare, Marvel Mystery, Marvel Super-Action, Marvel Super Heroes V2#3, Marvel Team-
Up, Marvel Treasury Special, Power Record Comics, USA Comics, Young Allies & Young Men)

CAPTAIN AMERICA (Formerly Tales of Suspense #1-99) (Captain America and
the Falcon #134-223 & Steve Rogers: Captain America #444-454 appears on
cover only)

Marvel Comics Group: No. 100, Apr, 1968 - No. 454, Aug, 1996

100-Flashback on Cap's revival with Avengers & Sub-Mariner; story continued from Tales of Suspense #99; Kirby-c/a begins	37	111	278	500
101-The Sleeper/story; Red Skull app.	7	21	53	85
102-104: 102-Sleeper-c/s. 103,104-Red Skull-c/sty	5	15	38	60
105-108	4	12	30	50
109-Origin Capt. America retold	7	21	50	80
110,111,113-Classic Steranko-c/a: 110-Rick becomes Cap's partner; Hulk x-over; 1st app. Viper. 111-Death of Steve Rogers. 113-Cap's funeral	6	18	45	75
112-Origin retold; last Kirby-c/a	4	12	26	40
114,115: 115-Last 12¢ issue	3	9	19	28
116,118-120	2	6	15	22
117-1st app. The Falcon (9/69)	6	18	40	65
121-136,139,140: 121-Falcon's origin. 133-The Falcon becomes Cap's partner; origin Modok. 140-Origin Grey Gargoyle retold	2	6	11	15
137,138-Spider-Man x-over	2	6	12	18

	GD2.0	FN6.0	VF8.0	NM9.4

141,142: 142-Last 15¢ issue	2	6	10	14
143-(52 pgs).	2	6	12	18
144-153: 144-New costume Falcon. 153-1st app. (cameo) Jack Monroe	2	6	9	12
154-1st full app. Jack Monroe (Nomad)(10/72)	2	6	11	15
155-Origin; redrawn w/Falcon added; origin Jack Monroe	2	6	11	15
156-171,176-179: 155-158-Cap's strength increased. 160-1st app. Solarr. 164-1st app. Nightshade. 176-End of Capt. America.	1	4	7	10
172-175: X-Men x-over	2	6	11	15
180-Intro/origin of Nomad (Steve Rogers)	2	6	11	15
181-Intro/origin new Cap.	2	6	9	12
182,184-192: 186-True origin The Falcon	1	3	5	7
183-Death of new Cap; Nomad becomes Cap	1	4	7	10
193-Kirby-c/a begins	2	6	12	18
194-199-(Regular 25¢ edition)(4-7/76)	2	6	9	12
196-199-(30¢-c variants, limited distribution)	2	6	12	18
200-(Regular 25¢ edition)(8/76)	2	6	11	15
200-(30¢-c variant, limited distribution)	2	6	15	22
201-214-Kirby-c/a	1	4	7	10
210-214-(35¢-c variants, limited dist.)(6-10/77)	2	6	11	15
215,216,218-229,231-234,236-240,242-246: 215-Retells Cap's origin. 216-r/story from Strange Tales #114. 229-Marvel Man app. 233-Death of Sharon Carter. 234-Daredevil x-over. 244,245-Miller-c				4.00
217,230,235: 217-1st app. Marvel Man (later Quasar). 230-Battles Hulk-c/story cont'd in Hulk #232. 235-(7/79) Daredevil x-over; Miller-a(p)				6.00
241-Punisher app.; Miller-c.	2	6	9	12
241-2nd print				2.50
247-255-Byrne-a. 255-Origin; Miller-c.				6.00
256-281,284,285,289-322,324-326,328-331: 264-Old X-Men cameo in flash-back. 265,266-Nick Fury & Spider-Man. 267-1st app. Everyman. 269-1st Team America. 279-(3/83)-Contains Tattooz skin decals. 281-1950s Bucky returns. 284-Patriot (Jack Mace) app. 285-Death of Patriot. 298-Origin Red Skull. 328-Origin & 1st app. D-Man				3.00
282-Bucky becomes new Nomad (Jack Monroe)				4.00
282-Silver ink 2nd print (with $1.75) w/original date (6/83)				2.25
283,327,333-340: 283-2nd app. Nomad. 327-Capt. Amer. battles Super Patriot. 333-Intro & origin new Captain (Super Patriot) 339-Fall of the Mutants tie-in				4.00
286-288-Deathlok app.				4.00
323-1st app. new Super Patriot (see Nick Fury)				4.00
332-Old Cap resigns				6.00
341-343,345-349				3.00
344-($1.50, 52 pgs.)-Ronald Reagan cameo				4.00
350-($1.75, 68 pgs.)-Return of Steve Rogers (original Cap) to original costume				4.00
351-382,384-396: 351-Nick Fury app. 354-1st app. U.S. Agent (6/89, see Avengers West Coast)373-Bullseye app. 375-Daredevil app. 386-U.S. Agent app. 387-389-Red Skull back-up stories. 396-Last $1.00-c. 396,397-1st app. all new Jack O'Lantern				2.50
383-($2.00, 68 pgs.)-50th anniversary issue; Red Skull story; Jim Lee-c(i)				4.00
397-399,401-424,425: 402-Begin 6 part Man-Wolf story w/Wolverine in #403-407. 405-410-New Jack O'Lantern app. in back-up story. 406-Cable & Shatterstar cameo. 407-Capwolf vs. Cable-c/story. 408-Infinity War x-over; Falcon solo back-up. 423-Vs. Namor-c/story				2.25
400-($2.25, 84 pgs.)-Flip book format w/double gatefold-c; r/Avengers #4 plus-c; contains cover pin-ups.				3.00
425-($2.95, 52 pgs.)-Embossed Foil-c ed.n; Fighting Chance Pt. 1				3.00
426-443,446,447,449-453: 427-Begin $1.50-c; bound-in trading card sheet. 449-Thor app. 450-"Man Without A Country" storyline begins, ends #453; Bill Clinton app; variant-c exists. 451-1st app.Cap's new costume. 452-Machinesmith app. 453-Cap gets old costume back; Bill Clinton app.				2.25
444-Mark Waid scripts & Ron Garney-c/a(p) begins, ends #454; Avengers app.				5.00
445,454: 445-Sharon Carter & Red Skull return.				4.00
448-($2.95, double-issue)-Waid script & Garney-c/a; Red Skull "dies"				4.00
Special 1(1/71)-Origin retold	4	12	26	40
Special 2(1/72, 52 pgs.)-Colan-r/Not Brand Echh; all-r	2	6	15	22
Annual 3('76, 52 pgs.)-Kirby-c/a(new)	2	6	11	15
Annual 4('77, 34 pgs.)-Magneto-c/story	2	6	11	15

Captain America Annual 2001 © MAR

Captain America Comics #7 © MAR

Captain America: Sentinel of Liberty #5 © MAR

	GD2.0	FN6.0	VF8.0	NM9.4
Annual 5-7: (52 pgs.)('81-'83)				5.00
Annual 8(9/86)-Wolverine-c/story	3	9	17	24
Annual 9-13('90-'94, 68 pgs.)-9-Nomad back-up. 10-Origin retold (2 pgs.). 11-Falcon solo story. 12-Bagged w/card. 13-Red Skull-c/story				3.00
...Ashcan Edition ('95, 75¢)				2.25
...Deathlok Lives! nn(10/93, $4.95)-r/#286-288				5.00
...Drug War 1-(1994, $2.00, 52 pgs.)-New Warriors app.				2.25
...Man Without a Country(1998, $12.99, TPB)-r/#450-453				13.00
...Medusa Effect 1 (1994, $2.95, 68 pgs.)-Origin Baron Zemo				3.00
...Operation Rebirth (1996, $9.95)-r/#445-448				10.00
...Streets of Poison ($15.95)-r/#372-378				16.00
...: The Movie Special nn (5/92, $3.50, 52 pgs.)-Adapts movie; printed on coated stock; The Red Skull app.				3.50

NOTE: **Austin** c-225i, 239i, 246i. **Buscema** a-115p, 217p; c-136p, 217, 297. **Byrne** c-223(part), 238, 239, 247p-254p, 255, 313p, 350. **Colan** a(p)-116-137, 256, Annual 5; c(p)-116-123, 126, 129. **Everett** a-136i, 137i; c-126i. **Gil Kane** a(p)-444-454. **Gil Kane** 145p; c-147p, 149p, 150i, 170p, 172-174, 180, 181p, 183-190p, 215, 216, 220, 221. **Kirby** a(p)-100-109, 112, 193-214, 216, Special 1, 2(layouts), Annual 3, 4; c-100-109, 112, 126p, 193-214. **Ron Lim** a(p)-366, 368-386; c-366p, 368-378p, 379, 380-393p. **Miller** c-241p, 244p, 245p, 255p, Annual 5. **Mooney** a-149i. **Morrow** a-243p, 246p. **Robbins** c(p)-183-187, 189-192, 225. **Roussos** a-140i, 168i. **Starlin/Sinnott** c-162. **Sutton** a-244i. **Tuska** a-112i, 215p, Special 2. **Waid** scripts-444-454. **Williamson** a-313i. **Wood** a-127i. **Zeck** a-263-289; c-300.

CAPTAIN AMERICA (Volume Two)
Marvel Comics: V2#1, Nov, 1996 - No. 13, Nov, 1997($2.95/$1.95/$1.99)
(Produced by Extreme Studios)

	GD2.0	FN6.0	VF8.0	NM9.4
1-($2.95)-Heroes Reborn begins; Rob Liefeld-c/a; Jeph Loeb scripts; reintro Nick Fury				6.00
1-($2.95)-(Variant(all)-Liefeld-c/a				6.00
1-(7/96, $2.95)-(Exclusive Comicon Ed.)-Liefeld-c/a. 1	3	6	8	
2-11,13: 5-Two-c. 6-Cable-c/app. 13-"World War 3"-pt. 4, x-over w/Image				3.00
12-($2.99) "Heroes Reunited"-pt. 4				4.00

CAPTAIN AMERICA (Vol. Three) (Also see Capt. America: Sentinel of Liberty)
Marvel Comics: Jan, 1998 - Present ($2.99/$1.99/$2.25)

1-($2.99) Mark Waid-s/Ron Garney-a			4.00
1-Variant cover			6.00
2-($1.99): 2-Two covers			3.00
3-11: 3-Returns to old shield. 4-Hawkeye-c/app. 5-Thor-c/app. 7-Andy Kubert-c/a begin. 9-New shield			2.50
12-($2.99) Battles Nightmare; Red Skull back-up story			3.50
13-17,19-Red Skull returns			2.25
18-($2.99) Cap vs. Korvac in the Future			3.00
20-24,26-29: 20,21-Sgt. Fury back-up story painted by Evans			2.25
25-($2.99) Cap & Falcon vs. Hatemonger			3.00
30-49: 30-Begin $2.25-c. 32-Ordway-a. 33-Jurgens-s/a begins; U.S. Agent app.			2.25
36-Maximum Security x-over. 41,46-Red Skull app.			3.50
...Citizen V '98 Annual ($3.50) Busiek & Kesel-s			3.50
1999 Annual ($3.50) Flag Smasher app.			3.50
2000 Annual ($3.50) Continued from #35 vs. Protocide; Jurgens-s			3.50
2001 Annual ($2.99) Golden Age flashback; Invaders app.			3.00

CAPTAIN AMERICA COMICS
Timely/Marvel Comics (TCI 1-20/CmPS 21-68/MjMC 69-75/Atlas Comics (PrPl 76-78): Mar, 1941 - No. 75, Feb, 1950; No. 76, 5/54 - No. 78, 9/54 (No. 74 & 75 titled Capt. America's Weird Tales)

	GD2.0	FN6.0	VF8.0	NM9.4
1-Origin & 1st app. Captain America & Bucky by S&K; Hurricane, Tuk the Caveboy begins by S&K; 1st app. Red Skull (by Simon?); intro of the "Capt. America Sentinels of Liberty Club" (advertised on inside front-c.); indicia states Vol. 1, Number 1	6450	19,350	45,150	100,000
2-S&K Hurricane; Tuk by Avison (Kirby splash); classic Hitler-c	1071	3214	7500	15,000
3-Classic Red Skull-c & app; Stan Lee's 1st text (1st work for Marvel)	923	2769	6000	12,000
4-1st full pg. panel in comics	615	1845	4000	8000
5	538	1614	3500	7000
6-Origin Father Time; Tuk the Caveboy ends	477	1431	3100	6200
7-Red Skull app.; classic-c	554	1662	3600	7200
8-10-Last S&K issue, (S&K centerfold #6-10)	417	1250	2604	5000
11-Last Hurricane, Headline Hunter; Al Avison Captain America begins, ends #20; Avison-c(p)	350	1050	2188	4200
12-The Imp begins, ends #16; last Father Time	333	1000	2083	4000
13-Origin The Secret Stamp; classic-c	358	1074	2238	4300

	GD2.0	FN6.0	VF8.0	NM9.4
14,15	333	1000	2083	4000
16-Red Skull unmasks Cap; Red Skull-c	400	1200	2500	4800
17-The Fighting Fool only app.	300	900	1875	3300
18-Classic-c	300	900	1875	3300
19-Human Torch begins #19	241	723	1506	2650
20-Sub-Mariner app.; no H. Torch	241	723	1506	2650
21-25: 25-Cap drinks liquid opium	227	681	1420	2500
26-30: 27-Last Secret Stamp; last 68 pg. issue. 28-60 pg. issues begin.	214	642	1338	2350
31-35,38-40: 34-Centerfold poster of Cap	182	546	1136	2000
36-Classic Hitler-c	282	846	1763	3100
37-Red Skull app.	227	681	1420	2500
41-45,47: 41-Last Jap War-c. 47-Last German War-c	164	492	1023	1800
46-German Holocaust-c; classic	200	600	1250	2200
48-58,60	127	381	795	1400
59-Origin retold	300	900	1875	3300
61-Red Skull-c/story	245	735	1534	2700
62,64,65: 65-Kurtzman's "Hey Look"	164	492	1023	1800
63-Intro/origin Asbestos Lady	168	505	1050	1850
66-Bucky is shot; Golden Girl teams up with Captain America & learns his i.d; origin Golden Girl	177	531	1106	1950
67-73: 67-Captain America/Golden Girl team-up; Mxyztplk swipe; last Toro in Human Torch. 68,70-Sub-Mariner/Namora, and Captain America/Golden Girl team-up in each. 69-Human Torch/Sun Girl team-up. 70-Science fiction-c/story. 71-Anti Wertham editorial; The Witness, Bucky app.	173	519	1080	1900
74-(Scarce)(10/49)-Titled "Captain America's Weird Tales"; Red Skull-c & app.; classic-c	462	1380	3000	6000
75(2/50)-Titled "C.A.'s Weird Tales"; no C.A. app.; horror comic/stories	173	519	1080	1900
76-78(1954): Human Torch/Toro stories; all have communist-c/stories	100	300	625	1100
132-Pg. Issue (B&W-1942)(Canadian)-Very rare. Has blank inside-and back-c; contains Marvel Mystery #33 & Captain America #18 w/cover from Captain America #22; same contents as Marvel Mystery annual	2800	8400	18,000	—

NOTE: **Crandall** a-2i, 3i, 9i, 10i. **Kirby** c-1, 2, 5-8p. **Rico** c-77, 78. **Romita** c-77, 78. **Schomburg** c-3, 4, 26-29, 31, 33, 37-39, 41, 42, 45-54, 58. **Sekowsky** c-55, 56. **Shores** c-1i, 2i, 5-7i, 11i, 20-25, 30, 32, 34, 35, 40, 57, 59-67. **S&K** c-9, 10. **Bondage** c-3, 7, 15, 16, 34, 38.

CAPTAIN AMERICA/NICK FURY: BLOOD TRUCE
Marvel Comics: Feb, 1995 ($5.95, one-shot, squarebound)

nn-Chaykin story			6.00

CAPTAIN AMERICA/NICK FURY: THE OTHERWORLD WAR
Marvel Comics: Oct, 2001 ($6.95, one-shot, squarebound)

nn-Manco-a; Bucky and Red Skull app.			7.00

CAPTAIN AMERICA, SENTINEL OF LIBERTY (See Fireside Book Series)

CAPTAIN AMERICA: SENTINEL OF LIBERTY
Marvel Comics: Sept, 1998 - No. 12, Aug, 1999 ($1.99)

1-Waid-s/Garney-a			3.00
1-Rough Cut ($2.99) Features original script and pencil pages			3.00
2-5: 2-Two-c; Invaders WW2 story			2.25
6-($2.99) Iron Man-c/app.			3.00
7-11: 8-Falcon-c/app. 9-Falcon poses as Cap			2.25
12-($2.99) Final issue; Bucky-c/app.			3.00

CAPTAIN AMERICA SPECIAL EDITION
Marvel Comics: Feb, 1984 - No. 2, Mar, 1984 ($2.00, Baxter paper)

1-Steranko-c/a(r) in both; r/ Captain America #110,111			4.00
2-Reprints the scarce Our Love Story #5, and C.A. #113			6.00

CAPTAIN AMERICA: THE CLASSIC YEARS
Marvel Comics: Jun, 1998 - Present (trade paperbacks)

1-($19.95) Reprints Captain America Comics #1-5			25.00
2-($24.95) Reprints Captain America Comics #6-10			25.00

CAPTAIN AMERICA: THE LEGEND
Marvel Comics: Sept, 1996 ($3.95, one-shot)

1-Tribute issue; wraparound-c			4.00

Captain Battle Jr. #1 © LEV

Captain Carrot and his Amazing Zoo Crew #13 © DC

Captain Easy #14 © NEA

CAPTAIN AND THE KIDS, THE (See Famous Comics Cartoon Books)

CAPTAIN AND THE KIDS, THE (See Comics on Parade, Katzenjammer Kids, Okay Comics & Sparkler Comics)
United Features Syndicate/Dell Publ. Co.: 1938 -12/39; Sum, 1947 - No. 32, 1955; Four Color No. 881, Feb, 1958

	GD2.0	FN6.0	VF8.0	NM9.4
Single Series 1(1938)	91	273	568	1000
Single Series 1(Reprint)(12/39- "Reprint" on-c)	47	141	286	500
1(Summer, 1947-UFS)-Katzenjammer Kids	16	48	83	140
2	9	27	49	70
3-10	7	21	38	55
11-20	6	18	28	38
21-32 (1955)	5	15	24	32
50th Anniversary issue-(1948)-Contains a 2 pg. history of the strip, including an account of the famous Supreme Court decision allowing both Pulitzer & Hearst to run the same strip under different names	10	30	55	85
Special Summer issue, Fall issue (1948)	7	21	38	55
Four Color 881 (Dell)	4	12	26	40

CAPTAIN ATOM
Nationwide Publishers: 1950 - No. 7, 1951 (5¢, 5x7-1/4", 52 pgs.)

1-Science fiction	40	120	232	400
2-7	22	66	116	200

CAPTAIN ATOM (Formerly Strange Sus. Stories #77)(Also see Space Adv.)
Charlton Comics: V2#78, Dec, 1965 - V2#89, Dec, 1967

V2#78-Origin retold; Nightshade-a (3 pgs.)	9	27	63	105
79-82: 79-1st app. Dr. Spectro. 3 pg. Ditko cut & paste /Space Adventures #24. 81(9/66)-1st app. new Captain Atom	5	15	38	60
83-86: Ted Kord Blue Beetle in all. 83-(11/66)-1st app. Ted Kord. 84-1st app. new Captain Atom	5	15	34	55
87-89: Nightshade by Aparo in all	5	15	34	55
83-85(Modern Comics-1977)-reprints	1	3	5	7

NOTE: *Aparo a-87-89. Ditko c/a(p) 78-89. #90 only published in fanzine 'The Charlton Bullseye' #1, 2.*

CAPTAIN ATOM (Also see Americomics & Crisis On Infinite Earths)
DC Comics: Mar, 1987 - No. 57, Sept, 1991 (Direct sales only #35 on)

1-(44 pgs.)-Origin/1st app. with new costume				4.00
2-49: 5-Firestorm x-over. 6-Intro. new Dr. Spectro. 11-Millennium tie-in 14-Nightshade app. 16-Justice League app. 17-$1.00-c begins; Swamp Thing x-over. 20-Blue Beetle x-over. 24,25-Invasion tie-in				2.50
51-57: 50-($2.00, 52 pgs.). 57-War of the Gods x-over				2.50
Annual 1,2 ('88, '89)-1-Intro Major Force				3.00

CAPTAIN BATTLE (Boy Comics #3 on) (See Silver Streak Comics)
New Friday Publ./Comic House: Summer, 1941 - No. 2, Fall, 1941

1-Origin Blackout by Rico; Captain Battle begins (1st appeared in Silver Streak #10, 5/41)	127	381	795	1400
2	80	240	500	875

CAPTAIN BATTLE (2nd Series)
Magazine Press/Picture Scoop No. 5: No. 3, Wint, 1942-43; No. 5, Sum, 1943 (No #4)

3-Origin Silver Streak-r/SS#3; origin Lance Hale-r/Silver Streak; Simon-a(r) (52 pgs., nd)	68	205	426	750
5-Origin Blackout retold (68 pgs.)	50	150	300	525

CAPTAIN BATTLE, JR.
Comic House (Lev Gleason): Fall, 1943 - No. 2, Winter, 1943-44

1-The Claw vs. The Ghost	105	315	656	1150
2-Wolverton's Scoop Scuttle; Don Rico-c/a; The Green Claw story is reprinted from Silver Streak #6	80	240	500	875

CAPTAIN BEN DIX (See Promotional Comics section)

CAPTAIN BRITAIN (Also see Marvel Team-Up No. 65, 66)
Marvel Comics International: Oct. 13, 1976 - No. 39, July 6, 1977 (Weekly)

1-Origin; with Capt. Britain's face mask inside	2	6	10	14
2-Origin, part II; Capt. Britain's Boomerang inside	1	3	6	8
3-11: 3,8-Vs. Bank Robbers. 4-7-Vs. Hurricane. 9-11: Vs. Dr. Synne				4.00
12-23,25-27: (scarce)-12,13-Vs. Dr. Synne. 14,15-Vs. Mastermind. 16-23,25,26-With Capt. America. 17 misprinted & color section reprinted in #18.				

27-Origin retold	2	6	9	12
24-With C.B.'s Jet Plane inside	2	6	11	16
28-32,36-39: 28-32-Vs. Lord Hawk. 36-Star Sceptre. 37-39-Vs. Highwayman & Munipulator				3.50
33-35-More on origin				4.00
Annual (1978, Hardback, 64 pgs.)-Reprints #1-7 with pin-ups of Marvel characters	2	6	9	12
Summer Special (1980, 52 pgs.)-Reprints				4.00

NOTE: *No. 1, 2, & 24 are rarer in mint due to inserts. Distributed in Great Britain only. Nick Fury-r by Steranko in 1-20, 24-31, 35-37. Fantastic Four-r by J. Buscema in all. New Buscema-a in 24-30. Story from No. 39 continues in Super Spider-Man (British weekly) No. 231-247. Following cancellation of this series, new Captain Britain stories appeared in "Super Spider-Man" (British weekly) No. 231-247. Captain Britain stories which appear in Super-Spider-Man No 248-253 are reprints of Marvel Team-Up No. 65&66. Capt. Britain strips also appeared in Hulk Comic (weekly) 1, 3-30, 42-55, 57-60, in Marvel Superheroes (monthly) 377-388, in Daredevils (monthly) 1-11, Mighty World of Marvel (monthly) 7-16 & Captain Britain (monthly) 1-14. Issues 1-23 have B&W & color, paper-c, & are 32 pgs. Issues 24 on are all B&W w/glossy-c & are 36 pgs.*

CAPTAIN CANUCK
Comely Comix (Canada) (All distr. in U. S.): 7/75 - No. 4, 7/77; No. 4, 7-8/79 - No. 14, 3-4/81

1-1st app. Bluefox				5.00
2,3(5-7/76)-2-1st app. Dr. Walker, Redcoat & Kebec. 3-1st app. Heather				4.00
4(1st printing-2/77)-10x14-1/2"; (5.00); B&W; 300 copies serially numbered and signed with one certificate of authenticity	8	24	56	90
4(2nd printing-7/77)-11x17", B&W; only 15 copies printed; signed by creator Richard Comely, serially #'d and two certificates of authenticity inserted; orange cardboard covers (Very Rare)	10	30	70	120
4-14: 4(7-8/79)-1st app. Tom Evans & Mr. Gold; origin The Catman. 5-Origin Capt. Canuck's powers; 1st app. Earth Patrol & Chaos Corps. 8-Jonn 'The Final Chapter'. 9-1st World Beyond. 11-1st 'Chariots of Fire' story				3.00
Special Collectors Pack (polybagged)	1	3	6	9
Summer Special 1(7-9/80, 95¢, 64 pgs.)				3.00

NOTE: *30,000 copies of No. 4 were destroyed in Winnipeg.*

CAPTAIN CARROT AND HIS AMAZING ZOO CREW (Also see New Teen Titans & Oz-Wonderland War)
DC Comics: Mar, 1982 - No. 20, Nov, 1983

1-20: 1-Superman app. 3-Re-intro Dodo & The Frog. 9-Re-intro Three Mouseketeers, the Terrific Whatzit. 10,11- Pig Iron reverts back to Peter Porkchops. 20-The Changeling app.				3.00

CAPTAIN CARVEL AND HIS CARVEL CRUSADERS (See Carvel Comics)

CAPTAIN CONFEDERACY
Marvel Comics (Epic Comics): Nov, 1991 - No. 4, Feb, 1992 ($1.95)

1-4: All new stories				2.25

CAPTAIN COURAGEOUS COMICS (Banner #3-5; see Four Favorites #5)
Periodical House (Ace Magazines): No. 6, March, 1942

6-Origin & 1st app. The Sword; Lone Warrior, Capt. Courageous app.; Capt. moves to Four Favorites #5 in May	77	231	483	850

CAPT'N CRUNCH COMICS (See Cap'n...)

CAPTAIN DAVY JONES
Dell Publishing Co.: No. 598, Nov, 1954

Four Color 598	4	12	30	50

CAPTAIN EASY (See The Funnies & Red Ryder #3-32)
Hawley/Dell Publ./Standard(Visual Editions)/Argo: 1939 - No. 17, Sept, 1949; April, 1956

nn-Hawley(1939)-Contains reprints from The Funnies & 1938 Sunday strips by Roy Crane	89	267	556	975
Four Color 24 (1943)	42	125	294	550
Four Color 111(6/46)	14	42	98	185
10(Standard-10/47)	12	36	61	105
11,12,14,15,17: 11-17 all contain 1930s & '40s strip-r	10	30	55	80
13,16: Schomburg-c	11	33	55	90
Argo 1(4/56)-Reprints	7	21	36	50

CAPTAIN EASY & WASH TUBBS (See Famous Comics Cartoon Books)

CAPTAIN ELECTRON
Brick Computer Science Institute: Aug, 1986 ($2.25)

1-Disbrow-a				2.50

Captain Flight Comics #8 © Four Star Pub.

Captain Gallant #2 © CC

Captain Marvel #8 © MAR

	GD2.0	FN6.0	VF8.0	NM9.4

	GD2.0	FN6.0	VF8.0	NM9.4

CAPTAIN EO 3-D (Disney)
Eclipse Comics: July, 1987 (Eclipse 3-D Special #18, $3.50, Baxter)

1-Adapts 3-D movie				4.00
1-2-D limited edition				6.00
1-Large size (11x17", 8/87)-Sold only at Disney Theme parks ($6.95)				
	2	6	11	16

CAPTAIN FEARLESS COMICS (Also see Holyoke One-Shot #6, Old Glory
Comics & Silver Streak #1)
Helnit Publishing Co. (Holyoke Publ. Co.): Aug, 1941 - No. 2, Sept, 1941

1-Origin Mr. Miracle, Alias X, Captain Fearless, Citizen Smith Son of the Unknown Soldier; Miss Victory (1st app.) begins (1st patriotic heroine? before Wonder Woman)	86	258	540	950
2-Grit Grady, Captain Stone app.	55	165	330	575

CAPTAIN FLAG (See Blue Ribbon Comics #16)

CAPTAIN FLASH
Sterling Comics: Nov, 1954 - No. 4, July, 1955

1-Origin; Sekowsky-a; Tomboy (female super hero) begins; only pre-code issue; atomic rocket-c	40	120	240	420
2-4: 4-Flying saucer invasion-c	24	72	127	220

CAPTAIN FLEET (Action Packed Tales of the Sea)
Ziff-Davis Publishing Co.: Fall, 1952

1-Painted-c	16	48	83	140

CAPTAIN FLIGHT COMICS
Four Star Publications: Mar, 1944 - No. 10, Dec, 1945; No. 11, Feb-Mar, 1947

nn	41	123	246	425
2-4: 4-Rock Raymond begins, ends #7	25	75	130	225
5-Bondage, classic torture-c; Red Rocket begins; the Grenade app. (scarce)	105	315	656	1150
6	23	69	121	210
7-10: 7-L. B. Cole covers begin, end #11. 8-Yankee Girl begins; intro. Black Cobra & Cobra Kid & begins. 9-Torpedoman app.; last Yankee Girl; Kinstler-a. 10-Deep Sea Dawson, Zoom of the Jungle, Rock Raymond, Red Rocket, & Black Cobra app; bondage-c	50	150	300	525
11-Torpedoman, Blue Flame (Human Torch clone) app.; last Black Cobra, Red Rocket; classic L. B. Cole robot-c (scarce)	105	315	656	1150

CAPTAIN GALLANT (...of the Foreign Legion) (TV) (Texas Rangers in Action No. 5 on?)
Charlton Comics: 1955; No. 2, Jan, 1956 - No. 4, Sept, 1956

Non-Heinz version (#1)-Buster Crabbe photo on-c; full page Buster Crabbe photo inside front-c	10	30	55	80
(Heinz version is listed in the Promotional Comics section)				
2-4: Buster Crabbe in all	9	27	49	70

CAPTAIN GLORY
Topps Comics: Apr, 1993 ($2.95) (Created by Jack Kirby)

1-Polybagged w/Kirbychrome trading card; Ditko-a & Kirby-c; has coupon for Amberchrome Secret City Saga #0				3.00

CAPTAIN HERO (See Jughead as...)

CAPTAIN HERO COMICS DIGEST MAGAZINE
Archie Publications: Sept, 1981

1-Reprints of Jughead as Super-Guy	2	6	9	12

CAPTAIN HOBBY COMICS
Export Publication Ent. Ltd. (Dist. in U.S. by Kable News Co.): Feb, 1948
(Canadian)

1	7	21	38	55

CAPT. HOLO IN 3-D (See Blackthorne 3-D Series #65)

CAPTAIN HOOK & PETER PAN (Movie)(Disney)
Dell Publishing Co.: No. 446, Jan, 1953

Four Color 446	9	27	63	110

CAPTAIN JET (Fantastic Fears No. 7 on)
Four Star Publ./Farrell/Comic Media: May, 1952 - No. 5, Jan, 1953

1-Bakerish-a	21	63	110	190
2	12	36	61	100
3-5,6(?)	10	30	55	85

CAPTAIN JOHNER & THE ALIENS
Valiant: May, 1995 - No. 2, May, 1995 ($2.95, shipped in same month)

1,2: Reprints Magnus Robot Fighter 4000 A.D. back-up stories; new Paul Smith-c				3.00

CAPTAIN JUSTICE (TV)
Marvel Comics: Mar, 1988 - No. 2, Apr, 1988 (limited series)

1,2-Based on True Colors television series.				2.25

CAPTAIN KANGAROO (TV)
Dell Publishing Co.: No. 721, Aug, 1956 - No. 872, Jan, 1958

Four Color 721 (#1)-Photo-c	16	48	112	210
Four Color 780, 872-Photo-c	13	39	91	170

CAPTAIN KIDD (Formerly Dagar; My Secret Story #26 on)(Also see Comic Comics & Fantastic Comics)
Fox Feature Syndicate: No. 24, June, 1949 - No. 25, Aug, 1949

24,25: 24-Features Blackbeard the Pirate	15	45	77	130

CAPTAIN MARVEL (See All Hero, All-New Collectors' Ed., America's Greatest, Fawcett Miniature, Gift, Legends, Limited Collectors' Ed., Marvel Family, Master No. 21, Mighty Midget Comics, Power of Shazam!, Shazam, Special Edition Comics, Whiz, Wisco (in Promotional Comics section), World's Finest #253 and XMas Comics)

CAPTAIN MARVEL (Marvel's Space-Born Super-Hero! Captain Marvel #1-6; see Giant-Size..., Life Of..., Marvel Graphic Novel #1, Marvel Spotlight V2#1 & Marvel Super-Heroes #12)
M. F. Enterprises: April, 1966 - No. 4, Nov, 1966 (25¢ Giants)

nn-(#1 on pg 5)-Origin; created by Carl Burgos	4	12	26	40
2-4: 3-(#3 on pg 4)-Fights the Bat	3	9	17	25

CAPTAIN MARVEL
Marvel Comics Group: May, 1968 - No. 19, Dec, 1969; No. 20, June, 1970 - No. 21, Aug, 1970; No. 22, Sept, 1972 - No. 62, May, 1979

1	10	30	73	125
2-Super Skrull-c/story	4	12	26	40
3-5: 4-Captain Marvel battles Sub-Mariner	3	9	17	25
6-11: 11-Capt. Marvel given great power by Zo the Ruler; Smith/Trimpe-c; Death of Una	2	6	11	15
12,13,15-20: 16,17-New costume	1	4	7	10
14,21: 14-Capt. Marvel vs. Iron Man; last 12¢ issue. 21-Capt. Marvel battles Hulk; last 15¢ issue	2	6	13	20
22-24	1	4	7	10
25,26: 25-Starlin-c/a begins; Starlin's 1st Thanos saga begins (3/73), ends #34; Thanos cameo (5 panels). 26-Minor Thanos app. (see Iron Man #55); 1st Thanos-c	5	15	—	22
27,28: 1st & 2nd full app. Thanos. 28-Thanos-c/s	2	6	12	18
29,30-Thanos cameos. 29-C.M. gains more powers	2	6	9	12
31,32: Thanos app. 31-Last 20¢ issue. 32-Thanos-c	2	6	11	15
33-Thanos-c & app.; Capt. Marvel battles Thanos; 1st origin Thanos	2	6	12	18
34-1st app. Nitro; C.M. contracts cancer which eventually kills him; last Starlin-c/a	2	6	9	12
35,37-40,42,46-48,50,53-56,58-62: 39-Origin Watcher. 58-Thanos cameo				5.00
36,41,43,49: 36-R-origin/1st app. Capt. Marvel from Marvel Super-Heroes #12.				
41,43-Wrightson part inks; #43-c(i). 49-Starlin & Weiss-p assists				6.00
44,45-(Regular 25¢ editions)(5,7/76)				5.00
44,45-(30¢-c variants, limited distribution)	1	3	6	8
51,52-(Regular 30¢ editions)(7,9/77)				5.00
51,52-(35¢-c variants, limited distribution)	1	3	6	8
57-Thanos appears in flashback	1	3	6	8

NOTE: Alcala a-35. Austin a-46i, 49-53i; c-52i. Buscema a-18p-21p. Colan a(p)-1-4; c(p)-1-4, 8, 9. Heck a-5-10p, 16p. Gil Kane a-17-21p; c-17-24p, 37p, 53. Starlin a-36. McWilliams a-40i. #25-34 were reprinted in The Life of Captain Marvel.

CAPTAIN MARVEL
Marvel Comics: Nov, 1989 ($1.50, one-shot, 52 pgs.)

1-Super-hero from Avengers; new powers				3.00

CAPTAIN MARVEL
Marvel Comics: Feb, 1994 ($1.75, 52 pgs.)

1-(Indicia reads Vol 2 #2)-Minor Captain America app.				2.50

CAPTAIN MARVEL
Marvel Comics: Dec, 1995 - No. 6, May, 1996 ($2.95/$1.95)

Captain Marvel V3 #4 © MAR

Captain Marvel Adventures #27 © FAW

Captain Marvel, Jr. #9 © FAW

	GD2.0	FN6.0	VF8.0	NM9.4

	GD2.0	FN6.0	VF8.0	NM9.4
1 ($2.95)-Advs. of Mar-Vell's son begins; Fabian Nicieza scripts; foil-c				3.50
2-6: 2-Begin $1.95-c				2.50

CAPTAIN MARVEL (Vol. 3) (See Avengers Forever)
Marvel Comics: Jan, 2000 - Present ($2.50)

	GD2.0	FN6.0	VF8.0	NM9.4
1-26: 1-Peter David-s. 2-Two covers; Hulk app. 9-Silver Surfer app.				
12-Maximum Security x-over. 17,18-Starlin-a				2.50
Wizard #0-Preview and history of Rick Jones				2.25
...: First Contact (8/01, $16.95, TPB) r/#0,1-6				17.00

CAPTAIN MARVEL ADVENTURES (See Special Edition Comics for pre #1)
Fawcett Publications: 1941 (March) - No. 150, Nov, 1953
(#1 on stands 1/16/41)

	GD2.0	FN6.0	VF8.0	NM9.4
nn(#1)-Captain Marvel & Sivana by Jack Kirby. The cover was printed on unstable paper stock and is rarely found in Fine or Mint condition; blank back inside-c	2575	7725	18,025	36,000
2-(Advertised as #3, which was counting Special Edition Comics as the real #1); Tuska-a	400	1200	2500	4800
3-Metallic silver-c	273	819	1705	3000
4-Three Lt. Marvels app.	191	573	1194	2100
5	150	450	938	1650
6-10: 9-1st Otto Binder scripts on Capt. Marvel	114	342	713	1250
11-15: 12-Capt. Marvel joins the Army. 13-Two pg. Capt. Marvel pin-up.				
15-Comic cards on back-c begin, end #26	89	267	556	975
16,17: 17-Painted-c	84	252	525	925
18-Origin & 1st app. Mary Marvel & Marvel Family (12/11/42); painted-c; Mary Marvel by Marcus Swayze	209	627	1307	2300
19-Mary Marvel x-over; Christmas-c	70	210	438	775
20,21-Attached to the cover, each has a miniature comic just like the Mighty Midget Comics #11, except that each has a full color promo ad on the back cover. Most copies were circulated without the miniature comic. These issues with miniatures attached are very rare, and should not be mistaken for copies with the similar Mighty Midget glued in its place. The Mighty Midgets had blank back covers except for a small victory stamp seal. Only the Capt. Marvel, Captain Marvel Jr. and Golden Arrow No. 11 miniatures have been positively documented as having been affixed to these covers. Each miniature was only partially glued by its back cover to the Captain Marvel comic making it easy to see if it's the genuine miniature rather than a Mighty Midget.				
with comic attached....	350	1050	2188	4200
20-Without miniature	66	198	413	725
21-Without miniature; Hitler-c	86	258	540	950
22-Mr. Mind serial begins; 1st app. Mr. Mind	91	273	568	1000
23-25	64	192	398	700
26-30: 26-Flag-c. 27-1st Mr. Mind app. (his voice was heard over the radio before now)(11/43). 29-1st Mr. Mind-c	55	165	330	575
31-35: 35-Origin Radar (5/44, see Master #50)	50	150	300	525
36-40: 37-Mary Marvel x-over	45	135	270	475
41-46: 42-Christmas-c. 43-Capt. Marvel 1st meets Uncle Marvel; Mary Batson cameo. 46-Mr. Mind serial ends	40	120	217	375
47-50	37	111	197	340
51-53,55-60: 51-63-Bi-weekly issues. 52-Origin & 1st app. Sivana Jr.; Capt. Marvel Jr. x-over	31	93	168	290
54-Special oversize 68 pg. issue	33	99	174	300
61-The Cult of the Curse serial begins	36	100	191	330
62-65-Serial cont.; Mary Marvel x-over in #65	31	93	168	290
66-Serial ends; Atomic War-c	35	105	188	325
67-77,79: 69-Billy Batson's Christmas; Uncle Marvel, Mary Marvel, Capt. Marvel x-over. 71-Three Lt. Marvels app. 79-Origin Mr. Tawny	27	81	145	250
78-Origin Mr. Atom	31	81	165	285
80-Origin Capt. Marvel retold	59	177	369	650
81-84,86-90: 81,90-Mr. Atom app. 82-Infinity-c. 82,86,89,90-Mr. Tawny app.	26	78	139	240
85-Freedom Train issue	31	93	165	285
91-99: 92-Mr. Tawny app. 96-Gets 1st name "Tawky"	25	75	133	230
100-Origin retold; silver metallic-c	45	135	270	475
101-115,117-120	24	72	127	220
116-Flying Saucer issue (1/51)	27	81	145	250
121-Origin retold	33	99	174	300
122-137,139-149: 141-Pre-code horror story "The Hideous Head-Hunter". 142-used in **POP**, pgs. 92,96	23	69	121	210
138-Flying Saucer issue (11/52)	27	81	145	250
150-(Low distribution)	40	120	232	400

NOTE: Swayze a-12, 14, 15, 18, 19, 40; c-12, 15, 19.

	GD2.0	FN6.0	VF8.0	NM9.4

CAPTAIN MARVEL AND THE GOOD HUMOR MAN (Movie)
Fawcett Publications: 1950

	GD2.0	FN6.0	VF8.0	NM9.4
nn-Partial photo-c w/Jack Carson & the Captain Marvel Club Boys	47	142	286	500

CAPTAIN MARVEL COMIC STORY PAINT BOOK (See Comic Story...)

CAPTAIN MARVEL, JR. (See Fawcett Miniatures, Marvel Family, Master Comics, Mighty Midget Comics, Shazam & Whiz Comics)

CAPTAIN MARVEL, JR.
Fawcett Publications: Nov, 1942 - No. 119, June, 1953 (No #34)

	GD2.0	FN6.0	VF8.0	NM9.4
1-Origin Capt. Marvel Jr. retold (Whiz #25); Capt. Nazi app. Classic Raboy-c	500	1500	3250	6500
2-Vs. Capt. Nazi; origin Capt. Nippon	191	573	1194	2100
3	109	327	682	1200
4-Classic Raboy-c	116	348	725	1275
5-Vs. Capt. Nazi	95	285	597	1050
6-8: 8-Vs. Capt. Nazi	77	231	483	850
9-Classic flag-c	82	246	511	900
10-Hitler-c	91	273	568	1000
11,12,15-Capt. Nazi app.	66	198	413	725
13-Classic Hitler, Tojo and Mussolini football-c	86	258	540	950
14,16-20: 14-X-mas-c. 16-Capt. Marvel & Sivana x-over.				
19-Capt. Nazi & Capt. Nippon app.	55	165	341	600
21-30: 25-Flag-c	45	135	270	475
31-33,36-40: 37-Infinity-c	33	99	174	300
35-#34 on inside; cover shows origin of Sivana Jr. which is not on inside. Evidently the cover #35 was printed out of sequence and bound with contents to #34	33	99	174	300
41-70: 42-Robot-c. 53-Atomic Bomb-c/story	25	75	133	230
71-99,101-104: 87-Robot-c. 104-Used in **POP**, pg. 89	18	54	94	160
100	21	63	110	190
105-114,116-118: 116-Vampira, Queen of Terror app.	16	48	83	140
115-Injury to eye-c; Eyeball story w/injury-to-eye panels	33	99	174	300
119-Electric chair-c (scarce)	38	114	203	350

NOTE: Mac Raboy c-1-28, 30-32, 57, 59 among others.

CAPTAIN MARVEL PRESENTS THE TERRIBLE FIVE
M. F. Enterprises: Aug, 1966; V2#5, Sept, 1967 (No #2-4) (25¢)

	GD2.0	FN6.0	VF8.0	NM9.4
1	4	12	26	40
V2#5-(Formerly Captain Marvel)	3	9	17	25

CAPTAIN MARVEL'S FUN BOOK
Samuel Lowe Co.: 1944 (1/2" thick) (cardboard covers)(25¢)

	GD2.0	FN6.0	VF8.0	NM9.4
nn-Puzzles, games, magic, etc.; infinity-c	36	108	191	330

CAPTAIN MARVEL SPECIAL EDITION (See Special Edition)

CAPTAIN MARVEL STORY BOOK
Fawcett Publications: Summer, 1946 - No. 4, Summer?, 1948

	GD2.0	FN6.0	VF8.0	NM9.4
1-Half text	55	165	341	600
2-4	40	120	270	380

CAPTAIN MARVEL THRILL BOOK (Large-Size)
Fawcett Publications: 1941 (B&W w/color-c)

	GD2.0	FN6.0	VF8.0	NM9.4
1-Reprints from Whiz 8,10, & Special Edition #1 (Rare)	275	825	2750	–

NOTE: Rarely found in Fine or Mint condition.

CAPTAIN MIDNIGHT (TV, radio, films) (See The Funnies, Popular Comics & Super Book of Comics)(Becomes Sweethearts No. 68 on)
Fawcett Publications: Sept, 1942 - No. 67, Fall, 1948 (#1-14: 68 pgs.)

	GD2.0	FN6.0	VF8.0	NM9.4
1-Origin Captain Midnight, star of radio and movies; Captain Marvel cameo on cover	300	900	1875	3500
2-Smashes the Jap Juggernaut	136	408	852	1500
3-5: Grapples the Gremlins	100	300	625	1100
6-10: 9-Raboy-c. 10-Raboy Flag-c	73	219	455	800
11-20: 11,17,18-Raboy-c. 16 (1/44)	55	165	330	575
21-30: 22-War savings stamp-c. 24-Jap flag sunburst-c.				
	43	129	257	450
31-40	33	99	174	300

Captain Planet and the Planeteers #9 © TBS Prod.

Captain Science #7 © YM

Captain Victory and the Galactic Rangers #1 © Jack Kirby

	GD2.0	FN6.0	VF8.0	NM9.4
41-59,61-67: 50-Sci/fi theme begins?	27	81	145	250
60-Flying Saucer issue (2/48)-3rd of this theme; see The Spirit 9/28/47(1st), Shadow Comics V7#10 (2nd, 1/48) & Boy Commandos #26 (4th, 3-4/48)	34	102	179	310

CAPTAIN NICE (TV)
Gold Key: Nov, 1967 (one-shot)

1(10211-711)-Photo-c	7	21	49	85

CAPTAIN N: THE GAME MASTER (TV)
Valiant Comics: 1990 - No. 6? ($1.95, thick stock, coated-c)

1-6: 4-6-Layton-c				3.00

CAPTAIN PARAGON (See Bill Black's Fun Comics)
Americomics: Dec, 1983 - No. 4, 1985

1-Intro/1st app. Ms. Victory				4.00
2-4				3.00

CAPTAIN PARAGON AND THE SENTINELS OF JUSTICE
AC Comics: April, 1985 - No. 6, 1986 ($1.75)

1-6: 1-Capt. Paragon, Commando D., Nightveil, Scarlet Scorpion, Stardust & Atoman begin				3.00

CAPTAIN PLANET AND THE PLANETEERS (TV cartoon)
Marvel Comics: Oct, 1991 - No. 12, Oct, 1992 ($1.00/$1.25)

1-N. Adams painted-c				4.00
2-12: 3-Romita-c				3.00

CAPTAIN POWER AND THE SOLDIERS OF THE FUTURE (TV)
Continuity Comics: Aug, 1988 - No. 2, 1988 ($2.00)

1,2: 1-Neal Adams-c/layouts/inks; variant-c exists.				3.00

CAPTAIN PUREHEART (See Archie as...)

CAPTAIN ROCKET
P. L. Publ. (Canada): Nov, 1951

1	43	129	257	450

CAPT. SAVAGE AND HIS LEATHERNECK RAIDERS (...And His Battlefield Raiders #9 on)
Marvel Comics Group (Animated Timely Features): Jan, 1968 - No. 19, Mar, 1970 (See Sgt. Fury No. 10)

1-Sgt. Fury & Howlers cameo	4	12	26	40
2,7,11: 2-Origin Hydra. 1-5,7-Ayers/Shores-a. 7-Pre-"Thing" Ben Grimm story.				
11-Sgt. Fury app.	2	6	13	20
3-6,8-10,12-14: 14-Last 12¢ issue	2	6	12	18
15-19	2	6	11	15

CAPTAIN SCIENCE (Fantastic No. 8 on)
Youthful Magazines: Nov, 1950 - No. 7, Dec, 1951

1-Wood-a; origin; 2 pg. text w/ photos of George Pal's "Destination Moon."	84	252	525	925
2	43	129	257	450
3,6,7; 3/6-Bondage c-swipes/Wings #94,91	40	120	232	400
4,5-Wood/Orlando-c/a(2) each	80	240	500	875

NOTE: *Fass a-4. Bondage c-3, 6, 7.*

CAPTAIN SILVER'S LOG OF SEA HOUND (See Sea Hound)

CAPTAIN SINBAD (Movie Adaptation) (See Fantastic Voyages of... & Movie Comics)

CAPTAIN STERNN: RUNNING OUT OF TIME
Kitchen Sink Press: Sept, 1993 - No. 5, 1994 ($4.95, limited series, coated stock, 52 pgs.)

1-5: Berni Wrightson-c/a/scripts				6.00
1-Gold ink variant				10.00

CAPTAIN STEVE SAVAGE (...& His Jet Fighters, No. 2-13)
Avon Periodicals: 1950 - No. 8, 1/53; No. 9, 5-10/54 - No. 13, 5-6/56

nn(1st series)-Wood-a, 22 pgs. (titled "...Over Korea")	39	117	208	360
1(4/51)-Reprints nn issue (Canadian)	16	48	83	140
2-Kamen-a	11	33	55	95
3-11 (#6, 9-10/54, last precode)	8	24	42	60
12-Wood-a (6 pgs.)	12	36	61	100
13-Check, Lawrence-a	8	24	41	65

	GD2.0	FN6.0	VF8.0	NM9.4

NOTE: *Kinstler c-2-5, 7-9, 11. Lawrence a-8. Ravielli a-5, 9.*

5(9-10/54-2nd series)(Formerly Sensational Police Cases)				
	8	24	42	60
6-Reprints nn issue; Wood-a	10	30	55	80
7-13: 9,10-Kinstler-c. 10-r/cover #2 (1st series). 13-r/cover #8 (1st series)				
	6	18	29	40

CAPTAIN STONE (See Holyoke One-Shot No. 10)

CAPT. STORM (Also see G. I. Combat #138)
National Periodical Publications: May-June, 1964 - No. 18, Mar-Apr, 1967 (Grey tone c-8)

1-Origin	5	15	38	60
2-18: 3,6,13-Kubert-a. 4-Colan-a. 12-Kubert-c	4	12	26	40

CAPTAIN 3-D (Super hero)
Harvey Publications: December, 1953 (25¢, came with 2 pairs of glasses)

1-Kirby/Ditko-a (Ditko's 3rd published work tied with Strange Fantasy #9, see also Daring Love #1 & Black Magic V4 #3); shows cover in 3-D on inside; Kirby/Meskin-c	12	36	61	100

NOTE: *Half price without glasses*

CAPTAIN THUNDER AND BLUE BOLT
Hero Comics: Sept, 1987 - No. 10, 1988 ($1.95)

1-10: 1-Origin Blue Bolt. 3-Origin Capt. Thunder. 6-1st app. Wicket.				
8-Champions x-over				2.25

CAPTAIN TOOTSIE & THE SECRET LEGION (Advs. of...)(Also see Monte Hale #30,39 & Real Western Hero)
Toby Press: Oct, 1950 - No. 2, Dec, 1950

1-Not Beck-a; both have sci/fi covers	33	99	174	300
2-The Rocketeer Patrol app.; not Beck-a	20	60	105	175

CAPTAIN TRIUMPH (See Crack Comics #27)

CAPTAIN VENTURE & THE LAND BENEATH THE SEA (See Space Family Robinson)
Gold Key: Oct, 1968 - No. 2, Oct, 1969

1-r/Space Family Robinson serial; Spiegle-a	4	12	30	50
2-Spiegle-a	4	12	29	45

CAPTAIN VICTORY AND THE GALACTIC RANGERS
Pacific Comics: Nov, 1981 - No. 13, Jan, 1984 ($1.00, direct sales, 36-48 pgs.) (Created by Jack Kirby)

1-1st app. Mr. Mind				4.00
2-13: 3-N. Adams-a				3.00
Special 1-(10/83)-Kirby c/a(p)				4.00

NOTE: *Conrad a-10, 11. Ditko a-6. Kirby a-1-3p; c-1-13.*

CAPTAIN VICTORY AND THE GALACTIC RANGERS
Jack Kirby Comics: July, 2000 ($2.95, B&W)

1-New Jeremy Kirby-s with reprinted Jack Kirby-a; Liefeld pin-up art				3.00

CAPTAIN VIDEO (TV) (See XMas Comics)
Fawcett Publications: Feb, 1951 - No. 6, Dec, 1951 (No. 1,5,6-36pgs.; 2-4, 52pgs.) (All photo-c)

1-George Evans-a(2); 1st TV hero comic	114	342	713	1250
2-Used in SOTI, pg. 382	75	225	469	825
3-6-All Evans except #5 mostly Evans	64	192	398	700

NOTE: *Minor Williamson assists on most issues. Photo c-1, 5, 6; painted c-2-4.*

CAPTAIN WILLIE SCHULTZ (Also see Fightin' Army)
Charlton Comics: No. 76, Oct, 1985 - No. 77, Jan, 1986

76,77-Low print run				5.00

CAPTAIN WIZARD COMICS (See Meteor, Red Band & Three Ring Comics)
Rural Home: 1946

1-Capt. Wizard dons new costume; Impossible Man, Race Wilkins app.				
	31	93	168	290

CARE BEARS (TV, Movie)(See Star Comics Magazine)
Star Comics/Marvel Comics No. 15 on: Nov, 1985 - No. 20, Jan, 1989

1-20: Post-a begins. 11-$1.00-c begins. 13-Madballs app.				4.00

CAREER GIRL ROMANCES (Formerly Three Nurses)
Charlton Comics: June, 1964 - No. 78, Dec, 1973

Carnage: Mind Bomb #1 © MAR

Cartoon Network Starring #14 © Cartoon Network

Casey - Crime Photographer #2 © MAR

	GD2.0	FN6.0	VF8.0	NM9.4
V4#24-31	2	6	13	20

32-Elvis Presley, Herman's Hermits, Johnny Rivers line drawn-c

	10	30	73	125
33-50	2	6	11	16
51-78	2	6	9	12

CAR 54, WHERE ARE YOU? (TV)
Dell Publishing Co.: Mar-May, 1962 - No. 7, Sept-Nov, 1963; 1964 - 1965
(All photo-c)

Four Color 1257(#1, 3-5/62)	8	24	56	100
2(6-8/62)-7	5	15	34	55
2,3(10-12/64), 4(1-3/65)-Reprints #2,3,&4 of 1st series				
	3	9	21	32

CARL BARKS LIBRARY OF WALT DISNEY'S GYRO GEARLOOSE COMICS AND FILLERS IN COLOR, THE
Gladstone: 1993 ($7.95, 8-1/2x11", limited series, 52 pgs.)

1-6: Carl Barks reprints	1	4	7	10

CARL BARKS LIBRARY OF WALT DISNEY'S COMICS AND STORIES IN COLOR, THE
Gladstone: Jan, 1992 - No. 51, Mar, 1996 ($8.95, 8-1/2x11", 60 pgs.)

1,2,6,8-51: 1-Barks Donald Duck-r/WDC&S #31-35; 2-r/#36,38-41; 6-r/#57-61; 8-r/#67-71; 9-r/#72-76; 10-r/#77-81; 11-r/#82-86; 12-r/#87-91; 13-r/#92-96; 14-r/#97-101; 15-r/#102-106; 16-r/#107-111; 17-r/#112,114,117,124,125; 18-r/#126-130; 19-r/#131,132(2),133,134; 20-r/#135-139; 21-r/#140-144; 22-r/#145-149; 23-r/#150-154; 24-r/#155-159; 25-r/#160-164; 26-r/#165-169; 27-r/#170-174;28-r/#175-179; 29-r/#180-184; 30-r/#185-189; 31-r/#190-194; 32-r/#195-199;33-r/#200-204; 34-r/#205-209; 35-r/#210-214; 36-r/#215-219; 37-r/#220-224; 38-r/#225-229; 39-r/#230-234; 40-r/#235-239; 41-r/#240-244; 42/#245-249; 43-r/#250-254; 44-50; All contain one Heroes & Villains trading

card each	1	4	7	10
3,4,7: 3-r/#42-46. 4-r/#47-51. 7-r/#62-66.	2	6	11	15
5-r/#52-56	2	6	13	20

CARL BARKS LIBRARY OF WALT DISNEY'S DONALD DUCK ADVENTURES IN COLOR, THE
Gladstone: Jan, 1994 - No. 25, Jan, 1996 ($7.95-$9.95, 44-68 pgs., 8-1/2"x11")
(all contain one Donald Duck trading card each)

1-5,7,25-Carl Barks-r: 1-r/FC #9; 2-r/FC #29; 3-r/FC #62; 4-r/FC #108; 5-r/FC #147 & #79(Mickey Mouse); 7-r/FC #159. 8-r/FC #178 & 189. 9-r/FC #199 & 203; 10-r/FC 223 & 238; 11-r/Christmas Parade #1 & 2; 12-r/FC #296; 13-r/FC #263; 14-r/MOC #20 & 41; 15-r/FC 275 & 282; 16-r/FC #291&300; 17-r/FC #308 & 318; 18-r/Vac. Parade #1 & Summer Fun #2;

19-r/FC #328 & 367	2	6	9	12
6-r/MOC #4, Cheerios "Atom Bomb," D.D. Tells About Kites				
	2	6	13	20

CARL BARKS LIBRARY OF WALT DISNEY'S DONALD DUCK CHRISTMAS STORIES IN COLOR, THE
Gladstone: 1992 ($7.95, 44pgs., one-shot)

nn-Reprints Firestone giveaways 1945-1949	2	6	11	15

CARL BARKS LIBRARY OF WALT DISNEY'S UNCLE SCROOGE COMICS ONE PAGERS IN COLOR, THE
Gladstone: 1992 - No. 2, 1993 ($8.95, limited series, 60 pgs, 8-1/2x11")

1-Carl Barks one pg. reprints	3	9	17	25
2-Carl Barks one pg. reprints	2	6	11	15

CARNAGE: IT'S A WONDERFUL LIFE
Marvel Comics: Oct, 1996 ($1.95, one-shot)

1-David Quinn scripts				3.00

CARNAGE: MIND BOMB
Marvel Comics: Feb, 1996 ($2.95, one-shot)

1-Warren Ellis script; Kyle Hotz-a				3.00

CARNATION MALTED MILK GIVEAWAYS (See Wisco)

CARNEYS, THE
Archie Comics: Summer, 1994 ($2.00, 52 pgs)

1-Bound-in pull-out poster				2.50

CARNIVAL COMICS (Formerly Kayo #12; becomes Red Seal Comics #14)
Harry 'A' Chesler/Pershing Square Publ. Co.: 1945

nn (#13)-Guardineer-a	17	51	88	150

CAROLINE KENNEDY
Charlton Comics: 1961 (one-shot)

nn-Interior photo covers of Kennedy family	9	27	63	105

CAROUSEL COMICS
F. E. Howard, Toronto: V1#8, April, 1948

V1#8	6	18	32	45

CARTOON CARTOONS (Anthology)
DC Comics: Mar, 2001 - Present ($1.99)

1-8-Short stories of Cartoon Network characters. 3,6-Space Ghost				2.00

CARTOON KIDS
Atlas Comics (CPS): 1957 (no month)

1-Maneely-c/a; Dexter The Demon, Willie The Wise-Guy, Little Zelda app.				
	10	30	55	85

CARTOON NETWORK PRESENTS
DC Comics: Aug, 1997 - No. 24, Aug, 1999 ($1.75-$1.99, anthology)

1-24: 1-Dexter's Lab. 2-Space Ghost. 12-Bizarro World				2.25
1-Platinum Edition				5.00

CARTOON NETWORK PRESENTS SPACE GHOST
Archie Comics: Mar, 1997 ($1.50)

1-Scott Rosema-p				3.00

CARTOON NETWORK STARRING... (Anthology)
DC Comics: Sept, 1999 - No. 18, Feb, 2001 ($1.99)

1-Powerpuff Girls				4.00
2-18: 2,8,11,14,17-Johnny Bravo. 12,15,18-Space Ghost				2.25

CARTOON TALES (Disney's...)
W.D. Publications (Disney): nd, nn (1992) ($2.95, 6-5/8x9-1/2", 52 pgs.)

nn-Ariel & Sebastian-Serpent Teen; Beauty and the Beast; A Tale of Enchantment; Darkwing Duck - Just Us Justice Ducks; 101 Dalmatians - Canine Classics;

Tale Spin - Surprise in the Skies; Uncle Scrooge - Blast to the Past				4.00

CARVERS
Image Comics (Flypaper Press): 1998 - No. 3, 1999 ($2.95)

1-3-Pander Bros.-a/Fleming-s				3.00

CAR WARRIORS
Marvel Comics (Epic): June, 1991 - No. 4, Sept, 1991 ($2.25, lim. series)

1-4: 1-Says April in indicia				2.25

CASE OF THE SHOPLIFTER'S SHOE (See Perry Mason, Feature Book No.50)

CASE OF THE WINKING BUDDHA, THE
St. John Publ. Co.: 1950 (132 pgs.; 25¢; B&W; 5-1/2x7-5-1/2x8")

nn-Charles Raab-a; reprinted in Authentic Police Cases No. 25				
	29	87	153	265

CASEY-CRIME PHOTOGRAPHER (Two-Gun Western No. 5 on)(Radio)
Marvel Comics (BFP): Aug, 1949 - No. 4, Feb, 1950

1-Photo-c; 52 pgs.	25	75	130	225
2-4: Photo-c	17	51	88	150

CASEY JONES (TV)
Dell Publishing Co.: No. 915, July, 1958

Four Color 915-Alan Hale photo-c	5	15	35	60

CASEY JONES & RAPHAEL (See Bodycount)
Mirage Studios: Oct, 1994 ($2.75, unfinished limited series)

1-Bisley-c; Eastman story & pencils				2.75

CASEY JONES: NORTH BY DOWNEAST
Mirage Studios: May, 1994 - No. 2, July, 1994 ($2.75, limited series)

1,2-Rick Veitch script & pencils; Kevin Eastman story & inks				2.75

CASPER ADVENTURE DIGEST
Harvey Comics: V2#1, Oct, 1992 - V2#8, Apr, 1994 ($1.75/$1.95, digest-size)

V2#1: Casper, Richie Rich, Spooky, Wendy				5.00
2-8				3.50

CASPER AND...

Casper and Nightmare #14 © Paramount

Casper Spaceship #2 © Paramount

Casper, The Friendly Ghost #9 © Paramount

	GD2.0	FN6.0	VF8.0	NM9.4

	GD2.0	FN6.0	VF8.0	NM9.4

Harvey Comics: Nov., 1987 - No. 12, June, 1990 (.75/$1.00, all reprints)

1-Ghostly Trio				5.00
2-12: 2-Spooky; begin $1.00-c. 3-Wendy. 4-Nightmare. 5-Ghostly Trio. 6-Spooky. 7-Wendy. 8-Hot Stuff. 9-Baby Huey. 10-Wendy.11-Ghostly Trio. 12-Spooky				3.00

CASPER AND FRIENDS
Harvey Comics: Oct, 1991 - No. 5, July, 1992 ($1.00/$1.25)

1-Nightmare, Ghostly Trio, Wendy, Spooky				4.00
2-5				3.00

CASPER AND FRIENDS MAGAZINE: Mar, 1997 - No. 3, July, 1997 ($3.99)

1-3				4.00

CASPER AND NIGHTMARE (See Harvey Hits# 37, 45, 52, 56, 59, 62, 65, 68,71, 75)

CASPER AND NIGHTMARE (Nightmare & Casper No. 1-5)
Harvey Publications: No. 6, 11/64 - No. 44, 10/73; No. 45, 6/74 - No. 46, 8/74 (25¢)

6: 68 pg. Giants begin, ends #32	4	12	29	45
7-10	3	9	21	32
11-20	2	6	15	22
21-37: 33-37-(52 pg. Giants)	2	6	12	18
38-46	1	4	7	10

NOTE: Many issues contain reprints.

CASPER AND SPOOKY (See Harvey Hits No. 20)
Harvey Publications: Oct, 1972 - No. 7, Oct, 1973

1	3	9	19	28
2-7	2	6	10	14

CASPER AND THE GHOSTLY TRIO
Harvey Pub.: Nov, 1972 - No. 7, Nov, 1973; No. 8, Aug, 1990 - No. 10, Dec, 1990

1	3	9	19	28
2-7	2	6	10	14
8-10				4.00

CASPER AND WENDY
Harvey Publications: Sept, 1972 - No. 8, Nov, 1973

1: 52 pg. Giant	3	9	19	28
2-8	2	6	10	14

CASPER BIG BOOK
Harvey Comics: V2#1, Aug, 1992 - No. 3, May, 1993 ($1.95, 52 pgs.)

V2#1-Spooky app.				4.00
2,3				3.00

CASPER CAT (See Dopey Duck)
I. W. Enterprises/Super: 1958; 1963

1,7:1-Wacky Duck #?.7-Reprint, Super No. 14('63)	2	6	10	14

CASPER DIGEST (...Magazine #?; ...Halloween Digest #8, 10)
Harvey Publications: Oct, 1986 - No. 18, Jan, 1991 ($1.25/$1.75, digest-size)

1	1	3	6	9
2-18: 11-Valentine-c. 18-Halloween-c				6.00

CASPER DIGEST (...Magazine #? on)
Harvey Comics: V2#1, Sept, 1991 - V2#14, Nov, 1994 ($1.75/$1.95, digest-size)

V2#1				5.00
2-14				3.50

CASPER DIGEST STORIES
Harvey Publications: Feb, 1980 - No. 4, Nov, 1980 (95¢, 132 pgs., digest size)

1	2	6	11	15
2-4	1	3	6	8

CASPER DIGEST WINNERS
Harvey Publications: Apr, 1980 - No. 3, Sept, 1980 (95¢, 132 pgs., digest size)

1	2	6	11	15
2,3	1	3	6	8

CASPER ENCHANTED TALES DIGEST
Harvey Comics: May, 1992 - No. 10, Oct, 1994 ($1.75, digest-size, 98 pgs.)

1-Casper, Spooky, Wendy stories				5.00
2-10				3.50

CASPER GHOSTLAND
Harvey Comics: May, 1992 ($1.25)

1				3.00

CASPER GIANT SIZE
Harvey Comics: Oct, 1992 - No. 4, Nov, 1993 ($2.25, 68 pgs.)

V2#1-Casper, Wendy, Spooky stories				5.00
2-4				4.00

CASPER HALLOWEEN TRICK OR TREAT
Harvey Publications: Jan, 1976 (52 pgs.)

1	3	9	19	28

CASPER IN SPACE (Formerly Casper Spaceship)
Harvey Publications: No. 6, June, 1973 - No. 8, Oct, 1973

6-8	2	6	10	14

CASPER'S GHOSTLAND
Harvey Publications: Winter, 1958-59 - No. 97, 12/77; No. 98, 12/79 (25¢)

1-84 pgs. begin, ends #10	17	51	118	210
2	9	27	63	105
3-10	7	21	50	80
11-20: 11-68 pgs. begin, ends #61. 13-X-Mas-c	5	15	38	60
21-40	4	12	27	42
41-61	3	9	17	24
62-77: 62-52 pgs. begin	2	6	10	14
78-98: 94-X-Mas-c	1	3	6	8

NOTE: Most issues contain reprints w/new stories.

CASPER SPACESHIP (Casper in Space No. 6 on)
Harvey Publications: Aug, 1972 - No. 5, April, 1973

1: 52 pg. Giant	3	9	20	30
2-5	2	6	11	15

CASPER STRANGE GHOST STORIES
Harvey Publications: October, 1974 - No. 14, Jan, 1977 (All 52 pgs.)

1	3	9	19	28
2-14	2	6	11	15

CASPER, THE FRIENDLY GHOST (See America's Best TV Comics, Famous TV Funday Funnies, The Friendly Ghost..., Nightmare &..., Richie Rich and..., Tastee-Freez, Treasury of Comics, Wendy the Good Little Witch & Wendy Witch World)

CASPER, THE FRIENDLY GHOST (Becomes Harvey Comics Hits No. 61 (No. 6), and then continued with Harvey issue No. 7)(1st Series)
St. John Publishing Co.: Sept, 1949 - No. 5, Aug, 1951

1(1949)-Origin & 1st app. Baby Huey & Herman the Mouse (1st time the name Casper app. in any media, even films)	164	492	1023	1800
2,3 (2/50 & 8/50)	68	205	426	750
4,5 (3/51 & 8/51)	55	165	330	575

CASPER, THE FRIENDLY GHOST (Paramount Picture Star...)(2nd Series)
Harvey Publications (Family Comics): No. 7, Dec, 1952 - No. 70, July, 1958
Note: No. 6 is Harvey Comics Hits No. 61 (10/52)

7-Baby Huey begins, ends #9	31	93	222	400
8,9	18	54	123	220
10-Spooky begins (1st app., 6/53), ends #70?	20	60	140	250
11-18: Alfred Harvey app. in story	11	33	77	130
19-1st app. Nightmare (4/54)	16	48	112	200
20-Wendy the Witch begins (1st app., 5/54)	21	63	146	260
21-30: 24-Infinity-c	9	27	63	105
31-40	6	18	45	75
41-50	5	15	34	55
51-70 (Continues as Friendly Ghost... 8/58)	4	12	30	50

CASPER THE FRIENDLY GHOST (Formerly The Friendly Ghost...)(3rd Series)
Harvey Comics: No. 254, July, 1990 - No. 260, Jan, 1991 ($1.00)

254-260				3.00

CASPER THE FRIENDLY GHOST (4th Series)
Harvey Comics: Mar, 1991 - No. 28, Nov, 1994 ($1.00/$1.25/$1.50)

1-Casper becomes Mighty Ghost; Spooky & Wendy app.				5.00
2-10: 7,8-Post-a				3.00
11-28-($1.50)				2.50

Casual Heroes #1 © Motown Animation

Catman Comics #17 © HOKE

Catwoman #19 © DC

	GD2.0	FN6.0	VF8.0	NM9.4

CASPER T.V. SHOWTIME
Harvey Comics: Jan, 1980 - No. 5, Oct, 1980
1 .... 2 6 9 12
2-5 .... 6.00

CASSETTE BOOKS (Classics Illustrated)
Cassette Book Co./I.P.S. Publ.: 1984 (48 pgs, b&w comic with cassette tape)
NOTE: This series was illegally obtained, and the Classics Illustrated copyright owner, Twin Circle Publ. sued to get an injunction to prevent the continued sale of this series. Many C.I. collectors obtained copies before the 1987 injunction, but these are already scarce. Here again the market is just developing, but sealed mint copies of comic and tape should be worth at least $25.
1001 (CI#1-A2)New-PC 1002(CI#3-A2)CI-PC 1003(CI#13-A2)CI-PC
1004(CI#25)CI-LDC 1005(CI#10-A2)New-PC 1006(CI#64)CI-LDC

CASTILIAN (See Movie Classics)

CASTLE WAITING
Olio: 1997 - No. 7, 1999 ($2.95, B&W)
Cartoon Books: Vol. 2, Aug, 2000 - Present ($2.95, B&W)
1-Linda Medley-s/a in all 1 3 6 8
2 .... 4.00
3-7 .... 3.00
The Lucky Road TPB r/#1-7 .... 17.00
Hiatus Issue (1999) Crilley-c; short stories and previews 3.00
Vol. 2 #1-6 .... 3.00

CASUAL HEROES
Image Comics (Motown Machineworks): Apr, 1996 ($2.25, unfinished lim. series)
1-Steve Rude-c 2.25

CAT, T.H.E. (TV) (See T.H.E. Cat)

CAT, THE (See Movie Classics)

CAT, THE (Female hero)
Marvel Comics Group: Nov, 1972 - No. 4, June, 1973
1-Origin & 1st app. The Cat (who later becomes Tigra); Mooney-a(i);
  Wood-c(i)/a(i) 3 9 20 30
2,3: 2-Marie Severin/Mooney-a. 3-Everett inks 2 6 11 16
4-Starlin/Weiss-a/p 2 6 12 18

CATALYST: AGENTS OF CHANGE (Also see Comics' Greatest World)
Dark Horse Comics: Feb, 1994 - No.7, Nov, 1994 ($2.00, limited series)
1-7: Foil stamped logo 2.50

CAT & MOUSE
EF Graphics (Silverline): Dec, 1988 ($1.75, color w/part B&W)
1-1st printing (12/88, 32 pgs.), 1-2nd printing (5/89, 36 pgs.) 2.25

CAT FROM OUTER SPACE (See Walt Disney Showcase #46)

CATHOLIC COMICS (See Heroes All Catholic...)
Catholic Publications: June, 1946 - V3#10, July, 1949
1 .... 31 93 165 285
2 .... 16 48 83 140
3-13(7/47) 14 42 72 120
V2#1-10 .... 10 30 55 85
V3#1-10: Reprints 10-part Treasure Island serial from Target V2#2-11
  (see Key Comics #5) 11 33 55 90

CATHOLIC PICTORIAL
Catholic Guild: 1947
1-Toth-a(2) (Rare) 40 120 232 400

CATMAN COMICS (Formerly Crash Comics No. 1-5)
Holyoke Publishing Co./Continental Magazines V2#12, 7/44 on:
5/41 - No. 17, 1/43; No. 18, 7/43 - No. 22, 12/43; No. 23, 3/44 - No. 26,
11/44; No. 27, 4/45 - No. 30, 12/45; No. 31, 6/46 - No. 32, 8/46
1(V1#6)-Origin The Deacon & Sidekick Mickey, Dr. Diamond & Rag-Man; The
  Black Widow app.; The Catman by Chas. Quinlan & Blaze Baylor begin
  .... 350 1050 2188 4200
2(V1#7) 127 381 795 1400
3(V1#8)-The Pied Piper begins; classic Hitler, Stalin & Mussolini-c
  .... 109 327 682 1200
4(V1#9) 91 273 568 1000

5(V2#10)-1st app. Kitten; The Hood begins (c-redated), 6,7(V2#11,12)
  .... 77 231 483 850
8(V2#13,3/42)-Origin Little Leaders; Volton by Kubert begins (his 1st comic
  book work) 91 273 568 1000
9,10(V2#14,15): 10-Origin Blackout retold; Phantom Falcon begins
  .... 64 192 398 700
11 (V3#1)-Kubert-a 64 192 398 700
12 (V3#2), 14, 15, 17, 18(V3#8, 7/43) 55 165 330 575
13-(scarce) 82 246 511 900
16 (V3#5)-Hitler, Tojo, Mussolini, Stalin-c 73 219 455 800
19,20: 19 (V2#6)-Hitler, Tojo, Mussolini-c. 20 (V2#7): Classic Hitler-c
  .... 77 231 483 850
21-23 (V3#10, 3/44) 49 147 294 515
nn(V3#13, 5/44)-Rico-a; Schomburg bondage-c 49 147 294 515
nn(V2#12, 7/44), nn(V3#1, 9/44)-Origin The Golden Archer; Leatherface app.
  .... 45 135 270 475
nn(V3#2, 11/44)-L. B. Cole-c 77 231 483 850
27-Origins Catman & Kitten retold; L. B. Cole Flag-c; Infantino-a
  .... 86 258 540 950
28-Catman learns Kitten's I.D.; Dr. Macabre, Deacon app.; L. B. Cole c/a
  .... 91 273 568 1000
29-32-L. B. Cole-c; bondage-#30 .... 80 240 500 875
NOTE: **Fuje** a-11, 29(3), 30. **Palais** a-11, 29(2), 30(2), 32; c-25(7/44). **Rico** a-11(2).

CATSEYE
Hyperwerks Comics: Dec, 1998 - No. 4, June, 1999 ($2.95)
1-4-Altstaetter-s/a 3.00

CAT TALES (3-D)
Eternity Comics: Apr, 1989 ($2.95)
1-Felix the Cat-r in 3-D 5.00

CATWOMAN (Also see Action Comics Weekly #611, Batman #404-407,
  Detective Comics, & Superman's Girlfriend Lois Lane #70, 71)
DC Comics: Feb, 1989 - No. 4, May, 1989 ($1.50, limited series, mature)
1 .... 1 4 7 10
2-4: 3-Batman cameo. 4-Batman app. 1 3 6 9
Her Sister's Keeper (1991, $9.95, trade paperback)-r/#1-4 .... 10.00

CATWOMAN (Also see Showcase '93, Showcase '95 #4, & Batman #404-407)
DC Comics: Aug, 1993 - No. 94, Jul, 2001 ($1.50-$2.25)
0-(10/94)-Zero Hour; origin retold. Released between #14&15 .... 3.00
1-($1.95)-Embossed-c; Bane app.; Balent c-1-10; a-1-10p 4.00
2-20: 3-Bane flashback cameo. 4-Brief Bane app. 6,7-Knightquest tie-ins;
  Batman (Azrael) app. 8-1st app. Zephyr. 12-KnightsEnd pt. 6. 13-new Knights
  End Aftermath.14-(9/94)-Zero Hour 3.00
21-24, 26-30, 33-49: 21-$1.95-c begins. 28,29-Penguin cameo app.
  36-Legacy pt. 2. 38-40-Year Two; Batman, Joker, Penguin & Two-face app.
  46-Two-Face app. 2.50
25,31,32: 25-($2.95)-Robin app. 31-Contagion pt. 4 (Reads pt. 5 on-c). 32-
  Contagion pt. 9. .... 3.00
50-($2.95, 48 pgs.)-New armored costume 3.00
50-($2.95, 48 pgs.)-Collector's Ed.w/metallic ink-c 3.00
51-77: 51-Huntress-c/app. 54-Grayson-s begins. 56-Cataclysm pt.6. 57-Poison
  Ivy-c/app.63-65-Joker-c/app. 72-No Man's Land; Ostrander-s begins 2.50
78-82: 80-Catwoman goes to jail 2.25
83-94: 83-Begin $2.25-c. 83,84,89-Harley Quinn-c/app. 2.25
#1,000,000 (11/98) 853rd Century x-over 2.25
Annual 1 (1994, $2.95, 68 pgs.)-Elseworlds story; Batman app.; no Balent-a 3.00
Annual 2,4 ('95, '97, $3.95)-2-Year One story. 4-Pulp Heroes 4.00
Annual 3 (1996, $2.95)-Legends of the Dead Earth story 3.00
...Plus 1 (11/97, $2.95) Screamqueen (Scare Tactics) app. 3.00
TPB ($9.95) r/#15-19, Balent-c 10.00

CATWOMAN
DC Comics: Jan, 2002 - Present ($2.50)
1,2-Darwyn Cooke & Mike Allred-a; Ed Brubaker-s 2.50

CATWOMAN/ GUARDIAN OF GOTHAM
DC Comics: 1999 - No. 2, 1999 ($5.95, limited series)
1,2-Elseworlds; Moench-s/Balent-a 6.00

Cave Kids #5 © H-B

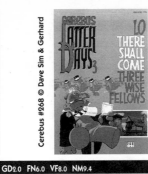

Cerebus #268 © Dave Sim & Gerhard

The Challenger #4 © Interfaith

CH

	GD2.0	FN6.0	VF8.0	NM9.4

CATWOMAN/VAMPIRELLA: THE FURIES
DC Comics/Harris Publ.: Feb, 1997 ($4.95, squarebound, one-shot, 46 pgs.)
(1st DC/Harris x-over)
nn-Reintro Pantha; Chuck Dixon scripts; Jim Balent-c/a 5.00

CATWOMAN/WILDCAT
DC Comics: Aug, 1998 - No. 4, Nov, 1998 ($2.50, limited series)
1-4-Chuck Dixon & Beau Smith-s; Stelfreeze-c 3.00

CAUGHT
Atlas Comics (VPI): Aug, 1956 - No. 5, Apr, 1957

1	22	66	116	200
2-4: 3-Maneely, Pakula, Torres-a. 4-Maneely-a	12	36	61	100
5-Crandall, Krigstein-a	13	39	66	110

NOTE: *Drucker a-2. Heck a-4. Severin c-1, 2, 4, 5. Shores a-4.*

CAVALIER COMICS
A. W. Nugent Publ. Co.: 1945; 1952 (Early DC reprints)

2(1945)-Speed Saunders, Fang Gow	22	66	116	200
2(1952)	12	36	61	100

CAVE GIRL (Also see Africa)
Magazine Enterprises: No. 11, 1953 - No. 14, 1954

11(A-1 82)-Origin; all Cave Girl stories	45	135	270	475
12(A-1 96), 13(A-1 116), 14(A-1 125)-Thunda by Powell in each	36	108	191	330

NOTE: *Powell c/a in all.*

CAVE GIRL
AC Comics: 1988 ($2.95, 44 pgs.) (16 pgs. of color, rest B&W)
1-Powell-r/Cave Girl #11; Nyoka photo back-c from movie; Powell/Bill
Black-c; Special Limited Edition on-c 4.00

CAVE KIDS (TV) (See Comic Album #16)
Gold Key: Feb, 1963 - No. 16, Mar, 1967 (Hanna-Barbera)

1	7	21	49	85
2-5	4	12	26	40
6-16: 7,12-Pebbles & Bamm Bamm app. 16-1st Space Kidettes	3	9	20	30

CAVEWOMAN
Basement Comics: Jan, 1994 - No. 6, 1995 ($2.95)

1	3	9	20	30
2	2	6	11	15
3-6	1	3	6	8
...: Meets Explorers ('97, $2.95)				3.00
...: One-Shot Special (7/00, $2.95) Massey-s/a				3.00

CELESTINE (See Violator Vs. Badrock #1)
Image Comics (Extreme): May, 1996 - No. 2, June, 1996 ($2.50, limited series)
1,2: Warren Ellis scripts 2.50

CENTURION OF ANCIENT ROME, THE
Zondervan Publishing House: 1958 (no month listed) (B&W, 36 pgs.)
(Rare) All by Jay Disbrow 38 114 203 350

CENTURIONS (TV)
DC Comics: June, 1987 - No. 4, Sept, 1987 (75¢, limited series)
1-4 2.50

CENTURY: DISTANT SONS
Marvel Comics: Feb, 1996 ($2.95, one-shot)
1-Wraparound-c 3.00

CENTURY OF COMICS (See Promotional Comics section)

CEREBUS BI-WEEKLY
Aardvark-Vanaheim: Dec. 2, 1988 - No. 26, Nov. 11, 1989 ($1.25, B&W)
Reprints Cerebus The Aardvark#1-26

1-16, 18, 19, 21-26:				3.00
17-Hepcats app.	2	6	9	12
20-Milk & Cheese app.	2	6	11	15

CEREBUS: CHURCH & STATE
Aardvark-Vanaheim: Feb, 1991 - No. 30, Apr, 1992 ($2.00, B&W, bi-weekly)

1-30: r/Cerebus #51-80				3.00

CEREBUS: HIGH SOCIETY
Aardvark-Vanaheim: Feb, 1990 - No. 25, 1991 ($1.70, B&W)

1-25: r/Cerebus #26-50				3.00

CEREBUS JAM
Aardvark-Vanaheim: Apr, 1985
1-Eisner, Austin, Dave Sim-a (Cerebus vs. Spirit) 6.00

CEREBUS THE AARDVARK (See A-V in 3-D, Nucleus, Power Comics)
Aardvark-Vanaheim: Dec, 1977 - Present ($1.70/$2.00/$2.25, B&W)

0				3.00
0-Gold				20.00
1-1st app. Cerebus; 2000 print run; most copies poorly printed	28	84	196	350

Note: *There is a counterfeit version known to exist. It can be distinguished from the original in the following ways: inside cover is glossy instead of flat, black background on the front cover is blotted or spotty. Reports show that a counterfeit #2 also exists.*

2-Dave Sim art in all	8	24	60	100
3-Origin Red Sophia	8	24	56	90
4-Origin Elrod the Albino	5	15	38	60
5,6	4	12	30	50
7-10	3	10	23	35
11,12: 11-Origin The Cockroach	3	9	17	24
13-15: 14-Origin Lord Julius	2	6	11	15
16-20	1	4	7	10
23-30: 23-Preview of Wandering Star by Teri S. Wood. 26-High Society begins,ends #50	1	3	6	8
21-B. Smith letter in letter column	3	10	23	35
22-Low distribution; no cover price	2	6	11	16
31-Origin Moonroach	1	4	7	10
32-40, 53-Intro. Wolveroach (cameo)				6.00
41-50,52: 52-Church & State begins, ends #111; Cutey Bunny app.				5.00
51,54: 51-Cutey Bunny app. 54-1st full Wolveroach story	1	3	6	8
55,56-Wolveroach app.; Normalman back-ups by Valentino				5.00
57-100: 61,62: Flaming Carrot app. 65-Gerhard begins				4.00
101-160: 104-Flaming Carrot app. 112/113-Double issue. 114-Jaka's Story begins, ends #136. 139-Melmoth begins, ends #150. 151-Mothers & Daughters begins, ends #200				3.00
161-Bone app.	1	3	6	8
162-231: 175-($2.25, 44 pgs.) 201-Guys storyline begins; Eddie Campbell's Bacchus app. 220-231-Rick's Story				2.50
232-265-Going Home				2.25
266-273-Latter Days: 267-Five-Bar Gate				2.25
Free Cerebus (Giveaway, 1991-92?, 36 pgs.)-All-r				2.25

CHAIN GANG WAR
DC Comics: July, 1993 - No. 12, June, 1994 ($1.75)

1-($2.50)-Embossed silver foil-c, Dave Johnson-c/a				3.00
2-4,6-12: 3-Deathstroke app. 4-Brief Deathstroke app. 6-New Batman (Azrael) cameo. 11-New Batman-c/story. 12-New Batman app.				2.25
5-($2.50)-Foil-c; Deathstroke app; new Batman cameo (1 panel)				3.00

CHAINS OF CHAOS
Harris Comics: Nov, 1994 - No. 3, Jan, 1995 ($2.95, limited series)
1-3-Re-Intro of The Rook w/ Vampirella 3.00

CHALLENGE OF THE UNKNOWN (Formerly Love Experiences)
Ace Magazines: No. 6, Sept, 1950 (See Web Of Mystery No. 19)
6- "Villa of the Vampire" used in N.Y. Joint Legislative Comm. Publ;
Sekowsky-a 31 93 168 290

CHALLENGER, THE
Interfaith Publications/T.C. Comics: 1945 - No. 4, Oct-Dec, 1946

nn; nd; 32 pgs.; Origin the Challenger Club; Anti-Fascist with funny animal filler	40	120	240	420
2-4: Kubert-a; 4-Fuje-a	33	99	174	300

CHALLENGERS OF THE FANTASTIC
Marvel Comics (Amalgam): June 1997 ($1.95, one-shot)
1-Karl Kesel-s/Tom Grummett-a 2.50

CHALLENGERS OF THE UNKNOWN (See Showcase #6, 7, 11, 12, Super

Challengers of the Unknown #79 © DC

Chamber of Chills #23 © HARV

Champion Comics #7 © HARV

	GD2.0	FN6.0	VF8.0	NM9.4

DC Giant, and Super Team Family)
National Per. Publ./DC Comics: 4-5/58 - No. 77, 12-1/70-71; No. 78, 2/73 - No. 80, 6-7/73; No. 81, 6-7/77 - No. 87, 6-7/78

1-(4-5/58)-Kirby/Stein-a(2); Kirby-c	176	528	1500	3000
2-Kirby/Stein-a(2)	66	198	558	1050
3-Kirby/Stein-a(2)	56	169	478	900
4-8-Kirby/Wood-a plus cover to #8	45	135	359	650
9,10	27	81	190	340
11-15: 11-Grey tone-c. 14-Origin/1st app. Multi-Man (villain)				
	18	54	126	225
16-22: 18-Intro. Cosmo, the Challengers Spacepet. 22-Last 10¢ issue				
	13	39	91	155
23-30	7	21	50	80
31-Retells origin of the Challengers	7	21	53	85
32-40	4	12	26	40
41-47,49,50,52-60: 43-New look begins. 49-Intro. Challenger Corps. 55-Death of Red Ryan. 60-Red Ryan returns	3	9	19	28
48,51: 48-Doom Patrol app. 51-Sea Devils app.	3	9	21	32
61-68: 64,65-Kirby origin-r, parts 1 & 2. 66-New logo. 68-Last 12¢ issue.				
	2	6	11	15
69-73,75-80: 69-1st app. Corinna. 77-Last 15¢ issue	1	4	7	10
74-Deadman by Tuska/Adams; 1 pg. Wrightson-a	3	9	19	28
81,83-87: 81-(6-7/77). 83-87-Swamp Thing app.	1	3	6	8
82-Swamp Thing begins, c/s	1	4	7	10

NOTE: *N. Adams* a-c67, 68, 70, 72, 74i, 81i. *Buckler* c-83-86p. *Giffen* a-83-87p. *Kirby* a-75-80r; c-75, 77, 78. *Kubert* c-64, 66, 69, 76, 79. *Nasser* c/a-81p, 82p. *Tuska* a-73. *Wood* r-76-80r.

CHALLENGERS OF THE UNKNOWN
DC Comics: Mar, 1991 - No. 8, Oct, 1991 ($1.75, limited series)

1-Jeph Loeb scripts & Tim Sale-a in all (1st work together); Bolland-c				3.00
2-8: 2-Superman app. 3-Dr. Fate app. 6-G. Kane-c(p). 7-Steranko-c/swipe by Art Adams				2.50

NOTE: *Art Adams* c-7. *Hempel* c-5. *Gil Kane* c-6p. *Sale* a-1; c-3, 8. *Wagner* c-4.

CHALLENGERS OF THE UNKNOWN
DC Comics: Feb, 1997 - No. 18, July, 1998 ($2.25)

1-18: 1-Intro new team; Leon-c/a(c) begins. 4-Origin of new team. 11,12-Batman app. 15-Millennium Giants x-over; Superman-c/app.				2.50

CHALLENGE TO THE WORLD
Catechetical Guild: 1951 (10¢, 36 pgs.)

nn	5	14	21	28

CHAMBER OF CHILLS (Formerly Blondie Comics #20; ...of Clues No. 27 on)
Harvey Publications/Witches Tales: No. 21, June, 1951 - No. 26, Dec, 1954

21 (#1)	43	129	257	450
22,24 (#2,4)	29	87	156	270
23-Excessive violence; eyes torn out	33	99	174	300
5(2/52)-Decapitation, acid in face scene	33	99	174	300
6-Woman melted alive	31	93	168	290
7-Used in SOTI, pg. 389; decapitation/severed head panels				
	29	87	156	270
8-10: 8-Decapitation panels	25	75	130	225
11,12,14	20	60	105	175
13,15-Nostrand-a in all. 13,21-Decapitation panels. 18-Atom bomb panels.				
20-Nostrand-c	26	78	136	235
25,26	16	48	83	140

NOTE: *About half the issues contain bondage, torture, sadism, perversion, gore, cannabalism, eyes ripped out, acid in face, etc.* **Elias** *c-4-11, 14-19, 21-26.* **Kremer** *a-12, 17.* **Palais** *a-21(1), 23. Nostrand/Powell a-13, 15, 16.* **Powell** *a-21, 23, 24('51), 5-8, 11, 13, 18-21, 23-25. Bondage-c-21, 24('51), 7. 25-r/#5; 26-r/#9.*

CHAMBER OF CHILLS
Marvel Comics Group: Nov, 1972 - No. 25, Nov, 1976

1-Harlan Ellison adaptation	3	9	17	25
2-5: 2-1st app. John Jakes (Brak the Barbarian)	2	6	11	15
6-25: 22,23-(Regular 25¢ editions)	2	6	9	12
22,23-(30¢-c variants, limited distribution)(5,7/76)	2	6	12	18

NOTE: *Adkins a-1i, 2i. Brunner a-2-4; c-4. Chaykin a-4. Ditko r-14, 16, 19, 23, 24. Everett a-3i, 11r,21r. Heath a-1r. Gil Kane c-2p. Kirby r-11, 18, 19, 22. Powell a-13r. Russell a-1p, 2p. Williamson/Mayo a-13r. Robert E. Howard horror story adaptation-2, 3.*

CHAMBER OF CLUES (Formerly Chamber of Chills)
Harvey Publications: No. 27, Feb, 1955 - No. 28, April, 1955

	GD2.0	FN6.0	VF8.0	NM9.4

27-Kerry Drake-r/#19; Powell-a; last pre-code	7	21	36	50
28-Kerry Drake	6	18	29	40

CHAMBER OF DARKNESS (Monsters on the Prowl #9 on)
Marvel Comics Group: Oct, 1969 - No. 8, Dec, 1970

1-Buscema-a(p)	5	15	38	60
2,3: 2-Neal Adams scripts. 3-Smith, Buscema-a	3	9	20	30
4-A Conan-esque tryout by Smith (4/70); reprinted in Conan #16; Marie Severin/Everett-a	5	15	38	60
5,8: 5-H.P. Lovecraft adaptation. 8-Wrightson-c	2	6	15	22
6	2	6	12	18
7-Wrightson-c/a, 7pgs. (his 1st work at Marvel); Wrightson draws himself in 1st & last panels; Kirby/Ditko-r, last 15¢-c	3	9	20	30
1-(1/72, 25¢ Special, 52 pgs.)	3	9	20	30

NOTE: *Adkins/Everett a-8. Buscema a-Special 1r. Craig a-5. Ditko a-6-8r. Heck a-1, 2, 8, Special 1r. Kirby a(p)-4, 5, 7r. Kirby/Everett c-5. Severin/Everett c-6. Shores a-2, 3i, Special 1r. Sutton a-1, 2i, 4, 7, Special 1r. Wrightson c-7.*

CHAMP COMICS (Formerly Champion No. 1-10)
Worth Publ. Co./Harvey Publ./Family Comics(Harvey Publ.): No. 11, Oct, 1940 - No. 24, Dec, 1942; No. 25, April, 1943

11-Human Meteor cont'd from Champion	86	258	540	950
12-17,20: 14,15-Crandall-a. 20-The Green Ghost app.				
	66	198	413	725
18,19-Simon-c. 19-The Wasp app.	82	246	511	900
21-23,25: 22-The White Mask app. 23-Flag-c	52	157	314	550
24-Hitler, Tojo & Mussolini-c	55	165	341	600

CHAMPION (See Gene Autry's...)

CHAMPION COMICS (Formerly Speed Comics #1?; Champ Comics No. 11 on)
Worth Publ. Co.(Harvey Publications): No. 2, Dec, 1939 - No. 10, Aug, 1940 (no No.1)

2-The Champ, The Blazing Scarab, Neptina, Liberty Lads, Jungleman, Bill Handy, Swingtime Sweetie begin	173	519	1080	1900
3-7: 7-The Human Meteor begins?	77	231	483	850
8-10: 8-Simon-c. 9-1st S&K-c (1st collaboration together). 10-Bondage-c by Kirby	136	408	852	1500

CHAMPIONS, THE
Marvel Comics Group: Oct, 1975 - No. 17, Jan, 1978

1-Origin & 1st app. The Champions (The Angel, Black Widow, Ghost Rider, Hercules, Iceman); Venus x-over	3	9	17	24
2-4,8-10,16: 2,3-Venus x-over	1	4	7	10
5-7-(Regular 25¢ edition)(4-8/76) 6-Kirby-c	1	4	7	10
5-7-(30¢-c variants, limited distribution)	2	6	11	15
11-14,17-Byrne-a. 14-(Regular 30¢ edition)	1	4	7	10
14,15-(35¢-c variant, limited distribution)	2	6	11	15
15-(Regular 30¢ edition)(9/77)-Byrne-a	1	4	7	10

NOTE: *Buckler/Adkins c-3. Byrne a-11-15, 17. Kane/Adkins c-1. Kane/Layton c-11. Tuska a-3p, 4p, 6p, 7p. Ghost Rider c-1-4, 7, 8, 10, 14, 16, 17 (4, 10, 14 are more prominent).*

CHAMPIONS (Game)
Eclipse Comics: June, 1986 - No. 6, Feb, 1987 (limited series)

1-6: 1-Intro Flare; based on game. 5-Origin Flare				2.50

CHAMPIONS (Also see The League of Champions)
Hero Comics: Sept, 1987 - No. 12, 1989 ($1.95)

1-12: 1-Intro The Marksman & The Rose. 14-Origin Malice				2.25
Annual 1(1988, $2.75, 52pgs.)-Origin of Giant				2.75

CHAMPION SPORTS
National Periodical Publications: Oct-Nov, 1973 - No. 3, Feb-Mar, 1974

1	3	9	19	28
2,3	2	6	10	14

CHANNEL ZERO
Image Comics: Feb, 1998 - No. 5 ($2.95, B&W, limited series)

1-5, ...Dupe (1/99)-Brian Wood-s/a				3.00

CHAOS (See The Crusaders)

CHAOS! BIBLE
Chaos! Comics: Nov, 1995 ($3.30, one-shot)

1-Profiles of characters & creators				3.50

Charlie Chan #8 © PRIZE

Charlton Bullseye #4 © CC

Chase #1 © DC

	GD2.0	FN6.0	VF8.0	NM9.4

		4	12	26	40

CHAOS! CHRONICLES
Chaos! Comics: Feb, 2000 ($3.50, one-shot)

1-Profiles of characters, checklist of Chaos! comics and products	3.50

CHAOS EFFECT, THE
Valiant: 1994

Alpha (Giveaway w/trading card checklist)	2.25
Alpha-Gold variant, Omega-Gold variant	5.00
Omega (11/94, $2.25); Epilogue Pt. 1, 2 (12/94, 1/95; $2.95)	3.00

CHAOS! GALLERY
Chaos! Comics: Aug, 1997 ($2.95, one-shot)

1-Pin-ups of characters	3.00

CHAOS! QUARTERLY
Chaos! Comics: Oct, 1995 -No. 3, May, 1996 ($4.95, quarterly)

1-3: 1-anthology. Lady Death-c by Julie Bell. 2-Boris "Lady Demon"-c	5.00
1-Premium Edition (7,500)	25.00

CHAPEL (Also see Youngblood & Youngblood Strikefile #1-3)
Image Comics (Extreme Studios): No. 1 Feb, 1995 - No. 2, Mar, 1995 ($2.50, limited series)

1,2	2.50

CHAPEL (Also see Youngblood & Youngblood Strikefile #1-3)
Image Comics (Extreme Studios): V2 #1, Aug, 1995 - No. 7, Apr, 1996 ($2.50)

V2#1-7: 4-Babewatch x-over. 5-vs. Spawn. 7-Shadowhawk-c/app; Shadowhunt x-over	2.50
#1-Quesada & Palmiotti variant-c	2.50

CHAPEL (Also see Youngblood & Youngblood Strikefile #1-3)
Awesome Entertainment: Sept, 1997 ($2.99, one-shot)

1 (Reg. & alternate covers)	3.00

CHARLEMAGNE (Also see War Dancer)
Defiant Comics: Mar, 1994 - No. 5, July, 1994 ($2.50)

1/2 (Hero Illustrated giveaway)-Adam Pollina-c/a.	
1-(3/94, $3.50, 52 pgs.)-Adam Pollina-c/a.	3.50
2,3,5: Adam Pollina-c/a. 2-War Dancer app. 5-Pre-Schism issue.	2.50
4-($3.25, 52 pgs.)	3.25

CHARLIE CHAN (See Big Shot Comics, Columbia Comics, Feature Comics & The New Advs. of...)

CHARLIE CHAN (The Adventures of...) (Zaza The Mystic No. 10 on) (TV)
Crestwood(Prize) No. 1-5; Charlton No. 6(6/55) No. 6-7/48 - No. 5, 2-3/49; No.6, 6/55 - No. 9, 3/56

1-S&K-c, 2 pgs.; Infantino-a	77	231	483	850
2-5-S&K-c: 3-S&K-c/a	50	150	300	525
6 (6/55-Charlton)-S&K-c	37	111	197	340
7-9	19	57	99	170

CHARLIE CHAN
Dell Publishing Co.: Oct-Dec, 1965 - No. 2, Mar, 1966

1-Springer-a	5	15	34	55
2	3	9	21	32

CHARLIE McCARTHY (See Edgar Bergen Presents...)
Dell Publishing Co.: No. 171, Nov, 1947 - No. 571, July, 1954 (See True Comics #14)

Four Color 171	26	78	182	340
Four Color 196-Part photo-c; photo back-c	17	50	119	220
1(3-5/49)-Part photo-c; photo back-c	15	45	105	190
2-9(7/52; #5,6-52 pgs.)	7	21	49	90
Four Color 445,478,527,571	5	15	35	60

CHARLTON BULLSEYE
CPL/Gang Publications: 1975 - No. 5, 1976 ($1.50, B&W, bi-monthly, magazine format)

1: 1 & 2 are last Capt. Atom by Ditko/Byrne intended for the never published Capt. Atom #90; Nightshade app.; Jeff Jones-a	5	15	34	55
2-Part 2 Capt. Atom story by Ditko/Byrne	3	10	23	35
3-Wrong Country by Sanho Kim	2	6	12	18
4-Doomsday + 1 by John Byrne	3	9	17	24
5-Doomsday + 1 by Byrne, The Question by Toth; Neal Adams back-c; Toth-a				

CHARLTON BULLSEYE
Charlton Publications: June, 1981 - No. 10, Dec, 1982; Nov, 1986

1-Blue Beetle, The Question app.; 1st app. Rocket Rabbit	6.00
2-5: 2-1st app. Neil The Horse; Rocket Rabbit app. 4-Vanguards	4.00
6-10: Low print run. 6-Origin & 1st app. Thunderbunny	6.00
Special 1,2: 1(11/86) (Half in B&W). 2-Atomic Mouse app. (1987)	5.00

CHARLTON CLASSICS
Charlton Comics: Apr, 1980 - No. 9, Aug, 1981

1-Hercules-r by Glanzman in all	6.00
2-9	5.00

CHARLTON CLASSICS LIBRARY (1776)
Charlton Comics: V10 No.1, Mar, 1973 (one-shot)

1776 (title) - Adaptation of the film musical "1776"; given away at movie theatres	2	6	12	18

CHARLTON PREMIERE (Formerly Marine War Heroes)
Charlton Comics: V1#19, July, 1967; V2#1, Sept, 1967 - No. 4, May, 1968

V1#19, V2#1,2,4: V1#19-Marine War Heroes. V2#1-Trio; intro. Shape, Tyro Team & Spookman. 2-Children of Doom; Boyette classic-a. 4-Unlikely Tales; Aparo, Ditko-a	3	9	17	24
V2#3-Sinistro Boy Fiend; Blue Beetle & Peacemaker x-over	3	9	19	28

CHARLTON SPORT LIBRARY - PROFESSIONAL FOOTBALL
Charlton Comics: Winter, 1969-70 (Jan. on cover) (68 pgs.)

1	3	9	21	32

CHARM SCHOOL (See Action Girl Comics #13)
Slave Labor Graphics: Apr, 2000 - Present ($2.95, B&W)

1-4-Elizabeth Watasin-s/a	3.00

CHASE (See Batman #550 for 1st app.)
DC Comics: Feb, 1998 - No. 9, Oct, 1998; #1,000,000 Nov, 1998 ($2.50)

1-9: Williams III & Gray-a. 1-Includes 4 Chase cards. 4-Teen Titans app. 7,8-Batman app. 9-GL Hal Jordan-c/app.	2.50
#1,000,000 (11/98) Final issue; 853rd Century x-over	2.50

CHASING DOGMA (See Jay and Silent Bob)

CHASSIS
Millenium Publications: 1996 - No. 3 ($2.95)

1-3: 1-Adam Hughes-c. 2-Conner var-c	3.00

CHASSIS
Hurricane Entertainment: 1998 - No. 3 ($2.95)

0,1-3: 1-Adam Hughes-c. 0-Green var-c	3.00

CHASSIS (Vol. 3)
Image Comics: Nov, 1999 - Present ($2.95, limited series)

1-4: 1-Two covers by O'Neil and Green. 2-Busch var-c	3.00
1-($6.95) DF Edition alternate-c by Wieringo	7.00

CHASTITY
Chaos! Comics: (one-shots)

#1/2 (1/01, $2.95) Batista-a	3.00
Love Bites (3/01, $2.99) Vale-a/Romano-c	3.00
Reign of Terror 1 (10/00, $2.95) Grant-s/Ross-a/Rio-c	3.00

CHASTITY: LUST FOR LIFE
Chaos! Comics: May, 1999 - No. 3, July, 1999 ($2.95, limited series)

1-3-Nutman-s/Benes-c/a	3.00

CHASTITY: ROCKED
Chaos! Comics: Nov, 1998 - No. 4, Feb, 1999 ($2.95, limited series)

1-4-Nutman-s/Justiniano-c/a	3.00

CHASTITY: SHATTERED
Chaos! Comics: Jun, 2001 - No. 3, Sept, 2001 ($2.99, limited series)

1-3-Kaminski & Pulido-s/Batista-c/a	3.00

CHASTITY: THEATER OF PAIN
Chaos! Comics: Feb, 1997 - No. 3, June, 1997 ($2.95, limited series)

Cheryl Blossom #30 © AP

Cheval Noir #32 © DH

Childhood's End #1 © Bourne/Califiore

	GD2.0	FN6.0	VF8.0	NM9.4
1-3-Pulido-s/Justiniano-c/a				3.00
TPB (1997, $9.95) r/#1-3				10.00

CHECKMATE (TV)
Gold Key: Oct, 1962 - No. 2, Dec, 1962

	GD2.0	FN6.0	VF8.0	NM9.4
1-Photo-c on both	5	15	35	65
2	5	15	34	55

CHECKMATE! (See Action Comics #598)
DC Comics: Apr, 1988 - No. 33, Jan, 1991 ($1.25)

1-33: 13: New format begins				2.50

NOTE: *Gil Kane c-2, 4, 7, 8, 10, 11, 15-19.*

CHERYL BLOSSOM (See Archie's Girls, Betty and Veronica #320 for 1st app.)
Archie Publications: Sept, 1995 - No. 3, Nov, 1995 ($1.50, limited series)

1-3				4.00
Special 1-4 ('95, '96, $2.00)				4.00

CHERYL BLOSSOM (Cheryl's Summer Job)
Archie Publications: July, 1996 - No. 3, Sept, 1996 ($1.50, limited series)

1-3				3.00

CHERYL BLOSSOM (...Goes Hollywood)
Archie Publications: Dec, 1996 - No. 3, Feb, 1997 ($1.50, limited series)

1-3				3.00

CHERYL BLOSSOM
Archie Publications: Apr, 1997 - No. 37, Mar, 2001 ($1.50/$1.75/$1.79/$1.99)

1-Dan DeCarlo-c/a				3.00
2-37: 2-7-Dan DeCarlo-c/a. 32-Begin $1.99-c. 34-Sabrina app.				2.25

CHESTY SANCHEZ
Antarctic Press: Nov, 1995 - No. 2, Mar, 1996 ($2.95, B&W)

1,2				3.00
...Super Special (2/99, $5.99)				6.00

CHEVAL NOIR
Dark Horse Comics: 1989 - No. 48, Nov, 1993 ($3.50, B&W, 68 pgs.)

1-8,10 ($3.50): 6-Moebius poster insert				3.50
9,11,13,15,17,20,22 ($4.50, 84 pgs.)				4.50
12,18,19,21,23,25,26 ($3.95): 12-Geary-a; Mignola-c. 26-Moebius-a begins				4.00
14 ($4.95, 76 pgs.)(7 pgs. color)				5.00
16,24 ($3.75): 16-19-Contain trading cards				3.75
27-48 ($2.95): 33-Snyder III-c				3.00

NOTE: *Bolland a-2, 6, 7, 13, 14. Bolton a-2, 4, 45; c-4, 20. Chadwick c-13. Dorman painted c-16. Geary a-13, 14. Kelley Jones c-27. Kaluta a-6; c-6, 18. Moebius c-5, 9, 26. Dave Stevens c-1, 7. Sutton painted c-36.*

CHEYENNE (TV)
Dell Publishing Co.: No. 734, Oct, 1956 - No. 25, Dec-Jan, 1961-62

	GD2.0	FN6.0	VF8.0	NM9.4
Four Color 734(#1)-Clint Walker photo-c	17	51	119	220
Four Color 772,803: Clint Walker photo-c	8	24	56	105
4(8-10/57) - 20: 4-9,13-20-Clint Walker photo-c. 10-12-Ty Hardin photo-c	5	15	35	60
21-25-Clint Walker photo-c on all	5	15	36	65

CHEYENNE AUTUMN (See Movie Classics)

CHEYENNE KID (Formerly Wild Frontier No. 1-7)
Charlton Comics: No. 8, July, 1957 - No. 99, Nov, 1973

	GD2.0	FN6.0	VF8.0	NM9.4
8 (#1)	7	21	36	50
9,15-19	5	15	24	32
10-Williamson/Torres-a(3); Ditko-c	11	33	55	90
11-(68 pgs.)-Cheyenne Kid meets Geronimo	10	30	55	85
12-Williamson/Torres-a(2)	10	30	55	85
13-Williamson/Torres-a (5 pgs.)	7	21	38	55
14-Williamson-a (5 pgs.?)	7	21	36	50
20-22,24,25-Severin c/a(3) each	3	10	23	35
23,27-29	2	6	13	20
26,30-Severin-a	3	9	17	25
31-59	2	6	11	16
60-65,67-80	2	6	9	12
66-Wander by Aparo begins, ends #87	2	6	10	14
81-99: Apache Red begins #88, origin in #89	1	3	6	9

Modern Comics Reprint 87,89(1978)				4.00

CHIAROSCURO (THE PRIVATE LIVES OF LEONARDO DA VINCI)
DC Comics (Vertigo): July, 1995 - No. 10, Apr, 1996 ($2.50/$2.95, limited series, mature)

1-9				2.50
10-($2.95)				3.00

CHICAGO MAIL ORDER (See C-M-O Comics)

CHI-CHIAN
Sirius Entertainment: 1997 - No. 6, 1998 ($2.95, limited series)

1-6-Voltaire-s/a				3.00

CHIEF, THE (Indian Chief No. 3 on)
Dell Publishing Co.: No. 290, Aug, 1950 - No. 2, Apr-June, 1951

	GD2.0	FN6.0	VF8.0	NM9.4
Four Color 290(#1)	6	18	42	75
2	5	15	35	60

CHIEF CRAZY HORSE (See Wild Bill Hickok #21)
Avon Periodicals: 1950 (Also see Fighting Indians of the Wild West!)

	GD2.0	FN6.0	VF8.0	NM9.4
nn-Fawcette-c	21	63	110	185

CHIEF VICTORIO'S APACHE MASSACRE (See Fight Indians of/Wild West!)
Avon Periodicals: 1951

	GD2.0	FN6.0	VF8.0	NM9.4
nn-Williamson/Frazetta-a (7 pgs.); Larsen-a; Kinstler-c				
	43	129	257	450

CHILDHOOD'S END
Image Comics: Oct, 1997 ($2.95, B&W)

1-Bourne-s/Calafiore-a				3.00

CHILDREN OF FIRE
Fantagor Press: Nov, 1987 - No. 3, 1988 ($2.00, limited series)

1-3: by Richard Corben				4.00

CHILDREN OF THE VOYAGER (See Marvel Frontier Comics Unlimited)
Marvel Frontier Comics: Sept, 1993 - No. 4, Dec, 1993 ($1.95, limited series)

1-($2.95)-Embossed glow-in-the-dark-c; Paul Johnson-c/a				3.00
2-4				2.25

CHILDREN'S BIG BOOK
Dorene Publ. Co.: 1945 (25¢, stiff-c, 68 pgs.)

	GD2.0	FN6.0	VF8.0	NM9.4
nn-Comics & fairy tales; David Icove-a	12	36	61	100

CHILDREN'S CRUSADE, THE
DC Comics (Vertigo): Dec, 1993 - No. 2, Jan, 1994 ($3.95, limited series)

1,2-Neil Gaiman scripts & Chris Bachalo-a; framing issues for Children's Crusade x-over				4.00

CHILD'S PLAY: THE SERIES (Movie)
Innovation Publishing: May, 1991 - #3, 1991 ($2.50, 28pgs.)

1-3				2.50

CHILD'S PLAY 2 THE OFFICIAL MOVIE ADAPTATION (Movie)
Innovation Publishing: 1990 - No. 3, 1990 ($2.50, bi-weekly limited series)

1-3: Adapts movie sequel				2.50

CHILI (Millie's Rival)
Marvel Comics Group: 5/69 - No. 17, 9/70; No. 18, 8/72 - No. 26, 12/73

	GD2.0	FN6.0	VF8.0	NM9.4
1	6	18	40	65
2-5	3	9	21	32
6-17	2	6	13	20
18-26	2	6	11	15
Special 1(12/71, 52 pgs.)	4	12	25	38

CHILLER
Marvel Comics (Epic): Nov, 1993 - No. 2, Dec, 1993 ($7.95, lim. series)

	GD2.0	FN6.0	VF8.0	NM9.4
1,2-(68 pgs.)	1	3	6	8

CHILLING ADVENTURES IN SORCERY (...as Told by Sabrina #1, 2)
(Red Circle Sorcery No. 6 on)
Archie Publications (Red Circle Productions): 9/72 - No. 2, 10/72; No. 3, 10/73 - No. 5, 2/74

	GD2.0	FN6.0	VF8.0	NM9.4
1-Sabrina cameo as narrator	4	12	26	40
2-Sabrina cameo as narrator	2	6	13	20

Chilling Adventures in Sorcery #1 © AP

Christmas Carnival nn © Z-D

Chroma-Tick #6 © Ben Edlund

	GD2.0	FN6.0	VF8.0	NM9.4

3-5: Morrow-c/a, all. 4,5-Alcazar-a   2   6   9   12

CHILLING TALES (Formerly Beware)
Youthful Magazines: No. 13, Dec, 1952 - No. 17, Oct, 1953

	GD2.0	FN6.0	VF8.0	NM9.4
13(No.1)-Harrison-a; Matt Fox-c/a	55	165	330	575
14-Harrison-a	39	117	208	360
15-Has #14 on-c; Matt Fox-c; Harrison-a	43	129	257	450
16-Poe adapt.-'Metzengerstein'; Rudyard Kipling adapt.-'Mark of the Beast', by Kiefer; bondage-a	33	99	174	300
17-Matt Fox-c; Sir Walter Scott & Poe adapt.	40	120	220	380

CHILLING TALES OF HORROR (Magazine)
Stanley Publications: V1#1, 6/69 - V1#7, 12/70; V2#2, 2/71 - V2#5, 10/71 (50¢, B&W, 52 pgs.)

	GD2.0	FN6.0	VF8.0	NM9.4
V1#1	5	15	34	55
2-7: 2-Two different #2 issues exist (2/71 & 4/71). 7-Cameron-a	4	12	25	38
V2#2-5: 2-(2/71) Spirit of Frankenstein-r/Adventures into the Unknown #16.				
4-(8/71) different from other V2#4(6/71)	3	9	21	32
V2#4-(6/71) r/9 pg. Feldstein-a from Adventures into the Unknown #3				
	4	12	25	38

NOTE: *Two issues of V2#2 exist, Feb, 1971 and April, 1971. Two issues of V2#4 exist, Jun, 1971 and Aug, 1971.*

CHILLY WILLY
Dell Publ. Co.: No. 740, Oct, 1956 - No. 1281, Apr-June, 1962 (Walter Lantz)

	GD2.0	FN6.0	VF8.0	NM9.4
Four Color 740 (#1)	5	15	35	60
Four Color 852 (2/58),967 (2/59),1017 (9/59),1074 (2-4/60),1122 (8/60), 1177 (4-6/61), 1212 (7-9/61), 1281	4	12	26	40

CHINA BOY (See Wisco)

CHIP 'N' DALE (Walt Disney)(See Walt Disney's C&S #204)
Dell Publishing Co/Gold Key/Whitman No. 65 on: Nov, 1953 - No. 30, June-Aug, 1962; Sept, 1967 - No. 83, July, 1984

	GD2.0	FN6.0	VF8.0	NM9.4
Four Color 517(#1)	9	27	63	120
Four Color 581,636	5	15	35	60
4(12/55-2/56)-10	5	15	34	55
11-30	4	12	26	40
1(Gold Key, 1967)-Reprints	3	9	19	28
2-10	2	6	10	14
11-20	1	3	6	9
21-40	1	3	5	7
41-64,70-77: 75(2/82), 76(2-3/82), 77(3/82)				6.00
65,66 (Whitman)	1	3	5	7
67-69 (3-pack) 1980)(scarce)	2	6	10	14
78-83 (All #90214; 3-pack, nd, no code): 78(4/83), 79(5/83), 80(7/83), 81(8/83), 82(5/84), 83(7/84)	1	4	7	10

NOTE: *All Gold Key/Whitman issues have reprints except No. 32-35, 38-41, 45-47. No. 23-28, 30-42, 45-47, 49 have new covers.*

CHIP 'N DALE RESCUE RANGERS
Disney Comics: June, 1990 - No. 19, Dec, 1991 ($1.50)

1-New stories; origin begins				3.00
2-19: 2-Origin continued				2.50

CHITTY CHITTY BANG BANG (See Movie Comics)

C.H.I.X.
Image Comics (Studiosaurus): Jan, 1998 ($2.50)

1-Dodson, Haley, Lopresti, Randall, and Warren-s/c/a				3.00
1-($5.00) "X-Ray Variant" cover				5.00
C.H.I.X. That Time Forgot 1 (8/98, $2.95)				3.00

CHOICE COMICS
Great Publications: Dec, 1941 - No. 3, Feb, 1942

	GD2.0	FN6.0	VF8.0	NM9.4
1-Origin Secret Circle; Atlas the Mighty app.; Zomba, Jungle Fight, Kangaroo Man, & Fire Eater begin	164	492	1023	1800
2	84	252	525	925
3-Double feature; Features movie "The Lost City" (classic cover); continued from Great Comics #3	118	354	738	1300

CHOO CHOO CHARLIE
Gold Key: Dec, 1969

	GD2.0	FN6.0	VF8.0	NM9.4
1-John Stanley-a (scarce)	10	30	70	125

CHRISTIAN (See Asylum)
Maximum Press: Jan, 1996 ($2.99, one-shot)

1-Pop Mhan-a				3.00

CHRISTIAN HEROES OF TODAY
David C. Cook: 1964 (36 pgs.)

	GD2.0	FN6.0	VF8.0	NM9.4
nn	2	6	12	18

CHRISTMAS (Also see A-1 Comics)
Magazine Enterprises: No. 28, 1950

	GD2.0	FN6.0	VF8.0	NM9.4
A-1 28	6	18	29	40

CHRISTMAS ADVENTURE, A (See Classics Comics Giveaways, 12/69)

CHRISTMAS ALBUM (See March of Comics No. 312)

CHRISTMAS ANNUAL
Golden Special: 1975 ($1.95, 100 pgs., stiff-c)

	GD2.0	FN6.0	VF8.0	NM9.4
nn-Reprints Mother Goose stories with Walt Kelly-a	4	12	25	38

CHRISTMAS & ARCHIE
Archie Comics: Jan, 1975 ($1.00, 68 pgs., 10-1/4x13-1/4" treasury-sized)

	GD2.0	FN6.0	VF8.0	NM9.4
1	4	12	30	50

CHRISTMAS BELLS (See March of Comics No. 297)

CHRISTMAS CARNIVAL
Ziff-Davis Publ. Co./St. John Publ. Co. No. 2: 1952 (25¢, one-shot, 100 pgs.)

	GD2.0	FN6.0	VF8.0	NM9.4
nn	33	99	174	300
2-Reprints Ziff-Davis issue plus-c	17	51	88	150

CHRISTMAS CAROL, A (See March of Comics No. 33)

CHRISTMAS EVE, A (See March of Comics No. 212)

CHRISTMAS IN DISNEYLAND (See Dell Giants)

CHRISTMAS PARADE (See Dell Giant No. 26, Dell Giants, March of Comics No. 284, Walt Disney Christmas Parade & Walt Disney's...)

CHRISTMAS PARADE (Walt Disney's)
Gold Key: 1962 (no month listed) - No. 9, Jan, 1972 (#1,5: 80 pgs.; #2-4,7-9: 36 pgs.)

	GD2.0	FN6.0	VF8.0	NM9.4
1 (30018-301)-Giant	8	24	56	105
2-6: 2-r/F.C. 367 by Barks. 3-r/F.C. #178 by Barks. 4-r/F.C. #203 by Barks. 5-r/Christ. Parade #1 (Dell) by Barks; giant. 6-r/Christmas Parade #2 (Dell) by Barks (64 pgs.); giant	6	18	42	80
7-Pull-out poster (half price w/o poster)	5	15	34	55
8-r/F.C. 367 by Barks; pull-out poster	6	18	42	80
9	4	12	26	40

CHRISTMAS PARTY (See March of Comics No. 256)

CHRISTMAS STORIES (See Little People No. 959, 1062)

CHRISTMAS STORY (See March of Comics No. 326)

CHRISTMAS STORY BOOK (See Woolworth's Christmas Story Book)

CHRISTMAS TREASURY, A (See Dell Giants & March of Comics No. 227)

CHRISTMAS WITH ARCHIE
Spire Christian Comics (Fleming H. Revell Co.): 1973, 1974 (49¢, 52 pgs.)

	GD2.0	FN6.0	VF8.0	NM9.4
nn-Low print run	2	6	10	14

CHRISTMAS WITH MOTHER GOOSE
Dell Publishing Co.: No. 90, Nov, 1945 - No. 253, Nov, 1949

	GD2.0	FN6.0	VF8.0	NM9.4
Four Color 90 (#1)-Kelly-a	18	54	126	230
Four Color 126 (46), 172 (11/47)-By Walt Kelly	13	40	91	175
Four Color 201 (10/48), 253-By Walt Kelly	12	36	84	155

CHRISTMAS WITH SANTA (See March of Comics No. 92)

CHRISTMAS WITH THE SUPER-HEROES (See Limited Collectors' Edition)
DC Comics: 1988; No. 2, 1989 ($2.95)

1,2: 1-(100 pgs.)-All reprints; N. Adams-r, Byrne-c; Batman, Superman, JLA, LSH Christmas stories; r-Miller's 1st Batman/DC Special Series #21. 2-(68 pgs.)-Superman by Chadwick; Batman, Wonder Woman, Deadman, Gr. Lantern, Flash app.; Morrow-a; Enemy Ace by Byrne; all new-a				5.00

CHROMA-TICK, THE (...Special Edition, #1,2) (Also see The Tick)
New England Comics Press: Feb, 1992 - No. 8, Sept, 1993 ($3.95/$3.50, 44 pgs.)

Cinderella Love #11 © Z-D

Circus Comics #1 © D.S. Pub.

City of the Living Dead © AVON

	GD2.0	FN6.0	VF8.0	NM9.4

1,2-Includes serially numbered trading card set — 5.00
3-8 ($3.50, 36 pgs.): 6-Bound-in card — 4.00

CHROME
Hot Comics: 1986 - No. 3, 1986 ($1.50, limited series)
1-3 — 2.25

CHROMIUM MAN, THE
Triumphant Comics: Aug, 1993 - No.10, May, 1994 ($2.50)
1-1st app. Mr. Death; all serially numbered — 2.50
2-10: 2-1st app. Prince Vandal. 3-1st app. Candi, Breaker & Coil.
4,5-Triumphant Unleashed x-over. 8,9-(3/94). 10-(5/94) — 2.50
0-(4/94)-Four color-c, 0-All pink-c & all blue-c; no cover price — 2.50

CHROMIUM MAN: VIOLENT PAST, THE
Triumphant Comics: Jan, 1994 - No. 2, Jan, 1994 ($2.50, limited series)
1,2-Serially numbered to 22,000 each — 2.50

CHRONICLES OF CORUM, THE (Also see Corum...)
First Comics: Jan, 1987 - No. 12, Nov, 1988 ($1.75/$1.95, deluxe series)
1-12 Adapts Michael Moorcock's novel — 2.50

CHRONOS
DC Comics: Mar, 1998 - No. 11, Feb. 1999 ($2.50)
1-11-J.F. Moore-s/Guinan-a — 2.50
#1,000,000 (11/98) 853rd Century x-over — 2.50

CHRONOWAR (Manga)
Dark Horse Comics: Aug, 1996 - No. 9, Apr, 1997 ($2.95, limited series)
1-9 — 3.00

CHUCKLE, THE GIGGLY BOOK OF COMIC ANIMALS
R. B. Leffingwell Co.: 1945 (132 pgs., one-shot)
1-Funny animal — 21 — 63 — 110 — 185

CHUCK NORRIS (TV)
Marvel Comics (Star Comics): Jan, 1987 - No. 4, July, 1987
1-3: Ditko-a — 3.50
4-No Ditko-a (low print run) — 5.00

CHUCK WAGON (See Sheriff Bob Dixon's...)

CHYNA (WWF Wrestling)
Chaos! Comics: Sept, 2000; July, 2001 ($2.95/$2.99, one-shots)
1-Grant-s/Barrows-a; photo-c — 3.00
1-($9.95) Premium Edition; Cleavenger-c — 10.00
II -(7/01, $2.99) Deodato-a; photo-c — 3.00

CICERO'S CAT
Dell Publishing Co.: July-Aug, 1959 - No. 2, Sept-Oct, 1959
1-Cat from Mutt & Jeff — 4 — 12 — 30 — 50
2 — 4 — 12 — 27 — 42

CIMARRON STRIP (TV)
Dell Publishing Co.: Jan, 1968
1-Stuart Whitman photo-c — 4 — 12 — 27 — 42

CINDER AND ASHE
DC Comics: May, 1988 - No. 4, Aug, 1988 ($1.75, limited series)
1-4: Mature readers — 2.25

CINDERELLA (Disney) (See Movie Comics)
Dell Publishing Co.: No. 272, Apr, 1950 - No. 786, Apr, 1957
Four Color 272 — 11 — 33 — 77 — 140
Four Color 786-Partial-r 272 — 6 — 18 — 42 — 80

CINDERELLA
Whitman Publishing Co.: Apr, 1982
nn-Reprints 4-Color #272 — 5.00

CINDERELLA LOVE
Ziff-Davis/St. John Publ. Co. No. 12 on: No. 10, 1950; No. 11, 4-5/51; No. 12, 9/51; No. 4, 10-11/51 - No. 11, Fall, 1952; No. 12, 10/53 - No. 15, 8/54; No. 25, 12/54 - No. 29, 10/55 (No #16-24)
10(#1)(1st Series, 1950)-Painted-c — 15 — 45 — 77 — 130
11(#2, 4-5/51)-Crandall-a; Saunders painted-c — 10 — 30 — 55 — 80

12(#3, 9/51)-Photo-c	8	24	42	60
4-8: 4,6,7-Photo-c	7	21	36	50
9-Kinstler-a; photo-c	8	24	45	65
10,11(Fall/'52), 14: 10,11-Photo-c. 14-Baker-a	8	24	42	60
12(St. John-10/53)-#13:13-Painted-c.	6	18	32	45
15(8/54)-Matt Baker-c	9	27	49	70
25(2nd Series)(Formerly Romantic Marriage)	6	18	32	45
26-Baker-c; last precode (2/55)	9	27	49	70
27,29: Both Matt Baker-c	9	27	49	70
28	5	15	25	35

CINDY COMICS (...Smith No. 39, 40; Crime Can't Win No. 41 on)(Formerly Krazy Komics) (See Junior Miss & Teen Comics)
Timely Comics: No. 27, Fall, 1947 - No. 40, July, 1950
27-Kurtzman-a, 3 pgs: Margie, Oscar begin	21	63	110	185
28-31-Kurtzman-a	13	39	66	110
32-40: 33-Georgie story; anti-Wertham editorial	9	27	49	70
NOTE: Kurtzman's "Hey Look"-#27(3), 29(2), 30(2), 31; "Giggles 'n' Grins"-28.

CIRCUS (...the Comic Riot)
Globe Syndicate: June, 1938 - No. 3, Aug, 1938
1-(Scarce)-Spacehawks (2 pgs.), & Disk Eyes by Wolverton (2 pgs.), Pewee Throttle by Cole (2nd comic book work; see Star Comics V1#11), Beau Gus, Ken Craig & The Lords of Crillon, Jack Hinton by Eisner, Van Bragger by Kane — 800 — 2400 — 4400 — 7200
2,3-(Scarce)-Eisner, Cole, Wolverton, Bob Kane-a in each — 400 — 1200 — 2200 — 3600

CIRCUS BOY (TV) (See Movie Classics)
Dell Publishing Co.: No. 759, Dec, 1956 - No. 813, July, 1957
Four Color 759 (#1)-The Monkees' Mickey Dolenz photo-c — 13 — 39 — 91 — 170
Four Color 785 (4/57),813-Mickey Dolenz photo-c — 11 — 33 — 77 — 140

CIRCUS COMICS
Farm Women's Pub. Co./D. S. Publ.: 1945 - No. 2, Jun, 1945; Wint., 1948-49
1-Funny animal — 13 — 39 — 66 — 110
2 — 9 — 27 — 49 — 70
1(1948)-D.S. Publ.; 2 pgs. Frazetta — 25 — 75 — 130 — 225

CIRCUS OF FUN COMICS
A. W. Nugent Publ. Co.: 1945 - No. 3, Dec, 1947 (A book of games & puzzles)
1 — 14 — 42 — 72 — 120
2,3 — 9 — 27 — 49 — 70

CISCO KID, THE (TV)
Dell Publishing Co.: July, 1950 - No. 41, Oct-Dec, 1958
Four Color 292(#1)-Cisco Kid, his horse Diablo, & sidekick Pancho & his horse Loco begin; painted-c begin — 24 — 72 — 168 — 315
2(1/51) — 12 — 36 — 84 — 150
3-5 — 10 — 30 — 70 — 130
6-10 — 8 — 24 — 56 — 100
11-20 — 7 — 21 — 49 — 90
21-36-Last painted-c — 5 — 15 — 35 — 65
37-41: All photo-c — 9 — 27 — 63 — 120
NOTE: Buscema a-40. Ernest Nordli painted c-5-16, 20, 35.

CISCO KID COMICS
Bernard Bailey/Swappers Quarterly: Winter, 1944 (one-shot)
1-Illustrated Stories of the Operas: Faust; Funnyman by Giunta; Cisco Kid (1st app.) & Superbaby begin; Giunta-a — 40 — 120 — 240 — 425

CITIZEN SMITH (See Holyoke One-Shot No. 9)

CITIZEN V AND THE V-BATTALION (See Thunderbolts)
Marvel Comics: June, 2001 - No. 3, Aug, 2001 ($2.99, limited series)
1-3-Nicieza-a; Michael Ryan-c/a — 3.00

CITY OF SILENCE
Image Comics: May, 2000 - No. 3, July, 2000 ($2.50)
1-3-Ellis-s/Erskine-a — 2.50

CITY OF THE LIVING DEAD (See Fantastic Tales No. 1)
Avon Periodicals: 1952
nn-Hollingsworth-c/a — 44 — 132 — 264 — 460

Clandestine #2 © MAR

Clash #1 © DC

Classic Comics #1 © GIL

	GD2.0	FN6.0	VF8.0	NM9.4		GD2.0	FN6.0	VF8.0	NM9.4

CITY PEOPLE NOTEBOOK
Kitchen Sink Press: 1989 ($9.95, B&W, magazine sized)
nn-Will Eisner-s/a 10.00
nn-(DC Comics, 2000) Reprint 10.00

CITY SURGEON (Blake Harper...)
Gold Key: August, 1963
1(10075-308)-Painted-c .... 4 .... 12 .... 26 40

CIVIL WAR MUSKET, THE (Kadets of America Handbook)
Custom Comics, Inc.: 1960 (25¢, half-size, 36 pgs.)
nn .... 3 .... 9 .... 19 28

CLAIRE VOYANT (Also see Keen Teens)
Leader Publ./Standard/Pentagon Publ.: 1946 - No. 4, 1947 (Sparling strip reprints)
nn .... 59 ...... 177 ...... 369 650
2,4: 2-Kamen-c. 4-Kamen bondage-c ... 47 ... 142 ... 286 ... 500
3-Kamen bridal-c; contents mentioned in Love and Death, a book by Gershom Legman(1949) referenced by Dr. Wertham in SOTI
.... 55 ...... 165 ...... 341 600

CLANDESTINE (Also see Marvel Comics Presents & X-Men: ClanDestine)
Marvel Comics: Oct, 1994 - No.12, Sept, 1995 ($2.95/$2.50)
1-($2.95)-Alan Davis-c/a(p)/scripts & Mark Farmer-c/a(i) begin, ends #8; Modok app.; Silver Surfer cameo; gold foil-c 3.00
2-12: 2-Wraparound-c. 2,3-Silver Surfer app. 5-Origin of ClanDestine.
6-Capt. America, Hulk, Spider-Man, Thing & Thor-c; Spider-Man cameo.
7-Spider-Man-c/app; Punisher cameo. 8-Invaders & Dr. Strange app.
9-12-Modok app. 10-Captain Britain-c/app. 11-Sub-Mariner app ... 2.50
Preview (10/94, $1.50) 2.50

CLASH
DC Comics: 1991 - No. 3, 1991 ($4.95, limited series, 52 pgs.)
Book One - Three: Adam Kubert-c/a 5.00

CLASSIC COMICS/ILLUSTRATED - INTRODUCTION
by Dan Malan

Further revisions have been made to help in understanding the **Classics** section. **Classics** reprint editions prior to 1963 had either incorrect dates or no dates listed. Those reprint editions should be identified only by the highest number on the reorder list (HRN). Past price guides listed what were calculated to be approximately correct dates, but many people found it confusing for the price guide to list a date not listed in the comic itself.

We have also attempted to clear up confusion about edition variations, such as color, printer, etc. Such variations will be identified by letters. Editions will now be determined by three categories. Original edition variations will be Edition 1A, 1B, etc. All reprint editions prior to 1963 will be identified by HRN only. All reprint editions from 9/63 on will be identified by the correct date listed in the comic.

We have also included new information on four recent reprintings of **Classics** not previously listed. From 1968-1976 Twin Circle, the Catholic newspaper, serialized over 100 **Classics** titles. That list can be found under non-series items at the end of this section. In 1972 twelve **Classics** were reissued as **Now Age Books Illustrated**. They are listed under **Pendulum Illustrated Classics**. In 1982, 20 **Classics** were reissued, adapted for teaching English as a second language. They are listed under **Regents Illustrated Classics**. Then in 1984, six **Classics** were reissued with cassette tapes. See the listing under **Cassette Books**.

UNDERSTANDING CLASSICS ILLUSTRATED
by Dan Malan

Since **Classics Illustrated** is the most complicated comic book series, with all its reprint editions and variations, with changes in covers and artwork, with a variety of means of identifying editions, and with the most extensive worldwide distribution of any comic-book series; therefore this introductory section is provided to assist you in gaining expertise about this series.

THE HISTORY OF CLASSICS
The **Classics** series was the brainchild of Albert L. Kanter, who saw in the new comic-book medium a means of introducing children to the great classics of literature. In October of 1941 his Gilberton Co. began the **Classic Comics** series with **The Three Musketeers**, with 64 pages of storyline. In those early years, the struggling series saw irregular schedules and numerous printers, not to mention

variable art quality and liberal story adaptations. With No.13 the page total was reduced to 56 (except for No. 33, originally scheduled to be No. 9), and with No. 15 the coming-next ad on the outside back cover moved inside. In 1945 the Jerry Iger Shop began producing all new CC titles, beginning with No. 23. In 1947 the search for a classier logo resulted in **Classics Illustrated**, beginning with No. 35, **Last Days of Pompeii**. With No. 45 the page total dropped again to 48, which was to become the standard.

Two new developments in 1951 had a profound effect upon the success of the series. One was the introduction of painted covers, instead of the old line drawn covers, beginning with No. 81, **The Odyssey**. The second was the switch to the major national distributor Curtis. They raised the cover price from 10 to 15 cents, making it the highest priced comic-book, but it did not slow the growth of the series, because they were marketed as books, not comics. Because of this higher quality image, **Classics** flourished during the fifties while other comic series were reeling from outside attacks. They diversified with their new **Juniors**, **Specials**, and **World Around Us** series.

Classics artwork can be divided into three distinct periods. The pre-Iger era (1941-44) was mentioned above for its variable art quality. The Iger era (1945-53) was a major improvement in art quality and adaptations. It came to be dominated by artists Henry Kiefer and Alex Blum, together accounting for some 50 titles. Their styles gave the first real personality to the series. The EC era (1954-62) resulted from the demise of the EC horror series, when many of their artists made the major switch to classical art.

But several factors brought the production of new CI titles to a complete halt in 1962. Gilberton lost its 2nd class mailing permit. External factors like television, cheap paperback books, and Cliff Notes were all eating away at their market. Production halted with No.167, **Faust**, even though many more titles were already in the works. Many of those found their way into foreign series, and are very desirable to collectors. In 1967, **Classics** was sold to Patrick Frawley and his Catholic publication, Twin Circle. They issued two new titles in 1969 as part of an attempted revival, but succumbed to major distribution problems in 1971. In 1988, the trio: First Publishing, Berkley Press, and Classics Media Group acquired the use rights for the old CI series art, logo, and name from the Frawley Group. So far they have used only the name in the new series, but do have plans to reprint the old CI.

One of the unique aspects of the **Classics Illustrated** (CI) series was the proliferation of reprint variations. Some titles had as many as 25 editions. Reprinting began in 1943. Some **Classic Comics** (CC) reprints (r) had the logo format revised to a banner logo, and added a motto under the banner. In 1947 CC titles changed to the CI logo, but kept their line drawn covers (LDC). In 1948, Nos. 13, 18, 29 and 41 received second covers (LDC2), replacing covers considered too violent, and reprints of Nos. 13-44 had pages reduced to 48, except for No. 26, which had 48 pages to begin with.

Starting in the mid-1950s, 70 of the 80 LDC titles were reissued with new painted covers (PC). Thirty of them also received new interior artwork (A2). The new artwork was generally higher quality with larger art panels and more faithful but abbreviated storylines. Later on, there were 29 second painted covers (PC2), mostly by Twin Circle. Altogether there were 199 interior art variations (169 (O)s and 30 A2 editions) and 272 different covers (169 (O)s, four LDC2s, 70 new PCs of LDC (O)s, and 29 PC2s). It is really astounding to realize that there are nearly 1400 different editions in the U.S. CI series.

FOREIGN CLASSICS ILLUSTRATED
If U.S. Classics variations are mildly astounding, the veritable plethora of foreign CI variations will boggle your imagination. While we still anticipate additional discoveries, we presently know about series in 25 languages and 27 countries. There were 250 new CI titles in foreign series, and nearly 400 new foreign covers of U.S. titles. The 1400 U.S. CI editions pale in comparison to the 4000 plus foreign editions. The very nature of CI lent itself to flourishing as an international series. Worldwide, they published over one billion copies! The first foreign CI series consisted of six Canadian Classic Comic reprints in 1946.

The following chart shows when CI series first began in each country:
1946: Canada. 1947: Australia. 1948: Brazil/The Netherlands. 1950: Italy. 1951: Greece/Japan/Hong Kong(?)/England/Argentina/Mexico. 1952: West Germany. 1954: Norway. 1955: New Zealand/South Africa. 1956: Denmark/Sweden/Iceland. 1957: Finland/France. 1962: Singapore(?). 1964: India (8 languages). 1971: Ireland (Gaelic). 1973: Belgium(?) /Philippines(?) & Malaysia(?).

Significant among the early series were Brazil and Greece. In 1950, Brazil was the first country to begin doing its own new titles. They issued nearly 80 new CI titles by Brazilian authors. In Greece in 1951 they actually had debates in parlia-

Classic Comics #2 © GIL

Classic Comics #3 © GIL

Classic Comics #4 © GIL

ment about the effects of Classics Illustrated on Greek culture, leading to the inclusion of 88 new Greek History & Mythology titles in the CI series.

But by far the most important foreign CI development was the joint European series which began in 1956 in 10 countries simultaneously. By 1960, CI had the largest European distribution of any American publication, not just comics! So when all the problems came up with U.S. distribution, they literally moved the CI operation to Europe in 1962, and continued producing new titles in all four CI series. Many of them were adapted and drawn in the U.S., the most famous of which was the British CI #158A. Dr. No, drawn by Norman Nodel. Unfortunately, the British CI series ended in late 1963, which limited the European CI titles available in English to 15. Altogether there were 82 new CI art titles in the joint European series, which ran until 1976.

IDENTIFYING CLASSICS EDITIONS

HRN: This is the highest number on the reorder list. It should be listed in ( ) after the title number. It is crucial to understanding various CI editions.

ORIGINALS (O): This is the all-important First Edition. To determine (O)s, there is one primary rule and two secondary rules (with exceptions):

Rule No. 1: All (O)s and only (O)s have coming-next ads for the next number. Exceptions: No. 14(15) (reprint) has an ad on the last inside text page only. No. 14(0) also has a full-page outside back cover ad (also rule 2). Nos.55(75) and 57(75) have coming-next ads. (Rules 2 and 3 apply here). Nos. 168(0) and 169(0) do not have coming-next ads. No.168 was never reprinted; No. 169(0) has HRN (166). No. 169(169) is the only reprint.

Rule No. 2: On nos.1-80, all (O)s and only (O)s list 10c on the front cover. Exceptions: Reprint variations of Nos. 37(62), 39(71), and 46(62) list 10c on the front cover. (Rules 1 and 3 apply here.)

Rule No. 3: All (O)s have HRN close to that title No. Exceptions: Some reprints also have HRNs close to that title number: a few CC(r)s, 58(62), 60(62), 149(149), 152(149) 153(149), and title nos. in the 160's. (Rules 1 and 2 apply here.)

DATES: Many reprint editions list either an incorrect date or no date. Since Gilberton apparently kept track of CI editions by HRN, they often left the (O) date on reprints. Often, someone with a CI collection for sale will swear that all their copies are originals. That is why we are so detailed in pointing out how to identify original editions. Except for original editions, which should have a coming-next ad, etc., all CI dates prior to 1963 are incorrect! So you want to go by HRN only if it is (165) or below, and go by listed date if it is 1963 or later. There are a few (167) editions with incorrect dates. They could be listed either as (167) or (62/3), which is meant to indicate that they were issued sometime between late 1962 and early 1963.

COVERS: A change from CC to LDC indicates a logo change, not a cover change; while a change from LDC to LDC, LDC to PC, or from PC to PC2 does indicate a new cover. New PCs can be identified by HRN, and PC2s can be identified by HRN and date. Several covers had color changes, particularly from purple to blue.

Notes: If you see 15 cents in Canada on a front cover, it does not necessarily indicate a Canadian edition. Editions with an HRN between 44 and 75, with 15 cents on the cover are Canadian. Check the publisher's address. An HRN listing two numbers with a / between them indicates that there are two different reorder lists in the front and back covers. Official Twin Circle editions have a full-page back cover ad for their TC magazine, with no CI reorder list. Any CI with just a Twin Circle sticker on the front is not an official TC edition.

TIPS ON LISTING CLASSICS FOR SALE

It may be easy to just list Edition 17, but Classics collectors keep track of CI editions in terms of HRN and/or date, (O) or (r), CC or LDC, PC or PC2, A1 or A2, soft or stiff cover, etc. Try to help them out. For originals, just list (0), unless there are variations such as color (Nos. 10 and 61), printer (Nos. 18-22), HRN (Nos. 95, 108, 160), etc. For reprints, just list HRN if its (165) or below. Above that, list HRN and date. Also, please list type of logo/cover/art for the convenience of buyers. They will appreciate it.

CLASSIC COMICS (Also see Best from Boys Life, Cassette Books, Famous Stories, Fast Fiction, Golden Picture Classics, King Classics, Marvel Classics Comics, Pendulum Illustrated Classics, Picture Parade, Picture Progress, Regents Ill. Classics, Spitfire, Stories by Famous Authors, Superior Stories, and World Around Us.)

CLASSIC COMICS (Classics Illustrated No. 35 on)
Elliot Publishing #1-3 (1941-1942)/Gilberton Publications #4-167 (1942-1967) /Twin Circle Pub. (Frawley). (1968-1969):
10/41 - No. 34, 2/47; No. 35, 3/47 - No. 169, Spring 1969

(Reprint Editions of almost all titles 5/43 - Spring 1971)
(Painted Covers (0)s No. 81 on, and (r)s of most Nos. 1-80)

Abbreviations:
A–Art; C or c–Cover; CC–Classic Comics; CI–Classics Ill.; Ed–Edition; LDC–Line Drawn Cover; PC–Painted Cover; r–Reprint

1. The Three Musketeers

Ed	HRN	Date	Details	A	C				
1	–	10/41	Date listed-1941; Elliot Pub; 68 pgs.	1	1	438	1314	2847	5700
2	10	–	10¢ price removed on all (r)s; Elliot Pub; CC-r	1	1	37	111	197	340
3	15	–	Long Isl. Ind. Ed.; CC-r	1	1	27	81	142	245
4	18/20	–	Sunrise Times Ed.; CC-r	1	1	19	57	99	165
5	21	–	Richmond Courier Ed.; CC-r	1	1	17	51	88	150
6	28	1946	CC-r	1	1	14	42	72	120
7	36	–	LDC-r	1	1	8	24	42	60
8	60	–	LDC-r	1	1	6	18	28	38
9	64	–	LDC-r	1	1	5	15	23	30
10	78	–	C-price 15¢;LDC-r	1	1	4	13	19	26
11	93	–	LDC-r	1	1	4	13	19	26
12	114	–	Last LDC-r	1	1	3	9	15	22
13	134	–	New-c; old-a; 64 pg. PC-r	1	2	3	9	17	26
14	143	–	Old-a; PC-r; 64 pg.	1	2	3	9	14	20
15	150	–	New-a; PC-r; Evans/Crandall-a	2	2	3	9	17	24
16	149	–	PC-r	2	2	2	6	9	12
17	167	–	PC-r	2	2	2	6	9	12
18	167	4/64	PC-r	2	2	2	6	9	12
19	167	1/65	PC-r	2	2	2	6	9	12
20	167	3/66	PC-r	2	2	2	6	9	12
21	166	11/67	PC-r	2	2	2	6	9	12
22	166	Spr/69	C-price 25¢ ; stiff-c; PC-r	2	2	2	6	9	12
23	169	Spr/71	PC-r; stiff-c	2	2	2	6	9	12

2. Ivanhoe

Ed	HRN	Date	Details	A	C				
1	(O)	12/41?	Date listed-1941; Elliot Pub; 68 pgs.	1	1	227	681	1420	2500
2	10	–	Price & 'Presents' removed; Elliot Pub; CC-r	1	1	33	99	174	300
3	15	–	Long Isl. Ind. ed.; CC-r	1	1	21	63	110	185
4	18/20	–	Sunrise Times ed.; CC-r	1	1	19	57	99	165
5	21	–	Richmond Courier ed.; CC-r	1	1	17	51	88	150
6	28	1946	Last 'Comics'-r	1	1	14	42	72	120
7	36	–	1st LDC-r	1	1	9	27	49	70
8	60	–	LDC-r	1	1	6	18	28	38
9	64	–	LDC-r	1	1	5	15	23	30
10	78	–	C-price 15¢; LDC-r	1	1	4	13	19	26
11	89	–	LDC-r	1	1	4	12	18	24
12	106	–	LDC-r	1	1	3	9	14	20
13	121	–	Last LDC-r	1	1	3	9	14	20
14	136	–	New-c&a; PC-r	2	2	4	12	19	28
15	142	–	PC-r	2	2	2	6	10	14
16	153	–	PC-r	2	2	2	6	10	14
17	149	–	PC-r	2	2	2	6	9	12
18	167	–	PC-r	2	2	2	6	9	12
19	167	5/64	PC-r	2	2	2	6	9	12
20	167	1/65	PC-r	2	2	2	6	9	12

Classic Comics #5 © GIL   Classic Comics #6 © GIL   Classic Comics #7 © GIL

				GD2.0	FN6.0	VF8.0	NM9.4
1	167	3/66	PC-r	2 2	2	6	9	12

#	HRN	Date	Details	A C	GD2.0	FN6.0	VF8.0	NM9.4
1	167	3/66	PC-r	2 2	2	6	9	12
2A	166	9/67	PC-r	2 2	2	6	9	12
2B	166	–	Center ad for Children's Digest & Young Miss; rare; PC-r	2 2	10	30	63	100
3	166	R/68	C-Price 25¢; PC-r	2 2	2	6	9	12
4	169	Win/69	Stiff-c	2 2	2	6	9	12
5	169	Win/71	PC-r; stiff-c	2 2	2	6	9	12

The Count of Monte Cristo

Ed	HRN	Date	Details	A C	GD2.0	FN6.0	VF8.0	NM9.4
1	(O)	3/42	Elliot Pub; 68 pgs.	1 1	141	423	881	1550
2	10	–	Conray Prods; CC-r	1	28	84	148	255
3	15	–	Long Isl. Ind. ed.; CC-r	1 1	22	66	116	195
4	18/20		Sunrise Times ed.;	1 1	20	60	105	175
5	20	–	Sunrise Times ed.;	1 1	18	54	94	155
6	21	–	Richmond Courier ed.; CC-r	1 1	17	51	88	150
7	28	1946	CC-r; new Banner logo	1 1	14	42	72	120
8	36	–	1st LDC-r	1 1	9	27	49	70
9	60	–	LDC-r	1 1	6	18	28	38
10	62	–	LDC-r	1 1	6	18	30	42
11	71	–	LDC-r	1 1	5	14	21	28
12	87	–	C-price 15¢; LDC-r	1 1	4	12	19	26
13	113	–	LDC-r	1 1	3	9	14	20
14	135	–	New-c&a; PC-r; Cameron-a	2 2	3	9	17	26
15	143	–	PC-r	2 2	2	6	10	14
16	153	–	PC-r	2 2	2	6	10	14
17	161	–	PC-r	2 2	2	6	10	14
18	167	–	PC-r	2 2	2	6	9	12
19	167	7/64	PC-r	2 2	2	6	9	12
20	167	7/65	PC-r	2 2	2	6	9	12
21	167	7/66	PC-r	2 2	2	6	9	12
22	166	R/68	C-price 25¢; PC-r	2 2	2	6	9	12
23	169	Win/69	Stiff-c; PC-r	2 2	2	6	9	12

The Last of the Mohicans

Ed	HRN	Date	Details	A C	GD2.0	FN6.0	VF8.0	NM9.4
1	(O)	8/42	Date listed-1942; Gilberton #4(0) on; 68 pgs.	1 1	118	354	738	1300
2	12	–	Elliot Pub; CC-r	1 1	28	84	148	255
3	15	–	Long Isl. Ind. ed.; CC-r	1 1	22	66	116	195
4	20	–	Long Isl. Ind. ed.; banner logo	1 1	19	57	99	165
5	21	–	Queens Home News ed.; CC-r	1 1	17	51	88	150
6	28	1946	Last CC-r; new	1 1	14	42	72	120
7	36	–	1st LDC-r	1 1	9	27	49	70
8	60	–	LDC-r	1 1	6	18	28	38
9	64	–	LDC-r	1 1	5	14	21	28
10	78	–	C-price 15¢; LDC-r	1 1	5	14	21	28
11	89	–	LDC-r	1 1	4	12	18	24
12	117	–	Last LDC-r	1 1	3	9	14	20
13	135	–	New-c; PC-r	1 2	3	9	17	26
14	141	–	PC-r	1 2	2	6	11	16
15	150	–	New-a; PC-r; Severin, L.B. Cole-a	2 2	4	12	19	28
16	161	–	PC-r	2 2	2	6	9	12
17	167	–	PC-r	2 2	2	6	9	12
18	167	6/64	PC-r	2 2	2	6	9	12
19	167	8/65	PC-r	2 2	2	6	9	12
20	167	8/66	PC-r	2 2	2	6	9	12
21	166	R/67	C-price 25¢; PC-r	2 2	2	6	9	12
22	169	Spr/69	Stiff-c; PC-r	2 2	2	6	9	12

5. Moby Dick

Ed	HRN	Date	Details	A C	GD2.0	FN6.0	VF8.0	NM9.4
1A	(O)	9/42	Date listed-1942; Gilberton; 68 pgs.	1 1	150	450	938	1650
1B			inside-c, rare free promo		227	681	1420	2500
2	10	–	Conray Prods; Pg. 64 changed from 105 title list to letter from Editor; CC-r	1 1	30	90	159	275
3	15	–	Long Isl. Ind. ed.; Pg. 64 changed from Letter to the Editor to Ill. poem-Concord Hymn; CC-r	1 1	25	75	130	225
4	18/20	–	Sunrise Times ed.; CC-r	1 1	20	60	105	175
5	20	–	Sunrise Times ed.; CC-r	1 1	19	57	99	165
6	21	–	Sunrise Times ed.; CC-r	1 1	17	51	88	150
7	28	1946	CC-r; new banner logo	1 1	15	45	77	130
8	36	–	1st LDC-r	1 1	9	27	49	70
9	60	–	LDC-r	1 1	6	18	28	38
10	62	–	LDC-r	1 1	6	18	30	42
11	71	–	LDC-r	1 1	5	14	23	30
12	87	–	C-price 15¢; LDC-r	1 1	5	14	21	28
13	118	–	LDC-r	1 1	3	9	17	24
14	131	–	New-c&a; PC-r	2 2	4	12	19	28
15	138	–	PC-r	2 2	2	6	10	14
16	148	–	PC-r	2 2	2	6	10	14
17	158	–	PC-r	2 2	2	6	10	14
18	167	–	PC-r	2 2	2	6	9	12
19	167	6/64	PC-r	2 2	2	6	9	12
20	167	7/65	PC-r	2 2	2	6	9	12
21	167	3/66	PC-r	2 2	2	6	9	12
22	166	9/67	PC-r	2 2	2	6	9	12
23	166	Win/69	New-c & c-price 25¢; Stiff-c; PC-r	2 3	3	9	15	22
24	169	Win/71	PC-r	2 3	3	9	14	20

6. A Tale of Two Cities

Ed	HRN	Date	Details	A C	GD2.0	FN6.0	VF8.0	NM9.4
1	(O)	10/42	Date listed-1942; 68 pgs. Zeckerberg c/a	1 1	118	354	738	1300
2	14	–	Elliot Pub; CC-r	1 1	27	81	142	245
3	18	–	Long Isl. Ind. ed.; CC-r	1 1	21	63	110	185
4	20	–	Sunrise Times ed.; CC-r	1 1	19	57	99	165
5	28	1946	Last CC-r; new banner logo	1 1	14	42	72	120
6	51	–	1st LDC-r	1 1	8	24	42	60
7	64	–	LDC-r	1 1	5	15	24	32
8	78	–	C-price 15¢; LDC-r	1 1	5	14	21	28
9	89	–	LDC-r	1 1	3	9	14	20
10	117	–	LDC-r	1 1	3	9	14	20
11	132	–	New-c&a; PC-r; Joe Orlando-a	2 2	4	12	19	28
12	140	–	PC-r	2 2	2	6	9	12
13	147	–	PC-r	2 2	2	6	9	12
14	152	–	PC-r; very rare	2 2	19	56	108	175
15	153	–	PC-r	2 2	2	6	10	14
16	149	–	PC-r	2 2	2	6	10	14
17	161	–	PC-r	2 2	2	6	9	12
18	167	6/64	PC-r	2 2	2	6	9	12
19	167	8/65	PC-r	2 2	2	6	9	12
20	167	8/66	PC-r	2 2	2	6	9	12
21	166	Fall/68	New-c & 25¢; PC-r	2 3	3	9	17	24

Classic Comics #8 © GIL Classic Comics #9 © GIL Classic Comics #10 © GIL

						GD2.0	FN6.0	VF8.0	NM9.4
22	169	Sum/70	Stiff-c; PC-r	2	3	3	9	14	20

7. Robin Hood

Ed	HRN	Date	Details	A	C	GD2.0	FN6.0	VF8.0	NM9.4
1	(O)	12/42	Date listed-1942; first Gift Box ad-bc; 68 pgs.	1	1	84	253	525	925
2	12	–	Elliot Pub; CC-r	1	1	26	78	136	235
3	18	–	Long Isl. Ind. ed.; CC-r	1	1	20	60	105	175
4	20	–	Nassau Bulletin ed.; CC-r	1	1	19	57	99	165
5	22	–	Queens Cty. Times ed.; CC-r	1	1	17	51	88	150
6	28	–	CC-r	1	1	15	45	77	130
7	51	–	LDC-r	1	1	8	24	42	60
8	64	–	LDC-r	1	1	5	15	25	35
9	78	–	LDC-r	1	1	4	13	19	26
10	97	–	LDC-r	1	1	4	12	18	24
11	106	–	LDC-r	1	1	3	9	14	20
12	121	–	LDC-r	1	1	3	9	14	20
13	129	–	New-c; PC-r	1	2	4	12	19	28
14	136	–	New-a; PC-r	2	2	4	12	19	28
15	143	–	PC-r	2	2	2	6	10	14
16	153	–	PC-r	2	2	2	6	10	14
17	164	–	PC-r	2	2	2	6	9	12
18	167	–	PC-r	2	2	2	6	9	12
19	167	6/64	PC-r	2	2	2	6	9	12
20	167	5/65	PC-r	2	2	2	6	9	12
21	167	7/66	PC-r	2	2	2	6	9	12
22	166	12/67	PC-r	2	2	2	6	9	12
23	169	Sum/69	Stiff-c; c-price 25¢; PC-r	2	2	2	6	9	12

8. Arabian Nights

Ed	HRN	Date	Details	A	C	GD2.0	FN6.0	VF8.0	NM9.4
1	(O)	2/43	Original; 68 pgs. Lilian Chestney-c/a	1	1	150	450	938	1650
2	17	–	Long Isl. ed.; pg. 64 changed from Gift Box ad to Letter from British Medical Worker; CC-r	1	1	55	165	331	580
3	20	–	Nassau Bulletin; Pg. 64 changed from letter to article-Three Men Named Smith; CC-r	1	1	44	133	264	465
4A	28	1946	CC-r; new banner logo, slick-c	1	1	34	102	179	310
4B	28	1946	Same, but w/stiff-c	1	1	34	102	179	310
5	51	–	LDC-r	1	1	24	72	127	215
6	64	–	LDC-r	1	1	20	60	105	175
7	78	–	LDC-r	1	1	19	57	99	165
8	164	–	New-c&a; PC-r	2	2	15	45	92	150

9. Les Miserables

Ed	HRN	Date	Details	A	C	GD2.0	FN6.0	VF8.0	NM9.4
1A	(O)	3/43	Original; slick paper cover; 68 pgs.	1	1	84	254	525	925
1B	(O)	3/43	Original; rough, pulp type-c; 68 pgs.	1	1	105	316	656	1150
2	14	–	Elliot Pub; CC-r	1	1	28	84	148	255
3	18	3/44	Nassau Bul. Pg. 64 changed from Gift Box ad to Bill of Rights article; CC-r	1	1	24	72	127	215
4	20	–	Richmond Courier ed.; CC-r	1	1	20	60	105	175
5	28	1946	Gilberton; pgs. 60-64 rearranged/ illos added; CC-r	1	1	15	45	77	130

						GD2.0	FN6.0	VF8.0	NM
6	51	–	LDC-r	1	1	9	27	49	7
7	71	–	LDC-r	1	1	6	18	30	4
8	87	–	C-price 15¢; LDC-r	1	1	6	18	28	3
9	161	–	New-c&a; PC-r	2	2	5	15	27	4
10	167	9/63	PC-r	2	2	3	9	14	2
11	167	12/65	PC-r	2	2	3	9	14	2
12	166	R/1968	New-c & price 25¢; PC-r	2	3	3	9	17	2

10. Robinson Crusoe (Used in SOTI, pg. 142)

Ed	HRN	Date	Details	A	C	GD2.0	FN6.0	VF8.0	NM
1A	(O)	4/43	Original; Violet-c; 68 pgs; Zuckerberg c/a	1	1	73	219	455	80
1B	(O)	4/43	Original; blue-grey-c, 68 pgs.	1	1	82	246	511	90
2A	14	–	Elliot Pub; violet-c; 68 pgs; CC-r	1	1	30	90	159	27
2B	14	–	Elliot Pub; blue-grey-c; CC-r	1	1	27	81	142	24
3	18	–	Nassau Bul. Pg. 64 changed from Gift Box ad to Bill of Rights article; CC-r	1	1	20	60	105	17
4	20	–	Queens Home News ed.; CC-r	1	1	17	51	88	15
5	28	1946	Gilberton; pg. 64 changes from Bill of Rights to WWII article-One Leg Shot Away; last CC-r	1	1	14	42	72	12
6	51	–	LDC-r	1	1	8	24	42	6
7	64	–	LDC-r	1	1	6	18	28	3
8	78	–	C-price 15¢; LDC-r	1	1	5	14	21	2
9	97	–	LDC-r	1	1	4	13	19	2
10	114	–	PC-r	1	1	3	9	14	2
11	130	–	New-c; PC-r	1	2	4	12	19	2
12	140	–	New-a; PC-r	2	2	4	12	19	2
13	153	–	PC-r	2	2	2	6	9	1
14	164	–	PC-r	2	2	2	6	9	1
15	167	–	PC-r	2	2	2	6	9	1
16	167	7/64	PC-r	2	2	2	6	11	1
17	167	5/65	PC-r	2	2	2	6	11	1
18	167	6/66	PC-r	2	2	2	6	9	1
19	166	Fall/68	C-price 25¢; PC-r	2	2	2	6	9	1
20	166	R/68	(No Twin Circle ad)	2	2	2	6	10	1
21	169	Sm/70	Stiff-c; PC-r	2	2	2	6	11	1

11. Don Quixote

Ed	HRN	Date	Details	A	C	GD2.0	FN6.0	VF8.0	NM
1	10	5/43	First (O) with HRN list; 68 pgs.	1	1	80	240	500	87
2	18	–	Nassau Bulletin ed.; CC-r	1	1	25	75	130	22
3	21	–	Queens Home News ed.; CC-r	1	1	20	60	105	17
4	28	–	CC-r	1	1	15	45	77	13
5	110	–	New-PC; PC-r	1	2	5	15	26	4
6	156	–	Pgs. reduced 68 to 52; PC-r	1	2	3	9	14	2
7	165	–	PC-r	1	2	2	6	10	1
8	167	1/64	PC-r	1	2	2	6	10	1
9	167	11/65	PC-r	1	2	2	6	10	1
10	166	R/1968	New-c & price 25¢; PC-r	1	3	4	12	19	2

12. Rip Van Winkle and the Headless Horseman

Ed	HRN	Date	Details	A	C	GD2.0	FN6.0	VF8.0	NM
1	11	6/43	Original; 68 pgs.	1	1	80	240	500	87
2	15	–	Long Isl. Ind. ed.; CC-r	1	1	25	75	130	22
3	20	–	Long Isl. Ind. ed.;	1	1	20	60	105	17
4	22	–	Queens Cty.	1	1	17	51	88	15

Classic Comics #11 © GIL   Classic Comics #13 © GIL   Classic Comics #15 © GIL

Ed	HRN	Date	Details	A	C	GD2.0	FN6.0	VF8.0	NM9.4
			Times ed.; CC-r						
5	28	–	CC-r	1	1	14	42	72	120
6	60	–	1st LDC-r	1	1	7	21	38	55
7	62	–	LDC-r	1	1	5	15	24	32
8	71	–	LDC-r	1	1	4	13	19	26
9	89	–	C-price 15¢; LDC-r	1	1	4	12	18	24
10	118	–	LDC-r	1	1	3	9	14	20
11	132	–	New-c; PC-r	1	2	4	12	19	28
12	150	–	New-a; PC-r	2	2	4	12	19	28
13	158	–	PC-r	2	2	2	6	10	14
14	167	–	PC-r	2	2	2	6	10	14
15	167	12/63	PC-r	2	2	2	6	9	12
16	167	4/65	PC-r	2	2	2	6	9	12
17	167	4/66	PC-r	2	2	2	6	9	12
18	166	R/1968	New-c&price 25¢; PC-r; stiff-c	2	3	3	9	14	20
19	169	Sm/70	PC-r; stiff-c	2	3	2	6	11	16

3. Dr. Jekyll and Mr. Hyde (Used in SOTI, pg. 143)(1st horror comic?)

Ed	HRN	Date	Details	A	C	GD2.0	FN6.0	VF8.0	NM9.4
1	12	8/43	Original 60 pgs.	1	1	118	354	738	1300
2	15	–	Long Isl. Ind. ed.; CC-r	1	1	35	105	185	320
3	20	–	Long Isl. Ind. ed.; CC-r	1	1	25	75	130	225
4	28	–	No c-price; CC-r	1	1	19	57	99	165
5	60	–	New-c; Pgs. reduced from 60 to 52; H.C. Kiefer-c; LDC-r	1	2	7	21	38	55
6	62	–	LDC-r	1	2	6	18	28	38
7	71	–	LDC-r	1	2	5	15	23	30
8	87	–	Date returns (erroneous); LDC-r	1	2	5	14	21	28
9	112	–	New-c&a; PC-r; Cameron-a	2	3	5	15	25	38
10	153	–	PC-r	2	3	2	6	10	14
11	161	–	PC-r	2	3	2	6	10	14
12	167	–	PC-r	2	3	2	6	9	12
13	167	8/64	PC-r	2	3	2	6	9	12
14	167	11/65	PC-r	2	3	2	6	9	12
15	166	R/68	C-price 25¢; PC-r	2	3	2	6	9	12
16	169	Wn/69	PC-r; stiff-c	2	3	2	6	9	12

4. Westward Ho!

Ed	HRN	Date	Details	A	C	GD2.0	FN6.0	VF8.0	NM9.4
1	13	9/43	Original; last outside bc coming-next ad; 60 pgs.	1	1	191	573	1194	2100
2	15	–	Long Isl. Ind. ed.; CC-r	1	1	55	165	331	580
3	21	–	Queens Home News; Pg. 56 changed from coming-next ad to Three Men Named Smith; CC-r	1	1	43	129	257	450
4	28	1946	Gilberton; Pg. 56 changed again to WWII article-Speaking for America; last CC-r	1	1	39	117	208	360
5	53	–	Pgs. reduced from 60 to 52; LDC-r	1	1	35	105	185	320

5. Uncle Tom's Cabin (Used in SOTI, pgs. 102, 103)

Ed	HRN	Date	Details	A	C	GD2.0	FN6.0	VF8.0	NM9.4
1	14	11/43	Original; Outside-bc ad: 2 Gift Boxes; 60 pgs.; color var. on-c; green trunk,root on left & brown trunk, root on left; listed- bottom inside-fc; also Gilberton listed bottom-pg. 1; CC-r; green root vs. brown root var. occurs again	1	1	66	198	413	725
2	15	–	Long Isl. Ind.	1	1	27	81	142	245
3	21	–	Nassau Bulletin ed.; CC-r	1	1	21	63	110	185
4	28	–	No c-price; CC-r	1	1	15	45	77	130
5	53	–	Pgs. reduced 60 to 52; LDC-r	1	1	8	24	42	60
6	71	–	LDC-r	1	1	6	18	28	38
7	89	–	C-price 15¢; LDC-r	1	1	5	15	25	35
8	117	–	New-c/lettering changes; PC-r	1	2	4	12	19	28
9	128	–	'Picture Progress' promo; PC-r	1	2	2	6	11	16
10	137	–	PC-r	1	2	2	6	10	14
11	146	–	PC-r	1	2	2	6	10	14
12	154	–	PC-r	1	2	2	6	10	14
13	161	–	PC-r	1	2	2	6	9	12
14	167	–	PC-r	1	2	2	6	9	12
15	167	6/64	PC-r	1	2	2	6	9	12
16	167	5/65	PC-r	1	2	2	6	9	12
17	166	5/67	PC-r	1	2	2	6	9	12
18	166	Wn/69	New-stiff-c; PC-r	1	3	3	9	14	20
19	169	Sm/70	PC-r; stiff-c	1	3	2	6	11	16

16. Gullivers Travels

Ed	HRN	Date	Details	A	C	GD2.0	FN6.0	VF8.0	NM9.4
1	15	12/43	Original-Lilian Chestney c/a; 60 pgs.	1	1	68	205	426	750
2	18/20	–	Price deleted; Queens Home News; CC-r	1	1	24	72	127	215
3	22	–	Queens Cty. Times ed.; CC-r	1	1	19	57	99	165
4	28	–	CC-r	1	1	14	42	72	120
5	60	–	Pgs. reduced to 48; LDC-r	1	1	6	18	32	45
6	62	–	LDC-r	1	1	5	15	24	32
7	78	–	C-price 15¢; LDC-r	1	1	5	14	21	28
8	89	–	LDC-r	1	1	4	12	18	24
9	155	–	New-c; PC-r	1	2	4	12	19	28
10	165	–	PC-r	1	2	2	6	9	12
11	167	5/64	PC-r	1	2	2	6	9	12
12	167	11/65	PC-r	1	2	2	6	9	12
13	166	R/1968	C-price 25¢; PC-r	1	2	2	6	9	12
14	169	Wn/69	PC-r; stiff-c	1	2	2	6	9	12

17. The Deerslayer

Ed	HRN	Date	Details	A	C	GD2.0	FN6.0	VF8.0	NM9.4
1	16	1/44	Original; Outside-bc ad: 3 Gift Boxes; 60 pgs.	1	1	59	177	369	650
2A	18	–	Queens Cty Times (inside-fc); CC-r	1	1	25	75	130	225
2B	18	–	Gilberton (bottom-pg. 1); CC-r; Scarce	1	1	35	105	185	320
3	22	–	Queens Cty. Times ed.; CC-r	1	1	20	60	105	175
4	28	–	CC-r	1	1	15	45	77	130
5	60	–	Pgs.reduced to 52; LDC-r	1	1	7	21	38	55
6	64	–	LDC-r	1	1	5	15	23	30
7	85	–	C-price 15¢; LDC-r	1	1	4	12	18	24
8	118	–	LDC-r	1	1	3	9	14	20
9	132	–	LDC-r	1	1	3	9	14	20
10	167	11/66	Last LDC-r	1	1	3	9	14	20
11	166	R/1968	New-c & price 25¢; PC-r	1	2	3	9	17	26
12	169	Spr/71	Stiff-c; letters from parents & educators; PC-r	1	2	2	6	12	18

			GD2.0	FN6.0	VF8.0	NM9.4

18. The Hunchback of Notre Dame

Ed	HRN	Date	Details	A	C	GD2.0	FN6.0	VF8.0	NM9.4
1A	17	3/44	Orig.; Gilberton ed; 60 pgs.	1	1	77	231	483	850
1B	17	3/44	Orig.; Island Pub. Ed.; 60 pgs.	1	1	68	205	426	750
2	18/20	–	Queens Home News ed.; CC-r	1	1	27	81	142	245
3	22	–	Queens Cty. Times ed.; CC-r	1	1	20	60	105	175
4	28	–	CC-r	1	1	17	51	88	150
5	60	–	New-c; 8pgs. deleted; Kiefer-c; LDC-r	1	2	7	21	38	55
6	62	–	LDC-r	1	2	5	15	23	30
7	78	–	C-price 15¢; LDC-r	1	2	5	14	21	28
8A	89	–	H.C.Kiefer on bottom right-fc; LDC-r	1	2	4	13	19	26
8B	89	–	Name omitted; LDC-r	1	2	5	15	25	35
9	118	–	LDC-r	1	2	3	9	17	24
10	140	–	New-c; PC-r	1	3	5	15	25	38
11	146	–	PC-r	1	3	3	9	17	26
12	158	–	New-c&a; PC-r; Evans/Crandall-a	2	4	4	12	19	28
13	165	–	PC-r	2	4	2	6	10	14
14	167	9/63	PC-r	2	4	2	6	10	14
15	167	10/64	PC-r	2	4	2	6	10	14
16	167	4/66	PC-r	2	4	2	6	9	12
17	166	R/1968	New price 25¢; PC-r	2	4	2	6	9	12
18	169	Sp/70	Stiff-c; PC-r	2	4	2	6	9	14

19. Huckleberry Finn

Ed	HRN	Date	Details	A	C	GD2.0	FN6.0	VF8.0	NM9.4
1A	18	4/44	Orig.; Gilberton ed.; 60 pgs.	1	1	50	150	300	525
1B	18	4/44	Orig.; Island Pub.; 60 pgs.	1	1	55	165	331	580
2	18	–	Nassau Bulletin ed.; fc-price 15¢-Canada; no coming-next ad; CC-r	1	1	25	75	130	225
3	22	–	Queens City Times ed.; CC-r	1	1	20	60	105	175
4	28	–	CC-r	1	1	14	42	72	120
5	60	–	Pgs. reduced to 48; LDC-r	1	1	6	18	32	45
6	62	–	LDC-r	1	1	5	15	24	32
7	78	–	LDC-r	1	1	4	13	19	26
8	89	–	LDC-r	1	1	4	12	18	24
9	117	–	LDC-r	1	1	3	9	14	20
10	131	–	New-c&a; PC-r	2	2	3	9	17	26
11	140	–	PC-r	2	2	2	6	10	14
12	150	–	PC-r	2	2	2	6	10	14
13	158	–	PC-r	2	2	2	6	10	14
14	165	–	PC-r (scarce)	2	2	3	9	17	24
15	167	–	PC-r	2	2	2	6	9	12
16	167	6/64	PC-r	2	2	2	6	9	12
17	167	6/65	PC-r	2	2	2	6	9	12
18	167	10/66	PC-r	2	2	2	6	9	12
19	166	9/67	PC-r	2	2	2	6	9	12
20	166	Win/69	C-price 25¢; PC-r; stiff-c	2	2	2	6	9	12
21	169	Sm/70	PC-r; stiff-c	2	2	2	6	9	12

20. The Corsican Brothers

Ed	HRN	Date	Details	A	C	GD2.0	FN6.0	VF8.0	NM9.4
1A	20	6/44	Orig.; Gilberton ed.; bc-ad: 4 Gift Boxes; 60 pgs.	1	1	43	129	257	450
1B	20	6/44	Orig.; Courier ed.; 60 pgs.	1	1	40	120	220	380
1C	20	6/44	Orig.; Long Island Ind. ed.; 60 pgs.	1	1	40	120	220	380
2	22	–	Queens Cty. Times ed.; white logo banner; CC-r	1	1	21	63	110	18
3	28	–	CC-r	1	1	20	60	105	175
4	60	–	CI logo; no price; 48 pgs.; LDC-r	1	1	17	51	88	15
5A	62	–	LDC-r; Classics Ill. logo at top of pgs.	1	1	15	45	77	13
5B	62	–	w/o logo at top of pg. (scarcer)	1	1	16	48	83	14
6	78	–	C-price 15¢; LDC-r	1	1	14	42	72	12
7	97	–	LDC-r	1	1	13	39	66	11

21. 3 Famous Mysteries ("The Sign of the 4", "The Murders in the Rue Morgue", "The Flayed Hand")

Ed	HRN	Date	Details	A	C	GD2.0	FN6.0	VF8.0	NM9.4
1A	21	7/44	Orig.; Gilberton ed.; 60 pgs.	1	1	89	268	556	97
1B	21	7/44	Orig.; Island Pub. Co.; 60 pgs.	1	1	93	279	581	102
1C	21	7/44	Original; Courier Ed.; 60 pgs.	1	1	77	231	483	85
2	22	–	Nassau Bulletin ed.; CC-r	1	1	39	117	208	36
3	30	–	CC-r	1	1	30	90	159	27
4	62	–	LDC-r; 8 pgs. deleted; LDC-r	1	1	24	72	127	21
5	70	–	LDC-r	1	1	22	66	116	19
6	85	–	C-price 15¢; LDC-r	1	1	19	57	99	16
7	114	–	New-c; PC-r	1	2	19	57	99	16

22. The Pathfinder

Ed	HRN	Date	Details	A	C	GD2.0	FN6.0	VF8.0	NM9.4
1A	22	10/44	Orig.; No printer listed; ownership statement inside fc lists Gilberton & date; 60 pgs.	1	1	43	129	257	45
1B	22	10/44	Orig.; Island Pub. ed.; 60 pgs.	1	1	40	120	220	38
1C	22	10/44	Orig.; Queens City Times ed. 60 pgs.	1	1	40	120	220	38
2	30	–	C-price removed; CC-r	1	1	15	45	77	13
3	60	–	Pgs. reduced to 52; LDC-r	1	1	6	18	28	3
4	70	–	LDC-r	1	1	5	15	23	3
5	85	–	C-price 15¢; LDC-r	1	1	4	13	19	2
6	118	–	LDC-r	1	1	3	9	17	2
7	132	–	LDC-r	1	1	3	9	14	2
8	146	–	LDC-r	1	1	3	9	14	2
9	167	11/63	New-c; PC-r	1	2	5	15	25	3
10	167	12/65	PC-r	1	2	3	9	14	2
11	166	8/67	PC-r	1	2	3	9	14	2

23. Oliver Twist (1st Classic produced by the Iger Shop)

Ed	HRN	Date	Details	A	C	GD2.0	FN6.0	VF8.0	NM9.4
1	23	7/45	Original; 60 pgs.	1	1	40	120	240	42
2A	30	–	Printers Union logo on bottom left-fc same as 23(Orig.) (very rare); CC-r	1	1	33	99	174	30
2B	30	–	Union logo omitted; CC-r	1	1	14	42	72	12
3	60	–	Pgs. reduced to 48; LDC-r	1	1	6	18	30	4
4	62	–	LDC-r	1	1	5	15	24	3
5	71	–	LDC-r	1	1	5	14	21	2
6	85	–	C-price 15¢; LDC-r	1	1	4	13	19	2

Classic Comics #25 © GIL

Classic Comics #29 © GIL

Classic Comics #31 © GIL

Ed	HRN	Date	Details	A	C	GD2.0	FN6.0	VF8.0	NM9.4
7	94	–	LDC-r	1	1	3	9	14	20
8	118	–	LDC-r	1	1	3	9	14	20
9	136	–	New-PC, old-a; PC-r	1	2	3	9	17	26
10	150	–	Old-a; PC-r	1	2	3	9	14	20
11	164	–	Old-a; PC-r	1	2	3	9	15	22
12	164	–	New-a; PC-r; Evans/Crandall-a	2	2	5	15	25	38
13	167	–	PC-r	2	2	3	9	14	20
14	167	8/64	PC-r	2	2	2	6	9	12
15	167	12/65	PC-r	2	2	2	6	9	12
16	166	R/1968	New 25¢; PC-r	2	2	2	6	9	12
17	169	Win/69	Stiff-c; PC-r	2	2	2	6	9	12

4. A Connecticut Yankee in King Arthur's Court

Ed	HRN	Date	Details	A	C	GD2.0	FN6.0	VF8.0	NM9.4
1	–	9/45	Original	1	1	40	120	220	380
2	30	–	No price circle; CC-r	1	1	14	42	72	120
3	60	–	8 pgs. deleted; LDC-r	1	1	6	18	28	38
4	62	–	LDC-r	1	1	5	15	24	32
5	71	–	LDC-r	1	1	5	15	23	30
6	87	–	C-price 15¢; LDC-r	1	1	4	13	19	26
7	121	–	LDC-r	1	1	3	9	17	24
8	140	–	New-c&a; PC-r	2	2	4	12	19	28
9	153	–	PC-r	2	2	2	6	10	14
10	164	–	PC-r	2	2	2	6	9	12
11	167	–	PC-r	2	2	2	6	9	12
12	167	7/64	PC-r	2	2	2	6	9	12
13	167	6/66	PC-r	2	2	2	6	9	12
14	166	R/1968	C-price 25¢; PC-r	2	2	2	6	9	12
15	169	Spr/71	PC-r; stiff-c	2	2	2	6	9	12

5. Two Years Before the Mast

Ed	HRN	Date	Details	A	C	GD2.0	FN6.0	VF8.0	NM9.4
1	–	10/45	Original; Webb/Heames-a&c	1	1	40	120	220	380
2	30	–	Price circle blank; CC-r	1	1	14	42	72	120
3	60	–	8 pgs. deleted; LDC-r	1	1	6	18	28	38
4	62	–	LDC-r	1	1	5	15	24	32
5	71	–	LDC-r	1	1	4	13	19	26
6	85	–	C-price 15¢; LDC-r	1	1	4	12	18	24
7	114	–	LDC-r	1	1	3	9	14	20
8	156	–	3 pgs. replaced by fillers; new-c; PC-r	1	2	4	12	19	28
9	167	12/63	PC-r	1	2	2	6	9	12
10	167	12/65	PC-r	1	2	2	6	9	12
11	167	9/67	PC-r	1	2	2	6	9	12
12	169	Win/69	C-price 25¢; stiff-c; PC-r	1	2	2	6	9	12

6. Frankenstein (2nd horror comic?)

Ed	HRN	Date	Details	A	C	GD2.0	FN6.0	VF8.0	NM9.4
1	26	12/45	Orig.; Webb/Brewster a&c; 52 pgs.	1	1	95	285	597	1050
2A	30	–	Price circle blank, no indicia; CC-r	1	1	30	90	159	275
2B	30	–	With indicia; scarce; CC-r	1	1	35	105	185	320
3	60	–	LDC-r	1	1	17	51	88	150
4	62	–	LDC-r	1	1	15	45	77	130
5	71	–	LDC-r	1	1	7	21	36	50
6A	82	–	C-price 15¢; soft-c; LDC-r	1	1	6	18	29	40
6B	82	–	Stiff-c; LDC-r	1	1	7	21	36	50
7	117	–	LDC-r	1	1	3	9	17	25
8	146	–	New Saunders-c; PC-r	1	2	4	12	21	32
9	152	–	Scarce; PC-r	1	2	7	21	38	55

Ed	HRN	Date	Details	A	C	GD2.0	FN6.0	VF8.0	NM9.4
10	153	–	PC-r	1	2	2	6	10	14
11	160	–	PC-r	1	2	2	6	10	14
12	165	–	PC-r	1	2	2	6	9	12
13	167	–	PC-r	1	2	2	6	9	12
14	167	6/64	PC-r	1	2	2	6	9	12
15	167	6/65	PC-r	1	2	2	6	9	12
16	167	10/65	PC-r	1	2	2	6	9	12
17	166	9/67	PC-r	1	2	2	6	9	12
18	169	Fall/69	C-price 25¢; stiff-c; PC-r	1	2	2	6	9	12
19	169	Spr/71	PC-r; stiff-c	1	2	2	6	9	12

27. The Adventures of Marco Polo

Ed	HRN	Date	Details	A	C	GD2.0	FN6.0	VF8.0	NM9.4
1	–	4/46	Original	1	1	40	120	232	400
2	30	–	Last 'Comics' reprint; CC-r	1	1	14	42	72	120
3	70	–	8 pgs. deleted; no c-price; LDC-r	1	1	5	15	25	35
4	87	–	C-price 15¢; LDC-r	1	1	4	13	19	26
5	117	–	LDC-r	1	1	3	9	14	20
6	154	–	New-c; PC-r	1	2	3	9	17	26
7	165	–	PC-r	1	2	2	6	9	12
8	167	4/64	PC-r	1	2	2	6	9	12
9	167	6/66	PC-r	1	2	2	6	9	12
10	169	Spr/70	New price 25¢; stiff-c; PC-r	1	2	2	6	9	12

28. Michael Strogoff

Ed	HRN	Date	Details	A	C	GD2.0	FN6.0	VF8.0	NM9.4
1	–	6/46	Original	1	1	43	129	237	410
2	51	–	8 pgs. cut; LDC-r	1	1	14	42	72	120
3	115	–	New-c; PC-r	1	2	5	15	25	35
4	155	–	PC-r	1	2	3	9	14	20
5	167	11/63	PC-r	1	2	2	6	11	16
6	167	7/66	PC-r	1	2	2	6	11	16
7	169	Sm/69	C-price 25¢; stiff-c; PC-r	1	3	3	9	15	22

29. The Prince and the Pauper

Ed	HRN	Date	Details	A	C	GD2.0	FN6.0	VF8.0	NM9.4
1	–	7/46	Orig.; "Horror"-c	1	1	55	165	341	600
2	60	–	8 pgs. cut; new-c by Kiefer; LDC-r	1	2	7	21	38	55
3	70	–	LDC-r	1	2	5	15	25	35
4	71	–	LDC-r	1	2	4	13	19	26
5	93	–	LDC-r	1	2	4	12	18	24
6	114	–	LDC-r	1	2	3	9	14	20
7	128	–	New-c; PC-r	1	3	3	9	17	26
8	138	–	PC-r	1	3	2	6	10	14
9	150	–	PC-r	1	3	2	6	10	14
10	164	–	PC-r	1	3	2	6	9	12
11	167	–	PC-r	1	3	2	6	9	12
12	167	7/64	PC-r	1	3	2	6	9	12
13	167	11/65	PC-r	1	3	2	6	9	12
14	166	R/68	C-price 25¢; PC-r	1	3	2	6	9	12
15	169	Spr/71	PC-r; stiff-c	1	3	2	6	9	12

30. The Moonstone

Ed	HRN	Date	Details	A	C	GD2.0	FN6.0	VF8.0	NM9.4
1	–	9/46	Original; Rico-c/a	1	1	40	120	232	400
2	60	–	LDC-r; 8pgs. cut	1	1	7	21	38	55
3	70	–	LDC-r	1	1	7	21	36	50
4	155	–	New L.B. Cole-c;	1	2	6	18	36	55
5	165	–	PC-r; L.B. Cole-c	1	2	4	12	18	26
6	167	1/64	PC-r; L.B. Cole-c	1	2	2	6	11	15
7	167	9/65	PC-r; L.B. Cole-c	1	2	2	6	9	12
8	166	R/1968	C-price 25¢; PC-r	1	2	2	6	9	12

31. The Black Arrow

Ed	HRN	Date	Details	A	C	GD2.0	FN6.0	VF8.0	NM9.4
1	–	10/46	Original	1	1	33	99	174	300
2	51	–	CI logo; LDC-r	1	1	6	18	30	42

Classic Comic #33 © GIL

Classics Illustrated #37 © GIL

Classics Illustrated #39 © GIL

				GD2.0	FN6.0	VF8.0	NM9.4					GD2.0	FN6.0	VF8.0	NM9
			8pgs. deleted					4	167	7/66	PC-r 2 2	3	9	17	24
3	64	–	LDC-r 1 1	4	13	19	26	5	169	Spr/70	New price 25¢; 2 2	3	9	17	24
4	87	–	C-price 15¢; LDC-r 1 1	4	12	18	24				stiff-c; PC-r				

36. Typee

Ed	HRN	Date	Details A C	GD2.0	FN6.0	VF8.0	NM9
5	108	–	LDC-r 1 1	3	9	14	20
6	125	–	LDC-r 1 1	3	9	14	20
7	131	–	New-c; PC-r 1 2	3	9	17	26
8	140	–	PC-r 1 2	2	6	10	14

36. Typee

Ed	HRN	Date	Details	A C	GD2.0	FN6.0	VF8.0	NM9
1	–	4/47	Original	1 1	24	72	127	215
2	64	–	No c-price; 8 pg. ed.; LDC-r	1 1	7	21	36	50
3	155	–	New-c; PC-r	1 2	4	12	19	28
4	167	9/63	PC-r	1 2	2	6	11	15
5	167	7/65	PC-r	1 2	2	6	11	15
6	169	Sm/69	C-price 25¢; stiff-c PC-r	1 2	2	6	11	15

				GD2.0	FN6.0	VF8.0	NM9.4
9	148	–	PC-r 1 2	2	6	10	14
10	161	–	PC-r 1 2	2	6	9	12
11	167	–	PC-r 1 2	2	6	9	12
12	167	7/64	PC-r 1 2	2	6	9	12
13	167	11/65	PC-r 1 2	2	6	9	12
14	167	R/1968	C-price 25¢; PC-r 1 2	2	6	9	12

32. Lorna Doone

Ed	HRN	Date	Details	A C	GD2.0	FN6.0	VF8.0	NM9.4
1	–	12/46	Original; Matt Baker c&a	1 1	40	120	220	380
2	53/64	–	8 pgs. deleted; LDC-r	1 1	8	24	42	60
3	85	1951	C-price 15¢; LDC-r; Baker c&a	1 1	6	18	32	45
4	118	–	LDC-r	1 1	3	9	17	26
5	138	–	New-c; old-c becomes new title pg.; PC-r	1 2	4	12	20	30
6	150	–	PC-r	1 2	2	6	9	12
7	165	–	PC-r	1 2	2	6	9	12
8	167	1/64	PC-r	1 2	2	6	10	14
9	167	11/65	PC-r	1 2	2	6	10	14
10	166	R/1968	New-c; PC-r	1 3	4	12	19	28

33. The Adventures of Sherlock Holmes

Ed	HRN	Date	Details	A C	GD2.0	FN6.0	VF8.0	NM9.4
1	33	1/47	Original; Kiefer-c; contains Study in Scarlet & Hound of the Baskervilles; 68 pgs.	1 1	118	354	738	1300
2	53	–	"A Study in Scarlet" (17 pgs.) deleted; LDC-r	1 1	44	132	264	460
3	71	–	LDC-r	1 1	37	111	197	340
4A	89	–	C-price 15¢; LDC-r	1 1	30	90	159	275
4B	89	–	Kiefer's name omitted from-c	1 1	31	93	165	285

34. Mysterious Island (Last "Classic Comic")

Ed	HRN	Date	Details	A C	GD2.0	FN6.0	VF8.0	NM9.4
1	–	2/47	Original; Webb-Heames-c/a	1 1	40	120	232	400
2	60	–	8 pgs. deleted; LDC-r	1 1	6	18	32	45
3	62	–	LDC-r	1 1	5	15	24	32
4	71	–	LDC-r	1 1	6	18	32	45
5	78	–	C-price 15¢ in circle; LDC-r	1 1	5	14	21	28
6	92	–	LDC-r	1 1	4	13	19	26
7	117	–	LDC-r	1 1	3	9	14	20
8	140	–	New-c; PC-r	1 2	3	9	17	26
9	156	–	PC-r	1 2	2	6	10	14
10	167	10/63	PC-r	1 2	2	6	9	12
11	167	5/64	PC-r	1 2	2	6	9	12
12	167	6/66	PC-r	1 2	2	6	9	12
13	166	R/1968	C-price 25¢; PC-r	1 2	2	6	9	12

35. Last Days of Pompeii (First "Classics Illustrated")

Ed	HRN	Date	Details	A C	GD2.0	FN6.0	VF8.0	NM9.4
1	–	3/47	Original; LDC; Kiefer-c/a	1 1	40	120	232	400
2	161	–	New c&a; 15¢; PC-r; Kirby/Ayers-a	2 2	5	15	29	45
3	167	1/64	PC-r	2 2	3	9	17	24

37. The Pioneers

Ed	HRN	Date	Details	A C	GD2.0	FN6.0	VF8.0	NM9
1	37	5/47	Original; Palais-c/a	1 1	22	66	116	200
2A	62	–	8 pgs. cut; LDC-r; price circle blank	1 1	5	15	24	32
2B	62	–	10¢; LDC-r;	1 1	26	78	136	235
3	70	–	LDC-r	1 1	4	12	18	24
4	92	–	15¢; LDC-r	1 1	4	11	17	22
5	118	–	LDC-r	1 1	3	9	14	20
6	131	–	LDC-r	1 1	3	9	14	20
7	132	–	LDC-r	1 1	3	9	14	20
8	153	–	LDC-r	1 1	3	9	14	20
9	167	5/64	LDC-r	1 1	2	6	10	14
10	167	6/66	LDC-r	1 1	2	6	10	14
11	166	R/1968	New-c; 25¢; PC-r	1 2	3	9	19	28

38. Adventures of Cellini

Ed	HRN	Date	Details	A C	GD2.0	FN6.0	VF8.0	NM9
1	–	6/47	Original; Froehlich c/a	1 1	30	90	159	275
2	164	–	New-c&a; PC-r	2 2	4	12	19	28
3	167	12/63	PC-r	2 2	2	6	11	15
4	167	7/66	PC-r	2 2	2	6	11	15
5	169	Spr/70	Stiff-c; new price 25¢; PC-r	2 2	2	6	11	16

39. Jane Eyre

Ed	HRN	Date	Details	A C	GD2.0	FN6.0	VF8.0	NM9
1	–	7/47	Original	1 1	29	87	153	265
2	60	–	No c-price; 8 pgs. cut; LDC-r	1 1	6	18	29	40
3	62	–	LDC-r	1 1	5	15	25	35
4	71	–	LDC-r; c-price 10¢	1 1	5	15	23	30
5	92	–	C-price 15¢; LDC-r	1 1	4	13	19	26
6	118	–	LDC-r	1 1	3	9	17	26
7	142	–	New-c; old-a; PC-r	1 2	4	12	20	30
8	154	–	Old-a; PC-r	1 2	3	9	17	24
9	165	–	New-a; PC-r	2 2	4	12	19	28
10	167	12/63	PC-r	2 2	3	9	17	24
11	167	4/65	PC-r	2 2	3	9	15	22
12	167	8/66	PC-r	2 2	3	9	15	22
13	166	R/1968	New-c; PC-r	2 3	7	21	40	60

40. Mysteries ("The Pit and the Pendulum", "The Advs. of Hans Pfall" & "The Fall of the House of Usher")

Ed	HRN	Date	Details	A C	GD2.0	FN6.0	VF8.0	NM9
1	–	8/47	Original; Kiefer-c/a, Froehlich, Griffiths-a	1 1	59	177	369	650
2	62	–	LDC-r; 8pgs. cut	1 1	26	78	136	235
3	75	–	LDC-r	1 1	22	66	116	195
4	92	–	C-price 15¢; LDC-r	1 1	19	57	99	165

41. Twenty Years After

Ed	HRN	Date	Details	A C	GD2.0	FN6.0	VF8.0	NM9
1	–	9/47	Original; 'horror'-c	1 1	40	120	232	400
2	62	–	New-c; no c-price 8 pgs. cut; LDC-r; Kiefer-c	1 2	6	18	32	45

				A	C	GD2.0	FN6.0	VF8.0	NM9.4
3	78	–	C-price 15¢; LDC-r	1	2	5	15	24	32
4	156	–	New-c; PC-r	1	3	3	9	17	26
5	167	12/63	PC-r	1	3	2	6	9	12
6	167	11/66	PC-r	1	3	2	6	9	12
7	169	Spr/70	New price 25¢; stiff-c; PC-r	1	3	2	6	9	12

2. Swiss Family Robinson

Ed	HRN	Date	Details	A	C	GD2.0	FN6.0	VF8.0	NM9.4
1	42	10/47	Orig.; Kiefer-c&a;	1	1	22	66	116	200
2A	62	–	8 pgs. cut; outside bc: Gift Box ad; LDC-r	1	1	6	18	30	42
2B	62	–	8 pgs. cut; outside- bc: Reorder list; scarce; LDC-r	1	1	10	30	55	85
3	75	–	LDC-r	1	1	5	14	21	28
4	93	–	LDC-r	1	1	4	13	19	26
5	117	–	LDC-r	1	1	3	9	17	24
6	131	–	New-c; old-a; PC-r	1	2	3	9	17	26
7	137	–	Old-a; PC-r	1	2	2	6	12	18
8	141	–	Old-a; PC-r	1	2	2	6	12	18
9	152	–	New-a; PC-r	2	2	3	9	17	26
0	158	–	PC-r	2	2	2	6	9	12
1	165	–	PC-r	2	2	3	9	17	26
2	167	12/63	PC-r	2	2	2	6	10	14
3	167	4/65	PC-r	2	2	2	6	9	12
4	167	5/66	PC-r	2	2	2	6	9	12
5	166	11/67	PC-r	2	2	2	6	9	12
6	169	Spr/69	PC-r; stiff-c	2	2	2	6	9	12

3. Great Expectations (Used in **SOTI**, pg. 311)

Ed	HRN	Date	Details	A	C	GD2.0	FN6.0	VF8.0	NM9.4
1	42	11/47	Original; Kiefer-a/c	1	1	86	258	540	950
2	62	–	No c-price; 8 pgs. cut; LDC-r	1	1	55	165	341	600

4. Mysteries of Paris (Used in **SOTI**, pg. 323)

Ed	HRN	Date	Details	A	C	GD2.0	FN6.0	VF8.0	NM9.4
1A	44	12/47	Original; 56 pgs.; Kiefer-c/a	1	1	64	192	398	700
1B	44	12/47	Orig.; printed on white/heavier paper; (rare)	1	1	73	219	455	800
2A	62	–	8 pgs. cut; outside- bc: Gift Box ad; LDC-r	1	1	30	90	159	275
2B	62	–	8 pgs. cut; outside- bc: reorder list; LDC-r	1	1	30	90	159	275
3	78	–	C-price 15¢; LDC-r	1	1	25	75	130	225

5. Tom Brown's School Days

Ed	HRN	Date	Details	A	C	GD2.0	FN6.0	VF8.0	NM9.4
1	44	1/48	Original; 1st 48pg. issue	1	1	16	48	83	140
2	64	–	No c-price; LDC-r	1	1	6	18	32	45
3	161	–	New-c&a; PC-r	2	2	3	9	17	24
4	167	2/64	PC-r	2	2	2	6	10	14
5	167	8/66	PC-r	2	2	2	6	10	14
6	166	R/1968	C-price 25¢; PC-r	2	2	2	6	9	12

6. Kidnapped

Ed	HRN	Date	Details	A	C	GD2.0	FN6.0	VF8.0	NM9.4
1	47	4/48	Original; Webb-c/a	1	1	15	45	77	135
2A	62	–	Price circle blank; LDC-r	1	1	5	15	25	35
2B	62	–	C-price 10¢; rare; LDC-r	1	1	30	90	159	275
3	78	–	C-price 15¢; LDC-r	1	1	5	14	21	28
4	87	–	LDC-r	1	1	4	13	19	26
5	118	–	LDC-r	1	1	3	9	14	20
6	131	–	New-c; PC-r	1	2	3	9	17	24
7	140	–	PC-r	1	2	2	6	10	14
8	150	–	PC-r	1	2	2	6	10	14
9	164	–	Reduced pg.width;	1	2	2	6	9	12
10	167	–	PC-r	1	2	2	6	9	12
11	167	3/64	PC-r	1	2	2	6	9	12
12	167	6/65	PC-r	1	2	2	6	9	12
13	167	12/65	PC-r	1	2	2	6	9	12
14	166	9/67	PC-r	1	2	2	6	9	12
15	166	Win/69	New price 25¢; PC-r; stiff-c	1	2	2	6	9	12
16	169	Sm/70	PC-r; stiff-c	1	2	2	6	9	12

47. Twenty Thousand Leagues Under the Sea

Ed	HRN	Date	Details	A	C	GD2.0	FN6.0	VF8.0	NM9.4
1	47	5/48	Orig.; Kiefer-a&c;	1	1	16	48	83	140
2	64	–	No c-price; LDC-r	1	1	5	15	25	35
3	78	–	C-price 15¢; LDC-r	1	1	4	13	19	26
4	94	–	LDC-r	1	1	4	12	18	24
5	118	–	LDC-r	1	1	3	9	14	20
6	128	–	New-c; PC-r	1	2	3	9	17	26
7	133	–	PC-r	1	2	2	6	11	16
8	140	–	PC-r	1	2	2	6	10	14
9	148	–	PC-r	1	2	2	6	10	14
10	156	–	PC-r	1	2	2	6	10	14
11	165	–	PC-r	1	2	2	6	10	14
12	167	–	PC-r	1	2	2	6	10	14
13	167	3/64	PC-r	1	2	2	6	10	14
14	167	8/65	PC-r	1	2	2	6	10	14
15	167	10/66	PC-r	1	2	2	6	10	14
16	166	R/1968	C-price 25¢; new-c PC-r	1	3	2	6	12	18
17	169	Spr/70	Stiff-c; PC-r	1	3	3	9	14	20

48. David Copperfield

Ed	HRN	Date	Details	A	C	GD2.0	FN6.0	VF8.0	NM9.4
1	47	6/48	Original; Kiefer-c/a	1	1	15	45	77	135
2	64	–	Price circle re- placed by motif of boy reading; LDC-r	1	1	5	15	25	35
3	87	–	C-price 15¢; LDC-r	1	1	4	12	18	24
4	121	–	New-c; PC-r	1	2	3	9	15	22
5	130	–	PC-r	1	2	2	6	10	14
6	140	–	PC-r	1	2	2	6	10	14
7	148	–	PC-r	1	2	2	6	10	14
8	156	–	PC-r	1	2	2	6	10	14
9	167	–	PC-r	1	2	2	6	9	12
10	167	4/64	PC-r	1	2	2	6	9	12
11	167	6/65	PC-r	1	2	2	6	9	12
12	166	5/67	PC-r	1	2	2	6	9	12
13	166	R/67	PC-r; C-price 25¢	1	2	2	6	11	16
14	166	Spr/69	C-price 25¢; stiff-c PC-r	1	2	2	6	9	12
15	169	Win/69	Stiff-c; PC-r	1	2	2	6	9	12

49. Alice in Wonderland

Ed	HRN	Date	Details	A	C	GD2.0	FN6.0	VF8.0	NM9.4
1	47	7/48	Original; 1st Blum a & c	1	1	20	60	105	180
2	64	–	No c-price; LDC-r	1	1	7	21	36	50
3A	85	–	C-price 15¢; soft-c LDC-r	1	1	6	18	29	40
3B	85	–	Stiff-c; LDC-r	1	1	6	18	32	45
4	155	–	New PC, similar to orig.; PC-r	1	2	4	12	25	40
5	165	–	PC-r	1	2	4	12	19	28
6	167	3/64	PC-r	1	2	3	9	17	24
7	167	6/66	PC-r	1	2	3	9	17	24
8A	166	Fall/68	New-c; soft-c; 25¢	1	3	4	12	25	40
8B	166	Fall/68	New-c; stiff-c; 25¢ c-price; PC-r	1	3	9	27	50	80

50. Adventures of Tom Sawyer (Used in **SOTI**, pg. 37)

Ed	HRN	Date	Details	A	C	GD2.0	FN6.0	VF8.0	NM9.4
1A	51	8/48	Orig.; Aldo Rubano a&c	1	1	15	45	77	135
1B	51	9/48	Orig.; Rubano c&a	1	1	15	45	77	135
1C	51	9/48	Orig.; outside-bc: blue & yellow only; rare	1	1	22	66	116	200
2	64	–	No c-price; LDC-r	1	1	5	15	23	30
3	78	–	C-price 15¢; LDC-r	1	1	4	12	18	24
5	117	–	LDC-r	1	1	2	6	12	18
6	132	–	LDC-r	1	1	2	6	12	18
7	140	–	New-c; PC-r	1	1	3	9	17	26
8	150	–	PC-r	1	2	2	6	10	14
9	164	–	New-a; PC-r	2	2	3	9	17	26
10	167	–	PC-r	2	2	2	6	10	14
11	167	1/65	PC-r	2	2	2	6	9	12
12	167	5/66	PC-r	2	2	2	6	9	12
13	166	12/67	PC-r	2	2	2	6	9	12
14	169	Fall/69	C-price 25¢; stiff-c; PC-r	2	2	2	6	9	12
15	169	Win/71	PC-r	2	2	2	6	9	12

51. The Spy

Ed	HRN	Date	Details	A	C	GD2.0	FN6.0	VF8.0	NM9.4
1A	51	9/48	Original; inside-bc illo: Christmas Carol	1	1	14	42	72	125
1B	51	9/48	Original; inside-bc illo: Man in Iron Mask	1	1	14	42	72	125
1C	51	8/48	Original; outside-bc: full color	1	1	14	42	72	125
1D	51	8/48	Original; outside-bc: blue & yellow only; scarce	1	1	17	51	88	150
2	89	–	C-price 15¢; LDC-r	1	1	5	14	21	28
3	121	–	LDC-r	1	1	3	9	17	24
4	139	–	New-c; PC-r	1	2	3	9	17	26
5	156	–	PC-r	1	2	2	6	10	14
6	167	11/63	PC-r	1	2	2	6	9	12
7	167	7/66	PC-r	1	2	2	6	9	12
8A	166	Win/69	C-price 25¢; soft-c; scarce; PC-r	1	2	4	13	19	26
8B	166	Win/69	C-price 25¢; stiff-c; PC-r	1	2	2	6	9	12

52. The House of the Seven Gables

Ed	HRN	Date	Details	A	C	GD2.0	FN6.0	VF8.0	NM9.4
1	53	10/48	Orig.; Griffiths a&c	1	1	14	42	72	125
2	89	–	C-price 15¢; LDC-r	1	1	5	14	21	28
3	121	–	LDC-r	1	1	3	9	17	24
4	142	–	New-c&a; PC-r; Woodbridge-a	2	2	4	12	19	28
5	156	–	PC-r	2	2	2	6	10	14
6	165	–	PC-r	2	2	2	6	9	12
7	167	5/64	PC-r	2	2	2	6	10	14
8	167	3/66	PC-r	2	2	2	6	9	12
9	166	R/1968	C-price 25¢; PC-r	2	2	2	6	9	12
10	169	Spr/70	Stiff-c; PC-r	2	2	2	6	9	12

53. A Christmas Carol

Ed	HRN	Date	Details	A	C	GD2.0	FN6.0	VF8.0	NM9.4
1	53	11/48	Original & only ed; Kiefer-c/a	1	1	20	60	105	180

54. Man in the Iron Mask

Ed	HRN	Date	Details	A	C	GD2.0	FN6.0	VF8.0	NM9.4
1	55	12/48	Original; Froehlich-a, Kiefer-c	1	1	14	42	72	125
2	93	–	C-price 15¢; LDC-r	1	1	5	15	24	32
3A	111	–	(O) logo lettering; scarce; LDC-r	1	1	5	15	29	45
3B	111	–	New logo as PC; LDC-r	1	1	4	12	20	30
4	142	–	New-c&a; PC-r	2	2	4	12	19	2
5	154	–	PC-r	2	2	2	6	10	1
6	165	–	PC-r	2	2	2	6	9	1
7	167	5/64	PC-r	2	2	2	6	9	1
8	167	4/66	PC-r	2	2	2	6	9	1
9A	166	Win/69	C-price 25¢; soft-c	2	2	4	13	19	2
9B	166	Win/69	Stiff-c	2	2	2	6	9	1

55. Silas Marner (Used in SOTI, pgs. 311, 312)

Ed	HRN	Date	Details	A	C	GD2.0	FN6.0	VF8.0	NM9.4
1	55	1/49	Original-Kiefer-c	1	1	14	42	72	12
2	75	–	Price circle blank; 'Coming Next' ad; LDC-r	1	1	5	15	25	3
3	97	–	LDC-r	1	1	3	9	17	2
4	121	–	New-c; PC-r	1	2	3	9	17	2
5	130	–	PC-r	1	2	2	6	10	1
6	140	–	PC-r	1	2	2	6	10	1
7	154	–	PC-r	1	2	2	6	9	1
8	165	–	PC-r	1	2	2	6	9	1
9	167	2/64	PC-r	1	2	2	6	9	1
10	167	6/65	PC-r	1	2	2	6	9	1
11	166	5/67	PC-r	1	2	2	6	9	1
12A	166	Win/69	C-price 25¢; soft-c	1	2	4	13	19	2
12B	166	Win/69	C-price 25¢; stiff-c	1	2	2	6	9	1

56. The Toilers of the Sea

Ed	HRN	Date	Details	A	C	GD2.0	FN6.0	VF8.0	NM9.4
1	55	2/49	Original; A.M. Froehlich-c/a	1	1	24	72	127	21
2	165	–	New-c&a; PC-r; Angelo Torres-a	2	2	5	15	29	4
3	167	3/64	PC-r	2	2	3	9	17	2
4	167	10/66	PC-r	2	2	3	9	17	2

57. The Song of Hiawatha

Ed	HRN	Date	Details	A	C	GD2.0	FN6.0	VF8.0	NM9.4
1	55	3/49	Original; Alex Blum-c/a	1	1	14	42	72	12
2	75	–	No c-price w/15¢ sticker; 'Coming Next' ad; LDC-r	1	1	5	15	25	3
3	94	–	C-price 15¢; LDC-r	1	1	5	14	21	2
4	118	–	LDC-r	1	1	3	9	17	2
5	134	–	New-c; PC-r	1	2	3	9	17	2
6	139	–	PC-r	1	2	2	6	10	1
7	154	–	PC-r	1	2	2	6	10	1
8	167	–	Has orig.date; PC-r	1	2	2	6	9	1
9	167	9/64	PC-r	1	2	2	6	9	1
10	167	10/65	PC-r	1	2	2	6	9	1
11	166	F/1968	C-price 25¢; PC-r	1	2	2	6	9	1

58. The Prairie

Ed	HRN	Date	Details	A	C	GD2.0	FN6.0	VF8.0	NM9.4
1	60	4/49	Original; Palais c/a	1	1	14	42	72	12
2A	62	–	No c-price; no coming-next ad; LDC-r	1	1	8	24	42	6
2B	62	–	10¢ (rare)	1	1	17	51	88	15
3	78	–	C-price 15¢ in dbl. circle; LDC-r	1	1	5	14	21	2
4	114	–	LDC-r	1	1	3	9	17	2
5	131	–	LDC-r	1	1	3	9	14	2
6	132	–	LDC-r	1	1	3	9	14	2
7	146	–	New-c; PC-r	1	2	3	9	17	2
8	155	–	PC-r	1	2	2	6	10	1
9	167	5/64	PC-r	1	2	2	6	9	1
10	167	4/66	PC-r	1	2	2	6	9	1
11	169	Sm/69	New price 25¢;	1	2	2	6	9	1

Classics Illustrated #61 © GIL

Classics Illustrated #64 © GIL

Classics Illustrated #68 © GIL

				GD2.0	FN6.0	VF8.0	NM9.4

stiff-c; PC-r

59. Wuthering Heights

Ed	HRN	Date	Details	A	C	GD2.0	FN6.0	VF8.0	NM9.4
1	60	5/49	Original; Kiefer-c/a	1	1	15	45	77	130
2	85	–	C-price 15¢; LDC-r	1	1	6	18	29	40
3	156	–	New-c; PC-r	1	2	4	12	19	28
4	167	1/64	PC-r	1	2	2	6	10	14
5	167	10/66	PC-r	1	2	2	6	10	14
6	169	Sm/69	C-price 25¢; stiff-c; PC-r	1	2	2	6	10	14

60. Black Beauty

Ed	HRN	Date	Details	A	C	GD2.0	FN6.0	VF8.0	NM9.4
1	62	6/49	Original; Froehlich-c/a	1	1	14	42	72	125
2	62	–	No c-price; no coming-next ad; LDC-r (rare)	1	1	16	48	83	140
3	85	–	C-price 15¢; LDC-r	1	1	5	15	24	32
4	158	–	New L.B. Cole-c/a; PC-r	2	2	5	15	25	38
5	167	2/64	PC-r	2	2	3	9	13	20
6	167	3/66	PC-r	2	2	3	9	13	20
7	166	R/1968	New-c&price, 25¢; PC-r	2	3	7	21	40	60

61. The Woman in White

Ed	HRN	Date	Details	A	C	GD2.0	FN6.0	VF8.0	NM9.4
1A	62	7/49	Original; Blum-c/a fc-purple; bc: top illos light blue	1	1	15	45	77	130
1B	62	7/49	Original; Blum-c/a fc-pink; bc: top illos light violet	1	1	15	45	77	130
2	156	–	New-c; PC-r	1	2	4	12	20	30
3	167	1/64	PC-r	1	2	3	9	14	20
4	166	R/1968	C-price 25¢; PC-r	1	2	3	9	14	20

62. Western Stories ("The Luck of Roaring Camp" and "The Outcasts of Poker Flat")

Ed	HRN	Date	Details	A	C	GD2.0	FN6.0	VF8.0	NM9.4
1	62	8/49	Original; Kiefer-c/a	1	1	13	39	66	110
2	89	–	C-price 15¢; LDC-r	1	1	5	15	24	32
3	121	–	LDC-r	1	1	3	9	17	26
4	137	–	New-c; PC-r	1	2	3	9	17	26
5	152	–	PC-r	1	2	2	6	9	12
6	167	10/63	PC-r	1	2	2	6	9	12
7	167	6/64	PC-r	1	2	2	6	9	12
8	167	11/66	PC-r	1	2	2	6	9	12
9	166	R/1968	New-c&price 25¢; PC-r	1	3	3	9	17	26

63. The Man Without a Country

Ed	HRN	Date	Details	A	C	GD2.0	FN6.0	VF8.0	NM9.4
1	62	9/49	Original; Kiefer-c/a	1	1	14	42	72	120
2	78	–	C-price 15¢ in double circle; LDC-r	1	1	5	15	24	32
3	156	–	New-c, old-a; PC-r	1	2	5	15	23	30
4	165	–	New-a & text pgs.; PC-r; A. Torres-a	2	2	4	12	19	28
5	167	3/64	PC-r	2	2	2	6	9	12
6	167	8/66	PC-r	2	2	2	6	9	12
7	169	Sm/69	New price 25¢; stiff-c; PC-r	2	2	2	6	9	12

64. Treasure Island

Ed	HRN	Date	Details	A	C	GD2.0	FN6.0	VF8.0	NM9.4
1	62	10/49	Original; Blum-c/a	1	1	14	42	72	125
2A	82	–	C-price 15¢; soft-c LDC-r	1	1	5	15	23	30
2B	82	–	Stiff-c; LDC-r	1	1	5	15	24	32
3	117	–	LDC-r	1	1	3	9	17	26
4	131	–	New-c; PC-r	1	2	3	9	17	26
5	138	–	PC-r	1	2	2	6	10	14
6	146	–	PC-r	1	2	2	6	10	14
7	158	–	PC-r	1	2	2	6	10	14
8	165	–	PC-r	1	2	2	6	9	12
9	167	–	PC-r	1	2	2	6	9	12
10	167	6/64	PC-r	1	2	2	6	9	12
11	167	12/65	PC-r	1	2	2	6	9	12
12A	166	10/67	PC-r	1	2	2	6	9	12
12B	166	10/67	w/Grit ad stapled in book	1	2	10	30	70	120
13	169	Spr/69	New price 25¢; stiff-c; PC-r	1	2	2	6	10	14
14	–	1989	Long John Silver's Seafood Shoppes; $1.95, First/Berkley Publ.; Blum-r	1	2				5.00

65. Benjamin Franklin

Ed	HRN	Date	Details	A	C	GD2.0	FN6.0	VF8.0	NM9.4
1	64	11/49	Original; Kiefer-c; Iger Shop-a	1	1	14	42	72	125
2	131	–	New-c; PC-r	1	2	4	12	19	28
3	154	–	PC-r	1	2	2	6	11	15
4	167	2/64	PC-r	1	2	2	6	10	14
5	167	4/66	PC-r	1	2	2	6	10	14
6	169	Fall/69	New price 25¢; stiff-c; PC-r	1	2	2	6	10	14

66. The Cloister and the Hearth

Ed	HRN	Date	Details	A	C	GD2.0	FN6.0	VF8.0	NM9.4
1	67	12/49	Original & only ed; Kiefer-a & c	1	1	29	87	153	265

67. The Scottish Chiefs

Ed	HRN	Date	Details	A	C	GD2.0	FN6.0	VF8.0	NM9.4
1	67	1/50	Original; Blum-a&c	1	1	12	36	61	100
2	85	–	C-price 15¢; LDC-r	1	1	5	15	24	32
3	118	–	LDC-r	1	1	3	9	17	26
4	136	–	New-c; PC-r	1	2	3	9	19	28
5	154	–	PC-r	1	2	2	6	10	14
6	167	11/63	PC-r	1	2	2	6	11	16
7	167	8/65	PC-r	1	2	2	6	10	14

68. Julius Caesar (Used in SOTI, pgs. 36, 37)

Ed	HRN	Date	Details	A	C	GD2.0	FN6.0	VF8.0	NM9.4
1	70	2/50	Original; Kiefer-c/a	1	1	12	36	61	100
2	85	–	C-price 15¢; LDC-r	1	1	5	15	23	30
3	108	–	LDC-r	1	1	3	9	17	26
4	156	–	New L.B. Cole-c; PC-r	1	2	4	12	20	30
5	165	–	New-a by Evans, Crandall; PC-r	2	2	4	12	20	30
6	167	2/64	PC-r	2	2	2	6	9	12
7	167	10/65	Tarzan books inside cover; PC-r	2	2	2	6	9	12
8	166	R/1967	PC-r	2	2	2	6	9	12
9	169	Win/69	PC-r; stiff-c	2	2	2	6	9	12

69. Around the World in 80 Days

Ed	HRN	Date	Details	A	C	GD2.0	FN6.0	VF8.0	NM9.4
1	70	3/50	Original; Kiefer-c/a	1	1	12	36	61	100
2	87	–	C-price 15¢; LDC-r	1	1	5	15	23	30
3	125	–	LDC-r	1	1	3	9	17	26
4	136	–	New-c; PC-r	1	2	4	12	19	28
5	146	–	PC-r	1	2	2	6	10	14
6	152	–	PC-r	1	2	2	6	10	14
7	164	–	PC-r	1	2	2	6	9	12
8	167	–	PC-r	1	2	2	6	9	12
9	167	7/64	PC-r	1	2	2	6	9	12
10	167	11/65	PC-r	1	2	2	6	9	12
11	166	7/67	PC-r	1	2	2	6	9	12
12	169	Spr/69	C-price 25¢; stiff-c; PC-r	1	2	2	6	9	12

Classics Illustrated #72 © GIL

Classics Illustrated #77 © GIL

Classics Illustrated #78 © GIL

70. The Pilot

Ed	HRN	Date	Details	A	C	GD2.0	FN6.0	VF8.0	NM9.4
1	71	4/50	Original; Blum-c/a	1	1	11	33	55	90
2	92	–	C-price 15¢; LDC-r	1	1	5	15	24	32
3	125	–	LDC-r	1	1	3	9	17	26
4	156	–	New-c; PC-r	1	2	4	12	20	30
5	167	2/64	PC-r	1	2	3	9	14	20
6	167	5/66	PC-r	1	2	2	6	11	16

71. The Man Who Laughs

Ed	HRN	Date	Details	A	C	GD2.0	FN6.0	VF8.0	NM9.4
1	71	5/50	Original; Blum-c/a	1	1	17	51	88	150
2	165	–	New-c&a; PC-r	2	2	11	33	55	90
3	167	4/64	PC-r	2	2	10	30	55	80

72. The Oregon Trail

Ed	HRN	Date	Details	A	C	GD2.0	FN6.0	VF8.0	NM9.4
1	73	6/50	Original; Kiefer-c/a	1	1	10	30	55	85
2	89	–	C-price 15¢; LDC-r	1	1	5	15	24	32
3	121	–	LDC-r	1	1	3	9	17	26
4	131	–	New-c; PC-r	1	2	4	12	19	28
5	140	–	PC-r	1	2	2	6	10	14
6	150	–	PC-r	1	2	2	6	10	14
7	164	–	PC-r	1	2	2	6	9	12
8	167	–	PC-r	1	2	2	6	9	12
9	167	8/64	PC-r	1	2	2	6	9	12
10	167	10/65	PC-r	1	2	2	6	9	12
11	166	R/1968	C-price 25¢; PC-r	1	2	2	6	9	12

73. The Black Tulip

Ed	HRN	Date	Details	A	C	GD2.0	FN6.0	VF8.0	NM9.4
1	75	7/50	1st & only ed.; Alex Blum-c/a	1	1	35	105	185	320

74. Mr. Midshipman Easy

Ed	HRN	Date	Details	A	C	GD2.0	FN6.0	VF8.0	NM9.4
1	75	8/50	1st & only edition	1	1	35	105	185	320

75. The Lady of the Lake

Ed	HRN	Date	Details	A	C	GD2.0	FN6.0	VF8.0	NM9.4
1	75	9/50	Original; Kiefer-c/a	1	1	10	30	55	85
2	85	–	C-price 15¢; LDC-r	1	1	5	15	25	35
3	118	–	LDC-r	1	1	4	12	19	28
4	139	–	New-c; PC-r	1	2	4	12	19	28
5	154	–	PC-r	1	2	2	6	10	14
6	165	–	PC-r	1	2	2	6	9	12
7	167	4/64	PC-r	1	2	2	6	9	12
8	167	5/66	PC-r	1	2	2	6	9	12
9	169	Spr/69	New price 25¢; stiff-c; PC-r	1	2	2	6	9	12

76. The Prisoner of Zenda

Ed	HRN	Date	Details	A	C	GD2.0	FN6.0	VF8.0	NM9.4
1	75	10/50	Original; Kiefer-c/a	1	1	10	30	55	80
2	85	–	C-price 15¢; LDC-r	1	1	5	15	24	32
3	111	–	LDC-r	1	1	3	9	17	26
4	128	–	New-c; PC-r	1	2	3	9	17	26
5	152	–	PC-r	1	2	2	6	10	14
6	165	–	PC-r	1	2	2	6	9	12
7	167	4/64	PC-r	1	2	2	6	9	12
8	167	9/66	PC-r	1	2	2	6	9	12
9	169	Fall/69	New price 25¢; stiff-c; PC-r	1	2	2	6	9	12

77. The Iliad

Ed	HRN	Date	Details	A	C	GD2.0	FN6.0	VF8.0	NM9.4
1	78	11/50	Original; Blum-c/a	1	1	10	30	55	80
2	87	–	C-price 15¢; LDC-r	1	1	5	15	25	35
3	121	–	LDC-r	1	1	3	9	17	26
4	139	–	New-c; PC-r	1	2	3	9	17	24
5	150	–	PC-r	1	2	2	6	10	14
6	165	–	PC-r	1	2	2	6	9	12
7	167	10/63	PC-r	1	2	2	6	9	12
8	167	7/64	PC-r	1	2	2	6	9	12
9	167	5/66	PC-r	1	2	2	6	9	12
10	166	R/1968	C-price 25¢; PC-r	1	2	2	6	9	12

78. Joan of Arc

Ed	HRN	Date	Details	A	C	GD2.0	FN6.0	VF8.0	NM9.4
1	78	12/50	Original; Kiefer-c/a	1	1	10	30	55	80
2	87	–	C-price 15¢; LDC-r	1	1	5	15	24	32
3	113	–	LDC-r	1	1	3	9	17	26
4	128	–	New-c; PC-r	1	2	3	9	17	26
5	140	–	PC-r	1	2	2	6	10	14
6	150	–	PC-r	1	2	2	6	10	14
7	159	–	PC-r	1	2	2	6	10	14
8	167	–	PC-r	1	2	2	6	9	12
9	167	12/63	PC-r	1	2	2	6	9	12
10	167	6/65	PC-r	1	2	2	6	9	12
11	166	6/67	PC-r	1	2	2	6	9	12
12	166	Win/69	New-c&price, 25¢; PC-r; stiff-c	1	3	4	12	19	28

79. Cyrano de Bergerac

Ed	HRN	Date	Details	A	C	GD2.0	FN6.0	VF8.0	NM9.4
1	78	1/51	Orig.; movie promo inside front-c; Blum-c/a	1	1	10	30	55	80
2	85	–	C-price 15¢; LDC-r	1	1	5	15	24	32
3	118	–	LDC-r	1	1	3	9	17	26
4	133	–	New-c; PC-r	1	2	3	9	17	26
5	156	–	PC-r	1	2	3	9	14	20
6	167	8/64	PC-r	1	2	3	9	14	20

80. White Fang (Last line drawn cover)

Ed	HRN	Date	Details	A	C	GD2.0	FN6.0	VF8.0	NM9.4
1	79	2/51	Orig.; Blum-c/a	1	1	10	30	55	80
2	87	–	C-price 15¢; LDC-r	1	1	5	15	25	35
3	125	–	LDC-r	1	1	3	9	17	26
4	132	–	New-c; PC-r	1	2	3	9	17	24
5	140	–	PC-r	1	2	2	6	10	14
6	153	–	PC-r	1	2	2	6	10	14
7	167	–	PC-r	1	2	2	6	9	12
8	167	9/64	PC-r	1	2	2	6	9	12
9	167	7/65	PC-r	1	2	2	6	9	12
10	166	6/67	PC-r	1	2	2	6	9	12
11	169	Fall/69	New price 25¢; PC-r; stiff-c	1	2	2	6	9	12

81. The Odyssey (1st painted cover)

Ed	HRN	Date	Details	A	C	GD2.0	FN6.0	VF8.0	NM9.4
1	82	3/51	First 15¢ Original; Blum-c	1	1	10	30	55	80
2	167	8/64	PC-r	1	1	3	9	14	20
3	167	10/66	PC-r	1	1	3	9	14	20
4	169	Spr/69	New, stiff-c; PC-r	1	2	4	12	19	28

82. The Master of Ballantrae

Ed	HRN	Date	Details	A	C	GD2.0	FN6.0	VF8.0	NM9.4
1	82	4/51	Original; Blum-c	1	1	8	24	42	60
2	167	8/64	PC-r	1	1	3	9	17	24
3	166	Fall/68	New, stiff-c; PC-r	1	2	4	12	19	28

83. The Jungle Book

Ed	HRN	Date	Details	A	C	GD2.0	FN6.0	VF8.0	NM9.4
1	85	5/51	Original; Blum-c Bossert/Blum-a	1	1	8	24	42	60
2	110	–	PC-r	1	1	2	6	11	16
3	125	–	PC-r	1	1	2	6	10	14
4	134	–	PC-r	1	1	2	6	10	14
5	142	–	PC-r	1	1	2	6	10	14
6	150	–	PC-r	1	1	2	6	10	14
7	159	–	PC-r	1	1	2	6	10	14
8	167	–	PC-r	1	1	2	6	9	12
9	167	3/65	PC-r	1	1	2	6	9	12
10	167	11/65	PC-r	1	1	2	6	9	12
11	167	5/66	PC-r	1	1	2	6	9	12
12	166	R/1968	New c&a; stiff-c; PC-r	2	2	4	12	19	28

Classics Illustrated #87 © GIL

Classics Illustrated #89 © GIL

Classics Illustrated #91 © GIL

					GD2.0	FN6.0	VF8.0	NM9.4						GD2.0	FN6.0	VF8.0	NM9.4

84. The Gold Bug and Other Stories ("The Gold Bug", "The Tell-Tale Heart", "The Cask of Amontillado")

Ed	HRN	Date	Details	A	C				
1	85	6/51	Original; Blum-c/a; Palais, Laverly-a	1	1	12	36	61	100
2	167	7/64	PC-r	1	1	10	30	55	80

85. The Sea Wolf

Ed	HRN	Date	Details	A	C				
1	85	7/51	Original; Blum-c/a	1	1	7	21	36	50
2	121	–	PC-r	1	1	2	6	10	14
3	132	–	PC-r	1	1	2	6	10	14
4	141	–	PC-r	1	1	2	6	10	14
5	161	–	PC-r	1	1	2	6	9	12
6	167	2/64	PC-r	1	1	2	6	9	12
7	167	11/65	PC-r	1	1	2	6	9	12
8	169	Fall/69	New price 25¢; stiff-c; PC-r	1	1	2	6	9	12

86. Under Two Flags

Ed	HRN	Date	Details	A	C				
1	87	8/51	Original; first delBourgo-a	1	1	6	18	32	45
2	117	–	PC-r	1	1	2	6	11	16
3	139	–	PC-r	1	1	2	6	10	14
4	158	–	PC-r	1	1	2	6	10	14
5	167	2/64	PC-r	1	1	2	6	9	12
6	167	8/66	PC-r	1	1	2	6	9	12
7	169	Sm/69	New price 25¢; stiff-c; PC-r	1	1	2	6	9	12

87. A Midsummer Nights Dream

Ed	HRN	Date	Details	A	C				
1	87	9/51	Original; Blum c/a	1	1	6	18	33	48
2	161	–	PC-r	1	1	2	6	10	14
3	167	4/64	PC-r	1	1	2	6	9	12
4	167	5/66	PC-r	1	1	2	6	9	12
5	169	Sm/69	New price 25¢; stiff-c; PC-r	1	1	2	6	9	12

88. Men of Iron

Ed	HRN	Date	Details	A	C				
1	89	10/51	Original	1	1	6	18	33	48
2	154	–	PC-r	1	1	2	6	10	14
3	167	1/64	PC-r	1	1	2	6	9	12
4	166	R/1968	C-price 25¢; PC-r	1	1	2	6	9	12

89. Crime and Punishment (Cover illo. in POP)

Ed	HRN	Date	Details	A	C				
1	89	11/51	Original; Palais-a	1	1	7	21	36	50
2	152	–	PC-r	1	1	2	6	10	14
3	167	4/64	PC-r	1	1	2	6	9	12
4	167	5/66	PC-r	1	1	2	6	9	12
5	169	Fall/69	New price 25¢; stiff-c; PC-r	1	1	2	6	9	12

90. Green Mansions

Ed	HRN	Date	Details	A	C				
1	89	12/51	Original; Blum-c/a	1	1	6	18	33	48
2	148	–	New L.B. Cole-c; PC-r	1	2	3	9	15	22
3	165	–	PC-r	1	2	2	6	9	12
4	167	4/64	PC-r	1	2	2	6	9	12
5	167	9/66	PC-r	1	2	2	6	9	12
6	169	Sm/69	New price 25¢; stiff-c; PC-r	1	2	2	6	9	12

91. The Call of the Wild

Ed	HRN	Date	Details	A	C				
1	92	1/52	Orig.; delBourgo-a	1	1	6	18	33	48
2	112	–	PC-r	1	1	2	6	10	14
3	125	–	'Picture Progress' on back-c; PC-r	1	1	2	6	10	14
4	134	–	PC-r	1	1	2	6	10	14
5	143	–	PC-r	1	1	2	6	10	14

6	165	–	PC-r	1	1	2	6	10	14
7	167	–	PC-r	1	1	2	6	9	12
8	167	4/65	PC-r	1	1	2	6	9	12
9	167	3/66	PC-r	1	1	2	6	9	12
10	166	11/67	PC-r	1	1	2	6	9	12
11	169	Spr/70	New price 25¢; stiff-c; PC-r	1	1	2	6	9	12

92. The Courtship of Miles Standish

Ed	HRN	Date	Details	A	C				
1	92	2/52	Original; Blum-c/a	1	1	6	18	32	45
2	165	–	PC-r	1	1	2	6	10	14
3	167	3/64	PC-r	1	1	2	6	10	14
4	166	5/67	PC-r	1	1	2	6	10	14
5	169	Win/69	New price 25¢ stiff-c; PC-r	1	1	2	6	10	14

93. Pudd'nhead Wilson

Ed	HRN	Date	Details	A	C				
1	94	3/52	Orig.; Kiefer-c/a;	1	1	6	18	33	48
2	165	–	New-c; PC-r	1	2	2	6	12	18
3	167	3/64	PC-r	1	2	2	6	10	14
4	166	R/1968	New price 25¢; soft-c; PC-r	1	2	2	6	10	14

94. David Balfour

Ed	HRN	Date	Details	A	C				
1	94	4/52	Original; Palais-a	1	1	6	18	33	48
2	167	5/64	PC-r	1	1	3	9	14	20
3	166	R/1968	C-price 25¢; PC-r	1	1	3	9	14	20

95. All Quiet on the Western Front

Ed	HRN	Date	Details	A	C				
1A	96	5/52	Orig.; del Bourgo-a	1	1	11	33	55	90
1B	99	5/52	Orig.; del Bourgo-a	1	1	9	27	49	70
2	167	10/64	PC-r	1	1	3	9	17	26
3	167	11/66	PC-r	1	1	3	9	17	26

96. Daniel Boone

Ed	HRN	Date	Details	A	C				
1	97	6/52	Original; Blum-a	1	1	6	18	30	42
2	117	–	PC-r	1	1	2	6	10	14
4	132	–	PC-r	1	1	2	6	10	14
5	134	–	"Story of Jesus" on back-c; PC-r	1	1	2	6	10	14
6	158	–	PC-r	1	1	2	6	10	14
7	167	1/64	PC-r	1	1	2	6	9	12
8	167	5/65	PC-r	1	1	2	6	9	12
9	167	11/66	PC-r	1	1	2	6	9	12
10	166	Win/69	New-c; price 25¢; PC-r; stiff-c	1	2	3	9	15	22

97. King Solomon's Mines

Ed	HRN	Date	Details	A	C				
1	96	7/52	Orig.; Kiefer-a	1	1	6	18	30	42
2	118	–	PC-r	1	1	2	6	10	14
3	131	–	PC-r	1	1	2	6	10	14
4	141	–	PC-r	1	1	2	6	10	14
5	158	–	PC-r	1	1	2	6	10	14
6	167	2/64	PC-r	1	1	2	6	9	12
7	167	9/65	PC-r	1	1	2	6	9	12
8	169	Sm/69	New price 25¢; stiff-c; PC-r	1	1	2	6	9	12

98. The Red Badge of Courage

Ed	HRN	Date	Details	A	C				
1	98	8/52	Original	1	1	6	18	32	45
2	118	–	PC-r	1	1	2	6	10	14
3	132	–	PC-r	1	1	2	6	10	14
4	142	–	PC-r	1	1	2	6	10	14
5	152	–	PC-r	1	1	2	6	10	14
6	161	–	PC-r	1	1	2	6	10	14
7	167	–	Has orig.date; PC-r	1	1	2	6	10	14
8	167	9/64	PC-r	1	1	2	6	10	14

Classics Illustrated #100 © GIL

Classics Illustrated #102 © GIL

Classics Illustrated #111 © GIL

						GD2.0	FN6.0	VF8.0	NM9.4
9	167	10/65	PC-r	1	1	2	6	10	14
10	166	R/1968	New-c&price 25¢; PC-r; stiff-c	1	2	3	9	17	24

99. Hamlet (Used in **POP**, pg. 102)

Ed	HRN	Date	Details	A	C				
1	98	9/52	Original; Blum-a	1	1	6	18	33	48
2	121	–	PC-r	1	1	2	6	10	14
3	141	–	PC-r	1	1	2	6	10	14
4	158	–	PC-r	1	1	2	6	10	14
5	167	–	Has orig.date; PC-r	1	1	2	6	9	12
6	167	7/65	PC-r	1	1	2	6	9	12
7	166	4/67	PC-r	1	1	2	6	9	12
8	169	Spr/69	New-c&price 25¢; PC-r; stiff-c	1	2	3	9	17	24

100. Mutiny on the Bounty

Ed	HRN	Date	Details	A	C				
1	100	10/52	Original	1	1	6	18	30	42
2	117	–	PC-r	1	1	2	6	10	14
3	132	–	PC-r	1	1	2	6	10	14
4	142	–	PC-r	1	1	2	6	10	14
5	155	–	PC-r	1	1	2	6	10	14
6	167	–	Has orig. date;PC-r	1	1	2	6	9	12
7	167	5/64	PC-r	1	1	2	6	9	12
8	167	3/66	PC-r	1	1	2	6	9	12
9	169	Spr/70	PC-r; stiff-c	1	1	2	6	9	12

101. William Tell

Ed	HRN	Date	Details	A	C				
1	101	11/52	Original; Kiefer-c delBourgo-a	1	1	6	18	30	42
2	118	–	PC-r	1	1	2	6	10	14
3	141	–	PC-r	1	1	2	6	10	14
4	158	–	PC-r	1	1	2	6	10	14
5	167	–	Has orig.date; PC-r	1	1	2	6	9	12
6	167	11/64	PC-r	1	1	2	6	9	12
7	166	4/67	PC-r	1	1	2	6	9	12
8	169	Win/69	New price 25¢; stiff-c; PC-r	1	1	2	6	9	12

102. The White Company

Ed	HRN	Date	Details	A	C				
1	101	12/52	Original; Blum-a	1	1	10	30	55	80
2	165	–	PC-r	1	1	4	12	19	28
3	167	4/64	PC-r	1	1	4	12	19	28

103. Men Against the Sea

Ed	HRN	Date	Details	A	C				
1	104	1/53	Original; Kiefer-c; Palais-a	1	1	6	18	33	48
2	114	–	PC-r	1	1	3	9	15	22
3	131	–	New-c; PC-r	1	2	4	12	19	28
4	158	–	PC-r	1	2	3	9	14	20
5	149	–	White reorder list; came after HRN-158; PC-r	1	2	4	12	20	30
6	167	3/64	PC-r	1	2	2	6	10	14

104. Bring 'Em Back Alive

Ed	HRN	Date	Details	A	C				
1	105	2/53	Original; Kiefer-c/a	1	1	6	18	30	42
2	118	–	PC-r	1	1	2	6	10	14
3	133	–	PC-r	1	1	2	6	10	14
4	150	–	PC-r	1	1	2	6	10	14
5	158	–	PC-r	1	1	2	6	10	14
6	167	10/63	PC-r	1	1	2	6	9	12
7	167	9/65	PC-r	1	1	2	6	9	12
8	169	Win/69	New price 25¢; stiff-c; PC-r	1	1	2	6	9	12

105. From the Earth to the Moon

Ed	HRN	Date	Details	A	C				
1	106	3/53	Original; Blum-a	1	1	6	18	30	42
2	118	–	PC-r	1	1	2	6	10	14

						GD2.0	FN6.0	VF8.0	NM9.4
3	132	–	PC-r	1	1	2	6	10	14
4	141	–	PC-r	1	1	2	6	10	14
5	146	–	PC-r	1	1	2	6	10	14
6	156	–	PC-r	1	1	2	6	10	14
7	167	–	Has orig. date; PC-r	1	1	2	6	9	12
8	167	5/64	PC-r	1	1	2	6	9	12
9	167	5/65	PC-r	1	1	2	6	9	12
10A	166	10/67	PC-r	1	1	2	6	9	12
10B	166	10/67	w/Grit ad stapled in book	1	1	8	24	60	100
11	169	Sm/69	New price 25¢; stiff-c; PC-r	1	1	2	6	9	12
12	169	Spr/71	PC-r	1	1	2	6	9	12

106. Buffalo Bill

Ed	HRN	Date	Details	A	C				
1	107	4/53	Orig.; delBourgo-a	1	1	6	18	29	40
2	118	–	PC-r	1	1	2	6	10	14
3	132	–	PC-r	1	1	2	6	10	14
4	142	–	PC-r	1	1	2	6	10	14
5	161	–	PC-r	1	1	2	6	9	12
6	167	3/64	PC-r	1	1	2	6	9	12
7	166	7/67	PC-r	1	1	2	6	9	12
8	169	Fall/69	PC-r; stiff-c	1	1	2	6	9	12

107. King of the Khyber Rifles

Ed	HRN	Date	Details	A	C				
1	108	5/53	Original	1	1	6	18	30	42
2	118	–	PC-r	1	1	2	6	10	14
3	146	–	PC-r	1	1	2	6	10	14
4	158	–	PC-r	1	1	2	6	10	14
5	167	–	Has orig.date; PC-r	1	1	2	6	9	12
6	167	–	PC-r	1	1	2	6	9	12
7	167	10/66	PC-r	1	1	2	6	9	12

108. Knights of the Round Table

Ed	HRN	Date	Details	A	C				
1A	108	6/53	Original; Blum-a	1	1	6	18	33	48
1B	109	6/53	Original; scarce	1	1	7	21	38	55
2	117	–	PC-r	1	1	2	6	10	14
3	165	–	PC-r	1	1	2	6	9	12
4	167	4/64	PC-r	1	1	2	6	9	12
5	166	4/67	PC-r	1	1	2	6	9	12
6	169	Sm/69	New price 25¢; stiff-c; PC-r	1	1	2	6	9	12

109. Pitcairn's Island

Ed	HRN	Date	Details	A	C				
1	110	7/53	Original; Palais-a	1	1	6	18	33	48
2	165	–	PC-r	1	1	2	6	10	14
3	167	3/64	PC-r	1	1	2	6	10	14
4	166	6/67	PC-r	1	1	2	6	10	14

110. A Study in Scarlet

Ed	HRN	Date	Details	A	C				
1	111	8/53	Original	1	1	12	36	61	100
2	165	–	PC-r	1	1	10	30	55	80

111. The Talisman

Ed	HRN	Date	Details	A	C				
1	112	9/53	Original; last H.C. Kiefer-a	1	1	6	18	33	48
2	165	–	PC-r	1	1	2	6	10	14
3	167	5/64	PC-r	1	1	2	6	10	14
4	166	Fall/68	C-price 25¢; PC-r	1	1	2	6	10	14

112. Adventures of Kit Carson

Ed	HRN	Date	Details	A	C				
1	113	10/53	Original; Palais-a	1	1	6	18	32	45
2	129	–	PC-r	1	1	2	6	10	14
3	141	–	PC-r	1	1	2	6	10	14
4	152	–	PC-r	1	1	2	6	10	14
5	161	–	PC-r	1	1	2	6	9	12

Classics Illustrated #118 © GIL

Classics Illustrated #123 © GIL

Classics Illustrated #124 © GIL

					GD2.0	FN6.0	VF8.0	NM9.4

Ed	HRN	Date	Details	A	C	GD2.0	FN6.0	VF8.0	NM9.4
6	167	–	PC-r	1	1	2	6	9	12
7	167	2/65	PC-r	1	1	2	6	9	12
8	167	5/66	PC-r	1	1	2	6	9	12
9	166	Win/69	New-c&price 25¢; PC-r; stiff-c	1	2	3	9	14	20

113. The Forty-Five Guardsmen

Ed	HRN	Date	Details	A	C	GD2.0	FN6.0	VF8.0	NM9.4
1	114	11/53	Orig.; delBourgo-a	1	1	9	27	49	70
2	166	7/67	PC-r	1	1	3	9	21	32

114. The Red Rover

Ed	HRN	Date	Details	A	C	GD2.0	FN6.0	VF8.0	NM9.4
1	115	12/53	Original	1	1	9	27	49	70
2	166	7/67	PC-r	1	1	3	9	21	32

115. How I Found Livingstone

Ed	HRN	Date	Details	A	C	GD2.0	FN6.0	VF8.0	NM9.4
1	116	1/54	Original	1	1	10	30	55	80
2	167	1/67	PC-r	1	1	4	12	29	45

116. The Bottle Imp

Ed	HRN	Date	Details	A	C	GD2.0	FN6.0	VF8.0	NM9.4
1	117	2/54	Orig.; Cameron-a	1	1	10	30	55	80
2	167	1/67	PC-r	1	1	4	12	29	45

117. Captains Courageous

Ed	HRN	Date	Details	A	C	GD2.0	FN6.0	VF8.0	NM9.4
1	118	3/54	Orig.; Costanza-a	1	1	9	27	49	70
2	167	2/67	PC-r	1	1	3	9	17	24
3	169	Fall/69	New price 25¢; stiff-c; PC-r	1	1	3	9	17	24

118. Rob Roy

Ed	HRN	Date	Details	A	C	GD2.0	FN6.0	VF8.0	NM9.4
1	119	4/54	Original; Rudy & Walter Palais-a	1	1	10	30	55	80
2	167	2/67	PC-r	1	1	4	12	29	45

119. Soldiers of Fortune

Ed	HRN	Date	Details	A	C	GD2.0	FN6.0	VF8.0	NM9.4
1	120	5/54	Schaffenberger-a	1	1	8	24	42	60
2	166	3/67	PC-r	1	1	3	9	17	24
3	169	Spr/70	New price 25¢; stiff-c; PC-r	1	1	3	9	17	24

120. The Hurricane

Ed	HRN	Date	Details	A	C	GD2.0	FN6.0	VF8.0	NM9.4
1	121	6/54	Orig.; Cameron-a	1	1	8	24	42	60
2	166	3/67	PC-r	1	1	3	9	21	32

121. Wild Bill Hickok

Ed	HRN	Date	Details	A	C	GD2.0	FN6.0	VF8.0	NM9.4
1	122	7/54	Original	1	1	6	18	28	38
2	132	–	PC-r	1	1	2	6	10	14
3	141	–	PC-r	1	1	2	6	10	14
4	154	–	PC-r	1	1	2	6	10	14
5	167	–	PC-r	1	1	2	6	9	12
6	167	8/64	PC-r	1	1	2	6	9	12
7	166	4/67	PC-r	1	1	2	6	9	12
8	169	Win/69	PC-r; stiff-c	1	1	2	6	9	12

122. The Mutineers

Ed	HRN	Date	Details	A	C	GD2.0	FN6.0	VF8.0	NM9.4
1	123	9/54	Original	1	1	6	18	33	48
2	136	–	PC-r	1	1	2	6	10	14
3	146	–	PC-r	1	1	2	6	10	14
4	158	–	PC-r	1	1	2	6	10	14
5	167	11/63	PC-r	1	1	2	6	9	12
6	167	3/65	PC-r	1	1	2	6	9	12
7	166	8/67	PC-r	1	1	2	6	9	12

123. Fang and Claw

Ed	HRN	Date	Details	A	C	GD2.0	FN6.0	VF8.0	NM9.4
1	124	11/54	Original	1	1	6	18	33	48
2	133	–	PC-r	1	1	2	6	10	14
3	143	–	PC-r	1	1	2	6	10	14
4	154	–	PC-r	1	1	2	6	10	14
5	167	–	Has orig.date; PC-r	1	1	2	6	9	12
6	167	9/65	PC-r	1	1	2	6	9	12

124. The War of the Worlds

Ed	HRN	Date	Details	A	C	GD2.0	FN6.0	VF8.0	NM9.4
1	125	1/55	Original; Cameron-c/a	1	1	8	24	45	65
2	131	–	PC-r	1	1	2	6	11	16
3	141	–	PC-r	1	1	2	6	11	16
4	148	–	PC-r	1	1	2	6	11	16
5	156	–	PC-r	1	1	2	6	11	16
6	165	–	PC-r	1	1	3	9	14	20
7	167	–	PC-r	1	1	2	6	10	14
8	167	11/64	PC-r	1	1	2	6	11	16
9	167	11/65	PC-r	1	1	2	6	10	14
10	166	R/1968	C-price 25¢; PC-r	1	1	2	6	10	14
11	169	Sm/70	PC-r; stiff-c	1	1	2	6	10	14

125. The Ox Bow Incident

Ed	HRN	Date	Details	A	C	GD2.0	FN6.0	VF8.0	NM9.4
1	–	3/55	Original; Picture Progress replaces reorder list	1	1	6	18	28	38
2	143	–	PC-r	1	1	2	6	10	14
3	152	–	PC-r	1	1	2	6	10	14
4	149	–	PC-r	1	1	2	6	10	14
5	167	–	PC-r	1	1	2	6	9	12
6	167	11/64	PC-r	1	1	2	6	9	12
7	166	4/67	PC-r	1	1	2	6	9	12
8	169	Win/69	New price 25¢; stiff-c; PC-r	1	1	2	6	9	12

126. The Downfall

Ed	HRN	Date	Details	A	C	GD2.0	FN6.0	VF8.0	NM9.4
1	5/55	–	Orig.; 'Picture Progress' replaces reorder list; Cameron-c/a	1	1	6	18	33	48
2	167	8/64	PC-r	1	1	3	9	14	20
3	166	R/1968	C-price 25¢; PC-r	1	1	3	9	14	20

127. The King of the Mountains

Ed	HRN	Date	Details	A	C	GD2.0	FN6.0	VF8.0	NM9.4
1	128	7/55	Original	1	1	6	18	33	48
2	167	6/64	PC-r	1	1	2	6	11	16
3	166	F/1968	C-price 25¢; PC-r	1	1	2	6	11	16

128. Macbeth (Used in POP, pg. 102)

Ed	HRN	Date	Details	A	C	GD2.0	FN6.0	VF8.0	NM9.4
1	128	9/55	Orig.; last Blum-a	1	1	6	18	33	48
2	143	–	PC-r	1	1	2	6	10	14
3	158	–	PC-r	1	1	2	6	10	14
4	167	–	PC-r	1	1	2	6	9	12
5	167	6/64	PC-r	1	1	2	6	9	12
6	166	4/67	PC-r	1	1	2	6	9	12
7	166	R/1968	C-Price 25¢; PC-r	1	1	2	6	9	12
8	169	Spr/70	Stiff-c; PC-r	1	1	2	6	9	12

129. Davy Crockett

Ed	HRN	Date	Details	A	C	GD2.0	FN6.0	VF8.0	NM9.4
1	129	11/55	Orig.; Cameron-a	1	1	12	36	61	100
2	167	9/66	PC-r	1	1	9	27	51	80

130. Caesar's Conquests

Ed	HRN	Date	Details	A	C	GD2.0	FN6.0	VF8.0	NM9.4
1	130	1/56	Original; Orlando-a	1	1	7	21	36	50
2	142	–	PC-r	1	1	2	6	10	14
3	152	–	PC-r	1	1	2	6	10	14
4	149	–	PC-r	1	1	2	6	10	14
5	167	–	PC-r	1	1	2	6	9	12
6	167	10/64	PC-r	1	1	2	6	9	12
7	166	4/66	PC-r	1	1	2	6	9	12

131. The Covered Wagon

Ed	HRN	Date	Details	A	C	GD2.0	FN6.0	VF8.0	NM9.4
1	131	3/56	Original	1	1	4	12	25	38

Classics Illustrated #138 © GIL

Classics Illustrated #140 © GIL

Classics Illustrated #146 © GIL

Ed	HRN	Date	Details	A	C	GD2.0	FN6.0	VF8.0	NM9.4
2	143	–	PC-r	1	1	2	6	10	14
3	152	–	PC-r	1	1	2	6	10	14
4	158	–	PC-r	1	1	2	6	10	14
5	167	–	PC-r	1	1	2	6	9	12
6	167	11/64	PC-r	1	1	2	6	9	12
7	167	4/66	PC-r	1	1	2	6	9	12
8	169	Win/69	New price 25¢; stiff-c; PC-r	1	1	2	6	9	12

132. The Dark Frigate

Ed	HRN	Date	Details	A	C	GD2.0	FN6.0	VF8.0	NM9.4
1	132	5/56	Original	1	1	5	15	31	48
2	150	–	PC-r	1	1	2	6	11	15
3	167	1/64	PC-r	1	1	2	6	10	14
4	166	5/67	PC-r	1	1	2	6	10	14

133. The Time Machine

Ed	HRN	Date	Details	A	C	GD2.0	FN6.0	VF8.0	NM9.4
1	132	7/56	Orig.; Cameron-a	1	1	5	15	32	50
2	142	–	PC-r	1	1	2	6	11	16
3	152	–	PC-r	1	1	2	6	11	16
4	158	–	PC-r	1	1	2	6	11	16
5	167	–	PC-r	1	1	2	6	10	14
6	167	6/64	PC-r	1	1	2	6	11	16
7	167	3/66	PC-r	1	1	2	6	10	14
8	166	12/67	PC-r	1	1	2	6	10	14
9	169	Win/71	New price 25¢; stiff-c; PC-r	1	1	2	6	10	14

134. Romeo and Juliet

Ed	HRN	Date	Details	A	C	GD2.0	FN6.0	VF8.0	NM9.4
1	134	9/56	Original; Evans-a	1	1	5	15	31	48
2	161	–	PC-r	1	1	2	6	10	14
3	167	9/63	PC-r	1	1	2	6	9	12
4	167	5/65	PC-r	1	1	2	6	9	12
5	166	6/67	PC-r	1	1	2	6	9	12
6	166	Win/69	New c&price 25¢; PC-r	1	2	3	9	17	26

135. Waterloo

Ed	HRN	Date	Details	A	C	GD2.0	FN6.0	VF8.0	NM9.4
1	135	11/56	Orig.; G. Ingels-a	1	1	5	15	31	48
2	153	–	PC-r	1	1	2	6	10	14
3	167	–	PC-r	1	1	2	6	9	12
4	167	9/64	PC-r	1	1	2	6	9	12
5	166	R/1968	C-price 25¢; PC-r	1	1	2	6	9	12

136. Lord Jim

Ed	HRN	Date	Details	A	C	GD2.0	FN6.0	VF8.0	NM9.4
1	136	1/57	Original; Evans-a	1	1	5	15	31	48
2	165	–	PC-r	1	1	2	6	9	12
3	167	3/64	PC-r	1	1	2	6	9	12
4	167	9/66	PC-r	1	1	2	6	9	12
5	169	Sm/69	New price 25 ¢; PC-r	1	1	2	6	9	12

137. The Little Savage

Ed	HRN	Date	Details	A	C	GD2.0	FN6.0	VF8.0	NM9.4
1	136	3/57	Original; Evans-a	1	1	5	15	31	48
2	148	–	PC-r	1	1	2	6	10	14
3	156	–	PC-r	1	1	2	6	10	14
4	167	–	PC-r	1	1	2	6	9	12
5	167	10/64	PC-r	1	1	2	6	9	12
6	166	8/67	PC-r	1	1	2	6	9	12
7	169	Spr/70	New price 25¢; stiff-c; PC-r	1	1	2	6	9	12

138. A Journey to the Center of the Earth

Ed	HRN	Date	Details	A	C	GD2.0	FN6.0	VF8.0	NM9.4
1	136	5/57	Original	1	1	7	21	43	65
2	146	–	PC-r	1	1	2	6	12	18
3	156	–	PC-r	1	1	2	6	12	18
4	158	–	PC-r	1	1	2	6	12	18
5	167	–	PC-r	1	1	2	6	10	14
6	167	6/64	PC-r	1	1	3	9	14	20
7	167	4/66	PC-r	1	1	3	9	14	20
8	166	R/68	C-price 25¢; PC-r	1	1	2	6	11	16

139. In the Reign of Terror

Ed	HRN	Date	Details	A	C	GD2.0	FN6.0	VF8.0	NM9.4
1	139	7/57	Original; Evans-a	1	1	4	12	25	38
2	154	–	PC-r	1	1	2	6	10	14
3	167	–	Has orig.date; PC-r	1	1	2	6	9	12
4	167	7/64	PC-r	1	1	2	6	9	12
5	166	R/1968	C-price 25¢; PC-r	1	1	2	6	9	12

140. On Jungle Trails

Ed	HRN	Date	Details	A	C	GD2.0	FN6.0	VF8.0	NM9.4
1	140	9/57	Original	1	1	4	12	25	38
2	150	–	PC-r	1	1	2	6	10	14
3	160	–	PC-r	1	1	2	6	10	14
4	167	9/63	PC-r	1	1	2	6	9	12
5	167	9/65	PC-r	1	1	2	6	9	12

141. Castle Dangerous

Ed	HRN	Date	Details	A	C	GD2.0	FN6.0	VF8.0	NM9.4
1	141	11/57	Original	1	1	6	18	36	55
2	152	–	PC-r	1	1	2	6	10	14
3	167	–	PC-r	1	1	2	6	10	14
4	166	7/67	PC-r	1	1	2	6	10	14

142. Abraham Lincoln

Ed	HRN	Date	Details	A	C	GD2.0	FN6.0	VF8.0	NM9.4
1	142	1/58	Original	1	1	5	15	32	50
2	154	–	PC-r	1	1	2	6	10	14
3	158	–	PC-r	1	1	2	6	10	14
4	167	10/63	PC-r	1	1	2	6	9	12
5	167	7/65	PC-r	1	1	2	6	9	12
6	166	11/67	PC-r	1	1	2	6	9	12
7	169	Fall/69	New price 25¢; stiff-c; PC-r	1	1	2	6	9	12

143. Kim

Ed	HRN	Date	Details	A	C	GD2.0	FN6.0	VF8.0	NM9.4
1	143	3/58	Original; Orlando-a	1	1	4	12	27	42
2	165	–	PC-r	1	1	2	6	9	12
3	167	11/63	PC-r	1	1	2	6	9	12
4	167	8/65	PC-r	1	1	2	6	9	12
5	169	Win/69	New price 25¢; stiff-c; PC-r	1	1	2	6	9	12

144. The First Men in the Moon

Ed	HRN	Date	Details	A	C	GD2.0	FN6.0	VF8.0	NM9.4
1	143	5/58	Original; Woodbridge/Williamson/Torres-a	1	1	5	15	32	50
2	152	–	(Rare)-PC-r	1	1	8	24	45	65
3	153	–	PC-r	1	1	2	6	10	14
4	161	–	PC-r	1	1	2	6	9	12
5	167	–	PC-r	1	1	2	6	9	12
6	167	12/65	PC-r	1	1	2	6	9	12
7	166	Fall/68	New-c&price 25¢; PC-r; stiff-c	1	2	3	9	15	22
8	169	Win/69	Stiff-c; PC-r	1	2	2	6	12	18

145. The Crisis

Ed	HRN	Date	Details	A	C	GD2.0	FN6.0	VF8.0	NM9.4
1	143	7/58	Original; Evans-a	1	1	5	15	31	48
2	156	–	PC-r	1	1	2	6	10	14
3	167	10/63	PC-r	1	1	2	6	9	12
4	167	3/65	PC-r	1	1	2	6	9	12
5	166	R/68	C-price 25¢; PC-r	1	1	2	6	9	12

146. With Fire and Sword

Ed	HRN	Date	Details	A	C	GD2.0	FN6.0	VF8.0	NM9.4
1	143	9/58	Original; Woodbridge-a	1	1	5	15	32	50
2	156	–	PC-r	1	1	2	6	11	16
3	167	11/63	PC-r	1	1	2	6	10	14
4	167	3/65	PC-r	1	1	2	6	10	14

Classics Illustrated #148 © GIL

Classics Illustrated #150 © GIL

Classics Illustrated #152 © GIL

			GD2.0	FN6.0	VF8.0	NM9.4

147. Ben-Hur

Ed	HRN	Date	Details	A	C	GD2.0	FN6.0	VF8.0	NM9.4
1	147	11/58	Original; Orlando-a	1	1	4	12	27	42
2	152	–	Scarce; PC-r	1	1	5	15	32	50
3	153	–	PC-r	1	1	2	6	10	14
4	158	–	PC-r	1	1	2	6	10	14
5	167	–	Orig.date; but PC-r	1	1	2	6	9	12
6	167	2/65	PC-r	1	1	2	6	9	12
7	167	9/66	PC-r	1	1	2	6	9	12
8A	166	Fall/68	New-c&price 25¢; PC-r; soft-c	1	2	3	9	17	26
8B	166	Fall/68	New-c&price 25¢; PC-r; stiff-c; scarce	1	2	4	12	27	42

148. The Buccaneer

Ed	HRN	Date	Details	A	C	GD2.0	FN6.0	VF8.0	NM9.4
1	148	1/59	Orig.; Evans/Jenny-a; Saunders-c	1	1	4	12	27	42
2	568	–	Juniors list only PC-r	1	1	2	6	10	14
3	167	–	PC-r	1	1	2	6	9	12
4	167	9/65	PC-r	1	1	2	6	9	12
5	169	Sm/69	New price 25¢; PC-r; stiff-c	1	1	2	6	9	12

149. Off on a Comet

Ed	HRN	Date	Details	A	C	GD2.0	FN6.0	VF8.0	NM9.4
1	149	3/59	Orig.;G.McCann-a; blue reorder list	1	1	5	15	31	48
2	155	–	PC-r	1	1	2	6	10	14
3	149	–	PC-r; white reorder list; no coming-next ad	1	1	2	6	10	14
4	167	12/63	PC-r	1	1	2	6	9	12
5	167	2/65	PC-r	1	1	2	6	9	12
6	167	10/66	PC-r	1	1	2	6	9	12
7	166	Fall/68	New-c & price 25¢; PC-r	1	2	3	9	17	24

150. The Virginian

Ed	HRN	Date	Details	A	C	GD2.0	FN6.0	VF8.0	NM9.4
1	150	5/59	Original	1	1	6	18	36	55
2	164	–	PC-r	1	1	3	9	14	20
3	167	10/63	PC-r	1	1	3	9	17	26
4	167	12/65	PC-r	1	1	3	9	14	20

151. Won By the Sword

Ed	HRN	Date	Details	A	C	GD2.0	FN6.0	VF8.0	NM9.4
1	150	7/59	Original	1	1	5	15	32	50
2	164	–	PC-r	1	1	2	6	11	16
3	167	10/63	PC-r	1	1	2	6	11	16
4	166	7/67	PC-r	1	1	2	6	11	16

152. Wild Animals I Have Known

Ed	HRN	Date	Details	A	C	GD2.0	FN6.0	VF8.0	NM9.4
1	152	9/59	Orig.; L.B. Cole c/a	1	1	6	18	38	60
2A	149	–	PC-r; white reorder list; no coming-next ad; IBC: Jr. list #572	1	1	2	6	10	14
2B	149	–	PC-r; inside-bc: Jr. list to #555	1	1	2	6	11	15
2C	149	–	PC-r; inside-bc: has World Around Us ad; scarce	1	1	3	9	17	26
3	167	9/63	PC-r	1	1	2	6	9	12
4	167	8/65	PC-r	1	1	2	6	9	12
5	169	Fall/69	New price 25¢; stiff-c; PC-r	1	1	2	6	9	12

153. The Invisible Man

Ed	HRN	Date	Details	A	C	GD2.0	FN6.0	VF8.0	NM9.4
1	153	11/59	Original	1	1	7	21	43	65
2A	149	–	PC-r; white reorder list; no coming-next ad; inside-bc: Jr. list to #572	1	1	2	6	12	18
2B	149	–	PC-r; inside-bc: Jr. list to #555	1	1	3	9	14	20
3	167	–	PC-r	1	1	2	6	11	15
4	167	2/65	PC-r	1	1	2	6	11	15
5	167	9/66	PC-r	1	1	2	6	11	15
6	166	Win/69	New price 25¢; PC-r; stiff-c	1	1	2	6	11	15
7	169	Spr/71	Stiff-c; letters spelling 'Invisible Man' are 'solid' not 'invisible;' PC-r	1	1	2	6	11	15

154. The Conspiracy of Pontiac

Ed	HRN	Date	Details	A	C	GD2.0	FN6.0	VF8.0	NM9.4
1	154	1/60	Original	1	1	6	18	36	55
2	167	11/63	PC-r	1	1	3	9	14	20
3	167	7/64	PC-r	1	1	3	9	14	20
4	166	12/67	PC-r	1	1	3	9	14	20

155. The Lion of the North

Ed	HRN	Date	Details	A	C	GD2.0	FN6.0	VF8.0	NM9.4
1	154	3/60	Original	1	1	5	15	32	50
2	167	1/64	PC-r	1	1	2	6	12	18
3	166	R/1967	C-price 25¢; PC-r	1	1	2	6	11	15

156. The Conquest of Mexico

Ed	HRN	Date	Details	A	C	GD2.0	FN6.0	VF8.0	NM9.4
1	156	5/60	Orig.; Bruno Premiani-c/a	1	1	5	15	32	50
2	167	1/64	PC-r	1	1	2	6	11	15
3	166	8/67	PC-r	1	1	2	6	11	15
4	169	Spr/70	New price 25¢; stiff-c; PC-r	1	1	2	6	9	12

157. Lives of the Hunted

Ed	HRN	Date	Details	A	C	GD2.0	FN6.0	VF8.0	NM9.4
1	156	7/60	Orig.; L.B. Cole-c	1	1	6	18	36	55
2	167	2/64	PC-r	1	1	3	9	14	20
3	166	10/67	PC-r	1	1	3	9	14	20

158. The Conspirators

Ed	HRN	Date	Details	A	C	GD2.0	FN6.0	VF8.0	NM9.4
1	156	9/60	Original	1	1	6	18	36	55
2	167	7/64	PC-r	1	1	3	9	14	20
3	166	10/67	PC-r	1	1	3	9	14	20

159. The Octopus

Ed	HRN	Date	Details	A	C	GD2.0	FN6.0	VF8.0	NM9.4
1	159	11/60	Orig.; Gray Morrow-a; L.B. Cole-c	1	1	6	18	36	55
2	167	2/64	PC-r	1	1	3	9	14	20
3	166	R/1967	C-price 25¢; PC-r	1	1	3	9	14	20

160. The Food of the Gods

Ed	HRN	Date	Details	A	C	GD2.0	FN6.0	VF8.0	NM9.4
1A	159	1/61	Original	1	1	6	18	38	60
1B	160	1/61	Original; same, except for HRN	1	1	6	18	36	55
2	167	1/64	PC-r	1	1	3	9	14	20
3	166	6/67	PC-r	1	1	3	9	14	20

161. Cleopatra

Ed	HRN	Date	Details	A	C	GD2.0	FN6.0	VF8.0	NM9.4
1	161	3/61	Original	1	1	6	18	36	55
2	167	1/64	PC-r	1	1	3	9	15	22
3	166	8/67	PC-r	1	1	3	9	15	22

162. Robur the Conqueror

Ed	HRN	Date	Details	A	C	GD2.0	FN6.0	VF8.0	NM9.4
1	162	5/61	Original	1	1	6	18	36	55
2	167	7/64	PC-r	1	1	3	9	14	20
3	166	8/67	PC-r	1	1	3	9	14	20

163. Master of the World

Classics Illustrated #168 © GIL

Classics Illustrated Giants - An Illustrated History of Great Indian Stories @ GIL

Classics Illustrated Junior #502 © GIL

					GD2.0	FN6.0	VF8.0	NM9.4

	Ed	HRN	Date	Details	A	C				
	1	163	7/61	Original; Gray Morrow-a	1	1	6	18	36	55
	2	167	1/65	PC-r	1	1	3	9	14	20
	3	166	R/1968	C-price 25¢; PC-r	1	1	3	9	14	20

164. The Cossack Chief

Ed	HRN	Date	Details	A	C				
1	164	(1961)	Orig.; nd(10/61?)	1	1	6	18	36	55
2	167	4/65	PC-r	1	1	3	9	14	20
3	166	Fall/68	C-price 25¢; PC-r	1	1	3	9	14	20

165. The Queen's Necklace

Ed	HRN	Date	Details	A	C				
1	164	1/62	Original; Morrow-a	1	1	6	18	36	55
2	167	4/65	PC-r	1	1	3	9	14	20
3	166	Fall/68	C-price 25¢; PC-r	1	1	3	9	14	20

166. Tigers and Traitors

Ed	HRN	Date	Details	A	C				
1	165	5/62	Original	1	1	9	27	58	90
2	167	2/64	PC-r	1	1	4	12	21	32
3	167	11/66	PC-r	1	1	4	12	21	32

167. Faust

Ed	HRN	Date	Details	A	C				
1	165	8/62	Original	1	1	13	39	84	130
2	167	2/64	PC-r	1	1	6	18	36	55
3	166	6/67	PC-r	1	1	6	18	36	55

168. In Freedom's Cause

Ed	HRN	Date	Details	A	C				
1	169	Win/69	Original; Evans/ Crandall-a; stiff-c; 25¢; no coming- next ad;	1	1	16	48	106	165

169. Negro Americans The Early Years

Ed	HRN	Date	Details	A	C				
1	166	Spr/69	Orig. & last issue; 25¢; Stiff-c; no coming-next ad; other sources indicate publication date of 5/69	1	1	13	39	89	140
2	169	Spr/69	Stiff-c	1	1	6	18	40	65

NOTE: Many other titles were prepared or planned but were only issued in British/European series.

CLASSIC PUNISHER (Also see Punisher)
Marvel Comics: Dec, 1989 ($4.95, B&W, deluxe format, 68 pgs.)

1-Reprints Marvel Super Action #1 & Marvel Preview #2 plus new story 5.00

CLASSICS ILLUSTRATED
First Publishing/Berkley Publishing: Feb, 1990 - No. 27, July, 1991 ($3.75/$3.95, 52 pgs.)

1-27: 1-Gahan Wilson-c/a. 4-Sienkiewicz painted-c/a. 6-Russell scripts/layouts. 7-Spiegle-a. 9-Ploog-c/a. 16-Staton-a. 18-Gahan Wilson-c/a; 20-Geary-a. 26-Aesop's Fables (6/91). 26,27-Direct sale only 5.00

CLASSICS ILLUSTRATED
Acclaim Books/Twin Circle PublishingCo.: Feb, 1997 - Present ($4.99, digest-size) (Each book contains study notes)

A Christmas Carol-(12/97), A Connecticut Yankee in King Arthur's Court-(5/97), All Quiet on the Western Front-(1/98), A Midsummer's Night Dream-(4/97), Around the World in 80 Days-(1/98), A Tale of Two Cities-(1/98)Joe Orlando-r, Captains Courageous-(11/97), Crime and Punishment-(3/97), Dr. Jekyll and Mr. Hyde-(10/97), Don Quixote-(12/97), Frankenstein-(10/97), Great Expectations-(4/97), Hamlet-(3/97), Huckleberry Finn-(3/97), Jane Eyre-(2/97), Kidnapped-(1/98), Les Miserables-(5/97), Lord Jim-(9/97), Macbeth-(5/97), Moby Dick-(4/97), Oliver Twist-(5/97), Robinson Crusoe-(9/97), Romeo & Juliet-(2/97), Silas Marner-(11/97), The Call of the Wild-(9/97), The Count of Monte Cristo-(1/98), The House of the Seven Gables-(9/97), The Iliad-(12/97), The Invisible Man-(10/97), The Last of the Mohicans-(12/97), The Master of Ballantrae-(11/97), The Odyssey-(3/97), The Prince and the Pauper-(4/97), The Red Badge Of Courage-(9/97), Tom Sawyer-(2/97)

Wuthering Heights-(11/97) 5.00
NOTE: Stories reprinted from the original Gilberton Classic Comics and Classics Illustrated.

CLASSICS ILLUSTRATED GIANTS
Gilberton Publications: Oct, 1949 (One-Shots - "OS")

These Giant Editions, all with new front and back covers, were advertised from 10/49 to 2/52. They were 50¢ on the newsstand and 60¢ by mail. They are actually four Classics in one volume. All the stories are reprints of the Classics Illustrated Series. NOTE: There were also British hardback Adventure & Indian Giants in 1952, with the same covers but different contents: Adventure - 2, 7, 10; Indian - 17, 22, 37, 58. They are also rare.

"An Illustrated Library of Great Adventure Stories" - reprints of No. 6,7,8,10			
(Rare); Kiefer-c	136	408	852	1500
"An Illustrated Library of Exciting Mystery Stories" - reprints of No. 30,21,40,			
13 (Rare); Blum-c	150	450	938	1650
"An Illustrated Library of Great Indian Stories" - reprints of No. 4,17,22,37			
(Rare); Blum-c	136	408	852	1500

INTRODUCTION TO CLASSICS ILLUSTRATED JUNIOR

Collectors of Juniors can be put into one of two categories: those who want any copy of each title, and those who want all the originals. Those seeking every original and reprint edition are a limited group, primarily because Juniors have no changes in art or covers to spark interest, and because reprints are so low in value it is difficult to get dealers to look for specific reprint editions.

In recent years it has become apparent that most serious Classics collectors seek Junior originals. Those seeking reprints seek them for low cost. This has made the previous note about the comparative market value of reprints inadequate. Three particular reprint editions are worth even more. For the 535-Twin Circle edition, see Giveaways. There are also reprint editions of 501 and 503 which have a full-page bc ad for the very rare Junior record. Those may sell as high as $10-15 in mint. Original editions of 557 and 558 also have that ad.

There are no reprints of 577. The only edition, from 1969, is a 25 cent stiff-cover edition with no ad for the next issue. All other original editions have coming-next ad. But 577, like C.I. #168, was prepared in 1962 but not issued. Copies of 577 can be found in 1963 British/European series, which then continued with dozens of additional new Junior titles.

PRICES LISTED BELOW ARE FOR ORIGINAL EDITIONS, WHICH HAVE AN AD FOR THE NEXT ISSUE.
NOTE: Non HRN 576 copies- many are written on or colored . Reprints with 576 HRN are worth about 1/3 original prices. All other HRN #'s are 1/2 original price

CLASSICS ILLUSTRATED JUNIOR
Famous Authors Ltd. (Gilberton Publications): Oct, 1953 - Spring, 1971

501-Snow White & the Seven Dwarfs; Alex Blum-a	11	33	55	90
502-The Ugly Duckling	8	24	42	60
503-Cinderella	6	18	29	40
504-512: 504-The Pied Piper. 505-The Sleeping Beauty. 506-The Three Little				
Pigs. 507-Jack & the Beanstalk. 508-Goldilocks & the Three Bears. 509-				
Beauty and the Beast. 510-Little Red Riding Hood. 511-Puss-N Boots.				
512-Rumpelstiltskin	5	15	23	30
513-Pinocchio	6	18	29	40
514-The Steadfast Tin Soldier	8	24	42	60
515-Johnny Appleseed	5	15	23	30
516-Aladdin and His Lamp	5	15	25	35
517-519: 517-The Emperor's New Clothes. 518-The Golden Goose.				
519-Paul Bunyan	5	15	23	30
520-Thumbelina	6	18	28	38
521-King of the Golden River	5	15	23	30
522,523,530: 522-The Nightingale. 523-The Gallant Tailor. 530-The Golden Bird				
	5	14	21	28
524-The Wild Swans	5	15	25	35
525,526: 525-The Little Mermaid. 526-The Frog Prince	5	15	25	35
527-The Golden-Haired Giant	5	15	23	30
528-The Penny Prince	5	15	23	30
529-The Magic Servants	5	15	23	30
531-Rapunzel	5	15	23	30
532-534: 532-The Dancing Princesses. 533-The Magic Fountain. 534-The				
Golden Touch	4	12	19	25
535-The Wizard of Oz	7	21	38	55
536-The Chimney Sweep	5	15	23	30
537-The Three Fairies	5	15	24	32
538-Silly Hans	4	12	19	25

Classics Illustrated Special Issue #162A © GIL

Classic Star Wars #1 © Lucasfilm

ARCHIE GOODWIN • AL WILLIAMSON

Claw the Unconquered #10 © DC

	GD2.0	FN6.0	VF8.0	NM9.4

539-The Enchanted Fish — 6 18 28 38
540-The Tinder-Box — 6 18 28 38
541-Snow White & Rose Red — 5 14 21 28
542-The Donkey's Tale — 5 14 21 28
543-The House in the Woods — 5 15 23 30
544-The Golden Fleece — 6 18 29 40
545-The Glass Mountain — 5 14 21 28
546-The Elves & the Shoemaker — 5 14 21 28
547-The Wishing Table — 5 15 23 30
548-551: 548-The Magic Pitcher. 549-Simple Kate. 550-The Singing Donkey.
551-The Queen Bee — 4 12 19 25
552-The Three Little Dwarfs — 5 15 23 30
553,556: 553-King Thrushbeard. 556-The Elf Mound — 4 12 19 25
554-The Enchanted Deer — 5 15 25 35
555-The Three Golden Apples — 5 14 21 28
557-Silly Willy — 5 15 24 32
558-The Magic Dish; L.B. Cole-c; soft and stiff-c exist on original
— 6 18 32 45
559-The Japanese Lantern; 1 pg. Ingels-a; L.B. Cole-c
— 6 18 32 45
560-The Doll Princess; L.B. Cole-c — 6 18 32 45
561-Hans Humdrum; L.B. Cole-c — 5 15 25 35
562-The Enchanted Pony; L.B. Cole-c — 6 18 32 45
563,565-567,570: 563-The Wishing Well; L.B. Cole-c. 565-The Silly Princess;
L.B. Cole-c. 566-Clumsy Hans; L.B. Cole-c. 567-The Bearskin Soldier;
L.B. Cole-c. 570-The Pearl Princess — 5 15 23 30
564-The Salt Mountain; 568-The Happy Hedgehog; L.B. Cole-c.
— 5 15 24 32
569,573: 569-The Three Giants.573-The Crystal Ball — 5 14 21 28
571,572: 571-How Fire Came to the Indians. 572-The Drummer Boy
— 6 18 28 38
574-Brightboots — 5 14 21 28
575-The Fearless Prince — 5 15 24 32
576-The Princess Who Saw Everything — 6 18 29 40
577-The Runaway Dumpling — 7 21 38 55
NOTE: Prices are for original editions. Last reprint - Spring, 1971. Costanza & Schaffenberger art in many issues.

CLASSICS ILLUSTRATED SPECIAL ISSUE
Gilberton Co.: (Came out semi-annually) Dec, 1955 - Jul, 1962 (35¢, 100 pgs.)
129-The Story of Jesus (titled …Special Edition) "Jesus on Mountain" cover
— 10 30 55 80
"Three Camels" cover (12/58) — 12 36 61 100
"Mountain" cover (no date)-Has checklist on inside b/c to HRN #161 &
different testimonial on back-c — 8 24 42 60
"Mountain" cover (1968 re-issue; has white 50¢ circle)
— 7 21 38 55
132A-The Story of America (6/56); Cameron-a — 8 24 45 65
135A-The Ten Commandments(12/56) — 7 21 38 55
138A-Adventures in Science(6/57); HRN to 137 — 7 21 36 50
138A-(12/61)-2nd version w/HRN to 149 — 5 15 25 35
138A-(12/61)-3rd version w/HRN to 149 — 6 18 32 45
141A-The Rough Rider (Teddy Roosevelt)(12/57); Evans-a
— 7 21 38 55
144A-Blazing the Trails West(6/58)- 73 pgs. of Crandall/Evans plus
Severin-a — 7 21 38 55
147A-Crossing the Rockies(12/58)-Crandall/Evans-a — 7 21 38 55
150A-Royal Canadian Police(6/59)-Ingels, Sid Check-a
— 7 21 38 55
153A-Men, Guns & Cattle (12/59)-Evans-a (26 pgs.); Kinstler-a
— 7 21 38 55
156A-The Atomic Age(6/60)-Crandall/Evans, Torres-a
— 7 21 38 55
159A-Rockets, Jets and Missiles(12/60)-Evans, Morrow-a
— 7 21 38 55
162A-War Between the States(6/61)-Kirby & Crandall/Evans-a; Ingels-a
— 14 42 72 125
165A-To the Stars(12/61)-Torres, Crandall, Evans, Kirby-a
— 8 24 45 65
166A-World War II('62)-Torres, Crandall, Evans, Kirby-a
— 11 33 55 90

167A-Prehistoric World(7/62)-Torres & Crandall/Evans-a; two versions exist
(HRN to 165 & HRN to 167) — 11 33 55 90
nn Special Issue-The United Nations (1964; 50¢; scarce); this is actually part of
the European Special Series, which cont'd on after the U.S. series stopped
issuing new titles in 1962. This English edition was prepared specifically for
sale at the U.N. It was printed in Norway — 33 99 174 300
NOTE: There was another U.S. Special Issue prepared in 1962 with artwork by Torres entitled
World War I. Unfortunately, it was never issued in any English-language edition. It was issued in
1964 in West Germany, The Netherlands, and some Scandinavian countries, with another edition
in 1974 with a new cover.

CLASSICS LIBRARY (See King Classics)

CLASSIC STAR WARS (Also see Star Wars)
Dark Horse Comics: Aug, 1992 - No. 20, June, 1994 ($2.50)
1-Begin Star Wars strip-r by Williamson; Williamson redrew portions of the
panels to fit comic book format — 6.00
2-10: 8-Polybagged w/Star Wars Galaxy trading card. 8-M. Schultz-c — 4.00
11-19: 13-Yeates-c. 17-M. Schultz-c. 19-Evans-c — 3.00
20-($3.50, 52 pgs.)-Polybagged w/trading card — 3.50
Escape to Hoth TPB ($16.95) r/#15-20 — 17.00
The Rebel Storm TPB - r/#8-14 — 17.00
Trade paperback ($29.95, slip-cased)-Reprints all movie adaptations — 30.00
NOTE: Williamson c-1-5,7,9,10,14,15,20.

CLASSIC STAR WARS: (Title series). Dark Horse Comics
—A NEW HOPE, 6/94 - No. 2, 7/94 ($3.95)
1,2: 1-r/Star Wars #1-3, 7-9 publ; 2-r/Star Wars #4-6, 10-12 publ. by Marvel
Comics — 4.00
—DEVILWORLDS, 8/96 - No.2, 9/96 ($2.50s)1,2: r/Alan Moore-s — 2.50
—HAN SOLO AT STARS' END, 3/97 - No.3, 5/97 ($2.95s)
1-3: r/strips by Alfredo Alcala — 3.00
—RETURN OF THE JEDI, 10/94 - No.2, 11/94 ($3.50)
1,2: r/1983-84 Marvel series; polybagged w/trading card — 3.50
—THE EARLY ADVENTURES, 8/94 - No. 9, 4/95 ($2.50)1-9 — 2.50
—THE EMPIRE STRIKES BACK, 8/94 - No. 2, 9/94 ($3.95)
1-r/Star Wars #39-44 publ. by Marvel Comics — 4.00

CLASSIC X-MEN (Becomes X-Men Classic #46 on)
Marvel Comics Group: Sept, 1986 - No. 45, Mar, 1990
1-Begins-r of New X-Men — 5.00
2-10: 10-Sabretooth app. — 4.00
11-45: 11-1st origin of Magneto in back-up story. 17-Wolverine-c. 27-r/X-Men
#121. 26-r/X-Men #120; Wolverine-c/app. 35-r/X-Men #129. 39-New Jim
Lee back-up story (2nd-a on X-Men). 43-Byrne-c/a(r); $1.75, double-size
— 3.00
NOTE: Art Adams c(p)-1-10, 12-16, 18-23. Austin c-10,15-21,24-28i. Bolton back up stories in 1-28,30-35. Williamson c-12-14i.

CLAW (See Capt. Battle, Jr. Daredevil Comics & Silver Streak Comics)

CLAW THE UNCONQUERED (See Cancelled Comic Cavalcade)
National Periodical Publications/DC Comics: 5-6/75 - No. 9, 9-10/76; No. 10, 4-5/78 - No. 12, 8-9/78
1-1st app. Claw — 1 4 7 10
2-12: 3-Nudity panel. 9-Origin — 6.00
NOTE: Giffen a-8-12p. Kubert c-10-12. Layton a-9i, 12i.

CLAY CODY, GUNSLINGER
Pines Comics: Fall, 1957
1-Painted-c — 6 18 29 40

CLEAN FUN, STARRING "SHOOGAFOOTS JONES"
Specialty Book Co.: 1944 (10¢, B&W, oversized covers, 24 pgs.)
nn-Humorous situations involving Negroes in the Deep South
White cover issue… — 10 30 55 80
Dark grey cover issue… — 11 33 55 90

CLEMENTINA THE FLYING PIG (See Dell Jr. Treasury)

CLEOPATRA (See Ideal, a Classical Comic No. 1)

CLERKS: THE COMIC BOOK (Also see Oni Double Feature #1)
Oni Press: Feb, 1998 ($2.95, B&W, one-shot)
1-Kevin Smith-s — 2 6 11 15

Clive Barker's Hellraiser #11 © MAR

Cloak and Dagger #3 © MAR

Clue Comics #4 © HILL

	GD2.0	FN6.0	VF8.0	NM9.4

	GD2.0	FN6.0	VF8.0	NM9.4

1-Second printing | | | | 4.00
...Holiday Special (12/98, $2.95) Smith-s | | | | 5.00
...The Lost Scene (12/99, $2.95) Smith-s/Hester-a | | | | 5.00

CLIFFHANGER (See Battle Chasers, Crimson, and Danger Girl)
WildStorm Prod./Wizard Press: 1997 (Wizard supplement)

0-Sketchbook preview of Cliffhanger titles | | | | 6.00

CLIMAX! (Mystery)
Gillmor Magazines: July, 1955 - No. 2, Sept, 1955

1	16	48	83	140
2	14	42	72	120

CLINT (Also see Adolescent Radioactive Black Belt Hamsters)
Eclipse Comics: Sept, 1986 - No. 2, Jan, 1987 ($1.50, B&W)

1,2 | | | | 2.25

CLINT & MAC (TV, Disney)
Dell Publishing Co.: No. 889, Mar, 1958

Four Color 889-Alex Toth-a, photo-c | 13 | 39 | 91 | 165

CLIVE BARKER'S BOOK OF THE DAMNED: A HELLRAISER COMPANION
Marvel Comics (Epic): Oct, 1991 - No. 3, Nov, 1992 ($4.95, semi-annual)

Volume 1-3-(52 pgs.): 1-Simon Bisley-c. 2-(4/92). 3-(11/92)-McKean-a (1 pg.) | | | | 5.00

CLIVE BARKER'S HELLRAISER (Also see Epic, Hellraiser Nightbreed –Jihad, Revelations, Son of Celluloid, Tapping the Vein & Weaveworld)
Marvel Comics (Epic Comics): 1989 - No. 20, 1993 ($4.50-6.95, mature readers, quarterly, 68 pgs.)

Book 1-4,10-16,18,19: Based on Hellraiser & Hellbound movies; Bolton-c/a; Spiegle & Wrightson-a (graphic album). 10-Foil-c. 12-Sam Kieth-a | | | | 6.00
Book 5-9 ($5.95): 7-Bolton-a. 8-Morrow-a | | | | 6.00
Book 17-Alex Ross-a, 34 pgs. | 2 | 6 | 9 | 12
Book 20-By Gaiman/McKean | 1 | 3 | 6 | 8
...Dark Holiday Special ('92, $4.95)-Conrad-a | | | | 6.00
...Spring Slaughter 1 ('94, $6.95, 52 pgs.)-Painted-c | | | | 7.00
...Summer Special 1 ('92, $5.95, 68 pgs.) | | | | 6.00

CLIVE BARKER'S NIGHTBREED (Also see Epic)
Marvel Comics (Epic Comics): Apr, 1990 - No. 25, Mar, 1993 ($1.95/$2.25/$2.50, mature readers)

1-25: 1-4-Adapt horror movie. 5-New stories; Guice-a(p) | | | | 2.50

CLIVE BARKER'S THE HARROWERS
Marvel Comics (Epic Comics): Dec, 1993 - No. 6, May, 1994 ($2.50)

1-($2.95)-Glow-in-the-dark-c; Colan-c/a in all | | | | 3.00
2-6 | | | | 2.50
NOTE: *Colan* a(p)-1-6; c-1-3, 4p, 5p. *Williamson* a(i)-2, 4, 5(part).

CLOAK AND DAGGER
Ziff-Davis Publishing Co.: Fall, 1952

1-Saunders painted-c | 27 | 81 | 142 | 245

CLOAK AND DAGGER (Also see Marvel Fanfare)
Marvel Comics Group: Oct, 1983 - No. 4, Jan, 1984 (Mini-series)
(See Spectacular Spider-Man #64)

1-4-Austin-c/a(i) in all. 4-Origin | | | | 3.00

CLOAK AND DAGGER (2nd Series)(Also see Marvel Graphic Novel #34 & Strange Tales)
Marvel Comics Group: July, 1985 - No. 11, Jan, 1987

1-11: 9-Art Adams-p | | | | 2.50
...And Power Pack (1990, $7.95, 68 pgs.) | | | | 8.00
NOTE: *Mignola* c-7, 8.

CLOAK AND DAGGER (3rd Series listed as Mutant Misadventures Of...)

CLOBBERIN' TIME
Marvel Comics: Sept, 1995 ($1.95) (Based on card game)

nn-Overpower game guide; Ben Grimm story | | | | 2.25

CLONEZONE SPECIAL
Dark Horse Comics/First Comics: 1989 ($2.00, B&W)

1-Back-up series from Badger & Nexus | | | | 2.25

CLOSE ENCOUNTERS (See Marvel Comics Super Special & Marvel Special Edition)

CLOSE SHAVES OF PAULINE PERIL, THE (TV cartoon)
Gold Key: June, 1970 - No. 4, March, 1971

1	3	9	20	30
2-4	2	6	13	20

CLOWN COMICS (No. 1 titled Clown Comic Book)
Clown Comics/Home Comics/Harvey Publ.: 1945 - No. 3, Win, 1946

nn (#1)	12	36	61	100
2,3	8	24	42	60

CLOWNS, THE (I Pagliacci)
Dark Horse Comics: 1998 ($2.95, B&W, one-shot)

1-Adaption of the opera; P. Craig Russell-script | | | | 3.00

CLUBHOUSE RASCALS (#1 titled ...Presents?) (Also see Three Rascals)
Sussex Publ. Co. (Magazine Enterprises): June, 1956 - No. 2, Oct, 1956

1-The Brain app. in both	7	21	36	50
2	6	18	32	45

CLUB "16"
Famous Funnies: June, 1948 - No. 4, Dec, 1948

1-Teen-age humor	12	36	61	100
2-4	7	21	38	55

CLUE COMICS (Real Clue Crime V2#4 on)
Hillman Periodicals: Jan, 1943 - No. 15(V2#3), May, 1947

1-Origin The Boy King, Nightmare, Micro-Face, Twilight, & Zippo	114	342	713	1250
2	55	165	341	600
3-5	40	120	217	375
6,8,9: 8-Palais-c/a(2)	30	90	159	275
7-Classic torture-c	43	129	257	450
10-Origin/1st app. The Gun Master & begin series; content changes to crime	30	90	159	275
11	22	66	116	200
12-Origin Rackman; McWilliams-a, Guardineer-a(2)	28	84	151	260
V2#1-Nightmare new origin; Iron Lady app.; Simon & Kirby-a	47	141	286	500
V2#2-S&K-a(2)-Bondage/torture-c; man attacks & kills people with electric iron. Infantino-a	64	192	398	700
V2#3-S&K-a(3)	50	150	300	525

CLUELESS SPRING SPECIAL (TV)
Marvel Comics: May, 1997 ($3.99, magazine sized, one-shot)

1-Photo-c from TV show | | | | 4.00

CLUTCHING HAND, THE
American Comics Group: July-Aug, 1954

1	38	114	203	350

CLYDE BEATTY COMICS (Also see Crackajack Funnies)
Commodore Productions & Artists, Inc.: October, 1953 (84 pgs.)

1-Photo front/back-c; movie scenes and comics | 28 | 84 | 148 | 255

CLYDE CRASHCUP (TV)
Dell Publishing Co.: Aug-Oct, 1963 - No. 5, Sept-Nov, 1964

1-All written by John Stanley	13	39	91	170
2-5	12	36	84	150

COBALT BLUE (Also see Power Comics)
Innovation Publishing: Sept, 1989 - No. 2, Oct, 1989 ($1.95, 28 pgs.)

1,2-Gustovich-c/a/scripts | | | | 2.25
The Graphic Novel ($6.95, color, 52 pgs.)-r/1,2 | | | | 7.00

CODE BLUE
Image Comics (Jet-Black): Apr, 1998 ($2.95, B&W)

1-Jimmie Robinson-s/a | | | | 3.00

CODE NAME: ASSASSIN (See 1st Issue Special)

CODENAME: DANGER
Lodestone Publishing: Aug, 1985 - No. 4, May, 1986 ($1.50)

1-4 | | | | 2.25

Codename: Knockout #0
© Robert Rodi & Louis Small Jr.

Codename: Stryke Force #10 © TCOW

The Coffin #3
© Phil Hester & Mike Huddleston

CO

	GD2.0	FN6.0	VF8.0	NM9.4

CODENAME: FIREARM (Also see Firearm)
Malibu Comics (Ultraverse): June, 1995 - No. 5, Sept, 1995 ($2.95, bimonthly limited series)
0-5: 0-2-Alec Swan back-up story by James Robinson — 3.00
NOTE: *Perez c-0.*

CODENAME: GENETIX
Marvel Comics UK: Jan, 1993 - No. 4, May, 1993 ($1.75, limited series)
1-4: Wolverine in all — 3.00

CODENAME: KNOCKOUT
DC Comics (Vertigo): No. 0, Jun, 2001 - Present ($2.50)
0-8: Rodi-s/Small Jr. -a. 1-Two covers by Chiodo & Cho. 7,8-Paquette-a — 2.50

CODENAME SPITFIRE (Formerly Spitfire And The Troubleshooters)
Marvel Comics Group: No. 10, July, 1987 - No. 13, Oct, 1987
10-13: 10-Rogers-c/a (low printing) — 3.00

CODENAME: STRYKE FORCE (Also See Cyberforce V1#4 & Cyberforce/Stryke Force: Opposing Forces ($1.95-$2.25)
Image Comics (Top Cow Productions): Jan, 1994 - No. 14, Sept, 1995
0,1-14: 1-12-Silvestri stories, Peterson-a. 4-Stormwatch app. 14-Story continues in Cyberforce/Stryke Force: Opposing Forces; Turner-a — 2.25
1-Gold, 1-Blue — 4.00

CODE NAME: TOMAHAWK
Fantasy General Comics: Sept, 1986 ($1.75, high quality paper)
1-Sci/fi — 2.25

CODE OF HONOR
Marvel Comics: Feb, 1997 - No. 4, May, 1997 ($5.95, limited series)
1-4-Fully painted by various; Dixon-s — 6.00

CODY OF THE PONY EXPRESS (See Colossal Features Magazine)
Fox Features Syndicate: Sept, 1950 (See Women Outlaws)(One shot)
1-Painted-c — 14 | 42 | 72 | 120

CODY OF THE PONY EXPRESS (Buffalo Bill…) (Outlaws of the West #11 on; Formerly Bullseye)
Charlton Comics: No. 8, Oct, 1955; No. 9, Jan, 1956; No. 10, June, 1956
8-Bullseye on splash pg; not S&K-a — 7 | 21 | 38 | 55
9,10: Buffalo Bill app. in all — 5 | 15 | 25 | 35

CODY STARBUCK (1st app. in Star Reach #1)
Star Reach Productions: July, 1978
nn-Howard Chaykin-c/a — 1 | 3 | 6 | 9
2nd printing — 6.00
NOTE: *Both printings say First Printing. True first printing is on lower-grade paper, somewhat off-register, and snow in snow sequence has green tint.*

CO-ED ROMANCES
P. L. Publishing Co.: November, 1951
1 — 7 | 21 | 36 | 50

COFFEE WORLD
World Comics: Oct, 1995 ($1.50, B&W, anthology)
1-Shannon Wheeler's Too Much Coffee Man story — 3.00

COFFIN, THE
Oni Press: Sept, 2000 - No. 4, May, 2001 ($2.95, B&W, limited series)
1-4-Hester-s/Huddleston-a — 3.00
TPB (8/01, $11.95, TPB) r/#1-4 — 12.00

COLLECTORS DRACULA, THE
Millennium Publications: 1994 - No. 2, 1994 ($3.95, color/B&W, 52 pgs., limited series)
1,2-Bolton-a (7 pgs.) — 4.00

COLLECTORS ITEM CLASSICS (See Marvel Collectors Item Classics)

COLONIA
Colonia Press: 1998 ($2.95, B&W)
1-5-Jeff Nicholson-s/a — 3.00

COLORS IN BLACK
Dark Horse Comics: Mar, 1995 - No. 4, June, 1995 ($2.95, limited series)

1-4 — 3.00

COLOSSAL FEATURES MAGAZINE (Formerly I Loved) (See Cody of the Pony Express)
Fox Features Syndicate: No. 33, 5/50 - No. 34, 7/50; No. 3, 9/50 (Based on Columbia serial)
33,34: Cody of the Pony Express begins. 33-Painted-c. 34-Photo-c — 14 | 42 | 72 | 120
3-Authentic criminal cases — 14 | 42 | 72 | 120

COLOSSAL SHOW, THE (TV)
Gold Key: Oct, 1969
1 — 5 | 15 | 34 | 55

COLOSSUS (See X-Men)
Marvel Comics: Oct, 1997 ($2.99, 48 pgs., one-shot)
1-Raab-s/Hitch & Neary-a, wraparound-c — 3.00

COLOSSUS COMICS (See Green Giant & Motion Picture Funnies Weekly)
Sun Publications (Funnies, Inc.?): March, 1940
1-(Scarce)-Tulpa of Tsang(hero); Colossus app. — 462 | 1386 | 3000 | 6000
NOTE: *Cover by artist that drew Colossus in Green Giant Comics.*

COLOUR OF MAGIC, THE (Terry Pratchett's…)
Innovation Publishing: 1991 - No. 4, 1991 ($2.50, limited series)
1-4: Adapts 1st novel of the Discworld series — 3.00

COLT .45 (TV)
Dell Publishing Co.: No. 924, 8/58 - No. 1058, 11-1/59-60; No. 4, 2-4/60 - No. 9, 5-7/61
Four Color 924(#1)-Wayde Preston photo-c on all — 10 | 30 | 70 | 130
Four Color 1004,1058, #4,5,7-9: 1004-Photo-b/c — 8 | 24 | 56 | 105
6-Toth-a — 9 | 27 | 63 | 115

COLUMBIA COMICS
William H. Wise Co.: 1943
1-Joe Palooka, Charlie Chan, Capt. Yank, Sparky Watts, Dixie Dugan app. — 29 | 87 | 153 | 265

COLUMBUS
Dark Horse Comics: Sept, 1992 ($2.50, B&W, one-shot)
1-Yeates painted-a — 2.50

COMANCHE (See Four Color No. 1350)

COMANCHEROS, THE
Dell Publishing Co.: No. 1300, Mar-May, 1962
Four Color 1300-Movie, John Wayne photo-c — 16 | 48 | 112 | 210

COMBAT
Atlas Comics (ANC): June, 1952 - No. 11, April, 1953
1 — 24 | 72 | 127 | 220
2-Heath-c/a — 13 | 39 | 66 | 110
3,5-9,11: 9-Robert Q. Sale-a — 10 | 30 | 55 | 80
4-Krigstein-a — 10 | 30 | 55 | 85
10-B&W and color illos. in POP — 10 | 30 | 55 | 80
NOTE: *Combat Casey in 7-11. Heath c-1, 2, 9. Maneely a-1; c-3. Pakula a-1. Reinman a-1.*

COMBAT
Dell Publishing Co.: Oct-Nov, 1961 - No. 40, Oct, 1973 (No #9)
1 — 5 | 15 | 34 | 55
2,3,5: — 3 | 9 | 21 | 32
4-John F. Kennedy c/story (P.T. 109) — 4 | 12 | 27 | 42
6,7,8(4-6/63), 8(7-9/63) — 3 | 9 | 19 | 28
10-26: 26-Last 12¢ issue — 2 | 6 | 13 | 20
27-40(reprints #1-14). 30-r/#4 — 2 | 6 | 11 | 16
NOTE: *Glanzman c/a-1-27, 28-40r.*

COMBAT CASEY (Formerly War Combat)
Atlas Comics (SAI): No. 6, Jan, 1953 - No. 34, July, 1957
6 (Indicia shows 1/52 in error) — 15 | 45 | 77 | 130
7 — 9 | 27 | 49 | 70
8-Used in POP, pg. 94 — 8 | 24 | 42 | 60
9 — 7 | 21 | 38 | 55
10,13-19-Violent art by R. Q. Sale; Battle Brady x-over #10

Combat Kelly #1 © MAR

Comedy Comics #25 © MAR

Comic Cavalcade #11 © DC

	GD2.0	FN6.0	VF8.0	NM9.4
	11	33	55	90
11,12,20-Last Precode (2/55)	7	21	38	55
21-34	7	21	36	50

NOTE: *Everett a-6. Heath c-10, 17, 19, 30. Maneely c-6. Powell a-29(5), 30(5), 34. Severin c-26, 33.*

COMBAT KELLY
Atlas Comics (SPI): Nov, 1951 - No. 44, Aug, 1957

1-1st app. Combat Kelly; Heath-a	29	87	156	270
2	14	42	72	125
3-10	11	33	55	90
11-Used in **POP**, pgs. 94,95 plus color illo.	9	27	49	70
12-Color illo. in **POP**	9	27	49	70
13-16	8	24	42	60
17-Violent art by R. Q. Sale; Combat Casey app.	11	33	55	90
18-20,22-44: 18-Battle Brady app. 28-Last precode (1/55). 38-Green Berets story (8/56)	7	21	36	50
21-Transvestism-c	7	21	38	55

NOTE: *Berg a-8, 12-14, 16, 17, 19-23, 25, 26, 28, 31-36, 42-44; c-2. Colan a-42. Heath a-4; c-31. Lawrence a-23. Maneely a-4(2), 6, 7(3), 8; c-4, 5, 7, 8, 10, 25. R.Q. Sale a-17, 25. Severin c-41, 42. Whitney a-5.*

COMBAT KELLY (...and the Deadly Dozen)
Marvel Comics Group: June, 1972 - No. 9, Oct, 1973

1-Intro & origin new Combat Kelly; Ayers/Mooney-a; Severin-c (20¢)	2	6	15	22
2,5-8	2	6	9	12
3,4: 3-Origin. 4-Sgt. Fury-c/s	2	6	11	16
9-Death of the Deadly Dozen	2	6	12	18

COMBINED OPERATIONS (See The Story of the Commandos)

COMEBACK (See Zane Grey 4-Color 357)

COMEDY CARNIVAL
St. John Publishing Co.: no date (1950's) (100 pgs.)

nn-Contains rebound St. John comics	35	105	185	320

COMEDY COMICS (1st Series) (Daring Mystery #1-8) (Becomes Margie Comics #35 on)
Timely Comics (TCI 9,10): No. 9, April, 1942 - No. 34, Fall, 1946

9-(Scarce)-The Fin by Everett, Capt. Dash, Citizen V, & The Silver Scorpion app.; Wolverton-a; 1st app. Comedy Kid; satire on Hitler & Stalin; The Fin, Citizen V & Silver Scorpion cont. from Daring Mystery	255	765	1591	2800
10-(Scarce)-Origin The Fourth Musketeer, Victory Boys; Monstro, the Mighty app.	191	573	1194	2100
11-Vagabond, Stuporman app.	52	157	314	550
12,13	15	45	77	130
14-Origin/1st app. Super Rabbit (3/43) plus-c	52	157	314	550
15-20	14	42	72	125
21-32	10	30	55	85
33-Kurtzman-a (5 pgs.)	13	39	66	110
34-Intro Margie; Wolverton-a (5 pgs.)	20	60	105	175

COMEDY COMICS (2nd Series)
Marvel Comics (ACI): May, 1948 - No. 10, Jan, 1950

1-Hedy, Tessie, Millie begin; Kurtzman's "Hey Look" (he draws himself)	34	102	179	310
2	14	42	72	125
3,4-Kurtzman's "Hey Look" (?&3)	15	45	77	130
5-10	8	24	45	65

COMET, THE (See The Mighty Crusaders & Pep Comics #1)
Red Circle Comics (Archie): Oct, 1983 - No. 2, Dec, 1983

1-Re-intro & origin The Comet; The American Shield begins. Nino & Infantino art in both. Hangman in both.	5.00
2-Origin continues.	4.00

COMET, THE
DC Comics (Impact Comics): July, 1991 - No. 18, Dec, 1992 ($1.00/$1.25)

1	3.00
2-18: 4-Black Hood app. 6-Re-intro Hangman. 8-Web x-over. 10-Contains Crusaders trading card. 4-Origin. Netzer(Nasser) c(p)-11,14-17	2.50
Annual 1 (1992, $2.50, 68 pgs.)-Contains Impact trading card; Shield back-up	

	GD2.0	FN6.0	VF8.0	NM9.4
story				2.50

COMET MAN, THE (Movie)
Marvel Comics Group: Feb, 1987 - No. 6, July, 1987 (limited series)

1-6: 3-Hulk app. 4-She-Hulk shower scene c/s. Fantastic 4 app. 5-Fantastic 4 app.	2.50

NOTE: *Kelley Jones a-1-6p.*

COMIC ALBUM (Also see Disney Comic Album)
Dell Publishing Co.: Mar-May, 1958 - No. 18, June-Aug, 1962

1-Donald Duck	8	24	56	100
2-Bugs Bunny	4	12	30	50
3-Donald Duck	6	18	42	80
4-6,8-10: 4-Tom & Jerry. 5-Woody Woodpecker. 6,10-Bugs Bunny. 8-Tom & Jerry. 9-Woody Woodpecker	4	12	26	40
7,11,15: Popeye. 11-(9-11/60)	4	12	30	50
12-14: 12-Tom & Jerry. 13-Woody Woodpecker. 14-Bugs Bunny	4	12	26	40
16-Flintstones (12-2/61-62)-3rd app. Early Cave Kids app.	7	21	49	90
17-Space Mouse (3rd app.)	4	12	30	50
18-Three Stooges; photo-c	7	21	49	90

COMIC BOOK
Marvel Comics-#1/Dark Horse Comics-#2: 1995 ($5.95, oversize)

1-Spumco characters by John K.	1	3	5	7
2-(Dark Horse)				6.00

COMIC CAPERS
Red Circle Mag./Marvel Comics: Fall, 1944 - No. 6, Summer, 1946

1-Super Rabbit, The Creeper, Silly Seal, Ziggy Pig, Sharpy Fox begin	26	78	139	240
2	14	42	72	120
3-6	11	33	55	95

COMIC CAVALCADE
All-American/National Periodical Publications: Winter, 1942-43 - No. 63, June-July, 1954 (Contents change with No. 30, Dec-Jan, 1948-49 on)

1-The Flash, Green Lantern, Wonder Woman, Wildcat, The Black Pirate by Moldoff (also #2), Ghost Patrol, and Red White & Blue begin; Scribbly app.; Minute Movie	1833	5500	5500	11,000
2-Mutt & Jeff begin; last Ghost Patrol & Black Pirate; Minute Movies	236	708	1477	2600
3-Hop Harrigan & Sargon, the Sorcerer begin; The King app.	164	492	1023	1800
4,5: 4-The Gay Ghost, The King, Scribbly, & Red Tornado app. 5-Christmas-c. 5-Prints ad for Jr. JSA membership kit that includes "The Minute Man Answers The Call"	145	435	909	1600
6-10: 7-Red Tornado & Black Pirate app.; last Scribbly. 9-Fat & Slat app. X-Mas-c	109	327	682	1200
11,12,14,16-20: 12-Last Red White & Blue. 19-Christmas-c	91	273	568	1000
13-Solomon Grundy app.; X-Mas-c	150	450	938	1650
15-Johnny Peril begins (1st app.,6-7/46), ends #29 (See Danger Trail & Sensation Mystery)	100	300	625	1100
21-23: 23-Harry Lampert-c (Toth swipes)	84	253	525	925
25-28: 25-Black Canary app.; X-Mas-c. 26-28-Johnny Peril app. 28-Last Mutt & Jeff	75	225	469	825
29-(10-11/48)-Last Flash, Wonder Woman, Green Lantern & Johnny Peril; Wonder Woman invents "Thinking Machine"; 2nd computer in comics (after Flash Comics #52); Leave it to Binky story app.)	84	253	525	925
30-(12-1/48-49)-The Fox & the Crow, Dodo & the Frog & Nutsy Squirrel begin	40	120	232	400
31-35	24	72	127	215
36-49	17	51	88	150
50-62(Scarce)	21	63	110	185
63(Rare)	34	102	179	310

NOTE: *Grossman a-30-63. E.E. Hibbard c-(Flash only)-1-4, 7-14, 16-19, 21. Sheldon Mayer a(2-3)-40-63. Moulson c(G.L.)-7, 15. Nodell c(G.L.)-3, 19, 24. H.G. Peter c(W. Woman only)-1, 3-21, 24. Post a-31, 36. Purcell c(G.L.)-2-5, 10. Reinman a(Green Lantern)-4-6, 8, 9, 13, 15-21; c(Gr. Lantern)-6, 8, 19. Toth a(Green Lantern)-26-28; c-27. Atom app.-22, 23.*

The Comics #8 © DELL

Comics Greatest World: X © DH

Comics Greatest World: X © DH

Comics on Parade #57 © UFS

	GD2.0	FN6.0	VF8.0	NM9.4

	GD2.0	FN6.0	VF8.0	NM9.4

COMIC COMICS
Fawcett Publications: Apr, 1946 - No. 10, Feb, 1947

1-Captain Kid; Nutty Comics #1 in indicia	14	42	72	120
2-10-Wolverton-a, 4 pgs. each. 5-Captain Kidd app. Mystic Moot by				
Wolverton in #2-10?	15	45	77	130

COMIC CUTS (Also see The Funnies)
H. L. Baker Co., Inc.: 5/19/34 - 7/28/34 (5¢, 24 pgs.) (Tabloid size in full color)
(Not reprints; published weekly; created for newsstand sale)

V1#1 - V1#7(6/30/34), V1#8(7/14/34), V1#9(7/28/34)-Idle Jack strips				
	11	33	55	90

COMIC LAND
Fact and Fiction Publ.: March, 1946

1-Sandusky & the Senator, Sam Stupor, Sleuth, Marvin the Great, Sir Passer,				
Phineas Gruff app.; Irv Tirman & Perry Williams art				
	15	45	77	130

COMICO CHRISTMAS SPECIAL
Comico: Dec, 1988 ($2.50, 44pgs.)

1-Rude/Williamson-a; Dave Stevens-c				4.00

COMICO COLLECTION (Also see Grendel)
Comico: 1987 ($9.95, slipcased collection)

nn-Contains exclusive Grendel: Devil's Vagary, 9 random Comico comics, a				
poster and newsletter in black slipcase w/silver ink				25.00

COMICO PRIMER (See Primer)

COMIC PAGES (Formerly Funny Picture Stories)
Centaur Publications: V3#4, July, 1939 - V3#6, Dec, 1939

V3#4-Bob Wood-a	55	165	341	600
5,6: 6-Schwab-c	43	129	257	450

COMICS (See All Good)

COMICS, THE
Dell Publ. Co.: Mar, 1937 - No. 11, Nov, 1938 (Newspaper strip-r; bi-monthly)

1-1st app. Tom Mix in comics; Wash Tubbs, Tom Beatty, Myra North, Arizona				
Kid, Erik Noble & International Spy w/Doctor Doom begin				
	182	546	1136	2000
2	82	245	511	900
3-11: 3-Alley Oop begins	68	205	426	750

COMICS AND STORIES (See Walt Disney's Comics and Stories)

COMICS & STORIES (Also see Wolf & Red)
Dark Horse Comics: Apr, 1996 - No. 4, July, 1996 ($2.95, limited series)
(Created by Tex Avery)

1-4: Wolf & Red app; reads Comics and Stories on-c. 1-Terry Moore-a. 2-Reed				
Waller-a.				3.00

COMICS CALENDAR, THE (The 1946...)
True Comics Press (ordered through the mail): 1946 (25¢, 116 pgs.)
(Stapled at top)

nn-(Rare) Has a "strip" story for every day of the year in color				
	40	120	232	400

COMICS DIGEST (Pocket size)
Parents' Magazine Institute: Winter, 1942-43 (B&W, 100 pgs)

1-Reprints from True Comics (non-fiction World War II stories)				
	10	30	55	80

COMICS EXPRESS
Eclipse Comics: Nov, 1989 - No. 2, Jan, 1990 ($2.95, B&W, 68pgs.)

1,2: Collection of strip-r; 2(12/89-c, 1/90 inside)				3.00

COMICS FOR KIDS
London Publ. Co./Timely: 1945 (no month); No. 2, Sum, 1945 (Funny animal)

1,2-Puffy Pig, Sharpy Fox	15	45	77	130

COMICS' GREATEST WORLD
Dark Horse Comics: Jun, 1993 - V4#4, Sept, 1993 ($1.00, weekly, lim. series)

Arcadia (Wk 1): V1#1,2,4: 1-X: Frank Miller-c. 2-Pit Bulls. 4-Monster.				2.25
1-B&W Press Proof Edition (1500 copies)	1	4	7	10
1-Silver-c; distr. retailer bonus w/print & cards	1	3	6	8

3-Ghost, Dorman-c; Hughes-a				4.00
Retailer's Prem. Emb. Silver Foil Logo-r/V1#1-4	1	4	7	10

Golden City (Wk 2): V2#1-4: 1-Rebel; Ordway-c. 2-Mecha; Dave Johnson-c.

3-Titan; Walt Simonson-c. 4-Catalyst; Perez-c.				2.25
1-Gold-c; distr. retailer bonus w/print & cards.				6.00
Retailer's Prem. Embos. Gold Foil Logo-r/V2#1-4	1	3	6	8

Steel Harbor (Week 3): V3#1-Barb Wire; Dorman-c; Gulacy-a(p)

				4.00
2-4: 2-The Machine. 3-Wolfgang. 4-Motorhead				2.25
1-Silver-c; distr. retailer bonus w/print & cards	1	3	6	8
Retailer's Prem. Emb. Red Foil Logo-r/V3#1-4.	1	4	7	10

Vortex (Week 4): V4#1-4: 1-Division 13; Dorman-c. 2-Hero Zero; Art Adams-c.

3-King Tiger; Chadwick-a(p); Darrow-c. 4-Vortex; Miller-c.				2.25
1-Gold-c; distr. retailer bonus w/print & cards.				6.00
Retailer's Prem. Emb. Blue Foil Logo-r/V4#1-4.	1	3	6	8

COMICS' GREATEST WORLD: OUT OF THE VORTEX (See Out of The Vortex)

COMICS HITS (See Harvey Comics Hits)

COMICS MAGAZINE, THE (...Funny Pages #3)(Funny Pages #6 on)
Comics Magazine Co. (1st Comics Mag./Centaur Publ.): May, 1936 - No. 5, Sept, 1936 (Paper covers)

1-1st app. Dr. Mystic (a.k.a. Dr. Occult) by Siegel & Shuster (the 1st app. of a				
Superman prototype in comics). Dr. Mystic is not in costume but later				
appears in costume as a more pronounced prototype in More Fun #14-17.				
(1st episode of "The Koth and the Seven"; continues in More Fun #14;				
originally scheduled for publication at DC). 1 pg. Kelly-a; Sheldon Mayer-a				
	1350	4050	11,000	–
2-Federal Agent (a.k.a. Federal Men) by Siegel & Shuster; 1 pg. Kelly-a				
	275	825	1500	2400
3-5	225	675	1200	2000

COMICS NOVEL (Anarcho, Dictator of Death)
Fawcett Publications: 1947

1-All Radar; 51 pg anti-fascism story	31	93	165	285

COMICS ON PARADE (No. 30 on are a continuation of Single Series)
United Features Syndicate: Apr, 1938 - No. 104, Feb, 1955

1-Tarzan by Foster; Captain & the Kids, Little Mary Mixup, Abbie & Slats, Ella				
Cinders, Broncho Bill, Li'l Abner app.	350	1050	2188	4200
2 (Tarzan & others app. on-c of #1-3,17)	127	381	795	1400
3	100	300	625	1100
4,5	75	225	469	825
6-10	55	165	330	575
11-16,18-20	43	129	257	450
17-Tarzan-c	50	150	300	525
21-29: 22-Son of Tarzan begins. 22,24,28-Tailspin Tommy-c. 29-Last Tarzan				
issue	39	117	208	360
30-Li'l Abner	24	72	127	215
31-The Captain & the Kids	17	51	88	150
32-Nancy & Fritzi Ritz	14	42	72	125
33,36,39,42-Li'l Abner	20	60	105	175
34,37,40-The Captain & the Kids (10/41,6/42,3/43)	17	51	88	150
35,38-Nancy & Fritzi Ritz. 38-Infinity-c	14	42	72	125
41-Nancy & Fritzi Ritz	11	33	55	90
43-The Captain & the Kids	17	51	88	150
44 (3/44),47,50: Nancy & Fritzi Ritz	11	33	55	90
45-Li'l Abner	17	51	88	150
46,49-The Captain & the Kids	14	42	72	120
48-Li'l Abner (3/45)	17	51	88	150
51,54-Li'l Abner	14	42	72	120
52-The Captain & the Kids (3/46)	11	33	55	80
53,55,57-Nancy & Fritzi Ritz	11	33	55	80
56-The Captain & the Kids (r/Sparkler)	11	33	55	80
58-Li'l Abner; continues as Li'l Abner #61?	14	42	72	120
59-The Captain & the Kids	8	24	42	60
60-70-Nancy & Fritzi Ritz	7	21	38	55
71-99,101-104-Nancy & Sluggo: 71-76-Nancy only	6	18	33	48
100-Nancy & Sluggo	8	24	42	60
Special Issue, 7/46; Summer, 1948 - The Captain & the Kids app.				
	6	18	33	48

NOTE: Bound Volume (Very Rare) includes No. 1-12; bound by publisher in pictorial comic boards & distributed at the 1939 World's Fair and through mail order from ads in comic books

Commander Battle and the Atomic Sub #7 © ACG

Conan Classic #5 © Conan Properties

Conan Saga #45 © Conan Properties

	GD2.0	FN6.0	VF8.0	NM9.4

(also see Tip Top) 255 765 1591 2800
NOTE: Li'l Abner reprinted from Tip Top.

COMICS READING LIBRARIES (See the Promotional Comics section)

COMICS REVUE
St. John Publ. Co. (United Features Synd.): June, 1947 - No. 5, Jan, 1948

1-Ella Cinders & Blackie	11	33	55	90
2,4: 2-Hap Hopper (7/47). 4-Ella Cinders (9/47)	8	24	45	65
3,5: 3-Iron Vic (8/47). 5-Gordo No. 1 (1/48)	8	24	42	60

COMIC STORY PAINT BOOK
Samuel Lowe Co.: 1943 (Large size, 68 pgs.)

1055-Captain Marvel & a Captain Marvel Jr. story to read & color; 3 panels in color per pg. (reprints) 75 225 469 825

COMIX BOOK
Marvel Comics Group/Krupp Comics Works No. 4,5: 1974 - No. 5, 1976 ($1.00, B&W, magazine)

1-Underground comic artists; 2 pgs. Wolverton-a	3	9	17	25
2,3: 2-Wolverton-a (1 pg.)	2	6	15	22
4(2/76), 4(5/76), 5 (Low distribution)	3	9	17	24
NOTE: Print run No. 1-3: 200-250M; No. 4&5: 10M each.

COMIX INTERNATIONAL
Warren Magazines: Jul, 1974 - No. 5, Spring, 1977 (Full color, stiff-c, mail only)

1-Low distribution; all Corben story remainders from Warren; Corben-c on all		8	24	56	90
2,4: 2-Two Dracula stories; Wood, Wrightson-r; Crandall-a; Maroto-a.				
4-Printing w/ 3 Corben sty	3	10	23	35
3-5: 3-Dax story. 4-(printing without Corben story). 4-Crandall-a. 4,5-Vampirella				
stories. 5-Spirit story; Eisner-a	3	9	20	30
NOTE: No. 4 had two printings with extra Corben story in one. No. 3 may also have a variation. No. 3 has two Jeff Jones reprints from Vampirella.

COMMANDER BATTLE AND THE ATOMIC SUB
Amer. Comics Group (Titan Publ. Co.): Jul-Aug, 1954 - No. 7, Aug-Sep, 1955

1 (3-D effect)-Moldoff flying saucer-c	47	140	286	500
2,4-7: 2-Moldoff-c. 4-(1-2/55)-Last pre-code; Landau-a. 5-3-D effect story				
(2 pgs.). 6,7-Landau-a. 7-Flying saucer-c	33	99	174	300
3-H-Bomb-c; Atomic Sub becomes Atomic Spaceship				
	34	102	179	310

COMMANDO ADVENTURES
Atlas Comics (MMC): June, 1957 - No. 2, Aug, 1957

1-Severin-c	12	36	61	100
2-Severin-c; Drucker-a?	10	30	55	80

COMMANDO YANK (See The Mighty Midget Comics & Wow Comics)

COMPLETE BOOK OF COMICS AND FUNNIES
William H. Wise & Co.: 1944 (25¢, one-shot, 196 pgs.)

1-Origin Brad Spencer, Wonderman; The Magnet, The Silver Knight by Kinstler, & Zudo the Jungle Boy app. 40 120 232 400

COMPLETE BOOK OF TRUE CRIME COMICS
William H. Wise & Co.: No date (Mid 1940's) (25¢, 132 pgs.)

nn-Contains Crime Does Not Pay rebound (includes #22)
109 327 682 1200

COMPLETE COMICS (Formerly Amazing Comics No. 1)
Timely Comics (EPC): No. 2, Winter, 1944-45

2-The Destroyer, The Whizzer, The Young Allies & Sergeant Dix; Schomburg-c 150 450 938 1650

COMPLETE GUIDE TO THE DEADLY ARTS OF KUNG FU AND KARATE
Marvel Comics: 1974 (68 pgs., B&W magazine)

V1#1-Bruce Lee-c and 5 pg. story (scarce) 4 12 26 40

COMPLETE LOVE MAGAZINE (Formerly a pulp with same title)
Ace Periodicals (Periodical House): V26#2, May-June, 1951 - V32#4(#191), Sept, 1956

V26#2-Painted-c (52 pgs.)	6	18	32	45
V26#3-6(2/52), V27#1(4/52)-6(1/53)	5	15	24	32
V28#1(3/53), V28#2(5/53), V29#3(7/53)-6(12/53)	4	13	19	26
V30#1(2/54), V30#1(#176, 4/54),2,4-6(#181, 1/55)	4	13	19	26

V30#3(#178)-Rock Hudson photo-c	5	15	24	32
V31#1(#182, 3/55)-Last precode	4	13	19	26
V31#2(5/55)-6(#187, 1/56)	4	11	17	22
V32#1(#188, 3/56)-4(#191, 9/56)	4	11	17	22
NOTE: (34 total issues). Photo-c V27#5-on. Painted-c V26#3.

COMPLETE MYSTERY (True Complete Mystery No. 5 on)
Marvel Comics (PrPI): Aug, 1948 - No. 4, Feb, 1949 (Full length stories)

1-Seven Dead Men	45	135	270	475
2-4: 2-Jigsaw of Doom! 3-Fear in the Night; Burgos-c/a (28 pgs.). 4-A Squealer				
Dies Fast	40	120	220	380

COMPLETE ROMANCE
Avon Periodicals: 1949

1-(Scarce)-Reprinted as Women to Love 40 120 220 380

CONAN (See Chamber of Darkness #4, Giant-Size..., Handbook of..., King Conan, Marvel Graphic Novel #19, 28, Marvel Treasury Ed., Power Record Comics, Robert E. Howard's.., Savage Sword of Conan, and Savage Tales)

CONAN: (Title Series): Marvel Comics

CONAN, 8/95 - No. 11, 6/96 ($2.95), 1-11: 4-Malibu Comic's Rune app. 3.00

...CLASSIC, 6/94 - No. 11, 4/95 ($1.50), 1-11: 1-r/Conan #1 by B. Smith, r/covers w/changes. 2-11-r/Conan #2-11 by Smith. 2-Bound w/cover to Conan The Adventurer 2.25

...DEATH COVERED IN GOLD, 9/99 - No. 3, 11/99 ($2.99), 1-3-Roy Thomas-s/John Buscema-a 3.00

...FLAME AND THE FIEND, 8/00 - No. 3, 10/00 ($2.99), 1-3-Thomas-s 3.00

...RETURN OF STYRM, 9/98 - No. 3, 11/98 ($2.99), 1-3-Parente & Soresina-a; painted-c 3.00

...RIVER OF BLOOD, 6/98 - No. 3, 8/98 ($2.50), 1-3 2.50

...SCARLET SWORD, 12/98 - No. 3, 2/99 ($2.99), 1-3-Thomas-s/Raffaele-a
3.00

CONAN SAGA, THE
Marvel Comics: June, 1987 - No. 97, Apr, 1995 ($2.00/$2.25, B&W, magazine)

1-Barry Smith-r; new Smith-c	6.00
2-27: 2-9,11-new Barry Smith-c. 13,15-Boris-c. 17-Adams-r.18,25-Chaykin-r.	
22-r/Giant-Size Conan 1,2	4.00
28-97: 28-Begin $2.25-c. 31-Red Sonja-r by N. Adams/SSOC #1; 1 pg. Jeff	
Jones-r. 32-Newspaper strip-r begin by Buscema. 33-Smith/Conrad-a.	
39-r/Kull #1('71) by Andru/Wood. 44-Swipes-c/Savage Tales #1.	
57-Brunner-r/SSOC #30. 66-r/Conan Annual #2 by Buscema. 79-r/Conan	
#43-45 w/Red Sonja. 85-Based on Conan #57-63	3.00
NOTE: J. Buscema r-32-on; c-86. Chaykin r-34. Chiodo painted c-63, 65, 66, 82. G. Colan a-47p. Jusko painted c-64, 83. Kaluta c-84. Nino a-37. Ploog a-50. N. Redondo painted c-48, 50, 51, 53, 57, 62. Simonson r-50-54, 56. B. Smith r-51. Starlin c-34. Williamson r-50i.

CONAN THE ADVENTURER
Marvel Comics: June, 1994 - No. 14, July, 1995 ($1.50)

1-($2.50)-Embossed foil-c; Kayaran-a	3.00
2-14	2.50
2-Contents are Conan Classics #2 by mistake	2.50

CONAN THE BARBARIAN
Marvel Comics: Oct, 1970 - No. 275, Dec, 1993

1-Origin/1st app. Conan (in comics) by Barry Smith; 1st app. Kull (cameo);				
#1-9 are 15¢ issues	24	72	168	300
2	8	24	60	100
3-(Low distribution in some areas)	14	42	102	175
4,5	6	18	42	70
6-9: 8-Hidden panel message, pg. 14. 9-Last 15¢-c	4	12	30	50
10,11 (25¢ 52 pg. giants): 10-Black Knight-r; Kull story by Severin				
	6	18	40	65
12,13: 12-Wrightson-c(i)	4	12	26	40
14,15-Elric app.	4	12	30	50
16,19,20: 16-Conan-r/Savage Tales #1	3	10	23	35
17,18-No Barry Smith-a	2	6	13	20
21,22: 22-Has reprint from #1	4	12	26	40
23-1st app. Red Sonja (2/73)	3	10	23	35
24-1st full Red Sonja story; last Smith-a	3	10	23	35
25-John Buscema-c/a begins	2	6	11	15

Conan The Barbarian #150
© Conan Properties

Concrete: Eclectica #1
© Paul Chadwick

Confessions of Love #14 © STAR

	GD2.0	FN6.0	VF8.0	NM9.4

26-30	2	6	9	12
31-36,38-40	1	3	6	9
37-Neal Adams-c/a; last 20¢ issue; contains pull-out subscription form				
	2	6	11	16
41-43,46-50: 48-Origin retold	1	3	5	7
44,45-N. Adams-i(Crusty Bunkers). 45-Adams-c	1	4	7	10
51-57,59,60: 59-Origin Belit				5.00
58-2nd Belit app. (see Giant-Size Conan #1)				6.00
61-65-(Regular 25¢ editions)(4-8/76)				4.00
61-65-(30¢-c variants, limited distribution)				6.00
66-99: 68-Red Sonja story cont'd from Marvel Feature #7. 75-79-(Reg. 30¢-c).				
84-Intro. Zula. 85-Origin Zula. 87-r/Savage Sword of Conan #3 in color				3.50
75-79-(35¢-c variants, limited distribution)				6.00
100-(52 pg. Giant)-Death of Belit				5.00
101-114,116-199,201-231,233-249: 116-r/Power Record Comic PR31.				
244-Return of Zula				2.25
115-Double size				3.00
200,232: 200-(52 pgs.). 232-Young Conan storyline begins; Conan is born				4.00
250-(60 pgs.)				3.00
251-274: 262-Adapted from R.E. Howard story				2.50
275-($2.50, 68 pgs.)-Final issue; painted-c				4.00
King Size 1(1973, 35¢)-Smith-r/#2,4; Smith-c	2	6	12	18
Annual 2(1976, 50¢)-New full length story	1	3	6	8
Annual 3,4: 3('78)-Chaykin/N. Adams-r/SSOC #2. 4('78)-New full length story				
	1	3	5	7
Annual 5,6: 5(1979)-New full length Buscema story & part-c, 6(1981)-Kane-c/a				
				4.00
Annual 7-12: 7('82)-Based on novel "Conan of the Isles" (new-a). 8(1984).				
9(1984). 10(1986). 11(1986). 12(1987)				3.00
Special Edition 1 (Red Nails)				4.00

NOTE: *Arthur Adams* c-248, 249. *Neal Adams* a-116r(i); c-49i. *Austin* a-125, 126; c-125i, 126i. *Brunner* c-17i. c-40. *Buscema* a-25-36p, 38, 39, 41-56p, 58-63p, 65-67p, 68, 70-78p, 84-86p, 88-91p, 93-126p, 136p, 140, 141-144p, 146-158p, 159, 161, 162, 163p, 165-185p, 187-190p, Annual 2(3pgs.), 3-5p, 7p; c(p)-26, 36, 44, 46, 52, 56, 58, 59, 64, 65, 72, 78-80, 83-91, 93-103, 105-126, 136-151, 155-159, 161, 162, 168, 169, 171, 172, 174, 175, 178-185, 188, 189, Annual 4, 5, 7. *Chaykin* a-79-83i. *Golden* c-152. *Kaluta* c-16? *Gil Kane* a-12p, 17p, 18p, 127-130, 131-134p; c-12p, 17p, 18p, 23, 25-27,32-34, 35, 36, 38, 39, 41-43, 45-51, 53-55, 57, 60-63, 65-71, 73p, 76p, 127-134. *Jim Lee* c-242. *McFarlane* c-241p. *Ploog* a-57. *Russell* a-21; c-251i. *Simonson* c-135. *B. Smith* a-1-11p, 12, 13-15p, 16, 19-21, 23, 24; c-1-11, 13-16, 19-24p. *Starlin* a-64. *Wood* a-47r. Issue Nos. 3-5, 7-9, 11, 16-18, 21, 23, 25, 27-30, 35, 37, 38, 42, 45, 52, 57, 58, 65, 69-71, 73, 79-83, 99, 100, 104, 114, Annual 2 have original Robert E. Howard stories adapted. Issues #32-34 adapted from Norvell Page's novel *Flame Winds*.

CONAN THE BARBARIAN (Volume 2)
Marvel Comics: July, 1997 - No. 3, Oct, 1997 ($2.50, limited series)
1-3-Castellini-a				2.50

CONAN THE BARBARIAN MOVIE SPECIAL (Movie)
Marvel Comics Group: Oct, 1982 - No. 2, Nov, 1982
1,2-Movie adaptation; Buscema-a				3.00

CONAN THE BARBARIAN: THE USURPER
Marvel Comics: Dec, 1997 - No. 3, Feb, 1998 ($2.50, limited series)
1-3-Dixon-s				2.50

CONAN THE DESTROYER (Movie)
Marvel Comics Group: Jan, 1985 - No. 2, Mar, 1985
1,2-r/Marvel Super Special				2.50

CONAN THE KING (Formerly King Conan)
Marvel Comics Group: No. 20, Jan, 1984 - No. 55, Nov, 1989
20-55				3.00
NOTE: *Kaluta* c-20-23, 24i, 26, 27, 30, 50, 52. *Williamson* a-37i; c-37i, 38i.

CONAN: THE LORD OF THE SPIDERS
Marvel Comics: Mar, 1998 - No. 3, May, 1998 ($2.50, limited series)
1-3-Roy Thomas-s/Raffaele-a				2.50

CONAN THE SAVAGE
Marvel Comics: Aug, 1995 - No. 10, May, 1996 ($2.95, B&W, Magazine)
1-10: 1-Bisley-c. 4-vs. Malibu Comic's Rune. 5,10-Brereton-c				3.00

CONAN VS. RUNE (Also See Conan #4)
Marvel Comics: Nov, 1995 ($2.95, one-shot)
1-Barry Smith-c/a/scripts				3.00

CONCRETE (Also see Dark Horse Presents & Within Our Reach)
Dark Horse Comics: March, 1987 - No. 10, Nov, 1988 ($1.50, B&W)
1-Paul Chadwick-c/a in all	1	4	7	10
1-2nd print				3.00
2				6.00
3-Origin				5.00
4-10				4.00
A New Life 1 (1989, $2.95, B&W)-r/#3,4 plus new-a (11 pgs.)				3.00
Celebrates Earth Day 1990 ($3.50, 52 pgs.)				6.00
Color Special 1 (2/89, $2.95, 44 pgs.)-r/1st two Concrete apps. from Dark				
Horse Presents #1,2 plus new-a				6.00
Land And Sea 1 (2/89, B&W)-r/#1,2				6.00
Odd Jobs 1 (7/90, $3.50)-r/5,6 plus new-a				3.50

CONCRETE: (Title series), Dark Horse Comics
--ECLECTICA, 4/93 - No. 2, 5/93 ($2.95) 1,2				3.00
--FRAGILE CREATURE, 6/91 - No. 4, 2/92 ($2.50) 1-4				3.00
--KILLER SMILE, (Legend), 7/94 - No. 4, 10/94 ($2.9) 1-4				3.00
--STRANGE ARMOR, 12/97 - No. 5, 5/98 ($2.95, color) 1-5-Chadwick-s/c/a; retells origin				3.00
--THINK LIKE A MOUNTAIN, (Legend), 3/96 - No. 6, 8/96 ($2.95)				
1-6: Chadwick-a/scripts & Darrow-c in all				3.00

CONDORMAN (Walt Disney)
Whitman Publishing: Oct, 1981 - No. 3, Jan, 1982
1-3: 1,2-Movie adaptation; photo-c	1	3	6	8

CONEHEADS
Marvel Comics: June, 1994 - No. 4, 1994 ($1.75, limited series)
1-4				2.50

CONFESSIONS ILLUSTRATED (Magazine)
E. C. Comics: Jan-Feb, 1956 - No. 2, Spring, 1956
1-Craig, Kamen, Wood, Orlando-a	17	51	88	150
2-Craig, Crandall, Kamen, Orlando-a	15	45	77	130

CONFESSIONS OF LOVE
Artful Publ.: Apr, 1950 - No. 2, July, 1950 (25¢, 7-1/4x5-1/4", 132 pgs.)
1-Bakerish-a	28	84	151	260
2-Art & text; Bakerish-a	16	48	83	140

CONFESSIONS OF LOVE (Formerly Startling Terror Tales #10; becomes Confessions of Romance No. 7 on)
Star Publications: No. 11, 7/52 - No. 14, 1/53; No. 4, 3/53- No. 6, 8/53
11-13: 12,13-Disbrow-a	16	48	83	140
14,5,6	12	36	61	100
4-Disbrow-a	13	39	66	110
NOTE: *All have L. B. Cole covers.*

CONFESSIONS OF ROMANCE (Formerly Confessions of Love)
Star Publications: No. 7, Nov, 1953 - No. 11, Nov, 1954
7	16	48	83	140
8	12	36	61	100
9-Wood-a	14	42	72	120
10,11-Disbrow-a	13	39	66	110
NOTE: *All have L. B. Cole covers.*

CONFESSIONS OF THE LOVELORN (Formerly Lovelorn)
American Comics Group (Regis Publ./Best Synd. Features): No. 52, Aug, 1954 - No. 114, June-July, 1960
52 (3-D effect)	29	87	153	265
53,55	9	27	49	70
54 (3-D effect)	29	87	153	265
56-Anti-communist propaganda story, 10 pgs; last pre-code (2/55)				
	11	33	55	90
57-90,100	6	18	29	40
91-Williamson-a	9	27	49	70
92-99,101-114	5	15	24	32
NOTE: *Whitney* a-most issues; c-52, 53. Painted c-106, 107.

CONFIDENTIAL DIARY (Formerly High School Confidential Diary; Three Nurses #18 on)
Charlton Comics: No. 12, May, 1962 - No. 17, Mar, 1963

Congo Bill ('99) #1 © DC

Coo Coo Comics #40 © STD

Cookie #5 © ACG

	GD2.0	FN6.0	VF8.0	NM9.4

	GD2.0	FN6.0	VF8.0	NM9.4

12-17 ... 2 6 13 20

CONGO BILL (See Action Comics & More Fun Comics #56)
National Periodical Publication: Aug-Sept, 1954 - No. 7, Aug-Sept, 1955

1 (Scarce)	125	375	1000	–
2,7 (Scarce)	100	300	800	–
3-6 (Scarce). 4-Last pre-code issue	75	225	600	–

NOTE: (Rarely found in fine to mint condition.) *Nick Cardy* c-1-7.

CONGO BILL
DC Comics (Vertigo): Oct, 1999 - No. 4, Jan, 2000 ($2.95, limited series)

1-4-Corben-c ... 3.00

CONGORILLA (Also see Actions Comics #224)
DC Comics: Nov, 1992 - No. 4, Feb, 1993 ($1.75, limited series)

1-4: 1,2-Brian Bolland-c ... 3.00

CONJURORS
DC Comics: Apr, 1999 - No. 3, Jun, 1999 ($2.95, limited series)

1-3-Elseworlds; Phantom Stranger app.; Barreto-c/a ... 3.00

CONNECTICUT YANKEE, A (See King Classics)

CONQUEROR, THE
Dell Publishing Co.: No., 690, Mar, 1956

Four Color 690-Movie, John Wayne photo-c ... 17 51 119 220

CONQUEROR COMICS
Albrecht Publishing Co.: Winter, 1945

nn ... 20 60 105 180

CONQUEROR OF THE BARREN EARTH (See The Warlord #63)
DC Comics: Feb, 1985 - No. 4, May, 1985 (Limited series)

1-4: Back-up series from Warlord ... 2.50

CONQUEST
Store Comics: 1953 (6¢)

1-Richard the Lion Hearted, Beowulf, Swamp Fox ... 6 18 29 40

CONQUEST
Famous Funnies: Spring, 1955

1-Crandall-a, 1 pg.; contains contents of 1953 ish. ... 4 11 17 22

CONSPIRACY
Marvel Comics: Feb, 1998 - No. 2, Mar, 1998 ($2.99, limited series)

1,2-Painted art by Korday/Abnett-s ... 3.00

CONSTRUCT
Caliber (New Worlds): 1996 - No. 6, 1997 ($2.95, B&W)

1-6: Paul Jenkins scripts ... 3.00

CONTACT COMICS
Aviation Press: July, 1944 - No. 12, May, 1946

nn-Black Venus, Flamingo, Golden Eagle, Tommy Tomahawk begin	50	150	300	525
2-5: 3-Last Flamingo. 3,4-Black Venus by L. B. Cole. 5-The Phantom Flyer app.	40	120	220	380
6,11-Kurtzman's Black Venus; 11-Last Golden Eagle, last Tommy Tomahawk; Feldstein-a	43	129	257	450
7-10	39	117	208	360
12-Sky Rangers, Air Kids, Ace Diamond app.; L.B. Cole sci-fi cover	73	219	455	800

NOTE: *L. B. Cole* a-3, 9; c-1-12. *Giunta* a-3. *Hollingsworth* a-5, 7, 10. *Palais* a-11, 12.

CONTEMPORARY MOTIVATORS
Pendelum Press: 1977 - 1978 ($1.45, 5-3/8x8", 31 pgs., B&W)

14-3002 The Caine Mutiny; 14-3010 Banner in the Sky; 14-3029 God Is My
Co-Pilot; 14-3037 Guadalcanal Diary; 14-3045 Hiroshima; 14-3053 Hot Rod;
14-3061 Just Dial a Number; 14-3088 The Diary of Anne Frank; 14-3096
Lost Horizon ... 1 3 6 8

NOTE: Also see Pendulum Illustrated Classics. Above may have been distributed the same.

CONTEST OF CHAMPIONS (See Marvel Super-Hero...)

CONTEST OF CHAMPIONS II
Marvel Comics: Sept, 1999 - No. 5 ($2.50, limited series)

1-5-Claremont-s/Jimenez-a ... 2.50

CONTRACTORS
Eclipse Comics: June, 1987 ($2.00, B&W, one-shot)

1-Funny animal ... 2.25

CONTRACT WITH GOD, A
Baronet Publishing Co./Kitchen Sink Press: 1978 ($7.95, B&W, graphic novel)

nn-Will Eisner-s/a	2	6	12	18
Reprint (DC Comics, 2000, $12.95)				13.00

CONVOCATIONS: A MAGIC THE GATHERING GALLERY
Acclaim Comics (Armada): Jan, 1996 ($2.50, one-shot)

1-pin-ups by various artists including Kaluta, Vess, and Dringenberg ... 2.50

COO COO COMICS (...the Bird Brain No. 57 on)
Nedor Publ. Co./Standard (Animated Cartoons): Oct, 1942 - No. 62, Apr, 1952

1-Origin/1st app. Super Mouse & begin series (cloned from Superman); the first funny animal super hero series (see Looney Tunes #5 for 1st funny animal super hero)	31	93	165	285
2	14	42	72	120
3-10: 10-(3/44)	9	27	49	70
11-33: 33-1 pg. Ingels-a	7	21	36	50
34-40,43-46,48-Text illos by Frazetta in all. 36-Super Mouse covers begin	10	30	55	85
41-Frazetta-a (6-pg. story & 3 text illos)	19	57	99	165
42,47-Frazetta-a & text illos.	14	42	72	120
49-(1/50)-3-D effect story; Frazetta text illo	11	33	55	90
50,51-3-D effect-c only. 50-Frazetta text illo	10	30	55	85
52-62: 56-Last Supermouse?	6	18	29	40

"COOKIE" (Also see Topsy-Turvy)
Michel Publ./American Comics Group(Regis Publ.): Apr, 1946 - No. 55, Aug-Sept, 1955

1-Teen-age humor	21	63	110	185
2	11	33	55	90
3-10	8	24	42	60
11-20	6	18	33	48
21-23,26,28-30	5	15	25	35
24,25,27-Starlett O'Hara stories	6	18	29	40
31-34,37-50,52-55	5	15	24	32
35,36-Starlett O'Hara stories	5	15	25	35
51-(10-11/54) 8pg. TrueVision 3-D effect story	9	27	49	70

COOL CAT (Formerly Black Magic)
Prize Publications: V8#6, Mar-Apr, 1962 - V9#2, July-Aug, 1962

V8#6, nn(V9#1, 5-6/62), V9#2 ... 3 9 20 30

COOL WORLD (Movie)
DC Comics: Apr, 1992 - No. 4, Sept, 1992 ($1.75, limited series)

1-4: Prequel to animated/live action movie by Ralph Bakshi. 1-Bakshi-c. Bill Wray inks in all				2.25
Movie Adaptation nn ('92, $3.50, 68pg.)-Bakshi-c				3.50

COPPER CANYON (See Fawcett Movie Comics)

COPS (TV)
DC Comics: Aug, 1988 - No. 15, Aug, 1989 ($1.00)

1 ($1.50, 52 pgs.)-Based on Hasbro Toys				3.00
2-15: 14-Orlando-c(p)				2.25

COPS: THE JOB
Marvel Comics: June, 1992 - No. 4, Sept, 1992 ($1.25, limited series)

1-4: All have Jusko scripts & Golden-c ... 2.25

CORBEN SPECIAL, A
Pacific Comics: May, 1984 (one-shot)

1-Corben-c/a; E.A. Poe adaptation ... 5.00

CORKY & WHITE SHADOW (Disney, TV)
Dell Publishing Co.: No. 707, May, 1956 (Mickey Mouse Club)

Four Color 707-Photo-c ... 7 21 49 90

CORLISS ARCHER (See Meet Corliss Archer)

CORMAC MAC ART (Robert E. Howard's...)
Dark Horse Comics: 1990 - No. 4, 1990 ($1.95, B&W, mini-series)

Cosmic Odyssey #2 © DC

Countdown #1 © DC

Coven #2 © Awesome Ent.

	GD2.0	FN6.0	VF8.0	NM9.4

1-4: All have Bolton painted-c; Howard adapts. — 3.00

CORNY'S FETISH
Dark Horse Comics: Apr, 1998 ($4.95, B&W, one-shot)
1-Renée French-s/a; Bolland-c — 5.00

CORPORAL RUSTY DUGAN (See Holyoke One-Shot #2)

CORPSES OF DR. SACOTTI, THE (See Ideal a Classical Comic)

CORSAIR, THE (See A-1 Comics No. 5, 7, 10 under Texas Slim)

CORTEZ AND THE FALL OF THE AZTECS
Tome Press: 1993 ($2.95, B&W, limited series)
1,2 — 3.00

CORUM: THE BULL AND THE SPEAR (See Chronicles Of Corum)
First Comics: Jan, 1989 - No. 4, July, 1989 ($1.95)
1-4: Adapts Michael Moorcock's novel — 2.50

COSMIC BOOK, THE
Ace Comics: Dec, 1986 - No. 1, 1987 ($1.95)
1,2: 1-(44pgs.)-Wood, Toth-a. 2-(B&W) — 2.25

COSMIC BOY (Also see The Legion of Super-Heroes)
DC Comics: Dec, 1986 - No. 4, Mar, 1987 (limited series)
1-4: Legends tie-ins all issues — 2.50

COSMIC HEROES
Eternity/Malibu Graphics: Oct, 1988 - No. 11, Dec, 1989 ($1.95, B&W)
1-11: Reprints 1934-1936's Buck Rogers newspaper strips #1-728 — 2.00

COSMIC ODYSSEY
DC Comics: 1988 - No. 4, 1988 ($3.50, limited series, squarebound)
1-4: Reintro. New Gods into DC continuity; Superman, Batman, Green Lantern (John Stewart) app; Starlin scripts, Mignola-c/a in all. 2-Darkseid merges Demon & Jason Blood (separated in Demon limited series #4); John Stewart responsible for the death of a star system. — 5.00
Trade paperback-r/#1-4. — 20.00

COSMIC POWERS
Marvel Comics: Mar, 1994 - No. 6, Aug, 1994 ($2.50, limited series)
1-6: 1-Ron Lim-c/a(p). 1,2-Thanos app. 2-Terrax. 3-Ganymede & Jack of Hearts app. — 2.50

COSMIC POWERS UNLIMITED
Marvel Comics: May, 1995 - No. 5, May, 1996 ($3.95, quarterly)
1-5 — 4.00

COSMIC RAY
Image Comics: June, 1999 - No. 2 ($2.95, B&W)
1,2-Steven Blue-s/a — 3.00

COSMIC SLAM
Ultimate Sports Entertainment: 1999 ($3.95, one-shot)
1-McGwire, Sosa, Bagwell, Justice battle aliens; Sienkiewicz-c — 4.00

COSMO CAT (Becomes Sunny #11 on; also see All Top & Wotalife Comics)
Fox Features/Green Publ. Co./Norlen Mag.: July-Aug, 1946 - No. 10, Oct, 1947; 1957; 1959

1	29	87	153	265
2	15	45	77	130
3-Origin (11-12/46)	20	60	105	175
4-10: 4-Robot-c	10	30	55	80
2-4(1957-Green Publ. Co.)	5	15	25	35
2-4(1959-Norlen Mag.)	5	15	23	30
I.W. Reprint #1	2	6	12	18

COSMO THE MERRY MARTIAN
Archie Publications (Radio Comics): Sept, 1958 - No. 6, Oct, 1959

1-Bob White-a in all	15	45	77	130
2-6	10	30	55	85

COTTON WOODS
Dell Publishing Co.: No. 837, Sept, 1957

Four Color 837	4	12	25	38

COUGAR, THE (Cougar No. 2)

Seaboard Periodicals (Atlas): April, 1975 - No. 2, July, 1975
1,2: 1-Vampire; Adkins-a(p). 2-Cougar origin; werewolf-s; Buckler-c(p) — 6.00

COUNTDOWN (See Movie Classics)

COUNTDOWN
DC Comics (WildStorm): June, 2000 - No. 8, Jan, 2001 ($2.95)
1-8-Mariotte-s/Lopresti-a — 3.00

COUNT DUCKULA (TV)
Marvel Comics: Nov, 1988 - No. 15, Jan, 1991 ($1.00)
1-Dangermouse back-up — 6.00
2-15: 8-2,7,9-15: Dangermouse back-ups. 8-Geraldo Rivera photo-c/& app.; Sienkiewicz-a(i) — 5.00

COUNT OF MONTE CRISTO, THE
Dell Publishing Co.: No. 794, May, 1957

Four Color 794-Movie, Buscema-a	9	27	63	110

COURAGE COMICS
J. Edward Slavin: 1945

1,2,77	11	33	55	90

COURTSHIP OF EDDIE'S FATHER (TV)
Dell Publishing Co.: Jan, 1970 - No. 2, May, 1970

1-Bill Bixby photo-c on both	4	12	30	50
2	4	12	26	40

COVEN
Awesome Entertainment: Aug, 1997 - No. 5, Mar, 1998 ($2.50)

Preview	1	3	6	8
1-Loeb-s/Churchill-a; Churchill-c	1	3	6	8
1-Liefeld variant-c	1	3	5	7
1-Pollina variant-c	1	3	6	8
1-American Entertainment Ed.	1	3	6	8
1-American Entertainment Gold Ed.				10.00
1-Fan Appreciation Ed.(3/98); new Churchill-c				3.00
1-Fan Appreciation Gold Ed.				10.00
1+ :Includes B&W art from Kaboom	1	4	7	10
1+ :Gold Ed.				8.00
1+ :Red Foil cover				12.00
2-Regular-c w/leaping Fantom				6.00
2-Variant-c w/circle of candles	1	3	6	8
2-American Entertainment Gold Ed.				8.00
2-Dynamic Forces Gold Ed.				10.00
3-6-Contains flip book preview of ReGex				3.00
3-White variant-c	1	3	5	7
3,4: 3-Halloween wraparound-c. 4-Purple variant-c				3.00
4-Dynamic Forces Ed.				5.00
4,5-Dynamic Forces Gold Ed.	1	3	6	8
5-Dynamic Forces Ed.				4.00
...Black & White (9/98) Short stories				3.00
...Fantom Special (2/98) w/sketch pages				5.00
...Fantom Special Gold Ed.				10.00

COVEN
Awesome Entertainment: Jan, 1999 - Present ($2.50)
1-3: 1-Loeb-s/Churchill-a; 6 covers by various. 2-Supreme-c/app. 3-Flip book w/Kaboom preview — 2.50
... Dark Origins (7/99, 2.50) w/Lionheart gallery — 2.50

COVERED WAGONS, HO (Disney, TV)
Dell Publishing Co.: No. 814, June, 1957 (Donald Duck)

Four Color 814-Mickey Mouse app.	5	15	35	60

COWBOY ACTION (Formerly Western Thrillers No. 1-4; Becomes Quick-Trigger Western No. 12 on)
Atlas Comics (ACI): No. 5, March, 1955 - No. 11, March, 1956

5	14	42	72	120
6-10: 6-8-Heath-c	10	30	55	80
11-Williamson-a (4 pgs.); Baker-a	11	33	55	90

NOTE: Ayers a-8. Drucker a-6. Maneely c/a-5, 6. Severin c-10. Shores a-7.

COWBOY COMICS (Star Ranger #12, Stories #14)(Star Ranger Funnies #15)
Centaur Publishing Co.: No. 13, July, 1938 - No. 14, Aug, 1938

Cowgirl Romances #9 © FH

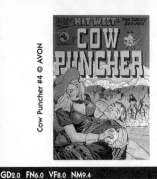

Cow Puncher #4 © AVON

Crackajack Funnies #3 © DELL

	GD2.0	FN6.0	VF8.0	NM9.4

13-(Rare)-Ace and Deuce, Lyin Lou, Air Patrol, Aces High, Lee Trent,
Trouble Hunters begin ... 123 369 769 1350
14-Filchock-c ... 84 253 525 925
NOTE: *Guardineer* a-13, 14. **Gustavson** a-13, 14.

COWBOY IN AFRICA (TV)
Gold Key: Mar, 1968
1(10219-803)-Chuck Connors photo-c ... 4 12 30 50

COWBOY LOVE (Becomes Range Busters?)
Fawcett Publications/Charlton Comics No. 28 on: 7/49 - V2#10, 6/50; No. 11, 1951; No. 28, 2/55 - No. 31, 8/55
V1#1-Rocky Lane photo back-c ... 20 60 105 175
2 ... 8 24 42 60
V1#3,4,6 (12/49) ... 7 21 36 50
5-Bill Boyd photo back-c (11/49) ... 8 24 45 65
V2#7-Williamson/Evans-a ... 10 30 55 80
V2#8-11 ... 6 18 29 40
V1#28 (Charlton)-Last precode (2/55) (Formerly Romantic Story?)
... 6 18 29 40
V1#29-31 (Charlton; becomes Sweetheart Diary #32 on)
... 5 15 25 35
NOTE: *Powell* a-10. *Marcus Swayze* a-2, 3. Photo c-1-11. No. 1-3, 5-7, 9, 10 are 52 pgs.

COWBOY ROMANCES (Young Men No. 4 on)
Marvel Comics (IPC): Oct, 1949 - No. 3, Mar, 1950 (All photo-c & 52 pgs.)
1-Photo-c ... 24 72 127 215
2-William Holden, Mona Freeman "Streets of Laredo" photo-c
... 16 48 83 140
3-Photo-c ... 14 42 72 120

COWBOYS 'N' INJUNS (...and Indians No. 6 on)
Com No. 1-5/Magazine Enterprises No. 6 on: 1946 - No. 5, 1947; No. 6, 1949 - No. 8, 1952
1 ... 12 36 61 105
2-5-All funny animal western ... 9 27 49 70
6(A-1 23)-Half violent, half funny; Ayers-a ... 10 30 55 85
7(A-1 41, 1950), 8(A-1 48)-All funny ... 8 24 42 60
I.W. Reprint No. 1,7 (Reprinted in Canada by Superior, No. 7)
... 2 6 12 18
Super Reprint No. 10 (1963) ... 2 6 12 18

COWBOY WESTERN COMICS (TV)(Formerly Jack In The Box; Becomes Space Western No. 40-45 & Wild Bill Hickok & Jingles No. 68 on; title:Cowboy Western Heroes No. 47 & 48; Cowboy Western No. 49 on)
Charlton (Capitol Stories): No. 17, 7/48 - No. 39, 8/52; No. 46, 10/53; No. 47, 12/53; No. 48, Spr, '54;
No. 49, 5-6/54 - No. 67, 3/58 (nn 40-45)
17-Jesse James, Annie Oakley, Wild Bill Hickok begin; Texas Rangers app.
... 20 60 105 175
18,19-Orlando-c/a. 18-Paul Bunyan begins. 19-Wyatt Earp story
... 12 36 61 100
20-25: 21-Buffalo Bill story. 22-Texas Rangers-c/story. 24-Joel McCrea photo-c & adaptation from movie "Three Faces West". 25-James Craig photo-c & adaptation from movie "Northwest Stampede" ... 10 30 55 85
26-George Montgomery photo-c and adaptation from movie "Indian Scout"; 1 pg. bio on Will Rogers ... 13 39 66 110
27-Sunset Carson photo-c and adaptation from movie "Sunset Carson Rides Again" plus 1 other Sunset Carson story ... 61 183 381 675
28-Sunset Carson line drawn-c; adapts movies "Battling Marshal" & "Fighting Mustangs" starring Sunset Carson ... 34 102 179 310
29-Sunset Carson line drawn-c; adapts movies "Rio Grande" with Sunset Carson & "Winchester '73" w/James Stewart plus 5 pg. life history of Sunset Carson featuring Tom Mix ... 34 102 179 310
30-Sunset Carson photo-c; adapts movie "Deadline" starring Sunset Carson plus 1 other Sunset Carson story ... 59 177 369 650
31-34,38,39,47-50 (no #40-45): 50-Golden Arrow, Rocky Lane & Blackjack (r?) stories ... 9 27 49 70
35,36-Sunset Carson-c/stories (2 in each). 35-Inside front-c photo of Sunset Carson plus photo on-c ... 34 102 179 310
37-Sunset Carson stories (2) ... 22 66 116 200
46-(Formerly Space Western)-Space western story 21 63 110 185

	GD2.0	FN6.0	VF8.0	NM9.4

51-57,59-66: 51-Golden Arrow(r?) & Monte Hale-r renamed Rusty Hall.
53,54-Tom Mix-r. 55-Monte Hale story(r?). 66-Young Eagle story. 67-Wild
Bill Hickok and Jingles-c/story ... 7 21 36 50
58-(1/56, 15¢, 68 pgs.)-Wild Bill Hickok, Annie Oakley & Jesse James stories;
Forgione-a ... 9 27 49 70
67-(15¢, 68 pgs.)-Williamson/Torres-a, 5 pgs. ... 10 30 55 85
NOTE: *Many issues trimmed 1" shorter*. *Maneely* a-67(5). Inside front/back photo c-29.

COWGIRL ROMANCES (Young Men No. 4 on)
Marvel Comics (CCC): No. 28, Jan, 1950 (52 pgs.)
28(#1)-Photo-c ... 21 63 110 185

COWGIRL ROMANCES
Fiction House Magazines: 1950 - No. 12, Winter, 1952-53 (No. 1-3: 52 pgs.)
1-Kamen-a ... 35 105 185 320
2 ... 18 54 94 160
3-5: 5-12-Whitman-c (most) ... 16 48 83 140
6-9,11,12 ... 15 45 77 130
10-Frazetta?/Williamson?-a; Kamen?/Baker-a; r/Mitzi story from Movie Comics #4 w/all new dialogue ... 32 96 171 295

COW PUNCHER (...Comics)
Avon Periodicals: Jan, 1947; No. 2, Sept, 1947 - No. 7, 1949
1-Clint Cortland, Texas Ranger, Kit West, Pioneer Queen begin; Kubert-a;
Alabam stories begin ... 40 120 232 400
2-Kubert, Kamen/Feldstein-a; Kamen-a ... 36 108 191 330
3-5,7: 3-Kiefer story ... 26 78 136 235
6-Opium drug mention story; bondage, headlight-c; Reinman-a
... 33 99 174 300

COWPUNCHER
Realistic Publications: 1953 (nn) (Reprints Avon's No. 2)
nn-Kubert-a ... 11 33 55 90

COWSILLS, THE (See Harvey Pop Comics)

COW SPECIAL, THE
Image Comics (Top Cow): Spring-Summer 2000; 2001 ($2.95)
1-Previews upcoming Top Cow projects; Yancy Butler photo-c ... 3.00
Vol. 2 #1-Witchblade-c; previews and interviews ... 3.00

COYOTE
Marvel Comics (Epic Comics): June, 1983 - No. 16, Mar, 1986
1-10,15: 7-10-Ditko-a ... 2.50
11-1st McFarlane-a. ... 6.00
12-14,16: 12-14-McFarlane-a. 14-Badger x-over. 16-Reagan c/app. ... 4.00

CRACKAJACK FUNNIES (Also see The Owl)
Dell Publishing Co.: June, 1938 - No. 43, Jan, 1942
1-Dan Dunn, Freckles, Myra North, Wash Tubbs, Apple Mary, The Nebbs,
Don Winslow, Tom Mix, Buck Jones, Major Hoople, Clyde Beatty, Boots
begin ... 245 735 1534 2700
2 ... 100 300 625 1100
3 ... 73 219 455 800
4 ... 55 165 330 575
5-Nude woman on cover ... 55 165 341 600
6-8,10: 8-Speed Bolton begins (1st app.) ... 43 129 257 450
9-(3/39)-Red Ryder strip-r begin by Harman; 1st app. in comics and 1st cover
app. ... 136 408 852 1500
11-14 ... 40 120 240 420
15-Tarzan text feature begins by Burroughs (8/39); not in #26,35
... 44 132 264 465
16-24: 18-Stratosphere Jim begins (1st app., 12/39). 23-Ellery Queen begins
plus-c (1st comic book app., 5/40) ... 35 105 185 320
25-The Owl begins (1st app., 7/40); in new costume #26 by Frank Thomas
(also see Popular Comics #72) ... 77 231 483 850
26-30: 28-Part Owl-c ... 55 165 330 575
31-Owl covers begin, end #42 ... 55 165 341 600
32-Origin Owl Girl ... 59 177 369 650
33-38: 36-Last Tarzan issue. 37-Cyclone & Midge begin (1st app.)
... 50 150 300 525
39-Andy Panda begins (intro/1st app., 9/41) ... 55 165 341 600
40-42: 42-Last Owl-c. ... 40 120 232 400
43-Terry & the Pirates-r ... 37 111 197 340

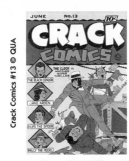

Crack Comics #13 © QUA

Cracked #250 © Globe Comm. Corp.

Cracked #323 © Globe Comm. Corp.

	GD2.0	FN6.0	VF8.0	NM9.4

NOTE: **McWilliams** art in most issues.

CRACK COMICS (Crack Western No. 63 on)
Quality Comics Group: May, 1940 - No. 62, Sept, 1949

1-Origin & 1st app. The Black Condor by Lou Fine, Madame Fatal, Red Torpedo, Rock Bradden & The Space Legion; The Clock, Alias the Spider (by Gustavson), Wizard Wells, & Ned Brant begin; Powell-a; Note: Madame Fatal is a man dressed as a woman	462	1386	3000	6000
2	236	708	1477	2600
3	164	492	1023	1800
4	136	408	852	1500
5-10: 5-Molly The Model begins. 10-Tor, the Magic Master begins	105	315	656	1150
11-20: 13-1 pg. J. Cole-a. 15-1st app. Spitfire	91	273	568	1000
21-24: 23-Pen Miller begins; continued from National Comics #22. 24-Last Fine Black Condor	68	205	426	750
25,26: 26-Flag-c	55	165	341	600
27-(1/43)-Intro & origin Captain Triumph by Alfred Andriola (Kerry Drake artist) & begin series	105	315	656	1150
28-30	47	140	286	500
31-39: 31-Last Black Condor	30	90	159	275
40-46	22	66	116	195
47-57,59,60-Capt. Triumph by Crandall	24	72	127	215
58,61,62-Last Captain Triumph	16	48	83	140

NOTE: Black Condor by **Fine**: No. 1, 2, 4-6, 8, 10-24; by **Sultan**: No. 3, 7; by **Fugitani**: No. 9. Cole a-34. **Crandall** a-61(unsigned); c-48, 49, 51-61. **Guardineer** a-17. **Gustavson** a-1, 13, 17. **McWilliams** a-15-27. Black Condor c-2, 4, 6, 8, 10, 12, 14, 16, 18, 20-26. Capt. Triumph c-27-62. The Clock c-1, 3, 5, 7, 9, 11, 13, 15, 17, 19.

CRACKED (Magazine) (Satire) (Also see The 3-D Zone #19)
Major Magazines(#1-212)/Globe Communications(#213-346/American Media #347 on): Feb-Mar, 1958 - Present

1-One pg. Williamson-a; Everett-c; Gunsmoke-s	14	42	98	165
2-1st Shut-Ups & Bonus Cut-Outs; Superman parody-c by Severin (his 1st cover on the title) Frankenstein-s	7	21	50	80
3-5	5	15	38	60
6-10: 7-Reprints 1st 6 covers on-c. 8-Frankenstein-s. 10-Wolverton-a	4	12	30	50
11-12, 13(nn,3/60),	4	12	26	40
14-Kirby-a	4	12	29	45
15-17, 18(nn,2/61), 19,20	4	12	25	38
21-27(11/62), 27(No.28, 2/63; mis-#d), 29(5/63)	3	10	23	35
30-40(11/64): 37-Beatles and Superman cameos	3	9	21	32
41-45,47,56,59,60: 47,49,52-Munsters. 51-Beatles inside-c				
59-Laurel and Hardy photos	4	12	30	50
46,57,58: 46,58-Man From U.N.C.L.E. 46-Beatles. 57-Rolling Stones	3	9	20	30
61-80: 62-Beatles cameo. 69-Batman, Superman app. 70-(8/68) Elvis cameo.				
71-Garrison's Gorillas, W.C. Fields photos	2	6	13	20
81-99: 98-Alfred E. Neuman on-c	2	6	12	18
100	3	9	19	28
101-119: 104-Godfather-c/s. 108-Archie Bunker-s. 112,119-Kung Fu (TV) 113-Tarzan-s. 115-MASH. 117-Cannon. 118-The Sting-c/s				
	2	6	9	12
120(12/74) Six Million Dollar Man-c/s; Ward-a	2	6	11	16
121,122,124-126,128-133,136-140: 121-American Graffiti. 122-Korak-c/s. 124,131-Godfather-c/s. 128-Capone-s. 129,131-Jaws. 132-Baretta-s. 133-Space 1999. 136-Laverne and Shirley/Fonz-c. 137-Travolta/Kotter-c/s. 138-Travolta/Laverne and Shirley/Fonz-c. 139-Barney Miller-c/s. 140-King Kong-c/s; Fonz-s	2	6	9	12
123-Planet of the Apes-c/s; Six Million Dollar Man	2	6	11	16
127,134,135: 127-Star Trek-c/s; Ward-a. 134-Fonz-c/s; Starsky and Hutch. 135-Bionic Woman/C; Ward-a	2	6	10	14
141,151-Charlie's Angels-c/s. 151-Frankenstein	2	6	10	14
142,143,150,152-155,157: 142-MASH-c/s; Ward-a. 143-Rocky-c/s; King Kong-s. 150-(5/78) Close Encounters-c/s. 152-Close Enc./Fonz-c/s. 153-Close Enc./Fonz-c/s. 154-Jaws II-c/s; Star Wars-s. 155-Star Wars/Fonz-c				
	2	6	9	12
144,149,156,158-160: 144-Fonz/Happy Days-c. 149-Star Wars/Six Mil.$ Man-c/s. 156-Grease/Travolta-c/s. 158-Mork & Mindy. 159-Battlestar Galactica-c/s; MASH-s. 160-Superman-c/s	2	6	10	14
145,147-Both have insert postcards: 145-Fonz/Rocky/L&S-c/s. 147-Star Wars-s;				

	GD2.0	FN6.0	VF8.0	NM9.4

Farrah photo page (missing postcards-1/2 price)	2	6	13	20
146,148: 46-Star Wars-c/s with stickers insert (missing stickers-1/2 price).				
148-Star Wars-c/s with inside-c color poster	3	9	17	24
161,170-Ward-a: 161-Mork & Mindy-c/s. 170-Dukes of Hazzard-c/s				
	1	3	6	9
162,165-168,171,172,175-178,180-Ward-a: 162-Sherlock Holmes-s. 165-Dracula-c/s. 167-Mork-c/s. 168,175-MASH-c/s. 168-Mork-c. 172-Dukes of Hazzard/CHiPs-c/s. 176-Barney Miller-c/s	1	3	6	8
163,179:163-Postcard insert; Mork & Mindy-c/s. 179-Insult cards insert; Popeye, Dukes of Hazzard-c/s	2	6	12	18
164,169,173,174: 164-Alien movie-c/s; Mork & Mindy-s. 169-Star Trek. 173,174-Star Wars-Empire Strikes Back. 173-SW poster	2	6	9	12
181,182,185-191,193,194,196-198-most Ward-c/s: 182-MASH-c/s. 185-Dukes of Hazzard-c/s; Jefferson-s. 187-Love Boat. 188-Fall Guy-s. 189-Fonz/Happy Days-c. 190,194-MASH-c/s. 191-Magnum P.I./Rocky-c; Magnum-s.				
193-Knight Rider-c/s. 196-Dukes of Hazzard/Knight Rider-c/s. 198-Jaws III-c/s; Fall Guy-s	1	3	5	7
183,184,192,195,199,200-Ward-a in all: 183-Superman-c/s. 184-Star Trek-c/s. 192-E.T.-c/s; Rocky-s. 195-E.T.-c/s. 199-Jabba-c/s; Star Wars-s. 200-(12/83)				
	1	3	6	8
201,203,210-A-Team-c/s				6.00
202-204-206,211-224,226,227,230-233: 202-Knight Rider-s. 204-Magnum P.I.; A-Team-s. 206-Michael Jackson/Mr. T-c/s. 212-Prince-s; Cosby's. 213-Monsters issue-c/s. 215-Hulk Hogan/Mr. T-c/s. 216-Miami Vice-s; James Bond-s. 217-Rambo-s; Cosby-s; A-Team-s. 218-Rocky-c/s. 219-Arnold/Commando-c/s; Rocky-s; Godzilla. 220-Rocky-c/s. 221-Stephen King Poster. 223-Miami Vice-s. 224-Cosby-s. 226-29th Anniv.; Tarzan-s; Aliens-s; Family Ties-s. 227-Cosby, Family Ties, Miami Vice-s. 230-Monkees-c/s; Elvis on-c; Gumby-s. 232-Alf, Cheers, StarTrek-s. 233-Superman/James Bond-c/s; Robocop, Predator-s				5.00
207-209,225,234: 207-Michael Jackson-c/s. 208-Indiana Jones-c/s. 209-Michael Jackson/Gremlins-c/s; Star Trek III-s. 225-Schwarzenegger/Stallone/G.I. Joe-c/s. 234-Don Martin-a begins; Batman/Robocop/Clint Eastwood-c/s				6.00
228,229: 228-Star Trek-c/s; Alf, Pee Wee Herman-s. 229-Monsters issue-c/s; centerfold with many superheroes				6.00
235,239,243,249: 235-1st Martin-c; Star Trek:TNG-s; Alf-s. 239-Beetlejuice-c/s; Mike Tyson-s. 243-X-Men and other heroes app. 249-Batman/Indiana Jones/Ghostbusters-c/s				6.00
236,244,245,248: 236-Madonna/Stallone-c/s; Twilight Zone-s. 244-Elvis-c/s; Martin-s. 245-Roger Rabbit-c/s. 248-Batman issue				6.00
237,238,240-242,246,247,250: 237-Robocop-s. 238-Rambo-c/s; Star Trek-s. 242-Dirty Harry-s, Ward-a. 246-Alf-s; Star Trek-s., Ward-a 247-Star Trek-s. 250-Batman/Ghostbusters-s				4.00
251-253,255,256,259,261-265,275-278,281,284,286-297,299: 252-Star Trek-s. 253-Back to the Future-c/s. 255-TMNT-c/s. 256-TMNT-s; Batman, Bart Simpson on-c. 259-Die Hard II, Robocop-s. 261-TMNT, Twin Peaks-s. 262-Rocky-c/s; Rocky Horror-c-s. 265-TMNT-s. 276-Aliens III, Batman-s. 277-Clinton-c. 284-Bart Simpson-c/s; 90210-s. 297-Van Damme-s/photo-c. 299-Dumb & Dumber-c/s				4.00
254,257,266,267,272,280,282,285,298,300: 254-Back to the Future, Punisher-s; Wolverton-a, Batman-s, Ward-a. 257-Batman, Simpsons-s; Spider-Man and other heroes app. 266-Terminator-s. 267-Toons-c/s. 272-Star Trek VI-s. 280-Swimsuit issue. 282-Cheers-c/s. 285-Jurassic Park-c/s. 298-Swimsuit issue; Martin-s. 300-(8/95) Brady Bunch-c/s				5.00
258,260,274,279,283: 258-Simpsons-c/s; Back to the Future-s. 260-Spider-Man -c/s; Simpsons-s. 274-Batman-c/s. 279-Madonna-c/s. 283-Jurassic Park, Wolverine app. inside back-c				5.00
301-305,307-348				2.50
306-Toy Story-c/s				4.00
Biggest... (Winter, 1977)	2	6	11	16
Biggest, Greatest... nn('65)	3	10	23	35
Biggest, Greatest... 2('66) - #5('69)	3	9	17	24
Biggest, Greatest... 6('70) - #12('76)	2	6	12	18
Biggest, Greatest... 13('77) - #21(Wint. '86)	1	4	7	10
...Blockbuster 1(Sum '87), 2('88)	1	3	6	8
...Digest 1(Fall, '86, 148 pgs.) - #5	1	3	6	8
...Collectors' Edition 4 ('73; formerly ...Special)				
5-10	2	6	10	14
11-30: 23-Ward-a	1	4	7	10
31-50	1	3	6	8

Crack Western #71 © QUA

Crash Comics #3 © Tem. Pub. Co.

Crazy #4 © MAR

	GD2.0	FN6.0	VF8.0	NM9.4

	GD2.0	FN6.0	VF8.0	NM9.

51-70 6.00
71-84: 83-Elvis, Batman parodies 4.00
...Party Pack 1,2('88) 4.00

...Shut-Ups (2/72-'72; Cracked Spec. #3) 1	3	9	17	24
2	2	6	10	14

...Special 3('73; formerly Cracked Shut-Ups; ...Collectors' Edition#4 on)

	2	6	9	12
Extra Special... 1('76)	2	6	11	15
Extra Special... 2('76)	2	6	9	12
Giant... nn('65)	4	12	29	45
Giant... 2('66)-5('69)	3	9	20	30
Giant...6('70)-12('76)	3	9	17	24
Giant...nn(9/77)-24	2	6	11	16
Giant...25-35	2	6	9	12
Giant...36-48('87)	1	3	6	8
King Sized... 1('67)	4	12	29	45
King Sized... 2('68)-5('71)	3	9	19	28
King Sized... 6('72)-11('77)	2	6	15	22
King Sized... 12-17	2	6	9	12
King Sized... 18-22 (Sum/'86)	1	3	6	8
Super... 1('68)	4	12	25	38
Super... 2('69)-5	3	9	20	30
Super... 6-10	3	9	17	24
Super... 11-16	2	6	11	16
Super... 17-24('88)	2	6	9	12
Super... 1('87, 100 pgs.)-Severin & Elder-a	1	3	6	8

NOTE: *Burgos* a-1-10. *Colan* a-257. *Davis* a-5, 11-17, 24, 40, 80; c-12-14, 16. *Elder* a-5, 6, 10-13; c-10. *Everett* a-1-10, 23-25, 61; c-1. *Heath* a-1-3, 6, 13, 14, 17, 110; c-6. *Jaffee* a-5, 6. *Don Martin* c-235, 244, 247, 259, 261, 264. *Morrow* a-8-10. *Reinman* a-1-4. *Severin* c/a-in most all issues. *Shores* a-3-7. *Torres* a-7-10. *Ward* a-22-24, 27, 35, 40, 120-193, 195, 197-205, 242, 244, 246, 247, 250, 252-257. *Williamson* a-1 (1 pg.). *Wolverton* a-10 (2 pgs.). *Giant* nn('65). *Wood* a-27, 35, 40. Alfred E. Neuman a-177, 200, 202. Batman a-234, 248, 249, 256, 274. Captain America a-256. Christmas-c-234, 243. Spider-Man c-260. Star Trek c-127, 169, 207, 228. Star Wars c-145, 146, 148, 149, 152, 155, 173, 174, 199. Superman c-183, 233. #144, 146 have free full-color pre-glued stickers. #145, 147, 155, 163 have free full-color postcards. #123, 137, 154, 157 have free iron-ons.

CRACKED MONSTER PARTY
Globe Communications: July, 1988 - No. 26, 1990?

1	2	6	10	14
2-10	1	3	6	9
11-26				5.00

CRACKED'S FOR MONSTERS ONLY
Major Magazines: Sept, 1969 - No. 9, Sept, 1969

1	3	10	23	35
2-9	2	6	12	18

CRACKED SPACED OUT
Globe Communications: Fall, 1993 - No. 4, 1994?

1-4 3.00

CRACK WESTERN (Formerly Crack Comics; Jonesy No. 85 on)
Quality Comics Group: No. 63, Nov, 1949 - No. 84, May, 1953
(36 pgs., 63-68,74-on)

63(#1)-Ward-c; Two-Gun Lil (origin & 1st app.)(ends #84), Arizona Ames, his horse Thunder (with sidekick Spurs & his horse Calico), Frontier Marshal (ends #70), & Dead Canyon Days (ends #69) begin; Crandall-a	23	69	121	210
64,65: 64-Ward-c. Crandall-a in both.	17	51	88	150
66,68-Photo-c. 66-Arizona Ames becomes A. Raines (ends #84)	15	45	77	130
67-Randolph Scott photo-c; Crandall-a	17	51	88	150
69(52pgs.)-Crandall-a	15	45	77	130
70(52pgs.)-The Whip (origin & 1st app.) & his horse Diablo begin (ends #84); Crandall-a	15	45	77	130
71(52pgs.)-Frontier Marshal becomes Bob Allen F. Marshal (ends #84); Crandall-c/a	17	51	88	150
72(52pgs.)-Tim Holt photo-c	14	42	72	120
73(52pgs.)-Photo-c	10	30	55	80
74-76,78,79,81,83-Crandall-a	13	39	66	110
77,80,82	9	27	49	70
84-Crandall-a	14	42	72	120

NOTE: *Crandall* c-71p, 74-81, 83p(w/*Cuidera-i*).

CRASH COMICS (Catman Comics No. 6 on)
Tem Publishing Co.: May, 1940 - No. 5, Nov, 1940

1-The Blue Streak, Strongman (origin), The Perfect Human, Shangra begin (1st app. of each); Kirby-a	300	900	1875	3500
2-Simon & Kirby-a	150	450	938	1650
3,5-Simon & Kirby-a	127	381	795	1400
4-Origin & 1st app. The Catman; S&K-a	300	900	1875	3500

NOTE: *Solar Legion by Kirby* No. 1-5 (5 pgs. each). Strongman c-1-4. Catman c-5.

CRASH DIVE (See Cinema Comics Herald)

CRASH METRO AND THE STAR SQUAD
Oni Press: May, 1999 ($2.95, B&W, one-shot)

1-Allred-s/Ontiveros-a 3.00

CRASH RYAN (Also see Dark Horse Presents #44)
Marvel Comics (Epic): Oct, 1984 - No. 4, Jan, 1985 (Baxter paper, lim. series)

1-4 2.25

CRAZY (Also see This Magazine is Crazy)
Atlas Comics (CSI): Dec, 1953 - No. 7, July, 1954

1-Everett-c/a	27	81	145	250
2	20	60	105	175
3-7: 4-I Love Lucy satire. 5-Satire on censorship	16	48	83	140

NOTE: *Ayers* a-5. *Berg* a-1, 2. *Burgos* c-5, 6. *Drucker* a-6. *Everett* a-1-4. *Al Hartley* a-4. *Heath* a-3, 7; c-7. *Maneely* a-1-7, c-3, 4. *Post* a-3-6. Funny monster c-1-4.

CRAZY (Satire)
Marvel Comics Group: Feb, 1973 - No. 3, June, 1973

1-Not Brand Echh-r; Beatles cameo (r)	2	6	15	22
2,3-Not Brand Echh-r; Kirby-a	2	6	11	15

CRAZY MAGAZINE (Satire)
Oct, 1973 - No. 94, Apr, 1983 (40-90¢, B&W magazine)
Marvel Comics (#1, 44 pgs, #2-90, reg. issues, 52 pgs; #92-95, 68 pgs)'

1-Wolverton(1pg.), Bode-a; 3 pg. photo story of Neal Adams & Dick Giordano; Harlan Ellison story; TV Kung Fu sty.	3	10	23	35
2-"Live & Let Die" c/s; 8pgs; Adams/Buscema-a; McCloud w5 pgs. Adams-a; Kurtzman's "Hey Look" 2 pg.-r	3	9	17	24
3-5: 3-"High Plains Drifter" w/Clint Eastwood c/s; Waltons app; Drucker, Reese-a. 4-Shaft-c/s; Ploog-a; Nixon 3 pg. app; Freas-a. 5-Michael Crichton's "Westworld" c/s; Nixon app.	2	6	13	20
6,7,18: 6-Exorcist c/s; Nixon app. 7-TV's Kung Fu c/s; Nixon app., Ploog & Freas-a. 18-Six Million Dollar Man/Bionic Woman c/s; Welcome Back Kotter story	1	4	7	11
8-10: 8-Serpico c/s; Casper parody. 9-Joker cameo; Chinatown story; Eisner s/a begins; Has 1st 8 covers on-c. 10-Playboy Bunny-c; M. Severin-a; Lee Marrs-a begins; "Deathwish" story	2	6	10	14
11-17,19: 11-Towering Inferno. 12-Rhoda. 13-"Tommy" the Who Rock Opera. 14-Mandingo. 15-Jaws story. 16-Santa-Xmas-c; "Good Times" TV story; Jaws. 17-Bi-Centennial ish; Baretta; Woody Allen. 19-King Kong-c; Reagan, J. Carter, Howard the Duck cameos, "Laverne & Shirley"	1	4	7	10
20,24,27: 20-Bi-Centennial-c; Space 1999 sty; Superheroes song sheet, 4pgs. 24-Charlies Angels. 27-Charlies Angels/Travolta/Fonz-c; Bionic Woman sty	2	6	11	15
21-23,25,26,28-30: 21-Starsky & Hutch. 22-Mount Rushmore/J. Carter's/ TV's Barney Miller; Superheroes spoof. 23-Santa/Xmas-c; "Happy Days" sty; "Omen" sty. 25-J. Carter-c/s; Grandenetti-a begins; TV's Alice; Logan's Run. 26-TV Stars-c; Mary Hartman, King Kong. 28-Donny & Marie Osmond-c/s; Marathon Man. 29-Travolta/Kotter-c; "One Day at a Time", Gong Show. 30-1977, 84 pgs. w/bonus; Jaws, Baretta, King Kong, Happy Days	1	3	6	9
31,33-35,38,40: 31-"Rocky"-c/s; TV game shows. 33-Peter Benchley's "Deep". 34-J. Carter-c; TV's "Fish". 35-Xmas-c with Fonz/Six Million Dollar Man/ Wonder Woman/Darth Vader/Travolta, TV's "Mash" & "Family Matters". 38-Close Encounters of the Third Kind-c/s; 40-"Three's Company-c/s	1	3	5	7
32-Star Wars/Darth Vader-c/s; "Black Sunday"	2	6	11	16

36,42,47,49: 36-Farrah Fawcett/Six Million Dollar Man-c; TV's Nancy Drew & Hardy Boys. 42-Howard The Duck in Crazy, 2 pgs. 42-84 pgs. w/bonus; TV Hulk/Spider-Man-c; Mash, Gong Show, One Day at a Time, Disco, Alice. 47-Battlestar Galactica xmas-c; movie "Foul Play". 49-1979, 84 pgs. w/bonus;

Crazy #53 © MAR

Crazy #82 © MAR

Creature Commandos #3 © DC

	GD2.0	FN6.0	VF8.0	NM9.4

Mork & Mindy-c; Jaws, Saturday Night Fever, Three's Company

	1	3	6	9

37-1978, 84 pgs. w/bonus. Darth Vader-c; Barney Miller, Laverne & Shirley, Good Times, Rocky, Donny & Marie Osmond, Bionic Woman

	2	6	10	14

39,44: 39-Saturday Night Fever-c/s. 44-"Grease"-c by Travolta/O. Newton-John

	2	6	9	12

41-Kiss-c & 1pg. photos; Disaster movies, TV's "Family", Annie Hall

	3	10	23	35

43,45,46,48,51: 43-Jaws-c; Saturday Night Fever; Stallone's "Fist".43-E.C. swipe from Mad #131 45-Travolta/O. Newton-John & Carter-c; Eight is Enough. 46-TV Hulk-c/s; Punk Rock. 48-"Wiz"-c, Battlestar Galactica-s. 51-Grease/Mork & Mindy/D&M Osmond-s, Mork & Mindy-sty. "Boys from Brazil"

	1	3	5	7

50,58: 50-Superman movie-c/sty, Playboy Mag., TV Hulk, Fonz; Howard the Duck, 1 pg. 58-1980, 84 pgs. w/32 pg. color comic bonus insert-Full reprint of Crazy Comic #1, Battlestar Galactica, Charlie's Angels, Starsky & Hutch

	2	6	10	14

52,59,60,64: 52-1979, 84 pgs. w/bonus. Marlon Brando-c; TV Hulk, Grease. Kiss, 1 pg. photos. 59-Santa Ptd-c by Larkin; "Alien", "Moonraker", Rocky-2, Howard the Duck, 1 pg. 60-Star Trek w/Muppets-c; Star Trek sty; 1st app/ori gin Teen Hulk; Severin-a. 64-84 pgs. w/bonus Monopoly game satire. "Empire Strikes Back", 8 pgs.,One Day at a Time.

	2	6	10	14

53,54,65,67-70: 53-"Animal House"-c/sty; TV's "Vegas", Howard the Duck, 1 pg. 54-Love at First Bite-c/sty, Fantasy Island-sty, Howard the Duck, 1 pg. 65-(Has #66 on-c, Aug/'80). "Black Hole" w/Janson-a; Kirby,Wood/Severin-a(r), 5 pgs. Howard the Duck, 3 pgs.; Broderick-a; Buck Rogers, Mr. Rogers. 67-84 pgs. w/bonus; TV's Kung Fu, Exorcist; Ploog-a(r). 68-American Gigalo, Dukes of Hazzard, Howard the Duck; Howard the Duck, 3 pgs. Broderick-a; Monster sty/5 pg. Ditko-a(r). 69-Obnoxio the Clown-c/sty; Stephen King's "Shining", Teen Hulk, Richie Rich, Howard the Duck, 3pgs; Broderick-a. 70-84 pgs. Towering Inferno, Daytime TV; Trina Robbins-a

	1	3	5	7

55-57,61,63: 55-84 pgs. w/bonus; Love Boat, Mork & Mindy, Fonz, TV Hulk. 56-Mork/Rocky/J. Carter-c; China Syndrome. 57-TV Hulk with Miss Piggy-c, Dracula, Taxi, Muppets. 61-1980, 84 pgs. Adams-a(r), McCloud, Pro wrestling, Casper, TV's Police Story. 63-Apocalypse Now-Coppola's cult movie; 3rd app. Teen Hulk, Howard the Duck, 3 pgs.

	1	3	6	9

62-Kiss Ptd-c & 2 pg. app; Quincy, 2nd app. Teen Hulk

	3	9	20	30

66-Sept/'80, Empire Strikes Back-c/sty; Teen Hulk by Severin, Howard the Duck, 3pgs. by Broderick

	2	6	9	12

71,72,75-77,79: 71-Blues Brothers parody, Teen Hulk, Superheroes parody, WKRP in Cincinnati, Howard the Duck, 3pgs. by Broderick. 72-Jackie Gleason/Smokey & the Bandit II-c/sty, Shogun, Teen Hulk. Howard the Duck, 3pgs. by Broderick. 75-Flash Gordon movie c/sty; Teen Hulk, Cat in the Hat, Howard the Duck 3pgs. by Broderick. 76-84 pgs. w/bonus; Monster-sty w/ Crandall-a(r), Monster-story(2) w/Kirby-a(r), 5pgs. ea; Teen Hulk, Chinatown. 77-Popeye movie-Rs. Williams-c/sty; Teen Hulk, Love Boat, Howard the Duck 3 pgs. 79-84 pgs. w/bonus color stickers; has new materi al; "9 to 5" w/Dolly Parton, Teen Hulk, Magnum P.I., Monster-sty w/5pgs, Ditko-a(r), "Rat" w/Sutton-a(r), Everett-a, 4 pgs.(r)

	1	3	5	7

73,74,78,80: 73-84 pgs. w/bonus Hulk/Spiderman Finger Puppets-c & bonus; "Live & Let Die, Jaws, Fantasy Island. 74-Dallas/"Who Shot J.R."-c/sty; Elephant Man, Howard the Duck 3pgs. by Broderick. 78-Clint Eastwood-c/sty; Teen Hulk, Superheroes parody, Lou Grant. 80-Star Wars, 2 pg. app; "Howling", TV's "Greatest American Hero"

	1	3	5	7

81,84,86,87,89: 81-Superman movie II-c/sty; Wolverine cameo, Mash, Teen Hulk. 84-American Werewolf in London, Johnny Carson app; Teen Hulk. 86-Time Bandits-c/sty; Private Benjamin. 87-Rubix Cube-c; Hill Street Blues, "Ragtime", Origin Obnoxio the Clown; Teen Hulk. 89-Burt Reynolds "Sharkeys Machine", Teen Hulk

	1	3	5	7

82-X-Men-c w/new Byrne-a, 84 pgs. w/new material; Fantasy Island, Teen Hulk, "For Your Eyes Only", Spiderman/Human Torch-r by Kirby/Ditko; Sutton-a(r); Rogers-a; Hunchback of Notre Dame, 5 pgs.

	2	6	11	15

83-Raiders of the Lost Ark-c/sty; Hart to Hart; Reese-a; Teen Hulk

	2	6	9	12

85,88: 85-84 pgs; Escape from New York, Teen Hulk; Kirby-a(r), 5 pgs. Posieden Adventure, Flintstones, Sesame Street. 88-84 pgs. w/bonus Dr. Strange Game; some new material; Jeffersons, X-Men/Wolverine, 10 pgs.;

Byrne-a; Apocalypse Now, Teen Hulk

	1	3	6	9

90-94: 90-Conan-c/sty; M. Severin-a; Teen Hulk. 91-84 pgs, some new materi al; Bladerunner-c/sty, "Deathwish-II, Teen Hulk, Black Knight, 10 pgs.-'50s-r w/Maneely-a. 92-Wrath of Khan Star Trek-c/sty; Joanie & Chachi, Teen Hulk. 93-"E.T."-c/sty, Teen Hulk, Archie Bunkers Place, Dr. Doom Game. 94-Poltergeist, Smurfs, Teen Hulk, Casper, Avengers parody-8pgs. Adams-a.

	2	6	10	14

Crazy Summer Special #1 (Sum, '75, 100 pgs.)-Nixon, TV Kung Fu, Babe Ruth, Joe Namath, Waltons, McCloud, Chariots of the Gods

	3	9	15	20

NOTE: **N. Adams**-a-2, 61r, 94p. **Austin**-a-82i. **Buscema**-a-2, 82. **Byrne**-c-82p. **Nick Cardy** c-7, 8, 10, 12-16, Super Special 1. **Crandall** a-76r. **Ditko** a-68r, 79r, 82r. **Drucker** a-3. **Eisner** a-9-16. **Kelly Freas** c-1-6, 9, 11; a-7. **Kirby/Wood** a-66r. **Ploog** a-1, 4, 7, 67r; 73r. **Rogers** a-82r. **Sparling** a-92r. **Wood**-a-65r. Howard the Duck in 36, 50, 51, 53, 54, 59, 63, 65, 66, 68, 69, 71, 72, 74, 75, 77. Hulk in 46, c-42, 46, 57, 73. Star Wars in 32, 66; c-37.

CRAZYMAN
Continuity Comics: Apr, 1992 - No. 3, 1992 ($2.50, high quality paper)

1-($3.95, 52 pgs.)-Embossed-c; N. Adams part-i				4.00
2,3 ($2.50): 2-N. Adams/Bolland-c				2.50

CRAZYMAN
Continuity Comics: V2#1, 5/93 - No. 4, 1/94 ($2.50, high quality paper)

V2#1-4: 1-Entire book is die-cut. 2-(12/93)-Adams-c(p) & part scripts. 3-(12/93). 4-Indicia says #3, Jan. 1993				2.50

CRAZY, MAN, CRAZY (Magazine) (Becomes This Magazine is...?)
(Formerly From Here to Insanity)
Humor Magazines (Charlton): V2#1, Dec, 1955 - V2#2, June, 1956

V2#1,V2#2-Satire; Wolverton-a, 3 pgs.	14	42	72	120

CREATURE, THE (See Movie Classics)

CREATURE
Antarctic Press: Oct, 1997 - No. 2 ($2.95, B&W)

1,2-Don Walker-s/a				3.00

CREATURE COMMANDOS
DC Comics: May, 2000 - No. 8, Dec, 2000 ($2.50, limited series)

1-8: Truman-s/Eaton-a				2.50

CREATURES OF THE ID
Caliber Press: 1990 ($2.95, B&W)

1-Frank Einstein (Madman) app.-Allred-a	3	9	20	30

CREATURES ON THE LOOSE (Formerly Tower of Shadows No. 1-9)(See Kull)
Marvel Comics: No. 10, March, 1971 - No. 37, Sept, 1975 (New-a & reprints)

10-(15¢)-1st full app. King Kull; see Kull the Conqueror; Wrightson-a				
	4	12	29	45
11-15: 15-Last 15¢ issue	2	6	12	18
16-Origin Warrior of Mars (begins, ends #21)	2	6	9	12
17-20	1	3	6	9
21-Steranko-c	2	6	9	12
22-Steranko-c; Thongor stories begin	2	6	9	14
23-29-Thongor-c/stories				6.00
30-Manwolf begins	2	6	12	18
31-33	2	6	9	12
34-37	1	3	6	9

NOTE: **Crandall**-a-13. **Ditko** r-15, 17, 18, 20, 22, 24, 28. **Everett** a-16i(new). **Matt Fox** r-21i. **Howard** a-26i. **Gil Kane** a-16p, 17p, 19i; c-16, 17, 19, 20, 25, 29, 33p, 35p, 36p. **Kirby** a-10-15r, 16(2)r, 17r, 19r. **Morrow** a-20, 21. **Perez** a-33-37; c-34p. **Shores** a-11. **innott** r-21. **Sutton** c-10. **Tuska** a-31p, 32p.

CREECH, THE
Image Comics: Oct, 1997 - No. 3, Dec, 1997 ($1.95/$2.50, limited series)

1-3: 1-Capullo-s/c(a/p)				2.50
TPB (1999, $9.95) r/#1-3, McFarlane intro.				10.00
Out for Blood 1-3 (7/01 - No. 3, 11/01; $4.95) Capullo-s/c/a				5.00

CREED
Hall of Heroes Comics: Dec, 1994 - No. 2, Jan, 1995 ($2.50, B&W)

1	2	6	11	15
2	2	6	9	12

CREED
Lightning Comics: June, 1995 - Present ($2.75/$3.00, B&W/color)

The Creeper #9 © DC

Creepy #25 © WP

Crime and Justice #9 © CC

	GD2.0	FN6.0	VF8.0	NM9.4
1-($2.75)				4.00
1-($3.00, color)				5.00
1-($9.95)-Commemorative Edition				10.00
1-TwinVariant Edition (1250? print run)				10.00
1-Special Edition; polybagged w/certificate				4.00
1 Gold Collectors Edition; polybagged w/certificate				3.00
2,3-($3.00, color)-Butt Naked Edition & regular-c				3.00
3-($9.95)-Commemorative Edition; polybagged w/certificate & card				10.00

CREED: APPLE TREE
Gearbox Press: Dec, 2000 - No. 2 ($2.95, B&W)

1,2-Kaniuga-s/c/a				3.00

CREED: CRANIAL DISORDER
Lightning Comics: Oct, 1996 ($3.00, one-shot)

1-3-Two covers				3.00
1-($5.95)-Platinum Edition				6.00
2,3-($9.95)Ltd.l Edition				10.00

CREED: MECHANICAL EVOLUTION
Gearbox Press: Sept, 2000 - No. 2, Oct, 2000 ($2.95, B&W)

1,2-Kaniuga-s/c/a				3.00

CREED/TEENAGE MUTANT NINJA TURTLES
Lightning Comics: May, 1996 ($3.00, one-shot)

1-Kaniuga-a(p)/scripts; Laird-c; variant-c exists				3.00
1-($9.95)-Platinum Edition				10.00
1-Special Edition; polybagged w/certificate				5.00

CREED: USE YOUR DELUSION
Avatar Press: Jan, 1998 - No. 2, Feb, 1998 ($3.00, B&W)

1,2-Kaniuga-s/c/a				3.00
1,2-($4.95) Foil cover				5.00

CREEPER, THE (See Beware... , Showcase #73 & 1st Issue Special #7)
DC Comics: Dec, 1997 - No. 11, Nov, 1998 ($2.50)

1-11-Kaminski/Martinbrough(p). 7,8-Joker-c/app.				3.00
#1,000,000 (11/98) 853rd Century x-over				3.00

CREEPS
Image Comics: Oct, 2001 - Present ($2.95)

1,2-Mandrake-a/Mishkin-s				3.00

CREEPSHOW
Plume/New American Library Pub.: July, 1982 (softcover graphic novel)

1st edition-nn-(68 pgs.) Kamen-c/Wrightson-a; screenplay by Stephen King for the George Romero movie	2	6	13	20
Later editions	2	6	11	15

CREEPSVILLE
Laughing Reindeer Press: V2#1, Winter, 1995 ($4.95)

V2#1-Comics w/text				5.00

CREEPY (See Warren Presents)
Warren Publishing Co./Harris Publ. #146: 1964 - No. 145, Feb, 1983; No. 146, 1985 (B&W, magazine) (#1-70 scarce in strict NM)

1-Frazetta-a (his last story in comics?); Jack Davis-c; 1st Warren all comics magazine; 1st app. Uncle Creepy	10	30	68	115
2-Frazetta-c & 1 pg. strip	6	18	40	65
3-8,11-13,15-17: 3-7,9-11,15-17-Frazetta-c. 7-Frazetta-c 1 pg. strip. 15,16-Adams-a. 16-Jeff Jones-a	3	9	20	30
9-Creepy fan club sketch by Wrightson (1st published-a); has 1/2 pg. anti-smoking strip by Frazetta; Frazetta-c; 1st Wood and Ditko art on this title; Toth-a	5	15	34	55
10-Brunner fan club sketch (1st published work)	4	12	25	38
14-Neal Adams 1st Warren work	3	10	23	35
18-28,30,31: 27-Frazetta-c	3	9	17	26
29,34: 29-Jones-a	3	9	20	30
32-(scarce) Frazetta-c; Harlan Ellison sty	4	12	30	50
33,35,37,39,40,42-47,49: 35-Hitler/Nazi-s. 39-1st Uncle Creepy solo-c; Cousin Eerie app.; early Brunner-a. 42-1st San Julian-c. 44-1st Ploog-a. 46-Corben-a	3	9	17	24
36-(11/70)1st Corben art at Warren	3	9	20	30
38,41-(scarce): 38-1st Kelly-c. 41-Corben-a	4	12	25	38

	GD2.0	FN6.0	VF8.0	NM9.
48,55,65-(1972, 1973, 1974 Annuals) #55 & 65 contain an 8 pg. slick comic insert. 48-(84 pgs.). 55-Color poster bonus (1/2 price if missing). 65-(100 pgs.) Summer Giant	3	9	21	32
50-Vampirella/Eerie/Creepy-c	3	10	23	35
51,54,56-61,64: All contain an 8 pg. slick comic insert in middle. 59-Xmas horror. 54,64-Chaykin-a	3	9	17	26
52,53,66,71,72,75,76,78-80: 71-All Bermejo-a; Space & Time issue. 72-Gual-a. 78-Fantasy issue. 79,80-Monsters issue	2	6	11	15
62,63-1st & 2nd full Wrightson story art; Corben-a; 8 pg. color comic insert	3	9	19	28
67,68,73	2	6	15	22
69,70-Edgar Allan Poe issues; Corben-a	2	6	13	20
74,77: 74-All Crandell-a. 77-Xmas Horror issue; Corben-a,Wrightson-a	3	9	17	24
81,84,85,88-90,92-94,96-99,102,104-112,114-118,120-130: 84,93-Sports issue. 85,97,102-Monster issue. 89-All war issue; Nino-a. 94-Weird Children issue. 96,109-Aliens issue. 99-Disasters. 103-Corben-a. 104-Robots issue. 106-Sword & Sorcery.107-Sci-fi. 116-End of Man. 125-Xmas Horror	1	3	6	9
82,100,101: 82-All Maroto issue. 100-(8/78) Anniversary. 101-Corben-a	2	6	11	16
83,95-Wrightson-a. 83-Corben-a. 95-Gorilla/Apes.	2	6	9	12
86,87,91,103-Wrightson-a. 86-Xmas Horror	2	6	9	12
113-All Wrightson-r issue	2	6	13	20
119,121: 119-All Nino issue.121-All Severin-r issue	2	6	9	12
131,133-136,138,140: 135-Xmas issue	2	6	9	12
132,137,139: 132-Corben. 137-All Williamson-r issue. 139-All Toth-r issue	2	6	11	15
141,143,144 (low dist.): 144-Giant, $2.25; Frazetta-c	3	10	23	20
142,145 (low dist.): 142-(10/82, 100 pgs.) All Torres issue. 145-(2/83) last Warren issue	2	6	13	20
146 ($2.95)-1st from Harris; resurrection issue	6	18	45	75
Year Book '68-'70: '70-Neal Adams, Ditko-a(r)	4	12	26	40
Annual 1971,1972	3	10	23	35
1993 Fearbook ($3.95)-Harris Publ.; Brereton-c; Vampirella by Busiek-s/Art Adams-a; David-s; Paquette-a	3	10	23	35
...:The Classic Years TPB (Harris/Dark Horse,'91, $12.95) Kaluta-c; art by Frazetta,Torres, Crandall, Ditko, Morrow, Williamson, Wrightson				25.00

NOTE: All issues contain many good artists works: Neal Adams, Brunner, Corben, Craig (Taycee), Crandall, Ditko, Evans, Frazetta, Heath, Jeff Jones, Krenkel, McWilliams, Morrow, Nino, Orlando, Ploog, Severin, Torres, Toth, Williamson, Wood, & Wrightson; covers by Crandall, Davis, Frazetta, Morrow, San Julian, Todd/Bode; Otto Binder's "Adam Link" stories in No. 2, 4, 6, 8, 9, 12, 13, 15 with Orlando art. Frazetta c-2-7, 9-11, 15-17, 27, 32, 63r, 89r, 91r. E.A. Poe adaptations in 66, 69, 70.

CREEPY (Mini-series)
Harris Comics/Dark Horse: 1992 - Book 4, 1992 (48 pgs, B&W, squarebound)

Book 1-4: Brereton painted-c on all. Stories and art by various incl. David (all), Busiek(2), Infantino(2), Guice(3), Colan(1)	2	6	9	12

CREEPY THINGS
Charlton Comics: July, 1975 - No. 6, June, 1976

1	2	6	11	16
2-6: Ditko in 3,5. Sutton c-3,4	1	3	6	9
Modern Comics Reprint 2-6(1977)				4.00

NOTE: Larson a-2,6. Sutton a-1,2,4,6. Zeck a-2.

CREMATOR
Chaos! Comics: Dec, 1998 - No. 5, May, 1999 ($2.95, limited series)

1-5-Leonardo Jimenez-s/a				3.00

CRIME AND JUSTICE (Badge Of Justice #22 on; Rookie Cop? on)
Capitol Stories/Charlton Comics: March, 1951 - No. 21; No. 23 - No. 26, Sept, 1955 (No #22)

1	33	99	174	300
2	12	36	61	100
3-8,10-13: 6-Negligee panels	10	30	55	85
9-Classic story "Comics Vs. Crime"	24	72	127	215
14-Color illos in POP; gory story of man who beheads women	19	57	99	165
15-17,19-21,23-26: 15-Negligee panels. 23-26 (exist?)	7	21	38	55
18-Ditko-a	25	75	130	225

Crime Can't Win #43 © MAR   Crime Clinic #5 © Z-D   Crime Does Not Pay #32 © LEV

	GD2.0	FN6.0	VF8.0	NM9.4

NOTE: **Alascia** c-20. **Ayers** a-17. **Shuster** a-19-21; c-19. Bondage c-11, 12.

CRIME AND PUNISHMENT (Title inspired by 1935 film)
Lev Gleason Publications: April, 1948 - No. 74, Aug, 1955

1-Mr. Crime app. on-c	33	99	174	300
2	17	51	88	150
3-Used in **SOTI**, pg. 112; injury-to-eye panel; Fuje-a				
	20	60	105	175
4,5	13	39	66	110
6-10	11	33	55	90
11-20	10	30	55	80
21-30	8	24	42	60
31-38,40-44,46: 46-One pg. Frazetta-a	7	21	36	50
39-Drug mention story "The 5 Dopes"	10	30	55	80
45- "Hophead Killer" drug story	10	30	55	80
47-57,60-65,70-74:	6	18	32	45
58-Used in **POP**, pg. 79	7	21	36	50
59-Used in **SOTI**, illo "What comic-book America stands for"				
	29	87	153	265
66-Toth-c/a(4); 3-D effect issue (3/54); 1st "Deep Dimension" process				
	38	114	203	350
67- "Monkey on His Back" heroin story; 3-D effect issue				
	33	99	174	300
68-3-D effect issue; Toth-c (7/54)	28	84	151	260
69- "The Hot Rod Gang" dope crazy kids	10	30	55	80

NOTE: **Biro** c-most. **Everett** a-31. **Fuje** a-3, 4, 12, 13, 17, 18, 20, 26, 27. **Guardineer** a-2-4, 10, 14, 17, 18, 20, 26-28, 32, 38-44,54. **Kinstler** c-69. **McWilliams** a-41, 48, 49. **Tuska** a-28, 30, 51, 64, 70.

CRIME AND PUNISHMENT: MARSHALL LAW TAKES MANHATTAN
Marvel Comics (Epic Comics): 1989 ($4.95, 52 pgs., direct sales only, mature)

nn-Graphic album featuring Marshall Law				5.00

CRIME CAN'T WIN (Formerly Cindy Smith)
Marvel/Atlas Comics (TCI 41/CCC 42,43,4-12): No. 41, 9/50 - No. 43, 2/51; No. 4, 4/51 - No. 12, 9/53

41(#1)	26	78	136	235
42(#2)	15	45	77	130
43(#3)-Horror story	18	54	94	155
4(4/51),5-12: 10-Possible use in **SOTI**, pg. 161	12	36	61	100

NOTE: **Robinson** a-9-11. **Tuska** a-43.

CRIME CASES COMICS (Formerly Willie Comics)
Marvel/Atlas Comics(CnPC No.24-8/MJMC No.9-12): No. 24, 8/50 - No. 27, 3/51; No. 5, 5/51 - No. 12, 7/52

24 (#1, 52 pgs.)-True police cases	17	51	88	150
25-27(#2-4): 27-Morisi-a	12	36	61	100
5-12: 11-Robinson-a. 12-Tuska-a	10	30	55	85

CRIME CLINIC
Ziff-Davis Publishing Co.: No. 10, July-Aug, 1951 - No. 5, Summer, 1952

10(#1)-Painted-c; origin Dr. Tom Rogers	28	84	148	255
11(#2),4,5: 4,5-Painted-c	20	60	105	175
3-Used in **SOTI**, pg. 18	21	63	110	185

NOTE: All have painted covers by **Saunders**. **Starr** a-10.

CRIME CLINIC
Slave Labor Graphics: May, 1995 - No. 2, Oct, 1995 ($2.95, B&W, limited series)

1,2				3.00

CRIME DETECTIVE COMICS
Hillman Periodicals: Mar-Apr, 1948 - V3#8, May-June, 1953

V1#1-The Invisible 6, costumed villains app; Fuje-c/a, 15 pgs.				
	27	81	145	250
2,5: 5-Krigstein-a	12	36	61	100
3,4,6,7,10-12: 6-McWilliams-a	10	30	55	85
8-Kirbyish by McCann	10	30	55	85
9-Used in **SOTI**, pg. 16 & "Caricature of the author in a position comic book publishers wish he were in permanently" illo.	36	108	191	330
V2#1,4,7-Krigstein-a: 1-Tuska-a	10	30	55	85
2,3,5,6,8-12 (1-2/52)	8	24	42	60
V3#1-Drug use-c	8	24	45	65
2-8	6	18	32	45

	GD2.0	FN6.0	VF8.0	NM9.4

NOTE: **Briefer** a-11, V3#1. **Kinstler**ish-a by **McCann**-V2#7, V3#2. **Powell** a-10, 11. **Starr** a-10.

CRIME DETECTOR
Timor Publications: Jan, 1954 - No. 5, Sept, 1954

1	20	60	105	180
2	11	33	55	90
3,4	10	30	55	85
5-Disbrow-a (classic)	22	66	116	195

CRIME DOES NOT PAY (Formerly Silver Streak Comics No. 1-21)
Comic House/Lev Gleason/Golfing (Title inspired by film):
No. 22, June, 1942 - No. 147, July, 1955 (1st crime comic)

22 (23 on cover, 22 on indicia)-Origin The War Eagle & only app.; Chip Gardner begins; #22 was rebound in Complete Book of True Crime (Scarce)	236	708	1477	2600
23 (Scarce)	127	381	795	1400
24-Intro. & 1st app. Mr. Crime (Scarce).	102	306	638	1125
25,26,28-30: 30-Wood and Biro app.	55	165	341	600
27-Classic Biro-c	61	183	381	675
31,32,34-40	40	120	217	375
33-Classic Biro Hanging & hatchet-c	41	123	246	425
41-Origin & 1st app. Officer Common Sense	29	87	153	265
42-Electrocution-c	35	105	185	320
43-46,48-50: 44,45,50 are 68 pg. issues; 44- "legs" diamond story				
	19	57	99	170
47-Electric chair-c	33	99	174	300
51-70: 63,64-Possible use in **SOTI**, pg. 306. 63-Contains Biro & Gleason's self censorship code of 12 listed restrictions (5/48)	17	51	88	150
71-99: 87-Chip Gardner begins, ends #100	14	42	72	125
100	15	45	77	135
101-104,107-110: 102-Chip Gardner app	11	33	55	90
105-Used in **POP**, pg. 84	12	36	61	100
106,114-Frazetta-a, 1 pg.	11	33	55	90
111-Used in **POP**, pgs. 80 & 81; injury-to-eye stly illo	11	33	55	90
112,113,115-130	8	24	45	65
131-140	7	21	36	50
141,142-Last pre-code issue; Kubert-a(1)	10	30	55	80
143-Kubert-a in one story	10	30	55	80
144-146	7	21	36	50
147-Last issue (scarce); Kubert-a	14	42	72	120
1(Golfing-1945)	7	21	36	50
The Best of...(1944, 128 pgs.)-Series contains 4 rebound issues				
	77	231	483	850
...1945 issue	59	177	369	650
...1946-48 issues	43	129	257	450
...1949-50 issues	40	120	232	400
...1951-53 issues	34	102	179	310

NOTE: Many issues contain violent covers and stories. Who Dunnit by **Guardineer**-39-42, 44-105, 108-110; Chip Gardner by **Bob Fujitani** (**Fuje**)-88-103. **Alderman** a-29, 41-44, 49. **Dan Barry** a-67, 75. **Biro** c-1-76, 122, 142. **Briefer** a-29(2), 30, 31, 33, 37, 39. **G. Colan** a-105. **Fuje** c-88, 89, 91-94, 96, 98, 99, 102, 103. **Guardineer** a-57, 67, 68, 71, 74. **Kubert** c-143. **Landau** a-118. **Maurer** a-29, 39, 41, 42. **McWilliams** a-91, 93, 95, 100-103. **Palais** a-30, 33, 37, 39, 41-43, 44(2), 46, 49. **Powell** a-146, 147. **Tuska** a-48, 50(2), 51, 52, 56, 57(2), 60-64, 66, 67, 68, 71, 74. Painted c-87-102. Bondage c-43, 62, 98.

CRIME EXPOSED
Marvel Comics (PPI)/Marvel Atlas Comics (PrPI): June, 1948; Dec, 1950 - No. 14, June, 1952

1(6/48)	33	99	174	300
1(12/50)	20	60	105	175
2	14	42	72	120
3-9,11,14	11	33	55	90
10-Used in **POP**, pg. 81	12	36	61	100
12-Krigstein & Robinson-a	12	36	61	100
13-Used in **POP**, pg. 81; Krigstein-a	12	36	61	105

NOTE: **Maneely** c-8. **Robinson** a-11, 12. **Tuska** a-3, 4.

CRIMEFIGHTERS
Marvel Comics (CmPS 1-3/CCC 4-10): Apr, 1948 - No. 10, Nov, 1949

1-Some copies are undated & could be reprints	25	75	130	225
2,3: 3-Morphine addict story	14	42	72	120
4-10: 6-Anti-Wertham editorial. 9,10-Photo-c	12	36	61	100

CRIME FIGHTERS (...Always Win)

Crime Fighters #9 © MAR

Crime Mysteries #11 © Ribage

Crime Reporter #1 © STJ

Atlas Comics (CnPC): No. 11, Sept, 1954 - No. 13, Jan, 1955

11-13: 11-Maneely-a,13-Pakula, Reinman, Severin-a

12	36	61	100

CRIME-FIGHTING DETECTIVE (Shock Detective Cases No. 20 on; formerly Criminals on the Run)
Star Publications: No. 11, Apr-May, 1950 - No. 19, June, 1952
(Based on true crime cases)

11-L. B. Cole-c/a (2 pgs.); L. B. Cole-c on all	20	60	105	175
12,13,15-19: 17-Young King Cole & Dr. Doom app.	15	45	77	130
14-L. B. Cole-c/a, r/Law-Crime #2	17	51	88	150

CRIME FILES
Standard Comics: No. 5, Sept, 1952 - No. 6, Nov, 1952

5-1pg. Alex Toth-a; used in SOTI, pg. 4 (text)	25	75	130	225
6-Sekowsky-a	13	39	66	110

CRIME ILLUSTRATED (Magazine)
E. C. Comics: Nov-Dec, 1955 - No. 2, Spring, 1956 (25¢, Adult Suspense Stories on-c)

1-Ingels & Crandall-a	15	45	77	135
2-Ingels & Crandall-a	13	39	66	110

NOTE: *Craig a-2. Crandall a-1, c-2. Evans a-1. Davis a-2. Ingels a-1, 2. Krigstein/ Crandall a-1. Orlando a-1, 2; c-1.*

CRIME INCORPORATED (Formerly Crimes Incorporated)
Fox Features Syndicate: No. 2, Aug, 1950; No. 3, Aug, 1951

2	27	81	145	250
3(1951)-Hollingsworth-a	20	60	105	175

CRIME MACHINE (Magazine)
Skywald Publications: Feb, 1971 - No. 2, May, 1971 (B&W)

1-Kubert-a(2)(r)(Avon)	5	15	38	60
2-Torres, Wildey-a; violent-c/a	3	10	23	35

CRIME MUST LOSE! (Formerly Sports Action?)
Sports Action (Atlas Comics): No. 4, Oct, 1950 - No. 12, April, 1952

4-Ann Brewster-a in all; c-used in N.Y. Legis. Comm. documents				
	19	57	99	165
5-12: 9-Robinson-a. 11-Used in POP, pg. 89	13	39	66	110

CRIME MUST PAY THE PENALTY (Formerly Four Favorites; Penalty #47, 48)
Ace Magazines (Current Books): No. 33, Feb, 1948; No. 2, Jun, 1948 - No. 48, Jan, 1956

33(#1, 2/48)-Becomes Four Teeners #34?	33	99	174	300
2(6/48)-Extreme violence; Palais-a?	21	63	110	185
3,4,8- "Frisco Mary" story used in Senate Investigation report, pg. 7. 4,8-Transvestism stories	15	45	77	130
5-7,9,10	11	33	55	90
11-20-Drug story "Dealers in White Death"	10	30	55	80
21-32,34-40,42-48	7	21	36	50
33(7/53)- "Dell Fabry-Junk King" drug story; mentioned in Love and Death				
	10	30	55	80
41-reprints "Dealers in White Death"	8	24	42	60

NOTE: *Cameron a-29-31, 34, 35, 39-41. Colan a-20, 31. Kremer a-3, 37t. Larsen a-32. Palais a-5?,37.*

CRIME MUST STOP
Hillman Periodicals: October, 1952 (52 pgs.)

V1#1(Scarce)-Similar to Monster Crime; Mort Lawrence, Krigstein-a				
	64	192	398	700

CRIME MYSTERIES (Secret Mysteries #16 on; combined with Crime Smashers #7 on)
Ribage Publ. Corp. (Trojan Magazines): May, 1952 - No. 15, Sept, 1954

1-Transvestism story; crime & terror stories begin	55	165	331	580
2-Marijuana story (7/52)	40	120	220	380
3-One pg. Frazetta-a	36	108	191	330
4-Cover shows girl in bondage having her blood drained; 1 pg. Frazetta-a				
	55	165	331	580
5-10	30	90	159	275
11,12,14	28	84	148	255
13-(5/54)-Angelo Torres 1st comic work (inks over Check's pencils); Check-a				
	34	102	179	310

15-Acid in face-c	40	120	232	400

NOTE: *Fass a-13; c-4, 10. Hollingsworth a-10-13, 15; c-2, 12, 13, 15. Kiefer a-4. Woodbridge a-13? Bondage-c-1, 8, 12.*

CRIME ON THE RUN (See Approved Comics #8)

CRIME ON THE WATERFRONT (Formerly Famous Gangsters)
Realistic Publications: No. 4, May, 1952 (Painted cover)

4	30	90	159	275

CRIME PATROL (Formerly International #1-5; International Crime Patrol #6; becomes Crypt of Terror #17 on)
E. C. Comics: No. 7, Summer, 1948 - No. 16, Feb-Mar, 1950

7-Intro. Captain Crime	64	192	398	700
8-14: 12-Ingels-a	56	168	350	620
15-Intro. of Crypt Keeper (inspired by Witches Tales radio show) & Crypt of Terror (see Tales From the Crypt #33 for origin); used by N.Y. Legis. Comm.; last pg. Feldstein-a	240	720	1680	3000
16-2nd Crypt Keeper app.; Roussos-a	160	480	1120	2000

NOTE: *Craig c/a on most issues. Feldstein a-9-16. Kiefer a-8, 10, 11. Moldoff a-7.*

CRIME PATROL
Gemstone Publishing: Apr, 2000 - No. 10, Jan, 2001 ($2.50)

1-10: E.C. reprints				2.50
Volume 1,2 (2000, $13.50) 1-r/#1-5. 2-r/#6-10				14.00

CRIME PHOTOGRAPHER (See Casey...)

CRIME REPORTER
St. John Publ. Co.: Aug, 1948 - No. 3, Dec, 1948 (Indicia shows Oct.)

1-Drug club story	50	150	300	525
2-Used in SOTI, illo- "Children told me what the man was going to do with the red-hot poker;" r/Dynamic #17 with editing; Baker-c; Tuska-a				
	68	205	426	750
3-Baker-c; Tuska-a	40	120	232	400

CRIMES BY WOMEN
Fox Features Syndicate: June, 1948 - No. 15, Aug, 1951; 1954
(True crime cases)

1-True story of Bonnie Parker	127	381	795	1400
2,3: 3-Used in SOTI, pg. 234	66	197	413	725
4,5,7,9,11-15: 8-Used in POP	59	177	369	650
6-Classic girl fight-c; acid-in-face panel	64	192	398	700
10-Used in SOTI, pg. 72; girl fight-c	61	183	381	675
54(M.S. Publ.-'54)-Reprint; (formerly My Love Secret)				
	27	81	142	245

CRIMES INCORPORATED (Formerly My Past)
Fox Features Syndicate: No. 12, June, 1950 (Crime Incorporated No. 2 on)

12	15	45	77	130

CRIMES INCORPORATED (See Fox Giants)

CRIME SMASHER (See Whiz #76)
Fawcett Publications: Summer, 1948 (one-shot)

1-Formerly Spy Smasher	44	132	264	460

CRIME SMASHERS (Becomes Secret Mysteries No. 16 on)
Ribage Publishing Corp.(Trojan Magazines): Oct, 1950 - No. 15, Mar, 1953

1-Used in SOTI, pg. 19,20, & illo "A girl raped and murdered;" Sally the Sleuth begins	82	246	511	900
2-Kubert-c	45	135	270	475
3,4	37	111	197	340
5-Wood-a	43	129	257	450
6,8-11: 8-Lingerie panel	29	87	153	265
7-Female heroin junkie story	30	90	162	280
12-Injury to eye panel; 1 pg. Frazetta-a	31	93	168	290
13-Used in POP, pgs. 79,80; 1 pg. Frazetta-a	31	93	168	290
14,15	25	75	130	225

NOTE: *Hollingsworth a-14. Kiefer a-15. Bondage c-7, 9.*

CRIME SUSPENSTORIES (Formerly Vault of Horror No. 12-14)
E. C. Comics: No. 15, Oct-Nov, 1950 - No. 27, Feb-Mar, 1955

15-Identical to #1 in content; #1 printed on outside front cover. #15 (formerly "The Vault of Horror" printed and blackened out on inside front cover with Vol. 1, No. 1 printed over it. Evidently, several of No. 15 were printed before a decision was made not to drop the Vault of Horror and Haunt of Fear series. The print run was stopped on No. 15 and continued on No. 1. All of No. 15 were changed a

Crime Suspenstories #16 © WMG

Crimson #24 © Humberto Ramos

Crisis on Infinite Earths #12 © DC

CR

	GD2.0	FN6.0	VF8.0	NM9.4

described above.

	136	408	952	1700
1	100	300	700	1250
2	54	162	378	675
3-5: 3-Poe adaptation. 3-Old Witch stories begin	38	114	266	475
6-10	31	93	217	385
11,12,14,15: 15-The Old Witch guest stars	24	72	168	300
13,16-Williamson-a	26	78	182	325
17-Williamson/Frazetta-a (6 pgs.)	30	90	210	375
18,19: 19-Used in SOTI, pg. 235	20	60	140	250
20-Cover used in SOTI, illo "Cover of a children's comic book"				
	26	78	182	320
21,24-27: 24- "Food For Thought" similar to "Cave In" in Amazing Detective				
Cases #13 (1952)	14	42	98	175
22,23-Used in Senate investigation on juvenile delinquency. 22-Ax				
decapitation-c	20	60	140	250

NOTE: Craig a-1-21; c-1-18, 20-22. Crandall a-18-26. Davis a-4, 5, 7, 9-12, 20. Elder a-17,18. Evans a-15, 19, 21, 23, 25, 27; c-23, 24. Feldstein c-19. Ingels a-1-12, 14, 15, 27. Kamen a-2, 4-18, 20-27; c-25-27. Krigstein a-22, 24, 25, 27. Kurtzman a-1, 3. Orlando a-16, 22, 24, 26. Wood a-1, 3. Issues No. 11-15 have E. C. "quickie" stories. No. 25 contains the famous "Are You a Red Dupe?" editorial. Ray Bradbury adaptations-15, 17.

CRIME SUSPENSTORIES
Russ Cochran/Gemstone Publ.: Nov, 1992 - No. 24 ($1.50/$2.00/$2.50)

1-24: Reprints Crime SuspenStories series				3.00

CRIMINALS ON THE RUN (Formerly Young King Cole)
Crime Fighting Detective No. 11 on)
Premium Group (Novelty Press): V4#1, Aug-Sep, 1948-#10, Dec-Jan, 1949-50

V4#1-Young King Cole continues	31	93	165	285
2-6: 6-Dr. Doom app.	27	81	145	250
7-Classic "Fish in the Face" c by L. B. Cole	54	162	324	570
V5#1,2 (#8,9),10: 9,10-L. B. Cole-c	25	75	130	225

NOTE: Most issues have L. B. Cole covers. McWilliams a-V#4,6, 7, V5#2; c-V4#5.

CRIMSON (Also see Cliffhanger #0)
Image Comics (Cliffhanger Productions): May, 1998 - No. 7, Dec, 1998;
DC Comics (Cliffhanger Prod.): No. 8, Mar, 1999 - No. 24, Apr, 2001 ($2.50)

1-Humberto Ramos-a/Augustyn-s				5.00
1-Variant-c by Warren				8.00
1-Chromium-c				30.00
2-Ramos-c with street crowd, 2-Variant-c by Art Adams				3.00
2-Dynamic Forces CrimsonChrome cover				12.00
3-7: 3-Ramos Moon background-c. 7-3 covers by Ramos, Madureira,				
& Campbell				3.00
8-23: 8-First DC issue				2.50
24-($3.50) Final issue; wraparound-c				3.50
DF Premiere Ed. 1998 ($6.95) covers by Ramos and Jae Lee				7.00
Crimson: Scarlet X Blood on the Moon (10/99, $3.95)				4.00
Crimson Sourcebook (11/99, $2.95) Pin-ups and info				3.00
Earth Angel TPB (2001, $14.95) r/#13-18				15.00
Heaven and Earth TPB (1/00, $14.95) r/#7-12				15.00
Loyalty and Loss TPB ('99, $12.95) r/#1-6				13.00
Redemption TPB ('01, $14.95) r/#19-24				15.00

CRIMSON AVENGER, THE (See Detective Comics #20 for 1st app.)(Also see Leading Comics #1 & World's Best/Finest Comics)
DC Comics: June, 1988 - No. 4, Sept, 1988 ($1.00, limited series)

1-4				2.50

CRIMSON NUN
Antarctic Press: May, 1997 - No. 4, Nov, 1997 ($2.95, limited series)

1-4				3.00

CRIMSON PLAGUE
Event Comics: June, 1997 ($2.95, unfinished mini-series)

1-George Perez-a				3.00

CRIMSON PLAGUE (George Pérez's...)
Image Comics (Gorilla): June, 2000 - Present ($2.95, mini-series)

1-George Perez-a; reprints 6/97 issue with 16 new pages				3.00
2-($2.50)				2.50

CRIMSON SKIES
Image Comics (Top Cow): Winter, 2000

Preview-Comic and Microsoft video game preview 3.00

CRISIS ON INFINITE EARTHS (Also see Official... Index and Legends of the DC Universe)
DC Comics: Apr, 1985 - No. 12, Mar, 1986 (maxi-series)

		GD2.0	FN6.0	VF8.0	NM9.4
1-1st DC app. Blue Beetle & Detective Karp from Charlton; Pérez-c on all					
		2	6	11	15
2-6: 6-Intro Charlton's Capt. Atom, Nightshade, Question, Judomaster,					
Peacemaker & Thunderbolt into DC Universe		1	4	7	10
7-Double size; death of Supergirl		2	6	12	18
8-Death of the Flash (Barry Allen)		2	6	12	18
9-11: 9-Intro. Charlton's Ghost into DC Universe. 10-Intro. Charlton's					
Banshee, Dr. Spectro, Image, Punch & Jewellee into DC Universe; Starman					
(Prince Gavyn) dies.		1	4	7	10
12-(52 pgs.)-Deaths of Dove, Kole, Lori Lemaris, Sunburst, G.A. Robin &					
Huntress; Kid Flash becomes new Flash; 3rd & final DC app. of the 3 Lt.					
Marvels; Green Fury gets new look (becomes Green Flame in Infinity, Inc.					
#32)		2	6	9	12
Slipcased Hardcover (1998, $99.95) Wraparound dust-jacket cover by Pérez					
and Alex Ross; sketch pages by Pérez; intro by Wolfman					125.00
TPB (2000, $29.95) Wraparound-c by Pérez and Ross					30.00

NOTE: Crossover issues: All Star Squadron 50-56,60; Amethyst 13; Blue Devil 17,18; DC Comics Presents 78,86-88,95; Detective Comics 558; Fury of Firestorm 41,42; G.I. Combat 274; Green Lantern 194-196,198; Infinity, Inc. 18-25 & Annual 1, Justice League of America 244,245 & Annual 3; Legion of Super-Heroes 16,18; Losers Special 1; New Teen Titans 13,14; Omega Men 31,33; Superman 413-415; Swamp Thing 44,46; Wonder Woman 327-329.

CRITICAL MASS (See A Shadowline Saga: Critical Mass)

CRITTERS (Also see Usagi Yojimbo Summer Special)
Fantagraphics Books: 1986 - No. 50, 1990 ($1.70/$2.00, B&W)

1-Cutey Bunny, Usagi Yojimbo app.				6.00
2,4,5,8,9				5.00
3,6,7,10-Usagi Yojimbo app.				5.00
11-22,24-37,39-49: 11,14-Usagi Yojimbo app. 11-Christmas Special (68				
pgs.); Usagi Yojimbo. 22-Watchmen parody; two diff. covers exist				2.50
23-With Alan Moore Flexi-disc ($3.95)				5.00
38-($2.75-c) Usagi Yojimbo app.				3.00
50 ($4.95, 84 pgs.)-Neil the Horse, Capt. Jack, Sam & Max & Usagi Yojimbo				
app.; Quagmire, Shaw-a				5.00
Special 1 (1/88, $2.00)				2.50

CROSS
Dark Horse Comics: No. 0, Oct, 1995 - No. 6, Apr, 1995 ($2.95, limited series, mature)

0-6: Darrow-c & Vachss scripts in all				3.00

CROSS AND THE SWITCHBLADE, THE
Spire Christian Comics (Fleming H. Revell Co.): 1972 (35-49¢)

1-Some issues have nn	1	3	5	7

CROSSFIRE
Spire Christian Comics (Fleming H. Revell Co.): 1973 (39/49¢)

nn	1	3	5	7

CROSSFIRE (Also see DNAgents)
Eclipse Comics: 5/84 - No. 17, 3/86; No. 18, 1/87 - No. 26, 2/88 ($1.50, Baxter paper)(#18-26 (B&W)

1-11,14-26: 1-DNAgents x-over; Spiegle-c/a begins				2.50
12,13-Death of Marilyn Monroe. 12-Dave Stevens-c				4.00

CROSSFIRE AND RAINBOW (Also see DNAgents)
Eclipse Comics: June, 1986 - No. 4, Sept, 1986 ($1.25, deluxe format)

1-3: Spiegle-a. 4-Dave Stevens-c				2.25

CROSSGEN...
CrossGeneration Comics

CrossGenesis (1/00) Previews CrossGen universe; cover gallery				3.00
...Primer (1/00) Wizard supplement; intro. to the CrossGen universe				1.00
...Sampler (2/00) Retailer preview book				3.00

CROSSGEN CHRONICLES
CrossGeneration Comics: June, 2000 - Present ($3.95)

1-Intro. to CrossGen characters & company				4.00
1-(no cover price) same contents, customer preview				4.00

CrossGen Chronicles #2 © CRO

The Crow #9 © Crowvision, Inc.

The Crusades #2 © Steven Seagle & Kelley Jones

2-(3/01) George Pérez-c/a				5.00
3-5-Pérez-a/Waid-s				4.00

CROSSING THE ROCKIES (See Classics Illustrated Special Issue)

CROSSROADS
First Comics: July, 1988 - No. 5, Nov, 1988 ($3.25, lim. series, deluxe format)

1-5				3.25

CROW, THE (Also see Caliber Presents)
Caliber Press: Feb, 1989 - No. 4, 1989 ($1.95, B&W, limited series)

1-James O'Barr-c/a/scripts	4	12	26	40
1-3-2nd printing				5.00
2-4	2	6	13	20
2-3rd printing				3.00

CROW, THE
Tundra Publishing, Ltd.: Jan, 1992 - No. 3, 1992 ($4.95, B&W, 68 pgs.)

1-3: 1-r/#1,2 of Caliber series. 2-r/#3 of Caliber series w/new material. 3-All new material	1	3	6	8

CROW, THE
Kitchen Sink Press: 1/96 - No. 3, 3/96 ($2.95, B&W)

1-3: James O'Barr-c/scripts				3.50
#0-A Cycle of Shattered Lives (12/98, $3.50) new story by O'Barr				3.50

CROW, THE
Image Comics (Todd McFarlane Prod.): Feb, 1999 - No. 10, Nov, 1999 ($2.50)

1-10: 1-Two covers by McFarlane and Kent Williams; Muth-s in all. 2-6,10-Paul Lee-a. 9-Tollagson-a				3.00
Book 1 - Vengeance (2000, $10.95, TPB) r/#1-3,5,6				11.00
Book 2 - Evil Beyond Reach (2000, $10.95, TPB) r/#4,7-10				11.00
Todd McFarlane Presents The Crow Magazine 1 (3/00, $4.95)				5.00

CROW, THE: CITY OF ANGELS (Movie)
Kitchen Sink Press: July, 1996 - No. 3, Sept, 1996 ($2.95, limited series)

1-3: Adaptation of film; two-c (photo & illos.). 1-Vincent Perez interview				3.00

CROW, THE: FLESH AND BLOOD
Kitchen Sink Press: May, 1996 - No. 3, July, 1996 ($2.95, limited series)

1-3-O'Barr-c				3.00

CROW, THE: RAZOR - KILL THE PAIN
London Night Studios: Apr, 1998 - No.3, July, 1998 ($2.95, B&W, lim. series)

1-3-Hartsoe-s/O'Barr-painted-c				3.00
0(10/98) Dorien painted-c, Finale (2/99)				3.00
The Lost Chapter (2/99, $4.95), Tour Book-(12/97) pin-ups; 4 diff.-c				5.00

CROW, THE: WAKING NIGHTMARES
Kitchen Sink Press: Jan, 1997 - No.4, 1998 ($2.95, B&W, limited series)

1-4-Miran Kim-c				3.00

CROW, THE: WILD JUSTICE
Kitchen Sink Press: Oct, 1996 - No. 3, Dec, 1996 ($2.95, B&W, limited series)

1-3-Prosser-s/Adlard-a				3.00

CROWN COMICS
Golfing/McCombs Publ.: Wint, 1944-45; No. 2, Sum, 1945 - No. 19, July, 1949

1- "The Oblong Box" E.A. Poe adaptation	36	108	191	330
2,3-Baker-a; 3-Voodah by Baker	25	75	130	225
4-6-Baker-c/a; Voodah app. #4,5	28	84	148	255
7-Feldstein, Baker, Kamen-a; Baker-c	28	84	151	260
8-Baker-a; Voodah app.	24	72	127	215
9-11,13-19: Voodah in #10-19. 13-New logo	15	45	77	130
12-Master Marvin by Feldstein, Starr-a; Voodah-c	15	45	77	135

NOTE: **Bolle** a-11, 13-16, 18, 19; c-11p, 15. **Powell** a-19. **Starr** a-11-13; c-11l.

CRUCIBLE
DC Comics (Impact): Feb, 1993 - No. 6, July, 1993 ($1.25, limited series)

1-6: 1-(99¢)-Neon ink-c. 1,2-Quesada-c(p). 1-4-Quesada layouts				2.50

CRUEL AND UNUSUAL
DC Comics (Vertigo): June, 1999 - No. 4, Sept, 1999 ($2.95, limited series)

1-4-Delano & Peyer-s/McCrea-c/a				3.00

CRUSADER FROM MARS (See Tops in Adventure)

Ziff-Davis Publ. Co.: Jan-Mar, 1952 - No. 2, Fall, 1952 (Painted-c)

1-Cover is dated Spring	73	219	455	800
2-Bondage-c	55	165	341	600

CRUSADER RABBIT (TV)
Dell Publishing Co.: No. 735, Oct, 1956 - No. 805, May, 1957

Four Color 735 (#1)	32	96	224	420
Four Color 805	25	75	175	325

CRUSADERS, THE (Religious)
Chick Publications: 1974 - Vol. 17, 1988 (39/69¢, 36 pgs.)

Vol.1-Operation Bucharest ('74). Vol.2-The Broken Cross ('74). Vol.3-Scarface ('74). Vol.4-Exorcists ('75). Vol.5-Chaos ('75)	1	3	6	8
Vol.6-Primal Man? ('76)-(Disputes evolution theory). Vol.7-The Ark-(claims proof of existence, destroyed by Bolsheviks). Vol.8-The Gift-(Life story of Christ). Vol.9-Angel of Light-(Story of the Devil). Vol.10-Spellbound?-(Tells how rock music is Satanic & produced by witches). 11-Sabotage?. 12-Alberto 13-Double Cross. 14-The Godfathers. (No. 6-14 low in distribution; loaded in religious propaganda.). 15-The Force. 16-The Four Horsemen	1	3	6	8
Vol. 17-The Prophet (low print run)	1	3	6	9

CRUSADERS (Southern Knights No. 2 on)
Guild Publications: 1982 (B&W, magazine size)

1-1st app. Southern Knights	1	3	5	7

CRUSADERS, THE (Also see Black Hood, The Jaguar, The Comet, The Fly, Legend of the Shield, The Mighty… & The Web)
DC Comics (Impact): May, 1992 - No. 8, Dec, 1992 ($1.00/$1.25)

1-8-Contains 3 Impact trading cards				2.50

CRUSADES, THE
DC Comics (Vertigo): 2001 - Present ($3.95, $2.50)

…: Urban Decree ('01, $3.95) Intro. the Knight; Seagle-s/Kelley Jones-c/a				4.00
1-(5/01, $2.50) Sienkiewicz-c				2.50
2-11: 2-Moeller-c				2.50

CRUSH, THE
Image Comics (Motown Machineworks): Jan, 1996 - No. 5, July, 1996 ($2.25, limited series)

1-5: Baron scripts				3.00

CRUX
CrossGeneration Comics: May, 2001 - Present ($2.95)

1-9: 1-Waid-s/Epting & Magyar-a/c. 6-Pelletier-a				3.00

CRY FOR DAWN
Cry For Dawn Pub.: 1989 - No. 9 ($2.25, B&W, mature)

1	8	24	60	100
1-2nd printing	3	9	20	30
1-3rd printing	2	6	13	20
2	4	12	29	45
2-2nd printing	1	3	6	9
3	3	9	20	30
4-6	2	6	12	18
5-2nd printing				5.00
7-9	2	6	10	14
4-9-Signed & numbered editions	3	9	17	25
…Calendar (1993)				35.00

CRYIN' LION COMICS
William H. Wise Co.: Fall, 1944 - No. 3, Spring, 1945

1-Funny animal	15	45	77	130
2-Hitler app.	13	39	66	110
3	10	30	55	80

CRYPT
Image Comics (Extreme): Aug, 1995 - No.2, Oct. 1995 ($2.50, limited series)

1,2-Prophet app.				2.50

CRYPTIC WRITINGS OF MEGADETH
Chaos! Comics: Sept, 1997 - Present ($2.95, quarterly)

1-4-Stories based on song lyrics by Dave Mustaine				3.00

Crypt of Shadows #1 © MAR

Curse of the Spawn #17 © TMP

Cyberforce V2 #20 © TCOW

	GD2.0	FN6.0	VF8.0	NM9.4

CRYPT OF DAWN (see Dawn)
Sirius: 1996 ($2.95, B&W, limited series)

1-Linsner-c/s; anthology.				5.00
2, 3 (2/98)				4.00
4,5: 4- (6/98), 5-(11/98)				3.00
Ltd. Edition				20.00

CRYPT OF SHADOWS
Marvel Comics Group: Jan, 1973 - No. 21, Nov, 1975 (#1-9 are 20¢)

1-Wolverton-r/Advs. Into Terror #7	2	6	13	20
2-10: 2-Starlin/Everett-c	2	6	11	15
11-21: 18,20-Kirby-a	1	4	7	10

NOTE: *Briefer a-2r. Ditko a-13r, 18-20r. Everett a-6, 14r; c-2i. Heath a-1r. Gil Kane c-1, 6. Mort Lawrence a-1r, 8r. Maneely a-2r. Moldoff a-8. Powell a-12r, 14r. Tuska a-2r.*

CRYPT OF TERROR (Formerly Crime Patrol; Tales From the Crypt No. 20 on)
E. C. Comics: No. 17, Apr-May, 1950 - No. 19, Aug-Sept, 1950

17-1st New Trend to hit stands	264	792	1848	3300
18,19	152	456	1064	1900

NOTE: *Craig c/a-17-19. Feldstein a-17. Ingels a-19. Kurtzman a-18. Wood a-18. Canadian reprints known; see Table of Contents.*

C•23 (Jim Lee's...) (Based on Wizards of the Coast card game)
Image Comics: Apr, 1998 - No. 8, Nov, 1998 ($2.50)

1-8: 1,2-Choi & Mariotte-s/ Charest-c. 2-Variant-c by Jim Lee. 4-Ryan Benjamin-c. 5,8-Corben var-c. 6-Flip book with Planetary preview; Corben-c				3.00

CUD
Fantagraphics Books: 8/92 - No. 8, 12/94 ($2.25-$2.75, B&W, mature)

1-8: Terry LaBan scripts & art in all. 6-1st Eno & Plum				3.00

CUD COMICS
Dark Horse Comics: Jan, 1995 - Present ($2.95, B&W)

1-8: Terry LaBan-c/a/scripts. 5-Nudity; marijuana story				3.00
Eno and Plum TPB (1997, $12.95) r/#1-4, DHP #93-95				13.00

CUPID
Marvel Comics (U.S.A.): Dec, 1949 - No. 2, Mar, 1950

1-Photo-c	14	42	72	125
2-Bettie Page ('50s pin-up queen) photo-c; Powell-a (see My Love #4)	33	99	174	300

CURIO
Harry 'A' Chesler: 1930's(?) (Tabloid size, 16-20 pgs.)

nn	21	63	110	185

CURLY KAYOE COMICS (Boxing)
United Features Syndicate/Dell Publ. Co.: 1946 - No. 8, 1950; Jan, 1958

1 (1946)-Strip-r (Fritzi Ritz); biography of Sam Leff, Kayoe's artist	18	54	94	160
2	10	30	55	80
3-8	8	24	42	60
United Presents...(Fall, 1948)	8	24	42	60
Four Color 871 (Dell, 1/58)	3	9	20	30

CURSE OF DRACULA, THE
Dark Horse Comics: July, 1998 - No. 3, Sept, 1998 ($2.95, limited series)

1-3-Wolfman-s/Colan-a				3.00

CURSE OF DREADWOLF
Lightning Comics: Sept, 1994 ($2.75, B&W)

1				2.75

CURSE OF RUNE (Becomes Rune, 2nd Series)
Malibu Comics (Ultraverse): May, 1995 - No. 4, Aug, 1995 ($2.50, lim. series)

1-4: 1-Two covers form one image				2.50

CURSE OF THE SPAWN
Image Comics (Todd McFarlane Prod.): Sept, 1996 - No. 29, Mar, 1999 ($1.95)

1-Dwayne Turner-a(p)				6.00
1-B&W Edition	2	6	11	16
2-3				4.00
4-29: 12-Movie photo-c of Melinda Clarke (Priest)				2.50
Blood and Sutures ('99, $9.95, TPB) r/#5-8				10.00

Lost Values ('00, $10.95, TPB) r/#12-14,22; Ashley Wood-c				11.00
Sacrifice of the Soul ('99, $9.95, TPB) r/#1-4				10.00
Shades of Gray ('00, $9.95, TPB) r/#9-11,29				10.00

CURSE OF THE WEIRD
Marvel Comics: Dec, 1993 - No. 4, Mar, 1994 ($1.25, limited series)
(Pre-code horror-r)

1-4: 1,3,4-Wolverton-r(1-Eye of Doom; 3-Where Monsters Dwell; 4-The End of the World). 2-Orlando-r. 2-Zombie by Everett; painted-c				3.00

NOTE: *Briefer r-2. Jack Davis a-4r. Ditko a-1r, 2r, 4r; c-1r. Everett r-1. Heath r-1-3. Kubert r-3. Wolverton a-1r, 3r, 4r.*

CUSTER'S LAST FIGHT
Avon Periodicals: 1950

nn-Partial reprint of Cowpuncher #1	18	54	94	155

CUTEY BUNNY (See Army Surplus Komikz Featuring...)

CUTIE PIE
Junior Reader's Guild (Lev Gleason): May, 1955 - No. 3, Dec, 1955; No. 4, Feb, 1956; No. 5, Aug, 1956

1	7	21	36	50
2-5: 4-Misdated 2/55	5	15	23	30

CUTTING EDGE
Marvel Comics: Dec, 1995 ($2.95)

1-Hulk-c/story; Messner-Loebs scripts				3.00

CYBERCITY
CPM Comics: Sept, 1995- Present ($2.95, bi-monthly)

Part One #1,2; Part Two #1,2; Part Three #1,2				3.00

CYBERELLA (Helix)
DC Comics (Helix): Sept, 1996 - No. 12, Aug, 1997 ($2.25/$2.50)
(1st Helix series)

1-12: 1-5-Chaykin & Cameron-a. 1,2-Chaykin-c. 3-5-Cameron-c				2.50

CYBERFORCE
Image Comics (Top Cow Productions): Oct, 1992 - No. 4, 1993; No. 0, Sept, 1993 ($1.95, limited series)

1-Silvestri-c/a in all; coupon for Image Comics #0; 1st Top Cow Productions title.				6.00
1-With coupon missing				2.25
2-4,0: 2-(3/93). 3-Pitt-c/story. 4-Codename: Stryke Force back-up (1st app.); foil-c. 0-(9/93)-Walt Simonson-c/a/scripts				3.00

CYBERFORCE
Image Comics (Top Cow Productions)/Top Cow Comics No. 28 on:
V2#1, Nov, 1993 - No. 35, Sept. 1997 ($1.95)

V2#1-24: 1-7-Marc Silvestri/Keith Williams-a. 8-McFarlane-c/a. 10-Painted variant-c exists. 18-Variant-c exists. 23-Velocity-c.				2.50
1-3: 1-Gold Logo-c. 2-Silver embossed-c. 3-Gold embossed-c				10.00
1-(99¢, 3/96, 2nd printing)				2.25
25-($3.95)-Wraparound, foil-c				4.00
26-35: 28-(11/96)-1st Top Cow Comics iss. Quesada & Palmiotti's Gabriel app.				
27-Quesada & Palmiotti's Ash app.				2.50
Annual 1,2 (3/95, 8/96, $2.50, $2.95)				3.00

NOTE: *Annuals read Volume One in the indica.*

CYBERFORCE ORIGINS
Image Comics (Top Cow Productions): Jan, 1995 - No. 3, Nov, 1995 ($2.50)

1-Cyblade (1/95)				5.00
1-Cyblade (3/96, 99¢, 2nd printing)				2.25
1A-Exclusive Ed.; Tucci-c				4.00
2,3: 2-Stryker (2/95)-1st Mike Turner-a. 3-Impact				2.50
(#4) Misery (12/95, $2.95)				3.00

CYBERFORCE/STRYKEFORCE: OPPOSING FORCES (See Codename: Stryke Force #15)
Image Comics (Top Cow Productions): Sept, 1995 - No.2, Oct, 1995 ($2.50, limited series)

1,2: 2-Stryker disbands Strykeforce.				2.50

CYBERFORCE UNIVERSE SOURCEBOOK
Image Comics (Top Cow Productions): Aug, 1994/Feb, 1995 ($2.50)

Cyclone Comics #1 © Bilbara

Cyclops #1 © MAR

Dagar, Desert Hawk #16 © FOX

			GD2.0	FN6.0	VF8.0	NM9

1,2-Silvestri-c — 2.50

CYBERFROG
Hall of Heroes: June, 1994 - No. 2, Dec, 1994 ($2.50, B&W, limited series)
1,2 — 3.00

CYBERFROG
Harris Comics: Feb, 1996 - No. 3, Apr, 1996 ($2.95)
0-3: Van Sciver-c/a/scripts. 2-Variant-c exists — 5.00

CYBERFROG: (Title series), **Harris Comics**
--RESERVOIR FROG, 9/96 - No. 2, 10/96 ($2.95) 1,2: Van Sciver-c/a/scripts; wraparound-c — 3.00
--3RD ANNIVERSARY SPECIAL, 1/97 - #2, ($2.50, B&W) 1,2 — 3.00
--VS. CREED, 7/97 ($2.95, B&W)1 — 3.00

CYBERNARY (See Deathblow #1)
Image Comics (WildStorm Productions): Nov, 1995 - No.5, Mar, 1996 ($2.50)
1-5 — 2.50

CYBERNARY 2.0
DC Comics (WildStorm): Sept, 2001 - No. 6 ($2.95, limited series)
1-5: Joe Harris-s/Eric Canete-a — 3.00

CYBERPUNK
Innovation Publishing: Sept, 1989 - No. 2, Oct, 1989 ($1.95, 28 pgs.) Book 2, #1, May, 1990 - No 2, 1990 ($2.25, 28 pgs.)
1,2, Book 2 #1,2:1,2-Ken Steacy painted-covers (Adults) — 2.25

CYBERPUNK: THE SERAPHIM FILES
Innovation Publishing: Nov, 1990 - No. 2, Dec, 1990 ($2.50, 28 pgs., mature)
1,2: 1-Painted-c; story cont'd from Seraphim — 2.50

CYBERPUNX
Image Comics (Extreme Studios): Mar, 1996 ($2.50)
1 — 3.00

CYBERRAD
Continuity Comics: 1991 - No. 7, 1992 ($2.00)(Direct sale & newsstand-c variations)
V2#1, 1993 ($2.50)
1-7: 5-Glow-in-the-dark-c by N. Adams (direct sale only). 6-Contains 4 pg. fold-out poster; N. Adams layouts — 2.50
V2#1-($2.95, direct sale ed.)-Die-cut-c w/B&W hologram on-c; Neal Adams sketches — 3.00
V2#1-($2.50, newsstand ed.)-Without sketches — 2.50

CYBERRAD DEATHWATCH 2000 (Becomes CyberRad w/#2, 7/93)
Continuity Comics: Apr, 1993 - No. 2, 1993 ($2.50)
1,2: 1-Bagged w/2 cards; Adams-c & layouts & plots. 2-Bagged w/card; Adams scripts — 2.50

CYBER 7
Eclipse Comics: Mar, 1989 - #7, Sept, 1989; V2#1, Oct, 1989 - #10, 1990 ($2.00, B&W)
1-7, Book 2 #1-10: Stories translated from Japanese — 2.50

CYBLADE/ GHOST RIDER
Marvel Comics /Top Cow Productions: Jan 1997 ($2.95, one-shot)
1-Devil's Reign pt. 2 — 4.00

CYBLADE/SHI (Also see Battle For The Independents & Shi/Cyblade: The Battle For The Independents)
Image Comics (Top Cow Productions): 1995 ($2.95, one-shot)

	GD2.0	FN6.0	VF8.0	NM9.4
San Diego Preview	3	9	17	25
1-($2.95)-1st app. Witchblade	2	6	13	20
1-($2.95)-variant-c; Tucci-a	2	6	11	15

CYBRID
Maximum Press: July, 1995; No. 0, Jan, 1997 ($2.95/$3.50)
1-(7/95) — 3.50
0-(1/97)-Liefeld-a/script; story cont'd in Avengelyne #4 — 3.50

CYCLONE COMICS (Also see Whirlwind Comics)
Bilbara Publishing Co.: June, 1940 - No. 5, Nov, 1940

	GD2.0	FN6.0	VF8.0	NM9
1-Origin Tornado Tom; Volton (the human generator), Tornado Tom, Kingdom of the Moon, Mister Q begin (1st app. of each)	155	465	966	1700
2	77	231	483	850
3-Classic-c (scarce)	100	300	625	1100
4	61	183	381	675
5-(Scarce)	58	174	454	800

CYCLOPS (X-Men)
Marvel Comics: Oct, 2001 - No. 4, Jan, 2002 ($2.50, limited series)
1-4-Texeira-c/a. 1,2-Black Tom and Juggernaut app. — 2.50

CYCLOPS: RETRIBUTION
Marvel Comics: 1994 ($5.95, trade paperback)
nn-r/Marvel Comics Presents #17-24 — 6.00

CY-GOR (See Spawn #38 for 1st app.)
Image Comics (Todd McFarlane Prod.): July, 1999 - No. 6, Dec, 1999 ($2.50)
1-6-Veitch-s — 2.50

CYNTHIA DOYLE, NURSE IN LOVE (Formerly Sweetheart Diary)
Charlton Publications: No. 66, Oct, 1962 - No. 74, Feb, 1964

	GD2.0	FN6.0	VF8.0	NM9
66-74	2	6	12	18

DAEMONSTORM
Caliber Comics: 1997 ($3.95, one-shot)
1-McFarlane-c — 4.00

DAEMONSTORM: STORMWALKER
Caliber Comics: 1997 ($3.95, B&W, one-shot)
nn — 4.00

DAFFY (Daffy Duck No. 18 on)(See Looney Tunes)
Dell Publishing Co./Gold Key No. 31-127/Whitman No. 128 on: #457, 3/53 - #30, 7-9/62; #31, 10-12/62 - #145, 6/84 (No #132,133)

	GD2.0	FN6.0	VF8.0	NM9
Four Color 457(#1)-Elmer Fudd x-overs begin	9	27	63	110
Four Color 536,615('55)	5	15	34	55
4(1-3/56)-11('57)	4	12	26	40
12-19(1958-59)	3	9	19	28
20-40(1960-64)	2	6	13	20
41-60(1964-68)	2	6	12	18
61-90(1969-74)-Road Runner in most	1	4	7	10
91-110	1	3	6	9
111-127	1	3	5	7
128,134-141: 139(2/82), 140(2-3/82), 141(4/82)	1	3	6	8
129(8/80), 130,131 (pre-pack?) (scarce)	2	6	11	15
142-145(#90029 on-c; nd, nd code, pre-pack): 142(6/83), 143(8/83), 144(3/84), 145(6/84)	2	6	9	12
Mini-Comic 1 (1976; 3-1/4x6-1/2")				6.00

NOTE: Reprint issues-No.41-46, 48, 50, 53-55, 58, 59, 65, 67, 69, 73, 81, 96, 103-108; 136-144, 145(1/3-2/3-r). (See March of Comics No. 277, 288, 303, 313, 331, 347, 357,375, 387, 39 402, 413, 425, 437, 460).

DAFFY TUNES COMICS
Four-Star Publications: June, 1947; No. 12, Aug, 1947

	GD2.0	FN6.0	VF8.0	NM9
nn	8	24	45	65
12-Al Fago-c/a; funny animal	7	21	38	55

DAGAR, DESERT HAWK (Captain Kidd No. 24 on; formerly All Great)
Fox Features Syndicate: No. 14, Feb, 1948 - No. 23, Apr, 1949 (No #17,18)

	GD2.0	FN6.0	VF8.0	NM9
14-Tangi & Safari Cary begin; Good bondage-c/a	77	231	483	850
15,16-E. Good-a; 15-Bondage-c	47	142	286	500
19,20,22: 19-Used in SOTI, pg. 180 (Tangi)	40	120	240	420
21,23: 21- "Bombs & Bums Away" panel in "Flood of Death" story used in SOTI.				
23-Bondage-c	45	135	270	475

NOTE: Tangi by Kamen-14-16, 19, 20; c-20, 21.

DAGAR THE INVINCIBLE (Tales of Sword & Sorcery...) (Also see Dan Curtis Giveaways & Gold Key Spotlight)
Gold Key: Oct, 1972 - No. 18, Dec, 1976; No. 19, Apr, 1982

	GD2.0	FN6.0	VF8.0	NM9
1-Origin; intro. Villains Olstellon & Scor	3	9	20	30
2-5: 2-Intro. Graylin, Dagar's woman; Jarn x-over	2	6	9	12
6-1st Dark Gods story	1	4	7	10
7-10: 9-Intro. Torgus. 10-1st Three Witches story	1	4	7	10
11-18: 13-Durak & Torgus x-over; story continues in Dr. Spektor #15.				
14-Dagar's origin retold. 18-Origin retold	1	3	6	8

Dale Evans Comics #3 © DC

Dalton Boys #1 © AVON

Danger #10 © Comic Media

	GD2.0	FN6.0	VF8.0	NM9.4

19(4/82)-Origin-r/#18 — 6.00
NOTE: *Durak app. in 7, 12, 13. Tragg app. in 5, 11.*

DAGWOOD (Chic Young's) (Also see Blondie Comics)
Harvey Publications: Sept, 1950 - No. 140, Nov, 1965

1	13	39	94	160
2	7	21	50	80
3-10	5	15	38	60
11-20	4	12	30	50
21-30	4	12	29	45
31-50	4	12	25	38
51-70	3	9	19	28
71-100	2	6	13	20
101-128,130,135	2	6	11	16
129,131-134,136-140-All are 68-pg. issues	3	9	19	28

NOTE: *Popeye and other one page strips appeared in early issues.*

DAI KAMIKAZE!
Now Comics: June, 1987 - No. 12, Aug, 1988 ($1.75)

1-12: 1-1st app. Speed Racer; 2nd print exists — 2.50

DAILY BUGLE (See Spider-Man)
Marvel Comics: Dec, 1996 - No. 3, Feb, 1997 ($2.50, B&W, limited series)

1-3-Paul Grist-s — 2.50

DAISY AND DONALD (See Walt Disney Showcase No. 8)
Gold Key/Whitman No. 42 on: May, 1973 - No. 59, Feb, 1984 (no No. 48)

1-Barks-r/WDC&S #280,308	3	9	20	30
2-5: 4-Barks-r/WDC&S #224	2	6	11	16
6-10	2	6	9	12
11-20	1	3	6	9
21-41: 32-r/WDC&S #308				6.00
42-44 (Whitman)	1	3	6	9
45 (8/80),46-(pre-pack?)(scarce)	3	9	17	24
47-(12/80)-Only distr. in Whitman 3-pack (scarce)	4	12	29	45
48(3/81)-50(8/81): 50-r/#3	2	6	10	14
51-54: 51-Barks-r/4-Color #1150. 52-r/#2. 53(2/82), 54(4/82)				
	2	6	9	12
55-59-(all #90284 on-c, nd, nd code, pre-pack): 55(5/83), 56(7/83), 57(8/83), 58(8/83), 59(7/84)				
	2	6	11	16

DAISY & HER PUPS (Dagwood & Blondie's Dogs)(Formerly Blondie Comics #20)
Harvey Publications: No. 21, 7/51 - No. 27, 7/52; No. 8, 9/52 - No. 18, 5/54

21 (#1)-Blondie's dog Daisy and her 5 pups led by Elmer begin. Rags Rabbit app.	5	15	34	55
22-27 (#2-7): 26 has No. 6 on cover but No. 26 on inside. 23,25-The Little King app. 24-Bringing Up Father by McManus app. 25-27-Rags Rabbit app.	3	10	23	35
8-18: 8,9-Rags Rabbit app. 8,17-The Little King app. 11-The Flop Family Swan begins. 22-Cookie app. 11-Felix The Cat app. by 17,18-Popeye app.	3	9	19	28

DAISY DUCK & UNCLE SCROOGE PICNIC TIME (See Dell Giant #33)

DAISY DUCK & UNCLE SCROOGE SHOW BOAT (See Dell Giant #55)

DAISY DUCK'S DIARY (See Dynabrite Comics, & Walt Disney's C&S #298)
Dell Publishing Co.: No. 600, Nov, 1954 - No. 1247, Dec-Feb, 1961-62 (Disney)

Four Color 600 (#1)	7	21	49	65
Four Color 659, 743 (11/56)	5	15	35	65
Four Color 858 (11/57), 948 (11/58), 1247 (12-2/61-62)				
	5	15	34	55
Four Color 1055 (11-1/59-60), 1150 (12-1/60-61)-By Carl Barks	9	27	65	120

DAISY HANDBOOK
Daisy Manufacturing Co.: 1946; No. 2, 1948 (10¢, pocket-size, 132 pgs.)

1-Buck Rogers, Red Ryder; Wolverton-a(2 pgs.)	40	120	220	380
2-Captain Marvel & Ibis the Invincible, Red Ryder, Boy Commandos & Robotman; Wolverton-a (2 pgs.); contains 8 pg. color catalog				
	40	120	220	380

DAISY MAE (See Oxydol-Dreft)

DAISY'S RED RYDER GUN BOOK
Daisy Manufacturing Co.: 1955 (25¢, pocket-size, 132 pgs.)

	GD2.0	FN6.0	VF8.0	NM9.4

nn-Boy Commandos, Red Ryder; 1pg. Wolverton-a	27	81	145	250

DAKKON BLACKBLADE ON THE WORLD OF MAGIC: THE GATHERING
Acclaim Comics (Armada): June, 1996 ($5.95, one-shot)

1-Jerry Prosser scripts; Rags Morales-c/a. — 6.00

DAKOTA LIL (See Fawcett Movie Comics)

DAKOTA NORTH
Marvel Comics Group: June, 1986 - No. 5, Feb, 1987

1-5 — 2.25

DAKTARI (Ivan Tors) (TV)
Dell Publishing Co.: July, 1967 - No. 3, Oct, 1968; No. 4, Sept, 1969
(All have photo-c)

1	4	12	26	40
2-4	3	9	19	28

DALE EVANS COMICS (Also see Queen of the West…)(See Boy Commandos #32)
National Periodical Publications: Sept-Oct, 1948 - No. 24, July-Aug, 1952 (No. 1-19: 52 pgs.)

1-Dale Evans & her horse Buttermilk begin; Sierra Smith begins by Alex Toth	100	300	625	1100
2-Alex Toth-a	47	142	286	500
3-11-Alex Toth-a	34	102	179	310
12-20: 12-Target-c	18	54	94	160
21-24	19	57	99	170

NOTE: *Photo-c-1, 2, 4-14.*

DALGODA
Fantagraphics Books: Aug, 1984 - No. 8, Feb, 1986 (High quality paper)

1- Fujitake-c/a in all — 3.00
2-7: 2,3-Debut Grimwood's Daughter. 8-Alan Moore story — 2.25

DALTON BOYS, THE
Avon Periodicals: 1951

1-(Number on spine)-Kinstler-c	17	51	88	150

DAMAGE
DC Comics: Apr, 1994 - No. 20, Jan, 1996 ($1.75/$1.95/$2.25)

1-20: 6-(9/94)-Zero Hour. 0-(10/94). 7-(11/94). 14-Ray app. — 3.00

DAMAGE CONTROL (See Marvel Comics Presents #19)
Marvel Comics: 5/89 - No. 4, 8/89; V2#1, 12/89 - No. 4, 2/90 ($1.00)
V3#1, 6/91 - No. 4, 9/91 ($1.25, all are limited series)

V1#1-4,V2#1-4,V3#1-4: V1#4-Wolverine app. V2#2,4-Punisher app. 1-Spider-Man app. 2-New Warriors app. 3,4-Silver Surfer app. 4-Infinity Gauntlet parody — 2.50

DAMNED
Image Comics (Homage Comics): June, 1997 - No. 4, Sept, 1997 ($2.50, limited series)

1-4-Steven Grant-s/Mike Zeck-c/a in all — 2.50

DANCES WITH DEMONS (See Marvel Frontier Comics Unlimited)
Marvel Frontier Comics: Sept, 1993 - No. 4, Dec, 1993 ($1.95, limited series)

1-($2.95)-Foil embossed-c; Charlie Adlard & Rod Ramos-a — 3.00
2-4 — 2.25

DANDEE: Four Star Publications: 1947 (Advertised, not published)

DAN DUNN (See Crackajack Funnies, Detective Dan, Famous Feature Stories & Red Ryder)

DANDY COMICS (Also see Happy Jack Howard)
E. C. Comics: Spring, 1947 - No. 7, Spring, 1948

1-Funny animal; Vince Fago-a in all; Dandy in all	36	180	194	335
2	26	78	136	235
3-7: 3-Intro Handy Andy who is c-feature #3 on	20	60	105	175

DANGER
Comic Media/Allen Hardy Assoc.: Jan, 1953 - No. 11, Aug, 1954

1-Heck-c/a	20	60	105	180
2,3,5,7,9-11-Heck-c	11	33	55	90
4-Marijuana cover/story	14	42	72	120
6- "Narcotics" story; begin spy theme	12	36	61	100
8-Bondage/torture/headlights panels	15	45	77	130

Danger Girl #5 © Atomico

Danny Blaze #1 © CC

Daredevil #10 © MAR

	GD2.0	FN6.0	VF8.0	NM9.4

NOTE: *Morisi a-2, 5, 6(3), 10; c-2. Contains some reprints from Danger & Dynamite.*

DANGER (Formerly Comic Media title)
Charlton Comics Group: No. 12, June, 1955 - No. 14, Oct, 1955

12(#1)	10	30	55	80
13,14: 14-r/#12	8	24	42	60

DANGER
Super Comics: 1964

Super Reprint #10-12 (Black Dwarf; #10-r/Great Comics #1 by Novack. #11-r/Johnny Danger #1. #12-r/Red Seal #14), #15-r/Spy Cases #26. #16-Unpublished Chesler material (Yankee Girl), #17-r/Scoop #8 (Capt. Courage & Enchanted Dagger), #18(nd)-r/Guns Against Gangsters #5 (Gun-Master, Annie Oakley, The Chameleon; L.B. Cole-r)

	2	6	12	18

DANGER AND ADVENTURE (Formerly This Magazine Is Haunted; Robin Hood and His Merry Men No. 28 on)
Charlton Comics: No. 22, Feb, 1955 - No. 27, Feb, 1956

22-Ibis the Invincible-c/story; Nyoka app.; last pre-code issue				
	11	33	55	90
23-Lance O'Casey-c/sty; Nyoka app.; Ditko-a thru #27				
	13	39	66	110
24-27: 24-Mike Danger & Johnny Adventure begin	9	27	49	70

DANGER GIRL (Also see Cliffhanger #0)
Image Comics (Cliffhanger Productions): Mar, 1998 - No. 4, Dec, 1998;
DC Comics (Cliffhanger Prod.): No. 5, July, 1999 - No. 7, Feb, 2001

Preview-Bagged in DV8 #14 Voyager Pack				4.00
Preview Gold Edition				8.00
1-($2.95) Hartnell & Campbell-s/Campbell/Garner-a	1	3	6	8
1-($4.95) Chromium cover				35.00
1-American Entertainment Ed.				8.00
1-American Entertainment Gold Ed., 1-Tourbook edition				10.00
1-"Danger-sized" ed.; over-sized format	3	9	20	30
2-($2.50)				4.00
2-Smoking Gun variant cover, 2-Platinum Ed., 2-Dynamic Forces Omnichrome variant-c	2	6	11	15
2-Gold foil cover				9.00
2-Ruby red foil cover				50.00
3,4: 3-c by Campbell, Charest and Adam Hughes. 4-Big knife variant-c				3.00
3,5: 3-Gold foil cover. 5-DF Bikini variant-c				10.00
4-6				3.00
7-($5.95) Wraparound gatefold-c; Last issue				6.00
San Diego Preview (8/98, B&W) flip book w/Wildcats preview				6.00
Sketchbook (2001, $6.95) Campbell-a: sketches for comics, toys, games				7.00
...Special (2/00, $3.50) art by Campbell, Chiodo, and Art Adams				3.50
...: The Dangerous Collection nn(8/98; r-#1)				6.00
...: The Dangerous Collection 2,3: 2-(11/98, $5.95) r/#2,3. 3-('99) r/#4,5				6.00
...: The Dangerous Collection nn, 2-($10.00) Gold foil logo				10.00
...: The Ultimate Collection HC ($29.95) r/#1-7; intro by Bruce Campbell				30.00

DANGER GIRL KAMIKAZE
DC Comics (Cliffhanger): Nov, 2001 - No. 2, Dec., 2001 ($2.95, lim. series)

1,2-Tommy Yune-s/a				3.00

DANGER IS OUR BUSINESS!
Toby Press: 1953(Dec.) - No. 10, June, 1955

1-Captain Comet by Williamson/Frazetta-a, 6 pgs. (science fiction)				
	44	132	264	460
2	13	39	66	110
3-10	11	33	55	90
I.W. Reprint #9('64)-Williamson/Frazetta-r/#1; Kinstler-c				
	9	27	63	105

DANGER IS THEIR BUSINESS (Also see A-1 Comic)
Magazine Enterprises: No. 50, 1952

A-1 50-Powell-a	14	42	72	120

DANGER MAN (TV)
Dell Publishing Co.: No. 1231, Sept-Nov, 1961

Four Color 1231-Patrick McGoohan photo-c	11	33	77	140

DANGER TRAIL (Also see Showcase #50, 51)
National Periodical Publ.: July-Aug, 1950 - No. 5, Mar-Apr, 1951 (52 pgs.)

1-King Faraday begins, ends #4; Toth-a in all	118	354	738	1300

	GD2.0	FN6.0	VF8.0	NM9.
2	84	252	525	925
3-(Rare) one of the rarest early '50s DCs	118	354	738	1300
4,5: 5-Johnny Peril-c/story (moves to Sensation Comics #107); new logo (also see Comic Cavalcade #15-29)	68	205	426	750

DANGER TRAIL
DC Comics: Apr, 1993 - No. 4, July, 1993 ($1.50, limited series)

1-4: Gulacy-c on all				2.25

DANGER UNLIMITED (See San Diego Comic Con Comics #2 & Torch of Liberty Special)

DANGER UNLIMITED (Legend): Feb, 1994 - No. 4, May, 1994 ($2.00, limited series)

1-4: Byrne-c/a/scripts in all; origin stories of both original team (Doc Danger, Thermal, Miss Mirage, & Hunk) & future team (Thermal, Belebet, & Caucus). 1-Intro Torch of Liberty & Golgotha (cameo) in back-up story. 4-Hellboy & Torch of Liberty cameo in lead story				2.50
TPB (1995, $14.95) r/#1-4; includes last pg. originally cut from #4				15.00

DAN HASTINGS (See Syndicate Features)

DANIEL BOONE (See The Exploits of..., Fighting... Frontier Scout...,The Legends of... & March of Comics No. 306)
Dell Publishing Co.: No. 1163, Mar-May, 1961

Four Color 1163-Marsh-a	5	15	35	60

DANIEL BOONE (TV) (See March of Comics No. 306)
Gold Key: Jan, 1965 - No. 15, Apr, 1969 (All have Fess Parker photo-c)

1	9	27	63	110
2	5	15	34	55
3-5	4	12	29	45
6-15	3	9	20	30

DAN'L BOONE
Sussex Publ. Co.: Sept, 1955 - No. 8, Sept, 1957

1	15	45	77	130
2	10	30	55	80
3-8	7	21	38	55

DANNY BLAZE (...Firefighter) (Nature Boy No. 3 on)
Charlton Comics: Aug, 1955 - No. 2, Oct, 1955

1	11	33	55	90
2	9	27	49	70

DANNY DINGLE (See Sparkler Comics)
United Features Syndicate: No. 17, 1940

Single Series 17	26	78	136	235

DANNY THOMAS SHOW, THE (TV)
Dell Publishing Co.: No. 1180, Apr-June, 1961 - No. 1249, Dec-Feb, 1961-62

Four Color 1180-Toth-a, photo-c	17	51	119	220
Four Color 1249-Manning-a, photo-c	16	48	112	205

DARBY O'GILL & THE LITTLE PEOPLE (Movie)(See Movie Comics)
Dell Publishing Co.: 1959 (Disney)

Four Color 1024-Toth-a; photo-c	10	30	70	150

DAREDEVIL (...& the Black Widow #92-107 on-c only; see Giant-Size...,Marvel Advs., Marvel Graphic Novel #24, Marvel Super Heroes, '66 & Spider-Man &...)
Marvel Comics Group: Apr, 1964 - No. 380, Oct, 1998

1-Origin/1st app. Daredevil; reprinted in Marvel Super Heroes #1 (1966); death of Battling Murdock; intro Foggy Nelson & Karen Page; Everett-c/a				
	159	477	1350	2700
2-Fantastic Four cameo; 2nd app. Electro (Spidey villain); Thing guest star				
	45	135	359	650
3-Origin & 1st app. The Owl (villain)	31	93	222	400
4-The Purple Man app.	29	87	202	360
5-Minor costume change; Wood-a begins	20	60	140	250
6,8-10: 9-Origin/1st app. Stilt-Man	14	42	100	170
7-Daredevil battles Sub-Mariner & dons new red costume (4/65)				
	28	84	196	350
11-15: 12-1st app. Plunderer; Ka-Zar app. 13-Facts about Ka-Zar's origin; Kirby-a	7	21	53	85
16,17-Spider-Man x-over. 16-1st Romita-a on Spider-Man (5/66)				
	10	30	70	120

Daredevil #98 © MAR

Daredevil #230 © MAR

Daredevil V2 #2 © MAR

	GD2.0	FN6.0	VF8.0	NM9.4
18-Origin & 1st app. Gladiator	6	18	45	75
19,20	5	15	38	60
21-26,28-30: 24-Ka-Zar app.	4	12	27	42
27-Spider-Man x-over	4	12	29	45
31-40: 38-Fantastic Four x-over; cont'd in F.F. #73. 39-1st Exterminator (later				
becomes Death-Stalker)	3	10	30	35
41,42,44-49: 41-Death Mike Murdock. 42-1st app. Jester. 45-Statue of Liberty				
photo-c	3	9	17	25
43,50-53: 43-Daredevil battles Captain America; origin partially retold. 50-52-B.				
Smith-a. 53-Origin retold; last 12¢ issue	3	9	20	30
54-56,58-60: 54-Spider-Man cameo. 56-1st app. Death's Head (9/69); story				
cont'd in #57 (not same as new Death's Head)	2	6	13	20
57-Reveals i.d. to Karen Page; Death's Head app.	2	6	15	22
61-76,78-80: 79-Stan Lee cameo. 80-Last 15¢ issue	2	6	12	18
77-Spider-Man x-over	2	6	15	22
81-(52 pgs.) Black Widow begins (11/71).	3	9	19	28
82,84-99: 87-Electro-c/story	2	6	11	15
83-B. Smith layouts/Weiss-p	2	6	12	18
100-Origin retold	3	9	19	28
101-104,106-120: 107-Starlin-c; Thanos cameo. 113-1st app. Deathstalker				
(cameo). 114-1st full app. Deathstalker	2	6	9	12
105-Origin Moondragon by Starlin (12/73); Thanos cameo in flashback (early				
app.)	2	6	11	15
121-130,137: 124-1st app. Copperhead; Black Widow leaves. 126-1st				
new Torpedo	1	3	6	8
131-Origin/1st app. new Bullseye (see Nick Fury #15)				
	3	9	17	25
132-136-(Regular 25¢ editions). 132-Bullseye app.	1	3	6	8
132-136-(30¢-c variants, limited distribution)(4-8/76)	2	6	9	12
138-Ghost Rider-c/story; Death's Head is reincarnated; Byrne-a				
	1	4	7	10
139-157: 142-Nova cameo. 146-148-(Reg. 30¢-c). 146-Bullseye app. 150-1st app.				
Paladin. 151-Reveals i.d. to Heather Glenn. 155-Black Widow returns.				
156-The 1960s Daredevil app.	1	3	5	7
146-148-(35¢-c variants, limited distribution)	1	3	5	7
158-Frank Miller art begins (5/79); origin/death of Deathstalker (see Captain				
America #235 & Spectacular Spider-Man #27	4	12	30	50
159	3	9	19	28
160,161,163,164,169: 163-Hulk cameo. 164-Origin retold. 169-Electra app.				
	2	6	12	18
162-Ditko-a; no Miller-a	1	3	5	7
165-167,170	2	6	9	12
168-Origin/1st app. Elektra	5	15	34	55
171-175: 174-Elektra app.	1	3	6	9
176-180-Elektra app. 178-Cage app. 179-Anti-smoking issue mentioned in the				
Congressional Record	1	3	6	8
181-(52 pgs.)-Death of Elektra; Punisher cameo out of costume				
	2	6	11	15
182-184-Punisher app. by Miller (drug issues)	1	3	5	7
185-191: 187-New Black Widow. 189-Death of Stick. 190-($1.00, 52 pgs.)-Elek-				
tra returns, part origin. 191-Last Miller Daredevil				6.00
192-195,197-199,201-207,209-218,220-226,234-237: 197-Bullseye app.				
226-Frank Miller plots begin				3.00
196-Wolverine app.	2	6	9	12
200,208,219,228-233,238: 200-Bullseye app. 208-Harlan Ellison scripts borrowed				
from Avengers TV episode "House that Jack Built". 219-Miller-c/script.				
228-233-Last Miller scripts. 238-Mutant Massacre; Sabretooth app.				4.00
227-Miller scripts begin				5.00
239,240,242-247				3.00
241-Todd McFarlane-a(p)				4.00
248,249-Wolverine app.				5.00
250,251,253,258: 250-1st app. Bullet. 258-Intro The Bengal (a villain)				3.00
252,260: 252-Fall of the Mutants. 260-Typhoid Mary app.				4.00
254-Origin & 1st app. Typhoid Mary (5/88)				6.00
255,256: 255,256-2nd/3rd app. Typhoid Mary. 259-Typhoid Mary app.				4.00
257-Punisher app. (x-over w/Punisher #10)				5.00
261-281,283-294,296-299,301-304,307-318: 270-1st app. Black Heart. 272-Intro				
Shotgun (villain). 281-Silver Surfer cameo. 283-Capt. America app.				
297-Typhoid Mary app.; Kingpin storyline begins. 292-D.G. Chichester scripts				
begin. 293-Punisher app. 303-Re-intro the Owl. 304-Garney-c/a.				

	GD2.0	FN6.0	VF8.0	NM9.4
309-Punisher-c.; Terror app. 310-Calypso-c.				2.50
282,295,300,305,306: 282-Silver Surfer app. 295-Ghost Rider app. 300-($2.00,				
52 pgs.)-Kingpin story ends. 305,306-Spider-Man-c				3.00
319-Prologue to Fall From Grace; Elektra returns				4.00
319-2nd printing w/black-c				2.50
320-Fall From Grace Pt 1				4.00
321-Fall From Grace regular ed.; Pt 2; new costume; Venom app.				3.00
321-($2.00)-Wraparound Glow-in-the-dark-c ed.				4.00
322-Fall From Grace Pt 3; Eddie Brock app.				3.50
323,324-Fall From Grace Pt. 4 & 5: 323-Vs. Venom-c/story. 324-Morbius-c/				
story				3.00
325-($2.50, 52 pgs.)-Fall From Grace ends; contains bound-in poster				3.50
326-349,351-353: 326-New logo. 328-Bound-in trading card sheet. 330-Gambit				
app. 348-1st Cary Nord art in DD (1/96);"Dec" on-c. 353-Karl Kesel scripts;				
Nord-c/a begins; Mr. Hyde/app.				2.50
350-($2.95)-Double-sized				3.00
350-($3.50)-Double-sized; gold ink-c				3.50
354-374,376-379: Kesel scripts, Nord-c/a in all. 354-$1.50-c begins. 355-Larry				
Hama layouts; Pyro app. 358-Mysterio-c/app. 359-Absorbing Man cameo.				
360-Absorbing Man-c/app. 361-Black Widow-c/app. 363-Gene Colan-a(p)				
begins. 368-Omega Red-c/app. 372-Ghost Rider-c/app. 376-379-"Flying				
Blind", DD goes undercover for S.H.I.E.L.D.				2.50
375-($2.99)-Wraparound-c; Mr. Fear-c/app.				3.00
380-($2.99) Final issue; flashback story				4.00
Special 1(9/67, 25¢, 68 pgs.)-New art/story	4	12	30	50
Special 2,3: 2(2/71, 25¢, 52 pgs.)-Entire book has Powell/Wood-r; Wood-c.				
3(1/72, 52 pgs.)-Reprints	2	6	12	18
Annual 4(10/76)				6.00
Annual 4(#5)-10: ('89-94 68 pgs.)-5-Atlantis Attacks. 6-Sutton-a. 7-Guice-a				
(7 pgs.). 8-Deathlok-c/story. 9-Polybagged w/card. 10				3.00
...:Born Again TPB ($17.95)-r/#227-233; Miller's/Mazzucchelli-a & new-c				20.00
.../Deadpool: (Annual '97, $2.99)-Wraparound-c				3.00
...:Fall From Grace TPB ($19.95)-r/#319-325				20.00
... :Gang War TPB ($15.95)-r/#169-172,180; Miller-s/a(p)				16.00
.../Punisher TPB (1988, $4.95)-r/D.D. #182-184 (all printings)				5.00
...Visionaries: Frank Miller Vol. 1 TPB ($17.95)-r/#158-161,163-167				18.00
...Visionaries: Frank Miller Vol. 2 TPB ($24.95)-r/#168-182; new Miller-c				25.00
...Visionaries: Frank Miller Vol. 3 TPB ($24.95)-r/#183-191, What If? #28,35 &				
Bizarre Adventures #28; new Miller-c				25.00

NOTE: **Art Adams** c-238b, 239. **Austin** a-191c c-151i, 200i. **John Buscema** a-136, 137b, 234b, 235p; c-86p, 136i, 137p, 142, 219. **Byrne** c-200p, 201, 203, 223. **Capullo** a-286p. **Colan** a(p)-20-49, 53-82, 84-98, 100, 110, 112, 124, 153, 154, 156, 157, Spec. 1p; c(p)-20-42, 44-49, 53-60, 71, 92, 98, 138, 153, 154, 156, 157, Annual 1. **Craig** a-50i, 52i. **Ditko** a-162, 234p, 235p, 264p; c-162. **Everett** c/a-1; inks-21, 83. **Garney** a-c-304. **Gil Kane** a-141p, 146-148p, 151p; c(p)-85, 90, 91, 93, 94, 115, 116, 119, 120, 125, 126, 133, 135, 147, Annual 1. **Kirby** c-2-4, 5p, 12p, 3a, 4. **Layton** c-202. **Miller** scripts-168-182, 183(part), 184-191, 219, 227-233; a-158-161p, 163-184p, 191p; c-158-161p, 163-184p, 191p, 219. **Orlando** a-2-4p. **Powell** a-9p, 11p, Special 1r, 2r. **Simonson** c-199, 236p. **B. Smith** a-236p; c-51p, 52p, 217. **Starlin** a-105p. **Steranko** c-44i. **Tuska** a-39i, 145p. **Williamson** a(i)-237, 239, 240, 243, 248-257, 259-282, 283(part), 284, 285, 287, 288(part), 289(part), 293-300; c(i)-237, 243, 244, 248-257, 259-278, 280-289, Annual 8. **Wood** a-5-8, 9i, 10, 11i. Spec. 2i; c-5i, 6-11, 164i.

DAREDEVIL (Volume 2) (Marvel Knights)
Marvel Comics: Nov, 1998 - Present ($2.50)

1-Kevin Smith-s/Quesada & Palmiotti-a				6.00
1-($6.95) DF Edition w/Quesada & Palmiotti var.-c				7.00
1-($6.00) DF Sketch Ed. w/B&W-c				6.00
2-Two covers by Campbell and Quesada/Palmiotti				5.00
3-8: 4,5-Bullseye app. 8-Spider-Man-c/app.; last Smith-s				3.00
9-11-David Mack-s; intro Echo				3.00
12-15: 12-Begin $2.99-c; Haynes-a. 13,14-Quesada-a				3.00
16-19-Direct editions; David Mack-c/painted-a				3.00
18-22-Newsstand editions with variant cover logo "Marvel Unlimited Featuring..."				
				3.00
20-($3.50) Gale-s/Winslade-a; back-up by Stan Lee-s/Colan-a; Mack-c				3.50
21-25-($2.99) Gale-s				3.00
26-28-Bendis/Maleev-a				3.00
TPB ($9.95) r/#1-3				10.00
Visionaries TPB ($19.95) r/#1-8; Ben Affleck intro.				20.00

DAREDEVIL / BATMAN (Also see Batman/Daredevil)
Marvel Comics/ DC Comics: 1997 ($5.99, one-shot)

nn-McDaniel-c/a				6.00

Daredevil: Yellow #1 © MAR

Daredevil Comics #2 © LEV

Daring Mystery Comics #2 © MAR

DAREDEVIL: NINJA
Marvel Comics: Dec, 2000 - No. 3, Feb, 2001 ($2.99, limited series)

1-3: Bendis-s/Haynes-a		3.00
TPB (7/01, $12.95) r/#1-3 with cover and sketch gallery		13.00

DAREDEVIL/ SHI (See Shi/ Daredevil)
Marvel Comics/ Crusade Comics: Feb,1997 ($2.95, limited series)

1		3.00

DAREDEVIL/ SPIDER-MAN
Marvel Comics: Jan, 2001 - No. 4, Apr, 2001 ($2.99, limited series)

1-4-Jenkins-s/Winslade-a/Alex Ross-c; Stilt Man app.		3.00
TPB (8/01, $12.95) r/#1-4; Ross-c		13.00

DAREDEVIL THE MAN WITHOUT FEAR
Marvel Comics: Oct, 1993 - No. 5, Feb, 1994 ($2.95, limited series), (foil embossed covers)

1-5: Miller scripts; Romita, Jr./Williamson-c/a		4.00
Hardcover		100.00
Trade paperback		20.00

DAREDEVIL: YELLOW
Marvel Comics: Aug, 2001 - No. 6, Jan, 2002 ($3.50, limited series)

1-6-Jeph Loeb-s/Tim Sale-a/c; origin & yellow costume days retold		3.50

DAREDEVIL COMICS (See Silver Streak Comics)
Lev Gleason Publications (Funnies, Inc. No. 1): July, 1941 - No. 134, Sept, 1956 (Charles Biro stories)

1-No. 1 titled "Daredevil Battles Hitler"; The Silver Streak, Lance Hale, Cloud Curtis, Dickey Dean, Pirate Prince team up w/Daredevil and battle Hitler; Daredevil battles the Claw; Origin of Hitler feature story. Hitler photo app. on-c	1035	3105	7245	14,500
2-London, Pat Patriot (by Reed Crandall), Nightro, Real American No. 1 (by Briefer #2-11), Dickie Dean, Pirate Prince, & Times Square begin; intro. & only app. The Pioneer, Champion of America	300	900	1875	3500
3-Origin of 13	190	570	1188	2100
4	164	492	1023	1800
5-Intro. Sniffer & Jinx; Ghost vs. Claw begins by Bob Wood, ends #20	127	381	795	1400
6-(#7 in indicia)	109	327	682	1200
7-10: 8-Nightro ends	91	273	568	1000
11-London, Pat Patriot end; classic bondage/torture-c	114	342	712	1250
12-Origin of The Claw; Scoop Scuttle by Wolverton begins (2-4 pgs.), ends #22, not in #21	141	423	881	1550
13-Intro. of Little Wise Guys (10/42)	118	354	738	1300
14	64	192	398	700
15-Death of Meatball	93	279	581	1025
16,17	54	177	369	650
18-New origin of Daredevil (not same as Silver Streak #6). Hitler, Mussolini Tojo and Mickey Mouse app. on-c	127	381	795	1400
19,20	50	150	300	525
21-Reprints cover of Silver Streak #6 (on inside) plus intro. of The Claw from Silver Streak #1	88	264	550	975
22-30: 27-Bondage/torture-c	40	120	232	400
31-Death of The Claw	80	240	500	875
32-37,39-41: 35-Two Daredevil stories begin, end #68 (35-41 are 64 pgs.)	31	93	165	285
38-Origin Daredevil retold from #18	43	129	257	450
42-50: 42-Intro. Kilroy in Daredevil	25	75	130	225
51-69-Last Daredevil issue (12/50)	18	54	94	160
70-Little Wise Guys take over book; McWilliams-a; Hot Rock Flanagan begins, ends #80	11	33	55	90
71-79,81: 79-Daredevil returns	9	27	49	70
80-Daredevil x-over	9	27	51	75
82,90,100: 82,90-One pg. Frazetta ad in both	9	27	49	70
83-89,91-99,101-134	8	24	42	60

NOTE: *Biro* c/a-all? *Bolle* a-125. *Maurer* a-75. *McWilliams* a-73, 75, 79, 80.

DARIA JONTAK
JMJ Media Group: Jan, 2001 - Present ($4.99)

1-Matt Busch-s/a		5.00

DARING ADVENTURES (Also see Approved Comics)
St. John Publishing Co.: Nov, 1953 (25¢, 3-D, came w/glasses)

1 (3-D)-Reprints lead story from Son of Sinbad #1 by Kubert	36	108	191	330

DARING ADVENTURES
I.W. Enterprises/Super Comics: 1963 - 1964

I. W. Reprint #8-r/Fight Comics #53; Matt Baker-a	5	15	38	60
I.W. Reprint #9-r/Blue Bolt #115; Disbrow-a(3)	6	18	40	65
Super Reprint #10,11('63)-r/Dynamic #24,16; 11-Marijuana story; Yankee Boy app.; Mac Raboy-a	4	12	26	40
Super Reprint #12('64)-Phantom Lady from Fox (r/#14 only? w/splash pg. omitted); Matt Baker-a	13	39	91	155
Super Reprint #15('64)-r/Hooded Menace #1	8	24	56	90
Super Reprint #16('64)-r/Dynamic #12	3	10	23	35
Super Reprint #17('64)-r/Green Lama #3 by Raboy	4	12	30	50
Super Reprint #18-Origin Atlas from unpublished Atlas Comics #1	4	12	29	45

DARING COMICS (Formerly Daring Mystery) (Jeanie Comics No. 13 on)
Timely Comics (HPC): No. 9, Fall, 1944 - No. 12, Fall, 1945

9-Human Torch, Toro & Sub-Mariner begin	118	354	738	1300
10-12: 10-The Angel only app. 11,12-The Destroyer app.	95	285	597	1050

NOTE: *Schomburg* c-9-11. *Sekowsky* c-12? Human Torch, Toro & Sub-Mariner c-9-12.

DARING CONFESSIONS (Formerly Youthful Hearts)
Youthful Magazines: No. 4, 11/52 - No. 7, 5/53; No. 8, 10/53

4-Doug Wildey-a; Tony Curtis story	16	48	83	140
5-8: 5-Ray Anthony photo on-c. 6,8-Wildey-a	12	36	61	100

DARING ESCAPES
Image Comics: Sept, 1998 - No. 4, Mar, 1999 ($2.95/$2.50, mini-series)

1-Houdini; following app. in Spawn #19,20		3.00
2-4-($2.50)		2.50

DARING LOVE (Radiant Love No. 2 on)
Gilmor Magazines: Sept-Oct, 1953

1-Steve Ditko's 1st published work (1st drawn was Fantastic Fears #5)(Also see Black Magic #27)(scarce)	43	129	257	450

DARING LOVE (Formerly Youthful Romances)
Ribage/Pix: No. 15, 12/52; No. 16, 2/53-c, 4/53-Indicia; No. 17-4/53-c & indicia

15	11	33	55	90
16,17: 17-Photo-c	10	30	55	80

NOTE: *Colletta* a-15. *Wildey* a-17.

DARING LOVE STORIES (See Fox Giants)

DARING MYSTERY COMICS (Comedy Comics No. 9 on; title changed to Daring Comics with No. 9)
Timely Comics (TPI 1-6/TCI 7,8): 1/40 - No. 5, 6/40; No. 6, 9/40; No. 7, 4/41 - No. 8, 1/42

1-Origin The Fiery Mask (1st app.) by Joe Simon; Monako, Prince of Magic (1st app.), John Steele, Soldier of Fortune (1st app.), Doc Denton (1st app.) begin; Flash Foster & Barney Mullen, Sea Rover only app; bondage-c	1785	5355	12,500	25,000
2-(Rare)-Origin The Phantom Bullet (1st & only app.); The Laughing Mask & Mr. E only app.; Trojak the Tiger Man begins, ends #6; Zephyr Jones & K-4 & His Sky Devils app., also #4	731	2193	4750	9500
3-The Phantom Reporter, Dale of FBI, Captain Strong only app.; Breeze Barton Marvex the Super-Robot, The Purple Mask begin	462	1386	3000	6000
4,5: 4-Last Purple Mask; Whirlwind Carter begins; Dan Gorman, G-Man app. 5-The Falcon begins (1st app.); The Fiery Mask, Little Hercules app. by Sagendorf in the Segar style; bondage-c	300	900	1875	3600
6-Origin & only app. Marvel Boy by S&K; Flying Flame, Dynaman, & Stuporman only app.; The Fiery Mask by S&K; S&K-c	400	1200	2500	4800
7-Origin The Blue Diamond, Captain Daring by S&K, The Fin by Everett, The Challenger, The Silver Scorpion & The Thunderer by Burgos; Mr. Millions app	317	951	1979	3800
8-Origin Citizen V; Last Fin, Silver Scorpion, Capt. Daring by Borth, Blue				

Dark Angel: Phoenix Resurrected #1
© Image

Darkchylde #2
© Randy Queen & Majesty Graphics

Darkhawk #6 © MAR

DA

Diamond & The Thunderer; Kirby & part solo Simon-c; Rudy the Robot only
app.; Citizen V, Fin & Silver Scorpion continue in Comedy #9

		273	819	1705	3000

)TE: **Schomburg** c-1-4, 7. **Simon** a-2, 3, 5. Cover features: 1-Fiery Mask; 2-Phantom Bullet; 3-
urple Mask; 4-G-Man; 5-The Falcon; 6-Marvel Boy; 7, 8-Multiple characters.

ARING NEW ADVENTURES OF SUPERGIRL, THE
C Comics: Nov, 1982 - No. 13, Nov, 1983 (Supergirl No. 14 on)

		1	3	6	8
1-Origin retold; Lois Lane back-ups in #2-12		1	3	6	8
2-13: 8,9-Doom Patrol app. 13-New costume; flag-c					4.00

)TE: **Buckler** c-1p, 2p. **Giffen** c-3p, 4p. **Gil Kane** c-6, ,8, 9, 11-13.

ARK, THE
ontinuum Comics: Nov, 1990 - No. 4, Feb, 1993; V2#1, May, 1993 - V2#7, Apr?,
994 ($1.95)

1-4: 1-Bright-p; Panosian, Hanna-i; Stroman-a. 2-(1/92)-Stroman-c/a(p).				
4-Perez-c & part-i				3.00
2#1,V2#2-6: V2#1-Red foil Bart Sears-c. V2#1-Red non-foil variant-c.				
V2#1-2nd printing w/blue foil Bart Sears-c. V2#2-Stroman/Bryant-a. 3-Perez-				
c(i). 3-6-Foil-c. 4-Perez-c & part-i;bound-in trading cards. 5,6-(2,3/94)-Perez-				
c(i). 7-(B&W)-Perez-c(i)				2.25
onvention Book 1 ,2(Fall/94, 10/94)-Perez-c				2.25

ARK ANGEL (Formerly Hell's Angel)
larvel Comics UK, Ltd.: No. 6, Dec, 1992 - No. 16, Dec, 1993 ($1.75)

| 6-8,13-16: 6-Excalibur-c/story. 8-Psylocke app. | | | | 2.25 |
| 9-12-Wolverine/X-Men app. | | | | 3.00 |

ARK ANGEL: PHOENIX RESURRECTION (Kia Asamiya's...)
nage Comics: May, 2000 - Present ($2.95)

| 1-4-Kia Asamiya-s/a. 3-Van Fleet variant-c | | | | 3.00 |

ARKCHYLDE (Also see Dreams of the Darkchylde)
aximum Press #1-3/ Image Comics #4 on: June, 1996 - No. 5, Sept, 1997
i2.95/ $2.50)

1-Randy Queen-c/a/scripts; "Roses" cover				6.00
1-American Entertainment Edition-wraparound-c				6.00
1-"Fashion magazine-style" variant-c		1	3	5	7
1-Special Comicon Edition (contents of #1) Winged devil variant-c			5.00	
1-($2.50)-Remastered Ed.-wraparound-c				4.00
2(Reg-c),2-Spiderweb and Moon variant-c				4.00
3(Reg-c),3-"Kalvin Klein" variant-c by Drew				3.00
4(Reg-c), 4-Variant-c				4.00
5				4.00
5-B&W Edition, 5-Dynamic Forces Gold Ed.				8.00
)-(3/98, $2.50)				2.50
)-American Entertainment Ed.				4.00
)-Dynamic Forces Ed.				5.00
)-Dynamic Forces Gold Ed.				7.00
)-Remastered (1/01, $2.95) includes Darkchylde: Redemption preview				3.00
#2-WIzard offer				4.00
#2 Variant-c				4.00
#2 Gold Ed.				9.00
The Descent TPB ('98, $19.95) r/#1-5; bagged with Darkchylde The Legacy				
Preview Special 1998; listed price is for TPB only				20.00

ARKCHYLDE REDEMPTION
arkchylde Entertainment: Feb, 2001 - No. 3 ($2.95)

| 1,2: 1-Wraparound-c | | | | 3.00 |

ARKCHYLDE SKETCH BOOK
nage Comics (Dynamic Forces): 1998

| 1-Regular-c | | | | 8.00 |
| 1-DarkChrome cover | | | | 16.00 |

ARKCHYLDE SUMMER SWIMSUIT SPECTACULAR
C Comics (WildStorm): Aug, 1999 ($3.95, one-shot)

| 1-Pin-up art by various | | | | 4.00 |

ARKCHYLDE SWIMSUIT ILLUSTRATED
nage Comics: 1998 ($2.50, one-shot)

#-Pin-up art by various				2.50
#-(6.95) Variant cover				7.00
1-American Entertainment Ed.				3.00

1-Dynamic Forces Ed.				4.00
1-Dynamic Forces Gold Ed.				6.00
1-Chromium cover				15.00

DARKCHYLDE THE DIARY
Image Comics: June, 1997 ($2.50, one-shot)

1-Queen-c/s/ art by various				2.50
1-Variant-c				5.00
1-Holochrome variant-c				8.00

DARKCHYLDE THE LEGACY
Image Comics/DC (WildStorm) #3 on: Aug, 1998 - No. 3 ($2.50)

| 1-3: 1-Queen-c. 2-Two covers by Queen and Art Adams | | | | 2.50 |

DARK CLAW ADVENTURES
DC Comics (Amalgam): June, 1997 ($1.95, one-shot)

| 1-Templeton-c/s/a & Burchett-a | | | | 2.50 |

DARK CROSSINGS: DARK CLOUDS RISING
Image Comics (Top Cow): June, 2000; Oct, 2000 ($5.95, limited series)

| 1-Witchblade, Darkness, Tomb Raider crossover; Dwayne Turner-a | | | | 6.00 |
| 1-(Dark Clouds Overhead) | | | | 6.00 |

DARK CRYSTAL, THE (Movie)
Marvel Comics Group: April, 1983 - No. 2, May, 1983

| 1,2-Adaptation of film | | | | 3.00 |

DARKDEVIL (See Spider-Girl)
Marvel Comics: Nov, 2000 - No. 3, Jan, 2001 ($2.99, limited series)

| 1-3: 1-Origin of Darkdevil; Kingpin-c/app. | | | | 3.00 |

DARK DOMINION
Defiant: Oct, 1993 - No. 10, July, 1994 ($2.50)

| 1-10-Len Wein scripts begin. 4-Free extra 16 pgs. 7-9-J.G. Jones-c/a. 10-Pre- | | | | |
| Schism issue; Shooter/Wein script; John Ridgway-a | | | | 2.50 |

DARKER IMAGE (Also see Deathblow, The Maxx, & Bloodwulf)
Image Comics: Mar, 1993 ($1.95, one-shot)

1-The Maxx by Sam Kieth begins; Bloodwulf by Rob Liefeld & Deathblow by				
Jim Lee begin (both 1st app.); polybagged w/1 of 3 cards by Kieth, Lee or				
Liefeld				2.50
1-B&W interior pgs. w/silver foil logo				6.00

DARKEWOOD
Aircel Publishing: 1987 - No. 5, 1988 ($2.00, 28pgs, limited series)

| 1-5 | | | | 2.25 |

DARK FANTASIES
Dark Fantasy: 1994 - No. 8, 1995 ($2.95)

1-Test print Run (3,000)-Linsner-c		1	3	6	8
1-Linsner-c					5.00
2-8: 2-4 (Deluxe), 2-4 (Regular), 5-8 (Deluxe; $3.95)					4.00
5-8 (Regular; $3.50)					3.50

DARK GUARD
Marvel Comics UK: Oct, 1993 - No. 4, Jan, 1994 ($1.75)

| 1-($2.95)-Foil stamped-c | | | | 3.00 |
| 2-4 | | | | 2.25 |

DARKHAWK
Marvel Comics: Mar, 1991 - No. 50, Apr, 1995 ($1.00/$1.25/$1.50)

1-Origin/1st app. Darkhawk; Hobgoblin cameo				4.00
2,3,13,14: 2-Spider-Man & Hobgoblin app. 3-Spider-Man & Hobgoblin app.				
13,14-Venom-c/story				3.00
4-12,15-24,26-49: 6-Capt. America & Daredevil x-over. 9-Punisher app.				
11,12-Tombstone app. 19-Spider-Man & Brotherhood of Evil Mutants-c/story.				
20-Spider-Man app. 22-Ghost Rider-c/story. 23-Origin begins, ends #25.				
27-New Warriors-c/story. 35-Begin 3 part Venom story. 39-Bound-in trading				
card sheet				2.25
25,50: (52 pgs.)-Red holo-grafx foil-c w/double gatefold poster; origin of				
Darkhawk armor revealed.				3.00
Annual 1-3 ('92-'94,68 pgs.)-1-Vs. Iron Man. 2 -Polybagged w/card				3.00

DARKHOLD: PAGES FROM THE BOOK OF SINS (See Midnight Sons Unltd)
Marvel Comics (Midnight Sons imprint #15 on): Oct, 1992 - No. 16, Jan, 1994

	GD2.0	FN6.0	VF8.0	NM9.4

1-($2.75, 52 pgs.)-Polybagged w/poster by Andy & Adam Kubert; part 4 of
   Rise of the Midnight Sons storyline 3.00
2-10,12-16: 3-Reintro Modred the Mystic (see Marvel Chillers #1). 4-
   Sabertooth-c/sty. 5-Punisher & Ghost Rider app. 15-Spot varnish-c. 15,16-
   Siege of Darkness part 4&12 2.25
11-($2.25)-Outer-c is a Darkhold envelope made of black parchment w/gold ink
   2.50

DARK HORSE CLASSICS (Title series), **Dark Horse Comics**
1992 ($3.95, B&W, 52 pgs. nn's: The Last of the Mohicans. 20,000 Leagues
   Under the Sea 4.00

DARK HORSE CLASSICS, 5/96 ($2.95) 1-r/Predator: Jungle Tales 3.00
--**ALIENS VERSUS PREDATOR,** 2/97 - No. 6, 7/97 ($2.95.) 1-6: r/Aliens Versus
   Predator 3.00
--**GODZILLA: KING OF THE MONSTERS,** 4/98 ($2.95) 1-6: 1-r/Godzilla: Color
   Special; Art Adams-a 3.00
--**STAR WARS: DARK EMPIRE,** 3/97 - No. 6, 8/97 ($2.95) 1-6: r/Star Wars:
   Dark Empire 3.00
--**TERROR OF GODZILLA,** 8/98 - No. 6, 1/99 ($2.95) 1-6-r/manga Godzilla in
   color; Art Adams-c 3.00

DARK HORSE COMICS
Dark Horse Comics: Aug, 1992 - No. 25, Sept, 1994 ($2.50)
1-Dorman double gategold painted-c; Predator, Robocop, Timecop (3-part) &
   Renegade stories begin 3.00
2-6,11-25: 2-Mignola-c. 3-Begin 3-part Aliens story; Aliens-c. 4-Predator-c.
   6-Begin 4 part Robocop story. 12-Begin 2-part Aliens & 3-part Predator
   stories. 13-Thing From Another World begins w/Nino-a(i). 15-Begin 2-part
   Aliens: Cargo story. 16-Begin 3-part Predator story. 18-Begin 3-part Star
   Wars: Droids story & 3-part Aliens: Alien story; Droids-c. 19-Begin 2-part X
   story; X cover 2.50
7-Begin Star Wars: Tales of the Jedi story   1   3   5   7
8-1st app. X and begins; begin 4-part James Bond 6.00
9,10: 9-Star Wars ends. 10-X ends; Begin 3-part Predator & Godzilla stories
   4.00
NOTE: *Art Adams c-11.*

DARK HORSE DOWN UNDER
Dark Horse Comics: June, 1994 - No. 3, Oct, 1994 ($2.50, B&W, limited series)
1-3 2.50

DARK HORSE MAVERICK
Dark Horse Comics: July, 2000; July, 2001 (B&W, annual)
2000-($3.95) Short stories by Miller, Chadwick, Sakai, Pearson 4.00
2001-($4.99) Short stories by Sakai, Wagner and others; Miller-c 5.00

DARK HORSE MONSTERS
Dark Horse Comics: Feb, 1997 ($2.95, one-shot)
1-reprints 3.00

DARK HORSE PRESENTS
Dark Horse Comics: July, 1986 - No. 157, Sept, 2000 ($1.50-$2.95, B&W)
1-1st app. Concrete by Paul Chadwick   1   4   7   10
1-2nd printing (1988, $1.50) 2.25
1-Silver ink 3rd printing (1992, $2.25)-Says 2nd printing inside 2.25
2-9: 2-6,9-Concrete app. 4.00
10-1st app. The Mask; Concrete app.   1   4   7   10
11-19,21-23: 11-19,21-Mask stories. 12,14,16,18,22-Concrete app. 15(2/88).
   17-All Roachmill issue 3.00
20-(68 pgs.)-Concrete, Flaming Carrot, Mr. Monster app.   1   4   7   10
24-Origin Aliens-c/story (11/88); Mr. Monster app.   2   6   12   18
25-31,33,37-41,44,45,47-49: 28-(52 pgs.)-Concrete app.; Mr. Monster story
   (homage to Graham Ingels). 33-(44 pgs.). 38-Concrete. 40-(52 pgs.)-1st
   Argosy story. 44-Crash Ryan. 48,49-Contain 2 trading cards 3.00
32,34,35: 32-(68 pgs.)-Annual; Concrete, American. 34-Aliens-c/story.
   35-Predator-c/story 4.00
36-1st Aliens Vs. Predator story; painted-c, 36-Variant line drawn-c 5.00
42,43,46: 42,43-Aliens-c/stories. 46-Prequel to new Predator II mini-series 3.00
50-S/F story by Perez; contains 2 trading cards 3.00
51-53-Sin City by Frank Miller, parts 2-4; 51,53-Miller-c (see D.H.P. Fifth
   Anniv. Special for pt. 1) 3.00

54-62: 54-(9/91) The Next Men begins (1st app.) by Byrne; Miller-a/Morrow-c.
   Homocide by Morrow (also in #55). 55-2nd app. The Next Men; parts 5 & 6 of
   Sin City by Miller; Miller-c. 56-(68 pg. annual)-part 7 of Sin City by Miller; part
   prologue to Aliens: Genocide; Next Men by Byrne. 57-(52 pgs.)-Part 8 of Sin
   City by Miller; Next Men by Byrne; Byrne & Miller-c; Alien Fire story; swipes
   cover to Daredevil #1. 58,59-Part 9,10 Sin City by Miller; Alien Fire stories.
   60,61-Part 11,12 Sin City by Miller. 62-Last Sin City (entire book by Miller,
   c/a(52 pgs.) 4.00
63-66,68-79,81-84-($2.25): 64-Dr. Giggles begins (1st app.), ends #66; Boris
   the Bear story. 66-New Concrete-c/story by Chadwick. 71-Begin 3 part
   Dominque story by Jim Balent; Balent/-5. 72-(3/93)-Begin 3-part Eudaemon
   (1st app.) story by Nelson 3.00
67-($3.95, 68 pgs.)-Begin 8-part prelude to Predator: Race War mini-series;
   Oscar Wilde adapt. by Russell 4.00
80-Art Adams-c/a (Monkeyman & O'Brien) 4.00
85-87,92-99: 85-Begin $2.50-c. 92, 93, 95-Too Much Coffee Man 3.00
88-91-Hellboy by Mignola 4.00
NOTE: *There are 5 different Dark Horse Presents #100 issues*
100-1-Intro Lance Blastoff by Miller; Milk & Cheese by Evan Dorkin 4.00
100-2-100-5: 100-2-Hellboy-c by Wrightson; Hellboy story by Mignola; includes
   Roberta Gregory & Paul Pope stories. 100-3-Darrow-c, Concrete by
   Chadwick; Pekar story. 100-4-Gibbons-c; Miller story, Geary story/a. 100-5-
   Allred-c, Adams, Dorkin, Pope 3.00
101-125: 101-Aliens c/a by Wrightson, story by Paul Pope. 103-Kirby gatefold-c
   106-Big Blown Baby by Bill Wray. 107-Mignola-c/a. 109-Begin $2.95-c; Paul
   Pope-c. 110-Ed Brubaker-a/scripts. 114-Flip books begin; Lance Blastoff by
   Miller; Star Slammers by Simonson. 115-Miller-c. 117-Aliens-c/app. 118-Eva
   Dorkin-c/a. 119-Monkeyman & O'Brien. 124-Predator. 125-Nocturnals 3.00
126-($3.95, 48 pgs.)-Flip book: Nocturnals, Starship Troopers 4.00
127-134,136-140: 127-Nocturnals. 129-The Hammer. 132-134-Warren-a 3.00
135-($3.50) The Mark 3.50
141-All Buffy the Vampire Slayer issue 4.00
142-149: 142-Mignola-c. 143-Tarzan. 146,147-Aliens vs. Predator. 148-Xena
   3.00
150-($4.50) Buffy-c by Green; Buffy, Concrete, Fish Police app. 4.50
151-157: 151-Hellboy-c/app. 153-155-Angel flip-c. 156,157-Witch's Son 4.00
Annual 1997 ($4.95, 64 pgs.)-Flip book; Body Bags, Aliens. Pearson-c; stories
   by Allred & Stephens, Pope, Smith & Morrow   1   3   6
Annual 1998 ($4.95, 64 pgs.)-1st Buffy the Vampire Slayer comic app.;
   Hellboy story and cover by Mignola   1   3   5
Annual 1999 (7/99, $4.95) Stories of Xena, Hellboy, Ghost, Luke Skywalker,
   Groo, Concrete, the Mask and Usagi Yojimbo in their youth. 5.0
Annual 2000 ($4.95) Girl sidekicks; Chiodo-c and flip photo Buffy-c 5.0
...Aliens Platinum Edition (1992)-r/DHP #24,43,46,56 & Special 11.0
...Fifth Anniversary Special nn (4/91, $9.95)-Part 1 of Sin City by Frank Miller
   (c/a); Aliens, Aliens vs. Predator, Concrete, Roachmill, Give Me Liberty &
   The American stories 10.0
The One Trick Rip-off (1997, $12.95, TPB)-r/stories from #101-112 13.0
NOTE: *Geary a-59, 60. Miller a-Special, 51-53, 55-62; c-59-62, 100-1; c-51, 53, 55, 59-62,
100-1. Moebius a-63; c-63, 70. Vess a-78; c-75, 78.*

DARK KNIGHT (See Batman: The Dark Knight Returns & Legends of the...)
DARK KNIGHT STRIKES AGAIN, THE (Also see Batman: The Dark Knight Returns)
DC Comics: 2001 - No. 3 ($7.95, prestige format, limited series)
1-Frank Miller-s/a/c; sequel 3 years after Dark Knight Returns; 2 covers 8.0

DARKLON THE MYSTIC (Also see Eerie Magazine #79,80)
Pacific Comics: Oct, 1983 (one-shot)
1-Starlin-c/a(r) 4.0

DARKMAN (Movie)
Marvel Comics: Sept, 1990; Oct, 1990 - No. 3, Dec, 1990 ($1.50)
1 (9/90, $2.25, B&W mag., 68 pgs.)-Adaptation of film 3.0
1-3: Reprints B&W magazine 2.2

DARKMAN
Marvel Comics: V2#1, Apr, 1993 -No. 6, Sept, 1993 ($2.95, limited series)
V2#1 ($3.95, 52 pgs.) 4.0
2-6 3.0

DARK MANSION OF FORBIDDEN LOVE, THE (Becomes Forbidden Tales of
   Dark Mansion No. 5 on)

Dark Mysteries #24 © Merit Pub.

The Darkness #3 © TCOW

Dark Shadows #3 © Dan Curtis Prod.

	GD2.0	FN6.0	VF8.0	NM9.4

National Periodical Publ.: Sept-Oct, 1971 - No. 4, Mar-Apr, 1972 (52 pgs.)

1	14	42	102	175
2-4: 2-Adams-c. 3-Jeff Jones-c	6	18	40	65

DARKMINDS
Image Comics (Dreamwave Prod.): July, 1998 - No. 8, Apr, 1999 ($2.50)

1-Manga; Pat Lee-s/a; 2 covers	1	4	7	10
1-2nd printing				2.50
2, 0-(1/99, $5.00) Story and sketch pages				5.00
3-8, 1/2-(5/99, $2.50) Story and sketch pages				2.50
.. Collected 1,2 (1/99,3/99; $7.95) 1-r/#1-3. 2-r/#4-6				8.00
.. Collected 3 (5/99; $5.95) r/#7,8				6.00

DARKMINDS (Volume 2)
Image Comics (Dreamwave Prod.): Feb, 2000 - No. 10, Apr, 2001 ($2.50)

1-10-Pat Lee-c				2.50
0-(7/00) Origin of Mai Murasaki; sketchbook				2.50

DARKMINDS: MACROPOLIS (Volume 3)
Image Comics (Dreamwave Prod.):

Preview (8/01) Flip book w/Banished Knights preview				1.00

DARKMINDS / WITCHBLADE
Image Comics (Top Cow/Dreamwave Prod.): Aug, 2000 ($5.95, one-shot)

1-Wohl-s/Pat Lee-a; two covers by Silvestri and Lee				6.00

DARK MYSTERIES (Thrilling Tales of Horror & Suspense)
"Master" - "Merit" Publications: June-July, 1951 - No. 24, July, 1955

1-Wood-c/a (8 pgs.)	105	315	656	1150
2-Wood/Harrison-c/a (8 pgs.)	73	219	455	800
3-9: 7-Dismemberment, hypo blood drainage stys	40	120	232	400
10-Cannibalism story; witch burning-c	43	129	257	450
11-13,15-18: 11-Severed head panels. 13-Dismemberment-c/story. 17-The				
Old Gravedigger host	35	105	185	320
14-Several E.C. Craig swipes	35	105	188	325
19-Injury-to-eye panel; E.C. swipe; torture-c	40	120	240	420
20-Female bondage, blood drainage story	40	120	217	375
21,22: 21-Devil-c. 22-Last pre-code issue, misdated 3/54 instead of 3/55				
	25	75	130	225
23,24	20	60	105	175

NOTE: *Cameron* a-1, 2. *Myron Fass* c/a-21. *Harrison* a-3; 7; c-3. *Hollingsworth* a-7-17, 20, 21, 23. *Wildey* a-5. *Woodish* art by *Fleishman*-9; c-10, 14-17. Bondage c-10, 18, 19.

DARK NEMESIS (VILLAINS) (See Teen Titans)
DC Comics: Feb, 1998 ($1.95) one-shot)

1-Jurgens-s/Pearson-c				2.25

DARKNESS, THE (See Witchblade #10)
Image Comics (Top Cow Productions): Dec, 1996 - Present ($2.50)

Special Preview Edition-(7/96, B&W)-Ennis script; Silvestri-a(p)

	2	6	11	16
0	2	6	9	12
0-Gold Edition				16.00
1/2	1	4	7	10
1/2-Christmas-c	3	9	17	24
1/2-(3/01, $2.95) r/#1/2 w/new 6 pg. story & Silvestri-c				3.00
1-Ennis-s/Silvestri-a, 1-Black variant-c	2	6	9	12
1-Platinum variant-c				25.00
1,2: 1-Fan Club Ed.	1	3	5	7
3-5				4.00
6-10: 9,10-Witchblade "Family Ties" x-over pt. 2,3				3.50
7-Variant-c w/concubine	1	3	6	9
8-American Entertainment				6.00
8-American Entertainment Gold Ed.				12.00
9-American Entertainment Gold Ed.				7.00
10-American Entertainment Gold Ed.				7.00
11-Regular Ed.; Ennis-s/Silverstri & D-Tron-c				3.00
11-Nine (non-chromium) variant-c (Benitez, Cabrera, the Hildebrandts, Finch,				
Keown, Peterson, Portacio, Tan, Turner				5.00
11-Chromium-c by Silvestri & Batt				20.00
12-19: 13-Begin Benitez-a(p)				3.00
20-24,26-40: 34-Ripclaw app.				2.50
25-($3.99) Two covers (Benitez, Silvestri)				2.50

25-Chromium-c variant by Silvestri				6.00
Holiday Pin-up-American Entertainment				5.00
Holiday Pin-up Gold Ed.-American Entertainment				7.00
Infinity #1 (8/99, $3.50) Lobdell-s				3.50
Prelude-American Entertainment				4.00
Prelude Gold Ed.-American Entertainment				7.00
Wizard ACE Ed.- Reprints #1	1	3	6	9
...Collected Editions #1-4 ($4.95,TPB) 1-r/#1,2. 2-r/#3,4. 3- r/#5,6. 4- r/#7,8				6.00
...Collected Editions #5,6 ($5.95, TPB)5- r/#11,12. 6-r/#13,14				6.00
Deluxe Collected Editions #1 (12/98, $14.95, TPB) r/#1-6 & Preview				15.00
...: Heart of Darkness (2001, $14.95, TPB) r/ #7,8, 11-14				15.00

DARKNESS/ BATMAN
Image Comics (Top Cow Productions): Aug, 1999 ($5.95, one-shot)

1-Silvestri, Finch, Lansing-a(p)				6.00

DARK ONE'S THIRD EYE
Sirius Entertainment: 1996; Dec, 1998 ($4.95, B&W)

nn-Dark One-a; squarebound; pinups, Vol. 2-(12/98)				5.00

DARK OZ
Arrow Comics: 1997 - No. 5 ($2.75, B&W, limited series)

1-5-Bill Bryan-a				2.75

DARK REALM
Image Comics: Oct, 2000 -No. 4, June, 2001 ($2.95, limited series)

1-4-Taeson Chang-a. 3-Flip book w/Mech Destroyer prequel				3.00

DARKSEID (VILLAINS) (See Jack Kirby's New Gods and New Gods)
DC Comics: Feb, 1998 ($1.95, one-shot)

1-Byrne-s/Pearson-c				2.25

DARKSEID VS. GALACTUS: THE HUNGER
DC Comics: 1995 ($4.95, one-shot) (1st DC/Marvel x-over by John Byrne)

nn-John Byrne-c/a/script				5.00

DARK SHADOWS
Steinway Comic Publ. (Ajax)(America's Best): Oct, 1957 - No. 3, May, 1958

1	22	66	116	200
2,3	17	51	88	150

DARK SHADOWS (TV) (See Dan Curtis Giveaways)
Gold Key: Mar, 1969 - No. 35, Feb, 1976 (Photo-c: 1-7)

1(30039-903)-With pull-out poster (25¢)	30	90	190	330
1-With poster missing	10	30	70	120
2	8	24	56	100
3-With pull-out poster	15	45	100	165
3-With poster missing	6	18	42	80
4-7: 7-Last photo-c	7	21	49	90
8-10	5	15	35	65
11-20	5	15	34	55
21-35: 30-Last painted-c	4	12	29	45
Story Digest 1 (6/70, 148pp.)-Photo-c	9	27	65	110

DARK SHADOWS (TV) (See Nightmare on Elm Street)
Innovation Publishing: June, 1992 - No. 4, Spring, 1993 ($2.50, limited series, coated stock)

1-Based on 1991 NBC TV mini-series; painted-c				4.00
2-4				3.00

DARK SHADOWS: BOOK TWO
Innovation Publishing: 1993 - No. 4, July, 1993 ($2.50, limited series)

1-4-Painted-c. 4-Maggie Thompson scripts				3.00

DARK SHADOWS: BOOK THREE
Innovation Publishing: Nov, 1993 ($2.50)

1-(Whole #9)				3.00

DARKSIDE
Maximum Press: Oct, 1996 ($2.99, one-shot)

1-Avengelyne-c/app.				3.00

DARKSTARS, THE
DC Comics: Oct, 1992 - No. 38, Jan, 1996 ($1.75/$1.95)

1-1st app. The Darkstars				3.00

Date With Danger #5 © STD

David Cassidy #2 © CC

Dawn #5 © J.M. Linsner

	GD2.0	FN6.0	VF8.0	NM9.4

2-24,0,25-38: 5-Hawkman & Hawkwoman app. 18-20-Flash app.. 24-(9/94)-Zero Hour. 0-(10/94). 25-(11/94). 30-Green Lantern app. 31-...vs. Darkseid. 32-Green Lantern app. 2.50

NOTE: *Travis Charest* a(p)-4-7; c(p)-2-5; c-6-11. *Stroman* a-1-3; c-1.

DARK TOWN
Mad Monkey Press: 1995 ($3.95, magazine-size, quarterly)

1-Kaja Blackley scripts; Vanessa Chong-a 4.00

DARKWING DUCK (TV cartoon) (Also see Cartoon Tales)
Disney Comics: Nov, 1991 - No. 4, Feb, 1992 ($1.50, limited series)

1-4: Adapts hour-long premiere TV episode 2.50

DARLING LOVE
Close Up/Archie Publ. (A Darling Magazine): Oct-Nov, 1949 - No. 11, 1952 (no month) (52 pgs.)(Most photo-c)

1-Photo-c	18	54	94	155
2-Photo-c	11	33	55	90
3-8,10,11: 3-6-photo-c	9	27	49	70
9-Krigstein-a	10	30	55	80

DARLING ROMANCE
Close Up (MLJ Publications): Sept-Oct, 1949 - No. 7, 1951 (All photo-c)

1-(52 pgs.)-Photo-c	24	72	127	215
2	11	33	55	90
3-7	10	30	55	80

DARQUE PASSAGES (See Master Darque)
Acclaim (Valiant): April, 1998 ($2.50)

1-Christina Z.-s/Manco-c/a 2.50

DART (Also see Freak Force & Savage Dragon)
Image Comics (Highbrow Entertainment): Feb, 1996 - No. 3, May, 1996 ($2.50, limited series)

1-3 .... 3.00

DASTARDLY & MUTTLEY (See Fun-In No. 1-4, 6 and Kite Fun Book)
DATE WITH DANGER
Standard Comics: No. 5, Dec, 1952 - No. 6, Feb, 1953

5,6-Secret agent stories: 6-Atom bomb story   9   27   49   70

DATE WITH DEBBI (Also see Debbi's Dates)
National Periodical Publ.: Jan-Feb, 1969 - No. 17, Sept-Oct, 1971; No. 18, Oct-Nov, 1972

1-Teenage	4	12	30	50
2-5,17-(52 pgs) James Taylor sty.	3	9	17	25
6-12,18-Last issue	2	6	15	22
13-16-(68 pgs.): 14-1 pg. story on Jack Wild. 15-Marlo Thomas/"That Girl" sty	3	9	19	28

DATE WITH JUDY, A (Radio/TV, and 1948 movie)
National Periodical Publications: Oct-Nov, 1947 - No. 79, Oct-Nov, 1960 (No. 1-25: 52 pgs.)

1-Teenage	29	87	153	265
2	14	42	72	120
3-10	11	33	55	90
11-20	7	21	38	55
21-40	6	18	32	45
41-45: 45-Last pre-code (2-3/55)	6	18	28	38
46-79: 79-Drucker-c/a	5	15	23	30

DATE WITH MILLIE, A (Life With Millie No. 8 on)(Teenage)
Atlas/Marvel Comics (MPC): Oct, 1956 - No. 7, Aug, 1957; Oct, 1959 - No. 7, Oct, 1960

1(10/56)-(1st Series)-Dan DeCarlo-a in #1-7	26	78	139	240
2	14	42	72	120
3-7	10	30	55	80
1(10/59)-(2nd Series)	14	42	72	120
2-7	10	30	55	80

DATE WITH PATSY, A (Also see Patsy Walker)
Atlas Comics: Sept, 1957 (One-shot)

1-Starring Patsy Walker   11   33   55   90

DAVID AND GOLIATH (Movie)
Dell Publishing Co.: No. 1205, July, 1961

Four Color 1205-Photo-c   6   18   42   80

DAVID BORING (See Eightball)
Pantheon Books: 2000 ($24.95, hardcover w/dust jacket)

Hardcover - reprints David Boring stories from Eightball; Clowes-s/a 24.95

DAVID CASSIDY (TV)(See Partridge Family, Swing With Scooter #33 & Time For Love #30)
Charlton Comics: Feb, 1972 - No. 14, Sept, 1973

1-Most have photo covers	5	15	38	60
2-5	3	10	23	35
6-14	3	9	20	30

DAVID LADD'S LIFE STORY (See Movie Classics)
DAVY CROCKETT (See Dell Giants, Fightin..., Frontier Fighters, It's Game Time, Power Record Comics, Western Tales & Wild Frontier)
DAVY CROCKETT (Frontier Fighter...)
Avon Periodicals: 1951

nn-Tuska?, Reinman-a; Fawcette-c   19   57   99   165

DAVY CROCKETT (...King of the Wild Frontier No. 1,2)(TV)
Dell Publishing Co./Gold Key: 5/55 - No. 671, 12/55; No. 1, 12/63; No. 2, 11/69 (Walt Disney)

Four Color 631(#1)-Fess Parker photo-c	20	60	140	260
Four Color 639-Photo-c	16	48	112	210
Four Color 664,671(Marsh-a)-Photo-c	15	45	105	195
1(12/63-Gold Key)-Fess Parker photo-c; reprints	15	45	105	195
2(11/69)-Fess Parker photo-c; reprints	5	15	34	55

DAVY CROCKETT (...Frontier Fighter #1,2; Kid Montana #9 on)
Charlton Comics: Aug, 1955 - No. 8, Jan, 1957

1	10	30	55	80
2	6	18	32	45
3-8	5	15	24	32

DAWN
Sirius Entertainment: June, 1995 - No. 6, 1996 ($2.95)

1/2-w/certificate				6.00
1/2-Variant-c	2	6	11	15
1-Linsner-c/a	1	3	5	7
1-Black Light Edition	1	4	7	10
1-White Trash Edition	2	6	11	15
1-Look Sharp Edition	3	9	20	30
2-4: Linsner-c/a				4.00
2-Variant-c, 3-Limited Edition	2	6	11	15
4-6-Vibrato-c				3.00
4, 5-Limited Edition	1	4	7	10
6-Limited Edition	2	6	9	12
Genesis Edition ('99, Wizard supplement) previews Return of the Goddess				2.25
Lucifer's Halo TPB (11/97, $19.95) r/Drama, Dawn #1-6 plus 12 pages of new artwork				20.00
...: Tenth Anniversary Special(9/99, $2.95) Interviews				3.00
The Portable Dawn ($9.95, 5"x4", 64 pgs.) Pocket-sized cover gallery				10.00

DAWN: THE RETURN OF THE GODDESS
Sirius Entertainment: Apr, 1999 - No. 4, July, 2000 ($2.95, limited series)

1-4-Linsner-s/a 3.00

DAYDREAMERS (See Generation X)
Marvel Comics: Aug, 1997 - No. 3, Oct, 1997 ($2.50, limited series)

1-3-Franklin Richards, Howard the Duck, Man-Thing app. 2.50

DAY OF JUDGMENT
DC Comics: Nov, 1999 - No. 5, Nov, 1999 ($2.95/$2.50, limited series)

1-($2.95) Spectre possessed; Matt Smith-a		3.00
2-5: Parallax returns. 5-Hal Jordan becomes the Spectre		2.50
...Secret Files 1 (11/99, $4.95) Harris-a		5.00

DAYS OF THE DEFENDERS (See Defenders, The)
Marvel Comics: Mar, 2001 ($3.50, one-shot)

1-Reprints early team-ups of members, incl. Marvel Feature #1; Larsen-c 3.50

The Dazzler #35 © MAR

DC Graphic Novel #4 © DC

DC/Marvel: All Access #1 © DC/MAR

	GD2.0	FN6.0	VF8.0	NM9.4

	GD2.0	FN6.0	VF8.0	NM9.4

DAYS OF THE MOB (See In the Days of the Mob)

DAZEY'S DIARY
Dell Publishing Co.: June-Aug, 1962

01-174-208: Bill Woggon-c/a	4	12	27	42

DAZZLER, THE (Also see Marvel Graphic Novel & X-Men #130)
Marvel Comics Group: Mar, 1981 - No. 42, Mar, 1986

1,22,24,27,28,38: 1-X-Men app. 22 (12/82)-vs. Rogue Battle-c/sty. 24-Full app. Rogue w/Powerman (Iron Fist). 27-Rogue app. 28-Full app. Rogue; Mystique app. 38-Wolverine-c/app.; X-Men app. 4.00
2-21,23,25,26,29-37,39-41: 2-X-Men app. 10,11-Galactus app. 21-Double size; photo-c. 23-Rogue/Mystique 1 pg. app. 26-Jusko-c. 33-Michael Jackson thriller swipe-c/sty. 40-Secret Wars II 3.00
42-Beast-c/sty 4.00
NOTE: No. 1 distributed only through comic shops. **Alcala** a-1i, 2i. **Chadwick** a-38-42p; c(p)-39, 41, 42. **Guice** a-38i, 42i; c-38, 40.

DC CHALLENGE
DC Comics: Nov, 1985 - No. 12, Oct, 1986 ($1.25/$2.00, maxi-series)

1-11: 1-Colan-a. 2,8-Batman-c/app. 4-Gil Kane-c/a 2.50
12-($2.00-c) Giant; low print 3.00
NOTE: Batman app. in 4, 6-12. Joker app. in 7. **nfantino** a-3. **Ordway** c-12. **Swan/Austin** c-10.

DC COMICS PRESENTS
DC Comics: July-Aug, 1978 - No. 97, Sept, 1986 (Superman team-ups in all)

1-4th & final Superman/Flash race	2	6	11	15
1-(Whitman variant)	2	6	12	18
2-Part 2 of Superman/Flash race	1	4	7	10

2-4,10-12,14,15,19,21,22-(Whitman variants, low print run, none have issue # on cover) 4 9 12
3-10: 4-Metal Men. 6-Green Lantern. 8-Swamp Thing. 9-Wonder Woman 4.00
11-25,27,40-42,46-48,50-52,71-73,76-79,83: 13,43,80-Legion of Super-Heroes. 19-Batgirl. 31,58-Robin. 35-Man-Bat. 42-Sandman. 52-Doom Patrol. 82-Adam Strange. 83-Batman & Outsiders. 4.00

26-(10/80)-Green Lantern; intro Cyborg, Starfire, Raven (1st app. New Teen Titans in 16 pg. preview); Starlin-c/a; Sargon the Sorcerer back-up	2	6	13	20

41,72,77,78,97: 41-Superman/Joker-c/story. 72-Joker/Phantom Stranger-c.77,78-Animal Man app. (77-c also). 97-Phantom Zone 5.00
47-He-Man-c/s (1st app. in comics) 1 4 7 10
51,84,85: 51-Preview insert (16 pgs.) of He-Man (2nd app.). 84-Challengers of the Unknown; Kirby-c/s. 85-Swamp Thing; Alan Moore scripts 6.00
86-96: 86-88-Crisis x-over. 88-Creeper 4.00
Annual 2,3: 2(7/83)-Intro/origin Superwoman 4.00
Annual 1,4: 1(9/82)-G.A. Superman. 4(10/85)-Superman 4.00
Annual 2,3: 2(7/83)-Intro/origin Superwoman. 3(9/84)-Shazam. 4.00
NOTE: **Adkins** a-2, 54; c-2. **Buckler** a-33, 34; c-30, 33, 34. **Giffen** a-39; c-59. **Gil Kane** a-28, 35, Annual 3; c-48p, 56, 58, 60, 62, 64, 68, Annual 2, 3. **Kirby** c/a-84. **Kubert** c/a-66. **Morrow** c/a-65. **Newton** c/a-54p. **Orlando** c-53i. **Perez** a-26p, 61p; c-38, 61, 94. **Starlin** a-26-29p, 36p, 37p; c-26-29, 36, 37, 93. **Toth** a-84. **Williamson** i-79, 85, 87.

DC GRAPHIC NOVEL (Also see DC Science Fiction...)
DC Comics: Nov, 1983 - No. 7, 1986 ($5.95, 68 pgs.)

1-3,5,7: 1-Star Raiders 2-Warlords; not from regular Warlord series. 3-The Medusa Chain; Ernie Colon story/a. 5-Me and Joe Priest; Chaykin-c. 7-Space Clusters; Nino-c/a.	2	6	9	12
4-The Hunger Dogs by Kirby; Darkseid kills Himon from Mister Miracle & destroys New Genesis	3	9	21	32
6-Metalzoic; Sienkiewicz-a ($6.95)	2	6	9	12

DC/MARVEL: ALL ACCESS (Also see DC Versus Marvel & Marvel Versus DC)
DC Comics: Nov. 1996 - No. 4, 1997 ($2.95, limited series)

1-4: 1-Superman & Spider-Man app. 2-Robin & Jubilee app. 3-Dr. Strange & Batman-c/app., X-Men , JLA app. 4-X-Men vs JLA-c/app. rebirth of Amalgam 3.00

DC/MARVEL: CROSSOVER CLASSICS II
DC Comics: 1998 ($14.95, TPB)

1-Reprints Batman/Punisher: Lake of Fire, Punisher/Batman: Deadly Knights, Silver Surfer/Superman, Batman & Capt. America 15.00

DC 100 PAGE SUPER SPECTACULAR
(Title is 100 Page... No. 14 on)(Square bound) (Reprints, 50¢)
National Periodical Publications: No. 4, Summer, 1971 - No. 13, 6/72; No. 14, 2/73 - No. 22, 11/73 (No #1-3)

DC Comics: Nov. 1985 - No. 12, Oct, 1986 ($1.25/$2.00, maxi-series)

4-Weird Mystery Tales; Johnny Peril & Phantom Stranger; cover & splashes by Wrightson; origin Jungle Boy of Jupiter	16	48	112	200
5-Love Stories; Wood inks (7 pgs.)(scarcer)	41	123	331	600
6- "World's Greatest Super-Heroes"; JLA, JSA, Spectre, Johnny Quick, Vigilante & Hawkman; contains unpublished Wildcat story; N. Adams wrap-around-c; r/JLA #21,22	16	48	112	200
7-(Also listed as Superman #245) Air Wave, Kid Eternity, Hawkman-r; Atom-r/Atom #3	7	21	55	80
8-(Also listed as Batman #238) Batman, Legion, Aquaman-r; G.A. Atom, Sargon (r/Sensation #57), Plastic Man (r/Police #14) stories; Doom Patrol origin-r; N. Adams wraparound-c	9	27	65	110
9-(Also listed as Our Army at War #242) Kubert-a	8	24	60	100
10-(Also listed as Adventure Comics #416) Golden Age-reprints; r/1st app. Black Canary from Flash #86; no Zatanna	8	24	60	100
11-(Also listed as Flash #214) origin Metal Men-r/Showcase #37; never before pubbed G.A. Flash story.	6	18	45	75
12,14: 12-(Also listed as Superboy #185) Legion-c/story; Teen Titans, Kid Eternity (r/Hit #46), Star Spangled Kid-r(S.S. #55). 14-Batman-r/Detective #31,32,156; Atom-r/Showcase #34	4	12	30	50
13-(Also listed as Superman #252) Ray(r/Smash #17), Black Condor, (r/Crack #18), Hawkman(r/Flash #24); Starman-r/Adv. #67; Dr. Fate & Spectre-r/More Fun #57; N. Adams-c	7	21	50	80
15,16,18,19,21,22: 15-r/2nd Boy Commandos/Det. #64. 21-Superboy; r/Brave & the Bold #54. 22-r/All-Flash #13.	3	10	23	35
17,20: 17-JSA-r/All Star #37 (10-11/47, 38 pgs.), Sandman-r/Adv. #65 (8/41), JLA #23 (11/63) & JLA #43 (3/66). 20-Batman-r/Det. #66,68, Spectre; origin Two-Face	4	12	26	40
... : Love Stories Replica Edition (2000, $6.95) reprints #5				7.00

NOTE: **Anderson** r-11, 14, 18i, 22. **Bailly** r-18, 20. **Burnley** r-18, 20. **Crandall** r-14p, 20. **Drucker** r-4. **Grandenetti** a-22(2)r. **Heath** a-22r. **Infantino** r-17, 20, 22. **G. Kane** r-18. **Kirby** r-15. **Kubert** r-6, 7, 16, 17; c-16, 19. **Manning** a-19r. **Meskin** r-4, 22. **Mooney** r-15, 21. **Toth** r-17, 20.

DC ONE MILLION (Also see crossover #1,000,000 issues)
DC Comics: Nov, 1998 - No. 4, Nov, 1998 ($2.95/$1.99, weekly lim. series)

1-($2.95) JLA travels to the 853rd century; Morrison-s			3.00
2-4-($1.99)			2.25
... Eighty-Page Giant (8/99, $4.95)			5.00
TPB ('99, $14.95) r/#1-4 and several x-over stories			15.00

DC SCIENCE FICTION GRAPHIC NOVEL
DC Comics: 1985 - No. 7, 1987 ($5.95)

SF1-SF7: SF1-Hell on Earth by Robert Bloch; Giffen-p. SF2-Nightwings by Robert Silverberg; G. Colan-p. SF3-Frost & Fire by Bradbury. SF4-Merchants of Venus. SF5-Demon With A Glass Hand by Ellison; Rogers-a. SF6-The Magic Goes Away by Niven. SF7-Sandkings by George R.R. Martin	2	6		12

DC SILVER AGE CLASSICS
DC Comics: 1992 ($1.00, all reprints)

...Action Comics #252-r/1st Supergirl. Adventure Comics #247-r/1st Legion of S.H. The Brave and the Bold #28-r/1st JLA. Detective Comics #225-r/1st Martian Manhunter. Detective Comics #327-r/1st new look Batman. Green Lantern #76-r/Green Lantern/Gr. Arrow. House of Secrets #92-r/1st Swamp Thing. Showcase #4-r/1st S.A. Flash. Showcase #22-r/1st S.A. Green Lantern			2.50
...Sugar and Spike #99; 2 unpublished stories			4.00

DC SPECIAL (Also see Super DC Giant)
National Per. Publ.: 10-12/68 - No. 15, 11-12/71; No. 16, Spr/75 - No. 29, 8-9/77

1-All Infantino issue; Flash, Batman, Adam Strange-r; begin 68 pg. issues, end #21	6	18	42	70
2-Teen humor; Binky, Buzzy, Harvey app.	8	24	60	100
3-All-Girl issue; unpubl. GA Wonder Woman story	7	21	50	80
4-15: 4-Horror (1st Abel cameo). 8-All Kubert issue; Viking Prince, Sgt. Rock-r. 6-Western. 7,9,13-Strangest Sports. 11-Monsters. 12-Viking Prince; Kubert-c/a (r/B&B almost entirely). 15-G.A. Plastic Man origin-r/Police #1; origin Woozy by Cole; 14,15-(52 pgs.)	3	10	23	35
16-27: 16-Super Heroes Battle Super Gorillas; r/Capt. Storm #1, 1st Johnny Cloud/All-Amer. Men of War #82. 17-Early S.A. Green Lantern-r. 22-Origin Robin Hood. 26-Enemy Ace on-c only. 27-Captain Comet story	2	6	11	15
28,29: 28-Earth Shattering Disaster Stories; Legion of Super-Heroes story.				

	GD2.0	FN6.0	VF8.0	NM9.4

	GD2.0	FN6.0	VF8.0	NM9.4

29-New "The Untold Origin of the Justice Society"; Staton-a

	2	6	12	18

NOTE: **N. Adams** c-3, 4, 6, 11, 29. **Grell** a-20; c-17, 20. **Heath** a-12r. **G. Kane** a-6p, 13r, 17r, 19-21r. **Kirby** a-4,11. **Kubert** a-6r, 12r, 22. **Meskin** a-10. **Moreira** a-10. **Staton** a-29p. Toth a-13, 20r. #1-15: 25¢; 16-27: 50¢; 28, 29: 60¢. #1-13, 16-21: 68 pgs., 14, 15: 52 pgs.; 25-27: oversized.

DC SPECIAL BLUE RIBBON DIGEST
DC Comics: Mar-Apr, 1980 - No. 24, Aug, 1982

1,2,4,5: 1-Legion reprints. 2-Flash. 4-Green Lantern. 5-Secret Origins; new Zatara and Zatanna

	2	6	9	12

3-Justice Society 2 6 11 16

6,8-10: 6-Ghosts. 8-Legion. 9-Secret Origins. 10-Warlord-"The Deimos Saga"-Grell-s/c/a

	2	6	9	12

7-Sgt. Rock's Prize Battle Tales 2 6 13 20

11,16: 11-Justice League. 16-Green Lantern/Green Arrow-r; all Adams-a.

12-Haunted Tank; reprints 1st app. 2 6 13 20

13-15,17-19: 13-Strange Sports Stories. 14-UFO Invaders; Adam Strange app. 15-Secret Origins of Super Villains; JLA app. 17-Ghosts. 18-Sgt. Rock; Kubert front & back-c. 19-Doom Patrol; new Perez-c 2 6 11 15

20-Dark Mansion of Forbidden Love (scarce) 4 12 30 50

21-Our Army at War 3 9 17 25

22-24: 22-Secret Origins. 23-Green Arrow, w/new 7 pg. story. 24-House of Mystery; new Kubert wraparound-c

	2	6	13	20

NOTE: **N. Adams** a-16(6)r, 17r, 23r; c-16. **Aparo** a-6r, 24r; c-23. **Grell** a-8, 10; c-10. **Heath** a-14. **Infantino** a-15r. **Kaluta** a-17r. **Gil Kane** a-15r, 22r. **Kirby** a-5, 9, 23r. **Kubert** a-3, 18r, 21r; c-7, 12, 14, 17, 18, 21, 24. **Morrow** a-24r. **Orlando** a-17r, 22r; c-1, 20. **Toth** a-21r, 24r. **Wood** a-3, 17r, 24r. **Wrightson** a-16r, 17r, 24r.

DC SPECIAL SERIES
National Periodical Publications/DC Comics: 9/77 - No. 16, Fall, 1978; No. 17, 8/79 - No. 27, Fall, 1981 (No. 18, 19, 23, 24 - digest size, 100 pgs.; No. 25-27 - Treasury sized)

1-"5-Star Super-Hero Spectacular 1977"; Batman, Atom, Flash, Green Lantern, Aquaman, in solo stories, Kobra app.; N. Adams-c

	2	6	13	20

2(#1)-"The Original Swamp Thing Saga 1977"-r/Swamp Thing #1&2 by Wrightson; new Wrightson wraparound-c. 1 4 7 10

3,4,6,8: 3-Sgt Rock. 4-Unexpected. 6-Secret Society of Super Villains, Jones-a. 7-Ghosts Special. 8-Brave and Bold w/ new Batman, Deadman & Sgt Rock team-up 2 6 10 14

5-"Superman Spectacular 1977"-(84 pg, $1.00)-Superman vs. Braniac & Lex Luthor, new 63 pg. story 2 6 12 18

9-Wonder Woman; Ditko-a (11 pgs.) 2 6 13 20

10-"Secret Origins of Superheroes Special 1978"-(52 pgs.)-Dr. Fate, Lightray & Black Canary-c/new origin stories; Staton, Newton-a 2 6 10 14

11-"Flash Spectacular 1978"-(84 pgs.) Flash, Kid Flash, GA Flash & Johnny Quick vs. Grodd; Wood-i on Kid Flash chapter 2 6 10 14

12-"Secrets of Haunted House Special Spring 1978" 2 6 11 16

13-"Sgt. Rock Special Spring 1978", 50 pg new story 2 6 11 16

14,17,20-"Original Swamp Thing Saga", Wrightson-a: 14-Sum '78, r/#3,4. 17-Sum '79 r/#5-7. 20-Jan/Feb '80, r/#8-10 1 4 7 10

15-"Batman Spectacular Summer 1978", Ra's Al Ghul-app.; Golden-a. Rogers-a/front & back-c 2 6 12 18

16-"Jonah Hex Spectacular Fall 1978"; death of Jonah Hex, Heath-a; Bat Lash and Scalphunter stories 4 12 30 50

18,19-Digest size: 18-"Sgt. Rock's Prize Battle Tales Fall 1979". 19-"Secret Origins of Super-Heroes Fall 1979"; origins Wonder Woman (new-a),r/Robin, Batman-Superman team, Aquaman, Hawkman and others

	2	6	10	14

21-"Super-Star Holiday Spectacular Spring 1980", Frank Miller-a in "Batman--Wanted Dead or Alive" (1st Batman story); Jonah Hex, Sgt. Rock, Superboy &LSH and House of Mystery/Witching Hour-c/stories 3 9 17 24

22-"G.I. Combat Sept. 1980", Kubert-c. Haunted Tank-s 2 6 10 14

23,24-Digest size: 23-World's Finest-r. 24-Flash 2 6 10 14

V5#25-($2.95)-"Superman II, the Adventure Continues Summer 1981"; photos from movie & photo-c (see All-New Coll. C-62) 2 6 11 16

26-($2.50)-"Superman and His Incredible Fortress of Solitude Summer 1981"

	2	6	11	16

27-($2.50)-"Batman vs. The Incredible Hulk Fall 1981" 3 9 19 28

NOTE: **Aparo** c-8. **Heath** a-12i, 16. **Infantino** a-19r. **Kirby** a-23, 19r. **Kubert** c-13, 19r. **Nasser/Netzer** a-1, 10i, 15. **Newton** a-10. **Nino** a-4, 7. **Starlin** c-12. **Staton** a-1. **Tuska** a-19r. #25 & 26. were advertised as All-New Collectors' Edition C-63, C-64. #26 was originally planned as All-New Collectors' Edition C-30?; has C-630 & A.N.C.E. on cover.

DC SUPER-STARS
National Periodical Publications/DC Comics: March, 1976 - No. 18, Winter, 1978 (No.3-18: 52 pgs.)

1-(68 pgs.)-Re-intro Teen Titans (predates T. T. #44 (11/76); tryout iss.) plus r/Teen Titans; W.W. as girl was original Wonder Girl

	2	6	12	18

2-7,9,11,12,16: 2,4,6,8-Adam Strange; 2-(68 pgs.)-r/1st Adam Strange/ Hawkman team-up from Mystery in Space #90 plus Atomic Knights origin-r. 3-Legion issue. 4-r/Tales/Unexpected #45 1 4 7 10

8-r/1st Space Ranger from Showcase #15, Adam Strange-r/Mystery in Space #89 & Star Rovers-r/M.I.S. #80 2 6 9 12

10-Strange Sports Stories; Batman/Joker-c/story 2 6 9 12

13-Sergio Aragonés Special 2 6 12 18

14,15,18: 15-Sgt. Rock 2 6 9 12

17-Secret Origins of Super-Heroes (origin of The Huntress); origin Green Arrow by Grell; Legion app.; Earth II Batman & Catwoman marry (1st revealed; also see B&B #197 & Superman Family #211) 3 9 17 24

NOTE: **M. Anderson** r-2, 4, 6. **Aparo** c-7, 14, 18. **Austin** a-11i. **Buckler** a-14p; c-10. **Grell** a-17. **G. Kane** a-1r, 10r. **Kubert** c-15. **Layton** c/a-16i, 17i. **Mooney** a-4r, 6r. **Morrow** c/a-11r. **Nasser** a-7. **Newton** c/a-16p. **Staton** a-17; c-17. No. 10, 12-18 contain all new material; the rest are reprints. #1 contains new and reprint material.

DC 2000
DC Comics: Nov - No. 2, 2000 ($6.95, limited series)

1,2-JLA visit 1941 JSA; Semeiks-a 7.00

DCU HEROES SECRET FILES
DC Comics: Feb, 1999 ($4.95, one-shot)

1-Origin-s and pin-ups; new Star Spangled Kid app. 5.00

DC UNIVERSE CHRISTMAS, A
DC Comics: 2000 ($19.95)

TPB-Reprints DC Christmas stories by various 20.00

DC UNIVERSE HOLIDAY BASH
DC Comics: 1997- 1999 ($3.95)

I,II-(X-mas '96,'97) Christmas stories by various 5.00
III (1999, for Christmas '98, $4.95) 5.00

DC UNIVERSE: TRINITY
DC Comics: 1993 - No. 2, Sept, 1993 ($2.95, 52 pgs, limited series)

1,2-Foil-c; Green Lantern, Darkstars, Legion app. 3.50

DCU VILLAINS SECRET FILES
DC Comics: Apr, 1999 ($4.95, one-shot)

1-Origin-s and profile pages 5.00

DC VERSUS MARVEL (See Marvel Versus DC) (Also see Amazon, Assassins, Bruce Wayne: Agent of S.H.I.E.L.D., Bullets & Bracelets, Doctor Strangefate, JLX, Legend of the Dark Claw, Magneto & The Magnetic Men, Speed Demon, Spider-Boy, Super Soldier, X-Patrol)
DC Comics: No. 1, 1996, No. 4, 1996 ($3.95, limited series)

1,4: 1-Marz script, Jurgens-a(p); 1st app. of Access. 4.00
.../Marvel Versus DC ($12.95, trade paperback) r/1-4 13.00

D-DAY (Also see Special War Series)
Charlton Comics (no no. 3): Sum/63; No. 2, Fall/64; No. 4, 9/66; No. 5, 10/67; No. 6, 11/68

1,2: 1(1963)-Montes/Bache-c. 2(Fall '64)-Wood-a(4) 4 12 26 40
4-6('66-'68)-Montes/Bache-a #5 2 6 15 22

DEAD AIR
Slave Labor Graphics: July, 1989 ($5.95, graphic novel)

nn-Mike Allred's 1st published work 6.00

DEAD CORPSE
DC Comics (Helix): Sept, 1998 - No. 4, Dec, 1998 ($2.50, limited series)

1-4-Pugh-a/Hinz-s 2.50

DEAD END CRIME STORIES
Kirby Publishing Co.: April, 1949 (52 pgs.)

nn-(Scarce)-Powell, Roussos-a; painted-c 50 150 300 525

DEAD ENDERS
DC Comics (Vertigo): Mar, 2000 - No. 16, June, 2001 ($2.50)

Dead Enders #13 © Brubaker/Pleece

Dead-Eye Western Comics #2 © HILL

Deadman: Dead Again #1 © DC

	GD2.0	FN6.0	VF8.0	NM9.4

1-16-Brubaker-s/Pleece & Case-a ... 2.50
Stealing the Sun (2000, $9.95, TPB) r/#1-4, Vertigo Winter's Edge #3 ... 10.00

DEAD-EYE WESTERN COMICS
Hillman Periodicals: Nov-Dec, 1948 - V3#1, Apr-May, 1953

V1#1-(52 pgs.)-Krigstein, Roussos-a	19	57	99	170
V1#2,3-(52 pgs.)	10	30	55	85
V1#4-12-(52 pgs.)	7	21	36	50
V2#1,2,5-8,10-12: 1-7-(52 pgs.)	6	18	29	40
3,4-Krigstein-a	7	21	38	55
9-One pg. Frazetta ad	6	18	29	40
V3#1	6	18	29	40

NOTE: **Briefer** a-V1#8. Kinstleresque stories by **McCann**-12, V2#1, 2, V3#1. **McWilliams** a-V1#5. **Ed Moore** a-V1#4.

DEADFACE: DOING THE ISLANDS WITH BACCHUS
Dark Horse Comics: July, 1991 - No. 3, Sept, 1991 ($2.95, B&W, lim. series)

1-3: By Eddie Campbell ... 3.00

DEADFACE: EARTH, WATER, AIR, AND FIRE
Dark Horse Comics: July, 1992 - No. 4, Oct, 1992 ($2.50, B&W, limited series; British-r)

1-4: By Eddie Campbell ... 3.00

DEAD IN THE WEST
Dark Horse Comics: Oct, 1993 - No. 2, Mar, 1994 ($3.95, B&W, 52 pgs.)

1,2-Timothy Truman-c ... 4.00

DEAD KING (See Evil Ernie)
Chaos! Comics: May, 1998 - No. 4, Aug, 1998, ($2.95, limited series)

1-4-Fisher-s ... 3.00

DEADLIEST HEROES OF KUNG FU (Magazine)
Marvel Comics Group: Summer, 1975 (B&W)(76 pgs.)

1 -Bruce Lee vs. Carradine painted-c; TV Kung Fu, 4pgs. photos/article; Enter the Dragon, 24 pgs. photos/article w/ Bruce Lee; Bruce Lee photo pinup
| | 2 | 6 | 15 | 22 |

DEADLINE USA
Dark Horse Comics: Apr, 1992 - No. 8, Nov, 1992 ($3.95, B&W, 52 pgs.)

1-8: Johnny Nemo w/Milligan scripts in all ... 4.00

DEADLY DUO, THE
Image Comics (Highbrow Entertainment): Nov, 1994 - No. 3, Jan, 1995 ($2.50, limited series)

1-3: 1-1st app. of Kill Cat ... 2.50

DEADLY DUO, THE
Image Comics (Highbrow Entertainment): June, 1995 - No. 4, Oct, 1995 ($2.50, limited series)

1-4: 1-Spawn app. 2-Savage Dragon app. 3-Gen 13 app. ... 2.50

DEADLY FOES OF SPIDER-MAN (See Lethal Foes of...)
Marvel Comics: May, 1991 - No. 4, Aug, 1991 ($1.00, limited series)

1-4: 1-Punisher, Kingpin, Rhino app. ... 2.50

DEADLY HANDS OF KUNG FU, THE (See Master of Kung Fu)
Marvel Comics Group: April, 1974 - No. 33, Feb, 1977 (75¢) (B&W, magazine)

1(V1#4 listed in error)-Origin Sons of the Tiger; Shang-Chi, Master of Kung Fu begins (ties w/Master of Kung Fu #17 as 3rd app. Shang-Chi); Bruce Lee painted-c by Neal Adams; 2pg. memorial photo pinup w/8 pgs. photos/articles; TV Kung Fu, 9 pgs. photos/article. Starlin-a.
| | 3 | 10 | 23 | 35 |
2-Adams painted-c; 1st time origin of Shang-Chi, 34 pgs. by Starlin. TV Kung Fu, 6 pgs. ph/a w/2 pg. pinup. Bruce Lee, 11 pgs. ph/a
| | 3 | 9 | 19 | 28 |
3,4,7,10: 3-Adams painted-c; Gulacy-a. Enter the Dragon, photos/articles, 8 pgs. 4-TV Kung Fu painted-c by Neal Adams; TV Kung Fu 7 pg. article/art; Fu Manchu; Enter the Dragon, 10 pg. photos/article w/Bruce Lee. 7-Bruce Lee painted-c & 9 pgs. photos/articles-Return of Dragon plus 1 pg. photo pinup. 10-(3/75)-Iron Fist painted-c & 34 pg. sty-Early app.
| | 2 | 6 | 13 | 20 |
5,6: 5-1st app. Manchurian, 6 pgs. Gulacy-a. TV Kung Fu, 4 pg. article; re books w/Barry Smith-a. Capt. America-sty, 10 pgs. Kirby-a(r). 6-Bruce Lee

photos/article, 6 pgs.; 15 pgs. early Perez-a
| | 2 | 6 | 12 | 18 |
8,9,11: 9-Iron Fist, 2 pg. Preview pinup; Nebres-a. 11-Billy Jack painted-c by Adams; 17 pgs. photos/article
| | 2 | 6 | 11 | 16 |
12,13: 12-James Bond painted-c by Adams; 14 pg. photos/article. 13-16 pgs. early Perez-a; Piers Anthony, 7 pgs. photos/article
| | 2 | 6 | 10 | 14 |
14-Classic Bruce Lee painted-c by Adams. Lee pinup by Chaykin. Lee 16 pg. photos/article w/2 pgs. Green Hornet TV
| | 4 | 12 | 29 | 45 |
15,19: 15-Sum, '75 Giant Annual #1. 20pgs. Starlin-a. Bruce Lee photo pinup & 3 pg photos/article re book; Man-Thing app. Iron Fist-c/sty; Gulacy-a 18pgs. 19-Iron Fist painted-c & series begins; 1st White Tiger 2
| | 2 | 6 | 11 | 16 |
16,18,20: 16-1st app. Corpse Rider, a Samurai w/Sanho Kim-a. 20-Chuck Norris painted-c & 16 pgs. interview w/photos/article; Bruce Lee vs. C. Norris pinup by Ken Barr. Origin The White Tiger, Perez-a
| | 2 | 6 | 10 | 14 |
17-Bruce Lee painted-c by Adams; interview w/R. Clouse, director Enter Dragon 7 pgs. w/B. Lee app. 1st Giffen-a (1pg. 11/75)
| | 3 | 9 | 19 | 28 |
21-Bruce Lee 1pg. photos/article
| | 2 | 6 | 9 | 12 |
22,30-32: 22-1st app. Jack of Hearts (cameo). 1st Giffen sty-a (along w/Amazing Adv. #35, 3/76). 30-Swordquest-c/sty & conclusion; Jack of Hearts app. 31-Jack of Hearts app; Staton-a. 32-1st Daughters of the Dragon -c/sty, 21 pgs. M. Rogers-a/Claremont-sty; Iron Fist pinup
| | 2 | 6 | 12 | 18 |
23-26,29: 23-1st full app. Jack of Hearts. 24-Iron Fist-c & centerfold pinup. early Zeck-a. 25-1st app. Shimura, "Samurai", 20 pgs. Mantlo-sty/Broderick-a; "Swordquest"-c & begins 17 pg. sty by Sanho Kim; 11 pgs. photos/article; partly Bruce Lee 26-Bruce Lee painted-c & pinup; 16 pgs. interviews w/Kwon & Clouse; talk about B. Lee re-filming of B. Lee legend. 29-Ironfist vs. Shang Chi battle-c/sty; Jack of Hearts app.
| | 2 | 6 | 12 | 18 |
27
| | 2 | 6 | 9 | 12 |
28-All Bruce Lee Special Issue; (1st time in comics). Bruce Lee painted-c by Ken Barr & pinup. 36 pgs. comics chronicling Bruce Lee's life; 15 pgs. B. Lee photos/article (Rare in high grade)
| | 5 | 15 | 38 | 60 |
33-Shang Chi-c/sty; Classic Daughters of the Dragon, 21 pgs. M. Rogers-a/ Claremont-sty with Nudity; Bob Wall interview, photos/article, 14 pgs.
| | 2 | 6 | 12 | 18 |
...Special Album Edition 1(Summer, '74)-Iron Fist-c/story (early app., 3rd?); 10 pgs. Adams-i; Shang Chi/Fu Manchu, 10 pgs.; Sons of Tiger, 11 pgs.; TV Kung Fu, 6 pgs. photos/article
| | 2 | 6 | 11 | 16 |
NOTE: **Bruce Lee:** 1-7, 14, 15, 17, 25, 26, 28. **Kung Fu (TV):** 1, 2, 4. **Jack of Hearts:** 22, 23, 29-33. **Shang Chi Master of Kung Fu:** 1-9, 11-18, 29, 31, 33. **Sons of Tiger:** 1, 3, 4, 6-14, 16-19. **Swordquest:** 25-27, 29-33. **White Tiger:** 19-24, 26, 27, 29-33. **N. Adams** a-1(part), 2(r); c-1, 2-4, 11, 12, 14, 17. **Adams** a-22(p), 24p. **G. Kane** a-23p. **Kirby** a-5r. **Nasser** a-27p, 28. **Perez** a(p)-6-14, 16, 17, 19, 21. **Rogers** a-26, 32, 33. **Starlin** a-1, 2r, 15r. **Staton** a-28p, 31, 32.

DEADMAN (See The Brave and the Bold & Phantom Stranger #39)
DC Comics: May, 1985 - No. 7, Nov, 1985 ($1.75, Baxter paper)

1-7: 1-Deadman-r by Infantino, N. Adams in all. 5-Batman-c/story-r/Str. Advs. 7-Batman-r ... 3.00

DEADMAN
DC Comics: Mar, 1986 - No. 4, June, 1986 (75¢, limited series)

1-4: Lopez-c/a. 4-Byrne-c(p) ... 2.50

DEADMAN
DC Comics: Feb, 2002 - Present ($2.50)

1,2-Vance-s/Beroy-a ... 2.50

DEADMAN: DEAD AGAIN (Leads into 2002 series)
DC Comics: Oct, 2001 - No. 5, Oct, 2001 ($2.50, weekly limited series)

1-5: Deadman at the deaths of the Flash, Robin, Superman, Hal Jordan ... 2.50

DEADMAN: EXORCISM
DC Comics: 1992 - No. 2, 1992 ($4.95, limited series, 52 pgs.)

1,2: Kelley Jones-c/a in both ... 5.00

DEADMAN: LOVE AFTER DEATH
DC Comics: 1989 - No. 2, 1990 ($3.95, 52 pgs., limited series, mature)

Book One, Two: Kelley Jones-c/a in both: 1-contains nudity ... 4.00

DEAD OF NIGHT
Marvel Comics Group: Dec, 1973 - No. 11, Aug, 1975

1-Horror reprints
| | 2 | 6 | 13 | 20 |

Deadpool #55 © DC

Deathblow #11 © WSP

Deathlok #3 © DC

	GD2.0	FN6.0	VF8.0	NM9.4

2-10: 10-Kirby-a	2	6	9	12
11-Intro Scarecrow; Kane/Wrightson-c	3	9	17	25

NOTE: *Ditko* r-7, 10. *Everett* c-2. *Sinnott* r-1.

DEAD OR ALIVE - A CYBERPUNK WESTERN
Image Comics (Shok Studio): Apr, 1998 - No. 4, July, 1998 ($2.50, lim. series)

1-4				3.00

DEADPOOL (See New Mutants #98)
Marvel Comics: Aug, 1994 - No. 4, Nov, 1994 ($2.50, limited series)

1-4: Mark Waid's 1st Marvel work; Ian Churchill-c/a				3.00

DEADPOOL (... : Agent of Weapon X on cover #57-on)
Marvel Comics: Jan, 1997 - Present ($2.95/$1.95/$1.99)

1-($2.95)-Wraparound-c				4.00
2-Begin-$1.95-c.				3.00
3-10,12-22,24: 4-Hulk-c/app. 12-Variant-c. 14-Begin McDaniel-a. 22-Cable app.				2.50
11-($3.99)-Deadpool replaces Spider-Man from Amazing Spider-Man #47; Kraven, Gwen Stacy app.				5.00
23,25-($2.99) 23-Dead Reckoning pt. 1; wraparound-c				3.00
26-40: 27-Wolverine-c/app. 37-Thor app.				2.25
41-53,56-60: 41-Begin $2.25-c. 44-Black Panther-c/app. 46-49-Chadwick-a 51-Cover swipe of Detective #38. 57-60-BWS-c				2.25
54,55-Punisher-c/app. 54-Dillon-c. 55-Bradstreet-c				2.25
60-Funeral For a Freak				2.25
#(-1) Flashback (7/97) Lopresti-a; Wade Wilson's early days				2.25
...Death '98 Annual ($2.99) Kelly-s, ... Team-Up (12/98, $2.99) Widdle Wade-c/app., Baby's First Deadpool Book (12/98, $2.99), Encyclopædia Deadpoolica (12/98, $2.99) Synopses				3.00
Mission Improbable TPB (9/98, $14.95) r/#1-5				15.00
Wizard #0 ('98, bagged with Wizard #87)				2.25

DEADPOOL: THE CIRCLE CHASE (See New Mutants #98)
Marvel Comics: Aug, 1993 - No. 4, Nov, 1993 ($2.00, limited series)

1-($2.50)-Embossed-c				4.00
2-4				3.00

DEADSHOT (See Batman #59, Detective Comics #474, & Showcase '93 #8)
DC Comics: Nov, 1988 - No. 4, Feb, 1989 ($1.00, limited series)

1-4				2.50

DEADSIDE (See Shadowman)
Acclaim Comics: Feb, 1999 - No. 4, ($2.50, limited series)

1-3-Jenkins-s/Haselden-Wood-a				2.50

DEAD WHO WALK, THE (See Strange Mysteries, Super Reprint #15, 16)
Realistic Comics: 1952 (one-shot)

nn	50	150	300	525

DEADWORLD (Also see The Realm)
Arrow Comics/Caliber Comics: Dec, 1986 - No. 26 ($1.50/$1.95/#15-28: $2.50, B&W, mature)

1-26: 5-26-Graphic covers, 5-26: Tame covers				2.50
...Archives 1-3 (1992, $2.50)				2.50

DEAN MARTIN & JERRY LEWIS (See Adventures of...)

DEAR BEATRICE FAIRFAX
Best/Standard Comics (King Features): No. 5, Nov, 1950 - No. 9, Sept, 1951 (Vern Greene art)

5-All have Schomburg air brush-c	10	30	55	80
6-9	6	18	32	45

DEAR HEART (Formerly Lonely Heart)
Ajax: No. 15, July, 1956 - No. 16, Sept, 1956

15,16	6	18	29	40

DEAR LONELY HEART (...Illustrated No. 1-6)
Artful Publications: Mar, 1951; No. 2, Oct, 1951 - No. 8, Oct, 1952

1	17	51	88	150
2	8	24	45	65
3-Matt Baker Jungle Girl story	20	60	105	175
4-8	7	21	38	55

DEAR LONELY HEARTS (Lonely Heart #9 on)

	GD2.0	FN6.0	VF8.0	NM9.4

Harwell Publ./Mystery Publ. Co. (Comic Media): Aug, 1953 -No. 8, Oct, 1954

1	10	30	55	85
2-8	7	21	36	50

DEARLY BELOVED
Ziff-Davis Publishing Co.: Fall, 1952

1-Photo-c	17	51	88	150

DEAR NANCY PARKER
Gold Key: June, 1963 - No. 2, Sept, 1963

1-Painted-c on both	3	10	23	35
2	3	9	17	26

DEATHBLOW (Also see Darker Image)
Image Comics (WildStorm Productions): May (Apr. inside), 1993 - No. 29, Aug, 1996 ($1.75/$1.95/$2.50)

0-(8/96, $2.95, 32 pgs.)-r/Darker Image w/new story & art; Jim Lee & Trevor Scott-a; new Jim Lee-c				3.00
1-($2.50)-Red foil stamped logo on black varnish-c; Jim Lee-c/a; flip-book side has Cybernary r-c/story (#2 also)				3.00
1-($1.95)-Newsstand version w/o foil-c & varnish				2.25
2-29: 2-(8/93)-Lee-a; with bound-in poster. 2-($1.75)-Newsstand version w/o poster. 4-Jim Lee-c/Tim Sale-a begin. 13-W/pinup poster by Tim Sale & Jim Lee. 16 ($1.95, Newsstand) Wildstorm Rising Pt. 6. 16. ($2.50, Direct Market)-Wildstorm Rising Pt. 617-Variant "Chicago Comicon" edition exists. 20,21-Gen 13 app. 23-Backlash-c/app. 24,25-Grifter-c/app; Gen 13 & Dane from Wetworks app. 28-Deathblow dies. 29-Memorial issue				2.50
5-Alternate Portacio-c (Forms larger picture when combined with alternate-c for Gen 13 #5, Kindred #3, Stormwatch #10, Team 7 #1, Union #0, Wetworks #2 & WildC.A.T.S # 11)				6.00
....Sinners and Saints TPB ('99, $19.95) r/#1-12; Sale-c				20.00

DEATHBLOW BY BLOWS
DC Comics (WildStorm): Nov, 1999 - No. 3, Jan, 2000 ($2.95, limited series)

1-3-Alan Moore-s/Jim Baikie-a				3.00

DEATHBLOW/WOLVERINE
Image Comics (WildStorm Productions)/ Marvel Comics: Sept, 1996 - No. 2, Feb, 1997 ($2.50, limited series)

1,2: Wiesenfeld-s/Bennett-a				2.50
TPB (1997, $8.95) r/#1,2				9.00

DEATHDEALER
Verotik: July, 1995 - No. 4, July, 1997 ($5.95)

1-Frazetta-c; Bisley-a	1	3	6	8
1-2nd print, 2-4-($6.95)-Frazetta-c; embossed logo	1	3	5	7

DEATHLOK (Also see Astonishing Tales #25)
Marvel Comics: July, 1990 - No. 4, Oct, 1990 ($3.95, limited series, 52 pgs.)

1-4: 1,2-Guice-a(p). 3,4-Denys Cowan-a, c-4				4.00

DEATHLOK
Marvel Comics: July, 1991 - No. 34, Apr, 1994 ($1.75)

1-Silver ink cover; Denys Cowan-c/a(p) begins				3.00
2-18,20-24,26-34: 2-Forge (X-Men) app. 3-Vs. Dr. Doom. 5-X-Men & F.F. x-over. 6,7-Punisher x-over. 9,10-Ghost Rider-c/story. 16-Infinity War x-over. 17-Jae Lee-c. 22-Black Panther app. 27-Siege app.				2.25
19-($2.25)-Foil-c				2.50
25-($2.95, 52 pgs.)-Holo-grafx foil-c				3.00
Annual 1 (1992, $2.25, 68 pgs.)-Guice-p; Quesada-c(i)				3.00
Annual 2 (1993, $2.95, 68 pgs.)-Bagged w/card; intro Tracer				3.00

NOTE: *Denys Cowan* a(p)-9-13, 15, Annual 1; c-9-12, 13p, 14. *Guice/Cowan* c-8.

DEATHLOK
Marvel Comics: Sept, 1999 - No. 11, June, 2000 ($1.99)

1-11: 1-Casey-s/Manco-a. 2-Two covers. 4-Canete-a				2.25

DEATHLOK SPECIAL
Marvel Comics: May, 1991 - No. 4, June, 1991 ($2.00, bi-weekly lim. series)

1-4: r/1-4(1990) w/new Guice-c #1,2; Cowan c-3,4				2.50
1-2nd printing w/white-c				2.25

DEATHMARK
Lightning Comics: Dec, 1994 ($2.95, B&W)

Deathstroke: The Terminator #2 © DC

Death: The High Cost of Living #2 © DC

Debbie Dean, Career Girl #2 © Civil Serv. Pub.

DE

DEBBIE GETS IN DUTCH

| | GD2.0 | FN6.0 | VF8.0 | NM9.4 | | | GD2.0 | FN6.0 | VF8.0 | NM9.4 |

1   3.00

DEATHMATE
Valiant (Prologue/Yellow/Blue)/Image Comics (Black/Red/Epilogue):
Sept, 1993 - Epilogue (#6), Feb, 1994 ($2.95/$4.95, limited series):
Preview-(7/93, 8 pgs.)   2.25
Prologue (#1)–Silver foil; Jim Lee/Layton-c; B. Smith/Lee-a; Liefeld-a(p)
                                                             3.00
Prologue–Special gold foil ed. of silver ed.   4.00
Black (#2)-(9/93, $4.95, 52 pgs.)-Silvestri/Jim Lee-c; pencils by Peterson/Silves-
tri/Capullo/Jim Lee/Portacio; 1st story app. Gen 13 telling their rebellion
against the Troika (see WildC.A.T.S. Trilogy)   6.00
Black-Special gold foil edition   7.00
Yellow (#3)-(10/93, $4.95, 52 pgs)-Yellow foil-c; Indicia says Prologue Sept 1993
by mistake; 3rd app. Ninjak; Thibert-c(i)   5.00
Yellow-Special gold foil edition   6.00
Blue (#4)-(10/93, $4.95, 52 pgs.)-Thibert blue foil-c(i); Reese-a(i)   5.00
Blue-Special gold foil edition   6.00
Red (#5), Epilogue (#6)-(2/94, $2.95)-Silver foil Quesada/Silvestri; Silvestri-a(p)
                                                             3.00

DEATH METAL
Marvel Comics UK: Jan, 1994 - No. 4, Apr, 1994 ($1.95, limited series):
1-4: 1-Silver ink-c. Alpha Flight app.   2.25

DEATH METAL VS. GENETIX
Marvel Comics UK: Dec, 1993 - No. 2, Jan, 1994 (Limited series):
1-($2.95)-Polybagged w/2 trading cards   3.00
2-($2.50)-Polybagged w/2 trading cards   2.50

DEATH OF CAPTAIN MARVEL (See Marvel Graphic Novel #1)

DEATH OF MR. MONSTER, THE (See Mr. Monster #8)

DEATH OF SUPERMAN (See Superman, 2nd Series)

DEATH RACE 2020
Roger Corman's Cosmic Comics: Apr, 1995 - No. 8, Nov, 1995 ($2.50):
1-8: Sequel to the Movie   2.50

DEATH RATTLE (Formerly an Underground)
Kitchen Sink Press: V2#1, 10/85 - No. 18, 1988, 1994 ($1.95, Baxter paper,
mature); V3#1, 11/95 - No. 5, 6/96 ($2.95, B&W):
V2#1-7,9-18: 1-Corben-c. 2-Unpubbed Spirit story by Eisner. 5-Robot Woman-r
by Wolverton. 6-B&W issues begin. 10-Savage World-r by Williamson/
Torres/ Krenkel/Frazetta from Witzend #1. 16-Wolverton Spacehawk-r 3.00
8-(12/86)-1st app. Mark Schultz's Xenozoic Tales/Cadillacs & Dinosaurs 4.00
8-(1994)-r plus interview w/Mark Schultz   3.00
V3#1-5 ($2.95-c)   3.00

DEATH'S HEAD (See Daredevil #56, Dragon's Claws #5 & Incomplete...)
Marvel Comics: Dec, 1988 - No. 10, Sept, 1989 ($1.75):
1-Dragon's Claws spin-off   3.00
2-Fantastic Four app.; Dragon's Claws x-over   2.50
3-10: 8-Dr. Who app. 9-F. F. x-over; Simonson-c(p)   2.25

DEATH'S HEAD II (Also see Battletide)
Marvel Comics UK, Ltd.: Mar, 1992 - No. 4, June (May inside), 1992 ($1.75,
color, limited series):
1-4: 2-Fantastic Four app. 4-Punisher, Spider-Man , Daredevil, Dr. Strange,
Capt. America & Wolverine in the year 2020   2.25
1,2-Silver ink 2nd printiing   2.25

DEATH'S HEAD II (Also see Battletide)
Marvel Comics UK, Ltd.: Dec, 1992 - No. 16, Mar, 1994 ($1.75/$1.95):
V2#1-13,15,16: 1-Gatefold-c. 1-4-X-Men app.15-Capt. America
& Wolverine app.   2.25
14-($2.95)-Foil flip-c w/Death's Head II Gold #0   3.00
...Gold 1 (1/94, $3.95, 68 pgs.)-Gold foil-c   4.00

DEATH'S HEAD II & THE ORIGIN OF DIE CUT
Marvel Comics UK, Ltd.: Aug, 1993 - No. 2, Sept, 1993 (limited series):
1-($2.95)-Embossed-c   3.00
2 ($1.75)   2.25

DEATHSTROKE: THE TERMINATOR (Deathstroke: The Hunted #0-47;

Deathstroke #48-60) (Also see Marvel & DC Present, New Teen Titans #2,
New Titans, Showcase '93 #7,9 & Tales of the Teen Titans #42-44)
DC Comics: Aug, 1991 - No. 60, June, 1996 ($1.75-$2.25):
1-New Titans spin-off; Mike Zeck c-1-28   4.00
1-Gold ink 2nd printing ($1.75)   2.25
2   3.00
3-40,(10/94),41(11/94)-49,51-60: 6,8-Batman cameo. 7,9-Batman-c/story. 9-
1st new Vigilante (female) in cameo. 10-1st full app. new Vigilante; Perez-i.
13-Vs. Justice League; Deathstroke cameo on last pg. 14-Total Chaos, part 1;
TeamTitans-c/story cont'd in New Titans #90. 15-Total Chaos, part 4. 40-
(9/94). 0-(10/94)-Begin Deathstroke, The Hunted, ends #47.   2.50
50 ($3.50)   3.50
Annual 1-4 ('92-'95, 68 pgs.): 1-Nightwing & Vigilante app.; minor Eclipso app. 2-
Bloodlines Deathstorm; 1st app. Gunfire. 3-Elseworlds story. 4-Year One
story   4.00
NOTE: Golden a-12. Perez a-11i. Zeck c-Annual 1, 2.

DEATH: THE HIGH COST OF LIVING (See Sandman #8) (Also see the Books
of Magic limited & ongoing series)
DC Comics (Vertigo): Mar, 1993 - No. 3, May, 1993 ($1.95, limited series):
1-Bachalo/Buckingham-a; Dave McKean-c; Neil Gaiman scripts in all
                                                             6.00
1-Platinum edition   20.00
2   3.50
3-Pgs. 19 & 20 had wrong placement   3.00
3-Corrected version w/pgs. 19 & 20 facing each other; has no-c & ads for
Sebastion O & The Geek added   4.00
Death Talks About Life-giveaway about AIDS prevention   4.00
Hardcover (1994, $19.95)-r/#1-3 & Death Talks About Life; intro. by Tori Amos.
                                                             20.00
Trade paperback (6/94, $12.95, Titan Books)-r/#1-3 & Death Talks About Life;
prism-c   13.00

DEATH: THE TIME OF YOUR LIFE (See Sandman #8)
DC Comics (Vertigo): Apr, 1996 - No. 3, July, 1996 ($2.95, limited series):
1-3: Neil Gaiman story & Bachalo/Buckingham-a; Dave McKean-c. 2-(5/96).
                                                             3.00
Hardcover (1997, $19.95)-r/#1-3 w/3 new pages & gallery art by various   20.00
Trade paperback (1997, $12.95)-r/#1-3 & Visions of Death gallery;
Intro. by Claire Danes   13.00

DEATH 3
Marvel Comics UK: Sept, 1993 - No. 4, Dec, 1993 (limited series):
1-($2.95)-Embossed-c   3.00
2-4   2.25

DEATH VALLEY (Cowboys and Indians)
Comic Media: Oct, 1953 - No. 6, Aug, 1954

	11	33	55	90
1-Billy the Kid; Morisi-a; Andru/Esposito-c/a	11	33	55	90
2-Don Heck-c	7	21	36	50
3-6: 3,5-Morisi-a. 5-Discount-a	6	18	32	45

DEATH VALLEY (Becomes Frontier Scout, Daniel Boone No.10-13)
Charlton Comics: No. 7, 6/55 - No. 9, 10/55 (Cont'd from Comic Media series)

7-9: 8-Wolverton-a (half pg.)	6	18	29	40

DEATHWISH
DC Comics (Milestone Media): Dec, 1994 - No. 4, Mar, 1995 (2.50, lim. series):
1-4   2.50

DEATH WRECK
Marvel Comics UK: Jan, 1994 - No. 4, Apr, 1994 ($1.95, limited series):
1-4: 1-Metallic ink logo; Death's Head II app.   2.25

DEBBIE DEAN, CAREER GIRL
Civil Service Publ.: April, 1945 - No. 2, July, 1945

	14	42	72	120
1,2-Newspaper reprints by Bert Whitman	14	42	72	120

DEBBI'S DATES (Also see Date With Debbi)
National Periodical Publications: Apr-May, 1969 - No. 11, Dec-Jan, 1970-71

	4	12	30	50
1	4	12	30	50
2,3,5,7-11: 2-Last 12¢ issue	2	6	15	22
4-Neal Adams text illo	3	9	21	32

The Defenders #13 © MAR

The Defenders V2 #1 © MAR

Dell Giant Comics - Bugs Bunny's County Fair #1 © WB

	GD2.0	FN6.0	VF8.0	NM9.4

	GD2.0	FN6.0	VF8.0	NM9.4

6-Superman cameo — 4 12 30 50

DECADE OF DARK HORSE, A
Dark Horse Comics: Jul, 1996 - No. 4, Oct, 1996 ($2.95, B&W/color, lim. series)
1-4: 1-Sin City-c/story by Miller; Grendel by Wagner; Predator. 2-Star Wars wraparound-c. 3-Aliens-c/story; Nexus, Mask stories — 3.00

DECAPITATOR (Randy Bowen's...)
Dark Horse Comics: Jun, 1998 - No. 4, ($2.95)
1-4-Bowen-s/art by various. 1-Mahnke-c. 3-Jones-c — 4.00

DECEPTION, THE
Image Comics (Flypaper Press): 1999 - No. 3, 1999 ($2.95, B&W, mini-series)
1-3-Horley painted-c — 3.00

DEEP, THE (Movie)
Marvel Comics Group: Nov, 1977 (Giant)
1-Infantino-c/a — 6.00

DEEP DARK FANTASIES
Dark Fantasy Productions: Oct, 1995 ($4.50/$4.95, B&W)
1-($4.50)-Clive Barker-c, anthology — 4.50
1-($4.95)-Red foil logo-c — 5.00

DEFCON 4: Feb, 1996 - No. 4, Sept, 1996 ($2.50,
Image Comics (WildStorm Productions): limited series)
1/2 — 1 3 6 9
1/2 Gold-(1000 printed) — 14.00
1-Main Cover by Mat Broome & Edwin Rosell — 3.00
1-Hordes of Cymulants variant-c by Michael Golden — 5.00
1-Backs to the Wall variant-c by Humberto Ramos & Alex Garner — 5.00
1-Defcon 4-Way variant-c by Jim Lee — 1 3 5 7
2-4 — 2.50

DEFENDERS, THE (TV)
Dell Publishing Co.: Sept-Nov, 1962 - No. 2, Feb-Apr, 1963
12-176-211(#1) — 4 12 29 45
12-176-304(#2) — 3 10 23 35

DEFENDERS, THE (Also see Giant-Size..., Marvel Feature, Marvel Treasury Edition, Secret Defenders & Sub-Mariner #34, 35; The New...#140-on)
Marvel Comics Group: Aug, 1972 - No. 152, Feb, 1986
1-The Hulk, Doctor Strange, Sub-Mariner begin — 9 27 65 110
2-Silver Surfer x-over — 4 12 29 45
3-5: 3-Silver Surfer x-over. 4-Valkyrie joins — 3 9 20 30
6,7: 6-Silver Surfer x-over — 2 6 15 22
8,9,11: 8-11-Defenders vs. the Avengers (Crossover with Avengers #115-118)
8,11-Silver Surfer x-over — 3 9 20 30
10-Hulk vs. Thor battle — 4 12 26 40
12-14: 12-Last 20¢ issue — 2 6 9 12
15,16-Magneto & Brotherhood of Evil Mutants app. from X-Men
— 2 6 11 15
17-20: 17-Power Man x-over (11/74) — 1 3 6 9
21-25: 24,25-Son of Satan app. — 6.00
26-29-Guardians of the Galaxy app. (#26 is 8/75; pre-dates Marvel Presents #3): 28-1st full app. Starhawk (cameo #27). 29-Starhawk joins Guardians
— 3 6 8
30-33,39-50: 31,32-Origin Nighthawk. 44-Hellcat joins. 45-Dr. Strange leaves.
47-49-Early Moon Knight app. (5/77). 48-50-(Reg. 30¢-c) — 5.00
34-38-(Regular 25¢ editions): 35-Intro New Red Guardian — 5.00
34-38-(30¢-c variants, limited distribution)(4-8/76) — 1 3 5 7
48-52-(35¢-c variants, limited distribution)(6-10/77) — 1 3 5 7
51-60: 51,52-(Reg. 30¢-c). 53-1st app. Lunatik (cameo, Lobo lookalike). 55-Origin Red Guardian; Lunatik cameo. 56-1st full Lunatik story — 4.00
61-75: 61-Lunatik & Spider-Man app. 70-73-Lunatik (origin #71). 73-75-Foolkiller II app. (Greg Salinger). 74-Nighthawk resigns — 3.00
76-95,97-99,101-124,126-149,151: 77-Origin Omega. 78-Original Defenders return thru #101. 94-1st Gargoyle. 101-Silver Surfer-c & app. 104-The Beast joins. 105-Son of Satan joins. 106-Death of Nighthawk. 120,121-Son of Satan-c/stories. 122-Final app. Son of Satan (2 pgs.). 129-New Mutants cameo (3/84, early x-over) — 2.50
96-Ghost Rider app. — 4.00

100-(52 pgs.)-Hellcat (Patsy Walker) revealed as Satan's daughter — 5.00
125,150: 125-(52 pgs.)-Intro new Defenders. 150-(52 pgs.)-Origin Cloud — 4.00
152-(52 pgs.)-Ties in with X-Factor & Secret Wars II — 4.00
Annual 1 (1976, 52 pgs.)-New book-length story — 2 6 11 16
NOTE: **Art Adams** c-142p. **Austin** a-53i; c-65i, 119i, 145i. **Frank Bolle** a-7i, 11i. **Buckler** c(p)-34, 38, 76, 77, 79-86, 90, 91. **J. Buscema** a-66. **Giffen** a-42-49p, 50, 51-54p. **Golden** a-53p, 54p, c-94, 96. **Guice** c-129. **G. Kane** c(p)-13, 16, 18, 19, 21-26, 33-35, 37, 40, 41, 52, 55. **Kirby** c-42-45. **Mooney** a-3i, 31-34i, 62i, 63i, 85i. **Nasser** c-88p. **Perez** c(p)-51, 53, 54. **Rogers** c-98. **Starlin** c-110. **Tuska** a-57p. Silver Surfer in No. 2, 3, 6, 8-11, 92, 98-101, 107, 112-115, 122-125.

DEFENDERS, THE (Volume 2)
Marvel Comics: Mar, 2001 - Present ($2.99/$2.25)
1-Busiek & Larsen-s/Larsen & Janson-a/c — 3.00
2-11: 2-Two covers by Larsen & Art Adams; Valkyrie app. 4-Frenz-a — 2.25
12-($3.50) 'Nuff Said issue; back-ups Reis-a — 3.50

DEFENDERS OF DYNATRON CITY
Marvel Comics: Feb, 1992 - No. 6, July, 1992 ($1.25, limited series)
1-6-Lucasarts characters. 2-Origin — 3.00

DEFENDERS OF THE EARTH (TV)
Marvel Comics (Star Comics): Jan, 1987 - No. 4, July, 1987
1-4: The Phantom, Mandrake The Magician, Flash Gordon begin. 3-Origin Phantom. 4-Origin Mandrake — 4.00

DEFINITIVE DIRECTORY OF THE DC UNIVERSE, THE (See Who's Who...)

DEITY (Also see Kosmic Kat)
Hyperwerks Comics: Sept, 1997 - No. 6, Apr, 1998, ($2.95, limited series)
1-6, 0(5/98) — 4.00
1-Variant-c — 5.00
2-6,0-Variant covers — 4.00
0-NDC Edition — 4.00
0-NDC Silver Ed. — 8.00
0-NDC Gold Ed. — 12.00

DEITY (Volume 2)
Hyperwerks Comics: Sept, 1998 - No. 5 ($2.95)
Preview (6/98) Flip book with Lady Dragon preview — 3.00
1-5: 1-Flip book w/Catseye preview — 3.00

DEITY:REVELATIONS (Volume 3)
Hyperwerks Comics: July, 1999 - No. 4, Dec, 1999 ($2.95)
1-4-Alstaetter and Napton-s/a — 3.00

DELECTA OF THE PLANETS (See Don Fortune & Fawcett Miniatures)

DELLA VISION (...The Television Queen) (Patty Powers #4 on)
Atlas Comics: April, 1955 - No. 3, Aug, 1955
1-Al Hartley-c — 16 48 83 140
2,3 — 11 33 55 90

DELL GIANT COMICS
Dell Publishing began to release square bound comics in 1949 with a 132-page issue called Christmas Parade #1. The covers were of a heavier stock to accommodate the increased number of pages. The books proved profitable at 25 cents but the average number of pages was quickly reduced to 100. Ten years later they were converted to a numbering system similar to the Four Color Comics, for greater ease in distribution and the page counts cut back to mostly 84 pages. The label "Dell Giant" began to appear on the covers in 1954. Because of the size of the books and the heavier, less pliant cover stock, they are rarely found in high grade condition, and with the exception of a small quantity of copies released from Western Publishing's warehouse–are almost never found in near mint.
Abraham Lincoln Life Story 1/3(58) — 6 18 48 110
Bugs Bunny Christmas Funnies 1(11/50, 116pp) — 14 42 112 280
...Christmas Funnies 2(11/51, 116pp) — 9 27 72 180
...Christmas Funnies 3-5(11/52-11/54,)-Becomes Christmas Party #6
— 8 24 64 160
...Christmas Funnies 7-9(12/56-12/58) — 7 21 56 140
...Christmas Party 6(11/55)-Formerly Bugs Bunny Christmas Funnies
— 7 21 56 140
...County Fair 1(9/57) — 9 27 72 180
...Halloween Parade 1(10/53) — 9 27 72 180
...Halloween Parade 2(10/54)-Trick 'N' Treat Halloween Fun #3 on
— 8 24 64 150

	GD2.0	FN6.0	VF8.0	NM9.4			GD2.0	FN6.0	VF8.0	NM9.4

...Trick 'N' Treat Halloween Fun 3,4(10/55-10/56)-Formerly Halloween Parade
| #2 | 8 | 24 | 64 | 160 |
...Vacation Funnies 1(7/51, 112pp) | 14 | 42 | 112 | 280 |
...Vacation Funnies 2('52) | 11 | 33 | 88 | 220 |
...Vacation Funnies 3-5('53-'55) | 9 | 27 | 72 | 170 |
...Vacation Funnies 6-9('54-6/59) | 8 | 24 | 64 | 150 |
Cadet Gray of West Point 1(4/58)-Williamson-a, 10pgs.; Buscema-a; photo-c
| | 6 | 18 | 48 | 110 |
Christmas In Disneyland 1(12/57)-Barks-a, 18 pgs.
| | 21 | 63 | 168 | 420 |
Christmas Parade 1(11/49)(132 pgs.)(1st Dell Giant)-Donald Duck (25pgs. by
Barks, r-in G.K. Christmas Parade #5); Mickey Mouse & other film oriented
stories; Cinderella (prior to movie), 7 Dwarfs, Bambi & Thumper, So Dear To
My Heart, Flying Mouse, Dumbo, Cookieland & others
| | 48 | 144 | 384 | 960 |
Christmas Parade 2('50)-Donald Duck (132 pgs.) by Barks, r-in G.K.
Christmas Parade #6). Mickey, Pluto, Chip & Dale, etc. Contents shift to a
holiday expansion of W.D. C&S type format
| | 37 | 111 | 296 | 740 |
Christmas Parade 3-7('51-'55, #3-116pgs; #4-7, 100 pgs.)
| | 11 | 33 | 88 | 220 |
Christmas Parade 8(12/56)-Barks-a, 8 pgs. | 18 | 54 | 144 | 360 |
Christmas Parade 9(12/58)-Barks-a, 20 pgs. | 21 | 63 | 168 | 420 |
Christmas Treasury, A 1(11/54) | 7 | 21 | 56 | 140 |
Davy Crockett, King Of The Wild Frontier 1(9/55)-Fess Parker photo-c;
Marsh-a | 16 | 48 | 128 | 320 |
Disneyland Birthday Party 1(10/58)-Barks-a, 16 pgs. r-by Gladstone
| | 21 | 63 | 168 | 420 |
Donald and Mickey In Disneyland 1(5/58) | 9 | 27 | 72 | 180 |
Donald Duck Beach Party 1(7/54)-Has an Uncle Scrooge story (not by Barks)
that prefigures the later rivalry with Flintheart Glomgold and tells of Scrooge's
wild rivalry with another millionaire | 12 | 36 | 96 | 240 |
...Beach Party 2(1955)-Lady & Tramp | 9 | 27 | 72 | 180 |
...Beach Party 3-5(1956-58) | 9 | 27 | 72 | 180 |
...Beach Party 6(8/59, 84pp)-Stapled | 6 | 18 | 48 | 120 |
Donald Duck Fun Book 1(1953 & 10/54)-Games, puzzles, comics & cut-outs
(very rare in unused condition)(most copies commonly have defaced
interior pgs.) | 45 | 135 | 360 | 900 |
Donald Duck In Disneyland 1(9/55)-1st Disneyland Dell Giant
| | 11 | 33 | 88 | 220 |
Golden West Rodeo Treasury 1(10/57) | 8 | 24 | 64 | 150 |
Huey, Dewey and Louie Back To School 1(9/58)
| | 7 | 21 | 56 | 140 |
Lady and the Tramp 1(6/55) | 14 | 42 | 112 | 280 |
Life Stories of American Presidents 1(11/57)-Buscema-a
| | 5 | 15 | 40 | 90 |
Lone Ranger Golden West 3(8/55)-Formerly Lone Ranger Western Treasury
| | 15 | 45 | 120 | 300 |
Lone Ranger Movie Story nn(3/56)-Origin Lone Ranger in text; Clayton Moore
photo-c | 30 | 90 | 240 | 600 |
...Western Treasury 1(9/53)-Origin Lone Ranger, Silver, & Tonto; painted cover
| | 20 | 60 | 160 | 400 |
...Western Treasury 2(8/54)-Becomes Lone Ranger Golden West #3
| | 15 | 45 | 120 | 300 |
Marge's Little Lulu & Alvin Story Telling Time 1(3/59)-r/#2,5,3,11,30,10,21,17,8,
14,16; Stanley-a | 12 | 36 | 96 | 240 |
...& Her Friends 4(3/56)-Tripp-a | 10 | 30 | 80 | 200 |
...& Her Special Friends 3(3/55)-Tripp-a | 12 | 36 | 96 | 240 |
...& Tubby At Summer Camp 5,2: 5(10/57)-Tripp-a. 2(10/58)-Tripp-a
| | 10 | 30 | 80 | 200 |
...& Tubby Halloween Fun 6,2: 6(10/57)-Tripp-a. 2(10/58)-Tripp-a
| | 10 | 30 | 80 | 200 |
...& Tubby In Alaska 1(7/59)-Tripp-a | 10 | 30 | 80 | 200 |
...On Vacation 1(7/54)-r/4C-110,14,4C-146,4C-97,4,4C-158,3,1;Stanley-a
| | 21 | 63 | 168 | 420 |
...& Tubby Annual 1(3/53)-r/4C-165,4C-74,4C-146,4C-97,4C-158, 4C-139, 4C
-131; Stanley-a (1st Lulu Dell Gnt) | 25 | 75 | 200 | 500 |
...& Tubby Annual 2('54)-r/4C-139,6,4C-115,4C-74,5,4C-97,3,4C-146,18;
Stanley-a | 22 | 66 | 176 | 440 |
Marge's Tubby & His Clubhouse Pals 1(10/56)-1st app. Gran'pa Feeb;1st app.

Janie; written by Stanley; Tripp-a | 11 | 33 | 88 | 220 |
Mickey Mouse Almanac 1(12/57)-Barks-a, 8pgs. | 22 | 66 | 176 | 440 |
...Birthday Party 1(9/53)-r/entire 48pgs. of Gottfredson's "Mickey Mouse
in Love Trouble" from WDC&S 36-39. Quality equal to original. Also reprints
one story each from 4-Color 27, 29, & 181 plus 6 panels of highlights in
the career of Mickey Mouse | 26 | 78 | 208 | 520 |
...Club Parade 1(12/55)-r/4-Color 16 with some death trap scenes redrawn by
Paul Murry & recolored with night turned into day; quality less than original
| | 20 | 60 | 160 | 400 |
...In Fantasy Land 1(5/57) | 10 | 30 | 80 | 200 |
...In Frontier Land 1(5/56)-Mickey Mouse Club issue
| | 10 | 30 | 80 | 200 |
...Summer Fun 1(8/58)-Mobile cut-outs on back-c; becomes Summer
Fun with #2 | 10 | 30 | 80 | 200 |
Moses & The Ten Commandments 1(8/57)-Not based on movie; Dell's
adaptation; Sekowsky-a | 4 | 12 | 32 | 80 |
Nancy & Sluggo Travel Time 1(9/58) | 6 | 18 | 48 | 120 |
Peter Pan Treasure Chest 1(1/53, 212pp)-Disney; Donald & Mickey story
adaptation & other P. Pan stories; plus Donald & Mickey stories w/P. Pan; a 32-
page retelling of "D. Duck Finds Pirate Gold" with yellow beak, called "Capt.
Hook & the Buried Treasure" | 90 | 270 | 720 | 1800 |
Picnic Party 6,7(7/55-6/56)(Formerly Vacation Parade)-Uncle Scrooge,
Mickey & Donald | 9 | 27 | 72 | 180 |
Picnic Party 8(7/57)-Barks-a, 6pgs | 18 | 54 | 144 | 360 |
Pogo Parade 1(9/53)-Kelly-a(r-/Pogo from Animal Comics in this order:
#11,13,21,14,27,16,23,9,18,15,17) | 24 | 72 | 192 | 480 |
Raggedy Ann & Andy 1(2/55) | 16 | 48 | 128 | 320 |
Santa Claus Funnies 1(11/52)-Dan Noonan -A Christmas Carol adaptation
| | 7 | 21 | 56 | 140 |
Silly Symphonies 1(9/52)-Redrawing of Gottfredson's Mickey Mouse strip of "The
Brave Little Tailor;" 2 Good Housekeeping pages (from 1943); Lady and the
Two Siamese Cats, three years before "Lady & the Tramp;" a retelling of
Donald Duck's first app. in "The Wise Little Hen" & other stories based on
1930's Silly Symphony cartoons | 24 | 72 | 192 | 480 |
Silly Symphonies 2(9/53)-M. Mouse in "The Sorcerer's Apprentice", 2 Good
Housekeeping pages (from 1944); The Pelican & the Snipe, Elmer Elephant,
Peculiar Penguins, Little Hiawatha, & others
| | 21 | 63 | 168 | 420 |
Silly Symphonies 3(2/54)-r/Mickey & The Beanstalk (4-Color #157, 39pgs.),
Little Minnehaha, Pablo, The Flying Gauchito, Pluto, & Bongo, & 2 Good
Housekeeping pages (1944) | 18 | 54 | 144 | 360 |
Silly Symphonies 4(8/54)-r/Dumbo (4-Color 234), Morris The Midget
Moose, The Country Cousin, Bongo, & Clara Cluck
| | 18 | 54 | 144 | 360 |
Silly Symphonies 5-8: 5(2/55)-r/Cinderella (4-Color 272), Bucky Bug, Pluto,
Little Hiawatha, The 7 Dwarfs & Dumbo, Pinocchio. 6(8/55)-r/Pinocchio
(WDC&S 63), The 7 Dwarfs & Thumper (WDC&S 45), M. Mouse "Adventures
With Robin Hood" (40 pgs.), Johnny Appleseed, Pluto & Peter Pan, & Bucky
Bug; Cut-out on back-c. 7(2/57)-r/Reluctant Dragon, Ugly Duckling, M. Mouse
& Peter Pan, Jiminy Cricket, Peter & The Wolf, Brer Rabbit, Bucky Bug; Cut-
out on back-c. 8(2/58)-r/Thumper Meets The 7 Dwarfs (4-Color #19), Jiminy
Cricket, Niok, Brer Rabbit; Cut-out on back-c
| | 15 | 45 | 120 | 300 |
Silly Symphonies 9(2/59)-r/Paul Bunyan, Humphrey Bear, Jiminy Cricket, The
Social Lion, Goliath II; cut-out on back-c
| | 14 | 42 | 112 | 280 |
Sleeping Beauty 1(4/59) | 24 | 72 | 192 | 480 |
Summer Fun 2(8/59, 84pp, stapled binding)(Formerly Mickey Mouse...)-Barks-
a(2), 24 pgs. | 21 | 63 | 168 | 420 |
Tarzan's Jungle Annual 1(8/52)-Lex Barker photo on-c of #1,2
| | 11 | 33 | 88 | 220 |
...Annual 2(8/53) | 9 | 27 | 72 | 180 |
...Annual 3-7('54-9/58)(two No. 5s)-Manning-a-No. 3,5-7; Marsh-a in
No. 1-7 plus painted-c 1-7 | 7 | 21 | 56 | 140 |
Tom And Jerry Back To School 1(9/56) | 11 | 33 | 88 | 220 |
...Picnic Time 1(7/58) | 8 | 24 | 64 | 160 |
...Summer Fun 1(7/54)-Droopy written by Barks
| | 13 | 39 | 104 | 260 |
...Summer Fun 2-4(7/55-7/57) | 6 | 18 | 48 | 120 |
...Toy Fair 1(6/58) | 8 | 24 | 64 | 160 |

Dell Giant Comics - Tom & Jerry Winter Carnival #2 © DELL

Dell Giant #48 © H-B

The Demon (limited series) #1 © DC

	GD2.0	FN6.0	VF8.0	NM9.4

...Winter Carnival 1(12/52)-Droopy written by Barks

| | 18 | 54 | 144 | 360 |

...Winter Carnival 2(12/53)-Droopy written by Barks

| | 15 | 45 | 120 | 300 |

...Winter Fun 3(12/54) 6 18 48 120
...Winter Fun 4-7(12/55-11/58) 5 15 40 100
Treasury of Dogs, A 1(10/56) 5 15 40 100
Treasury of Horses, A (9/55) 5 15 40 100
Uncle Scrooge Goes To Disneyland 1(8/57p)-Barks-a, 20pgs.r-by Gladstone

| | 21 | 63 | 168 | 420 |

Vacation In Disneyland 1(8/58) 9 27 72 180
Vacation Parade 1(7/50, 132pp)-Donald Duck & Mickey Mouse; Barks-a, 55 pgs.

| | 70 | 210 | 560 | 1400 |

Vacation Parade 2(7/51,116pp) 22 66 176 440
Vacation Parade 3-5(7/52-7/54)-Becomes Picnic Party No. 6 on. #4-Robin Hood Advs.

| | 11 | 33 | 88 | 220 |

Western Roundup 1(6/52)-Photo-c; Gene Autry, Roy Rogers, Johnny Mack Brown, Rex Allen, & Bill Elliott begin; photo back-c begin, and No. 14,16,18

| | 20 | 60 | 160 | 400 |

Western Roundup 2(2/53)-Photo-c 11 33 88 220
Western Roundup 3-5(7-9/53 - 1-3/54)-Photo-c 9 27 72 180
Western Roundup 6-10(4-6/54 - 4-6/55)-Photo-c 8 24 64 160
Western Roundup 11-17,25-Photo-c; 11-13,16,17-Manning-a. 11-Flying A's Range Rider, Dale Evans begin 7 21 56 140
Western Roundup 18-Toth-a; last photo-c; Gene Autry ends

| | 8 | 24 | 64 | 160 |

Western Roundup 19-24-Manning-a. 19-Buffalo Bill Jr. begins (7-9/57; early app.). 19,20,22-Toth-a. 21-Rex Allen, Johnny Mack Brown end. 22-Jace Pearson's Texas Rangers, Rin Tin Tin, Tales of Wells Fargo (2nd app., 4-6/58) & Wagon Train (2nd app.) begin 7 21 56 140
Woody Woodpecker Back To School 1(10/52)

| | 8 | 24 | 64 | 160 |

...Back To School 2-4,6('53-10/57)-County Fair No. 5

| | 6 | 18 | 48 | 120 |

...County Fair 5(9/56)-Formerly Back To School

| | 6 | 18 | 48 | 120 |

...County Fair 2(11/58) 5 15 40 100

DELL GIANTS (Consecutive numbering)
Dell Publishing Co.: No. 21, Sept. 1959 - No. 55, Sept. 1961 (Most 84 pgs., 25¢)
21-(#1)-M.G.M.'s Tom & Jerry Picnic Time (84pp, stapled binding)-Painted-c

| | 9 | 27 | 72 | 180 |

22-Huey, Dewey & Louie Back to School (Disney; 10/59, 84pp, square binding begins) 7 21 56 140
23-Marge's Little Lulu & Tubby Halloween Fun (10/59)-Tripp-a

| | 9 | 27 | 72 | 180 |

24-Woody Woodpecker's Family Fun (11/59)(Walter Lantz)

| | 7 | 21 | 56 | 140 |

25-Tarzan's Jungle World(11/59)-Marsh-a; painted-c 9 27 72 180
26-Christmas Parade(Disney; 12/59)-Barks-a, 16pgs.; Barks draws himself on wanted poster pg. 13 18 54 144 360
27-Walt Disney's Man in Space (10/59) r-/4-Color 716,866, & 954 (100 pgs., 35¢)(TV) 8 24 64 160
28-Bugs Bunny's Winter Fun (2/60) 8 24 64 160
29-Marge's Little Lulu & Tubby in Hawaii (4/60)-Tripp-a

| | 9 | 27 | 72 | 180 |

30-Disneyland USA(Disney; 6/60) 7 21 56 140
31-Huckleberry Hound Summer Fun (7/60)(TV)(HannaBarbera)-Yogi Bear & Pixie & Dixie app. 11 33 88 220
32-Bugs Bunny Beach Party 5 15 40 100
33-Daisy Duck & Uncle Scrooge Picnic Time (Disney; 9/60)

| | 7 | 21 | 56 | 140 |

34-Nancy & Sluggo Summer Camp (8/60) 6 18 48 120
35-Huey, Dewey & Louie Back to School (Disney; 10/60)-1st app. Daisy Duck's Nieces, April, May & June 9 27 72 180
36-Marge's Little Lulu & Witch Hazel Halloween Fun (10/60)-Tripp-a

| | 9 | 27 | 72 | 180 |

37-Tarzan, King of the Jungle (11/60)-Marsh-a; painted-c

| | 8 | 24 | 64 | 160 |

38-Uncle Donald & His Nephews Family Fun (Disney; 11/60)-Cover painting

	GD2.0	FN6.0	VF8.0	NM9.

based on a pencil sketch by Barks 11 33 88 220
39-Walt Disney's Merry Christmas (Disney; 12/60)-Cover painting based on a pencil sketch by Barks 11 33 88 220
40-Woody Woodpecker Christmas Parade (12/60)(Walter Lantz)

| | 5 | 15 | 40 | 100 |

41-Yogi Bear's Winter Sports (12/60)(TV)(Hanna-Barbera)-Huckleberry Hound, Pixie & Dixie, Augie Doggie app. 11 33 88 220
42-Marge's Little Lulu & Tubby in Australia (4/61) 10 30 80 200
43-Mighty Mouse in Outer Space (5/61) 17 51 136 340
44-Around the World with Huckleberry and His Friends (7/61)(TV)(Hanna-Barbera)-Yogi Bear, Pixie & Dixie, Quick Draw McGraw, Augie Doggie app.; 1st app. Yakky Doodle 11 33 88 220
45-Nancy & Sluggo Summer Camp (8/61) 5 15 40 100
46-Bugs Bunny Beach Party (8/61) 5 15 40 100
47-Mickey & Donald in Vacationland (Disney; 8/61) 7 21 56 140
48-The Flintstones (No. 1)(Bedrock Bedlam)(7/61)(TV)(Hanna-Barbera) 1st app. in comics 16 48 128 320
49-Huey, Dewey & Louie Back to School (Disney; 9/61)

| | 7 | 21 | 56 | 140 |

50-Marge's Little Lulu & Witch Hazel Trick 'N' Treat (10/61)

| | 9 | 27 | 72 | 180 |

51-Tarzan, King of the Jungle by Jesse Marsh (11/61)-Painted-c

| | 6 | 18 | 48 | 120 |

52-Uncle Donald & His Nephews Dude Ranch (Disney; 11/61)

| | 6 | 18 | 48 | 120 |

53-Donald Duck Merry Christmas (Disney; 12/61) 6 18 48 120
54-Woody Woodpecker's Christmas Party (12/61)-Issued after No. 55

| | 6 | 18 | 48 | 120 |

55-Daisy Duck & Uncle Scrooge Showboat (Disney; 9/61)

| | 7 | 21 | 56 | 140 |

NOTE: All issues printed with & without ad on back cover.

DELL JUNIOR TREASURY
Dell Publishing Co.: June, 1955 - No. 10, Oct, 1957 (15¢) (All painted-c)
1-Alice in Wonderland; r/4-Color #331 (52 pgs.) 10 30 70 125
2-Aladdin & the Wonderful Lamp 7 21 49 90
3-Gulliver's Travels (1/56) 6 18 42 80
4-Adventures of Mr. Frog & Miss Mouse 7 21 49 90
5-The Wizard of Oz (7/56) 7 21 49 90
6-10: 6-Heidi (10/56). 7-Santa and the Angel. 8-Raggedy Ann and the Camel with the Wrinkled Knees. 9-Clementina the Flying Pig. 10-Adventures of Tom Sawyer 6 18 42 80

DEMOLITION MAN
DC Comics: Nov, 1993 - No. 4, Feb, 1994 ($1.75, color, limited series)
1-4-Movie adaptation 2.25

DEMON, THE (See Detective Comics No. 482-485)
National Periodical Publications: Aug-Sept, 1972 - V3#16, Jan, 1974
1-Origin; Kirby-c/a in all 4 12 26 40
2-5 2 6 12 18
6-16 2 6 9 12

DEMON, THE (1st limited series)(Also see Cosmic Odyssey #2)
DC Comics: Nov, 1986 - No. 4, Feb, 1987 (75¢, limited series)
(#2 has #4 of 4 on c.)

1-4: Matt Wagner-a(p) & scripts in all. 4-Demon & Jason Blood become separate entities. 3.00

DEMON, THE (2nd Series)
DC Comics: July, 1990 - No. 57, May, 1995 ($1.50/$1.75/$1.95)
1-Grant scripts begin, ends #39: 1-4-Painted-c 4.00
2-18,20-27,29-39,41,42,46,47: 3,8-Batman app. (cameo #4). 12-Bisley painted-c. 12-15,21-Lobo app. (1 pg. cameo #11). 23-Robin app. 29-Superman app. 31,33-39-Lobo app. 2.50
19,28,40: 19-($2.50, 44 pgs.)-Lobo poster stapled inside. 28-Superman-c/story; begin 1.95-c. 40-Garth Ennis scripts begin 4.00
43-45-Hitman app. 1 3 6 8
46-48 Return of The Haunted Tank-c/s. 48-Begin $1.95-c. 5.00
49,51,0-(10/94),55-57: 51-(9/94) 2.50
50 ($2.95, 52 pgs.) 3.00
52-54-Hitman-s 4.00

	GD2.0	FN6.0	VF8.0	NM9.4

Annual 1 (1992, $3.00, 68 pgs.)-Eclipso-c/story 3.00
Annual 2 (1993, $3.50, 68 pgs.)-1st app. of Hitman   2   6   11   16
NOTE: *Alan Grant* scripts in #1-16, 20, 21, 23-25, 30-39, Annual 1. *Wagner* a/scripts-22.

DEMON DREAMS
Pacific Comics: Feb, 1984 - No. 2, May, 1984
1,2-Mostly r-/Heavy Metal 2.25

DEMONGATE
Sirius Entertainment: May, 1996 - No. 10 ($2.50, B&W)
1-10-Bao Lin Hum/Steve Blevins-s/a 2.50

DEMON GUN
Crusade Ent.: June, 1996 - No. 3, Jan, 1997 ($2.95, B&W, limited series)
1-3: Gary Cohn scripts in all. 2-(10/96) 3.00

DEMON-HUNTER
Seaboard Periodicals (Atlas): Sept, 1975
1-Origin/1st app. Demon-Hunter; Buckler-c/a 6.00

DEMON KNIGHT: A GRIMJACK GRAPHIC NOVEL
First Publishing: 1990 ($8.95, 52 pgs.)
nn-Flint Henry-a 9.00

DEMONSLAYER
Image Comics: Nov, 1999 - No. 3, Jan, 2000 ($2.95)
1-3-Story & art by Mychaels & Mendoza 3.00

DEMONSLAYER: INTO HELL (Volume 2)
Image Comics: Apr, 2000 - No. 3, Aug, 2000 ($2.95)
1-3-Story & art by Mychaels 3.00
1-3 ($5.00) Variant cover editions 5.00

DENNIS THE MENACE (TV with 1959 issues) (Becomes ...Fun Fest Series; See The Best of... & The Very Best of...)(...Fun Fest on-c only to #156-166)
Standard Comics/Pines No.15-31/Hallden (Fawcett) No.32 on: 8/53 - #14, 1/56; #15, 3/56 - #31, 11/58; #32, 1/59 - #166, 11/79
1-1st app. Dennis, Mr. & Mrs. Wilson, Ruff & Dennis' mom & dad; Wiseman-a, written by Fred Toole-most issues   47   142   286   500
2   25   75   130   225
3-10: 8-Last pre-code issue   15   45   77   130
11-20   12   36   61   100
21-30: 22-1st app. Margaret w/blonde hair   8   24   45   65
31-1st app. Joey   9   27   49   70
32-40(1/60): 37-A-Bomb blast panel. 39-1st app. Gina (11/59)
   6   18   29   40
41-60(7/62)   3   9   19   28
61-80(9/65),100(1/69)   2   6   12   18
81-99   2   6   11   15
101-117: 102-Last 12¢ issue   1   4   7   10
118(1/72)-131 (All 52 pages)   2   6   9   12
132(1/74)-142,144-160 6.00
143(3/76) Olympic-c/s; low print   2   6   9   12
161-166   1   3   6   8
NOTE: *Wiseman* c/a-1-46, 53, 68, 69.

DENNIS THE MENACE (Giants) (No. 1 titled Giant Vacation Special; becomes Dennis the Menace Bonus Magazine No. 76 on)
(#1-8,18,23,25,30,38: 100 pgs.; rest to #41: 84 pgs.; #42-75: 68 pgs.)
Standard/Pines/Hallden(Fawcett): Summer, 1955 - No. 75, Dec, 1969
nn-Giant Vacation Special(Summ/55-Standard   18   54   94   155
nn-Christmas issue (Winter '55)   16   48   83   140
2-Giant Vacation Special (Summer '56-Pines   14   42   72   120
3-Giant Christmas issue (Winter '56-Pines   13   39   66   110
4-Giant Vacation Special (Summer '57-Pines   12   36   61   100
5-Giant Christmas issue (Winter '57-Pines   12   36   61   100
6-In Hawaii (Giant Vacation Special)(Summer '58-Pines
   11   33   55   90
6-In Hawaii (Summer '59-Hallden) says 3rd large printing on-c
6-In Hawaii (Summer '60)-3rd printing; says 4th large printing on-c
6-In Hawaii (Summer '62)-4th printing; says 5th large printing on-c
each....   8   24   42   60
6-Giant Christmas issue (Winter '58)   11   33   55   90
7-In Hollywood (Winter '59-Hallden)   5   15   34   55

7-In Hollywood (Summer '61)-2nd printing   4   12   26   40
8-In Mexico (Winter '60, 100 pgs.-Hallden/Fawcett)   5   15   34   55
8-In Mexico (Summer '62, 2nd printing)   4   12   25   38
9-Goes to Camp (Summer '61, 84 pgs.)-1st CCA approved issue
   5   15   34   55
9-Goes to Camp (Summer '62)-2nd printing   4   12   25   38
10-12: 10-X-Mas issue (Winter '61), 11-Giant Christmas issue (Winter '62), 12-Triple Feature (Winter '62)   6   18   40   65
13-17: 13-Best of Dennis the Menace (Spring '63)-Reprints, 14-And His Dog Ruff (Summer '63), 15-In Washington, D.C. (Summer '63), 16-Goes to Camp (Summer '63)-Reprints No. 9, 17-& His Pal Joey (Winter '63)
   3   10   23   35
18-In Hawaii (Reprints No. 6)   3   9   19   28
19-Giant Christmas issue (Winter '63)   4   12   25   38
20-Spring Special (Spring '64)   4   12   25   38
21-40 (Summer '66): 30-r/#6. #35-Xmas spec.Wint.'65
   3   9   17   26
41-60 (Fall '68)   2   6   12   18
61-75 (12/69): 68-Partial-r/#6   2   6   11   15
NOTE: *Wiseman* c/a-1-8, 12, 14, 15, 17, 20, 22, 27, 28, 31, 35, 36, 41, 49.

DENNIS THE MENACE
Marvel Comics Group: Nov, 1981 - No. 13, Nov, 1982
1-New-a   1   3   6   9
2-13: 2-New art. 3-Part-r. 4,5-r. 5-X-mas-c & issue, 7-Spider Kid-c/sty 6.00
NOTE: *Hank Ketcham* c-most; a-3, 12. *Wiseman* a-4, 5.

DENNIS THE MENACE AND HIS DOG RUFF
Hallden/Fawcett: Summer, 1961
1-Wiseman-c/a   5   15   34   55

DENNIS THE MENACE AND HIS FRIENDS
Fawcett Publ.: 1969; No. 5, Jan, 1970 - No. 46, April, 1980 (All reprints)
Dennis the Menace & Joey No. 2 (7/69)   2   6   12   18
Dennis the Menace & Ruff No. 2 (9/69)   2   6   12   18
Dennis the Menace & Mr. Wilson No. 1 (10/69)   3   9   17   24
Dennis & Margaret No. 1 (Winter '69)   3   9   17   24
5-20: 5-Dennis the Menace & Margaret. 6-...& Joey. 7-...& Ruff. 8-...& Mr. Wilson   1   4   7   10
21-37   1   3   6   9
38-46 (Digest size, 148 pgs.), 4/78, 95¢)   1   4   7   10
NOTE: *Titles rotate every four issues, beginning with No. 5.*

DENNIS THE MENACE AND HIS PAL JOEY
Fawcett Publ.: Summer, 1961 (10¢) (See Dennis the Menace Giants No. 45)
1-Wiseman-c/a   5   15   34   55

DENNIS THE MENACE AND THE BIBLE KIDS
Word Books: 1977 (36 pgs.)
1-6: 1-Jesus. 2-Joseph. 3-David. 4-The Bible Girls. 5-Moses. 6-More About Jesus   1   3   6   8
7-10-Low print run: 7-The Lord's Prayer. 8-Stories Jesus told. 9-Paul, God's Traveller. 10-In the Beginning   2   6   10   14
NOTE: *Ketcham c/a in all.*

DENNIS THE MENACE BIG BONUS SERIES
Fawcett Publications: No. 10, Feb, 1980 - No. 11, Apr, 1980
10,11 6.00

DENNIS THE MENACE BONUS MAGAZINE (Formerly Dennis the Menace Giants Nos. 1-75)(...Big Bonus Series on-c for #174-194)
Fawcett Publications: No. 76, 1/70 - No. 95, 7/71; No. 97, '71; No. 194, 10/79; (No. 76-124: 68 pgs.; No. 125-163: 52 pgs.; No. 164 on: 36 pgs.)
76-90(3/71)   2   6   9   12
91-95, 97-110(10/72): Two #95's with same date(7/71) A-Summer Games, and B-That's Our Boy. No #96   1   4   7   10
111-124   1   3   6   8
125-163-(52 pgs.)   1   3   5   7
164-194: 166-Indicia printed backwards 5.00

DENNIS THE MENACE COMICS DIGEST
Marvel Comics Group: April, 1982 - No. 3, Aug, 1982 ($1.25, digest-size)
1-3-Reprints   1   3   6   9
1-Mistakenly printed with DC emblem on cover   2   6   10   14

Dennis the Menace Triple Feature #1 © FAW

The Destructor #3 © Seaboard Pub.

Detective Comics #18 © DC

NOTE: *Ketcham* c-all. *Wiseman* a-all. A few thousand #1's were published with a DC emblem on cover.

DENNIS THE MENACE FUN BOOK
Fawcett Publications/Standard Comics: 1960 (100 pgs.)

1-Part Wiseman-a	6	18	42	70

DENNIS THE MENACE FUN FEST SERIES (Formerly Dennis the Menace #166)
Hallden (Fawcett): No. 16, Jan, 1980 - No. 17, Mar, 1980 (40¢)

16,17-By Hank Ketcham		5.00

DENNIS THE MENACE POCKET FULL OF FUN!
Fawcett Publications (Hallden): Spring, 1969 - No. 50, March, 1980 (196 pgs.) (Digest size)(Scarce in VF or better)

1-Reprints in all issues	4	12	29	45
2-10	3	9	20	30
11-20	2	6	12	18
21-28	2	6	9	12
29-50: 35,40,46-Sunday strip-r	1	3	6	8

NOTE: No. 1-28 are 196 pgs.; No. 29-36: 164 pgs.; No. 37: 148 pgs.; No. 38 on: 132 pgs. No. 8, 11, 15, 21, 25, 29 all contain strip reprints.

DENNIS THE MENACE TELEVISION SPECIAL
Fawcett Publ. (Hallden Div.): Summer, 1961 - No. 2, Spring, 1962 (Giant)

1	6	18	40	65
2	3	10	23	35

DENNIS THE MENACE TRIPLE FEATURE
Fawcett Publications: Winter, 1961 (Giant)

1-Wiseman-c/a	6	18	40	65

DEPUTY, THE (TV)
Dell Publishing Co.: No. 1077, Feb-Apr, 1960 - No. 1225, Oct-Dec, 1961 (all-Henry Fonda photo-c)

Four Color 1077 (#1)-Buscema-a	13	39	91	170
Four Color 1130 (9-11/60)-Buscema-a,1225	10	30	70	130

DEPUTY DAWG (TV) (Also see New Terrytoons)
Dell Publishing Co./Gold Key: Oct-Dec, 1961 - No. 1299, 1962; No. 1, Aug, 1965

Four Color 1238,1299	11	33	77	145
1(10164-508)(8/65)-Gold Key	11	33	77	145

DEPUTY DAWG PRESENTS DINKY DUCK AND HASHIMOTO-SAN (TV)
Gold Key: August, 1965

1(10159-508)	10	30	70	125

DESERT GOLD (See Zane Grey 4-Color 467)

DESIGN FOR SURVIVAL (Gen. Thomas S. Power's...)
American Security Council Press: 1968 (36 pgs. in color) (25¢)

nn-Propaganda against the Threat of Communism-Aircraft cover; H-Bomb panel		3	9	17	25
Twin Circle Edition-Cover shows panels from inside	2	6	11	15

DESPERADO (Becomes Black Diamond Western No. 9 on)
Lev Gleason Publications: June, 1948 - No. 8, Feb, 1949 (All 52 pgs.)

1-Biro-c on all; contains inside photo-c of Charles Biro, Lev Gleason & Bob Wood	15	45	77	130
2	8	24	45	65
3-Story with over 20 killings	9	27	49	70
4-8	6	18	32	45

NOTE: Barry a-2. Fuje a-4, 8. Guardineer a-5-7. Kida a-3-7. Ed Moore a-4.

DESPERADOES (Becomes Black Diamond Western No. 9 on)

DESPERADOES
Image Comics (Homage): Sept, 1997 - No. 5, June, 1998 ($2.50/$2.95)

1-5-Mariotte-s/Cassaday-c/a: 1-($2.50-c). 2-5-($2.95)		3.00
...: A Moment's Sunlight TPB ('98, $16.95) r/#1-5		17.00
...: Epidemic! (11/99, $5.95) Mariotte-s		6.00

DESPERADOES: QUIET OF THE GRAVE
DC Comics (Homage): Jul, 2001 - No. 5, Nov, 2001 ($2.95)

1-5-Jeff Mariotte-s/John Severin-c/a		3.00

DESPERATE TIMES (See Savage Dragon)
Image Comics: Jun, 1998 - No. 4, Dec, 1998; Nov, 2000 - Present ($2.95, B&W)

1-4-Chris Eliopoulos-s/a		3.00
(Vol. 2) 1-4		3.00

DESTINATION MOON (See Fawcett Movie Comics, Space Adventures #20, 23, & Strange Adventures #1)

DESTINY: A CHRONICLE OF DEATHS FORETOLD (See Sandman)
DC Comics (Vertigo): 1997 - No.3, 1998 ($5.95, limited series)

1-3-Kwitney-s in all: 1-Williams & Zulli-a, Williams painted-c. 2-Williams & Scott Hampton-painted-c/a. 3-Williams & Guay-a		6.00
TPB (2000, $14.95) r/series		14.95

DESTROY!!
Eclipse Comics: 1986 ($4.95, B&W, magazine-size, one-shot)

1		5.00
3-D Special 1-r-/#1 ($2.50)		5.00

DESTROYER, THE
Marvel Comics: Nov, 1989 - No. 9, Jun, 1990 ($2.25, B&W, magazine, 52 pgs.)

1-Based on Remo Williams movie, paperbacks		4.00
2-9: 2-Williamson part inks. 4-Ditko-a		3.00

DESTROYER, THE
Marvel Comics: V2#1, March, 1991 ($1.95, 52 pgs.)
V3#1, Dec, 1991 - No. 4, Mar, 1992 ($1.95, mini-series)

V2#1,V3#1-4: Based on Remo Williams paperbacks. V3#1-4-Simonson-c. 3-Morrow-a		2.50

DESTROYER, THE (Also see Solar, Man of the Atom)
Valiant: Apr, 1995 ($2.95, color, one-shot)

0-Indicia indicates #1		3.00

DESTROYER DUCK
Eclipse Comics: Feb, 1982 - No. 7, May, 1984 (#2-7: Baxter paper) ($1.50)

1-Origin Destroyer Duck; 1st app. Groo; Kirby-c/a(p) 1	4	7	10
2-5: 2-Starling back-up begins; Kirby-c/a(p) thru #5		5.00
6,7		4.00

NOTE: Neal Adams c-1i. Kirby c/a-1-5p. Miller c-7.

DESTRUCTOR, THE
Atlas/Seaboard: February, 1975 - No. 4, Aug, 1975

1-Origin/1st app.: Ditko/Wood-a; Wood-c(i)	1	3	6	8
2-4: 2-Ditko/Wood-a. 3,4-Ditko-a(p)				6.00

DETECTIVE COMICS (Also see other Batman titles)
National Periodical Publications/DC Comics: Mar, 1937 - Present

1-(Scarce)-Slam Bradley & Spy by Siegel & Shuster, Speed Saunders by Guardineer, Flat Foot Flannigan by Gustavson, Cosmo, the Phantom of Disguise, Buck Marshall, Bruce Nelson begin; Chin Lung in 'Claws of the Red Dragon' serial begin; Vincent Sullivan-c	8,333	25,000	55,000	–
2 (Rare)-Creig Flessel-c begin; new logo	2333	6999	15,500	–
3 (Rare)	1666	5000	11,000	–
4,5: 5-Larry Steele begins	1033	3099	5500	7200
6,7,9,10	750	2250	3500	5200
8-Mister Chang-c; classic-c	1133	3399	5200	7800
11-17,19: 17-1st app. Fu Manchu in Det.	566	1700	2600	4000
18-Fu Manchu-c; last Flessel-c	950	2850	4400	6600
20-The Crimson Avenger begins (1st app.)	866	2600	4000	6000
21,23-25	450	1350	2000	3100
22-1st Crimson Avenger-c by Chambers (12/38)	583	1749	2700	4100
26	400	1200	1800	2800
27-The Bat-Man & Commissioner Gordon begin by Bill Finger & Bob Kane (5/39); Batman-c (1st)(by Kane). Bat-Man's secret identity revealed as Bruce Wayne in 6pg. sty. Signed Rob't Kane (also see Det. Picture Stories #5 & Funny Pages V3#1)	30,000	90,000	165,000	300,000
27-Reprint, Oversize 13-1/2x10". WARNING: This comic is an exact duplicate reprint of the original except for its size. DC published it in 1974 with a second cover titling it as Famous First Edition. There have been many reported cases of the outer cover being removed and the interior sold as the original edition. The reprint with the new outer cover removed is practically worthless; see Famous First Edition for value.				
28-2nd app. The Batman (6 pg. story); non-Bat-Man-c; signed Rob't Kane	1607	4821	11,250	22,500
29-1st app. Doctor Death-c/story, Batman's 1st name villain. 1st 2 part story (10 pgs.). 2nd Batman-c by Kane	2643	7929	18,500	37,000

Detective Comics #73 © DC

Detective Comics #104 © DC

Detective Comics #267 © DC

	GD2.0	FN6.0	VF8.0	NM9.4

30-Dr. Death app. Story concludes from issue #29. Classic Batman splash panel by Kane. 615 1845 4000 8000

31-Classic Batman over castle cover; 1st app. The Monk & 1st Julie Madison (Bruce Wayne's 1st love interest); 1st Batplane (Bat-Gyro) and Batarang; 2nd 2-part Batman adventure. Gardner Fox takes over script from Bill Finger. 1st mention of locale (New York City) where Batman lives 2643 7929 18,500 37,000

32-Batman story concludes from issue #31. 1st app. Dala (Monk's assistant). Batman uses gun for 1st time to slay The Monk and Dala. This was the 1st time a costumed hero used a gun in comic books. 1st Batman head logo on cover 561 1683 3646 7300

33-Origin The Batman (2 pgs.)(1st told origin); Batman w/smoking gun holster-c; Batman story now 12 pgs. Classic Batman-c 3570 10,710 24,990 50,000

34-2nd Crimson Avenger by Creig Flessel and last non Batman-c. Story from issue #32 x-over as Bruce Wayne sees Julie Madison off to America from Paris. Classic Batman splash panel used later in Batman #1 for origin story. Steve Malone begins 438 1314 2847 5700

35-Classic Batman hypodermic needle-c that reflects story in issue #34. Classic Batman with smoking .45 automatic splash panel. Batman-c begin 923 2769 6000 12,000

36-Batman-c that reflects adventure in issue #35. Last app. of Dr. Hugo Strange (1st major villain, 2/40). 1st finned-gloves worn by Batman 646 1938 4200 8400

37-Last solo Golden-Age Batman adventure in Detective Comics. Panel at end of story reflects solo Batman adventure in Batman #1 that was originally planned for Detective #38. Cliff Crosby begins 600 1800 3900 7800

38-Origin/1st app. Robin the Boy Wonder (4/40); Batman and Robin-c begin; cover by Kane & Robinson taken from splash pg. 3214 9642 22,500 45,000

39-Opium-c 538 1614 3500 7000

40-Origin & 1st app. Clay Face (Basil Karlo) (6/40); 1st Joker cover app. Joker story intended for this issue was used in Batman #1 instead; cover is similar to splash pg. in 2nd Joker story in Batman #1 630 1890 4095 8200

41-Robin's 1st solo 333 1000 2083 4000

42-44: 44-Crimson Avenger-new costume 236 708 1477 2600

45-1st Joker story in Det. (3rd book app. & 4th story app. over all, 11/40) 333 1000 2083 4000

46-50: 46-Death of Hugo Strange. 48-1st time car called Batmobile (2/41); Gotham City 1st ment. in Det. (1st mentioned in Wow #1; also see Batman #4). 49-Last Clay Face 218 654 1364 2400

51-57 145 435 909 1600

58-1st Penguin app. (12/41); last Speed Saunders; Fred Ray-c 400 1200 2500 4800

59,60: 59-Last Steve Malone; 2nd Penguin; Wing becomes Crimson Avenger's aide. 60-Intro. Air Wave; Joker app. (2nd in Det.) 164 492 1023 1800

61,63: 63-Last Cliff Crosby; 1st app. Mr. Baffle 145 435 909 1800

62-Joker-c/story (2nd Joker-c, 4/42) 236 708 1477 2600

64-Origin & 1st app. Boy Commandos by Simon & Kirby (6/42); Joker app. 383 1149 2396 4600

65-1st Boy Commandos (S&K-a on Boy Commandos & Ray/Robinson-a on Batman & Robin on-c; 4 artists on one-c) 300 900 1875 3300

66-Origin & 1st app. Two-Face 350 1050 2188 4200

67-1st Penguin app. (9/42) 227 681 1420 2500

68-Two-Face-c/story; 1st Two-Face-c 164 492 1023 1800

69-Joker-c/story 164 492 1023 1800

70 118 354 738 1300

71-Joker-c/story 141 423 881 1550

72,74,75: 74-1st Tweedledum & Tweedledee plus+; S&K-a 105 315 656 1150

73-Scarecrow-c/story (1st Scarecrow-c) 127 381 795 1400

76-Newsboy Legion & The Sandman x-over in Boy Commandos; S&K-a; Joker-c/story 164 492 1023 1800

77-79: All S&K-a 113 339 706 1250

80-Two-Face-c/story; S&K-a 123 369 769 1350

81,82,84,86-90: 81-1st Cavalier-c & app. 89-1st Crimson Avenger; 2nd Cavalier-c & app. 77 231 568 1000

83-1st "skinny" Alfred (2/44)(see Batman #21; last S&K Boy Commandos (also #92,128); most issues #84 on signed S&K are not by them

	GD2.0	FN6.0	VF8.0	NM9.4

100 300 625 1100

85-Joker-c/story; last Spy; Kirby/Klech Boy Commandos 118 354 738 1300

91,102-Joker-c/story 113 339 706 1250

92-98: 96-Alfred's last name 'Beagle' revealed, later changed to 'Pennyworth' in #214 75 225 465 825

99-Penguin-c 113 339 706 1250

100 (6/45) 123 369 769 1350

101,103-108,110-113,115-117,119: 108-1st Bat-signal-c (2/46). 114-1st small logo (8/46) 73 219 455 800

109,114,118-Joker-c/stories 98 294 611 1075

120-Penguin-c (white-c, rare above fine) 164 492 1023 1800

121,123,125,127,129,130 68 205 426 750

122-1st Catwoman-c (4/47) 136 408 852 1500

124,128-Joker-c/stories 93 279 581 1025

126-Penguin-c 93 279 581 1025

131-134,136,139 59 177 369 650

135-Frankenstein-c/story 64 192 398 700

137-Joker-c/story; last Air Wave 77 231 483 850

138-Origin Robotman (see Star Spangled #7 for 1st app.); series ends #202 113 339 706 1250

140-The Riddler-c/story (1st app., 10/48) 430 1290 2795 5600

141,143-148,150: 150-Last Boy Commandos 59 177 369 650

142-2nd Riddler-c/story 116 348 725 1275

149-Joker-c/story 79 237 494 875

151-Origin & 1st app. Pow Wow Smith, Indian lawman (9/49) & begins series 73 219 455 800

152,154,155,157-160: 152-1st Slam Bradley 59 177 369 650

153-1st app. Roy Raymond TV Detective (11/49); origin The Human Fly 67 201 419 725

156(2/50)-The new classic Batmobile 84 252 525 925

161-167,169,170,172-176: Last 52 pg. issue 55 165 341 600

168-Origin the Joker 333 1000 2083 4000

171-Penguin-c 86 258 540 950

177-179,181-186,188,189,191,192,194-199,201,202,204,206-210,212,214-216: 184-1st app. Fire Fly. 185-Secret of Batman's utility belt. 187-Two-Face-c. 202-Last Robotman & Pow Wow Smith. 215-1st app. of Batmen of all Nations. 216-1st precode (2/55) 50 150 300 525

180,193-Joker-c/story 55 165 341 600

187-Two-Face-c/story 55 165 330 575

190-Origin Batman retold 73 219 455 800

200(1/53), 205: 205-Origin Batcave 67 201 419 725

203,211-Catwoman-c/stories 55 165 341 600

213-Origin & 1st app. Mirror Man 59 177 369 650

217-224: 218-Batman Jr. & Robin Sr. app. 43 129 257 450

225-(11/55)-1st app. Martian Manhunter, John Jones; later changed to J'onn J'onzz; origin begins; also see Batman #78 358 1074 3222 6800

226-Origin Martian Manhunter cont'd (2nd app.) 136 408 852 1500

227-229: Martian Manhunter stories in all 55 165 330 575

230-1st app. Mad Hatter; brief recap origin of Martian Manhunter 55 177 341 600

231-Brief origin recap Martian Manhunter 40 120 232 400

232,234,237-240: 239-Early DC grey tone-c 40 120 217 375

233-Origin app. 1st Batwoman (7/56) 127 381 790 1400

235-Origin Batman & his costume; tells how Bruce Wayne's father (Thomas Wayne) wore Bat costume & fought crime (reprinted in Batman #255) 64 192 398 700

236-1st S.A. issue; J'onn J'onzz talks to parents and Mars-1st since being stranded on Earth; 1st app. Bat-Tank? 42 127 252 440

241-260: 246-Intro. Diane Meade, John Jones' girl. 249-Batwoman-c/app. 253-1st app. The Terrible Trio. 254-Bat-Hound-c/story. 257-Intro. & 1st app. Whirly Bats. 259-1st app. The Calendar Man 33 99 174 300

261,264,266,268-271: 261-J. Jones tie-in to sci/fi movie "Incredible Shrinking Man"; 1st app. Dr. Double X. 262-Origin Joker Jackal. 268,271-Manhunter origin recap 25 75 133 230

265-Batman's origin retold with new facts 39 117 208 360

267-Origin & 1st app. Bat-Mite (5/59) 40 120 217 375

272,274,275,277-280 21 63 110 185

273-J'onn J'onzz i.d. revealed for 1st time 21 63 110 190

276-2nd app. Bat-Mite 23 69 121 210

		GD2.0	FN6.0	VF8.0	NM9.4

281-292, 294-297: 285,286,292-Batwoman-c/app. 287-Origin J'onn onzz retold. 289-Bat-Mite-c/story. 292-Last Roy Raymond. 297-Last 10¢ issue (11/61) 17 51 88 150

293-(7/61)-Aquaman begins (pre #1); ends #300 18 54 94 155

298-(12/61)-1st modern Clayface (Matt Hagen) 24 72 168 300

299, 300-(2/62)-Aquaman ends 10 30 73 125

301-(3/62)-J'onn onzz returns to Mars (1st time since stranded on Earth six years before) 9 27 65 110

302-317,319-321,323,324,326,329,330: 302,307,311,321-Batwoman-c/app. 311-Intro. Zook in John Jones; 1st app. Cat-Man. 321-2nd Terrible Trio. 326-Last J'onn J'onzz, story cont'd in H.O.M. #143; intro. Idol-Head of Diabolu 7 21 53 85

318,322,325: 318,325-Cat-Man-c/story (2nd & 3rd app.); also 1st & 2nd app. Batwoman as the Cat-Woman. 322-Bat-Girl's 1st/only app. in Det. (6th in all); Batman cameo in J'onn J'onzz (only hero to app. in series) 7 21 53 85

327-(5/64)-Elongated Man begins, ends #383; 1st new look Batman with new costume; Infantino/Giella new look-a begins; Batman with gun 11 33 80 135

328-Death of Alfred; Bob Kane biog, 2 pgs. 10 30 73 125

331,333-340,342-358,360,361,366-368,370: 334-1st app. The Outsider. 345-Intro Block Buster. 347-"What If" theme story (1/66). 351-Elongated Man new costume. 355-Zatanna x-over in Elongated Man. 356-Alfred brought back in Batman, 1st SA app.? 370-1st Neal Adams-a on Batman (cover only, 12/67) 5 15 34 55

332,341,365-Joker-c/stories 6 18 42 70

359-Intro/origin Batgirl (Barbara Gordon)-c/story (1/67); 1st Silver Age Killer Moth 11 33 80 135

362-364: 362,364-Riddler app. (early). 363-2nd app. new Batgirl 5 15 34 55

369(11/67)-N. Adams-a (Elongated Man); 3rd app. S.A. Catwoman (cameo); leads into Batman #197); 4th app. new Batgirl 6 18 45 75

371-(1/68) 1st new Batmobile from TV show; classic Batgirl-c 6 18 40 65

372-386,389,390: 375-New Batmobile-c. 377-S.A. Riddler app. 4 12 29 45

387-r/1st Batman story from #27 (30th anniversary, 5/69); Joker-c; 5 15 38 60

388-Joker-c/story; last 12¢ issue 5 15 34 55

391-394,396,398,399,401,403,405,406,409: 392-1st app. Jason Bard. 401-2nd Batgirl/Robin team-up 3 10 23 35

395,397,402,404,407,408,410-Neal Adams-a. 404-Tribute to Enemy Ace 4 12 29 45

400-(6/70)-Origin & 1st app. Man-Bat; 1st Batgirl/Robin team-up (cont'd in #401); Neal Adams-a 8 24 56 90

411-413: 413-Last 15¢ issue 3 9 20 30

414-424: All-25¢, 52 pgs. 418-Creeper x-over. 424-Last Batgirl 3 10 23 35

425-436: 426,430,436-Elongated Man app. 428,434-Hawkman begins, ends #467 2 6 13 20

437-New Manhunter begins (10-11/73, 1st app.) by Simonson, ends #443 3 10 23 35

438-445 (All 100 Page Super Spectaculars): 438-Kubert Hawkman-r. 439-Origin Manhunter. 440-G.A. Manhunter(Adv. #79) by S&K, Hawkman, Dollman, Gr. Lantern; Toth-a. 441-G.A. Plastic Man, Batman, Ibis-r. 442-G.A. Newsboy Legion, Black Canary, Elongated Man, Dr. Fate-r. 443-Origin The Creeper-r; death of Manhunter; G.A. Green Lantern, Spectre-r; Batman-r/Batman #18. 444-G.A. Kid Eternity-r. 445-G.A. Dr. Midnite-r 5 15 34 55

446-460: 457-Origin retold & updated 2 6 11 16

461-465,470,480: 480-(44 pgs.). 463-1st app. Black Spider. 464-2nd app. Black Spider 2 6 10 14

466-468,471-474,478,479-Rogers-a in all: 466-1st app. Signalman since Batman #139. 470,471-1st modern app. Hugo Strange. 474-1st app. new Deadshot. 478-1st app. 3rd Clayface (Preston Payne). 479-(44 pgs.)-Clayface app. 3 9 19 28

469-Intro Dr. Phosphorous; Simonson-a 3 9 17 25

475,476-Joker-c/stories; Rogers-a 4 12 30 50

477-Neal Adams-a(r); Rogers-a (3 pgs.) 3 9 17 25

481-(Combined with Batman Family, 12-1/78-79, begin $1.00, 68 pg. issues, ends #495); 481-495-Batgirl, Robin solo stories 2 6 12 18

482-Starlin/Russell, Golden-a; The Demon begins (origin-r), ends #485 (by Ditko #483-485) 2 6 11 15

483-40th Anniversary issue; origin retold; Newton Batman begins 2 6 12 18

484-495 (68 pgs): 484-Origin Robin. 485-Death of Batwoman. 487-The Odd Man by Ditko. 489-Robin/Batgirl team-up. 490-Black Lightning begins. 491-(#492 on inside) 2 6 9 12

496-499 1 3 6 8

500-($1.50, 52 pgs.)-Batman/Deadman team-up; new Hawkman story by Joe Kubert; incorrectly says 500th anniv. of Det. 2 6 11 15

501-503,505-523: 512-2nd app. new Dr. Death. 519-Last Batgirl. 521-Green Arrow series begins. 523-Solomon Grundy app. 6.00

504-Joker-c/story 1 4 7 10

524-2nd app. Jason Todd (cameo)(3/83) 1 3 6 8

525-3rd app. Jason Todd (See Batman #357) 1 3 6 8

526-Batman's 500th app. in Detective Comics ($1.50, 68 pgs.); Death of Jason Todd's parents, Joker-c/story (55 pgs.); Bob Kane pin-up 2 6 11 16

527-531,533,534,536-568,571,573: 538-Cat-Man-c/story cont'd from Batman #371. 542-Jason Todd as Robin (becomes Robin again #547). 549, 550-Alan Moore scripts (Green Arrow). 554-1st new Black Canary (9/85). 566-Batman villains profiled. 567-Harlan Ellison scripts. 5.00

532,569,570-Joker-c/stories 1 3 6 8

535-Intro new Robin (JasonTodd)-1st appeared in Batman. 6.00

572-(3/87, $1.25, 60 pgs.)-50th Anniv. of Det. Comics 6.00

574-Origin Batman & Jason Todd retold 6.00

575-Year 2 begins, ends #578 2 6 11 15

576-578: McFarlane-c/a. 578-Clay Face app. 2 6 9 12

579-597,601-610: 579-New bat wing logo. 583-1st app. villains Scarface & Ventriloquist. 589-595-(52 pgs.)-Each contain free 16 pg. Batman stories. 604-607-Mudpack storyline; 601-app. Batman mini-posters. 610-Faked death of Penguin; artists names app. on tombstone cover-c 3.00

598-($2.95, 84 pgs.)- "Blind Justice" storyline begins by Batman movie writer Sam Hamm, ends #600 4.00

599 3.00

600-(5/89, $2.95, 84 pgs.)-50th Anniv. of Batman in Det.; 1 pg. Neal Adams pin-up, among other artists 4.00

611-626,628-658: 612-1st new look Cat-Man; Catwoman app. 615- "The Penguin Affair" part 2 (See Batman #448,449). 617-Joker-c/story. 624-1st new Catwoman (w/death) & 1st new Batwoman. 626-Batman's 600th app. in Det. 642-Return of Scarface, part 2. 644-Last $1.00-c. 652,653-Huntress-c/ story w/new costume plus Travis Charest-c on both 3.00

627-($2.95, 84 pgs.)-Batman's 601st app. in Det.; reprints 1st story/#27 plus 3 versions (2 new) of same story 4.00

659-664: 659-Knightfall part 2; Kelley Jones-a. 660-Knightfall part 4; Bane-c by Sam Kieth. 661-Knightfall part 6; brief Joker & Riddler app. 662-Knightfall part 8; Riddler app.; Sam Kieth-c. 663-Knightfall part 10; Kelley Jones-a. 664-Knightfall part 12; Bane-c/story; Joker app.; continued in Showcase 93 #7 & #8; Jones-a 3.00

665,666-Knightfall parts 16 & 18; 666-Bane-c/story. 667-Knightquest: The Crusade & new Batman begins (1st app. inBatman #500). 669-Begin $1.50-c; Knightquest, cont'd in Robin #1. 671,673-Joker app. 2.50

675-($2.95)-Collectors edition w/foil-c 3.50

676-($2.50, 52 pgs.)-KnightsEnd Pt. 3 3.00

677,678: 677-KnightsEnd Pt. 9. 678-(9/94)-Zero Hour tie-in 2.50

679-685: 679-(11/94). 682-Troika Pt. 3 2.50

682-($2.50) Embossed-c Troika Pt. 3 3.00

686-699,701-719: 686-Begin $1.95-c. 693,694-Poison Ivy-c/app. 695-Contagion Pt. 2; Catwoman, Penguin app. 696-Contagion Pt. 8. 698-Two-Face-c/app. 701-Legacy Pt. 6; Batman vs. Bane-c/app. 702-Legacy Epilogue. 703-Final Night x-over. 705-707-Riddler-app. 714,715-Martian Manhunter-app. 2.50

700-($4.95, Collectors Edition)-Legacy Pt. 1; Ra's Al Ghul-c/app; Talia & Bane app; book displayed at shops in envelope 5.00

700-($2.95, Regular Edition)-Different-c 3.00

720-740: 720,721-Cataclysm Pts. 5,14. 723-Green Arrow app. 730-740-No Man's Land stories 2.50

741-($2.50) Endgame; Joker-c/app. 3.00

742-749,751-766: 742-New look Batman begins. 751,752-Poison Ivy apps. 756-Superman-c/app. 759-762-Catwoman back-up; Cooke-a 2.50

Detectives, Inc. #1 © Don McGregor & Marshall Rogers

Devil Dinosaur #6 © MAR

Dexter's Laboratory #25 © Cartoon Network

	GD2.0	FN6.0	VF8.0	NM9.4

750-($4.95, 64 pgs.) Ra's al Ghul-c ... 5.00
#0-(10/94) Zero Hour tie-in ... 2.50
#1,000,000 (11/98) 853rd Century x-over ... 2.50
Annual 1 (1988, $1.50) ... 5.00
Annual 2-7,9 ('89-'94, '96, 68 pgs.)-4-Painted-c. 5-Joker-c/story (54 pgs.)
  continued in Robin Annual #1; Sam Kieth-c; Eclipso story. 6-Azrael as Batman
  in new costume; intro Geist the Twilight Man; Bloodlines storyline. 7-
  Elseworlds story. 9-Legends of the Dead Earth story ... 3.00
Annual 8 (1995, $3.95, 68 pgs.)-Year One story ... 4.00
Annual 10 (1997, $3.95)-Pulp Heroes story ... 4.00
NOTE: Neal Adams c-370, 372, 383, 385, 389, 391, 392, 394-422, 439. Aparo a-437, 438, 444-
446, 500, 625-632p, 638-643p; c-430, 437, 440-446, 448, 468-470, 480, 484(back), 492-502,508,
509, 515, 518-522, 641, 716, 719, 722, 724. Austin a(i)-450, 451, 463-468, 471-476; c(i)-474-476,
478. Baily a-443r. Buckler a-434, 446p, 479p; c(p)-467, 482, 505-507, 511, 513-516, 518. Burnley
a(Batman)-65, 75, 78, 83, 100, 103, 125; c-62i, 63i, 64, 73i, 78, 83p, 96p, 103p, 105p, 106, 108,
121p, 123p, 125p. Chaykin a-441. Colan a(p)-510, 512, 517, 523, 528-538, 540-546, 555-567; c(p)-
510, 512, 528, 530-535, 537, 538, 540, 541, 543-545, 556-558, 560-564. J. Craig a-488. Ditko a-
443r, 483-485, 487. Golden a-482p; c-625, 626, 628-631, 633, 644-646. Alan Grant scripts-584-
597, 601-621, 641, 642, Annual 5. Grell a-445, 455, 463p, 464p; c-455. Guardineer c-23, 24, 26,
28, 30, 32. Gustavson a-441r. Infantino a-442(2)r, 500, 572. Infantino/Anderson c-333, 337-340,
343, 344, 347, 351, 352, 359, 361-368, 371. Kelley Jones c-651, 657i, 658i, 659i, 661, 663-675.
Kaluta c-423, 424, 426-428, 431, 434, 438, 484, 486, 572. Bob Kane a-early issues #27 on,
29??, 356r; c38-440r, 442r, 443r. Kane/Robinson c-33. Gil Kane a(p)-368, 370-374, 384, 385, 388-
407, 439r, 439r, 520. Kane/Anderson c-369. Sam Kieth c-654-656 (657, 658 w/Kelley Jones),
660, 662, Annual #5. Kubert a-438r, 439r, 500; c-348, 350. McFarlane c(a/p)-576-578. Meskin a-
420r. Mignola c-583. Moldoff c-233-354, 259, 266, 267, 275, 287, 289, 290, 297, 300.
Moldoff/Giella a-328, 330, 332, 334, 336, 338, 340, 342, 344, 346, 348, 350, 352, 354, 356.
Mooney a-444r. Moreira a-153-300, 419r, 444r, 445r. Nasser/Netzer a-654, 655, 657, 658. Newton
a(p)-480, 481, 489-499, 501-509, 511, 513-516, 518-520, 524, 526. Irv Novick c-375-
377. Robbins a-426p, 429p. Robinson a-part: 66, 68, 71-73; dir: 74-76, 79, 80; c-62, 64, 66, 68-74,
76, 79, 82, 86, 88, 442r, 443r. Rogers a-466-468, 471-479p, 481p; c-471p, 472p, 473, 474-479p.
Roussos Airwave-76-105(most); c(i)-71, 72, 74-76, 79, 107. Russell a-481i, 482i. Simon/Kirby a-
440r, 442r. Simonson a-437-443, 460, 469, 470, 500. Dick Sprang a-part 82, 84, 85, 87, 89-93, 95-
100, 102, 103i, 104i, 106, 108, 114, 117, 118, 122, 123, 128, 129, 131, 133, 135, 141, 148, 149,
168, 622-624. Starlin a-481p, 482p; c-503, 504, 567p. Starr a-442; c-414, 416, 418,
424, 440-441, 443, 444. Tuska a-486p, 490p. Matt Wagner c-647-649. Wrightson c-425.

DETECTIVE DAN, SECRET OP. 48 (Also see Adventures of Detective Ace
King and Bob Scully, The Two-Fisted Hick Detective)
Humor Publ. Co. (Norman Marsh): 1933 (10¢, 10x13", 36 pgs., B&W, one-shot)
(3 color, cardboard-c)

nn-By Norman Marsh, 1st comic w/ original-a; 1st newsstand-c; Dick Tracy
  look-alike; forerunner of Dan Dunn. (Title and Wu Fang character inspired
  Detective Eye #1 four years later.) (1st comic of a single theme)
                                  1500 4500 8000 –

DETECTIVE EYE (See Keen Detective Funnies)
Centaur Publications: Nov, 1940 - No. 2, Dec, 1940

1-Air Man (see Keen Detective) & The Eye Sees begins; The Masked Marvel
  & Dean Denton app. ... 218 654 1364 2400
2-Origin Don Rance and the Mysticape; Binder-a; Frank Thomas-c
                          127 381 795 1400

DETECTIVE PICTURE STORIES (Keen Detective Funnies No. 8 on?)
Comics Magazine Company: Dec, 1936 - No. 5, Apr, 1937
(1st comic of a single theme)

1 (all issues are very scarce) ... 550 1650 2800 4400
2-The Clock app. (1/37, early app.) ... 233 699 1200 1900
3,4-Eisner-a ... 150 450 800 1200
5-The Clock-c/story (4/37); 1st detective/adventure art by Bob Kane; Bruce
  Wayne prototype app.(see Funny Pages V3/1) 166 500 900 1400

DETECTIVES, THE (TV)
Dell Publishing Co.: No. 1168, Mar-May, 1961 - No. 1240, Oct-Dec, 1961

Four Color 1168 (#1)-Robert Taylor photo-c 10 30 70 130
Four Color 1219-Robert Taylor, Adam West photo-c 9 27 63 115
Four Color 1240-Tufts-a; Robert Taylor photo-c 9 27 63 115

DETECTIVES, INC. (See Eclipse Graphic Album Series)
Eclipse Comics: Apr, 1985 - No. 2, Apr, 1985 ($1.75, both w/April dates)

1,2: 2-Nudity ... 2.25

DETECTIVES, INC.: A TERROR OF DYING DREAMS
Eclipse Comics: Jun, 1987 - No. 3, Dec, 1987 ($1.75, B&W& sepia)

1-3: Colan-a ... 2.25
TPB ('99, $19.95) r/series ... 20.00

DETENTION COMICS
DC Comics: Oct, 1996 ($3.50, 56 pgs., one-shot)

1-Robin story by Dennis O'Neil & Norm Breyfogle; Superboy story by Ron Marz
  & Ron Lim; Warrior story by Ruben Diaz & Joe Phillips; Phillips-c ... 5.00

DETONATOR
Chaos! Comics: Dec, 1994 - No. 2, 1995 ($2.95, limited series)

1,2-Brian Pulido scripts; Steven Hughes-a ... 3.00

DEVASTATOR
Image Comics/Halloween: 1998 - No. 3 ($2.95, B&W, limited series)

1,2-Hudnall-s/Horn-c/a ... 3.00

DEVIL CHEF
Dark Horse Comics: July, 1994 ($2.50, B&W, one-shot)

nn ... 2.50

DEVIL DINOSAUR
Marvel Comics Group: Apr, 1978 - No. 9, Dec, 1978

1-Kirby/Royer-a in all; all have Kirby-c 2 6 11 15
2-9: 4-7-UFO/sci. fic. 8-Dinoriders-c/sty 1 3 6 8

DEVIL DINOSAUR SPRING FLING
Marvel Comics: June, 1997 ($2.99. one-shot)

1-(48pgs.) Moon-Boy-c/app. ... 3.00

DEVIL-DOG DUGAN (Tales of the Marines No. 4 on)
Atlas Comics (OPI): July, 1956 - No. 3, Nov, 1956

1-Severin-c 13 39 66 110
2-Iron Mike McGraw x-over; Severin-c 8 24 42 60
3 7 21 36 50

DEVIL DOGS
Street & Smith Publishers: 1942

1-Boy Rangers, U.S. Marines 29 87 176 265

DEVLIN (See Avengelyne/Glory)
Maximum Press: Apr, 1996 ($2.50, one-shot)

1-Avengelyne app. ... 2.50

DEVILINA (Magazine)
Atlas/Seaboard: Feb, 1975 - No. 2, May, 1975 (B&W)

1-Art by Reese, Marcos; "The Tempest" adapt. 2 6 12 18
2 (Low printing) 3 9 17 25

DEVIL KIDS STARRING HOT STUFF
Harvey Comics (Illustrated Humor): July, 1962 - No. 107, Oct, 1981
(Giant-Size #41-55)

1 (12¢ cover price #1-#41-9/69) 15 45 105 180
2 8 24 56 90
3-10 (1/64) 5 15 38 60
11-20 3 10 23 35
21-30 3 9 17 25
31-40: 40-(6/69) 2 6 13 20
41-50: All 68 pg. Giants 3 9 17 25
51-55: All 52 pg. Giants 2 6 13 20
56-70 2 6 9 12
71-90 1 3 5 7
91-107   5.00

DEVILMAN
Verotik: June, 1995 -No. 3 ($2.95, mature)

1-3: Go Nagai story and art. 3-Bisley-c ... 3.00

DEXTER COMICS
Dearfield Publ.: Summer, 1948 - No. 5, July, 1949

1-Teen-age humor 9 27 49 70
2-Junie Prom app. 7 21 36 50
3-5 5 15 25 35

DEXTER'S LABORATORY (Cartoon Network)
DC Comics: Sept, 1999 - Present ($1.99)

1-24: 2-McCracken-s ... 2.25
25-(50¢-c) Tartakovsky-s/a; Action Hank-c/app. ... .50

Diary of Horror #1 © AVON

Dickie Dare #3 © EAS

Dick Tracy #16 © Ny News Synd.

	GD2.0	FN6.0	VF8.0	NM9.4

26,27				2.00

DEXTER THE DEMON (Formerly Melvin The Monster)(See Cartoon Kids &
Peter the Little Pest)
Atlas Comics (HPC): No. 7, Sept, 1957

7	6	18	32	45

DHAMPIRE: STILLBORN
DC Comics (Vertigo): 1996 ($5.95, one-shot, mature)

1-Nancy Collins script; Paul Lee-c/a				6.00

DIABLO: TALES OF SANCTUARY (From the computer game)
Dark Horse Comics (Blizzard): Nov, 2001 ($5.95, 6.5 x 9", one-shot)

1-Francisco Ruiz-c/a				6.00

DIARY CONFESSIONS (Formerly Ideal Romance)
Stanmor/Key Publ.(Medal Comics): No. 9, May, 1955 - No. 14, Apr, 1955

9	7	21	36	50
10-14	5	15	25	35

DIARY LOVES (Formerly Love Diary #1; G. I. Sweethearts #32 on)
Quality Comics Group: No. 2, Nov, 1949 - No. 31, April, 1953

2-Ward-c/a, 9 pgs.	17	51	88	150
3 (1/50)-Photo-c begin, end #27?	7	21	36	50
4-Crandall-a	9	27	49	70
5-7,10	6	18	29	40
8,9-Ward-a 6,8 pgs. 8-Gustavson-a; Esther Williams photo-c				
	11	33	55	90
11,13,14,17-20	5	15	25	35
12,15,16-Ward-a 9,7,8 pgs.	10	30	55	85
21-Ward-a, 7 pgs.	9	27	49	70
22-31: Whitney-a	5	14	21	28

NOTE: Photo c-3-10, 12-27.

DIARY OF HORROR
Avon Periodicals: December, 1952

1-Hollingsworth-c/a; bondage-c	40	120	220	380

DIARY SECRETS (Formerly Teen-Age Diary Secrets)(See Giant Comics Ed.)
St. John Publishing Co.: No. 10, Feb, 1952 - No. 30, Sept, 1955

10-Baker-c/a most issues	19	57	99	165
11-16,18,19	14	42	72	120
17,20: Kubert-r/Hollywood Confessions #1. 17-r/Teen Age Romances #9				
	14	42	72	120
21-30: 22,27-Signed stories by Estrada. 28-Last precode (3/55)				
	10	30	55	80
nn-(25¢ giant, nd (1950?)-Baker-c & rebound St. John comics				
	47	141	286	500

DICK COLE (Sport Thrills No. 11 on)(See Blue Bolt & Four Most #1)
Curtis Publ./Star Publications: Dec-Jan, 1948-49 - No. 10, June-July, 1950

1-Sgt. Spook; L. B. Cole-c; McWilliams-a; Curt Swan's 1st work				
	34	102	179	310
2,5	16	48	83	140
3,4,6-10: All-L.B. Cole-c. 10-Joe Louis story	23	69	121	210
Accepted Reprint #7(V1#6 on-c)(1950's)-Reprints #7; L.B. Cole-c				
	8	24	42	60
Accepted Reprint #9(nd)-(Reprints #9 & #8-c)	8	24	42	60

NOTE: L. B. Cole c-1, 3, 4, 6-10. Al McWilliams a-6. Dick Cole in 1-9. Baseball c-10. Basketball c-9. Football c-8.

DICKIE DARE
Eastern Color Printing Co.: 1941 - No. 4, 1942 (#3 on sale 6/15/42)

1-Caniff-a, bondage-c by Everett	55	165	330	575
2	28	84	151	260
3,4-Half Scorchy Smith by Noel Sickles who was very influential in Milton Caniff's development	33	99	174	300

DICK POWELL (Also see A-1 Comics)
Magazine Enterprises: No. 22, 1949 (one shot)

A-1 22-Photo-c	26	78	136	235

DICK QUICK, ACE REPORTER (See Picture News #10)
DICKS

Caliber Comics: 1997 - No. 4, 1998 ($2.95, B&W)

1-4-Ennis-s/McCrea-c/a; r/Fleetway				3.00
TPB ('98, $12.95) r/series				13.00

DICK'S ADVENTURES
Dell Publishing Co.: No. 245, Sept, 1949

Four Color 245	5	15	35	60

DICK TRACY (See Famous Feature Stories, Harvey Comics Library, Limited Collectors' Ed., Mammoth Comics, Merry Christmas, The Original…, Popular Comics, Super Book No. 1, 7, 13, 25, Super Comics & Tastee-Freez)
DICK TRACY
David McKay Publications: May, 1937 - Jan, 1938

Feature Books nn - 100 pgs., partially reprinted as 4-Color No. 1 (appeared before Large Feature Comics, 1st Dick Tracy comic book) (Very Rare-five known copies; two incomplete)	630	1890	4095	8200
Feature Books 4 - Reprints nn ish. w/new-c	118	354	738	1300
Feature Books 6,9	86	258	540	950

DICK TRACY (…Monthly #1-24)
Dell Publishing Co.: No. 1 - No. 24, Dec, 1949

Large Feature Comic 1 (1939) -Dick Tracy Meets The Blank				
	150	465	969	1700
Large Feature Comic 4,8	86	258	537	950
Large Feature Comic 11,13,15	77	231	483	850
Four Color 1(1939)('35-r)	615	1845	4305	8000
Four Color 6(1940)('37-r)-(Scarce)	146	438	1022	1900
Four Color 8(1940)('38-'39-r)	73	219	511	950
Large Feature Comic 3(1941, Series II)	63	189	441	825
Four Color 21('41)('38-r)	61	183	427	800
Four Color 34('43)('39-'40-r)	42	125	294	550
Four Color 56('44)('40-r)	35	105	245	450
Four Color 96('46)('40-r)	25	75	175	325
Four Color 133('47)('40-'41-r)	20	60	140	260
Four Color 163('47)('41-r)	17	50	119	220
Four Color 215('48)-Titled "Sparkle Plenty", Tracy-r	10	30	70	130
1(1/48)('34-r)	40	120	280	525
2,3	22	65	154	290
4-10	20	60	140	260
11-18: 13-Bondage-c	15	45	105	190
19-1st app. Sparkle Plenty, B.O. Plenty & Gravel Gertie in a 3-pg. strip not by Gould	15	45	105	200
20-1st app. Sam Catchem; c/a not by Gould	14	42	98	180
21-24-Only 2 pg. Gould-a in each	13	39	91	175

NOTE: No. 19-24 have a 2 pg. biography of a famous villain illustrated by **Gould**: 19-Little Face; 20-Flattop; 21-Breathless Mahoney; 22-Measles; 23-Itchy; 24-The Brow.

DICK TRACY (Continued from Dell series)(…Comics Monthly #25-140)
Harvey Publications: No. 25, Mar, 1950 - No. 145, April, 1961

25-Flat Top-c(story (also #26,27)	18	54	126	225
26-28,30: 28-Bondage-c. 28,29-The Brow-c/stories	14	42	100	170
29-1st app. Gravel Gertie in a Gould-r	17	51	118	210
31,32,34,35,37-40: 40-Intro/origin 2-way wrist radio (6/51)				
	12	36	88	150
33- "Measles the Teen-Age Dope Pusher"	14	42	98	165
36-1st app. B.O. Plenty in a Gould-r	14	42	98	165
41-50	10	30	73	125
51-56,58-80: 51-2pgs Powell-a	9	27	65	110
57-1st app. Sam Catchem in a Gould-r	11	33	77	130
81-99,101-140	8	24	60	100
100, 141-145 (25¢)(titled "Dick Tracy")	9	27	63	105

NOTE: **Powell** a(1-2pgs.)-43, 44, 104, 108, 109, 146. No. 110-120, 141-145 are all reprints from earlier issues.

DICK TRACY
Blackthorne Publishing: 12/84 - No. 24, 6/89 (1-12: $5.95; 13-24: $6.95, B&W, 76 pgs.)

1-8-1st printings; hard-c ed. ($14.95)				15.00
1-3-2nd printings, 1986; hard-c ed.				15.00
1-12-1st & 2nd printings; squarebound. thick-c				7.00
13-24 ($6.95): 21,22-Regular-c & stapled				7.00

NOTE: Gould daily & Sunday strip-r in all. 1-12 r-12/31/45-4/5/49; 13-24 r-7/13/41-2/20/44.

Digimon Digital Monsters #2 © Toei

Dilly #1 © LEV

Dinosaurs For Hire #7 © Tom Mason

DI

	GD2.0	FN6.0	VF8.0	NM9.4		GD2.0	FN6.0	VF8.0	NM9.4

DICK TRACY (Disney)
WD Publications: 1990 - No. 3, 1990 (color) (Book 3 adapts 1990 movie)

Book One ($3.95, 52pgs.)-Kyle Baker-c/a				6.00
Book Two, Three ($5.95, 68pgs.)-Direct sale				6.00
Book Two, Three ($2.95, 68pgs.)-Newsstand				3.00

DICK TRACY ADVENTURES
Gladstone Publishing: May, 1991 ($4.95, 76 pgs.)

1-Reprints strips 2/1/42-4/18/42				5.00

DICK TRACY, EXPLOITS OF
Rosdon Books, Inc.: 1946 ($1.00, hard-c strip reprints)

1-Reprints the near complete case of "The Brow" from 6/12/44 to 9/24/44				
(story starts a few weeks late)	26	78	139	240
with dust jacket...	40	120	232	400

DICK TRACY MONTHLY/WEEKLY
Blackthorne Publishing: May, 1986 - No. 99, 1989 ($2.00, B&W)
(Becomes Weekly #26 on)

1-60: Gould-r. 30,31-Mr. Crime app.				3.00
61-90				4.00
91-95				5.00
96-99-Low print	1	3	5	7

NOTE: #1-10 reprint strips 3/10/40-7/13/41; #10(pg.8)-51 reprint strips 4/6/49-12/31/55; #52-99 reprint strips 12/26/56-4/26/64.

DICK TRACY SPECIAL
Blackthorne Publ.: Jan, 1988 - No. 3, Aug. (no month), 1989 ($2.95, B&W)

1-3: 1-Origin D. Tracy; 4/strips 10/12/31-3/30/32				3.00

DICK TRACY: THE EARLY YEARS
Blackthorne Publishing: Aug, 1987 - No. 4, Aug (no month) 1989 ($6.95, B&W, 76 pgs.)

1-3: 1-4-r/strips 10/12/31(1st daily)-8/31/32 & Sunday strips 6/12/32-8/28/32;				
Big Boy apps. in #1-3	1	3	5	7
4 ($2.95, 52pgs.)				3.00

DICK TRACY UNPRINTED STORIES
Blackthorne Publishing: Sept, 1987 - No. 4, June, 1988 ($2.95, B&W)

1-4: Reprints strips 1/1/56-12/25/56				3.00

DICK TURPIN (See Legend of Young...)

DIE-CUT
Marvel Comics UK, Ltd: Nov, 1993 - No. 4, Feb, 1994 ($1.75, limited series)

1-4: 1-Die-cut-c; The Beast app.				2.25

DIE-CUT VS. G-FORCE
Marvel Comics UK, Ltd: Nov, 1993 - No. 2, Dec, 1993 ($2.75, limited series)

1,2-($2.75)-Gold foil-c on both				2.75

DIE, MONSTER, DIE (See Movie Classics)

DIGIMON DIGITAL MONSTERS (TV)
Dark Horse Comics: May, 2000 - Present ($2.95)

1-12				3.00

DIGITEK
Marvel UK, Ltd: Dec, 1992 - No. 4, Mar, 1993 ($1.95/$2.25, mini-series)

1-4: 3-Deathlock-c/story				2.25

DILLY (Dilly Duncan from Daredevil Comics; see Boy Comics #57)
Lev Gleason Publications: May, 1953 - No. 3, Sept, 1953

1-Teenage; Biro-c	6	18	29	40
2,3-Biro-c	5	14	21	28

DILTON'S STRANGE SCIENCE (See Pep Comics #78)
Archie Comics: May, 1989 - No. 5, May, 1990 (75¢/$1.00)

1-5				3.00

DIME COMICS
Newsbook Publ. Corp.: 1945; 1951

1-Silver Streak-c/story; L. B. Cole-c	64	192	398	700
1(1951)	7	21	36	50

DINGBATS (See 1st Issue Special)

DING DONG
Compix/Magazine Enterprises: Summer?, 1946 - No. 5, 1947 (52 pgs.)

1-Funny animal	26	78	139	240
2 (9/46)	13	39	66	110
3 (Wint '46-'47) - 5	10	30	55	80

DINKY DUCK (Paul Terry's...) (See Approved Comics, Blue Ribbon, Giant Comics Edition #5A & New Terrytoons)
St. John Publishing Co./Pines No. 16 on: Nov, 1951 - No. 16, Sept, 1955; No. 16, Fall, 1956; No. 17, May, 1957 - No. 19, Summer, 1958

1-Funny animal	12	36	61	100
2	7	21	36	50
3-10	5	15	24	32
11-16(9/55)	4	12	19	25
16(Fall,'56) - 19	4	10	15	20

DINKY DUCK & HASHIMOTO-SAN (See Deputy Dawg Presents...)

DINO (TV)(The Flintstones)
Charlton Publications: Aug, 1973 - No. 20, Jan, 1977 (Hanna-Barbera)

1	3	9	20	30
2-10	2	6	12	18
11-20	2	6	9	12

DINO ISLAND
Mirage Studios: Feb, 1994 - No. 2, Mar, 1994 ($2.75, limited series)

1,2-By Jim Lawson				2.75

DINO RIDERS
Marvel Comics: Feb, 1989 - No. 3, 1989 ($1.00)

1-3: Based on toys				3.00

DINOSAUR REX
Upshot Graphics (Fantagraphics): 1986 - No. 3, 1986 ($2.00, limited series)

1-3				2.25

DINOSAURS, A CELEBRATION
Marvel Comics (Epic): Oct, 1992 - No. 4, Oct, 1992 ($4.95, lim. series, 52 pgs.)

1-4: 2-Bolton painted-c				5.00

DINOSAURS ATTACK! THE GRAPHIC NOVEL
Eclipse Comics: 1991 ($3.95, coated stock, stiff-c)

Book One- Based on Topps trading cards				4.00

DINOSAURS FOR HIRE
Malibu Comics: Feb, 1993 - No. 12, Feb, 1994 ($1.95/$2.50)

1-12: 1,10-Flip bk. 8-Bagged w/Skycap; Staton-c. 10-Flip book				2.50

DINOSAURS GRAPHIC NOVEL (TV)
Disney Comics: 1992 - No. 2, 1993 ($2.95, 52 pgs.)

1,2-Staton-a; based on Dinosaurs TV show				3.00

DINOSAURUS
Dell Publishing Co.: No. 1120, Aug, 1960

Four Color 1120-Movie, painted-c	8	24	56	100

DIPPY DUCK
Atlas Comics (OPI): October, 1957

1-Maneely-a; code approved	9	27	49	70

DIRECTORY TO A NONEXISTENT UNIVERSE
Eclipse Comics: Dec, 1987 ($2.00, B&W)

1				2.25

DIRTY DOZEN (See Movie Classics)

DIRTY PAIR (Manga)
Eclipse Comics: Dec, 1988 - No. 4, Apr, 1989 ($2.00, B&W, limited series)

1-4: Japanese manga with original stories				3.00
...: Start the Violence (Dark Horse, 9/99, $2.95) r/B&W stories in color from Dark Horse Presents #132-134; covers by Warren & Pearson				3.00

DIRTY PAIR: FATAL BUT NOT SERIOUS (Manga)
Dark Horse Comics: July, 1995 - No. 5, Nov, 1995 ($2.95, limited series)

1-5				3.00

DIRTY PAIR: RUN FROM THE FUTURE (Manga)

Dirty Pair II #5 © Haruka Takachiho

Disney's Aladdin #2 © WDC

Disney's Beauty and the Beast #4 © WDC

	GD2.0	FN6.0	VF8.0	NM9.4

Dark Horse Comics: Jan, 2000 - No. 4, Mar, 2000 ($2.95, limited series)
1-4-Warren-s/c/a. Var.-c by Hughes(1), Stelfreeze(2), Timm(3), Ramos(4) 3.00

DIRTY PAIR: SIM HELL (Manga)
Dark Horse Comics: May, 1993 - No. 4, Aug, 1993 ($2.50, B&W, limited series)
1-4 3.00
...Remastered #1-4 (5/01 - 8/01) reprints in color, with pin-up gallery 3.00

DIRTY PAIR II (Manga)
Eclipse Comics: June, 1989 - No. 5, Mar, 1990 ($2.00, B&W, limited series)
1-5: 3-Cover is misnumbered as #1 3.00

DIRTY PAIR III, THE (A Plague of Angels) (Manga)
Eclipse Comics: Aug, 1990 - No. 5, Aug, 1991 ($2.00/$2.25, B&W, lim. series)
1-5 3.00

DISAVOWED
DC Comics (Homage): Mar, 2000 - No. 6, Sept, 2000 ($2.50)
1-6: 1-3-Choi & Heisler-s/Edwards-a. 4,5-Lucas-a 2.50

DISCIPLES
Image Comics: Apr, 2001 - Present ($2.95)
1,2: 1-Wraparound-c 3.00
...: Wheel of Fortune (12/01, $4.95) 5.00

DISHMAN
Eclipse Comics: Sept, 1988 ($2.50, B&W, 52 pgs.)
1 2.50

DISNEY AFTERNOON, THE (TV)
Marvel Comics: Nov, 1994 - No. 10?, Aug, 1995 ($1.50)
1-10: 3-w/bound-in Power Ranger Barcode Card 3.00

DISNEY COMIC ALBUM
Disney Comics: 1990(no month, year) - No. 8, 1991 ($6.95/$7.95)
1,2 ($6.95): 1-Donald Duck and Gyro Gearloose by Barks(r). 2-Uncle Scrooge by Barks(r); Jr. Woodchucks app. 9.00
3-8: 3-Donald Duck-r/F.C. 308 by Barks; begin $7.95-c. 4-Mickey Mouse Meets the Phantom Blot; r/M.M Club Parade (censored 1956 version of story). 5-Chip `n' Dale Rescue Rangers; new-a. 6-Uncle Scrooge. 7-Donald Duck in Too Many Pets; Barks-r(4) including F.C. #29. 8-Super Goof; r/S.G. #1, D.D. #102 9.00

DISNEY COMIC HITS
Marvel Comics: Oct, 1995 - No. 16, Jan, 1997 ($1.50/$2.50)
1-16: 4-Toy Story. 6-Aladdin. 7-Pocahontas. 10-The Hunchback of Notre Dame (Same story in Disney's The Hunchback of Notre Dame) 13-Aladdin and the Forty Thieves 4.00

DISNEY COMICS
Disney Comics: June, 1990
Boxed set of #1 issues includes Donald Duck Advs., Ducktales, Chip 'n Dale Rescue Rangers, Roger Rabbit, Mickey Mouse Advs. & Goofy Advs.; limited to 10,000 sets 2 6 11 15

DISNEYLAND BIRTHDAY PARTY (Also see Dell Giants)
Gladstone Publishing Co.: Aug, 1985 ($2.50)
1-Reprints Dell Giant with new-photo-c 2 6 9 12
...Comics Digest #1-(Digest) 2 6 10 14

DISNEYLAND MAGAZINE
Fawcett Publications: Feb. 15, 1972 - ? (10-1/4"x12-5/8", 20 pgs, weekly)
1-One or two page painted art features on Dumbo, Snow White, Lady & the Tramp, the Aristocats, Brer Rabbit, Peter Pan, Cinderella, Jungle Book, Alice & Pinocchio. Most standard characters app. 3 9 17 25

DISNEYLAND, USA (See Dell Giant No. 30)

DISNEY MOVIE BOOK
Walt Disney Productions (Gladstone): 1990 ($7.95, 8-1/2"x11", 52 pgs.) (w/pull-out poster)
1-Roger Rabbit in Tummy Trouble; from the cartoon film strips adapted to the comic format. Ron Dias-c 2 6 9 12

DISNEY'S ACTION CLUB
Acclaim Books: 1997 - No. 4 ($4.50, digest size)

1-4: 1-Hercules. 4-Mighty Ducks 4.50

DISNEY'S ALADDIN (Movie)
Marvel Comics: Oct, 1994 - No. 11, 1995 ($1.50)
1-11 3.00

DISNEY'S BEAUTY AND THE BEAST (Movie)
Marvel Comics: Sept, 1994 - No. 13, 1995 ($1.50)
1-13 3.00

DISNEY'S BEAUTY AND THE BEAST HOLIDAY SPECIAL
Acclaim Books: 1997 ($4.50, digest size, one-shot)
1-Based on The Enchanted Christmas video 4.50

DISNEY'S COLOSSAL COMICS COLLECTION
Disney Comics: 1991 - No. 10, 1993 ($1.95, digest-size, 96/132 pgs.)
1-10: Ducktales, Talespin, Chip 'n Dale's Rescue Rangers. 4-r/Darkwing Duck #1-4. 6-Goofy begins. 8-Little Mermaid 5.00

DISNEY'S COMICS IN 3-D
Disney Comics: 1992 ($2.95, w/glasses, polybagged)
1-Infinity-c; Barks, Rosa, Gottfredson-r 5.00

DISNEY'S ENCHANTING STORIES
Acclaim Books: 1997 - No. 5 ($4.50, digest size)
1-5: 1-Hercules. 2-Pocahontas 4.50

DISNEY'S NEW ADVENTURES OF BEAUTY AND THE BEAST (Also see Beauty and the Beast & Disney's Beauty and the Beast)
Disney Comics: 1992 - No. 2, 1992 ($1.50, limited series)
1,2-New stories based on movie 3.00

DISNEY'S POCAHONTAS (Movie)
Marvel Comics: 1995 ($4.95, one-shot)
1-Movie adaptation 1 3 5 7

DISNEY'S TALESPIN LIMITED SERIES: "TAKE OFF" (TV) (See Talespin)
W. D. Publications (Disney Comics): Jan, 1991 - No. 4, Apr, 1991 ($1.50, limited series, 52 pgs.)
1-4: Based on animated series; 4 part origin 2.50

DISNEY'S TARZAN (Movie)
Dark Horse Comics: June, 1999 - No. 2, July, 1999 ($2.95, limited series)
1,2: Movie adaptation 3.00

DISNEY'S THE LION KING (Movie)
Marvel Comics: July, 1994 - No. 2, July, 1994 ($1.50, limited series)
1,2: 2-part movie adaptation 3.00
1-($2.50, 52 pgs.)-Complete story 5.00

DISNEY'S THE LITTLE MERMAID (Movie)
Marvel Comics: Sept, 1994 - No. 12, 1995 ($1.50)
1-12 4.00

DISNEY'S THE LITTLE MERMAID LIMITED SERIES (Movie)
Disney Comics: Feb, 1992 - No. 4, May, 1992 ($1.50, limited series)
1-4: Peter David scripts 3.00

DISNEY'S THE LITTLE MERMAID: UNDERWATER ENGAGEMENTS
Acclaim Books: 1997 ($4.50, digest size)
1-Flip book 4.50

DISNEY'S THE HUNCHBACK OF NOTRE DAME (Movie)(See Disney's Comic Hits #10)
Marvel Comics: July, 1996 ($4.95, squarebound, one-shot)
1-Movie adaptation. 1 3 5 7
NOTE: A different edition of this series was sold at Wal-Mart stores with new covers depicting scenes from the 1989 feature film. Inside contents and price were identical.

DISNEY'S THE THREE MUSKETEERS (Movie)
Marvel Comics: Jan, 1994 - No. 2, Feb, 1994 ($1.50, limited series)
1,2-Morrow-c; Spiegle-a; Movie adaptation 2.25

DISNEY'S TOY STORY (Movie)
Marvel Comics: Dec, 1995 ($4.95, one-shot)
nn-Adaptation of film 1 3 5 7

Distant Soil #20 © Colleen Doran

Divine Right #5 © WSP

Dizzy Don Comics #4 © Howard Pub.

	GD2.0	FN6.0	VF8.0	NM9.4

DISTANT SOIL, A (1st Series)
WaRP Graphics: Dec, 1983 - No. 9, Mar 1986 ($1.50, B&W)

1-9: 1-4 are magazine size				3.00

NOTE: Second printings exist of #1, 2, 3 & 6.

DISTANT SOIL, A
Donning (Star Blaze): Mar, 1989 ($12.95, trade paperback)

nn-new material				13.00

DISTANT SOIL, A (2nd Series)
Aria Press/Image Comics (Highbrow Entertainment) #15 on:
June, 1991 - Present ($1.75/$2.50/$2.95/$3.95, B&W)

1-27: 13-$2.95-c begins. 14-Sketchbook. 15-(8/96)-1st Image issue				3.00
29-33-($3.95)				4.00
The Aria ('01, $16.95,TPB) r/#26-31				17.00
The Ascendant ('98, $18.95,TPB) r/#13-25				19.00
The Gathering ('97, $18.95,TPB) r/#1-13; intro. Neil Gaiman				19.00

NOTE: Four separate printings exist for #1 and are clearly marked. Second printings exist of #2-4 and are also clearly marked.

DISTANT SOIL, A: IMMIGRANT SONG
Donning (Star Blaze): Aug, 1987 ($6.95, trade paperback)

nn-new material				7.00

DIVER DAN (TV)
Dell Publishing Co.: Feb-Apr, 1962 - No. 2, June-Aug, 1962

Four Color 1254(#1), 2	5	15	35	60

DIVINE RIGHT
Image Comics (WildStorm Prod.): Sept, 1997 - No. 12, Nov, 1999 ($2.50)

Preview				5.00
1,2: 1-Jim Lee-s/a(p)/c. 1-Variant-c by Charest				4.00
1-($3.50)-Voyager Pack w/Stormwatch preview				3.50
1-American Entertainment Ed.				6.00
2-Variant-c of Exotica & Blaze				5.00
3-5-Fairchild & Lynch app.				3.00
3-Chromium-c by Jim Lee				5.00
4,6-12: 4-American Entertainment Ed. 8-Two covers. 9-1st DC issue.				
11,12-Divine Intervention pt. 1,4				3.00
5-Pacific Comicon Ed.				6.00
6-Glow in the dark variant-c, European Tour Edition				20.00
...Collected Edition #1-3 ($5.95, TPB) 1-r/#1,2. 2-r/#3,4. 3-r/#5,6				6.00
Divine Intervention/Gen 13 (11/99, $2.50) Part 3; D'Anda-a				2.50
Divine Intervention/Wildcats (11/99, $2.50) Part 2; D'Anda-a				2.50

DIVISION 13 (See Comic's Greatest World)
Dark Horse Comics: Sept, 1994 - Jan, 1995 ($2.50, color)

1-4: Giffen story in all. 1-Art Adams-c				2.50

DIXIE DUGAN (See Big Shot, Columbia Comics & Feature Funnies)
McNaught Syndicate/Columbia/Publication Ent.: July, 1942 - No. 13, 1949
(Strip reprints in all)

1-Joe Palooka x-over by Ham Fisher	29	87	153	265
2	16	48	83	140
3	12	36	61	100
4,5(1945-46)-Bo strip-r	9	27	49	70
6-13(1/47-49): 6-Paperdoll cut-outs	7	21	38	55

DIXIE DUGAN
Prize Publications (Headline): V3#1, Nov, 1951 - V4#4, Feb, 1954

V3#1	9	27	49	70
2-4	6	18	30	42
V4#1-4(#5-8)	5	15	25	35

DIZZY DAMES
American Comics Group (B&M Distr. Co.): Sept-Oct, 1952 - No. 6, Jul-Aug, 1953

1-Whitney-c	14	42	72	125
2	9	27	49	70
3-6	7	21	36	50

DIZZY DON COMICS
F. E. Howard Publications/Dizzy Don Ent. Ltd (Canada): 1942 - No. 22, Oct, 1946; No. 3, Apr, 1947 (Most B&W)

1 (B&W)	12	36	61	100
2 (B&W)	7	21	36	50
4-21 (B&W)	6	18	32	45
22-Full color, 52 pgs.	13	39	66	115
3 (4/47)-Full color, 52 pgs.	13	39	66	115

DIZZY DUCK (Formerly Barnyard Comics)
Standard Comics: No. 32, Nov, 1950 - No. 39, Mar, 1952

32-Funny animal	10	30	55	80
33-39	5	15	25	35

DNAGENTS (The New DNAgents V2/1 on)(Also see Surge)
Eclipse Comics: March, 1983 - No. 24, July, 1985 ($1.50, Baxter paper)

1,24: 1-Origin. 4-Amber app. 24-Dave Stevens-c				3.00
2-23: 8-Infinity-c				2.25

DOBERMAN (See Sgt. Bilko's Private...)

DOBIE GILLIS (See the Many Loves of...)

DOC CHAOS: THE STRANGE ATTRACTOR
Vortex Comics: Apr, 1990 - #3, 1990 ($3.00, 32 pgs.)

1-3: The Lust For Order				3.00

DOC SAMSON (Also see Incredible Hulk)
Marvel Comics: Jan, 1996 - No. 4, Apr, 1996 ($1.95, limited series)

1-4: 1-Hulk c/app. 2-She-Hulk-c/app. 3-Punisher-c/app. 4-Polaris-c/app.				2.25

DOC SAVAGE
Gold Key: Nov, 1966

1-Adaptation of the Thousand-Headed Man; James Bama c-r/1964 Doc Savage paperback	10	30	73	125

DOC SAVAGE (Also see Giant-Size...)
Marvel Comics Group: Oct, 1972 - No. 8, Jan, 1974

1	2	6	13	20
2,3-Steranko-c	2	6	9	12
4-8	1	4	7	10

NOTE: Gil Kane c-5, 6. Mooney a-1i. No. 1, 2 adapts pulp story "The Man of Bronze"; No. 3 adapts "Death in Silver"; No. 5, 6 adapts "The Monsters"; No. 7, 8 adapts "The Brand of The Werewolf".

DOC SAVAGE (Magazine)
Marvel Comics Group: Aug, 1975 - No. 8, Spring, 1977 ($1.00, B&W)

1-Cover from movie poster; Ron Ely photo-c	2	6	10	14
2-5: 3-Buscema-a. 5-Adams-a(1 pg.), Rogers-a(1 pg)	1	3	6	8
6-8	1	4	7	10

DOC SAVAGE
DC Comics: Nov, 1987 - No. 4, Feb, 1988 ($1.75, limited series)

1-4				3.00

DOC SAVAGE
DC Comics: Nov, 1988 - No. 24, Oct, 1990 ($1.75/$2.00: #13-24)

1-16,19-24				3.00
17,18-Shadow x-over				4.00
Annual 1 (1989, $3.50, 68 pgs.)				4.00

DOC SAVAGE COMICS (Also see Shadow Comics)
Street & Smith Publications: May, 1940 - No. 20, Oct, 1943 (1st app. in Doc Savage pulp, 3/33)

1-Doc Savage, Cap Fury, Danny Garrett, Mark Mallory, The Whisperer; Captain Death, Billy the Kid, Sheriff Pete & Treasure Island begin; Norgil, the Magician app.	462	1386	3000	6000
2-Origin & 1st app. Ajax, the Sun Man; Danny Garrett, The Whisperer end	164	492	1023	1800
3	123	369	769	1350
4-Treasure Island ends; Tuska-a	100	300	625	1100
5-Origin & 1st app. Astron, the Crocodile Queen, not in #9 & 11; Norgi the Magician app.	77	231	483	850
6-10: 6-Cap Fury ends; origin & only app. Red Falcon in Astron story. 8-Mark Mallory ends; Charlie McCarthy app. on-c plus true life story. 10-Origin & only app. The Thunderbolt	61	182	381	675
11,12	52	157	314	550
V2#1-8(#13-20): 15-Origin of Ajax the Sun Man; Jack Benny on-c; Hitler app. 16-The Pulp Hero, The Avenger app.; Fanny Brice story. 17-Sun Man ends; Nick Carter begins; Duffy's Tavern part photo-c & story. 18-Huckleberry Finn				

Doctor Fate #1 © DC

Doctor Mid-Nite #2 © DC

Doctor Strange #56 © MAR

	GD2.0	FN6.0	VF8.0	NM9.4

	GD2.0	FN6.0	VF8.0	NM9.4

part-c/story. 19-Henny Youngman part photo-c & life story. 20-Only all funny-c w/Huckleberry Finn

	52	157	314	550

DOC SAVAGE: CURSE OF THE FIRE GOD
Dark Horse Comics: Sept, 1995 - No. 4, Dec, 1995 ($2.95, limited series)

| 1-4 | | | | 3.00 |

DOC SAVAGE: THE MAN OF BRONZE
Skylark Pub: Mar, 1979, 68pgs. (B&W comic digest, 5-1/4x7-5/8")

| 15406-0: Whitman-a, 60 pgs., new comics | 3 | 9 | 21 | 32 |

DOC SAVAGE: THE MAN OF BRONZE
Millennium Publications: 1991 - No. 4, 1991 ($2.50, limited series)

| 1-4: 1-Bronze logo | | | | 3.00 |
| ...: The Manual of Bronze 1 ($2.50, B&W, color, one-shot)-Unpublished proposed Doc Savage strip in color, B&W strip-r | | | | 3.00 |

DOC SAVAGE: THE MAN OF BRONZE, DOOM DYNASTY
Millennium Publ.: 1992 (Says 1991) - No. 2, 1992 ($2.50, limited series)

| 1,2 | | | | 3.00 |

DOC SAVAGE: THE MAN OF BRONZE - REPEL
Innovation Publishing: 1992 ($2.50)

| 1-Dave Dorman painted-c | | | | 3.00 |

DOC SAVAGE: THE MAN OF BRONZE THE DEVIL'S THOUGHTS
Millennium Publ.: 1992 (Says 1991) - No. 3, 1992 ($2.50, limited series)

| 1-3 | | | | 3.00 |

DOC STEARN...MR. MONSTER (See Mr. Monster)

DR. ANTHONY KING, HOLLYWOOD LOVE DOCTOR
Minoan Publishing Corp./Harvey Publications No. 4: 1952(Jan) - No. 3, May, 1953; No. 4, May, 1954

| 1 | 13 | 39 | 66 | 110 |
| 2-4: 4-Powell-a | 8 | 24 | 42 | 60 |

DR. ANTHONY'S LOVE CLINIC (See Mr. Anthony's...)

DR. BOBBS
Dell Publishing Co.: No. 212, Jan, 1949

| Four Color 212 | 4 | 12 | 30 | 50 |

DOCTOR BOOGIE
Media Arts Publishing: 1987 ($1.75)

| 1-Airbrush wraparound-c; Nick Cuti-i | | | | 2.25 |

DOCTOR CHAOS
Triumphant Comics: Nov, 1993 - No. 6, Mar, 1994 ($2.50)

| 1-6: 1,2-Triumphant Unleashed x-over. 2-1st app. War Dancer in pin-up. 3-Intro The Cry | | | | 2.50 |

DOCTOR CYBORG
Attention! Publishing: 1996 - No. 5 ($2.95, B&W)

| 1-5 | | | | 3.00 |
| The Clone Conspiracy TPB (1998, $14.95) r/#1-5 | | | | 15.00 |

DR. DOOM'S REVENGE
Marvel Comics: 1989 (Came w/computer game from Paragon Software)

| V1#1-Spider-Man & Captain America fight Dr. Doom | | | | 3.00 |

DR. FATE (See 1st Issue Special, The Immortal..., Justice League, More Fun #55, & Showcase)

DOCTOR FATE
DC Comics: July, 1987 - No. 4, Oct, 1987 ($1.50, limited series, Baxter paper)

| 1-4: Giffen-c/a in all | | | | 3.00 |

DOCTOR FATE
DC Comics: Winter, 1988-`89 - No. 41, June, 1992 ($1.25/$1.50 #5 on)

1,15: 15-Justice League app.				3.50
2-14				3.00
16-41: 25-1st new Dr. Fate. 36-Original Dr. Fate returns				2.50
Annual 1(1989, $2.95, 68 pgs.)-Sutton-a				3.50

DR. FU MANCHU (See The Mask of...)
I.W. Enterprises: 1964

| 1-r/Avon's "Mask of Dr. Fu Manchu"; Wood-a | 9 | 27 | 63 | 105 |

DR. GIGGLES (See Dark Horse Presents #64-66)
Dark Horse Comics: Oct, 1992 - No. 2, Oct, 1992 ($2.50, limited series)

| 1,2-Based on movie | | | | 2.50 |

DOCTOR GRAVES (Formerly The Many Ghosts of...)
Charlton Comics: No. 73, Sept, 1985 - No. 75, Jan, 1986

| 73-75-Low print run | | | | 6.00 |

DR. JEKYLL AND MR. HYDE (See A Star Presentation & Supernatural Thrillers #4)

DR. KILDARE (TV)
Dell Publishing Co.: No. 1337, 4-6/62 - No. 9, 4-6/65 (All Richard Chamberlain photo-c)

| Four Color 1337(#1, 1962) | 9 | 27 | 63 | 110 |
| 2-9 | 6 | 18 | 42 | 80 |

DR. MASTERS (See The Adventures of Young...)

DOCTOR MID-NITE (Also see All-American #25)
DC Comics: 1999 - No. 3, 1999 ($5.95, square-bound, limited series)

| 1-3-Matt Wagner-s/John K. Snyder III-painted art | | | | 6.00 |
| TPB (2000, $19.95) r/series | | | | 20.00 |

DR. ROBOT SPECIAL
Dark Horse Comics: Apr, 2000 ($2.95, one-shot)

| 1-Bernie Mireault-s/a; some reprints from Madman Comics #12-15 | | | | 3.00 |

DOCTOR SOLAR, MAN OF THE ATOM (Also see The Occult Files of Dr. Spektor #14 & Solar)
Gold Key/Whitman No. 28 on: 10/62 - No. 27, 4/69; No. 28, 4/81 - No. 31, 3/82 (1-27 have painted-c)

1-(#10000-210)-Origin/1st app. Dr. Solar (1st original Gold Key character)	19	57	133	250
2-Prof. Harbinger begins	8	24	56	100
3,4	5	15	35	65
5-Intro. Man of the Atom in costume	5	15	36	70
6-10	4	12	29	45
11-14,16-20	3	10	23	35
15-Origin retold	4	12	26	40
21-23: 23-Last 12¢ issue	3	9	19	28
24-27	3	9	17	25
28-31: 29-Magnus Robot Fighter begins. 31-(3/82)The Sentinel app.	2	6	11	15

NOTE: *Frank Bolle* a-6-19, 29-31; c-29i, 30i. *Bob Fugitani* a-1-5. *Spiegle* a-29-31. *Al McWilliams* a-20-23.

DOCTOR SOLAR, MAN OF THE ATOM
Valiant Comics: 1990 - No. 2, 1991 ($7.95, card stock-c, high quality, 96 pgs.)

| 1,2: Reprints Gold Key series | 1 | 3 | 6 | 8 |

DOCTOR SPEKTOR (See The Occult Files of..., & Spine-Tingling Tales)

DOCTOR STRANGE (Formerly Strange Tales #1-168) (Also see The Defenders, Giant-Size..., Marvel Fanfare, Marvel Graphic Novel, Marvel Premiere, Marvel Treasury Edition & Strange Tales, 2nd Series)
Marvel Comics Group: No. 169, 6/68 - No. 183, 11/69; 6/74 - No. 81, 2/87

169(#1)-Origin retold; panel swipe/M.D. #1-c	16	48	112	200
170-177: 177-New costume	4	12	29	45
178-183: 178-Black Knight app. 179-Spider-Man story-r. 180-Photo montage-c. 181-Brunner-c(part-i), last 12¢ issue	4	12	26	40
1(6/74, 2nd series)-Brunner-c/a	5	15	38	60
2	3	9	17	25
3-5	2	6	11	15
6-10	1	3	6	8
11-13,15-20: 13,15-17-(Regular 25¢ editions)				5.00
13-17-(30¢-c variants, limited distribution)	1	3	6	8
14-(5/76) Dracula app.; (regular 25¢ edition)				6.00
21-40: 21-Origin-r/Doctor Strange #169. 23-25-(Regular 30¢ editions). 31-Sub-Mariner-r				3.00
23-25-(35¢-c variants, limited distribution)(6,8,10/77) 1		3	6	8
41-57,63-77,79-81: 56-Origin retold				2.50
58-62: 58-Re-intro Hannibal King (cameo). 59-Hannibal King full app. 59-62-Dracula app. (Darkhold storyline). 61,62-Doctor Strange, Blade, Hannibal King & Frank Drake team-up to battle. Dracula. 62-Death of Dracula & Lilith				4.00
78-New costume				2.50

DO

Doctor Strange, Sorcerer Supreme #67 © MAR

Dr. Tomorrow #6 © Acclaim

Doll Man Quarterly #6 © QUA

	GD2.0	FN6.0	VF8.0	NM9.4

Annual 1(1976, 52 pgs.)-New Russell-a (35 pgs.) 1 4 7 10
...Silver Dagger Special Edition 1 (3/83, $2.50)-r/#1,2,4,5; Wrightson-c 3.00
...What Is It That Disturbs You, Stephen? #1 (10/97, $5.99, 48 pgs.)
Russell-a/Andreyko & Russell-s, retelling of Annual #1 story 6.00
NOTE: *Adkins* a-169, 170, 171i; c-169-171, 172i, 173. *Adams* a(i)-48-60, 66, 68, 70, 73; c169-171, 172i, 173. *Austin* a(i)-48-60, 66, 68, 70, 183, 6-18, 36-45, 47; c(p)-172, 174-183, 11-21, 23, 27, 35, 36, 47. *Ditko* a-179r; 3r. *Everett* c-183i. *Golden* a-46p, 55p; c-47-48. *G. Kane* c(p)-8-10. *Miller* c-46p. *Nebres* a-20, 22, 23, 24i, 26i, 32i; c-32i, 34. *Rogers* a-48-53p; c-47p-53p. *Russell* a-34i, Annual 1, *B. Smith* c-179. *Paul Smith* a-54p, 56p, 65, 66p, 69, 71-73; c-56, 65, 66, 68, 71. *Starlin* a-23p, 26; c-25, 26. *Sutton* a-27-29p, 31i, 33, 34p. *Painted* c-62, 63.

DOCTOR STRANGE (Volume 2)
Marvel Comics: Feb, 1999 - No. 4, May, 1999 ($2.99, limited series)
1-4: 1,2-Tony Harris-a/painted cover. 3,4-Chadwick-a 3.00

DOCTOR STRANGE CLASSICS
Marvel Comics Group: Mar, 1984 - No. 4, June, 1984 ($1.50, Baxter paper)
1-4: Ditko-r; Byrne-a. 4-New Golden pin-up 3.00
NOTE: *Byrne* c-1, 2-4.

DOCTOR STRANGEFATE (See Marvel Versus DC #3 & DC Versus Marvel #4)
DC Comics (Amalgam): Apr, 1996 ($1.95)
1-Ron Marz script w/Jose Garcia-Lopez-(p) & Kevin Nowlan-(i). Access & Charles Xavier app. 2.50

DOCTOR STRANGE MASTER OF THE MYSTIC ARTS (See Fireside Book Series)

DOCTOR STRANGE, SORCERER SUPREME
Marvel Comics (Midnight Sons imprint #60 on): Nov, 1988 - No. 90, June, 1996 ($1.25/$1.50/$1.75/$1.95, direct sales only, Mando paper)
1 ($1.25) 4.00
2-9,12-14,16-25,27,29-40,42-49,51-64: 3-New Defenders app. 5-Guice-c/a begins. 18-Morbius story line. 31-36-Morbius Inferno x-overs. 31-Silver Surfer app. 33-Thanos-c & cameo. 36-Warlock app. 37-Silver Surfer app. 40-Daredevil x-over. 41-Wolverine-c/story. 42-47-Infinity War x-overs. 47-Gamora app. 52,53-Morbius c/stories. 60,61-Siege of Darkness pt. 8 & 13. 60-Spot varnish-c. 61-New Doctor Strange begins (cameo, 1st app.). 62-Dr. Doom & Morbius app. 2.50
10,11,26,28,41: 10-Re-intro Morbius w/new costume (11/89). 11-Hobgoblin app. 26-Werewolf by Night app. 28-Ghost Rider-s cont'd from G.R. #12; published at same time as Doctor Strange/Ghost Rider Annual #1(4/91) 3.00
15-Unauthorized Amy Grant photo-c 4.00
50-($2.95, 52 pgs.)-Holo-grafx foil-c; Hulk, Ghost Rider & Silver Surfer app.; leads into new Secret Defenders series 3.00
65-74, 76-90: 65-Begin $1.95-c; bound-in card sheet. 72-Silver ink-c. 80-82-Ellis-s. 84-DeMatteis story begins. 87-Death of Baron Mordo. 2.50
75 ($2.50) 4.00
75 ($3.50)-Foil-c 4.00
Annual 2-4 ('92-'94, 68 pgs.)-2-Defenders app. 3-Polybagged w/card 3.00
Ashcan (1995, 75¢) 2.25
.../Ghost Rider Special 1 (4/91, $1.50)-Same book as D.S.S.S. #28 2.50
...Vs. Dracula 1 (3/94, $1.75, 52 pgs.)-r/Tomb of Dracula #44 & Dr. Strange #14 2.50
NOTE: *Colan* c/a-19. *Golden* c-28. *Guice* a-5-16, 18, 20-24; c-5-12, 20-24. See 1st series for Annual #1.

DR. TOM BRENT, YOUNG INTERN
Charlton Publications: Feb, 1963 - No. 5, Oct, 1963
1 2 6 13 20
2-5 2 6 9 12

DR. TOMORROW
Acclaim Comics (Valiant): Sept, 1997 - No. 12 ($2.50)
1-12: 1-Mignola-c 2.50

DR. VOLTZ (See Mighty Midget Comics)

DR. WEIRD
Big Bang Comics: Oct, 1994 - No. 2, May, 1995 ($2.95, B&W)
1,2: 1-Frank Brunner-c 4.00

DR. WEIRD SPECIAL
Big Bang Comics: Feb, 1994 ($3.95, B&W, 68 pgs.)
1-Origin-r by Starlin; Starlin-c. 4.00

DOCTOR WHO (Also see Marvel Premiere #57-60)

Marvel Comics Group: Oct, 1984 - No. 23, Aug, 1986 ($1.50, color, direct sales, Baxter paper)
1-15-British-r 4.00
16-23 5.00
Graphic Novel Voyager (1985, $8.95) color reprints of B&W comic pages from Doctor Who Magazine #88-99; Colin Baker afterword 12.00

DR. WHO & THE DALEKS (See Movie Classics)

DR. WONDER
Old Town Publishing: June, 1996 - No. 5 ($2.95, B&W)
1-5: 1-Intro & origin of Dr. Wonder; Dick Ayers-c/a; Irwin Hasen-a; contains profiles of the artists 3.00

DOCTOR ZERO
Marvel Comics (Epic Comics): Apr, 1988 - No. 8, Aug, 1989 ($1.25/$1.50)
1-8: 1-Sienkiewicz-c. 6,7-Spiegle-a 2.25
NOTE: *Sienkiewicz* a-3i, 4i; c-1. *Spiegle* a-6, 7.

DO-DO (Funny Animal Circus Stories)
Nation-Wide Publishers: 1950 - No. 7, 1951 (5¢, 5x7-1/4" Miniature)
1 (32 pgs.) 26 78 139 240
2-7 14 42 72 120

DODO & THE FROG, THE (Formerly Funny Stuff; also see It's Game Time #2)
National Periodical Publications: No. 80, 9-10/54 - No. 88, 1-2/56; No. 89, 8-9/56; No. 90, 10-11/56; No. 91, 9/57; No. 92, 11/57 (See Comic Cavalcade)
80-1st app. Doodles Duck by Sheldon Mayer 21 63 110 185
81-91-1st app. Doodles Duck by Mayer in #81,83-90 14 42 72 120
92-(Scarce)-Doodles Duck by S. Mayer 19 57 99 165

DOGFACE DOOLEY
Magazine Enterprises: 1951 - No. 5, 1953
1(A-1 40) 6 18 32 45
2(A-1 43), 3(A-1 49), 4(A-1 53), 5(A-1 64) 5 15 24 32
I.W. Reprint #1('64), Super Reprint #17 3 8 12 16

DOG MOON
DC Comics (Vertigo): 1996 ($6.95, one-shot)
1-Robert Hunter-scripts; Tim Truman-c/a 7.00

DOG OF FLANDERS, A
Dell Publishing Co.: No. 1088, Mar, 1960
Four Color 1088-Movie, photo-c 4 12 30 50

DOGPATCH (See Al Capp's... & Mammy Yokum)

DOGS OF WAR (Also see Warriors of Plasm)
Defiant: Apr, 1994 - No. 5, Aug, 1994 ($2.50)
1-5 2.50

DOGS-O-WAR
Crusade Comics: June, 1996 - No. 3, Jan, 1997 ($2.95, B&W, limited series)
1-3: 1,2-Photo-c 3.00

DOLLFACE & HER GANG (Betty Betz'...)
Dell Publishing Co.: No. 309, Jan, 1951
Four Color 309 5 15 35 60

DOLLMAN (Movie)
Eternity Comics: Sept, 1991 - No. 4, Dec, 1991 ($2.50, limited series)
1-4: Adaptation of film 2.50

DOLL MAN QUARTERLY, THE (Doll Man #17 on; also see Feature Comics #27 & Freedom Fighters)
Quality Comics: Fall, 1941 - No. 7, Fall, '43; No. 8, Spr, '46 - No. 47, Oct, 1953
1-Dollman (by Cassone), Justin Wright begin 317 951 1979 3800
2-The Dragon begins; Crandall-a(5) 136 408 852 1500
3,4 91 273 568 1000
5-Crandall-a 77 231 483 850
6,7(1943) 55 165 341 600
8(1946)-1st app. Torchy by Bill Ward 164 492 1025 1800
9 55 165 341 600
10-20 43 129 257 450
21-30: 28-Vs. The Flame 39 117 208 360
31-36,38,40: 31-(12/50)-Intro Elmo, the wonder dog (Dollman's faithful dog).

Dolly #10 © Z-D

Donald Duck Large Feature Comic #20 © WDC

Donald Duck Four Color #108 © WDC

	GD2.0	FN6.0	VF8.0	NM9.4		GD2.0	FN6.0	VF8.0	NM9.4

32-34-Jeb Rivers app.; 34 by Crandall(p) — 33 99 174 300
37-Origin & 1st app. Dollgirl; Dollgirl bondage-c — 43 129 257 450
39- "Narcotics...the Death Drug" c-/story — 35 105 185 320
41-47 — 23 69 121 210
Super Reprint #11('64, r/#20),15(r/#23),17(r/#28): 15,17-Torchy app.; Andru/
 Esposito-a — 4 12 25 38
NOTE: *Ward* Torchy in 8, 9, 11, 12, 14-24, 26, 27; by Fox-#30, 35-47. *Crandall* a-2, 5, 10, 13 &
Super #11, 17, 18. *Crandall/Cuidera* c-40-42. *Guardineer* a-3. Bondage c-27, 37, 38, 39.

DOLLS
Sirius: June, 1996 ($2.95, B&W, one-shot)
1 — 3.00

DOLLY
Ziff-Davis Publ. Co.: No. 10, July-Aug, 1951 (Funny animal)
10-Painted-c — 6 18 32 45

DOLLY DILL
Marvel Comics/Newsstand Publ.: 1945
1 — 16 48 83 140

DOLLZ, THE
Image Comics: Apr, 2001 - Present ($2.95)
1,2: 1-Four covers; Sniegoski & Green-s/Green-a — 3.00

DOMINATION FACTOR
Marvel Comics: Nov, 1999 - 4.8, Feb, 2000 ($2.50, interconnected mini- series)
1.1, 2.3, 3.5, 4.7-Fantastic Four; Jurgens-s/a — 2.50
1.2, 2.4, 3.6, 4.8-Avengers; Ordway-s/a — 2.50

DOMINION (Manga)
Eclipse Comics: Dec, 1990 - No. 6., July, 1990 ($2.00, B&W, limited series)
1-6 — 3.00

DOMINION: CONFLICT 1 (Manga)
Dark Horse Comics: Mar, 1996 - No. 6, Aug, 1996 ($2.95, B&W, limited series)
1-6: Shirow-c/a/scripts — 3.00

DOMINIQUE: KILLZONE
Caliber Comics: May, 1995 ($2.95, B&W)
1 — 3.00

DOMINO (See X-Force)
Marvel Comics: Jan, 1997 - No. 3, Mar, 1997 ($1.95, limited series)
1-3: 2-Deathstrike-c/app. — 2.25

DOMINO CHANCE
Chance Enterprises: May-June, 1982 - No. 9, May, 1985 (B&W)
1-9: 7-1st app. Gizmo, 2 pgs. 8-1st full Gizmo story,
1-Reprint, May, 1985 — 2.50

DONALD AND MICKEY IN DISNEYLAND (See Dell Giants)

DONALD AND SCROOGE
Disney Comics: 1992 ($8.95, squarebound, 100 pgs.)
nn-Don Rosa reprint special; r/U.S., D.D. Advs. — 1 4 7 10
1-3 (1992, $1.50)-r/D.D. Advs. (Disney) #1,22,24 & U.S. #261-263,269 — 3.00

DONALD AND THE WHEEL (Disney)
Dell Publishing Co.: No. 1190, Nov, 1961
Four Color 1190-Movie, Barks-c — 7 21 49 90

DONALD DUCK (See Adventures of Mickey Mouse, Cheerios, Donald & Mickey, Ducktales,
Dynabrite Comics, Gladstone Comic Album, Mickey & Donald, Mickey Mouse Mag., Story Hour
Series, Uncle Scrooge, Walt Disney's Comics & Stories, W. D.'s Donald Duck, Wheaties &
Whitman Comic Books, Wise Little Hen, The)

DONALD DUCK
Whitman Publishing Co./Grosset & Dunlap/K.K.: 1935, 1936 (All pages on
heavy linen-like finish cover stock in color;1st book ever devoted to Donald Duck;
see Advs. of Mickey Mouse for 1st app.) (9-1/2x13")
978(1935)-16 pgs.; Illustrated text story book — 350 1050 1925 3500
nn(1936)-36 pgs.plus hard cover & dust jacket. Story completely rewritten with
 B&W illos added. Mickey appears and his nephews are named Morty & Monty
Book only — 355 1065 1950 3200
Dust jacket only.... — 88 264 485 800

DONALD DUCK (Walt Disney's) (10¢)
Whitman/K.K. Publications: 1938 (8-1/2x11-1/2", B&W, cardboard-c)
(Has D. Duck with bubble pipe on-c)
nn-The first Donald Duck & Walt Disney comic book; 1936 & 1937 Sunday
 strip-r(in B&W); same format as the Feature Books; 1st strips with Huey,
 Dewey & Louie from 10/17/37 — 355 1065 1950 3200

DONALD DUCK (Walt Disney's...#262 on; see 4-Color listings for titles &
Four Color No. 1109 for origin story)
Dell Publ. Co./Gold Key #85-216/Whitman #217-245/Gladstone #246 on: 1940
- No. 84, Sept-Nov, 1962; No. 85, Dec, 1962 - No. 245, July, 1984; No. 246, Oct,
1986 - No. 279, May, 1990; No. 280, Sept, 1993 - No. 304, Sept, 1997
Four Color 4(1940)-Daily 1939 strip-r by Al Taliaferro
 — 867 2600 6070 13,000
Large Feature Comic 16(1/41?)-1940 Sunday strips-r in B&W
 — 400 1200 2800 6000
Large Feature Comic 20('41)-Comic Paint Book, r-single panels from Large
 Feature #16 at top of each pg. to color; daily strip-r across bottom of
 each pg. — 447 1341 3130 6700
Four Color 9('42)- "Finds Pirate Gold"; 64 pgs. by Carl Barks & Jack Hannah
 (pgs. 1,2,5,12-40 are by Barks, his 1st Donald Duck comic book art work;
 © 8/17/42) — 667 2000 4670 10,000
Four Color 29(9/43)- "Mummy's Ring" by Barks; reprinted in Uncle Scrooge &
 Donald Duck #1('65), W. D. Comics Digest #44('73) & Donald Duck
 Advs. #14 — 510 1530 3570 7650
Four Color 62(1/45)- "Frozen Gold"; 52 pgs. by Barks, reprinted in The Best of
 W.D. Comics & Donald Duck Advs. #4 — 160 480 1120 2400
Four Color 108(1946)- "Terror of the River"; 52 pgs. by Carl Barks; reprinted in
 Gladstone Comic Album #2 — 120 360 840 1800
Four Color 147(5/47)-in "Volcano Valley" by Barks — 80 240 560 1200
Four Color 159(8/47)-in "The Ghost of the Grotto";52 pgs. by Carl Barks;
 reprinted in Best of Uncle Scrooge & Donald Duck #1 ('66) & The Best of
 W.D. Comics & D.D. Advs. #9; two Barks stories 67 200 470 1000
Four Color 178(12/47)-1st app. Uncle Scrooge by Carl Barks; reprinted in Gold
 Key Christmas Parade #3 & The Best of Walt Disney Comics
 — 97 291 679 1450
Four Color 189(6/48)-by Carl Barks; reprinted in Best of Donald Duck & Uncle
 Scrooge #1('64) & D.D. Advs. #19 — 60 180 420 900
Four Color 199(10/48)-by Carl Barks; mentioned in Love and Death; r/in
 Gladstone Comic Album #5 — 67 200 470 1000
Four Color 203(12/48)-by Barks; reprinted as Gold Key Christmas Parade #4
 — 46 138 322 690
Four Color 223(4/49)-by Barks; reprinted as Best of Donald Duck #1 & Donald
 Duck Advs. #3 — 64 192 448 960
Four Color 238(8/49)-in "Voodoo Hoodoo" by Barks 46 138 322 690
Four Color 256(12/49)-by Barks; reprinted in Best of Donald Duck & Uncle
 Scrooge #2('67), Gladstone Comic Album #16 & W.D. Comics Digest 44('73)
 — 34 102 238 510
Four Color 263(2/50)-Two Barks stories; r-in D.D. #278
 — 32 96 224 475
Four Color 275(5/50), 282(7/50), 291(9/50), 300(11/50)-All by Carl Barks; 275,
 282 reprinted in W.D. Comics Digest #44('73). #275 r/in Gladstone Comic
 Album #10. #291 r/in D. Duck Advs. #16 30 90 210 450
Four Color 308(1/51), 318(3/51)-by Barks; #318-reprinted in W.D. Comics
 Digest #34 & D.D. Advs. #2,19 26 78 182 390
Four Color 328(5/51)-by Carl Barks 28 84 196 420
Four Color 339(7-8/51), 379-2nd Uncle Scrooge-c; art not by Barks.
 — 7 21 49 85
Four Color 348(9-10/51), 356,394-Barks-c only 15 45 105 200
Four Color 367(1-2/52)-by Barks; reprinted as Gold Key Christmas Parade #2 &
 #8 — 25 75 175 375
Four Color 408(7-8/52), 422(9-10/52)-All by Barks. #408-r-in Best of Donald
 Duck & Uncle Scrooge #1('64) & Gladstone Comic Album #13
 — 25 75 175 375
26(11-12/52)-In "Trick or Treat" (Barks-a, 36pgs.) 1st story r-in Walt Disney
 Digest #16 & Gladstone C.A. #23 26 78 182 385
27-30-Barks-c only 11 33 77 140
31-44,47-50 5 15 35 60
45-Barks-a (6 pgs.) 12 36 84 155
46- "Secret of Hondorica" by Barks, 24 pgs.; reprinted in Donald Duck #98

Donald Duck #31 © WDC

Donald Duck #264 © WDC

Don Rosa's Comics & Stories #2 © Don Rosa

	GD2.0	FN6.0	VF8.0	NM9.4

	GD2.0	FN6.0	VF8.0	NM9.4
& 154	18	55	126	240
51-Barks-a,1/2 pg.	5	15	35	65
52- "Lost Peg-Leg Mine" by Barks, 10 pgs.	13	39	91	165
53,55-59	5	15	34	55
54- "Forbidden Valley" by Barks, 26 pgs. (10¢ & 15¢ versions exist)	13	39	91	170
60- "Donald Duck & the Titanic Ants" by Barks, 20 pgs. plus 6 more pgs.	13	39	91	170
61-67,69,70	4	12	29	45
68-Barks-a, 5 pgs.	10	30	70	125
71-Barks-r, 1/2 pg.	4	12	29	45
72-78,80,82-97,99,100: 96-Donald Duck Album	4	12	29	45
79,81-Barks-a, 1pg.	4	12	29	45
98-Reprints #46 (Barks)	4	12	29	45
101,103-111,113-135: 120-Last 12¢ issue. 134-Barks-r/#52 & WDC&S 194. 135-Barks-r/WDC&S 198, 19 pgs.	3	9	21	32
102-Super Goof. 112-1st Moby Duck	3	10	23	35
136-153,155,156,158: 149-20¢-c begin	2	6	12	18
154-Barks-r(#46)	2	6	15	22
157,159,160,164: 157-Barks-r(#45); 25¢-c begin. 159-Reprints/WDC&S #192 (10 pgs). 160-Barks-r(#26). 164-Barks-r(#79)	2	6	12	18
161-163,165-173,175-187,189-191: 175-30¢-c begin. 187-Barks-r/#68.	2	6	10	14
174,188: 174-r/4-Color #394.	2	6	11	16
192-Barks-r(40 pgs.) from Donald Duck #60 & WDC&S #226,234 (52 pgs.)				
	2	6	13	20
193-200,202-207,209-211,213-216	1	4	7	10
201,208,212: 201-Barks-r/Christmas Parade #26, 16pgs. 208-Barks-r/#60 (6 pgs.). 212-Barks-r/WDC&S #130	1	4	7	10
217-219: 217 has 216 on-c. 219-Barks-r/WDC&S #106,107, 10 pgs. ea.				
	2	6	9	12
220,225-228: 228-Barks-r/F.C. #275	2	6	11	16
221,223,224: Scarce; only sold in pre-packs	3	9	20	30
222-(9-10/80)-(Very low distribution)	15	45	105	195
229-240: 229-Barks-r/F.C. #282. 230-Barks-r/ #52 & WDC&S #194. 236(2/82), 237(2-3/82), 238(3/82), 239(4/82), 240(5/82)	2	6	9	12
241-245: 241(4/83), 242(5/83), 243(3/84), 244(4/84), 245(7/84)	2	6	12	18
246-(1st Gladstone issue)-Barks-r/FC #422	2	6	13	20
247-249,251: 248,249-Barks-r/DD #54 & 26. 251-Barks-r/1945 Firestone				
	2	6	10	14
250-($1.50, 68 pgs.)-Barks-r/4-Color #9	2	6	11	16
252-277,282: 254-Barks-r/FC #328. 256-Barks-r/FC #147. 257-($1.50, 52 pgs.)-Barks-r/Vacacation Parade #1. 261-Barks-r/FC #300. 275-Kelly-r/FC #92.				
280 (#1, 2nd Series)	1	3	5	7
278,279,286: 278,279 ($1.95, 68 pgs.): 278-Rosa-a; Barks-r/FC #263.				
279-Rosa-c; Barks-r/MOC #4. 286-Rosa-a	1	3	6	8
281,282,284				6.00
283-Don Rosa-a, part-c & scripts	1	3	5	7
285,287-304				4.00
286 ($2.95, 68 pgs.)-Happy Birthday, Donald				5.00
Mini-Comic #1(1976)-(3-1/4x6-1/2"); r/D.D. #150	1	3	6	8

NOTE: *Carl Barks* wrote all issues but illustrated, but #117, 126, 138 contain his script only. Issues 4-Color #189, 199, 203, 223, 238, 256, 263, 275, 282, 308, 348, 356, 367, 394, 408, 422, 26-30, 35, 44, 46, 52, 55, 57, 60, 65, 70-73, 77-80, 83, 101, 103, 105, 106, 111, 126, 246r, 266r, 268r, 271r, 275r, 278r(F.C. 263) all have *Barks* covers. *Barks* r-263-267, 269-278-282, 284, 285. #96 titled "Comic Album", #99-"Christmas Album". New art issues (not reprints)-106-46, 148-63, 167, 169, 170, 172, 173, 175, 178, 179, 196, 209, 223, 225, 236. *Taliaferro* daily newspaper strips #258-260, 264, 284, 285; Sunday strips #247, 280-283.

DONALD DUCK ADVENTURES (See Walt Disney's Donald Duck Adventures)

DONALD DUCK ALBUM (See Comic Album No. 1,3 & Duck Album)
Dell Publishing Co./Gold Key: 5-7/59 - F.C. No. 1239, 10-12/61; 1962; 8/63 - No. 2, Oct, 1963

	GD2.0	FN6.0	VF8.0	NM9.4
Four Color 995 (#1)	5	15	35	70
Four Color 1182, 01204-207 (1962-Dell)	4	12	30	50
Four Color 1099,1140,1239-Barks-c	6	18	42	80
1(8/63-Gold Key)-Barks-c	5	15	35	65
2(10/63)	4	12	30	50

DONALD DUCK AND THE BOYS (Also see Story Hour Series)
Whitman Publishing Co.: 1948 (5-1/4x5-1/2", 100pgs., hard-c; art & text)

	GD2.0	FN6.0	VF8.0	NM9.4
845-(49) new illos by Barks based on his Donald Duck 10-pager in WDC&S #74, Expanded text not written by Barks; Cover not by Barks	50	150	350	650

(Prices vary widely on this book)

DONALD DUCK AND THE CHRISTMAS CAROL
Whitman Publishing Co.: 1960 (A Little Golden Book, 6-3/8"x7-5/8", 28 pgs.)

	GD2.0	FN6.0	VF8.0	NM9.4
nn-Story book pencilled by Carl Barks with the intended title "Uncle Scrooge's Christmas Carol." Finished art adapted by Norman McGary. (Rare)-Reprinted in Uncle Scrooge in Color.	30	90	135	200

DONALD DUCK BEACH PARTY (Also see Dell Giants)
Gold Key: Sept, 1965 (12¢)

	GD2.0	FN6.0	VF8.0	NM9.4
1(#10158-509)-Barks-r/WDC&S #45; painted-c	6	18	42	80

DONALD DUCK BOOK (See Story Hour Series)

DONALD DUCK COMICS DIGEST
Gladstone Publishing: Nov, 1986 - No. 5, July, 1987 ($1.25/$1.50, 96 pgs.)

	GD2.0	FN6.0	VF8.0	NM9.4
1,3: 1-Barks-c/a-r	1	3	6	9
2,4,5: 4,5-$1.50-c				6.00

DONALD DUCK FUN BOOK (See Dell Giants)

DONALD DUCK IN DISNEYLAND (See Dell Giants)

DONALD DUCK MARCH OF COMICS (See March of Comics #4,20,41,56,69,263)

DONALD DUCK MERRY CHRISTMAS (See Dell Giant No. 53)

DONALD DUCK PICNIC PARTY (See Picnic Party listed under Dell Giants)

DONALD DUCK TELLS ABOUT KITES (See Kite Fun Book)

DONALD DUCK, THIS IS YOUR LIFE (Disney, TV)
Dell Publishing Co.: No. 1109, Aug-Oct, 1960

	GD2.0	FN6.0	VF8.0	NM9.4
Four Color 1109-Gyro flashback to WDC&S #141; origin Donald Duck (1st told)	14	41	98	180

DONALD DUCK XMAS ALBUM (See regular Donald Duck No. 99)

DONALD IN MATHMAGIC LAND (Disney)
Dell Publishing Co.: No. 1051, Oct-Dec, 1959 - No. 1198, May-July, 1961

	GD2.0	FN6.0	VF8.0	NM9.4
Four Color 1051 (#1)-Movie	9	27	63	110
Four Color 1198-Reprint of above	6	18	42	80

DONATELLO, TEENAGE MUTANT NINJA TURTLE
Mirage Studios: Aug, 1986 ($1.50, B&W, one-shot, 44 pgs.)

1				4.00

DONDI
Dell Publishing Co.: No. 1176, Mar-May, 1961 - No. 1276, Dec, 1961

	GD2.0	FN6.0	VF8.0	NM9.4
Four Color 1176 (#1)-Movie; origin, photo-c	4	12	30	50
Four Color 1276	3	9	17	25

DON FORTUNE MAGAZINE
Don Fortune Publishing Co.: Aug, 1946 - No. 6, Feb, 1947

	GD2.0	FN6.0	VF8.0	NM9.4
1-Delecta of the Planets by C. C. Beck in all	24	72	127	220
2	14	42	72	120
3-6: 3-Bondage-c	12	36	61	100

DONKEY KONG (See Blip #1)

DONNA MATRIX
Reactor, Inc.: Aug, 1993 ($2.95, 52 pgs.)

1-Computer generated-c/a by Mike Saenz; 3-D effects				3.00

DON NEWCOMBE
Fawcett Publications: 1950 (Baseball)

	GD2.0	FN6.0	VF8.0	NM9.4
nn-Photo-c	40	120	232	400

DON ROSA'S COMICS AND STORIES
Fantagraphics Books (CX Comics): 1983 ($2.95)

	GD2.0	FN6.0	VF8.0	NM9.4
1,2: 1-(68 pgs.) Reprints Rosa's The Pertwillaby Papers episodes #128-133.				
2-(60 pgs.) Reprints episodes #134-138	2	6	10	14

DON SIMPSON'S BIZARRE HEROES (Also see Megaton Man)
Fiasco Comics: May, 1990 - No. 17, Sept, 1996 ($2.50/$2.95, B&W)

1-10,0,11-17: 0-Begin $2.95-c; r/Bizarre Heroes #1. 17-(9/96)-Indicia also reads Megaton Man #0; intro Megaton Man and the Fiascoverse to new readers				
				3.00

Don Winslow of the Navy #15 © FAW

Doom Patrol #1 © DC

Doom 2099 #19 © MAR

	GD2.0	FN6.0	VF8.0	NM9.4

DON'T GIVE UP THE SHIP
Dell Publishing Co.: No. 1049, Aug, 1959

Four Color 1049-Movie, Jerry Lewis photo-c	8	24	56	100

DON WINSLOW OF THE NAVY
Merwil Publishing Co.: Apr, 1937 - No. 2, May, 1937 (96 pgs.)(A pulp/comic book cross; stapled spine)

V1#1-Has 16 pgs. comics in color. Captain Colorful & Jupiter Jones by Sheldon

Mayer; complete Don Winslow novel	600	1800	4200	–
2-Sheldon Mayer-a	157	471	1100	–

DON WINSLOW OF THE NAVY (See Crackajack Funnies, Famous Feature Stories, Popular Comics & Super Book #5,6)
Dell Publishing Co.: No. 2, Nov, 1939 - No. 22, 1941

Four Color 2 (#1)-Rare	138	414	966	1800
Four Color 22	31	93	217	400

DON WINSLOW OF THE NAVY (See TV Teens; Movie, Radio, TV)
(Fightin' Navy No. 74 on)
Fawcett Publications/Charlton No. 70 on: 2/43 - #64, 12/48; #65, 1/51 - #69, 9/51; #70, 3/55 - #73, 9/55

1-(68 pgs.)-Captain Marvel on cover	109	327	682	1200
2	52	157	314	550
3	40	120	232	400
4-6: 6-Flag-c	34	102	179	310
7-10: 8-Last 68 pg. issue?	25	75	130	225
11-20	20	60	105	175
21-40	13	39	66	110
41-64: 51,60-Singapore Sal (villain) app. 64-(12/48)	11	33	55	90
65(1/51)-Flying Saucer attack; photo-c	15	45	77	130
66 - 69(9/51): All photo-c. 66-sci-fi story	14	42	72	120
70(3/55)-73: 70-73 r-/#26,58 & 59	10	30	55	80

DOOM
Marvel Comics: Oct, 2000 - No. 3, Dec, 2000 ($2.99, limited series)

1-3-Dr. Doom; Dixon/Manco-a				3.00

DOOM FORCE SPECIAL
DC Comics: July, 1992 ($2.95, 68 pgs., one-shot, mature) (X-Force parody)

1-Morrison scripts; Simonson, Steacy, & others-a; Giffen/Mignola-c				3.00

DOOM PATROL, THE (Formerly My Greatest Adventure No. 1-85; see Brave and the Bold, DC Special Blue Ribbon Digest 19, Official… Index & Showcase No. 94-96)
National Periodical Publications: No. 86, 3/64 - No. 121, 9-10/68; No. 122, 2/73 - No. 124, 6-7/73

86-1 pg. origin (#86-121 are 12¢ issues)	10	30	70	120
87-98: 88-Origin The Chief. 91-Intro. Mento	7	21	53	85
99-Intro. Beast Boy (later becomes the Changeling in New Teen Titans)	8	24	56	90
100-Origin Beast Boy; Robot-Maniac series begins (12/65)	8	24	56	90
101-110: 102-Challengers of the Unknown app. 105-Robot-Maniac series ends. 106-Negative Man begins (origin)	4	12	30	50
111-120	4	12	26	40
121-Death of Doom Patrol; Orlando-c.	9	27	65	110
122-124: All reprints	1	4	7	10

DOOM PATROL
DC Comics (Vertigo imprint #64 on): Oct, 1987 - No, 87, Feb, 1995 (75¢-$1.95, new format)

1-Wraparound-c; Lightle-a				5.00
2-18: 18-1st app. Lodestone. 4-1st app. Karma. 8,15,16-Art Adams-c(i). 18-Invasion tie-in.				3.00
19-(2/89)-Grant Morrison scripts begin, ends #63; 1st app Crazy Jane; $1.50-c & new format begins.				6.00
20-30: 29-Superman app. 30-Night Breed fold-out				4.00
31-49,51-56,58-60: 35-1st app. of Flex Mentallo (cameo). 36-1st full app. of Flex Mentallo. 39-World Without End preview.42-Origin of Flex Mentallo. 50,57 ($2.50, 52 pgs.)				2.50
61-87: 61,70-Photo-c. 73-Death cameo (2 panels)				2.50
…And Suicide Squad 1 (3/88, $1.50, 52 pgs.)-Wraparound-c				2.50

Annual 1 (1988, $1.50, 52 pgs.)				2.50
Annual 2 (1994, $3.95, 68 pgs.)-Children's Crusade tie-in.				4.00

NOTE: *Bisley* painted c-26-48, 55-58. *Bolland* c-64, 75. *Dringenberg* a-42(p). *Steacy* a-53.

DOOM PATROL
DC Comics: Dec, 2001 - Present ($2.50)

1-Intro. new team with Robotman; Tan Eng Huat-c/a; John Arcudi-s				3.00
2-4: 4-Metamorpho & Elongated Man app.				2.50

DOOM PATROL (See Tangent Comics/ Doom Patrol)

DOOMSDAY
DC Comics: 1995 ($3.95, one-shot)

1-Year One story by Jurgens, L. Simonson, Ordway, and Gil Kane; Darkseid, Superman app.				4.00

DOOMSDAY + 1 (Also see Charlton Bullseye)
Charlton Comics: July, 1975 - No. 6, June, 1976; No. 7, June, 1978 - No. 12, May, 1979

1: #1-5 are 25¢ issues	2	6	12	18
2-6: 4-Intro Lor. 5-Ditko-a(1 pg.) 6-Begin 30¢-c	1	4	7	10
V3#7-12 (reprints #1-6)				5.00
5 (Modern Comics reprint, 1977)				3.00

NOTE: *Byrne* c/a-1,12; Painted covers-2-7.

DOOMSDAY SQUAD, THE
Fantagraphics Books: Aug, 1986 - No. 7, 1987 ($2.00)

1-7: 1-New Byrne-c. 3-New Byrne-c. 3-Usagi Yojimbo app. (1st in color).4-N Adams-c. 5-7-Gil Kane-c				3.00

DOOM'S IV
Image Comics (Extreme): July, 1994 - No.4, Oct, 1994 ($2.50, limited series)

1-4-Liefeld story				2.50
1,2-Two alternate Liefeld-c each, 4 covers form 1 picture				5.00

DOOM: THE EMPEROR RETURNS
Marvel Comics: Jan, 2002 - No. 3, Mar, 2002 ($2.50, limited series)

1,2-Dixon-s/Manco-a; Franklin Richards app.				2.50

DOOM 2099 (See Marvel Comics Presents #118 & 2099: World of Tomorrow)
Marvel Comics: Jan, 1993 - No. 44, Aug, 1996 ($1.25/$1.50/$1.95)

1-24,26-44: 1-Metallic foil stamped-c. 4-Ron Lim-c(p). 17-bound-in trading card sheet. 40-Namor & Doctor Strange app. 41-Daredevil app., Namor-c/app. 44-Intro The Emissary; story contin'd in 2099: World of Tomorrow				2.25
1-2nd printing				2.25
18-Variant polybagged with Sega Sub-Terrania poster				4.00
25 ($2.25, 52 pgs.)				2.50
25 ($2.95, 52pgs.) Foil embossed cover				3.00
29 ($3.50)-acetate-c.				3.50

DOORWAY TO NIGHTMARE (See Cancelled Comic Cavalcade)
DC Comics: Jan-Feb, 1978 - No. 5, Sept-Oct, 1978

1-Madame Xanadu in all	1	4	7	10
2-5: 4-Craig-a	1	3	6	8

NOTE: *Kaluta* covers on all. Merged into The Unexpected with No. 190.

DOPEY DUCK COMICS (Wacky Duck No. 3) (See Super Funnies)
Timely Comics (NPP): Fall, 1945 - No. 2, Apr, 1946

1,2-Casper Cat, Krazy Krow	21	63	110	190

DORK
Slave Labor: June, 1993 - Present ($2.50-$2.95, B&W, mature)

1-7: Evan Dorkin-c/a/scripts in all. 1(8/95),2(1/96)-(2nd printing): Reads 2nd Print on bottom inside-c				3.00
8-($3.50)				3.50

DOROTHY LAMOUR (Formerly Jungle Lil)(Stage, screen, radio)
Fox Features Syndicate: No. 2, June, 1950 - No. 3, Aug, 1950

2,3-Wood-a(3) each, photo-c	27	81	142	245

DOT DOTLAND (Formerly Little Dot Dotland)
Harvey Publications: No. 62, Sept, 1974 - No. 63, Nov, 1974

62,63	1	4	7	10

DOTTY (…& Her Boy Friends)(Formerly Four Teeners; Glamorous Romances No. 41 on)

Double Comics 1941 © EP

Down With Crime #7 © FAW

Dracula Lives! Annual #1 © MAR

	GD2.0	FN6.0	VF8.0	NM9.4

Ace Magazines (A. A. Wyn): No. 35, June, 1948 - No. 40, May, 1949

35-Teen-age	7	21	36	50
36-40: 37-Transvestism story	5	14	21	28

DOTTY DRIPPLE (Horace & Dotty Dripple No. 25 on)
Magazine Ent.(Life's Romances)/Harvey No. 3 on: 1946 - No. 24, June, 1952
(Also see A-1 No. 1, 3-8, 10)

1 (nd) (10¢)	8	24	45	65
2	5	15	23	30
3-10: 3,4-Powell-a	4	11	17	22
11-24	3	8	12	16

DOTTY DRIPPLE AND TAFFY
Dell Publishing Co.: No. 646, Sept, 1955 - No. 903, May, 1958

Four Color 646 (#1)	4	12	26	40
Four Color 691,718,746,801,903	3	9	17	25

DOUBLE ACTION COMICS
National Periodical Publications: No. 2, Jan, 1940 (68 pgs., B&W)

2-Contains original stories(?); pre-hero DC contents; same cover as Adventure No. 37. (seven known copies, five in high grade) (not an ashcan)				

NOTE: The cover to this book was probably reprinted from Adventure #37. #1 exists as an ash can copy with B&W cover; contains a coverless comic on inside with 1st & last page missing. Two copies exist in fair & fine condition proving at least limited newsstand distribution.

DOUBLE COMICS
Elliot Publications: 1940 - 1944 (132 pgs.)

1940 issues; Masked Marvel-c & The Mad Mong vs. The White Flash covers known

	227	681	1420	2500

1941 issues; Tornado Tim-c, Nordac-c, & Green Light covers known

	155	466	966	1700
1942 issues	114	342	713	1250
1943,1944 issues	93	279	581	1025

NOTE: Double Comics consisted of an almost endless combination of pairs of remaindered, unsold issues of comics representing most publishers and usually mixed publishers in the same book; e.g., a Captain America with a Silver Streak, or a Feature with a Detective, etc., could appear inside the same cover. The actual contents would have to determine its price. Prices listed are for average contents. Any containing rare or first issues are worth much more. Covers also vary in same year. Value would be approximately 50 percent of contents.

DOUBLE-CROSS (See The Crusaders)

DOUBLE-DARE ADVENTURES
Harvey Publications: Dec, 1966 - No. 2, Mar, 1967 (35¢/25¢, 68 pgs.)

1-Origin Bee-Man, Glowing Gladiator, & Magic-Master; Simon/Kirby-a (last S&K art as a team?)	6	18	42	70
2-Williamson/Crandall-a; r/Alarming Adv. #3('63)	5	15	34	55

NOTE: Powell a-1. Simon/Sparling c-1, 2.

DOUBLE DRAGON
Marvel Comics: July, 1991 - No. 6, Dec, 1991 ($1.00, limited series)

1-6: Based on video game. 2-Art Adams-c				2.50

DOUBLE EDGE
Marvel Comics: Alpha, 1995; Omega, 1995 ($4.95, limited series)

Alpha ($4.95)- Punisher story, Nick Fury app.				5.00
Omega ($4.95)-Punisher, Daredevil, Ghost Rider app. Death of Nick Fury				5.00

DOUBLE IMAGE
Image Comics: Feb, 2001 - Present ($2.95)

1-5: 1-Flip covers of Codeflesh (Casey-s/Adlard-a) and The Bod (Young-s). 2-Two covers. 5-"Trust in Me" begins; Chaudhary-a				2.95

DOUBLE LIFE OF PRIVATE STRONG, THE
Archie Publications/Radio Comics: June, 1959 - No. 2, Aug, 1959

1-Origin & re-intro The Shield; Simon & Kirby-a, their re-entry into the super-hero genre; intro./1st app. The Fly; 1st S.A. super-hero for Archie Publ.	50	150	410	750
2-S&K-c/a; Tuska-a; The Fly app. (2nd or 3rd?)	33	99	250	450

DOUBLE TROUBLE
St. John Publishing Co.: Nov, 1957 - No. 2, Jan-Feb, 1958

1,2: Tuffy & Snuffy by Frank Johnson; dubbed "World's Funniest Kids"	6	18	29	40

DOUBLE TROUBLE WITH GOOBER
Dell Publishing Co.: No. 417, Aug, 1952 - No. 556, May, 1954

Four Color 417	3	10	23	35
Four Color 471,516,556	2	6	13	20

DOUBLE UP
Elliott Publications: 1941 (Pocket size, 200 pgs.)

1-Contains rebound copies of digest sized issues of Pocket Comics, Speed Comics, & Spitfire Comics	77	231	483	850

DOVER & CLOVER (See All Funny & More Fun Comics #93)

DOVER BOYS (See Adventures of the...)

DOVER THE BIRD
Famous Funnies Publishing Co.: Spring, 1955

1-Funny animal; code approved	6	18	32	45

DOWN WITH CRIME
Fawcett Publications: Nov, 1952 - No. 7, Nov, 1953

1	33	99	174	300
2,4,5: 2,4-Powell-a in each. 5-Bondage-c	17	51	88	150
3-Used in POP, pg. 106; "H is for Heroin" drug story	19	57	99	165
6,7: 6-Used in POP, pg. 80	14	42	72	120

DO YOU BELIEVE IN NIGHTMARES?
St. John Publishing Co.: Nov, 1957 - No. 2, Jan, 1958

1-Mostly Ditko-c/a	50	150	300	525
2-Ayers-a	30	90	159	275

D.P. 7
Marvel Comics Group (New Universe): Nov, 1986 - No. 32, June, 1989

1-20, Annual #1 (11/87)-Intro. The Witness				2.25
21-32-Low print				3.00

NOTE: Williamson a-9i, 11i; c-9i.

DRACULA (See Bram Stoker's Dracula, Giant-Size..., Little Dracula, Marvel Graphic Novel, Requiem for Dracula, Spider-Man Vs...., Tomb of ... & Wedding of...; also see Movie Classics under Universal Presents as well as Dracula)

DRACULA (See Movie Classics for #1)(Also see Frankenstein & Werewolf)
Dell Publ. Co.: No. 2, 11/66 - No. 4, 3/67; No. 6, 7/72 - No. 8, 7/73 (No #5)

2-Origin & 1st app. Dracula (11/66) (super hero)	4	12	26	40
3,4: 4-Intro. Fleeta ('67)	3	9	17	25
6-('72)-r/#2 w/origin	2	6	13	20
7,8-r/#3, #4	2	6	11	16

DRACULA (Magazine)
Warren Publishing Co.: 1979 (120 pgs., full color)

Book 1-Maroto art; Spanish material translated into English	5	15	34	55

DRACULA CHRONICLES
Topps Comics: Apr, 1995 - No. 3, June, 1995 ($2.50, limited series)

1-3-Linsner-c				3.00

DRACULA LIVES! (Magazine)(Also see Tomb of Dracula)
Marvel Comics Group: 1973(no month) - No. 13, July, 1975 (75¢, B&W) (76 pgs.)

1-Boris painted-c	4	12	30	50
2 (7/73)-1st time origin Dracula; Adams, Starlin-a	3	10	23	35
3-1st app. Robert E. Howard's Soloman Kane; Adams-c/a	3	10	23	35
4,5: 4-Ploog-a. 5-(V2#1)-Bram Stoker's Classic Dracula adapt. begins	2	6	15	22
6-9: 6-8-Bram Stoker adapt. 9-Bondage-c	3	9	17	25
10 (1/75)-16 pg. Lilith solo (1st?)	3	9	21	32
11-13: 11-21 pg. Lilith solo sty. 12-31 pg. Dracula sty	3	9	17	25
Annual 1(Summer, 1975, $1.25, 92 pgs.)-Morrow painted-c; 6 Dracula stories. 25 pgs. Adams-a(r)	3	9	19	28

NOTE: N. Adams a-2, 3i, 10i, Annual 1r(2, 3). Alcala a-9. Buscema a-3p, 6p, Annual 1p. Colan a(p)-1, 2, 5, 6, 8. Evans a-7. Gulacy a-9. Heath a-1r, 13. Pakula a-6r. Sutton a-13. Weiss r-Annual 1p. 4 Dracula stories each in 1, 609; 3 Dracula stories in 2, 4, 5,, 13.

DRACULA: LORD OF THE UNDEAD

The Dragon #5 © Erik Larsen

Dragon Ball Pt. 4 #1 © Bird Studios

Dragon Lines #2 © MAR

Marvel Comics: Dec, 1998 - No. 3, Dec, 1998 ($2.99, limited series)
1-3-Olliffe & Palmer-a 3.00

DRACULA: RETURN OF THE IMPALER
Slave Labor Graphics: July, 1993 - No. 4, Oct, 1994 ($2.95, limited series)
1-4 .... 3.00

DRACULA VERSUS ZORRO
Topps Comics: Oct, 1993 - No. 2, Nov, 1993 ($2.95, limited series)
1,2: 1-Spot varnish & red foil-c. 2-Polybagged w/16 pg. Zorro #0 .... 3.00

DRACULA VERSUS ZORRO
Dark Horse Comics: Sept, 1998 - No. 2, Oct, 1998 ($2.95, limited series)
1,2 .... 3.00

DRACULA: VLAD THE IMPALER (Also see Bram Stoker's Dracula)
Topps Comics: Feb, 1993 - No. 3, Apr, 1993 ($2.95, limited series)
1-3-Polybagged with 3 trading cards each; Maroto-c/a 3.00

DRAFT, THE
Marvel Comics: 1988 ($3.50, one-shot, squarebound)
1-Sequel to "The Pitt" 3.50

DRAG 'N' WHEELS (Formerly Top Eliminator)
Charlton Comics: No. 30, Sept, 1968 - No. 59, May, 1973

	4	12	29	45
30	4	12	29	45
31-40-Scot Jackson begins	3	9	20	30
41-50	3	9	17	25
51-59: Scot Jackson	2	6	11	15
Modern Comics Reprint 58('78)				5.00

DRAGON, THE (Also see The Savage Dragon)
Image Comics (Highbrow Ent.): Mar, 1996 - No. 5, July, 1996 (99¢, lim. series)
1-5: Reprints Savage Dragon limited series w/new story & art. 5-Youngblood
app; includes 5 pg. Savage Dragon story from 1984 .... 2.25

DRAGON ARCHIVES, THE (Also see The Savage Dragon)
Image Comics: Jun, 1998 - No. 4, Jan, 1999 ($2.95, B&W)
1-4 .... 3.00

DRAGON, THE: BLOOD & GUTS (Also see The Savage Dragon)
Image Comics (Highbrow Entertainment): Mar, 1995 - No. 3, May, 1995 ($2.50, limited series)
1-3: Jason Pearson-c/scripts 2.50

DRAGON BALL
Viz Comics: 1998 - Present ($2.95, B&W, Manga reprints read right to left)

Part 1: 1-Akira Toriyama-s/a	1	3	6	8
2-12				5.00
1-12 (2nd & 3rd printings)				3.00
Part 2: 1-15: 15-($3.50-c)				4.00
Part 3: 1-14				3.00
Part 4: 1-10				3.00

DRAGON BALL Z
Viz Comics: 1998 - Present ($2.95, B&W, Manga reprints read right to left)

Part 1: 1-Akira Toriyama-s/a	2	6	9	12
2-9				5.00
1-9 (2nd & 3rd printings)				3.00
Part 2: 1-14				4.00
Part 3: 1-10				3.00
Part 4: 1-15				3.00
Part 5: 1-12				3.00

DRAGON CHIANG
Eclipse Books: 1991 ($3.95, B&W, squarebound, 52 pgs.)
nn-Timothy Truman-c/a(p) 4.00

DRAGONFLIGHT
Eclipse Books: Feb, 1991 - No. 3, 1991 ($4.95, 52 pgs.)
Book One - Three: Adapts 1968 novel 5.00

DRAGONFLY (See Americomics #4)
Americomics: Sum, 1985 - No. 8, 1986 ($1.75/$1.95)
1 .... 3.00

2-8 .... 2.25

DRAGONFORCE
Aircel Publishing: 1988 - No. 13, 1989 ($2.00)
1-Dale Keown-c/a/scripts in #1-12 .... 3.00
2-13: 13-No Keown-a 2.25
...Chronicles Book 1-5 ($2.95, B&W, 60 pgs.): Dale Keown-r/Dragonring & Dragonforce 3.00

DRAGONHEART (Movie)
Topps Comics: May, 1996 - No. 2, June, 1996 ($2.95/$4.95, limited series)
1-($2.95, 24 pgs.)-Adaptation of the film; Hildebrandt Bros-c; Lim-a. 3.00
2-($4.95, 64 pgs.) 5.00

DRAGONLANCE (Also see TSR Worlds)
DC Comics: Dec, 1988 - No. 34, Sept, 1991 ($1.25/$1.50, Mando paper)
1, Annual 1 (1990, $2.95, 68 pgs.) 3.00
2-34: Based on TSR game. 30-32-Kaluta-c 2.50

DRAGON LINES
Marvel Comics (Epic Comics/Heavy Hitters): May, 1993 - No. 4, Aug, 1993 ($1.95, limited series)
1-($2.50)-Embossed-c; Ron Lim-c/a in all 3.00
2-4 .... 2.25

DRAGON LINES: WAY OF THE WARRIOR
Marvel Comics (Epic Comics/ Heavy Hitters): Nov, 1993 - No. 2, Jan, 1994 ($2.25, limited series)
1,2-Ron Lim-c/a(p) 2.25

DRAGONQUEST
Silverwolf Comics: Dec, 1986 - No. 2, 1987 ($1.50, B&W, 28 pgs.)
1,2-Tim Vigil-c/a in all 3.00

DRAGONRING
Aircel Publishing: 1986 - V2#15, 1988 ($1.70/$2.00, B&W/color)
1-6: 6-Last B&W issue, V2#1-15($2.00, color) 2.25

DRAGON'S CLAWS
Marvel UK, Ltd.: July, 1988 - No. 10, Apr, 1989 ($1.25/$1.50/$1.75, British)
1-10: 3-Death's Head 1 pg. strip on back-c (1st app.). 4-Silhouette of Death's
Head on last pg. 5-1st full app. new Death's Head 2.25

DRAGONSLAYER (Movie)
Marvel Comics Group: October, 1981 - No. 2, Nov, 1981
1,2-Paramount Disney movie adaptation 3.00

DRAGON'S STAR 2
Caliber Press: 1994 ($2.95, B&W)
1 .... 3.00

DRAGON STRIKE
Marvel Comics: Feb, 1994 ($1.25)
1-Based on TSR role playing game 2.25

DRAGOON WELLS MASSACRE
Dell Publishing Co.: No. 815, June, 1957

Four Color 815-Movie, photo-c	8	24	56	100

DRAGSTRIP HOTRODDERS (World of Wheels No. 17 on)
Charlton Comics: Sum, 1963; No. 2, Jan, 1965 - No. 16, Aug, 1967

1	6	18	42	70
2-5	4	12	26	40
6-16	3	9	21	32

DRAKUUN
Dark Horse Comics: Feb, 1997 - Present ($2.95, B&W, manga)
1-25; 1-6- Johji Manabe-s/a in all. Rise of the Dragon Princess series. 7-12-
Revenge of Gustav. 13-18-Shadow of the Warlock. 19-25-The Hidden War 3.00

DRAMA
Sirius: June, 1994 ($2.95, mature)
1-1st full color Dawn app. in comics 2 6 13 20
1-Limited edition (1400 copies); signed & numbered; fingerprint authenticity

Dreadstar #33 © FC

The Dreaming #54 © DC

Dreamwalker - Autumn Leaves #1 © Jenni Gregory

	GD2.0	FN6.0	VF8.0	NM9.4
	4	12	30	50

NOTE: Dawn's 1st full color app. was a pin-up in Amazing Heroes' Swimsuit Special #5.

DRAMA OF AMERICA, THE
Action Text: 1973 ($1.95, 224 pgs.)

1- "Students' Supplement to History"				5.00

DREADLANDS (Also see Epic)
Marvel Comics (Epic Comics): 1992 - No. 4, 1992 ($3.95, lim. series, 52 pgs.)

1-4: Stiff-c				4.00

DREADSTAR
Marvel Comics (Epic Comics)/First Comics No. 27 on: Nov, 1982 - No. 64, Mar, 1991

1				4.00
2-5,8-49				3.00
6,7,51-64: 6,7-1st app. Interstellar Toybox; 8pgs. ea.; Wrightson-a				4.00
50				5.00
Annual 1 (12/83)-r/The Price				4.00

DREADSTAR
Malibu Comics (Bravura): Apr, 1994 - No.6, Jan, 1995 ($2.50, limited series)

1-6-Peter David scripts: 1,2-Starlin-c				2.50

NOTE: Issues 1-6 contain Bravura stamps.

DREADSTAR AND COMPANY
Marvel Comics (Epic): July, 1985 - No. 6, Dec, 1985

1-6: 1,3,6-New Starlin-a: 2-New Wrightson-c; reprints of Dreadstar series				2.25

DREAM BOOK OF LOVE (Also see A-1 Comics)
Magazine Enterprises: No. 106, June-July, 1954 - No. 123, Oct-Nov, 1954

	GD2.0	FN6.0	VF8.0	NM9.4
A-1 106 (#1)-Powell, Bolle-a; Montgomery Clift, Donna Reed photo-c	12	36	61	100
A-1-114 (#2)-Guardineer, Bolle-a; Piper Laurie, Victor Mature photo-c	10	30	55	80
A-1 123 (#3)-Movie photo-c	9	27	49	70

DREAM BOOK OF ROMANCE (Also see A-1 Comics)
Magazine Enterprises: No. 92, 1954 - No. 124, Oct-Nov, 1954

	GD2.0	FN6.0	VF8.0	NM9.4
A-1 92 (#5)-Guardineer-a; photo-c	11	33	55	90
A-1 101 (#6)(4-6/54)-Marlon Brando photo-c; Powell, Bolle, Guardineer-a	19	57	99	165
A-1 109,110,124: 109 (#7)(7-8/54)-Powell-a; movie photo-c. 110 (#8)(1/54)-Movie photo-c. 124 (#8)(10-11/54)	9	27	49	70

DREAMER, THE
Kitchen Sink Press: 1986 ($6.95, B&W, graphic novel)

nn-Will Eisner-s/a				12.00
DC Comics Reprint ($7.95, 6/00)				8.00

DREAMERY, THE
Eclipse Comics: Dec, 1986 - No. 14, Feb, 1989 ($2.00, B&W, Baxter paper)

1-14: 2-7-Alice In Wonderland adapt.				2.25

DREAMING, THE (See Sandman, 2nd Series)
DC Comics (Vertigo): June, 1996 - No. 60, May, 2001 ($2.50)

1-McKean-c on all.; LaBan scripts & Snejbjerg-a				4.00
2-30,32-60: 2,3-LaBan scripts & Snejbjerg-a. 4-7-Hogan scripts; Parkhouse-a. 8-Zulli-a. 9-11-Talbot-a/Taylor-a(p). 41-Previews Sandman: The Dream Hunters. 50-Hempel, Fegredo, McManus, Totleben-a				2.50
31-($3.95) Art by various				4.00
...Beyond The Shores of Night TPB ('97, $19.95) r/#1-8				20.00
...Special (7/98, $5.95, one-shot) Trial of Cain				6.00
...Through The Gates of Horn and Ivory TPB ('99, $19.95) r/#15-19,22-25				20.00

DREAM OF LOVE
I. W. Enterprises: 1958 (Reprints)

	GD2.0	FN6.0	VF8.0	NM9.4
1,2,8: 1-r/Dream Book of Love #1; Bob Powell-a. 2-r/Great Lover's Romances #10. 8-r/Great Lover's Romances #1; also contains 2 Jon Juan stories by Siegel & Schomburg, Kinstler-c	2	6	11	16
9-Kinstler-c; 1pg. John Wayne interview & Frazetta illo from John Wayne Adv. Comics #2	2	6	11	16

DREAMS OF THE DARKCHYLDE
Darkchylde Entertainment: Oct, 2000 - No. 6, Sept, 2001 ($2.95)

1-6-Randy Queen-s in all. 1-Brandon Peterson-c/a				3.00

DREAM TEAM (See Battlezones: Dream Team 2)
Malibu Comics (Ultraverse): July, 1995 ($4.95, one-shot)

1-Pin-ups teaming up Marvel & Ultraverse characters by various artists including Allred, Romita, Darrow, Balent, Quesada & Palmiotti				5.00

DREAMWALKER
Dreamwalker Press: 1996 - No. 5, 1996 ($2.95, B&W)

1-5-Jenni Gregory-c/s/a				3.00

DREAMWALKER (Volume 2)
Caliber Comics (Tapestry): Dec, 1996 - No. 6, Jul, 1998 ($2.95, B&W)

1-6-Jenni Gregory-c/s/a				3.00

DREAMWALKER
Avatar Press: Jenni Gregory-c/s/a in all

#0 (11/98, $3.00)				3.00
--AUTUMN LEAVES, 9/99 - No. 2, 10/99 ($3.00) 1,2-wraparound-c				3.00
--CAROUSEL, 3/99 - No. 2, 4/99 ($3.00) 1,2				3.00
--SUMMER RAIN, 7/99 ($3.00, one-shot) 1				3.00

DRIFT FENCE (See Zane Grey 4-Color 270)

DRIFT MARLO
Dell Publishing Co.: May-July, 1962 - No. 2, Oct-Dec, 1962

	GD2.0	FN6.0	VF8.0	NM9.4
01-232-207 (#1)	4	12	30	50
2 (12-232-212)	4	12	29	45

DRISCOLL'S BOOK OF PIRATES
David McKay Publ. (Not reprints): 1934 (B&W, hardcover; 124 pgs, 7x9")

	GD2.0	FN6.0	VF8.0	NM9.4
nn-By Montford Amory	23	69	121	210

DROIDS (Also see Dark Horse Comics)
Marvel Comics (Star Comics): April, 1986 - No. 8, June, 1987
(Based on Saturday morning cartoon)

	GD2.0	FN6.0	VF8.0	NM9.4
1-R2D2 & C-3PO from Star Wars app. in all	2	6	13	20
2-8: 2,5,7,8-Williamson-a(i)	2	6	9	12

NOTE: Romita a-3p. Sinnott a-3i.

DROOPY (See Tom & Jerry #60)

DROOPY (Tex Avery's...)
Dark Horse Comics: Oct, 1995 - No. 3, Dec, 1995 ($2.50, limited series)

1-3: Characters created by Tex Avery; painted-c				2.50

DROPSIE AVENUE: THE NEIGHBORHOOD
Kitchen Sink Press: June, 1995 ($15.95/$24.95, B&W)

nn-Will Eisner (softcover)				16.00
nn-Will Eisner (hardcover)				25.00

DROWNED GIRL, THE
DC Comics (Piranha Press): 1990 ($5.95, 52 pgs, mature)

nn				6.00

DRUG WARS
Pioneer Comics: 1989 ($1.95)

1-Grell-c				2.25

DRUID
Marvel Comics: May, 1995 - No. 4, Aug, 1995 ($2.50, limited series)

1-4: Warren Ellis scripts.				2.50

DRUM BEAT
Dell Publishing Co.: No. 610, Jan, 1955

	GD2.0	FN6.0	VF8.0	NM9.4
Four Color 610-Movie, Alan Ladd photo-c	9	27	63	110

DRUMS OF DOOM
United Features Syndicate: 1937 (25¢)(Indian)(Text w/color illos.)

	GD2.0	FN6.0	VF8.0	NM9.4
nn-By Lt. F.A. Methot; Golden Thunder app.; Tip Top Comics ad in comic; nice-c	35	105	185	320

DRUNKEN FIST
Jademan Comics: Aug, 1988 - No. 54, Jan, 1993 ($1.50/$1.95, 68 pgs.)

1-54				2.50

DUCK ALBUM (See Donald Duck Album)
Dell Publishing Co.: No. 353, Oct, 1951 - No. 840, Sept, 1957

Dudley Do-Right #3 © Jay Ward

Durango Kid #4 © ME

DV8 #6 © WSP

Four Color 353 (#1)-Barks-c; 1st Uncle Scrooge-c (also appears on back-c).

	9	27	63	110
Four Color 450-Barks-c	6	18	42	80
Four Color 492,531,560,586,611,649,686,	5	15	35	60
Four Color 726,782,840	5	15	35	60

DUCKMAN
Dark Horse Comics: Sept, 1990 ($1.95, B&W, one-shot)

1-Story & art by Everett Peck   2.50

DUCKMAN
Topps Comics: Nov, 1994 - No. 5, May, 1995; No. 0, Feb, 1996 ($2.50)

0 (2/96, $2.95, B&W)-r/Duckman #1 from Dark Horse Comics   4.00
1-5: 1-w/ coupon #A for Duckman trading card. 2-w/Duckman 1st season
    episode guide   3.00

DUCKMAN: THE MOB FROG SAGA
Topps Comics: Nov, 1994 - No. 3, Feb, 1995 ($2.50, limited series)

1-3: 1-w/coupon #B for Duckman tradiing card, S. Shaw!-c   2.50

DUCKTALES
Gladstone Publ.: Oct, 1988 - No. 13, May, 1990 (1,2,9-11: 1.50; 3-8: 95¢)

1-Barks-r   6.00
2-11: 2-7,9-11-Barks-r   4.00
12,13 ($1.95, 68 pgs.)-Barks-r; 12-r/F.C. #495   5.00

DUCKTALES (TV)
Disney Comics: June, 1990 - No. 18, Nov, 1991 ($1.50)

1-All new stories   3.00
2-18   2.50
The Movie nn (1990, $7.95, 68 pgs.)-Graphic novel adapting animated movie
                                                           9.00

DUDLEY (Teen-age)
Feature/Prize Publications: Nov-Dec, 1949 - No. 3, Mar-Apr, 1950

1-By Boody Rogers	15	45	77	130
2,3	10	30	55	80

DUDLEY DO-RIGHT (TV)
Charlton Comics: Aug, 1970 - No. 7, Aug, 1971 (Jay Ward)

1	9	27	65	110
2-7	7	21	50	80

DUKE OF THE K-9 PATROL
Gold Key: Apr, 1963

1 (10052-304)	4	12	26	40

DUMBO (Disney; see Movie Comics, & Walt Disney Showcase #12)
Dell Publishing Co.: No. 17, 1941 - No. 668, Jan, 1958

Four Color 17 (#1)-Mickey Mouse, Donald Duck, Pluto app.				
	185	555	1295	2400
Large Feature Comic 19 ('41)-Part-r 4-Color 17	254	762	1778	3300
Four Color 234 ('49)	13	33	77	150
Four Color 668 (12/55)-1st of two printings. Dumbo on-c with starry sky.				
Same-c as #234	9	27	63	120
Four Color 668 (1/58)-2nd printing. Same cover altered with Timothy Mouse				
added. Same contents	6	18	42	80

DUMBO COMIC PAINT BOOK (See Dumbo, Large Feature Comic No. 19)

DUNC AND LOO (#1-3 titled "Around the Block with Dunc and Loo")
Dell Publishing Co.: Oct-Dec, 1961 - No. 8, Oct-Dec, 1963

1	9	27	63	120
2	6	18	42	80
3-8	5	15	35	60

NOTE: Written by John Stanley; Bill Williams art.

DUNCAN'S KINGDOM
Image Comics: 1999 - No. 2, 1999 ($2.95, B&W, limited series)

1,2-Gene Yang-s/Derek Kirk-a   3.00

DUNE (Movie)
Marvel Comics: Apr, 1985 - No. 3, June, 1985

1-3-r/Marvel Super Special; movie adaptation   3.00

DUNG BOYS, THE

Kitchen Sink Press: 1996 - No. 3, 1996 ($2.95, B&W, limited series)

1-3   3.00

DURANGO KID, THE (Also see Best of the West, Great Western & White
Indian) (Charles Starrett starred in Columbia's Durango Kid movies)
Magazine Enterprises: Oct-Nov, 1949 - No. 41, Oct-Nov, 1955 (All 36 pgs.)

1-Charles Starrett photo-c; Durango Kid & his horse Raider begin; Dan Brand
    & Tipi (origin) begin by Frazetta & continue through #16

	73	219	455	800
2-Starrett photo-c.	39	117	208	360
3-5-All have Starrett photo-c.	36	108	191	330
6-10: 7-Atomic weapon-c/story	20	60	105	175
11-16-Last Frazetta issue	14	42	72	120
17-Origin Durango Kid	20	60	105	175
18-30: 18-Fred Meagher-a on Dan Brand begins.19-Guardineer-c/a(3) begins,				
end #41. 23-Intro. The Red Scorpion	11	33	55	90
31-Red Scorpion returns	10	30	55	85
32-41-Bolle/Frazetta ish-a (Dan Brand; true in later issues?)				
	10	30	55	85

NOTE: #6, 8, 14, 15 contain Frazetta art not reprinted in White Indian. Ayers c-18. Guardineer
a(3)-19-41; c-19-41. Fred Meagher a-18-29 at least.

DURANGO KID, THE
AC Comics: 1990 - #2, 1990 ($2.50,$2.75, half-color)

1,2: 1-Starrett photo front/back-c; Guardineer-r. 2-B&W)-Starrett photo-c; White
    Indian-r by Frazetta; Guardineer-r (50th anniversary of films)   3.00

DUSTCOVERS: THE COLLECTED SANDMAN COVERS 1989-1997
DC Comics (Vertigo): 1997 ($39.95, Hardcover)

Reprints Dave McKean's Sandman covers with Gaiman text   40.00
Softcover (1998, $24.95)   30.00

DUSTY STAR
Image Comics (Desperado Studios): Apr, 1997 - Present ($2.95, B&W)

0,1-Pruett-s/Robinson-a   3.00

DV8 (See Gen 13)
Image Comics (WildStorm Productions): Aug, 1996 - No. 25, Dec, 1998;
DC Comics (WildStorm Prod.): No. 0, Apr, 1999 - No. 32, Nov, 1999 ($2.50)

1/2   6.00
1-Warren Ellis scripts & Humberto Ramos-c/a(p)   4.00
1-(7-variant covers, w/1 by Jim Lee...each   4.00
2-4: 3-No Ramos-a   3.00
5-32: 14-Regular-c, 14-Variant-c by Charest. 26-(5/99)-McGuinness-c 2.50
14-($3.50) Voyager Pack w/Danger Girl preview   5.00
0-(4/99, $2.95) Two covers (Rio and McGuinness)   3.00
Annual 1 (1/98, $2.95)   3.00
Annual 1999 ($3.50) Slipstream x-over with Gen13   3.50
Rave-(7/96, $1.75)-Ramos-c; pinups & interviews   3.00

DV8 VS. BLACK OPS
Image Comics (WildStorm): Oct, 1997 - No. 3, Dec, 1997 ($2.50, lim. series)

1-3-Bury-s/Norton-a   3.00

DWIGHT D. EISENHOWER
Dell Publishing Co.: December, 1969

01-237-912 - Life story	4	12	30	50

DYLAN DOG
Dark Horse (Bonelli Comics): Mar, 1999 - No. 6, Aug, 1999 ($4.95, B&W, digest
size)

1-6-Reprints Italian series in English; Mignola-c   5.00

DYNABRITE COMICS
Whitman Publishing Co.: 1978 - 1979 (69¢, 10x7-1/8", 48 pgs., cardboard-c)
(Blank inside covers)

11350 - Walt Disney's Mickey Mouse & the Beanstalk (4-C 157). 11350-1 - Mickey Mouse
Album (4-C 1057,1151,1246). 11351 - Mickey Mouse & His Sky Adventure (4-C 214, 343). 11354
- Goofy: A Gaggle of Giggles. 11354-1 - Super Goof Meets Super Thief. 11356 - (?). 11359 - Bugs
Bunny-r. 11360 - Winnie the Pooh Fun and Fantasy (Disney-r).

each....	1	3	6	8

11352 - Donald Duck (4-C 408, Donald Duck 45,52)-Barks-a. 11352-1 - Donald Duck (4-C 318,
10 pg. Barks/WDC&S 125,128)-Barks-c(r). 11353 - Daisy Duck's Diary (4-C 1055,1150) Barks-a.
11355 - Uncle Scrooge (Barks-a/U.S. 12,33). 11355-1 - Uncle Scrooge (Barks-a/U.S. 13,16) -

	GD2.0	FN6.0	VF8.0	NM9.4

Barks-c(r). 11357 - Star Trek (r/-Star Trek 33,41). 11358 - Star Trek (r/-Star Trek 34,36). 11361 - Gyro Gearloose & the Disney Ducks (r/4-C 1047,1184)-Barks-c(r).

each....	1	4	7	10

DYNAMIC ADVENTURES
I. W. Enterprises: No. 8, 1964 - No. 9, 1964

8-Kayo Kirby-r by Baker?/Fight Comics 53.	3	9	17	25
9-Reprints Avon's "Escape From Devil's Island"; Kinstler-c				
	3	9	19	28
nn (no date)-Reprints Risks Unlimited with Rip Carson, Senorita Rio; r/Fight #53				
	3	9	17	25

DYNAMIC CLASSICS (See Cancelled Comic Cavalcade)
DC Comics: Sept-Oct, 1978 (44 pgs.)

1-Neal Adams Batman, Simonson Manhunter-r	1	3	6	8

DYNAMIC COMICS (No #4-7)
Harry 'A' Chesler: Oct, 1941 - No. 3, Feb, 1942; No. 8, Mar, 1944 - No. 25, May, 1948

1-Origin Major Victory by Charles Sultan (reprinted in Major Victory #1), Dynamic Man & Hale the Magician; The Black Cobra only app.; Major Victory & Dynamic Man begin	173	579	1080	1900
2-Origin Dynamic Boy & Lady Satan; intro. The Green Knight & sidekick Lance Cooper	80	240	500	875
3-1st small logo, resumes with #10	68	204	426	750
8-Classic-c; Dan Hastings, The Echo, The Master Key, Yankee Boy begin; Yankee Doodle Jones app.; hypo story	77	231	483	850
9-Mr. E begins; Mac Raboy-c	68	204	426	750
10-Small logo begins	55	165	330	575
11-16: 15-The Sky Chief app. 16-Marijuana story	45	135	270	475
17(1/46)-Illustrated in SOTI, "The children told me what the man was going to do with the hot poker," but Wertham saw this in Crime Reporter #2				
	61	182	381	675
18,19,21,22,25: 21-Dinosaur-c; new logo	40	120	217	375
20-Bare-breasted woman-c	66	198	413	725
23,24-(68 pgs.): 23-Yankee Girl app.	40	120	232	400
I.W. Reprint #1,8('64): 1-r/#23. 8-Exist?	3	9	21	32

NOTE: Kinstler c-IW #1. Tuska art in many issues, #3, 9, 11, 12, 16, 19. Bondage c-16.

DYNAMITE (Becomes Johnny Dynamite No. 10 on)
Comic Media/Allen Hardy Publ.: May, 1953 - No. 9, Sept, 1954

1-Pete Morisi-a; Don Heck-c; r-as Danger #6	24	72	127	220
2	13	39	66	110
3-Marijuana story; Johnny Dynamite (1st app.) begins by Pete Morisi(c/a); Heck text-a; man shot in face at close range	16	48	83	140
4-Injury-to-eye, prostitution; Morisi-c/a	17	51	88	150
5-9-Morisi-c/a in all. 7-Prostitute story & reprints	12	36	61	100

DYNAMO (Also see Tales of Thunder & T.H.U.N.D.E.R. Agents)
Tower Comics: Aug, 1966 - No. 4, June, 1967 (25¢)

1-Crandall/Wood, Ditko/Wood-a; Weed series begins; NoMan & Lightning cameos; Wood-a	8	24	56	90
2-4: Wood-c/a in all	5	15	34	55

NOTE: Adkins/Wood a-2. Ditko a-4?. Tuska a-2, 3.

DYNAMO JOE (Also see First Adventures & Mars)
First Comics: May, 1986 - No. 15, Jan, 1988 (#12-15: $1.75)

1-15: 4-Cargonauts begin, Special 1(1/87)-Mostly-r/Mars				2.25

DYNOMUTT (TV)(See Scooby-Doo (3rd series))
Marvel Comics Group: Nov, 1977 - No. 6, Sept, 1978 (Hanna-Barbera)

1-The Blue Falcon, Scooby Doo in all	3	9	20	30
2-6-All newsstand only	2	6	13	20

EAGLE, THE (1st Series) (See Science Comics & Weird Comics #8)
Fox Features Syndicate: July, 1941 - No. 4, Jan, 1942

1-The Eagle begins; Rex Dexter of Mars app. by Briefer; all issues feature German war covers	182	546	1136	2000
2-The Spider Queen (origin)	84	254	525	925
3,4: 3-Joe Spook begins (origin)	68	205	426	750

EAGLE (2nd Series)
Rural Home Publ.: Feb-Mar, 1945 - No. 2, Apr-May, 1945

1-Aviation stories	43	129	257	450

2-Lucky Aces	26	78	139	240

NOTE: L. B. Cole c/a in each.

EAGLE
Crystal Comics/Apple Comics #17 on: Sept, 1986 - No. 23, 1989 ($1.50/1.75/1.95, B&W)

1-23: 12-Double size origin issue ($2.50)				2.50
1-Signed and limited				4.00

EAGLES DARE
Aager comics, Inc.: Aug, 1994 - Present? ($1.95, B&W, limited series)

1,2				2.25

EARTH 4 (Also see Urth 4)
Continuity Comics: Dec, 1993 - No. 4, Jan, 1994 ($2.50)

1-4: 1-3 all listed as Dec, 1993 in indicia				2.50

EARTH 4 DEATHWATCH 2000
Continuity Comics: Apr, 1993 - No. 3, Aug, 1993 ($2.50)

1-3				2.50

EARTH MAN ON VENUS (An...) (Also see Strange Planets)
Avon Periodicals: 1951

nn-Wood-a (26 pgs.); Fawcette-c	127	381	795	1400

EARTHWORM JIM (TV, cartoon)
Marvel Comics: Dec, 1995 - No. 3, Feb, 1996 ($2.25)

1-3: Based on video game and toys				2.25

EARTH X
Marvel Comics: No. 0, Mar, 1999 - No. 12, Apr, 2000 ($3.99/$2.99, lim. series)

nn- (Wizard supplement) Alex Ross sketchbook; painted-c				5.00
Sketchbook (2/99) New sketches and previews				5.00
0-(3/99)-Prelude; Leon-a(p)/Ross-c				5.00
1-(4/99)-Leon-a(p)/Ross-c				6.00
1-2nd printing				3.00
2-12				3.00
#X (6/00, $3.99)				4.00
TPB (12/00, $24.95) r/#0,1-12, X; foreward by Joss Whedon				25.00

EASTER BONNET SHOP (See March of Comics No. 29)

EASTER WITH MOTHER GOOSE
Dell Publishing Co.: No. 103, 1946 - No. 220, Mar, 1949

Four Color 103 (#1)-Walt Kelly-a	19	57	133	240
Four Color 140 ('47)-Kelly-a	15	45	105	190
Four Color 185 ('48),220-Kelly-a	13	39	91	165

EAST MEETS WEST
Innovation Publishing: Apr, 1990 - No. 2, 1990 ($2.50, limited series, mature)

1,2: 1-Stevens part-i; Redondo-c(i). 2-Stevens-c(i); 1st app. Cheech & Chong in comics				2.50

E. C. CLASSIC REPRINTS
East Coast Comix Co.: May, 1973 - No. 12, 1976 (E. C. Comics reprinted in color minus gale)

1-The Crypt of Terror #1 (Tales from the Crypt #46)	2	6	11	16
2-12: 2-Weird Science #15('52). 3-Shock SuspenStories #12. 4-Haunt of Fear #12. 5-Weird Fantasy #13('52). 6-Crime SuspenStories #25. 7-Vault of Horror #26. 8-Shock SuspenStories #6. 9-Two-Fisted Tales #34. 10-Haunt of Fear #23. 11-Weird Science #12(#1). 12-Shock SuspenStories #2				
		1	4	7	10

EC CLASSICS
Russ Cochran: Aug, 1985 - No. 12, 1986? (High quality paper; each-r 8 stories in color) (#2-12 were resolicited in 1990)($4.95, 56 pgs., 8x11")

1-12: 1-Tales From the Crypt. 2-Weird Science. 3-Two-Fisted Tales (r/31); Frontline Combat (r/9). 4-Shock SuspenStories. 5-Weird Fantasy. 6-Vault of Horror. 7-Weird Science-Fantasy(r/23,24). 8-Crime SuspenStories (r/17,18). 9-Haunt of Fear (r/14,15). 10-Panic (r/1,2). 11-Tales From the Crypt (r/23,24). 12-Weird Science (r/20,22)				6.00

ECHO
Image Comics (Dreamwave Prod.): Mar, 2000 - Present ($2.50)

1-5: 1-3-Pat Lee-c				2.50

Eclipso #10 © DC

Eddie Campbell's Bacchus #33 © Eddie Campbell

Edge #2 © Steven Grant & Gil Kane

	GD2.0	FN6.0	VF8.0	NM9.4

	GD2.0	FN6.0	VF8.0	NM9.4

0-(7/00) 2.50

ECHO OF FUTUREPAST
Pacific Comics/Continuity Com.: May, 1984 - No. 9, Jan, 1986 ($2.95, 52 pgs.)

1-9: Neal Adams-c/a in all? 6.00
NOTE: **N. Adams** a-1-6,7i,9i; c-1-3, 5p,7i,8,9i. **Golden** a-1-6 (Bucky O'Hare); c-6. **Toth** a-6,7.

ECLIPSE GRAPHIC ALBUM SERIES
Eclipse Comics: Oct, 1978 - 1989 (8-1/2x11") (B&W #1-5)

1-Sabre (10/78, B&W, 1st print.); Gulacy-a; 1st direct sale graphic novel
14.00
1-Sabre (2nd printing, 1/79) 8.00
1-Sabre (3rd printing, $5.95) 6.00
3,4: 3-Detectives, Inc. (5/80, B&W, $6.95)-Rogers-a. 4-Stewart The Rat (1980,
B&W)-G. Colan-a 9.00
5-The Price (10/81, B&W, Starlin-a) 15.00
2,6,7,13: 2-Night Music (11/79, B&W)-Russell-a. 6-I Am Coyote (11/84, color)-
Rogers-c/a. 7-The Rocketeer (2nd print, $7.95). 13-The Sisterhood of Steel ('87,
1991, $8.95). 13-The Sisterhood of Steel ('87, $8.95, color) 10.00
7-The Rocketeer (9/85, color)-Dave Stevens-a (r/chapters 1-5)(see Pacific
Presents & Starslayer); has 7 pgs. new-a 13.00
7-The Rocketeer, signed & limited HC 60.00
7-The Rocketeer, hardcover (1986, $19.95) 20.00
7-The Rocketeer, unsigned HC (3rd, $32.95) 33.00
8-Zorro In Old California ('86, color) 12.00
8,12-Hardcover 16.00
9,10: 9-Sacred And The Profane ('86)-Steacy-a. 10-Somerset Holmes ('86,
$15.95)-Adults, soft-c 16.00
9,10,12-Hardcover ($24.95). 12-signed & #'d 25.00
11,14,16,18,20,23,24: 11-Floyd Farland, Citizen of the Future ('87, $3.95, B&W)
14-Samurai, Son of Death ('87, $4.95, B&W). 16,18,20,23-See Airfighters
Classics #1-4. 24-Heartbreak ($4.95, B&W) 15.00
12,28,31,35: 12-Silverheels ('87, $7.95, color). 28-Miracleman Book I ($5.95)
31-Pigeons From Hell by R. E. Howard (11/88). 35-Rael: Into The Shadow of
the Sun ('88, $7.95) 9.00
14,17,21,14-Samurai, Son of Death ($3.95, 2nd printing). 17-Valkyrie, Prisoner
of the Past SC ('88, $3.95, color). 21-XYR-Multiple ending comic (`88, $3.95,
B&W) 5.00
15,22,27: 15-Twisted Tales (11/87, color)-Dave Stevens-c. 22-Alien Worlds #1
(5/88, $3.95, 52 pgs.)-Nudity. 27-Fast Fiction (She) ($5.95, B&W) 7.00
17-Valkyrie, Prisoner of the Past S&N Hardcover ('88, $19.95) 20.00
19-Scout: The Four Monsters ('88, $14.95, color)-r/Scout #1-7; soft-c 9.00
25,30,32-34: 25-Alex Toth's Zorro Vol. 1 ,2($10.95, B&W). 30-Brought To Light;
Alan Moore scripts ('89). 32-Teenaged Dope Slaves and Reform School
Girls. 33-Bogie. 34-Air Fighters Classics #5 12.00
29-Real Love: Best of Simon & Kirby Romance Comics(10/88, $12.95) 14.00
30,31: Limited hardcover ed. ($29.95). 31-signed 30.00
36-Dr. Watchstop: Adventures in Time and Space ('89, $8.95) 9.00

ECLIPSE MAGAZINE (Becomes Eclipse Monthly)
Eclipse Publishing: May, 1981 - No. 8, Jan, 1983 ($2.95, B&W, magazine)

1-8: 1-1st app. Cap'n Quick and a Foozle by Rogers, Ms. Tree by Beatty, and
Dope by Trina Robbins. 2-1st app. I Am Coyote by Rogers. 7-1st app.
Masked Man by Boyer 5.00
NOTE: **Colan** a-3, 5, 8. **Golden** c/a-2. **Gulacy** a-6, c-1, 6. **Kaluta** c/a-5. **Mayerik** a-2, 3. **Rogers**
a-1-8. **Starlin** a-1. **Sutton** a-6.

ECLIPSE MONTHLY
Eclipse Comics: Aug, 1983 - No. 10, Jul, 1984 (Baxter paper, $2.00/$1.50/$1.75)

1-10: ($2.00, 52 pgs.)-Cap'n Quick and a Foozle by Rogers, Static by Ditko,
Dope by Trina Robbins, Rio by Doug Wildey, The Masked Man by Boyer
begin. 3-Ragamuffins begins 3.00
NOTE: **Boyer** c-6. **Ditko** a-1-3. **Rogers** a-1-4; c/a-2, 4, 7. **Wildey** a-1, 2, 5, 9, 10; c-5, 10.

ECLIPSO (See Brave and the Bold #64, House of Secrets #61 & Phantom
Stranger, 1987)
DC Comics: Nov, 1992 - No. 18, Apr, 1994 ($1.25)

1-18: 1-Giffen plots/breakdowns begin. 10-Darkseid app. Creeper in #3-6,9,11-
13. 18-Spectre-c/s 2.25
Annual 1 (1993, $2.50, 68 pgs.)-Intro Prism 2.50

ECLIPSO: THE DARKNESS WITHIN
DC Comics: July, 1992 - No. 2, Oct, 1992 ($2.50, 68 pgs.)

1,2: 1-With purple gem attached to-c, 1-Without gem; Superman, Creeper app.,
2-Concludes Eclipso storyline from annuals 2.50

E. C. 3-D CLASSICS (See Three Dimensional...)

ECTOKID (See Razorline)
Marvel Comics: Sept, 1993 - No. 9, May, 1994 ($1.75/$1.95)

1-($2.50)-Foil embossed-c; created by C. Barker 3.00
2-9: 2-Origin. 5-Saint Sinner x-over 2.25
...: Unleashed! 1 (10/94, $2.95, 52 pgs.) 3.00

ED "BIG DADDY" ROTH'S RATFINK COMIX (Also see Ratfink)
World of Fandom/ Ed Roth: 1991 - No. 3, 1991 ($2.95)

1-3: Regular Ed., 1-Limited double cover	1	4	7	10

EDDIE CAMPBELL'S BACCHUS
Eddie Campbell Comics: May, 1995 - Present ($2.95, B&W)

1-Cerebus app. 6.00
1-2nd printing (5/97) 3.00
2-10: 9-Alex Ross back-c 4.00
11-60 3.00
Doing The Islands With Bacchus ('97, $17.95) 18.00
Earth, Water, Air & Fire ('98, $9.95) 10.00
King Bacchus ('99, $12.95) 13.00
The Eyeball Kid ('98, $8.50) 8.50

EDDIE STANKY (Baseball Hero)
Fawcett Publications: 1951 (New York Giants)

nn-Photo-c	35	105	185	320

EDEN MATRIX, THE
Adhesive Comics: 1994 ($2.95)

1,2-Two variant-c; alternate-c on inside back-c 3.00

EDGAR BERGEN PRESENTS CHARLIE McCARTHY
Whitman Publishing Co. (Charlie McCarthy Co.): No. 764, 1938
(36 pgs.; 15x10-1/2"; in color)

764	73	219	455	800

EDGAR RICE BURROUGHS' TARZAN: A TALE OF MUGAMBI
Dark Horse Comics: 1995 ($2.95, one-shot)

1 3.00

**EDGAR RICE BURROUGHS' TARZAN: IN THE LAND THAT TIME FORGOT
AND THE POOL OF TIME**
Dark Horse Comics: 1996 ($12.95, trade paperback)

nn-r/Russ Manning-a 13.00

EDGAR RICE BURROUGHS' TARZAN OF THE APES
Dark Horse Comics: May, 1999 ($12.95, trade paperback)

nn-reprints 13.00

EDGAR RICE BURROUGHS' TARZAN: THE LOST ADVENTURE
Dark Horse Comics: Jan, 1995 - No. 4, Apr, 1995 ($2.95, B&W, limited series)

1-4: ERB's last Tarzan story, adapted by Joe Lansdale 3.00
Hardcover (12/95, $19.95) 20.00
Limited Edition Hardcover ($99.95)-signed & numbered 100.00

EDGAR RICE BURROUGHS' TARZAN: THE RETURN OF TARZAN
Dark Horse Comics: May, 1997 - No. 3, July, 1997 ($2.95, limited series)

1-3 3.00

EDGAR RICE BURROUGHS' TARZAN: THE RIVERS OF BLOOD
Dark Horse Comics: Nov, 1999 - No. 4, Feb, 2000 ($2.95, limited series)

1-4-Kordey-c/a 3.00

EDGE
Malibu Comics (Bravura): July, 1994 - No. 3, Apr, 1995 ($2.50/$2.95, unfinished
limited series)

1,2-S. Grant-story & Gil Kane-c/a; w/Bravura stamp 2.50
3-($2.95-c) 3.00

EDGE OF CHAOS
Pacific Comics: July, 1983 - No. 3, Jan, 1984 (Limited series)

1-3-Morrow c/a; all contain nudity 2.25

Eerie #17 © AVON

Eerie (magazine) #15 © WP

Egypt #1 © Peter Milligan & Glyn Dillon

	GD2.0	FN6.0	VF8.0	NM9.4

ED WHEELAN'S JOKE BOOK STARRING FAT & SLAT (See Fat & Slat)

EERIE (Strange Worlds No. 18 on)
Avon Per.: No. 1, Jan, 1947; No. 1, May-June, 1951 - No. 17, Aug-Sept, 1954
1(1947)-1st supernatural comic; Kubert, Fugitani-a; bondage-c
    333 1000 2083 4000
1(1951)-Reprints story from 1947 #1 61 183 381 675
2-Wood-c/a; bondage-c 66 198 413 725
3-Wood-c; Kubert, Wood/Orlando-a 66 198 413 725
4,5-Wood-c 55 165 341 600
6,8,13,14: 6-Kinstler-a; bondage-c; Phantom Witch Doctor story
    31 93 165 285
7-Wood/Orlando-c; Kubert-a 43 130 257 450
9-Kubert-a; Check-a 36 108 191 330
10,11: 10-Kinstler-a. 11-Kinstlerish-a by McCann 31 93 165 285
12-Dracula story from novel, 25 pgs. 37 111 197 340
15-Reprints No. 1('51) minus-c(bondage) 24 72 127 220
16-Wood-a r-/No. 2 24 72 127 220
17-Wood/Orlando & Kubert-a; reprints #3 minus inside & outside Wood-c
    24 72 127 220
NOTE: *Hollingsworth a-9-11; c-10, 11.*

EERIE
I.W. Enterprises: 1964
I.W. Reprint #1('64)-Wood-c(r); r-story/Spook #1 4 12 26 40
I.W. Reprint #2,6,8: 8-Dr. Drew by Grandenetti from Ghost #9
    3 10 23 35
I.W. Reprint #9-r/Tales of Terror #1(Toby); Wood-c 4 12 29 45

EERIE (Magazine)(See Warren Presents)
Warren Publ. Co.: No. 1, Sept, 1965; No. 2, Mar, 1966 - No. 139, Feb, 1983
(#2-70 scarce in NM)

1-24 pgs., black & white, small size (5-1/4x7-1/4"), low distribution; cover from inside back cover of Creepy No. 2; stories reprinted from Creepy No. 7, 8. At least three different versions exist.
First Printing - B&W, 5-1/4" high, evenly trimmed. On page 18, panel 5, in the upper left-hand corner, the large rear view of a bald headed man blends into solid black and is unrecognizable. Overall printing quality is poor. 28 84 196 350
Second Printing - B&W, 5-1/4x7-1/4", with uneven, untrimmed edges (if one of these were trimmed evenly, the size would be less than as indicated). The figure of the bald headed man on page 18, panel 5 is clear and discernible. The staples have a 1/4" blue stripe.
    13 39 91 155
Other unauthorized reproductions for comparison's sake would be practically worthless. One known version was probably shot off a first printing copy with some loss of detail; the finer lines tend to disappear in this version which can be determined by looking at the lower right-hand corner of page one, first story. The roof of the house is shaded with straight lines. These lines are sharp and distinct on original, but broken on reprint.
NOTE: *The Overstreet Comic Book Price Guide recommends that, before buying a 1st issue, you consult an expert.*

2-Frazetta-c; Toth-a; 1st app. host Cousin Eerie 8 24 56 90
3-Frazetta-c & half pg. ad (rerun in #4); Toth, Williamson, Ditko-a
    6 18 48 65
4-8: 4-Frazetta-a (1/2 pg. ad). 5,7,8-Frazetta-c. Ditko-a in all.
    4 12 25 38
9-11,25: 9,10-Neal Adams-a, Ditko-a. 11-Karloff Mummy adapt.-Wood-s/a.
25-Steranko-a 4 12 26 40
12-16,18-22,24,32-35,40,45: 12,13,20-Poe-s. 12-Bloch-s. 12,15-Jones-a.
13-Lovecraft-s. 14,16-Toth-a. 16,19,24-Stoker-s. 16,32,33,43-Corben-a.
34-Early Boris-c. 35-Early Brunner-a. 35,40-Early Ploog-a. 40-Frankestein;
Ploog-a (6/72, 6 months before Marvel's series) 3 9 19 28
17 (scarce) 8 24 58 95
23-Frazetta-c; Adams-a(reprint) 4 12 29 45
24,31,36-38,43,44 3 9 21 33
39,41: 39-1st Dax the Warrior; Maroto-a. 41 (scarce) 4 12 25 38
42,51-42-('73 Annual, 84 pgs.) Spooktacular; Williamson-a. 51-('74 Annual, 76
pgs.) Color poster insert; Toth-a 3 10 23 34
46,48: 46-Dracula series by Sutton begins; 2pgs. Vampirella. 48-Begin "Mummy
Walks" and "Curse of the Werewolf" (both continue in #49,50,52,53)
    3 9 17 26
47,49,50,52,53: 47-Lilith. 49-Marvin the Dead Thing. 50-Satanna, Daughter of
Satan. 52-Hunter by Neary begins. 53-Adams-a 3 9 17 24
54,55-Color insert Spirit story by Eisner, reprints sections 12/21/47 & 6/16/46
54-Dr. Archaeus series begins 2 6 15 22

56,57,59,63,69,77,78: All have 8 pg. slick color insert. 56,57,77-Corben-a.
59-(100 pgs.) Summer Special, all Dax issue. 69-Summer Special, all Hunter
issue, Neary-a. 78-All Mummy issue 2 6 15 22
58,60,62,68,72,: 8 pg. slick color insert & Wrightson-a in all. 58,60,62-Corben-a.
60-Summer Giant (9/74, $1.25) 1st Exterminator One; Wood-a. 62-Mummies
Walk. 68-Summer Special (84 pgs.) 3 9 19 28
61,64-67,71: 61-Mummies Walk-s, Wood-a. 64-Corben-a. 64,65,67-Toth-a.
65,66-El Cid. 67-Hunter II. 71-Goblin-c/1st app. 2 6 13 20
70,73-75 2 6 11 15
76-1st app. Darklon the Mystic by Starlin-s/a 3 9 17 26
79,80-Origin Darklon the Mystic by Starlin 2 6 15 22
81,86,97: 81-Frazetta-c, King Kong; Corben-a. 86-(92 pgs.) All Corben issue.
97-Time Travel/Dinosaur issue; Corben,Adams-a 2 6 13 20
82-Origin/1st app. The Rook 3 9 17 24
83,85,88,89,91-93,98,99: 98-Rook (31 pgs.). 99-1st Horizon Seekers.
    2 6 9 12
84,87,90,96,100: 84,100-Starlin-a. 87-Hunter 3; Nino-a. 87,90-Corben-a.
96-Summer Special (92 pgs.). 100-(92 pgs.) Anniverary issue; Rook (30 pgs.)
    2 6 11 16
94,95-The Rook & Vampirella team-up. 95-Vampirella-c; 1st MacTavish
    2 6 15 17
101,106,112,115,118,120,121,128: 101-Return of Hunter II, Starlin-a. 106-Hard
John Nuclear Hit Parade Special, Corben-a. 112-All Maroto issue, Luana-s.
115-All José Ortiz issues. 118-1st Haggarth. 120-1st Zud Kamish.
121-Hunter/Darklon. 128-Starlin-a, Hsu-a 2 6 10 14
102-105,107-111,113,114,116,117,119,122-124,126,127,129: 104-Beast World.
103-105,109-111-Gulacy-a 2 6 9 12
125-(10/81, 84 pgs.) all Neal Adams issue 2 6 13 20
130-(76 pgs.) Vampirella-c/sty (54 pgs.); Pantha, Van Helsing, Huntress, Dax,
Schreck, Hunter, Exterminator One, Rook app. 2 6 15 22
131,135,137-139 (lower distr.): 131-All Wood issue. 135-(10/82, 100 pgs.) All
Ditko issue. 137-All Super-Hero issue. 138-Sherlock Holmes. 138,139-Color
comic insert 2 6 12 18
132-134,136: 132-Rook returns. 133-All Ramon Torrents-a issue. 134,136-Color
comic insert 2 6 10 14
Yearbook '70-Frazetta-c 4 12 29 45
Annual '71, '72-Reprints in both 4 12 25 38
NOTE: *The above books contain art by many good artists: **N. Adams, Brunner, Corben, Craig (Taycee), Crandall, Ditko, Eisner, Evans, Jeff Jones, Krenkel, McWilliams, Morrow, Orlando, Ploog, Severin, Starlin, Torres, Toth, Williamson, Wood,** and **Wrightson;** covers by **Bode', Corben, Davis, Frazetta, Morrow,** and **Orlando.** Frazetta c-2, 3, 7, 8, 23. Annuals from 1973-on are included in regular numbering. 1970-74 Annuals are complete reprints. Annuals from 1975-on are in the format of the regular issues.*

EERIE ADVENTURES (Also see Weird Adventures)
Ziff-Davis Publ. Co.: Winter, 1951 (Painted-c)
1-Powell-a(2), McCann-a; used in **SOTI**; bondage-c; Krigstein back-c
    40 120 220 380
NOTE: *Title dropped due to similarity to Avon's Eerie & legal action.*

EERIE TALES (Magazine)
Hastings Associates: 1959 (Black & White)
1-Williamson, Torres, Tuska-a, Powell(2), & Morrow(2)-a
    12 36 61 100

EERIE TALES
Super Comics: 1963-1964
Super Reprint No. 10,11,12,18: 10('63)-r/Spook #27. Purple Claw in #11,12
('63); #12-r/Avon's Eerie #1('51)-Kida-r 3 9 20 30
15-Wolverton-a, Spacehawk-r/Blue Bolt Weird Tales #113; Disbrow-a
    5 15 38 60

EGBERT
Arnold Publications/Quality Comics Group: Spring, 1946 - No. 20, 1950
1-Funny animal; intro Egbert & The Count 20 60 105 175
2 10 30 55 85
3-10 7 21 36 50
11-20 5 15 25 35

EGON
Dark Horse Comics: Jan, 1998 - No.2, Feb, 1998 ($2.95, limited series)
1,2-Horley-painted-c 3.00

EGYPT

80 Page Giant #9 © DC

Elektra V2 #2 © MAR

The Elementals #19 © Bill Willingham

	GD2.0	FN6.0	VF8.0	NM9.4

DC Comics (Vertigo): Aug, 1995 - No.7, Feb, 1996 ($2.50, lim. series, mature)

1-7: Milligan scripts in all.				3.00

EH! (...Dig This Crazy Comic) (From Here to Insanity No. 8 on)
Charlton Comics: Dec, 1953 - No. 7, Nov-Dec, 1954 (Satire)

1-Davis-ish-c/a by Ayers, Wood-ish-a by Giordano; Atomic Mouse app.				
	35	105	185	320
2-Ayers-c/a	21	63	110	185
3,5,7	19	57	99	165
4,6: Sexual innuendo-c. 6-Ayers-a	20	60	105	175

EIGHTBALL (Also see David Boring)
Fantagraphics Books: Oct, 1989 - Present ($2.75/$2.95/$3.95, semi-annually, mature)

1 (1st printing)	1	4	7	10
2,3				6.00
4-8				5.00
9-19: 17-(8/96)				4.00
20-($4.50)				4.50
21-($4.95) Concludes David Boring 3-parter				5.00
22-($5.95) 29 short stories				6.00

EIGHTH WONDER, THE
Dark Horse Comics: Nov, 1997 ($2.95, one-shot)

nn-Reprints stories from Dark Horse Presents #85-87				3.00

EIGHT IS ENOUGH KITE FUN BOOK (See Kite Fun Book)

80 PAGE GIANT (...Magazine No. 2-15)
National Periodical Publications: 8/64 - No. 15, 10/65; No. 16, 11/65 - No. 89, 7/71 (25¢)(All reprints) (#1-56: 84 pgs.; #57-89: 68 pgs.)

1-Superman Annual; originally planned as Superman Annual #9 (8/64)				
	38	114	304	575
2-Jimmy Olsen	22	66	176	325
3,4: 3-Lois Lane. 4-Flash-G.A.-r; Infantino-a	17	51	136	250
5-Batman; has Sunday newspaper strip; Catwoman-r; Batman's Life Story-r (25th anniversary special)	17	51	136	250
6-Superman	15	45	120	220
7-Sgt. Rock's Prize Battle Tales; Kubert-c/a	18	54	144	275
8-More Secret Origins-origins of JLA, Aquaman, Robin, Atom, & Superman; Infantino-a	32	96	256	475
9-15: 9-Flash (r/Flash #106,117,123 & Showcase #14); Infantino-a. 10-Superboy. 11-Superman; all Luthor issue. 12-Batman; has Sunday newspaper strip. 13-Jimmy Olsen. 14-Lois Lane. 15-Superman and Batman; Joker-c/story	14	42	112	210

Continued as part of regular series under each title in which that particular book came out, a Giant being published instead of the regular size. Issues No. 16 to No. 89 are listed for your information. See individual titles for prices.

16-JLA #39 (11/65), 17-Batman #176, 18-Superman #183, 19-Our Army at War #164, 20-Action #334, 21-Flash #160, 22-Superboy #129, 23-Superman #187, 24-Batman #182, 25-Jimmy Olsen #95, 26-Lois Lane #68, 27-Batman #185, 28-World's Finest #161, 29-JLA #48, 30-Batman #187, 31-Superman #193, 32-Our Army at War #177, 33-Action #347, 34-Flash #169, 35-Superboy #138, 36-Superman #197, 37-Batman #193, 38-Jimmy Olsen #104, 39-Lois Lane #77, 40-World's Finest #170, 41-JLA #58, 42-Superman #202, 43-Batman #198, 44-Our Army at War #190, 45-Action #360, 46-Flash #178, 47-Superboy #147, 48-Superman #207, 49-Batman #203, 50-Jimmy Olsen #113, 51-Lois Lane #86, 52-World's Finest #179, 53-JLA #67, 54-Superman #212, 55-Batman #208, 56-Our Army at War #203, 57-Action #373, 58-Flash #187, 59-Superboy #156, 60-Superman #217, 61-Batman #213, 62-Jimmy Olsen #122, 63-Lois Lane #95, 64-World's Finest #188, 65-JLA #76, 66-Superman #222, 67-Batman #218, 68-Our Army at War #216, 69-Adventure #390, 70-Flash #196, 71-Superboy #165, 72-Superman #227, 73-Batman #223, 74-Jimmy Olsen #131, 75-Lois Lane #104, 76-World's Finest #197, 77-JLA #85, 78-Superman #232, 79-Batman #228, 80-Our Army at War #229, 81-Adventure #403, 82-Flash #205, 83-Superboy #174, 84-Superman #239, 85-Batman #203, 86-Jimmy Olsen #140, 87-Lois Lane #113, 88-World's Finest #206, 89-JLA #93.

87TH PRECINCT (TV)
Dell Publishing Co.: Apr-June, 1962 - No. 2, July-Sept, 1962

Four Color 1309(#1)-Krigstein-a	10	30	70	130
2	9	27	63	115

EL BOMBO COMICS
Standard Comics/Frances M. McQueeny: 1946

nn(1946), 1(no date)	11	33	55	90

EL CID
Dell Publishing Co.: No. 1259, 1961

Four Color 1259-Movie, photo-c	7	21	49	90

EL DIABLO (See All-Star Western #2 & Weird Western Tales #12)
DC Comics: Aug, 1989 - No. 16, Jan, 1991 ($1.50-$1.75, color)

1 ($2.50, 52pgs.)-Masked hero				3.00
2-16				2.50

EL DIABLO
DC Comics (Vertigo): Mar, 2001 - No. 4, Jun, 2001 ($2.50, limited series)

1-4-Azzarello-s/Zezelj-a/Sale-c				2.50

EL DORADO (See Movie Classics)

ELECTRIC UNDERTOW (See Strikeforce Morituri: Electric Undertow)

ELECTRIC WARRIOR
DC Comics: May, 1986 - No. 18, Oct, 1987 ($1.50, Baxter paper)

1-18				2.25

ELECTROPOLIS
Image Comics: May, 2001 - Present ($2.95)

1-3-Dean Motter-s/a				3.00

ELEKTRA (Also see Daredevil #319-325)
Marvel Comics: Mar, 1995 - No. 4, June, 1995 ($2.95, limited series)

1-4-Embossed-c; Scott McDaniel-a				3.00

ELEKTRA (Also see Daredevil)
Marvel Comics: Nov, 1996 - No. 19, Jun, 1998 ($1.95)

1-Peter Milligan scripts; Deodato-c/a				3.00
1-Variant-c				5.00
2-19: 4-Dr. Strange-c/app. 10-Logan-c/app.				2.50
#(-1) Flashback (7/97) Matt Murdock-c/app.; Deodato-c/a				2.50
.../Cyblade (Image, 3/97,$2.95) Devil's Reign pt. 7				3.00

ELEKTRA (Vol. 2) (Marvel Knights)
Marvel Comics: Sept, 2001 - Present ($3.50/$2.99)

1-Bendis-s/Austen-a/Horn-c				5.00
2-6: 2-Two covers (Sienkiewicz and Horn) 3,4-Silver Samurai app.				3.00

ELEKTRA & WOLVERINE: THE REDEEMER
Marvel Comics: Jan, 2002 - No. 3 ($5.95, square-bound, limited series)

1-Greg Rucka-s/Yoshitaka Amano-a/c				6.00

ELEKTRA: ASSASSIN (Also see Daredevil)
Marvel Comics (Epic Comics): Aug, 1986 - No. 8, June, 1987 (Limited series, mature)

1-Miller scripts in all; Sienkiewicz-c/a.				6.00
2-8				5.00
Signed & numbered hardcover (Graphitti Designs, $39.95, 2000 print run)-reprints 1-8				50.00
TPB (2000, $24.95)				25.00

ELEKTRA LIVES AGAIN (Also see Daredevil)
Marvel Comics (Epic Comics): 1990 ($24.95, oversize, hardcover, 76 pgs.) (Produced by Graphitti Designs)

nn-Frank Miller-c/a/scripts; Lynn Varley painted-a; Matt Murdock & Bullseye app.; Elektra dies				30.00

ELEKTRA MEGAZINE
Marvel Comics: Nov, 1996 - No. 2, Dec, 1996 ($3.95, 96 pgs., reprints, limited series)

1,2: Reprints Frank Miller's Elektra stories in Daredevil				4.00

ELEKTRA SAGA, THE
Marvel Comics Group: Feb, 1984 - No. 4, June, 1984 ($2.00, limited series, Baxter paper)

1-4-r/Daredevil 168-190; Miller-c/a				3.00

ELEMENTALS, THE (See The Justice Machine & Morningstar Spec.)
Comico The Comic Co. : June, 1984 - No. 29, Sept, 1988; V2#1, Mar, 1989 - No. 28, 1994? ($1.50/$2.50, Baxter paper); V3#1, Dec, 1995 - No. 3 ($2.95)

1-Willingham-c/a, 1-8				5.00
2-29, V2#1-28: 9-Bissette-a(p). 10-Photo-c. V2#6-1st app. Strike Force America. 18-Prelude to Avalon mini-series. 27-Prequel to Strike Force America series				3.00
V3#1-3: 1-Daniel-a(p), bagged w/gaming card				3.00

Elflord V1 #3 © Aircel Pub.

Elfquest V2 #12 © Richard & Wendy Pini

Ellery Queen #1 © SUPR

EL

	GD2.0	FN6.0	VF8.0	NM9.4

_ingerie (5/96, $2.95) ... 3.00
Special 1,2 (3/86, 1/89)-1-Willingham-a(p) ... 3.00

ELEMENTALS: (Title series), Comico
--GHOST OF A CHANCE, 12/95 ($5.95)-graphic novel, nn-Ross-c. ... 6.00
--HOW THE WAR WAS WON, 6/996 - No. 2, 8/96 ($2.95) 1,2-Tony Daniel-a, & 1-Variant-c; no logo ... 3.00
--SEX SPECIAL, 5/97 - No. 2, 6/97 ($2.95 1-Tony Daniel, Jeff Moy-a, 2-Robb Phipps, Adam McDaniel-a ... 3.00
--SWIMSUIT SPECTACULAR 1996, 6/96 ($2.95), 1-pin-ups, 1-Variant-c; no logo ... 3.00
--THE VAMPIRE'S REVENGE, 6/96 - No. 2 8/96 ($2.95) 1,2-Willingham-s, 1-Variant-c; no logo ... 3.00

1111 (ELEVEN ELEVEN)
Crusade Entertainment: Oct, 1996 ($2.95, B&W, one-shot)
1-Wrightson-c/a ... 3.00

ELEVEN OR ONE
Sirius: Apr, 1995 ($2.95)

1-Linsner-c/a	1	3	6	8

1-(6/96) 2nd printing ... 3.00

ELFLORD
Aircel Publ.: 1986 - No. 6, Oct, 1989 ($1.70, B&W); V2#1- V2#31, 1995 ($2.00)
1 ... 3.00
2-4,V2#1-20,22-30: 4-6: Last B&W issue. V2#1-Color-a begin. 22-New cast.
25-Begin B&W ... 2.50
1,2-2nd printings ... 2.50
21-Double size ($4.95) ... 5.00

ELFLORD
Warp Graphics: Jan, 1997-No.4, Apr, 1997 ($2.95, B&W, mini-series)
1-4 ... 3.00

ELFLORD (CUTS LOOSE) (Vol. 2)
Warp Graphics: Sept, 1997 - No. 7, Apr, 1998 ($2.95, B&W, mini-series)
1-7 ... 3.00

ELFLORD: DRAGON'S EYE
Night Wynd Enterprises: 1993 ($2.50, B&W)
1 ... 2.50

ELFLORD: THE RETURN
Mad Monkey Press: 1996 ($6.95, magazine size)
1 ... 7.00

ELFQUEST (Also see Fantasy Quarterly & Warp Graphics Annual)
Warp Graphics, Inc.: No. 2, Aug, 1978 - No. 21, Feb, 1985 (All magazine size) No. 1, Apr, 1979
NOTE: _Elfquest_ was originally published as one of the stories in _Fantasy Quarterly #1._ When the publisher went out of business, the creative team, Wendy and Richard Pini, formed WaRP Graphics and continued the series, beginning with _Elfquest #2. Elfquest #1,_ which reprinted the story from _Fantasy Quarterly,_ was published about the same time _Elfquest #4_ was released. Thereafter, most issues were reprinted as demand warranted, until Marvel announced it would reprint the entire series under its Epic imprint (mid, 1985).

1(4/79)-Reprints Elfquest story from Fantasy Quarterly No. 1
1st printing ($1.00-c)	3	9	17	25
2nd printing ($1.25-c)	1	3	6	9
3rd printings ($1.50-c)				3.00
4th printing; different-c ($1.50-c)				2.50
2(8/78)-5: 1st printings ($1.00-c)	2	6	11	15
2nd printings ($1.25-c)				4.00
3rd & 4th printings ($1.50-c)(all 4th prints 1989)				2.50
6-9: 1st printings ($1.25-c)	1	3	6	8
2nd printings ($1.50-c)				3.00
3rd printings ($1.50-c)				2.50
10-21: ($1.50-c); 16-8pg. preview of A Distant Soil ... 5.00
10-14: 2nd printings ($1.50) ... 2.50

ELFQUEST
Marvel Comics (Epic Comics): Aug, 1985 - No. 32, Mar, 1988
1-Reprints in color the Elfquest epic by Warp Graphics ... 3.00

2-32 ... 2.50

ELFQUEST (Title series), Warp Graphics
'89 - No. 4, '89 ($1.50, B&W) 1-4: R-original Elfquest series ... 2.50

ELFQUEST (Volume 2),Warp Graphics: V2#1, 5/96 - No. 33, 2/99 ($4.95/$2.95, B&W)
V2#1-31: 1,3,5,8,10,12,13,18,21,23,25-Wendy Pini-c/a ... 5.00
32,33-($2.95-c) ... 3.00
--BLOOD OF TEN CHIEFS, 7/93 - No. 20, 9/95 ($2.00/$2.50) 1-20-By Richard & Wendy Pini ... 3.00
--HIDDEN YEARS, 5/92 - No. 29, 3/96 ($2.00/$2.25)1-9,9 1/2, 10-29 ... 3.00
--JINK, 11/94 - No. 12, 2/6 ($2.25/$2.50) 1-12-W. Pini/John Byrne-back-c ... 3.00
--KAHVI, 10/95 - No. 6,3/96 ($2.25, B&W) 1-6 ... 3.00
--KINGS CROSS, 11/97 - No. 2, 12/97 ($2.95, B&W) 1,2 ... 3.00
--KINGS OF THE BROKEN WHEEL, 6/90 - No. 9, 2/92 ($2.00, B&W) (3rd Elfquest saga) 1-9; 1-Color insert ... 3.00
1-2nd printing ... 2.50
--METAMORPHOSIS, 4/96 ($2.95, B&W) 1 ... 3.00
--NEW BLOOD (...Summer Special on-c #1 only), 8/92 - No. 35, 1/96 ($2.00-$2.50, color/B&W)
1-($3.95, 68 pgs.,....Summer Special on-c)-Byrne-a/scripts (16 pgs.) ... 4.00
2-35: Barry Blair-a in all ... 3.00
1993 Summer Special ($3.95) Byrne-a/scripts ... 4.00
--SHARDS, 8/94 - No. 16, 3/96 ($2.25/$2.50) 1-16 ... 3.00
--SIEGE AT BLUE MOUNTAIN, WaRP Graphics/Apple 3/87 - No. 8, 12/88 (1.75/ $1.95, B&W) 1-Staton-a(i) in all; 2nd Elfquest saga ... 4.00
1-3-2nd printing, 3-8 ... 2.50
2 ... 3.00
--THE REBELS, 11/94 - No. 12, 3/96 ($2.25/$2.50, B&W/color) 1-12 ... 3.00
--TWO-SPEAR, 10/95 - No. 5, 2/96 ($2.25, B&W) 1-5 ... 3.00
--WAVE DANCERS, 12/93 - No. 6, 3/96, 1-6: 1-Foil-c & poster ... 3.00
Special 1 ($2.95) ... 3.00
--WORLDPOOL, 7/97 ($2.95, B&W) 1-Richard Pini-s/Barry Blair-a ... 3.00

ELF-THING
Eclipse Comics: March, 1987 ($1.50, B&W, one-shot)
1 ... 2.25

ELIMINATOR (Also see The Solution #16 & The Night Man #16)
Malibu Comics (Ultraverse): Apr, 1995 - No. 3, Jul, 1995 ($2.95/$2.50, lim. series)
0-Mike Zeck-a in all ... 3.00
1-3-($2.50): 1-1st app. Siren ... 2.50
1-($3.95)-Black cover edition ... 4.00

ELIMINATOR FULL COLOR SPECIAL
Eternity Comics: Oct, 1991 ($2.95, one-shot)
1-Dave Dorman painted-c ... 3.00

ELLA CINDERS (See Comics On Parade, Comics Revue #1,4, Famous Comics Cartoon Book, Giant Comics Editions, Sparkler Comics, Tip Top & Treasury of Comics)
ELLA CINDERS
United Features Syndicate: 1938 - 1940
Single Series 3(1938)	40	120	232	400
Single Series 21(#2 on-c, #21 on inside), 28('40)	36	108	191	330

ELLA CINDERS
United Features Syndicate: Mar, 1948 - No. 5, Mar, 1949
1-(#2 on cover)	14	42	72	120
2	9	27	49	70
3-5	6	18	32	45

ELLERY QUEEN
Superior Comics Ltd.: May, 1949 - No. 4, Nov, 1949
1-Kamen-c; L.B. Cole-a; r-in Haunted Thrills	50	150	300	525
2-4: 3-Drug use stories(2)	40	120	214	370
NOTE: Iger shop art in all issues.

ELLERY QUEEN (TV)

Elric, Stormbringer #4 © Michael Moorcock

Elvira #100 © Queen 'B' Prods.

E-Man #5 © FC

	GD2.0	FN6.0	VF8.0	NM9.4

Ziff-Davis Publishing Co.: 1-3/52 (Spring on-c) - No. 2, Summer/52 (Saunders painted-c)

1-Saunders-c	44	132	264	460
2-Saunders bondage, torture-c	40	120	214	370

ELLERY QUEEN (Also see Crackajack Funnies No. 23)
Dell Publishing Co.: No. 1165, Mar-May, 1961 - No.1289, Apr, 1962

Four Color 1165 (#1)-	11	33	77	145
Four Color 1243 (11-1/61-61), 1289	9	27	63	115

ELMER FUDD (Also see Camp Comics, Daffy, Looney Tunes #1 & Super Book #10, 22)
Dell Publishing Co.: No. 470, May, 1953 - No. 1293, Mar-May, 1962

Four Color 470 (#1)	5	15	35	60
Four Color 558,628,689('56)	4	12	27	42
Four Color 725,783,841,888,938,977,1032,1081,1131,1171,1222,1293('62)	3	9	21	32

ELMO COMICS
St. John Publishing Co.: Jan, 1948 (Daily strip-r)

1-By Cecil Jensen	10	30	55	80

ELONGATED MAN (See Flash #112 & Justice League of America #105)
DC Comics: Jan, 1992 - No. 4, Apr, 1992 ($1.00, limited series)

1-4: 3-The Flash app.	2.25

ELRIC (Of Melnibone)(See First Comics Graphic Novel #6 & Marvel Graphic Novel #2)
Pacific Comics: Apr, 1983 - No. 6, Apr, 1984 ($1.50, Baxter paper)

1-6: Russell-c/a(i) in all	3.00

ELRIC
Topps Comics: 1996 ($2.95, one-shot)

0—One Life: Russell-c/a; adapts Neil Gaiman's short story "One Life--Furnished in Early Moorcock."	3.00

ELRIC, SAILOR ON THE SEAS OF FATE
First Comics: June, 1985 - No. 7, June, 1986 ($1.75, limited series)

1-7: Adapts Michael Moorcock's novel	3.00

ELRIC, STORMBRINGER
Dark Horse Comics/Topps Comics: 1997 - No. 7, 1997($2.95, limited series)

1-7: Russell-c/s/a; adapts Michael Moorcock's novel	3.00

ELRIC: THE BANE OF THE BLACK SWORD
First Comics: Aug, 1988 - No. 6, June, 1989 ($1.75/$1.95, limited series)

1-6: Adapts Michael Moorcock's novel	3.00

ELRIC: THE VANISHING TOWER
First Comics: Aug, 1987 - No. 6, June, 1988 ($1.75, limited series)

1-6: Adapts Michael Moorcock's novel	3.00

ELRIC: WEIRD OF THE WHITE WOLF
First Comics: Oct, 1986 - No. 5, June, 1987 ($1.75, limited series)

1-5: Adapts Michael Moorcock's novel	3.00

EL SALVADOR - A HOUSE DIVIDED
Eclipse Comics: March, 1989 ($2.50, B&W, Baxter paper, stiff-c, 52 pgs.)

1-Gives history of El Salvador	2.50

ELSEWHERE PRINCE, THE (Moebius' Airtight Garage)
Marvel Comics (Epic): May, 1990 - No. 6, Oct, 1990 ($1.95, limited series)

1-6: Moebius scripts & back-up-a in all	3.00

ELSEWORLDS 80-PAGE GIANT
DC Comics: Aug, 1999 ($5.95, one-shot)

1-Most copies destroyed by DC over content of the "Superman's Babysitter" story; some UK shipments sold before recall	150.00

ELSEWORLD'S FINEST
DC Comics: 1997 - No. 2, 1997 ($4.95, limited series)

1,2: Elseworld's story-Superman & Batman in the 1920's	5.00

ELSEWORLD'S FINEST: SUPERGIRL & BATGIRL
DC Comics: 1998 ($5.95, one-shot)

1-Haley-a				6.00

ELSIE THE COW
D. S. Publishing Co.: Oct-Nov, 1949 - No. 3, July-Aug, 1950

1-(36 pgs.)	24	72	127	220
2,3	19	57	99	165

ELSON'S PRESENTS
DC Comics: 1981 (100 pgs., no cover price)

Series 1-6: Repackaged 1981 DC comics; 1-DC Comics Presents #29, Flash #303, Batman #331. 2-Superman #335, Ghosts #96, Justice League of America #186. 3-New Teen Titans #3, Secrets of Haunted House #32, Wonder Woman #275. 4-Secrets of the LSH #1, Brave & the Bold #170, New Adv. of Superboy #13. 5-LSH #271, Green Lantern #136, Super Friends #40. 6-Action #515, Mystery in Space #115, Detective #498	2	6	9	12

ELVEN (Also see Prime)
Malibu Comics (Ultraverse): Oct, 1994 - No. 4, Feb, 1995 ($2.50, lim. series)

0 ($2.95)-Prime app.	3.00
1-4: 2,4-Prime app. 3-Primevil app.	2.50
1-Limited Foil Edition- no price on cover	3.00

ELVIRA MISTRESS OF THE DARK
Marvel Comics: Oct, 1988 ($2.00, B&W, magazine size)

1-Movie adaptation	5.00

ELVIRA MISTRESS OF THE DARK
Claypool Comics (Eclipse): May, 1993 - Present ($2.50, B&W)

1-Austin-a(i). Spiegle-a	6.00
2-6: Spiegle-a	4.00
7-99-Photo-c	2.50
100-(8/01) Kurt Busiek back-up-s; art by DeCarlo and others	2.50
TPB ($12.95)	13.00

ELVIRA'S HOUSE OF MYSTERY
DC Comics: Jan, 1986 - No. 11, Jan, 1987

1,11: 11-Dave Stevens-c	6.00
2-10: 9-Photo-c, Special 1 (3/87, $1.25)	4.00

ELVIS MANDIBLE, THE
DC Comics (Piranha Press): 1990 ($3.50, 52 pgs., B&W, mature)

nn	3.50

ELVIS PRESLEY (See Career Girl Romances #32, Go-Go, Howard Chaykin's American Flagg #10, Humbug #8, I Love You #60 & Young Lovers #18)

E-MAN
Charlton Comics: Oct, 1973 - No. 10, Sept, 1975 (Painted-c No. 7-10)

1-Origin & 1st app. E-Man; Staton c/a in all	2	6	13	20
2-4: 2-Ditko-a. 3-Howard-a	1	3	6	9
5-Miss Liberty Belle app. by Ditko	1	3	6	8
6-10: 6,7,9,10-Early Byrne-a (#6 is 1/75). 6-Disney parody. 8-Full-length story; Nova begins as E-Man's partner	2	6	9	12
1-4,9,10(Modern Comics reprints, '77)				4.00

NOTE: Killjoy app.-No. 2, 4. Liberty Belle app.-No. 5. Rog 2000 app.-No. 6, 7, 9, 10. Travis app.-No. 3. **Tom Sutton** a-1.

E-MAN
Comico: Sept, 1989 ($2.75, one-shot, no ads, high quality paper)

1-Staton-c/a; Michael Mauser story	2.75

E-MAN
Comico: V4#1, Jan, 1990 - No. 3, Mar, 1990 ($2.50, limited series)

1-3: Staton-c/a	2.50

E-MAN
Alpha Productions: Oct, 1993 ($2.75)

V5#1-Staton-c/a; 20th anniversary issue	2.75

E-MAN COMICS (Also see Michael Mauser & The Original E-Man)
First Comics: Apr, 1983 - No. 25, Aug, 1985 ($1.00/$1.25, direct sales only)

1-25: 2-X-Men satire. 3-X-Men/Phoenix satire. 6-Origin retold. 8-Cutey Bunny app. 10-Origin Nova Kane. 24-Origin Michael Mauser	2.50

NOTE: **Staton** a-1-5, 6-25p; c-1-25.

Elvira #100 © Queen 'B' Prods.

E-Man #5 © FC

	GD2.0	FN6.0	VF8.0	NM9.4

	GD2.0	FN6.0	VF8.0	NM9.4

E-MAN RETURNS
Alpha Productions: 1994 ($2.75, B&W)

1-Joe Staton-c/a(p)			2.75

EMERALD DAWN
DC Comics: 1991 ($4.95, trade paperback)

nn-Reprints Green Lantern: Emerald Dawn #1-6			5.00

EMERALD DAWN II (See Green Lantern...)

EMERGENCY (Magazine)
Charlton Comics: June, 1976 - No. 4, Jan, 1977 (B&W)

1-Neal Adams-c/a; Heath, Austin-a	3	9	21	32
2,3: 2-N. Adams-c. 3-N. Adams-a.	3	9	19	28
4-Alcala-a	2	6	13	20

EMERGENCY (TV)
Charlton Comics: June, 1976 - No. 4, Dec, 1976

1-Staton-c; early Byrne-a (22 pages)	3	9	19	28
2-4: 2-Staton-c. 2,3-Byrne text illos.	2	6	12	18

EMERGENCY DOCTOR
Charlton Comics: Summer, 1963 (one-shot)

1	3	9	20	30

EMIL & THE DETECTIVES (See Movie Comics)

EMMA PEEL & JOHN STEED (See The Avengers)

EMPEROR'S NEW CLOTHES, THE
Dell Publishing Co.: 1950 (10¢, 68 pgs., 1/2 size, oblong)

nn - (Surprise Books series)	4	12	19	25

EMPIRE
Image Comics (Gorilla): May, 2000 - Present ($2.50)

1,2: 1-Waid-s/a; w/Crimson Plague prologue			2.50

EMPIRE STRIKES BACK, THE (See Marvel Comics Super Special #16 & Marvel Special Edition)

EMPTY LOVE STORIES
Slave Labor #1 & 2/Funny Valentine Press: Nov, 1994 - Present ($2.95, B&W)

1,2: Steve Darnell scripts in all. 1-Alex Ross-c. 2-(8/96)-Mike Allred-c			4.00
1,2-2nd printing (Funny Valentine Press)			3.00
... 1999-Jeff Smith; Doran-a			3.00
..."Special" (2.95) Ty Templeton-c			3.00

ENCHANTED
Sirius Entertainment: 1997 - No. 3 ($2.50, B&W, limited series)

1-3-Robert Chang-s/a			2.50

ENCHANTED (Volume 2)
Sirius Entertainment: 1998 - No. 3 ($2.95, limited series)

1-Robert Chang-s/a			3.00

ENCHANTED APPLES OF OZ, THE (See First Comics Graphic Novel #5)

ENCHANTER
Eclipse Comics: Apr, 1987 - No. 3, Aug. 1987 ($2.00, B&W, limited series)

1-3			2.25

ENCHANTING LOVE
Kirby Publishing Co.: Oct, 1949 - No. 6, July, 1950 (All 52 pgs.)

1-Photo-c	14	42	72	120
2-Photo-c; Powell-a	8	24	42	60
3,4,6: 3-Jimmy Stewart photo-c	7	21	38	55
5-Ingels-a, 9 pgs.; photo-c	15	45	77	130

ENCHANTMENT VISUALETTES (Magazine)
World Editions: Dec, 1949 - No. 5, Apr, 1950 (Painted c-1)

1-Contains two romance comic strips each	15	45	77	130
2	11	33	55	90
3-5	10	30	55	80

ENEMY
Dark Horse Comics: May, 1994 - No. 5, Sept, 1994 ($2.50, limited series)

1-5			2.50

ENEMY ACE SPECIAL (Also see Our Army at War #151, Showcase #57, 58 & Star Spangled War Stories #138)
DC Comics: 1990 ($1.00, one-shot)

1-Kubert-r/Our Army #151,153; c-r/Showcase 57			5.00

ENEMY ACE: WAR IDYLL
DC Comics: 1990 (Graphic novel)

Hardcover-George Pratt-s/painted-a/c			30.00
Softcover (1991, $14.95)			15.00

ENEMY ACE: WAR IN HEAVEN
DC Comics: 2001 - No. 2, 2001 ($5.95, squarebound, limited series)

1,2-Ennis-s; Von Hammer in WW2. 1-Weston & Alamy-a. 2-Heath-a			6.00

ENIGMA
DC Comics (Vertigo): Mar, 1993 - No. 8, Oct, 1993 ($2.50, limited series)

1-8: Milligan scripts			2.50
Trade paperback ($19.95)-reprints			20.00

ENO AND PLUM (Also see Cud Comics)
Oni Press: Mar, 1998 ($2.95, B&W)

1-Terry LaBan-s/c/a			3.00

ENSIGN O'TOOLE (TV)
Dell Publishing Co.: Aug-Oct, 1963 - No. 2, 1964

1	3	9	20	30
2	3	9	17	25

ENSIGN PULVER (See Movie Classics)

EPIC
Marvel Comics (Epic Comics): 1992 - Book 4, 1992 ($4.95, lim. series, 52 pgs.)

Book One-Four: 2-Dorman painted-c			5.00

NOTE: Alien Legion in #3. Cholly & Flytrap by **Burden**(scripts) & **Suydam**(art) in 3, 4. Dinosaurs in #4. Dreadlands in #1. Hellraiser in #1. Nightbreed in #2. Sleeze Brothers in #2. Stalkers in #1-4. Wild Cards in #1.

EPIC ILLUSTRATED (Magazine)
Marvel Comics Group: Spring, 1980 - No. 34, Feb, 1986 ($2.00/$2.50, B&W/color, mature)

1-10: 1-Frazetta-c; Silver Surfer/Galactus-sty; Wendy Pini-s/a; Suydam-s/a; Metamorphosis Odyssey begins (thru #9) Starlin-a. 2-Bissette/Veitch-a; Goodwin-s. 3-Goodwin-s. 4-Ellison 15 pg. story w/art by Steacy; Hempel-s/a; Veitch-s/a. 5-Hildebrandts-c/interview; Jusko-a; Vess-s/a. 6-Ellison-s (26 pgs). 7-Adams-a(16 pgs.); BWS interview. 8-Suydam-s/a; Vess-s/a. 9-Conrad-c. 10-Marada the She-Wolf-c/sty(21 pgs.) by Claremont and Bolton				6.00
11-20: 11-Wood-a; Jusko-a. 12-Wolverton Spacehawk-r edited & recolored w/article on him; Muth-a. 13-Blade Runner preview by Williamson. 14-Elric of Melnibone by Russell; Revenge of the Jedi preview. 15-Vallejo-c & interview; 1st Dreadstar story (cont'd in Dreadstar #1). 16-B. Smith-c/a(2); Sim-s/a. 17-Starslammers preview. 18-Go Nagai; Williams-a. 19-Jabberwocky w/Hampton-a; Cheech Wizard-s. 20-The Sacred & the Profane begins by Ken Steacy; Elric by Gould; Williams-a	1	3	5	7
21-30: 21-Vess-s/a. 22-Frankenstein w/Wrightson-a. 26-Galactus series begins (thru #34); Cerebus the Aardvark story by Dave Sim. 27-Groo. 28-Cerebus. 29-1st Sheeva. 30-Cerebus; History of Dreadstar, Starlin-s/a; Williams-a; Vess-a	1	3	6	9
31-33: 31-Bolton-c/a. 32-Cerebus portfolio.	2	5	9	12
34-R.E.Howard tribute by Thomas-/Plunkett-a; Moore-s/Veitch-a; Cerebus; Cholly & Flytrap w/Suydam-a; BWS-a	2	6	12	18

NOTE: **N. Adams** a-7; c-6. **Austin** a-15-20i. **Bode** a-19, 23, 27r. **Bolton** a-7, 10-12, 15, 18, 22-25; c-10, 18, 22, 23. **Boris** c/a-15. **Brunner** c-12. **Buscema** a-1p; 9p, 11-13p, **Byrne/Austin** a-26-34. **Chaykin** a-2; c-6. **Conrad** a-2-5, 7-9, 25-34; c-17. **Corben** a-15; c-2. **Frazetta** c-1. **Golden** a-3r. **Gulacy** c/a-3. **Jeff Jones** c-1. **Kaluta** a-17r, 21, 24r, 26; c-4, 28. **Nebres** a-1. **Reese** a-12. **Russell** a-2-4, 9, 14, 33; c-14. **Simonson** a-17. **B. Smith** c/a-7, 16. **Starlin** a-1-9, 14, 15, 34. **Steranko** c-19. **Williamson** a-13, 27, 34. **Wrightson** a-13p, 22, 25, 27, 34; c-30.

EPIC LITE
Marvel Comics (Epic Comics): Sept, 1991 ($3.95, 52 pgs., one-shot)

1-Bob the Alien, Normalman by Valentino			4.00

EPICURUS THE SAGE
DC Comics (Piranha Press): Vol. 1, 1991 - Vol. 2, 1991 ($9.95, 8-1/8x10-7/8")

Volume 1,2-Sam Kieth-c/a			10.00

EPSILON WAVE
Independent Comics/Elite Comics No. 5 on: Oct, 1985 - V2#2, 1987

	GD2.0	FN6.0	VF8.0	NM9.4

($1.50/$1.25/$1.75)

1-8,V2#1,2: 1-3,6-Seadragon app. V2 (B&W)   2.25

ERADICATOR
DC Comics: Aug, 1996 - No. 3, Oct, 1996 ($1.75, limited series)

1-3: Superman app.   3.00

ERNIE COMICS (Formerly Andy Comics #21; All Love Romances #26 on)
Current Books/Ace Periodicals: No. 22, Sept, 1948 - No. 25, Mar, 1949

nn (9/48,11/48; #22,23)-Teenage humor	6	18	32	45
24,25	5	15	24	32

ESCAPADE IN FLORENCE (See Movie Comics)

ESCAPE FROM DEVIL'S ISLAND
Avon Periodicals: 1952

1-Kinstler-c; r/as Dynamic Adventures #9	39	117	208	360

ESCAPE FROM THE PLANET OF THE APES (See Power Record Comics)

ESCAPE TO WITCH MOUNTAIN (See Walt Disney Showcase No. 29)

ESPERS (Also see Interface)
Eclipse Comics: July, 1986 - No. 5, Apr, 1987 ($1.25/$1.75, Mando paper)

1-5-James Hudnall story & David Lloyd-a.   3.00

ESPERS
Halloween Comics: V2#1, 1996 - No. 6, 1997 ($2.95, B&W)
(1st Halloween Comics series)

V2#1-6: James D. Hudnall scripts	3.00
Undertow TPB ('98, $14.95) r/#1-6	15.00

ESPERS
Image Comics: V3#1, 1997 - Present ($2.95, B&W, limited series)

V3#1-7: James D. Hudnall scripts	3.00
Black Magic TPB ('98, $14.95) r/#1-4	15.00

ESPIONAGE (TV)
Dell Publishing Co.: May-July, 1964 - No. 2, Aug-Oct, 1964

1,2	3	9	21	32

ESSENTIAL (Title series), **Marvel Comics**

--AVENGERS, '98 (B&W- r) V1-R-Avengers #1-24; new Immonen-c   15.00
V2(6/00)-Reprints Avengers #25-46, King-Size Special #1; Immonen-c   15.00
V3(3/01)-Reprints Avengers #47-68, Annual #2; Immonen-c   15.00

--CAPTAIN AMERICA, '00 (B&W- r) V1-Reprints stories from Tales of Suspense
#59-99, Captain America #100-102; new Romita & Milgrom-c   15.00

--CONAN, '00 (B&W- r) V1-R-Conan the Barbarian#1-25; new Buscema-c 15.00

--FANTASTIC FOUR, '98 - Present (B&W-r)
V1-Reprints FF #1-20, Annual #1; new Alan Davis-c   15.00
V2-Reprints FF #21-40, Annual #2; Davis and Farmer-c   15.00
V3-Reprints FF #41-63, Annual #3,4; Davis-c   15.00

--HULK, '99 (B&W-r) V1-R-Incred. Hulk #1-6, Tales To Astonish stories; new
Bruce Timm-c   15.00
V2-Reprints Tales To Astonish #102-117, Annual #1   15.00

--IRON MAN, '00 (B&W-r) V1-Tales Of Suspense #39-72; new Timm-c and
back-c   15.00

--SILVER SURFER, '98 (B&W-r) V1-R-material from SS#1-18 and Fantastic Four
Annual #1   15.00

--SPIDER-MAN, '96 - Present (B&W-r)
V1-R-AF #15, Amaz. S-M #1-20, Ann. #1 (2 printings)   15.00
V2-R-Amaz. Spider-Man #21-43, Annual #2,3   15.00
V3-R-Amaz. Spider-Man #44-68   15.00
V4-R-Amaz. Spider-Man #69-89; Annual #4,5; new Timm-f&b-c   15.00

--THOR, '01 (B&W-r) V1-R-Journey Into Mystery #83-112   15.00

--UNCANNY X-MEN, '99 - Present (B&W reprints)
V1-Reprints X-Men (1st series) #1-24; Timm-c   15.00

ESSENTIAL VERTIGO: THE SANDMAN
DC Comics (Vertigo): Aug, 1996 - No. 32, Mar, 1999 ($1.95/$2.25, reprints)

1-13,15-31: Reprints Sandman, 2nd series	3.00
14-($2.95)	3.50

32-($4.50) Reprints Sandman Special #1   4.50

ESSENTIAL VERTIGO: SWAMP THING
DC Comics: Nov, 1996 - No. 24, Oct, 1998 ($1.95/$2.25,B&W, reprints)

1-11,13-24: 1-9-Reprints Alan Moore's Swamp Thing stories	3.00
12-($3.50) r/Annual #2	3.50

ESSENTIAL WOLVERINE
Marvel Comics: 1999 - Present (B&W reprints)

V1-r/#1-23, V2-r/#24-47, V3-R/#48-69   15.00

ESSENTIAL X-MEN
Marvel Comics: 1996 - Present (B&W reprints)

V1, V2-Reprints, V3--R-Uncanny X-Men #145-161, Ann. #3-5   15.00
V4-Uncanny X-Men #162-179, Ann. #6   15.00

ESTABLISHMENT, THE (Also see The Authority and The Monarchy)
DC Comics (WildStorm): Nov, 2001 - Present ($2.50)

1-4-Edginton-s/Adlard-a   2.50

ETC
DC Comics (Piranha Press): 1989 - No. 5, 1990 ($4.50, 60 pgs., mature)

Book 1-5: Conrad scripts/layouts in all   4.50

ETERNAL BIBLE, THE
Authentic Publications: 1946 (Large size) (16 pgs. in color)

1	15	45	77	130

ETERNALS, THE
Marvel Comics Group: July, 1976 - No. 19, Jan, 1978

1-(Regular 25¢ edition)-Origin & 1st app. Eternals	2	6	11	15
1-(30¢-c variant, limited distribution)	2	6	15	22
2-(Regular 25¢ edition)-1st app. Ajak & The Celestials	1	3	6	8
2-(30¢-c variant, limited distribution)	2	6	9	12
3-19: 14,15-Cosmic powered Hulk-c/story	1	3	6	8
12-16-(35¢-c variants, limited distribution)	2	6	9	12
Annual 1(10/77)	1	3	6	8

NOTE: *Kirby* c/a(p) in all.

ETERNALS, THE
Marvel Comics: Oct, 1985 - No. 12, Sept, 1986 (Maxi-series, mando paper)

1,12 (52 pgs.): 12-Williamson-a(i)	3.00
2-11	2.50

ETERNALS: THE HEROD FACTOR
Marvel Comics: Nov, 1991 ($2.50, 68 pgs.)

1   2.50

ETERNAL WARRIOR (See Solar #10 & 11)
Valiant/Acclaim Comics (Valiant): Aug, 1992 - No. 50, Mar, 1996 ($2.25/$2.50)

1-Unity x-over; Miller-c; origin Eternal Warrior & Aram (Armstrong)	4.00
1-Gold logo	5.00
1-Gold foil logo	6.00
2-8: 2-Unity x-over; Simonson-c. 3-Archer & Armstrong x-over. 4-1st app. Bloodshot (last pg. cameo); see Rai #0 for 1st full app.; Cowan-c. 5-2nd full app. Bloodshot (12/92; see Rai #0). 6,7: 6-2nd app. Master Darque. 8-Flip book w/Archer & Armstrong #8	3.00
9-25,27-34: 9-1st Book of Geomancer. 14-16-Bloodshot app. 18-Doctor Mirage cameo. 19-Doctor Mirage app. 22-W/bound-in trading card. 25-Archer & Armstrong app.; cont'd from A&A #25	2.50
26-($2.75, 44 pgs.)-Flip book w/Archer & Armstrong	2.75
35-50: 35-Double-c; $2.50-c begins. 50-Geomancer app.	2.50
Special 1 (2/96, $2.50)-Art Holcomb script	2.50
Yearbook 1 (1993, $3.95), 2(1994, $3.95)	4.00

ETERNAL WARRIORS: BLACKWORKS
Acclaim Comics (Valiant Heroes): Mar, 1998 ($3.50, one-shot)

1   3.50

ETERNAL WARRIORS: DIGITAL ALCHEMY
Acclaim Comics (Valiant Heroes): Vol. 2, Sep, 1997 ($3.95, one-shot, 64 pgs.)

Vol. 2-Holcomb-s/Eaglesham-a(p)   4.00

ETERNAL WARRIORS: FIST AND STEEL
Acclaim Comics (Valiant): May, 1996 - No. 2, June, 1996 ($2.50, lim. series)

Etta Kett #11 © KING

E.V.E. Protomecha #2 © Lusen & Lichtner

Everything's Archie #157 © AP

	GD2.0	FN6.0	VF8.0	NM9.4

1,2: Geomancer app. in both. 1-Indicia reads "June." 2-Bo Hampton-a 2.50

ETERNAL WARRIORS: TIME AND TREACHERY
Acclaim Comics (Valiant Heroes): Vol. 1, Jun, 1997 ($3.95, one-shot, 48 pgs.)
Vol. 1-Reintro Aram, Archer, Ivar the Timewalker, & Gilad the Warmaster;
1st app. Shalla Redburn; Art Holcomb script 4.00

ETERNITY SMITH
Renegade Press: Sept, 1986 - No. 5, May, 1987 ($1.25/$1.50, 36 pgs.)
1-5: 1st app. Eternity Smith. 5-Death of Jasmine 2.25

ETERNITY SMITH
Hero Comics: Sept, 1987 - No. 9, 1988 ($1.95)
V2#1-9: 8-Indigo begins 2.25

ETTA KETT
King Features Syndicate/Standard: No. 11, Dec, 1948 - No. 14, Sept, 1949

11-Teenage	9	27	49	70
12-14	6	18	32	45

EUDAEMON, THE (See Dark Horse Presents #72-74)
Dark Horse Comics: Aug, 1993 - No. 3, 1993 ($2.50, limited series)
1-3: Nelson-a, painted-c & scripts 2.50

EUROPA AND THE PIRATE TWINS
Powder Monkey Productions: Oct, 1996 - No. 2, ($2.50, B&W, limited series)
1,2: Two covers 2.50

EVANGELINE (Also see Primer)
Comico/First Comics V2#1 on/Lodestone Publ.: 1984 - #2, 6/84; V2#1, 5/87 -
V2#12, Mar, 1989 (Baxter paper)
1,2, V2#1 (5/87) - 12, Special #1 (1986, $2.00)-Lodestone Publ. 2.25

EVA THE IMP
Red Top Comic/Decker: 1957 - No. 2, Nov, 1957

1,2	4	12	18	24

E.V.E. PROTOMECHA
Image Comics (Top Cow): Mar, 2000 - No. 6, Sept, 2000 ($2.50)

Preview ($5.95) Flip book w/Soul Saga preview	2	6	9	12
1-6: 1-Covers by Finch, Madureira, Garza. 2-Turner var-c				3.00
1-Another Universe variant-c				5.00
TPB (5/01, $17.95) r/#1-6 plus cover galley and sketch pages				18.00

EVERYBODY'S COMICS (See Fox Giants)

EVERYMAN, THE
Marvel Comics (Epic Comics): Nov, 1991 ($4.50, one-shot, 52 pgs.)

1-Mike Allred-a	1	3	5	7

EVERYTHING HAPPENS TO HARVEY
National Periodical Publications: Sept-Oct, 1953 - No. 7, Sept-Oct, 1954

1	26	78	139	240
2	15	45	77	130
3-7	12	36	61	100

EVERYTHING'S ARCHIE
Archie Publications: May, 1969 - No. 157, Sept, 1991 (Giant issues No. 1-20)

1-(68 pages)	8	24	56	90
2-(68 pages)	5	15	38	60
3-5-(68 pages)	4	12	29	45
6-13-(68 pages)	3	9	20	30
14-31-(52 pages)	2	6	13	20
32 (7/74)-50 (8/76)	1	4	7	10
51-80 (12/79),100 (4/82)	1	3	6	8
81-99				6.00
101-120				5.00
121-156: 142,148-Gene Colan-a				4.00
157-Last issue				5.00

EVERYTHING'S DUCKY (Movie)
Dell Publishing Co.: No. 1251, 1961

Four Color 1251	4	12	30	50

EVIL ERNIE
Eternity Comics: Dec, 1991 - No. 5, 1992 ($2.50, B&W, limited series)

1-1st app. Lady Death by Steven Hughes (12,000 print run); Lady Death app. in all issues	4	12	30	50
2,3: 2-1st Lady Death-c. 2,3-(7,000 print run)	3	9	17	25
4-(8,000 print run)	2	6	13	20
5	2	6	11	16
Special Edition 1	3	9	17	25
Youth Gone Wild! ($9.95, trade paperback)-r/#1-5	1	4	7	10
Youth Gone Wild! Director's Cut ($4.95)-Limited to 15,000 copies, shows the making of the comic				5.00

EVIL ERNIE (Monthly series)
Chaos! Comics: July, 1998 - No. 10, Apr, 1999 ($2.95)

1-10-Pulido & Nutman-s/Brewer-a				3.00
1-($10.00) Premium Ed.				10.00

EVIL ERNIE: BADDEST BATTLES
Chaos! Comics: Jan, 1997 ($1.50, one-shot)
1-Pin-ups, 1-Variant-c 3.00

EVIL ERNIE: DEPRAVED
Chaos! Comics: Jul, 1999 - No. 3, Sept, 1999 ($2.95, limited series)
1-3-Pulido-s/Brewer-a 3.00

EVIL ERNIE: DESTROYER
Chaos! Comics: Oct, 1997 - No. 9, Jun, 1998 ($2.95, limited series)
Preview ($2.50), 1-9-Flip cover 3.00

EVIL ERNIE: PIECES OF ME
Chaos! Comics: Nov, 2000 ($2.95, B&W, one-shot)
1-Flashback story; Pulido-s/Beck-a 3.00

EVIL ERNIE: RETURNS
Chaos! Comics (Black Label Graphics): Oct, 2001 ($3.99, B&W, one-shot)
1-Pulido-s/Beck-a 4.00

EVIL ERNIE: REVENGE
Chaos! Comics: Oct, 1994 - No.4, Feb, 1995 ($2.95, limited series)

1: 1-Glow-in-the-dark-c; Lady Death app. 1-3-flip book w. Kilzone Preview (series of 3)				5.00
1-Commemorative-(4000 print run)	1	4	7	10
2-4				4.00
Trade paperback (10/95, $12.95)				13.00

EVIL ERNIE: STRAIGHT TO HELL
Chaos! Comics: Oct, 1995 - No. 5, May, 1996 ($2.95, limited series)

1-5-fold-out-c				3.00
1,3:1-($19.95) Chromium Ed. 3-Chastity Chase-c-(4000 printed)				20.00
Special Edition (10,000)				20.00

EVIL ERNIE: THE RESURRECTION
Chaos! Comics: 1993 - No. 4, 1994 (Limited series)

0				5.00
1	2	6	9	12
1A-Gold	3	9	20	30
2-4	1	3	6	8

EVIL ERNIE VS. THE MOVIE MONSTERS
Chaos! Comics: Mar, 1997 ($2.95, one-shot)

1				3.00
1-Variant-"Chaos-Scope•Terror Vision" card stock-c				5.00

EVIL ERNIE VS. THE SUPER HEROES
Chaos! Comics: Aug, 1995; Sept, 1998 ($2.95)

1-Lady Death poster				3.00
1-Foil-c variant (limited to 10,000)	2	6	13	20
1-Limited Edition (1000)	2	6	13	20
2-(9/98) Ernie vs. JLA and Marvel parodies				3.00

EVIL ERNIE: WAR OF THE DEAD
Chaos! Comics: Nov, 1999 - No. 3, Jan, 2000 ($2.95, limited series)
1-3-Pulido & Kaminski-s/Brewer-a. 3-End of Evil Ernie 3.00

EVIL EYE
Fantagraphics Books: June, 1998 - Present ($2.95/$3.50, B&W)
1-7-Richard Sala-s/a 3.00

Ewoks #5 © Lucasfilm

Excalibur #116 © MAR

Exciting Comics #10 © STD

	GD2.0	FN6.0	VF8.0	NM9.4

8-($3.50) 3.50

EWOKS (Star Wars) (TV) (See Star Comics Magazine)
Marvel Comics (Star Comics): June, 1985 - No. 14, Jul, 1987 (75¢/$1.00)

1,10: 10-Williamson-a (From Star Wars)	2	6	11	15
2-9	2	6	9	12
11-14: 14-($1.00-c)	2	6	10	14

EXCALIBUR (Also see Marvel Comics Presents #31)
Marvel Comics: Apr, 1988; Oct, 1988 - No. 125, Oct, 1998 ($1.50/1.75/$1.99)

Special Edition nn (The Sword is Drawn)(4/88, $3.25)-1st Excalibur comic 6.00
Special Edition nn (4/88)-no price on-c 1 4 7 10
Special Edition nn (2nd & print, 10/88, 12/89) 3.00
...The Sword is Drawn (Apr, 1992, $4.95) 5.00
1($1.50, 10/88)-X-Men spin-off; Nightcrawler, Shadowcat(Kitty Pryde), Capt.
Britain, Phoenix & Meggan begin 5.00
2-4 4.00
5-10 3.00
11-49,51-70,72-74,76: 10,11-Rogers/Austin-a; Austin-i. 21-Intro Crusader X. 22-
Iron Man x-over. 24-John Byrne app. in story. 26-Ron Lim-c/a. 27-B. Smith-
a(p). 37-Dr. Doom & Iron Man app. 41-X-Men (Wolverine) app.; Cable cameo
49-Neal Adams c-swipe. 52,57-X-Men(Cyclops, Wolverine) app. 53-Spider-
Man-c/story. 58-X-Men (Wolverine, Gambit, Cyclops, etc.)-c/story. 61-Phoenix
returns. 68-Starjammers c/story 2.50
50-($2.75, 56 pgs.)-New logo 3.00
71-($3.95, 52 pgs.)-Hologram on-c; 30th anniversary 5.00
75-($3.50, 52 pgs.)-Holo-grafx foil-c 4.00
75-($2.25, 52 pgs.)-Regular edition 2.50
77-81,83-86: 77-Begin $1.95-c; bound-in trading card sheet. 83-86-Deluxe
Editions and Standard Editions. 86-1st app. Pete Wisdom 2.50
82-($2.50)-Newsstand edition 4.00
82-($3.50)-Enhanced edition 4.00
87-89,91-99,101-110: 87-Return from Age of Apocalypse. 92-Colossus-c/app.
94-Days of Future Tense 95-X-Man-c/app. 96-Sebastian Shaw & the
Hellfire Club app. 99-Onslaught tie-in. 101-Onslaught tie-in. 102-w/card insert.
103-Last Warren Ellis scripts; Belasco app. 104,105-Hitch & Neary-c/a.
109-Spiral-c/app. 2.50
90,100-($2.95)-double-sized. 100-Onslaught tie-in; wraparound-c 4.00
111-124: 111-Begin $1.99-c, wraparound-c. 119-Calafiore-a 2.50
125-($2.99) Wedding of Capt. Britain and Meggan 4.00
Annual 1,2 ('93, '94, 68 pgs.)-1st app. Khaos. 2-X-Men & Psylocke app. 3.00
#(-1) Flashback (7/97) 2.50
...Air Apparent nn (12/91, $4.95)-Simonson-c 5.00
...Mojo Mayhem nn (12/89, $4.50)-Art Adams/Austin-c/a 5.00
...: The Possession nn (7/91, $2.95, 52 pgs.) 3.00
...: XX Crossing (7/92, 5/92-inside, $2.50)-vs. The X-Men 2.50

EXCALIBUR
Marvel Comics: Feb, 2001 - No. 4, May, 2001 ($2.99)

1-4-Return of Captain Britain; Raimondi-a 3.00

EXCITING COMICS
Nedor/Better Publications/Standard Comics: Apr, 1940 - No. 69, Sept, 1949

1-Origin & 1st app. The Mask, Jim Hatfield, Sgt. Bill King, Dan Williams begin; early Robot-c (see Smash #1)	375	1125	2344	4500
2-The Sphinx begins; The Masked Rider app.; Son of the Gods begins, ends #8	164	492	1023	1800
3-Robot-c	109	327	682	1200
4-6	73	219	455	800
7,8	59	177	369	650
9-Origin/1st app. of The Black Terror & sidekick Tim, begin series (5/41) (Black Terror c-9-21,23-52,54,55)	846	2538	5500	11,000
10-2nd app. Black Terror	273	819	1705	3000
11	136	408	852	1500
12,13	91	273	568	1000
14-Last Sphinx, Dan Williams	61	182	381	675
15-The Liberator begins (origin)	64	192	398	700
16-20: 20-The Mask ends	55	165	330	575
21,23-25: 25-Robot-c	45	135	270	475
22-Origin The Eaglet; The American Eagle begins	55	165	330	575
26,27,29,30: 26-Schomburg-c begin	55	165	341	600
28-(Scarce) Crime Crusader begins, ends #58	68	204	426	750

	GD2.0	FN6.0	VF8.0	NM9.4

31-38: 35-Liberator ends, not in 31-33	50	150	300	525
39-Origin Kara, Jungle Princess	61	182	381	675
40-50: 42-The Scarab begins. 45-Schomburg Robot-c. 49-Last Kara, Jungle Princess. 50-Last American Eagle	55	165	341	600
51-Miss Masque begins (1st app.)	61	182	381	675
52-54: Miss Masque ends. 53-Miss Masque-c	55	165	330	575
55-58: 55-Judy of the Jungle begins (origin), ends #69; 1 pg. Ingels-a; Judy of the Jungle c-56-66. 57,58-Airbrush-c	55	165	330	575
59-Frazetta art in Caniff style; signed Frank Frazeta (one t), 9 pgs.	55	165	341	600
60-66: 60-Rick Howard, the Mystery Rider begins. 66-Robinson/Meskin-a	50	150	300	525
67-69-All western covers	21	63	110	185

NOTE: **Schomburg (Xela)** c-26-68; airbrush c-57-66. Black Terror by **R. Moreira**-#65. **Rousso**s a-
62. Bondage-c 9, 12, 13, 20, 23, 25, 30, 59.

EXCITING ROMANCES
Fawcett Publications: 1949 (nd); No. 2, Spring, 1950 - No. 5, 10/50; No. 6 (1951, nd); No. 7, 9/51 -No. 12, 1/53

1,3: 1(1949). 3-Wood-a	14	42	72	120
2,4,5-(1950)	9	27	49	70
6-12	7	21	38	55

NOTE: **Powell** a-8-10. **Marcus Swayze** a-5, 6, 9. Photo c-1-7, 10-12.

EXCITING ROMANCE STORIES (See Fox Giants)

EXCITING WAR (Korean War)
Standard Comics (Better Publ.): No. 5, Sept, 1952 - No. 8, May, 1953; No. 9, Nov, 1953

5	9	27	49	70
6,7,9	6	18	29	40
8-Toth-a	8	24	42	60

EXCITING X-PATROL
Marvel Comics (Amalgam): June, 1997 ($1.95, one-shot)

1-Barbara Kesel-s/ Bryan Hitch-a 2.50

EXILES (Also see Break-Thru)
Malibu Comics (Ultraverse): Aug, 1993 - No. 4, Nov, 1993 ($1.95)

1,2,4: 1,2-Bagged copies of each exist. 2-Gustovich-c. 4-Team dies; story
cont'd in Break-Thru #1 2.25
3-($2.50, 40 pgs.)-Rune flip-c/story by B. Smith (3 pgs.) 2.50
1-Holographic-c edition 1 3 6 8

EXILES (All New, The) (2nd Series) (Also see Black September)
Malibu Comics (Ultraverse): Sept, 1995 - V2#11, Aug, 1996 ($1.50)

Infinity (9/95, $1.50)-Intro new team including Marvel's Juggernaut & Reaper. 2.25
Infinity (2000 signed), V2#1 (2000 signed) 1 4 7 10
V2#1-4,6-11: 1-(10/95, 64 pgs.)-Reprint of Ultraforce V2#1 follows lead story.
2-1st app. Hellblade. 8-Intro Maxis. 11-Vs. Maxis; Ripfire app.;
cont'd in Ultraforce #12 2.25
V2#5-($2.50) Juggernaut returns to the Marvel Universe. 2.50

EXILES (Also see X-Men titles)
Marvel Comics: Aug, 2001 - Present ($2.99/$2.25)

1-($2.99) Blink and parallel world X-Men; Winick-s/McKone & McKenna-a 3.00
2-8-($2.25) 2-Two covers (McKone & JH Williams III). 5-Alpha Flight app. 2.25

EXILES VS. THE X-MEN
Malibu Comics (Ultraverse): Oct, 1995 (one-shot)

0-Limited Super Premium Edition; signed w/certificate; gold foil logo,
0-Limited Premium Edition 1 4 7 10

EX-MUTANTS
Malibu Comics: Nov, 1992 - No. 18, Apr, 1994 ($1.95/$2.25/$2.50)

1-18: 1-Polybagged w/Skycap 2.50

EXORCISTS (See The Crusaders)

EXOSQUAD (TV)
Topps Comics: No. 0, Jan, 1994 ($1.25)

0-($1.00, 20 pgs.)-1st app.; Staton-a(p); wraparound-c 2.25

EXOTIC ROMANCES (Formerly True War Romances)
Quality Comics Group (Comic Magazines): No. 22, Oct, 1955-No. 31, Nov, 1956

Extinct! #1 © NEC

Extreme Justice #17 © DC

Fairy Tale Parade #5 © WEST

FA

	GD2.0	FN6.0	VF8.0	NM9.4

	GD2.0	FN6.0	VF8.0	NM9.4
22	10	30	55	80
23-26,29	6	18	29	40
27,31-Baker-c/a	14	42	72	120
28,30-Baker-a	11	33	55	90

EXPLOITS OF DANIEL BOONE
Quality Comics Group: Nov, 1955 - No. 6, Oct, 1956

1-All have Cuidera-c(i)	29	87	153	265
2	19	57	99	165
3-6	16	48	83	140

EXPLOITS OF DICK TRACY (See Dick Tracy)

EXPLORER JOE
Ziff-Davis Comic Group (Approved Comics): Win, 1951 - No. 2, Oct-Nov, 1952

1-2: Saunders painted covers; 2-Krigstein-a	14	42	72	120

EXPLORERS OF THE UNKNOWN (See Archie Giant Series #587, 599)
Archie Comics: June, 1990 - No. 6, Apr, 1991 ($1.00)

1-6: Featuring Archie and the gang				3.00

EXPOSED (...True Crime Cases; ...Cases in the Crusade Against Crime #5-9)
D. S. Publishing Co.: Mar-Apr, 1948 - No. 9, July-Aug, 1949

1	24	72	127	215
2-Giggling killer story with excessive blood; two injury-to-eye panels; electrocution panel	29	87	153	265
3,8,9	12	36	61	100
4-Orlando-a	13	39	66	110
5-Breeze Lawson, Sky Sheriff by E. Good	13	39	66	110
6,7: 6-Ingels-a; used in **SOTI**, illo. "How to prepare an alibi" 7-Illo. in **SOTI**, "Diagram for housebreakers," used by N.Y. Legis. Committee				
	37	111	197	340

EXPOSURE
Image Comics: 1999 - No. 4, 2000 ($2.50)

1-4: Al Rio-a/David Campiti-s. 1-Wraparound & photo covers				2.50
1-Variant-c				10.00
Prelude ($5.00)				5.00

EXPOSURE SECOND COMING
Avatar Press: Sept, 2000 ($3.50)

1-Al Rio-a/David Campiti-s; wraparound & photo covers				3.50

EXTINCT!
New England Comics Press: Wint, 1991-92 - No. 2, Fall, 1992 ($3.50, B&W)

1,2-Reprints and background info of "perfectly awful" Golden Age stories				3.50

EXTRA!
E. C. Comics: Mar-Apr, 1955 - No. 5, Nov-Dec, 1955

1-Not code approved	18	54	126	225
2-5	12	36	84	150

NOTE: *Craig, Crandall, Severin* art in all.

EXTRA!
Gemstone Publishing: Jan, 2000 - No. 5 ($2.50)

1-5-Reprints E.C. series				2.50

EXTRA COMICS
Magazine Enterprises: 1948 (25¢, 3 comics in one)

1-Giant; consisting of rebound ME comics. Two versions known; (1)- Funnyman by Siegel & Shuster, Space Ace, Undercover Girl, Red Fox by L.B. Cole, Trail Colt & (2)-All Funnyman	55	165	330	575

EXTREME
Image Comics (Extreme Studios): Aug, 1993 (Giveaway)

0				3.00

EXTREME DESTROYER
Image Comics (Extreme Studios): Jan, 1996 ($2.50)

Prologue 1-Polybagged w/card; Liefeld-c, Epilogue 1-Liefeld-c				2.50

EXTREME JUSTICE
DC Comics: No. 0, Jan, 1995 - No. 18, July, 1996 ($1.50/$1.75)

0-18				3.00

EXTREMELY YOUNGBLOOD

Image Comics (Extreme Studios): Sept, 1996 ($3.50, one-shot)

1				3.50

EXTREME SACRIFICE
Image Comics (Extreme Studios): Jan, 1995 ($2.50, limited series)

Prelude (#1)-Liefeld wraparound-c; polybagged w/ trading card				2.50
Epilogue (#2)-Liefeld wraparound-c; polybagged w/trading card				2.50
Trade paperback (6/95, $16.95)-Platt-a				17.00

EXTREME SUPER CHRISTMAS SPECIAL
Image Comics (Extreme Studios): Dec, 1994 ($2.95, one-shot)

1				3.00

EXTREMIST, THE
DC Comics (Vertigo): Sept, 1993 - No. 4, Dec, 1993 ($1.95, limited series)

1-4-Peter Milligan scripts; McKeever-c/a				2.25
1-Platinum Edition				5.00

EYE OF THE STORM
Rival Productions: Dec, 1994 - No. 7, June, 1995? ($2.95)

1-7: Computer generated comic				3.00

FACE
DC Comics (Vertigo): Jan, 1995 ($4.95, one-shot)

1				5.00

FACE, THE (Tony Trent, the Face No. 3 on) (See Big Shot Comics)
Columbia Comics Group: 1941 - No. 2, 1943

1-The Face; Mart Bailey-c	91	273	568	1000
2-Bailey-c	55	165	330	575

FACTOR X
Marvel Comics: Mar, 1995 - No. 4, July, 1995 ($1.95, limited series)

1-Age of Apocalypse				3.00
2-4				2.50

FACULTY FUNNIES
Archie Comics: June, 1989 - No. 5, May, 1990 (75¢/95¢ #2 on)

1-5: 1,2-The Awesome Four app.				3.00

FAFHRD AND THE GREY MOUSER (Also see Sword of Sorcery & Wonder Woman #202)
Marvel Comics: Oct, 1990 - No. 4, 1991 ($4.50, 52 pgs., squarebound)

1-4: Mignola/Williamson-a; Chaykin scripts				4.50

FAIRY TALE PARADE (See Famous Fairy Tales)
Dell Publishing Co.: June-July, 1942 - No. 121, Oct, 1946 (Most by Walt Kelly)

1-Kelly-a begins	123	369	861	1600
2(8-9/42)	50	150	350	650
3-5 (10-11/42 - 2-4/43)	36	108	252	475
6-9 (5-7/43 - 11-1/43-44)	27	80	189	350
Four Color 50('44),69('45), 87('45)	25	75	175	325
Four Color 104,114('46)-Last Kelly issue	18	55	126	240
Four Color 121('46)-Not by Kelly	11	33	77	145

NOTE: #1-9, 4-Color #50, 69 have *Kelly* c/a; 4-Color #87, 104, 114-*Kelly* art only. #9 has a redrawn version of The Reluctant Dragon. This series contains all the classic fairy tales from Jack In The Beanstalk to Cinderella.

FAIRY TALES
Ziff-Davis Publ. Co. (Approved Comics): No. 10, Apr-May, 1951 - No. 11, June-July, 1951

10,11-Painted-c	20	60	105	175

FAITH
DC Comics (Vertigo): Nov, 1999 - No. 5, Mar, 2000 ($2.50, limited series)

1-5-Ted McKeever-s/c/a				2.50

FAITHFUL
Marvel Comics/Lovers' Magazine: Nov, 1949 - No. 2, Feb, 1950 (52 pgs.)

1,2-Photo-c	10	30	55	80

FALCON (See Marvel Premiere #49)(Also see Avengers #181 & Captain America #117 & 133)
Marvel Comics Group: Nov, 1983 - No. 4, Feb, 1984 (Mini-series)

1-4: 1-Paul Smith-c/a(p). 2-Paul Smith-c				3.00

Famous Crimes #6 © FOX

Famous First Edition C-26 © DC

Famous Funnies #52 © EAS

| | GD2.0 | FN6.0 | VF8.0 | NM9.4 | | | GD2.0 | FN6.0 | VF8.0 | NM9.4 |

FALLEN ANGEL ON THE WORLD OF MAGIC: THE GATHERING
Acclaim (Armada): May, 1996 ($5.95, one-shot)

1-Nancy Collins story.				6.00

FALLEN ANGELS
Marvel Comics Group: April, 1987 - No. 8, Nov, 1987 (Limited series)

1-8				2.50

FALLING IN LOVE
Arleigh Pub. Co./National Per. Pub.: Sept-Oct, 1955 - No. 143, Oct-Nov, 1973

1	39	117	208	360
2	20	60	105	175
3-10	12	36	61	100
11-20	10	30	55	80
21-40	7	21	36	50
41-47: 47-Last 10¢ issue?	5	15	25	35
48-70	3	9	17	26
71-99,108: 108-Wood-a (4 pgs., 7/69)	2	6	13	20
100	3	10	23	35
101-107,109-124	2	6	11	16
134-143	2	6	10	14
125-133: 52 pgs.	3	9	19	28

NOTE: Colan c/a-75, 81. 52 pgs.-#125-133.

FALLING MAN, THE
Image Comics: Feb, 1998 ($2.95)

1-McCorkindale-s/Hester-a				3.00

FALL OF THE HOUSE OF USHER, THE (See A Corben Special & Spirit section 8/22/48)

FALL OF THE ROMAN EMPIRE (See Movie Comics)

FAMILY AFFAIR (TV)
Gold Key: Feb, 1970 - No. 4, Oct, 1970 (25¢)

1-With pull-out poster; photo-c	5	15	35	65
1-With poster missing	3	9	19	28
2-4: 3,4-Photo-c	3	10	23	35

FAMILY FUNNIES
Parents' Magazine Institute: No. 9, Aug-Sept, 1946

9	5	15	23	30

FAMILY FUNNIES (Tiny Tot Funnies No. 9)
Harvey Publications: Sept, 1950 - No. 8, Apr, 1951

1-Mandrake (has over 30 King Feature strips)	10	30	55	80
2-Flash Gordon, 1 pg.	7	21	36	50
3-8: 4,5,7-Flash Gordon, 1 pg.	6	18	30	42

FAMILY MAN
DC Comics (Paradox Press): 1995 - No. 3, 1995 ($4.95, B&W, digest-size, limited series)

1-3				5.00

FAMILY MATTER
Kitchen Sink Press: 1998 ($24.95/$15.95, graphic novel)

Hardcover ($24.95) Will Eisner-s/a				25.00
Softcover ($15.95)				16.00

FAMOUS AUTHORS ILLUSTRATED (See Stories by...)

FAMOUS CRIMES
Fox Features Syndicate/M.S. Dist. No. 51,52: June, 1948 - No. 19, Sept, 1950; No. 20, Aug, 1951; No. 51, 52, 1953

1-Blue Beetle app. & crime story-r/Phantom Lady #16	50	150	300	525
2-Has woman dissolved in acid; lingerie/panels	40	120	220	380
3-Injury-to-eye story used in SOTI, pg. 112; has two electrocution stories	47	142	286	500
4-6	23	69	121	210
7- "Tarzan, the Wyoming Killer" used in SOTI, pg. 44; drug trial/ possession story	40	120	220	380
8-20: 17-Morisi-a. 20-Same cover as #15	18	54	94	155
51(nd, 1953)	16	48	83	140
52 (Exist?)	10	30	55	80

FAMOUS FEATURE STORIES
Dell Publishing Co.: 1938 (7-1/2x11", 68 pgs.)

1-Tarzan, Terry & the Pirates, King of the Royal Mtd., Buck Jones, Dick Tracy, Smilin' Jack, Dan Dunn, Don Winslow, G-Man, Tailspin Tommy, Mutt & Jeff, Little Orphan Annie reprints - all illustrated text	68	205	426	750

FAMOUS FIRST EDITION (See Limited Collectors' Edition)
National Periodical Publications/DC Comics: ($1.00, 10x13-1/2", 72 pgs.) (No.6-8, 68 pgs.) 1974 - No. 8, Aug-Sept, 1975; C-61, 1979 (Hardbound editions with dust jackets are from Lyle Stuart, Inc.)

C-26-Action Comics #1; gold ink outer-c	4	12	26	40
C-26-Hardbound edition w/dust jacket	17	51	118	210
C-28-Detective #27; silver ink outer-c	6	18	40	65
C-28-Hardbound edition w/dust jacket	22	66	151	270
C-30-Sensation #1(1974); bronze ink outer-c	4	12	26	40
C-30-Hardbound edition w/dust jacket	17	51	118	210
F-4-Whiz Comics #2(#1)(10-11/74)-Cover not identical to original (dropped "Gangway for Captain Marvel" from cover); gold ink on outer-c	4	12	26	40
F-4-Hardbound edition w/dust jacket	17	51	118	210
F-5-Batman #1(F-6 inside); silver ink on outer-c	5	15	34	55
F-5-Hardbound edition w/dust jacket	17	51	118	210
V2#F-6-Wonder Woman #1	4	12	26	40
F-6-Wonder Woman #1 Hardbound w/dust jacket	17	51	118	210
F-7-All-Star Comics #3	4	12	26	40
F-8-Flash Comics #1(8-9/75)	4	12	26	40
V8#C61-Superman #1(1979, $2.00)	3	9	20	30

Warning: The above books are almost exact reprints of the originals that they represent except for the Giant-Size format. None of the originals are Giant-Size. The first five issues and C-61 were printed with two covers. Reprint information can be found on the outside cover, but not on the inside cover which was reprinted exactly like the original (inside and out).

FAMOUS FUNNIES
Eastern Color: 1934; July, 1934 - No. 218, July, 1955

A Carnival of Comics (See Promotional Comics section)

Series 1-(Very rare)(nd-early 1934)(68 pgs.) No publisher given (Eastern Color Printing Co.); sold in chain stores for 10¢. 35,000 print run. Contains Sunday strip reprints of Mutt & Jeff, Reg'lar Fellers, Nipper, Hairbreadth Harry, Strange As It Seems, Joe Palooka, Dixie Dugan, The Nebbs, Keeping Up with the Jones, and others. Inside front and back covers and pages 1-16 of Famous Funnies Series 1, #s 49-64 reprinted from **Famous Funnies, A Carnival of Comics**, and most of pages 17-48 reprinted from **Funnies on Parade**. This was the first comic book sold.

	4000	12000	25,000	–

No. 1 (Rare)(7/34-on stands 5/34) - Eastern Color Printing Co. First monthly newsstand comic book. Contains Sunday strip reprints of Toonerville Folks, Mutt & Jeff, Hairbreadth Harry, S'Matter Pop, Nipper, Dixie Dugan, The Bungle Family, Connie, Ben Webster, Tailspin Tommy, The Nebbs, Joe Palooka, & others.

	3000	9000	18,000	–
2 (Rare, 9/34)	525	1575	3600	–
3-Buck Rogers Sunday strip-r by Rick Yager begins, ends #218; 1st comic book app. of Buck Rogers; the number of the 1st strip reprinted is pg. 190, Series No. 1	680	2040	4600	–
4	215	645	1500	–
5-1st Christmas-c on a newsstand comic	185	555	1400	–
6-10	123	370	925	–
11,12,18-Four pgs. of Buck Rogers in each issue, completes stories in Buck Rogers #1 which lacks these pages. 18-Two pgs. of Buck Rogers reprinted in Daisy Comics #1	97	291	533	925
13-17,19,20: 14-Has two Buck Rogers panels missing. 17-2nd Christmas-c on a newsstand comic (12/35)	76	228	418	725
21,23-30: 27-(10/36)-War on Crime begins (4 pgs.); 1st true crime in comics (reprints). 29-X-Mas-c (12/36)	55	165	302	525
22-Four pgs. of Buck Rogers needed to complete stories in Buck Rogers #1	59	177	324	560
31,33,34,36,37,39,40: 33-Careers of Baby Face Nelson & John Dillinger traced	40	120	220	380
32-(3/37) 1st app. the Phantom Magician (costume hero) in Advs. of Patsy	44	132	242	420
35-Two pgs. Buck Rogers omitted in Buck Rogers #2	44	132	242	420
38-Full color portrait of Buck Rogers	42	126	231	400
41-60: 41,53-X-Mas-c. 55-Last bottom panel, pg. 4 in Buck Rogers redrawn in Buck Rogers #3	29	87	153	265
61,63,64,66,67,69,70	23	69	121	210

Famous Funnies #110 © EAS

Fan Boy #2 © Horse Feathers, Inc.

Fantastic Comics #5 © FOX

FA

	GD2.0	FN6.0	VF8.0	NM9.4
62,65,68,73-78-Two pgs. Kirby-a "Lightnin' & the Lone Rider".				
65,77-X-Mas-c	26	78	136	235
71,79,80: 80-(3/41)-Buck Rogers story continues from Buck Rogers #5	17	51	88	150
72-Speed Spaulding begins by Marvin Bradley (artist), ends #88. This series was written by Edwin Balmer & Philip Wylie (later appeared as film & book "When Worlds Collide")	19	57	99	170
81-Origin & 1st app. Invisible Scarlet O'Neil (4/41); strip begins #82, ends #167; 1st non-funny-c (Scarlet O'Neil)	19	57	99	170
82-Buck Rogers-c	19	57	99	170
83-87,90: 86-Connie vs. Monsters on the Moon-c. 87 has last Buck Rogers full page-c. 90-Bondage-c	14	42	72	125
88,89: 88-Buck Rogers in "Moon's End" by Calkins, 2 pgs.(not reprints). Beginning with #88, all Buck Rogers pgs. have rearranged panels. 89-Origin & 1st app. Fearless Flint, the Flint Man	15	45	77	135
91-93,95,96,98-99,101,103-110: 105-Series 2 begins (Strip Page #1)	13	39	66	110
94-Buck Rogers in "Solar Holocaust" by Calkins, 3 pgs.(not reprints)	14	42	72	120
97-War Bond promotion, Buck Rogers by Calkins, 2 pgs.(not reprints)	14	42	72	120
100-1st comic to reach #100; 100th Anniversary cover features 11 major Famous Funnies characters, including Buck Rogers	15	45	77	135
102-Chief Wahoo vs. Hitler,Tojo & Mussolini-c (1/43)	40	120	232	400
111-130: 113-X-Mas-c	10	30	55	80
131-150 (1/47): 137-Strip page No. 110 omitted	8	24	45	65
151-162,164-168	7	21	38	55
163-St. Valentine's Day-c	8	24	42	60
169,170-Two text illos. by Williamson, his 1st comic book work	11	33	55	90
171-190: 171-Strip pgs. 227,229,230, Series 2 omitted. 172-Strip Pg. 232 omitted. 190-Buck Rogers ends with start of strip pg. 302, Series 2; Oaky Doaks-c/story	7	21	36	50
191-197,199,201,203,206-208: No Buck Rogers. 191-Barney Carr, Space detective begins at #192.	6	18	32	45
198,200,202,205-One pg. Frazetta ads; no B. Rogers	7	21	36	50
204-Used in POP, 79,99; war-c begin, end #208	7	21	38	55
209-216: Frazetta-c. 209-Buck Rogers begins (12/53) with strip pg. 480, Series 2; 211-Buck Rogers ads by Anderson begins, ends #217. #215-Contains B. Rogers strip pgs. 515-518, series 2 followed by pgs.179-181, Series 3	114	342	712	1250
217,218-B. Rogers ends with pg. 199, Series 3. 218-Wee Three-c/story	7	21	36	50

NOTE: Rick Yager did the Buck Rogers Sunday strips reprinted in Famous Funnies. The Sundays were formerly done by Russ Keaton and Lt. Dick Calkins did the dailies, but would sometimes assist Yager on a panel or two from time to time. Strip No. 169 is Yager's first full Buck Rogers page. Yager did the strip until 1958 when *Murphy Anderson* took over. *Tuska* did the strip from 4/26/59 - 1965. Virtually every panel was rewritten for Famous Funnies. Not identical to the original Sunday page. The Buck Rogers reprints run continuously through Famous Funnies issue No. 190 (page No. 302) with no break in story line. The story line has no continuity after No. 190. The Buck Rogers newspaper strips came out in four series: Series 1, 3/30/30 - 9/21/41 (No. 1 - 600); Series 2, 9/28/41 -10/21/51 (No. 1 -525)(Strip No. 110-1/2 (1/2 pg.) published in only a few newspapers); Series 3, 10/28/51 -2/9/58 (No. 100-428)(No No. 110 - page No. 110); Series 4, 2/16/58 - 6/13/65 (No numbers). *Everett* c-85, 86. *Moulton* a-100. Chief Wahoo c-93, 97, 102, 116, 136, 139, 151. Dickie Dare c-83, 88. Fearless Flint c-89. Invisible Scarlet O'Neil c-81, 87, 95, 121(part), 132. Scorchy Smith c-84, 90.

FAMOUS FUNNIES
Super Comics: 1964

Famous Reprint Nos. 15-18:17-r/Double Trouble #1. 18-Space Comics #?	2	6	11	16

FAMOUS GANGSTERS (Crime on the Waterfront No. 4)
Avon Periodicals/Realistic No. 3: Apr, 1951 - No. 3, Feb, 1952

1-3: 1-Capone, Dillinger; c-/Avon paperback #329. 2-Dillinger Machine Gun Killer; Wood-a (1 pg.) = r/Saint #7 & retitled "Mike Strong". 3-Lucky Luciano & Murder, Inc; c-/Avon paperback #66	39	117	208	360

FAMOUS INDIAN TRIBES
Dell Publishing Co.: July-Sept, 1962; No. 2, July, 1972

12-264-209(#1) (The Sioux)	2	6	13	20
2(7/72)-Reprints above	1	3	6	8

FAMOUS STARS
Ziff-Davis Publ. Co.: Nov-Dec, 1950 - No. 6, Spring, 1952 (All have photo-c)

1-Shelley Winters, Susan Peters, Ava Gardner, Shirley Temple; Jimmy Stewart & Shelley Winters photo-c; Whitney-a	34	102	179	310
2-Betty Hutton, Bing Crosby, Colleen Townsend, Gloria Swanson; Betty Hutton photo-c; Everett-a(2)	23	69	121	210
3-Farley Granger, Judy Garland's ordeal (life story; she died 6/22/69 at the age of 47), Alan Ladd; Farley Granger photo-c; Whitney-a	26	78	139	240
4-Al Jolson, Bob Mitchum, Ella Raines, Richard Conte, Vic Damone; Bob Mitchum photo-c; Crandall-a, 6pgs.	20	30	105	180
5-Liz Taylor, Betty Grable, Esther Williams, George Brent, Mario Lanza; Liz Taylor photo-c; Krigstein-a	33	99	174	300
6-Gene Kelly, Hedy Lamarr, June Allyson, William Boyd, Janet Leigh, Gary Cooper; Gene Kelly photo-c	17	51	88	150

FAMOUS STORIES (...Book No. 2)
Dell Publishing Co.: 1942 - No. 2, 1942

1,2: 1-Treasure Island. 2-Tom Sawyer	31	93	165	285

FAMOUS TV FUNDAY FUNNIES
Harvey Publications: Sept, 1961 (25¢ Giant)

1-Casper the Ghost, Baby Huey, Little Audrey	5	15	38	60

FAMOUS WESTERN BADMEN (Formerly Redskin)
Youthful Magazines: No. 13, Dec, 1952 - No. 15, Apr, 1953

13-Redskin story	13	39	66	110
14,15: 15-The Dalton Boys story	10	30	55	80

FAN BOY
DC Comics: Mar, 1999 - No. 6, Aug, 1999 ($2.50, limited series)

1-6: 1-Art by Aragonés and various in all. 2-Green Lantern-c/a by Gil Kane. 3-JLA. 4-Sgt. Rock art by Heath, Marie Severin. 5-Batman art by Sprang, Adams, Miller, Timm. 6-Wonder Woman; art by Rude, Grell				2.50
TPB (2001, $12.95) r/#1-6				13.00

FANTASTIC (Formerly Captain Science; Beware No. 10 on)
Youthful Magazines: No. 8, Feb, 1952 - No. 9, Apr, 1952

8-Capt. Science by Harrison; decapitation, shrunken head panels	40	120	232	400
9-Harrison-a	33	99	174	300

FANTASTIC ADVENTURES
Super Comics: 1963 - 1964 (Reprints)

9,10,12,15,16,18: 9-r/? 10-r/He-Man #2(Toby). 11-Disbrow-a. 12-Unpublished Chesler material? 15-r/Spook #23. 16-r/Dark Shadows #2(Steinway); Briefer-a.18-r/Fantastic #8	3	9	21	32
11-Wood-a; r/Blue Bolt #118	4	12	30	48
17-Baker-a(2) r/Seven Seas #6	4	12	30	48

FANTASTIC COMICS
Fox Features Syndicate: Dec, 1939 - No. 23, Nov, 1941

1-Intro/origin Samson; Stardust, The Super Wizard, Sub Saunders by Kiefer), Space Smith, Capt. Kidd begin	446	1338	2900	5800
2-Powell text illos	236	708	1477	2600
3-Classic Lou Fine Robot-c; Powell text illos	1015	3045	5000	7000
4,5: Last Lou Fine-c	182	546	1136	2000
6,7-Simon-c	136	408	852	1500
8-10: 10-Intro/origin David, Samson's aide	95	285	597	1050
11-17,19,20: 16-Stardust ends	77	231	483	850
18,23: 18-1st app. Black Fury & sidekick Chuck; ends #23. 23-Origin The Gladiator	80	240	500	875
21-The Banshee begins(origin); ends #23; Hitler-c	84	253	525	925
22-Hitler-c (likeness of Hitler as furnace on cover)	91	273	568	1000

NOTE: Lou Fine c-1-5. Tuska a-3-5, 8. Bondage c-6, 8, 9. Issue #11 has indicia to Mystery Men Comics #15. All issues feature Samson covers.

FANTASTIC COMICS (Fantastic Fears #1-9; Becomes Samson #12)
Ajax/Farrell Publ.: No. 10, Nov-Dec, 1954 - No. 11, Jan-Feb, 1955

10 (#1)	20	60	105	175
11-Robot-a	23	69	121	210

FANTASTIC FABLES
Silverwolf Comics: Feb, 1987 - No. 2, 1987 ($1.50, 28 pgs., B&W)

1,2: 1-Tim Vigil-a (6 pgs.). 2-Tim Vigil-a (7 pgs.)				4.00

Fantastic Five #5 © MAR

Fantastic Four #27 © MAR

Fantastic Four #202 © MAR

	GD2.0	FN6.0	VF8.0	NM9.4

FANTASTIC FEARS (Formerly Captain Jet) (Fantastic Comics #10 on)
Ajax/Farrell Publ.: No. 7, May, 1953 - No. 9, Sept-Oct, 1954

	GD2.0	FN6.0	VF8.0	NM9.4
7(#1, 5/53)-Tales of Stalking Terror	43	129	257	450
8(#2, 7/53)	33	99	174	300
3,4	25	75	130	225
5-(1-2/54)-Ditko story (1st drawn) is written by Bruce Hamilton; r-in Weird V2#8 (1st pro work for Ditko but Daring Love #1 was published 1st)				
	80	240	500	875
6-Decapitation-girl's head w/paper cutter (classic)	52	157	314	550
7(5-6/54), 9(9-10/54)	25	75	130	225
8(7-8/54)-Contains story intended for Jo-Jo; name changed to Kaza; decapitation story	29	87	153	265

FANTASTIC FIVE
Marvel Comics: Oct, 1999 - No. 5, Feb, 2000 ($1.99)

1-5: 1-M2 Universe; recaps origin; Ryan-a. 2-Two covers			2.25

FANTASTIC FORCE
Marvel Comics: Nov, 1994 - No. 18, Apr, 1996 ($1.75)

1-($2.50)-Foil wraparound-c; intro Fantastic Force w/Huntara, Delvor, Psi-Lord & Vibraxas			3.00
2-18: 13-She-Hulk app.			2.25

FANTASTIC FOUR (See America's Best TV..., Fireside Book Series, Giant-Size..., Giant Size Super-Stars, Marvel Collectors Item Classics, Marvel Milestone Edition, Marvel's Greatest, Marvel Treasury Edition, Marvel Triple Action, Official Marvel Index to... & Power Record Comics)
Marvel Comics Group: Nov, 1961 - No. 416, Sept, 1996 (Created by Stan Lee & Jack Kirby)

	GD2.0	FN6.0	VF8.0	NM9.4
1-Origin & 1st app. The Fantastic Four (Reed Richards: Mr. Fantastic, Johnny Storm: The Human Torch, Sue Storm: The Invisible Girl, & Ben Grimm: The Thing–Marvel's 1st super-hero group since the G.A.; 1st app. S.A. Human Torch); origin/1st app. The Mole Man.				
	800	2400	8800	27,000
1-Golden Record Comic Set Reprint (1966)-cover not identical to original				
	15	45	105	180
with Golden Record	22	65	151	270
2-Vs. The Skrulls (last 10¢ issue)	278	834	2500	5000
3-Fantastic Four don costumes & establish Headquarters; brief 1pg. origin; intro. The Fantasti-Car; Human Torch drawn w/two left hands on-c				
	188	564	1600	3200
4-1st S. A. Sub-Mariner app. (5/62)	215	645	1900	3800
5-Origin & 1st app. Doctor Doom	233	700	2100	4200
6-Sub-Mariner, Dr. Doom team up; 1st Marvel villain team-up (2nd S.A. Sub-Mariner app.)	131	393	1113	2100
7-10: 7-1st app. Kurrgo. 8-1st app. Puppet-Master & Alicia Masters. 9-3rd Sub-Mariner app. 10-Stan Lee & Jack Kirby app. in story				
	72	216	612	1150
11-Origin/1st app. The Impossible Man (2/63)	56	169	478	900
12-Fantastic Four Vs. The Hulk (1st meeting); 1st Hulk x-over & ties w/Amazing Spider-Man #1 as 1st Marvel x-over; (3/63)	106	318	903	1700
13-Intro. The Watcher; 1st app. The Red Ghost	41	123	331	600
14-19: 14-Sub-Mariner x-over. 15-1st app. Mad Thinker. 16-1st app. Ant-Man x-over (7/63); Wasp cameo. 18-Origin/1st app. The Super Skrull. 19-Intro. Rama-Tut; Stan Lee and Kirby cameo	30	90	210	375
20-Origin/1st app. The Molecule Man	31	93	222	400
21-Intro. The Hate Monger; 1st Sgt. Fury x-over (12/63)				
	22	65	157	280
22-24: 22-Sue Storm gains more powers	16	48	112	200
25,26-The Hulk Vs. the Thing (their 1st battle). 25-3rd Avengers x-over (1st time w/Capt. America)(cameo, 4/64); 2nd S.A. app. Cap (takes place between Avengers #4 & 5. 26-4th Avengers x-over				
	37	111	278	500
27-1st Doctor Strange x-over (6/64)	17	51	118	210
28-Early X-Men x-over (7/64); same date as X-Men #6				
	28	84	196	350
29,30: 30-Intro. Diablo	18	54	113	180
31-40: 31-Early Avengers x-over (10/64). 33-1st app. Attuma; part photo-c. 35-Intro/1st app. Dragon Man. 36-Intro/1st app. Madam Medusa & the Frightful Four (Sandman, Wizard, Paste Pot Pete). 39-Wood inks on				

	GD2.0	FN6.0	VF8.0	NM9.4
Daredevil (early x-over)	10	30	73	125
41-44,47: 41-43-Frightful Four app. 44-Intro. Gorgon	8	24	58	95
45-Intro/1st app. The Inhumans (c/story, 12/65); also see Incredible Hulk Special #1 & Thor #146, & 147	10	30	73	125
46-1st Black Bolt-c (Kirby) & 1st full app.	9	27	65	110
48-Partial origin/1st app. The Silver Surfer & Galactus by Lee & Kirby; Galactus cameo in last panel; 1st of 3 part story	78	234	663	1250
49-2nd app./1st cover Silver Surfer & Galactus	27	81	190	340
50-Silver Surfer battles Galactus; full S.S.-c	28	84	196	350
51,54: 54-Inhumans cameo	6	18	45	75
52-1st app. The Black Panther (7/66)	14	42	102	175
53-Origin & 2nd app. The Black Panther	10	30	73	120
55-Thing battles Silver Surfer; 4th app. Silver Surfer	10	30	70	120
56-Silver Surfer cameo	7	21	50	80
57-60: Dr. Doom steals Silver Surfer's powers (See Silver Surfer: Loftier Than Mortals).				
59,60-Inhumans cameo	7	21	53	85
61-65,68-70: 61-Silver Surfer cameo; Sandman-c/s	5	15	38	60
66-Begin 2 part origin of Him (Warlock); does not app. (9/67)				
	10	30	68	115
67-Origin/1st app. Him (Warlock); 1 pg. cameo; see FF #165,166 for 1st full app.	11	33	77	130
71,78-80	4	12	30	50
72-Silver Surfer-c/story (pre-dates Silver Surfer #1)	6	18	40	65
73-Spider-Man, D.D., Thor x-over; cont'd from Daredevil #38				
	5	15	34	55
74-77: Silver Surfer app.(#77 is same date/S.S. #1)	5	15	38	60
81-88: 81-Crystal joins & dons costume. 82,83-Inhumans app.				
84-87-Dr. Doom app. 88-Last 12¢ issue	4	12	27	42
89-99,101: 94-Intro. Agatha Harkness.	3	10	23	35
100 (7/70)	9	27	65	110
102-104: F.F. vs. Sub-Mariner. 104-Magneto-c/story	4	12	25	38
105-109,111: 108-Last Kirby issue (not in #103-107)	3	9	17	25
110-Initial version w/green Thing and blue faces and pink uniforms on-c				
	4	12	26	40
110-Corrected-c w/accurately colored faces and uniforms and orange Thing				
	3	10	23	35
112-Hulk Vs. Thing (7/71)	8	24	60	100
113-115: 115-Last 15¢ issue	2	6	15	22
116 (52 pgs.)	3	9	20	30
117-120	2	6	12	18
121-Silver Surfer-c/stories. 122,123-Galactus	2	6	12	18
124,125,127,129-149: 129-Intro. Thundra. 130-Sue leaves F.F. 131-Quicksilver app. 132-Medusa joins. 133-Thundra Vs. Thing. 142-Kirbyish-a by Buckler begins. 143-Dr. Doom-c/story. 147-Sub-Mariner	2	6	11	15
126-Origin F.F. retold; cover swipe of F.F. #1	2	6	12	18
128-Four pg. insert of F.F. Friends & Foes	2	6	12	18
150-Crystal & Quicksilver's wedding	2	6	13	20
151-154,158-160: 151-Origin Thundra. 159-Medusa leaves; Sue rejoins				
	1	4	7	10
155-157: Silver Surfer in all	2	6	9	12
161-165,168-174,176-180: 164-The Crusader (old Marvel Boy) revived (origin #165); 1st app.Frankie Raye. 168-170-Cage app. 176-Re-intro Impossible Man; Marvel artists app. 180-r/#101 by Kirby	1	3	5	7
166,167-vs. Hulk	1	3	5	7
169-173 (Regular 25¢ edition)(4-8/75)	1	4	7	10
169-173-(30¢-c, limited distribution)	1	3	6	9
181-199: 189-G.A. Human Torch app. & origin retold. 190,191-Fantastic Four break up				6.00
183-187-(35¢-c variants, limited dist.)(6-10/77)	1	3	6	9
200-(11/78, 52 pgs.)-F.F. re-united vs. Dr. Doom	1	3	6	9
201-208,219,222-231: 207-Human Torch vs. Spider-Man-c/story. 211-1st app. Terrax. 224-Contains unused alternate-c for FF #3 and pin-ups				4.00
209-216,218,220,221-Byrne-a. 209-1st Herbie the Robot. 220-Brief return				5.00
217-Dazzler app. by Byrne				5.00
232-Byrne-a begins				5.00
233-235,237-249,251-260: All Byrne-a. 238-Origin Frankie Raye. 244-Frankie Raye becomes Nova, Herald of Galactus. 252-Reads sideways; Annihilus app.; contains skin "Tattooz" decals				4.00
236-20th Anniversary issue(11/81, 68 pgs., $1.00)-Brief origin F.F.; Byrne-c/a(p); new Kirby-a(p)				5.00

Fantastic Four #386 © MAR
Fantastic Four V3 #32 © MAR
Fantastic Four Big Town #3 © MAR

FA

	GD2.0	FN6.0	VF8.0	NM9.4

250-(52 pgs)-Spider-Man x-over; Byrne-a; Skrulls impersonate New X-Men 5.00
261-285: 261-Silver Surfer. 262-Origin Galactus; Byrne writes & draws himself
  into story. 264-Swipes-c of F.F. #1. 274-Spider-Man's alien costume app.
  (4th app., 1/85, 2 pgs.) 3.00
286-2nd app. X-Factor continued from Avengers #263; story continues in
  X-Factor #1 4.00
287-295: 292-Nick Fury app. 293-Last Byrne-a 3.00
296-($1.50)-Barry Smith-c/a; Thing rejoins 4.00
297-318,321-330: 300-Johnny Storm & Alicia Masters wed. 306-New team
  begins (9/87). 311-Re-intro The Black Panther. 312-X-Factor x-over. 327-Mr.
  Fantastic & Invisible Girl return 3.00
319,320: 319-Double size. 320-Thing vs. Hulk 4.00
331-346,351-357,359,360: 334-Simonson-c/scripts begin. 337-Simonson-a
  begins. 342-Spider-Man cameo. 356-F.F. vs. The New Warriors; Paul
  Ryan-c begins. 360-Last $1.00-c 2.50
347-Ghost Rider, Wolverine, Spider-Man, Hulk-c/stories thru #349; Arthur
  Adams-c/a(p) in each 4.00
347,348-Gold 2nd printing 2.50
348,349 3.00
350-($1.50, 52 pgs.)-Dr. Doom app. 3.00
358-(11/91, $2.25, 88 pgs.)-30th anniversary issue; gives history of F.F.;
  die cut-c; Art Adams back-up story-a 3.00
361-368,370,372-374,376-380,382-386: 362-Spider-Man app. 367-Wolverine
  app. (brief). 370-Infinity War x-over; Thanos & Magus app. 374-Secret
  Defenders (Ghost Rider, Hulk, Wolverine) x-over 2.25
369-Infinity War x-over; Thanos app. 2.50
371-All white embossed-c ($2.00) 4.00
371-All red 2nd printing ($2.00) 2.50
375-($2.95, 52 pgs.)-Holo-grafx foil-c; ann. issue 3.00
376-($2.50)-Variant polybagged w/Dirt Magazine #4 and music tape 5.00
381-Death of Reed Richards (Mister Fantastic) & Dr. Doom 4.00
387-Newsstand ed. ($1.25) 2.25
387-($2.95)-Collector's Ed. w/Die-cut foil-c 3.00
388-393,395-397: 388-bound-in trading card sheet. 394-($1.50-c) 2.25
394,398,399: 394 ($2.95)-Collector's Edition-polybagged w/16 pg. Marvel Action
  Hour book and acetate print; pink logo. 398,399-Rainbow Foil-c 3.00
400-Rainbow-Foil-c 4.00
401-415: 401,402-Atlantis Rising. 407,408-Return of Reed Richards.
  411-Inhumans app. 414-Galactus vs. Hyperstorm. 415-Onslaught tie-in;
  X-Men app. 2.25
416-($2.50)-Onslaught tie-in; Dr. Doom app.; wraparound-c 3.00

Annual 1('63)-Origin F.F.; Ditko-i; early Spidey cameo	59	178	505	950
Annual 2('64)-Dr. Doom origin & c/story	33	99	250	500
Annual 3('65)-Reed & Sue wed; r/#6,11	15	45	105	180

Special 4(11/66)-G.A. Torch x-over (1st S.A. app.) & origin retold; r/#25,26

(Hulk vs. Thing); Torch battle	10	30	70	120

Special 5(11/67)-New art; Intro. Psycho-Man; early Black Panther, Inhumans

& Silver Surfer (1st solo app.)	10	30	73	125

Special 6(11/68)-Intro. Annihilus; birth of Franklin Richards; new 48 pg. movie

length epic; last non-reprint annual	6	18	42	70
Special 7(11/69)-r/F.F. #1-5; Marvel staff photos	3	9	20	30

Special 8-10: All reprints. 8(12/70)-F.F. vs. Sub-Mariner plus gallery of F.F. foes.

9(12/71). 10('73)	2	6	13	20

Annual 11-14: 11(1976)-New art begins again. 12(1978). 13(1978). 14(1979)

	1	3	6	8

Annual 15-17: 15('80-'94, 68 pgs.)17(1983)-Byrne-c/a 5.00
Annual 18-27: 21(1988)-Evolutionary War x-over. 22-Atlantis Attacks x-over;
  Sub-Mariner & The Avengers app.; Buckler-a. 23-Byrne-c; Guice-p. 24-2-pg.
  origin recap of Fantastic Four; Guardians of the Galaxy x-over.
  25-Moondragon story. 26-Bagged w/card 3.00
Special Edition 1(5/84)/Annual #1; Byrne-c/a 3.00
...: Monsters Unleashed nn (1992, $5.95)-r/F.F. #347-349 w/new Arthur
  Adams-c 6.00
...: Nobody Gets Out Alive (1994, $15.95) TPB r/ #387-392 16.00
...: Visionaries (11/01, $19.95) r/#232-240 by John Byrne 20.00
NOTE: **Arthur Adams** c/a-347-349p. **Austin** c(i)-232-236, 238, 240-242, 250i, 286i. **Buckler** c-151,
168. **John Buscema** a(p)-107, 109-130, 132, 134-141, 160, 173-
175, 202, 296-309p, Annual 11, 13; c(p)-107-122, 124-129, 133-139, 202, Annual 12p, Special 10.
Byrne a-209-218p, 220p, 221p, 232-265, 266i, 267-273, 274-293p, Annual 17, 19; c-211-214p,
220p, 232-236p, 237, 238p, 239, 240-242p, 243-249, 250p, 251-267, 269-277, 278-281p, 283p,
284, 285, 298p, 286-293. **Ditko** a-13i, 14i(w/**Kirby**-p), Annual 16. **G. Kane** c-145p,
146p, 150p, 160p. **Kirby** a-1-102p, 108p, 180r, 189r, 236p, Special 1-10; c-1-101, 164, 167, 171-

177, 180, 181, 190, 200, Annual 11, Special 1-7, 9. **Marcos** a-Annual 14i. **Mooney** a-118i, 152i.
Perez a(p)-164-167, 170-172, 176-178, 184-188, 191p, 192p. Annual 14p, 15p; c(p)-183-188, 191,
192, 194-197. **Simonson** a-337-341, 343, 344p, 345p, 346, 350p, 352-354; c-212, 334-341, 342p,
343-346, 350, 353, 354. **Steranko** c-130-132p. **Williamson** c-357i.

FANTASTIC FOUR (Volume Two)
Marvel Comics: V2#1, Nov, 1996 - No. 13, Nov, 1997 ($2.95/$1.95/$1.99)
(Produced by WildStorm Productions)
1-($2.95)-Reintro Fantastic Four; Jim Lee-c/a; Brandon Choi scripts; Mole Man
  app. 5.00

1-($2.95)-Variant-c	1	3	5	7

2-9: 2-Namor-c/app. 3-Avengers-c/app. 4-Two covers; Dr. Doom cameo 3.00
10,11,13: All $1.99-c. 13-"World War 3"-pt. 1, x-over w/Image 3.00
12-($2.99) "Heroes Reunited"-pt. 1 4.00
...: Heroes Reborn (7/00, $17.95, TPB) r/#1-6 18.00

FANTASTIC FOUR (Volume Three)
Marvel Comics: V3#1, Jan, 1998 - Present ($2.99/$1.99/$2.25)
1-($2.99)-Heroes Return; Lobdell-s/Davis & Farmer-a 5.00

1-Alternate Heroes Return-c	1	3	5	7

2-4,12: 2-2-covers. 4-Claremont-s/Larroca begin; Silver Surfer c/app.12-
  ($2.99) Wraparound-c by Larroca 4.00
5-11: 6-Heroes For Hire app. 9-Spider-Man-c/app. 3.00
13-24: 13,14-Ronan-c/app. 2.50
25-($2.99) Dr. Doom returns 3.00
26-29: 27-Dr. Doom marries Sue 2.25
30-49: 30-Begin $2.25-c. 32,42-Namor-c/app. 35-Regular cover; Pacheco-s/a
  begins 37-Super-Skrull(3 app). 38-New Baxter Building 2.25
35-($3.25) Variant foil enhanced-c; Pacheco-s/a begins 3.25
...'98 Annual ($3.50) Immonen-a 3.50
...'99 Annual ($3.50) Ladronn-a 3.50
...'00 Annual ($3.50) Larocca-a; Marvel Girl back-up story 3.50
...'01 Annual ($2.99) Maguire-a; Thing back-up w/Yu-a 3.00
Fantastic 4th Voyage of Sinbad (9/01, $5.95) Claremont-s/Ferry-a 6.00
Flesh and Stone (8/01, $12.95, TPB) r/#35-39 13.00
Wizard 1/2 -Lima 10.00

FANTASTIC FOUR: ATLANTIS RISING
Marvel Comics: June, 1995 - No. 2, July, 1995 ($3.95, limited series)
1,2: Acetate-c 5.00
Collector's Preview (5/95, $2.25, 52 pgs.) 2.50

FANTASTIC FOUR: BIG TOWN
Marvel Comics: Jan, 2001 - No. 4, Apr, 2001 ($2.99, limited series)
1-4:"What If?" story; McKone-a/Englehart-s 3.00

FANTASTIC FOUR: FIREWORKS
Marvel Comics: Jan, 1999 - No. 3, Mar, 1999 ($2.99, limited series)
1-3-Remix; Jeff Johnson-a 3.00

FANTASTIC FOUR INDEX (See Official...)

FANTASTIC FOUR: 1 2 3 4
Marvel Comics: Oct, 2001 - No. 4, Jan, 2002 ($2.99, limited series)
1-4-Morrison-s/Jae Lee-a. 2-4-Namor-c/app. 3.00

FANTASTIC FOUR ROAST
Marvel Comics Group: May, 1982 (75¢, one-shot, direct sales)
1-Celebrates 20th anniversary of F.F.#1; X-Men, Ghost Rider & many others
  cameo; Golden, Miller, Buscema, Rogers, Byrne, Anderson art;
  Hembeck/Austin-c 4.00

FANTASTIC FOUR: THE LEGEND
Marvel Comics: Oct, 1996 ($3.95, one-shot)
1-Tribute issue 4.00

FANTASTIC FOUR 2099
Marvel Comics: Jan, 1996 - No. 8, Aug, 1996 ($3.95/$1.95)
1-($3.95)-Chromium-c; X-Nation preview 4.00
2-8: 6-Spider-Man 2099-c/app. 5-Doctor Strange app. 7-Thibert-c 2.25
NOTE: **Williamson** a-1i; c-1i.

FANTASTIC FOUR UNLIMITED
Marvel Comics: Mar, 1993 - No. 12, Dec, 1995 ($3.95, 68 pgs.)
1-12: 1-Black Panther app. 4-Thing vs. Hulk. 5-Vs. The Frightful Four. 6-Vs.

Fantastic Four: World's Greatest Comic Magazine #6 © MAR

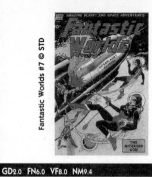
Fantastic Worlds #7 © STD

Fast Fiction #4 © Seaboard Pub.

x

	GD2.0	FN6.0	VF8.0	NM9.4

Namor. 7, 9-12-Wraparound-c 4.00

FANTASTIC FOUR UNPLUGGED
Marvel Comics: Sept, 1995 - No. 6, Aug 1996 (99¢, bi-monthly)
1-6 2.25

FANTASTIC FOUR VS. X-MEN
Marvel Comics: Feb, 1987 - No. 4, June, 1987 (Limited series)
1-4: 4-Austin-a(i) 4.00

FANTASTIC FOUR: WORLD'S GREATEST COMICS MAGAZINE
Marvel Comics: 2001 - No. 12 (Limited series)
1-12: Homage to Lee & Kirby era of F.F.; s/a by Larsen & various. 5-Hulk-c/app.
10-Thor app. 3.00

FANTASTIC GIANTS (Formerly Konga #1-23)
Charlton Comics: V2#24, Sept, 1966 (25¢, 68 pgs.)
V2#24-Special Ditko issue; origin Konga & Gorgo reprinted plus two new
Ditko stories 7 21 50 80

FANTASTIC TALES
I. W. Enterprises: 1958 (no date) (Reprint, one-shot)
1-Reprints Avon's "City of the Living Dead" 3 10 23 35

FANTASTIC VOYAGE (See Movie Comics)
Gold Key: Aug, 1969 - No. 2, Dec, 1969
1 (TV) 5 15 35 60
2 4 12 29 45

FANTASTIC VOYAGES OF SINDBAD, THE
Gold Key: Oct, 1965 - No. 2, June, 1967
1-Painted-c on both 5 15 35 70
2 5 15 34 55

FANTASTIC WORLDS
Standard Comics: No. 5, Sept, 1952 - No. 7, Jan, 1953
5-Toth, Anderson-a 36 108 191 330
6-Toth-c/a 31 93 165 285
7 20 60 105 175

FANTASY FEATURES
Americomics: 1987 - No. 2, 1987 ($1.75)
1,2 3.00

FANTASY ILLUSTRATED
New Media Publ.: Spring 1982 ($2.95, B&W magazine)
1-P. Craig Russell-c/a; art by Ditko, Sekowsky, Sutton; Englehart-s
1 3 5 7

FANTASY MASTERPIECES (Marvel Super Heroes No. 12 on)
Marvel Comics Group: Feb, 1966 - No. 11, Oct, 1967; V2#1, Dec, 1979 - No. 14,
Jan, 1981
1-Photo of Stan Lee (12¢-c #1,2) 6 18 42 70
2-r/1st Fin Fang Foom from Strange Tales #89 3 10 23 35
3-8: 3-G.A. Capt. America-r begin, end #11; 12¢ Giant; Colan-r. 3-6-Kirby-c
(p). 4-Kirby-c(p)(i). 7-Begin G.A. Sub-Mariner, Torch-r/M. Mystery. 8-Torch
battles the Sub-Mariner-r/Marvel Mystery #9 4 12 26 40
9-Origin Human Torch-r/Marvel Comics #1 4 12 29 45
10,11: 10-r/origin & 1st app. All Winners Squad from All Winners #19.
11-r/origin of Toro (H.T. #1) & Black Knight #1 4 12 26 40
V2#1(12/79, 75¢, 52 pgs.)-r/origin Silver Surfer from Silver Surfer #1 with
editing plus reprints cover; J. Buscema-a 5.00
2-14-Reprints Silver Surfer #2-14 w/covers 3.00
NOTE: **Buscema** c-V2#7-9(in part). **Ditko** r-1-3, 7, 9. **Everett** r-1,7-9. **Matt Fox** r-9i. **Kirby** r-1-11;
c(p)-3, 4i, 5, 6. **Starlin** r-8-13. Some direct sale V2#14's had a 50¢ cover price. #3-11 contain Capt.
America-r/Capt. America #3-10. #7-11 contain G.A.Human Torch & Sub-Mariner-r.

FANTASY QUARTERLY (Also see Elfquest)
Independent Publishers Syndicate: Spring, 1978 (B&W)
1-1st app. Elfquest; Dave Sim-a (6 pgs.) 6 18 40 65

FANTOMAN (Formerly Amazing Adventure Funnies)
Centaur Publications: No. 2, Aug, 1940 - No. 4, Dec, 1940
2-The Fantom of the Fair, The Arrow, Little Dynamite-r begin; origin The
Ermine by Filchock; Fantoman app. in 2-4; Burgos, J. Cole, Ernst,

	GD2.0	FN6.0	VF8.0	NM9.4

Gustavson-a 123 369 769 1350
3,4: Gustavson-r. 4-Red Blaze story 100 300 625 1100

FAREWELL MOONSHADOW (See Moonshadow)
DC Comics (Vertigo): Jan, 1997 ($7.95, one-shot)
nn-DeMatteis-s/Muth-c/a 8.00

FARGO KID (Formerly Justice Traps the Guilty)(See Feature Comics #47
Prize Publications: V11#3(#1), June-July, 1958 - V11#5, Oct-Nov, 1958
V11#3(#1)-Origin Fargo Kid; Severin-c/a; Williamson-a(2); Heath-a
20 60 105 175
V11#4,5-Severin-c/a 13 39 66 110

FARMER'S DAUGHTER, THE
Stanhall Publ./Trojan Magazines: Feb-Mar, 1954 - No. 3, June-July, 1954;
No. 4, Oct, 1954
1-Lingerie, nudity panel 22 66 116 200
2-4(Stanhall) 14 42 72 120

FASHION IN ACTION
Eclipse Comics: Aug, 1986 - Feb, 1987 (Baxter paper)
Summer Special 1, Winter Special 1, each Snyder III-c/a 2.25

FASTBALL EXPRESS (Major League Baseball)
Ultimate Sports Force: 2000 ($3.95, one-shot)
1-Polybagged with poster; Johnson, Maddux, Park, Nomo, Clemens app. 4.00

FASTEST GUN ALIVE, THE (Movie)
Dell Publishing Co.: No. 741, Sept, 1956 (one-shot)
Four Color 741-Photo-c 7 21 49 90

FAST FICTION (...Action) (Stories by Famous Authors Illustrated #6 on)
Seaboard Publ./Famous Authors Ill.: Oct, 1949 - No. 5, Mar, 1950
(All have Kiefer-c)(48 pgs.)
1-Scarlet Pimpernel; Jim Lavery-c/a 39 117 208 360
2-Captain Blood; H. C. Kiefer-c/a 35 105 185 320
3-She, by Rider Haggard; Vincent Napoli-a 40 120 232 400
4-(1/50, 52 pgs.)-The 39 Steps; Lavery-c/a 27 81 145 250
5-Beau Geste; Kiefer-c/a 27 81 145 250
NOTE: **Kiefer** a-2, 5; c-2, 3,5. **Lavery** c/a-1, 4. **Napoli** a-3.

FAST FORWARD
DC Comics (Piranha Press): 1992 - No. 3, 1993 ($4.95, 68 pgs.)
1-3: 1-Morrison scripts; McKean-c/a. 3-Sam Kieth-a 5.00

FAST WILLIE JACKSON
Fitzgerald Periodicals, Inc.: Oct, 1976 - No. 7, 1977
1 2 6 11 16
2-7 1 3 6 9

FAT ALBERT (...& the Cosby Kids) (TV)
Gold Key: Mar, 1974 - No. 29, Feb, 1979
1 3 9 21 32
2-10 2 6 11 16
11-29 2 6 9 12

FATALE (Also see Powers That Be #1 & Shadow State #1,2)
Broadway Comics: Jan, 1996 - No. 6, Aug, 1996 ($2.50)
1-6: J.G. Jones-c/a in all, Preview Edition 1 (11/95, B&W) 2.50

FAT AND SLAT (Ed Wheelan) (Becomes Gunfighter No. 5 on)
E. C. Comics: Summer, 1947 - No. 4, Spring, 1948
1-Intro/origin Voltage, Man of Lightning; "Comics" McCormick, the World's
No. 1 Comic Book Fan begins, ends #4 35 105 195 320
2-4: 4-Comics McCormick-c feature 24 72 127 215

FAT AND SLAT JOKE BOOK
All-American Comics (William H. Wise): Summer, 1944 (52 pgs., one-shot)
nn-by Ed Wheelan 26 78 139 240

FATE (See Hand of Fate & Thrill-O-Rama)

FATE
DC Comics: Oct, 1994 - No. 22, Sept, 1996 ($1.95/$2.25)
0,1-22: 8-Begin $2.25-c. 11-14-Alan Scott (Sentinel) app. 10,14-Zatanna app.
21-Phantom Stranger app. 22-Spectre app. 2.25

Fathom: Killian's Tide #1
© Michael Turner

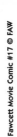

Fawcett Movie Comic #17 © FAW

Fawcett's Funny Animals #7 © FAW

	GD2.0	FN6.0	VF8.0	NM9.4

	GD2.0	FN6.0	VF8.0	NM9.4

FATHOM
Comico: May, 1987 - No. 3, July, 1987 ($1.50, limited series)

1-3				2.25

FATHOM
Image Comics (Top Cow Prod.): Aug, 1998 - Present ($2.50)

Preview				10.00
0-Wizard supplement				8.00
0-($6.95) DF Alternate				7.00
1-Turner-s/a; three covers; alternate story pages				6.00
1-Wizard World Ed.				35.00
2-12: 12-Witchblade-c/app.				3.00
... Collected Edition 1 (3/99, $5.95) r/Preview & all three #1's				6.00
... Collected Edition 2-4 (3-12/99, $5.95) 2-r/#2,3. 3-r/#4,5. 4-r/#6,7				6.00
... Collected Edition 5 (4/00, $5.95) 5-r/#8,9				6.00
... Swimsuit Special (5/99, $2.95) Pin-ups by various				3.00
... Swimsuit Special 2000 (12/00, $2.95) Pin-ups by various; Turner-c				3.00
Michael Turner's Fathom HC ('01, $39.95) r/#1-9, black-c w/silver foil				40.00

FATHOM: KILLIAN'S TIDE
Image Comics (Top Cow Prod.): Apr, 2001 - No. 4, Nov, 2001 ($2.95)

1-4-Caldwell-a(p); two covers by Caldwell and Turner. 2-Flip-book preview of Universe;				3.00

FATIMA...CHALLENGE TO THE WORLD
Catechetical Guild: 1951, 36 pgs. (15¢)

nn (not same as 'Challenge to the World')	4	10	15	20

FATMAN, THE HUMAN FLYING SAUCER
Lightning Comics(Milson Publ. Co.): April, 1967 - No. 3, Aug-Sept, 1967 (68 pgs.) (Written by Otto Binder)

1-Origin/1st app. Fatman & Tinman by Beck	6	18	40	65
2-C. C. Beck-a	4	12	29	45
3-(Scarce)-Beck-a	6	18	45	75

FAULTLINES
DC Comics (Vertigo): May, 1997 - No. 6, Oct, 1997 ($2.50, limited series)

1-6-Lee Marrs-s/Bill Koeb-a in all				2.50

FAUNTLEROY COMICS (Super Duck Presents...)
Close-Up/Archie Publications: 1950; No. 2, 1951; No. 3, 1952

1-Super Duck-c/stories by Al Fagaly in all	9	27	49	70
2,3	6	18	29	40

FAUST
Northstar Publishing/Rebel Studios #7 on: 1989 - No 11, 1997 ($2.00/$2.25, B&W, mature themes)

1-Decapitation-c; Tim Vigil-c/a in all	2	6	15	22
1-2nd - 4th printings				3.00
2	2	6	10	14
2-2nd & 3rd printings, 3,5-2nd printing				3.00
3	1	3	6	9
4-10: 7-Begin Rebel Studios series				5.00
11-($2.25)				3.00

FAWCETT MOTION PICTURE COMICS (See Motion Picture Comics)

FAWCETT MOVIE COMIC
Fawcett Publications: 1949 - No. 20, Dec, 1952 (All photo-c)

nn- "Dakota Lil"; George Montgomery & Rod Cameron (1949)				
	33	99	174	300
nn- "Copper Canyon"; Ray Milland & Hedy Lamarr (1950)				
	25	75	130	225
nn- "Destination Moon" (1950)	77	231	483	850
nn- "Montana"; Errol Flynn & Alexis Smith (1950)	25	75	130	225
nn- "Pioneer Marshal"; Monte Hale (1950)	25	75	130	225
nn- "Powder River Rustlers"; Rocky Lane (1950)	37	111	197	340
nn- "Singing Guns"; Vaughn Monroe, Ella Raines & Walter Brennan (1950)				
	22	66	116	195
7- "Gunmen of Abilene"; Rocky Lane; Bob Powell-a (1950)				
	27	81	142	245
8- "King of the Bullwhip"; Lash LaRue; Bob Powell-a (1950)				
	40	120	220	380

9- "The Old Frontier"; Monte Hale; Bob Powell-a (2/51; mis-dated 2/50)				
	26	78	136	235
10- "The Missourians"; Monte Hale (4/51)	26	78	136	235
11- "The Thundering Trail"; Lash LaRue (6/51)	34	102	179	310
12- "Rustlers on Horseback"; Rocky Lane (8/51)	27	81	142	245
13- "Warpath"; Edmond O'Brien & Forrest Tucker (10/51)				
	19	57	99	165
14- "Last Outpost"; Ronald Reagan (12/51)	40	120	232	400
15-(Scarce)- "The Man From Planet X"; Robert Clark; Schaffenberger-a (2/52)				
	218	654	1364	2400
16- "10 Tall Men"; Burt Lancaster	15	45	77	130
17- "Rose of Cimarron"; Jack Buetel & Mala Powers	12	36	61	105
18- "The Brigand"; Anthony Dexter & Anthony Quinn; Schaffenberger-a				
	12	36	61	105
19- "Carbine Williams"; James Stewart; Costanza-a; James Stewart photo-c				
	14	42	72	120
20- "Ivanhoe"; Robert Taylor & Liz Taylor photo-c	21	63	110	190

FAWCETT'S FUNNY ANIMALS (No. 1-26, 80-on titled "Funny Animals"; becomes Li'l Tomboy No. 92 on?)
Fawcett Publications/Charlton Comics No. 84 on: 12/42 - #79, 4/53; #80, 6/53 - #83, 12?/53; #84, 4/54 - #91, 2/56

1-Capt. Marvel on cover; intro. Hoppy The Captain Marvel Bunny, cloned from Capt. Marvel; Billy the Kid & Willie the Worm begin				
	55	165	341	600
2-Xmas-c	34	102	179	310
3-5: 3(2/43)-Spirit of '43-c	20	60	105	175
6,7,9,10	14	42	72	120
8-Flag-c	15	45	77	130
11-20: 14-Cover is a 1944 calendar	11	33	55	90
21-40: 25-Xmas-c. 26-St. Valentines Day-c	8	24	42	60
41-86,90,91	6	18	32	45
87-89(10-54-2/55)-Merry Mailman ish (TV/Radio)-part photo-c				
	8	24	42	60

NOTE: Marvel Bunny in all issues to at least No. 68 (not in 49-54).

FAZE ONE FAZERS
AC Comics: 1986 - No. 4, Sept, 1986 (Limited series)

1-4				2.25

F.B.I., THE
Dell Publishing Co.: Apr-June, 1965

1-Sinnott-a	3	9	19	28

F.B.I. STORY, THE (Movie)
Dell Publishing Co.: No. 1069, Jan-Mar, 1960

Four Color 1069-Toth-a; James Stewart photo-c	10	30	70	130

FEAR (Adventure into...)
Marvel Comics Group: Nov, 1970 - No. 31, Dec, 1975

1-Fantasy & Sci-Fi-r in early issues; 68 pg. Giant size; Kirby-a(r)				
	4	12	26	40
2-6: 2-4-(68 pgs.). 5,6-(52 pgs.) Kirby-a(r)	3	9	17	25
7-9-Kirby-a(r)	2	6	11	15
10-Man-Thing begins (10/72, 4th app.), ends #19; see Savage Tales #1 for 1st app.; 1st solo series; Chaykin/Morrow-c/a;	3	9	20	30
11,12: 11-N. Adams-c. 12-Starlin/Buckler-a	2	6	9	12
13,14,16-18: 17-Origin/1st app. Wundarr	1	4	7	10
15-1st full-length Man-Thing story (8/73)	2	6	9	12
19-Intro. Howard the Duck; Val Mayerik-a (12/73)	3	9	20	30
20-Morbius, the Living Vampire begins, ends #31; has history recap of Morbius with X-Men & Spider-Man	3	9	20	30
21-23,25	1	4	7	10
24-Blade-c/story	2	6	15	22
26-31	1	3	6	8

NOTE: Bolle a-13i. Brunner c-15-17. Buckler a-11p, 12i. Chaykin a-10i. Colan a-23r. Craig a-10p. Ditko a-6-8r. Evans a-30. Everett a-9, 10i, 21r. Gulacy a-20p. Heath a-12r. Heck a-8r, 13r. Gil Kane a-21p; c(p)-20, 21, 23-28, 31. Kirby a-1-9r. Maneely a-24r. Mooney a-11i, 26r. Morrow a-11i. Paul Reinman a-14r. Robbins a(p)-25-27, 31. Russell a-23p, 24p. Severin c-8. Starlin c-12p.

FEARBOOK
Eclipse Comics: April, 1986 ($1.75, one-shot, mature)

1-Scholastic Mag- r; Bissette-a				2.25

Feature Books #52 © KING

Feature Comics #54 © QUA

Feature Funnies #9 © QUA

	GD2.0	FN6.0	VF8.0	NM9.4

	GD2.0	FN6.0	VF8.0	NM9.4

FEAR EFFECT (Based on the video game)
Image Comics (Top Cow): May, 2000; March, 2001 ($2.95)

Retro Helix 1 (3/01), Special 1 (5/00)				3.00

FEAR IN THE NIGHT (See Complete Mystery No. 3)

FEARLESS FAGAN
Dell Publishing Co.: No. 441, Dec, 1952 (one-shot)

Four Color 441	4	12	27	42

FEATURE BOOK (Dell) (See Large Feature Comic)

FEATURE BOOKS (Newspaper-r, early issues)
David McKay Publications: May, 1937 - No. 57, 1948 (B&W)
(Full color, 68 pgs. mostly)

Note: See individual alphabetical listings for prices

nn-Popeye & the Jeep (#1, 100 pgs.);
reprinted as Feature Books #3 (Very
Rare; only 3 known copies, 1-VF, 2-in
low grade)

NOTE: Above books were advertised together with different covers from Feat. Books #3 & 4.

1-King of the Royal Mtd. (#1)
3-Popeye (7/37) by Segar;
4-Dick Tracy (8/37)-Same as
nn issue but a new cover added
6-Dick Tracy (10/37)
8-Secret Agent X-9 (12/37)
-Not by Raymond
9-Dick Tracy (1/38)
11-Little Annie Rooney (#1, 3/38)
13-Inspector Wade (5/38)
15-Barney Baxter (#1) (7/38)
17-Gangbusters (#1, 9/38) (1st app.)
20-Phantom (#1, 12/38)
22-Phantom
24-Lone Ranger (1941)
26-Prince Valiant (1941)-Hal Foster
-c/a; newspaper strips reprinted, pgs.
1-28,30-63; color & 68 pg. issues
begin; Foster cover is only original
comic book artwork by him
36('43),38,40('44),42,43,
45,47-Blondie
39-Phantom
46-Mandrake in the Fire World-(58 pgs.)
48-Maltese Falcon by Dashiell
Hammett('46)
51,54-Rip Kirby; Raymond-c/s;
origin-#51
53,56,57-Phantom

nn-Dick Tracy (#1)-Reprinted as
Feature Book #4 (100 pgs.) & in
part as 4-Color #1 (Rare, less in
than 10 known copies)

2-Popeye (6/37) by Segar
same as nn issue but a new
cover added
5-Popeye (9/37) by Segar
7-Little Orphan Annie (#1, 11/37)
(Rare)Perkins strips from
12/31/34 to 7/17/35
10-Popeye (2/38)
12-Blondie (#1) (4/38) (Rare)
14-Popeye (6/38) by Segar
16-Red Eagle (8/38)
18,19-Mandrake
21-Lone Ranger
23-Mandrake
25-Flash Gordon (#1)-Reprints
not by Raymond
27-29,31,34-Blondie
30-Katzenjammer Kids (#1, 1942)
32,35,41,44-Katzenjammer Kids
33(nn)-Romance of Flying; World
War II photos
37-Katzenjammer Kids; has photo
& biog. of Harold H.Knerr(1883-
1949) who took over strip from
Rudolph Dirks in 1914
49,50-Perry Mason; based on
Gardner novels
52,55-Mandrake

NOTE: All Feature Books through #25 are over-sized 8-1/2x11-3/8" comics with color covers and
black and white interiors. The covers are rough, heavy stock. The page counts, including covers, are
as follows: nn, #3, 4-100 pgs.; #1, 2-52 pgs.; #5-25 are all 76 pgs. #33 was found in bound set from
publisher.

FEATURE COMICS (Formerly Feature Funnies)
Quality Comics Group: No. 21, June, 1939 - No. 144, May, 1950

21-The Clock, Jane Arden & Mickey Finn continue from Feature Funnies

	68	204	375	575
22-26: 23-Charlie Chan begins (8/39, 1st app.)	47	141	260	400
26-(nn, nd)-Cover in one color, (10¢, 36 pgs.; issue No. blanked out. Two varia-				
tions exist, each contain half of the regular #26)	35	105	195	300
27-(Rare)-Origin/1st app. Doll Man by Eisner (scripts) & Lou Fine (art); Doll				
Man begins, ends #139	417	1250	2604	5000
28-2nd app. Doll Man by Lou Fine	164	492	1023	1800
29	95	285	597	1050
30-1st Doll Man-c	114	342	712	1250
31-Last Clock & Charlie Chan issue (4/40); Charlie Chan moves to Big Shot				
#1 following month (5/40)	75	225	469	825
32-37: 32-Rusty Ryan & Samar begin. 34-Captain Fortune app. 37-Last				
Fine Doll Man	55	165	341	600

Note: A 15¢ Canadian version of Feature Comics #37, made in the US, exists.

38-41: 38-Origin the Ace of Space. 39-Origin The Destroying Demon, ends

#40; X-Mas-c. 40-Bruce Blackburn in costume	43	129	257	450
42,43,45-50: 42-USA, the Spirit of Old Glory begins. 46-Intro. Boyville				
Brigadiers in Rusty Ryan. 47-Fargo Kid begins. 48-USA ends				
	34	102	179	310
44-Doll Man by Crandall begins, ends #63; Crandall-a(2)				
	45	135	270	475
51-60: 56-Marijuana story in Swing Sisson strip. 57-Spider Widow begins.				
60-Raven begins, ends #71	26	78	139	240
61-68 (5/43)	24	72	127	215
69-71-Phantom Lady x-over in Spider Widow	26	78	139	240
72-80,100: 72-Spider Widow ends	19	57	99	165
81-99	15	45	77	130
101-144: 139-Last Doll Man & last Doll Man-c. 140-Intro. Stuntman Stetson				
(Stuntman Stetson c-140-144)	13	39	66	110

NOTE: Celardo a-37-43. Crandall a-44-60, 62, 63-on(most). Gustavson a-(Rusty Ryan)- 32-134.
Powell a-34, 64-73. The Clock c-25, 28, 29. Doll Man c-30, 32, 34, 36, 38, 40, 42, 44, 46, 48, 50,
52, 54, 56, 58, 60, 62, 64, 66, 68, 70, 72, 74, 77-139. Joe Palooka c-21, 24, 27.

FEATURE FILMS
National Periodical Publ.: Mar-Apr, 1950 - No. 4, Sept-Oct, 1950 (All photo-c)

1- "Captain China" with John Payne, Gail Russell, Lon Chaney & Edgar				
Bergen	64	192	398	700
2- "Riding High" with Bing Crosby	68	205	426	750
3- "The Eagle & the Hawk" with John Payne, Rhonda Fleming & D. O'Keefe				
	64	192	398	700
4- "Fancy Pants"; Bob Hope & Lucille Ball	73	219	455	800

FEATURE FUNNIES (Feature Comics No. 21 on)
Harry 'A' Chesler: Oct, 1937 - No. 20, May, 1939

1(V9#1-indicia)-Joe Palooka, Mickey Finn (1st app.), The Bungles, Jane				
Arden, Dixie Dugan (1st app.), Big Top, Ned Brant, Strange As It Seems, &				
Off the Record strip reprints begin	318	954	1749	2700
2-The Hawk app. (11/37); Goldberg-c	147	441	809	1250
3-Hawks of Seas begins by Eisner, ends #12; The Clock begins;				
Christmas-c	115	345	632	975
4,5	85	255	468	725
6-12: 11-Archie O'Toole by Bud Thomas begins, ends #22				
	65	195	358	550
13-Espionage, Starring Black X begins by Eisner, ends #20				
	70	210	385	600
14-20	50	150	275	425

NOTE: Joe Palooka covers 1, 6, 9, 12, 15, 18.

FEATURE PRESENTATION, A (Feature Presentations Magazine #6)
(Formerly Women in Love) (Also see Startling Terror Tales #11)
Fox Features Syndicate: No. 5, April, 1950

5(#1)-Black Tarantula	40	120	232	400

FEATURE PRESENTATIONS MAGAZINE (Formerly A Feature Presentation
#5; becomes Feature Stories Magazine #3 on)
Fox Features Syndicate: No. 6, July, 1950

6(#2)-Moby Dick; Wood-c	33	99	174	300

FEATURE STORIES MAGAZINE (Formerly Feature Presentations Mag. #6)
Fox Features Syndicate: No. 3, Aug, 1950

3-Jungle Lil, Zegra stories; bondage-c	35	105	185	320

FEDERAL MEN COMICS (See Adventure Comics #32, The Comics Magazine,
New Adventure Comics, New Book of Comics, New Comics & Star Spangled
Comics #91)
Gerard Publ. Co.: No. 2, 1945 (DC reprints from 1930's)

2-Siegel/Shuster-a; cover redrawn from Det. #9	40	120	220	380

FEEDERS
Dark Horse Comics: Oct, 1999 ($2.95, one-shot)

1-Mike Allred-c/a/Shane Hawks-s				3.00

FELICIA HARDY: THE BLACK CAT
Marvel Comics: July, 1994 - No. 4, Oct, 1994 ($1.50, limited series)

1-4: 1,4-Spider-Man app.				2.25

FELIX'S NEPHEWS INKY & DINKY
Harvey Publications: Sept, 1957 - No. 7, Oct, 1958

1-Cover shows Inky's left eye with 2 pupils	10	30	55	80

Felix the Cat #13 © KING

Felon #1 © Greg Rucka & TCOW

F5 #2 © F5 Ent.

| | GD2.0 | FN6.0 | VF8.0 | NM9.4 | | GD2.0 | FN6.0 | VF8.0 | NM9.4 |

2-7 ... 6 18 29 40
NOTE: *Messmer* art in 1-6. *Oriolo* a-1-7.

FELIX THE CAT (See Cat Tales 3-D, The Funnies, March of Comics #24,36,51, New Funnies & Popular Comics)
Dell Publ. No. 1-19/Toby No. 20-61/Harvey No. 62-118/Dell No. 1-12:
1943 - No. 118, Nov, 1961; Sept-Nov, 1962 - No. 12, July-Sept, 1965

Four Color 15	73	219	511	950
Four Color 46('44)	41	123	287	535
Four Color 77('45)	39	117	273	510
Four Color 119('46)-All new stories begin	32	96	224	420
Four Color 135('46)	24	72	168	320
Four Color 162(9/47)	19	57	133	250
1(2-3/48)(Dell)	27	81	189	350
2	15	45	108	190
3-5	12	36	84	150
6-19(2-3/51-Dell)	8	24	56	110

20-30,32,33,36,38-61(6/55)-All Messmer issues.(Toby): 28-(2/52)-Some copies have #29 on cover, #28 on inside (Rare in high grade)
... 22 66 154 285
31,34,35-No Messmer-a; Messmer-c only 31,34 ... 9 27 63 120
37-(100 pgs., 25 ¢, 1/15/53, X-Mas-c, Toby; daily & Sunday-r (rare)
... 46 138 322 600

62(8/55)-80,100 (Harvey)	5	15	34	55
81-99	4	12	29	45
101-118(11/61): 101-117-Reprints. 118-All new-a	3	9	21	32
12-269-211(#1, 9-11/62)(Dell)-No Messmer	4	12	30	50
2-12(7-9/65)(Dell, TV)-No Messmer	3	10	23	35
3-D Comic Book 1(1953-One Shot)-w/glasses	40	120	220	380

Summer Annual nn ('53, 25¢, 100 pgs., Toby)-Daily & Sunday-r
... 42 126 294 500
Winter Annual 2 ('54, 25¢, 100 pgs., Toby)-Daily & Sunday-r
... 40 120 280 480

(Special note: Despite the covers on Toby 37 and the Summer Annual above proclaiming "all new stories," they were actually reformatted newspaper strips.)
NOTE: *Otto Messmer* went to work for Universal Film as an animator in 1915 and then worked for the Pat Sullivan animation studio in 1916. He created a black cat in the cartoon short, *Feline Follies* in 1919 that became known as Felix in the early 1920s. The Felix Sunday strip began Aug. 14, 1923 and continued until Sept. 19, 1943 whjen *Messmer* took the character to Dell (Western Publishing) and began doing Felix comic books, first adapting strips to the comic format. The first all new Felix comic was Four Color #119 in 1946 (#4 in the Dell run). The daily Felix was begun on May 9, 1927 by another artist, but by the following year, *Messmer* did too. King Features took the daily away from *Messmer* in 1954 and he began to do some of his most dynamic art for Toby Press. The daily was continued by *Joe Oriolo* who drew it until it was discontinued Jan. 9, 1967. *Oriolo* was *Messmer's* assistant for many years and inked some of the stories during the Toby run, as well as doing some of the stories by himself. Though *Messmer* continued to work for Harvey, his contribuitons were limited, and no all *Messmer* stories appeared after the Toby run until some early Toby reprints were published in the 1990s Harvey revival of the title. 4-Color Nos. 15, 46, 77 and the Toby Annuals are all daily or Sunday newspaper reprints from the 1930's-1940's drawn by *Otto Messmer*. #101-r/#64; 102-r/#65; 103-r/#67; 104-117-r/#68-81. *Messmer*-a in all Dell/Toby/Harvey issues except #34, 35, 97, 98, 100, 118. *Oriolo* a-20, 31-on.

FELIX THE CAT (Also see The Nine Lives of...)
Harvey Comics/Gladstone: Sept, 1991 - No. 7, Jan, 1993 ($1.25/$1.50, bi-monthly)
1: 1950s-r/Toby issues by Messmer begins. 1-Inky and Dinky back-up story (produced by Gladstone) ... 4.00
2-7, Big Book, V2#1 (9/92, $1.95, 52 pgs.) ... 3.00

FELIX THE CAT AND FRIENDS
Felix Comics: 1992 - No. 5, 1993 ($1.95)
1-5: 1-Contains Felix trading cards ... 3.00

FELIX THE CAT & HIS FRIENDS (Pat Sullivan's...)
Toby Press: Dec, 1953 - No. 3, 1954 (Indicia title for #2&3 as listed)
1 (Indicia title, "Felix and His Friends," #1 only) ... 31 93 165 285
2-3 ... 20 60 105 175

FELIX THE CAT DIGEST MAGAZINE
Harvey Comics: July, 1992 ($1.75, digest-size, 98 pgs.)
1-Felix, Richie Rich stories ... 5.00

FELIX THE CAT KEEPS ON WALKIN'
Hamilton Comics: 1991 ($15.95, 8-1/2"x11", 132 pgs.)
nn-Reprints 15 Toby Press Felix the Cat and Felix and His Friends stories in new computer color ... 16.00

FELON
Image Comics (Minotaur Press): Nov, 2001 - Present ($2.95, B&W)
1-Rucka-s/Clark-a/c ... 3.00

FEM FANTASTIQUE
AC Comics: Aug, 1988 ($1.95, B&W)
V2#1-By Bill Black; Betty Page pin-up ... 4.00

FEMFORCE (Also see Untold Origin of the Femforce)
Americomics: Apr, 1985 - No. 109 (1.75-/2.95, B&W #16-56)
1-Black-a in most; Nightveil, Ms. Victory begin ... 1 3 6 9
2-10 ... 4.00
11-43,45-63,65-99: 25-Origin/1st app. new Ms. Victory. 28-Colt leaves. 29,30-Camilla-r by Mayo from Jungle Comics. 36-(2.95, 52 pgs.) 50 (2.95, 52 pgs.)-Contains flexi-disc; origin retold; most AC characters app.
51-Photo-c from movie. 57-Begin color issues. 95-Photo-c ... 3.00
44,64: 44-W/mini-comic, Catman & Kitten #0. 64-Re-intro Black Phantom ... 5.00
100-($3.95) ... 5.00
100-($6.90)-Polybagged ... 1 3 6 8
101-109-($4.95) ... 5.00
Special 1 (Fall, '84)(B&W,52pgs.)-1st app. Ms. Victory, She-Cat, Blue Bulleteer, Rio Rita & Lady Luger ... 4.00
Bad Girl Backlash-(12/95, $5.00) ... 5.00
Frightbook 1 ('92, $2.95, B&W)-Halloween special, In the House of Horror 1 ('89, 2.50, B&W), Night of the Demon 1 ('90, 2.75, B&W), Out of the Asylum Special 1 ('87, B&W, $1.95), Pin-Up Portfolio ... 3.50
Pin-Up Portfolio (5 issues) ... 4.00

FEMFORCE UP CLOSE
AC Comics: Apr, 1992 - No. 11, 1995 ($2.75, quarterly)
1-11: 1-Stars Nightveil; inside f/c photo from Femforce movie. 2-Stars Stardust. 3-Stars Dragonfly. 4-Stars She-Cat ... 3.50

FERDINAND THE BULL (See Mickey Mouse Magazine V4#3)
Dell Publishing Co.: 1938 (10¢, large size, some color w/rest B&W)
nn ... 20 60 105 175

FERRET
Malibu Comics: Sept, 1992; May, 1993 - No. 10, Feb, 1994 ($1.95)
1-(1992, one-shot) ... 3.00
1-10: 1-Die-cut-c. 2-4-Collector's Ed. w/poster. 5-Polybagged w/Skycap ... 2.50
2-4-($1.95)-Newsstand Edition w/different-c ... 2.25

FEUD
Marvel Comics (Epic Comics/Heavy Hitters): July, 1993 - No. 4, Oct, 1993 ($1.95, limited series)
1-($2.50)-Embossed-c ... 3.00
2-4 ... 2.25

F5
Image Comics: Jan, 2000 - No. 4, Oct, 2000 ($2.50/$2.95)
Preview (1/00, $2.50) Character bios and b&w pages; Daniel-s/a ... 2.50
1-($2.95, 48 pgs.) Tony Daniel-s/a ... 3.00
1-($20.00) Variant bikini-c ... 20.00
2-4-($2.50) ... 2.50

FIBBER McGEE & MOLLY (Radio)(Also see A-1 Comics)
Magazine Enterprises: No. 25, 1949 (one-shot)
A-1 25 ... 10 30 55 85

55 DAYS AT PEKING (See Movie Comics)

FICTION ILLUSTRATED
Byron Preiss Visual Publ./Pyramid: No. 1, Jan, 1975 - No. 3, Aug, 1976 ($1.00, digest size, 132 pgs.)
1,2: 1-Schlomo Raven; Sutton-a. 2-Starwarn; Stephen Fabian-a.
... 2 6 11 16
3-($1.00-c, 4 3/4 x 6 1/2 digest size) Chandler; new Steranko-a
... 2 6 13 20
3-($4.95-c, 8 1/2 x 11" graphic novel; low print) same contents and indicia, but "Chandler" is the cover feature title ... 5 15 38 60

FIGHT AGAINST CRIME (Fight Against the Guilty #22, 23)
Story Comics: May, 1951 - No. 21, Sept, 1954

Fight Against Crime #2 © Story

Fight Comics #13 © FH

Fighting American #6 © DC

	GD2.0	FN6.0	VF8.0	NM9.4
1-True crime stories #1-4	37	111	197	340
2	20	60	105	175
3,5: 5-Frazetta-a, 1 pg.; content change to horror & suspense	17	51	88	150
4-Drug story "Hopped Up Killers"	18	54	94	160
6,7: 6-Used in POP, pgs. 83,84	14	42	72	125
8-Last crime format issue	13	39	66	115

NOTE: No. 9-21 contain violent, gruesome stories with blood, dismemberment, decapitation, E.C. style plot twists and several E.C. swipes. Bondage c-4, 6, 18, 19.

9-11,13	37	111	197	340
12-Morphine drug story "The Big Dope"	40	120	217	375
14-Tothish art by Ross Andru; electrocution-c	39	117	208	360
15-B&W & color illos in POP	37	111	197	340
16-E.C. story swipe/Haunt of Fear #19; Tothish-a by Ross Andru; bondage-c	40	120	217	375
17-Wildey E.C. swipe/Shock SuspenStories #9; knife through neck-c (1/54)	39	117	208	360
18,19: 19-Bondage/torture-c	35	105	185	320
20-Decapitation cover; contains hanging, ax murder, blood & violence	55	165	341	600
21-E.C. swipe	28	87	156	270

NOTE: Cameron a-4, 5, 8. Hollingsworth a-3-7, 9, 10, 13. Wildey a-6, 15, 16.

FIGHT AGAINST THE GUILTY (Formerly Fight Against Crime)
Story Comics: No. 22, Dec, 1954 - No. 23, Mar, 1955

22-Tothish-a by Ross Andru; Ditko-a; E.C. story swipe; electrocution-c (Last pre-code)	29	87	156	270
23-Hollingsworth-a	21	63	110	185

FIGHT COMICS
Fiction House Magazines: Jan, 1940 - No. 83, 11/52; No. 84, Wint, 1952-53; No. 85, Spring, 1953; No. 86, Summer, 1954

1-Origin Spy Fighter, Starring Saber; Jack Dempsey life story; Shark Brodie & Chip Collins begin; Fine-c; Eisner-a	300	900	1875	3500
2-Joe Louis life story; Fine/Eisner-c	114	342	712	1250
3-Rip Regan, the Power Man begins (3/40)	86	258	540	950
4,5: 4-Fine-c	64	192	398	700
6-10: 6,7-Powell-c	50	150	300	525
11-14: Rip Regan ends	43	129	257	450
15-1st app. Super American plus-c (10/41)	59	177	369	650
16-Captain Fight begins (12/41); Spy Fighter ends	59	177	369	650
17,18: Super American ends	45	135	270	475
19-Captain Fight ends; Senorita Rio begins (6/42, origin & 1st app.); Rip Carson, Chute Trooper begins	47	141	286	500
20	40	120	232	400
21-31: 31-Decapitation-c	33	99	174	300
32-Tiger Girl begins (6/44, 1st app.?)	40	120	220	380
33-50: 44-Capt. Fight returns. 48-Used in Love and Death by Legman. 49-Jungle-c begin, end #81	24	72	127	220
51-Origin Tiger Girl; Patsy Pin-Up app.	40	120	214	370
52-60,62-64-Last Baker issue	22	66	116	200
61-Origin Tiger Girl retold	24	72	127	220
65-78: 78-Used in POP, pg. 99	19	57	99	165
79-The Space Rangers app.	19	57	99	170
80-85: 81-Last jungle-c. 82-85-War-c/stories	16	48	83	140
86-Two Tigerman stories by Evans-r/Rangers Comics #40,41; Moreira-r/ Rangers Comics #45	16	48	83	145

NOTE: Bondage covers, Lingerie, headlights panels are common. Captain Fight by Kamen-51-66. Kayo Kirby by Baker-43-64, 67(not by Baker). Senorita Rio by Kamen-c-57-64; By Grandenetti-#65, 66. Tiger Girl by Baker-#36-60, 62-64; Eisner c-1-3, 5, 10, 11. Kamen a-54?, 57? Tuska a-1, 5, 8, 10, 21, 29, 34. Whitman c-73-84. Zolnerwich c-16, 17, 22. Power Man c-5, 6, 9. Super American c-15-17. Tiger Girl c-49-81.

FIGHT FOR LOVE
United Features Syndicate: 1952 (no month)

nn-Abbie & Slats newspaper-r	10	30	55	80

FIGHTING AIR FORCE (See United States Fighting Air Force)

FIGHTIN' AIR FORCE (Formerly Sherlock Holmes?; Never Again? War and Attack #54 on)
Charlton Comics: No. 3, Feb, 1956 - No. 53, Feb-Mar, 1966

V1#3	8	24	42	60
4-10	5	15	25	35

	GD2.0	FN6.0	VF8.0	NM9.4
11(3/58, 68 pgs.)	7	21	36	50
12 (100 pgs.)	11	33	55	90
13-30: 13,24-Glanzman-a. 24-Glanzman-c	3	9	19	28
31-50: 50-American Eagle begins	2	6	15	22
51-53	2	6	12	18

FIGHTING AMERICAN
Headline Publ./Prize (Crestwood): Apr-May, 1954 - No. 7, Apr-May, 1955

1-Origin & 1st app. Fighting American & Speedboy (Capt. America & Bucky clones); S&K-c/a(3); 1st super hero satire series	173	519	1080	1900
2-S&K-a(3)	80	240	500	875
3-5: 3,4-S&K-a(3). 5-S&K-a(2); Kirby/?-a	64	192	398	700
6-Origin-r (4 pgs.) plus 2 pgs. by S&K	61	182	381	675
7-Kirby-a	55	165	330	575

NOTE: Simon & Kirby covers on all. 6 is last pre-code issue.

FIGHTING AMERICAN
Harvey Publications: Oct, 1966 (25¢)

1-Origin Fighting American & Speedboy by S&K-r; S&K-c/a(3); 1 pg. Neal Adams ad	5	15	38	60

FIGHTING AMERICAN
DC Comics: Feb, 1994 - No. 6, 1994 ($1.50, limited series)

1-6				2.50

FIGHTING AMERICAN (Vol. 3)
Awesome Entertainment: Aug, 1997 - No. 2, Oct, 1997 ($2.50)

Preview-Agent America (pre-lawsuit)	1	3	5	7
1-Four covers by Liefeld, Churchill, Platt, McGuinness				2.50
1-Platinum Edition, 1-Gold foil Edition				10.00
1-Comic Cavalcade Edition, 2-American Ent. Spice Ed.				4.00
2-Platt-c, 2-Liefeld variant-c				2.50

FIGHTING AMERICAN: DOGS OF WAR
Awesome-Hyperwerks: Sept, 1998 - No. 3, May, 1999 ($2.50)

Limited Convention Special (7/98, B&W) Platt-a				2.50
1-3-Starlin-s/Platt-a/c				2.50

FIGHTING AMERICAN: RULES OF THE GAME
Awesome Entertainment: Nov, 1997 - No. 3, Mar, 1998 ($2.50, lim. series)

1-3: 1-Loeb-s/McGuinness-a/c. 2-Flip book with Swat! preview				2.50
1-Liefeld SPICE variant-c, 1-Dynamic Forces Ed.; McGuinness-c				2.50
1-Liefeld Fighting American & cast variant-c				2.50

FIGHTIN' ARMY (Formerly Soldier and Marine Comics) (See Captain Willy Schultz)
Charlton Comics: No. 16, 1/56 - No. 127, 12/76; No. 128, 9/77 - No. 172, 11/84

16	8	24	42	60
17-19,21-23,25-30	5	15	25	35
20-Ditko-a	8	24	42	60
24 (3/58, 68 pgs.)	6	18	32	45
31-45	3	9	17	24
46-60	2	6	15	22
61-74	2	6	11	16
75-1st The Lonely War of Willy Schultz	2	6	13	20
76-80: 76-92-The Lonely War of Willy Schultz. 79-Devil Brigade	2	6	11	15
81-88,91,93-99: 82,83-Devil Brigade	2	6	9	12
89,90,92-Ditko-a	2	6	12	18
100	2	6	11	16
101-127	1	3	6	9
128-140	1	3	5	7
141-165				5.00
166-172-Low print run				6.00
108(Modern Comics-1977)-Reprint				4.00

NOTE: Aparo c-154. Glanzman a-77-88. Montes/Bache a-48, 49, 51, 69, 75, 76, 170r.

FIGHTING CARAVANS (See Zane Grey 4-Color 632)

FIGHTING DANIEL BOONE
Avon Periodicals: 1953

nn-Kinstler-c/a, 22 pgs.	20	60	105	175
I.W. Reprint #1-Reprints #1 above; Kinstler-c/a; Lawrence/Alascia-a	2	6	15	22

Fighting Leathernecks #1 © TOBY

Fightin' Marines #9 © STJ

Fighting Yank #7 © Nedor

	GD2.0	FN6.0	VF8.0	NM9.4

FIGHTING DAVY CROCKETT (Formerly Kit Carson)
Avon Periodicals: No. 9, Oct-Nov, 1955

9-Kinstler-c	10	30	55	80

FIGHTIN' FIVE, THE (Formerly Space War) (Also see The Peacemaker)
Charlton Comics: July, 1964 - No. 41, Jan, 1967; No. 42, Oct, 1981 - No. 49, Dec, 1982

V2#28-Origin/1st app. Fightin' Five; Montes/Bache-a	5	15	38	60
29-39,41-Montes/Bache-a in all	3	9	19	28
40-Peacemaker begins (1st app.)	6	18	40	65
41-Peacemaker (2nd app.)	4	12	26	40
42-49: Reprints				5.00

FIGHTING FRONTS!
Harvey Publications: Aug, 1952 - No. 5, Jan, 1953

1	9	27	49	70
2-Extreme violence; Nostrand/Powell-a	10	30	55	85
3-5: 3-Powell-a	6	18	29	40

FIGHTING INDIAN STORIES (See Midget Comics)
FIGHTING INDIANS OF THE WILD WEST!
Avon Periodicals: Mar, 1952 - No. 2, Nov, 1952

1-Geronimo, Chief Crazy Horse, Chief Victorio, Black Hawk begin; Larsen-a; McCann-a(2)	17	51	88	150
2-Kinstler-c & inside-c only; Larsen, McCann-a	11	33	55	90
100 Pg. Annual (1952, 25¢)-Contains three comics rebound; Geronimo, Chief Crazy Horse, Chief Victorio; Kinstler-c	33	99	174	300

FIGHTING LEATHERNECKS
Toby Press: Feb, 1952 - No. 6, Dec, 1952

1- "Duke's Diary"; full pg. pin-ups by Sparling	14	42	72	125
2-5: 2- "Duke's Diary". 3-5- "Gil's Gals"; full pg. pin-ups	10	30	55	80
6-(Same as No. 3-5?)	10	30	55	80

FIGHTING MAN, THE (War)
Ajax/Farrell Publications(Excellent Publ.): May, 1952 - No. 8, July, 1953

1	14	42	72	120
2	7	21	36	50
3-8	6	18	29	40
Annual 1 (1952, 25¢, 100 pgs.)	24	72	127	220

FIGHTIN' MARINES (Formerly The Texan; also see Approved Comics)
St. John(Approved Comics)/Charlton Comics No. 14 on:
No. 15, 8/51 - No. 12, 3/53; No. 14, 5/55 - No. 132, 11/76; No. 133, 10/77 - No. 176, 9/84 (No #13?) (Korean War #1-3)

15(#1)-Matt Baker c/a "Leatherneck Jack"; slightly large size; Fightin' Texan No. 16 & 17?	40	120	232	400
2-1st Canteen Kate by Baker; slightly large size; partial Baker-c	43	129	257	450
3-9,11-Canteen Kate by Baker; Baker c-#2,3,5-11; 4-Partial Baker-c	25	75	130	225
10-Matt Baker-c	10	30	55	80
12-No Baker-c; Last St. John issue?	6	18	29	40
14 (5/55; 1st Charlton issue; formerly?)-Canteen Kate by Baker; all stories reprinted from #2	19	57	99	165
15-Baker-c	9	27	49	70
16,18-20-Not Baker-c	5	15	25	35
17-Canteen Kate by Baker	14	42	72	120
21-24	5	15	24	32
25-(68 pgs.)(3/58)-Check-a?	8	24	45	65
26-(100 pgs.)(8/58)-Check-a(5)	13	39	66	110
27-50	3	9	17	24
51-81: 78-Shotgun Harker & the Chicken series begin	2	6	12	18
82-(100 pgs.)	4	12	26	40
83-85: 85-Last 12¢ issue	2	6	11	16
86-94: 94-Last 15¢ issue	2	6	10	14
95-100,122: 122-(1975) Pilot issue for "War" title (Fightin' Marines Presents War)	2	6	9	12
101-121	1	3	6	8
123-140				6.00

141-170				5.00
171-176-Low print run	1	3	5	7
120(Modern Comics reprint, 1977)				4.00

NOTE: No. 14 & 16 (CC) reprint St. John issues; No. 16 reprints St. John insignia on cover. **Colan** a-3, 7. **Glanzman** c/a-92, 94. **Montes/Bache** a-48, 53, 55, 64, 65, 72-74, 77-83, 176r.

FIGHTIN' MARSHAL OF THE WILD WEST (See The Hawk)

FIGHTIN' NAVY (Formerly Don Winslow)
Charlton Comics: No. 74, 1/56 - No. 125, 4-5/66; No. 126, 8/83 - No. 133, 10/84

74	5	15	38	60
75-81	3	10	23	35
82-Sam Glanzman-a	4	12	25	38
83-(100 pgs.)	5	15	38	60
84-99,101: 101-UFO story	3	9	17	24
100	3	9	17	26
102-105,106-125('66)	2	6	12	18
126-133 (1984)-Low print run	1	3	5	7

NOTE: **Montes/Bache** a-109. **Glanzman** a-82, 92, 96, 98, 100, 131r.

FIGHTING PRINCE OF DONEGAL, THE (See Movie Comics)

FIGHTIN' TEXAN (Formerly The Texan & Fightin' Marines?)
St. John Publishing Co.: No. 16, Sept, 1952 - No. 17, Dec, 1952

16,17: Tuska-a each. 17-Cameron-c/a	8	24	42	60

FIGHTING UNDERSEA COMMANDOS (See Undersea Fighting...)
Avon Periodicals: May, 1952 - No. 5, April, 1953 (U.S. Navy frogmen)

1-Cover title is Undersea Fighting... #1 only	14	42	72	125
2	10	30	55	80
3-5: 1,3-Ravielli-a. 4-Kinstler-c	9	27	49	70

FIGHTING WAR STORIES
Men's Publications/Story Comics: Aug, 1952 - No. 5, 1953

1	10	30	55	80
2-5	6	18	29	40

FIGHTING YANK (See America's Best Comics & Startling Comics)
Nedor/Better Publ./Standard: Sept, 1942 - No. 29, Aug, 1949

1-The Fighting Yank begins; Mystico, the Wonder Man app; bondage-c	245	735	1534	2700
2	105	315	656	1150
3,4: 4-Schomburg-c begin	77	231	483	850
5-10: 7-Grim Reaper app. 8,10-Bondage/torture-c	59	177	369	650
11,13-20: 11-The Oracle app. 15-Bondage/torture-c. 18-The American Eagle app.	50	150	300	525
12-Hirohito bondage-c	55	165	341	600
21,24: 21-Kara, Jungle Princess app. 24-Miss Masque app.	45	135	270	475
22-Miss Masque-c/story	53	159	318	560
23-Classic Schomburg hooded vigilante-c	59	177	369	650
25-Robinson/Meskin-a; strangulation, lingerie panel; The Cavalier app.	53	159	318	560
26-29: All-Robinson/Meskin-a. 28-One pg. Williamson-a	44	132	264	460

NOTE: **Schomburg** (**Xela**) c-4-29; airbrush-c 28, 29. Bondage c-1, 4, 8, 10, 11, 12, 15, 17.

FIGHTMAN
Marvel Comics: June, 1993 ($2.00, one-shot, 52 pgs.)

1				2.25

FIGHT THE ENEMY
Tower Comics: Aug, 1966 - No. 3, Mar, 1967 (25¢, 68 pgs.)

1-Lucky 7 & Mike Manly begin	4	12	26	40
2-Boris Vallejo; McWilliams-a	3	9	21	32
3-Wood-a (1/2 pg.); McWilliams, Bolle-a	3	9	21	32

FILM FUNNIES
Marvel Comics (CPC): Nov, 1949 - No. 2, Feb, 1950 (52 pgs.)

1-Krazy Krow, Wacky Duck	19	57	99	165
2-Wacky Duck	14	42	72	120

FILM STARS ROMANCES
Star Publications: Jan-Feb, 1950 - No. 3, May-June, 1950 (True life stories of movie stars)

Fire #1 © Brian Michael Bendis

Firehair Comics #7 © FH

Fireside Book Series - Heart Throbs © DC

	GD2.0	FN6.0	VF8.0	NM9.4

1-Rudy Valentino & Gregory Peck stories; L. B. Cole-c; lingerie panels
43 129 257 450
2-Liz Taylor/Robert Taylor photo-c & true life story 41 123 246 425
3-Douglas Fairbanks story; photo-c 26 78 136 235

FINAL CYCLE, THE
Dragon's Teeth Productions: July, 1987 - No. 4, 1988 (Limited series)
1-4 2.25

FINAL NIGHT, THE (See DC related titles and Parallax: Emerald Night)
DC Comics: Nov, 1996 - No. 4, Nov, 1996 ($1.95, weekly limited series)
1-4: Kesel-s/Immonen-a(p) in all. 4-Parallax's final acts 3.50
Preview 2.25
TPB-(1998, $12.95) r/#1-4, Parallax: Emerald Night #1, and preview 13.00

FINALS
DC Comics (Vertigo): Sept, 1999 - No. 4, Dec, 1999 ($2.95, limited series)
1-4-Will Pfeifer-s/Jill Thompson-a 3.00

FIRE
Caliber Press: 1993 - No. 2, 1993 ($2.95, B&W, limited series, 52 pgs.)
1,2-Brian Michael Bendis-s/a 3.00
TPB (1999, 2001, $9.95) Restored reprints of series 10.00

FIREARM (Also see Codename: Firearm, Freex #15, Night Man #4 & Prime #10)
Malibu Comics (Ultraverse): Sept, 1993 - No. 18, Mar, 1995 ($1.95/$2.50)
0 ($14.95)-Came w/ video containing 1st half of story (comic contains 2nd half); 1st app. Duet 15.00
1,3-6: 1-James Robinson scripts begin; Cully Hamner-a; Howard Chaykin-c; 1st app Alec Swan. 3-Intro The Sportsmen; Chaykin-c. 4-Break-Thru x-over; Chaykin-c. 5-1st app. Ellen (Swan's girlfriend);2 pg. origin of Prime. 6-Prime app. (story cont'd in Prime #10);Brereton-c 2.50
1-($2.50)-Newsstand edition polybagged w/card 3.00
1-Ultra Limited silver foil-c 5.00
2 ($2.50, 44 pgs.)-Hardcase app.;Chaykin-a; Rune flip-c/story by B. Smith (3 pgs.) 3.00
7-10,12-17: 12-The Rafferty Saga begins, ends #18; 1st app. Rafferty 15-Night Man & Freex app. 17-Swan marries Ellen 2.50
11-($3.50, 68 pgs.)-Flip book w/Ultraverse Premiere #5 3.50
18-Death of Rafferty; Chaykin-c 3.00
NOTE: *Brereton* c-6. *Chaykin* c-1-4, 14, 18. *Hamner* a-1-4. *Herrera* a-12. *James Robinson* scripts-0-18.

FIRE BALL XL5 (See Steve Zodiac & The ...)

FIREBRAND (Also see Showcase '96 #4)
DC Comics: Feb, 1996 - No. 9, Oct, 1996 ($1.75)
1-9: Brian Augustyn scripts; Velluto-c/a in all. 9-Daredevil #319-c/swipe 2.25

FIRE FROM HEAVEN
Image Comics (WildStorm Productions): Mar, 1996 ($2.50)
1,2-Moore-s 2.50

FIREHAIR COMICS (Formerly Pioneer West Romances #3-6; also see Rangers Comics)
Fiction House Magazines (Flying Stories): Winter/48-49; No. 2, Wint/49-50; No. 7, Spr/51 - No. 11, Spr/52
1-Origin Firehair 55 165 331 580
2-Continues as Pioneer West Romances for #3-6 29 87 153 265
7-11 20 60 105 175
I.W. Reprint 8-(nd)-Kinstler-c; reprints Rangers #57; Dr. Drew story by Grandenetti 3 9 20 30

FIRESIDE BOOK SERIES (Hard and soft cover editions)
Simon and Schuster: 1974 - 1980 (130-260 pgs.), Square bound, color
Amazing Spider-Man, The, 1979, HC 8 24 60 100
130 pgs., $3.95, Bob Larkin-a SC 6 18 40 65
America At War–The Best of DC War HC 13 39 91 155
Comics, 1979, $6.95, 260 pgs, Kubert-c SC 8 24 58 95
Best of Spidey Super Stories (Electric SC 6 18 45 75
Company) 1978, $3.95,
Bring On The Bad Guys (Origins of the HC 8 24 58 95

Marvel Comics Villains) 1976, $6.95, SC 5 15 34 55
260 pgs.; Romita-c
Captain America, Sentinel of Liberty,1979, HC 8 24 60 100
130 pgs., $12.95, Cockrum-c SC 5 15 38 60
Doctor Strange Master of the Mystic HC 8 24 60 100
Arts, 1980, 130 pgs. SC 5 15 38 60
Fantastic Four, The, 1979, 130 pgs. HC 8 24 58 95
SC 5 15 34 55
Heart Throbs–The Best of DC Romance HC 18 54 123 220
Comics, 1979, 260 pgs., $6.,95 SC 11 33 77 130
Incredible Hulk, The, 1978, 260 pgs. HC 8 24 58 95
(8 1/4" x 11") SC 5 15 34 55
Marvel's Greatest Superhero Battles, HC 11 33 77 130
1978, 260 pgs., $6.95, Romita-a SC 6 18 45 75
Mysteries in Space, 1980, $7.95, HC 10 30 68 115
Anderson-c. r-DC sci/fi stories SC 6 18 42 70
Origins of Marvel Comics, 1974, 260 pgs., $5.95. r-covers & origins of Fantastic
Four, Hulk, Spider-Man, Thor, HC 8 24 58 95
& Doctor Strange SC 5 15 34 55
Silver Surfer, The, 1978, 130 pgs., HC 9 27 63 105
$4.95, Norem-c SC 6 18 45 75
Son of Origins of Marvel Comics, 1975, 260 pgs., $6.95, Romita-c. Reprints
covers & origins of X-Men, Iron Man, HC 8 24 58 95
Avengers, Daredevil, Silver Surfer SC 5 15 34 55
Superhero Women, The–Featuring the HC 11 33 77 130
Fabulous Females of Marvel Comics, SC 6 18 45 75
1977, 260 pgs., $6.95, Romita-a
Note: Prices listed are for 1st printings. Later printings are worth 30% less.

FIRESTAR
Marvel Comics Group: Mar, 1986 - No. 4, June, 1986 (75¢)(From Spider-Man TV series)
1,2: 1-X-Men & New Mutants app. 2-Wolverine-c (not real Wolverine?); Art Adams-a(p) 5.00
3,4: 3-Art Adams/Sienkiewicz-c. 4-B. Smith-c 3.00

FIRESTONE (See Donald And Mickey Merry Christmas)

FIRESTORM (See Cancelled Comic Cavalcade, DC Comics Presents, Flash #289, The Fury of... & Justice League of America #179)
DC Comics: March, 1978 - No. 5, Oct-Nov, 1978
1,5: 1-Origin & 1st app. 1 4 7 10
2-4: 2-Origin Multiplex. 3-Origin & 1st app. Killer Frost. 4-1st app. Hyena 6.00

FIRESTORM, THE NUCLEAR MAN (Formerly Fury of Firestorm)
DC Comics: No. 65, Nov, 1987 - No. 100, Aug, 1990
65-99: 66-1st app. Zuggernaut; Firestorm vs. Green Lantern. 71-Death of Capt. X. 67,68-Millennium tie-ins. 83-1st new look 2.50
100-($2.95, 68 pgs.) 4.00
Annual 5 (10/87)-1st app. new Firestorm 3.00

FIRST, THE
CrossGeneration Comics: Jan, 2001 - Present ($2.95)
1-14: 1-Barbara Kesel-s/Bart Sears & Andy Smith-a 3.00
Preview (11/00, free) 8 pg. intro 2.25
Two Houses Divided TPB (11/01, $19.95) r/#1-7; new Moeller-c 20.00

FIRST ADVENTURES
First Comics: Dec, 1985 - No. 5, Apr, 1986 ($1.25)
1-5: Blaze Barlow, Whisper & Dynamo Joe in all 2.25

FIRST AMERICANS, THE
Dell Publishing Co.: No. 843, Sept, 1957
Four Color 843-Marsh-a 9 27 63 110

FIRST CHRISTMAS, THE (3-D)
Fiction House Magazines (Real Adv. Publ. Co.): 1953 (25¢, 8-1/4x10-1/4", oversize)(Came w/glasses)
nn-(Scarce)-Kelly Freas painted-c; Biblical theme, birth of Christ; Nativity-c
34 102 179 310

First Issue Special #6 © DC

First Love Illustrated #11 © HARV

The Flame #1 © FOX

	GD2.0	FN6.0	VF8.0	NM9.4		GD2.0	FN6.0	VF8.0	NM9.4

FIRST COMICS GRAPHIC NOVEL
First Comics: Jan, 1984 - No. 21? (52pgs./176 pgs., high quality paper)

1,2: 1-Beowulf ($5.95)(both printings). 2-Time Beavers ... 8.00
3($11.95, 100 pgs.)-American Flagg! Hard Times (2nd printing exists) ... 14.00
4-Nexus ($6.95)-r/B&W 1-3 ... 11.00
5,7: 5-The Enchanted Apples of Oz ($7.95, 52 pgs.)-Intro by Harlan Ellison
  (1986). 7-The Secret Island Of Oz ($7.95) ... 9.00
6-Elric of Melnibone ($14.95, 176 pgs.)-Reprints with new color ... 17.00
8,10,14,18: Teenage Mutant Ninja Turtles Book I -IV ($9.95, 132 pgs.)-8-r/
  TMNT #1-3 in color w/12 pgs. new-a; origin. 10-r/TMNT #4-6 in color. 14-r/
  TMNT #7,8 in color plus new 12 pg. story. 18-r/TMNT #10,11 plus 3 pg. fold-
  out ... 11.00
9-Time 2: The Epiphany by Chaykin (11/86, $7.95, 52pgs. - indicia says #8)
  ... 9.00
11-Sailor On The Sea of Fate ($14.95) ... 16.00
nn-Time 2: The Satisfaction of Black Mariah (9/87) ... 9.00
12-American Flagg! Southern Comfort (10/87, $11.95) ... 14.00
13,15-17,19,21: 13-The Ice King Of Oz ($7.95). 15-Hex Breaker : Badger ($7.95). 16-
  The Forgotten Forest of Oz ($8.95). 17-Mazinger (68 pg., $8.95).19-The
  Original Nexus Graphic Novel ($7.95, 104 pgs.)-Reprints First Comics Graphic
  Novel #4 ($7.95). 21-Elric, The Weird of the White Wolf; r/#1-5 ... 10.00
20-American Flagg! State of the Union ($11.95, 96 pgs.); r/A.F. #7-9 ... 15.00
NOTE: Most or all issues have been reprinted.

1ST FOLIO (The Joe Kubert School Presents…)
Pacific Comics: Mar, 1984 ($1.50, one-shot)

1-Joe Kubert-c/a(2 pgs.); Adam & Andy Kubert-a ... 3.00

1ST ISSUE SPECIAL
National Periodical Publications: Apr, 1975 - No. 13, Apr, 1976 (Tryout series)

1,6: 1-Intro. Atlas; Kirby-c/a. 6-Dingbats	1	4	7	10
2,12: 2-Green Team (see Cancelled Comic Cavalcade). 12-Origin/1st app.				
"Blue" Starman (2nd app. in Starman, 2nd Series #3); Kubert-c	1	3	6	8
3-Metamorpho by Ramona Fradon	1	3	6	8
4,10,11: 4-Lady Cop. 10-The Outsiders. 11-Code Name: Assassin; Grell-c				
	1	3	5	7
5-Manhunter; Kirby-c/a/script	2	6	9	12
7,9: 7-The Creeper by Ditko (c/a). 9-Dr. Fate; Kubert-c				
	1	4	7	10
8,13: 8-Origin/1st app. The Warlord; Grell-c/a (11/75). 13-Return of the New				
Gods; Darkseid app.; 1st new costume Orion; predates New Gods #12 by				
more than a year	2	6	13	20

FIRST KISS
Charlton Comics: Dec, 1957 - No. 40, Jan, 1965

V1#1	4	12	29	45
V1#2-10	3	9	19	28
11-40	2	6	11	16

FIRST LOVE ILLUSTRATED
Harvey Publications(Home Comics)(True Love): 2/49 - No. 9, 6/50; No. 10,
1/51 - No. 86, 3/58; No. 87, 9/58 - No. 88, 11/58; No. 89, 11/62, No. 90, 2/63

1-Powell-a(2)	19	57	99	165
2-Powell-a	10	30	55	80
3-"Was I Too Fat To Be Loved" story	10	30	55	80
4-10	7	21	36	50
11-30: 13-"I Joined a Teen-age Sex Club" story. 30-Lingerie panel				
	5	15	25	35
31-34,37,39-49: 49-Last pre-code issue (2/55)	5	15	23	30
35-Used in SOTI, illo "The title of this comic book is First Love"				
	20	60	105	175
36-Communism story, "Love Slaves"	8	24	42	60
38-Nostrand-a	7	21	36	50
50-66,71-90	4	12	19	25
67-70-Kirby-a/c	5	15	25	35
NOTE: Disbrow a-13. Orlando c-87. Powell a-1, 3-5, 7, 10, 11, 13-17, 19-24, 26-29, 33,35-41,
43, 45, 46, 50, 54, 55, 57, 58, 61-63, 65, 71-73, 76, 79r, 82, 84, 88.

FIRSTMAN
Image Comics: June, 1997 ($2.50)

1 Snyder-s/ Andy Smith-a ... 2.50

FIRST MEN IN THE MOON (See Movie Comics)

FIRST ROMANCE MAGAZINE
Home Comics(Harvey Publ.)/True Love: 8/49 - #6, 6/50; #7, 6/51 - #50, 2/58;
#51, 9/58 - #52, 11/58

1	16	48	83	140
2	9	27	49	70
3-5	8	24	42	60
6-10,28: 28-Nostrand-a(Powell swipe)	6	18	32	45
11-20	5	15	25	35
21-27,29-32: 32-Last pre-code issue (2/55)	5	15	23	30
33-40,44-52	4	12	18	24
41-43-Kirby-c	5	15	25	35
NOTE: Powell a-1-5, 8-10, 14, 18, 20-22, 24, 25, 28, 36, 46, 48, 51.

FIRST TRIP TO THE MOON (See Space Adventures No. 20)

FIRST WAVE (Based on Sci-Fi Channel TV series)
Andromeda Entertainment: Dec, 2000 - Present ($2.99)

1-4-Kuhoric-s/Parsons-a/Busch-c ... 3.00

FISH POLICE (Inspector Gill of the...#2, 3)
Fishwrap Productions/Comico V2#5-17/Apple Comics #18 on:
Dec, 1985 - No. 11, Nov, 1987 ($1.50, B&W); V2#5, April, 1988 - V2#17, May,
1989 ($1.75, color) No. 18, Aug, 1989 - No. 26, Dec, 1990 ($2.25, B&W)

1-11, 1(5/86),2nd print, V2#5-17-(Color): V2#5-11. 12-17, new-a,	
18-26 ($2.25-c, B&W) 18-Origin Inspector Gill	2.50
Special 1($2.50, 7/87, Comico)	2.50
Graphic Novel: Hairballs (1987, $9.95, TPB) r/#1-4 in color	10.00

FISH POLICE
Marvel Comics: V2#1, Oct, 1992 - No. 6, Mar, 1993 ($1.25)

V2#1-6: 1-Hairballs Saga begins; r/#1 (1985) ... 2.50

5 CENT COMICS (Also see Whiz Comics)
Fawcett Publ.: Feb, 1940 (8 pgs., reg. size, B&W)

1-(nn-on-c) 1st app. Dan Dare	538	1614	3500	7000
NOTE: Only 2 known copies, in GD and NM condition. A promo comic, same as Flash & Thrill Comics.

5-STAR SUPER-HERO SPECTACULAR (See DC Special Series No. 1)

FLAME, THE (See Big 3 & Wonderworld Comics)
Fox Features Syndicate: Sum, 1940 - No. 8, Jan, 1942 (#1,2: 68 pgs; #3-8: 44 pgs.)

1-Flame stories reprinted from Wonderworld #5-9; origin The Flame; Lou				
Fine-a (18 pgs.), r/Wonderworld #3,10	317	951	1979	3800
2-Fine-a(2); Wing Turner by Tuska	136	408	852	1500
3-8: 3-Powell-a	91	273	568	1000

FLAME, THE (Formerly Lone Eagle)
Ajax/Farrell Publications (Excellent Publ.): No. 5, Dec-Jan, 1954-55 - No. 3,
April-May, 1955

5(#1)-1st app. new Flame	45	135	270	475
2,3	31	93	165	285

FLAMING CARROT (…Comics #6? on; see Anything Goes, Cerebus, Teenage
Mutant Ninja Turtles/Flaming Carrot/Flaming Carrot Crossover & Visions)
Aardvark-Vanaheim/Renegade Press #6-17/Dark Horse #18 on:
5/84 - No. 5, 1/85; No. 6, 3/85 - Present? ($1.70/$2.00, B&W)

1-Bob Burden story/art	4	12	30	50
2	3	9	17	25
3	2	6	11	16
4-6	2	6	9	12
7-9	1	3	6	9
10-12				6.00
13-15				4.00
15-Variant without cover price				6.00
16-(6/87) 1st app. Mystery Men	1	3	6	8
17-20: 18-1st Dark Horse issue				4.00
21-23,25: 25-Contains trading cards; TMNT app.				3.00
24-(2.50, 52 pgs.)-10th anniversary issue				4.00
26-28: 26-Begin $2.25-c, 26,27-Teenage Mutant Ninja Turtles x-over.				
27-Todd McFarlane-c				3.00
29-31-(2.50-c)				3.00
Annual 1(1/97, $5.00)				5.00
...:Fortune Favors the Bold (1998, $16.95, TPB) r/#19-24				17.00

	GD2.0	FN6.0	VF8.0	NM9.4
... :Men of Mystery (7/97, $12.95, TPB) r/#1-3, + new material				13.00
... 's Greatest Hits (4/98, $17.95, TPB) r/#12-18, + new material				18.00
... :The Wild Shall Wild Remain (1997, $17.95, TPB) r/#4-11, + new s/a				18.00

FLAMING CARROT COMICS (Also see Junior Carrot Patrol)
Killian Barracks Press: Summer-Fall, 1981 ($1.95, one shot) (Lg size, 8-1/2x11")

1-Bob Burden-c/a/scripts; serially #'ed to 6500	6	18	40	65

FLAMING LOVE
Quality Comics Group (Comic Magazines): Dec, 1949 - No. 6, Oct, 1950
(Photo covers #2-6) (52 pgs.)

1-Ward-c/a (9 pgs.)	39	117	208	360
2	18	54	94	155
3-Ward-a (9 pgs.); Crandall-a	27	81	142	245
4-6: 4-Gustavson-a	15	45	77	130

FLAMING WESTERN ROMANCES (Formerly Target Western Romances)
Star Publications: No. 3, Mar-Apr, 1950

3-Robert Taylor, Arlene Dahl photo on-c with biographies inside; L. B. Cole-c				
	40	120	220	380

FLARE (Also see Champions for 1st app. & League of Champions)
Hero Comics/Hero Graphics Vol. 2 on: Nov, 1988 - No. 3, Jan, 1989 ($2.75, color, 52 pgs.);V2#1, Nov, 1990 - No. 7, Nov, 1991 ($2.95/$3.50, color, mature, 52 pgs.);V2#8, Oct, 1992 - No. 16, Feb, 1994 ($3.50/$3.95, B&W, 36 pgs.)

V1#1-3, V2#1-16: 5-Eternity Smith returns. 6-Intro The Tigress				4.00
Annual 1(1992, $4.50, B&W, 52 pgs.)-Champions-r				4.50

FLARE ADVENTURES
Hero Graphics: Feb, 1992 - No. 12, 1993? ($3.50/$3.95)

1 (90¢, color, 20 pgs.)				2.50
2-12-Flip books w/Champions Classics				4.00

FLASH, THE (See Adventure Comics, The Brave and the Bold, Crisis On Infinite Earths, DC Comics Presents, DC Special, DC Special Series, The Greatest Flash Stories Ever Told, Green Lantern, Impulse, JLA, Justice League of America, Showcase, Speed Force, Super Team Family, Titans & World's Finest)

FLASH, THE (1st Series)(Formerly Flash Comics)(See Showcase #4,8,13,14)
National Periodical Publ./DC: No. 105, Feb-Mar, 1959 - No. 350, Oct, 1985

105-(2-3/59)-Origin Flash(retold), & Mirror Master (1st app.)				
	368	1104	3316	7000
106-Origin Grodd & Pied Piper; Flash's 1st visit to Gorilla City; begin Grodd				
the Super Gorilla trilogy (Scarce)	131	393	1113	2100
107-Grodd trilogy, part 2	69	207	584	1100
108-Grodd trilogy ends	58	174	493	925
109-2nd app. Mirror Master	45	135	359	650
110-Intro/origin Kid Flash who later becomes Flash in Crisis On Infinite Earths #12; begin Kid Flash trilogy, ends #112 (also in #114,116,118); 1st app. & origin of The Weather Wizard	109	327	926	1750
111-2nd Kid Flash tryout; Cloud Creatures	36	108	270	475
112-Origin & 1st app. Elongated Man (4-5/60); also apps. in #115,119,130				
	41	123	306	550
113-Origin & 1st app. Trickster	36	108	270	475
114-Captain Cold app. (see Showcase #8)	28	84	196	350
115,116,118-Elongated Man marries Sue Dearborn. 120-Flash & Kid Flash team-up for 1st time	22	66	157	280
117-Origin & 1st app. Capt. Boomerang; 1st & only S.A. app. Winky Blinky & Noddy	28	85	196	350
121,122: 122-Origin & 1st app. The Top	17	51	118	210
123-(9/61)-Re-intro. Golden Age Flash; origins of both Flashes; 1st mention of an Earth II where DC G. A. heroes live	106	318	903	1700
124-Last 10¢ issue	14	42	100	170
125-128,130: 127-Return of Grodd-c/story. 128-Origin & 1st app. Abra Kadabra				
130-(7/62)-1st Gauntlet of Super-Villains (Mirror Master, Capt. Cold, The Top, Capt. Boomerang & Trickster)	13	39	94	160
129-2nd G.A. Flash x-over; J.S.A. cameo in flashback (1st S.A. app. G.A. Green Lantern, Hawkman, Atom, Black Canary & Dr. Mid-Nite)				
	29	87	202	360
131-136,138,140: 131-Early Green Lantern x-over (9/62). 135-1st app. of Kid Flash's yellow costume (3/63). 136-1st Dexter Miles. 140-Origin & 1st app. Heat Wave	13	33	80	135
137-G.A. Flash x-over; J.S.A. cameo (1st S.A. app.)(1st real app. since 2-3/51); 1st S.A. app. Vandal Savage & Johnny Thunder; JSA team decides to re-				

	GD2.0	FN6.0	VF8.0	NM9
form	41	123	306	550
139-Origin & 1st app. Prof. Zoom	12	36	86	145
141-150: 142-Trickster app.	9	27	65	110
151-Engagement of Barry Allen & Iris West; G.A. Flash vs. The Shade.				
	12	36	86	145
152-159	8	24	56	90
160-(80-Pg. Giant G-21); G.A. Flash & Johnny Quick-r				
	10	30	73	125
161-164,166-168,170: 167-New facts about Flash's origin. 168-Green Lantern-c/app. 170-Dr. Mid-Nite, Dr. Fate, G.A. Flash x-over	7	21	50	80
165-Barry Allen weds Iris West	8	24	56	90
169-(80-Pg. Giant G-34)-New facts about origin	9	27	65	110
171-174,176,177,179,180: 171-JLA, Green Lantern, Atom flashbacks. 173-G.A. Flash x-over. 174-Barry Allen reveals I.D. to wife. 179-(5/68)-Flash travels to Earth-Prime and meets DC editor Julie Schwartz; 1st unnamed app. Earth-Prime (See Justice League of America #123 for 1st named app. & 3rd app. overall)	6	18	42	70
175-2nd Superman/Flash race (12/67) (See Superman #199 & World's Finest #198,199); JLA cameo; gold kryptonite used on J'onn J'onzz impersonating Superman)	16	48	112	200
178-(80-Pg. Giant G-46)	8	24	58	95
181-186,188,189: 186-Re-intro. Sargon. 189-Last 12¢-c				
	4	12	30	50
187,196: (68-Pg. Giants G-58, G-70)	6	18	40	65
190-195,197-199	4	12	26	40
200	4	12	30	50
201-204,206,207: 201-New G.A. Flash story. 206-Elongated Man begins				
207-Last 15¢ issue	3	9	20	30
205-(52-Pg. Giant G-82)	5	15	34	55
208-213-(52 pg.): 211-G.A. Flash origin-r/#104. 213-Reprints #137				
	3	10	23	35
214-DC 100 Page Super Spectacular DC-11; origin Metal Men-r/Showcase #37; never before published G.A. Flash story.				
(see DC 100 pg. Super Spec. #11 for price)				
215 (52 pgs.)-Flash-r/Showcase #4; G.A. Flash x-over, continued in #216				
	4	12	26	40
216,220: 220-1st app. Turtle since Showcase #4	3	9	17	25
217-219: Neal Adams-a in all. 217-Green Lantern/Green Arrow series begins (9/72); 2nd G.L. & G.A. team-up series (see Green Lantern #76). 219-Last Green Arrow	3	10	23	35
221-225,227,228,230,231,233: 222-G. Lantern x-over. 228-(7-8/74)-Flash writer Cary Bates travels to Earth-One & meets Flash, Iris Allen & Trickster; 2nd unnamed app. Earth-Prime (See Justice League of America #123 for 1st named app. & 3rd app. overall)	2	6	11	16
226-Neal Adams-p	2	6	13	20
229,232-(100 pg. issues)-G.A. Flash-r & new-a	4	12	29	45
234-250: 235-Green Lantern x-over. 243-Death of The Top. 245-Origin The Floronic Man in Green Lantern back-up, ends #246. 246-Last Green Lantern. 250-Intro Golden Glider	2	6	9	12
251-274: 256-Death of The Top retold. 265-267-(44 pgs.). 267-Origin of Flash's uniform. 270-Intro The Clown	1	3	5	8
268,273-276,278,283,286-(Whitman variants; low print run; no issue #s on cover				
	1.10	3.30	9.00	
275,276-Iris Allen dies	1	4	7	10
277-288,290: 286-Intro/origin Rainbow Raider	1	3	5	8
289-1st Perez DC art (Firestorm); new Firestorm back-up series begins (9/80), ends #304	1	3	6	8
291-299,301-305: 291-1st app. Saber-Tooth (villain). 295-Gorilla Grodd-c/story. 298-Intro/origin new Shade. 301-Atomic bomb-c. 303-The Top returns. 304-Intro/origin Colonel Computron; 305-G.A. Flash x-over				5.00
300-(52 pgs.)-Flash origin retold; 25th ann. issue				6.00
306-313-Dr. Fate by Giffen. 309-Origin Flash retold				5.00
314-349: 318-323-Creeper back-ups. 323,324-Two part Flash vs. Flash story. 324-Death of Reverse Flash (Professor Zoom). 328-Iris West Allen's death retold. 344-Origin Kid Flash				3.00
350-Double size ($1.25) Final issue				5.00
Annual 1 (10-12/63, 84 pgs.)-Origin Elongated Man & Kid Flash-r; origin Grodd; G.A. Flash-r	37	112	278	500
Annual 1 Replica Edition (2001, $6.95)-Reprints the entire 1963 Annual				7.00
The Flash Spectacular (See DC Special Series No. 11)				

The Flash (2nd series) #24 © DC

The Flash (2nd series) #134 © DC

Flash Comics #83 © DC

	GD2.0	FN6.0	VF8.0	NM9.4

The Life Story of the Flash (1997, $19.95, Hardcover) "Iris Allen's" chronicle of Barry Allen's life; comic panels w/additional text; Waid & Augustyn-s/ Kane & Staton-a/Orbik painted-c ... 20.00

The Life Story of the Flash (1998, $12.95, Softcover) New Orbik-c ... 13.00
NOTE: **N. Adams** a-194, 195, 203, 204, 206-208, 211, 213, 215, 226p, 246. **M. Anderson** c-165, (i)-195, 200-204, 206-208. Austin a-233i, 234i, 246i. **Buckler** a-271p, 272p; c(p)-247-250, 252, 253p, 255, 256p, 258, 262, 265-267, 269-271. **Giffen** a-306-313p; c-310p, 315. **Giordano** a-226i. **Sid Greene** a-167-174i, 229i(r). **Grell** a-237p, 238p, 240-243p; c-236. **Heck** a-198p. **Infantino/Anderson** a-135. c-135, 170-174, 192, 200, 201, 328-330. **Infantino/Giella** c-105-112, 163, 164, 166-168. **G. Kane** a-195p, 197-199p, 229r, 232r; c-197-199, 312p. **Kubert** a-108p, 215i(r); c-189-191. **Lopez** c-272. **Meskin** a-229r, 232r. **Perez** a-289-293p; c-293. **Starlin** a-294-296p. **Staton** c-263p, 264p. Green Lantern x-over-131, 143, 168, 171, 191.

FLASH (2nd Series) (See Crisis on Infinite Earths #12 and Justice League Europe)
DC Comics: June, 1987 - Present (75¢-$1.99)

1-Guice-c/a begins; New Teen Titans app.	1	4	7	10
2-10: 3-Intro. Kilgore. 5-Intro. Speed McGee. 7-1st app. Blue Trinity. 8,9-Millennium tie-ins. 9-1st app. The Chunk				4.00
11-61: 12-Free extra 16 pg. Dr. Light story. 19-Free extra 16 pg. Flash story. 28-Capt. Cold app. 29-New Phantom Lady app. 40-Dr. Alchemy app.				
50-($1.75, 52 pg.)				3.00
62-78,80: 62-Flash: Year One begins, ends #65. 65-Last $1.00-c. 66-Aquaman app. 69,70-Green Lantern app. 70-Gorilla Grodd story ends. 73-Re-intro Barry Allen & begin saga ("Barry Allen's" true ID revealed in #78). 76-Re-intro of Max Mercury (Quality Comics' Quicksilver), not in uniform until #77. 80-($1.25-c) Regular Edition				4.00
79,80 ($2.50): 79-(68 pgs.) Barry Allen saga ends. 80-Foil-c				5.00
81-91,93,94,0,95-99,101: 81,82-Nightwing & Starfire app. 84-Razer app. 94-Zero Hour. 0-(10/94). 95-"Terminal Velocity" begins, ends #100.				
96,98,99-Kobra app. 97-Origin Max Mercury; Chillblaine app.				4.00
92-1st Impulse	1	4	7	10
100 ($2.50)-Newstand edition; Kobra & JLA app.				4.00
100 ($3.50)-Foil-c edition; Kobra & JLA app.				5.00
102-131: 102-Mongul app.; begin-$1.75-c. 105-Mirror Master app. 107-Shazam app. 108-"Dead Heat" begins; 1st app. Savitar. 109-"Dead Heat" Pt. 2 (cont'd in Impulse #10). 110-"Dead Heat" Pt. 4 (cont'd in Impulse #11). 111-"Dead Heat" finale; Savitar disappears into the Speed Force; John Fox cameo (2nd app.). 112-"Race Against Time" begins, ends #118; re-intro John Fox; intro new Chillblaine. 113-Tornado Twins app. 119-Final Night x-over 127-129-Rogue's Gallery & Neron. 128,129-JLA-app. 130-Morrison & Millar-s begin				3.00
132-150: 135-GL & GA app. 142-Wally almost marries Linda; Waid-s return. 144-Cobalt Blue origin. 145-Chain Lightning begins.147-Professor Zoom app. 149-Barry Allen app. 150-($2.95) Final showdown with Cobalt Blue				3.00
151-162: 151-Casey-s. 152-New Flash-c. 154-New Flash ID revealed. 159-Wally marries Linda. 162-Last Waid-s.				2.50
163-181: 163-Begin $2.25-c. 164-181-Bolland-c.				2.25
#1,000,000 (11/98) 853rd Century x-over				2.50
Annual 1-7,9: 2-('87-'94,'96, 68 pgs). 3-Gives history of G.A.,S.A., & Modern Age Flash in text. 4-Armaggeddon 2001. 5-Eclipso-c/story. 7-Elseworlds story. 9-Legends of the Dead Earth story; J.H. Williams-a(p); Mick Gray-a(i)				3.00
Annual 8 (1995, $3.50)-Year One story				3.50
Annual 10 (1997, $3.95)-Pulp Heroes stories				4.00
Annual 11,12 ('98, '99)-Ghosts; Wrightson-c. 12-JLApe; Art Adams-c				3.00
Annual 13 ('00, $3.50) Planet DC; Alcatena-c/a				3.50
Dead Heat (2000, $14.95, TPB)-r/#108-111, Impulse #10,11				15.00
...80-Page Giant (8/98, $4.95) Flash family stories by Waid, Byrne, Millar, and others; Mhan-c				5.00
...80-Page Giant 2 (4/99, $4.95) Stories of Flash family, future Kid Flash, original Teen Titans, XS				5.00
...: Iron Heights (2001, $5.95)-Van Sciver-c/a; intro. Murmur				6.00
...: Our Worlds at War 1 (11/01, $2.95)-Jae Lee-c; Black Racer app.				3.00
...Plus 1 (1/1997, $2.95)-Nightwing-c/app.				3.00
Race Against Time (2001, $14.95, TPB)-r/#112-118				15.00
...Secret Files 1 (11/97, $4.95) Origin-s & pin-ups				5.00
...Secret Files 2,3 (11/99, 11/01; $4.95) 2-Origin of Replicant				5.00
Special 1 (1990, $2.95, 84 pgs.)-50th anniversary issue; Kubert-c; 1st Flash story by Mark Waid; 1st app. John Fox (27th Century Flash)				3.00
TV Special 1 (1991, $3.95, 76 pgs.)-Photo-c plus behind the scenes photos of TV show; Saltares-a, Byrne scripts				4.00
Terminal Velocity (1996, $12.95, TPB)-r/#95-100.				13.00
The Return of Barry Allen (1996, $12.95, TPB)-r/#74-79.				13.00

NOTE: **Guice** a-1-9p, 11p, Annual 1p; c-1-9p, Annual 1p. **Perez** c-15-17, Annual 2i. **Travest Charest** c/a-Annual 5p.

FLASH, THE (See Tangent Comics/ The Flash)

FLASH AND GREEN LANTERN: THE BRAVE AND THE BOLD
DC Comics: Oct, 1999 - No. 6, Mar, 2000 ($2.50, limited series)

1-6-Waid & Peyer-s/Kitson-a. 4-Green Arrow app.; Grindberg-a(p)		2.50
TPB (2001, $12.95) r/#1-6		13.00

FLASH/ GREEN LANTERN: FASTER FRIENDS (See Green Lantern/Flash...)
DC Comics: No. 2, 1997 ($4.95, continuation of Green Lantern/Flash: Faster Friends #1)

2-Waid/Augustyn-s ... 5.00

FLASH COMICS (Whiz Comics No. 2 on)
Fawcett Publications: Jan, 1940 (12 pgs., B&W, regular size)
(Not distributed to newsstands; printed for in-house use)

NOTE: **Whiz Comics** #2 was preceded by two books, **Flash Comics** and **Thrill Comics**, both dated Jan, 1940, (12 pgs, B&W, regular size) and were not distributed. These two books are identical except for the title, and were sent out to major distributors as ad copies to promote sales. It is believed that the complete 68 page issue of Fawcett's **Flash** and **Thrill Comics** #1 was finished and ready for publication with the January date. Since DC Comics would about to publish a book with the same date and title, Fawcett hurriedly printed up the black and white version of **Flash Comics** to secure copyright before DC. The inside covers are blank, with the covers and inside pages printed on a high quality uncoated paper stock. The eight page origin story of Captain Thunder is composed of pages 1-7 and 13 of the Captain Marvel story essentially as they appeared in the first issue of **Whiz Comics**. The balloon dialogue on page thirteen was relettered to tie the story into the end of page seven in **Flash** and **Thrill Comics** to produce a shorter version of the origin story for copyright purposes. Obviously, DC acquired the copyright and Fawcett dropped **Flash** as well as **Thrill** and came out with **Whiz Comics** a month later. Fawcett never used the cover to **Flash** and **Thrill** #1, designing a new cover for **Whiz Comics**. Fawcett also must have discovered that Captain Thunder had already been used by another publisher (Captain Terry Thunder by Fiction House), that all references to Captain Thunder were relettered to Captain Marvel before appearing in **Whiz**.

1 (nn on-c, #1 on inside)-Origin & 1st app. Captain Thunder. Eight copies of Flash and some copies of Thrill exist. All 3 copies of Thrill sold in 1986 for between $4,000-$10,000 each. A NM copy of Thrill sold in 1987 for $12,000. A vg copy of Thrill sold in 1987 for $9000 cash; another copy sold in 1987 for $2000 cash, $10,000 trade; cover by Leo O'Mealia		

FLASH COMICS (The Flash No. 105 on) (Also see All-Flash)
National Periodical Publ./All-American: Jan, 1940 - No. 104, Feb, 1949

1-The Flash (origin/1st app.) by Harry Lampert, Hawkman (origin/1st app.) by Gardner Fox, The Whip, & Johnny Thunder (origin/1st app.) by Stan Asch; Cliff Cornwall by Moldoff, Flash Picture Novelets (later Minute Movies w/#12) begin; Moldoff (Shelly) cover; 1st app. Shiera Sanders who later becomes Hawkgirl, #24; reprinted in Famous First Edition (on sale 11/10/39); The Flash-c	6071	18,215	42,500	85,000
1-Reprint, Oversize 13-1/2x10". WARNING: This comic is an exact reprint of the original except for its size. DC published in 1974 with a second cover titling it as a Famous First Edition. There have been many reported cases of the outer cover being removed and the interior sold as the original edition. The reprint with the new outer cover removed is practically worthless. See Famous First Edition for value.				
2-Rod Rian begins, ends #11; Hawkman-c	707	2121	4600	9200
3-King Standish begins (1st app.), ends #41 (called The King #16-37,39-41); E.E. Hibbard-a begins on Flash	500	1500	3250	6500
4-Moldoff (Shelly) Hawkman begins; The Whip-c	417	1250	2604	5000
5-The King-c	333	1000	2083	4000
6-2nd Flash-c (alternates w/Hawkman #6 on)	462	1386	3000	6000
7-2nd Hawkman-c; 1st Moldoff Hawkman-c	430	1290	2795	5600
8-New logo begins; classic Moldoff Flash-c	300	900	1875	3300
9,10: 9-Moldoff Hawkman-c; 10-Classic Moldoff Flash-c	308	924	1927	3700
11-13,15-20: 12-Les Watts begins; "Sparks" #16 on. 17-Last Cliff Cornwall	200	600	1250	2200
14-World War II cover	236	708	1477	2600
21-Classic Hawkman-c	191	573	1194	2100
22,23	168	505	1050	1850
24-Shiera becomes Hawkgirl (12/41); see All-Star Comics #5 for 1st app.	205	615	1281	2250
25-28,30: 28-Last Les Sparks	114	342	713	1250
29-Ghost Patrol begins (origin/1st app.), ends #104.	130	390	812	1425
31,33-Classic Hawkman-c. 33-Origin Shade	114	342	713	1250
32,34-40	105	315	656	1150

Flash Gordon (DC) #1 © KING

Flex Mentallo #4 © DC

Flinch #12 © DC

	GD2.0	FN6.0	VF8.0	NM9.4
41-50	93	279	581	1025
51-61: 52-1st computer in comics, c/s (4/44). 59-Last Minute Movies. 61-Last				
Moldoff Hawkman	84	252	525	925
62-Hawkman by Kubert begins	105	315	656	1150
63-85: 66-68-Hop Harrigan in all. 70-Mutt & Jeff app. 80-Atom begins, ends				
#104	75	225	469	825
86-Intro. The Black Canary in Johnny Thunder (8/47); see All-Star #38.				
	273	819	1705	3000
87,88,90: 87-Intro. The Foil. 88-Origin Ghost.	114	342	713	1250
89-Intro villain The Thorn	164	492	1023	1800
91,93-99: 98-Atom & Hawkman don new costumes				
	130	390	812	1425
92-1st solo Black Canary plus-c; rare in Mint due to black ink smearing on				
white-c	333	1000	2083	4000
100 (10/48),103(Scarce)-52 pgs. each	300	900	1875	3300
101,102(Scarce)	245	735	1534	2700
104-Origin The Flash retold (Scarce)	631	1893	4100	8200

NOTE: *Irwin Hasen* a-Wheaties Giveaway. c-97, Wheaties Giveaway. *E.E. Hibbard* c-6, 12, 20, 24, 26, 28, 30, 44, 46, 48, 50, 62, 66, 68, 69, 72, 74, 76, 78, 80, 82. *Infantino* a-86p, 90, 93-95, 99-104; c-90, 92, 93, 97, 99, 101, 103. *Kinstler* a-87, 89(Hawkman); c-87. *Chet Kozlak* c-77, 79, 81. *Krigstein* a-94. *Kubert* a-62-76, 83, 85, 86, 88-104; c-63, 65, 67, 70, 71, 73, 75, 83, 85, 86, 88, 89, 91, 94, 96, 98, 100, 104. *Moldoff* a-3; c-3, 7-11, 13-17, plus odd #'s 19-61. *Martin Naydell* c-52, 54, 56, 58, 60, 64, 84.

FLASH DIGEST, THE (See DC Special Series #24)

FLASH GORDON (See Defenders Of The Earth, Eat Right to Work..., Giant Comic Album, King Classics, King Comics, March of Comics #118, 133, 142, The Phantom #18, Street Comix & Wow Comics, 1st series)

FLASH GORDON
Dell Publishing Co.: No. 25, 1941; No. 10, 1943 - No. 512, Nov, 1953

Feature Books 25 (#1)(1941))-r-not by Raymond	90	270	630	1170
Four Color 10(1943)-by Alex Raymond; reprints "The Ice Kingdom"				
	96	288	672	1250
Four Color 84(1945)-by Alex Raymond; reprints "The Fiery Desert"				
	43	129	300	560
Four Color 173	16	48	112	205
Four Color 190-Bondage-c; "The Adventures of the Flying Saucers"; 5th Flying				
Saucer story (6/48)- see The Spirit 9/28/47(1st), Shadow Comics V7#10				
(2nd, 1/48), Captain Midnight #60 (3rd, 2/48) & Boy Commandos #26				
(4th, 3-4/48)	18	54	126	235
Four Color 204,247	12	36	84	160
Four Color 424-Painted-c	10	30	70	125
2(5-7/53-Dell)-Painted-c; Evans-a?	6	18	42	75
Four Color 512-Painted-c	6	18	42	75

FLASH GORDON (See Tiny Tot Funnies)
Harvey Publications: Oct, 1950 - No. 4, April, 1951

1-Alex Raymond-a; bondage-c; reprints strips from 7/14/40 to 12/8/40				
	35	105	188	325
2-Alex Raymond-a; r/strips 12/15/40-4/27/41	23	69	121	210
3,4-Alex Raymond-a; 3-bondage-c; r/strips 5/4/41-9/21/41. 4-r/strips				
10/24/37-3/27/38	22	66	116	195
5-(Rare)-Small size-5-1/2x8-1/2"; B&W; 32 pgs.; Distributed to some mail				
subscribers only	52	157	314	550
(Also see All-New 15, Boy Explorers No. 2, and Stuntman No. 3)				

FLASH GORDON
Gold Key: June, 1965

1 (1947 reprint)-Painted-c	5	15	35	60

FLASH GORDON (Also see Comics Reading Libraries in the Promotional Comics section)
King #1-11/Charlton #12-18/Gold Key #19-23/Whitman #28 on:
9/66 - #11, 12/67; #12, 2/69 - #18, 1/70; #19, 9/78 - #37, 3/82
(Painted covers No. 19-30, 34)

1-1st S.A. app Flash Gordon; Williamson c/a(2); E.C. swipe/Incredible S.F.				
#32; Mandrake story	5	15	38	60
1-Army giveaway(1968)("Complimentary" on cover)(Same as regular #1 minus				
Mandrake story & back-c)	4	12	26	40
2-8: 2-Bolle, Gil Kane-a(3). 3-Williamson-a. 4-Secret Agent X-9				
begins, Williamson-c/a(3). 5-Williamson-c/a(2). 6,8-Crandall-a. 7-Raboy-a				
(last in comics?). 8-Secret Agent X-9-r	3	10	23	35

	GD2.0	FN6.0	VF8.0	NM9.4
9-13: 9,10-Raymond-r. 10-Buckler's 1st pro work (11/67). 11-Crandall-a. 12-				
Crandall-c/a. 13-Jeff Jones-a (15 pgs.)	3	9	20	30
14,15: 15-Last 12¢ issue	2	6	15	22
16,17: 17-Brick Bradford story	2	6	12	18
18-Kaluta-a (3rd pro work?)(see Teen Confessions)	3	9	17	24
19(9/78, G.K.), 20-26	1	3	6	8
27-29,34-37: 34-37-Movie adaptation	1	4	7	10
30 (10/80) (scarce)	2	6	12	18
30 (7/81; re-issue), 31-33-single issues	1	3	6	8
31-33 (Bagged 3-pack): Movie adaptation; Williamson-a.				24.00

NOTE: *Aparo* a-8. *Bolle* a-21, 22. *Boyette* a-14-18. *Briggs* c-10. *Buckler* a-10. *Crandall* c-6. *Estrada* a-3. *Gene Fawcette* a-29, 30, 34, 37. *McWilliams* a-31-33, 36.

FLASH GORDON
DC Comics: June, 1988 - No. 9, Holiday, 1988-'89 ($1.25, mini-series)

1-9: 1,5-Painted-c				3.00

FLASH GORDON
Marvel Comics: June, 1995 - No. 2, July, 1995 ($2.95, limited series)

1,2: Schultz scripts; Williamson-a				3.00

FLASH GORDON THE MOVIE
Western Publishing Co.: 1980 (8-1/4 x 11", $1.95, 68 pgs.)

11294-Williamson-c/a; adapts movie	2	6	11	15
13743-Hardback edition	2	6	13	20

FLASHPOINT (Elseworlds Flash)
DC Comics: Dec, 1999 - No. 3, Feb, 2000 ($2.95, limited series)

1-3-Paralyzed Barry Allen; Breyfogle/McGreal-s				3.00

FLAT-TOP
Mazie Comics/Harvey Publ.(Magazine Publ.) No. 4 on: 11/53 - No. 3, 5/54; No. 4, 3/55 - No. 7, 9/55

1-Teenage; Flat-Top, Mazie, Mortie & Stevie begin	7	21	38	55
2,3	5	14	21	28
4-7	4	12	18	24

FLESH & BLOOD
Brainstorm Comics: Dec, 1995 ($2.95, B&W, mature)

1-Balent-c; foil-c.				3.00

FLESH AND BONES
Upshot Graphics (Fantagraphics Books): June, 1986 - No. 4, Dec, 1986 (Limited series)

1-4: Alan Moore scripts (r) & Dalgoda by Fujitake				3.00

FLESH CRAWLERS
Kitchen Sink Press: Aug, 1993 - No. 3, 1995 ($2.50, B&W, limited series, mature)

1-3				2.50

FLEX MENTALLO (Man of Muscle Mystery) (See Doom Patrol, 2nd Series)
DC Comics (Vertigo): Jun, 1996 - No. 4, Sept, 1996 ($2.50, lim. series, mature)

1-4: Grant Morrison scripts & Frank Quitely-c/a in all				3.00

FLINCH (Horror anthology)
DC Comics (Vertigo): Jun, 1999 - No. 16, Jan, 2001 ($2.50)

1-16: 1-Art by Jim Lee, Quitely, and Corben. 5-Sale-c. 11-Timm-a				2.50

FLINTSTONE KIDS, THE (TV) (See Star Comics Digest)
Star Comics/Marvel Comics #5 on: Aug, 1987 - No. 11, Apr, 1989

1-11				4.00

FLINTSTONES, THE (TV)(See Dell Giant #48 for No. 1)
Dell Publ. Co./Gold Key No. 7 (10/62) on: No. 2, Nov-Dec, 1961 - No. 60, Sept, 1970 (Hanna-Barbera)

2-2nd app. (TV show debuted on 9/30/60); 1st app. of Cave Kids;				
15¢-c thru #5	12	36	84	140
3-6(7-8/62): 3-Perry Gunnite begins. 6-1st 12¢-c	7	21	53	85
7 (10/62; 1st GK)	7	21	53	85
8-10	6	18	40	65
11-1st app. Pebbles (6/63)	9	27	65	110
12-15,17-20	4	12	30	50
16-1st app. Bamm-Bamm (1/64)	8	24	60	100
21-23,25-30,33: 33-Meet Frankenstein & Dracula	4	12	29	45

FL

	GD2.0	FN6.0	VF8.0	NM9.4

	GD2.0	FN6.0	VF8.0	NM9.4
24-1st app. The Grusomes	6	18	42	70
31,32,35-40: 31-Xmas-c. 39-Reprints	4	12	26	40
34-1st app. The Great Gazoo	6	18	42	70
41-60: 45-Last 12¢ issue	3	10	23	35

At N. Y. World's Fair ('64)-J.W. Books (25¢)-1st printing; no date on-c (29¢ version exists, 2nd print?) Most H-B characters app.) including Yogi Bear, Top Cat, Snagglepuss and the Jetsons 5 15 38 60

At N. Y. World's Fair (1965 on-c; re-issue; Warren Pub.). NOTE: Warehouse found in 1984 2 6 10 14

Bigger & Boulder 1(#30013-211) (Gold Key Giant, 11/62, 25¢, 84 pgs.) 8 24 60 100

Bigger & Boulder 2-(1966, 25¢)-Reprints B&B No. 1 7 21 53 85

...On the Rocks (9/61, $1.00, 6-1/4x9", cardboard-c, high quality paper,116 pgs.) B&W new material 9 27 65 110

...With Pebbles & Bamm Bamm (100 pgs., G.K.)-30028-511 (paper-c, 25¢) (11/65) 8 24 60 100

NOTE: (See Comic Album #16, Bamm-Bamm & Pebbles Flintstone, Dell Giant 48, Golden Comics Digest, March of Comics #229, 243, 271, 289, 299, 317, 327, 341, Pebbles Flintstone, Top Comics #2-4, and Whitman Comic Book.)

FLINTSTONES, THE (TV)(...& Pebbles)
Charlton Comics: Nov, 1970 - No. 50, Feb, 1977 (Hanna-Barbera)

1	8	24	58	95
2	4	12	29	45
3-7,9,10	3	9	20	30

8- "Flintstones Summer Vacation" (Summer, 1971, 52 pgs.) 6 18 40 65

11-20,36: 36-Mike Zeck illos (early work)	3	9	17	25
21-35,38-41,43-45	2	6	13	20
37-Byrne text illos (early work; see Nightmare #20)	3	9	19	28
42-Byrne-a (2 pgs.)	3	9	19	28
46-50	3	9	13	20

(Also see Barney & Betty Rubble, Dino, The Great Gazoo, & Pebbles Bamm-Bamm)

FLINTSTONES, THE (TV)(See Yogi Bear, 3rd series) (Newsstand sales only)
Marvel Comics Group: October, 1977 - No. 9, Feb, 1979 (Hanna-Barbera)

1,7,9: 1-(30¢-c). 7-9-Yogi Bear app.	3	9	17	25
1-(35¢-c variant, limited distribution)	3	9	20	30
2,3,5,6: Yogi Bear app.	2	6	13	20
4-The Jetsons app.	3	9	17	25

FLINTSTONES, THE (TV)
Harvey Comics: Sept, 1992 - No. 13, Jun, 1994 ($1.25/$1.50) (Hanna-Barbera)
V2#1-13	3.00
...Big Book 1,2 (11/92, 3/93; both $1.95, 52 pgs.)	3.50
...Giant Size 1-3 (10/92, 4/93, 11/93; $2.25, 68 pgs.)	3.50

FLINTSTONES, THE (TV)
Archie Publications: Sept, 1995 - No. 22, June, 1997 ($1.50)
1-22	2.50

FLINTSTONES AND THE JETSONS, THE (TV)
DC Comics: Aug, 1997 - No. 21, May, 1999 ($1.75/$1.95)
1-21-($1.99): 19-Bizarro Elroy-c	2.50

FLINTSTONES CHRISTMAS PARTY, THE (See The Funtastic World of Hanna-Barbera No. 1)

FLIP
Harvey Publications: April, 1954 - No. 2, June, 1954 (Satire)
1,2-Nostrand-a each. 2-Powell-a	23	69	121	210

FLIPPER (TV)
Gold Key: Apr, 1966 - No. 3, Nov, 1967 (All have photo-c)
1	6	18	42	75
2,3	4	12	30	50

FLIPPITY & FLOP
National Per. Publ. (Signal Publ. Co.): 12-1/51-52 - No. 46, 8-10/59; No. 47, 9-11/60

1-Sam dog & his pets Flippity The Bird and Flop The Cat begin; Twiddle and Twaddle begin 27 81 145 250

2	15	45	77	130
3-5	13	39	66	110
6-10	11	33	55	90
11-20: 20-Last precode (3/55)	10	30	55	80
21-47	9	27	49	70

FLOATERS
Dark Horse Comics: Sept, 1993 - No. 5, Jan, 1994 ($2.50, B&W, lim. series)
1-5	2.50

FLOOD RELIEF
Malibu Comics (Ultraverse): Jan, 1994 (36 pgs.)(Ordered thru mail w/$5.00 to Red Cross)
1-Hardcase, Prime & Prototype app.	5.00

FLOYD FARLAND (See Eclipse Graphic Album Series #11)

FLY, THE (Also see Adventures of..., Blue Ribbon Comics & Flyman)
Archie Enterprises, Inc.: May, 1983 - No. 9, Oct, 1984

1,2: 1-Mr. Justice app; origin Shield; Kirby-a; Steranko-a. 2-Ditko-a; Flygirl app. 5.00
3-9: Ditko-a in all. 4-8-Ditko-c(p) 4.00
NOTE: Ayers c-9. Buckler a-1, 2. Kirby a-1. Nebres c-3, 4, 5i, 6, 7i. Steranko c-1, 2.

FLY, THE
Impact Comics (DC): Aug, 1991 - No. 17, Dec, 1992 ($1.00)
1	3.00
2-17: 4-Vs. The Black Hood. 9-Trading card inside	2.50
Annual 1 ('92, $2.50, 68 pgs.)-Impact trading card	3.00

FLYBOY (Flying Cadets)(Also see Approved Comics #5)
Ziff-Davis Publ. Co. (Approved): Spring, 1952 - No. 2, Oct-Nov, 1952
1-Saunders painted-c	20	60	105	180
2-(10-11/52)-Saunders painted-c	14	42	72	120

FLYING ACES (Aviation stories)
Key Publications: July, 1955 - No. 5, Mar, 1956
1	7	21	36	50
2-5: 2-Trapani-a	5	14	21	28

FLYING A'S RANGE RIDER, THE (TV)(See Western Roundup under Dell Giants)
Dell Publishing Co.: #404, 6-7/52; #2, June-Aug, 1953 - #24, Aug, 1959 (All photo-c)
Four Color 404(#1)-Titled "The Range Rider"	11	33	77	140
2	7	21	49	85
3-10	5	15	35	65
11-16,18-24	5	15	34	55
17-Toth-a	5	15	35	70

FLYING CADET (WW II Plane Photos)
Flying Cadet Publ. Co.: Jan, 1943 - V2#8, 1947 (Half photos, half comics)
V1#1-Painted-c	15	45	77	130
2	8	24	45	65
3-9 (Two #6's, Sept. & Oct.): 5,6a,6b-Photo-c	7	21	38	55
V2#1-7(#10-16)	6	18	32	45
8(#17)-Bare-breasted woman-c	19	57	99	165

FLYING COLORS 10th ANNIVERSARY SPECIAL
Flying Colors Comics: Fall 1998 ($2.95, one-shot)
1-Dan Brereton-c; pin-ups by Jim Lee and Jeff Johnson	3.00

FLYIN' JENNY
Pentagon Publ. Co./Leader Enterprises #2: 1946 - No. 2, 1947 (1945 strip-r)
nn-Marcus Swayze strip-r (entire insides)	14	42	72	120
2-Baker-c; Swayze strip reprints	16	48	83	140

FLYING MODELS
H-K Publ. (Health-Knowledge Publs.): V61#3, May, 1954 (5¢, 16 pgs.)
V61#3 (Rare)	9	27	49	70

FLYING NUN (TV)
Dell Publishing Co.: Feb, 1968 - No. 4, Nov, 1968
1-Sally Field photo-c	5	15	35	65
2-4: 2-Sally Field photo-c	4	12	26	40

FLYING NURSES (See Sue & Sally Smith...)

FLYING SAUCERS (See The Spirit 9/28/47(1st app.), Shadow Comics V7#10 (2nd, 1/48), Captain Midnight #60 (3rd, 2/48), Boy Commandos #26 (4th, 3-4/48) & Flash Gordon Four Color 190 (5th, 6/48))

FOOM #15 © MAR

Football Thrills #1 © Z-D

Forbidden Worlds #9 © ACG

	GD2.0	FN6.0	VF8.0	NM9.4

FLYING SAUCERS
Avon Periodicals/Realistic: 1950; 1952; 1953

1(1950)-Wood-a, 21 pgs.; Fawcette-c	77	231	483	850
nn(1952)-Cover altered plus 2 pgs. of Wood-a not in original	45	135	270	475
nn(1953)-Reprints above	36	108	191	330

FLYING SAUCERS (Comics)
Dell Publishing Co.: April, 1967 - No. 4, Nov, 1967; No. 5, Oct, 1969

1	4	12	26	40
2-5	3	9	19	28

FLY MAN (Formerly Adventures of The Fly; Mighty Comics #40 on)
Mighty Comics Group (Radio Comics) (Archie):
No. 32, July, 1965 - No. 39, Sept, 1966 (Also see Mighty Crusaders)

32,33-Comet, Shield, Black Hood, The Fly & Flygirl x-over. 33-Re-intro Wizard, Hangman (1st S.A. appearances)	4	12	30	50
34-39: 34-Shield begins. 35-Origin Black Hood. 36-Hangman x-over in Shield; re-intro. & origin of Web (1st S.A. app.). 37-Hangman, Wizard x-over in Flyman; last Shield issue. 38-Web story. 39-Steel Sterling story (1st S.A. app.)	3	10	23	35

FOES
Ram Comics: 1989 - No. 3, 1989 ($1.95, limited series)

1-3				2.25

FOLLOW THE SUN (TV)
Dell Publishing Co.: May-July, 1962 - No. 2, Sept-Nov, 1962 (Photo-c)

01-280-207(No.1)	4	12	30	50
12-280-211(No.2)	4	12	29	45

FOODANG
Continum Comics: July, 1994 ($1.95, B&W, bi-monthly)

1				2.25

FOODINI (TV)(The Great...; see Jingle Dingle & Pinhead &...)
Continental Publ. (Holyoke): March, 1950 - No. 4, Aug, 1950 (All have 52 pgs.)

1-Based on TV puppet show (very early TV comic)	22	66	116	200
2-Jingle Dingle begins	12	36	61	100
3,4	10	30	55	80

FOOEY (Magazine) (Satire)
Scoff Publishing Co.: Feb, 1961 - No. 4, May, 1961

1	5	15	34	55
2-4	3	10	23	35

FOOFUR (TV)
Marvel Comics (Star Comics)/Marvel No. 5 on: Aug, 1987 - No. 6, Jun, 1988

1-6				3.00

FOOLKILLER (Also see The Amazing Spider-Man #225, The Defenders #73 Man-Thing #3 & Omega the Unknown #8)
Marvel Comics: Oct, 1990 - No. 10, Oct, 1991 ($1.75, limited series)

1-10: 1-Origin 3rd Foolkiller; Greg Salinger app; DeZuniga-a(i) in 1-4. 8-Spider-Man x-over				2.25

FOOM (Friends Of Ol' Marvel)
Marvel Comics: 1973 - No. 22, 1979 (Marvel fan magazine)

1	4	12	30	50
2-Hulk-c by Steranko	3	10	23	35
3,4	3	9	20	30
5-11: 11-Kirby-a and interview	3	9	17	25
12-15: 12-Vision-c. 13-Daredevil-c. 14-Conan. 15-Howard the Duck	2	6	13	20
16-20: 16-Marvel bullpen. 17-Stan Lee issue. 19-Defenders	2	6	11	15
21-Star Wars	2	6	13	20
22-Spider-Man-c; low print run final issue	4	12	26	40

FOOTBALL THRILLS (See Tops In Adventure)
Ziff-Davis Publ. Co.: Fall-Winter, 1951-52 - No. 2, Fall, 1952
(Edited by "Red" Grange)

1-Powell a(2); Saunders painted-c; Red Grange, Jim Thorpe stories	29	87	156	270
2-Saunders painted-c	20	60	105	180

FOOT SOLDIERS, THE
Dark Horse Comics: Jan, 1996 - No. 4, Apr, 1996 ($2.95, limited series)

1-4: Jim Krueger story & Michael Avon Oeming-a. in all. 1-Alex Ross-c. 4-John K. Snyder, III-c.				3.00

FOOT SOLDIERS, THE (Volume Two)
Image Comics: Sept, 1997 - No. 5, May, 1998 ($2.95, limited series)

1-5: 1-Yeowell-a. 2-McDaniel, Hester, Sienkiewicz, Giffen-a				3.00

FOR A NIGHT OF LOVE
Avon Periodicals: 1951

nn-Two stories adapted from the works of Emile Zola; Astarita, Ravielli-a; Kinstler-c	31	93	165	285

FORBIDDEN KNOWLEDGE: ADVENTURE BEYOND THE DOORWAY TO SOULS WITH RADICAL DREAMER (Also see Radical Dreamer)
Mark's Giant Economy Size Comics: 1996 ($3.50, B&W, one-shot, 48 pgs.)

nn-Max Wrighter app.; Wheatley-c/a/script; painted infinity-c				3.50

FORBIDDEN LOVE
Quality Comics Group: Mar, 1950 - No. 4, Sept, 1950 (52 pgs.)

1-(Scarce)-Classic photo-c; Crandall-a	73	219	455	800
2-(Scarce)-Classic photo-c	55	165	341	600
3-(Scarce)-Photo-c	40	120	220	380
4-(Scarce)-Ward/Cuidera-a; photo-c	40	120	232	400

FORBIDDEN LOVE (See Dark Mansion of...)

FORBIDDEN PLANET
Innovation Publishing: May, 1992 - No. 4, 1992 ($2.50, limited series)

1-4: Adapts movie; painted-c				2.50

FORBIDDEN TALES OF DARK MANSION (Formerly Dark Mansion of Forbidden Love #1-4)
National Periodical Publ.: No. 5, May-June, 1972 - No. 15, Feb-Mar, 1974

5-(52 pgs.)	4	12	29	45
6-15: 13-Kane/Howard-a	2	6	13	20

NOTE: *N. Adams* c-9. *Alcala* a-9-11, 13. *Chaykin* a-7,15. *Evans* a-14. *Heck* a-5. *Kaluta* a-7i, 8-12 c-7, 8, 13. *G. Kane* a-6. *Kirby* a-6. *Nino* a-8, 12, 15. *Redondo* a-14.

FORBIDDEN WORLDS
American Comics Group: 7-8/51 - No. 34, 10-11/54; No. 35, 8/55 - No. 145, 8/67 (No. 1-5: 52 pgs.; No. 6-8: 44 pgs.)

1-Williamson/Frazetta-a (10 pgs.)	150	450	938	1650
2	66	198	412	725
3-Williamson/Orlando-a (7 pgs.); Wood (2 panels); Frazetta (1 panel)	68	205	426	750
4	40	120	240	420
5-Krenkel/Williamson-a (8 pgs.)	55	165	331	580
6-Harrison/Williamson-a (8 pgs.)	47	142	286	500
7,8,10: 7-1st monthly issue	31	93	165	285
9-A-Bomb explosion story	34	102	179	310
11-20	22	66	116	200
21-33: 24-E.C. swipe by Landau	16	48	83	140
34(10-11/54)(Scarce)(becomes Young Heroes #35 on)-Last pre-code issue; A-Bomb explosion story	18	54	94	160
35(8/55)-Scarce	17	51	88	150
36-62	11	33	55	90
63,69,76,78-Williamson-a in all; w/Krenkel #69	11	33	55	95
64,66-68,70-72,74,75,77,79-85,87-90	9	27	49	70
65-"There's a New Moon Tonight" listed in #114 as holding 1st record fan mail response	11	33	55	95
73-1st app. Herbie by Ogden Whitney	39	117	208	360
86-Flying saucer-c by Schaffenberger	10	30	55	80
91-93,95-100	5	15	34	55
94-Herbie (2nd app.)	8	24	60	100
101-109,111-113,115,117-120	4	12	26	40
110,114,116-Herbie app. 114-1st Herbie-c; contains list of editor's top 20 ACG stories. 116-Herbie goes to Hell	6	18	42	70
121-123	3	10	23	35
124,126-130: 24-Magic Agent app.	4	12	26	40
125-Magic Agent app.; intro. & origin Magicman series, ends #141				

Force Works #6 © MAR

Forever People #4 © DC

Four Color (Series 1) #2 © FAW

	GD2.0	FN6.0	VF8.0	NM9.4		GD2.0	FN6.0	VF8.0	NM9.4

	5	15	38	60
131-139: 133-Origin/1st app. Dragonia in Magicman (1-2/66); returns in #138.				
136-Nemesis x-over in Magicman	3	10	23	35
140-Mark Midnight app. by Ditko	4	12	26	40
141-145	23	9	20	30

NOTE: *Buscema* a-75, 79, 81, 82, 140r. *Cameron* a-5. *Disbrow* a-10. *Ditko* a-137p, 138, 140. *Landau* a-24, 27-29, 31-34, 48, 86r, 96, 143-45. *Lazarus* a-18, 23, 24, 57. *Moldoff* a-27, 31, 139r. *Reinman* a-93. *Whitney* a-115, 116, 137; c-40, 46, 57, 60, 68, 78, 79, 90, 93, 94, 100, 102, 103, 106-108, 114, 129.

FORCE, THE (See The Crusaders)

FORCE OF BUDDHA'S PALM THE
Jademan Comics: Aug, 1988 - No. 55, Feb, 1993 ($1.50/$1.95, 68 pgs.)

1-55-Kung Fu stories				2.50

FORCE WORKS
Marvel Comics: July, 1994 - No. 22, Apr, 1996 ($1.50)

1-($3.95)-Fold-out pop-up-c; Iron Man, Wonder Man, Spider-Woman,U.S. Agent & Scarlet Witch (new costume)				4.00
2-11, 13-22: 5-Blue logo version & pink logo version. 9-Intro Dreamguard. 13-Avengers app.				2.25
5-Pink logo ($2.95)-polybagged w/ 16pg. Marvel Action Hour Preview & acetate print				3.00
12 ($2.50)-Flip book w/War Machine.				2.50

FORD ROTUNDA CHRISTMAS BOOK (See Christmas at the Rotunda)

FOREIGN INTRIGUES (Formerly Johnny Dynamite; becomes Battlefield Action #16 on)
Charlton Comics: No. 14, 1956 - No. 15, Aug, 1956

14,15-Johnny Dynamite continues	6	18	32	45

FOREMOST BOYS (See 4Most)

FOR ETERNITY
Antarctic Press: July, 1997 - No. 4, Jan, 1998 ($2.95, B&W)

1-4				3.00

FOREVER AMBER
Image Comics: July, 1999 - Oct, 1999 ($2.95, B&W)

1-4-Don Hudson-s/a				3.00

FOREVER DARLING (Movie)
Dell Publishing Co.: No. 681, Feb, 1956

Four Color 681-w/Lucille Ball & Desi Arnaz; photo-c	11	33	77	140

FOREVER PEOPLE, THE
National Periodical Publications: Feb-Mar, 1971 - No. 11, Oct-Nov, 1972 (Fourth World) (#1-3, 10-11 are 36 pgs.; #4-9 are 52 pgs.)

1-1st app. Forever People; Superman x-over; Kirby-c/a begins; 1st full app. Darkseid (3rd anywhere, 3 weeks before New Gods #1); Darkseid storyline begins, ends in 1-4,6,8; cameos in 5,11	6	18	40	65
2-9: 4-G.A. reprints thru #9. 9,10-Deadman app.	3	10	23	35
10,11:	2	6	15	22
Jack Kirby's Forever People TPB ('99, $14.95, B&W&Grey) r/#1-11 plus cover gallery of original series				15.00

NOTE: *Kirby* c/a(p)-1-11; #4-9 contain Sandman reprints from Adventure #85, 84, 75, 80, 77, 74 in that order.

FOREVER PEOPLE
DC Comics: Feb, 1988 - No. 6, July, 1988 ($1.25, limited series)

1-6				3.00

FOR GIRLS ONLY
Bernard Baily Enterprises: 11/53 - No. 2, 6/54 (100 pgs., digest size, 25¢)

1-25% comic book, 75% articles, illos, games	14	42	72	120
2-Eddie Fisher photo & story.	10	30	55	80

FORGOTTEN FOREST OF OZ, THE (See First Comics Graphic Novel #16)

FORGOTTEN REALMS (Also see Avatar & TSR Worlds)
DC Comics: Sept, 1989 - No. 25, Sept, 1991 ($1.50/$1.75)

1 , Annual 1 (1990, $2.95, 68 pgs.)				3.00
2-25: Based on TSR role-playing game. 18-Avatar story				2.25

FORLORN RIVER (See Zane Grey Four Color 395)

FOR LOVERS ONLY (Formerly Hollywood Romances)

Charlton Comics: No. 60, Aug, 1971 - No. 87, Nov, 1976

60	3	10	23	35
61-87	2	6	12	18

FORTUNE AND GLORY
Oni Press: Dec, 1999 - No. 3, Apr, 2000 ($4.95, B&W, limited series)

1-3-Brian Michael Bendis in Hollywood		5.00
TPB ($14.95)		15.00

40 BIG PAGES OF MICKEY MOUSE
Whitman Publ. Co.: No. 945, Jan, 1936 (10-1/4x12-1/2", 44 pgs., cardboard-c)

945-Reprints Mickey Mouse Magazine #1, but with a different cover; ads were eliminated and some illustrated stories had expanded text. The book is 3/4" shorter than Mickey Mouse Mag. #1, but the reprints are the same size (Rare)	155	465	966	1700

FOR YOUR EYES ONLY (See James Bond...)

FOUR COLOR
Dell Publishing Co.: Sept?, 1939 - No. 1354, Apr-June, 1962
(Series I are all 68 pgs.)

NOTE: Four Color only appears on issues #19-25, 1-99,101. Dell Publishing Co. filed these as Series I, #1-25, and Series II, #1-1354. Issues beginning with #710? were printed with and without ads on back cover. Issues without ads are worth more.

SERIES I:

1-(nn)-Dick Tracy	615	1845	4305	8000
2-(nn)-Don Winslow of the Navy (#1) (Rare) (11/39?)				
	138	414	966	1800
3-(nn)-Myra North (1/40?)	75	225	525	975
4-Donald Duck by Al Taliaferro (1940)(Disney)(3/40?)				
	867	2600	6070	13,000
(Prices vary widely on this book)				
5-Smilin' Jack (#1) (5/40?)	60	180	420	775
6-Dick Tracy (Scarce)	146	438	1022	1900
7-Gang Busters	36	108	252	475
8-Dick Tracy	73	219	511	950
9-Terry and the Pirates-r/Super #9-29	58	175	406	760
10-Smilin' Jack	52	156	364	675
11-Smitty (#1)	35	105	245	460
12-Little Orphan Annie; reprints strips from 12/19/37 to 6/4/38				
	48	144	336	625
13-Walt Disney's Reluctant Dragon('41)-Contains 2 pgs. of photos from film; 2 pg. foreword to Fantasia by Leopold Stokowski; Donald Duck, Goofy, Baby Weems & Mickey Mouse (as the Sorcerer's Apprentice) app. (Disney)	162	486	1134	2100
14-Moon Mullins (#1)	35	105	245	460
15-Tillie the Toiler (#1)	35	105	245	460
16-Mickey Mouse (#1) (Disney) by Gottfredson	1200	3600	12,000	–
17-Walt Disney's Dumbo, the Flying Elephant (#1)(1941)-Mickey Mouse, Donald Duck, & Pluto app. (Disney)	185	555	1295	2400
18-Jiggs and Maggie (#1)(1936-38-r)	38	115	266	500
19-Barney Google and Snuffy Smith (#1)-(1st issue with Four Color on the cover)	38	115	266	500
20-Tiny Tim	28	85	196	370
21-Dick Tracy	61	183	427	800
22-Don Winslow	31	93	217	400
23-Gang Busters	28	84	196	360
24-Captain Easy	42	125	294	550
25-Popeye (1942)	69	206	483	900

SERIES II:

1-Little Joe (1942)	52	156	364	675
2-Harold Teen	27	81	189	350
3-Alley Oop (#1)	50	150	350	650
4-Smilin' Jack	43	128	301	560
5-Raggedy Ann and Andy (#1)	50	150	350	650
6-Smitty	22	65	154	285
7-Smokey Stover (#1)	32	95	224	420
8-Tillie the Toiler	23	68	161	300
9-Donald Duck Finds Pirate Gold, by Carl Barks & Jack Hannah (Disney) (© 8/17/42)	667	2000	4670	10,000
10-Flash Gordon by Alex Raymond; reprinted from "The Ice Kingdom"				

Four Color (Series 2) #49 © WDC

Four Color #58 © NY News Synd.

Four Color #107 © News Synd. Co.

	GD2.0	FN6.0	VF8.0	NM9.4
11-Wash Tubbs	96	288	672	1250
12-Walt Disney's Bambi (#1)	30	90	210	385
13-Mr. District Attorney (#1)-See The Funnies #35 for 1st app.	59	177	413	775
14-Smilin' Jack	30	90	210	385
15-Felix the Cat (#1)	35	105	245	450
16-Porky Pig (#1)(1942)- "Secret of the Haunted House"	73	219	511	950
17-Popeye	85	255	595	1100
18-Little Orphan Annie's Junior Commandos; Flag-c; reprints strips from	50	150	350	650
6/14/42 to 11/21/42	38	113	266	500
19-Walt Disney's Thumper Meets the Seven Dwarfs (Disney); reprinted in Silly Symphonies	56	168	392	725
20-Barney Baxter	27	80	189	350
21-Oswald the Rabbit (#1)(1943)	50	150	350	650
22-Tillie the Toiler	18	54	126	230
23-Raggedy Ann and Andy	37	110	259	480
24-Gang Busters	28	84	196	360
25-Andy Panda (#1) (Walter Lantz)	54	162	378	700
26-Popeye	50	150	350	650
27-Walt Disney's Mickey Mouse and the Seven Colored Terror	85	255	595	1100
28-Wash Tubbs	21	63	147	275
29-Donald Duck and the Mummy's Ring, by Carl Barks (Disney) (9/43)	510	1530	3570	7650
30-Bambi's Children (1943)-Disney	56	168	392	725
31-Moon Mullins	19	57	133	240
32-Smitty	16	48	112	210
33-Bugs Bunny "Public Nuisance #1"	115	345	805	1500
34-Dick Tracy	42	125	294	550
35-Smokey Stover	17	50	119	220
36-Smilin' Jack	24	72	168	310
37-Bringing Up Father	19	57	133	250
38-Roy Rogers (#1, © 4/44)-1st western comic with photo-c (see Movie Comics #3)	219	657	1533	2850
39-Oswald the Rabbit (1944)	35	105	245	455
40-Barney Google and Snuffy Smith	22	66	154	290
41-Mother Goose and Nursery Rhyme Comics (#1)-All by Walt Kelly	22	65	154	290
42-Tiny Tim (1934-r)	17	50	119	220
43-Popeye (1938-'42-r)	32	96	224	420
44-Terry and the Pirates (1938-r)	40	119	280	520
45-Raggedy Ann	31	93	217	400
46-Felix the Cat and the Haunted Castle	41	123	287	535
47-Gene Autry (copyright 6/16/44)	43	129	301	560
48-Porky Pig of the Mounties by Carl Barks (7/44)	96	288	672	1250
49-Snow White and the Seven Dwarfs (Disney)	62	186	434	800
50-Fairy Tale Parade-Walt Kelly art (1944)	25	75	175	325
51-Bugs Bunny Finds the Lost Treasure	36	108	252	475
52-Little Orphan Annie; reprints strips from 6/18/38 to 11/19/38	30	90	210	385
53-Wash Tubbs	15	46	105	200
54-Andy Panda	30	90	210	400
55-Tillie the Toiler	13	40	91	175
56-Dick Tracy	35	105	245	450
57-Gene Autry	41	123	287	530
58-Smilin' Jack	24	72	168	310
59-Mother Goose and Nursery Rhyme Comics-Kelly-c/a	19	57	133	250
60-Tiny Folks Funnies	15	45	105	200
61-Santa Claus Funnies(11/44)-Kelly art	24	72	168	310
62-Donald Duck in Frozen Gold, by Carl Barks (Disney) (1/45)	160	480	1120	2400
63-Roy Rogers; color photo-all 4 covers	48	144	336	625
64-Smokey Stover	13	39	91	165
65-Smitty	13	39	91	165
66-Gene Autry	41	123	287	530
67-Oswald the Rabbit	18	54	126	230
68-Mother Goose and Nursery Rhyme Comics, by Walt Kelly				

	GD2.0	FN6.0	VF8.0	NM9.4
69-Fairy Tale Parade, by Walt Kelly	19	57	133	250
70-Popeye and Wimpy	25	75	175	325
71-Walt Disney's Three Caballeros, by Walt Kelly (© 4/45)-(Disney)	25	75	175	325
	80	240	560	1050
72-Raggedy Ann	25	75	175	325
73-The Gumps (#1)	12	36	84	160
74-Marge's Little Lulu (#1)	115	345	805	1500
75-Gene Autry and the Wildcat	31	93	217	400
76-Little Orphan Annie; reprints strips from 2/28/40 to 6/24/40	25	75	175	320
77-Felix the Cat	39	117	273	510
78-Porky Pig and the Bandit Twins	24	72	168	310
79-Walt Disney's Mickey Mouse in The Riddle of the Red Hat by Carl Barks (8/45)	108	324	756	1400
80-Smilin' Jack	15	45	105	195
81-Moon Mullins	11	33	77	140
82-Lone Ranger	42	125	294	550
83-Gene Autry in Outlaw Trail	31	93	217	400
84-Flash Gordon by Alex Raymond-Reprints from "The Fiery Desert"	43	129	300	560
85-Andy Panda and the Mad Dog Mystery	16	48	112	210
86-Roy Rogers; photo-c	35	106	245	460
87-Fairy Tale Parade by Walt Kelly; Dan Noonan-c	25	75	175	325
88-Bugs Bunny's Great Adventure (Sci/fi)	21	63	147	270
89-Tillie the Toiler	13	40	91	175
90-Christmas with Mother Goose by Walt Kelly (11/45)	18	54	126	230
91-Santa Claus Funnies (11/45)	18	54	126	230
92-Walt Disney's The Wonderful Adventures Of Pinocchio (1945); Donald Duck by Kelly, 16 pgs. (Disney)	60	180	420	775
93-Gene Autry in The Bandit of Black Rock	28	84	196	360
94-Winnie Winkle (1945)	12	36	84	155
95-Roy Rogers Comics; photo-c	35	106	245	460
96-Dick Tracy	25	75	175	325
97-Marge's Little Lulu (1946)	50	150	350	650
98-Lone Ranger, The	32	96	224	420
99-Smitty	11	33	77	140
100-Gene Autry Comics; 1st Gene Autry photo-c	31	93	217	400
101-Terry and the Pirates	26	78	182	340

NOTE: No. 101 is last issue to carry "Four Color" logo on cover; all issues beginning with No. 100 are marked "...O. S." (One Shot) which can be found in the bottom left-hand panel on the first page; the numbers following "O. S." relate to the year/month issued.

	GD2.0	FN6.0	VF8.0	NM9.4
102-Oswald the Rabbit-Walt Kelly art, 1 pg.	15	45	105	200
103-Easter with Mother Goose by Walt Kelly	19	57	133	240
104-Fairy Tale Parade by Walt Kelly	18	55	126	240
105-Albert the Alligator and Pogo Possum (#1) by Kelly (4/46)	71	213	497	925
106-Tillie the Toiler (5/46)	10	30	70	125
107-Little Orphan Annie; reprints strips from 11/16/42 to 3/24/43	21	63	147	275
108-Donald Duck in The Terror of the River, by Carl Barks (Disney) (© 4/16/46)	120	360	840	1800
109-Roy Rogers Comics; photo-c	27	80	189	350
110-Marge's Little Lulu	35	105	245	450
111-Captain Easy	14	42	98	185
112-Porky Pig's Adventure in Gopher Gulch	15	45	105	190
113-Popeye; all new Popeye stories begin	13	39	91	165
114-Fairy Tale Parade by Walt Kelly	18	55	126	240
115-Marge's Little Lulu	35	105	245	450
116-Mickey Mouse and the House of Many Mysteries (Disney)	23	69	161	300
117-Roy Rogers Comics; photo-c	21	63	147	275
118-Lone Ranger, The	32	96	224	420
119-Felix the Cat; all new Felix stories begin	32	96	224	420
120-Marge's Little Lulu	30	90	210	385
121-Fairy Tale Parade-(not Kelly)	11	33	77	145
122-Henry (#1) (10/46)	14	42	98	180
123-Bugs Bunny's Dangerous Venture	16	48	112	205
124-Roy Rogers Comics; photo-c	21	63	147	275

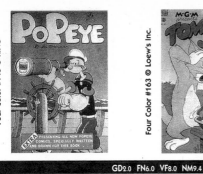

Four Color #145 © KING

Four Color #163 © Loew's Inc.

Four Color #208 © WDC

	GD2.0	FN6.0	VF8.0	NM9.4
125-Lone Ranger, The	22	66	154	280
126-Christmas with Mother Goose by Walt Kelly (1946)				
	13	40	91	175
127-Popeye	13	39	91	165
128-Santa Claus Funnies- "Santa & the Angel" by Gollub; "A Mouse in the				
House" by Kelly	14	41	98	180
129-Walt Disney's Uncle Remus and His Tales of Brer Rabbit (#1) (1946)-				
Adapted from Disney movie "Song of the South"	28	84	196	360
130-Andy Panda (Walter Lantz)	10	30	70	130
131-Marge's Little Lulu	30	90	210	385
132-Tillie the Toiler (1947)	10	30	70	125
133-Dick Tracy	20	60	140	260
134-Tarzan and the Devil Ogre; Marsh-c/a	65	195	455	845
135-Felix the Cat	24	72	168	320
136-Lone Ranger, The	22	66	154	280
137-Roy Rogers Comics; photo-c	21	63	147	275
138-Smitty	9	27	63	120
139-Marge's Little Lulu (1947)	28	84	196	360
140-Easter with Mother Goose by Walt Kelly	15	45	105	190
141-Mickey Mouse and the Submarine Pirates (Disney)				
	20	60	140	260
142-Bugs Bunny and the Haunted Mountain	16	48	112	205
143-Oswald the Rabbit and the Prehistoric Egg	9	27	63	120
144-Roy Rogers Comics (1947)-Photo-c	21	63	147	275
145-Popeye	13	39	91	165
146-Marge's Little Lulu	28	84	196	360
147-Donald Duck in Volcano Valley, by Carl Barks (Disney) (5/47)				
	80	240	560	1200
148-Albert the Alligator and Pogo Possum by Walt Kelly (5/47)				
	58	175	406	760
149-Smilin' Jack	10	30	70	130
150-Tillie the Toiler (6/47)	9	27	63	115
151-Lone Ranger, The	18	54	126	240
152-Little Orphan Annie; reprints strips from 1/2/44 to 5/6/44				
	14	42	98	175
153-Roy Rogers Comics; photo-c	19	57	133	250
154-Walter Lantz Andy Panda	10	30	70	130
155-Henry (7/47)	9	27	63	115
156-Porky Pig and the Phantom	10	30	70	135
157-Mickey Mouse & the Beanstalk (Disney)	20	60	140	260
158-Marge's Little Lulu	28	84	196	360
159-Donald Duck in the Ghost of the Grotto, by Carl Barks (Disney) (8/47)				
	67	200	470	1000
160-Roy Rogers Comics; photo-c	19	57	133	250
161-Tarzan and the Fires Of Tohr; Marsh-c/a	56	168	392	725
162-Felix the Cat (9/47)	19	57	133	250
163-Dick Tracy	17	50	119	220
164-Bugs Bunny Finds the Frozen Kingdom	16	48	112	205
165-Marge's Little Lulu	28	84	196	360
166-Roy Rogers Comics (52 pgs.)-Photo-c	19	57	133	250
167-Lone Ranger, The	18	54	126	240
168-Popeye (10/47)	13	39	91	165
169-Woody Woodpecker (#1)- "Manhunter in the North"; drug use story				
	16	48	112	210
170-Mickey Mouse on Spook's Island (11/47)(Disney)-reprinted in Mickey				
Mouse #103	17	50	119	220
171-Charlie McCarthy (#1) and the Twenty Thieves	26	78	182	340
172-Christmas with Mother Goose by Walt Kelly (11/47)				
	13	40	91	175
173-Flash Gordon	16	48	112	205
174-Winnie Winkle	7	21	49	95
175-Santa Claus Funnies by Walt Kelly (1947)	14	41	98	180
176-Tillie the Toiler (12/47)	9	27	63	115
177-Roy Rogers Comics (36 pgs.); Photo-c	19	57	133	250
178-Donald Duck "Christmas on Bear Mountain" by Carl Barks; 1st app.				
Uncle Scrooge (Disney)(12/47)	97	291	679	1450
179-Uncle Wiggily (#1)-Walt Kelly-c	15	45	105	200
180-Ozark Ike (#1)	10	30	70	130
181-Walt Disney's Mickey Mouse in Jungle Magic	17	50	119	220
182-Porky Pig in Never-Never Land (2/48)	10	30	70	135
183-Oswald the Rabbit (Lantz)	9	27	63	120
184-Tillie the Toiler	9	27	63	115
185-Easter with Mother Goose by Walt Kelly (1948)	13	39	91	165
186-Walt Disney's Bambi (4/48)-Reprinted as Movie Classic Bambi #3 (1956)				
	17	51	119	215
187-Bugs Bunny and the Dreadful Dragon	11	33	77	140
188-Woody Woodpecker (Lantz, 5/48)	10	30	70	135
189-Donald Duck in The Old Castle's Secret, by Carl Barks (Disney) (6/48)				
	60	180	420	900
190-Flash Gordon (6/48); bondage-c; "The Adventures of the Flying Saucers";				
5th Flying Saucer story- see The Spirit 9/28/47(1st), Shadow Comics V7#10				
(2nd, 1/48),Captain Midnight #60 (3rd, 2/48) & Boy Commandos #26				
(4th, 3-4/48)	18	54	126	235
191-Porky Pig to the Rescue	10	30	70	135
192-The Brownies (#1)-by Walt Kelly (7/48)	13	39	91	175
193-M.G.M. Presents Tom and Jerry (#1)(1948)	16	48	112	210
194-Mickey Mouse in The World Under the Sea (Disney)-Reprinted in				
Mickey Mouse #101	17	50	119	220
195-Tillie the Toiler	7	21	49	85
196-Charlie McCarthy in The Haunted Hide-Out; part photo-c				
	17	50	119	220
197-Spirit of the Border (#1) (Zane Grey) (1948)	11	33	77	145
198-Andy Panda	10	30	70	130
199-Donald Duck in Sheriff of Bullet Valley, by Carl Barks; Barks draws himself				
on wanted poster, last page; used in Love & Death (Disney) (10/48)				
	67	200	470	1000
200-Bugs Bunny, Super Sleuth (10/48)	11	33	77	140
201-Christmas with Mother Goose by W. Kelly	12	36	84	155
202-Woody Woodpecker	7	21	49	85
203-Donald Duck in the Golden Christmas Tree, by Carl Barks (12/48)				
	46	138	322	690
204-Flash Gordon (12/48)	12	36	84	160
205-Santa Claus Funnies by Walt Kelly	13	39	91	165
206-Little Orphan Annie; reprints strips from 11/10/40 to 1/11/41				
	7	21	49	95
207-King of the Royal Mounted (#1) (12/48)	15	45	105	190
208-Brer Rabbit Does It Again (Disney) (1/49)	12	36	84	150
209-Harold Teen	5	15	34	55
210-Tippie and Cap Stubbs	4	12	30	50
211-Little Beaver (#1)	8	24	56	105
212-Dr. Bobbs	4	12	30	50
213-Tillie the Toiler	7	21	49	85
214-Mickey Mouse and His Sky Adventure (2/49)(Disney)-Reprinted in				
Mickey Mouse #105	14	42	98	175
215-Sparkle Plenty (Dick Tracy-r by Gould)	10	30	70	130
216-Andy Panda and the Police Pup (Lantz)	7	21	49	85
217-Bugs Bunny in Court Jester	11	33	77	140
218-Three Little Pigs and the Wonderful Magic Lamp (Disney) (3/49)(#1)				
	12	36	84	150
219-Swee'pe	9	27	63	110
220-Easter with Mother Goose by Walt Kelly	13	39	91	165
221-Uncle Wiggily-Walt Kelly cover in part	9	27	63	120
222-West of the Pecos (Zane Grey)	6	18	42	80
223-Donald Duck "Lost in the Andes" by Carl Barks (Disney-4/49)				
(square egg story)	64	192	448	960
224-Little Iodine (#1), by Hatlo (4/49)	9	27	63	120
225-Oswald the Rabbit (Lantz)	5	15	35	70
226-Porky Pig and Spoofy, the Spook	8	24	56	100
227-Seven Dwarfs (Disney)	10	30	70	130
228-Mark of Zorro, The (#1) (1949)	21	63	147	275
229-Smokey Stover	5	15	35	65
230-Sunset Pass (Zane Grey)	6	18	42	80
231-Mickey Mouse and the Rajah's Treasure (Disney)				
	14	42	98	175
232-Woody Woodpecker (Lantz, 6/49)	7	21	49	85
233-Bugs Bunny, Sleepwalking Sleuth	11	33	77	140
234-Dumbo in Sky Voyage (Disney)	11	33	77	150
235-Tiny Tim	4	12	30	50
236-Heritage of the Desert (Zane Grey) (1949)	6	18	42	80
237-Tillie the Toiler	7	21	49	85

Four Color #252 © WDC

Four Color #282 © WDC

Four Color #310 © WDC

	GD2.0	FN6.0	VF8.0	NM9.4
238-Donald Duck in Voodoo Hoodoo, by Carl Barks (Disney) (8/49)				
	46	138	322	690
239-Adventure Bound (8/49)	5	15	35	60
240-Andy Panda (Lantz)	7	21	49	85
241-Porky Pig, Mighty Hunter	8	24	56	100
242-Tippie and Cap Stubbs	4	12	26	40
243-Thumper Follows His Nose (Disney)	10	30	70	135
244-The Brownies by Walt Kelly	10	30	70	130
245-Dick's Adventures (9/49)	5	15	35	60
246-Thunder Mountain (Zane Grey)	4	12	30	50
247-Flash Gordon	12	36	84	160
248-Mickey Mouse and the Black Sorcerer (Disney)	14	42	98	175
249-Woody Woodpecker in the "Globetrotter" (10/49)				
	7	21	49	85
250-Bugs Bunny in Diamond Daze; used in SOTI, pg. 309				
	12	36	84	150
251-Hubert at Camp Moonbeam	4	12	30	50
252-Pinocchio (Disney)-not by Kelly; origin	10	30	70	135
253-Christmas with Mother Goose by W. Kelly	12	36	84	155
254-Santa Claus Funnies by Walt Kelly; Pogo & Albert story by Kelly (11/49)				
	13	39	91	165
255-The Ranger (Zane Grey) (1949)	4	12	30	50
256-Donald Duck in "Luck of the North" by Carl Barks (Disney) (12/49)-Shows				
#257 on inside	34	102	238	510
257-Little Iodine	7	21	49	90
258-Andy Panda and the Balloon Race (Lantz)	7	21	49	85
259-Santa and the Angel (Gollub art-condensed from #128) & Santa at the				
Zoo (12/49)	4	12	30	50
260-Porky Pig, Hero of the Wild West (12/49)	8	24	56	100
261-Mickey Mouse and the Missing Key (Disney)	14	42	98	175
262-Raggedy Ann and Andy	7	21	49	95
263-Donald Duck in "Land of the Totem Poles" by Carl Barks (Disney)				
(2/50)-Has two Barks stories	32	96	224	475
264-Woody Woodpecker in the Magic Lantern (Lantz)				
	7	21	49	85
265-King of the Royal Mounted (Zane Grey)	8	24	56	100
266-Bugs Bunny on the "Isle of Hercules" (2/50)-Reprinted in Best of Bugs				
Bunny #1	9	27	63	110
267-Little Beaver; Harmon-c/a	4	12	30	50
268-Mickey Mouse's Surprise Visitor (1950) (Disney)				
	13	39	91	165
269-Johnny Mack Brown (#1)-Photo-c	23	69	161	300
270-Drift Fence (Zane Grey) (3/50)	4	12	30	50
271-Porky Pig in Phantom of the Plains	8	24	56	100
272-Cinderella (Disney) (4/50)	11	33	77	140
273-Oswald the Rabbit (Lantz)	5	15	35	70
274-Bugs Bunny, Hare-brained Reporter	9	27	63	110
275-Donald Duck in "Ancient Persia" by Carl Barks (Disney) (5/50)				
	30	90	210	450
276-Uncle Wiggily	8	24	56	100
277-Porky Pig in Desert Adventure (5/50)	8	24	56	100
278-Bill Elliott Comics (#1)-Photo-c	13	39	91	170
279-Mickey Mouse and Pluto Battle the Giant Ants (Disney); reprinted in				
Mickey Mouse #102 & 245	10	30	70	125
280-Andy Panda in The Isle Of Mechanical Men (Lantz)				
	7	21	49	85
281-Bugs Bunny in The Great Circus Mystery	9	27	63	110
282-Donald Duck and the Pixilated Parrot by Carl Barks (Disney)				
(© 5/23/50)	30	90	210	450
283-King of the Royal Mounted (7/50)	8	24	56	100
284-Porky Pig in The Kingdom of Nowhere	8	24	56	100
285-Bozo the Clown & His Minikin Circus (#1) (TV)	19	5	133	250
286-Mickey Mouse and the Uninvited Guest (Disney)	10	30	70	125
287-Gene Autry's Champion in The Ghost Of Black Mountain; photo-c				
	11	33	77	140
288-Woody Woodpecker in Klondike Gold (Lantz)	7	21	49	85
289-Bugs Bunny in "Indian Trouble"	9	27	63	110
290-The Chief (#1) (8/50)	6	18	42	75
291-Donald Duck in "The Magic Hourglass" by Carl Barks (Disney) (9/50)				
	30	90	210	450

	GD2.0	FN6.0	VF8.0	NM9.4
292-The Cisco Kid Comics (#1)	24	72	168	315
293-The Brownies-Kelly-c/a	10	30	70	130
294-Little Beaver	4	12	30	50
295-Porky Pig in President Porky (9/50)	8	24	56	100
296-Mickey Mouse in Private Eye for Hire (Disney)	10	30	70	125
297-Andy Panda in The Haunted Inn (Lantz, 10/50)	7	21	49	85
298-Bugs Bunny in Sheik for a Day	9	27	63	110
299-Buck Jones & the Iron Horse Trail (#1)	13	39	91	170
300-Donald Duck in "Big-Top Bedlam" by Carl Barks (Disney) (11/50)				
	30	90	210	450
301-The Mysterious Rider (Zane Grey)	4	12	30	50
302-Santa Claus Funnies (11/50)	5	15	35	60
303-Porky Pig in The Land of the Monstrous Flies	5	15	35	70
304-Mickey Mouse in Tom-Tom Island (Disney) (12/50)				
	8	24	56	100
305-Woody Woodpecker (Lantz)	5	15	34	55
306-Raggedy Ann	5	15	35	60
307-Bugs Bunny in Lumber Jack Rabbit	7	21	49	95
308-Donald Duck in "Dangerous Disguise" by Carl Barks (Disney) (1/51)				
	26	78	182	390
309-Betty Betz' Dollface and Her Gang (1951)	5	15	35	60
310-King of the Royal Mounted (1/51)	6	18	42	80
311-Porky Pig in Midget Horses of Hidden Valley	5	15	35	70
312-Tonto (#1)	10	30	70	125
313-Mickey Mouse in The Mystery of the Double-Cross Ranch (#1)				
(Disney) (2/51)	8	24	56	100
Note: Beginning with the above comic in 1951 Dell/Western began adding #1 in				
small print on the covers of several long running titles with the evident intention of				
switching these titles to their own monthly numbers, but when the conversions				
were made, there was no connection. It is thought that the post office may have				
stepped in and decreed the sequences should commence as though the first four				
colors printed had each begun with number one, or the first issues sold by sub-				
scription. Since the regular series' numbers don't correctly match to the numbers				
of earlier issues published, it's not known whether or not the numbering was in				
error.				
314-Ambush (Zane Grey)	4	12	30	50
315-Oswald the Rabbit (Lantz)	5	15	35	60
316-Rex Allen (#1)-Photo-c; Marsh-a	13	40	91	175
317-Bugs Bunny in Hair Today Gone Tomorrow (#1)	7	21	49	95
318-Donald Duck in "No Such Varmint" by Carl Barks (#1)-Indicia shows #317				
(Disney, © 1/23/51)	26	78	182	390
319-Gene Autry's Champion; painted-c	5	15	35	60
320-Uncle Wiggily (#1)	8	24	56	100
321-Little Scouts (#1) (3/51)	4	12	26	40
322-Porky Pig in Roaring Rockets (#1 on-c)	5	15	35	70
323-Susie Q. Smith (#1) (3/51)	4	12	29	45
324-I Met a Handsome Cowboy (3/51)	9	27	63	110
325-Mickey Mouse in The Haunted Castle (#2) (Disney) (4/51)				
	8	24	56	100
326-Andy Panda (#1) (Lantz)	5	15	34	55
327-Bugs Bunny and the Rajah's Treasure (#2)	7	21	49	95
328-Donald Duck in Old California (#2) by Carl Barks-Peyote drug use issue				
(Disney) (5/51)	28	84	196	420
329-Roy Roger's Trigger (#1)(5/51)-Painted-c	13	39	91	170
330-Porky Pig Meets the Bristled Bruiser (#2)	5	15	35	70
331-Alice in Wonderland (Disney) (1951)	14	42	98	185
332-Little Beaver	4	12	30	50
333-Wilderness Trek (Zane Grey) (5/51)	4	12	30	50
334-Mickey Mouse and Yukon Gold (Disney) (6/51)	8	24	56	100
335-Francis the Famous Talking Mule (#1, 6/51)-1st Dell non animated movie				
comic (all issues based on movie)	10	30	70	130
336-Woody Woodpecker (Lantz)	5	15	34	55
337-The Brownies-not by Walt Kelly	4	12	29	45
338-Bugs Bunny and the Rocking Horse Thieves	7	21	49	95
339-Donald Duck and the Magic Fountain-not by Carl Barks (Disney) (7-8/51)				
	7	21	49	85
340-King of the Royal Mounted (7/51)	8	18	42	80
341-Unbirthday Party with Alice in Wonderland (Disney) (7/51)				
	14	42	98	185
342-Porky Pig the Lucky Peppermint Mine; r/in Porky Pig #3				

Four Color #349 © Howard Garis

Four Color #359 © HILL

Four Color #487 © WP

	GD2.0	FN6.0	VF8.0	NM9.4
	4	12	30	50
343-Mickey Mouse in The Ruby Eye of Homar-Guy-Am (Disney)-Reprinted in				
Mickey Mouse #104	6	18	42	80
344-Sergeant Preston from Challenge of The Yukon (#1) (TV)				
	12	36	84	150
345-Andy Panda in Scotland Yard (8-10/51) (Lantz)	5	15	34	55
346-Hideout (Zane Grey)	4	12	30	50
347-Bugs Bunny the Frigid Hare (8-9/51)	7	21	49	85
348-Donald Duck "The Crocodile Collector"; Barks-c only (Disney) (9-10/51)				
	15	45	105	200
349-Uncle Wiggily	6	18	42	80
350-Woody Woodpecker (Lantz)	5	15	34	55
351-Porky Pig & the Grand Canyon Giant (9-10/51)	4	12	30	50
352-Mickey Mouse in The Mystery of Painted Valley (Disney)				
	6	18	42	80
353-Duck Album (#1)-Barks-c (Disney)	9	27	63	110
354-Raggedy Ann & Andy	5	15	35	60
355-Bugs Bunny Hot-Rod Hare	7	21	49	95
356-Donald Duck in "Rags to Riches"; Barks-c only	15	45	105	200
357-Comeback (Zane Grey)	4	12	26	40
358-Andy Panda (Lantz) (11-1/52)	5	15	34	55
359-Frosty the Snowman (#1)	9	27	63	110
360-Porky Pig in Tree of Fortune (11-12/51)	4	12	30	50
361-Santa Claus Funnies	5	15	35	60
362-Mickey Mouse and the Smuggled Diamonds (Disney)				
	6	18	42	80
363-King of the Royal Mounted	5	15	35	65
364-Woody Woodpecker (Lantz)	4	12	30	50
365-The Brownies-not by Kelly	4	12	29	45
366-Bugs Bunny Uncle Buckskin Comes to Town (12-1/52)				
	7	21	49	95
367-Donald Duck in "A Christmas for Shacktown" by Carl Barks (Disney)				
(1-2/52)	25	75	175	375
368-Bob Clampett's Beany and Cecil (#1)	26	78	182	340
369-The Lone Ranger's Famous Horse Hi-Yo Silver (#1); Silver's origin				
	9	27	63	120
370-Porky Pig in Trouble in the Big Trees	4	12	30	50
371-Mickey Mouse in The Inca Idol Case (1952) (Disney)				
	6	18	42	80
372-Riders of the Purple Sage (Zane Grey)	4	12	26	40
373-Sergeant Preston (TV)	7	21	49	90
374-Woody Woodpecker (Lantz)	4	12	30	50
375-John Carter of Mars (E. R. Burroughs)-Jesse Marsh-a; origin				
	25	75	175	320
376-Bugs Bunny, "The Magic Sneeze"	7	21	49	85
377-Susie Q. Smith	4	12	25	38
378-Tom Corbett, Space Cadet (#1) (TV)-McWilliams-a				
	17	50	119	225
379-Donald Duck in "Southern Hospitality"; Not by Barks (Disney)				
	7	21	49	85
380-Raggedy Ann & Andy	5	15	35	60
381-Marge's Tubby (#1)	21	63	147	270
382-Snow White and the Seven Dwarfs (Disney)-origin; partial reprint of				
4-Color #49 (Movie)	10	30	70	130
383-Andy Panda (Lantz)	3	9	21	40
384-King of the Royal Mounted (3/52)(Zane Grey)	5	15	35	65
385-Porky Pig inThe Isle of Missing Ships (3-4/52)	4	12	30	50
386-Uncle Scrooge (#1)-by Carl Barks (Disney) in "Only a Poor Old Man"				
(3/52)	92	275	672	1250
387-Mickey Mouse in High Tibet (Disney) (4-5/52)	6	18	42	80
388-Oswald the Rabbit (Lantz)	5	15	35	60
389-Andy Hardy Comics (#1)	4	12	29	45
390-Woody Woodpecker (Lantz)	4	12	30	50
391-Uncle Wiggily	6	18	42	80
392-Hi-Yo Silver	5	15	35	60
393-Bugs Bunny	7	21	49	95
394-Donald Duck in Malayalaya-Barks-c only (Disney)				
	15	45	105	200
395-Forlorn River(Zane Grey)-First Nevada (5/52)	4	12	26	40
396-Tales of the Texas Rangers(#1)(TV)-Photo-c	11	33	77	140

	GD2.0	FN6.0	VF8.0	NM9.4
397-Sergeant Preston of the Yukon (TV) (5/52)	7	21	49	90
398-The Brownies-not by Kelly	4	12	29	45
399-Porky Pig in The Lost Gold Mine	4	12	30	50
400-Tom Corbett, Space Cadet (TV)-McWilliams-c/a				
	10	30	70	125
401-Mickey Mouse and Goofy's Mechanical Wizard (Disney) (6-7/52)				
	5	15	34	55
402-Mary Jane and Sniffles	8	24	56	100
403-Li'l Bad Wolf (Disney) (6/52)(#1)	7	21	49	90
404-The Range Rider (#1) (TV)-Photo-c	11	33	77	140
405-Woody Woodpecker (Lantz) (6-7/52)	4	12	30	50
406-Tweety and Sylvester (#1)	9	27	63	110
407-Bugs Bunny, Foreign-Legion Hare	6	18	42	80
408-Donald Duck and the Golden Helmet by Carl Barks (Disney)				
(7-8/52)	25	75	175	375
409-Andy Panda (7-9/52)	3	9	21	40
410-Porky Pig in The Water Wizard (7/52)	4	12	30	50
411-Mickey Mouse and the Old Sea Dog (Disney) (8-9/52)				
	5	15	34	55
412-Nevada (Zane Grey)	4	12	26	40
413-Robin Hood (Disney-Movie) (8/52)-Photo-c (1st Disney movie four color				
book)	10	30	70	130
414-Bob Clampett's Beany and Cecil (TV)	16	48	112	210
415-Rootie Kazootie (#1) (TV)	10	30	70	130
416-Woody Woodpecker (Lantz)	4	12	30	50
417-Double Trouble with Goober (#1) (8/52)	3	10	23	35
418-Rusty Riley, a Boy, a Horse, and a Dog (#1)-Frank Godwin-a (strip				
reprints) (8/52)	4	12	30	50
419-Sergeant Preston (TV)	7	21	49	90
420-Bugs Bunny in The Mysterious Buckaroo (8-9/52)				
	6	18	42	80
421-Tom Corbett, Space Cadet(TV)-McWilliams-a	10	30	70	125
422-Donald Duck and the Gilded Man, by Carl Barks (Disney) (9-10/52)				
(#423 on inside)	25	75	175	375
423-Rhubarb, Owner of the Brooklyn Ball Club (The Millionaire Cat) (#1)-Painted				
cover	5	15	35	60
424-Flash Gordon-Test Flight in Space (9/52)	10	30	70	125
425-Zorro, the Return of	12	36	84	155
426-Porky Pig in The Scalawag Leprechaun	4	12	30	50
427-Mickey Mouse and the Wonderful Whizzix (Disney) (10-11/52)-Reprinted				
in Mickey Mouse #100	5	15	34	55
428-Uncle Wiggily	5	15	34	55
429-Pluto in "Why Dogs Leave Home" (Disney) (10/52)(#1)				
	9	27	63	110
430-Marge's Tubby, the Shadow of a Man-Eater	12	36	84	150
431-Woody Woodpecker (Lantz) (10/52) (Lantz)	4	12	30	50
432-Bugs Bunny and the Rabbit Olympics	6	18	42	80
433-Wildfire (Zane Grey) (11-1/52-53)	4	12	26	40
434-Rin Tin Tin "In Dark Danger" (#1) (TV) (11/52)-Photo-c				
	15	45	105	200
435-Frosty the Snowman (11/52)	5	15	34	55
436-The Brownies-not by Kelly (11/52)	4	12	26	40
437-John Carter of Mars (E. R. Burroughs)-Marsh-a	15	45	105	200
438-Annie Oakley (TV)	15	45	105	190
439-Little Hiawatha (Disney) (12/52)|(#1)	5	15	35	65
440-Black Beauty (12/52)	4	12	25	38
441-Fearless Fagan	4	12	27	42
442-Peter Pan (Disney) (Movie)	10	30	70	125
443-Ben Bowie and His Mountain Men (#1)	6	18	42	80
444-Marge's Tubby	12	36	84	150
445-Charlie McCarthy	5	15	35	60
446-Captain Hook and Peter Pan (Disney)(Movie)(1/53)				
	9	27	63	110
447-Andy Hardy Comics	3	9	21	32
448-Bob Clampett's Beany and Cecil (TV)	16	48	112	210
449-Tappan's Burro (Zane Grey) (2-4/53)	4	12	26	40
450-Duck Album; Barks-c (Disney)	6	18	42	80
451-Rusty Riley-Frank Godwin-a (strip-r) (2/53)	4	12	26	40
452-Raggedy Ann & Andy (1953)	5	15	35	60
453-Susie Q. Smith (2/53)	4	12	25	38

Four Color #492 © WDC

Four Color #521 © KING

Four Color #546 © DELL

	GD2.0	FN6.0	VF8.0	NM9.4
454-Krazy Kat Comics; not by Herriman	4	12	29	45
455-Johnny Mack Brown Comics(3/53)-Photo-c	6	18	42	80
456-Uncle Scrooge Back to the Klondike (#2) by Barks (3/53) (Disney)				
	60	180	420	775
457-Daffy (#1)	9	27	63	110
458-Oswald the Rabbit (Lantz)	4	12	26	40
459-Rootie Kazootie (TV)	7	21	49	90
460-Buck Jones (4/53)	5	15	35	60
461-Marge's Tubby	10	30	70	130
462-Little Scouts	3	9	17	24
463-Petunia (4/53)	4	12	27	42
464-Bozo (4/53)	9	27	63	110
465-Francis the Famous Talking Mule	5	15	35	65
466-Rhubarb, the Millionaire Cat; painted-c	4	12	30	50
467-Desert Gold (Zane Grey) (5-7/53)	4	12	26	40
468-Goofy (#1) (Disney)	12	36	84	160
469-Beetle Bailey (#1) (5/53)	9	27	63	120
470-Elmer Fudd	5	15	35	60
471-Double Trouble with Goober	2	6	13	20
472-Wild Bill Elliott (6/53)-Photo-c	4	12	30	50
473-Li'l Bad Wolf (Disney) (6/53)(#2)	4	12	30	50
474-Mary Jane and Sniffles	7	21	49	90
475-M.G.M.'s The Two Mouseketeers (#1)	7	21	49	90
476-Rin Tin Tin (TV)-Photo-c	8	24	56	100
477-Bob Clampett's Beany and Cecil (TV)	16	48	112	210
478-Charlie McCarthy	5	15	35	60
479-Queen of the West Dale Evans (#1)-Photo-c	22	65	154	290
480-Hardy Oldy Comics	3	9	21	32
481-Annie Oakley And Tagg (TV)	9	27	63	115
482-Brownies-and Kelly	4	12	26	40
483-Little Beaver (7/53)	4	12	26	40
484-River Feud (Zane Grey) (8-10/53)	4	12	26	40
485-The Little People-Walt Scott (#1)	6	18	42	80
486-Rusty Riley-Frank Godwin strip-r	4	12	26	40
487-Mowgli, the Jungle Book (Rudyard Kipling's)	5	15	35	65
488-John Carter of Mars (Burroughs)-Marsh-a; painted-c				
	15	45	105	200
489-Tweety and Sylvester	5	15	34	55
490-Jungle Jim (#1)	6	18	42	80
491-Silvertip (#1) (Max Brand)-Kinstler-a (8/53)	8	24	56	100
492-Duck Album (Disney)	5	15	35	60
493-Johnny Mack Brown; photo-c	6	18	42	80
494-The Little King (#1)	9	27	63	120
495-Uncle Scrooge (#3) (Disney)-by Carl Barks (9/53)				
	44	131	308	575
496-The Green Hornet; painted-c	25	75	175	320
497-Zorro (Sword of...)-Kinstler-a	13	39	91	165
498-Bugs Bunny's Album (9/53)	5	15	35	60
499-M.G.M.'s Spike and Tyke (9/53)	4	12	30	50
500-Buck Jones	5	15	35	60
501-Francis the Famous Talking Mule	4	12	30	50
502-Rootie Kazootie (TV)	7	21	49	90
503-Uncle Wiggily (10/53)	5	15	34	55
504-Krazy Kat; not by Herriman	4	12	29	45
505-The Sword and the Rose (Disney) (10/53)(Movie)-Photo-c				
	9	27	63	110
506-The Little Scouts	3	9	17	24
507-Oswald the Rabbit (Lantz)	4	12	26	40
508-Bozo (10/53)	9	27	63	110
509-Pluto (Disney) (10/53)	5	15	35	65
510-Son of Black Beauty	4	12	25	38
511-Outlaw Trail (Zane Grey)-Kinstler-a	4	12	30	50
512-Flash Gordon (11/53)	6	18	42	75
513-Ben Bowie and His Mountain Men	4	12	26	40
514-Frosty the Snowman (11/53)	5	15	34	55
515-Andy Hardy	3	9	21	32
516-Double Trouble With Goober	2	6	13	20
517-Chip 'N' Dale (#1) (Disney)	9	27	63	120
518-Rivets (11/53)	3	9	21	32
519-Steve Canyon (#1)-Not by Milton Caniff	9	27	63	110

	GD2.0	FN6.0	VF8.0	NM9.4
520-Wild Bill Elliott-Photo-c	4	12	30	50
521-Beetle Bailey (12/53)	5	15	35	60
522-The Brownies	4	12	26	40
523-Rin Tin Tin (TV)-Photo-c (12/53)	8	24	56	100
524-Tweety and Sylvester	5	15	34	55
525-Santa Claus Funnies	5	15	35	60
526-Napoleon	3	9	19	28
527-Charlie McCarthy	5	15	35	60
528-Queen of the West Dale Evans; photo-c	10	30	70	135
529-Little Beaver	4	12	26	40
530-Bob Clampett's Beany and Cecil (TV) (1/54)	16	48	112	210
531-Duck Album (Disney)	5	15	35	60
532-The Rustlers (Zane Grey) (2-4/54)	4	12	26	40
533-Raggedy Ann and Andy	5	15	35	60
534-Western Marshal(Ernest Haycox's)-Kinstler-a	5	15	35	65
535-I Love Lucy (#1) (TV) (2/54)-Photo-c	53	159	371	690
536-Daffy (3/54)	5	15	34	55
537-Stormy, the Thoroughbred... (Disney-Movie) on top 2/3 of each page; Pluto story on bottom 1/3 of each page (2/54)	4	12	25	38
538-The Mask of Zorro; Kinstler-a	13	39	91	165
539-Ben and Me (Disney) (3/54)	4	12	26	40
540-Knights of the Round Table (3/54) (Movie)-Photo-c				
	7	21	49	90
541-Johnny Mack Brown; photo-c	6	18	42	80
542-Super Circus Featuring Mary Hartline (TV) (3/54)				
	7	21	49	90
543-Uncle Wiggily (3/54)	5	15	34	55
544-Rob Roy (Disney-Movie)-Manning-a; photo-c	8	24	56	100
545-The Wonderful Adventures of Pinocchio-Partial reprint of 4-Color #92 (Disney-Movie)				
	7	21	49	90
546-Buck Jones	5	15	35	60
547-Francis the Famous Talking Mule	4	12	30	50
548-Krazy Kat; not by Herriman (4/54)	4	12	26	40
549-Oswald the Rabbit (Lantz)	4	12	26	40
550-The Little Scouts	3	9	17	24
551-Bozo (4/54)	9	27	63	110
552-Beetle Bailey	5	15	35	60
553-Susie Q. Smith	4	12	25	38
554-Rusty Riley (Frank Godwin strip-r)	4	12	26	40
555-Range War (Zane Grey)	4	12	26	40
556-Double Trouble With Goober (5/54)	2	6	13	20
557-Ben Bowie and His Mountain Men	4	12	26	40
558-Elmer Fudd (5/54)	4	12	27	42
559-I Love Lucy (#2) (TV)-Photo-c	32	96	224	415
560-Duck Album (Disney) (5/54)	5	15	35	60
561-Mr. Magoo (5/54)	11	33	77	145
562-Goofy (Disney)(#2)	7	21	49	90
563-Rhubarb, the Millionaire Cat (6/54)	4	12	30	50
564-Li'l Bad Wolf (Disney)(#3)	4	12	30	50
565-Jungle Jim	4	12	26	40
566-Son of Black Beauty	4	12	25	38
567-Prince Valiant (#1)-By Bob Fuje (Movie)-Photo-c				
	11	33	77	145
568-Gypsy Colt (Movie) (6/54)	4	12	30	50
569-Priscilla's Pop	4	12	25	38
570-Bob Clampett's Beany and Cecil (TV)	16	48	112	210
571-Charlie McCarthy	5	15	35	60
572-Silvertip (Max Brand) (7/54); Kinstler-a	4	12	30	50
573-The Little People by Walt Scott	4	12	29	45
574-The Hand of Zorro; Kinstler-a	13	39	91	165
575-Annie Oakley and Tagg (TV)-Photo-c	9	27	63	115
576-Angel (#1) (6/54)	3	9	19	28
577-M.G.M.'s Spike and Tyke	3	9	20	30
578-Steve Canyon (8/54)	5	15	35	60
579-Francis the Famous Talking Mule	4	12	30	50
580-Six Gun Ranch (Luke Short-8/54)	4	12	26	40
581-Chip 'N' Dale (#2) (Disney)	5	15	35	60
582-Mowgli Jungle Book (Kipling) (8/54)	4	12	30	50
583-The Lost Wagon Train (Zane Grey)	4	12	26	40
584-Johnny Mack Brown-Photo-c	6	18	42	80

FO

Four Color #602 © Columbia Pict.

Four Color #650 © KING

Four Color #676 © DELL

	GD2.0	FN6.0	VF8.0	NM9.4
585-Bugs Bunny's Album	5	15	35	60
586-Duck Album (Disney)	5	15	35	60
587-The Little Scouts	3	9	17	24
588-King Richard and the Crusaders (Movie) (10/54) Matt Baker-a; photo-c				
	10	30	70	130
589-Buck Jones	5	15	35	60
590-Hansel and Gretel; partial photo-c	6	18	42	80
591-Western Marshal(Ernest Haycox's)-Kinstler-a	5	15	35	60
592-Super Circus (TV)	6	18	42	80
593-Oswald the Rabbit (Lantz)	4	12	26	40
594-Bozo (10/54)	9	27	63	110
595-Pluto (Disney)	4	12	26	40
596-Turok, Son of Stone (#1)	60	180	420	775
597-The Little King	5	15	35	60
598-Captain Davy Jones	4	12	30	50
599-Ben Bowie and His Mountain Men	4	12	26	40
600-Daisy Duck's Diary (#1) (Disney) (11/54)	7	21	49	85
601-Frosty the Snowman	5	15	34	55
602-Mr. Magoo and Gerald McBoing-Boing	11	33	77	145
603-M.G.M.'s The Two Mouseketeers	4	12	30	50
604-Shadow on the Trail (Zane Grey)	4	12	26	40
605-The Brownies-not by Kelly (12/54)	4	12	26	40
606-Sir Lancelot (not TV)	7	21	49	90
607-Santa Claus Funnies	5	15	35	60
608-Silvertip- "Valley of Vanishing Men" (Max Brand)-Kinstler-a				
	4	12	30	50
609-The Littlest Outlaw (Disney-Movie) (1/55)-Photo-c				
	6	18	42	80
610-Drum Beat (Movie); Alan Ladd photo-c	9	27	63	110
611-Duck Album (Disney)	5	15	35	60
612-Little Beaver (1/55)	4	12	26	40
613-Western Marshal (Ernest Haycox's) (2/55)-Kinstler-a				
	5	15	35	60
614-20,000 Leagues Under the Sea (Disney) (Movie) (2/55)-Painted-c				
	9	27	63	120
615-Daffy	5	15	34	55
616-To the Last Man (Zane Grey)	4	12	26	40
617-The Quest of Zorro	12	36	84	155
618-Johnny Mack Brown; photo-c	6	18	42	80
619-Krazy Kat; not by Herriman	4	12	26	40
620-Mowgli Jungle Book (Kipling)	4	12	30	50
621-Francis the Famous Talking Mule (4/55)	4	12	26	40
622-Beetle Bailey	5	15	35	60
623-Oswald the Rabbit (Lantz)	3	10	23	35
624-Treasure Island(Disney-Movie)(4/55)-Photo-c	9	27	63	110
625-Beaver Valley (Disney)	6	18	42	80
626-Ben Bowie and His Mountain Men	4	12	26	40
627-Goofy (Disney) (5/55)	7	21	49	90
628-Elmer Fudd	4	12	27	42
629-Lady and the Tramp with Jock (Disney)	7	21	49	90
630-Priscilla's Pop	4	12	25	38
631-Davy Crockett, Indian Fighter (#1) (Disney) (5/55) (TV)-Fess Parker				
	20	60	140	260
632-Fighting Caravans (Zane Grey)	4	12	26	40
633-The Little People by Walt Scott (6/55)	4	12	29	45
634-Lady and the Tramp Album (Disney) (6/55)	5	15	34	55
635-Bob Clampett's Beany and Cecil (TV)	16	48	112	210
636-Chip 'N' Dale (Disney)	5	15	35	60
637-Silvertip (Max Brand)-Kinstler-a	4	12	30	50
638-M.G.M.'s Spike and Tyke (8/55)	3	9	20	30
639-Davy Crockett at the Alamo (Disney) (7/55) (TV)-Fess Parker photo-c				
	16	48	112	210
640-Western Marshal(Ernest Haycox's)-Kinstler-a	5	15	35	60
641-Steve Canyon (1955)-by Caniff	5	15	35	60
642-M.G.M.'s The Two Mouseketeers	4	12	30	50
643-Wild Bill Elliott; photo-c	4	12	26	40
644-Sir Walter Raleigh (5/55)-Based on movie "The Virgin Queen"; photo-c				
	7	21	49	85
645-Johnny Mack Brown; photo-c	6	18	42	80
646-Dotty Dripple and Taffy (#1)	4	12	26	40

	GD2.0	FN6.0	VF8.0	NM9.4
647-Bugs Bunny's Album (9/55)	5	15	35	60
648-Jace Pearson of the Texas Rangers (TV)-Photo-c				
	5	15	35	60
649-Duck Album (Disney)	5	15	35	60
650-Prince Valiant; by Bob Fuje	7	21	49	85
651-King Colt (Luke Short) (9/55)-Kinstler-a	4	12	26	40
652-Buck Jones	4	12	26	40
653-Smokey the Bear (#1) (10/55)	10	30	70	130
654-Pluto (Disney)	4	12	26	40
655-Francis the Famous Talking Mule	4	12	26	40
656-Turok, Son of Stone (#2) (10/55)	34	102	238	440
657-Ben Bowie and His Mountain Men	4	12	26	40
658-Goofy (Disney)	7	21	49	90
659-Daisy Duck's Diary (Disney)(#2)	5	15	35	65
660-Little Beaver	4	12	26	40
661-Frosty the Snowman	5	15	34	55
662-Zoo Parade (TV)-Marlin Perkins (11/55)	5	15	34	55
663-Winky Dink (TV)	8	24	56	100
664-Davy Crockett in the Great Keelboat Race (TV) (Disney) (11/55)-Fess Parker photo-c				
	15	45	105	195
665-The African Lion (Disney-Movie) (11/55)	5	15	35	60
666-Santa Claus Funnies	5	15	35	60
667-Silvertip and the Stolen Stallion (Max Brand) (12/55)-Kinstler-a				
	4	12	30	50
668-Dumbo (Disney) (12/55)-First of two printings. Dumbo on cover with starry sky. Reprints 4-Color #234?; same-c as #234	9	27	63	120
668-Dumbo (Disney) (1/58)-Second printing. Same cover altered, with Timothy Mouse added. Same contents as above	6	18	42	80
669-Robin Hood (Disney-Movie) (12/55)-Reprints #413 plus-c; photo-c				
	5	15	35	60
670-M.G.M.'s Mouse Musketeers (#1) (1/56)-Formerly the Two Mouseketeers				
	4	12	29	45
671-Davy Crockett and the River Pirates (TV) (Disney) (12/55)-Jesse Marsh-a; Fess Parker photo-c				
	15	45	105	195
672-Quentin Durward (1/56) (Movie)-Photo-c	7	21	49	85
673-Buffalo Bill, Jr. (#1) (TV)-James Arness photo-c	7	21	49	85
674-The Little Rascals (#1) (TV)	7	21	49	90
675-Steve Donovan, Western Marshal (#1) (TV)-Kinstler-a; photo-c				
	8	24	56	100
676-Will-Yum!	3	9	19	28
677-Little King	5	15	35	60
678-The Last Hunt (Movie)-Photo-c	8	24	56	100
679-Gunsmoke (#1) (TV)-Photo-c	17	51	119	220
680-Out Our Way with the Worry Wart (2/56)	3	9	19	28
681-Forever Darling (Movie) with Lucille Ball & Desi Arnaz (2/56)-; photo-c				
	11	33	77	140
682-The Sword & the Rose (Disney-Movie)-Reprint of #505; Renamed When Knighthood Was in Flower for the novel; photo-c	7	21	49	90
683-Hi and Lois (3/56)	4	12	26	40
684-Helen of Troy (Movie)-Buscema-a; photo-c	10	30	70	130
685-Johnny Mack Brown	6	18	42	80
686-Duck Album (Disney)	5	15	35	60
687-The Indian Fighter (Movie)-Kirk Douglas photo-c	8	24	56	100
688-Alexander the Great (Movie) (5/56)-Buscema-a; photo-c				
	7	21	49	85
689-Elmer Fudd (3/56)	4	12	27	42
690-The Conqueror (Movie) - John Wayne photo-c	17	51	119	220
691-Dotty Dripple and Taffy	3	9	17	25
692-The Little People-Walt Scott	4	12	29	45
693-Song of the South (Disney) (1956)-Partial reprint of #129				
	9	27	63	110
694-Super Circus (TV)-Photo-c	6	18	42	80
695-Little Beaver	4	12	26	40
696-Krazy Kat; not by Herriman (4/56)	4	12	26	40
697-Oswald the Rabbit (Lantz)	3	10	23	35
698-Francis the Famous Talking Mule (4/56)	4	12	26	40
699-Prince Valiant-by Bob Fuje	7	21	49	85
700-Water Birds and the Olympic Elk (Disney-Movie) (4/56)				
	5	15	35	60
701-Jiminy Cricket (#1) (Disney) (5/56)	9	27	63	110

Four Color #709 © WB

Four Color #752 © KING

Four Color #804 © Field Ent.

	GD2.0	FN6.0	VF8.0	NM9.4
702-The Goofy Success Story (Disney)	7	21	49	90
703-Scamp (#1) (Disney)	9	27	63	110
704-Priscilla's Pop (5/56)	4	12	25	38
705-Brave Eagle (#1) (TV)-Photo-c	6	18	42	80
706-Bongo and Lumpjaw (Disney) (6/56)	5	15	35	65
707-Corky and White Shadow (Disney) (5/56)-Mickey Mouse Club (TV); photo-c	7	21	49	90
708-Smokey the Bear	5	15	35	65
709-The Searchers (Movie) - John Wayne photo-c	27	81	189	350
710-Francis the Famous Talking Mule	4	12	26	40
711-M.G.M's Mouse Musketeers	3	9	20	30
712-The Great Locomotive Chase (Disney-Movie) (9/56)-Photo-c	7	21	49	90
713-The Animal World (Movie) (8/56)	3	9	21	38
714-Spin and Marty (#1) (TV) (Disney)-Mickey Mouse Club (6/56); photo-c	12	36	84	160
715-Timmy (8/56)	4	12	26	40
716-Man in Space (Disney)(A science feature from Tomorrowland)	9	27	63	110
717-Moby Dick (Movie)-Gregory Peck photo-c	9	27	63	110
718-Dotty Dripple and Taffy	3	9	17	25
719-Prince Valiant; by Bob Fuje (8/56)	7	21	49	85
720-Gunsmoke (TV)-James Arness photo-c	9	27	63	110
721-Captain Kangaroo (TV)-Photo-c	16	48	112	210
722-Johnny Mack Brown-Photo-c	6	18	42	80
723-Santiago (Movie)-Kinstler-a (9/56); Alan Ladd photo-c	10	30	70	130
724-Bugs Bunny's Album	4	12	30	50
725-Elmer Fudd (9/56)	3	9	21	32
726-Duck Album (Disney) (9/56)	5	15	35	60
727-The Nature of Things (TV) (Disney)-Jesse Marsh-a	5	15	35	60
728-M.G.M's Mouse Musketeers	3	9	20	30
729-Bob Son of Battle (11/56)	4	12	26	40
730-Smokey Stover	4	12	30	50
731-Silvertip and The Fighting Four (Max Brand)-Kinstler-a	4	12	30	50
732-Zorro, the Challenge of (10/56)	12	36	84	155
733-Buck Jones	4	12	26	40
734-Cheyenne (#1) (TV) (10/56)-Clint Walker photo-c	17	51	119	220
735-Crusader Rabbit (#1) (TV)	32	96	224	420
736-Pluto (Disney)	4	12	26	40
737-Steve Canyon-Caniff-a	5	15	35	60
738-Westward Ho, the Wagons (Disney-Movie)-Fess Parker photo-c	9	27	63	120
739-Bounty Guns (Luke Short)-Drucker-a	4	12	25	38
740-Chilly Willy (#1) (Walter Lantz)	5	15	35	60
741-The Fastest Gun Alive (Movie)(9/56)-Photo-c	7	21	49	90
742-Buffalo Bill, Jr. (TV)-Photo-c	5	15	34	55
743-Daisy Duck's Diary (Disney) (11/56)	5	15	35	65
744-Little Beaver	4	12	26	40
745-Francis the Famous Talking Mule	4	12	26	40
746-Dotty Dripple and Taffy	3	9	17	25
747-Goofy (Disney)	7	21	49	90
748-Frosty the Snowman (11/56)	4	12	30	50
749-Secrets of Life (Disney-Movie)-Photo-c	5	15	34	55
750-The Great Cat Family (Disney-TV/Movie)-Pinocchio & Alice app.	6	18	42	80
751-Our Miss Brooks (TV)-Photo-c	8	24	56	100
752-Mandrake, the Magician	10	30	70	135
753-Walt Scott's Little People (11/56)	4	12	29	45
754-Smokey the Bear	5	15	35	65
755-The Littlest Snowman (12/56)	4	12	30	50
756-Santa Claus Funnies	5	15	35	60
757-The True Story of Jesse James (Movie)-Photo-c	9	27	63	120
758-Bear Country (Disney-Movie)	5	15	35	60
759-Circus Boy (TV)-The Monkees' Mickey Dolenz photo-c (12/56)	13	39	91	170

	GD2.0	FN6.0	VF8.0	NM9.4
760-The Hardy Boys (#1) (TV) (Disney)-Mickey Mouse Club; photo-c	11	33	77	140
761-Howdy Doody (TV) (1/57)	10	30	70	130
762-The Sharkfighters (Movie) (1/57); Buscema-a	8	24	56	100
763-Grandma Duck's Farm Friends (#1) (Disney)	7	21	49	90
764-M.G.M's Mouse Musketeers	3	9	20	30
765-Will-Yum!	3	9	19	28
766-Buffalo Bill, Jr. (TV)-Photo-c	5	15	34	55
767-Spin and Marty (TV) (Disney)-Mickey Mouse Club (2/57)	9	27	63	120
768-Steve Donovan, Western Marshal (TV)-Kinstler-a; photo-c	6	18	42	80
769-Gunsmoke (TV)-James Arness photo-c	9	27	63	110
770-Brave Eagle (TV)-Photo-c	4	12	26	40
771-Brand of Empire (Luke Short)(3/57)-Drucker-a	4	12	25	38
772-Cheyenne-Clint Walker photo-c	8	24	56	105
773-The Brave One (Movie)-Photo-c	5	15	35	60
774-Hi and Lois (3/57)	3	9	17	25
775-Sir Lancelot and Brian (TV)-Buscema-a; photo-c	9	27	63	120
776-Johnny Mack Brown; photo-c	6	18	42	80
777-Scamp (Disney) (3/57)	6	18	42	80
778-The Little Rascals (TV)	5	15	34	55
779-Lee Hunter, Indian Fighter (3/57)	4	12	30	50
780-Captain Kangaroo (TV)-Photo-c	13	39	91	170
781-Fury (#1) (TV) (3/57)-Photo-c	8	24	56	100
782-Duck Album (Disney)	5	15	35	60
783-Elmer Fudd	3	9	21	32
784-Around the World in 80 Days (Movie) (2/57)-Photo-c	6	18	42	80
785-Circus Boy (TV) (4/57)-The Monkees' Mickey Dolenz photo-c	11	33	77	140
786-Cinderella (Disney) (3/57)-Partial-r of #272	6	18	42	80
787-Little Hiawatha (Disney) (4/57)(#2)	4	12	30	50
788-Prince Valiant; by Bob Fuje	7	21	49	85
789-Silvertip-Valley Thieves (Max Brand) (4/57)-Kinstler-a	4	12	30	50
790-The Wings of Eagles (Movie) (John Wayne) (John Wayne photo-c; 10¢ and 15¢ editions exist	15	45	105	190
791-The 77th Bengal Lancers (TV)-Photo-c	7	21	49	90
792-Oswald the Rabbit (Lantz)	3	10	23	35
793-Morty Meekle	3	9	19	28
794-The Count of Monte Cristo (5/57) (Movie)-Buscema-a	9	27	63	110
795-Jiminy Cricket (Disney)(#2)	6	18	42	80
796-Ludwig Bemelman's Madeleine and Genevieve	4	12	25	38
797-Gunsmoke (TV)-Photo-c	9	27	63	110
798-Buffalo Bill, Jr. (TV)-Photo-c	5	15	34	55
799-Priscilla's Pop	3	9	17	25
800-The Buccaneers (TV)-Photo-c	7	21	49	90
801-Dotty Dripple and Taffy	3	9	17	25
802-Goofy (Disney) (5/57)	7	21	49	90
803-Cheyenne (TV)-Clint Walker photo-c	8	24	56	105
804-Steve Canyon-Caniff-a (1957)	5	15	35	60
805-Crusader Rabbit (TV)	25	75	175	325
806-Scamp (Disney) (6/57)	6	18	42	80
807-Savage Range (Luke Short)-Drucker-a	4	12	25	38
808-Spin and Marty (TV)(Disney)-Mickey Mouse Club; photo-c	9	27	63	120
809-The Little People (Walt Scott)	4	12	29	45
810-Francis the Famous Talking Mule	3	10	23	35
811-Howdy Doody (TV) (7/57)	10	30	70	130
812-The Big Land (Movie); Alan Ladd photo-c	9	27	63	120
813-Circus Boy (TV)-The Monkees' Mickey Dolenz photo-c	11	33	77	140
814-Covered Wagons, Ho! (Disney)-Donald Duck (TV) (6/57); Mickey Mouse app.	5	15	35	60
815-Dragoon Wells Massacre (Movie)-photo-c	8	24	56	100
816-Brave Eagle (TV)-photo-c	4	12	26	40

Four Color #825 © DELL

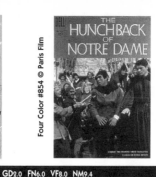

Four Color #854 © Paris Film

Four Color #911 © CBS

FO

	GD2.0	FN6.0	VF8.0	NM9.4
317-Little Beaver	4	12	26	40
318-Smokey the Bear (6/57)	5	15	35	65
319-Mickey Mouse in Magicland (Disney) (7/57)	4	12	29	45
320-The Oklahoman (Movie)-Photo-c	9	27	63	120
321-Wringle Wrangle (Disney)-Based on movie "Westward Ho, the Wagons"; Marsh-a; Fess Parker photo-c	8	24	56	100
322-Paul Revere's Ride with Johnny Tremain (TV) (Disney)-Toth-a	9	27	63	120
323-Timmy	3	9	19	28
324-The Pride and the Passion (Movie) (8/57)-Frank Sinatra & Cary Grant photo-c	9	27	63	110
325-The Little Rascals (TV)	5	15	34	55
326-Spin and Marty and Annette (TV) (Disney)-Mickey Mouse Club; Annette Funicello photo-c	24	72	168	310
327-Smokey Stover (8/57)	4	12	30	50
328-Buffalo Bill, Jr. (TV)-Photo-c	5	15	34	55
329-Tales of the Pony Express (TV) (8/57)-Painted-c	4	12	30	50
330-The Hardy Boys (TV) (Disney)-Mickey Mouse Club (8/57); photo-c	9	27	63	120
331-No Sleep 'Til Dawn (Movie)-Karl Malden photo-c	6	18	42	80
332-Lolly and Pepper (#1)	4	12	26	40
333-Scamp (Disney) (9/57)	6	18	43	80
334-Johnny Mack Brown; photo-c	6	18	42	80
335-Silvertip-The False Rider (Max Brand)	4	12	30	50
336-Man in Flight (Disney) (9/57)	7	21	49	90
337-All-American Athlete Cotton Woods	4	12	25	38
338-Bugs Bunny's Life Story Album (9/57)	4	12	30	50
339-The Vigilantes (Movie)	7	21	49	90
340-Duck Album (Disney) (9/57)	5	15	35	60
341-Elmer Fudd	3	9	21	32
342-The Nature of Things (Disney-Movie) ('57)-Jesse Marsh-a (TV series)	5	15	35	60
343-The First Americans (Disney) (TV)-Marsh-a	9	27	63	110
344-Gunsmoke (TV)-Photo-c	9	27	63	110
345-The Land Unknown (Movie)-Alex Toth-a	12	36	84	155
346-Gun Glory (Movie)-by Alex Toth; photo-c	9	27	63	120
347-Perri (squirrels) (Disney-Movie)-Two different covers published	5	15	35	60
348-Marauder's Moon (Luke Short)	4	12	25	38
349-Prince Valiant; by Bob Fuje	7	21	49	85
350-Buck Jones	4	12	26	40
351-The Story of Mankind (Movie) (1/58)-Hedy Lamarr & Vincent Price photo-c	7	21	49	90
352-Chilly Willy (2/58) (Lantz)	4	12	26	40
353-Pluto (Disney) (10/57)	4	12	26	40
354-The Hunchback of Notre Dame (Movie)-Photo-c	13	39	91	165
355-Broken Arrow (TV)-Photo-c	5	15	35	65
356-Buffalo Bill, Jr. (TV)-Photo-c	5	15	34	55
357-The Goofy Adventure Story (Disney) (11/57)	7	21	49	90
358-Daisy Duck's Diary (Disney) (11/57)	5	15	34	55
359-Topper and Neil (TV) (11/57)	4	12	30	50
360-Wyatt Earp (#1) (TV)-Manning-a; photo-c	10	30	70	130
361-Frosty the Snowman	4	12	30	50
362-The Truth About Mother Goose (Disney-Movie) (11/57)	7	21	49	90
363-Francis the Famous Talking Mule	3	10	23	35
364-The Littlest Snowman	4	12	30	50
365-Andy Burnett (TV) (Disney) (12/57)-Photo-c	9	27	63	120
366-Mars and Beyond (Disney-TV)(A science feature from Tomorrowland)	9	27	63	110
367-Santa Claus Funnies	5	15	35	60
368-The Little People (12/57)	4	12	29	45
369-Old Yeller (Disney-Movie)-Photo-c	5	15	35	60
370-Little Beaver (1/58)	4	12	26	40
371-Curly Kayoe	3	9	20	30
372-Captain Kangaroo (TV)-Photo-c	13	39	91	170
373-Grandma Duck's Farm Friends (Disney)	5	15	35	60
374-Old Ironsides (Disney-Movie with Johnny Tremain) (1/58)	6	18	42	80
375-Trumpets West (Luke Short) (2/58)	4	12	25	38

	GD2.0	FN6.0	VF8.0	NM9.4
876-Tales of Wells Fargo (#1)(TV)(2/58)-Photo-c	9	27	63	120
877-Frontier Doctor with Rex Allen (TV)-Alex Toth-a; Rex Allen photo-c	10	30	70	130
878-Peanuts (#1)-Schulz-c only (2/58)	15	45	105	200
879-Brave Eagle (TV) (2/58)-Photo-c	4	12	26	40
880-Steve Donovan, Western Marshal-Drucker-a (TV)-Photo-c	4	12	30	50
881-The Captain and the Kids (2/58)	4	12	26	40
882-Zorro (Disney)-1st Disney issue; by Alex Toth (TV) (2/58); photo-c	17	50	119	220
883-The Little Rascals (TV)	5	15	34	55
884-Hawkeye and the Last of the Mohicans (TV) (3/58); photo-c	7	21	49	90
885-Fury (TV) (3/58)-Photo-c	6	18	42	80
886-Bongo and Lumpjaw (Disney) (3/58)	4	12	28	50
887-The Hardy Boys (Disney) (TV)-Mickey Mouse Club (1/58)-Photo-c	9	27	63	120
888-Elmer Fudd (3/58)	3	9	21	32
889-Clint and Mac (Disney) (TV)-Alex Toth-a; photo-c	13	39	91	165
890-Wyatt Earp (TV)-by Russ Manning; photo-c	7	21	49	95
891-Light in the Forest (Disney-Movie) (3/58)-Fess Parker photo-c	8	24	56	100
892-Maverick (#1) (TV) (4/58)-James Garner photo-c	25	75	175	325
893-Jim Bowie (TV)-Photo-c	5	15	35	60
894-Oswald the Rabbit (Lantz)	3	10	23	35
895-Wagon Train (#1) (TV) (3/58)-Photo-c	12	36	84	150
896-The Adventures of Tinker Bell (Disney)	9	27	63	110
897-Jiminy Cricket (Disney)	6	18	42	80
898-Silvertip (Max Brand)-Kinstler-a (5/58)	4	12	30	50
899-Goofy (Disney)	5	15	34	55
900-Prince Valiant; by Bob Fuje	7	21	49	85
901-Little Hiawatha (Disney)	4	12	30	50
902-Will-Yum!	3	9	19	28
903-Dotty Dripple and Taffy	3	9	17	25
904-Lee Hunter, Indian Fighter	4	12	25	38
905-Annette (Disney) (TV) (5/58)-Mickey Mouse Club; Annette Funicello photo-c	28	84	196	365
906-Francis the Famous Talking Mule	3	10	23	35
907-Sugarfoot (#1) (TV)Toth-a; photo-c	13	39	91	165
908-The Little People and the Giant-Walt Scott (5/58)	4	12	29	45
909-Smitty	3	10	23	35
910-The Vikings (Movie)-Buscema-a; Kirk Douglas photo-c	9	27	63	110
911-The Gray Ghost (TV)-Photo-c	9	27	63	110
912-Leave It to Beaver (#1) (TV)-Photo-c	18	54	126	230
913-The Left-Handed Gun (Movie) (7/58); Paul Newman photo-c	10	30	70	130
914-No Time for Sergeants (Movie)-Andy Griffith photo-c; Toth-a	10	30	70	125
915-Casey Jones (TV)-Alan Hale photo-c	5	15	35	60
916-Red Ryder Ranch Comics (7/58)	4	12	29	45
917-The Life of Riley (TV)-Photo-c	12	36	84	150
918-Beep Beep, the Roadrunner (#1) (7/58)-Published with two different back covers	9	27	63	120
919-Boots and Saddles (#1) (TV)-Photo-c	8	24	56	100
920-Zorro (Disney) (6/58)Toth-a; photo-c	12	36	84	155
921-Wyatt Earp (TV)-Manning-a; photo-c	7	21	49	95
922-Johnny Mack Brown by Russ Manning; photo-c	7	21	49	85
923-Timmy	3	9	19	28
924-Colt .45 (#1) (TV) (8/58)-W. Preston photo-c	10	30	70	130
925-Last of the Fast Guns (Movie) (8/58)-Photo-c	7	21	49	90
926-Peter Pan (Disney)-Reprint of #442	4	12	30	50
927-Top Gun (Luke Short) Buscema-a	4	12	25	38
928-Sea Hunt (#1) (9/58) (TV)-Lloyd Bridges photo-c	12	36	84	160
929-Brave Eagle (TV)-Photo-c	4	12	26	40
930-Maverick (TV) (7/58)-James Garner photo-c	11	33	77	140

	GD2.0	FN6.0	VF8.0	NM9.4
931-Have Gun, Will Travel (#1) (TV)-Photo-c	14	41	98	180
932-Smokey the Bear (His Life Story)	5	15	35	65
933-Zorro (Disney, 9/58) (TV)-Alex Toth-a; photo-c	12	36	84	155
934-Restless Gun (#1) (TV)-Photo-c	12	36	84	150
935-King of the Royal Mounted	4	12	27	42
936-The Little Rascals (TV)	5	15	34	55
937-Ruff and Reddy #1 (9/58) (TV) (1st Hanna-Barbera comic book)	13	39	91	170
938-Elmer Fudd (9/58)	3	9	21	32
939-Steve Canyon - not by Caniff	5	15	35	60
940-Lolly and Pepper (10/58)	3	9	19	28
941-Pluto (Disney) (10/58)	4	12	26	40
942-Pony Express (TV)	4	12	30	50
943-White Wilderness (Disney-Movie) (10/58)	6	18	42	80
944-The 7th Voyage of Sinbad (Movie) (9/58)-Buscema-a; photo-c	13	39	91	165
945-Maverick (TV)-James Garner/Jack Kelly photo-c	11	33	77	140
946-The Big Country (Movie)-Photo-c	7	21	49	90
947-Broken Arrow (TV)-Photo-c (11/58)	5	15	34	55
948-Daisy Duck's Diary (Disney) (11/58)	5	15	34	55
949-High Adventure(Lowell Thomas')(TV)-Photo-c	5	15	35	65
950-Frosty the Snowman	4	12	30	50
951-The Lennon Sisters Life Story (TV)-Toth-a, 32 pgs.; photo-c	14	42	98	185
952-Goofy (Disney) (11/58)	5	15	34	55
953-Francis the Famous Talking Mule	3	10	23	35
954-Man in Space-Satellites (TV)	7	21	49	90
955-Hi and Lois (11/58)	3	9	17	25
956-Ricky Nelson (#1) (TV)-Photo-c	19	57	133	245
957-Buffalo Bee (#1) (TV)	9	27	63	120
958-Santa Claus Funnies	5	15	34	55
959-Christmas Stories-(Walt Scott's Little People) (1951-56 strip reprints)	4	12	29	45
960-Zorro (Disney) (TV) (12/58)-Toth art; photo-c	12	36	84	155
961-Jace Pearson's Tales of the Texas Rangers (TV)-Spiegle-a; photo-c	5	15	34	55
962-Maverick (TV) (1/59)-James Garner/Jack Kelly photo-c	11	33	77	140
963-Johnny Mack Brown; photo-c	6	18	42	80
964-The Hardy Boys (TV) (Disney) (1/59)-Mickey Mouse Club;	9	27	63	120
965-Grandma Duck's Farm Friends (Disney)(1/59)	4	12	30	50
966-Tonka (starring Sal Mineo; Disney-Movie)-Photo-c	8	24	56	100
967-Chilly Willy (2/59) (Lantz)	4	12	26	40
968-Tales of Wells Fargo (TV)-Photo-c	9	27	63	110
969-Peanuts (2/59)	10	30	70	135
970-Lawman (#1) (TV)-Photo-c	13	39	91	165
971-Wagon Train (TV)-Photo-c	7	21	49	85
972-Tom Thumb (Movie)-George Pal (1/59)	9	27	63	120
973-Sleeping Beauty and the Prince(Disney)(5/59)	12	36	84	150
974-The Little Rascals (TV) (3/59)	5	15	34	55
975-Fury (TV)	6	18	42	80
976-Zorro (Disney)(TV)-Toth-a; photo-c	12	36	84	155
977-Elmer Fudd (3/59)	3	9	21	32
978-Lolly and Pepper	3	9	19	28
979-Oswald the Rabbit (Lantz)	3	10	23	35
980-Maverick (TV) (4-6/59)-James Garner/Jack Kelly photo-c	11	33	77	140
981-Ruff and Reddy (TV) (Hanna-Barbera)	8	24	56	105
982-The New Adventures of Tinker Bell (TV) (Disney)	8	24	56	100
983-Have Gun, Will Travel (TV) (4-6/59)-Photo-c	9	27	63	115
984-Sleeping Beauty's Fairy Godmothers (Disney)	9	27	63	110
985-Shaggy Dog (Disney-Movie)-Photo-all four covers; Annette on back-c(5/59)	7	21	49	90
986-Restless Gun (TV)-Photo-c	8	24	56	105
987-Goofy (Disney) (7/59)	5	15	34	55
988-Little Hiawatha (Disney)	4	12	30	50
989-Jiminy Cricket (Disney) (5-7/59)	6	18	42	80
990-Huckleberry Hound (#1)(TV)(Hanna-Barbera); 1st app. Huck, Yogi Bear, & Pixie & Dixie & Mr. Jinks	12	36	84	160
991-Francis the Famous Talking Mule	3	10	23	35
992-Sugarfoot (TV)-Toth-a; photo-c	12	36	84	155
993-Jim Bowie (TV)-Photo-c	5	15	35	60
994-Sea Hunt (TV)-Lloyd Bridges photo-c	8	24	56	105
995-Donald Duck Album (Disney) (5-7/59)(#1)	5	15	35	70
996-Nevada (Zane Grey)	4	12	26	40
997-Walt Disney Presents-Tales of Texas John Slaughter (#1) (TV) (Disney)-Photo-c; photo of W. Disney inside-c	7	21	49	90
998-Ricky Nelson (TV)-Photo-c	19	57	133	245
999-Leave It to Beaver (TV)-Photo-c	15	45	105	190
1000-The Gray Ghost (TV) (6-8/59)-Photo-c	9	27	63	110
1001-Lowell Thomas' High Adventure (TV) (8-10/59)-Photo-c	5	15	35	60
1002-Buffalo Bee (TV)	7	21	49	85
1003-Zorro (TV) (Disney)-Toth-a; photo-c	12	36	84	155
1004-Colt .45 (6-8/59)-Photo-c	8	24	56	105
1005-Maverick (TV)-James Garner/Jack Kelly photo-c	11	33	77	140
1006-Hercules (Movie)-Buscema-a; photo-c	9	27	63	120
1007-John Paul Jones (Movie)-Robert Stack photo-c	5	15	35	60
1008-Beep Beep, the Road Runner (7-9/59)	5	15	35	60
1009-The Rifleman (#1) (TV)-Photo-c	25	75	175	320
1010-Grandma Duck's Farm Friends (Disney)-by Carl Barks	13	39	91	165
1011-Buckskin (#1) (TV)-Photo-c	7	21	49	90
1012-Last Train from Gun Hill (Movie) (7/59)-Photo-c	9	27	63	110
1013-Bat Masterson (#1) (TV) (8/59)-Gene Barry photo-c	12	36	84	160
1014-The Lennon Sisters (TV)-Toth-a; photo-c	13	40	91	175
1015-Peanuts-Schulz-c	10	30	70	135
1016-Smokey the Bear Nature Stories	4	12	26	40
1017-Chilly Willy (Lantz)	4	12	26	40
1018-Rio Bravo (Movie)(6/59)-John Wayne; Toth-a; John Wayne, Dean Martin & Ricky Nelson photo-c	23	68	161	300
1019-Wagon Train (TV)-Photo-c	7	21	49	90
1020-Jungle Jim-McWilliams-a	3	10	23	35
1021-Jace Pearson's Tales of the Texas Rangers (TV)-Photo-c	5	15	34	55
1022-Timmy	3	9	19	28
1023-Tales of Wells Fargo (TV)-Photo-c	9	27	63	110
1024-Darby O'Gill and the Little People (Disney-Movie)-Toth-a; photo-c	10	30	70	130
1025-Vacation in Disneyland (8-10/59)-Carl Barks-a(24pgs.) (Disney)	19	57	133	240
1026-Spin and Marty (TV) (Disney) (9-11/59)-Mickey Mouse Club; photo-c	8	24	56	100
1027-The Texan (#1)(TV)-Photo-c	9	27	63	110
1028-Rawhide (#1) (TV) (9-11/59)-Clint Eastwood photo-c; Tufts-a	23	68	161	300
1029-Boots and Saddles (9/59)-Photo-c	5	15	35	60
1030-Spanky and Alfalfa, the Little Rascals (TV)	5	15	34	55
1031-Fury (TV)-Photo-c	6	18	42	80
1032-Elmer Fudd	3	9	21	32
1033-Steve Canyon-not by Caniff; photo-c	5	15	35	60
1034-Nancy and Sluggo Summer Camp (9-11/59)	4	12	29	45
1035-Lawman (TV)-Photo-c	7	21	49	90
1036-The Big Circus (Movie)-Photo-c	6	18	42	80
1037-Zorro (Disney) (TV)-Tufts-a; Annette Funicello photo-c	15	45	105	190
1038-Ruff and Reddy (TV)(Hanna-Barbera)(1959)	8	24	56	105
1039-Pluto (Disney) (11-1/60)	4	12	26	40
1040-Quick Draw McGraw (#1) (TV) (Hanna-Barbera) (12-2/60)	14	42	98	180
1041-Sea Hunt (TV) (10-12/59)-Toth-a; Lloyd Bridges photo-c	9	27	63	110
1042-The Three Chipmunks (Alvin, Simon & Theodore) (#1) (TV) (10-12/59)	5	15	35	70

Four Color #1066 © WB

Four Color #1126 © DELL

Four Color #1162 © H-B

	GD2.0	FN6.0	VF8.0	NM9.4
043-The Three Stooges (#1)-Photo-c	21	63	147	275
044-Have Gun, Will Travel (TV)-Photo-c	9	27	63	115
045-Restless Gun (TV)-Photo-c	8	24	56	105
046-Beep Beep, the Road Runner (11-1/60)	5	15	35	60
047-Gyro Gearloose (#1) (Disney)-All Barks-c/a	18	54	126	240
048-The Horse Soldiers (Movie) (John Wayne)-Sekowsky-a; painted cover featuring John Wayne	14	42	98	180
049-Don't Give Up the Ship (Movie) (8/59)-Jerry Lewis photo-c	8	24	56	100
050-Huckleberry Hound (TV) (Hanna-Barbera) (10-12/59)	8	24	56	105
051-Donald in Mathmagic Land (Disney-Movie)	9	27	63	110
052-Ben-Hur (Movie) (11/59)-Manning-a	10	30	70	130
053-Goofy (Disney) (11-1/60)	5	15	34	55
054-Huckleberry Hound Winter Fun (TV) (Hanna-Barbera) (12/59)	8	24	56	105
055-Daisy Duck's Diary (Disney)-by Carl Barks (11-1/60)	9	27	63	120
056-Yellowstone Kelly (Movie)-Clint Walker photo-c	5	15	35	65
057-Mickey Mouse Album (Disney)	4	12	27	42
058-Colt .45 (TV)-Photo-c	8	24	56	105
059-Sugarfoot (TV)-Photo-c	9	27	63	110
060-Journey to the Center of the Earth (Movie)-Pat Boone & James Mason photo-c	12	36	84	150
061-Buffalo Bee (TV)	7	21	49	85
062-Christmas Stories (Walt Scott's Little People strip-r)	4	12	29	45
063-Santa Claus Funnies	5	15	34	55
064-Bugs Bunny's Merry Christmas (12/59)	4	12	30	50
065-Frosty the Snowman	4	12	30	50
066-77 Sunset Strip (#1) (TV)-Toth-a (1-3/60)-Efrem Zimbalist, Jr. & Edd "Kookie" Byrnes photo-c	12	36	84	150
067-Yogi Bear (#1) (TV) (Hanna-Barbera)	12	36	84	150
068-Francis the Famous Talking Mule	10	30	70	130
069-The FBI Story (Movie)-Toth-a; James Stewart photo on-c	10	30	70	130
070-Solomon and Sheba (Movie)-Sekowsky-a; photo-c	9	27	63	120
071-The Real McCoys (#1) (TV) (1-3/60)-Toth-a; Walter Brennan photo-c	9	27	63	120
072-Blythe (Marge's)	5	15	35	60
073-Grandma Duck's Farm Friends-Barks-c/a (Disney)	13	39	91	165
074-Chilly Willy (Lantz)	4	12	26	40
075-Tales of Wells Fargo (TV)-Photo-c	9	27	63	110
076-The Rebel (#1) (TV)-Sekowsky-a; photo-c	10	30	70	130
077-The Deputy (#1) (TV)-Buscema-a; Henry Fonda photo-c	13	39	91	170
078-The Three Stooges (2-4/60)-Photo-c	11	33	77	140
079-The Little Rascals (TV) (Spanky & Alfalfa)	5	15	34	55
080-Fury (TV) (2-4/60)-Photo-c	6	18	42	80
081-Elmer Fudd	3	9	21	32
082-Spin and Marty (Disney) (TV)-Photo-c	8	24	56	100
083-Men into Space (TV)-Anderson-a; photo-c	5	15	35	60
084-Speedy Gonzales	5	15	34	55
085-The Time Machine (H.G. Wells) (Movie) (3/60)-Alex Toth-a; Rod Taylor photo-c	15	45	105	190
086-Lolly and Pepper	3	9	19	28
087-Peter Gunn (TV)-Photo-c	9	27	63	120
088-A Dog of Flanders (Movie)-Photo-c	4	12	30	50
089-Restless Gun (TV)-Photo-c	8	24	56	105
090-Francis the Famous Talking Mule	3	10	23	35
091-Jacky's Diary (4-6/60)	4	12	30	50
092-Toby Tyler (Disney-Movie)-Photo-c	6	18	42	80
093-MacKenzie's Raiders (Movie/TV)-Richard Carlson photo-c from TV show	6	18	42	80
094-Goofy (Disney)	5	15	34	55
095-Gyro Gearloose (Disney)-All Barks-c/a	10	30	70	130
096-The Texan (Movie)-Rory Calhoun photo-c	8	24	56	100
097-Rawhide (TV)-Manning-a; Clint Eastwood photo-c				

	GD2.0	FN6.0	VF8.0	NM9.4
	14	41	98	180
1098-Sugarfoot (TV)-Photo-c	9	27	63	110
1099-Donald Duck Album (Disney) (5-7/60)-Barks-c	6	18	42	80
1100-Annette's Life Story (Disney-Movie) (5/60)-Annette Funicello photo-c	23	69	161	300
1101-Robert Louis Stevenson's Kidnapped (Disney-Movie) (5/60); photo-c	6	18	42	80
1102-Wanted: Dead or Alive (#1) (TV) (5-7/60); Steve McQueen photo-c	13	39	91	170
1103-Leave It to Beaver (TV)-Photo-c	15	45	105	190
1104-Yogi Bear Goes to College (TV) (Hanna-Barbera) (6-8/60)	7	21	49	95
1105-Gale Storm (Oh! Susanna) (TV)-Toth-a; photo-c	13	39	91	165
1106-77 Sunset Strip (6-8/60)-Toth-a; photo-c	9	27	63	120
1107-Buckskin (TV)-Photo-c	6	18	42	80
1108-The Troubleshooters (TV)-Keenan Wynn photo-c	5	15	35	60
1109-This Is Your Life, Donald Duck (Disney) (TV) (8-10/60)-Gyro flashback to WDC&S #141; origin Donald Duck (1st told)	14	41	98	180
1110-Bonanza (TV) (6-8/60)-Photo-c	37	111	259	480
1111-Shotgun Slade (TV)-Photo-c	6	18	42	80
1112-Pixie and Dixie and Mr. Jinks (#1) (TV) (Hanna-Barbera) (7-9/60)	7	21	49	95
1113-Tales of Wells Fargo (TV)-Photo-c	9	27	63	110
1114-Huckleberry Finn (Movie) (7/60)-Photo-c	5	15	35	60
1115-Ricky Nelson (TV)-Manning-a; photo-c	15	45	105	190
1116-Boots and Saddles (TV) (8/60)-Photo-c	5	15	35	60
1117-Boy and the Pirates (Movie)-Photo-c	6	18	42	80
1118-The Sword and the Dragon (Movie) (6/60)-Photo-c	8	24	56	100
1119-Smokey the Bear Nature Stories	4	12	26	40
1120-Dinosaurus (Movie)-Painted-c	8	24	56	100
1121-Hercules Unchained (Movie) (8/60)-Crandall/Evans-a	9	27	63	120
1122-Chilly Willy (Lantz)	4	12	26	40
1123-Tombstone Territory (TV)-Photo-c	9	27	63	120
1124-Whirlybirds (TV)-Photo-c	9	27	63	110
1125-Laramie (#1) (TV)-Photo-c; G. Kane/Heath-a	9	27	63	120
1126-Sundance (TV) (8-10/60)-Earl Holliman photo-c	6	18	42	80
1127-The Three Stooges-Photo-c (8-10/60)	11	33	77	140
1128-Rocky and His Friends (#1) (TV) (Jay Ward) (8-10/60)	37	110	259	480
1129-Pollyanna (Disney-Movie)-Hayley Mills photo-c	8	24	56	100
1130-The Deputy (TV)-Buscema-a; Henry Fonda photo-c	10	30	70	130
1131-Elmer Fudd (9-11/60)	3	9	21	32
1132-Space Mouse (Lantz) (8-10/60)	4	12	30	50
1133-Fury (TV)-Photo-c	6	18	42	80
1134-Real McCoys (TV)-Toth-a; photo-c	9	27	63	120
1135-M.G.M.'s Mouse Musketeers (9-11/60)	3	9	19	28
1136-Jungle Cat (Disney-Movie)-Photo-c	6	18	42	80
1137-The Little Rascals (TV)-Photo-c	5	15	34	55
1138-The Rebel (TV)-Photo-c	9	27	63	110
1139-Spartacus (Movie) (11/60)-Buscema-a; Kirk Douglas photo-c	13	39	91	165
1140-Donald Duck Album (Disney)-Barks-c	6	18	42	80
1141-Huckleberry Hound for President (TV) (Hanna-Barbera) (10/60)	8	24	56	100
1142-Johnny Ringo (TV)-Photo-c	7	21	49	90
1143-Pluto (Disney) (11-1/61)	4	12	26	40
1144-The Story of Ruth (Movie)-Photo-c	9	27	63	120
1145-The Lost World (Movie)-Gil Kane-a; photo-c; 1 pg. Conan Doyle biography by Torres	10	30	70	130
1146-Restless Gun (TV)-Photo-c; Wildey-a	8	24	56	105
1147-Sugarfoot (TV)-Photo-c	9	27	63	110
1148-I Aim at the Stars-the Wernher Von Braun Story (Movie) (11-1/61)-Photo-c	7	21	49	90

Four Color #1173 © CBS

Four Color #1195 © DELL

Four Color #1268 © Walter Lantz

	GD2.0	FN6.0	VF8.0	NM9.4

	GD2.0	FN6.0	VF8.0	NM9.

1149-Goofy (Disney) (11-1/61) 5 15 34 55
1150-Daisy Duck's Diary (Disney) (12-1/61) by Carl Barks
9 27 63 120
1151-Mickey Mouse Album (Disney) (11-1/61) 4 12 27 42
1152-Rocky and His Friends (TV) (Jay Ward) (12-2/61)
23 69 161 300
1153-Frosty the Snowman 4 12 30 50
1154-Santa Claus Funnies 5 15 34 55
1155-North to Alaska (Movie)-John Wayne photo-c 17 51 119 220
1156-Walt Disney Swiss Family Robinson (Movie) (12/60)-Photo-c
7 21 49 90
1157-Master of the World (Movie) (7/61) 5 15 35 60
1158-Three Worlds of Gulliver (2 issues exist with different covers) (Movie)-
Photo-c 7 21 49 85
1159-77 Sunset Strip (TV)-Toth-a; photo-c 9 27 63 120
1160-Rawhide (TV)-Clint Eastwood photo-c 14 41 98 180
1161-Grandma Duck's Farm Friends (Disney) by Carl Barks (2-4/61)
13 39 91 165
1162-Yogi Bear Joins the Marines (TV) (Hanna-Barbera) (5-7/61)
7 21 49 95
1163-Daniel Boone (3-5/61); Marsh-a 5 15 35 60
1164-Wanted: Dead or Alive (TV)-Steve McQueen photo-c
10 30 70 130
1165-Ellery Queen (#1) (3-5/61) 11 33 77 145
1166-Rocky and His Friends (TV) (Jay Ward) 23 69 161 300
1167-Tales of Wells Fargo (TV)-Photo-c 8 24 56 100
1168-The Detectives (TV)-Robert Taylor photo-c 10 30 70 130
1169-New Adventures of Sherlock Holmes 16 48 112 210
1170-The Three Stooges (3-5/61)-Photo-c 11 33 77 140
1171-Elmer Fudd 3 9 21 32
1172-Fury (TV)-Photo-c 6 18 42 80
1173-The Twilight Zone (#1) (TV) (5/61)-Crandall/Evans-c/a; Crandall tribute to
Ingles 21 63 147 270
1174-The Little Rascals (TV) 4 12 29 45
1175-M.G.M.'s Mouse Musketeers (3-5/61) 3 9 19 28
1176-Dondi (Movie)-Origin; photo-c 4 12 30 50
1177-Chilly Willy (Lantz) (4-6/61) 4 12 26 40
1178-Ten Who Dared (Disney-Movie) (12/60)-Painted-c; cast member photo
on back-c 7 21 49 90
1179-The Swamp Fox (TV) (Disney)-Leslie Nielson photo-c
9 27 63 110
1180-The Danny Thomas Show (TV)-Toth-a; photo-c
17 51 119 220
1181-Texas John Slaughter (TV) (Disney) (4-6/61)-Photo-c
7 21 49 90
1182-Donald Duck Album (Disney) (5-7/61) 4 12 30 50
1183-101 Dalmatians (Disney-Movie) (3/61) 10 30 70 130
1184-Gyro Gearloose; All Barks-c/a (Disney) (5-7/61) Two variations exist
10 30 70 130
1185-Sweetie Pie 4 12 29 45
1186-Yak Yak (#1) by Jack Davis (2 versions - one minus 3-pg. Davis-c/a)
9 27 63 110
1187-The Three Stooges (6-8/61)-Photo-c 11 33 77 140
1188-Atlantis, the Lost Continent (Movie) (5/61)-Photo-c
11 33 77 140
1189-Greyfriars Bobby (Disney-Movie) (11/61)-Photo-c (scarce)
7 21 49 90
1190-Donald and the Wheel (Disney-Movie) (11/61); Barks-c
7 21 49 90
1191-Leave It to Beaver (TV)-Photo-c 15 45 105 190
1192-Ricky Nelson (TV)-Manning-a; photo-c 15 45 105 190
1193-The Real McCoys (TV) (6-8/61)-Photo-c 9 27 63 110
1194-Pepe (Movie) (4/61) 3 9 17 25
1195-National Velvet (#1) (TV)-Photo-c 6 18 42 80
1196-Pixie and Dixie and Mr. Jinks (TV) (Hanna-Barbera) (7-9/61)
5 15 35 65
1197-The Aquanauts (TV) (5-7/61)-Photo-c 7 21 49 90
1198-Donald in Mathmagic Land (Disney-Movie)-Reprint of #1051
6 18 42 80
1199-The Absent-Minded Professor (Disney-Movie) (4/61)-Photo-c

1200-Hennessey (TV) (8-10/61)-Gil Kane-a; photo-c 7 21 49 90
1201-Goofy (Disney) (8-10/61) 5 15 34 55
1202-Rawhide (TV)-Clint Eastwood photo-c 14 41 98 180
1203-Pinocchio (Disney) (3/62) 5 15 35 60
1204-Scamp (Disney) 4 12 29 45
1205-David and Goliath (Movie) (7/61)-Photo-c 6 18 42 80
1206-Lolly and Pepper (9-11/61) 3 9 19 28
1207-The Rebel (TV)-Sekowsky-a; photo-c 9 27 63 110
1208-Rocky and His Friends (Jay Ward) (TV) 23 69 161 300
1209-Sugarfoot (TV)-Photo-c (10-12/61) 9 27 63 110
1210-The Parent Trap (Disney-Movie) (8/61)-Hayley Mills photo-c
9 27 63 120
1211-77 Sunset Strip (TV)-Manning-a; photo-c 9 27 63 110
1212-Chilly Willy (Lantz) (7-9/61) 4 12 26 40
1213-Mysterious Island (Movie)-Photo-c 9 27 63 110
1214-Smokey the Bear 4 12 26 40
1215-Tales of Wells Fargo (TV) (10-12/61)-Photo-c 8 24 56 100
1216-Whirlybirds (TV)-Photo-c 8 24 56 100
1218-Fury (TV)-Photo-c 6 18 42 80
1219-The Detectives (TV)-Robert Taylor & Adam West photo-c
9 27 63 115
1220-Gunslinger (TV)-Photo-c 9 27 63 110
1221-Bonanza (TV) (9-11/61)-Photo-c 18 54 126 235
1222-Elmer Fudd (9-11/61) 3 9 21 32
1223-Laramie (TV)-Gil Kane-a; photo-c 6 18 42 80
1224-The Little Rascals (TV) (10-12/61) 4 12 29 40
1225-The Deputy (TV)-Henry Fonda photo-c 10 30 70 130
1226-Nikki, Wild Dog of the North (Disney-Movie) (9/61)-Photo-c
5 15 35 60
1227-Morgan the Pirate (Movie) 8 24 56 100
1229-Thief of Baghdad (Movie)-Crandall/Evans-a; photo-c
7 21 49 85
1230-Voyage to the Bottom of the Sea (#1) (Movie)-Photo insert on-c
10 30 70 135
1231-Danger Man (TV) (9-11/61)-Patrick McGoohan
11 33 77 140
1232-On the Double (Movie) 4 12 30 50
1233-Tammy Tell Me True (Movie) (1961) 6 18 42 80
1234-The Phantom Planet (Movie) (1961) 7 21 49 90
1235-Mister Magoo (12-2/62) 9 27 63 110
1235-Mister Magoo (3-5/65) 2nd printing; reprint of 12-2/62 issue
6 18 42 75
1236-King of Kings (Movie)-Photo-c 8 24 56 100
1237-The Untouchables (#1) (TV)-Not by Toth; photo-c
23 68 161 300
1238-Deputy Dawg (TV) 11 33 77 145
1239-Donald Duck Album (Disney) (10-12/61)-Barks-c
6 18 42 80
1240-The Detectives (TV)-Tufts-a; Robert Taylor photo-c
9 27 63 115
1241-Sweetie Pie 3 10 23 35
1242-King Leonardo and His Short Subjects (#1) (TV) (11-1/62)
14 42 98 175
1243-Ellery Queen 9 27 63 115
1244-Space Mouse (Lantz) (11-1/62) 4 12 30 50
1245-New Adventures of Sherlock Holmes 15 45 105 190
1246-Mickey Mouse Album (Disney) 4 12 27 42
1247-Daisy Duck's Diary (Disney) (12-2/62) 5 15 34 55
1248-Pluto (Disney) 4 12 26 42
1249-The Danny Thomas Show (TV)-Manning-a; photo-c
16 48 112 205
1250-The Four Horsemen of the Apocalypse (Movie)-Photo-c
6 18 42 80
1251-Everything's Ducky (Movie) (1961) 4 12 30 50
1252-The Andy Griffith Show (TV)-Photo-c; 1st show aired 10/3/60
35 105 245 450
1253-Space Man (#1) (1-3/62) 7 21 49 90
1254-"Diver Dan" (#1) (TV) (2-4/62)-Photo-c 5 15 35 60
1255-The Wonders of Aladdin (Movie) (1961) 6 18 42 80

Four Color #1309 © DELL

Four Favorites #12 © ACE

4Most V1 #3 © Prem. Serv.

	GD2.0	FN6.0	VF8.0	NM9.4
1256-Kona, Monarch of Monster Isle (#1) (2-4/62)-Glanzman-a				
	7	21	49	90
1257-Car 54, Where Are You? (#1) (TV) (3-5/62)-Photo-c				
	8	24	56	100
1258-The Frogmen (#1)-Evans-a	7	21	49	95
1259-El Cid (Movie) (1961)-Photo-c	7	21	49	90
1260-The Horsemasters (TV, Movie) (Disney) (12-2/62)-Annette Funicello				
photo-c	12	36	84	160
1261-Rawhide (TV)-Clint Eastwood photo-c	14	41	98	180
1262-The Rebel (TV)-Photo-c	9	27	63	110
1263-77 Sunset Strip (TV) (12-2/62)-Manning-a; photo-c				
	9	27	63	110
1264-Pixie and Dixie and Mr. Jinks (TV) (Hanna-Barbera)				
	5	15	35	65
1265-The Real McCoys (TV)-Photo-c	9	27	63	110
1266-M.G.M.'s Spike and Tyke (12-2/62)	3	9	17	25
1267-Gyro Gearloose; Barks-c/a, 4 pgs. (Disney) (12-2/62)				
	7	21	49	95
1268-Oswald the Rabbit (Lantz)	3	10	23	35
1269-Rawhide (TV)-Clint Eastwood photo-c	14	41	98	180
1270-Bullwinkle and Rocky (#1) (TV) (Jay Ward) (3-5/62)				
	20	60	140	260
1271-Yogi Bear Birthday Party (TV) (Hanna-Barbera) (11/61) (Given away				
for 1 box top from Kellogg's Corn Flakes)	5	15	35	65
1272-Frosty the Snowman	4	12	30	50
1273-Hans Brinker (Disney-Movie)-Photo-c (2/62)	6	18	42	80
1274-Santa Claus Funnies (12/61)	5	15	34	55
1275-Rocky and His Friends (Jay Ward)	23	69	161	300
1276-Dondi	3	9	17	25
1278-King Leonardo and His Short Subjects (TV)	14	42	98	175
1279-Grandma Duck's Farm Friends (Disney)	4	12	30	50
1280-Hennessey (TV)-Photo-c	6	18	42	80
1281-Chilly Willy (Lantz) (4-6/62)	4	12	26	40
1282-Babes in Toyland (Disney-Movie) (1/62); Annette Funicello photo-c				
	13	39	91	170
1283-Bonanza (TV) (2-4/62)-Photo-c	18	54	126	235
1284-Laramie (TV)-Heath-a; photo-c	6	18	42	80
1285-Leave It to Beaver (TV)-Photo-c	15	45	105	190
1286-The Untouchables (TV)-Photo-c	16	48	112	210
1287-Man from Wells Fargo (TV)-Photo-c	5	15	35	65
1288-Twilight Zone (TV) (4/62)-Crandall/Evans-a/c	12	36	84	150
1289-Ellery Queen	9	27	63	115
1290-M.G.M.'s Mouse Musketeers	3	9	19	28
1291-77 Sunset Strip (TV)-Manning-a; photo-c	9	27	63	110
1293-Elmer Fudd (3-5/62)	3	9	21	32
1294-Ripcord (TV)	7	21	49	90
1295-Mister Ed, the Talking Horse (#1) (3-5/62)-Photo-c				
	13	39	91	175
1296-Fury (TV) (3-5/62)-Photo-c	6	18	42	80
1297-Spanky, Alfalfa and the Little Rascals (TV)	4	12	29	45
1298-The Hathaways (TV)-Photo-c	4	12	30	50
1299-Deputy Dawg (TV)	11	33	77	145
1300-The Comancheros (Movie) (1961)-John Wayne photo-c				
	16	48	112	210
301-Adventures in Paradise (TV) (2-4/62)	5	15	35	65
302-Johnny Jason, Teen Reporter (2-4/62)	5	15	25	38
303-Lad: A Dog (Movie)-Photo-c	4	12	29	45
304-Nellie the Nurse (3-5/62)-Stanley-a	7	21	49	90
305-Mister Magoo (3-5/62)	9	27	63	110
306-Target: The Corruptors (#1) (3-5/62)-Photo-c				
	5	15	35	65
307-Margie (3-5/62)	5	15	35	65
308-Tales of the Wizard of Oz (TV) (3-5/62)	12	36	84	150
309-87th Precinct (#1) (4-6/62)-Krigstein-a; photo-c				
	10	30	70	130
310-Huck and Yogi Winter Sports (TV) (Hanna-Barbera) (3/62)				
	9	27	63	115
311-Rocky and His Friends (TV) (Jay Ward)	23	69	161	300
312-National Velvet (TV)-Photo-c	4	12	26	40
313-Moon Pilot (Disney-Movie)-Photo-c	7	21	49	90

	GD2.0	FN6.0	VF8.0	NM9.4
1328-The Underwater City (Movie) (1961)-Evans-a; photo-c				
	7	21	49	90
1329-See Gyro Gearloose #01329-207				
1330-Brain Boy (#1)-Gil Kane-a	13	39	91	170
1332-Bachelor Father (TV)	8	24	56	100
1333-Short Ribs (4-6/62)	5	15	35	60
1335-Aggie Mack (4-6/62)	3	9	21	40
1336-On Stage; not by Leonard Starr	4	12	30	50
1337-Dr. Kildare (#1) (TV) (4-6/62)-Photo-c	9	27	63	110
1341-The Andy Griffith Show (TV) (4-6/62)-Photo-c	35	105	245	450
1348-Yak Yak (#2)-Jack Davis-c/a	8	24	56	100
1349-Yogi Bear Visits the U.N. (TV) (Hanna-Barbera) (1/62)-Photo-c				
	9	27	63	120
1350-Comanche (Disney-Movie)(1962)-Reprints 4-Color #966 (title change				
from "Tonka" to "Comanche") (4-6/62)-Sal Mineo photo-c				
	5	15	35	60
1354-Calvin & the Colonel (#1) (TV) (4-6/62)	9	27	63	115
NOTE: Missing numbers probably do not exist.				

4-D MONKEY, THE (Adventures of... #? on)
Leung's Publications: 1988 - No. 11, 1990 ($1.80/$2.00, 52 pgs.)

1-11: 1-Karate Pig, Ninja Flounder & 4-D Monkey (48 pgs., centerfold is a				
Christmas card). 2-4 (52pgs.)				2.50

FOUR FAVORITES (Crime Must Pay the Penalty No. 33 on)
Ace Magazines: Sept, 1941 - No. 32, Dec, 1947

1-Vulcan, Lash Lightning (formerly Flash Lightning in Sure-Fire), Magno the				
Magnetic Man & The Raven begin; flag/Hitler-c	155	465	966	1700
2-The Black Ace only app.	55	165	341	600
3-Last Vulcan	47	142	286	500
4,5: 4-The Raven & Vulcan end; Unknown Soldier app. (see Our Flag), ends				
#28. 5-Captain Courageous begins (5/42), ends #28 (moves over from				
Captain Courageous #6); not in #6	43	129	257	450
6-8: 6-The Flag app.; Mr. Risk begins (7/42)	40	120	232	400
9-Kurtzman-a (Lash Lightning); robot-c	43	129	257	450
10-Classic Kurtzman-c/a (Magno & Davey)	50	150	300	525
11-Kurtzman-a; Hitler, Mussolini, Hirohito-c; L.B. Cole-a; Unknown Soldier by				
Kurtzman	55	165	341	600
12-L.B. Cole-a	35	105	188	325
13-20: 18,20-Palais-c/a	29	87	153	265
21-No Unknown Soldier; The Unknown app.	22	66	116	200
22-26: 22-Captain Courageous drops costume. 23-Unknown Soldier drops				
costume. 25-29-Hap Hazard app. 26-Last Magno	22	66	116	200
27-29: 27-Hap Hazard app. in all	17	51	88	150
30-32: 30-Funny-c begin (teen humor), end #32	14	42	72	120
NOTE: Dave Berg c-5. Jim Mooney a-6; c-1-3. Palais a-18-20; c-18-25. Torture chamber c-5.				

FOUR HORSEMEN, THE (See The Crusaders)

FOUR HORSEMEN
DC Comics (Vertigo): Feb, 2000 - No. 4, May, 2000 ($2.50, limited series)

1-4-Essad Ribic-c/a; Robert Rodi-s				2.50

FOUR HORSEMEN OF THE APOCALYPSE, THE (Movie)
Dell Publishing Co.: No. 1250, Jan-Mar, 1962 (one-shot)

Four Color 1250-Photo-c	6	18	42	80

4MOST (Foremost Boys No. 32-40; becomes Thrilling Crime Cases #41 on)
Novelty Publications/Star Publications No. 37-on:
Winter, 1941-42 - V8#5(#36), 9-10/49; #37, 11-12/49 - #40, 4-5/50

V1#1-The Target by Sid Greene, The Cadet & Dick Cole begin with origins				
retold; produced by Funnies Inc.; quarterly issues begin, end V6#3				
	127	381	795	1400
2-Last Target (Spr/42)	50	150	300	525
3-Dan'l Flannel begins; flag-c	40	120	232	400
4-1pg. Dr. Seuss (signed) (Aut/42)	39	117	208	360
V2#1-3	15	45	77	130
4-Hitler, Tojo & Mussolini app. as pumpkins on-c	23	69	121	210
V3#1-4	13	39	66	110
V4#1-4: 2-Walter Johnson-c	11	33	55	90
V5#1-4: 1-The Target & Targeteers app.	10	30	55	80
V6#1-4	9	27	49	70
5-L. B. Cole-c	20	60	105	175

Four Women #1 © I Before E

Fox Giant - Burning Romances © FOX

Foxy Fagan Comics #4 © Dearfield

	GD2.0	FN6.0	VF8.0	NM9.4
V7#1,3,5, V8#1, 37	9	27	49	70
2,4,6-L. B. Cole-c. 6-Last Dick Cole	20	60	105	175
V8#2,3,5-L. B. Cole-c/a	23	69	121	210
4-L. B. Cole-a	14	42	72	120
38-40: 38-Johnny Weismuller (Tarzan) life story & Jim Braddock (boxer) life story. 38-40-L.B. Cole-c. 40-Last White Rider	17	51	88	150
Accepted Reprint 38-40 (nd): 40-r/Johnny Weismuller life story; all have L.B. Cole-c	10	30	55	80

FOUR-STAR BATTLE TALES
National Periodical Publications: Feb-Mar, 1973 - No. 5, Nov-Dec, 1973

1-reprints begin	3	9	20	30
2-5	2	6	11	16
NOTE: *Drucker* r-1, 3-5. *Heath* r-2, 5; c-1. *Krigstein* r-5. *Kubert* r-4; c-2.

FOUR STAR SPECTACULAR
National Periodical Publications: Mar-Apr, 1976 - No. 6, Jan-Feb, 1977

1	2	6	11	15
2-6: Reprints in all. 2-Infinity cover	1	3	6	8
NOTE: All contain DC Superhero reprints. #1 has 68 pgs.; #2-6, 52 pgs. #1, 4-Hawkman app.; #2-Kid Flash app.; #3-Green Lantern app. #2, 4, 5-Wonder Woman, Superboy app; #5-Green Arrow, Vigilante app; #6-Blackhawk G.A.-r.

FOUR TEENERS (Formerly Must Pay The Penalty; Dotty No. 35 on)
A. A. Wyn: No. 34, April, 1948 (52 pgs.)

34-Teen-age comic; Dotty app.; Curly & Jerry continue from Four Favorites	6	18	29	40

FOURTH WORLD GALLERY, THE (Jack Kirby's…)
DC Comics: 1996 (9/96) ($3.50, one-shot)

nn-Pin-ups of Jack Kirby's Fourth World characters (New Gods, Forever People & Mister Miracle) by John Byrne, Rick Burchett, Dan Jurgens, Walt Simonson & others				3.50

FOUR WOMEN
DC Comics (Homage): Dec, 2001 - No. 5 ($2.95, limited series)

1-4-Sam Kieth-s/a				2.95

FOX AND THE CROW (Stanley & His Monster No. 109 on) (See Comic Cavalcade & Real Screen Comics)
National Periodical Publications: Dec-Jan, 1951-52 - No. 108, Feb-Mar, 1968

1	105	315	656	1150
2(Scarce)	50	150	300	525
3-5	35	105	188	325
6-10	25	75	130	225
11-20	19	57	99	165
21-30: 22-Last precode issue (2/55)	13	39	66	110
31-40	11	33	55	90
41-60	6	18	45	75
61-80	4	12	30	50
81-94: 94-(11/65)-The Brat Finks begin	3	10	23	35
95-Stanley & His Monster begins (origin & 1st app)	4	12	30	50
96-99,101-108	3	9	17	25
100 (10-11/66)	3	9	20	30
NOTE: Many covers by *Mort Drucker.*

FOX AND THE HOUND, THE (Disney)(Movie)
Whitman Publishing Co.: Aug, 1981 - No. 3, Oct, 1981

11292(#1),2,3-Based on animated movie	1	3	6	8

FOXFIRE (See The Phoenix Resurrection)
Malibu Comics (Ultraverse): Feb, 1996 - No. 4, May, 1996 ($1.50)

1-4: Sludge, Ultraforce app. 4-Punisher app.				2.25

FOX GIANTS (Also see Giant Comics Edition)
Fox Features Syndicate: 1944 - 1950 (25¢, 132 - 196 pgs.)

Album of Crime nn(1949, 132p)	43	129	257	450
Album of Love nn(1949, 132p)	40	120	220	380
All Famous Crime Stories nn('49, 132p)	43	129	257	450
All Good Comics 1(1944, 132p)(R.W. Voigt)(The Bouncer, Purple Tigress,Rick Evans, Puppeteer, Green Mask; Infinity-c	40	120	217	375
All Great nn(1944, 132p)-Capt. Jack Terry, Rick Evans, Jaguar Man	40	120	217	375
All Great nn(Chicago Nite Life News)(1945, 132p)-Green Mask, Bouncer,				

	GD2.0	FN6.0	VF8.0	NM9.4
Puppeteer, Rick Evans, Rocket Kelly	40	120	226	390
All-Great Confessions nn(1949, 132p)	39	117	208	360
All Great Crime Stories nn('49, 132p)	43	129	257	450
All Great Jungle Adventures nn('49, 132p)	47	141	286	500
All Real Confession Magazine 3 (3/49, 132p)	39	117	208	360
All Real Confession Magazine 4 (4/49, 132p)	39	117	208	360
All Your Comics 1(1944, 132p)-The Puppeteer, Red Robbins, & Merciless the Sorcerer	40	120	220	380
Almanac Of Crime nn(1948, 148p)-Phantom Lady	45	135	270	475
Almanac Of Crime 1(1950, 132p)	40	120	240	420
Book Of Love nn(1950, 132p)	36	108	191	330
Burning Romances 1(1949, 132p)	41	122	246	435
Crimes Incorporated nn(1950, 132p)	40	120	232	400
Daring Love Stories nn(1950, 132p)	37	111	197	340
Everybody's Comics 1(1944, 50¢, 196p)-The Green Mask, The Puppeteer, The Bouncer, Rocket Kelly, Rick Evans	43	129	257	450
Everybody's Comics 1(1946, 196p)-Green Lama, The Puppeteer	37	111	197	340
Everybody's Comics 1(1946, 196p)-Same as 1945 Ribtickler	29	87	156	270
Everybody's Comics nn(1947, 132p)-Jo-Jo, Purple Tigress, Cosmo Cat, Bronze Man	35	105	188	325
Exciting Romance Stories nn(1949, 132p)	36	108	191	330
Famous Love nn(1950, 132p)	36	108	191	330
Intimate Confessions nn(1950, 132p)	37	111	197	340
Journal Of Crime nn(1949, 132p)	43	129	257	450
Love Problems nn(1949, 132p)	39	117	208	360
Love Thrills nn(1950, 132p)	39	117	208	360
March of Crime nn('48, 132p)-Female w/rifle-c	40	120	232	400
March of Crime nn('49, 132p)-Cop w/pistol-c	40	120	226	390
March of Crime nn(1949, 132p)-Coffin & man w/machine-gun-c	40	120	226	390
Revealing Love Stories nn(1950, 132p)	37	111	197	340
Ribtickler nn(1945, 50¢, 196p)-Chicago Nite Life News; Marvel Mutt, Cosmo Cat, Flash Rabbit, The Nebbs app.	35	105	185	320
Romantic Thrills nn(1950, 132p)	36	108	191	330
Secret Love Stories nn(1949, 132p)	36	108	191	330
Strange Love nn(1950, 132p)-Photo-c	40	120	232	400
Sweetheart Scandals nn(1950, 132p)	36	108	191	330
Teen-Age Love nn(1950, 132p)	36	108	191	330
Throbbing Love nn(1950, 132p)-Photo-c; used in **POP**, pg. 107	40	120	232	400
Truth About Crime nn(1949, 132p)	43	129	257	450
Variety Comics 1(1946, 132p)-Blue Beetle, Jungle Jo	40	120	217	375
Variety Comics nn(1950, 132p)-Jungle Jo, My Secret Affair(w/Harrison/Wood-a), Crimes by Women & My Story	39	117	208	360
Western Roundup nn('50, 132p)-Hoot Gibson; Cody of the Pony Express app.	40	120	214	370
NOTE: Each of the above usually contain four remaindered Fox books minus covers. Since these missing covers often had the first page of the first story, most Giants therefore are incomplete. Approximate values are listed. Books with appearances of Phantom Lady, Rulah, Jo-Jo, etc. could bring more.

FOXHOLE (Becomes Never Again #8?)
Mainline/Charlton No. 5 on: 9-10/54 - No. 4, 3-4/55; No. 5, 7/55 - No. 7, 3/56

1-Classic Kirby-c	43	129	257	450
2-Kirby-c/a(2); Kirby scripts based on his war time experiences	33	99	174	300
3-5-Kirby-c only	18	54	94	160
6-Kirby-c/a(2)	27	81	145	250
7	9	27	49	70
Super Reprints #10,15-17: 10-r/? 15,16-r/United States Marines #5,8. 17-r/Monty Hall #?	2	6	13	20
11,12,18-r/Foxhole #1,2,3; Kirby-c	3	9	20	30
NOTE: *Kirby* a(r)-Super #11, 12. *Powell* a(r)-Super #15, 16. Stories by actual veterans.

FOX KIDS FUNHOUSE (TV)
Acclaim Books: 1997 ($4.50, digest size)

1-The Tick				4.50

FOXY FAGAN COMICS (Funny Animal)
Dearfield Publishing Co.: Dec, 1946 - No. 7, Summer, 1948

Frankenstein #2 © MAR

Frankenstein Comics #10 © PRIZE

Fray #1 © Joss Whedon

FR

	GD2.0	FN6.0	VF8.0	NM9.4
1-Foxy Fagan & Little Buck begin	13	39	66	110
2	7	21	38	55
3-7: 6-Rocket ship-c	7	21	36	50

FRACTURED FAIRY TALES (TV)
Gold Key: Oct, 1962 (Jay Ward)

1 (10022-210)-From Bullwinkle TV show	12	36	84	150

FRAGGLE ROCK (TV)
Marvel Comics (Star Comics)/Marvel V2#1 on: Apr, 1985 - No. 8, Sept, 1986; V2#1, Apr, 1988 - No. 6, Sept, 1988

1-8: 1-6 (75¢-c)				5.00
V2#1-6-($1.00): Reprints 1st series				2.25

FRANCIS, BROTHER OF THE UNIVERSE
Marvel Comics Group: 1980 (75¢, 52 pgs., one-shot)

nn-Buscema/Marie Severin-a; story of Francis Bernadone celebrating his 800th birthday in 1982				4.00

FRANCIS THE FAMOUS TALKING MULE (All based on movie)
Dell Publishing Co.: No. 335 (#1), June, 1951 - No. 1090, March, 1960

Four Color 335 (#1)	10	30	70	130
Four Color 465	5	15	35	65
Four Color 501,547,579	4	12	30	50
Four Color 621,655,698,710,745	4	12	26	40
Four Color 810,863,906,953,991,1068,1090	3	10	23	35

FRANK
Nemesis Comics (Harvey): Apr (Mar inside), 1994 - No. 4, 1994 ($1.75/$2.50, limited series)

1-4-($2.50, direct sale): 1-Foil-c Edition				3.00
1-4-($1.75)-Newsstand Editions; Cowan-a in all				2.25

FRANK
Fantagraphics Books: Sept, 1996 ($2.95, B&W)

1-Woodring-c/a/scripts				3.00

FRANK BUCK (Formerly My True Love)
Fox Features Syndicate: No. 70, May, 1950 - No. 3, Sept, 1950

70-Wood a(p)(3 stories)-Photo-c	34	102	179	310
71-Wood-a (9 pgs.); photo/painted-c	18	54	94	155
3: 3-Photo/painted-c	14	42	72	120

NOTE: Based on "Bring 'Em Back Alive" TV show.

FRANKENSTEIN (See Dracula, Movie Classics & Werewolf)
Dell Publishing Co.: Aug-Oct, 1964; No. 2, Sept, 1966 - No. 4, Mar, 1967

1(12-283-410)(1964)	5	15	35	65
2-Intro. & origin super-hero character (9/66)	4	12	26	40
3,4	3	9	17	25

FRANKENSTEIN (The Monster of...; also see Monsters Unleashed #2, Power Record Comics, Psycho & Silver Surfer #7)
Marvel Comics Group: Jan, 1973 - No. 18, Sept, 1975

1-Ploog-c/a begins, ends #6	4	12	30	50
2	3	9	20	30
3-5	2	6	15	22
6,7,10: 7-Dracula cameo	2	6	12	18
8,9-Dracula c/sty. 9-Death of Dracula	3	10	23	35
11-17	2	6	9	12
18-Wrightson-c(i)	2	6	11	15

NOTE: Adkins c-17i. Buscema a-7-10p. Ditko a-12r. G. Kane c-15p. Orlando a-8r. Ploog a-1-3, 4p, 5p, 6; c-1-6. Wrightson c-18i.

FRANKENSTEIN (Mary Wollstonecraft Shelley's...; A Marvel Illustrated Novel)
Marvel Pub.: 1983 ($8.95, B&W, 196 pgs., 8x11" TPB)

nn-Wrightson-a; 4 pg. intro. by Stephen King	4	12	29	45

FRANKENSTEIN COMICS (Also See Prize Comics)
Prize Publ. (Crestwood/Feature): Sum, 1945 - V5#5(#33), Oct-Nov, 1954

1-Frankenstein begins by Dick Briefer (origin); Frank Sinatra parody	105	315	656	1150
2	52	157	314	550
3-5	40	120	232	400
6-10: 7-S&K a(r)/Headline Comics. 8(7-8/47)-Superman satire				

	GD2.0	FN6.0	VF8.0	NM9.4
	36	108	191	330
11-17(1-2/49)-11-Boris Karloff parody-c/story. 17-Last humor issue				
	31	93	165	285
18(3/52)-New origin, horror series begins	40	120	232	400
19,20(V3#4, 8-9/52)	27	81	145	250
21(V3#5), 22(V3#6), 23(V4#1) - #28(V4#6)	24	72	127	220
29(V5#1) - #33(V5#5)	24	72	127	220

NOTE: Briefer c/a-all. Meskin a-21, 29.

FRANKENSTEIN/DRACULA WAR, THE
Topps Comics: Feb, 1995 - No. 3, May, 1995 ($2.50, limited series)

1-3				3.00

FRANKENSTEIN, JR. (...& the Impossibles) (TV)
Gold Key: Jan, 1966 (Hanna-Barbera)

1-Super hero (scarce)	11	33	77	140

FRANKENSTEIN: OR THE MODERN PROMETHEUS
Caliber Press: 1994 ($2.95, one-shot)

1				3.00

FRANK FRAZETTA FANTASY ILLUSTRATED (Magazine)
Quantum Cat Entertainment: Spring 1998 - No. 8 ($5.95, quarterly)

1-Anthology; art by Corben, Horley, Jusko				6.00
1-Linsner variant-c				10.00
2-Battle Chasers by Madureira; Harris-a				8.00
2-Madureira Battle Chasers variant-c				12.00
3-8-Frazetta-c				6.00
3-Tony Daniel variant-c				15.00
5,6-Portacio variant-c, 7,8-Alex Nino variant-c				10.00
8-Alex Ross Chicago Comicon variant-c				10.00

FRANK FRAZETTA'S THUN'DA TALES
Fantagraphics Books: 1987 ($2.00, one-shot)

1-Frazetta-r				4.00

FRANK FRAZETTA'S UNTAMED LOVE (Also see Untamed Love)
Fantagraphics Books: Nov, 1987 ($2.00, one-shot)

1-Frazetta-r from 1950's romance comics				4.00

FRANKIE COMICS (...& Lana No. 13-15) (Formerly Movie Tunes; becomes Frankie Fuddle No. 16 on)
Marvel Comics (MgPC): No. 4, Wint, 1946-47 - No. 15, June, 1949

4-Mitzi, Margie, Daisy app.	13	39	66	110
5-9	8	24	42	60
10-15: 13-Anti-Wertham editorial	7	21	36	50

FRANKIE DOODLE (See Sparkler, both series)
United Features Syndicate: No. 7, 1939

Single Series 7	33	99	174	300

FRANKIE FUDDLE (Formerly Frankie & Lana)
Marvel Comics: No. 16, Aug, 1949 - No. 17, Nov, 1949

16,17	7	21	36	50

FRANK LUTHER'S SILLY PILLY COMICS (See Jingle Dingle...)
Children's Comics (Maltex Cereal): 1950 (10¢)

1-Characters from radio, records, & TV	7	21	36	50

FRANK MERRIWELL AT YALE (Speed Demons No. 5 on?)
Charlton Comics: June, 1955 - No. 4, Jan, 1956 (See Shadow Comics)

1	6	18	32	45
2-4	5	15	24	32

FRANTIC (Magazine) (See Ratfink & Zany)
Pierce Publishing Co.: Oct, 1958 - V2#2, Apr, 1959 (Satire)

V1#1	10	30	55	80
2	8	24	42	60
V2#1,2: 1-Burgos-a, Severin-c/a; Powell-a?	6	18	29	40

FRAY
Dark Horse Comics: June, 2001 - No. 8 ($2.99, limited series)

1-Joss Whedon-s/Moline & Owens-a				4.00
2-5				3.00

FREAK FORCE (Also see Savage Dragon)

Freedom Fighters #3 © DC

Friendly Ghost Casper #4 © HARV

Frisky Fables V2 #1 © STAR

	GD2.0	FN6.0	VF8.0	NM9.4

Image Comics (Highbrow Ent.): Dec, 1993 - No. 18, July, 1995 ($1.95/$2.50)

1-18-Superpatriot & Mighty Man in all; Erik Larsen scripts in all. 4-Vanguard app. 8-Begin $2.50-c. 9-Cyberforce-c & app. 13-Variant-c — 3.00

FREAK FORCE
Image Comics: Apr, 1997 - No. 3, July, 1997 ($2.95)

1-3-Larsen-s — 3.00

FRECKLES AND HIS FRIENDS (See Crackajack Funnies, Famous Comics Cartoon Book, Honeybee Birdwhistle... & Red Ryder)

FRECKLES AND HIS FRIENDS
Standard Comics/Argo: No. 5, 11/47 - No. 12, 8/49; 11/55 - No. 4, 6/56

5-Reprints	8	24	42	60
6-12-Reprints. 7-9-Airbrush-c (by Schomburg?). 11-Lingerie panels				
	5	15	25	35

NOTE: Some copies of No. 8 & 9 contain a printing oddity. The negatives were elongated in the engraving process, probably to conform to page dimensions on the filler pages. Those pages only look normal when viewed at a 45 degree angle.

1(Argo,'55)-Reprints (NEA Service)	5	15	25	35
2-4	4	12	19	25

FREDDY (Formerly My Little Margie's Boy Friends) (Also see Blue Bird)
Charlton Comics: V2#12, June, 1958 - No. 47, Feb, 1965

V2#12	3	10	23	35
13-15	2	6	15	22
16-47	2	6	11	16

FREDDY
Dell Publishing Co.: May-July, 1963 - No. 3, Oct-Dec, 1964

1	3	9	19	28
2,3	2	6	14	18

FREDDY KRUEGER'S A NIGHTMARE ON ELM STREET
Marvel Comics: Oct, 1989 - No. 2, Dec, 1989 ($2.25, B&W, movie adaptation)

1,2: Origin Freddy Krueger; Buckler/Alcala-a — 3.00

FREDDY'S DEAD: THE FINAL NIGHTMARE
Innovation Publishing: Oct, 1991 - No. 3, Dec 1991 ($2.50, color mini-series, adapts movie)

1-3: Dismukes (film poster artist) painted-c — 3.00

FRED HEMBECK DESTROYS THE MARVEL UNIVERSE
Marvel Comics: July, 1989 ($1.50, one-shot)

1-Punisher app.; Staton-i (5 pgs.) — 2.50

FRED HEMBECK SELLS THE MARVEL UNIVERSE
Marvel Comics: Oct, 1990 ($1.25, one-shot)

1-Punisher, Wolverine parodies; Hembeck/Austin-c — 2.50

FREEDOM AGENT (Also see John Steele)
Gold Key: Apr, 1963 (12¢)

1 (10054-304)-Painted-c	4	12	26	40

FREEDOM FIGHTERS (See Justice League of America #107,108)
National Periodical Publ./DC Comics: Mar-Apr, 1976 - No. 15, July-Aug, 1978

1-Uncle Sam, The Ray, Black Condor, Doll Man, Human Bomb, & Phantom Lady begin (all former Quality characters)	2	6	11	15
2-9: 4,5-Wonder Woman x-over. 7-1st app. Crusaders 1	3	6	9
10-15: 10-Origin Doll Man; Cat-Man-c/story (4th app; 1st revival since Det. #325). 11-Origin The Ray. 12-Origin Firebrand. 13-Origin Black Condor. 14-Batgirl & Batwoman app. 15-Batgirl & Batwoman app.; origin Phantom Lady				
	1	4	7	10

NOTE: *Buckler* c-5-11p, 13p, 14p.

FREE SPEECHES
Oni Press: Aug, 1998 ($2.95, one-shot)

1-Speeches against comic censorship; Frank Miller-c — 3.00

FREEX
Malibu Comics (Ultraverse): July, 1993 - No. 18, Mar, 1995 ($1.95)

1-3,5-14,16-18: 1-Polybagged w/trading card. 2-Some were polybagged w/card. 6-Nightman-c/story. 7-2 pg. origin Hardcase by Zeck. 17-Rune app.				
				2.25
1-Holographic-c edition				6.00
1-Ultra 5,000 limited silver ink-c				3.00

4-($2.50, 48 pgs.)-Rune flip-c/story by B. Smith (3 pgs.); 3 pg. Night Man preview				2.50
15 ($3.50)-w/Ultraverse Premiere #9 flip book; Alec Swan & Rafferty app.				3.50
Giant Size 1 (1994, $2.50)-Prime app.				2.50

NOTE: *Simonson* c-1.

FRENZY (Magazine) (Satire)
Picture Magazine: Apr, 1958 - No. 6, Mar, 1959

1	10	30	55	80
2-6	6	18	32	45

FRIDAY FOSTER
Dell Publishing Co.: October, 1972

1	3	9	21	32

FRIENDLY GHOST, CASPER, THE (Becomes Casper... #254 on)
Harvey Publications: Aug, 1958 - No. 224, Oct, 1982; No. 225, Oct, 1986 - No. 253, June, 1990

1-Infinity-c	29	87	202	360
2	13	39	94	160
3-10: 6-X-Mas-c	7	21	50	80
11-20: 18-X-Mas-c	5	15	34	55
21-30	3	10	23	35
31-50	3	9	17	25
51-70,100: 54-X-Mas-c	2	6	15	22
71-99	2	6	12	18
101-131: 131-Last 12¢ issue	2	6	11	16
132-159	2	6	10	14
160-163: All 52 pg. Giants	2	6	13	20
164-199: 173,179,185-Cub Scout Specials	1	3	6	9
200	1	4	7	10
201-224	1	3	5	7
225-237: 230-X-mas-c. 232-Valentine's-c				5.00
238-253: 238-Begin $1.00-c. 238,244-Halloween-c. 243-Last new material				3.00

FRIENDS OF MAXX (Also see Maxx)
Image Comics (I Before E): Apr, 1996 ($2.95)

1-Featuring Dude Japan; Sam Kieth-c/a/scripts — 3.00

FRIGHT
Atlas/Seaboard Periodicals: June, 1975 (Aug on inside)

1-Origin/1st app. The Son of Dracula; Frank Thorne-c/a — 6.00

FRIGHT NIGHT
Now Comics: Oct, 1988 - No. 22, 1990 ($1.75)

1-22: 1,2 Adapts movie. 8,9-Evil Ed horror photo-c from movie — 2.25

FRIGHT NIGHT II
Now Comics: 1989 ($3.95, 52 pgs.)

1-Adapts movie sequel — 4.00

FRISKY ANIMALS (Formerly Frisky Fables; Super Cat #56 on)
Star Publications: No. 44, Jan, 1951 - No. 55, Sept, 1953

44-Super Cat; L.B. Cole	24	72	127	215
45-Classic L. B. Cole-c	34	102	179	310
46-51,53-55: Super Cat. 54-Super Cat-c begin	22	66	116	195
52-L. B. Cole-c/a, 3 1/2 pgs.; X-Mas-c	24	72	127	215

NOTE: All have *L. B. Cole-c.* No. 47-No Super Cat. *Disbrow* a-49, 52. *Fago* a-51.

FRISKY ANIMALS ON PARADE (Formerly Parade Comics; becomes Superspook)
Ajax-Farrell Publ. (Four Star Comic Corp.): Sept, 1957 - No. 3, Dec-Jan, 1957-1958

1-L. B. Cole-c	20	60	105	175
2-No L. B. Cole-c	9	27	49	70
3-L. B. Cole-c	17	51	88	150

FRISKY FABLES (Frisky Animals No. 44 on)
Premium Group/Novelty Publ./Star Publ. V5#4 on: Spring, 1945 - No. 43, Oct, 1950

V1#1-Funny animal; Al Fago-c/a #1-38	21	63	110	190
2,3(Fall & Winter, 1945)	11	33	55	90
V2#1(#4, 4/46) - 9,11,12(#15, 3/47): 4-Flag-c	8	24	45	65
10-Christmas-c	9	27	49	70

Frogman Comics #11 © HILL

From Hell #11
© Alan Moore and Eddie Campbell

Frontline Combat #8 © WMG

FR

	GD2.0	FN6.0	VF8.0	NM9.4

V3#1(#16, 4/47) - 12(#27, 3/48): 4-Flag-c. 7,9-Infinity-c. 10-X-Mas-c

	7	21	36	50
V4#1(#28, 4/48) - 7(#34, 2-3/49)	7	21	36	50
V5#1(#35, 4-5/49) - 4(#38, 10-11/49)	7	21	36	50
39-43-L. B. Cole-c; 40-Xmas-c	23	69	121	210
Accepted Reprint No. 43 (nd); L.B. Cole-c	9	27	49	70

FRITZI RITZ (See Comics On Parade, Single Series #5, 1(reprint), Tip Top & United Comics)

FRITZI RITZ (United Comics No. 8-26)

United Features Synd./St. John No. 37-55/Dell No. 56 on:
Fall, 1948; No. 3, 1949 - No. 7, 1949; No. 27, 3-4/53 - No. 36, 9-10/54; No. 42, 1/56; No. 43, 6/56 - No. 55, 12-2/57-58 - No. 59, 9-11/58

nn(1948)-Special Fall issue; by Ernie Bushmiller	15	45	77	130
3(#1)	9	27	49	70
4-7(1949): 6-Abbie & Slats app.	7	21	38	55
27-29(1953): 29-Five pg. Abbie & Slats; 1 pg. Mamie by Russell Patterson	6	18	29	40
30,32-42,44-57 (38-41 exist?): 36-1 pg. Mamie by Patterson	5	15	25	35
31,43,58,59-Peanuts by Schulz. 31-(11-12/53)	6	18	32	45

NOTE: Abbie & Slats in #6,7, 27-31. Li'l Abner in #33, 35, 36.

FROGMAN COMICS
Hillman Periodicals: Jan-Feb, 1952 - No. 11, May, 1953

1	14	42	72	120
2	8	24	45	65
3,4,6-11: 4-Meskin-a	7	21	36	50
5-Krigstein-a	8	24	42	60

FROGMEN, THE
Dell Publishing Co.: No. 1258, Feb-Apr, 1962 - No. 11, Nov-Jan, 1964-65 (Painted-c)

Four Color 1258(#1)-Evans-a	7	21	49	95
2,3-Evans-a; part Frazetta inks in #2,3	5	15	35	65
4,6-11	3	10	23	35
5-Toth-a	4	12	29	45

FROM BEYOND THE UNKNOWN
National Periodical Publications: 10-11/69 - No. 25, 11-12/73

1	4	12	30	50
2-6	3	9	17	25
7-11: (64 pgs.) 7-Intro Col. Glenn Merrit	3	9	20	30
12-17: (52 pgs.) 13-Wood-a(i)(r). 17-Pres. Nixon-c	3	9	17	25
18-25: Star Rovers-r begin #18,19. Space Museum in #23-25	2	6	11	16

NOTE: **N. Adams** c-3, 6, 8, 9. **Anderson** c-2, 4, 5, 10, 11i, 15-17, 22; reprints-3, 4, 6-8, 10, 11, 13-16, 24, 25. **Infantino** r-1-5, 7-19, 23-25; c-11p. **Kaluta** c-18, 19. **Gil Kane** a-9r. **Kubert** c-1, 7, 12-14. **Toth** a-9, 13i. Photo c-22.

FROM DUSK TILL DAWN (Movie)
Big Entertainment: 1996 ($4.95, one-shot)

nn-Adaptation of the film; Brereton-c				5.00
nn-($9.95)Deluxe Ed. w/ new material				10.00

FROM HELL
Mad Love/Tundra Publishing/Kitchen Sink: 1991 - No. 11, Sept, 1998 (B&W)

1-Alan Moore and Eddie Campbell's Jack The Ripper story collected from the Taboo anthology series	2	6	13	20
1-(2nd printing)	2	6	11	15
1-(3rd printing)	1	3	6	8
2	1	3	6	9
2-(2nd printing)				6.00
2-(3rd printing)				4.00
3-1st Kitchen Sink Press issue	1	4	7	10
3-(2nd printing)				5.00
4-10: 10-(8/96)				6.00
11-Dance of the Gull Catchers (9/98, $4.95) Epilogue	2	6	11	15
Tundra Publishing reprintings 1-5 ('92)	1	3	5	7
HC				125.00
HC Ltd. Edition of 1,000 (signed and numbered)				225.00
TPB-1st printing (11/99)				60.00
TPB-2nd printing (3/00)				50.00
TPB-3rd printing (11/00)				40.00

	GD2.0	FN6.0	VF8.0	NM9.4

TPB-4th printing (7/01) Regular and movie covers				35.00

FROM HERE TO INSANITY (Satire) (Formerly Eh! #1-7)
(See Frantic & Frenzy)
Charlton Comics: No. 8, Feb, 1955 - V3#1, 1956

8	17	51	88	150
9	15	45	77	130
10-Ditko-c/a (3 pgs.)	24	72	127	215
11,12-All Kirby except 4 pgs.	33	99	174	300
V3#1(1956)-Ward-c/a(2) (signed McCartney); 5 pgs. Wolverton-a; 3 pgs. Ditko-a; magazine format (cover says "Crazy, Man, Crazy" and becomes Crazy, Man, Crazy with V2#2)	40	120	232	400

FROM THE PIT
Fantagor Press: 1994 ($4.95, one-shot, mature)

1-R. Corben-a; HP Lovecraft back-up story				6.00

FRONTIER DOCTOR (TV)
Dell Publishing Co.: No. 877, Feb, 1958 (one-shot)

Four Color 877-Toth-a, Rex Allen photo-c	10	30	70	130

FRONTIER FIGHTERS
National Periodical Publications: Sept-Oct, 1955 - No. 8, Nov-Dec, 1956

1-Davy Crockett, Buffalo Bill (by Kubert), Kit Carson begin (Scarce)	59	177	369	650
2	40	120	240	420
3-8	40	120	220	380

NOTE: Buffalo Bill by **Kubert** in all.

FRONTIER ROMANCES
Avon Periodicals/I. W.: Nov-Dec, 1949 - No. 2, Feb-Mar, 1950 (Painted-c)

1-Used in SOTI, pg. 180 (General reference) & illo. "Erotic spanking in a western comic book"	47	141	286	500
2 (Scarce)-Woodish-a by Stallman	39	117	208	360
I.W. Reprint #1-Reprints Avon's #1	4	12	26	40
I.W. Reprint #9-Reprints ?	3	9	17	25

FRONTIER SCOUT: DAN'L BOONE (Formerly Death Valley; The Masked Raider No. 14 on)
Charlton Comics: No. 10, Jan, 1956 - No. 13, Aug, 1956; V2#14, Mar, 1965

10	10	30	55	80
11-13(1956)	6	18	29	40
V2#14(3/65)	4	12	19	25

FRONTIER TRAIL (The Rider No. 1-5)
Ajax/Farrell Publ.: No. 6, May, 1958

6	5	15	25	35

FRONTIER WESTERN
Atlas Comics (PrPI): Feb, 1956 - No. 10, Aug, 1957

1	20	60	105	175
2,3,6-Williamson-a, 4 pgs. each	14	42	72	120
4,7,9,10-Check-a	9	27	49	70
5-Crandall, Baker, Davis-a; Williamson text illos	13	39	66	110
8-Crandall, Morrow, & Wildey-a	9	27	51	75

NOTE: **Baker** a-9. **Colan** a-6. **Drucker** a-3, 4. **Heath** c-5. **Maneely** c/a-2, 7, 9. **Maurera** a-3. **Romita** a-7. **Severin** a-2-8, 10. **Tuska** a-2. **Wildey** a-5, 8. Ringo Kid in No. 4.

FRONTLINE COMBAT
E. C. Comics: July-Aug, 1951 - No. 15, Jan, 1954

1-Severin/Kurtzman-a	56	168	392	700
2	35	105	245	435
3	28	78	182	325
4-Used in SOTI, pg. 257; contains "Airburst" by Kurtzman which is his personal all-time favorite story	24	72	168	300
5	21	63	147	260
6-10	17	51	119	210
11-15	12	36	84	150

NOTE: **Davis** a-in all; c-11, 12. **Evans** a-10-15. **Heath** a-1. **Kubert** a-14. **Kurtzman** a-1-5; c-1-10. **Severin** a-5-7, 9, 13, 15. **Severin/Elder** a-2-11; c-10. **Toth** a-8, 12. **Wood** a-1-4, 6-10, 12-15; c-13-15. Special issues: No. 7 (Two Jima), No. 9 (Civil War), No. 12 (Air Force). (Canadian reprints known; see Table of Contents.)

FRONTLINE COMBAT
Russ Cochran/Gemstone Publishing: Aug, 1995 - No. 14 ($2.00/$2.50)

Fugitives From Justice #3 © STJ

Fun Comics #9 © STAR

The Funnies #51 © DELL

	GD2.0	FN6.0	VF8.0	NM9.4

	GD2.0	FN6.0	VF8.0	NM9.4

1-14-E.C. reprints in all   3.00

FRONT PAGE COMIC BOOK
Front Page Comics (Harvey): 1945

1-Kubert-a; intro. & 1st app. Man in Black by Powell; Fuje-c	40	120	220	380

FROST AND FIRE (See DC Science Fiction Graphic Novel)

FROSTY THE SNOWMAN
Dell Publishing Co.: No. 359, Nov, 1951 - No. 1272, Dec-Feb?/1961-62

Four Color 359 (#1)	9	27	63	110
Four Color 435,514,601,661	5	15	34	55
Four Color 748,861,950,1065,1153,1272	4	12	30	50

FRUITMAN SPECIAL
Harvey Publications: Dec, 1969 (68 pgs.)

1-Funny super hero	3	9	21	32

F-TROOP (TV)
Dell Publishing Co.: Aug, 1966 - No. 7, Aug, 1967 (All have photo-c)

1	9	27	63	120
2-7	5	15	35	65

FUGITIVES FROM JUSTICE
St. John Publishing Co.: Feb, 1952 - No. 5, Oct, 1952

1	22	66	116	195
2-Matt Baker-r/Northwest Mounties #2; Vic Flint strip reprints begin	22	66	116	195
3-Reprints panel from Authentic Police Cases that was used in **SOTI** with changes; Tuska-a	21	63	110	185
4	10	30	55	80
5-Last Vic Flint-r; bondage-c	12	36	61	100

FUGITOID
Mirage Studios: 1985 (B&W, magazine size, one-shot)

1-Ties into Teenage Mutant Ninja Turtles #5				4.00

FULL OF FUN
Red Top (Decker Publ.)(Farrell)/I. W. Enterprises: Aug, 1957 - No. 2, Nov, 1957; 1964

1(1957)-Funny animal; Dave Berg-a	7	21	36	50
2-Reprints Bingo, the Monkey Doodle Boy	5	15	23	30
8-I.W. Reprint('64)	2	6	11	15

FUN AT CHRISTMAS (See March of Comics No. 138)

FUN CLUB COMICS (See Interstate Theatres...)

FUN COMICS (Formerly Holiday Comics #1-8; Mighty Bear #13 on)
Star Publications: No. 9, Jan, 1953 - No. 12, Oct, 1953

9-(25¢ Giant)-L. B. Cole X-Mas-c; X-Mas issue	23	69	121	210
10-12-L. B. Cole-c. 12-Mighty Bear-c/story	20	60	105	175

FUNDAY FUNNIES (See Famous TV..., and Harvey Hits No. 35,40)

FUN-IN (TV)(Hanna-Barbera)
Gold Key: Feb, 1970 - No. 10, Jan, 1972; No. 11, 4/74 - No. 15, 12/74

1-Dastardly & Muttley in Their Flying Machines; Perils of Penelope Pitstop in #1-4; It's the Wolf in all	6	18	42	75
2-4,6-Cattanooga Cats in 2-4	3	10	23	35
5,7-Motormouse & Autocat, Dastardly & Muttley in both; It's the Wolf in #7	4	12	26	40
8,10-The Harlem Globetrotters, Dastardly & Muttley in #10	4	12	26	40
9-Where's Huddles?, Dastardly & Muttley, Motormouse & Autocat app.	4	12	26	40
11-Butch Cassidy	3	9	21	32
12-15: 12,15-Speed Buggy. 13-Hair Bear Bunch. 14-Inch High Private Eye	3	9	20	30

FUNKY PHANTOM, THE (TV)
Gold Key: Mar, 1972 - No. 13, Mar, 1975 (Hanna-Barbera)

1	5	15	34	55
2-5	3	9	19	28
6-13	2	6	13	20

FUNLAND
Ziff-Davis (Approved Comics): No date (1940s) (25¢)

nn-Contains games, puzzles, cut-outs, etc.	18	54	94	160

FUNLAND COMICS
Croyden Publishers: 1945

1-Funny animal	16	48	83	140

FUNNIES, THE (New Funnies No. 65 on)
Dell Publishing Co.: Oct, 1936 - No. 64, May, 1942

1-Tailspin Tommy, Mutt & Jeff, Alley Oop (1st app?), Capt. Easy (1st app.), Don Dixon begin	355	1065	1952	3200
2 (11/36)-Scribbly by Mayer begins (see Popular Comics #6 for 1st app.)	167	501	918	1500
3	116	348	638	1050
4,5: 4(1/37)-Christmas-c	89	267	490	800
6-10	67	201	368	600
11-20: 16-Christmas-c	61	183	335	550
21-29: 25-Crime Busters by McWilliams(4pgs.)	47	141	258	425
30-John Carter of Mars (origin/1st app.) begins by Edgar Rice Burroughs; Warner Bros.' Bosko-c (4/39)	127	381	795	1400
31-44: 33-John Coleman Burroughs art begins on John Carter. 34-Last funny-c. 35-(9/39)-Mr. District Attorney begins; based on radio show; 1st cover app. John Carter of Mars	75	225	469	825
45-Origin/1st app. Phantasmo, the Master of the World (Dell's 1st super-hero, 7/40) & his sidekick Whizzer McGee	82	246	511	900
46-50: 46-The Black Knight begins, ends #62	50	150	300	525
51-56-Last ERB John Carter of Mars	45	135	270	475
57-Intro. & origin Captain Midnight (7/41)	300	900	1875	3500
58-60: 58-Captain Midnight-c begin, end #63	91	273	568	1000
61-Andy Panda begins by Walter Lantz	64	192	398	700
62,63: 63-Last Captain Midnight-c; bondage-c	64	192	398	700
64-Format change; Oswald the Rabbit, Felix the Cat, Li'l Eight Ball app.; origin & 1st app. Woody Woodpecker in Oswald; last Capt. Midnight; Oswald, Andy Panda, Li'l Eight Ball-c	114	342	712	1250

NOTE: Mayer c-26, 48. **McWilliams** art in many issues on "Rex King of the Deep". Alley Oop c-17, 20. Captain Midnight c-57(1/2), 58-63. John Carter c-35-37, 40. Phantasmo c-45-56, 57(1/2), 58-61(part). Rex King c-38, 39, 42. Tailspin Tommy c-41.

FUNNIES ANNUAL, THE
Avon Periodicals: 1959 ($1.00, approx. 7x10", B&W; tabloid-size)

1-(Rare)-Features the best newspaper comic strips of the year: Archie, Snuffy Smith, Beetle Bailey, Henry, Blondie, Steve Canyon, Buz Sawyer, The Little King, Hi & Lois, Popeye, & others. Also has a chronological history of the comics from 2000 B.C. to 1959.	43	129	257	450

FUNNIES ON PARADE (See Promotional Comics section)

FUNNY ANIMALS (See Fawcett's Funny Animals)
Charlton Comics: Sept, 1984 - No. 2, Nov, 1984

1,2-Atomic Mouse-r; low print				5.00

FUNNYBONE (... The Laugh-Book of Comical Comics)
La Salle Publishing Co.: 1944 (25¢, 132 pgs.)

nn	29	87	156	270

FUNNY BOOK (...Magazine for Young Folks) (Hocus Pocus No. 9)
Parents' Magazine Press (Funny Book Publishing Corp.): Dec, 1942 - No. 9, Aug-Sept, 1946 (Comics, stories, puzzles, games)

1-Funny animal; Alice In Wonderland app.	15	45	77	130
2-Gulliver in Giant-Land	9	27	49	70
3-9: 4-Advs. of Robin Hood. 9-Hocus-Pocus strip	7	21	36	50

FUNNY COMICS
Modern Store Publ.: 1955 (7¢, 5x7", 36 pgs.)

1-Funny animal	3	10	23	35

FUNNY COMIC TUNES (See Funny Tunes)

FUNNY FABLES
Decker Publications (Red Top Comics): Aug, 1957 - V2#2, Nov, 1957

V1#1	6	18	29	40
V1#2,V2#1,2: V1#2 (11/57)-Reissue of V1#1	4	12	19	25

FUNNY FILMS (Features funny animal characters from films)
American Comics Group(Michel Publ./Titan Publ.): Sept-Oct, 1949 - No. 29,

Funnyman #3 © ME

Funny Pages #5 © CEN

Funny Stuff #18 © DC

	GD2.0	FN6.0	VF8.0	NM9.4

May-June, 1954 (No. 1-4: 52 pgs.)

	GD2.0	FN6.0	VF8.0	NM9.4
1-Puss An' Boots, Blunderbunny begin	20	60	105	180
2	11	33	55	90
3-10: 3-X-Mas-c	8	24	42	60
11-20	6	18	29	40
21-29	5	15	23	30

FUNNY FOLKS (Hollywood… on cover only No. 16-26; becomes Hollywood Funny Folks No. 27 on)
National Periodical Publications: April-May, 1946 - No. 26, June-July, 1950 (52 pgs., #16 on)

1-Nutsy Squirrel begins (1st app.) by Rube Grossman	40	120	220	380
2	20	60	105	175
3-5: 4-1st Nutsy Squirrel-c	15	45	77	130
6-10: 6,9-Nutsy Squirrel-c begin	11	33	55	90
11-26: 16-Begin 52 pg. issues (10-11/48)	10	30	55	80

NOTE: **Sheldon Mayer** a-in some issues. **Post** a-18. Christmas c-12.

FUNNY FROLICS
Timely/Marvel Comics (SPI): Summer, 1945 - No. 5, Dec, 1946

1-Sharpy Fox, Puffy Pig, Krazy Krow	23	69	121	210
2	13	39	66	110
3,4	10	30	55	80
5-Kurtzman-a	11	33	55	90

FUNNY FUNNIES
Nedor Publishing Co.: April, 1943 (68 pgs.)

1-Funny animals; Peter Porker app.	20	60	105	175

FUNNYMAN (Also see Cisco Kid Comics & Extra Comics)
Magazine Enterprises: No. 1, Jan, 1948 - No. 6, Aug, 1948

nn(12/47)-Prepublication B&W undistributed copy by Siegel & Shuster-(5-3/4x8"), 16 pgs.; Sold at auction in 1997 for $575.00				
1-Siegel & Shuster-a in all; Dick Ayers 1st pro work (as assistant) on 1st few issues	45	135	270	475
2	29	87	153	265
3-6	24	72	127	215

FUNNY MOVIES (See 3-D Funny Movies)

FUNNY PAGES (Formerly The Comics Magazine)
Comics Magazine Co./Ultem Publ.(Chesler)/Centaur Publications:
No. 6, Nov, 1936 - No. 42, Oct, 1940

V1#6 (nn, nd)-The Clock begins (2 pgs., 1st app.), ends #11; The Clock is the 1st masked comic book hero	218	654	1364	2400
7-11	86	258	540	950
V2#1-V2#3: V2#1 (9/37)(V2#2 on-c; V2#1 in indicia). V2#2 (10/37)(V2#3 on-c; V2#2 in indicia). V2#3(11/37)-5	59	177	369	650
6(1st Centaur, 3/38)	86	258	540	950
7-9	61	182	381	675
10(Scarce, 9/38)-1st app. of The Arrow by Gustavson (Blue costume)	300	900	1875	3300
11,12	114	342	712	1250
V3#1-Bruce Wayne prototype in "Case of the Missing Heir" by Bob Kane, 3 months before app. Batman (See Det. Pic. Stories #5)	118	354	738	1300
2-6: 6,8-Last funny covers	105	315	656	1150
7-1st Arrow-c	218	654	1364	2400
8,9: 9-Tarpe Mills jungle-c	109	327	682	1200
10-2nd Arrow-c	173	519	1080	1900
V4#1(1/40, Arrow-c)-(Rare)-The Owl & The Phantom Rider app.; origin Mantoka, Maker of Magic by Jack Cole. Mad Ming begins, ends #42; Tarpe Mills-a	218	654	1364	2400
35-Classic Arrow-c	218	654	1364	2400
36-38-Mad Ming-c	105	315	656	1150
39-41-Arrow-c	164	492	1023	1800
42 (Scarce,10/40)-Last Arrow; Arrow-c	173	519	1080	1900

NOTE: **Biro** c-V2#9. **Burgos** c-V3#10. **Jack Cole** a-V2#3, 7, 8, 10, 11, V3#2, 6, 9, 10, V4#1, 37; c-V3#2, 4. **Eisner** a-V1#7, 8?, 10. **Ken Ernst** a-V1#7, 8. **Everett** a-V2#11 (illos). **Filchock** c-V2#10, V3#6. **Gill Fox** a-V2#11. **Sid Greene** a-39. **Guardineer** a-V2#2, 3, 5. **Gustavson** a-V2#5, 11, 12, V3#1-10, 35, 38-42; c-V3#7, 35, 39-42. **Bob Kane** a-V3#1. **McWilliams** a-V2#12, V4#1. **Tarpe Mills** a-V3#8-10, V4#1; c-V3#9. **Ed Moore Jr.** a-V2#12. **Schwab** c-V3#1. **Bob Wood**

a-V2#2, 3, 8, 11, V3#6, 9, 10; c-V2#6, 7. Arrow c-V3#7, 10, V4#1, 35, 40-42.

FUNNY PICTURE STORIES (Comic Pages V3#4 on)
Comics Magazine Co./Centaur Publications: Nov, 1936 - V3#3, May, 1939

V1#1-The Clock begins (c-feature)(see Funny Pages for 1st app.)	308	924	1927	3700
2	114	342	712	1250
3-7(6/37): 4-Eisner-a; X-Mas-c. 7-Racial humor-c	77	231	483	850
V2#1 (9/37; V1#10 on-c; V2#1 in indicia)-Jack Strand begins	55	165	330	575
2 (10/37; V1#11 on-c; V2#2 in indicia)	55	165	330	575
3-5,7-11(11/38): 4-Xmas-c	45	135	270	475
6(1st Centaur, 3/38)	77	231	483	850
V3#1(1/39)-3	43	129	257	450

NOTE: **Biro** a-V1#1, 8, 9, 11. **Guardineer** a-V1#11; c-V2#6, V3#5. **Bob Wood** c/a-V1#11, V2#2; c-V2#3, 5.

FUNNY STUFF (Becomes The Dodo and the Frog No. 80)
All-American/National Periodical Publications No. 7 on: Summer, 1944 - No. 79, July-Aug, 1954 (#1-7 are quarterly)

1-The Three Mouseketeers (ends #28) & The "Terrific Whatzit" begin; Sheldon Mayer-a	91	273	568	1000
2-Sheldon Mayer-a	43	129	257	450
3-5: 3-Flash parody. 5-All Mayer-a/scripts issue	16	93	165	285
6-10 10-(6/46)	21	63	110	185
11-17,19	16	48	83	140
18-The Dodo & the Frog (2/47, 1st app?) begin?; X-Mas-c	29	87	153	265
20-1st Dodo and the Frog-c (4/47)	19	57	99	165
21,23-30: 24-Infinity-c	11	33	55	90
22-Superman cameo	40	120	232	400
31-79: 70-1st Bo Bunny by Mayer & begins	10	30	55	80

NOTE: **Mayer** a-1-8, 55, 57, 58, 61, 62, 64, 65, 68, 70, 72, 74-79; c-2, 5, 6, 8.

FUNNY STUFF STOCKING STUFFER
DC Comics: Mar, 1985 ($1.25, 52 pgs.)

1-Almost every DC funny animal featured				3.00

FUNNY 3-D
Harvey Publications: December, 1953 (25¢, came with 2 pair of glasses)

1-Shows cameo in 3-D on inside	12	36	61	100

FUNNY TUNES (Animated Funny Comic Tunes 16-22; Funny Comic Tunes No. 23, on covers only; formerly Krazy Komics #15; Oscar 24 on)
U.S.A. Comics Magazine Corp. (Timely): No. 16, Summer, 1944 - No. 23, Fall, 1946

16-Silly Seal, Ziggy Pig, Krazy Krow begin	15	45	77	130
17 (Fall/44)-Becomes Gay Comics #18 on?	12	36	61	100
18-22: 21-Super Rabbit app.	10	30	55	80
23-Kurtzman-a	11	33	55	90

FUNNY TUNES (Becomes Space Comics #4 on)
Avon Periodicals: July, 1953 - No. 3, Dec-Jan, 1953-54

1-Space Mouse, Peter Rabbit, Merry Mouse, Spotty the Pup, Cicero the Cat begin; all continue in Space Comics	11	33	55	90
2,3	8	24	42	60

FUNNY WORLD
Marbak Press: 1947 - No. 3, 1948

1-The Berrys, The Toodles & other strip-r begin	8	24	42	60
2,3	6	18	32	45

FUNTASTIC WORLD OF HANNA-BARBERA, THE (TV)
Marvel Comics Group: Dec, 1977 - No. 3, June, 1978 ($1.25, oversized)

1-3: 1-The Flintstones Christmas Party(12/77). 2-Yogi Bear's Easter Parade(3/78). 3-Laff-a-lympics(6/78)	4	12	29	45

FUN TIME
Ace Periodicals: Spring, 1953 - No. 2, Sum, 1953; No. 3(nn), Fall, 1953; No. 4, Wint, 1953-54

1-(25¢, 100 pgs.)-Funny animal	18	54	94	160
2-4 (All 25¢, 100 pgs.)	15	45	77	130

FUN WITH SANTA CLAUS (See March of Comics No. 11, 108, 325)

	GD2.0	FN6.0	VF8.0	NM9.4

	GD2.0	FN6.0	VF8.0	NM9.4

FURTHER ADVENTURES OF CYCLOPS AND PHOENIX (Also see Adventures of Cyclops and Phoenix, Uncanny X-Men & X-Men)
Marvel Comics: June, 1996 - No. 4, Sept, 1996 ($1.95, limited series)

1-4: Origin of Mr. Sinister; Peter Milligan scripts; John Paul Leon-c/a(p).				
2-4-Apocalypse app.				3.00
Trade Paperback (1997, $14.99) r/1-4				15.00

FURTHER ADVENTURES OF INDIANA JONES, THE (Movie) (Also see Indiana Jones and the Last Crusade & Indiana Jones and the Temple of Doom)
Marvel Comics Group: Jan, 1983 - No. 34, Mar, 1986

1-Byrne/Austin-a; Austin-c				4.00
2-34: 2-Byrne/Austin-c/a				2.50

NOTE: *Austin* a-1i, 2i, 6i, 9i; c-1, 2i, 6i, 9i. *Byrne* a-1p, 2p; c-2p. *Chaykin* a-6p; c-6p, 8p-10p. *Ditko* a-21p, 25-28, 34. *Golden* c-24, 25. *Simonson* c-9. Painted c-14.

FURTHER ADVENTURES OF NYOKA, THE JUNGLE GIRL, THE (See Nyoka)
AC Comics: 1988 - No. 5, 1989 ($1.95, color; $2.25/$2.50, B&W)

1-5 : 1,2-Bill Black-a plus reprints. 3-Photo-c. 4-Krigstein-r. 5-(B&W)-Reprints plus movie photos				2.50

FURY (Straight Arrow's Horse...) (See A-1 No. 119)

FURY (TV) (See March Of Comics #200)
Dell Publishing Co./Gold Key: No. 781, Mar, 1957 - Nov, 1962 (All photo-c)

Four Color 781	8	24	56	100
Four Color 885,975,1031,1080,1133,1172,1218,1296, 01292-208(#1-'62), 10020-211(11/62-G.K.)	6	18	42	80

FURY
Marvel Comics: May, 1994 ($2.95, one-shot)

1-Iron Man, Red Skull, FF, Hatemonger, Logan app.; Origin Nick Fury				3.00

FURY (Volume 3)
Marvel Comics (MAX): Nov, 2001 - Present ($2.99, mature content)

1-4-Ennis-s/Robertson-a				3.00

FURY/ AGENT 13
Marvel Comics: June, 1998 - No. 2, July, 1998 ($2.99, limited series)

1,2-Nick Fury returns				3.00

FURY OF FIRESTORM, THE (Becomes Firestorm The Nuclear Man on cover with #50, in indicia with #65) (Also see Firestorm)
DC Comics: June, 1982 - No. 64, Oct, 1987 (75¢ on)

1-Intro The Black Bison; brief origin				5.00
2-40,43-64: 4-JLA x-over. 17-1st app. Firehawk. 21-Death of Killer Frost. 22-Origin. 23-Intro. Byte. 24-(6/84)-1st app. Blue Devil & Bug (origin); origin Byte. 34-1st app./origin Killer Frost II. 39-Weasel's ID revealed. 48-Intro. Moonbow. 53-Origin/1st app. Silver Shade. 55,56-Legends x-over.				
58-1st app./origin new Parasite				2.50
41,42-Crisis x-over				3.00
61-Test cover variant; Superman logo	3	10	23	35
Annual 1-4: 1(1983), 2(1984), 3(1985), 4(1986)				3.00

NOTE: *Colan* a-19p, Annual 4p. *Giffen* a-Annual 4p. *Gil Kane* c-30. *Nino* a-37. *Tuska* a-(p)-17, 18, 32, 45.

FURY OF SHIELD
Marvel Comics: Apr, 1995 - No. 4, July, 1995 ($2.50/$1.95, limited series)

1 ($2.50)-Foil-c				3.00
2-4: 4-Bagged w/ decoder				2.50

FUSION
Eclipse Comics: Jan, 1987 - No. 17, Oct, 1989 ($2.00, B&W, Baxter paper)

1-17: 11-The Weasel Patrol begins (1st app.?)				2.25

FUTURAMA (TV)
Bongo Comics: 2000 - Present ($2.50, bi-monthly)

1-Based on the FOX-TV animated series; Groening/Morrison-c				2.50
1-San Diego Comic-Con Premiere Edition				4.00
2-6				2.50

FUTURE COMICS
David McKay Publications: June, 1940 - No. 4, Sept, 1940

1-(6/40, 64 pgs.)-Origin The Phantom (1st in comics) (4 pgs.); The Lone Ranger (8 pgs.) & Saturn Against the Earth (4 pgs.) begin				
	255	765	1591	2800

2	123	369	739	1350
3,4	100	300	625	1100

FUTURE COP L.A.P.D. (Electronic Arts video game) (Also see Promotional Comics section)
DC Comics (WildStorm): Jan, 1999 ($4.95, magazine sized)

1-Stories & art by various				5.00

FUTURETECH
Mushroom Comics: Jan, 1996 ($2.50, limited series)

1-Flipbook w/SWARM				2.50

FUTURE WORLD COMICS
George W. Dougherty: Summer, 1946 - No. 2, Fall, 1946

1,2: H. C. Kiefer-c; preview of the World of Tomorrow	33	99	174	300

FUTURE WORLD COMIX (Warren Presents...)
Warren Publications: Sept, 1978 (B&W magazine, 84 pgs.)

1-Corben, Maroto, Morrow, Nino, Sutton-a; Todd-c/a; contains nudity panels				
	2	6	9	12

FUTURIANS, THE (See Marvel Graphic Novel #9)
Lodestone Publishing/Eternity Comics: Sept, 1985 - No. 3, 1985 ($1.50)

1-3: Indicia title "Dave Cockrum's..."				2.25
Graphic Novel 1 ($9.95, Eternity)-r/#1-3, plus never published #4 issue				10.00

G-8 (Listed at G-Eight)

GABBY (Formerly Ken Shannon) (Teen humor)
Quality Comics Group: No. 11, Jul, 1953; No. 2, Sep, 1953 - No. 9, Sep, 1954

11(#1)(7/53)	8	24	42	60
2	5	15	25	35
3-9	5	14	21	28

GABBY GOB (See Harvey Hits No. 85, 90, 94, 97, 100, 103, 106, 109)

GABBY HAYES ADVENTURE COMICS
Toby Press: Dec, 1953

1-Photo-c	16	48	83	140

GABBY HAYES WESTERN (Movie star) (See Monte Hale, Real Western Hero & Western Hero)
Fawcett Comics/Charlton Comics No. 51 on: Nov, 1948 - No. 50, Jan, 1953; No. 51, Dec, 1954 - No. 59, Jan, 1957

1-Gabby & his horse Corker begin; photo front/back-c begin	50	150	300	525
2	26	78	139	240
3-5	18	54	94	160
6-10: 9-Young Falcon begins	15	45	77	135
11-20: 19-Last photo back-c	12	36	61	105
21-49: 20,22,24,26,28,29-(52 pgs.)	10	30	55	80
50-(1/53)-Last Fawcett issue; last photo-c?	11	33	55	90
51-(12/54)-1st Charlton issue; photo-c	11	33	55	95
52-59(1955-57): 53,55-Photo-c. 58-Swayze-a	7	21	38	55

GAGS
United Features Synd./Triangle Publ. No. 9 on: July, 1937 - V3#10, Oct, 1944 (13-3/4x10-3/4")

1(7/37)-52 pgs.; 20 pgs. Grin & Bear It, Fellow Citizen	8	24	42	60
V1#9 (36 pgs.) (7/42)	5	15	25	35
V3#10	5	15	23	30

GALACTICA: THE NEW MILLENNIUM
Realm Press: Sept, 1999 ($2.99)

1-Stories by Shooter, Braden, Kuhoric				3.00

GALACTIC GUARDIANS
Marvel Comics: July, 1994 - No. 4, Oct, 1994 ($1.50, limited series)

1-4				2.25

GALACTIC WARS COMIX (Warren Presents... on cover)
Warren Publications: Dec, 1978 (B&W magazine, 84 pgs.)

nn-Wood, Williamson-r; Battlestar Galactica/Flash Gordon photo/text stories				
	2	6	9	12

Gambit V2 #11 © MAR

Gandy Goose #4 © STJ

Gang Busters #12 © DC

	GD2.0	FN6.0	VF8.0	NM9.4

GALACTUS THE DEVOURER
Marvel Comics: Sept, 1999 - No. 6, Mar, 2000 ($3.50/$2.50, limited series)

1-($3.50) L. Simonson-s/Muth & Sienkiewicz-a				3.50
2-5-($2.50) Buscema & Sienkiewicz-a				2.50
6-($3.50) Death of Galactus; Buscema & Sienkiewicz-a				3.50

GALLANT MEN, THE (TV)
Gold Key: Oct, 1963 (Photo-c)

1(1008-310)-Manning-a	3	9	20	30

GALLEGHER, BOY REPORTER (Disney, TV)
Gold Key: May, 1965

1(10149-505)-Photo-c	3	9	17	24

GAMBIT (See X-Men #266 & X-Men Annual #14)
Marvel Comics: Dec, 1993 - No. 4, Mar, 1994 ($2.00, limited series)

1-($2.50)-Lee Weeks-c/a in all; gold foil stamped-c				5.00
1 (Gold)	2	6	11	15
2-4				3.00

GAMBIT
Marvel Comics: Sept, 1997 - No. 4, Dec, 1997 ($2.50, limited series)

1-4-Janson-a/ Mackie & Kavanagh-s				3.00

GAMBIT
Marvel Comics: Feb, 1999 - No. 25, Feb, 2001 ($2.99/$1.99)

1-($2.99) Five covers; Nicieza-s/Skroce-a				4.00
2-11,13-16-($1.99): 2-Two covers (Skroce & Adam Kubert)				2.50
12-($2.99)				3.50
17-24: 17-Begin $2.25-c. 21-Mystique-c/app.				2.25
25-($2.99) Leads into "Gambit & Bishop"				3.00
...1999 Annual ($3.50) Nicieza-s/McDaniel-a				3.50
...2000 Annual ($3.50) Nicieza-s/Derenick & Smith-a				3.50

GAMBIT & BISHOP (... : Sons of the Atom on cover)
Marvel Comics: Feb, 2001 - No. 6, May, 2001 ($2.25, bi-weekly limited series)

Alpha (2/01) Prelude to series; Nord-a				2.25
1-6-Jeanty-a/Williams-c				2.25
Genesis (3/01, $3.50) reprints their first apps. and first meeting				3.50

GAMBIT AND THE X-TERNALS
Marvel Comics: Mar, 1995 - No. 4, July, 1995 ($1.95, limited series)

1-4-Age of Apocalypse				2.50

GAMEBOY (Super Mario covers on all)
Valiant: 1990 - No. 5 ($1.95, coated-c)

1-5: 3,4-Layton-a. 4-Morrow-a. 5-Layton-a(i)				4.00

GAMERA
Dark Horse Comics: Aug, 1996 - No. 4, Nov, 1996 ($2.95, limited series)

1-4				3.00

GAMMARAUDERS
DC Comics: Jan, 1989 - No. 10, Dec, 1989 ($1.25/$1.50/$2.00)

1-10-Based on TSR game				2.25

GAMORRA SWIMSUIT SPECIAL
Image Comics (WildStorm Productions): June, 1996 ($2.50, one-shot)

1-Campbell wraparound-c; pinups				2.50

GANDY GOOSE (Movies/TV)(See All Surprise, Giant Comics Edition #5A &10, Paul Terry's Comics & Terry-Toons)
St. John Publ. Co./Pines No.5,6: Mar, 1953 - No. 5, Nov, 1953; No. 5, Fall, 1956 - No. 6, Sum/58

1-All St. John issues are pre-code	10	30	55	80
2	6	18	29	40
3-5(1953)(St. John)	5	15	25	35
5,6(1956-58)(Pines)-CBS Televison Presents...	4	13	19	26

GANG BUSTERS (See Popular Comics #38)
David McKay/Dell Publishing Co.: 1938 - 1943

Feature Books 17(McKay)('38)-1st app.	52	156	364	675
Large Feature Comic 10('39)-(Scarce)	52	156	364	675
Large Feature Comic 17('41)	32	96	224	425

Four Color 7(1940)	36	108	252	475
Four Color 23,24('42-43)	28	84	196	360

GANG BUSTERS (Radio/TV)(Gangbusters #14 on)
National Periodical Publications: Dec-Jan, 1947-48 - No. 67, Dec-Jan, 1958-59 (No. 1-23: 52 pgs.)

1	86	258	540	950
2	40	120	240	420
3-5	33	99	174	300
6-10: 9-Dan Barry-a. 9,10-Photo-c	25	75	133	230
11-13-Photo-c	21	63	110	190
14,17-Frazetta-a, 8 pgs. each. 14-Photo-c	40	120	220	380
15,16,18-20,26: 26-Kirby-a	15	45	77	135
21-25,27-30	14	42	72	120
31-44: 44-Last Pre-code (2-3/55)	12	36	61	100
45-67	10	30	55	80

NOTE: *Barry* a-6, 8, 10. *Drucker* a-51. *Moreira* a-48, 50, 59. *Roussos* a-8.

GANGLAND
DC Comics (Vertigo): Jun, 1998 - No. 4, Sept, 1998 ($2.95, limited series)

1-4:Crime anthology by various. 2-Corben-a				3.00
TPB-(2000, $12.95) r/#1-4; Bradstreet-c				13.00

GANGSTERS AND GUN MOLLS
Avon Per./Realistic Comics: Sept, 1951 - No. 4, June, 1952 (Painted c-1-3)

1-Wood-a, 1 pg; c-/Avon paperback #292	47	142	286	500
2-Check-a, 8 pgs.; Kamen-a; Bonnie Parker story	40	120	220	380
3-Marijuana mentioned; used in *POP*, pg. 84,85	37	111	197	340
4-Syd Shores-c	29	87	153	265

GANGSTERS CAN'T WIN
D. S. Publishing Co.: Feb-Mar, 1948 - No. 9, June-July, 1949 (All 52 pgs?)

1-True crime stories	35	105	185	320
2	18	54	94	160
3,5,6	16	48	83	140
4-Acid in face story	20	60	105	175
7-9	12	36	61	105

NOTE: *Ingles* a-5, 6. *McWilliams* a-5, 7. *Reinman* c-6.

GANG WORLD
Standard Comics: No. 5, Nov, 1952 - No. 6, Jan, 1953

5-Bondage-c	20	60	105	175
6	15	45	77	130

GARGOYLE (See The Defenders #94)
Marvel Comics Group: June, 1985 - No. 4, Sept, 1985 (75¢, limited series)

1-Wrightson-c; character from Defenders				3.50
2-4				2.50

GARGOYLES (TV cartoon)
Marvel Comics: Feb, 1995 - No. 17, June, 1996 ($2.50)

1-17: Based on animated series				3.00

GARRISON'S GORILLAS (TV)
Dell Publishing Co.: Jan, 1968 - No. 4, Oct, 1968; No. 5, Oct, 1969 (Photo-c)

1	4	12	30	50
2-5: 5-Reprints #1	3	9	21	32

GARY GIANNI'S THE MONSTERMEN
Dark Horse Comics: Aug, 1999 ($2.95, one-shot)

1-Gianni-s/c/a; back-up Hellboy story by Mignola				3.00

GASM
Stories, Layouts & Press, Inc.: Nov, 1977 - nn(No. 4), Jun, 1978 (B&W/color)

1-Mark Wheatley-s/a; Gene Day-s/a; Workman-a	2	6	12	18
nn(#2, 2/78) Day-s/a; Wheatley-a; Workman-a	2	6	9	12
nn(#3, 4/78) Day-s/a; Wheatley-a; Corben-a	2	6	13	20
nn(#4, 6/78) Hempel-a; Howarth-a; Corben-a	2	6	15	24

GASOLINE ALLEY (Top Love Stories No. 3 on?)
Star Publications: Sept-Oct, 1950 - No. 2, Dec, 1950 (Newspaper-r)

1-Contains 1 pg. intro. history of the strip (The Life of Skeezix); reprints 15 scenes of highlights from 1921-1935, plus an adventure from 1935 and 1936 strips; a 2-pg. filler is included on the life of the creator Frank King, with photo of the cartoonist.				
	22	66	116	200

Gatecrasher (Mini-series) #1 © Black Bull Ent.

Gay Comics #24 © MAR

Geeksville V2 #3 © Rich Koslowski & Gary Sassaman

	GD2.0	FN6.0	VF8.0	NM9.4

	GD2.0	FN6.0	VF8.0	NM9.4
2-(1936-37 reprints)-L. B. Cole-c	26	78	136	235

(See Super Book No. 21)

GASP!
American Comics Group: Mar, 1967 - No. 4, Aug, 1967 (12¢)

1	4	12	26	40
2-4	3	9	17	24

GATECRASHER
Black Bull Entertainment: Mar, 2000 - No. 4, Jun, 2000 ($2.50, limited series)

1,2-Waid-s/Conner & Palmiotti-c/a; 1,2-variant-c by J.G. Jones			2.50
3,4- 3-Jusko var-c. 4-Linsner-c			2.50
... Ring of Fire TPB (11/00, $12.95) r/#1-4; Hughes-c; Ennis intro.			13.00

GATECRASHER (Regular series)
Black Bull Entertainment: Aug, 2000 - Present ($2.50)

1-6-Waid-s/Conner & Palmiotti-c/a; 1-3-Variant-c by Fabry. 4-Hildebrandts variant-c. 5-Art Adams var-c. 6-Texeira var-c			2.50

GAY COMICS (Honeymoon No. 41)
Timely Comics/USA Comic Mag. Co. No. 18-24: Mar, 1944 (no month);
No. 18, Fall, 1944 - No. 40, Oct, 1949

	GD2.0	FN6.0	VF8.0	NM9.4
1-Wolverton's Powerhouse Pepper; Tessie the Typist begins; 1st app. Willie (one shot)	47	141	286	500
18-(Formerly Funny Tunes #17?)-Wolverton-a	29	87	153	265
19-29: Wolverton-a in all. 21,24-6 pg., 7 pg. Powerhouse Pepper; additional 2 pg. story in 24). 23-7 pg Wolverton story & 2 two pg stories(total of 11pgs).				
24,29-Kurtzman-a (24-"Hey Look"(2))	23	69	121	210
30,33,36,37-Kurtzman's "Hey Look" begins	10	30	55	80
31-Kurtzman's "Hey Look" (1), Giggles 'N' Grins (1-1/2)	10	30	55	80
32,35,38-40: 35-Nellie The Nurse begins?	9	27	49	70
34-Three Kurtzman's "Hey Look"	10	30	55	85

GAY COMICS (Also see Smile, Tickle, & Whee Comics)
Modern Store Publ.: 1955 (7¢, 5x7-1/4", 52 pgs.)

1	3	10	23	35

GAY PURR-EE (See Movie Comics)

GAZILLION
Image Comics: Nov, 1998 ($2.50, one-shot)

1-Howard Shum-s/ Keron Grant-a			2.50

GEAR STATION, THE
Image Comics: Mar, 2000 - Present ($2.50)

1-Four covers by Ross, Turner, Pat Lee, Fraga			2.50
1-($6.95) DF Cover			7.00
2-5: 2-Two covers by Fraga and Art Adams			2.50

GEEK, THE (See Brother Power... & Vertigo Visions)

GEEKSVILLE (Also see 3 Geeks, The)
3 Finger Prints/ Image: Aug, 1999 - No. 6, Mar, 2001 ($2.75/$2.95, B&W)

1,2,4,6-The 3 Geeks by Koslowski; Innocent Bystander by Sassaman			3.00
3-Includes "Babes & Blades" mini-comic			5.00
0-(3/00) First Image issue			3.00
(Vol. 2) 1-4-($2.95) 3-Mini-comic insert by the Geeks			3.00

G-8 AND HIS BATTLE ACES (Based on pulps)
Gold Key: Oct, 1966

1 (10184-610)-Painted-c	4	12	26	40

G-8 AND HIS BATTLE ACES
Blazing Comics: 1991 ($1.50, one-shot)

1-Glanzman-a; Truman-c			2.25

NOTE: Flip book format with "The Spider's Web" #1 on other side w/*Glanzman*-a, *Truman*-c.

GEISHA
Oni Press: Sept, 1998 - No. 4, Dec, 1998 ($2.95, limited series)

1-4-Andi Watson-s/a. 2-Adam Warren-c			3.00
...One Shot (5/00, $4.50)			4.50

GEM COMICS
Spotlight Publishers: Apr, 1945 (52 pgs)

1-Little Mohee, Steve Strong app.; Jungle bondage-c			

	GD2.0	FN6.0	VF8.0	NM9.4
	43	129	257	450

GEMINAR
Image Comics: July, 2000 ($4.95, B&W)

1-(72-Page Special) Terry Collins-s/Al Bigley-a			5.00

GEMINI BLOOD
DC Comics (Helix): Sept, 1996 - No. 9, May, 1997 ($2.25, limited series)

1-9: 5-Simonson-c			2.25

GEN ACTIVE
DC Comics (WildStorm): May, 2000 - No. 6, Aug, 2001 ($3.95)

1-6: 1-Covers by Campbell and Madureira; Gen 13 & DV8 app. 5-Mahfood-a; Quitely and Stelfreeze-a/c. 6-Portacio-a/c			4.00

GENE AUTRY (See March of Comics No. 25, 28, 39, 54, 78, 90, 104, 120, 135, 150 & Western Roundup under Dell Giants)

GENE AUTRY COMICS (Movie, Radio star; singing cowboy)
Fawcett Publications: 1941 (On sale 12/31/41) - No. 10, 1943 (68 pgs.)
(Dell takes over with No. 11)

	GD2.0	FN6.0	VF8.0	NM9.4
1 (Rare)-Gene Autry & his horse Champion begin				
	731	2193	4750	9500
2-(1942)	150	450	938	1650
3-5: 3-(11/1/42)	95	285	597	1050
6-10	79	237	494	875

GENE AUTRY COMICS (...& Champion No. 102 on)
Dell Publishing Co.: No. 11, 1943 - No. 121, Jan-Mar, 1959 (TV - later issues)

	GD2.0	FN6.0	VF8.0	NM9.4
11 (1943, 60 pgs.)-Continuation of Fawcett series; photo back-c; first Dell issue				
	58	174	406	750
12 (2/44, 60 pgs.)	52	156	364	675
Four Color 47 (1944, 60 pgs.)	43	129	301	560
Four Color 57 (11/44),66('45)(52 pgs. each)	41	123	287	530
Four Color 75,83 ('45, 36 pgs. each)	31	93	217	400
Four Color 93 ('45, 36 pgs.)	28	84	196	360
Four Color 100 ('46, 36 pgs.) First Gene Autry photo-c				
	31	93	217	400
1 (5-6/46, 52 pgs.)	43	129	301	560
2 (7-8/46)-Photo-c begin, end #111	24	72	168	310
3-5: 4-Intro Flapjack Hobbs	18	54	126	230
6-10	15	45	105	195
11-20: 20-Panhandle Pete begins	12	36	84	160
21-29 (36pgs.)	10	30	70	130
30-40 (52pgs.)	8	24	56	110
41-56 (52pgs.)	7	21	49	90
57-66 (36pgs.): 58-X-mas-c	6	18	42	75
67-80 (52pgs.)	5	15	35	65
81-90 (52pgs.): 82-X-mas-c. 87-Blank inside-c	5	15	34	55
91-99 (36pgs. No. 91-on). 94-X-mas-c	4	12	30	50
100	5	15	34	55
101-111-Last Gene Autry photo-c	4	12	29	45
112-121-All Champion painted-c, most by Savitt	4	12	26	40

NOTE: Photo back covers 4-18, 20-45, 48-65. *Manning* a-118. *Jesse Marsh* art: 4-Color No. 66, 75, 93, 100, No. 1-25, 27-37, 39, 40.

GENE AUTRY'S CHAMPION (TV)
Dell Publ. Co.: No. 287, 8/50; No. 319, 2/51; No. 3, 8-10/51 - No. 19, 8-10/55

	GD2.0	FN6.0	VF8.0	NM9.4
Four Color 287(#1)('50, 52pgs.)-Photo-c	11	33	77	140
Four Color 319(#2, '51), 3; 2-Painted-c begin, most by Sam Savitt				
	5	15	35	60
4-19: 19-Last painted-c	4	12	29	45

GENE DOGS
Marvel Comics UK: Oct, 1993 - No. 4, Jan, 1994 ($1.75, limited series)

1-($2.75)-Polybagged w/4 trading cards			3.00
2-4: 2-Vs. Genetix			2.25

GENERAL DOUGLAS MACARTHUR
Fox Features Syndicate: 1951

	GD2.0	FN6.0	VF8.0	NM9.4
nn-True life story	21	63	110	190

GENERIC COMIC, THE
Marvel Comics Group: Apr, 1984 (one-shot)

1			3.00

Generation X #39 © MAR

Gene Roddenberry's Lost World #6 © Tekno Comix

Gen 13 #50 © WSP

	GD2.0	FN6.0	VF8.0	NM9.4

GENERATION HEX
DC Comics (Amalgam): June, 1997 ($1.95, one-shot)
1-Milligan-s/ Pollina & Morales-a   2.50

GENERATION NEXT
Marvel Comics: Mar, 1995 - No. 4, June, 1995 ($1.95, limited series)
1-4-Age of Apocalypse; Scott Lobdell scripts & Chris Bachalo-c/a   2.50

GENERATION X (See Gen ¹³/ Generation X)
Marvel Comics: Oct, 1994 - No. 75, June, 2001 ($1.50/$1.95/$1.99/$2.25)
Collectors Preview ($1.75), "Ashcan" Edition   2.25
-1(7/97) Flashback story   3.00
1/2 (San Diego giveaway)   2   6   9   12
1-($3.95)-Wraparound chromium-c; Scott Lobdell scripts & Chris Bachalo-c/a
begins.   6.00
2-($1.95)-Deluxe edition, Bachalo-a   4.00
3,4-($1.95)-Deluxe Edition; Bachalo-a   3.00
2-10: 2-4-Standard Edition. 5-Returns from "Age of Apocalypse", begin $1.95-c.
6-Bachalo-a(p) ends, returns #17. 7-Roger Cruz-a(p). 10-Omega Red-c/app.
22-Nightmare app.   3.00
11-24, 26-28: 13,14-Bishop-app. 17-Stan Lee app. (Stan Lee scripts own
dialogue); Bachalo/Buckingham-a; Onslaught update. 18-Toad cameo.
20-Franklin Richards app; Howard the Duck cameo. 21-Howard the Duck app.
25-($2.99)-Wraparound-c. Black Tom, Howard the Duck app.   3.50
29-37: 29-Begin $1.99-c, "Operation Zero Tolerance". 33-Hama-s   2.50
38-49: 38-Dodson-a begins. 40-Penance ID revealed. 49-Maggott app.   2.50
50,57-($2.99): 50-Crossover w/X-Man #50   3.50
51-56, 58-62: 59-Avengers & Spider-Man app.   2.25
63-74: 63-Ellis-s begin. 64-Begin $2.25-c. 69-71-Art Adams-c   2.25
75-($2.99) Final issue; Chamber joins the X-Men; Lim-a   3.00
'95 Special ($3.95)   4.00
'96 Special-($2.95)-Wraparound-c; Jeff Johnson-c/a   3.50
'97 Special-($2.99)-Wraparound-c;   3.50
'98 Annual-($3.50)-vs. Dracula   3.50
'99 Annual-($3.50)-Monet leaves   3.50
75¢ Ashcan Edition   3.00
...Holiday Special 1 (3/99, $3.50) Pollina-a   3.50
...Underground Special 1 (5/98, $2.50, B&W) Mahfood-a   2.50

GENERATION X/ GEN ¹³ (Also see Gen ¹³/ Generation X)
Marvel Comics: 1997 ($3.99, one-shot)
1-Robinson-s/Larroca-a(p)   4.00

GENE RODDENBERRY'S LOST UNIVERSE
Tekno Comix: Apr, 1995 - No. 7, Oct, 1995 ($1.95)
1-7: 1-3-w/ bound-in game piece & trading card. 4-w/bound-in trading card   2.25

GENE RODDENBERRY'S XANDER IN LOST UNIVERSE
Tekno Comix: No. 0, Nov, 1995; No. 1, Dec, 1995 - No. 8, July, 1996 ($2.25)
0,1-8: 1-5-Jae Lee-c. 6-Polybagged. 8-Pt. 5 of The Big Bang x-over   2.25

GENESIS (See DC related titles)
DC Comics: Oct, 1997 - No. 4, Oct, 1997 ($1.95, weekly limited series)
1-4: Byrne-s/Wagner-a(p) in all.   3.00

GENESIS: THE #1 COLLECTION (WildStorm Archives)
WildStorm Productions: 1998 ($9.99, TPB, B&W)
nn-Reprints #1 issues of WildStorm titles and pin-ups   10.00

GENETIX
Marvel Comics UK: Oct, 1993 - No. 6, Mar, 1994 ($1.75, limited series)
1-($2.75)-Polybagged w/4 cards; Dark Guard app.   3.00
2-6: 2-Intro Tektons. 4-Vs. Gene Dogs   2.25

GEN ¹² (Also see Gen¹³ and Team 7)

GEN ¹³ (Also see Wild C.A.T.S. #1 & Deathmate Black #2)
Image Comics (WildStorm Productions): Feb, 1994 - No. 5, July 1994 ($1.95, limited series)

0 (8/95, $2.50)-Ch. 1 w/Jim Lee-p; Ch.4 w/Charest-p   3.00
1/2   1   3   5   7
1-($2.50)-Created by Jim Lee   1   4   7   10
1-2nd printing   2.50
1-"3-D" Edition (9/97, $4.95)-w/glasses   5.00
2-($2.50)   1   3   5   7
3-Pitt-c & story   4.00
4-Pitt-c & story; wraparound-c   3.00
5   4.00
5-Alternate Portacio-c; see Deathblow #5   6.00
...Collected Edition ('94, $12.95)-r/#1-5   13.00
...Rave ($1.50, 3/95)-wraparound-c   3.00
NOTE: Issues 1-4 contain coupons redeemable for the ashcan edition of Gen 13 #0. Price listed is for a complete book.

GEN ¹³
Image Comics (WildStorm Productions): Mar, 1995 - No. 36, Dec, 1998;
DC Comics (WildStorm Prod.): No. 37, Mar, 1999 - Present ($2.95/$2.50)
1-A (Charge)-Campbell/Gardner-c   4.00
1-B (Thumbs Up)-Campbell/Gardner-c   4.00
1-C-1-K,1-M: 1-C (Lil' GEN 13)-Art Adams-c. 1-D (Barbari-GEN)-Simon Bisley-c
1-E (Your Friendly Neighborhood Grunge)-John Cleary-c. 1-F (GEN 13 Goes
Madison Ave.)-Michael Golden-c. 1-G (Lin-GEN-re)-Michael Lopez-c. 1-H
(GEN-et Jackson)-Jason Pearson-c. 1-I (That's the way we became GEN
13)-Campbell/Gibson-c. 1-J (All Dolled Up)-Campbell/McWeeney-c. 1-K
(Verti-GEN)-Dunn-c. 1-L (Picto-Fiction). 1-M (Do it Yourself Cover)   6.00
1-"3-D" Edition (2/98, $4.95)-w/glasses   5.00
2 ($1.95, Newsstand)-WildStorm Rising Pt. 4; bound-in card   2.50
2-12: ($2.50, Direct Market)-WildStorm Rising Pt. 4, bound-in card. 6,7-Jim
Lee-c/a(p). 9-Ramos-a. 10,11-Fire From Heaven Pt. 3. & Pt.9   3.00
11-($4.95)-Special European Tour Edition; chromium-c   8.00
13A,13B,13C-($1.30, 1 pgs.): 13A-Archie & Friends app. 13B-Bone-c/app.;
Teenage Mutant Ninja Turtles, Madman, Spawn & Jim Lee app.   3.00
14-24: 20-Last Campbell-a   2.50
25-($3.50)-Two covers by Campbell and Charest   3.50
25-($3.50)-Voyager Pack w/Danger Girl preview   3.50
26-32,34: 26-Arcudi-s/Frank-a begins. 34-Back-up story by Art Adams   2.50
33-Flip book w/Planetary preview   4.00
35-49: 36,38,40-Two covers. 37-First DC issue. 41-Last Frank-a   2.50
50-($3.95) Two covers by Lee and Benes; art by various   4.00
51-72: 51-Moy-a; Fairchild loses her powers. 60-Warren-a/a. 66-Art by various
incl. Campbell (3 pgs.). 70-Mays-a   2.50
Annual 1 (1997, $2.95) Ellis-s/ Dillon-c/a.   3.50
Annual 1999 ($3.50, DC) Slipstream x-over w/ DV8   3.50
Annual 2000 ($3.50) Devil's Night x-over w/WildStorm titles; Bermejo-c   3.50
...: A Christmas Caper (1/00, $5.95, one-shot) McWeeney-s/a   6.00
...: Archives (4/98, $12.95) B&W reprints of mini-series, #0,1/2,1-13ABC;
includes cover gallery and sourcebook   13.00
...: Carny Folk (2/00, $3.50) Collect back-up stories   3.50
... European Vacation TPB ($6.95) r/#6,7   7.00
.../ Fantastic Four (2001, $5.95) Maguire-s/c/a(p)   6.00
...: Going West (6/99, $2.50, one-shot) Pruett-s   2.50
...: Grunge Saves the World (5/99, $5.95, one-shot) Altieri-c/a   6.00
... I Love New York TPB ($9.95) r/part #25, 26-29; Frank-c   10.00
... London, New York, Hell TPB ($6.95) r/Annual #1 & Bootleg Ann. #1   7.00
... Lost in Paradise TPB ($6.95) r/#3-5   7.00
.../ Maxx (12/95, $3.50, one-shot) Messner-Loebs-s, 1st Coker-c/a.   3.50
...: Medicine Song (2001, $5.95) Brent Anderson-c/a(p)/Raab-s   6.00
... Science Friction (2001, $5.95) Haley & Lopresti-a   6.00
... Starting Over TPB ($14.95) r/#1-7   15.00
... #13 A,B&C Collected Edition ($6.95, TPB) r/#13A,B&C   7.00
...: 3-D Special (1997, $4.95, one-shot) Art Adams-s/a(p)   5.00
...: The Unreal World (7/96, $2.95, one-shot) Humberto Ramos-c/a   3.00
... We'll Take Manhattan TPB ($14.95) r/#45-50; new Benes-c   15.00
...: Wired (4/99, $2.50, one-shot) Richard Bennett-c/a   2.50
...: 'Zine (12/96, $1.95, B&W, digest size) Campbell/Garner-c   2.25
Variant Collection-Four editions (all 13 variants w/Chromium variant-limited,
signed)   100.00

GEN ¹³ BOOTLEG
Image Comics (WildStorm): Nov, 1996 - No. 20, Jul, 1998 ($2.50)

GEN ¹² (Also see Gen¹³ and Team 7)
Image Comics (WildStorm Productions): Feb, 1998 - No. 5, June, 1998 ($2.50, limited series)
1-5: 1-Team 7 & Gen¹³ app.; wraparound-c   3.00

Gen 13 / Monkeyman & O'Brien #2 © WSP

Georgie Comics #11 © MAR

Ghost #3 © FH

1-Alan Davis-a; alternate costumes-c				2.50		26-Logo design swipe from Archie Comics	7	21	36	50
1-Team falling variant-c				3.00		**GERALD McBOING-BOING AND THE NEARSIGHTED MR. MAGOO** (TV)				
2-7: 2-Alan Davis-a. 5,6-Terry Moore-s. 7-Robinson-s/Scott Hampton-a.				2.50		(Mr. Magoo No. 6 on)				
8-10-Adam Warren-s/a				4.00		**Dell Publishing Co.:** Aug-Oct, 1952 - No. 5, Aug-Oct, 1953				
11-20: 11,12-Lopresti-s/a & Simonson-s. 13-Wieringo-s/a. 14-Mariotte-s/Phillips-						1	13	39	91	175
a. 15,16-Strnad-s/Shaw-a. 18-Altieri-s/a(p)/c, 18-Variant-c by Bruce Timm						2-5	11	33	77	140
				2.50		**GERONIMO** (See Fighting Indians of the Wild West!)				
Annual 1 (2/98, $2.95) Ellis-s/Dillon-c/a				3.00		**Avon Periodicals:** 1950 - No. 4, Feb, 1952				
... Grunge: The Movie (12/97, $9.95) r/#8-10, Warren-c				10.00		1-Indian Fighter; Maneely-a; Texas Rangers-r/Cowpuncher #1; Fawcette-c				
...Vol. 1 TPB (10/98, $11.95) r/#1-4				12.00			19	57	99	165
GEN 13/ GENERATION X (Also see Generation X / Gen 13)						2-On the Warpath; Kit West app.; Kinstler-c/a	12	36	61	100
Image Comics (WildStorm Publications): July, 1997 ($2.95, one-shot)						3-And His Apache Murderers; Kinstler-c/a(2); Kit West-r/Cowpuncher #6				
1-Choi-s/ Art Adams-p/Garner-i. Variant covers by Adams/Garner							12	36	61	100
and Campbell/McWeeney				3.00		4-Savage Raids of; Kinstler-c & inside front-c; Kinstlerish-a by McCann(3)				
1-($4.95) 3-D Edition w/glasses; Campbell-c				5.00			11	33	55	90
GEN 13 INTERACTIVE						**GERONIMO JONES**				
Image Comics (WildStorm): Oct, 1997 - No. 3, Dec, 1997 ($2.50, lim. series)						**Charlton Comics:** Sept, 1971 - No. 9, Jan, 1973				
1-3-Internet voting used to determine storyline				2.50		1	2	6	13	20
... Plus! (7/98, $11.95) r/series & 3-D Special (in 2-D)				12.00		2-9	1	4	7	10
GEN 13 : MAGICAL DRAMA QUEEN ROXY						Modern Comics Reprint #7('78)				4.00
Image Comics (WildStorm): Oct, 1998 - No. 3, Dec, 1998 ($3.50, lim. series)						**GETALONG GANG, THE** (TV)				
1-3-Adam Warren-s/c/a; manga style, 2-Variant-c by Hiroyuki Utatane				3.50		**Marvel Comics (Star Comics):** May, 1985 - No. 6, Mar, 1986				
1-($6.95) Dynamic Forces Ed. w/variant Warren-c				7.00		1-6: Saturday morning TV stars				3.00
GEN 13 /MONKEYMAN & O'BRIEN						**GET LOST**				
Image Comics (WildStorm): June, 1998 - No. 2, July, 1998 ($2.50, lim. series)						**Mikeross Publications/New Comics:** Feb-Mar, 1954 - No. 3, June-July, 1954				
1,2-Art Adams-s/a(p); 1-Two covers				2.50		(Satire)				
1-($4.95) Chromium-c				5.00		1-Andru/Esposito-a in all?	31	93	165	285
1-($6.95) Dynamic Forces Ed.				7.00		2-Andru/Esposito-c; has 4 pg. E.C. parody featuring "The Sewer Keeper"				
GEN 13: ORDINARY HEROES							21	63	110	185
Image Comics (WildStorm Publications): Feb, 1996 - No. 2, July, 1996 ($2.50,						3-John Wayne 'Hondo' parody	17	51	88	150
limited series)						1,2 (10,12/87-New Comics)-B&W r-original				2.25
1,2-Adam Hughes-c/a/scripts				3.00		**GET SMART** (TV)				
GENTLE BEN (TV)						**Dell Publ. Co.:** June, 1966 - No. 8, Sept, 1967 (All have Don Adams photo-c)				
Dell Publishing Co.: Feb, 1968 - No. 5, Oct, 1969 (All photo-c)						1	10	30	70	125
1	4	12	26	40		2,3-Ditko-a	7	21	49	85
2-5: 5-Reprints #1	3	6	15	22		4-8: 8-Reprints #1 (cover and insides)	5	15	35	65
GEOMANCER (Also see Eternal Warrior: Fist & Steel)						**GHOST** (...Comics #9)				
Valiant: Nov, 1994 - No. 8, June, 1995 ($3.75/$2.25)						**Fiction House Magazines:** 1951(Winter) - No. 11, Summer, 1954				
1 ($3.75)-Chromium wraparound-c; Eternal Warrior app.				3.75		1-Most covers by Whitman	69	207	431	765
2-8				2.25		2-Ghost Gallery & Werewolf Hunter stories	39	117	208	360
GEORGE OF THE JUNGLE (TV)(See America's Best TV Comics)						3-9: 3,6,7,9-Bondage-c. 9-Abel, Discount-a	33	99	174	300
Gold Key: Feb, 1969 - No. 2, Oct, 1969 (Jay Ward)						10,11-Dr. Drew by Grandenetti in each, reprinted from Rangers; 11-Evans-r/				
1	12	36	84	160		Rangers #39; Grandenetti-r/Rangers #49	29	87	153	265
2	8	24	56	105		**GHOST** (See Comic's Greatest World)				
GEORGE PAL'S PUPPETOONS (Funny animal puppets)						**Dark Horse Comics:** Apr, 1995 - No. 36, Apr, 1998 ($2.50/$2.95)				
Fawcett Publications: Dec, 1945 - No. 18, Dec, 1947; No. 19, 1950						1-Adam Hughes-a	1	3	6	8
1-Captain Marvel-c	41	123	246	425		2,3-Hughes-a				4.00
2	23	69	121	210		4-24: 4-Barb Wire app. 5,6-Hughes-c. 12-Ghost/Hellboy preview. 15,21-X app.				
3-10	14	42	72	125		18,19-Barb Wire app.				3.00
11-19	12	36	61	100		25-($3.50)-48 pgs. special				3.50
GEORGIE COMICS (...& Judy Comics #20-35?; see All Teen & Teen Comics)						26-36: 26-Begin $2.95-c. 29-Flip book w/Timecop. 33-36-Jade Cathedral;				
Timely Comics/GPI No. 1-34: Spr, 1945 - No. 39, Oct, 1952 (#1-3 are quarterly)						Harris painted-c				3.00
1-Dave Berg-a	24	72	127	215		Special 1 (7/94, $3.95, 48 pgs.)	1	3	5	7
2	12	36	61	105		Special 2 (6/98, $3.95) Barb Wire app.				4.00
3-5,7,8	10	30	55	85		...Black October (1/99, $14.95, trade paperback)-r/#6-9,26,27				15.00
6-Georgie visits Timely Comics	13	39	66	110		...Nocturnes (1996, $9.95, trade paperback)-r/#1-3 & 5				10.00
9,10-Kurtzman's "Hey Look" (1 & ?); Margie app.	11	33	55	90		...Stories (1995, $9.95, trade paperback)-r/Early Ghost app.				10.00
11,12: 11-Margie, Millie app.	8	24	42	60		**GHOST** (Volume 2)				
13-Kurtzman's "Hey Look", 3 pgs.	9	27	49	70		**Dark Horse Comics:** Sept, 1998 - No. 22, Aug, 2000 ($2.95)				
14-Wolverton-a(1 pg.); Kurtzman's "Hey Look"	10	30	55	80		1-22: 1-4-Ryan Benjamin-c/Zanier-a				3.00
15,16,18-20	7	21	36	50		Handbook (8/99, $2.95) guide to issues and characters				3.00
17,29-Kurtzman's "Hey Look", 1 pg.	8	24	42	60		Special 3 (12/98, $3.95)				4.00
21-24,27,28,30-39: 21-Anti-Wertham editorial	6	18	32	45		**GHOST AND THE SHADOW**				
25-Painted-c by classic pin-up artist Peter Driben	10	30	55	80		**Dark Horse Comics:** Dec, 1995 ($2.95, one-shot)				

Ghost V2 #1 © DH

Ghostly Tales #121 © CC

Ghost Manor #57 © CC

	GD2.0	FN6.0	VF8.0	NM9.4
1-Moench scripts				3.00

GHOST/BATGIRL
Dark Horse Comics: Aug, 2000 - No. 4, Dec, 2000 ($2.95, limited series)

1-4-New Batgirl; Oracle & Bruce Wayne app.; Benjamin-c/a				3.00

GHOST/HELLBOY
Dark Horse Comics: May, 1996 - No. 2, June, 1996 ($2.50, limited series)

1,2: Mike Mignola-c/scripts & breakdowns; Scott Benefiel finished-a				3.00

GHOST BREAKERS (Also see Racket Squad in Action, Red Dragon & (CC)
Street & Smith Publications: Sept, 1948 - No. 2, Dec, 1948 (52 pgs.)

1-Powell-c/a(3); Dr. Neff (magician) app.	40	120	240	420
2-Powell-c/a(2); Maneely-a	35	105	185	320

GHOSTBUSTERS (TV) (Also, see Real...and Slimer)
First Comics: Feb, 1987 - No. 6, Aug, 1987 ($1.25)

1-6: Based on new animated TV series				3.00

GHOSTBUSTERS II
Now Comics: Oct, 1989 - No. 3, Dec, 1989 ($1.95, mini-series)

1-3: Movie Adaptation				3.00

GHOST CASTLE (See Tales of...)

GHOSTDANCING
DC Comics (Vertigo): Mar, 1995 - No. 6, Sept, 1995 ($1.95, limited series)

1-6: Case-c/a				2.25

GHOST IN THE SHELL (Manga)
Dark Horse: Mar, 1995 - No. 8, Oct, 1995 ($3.95, B&W/color, lim. series)

1	2	6	13	20
2	2	6	15	22
3	2	6	9	12
4-8	1	3	6	8

GHOSTLY HAUNTS (Formerly Ghost Manor)
Charlton Comics: #20, 9/71 - #53, 12/76; #54, 9/77 - #55, 10/77; #56, 1/78 - #58, 4/78

20	3	9	17	24
21	2	6	10	14
22-25,27,31-34,36,37-Ditko-c/a. 27-Dr. Graves x-over. 32-New logo. 33-Back to old logo	2	6	12	18
26,29,30,35-Ditko-c	2	6	10	14
28,38-40-Ditko-a. 39-Origin & 1st app. Destiny Fox	2	6	10	14
41,42: 41-Sutton-c; Ditko-a. 42-Newton-c/a	2	6	11	15
43-46,48,50,52-Ditko-a	2	6	9	12
47,54,56-Ditko-a. 56-Ditko-a(r).	2	6	11	15
49,51,53,55,57	1	3	6	9
40,41(Modern Comics-r, 1977, 1978)				4.00
58 (4/78) Last issue	2	6	12	18

NOTE: Ditko a-22-25, 27, 28, 31-34, 36-41, 43-48, 50, 52, 54, 56r; c-22-27, 29, 30, 33-37, 47, 54, 56. Glanzman a-20. Howard a-27, 30, 35, 40-43, 48, 54, 57. Kim a-38, 41, 57. Larson a-48, 50. Newton (a-42. Staton a-32, 35; c-28, 46. Sutton c-33, 37, 39, 41.

GHOSTLY TALES (Formerly Blue Beetle No. 50-54)
Charlton Comics: No. 55, 4-5/66 - No. 124, 12/76; No. 125, 9/77 - No. 169, 10/84

55-Intro. & origin Dr. Graves; Ditko-a	4	12	30	50
56-58,60,61,70,71-Ditko-a. 70-Dr. Graves ends. 71-Last 12¢ issue	3	9	17	25
59,62-66,68	2	6	13	20
67,69-Ditko-c/a	3	9	18	28
72,75,76,79-82,85-Ditko-c/a	2	6	11	16
73,77,78,83,84,86-90,92-95,97,99-Ditko-c/a	2	6	13	20
74,91,98,119,123,124,127-130: 127,130-Sutton-a	2	6	9	12
96-Ditko-c	2	6	11	16
100-Ditko-c; Sutton-a	2	6	11	16
101,103-105-Ditko-a	2	6	10	14
102,109-Ditko-c/a	2	6	12	18
110,113-Sutton-c; Ditko-a	2	6	10	14
106-Ditko & Sutton-a; Sutton-c	2	6	10	14
107-Ditko, Wood, Sutton-a	2	6	12	15
108,116,117,126-Ditko-a	2	6	10	14

111,118,120-122,125-Ditko-c/a	2	6	11	16
112,114,115: 112,114-Ditko, Sutton-a. 114-Newton-a. 115-Newton, Ditko-a.				
	2	6	11	14
131-133,163-Ditko-c/a	2	6	9	12
134,135,142,145-151,153,154,156-160	1	3	5	7
136-141,143,144,152,155-Ditko-a	1	3	6	9
161,162,164-168-Lower print run. 162-Nudity panel	2	6	9	12
169 (10/84) Last issue; lower print run	2	6	12	18

NOTE: Aparo a-65, 66, 68, 72, 141r, 142r; c-71, 72, 74-76, 81, 146r. Ditko a-55-58, 60, 61, 67, 69-73, 75-90, 92-95, 97, 99-118, 120-122, 125r, 126r, 131-133r, 136-141r, 143r, 144r, 152, 155, 161, 163; c-67, 69, 73, 77, 78, 83, 84, 86-90, 92-97, 99, 102, 109, 111, 118, 120-122, 125, 131-133, 163. Glanzman a-167. Howard a-95, 98, 99, 108, 117, 129; c-98, 107, 120, 121, 161. Larson a-117, 119. Morisi a-83, 84, 86. Newton a-114; c-115(painted). Palais a-61. Staton a-61; c-117. Sutton a-106, 107, 111-114, 127, 130, 162; c-100, 106, 110, 113(painted). Wood a-107.

GHOSTLY WEIRD STORIES (Formerly Blue Bolt Weird)
Star Publications: No. 120, Sept, 1953 - No. 124, Sept, 1954

120-Jo-Jo-r	40	120	220	380
121-124: 121-Jo-Jo-r. 122-The Mask-r/Capt. Flight #5; Rulah-r; has 1pg. story 'Death and the Devil Pills'-r/Western Outlaws #17. 123-Jo-Jo; Disbrow-a(2).				
124-Torpedo Man	35	105	185	320

NOTE: Disbrow a-120-124. L. B. Cole covers-all issues (#122 as a sci-fi cover).

GHOST MANOR (Ghostly Haunts No. 20 on)
Charlton Comics: July, 1968 - No. 19, July, 1971

1	4	12	29	45
2-6: 6-Last 12¢ issue	3	9	17	25
7-12,17: 17-Morisi-a	2	6	13	20
13,14,16-Ditko-a	3	9	17	25
15,18,19-Ditko-c/a	3	9	20	30

GHOST MANOR (2nd Series)
Charlton Comics: Oct, 1971-No. 32, Dec, 1976; No. 33, Sept, 1977-No. 77, 11/84

1	3	10	23	35
2,3,5-7,9-Ditko-c	2	6	11	16
4,10-Ditko-c/a	2	6	13	20
8-Wood, Ditko-a; Sutton-c	2	6	15	22
11,14-Ditko-c/a	2	6	12	18
12,17,27,30	2	6	9	12
13,15,16,19-21,23-26,29: 13-Ditko-a. 15,16-Ditko-c. 19-Newton, Sutton-a; nudity panels. Ditko-a. 23-Sutton-a. 24-26,29-Ditko-a. 25-Sutton-a. 26-Early Zeck-a; Boyette-c	2	6	10	14
18-Newton's 1st pro art; Ditko-a; Sutton-c	2	6	13	20
22-Newton-c/a; Ditko-a	2	6	11	16
28,31,37,38-Ditko-c/a: 28-Nudity panels	2	6	11	16
32-36,39,41,45,48-50,53	1	3	6	8
40-Ditko-c; torture & drug use	2	6	10	14
42,43,46,47,51,52,60,62-Ditko-c/a	2	6	9	12
44,54,71-Ditko-a	1	4	7	10
55,56,58,59,61,63,65-70				6.00
57-Wood, Ditko, Howard-a	2	6	9	12
64-Ditko & Newton-a	1	4	7	10
71-76				6.00
77-(11/84) Last issue Aparo-r/Space Adventures V3#60 (Paul Mann)				
	2	6	11	15
19 (Modern Comics reprint, 1977)				4.00

NOTE: Ditko a-4, 8, 10, 11(2), 13, 14, 18, 20-22, 24-26, 28, 29, 31, 37r, 38r, 40r, 42-44r, 46r, 47, 51r, 52r, 54r, 57, 60, 62, 64r, 71; c-2-7, 9-11, 14-16, 28, 31, 37, 38, 42, 43, 46, 47, 51, 52, 60, 62, 64. Howard a-4, 8, 12, 17, 19-21, 31, 41, 45, 57. Newton a-18-20, 22, 64; c-22. Staton a-13, 18, 44, 45. Staton a-19, 23, 25, 45;c-8, 18.

GHOST RIDER (See A-1 Comics, Best of the West, Black Phantom, Bobby Benson, Great Western, Red Mask & Tim Holt)
Magazine Enterprises: 1950 - No. 14, 1954

NOTE: The character was inspired by Vaughn Monroe's "Ghost Riders in the Sky," and Disney's movie "The Headless Horseman".

1(A-1 #27)-Origin Ghost Rider	77	231	483	850
2-5: 2(A-1 #29), 3(A-1 #31), 4(A-1 #34), 5(A-1 #37)-All Frazetta-c only	64	192	398	700
6,7: 6(A-1 #44)-Loco weed story, 7(A-1 #51)	29	87	156	270
8,9: 8(A-1 #57)-Drug use story, 9(A-1 #69)	25	75	130	225
10(A-1 #71)-Vs. Frankenstein	26	78	139	240
11-14: 11(A-1 #75). 12(A-1 #80)-Bondage-c; one-eyed Devil-c. 13(A-1 #84).				

Ghost Rider #10 © MAR

Ghost Rider V2 #53 © MAR

Ghosts #40 © DC

	GD2.0	FN6.0	VF8.0	NM9.4

	GD2.0	FN6.0	VF8.0	NM9

14(A-1 #112) — 22 — 66 — 116 — 195
NOTE: *Dick Ayers* art in all; c-1, 6-14.

GHOST RIDER, THE (See Night Rider & Western Gunfighters)
Marvel Comics Group: Feb, 1967 - No. 7, Nov, 1967 (Western hero)(12¢)

1-Origin & 1st app. Ghost Rider; Kid Colt-reprints begin	8	24	56	90
2	4	12	29	45
3-7: 6-Last Kid Colt-r; All Ayers-c/a(p)	3	10	23	35

GHOST RIDER (See The Champions, Marvel Spotlight #5, Marvel Team-Up #15, 58, Marvel Treasury Edition #18, Marvel Two-In-One #8, The Original Ghost Rider & The Original Ghost Rider Rides Again)
Marvel Comics Group: Sept, 1973 - No. 81, June, 1983 (Super-hero)

1-Johnny Blaze, the Ghost Rider begins; 1st app. Daimon Hellstrom (Son of Satan) in cameo	7	21	50	80
2-1st full app. Daimon Hellstrom; gives glimpse of costume (1 panel); story continues in Marvel Spotlight #12	3	9	20	30
3-5: 3-Ghost Rider gets new cycle; Son of Satan app.	3	9	17	25
6-10: 10-Reprints origin/1st app. from Marvel Spotlight #5; Ploog-a	2	6	12	18
11-16	1	4	7	10
17,19-(Reg. 25¢ editions)(4,8/76)	1	4	7	10
17,19-(30¢-c variants, limited distribution)	2	6	11	15
18-(Reg. 25¢ edition)(6/76). Spider-Man & app.	2	6	9	12
18-(30¢-c variant, limited distribution)	2	6	12	18
20-Daredevil x-over; ties into D.D. #138; Byrne-a	2	6	11	16
21-30: 22-1st app. Enforcer. 29,30-Vs. Dr. Strange				6.00
24-26-(35¢-c variants, limited distribution)	1	3	6	9
31-34,36-49				5.00
35-Death Race classic; Starlin-c/a/sty	1	4	7	10
50-Double size	1	3	5	7
51-76,78-80: 80-Brief origin recap. 68,77-Origin retold				4.00
81-Death of Ghost Rider (Demon leaves Blaze)	2	6	9	12

NOTE: *Anderson* c-64¢. *Infantino* a(p)-43, 44, 51. *G. Kane* a-21p; c(p)-1, 2, 4, 5, 8, 9, 11-13, 19, 20, 24, 25. *Kirby* c-21-23. *Mooney* a-2-9p, 30i. *Nebres* c-26i. *Newton* a-23i. *Perez* c-26p. *Shores* a-2i. *J. Sparling* a-62p, 64p, 65i. *Starlin* a(p)-35. *Sutton* a-1p, 44i, 64i, 65i, 66, 67i. *Tuska* a-13p, 14p, 16p.

GHOST RIDER (Volume 2) (Also see Doctor Strange/Ghost Rider Special, Marvel Comics Presents & Midnight Sons Unlimited)
Marvel Comics (Midnight Sons imprint #44 on): V2#1, May, 1990 - No. 93, Feb, 1998 ($1.50/$1.75/$1.95)

1-($1.95, 52 pgs.)-Origin/1st app. new Ghost Rider; Kingpin app.		6.00
1-2nd printing (not gold)		2.50
2-5: 3-Kingpin app. 5-Punisher app.; Jim Lee-c		3.00
5-Gold background 2nd printing		3.00
6-14,16-24,29,30,32-39: 6-Punisher app. 6,17-Spider-Man/Hobgoblin-c/story. 9-X-Factor app. 10-Reintro Johnny Blaze on the last pg. 11-Stroman-c/a(p). 12,13-Dr. Strange x-over cont'd in D.S. #28. 13-Painted-c. 14-Johnny Blaze vs. Ghost Rider; origin recap 1st Ghost Rider (Blaze). 18-Painted-c by Nelson. 29-Wolverine-c/story. 32-Dr. Strange x-over; Johnny Blaze app. 34-Williamson-a(i). 36-Daredevil app. 37-Archangel app.		2.50
15-Glow in the dark-c		3.00
25-27: 25-($2.75)-Contains pop-up scene insert. 26,27-X-Men x-over; Lee/Williams-c on both		3.00
28,31-($2.50, 52 pgs.)-Polybagged w/poster; part 1 & part 6 of Rise of the Midnight Sons storyline (see Ghost Rider/Blaze #1)		3.00
40-Outer-c is Darkhold envelope made of black parchment w/gold ink; Midnight Massacre; Demogoblin app.		3.00
41-48: 41-Lilith & Centurious app.; begin $1.75-c. 43-42-Neon ink-c. 43-Has free extra 16 pg. insert on Siege of Darkness. 44,45-Siege of Darkness parts 2 & 10. 44-Spot varnish-c. 46-Intro new Ghost Rider. 48-Spider-Man app.		2.25
49,51-60,62-74: 49-Begin $1.95-c; bound-in trading card sheet; Hulk app. 55-Werewolf by Night app. 65-Punisher app. 67,68-Gambit app. 68-Wolverine app. 73,74-Blaze, Vengeance app.		2.25
50,61: 50-($2.50, 52 pgs.)-Punisher app.		2.50
50-($2.95, 52 pgs.)-Collectors Ed. die cut foil-c		3.00
75-92: 76-Vs. Vengeance. 77,78-Dr. Strange-app. 78-New costume		2.25
93-($2.99)-Saltares & Texeira-a		3.00

#(-1) Flashback (7/97) Saltares-a — 2.00
Annual 1,2 ('93, '94, $2.95, 68 pgs.) 1-Bagged w/card — 3.00
...And Cable 1 (9/92, $3.95, stiff-c, 68 pgs.)-Reprints Marvel Comics Presents #90-98 w/new Kieth-c — 4.00
...:Crossroads (11/95, $3.95) Die cut cover; Nord-a — 5.00
Highway to Hell (2001, $3.50) Reprints origin from Marvel Spotlight #5 — 3.50
...: Resurrected TPB (2001, $12.95) r/#1-7 — 13.00
NOTE: *Andy & Joe Kubert* c/a-28-31. *Quesada* c-21. *Williamson* a(i)-33-35; c-33i.

GHOST RIDER (Volume 3)
Marvel Comics: Aug, 2001 - No. 6, Jan, 2002 ($2.99, limited series)

1-6-Grayson-s/Kaniuga-a/c — 3.00

GHOST RIDER/BALLISTIC
Marvel Comics: Feb, 1997 ($2.95, one-shot)

1-Devil's Reign pt. 3 — 3.00

GHOST RIDER/BLAZE: SPIRITS OF VENGEANCE (Also see Blaze)
Marvel Comics (Midnight Sons imprint #17 on): Aug, 1992 - No. 23, June, 1994 ($1.75)

1-($2.75, 52 pgs.)-Polybagged w/poster; part 2 of Rise of the Midnight Sons storyline; Adam Kubert-c/a begins — 3.00
2-11,14-21: 4-Art Adams & Joe Kubert-p. 5,6-Spirits of Venom parts 2 & 4 cont'd from Web of Spider-Man #95,96 w/Demogoblin. 14-17-Neon ink-c. 15-Intro Blaze's new costume & power. 17,18-Siege of Darkness parts 8 & 13. 17-Spot varnish-c — 2.25
12-($2.95)-Glow-in-the-dark-c — 3.00
13-($3.25)-Outer-c is Darkhold envelope made of black parchment w/gold ink; Midnight Massacre x-over — 2.50
22,23: 22-Begin $1.95-c; bound-in trading card sheet — 2.25
NOTE: *Adam & Joe Kubert* c-7, 8. *Adam Kubert/Steacy* c-6. *J. Kubert* a-13p(6 pgs.)

GHOST RIDER/CAPTAIN AMERICA: FEAR
Marvel Comics: Oct, 1992 ($4.95, 52 pgs.)

nn-Wraparound gatefold-c; Williamson inks — 6.00

GHOST RIDER 2099
Marvel Comics: May, 1994 - No. 25, May, 1996 ($1.50/$1.95)

1 ($2.25)-Collector's Edition w/prismatic foil-c — 3.00
1 ($1.50)-Regular Edition; bound-in trading card sheet — 2.25
2-24: 7-Spider-Man 2099 app. — 2.25
2-(Variant; polybagged with Sega Sub-Terrania poster) — 5.00
25 ($2.95) — 3.00

GHOST RIDER, WOLVERINE, PUNISHER: THE DARK DESIGN
Marvel Comics: Dec, 1994 ($5.95, one-shot)

nn-Gatefold-c — 6.00

GHOST RIDER; WOLVERINE; PUNISHER: HEARTS OF DARKNESS
Marvel Comics: Dec, 1991 ($4.95, one-shot, 52 pgs.)

1-Double gatefold-c; John Romita, Jr.-c/a(p) — 5.00

GHOSTS (Ghost No. 1)
National Periodical Publications/DC Comics: Sept-Oct, 1971 - No. 112, May, 1982 (No. 1-5: 52 pgs.)

1-Aparo-a	10	30	73	125
2-Wood-a(i)	5	15	38	60
3-5	4	12	29	45
6-10	3	9	17	25
11-20	2	6	11	16
21-39	2	6	9	12
40-(68 pgs.)	2	6	13	20
41-60	1	3	6	
61-96				6.00
97-99-The Spectre vs. Dr. 13 by Aparo. 97,98-Spectre-c by Aparo.	2	6	9	12
100-Infinity-c	1	3	5	
101-112				5.00

NOTE: *B. Baily* a-77. *Buckler* c-99, 100. *J. Craig* a-108. *Ditko* a-77, 111. *Giffen* a-104p, 106p, 111p. *Glanzman* a-2. *Golden* a-88. *Infantino* a-8. *Kaluta* a-c-7, 93, 101. *Kubert* a-c-89, 105-108, 111. *Mayer* a-111. *McWilliams* a-99. *Win Mortimer* a-89, 91, 94. *Nasser/Netzer* a-97. *Newton* a-92p, 94p. *Nino* a-35, 37, 57. *Orlando* a-74i; c-80. *Redondo* a-8, 13, 45. *Sparling* a(p)-90, 93, 94. *Spiegle* a-103, 105. *Tuska* a-2i. Dr. 13, the Ghostbreaker back-ups in 95-99, 101.

GHOSTS SPECIAL (See DC Special Series No. 7)

Giant Comics Edition #12 © STJ

Giantkiller #2 © Dan Brereton

Giant-Size Invaders #1 © MAR

	GD2.0	FN6.0	VF8.0	NM9.4

GHOST STORIES (See Amazing Ghost Stories)

GHOST STORIES
Dell Publ. Co.: Sept-Nov, 1962; No. 2, Apr-June, 1963 - No. 37, Oct, 1973

1-295-211(#1)-Written by John Stanley	5	15	35	60
2	3	9	20	30
3-10: Two No. 6's exist with different c/a(12-295-406 & 12-295-503)				
#12-295-503 is actually #9 with indicia to #6	3	9	17	25
11-21: 21-Last 12¢ issue	2	6	13	20
22-37	2	6	11	15

NOTE: #21-34, 36, 37 all reprint earlier issues.

GHOUL TALES (Magazine)
Stanley Publications: Nov, 1970 - No. 5, July, 1971 (52 pgs.) (B&W)

1-Aragon pre-code reprints; Mr. Mystery as host; bondage-c	6	18	45	75
2,3: 2-(1/71)Reprint/Climax #1. 3-(3/71)	3	10	23	35
4-(5/71)Reprints story "The Way to a Man's Heart" used in SOTI	4	12	29	45
5-ACG reprints	3	9	20	30

NOTE: No. 1-4 contain pre-code Aragon reprints.

GIANT BOY BOOK OF COMICS (Also see Boy Comics)
Newsbook Publications (Gleason): 1945 (240 pgs., hard-c)

1-Crimebuster & Young Robin Hood; Biro-c	91	273	568	1000

GIANT COMIC ALBUM
King Features Syndicate: 1972 (59¢, 11x14", 52 pgs., B&W, cardboard-c)

Newspaper reprints: Barney Google, Little Iodine, Katzenjammer Kids, Henry, Beetle Bailey, Blondie, & Snuffy Smith each...

each...	3	9	20	30
Flash Gordon ('68-69 Dan Barry)	4	12	26	40
Mandrake the Magician ('59 Falk), Popeye	3	10	23	30

GIANT COMICS
Charlton Comics: Summer, 1957 - No. 3, Winter, 1957 (25¢, 100 pgs.)

1-Atomic Mouse, Hoppy app.	22	66	116	200
2,3: 2-Romance. 3-Christmas Book; Atomic Mouse, Atomic Rabbit, Li'l Genius, Li'l Tomboy & Atom the Cat stories	16	48	83	140

NOTE: The above may be rebound comics; contents could vary.

GIANT COMICS (See Wham-O Giant Comics)

GIANT COMICS EDITION (See Terry-Toons) (Also see Fox Giants)
St. John Publishing Co.: 1947 - No. 17, 1950 (25¢, 100-164 pgs.)

1-Mighty Mouse	44	132	275	525
2-Abbie & Slats	21	63	131	250
3-Terry-Toons Album; 100 pgs.	33	100	206	400
4-Crime comics; contains Red Seal No. 16, used & illo. in SOTI	50	150	312	600
5-Police Case Book (4/49, 132 pgs.)-Contents varies; contains remaindered St. John books - some volumes contain 5 copies rather than 4, with 160 pages; Matt Baker-a	48	144	300	575
5A-Terry-Toons Album (132 pgs.)-Mighty Mouse, Heckle & Jeckle, Gandy Goose & Dinky stories	30	90	188	360
6-Western Picture Stories; Baker-c/a(3); Tuska-a; The Sky Chief, Blue Monk, Ventrilo app., 132 pgs.	46	148	288	550
7-Contains a teen-age romance plus 3 Mopsy comics	27	80	169	325
8-The Adventures of Mighty Mouse (10/49)	30	90	188	360
9-Romance and Confession Stories; Kubert-a(4); Baker-a; photo-c (132 pgs.)	49	147	306	585
10-Terry-Toons Album (132 pgs.)-Mighty Mouse, Heckle & Jeckle, Gandy Goose stories	30	90	188	360
11-Western Picture Stories-Baker-c/a(4); The Sky Chief, Desperado, & Blue Monk app.; another version with Son of Sinbad by Kubert (132 pgs.)	44	132	275	525
12-Diary Secrets; Baker prostitute-c; 4 St. John romance comics; Baker-a	92	276	575	1100
13-Romances; Baker, Kubert-a	44	132	275	525
14-Mighty Mouse Album (132 pgs.)	30	90	188	360
15-Romances (4 love comics)-Baker-c	50	150	312	600
16-Little Audrey; Abbott & Costello, Casper	31	93	194	375
17(nn)-Mighty Mouse Album (nn, no date, but did follow No. 16); 100 pgs.				

---

on cover but has 148 pgs.	30	90	188	360

NOTE: The above books contain remaindered comics and contents could vary with each issue. No. 11, 12 have part photo magazine insides.

GIANT COMICS EDITIONS
United Features Syndicate: 1940's (132 pgs.)

1-Abbie & Slats, Abbott & Costello, Jim Hardy, Ella Cinders, Iron Vic, Gordo, & Bill Bumlin	40	120	217	375
2-Jim Hardy, Ella Cinders, Elmo & Gordo	30	90	159	275

NOTE: Above books contain rebound copies; contents can vary.

GIANT GRAB BAG OF COMICS (See Archie All-Star Specials under Archie Comics)

GIANTKILLER
DC Comics: Aug, 1999 - No. 6, Jan, 2000 ($2.50, limited series)

1-6-Story and painted art by Dan Brereton				2.50
...A to Z: A Field Guide to Big Monsters (8/99)				2.50

GIANTS (See Thrilling True Story of the Baseball...)

GIANT-SIZE...
Marvel Comics Group: May, 1974 - Dec, 1975 (35/50¢, 52/68 pgs.)
(Some titles quarterly) (Scarce in strict NM or better due to defective cutting, gluing and binding; warping, splitting and off-center pages are common)

Avengers 1(8/74)-New-a plus G.A. H. Torch-r; 1st modern app. The Whizzer; 1st & only modern app. Miss America; 2nd app. Invaders; Kang, Rama-Tut, Mantis app.	3	10	23	35
Avengers 2,3,5: 2(11/74)-Death of the Swordsman; origin of Rama-Tut. 3(2/75). 5(12/75)-Reprints Avengers Special #1	2	6	13	20
Avengers 4 (6/75)-Vision marries Scarlet Witch.	2	6	11	15
Captain America 1(12/75)-r/stories T.O.S. 59-63 by Kirby (#63 reprints origin)	3	9	17	25
Captain Marvel 1(12/75)-r/Capt. Marvel #17, 20, 21 by Gil Kane (p)	2	6	12	18
Chillers 1(6/74, 52 pgs)-Curse of Dracula; origin/1st app. Lilith, Dracula's daughter; Heath-r, Colan-c/a(p); becomes Giant-Size Dracula #2 on	4	12	26	40
Chillers 1(2/75, 50¢, 68 pgs.)-Alacala-a	2	6	15	22
Chillers 2(5/75)-All-r; Everett-r from Advs. into Weird Worlds	2	6	11	16
Chillers 3(8/75)-Wrightson-c(new)/a(r); Colan, Kirby, Smith-r	2	6	13	20
Conan 1(9/74)-B. Smith-r/#3; start adaptation of Howard's "Hour of the Dragon" and new-a plus Belit; new-a begins 2	6	15	22
Conan 2(12/74)-B. Smith-r/#5; Sutton-a(i) (#1 also); Buscema-c	2	6	11	16
Conan 3-5: 3(4/75)-B. Smith-r/#6; Sutton-a(i). 4(6/75)-B. Smith-r/#7. 5(1975)-B. Smith-r/#14,15; Kirby-c	2	6	10	14
Creatures 1(5/74, 52 pgs.)-Werewolf app; 1st app. Tigra (formerly Cat); Crandall-r; becomes Giant-Size Werewolf w/#2	3	9	20	30
Daredevil 1(1975)-Reprints Daredevil Annual #1	2	6	11	16
Defenders 1(7/74)-Silver Surfer app.; Starlin-a; Ditko, Everett & Kirby reprints	3	9	19	28
Defenders 2(10/74, 68 pgs.)-New G. Kane-c/a(p); Son of Satan app.; Sub-Mariner-r by Everett; Ditko-r/Strange Tales #119 (Dr. Strange); Maneely-r	2	6	12	18
Defenders 3-5: 3(1/75)-1st app. Korvac.; Newton, Starlin-a; Ditko, Everett-r. 4(4/75)-Ditko, Everett-r. G. Kane-c. 5(7/75)-Guardians app.	2	6	11	15
Doc Savage 1(1975, 68 pgs.)-r/#1,2; Mooney-r	2	6	10	14
Doctor Strange 1(11/75)-Reprints stories from Strange Tales #164-168; Lawrence, Tuska-r	2	6	12	18
Dracula 2(9/74, 50¢)-Formerly Giant-Size Chillers	2	6	13	20
Dracula 3(12/74)-Fox-r/Uncanny Tales #6	2	6	12	18
Dracula 4(6/75)-Ditko-r(2)	2	6	12	18
Dracula 5(6/75)-1st Byrne art at Marvel	3	10	23	35
Fantastic Four 2-4: 2(8/74)-Formerly Giant-Size Super-Stars; Ditko-r. 3(11/74). 4(2/75)-1st Madrox; 2-4-All have Buscema-a	2	6	13	20
Fantastic Four 5,6: 5(5/75)-All-r; Kirby, G. Kane-a. 6(10/75)-All-r; Kirby-r	1	6	11	16
Hulk 1(1975) r/Hulk Special #1	3	9	17	24
Invaders 1(1975)-Origin; G.A. Sub-Mariner-r/Sub-Mariner #1; intro Master Man	2	6	15	22

	GD2.0	FN6.0	VF8.0	NM9.4
Iron Man 1(1975)-Ditko reprint	3	6	13	20
Kid Colt 1-3: 1(1/75). 2(4/75). 3(7/75)-new Ayers-a	4	12	30	50
Man-Thing 1(8/74)-New Ploog-c/a (25 pgs.); Ditko-r/Amazing Adv. #11; Kirby-r/ Strange Tales Ann. #2 & T.O.S. #15; (#1-5 all have new Man-Thing stories, pre-hero-r & are 68 pgs.)	3	9	17	25
Man-Thing 2,3: 2(11/74)-Buscema-c/a(p); Kirby, Powell-r. 3(2/75)-Alcala-a; Ditko, Kirby, Sutton-r; Gil Kane-c	2	6	11	16
Man-Thing 4,5: 4(5/75)-Howard the Duck by Brunner-c/a; Ditko-r. 5(8/75)- Howard the Duck by Brunner (p); Dracula cameo in Howard the Duck; Buscema-a(p); Sutton-a(i); G. Kane-c	2	6	13	22
Marvel Triple Action 1,2: 1(5/75). 2(7/75)	2	6	11	16
Master of Kung Fu 1(9/74)-Russell-a; Yellow Claw-r in #1-4; Gulacy-a in #1,2				
Master of Kung Fu 2-4: 2-(12/74)-r/Yellow Claw #1. 3(3/75)-Gulacy-a; Kirby-a. 4(6/75)-Kirby-a	2	6	11	16
Power Man 1(1975)	2	6	11	16
Spider-Man 1(7/74)-Spider-Man /Human Torch-r by Kirby/Ditko; Byrne-a plus new-a (Dracula-c/story)	5	15	34	55
Spider-Man 2,3: 2(10/74)-Shang-Chi-c/app. 3(1/75)-Doc Savage-c/app.; Daredevil/Spider-Man-r w/Ditko-a	3	9	21	32
Spider-Man 4(4/75)-3rd Punisher app.; Byrne, Ditko-r	8	24	56	90
Spider-Man 5,6: 5(7/75)-Man-Thing/Lizard-c. 6(9/75)	3	9	17	25
Super-Heroes Featuring Spider-Man 1(6/74, 35¢, 52 pgs.)-Spider-Man vs. Man-Wolf; Morbius, the Living Vampire app.; Ditko-r; G. Kane-a(p); Spidey villains app.	5	15	38	60
Super-Stars 1(7/74, 35¢, 52 pgs.)-Fantastic Four; Thing vs. Hulk; Kirbyish-c/a by Buckler/Sinnott; F.F. villains profiled; becomes Giant-Size Fantastic Four #2 on	10	20	33	35
Super-Villain Team-Up 1(3/75, 68 pgs.)-Craig-r(i) (Also see Fantastic Four #6 for 1st super-villain team-up)	2	6	12	18
Super-Villain Team-Up 2(6/75, 68 pgs.)-Dr. Doom, Sub-Mariner app.; Spider-Man-r/Amazing Spider-Man #8 by Ditko, Sekowsky-a(p)	2	6	11	18
Thor 1(7/75)	3	9	17	25
Werewolf 2(10/74, 68 pgs.)-Formerly Giant-Size Creatures; Ditko-r; Frankenstein app.	2	6	12	18
Werewolf 3,5: 3(1/75, 68 pgs.). 5(7/75, 68 pgs.)	2	6	12	18
Werewolf 4(4/75, 68 pgs.)-Morbius the Living Vampire app.	2	6	15	22
X-Men 1(Summer, 1975, 50¢, 68 pgs.)-1st app. new X-Men; intro Nightcrawler, Storm, Colossus & Thunderbird; 2nd full app. Wolverine after Incredible Hulk #181	69	207	584	1100
X-Men 2 (11/75)-N. Adams-r (51 pgs)	6	18	45	75

GIANT SPECTACULAR COMICS (See Archie All-Star Special under Archie Comics)

GIANT SUMMER FUN BOOK (See Terry-Toons...)

G. I. COMBAT
Quality Comics Group: Oct, 1952 - No. 43, Dec, 1956

1-Crandall-c; Cuidera a-1-43i	64	192	398	700
2	33	99	174	300
3-5,10-Crandall-c/a	29	87	153	265
6-Crandall-a	26	78	136	235
7-9	22	66	116	200
11-20	17	51	88	150
21-31,33,35-43: 41-1st S.A. issue	14	42	72	125
32-Nuclear attack-c/story "Atomic Rocket Assault"	17	51	88	150
34-Crandall-a	15	45	77	135

G. I. COMBAT (See DC Special Series #22)
National Periodical Publ./DC Comics: No. 44, Jan, 1957 - No. 288, Mar, 1987

44-Grey tone-c	47	141	376	675
45	27	81	188	335
46-50	21	63	146	260
51-Grey tone-c	21	63	148	265
52-54,59,60	17	51	118	210
55-minor Sgt. Rock prototype by Finger	18	54	126	225
56-Sgt. Rock prototype by Kanigher/Kubert	21	63	146	260
57,58-Pre-Sgt. Rock Easy Co. stories	20	60	140	250
61-65,69-74	13	39	94	160

66-Pre-Sgt. Rock Easy Co. story	18	54	126	225
67-1st Tank Killer	20	60	140	250
68-(1/59) Introduces "The Rock", Sgt. Rock prototype by Kanigher/Kubert; once considered his actual 1st app. (see Our Army at War #82,83)	47	141	376	675
75-80: 75-Greytone-c begin, end #109	15	45	105	180
81,82,84-86	12	36	84	140
83-1st Big Al, Little Al, & Charlie Cigar	14	42	100	170
87-1st Haunted Tank; series begins	47	141	376	675
88-2nd Haunted Tank	18	54	129	230
89,90: 90-Last 10¢ issue	12	36	84	140
91-1st Haunted Tank-c	14	42	102	175
92-99	9	27	65	110
100,108: 108-1st Sgt. Rock x-over	10	30	73	125
101-107,109: 109-Grey tone-c	8	24	56	90
110-112,115-120	6	18	40	65
113-Grey tone-c	6	18	45	75
114-Origin Haunted Tank	12	36	88	150
121-136: 121-1st app. Sgt. Rock's father. 136-Last 12¢ issue	4	12	29	45
137,139,140	3	10	23	35
138-Intro. The Losers (Capt. Storm, Gunner/Sarge, Johnny Cloud) in Haunted Tank (10-11/69)	8	24	60	100
141-143	2	6	15	22
144-148 (68pgs.)	3	9	20	22
149,151-154 (52 pgs.): 151-Capt. Storm story. 151,153-Medal of Honor series by Maurer	2	6	15	22
150- (52 pgs.) Ice Cream Soldier story (tells how he got his name); Death of Haunted Tank-c/s	3	9	20	30
155-167,169,170,200	2	6	9	12
168-Neal Adams-c	2	6	12	18
171-199	1	4	7	10
201,202 ($1.00 size) Neal Adams-c	2	6	11	15
203-210 ($1.00 size)	2	6	9	12
211-230 ($1.00 size)	1	3	6	9
231-259 ($1.00 size).232-Origin Kana the Ninja. 244-Death of Slim Stryker; 1st app. The Mercenaries. 246-(76 pgs., $1.50)-30th Anniversary issue.	2	6		8
257-Intro. Stuart's Raiders	2	6		8
260-281: 260-Begin $1.25, 52 pg. issues, end #281. 264-Intro Sgt. Bullet; origin Kana. 269-Intro. The Bravos of Vietnam. 274-Cameo of Monitor from Crisis on Infinite Earths x-over				5.00
282-288 (75¢): 282-New advs. begin				5.00

NOTE: **N. Adams** c-168, 201, 202. **Check** a-168, 173. **Drucker** a-48, 61, 63, 66, 71, 72, 76, 140, 141, 144, 147, 148, 153. **Evans** a-135, 138, 158, 164, 166, 201, 202, 204, 205, 215, 25 Giffen a-281. **Glanzman** a-most issues. **Kubert/Heath** a-most issues; **Kubert** covers most issues. **Morrow** a-159-161(2 pgs.). **Redondo** a-189, 240i, 243i. **Sekowsky** a-162p. **Severin** a-147, 15 154. **Simonson** c-169. **Thorne** a-152, 156. **Wildey** a-153. Johnny Cloud app.-112, 115, 120. Mike Marie app.-123, 132, 200. Sgt. Rock app.-111-113, 115, 120, 125, 141, 146, 147, 149, 200. US Stevens by **Glanzman**-145, 150-153, 157. **Grandenetti** c-44-48.

GIDGET (TV)
Dell Publishing Co.: Apr, 1966 - No. 2, Dec, 1966

1-Sally Field photo-c	9	27	63	120
2	6	18	42	80

GIFT (See The Crusaders)

GIFT COMICS
Fawcett Publications: 1942 - No. 4, 1949 (50¢/25¢, 324 pgs./152 pgs.)

1-Captain Marvel, Bulletman, Golden Arrow, Ibis the Invincible, Mr. Scarlet, & Spy Smasher begin; not rebound, remaindered comics, printed at same time as originals; 50¢-c & 324 pgs. begin, end #3.	255	765	1591	2800
2-Commando Yank, Phantom Eagle, others app.	159	477	994	1750
3	109	327	682	1200
4-(25¢, 152 pgs.)-The Marvel Family, Captain Marvel, etc.; each issue can vary in contents	68	204	426	750

GIFTS FROM SANTA (See March of Comics No. 137)

GIFTS OF THE NIGHT
DC Comics (Vertigo): Feb, 1999 - No. 4, May, 1999 ($2.95, limited series)

1-4-Bolton-c/a; Chadwick-s				3.00

Giggle Comics #1 © ACG

G.I. Jane #1 © Stanhall

G.I. Joe #1 © Hasbro

	GD2.0	FN6.0	VF8.0	NM9.4

GIGGLE COMICS (Spencer Spook No. 100) (Also see Ha Ha Comics)
Preston No.1-63/American Comics Group No. 64 on; Oct, 1943 - No. 99, Jan-Feb, 1955

	GD2.0	FN6.0	VF8.0	NM9.4
1-Funny animal	33	99	174	300
2	16	48	83	140
3-5: Ken Hultgren-a begins?	12	36	61	100
6-10: 9-1st Superkatt (6/44)	10	30	55	80
11-20	8	24	42	60
21-40: 32-Patriotic-c. 37,61-X-Mas-c. 39-St. Valentine's Day-c	7	21	36	50
41-54,56-59,61-99: 95-Spencer Spook begins?	6	18	29	40
55,60-Milt Gross-a	7	21	36	50

G-I IN BATTLE (G-I No. 1 only)
Ajax-Farrell Publ./Four Star: Aug, 1952 - No. 9, July, 1953; Mar, 1957 - No. 6, May, 1958

	GD2.0	FN6.0	VF8.0	NM9.4
1	11	33	55	90
2	6	18	32	45
3-9	6	18	29	40
Annual 1(1952, 25¢, 100 pgs.)	25	75	133	230
1(1957-Ajax)	7	21	36	50
2-6	5	15	24	32

G. I. JANE
Stanhall/Merit No. 11: May, 1953 - No. 11, Mar, 1955 (Misdated 3/54)

	GD2.0	FN6.0	VF8.0	NM9.4
1-PX Pete begins; Bill Williams-c/a	13	39	66	110
2-7(5/54)	7	21	38	55
8-10(12/54, Stanhall)	6	18	32	45
11 (3/55, Merit)	6	18	29	40

G. I. JOE (Also see Advs. of…, Showcase #53, 54 & The Yardbirds)
Ziff-Davis Publ. Co. (Korean War): No. 10, 1950; No. 11, 4-5/51 - No. 51, 6/55.: 10-14,6-17?)

	GD2.0	FN6.0	VF8.0	NM9.4
10(#1, 1950)-Saunders painted-c begin	15	45	77	135
11-14(#2-5, 10/51): 11-New logo. 12-New logo	10	30	55	85
12#6(12/51)-17-(11/52; Last 52 pgs.?)	10	30	55	80
18-(25¢, 100 pg. Giant, 12-1/52-53)	23	69	121	210
19-30: 20-22,24,28-31-The Yardbirds app.	8	24	45	65
31-47,49-51	8	24	42	60
48-Atom bomb story	8	24	45	65

NOTE: Powell a-V2#7, 8, 11. Norman Saunders painted c-10-14, V2#6-14, 26, 30, 31, 35, 38, 39. Iuska a-7. Bondage c-29, 35, 38.

G. I. JOE (America's Movable Fighting Man)
Custom Comics: 1967 (5-1/8x8-3/8", 36 pgs.)

	GD2.0	FN6.0	VF8.0	NM9.4
n-Schaffenberger-a; based on Hasbro toy	3	10	23	35

G.I. JOE
Dark Horse Comics: Dec, 1995 - No. 4, Apr, 1996 ($1.95, limited series)

1-4: Mike W. Barr scripts. 1,2-Miller-a. 3-Simonson-c				3.00

G.I. JOE
Dark Horse Comics: V2#1, June, 1996 - V2#4, Sept, 1996 ($2.50)

V2#1-4: Mike W. Barr scripts. 4-Painted-c				3.00

G.I. JOE
Image Comics: 2001 - Present ($2.95)

1-Campbell-c; back-c painted by Beck				6.00
1-2nd printing with front & back covers switched				4.00
2				3.00

G. I. JOE AND THE TRANSFORMERS
Marvel Comics Group: Jan, 1987 - No. 4, Apr, 1987 (Limited series)

1-4				4.00

G. I. JOE, A REAL AMERICAN HERO (…Starring Snake-Eyes on-c #135 on)
Marvel Comics Group: June, 1982 - No. 155, Dec, 1994

	GD2.0	FN6.0	VF8.0	NM9.4
1-Printed on Baxter paper; based on Hasbro toy	2	6	11	15
2-Printed on reg. paper	2	6	11	15
3-10	1	4	7	10
11-20: 11-Intro Airborne	1	3	6	8
21-1st Storm Shadow	1	4	7	10
2,26,27: 26,27-Origin Snake-Eyes parts 1 & 2	1	3	5	7

	GD2.0	FN6.0	VF8.0	NM9.4
23-25,28-30,60: 60-Todd McFarlane-a				5.00
31-59,61-90: 33-New headquarters				3.00
91,92,94-99				4.00
93-Snake-Eyes' face first revealed	1	4	7	10
100,135-142: 135-138-($1.75)-Bagged w/trading card. 139-142-New Transformers app.				6.00
101-134: 110-1st Ron Garney-a				4.00
143-149: 144-Origin Snake-Eyes				5.00
150-Low print thru #155	2	6	10	14
151-154	1	4	9	12
155-Last issue	2	6	11	16
All 2nd printings				2.25
Special Treasury Edition (1982)-r/#1	2	6	13	20
Yearbook 1-4: (3/85-3/88)-r/#1; Golden-c. 2-Golden-c/a				4.00

NOTE: Garney a(p)-110. Golden c-23, 29, 34, 36. Heath a-24. Rogers a(p)-75, 77-82, 84, 86; c-77.

G. I. JOE COMICS MAGAZINE
Marvel Comics Group: Dec, 1986 - No. 13, 1988 ($1.50, digest-size)

	GD2.0	FN6.0	VF8.0	NM9.4
1-13: G.I. Joe-r	1	3	6	8

G.I. JOE EUROPEAN MISSIONS (Action Force in indicia)
Marvel Comics Ltd. (British): Jun, 1988 - No. 15, Dec, 1989 ($1.50/$1.75)

1-15: Reprints Action Force				3.00

G. I. JOE ORDER OF BATTLE, THE
Marvel Comics Group: Dec, 1986 - No. 4, Mar, 1987 (limited series)

1-4				4.00

G. I. JOE SPECIAL MISSIONS (Indicia title: Special Missions)
Marvel Comics Group: Oct, 1986 - No. 28, Dec, 1989 ($1.00)

1-20				3.00
21-28				4.00

G. I. JUNIORS (See Harvey Hits No. 86,91,95,98,101,104,107,110,112,114,116,118,120,122)

GILGAMESH II
DC Comics: 1989 - No. 4, 1989 ($3.95, limited series, prestige format, mature)

1-4: Starlin-c/a/scripts				4.00

GIL THORP
Dell Publishing Co.: May-July, 1963

	GD2.0	FN6.0	VF8.0	NM9.4
1-Canniffish-a	4	12	25	38

GINGER
Archie Publications: 1951 - No. 10, Summer, 1954

	GD2.0	FN6.0	VF8.0	NM9.4
1-Teenage humor	14	42	72	120
2-(1952)	9	27	49	70
3-6: 6-(Sum/53)	7	21	36	50
7-10-Katy Keene app.	9	27	51	75

GINGER FOX (Also see The World of Ginger Fox)
Comico: Sept, 1988 - No. 4, Dec, 1988 ($1.75, limited series)

1-4: Part photo-c on all				2.25

G.I. R.A.M.B.O.T.
Wonder Color Comics/Pied Piper #2: Apr, 1987 - No. 2? ($1.95)

1,2: 2-Exist?				2.00

GIRL
DC Comics (Vertigo Verite): Jul, 1996 - No. 3, 1996 ($2.50, lim. series, mature)

1-3: Peter Milligan scripts; Fegredo-c/a				2.50

GIRL COMICS (Becomes Girl Confessions No. 13 on)
Marvel/Atlas Comics(CnPC): Oct, 1949 - No. 12, Jan, 1952 (#1-4: 52 pgs.)

	GD2.0	FN6.0	VF8.0	NM9.4
1-Photo-c	22	66	116	200
2-Kubert-a; photo-c	13	39	66	110
3-Everett-a; Liz Taylor photo-c	20	60	105	175
4-11: 4-Photo-c. 10-12-Sol Brodsky-c	10	30	55	80
12-Krigstein-a; Al Hartley-c	10	30	55	85

GIRL CONFESSIONS (Formerly Girl Comics)
Atlas Comics (CnPC/ZPC): No. 13, Mar, 1952 - No. 35, Aug, 1954

	GD2.0	FN6.0	VF8.0	NM9.4
13-Everett-a	12	36	61	100
14,15,19,20	8	24	45	65

Girls' Love Stories #1 © DC

The Girl Who Would Be Death #4 © DC

Gizmo #1 © MS

	GD2.0	FN6.0	VF8.0	NM9.4
16-18-Everett-a	10	30	55	80
21-35: Robinson-a	6	18	32	45

GIRL CRAZY
Dark Horse Comics: May, 1996 - No. 3, July, 1996 ($2.95, B&W, limited series)

1-3: Gilbert Hernandez-a/scripts.				3.00

GIRL FROM U.N.C.L.E., THE (TV) (Also see The Man From…)
Gold Key: Jan, 1967 - No. 5, Oct, 1967

1-McWilliams-a; Stephanie Powers photo front/back-c & pin-ups (no ads, 12¢)	9	27	63	120
2-5-Leonard Swift-Courier No. 5	6	18	42	80

GIRLS' FUN & FASHION MAGAZINE (Formerly Polly Pigtails)
Parents' Magazine Institute: V5#44, Jan, 1950 - V5#48, Sept., 1950

V5#44	5	15	25	35
45-48	4	12	19	25

GIRLS IN LOVE
Fawcett Publications: May, 1950 - No. 2, July, 1950

1-Photo-c	12	36	61	100
2-Photo-c	10	30	55	80

GIRLS IN LOVE (Formerly G. I. Sweethearts No. 45)
Quality Comics Group: No. 46, Sept, 1955 - No. 57, Dec, 1956

46	8	24	42	60
47-53,55,56	6	18	29	40
54- 'Commie' story	6	18	32	45
57-Matt Baker-c/a	9	27	49	70

GIRLS IN WHITE (See Harvey Comics Hits No. 58)

GIRLS' LIFE (Patsy Walker's Own Magazine For Girls!)
Atlas Comics (BFP): Jan, 1954 - No. 6, Nov, 1954

1	11	33	55	90
2-Al Hartley-c	7	21	36	50
3-6	6	18	29	40

GIRLS' LOVE STORIES
National Comics(Signal Publ. 9-65/Arleigh No. 83-117): Aug-Sept, 1949 - No. 180, Nov-Dec, 1973 (No. 1-13: 52 pgs.)

1-Toth, Kinstler-a, 8 pgs. each; photo-c	55	165	330	575
2-Kinstler-a?	32	96	171	295
3-10: 1-9-Photo-c. 7-Infantino-c(p)	22	66	116	195
11-20	17	51	88	150
21-33: 21-Kinstler-a. 33-Last pre-code (1-2/55)	11	33	55	90
34-50	9	27	49	70
51-70	5	15	38	60
71-99: 83-Last 10¢ issue	4	12	26	40
100	4	12	29	45
101-146: 113-117-April O'Day app.	3	9	19	28
147-151- "Confessions" serial. 150-Wood-a	3	9	19	28
152-160,171-179	2	6	12	18
161-170 (52 pgs.)	3	9	21	32
180 Last issue	3	9	19	28

GIRLS' ROMANCES
National Periodical Publ.(Signal Publ. No. 7-79/Arleigh No. 84): Feb-Mar, 1950 - No. 160, Oct, 1971 (No. 1-11: 52 pgs.)

1-Photo-c	53	159	318	560
2-Photo-c; Toth-a	31	93	165	285
3-10: 3-6-Photo-c	22	66	116	195
11,12,14-20	15	45	77	135
13-Toth-c	16	48	83	140
21-31: 31-Last pre-code (2-3/55)	10	30	55	85
32-50	6	18	40	65
51-99: 80-Last 10¢ issue	4	12	26	40
100	4	12	29	45
101-108,110-120	3	9	19	28
109-Beatles-c/story	12	36	88	150
121-133,135-140	2	6	15	22
134-Neal Adams-c (splash pg. is same as-c)	4	12	29	45
141-158	2	6	12	18
159,160-52 pgs.	3	9	21	32

	GD2.0	FN6.0	VF8.0	NM9.4

GIRL WHO WOULD BE DEATH, THE
DC Comics (Vertigo): Dec, 1998 - No. 4, March, 1999 ($2.50, lim. series)

1-4-Kiernan-s/Ormston-a				2.50

G. I. SWEETHEARTS (Formerly Diary Loves; Girls In Love #46 on)
Quality Comics Group: No. 32, June, 1953 - No. 45, May, 1955

32	8	24	42	60
33-45: 44-Last pre-code (3/55)	6	18	29	40

G.I. TALES (Formerly Sgt. Barney Barker No. 1-3)
Atlas Comics (MCI): No. 4, Feb, 1957 - No. 6, July, 1957

4-Severin-a(4)	8	24	45	65
5	6	18	32	45
6-Orlando, Powell, & Woodbridge-a	7	21	36	50

GIVE ME LIBERTY (Also see Dark Horse Presents Fifth Anniversary Special, Dark Horse Presents #100-4, Happy Birthday Martha Washington, Martha Washington Goes to War, Martha Washington Stranded In Space & San Diego Comicon Comics #2)
Dark Horse Comics: June, 1990 - No. 4, 1991 ($4.95, limited series, 52 pgs.)

1-4: 1st app. Martha Washington; Frank Miller scripts, Dave Gibbons-c/a in all.				5.00

G. I. WAR BRIDES
Superior Publishers Ltd.: Apr, 1954 - No. 8, June, 1955

1	8	24	45	65
2	5	15	25	35
3-8: 4-Kamenesque-a; lingerie panels	5	15	23	30

G. I. WAR TALES
National Periodical Publications: Mar-Apr, 1973 - No. 4, Oct-Nov, 1973

1-Reprints in all; dinosaur-c/s	3	9	17	25
2-N. Adams-a(r)	2	6	12	18
3,4: 4-Krigstein-a(r)	2	6	11	16

NOTE: **Drucker** a-3r, 4r. **Heath** a-4r. **Kubert** a-2, 3; c-4r.

GIZMO (Also see Domino Chance)
Chance Ent.: May-June, 1985 (B&W, one-shot)

1				4.00

GIZMO
Mirage Studios: 1986 - No. 6, July, 1987 ($1.50, B&W)

1-6				2.50

GLADSTONE COMIC ALBUM
Gladstone: 1987 - No. 28, 1990 ($5.95/$9.95, 8-1/2x11")(All Mickey Mouse albums are by Gottfredson)

1-10: 1-Uncle Scrooge; Barks-r; Beck-c. 2-Donald Duck. 3-Mickey Mouse-r by Gottfredson. 4-Uncle Scrooge; r/F.C. #456 by Barks w/ unedited story. 5-Donald Duck Advs.; r/F.C. #199. 6-Uncle Scrooge-r by Barks. 7-Donald Duck-r by Barks. 8-Mickey Mouse-r. 9-Bambi; r/F.C. #186? 10-Donald Duck Advs.; r/F.C. #275	1	4	7	10
11-20: 11-Uncle Scrooge; r/U.S. #4. 12-Donald And Daisy; r/F.C. #1055, WDC&S. 13-Donald Duck Advs.; r/F.C. #408. 14-Uncle Scrooge; Barks-r/ U.S #21. 15-Donald And Gladstone; Barks-r. 16-Donald Duck Advs.; r/F.C. #238. 17-Mickey Mouse (The World of Tomorrow, The Pirate Ghost Ship). 18-Donald Duck and the Junior Woodchucks; Barks-r. 19-Uncle Scrooge; r/U.S. #12; Rosa-c. 20-Uncle Scrooge; r/F.C. #386; Barks-c/a(r)	1	4	7	10
21-25: 21-Donald Duck Family; Barks-c/a(r). 22-Mickey Mouse strip-r. 23-Donald Duck; Barks-r/D.D. #26 w/unedited story. 24-Uncle Scrooge; Barks-r; Rosa-c. 25-D. Duck; Barks-c/a-r/F.C. #367	1	4	7	10
26-28: All have $9.95-c. 26-Mickey and Donald; Gottfredson-c/a(r). 27-Donald Duck; r/WDC&S by Barks; Barks painted-c. 28-Uncle Scrooge & Donald Duck; Rosa-c/a (4 stories)	1	4	7	10
Special 1-7: 1 ('89-'90, $9.95/13.95)-1-Donald Duck Finds Pirate Gold; r/F.C. #9 2 ('89, $8.95)-Uncle Scrooge and Donald Duck; Barks-r/Uncle Scrooge #5; Rosa-c. 3 ('89, $8.95)-Mickey Mouse strip-r. 4 ('89, $11.95)-Uncle Scrooge; Rosa-c/a-r/Son of the Sun from U.S. #219 plus Barks-r/U.S. 5 ('90, $11.95)-Donald Duck Advs.; Barks-r/F.C. #282 & 422 plus Barks painted-c. 6 ('90, $12.95)-Uncle Scrooge; Barks-c/a-r/Uncle Scrooge. 7 ('90, $13.95)-Mickey Mouse; Gottfredson strip-r	2	6	10	14

Glamorous Romances #41 © ACE

Glory #6 © Rob Liefeld

Godzilla #12 © Toho Co. Ltd.

	GD2.0	FN6.0	VF8.0	NM9.4

GLADSTONE COMIC ALBUM (2nd Series)(Also see The Original Dick Tracy)
Gladstone Publishing: 1990 ($5.95, 8-1/2 x 11," stiff-c, 52 pgs.)

1,2-The Original Dick Tracy. 2-Origin of the 2-way wrist radio				6.00
3-D Tracy Meets the Mole-r by Gould ($6.95).	1	3	6	8

(Photo-c 68-90)

GLAMOROUS ROMANCES (Formerly Dotty)
Ace Magazines (A. A. Wyn): No. 41, July, 1949 - No. 90, Oct, 1956
(Photo-c 68-90)

41-Dotty app.	8	24	45	65
42-72,74-80: 44-Begin 52 pg. issues. 45,50-61-Painted-c. 80-Last pre-code				
(2/55)	6	18	29	40
73-L.B. Cole-r/All Love #27	6	18	32	45
81-90	5	15	25	35

GLOBAL FORCE
Silverline Comics: 1987 - No. 2 ($1.95)

1,2				2.25

GLOOM COOKIE
SLG Publishing: June, 1999 - Present ($2.95, B&W)

1-10-Serena Valentino-s/Ted Naifeh-a. 10-Gebbia-a				3.00

GLORY
Image Comics (Extreme Studios)/Maximum Press: Mar, 1995 - No. 22, Apr, 1997 ($2.50)

0-Deodato-c/a, 1-(3/95)-Deodato-a				2.50
1A-Variant-c				4.00
2-11,13-22: 4-Variant-c by Quesada & Palmiotti. 5-Bagged w/Youngblood gaming card. 7,8-Deodato-c/a(p). 8-Babewatch x-over. 9-Cruz-c; Extreme Destroyer Pt. 5; polybagged w/card. 10-Angela/c/app. 11-Deodato-c.				2.50
12-($3.50)-Photo-c				3.50
Trade Paperback (1995, $9.95)-r/#1-4				10.00

GLORY
Awesome Comics: Mar, 1999 ($2.50)

0-Liefeld-c; story and sketch pages				2.50

GLORY
Avatar Press: Sept, 2001 ($1.99)
Preview-B&W pages and cover art; Alan Moore-s

				2.00

GLORY & FRIENDS BIKINI FEST
Image Comics (Extreme): Sept, 1995 - No. 2, Oct, 1995 ($2.50, limited series)

1,2: 1-Photo-c; centerfold photo; pin-ups				2.50

GLORY & FRIENDS CHRISTMAS SPECIAL
Image Comics (Extreme Studios): Dec, 1995 ($2.50, one-shot)

1-Deodato-c				2.50

GLORY & FRIENDS LINGERIE SPECIAL
Image Comics (Extreme Studios): Sept, 1995 ($2.95, one-shot)

1-Pin-ups w/photos; photo-c; varant-c exists				3.00

GLORY/ANGELA: ANGELS IN HELL (See Angela/Glory: Rage of Angels)
Image Comics (Extreme): Apr, 1996 ($2.50, one-shot)

1-Flip book w/Darkchylde #1				2.50

GLORY/AVENGELYNE
Image Comics (Extreme Studios): Oct, 1995 ($3.95, one-shot)

1-Chromium-c, 1-Regular-c				4.00

GLORY/CELESTINE: DARK ANGEL
Image Comics/Maximum Press (Extreme Studios): Sept, 1996 - No. 3, Nov, 1996 ($2.50, limited series)

1-3				2.50

GNOME MOBILE, THE (See Movie Comics)

GOBBLEDYGOOK
Mirage Studios: 1984 - No. 2, 1984 (B&W)(1st Mirage comics, published at same time)

1-(24 pgs.)-1st Teenage Mutant Ninja Turtles	20	60	140	250
2-(24 pgs.)	19	57	132	235

GOBBLEDYGOOK
Mirage Studios: Dec, 1986 ($3.50, B&W, one-shot, 100 pgs.)

1-New 8 pg. TMNT story plus a Donatello/Michaelangelo 7 pg. story & a Gizmo story; Corben-i(r)/TMNT #7				5.00

GOBLIN, THE
Warren Publishing Co.: June, 1982 - No. 3, Dec, 1982 ($2.25, B&W magazine with 8 pg. color insert comic in all)

1-The Gremlin app. Philo Photon & the Troll Patrol, Micro-Buccaneers & Wizard Wormglow begin & app. in all. Tin Man app. Golden-a(p). Nebres-c/a in all				
		2	6	13	20
2,3: 2-1st Hobgoblin. 3-Tin Man app.		2	6	9	12

NOTE: **Bermejo** a-1-3. **Elias** a-1-3. **Laxamana** a-1-3. **Nino** a-3.

GODDESS
DC Comics (Vertigo): June, 1995 - No. 8, Jan, 1996 ($2.95, limited series)

1-Garth Ennis scripts; Phil Winslade-c/a in all				5.00
2-8				4.00

GODFATHERS, THE (See The Crusaders)

GOD IS
Spire Christian Comics (Fleming H. Revell Co.): 1973, 1975 (35-49¢)

nn-By Al Hartley	1	3	6	8

GODS AND TULIPS
Westhampton House: Aug, 1999 ($3.00, B&W, one-shot for the CBLDF)

nn-Neil Gaiman speeches; Kaluta-c				3.00

GOD'S COUNTRY (Also see Marvel Comics Presents)
Marvel Comics: 1994 ($6.95)

nn-P. Craig Russell-a; Colossus story; r/Marvel Comics Presents #10-17				7.00

GODS FOR HIRE
Hot Comics: Dec, 1986 - No. 3 ($1.50)

1-3: Barry Crain-c/a(p)				2.25

GOD'S HEROES IN AMERICA
Catechetical Guild Educational Society: 1956 (nn) (25¢/35¢, 68 pgs.)

307	4	10	15	20

GOD'S SMUGGLER (Religious)
Spire Christian Comics/Fleming H. Revell Co.: 1972 (39¢/40¢)

1-Two variations exist	1	3	6	8

GODWHEEL
Malibu Comics (Ultraverse): No. 0, Jan, 1995 - No. 3, Feb, 1995 ($2.50, limited series)

0-3: 0-Flip-c. 1-1st app. of Primevil; Thor cameo (1 panel). 3-Perez-a in Chapter 3, Thor app.				2.50

GODZILLA (Movie)
Marvel Comics : August, 1977 - No. 24, July, 1979 (Based on movie series)

1-(Regular 30¢ edition)-Mooney-i	2	6	13	20
1-(35¢-c variant, limited distribution)	3	9	20	30
2-(Regular 30¢ edition)-Tuska-i.	1	4	7	10
2,3-(35¢-c variant, limited distribution)	2	6	11	15
3-(30¢-c) Champions app.(w/o Ghost Rider)	2	6	9	12
4-10: 4,5-Sutton-a.	1	3	6	9
11-23: 14-Shield app. 20-F.F. app. 21,22-Devil Dinosaur app.				
	1	3	6	8
24-Last issue	1	3	6	9

GODZILLA (Movie)
Dark Horse Comics: May, 1988 - No. 6, 1988 ($1.95, B&W, limited series) (Based on movie series)

1				6.00
2-6				4.00
...Collection (1990, $10.95)-r/1-6 with new-c				11.00
...Color Special 1 (Sum, 1992, $3.50, color, 44 pgs.)-Arthur Adams wrap-around-c/a & part scripts				5.00
...King Of The Monsters Special (8/87, $1.50)-Origin; Bissette-c/a				4.00
...Vs. Barkley nn (12/93, $2.95, color)-Dorman painted-c				4.00

GODZILLA (King of the Monsters) (Movie)
Dark Horse Comics: May, 1995 - No. 16, Sept, 1996 ($2.50) (Based on movies)

0-16: 0-r/Dark Horse Comics #10,11. 1-3-Kevin Maguire scripts.				

Go Girl! #4 © Trina Robbins

Go-Go #3 © CC

The Golden Age #2 © DC

3-8-Art Adams-c				4.00
...Vs. Hero Zero ($2.50)				3.00

GOG (VILLAINS) (See Kingdom Come)
DC Comics: Feb, 1998 ($1.95, one-shot)

1-Waid-s/Ordway-a(p)/Pearson-c				3.00

GO GIRL!
Image Comics: Aug, 2000 - Present ($3.50, B&W, quarterly)

1-5-Trina Robbins-s/Anne Timmons-a; pin-up gallery				3.50

GO-GO
Charlton Comics: June, 1966 - No. 9, Oct, 1967

	GD2.0	FN6.0	VF8.0	NM9.4
1-Miss Bikini Luv begins w/Jim Aparo's 1st published work; Rolling Stones, Beatles, Elvis, Sonny & Cher, Bob Dylan, Sinatra, parody; Herman's Hermits pin-ups; D'Agostino-c/a in #1-8	7	21	53	85
2-Ringo Starr, David McCallum & Beatles photos on cover; Beatles story and photos	7	21	53	85
3,4: 3-Blooperman begins, ends #6; 1 pg. Batman & Robin satire; photo pin-ups Lovin' Spoonful & The Byrds	4	12	29	45
5,7,9: 5 (2/67)-Super Hero & TV satire by Jim Aparo & Grass Green begins. 6-8-Aparo-a. 7-Photo of Brian Wilson of Beach Boys on-c & Beach Boys photo inside f/b-c. 9-Aparo-c/a	4	12	29	45
6-Parody of JLA & DC heroes vs. Marvel heroes; Aparo-a; Elvis parody; Petula Clark photo-c	5	15	34	55
8-Monkees photo on-c & photo inside f/b-c	5	15	38	60

GO-GO AND ANIMAL (See Tippy's Friends...)

GOING STEADY (Formerly Teen-Age Temptations)
St. John Publ. Co.: No. 10, Dec, 1954 - No. 13, June, 1955; No. 14, Oct, 1955

10(1954)-Matt Baker-c/a	21	63	110	185
11(2/55, last precode), 12(4/55)-Baker-c	12	36	61	100
13(6/55)-Baker-c/a	15	45	77	130
14(10/55)-Matt Baker-c/a, 25 pgs.	17	51	88	150

GOING STEADY (Formerly Personal Love)
Prize Publications/Headline: V3#3, Feb, 1960 - V3#6, Aug, 1960; V4#1, Sept-Oct, 1960

V3#3-6, V4#1	3	9	17	25

GOING STEADY WITH BETTY (Becomes Betty & Her Steady No. 2)
Avon Periodicals: Nov-Dec, 1949

1	15	45	77	130

GOLDEN AGE, THE
DC Comics (Elseworlds): 1993 - No. 4, 1994 ($4.95, limited series)

1-4: James Robinson scripts; Paul Smith-c/a; gold foil embossed-c				6.00
Trade Paperback (1995, $19.95)				20.00

GOLDEN AGE SECRET FILES
DC Comics: Feb, 2001 ($4.95, one-shot)

1-Origins and profiles of JSA members and other G.A. heroes; Lark-c				5.00

GOLDEN ARROW (See Fawcett Miniatures, Mighty Midget & Whiz Comics)
GOLDEN ARROW (...Western No. 6)
Fawcett Publications: Spring, 1942 - No. 6, Spring, 1947 (68 pgs.)

1-Golden Arrow begins	84	253	525	925
2-(1943)	42	125	252	440
3-5: 3-(Win/45-46). 4-(Spr/46). 5-(Fall/46)	34	101	182	315
6-Krigstein-a	36	108	194	335

GOLDEN COMICS DIGEST
Gold Key: May, 1969 - No. 48, Jan, 1976
NOTE: *Whitman editions exist of many titles and are generally valued the same.*

1-Tom & Jerry, Woody Woodpecker, Bugs Bunny	4	12	30	50
2-Hanna-Barbera TV Fun Favorites; Space Ghost, Flintstones, Atom Ant, Jetsons, Yogi Bear, Banana Splits, others app.	6	18	45	75
3-Tom & Jerry, Woody Woodpecker	2	6	15	22
4-Tarzan; Manning & Marsh-a	4	12	29	45
5,8-Tom & Jerry, W. Woodpecker, Bugs Bunny	2	6	13	20
6-Bugs Bunny	2	6	13	20
7-Hanna-Barbera TV Fun Favorites	4	12	30	50
9-Tarzan	4	12	29	45

	GD2.0	FN6.0	VF8.0	NM9.4
10,12-17: 10-Bugs Bunny. 12-Tom & Jerry, Bugs Bunny, W. Woodpecker Journey to the Sun. 13-Tom & Jerry. 14-Bugs Bunny Fun Packed Funnies. 15-Tom & Jerry, Woody Woodpecker, Bugs Bunny. 16-Woody Woodpecker Cartoon Special. 17-Bugs Bunny	2	6	13	20
11-Hanna-Barbera TV Fun Favorites	4	12	30	50
18-Tom & Jerry; Barney Bear-r by Barks	2	6	15	22
19-Little Lulu	4	12	25	38
20-22: 20-Woody Woodpecker Falltime Funtime. 21-Bugs Bunny Showtime. 22-Tom & Jerry Winter Wingding	2	6	13	20
23-Little Lulu & Tubby Fun Fling	4	12	25	38
24-26,28: 24-Woody Woodpecker Fun Festival. 25-Tom & Jerry. 26-Bugs Bunny Halloween Hulla-Boo-Loo; Dr. Spektor article, also #25. 28-Tom & Jerry	2	6	12	18
27-Little Lulu & Tubby in Hawaii	3	10	23	35
29-Little Lulu & Tubby	3	10	23	35
30-Bugs Bunny Vacation Funnies	2	6	12	18
31-Turok, Son of Stone; r/4-Color #596,656; c-r/#9	4	12	26	40
32-Woody Woodpecker Summer Fun	2	6	12	18
33,36: 33-Little Lulu & Tubby Halloween Fun; Dr. Spektor app. 36-Little Lulu & Her Friends	3	10	23	35
34,35,37-39: 34-Bugs Bunny Winter Funnies. 35-Tom & Jerry Snowtime Funtime. 37-Woody Woodpecker County Fair. 39-Bugs Bunny Summer Fun	2	6	12	18
38-The Pink Panther	2	6	15	22
40,43: 40-Little Lulu & Tubby Trick or Treat; all by Stanley. 43-Little Lulu in Paris	3	10	23	35
41,42,44,47: 41-Tom & Jerry Winter Carnival. 42-Bugs Bunny. 44-Woody Woodpecker Family Fun Festival. 47-Bugs Bunny	2	6	11	16
45-The Pink Panther	2	6	15	22
46-Little Lulu & Tubby	3	9	20	30
48-The Lone Ranger	3	9	17	24

NOTE: *#1-30, 164 pgs.; #31 on, 132 pgs..*

GOLDEN LAD
Spark/Fact & Fiction Publ.: July, 1945 - No. 5, June, 1946 (#4, 5: 52 pgs.)

1-Origin & 1st app. Golden Lad & Swift Arrow; Sandusky and the Senator begins	73	219	455	800
2-Mort Meskin-c/a	39	117	208	360
3,4-Mort Meskin-c/a	35	105	185	320
5-Origin/1st Golden Girl; Shaman & Flame app.	39	117	208	360

NOTE: *All have Robinson, and Roussos art plus Meskin covers and art.*

GOLDEN LEGACY
Fitzgerald Publishing Co.: 1966 - 1972 (Black History) (25¢)

1-Toussaint L'Ouverture (1966), 2-Harriet Tubman (1967), 3-Crispus Attucks & the Minutemen (1967), 4-Benjamin Banneker (1968), 5-Matthew Henson (1969), 6-Alexander Dumas & Family (1969), 7-Frederick Douglass, Part 1 (1969), 8-Frederick Douglass, Part 2 (1970), 9-Robert Smalls (1970), 10-J. Cinque & the Amistad Mutiny (1970), 11-Men in Action: White, Marshall J. Wilkins (1970), 12-Black Cowboys (1972), 13-The Life of Martin Luther King, Jr. (1972), 14-The Life of Alexander Pushkin (1971), 15-Ancient African Kingdoms (1972), 16-Black Inventors (1972) each....	2	6	11	15
1-10,12,13,15,16(1976)-Reprints				6.00

GOLDEN LOVE STORIES (Formerly Golden West Love)
Kirby Publishing Co.: No. 4, April, 1950

4-Powell-a; Glenn Ford/Janet Leigh photo-c	16	48	83	140

GOLDEN PICTURE CLASSIC, A
Western Publishing Co. (Simon & Schuster): 1956-1957 (Text stories w/illustrations in color; 100 pgs. each)

CL-401: Treasure Island	10	30	55	80
CL-402,403: 402: Tom Sawyer. 403: Black Beauty	8	24	45	65
CL-404, 405: CL-404: Little Women. CL-405: Heidi	8	24	45	65
CL-406: Ben Hur	6	18	32	45
CL-407: Around the World in 80 Days	6	18	32	45
CL-408: Sherlock Holmes	7	21	38	55
CL-409: The Three Musketeers	6	18	32	45
CL-410: The Merry Advs. of Robin Hood	6	18	32	45
CL-411,412: 411: Hans Brinker. 412: The Count of Monte Cristo	7	21	38	55

(Both soft & hardcover editions are valued the same)
NOTE: *Recent research has uncovered new information. Apparently #1-6 were issued in 1956 and #7-12 in 1957. But they can be found in five different series listings: CL-1 to CL-12 (softbound); CL-*

Gomer Pyle #1 © GK

Gon Book 3 © Kodansha Ltd.

Good Guys #1 © EEP, L.P.

	GD2.0	FN6.0	VF8.0	NM9.4

401 to CL-412 (also softbound); CL-101 to CL-112 (hardbound); plus two new series discoveries: A Golden Reading Adventure, publ. by Golden Press; edited down to 60 pages and reduced in size to 6x9"; only #s discovered so far are #381 (CL-4), #382 (CL-6) & #387 (CL-3). They have no reorder list and some have covers different from GPC. There have also been found British hardbound editions of GPC with dust jackets. Copies of all five listed series vary from scarce to very rare. Some editions of some series have not yet been found at all.

GOLDEN PICTURE STORY BOOK
Racine Press (Western): Dec, 1961 (50¢, Treasury size, 52 pgs.)
(All are scarce)

ST-1-Huckleberry Hound (TV); Hokey Wolf, Pixie & Dixie, Quick Draw McGraw, Snooper and Blabber, Augie Doggie app.	20	60	140	250
ST-2-Yogi Bear (TV); Snagglepuss, Yakky Doodle, Quick Draw McGraw, Snooper and Blabber, Augie Doggie app.	20	60	140	250
ST-3-Babes in Toyland (Walt Disney's...)-Annette Funicello photo-c	24	72	168	300
ST-4-(...of Disney Ducks)-Walt Disney's Wonderful World of Ducks (Donald Duck, Uncle Scrooge, Donald's Nephews, Grandma Duck, Ludwig Von Drake, & Gyro Gearloose stories)	24	72	168	300

GOLDEN RECORD COMIC (See Amazing Spider-Man #1, Avengers #4, Fantastic Four #1, Journey Into Mystery #83)

GOLDEN STORY BOOKS
Western Printing Co. (Simon & Shuster): 1949 (Heavy covers, digest size, 128 pgs.) (Illustrated text in color)

7-Walt Disney's Mystery in Disneyville, a book-length adventure starring Donald and Nephews, Mickey and Nephews, and with Minnie, Daisy and Goofy. Art by Dick Moores & Manuel Gonzales (scarce)	28	84	160	270
10-Bugs Bunny's Treasure Hunt, a book-length adventure starring Bugs & Porky Pig, with Petunia Pig & Nephew, Cicero. Art by Tom McKimson (scarce)	19	56	105	180

GOLDEN WEST LOVE (Golden Love Stories No. 4)
Kirby Publishing Co.: Sept-Oct, 1949 - No. 3, Feb, 1950 (All 52 pgs.)

1-Powell-a in all; Roussos-a; painted-c	22	66	116	200
2,3-Photo-c	16	48	83	140

GOLDEN WEST RODEO TREASURY (See Dell Giants)

GOLDFISH (See A.K.A. Goldfish)

GOLDILOCKS (See March of Comics No. 1)

GOLD KEY CHAMPION
Gold Key: Mar, 1978 - No. 2, May, 1978 (50¢, 52pgs.)

1,2: 1-Space Family Robinson; half-r. 2-Mighty Samson; half-r	1	3	6	8

GOLD KEY SPOTLIGHT
Gold Key: May, 1976 - No. 11, Feb, 1978

1-Tom, Dick & Harriet	1	3	6	9
2-11: 2-Wacky Advs. of Cracky. 3-Wacky Witch. 4-Tom, Dick & Harriet. 5-Wacky Advs. of Cracky. 6-Dagar the Invincible; Santos-a; origin Demonomicon. 7-Wacky Witch & Greta Ghost 10-O. G. Whiz.11-Tom, Dick & Harriet. 8-The Occult Files of Dr. Spektor, Simbar, Lu-sai; Santos-a. 9-Tragg	1	3	5	7

GOLD MEDAL COMICS
Cambridge House: 1945 (25¢, one-shot, 132 pgs.)

nn-Captain Truth by Fugitani, Crime Detector, The Witch of Salem, Luckyman, others app.	29	87	156	270

GOMER PYLE (TV)
Gold Key: July, 1966 - No. 3, Jan, 1967

1-Photo front/back-c	8	24	56	100
2,3	5	15	35	65

GON
DC Comics (Paradox Press): July, 1996 - No. 4, Oct, 1996; No. 5, 1997 ($5.95, B&W, digest-size, limited series)

1-5: Misadventures of baby dinosaur; 1-Gon again. 2-Gon Again. 3-Gon: Here Today, Gone Tomorrow. 4-Gon: Going, Going...Gon. 5-Gon Swimmin'. Tanaka-c/a/scripts in all.	1	3	6	8

GON COLOR SPECTACULAR
DC Comics (Paradox Press): 1998 ($5.95, square-bound)

nn-Tanaka-c/a/scripts	1	3	6	8

GON ON SAFARI
DC Comics (Paradox Press): 2000 ($7.95, B&W, digest-size)

nn-Tanaka-c/a/scripts	1	3	6	8

GON UNDERGROUND
DC Comics (Paradox Press): 1999 ($7.95, B&W, digest-size)

nn-Tanaka-c/a/scripts	1	3	6	8

GON WILD
DC Comics (Paradox Press): 1997 ($9.95, B&W, digest-size)

nn-Tanaka-c/a/scripts in all. (Rep. Gon #3,4)	1	4	7	10

GOODBYE, MR. CHIPS (See Movie Comics)

GOOD GIRL ART QUARTERLY
AC Comics: Summer, 1990 - No. 15, Spring, 1994 (B&W/color, 52 pgs.)

1,3-15 ($3.50)-All have one new story (often FemForce) & rest reprints by Baker, Ward & other "good girl" artists				4.00
2 ($3.95)				4.00

GOOD GIRL COMICS (Formerly Good Girl Art Quarterly)
AC Comics: No. 16, Summer, 1994 - No. 18, 1995 (B&W)

16-18				4.00

GOOD GUYS, THE
Defiant: Nov, 1993 - No. 9, July, 1994 ($2.50/$3.25/$3.50)

1-($3.50, 52 pgs.)-Glory x-over from Plasm				3.50
2,3,5-9: 9-Pre-Schism issue				2.50
4-($3.25, 52 pgs.)				3.25

GOOD TRIUMPHS OVER EVIL! (Also see Narrative Illustration)
M.C. Gaines: 1943 (12 pgs., 7-1/4"x10", B&W) (not a comic book) (Rare)

nn-A pamphlet, sequel to Narrative Illustration	91	273	568	1000

GOOFY (Disney)(See Dynabrite Comics, Mickey Mouse Magazine V4#7, Walt Disney Showcase #35 & Wheaties)
Dell Publishing Co.: No. 468, May, 1953 - Sept-Nov, 1962

Four Color 468 (#1)	12	36	84	160
Four Color 562,627,658,702,747,802,857	7	21	49	90
Four Color 899,952,987,1053,1094,1149,1201	5	15	34	55
12-308-211(Dell, 9-11/62)	5	15	34	55

GOOFY ADVENTURES
Disney Comics: June, 1990 - No. 17, 1991 ($1.50)

1-17: Most new stories. 3-Joshua Quagmire-a w/free poster. 7-WDC&S-r plus new-a. 9-Gottfredson-r. 14-Super Goof story. 15-All Super Goof issue. 17-Gene Colan-a(p)				3.00

GOOFY ADVENTURE STORY (See Goofy No. 857)

GOOFY COMICS (Companion to Happy Comics)(Not Disney)
Nedor Publ. Co. No. 1-14/Standard No. 14-48: June, 1943 - No. 48, 1953 (Animated Cartoons)

1-Funny animal; Oriolo-c	29	87	156	270
2	15	45	77	135
3-10	12	36	61	100
11-19	10	30	55	80
20-35-Frazetta text illos in all	11	33	55	90
36-48	8	24	42	60

GOOFY SUCCESS STORY (See Goofy No. 702)

GOOSE (Humor magazine)
Cousins Publ. (Fawcett): Sept, 1976 - No. 3, 1976 (75¢, 52 pgs., B&W)

1-Nudity in all	2	6	13	20
2,3: 2-(10/76) Fonz-c/s; Lone Ranger story. 3-Wonder Woman, King Kong, Six Million Dollar Man stories	2	6	10	14

GORDO (See Comics Revue No. 5 & Giant Comics Edition)

GORGO (Based on M.G.M. movie) (See Return of...)
Charlton Comics: May, 1961 - No. 23, Sept, 1965

1-Ditko-a, 22 pgs.	23	69	160	285
2,3-Ditko-c/a	12	36	84	140
4-Ditko-c	7	21	53	85

Gotham Nights #4 © DC

Gravestone #1 © MAL

Great Comics #1 © Novack

	GD2.0	FN6.0	VF8.0	NM9.4
5-11,13-16: 11,13-16-Ditko-a	7	21	50	80
12,17-23: 12-Reptilasaur x-over; Montes/Bache-a-No. 17-23. 20-Giordano-c				
	4	12	26	40
	5	15	34	55

GOSPEL BLIMP, THE
Spire Christian Comics (Fleming H. Revell Co.): 1973,1974 (35¢/39¢, 36 pgs.)

nn	1	3	6	8

G.O.T.H.
Verotik: Dec, 1995 - No. 3, June, 1996 ($2.95, limited series, mature)

1-3: Danzig scripts; Liam Sharpe-a.				3.00

GOTHAM BY GASLIGHT (A Tale of the Batman)(See Batman: Master of...)
DC Comics: 1989 ($3.95, one-shot, squarebound, 52 pgs.)

nn-Mignola/Russell-a; intro by Robert Bloch				4.00

GOTHAM NIGHTS (See Batman: Gotham Nights II)
DC Comics: Mar, 1992 - No. 4, June, 1992 ($1.25, limited series)

1-4: Featuring Batman				2.25

GOTHIC ROMANCES
Atlas/Seaboard Publ.: Dec, 1974 (75¢, B&W, magazine, 76 pgs.)

1-Text w/ illos by N. Adams, Chaykin, Heath (2 pgs. ea.); painted cover (scarce)	8	24	56	90

GOTHIC TALES OF LOVE (Magazine)
Marvel Comics: Apr, 1975 - No. 2, Jun, 1975 (B&W, 76 pgs.)

1,2-painted-c/a (scarce)	6	18	42	70

GOVERNOR & J. J., The (TV)
Gold Key: Feb, 1970 - No. 3, Aug, 1970 (Photo-c)

1	4	12	29	45
2,3	3	9	20	30

GRACKLE, THE
Acclaim Comics: Jan, 1997 - No. 4, Apr, 1997 ($2.95, B&W)

1-4: Mike Baron scripts & Paul Gulacy-c/a. 1-4-Doublecross				3.00

GRAFIK MUSIK
Caliber Press: Nov, 1990 - No. 4, Aug, 1991 ($3.50/$2.50)

1-($3.50, 48 pgs., color) Mike Allred-c/a/scripts-1st app. in color of Frank Einstein (Madman)	2	6	11	15
2-($2.50, 24 pgs., color)	1	3	6	8
3,4-($2.50, 24 pgs., B&W)				6.00

GRANDMA DUCK'S FARM FRIENDS(See Walt Disney's C&S 293 & Wheaties)
Dell Publishing Co.: No. 763, Jan, 1957 - No. 1279, Feb, 1962 (Disney)

Four Color 763 (#1)	7	21	49	90
Four Color 873	5	15	35	60
Four Color 965,1279	4	12	30	50
Four Color 1010,1073,1161-Barks-a; 1073,1161-Barks c/a				
	13	39	91	165

GRAND PRIX (Formerly Hot Rod Racers)
Charlton Comics: No. 16, Sept, 1967 - No. 31, May, 1970

16-Features Rick Roberts	3	10	23	35
17-20	3	9	19	28
21-31	2	6	15	22

GRAPHIQUE MUSIQUE
Slave Labor Graphics: Dec, 1989 - No. 3, May, 1990 ($2.95, 52 pgs.)

1-Mike Allred-c/a/scripts	4	12	26	40
2,3	3	9	20	30

GRAVEDIGGERS
Acclaim Comics: Nov, 1996 - No. 4, Feb, 1997 ($2.95, B&W)

1-4: Moretti scripts				3.00

GRAVESTONE
Malibu Comics: July, 1993 - No. 7, Feb, 1994 ($2.25)

1-6: 3-Polybagged w/Skycap				2.25
7-($2.50)				2.50

GRAVE TALES
Hamilton Comics: Oct, 1991 - No. 3, Feb, 1992 ($3.95, B&W, mag., 52 pgs.)

	GD2.0	FN6.0	VF8.0	NM9.4
1-Staton-c/a	1	3	6	8
2,3: 2-Staton-a; Morrow-c				6.00

GRAY GHOST, THE
Dell Publishing Co.: No. 911, July, 1958; No. 1000, June-Aug, 1959

Four Color 911 (#1), 1000-Photo-c each	9	27	63	110

GREASE MONKEY
Image Comics: Jan, 1998 - Present ($2.95, B&W)

1,2-Tim Eldred-s/a				3.00

GREAT ACTION COMICS
I. W. Enterprises: 1958 (Reprints with new covers)

1-Captain Truth reprinted from Gold Medal #1	3	9	20	30
8,9-Reprints Phantom Lady #15 & 23	9	27	63	105

GREAT AMERICAN COMICS PRESENTS - THE SECRET VOICE
Peter George 4-Star Publ./American Features Syndicate: 1945 (10¢)

1-Anti-Nazi; "What Really Happened to Hitler"	33	99	174	300

GREAT AMERICAN WESTERN, THE
AC Comics: 1987 - No. 4, 1990? ($1.75/$2.95/$3.50, B&W with some color)

1-4: 1-Western-r plus Bill Black-a. 2-Tribute to ME comics; Durango Kid photo-c 3-Tribute to Tom Mix plus Roy Rogers, Durango Kid; Billy the Kid-r by Severin; photo-c 4- ($3.50, 52 pgs., 16 pgs. color)-Tribute to Lash LaRue; photo-c & interior photos; Fawcett-r				4.00
...Presents 1 (1991, $5.00) New Sunset Carson; film history				5.00

GREAT CAT FAMILY, THE (Disney-TV/Movie)
Dell Publishing Co.: No. 750, Nov, 1956 (one-shot)

Four Color 750-Pinocchio & Alice app.	6	18	42	80

GREAT COMICS
Great Comics Publications: Nov, 1941 - No. 3, Jan, 1942

1-Origin/1st app. The Great Zarro; Madame Strange & Guy Gorham, Wizard of Science & The Great Zarro begin	127	381	795	1400
2-Buck Johnson, Jungle Explorer app.; X-Mas-c	64	192	398	700
3-Futuro Takes Hitler to Hell-c/s; "The Lost City" movie story (starring William Boyd); continues in Choice Comics #3	227	681	1420	2500

GREAT COMICS
Novack Publishing Co./Jubilee Comics/Knockout/Barrel O' Fun: 1945

1-(Four publ. variations: Barrel O-Fun, Jubilee, Knockout & Novack)-The Defenders, Capt. Power app.; L. B. Cole-c	40	120	240	420
1-(Jubilee)-Same cover; Boogey Man, Satanas, & The Sorcerer & His Apprentice	31	93	165	285
1-(Barrel O' Fun)-L. B. Cole-c; Barrel O' Fun overprinted in indicia; Li'l Cactus, Cuckoo Sheriff (humorous)	20	60	105	175

GREAT DOGPATCH MYSTERY (See Mammy Yokum & the...)

GREATEST BATMAN STORIES EVER TOLD, THE
DC Comics:

Hardcover ($24.95)				40.00
Softcover ($15.95) "Greatest DC Stories Vol. 2" on spine				17.00
Vol. 2 softcover (1992, $16.95)"Greatest DC Stories Vol. 7" on spine				17.00

GREATEST FLASH STORIES EVER TOLD, THE
DC Comics: 1991

nn-Hardcover ($29.95); Infantino-c				30.00
nn-Softcover ($14.95)				15.00

GREATEST GOLDEN AGE STORIES EVER TOLD, THE
DC Comics: 1990 ($24.95, hardcover)

nn-Ordway-c				45.00

GREATEST JOKER STORIES EVER TOLD, THE (See Batman)
DC Comics: 1983

Hardcover ($19.95)-Kyle Baker painted-c				35.00
Softcover ($14.95)				15.00
Stacked Deck...Expanded Edition (1992, $29.95)-Longmeadow Press Publ.				30.00

GREATEST 1950s STORIES EVER TOLD, THE
DC Comics: 1990

Great Lover Romances #3 © TOBY

Green Arrow #11 © DC

Green Arrow #2 © DC

		GD2.0	FN6.0	VF8.0	NM9.4

		GD2.0	FN6.0	VF8.0	NM9.4

Hardcover ($29.95)-Kubert-c — 45.00
Softcover ($14.95) "Greatest DC Stories Vol. 5" on spine — 16.00

GREATEST TEAM-UP STORIES EVER TOLD, THE
DC Comics: 1989

Hardcover ($24.95)-DeVries and Infantino painted-c — 45.00
Softcover ($14.95) "Greatest DC Stories Vol. 4" on spine; Adams-c — 16.00

GREATEST SUPERMAN STORIES EVER TOLD, THE
DC Comics: 1987

Hardcover ($24.95) — 40.00
Softcover ($15.95) — 18.00

GREAT EXPLOITS
Decker Publ./Red Top: Oct, 1957

1-Krigstein-a(2) (re-issue on cover); reprints Daring Advs. #6 by Approved
  Comics .... 8 ... 24 ... 42 ... 60

GREAT FOODINI, THE (See Foodini)

GREAT GAZOO, THE (The Flintstones)(TV)
Charlton Comics: Aug, 1973 - No. 20, Jan, 1977 (Hanna-Barbera)

1 .... 3 ... 10 ... 23 ... 35
2-10 .... 2 ... 6 ... 12 ... 18
11-20 .... 2 ... 6 ... 9 ... 12

GREAT GRAPE APE, THE (TV)(See TV Stars #1)
Charlton Comics: Sept, 1976 - No. 2, Nov, 1976 (Hanna-Barbera)

1 .... 3 ... 9 ... 17 ... 25
2 .... 2 ... 6 ... 11 ... 15

GREAT LOCOMOTIVE CHASE, THE (Disney)
Dell Publishing Co.: No. 712, Sept, 1956 (one-shot)

Four Color 712-Movie, photo-c .... 7 ... 21 ... 49 ... 90

GREAT LOVER ROMANCES (Young Lover Romances #4,5)
Toby Press: 3/51; #2, 1951(nd); #3, 1952 (nd); #6, Oct?, 1952 - No. 22, May,
1955 (Photo-c #1-5, 10 ,13, 15, 17) (no #4, 5)

1-Jon Juan story-r/Jon Juan #1 by Schomburg; Dr. Anthony King app.
  .... 17 ... 51 ... 88 ... 150
2-Jon Juan, Dr. Anthony King app. .... 10 ... 30 ... 55 ... 80
3,7,9-14,16-22: 10-Rita Hayworth & Aldo Ray
  photo-c .... 6 ... 18 ... 32 ... 45
6-Kurtzman-a (10/52) .... 10 ... 30 ... 55 ... 80
8-Five pgs. of "Pin-Up Pete" by Sparling .... 10 ... 30 ... 55 ... 80
15-Liz Taylor photo-c .... 14 ... 42 ... 72 ... 120

GREAT RACE, THE (See Movie Classics)

GREAT SCOTT SHOE STORE (See Bulls-Eye)

GREAT WEST (Magazine)
M. F. Enterprises: 1969 (B&W, 52 pgs.)

V1#1 .... 2 ... 6 ... 11 ... 16

GREAT WESTERN
Magazine Enterprises: No. 8, Jan-Mar, 1954 - No. 11, Oct-Dec, 1954

8(A-1 93)-Trail Colt by Guardineer; Powell Red Hawk-r/Straight Arrow begins,
  ends #11; Durango Kid story .... 22 ... 66 ... 116 ... 195
9(A-1 105), 11(A-1 127)-Ghost Rider, Durango Kid app. in each. 9-Red
  Mask-c, but no app. .... 14 ... 42 ... 72 ... 120
10(A-1 113)-The Calico Kid by Guardineer-r/Tim Holt #8; Straight Arrow,
  Durango Kid app. .... 14 ... 42 ... 72 ... 120
I.W. Reprint #1,2 9: 1,2-r/Straight Arrow #36,42. 9-r/Straight Arrow #?
  .... 3 ... 9 ... 17 ... 26
I.W. Reprint #8-Origin Ghost Rider(r/Tim Holt #11); Tim Holt app.; Bolle-a
  .... 3 ... 9 ... 20 ... 30

NOTE: *Guardineer c-8. Powell a(r)-8-11 (from Straight Arrow).*

GREEN ARROW (See Action #440, Adventure, Brave & the Bold, DC Super Stars #17,
Detective #521, Flash #217, Green Lantern #76, Justice League of America #4, Leading Comics,
More Fun #73 (1st app.), Showcase '95 #9 & World's Finest Comics)

GREEN ARROW
DC Comics: May, 1983 - No. 4, Aug, 1983 (limited series)

1-Origin; Speedy cameo; Mike W. Barr scripts, Trevor Von Eeden-c/a — 5.00
2-4 — 4.00

GREEN ARROW
DC Comics: Feb, 1988 - No. 137, Oct, 1998 ($1.00-$2.50) (Painted-c #1-3)

1-Mike Grell scripts begin, ends #80 — 5.00
2-49,51-74,76-86: 27,28-Warlord app. 35-38-Co-stars Black Canary; Bill
  Wray-i. 40-Grell-a. 47-Begin $1.50-c. 63-No longer has mature readers on-c.
  63-66-Shado app. 81-Aparo-a begins, ends #100. Nuklon app. 82-Intro &
  death of Rival. 83-Huntress-c/story. 84-Deathstroke cameo. 85-Deathstroke-
  c/app. 86-Catwoman-c/story w/Jim Balent layouts — 2.50
50,75-($2.50, 52 pgs.): Anniversary issues. 75-Arsenal (Roy Harper) & Shado
  app. — 3.00
0,87-96: 87-$1.95-c begins. 88-Guy Gardner, Martian Manhunter, &
  Wonder Woman-c/app.; Flash-c. 89-Anarky app. 90-(9/94)-Zero Hour tie-in.
  0-(10/94)-1st app. Connor Hawke; Aparo(a). 91-(11/94). 93-1st app.
  Camorouge. 95-Hal Jordan cameo. 96-Intro new Force of July; Hal Jordan
  (Parallax) app; Oliver Queen learns that Connor Hawke is his son — 2.50
97-99,102-109: 97-Begin $2.25-c; no Aparo-a. 98-Arsenal app. 102,103-
  Underworld Unleashed x-over. 104-GL(Kyle Rayner)-c/app. 105-Robin-c/app.
  107-109-Thorn app. 109-Lois Lane cameo; Weeks-c. — 2.50
100-($3.95)-Foil-c; Superman app. — 5.00
101-Death of Oliver Queen; Superman app. ... 2 ... 6 ... 9 ... 12
110,111-124: 110,111-GL x-over. 110-Intro Hatchet. 114-Final Night. 115-117-
  Black Canary & Oracle app. — 2.50
125-($3.50, 48 pgs)-GL x-over cont. in GL #92 — 3.50
126-136: 126-Begin $2.50-c. 130-GL & Flash x-over. 132,133-JLA app.
  134,135-Brotherhood of the Fist pts. 1,5. 136-Hal Jordan-c/app. — 2.50
137-Last issue; Superman app.; last panel cameo of Oliver Queen — 6.00
#1,000,000 (11/98) 853rd Century x-over — 2.50
Annual 1-6 ('88-'94, 68 pgs.)-1-No Grell scripts. 2-No Grell scripts; recaps origin
  Green Arrow,Speedy, Black Canary & others. 3-Bill Wray-a. 4-50th anniver
  sary issue. 5-Batman, Eclipso app. 6-Bloodlines; Hook app. — 3.50
7-('95, $3.95)-Year One story — 4.00
NOTE: *Aparo a-0, 81-85, 86 (partial),87p, 88p, 91-95, 96i, 98-100p, 109p; c-81,98-100p. Austin
c-96i. Balent layouts-86. Burchett c-91-95. Campanella a-100-108i, 110-113i; c-99i, 101-
108i,110-113i. Denys Cowan a-39p, 41-43p, 47p, 48p, 60p; c-41-43. Damaggio a(p)-97p, 100-
108p, 110-112p; c-97-99p, 101-108p, 110-113p. Mike Grell a-1-4, 10p, 11, 39, 40, 44, 45, 47-80,
Annual 4, 5. Nasser/Netzer a-89, 96. Sienkiewicz a-109i. Springer a-67, 68. Weeks c-109.*

GREEN ARROW
DC Comics: Apr, 2001 - Present ($2.50)

1-Oliver Queen returns; Kevin Smith-s/Hester-a/Wagner-painted-c — 10.00
1-2nd-4th printings — 2.50
2-Batman cameo — 5.00
2-2nd printing — 2.50
3-10: 4-JLA app. 7-Barry Allen & Hal Jordan app. 9,10-Stanley & his Monster
  app. 10-Oliver regains his soul — 2.50

GREEN ARROW: THE LONG BOW HUNTERS
DC Comics: Aug, 1987 - No. 3, Oct, 1987 ($2.95, limited series, mature)

1-Grell-c/a in all — 6.00
1,2-2nd printings — 3.00
2,3 — 4.00
Trade paperback (1989, $12.95)-r/#1-3 — 13.00

GREEN ARROW: THE WONDER YEAR
DC Comics: Feb, 1993 - No. 4, May, 1993 ($1.75, limited series)

1-4: Mike Grell-a(p)/scripts & Gray Morrow-a(i) — 2.50

GREEN BERET, THE (See Tales of...)

GREEN CANDLES
DC Comics (Paradox Press): Sept, 1995 - No. 3, Dec, 1995 ($5.95, B&W, limit-
ed series, digest size)

1-3 — 6.00
Paperback ($9.95) — 10.00

GREEN GIANT COMICS (Also see Colossus Comics)
Pelican Publ. (Funnies, Inc.): 1940 (No price on cover; distributed in New York
City only)

1-Dr. Nerod, Green Giant, Black Arrow, Mundoo & Master Mystic app.;
  origin Colossus (Rare) .... 1000 ... 3000 ... 6500 ... 13,000
NOTE: *The idea for this book came from George Kapitan. Printed by Moreau Publ. of Orange, N.J.
as an experiment to see if they could profitably use the idle time of their 40-page Hoe color press.
The experiment failed due to the difficulty of obtaining good quality color registration and Mr. Moreau
believes the book never reached the stands. The book has no price or date which lends credence*

Green Hornet Comics #4 © HARV

Green Lama #2 © Spark Pub.

Green Lantern #7 © DC

	GD2.0	FN6.0	VF8.0	NM9.4

to this. Contains five pages reprinted from Motion Picture Funnies Weekly.

GREEN GOBLIN
Marvel Comics: Oct, 1995 - No. 13, Oct, 1996 ($2.95/$1.95)

1-($2.95)-Scott McDaniel-c/a begins, ends #7; foil-c				3.50
2-13: 2-Begin $1.95-c. 4-Hobgoblin-c/app; Thing app. 6-Daredevil-c/app. 8-Darrick Robertson-a; McDaniel-c. 10-Arcade app. 12,13-Onslaught x-over. 13-Green Goblin quits; Spider-Man app.				2.25

GREENHAVEN
Aircel Publishing: 1988 - No. 3, 1988 ($2.00, limited series, 28 pgs.)

1-3				2.25

GREEN HORNET, THE (TV)
Dell Publishing Co./Gold Key: Sept, 1953; Feb, 1967 - No. 3, Aug, 1967

Four Color 496-Painted-c.	25	75	175	320
1-All have Bruce Lee photo-c	21	63	147	275
2,3	14	42	98	185

GREEN HORNET, THE (Also see Kato of the… & Tales of the…)
Now Comics: Nov, 1989 - No. 14, Feb, 1991 ($1.75)
V2#1, Sept, 1991 - V2#40, Jan, 1995 ($1.95)

1 ($2.95, double-size)-Steranko painted-c; G.A. Green Hornet		5.00
1,2: 1-2nd printing ('90, $3.95)-New Butler-c		4.00
3-14: 5-Death of original ('30s) Green Hornet. 6-Dave Dorman painted-c. 11-Snyder-c		3.00
V2#1-11,13-21,24-26,28-30,32-37,39,40: 1-Butler painted-c. 9-Mayerik-c		2.50
12-($2.50)-Color Green Hornet button polybagged inside		3.00
22,23-($2.95)-Bagged w/color hologravure card		3.00
27-($2.95)-Newsstand ed. polybagged w/multi-dimensional card (1993 Anniversary Special on cover), 27-($2.95)-Direct Sale ed. polybagged w/multi-dimensional card; cover variations		3.00
31,38: 31-($2.50)-Polybagged w/trading card		2.50
1-($2.50)-Polybagged w/button (same as #12)		2.50
2,3-($1.95)-Same as #13 & 14		2.25
Annual 1 (12/92, $2.50), Annual 1994 (10/94, $2.95)		3.00

GREEN HORNET: DARK TOMORROW
Now Comics: Jun, 1993 - No. 3, Aug, 1993 ($2.50, limited series)

1-3: Future Green Hornet		2.50

GREEN HORNET: SOLITARY SENTINEL, THE
Now Comics: Dec, 1992 - No. 3, 1993 ($2.50, limited series)

1-3		2.50

GREEN HORNET COMICS (…Racket Buster #44) (Radio, movies)
Helnit Publ. Co.(Holyoke) No. 1-6/Family Comics(Harvey) No. 7-on: Dec, 1940 - No. 47, Sept, 1949 (See All New #13,14)(Early issues: 68 pgs.)

1-1st app. Green Hornet & Kato; origin of Green Hornet on inside front-c; intro the Black Beauty (Green Hornet's car); painted-c	462	1386	3000	6000
2-Early issues based on radio adventures	182	546	1136	2000
3	136	408	852	1500
4-6: 6-(8/41)	109	327	682	1200
7 (6/42)-Origin The Zebra & begins; Robin Hood, Spirit of '76, Blonde Bomber & Mighty Midgets begin; new logo	91	273	568	1000
8,10	77	231	483	850
9-Kirby-c	95	285	597	1050
11,12-Mr. Q in both	77	231	483	850
13-1st Nazi-c; shows Hitler poster on-c	84	253	525	925
14-19	59	177	369	650
20-Classic-c	64	192	398	700
21-23,25-30	47	142	286	500
24-Sci-Fi-c	50	150	300	525
31-The Man in Black Called Fate begins (11-12/45, early app.)	49	147	294	520
32-36	40	120	232	400
37,38: Shock Gibson app. by Powell. 37-S&K Kid Adonis reprinted from Stuntman #3. 38-Kid Adonis app.	40	120	232	400
39-Stuntman story by S&K	50	150	300	525
40-47: 42-47-Kerry Drake in all. 45-Boy Explorers on-c only. 46- "Case of the Marijuana Racket" cover/story; Kerry Drake app.	35	105	188	325

NOTE: **Fuje** a-23, 24, 26. **Henkle** c-7-9. **Kubert** a-20, 30. **Powell** a-7-10, 12, 14, 16-21, 30, 31(2),

32(3), 33, 34(3), 35, 36, 37(2), 38. **Robinson** a-27. **Schomburg** c-15, 17-23. Kirbyish c-7, 15. Bondage c-8, 14, 18, 26, 36.

GREEN JET COMICS, THE (See Comic Books, Series 1)

GREEN LAMA (Also see Comic Books, Series 1, Daring Adventures #17 & Prize Comics #7)
Spark Publications/Prize No. 7 on: Dec, 1944 - No. 8, Mar, 1946

1-Intro. Lt. Hercules & The Boy Champions; Mac Raboy-c/a #1-8	127	381	795	1400
2-Lt. Hercules borrows the Human Torch's powers for one panel	75	225	469	825
3-6,8: 4-Dick Tracy take-off in Lt. Hercules story by H. L. Gold (science fiction writer). 5-Lt. Hercules story; Little Orphan Annie, Smilin' Jack & Snuffy Smith take-off (5/45)	61	182	381	675
7-X-mas-c; Raboy craft tint-c/a (note: a small quantity of NM copies surfaced)	40	120	220	380

NOTE: **Robinson** a-3-5, 8. **Roussos** a-8. Formerly a pulp hero who began in 1940.

GREEN LANTERN (1st Series) (See All-American, All Flash Quarterly, All Star Comics, The Big All-American & Comic Cavalcade)
National Periodical Publications/All-American: Fall, 1941 - No. 38, May-June, 1949 (#1-18 are quarterly)

1-Origin retold; classic Purcell-c	2800	8400	21,000	42,000
2-1st book-length story	630	1890	4100	8200
3-Classic German war-c by Mart Nodell	462	1386	3000	6000
4-Green Lantern & Doiby Dickles join the Army	400	1200	2500	4800
5	273	819	1705	3000
6,8: 8-Hop Harrigan begins; classic-c	214	642	1337	2350
7-Robot-c	232	695	1450	2550
9,10: 10-Origin/1st app. Vandal Savage	186	558	1162	2050
11-17,19,20: 12-Origin/1st app. Gambler	129	387	806	1425
18-Christmas-c	143	429	894	1575
21-26,28	118	355	738	1300
27-Origin/1st app. Sky Pirate	123	369	769	1350
29-All Harlequin issue; classic Harlequin-c	127	381	795	1400
30-Origin/1st app. Streak the Wonder Dog by Toth (2-3/48) (scarce)	136	408	852	1500
31-35: 35-Kubert-c. 35-38-New logo	100	300	625	1100
36-38: 37-Sargon the Sorcerer app.	123	369	769	1350

NOTE: Book-length stories #2-7. **Mayer/Moldoff** c-9. **Mayer/Purcell** c-8. **Purcell** c-1. **Mart Nodell** c-2, 3, 7. **Paul Reinman** c-11, 12, 15-22. **Toth** a-28, 30, 31, 34-38; c-28, 30, 34p, 36-38p. Cover to #8 says Fall while the indicia says Summer Issue. Streak the Wonder Dog c-30 (w/Green Lantern) 34, 36, 38.

GREEN LANTERN (See Action Comics Weekly, Adventure Comics, Brave & the Bold, DC Special, DC Special Series, Flash, Guy Gardner, Guy Gardner Reborn, Justice League of America, Parallax: Emerald Night, Showcase, Showcase '93 #12 & Tales of The…Corps)

GREEN LANTERN (2nd Series)(Green Lantern Corps #206 on) (See Showcase #22-24)
National Periodical Publ./DC Comics: 7-8/60 - No. 89, 4-5/72; No. 90, 8-9/76 - No. 205, 10/86

1-(7-8/60)-Origin retold; Gil Kane-c/a continues; 1st app. Guardians of the Universe	222	666	2000	4000
2-1st Pieface	59	177	505	950
3-Contains readers poll	39	117	292	525
4,5: 5-Origin/1st app. Hector Hammond	31	93	222	400
6-Intro Tomar-Re the alien G.L.	29	88	202	360
7-Origin/1st app. Sinestro (7-8/61)	26	78	185	330
8-10: 8-1st 5700 A.D. story; grey tone-c. 9-1st Jordan Brothers; last 10¢ issue	23	69	160	285
11,12	16	48	112	200
13-Flash x-over	19	57	134	240
14-20: 14-Origin/1st app. Sonar. 16-Origin & 1st app. Star Sapphire. 20-Flash x-over	14	42	98	165
21-30: 21-Origin & 1st app. Dr. Polaris. 23-1st Tattooed Man. 24-Origin & 1st app. Shark. 29-JLA cameo; 1st Blackhand	12	36	84	140
31-39: 39-1st app. Evil Star (villain)	10	30	68	115
40-1st app. Crisis (10/65); 2nd solo G.A. Green Lantern in Silver Age (see Showcase #55); origin The Guardians; Doiby Dickles app.	43	129	344	625
41-44,46-50: 42-Zatanna x-over. 43-Flash x-over	8	24	58	95
45-2nd S.A. app. G.A. Green Lantern in title (6/66)	14	42	98	165

	GD2.0	FN6.0	VF8.0	NM9.4

Green Lantern #92 © DC

Green Lantern (3rd series) #19 © DC

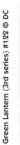

Green Lantern (3rd series) #122 © DC

	GD2.0	FN6.0	VF8.0	NM9.4

51,53-58 — 6, 18, 45, 75
52-G.A. Green Lantern x-over — 9, 27, 63, 105
59-1st app. Guy Gardner (3/68) — 20, 60, 140, 250
60,62-69: 69-Wood inks; last 12¢ issue — 5, 15, 34, 55
61-G.A. Green Lantern x-over — 6, 18, 42, 70
70-75 — 4, 12, 26, 40
76-(4/70)-Begin Green Lantern/Green Arrow series (by Neal Adams #76-89) ends #122 (see Flash #217 for 2nd series) — 20, 60, 140, 250
77 — 7, 21, 50, 80
78-80 — 5, 15, 38, 60
81-84: 82-Wrightson-i(1 pg.). 83-G.L. reveals i.d. to Carol Ferris. 84-N. Adams/ Wrightson-a(22 pgs.); last 15¢-c; partial photo-c — 5, 15, 34, 55
85,86-(52 pgs.)-Anti-drug issues. 86-G.A. Green Lantern-r; Toth-a — 6, 18, 45, 75
87-(52 pgs.): 2nd app. Guy Gardner (cameo); 1st app. John Stewart (12-1/ 71-72) (becomes 3rd Green Lantern in #182) — 4, 12, 29, 45
88-(2-3/72, 52 pgs.)-Unpubbed G.A. Green Lantern story; Green Lantern-r/ Showcase #23. N. Adams-c/a (1 pg.) — 3, 9, 17, 25
89-(4-5/72, 52 pgs.)-G.A. Green Lantern-r; Green Lantern & Green Arrow move to Flash #217 (2nd team-up series) — 4, 12, 29, 45
90 (8-9/76)-Begin 3rd Green Lantern/Green Arrow team-up series; Mike Grell-c/a begins, ends #111 — 2, 6, 12, 18
91-99 — 1, 3, 6, 9
100-(1/78, Giant)-1st app. Air Wave II — 2, 6, 11, 16
101-107,111,113-115,117-119: 107-1st Tales of the G.L. Corps story — 1, 3, 5, 7
108-110-(44 pgs)-G.A. Green Lantern back-ups in each. 111-Origin retold; G.A. Green Lantern origin retold — 1, 3, 6, 8
112-G.A. Green Lantern origin retold — 2, 6, 10, 14
116-1st app. Guy Gardner as G.L. (5/79) — 3, 10, 23, 35
117-119,121-(Whitman variants; low print run; none have issue # on cover) — 1, 3, 6, 9
120-122,124-150: 22-Last Green Lantern/Green Arrow team-up. 130-132-Tales of the G.L. Corps. 132-Adam Strange series begins, ends147. 136,137-1st app. Citadel; Space Ranger app. 141-1st app. Omega Men (6/81). 142,143-Omega Men app.;Perez-c. 144-Omega Men cameo. 148-Tales of the G.L. Corps begins, ends #173. 150-Anniversary issue, 52 pgs.; no G.L. Corps — 4.00
123-Green Lantern back to solo story; 2nd app. Guy Gardner as Green Lantern — 5.00
151-180,183,184,186,187: 159-Origin Evil Star. 160,161-Omega Men app. — 3.00
181,182,185,188: 181-Hal Jordan resigns as G.L. 182-John Stewart becomes new G.L.; origin recap of Hal Jordan as G.L. 185-Origin new G.L. (John Stewart).188-I.D. revealed; Alan Moore back-up scripts. — 3.00
189-193,196-199,201-205: 191-Re-intro Star Sapphire (cameo). 192-Re-intro Star Sapphire (1st full app.). 194,198-Crisis x-over. 199-Hal Jordan returns as a member of G.L. Corps (3 G.L.s now). 201-Green Lantern Corps begins (is cover title, issue premiere issue) — 3.00
194-Hal Jordan/Guy Gardner battle; Guardians choose Guy Gardner to become new Green Lantern — 4.00
195-Guy Gardner becomes Green Lantern; Crisis x-over — 1, 3, 6, 9
200-Double-size — 4.00
Annual 1 (Listed as Tales Of The Green Lantern Corps Annual 1) — 3.00
Annual 2,3 (See Tales of Green Lantern Corps Annual #2,3) — 3.00
Special 1 (1988), 2 (1989)-(Both $1.50, 52 pgs.) — 3.00
NOTE: **N. Adams** a-76, 77-87p, 89; c-63, 76-89. **M. Anderson** a-137i. **Austin** a-93i, 94i, 171i. **Haykin** c-196. **Greene** a-39-49i, 58-63i; c-54-58i. **Grell** a-90-106, 108-111; c-90-106, 108-112. **Heck** a-120-122p. **Infantino** a-137p, 145-147p, 151, 152p. **Gil Kane** a-1-49p, 50-57, 58-61p, 68-85p, 85p(r), 87p(r), 88p(r), 156, 177, 184p; c-1-52, 54-61p, 67-75, 123, 154, 156, 165-171, 177, 184. **Newton** a-148p, 149p, 181. **Perez** c-132p, 141-144. **Sekowsky** a-65p, 170p. **Simonson** c-200. **Sparling** a-63p. **Starlin** c-129, 133. **Staton** a-117p, 123-127p, 128, 129-131p, 132-139p, 140p, 141-146, 147p, 148-150, 151-155p; c-107p, 117p, 135(i), 136p, 145p, 146, 147, 148-152p, 155p. **Toth** a-86r, 171p. **Tuska** a-166-168p, 170p.

GREEN LANTERN (3rd Series)
DC Comics: June, 1990 - Present ($1.00/$1.25/$1.50/$1.75/$1.95/$1.99 $2.25)

1-Hal Jordan, John Stewart & Guy Gardner return; Batman app. — 5.00
2-26: 2-Guy Gardner solo story. 13-(52 pgs.). 18-Guy Gardner solo story. 19-($1.75, 52 pgs.)-50th anniversary issue; Mart Nodell (original G.A. artist) part-p on G.A. Gr. Lantern; G. Kane-c. 25-($1.75, 52 pgs.)-Hal Jordan/Guy Gardner battle — 4.00

	GD2.0	FN6.0	VF8.0	NM9.4

27-45,47: 30,31-Gorilla Grodd-c/story(see Flash #69). 38,39-Adam Strange-c/ story. 42-Deathstroke-c/s. 47-Green Arrow x-over — 3.00
46,48,49,50: 46-Superman app. cont'd in Superman #82. 48-Emerald Twilight part 1. 50-($2.95, 52 pgs.)-Glow-in-the-dark-c — 6.00
0, 51-62: 51-1st app. New Green Lantern (Kyle Rayner) with new costume. 53-Superman-c/story. 55-(9/94)-Zero Hour. 0-(10/94). 56-(11/94) — 4.00
63,64-Kyle Rayner vs. Hal Jordan. — 4.00
65-80,82-92: 63-Begin $1.75-c. 65-New Titans app. 66,67-Flash app. 71-Batman & Robin app. 72-Shazam!-c/app. 73-Wonder Woman-c/app. 73-75-Adam Strange app. 76,77-Green Arrow x-over. 80-Final Night x-over. 87-JLA app. 91-Genesis x-over. 92-Green Arrow x-over. — 3.00
81-(Regular Ed.)-Memorial for Hal Jordan (Parallax); most DC heroes app. — 5.00
81-($3.95, Deluxe Edition)-Embossed prism-c — 6.00
93-99: 93-Begin $1.95-c; Deadman app. 94-Superboy app. 95-Starlin-a(p). 98,99-Legion of Super-Heroes-c/app. — 2.50
100-($2.95) Two covers (Jordan & Rayner); vs. Sinestro — 5.00
101-106: 101-106-Hal Jordan-c/app. 103-JLA-c/app. 104-Green Arrow app. 105,106-Parallax app. — 3.00
107-126: 107-Jade becomes a Green Lantern. 119-Hal Jordan/Spectre app. 125-JLA app. — 2.25
127-143: 127-Begin $2.25-c. 129-Winick-s begin. 134-136-JLA-c/app. 143-Joker: Last Laugh; Lee-c. 145-Kyle becomes The Ion — 2.25
#1,000,000 (11/98) 853rd Century x-over — 2.25
Annual 1-3: ('92-'94, 68 pgs.)-1-Eclipso app. 2 -Intro Nightblade. 3-Elseworlds story — 3.50
Annual 4 (1995, $3.50)-Year One story — 4.00
Annual 5,7,8 ('96, '98, '99, $2.95): 5-Legends of the Dead Earth. 7-Ghosts; Wrightson-c. 8-JLApe; Art Adams-c — 3.00
Annual 6 (1997, $3.95)-Pulp Heroes story — 5.00
Annual 9 (2000, $3.50) Planet DC — 3.50
...80 Page Giant (12/98, $4.95) Stories by various — 5.00
...80 Page Giant 2 (6/99, $4.95) Team-ups — 5.00
...80 Page Giant 3 (8/00, $5.95) Darkseid vs. the GL Corps — 6.00
...: 1001 Emerald Nights (2001, $6.95) Elseworlds; Guay-a/c; LaBan-s — 7.00
...-3-D #1 (12/98, $3.95) Jeanty-a — 4.00
...: A New Dawn TPB (1998, $9.95)-r/#50-55 — 10.00
...: Baptism of Fire TPB (1999, $12.95)-r/#59,66,67,70-75 — 13.00
...: Emerald Allies TPB (2000, $14.95)-r/GL/GA team-ups — 15.00
...: Emerald Knights TPB (1998, $12.95)-r/Hal Jordan's return — 13.00
...: Emerald Twilight nn (1994, $5.95)-r/#48-50 — 6.00
...: Ganthet's Tale nn (1992, $5.95, 68 pgs.)-Silver foil stamped logo; Larry Niven scripts; Byrne-c/a — 6.00
.../Green Arrow Collection, Vol. 2-r/Gl #84-87,89 & Flash #217-219 & GL/GA #5-7 by O'Neil/Adams/Wrightson — 13.00
...: New Journey, Old Path TPB (2001, $12.95)-r/#129-136 — 13.00
...: Our Worlds at War (8/01, $2.95) Jae Lee-c; prelude to x-over — 3.00
...Plus 1 (12/1996, $2.95)-The Ray & Polaris-c/app. — 3.00
...Secret Files 1,2- (7/98-6/99, $4.95)1- Origin stories & profiles. 2-Grell-c — 5.00
.../Superman: Legend of the Green Flame (2000, $5.95) 1988 unpub. Neil Gaiman story of Hal Jordan with new art by various; Frank Miller-c — 6.00
...The Road Back nn (1992, $8.95)-r/1-8 w/covers — 9.00
...: Traitor TPB (2001, $12.95) r/Legends of the DCU #20,21,28,29,37,38 — 13.00
...: Willworld (2001, $24.95, HC) Seth Fisher-a/DeMatteis-s; Hal Jordan — 25.00
NOTE: Staton a(p)-9-12; c-9-12.

GREEN LANTERN (See Tangent Comics/ Green Lantern)

GREEN LANTERN ANNUAL NO. 1, 1963
DC Comics: 1998 ($4.95, one-shot)
1-Reprints Golden Age & Silver Age stories in 1963-style 80 pg. Giant format; new Gil Kane sketch art — 5.00

GREEN LANTERN: CIRCLE OF FIRE
DC Comics: Early Oct., 2000 - No. 2, Late Oct, 2000 (limited series)
1-($4.95) Intro. other Green Lanterns — 5.00
2-($3.75) — 4.00
Green Lantern (x-overs)- .../Adam Strange; .../Atom; .../Firestorm; ... /Green Lantern, Winick-s; .../Power Girl (all $2.50-c) — 2.50

GREEN LANTERN CORPS, THE (Formerly Green Lantern; see Tales of...)
DC Comics: No. 206, Nov, 1986 - No. 224, May, 1988
206-223: 220,221-Millennium tie-ins — 3.00

Green Lantern / Sentinel: Heart of Darkness #1 © DC

Green Mask #1 © FOX

Grendel - Black, White, and Red #1 © Matt Wagner

	GD2.0	FN6.0	VF8.0	NM9.4		GD2.0	FN6.0	VF8.0	NM9.

224-Double-size last issue 4.00
...Corps Annual 2,3- (12/86,8/87) 1-Formerly Tales of ...Annual #1; Alan Moore scripts. 3-Indicia says Green Lantern Annual #3; Moore scripts; Byrne-a 3.00
NOTE: **Austin** a-Annual 3i. **Gil Kane** a-223, 224p; c-223, 224, Annual 2. **Russell** a-Annual 3i. **Staton** a-207-213p, 217p, 221p, 222p, Annual 3; c-207-213p, 217p, 221p, 222p. **Willingham** a-213p, 219p, 220p, 218p, 219p, Annual 2, 3p; c-218p, 219p.

GREEN LANTERN CORPS QUARTERLY
DC Comics: Summer, 1992 - No. 8, Spring, 1994 ($2.50/$2.95, 68 pgs.)
1,7,8: 1-G.A. Green Lantern story; Staton-a(p). 7-Painted-c; Tim Vigil-a.
8-Lobo-c/s 3.50
2-6: 2-G.A. G.L.-c/story; Austin-c(i). Gulacy-a(p). 3-G.A. G.L. story. 4-Austin-i 3.00

GREEN LANTERN: DRAGON LORD
DC Comics: 2001 - No. 3, 2001 ($4.95, squarebound, limited series)
1-3: A G.L. in ancient China; Moench-s/Gulacy-c/a 5.00

GREEN LANTERN: EMERALD DAWN (Also see Emerald Dawn)
DC Comics: Dec, 1989 - No. 6, May, 1990 ($1.00, limited series)
1-Origin retold; Giffen plots in all 5.00
2-6 4.00

GREEN LANTERN: EMERALD DAWN II (Emerald Dawn II #1 & 2)
DC Comics: Apr, 1991 - No. 6, Sept, 1991 ($1.00, limited series)
1-6 2.50

GREEN LANTERN: FEAR ITSELF
DC Comics: 1999 (Graphic novel)
Hardcover ($24.95) Ron Marz/Brad Parker painted-a 25.00
Softcover ($14.95) 15.00

GREEN LANTERN/FLASH: FASTER FRIENDS (See Flash/Green Lantern...)
DC Comics: 1997 ($4.95, limited series)
1-Marz-s 5.00

GREEN LANTERN GALLERY
DC Comics: Dec, 1996 ($3.50, one-shot)
1-Wraparound-c; pin-ups by various 3.50

GREEN LANTERN/GREEN ARROW (Also see The Flash #217)
DC Comics: Oct, 1983 - No. 7, April, 1984 (52-60 pgs.)
1-7- r-Green Lantern #76-89 4.00
NOTE: **Neal Adams** r-1-7; c-1-4. **Wrightson** r-4, 5.

GREEN LANTERN: MOSAIC (Also see Cosmic Odyssey #2)
DC Comics: June, 1992 - No. 18, Nov, 1993 ($1.25)
1-18: Featuring John Stewart. 1-Painted-c by Cully Hamner 2.25

GREEN LANTERN/SENTINEL: HEART OF DARKNESS
DC Comics: Mar, 1998 - No. 3, May, 1998 ($1.95, limited series)
1-3-Marz-s/Pelletier-a 3.00

GREEN LANTERN/SILVER SURFER: UNHOLY ALLIANCES
DC Comics: 1995 ($4.95, one-shot)(Prelude to DC Versus Marvel)
nn-Hal Jordan app. 5.00

GREEN LANTERN: THE NEW CORPS
DC Comics: 1999 - No. 2, 1999 ($4.95, limited series)
1,2-Kyle recruits new GLs; Eaton-a 5.00

GREEN LANTERN VS. ALIENS
Dark Horse Comics: Sept, 2000 - No. 4, Dec, 2000 ($2.95, limited series)
1-4: 1-Hal Jordan and GL Corps vs. Aliens; Leonardi-p. 2-4-Kyle Rayner 3.00

GREEN MASK, THE (See Mystery Men)
Summer, 1940 - No. 9, 2/42; No. 10, 8/44 - No. 11, 11/44;
Fox Features Syndicate: V2#1, Spring, 1945 - No. 6, 10-11/46

V1#1-Origin The Green Mask & Domino; reprints/Mystery Men #1-3,5-7; Lou Fine-c	375	1125	2344	4500
2-Zanzibar The Magician by Tuska	136	408	852	1500
3-Powell-a; Marijuana story	84	253	525	925
4-Navy Jones begins, ends #6	68	205	426	750
5	55	165	341	600
6-The Nightbird begins, ends #9; bondage/torture-c				

7-9: 9(2/42)-Becomes The Bouncer #10(nn) on? & Green Mask #10 on	45	135	270	475
10,11: 10-Origin One Round Hogan & Rocket Kelly	40	120	220	380
	33	99	174	300
V2#1	25	75	130	225
2-6	21	63	110	185

GREEN PLANET, THE
Charlton Comics: 1962 (one-shot) (12¢)
nn-Giordano-c; sci-fi	7	21	50	80

GREEN TEAM (See Cancelled Comic Cavalcade & 1st Issue Special)

GREETINGS FROM SANTA (See March of Comics No. 48)

GRENDEL (Also see Primer #2, Mage and Comico Collection)
Comico: Mar, 1983 - No. 3, Feb, 1984 ($1.50, B&W)(#1 has indicia to Skrog #1)
1-Origin Hunter Rose	10	30	73	125
2,3: 2-Origin Argent	8	24	56	90

GRENDEL
Comico: Oct, 1986 - No. 40, Feb, 1990 ($1.50/$1.95/$2.50, mature)
1				6.00
1,2: 2nd printings				2.50
2,3,5-15,17-40: 13-15-Ken Steacy-c. 24-25,27-28,30-31-Snyder-c/a				5.00
4,16: 4-Dave Stevens-c(i). 16-Re-intro Mage (series begins, ends #19)				
Devil by the Deed (Graphic Novel, 10/86, $5.95, 52 pgs.)-r/Grendel back-ups/				
Mage 6-14; Alan Moore intro.	1	3	5	7
Devil's Legacy ($14.95, 1988, Graphic Novel)	2	6	11	15
Devil's Vagary (10/87, B&W & red)-No price; included in Comico Collection				
	2	6	9	12

GRENDEL (Title series): **Dark Horse Comics**
--**BLACK, WHITE, AND RED,** 11/98 - No. 4, 2/99 ($3.95, anthology)
1-Wagner-s in all. Art by Sale, Leon and others 5.00
2-4: 2-Mack, Chadwick-a. 3-Allred, Kristensen-a. 4-Pearson, Sprouse-a 4.00
--**CLASSICS,** 7/95 - 8/95 ($3.95, mature) 1,2-reprints; new Wagner-c 4.00
--**CYCLE,** 10/95 ($5.95) 1-nn-history of Grendel by M. Wagner & others 6.00
--**DEVIL BY THE DEED,** 7/93 ($3.95, varnish-c) 1-nn-M. Wagner-c/a/scripts; r/Grendel back-ups from Mage #6-14 4.00
Reprint (12/97, $3.95) w/pin-ups by various 4.00
--**DEVIL CHILD,** 6/99 - No. 2, 7/99 ($2.95, mature) 1,2-Sale & Kristiansen-a/ Diane Schutz-s 3.00
--**DEVIL QUEST,** 11/95 ($4.95) 1-nn-Prequel to Batman/Grendel II; M. Wagner story & art; r/back-up story from Grendel Tales series. 5.00
--**DEVILS AND DEATHS,** 10/94 - 11/94 ($2.95, mature) 1,2 3.00
: **DEVIL'S LEGACY,** 3/00 - No. 12, 2/01 ($2.95, reprints 1986 series, recolored)
1-12-Wagner-s/c; Pander Bros.-a 3.00
--**TALES: DEVIL'S CHOICES,** 3/95 - 6/95 ($2.95, mature) 1-4 3.00
--**TALES: FOUR DEVILS, ONE HELL,** 8/93 - 1/94 ($2.95, mature)
1-6-Wagner painted-c 3.00
TPB (12/94, $17.95) r/#1-6 18.00
--**TALES: HOMECOMING,** 12/94 - 2/95 ($2.95, mature) 1-3 3.00
--**TALES: THE DEVIL IN OUR MIDST,** 5/94 - 9/95 ($2.95, mature) 1-5-Wagner painted-c. in all 3.00
--**TALES: THE DEVIL MAY CARE,** 12/95 - No. 6, 5/96 ($2.95, mature)
1-6-Terry LaBan scripts. 5-Batman/Grendel II preview 3.00
--**TALES: THE DEVIL'S APPRENTICE,** 9/97 - No. 3, 11/97 ($2.95, mature)
1-3 3.00
: **THE DEVIL INSIDE,** 9/01 - No. 3 ($2.99) r/#13-15 with new Wagner-c 3.00

GRENDEL: WAR CHILD
Dark Horse Comics: Aug, 1992 - No. 10, Jun, 1993 ($2.50, lim. series, mature)
1-9: 1-4-Bisley painted-c; Wagner-i & scripts in all 3.00
10-($3.50, 52 pgs.) Wagner-c 4.00
Limited Edition Hardcover ($99.95) 100.00

GREYFRIARS BOBBY (Disney)(Movie)

Grifter #3 © WSP

Grimm's Ghost Stories #48 © GK

Groo #65 © Sergio Aragonés

	GD2.0	FN6.0	VF8.0	NM9.4

Dell Publishing Co.: No. 1189, Nov, 1961 (one-shot)

Four Color 1189-Photo-c (scarce)	7	21	49	90

GREYLORE
Sirius: 12/85 - No. 5, Sept, 1986 ($1.50/$1.75, high quality paper)

1-5: Bo Hampton-a in all				2.25

GREYSHIRT: INDIGO SUNSET (Also see Tomorrow Stories)
America's Best Comics: Dec, 2001 - No. 6 ($3.50, limited series)

1-3-Veitch-s/a				3.50

GRIDIRON GIANTS
Ultimate Sports Ent.: 2000 - No. 3 ($3.95, cardstock covers)

1,2-NFL players Sanders, Marino, Plummer, T. Davis battle evil				4.00

GRIFFIN, THE
DC Comics: 1991 - No. 6, 1991 ($4.95, limited series, 52 pgs.)

Book 1-6: Matt Wagner painted-c				5.00

GRIFTER (Also see Team 7 & WildC.A.T.S)
Image Comics (WildStorm Prod.): May, 1995 - No. 10, Mar, 1996 ($1.95)

1 ($1.95, Newsstand)-WildStorm Rising Pt. 5				2.50
1-10:1 ($2.50, Direct)-WildStorm Rising Pt. 5, bound-in trading card				3.00

GRIFTER
Image Comics (WildStorm Prod.): V2#1, July, 1996 - No. 14, Aug, 1997 ($2.50)

V2#1-14: Steven Grant scripts				3.00

GRIFTER AND THE MASK
Dark Horse Comics: Sept, 1996 - No. 2, Oct, 1996 ($2.50, limited series)
1st Dark Horse Comics/Image x-over)

1,2: Steve Seagle scripts				3.00

GRIFTER/BADROCK (Also see WildC.A.T.S & Youngblood)
Image Comics (Extreme Studios): Oct, 1995 - No.2, Nov, 1995 ($2.50, unfinished limited series)

1,2: 2-Flip book w/Badrock #2				2.50

GRIFTER: ONE SHOT
Image Comics (WildStorm Productions): Jan, 1995 ($4.95, one-shot)

1-Flip-c				5.00

GRIFTER/SHI
Image Comics (WildStorm Productions): Apr, 1996 - No. 2, May, 1996 ($2.95, limited series)

1,2: 1-Jim Lee-c/a(p); Travis Charest-a(p). 2-Billy Tucci-c/a(p); Travis Charest-a(p)				3.00

GRIM GHOST, THE
Atlas/Seaboard Publ.: Jan, 1975 - No. 3, July, 1975

1-3: Fleisher-s in all. 1-Origin. 2-Son of Satan; Colan-a. 3-Heath-c				6.00

GRIMJACK (Also see Demon Knight & Starslayer)
First Comics: Aug, 1984 - No. 81, Apr, 1991 ($1.00/$1.95/$2.25)

1-John Ostrander scripts & Tim Truman-c/a begins.				3.00
2-25: 20-Sutton-c/a begins. 22-Bolland-a.				2.25
26-2nd color Teenage Mutant Ninja Turtles				2.50
27-74,76-81 (Later issues $1.95, $2.25): 30-Dynamo Joe x-over; 31-Mandrake-c/a begins. 73,74-Kelley Jones-a				2.25
75-(\$5.95, 52 pgs.)-Fold-out map; coated stock				6.00
NOTE: *Truman c/a-1-17.*				

GRIMJACK CASEFILES
First Comics: Nov, 1990 - No. 5, Mar, 1991 ($1.95, limited series)

1-5 Reprints 1st stories from Starslayer #10 on				2.25

GRIMM'S GHOST STORIES (See Dan Curtis)
Gold Key/Whitman No. 55 on: Jan, 1972 - No. 60, June, 1982 (Painted-c #1-42,44,46-56)

1	3	9	20	30
2-5,8: 5,8-Williamson-a	2	6	11	16
6,7,9,10	2	6	9	12
11-20	1	3	6	9
21-42,45-54: 32,34-Reprints. 45-Photo-c	1	3	5	7
43,44,55-60: 43,44-(52 pgs.). 43-Photo-c. 58(2/82). 59(4/82)-Williamson-a(r/#8).				

60(6/82)	1	3	6	9
Mini-Comic No. 1 (3-1/4x6-1/2", 1976)	1	3	6	8

NOTE: *Reprints-#32?, 34?, 39, 43, 44, 47?, 53; 56-60(1/3). Bolle a-8, 17, 22-25, 27, 29(2), 33, 35, 41, 43r, 45(2), 48(2), 50, 52. Celardo a-17, 26, 28p, 30, 31, 43(2), 45. Lopez a-24, 25. McWilliams a-33, 44r, 48, 54(2), 57, 58. Win Mortimer a-31, 33, 49, 51, 55, 56, 58(2), 59, 60. Roussos a-25, 30. Sparling a-23, 24, 28, 30, 31, 33, 43r, 44, 45, 51(2), 52, 56, 58, 59(2), 60. Spiegle a-44.*

GRIN (The American Funny Book) (Satire)
APAG House Pubs: Nov, 1972 - No. 3, April, 1973 (Magazine, 52 pgs.)

1-Parodies-Godfather, All in the Family	3	9	17	25
2,3	2	6	11	15

GRIN & BEAR IT (See Gags)
Dell Publishing Co.: No. 28, 1941

Large Feature Comic 28	11	33	77	140

GRIPS (Extreme violence)
Silverwolf Comics: Sept, 1986 - No. 4, Dec, 1986 ($1.50, B&W, mature)

1-Tim Vigil-c/a in all				6.00
2-4				4.00

GRIP: THE STRANGE WORLD OF MEN
DC Comics (Vertigo): Jan, 2002 - No. 5 ($2.50, limited series)

1,2-Gilbert Hernandez-c/a				2.50

GRIT GRADY (See Holyoke One-Shot No. 1)

GROO (Sergio Aragonés'...)
Image Comics: Dec, 1994 - No. 12, Dec, 1995 ($1.95)

1-12: 2-Indicia reads #1, Jan, 1995; Aragonés-c/a in all				3.50

GROO (Sergio Aragonés'...)
Dark Horse Comics: Jan, 1998 - No. 4, Apr, 1998 ($2.95)

1-4: Aragonés-c/a in all				4.00

GROO CHRONICLES, THE (Sergio Aragonés)
Marvel Comics (Epic Comics): June, 1989 - No. 6, Feb, 1990 ($3.50)

Book 1-6: Reprints early Pacific issues				3.50

GROO SPECIAL
Eclipse Comics: Oct, 1984 ($2.00, 52 pgs., Baxter paper)

1-Aragonés-c/a	2	6	11	16

GROO THE WANDERER (See Destroyer Duck #1 & Starslayer #5)
Pacific Comics: Dec, 1982 - No. 8, Apr, 1984

1-Aragonés-c/a(p) in all; Aragonés bio., photo	2	6	13	20
2-5: 5-Deluxe paper (1.00-c)	2	6	9	12
6-8	2	6	10	14

GROO THE WANDERER (Sergio Aragonés'...) (See Marvel Graphic Novel #32)
Marvel Comics (Epic Comics): March, 1985 - No. 120, Jan, 1995

1-Aragonés-c/a in all	2	6	9	12
2-10				5.00
11-20,50-($1.50, double size)				4.00
21-49,51-99: 87-direct sale only, high quality paper				3.00
100-($2.95, 52 pgs.)				4.00
101-120				3.00
Groo Carnival, The (12/91, $8.95)-r/#9-12				11.00
Groo Garden, The (4/94, $10.95)-r/#25-28				11.00

GROOVY (Cartoon Comics - not CCA approved)
Marvel Comics Group: March, 1968 - No. 3, July, 1968

1-Monkees, Ringo Starr, Sonny & Cher, Mamas & Papas photos	8	24	56	90
2,3	5	15	38	60

GROSS POINT
DC Comics: Aug, 1997 - No. 14, Aug, 1998 ($2.50)

1-14: 1-Waid/Augustyn-s				2.50

GROUP LARUE, THE
Innovation Publishing: 1989 - No. 4, 1990 ($1.95, mini-series)

1-4-By Mike Baron				2.25

GRRL SCOUTS (Jim Mahfood's...)
Oni Press: Mar,1999 - No. 4, Dec, 1999 ($2.95, B&W, limited series)

Guardians of Metropolis #1 © DC

Guardians of the Galaxy #8 © MAR

Gun Runner #6 © MAR

	GD2.0	FN6.0	VF8.0	NM9.4

1-4-Mahfood-s/c/a — 3.00

GUADALCANAL DIARY (See American Library)

GUARDIANS OF JUSTICE & THE O-FORCE
Shadow Comics: 1990 (no date) ($1.50, 7-1/2 x10-1/4)
1-Super-hero group — 2.25

GUARDIANS OF METROPOLIS
DC Comics: Nov, 1995 - Feb, 1995 ($1.50, limited series)
1-4: 1-Superman & Granny Goodness app. — 2.25

GUARDIANS OF THE GALAXY (Also see The Defenders #26, Marvel Presents #3, Marvel Super-Heroes #18, Marvel Two-In-One #5)
Marvel Comics: June, 1990 - No. 62, July, 1995 ($1.00/$1.25)
1-Valentino-c/a(p) begin. — 3.00
2-16: 2-Zeck-c(i). 5-McFarlane-c(i). 7-Intro Malevolence (Mephisto's daughter); Perez-c(i). 8-Intro Rancor (descendant of Wolverine) in cameo. 9-1st full app. Rancor; Rob Liefeld-c(i). 10-Jim Lee-c(i). 13,14-1st app. Spirit of Vengeance (futuristic Ghost Rider). 14-Spirit of Vengeance vs. The Guardians. 15-Starlin-c(i). 16-($1.50, 52 pgs.)-Starlin-c(i) — 2.50
17-24,26-38,40-47: 17-20-31st century Punishers storyline. 20-Last $1.00-c. 21-Rancor app. 22-Reintro Starhawk. 24-Silver Surfer-c/story; Ron Lim-c. 26-Origin retold. 27-28-Infinity War x-over; 27-Inhumans app. 43-Intro Wooden (son of Thor) — 2.25
25-($2.50)-Prism foil-c; Silver Surfer/Galactus-c/s — 3.00
25-($2.50)-Without foil-c; newsstand edition — 2.50
39-($2.95, 52 pgs.)-Embossed & holo-grafx foil-c; Dr. Doom vs. Rancor — 2.25
48,49,51-62: 48-bound-in trading card sheet — 2.25
50-($2.00, 52 pgs.)-Newsstand edition — 2.25
50-($2.95, 52 pgs.)-Collectors ed. w/foil embossed-c — 3.00
Annual 1-4: ('91-'94, 68 pgs.)-1-2 pg. origin. 2-Spirit of Vengeance-c/story. 3-Bagged w/card — 3.00

GUERRILLA WAR (Formerly Jungle War Stories)
Dell Publishing Co.: No. 12, July-Sept, 1965 - No. 14, Mar, 1966

12-14	2	6	13	20

GUFF
Dark Horse Comics: Apr, 1998 ($1.95, B&W)
1-Flip book; Aragonés-c — 2.25

GUILTY (See Justice Traps the Guilty)

GULLIVER'S TRAVELS (See Dell Jr. Treasury No. 3)
Dell Publishing Co.: Sept-Nov, 1965 - No. 3, May, 1966

1	5	15	35	60
2,3	4	12	27	42

GUMBY'S SUMMER FUN SPECIAL
Comico: July, 1987 ($2.50)
1-Art Adams-c/a; B. Burden scripts — 3.00

GUMBY'S WINTER FUN SPECIAL
Comico: Dec, 1988 ($2.50, 44 pgs.)
1-Art Adams-c/a — 3.00

GUMPS, THE (See Merry Christmas…, Popular & Super Comics)
Dell Publ. Co./Bridgeport Herald Corp.: No. 73, 1945; Mar-Apr, 1947 - No. 5, Nov-Dec, 1947

Four Color 73 (Dell)(1945)	12	36	84	160
1 (3-4/47)	16	48	83	140
2-5	10	30	55	85

GUNFIGHTER (Fat & Slat #1-4) (Becomes Haunt of Fear #15 on)
E. C. Comics (Fables Publ. Co.): No. 5, Sum, 1948 - No. 14, Mar-Apr, 1950

5,6-Moon Girl in each	55	165	330	575
7-14: 14-Bondage-c	40	120	232	400

NOTE: Craig & H. C. Kiefer art in most issues. Craig c-5, 6, 13, 14. Feldstein/Craig a-10. Feldstein a-7-11. Harrison/Wood a-13, 14. Ingels a-5-14; c-7-12.

GUNFIGHTERS, THE
Super Comics (Reprints): 1963 - 1964
10-12,15,16,18: 10,11-r/Billy the Kid #s? 12-r/The Rider #5(Swift Arrow). 15-r/Straight Arrow #42; Powell-r. 16-r/Billy the Kid #?(Toby). 18-r/The Rider #3; Severin-c

	2	6	11	16

	GD2.0	FN6.0	VF8.0	NM9.

GUNFIGHTERS, THE (Formerly Kid Montana)
Charlton Comics: No. 51, 10/66 - No. 52, 10/67; No. 53, 6/79 - No. 85, 7/84

51,52	2	6	13	20
53,54,56:53,54-Williamson/Torres-r/Six Gun Heroes #47,49. 56-Williamson/Severin-c; Severin-r/Sheriff of Tombstone #1	1	3	6	9
55,57-80				6.00
81-84-Lower print run	1	3	5	7
85-S&K-r/1955 Bullseye	1	3	6	8

GUNFIRE (See Deathstroke Annual #2 & Showcase 94 #1,2)
DC Comics: May, 1994 - No. 13, June, 1995 ($1.75/$2.25)
1-5,0,6-13: 2-Ricochet-c/story. 5-(9/94). 0-(10/94). 6-(11/94) — 2.25

GUN GLORY (Movie)
Dell Publishing Co.: No. 846, Oct, 1957 (one-shot)

Four Color 846-Toth-a, photo-c.	9	27	63	120

GUNHAWK, THE (Formerly Whip Wilson)(See Wild Western)
Marvel Comics/Atlas (MCI): No. 12, Nov, 1950 - No. 18, Dec, 1951
(Also see Two-Gun Western #5)

12	20	60	105	175
13-18: 13-Tuska-a. 16-Colan-a. 18-Maneely-c	14	42	72	120

GUNHAWKS (Gunhawk No. 7)
Marvel Comics Group: Oct, 1972 - No. 7, October, 1973

1,6: 1-Reno Jones, Kid Cassidy; Shores-c/a(p). 6-Kid Cassidy dies	2	6	13	20
2-5,7: 7-Reno Jones solo	2	6	11	15

GUNHED
Vix Comics: 1990 - No. 3, 1991? ($4.95, 7-1/8 x 9-1/8, 52 pgs., bi-monthly)
1-3: Japanese sci-fi based on 1991 movie — 5.00

GUNMASTER (Becomes Judo Master #89 on)
Charlton Comics: 9/64 - No. 4, 1965; No. 84, 7/65 - No. 88, 3-4/66; No. 89, 10/67

V1#1	3	10	23	35
2,4, V5#84-86: 84-Formerly Six-Gun Heroes	2	6	15	22
V5#87-89	2	6	11	16

NOTE: Vol. 5 was originally cancelled with #88 (3-4/66). #89 on, became Judo Master, then later in 1967, Charlton issued #89 as a Gunmaster one-shot.

GUN RUNNER
Marvel Comics UK: Oct, 1993 - No. 6, Mar, 1994 ($1.75, limited series)
1-($2.75)-Polybagged w/4 trading cards; Spirits of Vengeance app. — 3.00
2-6: 2-Ghost Rider & Blaze app. — 2.25

GUNS AGAINST GANGSTERS (True-To-Life Romances #8 on)
Curtis Publications/Novelty Press: Sept-Oct, 1948 - No. 6, July-Aug, 1949; V2#1, Sept-Oct, 1949

1-Toni & Greg Gayle begins by Schomburg; L.B. Cole-c	39	117	208	360
2-L.B. Cole-c	29	87	156	270
3-6, V2#1: 6-Toni Gayle-c	25	75	130	225

NOTE: L. B. Cole c-1-6, V2#1, 2; a-1, 2, 3(2), 4-6.

GUNSLINGER
Dell Publishing Co.: No. 1220, Oct-Dec, 1961 (one-shot)

Four Color 1220-Photo-c	9	27	63	110

GUNSLINGER (Formerly Tex Dawson…)
Marvel Comics Group: No. 2, Apr, 1973 - No. 3, June, 1973

2,3	2	6	11	16

GUNSLINGERS
Marvel Comics: Feb, 2000 ($2.99)
1-Reprints stories of Two-Gun Kid, Rawhide Kid and Caleb Hammer — 3.00

GUNSMITH CATS: (Title series), **Dark Horse Comics**
--BAD TRIP (Manga), 6/98 - No. 6, 11/98 ($2.95, B&W) 1-6 — 3.00
--BEAN BANDIT (Manga), 1/99 - No. 9 ($2.95, B&W, limited series) 1-9 — 3.00
--GOLDIE VS. MISTY (Manga), 11/97 - No. 7, 5/98 ($2.95, B&W) 1-7 — 3.00
--KIDNAPPED (Manga), 11/99 - No. 10, 8/00 ($2.95, B&W) 1-10 — 3.00

Gunsmoke Western #68 © ATL

The Gunwitch: Outskirts of Doom #1 © Dan Brereton

Halloween II The Blackest Eyes © Chaos!

HA

-MISTER V (Manga), 10/00 - No. 11, 8/01 ($3.50/$2.99), B&W) 1-7,9-11   3.50
8-($2.99)   3.00
-THE RETURN OF GRAY (Manga), 8/96 - No. 7, 2/97 ($2.95, B&W) 1-7   3.00
-SHADES OF GRAY (Manga), 5/97 - No. 5, 9/97 ($2.95, B&W) 1-5   3.00
-SPECIAL (Manga) Nov, 2001 ($2.99, B&W, one-shot)   3.00

GUNSMOKE (Blazing Stories of the West)
Western Comics (Youthful Magazines): Apr-May, 1949 - No. 16, Jan, 1952

1-Gunsmoke & Masked Marvel begin by Ingels; Ingels bondage-c	40	120	240	420
2-Ingels-c/a(2)	29	87	153	265
3-Ingels bondage-c/a	24	72	127	215
4-6: Ingels-c/s	19	57	99	165
7-10	11	33	55	90
11-16: 15,16-Western/horror stories	10	30	55	80

NOTE: Stallman a-11, 14. Wildey a-15, 16.

GUNSMOKE (TV)
Dell Publishing Co./Gold Key (All have James Arness photo-c): No. 679, Feb, 1956 - No. 27, Feb, 1969 - No. 6, Feb, 1970

Four Color 679(#1)	17	51	119	220
Four Color 720,769,797,844 (#2-5),6(11-1/57-58)	9	27	63	110
7,8,9,11,12-Williamson-a in all, 4 pgs. each	9	27	63	115
10-Williamson/Crandall-a, 4 pgs.	9	27	63	115
13-27	7	21	49	90
1 (Gold Key)	5	15	35	65
2-6('69-70)	3	10	23	35

GUNSMOKE TRAIL
Ajax-Farrell Publ./Four Star Comic Corp.: June, 1957 - No. 4, Dec, 1957

1	11	33	55	90
2-4	6	18	32	45

GUNSMOKE WESTERN (Formerly Western Tales of Black Rider)
Atlas Comics No. 32-35(CPS/NPI); Marvel No. 36 on: No. 32, Dec, 1955 - No. 77, July, 1963

32-Baker & Drucker-a	17	51	88	150
33,35,36-Williamson-a in each: 5,6 & 4 pgs. plus Drucker-a #33. 33-Kinstler-a?	14	42	72	120
34-Baker-a, 4 pgs.; Kirby-c	12	36	61	100
37-Davis-a(2); Williamson text illo	11	33	55	90
38,39: 39-Williamson text illo (unsigned)	9	27	49	70
40-Williamson/Mayo-a (4 pgs.)	9	27	49	70
41,42,45,46,48,49,52-54,57,58,60: 49,52-Kirby-a from Texas story. 57-1st Two Gun Kid by Severin. 60-Sam Hawk app. in Kid Colt	7	21	36	50
44-Torres-a	7	21	36	50
47,51,59,61: 47,51,59-Kirby-a. 61-Crandall-a	8	24	45	65
50-Kirby, Crandall-a	10	30	55	80
55,56-Matt Baker-a	9	27	49	70
62-67,69,71-73,77-Kirby-a. 72-Origin Kid Colt	5	15	34	55
68,70,74-76: 68-(10¢-c)	4	12	26	40
68-(10¢ cover price blacked out, 12¢ printed on)	7	21	50	80

NOTE: Colan a-35-37, 39, 72, 76. Davis a-37, 52, 54, 55; c-50, 54. Ditko a-66; c-56p. Drucker a-32-34. Heath c-33. Jack Keller a-35, 40, 60, 72; c-72. Kirby a-47, 50, 51, 59, 62(3), 63-67, 69, 71, 73, 77; c-34(w/Ditko),57, 58, 60, 61(w/Ayers), 62, 63, 66, 68, 69, 71-77. Robinson a-35. Severin a-35, 59-61; c-34, 35, 39, 42, 43. Tuska a-34. Wildey a-10, 37, 42, 56, 57. Kid Colt in all. Two-Gun Kid in No. 57, 59, 60-63. Wyatt Earp in No. 45, 48, 49, 52, 54, 55, 58.

GUNS OF FACT & FICTION (Also see A-1 Comics)
Magazine Enterprises: No. 13, 1948 (one-shot)

A-1 13-Used in SOTI, pg. 19; Ingels & J. Craig-a	30	90	159	275

GUNS OF THE DRAGON
DC Comics: Oct, 1998 - No. 4, Jan, 1999 ($2.50, limited series)

1-4-DCU in the 1920's; Enemy Ace & Bat Lash app.   2.50

GUNWITCH, THE : OUTSKIRTS OF DOOM (See The Nocturnals)
Oni Press: June, 2001 - No. 3, Oct, 2001 ($2.95, B&W, limited series)

1-3-Brereton-s/a   3.00

GUY GARDNER (Guy Gardner: Warrior #17 on)(Also see Green Lantern #59)
DC Comics: Oct, 1992 - No. 44, July, 1996 ($1.25/$1.50/$1.75)

1-24,0,26-30: 1-Staton-c/a(p) begins. 6-Guy vs. Hal Jordan. 8-Vs. Lobo-c/story.

5-JLA x-over, begin $1.50-c. 18-Begin 4-part Emerald Fallout story; splash page x-over GL #50. 18-21-Vs. Hal Jordan. 24-(9/94)-Zero Hour.

0-(10/94)				2.50
25 (11/94, $2.50, 52 pgs.)				3.00
29 ($2.95)-Gatefold-c				3.50
29-Variant-c (Edward Hopper's Nighthawks)				2.50
31-44: 31-$1.75-c begins. 40-Gorilla Grodd-c/app. 44-Parallax-app. (1 pg.)				2.50
Annual 1 (1995, $3.50)-Year One story				4.00
Annual 2 (1996, $2.95)-Legends of the Dead Earth story				3.00

GUY GARDNER REBORN
DC Comics: 1992 - Book 3, 1992 ($4.95, limited series)

1-3: Staton-c/a(p). 1-Lobo-c/cameo. 2,3-Lobo-c/s   5.00

GYPSY COLT
Dell Publishing Co.: No. 568, June, 1954 (one-shot)

Four Color 568--Movie	4	12	30	50

GYRO GEARLOOSE (See Dynabrite Comics, Walt Disney's C&S #140 & Walt Disney Showcase #18)
Dell Publishing Co.: No. 1047, Nov-Jan/1959-60 - May-July, 1962 (Disney)

Four Color 1047 (No. 1)-All Barks-c/a	18	54	126	240
Four Color 1095,1184-All by Carl Barks	10	30	70	130
Four Color 1267-Barks c/a, 4 pgs.	7	21	49	95
01329-207 (#1, 5-7/62)-Barks-c only (intended as 4-Color 1329?)	5	15	35	65

HACKER FILES, THE
DC Comics: Aug, 1992 - No. 12, July, 1993 ($1.95)

1-12: 1-Sutton-a(p) begins; computer generated-c   2.25

HAGAR THE HORRIBLE (See Comics Reading Libraries in the Promotional Comics section)

HA HA COMICS (Teepee Tim No. 100 on; also see Giggle Comics)
Scope Mag.(Creston Publ.) No. 1-80/American Comics Group: Oct, 1943 - No. 99, Jan, 1955

1-Funny animal	33	99	174	300
2	16	48	83	140
3-5: Ken Hultgren-a begins?	12	36	61	100
6-10	10	30	55	80
11-20: 14-Infinity-c	8	24	42	60
21-40	7	21	36	50
41-94,96-99: 49-X-mas-c	6	18	29	40
95-3-D effect-c	15	45	77	130

HAIR BEAR BUNCH, THE (TV) (See Fun-In No. 13)
Gold Key: Feb, 1972 - No. 9, Feb, 1974 (Hanna-Barbera)

1	4	12	26	40
2-9	3	9	17	24

HALLELUJAH TRAIL, THE (See Movie Classics)

HALL OF FAME FEATURING THE T.H.U.N.D.E.R. AGENTS
JC Productions(Archie Comic Group): May, 1983 - No. 3, Dec, 1983

1-3: Thunder Agents-r(Crandall, Kane, Tuska, Wood-a). 2-New Ditko-c   3.00

HALLOWEEN (Movie)
Chaos! Comics: Nov, 2000; Apr, 2001 ($2.95/$2.99, one-shots)

1-Brewer-a; Michael Myers childhood at the Sanitarium   3.00
...II: The Blackest Eyes (4/01, $2.99) Beck-a   3.00
...III: The Devil's Eyes (11/01, $2.99) Justiniano-a   3.00

HALLOWEEN HORROR
Eclipse Comics: Oct, 1987 (Seduction of the Innocent #7)($1.75)

1-Pre-code horror-r   3.00

HALLOWEEN MEGAZINE
Marvel Comics: Dec, 1996 ($3.95, one-shot, 96 pgs.)

1-Reprints Tomb of Dracula   4.00

HALO, AN ANGEL'S STORY
Sirius Entertainment: Apr, 1996 - No. 4, Sept, 1996 ($2.95, limited series)

1-4: Knowles-c/a/scripts   3.00
TPB ($12.95) r/#1-4   13.00

Hammer of the Gods #1
© Michael Oeming & Mark Wheatley

Hand of Fate #24 © ACE

Hangman Comics #3 © MLJ

HALO JONES (See The Ballad of...)

HAMMER, THE
Dark Horse Comics: Oct, 1997 - No. 4, Jan, 1998 ($2.95, limited series)
1-4-Kelley Jones-s/c/a, ...: Uncle Alex (8/98, $2.95)	3.00

HAMMER, THE: THE OUTSIDER
Dark Horse Comics: Feb, 1999 - No. 3, Apr, 1999 ($2.95, limited series)
1-3-Kelley Jones-s/c/a	3.00

HAMMERLOCKE
DC Comics: Sept, 1992 - No. 9, May, 1993 ($1.75, limited series)
1-($2.50, 52 pgs.)-Chris Sprouse-c/a in all	3.00
2-9	2.25

HAMMER OF GOD (Also see Nexus)
First Comics: Feb, 1990 - No. 4, May, 1990 ($1.95, limited series)
1-4	2.50

HAMMER OF GOD: BUTCH
Dark Horse Comics: May, 1994 - No. 4, Aug, 1994 ($2.50, limited series)
1-3	2.50

HAMMER OF GOD: PENTATHLON
Dark Horse Comics: Jan, 1994 ($2.50, one shot)
1-character from Nexus	2.50

HAMMER OF GOD: SWORD OF JUSTICE
First Comics: Feb 1991 - Mar 1991 ($4.95, lim. series, squarebound, 52 pgs.)
V2#1,2	5.00

HAMMER OF THE GODS
Insight Studio Groups: 2001 - No. 5, 2001 ($2.95, limited series)
1-Michael Oeming & Mark Wheatley-s/a; Frank Cho-c	6.00
2-5: 3-Hughes-c. 5-Dave Johnson-c	3.00

HANDBOOK OF THE CONAN UNIVERSE, THE
Marvel Comics: June, 1985 ($1.25, one-shot)
1-Kaluta-c.	3.00

HAND OF FATE (Formerly Men Against Crime)
Ace Magazines: No. 8, Dec, 1951 - No. 25, Dec, 1954 (Weird/horror stories)
(Two #25's)
8-Surrealistic text story	40	120	232	400
9,10,21-Necronomicon sty; drug belladonna used	24	72	127	215
11-18,20,22,23	20	60	105	175
19-Bondage, hypo needle scenes	21	63	110	185
24-Electric chair-c	31	93	165	285
25a(11/54), 25b(12/54)-Both have Cameron-a	16	48	83	140

NOTE: Cameron a-9, 10, 19-25a, 25b; c-13. Sekowsky a-8, 9, 13, 14.

HAND OF FATE
Eclipse Comics: Feb, 1988 - No. 3, Apr, 1988 ($1.75/$2.00, Baxter paper)
1-3; 3-B&W	2.25

HANDS OF THE DRAGON
Seaboard Periodicals (Atlas): June, 1975
1-Origin/1st app.; Craig-a(p)/Mooney inks	1	3	5	7

HANGMAN COMICS (Special Comics No. 1; Black Hood No. 9 on)
(Also see Flyman, Mighty Comics, Mighty Crusaders & Pep Comics)
MLJ Magazines: No. 2, Spring, 1942 - No. 8, Fall, 1943
2-The Hangman, Boy Buddies begin	191	573	1194	2100
3-Beheading splash pg.; 1st Nazi war-c	123	369	769	1350
4-8: 5-1st Jap war-c. 8-2nd app. Super Duck (ties w/Jolly Jingles #11)	107	321	669	1175

NOTE: Fuje a-7(3), 8(3); c-3. Reinman c/a-3. Bondage a-3. Sahle c-6.

HANK
Pentagon Publishing Co.: 1946
nn-Coulton Waugh's newspaper reprint	8	24	42	60

HANNA-BARBERA (See Golden Comics Digest No. 2, 7, 11)

HANNA-BARBERA ALL-STARS
Archie Publications: Oct, 1995 - No. 6, Sept, 1996 ($1.50, bi-monthly)
1-6	3.00

HANNA-BARBERA BANDWAGON (TV)
Gold Key: Oct, 1962 - No. 3, Apr, 1963
1-Giant, 84 pgs. 1-Augie Doggie app.; 1st app. Lippy the Lion, Touché Turtle & Dum Dum, Wally Gator, Loopy de Loop,	13	39	94	160
2-Giant, 84 pgs.; Mr. & Mrs. J. Evil Scientist (1st app.) in Snagglepuss story; Yakky Doodle, Ruff and Reddy and others app.	10	30	70	120
3-Regular size; Mr. & Mrs. J. Evil Scientist app. (pre-#1), Snagglepuss, Wally Gator and others app.	7	21	53	85

HANNA-BARBERA GIANT SIZE
Harvey Comics: Oct, 1992 - No. 3 ($2.25, 68 pgs.)
V2#1-3:Flintstones, Yogi Bear, Magilla Gorilla, Huckleberry Hound, Quick Draw McGraw, Yakky Doodle & Chopper, Jetsons & others	4.00

HANNA-BARBERA HI-ADVENTURE HEROES (See Hi-Adventure...)

HANNA-BARBERA PARADE (TV)
Charlton Comics: Sept, 1971 - No. 10, Dec, 1972
1	8	24	56	90
2,4-10	4	12	29	45
3-(52 pgs.)- "Summer Picnic"	6	18	42	70

NOTE: No. 4 (1/72) went on sale late in 1972 with the January 1973 issues.

HANNA-BARBERA PRESENTS
Archie Publications: Nov, 1995 - No. 6 ($1.50, bi-monthly)
1-8: 1-Atom Ant & Secret Squirrel. 2-Wacky Races. 3-Yogi Bear. 4-Quick Draw McGraw & Magilla Gorilla. 5-A Pup Named Scooby-Doo. 6-Superstar Olympics. 7-Wacky Races. 8-Frankenstein Jr. & the Impossibles	3.00

HANNA-BARBERA SPOTLIGHT (See Spotlight)

HANNA-BARBERA SUPER TV HEROES (TV)
Gold Key: Apr, 1968 - No. 7, Oct, 1969 (Hanna-Barbera)
1-The Birdman, The Herculoids(ends #6; not in #2), Moby Dick, Young Samson & Goliath(ends #2,4), and The Mighty Mightor begin; Spiegle-a in all	18	54	126	225
2-The Galaxy Trio app.; Shazzan begins; 12¢ & 15¢ versions exist	12	36	88	150
3,6,7-The Space Ghost app.	12	36	84	140
4,5	10	30	70	120

NOTE: Birdman in #1,2,4,5. Herculoids in #2,4-7. Mighty Mightor in #1,2,4-7. Moby Dick in all. Shazzan in #2-5. Young Samson & Goliath in #1,3.

HANNA-BARBERA TV FUN FAVORITES (See Golden Comics Digest #2,7,11)

HANNA-BARBERA (TV STARS) (See TV Stars)

HANS BRINKER (Disney)
Dell Publishing Co.: No. 1273, Feb, 1962 (one-shot)
Four Color 1273-Movie, photo-c	6	18	42	80

HANS CHRISTIAN ANDERSEN
Ziff-Davis Publ. Co.: 1953 (100 pgs., Special Issue)
nn-Danny Kaye (movie)-Photo-c; fairy tales	17	51	88	150

HANSEL & GRETEL
Dell Publishing Co.: No. 590, Oct, 1954 (one-shot)
Four Color 590-Partial photo-c	6	18	42	80

HANSI, THE GIRL WHO LOVED THE SWASTIKA
Spire Christian Comics (Fleming H. Revell Co.): 1973, 1976 (39¢/49¢)
nn	2	6	15	22

HAP HAZARD COMICS (Real Love No. 25 on)
Ace Magazines (Readers' Research): Summer, 1944 - No. 24, Feb, 1949
(#1-6 are quarterly issues)
1	15	45	77	130
2	8	24	45	65
3-10	7	21	36	50
11-13,15-24	6	18	29	40
14-Feldstein-c (4/47)	9	27	49	70

HAP HOPPER (See Comics Revue No. 2)

HAPPIEST MILLIONAIRE, THE (See Movie Comics)

HAPPI TIM (See March of Comics No. 182)

HAPPY BIRTHDAY MARTHA WASHINGTON (Also see Give Me Liberty,

Happy Comics #11 © STD

Hardcase #21 © MAL

Harley Quinn #3 © DC

	GD2.0	FN6.0	VF8.0	NM9.4

Martha Washington Goes To War, & Martha Washington Stranded In Space)
Dark Horse Comics: Mar, 1995 ($2.95, one-shot)

1-Miller script; Gibbons-c/a ... 3.00

HAPPY COMICS (Happy Rabbit No. 41 on)
Nedor Publ./Standard Comics (Animated Cartoons): Aug, 1943 - No. 40, Dec, 1950 (Companion to Goofy Comics)

	GD2.0	FN6.0	VF8.0	NM9.4
1-Funny animal	27	81	145	250
2	14	42	72	125
3-10	10	30	55	80
11-19	8	24	42	60
20-31,34-37-Frazetta text illos in all (2 in #34&35, 3 in #27,28,30). 27-Al Fago-a	10	30	55	80
32-Frazetta-a, 7 pgs. plus 2 text illos; Roussos-a	21	63	110	185
33-Frazetta-a(2), 6 pgs. each (Scarce)	29	87	153	265
38-40	6	18	32	45

HAPPYDALE: DEVILS IN THE DESERT
DC Comics (Vertigo): 1999 - No. 2, 1999 ($6.95, limited series)

1,2-Andrew Dabb-s/Seth Fisher-a ... 7.00

HAPPY DAYS (TV)(See Kite Fun Book)
Gold Key: Mar, 1979 - No. 6, Feb, 1980

1-Photo-c of TV cast; 35¢-c	2	6	13	20
2-6-(40¢-c)	1	4	7	10

HAPPY HOLIDAY (See March of Comics No. 181)

HAPPY HOULIHANS (Saddle Justice No. 3 on; see Blackstone, The Magician Detective)
E. C. Comics: Fall, 1947 - No. 2, Winter, 1947-48

1-Origin Moon Girl (same date as Moon Girl #1)	47	141	286	500
2	29	87	156	270

HAPPY JACK
Red Top (Decker): Aug, 1957 - No. 2, Nov, 1957

V1#1,2	5	15	23	30

HAPPY JACK HOWARD
Red Top (Farrell)/Decker: 1957

nn-Reprints Handy Andy story from E. C. Dandy Comics #5, renamed "Happy Jack"	5	15	23	30

HAPPY RABBIT (Formerly Happy Comics)
Standard Comics (Animated Cartoons): No. 41, Feb, 1951 - No. 48, Apr, 1952

41-Funny animal	6	18	29	40
42-48	5	14	21	28

HARBINGER (Also see Unity)
Valiant: Jan, 1992 - No. 41, June, 1995 ($1.95/$2.50)

0-(Advance), 1-1st print run ... 6.00
2-4: 4-Low print run ... 5.00
5-24,26-41: 8,9-Unity x-overs. 8-Miller-c. 9-Simonson-c. 10-1st app. H.A.R.D Corps 10/92). 14-1st app. Stronghold18-Intro Screen. 19-1st app. Stunner. 22-Archer & Armstrong app. 24-Cover similar to #1. 26-Intro New Harbingers. 29-Bound-in trading card. 30-H.A.R.D. Corps app. 32-Eternal Warrior app. 33-Dr. Eclipse app. ... 2.50
25-($3.50, 52 pgs.)-Harada vs. Sting ... 3.50
...Files 1,2 (8/94,2/95 $2.50) ... 2.50
Trade paperback nn (11/92, $9.95)-Reprints #1-4 & comes polybagged with a copy of Harbinger #0 w/new-c. ... 10.00
NOTE: Issues 1-6 have coupons with origin of Harada and are redeemable for Harbinger #0.

HARD BOILED
Dark Horse Comics: Sept, 1990 - No. 3, Mar, 1992 ($4.95/$5.95, 8 1/2x11", lim. ser.)

1-3-Miller-s; Darrow-c/a; sexually explicit & violent	1	3	5	7
TPB (5/93, $15.95)				16.00
Big Damn Hard Boiled (12/97, $29.95, B&W) r/#1-3				30.00

HARDCASE (See Break Thru, Flood Relief & Ultraforce, 1st Series)
Malibu Comics (Ultraverse): June, 1993 - No. 26, Aug, 1995 ($1.95/$2.50)

1-Intro Hardcase; Dave Gibbons-c; has coupon for Ultraverse Premiere #0; Jim Callahan-a(p) begin, ends #3 ... 3.00
1-With coupon missing ... 2.25

	GD2.0	FN6.0	VF8.0	NM9.4

1-Platinum Edition ... 4.00
1-Holographic Cover Edition; 1st full-c holograph tied w/Prime 1 & Strangers 1 ... 7.00
1-Ultra Limited silver foil-c ... 4.00
2,3-Callahan-a. 2-($2.50)-Newsstand edition bagged w/trading card ... 2.50
4,6-15, 17-19: 4-Strangers app. 7-Break-Thru x-over. 8-Solution app. 9-Vs. Turf. 12-Silver foil logo, wraparound-c. 17-Prime app. ... 2.50
5-($2.50, 48 pgs.)-Rune flip-c/story by B. Smith (3 pgs.) ... 2.50
16 ($3.50, 68 pgs.)-Rune pin-up ... 3.50
20-26: 23-Loki app. ... 2.50
NOTE: *Perez* a-8(2); c-20i.

HARDCORE STATION
DC Comics: July, 1998 - No. 6, Dec, 1998 ($2.50, limited series)

1-6-Starlin-s/a(p). 3-Green Lantern-c/app. 5,6-JLA-c/app. ... 3.00

H.A.R.D. CORPS, THE (See Harbinger #10)
Valiant: Dec, 1992 - No. 30, Feb, 1995 ($2.25) (Harbinger spin-off)

1-(Advance) ... 3.00
1-($2.50)-Gatefold-c by Jim Lee & Bob Layton ... 3.00
1-Gold variant ... 5.00
2-30: 5-Bloodshot-c/story cont'd from Bloodshot #3. 5-Variant edition; came w/Comic Defense System. 10-Turok app. 17-vs. Armorines. 18-Bound-in trad ing card. 20-Harbinger app. ... 2.25

HARDWARE
DC Comics (Milestone): Apr, 1993 - No. 50, Apr, 1997 ($1.50/$1.75/$2.50)

1-($2.50)-Collector's Edition polybagged w/poster & trading card (direct sale only) ... 4.00
1-Platinum Edition ... 5.00
1-15,17-19: 11-Shadow War x-over. 11,14-Simonson-c. 12-Buckler-a(p). 17-Worlds Collide Pt. 2. 18-Simonson-c; Worlds Collide Pt. 9. 15-1st Humberto Ramos DC work ... 2.50
16,50-($3.95, 52 pgs.)-16-Collector's Edition w/gatefold 2nd cover by Byrne; new armor; Icon app. ... 4.00
16,20-24,26-49: 16-($2.50, 52 pgs.)-Newsstand Ed. 49-Moebius-c ... 2.50
25-($2.95, 52 pgs.) ... 3.00

HARDY BOYS, THE, (Disney)
Dell Publ. Co.: No. 760, Dec, 1956 - No. 964, Jan, 1959 (Mickey Mouse Club)

Four Color 760 (#1)-Photo-c	11	33	77	140
Four Color 830(8/57), 887(1/58), 964-Photo-c	9	27	63	120

HARDY BOYS, THE (TV)
Gold Key: Apr, 1970 - No. 4, Jan, 1971

1	4	12	29	45
2-4	3	9	19	28

HARLAN ELLISON'S DREAM CORRIDOR
Dark Horse Comics: Mar, 1995 - No. 5, July, 1995 ($2.95, anthology)

1-5: Adaptation of Ellison stories. 1-4-Byrne-a. ... 3.00
Special (1/95, $4.95) ... 5.00
Trade paperback-(1996, $18.95, 192 pgs)-r/#1-5 & Special #1 ... 19.00

HARLAN ELLISON'S DREAM CORRIDOR QUARTERLY
Dark Horse Comics: V2#1, Aug, 1996 ($5.95, anthology, squarebound)

V2#1-Adaptations of Ellison's stories w/new material; Neal Adams-a ... 6.00

HARLEM GLOBETROTTERS (TV) (See Fun-In No. 8, 10)
Gold Key: Apr, 1972 - No. 12, Jan, 1975 (Hanna-Barbera)

1	3	10	23	35
2-5	2	6	13	20
6-12	2	6	11	16
NOTE: #4, 8, and 12 contain 16 extra pages of advertising.

HARLEY QUINN
DC Comics: Dec, 2000 - Present ($2.95/$2.25)

1-Joker and Poison Ivy app.; Terry & Rachel Dodson-a/c ... 4.00
2-11-($2.25). 2-Two-Face-c/app. 3-Slumber party. 6,7-Riddler app. ... 2.25
12-($2.95) Batman app. ... 3.00
13-16: 13-Joker: Last Laugh ... 2.25
Harley & Ivy: Love on the Lam (2001, $5.95) Winick-s/Chiodo-c/a ... 6.00
...: Our Worlds at War (10/01, $2.95) Jae Lee-c; art by various ... 3.00

	GD2.0	FN6.0	VF8.0	NM9.4

	GD2.0	FN6.0	VF8.0	NM9.

HAROLD TEEN (See Popular Comics, & Super Comics)
Dell Publishing Co.: No. 2, 1942 - No. 209, Jan, 1949

Four Color 2	27	81	189	350
Four Color 209	5	15	34	55

HARRIERS
Entity Comics: June, 1995 - No. 3, 1995 ($2.50)

1-Foil-c; polybagged w/PC game, 1-3 ($2.50)				3.00

HARROWERS, THE (See Clive Barker's...)

HARSH REALM (Inspired 1999 TV series)
Harris Comics: 1993- No. 6, 1994 ($2.95, limited series)

1-6: Painted-c. Hudnall-s/Paquette & Ridgway-a				3.50
TPB (2000, $14.95) r/series				15.00

HARVEY
Marvel Comics: Oct, 1970; No. 2, 12/70; No. 3, 6/72 - No. 6, 12/72

1	8	24	56	90
2-6	5	15	34	55

HARVEY COLLECTORS COMICS (Richie Rich Collectors Comics #10 on, cover title only)
Harvey Publ.: Sept, 1975 - No. 15, Jan, 1978; No. 16, Oct, 1979 (52 pgs.)

1-Reprints Richie Rich #1,2	2	6	11	16
2-10: 7-Splash pg. shows cover to Friendly Ghost Casper #1	1	3	6	9
11-16: 16-Sad Sack-r	1	3	5	7

NOTE: All reprints: Casper-#2, 7, Richie Rich-#1, 3, 5, 6, 8-15, Sad Sack-#16. Wendy-#4. #6 titled 'Richie Rich...'on inside.

HARVEY COMICS HITS (Formerly Joe Palooka #50)
Harvey Publications: No. 51, Oct, 1951 - No. 62, Apr, 1953

51-The Phantom	31	93	165	285
52-Steve Canyon's Air Power(Air Force sponsored)	13	39	66	110
53-Mandrake the Magician	23	69	121	210
54-Tim Tyler's Tales of Jungle Terror	13	39	66	110
55-Love Stories of Mary Worth	8	24	42	60
56-The Phantom; bondage-c	26	78	136	235
57-Rip Kirby Exposes the Kidnap Racket; entire book by Alex Raymond	16	48	83	140
58-Girls in White (nurses stories)	8	24	42	60
59-Tales of the Invisible featuring Scarlet O'Neil	12	36	61	100
60-Paramount Animated Comics #1 (9/52) (3rd app. Baby Huey); 2nd Harvey app. Baby Huey & Casper the Friendly Ghost (1st in Little Audrey #25 (8/52)); 1st app. Herman & Catnip (c/story) & Buzzy the Crow	40	120	220	380
61-Casper the Friendly Ghost #6 (3rd Harvey Casper, 10/52)-Casper-c	40	120	240	420
62-Paramount Animated Comics #2; Herman & Catnip, Baby Huey & Buzzy the Crow	15	45	77	130

HARVEY COMICS LIBRARY
Harvey Comics: Apr, 1952 - No. 2, 1952

1-Teen-Age Dope Slaves as exposed by Rex Morgan, M.D.; drug propaganda story; used in SOTI, pg. 27	100	300	625	1100
2-Dick Tracy Presents Sparkle Plenty in "Blackmail Terror"	23	69	121	210

HARVEY COMICS SPOTLIGHT
Harvey Comics: Sept, 1987 - No. 4, Mar, 1988 (75¢/$1.00)

1-New material; begin 75¢, ends #3; Sand Sack				5.00
2-4: 2,4-All new material. 2-Baby Huey. 3-Little Dot; contains reprints w/5 pg. new story. 4-$1.00-c; Little Audrey				4.00

NOTE: No. 5 was advertised but not published.

HARVEY HITS
Harvey Comics: Sept, 1957 - No. 122, Nov, 1967

1-The Phantom	26	78	182	325
2-Rags Rabbit (10/57)	4	12	29	45
3-Richie Rich (11/57)-r/Little Dot; 1st book devoted to Richie Rich; see Little Dot for 1st app.	72	216	612	1150
4-Little Dot's Uncles (12/57)	15	45	107	185
5-Stevie Mazie's Boy Friend (1/58)	3	10	23	35

6-The Phantom (2/58); Kirby-c; 2pg. Powell-a	18	54	126	225
7-Wendy the Good Little Witch (3/58, pre-dates Wendy #1; 1st book devoted to Wendy)	19	57	134	240
8-Sad Sack's Army Life; George Baker-c	6	18	45	75
9-Richie Rich's Golden Deeds; reprints (2nd book devoted to Richie Rich)	37	111	278	500
10-Little Lotta's Lunch Box	10	30	68	115
11-Little Audrey Summer Fun (7/58)	8	24	56	90
12-The Phantom; Kirby-c; 2pg. Powell-a (8/58)	15	45	105	180
13-Little Dot's Uncles (9/58); Richie Rich 1pg.	10	30	68	115
14-Herman & Katnip (10/58, TV/movies)	3	9	20	30
15-The Phantom (12/58)-1 pg. origin	15	45	105	180
16-Wendy the Good Little Witch (1/59); Casper app.	10	30	68	115
17-Sad Sack's Army Life (2/59)	5	15	38	60
18-Buzzy & the Crow	3	10	23	35
19-Little Audrey (4/59)	5	15	34	55
20-Casper & Spooky	6	18	45	75
21-Wendy the Witch	6	18	45	75
22-Sad Sack's Army Life	4	12	29	45
23-Wendy the Witch (8/59)	6	18	45	75
24-Little Dot's Uncles (9/59); Richie Rich 1pg.	8	24	56	90
25-Herman & Katnip (10/59)	3	9	17	25
26-The Phantom (11/59)	12	35	84	140
27-Wendy the Good Little Witch (12/59)	6	18	45	75
28-Sad Sack's Army Life (1/60)	3	9	20	30
29-Harvey-Toon (No.1)('60); Casper, Buzzy	4	12	29	45
30-Wendy the Witch (3/60)	6	18	45	75
31-Herman & Katnip (4/60)	3	9	17	25
32-Sad Sack's Army Life (5/60)	3	9	19	28
33-Wendy the Witch (6/60)	6	18	45	75
34-Harvey-Toon (7/60)	3	9	20	30
35-Funday Funnies (8/60)	3	9	17	25
36-The Phantom (1960)	10	30	73	125
37-Casper & Nightmare	5	15	34	55
38-Harvey-Toon	3	9	20	30
39-Sad Sack's Army Life (12/60)	3	9	19	28
40-Funday Funnies (1/61)	2	6	15	22
41-Herman & Katnip	3	9	17	25
42-Harvey-Toon (3/61)	3	9	17	25
43-Sad Sack's Army Life (4/61)	3	9	17	25
44-The Phantom (5/61)	10	30	70	120
45-Casper & Nightmare	4	12	26	40
46-Harvey-Toon (7/61)	2	6	15	22
47-Sad Sack's Army Life (8/61)	2	6	15	22
48-The Phantom (9/61)	10	30	70	120
49-Stumbo the Giant (1st app. in Hot Stuff)	9	27	65	110
50-Harvey-Toon (11/61)	2	6	13	20
51-Sad Sack's Army Life (12/61)	2	6	13	20
52-Casper & Nightmare	4	12	26	40
53-Harvey-Toons (2/62)	2	6	12	18
54-Stumbo the Giant	5	15	34	55
55-Sad Sack's Army Life (4/62)	2	6	13	20
56-Casper & Nightmare	4	12	25	38
57-Stumbo the Giant	5	15	34	55
58-Sad Sack's Army Life	2	6	13	20
59-Stumbo the Giant (7/62)	4	12	25	38
60-Stumbo the Giant (9/62)	5	15	34	55
61-Sad Sack's Army Life	2	6	12	18
62-Casper & Nightmare	3	9	21	32
63-Stumbo the Giant	4	12	29	45
64-Sad Sack's Army Life (1/63)	2	6	12	18
65-Casper & Nightmare	3	9	21	32
66-Stumbo The Giant (3/63)	4	12	29	45
67-Sad Sack's Army Life (4/63)	2	6	12	18
68-Casper & Nightmare	3	9	21	32
69-Stumbo the Giant (6/63)	4	12	29	45
70-Sad Sack's Army Life (7/63)	2	6	12	18
71-Casper & Nightmare (8/63)	3	9	19	28
72-Stumbo the Giant	4	12	29	45
73-Little Sad Sack (10/63)	2	6	12	18

Hate Annual #1 © Peter Bagge

Haunted Thrills #2 © AJAX

Haunt of Fear #19 © WMG

HA

	GD2.0	FN6.0	VF8.0	NM9.4
74-Sad Sack's Muttsy… (11/63)	2	6	12	18
75-Casper & Nightmare	3	9	17	25
76-Little Sad Sack	2	6	12	18
77-Sad Sack's Muttsy…	2	6	12	18
78-Stumbo the Giant (3/64); JFK caricature	4	12	29	45
79-87: 79-Little Sad Sack (4/64). 80-Sad Sack's Muttsy… (5/64). 81-Little Sad Sack. 82-Sad Sack's Muttsy… 83-Little Sad Sack(8/64). 84-Sad Sack's Muttsy… 85-Gabby Gob (#1)(10/64). 86-G. I. Juniors (#1)(11/64). 87-Sad Sack's Muttsy… (12/64)	2	6	12	18
88-Stumbo the Giant (1/65)	4	12	29	45
89-122: 89-Sad Sack's Muttsy… 90-Gabby Gob. 91-G. I. Juniors. 92-Sad Sack's Muttsy… (5/65). 93-Sadie Sack (6/65). 94-Gabby Gob. 95-G. I. Juniors (8/65). 96-Gabby Gob (#1)… (9/65). 97-Gabby Gob (10/65). 98-G. I. Juniors (11/65). 99-Sad Sack's Muttsy… (12/65). 100-Gabby Gob(1/66). 101-G. I. Juniors (2/66). 102-Sad Sack's Muttsy… (3/66). 103-Gabby Gob. 104- G. I. Juniors. 105-Sad Sack's Muttsy… 106-Gabby Gob (7/66). 107-G. I. Juniors (8/66). 108-Sad Sack's Muttsy… 109-Gabby Gob. 110-G. I. Juniors (11/66). 111-Sad Sack's Muttsy… (12/66). 112-G. I. Juniors. 113-Sad Sack's Muttsy… 114-G. I. Juniors. 115-Sad Sack's Muttsy… 116-G. I. Juniors (5/67). 117-Sad Sack's Muttsy… 118-G. I. Juniors. 119-Sad Sack's Muttsy… (8/67). 120-G. I. Juniors (9/67). 121-Sad Sack's Muttsy… (10/67). 122-G. I. Juniors (11/67)	2	6	9	12

HARVEY HITS COMICS
Harvey Publications: Nov, 1986 - No. 6, Oct, 1987

1-Little Lotta, Little Dot, Wendy & Baby Huey				6.00
2-6: 3-Xmas-c				4.00

HARVEY POP COMICS (Rock Happening) (Teen Humor)
Harvey Publications: Oct, 1968 - No. 2, Nov, 1969 (Both are 68 pg. Giants)

1-The Cowsills	5	15	35	60
2-Bunny	4	12	30	50

HARVEY 3-D HITS (See Sad Sack)

HARVEY-TOON (…S) (See Harvey Hits Comics Nos. 29, 34, 38, 42, 46, 50, 53)

HARVEY WISEGUYS (…Digest #? on)
Harvey Comics: Nov, 1987; #2, Nov, 1988; #3, Apr, 1989 - No. 4, Nov, 1989 (98 pgs., digest-size, $1.25/$1.75)

1-Hot Stuff, Spooky, etc.				6.00
2-4: 2 (68 pgs.)				4.00

HATARI (See Movie Classics)

HATE
Fantagraphics Books: Spr, 1990 - No. 30, 1998 ($2.50/$2.95, B&W/color)

1	2	6	11	15
2-3	1	3	6	8
4-10				5.00
11-20: 16- color begins				4.00
21-29				3.00
30-($3.95) Last issue				4.00
Annual 1 (2/01, $3.95) Peter Bagge-s/a				4.00
Annual 2 (12/01, $4.95) Peter Bagge-s/a				5.00
Buddy Bites the Bullet! (2001, $16.95) r/Buddy stories in color				17.00
Buddy Go Home! (1997, $16.95) r/Buddy stories in color				17.00
Hate-Ball Special Edition ($3.95, giveaway)-reprints				4.00
Hate Jamboree (10/98, $4.50) old & new cartoons				4.50

HATHAWAYS, THE (TV)
Dell Publishing Co.: No. 1298, Feb-Apr, 1962 (one-shot)

Four Color 1298-Photo-c	4	12	30	50

HAUNTED (See This Magazine Is Haunted)

HAUNTED (Baron Weirwulf's Haunted Library on-c #21 on)
Charlton Comics: 9/71 - No. 18, 11/76; No. 31, 9/77 - No. 75, 9/84

1-All Ditko issue	4	12	25	38
2-7-Ditko-c/a	2	6	13	20
8,12,28-Ditko-a	2	6	11	15
9,19	2	6	9	12
10,20,15,18: 10.20-Sutton-a. 15,18-Sutton-a.	2	6	9	12
1,13,14,16-Ditko-c/a	2	6	12	18
17-Sutton-c/a; Newton-a	2	6	10	14

	GD2.0	FN6.0	VF8.0	NM9.4
21-Newton-c/a; Sutton-a; 1st Baron Weirwulf	2	6	15	22
22-Newton-c; Sutton-a	2	6	11	15
23,24-Sutton-c; Ditko-a	2	6	11	15
25-27,29,32,33	1	4	7	10
30,41,47,49-52,74-Ditko-c/a: 51-Reprints	2	6	11	15
31,35,37,38-Sutton-a	1	4	7	10
34,36,39,40,42,57,60-Ditko-a	2	6	9	12
43-46,48,53-56,58,59,61-73: 59-Newton-a. 64-Sutton-c. 71-73-Low print	1	3	6	8
75-(9/84) Last issue; low print	2	6	11	15

NOTE: Aparo c-45. Ditko a-1-8, 11-16, 18, 23, 24, 28, 30, 34r, 36r, 39-42r, 47r, 49-52r, 57, 60, 74. c-1-7, 11, 13, 14, 16, 30, 41, 47, 49-52, 74. Howard a-6, 9, 18, 22, 25, 32. Kim a-9, 19. Morisi a-13. Newton a-17, 21, 59r; c-21, 22(painted). Staton a-11, 12, 18, 21, 22, 30, 33, 35, 38; c-18, 33. Sutton a-10, 17, 20-22, 31, 35, 37, 38; c-15, 17, 18, 23(painted), 24(painted), 64r. #49 reprints Tales of the Mysterious Traveler #4.

HAUNTED, THE
Chaos! Comics: Jan, 2002 - No. 4 ($2.99, limited series)

1-Peter David-s/Nat Jones-a				3.00

HAUNTED LOVE
Charlton Comics: Apr, 1973 - No. 11, Sept, 1975

1-Tom Sutton-a (16 pgs.)	4	12	30	50
2,3,6,7,10,11	2	6	15	22
4,5-Ditko-a	3	9	19	28
8,9-Newton-c	3	9	17	24
Modern Comics #1(1978)	2	6	9	12

NOTE: Howard a-8i. Kim a-7-9. Newton c-8, 9. Staton a-1-6. Sutton a-1, 3-5, 10, 11.

HAUNTED MAN, THE
Dark Horse Comics: Mar, 2000 ($2.95, unfinished limited series)

1-Gerald Jones-s/Mark Badger-a				3.00

HAUNTED THRILLS (Tales of Horror and Terror)
Ajax/Farrell Publications: June, 1952 - No. 18, Nov-Dec, 1954

1-r/Ellery Queen #1	43	129	257	450
2-L. B. Cole-a /Ellery Queen #1	34	102	179	310
3-5: 3-Drug use story	29	87	153	265
6-10,12: 7-Hitler story	24	72	127	215
11-Nazi death camp story	25	75	130	225
13-18: 18-Lingerie panels. 14-Jesus Christ apps. in story by Webb. 15-Jo-Jo-r	20	60	105	175

NOTE: Kamenish art in most issues. Webb a-12.

HAUNT OF FEAR (Formerly Gunfighter)
E. C. Comics: No. 15, May-June, 1950 - No. 28, Nov-Dec, 1954

15(#1, 1950)(Scarce)	264	792	1848	3300
16-1st issue "The Witches Cauldron" & the Old Witch (as Kamen) begin series as hostess of HOF	112	336	784	1400
17-Origin of Crypt of Terror, Vault of Horror, & Haunt of Fear; used in SOTI, pg. 43; last pg. Ingels-a used by N.Y. Legis. Comm.; story "Monster Maker" based on Frankenstein. Old Witch by Feldstein	112	336	784	1400
4-Ingels becomes regular artist for Old Witch. 1st Vault Keeper & Crypt Keeper app. in HOF; begin series	68	204	476	850
5-Injury-to-eye panel, pg. 4 of Wood story	52	156	364	650
6,7,9,10: 6-Crypt Keeper by Feldstein begins. 9-Crypt Keeper & Davis begins. 10-Feldstein-c	39	117	273	490
8-Classic Feldstein Shrunken Head-c	42	126	294	525
11,12: Classic Ingels-c; 11-Kamen biog. 12-Feldstein biog.	31	93	217	390
13,15,16,18,20: 11-Kamen biog. 12-Feldstein biog. 16,18-Ray Bradbury adaptations. 18-Ray Bradbury biography. 20-Feldstein-r/Vault of Horror #12	29	87	203	360
14-Origin Old Witch by Ingels; classic-ingels-c	44	132	308	550
17-Classic Ingels-c	30	90	210	380
19-Used in SOTI, ill. "A comic book baseball game" & Senate investigation on juvenile delinq. bondage/decapitation-c	39	117	273	490
21-27: 23-Used in SOTI, pg. 241. 24-Used in Senate Investigative Report, pg.8. 26-Contains anti-censorship editorial, 'Are you a Red Dupe?' 27-Cannibalism story; Wertham cameo	20	60	140	250
28-Low distribution	28	84	196	350

NOTE: (Canadian reprints known; see Table of Contents) Craig a-15-17, 5, 7, 10, 12, 13; c-15-17, 5-7, Crandall a-20, 21, 26, 27. Davis a-4-26, 28. Evans a-15-19, 22-25, 27. Feldstein a-15-17, 20; 4, 6-8, 10. Ingels a-16, 17, 4-28; c-11-28. Kamen a-16, 4, 6, 7, 9-11, 13-19, 21-28.

The Hawk #4 © Z-D

Hawk and the Dove #6 © DC

Hawkman #7 © DC

	GD2.0	FN6.0	VF8.0	NM9.4

Krigstein a-28. Kurtzman a-15(#1), 17(#3). Orlando a-9, 12. Wood a-15, 16, 4-6.

HAUNT OF FEAR, THE
Gladstone Publishing: May, 1991 - No. 2, July, 1991 ($2.00, 68 pgs.)

1,2: 1-Ghastly Ingels-c(r); 2-Craig-c(r)   3.00

HAUNT OF FEAR
Russ Cochran/Gemstone Publ.: Sept, 1991 - No. 5, 1992 ($2.00, 68 pgs.); Nov, 1992 - Present ($1.50/$2.00/$2.50)

1-25: 1-Ingels-c(r). 1-3-r/HOF #15-17 with original-c. 4,5-r/HOF #4,5 with original-c   2.50
Annual 1-5: 1- r/#1-5. 2- r/#6-10. 3- r/#11-15. 4- r/#16-20. 5- r/#21-25   14.00
Annual 6-r/#26-28   9.00

HAUNT OF HORROR, THE (Digest)
Marvel Comics: Jun, 1973 - No. 2, Aug, 1973 (164 pgs.; text and art)

1-Morrow painted skull-c; stories by Ellison, Howard, and Leiber; Brunner-a   3   9   20   30
2-Kelly Freas painted bondage-c; stories by McCaffrey, Goulart, Leiber, Ellison; art by Simonson, Brunner, and Buscema   3   6   15   22

HAUNT OF HORROR, THE (Magazine)
Cadence Comics Publ. (Marvel): May, 1974 - No. 5, Jan, 1975 (75¢) (B&W)

1,2: 2-Origin & 1st app. Gabriel the Devil Hunter; Satana begins   2   6   10   14
3-5: 4-Neal Adams-a. 5-Evans-a(2)   2   6   12   18
NOTE: Alcala a-2. Colan a-2p. Heath r-1. Krigstein r-3. Reese a-1. Simonson a-1.

HAVE GUN, WILL TRAVEL (TV)
Dell Publishing Co.: No. 931, 8/58 - No. 14, 7-9/62 (All Richard Boone photo-c)

Four Color 931 (#1)   14   41   98   180
Four Color 983,1044 (#2,3)   9   27   63   115
4 (1-3/60) - 10   7   21   49   95
11-14   8   24   56   95

HAVEN: THE BROKEN CITY (See JLA/Haven: Arrival)
DC Comics: Feb, 2002 - No. 9 ($2.50, limited series)

1-Olivetti-c/a; JLA app.   2.50

HAVOK & WOLVERINE - MELTDOWN (See Marvel Comics Presents #24)
Marvel Comics (Epic Comics): Mar, 1989 - No. 4, Oct, 1989 ($3.50, mini-series, squarebound, mature)

1-4: Violent content   4.00

HAWAIIAN EYE (TV)
Gold Key: July, 1963 (Troy Donahue, Connie Stevens photo-c)

1 (10073-307)   5   15   34   55

HAWAIIAN ILLUSTRATED LEGENDS SERIES
Hogarth Press: 1975 (B&W)(Cover printed w/blue, yellow, and green)

1-Kalelealuaka, the Mysterious Warrior   2.50

HAWK, THE (Also see Approved Comics)
Ziff-Davis/St. John Publ. Co. No. 4 on: Wint/51 - No. 3, 11-12/52; No. 4, 1-2/53; No. 8, 9/54 - No. 12, 5/55 (Painted c-1-4)(#5-7 don't exist)

1-Anderson-a   21   63   110   185
2 (Sum, '52)-Kubert, Infantino-a   12   36   61   100
3-4,11: 11-Buckskin Belle & The Texan app.   10   30   55   80
8-10,12: 8(9/54)-Reprints #3 w/different-c by Baker. 9-Baker-c/a; Kubert-a(r)/#2. 10-Baker-c/a; r/one story from #2. 12-Baker-c/a; Buckskin Belle app.   13   39   66   110
3-D 1(11/53, 25¢)-Came w/glasses; Baker-c   35   105   185   320
NOTE: Baker c-8-12. Larsen a-10. Tuska a-1, 9, 12. Painted c-1, 4, 7.

HAWK AND THE DOVE, THE (See Showcase #75 & Teen Titans) (1st series)
National Periodical Publications: Aug-Sept, 1968 - No. 6, June-July, 1969

1-Ditko-c/a   8   24   56   90
2-6: 5-Teen Titans cameo   5   15   34   55
NOTE: Ditko c/a-1, 2. Gil Kane a-3p, 4p, 5, 6p; c-3-6.

HAWK AND DOVE (2nd series)
DC Comics: Oct, 1988 - No. 5, Feb, 1989 ($1.00, limited series)

1-Rob Liefeld-c/a(p) in all   4.00
2-5   3.00
Trade paperback ('93, $9.95)-Reprints #1-5   10.00

HAWK AND DOVE
DC Comics: June, 1989 - No. 28, Oct, 1991 ($1.00)

1-28   2.50
Annual 1,2 ('90, '91; $2.00) 1-Liefeld pin-up. 2-Armageddon 2001 x-over   3.00

HAWK AND DOVE
DC Comics: Nov, 1997 - No.5, Mar, 1998 ($2.50, limited series)

1-5-Baron-s/Zachary & Giordano-a   2.50

HAWK AND WINDBLADE (See Elflord)
Warp Graphics: Aug, 1997 - No.2, Sept, 1997 ($2.95, limited series)

1,2-Blair-s/Chan-c/a   3.00

HAWKEYE (See The Avengers #16 & Tales Of Suspense #57)
Marvel Comics Group: Sept, 1983 - No. 4, Dec, 1983 ($2.50, limited series)

1-4: Mark Gruenwald-a/scripts. 1-Origin Hawkeye. 3-Origin Mockingbird. 4-Hawkeye & Mockingbird elope   3.00

HAWKEYE
Marvel Comics: Jan, 1994 - No. 4, Apr, 1994 ($1.75, limited series)

1-4   2.00

HAWKEYE & THE LAST OF THE MOHICANS (TV)
Dell Publishing Co.: No. 884, Mar, 1958 (one-shot)

Four Color 884-Photo-c   7   21   49   90

HAWKEYE: EARTH'S MIGHTIEST MARKSMAN
Marvel Comics: Oct, 1998 ($2.99, one-shot)

1-Justice and Firestar app.; DeFalco-s   3.00

HAWKMAN (See Atom & Hawkman, The Brave & the Bold, DC Comics Presents, Detective, Flash Comics, Hawkworld, JSA, Justice League of America #31, Legend of the Hawkman, Mystery in Space, Shadow War Of..., Showcase, & World's Finest #256)
HAWKMAN (1st Series) (Also see The Atom #7 & Brave the Bold #34-36, 42-44, 51)
National Periodical Publications: Apr-May, 1964 - No. 27, Aug-Sept, 1968

1-(4-5/64)-Anderson-c/a begins, ends #21   50   150   410   750
2   21   63   148   265
3,5: 5-2nd app. Shadow Thief   12   36   88   150
4-Origin & 1st app. Zatanna (10-11/64)   17   51   118   210
6   11   33   77   130
7   10   30   68   115
8-10: 9-Atom cameo; Hawkman & Atom learn each other's I.D.; 3rd app. Shadow Thief   9   27   63   105
11-15   6   18   45   75
16,17-27: 18-Adam Strange x-over (cameo #19). 25-G.A. Hawkman-r by Moldoff. 26-Kirby-a(r). 27-Kubert-c   5   15   34   55

HAWKMAN (2nd Series)
DC Comics: Aug, 1986 - No. 17, Dec, 1987

1-17: 10-Byrne-c, Special #1 (1986, $1.25)   2.50
Trade paperback (1989, $19.95)-r/Brave and the Bold #34-36,42-44 by Kubert; Kubert-c   20.00

HAWKMAN (4th Series)(See both Hawkworld limited & ongoing series)
DC Comics: Sept, 1993 - No. 33, July, 1996 ($1.75/$1.95/$2.25)

1-($2.50)-Gold foil embossed-c; storyline cont'd from Hawkworld ongoing series; new costume & powers.   3.00
2-13,0,14-33: 2-Green Lantern x-over. 3-Airstryke app. 4,6-Won. Woman app. 13-(9/94)-Zero Hour. 0-(10/94). 14-(11/94). 15-Aquaman-c & app. 23-Wonder Woman app. 25-Kent Williams-c. 29,30-Chaykin-c. 32-Breyfogle-c   2.50
Annual 1 (1993, $2.50, 68 pgs.)-Bloodlines Earthplague   3.00
Annual 2 (1995, $3.95)-Year One story   4.00

HAWKMOON: THE JEWEL IN THE SKULL
First Comics: May, 1986 - No. 4, Nov, 1986 ($1.75, limited series, Baxter paper)

1-4: Adapts novel by Michael Moorcock   2.50

HAWKMOON: THE MAD GOD'S AMULET
First Comics: Jan, 1987 - No. 4, July, 1987 ($1.75, limited series, Baxter paper)

1-4: Adapts novel by Michael Moorcock   2.50

HAWKMOON: THE RUNESTAFF
First Comics: Jun, 1988 -No. 4, Dec, 1988 ($1.75-$1.95, lim. series, Baxter paper)

Hawkmoon: The Jewel in the Skull #2 © FC

Headline Comics #5 © PRIZE

Heart Throbs #5 © QUA

	GD2.0	FN6.0	VF8.0	NM9.4

1-4: ($1.75) Adapts novel by Michael Moorcock. 3,4 ($1.95)   2.50

HAWKMOON: THE SWORD OF DAWN
First Comics: Sept, 1987 - No. 4, Mar, 1988 ($1.75, lim. series, Baxter paper)
1-4: Dorman painted-c; adapts Moorcock novel   2.50

HAWKWORLD
DC Comics: 1989 - No. 3, 1989 ($3.95, prestige format, limited series)
Book 1-3: 1-Tim Truman story & art in all; Hawkman dons new costume; reintro
   Byth.   4.00
TPB (1991, $16.95) r/#1-3   17.00

HAWKWORLD (3rd Series)
DC Comics: June, 1990 - No. 32, Mar, 1993 ($1.50/$1.75)
1-Hawkman spin-off; story cont'd from limited series   3.00
2-32: 15,16-War of the Gods x-over. 22-J'onn J'onzz app.   2.25
Annual 1-3 ('90-'92, $2.95, 68 pgs.), 2-2nd printing with silver ink-c   3.00
NOTE: *Truman* a-30-32; c-27-32, Annual 1.

HAYWIRE
DC Comics: Oct, 1988 - No. 13, Sept, 1989 ($1.25, mature)
1-13   2.25

HAZARD
Image Comics (WildStorm Prod.): June, 1996 - No. 7, Nov, 1996 ($1.75)
1-7: 1-Intro Hazard; Jeff Mariotte scripts begin; Jim Lee-c(p)   3.00

HEADHUNTERS
Image Comics: Apr, 1997 - No. 3, June, 1997 ($2.95, B&W)
1-3: Chris Marrinan-s/a   3.00

HEADLINE COMICS (...For the American Boy) (...Crime No. 32-39)
Prize Publ./American Boys' Comics: Feb, 1943 - No. 22, Nov-Dec, 1946; No.
23, 1947 - No. 77, Oct, 1956

1-Junior Rangers-c/stories begin; Yank & Doodle x-over in Junior Rangers (Junior Rangers are Uncle Sam's nephews)	47	142	286	500
2	25	75	130	225
3-Used in POP, pg. 84	20	60	105	175
4-7,9,10: 4,9,10-Hitler stories in each	17	51	88	150
8-Classic Hitler-c	47	141	286	500
11,12	14	42	72	125
13-15-Blue Streak in all	17	51	88	150
16-Origin & 1st app. Atomic Man (11-12/45)	27	81	145	250
17,18,20,21: 21-Atomic Man ends (9-10/46)	14	42	72	120
19-S&K-a	31	93	165	285
22-Last Junior Rangers; Kiefer-c	11	33	55	90
23,24: (All S&K-a). 23-Valentine's Day Massacre story; content changes to true crime. 24-Dope-crazy killer story	29	87	153	265
25-35-S&K-c/a. 25-Powell-a	27	81	142	245
36-S&K-a; photo-c begin	21	63	110	185
37-1 pg. S&K, Severin-a; rare Kirby photo-c app.	21	63	110	185
38,40-Meskin-a	8	24	45	65
39,41-43,46-50,52-55: 41-J. Edgar Hoover 26th Anniversary Issue with photo on-c. 43,49-Meskin-a	7	21	36	50
44-S&K-c; Severin/Elder, Meskin-a	13	39	66	110
45-Kirby-a	11	33	55	90
51-Kirby-c	7	21	38	55
56-S&K-a	13	39	66	110
57-77: 72-Meskin-c/a(i)	5	15	25	35

NOTE: *Hollingsworth* a-30. Photo c-36-43. **H. C. Kiefer** c-12-16, 22. Atomic Man c-17-19.

HEADMAN
Innovation Publishing: 1990 ($2.50, mature)
1-Sci/fi   2.50

HEAP, THE
Skywald Publications: Sept, 1971 (52 pgs.)

1-Kinstler-r/Strange Worlds #8	3	9	17	25

HEART AND SOUL
Mikeross Publications: April-May, 1954 - No. 2, June-July, 1954

1,2	7	21	35	50

HEARTBREAKERS (Also see Dark Horse Presents)
Dark Horse Comics: Apr, 1996 - No. 4, July, 1996 ($2.95, limited series)

1-4: 1-W/paper doll & pin-up. 2-Ross pin-up. 3-Evan Dorkin pin-ups. 4-Brereton-c; Matt Wagner pin-up				3.00
...Superdigest (7/98, $9.95, digest-size) new stories				10.00

HEARTLAND (See Hellblazer)
DC Comics (Vertigo): Mar, 1997 ($4.95, one-shot, mature)
1-Garth Ennis-s/Steve Dillon-c/a   5.00

HEART OF DARKNESS
Hardline Studios: 1994 ($2.95)
1-Brereton-c   3.00

HEART OF EMPIRE
Dark Horse Comics: Apr, 1999 - No. 9, Dec, 1999 ($2.95, limited series)
1-9-Bryan Talbot-s/a   3.00

HEART OF THE BEAST, THE
DC Comics (Vertigo): 1994 ($19.95, hardcover, mature)
1-Dean Motter scripts   20.00

HEARTS OF DARKNESS (See Ghost Rider; Wolverine; Punisher: Hearts of...)

HEART THROBS (Love Stories No. 147 on)
Quality Comics/National Periodical #47(4-5/57) on (Arleigh #48-101):
8/49 - No. 8, 10/50; No. 9, 3/52 - No. 146, Oct, 1972

1-Classic Ward-c, Gustavson-a, 9 pgs.	40	120	240	420
2-Ward-c/a (9 pgs); Gustavson-a	26	78	139	240
3-Gustavson-a	10	30	55	80
4,6,8-Ward-a, 8-9 pgs.	14	42	72	120
5,7	7	21	38	55
9-Robert Mitchum, Jane Russell photo-c	11	33	55	90
10,15-Ward-a	11	33	55	90
11-14,16-20: 12 (7/52)	6	18	32	45
21-Ward-c	10	30	55	80
22,23-Ward-a(p)	7	21	38	55
24-33: 33-Last pre-code (3/55)	6	18	29	40
34-39,41-46 (12/56; last Quality issue)	5	15	25	35
40-Ward-a; r-7 pgs./#21	6	18	32	45
47-(4-5/57; 1st DC issue)	23	68	160	285
48-60, 100	9	27	63	105
61-70	6	18	42	70
71-99: 74-Last 10 cent issue	5	15	34	55
101-The Beatles app. on-c	14	42	98	165
102-120: 102-123-(Serial)-Three Girls, Their Lives, Their Loves	3	9	19	28
121-132,143-146	2	6	15	22
133-142-(52 pgs.)	3	9	21	32

NOTE: *Gustavson* a-8. *Tuska* a-128. Photo c-4, 5, 8-10, 15, 17.

HEART THROBS - THE BEST OF DC ROMANCE COMICS (See Fireside Book Series)

HEART THROBS
DC Comics (Vertigo): Jan, 1999 - No. 4, Apr, 1999 ($2.95, lim. series)
1-4-Romance anthology. 1-Timm-c. 3-Corben-a   3.00

HEATHCLIFF (See Star Comics Magazine)
Marvel Comics (Star Comics)/Marvel Comics No. 23 on: Apr, 1985 - No. 56,
Feb, 1991 (#16-on, $1.00)
1-Post-a most issues   6.00
2-10   4.00
11-56: 43-X-Mas issue. 47-Batman parody (Catman vs. the Soaker)   3.00
Annual 1 ('87)   3.00

HEATHCLIFF'S FUNHOUSE
Marvel Comics (Star Comics)/Marvel No. 6 on: May, 1987 - No. 10, 1988
1   4.00
2-10   3.00

HEAVY HITTERS
Marvel Comics (Epic Comics): 1993 ($3.75, 68 pgs.)
1-Bound w/trading card; Lawdog, Feud, Alien Legion, Trouble With Girls,
  & Spyke   3.75

HEAVY LIQUID
DC Comics (Vertigo): Oct, 1999 - No. 5, Feb, 2000 ($5.95, limited series)

Heckle and Jeckle #25 © CBS

Hellblazer #125 © DC

Hellboy: Conqueror Worm #4 © Michael Mignola

	GD2.0	FN6.0	VF8.0	NM9.4

1-5-Paul Pope-s/a; flip covers				6.00
TPB (2001, $29.95) r/#1-5				30.00

HECKLE AND JECKLE (Paul Terry's...)(See Blue Ribbon, Giant Comics Edition #5A & 10, Paul Terry's, Terry-Toons Comics)
St. John Publ. Co. No. 1-24/Pines No. 25 on: No. 3, 2/52 - No. 24, 10/55; No. 25, Fall/56 - No. 34, 6/59

3(#1)-Funny animal	26	78	136	235
4(6/52), 5	12	36	61	100
6-10(4/53)	8	24	42	60
11-20	7	21	36	50
21-34: 25-Begin CBS Television Presents on-c	5	15	25	35

HECKLE AND JECKLE (TV) (See New Terrytoons)
Gold Key/Dell Publ. Co.: 11/62 - No. 4, 8/63; 5/66; No. 2, 10/66; No. 3, 8/67

1 (11/62; Gold Key)	6	18	42	80
2-4	3	10	23	35
1 (5/66; Dell)	4	12	29	45
2,3	3	9	20	30
(See March of Comics No. 379, 472, 484)				

HECKLE AND JECKLE 3-D
Spotlight Comics: 1987 - No. 2?, 1987 ($2.50)

1,2				3.50

HECKLER, THE
DC Comics: Sept, 1992 - No. 6, Feb, 1993 ($1.25)

1-6-T&M Bierbaum-s/Keith Giffen-c/a				2.25

HECTIC PLANET
Slave Labor Graphics 1998 ($12.95/$14.95)

Book 1,2-r-Dorkin-s/a from Pirate Corp$ Vol. 1 & 2				15.00

HECTOR COMICS (The Keenest Teen in Town)
Key Publications: Nov, 1953 - No. 3, 1954

1-Teen humor	5	15	25	35
2,3	4	10	15	20

HECTOR HEATHCOTE (TV)
Gold Key: Mar, 1964

1 (10111-403)	7	21	49	90

HECTOR THE INSPECTOR (See Top Flight Comics)

HEDY DEVINE COMICS (Formerly All Winners #21? or Teen #22?(6/47); Hedy of Hollywood #36 on; also see Annie Oakley, Comedy & Venus)
Marvel Comics (RCM)/Atlas #50: No. 22, Aug, 1947 - No. 50, Sept, 1952

22-1st app. Hedy Devine (also see Joker #32)	25	75	130	225
23,24,27-30: 23-Wolverton-a, 1 pg; Kurtzman's "Hey Look", 2 pgs. 24,27-30-"Hey Look" by Kurtzman, 1-3 pgs.	17	51	88	150
25-Classic "Hey Look" by Kurtzman, "Optical Illusion"	19	57	99	165
26- "Giggles 'n' Grins" by Kurtzman	14	42	72	120
31-34,36-50: 32-Anti-Wertham editorial	10	30	55	80
35-Four pgs. "Rusty" by Kurtzman	14	42	72	125

HEDY-MILLIE-TESSIE COMEDY (See Comedy Comics)

HEDY WOLFE (Also see Patsy & Hedy & Miss America Magazine V1#2)
Atlas Publishing Co. (Emgee): Aug, 1957

1-Patsy Walker's rival; Al Hartley-c	11	33	55	90

HEE HAW (TV)
Charlton Press: July, 1970 - No. 7, Aug, 1971

1	4	12	26	40
2-7	3	9	17	25

HEIDI (See Dell Jr. Treasury No. 6)

HELEN OF TROY (Movie)
Dell Publishing Co.: No. 684, Mar, 1956 (one-shot)

Four Color 684-Buscema-a, photo-c	10	30	70	130

HELLBLAZER (John Constantine) (See Saga of Swamp Thing #37) (Also see Books of Magic limited series)
DC Comics (Vertigo #63 on): Jan, 1988 - Present ($1.25/$1.50/$1.95/$2.25)

1-(44 pgs.)-John Constantine; McKean-c thru #21	2	6	10	14
2-5	1	3	6	9
6-8,10: 10-Swamp Thing cameo				6.00
9,19: 9-X-over w/Swamp Thing #76. 19-Sandman app.	1	3	5	7
11-18,20				5.00
21-26,28-30: 22-Williams-c. 24-Contains bound-in Shocker movie poster. 25,26-Grant Morrison scripts.				5.00
27-Gaiman scripts; Dave McKean-a; low print run	2	6	11	15
31-39: 36-Preview of World Without End.				4.00
40-($2.25, 52 pgs.)-Dave McKean-a & colors; preview of Kid Eternity				4.00
41-Ennis scripts begin; ends #83				5.00
42-120: 44,45-Sutton-a(i). 50-($3.00, 52 pgs.). 52-Glenn Fabry painted-c begin. 62-Special Death insert by McKean. 63-Silver metallic ink on-c. 77-Totleben-c. 84-Sean Phillips-c/a begins; Delano story. 85-88-Eddie Campbell story. 75-($2.95, 52 pgs.). 89-Paul Jenkins scripts begin; 108-Adlard-a. 100,120 ($3.50,48 pgs.)				3.50
121-169: 129-Ennis-s, begin $2.50-c. 141-Bradstreet-a. 146-150-Corben-a				2.50
Annual 1 (1989, $2.95, 68 pgs.)-Bryan Talbot's 1st work in American comics				6.00
Special 1 (1993, $3.95, 68 pgs.)-Ennis-story; w/pin-ups.				6.00
...Damnation's Flame (1999, $16.95, TPB) r/#72-77				17.00
...Dangerous Habits (1997, $14.95, TPB) r/#41-46				15.00
...Fear and Loathing (1997, $14.95, TPB) r/#62-67				18.00
...Fear and Loathing (2nd printing, $17.95)				18.00
...Hard Time (2001, $9.95, TPB) r/#146-150				10.00
...Original Sins (1993, $19.95, TPB) r/#1-9				20.00
...Tainted Love (1998, $16.95, TPB) r/#68-71, Vertigo Jam #1 and Hellblazer Special #1				17.00

NOTE: **Alcala** a-8i, 9i, 18-22i. **Gaiman** scripts-27. **McKean** a-27,40; c-1-21. **Sutton** a-44i, 45i. **Talbot** a-Annual 1.

HELLBLAZER SPECIAL: BAD BLOOD
DC Comics (Vertigo): Sept, 2000 - No. 4 ($2.95, mini-series)

1-4-Delano-s/Bond-a; Constantine in 2025 London				3.00

HELLBLAZER/THE BOOKS OF MAGIC
DC Comics (Vertigo): Dec, 1997 - No. 2, Jan, 1998 ($2.50, mini-series)

1,2-John Constantine and Tim Hunter				2.50

HELLBOY (Also see Dark Horse Presents, John Byrne's Next Men. San Diego Comic Con #2, Danger Unlimited #4, Gen[13] #13B, Ghost/Hellboy, & Savage Dragon)

HELLBOY: ALMOST COLOSSUS
Dark Horse Comics (Legend): Jun, 1997 - No. 2, Jul, 1997 ($2.95, lim. series)

1,2-Mignola-s/a				3.00

HELLBOY: BOX FULL OF EVIL
Dark Horse Comics: Aug, 1999 - No. 2, Sept, 1999 ($2.95, lim. series)

1,2-Mignola-s/a; back-up story w/ Matt Smith-a				3.00

HELLBOY CHRISTMAS SPECIAL
Dark Horse Comics: Dec, 1997 ($3.95, one-shot)

nn-Christmas stories by Mignola, Gianni, Darrow, Purcell				4.00

HELLBOY: CONQUEROR WORM
Dark Horse Comics: May, 2001 - No. 4, Aug, 2001 ($2.99, lim. series)

1-4-Mignola-s/a/c				3.00

HELLBOY, JR.
Dark Horse Comics: Oct, 1999 - No. 2, Nov, 1999 ($2.95, limited series)

1,2-Stories and art by various				3.00

HELLBOY, JR., HALLOWEEN SPECIAL
Dark Horse Comics: Oct, 1997 ($3.95, one-shot)

nn-"Harvey" style renditions of Hellboy characters; Bill Wray, Mike Mignola & various-a; wraparound-c by Wray				4.00

HELLBOY: SEED OF DESTRUCTION
Dark Horse Comics: Mar, 1994 - No. 4, Jun, 1994 ($2.50, lim. series)

1-4-Mignola-a w/Byrne scripts; Monkeyman & O'Brien back-up story (origin) by Art Adams.				3.00
Trade paperback (1994, $17.95)-collects all four issues plus r/Hellboy's 1st app. in San Diego Comic Con #2 & pin-ups				18.00
Limited edition hardcover (1995, $99.95)-includes everything in trade paperback plus additional material.				100.00

Hell's Angel #4 © MAR

Hellspawn #9 © TMP

Henry Aldrich Comics #2 © DELL

	GD2.0	FN6.0	VF8.0	NM9.4

HELLBOY: THE CHAINED COFFIN AND OTHERS
Dark Horse Comics (Legend): Aug, 1998 ($17.95, TPB)
nn-Mignola-c/a/s; reprints out-of-print one shots; pin-up gallery ... 18.00

HELLBOY: THE CORPSE AND THE IRON SHOES
Dark Horse Comics (Legend): Jan, 1996 ($2.95, one-shot)
nn-Mignola-c/a/scripts; reprints "The Corpse" serial from Capitol City's Advance
Comics catalog w/new story ... 3.00

HELLBOY: THE RIGHT HAND OF DOOM
Dark Horse Comics (Legend): Apr, 2000 ($17.95, TPB)
nn-Mignola-c/a/s; reprints ... 18.00

HELLBOY: THE WOLVES OF ST. AUGUST
Dark Horse Comics (Legend): 1995 ($4.95, squarebound, one-shot)
nn-Mignola--c/a/scripts; r/Dark Horse Presents #88-91 with additional story 5.00

HELLBOY: WAKE THE DEVIL (Sequel to Seed of Destruction)
Dark Horse Comics (Legend): Jun, 1996 - No. 5, Oct, 1996 ($2.95, lim. series)
1-5: Mignola-c/a & scripts; The Monstermen back-up story by Gary Gianni 3.00
TPB (1997, $17.95) r/#1-5 ... 18.00

HELLCAT
Marvel Comics: Sept, 2000 - No. 3, Nov, 2000 ($2.99)
1-3-Englehart-s/Breyfogle-a; Hedy Wolfe app. ... 3.00

HELLCOP
Image Comics (Avalon Studios): Aug, 1998 - Present ($2.50)
1-4: 1-(Oct. on-c) Casey-s ... 2.50

HELL ETERNAL
DC Comics (Vertigo Verité): 1998 ($6.95, squarebound, one-shot)
1-Delano-s/Phillips-a ... 7.00

HELLHOLE
Image Comics: July, 1999 - No. 3, Oct, 1999 ($2.50)
1-3-Lobdell-s/Polina-a ... 2.50

HELLHOUNDS (...: Panzer Cops #3-6)
Dark Horse Comics: 1994 - No. 6, July, 1994 ($2.50, B&W, limited series)
1-6: 1-Hamner-c. 3-(4/94). 2-Joe Phillips-c ... 3.00

HELLHOUND, THE REDEMPTION QUEST
Marvel Comics (Epic Comics): Dec, 1993 - No. 4, Mar, 1994 ($2.25, limited series, coated stock)
1-4 ... 2.25

HELLO, I'M JOHNNY CASH
Spire Christian Comics (Fleming H. Revell Co.): 1976 (39/49¢)
nn ... 1 3 6 8

HELL ON EARTH (See DC Science Fiction Graphic Novel)

HELLO PAL COMICS (Short Story Comics)
Harvey Publications: Jan, 1943 - No. 3, May, 1943 (Photo-c)
1-Rocketman & Rocketgirl begin; Yankee Doodle Jones app.; Mickey
Rooney photo-c ... 64 192 398 700
2-Charlie McCarthy photo-c (scarce) ... 53 158 318 560
3-Bob Hope photo-c (scarce) ... 55 165 341 600

HELLRAISER/NIGHTBREED – JIHAD (Also see Clive Barker's...)
Epic Comics (Marvel Comics): 1991 - Book 2, 1991 ($4.50, 52 pgs.)
Book 1,2 ... 4.50

HELL-RIDER (Magazine)
Skywald Publications: Aug, 1971 - No. 2, Oct, 1971 (B&W)
1-Origin & 1st app.; Butterfly & Wildbunch begins ... 4 12 30 50
2 ... 3 10 23 35
NOTE: #3 advertised in Psycho #5 but did not come out. **Buckler** a-1, 2. **Morrow** c-3.

HELL'S ANGEL (Becomes Dark Angel #6 on)
Marvel Comics UK: July, 1992 - No. 5, Nov, 1993 ($1.75)
1-5: X-Men (Wolverine, Cyclops)-c/stories. 1-Origin. 3-Jim Lee cover swipe ... 2.25

HELLSHOCK
Image Comics: July, 1994 - No. 4, Nov, 1994 ($1.95, limited series)

1-4-Jae Lee-c/a & scripts. 4-variant-c. ... 2.50

HELLSHOCK
Image Comics: Jan, 1997 - No.2, Feb, 1997 ($2.95/$2.50, limited series)
1-($2.95)-Jae Lee-c/s/a, Villarrubia-painted-a ... 4.00
2-($2.50) ... 2.50

HELLSHOCK BOOK THREE: THE SCIENCE OF FAITH
Image Comics: Jan, 1998 ($2.50)
1-Jae Lee-c/s/a, Villarrubia-painted-a ... 2.50

HELLSPAWN
Image Comics: Aug, 2000 - Present ($2.50)
1-Bendis-s/Ashley Wood-c/a; Spawn and Clown app. ... 2.50
2-10: 6-Last Bendis-s. 7-Niles-s ... 2.50

HELLSTORM: PRINCE OF LIES (See Ghost Rider #1 & Marvel Spotlight #12)
Marvel Comics: Apr, 1993 - No. 21, Dec, 1994 ($2.00)
1-($2.95)-Parchment-c w/red thermographic ink ... 3.00
2-21: 14-Bound-in trading card sheet. 18-P. Craig Russell-c ... 2.50

HE-MAN (See Masters Of The Universe)

HE-MAN (Also see Tops In Adventure)
Ziff-Davis Publ. Co. (Approved Comics): Fall, 1952
1-Kinstler painted-c; Powell-a ... 17 51 88 150

HE-MAN
Toby Press: May, 1954 - No. 2, July, 1954 (Painted-c by B. Safran)
1 ... 16 48 83 140
2 ... 14 42 72 120

HENNESSEY (TV)
Dell Publishing Co.: No. 1200, Aug-Oct, 1961 - No. 1280, Mar-May, 1962
Four Color 1200-Gil Kane-a, photo-c ... 7 21 49 90
Four Color 1280-Photo-c ... 6 18 42 80

HENRY (Also see Little Annie Rooney)
David McKay Publications: 1935 (52 pgs.) (Daily B&W strip reprints)(10"x10" cardboard)
1-By Carl Anderson ... 40 120 220 380

HENRY (See King Comics & Magic Comics)
Dell Publishing Co.: No. 122, Oct, 1946 - No. 65, Apr-June, 1961
Four Color 122-All new stories begin ... 14 42 98 180
Four Color 155 (7/47), 1 (1-3/48)-All new stories ... 9 27 63 115
2 ... 5 15 34 55
3-10 ... 4 12 29 45
11-20: 20-Infinity-c ... 3 9 20 30
21-30 ... 3 9 17 25
31-40 ... 2 6 12 18
41-65 ... 2 6 10 14

HENRY (See Giant Comic Album and March of Comics No. 43, 58, 84, 101, 112, 129, 147, 162, 178, 189)

HENRY ALDRICH COMICS (TV)
Dell Publishing Co.: Aug-Sept, 1950 - No. 22, Sept-Nov, 1954
1-Part series written by John Stanley; Bill Williams-a ... 8 24 56 110
2 ... 5 15 34 55
3-5 ... 4 12 29 45
6-10 ... 4 12 25 38
11-22 ... 3 9 19 28

HENRY BREWSTER
Country Wide (M.F. Ent.): Feb, 1966 - V2#7, Sept, 1967 (All 25¢ Giants)
1 ... 3 9 19 28
2-6(12/66), V2#7-Powell-a in most ... 2 6 10 14

HEPCATS
Antarctic Press: Nov, 1996 - No. 12 ($2.95, B&W)
0-12-Martin Wagner-c/s/a: 0-color ... 3.00
0-($9.95) CD Edition ... 10.00

HERBIE (See Forbidden Worlds & Unknown Worlds)
American Comics Group: April-May, 1964 - No. 23, Feb, 1967 (All 12¢)

Here's Howie Comics #1 © DC

Heroes © MAR

Heroes For Hire #13 © MAR

	GD2.0	FN6.0	VF8.0	NM9.4

	GD2.0	FN6.0	VF8.0	NM9.4
1-Whitney-c/a in most issues	17	51	118	210
2-4	9	27	63	105
5-Beatles, Dean Martin, F. Sinatra app.	10	30	73	125
6,7,9,10	7	21	53	85
8-Origin & 1st app. The Fat Fury	9	27	63	105
11-23: 14-Nemesis & Magicman app. 17-r/2nd Herbie from Forbidden Worlds				
#94. 23-r/1st Herbie from F.W. #73	5	15	38	60

HERBIE
Dark Horse Comics: Oct, 1992 - No. 12, 1993 ($2.50, limited series)

| 1-Whitney-r plus new-c/a in all; Byrne-c/a & scripts. | | | | |
| 2-6: 3-Bob Burden-c/a. 4-Art Adams-c | | | | 2.50 |

HERBIE GOES TO MONTE CARLO, HERBIE RIDES AGAIN (See Walt Disney Showcase No. 24, 41)

HERCULES (See Hit Comics #1-21, Journey Into Mystery Annual, Marvel Graphic Novel #37, Marvel Premiere #26 & The Mighty...)

HERCULES (See Charlton Classics)
Charlton Comics: Oct, 1967 - No. 13, Sept, 1969; Dec, 1968

1-Thane of Bagarth begins; Glanzman-a in all	3	10	23	35
2-13: 1-5,7-10-Aparo-a. 8-(12¢-c)	2	6	13	20
8-(Low distribution)(12/68, 35¢, B&W); magazine format; new Hercules story				
plus-r story/#1; Thane-r/#1-3	5	15	34	55
Modern Comics reprint 10('77), 11('78)				6.00

HERCULES (Prince of Power) (Also see The Champions)
Marvel Comics Group: V1#1, 9/82 - V1#4, 12/82; V2#1, 3/84 - V2#4, 6/84 (color, both limited series)

| 1-4, V2#1-4: Layton-c/a-2. 4-Death of Zeus. | | | | 3.00 |
NOTE: Layton a-1, 2, 3p, 4p, V2#1-4; c-1-4, V2#1-4.

HERCULES: HEART OF CHAOS
Marvel Comics: Aug, 1997 - No. 3, Oct, 1997 ($2.50, limited series)

| 1-3-DeFalco-s, Frenz-a | | | | 2.50 |

HERCULES: OFFICIAL COMICS MOVIE ADAPTION
Acclaim Books: 1997 ($4.50, digest size)

| nn-Adaption of the Disney animated movie | | | | |
4.50

HERCULES: THE LEGENDARY JOURNEYS (TV)
Topps Comics: June, 1996 - No. 5, Oct, 1996 ($2.95)

1-2: 1-Golden-c				3.00
3-Xena-c/app.	1	3	5	7
3-Variant-c	2	6	11	15
4,5: Xena-c/app.				5.00

HERCULES UNBOUND
National Periodical Publications: Oct-Nov, 1975 - No. 12, Aug-Sept, 1977

| 1-Wood-i begins | 1 | 4 | 7 | 10 |
| 2-12: 7-Adams ad. 10-Atomic Knights x-over | | | | 6.00 |
NOTE: Buckler c-7p. Layton inks-No. 9, 10. Simonson a-7-10p, 11, 12; c- 8p, 9-12. Wood a-1-8i; c-7i, 8i.

HERCULES (...Unchained #1121) (Movie)
Dell Publishing Co.: No. 1006, June-Aug, 1959 - No.1121, Aug, 1960

| Four Color 1006-Buscema-a, photo-c | 9 | 27 | 63 | 120 |
| Four Color 1121-Crandall/Evans-a | 9 | 27 | 63 | 120 |

HERE COMES SANTA (See March of Comics No. 30, 213, 340)

HERE'S HOWIE COMICS
National Periodical Publications: Jan-Feb, 1952 - No. 18, Nov-Dec, 1954

1	25	75	130	225
2	13	39	66	110
3-5: 5-Howie in the Army issues begin (9-10/52)	10	30	55	80
6-10	8	24	45	65
11-18	7	21	38	55

HERETIC, THE (Blanc Noir) Nov, 1996 - No. 4, Mar, 1997 ($2.95, lim. series)
Dark Horse Comics:

| 1-4:-w/back-up story | | | | 3.00 |

HERITAGE OF THE DESERT (See Zane Grey, 4-Color 236)

HERMAN & KATNIP (See Harvey Comics Hits #60 & 62, Harvey Hits #14,25,31,41 &

	GD2.0	FN6.0	VF8.0	NM9.

Paramount Animated Comics #1)

HERMES VS. THE EYEBALL KID
Dark Horse Comics: Dec, 1994 - No. 3,Feb, 1995 ($2.95, B&W, limited series)

| 1-3: Eddie Campbell-c/a/scripts | | | | 3.00 |

HERO (Warrior of the Mystic Realms)
Marvel Comics: May, 1990 - No. 6, Oct, 1990 ($1.50, limited series)

| 1-6: 1-Portacio-i | | | | 2.25 |

HERO ALLIANCE, THE
Sirius Comics: Dec, 1985 - No. 2, Sept, 1986 (B&W)

| 1,2: 2-($1.50), Special Edition 1 (7/86, color) | | | | 2.25 |

HERO ALLIANCE
Wonder Color Comics: May, 1987 ($1.95)

| 1-Ron Lim-a | | | | 2.25 |

HERO ALLIANCE
Innovation Publishing: V2#1, Sept, 1989 - V2#17, Nov, 1991 ($1.95, 28 pgs.)

V2#1-17: 1,2-Ron Lim-a				2.25
Annual 1 (1990, $2.75, 36 pgs.)-Paul Smith-c/a				2.75
Special 1 (1992, $2.50, 32 pgs.)-Stuart Immonen-a (10 pgs.)				2.50

HERO ALLIANCE: END OF THE GOLDEN AGE
Innovation Publ.: July, 1989 - No. 3, Aug, 1989 ($1.75, bi-weekly lim. series)

| 1-3: Bart Sears & Ron Lim-c/a; reprints & new-a | | | | 2.25 |

HEROES
Marvel Comics: Dec, 2001 ($3.50, magazine-size, one-shot)

1-Pin-up tributes to the rescue workers of the Sept. 11 tragedy; art and text by				
various; cover by Alex Ross				3.50
1-2nd and 3rd printings				3.50

HEROES (Also see Shadow Cabinet & Static)
DC Comics (Milestone): May, 1996 - No. 6, Nov, 1996 ($2.50, limited series)

| 1-6: 1-Intro Heroes (Iota, Donner, Blitzen, Starlight, Payback & Static) | | | | 2.50 |

HEROES AGAINST HUNGER
DC Comics: 1986 ($1.50; one-shot for famine relief)

| 1-Superman, Batman app.; Neal Adams-c(p); includes many artists work; | | | | |
| Jeff Jones assist (2 pg.) on B. Smith-a; Kirby-a | | | | 4.00 |

HEROES ALL CATHOLIC ACTION ILLUSTRATED
Heroes All Co.: 1943 - V6#5, Mar 10, 1948 (paper covers)

V1#1-(16 pgs., 8x11")	23	69	121	210
V1#2-(16 pgs., 8x11")	20	60	105	175
V2#1(1/44)-3(3/44)-(16 pgs., 8x11")	17	51	88	150
V3#1(1/45)-10(12/45)-(16 pgs., 8x11")	15	45	77	130
V4#1-35 (12/20/46)-(16 pgs.)	13	39	66	110
V5#1(1/10/47)-8(2/28/47)-(16 pgs.), V5#9(3/7/47)-20(11/25/47)-(32 pgs.),				
V6#1(1/10/48)-5(3/10/48)-(32 pgs.)	11	33	55	90

HEROES FOR HIRE
Marvel Comics: July, 1997 - No. 19, Jan, 1999 ($2.99/$1.99)

1-($2.99)-Wraparound cover				5.00
2-19: 2-Variant cover. 7-Thunderbolts app. 9-Punisher-c/app. 10,11				
Deadpool-c/app. 18,19-Wolverine-c/app.				3.00
.../Quicksilver '98 Annual ($2.99) Siege of Wundagore pt.5				3.00

HEROES FOR HOPE STARRING THE X-MEN
Marvel Comics Group: Dec, 1985 ($1.50, one-shot, 52pgs., proceeds donated to famine relief)

| 1-Stephen King scripts; Byrne, Miller, Corben-a; Wrightson/J. Jones-a (3 pgs.); | | | | |
| Art Adams-c; Starlin back-c | | | | 5.00 |

HEROES, INC. PRESENTS CANNON
Wally Wood/CPL/Gang Publ.:1969 - No. 2, 1976 (Sold at Army PX's)

nn-Ditko, Wood-a; Wood-c; Reese-a(p)	2	6	11	15
2-Wood-c; Ditko, Byrne, Wood-a; 8-1/2x10-1/2"; B&W; $2.00				
	2	6	15	22
NOTE: First issue not distributed by publisher; 1,800 copies were stored and 900 copies were stolen many years ago. Many copies have surfaced in recent years.

HEROES OF THE WILD FRONTIER (Formerly Baffling Mysteries)
Ace Periodicals: No. 27, Jan, 1956 - No. 2, Apr, 1956

Heroes Reborn: The Return #2 © MAR

Heroic Comics #4 © EAS

Hex #1 © DC

	GD2.0	FN6.0	VF8.0	NM9.4
27(#1),2-Davy Crockett, Daniel Boone, Buffalo Bill	5	15	25	35

HEROES REBORN (one-shots)
Marvel Comics: Jan, 2000 ($1.99)

...:Ashema; ...:Doom; ...:Doomsday; ...:Masters of Evil; ...:Rebel; ...:Remnants;
...:Young Allies ... 2.25

HEROES REBORN: THE RETURN
Marvel Comics: Dec, 1997 - No. 4 ($2.50, weekly mini-series)

1-4-Avengers, Fantastic Four, Iron Man & Captain America rejoin regular Marvel Universe; Peter David-s/Larocca-c/a				4.00
1-4-Variant-c for each				6.00
Wizard 1/2	1	3	6	9
Return of the Heroes TPB ('98, $14.95) r/#1-4				15.00

HERO FOR HIRE (Power Man No. 17 on; also see Cage)
Marvel Comics Group: June, 1972 - No. 16, Dec, 1973

1-Origin & 1st app. Luke Cage; Tuska(p)	6	18	42	70
2-Tuska-a(p)	3	9	19	28
3-5: 3-1st app. Mace. 4-1st app. Phil Fox of the Bugle	2	6	13	20
6-10: 8,9-Dr. Doom app. 9-F.F. app.	2	6	9	14
11-16: 14-Origin retold. 15-Everett Subby-r('53). 16-Origin Stilletto; death of Rackham	1	3	6	9

HERO HOTLINE (1st app. in Action Comics Weekly #637)
DC Comics: April, 1989 - No. 6, Sept, 1989 ($1.75, limited series)

1-6: Super-hero humor; Schaffenberger-i				2.25

HEROIC ADVENTURES (See Adventures)

HEROIC COMICS (Reg'lar Fellers...#1-15; New Heroic #41 on)
Eastern Color Printing Co/Famous Funnies(Funnies, Inc. No. 1):
Aug, 1940 - No. 97, June, 1955

1-Hydroman (origin) by Bill Everett, The Purple Zombie (origin) & Mann of India by Tarpe Mills begins (all 1st apps.)	164	492	1023	1800
2	73	219	455	800
3,4	50	150	300	525
5,6	40	120	240	420
7-Origin 1st app. Man O'Metal (1 pg.)	44	132	264	460
8-10: 10-Lingerie panels	34	102	179	310
11,13: 13-Crandall/Fine-a	31	93	165	285
12-Music Master (origin/1st app.) begins by Everett, ends No. 31; last Purple Zombie & Mann of India	35	105	185	320
14,15-Hydroman x-over in Rainbow Boy. 14-Origin & 1st app. Rainbow Boy (super hero). 15-1st app. Downbeat	34	102	179	310
16-20: 16-New logo. 17-Rainbow Boy x-over in Hydroman. 19-Rainbow Boy x-over in Hydroman & vice versa	24	72	127	220
21-30:25-Rainbow Boy x-over in Hydroman. 28-Last Man O'Metal. 29-Last Hydroman	16	48	83	140
31,34,38	6	18	32	45
32,36,37-Toth-a (3-4 pgs. each)	8	24	42	60
33,35-Toth-a (8 & 9 pgs.)	8	24	45	65
39-42-Toth, Ingels-a	8	24	45	65
43,46,47,49-Toth-a (2-4 pgs. each). 47-Ingels-a	7	21	38	55
44,45,50-Toth-a (6-9 pgs. each)	8	24	42	60
48,53,54	6	18	29	40
51-Williamson-a	8	24	42	60
52-Williamson-a (3 pg. story)	6	18	32	45
55-Toth-c/a	7	21	38	55
56-60-Toth-c/a. 60-Everett-a	6	18	30	42
61-Everett-a	6	18	32	45
62,64-Everett-c/a	6	18	32	45
63-Everett-a	6	18	30	42
65-Williamson/Frazetta-a; Evans-a (2 pgs.)	10	30	55	80
66,75,94-Frazetta-a (2 pgs. each)	6	18	32	45
67,73-Frazetta-a (4 pgs. each)	7	21	38	55
68,74,76-80,84,85,88-93,95-97: 95-Last pre-code	5	15	25	35
69,72-Frazetta-a (6 & 8 pgs. each); 1st (?) app. Frazetta Red Cross ad	9	27	49	70
70,71,86,87-Frazetta, 3-4 pgs. 1 pg. ad by Frazetta in #70	6	18	32	45
81,82-Frazetta art (1 pg. each): 81-1st (?) app. Frazetta Boy Scout ad (tied w/				

	GD2.0	FN6.0	VF8.0	NM9.4
Buster Crabbe #9	6	18	28	38
83-Frazetta-a (1/2 pg.)	6	18	28	38

NOTE: *Evans* a-64, 65. *Everett* a-(Hydroman-c/a-No. 1-9), 44, 60-64; c-1-9, 62-64. *Harvey Fuller* c-28-35. *Sid Greene* a-38-43, 46. *Guardineer* a-42(3), 43, 44, 45(2), 49(3), 50, 60, 61(2), 65, 67(2) 70-72. *Ingels* c-41. *Kiefer* a-46, 48; c-19-22, 24, 44, 46, 48, 51-53, 65, 67-69, 71-74, 76, 77, 79, 80, 82, 85, 86, 88, 89, 94, 95. *Mort Lawrence* a-45. *Tarpe Mills* a-2(2), 3(2), 10. *Ed Moore* a-49, 52-54, 56-63, 65-69, 72-74, 76, 77. *H.G. Peter* a-58-74, 76, 77, 87. *Paul Reinman* a-49. *Rico* a-31. *Captain Tootsie* by *Beck*-31, 32. Painted-c #16 on. Hydroman c-1-11. Music Master c-12, 13, 15. Rainbow Boy c-14.

HERO ZERO (Also see Comics' Greatest World & Godzilla Versus Hero Zero)
Dark Horse Comics: Sept, 1994 ($2.50)

0				2.50

HEX (Replaces Jonah Hex)
DC Comics: Sept, 1985 - No. 18, Feb, 1987 (Story cont'd from Jonah Hex #92)

1-Hex in post-atomic war world; origin	1	3	6	8
2-18: 6-Origin Stiletta. 11-13: All contain future Batman storyline. 13-Intro The Dogs of War (origin #15)				5.00

NOTE: *Giffen* a(p)-15-18; c(p)-15,17,18. *Texeira* a-1, 2p, 3p, 5-7p, 9p, 11-14p; c(p)-1, 2, 4-7, 12.

HEXBREAKER (See First Comics Graphic Novel #15)

HEY THERE, IT'S YOGI BEAR (See Movie Comics)

HI-ADVENTURE HEROES (TV)
Gold Key: May, 1969 - No. 2, Aug, 1969 (Hanna-Barbera)

1-Three Musketeers, Gulliver, Arabian Knights	5	15	34	55
2-Three Musketeers, Micro-Venture, Arabian Knights	4	12	29	45

HI AND LOIS
Dell Publishing Co.: No. 683, Mar, 1956 - No. 955, Nov, 1958

Four Color 683	4	12	26	40
Four Color 774(3/57),955	3	9	17	25

HI AND LOIS
Charlton Comics: Nov, 1969 - No. 11, July, 1971

1	3	9	17	24
2-11	2	6	10	14

HICKORY (See All Humor Comics)
Quality Comics Group: Oct, 1949 - No. 6, Aug, 1950

1-Sahl-c/a in all; Feldstein?-a	17	51	88	150
2	10	30	55	80
3-6	9	27	49	70

HIDDEN CREW, THE (See The United States Air Force Presents:...)

HIDE-OUT (See Zane Grey, Four Color No. 346)

HIDING PLACE, THE
Spire Christian Comics (Fleming H. Revell Co.): 1973 (39¢/49¢)

nn	1	3	6	8

HIEROGLYPH
Dark Horse Comics: Nov, 1999 - No. 4, Feb, 2000 ($2.95, limited series)

1-4-Ricardo Delgado-s/a				3.00

HIGH ADVENTURE
Red Top(Decker) Comics (Farrell): Oct, 1957

1-Krigstein-r from Explorer Joe (re-issue on-c)	5	15	24	32

HIGH ADVENTURE (TV)
Dell Publishing Co.: No. 949, Nov, 1958 - No. 1001, Aug-Oct, 1959 (Lowell Thomas)

Four Color 949 (#1)-Photo-c	5	15	35	65
Four Color 1001-Lowell Thomas'...(#2)	5	15	35	60

HIGH CHAPPARAL (TV)
Gold Key: Aug, 1968 (Photo-c)

1 (10226-808)-Tufts-a	5	15	34	55

HIGH SCHOOL CONFIDENTIAL DIARY (Confidential Diary #12 on)
Charlton Comics: June, 1960 - No. 11, Mar, 1962

1	4	12	29	45
2-11	3	9	19	28

HIGH VOLTAGE

Hi-Ho Comics #2 © Four Star Pub.

Hit Comics #13 © QUA

Hitman #3 © DC

	GD2.0	FN6.0	VF8.0	NM9.4

Blackout Comics: 1996 ($2.95)

0-Mike Baron-s				3.00

HI-HO COMICS
Four Star Publications: nd (2/46?) - No. 3, 1946

1-Funny Animal; L. B. Cole-c	39	117	208	360
2,3: 2-L. B. Cole-c	22	66	116	200

HI-JINX (Teen-age Animal Funnies)
La Salle Publ. Co./B&I Publ. Co. (American Comics Group)/Creston: 1945; July-Aug, 1947 - No. 7, July-Aug, 1948

nn-(© 1945, 25 cents, 132 Pgs.)(La Salle)	23	69	121	210
1-Teen-age, funny animal	17	51	88	150
2,3	10	30	55	85
4-7-Milt Gross. 4-X-Mas-c	15	45	77	130

HI-LITE COMICS
E. R. Ross Publishing Co.: Fall, 1945

1-Miss Shady	20	60	105	180

HILLBILLY COMICS
Charlton Comics: Aug, 1955 - No. 4, July, 1956 (Satire)

1-By Art Gates	9	27	49	70
2-4	6	18	29	40

HILLY ROSE'S SPACE ADVENTURES
Astro Comics: May, 1995 - Present ($2.95, B&W)

1	1	3	6	9
2-5				5.00
6-9				3.00
Trade Paperback (1996, $12.95)-r/#1-5				13.00

HIP-IT-TY HOP (See March of Comics No. 15)

HI-SCHOOL ROMANCE (...Romances No. 41 on)
Harvey Publ./True Love(Home Comics): Oct, 1949 - No. 5, June, 1950; No. 6, Dec, 1950 - No. 73, Mar, 1958; No. 74, Sept, 1958 - No. 75, Nov, 1958

1-Photo-c	15	45	77	135
2-Photo-c	9	27	49	70
3-9: 3,5-Photo-c	7	21	36	50
10-Rape story	9	27	49	70
11-20	5	15	25	35
21-31	5	14	21	28
32- "Unholy passion" story	7	21	36	50
33-36: 36-Last pre-code (2/55)	4	12	18	24
37-75: 54-58,73-Kirby-c	4	9	14	19

NOTE: *Powell* a-1-3, 5, 8, 12-16, 18, 21-23, 25-27, 30-34, 36, 37, 39, 45-48, 50-52, 57, 58, 60, 64, 65, 67, 69.

HI-SCHOOL ROMANCE DATE BOOK
Harvey Publications: Nov, 1962 - No. 3, Mar, 1963 (25¢ Giants)

1-Powell, Baker-a	4	12	30	50
2,3	3	9	20	30

HIS NAME IS SAVAGE (Magazine format)
Adventure House Press: June, 1968 (35¢, 52 pgs.)

1-Gil Kane-a	4	12	29	45

HI-SPOT COMICS (Red Ryder No. 1 & No. 3 on)
Hawley Publications: No. 2, Nov, 1940

2-David Innes of Pellucidar; art by J. C. Burroughs; written by Edgar Rice Burroughs	118	354	738	1300

HISTORY OF THE DC UNIVERSE (Also see Crisis on Infinite Earths)
DC Comics: Sept, 1986 - No. 2, Nov, 1986 ($2.95, limited series)

1,2: 1-Perez-c/a				3.00
Limited Edition hardcover	4	12	30	50

HISTORY OF VIOLENCE, A
DC COMICS (Paradox Press) 1998?

nn-Paperback ($9.95)				10.00

HITCHHIKERS GUIDE TO THE GALAXY (See Life, the Universe and Everything & Restaraunt at the End of the Universe)
DC Comics: 1993 - No. 3, 1993 ($4.95, limited series)

1-3: Adaptation of Douglas Adams book				5.00
TPB (1997, $14.95) r/#1-3				15.00

HIT COMICS
Quality Comics Group: July, 1940 - No. 65, July, 1950

1-Origin/1st app. Neon, the Unknown & Hercules; intro. The Red Bee; Bob & Swab, Blaze Barton, the Strange Twins, X-5 Super Agent, Casey Jones & Jack & Jill (ends #7) begin	600	1800	3900	7800
2-The Old Witch begins, ends #14	255	765	1591	2800
3-Casey Jones ends; transvestism story "Jack & Jill"	236	708	1477	2600
4-Super Agent (ends #17), & Betty Bates (ends #65) begin; X-5 ends	214	642	1338	2350
5-Classic Lou Fine cover	508	1524	3300	6600
6-10: 10-Old Witch by Crandall (4 pgs.); 1st work in comics (4/41)	186	558	1162	2050
11-Classic cover	164	492	1023	1800
12-17: 13-Blaze Barton ends. 17-Last Neon; Crandall Hercules in all; Last Lou Fine-c	114	342	712	1250
18-Origin & 1st app. Stormy Foster, the Great Defender (12/41); The Ghost of Flanders begins; Crandall-a	125	375	781	1375
19,20	100	300	625	1100
21-24: 21-Last Hercules. 24-Last Red Bee & Strange Twins	95	285	594	1050
25-Origin & 1st app. Kid Eternity and begins by Moldoff (12/42); 1st app. The Keeper (Kid Eternity's aide)	182	546	1136	2000
26-Blackhawk x-over in Kid Eternity	100	300	625	1100
27-29	50	150	300	525
30,31- "Bill the Magnificent" by Kurtzman, 11 pgs. in each	45	135	270	475
32-40: 32-Plastic Man x-over. 34-Last Stormy Foster	29	87	153	265
41-50	21	63	110	185
51-60-Last Kid Eternity	20	60	105	175
61-63-Crandall-c/a; 61-Jeb Rivers begins	21	63	110	185
64,65-Crandall-a	20	60	105	175

NOTE: *Crandall* a-11-17(Hercules), 23, 24(Stormy Foster); c-18-20, 23, 24. *Fine* c-1-14, 16, 17(most). *Ward* c-33. Bondage c-7, 64. Hercules c-3, 10-17. Jeb Rivers c-61-65. Kid Eternity c-25-60 (w/Keeper-28-34, 36, 39-43, 45-55). Neon the Unknown c-2, 4, 8, 9. Red Bee c-1, 5-7. Stormy Foster c-18-24.

HITLER'S ASTROLOGER (See Marvel Graphic Novel #35)

HITMAN (Also see Bloodbath #2, Batman Chronicles #4, Demon #43-45 & Demon Annual #2)
DC Comics: May, 1996 - No. 60, Apr, 2001 ($2.25/$2.50)

1-Garth Ennis-s & John McCrea-c/a begin; Batman app.	1	3	6	9
2-Joker-c;Two Face, Mad Hatter, Batman app.				6.00
3-5: 3-Batman-c/app.; Joker app. 4-1st app. Nightfist				4.00
6-20: 8-Final Night x-over. 10-GL cameo. 11-20: 11,12-GL-c/app. 15-20-"Ace of Killers". 16-18-Catwoman app. 17-19-Demon-app.				3.00
21-59: 34-Superman-c/app.				2.50
60-($3.95) Final issue; includes pin-ups by various				4.00
#1,000,000 (11/98) Hitman goes to the 853rd Century				2.50
Annual 1 (1997, $3.95) Pulp Heroes				4.00
.../Lobo: That Stupid Bastich (7/00, $3.95) Ennis-s/Mahnke-a				4.00
TPB-(1997, $9.95) r/#1-3, Demon Ann. #2, Batman Chronicles #4				10.00
Ace of Killers TPB ('00, $17.95) r/#15-22				18.00
Local Heroes TPB ('99, $17.95) r/#9-14 & Annual #1				18.00
10,000 Bullets TPB ('98, $9.95) r/#4-8				10.00
Who Dares Wins TPB ('01, $12.95) r/#23-28				13.00

HI-YO SILVER (See Lone Ranger's Famous Horse... and also see The Lone Ranger and March of Comics No. 215)

HOBBIT, THE
Eclipse Comics: 1989 - No. 3, 1990 ($4.95, squarebound, 52 pgs.)

Book 1-3: Adapts novel; Wenzel-a				7.00
Book 1-Second printing				5.00
Graphic Novel (1990, Ballantine)-r/#1-3				20.00

HOCUS POCUS (Formerly Funny Book)
Parents' Magazine Press: No. 9, Aug-Sept, 1946

Hobbit Book 2 © Tolkien Estate

Hollywood Diary #2 © QUA

Holyoke One-Shot #3 © HOKE

	GD2.0	FN6.0	VF8.0	NM9.4

9

	6	18	29	40

HOGAN'S HEROES (TV)
Dell Publishing Co.: June, 1966 - No. 8, Sept, 1967; No. 9, Oct, 1969

	GD2.0	FN6.0	VF8.0	NM9.4
1: #1-7 photo-c	8	24	56	100
2,3-Ditko-a(p)	5	15	35	60
4-9: 9-Reprints #1	4	12	29	45

HOKUM & HEX (See Razorline)
Marvel Comics (Razorline): Sept, 1993 - No. 9, May, 1994 ($1.75/$1.95)

1-($2.50)-Foil embossed-c; by Clive Barker				3.00
2-9: 5-Hyperkind x-over				2.25

HOLIDAY COMICS
Fawcett Publications: 1942 (25¢, 196 pgs.)

1-Contains three Fawcett comics plus two page portrait of Captain Marvel; Capt. Marvel, Nyoka #1, & Whiz. Not rebound, remaindered comics; printed at the same time as originals	155	465	966	1700

HOLIDAY COMICS (Becomes Fun Comics #9-12)
Star Publications: Jan, 1951 - No. 8, Oct, 1952

1-Funny animal contents (Frisky Fables) in all; L. B. Cole X-mas-c	36	108	191	330
2-Classic L. B. Cole-c	39	117	208	360
3-8: 5,8-X-Mas-c; all L.B. Cole-c	25	75	130	225
Accepted Reprint 4 (nd)-L.B. Cole-c	11	33	55	90

HOLIDAY DIGEST
Harvey Comics: 1988 ($1.25, digest-size)

1	1	3	5	7

HOLIDAY PARADE (Walt Disney's...)
W. D. Publications (Disney): Winter, 1990-91(no yr. given) - No. 2, Winter, 1990-91 ($2.95, 68 pgs.)

1-Reprints 1947 Firestone by Barks plus new-a				4.00
2-Barks-r plus other stories				4.00

HOLI-DAY SURPRISE (Formerly Summer Fun)
Charlton Comics: V2#55, Mar, 1967 (25¢ Giant)

V2#55	3	10	23	35

HOLLYWOOD COMICS
New Age Publishers: Winter, 1944 (52 pgs.)

1-Funny animal	19	57	99	165

HOLLYWOOD CONFESSIONS
St. John Publishing Co.: Oct, 1949 - No. 2, Dec, 1949

1-Kubert-c/a (entire book)	29	87	153	265
2-Kubert-c/a (entire book) (Scarce)	35	105	185	320

HOLLYWOOD DIARY
Quality Comics Group: Dec, 1949 - No. 5, July-Aug, 1950

1-No photo-c	20	60	105	175
2-Photo-c	13	39	66	110
3-5-Photo-c. 5-June Allyson/Peter Lawford photo-c	11	33	55	90

HOLLYWOOD FILM STORIES
Feature Publications/Prize: April, 1950 - No. 4, Oct, 1950 (All photo-c; "Fumetti" type movie comic)

1-June Allyson photo-c	20	60	105	180
2-4: 2-Lizabeth Scott photo-c. 3-Barbara Stanwick photo-c. 4-Betty Hutton photo-c	15	45	77	130

HOLLYWOOD FUNNY FOLKS (Formerly Funny Folks; Becomes Nutsy Squirrel #61 on)
National Periodical Publ.: No. 27, Aug-Sept, 1950 - No. 60, July-Aug, 1954

27	14	42	72	120
28-40	10	30	55	80
41-60	9	27	49	70

NOTE: **Sheldon Mayer** a-27-35, 37-40, 43-46, 48-51, 53, 56, 57, 60.

HOLLYWOOD LOVE DOCTOR (See Doctor Anthony King...)

HOLLYWOOD PICTORIAL (...Romances on cover)
St. John Publishing Co.: No. 3, Jan, 1950

3-Matt Baker-a; photo-c	24	72	127	215

(Becomes a movie magazine - Hollywood Pictorial Western with No. 4.)

HOLLYWOOD ROMANCES (Formerly Brides In Love; becomes For Lovers Only #60 on)
Charlton Comics: V2#46, 11/66; #47, 10/67; #48, 11/68;V3#49,11/69-V3#59, 6/71

V2#46-Rolling Stones-c/story	9	27	63	105
V2#47-V3#59: 56- "Born to Heart Break" begins	2	6	11	15

HOLLYWOOD SECRETS
Quality Comics Group: Nov, 1949 - No. 6, Sept, 1950

1-Ward-c/a (9 pgs.)	34	102	179	310
2-Crandall-a, Ward-a (9 pgs.)	23	69	121	210
3-6: All photo-c. 5-Lex Barker (Tarzan)-c	12	36	61	105
...of Romance, I.W. Reprint #9; r/#2 above w/Kinstler-c	2	6	12	18

HOLLYWOOD SUPERSTARS
Marvel Comics (Epic Comics): Nov, 1990 - No. 5, Apr, 1991 ($2.25)

1-($2.95, 52 pgs.)-Spiegle-c/a in all; Aragones-a, inside front-c plus 2-4 pgs.				3.00
2-5 ($2.25)				2.25

HOLO-MAN (See Power Record Comics)

HOLYOKE ONE-SHOT
Holyoke Publishing Co. (Tem Publ.): 1944 - No. 10, 1945 (All reprints)

1,2: 1-Grit Grady (on cover only), Miss Victory, Alias X (origin)-All reprints from Captain Fearless. 2-Rusty Dugan (Corporal); Capt. Fearless (origin), Mr. Miracle app.	14	42	72	125
3-Miss Victory; r/Crash #4; Cat Man (origin), Solar Legion by Kirby app.; Miss Victory on cover only (1945)	27	81	145	250
4,6,8: 4-Mr. Miracle; The Blue Streak app. 6-Capt. Fearless, Alias X, Capt. Stone (splash used as-c to #10); Diamond Jim & Rusty Dugan (splash from cover of #2). 8-Blue Streak, Strong Man (story matches cover to #7)-Crash reprints	12	36	61	105
5,7: 5-U.S. Border Patrol Comics (Sgt. Dick Carter of the...), Miss Victory (story matches cover to #3); Citizen Smith, & Mr. Miracle app. 7-Secret Agent Z-2, Strong Man, Blue Streak (story matches cover to #8); Reprints from Crash #2	14	42	72	125
9-Citizen Smith, The Blue Streak, Solar Legion by Kirby & Strongman, the Perfect Human app.; reprints from Crash #4 & 5; Citizen Smith on cover only-from story in #5 (1944-before #3)	19	57	99	170
10-Captain Stone; r/Crash; Solar Legion by S&K	19	57	99	170

HOMER COBB (See Adventures of...)

HOMER HOOPER
Atlas Comics: July, 1953 - No. 4, Dec, 1953

1-Teenage humor	10	30	55	80
2-4	7	21	36	50

HOMER, THE HAPPY GHOST (See Adventures of...)
Atlas(ACI/PPI/WPI)/Marvel: 3/55 - No. 22, 11/58; V2#1, 11/69 - V2#4, 5/70

V1#1-Dan DeCarlo-c/a begins, ends #22	20	60	105	180
2-1st code approved issue	11	33	55	90
3-10	9	27	49	70
11-22	8	24	42	60
V2#1 (11/69)	9	27	65	110
2-4	5	15	34	55

HOME RUN (Also see A-1 Comics)
Magazine Enterprises: No. 89, 1953 (one-shot)

A-1 89 (#3)-Powell-a; Stan Musial photo-c	13	39	66	110

HOMICIDE (Also see Dark Horse Presents)
Dark Horse Comics: Apr, 1990 ($1.95, B&W, one-shot)

1-Detective story				2.25

HONEYMOON (Formerly Gay Comics)
A Lover's Magazine(USA) (Marvel): No. 41, Jan, 1950

41-Photo-c; article by Betty Grable	10	30	55	80

HONEYMOONERS, THE (TV)
Lodestone: Oct, 1986 ($1.50)

1-Photo-c				4.00

Hong Kong Phooey #1 © H-B

Hopalong Cassidy #20 © FAW

Hopeless Savages #1 © Jen Van Meter

	GD2.0	FN6.0	VF8.0	NM9.4

HONEYMOONERS, THE (TV)
Triad Publications: Sept, 1987 - No. 13? ($2.00)

1-13				4.00

HONEYMOON ROMANCE
Artful Publications (Canadian): Apr, 1950 - No. 2, July, 1950 (25¢, digest size)

1,2-(Rare)	37	111	197	340

HONEY WEST (TV)
Gold Key: Sept, 1966 (Photo-c)

1 (10186-609)	10	30	70	130

HONG KONG PHOOEY (TV)
Charlton Comics: June, 1975 - No. 9, Nov, 1976 (Hanna-Barbera)

1	5	15	34	55
2	3	9	19	28
3-9	2	6	13	20

HONG ON THE RANGE
Image/Flypaper Press: Dec, 1997 - No. 3, Feb, 1998 ($2.50, lim. series)

1-3: Wu-s/Lafferty-a				2.50

HOODED HORSEMAN, THE (Formerly Blazing West)
American Comics Group (Michel Publ.): No. 21, 1-2/52 - No. 27, 1-2/54; No. 18, 12-1/54-55 - No. 22, 8-9/55

21(1-2/52)-Hooded Horseman, Injun Jones cont.	15	45	77	130
22	10	30	55	80
23,24,27(1-2/54)	8	24	45	65
25 (9-10/53)-Cowboy Sahib on cover only; Hooded Horseman i.d. revealed	9	27	49	70
26-Origin/1st app. Cowboy Sahib by L. Starr	11	33	55	90
18(12-1/54-55)(Formerly Out of the Night)	10	30	55	80
19,21,22: 19-Last precode (1-2/55)	8	24	42	60
20-Origin Johnny Injun	9	27	49	70

NOTE: *Whitney c/a-21(`52), 20-22.*

HOODED MENACE, THE (Also see Daring Adventures)
Realistic/Avon Periodicals: 1951 (one-shot)

nn-Based on a band of hooded outlaws in the Pacific Northwest, 1900-1906; reprinted in Daring Advs. #15	47	141	286	500

HOODS UP
Fram Corp.: 1953 (15¢, distributed to service station owners, 16 pgs.)

1-(Very Rare; only 2 known); Eisner-c/a in all.	47	141	286	500
2-6-(Very Rare; only 1 known of #3, 4, 2 known of #2)	47	141	286	500

NOTE: *Convertible Connie gives tips for service stations, selling Fram oil filters.*

HOOK (Movie)
Marvel Comics: Early Feb, 1992 - No. 4, Late Mar, 1992 ($1.00, limited series)

1-4: Adapts movie; Vess-c; 1-Morrow-a(p)				2.25
nn (1991, $5.95, 84 pgs.)-Contains #1-4; Vess-c				6.00
1 (1991, $2.95, magazine, 84 pgs.)-Contains #1-4; Vess-c (same cover as nn issue)				3.00

HOOT GIBSON'S WESTERN ROUNDUP (See Western Roundup under Fox Giants)

HOOT GIBSON WESTERN (Formerly My Love Story)
Fox Features Syndicate: No. 5, May, 1950 - No. 3, Sept, 1950

5,6(#1,2): 5-Photo-c. 6-Photo/painted-c	29	87	153	265
3-Wood-a; painted-c	31	93	165	285

HOPALONG CASSIDY (Also see Bill Boyd Western, Master Comics, Real Western Hero, Six Gun Heroes & Western Hero; Bill Boyd starred as H. Cassidy in the movies; H. Cassidy in movies, radio & TV)
Fawcett Publications: Feb, 1943; No. 2, Summer, 1946 - No. 85, Nov, 1953

1 (1943, 68 pgs.)-H. Cassidy & his horse Topper on (on sale 1/8/43)-Captain Marvel app. on-c	462	1386	3000	6000
2-(Sum, '46)	77	231	483	850
3,4: 3-(Fall, '46, 52 pgs. begin)	40	120	232	400
5- "Mad Barber" story mentioned in **SOTI**, pgs. 308,309; photo-c	33	99	174	300
6-10: 8-Photo-c	27	81	145	250

11-19: 11,13-19-Photo-c	21	63	110	185
20-29 (52 pgs.)-Painted/photo-c	17	51	88	150
30,31,33,34,37-39,41 (52 pgs.)-Painted-c	12	36	61	100
32,40 (36pgs.)-Painted-c	10	30	55	85
35,42,43,45-47,49-51,53,54,56 (52 pgs.)-Photo-c	11	33	55	90
36,44,48 (36 pgs.)-Photo-c	10	30	55	80
52,55,57-70 (36 pgs.)-Photo-c	9	27	49	70
71-84-Photo-c	7	21	38	55
85-Last Fawcett issue; photo-c	9	27	49	70

NOTE: *Line-drawn c-1-4, 6, 7, 9, 10, 12.*

... & The 5 Men of Evil (AC Comics, 1991, $12.95) r/newspaper strips and Fawcett story "Signature of Death"				13.00

HOPALONG CASSIDY
National Periodical Publications: No. 86, Feb, 1954 - No. 135, May-June, 1959 (All-36 pgs.)

86-Gene Colan-a begins, ends #117; photo covers continue	40	120	220	380
87	23	69	121	210
88-91: 91-1 pg. Superboy-sty (6/54)	15	45	77	130
92-99 (98 has #93 on-c; last precode issue, 2/55). 95-Reversed photo-c to #52. 98-Reversed photo-c to #61. 99-Reversed photo-c to #60	14	42	72	120
100-Same cover as #50	15	45	77	130
101-108: 105-Same photo-c as #54. 107-Same photo-c as #51. 108-Last photo-c	7	21	53	85
109-130: 118-Photo-c begins. 123-Kubert-a (2 pgs.). 124-Painted-c	6	18	45	75
131-135	7	21	50	80

HOPELESS SAVAGES
Oni Press: Aug, 2001 - No. 4, Nov, 2001 ($2.95, B&W, limited series)

1-4-Van Meter-s/Norrie-a/Clugston-Major-a/Watson-c				3.00

HOPE SHIP
Dell Publishing Co.: June-Aug, 1963

1	2	6	13	20

HOPPY THE MARVEL BUNNY (See Fawcett's Funny Animals)
Fawcett Publications: Dec, 1945 - No. 15, Sept, 1947

1	30	90	159	275
2	15	45	77	130
3-15: 7-Xmas-c	13	39	66	110

HORACE & DOTTY DRIPPLE (Dotty Dripple No. 1-24)
Harvey Publications: No. 25, Aug, 1952 - No. 43, Oct, 1955

25-43	3	8	12	15

HORIZONTAL LIEUTENANT, THE (See Movie Classics)

HOROBI
Viz Premiere Comics: 1990 - No. 8, 1990 ($3.75, B&W, mature readers, 84 pgs.)
V2#1, 1990 - No. 7, 1991 ($4.25, B&W, 68 pgs.)

1-8: Japanese manga, Part Two, #1-7				4.50

HORRIFIC (Terrific No. 14 on)
Artful/Comic Media/Harwell/Mystery: Sept, 1952 - No. 13, Sept, 1954

1	43	129	257	450
2	26	78	139	240
3-Bullet in head-c	45	135	270	475
4,5,7,9,10: 4-Shrunken head-c. 7-Guillotine-c	22	66	116	200
6-Jack The Ripper story	23	69	121	210
8-Origin & 1st app. The Teller (E.C. parody)	26	78	139	240
11-13: 11-Swipe/Witches Tales #6,27; Devil-c	18	54	94	160

NOTE: *Don Heck a-8; c-3-13. Hollingsworth a-4. Morisi a-8. Palais a-5, 7-12.*

HORROR FROM THE TOMB (Mysterious Stories No. 2 on)
Premier Magazine Co.: Sept, 1954

1-Woodbridge/Torres, Check-a; The Keeper of the Graveyard is host	40	120	232	400

HORRORIST, THE (Also see Hellblazer)
DC Comics (Vertigo): Dec, 1995 - No. 2, Jan, 1996 ($5.95, lim. series, mature)

1,2: Jamie Delano scripts; David Lloyd-c/a; John Constantine (Hellblazer) app.				

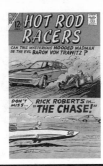

Horrific #5 © Comic Media

Hot Rod Racers #12 © CC

Hot Rods & Racing Cars #2 © CC

	GD2.0	FN6.0	VF8.0	NM9.4
				6.00

HORROR OF COLLIER COUNTY
Dark Horse Comics: Oct, 1999 - No. 5, Feb, 2000 ($2.95, B&W, limited series)

1-5-Rich Tommaso-s/a				3.00

HORRORS, THE (Formerly Startling Terror Tales #10)
Star Publications: No. 11, Jan, 1953 - No. 15, Apr, 1954

	GD2.0	FN6.0	VF8.0	NM9.4
11-Horrors of War; Disbrow-a(2)	31	93	165	285
12-Horrors of War; color illo in **POP**	29	87	153	265
13-Horrors of Mystery; crime stories	27	81	142	245
14,15-Horrors of the Underworld; crime stories	29	87	153	265

NOTE: All have **L. B. Cole** covers; a-12. **Hollingsworth** a-13. **Palais** a-13r.

HORROR TALES (Magazine)
Eerie Publications: V1#7, 6/69 - V6#6, 12/74; V7#1, 2/75; V7#2, 5/76 - V8#5, 1977; V9#1-3, 8/78; V10#1(2/79) (V1-V6: 52 pgs.; V7, V8#2: 112 pgs.; V8#4 on: 68 pgs.) (No V5#3, V8#1,3)

	GD2.0	FN6.0	VF8.0	NM9.4
V1#7	4	12	29	45
V1#8,9	3	9	20	30
V2#1-6('70), V3#1-6('71), V4#1-3,5-7('72)	3	9	18	26
V4#4-LSD story reprint/Weird V3#5	4	12	25	38
V5#1,2,4,5(6/73),5(10/73),6(12/73),V6#1-6('74),V7#1,2,4('76),V7#3('76)-				
Giant issue,V8#2,4,5('77)	3	9	18	26
V9#1-3(11/78, $1.50), V10#1(2/79)	3	9	21	32

NOTE: Bondage-c-V6#1, 3, V7#2.

HORSE FEATHERS COMICS
Lev Gleason Publ.: Nov, 1945 - No. 4, July(Summer on-c), 1948 (52 pgs.)

	GD2.0	FN6.0	VF8.0	NM9.4
1-Wolverton's Scoop Scuttle, 2 pgs.	20	60	105	175
2	10	30	55	80
3,4: 3-(5/48)	8	24	42	60

HORSEMAN
Crusade Comics/Kevlar Studios: Mar, 1996 - No. 3, Nov, 1997 ($2.95)

0-1st Kevlar Studios issue, 1-(3/96)-Crusade issue; Shi-c/app.,				
1-(11/96)-3-(11/97)-Kevlar Studios				3.00

HORSEMASTERS, THE (Disney)(TV, Movie)
Dell Publishing Co.: No. 1260, Dec-Feb, 1961/62

	GD2.0	FN6.0	VF8.0	NM9.4
Four Color 1260-Annette Funicello photo-c	12	36	84	160

HORSE SOLDIERS, THE
Dell Publishing Co.: No. 1048, Nov-Jan, 1959/60 (John Wayne movie)

	GD2.0	FN6.0	VF8.0	NM9.4
Four Color 1048-Painted-c, Sekowsky-a	14	42	98	180

HORSE WITHOUT A HEAD, THE (See Movie Comics)

HOT DOG
Magazine Enterprises: June-July, 1954 - No. 4, Dec-Jan, 1954-55

	GD2.0	FN6.0	VF8.0	NM9.4
1(A-1 #107)	8	24	42	60
2,3(A-1 #115),4(A-1 #136)	6	18	29	40

HOT DOG (See Jughead's Pal, Hotdog)

HOTEL DEPAREE - SUNDANCE (TV)
Dell Publishing Co.: No. 1126, Aug-Oct, 1960 (one-shot)

	GD2.0	FN6.0	VF8.0	NM9.4
Four Color 1126-Earl Holliman photo-c	6	18	42	80

HOT ROD AND SPEEDWAY COMICS
Hillman Periodicals: Feb-Mar, 1952 - No. 5, Apr-May, 1953

	GD2.0	FN6.0	VF8.0	NM9.4
1	27	81	145	250
2-Krigstein-a	20	60	105	175
3-5	11	33	55	90

HOT ROD COMICS (...Featuring Clint Curtis) (See XMas Comics)
Fawcett Publications: Nov, 1951 (no month given) - V2#7, Feb, 1953

	GD2.0	FN6.0	VF8.0	NM9.4
nn (V1#1)-Powell-c/a in all	33	99	174	300
2 (4/52)	19	57	99	165
3-6, V2#7	14	42	72	120

HOT ROD KING (Also see Speed Smith the Hot Rod King)
Ziff-Davis Publ. Co.: Fall, 1952

	GD2.0	FN6.0	VF8.0	NM9.4
1-Giacoia-a; Saunders painted-c	27	81	145	250

HOT ROD RACERS (Grand Prix No. 16 on)
Charlton Comics: Dec, 1964 - No. 15, July, 1967

	GD2.0	FN6.0	VF8.0	NM9.4
1	8	24	56	90
2-5	5	15	34	55
6-15	4	12	26	40

HOT RODS AND RACING CARS
Charlton Comics (Motor Mag. No. 1): Nov, 1951 - No. 120, June, 1973

	GD2.0	FN6.0	VF8.0	NM9.4
1-Speed Davis begins; Indianapolis 500 story	29	87	153	265
2	15	45	77	130
3-10	10	30	55	85
11-20	9	27	49	70
21-34,36-40	7	21	38	55
35 (6/58, 68 pgs.)	10	30	55	80
41-60	6	18	29	40
61-80	3	9	19	28
81-100	2	6	13	20
101-120	2	6	11	16

HOT SHOT CHARLIE
Hillman Periodicals: 1947 (Lee Elias)

	GD2.0	FN6.0	VF8.0	NM9.4
1	10	30	55	80

HOT SHOTS: AVENGERS
Marvel Comics: Oct, 1995 ($2.95, one-shot)

nn-pin-ups				3.00

HOTSPUR
Eclipse Comics: Jun, 1987 - No. 3, Sep, 1987 ($1.75, lim. series, Baxter paper)

1-3				2.25

HOT STUFF (See Stumbo Tinytown)
Harvey Comics: V2#1, Sept, 1991 - No. 12, June, 1994 ($1.00)

V2#1-Stumbo back-up story				4.00
2-12 ($1.50)				3.00
...Big Book 1 (11/92), 2 (6/93) (Both $1.95, 52 pgs.)				4.00

HOT STUFF CREEPY CAVES
Harvey Publications: Nov, 1974 - No. 7, Nov, 1975

	GD2.0	FN6.0	VF8.0	NM9.4
1	3	10	23	35
2-7	2	6	13	20

HOT STUFF DIGEST
Harvey Comics: July, 1992 - No. 5, Nov, 1993 ($1.75, digest-size)

V2#1-Hot Stuff, Stumbo, Richie Rich stories				3.50
2-5				2.50

HOT STUFF GIANT SIZE
Harvey Comics: Oct, 1992 - No. 3, Oct, 1993 ($2.25, 68 pgs.)

V2#1-Hot Stuff & Stumbo stories				4.00
2,3				3.00

HOT STUFF SIZZLERS
Harvey Publications: July, 1960 - No. 59, Mar, 1974; V2#1, Aug, 1992

	GD2.0	FN6.0	VF8.0	NM9.4
1- 84 pgs. begin, ends #5; Hot Stuff, Stumbo begin	13	39	94	160
2-5	6	18	42	70
6-10: 6-68 pgs. begin, ends #45	4	12	29	45
11-20	3	10	23	35
21-45	3	9	17	25
46-52: 52 pgs. begin	2	6	12	18
53-59	2	6	9	12
V2#1-(8/92, $1.25)-Stumbo back-up				4.00

HOT STUFF, THE LITTLE DEVIL (Also see Devil Kids & Harvey Hits)
Harvey Publications (Illustrated Humor): 10/57 - No. 141, 7/77; No. 142, 2/78 - No. 164, 8/82; No. 165, 10/86 - No. 171, 11/87; No. 172, 11/88; No. 173, Sept, 1990 - No. 177, 1/91

	GD2.0	FN6.0	VF8.0	NM9.4
1	36	108	270	475
2-1st app. Stumbo the Giant (12/57)	18	54	129	230
3-5	13	39	94	160
6-10	8	24	58	95
11-20	6	18	42	70
21-40	4	12	29	45
41-60	3	9	20	30
61-80	2	6	15	22

Hot Wheels #5 © DC

Hourman #25 © DC

House of Mystery #2 © DC

	GD2.0	FN6.0	VF8.0	NM9.4

	GD2.0	FN6.0	VF8.0	NM9.4
81-105	2	6	11	16
106-112: All 52 pg. Giants	2	6	15	22
113-125	1	3	6	9
126-141	1	3	5	7
142-177: 172-177-($1.00)				5.00

HOT WHEELS (TV)
National Periodical Publications: Mar-Apr, 1970 - No. 6, Jan-Feb, 1971

1	9	27	65	110
2,4,5	5	15	34	55
3-Neal Adams-c	5	15	38	60
6-Neal Adams-c/a	7	21	50	80
NOTE: *Toth* a-1p, 2-5; c-1p, 5.

HOURMAN (Justice Society member, see Adventure Comics #48)

HOURMAN (See JLA and DC One Million)
DC Comics: Apr, 1999 - No. 25, Apr, 2001 ($2.50)

1-25: 1-JLA app.; McDaniel-c. 2-Tomorrow Woman-c/app. 6,7-Amazo app. 11-13-Justice Legion A app. 16-Silver Age flashback. 18,19-JSA-c/app. 22-Harris-c/a. 24-Hourman Vs. Rex Tyler				2.50

HOUSE OF MYSTERY (See Brave and the Bold #93, Elvira's House of Mystery, Limited Collectors' Edition & Super DC Giant)

HOUSE OF MYSTERY, THE
National Periodical Publications/DC Comics: Dec-Jan, 1951-52 - No. 321, Oct, 1983 (No. 194-203: 52 pgs.)

1-DC's first horror comic	218	654	1364	2400
2	88	264	550	975
3	64	192	398	700
4,5	50	150	300	525
6-10	43	.129	257	450
11-15	39	117	208	360
16(7/53)-25	29	87	156	270
26-35(2/55)-Last pre-code issue; 30-Woodish-a	23	69	121	210
36-50: 50-Text story of Orson Welles' War of the Worlds broadcast	14	42	100	170
51-60: 55-1st S.A. issue	11	33	77	130
61,63,65,66,70,72,76,85-Kirby-a	12	36	88	150
62,64,67-69,71,73-75,77-83,86-99	9	27	65	110
84-Prototype of Negative Man (Doom Patrol)	13	39	94	160
100 (7/60)	10	30	70	120
101-116: 109-Toth, Kubert-a. 116-Last 10¢ issue	9	27	63	105
117-130: 117-Swipes-c to HOS #20. 120-Toth-a	8	24	56	90
131-142	6	18	45	75
143-J'onn J'onzz, Manhunter begins (6/64), ends #173; story continues from Detective #326; intro. Idol-Head of Diabolu	22	66	151	270
144	10	30	70	120
145-155,157-159: 149-Toth-a. 155-The Human Hurricane app. (12/65), Red Tornado prototype. 158-Origin Diabolu Idol-Head	7	21	50	80
156-Robby Reed begins (origin/1st app.), ends #173	9	27	63	105
160-(7/66)-Robby Reed becomes Plastic Man in this issue only; 1st S.A. app. Plastic Man; intro Marco Xavier (Martian Manhunter) & Vulture Crime Organization; ends #173	12	36	84	140
161-173: 169-Origin/1st app. Gem Girl	5	15	34	55
174-Mystery format begins.	6	18	45	75
175-1st app. Cain (House of Mystery host)	5	15	34	55
176,177	4	12	30	50
178-Neal Adams-a (2/68)	5	15	38	60
179-N. Adams/Orlando, Wrightson-a (1st pro work, 3 pgs.)	8	24	56	90
180,181,183: Wrightson-a (3,10, & 3 pgs.). 180-Last 12¢ issue; Kane/ Wood-a(2). 183-Wood-a	4	12	30	50
182,184: 182-Toth-a. 184-Kane/Wood, Toth-a	3	9	20	30
185-Williamson/Kaluta-a; Howard-a (3 pgs.)	3	10	23	35
186-N. Adams-c/a; Wrightson-a (10 pgs.)	4	12	29	45
187,190: Adams-c. 187-Toth-a. 190-Toth-a(r)	3	9	17	25
188-Wrightson-a (8 & 3pgs.); Adams-a	4	12	26	40
189,192,197: Adams-c on all. 189-Wood-a(i). 192-Adams 15¢-c	3	9	17	25
191-Wrightson-a (8 & 3pgs.); Adams-c	4	12	26	40
193-Wrightson-c	3	9	19	28
194-Wrightson-c; 52 pgs begin, end #203; Toth,Kirby-a	4	12	25	38
195: Wrightson-c. Swamp creature story by Wrightson similar to Swamp Thing (10 pgs.)(10/71)	5	15	34	55
196,198	3	9	20	30
199-Adams-c; Wood-a(8pgs.); Kirby-a	3	10	23	35
200-(25¢, 52 pgs.)-One third-r (3/72)	4	12	25	38
201-203-(25¢, 52 pgs.)-One third-r	3	9	21	32
204-Wrightson-c/a, 9 pgs.	3	9	19	28
205,206,208,210,212,215,216,218	2	6	11	15
207-Wrightson c/a; Starlin, Redondo-a	3	9	17	25
209,211,213,214,217,219-Wrightson-c	2	6	13	20
220,222,223	2	6	9	12
221-Wrightson/Kaluta-a(8 pgs.)	3	9	17	25
224-229: 224-Wrightson-r from Spectre #9; Dillin/Adams-r from House of Secrets #82; begin 100 pg. issues; Phantom Stranger-r. 225,227-(100 pgs.): 225-Spectre app. 226-Wrightson/Redondo-a Phantom Stranger-r. 228-N. Adams inks; Wrightson-r. 229-Wrightson-a(r); Toth-r; last 100 pg. issue.	4	12	29	45
230,232-235,237-250	1	3	6	9
231-Classic Wrightson-c	2	6	13	20
236-Wrightson-c; Ditko-a(p); N. Adams-i	2	6	9	12
251-254-(84 pgs.)-Adams-c. 251-Wood-a	2	6	11	16
255,256-(84 pgs.)-Wrightson-c	2	6	11	16
257-259-(84 pgs.)	2	6	10	14
260-289,291-299: 282-(68 pgs.)-Has extra story "The Computers That Saved Metropolis" Radio Shack giveaway by Jim Starlin	1	3	5	7
290-1st "I, Vampire"	2	6	11	16
300,319,321: Death of "I, Vampire"	2	6	9	12
301-318,320: 301-318-"I, Vampire"	1	3	5	7
Welcome to the House of Mystery (7/98, $5.95) reprints stories with new framing intro by Gaiman and Aragonés				6.00

NOTE: *Neal Adams* a-236i; c-175-192, 197, 199, 251-254. *Alcala* a-209, 217, 219, 224, 227. *M. Anderson* a-212; c/a-37. *Aparo* a-209. *Aragones* a-185, 186, 194, 196, 200, 202, 229, 251. *Baily* a-279p. *Cameron* a-76, 79. *Colan* a-202r. *Craig* a-263, 275, 295, 300. *Dillin/Adams* r-224. *Ditko* a-236p, 247, 254, 258, 276; c-277. *Drucker* a-37. *Evans* c-218. *Fraden* a-251. *Giffen* a-284. *Giunta* a-199, 227r. *Golden* c-257, 259. *Heath* a-194r; c-203. *Howard* a-182, 185, 187, 196, 229r, 247i, 254, 279i. *Kaluta* a-195, 200, 250r; c-200-202, 210, 212, 233, 260, 261, 263, 265, 267, 268, 273, 276, 284, 287, 288, 293-295, 300, 302, 304, 305, 309-319, 321. *Bob Kane* a-84. *Gil Kane* a-196p, 253p, 300p. *Kirby* a-194r, 199r; c-65, 76, 78, 79, 85. *Kubert* c-282, 283, 285, 286, 289-292, 297-299, 301, 303, 306-308. *Maneely* a-68, 227r. *Mayer* a-317p. *Meskin* a-52-144 (most), 195r, 224r, 229r; c-63, 66, 124, 127. *Mooney* a-24, 159, 160. *Moreira* a-3, 4, 20-50, 58, 59, 62, 68, 77, 79, 90, 108, 113, 123, 201r; 228; c-4-28, 44, 47, 50, 54, 59, 62, 64, 68, 70, 73. *Morrow* a-192, 196, 255, 320i. *Mortimer* a-204(3 pgs.). *Nasser* a-276. *Newton* a-259, 272. *Nino* a-204, 212, 213, 220, 224, 225, 245, 250, 252-256, 283. *Orlando* a-175(2 pgs.), 178, 240i; c-240-259, 262, 264p, 270p, 271, 272, 274, 275, 278, 296i. *Redondo* a-194, 195, 197, 202, 203, 207, 211, 214, 217, 219, 226, 227, 229, 235, 241, 287(layout), 302p, 303i, 308; c-229. *Reese* a-195, 200, 205i. *Rogers* a-254, 274, 277. *Roussos* a-65, 84, 224i. *Sekowsky* a-282p. *Sparling* a-203. *Starlin* a-207(2 pgs.), 282p; c-281. *Leonard Starr* a-9. *Staton* a-300p. *Sutton* a-189, 277, 290, 291, 293, 295, 297-299, 302, 303, 306-309, 310-313i, 314. *Tuska* a-293p, 294p, 316p. *Wrightson* c-193-195, 204, 207, 209, 211, 213, 214, 217, 219, 221, 231, 236, 255, 256; r-224.

HOUSE OF SECRETS (Combined with The Unexpected after #154)
National Periodical Publications/DC Comics: 11-12/56 - No. 80, 9-10/66; No. 81, 8-9/69 - No. 140, 2-3/76; No. 141, 8-9/76 - No. 154, 10-11/78

1-Drucker-a; Moreira-c	109	327	926	1750
2-Moreira-a	41	123	331	600
3-Kirby-c/a	37	111	278	500
4-Kirby-a	29	88	202	360
5-7	19	57	134	240
8-Kirby-a	23	69	160	285
9-11: 11-Lou Cameron-a (unsigned)	17	51	118	210
12-Kirby-c/a; Lou Cameron-a	19	57	134	240
13-15: 14-Flying saucer-c	13	39	94	160
16-20	12	36	84	140
21,22,24-30	10	30	70	120
23-1st app. Mark Merlin & begin series (8/59)	12	36	84	140
31-50: 48-Toth-a. 50-Last 10¢ issue	9	27	63	105
51-60: 58-Origin Mark Merlin	8	24	56	90
61-First Eclipso (7-8/63) and begin series	17	51	118	210
62	9	27	63	105
63-65-Toth-a on Eclipso (see Brave and the Bold #64)	7	21	50	80
66-1st Eclipso-c (also #67,70,78,79); Toth-a	9	27	63	105

House of Secrets #76 © DC

Howard the Duck #26 © MAR

Howdy Doody #5 © Cal. Nat. Prod.

	GD2.0	FN6.0	VF8.0	NM9.4

67,73: 67-Toth-a on Eclipso. 73-Mark Merlin becomes Prince Ra-Man (1st app.)
| | 8 | 24 | 56 | 90 |
68-72,74-80: 76-Prince Ra-Man vs. Eclipso. 80-Eclipso, Prince Ra-Man end
| | 7 | 21 | 50 | 80 |
81-Mystery format begins; 1st app. Abel (House Of Secrets host);
(cameo in DC Special #4)
| | 6 | 18 | 42 | 70 |
82-84: 82-Neal Adams-c(i) | 1 | 3 | 10 | 23 | 35 |
85,90: 85-N. Adams-a(i). 90-Buckler (early work)/N. Adams-a(i)
| | 4 | 12 | 26 | 40 |
86,88,89,91 | 3 | 9 | 19 | 28 |
87-Wrightson & Kaluta-a | 4 | 12 | 29 | 45 |
92-1st app. Swamp Thing-c/story (8 pgs.)(6-7/71) in Berni Wrightson(p)
w/Jeff.Jones/Kaluta/Weiss ink assists; classic-c. 48 | 144 | 386 | 700 |
93,95,97,98-(52 pgs.)-Wrightson-c | 3 | 9 | 21 | 32 |
94,96-(52 pgs.)-Wrightson-c. 94-Wrightson-a(i); 96-Wood-a
| | 3 | 9 | 21 | 32 |
99-Wrightson splash pg. | 3 | 9 | 17 | 25 |
100-Classic Wrightson-c | 3 | 10 | 23 | 35 |
101,102,104,105,108-120 | 2 | 6 | 10 | 14 |
103,106,107-Wrightson-c | 2 | 6 | 12 | 18 |
121-133 | 1 | 3 | 6 | 9 |
134-136,139-Wrightson-a | 2 | 6 | 9 | 12 |
137,138,141-154 | 1 | 3 | 5 | 7 |
140-1st solo origin of the Patchworkman (see Swamp Thing #3)
| | 2 | 6 | 13 | 20 |
NOTE: Neal Adams c-81, 82, 84-88, 90, 91. Alcala a-104-107. Anderson a-91. Aparo a-93, 97, 105. B. Bailey a-107. Cameron a-13, 15. Colan a-63. Ditko a-139p, 148. Elias a-58. Evans a-118. Finlay a-7r(Real Fact?). Glanzman a-91. Golden a-151. Heath a-31. Heck a-85. Kaluta a-87, 98, 99; c-98, 99, 101, 102, 105, 149, 151, 154. Bob Kane a-18, 21. G. Kane a-85p. Kirby c-3, 11, 12. Kubert a-39. Meskin a-2-68 (most), 94r; c-55-60. Moreira a-7, 8, 51, 54, 102-104, 106, 108, 113, 116, 118, 121, 123, 127; c-1, 2, 4-10, 20. Morrow a-86, 89, 90r; c-89, 146-148. Nino a-101, 103, 106, 109, 115, 117, 126, 128, 131, 147, 153. Redondo a-95, 99, 102, 104p, 113, 116, 134, 136, 139, 140. Reese a-85. Severin a-91. Starlin c-150. Sutton a-154. Toth a-63-67, 83, 93r, 94r, 96r-98r, 123. Tuska a-90, 104. Wrightson a-134; c-92-94, 96, 100, 103, 106, 107, 135, 136, 139.

HOUSE OF SECRETS
DC Comics (Vertigo): Oct, 1996 - No. 25, Dec, 1998 ($2.50) (Creator-owned series)
1-Steven Seagle-s/Kristiansen-c/a. | | | | 3.50
2-25: 5,7-Kristiansen-c/a. 6-Fegrado-a | | | | 3.00
TPB-(1997, $14.95) r/1-5 | | | | 15.00

HOUSE OF SECRETS: FACADE
DC Comics (Vertigo): 2001 - No. 2, 2001 ($5.95, limited series)
1,2-Steven Seagle-s/Teddy Kristiansen-c/a. | | | | 6.00

HOUSE OF TERROR (3-D)
St. John Publishing Co.: Oct, 1953 (25¢, came w/glasses)
1-Kubert, Baker-a | 34 | 102 | 179 | 310 |

HOUSE OF YANG, THE (See Yang)
Charlton Comics: July, 1975 - No. 6, June, 1976; 1978
1-Sanho Kim-a in all | 2 | 6 | 11 | 15 |
2-6 | 1 | 3 | 6 | 8 |
Modern Comics 1,2(1978) | | | | 4.00

HOUSE ON THE BORDERLAND
DC Comics (Vertigo): 2000 ($29.95, hardcover, one-shot)
HC-Adaption of William Hope Hodgson book; Corben-a | | | | 30.00

HOUSE II: THE SECOND STORY
Marvel Comics: Oct, 1987 (One-shot)
1-Adapts movie | | | | 2.50

HOWARD CHAYKIN'S AMERICAN FLAGG (See American Flagg!)
First Comics: V2#1, May, 1988 - V2#12, Apr, 1989 ($1.75/$1.95, Baxter paper)
V2#1-9,11,12-Chaykin-c/p in all | | | | 2.25
10-Elvis Presley photo-c | | | | 3.00

HOWARD THE DUCK (See Bizarre Adventures #34, Crazy Magazine, Fear, Man-Thing, Marvel Treasury Edition & Sensational She-Hulk #14-17)
Marvel Comics: Jan, 1976 - No. 31, May, 1979; No. 32, Jan, 1986; No. 33, Sept, 1986
1-Brunner-c/a; Spider-Man x-over (low distr.) | 2 | 6 | 13 | 20 |

2-Brunner-c/a | 1 | 3 | 6 | 8 |
3,4-(Regular 25¢ edition). 3-Buscema-a(p), (7/76) | 1 | 3 | 5 | 7 |
3,4-(30¢-c, limited distribution) | 1 | 4 | 7 | 10 |
5 | 1 | 3 | 5 | 7 |
6-11: 8-Howard The Duck for president. 9-1st Sgt. Preston Dudley of RCMP.
10-Spider-Man-c/sty | | | | 5.00
12-1st app. Kiss (cameo, 3/77) | 2 | 6 | 13 | 20 |
13-(30¢-c) Kiss app. (1st full story, 6/77); Daimon Hellstrom app. plus cameo of Howard as Son of Satan | 3 | 9 | 17 | 25 |
13-(35¢-c, limited distribution) | 3 | 9 | 20 | 30 |
14-32: 14-17-(Regular 30¢-c). 14-Howard as Son of Satan-c/story; Son of Satan app. 16-Album issue; 3 pgs. comics. 22,23-Man-Thing-c/stories; Star Wars parody. 30,32-P. Smith-a | | | | 4.00
14-17-(35¢-c, limited distribution) | | | | 5.00
33-Last issue; low print run | | | | 5.00
Annual 1(1977, 52 pgs.)-Mayerik-a | | | | 5.00
NOTE: Austin c-29i. Bolland c-33. Brunner a-1p, 2p; c-1, 2. Buckler c-3p. Buscema a-3p. Colan a(p)-4-15, 17-20, 24-27, 30, 31; c(p)-4-31, Annual 1p. Leialoha a-1-13i; c(i)-3-5, 8-11. Mayerik a-22, 23, 31. Paul Smith a-30p, 32. Man-Thing app. in #22, 23.

HOWARD THE DUCK (Magazine)
Marvel Comics Group: Oct, 1979 - No. 9, Mar, 1981 (B&W, 68 pgs.)
1-Art by Colan, Janson, Golden. Kidney Lady app. 1 | 3 | 5 | 7 |
2,3,5-9 (nudity in most): 2-Mayerick-a. 3-Xmas issue; Jack Davis-c; Duck World flashback. 5-Dracula app. 6-1st Street People back-up story. 7-Has poster by Byrne; Man-Thing-c/s(46 pgs.). 8-Batman parody w/Marshall Rogers-a; Dave Sim-a (1 pg.). 9-Marie Severin-a; John Pound painted-c | | | | 5.00
4-Beatles, John Lennon, Elvis, Kiss & Devo cameos; Hitler app. | | 1 | 3 | 5 | 7 |
NOTE: Buscema a-4p. Colan a-1-5p, 7-9p. Jack Davis c-3. Golden a(p)-1, 5, 6(51pgs.). Rogers a-7, 8. Simonson a-7.

HOWARD THE DUCK HOLIDAY SPECIAL
Marvel Comics: Feb, 1997 ($2.50, one-shot)
1-Wraparound-c; Hama-s | | | | 2.50

HOWARD THE DUCK: THE MOVIE
Marvel Comics Group: Dec, 1986 - No. 3, Feb, 1987 (Limited series)
1-3: Movie adaptation; r/Marvel Super Special | | | | 2.25

HOW BOYS AND GIRLS CAN HELP WIN THE WAR
The Parents' Magazine Institute: 1942 (10¢, one-shot)
1-All proceeds used to buy war bonds | 26 | 78 | 136 | 235 |

HOWDY DOODY (TV)(See Jackpot of Fun-- & Poll Parrot)
Dell Publishing Co.: 1/50 - No. 38, 7-9/56; No. 761, 1/57; No. 811, 7/57
1-(Scarce)-Photo-c; 1st TV comic | 92 | 276 | 644 | 1200 |
2-Photo-c | 38 | 114 | 266 | 500 |
3-5: All photo-c | 21 | 63 | 147 | 280 |
6-Used in SOTI, pg. 309; classic-c; painted covers begin | 20 | 60 | 140 | 260 |
7-10 | 15 | 45 | 105 | 190 |
11-20: 13-X-mas-c | 12 | 36 | 84 | 160 |
21-38, Four Color 761,811 | 10 | 30 | 70 | 130 |

HOW IT BEGAN
United Features Syndicate: No. 15, 1939 (one-shot)
Single Series 15 | 34 | 102 | 179 | 310 |

HOW SANTA GOT HIS RED SUIT (See March of Comics No. 2)

HOW THE WEST WAS WON (See Movie Comics)

HOW TO DRAW FOR THE COMICS
Street and Smith: No date (1942?) (10¢, 64 pgs., B&W & color, no ads)
nn-Art by Robert Winsor McCay (recreating his father's art), George Marcoux (Supersnipe artist), Vernon Greene (The Shadow artist), Jack Binder (with biog.), Thorton Fisher, Jon Small, & Jack Farr; has biographies of each artist
| | 29 | 87 | 153 | 265 |

H. P. LOVECRAFT'S CTHULHU
Millennium Publications: Dec, 1991 - No. 3, May, 1992 ($2.50, limited series)
1-3: Contains trading cards on thin stock | | | | 3.00

H. R. PUFNSTUF (TV) (See March of Comics #360)
Gold Key: Oct, 1970 - No. 8, July, 1972

Huckleberry Hound #5 © H-B

Huey, Dewey, and Louie Junior Woodchucks #24 © WDC

Hulk Smash #1 © MAR

	GD2.0	FN6.0	VF8.0	NM9.4
1-Photo-c	20	60	140	250
2-8-Photo-c on all	10	30	73	125

HUBERT AT CAMP MOONBEAM
Dell Publishing Co.: No. 251, Oct, 1949 (one shot)

Four Color 251	4	12	30	50

HUCK & YOGI JAMBOREE (TV)
Dell Publishing Co.: Mar, 1961 ($1.00, 6-1/4x9", 116 pgs., cardboard-c, high quality paper) (B&W original material)

nn (scarce)	9	27	63	120

HUCK & YOGI WINTER SPORTS (TV)
Dell Publishing Co.: No. 1310, Mar, 1962 (Hanna-Barbera) (one-shot)

Four Color 1310	9	27	63	115

HUCK FINN (See The New Adventures of... & Power Record Comics)

HUCKLEBERRY FINN (Movie)
Dell Publishing Co.: No. 1114, July, 1960

Four Color 1114-Photo-c	5	15	35	60

HUCKLEBERRY HOUND (See Dell Giant #31,44, Golden Picture Story Book, Kite Fun Book, March of Comics #199, 214, 235, Spotlight #1 & Whitman Comic Books)

HUCKLEBERRY HOUND (TV)
Dell/Gold Key No. 18 (10/62) on: No. 990, 5-7/59 - No. 43, 10/70 (Hanna-Barbera)

Four Color 990(#1)-1st app. Huckleberry Hound, Yogi Bear, & Pixie & Dixie & Mr. Jinks	12	36	84	160
Four Color 1050,1054 (12/59)	8	24	56	105
3(1-2/60) - 7 (9-10/60), Four Color 1141 (10/60)	8	24	56	100
8-10	6	18	42	75
11,13-17 (6-8/62)	4	12	30	50
12-1st Hokey Wolf & Ding-a-Ling	5	15	38	60
18,19 (84pgs.; 18-20 titled ...Chuckleberry Tales)	8	24	56	100
20-Titled Chuckleberry Tales	4	12	29	45
21-30; 28-30-Reprints	4	12	25	38
31-43; 31,32,35,37-43-Reprints	3	9	19	28

HUCKLEBERRY HOUND (TV)
Charlton Comics: Nov, 1970 - No. 8, Jan, 1972 (Hanna-Barbera)

1	5	15	34	55
2-8	3	9	19	28

HUEY, DEWEY, & LOUIE (See Donald Duck, 1938 for 1st app. Also see Mickey Mouse Magazine V4#2, V5#7 & Walt Disney's Junior Woodchucks Limited Series)
HUEY, DEWEY, & LOUIE BACK TO SCHOOL (See Dell Giant #22, 35, 49 & Dell Giants)

HUEY, DEWEY, AND LOUIE JUNIOR WOODCHUCKS (Disney)
Gold Key No. 1-61/Whitman No. 62 on: Aug, 1966 - No. 81, July, 1984 (See Walt Disney's Comics & Stories #125)

1	5	15	35	60
2,3(12/68)	3	10	23	35
4,5(4/70)-r/two WDC&S D.Duck stories by Barks	3	9	21	32
6-17	3	9	19	28
18,27-30	2	6	13	20
19-23,25-New storyboarded scripts by Barks, 13-25 pgs. per issue	3	9	20	30
24,26: 26-r/Barks Donald Duck WDC&S stories	2	6	13	20
31-57,60,61: 35,41-r/Barks J.W. scripts	1	4	7	10
58,59: 58-r/Barks Donald Duck WDC&S stories	2	6	9	12
62-64 (Whitman)	2	6	9	12
65-(9/80), 66 (Pre-pack? scarce)	3	9	13	20
67 (1/81),68	2	6	11	15
69-74: 72(2/82), 73(2-3/82), 74(3/82)	2	6	10	14
75-81 (all #90183; pre-pack; nd, nd code; scarce): 75(4/83), 76(5/83), 77(7/83), 78(8/83), 79(4/84), 80(5/84), 81(7/84)	2	6	11	15

HUGGA BUNCH (TV)
Marvel Comics (Star Comics): Oct, 1986 - No. 6, Aug, 1987

1-6				4.00

HULK (Magazine)(Formerly The Rampaging Hulk)(Also see The Incredible Hulk)
Marvel Comics: No. 10, Aug., 1978 - No. 27, June, 1981 ($1.50)

	GD2.0	FN6.0	VF8.0	NM9.4
10-18: 10-Bill Bixby interview. 11-Moon Knight begins. 12-15,17,18-Moon Knight stories. 12-Lou Ferrigno interview.	1	3	6	9
19-27: 20-Moon Knight story. 23-Last full color issue; Banner is attacked. 24-Part color, Lou Ferrigno interview. 25-Part color. 26,27-are B&W				6.00

NOTE: #10-20 have fragile spines which split easily. **Alcala** a(i)-15, 17-20, 22, 24-27. **Buscema** a-23; c-26. **Chaykin** a-21-25. **Colan** a(p)-11, 19, 24-27. **Jusko** painted c-12. **Nebres** a-16. **Severin** a-19i. Moon Knight by **Sienkiewicz** in 13-15, 17, 18, 20. **Simonson** a-27; c-23. Dominic Fortune appears in #21-24.

HULK (Becomes Incredible Hulk Vol. 2 with issue #12)
Marvel Comics: Apr, 1999 - No. 11, Feb, 2000 ($2.99/$1.99)

1-($2.99) Byrne-s/Garney-a				4.00
1-Variant-c				8.00
1-Gold foil variant				8.00
2-11-($1.99): 2-Two covers. 5-Art by Jurgens, Buscema & Texeira. 7-Avengers app. 11-She-Hulk app.				2.50
1999 Annual ($3.50) Chapter One story; Byrne-s/Weeks-a				3.50
Hulk Vs. The Thing (12/99, $3.99, TPB) reprints their notable battles				4.00

HULK: FUTURE IMPERFECT
Marvel Comics: Jan, 1993 - No. 2, Dec, 1992 (In error) ($5.95, 52 pgs., square-bound, limited series)

1,2: Embossed-c; Peter David story & George Perez-c/a. 1-1st app. Maestro.	1	3	6	8

HULK/ PITT
Marvel Comics: 1997 ($5.99, one-shot)

1-David-s/Keown-c/a				6.00

HULK SMASH
Marvel Comics: Mar, 2001 - No. 2, Apr, 2001 ($2.99, limited series)

1,2-Ennis-s/McCrea & Janson-a/Nowlan painted-c				3.00

HULK 2099
Marvel Comics: Dec, 1994 - No. 10, Sept, 1995 ($1.50/$1.95)

1-($2.50)-Green foil-c				3.00
2-10: 2-A. Kubert-c				2.25

HUMAN FLY
I.W. Enterprises/Super: 1963 - 1964 (Reprints)

I.W. Reprint #1-Reprints Blue Beetle #44('46)	2	6	13	20
Super Reprint #10-R/Blue Beetle #46('47)	2	6	13	20

HUMAN FLY, THE
Marvel Comics Group: Sept, 1977 - No. 19, Mar, 1979

1,2,9,19: 1,2-(Regular 30¢-c). 1-Origin; Spider-Man x-over. 2-Ghost Rider app. 9-Daredevil x-over; Byrne-c(p). 19-Last issue	1	3	6	8
1,2-(35¢-c, limited distribution)	1	4	7	10
3-8,10-18				4.00

NOTE: **Austin** c-4i, 9i. **Elias** a-1, 3p, 4p, 7p, 10-12p, 15p, 18p, 19p. **Layton** c-19.

HUMAN TARGET
DC Comics (Vertigo): Apr, 1999 - No. 4, July, 1999 ($2.95, limited series)

1-4-Milligan-s/Bradstreet-c/Biukovic-a				3.00
TPB (2000, $12.95) new Bradstreet-c				13.00

HUMAN TARGET SPECIAL (TV)
DC Comics: Nov, 1991 ($2.00, 52 pgs., one-shot)

1				3.00

HUMAN TORCH, THE (Red Raven #1)(See All-Select, All Winners, Marvel Mystery, Men's Adventures, Mystic Comics (2nd series), Sub-Mariner, USA & Young Men)
Timely/Marvel Comics (TP 2,3/TCI 4-9/SePI 10/SnPC 11-25/CnPC 26-35/Atlas Comics (CPC 36-38)): No. 2, Fall, 1940 - No. 15, Spring, 1944; No. 16, Fall, 1944 - No. 35, Mar, 1949 (Becomes Love Tales #36 on); No. 36, April, 1954 - No. 38, Aug, 1954

2(#1)-Intro & Origin Toro; The Falcon, The Fiery Mask, Mantor the Magician, & Microman only app.; Human Torch by Burgos, Sub-Mariner by Everett begin (origin of each in text)	2500	7500	17,500	35,000
3(#2)-40 pg. H.T. story; H.T. & S.M. battle over who is best artist in text-Everett or Burgos	1330	3100	6200
4(#3)-Origin The Patriot in text; last Everett Sub-Mariner; Sid Greene-a	400	1200	2500	4800

Human Torch #28 © MAR

Humphrey Comics #1 © HARV

Hunter: The Age of Magic #3 © DC

	GD2.0	FN6.0	VF8.0	NM9.4

5(#4)-The Patriot app; Angel x-over in Sub-Mariner (Summer, 1941);

1st Nazi war-c this title	300	900	1875	3600

5-Human Torch battles Sub-Mariner (Fall, '41); 60 pg. story

	462	1386	3000	6000
6,9	209	627	1307	2300
7-1st Japanese war-c	218	654	1364	2400

8-Human Torch battles Sub-Mariner; 52 pg. story; Wolverton-a, 1 pg.

	308	924	1927	3700

10-Human Torch battles Sub-Mariner, 45 pg. story; Wolverton-a, 1 pg.

	282	846	1762	3100

11,13-15: 14-1st Atlas Globe logo (Winter, 1943-44; see All Winners #11 also)

	168	504	1050	1850
12-Classic-c	291	873	1818	3200
16-20: 20-Last War issue	118	354	738	1300
21,22,24-30:	107	321	669	1175

23 (Sum/46)-Becomes Junior Miss 24? Classic Schomburg Robot-c

	123	369	769	1350

31,32: 31-Namora x-over in Sub-Mariner (also #30); last Toro. 32-Sungirl,

Namora app.; Sungirl-c	95	273	568	1000
33-Capt. America x-over	95	285	597	1050
34-Sungirl solo	84	252	525	925
35-Captain America & Sungirl app. (1949)	91	273	568	1000
36-38(1954)-Sub-Mariner in all	84	252	525	925

NOTE: *Ayers* Human Torch in 36(3). *Brodsky* c-25, 31-33?, 37, 38, *Burgos* c-36. *Everett* a-1-3, 27, 28, 30, 37, 38. *Powell* a-36(Sub-Mariner). *Schomburg* c-1-3, 5-8, 10-23. *Sekowsky* c-28, 34?, 35? *Shores* c-24, 26, 27, 29, 30. *Mickey Spillane* text 4-6. Bondage c-2, 12, 19.

HUMAN TORCH, THE (Also see Avengers West Coast, Fantastic Four, The Invaders, Saga of the Original... & Strange Tales #101)
Marvel Comics Group: Sept, 1974 - No. 8, Nov, 1975

1: 1-8-r/stories from Strange Tales #101-108	2	6	11	16
2-8: 1st H.T. title since G.A. 7-vs. Sub-Mariner	1	3	6	9

NOTE: Golden Age & Silver Age Human Torch-r #1-8. *Ayers* r-6, 7. *Kirby/Ayers* r-1-5, 8.

HUMBUG (Satire by Harvey Kurtzman)
Humbug Publications: Aug, 1957 - No. 9, May, 1958; No. 10, June, 1958; No. 11, Oct, 1958

1-Wood-a (intro pgs. only)	29	87	153	265
2	14	42	72	120
3-9: 8-Elvis in Jailbreak Rock	12	36	61	100
10,11-Magazine format. 10-Photo-c	16	48	83	140
Bound Volume(#1-9)(extremely rare)	64	192	398	700

NOTE: *Davis* a-1-11. *Elder* a-2-4, 6-9, 11. *Heath* a-2, 4-8, 10. *Jaffee* a-2, 4-9. *Kurtzman* a-11.

HUMDINGER (Becomes White Rider and Super Horse #3 on?)
Novelty Press/Premium Group: May-June, 1946 - V2#2, July-Aug, 1947

1-Jerkwater Line, Mickey Starlight by Don Rico, Dink begin	36	108	191	330
2	16	48	83	140
3-6, V2#1,2	11	33	55	90

HUMONGOUS MAN
Alternative Press (Ikon Press): Sept, 1997 -No. 3 ($2.25, B&W)

1-3-Stepp & Harrison-c/s/a.				2.25

HUMOR (See All Humor Comics)

HUMPHREY COMICS (Joe Palooka Presents...; also see Joe Palooka)
Harvey Publications: Oct, 1948 - No. 22, Apr, 1952

1-Joe Palooka's pal (r); (52 pgs.)-Powell-a	13	39	66	110
2,3: Powell-a	7	21	38	55
4-Boy Heroes app.; Powell-a	8	24	42	60
5-8,10: 5,6-Powell-a. 7-Little Dot app.	6	18	29	40
9-Origin Humphrey	7	21	38	55
11-22	5	15	25	35

HUNCHBACK OF NOTRE DAME, THE
Dell Publishing Co.: No. 854, Oct, 1957 (one shot)

Four Color 854-Movie, photo-c	13	39	91	165

HUNGER DOGS, THE (See DC Graphic Novel #4)

HUNK
Charlton Comics: Aug, 1961 - No. 11, 1963

1	4	12	26	40

	GD2.0	FN6.0	VF8.0	NM9.4
2-11	2	6	13	20

HUNTED (Formerly My Love Memoirs)
Fox Features Syndicate: No. 13, July, 1950; No. 2, Sept, 1950

13(#1)-Used in **SOTI**, pg. 42 & illo. "Treating police contemptuously"

(lower left); Hollingsworth bondage-c	36	108	191	330
2	16	48	83	140

HUNTER'S HEART
DC Comics: June, 1995 - No. 3, Aug, 1995 ($5.95, B&W, limited series)

1-3				6.00

HUNTER: THE AGE OF MAGIC (See Books of Magic)
DC Comics (Vertigo): Sept, 2001 - Present ($2.50)

1-6: Horrocks-s/Case-a/Bolton-c				2.50

HUNTRESS, THE (See All-Star Comics #69, Batman Family, Brave & the Bold #62, DC Super Stars #17, Detective #652, Infinity, Inc. #1, Sensation Comics #68 & Wonder Woman #271)
DC Comics: Apr, 1989 - No. 19, Oct, 1990 ($1.00, mature)

1-16: Staton-c/a(p) in all				2.50
17-19-Batman-c/stories				3.00

HUNTRESS, THE
DC Comics: June, 1994 - No. 4, Sept, 1994 ($1.50, limited series)

1-4-Netzer-c/a: 2-Batman app.				2.25

HURRICANE COMICS
Cambridge House: 1945 (52 pgs.)

1-(Humor, funny animal)	24	72	127	215

HYBRIDS
Continuity Comics: Jan, 1994 ($2.50, one-shot)

1-Neal Adams-c(p) & part-a(i); embossed-c.				2.50

HYBRIDS DEATHWATCH 2000
Continuity Comics: Apr, 1993 - No. 3, Aug, 1993 ($2.50)

0-(Giveaway)-Foil-c; Neal Adams-c(i) & plots (also #1,2)				2.50

1-3: 1-Polybagged w/card; die-cut-c. 2-Thermal-c. 3-Polybagged w/card;

indestructible-c; Adams plot				2.50

HYBRIDS ORIGIN
Continuity Comics: 1993 - No. 5, Jan, 1994 ($2.50)

1-5: 2,3-Neal Adams-c. 4,5-Valeria the She-Bat app. Adams-c(i)				2.50

HYDE-25
Harris Publications: Apr, 1995 ($2.95, one-shot)

0-coupon for poster; r/Vampirella's 1st app.				3.00

HYDROMAN (See Heroic Comics)

HYPERKIND (See Razorline)
Marvel Comics: Sept, 1993 - No. 9, May, 1994 ($1.75/$1.95)

1-($2.50)-Foil embossed-c; by Clive Barker				3.00
2-9				2.25

HYPERKIND UNLEASHED
Marvel Comics: Aug, 1994 ($2.95, 52 pgs., one-shot)

1				3.00

HYPER MYSTERY COMICS
Hyper Publications: May, 1940 - No. 2, June, 1940 (68 pgs.)

1-Hyper, the Phenomenal begins; Calkins-a	200	600	1250	2200
2	107	321	669	1175

HYPERSONIC
Dark Horse Comics: Nov, 1997 - No. 4, Feb, 1998 ($2.95, limited series)

1-4: Abnett & White/Erskine-a				3.00

I AIM AT THE STARS (Movie)
Dell Publishing Co.: No. 1148, Nov-Jan/1960-61 (one-shot)

Four Color 1148-The Werner Von Braun Sty-photo-c	7	21	49	90

I AM COYOTE (See Eclipse Graphic Album Series & Eclipse Magazine #2)

I AM LEGEND
Eclipse Books: 1991 - No. 4, 1991 ($5.95, B&W, squarebound, 68 pgs.)

Ibis, The Invincible #5 © FAW

Iceman #1 © MAR

Icon #17 © Millestone Media

	GD2.0	FN6.0	VF8.0	NM9.4
1-4: Based on 1954 novel				6.00

IBIS, THE INVINCIBLE (See Fawcett Miniatures, Mighty Midget & Whiz)
Fawcett Publications: 1942 (Fall?); #2, Mar.,1943; #3, Wint, 1945 - #5, Fall, 1946; #6, Spring, 1948

	GD2.0	FN6.0	VF8.0	NM9.4
1-Origin Ibis; Raboy-c; on sale 1/2/43	191	573	1312	2100
2-Bondage-c (on sale 2/5/43)	91	273	568	1000
3-Wolverton-a #3-6 (4 pgs. each)	73	219	455	800
4-6: 5-Bondage-c	50	150	300	525

NOTE: *Mac Raboy* c(p)-3-5. *Shaffenberger* c-6.

I–BOTS (See Isaac Asimov's I-BOTS)

ICE AGE ON THE WORLD OF MAGIC: THE GATHERING (See Magic The Gathering)

ICE KING OF OZ, THE (See First Comics Graphic Novel #13)

ICEMAN (Also see The Champions & X-Men #94)
Marvel Comics Group: Dec, 1984 - No. 4, June, 1985 (Limited series)

	GD2.0	FN6.0	VF8.0	NM9.4
1,2,4: Zeck covers on all				2.50
3-The Defenders, Champions (Ghost Rider) & the original X-Men x-over				3.50

ICEMAN (X-Men)
Marvel Comics: Dec, 2001 - No. 4, ($2.50, limited series)

	GD2.0	FN6.0	VF8.0	NM9.4
1-3-Abnett & Lanning-s/Kerschl-a				2.50

ICON
DC Comics (Milestone): May, 1993 - No. 42, Feb, 1997($1.50/$1.75/$2.50)

	GD2.0	FN6.0	VF8.0	NM9.4
1-($2.95)-Collector's Edition polybagged w/poster & trading card (direct sale only)				3.00
1-24,30-42: 9-Simonson-c. 15,16-Worlds Collide Pt. 4 & 11. 15-Superboy app. 16-Superman-c/story. 40-Vs. Blood Syndicate				2.50
25-($2.95, 52 pgs.)				3.00

IDAHO
Dell Publishing Co.: June-Aug, 1963 - No. 8, July-Sept, 1965

	GD2.0	FN6.0	VF8.0	NM9.4
1	3	9	17	24
2-8: 5-7-Painted-c	2	6	10	14

IDEAL (... a Classical Comic) (2nd Series) (Love Romances No. 6 on)
Timely Comics: July, 1948 - No. 5, March, 1949 (Feature length stories)

	GD2.0	FN6.0	VF8.0	NM9.4
1-Antony & Cleopatra	36	108	191	330
2-The Corpses of Dr. Sacotti	31	93	165	285
3-Joan of Arc; used in SOTI, pg. 308 'Boer War'	29	87	153	265
4-Richard the Lion-hearted; titled "...the World's Greatest Comics"; The Witness app.	40	120	232	400
5-Ideal Love & Romance; change to love; photo-c	19	57	99	165

IDEAL COMICS (1st Series) (Willie Comics No. 5 on)
Timely Comics (MgPC): Fall, 1944 - No. 4, Spring, 1946

	GD2.0	FN6.0	VF8.0	NM9.4
1-Funny animal; Super Rabbit in all	23	69	121	210
2	14	42	72	120
3,4	13	39	66	110

IDEAL LOVE & ROMANCE (See Ideal, A Classical Comic)

IDEAL ROMANCE (Formerly Tender Romance)
Key Publ.: No. 3, April, 1954 - No. 8, Feb, 1955 (Diary Confessions No. 9 on)

	GD2.0	FN6.0	VF8.0	NM9.4
3-Bernard Baily-c	9	27	49	70
4-8: 4,5-B. Baily-c	6	18	29	40

IDEALS (Secret Stories)
Ideals Publ., USA: 1981 (68 pgs, graphic novels, 7x10", stiff-c)

	GD2.0	FN6.0	VF8.0	NM9.4
Captain America - Star Spangled Super Hero	3	9	20	30
Fantastic Four - Cosmic Quartet	3	9	20	30
Incredible Hulk - Gamma Powered Goliath	3	9	20	30
Spider-Man - World Famous Wall Crawler	4	12	26	40

I DIE AT MIDNIGHT (Vertigo V2K)
DC Comics (Vertigo): 2000 ($6.95, prestige format, one-shot)

	GD2.0	FN6.0	VF8.0	NM9.4
1-Kyle Baker-s/a				7.00

IDOL
Marvel Comics (Epic Comics): 1992 - No. 3, 1992 ($2.95, mini-series, 52 pgs.)

	GD2.0	FN6.0	VF8.0	NM9.4
Book 1-3				3.00

I DREAM OF JEANNIE (TV)

Dell Publishing Co.: Apr, 1965 - No. 2, Dec, 1966 (Photo-c)

	GD2.0	FN6.0	VF8.0	NM9.4
1-Barbara Eden photo-c, each	15	45	105	200
2	12	36	84	150

I FEEL SICK
Slave Labor Graphics: Aug, 1999 - No. 2, May, 2000 ($3.95, limited series)

	GD2.0	FN6.0	VF8.0	NM9.4
1,2-Jhonen Vasquez-s/a				4.00

ILLUMINATOR
Marvel Comics/Nelson Publ.: 1993 - No. 4, 1993 ($4.99/$2.95, 52 pgs.)

	GD2.0	FN6.0	VF8.0	NM9.4
1,2-($4.99) Religious themed				5.00
3,4				3.00

ILLUSTRATED GAGS
United Features Syndicate: No. 16, 1940

	GD2.0	FN6.0	VF8.0	NM9.4
Single Series 16	17	51	88	150

ILLUSTRATED LIBRARY OF..., AN (See Classics Illustrated Giants)

ILLUSTRATED STORIES OF THE OPERAS
Baily (Bernard) Publ. Co.: 1943 (16 pgs.; B&W) (25 cents) (cover-B&W & red)

	GD2.0	FN6.0	VF8.0	NM9.4
nn-(Rare)(4 diff. issues)-Faust (part-r in Cisco Kid #1); nn-Aida, nn-Carmen; Baily-a, nn-Rigoleito	55	165	341	600

ILLUSTRATED STORY OF ROBIN HOOD & HIS MERRY MEN, THE (See Classics Giveaways, 12/44)

ILLUSTRATED TARZAN BOOK, THE (See Tarzan Book)

I LOVED (Formerly Rulah; Colossal Features Magazine No. 33 on)
Fox Features Syndicate: No. 28, July, 1949 - No. 32, Mar, 1950

	GD2.0	FN6.0	VF8.0	NM9.4
28	10	30	55	80
29-32	7	21	38	55

I LOVE LUCY
Eternity Comics: 6/90 - No. 6, 1990;V2#1, 11/90 - No. 6, 1991 ($2.95, B&W, mini-series)

	GD2.0	FN6.0	VF8.0	NM9.4
1-6: Reprints 1950s comic strip; photo-c				4.00
Book II #1-6: Reprints comic strip; photo-c				4.00
...In Full Color (1991, $5.95, 52 pgs.)-Reprints I Love Lucy Comics #4,5,8,16; photo-c with embossed logo (2 versions exist, one with pgs. 18 & 19 reversed, the other corrected)	1	3	6	8
...In 3-D (1991, $3.95, w/glasses)-Reprints I Love Lucy Comics; photo-c sealed in plastic bag				6.00

I LOVE LUCY COMICS (TV) (Also see The Lucy Show)
Dell Publishing Co.: No. 535, Feb, 1954 - No. 35, Apr-June, 1962 (Lucille Ball photo-c on all)

	GD2.0	FN6.0	VF8.0	NM9.4
Four Color 535(#1)	53	159	371	690
Four Color 559(#2, 5/54)	32	96	224	415
3 (8-10/54) - 5	19	57	133	250
6-10	15	45	105	195
11-20	11	33	77	140
21-35	9	27	63	115

I LOVE YOU
Fawcett Publications: June, 1950 (one-shot)

	GD2.0	FN6.0	VF8.0	NM9.4
1-Photo-c	15	45	77	130

I LOVE YOU (Formerly In Love)
Charlton Comics: No. 7, 9/55 - No. 121, 12/76; No. 122, 3/79 - No. 130, 5/80

	GD2.0	FN6.0	VF8.0	NM9.4
7-Kirby-c; Powell-a	9	27	63	105
8-10	4	12	26	40
11-16,18-20	3	10	23	35
17-(68 pg. Giant)	6	18	45	75
21-50: 26-No Torres-a	3	9	19	28
51-59	2	6	12	18
60-(1/66)-Elvis Presley line drawn c/story	14	42	102	175
61-85	2	6	10	14
86-110	1	3	6	9
111-130				6.00

I, LUSIPHER (Becomes Poison Elves, 1st series #8 on)
Mulehide Graphics: 1991 - No. 7, 1992 (B&W, magazine size)

	GD2.0	FN6.0	VF8.0	NM9.4
1-Drew Hayes-c/a/scripts	4	12	29	45
2,4,5	2	6	13	20

IN

	GD2.0	FN6.0	VF8.0	NM9.4

3-Low print run | 4 | 12 | 30 | 50
6,7 | 2 | 6 | 9 | 12
Poison Elves: Requiem For An Elf (Sirius Ent., 6/96, $14.95, trade paperback)-
Reprints I, Lusiphur #1,2 as text, and 3-6 | | | | 15.00

I'M A COP
Magazine Enterprises: 1954 - No. 3, 1954?
1(A-1 #111)-Powell-c/a in all | 16 | 48 | 83 | 140
2(A-1 #126), 3(A-1 #128) | 10 | 30 | 55 | 80

IMAGE GRAPHIC NOVEL
Image Int.: 1984 ($6.95)(Advertised as Pacific Comics Graphic Novel #1)
1-The Seven Samuroid; Brunner-c/a | | | | 7.00

IMAGE INTRODUCES...
Image Comics: Oct, 2001 - Present ($2.95, anthology)
Believer #1-Schamberger-s/Thurman & Molder-a; Legend of Isis preview | | | | 3.00
Primate #1-Two covers; Beau Smith & Bernhardt-s/Byrd-a | | | | 3.00

IMAGES OF A DISTANT SOIL
Image Comics: Feb, 1997 ($2.95, B&W, one-shot)
1-Sketches by various | | | | 3.00

IMAGES OF SHADOWHAWK (Also see Shadowhawk)
Image Comics: Sept, 1993 - No. 3, 1994 ($1.95, limited series)
1-3: Keith Giffen-c/a; Trencher app. | | | | 2.25

IMAGE TWO-IN-ONE
Image Comics: Mar, 2001 ($2.95, 48 pgs., B&W, one-shot)
1-Two stories; 24 pages produced in 24 hrs. by Larsen and Eliopoulos | | | | 3.00

IMAGE ZERO
Image Comics: 1993 (Received through mail w/coupons from Image books)
0-Savage Dragon, StormWatch, Shadowhawk, Strykeforce; 1st app. Troll; 1st
app. McFarlane's Freak, Blotch, Sweat and Bludd | | | | 5.00

I'M DICKENS - HE'S FENSTER (TV)
Dell Publishing Co.: May-July, 1963 - No. 2, Aug-Oct, 1963 (Photo-c)
1 | 5 | 15 | 35 | 60
2 | 5 | 15 | 34 | 55

I MET A HANDSOME COWBOY
Dell Publishing Co.: No. 324, Mar, 1951
Four Color 324 | 9 | 27 | 63 | 110

IMMORTAL DOCTOR FATE, THE
DC Comics: Jan, 1985 - No. 3, Mar, 1985 ($1.25, limited series)
1-3: 1-Simonson-c/a. 2-Giffen-c/a(p) | | | | 4.00

IMMORTALIS (See Mortigan Goth: Immortalis)

IMMORTAL II
Image Comics: Apr, 1997 - No. 5, Feb, 1998 ($2.50, B&W&Grey, lim. series)
1-5: 1-B&W w/ color pull-out poster | | | | 2.50

IMPACT
E. C. Comics: Mar-Apr, 1955 - No. 5, Nov-Dec, 1955
1-Not code approved | 15 | 45 | 105 | 190
2 | 10 | 30 | 70 | 120
3-5: 4-Crandall-a | 8 | 24 | 56 | 100
NOTE: Crandall a-1-4. Davis a-2-4; c-1-5. Evans a-1, 4, 5. Ingels a-in all. Kamen a-3.
Krigstein a-1, 5. Orlando a-2, 5.

IMPACT
Gemstone Publishing: Apr, 1999 - No. 5, Aug, 1999 ($2.50)
1-5-Reprints E.C. series | | | | 2.50

IMPACT CHRISTMAS SPECIAL
DC Comics (Impact Comics): 1991 ($2.50, 68 pgs.)
1-Gift of the Magi by Infantino/Rogers; The Black Hood, The Fly, The
Jaguar, & The Shield stories | | | | 2.50

IMPOSSIBLE MAN SUMMER VACATION SPECTACULAR, THE
Marvel Comics: Aug, 1990; No. 2, Sept, 1991 ($2.00, 68 pgs.) (See Fantastic
Four#11)
1-Spider Man, Quasar, Dr. Strange, She-Hulk, Punisher & Dr. Doom stories;

Barry Crain, Guice-a; Art Adams-c(i) | | | | 2.50
2-Ka Zar & Thor app.; Cable Wolverine-c app. | | | | 2.50

IMPERIAL GUARD
Marvel Comics: Jan, 1997 - No. 3, Mar, 1997 ($1.95, limited series)
1-3: Augustyn-s in all; 1-Wraparound-c | | | | 2.25

IMPULSE (See Flash #92, 2nd Series for 1st app.) (Also see Young Justice)
DC Comics: Apr, 1995 - Present ($1.50/$1.75/$1.95/$2.25/$2.50)
1-Mark Waid scripts & Humberto Ramos-c/a(p) begin; brief retelling of origin | | | | 6.00
2-12: 9-XS from Legion (Impulse's cousin) comes to the 20th Century,
returns to the 30th Century in #12. 10-Dead Heat Pt. 3 (cont'd in Flash #110).
11-Dead Heat Pt. 4 (cont'd in Flash #111); Johnny Quick dies. | | | | 3.00
13-25: 14-Trickster app. 17-Zatanna-c/app. 21-Legion-c/app. 22-Jesse Quick-
c/app. 24-Origin; Flash app. 25-Last Ramos-a. | | | | 2.50
26-55: 26-Rousseau-a begins. 28-1st new Arrowette (see World's Finest #113).
30-Genesis x-over.41-Arrowette-c/app. 47-Superman-c/app. 50-Batman &
Joker-c/app. Van Sciver-a begins. 52,53-Simonson art pages | | | | 2.50
56-62-Young Justice app. | | | | 2.50
63-81: 63-Begin $2.50-c. 66-JLA,JSA-c/app. 68,69-Adam Strange, GL app.
77-Our Worlds at War x-over; Young Justice-c/app.79-Amancio-a | | | | 2.50
#1,000,000 (11/98) John Fox app. | | | | 3.00
Annual 1 (1996, $2.95)-Legends of the Dead Earth; Parobeck-a | | | | 4.00
Annual 2 (1997, $3.95)-Pulp Heroes stories; Orbik painted-c | | | | 4.00
.../Atom Double-Shot 1(2/98, $1.95) Jurgens-s/Mhan-a | | | | 3.00
...: Bart Saves the Universe (4/99, $5.95) JSA app. | | | | 6.00
...Plus(9/97, $2.95) w/Gross Out (Scare Tactics)-c/app. | | | | 3.00
...Reckless Youth (1997, $14.95, TPB) r/Flash #92-94, Impulse #1-6 | | | | 15.00

INCAL, THE
Marvel Comics (Epic): Nov, 1988 - No. 3, Jan, 1989 ($10.95/$12.95, mature)
1-3: Moebius-c/a in all; sexual content | | | | 14.00

INCOMPLETE DEATH'S HEAD (Also see Death's Head)
Marvel Comics UK: Jan, 1993 - No. 12, Dec, 1993 ($1.75, limited series)
1-($2.95, 56 pgs.)-Die-cut cover | | | | 3.00
2-11: 2-Re-intro original Death's Head. 3-Original Death's Head vs. Dragon's
Claws | | | | 2.25
12-($2.50, 52 pgs.)-She Hulk app. | | | | 2.50

INCREDIBLE HULK, THE (See Aurora, The Avengers #1, The Defenders #1, Giant-
Size..., Hulk, Marvel Collectors Item Classics, Marvel Comics Presents #26, Marvel Fanfare,
Marvel Treasury Edition, Power Record Comics, Rampaging Hulk, She-Hulk & 2099 Unlimited)

INCREDIBLE HULK, THE
Marvel Comics: May, 1962 - No. 6, Mar, 1963; No. 102, Apr, 1968 - No. 474, Mar,
1999
1-Origin & 1st app. (skin is grey colored); Kirby pencils begin, end #5 | 600 | 1800 | 6000 | 17,000
2-1st green skinned Hulk; Kirby/Ditko-a | 188 | 564 | 1600 | 3200
3-Origin retold; 1st app. Ringmaster & Hercules (9/62) | 125 | 375 | 1062 | 2000
4,5: 4-Brief origin retold | 113 | 339 | 956 | 1800
6-(3/63) Intro. Teen Brigade; all Ditko-a | 156 | 468 | 1326 | 2650
102-(4/68) (Formerly Tales to Astonish)-Origin retold; story continued from
Tales to Astonish #101 | 22 | 66 | 154 | 275
103 | 9 | 27 | 65 | 110
104-Rhino app. | 9 | 27 | 65 | 110
105-108: 105-1st Missing Link. 107-Mandarin app.(9/68). 108-Mandarin & Nick
Fury app. (10/68). | 6 | 18 | 45 | 75
109,110: 109-Ka-Zar app. | 5 | 15 | 34 | 55
111-117: 117-Last 12¢ issue | 4 | 12 | 29 | 45
118-Hulk vs. Sub-Mariner | 4 | 12 | 30 | 50
119-121,123-125 | 3 | 9 | 20 | 30
122-Hulk battles Psyklop (12/69) | 3 | 15 | 38 | 60
126-1st Barbara Norriss (Valkyrie) | 3 | 10 | 23 | 35
127-139: 131-Hulk vs. Iron Man; 133-1st Jim Wilson, Hulk's new sidekick. 136-1st
Xeron, The Star-Slayer | 2 | 6 | 13 | 20
140-Written by Harlan Ellison; 1st Jarella, Hulk's love | 3 | 9 | 17 | 25
141-1st app. Doc Samson (7/71) | 4 | 12 | 29 | 45
142-144: 144-Last 15¢ issue | 2 | 6 | 11 | 16
145-(52 pgs.)-Origin retold | 3 | 9 | 17 | 24

Incredible Hulk #207 © MAR

Incredible Hulk #418 © MAR

Incredible Hulk V2 #34 © MAR

	GD2.0	FN6.0	VF8.0	NM9.4

146-160: 149-1st app. The Inheritor. 155-1st app. Shaper. 158-Warlock
cameo(12/72) | 2 | 6 | 9 | 12
161-The Mimic dies; Beast app. | 2 | 6 | 12 | 18
162-1st app. The Wendigo (4/73); Beast app. | 2 | 6 | 13 | 20
163-171,173-176: 163-1st app. The Gremlin. 164-1st Capt. Omen & Colonel
John D. Armbruster. 166-1st Zzzax. 168-1st The Harpy; nudity panels of
Betty Brant. 169-1st app. Bi-Beast.176-Warlock cameo (2 panels only); same
date as Strange Tales #178 (6/74) | 1 | 4 | 7 | 10
172-X-Men cameo; origin Juggernaut retold | 3 | 9 | 17 | 24
177-1st actual death of Warlock (last panel only) | 2 | 6 | 11 | 15
178-Rebirth of Warlock | 2 | 6 | 11 | 15
179 | 1 | 4 | 7 | 10
180-(10/74)-1st app. Wolverine (cameo last pg.) | 10 | 30 | 70 | 120
181-(11/74)-1st full Wolverine story; Trimpe-a | 69 | 207 | 584 | 1100
182-Wolverine app.; see Giant-Size X-Men #1 for next app.; 1st Crackajack
Jackson | 8 | 24 | 60 | 100
183-199: 185-Death of Col. Armbruster | 1 | 3 | 6 | 9
198,199, 201,202-(30¢-c variants, lim. distribution) | 2 | 6 | 10 | 14
200-(25¢-c) Silver Surfer app.; anniversary issue | 3 | 9 | 19 | 28
200-(30¢-c variant, limited distribution)(6/76) | 4 | 12 | 27 | 42
201-220: 201-Conan swipe-c/sty. 212-1st app. The Constrictor | | | | 6.00
212-216-(35¢-c variant, limited distribution) | 1 | 3 | 6 | 9
221-249: 227-Original Avengers app. 232-Capt. America x-over from C.A. #230.
233-Marvel Man app. 234-(4/79)-1st app. Quasar (formerly Marvel Man &
changes name to Quasar). 243-Cage app. | | | | 5.00
250-Giant size; Silver Surfer app. | | | | 4.00
251-277,280-299: 271-Rocket Raccoon app. 272-Sasquatch & Wendigo app.;
Wolverine & Alpha Flight cameo in flashback. 282-284-She-Hulk app.
293-F.F. battle | | | | 4.00
278,279-Most Marvel characters app. (Wolverine in both). 279-X-Men & Alpha
Flight cameos | | | | 5.00
300-(11/84, 52 pgs.)-Spider-Man app in new black costume on-c & 2 pg. cameo | | | | 6.00
301-313: 312-Origin Hulk retold | | | | 3.00
314-Byrne-c/a begins, ends #319 | | | | 4.00
315-319: 319-Bruce Banner & Betty Talbot wed | | | | 3.00
320-323,325,327-329 | | | | 3.00
324-1st app. Grey Hulk since #1 (c-swipe of #1) | 1 | 4 | 7 | 10
326-Grey vs. Green Hulk | | | | 4.00
330,331: 330-1st McFarlane ish (4/87); Thunderbolt Ross dies. 331-Grey Hulk
series begins | 2 | 6 | 12 | 18
332-334,336-339: 336,337-X-Factor app. | 1 | 4 | 7 | 10
335-No McFarlane-a | | | | 4.00
340-Hulk battles Wolverine by McFarlane | 3 | 9 | 20 | 30
341-346: 345-($1.50, 52 pgs.). 346-Last McFarlane issue | | | | 6.00
347-349,351-358,360-366: 347-1st app. Marlo | | | | 3.00
350-Hulk/Thing battle | | | | 5.00
359-Wolverine app. (illusion only) | | | | 3.00
367,372,377: 367-1st Dale Keown-a on Hulk (3/90). 372-Green Hulk app.;Keown
-c/a. 377-1st all new Hulk; fluorescent-c; Keown-c/a | 1 | 3 | 5 | 7
368-371,373-376: 368-Sam Kieth-c/a, 1st app. Pantheon. 369,370-Dale Keown-
c/a. 370,371-Original Defenders app. 371,373-376: Keown-c/a. 376-Green vs.
Grey Hulk | | | | 4.00
377-Fluorescent green logo 2nd printing | | | | 3.00
378,380,389: No Keown-a. 380-Doc Samson app. | | | | 3.00
379,381-388,390-393-Keown-a. 385-Infinity Gauntlet x-over. 389-Last $1.00-c.
392-X-Factor app. 393-($2.50, 72 pgs.)-30th anniversary issue; green foil
stamped-c; swipes-c to #1; has pin-ups of classic battles; Keown-c/a | | | | 4.00
393-2nd printing | | | | 2.50
394-399: 394-No Keown-c/a; intro Trauma. 395,396-Punisher-c/stories; Keown-
c/a. 397-Begin "Ghost of the Past" 4-part sty; Keown c/a. 398-Last Keown-c/a | | | | 2.50
400-($2.50, 68 pgs.)-Holo-grafx foil-c & r/TTA #63 | | | | 3.00
400-416: 400-2nd print-Diff. color foil-c. 402-Return of Doc Samson | | | | 2.50
417-424: 417-Begin $1.50-c; Rick Jones's bachelor party; Hulk returns from
"Future Imperfect"; bound-in trading card sheet. 418-(Regular edition)-Rick
Jones marries Marlo; includes cameo apps of various Marvel characters
as well as DC's Death & Peter David. 420-Death of Jim Wilson | | | | 2.50
418-($2.50)-Collector's Edition w/gatefold die-cut-c | | | | 3.00

425 ($2.25, 52 pgs.) | | | | 2.50
425 ($3.50, 52 pgs.)-Holographic-c | | | | 4.00
426-434, 436-442: 426-Begin $1.95-c. 427, 428-Man-Thing app. 431,432-
Abomination app. 434-Funeral for Nick Fury. 436-Ghosts of the Future begins,
ends #440. 439-Hulk becomes Maestro, Avengers app. 440-Thor-c/app.
441,442-She-Hulk-c/app. 442-Molecule Man app. | | | | 2.50
435-($2.50)-Rhino-app; excerpt from "What Savage Beast" | | | | 3.00
443,446-448: 443-Begin $1.50-c; re-app. of Hulk. 446-w/card insert. 447-Begin
Deodato-c/a(p) | | | | 2.50
444,445: 444-Cable-c/app.; "Onslaught". 445-"Onslaught" | | | | 4.00
447-Variant cover | | | | 4.00
449-1st app. Thunderbolts | | | | 6.00
450-($2.95)-Thunderbolts app.; 2 stories; Heroes Reborn-c/app. | | | | 5.00
451-473: 455-X-Men-c/app. 460-Bruce Banner returns. 464-Silver Surfer-c/app.
466,467: Betty dies. 467-Last Peter David/Kubert-a. 468-Casey-s/Pulido-a
begin | | | | 2.50
474-($2.99) Last issue; Abomination app. | | | | 4.00
#(-1) Flashback (7/97) Kubert-a | | | | 2.50
Special 1 (10/68, 25¢, 68 pg.)-New 51 pg. story, Hulk battles The Inhumans
(early app.); Steranko-c | 9 | 27 | 63 | 105
Special 2 (10/69, 25¢, 68 pg.)-Origin issue | 5 | 15 | 34 | 55
Special 3,4: 3-(1/71, 25¢, 68 pg.). 4-(1/72, 52pgs.) | 2 | 6 | 12 | 18
Annual 5 (1976) | 2 | 6 | 9 | 12
Annual 6-8 ('77-79)-7-Byrne/Layton-c/a; Iceman & Angel app. in book-length
story. 8-Book-length Sasquatch-c/sty | 1 | 3 | 6 | 8
Annual 9,10: 9('80). 10 ('81) | | | | 5.00
Annual 11('82)-Doc Samson back-up by Miller(p)(5 pgs.); Spider-Man & Avengers
app. Buckler-a(p) | | | | 3.50
Annual 12-17: 12 ('83). 13('84). 14('85). 15('86). 16('90, $2.00, 68 pgs.)-She-Hulk
app. 17(1991, $2.00)-Origin retold | | | | 3.00
Annual 18-20 ('92-'94 68 pgs.)-18-Return of the Defenders, Pt. I; no Keown-c/a
19-Bagged w/card | | | | 3.00
...'97 ($2.99) Pollina-c | | | | 3.00
...And Wolverine 1 (10/86, $2.50)-r/1st app. #180-181 1.25 3.75 | | | | 10.00
...: Beauty and the Behemoth (10/98, $19.95, TPB) r/Bruce & Betty stories | | | | 20.00
...Ground Zero ('95, $12.95) r/#340-346 | | | | 13.00
...Hercules Unleashed (10/96, $2.50) David-s/Deodato-c/a | | | | 2.50
.../Sub-Mariner 1998 (11/98, $2.50) r/4, cont'd. Annual 5 | | | | 3.00
...Versus Quasimodo 1 (3/83, one-shot)-Based on Saturday morning cartoon | | | | 4.00
...Vs. Superman 1 (7/99, $5.95, one-shot)-painted-c by Rude | | | | 6.00
...Versus Venom 1 (4/94, $2.50, one-shot)-red foil logo | | | | 3.00
Wizard #181 Ace Edition - Reprints #181 with new Chen-c | | | | 13.00
(Also see titles listed under **Hulk**)

NOTE: **Adkins** a-111-116i. **Austin** a(i)-350, 351, 353, 354; c-302i, 350i. **Ayers** a-3-5i. **Buckler**-a-
Annual 5; c-252. **John Buscema** a-202p. **Byrne** a-314-319p; c-314-316, 318, 319, 359, Annual
14i. **Colan** c-363. **Ditko** a-3-5i, 249. Annual 2r(5), 3r, 9p; c-2i, 6, 235, 249. **Everett** c-133i.
Golden c-248, 251. **Kane** c(p)-193, 194, 196, 198. **Dale Keown** a(p)-367, 369-377, 379, 381-388,
390-393, 395-398; c-369-377p, 381, 382p, 384, 385, 386, 387p, 388, 390p, 391-393, 395p, 396,
397p, 398. **Kirby** a-1-5p. Special 2, 3p. Annual 5p; c-1-5, Annual 5. **McFarlane** a-330-334p, 336-
339p, 340-343, 344-346p; c-330p, 340p, 341-343, 344p, 345, 346p. **Mignola** a-302, 305, 313.
Miller c-258p, 261, 264, 268. **Mooney** a-230p, 287i, 288i. **Powell** a-Special 3r(2). **Romita** a-
Annual 17p. **Severin** a(i)-108-110, 131-133, 141-151, 153-155; c(i)-109, 110, 132, 142, 144-155.
Simonson c-283, 364-367. **Starlin** a-222p; c-217. **Staton** a(i)-187-189, 191-209. **Tuska** a-102i,
105i, 106i, 218p. **Williamson** a-310i; c-310i, 311i. **Wrightson** c-197.

INCREDIBLE HULK (Vol. 2) (Formerly Hulk #1-11)
Marvel Comics: No. 12, Mar, 2000 - Present ($1.99-$3.50)

12-Jenkins-s/Garney & McKone-a | | | | 3.00
13,14-($1.99) Garney & Buscema-a | | | | 2.50
15-24,26-32: 15-Begin $2.25-c. 21-Maximum Security x-over. 24-($1.99-c) | | | | 2.25
25-($2.99) Hulk vs. The Abomination; Romita Jr.-a | | | | 3.00
33-($3.50, 100 pgs.) new Bogdanove-a/Priest-s; reprints | | | | 3.50
34,35: 34-Bruce Jones-s begin; Romita Jr.-a | | | | 2.25
Annual 2000 ($3.50) Texeira-a/Jenkins-s; Avengers app. | | | | 3.50
Annual 2001 ($2.99) Thor-c/app.; Larsen-s/Williams III-c-a | | | | 3.00
Dogs of War (6/01, $19.95, TPB) r/#12-20 | | | | 20.00

INCREDIBLE MR. LIMPET, THE (See Movie Classics)

INCREDIBLE SCIENCE FICTION (Formerly Weird Science-Fantasy)
E. C. Comics: No. 30, July-Aug, 1955 - No. 33, Jan-Feb, 1956

30,33: 33-Story-r/Weird Fantasy #18 | 36 | 108 | 252 | 450
31-Williamson/Krenkel-a, Wood-a(2) | 37 | 111 | 259 | 460

Indiana Jones and the Iron Phoenix #2 © Lucasfilm

Indians #3 © FH

Inferior Five #7 © DC

	GD2.0	FN6.0	VF8.0	NM9.4

32-Williamson/Krenkel-a   37   111   259   460
NOTE: *Davis* a-30, 32, 33; c-30-32. **Krigstein** a-in all. *Orlando* a-30, 32, 33("Judgement Day" reprint). *Wood* a-30, 31, 33; c-33.

INCREDIBLE SCIENCE FICTION (Formerly Weird Science-Fantasy)
EC Comics/Gemstone Publ.: No. 8, Aug, 1994 - No. 11, May, 1995 ($2.00)

8-11: Reprints #30-33 of E.C. series   2.50

INDEPENDENCE DAY (Movie)
Marvel Comics: No. 0, June, 1996 - No. 2, Aug, 1996 ($1.95, limited series)

0-Special Edition; photo-c   5.00
0-2   2.50

INDEPENDENT VOICES
Peregrine Entertainment: Sept, 1998; Sept, 1999 ($1.95/$2.95, B&W)

1-Sampler of Indy titles for CBLDF   2.25
2-(9/99, $2.95); 2nd printing-(5/00)   3.00

INDIANA JONES (Title series), **Dark Horse Comics**

--AND THE ARMS OF GOLD, 2/94 - 5/94 ($2.50) 1-4   2.50
--AND THE FATE OF ATLANTIS, 3/91 - 9/91 ($2.50) 1-4-Dorman painted-c on all; contain trading cards (#1 has a 2nd printing, 10/91)   2.50
--AND THE GOLDEN FLEECE, 6/94 - 7/94 ($2.50) 1,2   2.50
--AND THE IRON PHOENIX, 12/94 - 3/95 ($2.50) 1-4   2.50

INDIANA JONES AND THE LAST CRUSADE
Marvel Comics: 1989 - No. 4, 1989 ($1.00, limited series, movie adaptation)

1-4: Williamson-i assist   3.00
1-(1989, $2.95, B&W mag., 80 pgs.)   4.00
--AND THE SHRINE OF THE SEA DEVIL: Dark Horse, 9/94 ($2.50, one shot)
1-Gary Gianni   2.50
--AND THE SPEAR OF DESTINY: Dark Horse, 4/95 - 8/95 ($2.50) 1-4   2.50
--THUNDER IN THE ORIENT: Dark Horse, 9/93 - '94 ($2.50)
1-6: Dan Barry story & art in all; 1-Dorman painted-c   2.50

INDIANA JONES AND THE TEMPLE OF DOOM
Marvel Comics Group: Sept, 1984 - No. 3, Sept, 1984 (Movie adaptation)

1-3-r/Marvel Super Special; Guice-a   3.00

INDIAN BRAVES (Baffling Mysteries No. 5 on)
Ace Magazines: March, 1951 - No. 4, Sept, 1951

1-Green Arrowhead begins, ends #3   13   39   66   110
2   7   21   38   55
3,4   6   18   32   45
I.W. Reprint #1 (nd)-r/Indian Braves #4   2   6   11   15

INDIAN CHIEF (White Eagle...) (Formerly The Chief, Four Color 290)
Dell Publ. Co.: No. 3, July-Sept, 1951 - No. 33, Jan-Mar, 1959 (All painted-c)

3   4   12   29   45
4-11: 6-White Eagle app.   3   10   23   35
12-1st White Eagle(10-12/53)-Not same as earlier character
   4   12   29   45
13-29   3   9   19   28
30-33-Buscema-a   3   9   20   30

INDIAN CHIEF (See March of Comics No. 94, 110, 127, 140, 159, 170, 187)

INDIAN FIGHTER, THE (Movie)
Dell Publishing Co.: No. 687, May, 1956 (one-shot)

Four Color 687-Kirk Douglas photo-c   8   24   56   100

INDIAN FIGHTER
Youthful Magazines: May, 1950 - No. 11, Jan, 1952

1   13   39   66   110
2-Wildey-a/c(bondage)   9   27   49   70
3-11: 3,4-Wildey-a   6   18   32   45
NOTE: *Walter Johnson* c-1, 3, 4, 6. *Palais* a-10. *Stallman* a-7. *Wildey* a-2-4; c-2, 5.

INDIAN LEGENDS OF THE NIAGARA (See American Graphics)

INDIANS
Fiction House Magazines (Wings Publ. Co.): Spring, 1950 - No. 17, Spring, 1953 (1-8: 52 pgs.)

1-Manzar The White Indian, Long Bow & Orphan of the Storm begin

   29   87   153   265
2-Starlight begins   15   45   77   130
3-5: 5-17-Most-c by Whitman   13   39   66   110
6-10   11   33   55   90
11-17   10   30   55   80

INDIANS OF THE WILD WEST
I. W. Enterprises: Circa 1958? (no date) (Reprints)

9-Kinstler-c; Whitman-a; r/Indians #?   2   6   11   16

INDIANS ON THE WARPATH
St. John Publishing Co.: No date (Late 40s, early 50s) (132 pgs.)

nn-Matt Baker-c; contains St. John comics rebound. Many combinations possible   34   102   179   310

INDIAN TRIBES (See Famous Indian Tribes)

INDIAN WARRIORS (Formerly White Rider and Super Horse; becomes Western Crime Cases #9)
Star Publications: No. 7, June, 1951 - No. 8, Sept, 1951

7-White Rider & Superhorse continue; "Last of the Mohicans" serial begins; L.B. Cole-c   19   57   99   165
8-L. B. Cole-c   17   51   88   150
3-D 1(12/53, 25¢)-Came w/glasses; L. B. Cole-c   40   120   220   380
Accepted Reprint(nn)(inside cover shows White Rider & Superhorse #11)-r/cover to #7; origin White Rider &...; L. B. Cole-c   7   21   36   50
Accepted Reprint #8 (nd); L.B.Cole-c (r-cover to #8) 7   21   36   50

INDOORS-OUTDOORS (See Wisco)

INDOOR SPORTS
National Specials Co.: nd (6x9", 64 pgs., B&W-r, hard-c)

nn-By Tad   5   15   25   35

INDUSTRIAL GOTHIC
DC Comics (Vertigo): Dec, 1995 - No. 5, Apr, 1996 ($2.50, limited series)

1-5: Ted McKeever-c/a/scripts   2.50

INFERIOR FIVE, THE (Inferior 5 #11, 12) (See Showcase #62, 63, 65)
National Periodical Publications (#1-10: 12¢): 3-4/67 - No. 10, 9-10/68; No. 11, 8-9/72 - No. 12, 10-11/72

1-(3-4/67)-Sekowsky-a(p); 4th app.   5   15   34   55
2-5: 2-Plastic Man, F.F. app. 4-Thor app.   3   9   19   28
6-9: 6-Stars DC staff   2   6   13   20
10-Superman x-over; F.F., Spider-Man & Sub-Mariner app.
   3   9   17   25
11,12: Orlando-c/a; both r/Showcase #62,63   2   6   12   18

INFERNO
Caliber Comics: 1995 - No. 5 ($2.95, B&W)

1-5   3.00

INFERNO (See Legion of Super-Heroes)
DC Comics: Oct, 1997 - No. 4, Feb, 1998 ($2.50, limited series)

1-Immonen-s/c/a in all   4.00
2-4   3.00

INFERNO: HELLBOUND
Image Comics (Top Cow): Jan, 2002 - Present ($2.50)

1-Seven covers; Silvestri-a/Silvestri and Wohl-s   2.50
Wizard #0- Previews series; bagged with Wizard Top Cow Special mag   1.00

INFINITY CRUSADE
Marvel Comics: June, 1993 - No. 6, Nov, 1993 ($2.50, limited series, 52 pgs.)

1-6: By Jim Starlin & Ron Lim   2.50

INFINITY GAUNTLET (The... #2 on; see Infinity Crusade, The Infinity War & Warlock & the Infinity Watch)
Marvel Comics: July, 1991 - No. 6, Dec, 1991 ($2.50, limited series)

1-6:Thanos-c/stories in all; Starlin scripts in all; 5,6-Ron Lim-c/a   3.00
TPB (4/99, $24.95) r/#1-6   25.00
NOTE: *Lim* a-3p(part), 5p, 6p; c-5i, 6i. *Perez* a-1-3p, 4p(part) (painted), 2-4, 5i, 6i.

INFINITY, INC. (See All-Star Squadron #25)
DC Comics: Mar, 1984 - No. 53, Aug, 1988 ($1.25, Baxter paper, 36 pgs.)

1-Brainwave, Jr., Fury, The Huntress, Jade, Northwind, Nuklon, Obsidian,

Infinity, Inc. #3 © DC

The Inhumans V2 #2 © MAR

The Inspector #3 © GK

Power Girl, Silver Scarab & Star Spangled Kid begin				4.00
2-13,38-49,51-53: 2-Dr. Midnite, G.A. Flash, W. Woman, Dr. Fate, Hourman, Green Lantern, Wildcat app. 5-Nudity panels. 46,47-Millennium tie-ins				3.00
14-Todd McFarlane-a (5/85, 2nd full story)	1	3	6	9
15-37-McFarlane-a (20,23,24: 5 pgs. only; 33: 2 pgs.); 18-24-Crisis x-over.				
21-Intro new Hourman & Dr. Midnight. 26-New Wildcat app. 31-Star Spangled Kid becomes Skyman. 32-Green Fury becomes Green Flame. 33-Origin Obsidian. 35-1st modern app. G.A. Fury				4.00
50 ($2.50, 52 pgs.)				3.00
Annual 1,2: 1(12/85)-Crisis x-over. 2('88, $2.00), Special 1 ('87, $1.50)				3.00

NOTE: *Kubert* r-4. *McFarlane* a-14-37p, Annual 1p; c(p)-14-19, 22, 25, 26, 31-33, 37, Annual 1. *Tuska* a-12p, 13p(last work 4/85). *JSA* app. 3-10.

INFINITY WAR, THE (Also see Infinity Gauntlet & Warlock and the Infinity…)
Marvel Comics: June, 1992 - No. 6, Nov, 1992 ($2.50, mini-series)

1-Starlin scripts, Lim-c/a(p), Thanos app. in all	2.50
2-6: All have wraparound gatefold covers	2.50

INFORMER, THE
Feature Television Productions: April, 1954 - No. 5, Dec, 1954

1-Sekowsky-a begins	12	36	61	100
2	8	24	45	65
3-5	7	21	38	55

IN HIS STEPS
Spire Christian Comics (Fleming H. Revell Co.): 1973, 1977 (39/49¢)

nn	1	3	6	8

INHUMANOIDS, THE (TV)
Marvel Comics (Star Comics): Jan, 1987 - No. 4, July 1987

1-4: Based on Hasbro toys	3.00

INHUMANS, THE (See Amazing Adventures, Fantastic Four #54 & Special #5, Incredible Hulk Special #1, Marvel Graphic Novel & Thor #146)
Marvel Comics Group: Oct, 1975 - No. 12, Aug, 1977

1: #1-4,6 are 25¢ issues	2	6	11	16
2-12: 9-Reprints Amazing Adventures #1,2('70). 12-Hulk app.	1	3	6	8
4,6-(30¢-c variants, limited distribution)(4,8/76)	2	6	9	12
11,12-(35¢-c variants, limited distribution)	2	6	9	12
Special (4/90, $1.50, 52 pgs.)-F.F. cameo				3.00

NOTE: *Buckler* c-2-4p, 5. *Gil Kane* a-5-7p; c-1p, 7p, 8p. *Kirby* a-9r. *Mooney* a-11i. *Perez* a-1-4p, 8p.

INHUMANS (Marvel Knights)
Marvel Comics: Nov, 1998 - No. 12, Oct, 1999 ($2.99, limited series)

1-Jae Lee-c/a; Paul Jenkins-s	10.00
1-($6.95) DF Edition; Jae Lee variant-c	7.00
2-Two covers by Lee and Darrow	4.00
3-12	3.00
TPB (10/00, $24.95) r/#1-12	25.00

INHUMANS (Volume 3)
Marvel Comics: Jun, 2000 - No. 4, Oct, 2000 ($2.99, limited series)

1-4-Ladronn-c/Pacheco & Marin-s. 1-3-Ladronn-a. 4-Lucas-a	3.00

INHUMANS: THE GREAT REFUGE
Marvel Comics: May, 1995 ($2.95, one-shot)

1	3.00

INKY & DINKY (See Felix's Nephews…)

IN LOVE (…Magazine on-c; I Love You No. 7 on)
Mainline/Charlton No. 5 (5/55)-on: Aug-Sept, 1954 - No. 6, July, 1955 ('Adult Reading' on-c)

1-Simon & Kirby-a; book-length novel in all issues	39	117	208	360
2,3-S&K-a. 3-Last pre-code (12-1/54-55)	23	69	121	210
4-S&K-a.(Rare)	24	72	127	220
5-S&K-c only	10	30	55	80
6-No S&K-a	7	21	36	50

INNOVATION SPECTACULAR
Innovation Publishing: 1991 - No. 2, 1991 ($2.95, squarebound, 100 pgs.)

1,2: Contains rebound comics w/o covers	3.00

INNOVATION SUMMER FUN SPECIAL

Innovation Publishing: 1991 ($3.50, B&W/color, squarebound)

1-Contains rebound comics (Power Factory)	3.50

INSANE
Dark Horse Comics: Feb, 1988 - No. 2 ($1.75, B&W)

1,2: 1-X-Men, Godzilla parodies. 2-Concrete	2.25

INSANE CLOWN POSSE
Chaos! Comics: June, 1999 - No. 3, Nov, 1999 ($2.95)

1-3-McCann-s	4.00
TPB ('00, $8.95) r/#1-3	9.00

INSANE CLOWN POSSE: THE PENDULUM
Chaos! Comics: Jan, 2000 - No. 12 ($2.95)

1-10-($5.95) polybagged w/CD	6.00
…: Hallowicked 1 (11/01, $2.99)	3.00

IN SEARCH OF THE CASTAWAYS (See Movie Comics)

INSIDE CRIME (Formerly My Intimate Affair)
Fox Features Syndicate (Hero Books): No. 3, July, 1950 - No. 2, Sept, 1950

3-Wood-a (10 pgs.); L. B. Cole-c	29	87	153	265
2-Used in SOTI, pg. 182,183; r/Spook #24	23	69	121	210
nn(no publ. listed, nd)	10	30	55	80

INSPECTOR, THE (TV) (Also see The Pink Panther)
Gold Key: July, 1974 - No. 19, Feb, 1978

1	3	9	20	30
2-5	2	6	12	18
6-9	2	6	11	15
10-19: 11-Reprints	1	4	7	10

INSPECTOR GILL OF THE FISH POLICE (See Fish Police)

INSPECTOR WADE
David McKay Publications: No. 13, May, 1938

Feature Books 13	19	57	133	250

INSTANT PIANO
Dark Horse Comics: Aug, 1994 - No. 4, Feb, 1995 ($3.95, B&W, bimonthly, mature)

1-4	4.00

INTERFACE
Marvel Comics (Epic Comics): Dec, 1989 - No. 8, Dec, 1990 ($1.95, mature, coated paper)

1-8: Cont. from 1st ESPers series; painted-c/a	2.25
Espers: Interface TPB ('98, $16.95) r/#1-6	17.00

INTERNATIONAL COMICS (…Crime Patrol No. 6)
E. C. Comics: Spring, 1947 - No. 5, Nov-Dec, 1947

1-Schaffenberger-a begins, ends #4	55	165	341	600
2	42	126	252	440
3-5	40	120	217	375

INTERNATIONAL CRIME PATROL (Formerly International Comics #1-5; becomes Crime Patrol No. 7)
E. C. Comics: No. 6, Spring, 1948

6-Moon Girl app.	55	165	341	600

IN THE DAYS OF THE MOB (Magazine)
Hampshire Dist. Ltd. (National): Fall, 1971 (B&W)

1-Kirby-a; John Dillinger wanted poster inside	8	24	56	90

IN THE PRESENCE OF MINE ENEMIES
Spire Christian Comics/Fleming H. Revell Co.: 1973 (35/49¢)

nn	1	3	6	8

INTIMATE
Charlton Comics: Dec, 1957 - No. 3, May, 1958

1	5	15	23	30
2,3	4	10	15	20

INTIMATE CONFESSIONS (See Fox Giants)

INTIMATE CONFESSIONS
Realistic Comics: July-Aug, 1951 - No. 7, Aug, 1952; No. 8, Mar, 1953 (All paint-

Intimate Confessions #7
© Realistic Comics

The Invaders #4 © MAR

The Invisibles #9 © Grant Morrison

	GD2.0	FN6.0	VF8.0	NM9.4

ed-c)

1-Kinstler-c/a; c/Avon paperback #222	74	221	469	825
2	20	60	110	185
3-c/Avon paperback #250; Kinstler-c/a	23	68	125	215
4-8: 4-c/Avon paperback #304; Kinstler-c. 6-c/Avon paperback #120.				
8-c/Avon paperback #375; Kinstler-a	20	60	110	185

INTIMATE CONFESSIONS
I. W. Enterprises/Super Comics: 1964

I.W. Reprint #9,10, Super Reprint #10,12,18	2	6	12	18

INTIMATE LOVE
Standard Comics: No. 5, 1950 - No. 28, Aug, 1954

5-8: 6-8-Severin/Elder-a	8	24	45	65
9	5	15	25	35
10-Jane Russell, Robert Mitchum photo-c	10	30	55	80
11-18,20,23,25,27,28	5	15	23	30
19,21,22,24,26-Toth-a	6	18	32	45

NOTE: *Celardo* a-8, 10. *Colletta* a-23. *Moreira* a-13(2). Photo-c-6, 7, 10, 12, 14, 15, 18-20, 24, 26, 27.

INTIMATE SECRETS OF ROMANCE
Star Publications: Sept, 1953 - No. 2, Apr, 1954

1,2-L. B. Cole-c	20	60	105	175

INTRIGUE
Quality Comics Group: Jan, 1955

1-Horror; Jack Cole reprint/Web of Evil	33	99	174	300

INTRIGUE
Image Comics: Aug, 1999 - Present ($2.50/$2.95)

1,2: 1-Two covers (Andrews, Wieringo); Shum-s/Andrews-a				2.50
3-($2.95)				3.00

INTRUDER
TSR, Inc.: 1990 - No. 10, 1991 ($2.95, 44 pgs.)

1-10				3.00

INVADERS, THE (TV)
Gold Key: Oct, 1967 - No. 4, Oct, 1968 (All have photo-c)

1-Spiegle-a in all	10	30	70	135
2-4	7	21	49	90

INVADERS, THE (Also see The Avengers #71 & Giant-Size Invaders)
Marvel Comics Group: August, 1975 - No. 40, May, 1979; No. 41, Sept, 1979

1-Captain America & Bucky, Human Torch & Toro, & Sub-Mariner begin; cont'd. from Giant Size Invaders #1; #1-7 are 25¢ issues	4	12	26	40
2-5: 2-1st app. Brain-Drain. 3-Battle issue; Cap vs. Namor vs. Torch; into U-Man	2	6	11	16
6-10: 6,7-(Regular 25¢ edition). 6-(7/76) Liberty Legion app. 7-Intro Baron Blood & intro/1st app. Union Jack; Human Torch origin retold. 8-Union Jack-c/story. 9-Origin Baron Blood. 10-G.A. Capt. America-r/C.A #22	2	6	9	12
6,7-(30¢-c variants, limited distribution)	2	6	12	18
11-19: 11-Origin Spitfire; intro The Blue Bullet. 14-1st app. The Crusaders. 16-Re-intro The Destroyer. 17-Intro Warrior Woman. 18-Re-intro The Destroyer w/new origin. 19-Hitler-c/story	1	3	6	8
17-19,21-(35¢-c variants, limited distribution)	2	6	9	12
20-(Regular 30¢-c) Reprints origin/1st app. Sub-Mariner from Motion Picture Funnies Weekly with color added & brief write-up about MPFW; 1st app. new Union Jack II	1	4	7	10
20-(35¢-c variant, limited distribution)	2	6	10	14
21-(Regular 30¢-c edition)-r/Marvel Mystery #10 (battle issue)	1	3	5	7
22-39,34-40: 22-New origin Toro. 24-r/Marvel Mystery #17 (team-up issue; all-r). 25-All new-a begins. 28-Intro new Human Top & Golden Girl. 29-Intro Teutonic Knight. 34-Mighty Destroyer apps. 35-The Whizzer app.				6.00
31-33: 31-Frankenstein-c/sty. 32,33-Thor app.	1	3	6	8
41-Double size last issue	1	4	7	10
Annual 1 (9/77)-Schomburg, Rico stories (new); Schomburg-a/a (1st for Marvel in 30 years); Avengers app.; re-intro The Shark & The Hyena	3	9	17	25

NOTE: *Buckler* a-5. *Everett* r-20(`39), 21(1940), 24, Annual 1. *Gil Kane* c(p)-13, 17, 18, 20-27. *Kirby* c(p)-3-12, 14-16, 32, 33. *Mooney* a-5i, 16, 22. *Robbins* a-1-4, 6-9, 10(3 pg.), 11-15, 17-21, 23, 25-28; c-28.

INVADERS (See Namor, the Sub-Mariner #12)
Marvel Comics Group: May, 1993 - No. 4, Aug, 1993 ($1.75, limited series)

1-4				2.50

INVADERS FROM HOME
DC Comics (Piranha Press): 1990 - No. 6, 1990 ($2.50, mature)

1-6				2.50

INVASION
DC Comics: Holiday, 1988-'89 - No. 3, Jan, 1989 ($2.95, lim. series, 84 pgs.)

1-3:1-McFarlane/Russell-a. 2-McFarlane/Russell & Giffen/Gordon-a				3.00

INVINCIBLE FOUR OF KUNG FU & NINJA
Leung Publications: April, 1988 - No. 6, 1989 ($2.00)

1-($2.75)				3.00
2-6: 2-Begin $2.00-c				2.25

INVISIBLE BOY (See Approved Comics)

INVISIBLE MAN, THE (See Superior Stories #1 & Supernatural Thrillers #2)

INVISIBLE PEOPLE
Kitchen Sink Press: 1992 (B&W, lim. series)

Book One: Sanctum; Book Two: "The Power"; Will Eisner-s/a in all				2.25
Book Three: "Mortal Combat"				4.00
Hardcover ($34.95)				35.00
TPB (DC Comics, 9/00, $12.95) reprints series				13.00

INVISIBLES, THE (1st Series)
DC Comics (Vertigo): Sept, 1994 - No. 25, Oct, 1996 ($1.95/$2.50, mature)

1-($2.95, 52 pgs.)-Intro King Mob, Ragged Robin, Boy, Lord Fanny & Dane (Jack Frost); Grant Morrison scripts in all				6.00
2-8: 4-Includes bound-in trading cards. 5-1st app. Orlando; brown paper-c				4.00
9-25: 10-Intro Jim Crow. 13-15-Origin Lord Fanny. 19-Origin King Mob; polybagged. 20-Origin Boy. 25-Intro Division X				2.50
Apocalipstick (2001, $19.95, TPB)-r/#9-16; Bolland-c				20.00
Entropy in the U.K. (2001, $19.95, TPB)-r/#17-25; Bolland-c				20.00
Say You Want A Revolution (1996, $17.50, TPB)-r/#1-8				18.00

NOTE: *Buckingham* a-25p. *Rian Hughes* c-1, 5. *Phil Jimenez* a-17p-19p. *Paul Johnson* a-16, 21. *Sean Phillips* c-2-4, 6-25. *Weston* a-10p. *Yeowell* a-1p-4p, 22p-24p.

INVISIBLES, THE (2nd Series)
DC Comics (Vertigo): V2#1, Feb, 1997 - No. 22, Feb, 1999 ($2.50, mature)

1-Intro Jolly Roger; Grant Morrison scripts, Phil Jimenez-a & Brian Bolland-c begins				4.00
2-22: 9,14-Weston-a				2.50
Bloody Hell in America TPB ('98, $12.95) r/#1-4				13.00
Counting to None TPB ('99, $19.95) r/#5-13				20.00
Kissing Mr. Quimper TPB ('00, $19.95) r/#14-22				20.00

INVISIBLES, THE (3rd Series) (Issue #'s go in reverse from #12 to #1)
DC Comics (Vertigo): V3#12, Apr, 1999 - No. 1, June, 2000 ($2.95, mature)

1-12-Bolland-c; Morrison-s on all. 1-Quitely-a. 2-4-Art by various. 5-8-Phillips-a. 9-12-Phillip Bond-a.				3.00

INVISIBLE SCARLET O'NEIL (Also see Famous Funnies #81 & Harvey Comics Hits #59)
Famous Funnies (Harvey): Dec, 1950 - No. 3, Apr, 1951
(2-3 pgs. of Powell-a in each issue.)

1	15	45	77	130
2,3	11	33	55	90

I, PAPARAZZI
DC Comics (Vertigo): 2001 ($29.95, HC, digitally manipulated photographic art)

nn-Pat McGreal-s/Steven Parke-digital-a/Stephen John Phillips-photos				30.00

IRON CORPORAL, THE (See Army War Heroes #22)
Charlton Comics: No. 23, Oct, 1985 - No. 25, Feb, 1986

23-25: Glanzman-a(r); low print				5.00

IRON FIST (See Deadly Hands of Kung Fu, Marvel Premiere & Power Man)
Marvel Comics: Nov, 1975 - No. 15, Sept, 1977

1-Iron Fist battles Iron Man (#1-6: 25¢)	4	12	29	45

Iron Fist #10 © MAR

Iron Man #109 © MAR

Iron Man #306 © MAR

	GD2.0	FN6.0	VF8.0	NM9.4
2		3	9	17	25

3-10: 4-6-(Regular 25¢ edition)(4-6/76). 8-Origin retold

		2	6	12	18
4-6-(30¢-c variant, limited distribution)	3	9	19	28
11,13: 13-(30¢-c)	2	6	9	12
12-Capt. America app.	2	6	11	15
13-(35¢-c variant, limited distribution)	2	6	11	15
14-1st app. Sabretooth (8/77)(see Power Man)	10	30	73	125
14-(35¢-c variant, limited distribution)	24	72	168	300
15-(Regular 30¢ ed.) X-Men app., Byrne-a	5	15	34	55
15-(35¢-c variant, limited distribution)	7	21	53	85

NOTE: **Adkins** a-8p, 10i, 13i; c-8i. **Byrne** a-1-15p; c-8p, 15p. **G. Kane** c-4-6p. **McWilliams** a-1i.

IRON FIST
Marvel Comics: Sept, 1996 - No. 2, Oct, 1996 ($1.50, limited series)

1,2				3.00

IRON FIST
Marvel Comics: Jul, 1998 - No. 3, Sept, 1998 ($2.50, limited series)

1-3: Jurgens-s/Guice-a				2.50

IRON FIST: WOLVERINE
Marvel Comics: Nov, 2000 - No. 4, Feb, 2001 ($2.99, limited series)

1-4-Igle-c/a; Kingpin app. 2-Iron Man app. 3,4-Capt. America app.				3.00

IRONHAND OF ALMURIC (Robert E. Howard's...)
Dark Horse Comics: Aug, 1991 - No. 4, 1991 ($2.00, B&W, mini-series)

1-4: 1-Conrad painted-c				2.25

IRON HORSE (TV)
Dell Publishing Co.: March, 1967 - No. 2, June, 1967

1-Dale Robertson photo covers on both	3	9	19	28
2	2	6	13	20

IRONJAW (Also see The Barbarians)
Atlas/Seaboard Publ.: Jan, 1975 - No. 4, July, 1975

1,2-Neal Adams-c. 1-1st app. Iron Jaw; Sekowsky-a(p); Fleisher-s				6.00
3,4-Marcos. 4-Origin				5.00

IRON LANTERN (Marvel Comics/Amalgam)
Marvel Comics (Amalgam): June, 1997 ($1.95, one-shot)

1-Kurt Busiek-s/Paul Smith & Al Williamson-a				2.50

IRON MAN (Also see The Avengers #1, Giant-Size..., Marvel Collectors Item Classics, Marvel Double Feature, Marvel Fanfare & Tales of Suspense #39)
Marvel Comics: May, 1968 - No. 332, Sept, 1996

1-Origin; Colan-c/a(p); story continued from Iron Man & Sub-Mariner #1

	41	123	306	550
2	14	42	100	170
3	8	24	56	90
4,5	6	18	45	75
6-10: 9-Iron Man battles green Hulk-like android	5	15	38	60
11-15: 15-Last 12¢ issue	4	12	29	45
16-20	3	9	20	30

21-24,26-30: 22-Death of Janice Cord. 27-Intro Fire Brand

	2	6	15	22
25-Iron Man battles Sub-Mariner	3	9	17	26

31-42: 33-1st app. Spymaster. 35-Nick Fury & Daredevil x-over.

42-Last 15¢ issue	2	6	12	18
43-Intro The Guardsman; 25¢ giant (52 pgs.)	3	9	17	26

44-46,48-50: 43-Giant-Man back-up by Ayers. 44-Ant-Man by Tuska. 46-The Guardsman dies. 50-Princess Python app.

		2	6	11	16
47-Origin retold; Barry Smith-a(p)	2	6	15	22
51-53: 53-Starlin part pencils	2	6	10	14

54-Iron Man battles Sub-Mariner; 1st app. Moondragon (1/73) as Madame MacEvil; Everett part-c

		3	9	17	26

55-1st app. Thanos (cameo), Drax the Destroyer, Mentor, Starfox & Kronos (2/73); Starlin-c/a

	9	27	63	105
56-Starlin-a	2	6	13	20

57-65,67-70: 59-Firebrand returns. 65-Origin Dr. Spectrum. 67-Last 20¢ issue.

68-Sunfire & Unicorn app.; origin retold; Starlin-c	2	6	9	12
66-Iron Man vs. Thor.	2	6	11	16

71-84: 72-Cameo portraits of N. Adams. 73-Rename Stark Industries to

---

Stark International; Brunner. 76-r/#9.

	1	3	6	9

85-89-(Regular 25¢ editions): 86-1st app. Blizzard. 87-Origin Blizzard. 88-Thanos app. 89-Daredevil app.; last 25¢-c

	1	3	6	8
85-89-(30¢-c variants, limited distribution)(4-8/76)	2	6	9	12
90-99: 96-1st app. new Guardsman	1	3	6	8
99,101-103-(35¢-c variants, limited dist.)	1	3	6	9
100-(7/77)-Starlin-c	2	6	13	20
100-(35¢-c variant, limited dist.)	3	9	17	24

101-117: 101-Intro DreadKnight. 109-1st app. new Crimson Dynamo; 1st app. Vanguard. 110-Origin Jack of Hearts retold; death of Count Nefaria.

114-Avengers app.				6.00
118-Byrne-a(p); 1st app. Jim Rhodes	1	3	6	8

119-127: 120,121-Sub-Mariner x-over. 122-Origin. 123-128-Tony Stark treated for alcohol problem. 125-Ant-Man app.

	1	3	5	7
128-Classic Tony Stark alcoholism cover	1	4	7	10
129,130,133-149				4.00
131,132-Hulk x-over				5.00
150-Double size				6.00

151-168: 152-New armor. 161-Moon Knight app. 167-Tony Stark alcohol problem resurfaces

				3.00
169-New Iron Man (Jim Rhodes replaces Tony Stark)				5.00
170,171				4.00

172-199: 172-Captain America x-over. 186-Intro Vibro. 190-Scarlet Witch app. 191-198-Tony Stark returns as original Iron Man. 192-Both Iron Men battle

				3.00

200-(11/85, $1.25, 52 pgs.)-Tony Stark returns as new Iron Man (red & white armor) thru #230

				4.00
201-213,215-224: 213-Intro new Dominic Fortune				3.00

214,225,228,231,234,247: 214-Spider-Woman app. in new black costume (1/87). 225-Double size ($1.25). 228-vs. Capt. America. 231-Intro new Iron Man.

234-Spider-Man x-over. 247-Hulk x-over				4.00

226,227,229,230,232,233,235-243,245,246,248,249: 233-Ant-Man app. 243-Tony Stark loses use of legs

				2.50
244-($1.50, 2 pgs.)-New Armor makes him walk				3.00
250-($1.50, 52 pgs.)-Dr. Doom-c/story				3.00

251-274,276-281,283,285-287,289,291-299: 258-277-Byrne scripts. 271-Fin Fang Foom app. 276-Black Widow-c/story; last $1.00-c. 281-1st app.; War Machine (cameo). 283-2nd full app. War Machine

				2.50
275-($1.50, 52 pgs.)				3.00
282-1st full app. War Machine (7/92)				4.00
284-Death of Iron Man (Tony Stark)				4.00
288-($2.50, 52pg.)-Silver foil stamped-c; Iron Man's 350th app. in comics				3.00
290-($2.95, 52pg.)-Gold foil stamped-c; 30th ann.				3.00

300-($3.95, 68 pgs.)-Collector's Edition w/embossed foil-c; anniversary issue; War Machine-c/story

				4.00
300-($2.50, 68 pgs.)-Newsstand Edition				2.50
301-303: 302-Venom-c/story (cameo #301)				2.50

304-316,318-324,326-331: 304-Begin $1.50-c; bound-in trading card sheet; Thunderstrike-c/story. 310-Orange logo. 312-w/bound-in Power Ranger Card. 319-Prologue to "The Crossing". 326-New Tony Stark; Pratt-c.

330-War Machine & Stockpile app; return of Morgan Stark				2.50

310,325: 310 ($2.95)-Polybagged w/ 16 pg. Marvel Action Hour preview & acetate print; white logo. 325-($2.95)-Wraparound-c

				3.00
317 ($2.50)-Flip book				2.50
332-Onslaught x-over				4.00
Special 1 (8/70)-Sub-Mariner x-over; Everett-c	3	10	23	35
Special 2 (11/71, 52 pgs.)-r/TOS #81,82,91 (all-r)	2	6	12	18
Annual 3 (1976)-Man-Thing app.	1	3	6	9
King Size 4 (8/77)-The Champions (w/Ghost Rider) app.; Newton-a(i)				7.00
Annual 5 ('82) New-a				5.00

Annual 6-15: ('83-'94) 6-New Iron Man (J. Rhodes) app. 8-X-Factor app. 10-Atlantis Attacks x-over; P. Smith-a; Layton/Guice-a; Sub-Mariner app. 11-(1990)-Origin of Mrs. Arbogast by Ditko (p&i). 12-1 pg. origin recap; Ant-Man back-up story. 13-Darkhawk & Avengers West Coast app.; Colan/Williamson-a. 14-Bagged w/card

				3.00
Manual 1 (1993, $1.75)-Operations handbook				2.50

Graphic Novel: Crash (1988, $12.95, Adults, 72 pgs)-Computer generated art & color; violence & nudity

				13.00
...Collector's Preview 1(11/94, $1.95)-wraparound-c; text & illos-no comics				2.50
...Vs. Dr. Doom (12/94, $12.95)-r/#149-150,250. Julie Bell-c				13.00

NOTE: **Austin** c-105i, 109-111i, 151i. **Byrne** a-118p; c-109p, 197, 253. **Colan** a-1p, 253, Special

Iron Man & Sub-Mariner #1 © MAR

Isis #2 © Filmation Assoc.

It Really Happened #6 © STD

	GD2.0	FN6.0	VF8.0	NM9.4

1p(3); c-1p. **Craig** a-1i, 2-4, 5-13i, 14, 15-19i, 24p, 25p, 26-28i; c-2-4. Ditko a-160p. Everett a-
Guice a-233-241p. **G. Kane** c(p)-52-54, 63, 67, 72-75, 77-79, 88, 98. Kirby a-Special 1p; c-13,
80p, 90, 92-95. Mooney a-40i, 43i, 47i. **Perez** a-103p. **Simonson** c-Annual 8. **B. Smith** a-232p,
243i; c-232. **P. Smith** a-159p, 245p, Annual 9p; c-159. Starlin a-53p(part), 55p, 56p; c-55p, 160,
163. Tuska a-5-13p, 15-23p, 24i, 32p, 38-46p, 48-54p, 57-61p, 63-69p, 70-72p, 78p, 86-92p, 95-
106p, Annual 4p. **Wood** a-Special 1i.

IRON MAN (The Invincible...) (Volume Two)
Marvel Comics: Nov, 1996 - No. 13, Nov, 1997 ($2.95/$1.95/$1.99)
(Produced by WildStorm Productions)

V2#1-3-Heroes Reborn begins; Scott Lobdell scripts & Whilce Portacio-c/a begin; new origin Iron Man & Hulk. 2-Hulk app. 3-Fantastic Four app.				4.00
1-Variant-c				5.00
4-11: 4-Two covers. 6-Fantastic Four app.; Industrial Revolution; Hulk app. 7-Return of Rebel. 11-($1.99) Dr. Doom-c/app.				3.00
12-($2.99) "Heroes Reunited"-pt. 3; Hulk-c/app.				3.50
13-($1.99) "World War 3"-pt. 3, x-over w/Image				3.00

IRON MAN (The Invincible...) (Volume Three)
Marvel Comics: Feb, 1998 - Present ($2.99/$1.99/$2.25)

V3#1-($2.99)-Follows Heroes Return; Busiek scripts & Chen-c/a begin; Deathsquad app.				5.00
1-Alternate Ed.	1	3	6	8
2-12: 2-Two covers. 6-Black Widow-c/app. 7-Warbird-c/app. 8-Black Widow app. 9-Mandarin returns				3.00
13-($2.99) battles the Controller				3.50
14-24: 14-Fantastic Four-c/app.				3.00
25-($2.99) Iron Man and Warbird battle Ultimo; Avengers app.				3.00
26-30-Quesada-s. 28-Whiplash killed. 29-Begin $2.25-c.				2.50
31-45,47-49: 35-Maximum Security x-over; FF-c/app. 41-Grant-a begins. 44-New armor debut. 48-Ultron-c/app.				2.25
46-($3.50, 100 pgs.) Sentient armor returns; r/V1#78,140,141				3.50
.../Captain America '98 Annual ($3.50) vs. Modok				3.50
1999, 2000 Annual ($3.50)				3.50
2001 Annual ($2.99) Claremont-s/Ryan-a				3.00
Mask in the Iron Man (5/01, $14.95, TPB) r/#26-30, #1/2				15.00

IRON MAN & SUB-MARINER
Marvel Comics Group: Apr, 1968 (12¢, one-shot) (Pre-dates Iron Man #1 & Sub-Mariner #1)

1-Iron Man story by Colan/Craig continued from Tales of Suspense #99 & continued in Iron Man #1; Sub-Mariner story by Colan continued from Tales to Astonish #101 & continued in Sub-Mariner #1; Colan/Everett-c	14	42	102	175

IRON MAN: BAD BLOOD
Marvel Comics: Sept, 2000 - No. 4, Dec, 2000 ($2.99, limited series)

1-4-Micheline-s/Layton-a				3.00

IRON MAN: THE IRON AGE
Marvel Comics: Aug, 1998 - No. 2, Sept, 1998 ($5.99, one-shot)

1,2-Busiek-s; flashback story from gold armor days				6.00

IRON MAN: THE LEGEND
Marvel Comics: Sept, 1996 ($3.95, one-shot)

1-Tribute issue				4.50

IRON MAN 2020 (Also see Machine Man limited series)
Marvel Comics: June, 1994 ($5.95, one-shot)

nn				6.00

IRON MAN/X-O MANOWAR: HEAVY METAL (See X-O Manowar/Iron Man: In Heavy Metal)
Marvel Comics: Sept, 1996 ($2.50, one-shot) (1st Marvel/Valiant x-over)

1-Pt. II of Iron Man/X-O Manowar x-over; Fabian Nicieza scripts; 1st app. Rand Banion				2.50

IRON MARSHALL
Jademan Comics: July, 1990 - No. 32, Feb, 1993 ($1.75, plastic coated-c)

1-32: Kung Fu stories. 1-Poster centerfold				2.25

IRON VIC (See Comics Revue No. 3 & Giant Comics Editions)
United Features Syndicate/St. John Publ. Co.: 1940

Single Series 22	34	102	179	310

IRON WINGS
Image Comics: Apr, 2000 - No. 2 ($2.50)

1,2: 1-Two covers				2.50

IRONWOLF
DC Comics: 1986 ($2.00, one shot)

1-r/Weird Worlds 8-10; Chaykin story & art				2.25

IRONWOLF: FIRES OF THE REVOLUTION (See Weird Worlds #8-10)
DC Comics: 1992 ($29.95, hardcover)

nn-Chaykin/Moore story, Mignola a w/Russell inks.				30.00

ISAAC ASIMOV'S I-BOTS
Tekno Comix: Dec, 1995 - No. 7, May, 1996 ($1.95)

1-7: 1-6-Perez-c/a. 2-Chaykin variant-c exists. 3-Polybagged. 7-Lady Justice-c/app.				2.25

ISAAC ASIMOV'S I-BOTS
BIG Entertainment: V2#1, June, 1996 - Present ($2.25)

V2#1-9: 1-Lady Justice-c/app. 6-Gil Kane-c				2.25

ISIS (TV) (Also see Shazam)
National Per.I Publ./DC Comics: Oct-Nov, 1976 - No. 8, Dec-Jan, 1977-78

1-Wood inks	2	6	11	15
2-8: 5-Isis new look. 7-Origin	1	3	6	8

ISLAND AT THE TOP OF THE WORLD (See Walt Disney Showcase #27)

ISLAND OF DR. MOREAU, THE (Movie)
Marvel Comics Group: Oct, 1977 (52 pgs.)

1-Gil Kane-c				6.00

I SPY (TV)
Gold Key: Aug, 1966 - No. 6, Sept, 1968 (All have photo-c)

1-Bill Cosby, Robert Culp photo covers	23	69	161	300
2-6: 3,4-McWilliams-a. 5-Last 12¢-c	13	40	91	175

IT! (See Astonishing Tales No. 21-24 & Supernatural Thrillers No. 1)

ITCHY & SCRATCHY COMICS (The Simpsons TV show)
Bongo Comics: 1993 - No. 3, 1993 ($1.95)

1-3: 1-Bound-in jumbo poster. 3-w/decoder screen trading card				3.00
Holiday Special ('94, 1.95)				3.00

IT REALLY HAPPENED
William H. Wise No. 1,2/Standard (Visual Editions): 1944 - No. 11, Oct, 1947

1-Kit Carson & Ben Franklin stories	20	60	105	180
2	11	33	55	90
3,4,6,9,11: 6-Joan of Arc story. 9-Captain Kidd & Frank Buck stories	10	30	55	90
5-Lou Gehrig & Lewis Carroll stories	16	48	83	140
7-Teddy Roosevelt story	11	33	55	90
8-Story of Roy Rogers	17	51	88	150
10-Honus Wagner & Mark Twain stories	13	39	66	110

NOTE: **Guardineer** a-7(2), 8(2), 11. **Schomburg** c-1-7, 9-11.

IT RHYMES WITH LUST (Also see Bold Stories & Candid Tales)
St. John Publishing Co.: 1950 (Digest size, 128 pgs.)

nn (Rare)-Matt Baker & Ray Osrin-a	59	177	369	650

IT'S ABOUT TIME (TV)
Gold Key: Jan, 1967

1 (10195-701)-Photo-c	4	12	29	45

IT'S A DUCK'S LIFE
Marvel Comics/Atlas(MMC): Feb, 1950 - No. 11, Feb, 1952

1-Buck Duck, Super Rabbit begin	15	45	77	130
2	8	24	45	65
3-11	7	21	38	55

IT'S GAMETIME
National Periodical Publications: Sept-Oct, 1955 - No. 4, Mar-Apr, 1956

1-(Scarce)-Infinity-c; Davy Crockett app. in puzzle	75	225	469	825
2,3 (Scarce): 2-Dodo & The Frog	59	177	369	650
4 (Rare)	61	182	381	675

IT'S LOVE, LOVE, LOVE

Jackie Gleason #2 © STJ

Jackpot Comics #4 © MLJ

Jack Kirby's Fourth World #16 © DC

	GD2.0	FN6.0	VF8.0	NM9.4

St. John Publishing Co.: Nov, 1957 - No. 2, Jan, 1958 (10¢)

1,2	5	15	25	35

IVANHOE (See Fawcett Movie Comics No. 20)

IVANHOE
Dell Publishing Co.: July-Sept, 1963

1 (12-373-309)	3	10	23	35

IWO JIMA (See Spectacular Features Magazine)

JACE PEARSON OF THE TEXAS RANGERS (Radio/TV)(4-Color #396 is titled Tales of the Texas Rangers; ...'s Tales of ... #11-on)(See Western Roundup under Dell Giants)
Dell Publishing Co.: No. 396, 5/52 - No. 1021, 8-10/59 (No #10) (All-Photo-c)

Four Color 396 (#1)	11	33	77	140
2(5-7/53) - 9(2-4/55)	6	18	42	80
11(11-2/55-56) - 14,17-20(6-8/58)	5	15	35	60
15,16-Toth-a	5	15	35	60
Four Color 961, 1021: 961-Spiegle-a	5	15	34	55

NOTE: Joel McCrea photo c-1-9, F.C. 648 (starred on radio show only); Willard Parker photo c-11-on (starred on TV series).

JACK ARMSTRONG (Radio)(See True Comics)
Parents' Institute: Nov, 1947 - No. 9, Sept, 1948; No. 10, Mar, 1949 - No. 13, Sept, 1949

1-(Scarce) (odd size) Cast intro. inside front-c	43	129	257	450
2	21	63	110	185
3-5	15	45	77	130
6-13: 7-Vic Hardy's Crime Lab begins?	12	36	61	105

JACK HUNTER
Blackthorne Publishing: July, 1987 - No. 3 ($1.25)

1-3		2.25

JACKIE CHAN'S SPARTAN X
Topps Comics: May, 1997 - No. 3 ($2.95, limited series)

1-3-Michael Golden-s/a; variant photo-c		3.00

JACKIE CHAN'S SPARTAN X: HELL BENT HERO FOR HIRE
Image Comics (Little Eva Ink): Mar, 1998 - No. 3 ($2.95, B&W)

1-3-Michael Golden-s/a: 1-variant photo-c		3.00

JACKIE GLEASON (TV) (Also see The Honeymooners)
St. John Publishing Co.: Sept, 1955 - No. 4, Dec, 1955?

1(1955)(TV)-Photo-c	59	177	369	650
2-4	40	120	240	420

JACKIE GLEASON AND THE HONEYMOONERS (TV)
National Periodical Publications: June-July, 1956 - No. 12, Apr-May, 1958

1-1st app. Ralph Kramden	86	258	540	950
2	53	160	318	560
3-11	40	120	240	420
12 (Scarce)	59	177	369	650

JACKIE JOKERS (Became Richie Rich &...)
Harvey Publications: March, 1973 - No. 4, Sept, 1973 (#5 was advertised, but not published)

1-1st app.	3	9	17	25
2-4: 2-President Nixon app.	2	6	9	12

JACKIE ROBINSON (Famous Plays of...) (Also see Negro Heroes #2 & Picture News #4)
Fawcett Publications: May, 1950 - No. 6, 1952 (Baseball hero) (All photo-c)

nn	91	273	568	1000
2	55	165	330	575
3-6	45	135	270	475

JACK IN THE BOX (Formerly Yellowjacket Comics #1-10; becomes Cowboy Western Comics #17 on)
Frank Comunale/Charlton Comics No. 11 on: Feb, 1946; No. 11, Oct, 1946 - No. 16, Nov-Dec, 1947

1-Stitches, Marty Mouse & Nutsy McKrow	14	42	72	125
11-Yellowjacket (early Charlton comic)	20	60	105	175

12,14,15	9	27	49	70
13-Wolverton-a	21	63	110	185
16-12 pg. adapt. of Silas Marner; Kiefer-a	11	33	55	90

JACK KIRBY'S FOURTH WORLD (See Mister Miracle & New Gods, 3rd Series)
DC Comics: Mar, 1997 - No. 20, Oct, 1998 ($1.95/$2.25)

1-20: 1-Byrne-a/scripts & Simonson-c begin; story cont'd from New Gods, 3rd Series #15; retells "The Pact" (New Gods, 1st Series #7); 1st DC app. Thor (cameo). 2-Thor vs. Big Barda; "Apokolips Then" back-up begins; Kirby-c/swipe (Thor #126) 8-Genesis x-over. 10-Simonson-s/a 13-Simonson back-up story. 20-Superman-c/app.		2.25

JACK KIRBY'S SECRET CITY SAGA
Topps Comics (Kirbyverse): No. 0, April, 1993; No. 1, May, 1993 - No. 4, Aug, 1993 ($2.95, limited series)

0-(No cover price, 20 pgs.)-Simonson-c/a		3.00
0-Red embossed-c (limited ed.)		5.00
1-4-Bagged w/3 trading cards: Ditko-c/a: 1-Ditko/Art Adams-c. 2-Ditko/Byrne-c; has coupon for Pres. Clinton holo-foil trading card. 3-Dorman poster; has coupon for Gore holo-foil trading card. 4-Ditko/Perez-c		3.00

NOTE: Issues #1-4 contain coupons redeemable for Kirbychrome version of #1

JACK KIRBY'S SILVER STAR (Also see Silver Star)
Topps Comics (Kirbyverse): Oct, 1993 ($2.95)(Intended as a 4-issue limited series)

1-Silver ink-c; Austin-a(i); polybagged w/3 cards		3.00

JACK KIRBY'S TEENAGENTS (See Satan's Six)
Topps Comics (Kirbyverse): Aug, 1993 - No. 3, Oct, 1993 ($2.95)(Intended as a 4-issue limited series)

1-3: Bagged with/3 trading cards; 1-3-Austin-c(i): 3-Liberty Project app.		3.00

JACK OF HEARTS (Also see The Deadly Hands of Kung Fu #22 & Marvel Premiere #44)
Marvel Comics Group: Jan, 1984 - No. 4, Apr, 1984 (60¢, limited series)

1-4		2.50

JACKPOT COMICS (Jolly Jingles #10 on)
MLJ Magazines: Spring, 1941 - No. 9, Spring, 1943

1-The Black Hood, Mr. Justice, Steel Sterling & Sgt. Boyle begin; Biro-c	300	900	1875	3300
2-S. Cooper-c	136	408	852	1500
3-Hubbell-c	100	300	625	1100
4-Archie begins (Win/41; on sale 12/41)-(also see Pep Comics #22); 1st app. Mrs. Grundy, the principal; Novick-c	350	1050	2188	4200
5-Hitler, Tojo, Mussolini-c by Montana; 1st definitive Mr. Weatherbee; 1st app. Reggie in 1 panel cameo	150	450	938	1650
6-9: 6,7-Bondage-c by Novick. 8,9-Sahle-c	105	315	656	1150

JACK Q FROST (See Unearthly Spectaculars)

JACK THE GIANT KILLER (See Movie Classics)

JACK THE GIANT KILLER (New Adventures of...)
Bimfort & Co.: Aug-Sept, 1953

V1#1-H. C. Kiefer-c/a	24	72	127	215

JACKY'S DIARY
Dell Publishing Co.: No. 1091, Apr-June, 1960 (one-shot)

Four Color 1091	4	12	30	50

JADE (Chaos! Presents: ...)
Chaos! Comics: May, 2001 - No. 4, Aug, 2001 ($2.99, limited series)

1-4-Lashley-a/Golden & Sniegoski-a		3.00
...Redemption 1 (12/01 - No. 4) Tortosa-a		3.00

JADEMAN COLLECTION
Jademan Comics: Dec, 1989 - No. 3, 1990 ($2.50, plastic coated-c, 68 pgs.)

1-3: 1-Wraparound-c w/fold-out poster		2.50

JADEMAN KUNG FU SPECIAL
Jademan Comics: 1988 ($1.50, 64 pgs.)

1		2.50

JADE WARRIORS (Mike Deodato's...)
Image Comics (Glass House Graphics): Nov, 1999 - Present ($2.50)

	GD2.0	FN6.0	VF8.0	NM9.4

1-3-Deodato-a				2.50
1-Variant-c				2.50

JAGUAR, THE (Also see The Adventures of...)
Impact Comics (DC): Aug, 1991 - No. 14, Oct, 1992 ($1.00)

1-14: 4-The Black Hood x-over. 7-Sienkiewicz-c. 9-Contains Crusaders trading card				2.25
Annual 1 (1992, $2.50, 68 pgs.)-With trading card				2.50

JAGUAR GOD
Verotik: Mar, 1995 - No. 7, June, 1997 ($2.95, mature)

0 (2/96, $3.50)-Embossed Frazetta-c; Bisley-a; w/pin-ups.				4.00
1-Frazetta-c.				4.00
2-7: 2-Frazetta-c. 3-Bisley-c. 4-Emond-c. 7-($2.95)-Frazetta-c				3.00

JAKE THRASH
Aircel Publishing: 1988 - No. 3, 1988 ($2.00)

1-3				2.25

JAM, THE (...Urban Adventure)
Slave Labor Nos. 1-5/Dark Horse Comics Nos. 6-8/Caliber Comics No. 9 on: Nov, 1989 - No. 14, 1997 ($1.95/$2.50/$2.95, B&W)

1-14: Bernie Mireault-c/a/scripts. 6-1st Dark Horse issue. 9-1st Caliber issue				3.00

JAMBOREE
Round Publishing Co.: Feb, 1946(no mo. given) - No. 3, Apr, 1946

1-Funny animal	26	78	139	240
2,3	16	48	83	140

JAMES BOND 007: A SILENT ARMAGEDDON
Dark Horse Comics/Acme Press: Mar, 1993 - Apr 1993 (limited series)

1,2				3.50

JAMES BOND 007: GOLDENEYE (Movie)
Topps Comics: Jan, 1996 ($2.95, unfinished limited series of 3)

1-Movie adaptation; Stelfreeze-a				3.00

JAMES BOND 007: SERPENT'S TOOTH
Dark Horse Comics/Acme Press: July 1992 - Aug 1992 ($4.95, limited series)

1-3-Paul Gulacy-c/a				5.00

JAMES BOND 007: SHATTERED HELIX
Dark Horse Comics: Jun 1994 - July 1994 ($2.50, limited series)

1,2				3.00

JAMES BOND 007: THE QUASIMODO GAMBIT
Dark Horse Comics: Jan 1995 - May 1995 ($3.95, limited series)

1-3				4.50

JAMES BOND FOR YOUR EYES ONLY
Marvel Comics Group: Oct, 1981 - No. 2, Nov, 1981

1,2-Movie adapt.; r/Marvel Super Special #19				3.00

JAMES BOND JR. (TV)
Marvel Comics: June, 1992 - No. 12, Dec, 1992 (#1: $1.00, #2-on: $1.25)

1-12: Based on animated TV show				2.25

JAMES BOND: LICENCE TO KILL (See Licence To Kill)

JAMES BOND: PERMISSION TO DIE
Eclipse Comics/ACME Press: 1989 - No. 3, 1991 ($3.95, limited series, square-bound, 52 pgs.)

1-3: Mike Grell-c/a/scripts in all. 3-($4.95)				5.00

JAM: THE SUPER COOL COLOR INJECTED TURBO ADVENTURE #1 FROM HELL!
Comico: May, 1988 ($2.50, 44 pgs., one-shot)

1				2.50

JANE ARDEN (See Feature Funnies & Pageant of Comics)
St. John (United Features Syndicate): Mar, 1948 - No. 2, June, 1948

1-Newspaper reprints	16	48	83	140
2	12	36	61	100

JANN OF THE JUNGLE (Jungle Tales No. 1-7)
Atlas Comics (CSI): No. 8, Nov, 1955 - No. 17, June, 1957

	GD2.0	FN6.0	VF8.0	NM9.4
8(#1)	34	102	179	310
9,11-15	20	60	105	175
10-Williamson/Colletta-c	20	60	105	180
16,17-Williamson/Mayo-a(3), 5 pgs. each	21	63	110	190

NOTE: *Everett c-15-17. Heck a-8, 15, 17. Maneely c-11. Shores a-8.*

JAR OF FOOLS
Penny Dreadful Press: 1994 ($5.95, B&W)

1-Jason Lutes-c/a/scripts				6.00

JAR OF FOOLS
Black Eye Productions: 1994 - No. 2, 1994 ($6.95, B&W)

1,2: 1-Reprints of earlier ed. Jason Lutes-c/a/scripts				7.00

JASON & THE ARGONAUTS (See Movie Classics)

JASON GOES TO HELL: THE FINAL FRIDAY (Movie)
Topps Comics: July, 1993 - No. 3, Sept, 1993 ($2.95, limited series)

1-3: Adaptation of film. 1-Glow-in-the-dark-c				3.00

JASON'S QUEST (See Showcase #88-90)

JASON VS. LEATHERFACE
Topps Comics: Oct, 1995 - No. 3, Jan, 1996 ($2.95, limited series)

1-3: Collins scripts; Bisley-c				3.00

JAWS 2 (See Marvel Comics Super Special, A)

JAY & SILENT BOB (See Clerks & Oni Double Feature)
Oni Press: July, 1998 - No. 4, Oct, 1999 ($2.95, B&W, limited series)

1-Kevin Smith-s/Fegredo-a; photo-c & Quesada/Palmiotti-a				8.00
1-San Diego Comic Con variant covers (2 different covers, came packaged with action figures)				10.00
1-2nd & 3rd printings, 2-4: 2-Allred-c. 3-Flip-c by Jaime Hernandez				3.00
Chasing Dogma TPB (1999, $11.95) r/#1-4: Alanis Morissette intro.				12.00
Chasing Dogma TPB (2001, $12.95) r/#1-4 in color; Morissette intro.				13.00
Chasing Dogma HC (2001, $69.95, S&N) r/#1-4 in color; Morissette intro.				70.00

JCP FEATURES
J.C. Productions (Archie): Feb, 1982-c; Dec, 1981-indicia ($2.00, one-shot, B&W magazine)

1-T.H.U.N.D.E.R. Agents; Black Hood by Morrow & Neal Adams; Texeira-a; 2 pgs. S&K-a from Fly #1	1	3	6	9

JEANIE COMICS (Formerly All Surprise; Cowgirl Romances #28)
Marvel Comics/Atlas(CPC): No. 13, April, 1947 - No. 27, Oct, 1949

13-Mitzi, Willie begin	18	54	94	160
14,15	13	39	66	110
16-Used in Love and Death by Legman; Kurtzman's "Hey Look"	15	45	77	130
17-19,22-Kurtzman's "Hey Look", (1-3 pgs. each)	11	33	55	90
20,21,23-27	10	30	55	80

JEEP COMICS (Also see G.I. Comics and Overseas Comics)
R. B. Leffingwell & Co.: Winter, 1944 - No. 3, Mar-Apr, 1948

1-Capt. Power, Criss Cross & Jeep & Peep (costumed) begin	52	157	314	550
2	35	105	188	325
3-L. B. Cole dinosaur-c	45	135	270	475

JEFF JORDAN, U.S. AGENT
D. S. Publishing Co.: Dec, 1947 - Jan, 1948

1	15	45	77	130

JEMM, SON OF SATURN
DC Comics: Sept, 1984 - No. 12, Aug, 1985 (Maxi-series, mando paper)

1-12: 3-Origin				2.50

NOTE: *Colan a-1-12p; c-1-5, 7-12p.*

JENNY FINN
Oni Press: June, 1999 - No. 2, Sept, 1999 ($2.95, B&W, unfinished lim. series)

1,2-Mignola & Nixey-s/Nixey-a/Mignola-c				3.00

JENNY SPARKS: THE SECRET HISTORY OF THE AUTHORITY
DC Comics (WildStorm): Aug, 2000 - No. 5, Mar, 2001 ($2.50, limited series)

1-Millar-s/McCrea & Hodgkins-a/Hitch & Neary-c				3.00
1-Variant-c by McCrea				5.00

	GD2.0	FN6.0	VF8.0	NM9.4
	GD2.0	FN6.0	VF8.0	NM9.4

2-5: 2-Apollo & Midnighter. 3-Jack Hawksmoor. 4-Shen. 5-Engineer 2.50
TPB (2001, $14.95) r/#1-5; Ellis intro. 15.00

JERRY DRUMMER (Formerly Soldier & Marine V2#9)
Charlton Comics: V2#10, Apr, 1957 - V3#12, Oct, 1957

V2#10, V3#11,12: 11-Whitman-c/a	6	18	29	40

JERRY IGER'S... (All titles, Blackthorne/First)(Value: cover or less)

JERRY LEWIS (See The Adventures of...)

JESSE JAMES (The True Story Of..., also seeThe Legend of...)
Dell Publishing Co.: No. 757, Dec, 1956 (one shot)

Four Color 757-Movie, photo-c	9	27	63	120

JESSE JAMES (See Badmen of the West & Blazing Sixguns)
Avon Periodicals: 8/50 - No. 9, 11/52; No. 15, 10/53 - No. 29, 8-9/56

1-Kubert Alabam-r/Cowpuncher #1	17	51	88	150
2-Kubert-a(3)	14	42	72	120
3-Kubert Alabam-r/Cowpuncher #2	13	39	66	110
4,9-No Kubert	7	21	36	50
5,6-Kubert Jesse James-a(3); 5-Wood-a(1pg.)	13	39	66	110
7-Kubert Jesse James-a(2)	11	33	55	90
8-Kinstler-a(3)	8	24	42	60
15-Kinstler-r/#3	6	18	29	40
16-Kinstler-r/#3 & story-r/Butch Cassidy #1	6	18	30	42

17-19,21: 17-Jesse James-r/#4; Kinstler-c idea from Kubert splash in #6.
18-Kubert Jesse James-r/#5. 19-Kubert Jesse James-r/#6. 21-Two Jesse

James-r/#4, Kinstler-r/#4	6	18	28	38

20-Williamson/Frazetta-a; r/Chief Vic. Apache Massacre; Kubert Jesse

James-r/#6; Kit West story by Larsen	40	120	214	370

22-29: 22,23-No Kubert. 24-New McCarty strip by Kinstler; Kinstler-r. 25-New
McCarty Jesse James strip by Kinstler; Jesse James-r/#7,9. 26,27-New
McCarty Jesse James strip plus a Kinstler/McCann Jesse James-r.
28-Reprints most of Red Mountain, Featuring Quantrells Raiders

	6	18	28	38

Annual nn (1952; 25¢, 100 pgs.)- "...Brings Six-Gun Justice to the West"-

3 earlier issues rebound; Kubert, Kinstler-a(3)	29	87	153	265

NOTE: Mostly reprints #10 on. **Fawcette** c-1, 3. **Kida** a-5. **Kinstler** a-3, 4, 7-9, 15r, 16r(2), 21-27;
c-3, 4, 9, 17-27. Painted c-5-8. 22 has 2 stories r/Sheriff Bob Dixon's Chuck Wagon #1 with name
changed to Sheriff Bob Trent.

JESSE JAMES
Realistic Publications: July, 1953

nn-Reprints Avon's #1; same-c, colors different	10	30	55	80

JEST (Formerly Snap; becomes Kayo #12)
Harry 'A' Chesler: No. 10, 1944; No. 11, 1944

10-Johnny Rebel & Yankee Boy app. in text	17	51	88	150
11-Little Nemo in Adventure Land	17	51	88	150

JESTER
Harry 'A' Chesler: No. 10, 1945

10	15	45	77	130

JESUS
Spire Christian Comics (Fleming H. Revell Co.): 1979 (49¢)

nn	1	3	6	8

JET (See Jet Powers)

JET (Crimson from Wildcore & Backlash)
DC Comics (WildStorm): Nov, 2000 - No. 4, Feb, 2001 ($2.50, limited series)

1-4-Nguyen-a/Abnett & Lanning-s				2.50

JET ACES
Fiction House Magazines: 1952 - No. 4, 1953

1	14	42	72	125
2-4	9	27	49	70

JETCAT CLUBHOUSE (Also see Land of Nod, The)
Oni Press: Apr, 2001 ($3.25)

1-3-Jay Stephens-s/a. 1-Wraparound-c				3.25

JET DREAM (...and Her Stunt-Girl Counterspies)(See The Man from Uncle #7)
Gold Key: June, 1968 (12¢)

1-Painted-c	4	12	28	38

JET FIGHTERS (Korean War)
Standard Magazines: No. 5, Nov, 1952 - No. 7, Mar, 1953

5,7-Toth-a. 5-Toth-c	12	36	61	100
6-Celardo-a	6	18	29	40

JET POWER
I.W. Enterprises: 1963

I.W. Reprint 1,2-r/Jet Powers #1,2	3	9	21	32

JET POWERS (American Air Forces No. 5 on)
Magazine Enterprises: 1950 - No. 4, 1951

1(A-1 #30)-Powell-c/a begins	34	102	179	310
2(A-1 #32)	24	72	127	215
3(A-1 #35)-Williamson/Evans-a	40	120	214	370
4(A-1 #38)-Williamson/Wood-a; "The Rain of Sleep" drug story	40	120	214	370

JET PUP (See 3-D Features)

JETSONS, THE (TV) (See March of Comics #276, 330, 348 & Spotlight #3)
Gold Key: Jan, 1963 - No. 36, Oct, 1970 (Hanna-Barbera)

1-1st comic book app.	25	75	175	320
2	12	36	84	150
3-10	9	27	63	110
11-20	6	18	42	80
21-36: 23-36-Reprints	5	15	35	60

JETSONS, THE (TV) (Also see Golden Comics Digest)
Charlton Comics: Nov, 1970 - No. 20, Dec, 1973 (Hanna-Barbera)

1	8	24	60	100
2	4	12	30	50
3-10	3	10	23	35
11-20	3	9	17	25

JETSONS, THE (TV)
Harvey Comics: V2#1, Sept, 1992 - No. 5, Nov, 1993 ($1.25/$1.50) (Hanna-Barbera)

V2#1-5				4.00
...Big Book V2#1,2,3 ($1.95, 52 pgs.): 1-(11/92). 2-(4/93). 3-(7/93)				4.00
...Giant Size 1,2,3 ($2.25, 68 pgs): 1-(10/92). 2-(4/93). 3-(10/93)				4.00

JETSONS, THE (TV)
Archie Comics: Sept, 1995 - No. 17, Aug, 1996 ($1.50)

1-17				2.50

JETTA OF THE 21ST CENTURY
Standard Comics: No. 5, Dec, 1952 - No. 7, Apr, 1953 (Teen-age Archie type)

5	23	69	121	210
6,7: 6-Robot-c	14	42	72	120

JEZEBEL JADE (Hanna-Barbara)
Comico: Oct, 1988 - No. 3, Dec, 1988 ($2.00, mini-series)

1-3: Johnny Quest spin-off				3.00

JEZEBELLE (See Wildstorm 2000 Annuals)
DC Comics (WildStorm): Mar, 2001 - No. 6, Aug, 2001 ($2.50, limited series)

1-6-Ben Raab-s/Steve Ellis-a				2.50

JIGGS & MAGGIE
Dell Publishing Co.: No. 18, 1941 (one shot)

Four Color 18 (#1)-(1936-38-r)	38	115	266	500

JIGGS & MAGGIE
Standard Comics/Harvey Publications No. 22 on: No. 11, 1949(June) - No. 21, 2/53; No. 22, 4/53 - No. 7, 2-3/54

11	12	36	61	100
12-15,17-21	7	21	38	55
16-Wood text illos.	8	24	45	65
22-24-Little Dot app.	6	18	32	45
25,27	6	18	29	40
26-Four pgs. partially in 3-D	14	42	72	120

NOTE: Sunday page reprints by McManus loosely blended into story continuity. Based on
Bringing Up Father strip. Advertised on covers as "All New."

JIGSAW (Big Hero Adventures)

Left margin labels: Jesse James #8 © AVON / The Jetsons #24 © H-B / Jezebelle #1 © WSP

JL

	GD2.0	FN6.0	VF8.0	NM9.4

Harvey Publ. (Funday Funnies): Sept, 1966 - No. 2, Dec, 1966 (36 pgs.)

1-Origin & 1st app.; Crandall-a (5 pgs.)	3	9	17	25
2-Man From S.R.A.M.	2	6	12	18

JIGSAW OF DOOM (See Complete Mystery No. 2)

JIM BOWIE (Formerly Danger?; Black Jack No. 20 on)
Charlton Comics: No. 16, 1955? - No. 19, Apr, 1957

16	7	21	38	55
17-19	5	15	25	35

JIM BOWIE (TV, see Western Tales)
Dell Publishing Co.: No. 893, Mar, 1958 - No. 993, May-July, 1959

Four Color 893 (#1)	5	15	35	60
993-Photo-c	5	15	35	60

JIM DANDY
Dandy Magazine (Lev Gleason): May, 1956 - No. 3, Sept, 1956 (Charles Biro)

1-Biro-c	8	24	42	60
2,3	5	15	25	35

JIM HARDY (See Giant Comics Eds., Sparkler & Treasury of Comics #2 & 5)
United Features Syndicate/Spotlight Publ.: 1939; 1942; 1947 - No. 2, 1947

Single Series 6 ('39)	40	120	232	400
Single Series 27('42)	36	108	191	330
1('47)-Spotlight Publ.	15	45	77	130
2	9	27	49	70

JIM HARDY
Spotlight/United Features Synd.: 1944 (25¢, 132 pgs.) (Tip Top, Sparkler-r)

nn-Origin Mirror Man; Triple Terror app.	40	120	232	400

JIMINY CRICKET (Disney,, see Mickey Mouse Mag. V5#3 & Walt Disney
Showcase #37)
Dell Publishing Co.: No. 701, May, 1956 - No. 989, May-July, 1959

Four Color 701	9	27	63	110
Four Color 795, 897, 989	6	18	42	80

JIMMY CORRIGAN (See Acme Novelty Library)

JIMMY DURANTE (Also see A-1 Comics)
Magazine Enterprises: No. 18, 1949 - No. 20, 1949

A-1 18,20-Photo-c	43	129	257	450

JIMMY OLSEN (See Superman's Pal...)

JIMMY WAKELY (Cowboy movie star)
National Per. Publ.: Sept-Oct, 1949 - No. 18, July-Aug, 1952 (1-13: 52pgs.)

1-Photo-c, 52 pgs. begin; Alex Toth-a; Kit Colby Girl Sheriff begins	114	342	712	1250
2-Toth-a	47	141	286	500
3,4,6,7-Frazetta in all, 3 pgs. each; Toth-a in all. 7-Last photo-c. 4-Kurtzman "Pot-Shot Pete", 1 pg; Toth-a	49	147	294	510
5,8-15,18-Toth-a; 12,14-Kubert-a (3 & 2 pgs.)	40	120	220	380
16,17	34	102	179	310

NOTE: *Gil Kane* c-10-19p.

JIM RAY'S AVIATION SKETCH BOOK
Vital Publishers: Mar-Apr, 1946 - No. 2, May-June, 1946

1-Picture stories about planes and pilots	39	117	208	360
2	27	81	145	250

JIM SOLAR (See Wisco/Klarer)

JINGLE BELLE
Oni Press: Nov, 1999 - No. 2, Dec, 1999 ($2.95, B&W, limited series)

1,2-Paul Dini-s. 2-Alex Ross flip-c	3.00
Paul Dini's Jingle Belle Jubilee (11/01, $2.95) Dini-s; art by Rolston, DeCarlo, Morrison and Bone; pin-ups by Thompson and Aragonés	3.00
Paul Dini's Jingle Belle: The Mighty Elves (7/01, $2.95) Dini-s/Bone-a	3.00
Paul Dini's Jingle Belle's All-Star Holiday Hullabaloo (11/00, $4.95) stories by various incl. Dini, Aragonés, Jeff Smith, Bill Morrison; Frank Cho-c	5.00
TPB (10/00, $8.95) r/#1&2, and app. from Oni Double Feature #13	

JINGLE BELLS (See March of Comics No. 65)

JINGLE DINGLE CHRISTMAS STOCKING COMICS (See Foodini #2)

	GD2.0	FN6.0	VF8.0	NM9.4

Stanhall Publications: V2#1, 1951 (no date listed) (25¢, 100 pgs.; giant-size) (Publ. annually)

V2#1-Foodini & Pinhead, Silly Pilly plus games & puzzles	18	54	94	160

JINGLE JANGLE COMICS (Also see Puzzle Fun Comics)
Eastern Color Printing Co.: Feb, 1942 - No. 42, Dec, 1949

1-Pie-Face Prince of Old Pretzleburg, Jingle Jangle Tales by George Carlson, Hortense, & Benny Bear begin	40	120	240	420
2-4: 2,3-No Pie-Face Prince. 4-Pie-Face Prince-c	21	63	110	185
5	20	60	105	175
6-10: 8-No Pie-Face Prince	15	45	77	130
11-15	12	36	61	100
16-30: 17,18-No Pie-Face Prince. 30-XMas-c	10	30	55	80
31-42: 36,42-Xmas-c	9	27	49	70

NOTE: *George Carlson* a-(2) in all except No. 2, 3, 8; c-1-6. *Carlson* 1 pg. puzzles in 9, 10, 12-15, 18, 20. *Carlson* illustrated a series of Uncle Wiggily books in 1930's.

JING PALS
Victory Publishing Corp.: Feb, 1946 - No. 4, Aug?, 1946 (Funny animal)

1-Wishing Willie, Puggy Panda & Johnny Rabbit begin	15	45	77	130
2-4	8	24	45	65

JINKS, PIXIE, AND DIXIE (See Kite Fun Book & Whitman Comic Books)

JINN
Image Comics (Avalon Studios): Mar, 2000 - No. 3, Oct, 2000 ($2.50)

1-3-Rearte-c/a	3.00

JINX
Caliber Press: 1996 - No. 7, 1996 ($2.95, B&W, 32 pgs.)

1-7: Brian Michael Bendis-c/a/scripts. 2-Photo-c	3.00

JINX (Volume 2)
Image Comics: 1997 - No. 5, 1998 ($2.95, B&W, bi-monthly)

1-4: Brian Michael Bendis-c/a/scripts.	3.00
5-($3.95) Brereton-c	4.00
...Buried Treasures ('98, $3.95) short stories, ...Confessions ('98, $3.95) short stories, ...Pop Culture Hoo-Hah ('98, $3.95) humor shorts	4.00
TPB (1997, $10.95) r/Vol 1,#1-4	11.00
...: The Definitive Collection ('01, $24.95) remastered #1-5, sketch pages, art gallery, script excerpts, Mack intro.	25.00

JINX: TORSO
Image Comics: 1998 - No. 6, 1999 ($3.95/$4.95, B&W)

1-6-Based on Eliot Ness' pursuit of America's first serial killer; Brian Michael Bendis & Marc Andreyko-s/Bendis-a. 3-6-($4.95)	5.00
Softcover (2000, $24.95) r/#1-6; intro. by Greg Rucka; photo essay of the actual murders and police documents	25.00
Hardcover (2000, $49.95) signed & numbered	50.00

JLA (See Justice League of America and Justice Leagues)
DC Comics: Jan, 1997 - Present ($1.95/$1.99/$2.25)

1-Morrison-s/Porter & Dell-a. The Hyperclan app.	2	6	11	15
2	1	4	7	10
3,4	1	3	6	8
5-Membership drive; Tomorrow Woman app.				6.00
6-9: 8-Green Arrow joins.				6.00
10-21: 10-Rock of Ages begins. 11-Joker and Luthor-c/app. 15-($2.95) Rock of Ages concludes. 16-New members join; Prometheus app. 17,20-Jorgensen-a. 18-21-Wald-s. 20,21-Adam Strange c/app.				5.00
22-40: 22-Begin $1.99-c; Sandman (Daniel) app. 27-Amazo app. 28-31-JSA app. 35-Hal Jordan/Spectre app. 36-40-World War 3				2.50
41-($2.99) Conclusion of World War 3; last Morrison-s				3.00
42-46: 43-Waid-s; Ra's al Ghul app. 44-Begin $2.25-c. 46-Batman leaves				2.25
47-49: 47-Hitch & Neary-a begins; JLA battles Queen of Fables				3.25
50-($3.75) JLA vs. Dr. Destiny; art by Hitch & various				3.75
51-61: 52-55-Hitch-a. 59-Mahnke-a. 61-Kelly-s/Mahnke-a				2.25
#1,000,000 (11/98) 853rd Century x-over				2.50
Annual 1 (1997, $3.95) Pulp Heroes; Augustyn-s/Olivetti & Ha-a				4.00
Annual 2 (1998, $2.95) Ghosts; Wrightson-a				4.00
Annual 3 (1999, $2.95) JLApe; Art Adams-c				3.00

JLA: The Nail #1 © DC

JLA: Tomorrow Woman #1 © DC

JLA: Year One #5 © DC

	GD2.0	FN6.0	VF8.0	NM9.4

	GD2.0	FN6.0	VF8.0	NM9.

Annual 4 (2000, $3.50) Planet DC x-over; Steve Scott-c/a — 3.50
...80-Page Giant 1 (7/98, $4.95) stories & art by various — 6.00
...80-Page Giant 2 (11/99, $4.95) Green Arrow & Hawkman app. Hitch-c — 6.00
...80-Page Giant 3 (10/00, $5.95) Pariah & Harbinger; intro. Moon Maiden — 6.00
...Foreign Bodies (1999, $5.95) Kobra app.; Semeiks-a — 6.00
...Gallery (1997, $2.95) pin-ups by various; Quitely-c — 3.00
...God & Monsters (2001, $6.95) Benefiel-a/c — 7.00
.../ Haven: Arrival (2001, $6.95) Leads into Haven: The Broken City — 7.00
...In Crisis Secret Files 1 (11/98, $4.95) recap of JLA in DC x-overs — 5.00
...: Our Worlds at War (9/01, $2.95) Aquaman presumed dead — 3.00
...Primeval (1999, $5.95) Abnett & Lanning-s/Olivetti-a — 6.00
...: Riddle of the Beast HC (2001, $24.95) Grant-s/painted-a by various — 25.00
...: Seven Caskets (2000, $5.95) Brereton-s/painted-c/a — 6.00
...Showcase 80-Page Giant (2/00, $4.95) Hitch-c — 5.00
...Superpower (1999, $5.95) Arcudi-s/Eaton-a; Mark Antaeus joins — 6.00
...Vs. Predator (DC/Dark Horse, 2000, $5.95) Nolan-c/a — 6.00
American Dreams (1998, $7.95, TPB) r/#1-4 — 8.00
Divided We Fall (2001, $17.95, TPB) r/#47-54 — 18.00
Justice For All (1999, $14.95, TPB) r/#24-33 — 15.00
New World Order (1997, $5.95, TPB) r/#1-4 — 6.00
Rock of Ages (1998, $9.95, TPB) r/#10-15 — 10.00
Strength in Numbers (1998, $12.95, TPB) r/#16-23, Secret Files #2 and Prometheus #1 — 13.00
Tower of Babel (2001, $12.95, TPB) r/#42-46, Secret Files #3, 80-Page Giant #1 — 13.00
World War III (2000, $12.95, TPB) r/#34-41 — 13.00

JLA: ACT OF GOD
DC Comics: 2000 - No. 3, 2001 ($4.95, limited series)
1-3-Elseworlds; metahumans lose their powers; Moench-s/Dave Ross-a — 5.00

JLA: A LEAGUE OF ONE
DC Comics: 2000 (Graphic novel)
Hardcover ($24.95) Christopher Moeller-s/painted-a — 25.00

JLA: BLACK BAPTISM
DC Comics: May, 2001 - No. 4, Aug, 2001 ($2.50, limited series)
1-4-Saiz-a(p)/Bradstreet-c; Zatanna app. — 2.50

JLA: CREATED EQUAL
DC Comics: 2000 - No. 2, 2000 ($5.95, limited series, prestige format)
1,2-Nicieza-s/Maguire-a; Elseworlds-Superman as the last man on Earth — 6.00

JLA: EARTH 2
DC Comics: 2000 (Graphic novel)
Hardcover ($24.95) Morrison-s/Quitely-a; Crime Syndicate app. — 25.00
Softcover ($14.95) — 15.00

JLA: GATEKEEPER
DC Comics: 2001 - No. 3, 2001 ($4.95, prestige format, limited series)
1-3-Truman-s/a — 5.00

JLA: HEAVEN'S LADDER
DC Comics: 2000 ($9.95, Treasury-size one-shot)
nn-Bryan Hitch & Paul Neary-c/a; Mark Waid-s — 10.00

JLA: INCARNATIONS
DC Comics: Jul, 2001 - No. 7, Feb, 2002 ($3.50, limited series)
1-7-Ostrander-s/Semeiks-a; different eras of the Justice League — 3.50

JLA PARADISE LOST
DC Comics: Jan, 1998 - No. 3, Mar, 1998 ($1.95, limited series)
1-3-Millar-s/Olivetti-a — 2.50

JLA SECRET FILES
DC Comics: Sept, 1997 - Present ($4.95)
1-Standard Ed. w/origin-s & pin-ups — 5.00
1-Collector's Ed. w/origin-s & pin-ups; cardstock-c — 6.00
2,3; 2-(8/98) origin-s of JLA #16's newer members. 3-(12/00) — 5.00

JLA: SECRET SOCIETY OF SUPER-HEROES
DC Comics: 2000 - No. 2, 2000 ($5.95, limited series, prestige format)
1,2-Elseworlds JLA; Chaykin and Tischman-s/McKone-a — 6.00

JLA: THE NAIL (Elseworlds)

DC Comics: Aug, 1998 - No. 3, Oct, 1998 ($4.95, prestige format)
1-3-JLA in a world without Superman; Alan Davis-s/a(p) — 5.00
TPB ('98, $12.95) r/series w/new Davis-c — 13.00

JLA / TITANS
DC Comics: Dec, 1998 - No. 3, Feb, 1999 ($2.95, limited series)
1-3-Grayson-s; P. Jimenez-c/a — 3.00
...:The Technis Imperative ('99, $12.95, TPB) r/#1-3; Titans Secret Files — 13.00

JLA: TOMORROW WOMAN (Girlfrenzy)
DC Comics: June, 1998 ($1.95, one-shot)
1-Peyer-s; story takes place during JLA #5 — 2.50

JLA/ WILDC.A.T.S
DC Comics: 1997 ($5.95, one-shot, prestige format)
1-Morrison-s/Semeiks & Conrad-a — 6.00

JLA/WITCHBLADE
DC Comics/Top Cow: 2000 ($5.95, prestige format, one-shot)
1-Pararillo-c/a — 6.00

JLA/ WORLD WITHOUT GROWN-UPS (See Young Justice)
DC Comics: Aug, 1998 - No. 2, Sept, 1998 ($4.95, prestige format)
1,2-JLA, Robin, Impulse & Superboy app.; Ramos & McKone-a — 6.00
TPB ('98, $9.95) r/series w/ Young Justice: The Secret #1 — 10.00

JLA: YEAR ONE
DC Comics: Jan, 1998 - No. 12, Dec, 1998 ($2.95/$1.95, limited series)
1-($2.95)-Waid & Augustyn-s/Kitson-a — 5.00
1-Platinum Edition — 10.00
2-8-($1.95): 5-Doom Patrol-c/app. 7-Superman app. — 4.00
9-12 — 3.00
TPB ('99, $19.95) r/#1-12; Busiek intro. — 20.00

JLX
DC Comics (Amalgam): Apr, 1996 ($1.95, one-shot)
1-Mark Waid scripts — 2.50

JLX UNLEASHED
DC Comics (Amalgam): June, 1997 ($1.95, one-shot)
1-Priest-s/ Oscar Jimenez & Rodriguez/a — 2.50

JOAN OF ARC (Also see A-1 Comics & Ideal a Classical Comic)
Magazine Enterprises: No. 21, 1949 (one shot)
A-1 21-Movie adaptation; Ingrid Bergman photo-covers & interior photos; Whitney-a — 29 — 87 — 153 — 265

JOE COLLEGE
Hillman Periodicals: Fall, 1949 - No. 2, Wint, 1950 (Teen-age humor, 52 pgs.)
1-Powell-a; Briefer-a — 12 — 36 — 61 — 100
2-Powell-a — 10 — 30 — 55 — 80

JOE JINKS
United Features Syndicate: No. 12, 1939
Single Series 12 — 31 — 93 — 165 — 285

JOE LOUIS (See Fight Comics #2, Picture News #6 & True Comics #5)
Fawcett Publications: Sept, 1950 - No. 2, Nov, 1950 (Photo-c) (Boxing champ) (See Dick Cole #10)
1-Photo-c; life story — 55 — 165 — 341 — 600
2-Photo-c — 40 — 120 — 220 — 380

JOE PALOOKA (1st Series)(Also see Big Shot Comics, Columbia Comics & Feature Funnies)
Columbia Comic Corp. (Publication Enterprises): 1942 - No. 4, 1944
1-1st to portray American president; gov't permission required — 82 — 246 — 511 — 900
2 (1943)-Hitler-c — 52 — 157 — 314 — 550
3,4: 3-Nazi Sub-c — 34 — 102 — 179 — 310

JOE PALOOKA (2nd Series) (Battle Adv. #68-74; ...Advs. #75, 77-81, 83-85, 87; Champ of the Comics #76, 82, 86, 89-93) (See All-New)
Harvey Publications: Nov, 1945 - No. 118, Mar, 1961
1 — 45 — 135 — 270 — 475
2 — 24 — 72 — 127 — 215

Joe Palooka #41 © HARV

John Byrne's Next Men #5 © John Byrne

John Carter Warlord of Mars #1 © ERB

	GD2.0	FN6.0	VF8.0	NM9.4

	GD2.0	FN6.0	VF8.0	NM9.4
3,4,6,7-1st Flyin' Fool, ends #25	15	45	77	135
5-Boy Explorers by S&K (7-8/46)	21	63	110	190
8-10	12	36	61	105
11-14,16,18-20: 14-Black Cat text-s(2). 18-Powell-a.; Little Max app.				
19-Freedom Train-c	10	30	55	85
15-Origin & 1st app. Humphrey (12/47); Super-heroine Atoma app. by Powell	15	45	77	135
17-Humphrey vs. Palooka-c/s; 1st app. Little Max	15	45	77	135
21-26,29,30: 22-Powell-a. 30-Nude female painting	8	24	45	65
27-Little Max app.; Howie Morenz-s	9	27	49	70
28-Babe Ruth 4 pg. sty.	9	27	49	70
31,39,51: 31-Dizzy Dean 4 pg. sty. 39-(12/49) Humphrey & Little Max begin; Sonny Baugh football-s; Sherlock Max-s. 51-Babe Ruth 2 pg. sty; Jake Lamotta 1/2 pg. sty	7	21	38	55
32-38,40-50,52-61: 35-Little Max-c/story(4 pgs.); Joe Louis 1 pg. sty. 36-Humphrey story. 41-Bing Crosby photo on-c. 44-Palooka marries Ann Howe. 50-(11/51)-Becomes Harvey Comics Hits #51	6	18	33	48
62-S&K Boy Explorers-r	7	21	38	55
63-65,73-80,100: 79-Story of 1st meeting with Ann	6	18	29	40
66,67-'Commie' torture story "Drug-Diet Horror"	8	24	42	60
68,70-72: 68,70-Joe vs. "Gooks"-c. 71-Bloody bayonets-c. 72-Tank-c	7	21	38	55
69-1st "Battle Adventures" issue; torture & bondage	8	24	42	60
81-99,101-115: 104,107-Humphrey & Little Max-s	5	15	25	35
116-S&K Boy Explorers-r (Giant, '60)	7	21	38	55
117-(84 pg. Giant) r/Commie issues #66,67; Powell-a	8	24	42	60
118-(84 pg. Giant) Jack Dempsey 2 pg. sty, Powell-a	7	21	38	55
..Visits the Lost City nn (1945)(One Shot)(50¢)-164 page continuous story strip reprint. Has biography & photo of Ham Fisher; possibly the single longest comic book story published in that era (159 pgs.?)	159	477	994	1750

NOTE: *Nostrand/Powell* a-73. *Powell* a-7, 8, 10, 12, 14, 17, 19, 26-45, 47-53, 70, 73 at least. *Black Cat* text stories #8, 12, 13, 19.

JOE PSYCHO & MOO FROG
Goblin Studios: 1996 - No. 5, 1997 ($2.50, B&W)

1-5: 4-Two covers				2.50
..Full Color Extravagarbonzo ($2.95, color)				3.00

JOE YANK (Korean War)
Standard Comics (Visual Editions): No. 5, Mar, 1952 - No. 16, 1954

	GD2.0	FN6.0	VF8.0	NM9.4
5-Toth, Celardo, Tuska-a	8	24	42	60
6-Toth, Severin/Elder-a	9	27	49	70
7	5	15	25	35
8-Toth-c	7	21	36	50
9-16: 9-Andru-c. 12-Andru-a	5	15	24	32

JOHN BOLTON'S HALLS OF HORROR
Eclipse Comics: June, 1985 - No. 2, June, 1985 ($1.75, limited series)

1,2-British-r; Bolton-c/a				3.00

JOHN BOLTON'S STRANGE WINK
Dark Horse Comics: Mar, 1998 - No. 3, May, 1998 ($2.95, B&W, limited series)

1-3-Anthology; Bolton-s/c/a				3.00

JOHN BYRNE'S NEXT MEN (See Dark Horse Presents #54)
Dark Horse Comics (Legend imprint #19 on): Jan, 1992 - No. 30, Dec, 1994 ($2.50, mature)

1-Silver foil embossed-c; Byrne-c/a/scripts in all				4.00
1-4: 1-2nd printing with gold ink logo				2.50
0-(2/92)-r/chapters 1-4 from DHP r/new Byrne-c				2.50
5-20,22-30: 7-10-MA #1-4 mini-series on flip side. 16-Origin of Mark IV. 17-Mother-c. 19-23-Faith storyline. 23-26-Power storyline. 27-30-Lies storyline Pt. 1-4.				2.50
21-1st Hellboy				6.00
...Parallel, Book 2 ($16.95)-TPB; r/#7-12				17.00
...Fame, Book 3($16.95)-TPB r/#13-18				17.00
..Faith, Book 4($14.95)-TPB r/#19-22				15.00

NOTE: Issues 1 through 6 contain certificates redeemable for an exclusive Next Men trading card set by Byrne. Prices are for complete books. *Cody* painted c-23-26. *Mignola* a-21(part); c-21.

JOHN BYRNE'S 2112

Dark Horse Comics (Legend): Oct, 1994 ($9.95, TPB)

1-Byrne-c/a/s				10.00

JOHN CARTER OF MARS (See The Funnies & Tarzan #207)
Dell Publishing Co.: No. 375, Mar-May, 1952 - No. 488, Aug-Oct, 1953 (Edgar Rice Burroughs)

	GD2.0	FN6.0	VF8.0	NM9.4
Four Color 375 (#1)-Origin; Jesse Marsh-a	25	75	175	320
Four Color 437, 488-Painted-c	15	45	105	200

JOHN CARTER OF MARS
Gold Key: Apr, 1964 - No. 3, Oct, 1964

	GD2.0	FN6.0	VF8.0	NM9.4
1(10104-404)-r/4-Color #375; Jesse Marsh-a	5	15	35	65
2(407), 3(410)-r/4-Color #437 & 488; Marsh-a	4	12	29	45

JOHN CARTER OF MARS
House of Greystroke: 1970 (10-1/2x16-1/2", 72 pgs., B&W, paper-c)

	GD2.0	FN6.0	VF8.0	NM9.4
1941-42 Sunday strip-r; John Coleman Burroughs-a	3	9	21	32

JOHN CARTER, WARLORD OF MARS (Also see Weird Worlds)
Marvel Comics: June, 1977 - No. 28, Oct, 1979

	GD2.0	FN6.0	VF8.0	NM9.4
1,18: 1-Origin. 18-Frank Miller-a(p)(1st publ. Marvel work)	1	3	5	7
1-(35¢ variant, limited dist.)	1	4	7	10
2-5-(35¢-c variants, limited dist.)				6.00
2-17,19-28: 11-Origin Dejah Thoris				4.00
Annuals 1-3: 1(1977). 2(1978). 3(1979)-All 52 pgs. with new book-length stories				4.00

NOTE: *Austin* c-24i. *Gil Kane* a-1-10p; c-1p, 2p, 3, 4-9p, 10, 15p, Annual 1p. *Layton* a-17i. *Miller* c-25, 26p. *Nebres* a-2-4i, 8-16i; c(i)-6-9, 11-22, 25, Annual 1. *Perez* c-24p. *Simonson* a-15p. *Sutton* a-7i.

JOHN F. KENNEDY, CHAMPION OF FREEDOM
Worden & Childs: 1964 (no month) (25¢)

	GD2.0	FN6.0	VF8.0	NM9.4
nn-Photo-c	8	24	56	90

JOHN F. KENNEDY LIFE STORY
Dell Publishing Co.: Aug-Oct, 1964; Nov, 1965; June, 1966 (12¢)

	GD2.0	FN6.0	VF8.0	NM9.4
12-378-410-Photo-c	6	18	42	75
12-378-511 (reprint, 11/65)	3	10	23	35
12-378-606 (reprint, 6/66)	3	9	20	30

JOHN FORCE (See Magic Agent)

JOHN HIX SCRAP BOOK, THE
Eastern Color Printing Co. (McNaught Synd.): Late 1930's (no date) (10¢, 68 pgs., regular size)

	GD2.0	FN6.0	VF8.0	NM9.4
1-Strange As It Seems (resembles Single Series books)				
	39	117	208	360
2-Strange As It Seems	27	81	145	250

JOHN JAKES' MULLKON EMPIRE
Tekno Comix: Sept, 1995 - No. 6, Feb, 1996 ($1.95)

1-6				2.25

JOHN LAW DETECTIVE (See Smash Comics #3)
Eclipse Comics: April, 1983 ($1.50, Baxter paper)

1-Three Eisner stories originally drawn in 1948 for the never published John Law #1; original cover pencilled in 1948 & inked in 1982 by Eisner				3.00

JOHNNY APPLESEED (See Story Hour Series)

JOHNNY CASH (See Hello, I'm...)

JOHNNY DANGER (See Movie Comics, 1946)
Toby Press: 1950 (Based on movie serial)

	GD2.0	FN6.0	VF8.0	NM9.4
1-Photo-c; Sparling-a	18	54	94	155

JOHNNY DANGER PRIVATE DETECTIVE
Toby Press: Aug, 1954 (Reprinted in Danger #11 by Super)

	GD2.0	FN6.0	VF8.0	NM9.4
1-Photo-c; Opium den story	14	42	72	120

JOHNNY DYNAMITE (Formerly Dynamite #1-9; Foreign Intrigues #14 on)
Charlton Comics: No. 10, June, 1955 - No. 12, Oct, 1955

	GD2.0	FN6.0	VF8.0	NM9.4
10-12	9	27	49	70

JOHNNY DYNAMITE
Dark Horse Comics: Sept, 1994 - Dec, 1994 ($2.95, B&W & red, limited series)

1-4: Max Allan Collins scripts in all.				3.00

Johnny Mack Brown #2 © JMB

John Wayne Adventure Comics #12 © TOBY

Joker Comics #1 © MAR

	GD2.0	FN6.0	VF8.0	NM9.4			GD2.0	FN6.0	VF8.0	NM9.

JOHNNY HAZARD
Best Books (Standard Comics) (King Features): No. 5, Aug, 1948 - No. 8, May, 1949; No. 35, date?

5-Strip reprints by Frank Robbins (c/a)	20	60	105	175
6,8-Strip reprints by Frank Robbins	17	51	88	150
7,35: 7-New art, not Robbins	11	33	55	90

JOHNNY JASON (...Teen Reporter)
Dell Publishing Co.: Feb-Apr, 1962 - No. 2, June-Aug, 1962

Four Color 1302, 2(01380-208)	4	12	25	38

JOHNNY LAW, SKY RANGER
Good Comics (Lev Gleason): Apr, 1955 - No. 3, Aug, 1955; No. 4, Nov, 1955

1-Edmond Good-c/a	10	30	55	80
2-4	6	18	32	45

JOHNNY MACK BROWN (Western star; see Western Roundup under Dell Giants)
Dell Publishing Co.: No. 269, Mar, 1950 - No. 963, Feb, 1959 (All Photo-c)

Four Color 269(#1)(3/50, 52pgs.)-Johnny Mack Brown & his horse Rebel begin; photo front/back-c begin; Marsh-a in #1-9	23	69	161	300
2(10-12/50, 52pgs.)	12	36	84	150
3(1-3/51, 52pgs.)	9	27	63	115
4-10 (9-11/52)(36pgs.), Four Color 455,493,541,584,618,645,685,722,776, 834,963	6	18	42	80
Four Color 922-Manning-a	7	21	49	85

JOHNNY NEMO
Eclipse Comics: Sept, 1985 - No. 3, Feb, 1986 (Mini-series)

1-3				2.50

JOHNNY PERIL (See Comic Cavalcade #15, Danger Trail #5, Sensation Comics #107 & Sensation Mystery)

JOHNNY RINGO (TV)
Dell Publishing Co.: No. 1142, Nov-Jan, 1960/61 (one shot)

Four Color 1142-Photo-c	7	21	49	90

JOHNNY STARBOARD (See Wisco)

JOHNNY THE HOMICIDAL MANIAC
Slave Labor Graphics: Aug, 1995 - No. 7, Jan, 1997 ($2.95, B&W, lim. series)

1-Jhonen Vasquez-c/s/a	1	4	7	10
1-Signed & numbered edition	2	6	11	15
2,3: 2-(11/95). 3-(2/96)				6.00
4-7: 4-(5/96). 5-(8/96)				4.00
Hardcover-($29.95) r/#1-7				30.00
TPB-($19.95)				20.00

JOHNNY THUNDER
National Periodical Publications: Feb-Mar, 1973 - No. 3, July-Aug, 1973

1-Johnny Thunder & Nighthawk-r. in all	2	6	12	18
2,3: 2-Trigger Twins app.	2	6	9	12

NOTE: All contain 1950s DC reprints from All-American Western. Drucker r-2, 3. G. Kane r-2, 3. Moriera r-1. Toth r-1, 3; c-1r, 3r. Also see All-American, All-Star Western, Flash Comics, Western Comics, World's Best & World's Finest.

JOHN PAUL JONES
Dell Publishing Co.: No. 1007, July-Sept, 1959 (one-shot)

Four Color 1007-Movie, Robert Stack photo-c	5	15	35	60

JOHN STEED & EMMA PEEL (See The Avengers, Gold Key series)

JOHN STEELE SECRET AGENT (Also see Freedom Agent)
Gold Key: Dec, 1964

1-Freedom Agent	8	24	56	105

JOHN WAYNE ADVENTURE COMICS (Movie star; See Big Tex, Oxydol-Dreft, Tim McCoy, & With The Marines...#1)
Toby Press: Winter, 1949-50 - No. 31, May, 1955 (Photo-c: 1-12,17,25-on)

1 (36pgs.)-Photo-c begin (1st time in comics on-c)	155	465	1240	2700
2-4: 2-(4/50, 36pgs.)-Williamson/Frazetta-a(2) 6 & 2 pgs. (one story-r/Billy the Kid #1); photo back-c. 3-(36pgs.)-Williamson/Frazetta-a(2), 16 pgs. total; photo back-c. 4-(52pgs.)-Williamson/Frazetta-a(2), 16 pgs. total	68	204	426	750
5 (52pgs.)-Kurtzman-a(Alfred "L" Newman in Potshot Pete				

	48	144	288	505
6 (52pgs.)-Williamson/Frazetta-a (10 pgs.); Kurtzman-a "Pot-Shot Pete", (5 pgs.); & "Genius Jones", (1 pg.)	59	177	369	650
7 (52pgs.)-Williamson/Frazetta-a (10 pgs.)	52	157	314	550
8 (36pgs.)-Williamson/Frazetta-a(2) (12 & 9 pgs.)	64	192	398	700
9-11: Photo western-c	38	114	203	350
12,14-Photo war-c. 12-Kurtzman-a(2 pg.) "Genius"	38	114	203	350
13,15: 13,15-Line-drawn-c begin, end #24	34	102	179	310
16-Williamson/Frazetta-r/Billy the Kid #1	37	111	197	340
17-Photo-c	37	111	197	340
18-Williamson/Frazetta-a (r/#4 & 8, 19 pgs.)	40	120	220	380
19-24: 23-Evans-a?	31	93	165	285
25-Photo-c resume; end #31; Williamson/Frazetta-r/Billy the Kid #3	40	120	214	370
26-28,30-Photo-c	35	105	185	320
29,31-Williamson/Frazetta-a in each (r/#4, 2)	39	117	208	360

NOTE: Williamsonish art in later issues by Gerald McCann.

JO-JO COMICS (...Congo King #7-29; My Desire #30 on)
(Also see Fantastic Fears and Jungle Jo)
Fox Feature Syndicate: 1945 - No. 29, July, 1949 (Two No.7's; no #13)

nn(1945)-Funny animal, humor	17	51	88	150
2(Sum,'46)-6(4-5/47)-Funny animal. 2-Ten pg. Electro story (Fall/46)	10	30	55	80
7(7/47)-Jo-Jo, Congo King begins (1st app.); Bronze Man & Purple Tigress app.	89	267	556	975
7(#8) (9/47)	64	192	398	700
8-10(#9-11): 8-Tanee begins	55	165	330	575
11,12(#12,13),14,16: 11,16-Kamen bondage-c	47	141	286	500
15,17: 15-Cited by Dr. Wertham in 5/47 Saturday Review of Literature.	55	165	330	575
17-Kamen bondage-c	50	150	300	525
18-20	47	141	286	500
21-29: 21-Hollingsworth-a(4 pgs.; 23-1 pg.)	40	120	232	400

NOTE: Many bondage-c/a by Baker/Kamen/Feldstein/Good. No. 7's have Princesses Gwenna, Geesa, Yolda, & Safra before settling down on Tanee.

JOKEBOOK COMICS DIGEST ANNUAL (...Magazine No. 5 on)
Archie Publications: Oct, 1977 - No. 13, Oct, 1983 (Digest Size)

1(10/77)-Reprints; Neal Adams-a	2	6	11	16
2(4/78)-5	2	6	9	12
6-11	1	3	6	9

JOKER, THE (See Batman #1, Batman: The Killing Joke, Brave & the Bold, Detective, Greatest Joker Stories & Justice League Annual #2)
National Periodical Publications: May, 1975 - No. 9, Sept-Oct, 1976

1-Two-Face app.	4	12	26	40
2,3: 3-The Creeper app.	2	6	13	20
4-9: 4-Green Arrow-c/sty. 6-Sherlock Holmes-c/sty. 7-Lex Luthor-c/story. 8-Scarecrow-c/story. 9-Catwoman-c/story	2	6	11	15

JOKER, THE (See Tangent Comics/ The Joker)

JOKER COMICS (Adventures Into Terror No. 43 on)
Timely/Marvel Comics No. 36 on (TCI/CDS): Apr, 1942 - No. 42, Aug, 1950

1-(Rare)-Powerhouse Pepper (1st app.) begins by Wolverton; Stuporman app. from Daring Comics	255	765	1591	2800
2-Wolverton-a; 1st app. Tessie the Typist & begin series	86	258	540	950
3-5-Wolverton-a	55	165	330	575
6-10-Wolverton-a. 6-Tessie-c begin	40	120	226	390
11-20-Wolverton-a	34	102	179	310
21,22,24-27,29,30-Wolverton cont'd. & Kurtzman's "Hey Look" in #23-27	29	87	153	265
23-1st "Hey Look" by Kurtzman; Wolverton-a	31	93	165	285
28,32,34,37-41: 28-Millie the Model begins. 32-Hedy begins. 41-Nellie the Nurse app.	10	30	55	80
31-Last Powerhouse Pepper; not in #28	22	66	116	200
33,35,36-Kurtzman's "Hey Look"	11	33	55	90
42-Only app. 'Patty Pinup', clone of Millie the Model	10	30	55	85

JOKER: DEVIL'S ADVOCATE
DC Comics: 1996 ($24.95/$12.95, one-shot)

nn-(Hardcover)-Dixon scripts/Nolan & Hanna-a				25.00

Joker: Last Laugh #1 © DC

Jonah Hex #39 © DC

Josie and the Pussycats #45 © DDC

	GD2.0	FN6.0	VF8.0	NM9.4

nn-(Softcover)				13.00

JOKER: LAST LAUGH
DC Comics: Dec, 2001 - No. 6, Jan, 2002 ($2.95, weekly limited series)
1-6: 1,6-Bolland-c				3.00
...Secret Files (12/01, $5.95) Short stories by various; Simonson-c				6.00

JOKER / MASK
Dark Horse Comics: May, 2000 - No. 4, Aug, 2000 ($2.95, limited series)
1-4-Batman, Harley Quinn, Poison Ivy app.				3.00

JOLLY CHRISTMAS, A (See March of Comics No. 269)

JOLLY COMICS: Four Star Publishing Co.: 1947 (Advertised, not published)

JOLLY JINGLES (Formerly Jackpot Comics)
MLJ Magazines: No. 10, Sum, 1943 - No. 16, Wint, 1944/45
10-Super Duck begins (origin & 1st app.); Woody The Woodpecker begins (not same as Lantz character)	39	117	208	360
11 (Fall, '43)-2nd Super Duck(see Hangman #8)	20	60	105	175
12-Hitler-c	23	69	121	210
13-16: 13-Sahle-c. 15-Vigoda-c	13	39	66	110

JONAH HEX (See All-Star Western, Hex and Weird Western Tales)
National Periodical Pub./DC Comics: Mar-Apr, 1977 - No. 92, Aug, 1985
1	8	24	60	100
2	4	12	26	40
3,4,9: 9-Wrightson-c.	3	10	23	35
5,6,10: 5-Rep 1st app. from All-Star Western #10	3	9	17	25
7,8-Explains Hex's face disfigurement (origin)	4	12	26	40
11-20: 12-Starlin-c	2	6	11	15
21-32: 31,32-Origin retold	1	4	7	10
33-50	1	3	5	7
51-80				5.00
81-91: 89-Mark Teixeira-a				4.00
92-Story cont'd in Hex #1	2	6	12	18
NOTE: **Ayers** a(p)-35-37, 40, 41, 44-53, 56, 58-82. **Buckler** c-11, 13-16. **Kubert** c-43-46.
Morrow a-90-92; c-10. **Spiegle(Tothish)** a-34, 38, 40, 49, 52. **Teixeira** a-89d. Batlash back-ups in 49, 52. El Diablo back-ups in 48, 56-60, 73-75. Scalphunter back-ups in 40, 41, 45-47.

JONAH HEX AND OTHER WESTERN TALES (Blue Ribbon Digest)
DC Comics: Sept-Oct, 1979 - No. 3, Jan-Feb, 1980 (100 pgs.)
1-3: 1-Origin Scalphunter-r, Ayers/Evans, Neal Adams-a.; painted-c. 2-Weird Western Tales-r; Neal Adams, Toth, Aragones-a. 3-Outlaw-r, Scalphunter-r; Gil Kane, Wildey-a	2	6	9	12

JONAH HEX: RIDERS OF THE WORM AND SUCH
DC Comics (Vertigo): Mar, 1995 - No. 5, July, 1995 ($2.95, limited series)
1-5-Lansdale story, Truman -a				4.00

JONAH HEX: SHADOWS WEST
DC Comics (Vertigo): Feb, 1999 - No. 3, Apr, 1999 ($2.95, limited series)
1-3-Lansdale-s/Truman -a				4.00

JONAH HEX SPECTACULAR (See DC Special Series No. 16)

JONAH HEX: TWO-GUN MOJO
DC Comics (Vertigo): Aug, 1993 - No. 5, Dec, 1993 ($2.95, limited series)
1-Lansdale scripts in all; Truman/Glanzman-a in all w/Truman-c				6.00
1-Platinum edition with no price on cover				20.00
2-5				4.00
TPB-(1994, $12.95) r/#1-5				13.00

JONESY (Formerly Crack Western)
Comic Favorite/Quality Comics Group: No. 85, Aug, 1953; No. 2, Oct, 1953 - No. 8, Oct, 1954
85(#1)-Teen-age humor	7	21	38	55
2	5	15	24	32
3-8	4	12	19	25

JON JUAN (Also see Great Lover Romances)
Toby Press: Spring, 1950
1-All Schomburg-a (signed Al Reid on-c); written by Siegel; used in **SOTI**, pg. 38 (Scarce)	59	177	369	650

JONNI THUNDER (...A.K.A. Thunderbolt)
DC Comics: Feb, 1985 - No. 4, Aug, 1985 (75¢, limited series)

1-4: 1-Origin & 1st app.				2.25

JONNY DEMON
Dark Horse Comics: May, 1994 - No. 3, July, 1994 ($2.50, limited series)
1-3				2.50

JONNY DOUBLE
DC Comics (Vertigo): Sept, 1998 - No. 4, Dec, 1998 ($2.95, limited series)
1-4-Azzarello-s				3.00

JONNY QUEST (TV)
Gold Key: Dec, 1964 (Hanna-Barbera)
1 (10139-412)	35	105	245	450

JONNY QUEST (TV)
Comico: June 1986 - No. 31, Dec, 1988 ($1.50/$1.75)(Hanna-Barbera)
1				5.00
2,3,5: 3,5-Dave Stevens-c				4.00
4,6-31: 30-Adapts TV episode				3.00
Special 1(9/88, $1.75), 2(10/88, $1.75)				4.00
NOTE: **M. Anderson** a-9. **Mooney** a-Special 1. **Pini** a-2. **Quagmire** a-31p. **Rude** a-1; c-2i.
Sienkiewicz c-11. **Spiegle** a-7, 12, 21; c-21 **Staton** a-2i, 11p. **Steacy** c-8. **Stevens** a-4i; c-3,5.
Wildey a-1, c-1, 7, 12. **Williamson** a-4i; c-4i.

JONNY QUEST CLASSICS (TV)
Comico: May, 1987 - No. 3, July, 1987 ($2.00) (Hanna-Barbera)
1-3-Wildey-c/a; 3-Based on TV episode				3.00

JON SABLE, FREELANCE (Also see Mike Grell's Sable & Sable)
First Comics: 6/83 - No. 56, 2/88 (#1-17, $1; #18-33, $1.25, #34-on, $1.75)
1-Mike Grell-c/a/scripts				3.00
2-56: 3-5-Origin, parts 1-3. 6-Origin, part 4. 11-1st app. of Maggie the Cat. 14-Mando paper begins. 16-Maggie the Cat app. 25-30-Shatter app. 34-Deluxe format begins ($1.75)				2.25
NOTE: **Aragones** a-33; c-33(part). **Grell** a-1-43;c-1-52, 53p, 54-56.

JOSEPH & HIS BRETHREN (See The Living Bible)

JOSIE (She's... #1-16) (...the Pussycats #45 on) (See Archie Giant Series Magazine #528, 540, 551, 562, 571, 584, 597, 610, 622)
Archie Publ./Radio Comics: Feb, 1963; No. 2, Aug, 1963 - No. 106, Oct, 1982
1	17	51	118	210
2	9	27	63	105
3-5	6	18	42	70
6-10	4	12	29	45
11-20	3	10	23	35
21, 23-30	3	9	17	25
22 (9/66)-Mighty Man & Mighty (Josie Girl) app.	4	12	26	40
31-44	2	6	13	20
45 (12/69)-Josie and the Pussycats begins (Hanna Barbera TV cartoon); 1st app. of the Pussycats	8	24	50	100
46-2nd app./1st cover Pussycats	6	18	40	65
47-3rd app. of the Pussycats	3	10	23	35
48,49-Pussycats band-c/s	4	12	29	45
50-J&P-c; go to Hollywood, meet Hanna & Barbera	5	15	38	60
51-54	3	9	19	28
55-74 (2/74)(52pg. issues)	3	9	17	25
75-90(8/76)	2	6	10	14
91-99	2	6	10	14
100 (10/79)	2	6	12	18
101-106	2	6	11	16

JOSIE & THE PUSSYCATS (TV)
Archie Comics: 1993 - No. 2, 1994 ($2.00, 52 pgs.)(Published annually)
1,2-Bound-in pull-out poster in each. 2-(Spr/94)				4.00

JOURNAL OF CRIME (See Fox Giants)

JOURNEY
Aardvark-Vanaheim #1-14/Fantagraphics Books #15-on: 1983 - No. 14, 9/84; No. 15, 4/85 - No. 27, 7/86 (B&W)
1				3.00
2-27: 20-Sam Kieth-a				2.25

JOURNEY INTO FEAR
Superior-Dynamic Publications: May, 1951 - No. 21, Sept, 1954

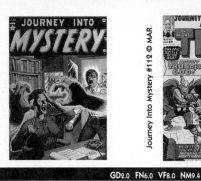

Journey Into Mystery #1 © MAR

Journey Into Mystery #112 © MAR

Journey Into Unknown Worlds #14 © MAR

	GD2.0	FN6.0	VF8.0	NM9.4
1-Baker-r(2)	62	186	388	685
2	43	129	257	450
3,4	40	120	217	375
5-10,15: 15-Used in **SOTI**, pg. 389	27	81	145	250
11-14,16-21	25	75	133	230

NOTE: *Kamenish 'headlight'-a most issues. Robinson a-10.*

JOURNEY INTO MYSTERY (1st Series) (Thor Nos. 126-502)
Atlas(CPS No. 1-48/AMI No. 49-68/Marvel No. 69 (6/61) on): 6/52 - No. 48, 8/57; No. 49, 11/58 - No. 125, 2/66; 503, 11/96 - No. 521, June, 1998

1-Weird/horror stories begin	300	900	1875	3500
2	103	309	644	1150
3,4	77	231	483	850
5-11	55	165	330	575
12-20,22: 15-Atomic explosion panel. 22-Davisesque-a; last pre-code issue (2/55)	42	126	252	440
21-Kubert-a; Tothish-a by Andru	43	129	257	450
23-32,35-38,40: 24-Torres?-a. 38-Ditko-a	30	90	159	275
33-Williamson-a; Ditko-a (his 1st for Atlas?)	34	102	179	310
34,39: 34-Krigstein-a. 39-1st S.A. issue; Wood-a	31	93	165	285
41-Crandall-a; Frazettaesque-a by Morrow	19	57	134	240
42,46,48: 42,48-Torres-a. 46-Torres & Krigstein-a	19	57	132	235
43,44-Williamson/Mayo-a in both	20	60	140	250
45,47,50,52-54: 50-Davis-a. 54-Williamson-a	18	54	123	220
49-Matt Fox, Check-a	19	57	132	235
51-Kirby/Wood-a	21	63	146	260
55-61,63-65,67-69,71,72,74,75: 74-Contents change to Fantasy. 75-Last 10¢ issue	55	165	330	575
75-Last 10¢ issue	42	126	252	440
62-Prototype ish. (The Hulk); 1st app. Xemnu (Titan) called "The Hulk"	28	84	196	350
66-Prototype ish. (The Hulk)-Return of Xemnu "The Hulk"	25	75	174	310
70-Prototype ish. (The Sandman)(7/61); similar to Spidey villain	24	72	165	295
73-Story titled "The Spider" where a spider is exposed to radiation & gets powers of a human and shoots webbing; a reverse prototype of Spider-Man's origin	35	105	262	475
76,77,80-82: 80-Anti-communist propaganda story	15	45	105	180
76-(10¢ cover price blacked out, 12¢ printed on)	31	93	222	400
78-The Sorcerer (Dr. Strange prototype) app. (3/62)	24	72	165	295
79-Prototype issue. (Mr. Hyde)	21	63	146	260
83-Origin & 1st app. The Mighty Thor by Kirby (8/62) and begin series; Thor-c also begin	331	993	2980	6300
83-Reprint from the Golden Record Comic Set	12	36	84	140
With the record (1966)	17	51	118	210
84-2nd app. Thor	88	264	744	1400
85-1st app. Loki & Heimdall; Odin cameo (1 panel)	56	169	478	900
86-1st full app. Odin	41	123	331	600
87-89: 89-Origin Thor retold	31	93	222	400
90-No Kirby-a	20	60	140	250
91,92,94,96-Sinnott-a	16	48	112	200
93,97-Kirby-a; Tales of Asgard series begins #97 (origin which concludes in #99) 97-Origin/1st app. Lava Man	18	54	129	230
95-Sinnott-a	17	51	120	215
98-100-Kirby/Heck-a. 98-Origin/1st app. The Human Cobra. 99-1st app. Surtur & Mr. Hyde	14	42	102	175
101,108: 101-(2/64)-2nd Avengers x-over (w/o Capt. America); see Tales of Suspense #49 for 1st x-over. 108-(9/64)-Early Dr. Strange & Avengers x-over; ten extra pgs. Kirby-a.	10	30	73	125
102,104-107,110: 102-Intro Sif. 105-109-Ten extra pgs. Kirby-a in each.				
107-1st app. Grey Gargoyle	9	27	65	110
103-1st app. Enchantress	10	30	70	120
109-Magneto-c & app. (1st x-over, 10/64)	13	39	94	160
111,113,116-123,125: 113-Origin Loki. 118-1st app. Destroyer. 119-Intro Hogun, Fandrall, Volstagg	8	24	60	100
112-Thor Vs. Hulk (1/65); Origin Loki	22	66	157	280
114-Origin/1st app. Absorbing Man	10	30	70	120
115-Detailed origin of Loki	10	30	73	125
124-Hercules-c/story	9	27	65	110
503-521: 503-(11/96, \$1.50)-The Lost Gods begin; Tom DeFalco scripts &				

Deodato Studios-c/a. 505-Spider-Man-c/app. 509-Loki-c/app. 514-516-Shang-Chi				2.50
#(-1) Flashback (7/97) Tales of Asgard Donald Blake app.				2.50
Annual 1(1965, 25¢, 72 pgs.)-New Thor vs. Hercules(1st app.)-c/story (see Incredible Hulk #3); Kirby-c/a; r/#85,93,95,97	18	54	129	230

NOTE: *Ayers a-14, 39, 64i, 71i, 74i, 80i. Bailey a-43. Briefer a-5, 12. Cameron a-35. Check a-17. Colan a-23. Ditko a-33, 38, 50-96; c-58, 67, 71, 88i. Kirby/Ditko a-50-83. Everett a-20, 48; c-4-7, 9, 36, 37, 39-42, 44, 45, 47. Forte a-19, 35, 40, 53. Heath a-4-6, 11, 14; c-1, 8, 11, 15, 51. Heck a-53, 73. Kirby a(p)-51, 52, 56, 57, 60, 62, 64, 66, 69, 71-74, 76, 79, 80-89, 93, 97, 98, 100(w/Heck). 101-125; c-50-57, 59-66, 68-70, 72-82, 88(w/Ditko), 83 & 84(w/Sinnott), 85-96(w/Ayers), 97-125p. Leiber/Fox a-93, 98-102. Maneely c-20-22. Morisi a-41, 42. Orlando a-30, 45, 57. Mac Pakula (Tothish) a-9, 35, 41. Powell a-20, 27, 34. Reinman a-39, 87, 92, 96i. Robinson a-9. Roussos a-39. Robert Sale a-14. Severin a-27; c-30. Sinnott a-41; c-10. Tuska a-11. Wildey a-16.*

JOURNEY INTO MYSTERY (2nd Series)
Marvel Comics: Oct, 1972 - No. 19, Oct, 1975

1-Robert Howard adaptation; Starlin/Ploog-a	3	9	17	25
2-5: 2,3,5-Bloch adapt. 4-H. P. Lovecraft adapt.	2	6	12	18
6-19: Reprints	2	6	9	12

NOTE: *N. Adams a-2i. Ditko r-7, 10, 12, 14, 15, 19; c-10. Everett r-9, 14i. G. Kane a-1p, 2p; c-1-3p. Kirby r-7, 13, 15, 18, 19; c-7. Mort Lawrence a-10. Maneely r-13. Orlando r-16. Reese a-1, 2i. Starlin a-1p, 3p. Torres r-16. Wildey r-9, 14.*

JOURNEY INTO UNKNOWN WORLDS (Formerly Teen)
Atlas Comics (WFP): No. 36, 9/50 - No. 38, 2/51; No. 4, 4/51 - No. 59, 8/57

36(#1)-Science fiction/weird; "End Of The Earth" c/story	227	681	1420	2500
37(#2)-Science fiction; "When Worlds Collide" c/story; Everett-c/a; Hitler story	100	300	625	1100
38(#3)-Science fiction	84	252	525	925
4-6,8,10-Science fiction/weird	55	165	330	575
7-Wolverton-a "Planet of Terror", 6 pgs; electric chair c-inset/story	89	267	556	975
9-Giant eyeball story	64	192	398	700
11,12-Krigstein-a	40	120	220	380
13,16,17,20	35	105	185	320
14-Wolverton-a "One of Our Graveyards Is Missing", 4 pgs; Tuska-a	66	198	413	725
15-Wolverton-a "They Crawl by Night", 5 pgs.; 2 pg. Maneely s/f story	66	198	413	725
18,19-Matt Fox-a	40	120	214	370
21-33: 21-Decapitation-c. 24-Sci/fic story. 26-Atom bomb panel. 27-Sid Check-a. 33-Last pre-code (2/55)	27	81	142	245
34-Kubert, Torres-a	21	63	110	185
35-Torres-a	17	51	99	165
36-45,48,50,53,55,59: 43-Krigstein-a. 44-Davis-a. 45,55,59-Williamson-a in all; with Mayo #55,59. 55-Crandall-a. 48,53-Crandall-a (4 pgs. #48). 48-Check-a. 50-Davis-Crandall-a	18	54	94	155
46,47,49,52,54,56-58: 54-Torres-a	16	48	83	140
51-Ditko, Wood-a	20	60	105	175

NOTE: *Ayers a-24, 43, Berg a-38(#3), 43. Lou Cameron a-33. Colan a-37(#2), 6, 17, 19, 20, 23, 39. Ditko a-45, 51. Drucker a-35, 58. Everett a-37(#2), 11, 14, 41, 55, 56i; c-37(#2), 11, 13, 14, 17, 22, 47, 48, 50, 53-55, 59. Forte a-49. Fox a-21i. Heath a-36(#1), 4, 6-8, 17, 20, 22, 36i; c-18. Keller a-15. Mort Lawrence a-38, 39. Maneely a-7, 8, 15, 16, 22, 49, 58; c-19, 25, 52. Morrow a-48. Orlando a-44, 57. Pakula a-36. Powell a-42, 53, 54. Reinman a-8. Rico a-21. Robert Sale a-24, 49. Sekowsky a-1. Severin a-38, 51; c-38, 48i, 56. Sinnott a-9, 21, 24. Tuska a-38(#3), 14. Wildey a-25, 43, 44.*

JOURNEYMAN
Image Comics: Aug, 1999 - No. 3, Oct, 1999 ($2.95, B&W, limited series)

1-3-Brandon McKinney-s/a				3.00

JOURNEY TO THE CENTER OF THE EARTH (Movie)
Dell Publishing Co.: No. 1060, Nov-Jan, 1959/60 (one-shot)

Four Color 1060-Pat Boone & James Mason photo-c	12	36	84	150

JSA (Justice Society of America) (Also see All Star Comics)
DC Comics: Aug, 1999 - Present ($2.50)

1-Robinson and Goyer-s; funeral of Wesley Dodds				4.00
2-5: 4-Return of the Dark				3.00
6-24: 6-Black Adam-c/app. 11,12-Kobra. 16-20-JSA vs. Johnny Sorrow. 19,20-Spectre app. 22-Hawkgirl origin. 23-Hawkman returns				2.50
25-($3.75) Hawkman rejoins the JSA				4.00
26-31: 27-Capt. Marvel app. 29-Joker: Last Laugh. 31-Snejbjerg-a				2.50

JSA #23 © DC

Judomaster #94 © CC

Jughead #20 © AP

	GD2.0	FN6.0	VF8.0	NM9.4

Annual 1 (10/00, $3.50) Planet DC; intro. Nemesis — 3.50
.: Our Worlds at War 1 (9/01, $2.95) Jae Lee-c; Saltares-a — 3.00
. Secret Files 1 (8/99, $4.95) Origin stories and pin-ups; death of Wesley Dodds
  (G.A. Sandman); intro Hawkgirl — 5.00
.. Secret Files 2 (9/01, $4.95) Short stories and profile pages — 5.00
ustice Be Done TPB (2000, $14.95) r/Secret Files & #1-5 — 15.00

SA: THE LIBERTY FILE (Elseworlds)
C Comics: Feb, 2000 - No. 2, Mar, 2000 ($6.95, limited series)
1,2-Batman, Dr. Mid-Nite and Hourman vs. WW2 Joker — 7.00

#2 (Also see A-Next and Juggernaut)
Marvel Comics: Oct, 1998 - No. 12, Sept, 1999 ($1.99)
1-Juggernaut's son; Lim-a — 2.50
2-12: 2-Two covers; X-People app. 3-J2 battles the Hulk — 2.25

UDE, THE FORGOTTEN SAINT
Catechetical Guild Education Soc.: 1954 (16 pgs.; 8x11"; full color; paper-c)
nn | 4 | 10 | 15 | 20

.U.D.G.E.: THE SECRET RAGE
Image Comics: Mar, 2000 - No. 3 ($2.95)
1-3-Greg Horn-s/c/a — 3.00

UDGE COLT
Gold Key: Oct, 1969 - No. 4, Sept, 1970
1 | 2 | 6 | 15 | 22
2-4 | 2 | 6 | 9 | 12

UDGE DREDD (...Classics #62 on; also see Batman - Judge Dredd, The Law
of Dredd & 2000 A.D. Monthly)
**Eagle Comics/IPC Magazines Ltd./Quality Comics #34-35, V2#1-37/
Fleetway #38 on:** Nov, 1983 - No. 35, 1986; V2#1, Oct, 1986 - No. 77, 1993
1-Bolland-c/a — 6.00
2-35 — 3.00
V2#1-77: 1-('86)-New look begins. 20-Begin $1.50-c. 21/22, 23/24-Two issue
  numbers in one. 28-1st app. Megaman (super-hero). 39-Begin $1.75-c.
  51-Begin $1.95-c. 53-Bolland-a. 57-Reprints 1st published Judge Dredd
  story — 2.50
Special 1 — 2.50
NOTE: *Bolland* a-1-6, 8, 10; c-1-10, 15. *Guice* c-V2#23/24, 26, 27.

UDGE DREDD (3rd Series)
DC Comics: Aug, 1994 - No. 18, Jan, 1996 ($1.95)
1-18: 1-Begin $2.25-c — 2.50
n ($5.95)-Movie adaptation, Sienkiewicz-c — 6.00

UDGE DREDD'S CRIME FILE
Eagle Comics: Aug, 1989 - No. 6, Feb, 1986 ($1.25, limited series)
1-6: 1-Byrne-a — 2.50

UDGE DREDD: LEGENDS OF THE LAW
C Comics: Dec, 1994 - No. 13, Dec, 1995 ($1.95)
1-13: 1-5-Dorman-c — 2.50

UDGE DREDD: THE EARLY CASES
Eagle Comics: Feb, 1986 - No. 6, Jul, 1986 ($1.25, Mega-series, Mando paper)
1-6: 2000 A.D.-r — 2.50

UDGE DREDD: THE JUDGE CHILD QUEST (Judge Child in indicia)
Eagle Comics: Aug, 1984 - No. 5, Oct, 1984 ($1.25, Lim. series, Baxter paper)
1-5: 2000A.D.-r; Bolland-c/a — 2.50

UDGE DREDD: THE MEGAZINE
Fleetway/Quality: 1991 - Present ($4.95, stiff-c, squarebound, 52 pgs.)
1-3 — 5.00

UDGE PARKER
Argo: Feb, 1956 - No. 2, 1956
1-Newspaper strip reprints | 6 | 18 | 32 | 45
2 | 5 | 15 | 23 | 30

UDGMENT DAY
Awesome Entertainment: June, 1997 - No. 3, Oct, 1997 ($2.50, limited series)
1-3: 1 Alpha-Moore-s/Liefeld-c/a(p) flashback art by various in all. 2 Omega.

3 Final Judgment, — 2.50
1-3-Variant cover by Dave Gibbons — 2.50
...Aftermath-($3.50) Moore-s/Kane-a; Youngblood, Glory, New Men, Maximage
  Allies and Spacehunter short stories — 3.50
...Aftermath-Variant cover by Dave Gibbons — 3.50

JUDO JOE
Jay-Jay Corp.: Aug, 1953 - No. 3, Dec, 1953 (Judo lessons in each issue)
1-Drug ring story | 9 | 27 | 49 | 70
2,3: 3-Hypo needle story | 6 | 18 | 32 | 45

JUDOMASTER (Gun Master #84-89) (Also see Crisis on Infinite Earths, Sarge
Steel #6 & Special War Series)
Charlton Comics: No. 89, May-June, 1966 - No. 98, Dec, 1967 (Two No. 89's)
89-3rd app. Judomaster | 4 | 12 | 27 | 42
90,92-98: 93-Intro. Tiger | 3 | 9 | 21 | 32
91-Sarge Steel begins | 3 | 10 | 23 | 35
93,94,96,98 (Modern Comics reprint, 1977) — 4.00
NOTE: *Morisi Thunderbolt* #90. #91 has 1 pg. biography on writer/artist Frank McLaughlin.

JUDY CANOVA (Formerly My Experience) (Stage, screen, radio)
Fox Features Syndicate: No. 23, May, 1950 - No. 3, Sept, 1950
23(#1)-Wood-c,a(p)? | 22 | 66 | 116 | 200
24-Wood-a(p) | 22 | 66 | 116 | 195
3-Wood-c; Wood/Orlando-a | 24 | 72 | 127 | 215

JUDY GARLAND (See Famous Stars)

JUDY JOINS THE WAVES
Toby Press: 1951 (For U.S. Navy)
nn | 6 | 18 | 34 | 45

JUGGERNAUT (See X-Men)
Marvel Comics: Apr, 1997, Nov, 1999 ($2.99, one-shots)
1-(4/97) Kelly-s/Casey-a — 3.00
1-(11/99) Casey-s; Eighth Day x-over; Thor, Iron Man, Spidey app. — 3.00

JUGHEAD (Formerly Archie's Pal...)
Archie Publications: No. 127, Dec, 1965 - No. 352, June, 1987
127-130 | 3 | 9 | 17 | 24
131,133,135-160(9/68) | 2 | 6 | 13 | 20
132,134: 132-Shield-c; The Fly & Black Hood app.; Shield cameo.
134-Shield-c | 3 | 9 | 20 | 30
161-180 | 2 | 6 | 11 | 16
181-199 | 2 | 6 | 9 | 12
200(1/72) | 2 | 6 | 10 | 14
201-240(5/75) | 1 | 3 | 6 | 9
241-270(11/77) | 1 | 3 | 5 | 7
271-299 | | | | 6.00
300(5/80)-Anniversary issue; infinity-c | 1 | 3 | 5 | 7
301-320(1/82) | | | | 4.00
321-324,326-352 | | | | 3.00
325-(10/82) Cheryl Blossom app. (not on cover); same month as intro. (Betty &
  story) in Archie's Girls, Betty & Veronica #320; Jason Blossom app.; DeCarlo-a
  | 2 | 6 | 15 | 22

JUGHEAD (2nd Series)(Becomes Archie's Pal Jughead Comics #46 on)
Archie Enterprises: Aug, 1987 - No. 45, May, 1993 (.75/$1.00/$1.25)
1 | 1 | 3 | 5 | 7
2-10 | | | | 4.00
11-45: 4-Xmas issue. 17-Colan-c/a | | | | 3.00

JUGHEAD AS CAPTAIN HERO (See Archie as Pureheart the Powerful,
Archie Giant Series Magazine #142 & Life With Archie)
Archie Publications: Oct, 1966 - No. 7, Nov, 1967
1-Super hero parody | 6 | 18 | 40 | 65
2 | 4 | 12 | 27 | 42
3-7 | 3 | 9 | 20 | 30

JUGHEAD JONES COMICS DIGEST, THE (...Magazine No. 10-64;
Jughead Jones Digest Magazine #65)
Archie Publ.: June, 1977 - No. 100, May, 1996 ($1.35/$1.50/$1.75, digest-size,
128 pgs.)
1-Neal Adams-a; Capt. Hero-r | 3 | 9 | 20 | 30

Jughead's Double Digest #78 © AP

Jughead's Folly #1 © AP

Jumbo Comics #167 © FH

	GD2.0	FN6.0	VF8.0	NM9.4
2(9/77)-Neal Adams-a	2	6	15	22
3-6,8-10	2	6	11	15
7-Origin Jaguar-r; N. Adams-a.	2	6	12	18
11-20: 13-r/1957 Jughead's Folly	1	4	7	10
21-50	1	3	5	7
51-70				5.00
71-100				3.00

JUGHEAD'S BABY TALES
Archie Comics: Spring, 1994 - No. 2, Wint. 1994 ($2.00, 52 pgs.)

1,2: 1-Bound-in pull-out poster				3.00

JUGHEAD'S DINER
Archie Comics: Apr, 1990 - No. 7, Apr, 1991 ($1.00)

1				4.00
2-7				2.50

JUGHEAD'S DOUBLE DIGEST (...Magazine #5)
Archie Comics: Oct, 1989 - Present ($2.25 - $3.29)

1	1	4	7	10
2-10: 2,5-Capt. Hero stories	1	3	5	7
11-25				4.00
26-82: 58-Begin $2.99-c. 66-Begin $3.19-c. 75-Begin $3.29-c				3.30

JUGHEAD'S EAT-OUT COMIC BOOK MAGAZINE (See Archie Giant Series Magazine No. 170)

JUGHEAD'S FANTASY
Archie Publications: Aug, 1960 - No. 3, Dec, 1960

1	18	54	123	220
2	12	36	84	140
3	10	30	70	120

JUGHEAD'S FOLLY
Archie Publications (Close-Up): 1957 (36 pgs.)(one-shot)

1-Jughead a la Elvis (Rare) (1st reference to Elvis in comics?)				
	50	150	300	525

JUGHEAD'S JOKES
Archie Publications: Aug, 1967 - No. 78, Sept, 1982
(No. 1-8, 38 on: reg. size; No. 9-23: 68 pgs.; No. 24-37: 52 pgs.)

1	7	21	50	80
2	4	12	26	40
3-8	3	9	19	28
9,10 (68 pgs.)	3	9	21	32
11-23(4/71) (68 pgs.)	3	9	17	25
24-37(1/74) (52 pgs.)	2	6	12	18
38-50(9/76)	1	3	6	8
51-78				4.00

JUGHEAD'S PAL HOT DOG (See Laugh #14 for 1st app.)
Archie Comics: Jan, 1990 - No. 5, Oct, 1990 ($1.00)

1				4.00
2-5				2.50

JUGHEAD'S SOUL FOOD
Spire Christian Comics (Fleming H. Revell Co.): 1979 (49 cents)

nn	2	6	9	12

JUGHEAD'S TIME POLICE
Archie Comics: July, 1990 - No. 6, May, 1991 ($1.00, bi-monthly)

1				4.00
2-6: Colan a-3-6p; c-3-6				2.50

JUGHEAD WITH ARCHIE DIGEST (...Plus Betty & Veronica & Reggie Too No. 1,2; ...Magazine #33-?, 101-on; ...Comics Digest Mag.)
Archie Pub.: Mar, 1974 - Present ($1.00/$1.25/$1.35/$1.50/$1.75/$1.95/$1.99)

1	5	15	34	55
2	3	10	23	35
3-10	3	9	17	25
11-13,15-17,19,20: Capt. Hero-r in #14-16; Capt. Pureheart #17,19				
	2	6	10	14
14,18,21,22-Pureheart the Powerful in #18,21,22	2	6	11	16
23-30: 29-The Shield-r. 30-The Fly-r	1	4	7	10
31-50,100		3	6	8

	GD2.0	FN6.0	VF8.0	NM9.4
51-99	1	3	5	7
101-121				4.00
122-171: 156-Begin $2.19-c				2.50

JUKE BOX COMICS
Famous Funnies: Mar, 1948 - No. 6, Jan, 1949

1-Toth-c/a; Hollingsworth-a	40	120	232	400
2-Transvestism story	27	81	142	245
3-6: 3-Peggy Lee story. 4-Jimmy Durante line drawn-c. 6-Features Desi Arnaz plus Arnaz line drawn-c	21	63	110	185

JUMBO COMICS (Created by S.M. Iger)
Fiction House Magazines (Real Adv. Publ. Co.): Sept, 1938 - No. 167, Mar, 1953 (No. 1-3: 68 pgs.; No. 4-8: 52 pgs.)(No. 1-8 oversized-10-1/2x14-1/2"; black & white)

1-(Rare)-Sheena Queen of the Jungle(1st app.) by Meskin, Hawks of the Seas (The Hawk #10 on; see Feature Funnies #3) by Eisner, The Hunchback by Dick Briefer (ends #8), Wilton of the West (ends #24), Inspector Dayton (ends #67) & ZX-5 (ends #140) begin; 1st comic art by Jack Kirby (Count of Monte Cristo & Wilton of the West); Mickey Mouse appears (1 panel) with brief biography of Walt Disney; 1st app. Peter Pupp by Bob Kane. Note: Sheena was created by Iger for publication in England as a newspaper strip. The early issues of Jumbo contain Sheena strip-r; multiple panel-c 1,2,7				
	1950	5850	19,500	–
2-(Rare)-Origin Sheena. Diary of Dr. Hayward by Kirby (also #3) plus 2 other stories; contains strip from Universal Film featuring Edgar Bergen & Charlie McCarthy plus-c (preview of film)	640	1920	6400	–
3-Last Kirby issue	440	1320	4400	–
4-(Scarce)-Origin The Hawk by Eisner; Wilton of the West by Fine (ends #14)(1st comic work); Count of Monte Cristo by Fine (ends #15); The Diary of Dr. Hayward by Fine (cont'd #8,9)	400	1200	4000	–
5-Christmas-c	350	1050	3500	–
6-8-Last B&W issue. #8 was a 1939 N.Y. World's Fair Special Edition; Frank Buck's Jungleland story	310	930	3100	–
9-Stuart Taylor begins by Fine (ends #140); Fine-c; 1st color issue (8-9/39)-1st Sheena (jungle) cover; 8-1/4x10-1/4" (oversized in width only)				
	280	840	2800	–
10-Regular size 68 pg. issues begin; Sheena dons new costume w/ origin costume; Stuart Taylor sci/fi-c; classic Lou Fine-c.				
	182	546	1136	2000
11-13: 12-The Hawk-c by Eisner. 13-Eisner-c	123	369	769	1350
14-Intro. Lightning (super-hero) on-c only	127	381	795	1400
15,17-20: 15-1st Lightning story and begins, ends #41. 17-Lightning part-c				
	77	231	483	850
16-Lightning-c	95	285	597	1050
21-30: 22-1st Tom, Dick & Harry; origin The Hawk retold. 25-Midnight the Black Stallion begins, ends #65	61	182	381	675
31-40: 31-(9/41)-1st app. Mars God of War in Stuart Taylor story (see Planet Comics #15. 35-Shows V2#11 (correct number does not appear)				
	50	150	300	525
41-50: 42-Ghost Gallery begins, ends #167	40	120	232	400
51-60: 52-Last Tom, Dick & Harry	36	108	191	330
61-70: 68-Sky Girl begins, ends #130; not in #79	27	81	142	245
71-93,95-99: 89-ZX5 becomes a private eye.	21	63	110	185
94-Used in Love and Death by Legman	23	69	121	210
100	23	69	121	210
101-140,150-158: 155-Used in POP, pg. 98	17	51	88	150
141-149-Two Sheena stories. 141-Long Bow, Indian Boy begins, ends #160				
	17	51	88	150
159-163: Space Scouts serial in all. 160-Last jungle-c (6/52). 161-Ghost Gallery covers begin, end #167. 163-Suicide Smith app.	16	48	83	140
164-The Star Pirate begins, ends #165	16	48	83	140
165-167: 165,167-Space Rangers app.	16	48	83	140

NOTE: Bondage covers, negligee panels, torture, etc. are common in this series. Hawks of the Seas, Inspector Dayton, Spies in Action, Sports Shorts, & Uncle Otto by Eisner, #1-7. Hawk by **Eisner**-#10-15. **Eisner** c-1-8, 12-14. 1pg. Patsy pin-ups in 92-97, 99-101. Sheena by **Meskin**-#1, 4; by **Powell**-#2, 3, 5-28; **Powell** c-14, 16, 17, 19. **Powell/Eisner** c-15. Sky Girl by **Matt Baker**-#69-78, 80-130. ZX-5 & Ghost Gallery by **Kamen**-#90-130. **Bailey** a-3-8. **Briefer** a-1-8, 10. Fine a-14; c-9-11. **Kamen** a-101, 105, 123, 132; c-105, 121-145. **Bob Kane** a-1-8. **Whitman** c-146-167(most). Jungle c-9, 13, 15, 17 on.

JUNGLE ACTION
Atlas Comics (IPC): Oct, 1954 - No. 6, Aug, 1955

Jungle Action #14 © ATL

Jungle Comics #11 © FH

Jungle Tales #1 © MAR

	GD2.0	FN6.0	VF8.0	NM9.4

1-Leopard Girl begins by Al Hartley (#1,3); Jungle Boy by Forte; Maneely-a
in all 39 117 208 360
2-(3-D effect cover) 39 117 208 360
3-6: 3-Last precode (2/55) 25 75 130 225
NOTE: *Maneely c-1, 2, 5, 6. Romita a-3, 6. Shores a-3; c-3, 4?.*

JUNGLE ACTION (...& Black Panther #18-21?)
Marvel Comics Group: Oct, 1972 - No. 24, Nov, 1976

1-Lorna, Jann-r (All reprints in 1-4) 2 6 13 20
2-4 .... 2 6 9 12
5-Black Panther begins (r/Avengers #62) 3 9 17 24
6,8: 6-New stories begin. 8-Origin Black Panther 2 6 11 16
7,9,10: 9-Contains pull-out centerfold ad by Mark Jewelers
.... 2 6 9 12
11-20,23,24: 19-23-KKK x-over. 23-r/#22. 24-1st Wind Eagle; sty contd in
Marvel Premiere #51-#53 .... 1 3 5 7
21,22-(Regular 25¢ edition)(5,7/76) 1 3 5 7
21,22-(30¢-c variant, limited distribution) 1 4 7 10
NOTE: *Buckler a-6-9p, 22; c-8p, 12p. Buscema a-5p; c-22. Byrne c-23. Gil Kane a-8p; c-2, 4, 10p, 11p, 13-17, 19, 24. Kirby c-18. Maneely r-1. Russell a-13i. Starlin c-3p.*

JUNGLE ADVENTURES
Super Comics: 1963 - 1964 (Reprints)

10,12,15,17,18: 10-r/Terrors of the Jungle #4 & #10(Rulah). 12-r/Zoot #14
(Rulah).15-r/Kaanga from Jungle #152 & Tiger Girl. 17-All Jo-Jo-r. 18-
Reprints/White Princess of the Jungle #1; no Kinstler-a; origin of both
White Princess & Cap'n Courage 4 12 25 38

JUNGLE ADVENTURES
Skywald Comics: Mar, 1971 - No. 3, June, 1971 (25¢, 52 pgs.)

1-Zangar origin; reprints of Jo-Jo, Blue Gorilla(origin)/White Princess #3,
Kinstler-r/White Princess #4 .... 2 6 15 22
2,3: 2-Zangar, Sheena-r/Sheena #17 & Jumbo #162, Jo-Jo, origin Slave Girl-r.
3-Zangar, Jo-Jo, Sheena, Rulah-r 2 6 11 15

JUNGLE BOOK (See King Louie and Mowgli, Movie Comics, Mowgli..., Walt Disney
Showcase #45 & Walt Disney's The Jungle Book)

JUNGLE CAT (Disney)
Dell Publishing Co.: No. 1136, Sept-Nov, 1960 (one shot)

Four Color 1136-Movie, photo-c 6 18 42 80

JUNGLE COMICS
Fiction House Magazines: 1/40 - No. 157, 3/53; No. 158, Spr, 1953 - No. 163,
Summer, 1954

1-Origin The White Panther, Kaanga, Lord of the Jungle, Tabu, Wizard of the
Jungle; Wambi, the Jungle Boy, Camilla & Capt. Terry Thunder begin (all
1st app.). Lou Fine-c 431 1293 3468 5600
2-Fantomah, Mystery Woman of the Jungle begins, ends #51; The Red
Panther begins, ends #26 .... 159 477 994 1750
3,4 .... 132 395 825 1450
5-Classic Eisner-c 143 429 894 1575
6-10: 7,8-Powell-c 75 225 469 825
11-20: 13-Tuska-c 55 165 330 575
21-30: 25-Shows V2#1 (correct number does not appear). #27-New origin
Fantomah, Daughter of the Pharoahs; Camilla dons new costume
.... 43 129 257 450
31-40 .... 35 105 185 320
41,43-50 .... 31 93 165 285
42-Kaanga by Crandall, 12 pgs. 34 102 179 310
51-60 .... 27 81 142 245
61-70: 67-Cover swipes Crandall splash pg. in #42 .... 23 69 121 210
71-80: 79-New origin Tabu 21 63 110 185
81-97,99,101-110 .... 17 51 99 165
98-Used in **SOTI**, pg. 185 & illo "In ordinary comic books, there are pictures
within pictures for children who know how to look;" used by N.Y. Legis.
Comm. 33 99 174 300
100 .... 23 69 121 210
111-163: 104-In Camilla story, villain is Dr. Wertham. 118-Clyde Beatty app.
135-Desert Panther begins in Terry Thunder (origin), not in #137; ends (dies)
#138. 139-Last 52 pg. issue. 141-Last Tabu. 143,145-Used in **POP**, pg. 99.
151-Last Camilla & Terry Thunder. 152-Tiger Girl begins. 158-Last Wambi;
Sheena app. 17 51 88 150

I.W. Reprint #1,9: 1-r/? 9-r/#151 .... 3 9 21 32
NOTE: *Bondage covers, negligee panels, torture, etc. are common to this series. Camilla by Fran
Hopper-#70-92; by Baker-#69, 100-113, 115, 116; by Lubbers-#97-99 by Tuska-#63, 65.
Kaanga by John Celardo-#80-113; by Larsen-#71, 75-79; by Moreira-#58, 60, 61, 63-70, 72-74;
by Tuska-#37, 62; by Whitman-#114-163. Tabu by Larsen-#59-75, 82-92; by Whitman-#93-113.
Terry Thunder by Hopper-#71, 72; by Celardo-#78, 79; by Lubbers-#80-85. Tiger Girl-r by
Baker-#152, 153, 155-157, 159. Wambi by Baker-#62-67, 74. Astarita c-45, 46. Celardo a-78; c-
98-113. Crandall c-67 from splash pg. Eisner c-2, 5, 6. Fine c-1. Larsen a-65, 66, 71, 72, 74, 75,
79, 83, 84, 87-90. Moriera c-43, 44. Morisi a-51. Powell c-7, 8. Sultan c-3, 4. Tuska c-13.
Whitman c-132-163(most). Zolnerowich c-11, 12, 18-41.*

JUNGLE COMICS
Blackthorne Publishing: May, 1988 - No. 4 ($2.00, B&W/color)

1-Dave Stevens-c; B. Jones scripts in all. 3.00
2-4: B&W-a begins 2.25

JUNGLE GIRL (See Lorna, the...)

JUNGLE GIRL (Nyoka, Jungle Girl No. 2 on)
Fawcett Publications: Fall, 1942 (one-shot)(No month listed)

1-Bondage-c; photo of Kay Aldridge who played Nyoka in movie serial app.
on-c. Adaptation of the classic Republic movie serial Perils of Nyoka. 1st
comic to devote entire contents to a movie serial adaptation
.... 127 381 795 1400

JUNGLE GIRLS
AC Comics: 1989 - No. 16, 1993 (B&W)

1-16: 1-4,10,13-16-New story & "good girl" reprints. 5-9,11,12-All g.g. reprints
(Baker, Powell, Lubbers, others) 3.00

JUNGLE JIM
Standard Comics (Best Books): No. 11, Jan, 1949 - No. 20, Apr, 1951

11 .... 10 30 55 80
12-20 .... 6 18 32 45

JUNGLE JIM
Dell Publishing Co.: No. 490, 8/53 - No. 1020, 8-10/59 (Painted-c)

Four Color 490(#1) 6 18 42 80
Four Color 565(#2, 6/54) 4 12 26 40
3(10-12/54)-5 .... 4 12 25 38
6-19(1-3/59), Four Color 1020(#20) 3 10 23 35

JUNGLE JIM
King Features Syndicate: No. 5, Dec, 1967

5-Reprints Dell #5; Wood-c 2 6 11 16

JUNGLE JIM (Continued from Dell series)
Charlton Comics: No. 22, Feb, 1969 - No. 28, Feb, 1970 (#21 was an overseas
edition only)

22-Dan Flagg begins; Ditko/Wood-a 3 10 23 35
23-26: 23-Last Dan Flagg; Howard-c. 24-Jungle People begin
.... 2 6 13 20
27,28: 27-Ditko/Howard-a. 28-Ditko-c 3 9 17 25
NOTE: *Ditko cover of #22 reprints story panels.*

JUNGLE JO
Fox Feature Syndicate (Hero Books): Mar, 1950 - No. 3, Sept, 1950

nn-Jo-Jo blanked out, leaving Congo King; came out after Jo-Jo #29
(intended as Jo-Jo #30?) 43 129 257 450
1-Tangi begins; part Wood-a 45 135 270 475
2,3 .... 37 111 197 340

JUNGLE LIL (Dorothy Lamour #2 on; also see Feature Stories Magazine)
Fox Feature Syndicate (Hero Books): April, 1950

1 .... 40 120 214 370

JUNGLE TALES (Jann of the Jungle No. 8 on)
Atlas Comics (CSI): Sept, 1954 - No. 7, Sept, 1955

1-Jann of the Jungle 39 117 208 360
2-7: 3-Last precode (1/55) 27 81 142 245
NOTE: *Heath c-4, 7. Maneely a-2; c-1, 3. Shores a-5-7; c-4, 6. Tuska a-2.*

JUNGLE TALES OF CAVEWOMAN
Basement Comics: 1998 ($2.95, B&W)

1-Budd Root-s/a 3.00

JUNGLE TALES OF TARZAN

Junior Miss #33 © MAR

Just A Pilgrim #1 © Black Ball Ent.

Justice, Inc. #2 © DC

	GD2.0	FN6.0	VF8.0	NM9.4

Charlton Comics: Dec, 1964 - No. 4, July, 1965

1	5	15	38	60
2-4	4	12	26	40

NOTE: Giordano c-3p. Glanzman a-1-3. Montes/Bache a-4.

JUNGLE TERROR (See Harvey Comics Hits No. 54)

JUNGLE THRILLS (Formerly Sports Thrills; Terrors of the Jungle #17 on)
Star Publications: No. 16, Feb, 1952; Dec, 1953; No. 7, 1954

16-Phantom Lady & Rulah story-reprint/All Top No. 15; used in POP, pg. 98,99;				
L. B. Cole-c	50	150	300	525
3-D 1(12/53, 25¢)-Came w/glasses; Jungle Lil & Jungle Jo appear; L. B. Cole-c				
	52	157	314	550
7-Titled 'Picture Scope Jungle Adventures;' (1954, 36 pgs, 15¢)-3-D effect				
c/stories; story & coloring book; Disbrow-a/script; L. B. Cole-c				
	49	147	294	510

JUNGLE TWINS, THE (Tono & Kono)
Gold Key/Whitman No. 18: Apr, 1972 - No. 17, Nov, 1975; No. 18, May, 1982

1	2	6	13	20
2-5	1	4	7	10
6-18: 18(Whitman, 5/82)-Reprints	1	3	5	7

NOTE: UFO c/story No. 13. Painted-c No. 1-17. Spiegle c-18.

JUNGLE WAR STORIES (Guerrilla War No. 12 on)
Dell Publishing Co.: July-Sept, 1962 - No. 11, Apr-June, 1965 (Painted-c)

01-384-209 (#1)	3	10	23	35
2-11	2	6	15	22

JUNIE PROM (Also see Dexter Comics)
Dearfield Publishing Co.: Winter, 1947-48 - No. 7, Aug, 1949

1-Teen-age	13	39	66	110
2	8	24	42	60
3-7	6	18	32	45

JUNIOR
Fantagraphics Books: June, 2000 - No. 5, Jan, 2001 ($2.95, B&W)

1-5-Peter Bagge-s/a				3.00

JUNIOR CARROT PATROL (Jr. Carrot Patrol #2)
Dark Horse Comics: May, 1989; No. 2, Nov, 1990 ($2.00, B&W)

1,2-Flaming Carrot spin-off. 1-Bob Burden-c(i)				2.50

JUNIOR COMICS (Formerly Li'l Pan; becomes Western Outlaws with #17)
Fox Feature Syndicate: No. 9, Sept, 1947 - No. 16, July, 1948

9-Feldstein-c/a; headlights-c	77	232	483	850
10-16-Feldstein-c/a; headlights-c on all	68	205	426	750

JUNIOR FUNNIES (Formerly Tiny Tot Funnies No. 9)
Harvey Publ. (King Features Synd.): No. 10, Aug, 1951 - No. 13, Feb, 1952

10-Partial reprints in all; Blondie, Dagwood, Daisy, Henry, Popeye, Felix,				
Katzenjammer Kids	5	15	24	32
11-13	5	14	21	28

JUNIOR HOPP COMICS
Stanmor Publ.: Feb, 1952 - No. 3, July, 1952

1-Teenage humor	10	30	55	80
2,3: 3-Dave Berg-a	6	18	29	40

JUNIOR MEDICS OF AMERICA, THE
E. R. Squire & Sons: No. 1359, 1957 (15¢)

1359	4	10	15	20

JUNIOR MISS
Timely/Marvel (CnPC): Wint, 1944; No. 24, Apr, 1947 - No. 39, Aug, 1950

1-Frank Sinatra & June Allyson life story	27	81	145	250
24-Formerly The Human Torch #23?	13	39	66	110
25-38: 29,31,34-Cindy-c/stories (others?)	8	24	42	60
39-Kurtzman-a	10	30	55	80

NOTE: Painted-c 35-37. 35, 37-all romance. 36, 38-mostly teen humor.

JUNIOR PARTNERS (Formerly Oral Roberts' True Stories)
Oral Roberts Evangelistic Assn.: No. 120, Aug, 1959 - V3#12, Dec, 1961

120(#1)	4	12	26	40
2(9/59)	3	9	19	28
3-12(7/60)	2	6	12	18
V2#1(8/60)-5(12/60)	2	6	10	14
V3#1(1/61)-12	1	4	7	10

JUNIOR TREASURY (See Dell Junior...)

JUNIOR WOODCHUCKS GUIDE (Walt Disney's...)
Danbury Press: 1973 (8-3/4"x5-3/4", 214 pgs., hardcover)

nn-Illustrated text based on the long-standing J.W. Guide used by Donald
Duck's nephews Huey, Dewey & Louie & Carl Barks. The guidebook was
a popular plot devise to enable the nephews to solve problems facing their
uncle or Scrooge McDuck (scarce)   5   15   34   55

JUNIOR WOODCHUCKS LIMITED SERIES (Walt Disney's...)
W. D. Publications (Disney): July, 1991 - No. 4, Oct, 1991 ($1.50, limited series;
new & reprint-a)

1-4: 1-The Beagle Boys app.; Barks-r				2.50

JUNIOR WOODCHUCKS (See Huey, Dewey & Louie...)

JUNK CULTURE
DC Comics (Vertigo): July, 1997 - No. 2, Aug, 1997 ($2.50, limited series)

1,2: Ted McKeever-s/a in all				2.50

JURASSIC PARK
Topps Comics: 6/93 - No. 4, 8/93; #5, 10/94 - #10, 2/95

1-($2.50)-Newsstand Edition; Kane/Perez-a in all; 1-4: movie adaptation				2.50
1-($2.95)-Collector's Ed.; polybagged w/3 cards				4.00
1-Amberchrome Edition w/no price or ads	1	3	5	7
2-4-($2.50)-Newsstand Edition				2.50
2,3-($2.95)-Collector's Ed.; polybagged w/3 cards				3.00
4-10: 4-($2.95)-Collector's Ed.; polybagged w/1 of 4 different action hologram				
trading card; Gil Kane/Perez-a. 5-becomes Advs. of				3.00
Annual 1 ($3.95, 5/95)				4.00
Trade paperback (1993, $9.95)-r/#1-4; bagged w/#0				10.00

JURASSIC PARK: RAPTOR
Topps Comics: Nov, 1993 - No. 2, Dec, 1993 ($2.95, limited series)

1,2: 1-Bagged w/3 trading cards & Zorro #0; Golden c-1,2				3.00

JURASSIC PARK: RAPTORS ATTACK
Topps Comics: Mar, 1994 - No. 4, June, 1994 ($2.50, limited series)

1-4-Michael Golden-c/frontispiece				2.50

JURASSIC PARK: RAPTORS HIJACK
Topps Comics: July, 1994 - No. 4, Oct, 1994 ($2.50, limited series)

1-4: Michael Golden-c/front piece				2.50

JUST A PILGRIM
Black Bull Entertainment: May, 2001 - Present ($2.99)

Limited Preview Edition (12/00, $7.00) Ennis & Ezquerra interviews				7.00
1-Ennis-s/Ezquerra-a/Texeira-c				3.00
1-Variant-c by JG Jones				3.00
2-5: 2-Fabry-c. 3-Nowlan-c. 4-Sienkiewicz-c				3.00
TPB (11/01, $12.99) r/#1-5; Waid intro.				13.00

JUSTICE
Marvel Comics Group (New Universe): Nov, 1986 - No. 32, June, 1989

1-32: 26-32-$1.50-c (low print run)				2.25

JUSTICE COMICS (Formerly Wacky Duck; Tales of Justice #53 on)
Marvel/Atlas Comics (NPP 7-9,4-19/CnPC 20-23/MjMC 24-38/Male 39-52):
No. 7, Fall/47 - No. 9, 6/48; No. 4, 8/48 - No. 52, 3/55

7(#1, 1947)	29	87	153	265
8(#2)-Kurtzman-a "Giggles 'n' Grins" (3)	20	60	105	175
9(#3, 6/48)	18	54	94	155
4	16	48	83	140
5(9/48)-9: 8-Anti-Wertham editorial	14	42	72	120
10-15-Photo-c	11	33	55	90
16-30	10	30	55	80
31-40,42-52: 35-Gene Colan-a. 48-Last precode; Pakula & Tuska-a.				
	9	27	49	70
41-Electrocution-c	17	51	88	150

NOTE: Heath a-24. Maneely c-44, 52. Pakula a-43, 45, 48. Louis Ravielli a-39. Robinson
a-22, 25, 41. Shores c-7(#1), 8(#2)? Tuska a-48. Wildey a-52.

Justice League #62 © DC

Justice League Adventures #1 © DC

Justice League Europe #5 © DC

JU

	GD2.0	FN6.0	VF8.0	NM9.4			GD2.0	FN6.0	VF8.0	NM9.4

JUSTICE: FOUR BALANCE
Marvel Comics: Sept, 1994 - No. 4, Dec, 1994 ($1.75, limited series)
1-4: 1-Thing & Firestar app.   2.25

JUSTICE, INC. (The Avenger) (Pulp)
National Periodical Publications: May-June, 1975 - No. 4, Nov-Dec, 1975

1-McWilliams-a, Kubert-c; origin	2	6	9	12
2-4: 3-Kirby-a(p), c-2,3p. 4-Kubert-c	1	4	7	10

NOTE: Adapted from Kenneth Robeson novel, creator of Doc Savage.

JUSTICE, INC. (Pulp)
DC Comics: 1989 - No. 2, 1989 ($3.95, 52 pgs., squarebound, mature)
1,2: Re-intro The Avenger; Andrew Helfer scripts & Kyle Baker-c/a 4.00

JUSTICE LEAGUE (...International #7-25; ...America #26 on)
DC Comics: May, 1987 - No. 113, Aug, 1996 (Also see Legends #6)
1-Batman, Green Lantern (Guy Gardner), Blue Beetle, Mr. Miracle, Capt.
   Marvel & Martian Manhunter begin   6.00
2,3: 3-Regular-c (white background)   4.00

3-Limited-c (yellow background, Superman logo)	4	12	29	45

4-10: 4-Booster Gold joins. 5-Origin Gray Man; Batman vs. Guy Gardner;
   Creeper app. 7-($1.25, 52 pgs.)-Capt. Marvel & Dr. Fate resign; Capt. Atom &
   Rocket Red join. 9,10-Millennium x-over   3.00
11-17,22,23,25-49,51-68,72-82: 16-Bruce Wayne-c/story. 31,32-J. L. Europe
   x-over. 58-Lobo app. 61-New team begins; swipes-c to J.L. of A. #1('60).
   70-Newsstand version w/o outer-c. 71-Direct sales version w/black outer-c.
   71-Newsstand version w/o outer-c.80-Intro new Booster Gold. 82,83-Guy
   Gardner-c/stories   2.50
18-21,24,50: 18-21-Lobo app. 24-($1.50)-1st app. Justice League Europe.
   50-($1.75, 52 pgs.)   3.00
69-Doomsday tie-in; takes place between Superman: The Man of Steel #18
   & Superman #74   5.00
69,70-2nd printings   2.25
70-Funeral for a Friend part 1; red 3/4 outer-c   4.00
83-99,101-113: 92-(9/94)-Zero Hour x-over; Triumph app. 113-Green Lantern,
   Flash & Hawkman app.   2.50
100 ($3.95)-Foil-c; 52 pgs.   4.00
100 ($2.95)-Newsstand   3.00
#0-(10/94) Zero Hour (publ between #92 & #93); new team begins (Hawkman,
   Wonder Woman, Flash, Metamorpho, Nuklon, Crimson Fox, Obsidian & Fire)
                                                                           2.50
Annual 1-8,10 ('87-'94, '96, 68 pgs.): 2-Joker-c/story; Batman cameo. 5-
   Armageddon 2001 x-over; Silver ink 2nd print. 7-Bloodlines x-over. 8-
   Elseworlds story. 10-Legends of the Dead Earth   3.00
Annual 9 (1995, $3.50)-Year One story   3.50
Special 1,2 ('90,'91, 52 pgs.): 1-Giffen plots. 2-Staton-a(p)   3.00
Spectacular 1 (1992, $1.50, 52 pgs.)-Intro new JLI & JLE teams; ties into
   JLI #61 & JLE #37; two interlocking covers by Jurgens   3.00
A New Beginning Trade Paperback (1989, $12.95)-r/#1-7   13.00
NOTE: Anderson c-61i. Austin a-1i, 60i; c-1i. Giffen a-13; c-21p. Guice a-62i. Maguire a-1-12,
16-19, 22, 23. Russell a-Annual 1i; c-54i. Willingham a-30p, Annual 2.

JUSTICE LEAGUE ADVENTURES (Based on Cartoon Network series)
DC Comics: Jan, 2002 - Present ($1.99)
1-3: 1-Timm & Ross-c. 3-Nicieza-s   2.00

JUSTICE LEAGUE: A MIDSUMMER'S NIGHTMARE
DC Comics: Sept, 1996 - No. 3, Nov, 1996 ($2.95, limited series, 38 pgs.)
1-3: Re-establishes Superman, Batman, Green Lantern, The Martian
   Manhunter, Flash, Aquaman & Wonder Woman as the Justice League; Mark
   Waid & Fabian Nicieza co-scripts; Jeff Johnson & Darick Robertson-a(p);
   Kevin Maguire-c.   5.00
TPB-(1997, $8.95) r/1-3   9.00

JUSTICE LEAGUE EUROPE (Justice League International #51 on)
DC Comics: Apr, 1989 - No. 68, Sept., 1994 (75¢/ $1.00/$1.25/$1.50)
1-Giffen plots in all, breakdowns in #1-8,13-30; Justice League #1-c/swipe 3.00
2-10: 7-9-Batman app. 7,8-JLA x-over. 8,9-Superman app.   2.50
11-49: 12-Metal Men app. 20-22-Rogers-c/a(s). 33,34-Lobo vs. Despero.
   34-New team begins; swipes-c to JLA #9; see JLA Spectacular   2.50
50-($2.50, 68 pgs.)-Battles Sonar   3.00
51-68: 68-Zero Hour x-over; Triumph joins Justice League Task Force
   (See JLTF #17)   2.25

Annual 1-5 ('90-'94, 68 pgs.)-1-Return of the Global Guardians; Giffen plots/
   breakdowns. 2-Armageddon 2001; Giffen-a(p); Rogers-a(p); Golden-a(i)
   3-Eclipso app. 4-Intro Lionheart. 5-Elseworlds story   3.00
NOTE: Phil Jimenez a-68p. Rogers c/a-20-22. Sears a-1-12, 14-19, 23-29; c-1-10, 12, 14-19,
23-29.

JUSTICE LEAGUE INTERNATIONAL (See Justice League Europe)

JUSTICE LEAGUE OF AMERICA (See Brave & the Bold #28-30, Mystery In
Space #75 & Official... Index)
National Periodical Publ./DC Comics: Oct-Nov, 1960 - No. 261, Apr, 1987 (#91-
99,139-157: 52 pgs.)

1-(10/11/60)-Origin & 1st app. Despero; Aquaman, Batman, Flash, Green
Lantern, J'onn J'onzz, Superman & Wonder Woman continue from Brave
and the Bold	278	834	2500	5000
2	63	189	531	1000
3-Origin/1st app. Kanjar Ro (see Mystery in Space #75)(scarce in high grade
due to black-c)	53	159	452	850
4-Green Arrow joins JLA	39	117	293	525
5-Origin & 1st app. Dr. Destiny	37	93	222	400
6-8,10: 6-Origin & 1st app. Prof. Amos Fortune. 7-(10-11/60)-Last 10¢
issue. 10-(3/62)-Origin & 1st app. Felix Faust; 1st app. Lord of Time.
28	74	196	350
9-(2/62)-Origin JLA (1st origin)	41	123	306	550
11-15: 12-(6/62)-Origin & 1st app. Dr. Light. 13-(8/62)-Speedy app.
14-(9/62)-Atom joins JLA.	19	57	134	240
16-20: 17-Adam Strange flashback	17	51	118	210
21-(8/63)-"Crisis on Earth-One"; re-intro of JSA in this title (see Flash #129)
(1st S.A. app. Hourman & Dr. Fate)	31	93	233	420
22- "Crisis on Earth-Two"; JSA x-over (story continued from #21)
28	84	196	350
23-28: 24-Adam Strange app. 27-Robin app.	12	36	88	150
29-JSA x-over; 1st S.A. app. Starman; "Crisis on Earth-Three"
16	48	110	190
30-JSA x-over	14	42	102	175
31-Hawkman joins JLA, Hawkgirl cameo (11/64)	11	33	77	130
32,34: 32-Intro & Origin Brain Storm. 34-Joker-c/sty	8	24	60	100
33,35,36,40,41: 40-3rd S.A. Penguin app. 41-Intro & origin The Key
7	21	53	85
37-39: 37,38-JSA x-over. 37-1st S.A. app. Mr. Terrific; Batman cameo.
38-"Crisis on Earth-A". 39-Giant G-16; r/B&B #28,30 & JLA #5
10	30	73	125
42-45: 42-Metamorpho app. 43-Intro. Royal Flush Gang
6	18	42	70
46-JSA x-over; 1st S.A. app. Sandman; 3rd S.A. app. of G.A. Spectre (8/66)
11	33	80	135
47-JSA x-over; 4th S.A. app of G.A. Spectre.	8	24	56	90
48-Giant G-29; r/JLA #2,3 & B&B #29	7	21	53	85
49-54,57,59,60	5	15	38	60
55-Intro. Earth 2 Robin (1st G.A. Robin in S.A.)	7	21	53	85
56-JLA vs. JSA (1st G.A. Wonder Woman in S.A.)	6	18	45	75
58-Giant G-41; r/JLA #6,8,1	6	18	45	75
61-63,66,68-72: 69-Wonder Woman quits. 71-Manhunter leaves.
72-Last 12¢ issue	4	12	29	45
64,65-JSA story. 64-(8/68)-Origin/1st app. S.A. Red Tornado
5	15	34	55
67-Giant G-53; r/JLA #4,14,31	6	18	42	70
73-1st S.A. app. of G.A. Superman.	5	15	34	55
74-Black Canary joins; 1st meeting of G.A. & S.A. Superman.
4	12	30	50
75-2nd app. Green Arrow in new costume (see Brave & the Bold #85)
4	12	29	45
76-Giant G-65	5	15	34	55
77-80: 78-Re-intro Vigilante (1st S.A. app?)	3	9	20	30
81-84,86-90: 82-1st S.A. app. of G.A. Batman (cameo). 83-Death of Spectre.
90-Last 15¢ issue	3	9	19	28
85,93-(Giant G-77,G-89; 68 pgs.)	4	12	29	45
91,92: 91-1st meeting of the G.A. & S.A. Robin; begin 25¢, 52 pgs. issues, ends
#99. 92-JLA, Robin tries on costume that is similar to that of G.A. Robin in
All Star Comics #58.	3	10	23	35
94-Reprints 1st Sandman story (Adv. #40) & origin/1st app. Starman (Adv.
#61); Deadman x-over; N. Adams-a (4 pgs.)	8	24	58	95

Justice League of America #107 © DC
 Justice League of America #148 © DC
 Justice Leagues: JLA #1 © DC

GD2.0 FN6.0 VF8.0 NM9.4   GD2.0 FN6.0 VF8.0 NM9.4

95,96: 95-Origin Dr. Fate & Dr. Midnight -r/ More Fun #67, All-American #25).

96-Origin Hourman (Adv. #48); Wildcat-r   4   12   25   38

97-99: 97-Origin JLA retold; Sargon, Starman-r. 98-G.A. Sargon, Starman-r. 99-
G.A. Sandman, Atom-r; last 52 pg. issue   3   9   20   30

100-(8/72)-1st meeting of G.A. & S.A. W. Woman   4   12   26   40

101,102: JSA x-overs. 102-Red Tornado dies   3   9   19   28

103-106,109: 103-Rutland Vermont Halloween x-over; Phantom Stranger joins.
105-Elongated Man joins. 106-New Red Tornado joins. 109-Hawkman resigns
2   6   12   18

107,108-G.A. Uncle Sam, Black Condor, The Ray, Dollman, Phantom Lady &
The Human Bomb (JSA) x-over, 1st S.A. app.   2   6   13   20

110-116: All 100 pgs. 111-JLA vs. Injustice Gang; Shining Knight, Green Arrow-r.
112-Amazo app; Crimson Avenger, Vigilante-r; origin Starman-r/Adv. #81.
115-Martian Manhunter app.   4   12   25   38

117-122,125-134: 117-Hawkman rejoins. 120,121-Adam Strange app. 125,126-
Two-Face-r/story. 128-Wonder Woman rejoins. 129-Destruction of Red
Tornado   2   6   9   12

123-(10/75),124: JLA/JSA x-over. DC editor Julie Schwartz & JLA writers Cary
Bates & Elliot S! Maggin appear in story as themselves. 1st named app.
Earth-Prime (3rd app. after Flash; 1st Series #179 & 228)
2   6   10   14

135-136: 135-137-G.A. Bulletman, Bulletgirl, Spy Smasher, Mr. Scarlet, Pinky &
Ibis x-over, 1st S.A. appearances   2   6   10   14

137-Superman battles G.A. Capt. Marvel   2   6   12   18

138,139-157: 138-Adam Strange app. w/c by Neal Adams; 1st app. Green
Lantern of the 73rd Century. 139-157-(52 pgs.): 139-Adam Strange app. 144-
Origin retold; origin J'onn J'onzz. 145-Red Tornado resurrected. 147,148-
Legion x-over   2   6   9   12

158-160-(44 pgs.)   1   3   6   8

158,160-162,168,169,171,172,176,179,181-(Whitman variants; low print run,
none have issue # on cover)   1   4   7   10

161-182: 161-Zatanna joins & new costume. 171-Mr. Terrific murdered.
178-Cover similar to #1; J'onn J'onzz app. 179-Firestorm joins. 181-Green
Arrow leaves JLA   5.00

183-185-JSA/New Gods/Darkseid/Mr.Miracle x-over   6.00

186-199: 192,193-Real origin Red Tornado. 193-1st app. All-Star Squadron
as free 16 pg. insert   4.00

200 ($1.50, Anniversary issue, 76pgs.)-JLA origin retold; Green Arrow rejoins;
Bolland, Aparo, Giordano, Gil Kane, Infantino, Kubert-a; Perez-c/a   5.00

201-206,209-243,246-259: 203-Intro/origin new Royal Flush Gang.
219,220-True origin Black Canary. 228-Re-intro Martian Manhunter.
228-230-War of the Worlds storyline; JLA Satellite destroyed by Martians.
233-Story cont'd from Annual #2. 243-Aquaman leaves. 250-Batman rejoins.
253-Origin Despero. 258-Death of Vibe. 258-261-Legends x-over   3.00

207,208-JSA, JLA, & All-Star Squadron team-up   4.00

244,245-Crisis x-over   4.00

260-Death of Steel   5.00

261-Last issue   1   3   5   7

Annual 1-3 ('83-'85), 2-Intro new J.L.A. (Aquaman, Martian Manhunter, Steel,
Gypsy,Vixen, Vibe, Elongated Man, & Zatanna). 3-Crisis x-over   3.00
NOTE: Neal Adams c-63, 66, 67, 70, 74, 79, 81, 82, 86-89, 91, 92, 94, 96-98, 138, 139. M.
Anderson c-1, 6, 7, 10, 12-14. Aparo a-200i. Austin a-200i. Baily a-200. Bolland a-200.
Buckler c-158, 163, 164. Burnley i-94, 98, 99. Greene a-46-61i, 64-73i, 110i(r). Grell c-117, 122.
Kaluta c-154p. Gil Kane a-200. Krigstein a-16r(Sensation #84). Kubert a-200; c-72, 73. Nino a-
228i, 230i. Orlando c-151i. Perez a-184-186p, 192-197p, 200p; c-184p, 186, 192-195, 196p,
197p, 199, 200, 201p, 202, 203-205p, 207-209, 212-215, 217, 219, 220. Reinman r-97. Roussos
a-62i. Sekowsky a-37, 38, 44-63p, 110-112p(r); c-46-48p, 51p. Sekowsky/Anderson c-5, 6, 9,
11, 15. B. Smith c-185i. Starlin c-178-180, 183, 185p. Staton a-244p; c-157p, 244p. Toth r-110.
Tuska a-153, 228p, 241-243p. JSA x-overs-21, 22, 29, 30, 37, 38, 46, 47, 55, 56, 64, 65, 73, 74,
82, 83, 91, 92, 100, 101, 102, 107, 108, 110, 113, 115, 123, 124, 135-137, 147, 148, 159, 160,
171, 172, 183-185, 195-197, 207-209, 219, 220, 231, 232, 244.

JUSTICE LEAGUE OF AMERICA SUPER SPECTACULAR
DC Comics: 1999 ($5.95, mimics format of DC 100 Page Super Spectaculars)

1-Reprints Silver Age JLA and Golden Age JSA   6.00

JUSTICE LEAGUE QUARTERLY (...International Quarterly #6 on)
DC Comics: Winter, 1990-91 - No. 17, Winter, 1994 ($2.95/$3.50, 84 pgs.)

1-12,14-17: 1-Intro The Conglomerate (Booster Gold, Praxis, Gypsy, Vapor,
Echo, Maxi-Man, & Reverb); Justice League #1-c/swipe. 1,2-Giffen plots/
breakdowns. 3-Giffen plot; 72 pg. story. 4-Rogers/Russell-a in back-up.
5,6-Waid scripts. 8,17-Global Guardians app. 12-Waid script   3.50

13-Linsner-c   5.00

NOTE: Phil Jimenez a-17p. Sprouse a-1p.

JUSTICE LEAGUES...
DC Comics: Mar, 2001 ($2.50, limited series)

JL?, Justice League of Amazons, Justice League of Atlantis, Justice League of
Arkham, Justice League of Aliens, JLA: JLA split by the Advance Man;
Perez-c in all; s&a by various   2.50

JUSTICE LEAGUE TASK FORCE
DC Comics: June, 1993 - No. 37, Aug, 1996 ($1.25/$1.50/$1.75)

1-16,0,17-37: Aquaman, Nightwing, Flash, J'onn J'onzz, & Gypsy form team.
5,6-Knight-quest tie-ins (new Batman cameo #5, 1 pg.). 15-Triumph cameo.
16-(9/94)-Zero Hour x-over;Triumph app. 0-(10/94). 17-(11/94)-Triumph
becomes part of Justice League Task Force (See JLE #68). 26-Impulse app.
35-Warlord app. 37-Triumph quits team   2.25

JUSTICE MACHINE, THE
Noble Comics: June, 1981 - No. 5, Nov, 1983 ($2.00, nos. 1-3 are mag. size)

1-Byrne-c(i)   3   9   17   24
2-Austin-c(i)   2   6   10   14
3   1   3   6   9
4,5, Annual 1 (1/84, 68 pgs.)(published by Texas Comics); 1st app. The
Elementals; Golden-c(p)   5.00

JUSTICE MACHINE (Also see The New Justice Machine)
Comico/Innovation Publishing: Jan, 1987 - No. 29, May 1989 ($1.50/$1.75)

1-29   2.25
Annual 1(6/89, $2.50, 36 pgs.)-Last Comico ish.   3.00
Summer Spectacular 1 ('89, $2.75)-Innovation Publ.; Byrne/Gustovich-c   3.00

JUSTICE MACHINE, THE
Innovation Publishing: 1990 - No. 4, 1990 ($1.95/$2.25, deluxe format, mature)

1-4: Gustovich-c/a in all   2.25

JUSTICE MACHINE FEATURING THE ELEMENTALS
Comico: May, 1986 - No. 4, Aug, 1986 ($1.50, limited series)

1-4   2.25

JUSTICE RIDERS
DC Comics: 1997 ($5.95, one-shot, prestige format)

1-Elseworlds; Dixon-s/Williams & Gray-a   6.00

JUSTICE SOCIETY OF AMERICA (See Adventure #461 & All-Star #3)
DC Comics: April, 1991 - No. 8, Nov, 1991 ($1.00, limited series)

1-8: 1-Flash. 2-Black Canary. 3-Green Lantern. 4-Hawkman. 5-Flash/
Hawkman. 6-Green Lantern/Black Canary. 7-JSA   2.50

JUSTICE SOCIETY OF AMERICA (Also see Last Days of the... Special)
DC Comics: Aug, 1992 - No. 10, May, 1993 ($1.50)

1-10   2.50

JUSTICE SOCIETY OF AMERICA 100-PAGE SUPER SPECTACULAR
DC Comics: 2000 ($6.95, mimics format of DC 100 Page Super Spectaculars)

1-"1975 Issue" reprints Flash team-up and Golden Age JSA   7.00

JUSTICE TRAPS THE GUILTY (Fargo Kid V11#3 #2)
Prize/Headline Publications: Oct-Nov, 1947 - V11#2(#92), Apr-May, 1958 (True
FBI Cases)

V2#1-S&K-c/a; electrocution-c   55   165   341   600
2-S&K-c/a   36   108   191   330
3-5-S&K-c/a   34   102   179   310
6-S&K-c/a; Feldstein-a   35   105   185   320
7,9-S&K-c/a. 7-9-V2#1-3 in indicia; #7-9 on-c   30   90   159   275
8,10-Frisch-S&K-a. 10-S&K-a   29   87   153   265
11,18,19-S&K-c   14   42   72   120
12,14-17,20-No S&K. 14-Severin/Elder-a (8pg.)   8   24   45   65
13-Used in SOTI, pg. 110-111   10   30   55   80
21,30-S&K-c   13   39   66   110
22,23,27-S&K-c   10   30   55   80
24-26,29,31-50: 32-Meskin story   7   21   36   50
28-Kirby-c   8   24   45   65
51-55,57,59-70   6   18   30   42
56-Ben Oda, Joe Simon, Joe Genola, Mort Meskin & Jack Kirby app. in
police line-up on classic-c   10   30   55   80

	GD2.0	FN6.0	VF8.0	NM9.4

58-Illo. in **SOTI**, "Treating police contemptuously" (top left); text on heroin

	27	81	142	245
71-92: 76-Orlando-a	5	15	25	35

NOTE: *Bailey* a-12, 13. *Elder* a-8. *Kirby* a-19p. *Meskin* a-22, 27, 63, 64; c-45, 46. *Robinson/Meskin* a-5, 19. *Severin* a-8, 11p. Photo c-12, 15-17.

JUST IMAGINE STAN LEE WITH... (Stan Lee re-invents DC icons)
DC Comics: 2001 - 2002 ($5.95, prestige format, one-shots)
(Adam Hughes back-c on all)(Michael Uslan back-up stories in all, diff. artists)

Joe Kubert Creating **Batman**- Back-up w/Kaluta-a	6.00
Kevin Maguire Creating **The Flash**- Back-up w/Aragonés-a	6.00
Dave Gibbons Creating **Green Lantern**- Back-up w/Giordano-a	6.00
Jerry Ordway Creating **JLA**	6.00
John Buscema Creating **Superman**- Back-up w/Kyle Baker-a	6.00
Jim Lee Creating **Wonder Woman**- Back-up w/Gene Colan-a	6.00

JUST MARRIED
Charlton Comics: January, 1958 - No. 114, Dec, 1976

1	6	18	45	75
2	4	12	25	38
3-10	3	9	19	28
11-30	2	6	13	20
31-50	2	6	11	15
51-70	2	6	9	12
71-90	1	3	6	9
91-114	1	3	6	8

JUSTY
Viz Comics: Dec 6, 1988 - No. 9, 1989 ($1.75, B&W, bi-weekly mini-series)

1-9: Japanese manga	2.50

KA'A'NGA COMICS (...Jungle King)(See Jungle Comics)
Fiction House Magazines (Glen-Kel Publ. Co.): Spring, 1949 - No. 20, Summer, 1954

1-Ka'a'nga, Lord of the Jungle begins	52	157	314	550
2 (Winter, '49-'50)	30	90	159	275
3,4	22	66	116	200
5-Camilla app.	17	51	88	150
6-10: 7-Tuska-a. 9-Tabu, Wizard of the Jungle app. 10-Used in **POP**, pg. 99				
	15	45	77	130
11-15: 15-Camilla-r by Baker/Jungle #106	12	36	61	105
16-Sheena app.	13	39	66	110
17-20	11	33	55	90
I.W. Reprint #1,8: 1-r/#18; Kinstler-c. 8-r/#10	3	9	17	25

NOTE: *Celardo* c-1. *Whitman* c-8-20(most).

KABOOM
Awesome Entertainment: Sept, 1997 - No. 3, Nov, 1997 ($2.50)

1-3: 1-Matsuda-a/Loeb-s; 4 covers exist (Matsuda, Sale, Pollina and McGuinness), 1-Dynamic Forces Edition, 2-Regular, 2-Alicia Watcher variant-c, 2-Gold logo variant -c, 3-Two covers by Liefeld & Matsuda, 3-Dynamic Forces Ed., Prelude ED.	2.50
Prelude Gold Edition	4.00

KABOOM (2nd series)
Awesome Entertainment: July, 1999 - No. 3, Dec, 1999 ($2.50)

1-3: 1-Grant-a(p); at least 4 variant covers	2.50

KABUKI
Caliber: Nov, 1994 ($3.50, B&W, one-shot)

nn-(Fear The Reaper) 1st app.; David Mack-c/a/scripts	1	3	6	8
Color Special (1/96, $2.95)-Mack-c/a/scripts; pin-ups by Tucci, Harris & Quesada				4.00
Gallery (8/95, $2.95)- pinups from Mack, Bradstreet, Paul Pope & others				3.00

KABUKI
Image Comics: Oct, 1997 - Present ($2.95, color)

1-David Mack-c/s/a	4.00
1-($10.00)-Dynamic Forces Edition	10.00
2-9	3.00
#1/2 (9/01, $2.95) r/Wizard 1/2; Eklipse Mag. article; bio	3.00
...Classics (2/99, $3.95) Reprints Fear the Reaper	4.00
...Classics 2 (3/99) $3.95) Reprints Dance of Dance	4.00

...Classics 3-5 (3-6/99, $4.95) Reprints Circle of Blood-Acts 1-3	5.00
...Classics 6-12 (7/99-3/00, $3.25) Various reprints	3.25
...Images (6/98, $4.95) r/#1 with new pin-ups	5.00
...Images 2 (1/99, $4.95) r/#1 with new pin-ups	5.00
...Metamorphosis TPB (10/00, $24.95) r/#1-9; Sienkiewicz intro.	25.00
...Reflections 1-3 (7/98, 12/98, 1/00, $4.95) new story plus art techniques	5.00

KABUKI AGENTS (SCARAB)
Image Comics: Aug, 1999 - No. 8, Aug, 2001 ($2.95, B&W)

1-8-David Mack-s/Rick Mays-a	3.00

KABUKI: CIRCLE OF BLOOD
Caliber Press: Jan, 1995 - No. 6, Nov, 1995 ($2.95, B&W)

1-David Mack story/a in all	5.00
2-6: 3-#1 on inside indicia.	3.00
6-Variant-c	3.00
TPB ($16.95) r/#1-6, intro. by Steranko	17.00
TPB (1997, $17.95) Image Edition-r/#1-6, intro. by Steranko	18.00
TPB ($24.95) Deluxe Edition	25.00

KABUKI: DANCE OF DEATH
London Night Studios: Jan, 1995 ($3.00, B&W, one-shot)

1-David Mack-c/a/scripts	1	3	6	8

KABUKI: DREAMS
Image Comics: Jan, 1998 ($4.95, TPB)

nn-Reprints Color Special & Dreams of the Dead	5.00

KABUKI: DREAMS OF THE DEAD
Caliber: July, 1996 ($2.95, one-shot)

nn-David Mack-c/a/scripts	3.00

KABUKI FAN EDITION
Gemstone Publ./Caliber: Feb, 1997 (mail-in offer, one-shot)

nn-David Mack-c/a/scripts	4.00

KABUKI: MASKS OF THE NOH
Caliber: May, 1996 - No. 4, Feb, 1997 ($2.95, limited series)

1-4: 1-Three-c (1A-Quesada, 1B-Buzz, &1C-Mack). 3-Terry Moore pin-up	3.00
TPB (4/98, $10.95) r/#1-4; intro by Terry Moore	11.00

KABUKI: SKIN DEEP
Caliber Comics: Oct, 1996 - No. 3, May, 1997 ($2.95)

1-3:David Mack-c/a/scripts 1-Two-c (1-Mack, 1-Ross)	3.00
TPB-(5/98, $9.95) r/#1-3; intro by Alex Ross	10.00

KAMANDI: AT EARTH'S END
DC Comics: June, 1993 - No. 6, Nov, 1993 ($1.75, limited series)

1-6: Elseworlds storyline	2.50

KAMANDI, THE LAST BOY ON EARTH (Also see Alarming Tales #1, Brave and the Bold #120 & 157 & Cancelled Comic Cavalcade)
National Periodical Publ./DC Comics: Oct-Nov, 1972 - 59, Sept-Oct, 1978

1-Origin & 1st app. Kamandi	5	15	38	60
2,3	3	9	20	30
4,5: 4-Intro. Prince Tuftan of the Tigers	2	6	13	20
6-10	2	6	11	16
11-20	2	6	9	12
21-28,30,31,33-40: 24-Last 20¢ issue. 31-Intro Pyra.	1	4	7	10
29,32: 29-Superman x-over. 32-(68 pgs.)-r/origin from #1 plus one new story; 4 pg. biog. of Jack Kirby with B&W photos	2	6	10	14
41-57	1	3	5	7
58-(44 pgs.)-Karate Kid x-over from LSH	2	6	9	12
59-(44 pgs.)-Cont'd in B&B #157; The Return of Omac back-up by Starlin-a(p)	2	6	9	12

NOTE: *Ayers* a(p)-48-59 (most). *Giffen* a-44p, 45p. *Kirby* a-1-40p; c-1-33. *Kubert* c-34-41. *Nasser* a-45p, 46p. *Starlin* a-59p; c-57, 59p.

KAMUI (Legend Of...#2 on)
Eclipse Comics/Viz Comics: May 12, 1987 - No. 37, Nov. 15, 1988 ($1.50, B&W, bi-weekly)

1-37: 1-3 have 2nd printings	2.50

KAOS MOON (Also see Negative Burn #34)
Caliber Comics: 1996 - No. 4, 1997 ($2.95, B&W)

Kathy #1 © MAR

Katy Keene #54 © AP

Ka-Zar V2 #2 © MAR

	GD2.0	FN6.0	VF8.0	NM9.4

	GD2.0	FN6.0	VF8.0	NM9.4

1-4-David Boller-s/a				3.00
3,4-Limited Alternate-c				4.00
3,4-Gold Alternate-c, Full Circle TPB ($5.95) r/#1,2				6.00

KARATE KID (See Action, Adventure, Legion of Super-Heroes, & Superboy)
National Periodical Publications/DC Comics: Mar-Apr, 1976 - No. 15, July-Aug, 1978 (Legion of Super-Heroes spin-off)

	2	6	9	12
1,15: 1-Meets Iris Jacobs; Estrada/Staton-a. 15-Continued into Kamandi #58				
2-14: 2-Major Disaster app. 14-Robin x-over	1	3	5	7

NOTE: *Grell* c-1-4, 5p, 6p, 7, 8. *Staton* a-1-9i. Legion x-over-No. 1, 2, 4, 6, 10, 12, 13. Princess Projectra x-over-#8, 9.

KATHY
Standard Comics: Sept, 1949 - No. 17, Sept, 1955

1-Teen-age	10	30	55	80
2-Schomburg-c	7	21	38	55
3-5	5	15	24	32
6-17: 17-Code approved	4	12	19	25

KATHY (The Teenage Tornado)
Atlas Comics/Marvel (ZPC): Oct, 1959 - No. 27, Feb, 1964

1-Teen-age	6	18	45	75
2	4	12	25	38
3-15	3	9	17	25
16-27	2	6	11	16

KAT KARSON
I. W. Enterprises: No date (Reprint)

1-Funny animals	2	6	11	15

KATO OF THE GREEN HORNET (Also see The Green Hornet)
Now Comics: Nov, 1991 - No. 4, Feb, 1992 ($2.50, mini-series)

1-4: Brent Anderson-c/a				2.50

KATO OF THE GREEN HORNET II (Also see The Green Hornet)
Now Comics: Nov, 1992 - No. 2, Dec, 1993 ($2.50, mini-series)

1,2-Baron-s/Mayerik & Sherman-a				2.50

KATY KEENE (Also see Kasco Komics, Laugh, Pep, Suzie, & Wilbur)
Archie Publ./Close-Up/Radio Comics: 1949 - No. 4, 1951; No. 5, 3/52 - No. 62, Oct, 1961 (50-53-Adventures of...on-c)

1-Bill Woggon-c/a begins; swipes-c to Mopsy #1	100	300	625	1100
2-(1950)	47	141	286	500
3-5: 3-(1951). 4-(1951)	40	120	220	380
6-10	34	102	179	310
11,13-21: 21-Last pre-code issue (3/55)	29	87	153	265
12-(Scarce)	34	102	179	310
22-40	21	63	110	185
41-62: 54-Wedding Album plus wedding pin-up. 62-Robot-c	17	51	88	150
Annual 1('54, 25¢)-All new stories; last pre-code	45	135	270	475
Annual 2-6('55-59, 25¢)-All new stories	29	87	153	265
3-D 1(1953, 25¢, large size)-Came w/glasses	40	120	220	380
Charm 1(9/58)-Woggon-c/a; new stories, and cut-outs	29	87	156	270
Glamour 1(1957)-Puzzles, games, cut-outs	29	87	156	270
Spectacular 1('56)	28	84	148	265

NOTE: Debby's Diary in #45, 47-49, 52, 57.

KATY KEENE COMICS DIGEST MAGAZINE
Close-Up, Inc. (Archie Ent.): 1987 - No. 10, July, 1990 ($1.25/$1.35/$1.50, digest size)

1	2	6	9	12
2-10	1	3	5	7

KATY KEENE FASHION BOOK MAGAZINE
Radio Comics/Archie Publications: 1955 - No. 13, Sum, '56 - N. 23, Wint, '58-59 (nn 3-10)

1-Bill Woggon-c/a	45	135	270	475
2	29	87	153	265
11-18: 18-Photo Bill Woggon	21	63	110	185
19-23	17	51	88	150

KATY KEENE HOLIDAY FUN (See Archie Giant Series Magazine No. 7, 12)

KATY KEENE PINUP PARADE
Radio Comics/Archie Publications: 1955 - No. 15, Summer, 1961 (25¢) (Cut-out & missing pages are common)

1-Cut-outs in all?; last pre-code issue	45	135	270	475
2-(1956)	27	81	145	250
3-5: 3-(1957)	24	72	127	220
6-10,12-14: 8-Mad parody. 10-Bill Woggon photo	20	60	105	180
11-Story of how comics get CCA approved, narrated by Katy	26	78	136	235
15(Rare)-Photo artist & family	40	120	232	400

KATY KEENE SPECIAL (Katy Keene #7 on; see Laugh Comics Digest)
Archie Ent.: Sept, 1983 - No. 33, 1990 (Later issues published quarterly)

1-10: 1-Woggon-r; new Woggon-c. 3-Woggon-r				5.00
11-25				6.00
26-32-(Low print run)	1	3	6	8
33	1	4	7	10

KATZENJAMMER KIDS, THE (See Captain & the Kids & Giant Comic Album)
David McKay Publ./Standard No. 12-21(Spring/'50 - 53)/Harvey No. 22, 4/53 on: 1945-1946; Summer, 1947 - No. 27, Feb-Mar, 1954

Feature Books 30	20	60	105	175
Feature Books 32,35('45),41,44('46)	17	51	88	150
Feature Book 37-Has photos & biography of Harold Knerr	19	57	99	165
1(1947)-All new stories begin	19	57	99	165
2	10	30	55	80
3-11	7	21	38	55
12-14(Standard)	6	18	29	40
-15-21(Standard)	5	15	25	35
22-25,27(Harvey): 22-24-Henry app.	5	15	25	35
26-Half in 3-D	17	51	88	150

KAYO (Formerly Bullseye & Jest; becomes Carnival Comics)
Harry 'A' Chesler: No. 12, Mar, 1945

12-Green Knight, Capt. Glory, Little Nemo (not by McCay)				
	16	48	95	150

KA-ZAR (Also see Marvel Comics #1, Savage Tales #6 & X-Men #10)
Marvel Comics Group: Aug, 1970 - No. 3, Mar, 1971 (Giant-Size, 68 pgs.)

1-Reprints earlier Ka-Zar stories; Avengers x-over in Hercules; Daredevil, X-Men app.; hidden profanity-c	3	9	20	30
2,3-Daredevil-r. 2-r/Daredevil #13 w/Kirby layouts; Ka-Zar origin, Angel-r from X-Men by Tuska. 3-Romita & Heck-a (no Kirby)	2	6	15	22

NOTE: *Buscema* r-2. *Colan* a-1p(r). *Kirby* c/a-1, 2. #1-Reprints X-Men #10 & Daredevil #24

KA-ZAR
Marvel Comics Group: Jan, 1974 - No. 20, Feb, 1977 (Regular Size)

1	2	6	11	16
2-10	1	3	6	8
11-14,16,18-20				5.00
15,17-(Regular 25¢ edition)(8/76)				5.00
15,17-(30¢-c variants, limited distribution)	1	3	5	7

NOTE: *Alcala* a-6i, 8i. *Brunner* c-4. *J. Buscema* a-6-10p; c-1, 5, 7. *Heath* a-12. *G. Kane* c(p)-3, 5, 8-11, 15, 20. *Kirby* c-12p. *Reinman* a-1.

KA-ZAR (Volume 2)
Marvel Comics: May, 1997 - No. 20, Dec, 1998 ($1.95/$1.99)

1-Waid-s/Andy Kubert-c/a. thru #4				3.00
1-2nd printing; new cover				2.25
2,4: 2-Two-c				2.50
3-Alpha Flight #1 preview				3.00
5-13,15-20: 8-Includes Spider-Man Cybercomic CD-ROM. 9-11-Thanos app. 15-Priest-s/Martinez & Rodriguez-a begin; Punisher app.				2.25
14-($2.99) Last Waid/Kubert issue; flip book with 2nd story previewing new creative team of Priest-s/Martinez & Rodriguez-a				3.00
'97 Annual ($2.99)-Wraparound-c				3.00

KA-ZAR OF THE SAVAGE LAND
Marvel Comics: Feb, 1997 ($2.50, one-shot)

1-Wraparound-c				2.50

KA-ZAR: SIBLING RIVALRY
Marvel Comics: July, 1997 ($1.95, one-shot)

Keen Detective Funnies V1 #10 © CEN

Ken Maynard Western #5 © FAW

Key Comics #2 © Consolidated Mags.

	GD2.0	FN6.0	VF8.0	NM9.4

(# -1) Flashback story w/Alpha Flight #1 preview				2.25

KA-ZAR THE SAVAGE (See Marvel Fanfare)
Marvel Comics Group: Apr, 1981 - No. 34, Oct, 1984 (Regular size)
(Mando paper #10 on)

1				4.00
2-20,24,27,28,30-34: 11-Origin Zabu. 12-One of two versions with panel				
missing on pg. 10. 20-Kraven the Hunter-c/story (also apps. in #21)				2.50
12-Version with panel on pg. 10 (1600 printed)				5.00
21-23, 25,26-Spider-Man app. 26-Photo-c.				3.00
29-Double size; Ka-Zar & Shanna wed				3.00
NOTE: *B. Anderson a-1-15p, 18, 19; c-1-17, 18p, 20(back). G. Kane a(back-up)-11, 12, 14.*

KEEN DETECTIVE FUNNIES (Formerly Detective Picture Stories?)
Centaur Publications: No. 8, July, 1938 - No. 24, Sept, 1940

V1#8-The Clock continues-r/Funny Picture Stories #1; Roy Crane-a (1st?)				
	218	654	1364	2400
9-Tex Martin by Eisner; The Gang Buster app.	84	252	525	925
10,11: 11-Dean Denton story (begins?)	75	225	469	825
V2#1,2-The Eye Sees by Frank Thomas begins; ends #23(Not in V2#3&5).				
2-Jack Cole-a	68	205	426	750
3-6: 3-TNT Todd begins. 4-Gabby Flynn begins. 5,6-Dean Denton story				
	64	192	398	700
7-The Masked Marvel by Ben Thompson begins (7/39, 1st app.)(scarce)				
	236	708	1477	2600
8-Nudist ranch panel w/four girls	84	252	525	925
9-11	73	219	455	800
12(12/39)-Origin The Eye Sees by Frank Thomas; death of Masked				
Marvel's sidekick ZL	91	273	568	1000
V3#1,2	68	205	426	750
18,19,21,22: 18-Bondage/torture-c	68	205	426	750
20-Classic Eye Sees-c by Thomas	95	285	597	1050
23-Air Man begins (intro); Air Man-c	75	273	568	1000
24-(scarce) Air Man-c	95	285	597	1050
NOTE: *Burgos a-V2#2. Jack Cole a-V2#2. Eisner a-10, V2#6r. Ken Ernst a-V2#4-7, 9, 10, 19, 21; c-V2#4. Everett a-V2#6, 7, 9, 11, 12, 20. Guardineer a-V2#5, 66. Gustavson a-V2#4-6. Simon (c-V3#1. Thompson c-V2#7, 9, 10, 22.*

KEEN KOMICS
Centaur Publications: V2#1, May, 1939 - V2#3, Nov, 1939

V2#1(Large size)-Dan Hastings (s/f), The Big Top, Bob Phantom the				
Magician, The Mad Goddess app.	95	285	597	1050
V2#2(Reg. size)-The Forbidden Idol of Machu Picchu; Cut Carson by Burgos				
begins	61	182	381	675
V2#3-Saddle Sniffl by Jack Cole, Circus Pays, Kings Revenge app.				
	61	182	381	675
NOTE: *Binder a-V2#2. Burgos a-V2#2, 3. Ken Ernst a-V2#2. Gustavson a-V2#2. Jack Cole a-V2#3.*

KEEN TEENS (Girls magazine)
Life's Romances Publ./Leader/Magazine Ent.: 1945 - No. 6, Aug-Sept, 1947

nn (#1)-14 pgs. Claire Voyant (cont'd. in other nn issue) movie photos, Dotty				
Dripple, Gertie O'Grady & Sissy; Van Johnson, Frank Sinatra photo-c				
	33	99	174	300
nn (#2, 1946)-16 pgs. Claire Voyant & 16 pgs. movie photos				
	27	81	142	245
3-6: 4-Glenn Ford photo-c. 5-Perry Como-c	11	33	55	90

KEIF LLAMA
Oni Press: Mar, 1999 ($2.95, B&W, one-shot)

1-Matt Howarth-s/a				3.00

KELLYS, THE (Formerly Rusty Comics; Spy Cases No. 26 on)
Marvel Comics (HPC): No. 23, Jan, 1950 - No. 25, June, 1950 (52 pgs.)

23-Teenage	12	36	61	100
24,25: 24-Margie app.	8	24	42	60

KELVIN MACE
Vortex Publications: 1986 - No. 2, 1986 ($2.00, B&W)

1,2: 1-(B&W). 1-2nd print (1/87, $1.75). 2-(Color)				2.25

KEN MAYNARD WESTERN (Movie star)(See Wow Comics, 1936)
Fawcett Publ.: Sept, 1950 - No. 8, Feb, 1952 (All 36 pgs; photo front/back-c)

1-Ken Maynard & his horse Tarzan begin	59	177	369	650

2	39	117	208	360
3-8: 6-Atomic bomb explosion panel	30	90	159	275

KEN SHANNON (Becomes Gabby #11 on) (Also see Police Comics #103)
Quality Comics Group: Oct, 1951 - No. 10, Apr, 1953 (A private eye)

1-Crandall-a	38	114	203	350
2-Crandall c/a(2)	31	93	165	285
3-5-Crandall-a. 3-Horror-c	22	66	116	195
6-Crandall-c/a; "The Weird Vampire Mob"-c/s	25	75	130	225
7,10: 7-Crandall-a. 10-Crandall-c	18	54	94	155
8,9: 8-Opium den drug use story	17	51	88	150
NOTE: *Crandall/Cuidera c-1-10. Jack Cole a-1-9. #1-15 published after title change to Gabby.*

KEN STUART
Publication Enterprises: Jan, 1949 (Sea Adventures)

1-Frank Borth-c/a	10	30	55	80

KENT BLAKE OF THE SECRET SERVICE (Spy)
Marvel/Atlas Comics(20CC): May, 1951 - No. 14, July, 1953

1-Injury to eye, bondage, torture; Brodsky-c	21	63	110	185
2-Drug use w/hypo scenes; Brodsky-c	15	45	77	130
3-14: 8-R.Q. Sale-a (2 pgs.)	9	27	49	70
NOTE: *Heath c-5, 7, 8. Infantino c-12. Maneely c-3. Sinnott a-2(3). Tuska a-8(3pg.).*

KENTS, THE
DC Comics: Aug, 1997 - No. 12, July, 1998 ($2.50, limited series)

1-12-Ostrander-s/art by Truman and Bair (#1-8), Mandrake (#9-12)				3.00
TPB ($19.95) r/#1-12				20.00

KERRY DRAKE (Also see A-1 Comics)
Argo: No. 2, March, 1956

1,2-Newspaper-r	8	24	45	65

KERRY DRAKE DETECTIVE CASES (...Racket Buster No. 32,33)
(Also see Chamber of Clues & Green Hornet Comics #42-47)
Life's Romances/Com/Magazine Ent.No.1-5/Harvey No.6: 1944 - No. 5, 1944; No. 6, Jan, 1948 - No. 33, Aug, 1952

nn(1944)(A-1 Comics)(slightly over-size)	29	87	156	270
2	19	57	99	165
3-5(1944)	16	48	83	140
6,8(1948): Lady Crime by Powell. 8-Bondage-c	11	33	55	90
7-Kubert-a; biog of Andriola (artist)	12	36	61	105
9,10-Two-part marijuana story; Kerry smokes marijuana in #10				
	16	48	83	140
11-15	10	30	55	80
16-33	8	24	42	60
NOTE: *Andiola c-6-9. Berg a-5. Powell a-10-23, 28, 29.*

KEWPIES
Will Eisner Publications: Spring, 1949

1-Feiffer-a; Kewpie Doll ad on back cover	45	135	270	475

KEY COMICS
Consolidated Magazines: Jan, 1944 - No. 5, Aug, 1946

1-The Key, Will-O-The-Wisp begin	40	120	240	420
2 (3/44)	23	69	121	210
3,4: 4-(5/46)-Origin John Quincy The Atom (begins); Walter Johnson c-3-5				
	20	60	105	175
5-4pg. Faust Opera adaptation; Kiefer-a; back-c advertises "Masterpieces				
Illustrated" by Lloyd Jacquet after he left Classic Comics (no copies of				
Masterpieces Illustrated known)	25	75	130	225

KEY RING COMICS
Dell Publishing Co.: 1941 (16 pgs.; two colors) (sold 5 for 10¢)

1-Sky Hawk, 1-Viking Carter, 1-Features Sleepy Samson, 1-Origin Greg Gilday-				
r/War Comics #2	7	21	36	50
1-Radior (Super hero)	8	24	42	60
NOTE: *Each book has two holes in spine to put in binder.*

KICKERS, INC.
Marvel Comics Group: Nov, 1986 - No. 12, Oct, 1987

1-12				2.25

KID CARROTS
St. John Publishing Co.: September, 1953

Kid Colt #2 © MAR

Kiddie Kapers #1 © Decker Pub.

Kid Komics #7 © MAR

	GD2.0	FN6.0	VF8.0	NM9.4

1-Funny animal   7   21   36   50

KID COLT OUTLAW (Kid Colt #1-4; ...Outlaw #5-on)(Also see All Western Winners, Best Western, Black Rider, Giant-Size..., Two-Gun Kid, Two-Gun Western, Western Winners, Wild Western, Wisco)
Marvel Comics(LCC) 1-16; Atlas(LMC) 17-102; Marvel 103-on: 8/48 - No. 139, 3/68; No. 140, 11/69 - No. 229, 4/79

1-Kid Colt & his horse Steel begin.	100	300	625	1100
2	50	150	300	525
3-5: 4-Anti-Wertham editorial; Tex Taylor app. 5-Blaze Carson app.				
	40	120	240	420
6-8: 6-Tex Taylor app; 7-Nimo the Lion begins, ends #10				
	29	87	153	265
9,10 (52 pgs.)	29	87	153	265
11-Werthm	33	99	174	300
12-20	21	63	110	190
21-32	17	51	88	150
33-45: Black Rider in all	13	39	66	110
46,47,49,50	11	33	55	90
48-Kubert-a	11	33	55	95
51-53,55,56	9	27	49	70
54-Williamson/Maneely-c	10	30	55	80
57-60,66: 4-pg. Williamson-a in all	7	21	53	85
61-63,67-78,80-86: 70-Severin-c. 73-Maneely-c. 86-Kirby-a(r).				
	5	15	34	55
64,65-Crandall-a	5	15	38	60
79,87: 79-Origin retold. 87-Davis-a(r)	5	15	38	60
88,89-Williamson-a in both (4 pgs.). 89-Redrawn Matt Slade #2				
	18	40	65	
90-99,101-106,108,109: 91-Kirby/Ayers-a. 95-Kirby/Ayers-c/story.				
102-Last 10¢ issue	4	12	29	45
100	4	12	30	50
107-Only Kirby sci-fi cover of title; Kirby -a.	4	12	30	50
110-(5/63)-1st app. Iron Mask (Iron Man type villain)	4	12	30	50
111-120: 114-(1/64)-2nd app. Iron Mask	3	10	23	35
121-129,133-139: 121-Rawhide Kid x-over. 125-Two-Gun Kid x-over				
139-Last 12¢ issue	3	9	17	25
130-132 (68 pgs.)-one new story each. 130-Origin	3	10	23	35
140-155: 140-Reprints begin (later issues all-r). 155-Last 15¢ issue				
	2	6	11	16
156-Giant; reprints (52 pgs.)	2	6	17	24
157-180,200: 170-Origin retold.	2	6	10	14
181-199	2	6	9	12
201-229: 229-Rawhide Kid-r	1	4	7	10
205-209(30¢-c variants, limited dist.)	2	6	9	12
218-220-(35¢-c variants, limited dist.)	2	6	9	12
...Album (no date; 1950's; Atlas Comics)-132 pgs.; random binding, cardboard cover, B&W stories; contents can vary (Rare)	77	231	483	850

NOTE: **Ayers** a-many. **Colan** a-52, 53; c(p)-223, 228, 229. **Crandall** a-140r, 167: **Everett** a-90, 137i, 225i(r). **Heath** a-8(2); c-34, 35, 39, 44, 46, 48, 49, 57, 64. **Heck** a-135, 139. **Jack Keller** a-25(2), 26-68(3-4), 78, 94p, 98, 99, 108, 110, 130, 132, 140-150r. **Kirby** a-86r, 93, 96, 107, 119, 176(part); c-87, 92-95, 97, 99-112, 114-117; 121-123, 197r; w/Ditko c-89. **Maneely** a-12, 68, 81; c-17, 19, 40-43, 47, 52, 53, 62, 65, 68, 78, 81, 142r, 150r. **Morrow** a-173r, 216r. **Rico** a-13, 18. **Severin** c-58, 59, 143, 148, 149i. **Shores** a-39, 41-43, 143r; c-1-10(most), 24. **Sutton** a-136, 137p, 225p(r). **Wildey** a-47, 54, 82, 144r. **Williamson** r-147, 170, 172, 216. **Woodbridge** a-64, 81. Black Rider in #33-45, 74, 86. Iron Mask in #110, 114, 121, 127. Sam Hawk in #84, 101, 111, 121, 146, 174, 181, 188.

KID COWBOY (Also see Approved Comics #4 & Boy Cowboy)
Ziff-Davis Publ./St. John (Approved Comics) #11,14: 1950 - No. 11, Wint, '52-'53; No. 14, June, 1954 (No #12,13)
(Painted covers #1-10, 14)

1-Lucy Belle & Red Feather begin	16	48	83	140
2-Maneely-c	10	30	55	80
3-11,14: (#3, spr. '51). 5-Berg-a. 14-Code approved	9	27	49	70

KID DEATH & FLUFFY HALLOWEEN SPECIAL
Event Comics: Oct, 1997 ($2.95, B&W, one-shot)

1-Variant-c by Cebollero & Quesada/Palmiotti   3.00

KID DEATH & FLUFFY SPRING BREAK SPECIAL
Event Comics: July, 1996 ($2.50, B&W, one-shot)

1-Quesada & Palmiotti-c/scripts   2.50

KIDDIE KAPERS
Kiddie Kapers Co., 1945/Decker Publ. (Red Top-Farrell): 1945?(nd); Oct, 1957; 1963 - 1964

1(nd, 1945-46?), 36 pgs.)-Infinity-c; funny animal	9	27	49	70
1(10/57)(Decker)-Little Bit-r from Kiddie Karnival	5	15	23	30
Super Reprint #7, 10('63), 12, 14('63), 15,17('64), 18('64): 10, 14-r/Animal Adventures #1. 15-Animal Adventures #? 17-Cowboys 'N' Injuns #?				
	2	6	9	12

KIDDIE KARNIVAL
Ziff-Davis Publ. Co. (Approved Comics): 1952 (25¢, 100 pgs.) (One Shot)

nn-Rebound Little Bit #1,2; painted-c   37   111   197   340

KID ETERNITY (Becomes Buccaneers) (See Hit Comics)
Quality Comics Group: Spring, 1946 - No. 18, Nov, 1949

1	86	258	540	950
2	40	120	232	400
3-Mac Raboy-a	40	120	237	410
4-10	25	75	130	225
11-18	20	60	105	175

KID ETERNITY
DC Comics: 1991 - No. 3, Nov, 1991 ($4.95, limited series)

1-3: Grant Morrison scripts   6.00

KID ETERNITY
DC Comics (Vertigo): May, 1993 - No. 16, Sept, 1994 ($1.95, mature)

1-16: 1-Gold ink-c. 6-Photo-c. All Sean Phillips-c/a except #15 (Phillips-c/i only)   2.25

KID FROM DODGE CITY, THE
Atlas Comics (MMC): July, 1957 - No. 2, Sept, 1957

1-Don Heck-c	10	30	55	80
2-Everett-c	6	18	32	45

KID FROM TEXAS, THE (A Texas Ranger)
Atlas Comics (CSI): June, 1957 - No. 2, Aug, 1957

1-Powell-a; Severin-c	10	30	55	85
2	6	18	32	45

KID KOKO
I. W. Enterprises: 1958

Reprint #1,2-(r/M.E.'s Koko & Kola #4, 1947)   2   6   10   14

KID KOMICS (Kid Movie Komics No. 11)
Timely Comics (USA 1,2/FCI 3-10): Feb, 1943 - No. 10, Spring, 1946

1-Origin Captain Wonder & sidekick Tim Mullrooney, & Subbie; intro the Sea-Going Lad, Pinto Pete, & Trixie Trouble; Knuckles & Whitewash Jones (from Young Allies) app.; Wolverton-a (7 pgs.)	400	1200	2500	4800
2-The Young Allies, Red Hawk, & Tommy Tyme begin; last Captain Wonder & Subbie	173	519	1080	1900
3-The Vision, Daredevils & Red Hawk app.	136	408	852	1500
4-The Destroyer begins; Sub-Mariner app.; Red Hawk & Tommy Tyme end	114	342	713	1250
5,6: 5-Tommy Tyme begins, ends #10	86	258	540	950
7-10: 7,10-The Whizzer app. Destroyer not in 7,8. 10-Last Destroyer, Young Allies & Whizzer	80	240	500	875

NOTE: **Brodsky** c-5. **Schomburg** c-2-4, 6-10. **Shores** c-1. Captain Wonder c-1, 2. The Young Allies c-3-10.

KID MONTANA (Formerly Davy Crockett Frontier Fighter; The Gunfighters No. 51 on)
Charlton Comics: V2#9, Nov, 1957 - No. 50, Mar, 1965

V2#9	5	15	34	55
10	4	12	25	38
11,12,14-20	3	9	17	26
13-Williamson-a	4	12	25	38
21-35	2	6	12	18
36-50	2	6	10	14

NOTE: Title change to Montana Kid on cover only #44 & 45; remained Kid Montana on inside.

KID MOVIE KOMICS (Formerly Kid Komics; Rusty Comics #12 on)
Timely Comics: No. 11, Summer, 1946

11-Silly Seal & Ziggy Pig; 2 pgs. Kurtzman "Hey Look" plus 6 pg. "Pigtales"

Killraven #1 © MAR

Killer Princesses #1
© Gail Simone & Lea Hernandez

King Comics #47 © DMP

	GD2.0	FN6.0	VF8.0	NM9.4
story	27	81	142	245

KIDNAPPED (Robert Louis Stevenson's...also see Movie Comics)(Disney)
Dell Publishing Co.: No. 1101, May, 1960

	GD2.0	FN6.0	VF8.0	NM9.4
Four Color 1101-Movie, photo-c	6	18	42	80

KIDNAP RACKET (See Harvey Comics Hits No. 57)

KID SLADE GUNFIGHTER (Formerly Matt Slade...)
Atlas Comics (SPI): No. 5, Jan, 1957 - No. 8, July, 1957

5-Maneely, Roth, Severin-a in all; Maneely-c	13	39	66	110
6,8-Severin-c	8	24	42	60
7-Williamson/Mayo-a, 4 pgs.	10	30	55	85

KID SUPREME (See Supreme)
Image Comics (Extreme Studios): Mar, 1996 - No. 3, July, 1996 ($2.50)

1-3: Fraga-a/scripts. 3-Glory-c/app.		2.50

KID TERRIFIC
Image Comics: Nov, 1998 ($2.95, B&W)

1-Snyder & Diliberto-s/a		3.00

KID ZOO COMICS
Street & Smith Publications: July, 1948 (52 pgs.)

1-Funny Animal	27	81	145	250

KILLER (...Tales By Timothy Truman)
Eclipse Comics: March, 1985 ($1.75, one-shot, Baxter paper)

1-Timothy Truman-c/a		2.50

KILLER INSTINCT (Video game)
Acclaim Comics: June, 1996 - No. 6 ($2.50, limited series)

1-6: 1-Bart Sears-a(p). 4-Special #1. 5-Special #2. 6-Special #3		3.00

KILLER PRINCESSES
Oni Press: Dec, 2001 - No. 3 ($2.95, limited series)

1-Gail Simone-s/Lea Hernandez-a	3.00	

KILLERS, THE
Magazine Enterprises: 1947 - No. 2, 1948 (No month)

1-Mr. Zin, the Hatchet Killer; mentioned in SOTI, pgs. 179,180; used by N.Y. Legis. Comm.; L. B. Cole-c	105	315	656	1150
2-(Scarce)-Hashish smoking story; "Dying, Dying, Dead" drug story; Whitney, Ingels-a; Whitney hanging-c	86	258	540	950

KILLING JOKE, THE (See Batman: The Killing Joke under Batman one-shots)

KILLPOWER: THE EARLY YEARS
Marvel Comics UK: Sept, 1993 - No. 4, Dec, 1993 ($1.75, mini-series)

1-($2.95)-Foil embossed-c		3.00
2-4: 2-Genetix app. 3-Punisher app.		2.25

KILLRAVEN (See Amazing Adventures #18 (5/73))
Marvel Comics: Feb, 2001 ($2.99, one-shot)

1-Linsner-s/a/c		3.00

KILLRAZOR
Image Comics (Top Cow Productions): Aug, 1995 ($2.50, one-shot)

1		2.50

KILL YOUR BOYFRIEND
DC Comics (Vertigo): June, 1995 ($4.95, one-shot)

1-Grant Morrison story		6.00
1($5.95, 1998) 2nd printing		6.00

KILROY (Volume 2)
Caliber Press: 1998 ($2.95, B&W)

1-Pruett-s		3.00

KILROY IS HERE
Caliber Press: 1995 ($2.95, B&W)

1-10		3.00

KILROYS, THE
B&I Publ. Co. No. 1-19/American Comics Group: June-July, 1947 - No. 54, June-July, 1955

1		23	69	121	210

	GD2.0	FN6.0	VF8.0	NM9.4
2	12	36	61	105
3-5: 5-Gross-a	10	30	55	80
6-10: 8-Milt Gross's Moronica	7	21	38	55
11-20: 14-Gross-a	7	21	36	50
21-30	6	18	29	40
31-47,50-54	5	15	25	35
48,49-(3-D effect-c/stories)	18	54	94	155

KILROY: THE SHORT STORIES
Caliber Press: 1995 ($2.95, B&W)

1		3.00

KIN
Image Comics (Top Cow): Mar, 2000 - Present ($2.95)

1-5-Gary Frank-s/c/a		3.00
1-($6.95) DF Alternate footprint cover		7.00
6-($3.95)		4.00

KINDRED, THE
Image Comics (WildStorm Productions): Mar, 1994 - No. 4, July, 1995 ($1.95, limited series)

1-($2.50)-Grifter & Backlash app. in all; bound-in trading card		2.50
2-4		2.50
2,3: 2-Variant-c. 3-Alternate-c by Portacio, see Deathblow #5		4.00
Trade paperback (2/95, $9.95)		10.00

NOTE: **Booth** c/a-1-4. The first four issues contain coupons redeemable for a Jim Lee Grifter/Backlash print.

KINDRED II, THE
DC Comics (WildStorm Productions): Mar, 2002 - No. 4 ($2.50, limited series)

1-Booth-s/Booth & Regla-a		2.50

KING ARTHUR AND THE KNIGHTS OF JUSTICE
Marvel Comics UK: Dec, 1993 - No. 3, Feb, 1994 ($1.25, limited series)

1-3: TV adaptation		2.25

KING CLASSICS
King Features : 1977 (36 pgs., cardboard-c)
(Printed in Spain for U.S. distr.)

1-Connecticut Yankee, 2-Last of the Mohicans, 3-Moby Dick, 4-Robin Hood, 5-Swiss Family Robinson, 6-Robinson Crusoe, 7-Treasure Island, 8-20,000 Leagues, 9-Christmas Carol, 10-Huck Finn, 11-Around the World in 80 Days, 12-Davy Crockett, 13-Don Quixote, 14-Gold Bug, 15-Ivanhoe, 16-Three Musketeers, 17-Baron Munchausen, 18-Alice in Wonderland, 19-Black Arrow, 20-Five Weeks in a Balloon, 21-Great Expectations, 22-Gulliver's Travels, 23-Prince & Pauper, 24-Lawrence of Arabia (Originals, 1977-78)				
each....	2	6	10	14
Reprints (1979; HRN-24)	1	3	6	8

NOTE: The first eight issues were not numbered. Issues No. 25-32 were advertised but not published. The 1977 originals have HRN 32a; the 1978 originals have HRN 32b.

KING COLT (See Luke Short's Western Stories)

KING COMICS (Strip reprints)
David McKay Publications/Standard #156-on: 4/36 - No. 155, 11-12/49; No. 156, Spr/50 - No. 159, 2/52 (Winter on-c)

1-1st app. Flash Gordon by Alex Raymond; Brick Bradford (1st app.), Popeye, Henry (1st app.) & Mandrake the Magician (1st app.) begin; Popeye-c begin	1200	3600	9000	–
2	344	1032	1892	3100
3	233	699	1282	2100
4	178	534	979	1600
5	128	384	704	1150
6-10: 9-X-Mas-c	89	267	490	800
11-20	69	207	380	625
21-30: 21-X-Mas-c	50	150	275	450
31-40: 33-Last Segar Popeye	40	120	220	360
41-50: 46-Text illos by Marge Buell contain characters similar to Lulu, Alvin & Tubby. 50-The Lone Ranger begins	34	102	179	310
51-60: 52-Barney Baxter begins?	23	69	121	210
61-The Phantom begins	25	75	130	225
62-80: 76-Flag-c. 79-Blondie begins	18	54	94	155
81-99	14	42	72	120
100	17	51	88	150
101-114: 114-Last Raymond issue (1 pg.); Flash Gordon by Austin Briggs begins, ends #155	13	39	66	110

KI

The Kingdom #1 © DC

KISS Psycho Circus #17 © KISS Catalog

Kissing Chaos © Arthur Dela Cruz

	GD2.0	FN6.0	VF8.0	NM9.4
115-145: 117-Phantom origin retold	10	30	55	80
146,147-Prince Valiant in both	8	24	45	65
148-155: 155-Flash Gordon ends (11-12/49)	8	24	45	65
156-159: 156-New logo begins (Standard)	8	24	42	60

NOTE: Marge Buell text illos in No. 24-46 at least.

KING CONAN (Conan The King No. 20 on)
Marvel Comics Group: Mar, 1980 - No. 19, Nov, 1983 (52 pgs.)

1				6.00
2-19: 4-Death of Thoth Amon. 7-1st Paul Smith-a, 1 pg. pin-up (9/81)				4.00

NOTE: J. Buscema a-1-9p, 17p; c(p)-1-5, 7-9, 14, 17. Kaluta c-19. Nebres a-17i, 18, 19i. Severin c-18. Simonson c-6.

KINGDOM, THE
DC Comics: Feb, 1999 - No. 2, Feb, 1999 ($2.95, limited series)

1,2-Waid-s; sequel to Kingdom Come; introduces Hypertime				4.00
...: Kid Flash 1 (2/99, $1.99) Waid-s/Pararillo-a, ...: Nightstar 1 (2/99, $1.99) Waid-s/Haley-a, ...: Offspring 1 (2/99, $1.99) Waid-s/Quitely-a, ...: Planet Krypton 1 (2/99, $1.99) Waid-s/Kitson-a, ...: Son of the Bat 1 (2/99, $1.99) Waid-s/Apthorp-a				2.25

KINGDOM COME
DC Comics: 1996 - No. 4, 1996 ($4.95, painted limited series)

1-Mark Waid scripts & Alex Ross-painted c/a in all; tells the last days of the DC Universe; 1st app. Magog	1	4	7	10
2-Superman forms new Justice League	1	4	7	10
3-Return of Capt. Marvel	1	3	6	8
4-Final battle of Superman and Capt. Marvel	1	3	6	8
Deluxe Slipcase Edition-($89.95) w/Revelations companion book, 12 new story pages, foil stamped covers, signed and numbered				160.00
Hardcover Edition-($29.95)-Includes 12 new story pages and artwork from Revelations, new cover artwork with gold foil inlay				35.00
Hardcover 2nd printing				30.00
Softcover Ed.-($14.95)-Includes 12 new story pgs. & artwork from Revelations, new c-artwork				15.00

KING KONG (See Movie Comics)

KING LEONARDO & HIS SHORT SUBJECTS (TV)
Dell Publishing Co./Gold Key: Nov-Jan, 1961-62 - No. 4, Sept, 1963

Four Color 1242,1278	14	42	98	175
01390-207(5-7/62)(Dell)	10	30	70	130
1 (10/62)	12	36	84	150
2-4	9	27	63	115

KING LOUIE & MOWGLI (See Jungle Book under Movie Comics)
Gold Key: May, 1968 (Disney)

1 (#10223-805)-Characters from Jungle Book	3	9	19	28

KING OF DIAMONDS (TV)
Dell Publishing Co.: July-Sept, 1962

01-391-209-Photo-c	4	12	27	42

KING OF KINGS (Movie)
Dell Publishing Co.: No. 1236, Oct-Nov, 1961

Four Color 1236-Photo-c	8	24	56	100

KING OF THE BAD MEN OF DEADWOOD
Avon Periodicals: 1950 (See Wild Bill Hickok #16)

nn-Kinstler-c; Kamen/Feldstein-r/Cowpuncher #2	16	48	83	140

KING OF THE ROYAL MOUNTED (See Famous Feature Stories, King Comics, Red Ryder #3 & Super Book #2, 6)

KING OF THE ROYAL MOUNTED (Zane Grey's...)
David McKay/Dell Publishing Co.: No. 1, May, 1937; No. 9, 1940; No. 207, Dec, 1948 - No. 935, Sept-Nov, 1958

Feature Books 1 (5/37)(McKay)	73	219	511	950
Large Feature Comic 9 (1940)	40	120	280	525
Four Color 207(#1, 12/48)	15	45	105	190
Four Color 265,283	8	24	56	100
Four Color 310,340	6	18	42	80
Four Color 363,384, 8(6-8/52)-10	5	15	35	65
11-20	5	15	34	55
21-28(3-5/58), Four Color 935(9-11/58)	4	12	27	42

NOTE: 4-Color No. 207, 265, 283, 310, 340, 363, 384 are all newspaper reprints with Jim Gary art. No. 8 on are all Dell originals. Painted c-No. 9-on.

KINGPIN
Marvel Comics: Nov, 1997 ($5.99, squarebound, one-shot)

nn-Spider-Man & Daredevil vs. Kingpin; Stan Lee-s/ John Romita Sr.-a				6.00

KING RICHARD & THE CRUSADERS
Dell Publishing Co.: No. 588, Oct, 1954

Four Color 588-Movie, Matt Baker-a, photo-c	10	30	70	130

KINGS OF THE NIGHT
Dark Horse Comics: 1990 - No. 2, 1990 ($2.25, limited series)

1,2-Robert E. Howard adaptation; Bolton-c				2.25

KING SOLOMON'S MINES (Movie)
Avon Periodicals: 1951

nn (#1 on 1st page)	40	120	220	380

KING TIGER & MOTORHEAD
Dark Horse Comics: Aug, 1996 - No. 2, Sept, 1996 ($2.95, limited series)

1,2-Chichester scripts				3.00

KIPLING, RUDYARD (See Mowgli, The Jungle Book)

KISS (See Crazy Magazine, Howard the Duck #12, 13, Marvel Comics Super Special #1, 5, Rock Fantasy Comics #10 & Rock N' Roll Comics #9)

KISS: THE PSYCHO CIRCUS
Image Comics: Aug, 1997 - No. 31, June, 2000 ($1.95/$2.25/$2.50)

1-Holguin-s/Medina-a(p)	1	4	7	10
1-2nd & 3rd printings				2.50
2				6.00
3,4: 4-Photo-c				4.00
5-8: 5-Begin $2.25-c				3.00
9-29				2.50
30,31: 30-Begin $2.50-c				2.50
Book 1 TPB ('98, $12.95) r/#1-6				13.00
Book 2 Destroyer TPB (8/99, $9.95) r/#10-13				10.00
Book 3 Whispered Scream TPB ('00, $9.95) r/#7-9,18				10.00
...Magazine 1 ($6.95) r/#1-3 plus interviews				7.00
...Magazine 2-5 ($4.95) 2-r/#4,5 plus interviews. 3-r/#6,7. 4-r/#8,9				5.00
Wizard 1/2 Edition ('98, supplement) Bios, tour preview and interviews				2.25

KISSING CHAOS
Oni Press: Sept, 2001 - No. 8 ($2.25, B&W, 6" x 9", limited series)

1-5-Arthur Dela Cruz-s/a				2.25

KISSYFUR (TV)
DC Comics: 1989 (Sept.) ($2.00, 52 pgs., one-shot)

1-Based on Saturday morning cartoon				4.00

KIT CARSON (Formerly All True Detective Cases No. 4; Fighting Davy Crockett No. 9; see Blazing Sixguns & Frontier Fighters)
Avon Periodicals: 1950; No. 2, 8/51 - No. 3, 12/51; No. 5, 11-12/54 - No. 8, 9/55 (No #4)

nn(#1) (1950)- "...Indian Scout"; r-Cowboys 'N' Injuns #?	14	42	72	120
2(8/51)	10	30	55	80
3(12/51)- "...Fights the Comanche Raiders"	8	24	45	65
5-6,8(11-12/54-9/55): 5-Formerly All True Detective Cases (last pre-code); titled "...and the Trail of Doom"	8	24	42	60
7-McCann-a?	8	24	42	60
I.W. Reprint #10('63)-r/Kit Carson #1; Severin-c	2	6	12	18

NOTE: Kinstler c-1-3, 5-8.

KIT CARSON & THE BLACKFEET WARRIORS
Realistic: 1953

nn-Reprint; Kinstler-c	10	30	55	80

KIT KARTER
Dell Publishing Co.: May-July, 1962

1	3	9	20	30

KITTY
St. John Publishing Co.: Oct, 1948

Knights of Pendragon #17 © MAR

Kobalt #15 © Milestone Media

Kong the Untamed #4 © DC

	GD2.0	FN6.0	VF8.0	NM9.4
1-Teenage; Lily Renee-c/a	7	21	38	55

KITTY PRYDE, AGENT OF S.H.I.E.L.D. (Also see Excalibur)
Marvel Comics: Dec, 1997 - No. 3, Feb, 1998 ($2.50, limited series)

1-3-Hama-s				2.50

KITTY PRYDE AND WOLVERINE (Also see Uncanny X-Men & X-Men)
Marvel Comics Group: Nov, 1984 - No. 6, Apr, 1985 (Limited series)

1-6: Characters from X-Men				4.50

KLARER GIVEAWAYS (See Wisco in the Promotional Comics section)

KNIGHTHAWK
Acclaim Comics (Windjammer): Sept, 1995 - No. 6, Nov, 1995 ($2.50, lim. series)

1-6: 6-origin				2.50

KNIGHTMARE
Antarctic Press: July, 1994 - May, 1995 ($2.75, B&W, mature readers)

1-6				2.75

KNIGHTMARE
Image Comics (Extreme Studios): Feb, 1995 - No. 5, June, 1995 ($2.50)

0 ($3.50)				3.50
1-5: 4-Quesada & Palmiotti variant-c, 5-Flip book w/Warcry				2.50

KNIGHTS OF PENDRAGON, THE (Also see Pendragon)
Marvel Comics Ltd.: July, 1990 - No. 18, Dec, 1991 ($1.95)

1-18: 1-Capt. Britain app. 2,8-Free poster inside. 9,10-Bolton-c. 11,18-Iron Man app.				2.25

KNIGHTS OF THE ROUND TABLE
Dell Publishing Co.: No. 540, Mar, 1954

Four Color 540-Movie, photo-c	7	21	49	90

KNIGHTS OF THE ROUND TABLE
Pines Comics: No. 10, April, 1957

10	5	15	23	30

KNIGHTS OF THE ROUND TABLE
Dell Publishing Co.: Nov-Jan, 1963-64

1 (12-397-401)-Painted-c	3	10	23	35

KNIGHTSTRIKE (Also see Operation: Knightstrike)
Image Comics (Extreme Studios): Jan, 1996 ($2.50)

1-Rob Liefeld & Eric Stephenson story; Extreme Destroyer Part 6.				2.50

KNIGHT WATCHMAN (See Big Bang Comics & Dr. Weird)
Image Comics: June, 1998 - No. 4, Oct, 1998 ($2.95/$3.50, B&W, lim. series)

1-3-Ben Torres-c/a in all				3.00
4-($3.50)				3.50

KNIGHT WATCHMAN: GRAVEYARD SHIFT
Caliber Press: 1994 ($2.95, B&W)

1,2-Ben Torres-a				3.00

KNOCK KNOCK (...Who's There?)
Whitman Publ./Gerona Publications: No. 801, 1936 (52 pgs.) (8x9", B&W)

801-Joke book; Bob Dunn-a	8	24	42	60

KNOCKOUT ADVENTURES
Fiction House Magazines: Winter, 1953-54

1-Reprints Fight Comics #53 w/Rip Carson-c/s	14	42	72	120

KNUCKLES (Spin-off of Sonic the Hedgehog)
Archie Publications: Apr, 1997 - Present ($1.50/$1.75/$1.79)

1-29				2.25

KNUCKLES' CHAOTIX
Archie Publications: Jan, 1996 ($2.00, annual)

1				2.25

KOBALT
DC Comics (Milestone): June, 1994 - No. 16, Sept, 1995 ($1.75/$2.50)

1-16: 1-Byrne-c. 4-Intro Page. 16-Kent Williams-c				2.50

KOBRA (See DC Special Series No. 1)
National Periodical Publications: Feb-Mar, 1976 - No. 7, Mar-Apr, 1977

	GD2.0	FN6.0	VF8.0	NM9.4
1-1st app.; Kirby-a redrawn by Marcos; only 25¢-c	1	4	7	10
2-7: (All 30¢ issues) 3-Giffen-a				6.00

NOTE: Austin a-3i. Buckler a-5p; c-5p. Kubert c-4. Nasser a-6p, 7; c-7.

KOKEY KOALA (...and the Magic Button)
Toby Press: May, 1952

1	11	33	55	90

KOKO AND KOLA (Also see A-1 Comics #16 & Tick Tock Tales)
Com/Magazine Enterprises: Fall, 1946 - No. 5, May, 1947; No. 6, 1950

1-Funny animal	11	33	55	90
2-X-Mas-c	7	21	36	50
3-6: 6(A-1 28)	6	18	29	40

KO KOMICS
Gerona Publications: Oct, 1945 (scarce)

1-The Duke of Darkness & The Menace (hero)	68	204	426	750

KOMIC KARTOONS
Timely Comics (EPC): Fall, 1945 - No. 2, Winter, 1945

1,2-Andy Wolf, Bertie Mouse	20	60	105	175

KOMIK PAGES (Formerly Snap; becomes Bullseye #11)
Harry 'A' Chesler, Jr. (Our Army, Inc.): Apr, 1945 (All reprints)

10(#1 on inside)-Land O' Nod by Rick Yager (2 pgs.), Animal Crackers, Foxy GrandPa, Tom, Dick & Mary, Cheerio Minstrels, Red Starr plus other 1-2 pg. strips; Cole-a	24	72	127	215

KONA (...Monarch of Monster Isle)
Dell Publishing Co.: Feb-Apr, 1962 - No. 21, Jan-Mar, 1967 (Painted-c)

Four Color 1256 (#1)	7	21	49	90
2-10: 4-Anak begins. 6-Gil Kane-c	4	12	27	42
11-21	3	9	20	30

NOTE: Glanzman a-all issues.

KONGA (Fantastic Giants No. 24) (See Return of...)
Charlton Comics: 1960; No. 2, Aug, 1961 - No. 23, Nov, 1965

1(1960)-Based on movie; Giordano-a	24	72	168	300
2-5: 2-Giordano-c; no Ditko-a	10	30	73	125
6-15	8	24	60	100
16-23	5	15	34	55

NOTE: Ditko a-1, 3-15; c-4, 6-9. Glanzman a-12. Montes & Bache a-16,23.

KONGA'S REVENGE (Formerly Return of...)
Charlton Comics: No. 2, Summer, 1963 - No. 3, Fall, 1964; Dec, 1968

2,3: 2-Ditko-c/a	6	18	42	70
1(12/68)-Reprints Konga's Revenge #3	3	9	20	30

KONG THE UNTAMED
National Periodical Publications: June-July, 1975 - V2#5, Feb-Mar, 1976

1-1st app. Kong; Wrightson-c; Alcala-a	1	3	6	8
2-5: 2-Wrightson-c. 2,3-Alcala-a				5.00

KOOKIE
Dell Publishing Co.: Feb-Apr, 1962 - No. 2, May-July, 1962 (15 cents)

1-Written by John Stanley; Bill Williams-a	8	24	56	105
2	7	21	49	95

KOOSH KINS
Archie Comics: Oct, 1991 - No. 3, Feb, 1992 ($1.00, bi-monthly, limited series)

1-3				2.25

NOTE: No. 4 was planned, but cancelled.

KORAK, SON OF TARZAN (Edgar Rice Burroughs)(See Tarzan #139)
Gold Key: Jan, 1964 - No. 45, Jan, 1972 (Painted-c No. 1-?)

1-Russ Manning-a	6	18	42	80
2-11-Russ Manning-a	4	12	26	40
12-23: 13-Warren Tufts-a. 14-Jon of the Kalahari ends. 15-Mabu, Jungle Boy begins. 21-Manning-a. 23-Last 12¢ issue	3	9	20	30
24-30	2	6	15	22
31-45	2	6	11	15

KORAK, SON OF TARZAN (Tarzan Family #60 on; see Tarzan #230)
National Periodical Publications: V9#46, May-June, 1972 - V12#56, Feb-Mar, 1974; No. 57, May-June, 1975 - No. 59, Sept-Oct, 1975 (Edgar Rice Burroughs)

	GD2.0	FN6.0	VF8.0	NM9.4		GD2.0	FN6.0	VF8.0	NM9.4

46-(52 pgs.)-Carson of Venus begins (origin), ends #56; Pellucidar feature;
| Weiss-a | 2 | 6 | 11 | 16 |
| 47-59: 49-Origin Korak retold | 1 | 3 | 5 | 7 |

NOTE: All have covers by **Joe Kubert. Manning** strip reprints-No. 57-59.
Murphy Anderson a-52. **Michael Kaluta** a-46-56. **Frank Thorne** a-46-51.

KORG: 70,000 B. C. (TV)
Charlton Publications: May, 1975 - No. 9, Nov, 1976 (Hanna-Barbera)

| 1,2: 1-Boyette-c/a. 2-Painted-c; Byrne text illos | 2 | 6 | 11 | 16 |
| 3-9 | 1 | 4 | 7 | 10 |

KORNER KID COMICS: Four Star Publications: 1947 (Advertised, not pub.)

KOSMIC KAT ACTIVITY BOOK (See Deity)
Image Comics: Aug, 1999 ($2.95, one-shot)

| 1-Stories and games by various | | | | 3.00 |

KRAZY KAT
Holt: 1946 (Hardcover)

| Reprints daily & Sunday strips by Herriman | 59 | 177 | 369 | 650 |
| dust jacket only | 45 | 135 | 270 | 475 |

KRAZY KAT (See Ace Comics & March of Comics No. 72, 87)

KRAZY KAT COMICS (...& Ignatz the Mouse early issues)
Dell Publ. Co/Gold Key: May-June, 1951 - F.C. #696, Apr, 1956; Jan, 1964
(None by Herriman)

1(1951)	7	21	49	90
2-5 (#5, 8-10/52)	4	12	30	50
Four Color 454,504	4	12	29	45
Four Color 548,619,696 (4/56)	4	12	26	40
1(10098-401)(1/64-Gold Key)(TV)	4	12	26	40

KRAZY KOMICS (1st Series) (Cindy Comics No. 27 on)
Timely Comics (USA No. 1-21/JPC No. 22-26): July, 1942 - No. 26, Spr, 1947
(Also see Ziggy Pig)

1-Toughy Tomcat, Ziggy Pig (by Jaffee) & Silly Seal begin				
	55	165	341	600
2	27	81	145	250
3-8,10	20	60	105	175
9-Hitler parody	21	63	110	185
11,13,14	14	42	72	120
12-Timely's entire art staff drew themselves into a Creeper story				
	26	78	136	235
15-(8-9/44)-Becomes Funny Tunes #16; has "Super Soldier" by Pfc. Stan Lee				
	14	42	72	120
16-24,26: 16-(10-11/44). 26-Super Rabbit-c/story	11	33	55	95
25-Wacky Duck-c/story & begin; Kurtzman-a (6pgs.)	14	42	72	120

KRAZY KOMICS (2nd Series)
Timely/Marvel Comics: Aug, 1948 - No. 2, Nov, 1948

1-Wolverton (10 pgs.) & Kurtzman (8 pgs.)-a; Eustice Hayseed begins				
(Li'l Abner swipe)	40	120	232	400
2-Wolverton-a (10 pgs.); Powerhouse Pepper cameo				
	33	99	174	300

KRAZY KROW (Also see Dopey Duck, Film Funnies, Funny Frolics & Movie Tunes)
Marvel Comics (ZPC): Summer, 1945 - No. 3, Wint, 1945/46

1	20	60	105	180
2,3	13	39	66	110
I.W. Reprint #1('57), 2('58), 7	2	6	13	20

KRAZYLIFE (Becomes Nutty Life #2)
Fox Feature Syndicate: 1945 (no month)

| 1-Funny animal | 17 | 51 | 88 | 150 |

KREE/SKRULL WAR STARRING THE AVENGERS, THE
Marvel Comics: Sept, 1983 - No. 2, Oct, 1983 ($2.50, 68 pgs., Baxter paper)

| 1,2 | | | | 3.50 |

NOTE: **Neal Adams** p-1r, 2. **Buscema** a-1r, 2r. **Simonson** a-1p; c-1p.

KROFFT SUPERSHOW (TV)
Gold Key: Apr, 1978 - No. 6, Jan, 1979

| 1-Photo-c | 2 | 6 | 15 | 22 |
| 2-6: 6-Photo-c | 2 | 6 | 11 | 15 |

KRULL
Marvel Comics Group: Nov, 1983 - No. 2, Dec, 1983

| 1,2-Adaptation of film; r/Marvel Super Special. 1-Photo-c from movie | | | | 2.50 |

KRUSTY COMICS (TV)(See Simpsons Comics)
Bongo Comics: 1995 - No. 3, 1995 ($2.25, limited series)

| 1-3 | | | | 2.50 |

KRYPTON CHRONICLES
DC Comics: Sept, 1981 - No. 3, Nov, 1981

| 1-3: 1-Buckler-c(p) | | | | 4.00 |

KULL AND THE BARBARIANS
Marvel Comics Group: May, 1975 - No. 3, Sept, 1975 ($1.00, B&W, magazine)

| 1-(84 pgs.) Andru/Wood-r/Kull #1; 2 pgs. Neal Adams; Gil Kane(p), Marie & John Severin-a(r); Krenkel text illo. | 2 | 6 | 10 | 14 |
| 2,3: 2-(84 pgs.) Red Sonja by Chaykin begins; Solomon Kane by Weiss/Adams; Gil Kane-a; Solomon Kane pin-up by Wrightson. 3-(76 pgs.) Origin Red Sonja by Chaykin; Adams-a; Solomon Kane app. | 1 | 3 | 6 | 9 |

KULL THE CONQUEROR (...the Destroyer #11 on; see Conan #1, Creatures on the Loose #10, Marvel Preview, Monsters on the Prowl)
Marvel Comics Group: June, 1971 - No. 2, Sept, 1971; No. 3, July, 1972 - No. 15, Aug, 1974; No. 16, Aug, 1976 - No. 29, Oct, 1978

1-Andru/Wood-a; 2nd app. & origin Kull; 15¢ issue	3	10	23	35
2-5: 2-3rd Kull app. Last 15¢ iss. 3-13: 20¢ issues	2	6	10	14
6-10	1	3	6	9
11-15: 11-15-Ploog-a. 14,15: 25¢ issues	1	3	5	7
16-(Regular 25¢ edition)(8/76)	1	3	5	7
16-(30¢-c variant, limited distribution)	1	4	7	10
17-29: 21-23-(Reg. 30¢ editions)				6.00
21-23-(35¢-c variants, limited distribution)	1	4	7	10

NOTE: No. 1, 2, 7-9, 11 are based on Robert E. Howard stories. **Alcala** a-17p, 18-20i; c-24. **Ditko** a-12r, 15r. **Gil Kane** c-15p, 21. **Nebres** a-22i-27i; c-25i, 27i. **Ploog** c-11, 12p, 13. **Severin** a-2-9i; c-2-10i, 19. **Starlin** c-14.

KULL THE CONQUEROR
Marvel Comics Group: Dec, 1982 - No. 2, Mar, 1983 (52 pgs., Baxter paper)

| 1,2: 1-Buscema-a(p) | | | | 4.00 |

KULL THE CONQUEROR (No. 9,10 titled "Kull")
Marvel Comics Group: 5/83 - No. 10, 6/85 (52 pgs., Baxter paper)

| V3#1-10: Buscema-a in #1-3,5-10 | | | | 3.00 |

NOTE: Bolton a-4. Golden painted c-3-8. Guice a-4p. Sienkiewicz c-2.

KUNG FU (See Deadly Hands of..., & Master of...)

KUNG FU FIGHTER (See Richard Dragon...)

KURT BUSIEK'S ASTRO CITY (Limited series)
Image Comics (Juke Box Productions): Aug, 1995 - No. 6, Jan, 1996 ($2.25)

1-Kurt Busiek scripts, Brent Anderson-a & Alex Ross front & back-c begins; 1st app. Samaritan & Honor Guard (Cleopatra, MHP, Beautie, The Black Rapier, Quarrel & N-Forcer)	2	6	9	12
2-6: 2-1st app. The Silver Agent, The Old Soldier, & the "original" Honor Guard (Max O'Millions, Starwoman, the "original" Cleopatra, the "original" N-Forcer, the bouncing Beatnik, Leopardman & Kitkat). 3-1st app. Jack-in-the-Box & The Deacon. 4-1st app. Winged Victory (cameo), The Hanged Man & The First Family. 5-1st app. Crackerjack, The Astro City Irregulars, Nightingale & Sunbird. 6-Origin Samaritan; 1st full app Winged Victory	1	4	7	10
Life In The Big City-(8/96, $19.95, trade paperback)-r/Image Comics limited series w/sketchbook & cover gallery; Ross-c				20.00
Life In The Big City-(8/96, $49.95, hardcover, 1000 print run)-r/Image Comics limited series w/sketchbook & cover gallery; Ross-c				50.00

KURT BUSIEK'S ASTRO CITY (1st Homage Comics series)
Image Comics (Homage Comics): V2#1, Sept, 1996 - No. 15, Dec, 1998;
DC Comics (Homage Comics): No. 16, Mar, 1999 - Present ($2.50)

1/2-(10/96)-The Hanged Man story; 1st app. The All-American & Slugger, The Lamplighter, The Time-Keeper & Eterneon	1	4	7	10
1/2-(1/98) 2nd printing w/new cover				2.50
1- Kurt Busiek scripts, Alex Ross-c, Brent Anderson-p & Will Blyberg-i begin; intro The Gentleman, Thunderhead & Helia.	1	3	6	8
1-(12/97, $4.95) "3-D Edition" w/glasses				5.00

Kurt Busiek's Astro City V2 #2 © Juke Box Prod.

Lady Death #6 © Chaos!

Lady Pendragon V3 #2 © Matt Hawkins

	GD2.0	FN6.0	VF8.0	NM9.4

2-Origin The First Family; Astra story	1	3	5	7
3-5: 4-1st app. The Crossbreed, Ironhorse, Glue Gun & The Confessor				
(cameo)				6.00
6-10				5.00
11-22: 14-20-Steeljack story arc. 16-(3/99) First DC issue				2.50
TPB-($19.95) Ross-c, r/#4-9, #1/2 w/sketchbook				20.00
Family Album TPB ($19.95) r/#1-3,10-13				20.00
The Tarnished Angel HC ($29.95) r/#14-20; new Ross dust jacket; sketch pages				
by Anderson & Ross; cover gallery with reference photos				30.00
The Tarnished Angel SC ($19.95) r/#14-20; new Ross-c				20.00

LABMAN
Image Comics: Nov, 1996 ($3.50, one-shot)

1-Allred-c				4.00

LABYRINTH
Marvel Comics Group: Nov, 1986 - No. 3, Jan, 1987 (Limited series)

1-3: David Bowie movie adaptation; r/Marvel Super Special #40				3.00

LA COSA NOSTROID (See Scud: The Disposible Assassin)
Fireman Press: Mar, 1996 - Present ($2.95, B&W)

1-9-Dan Harmon-s/Rob Schrab-c/a				3.00

LAD: A DOG (Movie)
Dell Publishing Co.: 1961 - No. 2, July-Sept, 1962

Four Color 1303	4	12	29	45
2	4	12	26	40

LADY AND THE TRAMP (Disney, See Dell Giants & Movie Comics)
Dell Publishing Co.: No. 629, May, 1955 - No. 634, June, 1955

Four Color 629 (#1)-..with Jock	7	21	49	90
Four Color 634-...Album	5	15	34	55

LADY COP (See 1st Issue Special)

LADY DEATH (See Evil Ernie)
Chaos! Comics: Jan, 1994 - No. 3, Mar, 1994 ($2.75, limited series)

1/2-S. Hughes-c/a in all, 1/2 Velvet	1	3	5	7
1/2 Gold	1	4	7	10
1/2 Signed Limited Edition	2	6	9	12
1-($3.50)-Chromium-c	2	6	12	18
1-Commemorative	2	6	11	16
1-(9/96, $2.95) "Encore Presentation"; r/#1				3.00
2	1	3	6	8
3				5.00
...And The Women of Chaos! Gallery #1 (11/96, $2.25) pin-ups by various				3.00
...Bad Kitty (9/01, $2.99) Mota-c/a				3.00
...By Steven Hughes (6/00, $2.95) Tribute issue to Steven Hughes				3.00
...By Steven Hughes Deluxe Edition(6/00, $15.95)				16.00
...Chastity (1/02, $2.99) Mota-c/a; Augustyn-s				3.00
...Death Becomes Her #0 (11/97, $2.95) Hughes-c/a				3.00
...FAN Edition: All Hallow's Eve #1 (1/97, mail-in)				5.00
...In Lingerie #1 (8/95, $2.95) pin-ups, wraparound-c				3.00
...In Lingerie #1-Leather Edition (10,000)				12.00
...In Lingerie #1-Micro Premium Edition; Lady Demon-c (2,000)				35.00
...: Love Bites (3/01, $2.99) Kaminski-s/Luke Ross-a				3.00
...Medieval Witchblade (8/01, $3.50) covers by Molenaar and Silvestri				3.50
...Medieval Witchblade Preview Ed. (8/01, $1.99) Molenaar-c				2.00
...: Mischief Night (11/01, $2.99) Ostrander-s/Reis-a				3.00
...: River of Fear (4/01, $2.99) Bennett-a(p)/Cleavenger-c				3.00
...Swimsuit Special #1-($2.50)-Wraparound-c				14.00
...Swimsuit Special #1-Red velvet-c				3.00
...Swimsuit 2001 #1-(2/01, $2.99)-Reis-c; art by various				7.00
...: The Reckoning (7/94, $6.95)-r/#1-3				
...: The Reckoning (8/95, $3.50)- new printing including Lady Death 1/2				
& Swimsuit Special #1				13.00
.../Vampirella (3/99, $3.50) Hughes-c/a				3.50
.../Vampirella 2 (3/00, $3.50) Deodato-a				3.50
...Vs. Purgatori (12/99, $3.50) Deodato-a				3.50
...Vs. Vampirella Preview (2/00, $1.00) Deodato-a/c				2.25

LADY DEATH (Ongoing series)
Chaos! Comics: Feb, 1998 - No. 16, May, 1999 ($2.95)

	GD2.0	FN6.0	VF8.0	NM9.4

1-16; 1-4: Pulido-s/Hughes-c/a. 5-8,13-16-Deodato-a. 9-11-Hughes-a				3.00
...Retribution (8/98, $2.95) Jadsen-a				3.00
...Retribution Premium Ed.				6.00

LADY DEATH: ALIVE
Chaos! Comics: May, 2001 - No. 4, Aug, 2001 ($2.99, limited series)

1-4-Ivan Reis-a; Lady Death becomes mortal				3.00

LADY DEATH: DARK MILLENNIUM
Chaos! Comics: Feb, 2000 - No. 3, Apr, 2000 ($2.95, limited series)

Preview (6/00, $5.00)				5.00
1-3-Ivan Reis-a				3.00

LADY DEATH: JUDGEMENT WAR
Chaos! Comics: Nov, 1999 - No. 3, Jan, 2000 ($2.95, limited series)

Prelude (10/99) two covers				3.00
1-3-Ivan Reis-a				3.00

LADY DEATH: LAST RITES
Chaos! Comics: Oct, 2001 - No. 4, ($2.99, limited series)

1-3-Ivan Reis-a/Ostrander-s				3.00

LADY DEATH: THE CRUCIBLE
Chaos! Comics: Nov, 1996 - No. 6, Oct, 1997 ($3.50/$2.95, limited series)

1/2				4.00
1/2 Cloth Edition				8.00
1-Wraparound silver foil embossed-c				4.00
1-($19.95)-Leather Edition				20.00
2-6-($2.95)				3.00

LADY DEATH: THE ODYSSEY
Chaos! Comics: Apr, 1996 - No. 4, Aug, 1996 ($3.50/$2.95)

1-($1.50)-Sneak Peek Preview				2.25
1-($1.50)-Sneak Peek Preview Micro Premium Edition (2500 print run)	2	6	9	12
1-($3.50)-Embossed, wraparound goil foil-c				5.00
1-Black Onyx Edition (200 print run)	7	21	50	80
1-($19.95)-Premium Edition (10,000 print run)				20.00
2-4-($2.95)				3.00

LADY DEATH: THE RAPTURE
Chaos! Comics: Jun, 1999 - No. 4, Sept, 1999 ($2.95, limited series)

1-4-Ivan Reis-c/a; Pulido-s				3.00

LADY DEATH: TRIBULATION
Chaos! Comics: Dec, 2000 - No. 4, Mar, 2001 ($2.95, limited series)

1-4-Ivan Reis-a; Kaminski-s				3.00

LADY DEATH II: BETWEEN HEAVEN & HELL
Chaos! Comics: Mar, 1995 - No. 4, July, 1995 ($3.50, limited series)

1-Chromium wraparound-c; Evil Ernie cameo				5.00
1-Commemorative (4,000), 1-Black Velvet-c	2	6	12	18
1-Gold	1	4	7	10
1-"Refractor" edition (5,000)	2	6	13	20
2-4				3.50
4-Lady Demon variant-c	1	3	6	9
Trade paperback-($12.95)-r/#1-4				13.00

LADY DEMON
Chaos! Comics: Mar, 2000 - No. 3, May, 2000 ($2.95, limited series)

1-3-Kaminski-s/Brewer-a				3.00
1-Premium Edition				10.00

LADY FOR A NIGHT (See Cinema Comics Herald)

LADY JUSTICE (See Neil Gaiman's)

LADY LUCK (Formerly Smash #1-85) (Also see Spirit Sections #1)
Quality Comics Group: No. 86, Dec, 1949 - No. 90, Aug, 1950

86(#1)	86	258	540	950
87-90	64	192	398	700

LADY PENDRAGON
Maximum Press: Mar, 1996 ($2.50)

1-Matt Hawkins script				2.50

LADY PENDRAGON

Lana #3 © MAR

Land of Nod #3 © Jay Stephens

Large Feature Comic #19 © WDC

	GD2.0	FN6.0	VF8.0	NM9.4

Image Comics: Nov, 1998 - No. 3, Jan, 1999 ($2.50, mini-series)
Preview (6/98) Flip book w/ Deity preview				3.00
1-3: 1-Matt Hawkins-s/Stinsman-a				3.00
1-($6.95) DF Ed. with variant-c by Jusko				7.00
2-($4.95)Variant edition				5.00
0-(3/99) Origin; flip book				2.50

LADY PENDRAGON (Volume 3)
Image Comics: Apr, 1999 - No. 9, Mar, 2000 ($2.50, mini-series)
1,2,4-6,8-10: 1-Matt Hawkins-s/Stinsman-a. 2-Peterson-c				2.50
3-Flip book w/Alley Cat preview (1st app.)				3.00
7-($3.95) Flip book; Stinsman-a/Cleavenger painted-a				4.00
Gallery Edition (10/99, $2.95) pin-ups				3.00
...Merlin (1/00, $2.95) Stinsman-a				3.00

LADY PENDRAGON/ MORE THAN MORTAL
Image Comics: May, 1999 ($2.50, one-shot)
Preview (2/99) Diamond Dateline suppl.				2.25
1-Scott-s/Norton-a; 2 covers by Norton & Finch				2.50

LADY RAWHIDE
Topps Comics: July, 1995 - No. 5, Mar, 1996 ($2.95, bi-monthly, limited series)
1-5: Don McGregor scripts & Mayhew-a. in all. 2-Stelfreeze-a. 3-Hughes-c.				
4-Golden-c. 5-Julie Bell-c.				3.00
It Can't Happen Here TPB (8/99, $16.95) r/#1-5				17.00
Mini Comic 1 (7/95) Maroto-a; Zorro app.				2.25
Special Edition 1 (6/95, $3.95)-Reprints				4.00

LADY RAWHIDE (Volume 2)
Topps Comics: Oct, 1996 -No. 5, June, 1997 ($2.95, limited series)
1-5: 1-Julie Bell-c.				3.00

LADY RAWHIDE OTHER PEOPLE'S BLOOD (ZORRO'S ...)
Image Comics: Mar, 1999 - No. 5, 1999 ($2.95, B&W)
1-5-Reprints Lady Rawhide series in B&W				3.00

LADY SUPREME (See Asylum)(Also see Supreme & Kid Supreme)
Image Comics (Extreme): May, 1996 - No. 2, June, 1996 ($2.50, limited series)
1,2-Terry Moore -s : 1-Terry Moore-c. 2-Flip book w/Newmen preview				2.50

LAFF-A-LYMPICS (TV)(See The Funtastic World of Hanna-Barbera)
Marvel Comics: Mar, 1978 - No. 13, Mar, 1979 (Newsstand sales only)
1-Yogi Bear, Scooby Doo, Pixie & Dixie, etc.	2	6	15	22
2-8	2	6	11	16
9-13: 11-Jetsons x-over; 1 pg. illustrated bio of Mighty Mightor, Herculoids,				
Shazzan, Galaxy Trio & Space Ghost	2	6	13	20

LAFFY-DAFFY COMICS
Rural Home Publ. Co.: Feb, 1945 - No. 2, Mar, 1945
1,2-Funny animal	10	30	55	80

LANA (Little Lana No. 8 on)
Marvel Comics (MjMC): Aug, 1948 - No. 7, Aug, 1949 (Also see Annie Oakley)
1-Rusty, Millie begin	21	63	110	185
2-Kurtzman's "Hey Look" (1); last Rusty	12	36	61	105
3-7: 3-Nellie begins	9	27	49	70

LANCELOT & GUINEVERE (See Movie Classics)

LANCELOT LINK, SECRET CHIMP (TV)
Gold Key: Apr, 1971 - No. 8, Feb, 1973
1-Photo-c	5	15	35	65
2-8: 2-Photo-c	3	10	23	35

LANCELOT STRONG (See The Shield)

LANCE O'CASEY (See Mighty Midget & Whiz Comics)
Fawcett Publications: Spring, 1946 - No. 3, Fall, 1946; No. 4, Summer, 1948
1-Captain Marvel app. on-c	36	108	191	330
2	23	69	121	210
3,4	17	51	88	150
NOTE: *The cover for the 1st issue was done in 1942 but was not published until 1946. The cover shows 68 pages but actually has only 36 pages.*

LANCER (TV)(Western)
Gold Key: Feb, 1969 - No. 3, Sept, 1969 (All photo-c)

	GD2.0	FN6.0	VF8.0	NM9.4
1	4	12	26	40
2,3	3	9	19	28

LAND OF NOD, THE
Dark Horse Comics: July, 1997 - No. 3, Feb, 1998 ($2.95, B&W)
1-3-Jetcat; Jay Stephens-s/a				3.00

LAND OF OZ
Arrow Comics: 1998 - Present ($2.95, B&W)
1-9-Bishop-s/Bryan-s/a				3.00

LAND OF THE GIANTS (TV)
Gold Key: Nov, 1968 - No. 5, Sept, 1969 (All have photo-c)
1	5	15	35	70
2-5	4	12	26	40

LAND OF THE LOST COMICS (Radio)
E. C. Comics: July-Aug, 1946 - No. 9, Spring, 1948
1	35	105	188	325
2	24	72	127	215
3-9	20	60	105	175

LAND UNKNOWN, THE (Movie)
Dell Publishing Co.: No. 845, Sept, 1957
Four Color 845-Alex Toth-a	12	36	84	155

LA PACIFICA
DC Comics (Paradox Press): 1994/1995 ($4.95, B&W, limited series, digest size, mature readers)
1-3				5.00

LARAMIE (TV)
Dell Publishing Co.: Aug, 1960 - July, 1962 (All photo-c)
Four Color 1125-Gil Kane/Heath-a	9	27	63	120
Four Color 1223,1284, 01-418-207 (7/62)	6	18	42	80

LAREDO (TV)
Gold Key: June, 1966
1 (10179-606)-Photo-c	4	12	25	38

LARGE FEATURE COMIC (Formerly called Black & White in previous guides)
Dell Publishing Co.: 1939 - No. 13, 1943
Note: See individual alphabetical listings for prices

1 (Series I)-Dick Tracy Meets the Blank
3-Heigh-Yo Silver! The Lone Ranger (text & ill.)(76 pgs.); also exists as a Whitman #710; based on radio
6-Terry & the Pirates & The Dragon Lady; reprints dailies from 1936
8-Dick Tracy the Racket Buster
9-King of the Royal Mounted (Zane Grey's...)
10-(Scarce)-Gang Busters (No. appears on inside front cover); first slick cover (based on radio program)
13-Dick Tracy and Scottie of Scotland Yard
15-Dick Tracy and the Kidnapped Princes
17-Gang Busters (1941)
18-Phantasmo (see The Funnies #45)
20-Donald Duck Comic Paint Book (rarer than #16) (Disney)
21,22: 21-Private Buck. 22-Nuts & Jolts
24-Popeye in "Thimble Theatre" by Segar
26-Smitty
28-Grin and Bear It
30-Tillie the Toiler
  2-Winnie Winkle (#1)
  3-Dick Tracy
  4-Tiny Tim (#1)
  6-Terry & the Pirates; Caniff-a

2-Terry and the Pirates (#1)
4-Dick Tracy Gets His Man
5-Tarzan of the Apes (#1) by Harold Foster (origin); reprints 1st Tarzan dailies from 1929
7-(Scarce, 52 pgs.)-Hi-Yo Silver the Lone Ranger to the Rescue; also exists as a Whitman #715, based on radio program
11-Dick Tracy Foils the Mad Doc Hump
12-Smilin' Jack; no number on-c
14-Smilin' Jack Helps G-Men Solve a Case!
16-Donald Duck; 1st app. Daisy Duck on back cover (6/41- Disney)
19-Dumbo Comic Paint Book (Disney); partial-r from 4-Color #17
23-The Nebbs
25-Smilin' Jack-1st issue to show title on-c
27-Terry and the Pirates; Caniff-c/a
29-Moon Mullins
  1 (Series II)-Peter Rabbit by Harrison Cady; arrival date- 3/27/42
  5-Toots and Casper
  7-Pluto Saves the Ship (#1)

Lash Larue Western #4 © FAW

The Last American #3 © MAR

Last Shot: First Draw #1 © Studio XD

	GD2.0	FN6.0	VF8.0	NM9.4

8-Bugs Bunny (#1)('42)   (Disney)-Written by Carl Barks,
9-Bringing Up Father   Jack Hannah, & Nick George
10-Popeye (Thimble Theatre)   (Barks' 1st comic book work)
11-Barney Google and Snuffy Smith   12-Private Buck
13-(nn)-1001 Hours Of Fun; puzzles
    & games; by A. W. Nugent. This book was
    bound as #13 with Large Feature Comics
    in publisher's files

NOTE: The Black & White Feature Books are oversized 8-1/2x11-3/8" comics with color covers and black and white interiors. The first nine issues all have rough, heavy thick covers and, except for #7, all have 76 pages, including covers. #7 and #10-on all have 52 pages. Beginning with #10 the covers are slick and thin and, because of their size, are difficult to handle without damaging. For this reason, they are seldom found in fine to mint condition. The paper stock, unlike Wow #1 and Capt. Marvel #1, is itself not unstable ...just thin.

LARRY DOBY, BASEBALL HERO
Fawcett Publications: 1950 (Cleveland Indians)

nn-Bill Ward-a; photo-c | 75 | 225 | 469 | 825

LARRY HARMON'S LAUREL AND HARDY (...Comics)
National Periodical Publ.: July-Aug, 1972 (Digest advertised, not published)

1-Low print run | 8 | 24 | 56 | 90

LARS OF MARS
Ziff-Davis Publishing Co.: No. 10, Apr-May, 1951 - No. 11, July-Aug, 1951
(Painted-c) (Created by Jerry Siegel, editor)

10-Origin; Anderson-a(3) in each; classic robot-c | 80 | 240 | 500 | 875
11-Gene Colan-a; classic-c | 64 | 192 | 398 | 700

LARS OF MARS 3-D
Eclipse Comics: Apr, 1987 ($2.50)

1-r/Lars of Mars 10,11 in 3-D plus new story | | | | 3.00
2-D limited edition (B&W, 100 copies) | | | | 5.00

LASER ERASER & PRESSBUTTON (See Axel Pressbutton &
Miracle Man 9)
Eclipse Comics: Nov, 1985 - No. 6, 1987 (95¢/$2.50, limited series)

1-6: 5,6-(95¢) | | | | 2.25
..In 3-D 1 (8/86, $2.50) | | | | 2.50
2-D 1 (B&W, limited to 100 copies signed & numbered) | | | | 4.00

LASH LARUE WESTERN (Movie star; king of the bullwhip)(See Fawcett
Movie Comic, Motion Picture Comics & Six-Gun Heroes)
Fawcett Publications: Sum, 1949 - No. 46, Jan, 1954 (36pgs., 1-7,9,13,16-on)

1-Lash & his horse Black Diamond begin; photo front/back-c begin
     | 107 | 321 | 669 | 1175
2(11/49) | 45 | 135 | 270 | 475
3-5 | 40 | 120 | 220 | 380
6,7,9: 6-Last photo back-c; intro. Frontier Phantom (Lash's twin brother)
     | 34 | 102 | 179 | 310
8,10 (52pgs.) | 35 | 105 | 185 | 320
11,12,14,15 (52pgs.) | 24 | 72 | 127 | 215
13,16-20 (36pgs.) | 21 | 63 | 110 | 185
21-30: 21-The Frontier Phantom app. | 18 | 54 | 94 | 155
31-45 | 15 | 45 | 77 | 130
46-Last Fawcett issue & photo-c | 16 | 48 | 83 | 140

LASH LARUE WESTERN (Continues from Fawcett series)
Charlton Comics: No. 47, Mar-Apr, 1954 - No. 84, June, 1961

47-Photo-c | 20 | 60 | 105 | 175
48 | 15 | 45 | 77 | 130
49-60, 67,68-(68 pgs.). 68-Check-a | 11 | 33 | 55 | 95
61-66,69,70: 52-r/#8; 53-r/#22 | 10 | 30 | 55 | 85
71-83 | 8 | 24 | 42 | 60
84-Last issue | 10 | 30 | 55 | 80

LASH LARUE WESTERN
AC Comics: 1990 ($3.50, 44 pgs) (24 pgs. of color, 16 pgs. of B&W)

1-Photo covers; r/Lash #6; r/old movie posters | | | | 3.50
Annual 1 (1990, $2.95, B&W, 44 pgs.)-Photo covers | | | | 3.00

LASSIE (TV)(M-G-M's... #1-36; see Kite Fun Book)
Dell Publ. Co./Gold Key No. 59 (10/62) on: June, 1950 - No. 70, July, 1969

1 (52 pgs.)-Photo-c; inside lists One Shot #282 in error

	GD2.0	FN6.0	VF8.0	NM9.4

  | 14 | 42 | 98 | 180
2-Painted-c begin | 6 | 18 | 42 | 80
3-10 | 5 | 15 | 34 | 55
11-19: 12-Rocky Langford (Lassie's master) marries Gerry Lawrence. 15-1st
    app. Timbu | 4 | 12 | 29 | 45
20-22-Matt Baker-a | 4 | 12 | 30 | 50
23-38,40: 33-Robinson-a. | 4 | 12 | 26 | 40
39-1st app. Timmy as Lassie picks up her TV family | 5 | 15 | 38 | 60
41-50 | 4 | 12 | 25 | 38
51-58 | 3 | 10 | 23 | 35
59 (10/62)-1st Gold Key | 4 | 12 | 29 | 45
60-70: 63-Last Timmy (10/63). 64-r/#19. 65-Forest Ranger Corey Stuart
    begins, ends #69. 70-Forest Rangers Bob Ericson & Scott Turner app.
    (Lassie's new masters) | 3 | 9 | 21 | 32
11193(1978, $1.95, 224 pgs., Golden Press)-Baker-r (92 pgs.)
     | 4 | 12 | 26 | 40

NOTE: Photo c-57, 63. (See March of Comics #210, 217, 230, 254, 266, 278, 296, 308, 324, 334, 346, 358, 370, 381, 394, 411, 432)

LAST AMERICAN, THE
Marvel Comics (Epic): Dec, 1990 - No. 4, March, 1991 ($2.25, mini-series)

1-4: Alan Grant scripts | | | | 2.25

LAST AVENGERS STORY, THE (Last Avengers #1)
Marvel Comics: Nov, 1995 - No. 2, Dec, 1995 ($5.95, painted, limited series)
(Alterniverse)

1,2: Peter David story; acetate-c in all. 1-New team (Hank Pym, Wasp, Human
    Torch, Cannonball, She-Hulk, Hotshot, Bombshell, Tommy Maximoff,
    Hawkeye, & Mockingbird) forms to battle Ultron 59, Kang the Conqueror,
    The Grim Reaper & Oddball | | | | 6.00

LAST DAYS OF THE JUSTICE SOCIETY SPECIAL
DC Comics: 1986 ($2.50, one-shot, 68 pgs.)

1-62 pg. JSA story plus unpubbed G.A. pg. | 1 | 3 | 5 | 7

LAST GENERATION, THE
Black Tie Studios: 1986 - No. 5, 1989 ($1.95, B&W, high quality paper)

1-5 | | | | 2.25
Book 1 (1989, $6.95)-By Caliber Press | | | | 7.00

LAST HUNT, THE
Dell Publishing Co.: No. 678, Feb, 1956

Four Color 678-Movie, photo-c | 8 | 24 | 56 | 100

LAST KISS
ACME Press (Eclipse): 1988 ($3.95, B&W, squarebound, 52 pgs.)

1-One story adapts E.A. Poe's The Black Cat | | | | 4.00

LAST OF THE COMANCHES (Movie) (See Wild Bill Hickok #28)
Avon Periodicals: 1953

nn-Kinstler-c/a, 21pgs.; Ravielli-a | 16 | 48 | 83 | 140

LAST OF THE ERIES, THE (See American Graphics)

LAST OF THE FAST GUNS, THE
Dell Publishing Co.: No. 925, Aug, 1958

Four Color 925-Movie, photo-c | 7 | 21 | 49 | 90

LAST OF THE MOHICANS (See King Classics & White Rider and...)

LAST OF THE VIKING HEROES, THE (Also see Silver Star #1)
Genesis West Comics: Mar, 1987 - No. 12 ($1.50/$1.95)

1-4,5A,5B,6-12: 4-Intro The Phantom Force, 1-Signed edition ($1.50), 5A-
    Kirby/Stevens-c. 5B,6 ($1.95). 7-Art Adams-c. 8-Kirby back-c. | | | | 4.00
Summer Special 1-3: 1-(1988)-Frazetta-c & illos. 2 (1990, $2.50)-A TMNT app.
    3 (1991, $2.50)-Teenage Mutant Ninja Turtles | | | | 4.00
Summer Special 1-Signed edition (sold for $1.95) | | | | 4.00
NOTE: Art Adams c-7. Byrne c-3. Kirby c-1p, 5p. Perez c-2i. Stevens c-5Ai.

LAST ONE, THE
DC Comics (Vertigo): July, 1993 - No. 6, Dec, 1993 ($2.50, lim. series, mature)

1-6 | | | | 2.50

LAST SHOT
Image Comics: Aug, 2001 - Present ($2.95)

1-3: 1-Wraparound-c; by Studio XD | | | | 3.00

Laugh Comics V2 #21 © AP

Laugh Comics Digest #167 © AP

Lawbreakers #9 © CC

	GD2.0	FN6.0	VF8.0	NM9.4

...: First Draw (5/01, $2.95) Introductory one-shot — 3.00

LAST STARFIGHTER, THE
Marvel Comics Group: Oct, 1984 - No. 3, Dec, 1984 (75¢, movie adaptation)

	GD2.0	FN6.0	VF8.0	NM9.4
1-3: r/Marvel Super Special; Guice-c				2.25

LAST TEMPTATION, THE
Marvel Comics: 1994 - No. 3, 1994 ($4.95, limited series)

	GD2.0	FN6.0	VF8.0	NM9.4
1-3-Alice Cooper story; Neil Gaiman scripts; McKean-c; Zulli-a: 1-Two covers.				5.00

LAST TRAIN FROM GUN HILL
Dell Publishing Co.: No. 1012, July, 1959

	GD2.0	FN6.0	VF8.0	NM9.4
Four Color 1012-Movie, photo-c	9	27	63	110

LATEST ADVENTURES OF FOXY GRANDPA (See Foxy Grandpa)

LATEST COMICS (Super Duper No. 3?)
Spotlight Publ./Palace Promotions (Jubilee): Mar, 1945 - No. 2, 1945?

	GD2.0	FN6.0	VF8.0	NM9.4
1-Super Duper	17	51	88	150
2-Bee-29 (nd); Jubilee in indicia blacked out	13	39	66	110

LAUGH
Archie Enterprises: June, 1987 - No. 29, Aug, 1991 (75¢/$1.00)

	GD2.0	FN6.0	VF8.0	NM9.4
V2#1				5.00
2-10,14,24: 5-X-Mas issue. 14-1st app. Hot Dog. 24-Re-intro Super Duck				4.00
11-13,15-23,25-29: 19-X-Mas issue				3.00

LAUGH COMICS (Teenage) (Formerly Black Hood #9-19) (Laugh #226 on)
Archie Publications (Close-Up): No. 20, Fall, 1946 - No. 400, Apr, 1987

	GD2.0	FN6.0	VF8.0	NM9.4
20-Archie begins; Katy Keene & Taffy begin by Woggon; Suzie & Wilbur also begin; Archie covers begin	61	182	381	675
21-23,25	35	105	185	320
24- "Pipsy" by Kirby (6 pgs.)	36	108	191	330
26-30	19	57	99	170
31-40	14	42	72	125
41-60: 41,54-Debbi by Woggon	11	33	55	90
61-80: 67-Debbi by Woggon	8	24	45	65
81-99	4	12	30	50
100	5	15	34	55
101-126: 125-Debbi app.	4	12	26	40
127-144: Super-hero app. in all (see note)	4	12	29	45
145-156,158-160	3	9	20	30
157-Josie app.(4/64)	4	12	25	38
161-165,167-180, 200 (12/67)	3	9	17	24
166-Beatles-c (1/65)	4	12	30	50
181-199	2	6	12	18
201-240(3/71)	2	6	9	12
241-280(7/74)	1	4	7	10
281-299	1	3	6	8
300(3/76)	1	3	6	9
301-340 (7/79)				6.00
341-370 (1/82)				5.00
371-380,385-399				4.00
381-384,400: 381-384-Katy Keene app.; by Woggon-381,382				5.00

NOTE: *The Fly app. in 128, 129, 132, 134, 138, 139. Flygirl app. in 136, 137, 143. Flyman app. in 137. The Jaguar app. in 127, 130, 131, 133, 135, 140-142, 144. Josie app. in 145, 160, 164. Katy Keene app. in 20-125, 129, 130, 133. Many issues contain paper dolls. Al Fagaly c-20-29. Montana c-33, 36, 37, 42. Bill Vigoda c-30, 50.*

LAUGH COMICS DIGEST (...Magazine #23-89; Laugh Digest Mag. #90 on)
Archie Publ. (Close-Up No. 1, 3 on): 8/74; No. 2, 9/75; No. 3, 3/76 - Present (Digest-size) (Josie and Sabrina app. in most issues)

	GD2.0	FN6.0	VF8.0	NM9.4
1-Neal Adams-a	4	12	29	45
2,7,8,19-Neal Adams-a	3	9	17	26
3-6,9,10	2	6	12	18
11-18,20	2	6	11	15
21-40	2	6	9	12
41-80	1	3	6	8
81-99				5.00
100				6.00
101-138				3.00
139-171: 139-Begin $1.95-c. 148-Begin $1.99-c. 156-Begin $2.19-c				2.25

NOTE: *Katy Keene in 23, 25, 27, 32-38, 40, 45-48, 50. The Fly in 19, 20. The Jaguar-r in 25, 27. Mr. Justice-r in 21. The Web-r in 23.*

LAUGH COMIX (Formerly Top Notch Laugh; Suzie Comics No. 49 on)
MLJ Magazines: No. 46, Summer, 1944 - No. 48, Winter, 1944-45

	GD2.0	FN6.0	VF8.0	NM9.4
46-Wilbur & Suzie in all; Harry Sahle-c	23	69	121	210
47,48: 47-Sahle-c. 48-Bill Vigoda-c	16	48	83	140

LAUGH-IN MAGAZINE (TV)(Magazine)
Laufer Publ. Co.: Oct, 1968 - No. 12, Oct, 1969 (50¢) (Satire)

	GD2.0	FN6.0	VF8.0	NM9.4
V1#1	4	12	30	50
2-12	3	10	23	35

LAUREL & HARDY (See Larry Harmon's... & March of Comics No. 302, 314)

LAUREL AND HARDY (...Comics)
St. John Publ. Co.: 3/49 - No. 3, 9/49; No. 26, 11/55 - No. 28, 3/56 (No #4-25)

	GD2.0	FN6.0	VF8.0	NM9.4
1	68	205	426	750
2	40	120	232	400
3	31	93	165	285
26-28 (Reprints)	17	51	88	150

LAUREL AND HARDY (TV)
Dell Publishing Co.: Oct, 1962 - No. 4, Sept-Nov, 1963

	GD2.0	FN6.0	VF8.0	NM9.4
12-423-210 (8-10/62)	5	15	35	65
2-4 (Dell)	4	12	29	45

LAUREL AND HARDY (Larry Harmon's...)
Gold Key: Jan, 1967 - No. 2, Oct, 1967

	GD2.0	FN6.0	VF8.0	NM9.4
1-Photo back-c	5	15	34	55
2	4	12	29	45

LAUREL AND HARDY DIGEST: DC Comics. 1972 (Advertised, not published)

L.A.W., THE (LIVING ASSAULT WEAPONS)
DC Comics: Sept, 1999 - No. 6, Feb, 2000 ($2.50, limited series)

	GD2.0	FN6.0	VF8.0	NM9.4
1-6-Blue Beetle, Question, Judomaster, Capt. Atom app.; Giordano-a				
5-JLA app.				2.50

LAW AGAINST CRIME (Law-Crime on cover)
Essenkay Publishing Co.: April, 1948 - No. 3, Aug, 1948 (Real Stories from Police Files)

	GD2.0	FN6.0	VF8.0	NM9.4
1-(#1-3 are half funny animal, half crime stories)-L. B. Cole-c/a in all; electrocution-c	71	213	444	780
2-L. B. Cole-c/a	54	162	324	570
3-Used in SOTI, pg. 180,181 & illo "The wish to hurt or kill couples in lovers' lanes;" reprinted in All-Famous Crime #9	67	201	419	740

LAW AND ORDER
Maximum Press: Sept, 1995 - No. 2, 1995 ($2.50, unfinished limited series)

	GD2.0	FN6.0	VF8.0	NM9.4
1,2				2.50

LAWBREAKERS (...Suspense Stories No. 10 on)
Law and Order Magazines (Charlton): Mar, 1951 - No. 9, Oct-Nov, 1952

	GD2.0	FN6.0	VF8.0	NM9.4
1	37	111	197	340
2	21	63	110	190
3,5,6,8,9	16	48	83	140
4- "White Death" junkie story	20	60	105	175
7- "The Deadly Dopesters" drug story	20	60	105	175

LAWBREAKERS ALWAYS LOSE!
Marvel Comics (CBS): Spring, 1948 - No. 10, Oct, 1949

	GD2.0	FN6.0	VF8.0	NM9.4
1-2pg. Kurtzman-a, "Giggles 'n' Grins"	35	105	185	320
2	19	57	99	165
3-5: 4-Vampire story	14	42	72	120
6(2/49)-Has editorial defense against charges of Dr. Wertham	15	45	77	130
7-Used in SOTI, illo "Comic-book philosophy"	31	93	165	285
8-10: 9,10-Photo-c	13	39	66	110

NOTE: *Brodsky c-4, 5. Shores c-1-3, 6-8.*

LAWBREAKERS SUSPENSE STORIES (Formerly Lawbreakers; Strange Suspense Stories No. 16 on)
Capitol Stories/Charlton Comics: No. 10, Jan, 1953 - No. 15, Nov, 1953

	GD2.0	FN6.0	VF8.0	NM9.4
10	38	114	203	350
11 (3/53)-Severed tongues-c/story & woman negligee scene	91	273	568	1000

Leading Comics #6 © DC

Leave It To Binky #5 © DC

Leave It To Chance #9
© James Robinson & Paul Smith

	GD2.0	FN6.0	VF8.0	NM9.4

	GD2.0	FN6.0	VF8.0	NM9.4

12-14: 13-Giordano begin, end #15

		22	66	116	200
12-14: 13-Giordano begin, end #15		22	66	116	200
15-Acid-in-face/story; hands dissolved in acid sty	47	142	286	500

LAW-CRIME (See Law Against Crime)

LAWDOG
Marvel Comics (Epic Comics): May, 1993 - No. 10, Feb, 1993

1-10				2.25

LAWDOG/GRIMROD: TERROR AT THE CROSSROADS
Marvel Comics (Epic Comics): Sept, 1993 ($3.50)

1				3.50

LAWMAN (TV)
Dell Publishing Co.: No. 970, Feb, 1959 - No. 11, Apr-June, 1962 (All photo-c)

Four Color 970(#1)	13	39	91	165
Four Color 1035('60), 3(2-4/60)-Toth-a	7	21	49	90
4-11	5	15	35	60

LAW OF DREDD, THE (Also see Judge Dredd)
Quality Comics/Fleetway #8 on: 1989 - No. 33, 1992 ($1.50/$1.75)

1-33: Bolland a-1-6,8,10-12,14(2 pg),15,19				2.50

LAWRENCE (See Movie Classics)

LAZARUS CHURCHYARD
Tundra Publishing: June, 1992 - No. 3, 1992 ($3.95, 44 pgs., coated stock)

1-3				4.00
The Final Cut (Image, 1/01, $14.95, TPB) Reprints Ellis/D'Israeli strips				15.00

LAZARUS FIVE
DC Comics: July, 2000 - No. 5, Nov, 2000 ($2.50, limited series)

1-5-Harris-c/Abell-a(p)				2.50

LEADING COMICS (...Screen Comics No. 42 on)
National Periodical Publications: Winter, 1941-42 - No. 41, Feb-Mar, 1950

1-Origin The Seven Soldiers of Victory; Crimson Avenger, Green Arrow & Speedy, Shining Knight, The Vigilante, Star Spangled Kid & Stripesy begin; The Dummy (Vigilante villain) 1st app.	423	1269	2750	5500
2-Meskin-a; Fred Ray-c	164	492	1023	1800
3	127	381	795	1400
4,5	91	273	568	1000
6-10	80	240	500	875
11,12,14(Spring, 1945)	55	165	341	600
13-Classic robot-c	89	267	556	975
15-(Sum,'45)-Contents change to funny animal	29	87	153	265
16-22,24-30: 16-Nero Fox-c begin, end #22	13	39	66	110
23-1st app. Peter Porkchops by Otto Feur & begins	29	87	153	265
31,32,34-41: 34-41-Leading Screen... on-c only	10	30	55	85
33-(Scarce)	21	63	110	185

NOTE: Rube Grossman-a(Peter Porkchops)-most #15-on; c-15-41. Post a-23-37, 39, 41.

LEADING SCREEN COMICS (Formerly Leading Comics)
National Periodical Publ.: No. 42, Apr-May, 1950 - No. 77, Aug-Sept, 1955

42-Peter Porkchops-c/stories continue	10	30	55	85
43-77	10	30	55	80

NOTE: Grossman a-most. Mayer a-45-48, 50, 54-57, 60, 62-74, 75(3), 76, 77.

LEAGUE OF CHAMPIONS, THE (Also see The Champions)
Hero Graphics: Dec, 1990 - No. 12, 1992 ($2.95, 52 pgs.)

1-12: 1-Flare app. 2-Origin Malice				3.00

LEAGUE OF EXTRAORDINARY GENTLEMEN, THE
America's Best Comics: Mar, 1999 - No. 6, Sept, 2000 ($2.95, limited series)

1-Alan Moore-s/Kevin O'Neill-a	1	3	6	8
1-DF Edition ($10.00) O'Neill-c				10.00
2,3				4.00
4-6				3.00
... Compendium 1,2: 1-r/#1,2. 2-r/#3,4				6.00
Hardcover (2000, $24.95) r/#1-6 plus cover gallery				25.00

LEAGUE OF JUSTICE
DC Comics (Elseworlds): 1996 - No. 2, 1996 ($5.95, 48 pgs., squarebound)

1,2: Magic-based alternate DC Universe story; Giordano-i				6.00

LEATHERFACE

Arpad Publishing: May (April on-c), 1991 - No. 4, May, 1992 ($2.75, painted-c)

1-4-Based on Texas Chainsaw movie; Dorman-c				3.00

LEATHERNECK THE MARINE (See Mighty Midget Comics)

LEAVE IT TO BEAVER (TV)
Dell Publishing Co.: No. 912, June, 1958; May-July, 1962 (All photo-c)

Four Color 912	18	54	126	230
Four Color 999,1103,1191,1285, 01-428-207	15	45	105	190

LEAVE IT TO BINKY (Binky No. 72 on) (Super DC Giant) (No. 1-22: 52 pgs.)
National Periodical Publications: 2-3/48 - #60, 10/58; #61, 6-7/68 - #71, 2-3/70 (Teen-age humor)

1-Lucy wears Superman costume	36	108	191	330
2	19	57	99	165
3,4	11	33	55	90
5-Superman cameo	18	54	94	155
6-10	10	30	55	80
11-14,16-22: Last 52 pg. issue	8	24	45	65
15-Scribbly story by Mayer	10	30	55	85
23-28,30-45: 45-Last pre-code (2/55)	6	18	30	42
29-Used in POP, pg. 78	6	18	32	45
46-60: 60-(10/58)	3	10	23	35
61 (6-7/68) 1950's reprints with art changes	4	12	30	50
62-69: 67-Last 12¢ issue	3	9	19	28
70-7pg. app. Bus Driver who looks like Ralph from Honeymooners	4	12	25	38
71-Last issue	3	9	21	32

NOTE: Aragones-a-61, 62, 67. Drucker a-28. Mayer a-1, 2, 15. Created by Mayer.

LEAVE IT TO CHANCE
Image Comics (Homage Comics): Sept, 1996 - No. 11, Sept, 1998;
DC Comics (Homage Comics): No. 12, Jun, 1999 - Present ($2.50/$2.95)

1-3: 1-Intro Chance Falconer & St. George; James Robinson scripts and Paul Smith-c/a begins				5.00
4-12				3.00
Shaman's Rain TPB (1997, $9.95) r/#1-4				10.00
Trick or Treat TPB (1997, $12.95) r/#5-8				13.00

LEE HUNTER, INDIAN FIGHTER
Dell Publishing Co.: No. 779, Mar, 1957; No. 904, May, 1958

Four Color 779 (#1)	4	12	30	50
Four Color 904	4	12	25	38

LEFT-HANDED GUN, THE (Movie)
Dell Publishing Co.: No. 913, July, 1958

Four Color 913-Paul Newman photo-c	10	30	70	130

LEGACY
Majestic Entertainment: Oct, 1993 - No. 2, Nov, 1993; No. 0, 1994 ($2.25)

1-2,0: 1-Glow-in-the-dark-c. 0-Platinum				2.25

LEGACY OF KAIN: SOUL REAVER
Top Cow Productions: Oct, 1999 (Diamond Dateline supplement)

1-Based on the Eidos video game; Benitez-c				2.25

LEGEND OF CUSTER, THE (TV)
Dell Publishing Co.: Jan, 1968

1-Wayne Maunder photo-c	3	9	19	28

LEGEND OF JESSE JAMES, THE (TV)
Gold Key: Feb, 1966

10172-602-Photo-c	3	9	19	28

LEGEND OF KAMUI, THE (See Kamui)

LEGEND OF LOBO, THE (See Movie Comics)

LEGEND OF MOTHER SARAH (Manga)
Dark Horse Comics: Apr, 1995 - No. 8, Nov, 1995 ($2.50, limited series)

1-8: Katsuhiro Otomo story				4.00

LEGEND OF MOTHER SARAH: CITY OF THE ANGELS (Manga)
Dark Horse Comics: Oct, 1996 - No. 9 ($3.95, B&W, limited series)

1(10/96), 2(12/97),3-9: Otomo scripts				4.00

LEGEND OF MOTHER SARAH: CITY OF THE CHILDREN (Manga)

Legend of the Shield #1 © AP

Legends of the DCU #14 © DC

Legion Lost #12 © DC

| | GD2.0 | FN6.0 | VF8.0 | NM9.4 | | GD2.0 | FN6.0 | VF8.0 | NM9.4 |

Dark Horse Comics: Jan, 1996 - No. 7, July, 1996 ($3.95, B&W, limited series)

1-7:Otomo scripts	4.00

LEGEND OF SUPREME
Image Comics (Extreme): Dec, 1994 - No. 3, Feb, 1995 ($2.50, limited series)

1-3	2.50

LEGEND OF THE ELFLORD
DavDez Arts: July, 1998 - No. 2, Sept, 1998 ($2.95)

1,2-Barry Blair & Colin Chin-s/a	3.00

LEGEND OF THE HAWKMAN
DC Comics: 2000 - No. 3, 2000 ($4.95, limited series)

1-3-Raab-s/Lark-c/a	5.00

LEGEND OF THE SAGE
Chaos Comics: Aug, 2001 - No. 4, Dec, 2001 ($2.99, limited series)

Preview Book (6/01, $1.99)	2.50
1-4-($2.99) Augustyn-s/Molenaar-a/c	3.00

LEGEND OF THE SHIELD, THE
DC Comics (Impact Comics): July, 1991 - No. 16, Oct, 1992 ($1.00)

1-16: 6,7-The Fly x-over. 12-Contains trading card	2.50
Annual 1 (1992, $2.50, 68 pgs.)-Snyder-a; w/trading card	2.50

LEGEND OF WONDER WOMAN, THE
DC Comics: May, 1986 - No. 4, Aug, 1986 (75¢, limited series)

1-4	4.00

LEGEND OF YOUNG DICK TURPIN, THE (Disney)(TV)
Gold Key: May, 1966

1 (10176-605)-Photo/painted-c	3	9	19	28

LEGEND OF ZELDA, THE (Link: The Legend... in indicia)
Valiant Comics: 1990 - No. 4, 1990 ($1.95, coated stiff-c)
V2#1, 1990 - No. 5, 1990 ($1.50)

1-4: 4-Layton-c(i)	3.00
V2#1-5	3.00

LEGENDS
DC Comics: Nov, 1986 - No. 6, Apr, 1987 (75¢, limited series)

1-5: 1-Byrne-c/a(p) in all; 1st app. new Capt. Marvel. 3-1st app. new Suicide Squad; death of Blockbuster	4.00
6-1st app. new Justice League	5.00

LEGENDS OF DANIEL BOONE, THE (...Frontier Scout)
National Periodical Publications: Oct-Nov, 1955 - No. 8, Dec-Jan, 1956-57

1 (Scarce)-Nick Cardy c-1-8	61	182	381	675
2 (Scarce)	44	132	264	460
3-8 (Scarce)	40	120	220	380

LEGENDS OF KID DEATH AND FLUFFY
Event Comics: Feb, 1997 ($2.95, B&W, one-shot)

1-Five covers	3.00

LEGENDS OF NASCAR, THE
Vortex Comics: Nov, 1990 - No. 14, 1992? (#1 3rd printing (1/91) says 2nd printing inside)

1-Bill Elliott biog.; Trimpe-a ($1.50)	5.00
1-2nd printing (11/90, $2.00)	2.25
1-3rd print; contains Maxx racecards ($3.00)	3.00
2-14: 2-Richard Petty. 3-Ken Schrader (7/91). 4-Bobby Allison; Spiegle-a(p); Adkins part-i. 5-Sterling Marlin. 6-Bill Elliott. 7-Junior Johnson; Spiegle-c/a. 8-Benny Parsons; Heck-a	3.00
1-13-Hologram cover versions. 2-Hologram shows Bill Elliott's car by mistake (all are numbered & limited)	5.00
2-Hologram corrected version	5.00
Christmas Special ($5.95)	6.00

LEGENDS OF THE DARK CLAW
DC Comics (Amalgam): Apr, 1996 ($1.95)

1-Jim Balent-c/a	3.00

LEGENDS OF THE DARK KNIGHT (See Batman: ...)

LEGENDS OF THE DC UNIVERSE
DC Comics: Feb, 1998 - No. 41, June, 2001 ($1.95/$1.99/$2.50)

1-13,15-21: 1-3-Superman; Robinson-s/Semeiks-a/Orbik-painted-c. 4,5-Wonder Woman; Deodato-a/Rude painted-c. 8-GL/GA, O'Neil-s. 10,11-Batgirl; Dodson-a. 12,13-Justice League. 15-17-Flash. 18-Kid Flash; Guice-a. 19-Impulse; prelude to JLApe Annuals. 20,21-Abin Sur	3.00
14-($3.95) Jimmy Olsen; Kirby-esque-c by Rude	4.00
22-27,30: 22,23-Superman; Rude-c/Ladronn-a. 26,27-Aquaman/Joker	2.50
28,29: Green Lantern & the Atom; Gil Kane-a; covers by Kane and Ross	2.50
31,32: 32-Begin $2.50-c; Wonder Woman; Texeira-a	2.50
33-36-Hal Jordan as The Spectre; DeMatteis-s/Zulli-a; Hale painted-c	2.50
37-41: 37,38-Kyle Rayner. 39-Superman. 40,41-Atom; Harris-c	2.50
...Crisis on Infinite Earths 1 (2/99, $4.95) Untold story during and after Crisis on I.E. #4; Wolfman-s/Ryan-a/Orbik-c	5.00
...80 Page Giant 1 (9/98, $4.95) Stories and art by various incl. Ditko, Perez, Gibbons, Mumy; Joe Kubert-c	5.00
...80 Page Giant 1 (5/00, $4.95) Stories and art by various incl. Challengers by Art Adams; Sean Phillips-c	5.00
...3-D Gallery (12/98, $2.95) Pin-ups w/glasses	3.00

LEGENDS OF THE LEGION (See Legion of Super-Heroes)
DC Comics: Feb, 1998 - No. 4, May, 1998 ($2.25, limited series)

1-4:1-Origin-s of Ultra Boy. 2-Spark. 3-Umbra. 4-Star Boy	3.00

LEGENDS OF THE STARGRAZERS (See Vanguard Illustrated #2)
Innovation Publishing: Aug, 1989 - No. 6, 1990 ($1.95, limited series, mature)

1-6: 1-Redondo part inks	2.25

LEGENDS OF THE WORLD'S FINEST (See World's Finest)
DC Comics: 1994 - No. 3, 1994 ($4.95, squarebound, limited series)

1-3: Simonson scripts; Brereton-c/a; embossed foil logos	6.00
TPB-(1995, $14.95) r/#1-3	15.00

L.E.G.I.O.N. (The # to right of title represents year of print)(Also see Lobo & R.E.B.E.L.S.)
DC Comics: Feb, 1989 - No. 70, Sept, 1994 ($1.50/$1.75)

1-Giffen plots/breakdowns in #1-12,28	5.00
2-22,24-47: 3-Lobo app. #3 on. 4-1st Lobo-c this title. 5-Lobo joins L.E.G.I.O.N. 13-Lar Gand app. 16-Lar Gand joins L.E.G.I.O.N., leaves #19. 31-Capt. Marvel app. 35-L.E.G.I.O.N. '92 begins	3.00
23,70-($2.50, 52 pgs.)-L.E.G.I.O.N. '91 begins. 70-Zero Hour	4.00
48,49,51-69: 48-Begin $1.75-c. 63-L.E.G.I.O.N. '94 begins; Superman x-over	3.00
50-($3.50, 68 pgs.)	4.00
Annual 1-5 ('90-94, 68 pgs.): 1-Lobo, Superman app. 2-Alan Grant scripts. 5-Elseworlds story; Lobo app.	4.00
NOTE: *Alan Grant scripts in #1-39, 51, Annual 1, 2.*

LEGION, THE (Continued from Legion Lost & Legion Worlds)
DC Comics: Dec, 2001 - Present ($2.50)

1-3-Abnett & Lanning-s; Coipel & Lanning-c/a	2.50

LEGION LOST (Continued from Legion of Super-Heroes [4th series] #125)
DC Comics: May, 2000 - No. 12, Apr, 2001 ($2.50, limited series)

1-12-Abnett & Lanning-s. Coipel-c/a in most. 4,9-Alixe-a	2.50

LEGIONNAIRES (See Legion of Super-Heroes #40, 41 & Showcase 95 #6)
DC Comics: Apr, 1992 - No. 81, Mar, 2000 ($1.25/$1.50/$2.25)

0-(10/94)-Zero Hour restart of Legion; released between #18 & #19	2.50
1-49,51-77: 1-(4/92)-Chris Sprouse-c/a; polybagged w/SkyBox trading card. 11-Kid Quantum joins. 18-(9/94)-Zero Hour. 19(11/94). 37-Valor (Lar Gand) becomes M'onel (5/96). 43-Legion tryouts; reintro Princess Projectra, Shadow Lass & others. 47-Forms one cover image with LSH #91. 60-Karate Kid & Kid Quantum join. 61-Silver Age & 70's Legion app. 76-Return of Wildfire. 79,80-Coipel-c/a; Legion vs. the Blight	2.50
50-($3.95) Pullout poster by Davis/Farmer	4.00
1,000,000 (11/98) Sean Phillips-a	2.50
Annual 1,3 ('94,'96 $2.95)-1-Elseworlds-s. 3-Legends of the Dead Earth-s	3.00
Annual 2 (1995, $3.95)-Year One-s	4.50

LEGIONNAIRES THREE
DC Comics: Jan, 1986 - No. 4, May, 1986 (75¢, limited series)

1-4	3.00

LEGION OF MONSTERS (Also see Marvel Premiere #28 & Marvel Preview #8)

Legionnaires #80 © DC

Legion of Super-Heroes #100 © DC

Legion Worlds #1 © DC

	GD2.0	FN6.0	VF8.0	NM9.4

Marvel Comics Group: Sept, 1975 ($1.00, B&W, magazine, 76 pgs.)

1-Origin & 1st app. Legion of Monsters; Neal Adams-c; Morrow-a; origin &
only app. The Manphibian; Frankenstein by Mayerik; Bram Stoker's
Dracula adaptation; Reese-a; painted-c (#2 was advertised with Morbius
& Satana, but was never published)   3   9   19   28

LEGION OF NIGHT, THE
Marvel Comics: Oct, 1991 - No. 2, Oct, 1991 ($4.95, 52 pgs.)

1,2-Whilce Portacio-c/a(p)   5.00

LEGION OF SUBSTITUTE HEROES SPECIAL (See Adventure Comics #306)
DC Comics: July, 1985 ($1.25, one-shot, 52 pgs.)

1-Giffen-c/a(p)   3.00

LEGION OF SUPER-HEROES (See Action, Adventure, All New Collectors
Edition, Legionnaires, Legends of the Legion, Limited Collectors Edition, Secrets
of the..., Superboy & Superman)
National Periodical Publications: Feb, 1973 - No. 4, July-Aug, 1973

1-Legion & Tommy Tomorrow reprints begin   3   9   19   28
2-4: 2-Forte-r. 3-r/Adv. #340. Action #240. 4-r/Adv. #341, Action #233;
   Mooney-r   2   6   11   15

LEGION OF SUPER-HEROES, THE (Formerly Superboy and...; Tales of The
Legion No. 314 on)
DC Comics: No. 259, Jan, 1980 - No. 313, July, 1984

259(#1)-Superboy leaves Legion   2   6   9   12
260-270,285-290,294: 265-Contains 28 pg. insert "Superman & the TRS-80
   computer"; origin Tyroc; Tyroc leaves Legion. 290-294-Great Darkness saga.
   294-Double size (52 pgs.)   1   3   5   7
261,263,264,266: (Whitman variants; low print run; no cover #'s)
    1   4   7   10
271-284,291-293: 272-Blok joins; origin; 20 pg. insert-Dial 'H' For Hero. 277-Intro
   Reflecto. 280-Superboy re-joins Legion. 282-Origin Reflecto. 283-Origin
   Wildfire   5.00
295-299,301-313: 297-Origin retold. 298-Free 16pg. Amethyst preview. 306-Brief
   origin Star Boy   3.00
300-(68 pgs., Mando paper)-Anniversary issue; has c/a by almost everyone at
   DC   5.00
Annual 1-3(82-84, 52 pgs.)-1-Giffen-c/a; 1st app./origin new Invisible Kid who
   joins Legion. 2-Karate Kid & Princess Projectra wed & resign   3.00
...The Great Darkness Saga (1989, $17.95, 196 pgs.)-r/LSH #287,290-294 &
   Annual #3; Giffen-c/a   2   6   12   18
NOTE: *Aparo* c-282, 283, 300(part). *Austin* c-268i. *Buckler* c-273p, 274p, 276z. *Colan* a-311p.
Ditko a(p)-267, 268, 272, 274, 276, 281. *Giffen* a-285-313p, Annual 1p; c-287p, 288p, 289, 290p,
291p, 292, 293, 294-299p, 300, 301-313p, Annual 1p, 2p. *Perez* c-268p, 277-280, 281p. *Starlin* a-
265. *Staton* a-259p, 260p, 280. *Tuska* a-308p.

LEGION OF SUPER-HEROES (3rd Series) (Reprinted in Tales of the Legion)
DC Comics: Aug, 1984 - No. 63, Aug, 1989 ($1.25/$1.75, deluxe format)

1-Silver ink logo   5.00
2-36,39-44,46-49,51-62: 4-Death of Karate Kid. 5-Death of Nemesis Kid. 12-
   Cosmic Boy, Lightning Lad, & Saturn Girl resign. 14-Intro new members:
   Tellus, Sensor Girl, Quislet. 15-17-Crisis tie-in. 18-Crisis x-over. 25-Sensor
   Girl i.d. revealed as Princess Projectra. 35-Saturn Girl rejoins. 42,43-
   Millennium tie-ins. 44-Origin Quislet   3.00
37,38-Death of Superboy   2   6   10   14
45,50: 45 ($2.95, 68 pgs.)-Anniversary ish. 50-Double size $2.50-c)   4.00
63-Final issue   4.00
Annual 1-4 (10/85-'88, 52 pgs.)-1-Crisis tie-in   3.00
NOTE: *Byrne* c-36p. *Giffen* a(p)-1, 2, 50-55, 57-63, Annual 1p; c-1-5p, 54p, Annual 1.
Orlando a-6p. *Steacy* c-45-50, Annual 3.

LEGION OF SUPER-HEROES (4th Series)
DC Comics: Nov, 1989 - No. 125, Mar, 2000 ($1.75/$1.95/$2.25)

0-(10/94)-Zero Hour restart of Legion; released between #61 & #62   2.50
1-Giffen-c/a(p)/scripts begin (4 pg.-a only #18)   4.00
2-20,26-49,51-53,55-58: 4-Mon-El (Lar Gand) destroys Time Trapper, changes
   reality. 5-Alt. reality story where Mordru rules all; Ferro Lad app. 6-1st app.
   of Laurel Gand (Lar Gand's cousin). 8-Origin. 10-Free poster by Giffen show
   ing new costumes. 15-(2/91)-1st reference of Lar Gand as Valor. 26-New map
   of headquarters. 34-Six pg. preview of Timber Wolf mini-series. 40-Minor
   Legionnaires app. 41-(3/93)-SW6 Legion renamed Legionnaires w/new
   costumes and some new code-names   3.00

21-25: 21-24-Lobo & Darkseid storyline. 24-Cameo SW6 younger Legion
   duplicates. 25-SW6 Legion full intro.   3.50
50-($3.50, 68 pgs.)   4.00
54-($2.95)-Die-cut & foil stamped-c   4.00
59-99: 61-(9/94)-Zero Hour. 62-(11/94). 75-XS travels back to the 20th Century
   (cont'd in Impulse #9). 77-Origin of Braniac 5. 81-Reintro Sun Boy. 85-Half of
   the Legion sent to the 20th century, Superman-c/app. 86-Final Night.
   87-Deadman-c/app. 88-Impulse-c/app. Adventure Comics #247 cover swipe.
   91-Forms one cover image with Legionnaires #47. 96-Wedding of Ultra Boy
   and Apparition. 99-Robin, Impulse, Superboy app.   2.50
100-($5.95, 96 pgs.)-Legionnaires return to the 30th Century; gatefold-c;
   5 stories-art by Simonson, Davis and others   1   3   5   7
101-125: 101-Armstrong-a(p) begins. 105-Legion past & present vs. Time Trapper. 109-Moder-a. 110-Thunder joins. 114,115-Bizarro Legion. 120,121-Coipel-
   Five. 122,123-Coipel-c/a. 125-Leads into "Legion Lost" maxi-series   2.50
#1,000,000 (11/98) Giffen-a   2.50
Annual 1-5 (1990-1994, $3.50, 68 pgs.): 4-Bloodlines. 5-Elseworlds story   3.50
Annual 6 (1995,$3.95)-Year One story   4.00
Annual 7 (1996, $3.50, 68 pgs.)-Legends of the Dead Earth story; intro 75th
   Century Legion of Super-Heroes; Wildfire app.   3.50
Legion: Secret Files 1 (1/98, $4.95) Retold origin & pin-ups   5.00
Legion: Secret Files 2 (6/99, $4.95) Story and profile pages   5.00
The Beginning of Tomorrow TPB ('99, $17.95) r/post-Zero Hour reboot   18.00
NOTE: *Giffen* a-1-24; breakdowns-26-32, 34-36; c-1-7, 8(part), 9-24. *Brandon Peterson* a(p)-
15(1st for DC), 16, 18, Annual 2(54 pgs.); c-Annual 2p. *Swan/Anderson* c-8(part).

LEGION: SCIENCE POLICE (See Legion of Super-Heroes)
DC Comics: Aug, 1998 - No. 4, Nov, 1998 ($2.25, limited series)

1-4-Ryan-a   2.50

LEGION WORLDS (Follows Legion Lost series)
DC Comics: Jun, 2001 - No. 6, Nov, 2001 ($3.95, limited series)

1-6-Abnett & Lanning-s; art by various. 5-Dillon-a. 6-Timber Wolf app.   4.00

LEMONADE KID, THE (See Bobby Benson's B-Bar-B Riders)
AC Comics: 1990 ($2.50, 28 pgs.)

1-Powell-c(r); Red Hawk-r by Powell; Lemonade Kid/Bobby Benson by
   Powell (2 stories)   2.50

LENNON SISTERS LIFE STORY, THE
Dell Publishing Co.: No. 951, Nov, 1958 - No. 1014, Aug, 1959

Four Color 951 (#1)-Toth-a, 32pgs., photo-c   14   42   98   185
Four Color 1014-Toth-a, photo-c   13   40   91   175

LENORE
Slave Labor Graphics: Feb, 1998 - Present ($2.95, B&W)

1-8: 1-Roman Dirge-s/a. 1,2-2nd printing   3.00
...: Noogies TPB ($11.95) r/#1-4   12.00
...: Wedgies TPB (2000, $13.95) r/#5-8   14.00

LEONARD NIMOY'S PRIMORTALS
Tekno Comix: Mar, 1995 - No. 15, May, 1996 ($1.95)

1-15: Concept by Leonard Nimoy & Isaac Asimov 1-3-w/bound-in game piece
   & trading card. 4-w/Teknophage Steel Edition coupon. 13,14-Art Adams-c.
   15-Simonson-c   2.25

LEONARD NIMOY'S PRIMORTALS
BIG Entertainment: V2#0, June, 1996 - No. 8, Feb, 1997 ($2.25)

V2#0-8: 0-Includes Pt. 9 of "The Big Bang" x-over. 0,1-Simonson-a. 3-Kelley
   Jones-c   2.25

LEONARD NIMOY'S PRIMORTALS ORIGINS
Tekno Comix: Nov, 1995 - No. 2, Dec, 1995 ($2.95, limited series)

1,2: Nimoy scripts; Art Adams-c; polybagged   3.00

LEONARDO (Also see Teenage Mutant Ninja Turtles)
Mirage Studios: Dec, 1986 ($1.50, B&W, one-shot)

1   4.00

LEO THE LION
I. W. Enterprises: No date(1960s) (10¢)

1-Reprint   2   6   11   15

LEROY (Teen-age)
Standard Comics: Nov, 1949 - No. 6, Nov, 1950

Lethargic Lad #1 © Greg Hyland

Liberty Meadows #18 © Creators Syndicate

Lidsville #1 © GK

	GD2.0	FN6.0	VF8.0	NM9.4
1	8	24	42	60
2-Frazetta text illo.	6	18	29	40
3-6: 3-Lubbers-a	5	15	25	35

LETHAL (Also see Brigade)
Image Comics (Extreme Studios): Feb, 1996 ($2.50, unfinished limited series)

1-Marat Mychaels-c/a.				2.50

LETHAL FOES OF SPIDER-MAN (Sequel to Deadly Foes of Spider-Man)
Marvel Comics: Sept, 1993 - No. 4, Dec, 1993 ($1.75, limited series)

1-4				2.50

LETHARGIC LAD
Crusade Ent.: June, 1996 - No. 3, Sept, 1996 ($2.95, B&W, limited series)

1,2				3.00
3-Alex Ross-c/swipe (Kingdom Come)				4.00

LETHARGIC LAD ADVENTURES
Crusade Ent./Destination Ent.#3 on: Oct, 1997 - No. 12, Sept./Oct. 1999 ($2.95, B&W)

1-12-Hyland-s/a. 9-Alex Ross sketch page & back-c				3.00

LET'S PRETEND (CBS radio)
D. S. Publishing Co.: May-June, 1950 - No. 3, Sept-Oct, 1950

1	17	51	88	150
2,3	13	39	66	110

LET'S READ THE NEWSPAPER
Charlton Press: 1974

nn-Features Quincy by Ted Sheares	1	4	7	10

LET'S TAKE A TRIP (TV) (CBS Television Presents)
Pines Comics: Spring, 1958

1-Marv Levy-c/a	5	15	23	30

LETTERS TO SANTA (See March of Comics No. 228)

LEX LUTHOR: THE UNAUTHORIZED BIOGRAPHY
DC Comics: 1989 ($3.95, 52 pgs., one-shot, squarebound)

1-Painted-c; Clark Kent app.				4.00

LIBERTY COMICS (Miss Liberty No. 1)
Green Publishing Co.: No. 5, May, '46 - No. 15, July, 1946 (MLJ & other-r)

5 (5/46)-The Prankster app; Starr-a	20	60	105	175
10-Hangman & Boy Buddies app.; Suzie & Wilbur begin; reprints Hangman story from Hangman #8	21	63	110	185
11(V2#2, 1/46)-Wilbur in women's clothes	17	51	88	150
12-Black Hood & Suzie app.; Skull-c	21	63	110	185
14,15-Patty of Airliner; Starr-a in both	12	36	61	105

LIBERTY GUARDS
Chicago Mail Order: No date (1946?)

nn-Reprints Man of War #1 with cover of Liberty Scouts #1; Gustavson-c	37	111	197	340

LIBERTY MEADOWS
Insight Studios Group: 1999 - Present ($2.95, B&W)

1-Frank Cho-s/a; reprints newspaper strips				6.00
2,3				4.00
4-24: 20-Adam Hughes-c. 22-Evil Brandy vs. Brandy				3.00

LIBERTY PROJECT, THE
Eclipse Comics: June, 1987 - No. 8, May, 1988 ($1.75, color, Baxter paper)

1-8: 6-Valkyrie app.				2.25

LIBERTY SCOUTS (See Liberty Guards & Man of War)
Centaur Publications: No. 2, June, 1941 - No. 3, Aug, 1941

2(#1)-Origin The Fire-Man, Man of War; Vapo-Man & Liberty Scouts begin; intro Liberty Scouts; Gustavson-c/a in both	127	381	795	1400
3(#2)-Origin & 1st app. The Sentinel	93	279	581	1025

LICENCE TO KILL (James Bond 007) (Movie)
Eclipse Comics: 1989 ($7.95, slick paper, 52 pgs.)

nn-Movie adaptation; Timothy Dalton photo-c	1	3	6	8
Limited Hardcover ($24.95)				25.00

	GD2.0	FN6.0	VF8.0	NM9.4

LIDSVILLE (TV)
Gold Key: Oct, 1972 - No. 5, Oct, 1973

1-Photo-c	4	12	30	50
2-5	3	9	20	30

LIEUTENANT, THE (TV)
Dell Publishing Co.: April-June, 1964

1-Photo-c	3	9	19	28

LIEUTENANT BLUEBERRY (Also see Blueberry)
Marvel Comics (Epic Comics): 1991 - No. 3, 1991 (Graphic novel)

1,2 ($8.95)-Moebius-a in all				9.00
3 ($14.95)				15.00

LT. ROBIN CRUSOE, U.S.N. (See Movie Comics & Walt Disney Showcase #26)

LIFE OF CAPTAIN MARVEL, THE
Marvel Comics Group: Aug, 1985 - No. 5, Dec, 1985 ($2.00, Baxter paper)

1-5: 1-All reprint Starlin issues of Iron Man #55, Capt. Marvel #25-34 plus Marvel Feature #12 (all with Thanos). 4-New Thanos back-c by Starlin				3.00

LIFE OF CHRIST, THE
Catechetical Guild Educational Society: No. 301, 1949 (35¢, 100 pgs.)

301-Reprints from Topix(1949)-V5#11,12	9	27	49	70

LIFE OF CHRIST: THE CHRISTMAS STORY, THE
Marvel Comics/Nelson: Feb, 1993 ($2.99, slick stock)

nn				4.00

LIFE OF CHRIST: THE EASTER STORY, THE
Marvel Comics/Nelson: 1993 ($2.99, slick stock)

nn				4.00

LIFE OF CHRIST VISUALIZED
Standard Publishers: 1942 - No. 3, 1943

1-3: All came in cardboard case, each...	7	21	36	50
Case only.....	9	27	51	75

LIFE OF CHRIST VISUALIZED
The Standard Publ. Co.: 1946? (48 pgs. in color)

nn	5	14	21	28

LIFE OF ESTHER VISUALIZED
The Standard Publ. Co.: No. 2062, 1947 (48 pgs. in color)

2062	5	14	21	28

LIFE OF JOSEPH VISUALIZED
The Standard Publ. Co.: No. 1054, 1946 (48 pgs. in color)

1054	5	14	21	28

LIFE OF PAUL (See The Living Bible)

LIFE OF POPE JOHN PAUL II, THE
Marvel Comics Group: Jan, 1983 ($1.50/$1.75)

1				6.00

LIFE OF RILEY, THE (TV)
Dell Publishing Co.: No. 917, July, 1958

Four Color 917-Photo-c	12	36	84	150

LIFE ON ANOTHER PLANET
Kitchen Sink Press: 1978 (B&W, graphic novel, magazine size)

nn-Will Eisner-s/a				13.00
Reprint (DC Comics, 5/00, $12.95)				13.00

LIFE'S LIKE THAT
Croyden Publ. Co.: 1945 (25¢, B&W, 68 pgs.)

nn-Newspaper strip-r by Neher	6	18	32	45

LIFE STORIES OF AMERICAN PRESIDENTS (See Dell Giants)

LIFE STORY
Fawcett Publications: Apr, 1949 - V8#46, Jan, 1953; V8#47, Apr, 1953 (All have photo-c?)

V1#1	14	42	72	120
2	7	21	38	55
3-6, V2#7-12	6	18	32	45

Life Story #45 © FAW

Life With Archie #283 © DC

Limited Collectors' Edition C-35 © DC

	GD2.0	FN6.0	VF8.0	NM9.4
V3#13-Wood-a	14	42	72	120
V3#14-18, V4#19-24, V5#25-30, V6#31-35	6	18	29	40
V6#36- "I sold drugs" on-c	7	21	36	50
V7#37,40-42, V8#44,45	5	15	25	35
V7#38, V8#43-Evans-a	6	18	29	40
V7#39-Drug Smuggling & Junkie story	6	18	32	45
V8#46,47 (Scarce)	6	18	32	45

NOTE: *Powell* a-13, 23, 24, 26, 28, 30, 32, 39. *Marcus Swayze* a-1-3, 10-12, 15, 16, 20, 21, 23-25, 31, 35, 37, 40, 44, 46.

LIFE, THE UNIVERSE AND EVERYTHING (See Hitchhikers Guide to the Galaxy & Restaurant at the End of the Universe)
DC Comics: 1996 - No. 3, 1996 ($6.95, squarebound, limited series)

1-3: Adaptation of novel by Douglas Adams.	1	3	5	7

LIFE WITH ARCHIE
Archie Publications: Sept, 1958 - No. 285, July, 1991

1	28	84	196	350
2-(9/59)	14	42	100	170
3-5: 3-(7/60)	9	27	65	110
6-10	7	21	50	80
11-20	5	15	38	60
21(7/63)-30	4	12	27	42
31-41	3	10	23	35
42-Pureheart begins (1st app.-c/s, 10/65)	6	18	45	75
43,44	4	12	27	42
45(1/66) 1st Man From R.I.V.E.R.D.A.L.E.	5	15	38	60
46-Origin Pureheart	4	12	27	42
47-49	3	10	23	35
50-United Teens begin: Pureheart (Archie), Superteen (Betty), Captain Hero (Jughead)	6	18	27	42
51-59: 59-Pureheart ends	3	10	23	35
60-Archie band begins, ends #66	4	12	27	42
61-66: 61-Man From R.I.V.E.R.D.A.L.E.-c/s	3	9	20	30
67-80	2	6	12	18
81-99	2	6	11	16
100 (8/70), 113-Sabrina & Salem app.	3	9	17	25
101-112, 114-130(2/73), 139(11/73)-Archie Band c/s	2	6	9	12
131,134-138,140-146,148-161,164-170(6/76)	1	3	6	9
132,133,147,163-all horror-c/s	2	6	10	14
162-UFO c/s	2	6	10	14
171,173-175,177-184,186,189,191-194,196	1	3	5	7
172,185,197 : 172-(9/77)-Bi-Cent. spec. ish, 185-2nd 24th cent.-c/s, 197-Time machine/TV c/s	1	3	6	8
176(12/76)-1st app. Capt. Archie of Starship Rivda, in 24th century c/s; 1st app. Stella the Robot	2	6	11	15
187,188,195,198,199-all horror-c/s	1	3	6	8
190-1st Dr. Doom-c/s	1	3	6	8
200 (12/78) Maltese Pigeon-s	1	3	6	
201-203,205-237,239,240(1/84): 208-Reintro Veronica.				5.00
204-Flying saucer-c/s	1	3	5	7
238-(9/83)-25th anniversary issue; Ol' Betsy (jalopy) replaced				6.00
241-278,280-284: 250-Comic book convention-s				4.00
279,285: 279-Intro Mustang Sally (TV-host, 7/90)				5.00

NOTE: *Gene Colan* a-272-279, 285, 286.

LIFE WITH MILLIE (Formerly A Date With Millie) (Modeling With Millie #21 on)
Atlas/Marvel Comics Group: No. 8, Dec, 1960 - No. 20, Dec, 1962

8-Teenage	7	21	53	85
9-11	5	15	34	55
12-20	4	12	29	45

LIFE WITH SNARKY PARKER (TV)
Fox Feature Syndicate: Aug, 1950

1-Early TV comic; photo-c from TV puppet show	25	81	145	250

LIGHT AND DARKNESS WAR, THE
Marvel Comics (Epic Comics): Oct, 1988 - No. 6, Dec, 1989 ($1.95, lim. series)

1-6				2.25

LIGHT FANTASTIC, THE (Terry Pratchett's)
Innovation Publishing: June, 1992 - No. 4, Sept, 1992 ($2.50, mini-series)

1-4: Adapts 2nd novel in Discworld series				2.50

LIGHT IN THE FOREST (Disney)
Dell Publishing Co.: No. 891, Mar, 1958

Four Color 891-Movie, Fess Parker photo-c	8	24	56	100

LIGHTNING COMICS (Formerly Sure-Fire No. 1-3)
Ace Magazines: No. 4, Dec, 1940 - No. 13(V3#1), June, 1942

4-Characters continue from Sure-Fire	100	300	625	1100
5,6: 6-Dr. Nemesis begins	68	204	426	750
V2#1-6: 2- "Flash Lightning" becomes "Lash…"	55	165	330	575
V3#1-Intro. Lightning Girl & The Sword	55	165	330	575

NOTE: *Anderson* a-V2#6. *Mooney* c-V1#5, 6, V2#1-6, V3#1. Bondage c-V2#6. Lightning-c on all.

LIGHTNING COMICS PRESENTS
Lightning Comics: May, 1994 ($3.50)

1-Red foil-c distr. by Diamond Distr., 1-Black/yellow/blue-c distrib. by Capital Distr., 1-Red/yellow-c distributed by H. World, 1-Platinum				3.50

LI'L ... (See Little ...)

LILI
Image Comics: No. 0, 1999 ($4.95, B&W, limited series)

0-Bendis & Yanover-s				5.00

LILLITH (See Warrior Nun...)
Antarctic Press: Sept, 1996 - No. 3, Feb, 1997 ($2.95, limited series)

1-3: 1-Variant-c				3.00

LIMITED COLLECTORS' EDITION (See Famous First Edition, Marvel Treasury #28, Rudolph The Red-Nosed Reindeer, & Superman Vs. The Amazing Spider-Man; becomes All-New Collectors' Edition)
National Periodical Publications/DC Comics:
(#21-34,51-59: 84 pgs.; #35-41: 68 pgs.; #42-50: 60 pgs.)

C-21, Summer, 1973 - No. C-59, 1978 ($1.00) (10x13-1/2")				
(Rudolph...C-20 (implied), 12/72)-See Rudolph The Red-Nosed Reindeer				
C-21: Shazam (TV); r/Captain Marvel Jr. #11 by Raboy; C.C. Beck-c, biog. & photo	3	9	21	32
C-22: Tarzan; complete origin reprinted from #207-210; all Kubert-c/a; Joe Kubert biography & photo inside	3	9	17	26
C-23: House of Mystery; Wrightson, N. Adams/Orlando, G. Kane/Wood, Toth, Aragones, Kaluta reprints	4	12	25	38
C-24: Rudolph The Red-Nosed Reindeer	8	24	56	90
C-25: Batman; Neal Adams-c/a(r); G.A. Joker-r; Batman/Enemy Ace-r; has photos from TV show	4	12	29	45
C-26: See Famous First Edition C-26 (same contents)				
C-27,C-29,C-31: C-27: Shazam (TV); G.A. Capt. Marvel & Mary Marvel-r; Beck-r. C-29: Tarzan; reprints "Return of Tarzan" from #219-223 by Kubert; Kubert-c. C-31: Superman; origin-r; N. Adams-a; photos of George Reeves from 1950s TV show on inside b/c; Burnley, Boring-r	3	9	17	24
C-32: Ghosts (new-a)	4	12	25	38
C-33: Rudolph The Red-Nosed Reindeer(new-a)	7	21	50	80
C-34: Christmas with the Super-Heroes; unpublished Angel & Ape story by Oksner & Wood; Batman & Teen Titans-r	3	9	17	24
C-35: Shazam (TV); photo cover features TV's Captain Marvel, Jackson Bostwick; Beck-r; TV photos inside b/c	6	15	22	
C-36: The Bible; all new adaptation beginning with Genesis by Kubert, Redondo & Mayer; Kubert-c	2	6	15	22
C-37: Batman; r-1946 Sundays; inside b/c photos of Batman TV show villains (all villain issue); r/G.A. Joker, Catwoman, Penguin, Two-Face, & Scarecrow stories plus 1946 Sundays-r	3	9	19	28
C-38: Superman; 1 pg. N. Adams; part photo-c; photos from TV show on inside back-c	2	6	15	22
C-39: Secret Origins of Super-Villains; N. Adams-i(r); collection reprints 1950's Joker origin, Luthor origin, Captain Cold origin from Showcase #8 among others; G.A. Batman-r; Beck-r.	2	6	15	22
C-40: Dick Tracy by Gould featuring Flattop; newspaper-r from 12/21/43 - 5/17/44; biog. of Chester Gould	2	6	15	22
C-41: Super Friends (TV); JLA-r(1965); Toth-c/a	3	9	17	24
C-42: Rudolph	5	15	34	55
C-43-C-47: C-43: Christmas with the Super-Heroes; Wrightson, S&K and Neal Adams-a. C-44: Batman; N. Adams-p(r) & G.A.-r; painted-c. C-45: More Secret Origins of Super-Villains; Flash-r/#105; G.A. Wonder Woman & Batman/Catwoman-r. C-46: Justice League of America(1963-r); 3 pgs. Toth-a				

Lionheart #2 © Awesome Ent.

Li'l Abner #65 © TOBY

Little Archie #40 © AP

	GD2.0	FN6.0	VF8.0	NM9.4		GD2.0	FN6.0	VF8.0	NM9.4

C-47: Superman Salutes the Bicentennial (Tomahawk interior); 2 pgs.

new-a	2	6	13	20

C-48,C-49: C-48: Superman Vs. The Flash (Superman/Flash race); swipes-c to Superman #199; r/Superman #199 & Flash #175; 6 pgs. Neal Adams-a. C-49

C-49: Superboy & the Legion of Super-Heroes 3 9 17 24
C-50: Rudolph The Red-Nosed Reindeer 5 5 34 55
C-51: Batman; Neal Adams-c/a 3 9 17 26
C-52,C-57: C-52: The Best of DC; Neal Adams-c/a; Toth, Kubert-a. C-57:
Welcome Back, Kotter-r(TV)(5/78) 3 9 17 24
C-59: Batman's Strangest Cases; N. Adams-r; Wrightson-r/Swamp Thing #7;
N. Adams/Wrightson-c 2 6 15 22
NOTE: All-r with exception of some special features and covers. *Aparo* a-52r; c-37. *Grell* c-49. *Infantino* a-25, 39, 44, 45, 52. *Bob Kane* r-25, 44. *Robinson* r-25, 44. *Sprang* r-44. Issues #21-31, 35-39, 45, 48 have back cover cut-outs.

LINDA (Everybody Loves...) (Phantom Lady No. 5 on)
Ajax-Farrell Publ. Co.: Apr-May, 1954 - No. 4, Oct-Nov, 1954
1-Kamenish-a 16 48 83 140
2-Lingerie panel 13 39 66 110
3,4 10 30 55 80

LINDA CARTER, STUDENT NURSE
Atlas Comics (AMI): Sept, 1961 - No. 9, Jan, 1963
1-Al Hartley-c 5 15 34 55
2-9 3 10 23 35

LINDA LARK
Dell Publishing Co.: Oct-Dec, 1961 - No. 8, Aug-Oct, 1963
1 3 9 20 30
2-8 2 6 12 18

LINUS, THE LIONHEARTED (TV)
Gold Key: Sept, 1965
1 (10155-509) 8 24 56 105

LION, THE (See Movie Comics)

LIONHEART
Awesome Comics: Sept, 1999 - No. 2 ($2.99/$2.50)
1-Ian Churchill-story/a, Jeph Loeb-s; Coven app. 3.00
2-Flip book w/Coven #4 2.50

LION OF SPARTA (See Movie Classics)

LIPPY THE LION AND HARDY HAR HAR (TV)
Gold Key: Mar, 1963 (12¢) (See Hanna-Barbera Band Wagon #1)
1 (10049-303) 9 27 63 120

LISA COMICS (TV)(See Simpsons Comics)
Bongo Comics: 1995 ($2.25)
1-Lisa in Wonderland 2.25

LI'L ABNER (See Comics on Parade, Sparkle, Sparkler Comics, Tip Top Comics & Tip Topper)
United Features Syndicate: 1939 - 1940
Single Series 4 ('39) 73 219 455 800
Single Series 18 ('40) (#18 on inside, #2 on-c) 59 177 369 650

LI'L ABNER (Al Capp's; continued from Comics on Parade #58)
Harvey Publ. No. 61-69 (2/49)/Toby Press No. 70 on - No. 61, Dec, 1947 - No. 97, Jan, 1955 (See Oxydol-Dreft in Promotional Comics section)
61(#1)-Wolverton & Powell-a 35 105 188 325
62-65: 63-The Wolf Girl app. 65-Powell-a 21 63 110 185
66,67,69,70 19 57 99 165
68-Full length Fearless Fosdick/story 20 60 105 175
71-74,76,80 15 45 77 130
75,77-79,86,91-All with Kurtzman art; 86-Sadie Hawkins Day. 91-r/#77
19 57 99 165
81-85,87-90,92-94,96,97: 83-Evil-Eye Fleegle & Double Whammy app. 88-Cou-
sin Weakeyes goes hunting. 94-Six lessons from Adam Lazonga. 96-Football
ish. 14 42 72 120
95-Full length Fearless Fosdick story 16 48 83 140

LI'L ABNER
Toby Press: 1951
1 19 57 99 165

LI'L ABNER'S DOGPATCH (See Al Capp's...)

LITTLE AL OF THE F.B.I.
Ziff-Davis Publications: No. 10, 1950 (no month) - No. 11, Apr-May, 1951
(Saunders painted-c)
10(1950) 17 51 88 150
11(1951) 14 42 72 120

LITTLE AL OF THE SECRET SERVICE
Ziff-Davis Publications: No. 10, 7-8/51; No, 2, 9-10/51; No. 3, Winter, 1951
(Saunders painted-c)
10(#1) 17 51 88 150
2,3 14 42 72 120

LITTLE AMBROSE
Archie Publications: September, 1958
1-Bob Bolling-c 15 45 77 130

LITTLE ANGEL
Standard (Visual Editions)/Pines: No. 5, Sept, 1954; No. 6, Sept, 1955 - No. 16, Sept, 1959
5-Last pre-code issue 7 21 36 50
6-16 5 15 23 30

LITTLE ANNIE ROONEY (Also see Henry)
David McKay Publ.: 1935 (25¢, B&W dailies, 48 pgs.)(10"x10", cardboard-c)
Book 1-Daily strip-r by Darrell McClure 39 117 208 360

LITTLE ANNIE ROONEY (See King Comics & Treasury of Comics)
David McKay/St. John/Standard: 1938; Aug, 1948 - No. 3, Oct, 1948
Feature Books 11 (McKay, 1938) 39 117 208 360
1 (St. John) 16 48 83 140
2,3 9 27 49 70

LITTLE ARCHIE (The Adventures of... #13-on) (See Archie Giant Series Mag. #527, 534, 538, 545, 549, 556, 560, 566, 570, 583, 594, 596, 607, 609, 619)
Archie Publications: 1956 - No. 180, Feb, 1983 (Giants No. 3-84)
1-(Scarce) 53 159 452 850
2 (1957) 26 78 179 320
3-5: 3-(1958)-Bob Bolling-c & giant issues begin 14 42 102 175
6-10 10 30 73 125
11-22 (84 pgs.) 7 21 50 80
23-39 (68 pgs.) 5 15 34 55
40 (Fall/66)-Intro. Little Pureheart-c/s (68 pgs.) 6 18 45 65
41,44-Intro Little Pureheart (68 pgs.) 4 12 30 50
42-Intro The Little Archies Band, ends #66 (68 pgs.) 5 15 38 60
43-1st Boy From R.I.V.E.R.D.A.L.E. (68 pgs.) 5 15 34 55
45-58 (68pgs.) 3 10 23 35
59 (68pgs.)-Little Sabrina begins 7 21 53 85
60-66 (68 pgs.) 3 10 23 35
67(9/71)-84: 84-Last 52pg. Giant-Size (2/74) 2 6 13 20
85-99 2 6 9 12
100 2 6 10 14
101-112,114-116,118-129 1 4 7 10
113,117,130: 113-Halloween Special issue(12/76). 117-Donny Osmond-c cameo
130-UFO cover (5/78) 1 4 7 10
131-150(1/80), 180(Last issue, 2/83) 6.00
151-179 4.00
...In Animal Land 1 (1957) 13 39 91 155
...In Animal Land 17 (Winter, 1957-58)-19 (Summer,1958)-Formerly Li'l Jinx
7 21 53 85
NOTE: *Little Archie Band* app. 42-66. *Little Sabrina* in 59-78,80-180

LITTLE ARCHIE CHRISTMAS SPECIAL (See Archie Giant Series #581)

LITTLE ARCHIE COMICS DIGEST ANNUAL (...Magazine #5 on)
Archie Publications: 10/77 - No. 48, 5/91 (Digest-size, 128 pgs., later issues $1.35-$1.50)
1(10/77)-Reprints 2 6 15 22
2(4/78,3(11/78)-Neal Adams-a. 3-The Fly-r by S&K 2 6 13 20
4(4/79) - 10 2 6 10 14
11-20 1 4 7 10
21-30: 28-Christmas-c 1 3 5 7
31-48: 40,46-Christmas-c 5.00

Little Audrey #2 © HARV

Little Dot #10 © HARV

The Little Endless Storybook © DC

	GD2.0	FN6.0	VF8.0	NM9.4

	GD2.0	FN6.0	VF8.0	NM9.4

NOTE: Little Archie, Little Jinx, Little Jughead & Little Sabrina in most issues.

LITTLE ARCHIE DIGEST MAGAZINE
Archie Comics: July, 1991 - No. 25 ($1.50/$1.79/$1.89, digest size, bi-annual)

V2#1				5.00
2-10				3.00
11-25				2.50

LITTLE ARCHIE MYSTERY
Archie Publications: Aug, 1963 - No. 2, Oct, 1963 (12¢ issues)

1	12	36	84	140
2	6	18	42	70

LITTLE ASPIRIN (See Little Lenny & Wisco)
Marvel Comics (CnPC): July, 1949 - No. 3, Dec, 1949 (52 pgs.)

1-Oscar app.; Kurtzman-a (4 pgs.)	17	51	88	150
2-Kurtzman-a (4 pgs.)	10	30	55	80
3-No Kurtzman-a	7	21	36	50

LITTLE AUDREY (Also see Playful...)
St. John Publ.: Apr, 1948 - No. 24, May, 1952

1-1st app. Little Audrey	40	120	240	420
2	23	69	121	210
3-5	15	45	77	130
6-10	11	33	55	90
11-20: 16-X-Mas-c	8	24	45	65
21-24	7	21	36	50

LITTLE AUDREY (See Harvey Hits #11, 19)
Harvey Publications: No. 25, Aug, 1952 - No. 53, April, 1957

25-(Paramount Pictures Famous Star... on-c); 1st Harvey Casper and Baby Huey (1 month earlier than Harvey Comic Hits #60(9/52))	13	39	94	160
26-30: 26-28-Casper app.	6	18	45	75
31-40: 32-35-Casper app.	5	15	38	60
41-53	4	12	26	40
...Clubhouse 1 (9/61, 68 pg. Giant)-New stories & reprints	8	24	58	95

LITTLE AUDREY
Harvey Comics: Aug, 1992 - No. 8, July, 1993 ($1.25/$1.50)

V2#1				3.00
2-8				2.25

LITTLE AUDREY (...Yearbook)
St. John Publishing Co.: 1950 (50¢, 260 pgs.)

Contains 8 complete 1949 comics rebound; Casper, Alice in Wonderland, Little Audrey, Abbott & Costello, Pinocchio, Moon Mullins, Three Stooges from Jubilee), Little Annie Rooney app. (Rare)

	64	192	398	700

(Also see All Good & Treasury of Comics)
NOTE: This book contains remaindered St. John comics; many variations possible.

LITTLE AUDREY & MELVIN (Audrey & Melvin No. 62)
Harvey Publications: May, 1962 - No. 61, Dec, 1973

1	9	27	65	110
2-5	5	15	34	55
6-10	4	12	26	40
11-20	3	9	17	25
21-40: 22-Richie Rich app.	2	6	12	18
41-50,55-61	2	6	10	14
51-54: All 52 pg. Giants	2	6	12	18

LITTLE AUDREY TV FUNTIME
Harvey Publ.: Sept, 1962 - No. 33, Oct, 1971 (#1-31: 68 pgs.; #32,33: 52 pgs.)

1-Richie Rich app.	8	24	60	100
2,3: Richie Rich app.	5	15	38	60
4,5: 5-25¢ & 35¢ issues exist	4	12	30	50
6-10	3	9	21	32
11-20	2	6	13	20
21-33	2	6	11	16

LITTLE BAD WOLF (Disney; seeWalt Disney's C&S #52, Walt Disney Showcase #21 & Wheaties)
Dell Publishing Co.: No. 403, June, 1952 - No. 564, June, 1954

Four Color 403 (#1)	7	21	49	90
Four Color 473 (6/53), 564	4	12	30	50

LITTLE BEAVER
Dell Publishing Co.: No. 211, Jan, 1949 - No. 870, Jan, 1958 (All painted-c)

Four Color 211('49)-All Harman-a	8	24	56	105
Four Color 267,294,332(5/51)	4	12	30	50
3(10-12/51)-8(1-3/53)	4	12	29	45
Four Color 483(8-10/53),529	4	12	26	40
Four Color 612,660,695,744,817,870	4	12	26	40

LITTLE BIT
Jubilee/St. John Publishing Co.: Mar, 1949 - No. 2, June, 1949

1	9	27	49	70
2	7	21	36	50

LITTLE DOT (See Humphrey, Li'l Max, Sad Sack, and Tastee-Freez Comics)
Harvey Publications: Sept, 1953 - No. 164, Apr, 1976

1-Intro./1st app. Richie Rich & Little Lotta	100	300	850	1500
2-1st app. Freckles & Pee Wee (Richie Rich's poor friends)	41	123	306	550
3	30	90	210	375
4	22	66	154	275
5-Origin dots on Little Dot's dress	30	90	210	375
6-Richie Rich, Little Lotta, & Little Dot all on cover; 1st Richie Rich cover featured	30	90	210	375
7-10: 9-Last pre-code issue (1/55)	15	45	107	185
11-20	10	30	73	125
21-30	9	27	51	75
31-40	8	24	42	60
41-50	6	18	32	45
51-60	6	18	28	38
61-80	3	9	19	28
81-100	2	6	15	22
101-141	2	6	11	15
142-145: All 52 pg. Giants	2	6	13	20
146-164	1	3	6	9

NOTE: Richie Rich & Little Lotta in all.

LITTLE DOT
Harvey Comics: Sept, 1992 - No. 7, June, 1994 ($1.25/$1.50)

V2#1-Little Dot, Little Lotta, Richie Rich in all				3.00
2-7 ($1.50)				2.50

LITTLE DOT DOTLAND (Dot Dotland No. 62, 63)
Harvey Publications: July, 1962 - No. 61, Dec, 1973

1-Richie Rich begins	10	30	73	125
2,3	5	15	38	60
4,5	5	15	34	55
6-10	3	10	23	35
11-20	3	9	19	28
21-30	2	6	12	18
31-50	2	6	11	16
51-54: All 52 pg. Giants	2	6	12	18
55-61	1	4	7	10

LITTLE DOT'S UNCLES & AUNTS (See Harvey Hits No. 4, 13, 24)
Harvey Enterprises: Oct, 1961; No. 2, Aug, 1962 - No. 52, Apr, 1974

1-Richie Rich begins; 68 pgs. begin	12	36	88	150
2,3	7	21	50	80
4,5	5	15	34	55
6-10	4	12	26	40
11-20	3	9	21	32
21-37: Last 68 pg. issue	2	6	15	22
38-52: All 52 pg. Giants	2	6	12	18

LITTLE DRACULA
Harvey Comics: Jan, 1992 - No. 3, May, 1992 ($1.25, quarterly, mini-series)

1-3				2.25

LITTLE ENDLESS STORYBOOK, THE (See The Sandman titles)
DC Comics: 2001 ($5.95, Prestige format, one-shot)

nn-Jill Thompson-s/painted-a/c; puppy Barnabas searches for Delirium				6.00

Little Giant Movie Funnies #1 © CEN

Li'l Jinx #3 © AP

Little Lizzie #4 © MAR

LITTLE EVA
St. John Publishing Co.: May, 1952 - No. 31, Nov, 1956

	GD2.0	FN6.0	VF8.0	NM9.4
1	16	48	83	140
2	9	27	49	70
3-5	7	21	36	50
6-10	6	18	29	40
11-31	5	15	25	35

3-D 1,2(10/53, 11/53, 25¢)-Both came w/glasses. 1-Infinity-c

	23	69	121	210

I.W. Reprint #1-3,6-8: 1-r/Little Eva #28. 2-r/Little Eva #29. 3-r/Little Eva #24

	2	6	9	12

Super Reprint #10,12('63),14,16,18('64): 18-r/Little Eva #25.

	2	6	9	12

LI'L GENIUS (Formerly Super Brat; Summer Fun No. 54) (See Blue Bird & Giant Comics #3)
Charlton Comics: 1954 - No. 52, 1/65; No. 53, 10/65; No. 54, 10/85 - No. 55, 1/86

5(#1?)	11	33	55	90
6-10	6	18	32	45
11-15,19,20	5	15	25	35
16,17-(68 pgs.)	7	21	36	50
18-(100 pgs., 10/58)	10	30	55	85
21-35	3	9	17	24
36-53	2	6	11	15
54,55 (Low print)				5.00

LI'L GHOST
St. John Publ. Co./Fago No. 1 on: 2/58; No. 2,1/59 - No. 3, Mar, 1959

1(St. John)	9	27	49	70
2,3	5	15	24	32

LITTLE GIANT COMICS
Centaur Publications: 7/38 - No. 3, 10/38; No. 4, 2/39 (132 pgs.) (6-3/4x4-1/2")

1-B&W with color-c; stories, puzzles, magic	64	192	398	700
2,3-B&W with color-c	55	165	341	600
4 (6-5/8x9-3/8")(68 pgs., B&W inside)	55	165	341	600

NOTE: *Filchock* c-2, 4. *Gustavson* a-1. *Pinajian* a-4. *Bob Wood* a-1.

LITTLE GIANT DETECTIVE FUNNIES
Centaur Publ.: Oct, 1938; No. 4, Jan, 1939 (6-3/4x4-1/2", 132 pgs., B&W)

1-B&W with color-c	75	225	469	825
4(1/39, B&W; color-c; 68 pgs., 6-1/2x9-1/2")-Eisner-r				
	55	165	341	600

LITTLE GIANT MOVIE FUNNIES
Centaur Publ.: Aug, 1938 - No. 2, Oct, 1938 (6-3/4x4-1/2", 132 pgs., B&W)

1-Ed Wheelan's "Minute Movies" reprints	75	225	469	825
2-Ed Wheelan's "Minute Movies" reprints	55	165	341	600

LITTLE GROUCHO (...the Red-Headed Tornado; ...Grouchy No. 2)
Reston Publ. Co.: No. 16; Feb-Mar, 1955 - No. 2, June-July, 1955
(See Tippy Terry)

16, 1 (2-3/55)	8	24	42	60
2(6-7/55)	5	15	25	35

LITTLE HIAWATHA (Disney; see Walt Disney's C&S #143)
Dell Publishing Co.: No. 439, Dec, 1952 - No. 988, May-July, 1959

Four Color 439 (#1)	5	15	35	65
Four Color 787 (4/57), 901 (5/58), 988	4	12	30	50

LITTLE IKE
St. John Publishing Co.: April, 1953 - No. 4, Oct, 1953

1	10	30	55	80
2	6	18	29	40
3,4	5	15	24	32

LITTLE IODINE (See Giant Comic Album)
Dell Publ. Co.: No. 224, 4/49 - No. 257, 1949: 3-5/50 - No. 56, 4-6/62 (1-4-52pgs.)

Four Color 224-By Jimmy Hatlo	9	27	63	120
Four Color 257	7	21	49	90
1(3-5/50)	9	27	63	110
2-5	4	12	29	45
6-10	3	10	23	35

11-20	3	9	17	25
21-30: 27-Xmas-c	2	6	15	22
31-40	2	6	12	18
41-56	2	6	11	15

LITTLE JACK FROST
Avon Periodicals: 1951

1	10	30	55	80

LI'L JINX (Little Archie in Animal Land #17) (Also see Pep Comics #62)
Archie Publications: No. 11, Nov, 1956 - No. 16, Sept, 1957

11-By Joe Edwards	13	39	66	110
12(1/57)-16	10	30	55	80

LI'L JINX (See Archie Giant Series Magazine No. 223)
LI'L JINX CHRISTMAS BAG (See Archie Giant Series Mag. No. 195, 206, 219)
LI'L JINX GIANT LAUGH-OUT (See Archie Giant Series Mag. No. 176, 185)
Archie Publications: No. 33, Sept, 1971 - No. 43, Nov, 1973 (52 pgs.)

33-43 (52 pgs.)	2	6	11	16

LITTLE JOE (See Popular Comics & Super Comics)
Dell Publishing Co.: No. 1, 1942

Four Color 1	52	156	364	675

LITTLE JOE
St. John Publishing Co.: Apr, 1953

1	5	14	21	28

LI'L KIDS (Also see Li'l Pals)
Marvel Comics Group: 8/70 - No. 2, 10/70; No. 3, 11/71 - No. 12, 6/73

1	5	15	38	60
2-9	3	9	21	32
10-12-Calvin app.	4	12	25	38

LITTLE KING
Dell Publishing Co.: No. 494, Aug, 1953 - No. 677, Feb, 1956

Four Color 494 (#1)	9	27	63	120
Four Color 597, 677	5	15	35	60

LITTLE LANA (Formerly Lana)
Marvel Comics (MjMC): No. 8, Nov, 1949; No. 9, Mar, 1950

8,9	8	24	45	65

LITTLE LENNY
Marvel Comics (CDS): June, 1949 - No. 3, Nov, 1949

1-Little Aspirin app.	12	36	61	100
2,3	7	21	38	55

LITTLE LIZZIE
Marvel Comics (PrPI)/Atlas (OMC): 6/49 - No. 5, 4/50; 9/53 - No. 3, Jan, 1954

1	13	39	66	110
2-5	8	24	42	60
1 (9/53, 2nd series by Atlas)-Howie Post-c	9	27	49	70
2,3	6	18	32	45

LITTLE LOTTA (See Harvey Hits No. 10)
Harvey Publications: 11/55 - No. 110, 11/73; No. 111, 9/74 - No. 120, 5/76
V2#1, Sept, 1992 - No. 4, July, 1993 ($1.25)

1-Richie Rich (r) & Little Dot begin	31	93	222	400
2,3	14	42	102	175
4,5	9	27	63	105
6-10	7	21	53	85
11-20	5	15	34	55
21-40	3	9	21	32
41-60	3	9	19	28
61-80: 62-1st app. Nurse Jenny	2	6	13	20
81-99	2	6	11	15
100-103: All 52 pg. Giants	2	6	12	18
104-120	1	3	6	9
V2#1-4 (1992-93)				2.50

NOTE: *No. 121 was advertised, but never released.*

LITTLE LOTTA FOODLAND
Harvey Publications: 9/63 - No. 14, 10/67; No. 15, 10/68 - No. 29, Oct, 1972

Little Lotta #1 © HARV

Little Monsters #18 © GK

Little Roquefort #2 © STJ

	GD2.0	FN6.0	VF8.0	NM9.4

	GD2.0	FN6.0	VF8.0	NM9.4

	GD2.0	FN6.0	VF8.0	NM9.4
1-Little Lotta, Little Dot, Richie Rich, 68 pgs. begin	12	36	88	150
2,3	8	24	56	90
4,5	5	15	38	60
6-10	4	12	29	45
11-20	3	9	20	30
21-26: 26-Last 68 pg. issue	2	6	15	22
27,28: Both 52 pgs.	2	6	13	20
29-(36 pgs.)	2	6	9	12

LITTLE LULU (Formerly Marge's Little Lulu)
Gold Key 207-257/Whitman 258 on: No. 207, Sept, 1972 - No. 268, Mar, 1984

207,209,220-Stanley-r. 207-1st app. Henrietta	2	6	10	14
208,210-219: 208-1st app. Snobbly, Wilbur's butler	1	4	7	10
221-240,242-249, 250(r/#166), 251-254(r/#206)	1	3	5	7
241,263-Stanley-r	1	3	6	8
255-257(Gold Key): 256-r/#212				6.00
258,259,262,264(2/82),265(3/82) (Whitman)	1	3	6	9
260,261	1	4	7	10
266-268 (All #90028 on-c; no date, no date code; 3-pack): 266(7/83). 267(8/83).				
268(3/84)-Stanley-r	2	6	11	15

LITTLE MARY MIXUP (See Comics On Parade)
United Features Syndicate: No. 10, 1939, - No. 26, 1940

Single Series 10, 26	36	108	191	330

LITTLE MAX COMICS (Joe Palooka's Pal; see Joe Palooka)
Harvey Publications: Oct, 1949 - No. 73, Nov, 1961

1-Infinity-c; Little Dot begins; Joe Palooka on-c	20	60	105	180
2-Little Dot app.; Joe Palooka on-c	11	33	55	90
3-Little Dot app.; Joe Palooka on-c	8	24	45	65
4-10: 5-Little Dot app., 1pg.	6	18	32	45
11-20	6	18	29	40
21-40: 23-Little Dot app. 38-r/#20	5	15	25	35
41-73: 64,66,67-73-Include new five pg. Richie Rich stories.				
70-73-Little Lotta app.	3	9	17	25

LI'L MENACE
Fago Magazine Co.: Dec, 1958 - No. 3, May, 1959

1-Peter Rabbit app.	8	24	42	60
2-Peter Rabbit (Vincent Fago's)	6	18	32	45
3	5	15	25	35

LITTLE MERMAID, THE (Walt Disney's...; also see Disney's...)
W. D. Publications (Disney): 1990 (no date given)($5.95, no ads, 52 pgs.)

nn-Adapts animated movie	1	3	5	7
nn-Comic version ($2.50)				3.00

LITTLE MERMAID, THE
Disney Comics: 1992 - No. 4, 1992 ($1.50, mini-series)

1-4: Based on movie				3.00
1-4: 2nd printings sold at Wal-Mart w/different-c				2.25

LITTLE MISS MUFFET
Best Books (Standard Comics)/King Features Synd.: No. 11, Dec, 1948 - No. 13, March, 1949

11-Strip reprints; Fanny Cory-c/a	8	24	42	60
12,13-Strip reprints; Fanny Cory-c/a	6	18	28	38

LITTLE MISS SUNBEAM COMICS
Magazine Enterprises/Quality Bakers of America: June-July, 1950 - No. 4, Dec-Jan, 1950-51

1	17	51	88	150
2-4	10	30	55	80
...Advs. In Space ('55)	6	18	30	42

LITTLE MONSTERS, THE (See March of Comics #423, Three Stooges #17)
Gold Key: Nov, 1964 - No. 44, Feb, 1978

1	6	18	40	65
2	3	9	21	32
3-10	3	9	17	25
11-20	2	6	13	20
21-30	2	6	11	15
31-44: 20,34-39,43-Reprints	1	3	6	9

LITTLE MONSTERS (Movie)
Now Comics: 1989 - No. 6, June, 1990 ($1.75)

1-6: Photo-c from movie				2.25

LITTLE NEMO (See Cocomalt, Future Comics, Help, Jest, Kayo, Punch, Red Seal, & Superworld; most by Winsor McCay Jr., son of famous artist) (Other McCay books: see Little Sammy Sneeze & Dreams of the Rarebit Fiend)

LITTLE NEMO (...in Slumberland)
McCay Features/Nostalgia Press('69): 1945 (11x7-1/4", 28 pgs., B&W)

1905 & 1911 reprints by Winsor McCay	10	30	55	85
1969-70 (Exact reprint)	2	6	10	14

LITTLE ORPHAN ANNIE (See Annie, Famous Feature Stories, Marvel Super Special, Merry Christmas..., Popular Comics, Super Book #7, 11, 23 & Super Comics)

LITTLE ORPHAN ANNIE
David McKay Publ./Dell Publishing Co.: No. 7, 1937 - No. 3, Sept-Nov, 1948; No. 206, Dec, 1948

Feature Books(McKay) 7-(1937) (Rare)	83	249	581	1075
Four Color 12(1941)	48	144	336	625
Four Color 18(1943)-Flag-c	38	113	266	500
Four Color 52(1944)	30	90	210	385
Four Color 76(1945)	25	75	175	320
Four Color 107(1946)	21	63	147	275
Four Color 152(1947)	14	42	98	175
1(3-5/48)-r/strips from 5/7/44 to 7/30/44	14	42	98	175
2-r/strips from 7/21/40 to 9/9/40	9	27	63	120
3-r/strips from 9/10/40 to 11/9/40	9	27	63	120
Four Color 206(12/48)	7	20	49	95

LI'L PALS (Also see Li'l Kids)
Marvel Comics Group: Sept, 1972 - No. 5, May, 1973

1	5	15	34	55
2-5	3	9	21	32

LI'L PAN (Formerly Rocket Kelly; becomes Junior Comics with #9)
Fox Features Syndicate: No. 6, Dec-Jan, 1946-47 - No. 8, Apr-May, 1947 (Also see Wotalife Comics)

6	10	30	55	80
7,8: 7-Atomic bomb story; robot-c	7	21	38	55

LITTLE PEOPLE (Also see Darby O'Gill & the...)
Dell Publishing Co.: No. 485, Aug-Oct, 1953 - No. 1062, Dec, 1959 (Walt Scott's)

Four Color 485 (#1)	6	18	42	80
Four Color 573(7/54), 633(6/55)	4	12	29	45
Four Color 692(3/56),753(11/56),809(7/57),868(12/57),908(5/58), 959(12/58), 1062	4	12	29	45

LITTLE RASCALS
Dell Publishing Co.: No. 674, Jan, 1956 - No. 1297, Mar-May, 1962

Four Color 674 (#1)	7	21	49	90
Four Color 778(3/57),825(8/57)	5	15	34	55
Four Color 883(3/58),936(9/58),974(3/59),1030(9/59),1079(2-4/60),1137 (9-11/60)	5	15	34	55
Four Color 1174(3-5/61),1224(10-12/61),1297	4	12	29	45

LI'L RASCAL TWINS (Formerly Nature Boy)
Charlton Comics: No. 6, 1957 - No. 18, Jan, 1960

6-Li'l Genius & Tomboy in all	6	18	29	40
7-18: 7-Timmy the Timid Ghost app.	4	12	18	24

LITTLE RED HOT: (CHANE OF FOOLS)
Image Comics: Feb, 1999 - No. 3, Apr, 1999 ($2.95/$3.50, B&W, limited series)

1-3-Dawn Brown-s/a, 2,3-($3.50-c)				3.50
The Foolish Collection TPB ($12.95) r/#1-3				13.00

LITTLE RED HOT: BOUND
Image Comics: July, 2001 - No. 3, Nov, 2001 ($2.95, color, limited series)

1-3-Dawn Brown-s/a.				3.00

LITTLE ROQUEFORT COMICS (See Paul Terry's Comics #105)
St. John Publishing Co.(all pre-code)/Pines No. 10: June, 1952 - No. 9, Oct, 1953; No. 10, Summer, 1958

Little Scouts Four Color #321 © Roland Coe

Lobo #4 © DC

Logan: Shadow Society nn © MAR

	GD2.0	FN6.0	VF8.0	NM9.4

	GD2.0	FN6.0	VF8.0	NM9.4
1-By Paul Terry	10	30	55	80
2	6	18	28	38
3-10: 10-CBS Television Presents on-c	5	15	23	30

LITTLE SAD SACK (See Harvey Hits No. 73, 76, 79, 81, 83)
Harvey Publications: Oct, 1964 - No. 19, Nov, 1967

1-Richie Rich app. on cover only	4	12	30	50
2-10	3	9	17	25
11-19	2	6	13	20

LITTLE SCOUTS
Dell Publishing Co.: No. 321, Mar, 1951 - No. 587, Oct, 1954

Four Color #321 (#1, 3/51)	4	12	26	40
2(10-12/51) - 6(10-12/52)	3	9	17	24
Four Color #462,506,550,587	3	9	17	24

LITTLE SHOP OF HORRORS SPECIAL (Movie)
DC Comics: Feb, 1987 ($2.00, 68 pgs.)

1-Colan-c/a				4.00

LITTLE SPUNKY
I. W. Enterprises: No date (1963?) (10¢)

1-r/Frisky Fables #1	2	6	9	12

LITTLE STOOGES, THE (The Three Stooges' Sons)
Gold Key: Sept, 1972 - No. 7, Mar, 1974

1-Norman Maurer cover/stories in all	3	9	21	32
2-7	2	6	12	18

LITTLEST OUTLAW (Disney)
Dell Publishing Co.: No. 609, Jan, 1955

Four Color 609-Movie, photo-c	6	18	42	80

LITTLEST SNOWMAN, THE
Dell Publishing Co.: No. 755, 12/56; No. 864, 12/57; 12-2/1963-64

Four Color 755,864, 1(1964)	4	12	30	50

LI'L TOMBOY (Formerly Fawcett's Funny Animals; see Giant Comics #3)
Charlton Comics: V14#92, Oct, 1956; No. 93, Mar, 1957 - No. 107, Feb, 1960

V14#92	5	15	23	30
93-107: 97-Atomic Bunny app.	4	12	19	25

LI'L WILLIE COMICS (Formerly & becomes Willie Comics #22 on)
Marvel Comics (MgPC): No. 20, July, 1949 - No. 21, Sept, 1949

20,21: 20-Little Aspirin app.	8	24	42	60

LITTLE WOMEN (See Power Record Comics)

LIVE IT UP
Spire Christian Comics (Fleming H. Revell Co.): 1973, 1976 (39-49 cents)

nn	1	3	6	8

LIVING BIBLE, THE
Living Bible Corp.: Fall, 1945 - No. 3, Spring, 1946

1-The Life of Paul; all have L. B. Cole-c	40	120	220	385
2-Joseph & His Brethren; Jonah & the Whale	30	90	159	275
3-Chaplains At War (classic-c)	40	120	232	400

LOBO
Dell Publishing Co.: Dec, 1965; No. 2, Oct, 1966

1-1st black character to have his own title	3	9	19	28
2	2	6	13	20

LOBO (Also see Action #650, Adventures of Superman, Demon (2nd series), Justice League, L.E.G.I.O.N., Mister Miracle, Omega Men #3 & Superman #41)
DC Comics: Nov, 1990 - No. 4, Feb, 1991 ($1.50, color, limited series)

1-(99¢)-Giffen plots/Breakdowns in all				4.00
1-2nd printing				2.50
2-4: 2-Legion '89 spin-off. 1-4 have Bisley painted covers & art				2.50
...: Blazing Chain of Love 1 (9/92, $1.50)-Denys Cowan-c/a; Alan Grant scripts, ...Convention Special 1 (1993, $1.75), ...Paramilitary Christmas Special 1 (1991, $2.39, 52 pgs.)-Bisley-c/a, ...: Portrait of a Victim 1 (1993, $1.75)				2.50

LOBO (Also see Showcase '95 #9)
DC Comics: Dec, 1993 - No. 64, Jul, 1999 ($1.75/$1.95/$2.25/$2.50, mature)

1 ($2.95)-Foil enhanced-c; Alan Grant scripts begin				3.00
2-9,10,11-64: 2-7-Alan Grant scripts. 9-(9/94). 0-(10/94)-Origin retold. 50-Lobo vs. the DCU. 58-Giffen-a				2.50
#1,000,000 (11/98) 853rd Century x-over				2.50
Annual 1 (1993, $3.50, 68 pgs.)-Bloodlines x-over				3.50
Annual 2 (1994, $3.50)-21 artists (20 listed on-c); Alan Grant script; Elseworlds story				3.50
Annual 3 (1995, $3.95)-Year One story				4.00
...Big Babe Spring Break Special (Spr, '95, $1.95)-Balent-a				2.50
...Bounty Hunting for Fun and Profit ('95)-Bisley-c				5.00
... Chained (5/97, $2.50)-Alan Grant story				2.50
.../Deadman: The Brave And The Bald (2/95, $3.50)				3.50
.../Demon: Helloween (12/96, $2.25)-Giarrano-a				2.50
...Fragtastic Voyage 1 ('97, $5.95)-Mejia painted-c/a				6.00
...Gallery (9/95, $3.50)-pin-ups				3.50
...In the Chair 1 (8/94, $1.95, 36 pgs.), ...I Quit-(12/95, $2.25)				2.50
.../Judge Dredd ('95, $4.95).				5.00
...Lobocop 1 (2/94, $1.95)-Alan Grant scripts; painted-c				2.50

LOBO: (Title Series), DC Comics

--A CONTRACT ON GAWD, 4/94 - 7/94 (mature) 1-4: Alan Grant scripts. 3-Groo cameo				2.50
--DEATH AND TAXES, 10/96 - No. 4, 1/97, 1-4-Giffen/Grant scripts				2.50
--GOES TO HOLLYWOOD, 8/96 ($2.25), 1-Grant scripts				2.50
--INFANTICIDE, 10/92 - 1/93 (mature), 1-4-Giffen-c/a; Grant scripts				2.50
~/ MASK, 2/97 - No. 2, 3/97 ($5.95), 1,2				6.00
~'S BACK, 5/92 - No. 4, 11/92 ($1.50, mature), 1-4: 1-Has 3 outer covers. Bisley painted-c 1,2; a-1-3. 3-Sam Kieth-a; all have Giffen plots/breakdown & Grant scripts				2.50
Trade paperback (1993, $9.95)-r/1-4				10.00
--THE DUCK, 6/97 ($1.95), 1-A. Grant-s/V. Semeiks & R. Kryssing-a				2.50
--UNAMERICAN GLADIATORS, 6/93 - 9/93 (mature), 1-4-Mignola-c; Grant/Wagner scripts				2.50

LOCKE!
Blackthorne Publishing: 1987 - No. 3, ($1.25, limited series)

1-3				2.25

LOCO (Magazine) (Satire)
Satire Publications: Aug, 1958 - V1#3, Jan, 1959

V1#1-Chic Stone-a	8	24	42	60
V1#2,3-Severin-a, 2 pgs. Davis; 3-Heath-a	6	18	32	45

LOGAN: PATH OF THE WARLORD
Marvel Comics: Feb, 1996 ($5.95, one-shot)

1-John Paul Leon-a				6.00

LOGAN: SHADOW SOCIETY
Marvel Comics: 1996 ($5.95, one-shot)

1				6.00

LOGAN'S RUN
Marvel Comics Group: Jan, 1977 - No. 7, July, 1977

1: 1-5-Based on novel & movie	1	4	7	10
2-5,7: 6,7-New stories adapted from novel				6.00
6-1st Thanos (also see Iron Man #55) solo story (back-up) by Zeck (6/77)	2	6	11	15
6-(35¢-c variant, limited distribution)	2	6	12	18
7-(35¢-c variant, limited distribution)	1	3	6	8

NOTE: *Austin* a-6i. *Gulacy* c-6. *Kane* c-7p. *Perez* a-1-5p; c-1-5p. *Sutton* a-6p, 7p.

LOIS & CLARK, THE NEW ADVENTURES OF SUPERMAN
DC Comics: 1994 ($9.95, one-shot)

1-r/Man of Steel #2, Superman Ann. 1, Superman #9 & 11, Action #600 & 655, Adventures of Superman #445, 462 & 466	1	4	7	10

LOIS LANE (Also see Daring New Adventures of Supergirl, Showcase #9,10 & Superman's Girlfriend...)
DC Comics: Aug, 1986 - No. 2, Sept, 1986 ($1.50, 52 pgs.)

1,2-Morrow-c/a in each				4.00

LOLLY AND PEPPER

The Lone Gunmen #1 © 20th Century Fox

The Lone Ranger #10 © Lone Ranger, Inc.

Long Bow #4 © FH

	GD2.0	FN6.0	VF8.0	NM9.4

Dell Publishing Co.: No. 832, Sept, 1957 - July, 1962

	GD2.0	FN6.0	VF8.0	NM9.4
Four Color 832(#1)	4	12	26	40
Four Color 940,978,1086,1206	3	9	19	28
01-459-207 (7/62)	3	9	17	25

LOMAX (See Police Action)

LONDON'S DARK
Escape/Titan: 1989 ($8.95, B&W, graphic novel)

	GD2.0	FN6.0	VF8.0	NM9.4
nn-James Robinson script; Paul Johnson-c/a	1	3	6	9

LONE EAGLE (The Flame No. 5 on)
Ajax/Farrell Publications: Apr-May, 1954 - No. 4, Oct-Nov, 1954

	GD2.0	FN6.0	VF8.0	NM9.4
1	13	39	66	110
2-4: 3-Bondage-c	9	27	49	70

LONE GUNMEN, THE (From the X-Files)
Dark Horse Comics: June, 2001 ($2.99, one-shot)

1-Paul Lee-a; photo-c				3.00

LONELY HEART (Formerly Dear Lonely Hearts; Dear Heart #15 on)
Ajax/Farrell Publ. (Excellent Publ.): No. 9, Mar, 1955 - No. 14, Feb, 1956

	GD2.0	FN6.0	VF8.0	NM9.4
9-Kamenesque-a; (Last precode)	10	30	55	80
10-14	6	18	32	45

LONE RANGER, THE (See Ace Comics, Aurora, Dell Giants,Future Comics, Golden Comics Digest #48, King Comics, Magic Comics & March of Comics #165, 174, 193, 208, 225, 236, 310, 322, 338, 350)

LONE RANGER, THE
Dell Publishing Co.: No. 3, 1939 - No. 167, Feb, 1947

	GD2.0	FN6.0	VF8.0	NM9.4
Large Feature Comic 3(1939)-Heigh-Yo Silver; text with illus. by Robert Weisman; also exists as a Whitman #710	127	381	795	1400
Large Feature Comic 7(1939)-Illustr. by Henry Vallely; Hi-Yo Silver the Lone Ranger to the Rescue; also exists as a Whitman #715	123	369	769	1350
Feature Book 21(1940), 24(1941)	80	240	500	875
Four Color 82(1945)	42	125	294	550
Four Color 98(1945),118(1946)	32	96	224	420
Four Color 125(1946),136(1947)	22	66	154	280
Four Color 151,167(1947)	18	54	126	240

LONE RANGER, THE (Movie, radio & TV; Clayton Moore starred as Lone Ranger in the movies; No. 1-37: strip reprints)(See Dell Giants)
Dell Publishing Co.: Jan-Feb, 1948 - No. 145, May-July, 1962

	GD2.0	FN6.0	VF8.0	NM9.4
1 (36 pgs.)-The Lone Ranger, his horse Silver, companion Tonto & his horse Scout begin	65	195	455	850
2 (52 pgs. begin, end #41)	29	87	203	375
3-5	22	66	154	280
6,7,9,10	18	54	126	230
8-Origin retold; Indian back-c begin, end #35	22	66	154	280
11-20: 11- "Young Hawk" Indian boy serial begins, ends #145	12	36	84	160
21,22,24-31: 51-Reprint. 31-1st Mask logo	10	30	70	125
23-Origin retold	13	39	91	165
32-37: 32-Painted-c begin. 36-Animal photo back-c begin, end #49. 37-Last newspaper-r issue; new outfit	8	24	56	100
38-41 (All 52 pgs.) 38-Paul S. Newman-s (wrote most of the stories #38-on)	7	21	49	95
42-50 (36 pgs.)	6	18	42	75
51-74 (52 pgs.): 56-One pg. origin story of Lone Ranger & Tonto. 71-Blank inside-c	6	18	42	75
75,77-99: 79-X-mas-c	5	15	35	65
76-Classic flag-c	6	18	42	75
100	7	21	49	85
101-111: Last painted-c	5	15	35	65
112-Clayton Moore photo-c begin, end #145	17	50	119	225
113-117	10	30	70	125
118-Origin Lone Ranger, Tonto, & Silver retold; Special anniversary issue	23	69	161	300
119-140: 139-Fran Striker-s	8	24	56	105
141-145	9	27	63	115

NOTE: **Hank Hartman** painted c(signed)-65, 66, 70, 75, 82; unsigned-64?, 67-69?, 71, 72, 73?, 74?, 76-78, 80, 81, 83-91, 92?, 93-111. **Ernest Nordli** painted c(signed)-42, 50, 52, 53, 56, 59, 60; unsigned-39-41, 44-49, 51, 54, 55, 57, 58, 61-63?

LONE RANGER, THE
Gold Key (Reprints in #13-20): 9/64 - No. 16, 12/69; No. 17, 11/72; No. 18, 9/74 - No. 28, 3/77

	GD2.0	FN6.0	VF8.0	NM9.4
1-Retells origin	5	15	35	70
2	3	10	23	35
3-10: Small Bear-r in #6-12. 10-Last 12¢ issue	3	9	20	30
11-17	2	6	13	20
18-28	2	6	11	15
Golden West 1(30029-610, 10/66)-Giant; r/most Golden West #3 including Clayton Moore photo front/back-c	7	21	49	85

LONE RANGER AND TONTO, THE
Topps Comics: Aug, 1994 - No. 4, Nov, 1994 ($2.50, limited series)

1-4: 3-Origin of Lone Ranger; Tonto leaves; Lansdale story, Truman-c/a in all.				2.50
1-4: Silver logo. 1-Signed by Lansdale and Truman				6.00
Trade paperback (1/95, $9.95)				10.00

LONE RANGER'S COMPANION TONTO, THE (TV)
Dell Publishing Co.: No. 312, Jan, 1951 - No. 33, Nov-Jan/58-59 (All painted-c)

	GD2.0	FN6.0	VF8.0	NM9.4
Four Color 312(#1, 1/51)	10	30	70	125
2(8-10/51),3: (#2 titled "Tonto")	5	15	35	65
4-10	5	15	34	65
11-20	4	12	29	45
21-33	3	10	23	35

NOTE: **Ernest Nordli** painted c(signed)-2, 7; unsigned-3-6, 8-11, 12?, 13, 14, 18?, 22-24? See Aurora Comic Booklets.

LONE RANGER'S FAMOUS HORSE HI-YO SILVER, THE (TV)
Dell Publishing Co.: No. 369, Jan, 1952 - No. 36, Oct-Dec, 1960 (All painted-c, most by Sam Savitt)

	GD2.0	FN6.0	VF8.0	NM9.4
Four Color 369(#1)-Silver's origin as told by The Lone Ranger	9	27	63	120
Four Color 392(#2, 4/52)	5	15	35	60
3(7-9/52)-10(4-6/52)	4	12	38	50
11-36	4	12	26	40

LONE RIDER (Also see The Rider)
Superior Comics(Farrell Publ.): Apr, 1951 - No. 26, Jul, 1955 (#3-on: 36 pgs.)

	GD2.0	FN6.0	VF8.0	NM9.4
1 (52 pgs.)-The Lone Rider & his horse Lightnin' begin; Kamenish-a begins	25	75	130	225
2 (52 pgs.)-The Golden Arrow begins (origin)	13	39	66	110
3-6: 6-Last Golden Arrow	12	36	61	100
7-Golden Arrow becomes Swift Arrow; origin of his shield	13	39	66	110
8-Origin Swift Arrow	14	42	72	120
9,10	9	27	51	75
11-14	7	21	38	50
15-Golden Arrow origin-r from #2, changing name to Swift Arrow	9	27	49	70
16-20,22-26: 23-Apache Kid app.	7	21	36	50
21-3-D effect-c	14	42	72	120

LONE WOLF AND CUB
First Comics: May, 1987 - No. 45, Apr, 1991 ($1.95-$3.25, B&W, deluxe size)

1-Frank Miller-c & intro.; reprints manga series by Koike & Kojima				8.00
1-2nd print, 3rd print, 2-2nd print				3.25
2-12: 6-72 pgs. origin issue				5.00
13-38,40,42-45: 40,42-Ploog-c				3.50
39-($5.95, 120 pgs.)-Ploog-c				6.00
41-($3.95, 84 pgs.)-Ploog-c				4.00
Deluxe Edition ($19.95, B&W)				20.00

NOTE: **Sienkiewicz** c-13-24. **Matt Wagner** c-25-30.

LONE WOLF AND CUB (Trade paperbacks)
Dark Horse Comics: Aug, 2000 - No. 28 ($9.95, B&W, 4" x 6", approx. 300 pgs.)

1-Collects First Comics reprint series; Frank Miller-c				18.00
1-(2nd printing)				12.00
1-(3rd-5th printings)				10.00
2,3-(1st printings)				12.00
2,3-(2nd printings)				10.00

Looney Tunes #72 © WB

Looney Tunes and Merrie Melodies #6 © WB

Lorna the Jungle Girl #11 © MAR

	GD2.0	FN6.0	VF8.0	NM9.4			GD2.0	FN6.0	VF8.0	NM9.4

4-15				10.00

LONG BOW (...Indian Boy)(See Indians & Jumbo Comics #141)
Fiction House Mag. (Real Adventures Publ.): 1951 - No. 9, Wint, 1952/53

1-Most covers by Maurice Whitman	17	51	88	150
2	10	30	55	85
3-9	9	27	49	70

LONG HOT SUMMER, THE
DC Comics (Milestone): Jul, 1995 - No. 3, Sept, 1995 ($2.95/$2.50, lim. series)

1-3: 1-($2.95-c). 2,3-($2.50-c)				3.00

LONG JOHN SILVER & THE PIRATES (Formerly Terry & the Pirates)
Charlton Comics: No. 30, Aug, 1956 - No. 32, March, 1957 (TV)

30-32: Whitman-c	10	30	55	80

LONGSHOT (Also see X-Men, 2nd Series #10)
Marvel Comics: Sept, 1985 - No. 6, Feb, 1986 (60¢, limited series)

1-6: 1-Art Adams/Whilce Portacio-c/a in all. 4-Spider-Man app. 6-Double size	1	3	5	7
Trade Paperback (1989, $16.95)-r/#1-6				17.00

LONGSHOT
Marvel Comics: Feb, 1998 ($3.99, one-shot)

1-DeMatteis-s/Zulli-a				4.00

LOONEY TUNES (2nd Series) (TV)
Gold Key/Whitman: April, 1975 - No. 47, June, 1984

1 -Reprints	3	9	20	30
2-10: 2,4-reprints	2	6	11	16
11-20: 16-reprints	1	4	7	10
21-30	1	3	6	8
31,32,36-42(2/82)				6.00
33-35('80) (Whitman, scarce)	2	6	11	15
43(4/82),44(6/83) (low distribution)	1	3	6	9
45-47 (All #90296 on-c; nd, nd code, pre-pack) 45(8/83), 46(3/84), 47(6/84)				
	2	6	10	14

LOONEY TUNES (3rd Series) (TV)
DC Comics: Apr, 1994 - Present ($1.50/$1.75/$1.95/$1.99)

1-10: 1-Marvin Martian-c/sty; Bugs Bunny, Roadrunner, Daffy begin				3.00
11-86: 69-23a/($1.75-c). 83-Super $1.99-c. 83-Giffen-s				2.25

LOONEY TUNES AND MERRIE MELODIES COMICS ("Looney Tunes" #166 (8/55) on)(Also see Porky's Duck Hunt)
Dell Publishing Co.: 1941 - No. 246, July-Sept, 1962

1-Porky Pig, Bugs Bunny, Daffy Duck, Elmer Fudd, Mary Jane & Sniffles, Pat Patsy and Pete begin (1st comic book app. of each). Bugs Bunny story by Win Smith (early Mickey Mouse artist)				
	1038	3115	7265	13,500
2 (11/41)	154	462	1078	2000
3-Kandi the Cave Kid begins by Walt Kelly; also in #4-6,8,11,15				
	123	369	861	1600
4-Kelly-a	123	369	861	1600
5-Bugs Bunny The Super-Duper Rabbit story (1st funny animal super hero, 3/42; also see Coo Coo); Kelly-a	96	288	672	1250
6,8-Kelly-a	69	206	483	900
7,9,10: 9-Painted-c. 10-Flag-c	54	162	378	700
11,15-Kelly-a; 15-X-Mas-c	54	162	378	700
12-14,16-19	38	114	266	500
20-25: Pat, Patsy & Pete by Walt Kelly in all	33	99	231	425
26-30	23	69	161	300
31-40: 33-War bond-c. 39-X-Mas-c	19	56	133	250
41-50	14	43	98	185
51-60	10	30	70	135
61-80	7	21	49	90
81-99: 87-X-Mas-c	5	15	35	70
100	6	18	42	80
101-120	5	15	34	55
121-150	4	12	29	45
151-200: 159-X-Mas-c	4	12	25	38
201-240	3	9	21	32
241-246	3	10	23	35

LOONY SPORTS (Magazine)
3-Strikes Publishing Co.: Spring, 1975 (68 pgs.)

1-Sports satire	2	6	9	12

LOOSE CANNON (Also see Action Comics Annual #5 & Showcase '94 #5)
DC Comics: June, 1995 - No. 4, Sept, 1995 ($1.75, limited series)

1-4: Adam Pollina-a. 1-Superman app.				2.50

LOOY DOT DOPE
United Features Syndicate: No. 13, 1939

Single Series 13	31	93	165	285

LORD JIM (See Movie Comics)

LORD PUMPKIN
Malibu Comics (Ultraverse): Oct, 1994 ($2.50, one-shot)

0-Two covers				2.50

LORD PUMPKIN/NECROMANTRA
Malibu Comics (Ultraverse): Apr, 1995 - No. 4, July, 1995 ($2.95, limited series, flip book)

1-4				3.00

LORDS OF MISRULE
Dark Horse Comics: Jan, 1997 - No. 6, Jun, 1997 ($2.95, B&W, limited series)

1-6: 1-Wraparound-c				3.00

LORDS OF THE ULTRA-REALM
DC Comics: June, 1986 - No. 6, Nov, 1986 (Mini-series)

1-6, Special 1(12/87, $2.25)				2.25

LORNA THE JUNGLE GIRL (...Jungle Queen #1-5)
Atlas Comics (NPI 1/OMC 2-11/NPI 12-26): July, 1953 - No. 26, Aug, 1957

1-Origin & 1st app.	39	117	208	360
2-Intro. & 1st app. Greg Knight	20	60	105	180
3-5	17	51	88	150
6-11: 11-Last pre-code (1/55)	14	42	72	120
12-17,19-26: 14-Colletta & Maneely-c	11	33	55	90
18-Williamson/Colletta-c	12	36	61	100

NOTE: *Brodsky* c-1-3, 5, 9. *Everett* c-21, 23-26. *Heath* c-6, 7. *Maneely* c-12, 15. *Romita* a-20, 22, 24, 26. *Shores* a-14-16, 24, 26; c-11, 13, 16. *Tuska* a-26.

LOSERS SPECIAL (See Our Fighting Forces #123)(Also see G.I. Combat & Our Fighting Forces)
DC Comics: Sept, 1985 ($1.25, one-shot)

1-Capt. Storm, Gunner & Sarge; Crisis x-over				5.00

LOST, THE
Chaos! Comics: Dec, 1997 - No. 3 ($2.95, B&W, unfinished limited series)

1-3-Andreyko-script: 1-Russell back-c				3.00

LOST CONTINENT
Eclipse Int'l: Sept, 1990 - No. 6, 1991 ($3.50, B&W, squarebound, 60 pgs.)

1-6: Japanese story translated to English				3.50

LOST HEROES
Davdez Arts: Mar, 1998 - No. 4 ($2.95)

0-4-Rob Prior-s/painted-a				3.00

LOST IN SPACE (Movie)
Dark Horse Comics: Apr, 1998 - No. 3, July, 1998 ($2.95, limited series)

1-3-Continuation of 1998 movie; Erskine-c				3.00

LOST IN SPACE (TV)(Also see Space Family Robinson)
Innovation Publishing: Aug, 1991 - No. 12, Jan, 1993 ($2.50, limited series)

1-12: Bill Mumy (Will Robinson) scripts in #1-9. 9-Perez-a				3.00
1,2-Special Ed.: r/#1,2 plus new art & new-c				3.00
Annual 1,2 (1991, 1992, $2.95, 52 pgs.)				3.00
...: Project Robinson (11/93, $2.50) 1st & only part of intended series				3.00

LOST IN SPACE: VOYAGE TO THE BOTTOM OF THE SOUL
Innovation Publishing: No. 13, Aug, 1993 - No. 18, 1994 ($2.50, limited series)

13(V1#1, $2.95)-Embossed silver logo edition; Bill Mumy scripts begin; painted-c				3.00
13(V1#1, $4.95)-Embossed gold logo edition bagged w/poster				5.00
14-18: Painted-c				3.00

Love and Marriage #3 © SUPR

Love and Rockets V2 #1 © Fantagraphics Books

Love Journal #10 © Our Publ. Co.

	GD2.0	FN6.0	VF8.0	NM9.4

NOTE: Originally intended to be a 12 issue limited series.

LOST ONES, THE
Image Comics: Mar, 2000 ($2.95)

1-Ken Penders-s/a				3.00

LOST PLANET
Eclipse Comics: 5/87 - No. 5, 2/88; No. 6, 3/89 (Mini-series, Baxter paper)

1-6-Bo Hampton-c/a in all				2.25

LOST WAGON TRAIN, THE (See Zane Grey Four Color 583)

LOST WORLD, THE
Dell Publishing Co.: No. 1145, Nov-Jan, 1960-61
Four Color 1145-Movie, Gil Kane-a, photo-c; 1pg. Conan Doyle biography by Torres

	10	30	70	130

LOST WORLD, THE (See Jurassic Park)
Topps Comics: May, 1997 - No. 4, Aug, 1997 ($2.95, limited series)

1-4-Movie adaption				3.00

LOST WORLDS (Weird Tales of the Past and Future)
Standard Comics: No. 5, Oct, 1952 - No. 6, Dec, 1952

5- "Alice in Terrorland" by Alex Toth; J. Katz-a	43	129	257	450
6-Toth-a	37	111	197	340

LOTS 'O' FUN COMICS
Robert Allen Co.: 1940's? (5¢, heavy stock, blue covers)
nn-Contents can vary; Felix, Planet Comics known; contents would determine value.
Similar to Up-To-Date Comics. Remainders - re-packaged.

LOU GEHRIG (See The Pride of the Yankees)

LOVE ADVENTURES (Actual Confessions #13)
Marvel (IPS)/Atlas Comics (MPI): Oct, 1949; No. 2, Jan, 1950; No. 3, Feb, 1951 - No. 12, Aug, 1952

1-Photo-c	17	51	88	150
2-Powell-a; Tyrone Power, Gene Tierney photo-c	15	45	77	130
3-8,10-12: 8-Robinson-a	8	24	45	65
9-Everett-a	9	27	49	70

LOVE AND MARRIAGE
Superior Comics Ltd. (Canada): Mar, 1952 - No. 16, Sept, 1954

1	13	39	66	115
2	7	21	38	55
3-10	6	18	30	42
11-16	5	15	25	35
I.W. Reprint #1,2,8,11,14: 8-r/Love and Marriage #3. 11-r/Love and Marriage #11.	2	6	11	17
Super Reprint #10('63),15,17('64):15-Love and Marriage #?	2	6	11	15

NOTE: All issues have Kamenish art.

LOVE AND ROCKETS
Fantagraphics Books: July, 1982 - No. 50, May, 1996 ($2.95/$2.50/$4.95, B&W, mature)

1-B&W-c (6/82, $2.95; small size, publ. by Hernandez Bros.)(800 printed)	3	9	17	25
1 (Fall, '82; color-c)	2	6	13	20
1-2nd & 3rd printing, 2-11,29-31: 2nd printings				3.00
2	1	3	5	7
3-10				5.00
11-49: 30 ($2.95, 52 pgs.)				3.00
50-($4.95)				5.00

LOVE AND ROCKETS (Volume 2)
Fantagraphics Books: Spring, 2001 - Present ($3.95, B&W, mature)

1-3-Gilbert, Jaime and Mario Hernandez-s/a				4.00

LOVE AND ROMANCE
Charlton Comics: Sept, 1971 - No. 24, Sept, 1975

1	3	9	19	28
2-10	2	6	11	16
11-24	1	4	7	10

LOVE AT FIRST SIGHT

	GD2.0	FN6.0	VF8.0	NM9.4

Ace Magazines (RAR Publ. Co./Periodical House): Oct, 1949 - No. 43, Nov, 1956 (Photo-c: 21-42)

1-Painted-c	14	42	72	120
2-Painted-c	8	24	42	60
3-10: 4-Painted-c	6	18	32	45
11-20	6	18	29	40
21-33: 33-Last pre-code	5	15	25	35
34-43	5	15	23	30

LOVE BUG, THE (See Movie Comics)

LOVE CLASSICS
A Lover's Magazine/Marvel: Nov, 1949 - No. 2, Feb, 1950 (Photo-c, 52 pgs.)

1,2: 2-Virginia Mayo photo-c; 30 pg. story "I Was a Small Town Flirt"	14	42	72	120

LOVE CONFESSIONS
Quality Comics: Oct, 1949 - No. 54, Dec, 1956 (Photo-c: 3,4,6,7,9,11-18,21)

1-Ward-c/a, 9 pgs; Gustavson-a	30	90	162	280
2-Gustavson-a; Ward-c	14	42	72	125
3	8	24	45	65
4-Crandall-a	10	30	55	80
5-Ward-a, 7 pgs.	12	36	61	100
6,7,9,11-13,15,16,18: 7-Van Johnson photo-c. 8-Robert Mitchum & Jane Russell photo-c	6	18	32	45
8,10-Ward-a(2 stories in #10)	12	36	61	100
14,17,19,22-Ward-a; 17-Faith Domergue photo-c	10	30	55	85
20-Ward-a(2)	12	36	61	100
21,23-28,30-38,40-42: Last precode, 4/55	5	15	25	35
29-Ward-a	10	30	55	80
39-Matt Baker-a	7	21	38	55
43,44,46,48,50-54: 47-Ward-c?	5	15	23	30
45-Ward-a	7	21	36	50
49-Baker-c/a	8	24	45	65

LOVE DIARY
Our Publishing Co./Toytown/Patches: July, 1949 - No. 48, Oct, 1955 (Photo-c: 1-24,27-29) (52 pgs. #1-11?)

1-Krigstein-a	18	54	94	160
2,3-Krigstein & Mort Leav-a in each	11	33	55	90
4-8	6	18	32	45
9,10-Everett-a	7	21	36	50
11-20: 16- Mort Leav-a, 3 pg. Baker-sty. Leav-a	6	18	29	40
21-30,32-48: 45-Leav-a. 47-Last precode(12/54)	5	15	25	35
31-John Buscema headlights-c	6	18	32	45

LOVE DIARY (Diary Loves #2 on; title change due to previously published title)
Quality Comics Group: Sept, 1949

1-Ward-c/a, 9 pgs	31	93	165	285

LOVE DIARY
Charlton Comics: July, 1958 - No. 102, Dec, 1976

1	9	27	49	70
2	6	18	30	42
3-5,7-10: 10-Photo-c	5	15	24	32
6-Torres-a	6	18	29	40
11-20: 20-Photo-c	3	9	17	24
21-40	2	6	13	20
41-60	2	6	11	15
61-80,100-102	1	4	7	10
81-99	1	3	6	8

LOVE DOCTOR (See Dr. Anthony King...)

LOVE DRAMAS (True Secrets No. 3 on?)
Marvel Comics (IPS): Oct, 1949 - No. 2, Jan, 1950

1-Jack Kamen-a; photo-c	18	54	94	160
2	13	39	66	110

LOVE EXPERIENCES (Challenge of the Unknown No. 6)
Ace Periodicals (A.A. Wyn/Periodical House): Oct, 1949 - No. 5, June, 1950; No. 6, Apr, 1951 - No. 38, June, 1956

1-Painted-c	12	36	61	105
2	7	21	36	50

Love Letters #32 © QUA

Love Mystery #2 © FAW

Love Scandals #2 © QUA

	GD2.0	FN6.0	VF8.0	NM9.4
3-5: 5-Painted-c	6	18	29	40
6-10	5	15	25	35
11-30: 30-Last pre-code (2/55)	5	14	21	28
31-38: 38-Indicia date-6/56; c-date-8/56	4	12	18	24

NOTE: Anne Brewster a-15. Photo c-4, 15-35, 38.

LOVE JOURNAL
Our Publishing Co.: No. 10, Oct, 1951 - No. 25, July, 1954

10	10	30	55	85
11-25: 19-Mort Leav-a	6	18	32	45

LOVELAND
Mutual Mag./Eye Publ. (Marvel): Nov, 1949 - No. 2, Feb, 1950 (52 pgs.)

1,2-Photo-c	10	30	55	85

LOVE LESSONS
Harvey Comics/Key Publ. No. 5: Oct, 1949 - No. 5, June, 1950

1-Metallic silver-c printed over the cancelled covers of Love Letters #1; indicia title is "Love Letters"	14	42	72	120
2-Powell-a; photo-c	7	21	38	55
3-5: 5-Photo-c	6	18	32	45

LOVE LETTERS (10/49, Harvey; advertised but never published; covers were printed before cancellation and were used as the cover to Love Lessions #1)

LOVE LETTERS (Love Secrets No. 32 on)
Quality Comics: 11/49 - #6, 9/50; #7, 3/51 - #31, 6/53; #32, 2/54 - #51, 12/56

1-Ward-c, Gustavson-a	24	72	127	220
2-Ward-c, Gustavson-a	20	60	105	175
3-Gustavson-a	14	42	72	120
4-Ward-a, 9 pgs.	19	57	99	165
5-8,10	7	21	36	50
9-One pg. Ward "Be Popular with the Opposite Sex"; Robert Mitchum photo-c	8	24	45	65
11-Ward-r/Broadway Romances #2 & retitled	8	24	45	65
12-15,18-20	6	18	30	42
16,17-Ward-a; 16-Anthony Quinn photo-c. 17-Jane Russell photo-c	11	33	55	95
21-29	6	18	28	38
30,31(6/53)-Ward-a	7	21	38	55
32(2/54)-39: 38-Crandall-a. 39-Last precode (4/55)	5	15	25	35
40-48	5	15	23	30
49,50-Baker-a	8	24	45	65
51-Baker-a	7	21	36	50

NOTE: Photo-c on most 3-28.

LOVE LIFE
P. L. Publishing Co.: Nov, 1951

1	10	30	55	80

LOVELORN (Confessions of the Lovelorn #52 on)
American Comics Group (Michel Publ./Regis Publ.): Aug-Sept, 1949 - No. 51, July, 1954 (No. 1-26: 52 pgs.)

1	15	45	77	135
2	9	27	49	70
3-10	7	21	36	50
11-20,22-48: 18-Drucker-a(2 pgs.). 46-Lazarus-a	6	18	29	40
21-Prostitution story	7	21	38	55
49-51-Has 3-D effect-c/stories	16	48	83	140

LOVE MEMORIES
Fawcett Publications: 1949 (no month) - No. 4, July, 1950 (All photo-c)

1	14	42	72	120
2-4: 2-(Win/49-50)	8	24	45	65

LOVE MYSTERY
Fawcett Publications: June, 1950 - No. 3, Oct, 1950 (All photo-c)

1-George Evans-a	21	63	110	190
2,3-Evans-a. 3-Powell-a	17	51	88	150

LOVE PROBLEMS (See Fox Giants)

LOVE PROBLEMS AND ADVICE ILLUSTRATED (see True Love...)

LOVE ROMANCES (Formerly Ideal #5)
Timely/Marvel/Atlas(TCI No. 7-71/Male No. 72-106): No. 6, May, 1949 - No. 106,

July, 1963

6-Photo-c	14	42	72	120
7-Photo-c; Kamen-a	9	27	49	70
8-Kubert-a; photo-c	9	27	49	70
9-20: 9-12-Photo-c	7	21	38	55
21,24-Krigstein-a	8	24	45	65
22,23,25-35,37,39,40	7	21	36	50
36,38-Krigstein-a	7	21	38	55
41-44,46,47: Last precode (2/55)	6	18	32	45
45,57-Matt Baker-a	8	24	45	65
48,50-52,54-56,58-74	4	12	25	38
49,53-Toth-a, 6 & ? pgs.	4	12	30	50
75,77,82-Matt Baker-a	5	15	34	55
76,78-81,86,88-90,92-95: 80-Heath-c. 95-Last 10¢-c?	3	10	23	35
83,84,87,91-Kirby-a. 83-Severin-a	5	15	34	55
85,96,97,99-106-Kirby-c/a	6	18	45	75
98-Kirby-c/a	7	21	50	80

NOTE: Anne Brewster a-67. Colletta a-37, 40, 42, 44, 67(2); c-42, 44, 49, 54, 80. Everett c-70. Heath a-67. Kirby c-80, 85, 88. Robinson a-29.

LOVERS (Formerly Blonde Phantom)
Marvel Comics No. 23,24/Atlas No. 25 on (ANC): No. 23, May, 1949 - No. 86, Aug?, 1957

23-Photo-c begin, end #28	14	42	72	120
24-Toth-ish plus Robinson-a	8	24	42	60
25,30-Kubert-a; 7, 10 pgs.	8	24	45	65
26-29,31-36,39,40	6	18	32	45
37-Krigstein-a	8	24	42	60
41-Everett-a(2)	8	24	42	60
42,44-65: 65-Last pre-code (1/55)	6	18	29	40
43-Frazetta 1 pg. ad	6	18	30	42
66,68-86	5	15	25	35
67-Toth-a	6	18	30	42

NOTE: Anne Brewster a-86. Colletta a-54, 59, 62, 64, 65, 69, 85; c-61, 64, 65, 75. Heath a-61. Maneely a-57. Powell a-27, 30. Robinson a-54, 56.

LOVERS' LANE
Lev Gleason Publications: Oct, 1949 - No. 41, June, 1954 (No. 1-18: 52 pgs.)

1-Biro-c	10	30	55	85
2-Biro-c	6	18	32	45
3-20: 3,4-Painted-c. 20-Frazetta 1 pg. ad	6	18	28	38
21-38,40,41	5	14	21	28
39-Story narrated by Frank Sinatra	6	18	32	45

NOTE: Briefer a-6, 21. Fuje a-4, 16; c-many. Guardineer a-1. Kinstler c-41. Tuska a-6. Painted a-3-18. Photo c-19-22, 26-28.

LOVE SCANDALS
Quality Comics: Feb, 1950 - No. 5, Oct, 1950 (Photo-c #2-5) (All 52 pgs.)

1-Ward-c/a, 9 pgs.	26	78	136	235
2,3: 2-Gustavson-a	10	30	55	85
4-Ward-a, 18 pgs; Gil Fox-a	21	63	110	185
5-C. Cuidera-a; tomboy story "I Hated Being a Woman"	11	33	55	90

LOVE SECRETS
Marvel Comics(IPC): Oct, 1949 - No. 2, Jan, 1950 (52 pgs., photo-c)

1	14	42	72	120
2	9	27	49	70

LOVE SECRETS (Formerly Love Letters #31)
Quality Comics Group: No. 32, Aug, 1953 - No. 56, Dec, 1956

32	10	30	55	80
33,35-39	5	18	29	40
34-Ward-a	10	30	55	80
40-Matt Baker-c	7	21	38	55
41-43: 43-Last precode (3/55)	6	18	28	38
44,47-50,53,54	5	15	23	30
45,46-Ward-a. 46-Baker-a	8	24	45	65
51,52-Ward(r). 52-r/Love Confessions #17	6	18	29	40
55,56: 55-Baker-a. 56-Baker-c	7	21	36	50

LOVE STORIES (See Top Love Stories)

Lucifer #6 © DC

Lucky Duck #6 © STD

Lynch Mob #2 © Chaos!

	GD2.0	FN6.0	VF8.0	NM9.4

LOVE STORIES (Formerly Heart Throbs)
National Periodical Publ.: No. 147, Nov, 1972 - No. 152, Oct-Nov, 1973

147-152	2	6	12	18

LOVE STORIES OF MARY WORTH (See Harvey Comics Hits #55 & Mary Worth)
Harvey Publications: Sept, 1949 - No. 5, May, 1950

1-1940's newspaper reprints-#1-4	8	24	42	60
2-5: 3-Kamen/Baker-a?	6	18	29	40

LOVE SUCKS
Ace Comics: 1995; Oct, 1996 - Present ($2.95, B&W)

1-5: 1-(1995) Hynes-s/Juch-a, 1-(10/96) Santiago-s/Juch-a	3.00

LOVE TALES (Formerly The Human Torch #35)
Marvel/Atlas Comics (ZPC No. 36-50/MMC No. 67-75): No. 36, 5/49 - No. 58, 8/52; No. 59, date? - No. 75, Sept, 1957

36-Photo-c	14	42	72	120
37	8	24	42	60
38-44,46-50: 39-41-Photo-c	7	21	36	50
45,51,52,69: 45-Powell-a. 51,69-Everett-a. 52-Krigstein-a	7	21	38	55
53-60: 60-Last pre-code (2/55)	6	18	28	40
61-68,70-75: 75-Brewster, Cameron, Colletta-a	5	15	24	32

LOVE THRILLS (See Fox Giants)

LOVE TRAILS (Western romance)
A Lover's Magazine (CDS)(Marvel): Dec, 1949 - No. 2, Mar, 1950 (52 pgs.)

1,2: 1-Photo-c	14	42	72	120

LOWELL THOMAS' HIGH ADVENTURE (See High Adventure)

LT. (See Lieutenant)

LUBA
Fantagraphics Books: Feb, 1998 - Present ($2.95/$3.50, B&W, mature)

1-4-Gilbert Hernandez-s/a	3.00
5-($3.50)	3.50

LUBA'S COMICS AND STORIES
Fantagraphics Books: Mar, 2000 - Present ($2.95/$3.50, B&W, mature)

1-Gilbert Hernandez-s/a	3.00
2-($3.50)	3.50

LUCIFER (See The Sandman #4)
DC Comics (Vertigo): Jun, 2000 - Present ($2.50)

1-21: 1-3-Carey-s/Weston-a/Fegredo-c. 5-13,15-19-Gross-a	2.50
Preview-16 pg. flip book w/Swamp Thing Preview	2.25
Children and Monsters TPB ('01, $17.95) r/#5-13	18.00
Devil in the Gateway TPB ('01, $14.95) r/#1-4 & Sandman Presents:..#1-3	15.00

LUCIFER'S HAMMER (Larry Niven & Jerry Pournelle's...)
Innovation Publishing: Nov, 1993 - No. 6, 1994 ($2.50, painted, limited series)

1-6: Adaptatin of novel, painted-c & art	2.50

LUCKY COMICS
Consolidated Magazines: Jan, 1944; No. 2, Sum, 1945 - No. 5, Sum, 1946

1-Lucky Starr & Bobbie begin	21	63	110	190
2-5: 5-Devil-c by Walter Johnson	12	36	61	100

LUCKY DUCK
Standard Comics (Literary Ent.): No. 5, Jan, 1953 - No. 8, Sept, 1953

5-Funny animal; Irving Spector-a	11	33	55	95
6-8-Irving Spector-a	10	30	55	80

NOTE: Harvey Kurtzman tried to hire Spector for Mad #1.

LUCKY "7" COMICS
Howard Publishers Ltd.: 1944 (No date listed)

1-Pioneer, Sir Gallagher, Dick Royce, Congo Raider, Punch Powers; bondage-c	39	117	208	360

LUCKY STAR (Western)
Nation Wide Publ. Co.: 1950 - No. 7, 1951; No. 8, 1953 - No. 14, 1955 (5x7-1/4"; full color, 5¢)

nn (#1)-(5¢, 52 pgs.)-Davis-a	16	48	83	140
2-3(5¢, 52 pgs.)-Davis-a	10	30	55	85

	GD2.0	FN6.0	VF8.0	NM9.4

4-7-(5¢, 52 pgs.)-Davis-a	9	27	49	70
8-14-(36 pgs.)(Exist?)	7	21	38	55

Given away with Lucky Star Western Wear by the Juvenile Mfg. Co.

	5	15	25	35

LUCY SHOW, THE (TV) (Also see I Love Lucy)
Gold Key: June, 1963 - No. 5, June, 1964 (Photo-c: 1,2)

1	13	39	91	170
2	7	21	49	90
3-5: Photo back c-1,2,4,5	6	18	42	80

LUCY, THE REAL GONE GAL (Meet Miss Pepper #5 on)
St. John Publishing Co.: June, 1953 - No. 4, Dec, 1953

1-Negligee panels	12	36	61	105
2	8	24	42	60
3,4: 3-Drucker-a	7	21	36	50

LUDWIG BEMELMAN'S MADELEINE & GENEVIEVE
Dell Publishing Co.: No. 796, May, 1957

Four Color 796	4	12	25	38

LUDWIG VON DRAKE (TV)(Disney)(See Walt Disney's C&S #256)
Dell Publishing Co.: Nov-Dec, 1961 - No. 4, June-Aug, 1962

1	7	21	49	85
2-4	5	15	34	55

LUFTWAFFE: 1946 (Volume 1)
Antarctic Press: July, 1996 - No. 4, Jan, 1997 ($2.95, B&W, limited series)

1-4-Ben Dunn & Ted Nomura-s/a, ...Special Ed.	3.00

LUFTWAFFE: 1946 (Volume 2)
Antarctic Press: Mar, 1997 - No. 18 ($2.95/$2.99, B&W, limited series)

1-18: 8-Reviews Tigers of Terra series	3.00
Annual 1 (4/98, $2.95)-Reprints early Nomura pages	3.00
...Color Special (4/98)	3.00
...Technical Manual 1,2 (2/98, 4/99)	4.00

LUGER
Eclipse Comics: Oct, 1986 - No. 3, Feb, 1987 ($1.75, miniseries, Baxter paper)

1-3: Bruce Jones scripts; Yeates-c/a	2.25

LUKE CAGE (See Cage & Hero for Hire)

LUKE SHORT'S WESTERN STORIES
Dell Publishing Co.: No. 580, Aug, 1954 - No. 927, Aug, 1958

Four Color 580(8/54), 651(9/55)-Kinstler-a	4	12	26	40
Four Color 739,771,807,848,875,927	4	12	25	38

LUNATIC FRINGE, THE
Innovation Publishing: July, 1989 - No. 2, 1989 ($1.75, deluxe format)

1,2	2.25

LUNATICKLE (Magazine) (Satire)
Whitstone Publ.: Feb, 1956 - No. 2, Apr, 1956

1,2-Kubert-a (scarce)	5	15	24	32

LUNATIK
Marvel Comics: Dec, 1995 - No. 3, Feb, 1996 ($1.95, limited series)

1-3	2.25

LUST FOR LIFE
Slave Labor Graphics: Feb, 1997 - No. 4, Jan, 1998 ($2.95, B&W)

1-4: 1-Jeff Levin-s/a	3.00

LYCANTHROPE LEO
Viz Communications: 1994 - No. 7($2.95, B&W, limited series, 44 pgs.)

1-7	3.00

LYNCH (See Gen[13])
Image Comics (WildStorm Productions): May, 1997 ($2.50, one-shot)

1-Helmut-c/app.	2.50

LYNCH MOB
Chaos! Comics: June, 1994 - No. 4, Sept, 1994 ($2.50, limited series)

1-4	2.50
1-Special edition full foil-c	5.00

Machine Man #7 © MAR

Mad #2 © E.C. Publ.

Mad #196 © E.C. Publ.

	GD2.0	FN6.0	VF8.0	NM9.4

LYNDON B. JOHNSON
Dell Publishing Co.: Mar, 1965

12-445-503-Photo-c	3	9	19	28

M
Eclipse Books: 1990 - No. 4, 1991 ($4.95, painted, 52 pgs.)

1-Adapts movie; contains flexi-disc ($5.95)		6.00
2-4		5.00

MACHINE, THE
Dark Horse Comics: Nov, 1994 - No. 4, Feb, 1995 ($2.50, limited series)

1-4		2.50

MACHINE MAN (Also see 2001, A Space Odyssey)
Marvel Comics Group: Apr, 1978 - No. 9, Dec, 1978; No. 10, Aug, 1979 - No. 19, Feb, 1981

1-Jack Kirby-c/a/scripts begin; end #9	2	6	11	16
2-9-Kirby-c/a/s. 9-(12/78)	1	3	6	8
10-17: 10-(8/79) Marv Wolfman scripts & Ditko-a begins				5.00
18-Wendigo, Alpha Flight-ties into X-Men #140	2	6	12	18
19-Intro/1st app. Jack O'Lantern (Macendale), later becomes 2nd Hobgoblin				
	2	6	10	14

NOTE: **Austin** c-7i, 19i. **Buckler** c-17p, 18p. **Byrne** c-14p. **Ditko** a-10-19; c-10-13, 14i, 15, 16. **Kirby** a-1-9p; c-1-5, 7-9p. **Layton** c-7i. **Miller** c-19p. **Simonson** c-6.

MACHINE MAN (Also see X-51)
Marvel Comics Group: Oct, 1984 - No. 4, Jan, 1985 (Limited-series)

1-4-Barry Smith-c/a(i) & colors in all		4.00
TPB (1988, $6.95) r/ #1-4; Barry Smith-c		7.00
.../Bastion '98 Annual ($2.99) wraparound-c		3.00

MACHINE MAN 2020
Marvel Comics: Aug, 1994 - Nov, 1994 ($2.00, 52 pgs., limited series)

1-4: Reprints Machine Man limited series; Barry Windsor-Smith-c/i(r)		2.25

MACK BOLAN: THE EXECUTIONER (Don Pendleton's...)
Innovation Publishing: July, 1993 ($2.50)

1-3-($2.50)		2.50
1-($3.95)-Indestructible Cover Edition		4.00
1-($2.95)-Collector's Gold Edition; foil stamped		3.00
1-($3.50)-Double Cover Edition; red foil outer-c		3.50

MACKENZIE'S RAIDERS (Movie, TV)
Dell Publishing Co.: No. 1093, Apr-June, 1960

Four Color 1093-Richard Carlson photo-c from TV show				
	6	18	42	80

MACROSS (Becomes Robotech: The Macross Saga #2 on)
Comico: Dec, 1984 ($1.50)(Low print run)

1-Early manga app.	2	6	15	22

MACROSS II
Viz Select Comics: 1992 - No. 10, 1993 ($2.75, B&W, limited series)

1-10: Based on video series		2.75

MAD (Tales Calculated to Drive You...)
E. C. Comics (Educational Comics): Oct-Nov, 1952 - Present (No. 24-on are magazine format)(Kurtzman editor No. 1-28, Feldstein No. 29 - No. ?)

1-Wood, Davis, Elder start as regulars	520	1560	3640	7000
2-Dick Tracy cameo	140	420	980	1750
3,4: 3-Stan Lee mentioned. 4-Reefer mention story "Flob Was a Slob" by Davis; Superman parody	84	252	588	1050
5-Low distr.; W.M. Gaines biog.	148	444	1036	1850
6-11: 6-Popeye cameo. 7,8- "Hey Look" reprints by Kurtzman. 11-Wolverton-a; Davis story was-r/Crime Suspenstories #12 w/new Kurtzman dialogue				
	60	180	420	750
12-15: 15,18-Pot Shot Pete-r by Kurtzman	48	143	336	600
16-23(5/55): 18-Alice in Wonderland by Jack Davis. 21-1st app. Alfred E. Neuman on-c in fake ad. 22-All by Elder plus photo-montages by Kurtzman. 23-Special cancel announcement	38	115	266	475
24(7/55)-1st magazine issue (25¢); Kurtzman logo & border on-c; 1st "What? Me Worry?" on-c; 2nd printing exists	90	270	630	1125
25-Jaffee starts as regular writer	40	120	280	500
26,27: 27-Jaffee starts as story artist; new logo	36	107	216	380

28-Last issue edited by Kurtzman; (three cover variations exist with different wording on contents banner on lower right of cover; value of each the same)				
	31	93	186	330
29-Kamen-a; Don Martin starts as regular; Feldstein editing begins				
	31	93	186	330
30-1st A. E. Neuman cover by Mingo; last Elder-a; Bob Clarke starts as regular; Disneyland & Elvis Presley spoof	46	138	276	480
31-Freas starts as regular; last Davis-a until #99	27	80	162	285
32,33: 32-Orlando, Drucker, Woodbridge start as regulars; Wood back-c				
33-Orlando back-c	24	73	144	255
34-Berg starts as regular	20	60	120	215
35-Mingo wraparound-c; Crandall-a	20	60	120	215
36-40 (7/58)	14	43	84	150
41-50: 42-Danny Kaye-s. 44-Xmas-c. 47-49-Sid Caesar-s. 48-Uncle Sam-c. 50 (10/59)-Peter Gunn-s	11	33	66	120
51-59: 52-Xmas-c; 77 Sunset Strip. 53-Rifleman-s. 55-Sid Caesar-s. 59-Strips of Superman, Flash Gordon, Donald Duck & others. 59-Halloween/Headless Horseman-c	10	30	60	110
60 (1/61)-JFK/Nixon flip-c; 1st Spy vs. Spy by Prohias, who starts as regular	15	35	72	130
61-70: 64-Rickard starts as regular. 65-JFK-s. 66-JFK-c. 68-Xmas-c by Martin.				
	7	20	42	75
70-Route 66-s	7	20	42	75
71-75,77-80 (7/63): 72-10th Anniv. special; 1/3 pg. strips of Superman, Tarzan & others. 73-Bonanza-s. 74-Dr. Kildare-s	5	15	34	55
76-Aragonés starts as regular	6	18	40	65
81-85: 81-Superman strip. 82-Castro-c. 85-Lincoln-c	4	12	29	45
86-1st Fold-in; commonly creased back makes these and later issues scarcer in NM	5	15	34	55
87,88	4	12	30	50
89,90: 89-One strip by Walt Kelly; Frankenstein-c; Fugitive-s. 90-Ringo back-c by Frazetta; Beatles app.	5	15	34	55
91,94,96,100: 91-Jaffee starts as story artist. 94-King Kong-c. 96-Man From U.N.C.L.E. 100-(1/66)-Anniversary issue	4	12	29	45
92,93,95,97-99: 99-Davis-a resumes	4	12	26	40
101,104,106,108,114,115,119,121: 101-Infinity-c; Voyage to the Bottom of the Sea-s. 104-Lost in Space-s. 106-Tarzan back-c by Frazetta; 2 pg. Batman by Aragonés. 108-Hogan's Heroes by Davis. 114-Rat Patrol-s. 115-Star Trek. 119-Invaders (TV). 121-Beatles-c; Ringo pin-up; flip-c of Sik-Teen; Flying Nun-s	3	9	21	32
102,103,107,109-113,116-118,120(7/68): 118-Beatles cameo				
	3	9	19	28
105-Batman-c/s, TV show parody (9/66)	4	12	26	40
122,124,126,128,129,131-134,136,137,139,140: 122-Ronald Reagan photo inside; Drucker & Mingo-c. 126-Family Affair-s. 128-Last Orlando. 131-Reagan photo back-c. 132-Xmas-c. 133-John Wayne/True Grit.				
136-Room 222	2	6	13	20
123-Three different covers	2	6	13	22
125,127,130,135,138: 125-2001 Space Odyssey; Hitler back-c. 127-Mod Squad-c/s. 130-Land of the Giants-s; Torres begins as reg. 135-Easy Rider-c by Davis. 138-Snoopy-c; MASH-s.	3	9	17	26
141-149,151-156,158-170: 141-Hawaii Five-0-s. 147-All in the Family-s. 153-Dirty Harry-s. 155-Godfather-c/s. 156-Columbo-s. 159-Clockwork Orange-c/s. 161-Tarzan-s. 164-Kung Fu (TV)-s. 165-James Bond-s; Dean Martin-c.				
169-Drucker-c; McCloud-s. 170-Exorcist-c	2	6	12	18
150-(4/72) Partridge Family-s	2	6	13	20
157-(4/72) Planet of the Apes-c/s	3	9	17	24
171-185,187,189-192,194,195,198,199: 172-Six Million Dollar Man-s; Hitler back-c. 178-Godfather II-c/s. 180-Jaws-c/s (1/76). 182-Bob Jones starts as regular.185-Starsky & Hutch-s. 187-Fonz/Happy Days-c/s; Harry North starts as regular. 189-Travolta/Kotter-c/s. 190-John Wayne-c/s. 192-King Kong-c/s. 194-Rocky-c/s; Laverne & Shirley-s. 199-James Bond-s.				
	2	6	11	15
186,188,197,200: 186-Star Trek-c/s. 188-Six Million Dollar Man/ Bionic Woman. 197-Spock-s; Star Wars-s. 200-Close Encounters-s	2	6	12	18
193,196: 193-Farrah/Charlie's Angels-s. 196-Star Wars-c/s				
	2	6	13	20
201,203,205,220: 201-Sat. Night Fever-c/s. 203-Star Wars. 205-Travolta/Grease. 220-Yoda-c, Empire Strikes Back-s	2	6	10	14
202,204,206,207,209,211-219,221-227,229,230: 204-Hulk TV show. 206-Tarzan. 208-Superman movie. 209-Mork & Mindy. 212-Spider-Man-s; Alien (movie)-s.				

Mad #343 © E.C. Publ.

Mad About Millie #14 © MAR

Mad Follies #1 © E.C. Publ.

	GD2.0	FN6.0	VF8.0	NM9.4

213-James Bond, Dracula, Rocky II-s 216-Star Trek. 219-Martin-c.
221-Shining-s. 223-Dallas-c/s. 225-Popeye. 226-Superman II. 229-James
Bond. 230-Star Wars   1   3   6   9

208,228: 208-Superman movie-c/s; Battlestar Galactica-s. 228-Raiders of the
   Lost Ark-c/s   2   6   9   12
210-Lord of the Rings   2   6   10   14
231-235,237-241,243-249,251-260: 233-Pac-Man-c. 234-MASH-c/s. 235-Flip-c
with Rocky III & Conan; Boris-a. 239-Mickey Mouse-c. 241-Knight Rider-s.
243-Superman III. 245- Last Rickard-a. 247-Seven Dwarfs-c. 253-Supergirl
movie-s; Prince/Purple Rain-s. 254-Rock stars-c. 255-Reagan-c; Cosby-s.
256-Last issue edited by Feldstein; Dynasty, Bev. Hills Cop. 259-Rambo.
260-Back to the Future-c/s; Honeymooners-s   1   3   5   7
236,242,250: 236-E.T.-c/s;Star Trek II-s. 242-Star Wars/A-Team-c/s.
250-Temple of Doom-c/s; Tarzan-s   1   3   6   8
261-267,269-276,278-288,290-297: 261-Miami Vice. 262-Rocky IV-c/s,
Leave It To Beaver-s. 263-Young Sherlock Holmes-s. 264-Hulk Hogan-c;
Rambo-s. 267-Top Gun. 271-Star Trek IV-c/s. 272-ALF-c; Get Smart-s.
273-Pee Wee Herman-c/s. 274-Last Martin-a. 281-California Raisins-c.
282-Star Trek:TNG-s; ALF-s. 283-Rambo III-c/s. 284-Roger Rabbit-c/s.
285-Hulk Hogan-c. 287-3 pgs. Easter-a. 291-TMNT-c; Indiana Jones-s.
292-Super Mario Bros.-c; Married with Children-s. 295-Back to the Future II.
297-Mike Tyson-c   6.00
268,277,289,298-300: 268-Aliens-c/s. 277-Michael Jackson-c; Robocop-s.
289-Batman movie parody. 298-Gremlins II-c; Robocop II. Batman-s.
299-Simpsons-c/story; Total Recall-s. 300-Dick Tracy-s, Casablanca-s, Dick Tracy-s,
Wizard of Oz-s, Gone With The Wind-s   1   3   5   7
300-303 (1/91-6/91)-Special Hussein Asylum Editions; only distributed to the
troops in the Middle East (see Mad Super Spec.) 1   3   6   8
301-310,312,313,315-320,322,324,326-334,337-349: 303-Home Alone-c/s.
305-Simpsons-s. 306-TMNT II movie. 308-Terminator II. 315-Tribute to
William Gaines. 316-Photo-c. 319-Dracula-c/s. 320-Disney's Aladdin-s.
322-Batman Animated series. 327-Seinfeld-s; X-Men-s. 331-Flintstones-c/s.
332-O.J. Simpson-c/s; Simpsons app. in Lion King. 334-Frankenstein-c/s.
338-Judge Dredd-c by Frazetta. 344-Pocahontas-s. 345-Beatles app. (1 pg.)
347-Broken Arrow & Mission Impossible   4.00
311,314,321,323,325,335,336,350,354,358: 311-Addams Family-c/story, Home
Improvement-s. 314-Batman Returns-c/story. 321-Star Trek DS9-c/s.
323-Jurassic Park-c/s. 325,336-Beavis & Butthead-c/s. 335-X-Files-s; Pulp
Fiction-s; Interview with the Vampire-s. 336-Lois & Clark-s. 350-Polybagged
w/CD Rom. 354-Star Wars; Beavis & Butthead-s. 358-X-Files   5.00
351-353,355-357,359-388   2.50
NOTE: Aragones a-210, 293. Davis c-2, 27, 135, 139, 173, 178, 212, 213, 219, 246, 260, 296,
308. Drucker c-22, 169, 176, 225, 234, 264, 266, 274, 280, 285, 297, 299, 303, 314, 315, 321.
Elder c-5, 259, 261, 268. Elder/Kurtzman a-258-274. Jules Feiffer a(r)-42. Freas c-39-59, 62-
67, 69-70, 72, 74. Heath a-14, 27. Jaffee c-171, 199, 217, 224, 258. Kamen a-12, 17,
24, 26. Kurtzman c-1, 3, 4, 6-10, 13, 16, 18. Martin c-68, 165, 229. Mingo c-30-37, 61, 71, 75-
80, 82-114, 117-124, 126, 129, 131, 133, 134, 136, 140, 143-148, 150-162, 164, 166-168, 171,
172, 174, 175, 177, 179, 181, 183, 185, 198, 206, 209, 211, 214, 218, 221, 222, 300. John
Severin a-1-6, 9, 10. Wolverton c-11; a-11, 17, 29, 31, 36, 40, 82, 137. Wood a-24-45, 59; c-26,
28, 29. Woodbridge a-43. Issues 1-23 are 36 pgs.; 24-28 are 58 pgs.; 29 on are 52 pgs.

MAD (See Mad Follies, ...Special, More Trash from..., and The Worst from...)

MAD ABOUT MILLIE (Also see Millie the Model)
Marvel Comics Group: April, 1969 - No. 16, Nov, 1970

1-Giant issue	7	21	50	80
2,3 (Giants)	4	12	30	50
4-10	3	9	20	30
11-16: 16-r	3	9	17	25
Annual 1(11/71, 52 pgs.)	3	9	20	30

MADAME XANADU
DC Comics: July, 1981 ($1.00, no ads, 36 pgs.)

1-Marshall Rogers-a(25 pgs.); Kaluta-c/a(2pgs.); pin-up   5.00

MADBALLS
Star Comics/Marvel Comics #9 on: Sept, 1986 - No. 3, Nov, 1986; No. 4, June,
1987 - No. 10, June, 1988

1-10: Based on toys. 9-Post-a   4.00

MAD DISCO
E.C. Comics: 1980 (one-shot, 36 pgs.)

1-Includes 30 minute flexi-disc of Mad disco music 2   6   12   18

MAD-DOG

Marvel Comics: May, 1993 - No. 6, Oct, 1993 ($1.25)

1-6-Flip book w/2nd story "created" by Bob Newhart's character from his TV
show "Bob" set at a comic book company; actual s/a-Ty Templeton   2.50

MAD DOGS
Eclipse Comics: Feb, 1992 - No. 3, July, 1992 ($2.50, B&W, limited series)

1-3   2.50

MAD 84 (Mad Extra)
E.C. Comics: 1984 (84 pgs.)

1	1	3	6	8

MAD FOLLIES (Special)
E. C. Comics: 1963 - No. 7, 1969

nn(1963)-Paperback book covers	24	72	168	310
2(1964)-Calendar	18	54	126	230
3(1965)-Mischief Stickers	13	40	91	175
4(1966)-Mobile; Frazetta-r/back-c Mad #90	10	30	70	130
5,6: 5(1967)-Stencils. 6(1968)-Mischief Stickers	7	21	49	95
7(1969)-Nasty Cards	7	21	49	95

(If bonus is missing, issue is half price)
NOTE: Clarke c-4. Frazetta r-4, 6 (1 pg. ea.). Mingo c-1-3. Orlando a-5.

MAD HATTER, THE (Costumed Hero)
O. W. Comics Corp.: Jan-Feb, 1946; No. 2, Sept-Oct, 1946

1-Freddy the Firefly begins; Giunta-c/a	89	267	556	975
2-Has ad for E.C.'s Animal Fables #1	42	126	252	440

MADHOUSE
Ajax/Farrell Publ. (Excellent Publ./4-Star): 3-4/54 - No. 4, 9-10/54; 6/57 - No. 4,
Dec?, 1957

1(1954)	31	93	168	290
2,3	17	51	88	150
4-Surrealistic-c	26	78	136	235
1(1957, 2nd series)	14	42	72	120
2-4 (#4 exist?)	10	30	55	80

MAD HOUSE (Formerly Madhouse Glads; ...Comics #104? on)
Red Circle Productions/Archie Publications: No. 95, 9/74 - No. 97, 1/75; No.
98, 8/75 - No. 130, 10/82

95,96-Horror stories through #97; Morrow-c	2	6	10	14
97-Intro. Henry Hobson; Morrow-a/c, Thorne-a	1	4	7	10
98,99,101-120-Satire/humor stories. 110-Sabrina app.,1pg.				
	1	3	6	8
100	1	3	6	9
121-130	1	3	6	9
Annual 8(1970-71)-Formerly Madhouse Ma-ad Annual; Sabrina app. (6 pgs.)				
	3	10	23	35
Annual 9- 12(1974-75): 11-Wood-a(r)	2	6	12	18
...Comics Digest 1(75-76)	2	6	11	15
2-8(8/82)(...Mag. #5 on)-Sabrina in many	2	6	9	12

NOTE: B. Jones a-96. McWilliams a-97. Wildey a-95, 96. See Archie Comics Digest #1, 13.

MADHOUSE GLADS (Formerly ...Ma-ad; Madhouse #95 on)
Archie Publ.: No. 73, May, 1970 - No. 94, Aug, 1974 (No. 78-92: 52 pgs.)

73-77,93,94: 74-1 pg. Sabrina	2	6	11	15
78-92 (52 pgs.)	2	6	12	18

MADHOUSE MA-AD (...Jokes #67-70; ...Freak-out #71-74)
(Formerly Archie's Madhouse) (Becomes Madhouse Glads #73 on)
Archie Publications: No. 67, April, 1969 - No. 72, Jan, 1970

67-71: 70-1 pg. Sabrina	2	6	12	18
72-6 pgs. Sabrina	3	9	19	28
...Annual 7(1969-70)-Formerly Archie's Madhouse Annual; becomes				
Madhouse Annual; 6 pgs. Sabrina	4	12	26	40

MADMAN (See Creatures of the Id #1)
Tundra Publishing: Mar, 1992 - No. 3, 1992 ($3.95, duotone, high quality, limited
series, 52 pgs.)

1-Mike Allred-c/a in all	2	6	9	12
1-2nd printing				4.00
2,3				6.00

MADMAN ADVENTURES

Mage #9 © Matt Wagner

Magic Comics #22 © DMP

Magic Pickle #1 © Scott Morse

Tundra Publishing: 1992 - No. 3, 1993 ($2.95, limited series)

1-Mike Allred-c/a in all	1	3	6	9
2,3				5.00

MADMAN COMICS (Also see The Atomics)
Dark Horse Comics (Legend No. 2 on): Apr, 1994 - No. 20, Dec, 2000 ($2.95/$2.99)

1-Allred-c/a; F. Miller back-c.	1	3	6	8
2-3: 3-Alex Toth back-c.				5.00
4-11: 4-Dave Stevens back-c. 6,7-Miller/Darrow's Big Guy app. 6-Bruce Timm back-c. 7-Darrow back-c. 8-Origin?; Bagge back-c. 10-Allred/Ross-c; Ross back-c. 11-Frazetta back-c				4.00
12-16: 12-(4/99)				3.00
17-20: 17-The G-Men From Hell #1 on cover; Brereton back-c. 18-(#2). 19,20-($2.99-c). 20-Clowes back-c				3.00
... Boogaloo TPB (6/99, $8.95) r/Nexus Meets Madman & Madman/The Jam				9.00
Ltd. Ed. Slipcover (1997, $99.95, signed and numbered) w/Vol.1 & Vol. 2.				
Vol.1- reprints #1-5; Vol. 2- reprints #6-10				100.00
The Complete Madman Comics: Volume 2 (11/96, $17.95, TPB) r/#6-10 plus new material				18.00
Yearbook '95 (1996, $17.95, TPB)-r/#1-5, intro by Teller				18.00

MADMAN / THE JAM
Dark Horse Comics: Jul, 1998 - No. 2, Aug, 1998 ($2.95, mini-series)

1,2-Allred & Mireault-s/a				3.00

MAD MONSTER PARTY (See Movie Classics)

MADNESS IN MURDERWORLD
Marvel Comics: (Came with computer game from Paragon Software)

V1#1-Starring The X-Men	2.25

MADRAVEN HALLOWEEN SPECIAL
Hamilton Comics: Oct, 1995 ($2.95, one-shot)

nn-Morrow-a	3.00

MAD SPECIAL (...Super Special)
E. C. Publications, Inc.: Fall, 1970 - Present (84 - 116 pgs.)
(If bonus is missing, issue is one half price)

Fall 1970(#1)-Bonus-Voodoo Doll; contains 17 pgs. new material	8	24	60	100
Spring 1971(#2)-Wall Nuts; 17 pgs. new material	5	15	34	55
3-Protest Stickers	5	15	34	55
4-8: 4-Mini Posters. 5-Mad Flag. 6-Mad Mischief Stickers. 7-Presidential candidate posters, Wild Shocking Message posters. 8-TV Guise	4	12	29	45
9(1972)-Contains Nostalgic Mad #1 (28 pgs.)	3	10	23	35
10-13: 10-Nonsense Stickers (Don Martin). 13-Sickie Stickers; 3 pgs. Wolverton-r/Mad #137. 11-Contains 33-1/3 RPM record . 12-Contains Nostalgic Mad #2 (36 pgs.); Davis, Wolverton-a	3	9	20	30
14,16-21,24: 4-Vital Message posters & Art Depreciation paintings. 16-Mad-hesive Stickers. 17-Don Martin posters. 20-Martin Stickers. 18-Contains Nostalgic Mad #4 (36 pgs.). 21,24-Contains Nostalgic Mad #5 (28 pgs.) & #6 (28 pgs.)	2	6	13	20
15-Contains Nostalgic Mad #3 (28 pgs.)	2	6	15	22
22,23,25,27-29,30: 22-Diplomas. 23-Martin Stickers. 25-Martin Posters.27-Mad Shock-Sticks. 28-Contains Nostalgic Mad #7 (36 pgs.). 29-Mad Collectable-Correctables Posters. 30-The Movies	2	6	10	14
26-Has 33-1/3 RPM record	2	6	12	18
31,33-35,37-50	2	6	9	12
32-Contains Nostalgic Mad #8. 36-Has 96 pgs. of comic book & comic strip spoofs: titles "The Comics" on-c	2	6	9	12
51-70	1	3	6	9
71-88,90-100: 71-Batman parodies-r by Wood, Drucker. 72-Wolverton-c r-from 1st panel in Mad #11; Wolverton-r/new dialogue. 83-All Star Trek spoof issue	1	3	5	7
76-(Fall, 1991)-Special Hussein Asylum Edition; distributed only to the troops in the Middle East (see Mad #300-303)	1	3	6	8
89-($3.95)-Polybagged w/1st of 3 Spy vs. Spy hologram trading cards (direct sale only issue)(other cards came w/card set)	1	3	5	7
101-135: 117-Sci-Fi parodies-r. Freas c-76. Mingo c-9, 11, 15, 19, 23.				4.00

NOTE: #28-30 have no number on cover. Freas c-76. Mingo c-9, 11, 15, 19, 23.

MAGDALENA, THE (See The Darkness)

Image Comics (Top Cow): Apr, 2000 - No. 3, Jan, 2001 ($2.50)

Preview Special ('00, $4.95) Flip book w/Blood Legacy preview	5.00
1-Benitez-c/a; variant covers by Silvestri & Turner	2.50
2,3: 2-Two covers	2.50
.../Angelus #1/2 (11/01, $2.95) Benitez-c/Ching-a	3.00

MAGE (The Hero Discovered...; also see Grendel #16)
Comico: Feb, 1984 (no month) - No. 15, Dec, 1986 ($1.50, Mando paper)

1-Comico's 1st color comic	2	6	10	14
2-5: 3-Intro Edsel				6.00
6-Grendel begins (1st in color)	3	9	17	25
7-1st new Grendel story	2	6	9	12
8-14: 13-Grendel dies. 14-Grendel story ends				6.00
15-($2.95) Double size w/pullout poster	1	3	6	8
TPB Volume 1-4 (Image, $5.95) 1- r/#1,2. 2- r/#3,4. 3- r/#5,6. 4- r/#7,8				7.00
TPB Volume 5-7 (Image, $6.95) 5- r/#9,10. 6- r/#11,12. 7- r/#13,14				7.00
TPB Volume 8 (Image, 9/99, $7.50) r/#15				7.50

MAGE (The Hero Defined)
Image Comics: July, 1997 - No. 15, Oct, 1999 ($2.50)

0-(7/97, $5.00) American Ent. Ed.	5.00
1-14:Matt Wagner-c/s/a in all. 13-Three covers	2.50
1-"3-D Edition" (2/98, $4.95) w/glasses	5.00
15-($5.95) Acetate cover	6.00
Volume 1,2 TPB ('98,'99, $9.95) 1- r/#1-4. 2- r/#5-8	10.00
Volume 3 TPB ('00, $12.95) r/#9-12	13.00
Volume 4 TPB ('01, $14.95) r/#13-15	15.00

MAGGIE AND HOPEY COLOR SPECIAL (See Love and Rockets)
Fantagraphics Books: May, 1997 ($3.50, one-shot)

1	3.50

MAGGIE THE CAT (Also see Jon Sable, Freelance #11 & Shaman's Tears #12)
Image Comics (Creative Fire Studio): Jan, 1996 - No. 2, Feb, 1996 ($2.50, unfinished limited series)

1,2: Mike Grell-c/a/scripts	2.50

MAGICA DE SPELL (See Walt Disney Showcase #30)

MAGIC AGENT (See Forbidden Worlds & Unknown Worlds)
American Comics Group: Jan-Feb, 1962 - No. 3, May-June, 1962

1-Origin & 1st app. John Force	4	12	26	40
2,3	3	9	19	28

MAGICAL POKÉMON JOURNEY
Viz Comics: 2000 - Present ($4.95, B&W, magazine-size)

1-4	5.00
Part 2: 1-3	5.00
Part 3: 1-4: 1-Includes color poster	5.00
Part 4: 1-4	5.00
Part 5: 1-4	5.00

MAGIC COMICS
David McKay Publications: Aug, 1939 - No. 123, Nov-Dec, 1949

1-Mandrake the Magician, Henry, Popeye , Blondie, Barney Baxter, Secret Agent X-9 (not by Raymond), Bunky by Billy DeBeck & Thornton Burgess text stories illustrated by Harrison Cady begin; Henry covers begin	333	1000	1830	3000
2	117	351	644	1050
3	89	267	490	800
4	69	206	380	625
5	53	158	292	480
6-10: 8-11,21-Mandrake/Henry-c	44	132	242	400
11-16,18,20: 12-Mandrake-c begin.	38	114	210	340
17-The Lone Ranger begins	41	123	226	370
19-Robot-c	44	132	242	400
21-30: 25-Only Blondie-c. 26-Dagwood-c begin	24	71	132	220
31-40: 36-Flag-c	18	54	99	165
41-50	14	42	77	130
51-60	12	36	66	110
61-70	10	30	55	90
71-99, 107,108-Flash Gordon app; not by Raymond	8	24	44	75
100	9	26	50	85

Magneto #1 © MAR

Magnus Robot Fighter #37 © GK

Major Bummer #4 © Arcudi & Mahnke

	GD2.0	FN6.0	VF8.0	NM9.4
101-106,109-123: 123-Last Dagwood-c	7	21	39	65

MAGIC FLUTE, THE (See Night Music #9-11)

MAGIC PICKLE
Oni Press: Sept, 2001 - No. 4, Dec, 2001 ($2.95, limited series)
| 1-4-Scott Morse-s/a; Mahfood-a (2 pgs.) | | | | 3.00 |

MAGIC SWORD, THE (See Movie Classics)

MAGIC THE GATHERING (Title Series), Acclaim Comics (Armada)
...ANTIQUITIES WAR,11/95 - 2/96 ($2.50), 1-4-Paul Smith-a(p)				2.50
...ARABIAN NIGHTS, 12/95 - 1/96 ($2.50), 1,2				2.50
...COLLECTION '95 ($4.95), 1,2-polybagged				5.00
...CONVOCATIONS, '95 ($2.50), 1-nn-pin-ups				2.50
...ELDER DRAGONS '95 ($2.50), 1,2-Doug Wheatley-a				2.50
...FALLEN ANGEL, '95 ($5.95), nn				6.00
...FALLEN EMPIRES ,9/95 - 10/95 ($2.75), 1,2				3.00
...Collection ($4.95)-polybagged				5.00
...HOMELANDS, '95 ($5.95), nn-polybagged w/card; Hildebrandts-c				6.00
...ICE AGE (On The World of...) ,7/5 -11/95 ($2.50), 1-4: 1,2-bound-in Magic Card. 3,4-bound-in insert				2.50
...LEGEND OF JEDIT OJANEN, '96 ($2.50), 1,2				2.50
...NIGHTMARE, '95 ($2.50, one shot), 1				2.50
...THE SHADOW MAGE, 7/95 - 10/95 ($2.50), 1-4--polybagged w/Magic The Gathering card				2.50
...Collection 1,2 (1995, $4.95)-Trade paperback; polybagged				5.00
...SHANDALAR, '96 ($2.50), 1,2				2.50
...WAYFARER ,11/95 - 2/96 ($2.50), 1-5				2.50

MAGIC: THE GATHERING: GERRARD'S QUEST
Dark Horse Comics: Mar, 1998 - No. 4, June, 1998 ($2.95, limited series)
| 1-4: Grell-s/Mhan-a | | | | 3.00 |

MAGIK (Illyana and Storm Limited Series)
Marvel Comics: Dec, 1983 - No. 4, Mar, 1984 (60¢, limited series)
| 1-4: 1-Characters from X-Men; Inferno begins; X-Men cameo (Buscema pencils in #1,2; c-1p. 2-4: 2-Nightcrawler app. & X-Men cameo | | | | 3.00 |

MAGIK (See Black Sun mini-series)

MAGIK
Marvel Comics: Dec, 2000 - No. 4, Mar, 2001 ($2.99, limited series)
| 1-4-Liam Sharp-a/Abnett & Lanning-s; Nightcrawler app. | | | | 3.00 |

MAGILLA GORILLA (TV) (See Kite Fun Book)
Gold Key: May, 1964 - No. 10, Dec, 1968 (Hanna-Barbera)
1-1st comic app.	10	30	70	130
2-4: 3-Vs. Yogi Bear for President. 4-1st Punkin Puss & Mushmouse, Ricochet Rabbit & Droop-a-Long	6	18	42	80
5-10: 10-Reprints	5	15	35	65

MAGILLA GORILLA (TV)(See Spotlight #4)
Charlton Comics: Nov, 1970 - No. 5, July, 1971 (Hanna-Barbera)
| 1 | 5 | 15 | 34 | 55 |
| 2-5 | 3 | 9 | 21 | 32 |

MAGNETIC MEN FEATURING MAGNETO
Marvel Comics (Amalgam): June, 1997 ($1.95, one-shot)
| 1-Tom Peyer-s/Barry Kitson & Dan Panosian-a | | | | 2.50 |

MAGNETO (See X-Men #1)
Marvel Comics: nd (Sept, 1993) (Giveaway) (one-shot)
| 0-Embossed foil-c by Sienkiewicz; r/Classic X-Men #19 & 12 by Bolton | | | | 5.00 |

MAGNETO
Marvel Comics: Nov, 1996 - No. 4, Feb, 1997 ($1.95, limited series)
| 1-4: Peter Milligan scripts & Kelley Jones-a(p) | | | | 2.50 |

MAGNETO AND THE MAGNETIC MEN
Marvel Comics (Amalgam): Apr, 1996 ($1.95, one-shot)
| 1-Jeff Matsuda-a(p) | | | | 2.50 |

MAGNETO ASCENDANT

	GD2.0	FN6.0	VF8.0	NM9.4

Marvel Comics: May, 1999 ($3.99, squarebound one-shot)
| 1-Reprints early Magneto appearances | | | | 4.00 |

MAGNETO: DARK SEDUCTION
Marvel Comics: Jun, 2000 - No. 4, Sept, 2000 ($2.99, limited series)
| 1-4: Nicieza-s/Cruz-a. 3,4-Avengers-c/app. | | | | 3.00 |

MAGNETO REX
Marvel Comics: Apr, 1999 - No. 3, July, 1999 ($2.50, limited series)
| 1-3-Rogue, Quicksilver app.; Peterson-a(p) | | | | 2.50 |

MAGNUS, ROBOT FIGHTER (...4000 A.D.)(See Doctor Solar)
Gold Key: Feb, 1963 - No. 46, Jan, 1977 (All painted covers except #5,31)
1-Origin & 1st app. Magnus; Aliens (1st app.) series begins	23	69	161	300
2,3	10	30	70	125
4-10: 10-Simonson fan club illo (5/65, 1st-a?)	6	18	42	75
11-20	4	12	30	50
21,24-28: 28-Aliens ends	3	10	23	35
22,23: 22-Origin-r/#1; last 12¢ issue	4	12	25	38
29-46-Mostly reprints	2	6	11	15
NOTE: *Manning* a-1-22, 28-43(r). *Spiegle* a-23, 44r.

MAGNUS ROBOT FIGHTER (Also see Vintage Magnus)
Valiant/Acclaim Comics: May, 1991 - No. 64, Feb, 1996 ($1.75/$1.95/$2.25/$2.50)
1-Nichols/Layton-c/a; 1-8 have trading cards				6.00
2-8: 4-Rai cameo. 5-Origin & 1st full app. Rai (10/91); 5-8 are in flip book format and back-c & half of book are Rai #1-4 mini-series. 6-1st Solar x-over. 7-Magnus vs. Rai-c/story; 1st X-O Armor				4.00
0-Origin issue; Layton-a; ordered through mail w/coupons from 1st 8 issues plus 50¢; B. Smith trading card				6.00
0-Sold thru comic shops without trading card				3.00
9-11				3.00
12-(3.25, 44 pgs.)-Turok-c/story (1st app. in Valiant universe, 5/92); has 8 pg. Magnus story insert	1	3	6	8
13-24,26-48, 50-63: 14-1st app. Isak. 15,16-Unity x-overs. 15-Miller-c. 16-Birth of Magnus. 24-Story cont'd in Rai & the Future Force #9. 33-Timewalker app.36-Bound-in trading cards. 37-Rai & Starwatchers app. 44-Bound-in sneak peek card. 21-New direction & new logo; Reese inks. 21-Gold ink variant				2.50
25-($2.95)-Embossed silver foil-c; new costume				3.00
49, 64 ($2.50): 64-Magnus dies?				3.00
...Invasion (1994, $9.95)-r/Rai #1-4 & Magnus #5-8				10.00
Yearbook (1994, $3.95, 52 pgs.)				4.00
NOTE: *Ditko/Reese* a-18. *Layton* a(i)-5; c-6-9i, 25; back(i)-5-8. *Reese* a(i)-22, 25, 28; c(i)-22, 24, 28. *Simonson* c-16. Prices for issues 1-8 are for trading cards and coupons intact.

MAGNUS ROBOT FIGHTER
Acclaim Comics (Valiant Heroes): V2#1, May, 1997 - No. 18, Jun, 1998 ($2.50)
| 1-18: 1-Reintro Magnus; Donavon Wylie (X-O Manowar) cameo; Tom Peyer scripts & Mike McKone-c/a begin; painted variant-c exists | | | | 2.50 |

MAGNUS ROBOT FIGHTER 4000 A.D.
Valiant: 1990 - No. 2?, 1991 ($7.95, high quality paper, card stock-c, 96 pgs.)
| 1,2: Russ Manning-r in all. 1-Origin | | | | 8.00 |

MAGNUS ROBOT FIGHTER/NEXUS
Valiant/Dark Horse Comics: Dec, 1993 - No. 2, Apr, 1994 ($2.95, lim. series)
| 1,2: Steve Rude painted-c & pencils in all | | | | 3.00 |

MAID OF THE MIST (See American Graphics)

MAI, THE PSYCHIC GIRL
Eclipse Comics: May, 1987 - No. 28, July, 1989 ($1.50, B&W, bi-weekly, 44pgs.)
| 1-28, 1,2-2nd print | | | | 2.50 |

MAJOR BUMMER
DC Comics: Aug, 1997 - No. 15, Oct, 1998 ($2.50)
| 1-15: 1-Origin and 1st app. Major Bummer | | | | 2.50 |

MAJOR HOOPLE COMICS (See Crackajack Funnies)
Nedor Publications: nd (Jan, 1943)
| 1-Mary Worth, Phantom Soldier app. by Moldoff | 40 | 120 | 240 | 420 |

	GD2.0	FN6.0	VF8.0	NM9.4

MAJOR VICTORY COMICS (Also see Dynamic Comics)
H. Clay Glover/Service Publ./Harry 'A' Chesler: 1944 - No. 3, Summer, 1945

1-Origin Major Victory (patriotic hero) by C. Sultan (reprint from Dynamic #1);				
1st app. Spider Woman	61	182	381	675
2-Dynamic Boy app.	40	120	232	400
3-Rocket Boy app.	39	117	208	360

MALIBU ASHCAN: RAFFERTY (See Firearm #12)
Malibu Comics (Ultraverse): Nov, 1994 (99¢, B&W w/color-c; one-shot)

1-Previews "The Rafferty Saga" storyline in Firearm; Chaykin-c   2.25

MALTESE FALCON
David McKay Publications: No. 48, 1946

Feature Books 48-by Dashiell Hammett	75	225	469	825

MALU IN THE LAND OF ADVENTURE
I. W. Enterprises: 1964 (See White Princess of Jungle #2)

1-r/Avon's Slave Girl Comics #1; Severin-c	5	15	38	60

MAMMOTH COMICS
Whitman Publishing Co.(K. K. Publ.): 1938 (84 pgs.) (B&W, 8-1/2x11-1/2")

1-Alley Oop, Terry & the Pirates, Dick Tracy, Little Orphan Annie, Wash				
Tubbs, Moon Mullins, Smilin' Jack, Tailspin Tommy, Don Winslow, Dan Dunn,				
Smokey Stover & other reprints (scarce)	200	600	1250	2200

MAN AGAINST TIME
Image Comics (Motown Machineworks): May, 1996 - No. 4, Aug, 1996 ($2.25, limited series)

1-4: 1-Simonson-c. 2,3-Leon-c. 4-Barreto & Leon-c   2.25

MAN-BAT (See Batman Family, Brave & the Bold, & Detective #400)
National Periodical Publications/DC Comics: Dec-Jan, 1975-76 - No. 2, Feb-Mar, 1976; Dec, 1984

1-Ditko-a(p); Aparo-c; Batman app.; 1st app. She-Bat?				
	2	6	12	18
2-Aparo-c	2	6	9	12
1 (12/84)-N. Adams-r(3)/Det.(Vs. Batman on-c)				4.00

MAN-BAT
DC Comics: Feb, 1996 - No. 3, Apr, 1996 ($2.25, limited series)

1-3: Dixon scripts in all. 2-Killer Croc-c/app.   2.25

MAN CALLED A-X, THE
Malibu Comics (Bravura): Nov, 1994 - No. 4, Jun, 1995 ($2.95, limited series)

0-4: Marv Wolfman scripts & Shawn McManus-c/a. 0-(2/95). 1-"1A" on cover   3.00

MAN CALLED A-X, THE
DC Comics: Oct, 1997 - No. 8, May, 1998 ($2.50)

1-8: Marv Wolfman scripts & Shawn McManus-c/a.   2.50

MAN COMICS
Marvel/Atlas Comics (NPI): Dec, 1949 - No. 28, Sept, 1953 (#1-6: 52 pgs.)

1-Tuska-a	23	69	121	210
2-Tuska-a	14	42	72	120
3-6	10	30	55	85
7,8	10	30	55	80
9-13,15: 9-Format changes to war	7	21	38	55
14-Henkel (3 pgs.); Pakula-a	8	24	45	65
16-21,23-28: 28-Crime issue (Bob Brant)	8	18	32	45
22-Krigstein-a, 5 pgs.	8	24	45	65

NOTE: **Berg** a-14, 15, 19. **Colan** a-9, 21. **Everett** a-8, 22; c-22, 25. **Heath** a-11, 17, 21. **Kubertish** a-by **Bob Brown**-3. **Maneely** a-11; c-10, 11. **Reinman** a-11. **Robinson** a-7, 10, 14. **Robert Sale** a-9, 11. **Sinnott** a-22, 23. **Tuska** a-1, 2.

MANDRAKE THE MAGICIAN (See Defenders Of The Earth, 123, 46, 52, 55, Giant Comic Album, King Comics, Magic Comics, The Phantom #21, Tiny Tot Funnies & Wow Comics, '36)

MANDRAKE THE MAGICIAN (See Harvey Comics Hits #53)
David McKay Publ./Dell/King Comics (All 12¢): 1938 - 1948; Sept, 1966 - No. 10, Nov, 1967 (Also see Four Color #752)

Feature Books 18,19,25 (1938)	57	171	356	625
Feature Books 46	41	124	246	425
Feature Books 52,55	35	105	188	325
Four Color 752 (11/56)	10	30	70	135

	GD2.0	FN6.0	VF8.0	NM9.4

1-Begin S.O.S. Phantom, ends #3	5	15	34	55

2-7,9: 4-Girl Phantom app. 5-Flying Saucer-c/story. 5,6-Brick Bradford app.

7-Origin Lothar. 9-Brick Bradford app.	3	9	20	30
8-Jeff Jones-a (4 pgs.)	3	10	23	35
10-Rip Kirby app.; Raymond-a (14 pgs.)	4	12	26	40

MANDRAKE THE MAGICIAN
Marvel Comics: Apr, 1995 - No. 2, May, 1995 ($2.95, unfinished limited series)

1,2: Mike Barr scripts   3.00

MAN-EATING COW (See Tick #7,8)
New England Comics: July, 1992 - No. 10, 1994? ($2.75, B&W, limited series)

1-10				3.00
Man-Eating Cow Bonanza (6/96, $4.95, 128 pgs.)-r/#1-4.				5.00

MAN FROM ATLANTIS (TV)
Marvel Comics: Feb, 1978 - No. 7, Aug, 1978

1-(84 pgs.)-Sutton-a(p), Buscema; origin & cast photos	1	3	6	8
2-7				4.00

MAN FROM PLANET X, THE
Planet X Productions: 1987 (no price; probably unlicensed)

1-Reprints Fawcett Movie Comic   2.25

MAN FROM U.N.C.L.E., THE (TV) (Also see The Girl From Uncle)
Gold Key: Feb, 1965 - No. 22, Apr, 1969 (All photo-c)

1	15	45	105	200
2-Photo back c-2-8	8	24	56	105
3-10: 7-Jet Dream begins (1st app., also see Jet Dream) (all new stories)				
	6	18	42	75
11-22: 19-Last 12¢ issue. 21,22-Reprint #10 & 7	5	15	35	65

MAN FROM U.N.C.L.E., THE (TV)
Entertainment Publishing: 1987 - No. 11 ($1.50/$1.75, B&W)

1-7 ($1.50), 8-11 ($1.75)   3.00

MAN FROM WELLS FARGO (TV)
Dell Publishing Co.: No. 1287, Feb-Apr, 1962 - May-July, 1962 (Photo-c)

Four Color 1287, #01-495-207	5	15	35	65

MANGA SHI (See Tomoe)
Crusade Entertainment: Aug, 1996 ($2.95)

1-Printed backwards (manga-style)   3.00

MANGA SHI 2000
Crusade Entertainment: Feb, 1997 - No. 3, June, 1997 ($2.95, mini-series)

1-3: 1-Two covers   3.00

MANGA ZEN (Also see Zen Intergalactic Ninja)
Zen Comics (Fusion Studios): 1996 - No. 3, 1996 ($2.50, B&W)

1-3   2.50

MANGAZINE
Antarctic Press: Aug, 1985 - No. 4, Sept, 1986 (B&W)

1-Soft paper-c	2	6	10	14
2-4	1	3	6	9

MANGLE TANGLE TALES
Innovation Publishing: 1990 ($2.95, deluxe format)

1-Intro by Harlan Ellison   3.00

MANHUNT! (Becomes Red Fox #15 on)
Magazine Enterprises: 10/47 - No. 11, 8/48; #13,14, 1953 (no #12)

1-Red Fox by L. B. Cole, Undercover Girl by Whitney, Space Ace begin (1st				
app.); negligee panels	47	140	286	500
2-Electrocution-c	40	120	217	375
3-6	34	102	179	310
7-10: 7-Space Ace ends. 8-Trail Colt begins (intro/1st app., 5/48) by				
Guardineer; Trail Colt-c. 10-G. Ingels-a	30	90	159	275
11(8/48)-Frazetta-a, 7 pgs.; The Duke, Scotland Yard begin				
	40	120	232	400
13(A-1 #63)-Frazetta, r-/Trail Colt #1, 7 pgs.	40	120	214	370
14(A-1 #77)-Bondage/hypo-c; last L. B. Cole Red Fox; Ingels-a				
	33	99	174	300

NOTE: **Guardineer** a-1-5; c-8. **Whitney** a-2-14; c-1-6, 10. Red Fox by **L. B. Cole**-#1-14. #15 was

Man-Thing #4 © MAR

Mantra #10 © MAL

Many Ghosts of Dr. Graves #49 © CC

| | GD2.0 | FN6.0 | VF8.0 | NM9.4 | | | GD2.0 | FN6.0 | VF8.0 | NM9.4 |

advertised but came out as Red Fox #15. Bondage c-6.

MANHUNTER (See Adventure #58, 73, Brave & the Bold, Detective Comics, 1st Issue Special, House of Mystery #143 and Justice League of America)
DC Comics: 1984 ($2.50, 76 pgs; high quality paper)
1-Simonson-c/a(r)/Detective; Batman app. 3.50

MANHUNTER
DC Comics: July, 1988 - No. 24, Apr, 1990 ($1.00)
1-24: 8,9-Flash app. 9-Invasion. 17-Batman-c/sty 2.25

MANHUNTER
DC Comics: No. 0, Nov, 1994 - No. 12, Nov, 1995 ($1.95/$2.25)
0-12 ..... 2.25

MANHUNTER: THE SPECIAL EDITION
DC Comics: 1999 ($9.95)
TPB-Reprints Detective Comics stories by Goodwin and Simonson 10.00

MAN IN BLACK (See Thrill-O-Rama) (Also see All New Comics, Front Page, Green Hornet #31, Strange Story & Tally-Ho Comics)
Harvey Publications: Sept, 1957 - No. 4, Mar, 1958

1-Bob Powell-c/a	18	54	94	160
2-4-Powell-c/a	14	42	72	120

MAN IN BLACK
Lorne-Harvey Publications (Recollections): 1990 - No. 2, July, 1991 (B&W)
1,2 ..... 2.25

MAN IN FLIGHT (Disney, TV)
Dell Publishing Co.: No. 836, Sept, 1957

Four Color 836	7	21	49	90

MAN IN SPACE (Disney, TV, see Dell Giant #27)
Dell Publishing Co.: No. 716, Aug, 1956 - No. 954, Nov, 1958

Four Color 716-A science feat. from Tomorrowland	9	27	63	110
Four Color 954-Satellites	7	21	49	90

MANKIND (WWF Wrestling)
Chaos Comics: Sept, 1999 ($2.95, one-shot)
1-Regular and photo-c 3.00
1-Premium Edition ($10.00) Dwayne Turner & Danny Miki-c 10.00

MANN AND SUPERMAN
DC Comics: 2000 ($5.95, prestige format, one-shot)
nn-Michael T. Gilbert-s/a 6.00

MAN OF STEEL, THE (Also see Superman: The Man of Steel)
DC Comics: 1986 (June release) - No. 6, 1986 (75¢, limited series)
1-6: 1-Silver logo; Byrne-c/a/scripts in all; origin, 1-Alternate-c for newsstand sales,1-Distr. to toy stores by So Much Fun, 2-6: 2-Intro. Lois Lane, Jimmy Olsen. 3-Intro/origin Magpie; Batman-c/story. 4-Intro. new Lex Luthor 4.00
1-6-Silver Editions (1993, $1.95)-r/1-6 ..... 3.00
...The Complete Saga nn-Contains #1-6, given away in contest 20.00
Limited Edition, softcover ..... 5 ..... 15 ..... 38 60
NOTE: *Issues 1-6 were released under Action #583 (9/86) & Action #584 (1/87) plus Superman #423 (9/86) & Advs. of Superman #424 (1/87).*

MAN OF THE ATOM (See Solar, Man of the Atom Vol. 2)

MAN OF WAR (See Liberty Guards & Liberty Scouts)
Centaur Publications: Nov, 1941 - No. 2, Jan, 1942

1-The Fire-Man, Man of War, The Sentinel, Liberty Guards, & Vapo-Man begin; Gustavson-c/a; Flag-c	164	492	1023	1800
2-Intro The Ferret; Gustavson-c/a	123	369	769	1350

MAN OF WAR
Eclipse Comics: Aug, 1987 - No. 3, Feb, 1988 ($1.75, Baxter paper)
1-3: Bruce Jones scripts 2.25

MAN OF WAR (See The Protectors)
Malibu Comics: 1993 - No. 8, Feb, 1994 ($1.95/$2.50/$2.25)
1-5 ($1.95)-Newsstand Editions w/different-c 2.25
1-8-1-5-Collector's Edi. w/poste.r. 6-8 ($2.25): 6-Polybagged w/Skycap. 8-Vs. Rocket Rangers 2.50

MAN O' MARS

Fiction House Magazines: 1953; 1964

1-Space Rangers; Whitman-c	40	120	240	420
I.W. Reprint #1-r/Man O'Mars #1 & Star Pirate; Murphy Anderson-a	5	15	38	60

MANTECH ROBOT WARRIORS
Archie Enterprises, Inc.: Sept, 1984 - No. 4, Apr, 1985 (75¢)
1-4: Ayers-c/a(p). 1-Buckler-c(i) 3.00

MAN-THING (See Fear, Giant-Size..., Marvel Comics Presents, Marvel Fanfare, Monsters Unleashed, Power Record Comics & Savage Tales)
Marvel Comics Group: Jan, 1974 - No. 22, Oct, 1975; V2#1, Nov, 1979 - V2#11, July, 1981

1-Howard the Duck(2nd app.) cont'd/Fear #19	4	12	26	40
2	2	6	12	18
3-1st app. original Foolkiller	2	6	10	14
4-Origin Foolkiller; last app. 1st Foolkiller	2	6	9	12
5-11-Ploog-a. 11-Foolkiller cameo (flashback)	2	6	9	12
12-22: 19-1st app. Scavenger. 20-Spidey cameo. 21-Origin Scavenger, Man-Thing. 22-Howard the Duck cameo	1	3	6	8
V2#1(1979)	1	3	5	7
V2#2-11: 4-Dr. Strange-c/app. 11-Mayerik-a				4.00

NOTE: *Alcala a-14. Brunner c-1. J. Buscema a-12p, 13p, 16p. Gil Kane c-4p, 10p, 12-20p, 21. Mooney a-17, 18, 19p, 20-22, V2#1-3p. Ploog Man-Thing-5p, 6p, 7, 8, 9-11p; c-5, 6, 8, 9, 11. Sutton a-13i. No. 19 says #10 in indicia.*

MAN-THING (Volume Three, continues in Strange Tales #1 (9/98))
Marvel Comics: Dec, 1997 - No. 8, July, 1998 ($2.99)
1-8-DeMatteis-s/Sharp-a. 2-Two covers. 6-Howard the Duck-c/app. 3.00

MANTRA
Malibu Comics (Ultraverse): July, 1993 - No. 24, Aug, 1995 ($1.95/$2.50)
1-Polybagged w/trading card & coupon 3.00
1-Newsstand edition w/o trading card or coupon 2.25
1-Full cover holographic edition ..... 1 ..... 4 ..... 7 10
1-Ultra-limited silver foil-c 5.00
2-9,11-24: 3-Intro Warstrike & Kismet. 6-Break-Thru x-over. 2-($2.50-Newsstand edition bagged w/card. 4-($2.50, 48 pgs.)-Rune flip-c/story by B. Smith (3 pgs.). 7-Prime app.; origin Prototype by Jurgens/Austin (2 pgs.). 11-New costume. 17-Intro NecroMantra & Pinnacle; prelude to Godwheel 2.50
10-($3.50, 68 pgs.)-Flip-c w/Ultraverse Premiere #2 ..... 3.50
Giant Size 1 (7/94, $2.50, 44 pgs.) 2.50
...Spear of Destiny 1,2 (4/95, $2.50, 36pgs.) 2.50

MANTRA (2nd Series) (Also See Black September)
Malibu Comics (Ultraverse): Infinity, Sept, 1995 - No. 7, Apr, 1996 ($1.50)
Infinity (9/95, $1.50)-Black September x-over, Intro new Mantra. 2.25
1-7: 5-(10/95). 5-Return of Eden (original Mantra). 6,7-Rush app. 2.25

MAN WITH THE X-RAY EYES (See X,... under Movie Comics)

MANY GHOSTS OF DR. GRAVES, THE (Doctor Graves #73 on)
Charlton Comics: 5/67 - No. 60, 12/76; No. 61, 9/77 - No. 62, 10/77; No. 63, 2/78 - No. 65, 4/78; No. 66, 6/81 - No. 72, 5/82

1-Ditko-a; Palais-a; early issues 12¢-c	4	12	30	50
2-6,8,10	2	6	15	22
7,9-Ditko-a	3	9	17	25
11-13,16-18-Ditko-c/a	2	6	11	16
14,19,23,25	1	4	7	10
15,20,21-Ditko-a	2	6	9	12
22,24,26,27,29-35,38,40-Ditko-c/a	2	6	9	12
28-Ditko-c	1	4	7	10
36,46,56,57,59,66-69,71	1	3	6	8
37,41,43,51,54,60,61,70,72-Ditko-a	1	4	7	10
39,58-Ditko-c. 39-Sutton-a. 58-Ditko-a	1	4	7	10
42,44,53-Ditko-a. 42-Sutton-a	1	4	7	10
45-1st Newton comic work (8 pgs.); new logo; Sutton-c	2	6	10	14
47-Newton, Sutton, Ditko-a	1	4	7	10
48-Ditko, Sutton-a	1	4	7	10
49-Newton-c/a; Sutton-a.	1	4	7	10
50-Sutton-a	1	3	6	8
52-Newton-c; Ditko-a	1	4	7	10

Marc Spector: Moon Knight #20 © MAR

Marge's Little Lulu #10 © Marjorie Buell

Margie Comics #40 © MAR

	GD2.0	FN6.0	VF8.0	NM9.4
55-Ditko-c; Sutton-a	1	4	7	10
62-65-Ditko-c/a. 65-Sutton-a	2	6	9	12
Modern Comics Reprint 12,25 (1978)				4.00

NOTE: *Aparo* a-4, 5, 7, 8, 66r, 69r; c-8, 14, 19, 66r, 67r. *Byrne* c-54. *Ditko* a-1, 7, 9, 11-13, 15-18, 20-22, 24, 26, 27, 29, 30-35, 37, 38, 40-44, 47, 48, 51-54, 58, 60r-65r, 70, 72; c-11-13, 16-18, 22, 24, 26-35, 38, 40, 55, 58, 62-65. *Howard* a-38, 39, 45i, 65; c-48. *Kim* a-36, 46, 52. *Larson* a-58. *Morisi* a-13, 14, 23, 26. *Newton* a-45, 47p, 49p; c-49, 52. *Staton* a-36, 37, 41, 43. *Sutton* a-39, 42, 47-50, 55, 65; c-42, 44, 45; painted c-53. *Zeck* a-56, 59.

MANY LOVES OF DOBIE GILLIS (TV)
National Periodical Publications: May-June, 1960 - No. 26, Oct, 1964

1-Most covers by Bob Oskner	24	72	168	300
2-5	13	39	94	160
6-10: 10-Last 10¢-c	9	27	63	105
11-26: 20-Drucker-a. 24-(3-4/64). 25-(9/64)	8	24	58	95

MARAUDER'S MOON (See Luke Short, Four Color #848)

MARCH OF COMICS (See Promotional Comics section)

MARCH OF CRIME (Formerly My Love Affair #1-6) (See Fox Giants)
Fox Features Synd.: No. 7, July, 1950 - No. 2, Sept, 1950; No. 3, Sept, 1951

7(#1)(7/50)-True crime stories; Wood-a	40	120	220	380
2(9/50)-Wood-a (exceptional)	39	117	208	360
3(9/51)	19	57	99	165

MARCO POLO
Charlton Comics Group: 1962 (Movie classic)

nn (Scarce)-Glanzman-c/a (25 pgs.)	11	33	80	135

MARC SPECTOR: MOON KNIGHT (Also see Moon Knight)
Marvel Comics: June, 1989 - No. 60, Mar, 1994 ($1.50/$1.75, direct sales)

1-24,26-49,51-54,58,59: 4-Intro new Midnight. 8,9-Punisher app. 15-Silver Sable app. 19-21-Spider-Man & Punisher app. 25-(52 pgs.)-Ghost Rider app. 32,33-Hobgoblin II (Macendale) & Spider-Man (in black costume) app. 35-38-Punisher story. 42-44-Infinity War x-over. 46-Demogoblin app. 51,53-Gambit app. 55-New look. 57-Spider-Man-c/story. 60-Moon Knight dies   2.50

50-(56 pgs.)-Special die-cut-c	3.00
55-57,60-Platt a	3.50
...: Divided We Fall ($4.95, 52 pgs.)	5.00
Special 1 (1992, $2.50)	2.50

NOTE: *Cowan* c(p) 20-23. *Guice* c-20. *Heath* c/a-4. *Platt* a-55-57,60; c-55-60.

MARGARET O'BRIEN (See The Adventures of...)

MARGE'S LITTLE LULU (Continues as Little Lulu from #207 on)
Dell Publishing Co./Gold Key: #165-206: No. 74, 6/45 - No. 164, 7-9/62; No. 165, 10/62 - No. 206, 8/72

Marjorie Henderson Buell, born in Philadelphia, Pa., in 1904, created Little Lulu, a cartoon character that appeared weekly in the Saturday Evening Post from Feb. 23, 1935 through Dec. 30, 1944. She was not responsible for any of the comic books. John Stanley did pencils only on all Little Lulu comics through at least #135 (1959). He did pencils and inks on Four Color #74 & 97. Irving Tripp began inking stories from #1 on, and remained the comic's illustrator throughout its entire run. Stanley did storyboards (layouts), pencils, and scripts in all cases and inking only on covers. His word balloons were in cursive. Tripp and occasionally other artists at Western Publ. in Poughkeepsie, N.Y. blew up the pencilled pages, inked the blowups, and lettered them. Arnold Drake did storyboards, pencils and scripts starting with #197, amidst reprinted issues. Buell sold her rights exclusively to Western Publ. in Dec., 1971. The earlier issues had to be approved by Buell prior to publication.

Four Color 74('45)-Intro Lulu, Tubby & Alvin	115	345	805	1500
Four Color 97(2/46)	50	150	350	650

(Above two books are all John Stanley - cover, pencils, and inks.)

Four Color 110('46)-1st Alvin Story Telling Time; 1st app. Willy; variant cover may exist	35	105	245	450
Four Color 115-1st app. Boys' Clubhouse	35	105	245	450
Four Color 120, 131: 120-1st app. Eddie	30	90	210	385
Four Color 139('47),146,158	28	84	196	360
Four Color 165 (10/47)-Smokes doll hair & has wild hallucinations. 1st Tubby detective story	28	84	196	360
1(1-2/48)-Lulu's Diary feature begins	62	186	434	800
2-1st app. Gloria; 1st Tubby story in a L.L. comic; 1st app. Miss Feeny	29	87	203	375
3-5	27	81	189	350
6-10: 7-1st app. Annie; Xmas-c	21	63	147	270
11-20: 18-X-Mas-c. 19-1st app. Wilbur. 20-1st app. Mr. McNabbem	18	54	126	230

	GD2.0	FN6.0	VF8.0	NM9.4
21-30: 26-r/F.C. 110. 30-Xmas-c	14	42	98	180
31-38,40: 35-1st Mumday story	12	36	84	155
39-Intro. Witch Hazel in "That Awful Witch Hazel"	13	39	91	170
41-60: 42-Xmas-c. 45-2nd Witch Hazel app. 49-Gives Stanley & others credit	11	33	77	145
61-80: 63-1st app. Chubby (Tubby's cousin). 68-1st app. Prof. Cleff.				
78-Xmas-c. 80-Intro. Little Itch (2/55)	8	24	56	105
81-99: 90-Xmas-c	7	21	49	85
100	7	21	49	90
101-130: 123-1st app. Fifi	5	15	35	65
131-164: 135-Last Stanley-p	5	15	34	55
165-Giant; ...in Paris ('62)	12	36	84	150
166-Giant; ...Christmas Diary (1962 - '63)	12	36	84	150
167-169	4	12	29	45
170,172,175,176,178-196,198-200-Stanley-r. 182-1st app. Little Scarecrow Boy	2	6	15	22
171,173,174,177,197	2	6	11	18
201,203,206-Last issue to carry Marge's name	2	6	11	15
202,204,205-Stanley-r	2	6	12	18
...& Tubby in Japan (12¢)(5-7/62) 01476-207	7	21	49	85
...Summer Camp 1(8/67-G.K.-Giant) '57-58-r	5	15	35	60
...Trick 'N' Treat 1(12¢)(12/62-Gold Key)	5	15	35	70

NOTE: *See Dell Giant Comics #23, 29, 36, 42, 50, & Dell Giants for annuals. All Giants not by Stanley from L.L. on Vacation (7/54) on. Irving Tripp a-#1-on. Christmas c-7, 18, 30, 42, 78, 90, 126, 166, 250. Summer Camp issues #173, 177, 181, 189, 197, 201, 206.*

MARGE'S LITTLE LULU (See Golden Comics Digest #19, 23, 27, 29, 33, 36, 40, 43, 46, & March of Comics #251, 267, 275, 293, 307, 323, 335, 349, 355, 369, 385, 406, 417, 427, 439, 456, 468, 475, 488)

MARGE'S TUBBY (Little Lulu)(See Dell Giants)
Dell Publishing Co./Gold Key: No. 381, Aug, 1952 - No. 49, Dec-Feb, 1961-62

Four Color 381(#1)-Stanley script; Irving Tripp-a	21	63	147	270
Four Color 430,444-Stanley-a	12	36	84	150
Four Color 461 (4/53)-1st Tubby & Men From Mars story; Stanley-a	10	30	70	130
5 (7-9/53)-Stanley-a	8	24	56	105
6-10	7	21	49	85
11-20	5	15	34	55
21-30	4	12	26	40
31-49	3	10	23	35
...& the Little Men From Mars No. 30020-410(10/64-G.K.)-25¢, 68 pgs.	7	21	49	95

NOTE: *John Stanley did all storyboards & scripts through at least #35 (1959). Lloyd White did all art except F.C. 381, 430, 444, 461 & #5.*

MARGIE (See My Little...)

MARGIE (TV)
Dell Publ. Co.: No. 1307, Mar-May, 1962 - No. 2, July-Sept, 1962 (Photo-c)

Four Color 1307(#1)	5	15	35	65
2	4	12	30	50

MARGIE COMICS (Formerly Comedy Comics; Reno Browne #50 on) (Also see Cindy Comics & Teen Comics)
Marvel Comics (ACI): No. 35, Winter, 1946-47 - No. 49, Dec, 1949

35	15	45	77	135
36-38,42,45,47-49	9	27	49	70
39,41,43(2),44,46-Kurtzman's "Hey Look"	10	30	55	85
40-Three "Hey Looks", three "Giggles 'n' Grins" by Kurtzman	12	36	61	100

MARINES (See Tell It to the...)

MARINES ATTACK
Charlton Comics: Aug, 1964 - No. 9, Feb-Mar, 1966

1-Glanzman-a begins	3	10	23	35
2-9	2	6	13	20

MARINES AT WAR (Formerly Tales of the Marines #4)
Atlas Comics (OPI): No. 5, Apr, 1957 - No. 7, Aug, 1957

5-7	8	24	42	60

NOTE: *Colan* a-5. *Drucker* a-5. *Everett* a-5. *Maneely* a-5. *Orlando* a-7. *Severin* c-5.

MARINES IN ACTION
Atlas News Co.: June, 1955 - No. 14, Sept, 1957

Marine War Heroes #1 © CC

The Marquis: Danse Macabre #2 © Guy Davis

Mars Attacks #2 © Topps

	GD2.0	FN6.0	VF8.0	NM9.4

1-Rock Murdock, Boot Camp Brady begin 11 33 55 90
2-14 8 24 42 60
NOTE: *Berg a-2, 8, 9, 11, 14. Heath c-2, 9. Maneely c-1. Severin a-4; c-7-11, 14.*

MARINES IN BATTLE
Atlas Comics (ACI No. 1-12/WPI No. 13-25): Aug, 1954 - No. 25, Sept, 1958
1-Heath-c; Iron Mike McGraw by Heath; history of U.S. Marine Corps. begins
 20 60 105 180
2-Heath-c 11 33 55 90
3-6,8-10: 4-Last precode (2/55) 8 24 45 65
7-Kubert/Moskowitz-a (6 pgs.) 9 27 49 70
11-16,18-21,24 8 24 42 60
17-Williamson-a (3 pgs.) 10 30 55 80
22,25-Torres-a 8 24 45 65
23-Crandall-a; Mark Murdock app. 9 27 49 70
NOTE: *Berg a-22. G. Colan a-22, 23. Drucker a-6. Everett a-4, 15; c-21. Heath c-1, 2, 4. Maneely c-23, 24. Orlando a-14. Pakula a-6, 23. Powell a-16. Severin a-22; c-12. Sinnott a-23. Tuska a-15.*

MARINE WAR HEROES (Charlton Premiere #19 on)
Charlton Comics: Jan, 1964 - No. 18, Mar, 1967
1-Montes/Bache-c/a 3 10 23 35
2-18: 14,18-Montes/Bache-a 2 6 13 20

MARK, THE (Also see Mayhem)
Dark Horse Comics: Dec, 1993 - No. 4, Mar, 1994 ($2.50, limited series)
1-4 2.50

MARK HAZZARD: MERC
Marvel Comics Group: Nov, 1986 - No. 12, Oct, 1987 (75¢)
1-12: Morrow-a, Annual 1 (11/87, $1.25) 2.25

MARK OF ZORRO (See Zorro, Four Color #228)

MARK 1 COMICS (Also see Shaloman)
Mark 1 Comics: Apr, 1988 - No. 3, Mar, 1989 ($1.50)
1-3: Early Shaloman app. 2-Origin 2.25

MARKSMAN, THE (Also see Champions)
Hero Comics: Jan, 1988 - No. 5, 1988 ($1.95)
1-5: 1-Rose begins. 1-3-Origin The Marksman 2.25
Annual 1 ('88, $2.75, 52pgs)-Champions app. 2.75

MARK TRAIL
Standard Magazines (Hall Syndicate)/Fawcett Publ. No. 5: Oct, 1955; No. 5, Summer, 1959
1(1955)-Sunday strip-r 7 21 36 50
5(1959) 5 14 21 28
...Adventure Book of Nature 1 (Summer, 1958, 25¢, Pines)-100 pg. Giant;
 Special Camp Issue; contains 78 Sunday strip-r 10 30 55 80

MARMADUKE MONK
I. W. Enterprises/Super Comics: No date; 1963 (10¢)
I.W. Reprint 1 (nd) 2 6 9 12
Super Reprint 14 (1963)-r/Monkeyshines Comics #? 2 6 9 12

MARMADUKE MOUSE
Quality Comics Group (Arnold Publ.): Spring, 1946 - No. 65, Dec, 1956 (Early issues: 52 pgs.)
1-Funny animal 18 54 94 160
2 10 30 55 80
3-10 7 21 38 55
11-30 6 18 30 42
31-65: Later issues are 36 pgs. 5 15 25 35
Super Reprint #14(1963) 2 6 10 14

MARQUIS, THE: DANSE MACABRE
Oni Press: May, 2000 - No. 5, Feb, 2001 ($2.95, B&W, limited series)
1-5-Guy Davis-s/a. 1-Wagner-c. 2-Mignola-c. 3-Vess-c. 5-K. Jones-c 3.00
TPB (8/2001, $18.95) r/1-5 & Les Preludes; Seagle intro. 19.00

MARRIAGE OF HERCULES AND XENA, THE
Topps Comics: July, 1998 ($2.95, one-shot)
1-Photo-c; Lopresti-a; Alex Ross pin-up, 1-Alex Ross painted-c 3.00
1-Gold foil logo-c 5.00

MARRIED ... WITH CHILDREN (TV)(Based on Fox TV show)
Now Comics: June, 1990 - No. 7, Feb, 1991(12/90 inside) ($1.75)
V2#1, Sept, 1991 - No. 12, 1992 ($1.95)
1-7: 2-Photo-c, 1,2-2nd printing, V2#1-12: 1,4,5,9-Photo-c 2.25
...Buck's Tale (6/94, $1.95) 2.25
...1994 Annual nn (2/94, $2.50, 52 pgs.)-Flip book format 2.50
Special 1 (7/92, $1.95)-Kelly Bundy photo-c/poster 2.25

MARRIED ... WITH CHILDREN: KELLY BUNDY
Now Comics: Aug, 1992 - No. 3, Oct, 1992 ($1.95, limited series)
1-3: Kelly Bundy photo-c & poster in each 2.25

MARRIED ... WITH CHILDREN: QUANTUM QUARTET
Now Comics: Oct, 1993 - No. 4, 1994, ($1.95, limited series)
1-4: Fantastic Four parody 2.25

MARRIED ... WITH CHILDREN: 2099
Now Comics: June, 1993 - No. 3, Aug, 1993 ($1.95, limited series)
1-3 2.25

MARS
First Comics: Jan, 1984 - No. 12, Jan, 1985 ($1.00, Mando paper)
nn: 1-12: Marc Hempel & Mark Wheatley story & art. 2-The Black Flame begins.
 10-Dynamo Joe begins 2.25

MARS & BEYOND (Disney, TV)
Dell Publishing Co.: No. 866, Dec, 1957
Four Color 866-A Science feat. from Tomorrowland 9 27 63 110

MARS ATTACKS
Topps Comics: May, 1994 - No. 5, Sept, 1994 ($2.95, limited series)
1-5-Giffen story; flip books 4.00
Special Edition 2 6 9 12
Trade paperback (12/94, $12.95)-r/limited series plus new 8 pg. story 13.00

MARS ATTACKS
Topps Comics: V2#1, 8/95 - V2#3, 10/95; V2#4, 1/96 - No. 7, 5/96($2.95, bi-monthly #6 on)
V2#1-7: 1-Counterstrike storyline begins. 4-(1/96). 5-(1/96). 5,7-Brereton-c.
 6-(3/96)-Simonson-c. 7-Story leads into Baseball Special #1
Baseball Special 1 (6/96, $2.95)-Bisley-c. 3.00

MARS ATTACKS HIGH SCHOOL
Topps Comics: May, 1997 - No. 2, Sept, 1997 ($2.95, B&W, limited series)
1,2-Stelfreeze-c 3.00

MARS ATTACKS IMAGE
Topps Comics: Dec, 1996 - No. 4, Mar, 1997 ($2.50, limited series)
1-4-Giffen-s/Smith/Sienkiewicz-a 3.00

MARS ATTACKS THE SAVAGE DRAGON
Topps Comics: Dec, 1996 - No. 4, Mar, 1997 ($2.95, limited series)
1-4: 1-w/bound-in card 3.00

MARSHAL BLUEBERRY (See Blueberry)
Marvel Comics (Epic Comics): 1991 ($14.95, graphic novel)
1-Moebius-a 15.00

MARSHAL LAW (Also see Crime And Punishment: Marshall Law...)
Marvel Comics (Epic Comics): Oct, 1987 - No. 6, May, 1989 ($1.95, mature)
1-6 2.25

M.A.R.S. PATROL TOTAL WAR (Formerly Total War #1,2)
Gold Key: No. 3, Sept, 1966 - No. 10, Aug, 1969 (All-Painted-c except #7)
3-Wood-a; aliens invade USA 5 15 35 65
4-10 3 10 23 35

MARTHA WASHINGTON (Also see Dark Horse Presents Fifth Anniversary Special, Dark Horse Presents #100-4, Give Me Liberty, Happy Birthday Martha Washington & San Diego Comicon Comics #2)

MARTHA WASHINGTON GOES TO WAR
Dark Horse Comics (Legend): May, 1994 - No. 5, Sep, 1994 ($2.95, lim. series)
1-5-Miller scripts; Gibbons-c/a 3.00
TPB ($17.95) r/#1-5 18.00

Martian Manhunter #99 © DC

Marvel Boy #2 © MAR

Marvel Classics Comics #24 © MAR

	GD2.0	FN6.0	VF8.0	NM9.4

MARTHA WASHINGTON SAVES THE WORLD
Dark Horse Comics: Dec, 1997 - No. 3, Feb, 1998 ($2.95/$3.95, lim. series)

1,2-Miller scripts; Gibbons-c/a in all				3.00
3-($3.95)				4.00

MARTHA WASHINGTON STRANDED IN SPACE
Dark Horse Comics: Nov, 1995 ($2.95, one-shot)

nn-Miller-s/Gibbons-a; Big Guy app.				3.00

MARTHA WAYNE (See The Story of...)

MARTIAN MANHUNTER (See Detective Comics & Showcase '95 #9)
DC Comics: May, 1988 - No. 4, Nov,. 1988 ($1.25, limited series)

1-4: 1,4-Batman app. 2-Batman cameo				2.50
Special 1-(1996, $3.50)				3.50

MARTIAN MANHUNTER (See JLA)
DC Comics: No. 0, Oct, 1998 - No. 36, Nov, 2001 ($1.99)

0-(10/98) Origin retold; Ostrander-s/Mandrake-c/a				3.00
1-36: 1-(12/98). 6-9-JLA app. 18,19-JSA app. 24-Mahnke-a				2.50
#1,000,000 (11/98) 853rd Century x-over				2.50
Annual 1,2 (1998,1999; $2.95) 1-Ghosts; Wrightson-c. 2-JLApe				3.00

MARTIAN MANHUNTER: AMERICAN SECRETS
DC Comics: 1992 - Book Three, 1992 ($4.95, limited series, prestige format)

1-3: Barreto-a				5.00

MARTIN KANE (William Gargan as... Private Eye)(Stage/Screen/Radio/TV)
Fox Features Syndicate (Hero Books): No. 4, June, 1950 - No. 2, Aug, 1950
(Formerly My Secret Affair)

4(#1)-True crime stories; Wood-c/a(2); used in SOTI, pg. 160; photo back-c				
	31	93	165	285
2-Wood/Orlando story, 5 pgs; Wood-a(2)	24	72	127	215

MARTIN MYSTERY
Dark Horse (Bonelli Comics): Mar, 1999 - No. 6, Aug, 1999 ($4.95, B&W, digest size)

1-6-Reprints Italian series in English; Gibbons-c on #1-3				5.00

MARTY MOUSE
I. W. Enterprises: No date (1958?) (10¢)

1-Reprint	2	6	10	14

MARVEL ACTION HOUR FEATURING IRON MAN (TV cartoon)
Marvel Comics: Nov, 1994 - No. 8, June, 1995 ($1.50/$2.95)

1-8: Based on cartoon series				2.25
1 ($2.95)-Polybagged w/16 pg Marvel Action Hour Preview & acetate print				3.00

MARVEL ACTION HOUR FEATURING THE FANTASTIC FOUR (TV cartoon)
Marvel Comics: Nov, 1994 - No. 8, June, 1995 ($1.50/$2.95)

1-8: Based on cartoon series				2.25
1-($2.95)-Polybagged w/ 16 pg. Marvel Action Hour Preview & acetate print				3.00

MARVEL ACTION UNIVERSE (TV cartoon)
Marvel Comics: Jan, 1989 ($1.00, one-shot)

1-r/Spider-Man And His Amazing Friends				2.50

MARVEL ADVENTURES
Marvel Comics: Apr, 1997 - No. 18, Sept, 1998 ($1.50)

1-18-"Animated style": 1,4,7-Hulk-c/app. 2,11-Spider-Man. 3,8,15-X-Men. 5-Spider-Man & X-Men. 6-Spider-Man & Human Torch. 9,12-Fantastic Four. 10,16-Silver Surfer. 13-Spider-Man & Silver Surfer. 14-Hulk & Dr. Strange 18-Capt. America				2.25

MARVEL ADVENTURES STARRING DAREDEVIL (...Adventure #3 on)
Marvel Comics Group: Dec, 1975 - No. 6, Oct, 1976

1	1	4	7	10
2-6-r/Daredevil #22-27 by Colan. 3-5-(25¢-c)				6.00
3-5-(30¢-c variants, limited distribution)(4,6,8/76)	1	3	6	9

MARVEL AND DC PRESENT FEATURING THE UNCANNY X-MEN AND THE NEW TEEN TITANS
Marvel Comics/DC Comics: 1982 ($2.00, 68 pgs., one-shot, Baxter paper)

1-3rd app. Deathstroke the Terminator; Darkseid app.; Simonson/Austin-c/a				
	2	6	12	18

MARVEL BOY (Astonishing #3 on; see Marvel Super Action #4)
Marvel Comics (MPC): Dec, 1950 - No. 2, Feb, 1951

1-Origin Marvel Boy by Russ Heath	105	315	656	1150
2-Everett-a	75	225	469	825

MARVEL BOY (Marvel Knights)
Marvel Comics: Aug, 2000 - No. 6, Mar, 2001 ($2.99, limited series)

1-Intro. Marvel Boy; Morrison-s/J.G. Jones-c/a				3.50
1-DF Variant-c				5.00
2-6				3.00
TPB (6/01, $15.95)				16.00

MARVEL CHILLERS (Also see Giant-Size Chillers)
Marvel Comics Group: Oct, 1975 - No. 7, Oct, 1976 (All 25¢ issues)

1-Intro. Modred the Mystic, ends #2; Kane-c(p)	2	6	9	12
2,4,5,7: 4-Kraven app. 5,6-Red Wolf app. 7-Kirby-c; Tuska-p	1	3	5	7
3-Tigra, the Were-Woman begins (origin), ends #7 (see Giant-Size Creatures #1). Chaykin/Wrightson-c.	2	6	12	18
4-6-(30¢-c variants, limited distribution)(4-8/76)	2	6	9	12
6-Byrne-a(p); Buckler/c(p)	1	3	6	9

NOTE: Bolle a-1. Buckler c-2. Kirby c-7.

MARVEL CLASSICS COMICS SERIES FEATURING... (Also see Pendulum Illustrated Classics)
Marvel Comics Group: 1976 - No. 36, Dec, 1978 (52 pgs., no ads)

1-Dr. Jekyll and Mr. Hyde	2	6	11	16
2-10,28: 28-1st Golden-c/a; Pit and the Pendulum	2	6	9	12
11-27,29-36	1	3	6	9

NOTE: Adkins c-1i, 4i, 12i. Alcala a-34i; c-34. Bolle a-35. Buscema c-17p, 19p, 26p. Golden c/a-28. Gil Kane c-1-16i, 21p, 22p, 24p, 32p. Nebres a-5; c-24i. Nino a-2, 8, 12. Redondo a-1, 9. No. 1-12 were reprinted from Pendulum Illustrated Classics.

MARVEL COLLECTIBLE CLASSICS: AVENGERS
Marvel Comics: 1998 ($10.00, reprints with chromium wraparound-c)

1-Reprints Avengers Vol.3, #1; Perez-c/a				10.00

MARVEL COLLECTIBLE CLASSICS: SPIDER-MAN
Marvel Comics: 1998 ($10.00, reprints with chromium wraparound-c)

1-Reprints Amazing Spider-Man #300; McFarlane-c				10.00
2-Reprints Spider-Man #1; McFarlane-c				10.00

MARVEL COLLECTIBLE CLASSICS: X-MEN
Marvel Comics: 1998 ($10.00, reprints with chromium wraparound-c)

1-6: 1-Reprints (Uncanny) X-Men #1 & 2; Adam Kubert-c. 2-Reprints Uncanny X-Men #141 & 142; Byrne-c. 3-Reprints (Uncanny) X-Men #137; Larroca-c. 4-Reprints X-Men #25; Andy Kubert-c. 5-Reprints Giant Size X-Men #1; Gary Frank-c. 6-Reprints X-Men V2#1; Ramos-c				10.00

MARVEL COLLECTOR'S EDITION
Marvel Comics: 1992 (Ordered thru mail with Charleston Chew candy wrapper)

1-Flip-book format; Spider-Man, Silver Surfer, Wolverine (by Sam Kieth), & Ghost Rider stories; Wolverine back-c by Kieth				3.00

MARVEL COLLECTORS' ITEM CLASSICS (Marvel's Greatest #23 on)
Marvel Comics Group(ATF): Feb, 1965 - No. 22, Aug, 1969 (25¢, 68 pgs.)

1-Fantastic Four, Spider-Man, Thor, Hulk, Iron Man-r begin				
	9	27	65	110
2 (4/66)	5	15	34	55
3,4	4	12	26	40
5-10	3	9	21	32
11-22: 22-r/The Man in the Ant Hill/TTA #27	3	9	17	24

NOTE: All reprints; Ditko, Kirby art in all.

MARVEL COMICS (Marvel Mystery Comics #2 on)
Timely Comics (Funnies, Inc.): Oct, Nov, 1939

NOTE: The first issue was originally dated October 1939. Most copies have a black circle stamped over the date (on cover and inside) with "November" printed over it. However, some copies do not have the November overprint and could have a higher value. Most No. 1's have printing defects, i.e., tilted pages which caused trimming into the panels usually on right side and bottom. Covers exist with and without gloss finish.

1-Origin Sub-Mariner by Bill Everett(1st newsstand app.); 1st 8 pgs. were pro-

Marvel Comics Presents #3 © MAR

Marvel Double Feature #15 © MAR

Marvel Family #10 © FAW

| | GD2.0 | FN6.0 | VF8.0 | NM9.4 | | GD2.0 | FN6.0 | VF8.0 | NM9.4 |

duced for Motion Picture Funnies Weekly #1 which was probably not distributed outside of advance copies; intro Human Torch by Carl Burgos, Kazar the Great (1st Tarzan clone), & Jungle Terror(only app.); intro. The Angel by Gustavson, The Masked Raider & his horse Lightning (ends #12); cover by sci/fi pulp illustrator Frank R. Paul   16,667   50,000   116,000   250,000

MARVEL COMICS PRESENTS

Marvel Comics (Midnight Sons imprint #143 on): Early Sept, 1988 - No. 175, Feb, 1995 ($1.25/$1.50/$1.75, bi-weekly)

1-Wolverine by Buscema in #1-10 ..... 6.00
2-5 ..... 4.00
6-10: 6-Sub-Mariner app. 10-Colossus begins 3.00
11-47,51-71: 17-Cyclops begins. 19-1st app. Damage Control. 24-Havok begins. 25-Origin/1st app. Nth Man. 26-Hulk begins by Rogers. 29-Quasar app. 31-Excalibur begins by Austin (i). 32-McFarlane-a(p). 37-Devil-Slayer app. 33-Capt. America; Jim Lee-a. 38-Wolverine begins by Buscema; Hulk app. 39-Spider-Man app. 46-Liefeld Wolverine-c. 51-53-Wolverine by Rob Liefeld. 54-61-Wolverine/Hulk story: 54-Werewolf by Night begins; The Shroud by Ditko. 58-Iron Man by Ditko. 59-Punisher. 62-Deathlok & Wolverine stories 63-Wolverine. 64-71-Wolverine/Ghost Rider 8-part story. 70-Liefeld Ghost Rider/Wolverine-c 2.50
48-50-Wolverine & Spider-Man team-up by Erik Larsen-c/a. 48-Wasp app. 49, 50-Savage Dragon prototype app. by Larsen. 50-Silver Surfer. 50-53-Comet Man; Bill Mumy scripts 4.00
72-Begin13-part Weapon-X story (Wolverine origin) by B. Windsor-Smith (prologue) 5.00
73-Weapon-X part 1; Black Knight, Sub-Mariner 4.00
74-84: 74-Weapon-X part 2; Black Knight, Sub-Mariner. 76-Death's Head story. 77-Mr. Fantastic story. 78-Iron Man by Steacy. 80,81-Capt. America by Ditko/Austin. 81-Daredevil by Rogers/Williamson. 82-Power Man. 83-Human Torch by Ditko(a&scripts); $1.00-c direct, $1.25 newsstand. 84-Last Weapon-X(24 pg. conclusion) 4.00
85-Begin 8-part Wolverine story by Sam Kieth (c/a); 1st Kieth-a on Wolverine; begin 8-part Beast story by Jae Lee(p) with Liefeld part pencils #85,86; 1st Jae Lee-a (assisted w/Liefeld, 1991) 4.00
86-90: 86-89-Wolverine, Beast stories continue. 90-Begin 8-part Ghost Rider & Cable story, ends #97; begin flip book format w/two-c 3.00
91-175: 93-Begin 6-part Wolverine story, ends #98. 98-Begin 2-part Ghost Rider story. 99-Spider-Man story. 101-Begin 6-part Ghost Rider/Dr. Strange story & begin 8-part Wolverine/Nightcrawler story by Colan/Williamson; Punisher story. 107-Begin 6-part Ghost Rider/Werewolf by Night story. 112-Demogoblin story by Colan/Williamson; Pip the Troll story w/Starlin scripts & Gamora cameo. 113-Begin 6-part Giant-Man & begin 6-part Ghost Rider/Iron Fist stories. 100-Full-length Ghost Rider/Wolverine story by Sam Kieth w/Tim Vigil assists; anniversary issue, non flip-book. 108-Begin 4-part Thanos story; Starlin scripts. 109-Begin 8 part Wolverine/Typhoid Mary story. 111-Iron Fist. 117-Preview of Ravage 2099 (1st app.). 118-Preview of Doom 2099 (1st app.). 119-Begin Ghost Rider/Cloak & Dagger story by Colan. 120,136,138-Spider-Man. 123-Begin 8-part Ghost Rider/Typhoid Mary story; begin 4-part She Hulk story; begin 8-part Wolverine/Lynx story. 125-Begin 6-part Iron Fist story. 129-Jae Lee back-c. 130-Begin 6-part Ghost Rider/ Cage story. 131-Begin 6-part Ghost Rider/ Cage story. 132-Begin 5-part Wolverine story. 133-136-Iron Fist vs. Sabretooth. 136-Daredevil. 137-Begin 6-part Wolverine story & 6-part Ghost Rider story. 147-Begin 2-part Vengeance-c/story w/new Ghost Rider. 149-Vengeance-c/story w/new Ghost Rider. 150-Silver ink-c; begin 2-part Bloody Mary story w/Typhoid Mary,Wolverine, Daredevil, new Ghost Rider; intro Steel Raven. 152-Begin 4-part Wolverine, 4-part War Machine, 4-part Vengeance, 3-part Moon Knight stories; same date as War Machine #1. 143-146: Siege of Darkness parts 3,6,11,14; all have spot-varnished-c. 143-Ghost Rider/Scarlet Witch; intro new Werewolf. 144-Ghost Rider story w/Morbius app. 145-Begin 2-part Nightstalkers story. 153-155-Bound-in Spider-Man trading card sheet 2.50
...Colossus: God's Country (1994, $6.95) r/#10-17 ..... 1 3 5 7
NOTE: *Austin* a-31-37; c(i)-48, 50, 99, 122. *Buscema* a-31-39, 38-47; c-6. *Byrne* a-79, c-71. *Colan* a(p)-36, 37, *Colan/Williamson* a-101-108. *Ditko* a-7p, 10, 56p, 58, 80, 81, 83. *Guice* a-62. *Sam Kieth* a-85-92, 117-122; c-85-98, 99p, 100-108, 117, 118, 120-122; back c-109-113, 117. *Jae Lee* c-129(back). *Liefeld* a-51, 52, 53p(2), 85p; c-46, 70. *McFarlane* c-32. *Mooney* a-73. *Rogers* a-26, 38, 46i, 81p. *Russell* a-10-14,16,17i; c-4,19, 30,31i. *Saltares* a-8p(early), 38-45p. *Simonson* c-1. *B. Smith* a-72-84; c-72-84. *P. Smith* c-34. *Sparling* a-33. *Starlin* a-89i. *Staton* a-74. *Steacy* a-78. *Sutton* a-101-105. *Williamson* c-62i. Two Gun Kid by Gil Kane in #116, 122.

MARVEL COMICS SUPER SPECIAL, A (Marvel Super Special #5 on)
Marvel Comics: Sept, 1977 - No. 41(?), Nov, 1986 (nn 7) ($1.50, magazine)

1-Kiss, 40 pgs. comics plus photos & features; Simonson-a(p); also see Howard the Duck #12; ink contains real KISS blood; Dr. Doom, Spider-Man, Avengers, Fantastic Four, Mephisto app.	12	36	84	140

1-Kiss, 40 pgs. comics plus photos & features; Simonson-a(p); also see Howard the Duck #12; ink contains real KISS blood; Dr. Doom, Spider-Man, Avengers, Fantastic Four, Mephisto app. 12 36 84 140
2-Conan (1978) 2 6 11 15
3-Close Encounters of the Third Kind (1978); Simonson-a 1 4 7 10
4-The Beatles Story (1978)-Perez/Janson-a; has photos & articles 4 12 26 40
5-Kiss (1978)-Includes poster 12 36 84 140
6-Jaws II (1978) 1 4 7 10
7-Sgt. Pepper; Beatles movie adaptation; withdrawn from U.S. distribution 12 36 84 140
8-Battlestar Galactica; tabloid size ($1.50, 1978); adapts TV show 2 6 12 18
8-Modern-r of tabloid size 2 6 12 18
8-Battlestar Galactica; publ. in regular magazine format; low distribution ($1.50, 8-1/2x11") 1 6 12 18
9-Conan 1 4 7 10
10-Star-Lord 1 4 7 10
11-13-Weirdworld begins #11; 25 copy special press run of each with gold seal and signed by artists (Proof quality), Spring-June, 1979 ..... 9 27 63 105
11-15: 11-13-Weirdworld (regular issues): 11-Fold-out centerfold. 14-Miller-c(p); adapts movie "Meteor." 15-Star Trek with photos & pin-ups ($1.50-c) 1 3 6 8
15-With $2.00 price (scarce); the price was changed at tail end of a 200,000 press run 1 4 7 10
16-Empire Strikes Back adaption; Williamson-a 1 4 7 10
17-20 (Movie adaptations):17-Xanadu. 18-Raiders of the Lost Ark. 19-For Your Eyes Only (James Bond). 20-Dragonslayer 6.00
21-26,28-30 (Movie adaptations): 21-Conan. 22-Blade Runner; Williamson-a; Steranko-c. 23-Annie. 24-The Dark Crystal. 25-Rock and Rule-photos; artwork is from movie. 26-Octopussy (James Bond). 28-Krull; photo-c. 29-Tarzan of the Apes (Greystoke movie). 30-Indiana Jones and the Temple of Doom 1 3 5 7
27,31-41: 27-Return of the Jedi. 31-The Last Star Fighter. 32-The Muppets Take Manhattan. 33-Buckaroo Banzai. 34-Sheena. 35-Conan The Destroyer. 36-Dune. 37-2010. 38-Red Sonja. 39-Santa Claus: The Movie. 40-Labyrinth. 41-Howard The Duck 1 3 6 8
NOTE: *J. Buscema* a-1, 2, 9, 11-13, 18p, 21, 35, 40; c-11(part). 12. *Chaykin* a-9, 19p; c-18, 19. *Colan* a(p)-6, 10, 14. *Morrow* a-34; c-1i, 34. *Nebres* a-11. *Spiegle* a-29. *Stevens* a-27. *Williamson* a-27. #22-28 contain photos from movies.

MARVEL COMICS: 2001
Marvel Comics: 2001 (no cover price, one-shot)

1-Previews new titles for Fall 2001; Wolverine-c 2.00

MARVEL DOUBLE FEATURE
Marvel Comics Group: Dec, 1973 - No. 21, Mar, 1977

1-Capt. America, Iron Man-r/T.O.S. begin 2 6 10 14
2-10: 3-Last 20¢ issue 1 3 6 8
11-17,20,21:17-Story-c/Iron Man & Sub-Mariner #1; last 25¢ issue 6.00
15-17-(30¢-c variants, limited distribution)(4,6,8/76) 1 3 6 9
18,19-Colan/Craig-r from Iron Man #1 in both 1 3 5 7
NOTE: *Colan* r-1-19p. *Craig* r-17-19i. *G. Kane* r-15p; c-15p. *Kirby* r-1-16p, 20, 21; c-17-20.

MARVEL FAMILY (Also see Captain Marvel Adventures No. 18)
Fawcett Publications: Dec, 1945 - No. 89, Jan, 1954

1-Origin Captain Marvel, Captain Marvel Jr., Mary Marvel, & Uncle Marvel retold; origin/1st app. Black Adam 164 492 1023 1800
2-The 3 Lt. Marvels & Uncle Marvel app. 75 225 469 825
3 ..... 55 165 330 575
4,5 ..... 43 129 257 450
6-10: 7-Shazam app. 39 117 208 360
11-20 ..... 29 87 156 270
21-30 ..... 25 75 130 225
31-40 ..... 23 63 110 190
41-46,48-50 ..... 17 51 88 150
47-Flying Saucer-c/story (5/50) 22 66 116 200
51-76,79,80,82-89: 79-Horror satire-c 15 45 77 135
77-Communist Threat-c 24 72 127 220

	GD2.0	FN6.0	VF8.0	NM9.4

	GD2.0	FN6.0	VF8.0	NM9.4

78,81-Used in **POP**, pg. 92,93.   16   48   83   140

MARVEL FANFARE (1st Series)
Marvel Comics Group: March, 1982 - No. 60, Jan, 1992 ($1.25/$2.25, slick paper, direct sales)

1-Spider-Man/Angel team-up; 1st Paul Smith-a (1st full story; see King Conan #7); Daredevil app.   6.00
2-Spider-Man, Ka-Zar, The Angel. F.F. origin retold   5.00
3,4-X-Men & Ka-Zar. 4-Deathlok, Spidey app.   4.00
5-14,16-23,25-32,34-44,46-50: 5-Dr. Strange, Capt. America. 6-Spider-Man, Scarlet Witch. 7-Incredible Hulk; D.D. back-up(see also 15). 8-Dr. Strange; Wolf Boy begins. 9-Man-Thing. 10-13-Black Widow. 14-The Vision. 16,17-Skywolf. 16-Sub-Mariner back-up. 17-Hulk back-up. 18-Capt. America by Miller. 19-Cloak and Dagger. 20-Thing/Dr. Strange. 21-Thing/Dr. Strange /Hulk. 22,23-Iron Man vs. Dr. Octopus. 25,26-Weirdworld. 27-Daredevil/Spider-Man. 28-Alpha Flight. 29-Hulk. 30-Moon Knight. 31,32-Capt. America. 34-37-Warriors Three. 38-Moon Knight/Dazzler. 39-Moon Knight/Hawkeye. 40-Angel/Rogue & Storm. 41-Dr. Strange. 42-Spider-Man. 43-Sub-Mariner/Human Torch. 44-Iron Man vs. Dr. Doom by Ken Steacy. 46-Fantastic Four. 47-Hulk. 48-She-Hulk/Vision. 49-Dr. Strange/Nick Fury. 50-X-Factor   2.50
15,24,33,45: 15-The Thing by Barry Smith, c/a. 24-Weirdworld; Wolverine back-up. 33-X-Men, Wolverine app.; Punisher pin-up. 45-All pin-up issue by Steacy, Art Adams & others   4.00
51-($2.95, 52 pgs.)-Silver Surfer; Fantastic Four & Capt. Marvel app.;
51,52-Colan/Williamson back-up (Dr. Strange)   3.00
52,53,56-60: 52,53-Black Knight; 53-Iron Man back up. 56-59-Shanna the She-Devil. 58-Vision & Scarlet Witch back-up. 60-Black Panther/Rogue/Daredevil stories   2.50
54,55-Wolverine back-ups. 54-Black Knight. 55-Power Pack   4.00
NOTE: **Art Adams** c-13. **Austin** a-1i, 4i, 33i, 38i; c-8i, 33i. **Buscema** a-51p. **Byrne** a-1p, 29, 48; c-29. **Chiodo** painted c-56-59. **Colan** a-51p. **Cowan/Simonson** c/a-60. **Golden** a-1, 2, 4p, 47; c-1, 2, 47. **Infantino** c/a(p)-8. **Gil Kane** a-3-11p. **Miller** a-18; c-17(Back-c), 18. **Perez** a-10, 11p, 12, 13p; c-10-13p. **Rogers** a-5p; c-5p. **Russell** a-5i, 6i, 8-11i, 43i; c-5i, 6. **Paul Smith** a-1p, 4p, 32, 60; c-4p. **Staton** c/a-50(p). **Williamson** a-30i, 51i.

MARVEL FANFARE (2nd Series)
Marvel Comics: Sept, 1996 - No. 6, Feb, 1997 (99¢)

1-6: 1-Capt. America & The Falcon-c/story; Deathlok app. 2-Wolverine & Hulk-c/app. 3-Ghost Rider & Vengeance-c/app. 5-Longshot-c/app. 6-Sabretooth, Power Man, & Iron Fist-c/app   2.25

MARVEL FEATURE (See Marvel Two-In-One)
Marvel Comics Group: Dec, 1971 - No. 12, Nov, 1973 (1,2: 25¢, 52 pg. giants) (#1-3: quarterly)

1-Origin/1st app. The Defenders (Sub-Mariner, Hulk & Dr. Strange); see Sub-Mariner #34,35 for prequel; Dr. Strange solo story (predates D.S. #1) plus 1950s Sub-Mariner-r; Neal Adams-c   15   45   105   180
2-2nd app. Defenders; 1950s Sub-Mariner-r. Rutland, Vermont Halloween x-over   7   21   50   80
3-Defenders begin   5   15   34   55
4-Re-intro Antman (1st app. since 1960s), begin series; brief origin; Spider-Man app.   3   9   17   25
5-7,9,10: 6-Wasp app. & begins team-ups. 9-Iron Man app.
10-Last Antman   2   6   9   12
8-Origin Antman & Wasp-r/TTA #44; Kirby-a   2   6   11   15
11-Thing vs. Hulk; 1st Thing solo book (9/73); origin Fantastic Four retold   4   12   30   50
12-Thing/Iron Man; early Thanos app.; occurs after Capt. Marvel #33;
Starlin-a(p)   5   15   22
NOTE: **Bolle** a-9i. **Everett** a-1i, 3i. **Hartley** r-10. **Kane** c-3p, 7p. **Russell** a-7-10p. **Starlin** a-8, 11, 12; c-8.

MARVEL FEATURE (Also see Red Sonja)
Marvel Comics: Nov, 1975 - No. 7, Nov, 1976 (Story cont'd in Conan #68)

1,7: 1-Red Sonja begins (pre-dates Red Sonja #1); adapts Howard short story; Adams-r/Savage Sword of Conan #1. 7-Battles Conan   1   3   6   8
2-6: Thorne-c/a in #2-7. 4,5-(Regular 25¢ edition)(5,7/76)   5.00
4,5-(30¢-c variants, limited distribution)   1   3   5   7

MARVEL FRONTIER COMICS UNLIMITED
Marvel Frontier Comics: Jan, 1994 ($2.95, 68 pgs.)

1-Dances with Demons, Immortalis, Children of the Voyager, Evil Eye, The

Fallen stories   3.00

MARVEL FUMETTI BOOK
Marvel Comics Group: Apr, 1984 ($1.00, one-shot)

1-All photos; Stan Lee photo-c; Art Adams touch-ups   4.00

MARVEL FUN & GAMES
Marvel Comics Group: 1979/80 (color comic for kids)

1,11: 1-Games, puzzles, etc. 11-X-Men-c   1   3   6   8
2-10,12,13: (beware marked pages)   6.00

MARVEL GRAPHIC NOVEL
Marvel Comics Group (Epic Comics): 1982 - No. 38, 1990? ($5.95/$6.95)

1-Death of Captain Marvel (2nd Marvel graphic novel); Capt. Marvel battles Thanos by Jim Starlin (c/a/scripts)   2   6   12   18
1 (2nd & 3rd printings)   1   3   6   8
2-Elric: The Dreaming City   2   6   9   12
3-Dreadstar; Starlin-c/a, 52 pgs.   2   6   9   12
4-Origin/1st app. The New Mutants (1982)   2   6   10   14
4,5-2nd printings   1   3   5   7
5-X-Men; book-length story (1982)   2   6   12   18
6-17,20,21,23-25,29-31: 6-The Star Slammers. 7-Killraven. 8-Super Boxers; Byrne scripts. 9-The Futurians. 10-Heartburst. 11-Void Indigo. 12-Dazzler. 13-Starstruck. 14-The Swords Of The Swashbucklers. 15-The Raven Banner (a tale of Asgard). 16-The Aladdin Effect (Storm, Tigra, Wasp, She-Hulk). 17-Revenge Of The Living Monolith (Spider-Man, Avengers, FF app.). 20-Greenberg the Vampire. 21-Marada the She-Wolf. 23-Dr. Strange. 24-Love and War (Daredevil); Miller scripts. 25-Alien Legion. 29-The Big Chance (Thing vs. Hulk). 30-A Sailor's Story. 31-Wolfpack
  1   3   6   9
18,19,26-28: 18-She Hulk. 19-Witch Queen of Acheron (Conan). 26-Dracula. 27-Avengers (Emperor Doom). 28-Conan the Reaver
  2   6   9   12
22-Amaz. Spider-Man in Hooky by Wrightson   2   6   10   14
32-Death of Groo   2   6   9   12
32-2nd printing ($5.95)   1   3   6   8
33,34,36,37: 33-Thor. 34-Predator & Prey (Cloak & Dagger). 36-Willow (movie adapt.). 37-Hercules   1   3   6   9
35-Hitler's Astrologer (The Shadow, $12.95, HC)   2   6   11   16
35-Soft-c reprint (1990, $10.95)   2   6   9   12
38-Silver Surfer (Judgement Day)($14.95, HC)   2   6   11   16
38-Soft-c reprint (1990, $10.95)   2   6   9   12
nn-Absolm Daak: Dalak Killer (1990, $8.95) Dr. Who   1   4   7   10
nn-Arena for Jove Jones (1989, $5.95) Dinosaurs   1   3   6   8
nn- A-Team Storybook Comics Illustrated (1983) r/ A-Team mini-series #1-3
  1   4   7   10
nn-Ax (1988, $5.95) Ernie Colan-s/a   1   4   7   10
nn-Black Widow Coldest War (4/90, $9.95)   2   6   9   12
nn-Chronicles of Genghis Grimtoad (1990, $8.95)-Alan Grant-s
  1   4   7   10
nn-Conan the Barbarian in the Horn of Azoth (1990, $8.95)
  2   6   9   12
nn-Conan of Isles ($8.95)   2   6   9   12
nn-Conan Ravagers of Time (1992, $9.95) Kull & Red Sonja app.
  2   6   9   12
nn-Conan -The Skull of Set   2   6   9   12
nn-Doctor Strange and Doctor Doom Triumph and Torment (1989, $17.95, HC)
  2   6   15   22
nn-Dreamwalker (1989, $6.95)-Morrow-a   1   3   6   9
nn-Excalibur Weird War III (1990, $9.95)   2   6   9   12
nn-G.I. Joe - The Trojan Gambit (1983, 68 pgs.)   1   4   7   10
nn-Harvey Kurtzman Strange Adventures (Epic, $19.95, HC) Aragonés, Crumb
  3   9   17   25
nn-Hearts and Minds (1990, $8.95) Heath-a   1   4   7   10
nn-Inhumans (1988, $7.95)-Williamson-i   1   3   6   9
nn-Jhereg (Epic, 1990, $8.95)   1   4   7   10
nn-Kazar-Guns of the Savage Land (7/90, $8.95)   1   4   7   10
nn-Kull-The Vale of Shadow ('89, $6.95)   1   4   7   10
nn-Last of the Dragons (1988, $9.95) Austin-a(i)   1   3   5   7
nn-Nightraven: House of Cards (1991, $14.95)   2   6   11   15
nn-Nightraven: The Collected Stories (1990, $9.95) Bolton-r/British Hulk mag.;

Marvel Knights #5 © MAR

Marvel Mystery Comics #7 © MAR

Marvel Mystery Comics #49 © MAR

	GD2.0	FN6.0	VF8.0	NM9.4

	GD2.0	FN6.0	VF8.0	NM9.4

David Lloyd-c/a 2 6 9 12
nn-Original Adventures of Cholly and Flytrap (Epic, 1991, $9.95)
Suydam-s/c/a 2 6 11 15
nn-Rick Mason Agent (1989, $9.95) 1 4 7 10
nn-Roger Rabbit In The Resurrection Of Doom (1989, $8.95)
    1 4 7 10
nn-A Sailor's Story Book II: Winds, Dreams and Dragons ('86, $6.95, softcover)
    1 4 7 10
nn-Squadron Supreme: Death of a Universe (1989, $9.95) Gruenwald-s;
    Ryan & Williamson-a 1 4 7 10
nn-Who Framed Roger Rabbit (1989, $6.95) 1 4 7 10
NOTE: **Aragones** a-27, 32. **Buscema** a-38. **Byrne** c/a-18. **Heath** a-35i. **Kaluta** a-13, 35p; c-13.
Miller a-24p. **Simonson** a-6; c-6. **Starlin** c/a-1,3. **Williamson** a-34. **Wrightson** c-29i.

MARVEL-HEROES & LEGENDS
Marvel Comics: Oct, 1996; 1997 ($2.95)
nn-Wraparound-c, ...1997 ($2.99) -Original Avengers story 3.00

MARVEL HOLIDAY SPECIAL
Marvel Comics: No. 1, 1991 ($2.25, 84 pgs.) - 1996
1-X-Men, Fantastic Four, Punisher, Thor, Capt. America, Ghost Rider, Capt.
    Ultra, Spidey stories; Art Adams-c/a 3.00
nn (1/93)-Wolverine, Thanos (by Starlin/Lim/Austin) 3.00
nn (1994)-Capt. America, X-Men, Silver Surfer 3.00
...1996-Spider-Man by Waid & Olliffe; X-Men, Silver Surfer 3.00
NOTE: **Art Adams** c-'93. **Golden** a-'93. **Perez** c-'94.

MARVEL ILLUSTRATED: SWIMSUIT ISSUE (See Marvel Swimsuit Spec.)
Marvel Comics: 1991 ($3.95, magazine, 52 pgs.)
V1#1-Parody of Sports Illustrated swimsuit issue; Mary Jane Parker
    centerfold pin-up by Jusko; 2nd print exists 1 3 5 7

MARVEL KNIGHTS (See Black Panther, Daredevil, Inhumans, & Punisher)
Marvel Comics: 1998 (Previews for upcoming series)
Sketchbook-Wizard suppl.; Quesada & Palmiotti-c 3.00
Tourbook-($2.99) Interviews and art previews 3.00

MARVEL KNIGHTS
Marvel Comics: July, 2000 - No. 15, Sept, 2001 ($2.99)
1-Daredevil, Punisher, Black Widow, Shang-Chi, Dagger app. 4.00
2-15: 2-Two covers by Barreto & Quesada 3.00
.../Marvel Boy Genesis Edition (6/00) Sketchbook preview 2.25
...: Millennial Visions (2/02, $3.99) Pin-ups by various; Harris-c 3.00

MARVEL KNIGHTS MAGAZINE
Marvel Comics: May, 2001 - No. 6, Oct, 2001 ($3.99, magazine size)
1-6-Reprints of recent Daredevil, Punisher, Black Widow, Inhumans 4.00

MARVEL MASTERPIECES COLLECTION, THE
Marvel Comics: May, 1993 - No. 4, Aug, 1993 ($2.95, coated paper, lim. series)
1-4-Reprints Marvel Masterpieces trading cards w/ new Jusko paintings in
    in each; Jusko painted-c/a 3.00

MARVEL MASTERPIECES 2 COLLECTION, THE
Marvel Comics: July, 1994 - No. 3, Sept, 1994 ($2.95, limited series)
1-3: 1-Kaluta-c; r/trading cards; new Steranko centerfold 3.00

MARVEL MILESTONE EDITION
Marvel Comics: 1991 - Present ($2.95, coated stock)(r/originals with original ads
w/silver ink-c)
...: X-Men #1-Reprints X-Men #1 (1991) 3.00
...: Giant Size X-Men #1-(1991, $3.95, 68 pgs.) 4.00
...: Fantastic Four #1 (11/91), ...: Incredible Hulk #1 (3/92, says 3/91 by error),
    ...: Amazing Fantasy #15 (3/92), ...: Fantastic Four #5 (11/92), ...: Amazing
    Spider-Man #129 (11/92), ...: Iron Man #55 (11/92), ...: Iron Fist #14 (11/92)
    ...: Amazing Spider-Man #1 (1/93) varia tion- no price on-c, ...: Tales of Suspense #39 (3/93), ...: Avengers #1 (9/93)
    ...: X-Men #9 (10/93), ...: Avengers #16 (10/93), ...:Amazing Spider-Man
    #149 (11/94, $2.95), ...:X-Men #28 (11/94, $2.95) 3.00
...:Captain America #1 (3/95, $3.95) 4.00
...:Amazing Spider-Man #3 (3/95, $2.95), ...:Avengers #4 (3/95, $2.95),
    ...:Strange Tales-r/Dr. Strange stories from #110, 111, 114, & 115 3.00
.....:Hulk #181 (8/99, $2.99) 3.00

MARVEL MINI-BOOKS (See Promotional Comics section)

MARVEL MOVIE PREMIERE (Magazine)
Marvel Comics Group: Sept, 1975 (B&W, one-shot)
1-Burroughs' "The Land That Time Forgot" adapt. 1 4 7 10

MARVEL MOVIE SHOWCASE FEATURING STAR WARS
Marvel Comics Group: Nov, 1982 - No. 2, Dec, 1982 ($1.25, 68 pgs.)
1,2-Star Wars movie adaptation; reprints Star Wars #1-6 by Chaykin,
    1-Reprints-c to Star Wars #1. 2-Stevens-r 4.00

MARVEL MOVIE SPOTLIGHT FEATURING RAIDERS OF THE LOST ARK
Marvel Comics Group: Nov, 1982 ($1.25, 68 pgs.)
1-Edited-r/Raiders of the Lost Ark #1-3; Buscema-c/a(p); movie adapt. 3.00

MARVEL MYSTERY COMICS (Formerly Marvel Comics) (Becomes Marvel Tales No. 93 on)
Timely /Marvel Comics (TP #2-17/TCI #18-54/MCI #55-92): No. 2, Dec, 1939 - No. 92, June, 1949

	GD2.0	FN6.0	VF8.0	NM9.4
2-(Rare)-American Ace begins, ends #3; Human Torch (blue costume) by Burgos, Sub-Mariner by Everett continue; 2 pg. origin recap of Human Torch	2107	6321	14,750	29,500
3-New logo from Marvel pulp begins; 1st app. of television in comics? in Human Torch story (1/40)	1071	3214	7500	15,000
4-Intro. Electro, the Marvel of the Age (ends #19), The Ferret, Mystery Detective (ends #9); 1st Sub-Mariner-c by Schomburg; 1st Nazi war-c on a comic book & 1st German flag (Swastika) on-c of a comic (2/40)	1000	3000	6500	13,000
5 Classic Schomburg-c (Scarce)	1700	5100	11,900	23,800
6,7-1st Sub-Mariner war story	577	1731	3750	7500
8-1st Human Torch & Sub-Mariner battle(6/40)	885	2655	5750	11,500
9-(Scarce)-Human Torch & Sub-Mariner battle (cover/story); classic-c	2000	6000	14,000	28,000
10-Human Torch & Sub-Mariner battle, conclusion; Terry Vance, the Schoolboy Sleuth begins, ends #57	600	1800	4200	7800
11	317	951	1979	3800
12-Classic Kirby-c	375	1125	2344	4500
13-Intro. & 1st app. The Vision by S&K (11/40); Sub-Mariner dons new costume, ends #15	446	1338	2900	5800
14-16: 14-Shows-c to Human Torch #1 on-c (12/40). 15-S&K Vision, Gustavson Angel story	236	708	1477	2600
17-Human Torch/Sub-Mariner team-up by Burgos/Everett; pin-up on back-c; shows-c to Human Torch #2 on-c	273	810	1705	3000
18	218	654	1364	2400
19,20: 19-Origin Toro in text; shows-c to Sub-Mariner #1 on-c. 20-Origin The Angel in text	227	681	1420	2500
21-The Patriot begins, (intro. in Human Torch #4 (#3)); not in #46-48; pin-up on back-c (7/41)	218	654	1364	2400
22-25: 23-Last Gustavson Angel; origin The Vision in text. 24-Injury-to-eye story	191	573	1194	2100
26-30: 27-Ka-Zar ends; last S&K Vision who battles Satan. 28-Jimmy Jupiter in the Land of Nowhere begins, ends #48; Sub-Mariner vs. The Flying Dutchman. 30-1st Japanese war-c	173	519	1080	1900
31-33,35,36,38,39: 31-Sub-Mariner by Everett ends, resumes #84. 32-1st app. The Boboes	155	465	966	1700
34-Everett, Burgos, Martin Goodman, Funnies, Inc. office appear in story & battles Hitler; last Burgos Human Torch	173	519	1080	1900
37-Classic Hitler-c	173	519	1080	1900
40-Classic Zeppelin-c	164	492	1023	1800
41-43,45,47,48: 48-Last Vision; flag-c	127	381	795	1400
44-Classic Super Plane-c	141	423	881	1550
46-Classic Hitler-c	141	423	881	1550
49-Origin Miss America	168	505	1050	1850
50-Mary becomes Miss Patriot (origin)	136	408	852	1500
51-60: 54-Bondage-c. 60-Last Japanese war-c	118	355	738	1300
61,62,64-Last German war-c	114	342	713	1250
63-Classic Hitler War-c; The Villainess Cat-Woman only app.	127	381	795	1400
65,66-Last Japanese War-c	114	342	713	1250
67-78: 74-Last Patriot. 75-Young Allies begin. 76-Ten Chapter Miss America serial begins, ends #85	105	315	735	1150
79-New cover format; Super Villains begin on cover; last Angel	107	321	669	1175

Marvel Premiere #36 © MAR

Marvel Preview #16 © MAR

Marvels Comics: Fantastic Four #1 © MAR

	GD2.0	FN6.0	VF8.0	NM9.4

80-1st app. Capt. America in Marvel Comics 127 387 795 1400
81-Captain America app. 100 300 625 1100
82-Origin & 1st app. Namora (5/47); 1st Sub-Mariner/Namora team-up;
Captain America app. 255 765 1591 2800
83,85: 83-Last Young Allies. 85-Last Miss America; Blonde Phantom app.
91 273 568 1000
84-Blonde Phantom begins (on-c of #84,88,89); Sub-Mariner by Everett begins;
Captain America app. 127 381 795 1400
86-Blonde Phantom i.d. revealed; Captain America app.; last Bucky app.
100 300 625 1100
87-1st Capt. America/Golden Girl team-up 107 321 669 1175
88-Golden Girl, Namora, & Sun Girl (1st in Marvel Comics) x-over; Captain
America, Blonde Phantom app.; last Toro 100 300 625 1100
89-1st Human Torch/Sun Girl team-up; 1st Captain America solo; Blonde
Phantom app. 100 300 625 1100
90,91: 90-Blonde Phantom un-masked; Captain America app. 91-Capt. America
app.; Blonde Phantom & Sub-Mariner end; early Venus app. (4/49)
(scarce) 118 354 738 1300
92-Feature story on the birth of the Human Torch and the death of Professor
Horton (his creator); 1st app. The Witness in Marvel Comics; Captain
America app. (scarce) 282 846 1763 3100
132 Pg. issue, B&W, 25¢ (1943-44)-printed in N. Y.; square binding, blank
inside covers; has Marvel No. 33-c in color; contains Capt. America #18 &
Marvel Mystery Comics #33; same contents as Captain America Annual
(Less than 5 copies known to exist) 3100 9300 20,000 –
NOTE: Brodsky c-49, 72, 86, 88-92. Crandall a-26i. Everett c-7-9, 27, 84. Gabrielle c-30-32.
Schomburg c-3-11, 13-29, 33-36, 39-48, 50-59, 63-69, 74, 76, 132 pg. issue. Shores c-37, 38,
75p, 77, 78p, 79p, 80, 81p, 82-84, 85p, 87p. Sekowsky c-73. Bondage covers-3, 4, 7, 12, 28, 29,
49, 50, 52, 56, 57, 58, 59, 65. Readit c-7. Remember Pearl Harbor issues-#30-32.

MARVEL MYSTERY COMICS
Marvel Comics: Dec, 1999 ($3.95, reprints)

1-Reprints original 1940s stories; Schomburg-c from #74 4.00

MARVEL NO-PRIZE BOOK, THE (The Official... on-c)
Marvel Comics Group: Jan, 1983 (one-shot, direct sales only)

1-Golden-c; Kirby-a 4.00

MARVEL PREMIERE
Marvel Comics Group: April, 1972 - No. 61, Aug, 1981 (A tryout book for new characters)

1-Origin Warlock (pre-#1) by Gil Kane/Adkins; origin Counter-Earth; Hulk &
Thor cameo (#1-14 are 20¢-c) 5 15 38 60
2-Warlock ends; Kirby Yellow Claw-r 3 9 19 28
3-Dr. Strange series begins (pre #1, 7/72), B. Smith-c(p)
4 12 30 50
4-Smith/Brunner-a 2 6 15 22
5-9: 8-Starlin-c/a(p) 2 6 10 14
10-Death of the Ancient One 2 6 12 18
11-14: 11-Dr. Strange origin-r by Ditko. 14-Last Dr. Strange (3/74), gets own
title 3 months later 1 3 7 10
15-Origin/1st app. Iron Fist (5/74), ends #25 6 18 45 75
16,25: 16-2nd app. Iron Fist; origin cont'd from #15; Hama's 1st Marvel-a. 25-
1st Byrne Iron Fist (moves to own title next) 3 9 19 28
17-24: Iron Fist in all 2 6 12 18
26-Hercules 1 3 5 7
27-Satana 1 3 6 9
28-Legion of Monsters (Ghost Rider, Man-Thing, Morbius, Werewolf)
2 6 12 18
29-46,49: 29,30-The Liberty Legion. 29-1st modern app. Patriot. 31-1st app.
Woodgod; last 25¢ issue. 32-1st app. Monark Starstalker. 33,34-1st color app.
Solomon Kane (Robert E. Howard adaptation "Red Shadows".) 35-Origin/1st
app. 3-D Man. 36,37-3-D Man. 38-1st Weirdworld. 39,40-Torpedo. 41-1st
Seeker 3000! 42-Tigra. 43-Paladin. 44-Jack of Hearts (1st solo book, 10/78).
45,46-Man-Wolf. 49-The Falcon (1st solo book, 8/79) 4.00
29-31-(30¢-c variants, limited distribution)(4,6,8/76) 6.00
36-38-(35¢-c variants, limited distribution)(6,8,10/77) 6.00
47,48-Byrne-a: 47-Origin/1st app. new Ant-Man. 48-Ant-Man
1 3 5 7
50-1st app. Alice Cooper; co-plotted by Alice 2 6 11 15
51-56,58-61: 51-53-Black Panther. 54-1st Caleb Hammer. 55-Wonder Man.
56-1st color app. Dominic Fortune. 58-60-Dr. Who. 61-Star Lord 3.00

57-Dr. Who (2nd U.S. app.-see Movie Classics) 5.00
NOTE: N. Adams (Crusty Bunkers) part inks-10, 12, 13. Austin a-50i, 56i; c-46i, 50i, 56i, 58.
Brunner a-4i, 6p, 9-14p; c-9-14. Byrne a-47p, 48p. Chaykin a-32-34; c-32, 33, 56. Giffen a-31p,
44p; c-44. Gil Kane a(p)-1, 2, 15; c(p)-1, 2, 15, 16, 22-24, 27, 36, 37. Kirby c-26, 29-31, 35.
Layton a-47i, 48i; c-47. McWilliams a-25i. Miller c-49p, 53p, 58p. Nebres a-44i; c-38i. Nino a-
38i. Perez c/a-38p, 45p, 46p. Ploog a-38; c-5-7. Russell a-7p. Simonson a-60(2pgs.); c-57.
Starlin a-8p; c-8. Sutton a-41, 43, 50p, 61; c-50p, 61. #57-60 publ'd w/two different prices on-c.

MARVEL PRESENTS
Marvel Comics: October, 1975 - No. 12, Aug, 1977 (#1-6 are 25¢ issues)

1-Origin & 1st app. Bloodstone 1 4 7 10
2-Origin Bloodstone continued; Kirby-c 6.00
3-Guardians of the Galaxy (1st solo book, 2/76) begins, ends #12
2 6 9 12
4-7,9-12: 9,10-Origin Starhawk 1 3 5 7
4-6-(30¢-c variants, limited distribution)(4-8/76) 1 4 7 10
8-r/story from Silver Surfer #2 plus 4 pgs. new-a 1 3 5 7
11,12-(35¢-c variants, limited distribution)(6,8/77) 1 4 7 10
NOTE: Austin a-6i. Buscema r-8p. Chaykin a-5p. Kane c-1p. Starlin layouts-10.

MARVEL PREVIEW (Magazine) (Bizarre Adventures #25 on)
Marvel Comics: Feb (no month), 1975 - No. 24, Winter, 1980 (B&W) ($1.00)

1-Man-Gods From Beyond the Stars; Crusty Bunkers (Neal Adams)-a(i) &
cover; Nino-a 2 6 9 12
2-1st origin The Punisher (see Amaz. Spider-Man #129 & Classic Punisher);
1st app. Dominic Fortune; Morrow-c 7 21 50 80
3,8,10: 3-Blade the Vampire Slayer. 8-Legion of Monsters; Morbius app. 10-
Thor the Mighty; Starlin frontispiece 2 6 10 14
4,5: 4-Star-Lord & Sword in the Star (origins & 1st app.). 5,6-Sherlock Holmes.
1 4 7 10
6,9: 6-Sherlock Holmes; N. Adams frontispiece. 9-Man-God; origin Star Hawk,
ends #20 1 3 5 7
7-Satana, Sword in the Star app. 1 3 6 9
11,16,19: 11-Star-Lord; Byrne-a; Starlin frontispiece. 16-Masters of Terror.
19-Kull 6.00
12-15,17,18,20-24: 12-Haunt of Horror. 14,15-Star-Lord. 14-Starlin painted-c.
16-Masters of Terror. 17-Blackmark by G. Kane (see SSOC #1-3).
18-Star-Lord. 20-Bizarre Advs. 21-Moon Knight (Spr/80)-Predates Moon
Knight #1; The Shroud by Ditko. 22-King Arthur. 23-Bizarre Advs.; Miller-a.
24-Debut Paradox 4.00
NOTE: N. Adams (C. Bunkers) r-20i. Buscema a-22, 23. Byrne a-11. Chaykin a-20r; c-20
(new). Colan a-8. Giffen a-7. Infantino a-14p. Kaluta c-12; c-
15. Miller a-20. Morrow a-8i; c-2-4. Perez a-20p. Ploog a-8. Starlin c-13, 14. Nudity in some
issues

MARVEL RIOT
Marvel Comics: Dec, 1995 ($1.95, one-shot)

1-"Age of Apocalypse" spoof; Lobdell script 2.25

MARVELS
Marvel Comics: Jan, 1994 - No. 4, Apr, 1994 ($5.95, painted lim. series)
No. 1 (2nd Printing), Apr, 1996 - No. 4 (2nd Printing), July, 1996 ($2.95)

1-4: Kurt Busiek scripts & Alex Ross painted-c/a in all; double-c w/acetate
overlay 1 3 6 8
Marvel Classic Collectors Pack ($11.90)-Issues #1 & 2 boxed (1st printings)
2 6 11 16
0-(8/94, $2.95)-no acetate overlay. 4.00
1-4-(2nd printing): r/original limited series w/o acetate overlay 3.00
Hardcover (1994, $59.95)-r/#0-4; w/intros by Stan Lee, John Romita, Sr., Kurt
Busiek & Scott McCloud. 60.00
Trade paperback ($19.95) 20.00

MARVEL SAGA, THE
Marvel Comics Group: Dec, 1985 - No. 25, Dec, 1987

1-25 2.25
NOTE: Williamson a(i)-9, 10; c(i)-7, 10-14, 16.

MARVELS COMICS: ... (Marvel-type comics read in the Marvel Universe)
Marvel Comics: Jul, 2000 ($2.25, one-shots)

...Captain America #1 -Frenz & Sinnott-a; ...Daredevil #1 -Isabella-s/Newell-a;
....Fantastic Four #1 -Kesel-s/Paul Smith-a; Spider-Man #1 -Oliff-a;
....Thor #1 -Templeton-s/Austin-a 2.25
...X-Men #1 -Millar-s/ Sean Phillips & Duncan Fegredo-a 2.25
The History of Marvels Comics (no cover price)-Faux history; previews titles 2.25

Marvels of Science #2 © CC

Marvel Spectacular #2 © MAR

Marvel Super-Heroes #71 © MAR

	GD2.0	FN6.0	VF8.0	NM9.4

MARVEL SELECTS:
Marvel Comics: Jan, 2000 - Present ($2.75/$2.99, reprints)
...Fantastic Four 1-6: Reprints F.F. #107-112; new Davis-c 2.75
...Spider-Man 1,2,4-6: Reprints AS-M #100,101,103,104,93; Wieringo-c 2.75
...Spider-Man 3 ($2.99): Reprints AS-M #102; new Wieringo-c 3.00

MARVEL'S GREATEST COMICS (Marvel Collectors' Item Classics #1-22)
Marvel Comics Group: No. 23, Oct, 1969 - No. 96, Jan, 1981

23-34 (Giants). Begin Fantastic Four-r/#30s?-116	2	6	12	18
35-37-Silver Surfer-r/Fantastic Four #48-50	1	3	6	9
38-50: 42-Silver Surfer-r/F.F.(others)-				6.00
51-70: 63,64-(25¢ editions)				4.00
63,64-(30¢-c variants, limited distribution)(5,7/76)				6.00
71-96: 71-73-(30¢ editions)				3.00
71-73-(35¢-c variants, limited distribution)(7,9-10/77)				5.00

NOTE: Dr. Strange, Fantastic Four, Iron Man, Watcher-#23, 24. Capt. America, Dr. Strange, Iron Man, Fantastic Four-#25-28. Fantastic Four-#38-96. Buscema r-85-92; c-87-92r. Ditko r-23-28. Kirby r-23-82; c-75, 77p, 80p. #81 reprints Fantastic Four #100.

MARVEL'S GREATEST SUPERHERO BATTLES (See Fireside Book Series)

MARVEL: SHADOWS AND LIGHT
Marvel Comics: Feb, 1997 ($2.95, B&W, one-shot)
1-Tony Daniel-c 3.00

MARVELS OF SCIENCE
Charlton Comics: March, 1946 - No. 4, June, 1946

1-A-Bomb story	23	69	121	210
2-4	14	42	72	120

MARVEL SPECIAL EDITION FEATURING... (Also see Special Collectors' Ed.)
Marvel Comics Group: 1975 - 1978 (84 pgs.) (Oversized)

1-The Spectacular Spider-Man ($1.50); r/Amazing Spider-Man #6,35, Annual 1; Ditko-a(r)	3	9	17	24
1,2-Star Wars ('77,'78; r/Star Wars #1-3 & #4-6	2	6	11	15
3-Star Wars ('78, $2.50, 116pgs.); r/S. Wars #1-6	2	6	12	18
3-Close Encounters of the Third Kind (1978, $1.50, 56 pgs.)-Movie adaptation; Simonson-a(p)	2	6	10	14
V2#2(Spring, 1980, $2.00, oversized)- "Star Wars: The Empire Strikes Back"; r/Marvel Comics Super Special #16	3	9	17	24

NOTE: Chaykin c/a(r)-1(1977), 2, 3. Stevens a(r)-2i, 3i. Williamson c/a(r)-V2#2.

MARVEL SPECTACULAR
Marvel Comics: Aug, 1973 - No. 19, Nov, 1975

1-Thor-r from mid-sixties begin by Kirby	1	4	7	10
2-19				5.00

MARVELS: PORTRAITS
Marvel Comics: Mar, 1995 - No. 4, June, 1995 ($2.95, limited series)
1-4:Different artists renditions of Marvel characters 3.00

MARVEL SPOTLIGHT (....& Son of Satan #19, 20, 23, 24)
Marvel Comics Group: Nov, 1971 - No. 33, Apr, 1977; V2#1, July, 1979 - V2#11, Mar, 1981 (A try-out book for new characters)

1-Origin Red Wolf (western hero)(1st solo book, pre-#1); Wood inks, Neal Adams-c; only 15¢ issue	3	10	23	35
2-(25¢, 52 pgs.)-Venus-r by Everett; origin/1st app. Werewolf By Night (begins) by Ploog; N. Adams-c	14	42	102	175
3,4: 4-Werewolf By Night ends (6/72); gets own title 9/72	5	15	34	55
5-Origin/1st app. Ghost Rider (8/72) & begins	10	30	70	120
6-8: 8-Origin G.R. retold. 8-Last Ghost Rider	4	12	27	42
9-11-Last Ghost Rider (gets own title next mo.)	3	9	21	32
12-Origin & 2nd full app. The Son of Satan (10/73); story cont'd from Ghost Rider #2 & into #3; series begins, ends #24	3	9	21	32
13-24: 13-Partial origin Son of Satan. 14-Last 20¢ issue. 22-Ghost Rider-c & cameo (5 panels). 24-Last Son of Satan (10/75); gets own title 12/75	1	3	6	9
25,27,30,31: 27-(Regular 25¢-c), Sub-Mariner app. 30-The Warriors Three. 31-Nick Fury				5.00
26-Scarecrow	1	4	7	10
27-(30¢-c variant, limited distribution)	1	3	6	8
28-(Regular 25¢-c) 1st solo app. Moon Knight app.	3	9	20	30
28-(30¢-c variant, limited distribution)	4	12	29	45

MARVEL SUPER ACTION (Magazine)
Marvel Comics Group: Jan, 1976 (B&W, 76 pgs.)

1-Origin/2nd app. Dominic Fortune(see Marvel Preview); early Punisher app.; Weird World & The Huntress; Evans, Ploog-a	5	15	34	55

MARVEL SUPER ACTION
Marvel Comics Group: May, 1977 - No. 37, Nov, 1981

1-Reprints Capt. America #100 by Kirby	1	4	7	10
2-13: 2,3,5-13 r/Capt. America #101,102,103-111. 11-Origin-r. 12,13-Classic Steranko-c/a(r). 4-Marvel Boy-r(origin)/M. Boy #1				6.00
2,3-(35¢-c variants, limited distribution)(6,8/77)	1	3	6	8
14-20: r/Avengers #55,56, Annual 2, others				4.00
21-37: 30-r/Hulk #6 from U.K.				4.00

NOTE: Buscema a(r)-14p, 15p; c-18-20, 22, 35r-37. Everett a-4. Heath a-4r. Kirby r-1-3, 5-11. B. Smith a-27r, 28r. Steranko a(r)-12p, 13p; c-12r, 13r.

MARVEL SUPER HERO CONTEST OF CHAMPIONS
Marvel Comics Group: June, 1982 - No. 3, Aug, 1982 (Limited series)

1-3: Features nearly all Marvel characters currently appearing in their comics; 1st Marvel limited series				6.00

MARVEL SUPER HEROES
Marvel Comics Group: October, 1966 (25¢, 68 pgs.) (1st Marvel one-shot)

1-r/origin Daredevil from D.D. #1; r/Avengers #2; G.A. Sub-Mariner-r/Marvel Mystery #8 (Human Torch app.). Kirby-a	10	30	70	120

MARVEL SUPER-HEROES (Formerly Fantasy Masterpieces #1-11)
(Also see Giant-Size Super Heroes) (#12-20: 25¢, 68 pgs.)
Marvel Comics: No. 12, 12/67 - No. 31, 11/71; No. 32, 9/72 - No. 105, 1/82

12-Origin & 1st app. Capt. Marvel of the Kree; G.A. Human Torch, Destroyer, Capt. America, Black Knight, Sub-Mariner-r (#12-20 all contain new stories and reprints)	10	30	73	125
13-2nd app. Capt. Marvel; G.A. Black Knight, Torch, Vision, Capt. America, Sub-Mariner-r	5	15	38	60
14-Amazing Spider-Man (5/68, new-a by Andru/Everett); G.A. Sub-Mariner, Torch, Mercury (1st Kirby-a at Marvel), Black Knight, Capt. America	8	24	56	90
15-17: 15-Black Bolt cameo in Medusa (new-a); Black Knight, Sub-Mariner, Black Marvel, Capt. America-r. 16-1st app. S. A. Phantom Eagle; G.A. Torch, Capt. America, Black Knight, Patriot, Sub-Mariner-r. 17-Origin Black Knight (new-a); G.A. Torch, Sub-Mariner-r; reprint from All-Winners Squad #21 (cover & story)	3	10	23	35
18-Origin/1st app. Guardians of the Galaxy (1/69); G.A. Sub-Mariner, All-Winners Squad-r	4	12	30	50
19-Ka-Zar (new-a); G.A. Torch, Marvel Boy, Black Knight, Sub-Mariner reprints; Smith-c(p); Tuska-a(r)	2	6	15	22
20-Doctor Doom (5/69); r/Young Men #24 w/-c	3	9	20	30
21-31: All-r issues. 21-X-Men, Daredevil, Iron Man-r begin, end #31. 31-Last Giant issue	2	6	10	14
32-50: 32-Hulk/Sub-Mariner-r begin from TTA				5.00
51-105: 56-r/origin Hulk/Inc. Hulk #102; Hulk-r begin				3.00
57,58-(30¢-c variants, limited distribution)(5,7/76)				4.00
65,66-(35¢-c variants, limited distribution)(7,9/77)				4.00

NOTE: Austin a-104. Colan a(p)-12, 13, 15, 18; c-12, 13, 15, 18. Everett a-14i(new); r-14, 15i, 18, 19, 33; c-85r(r). New Kirby c-22, 27; r-14, 15, 19. Maneely r-14, 15, 19. Severin r-83-85i, 100-102; c-100-102r. Starlin c-47. Tuska a-19p. Black Knight-r by Maneely in 12-16, 19. Sub-Mariner-r by Everett in 12-20.

MARVEL SUPER-HEROES
Marvel Comics: May, 1990 - V2#15, Oct, 1993 ($2.95/$2.50, quart., 68-84 pgs.)

29,32: 29-(Regular 25¢-c) (8/76) Moon Knight app.; last 25¢ issue.
32-1st app./partial origin Spider-Woman (2/77); Nick Fury app.

		2	6	15	22
29-(30¢-c variant, limited distribution)		3	10	23	35
33-Deathlok; 1st app. Devil-Slayer		1	3	5	7
V2#1-7,9-11: 1-4-Capt. Marvel. 5-Dragon Lord. 6,7-StarLord; origin #6. 9-11-Capt. Universe (see Micronauts #8)					3.00
1-Variant copy missing issue #1 on cover			1	4	7	10
8-Capt. Marvel; Miller-c/a(p)						5.00

NOTE: Austin c-V2#2i, 8. J. Buscema c/a-30p. Chaykin a-31; c-26, 31. Colan a-18p, 19p. Ditko a-V2#4, 5, 9-11; c-V2#4, 9,11. Kane c-21p, 32p. Kirby c-29p. McWilliams a-20i. Miller a-V2#8p; c(p)-V2#2, 5, 7, 8. Mooney a-8i, 10i, 14p, 15, 16p, 17p, 24p, 27, 32i. Nasser a-33p. Ploog a-2-5, 6-8p; c-3-9. Romita c-13. Sutton a-9-11p, V2#6, 7. #29-25¢ & 30¢ issues exist.

MARVEL SUPER-HEROES
Marvel Comics: Jan, 1976 (B&W, 76 pgs.)

Marvel Swimsuit Special #1 © MAR

Marvel Tales #125 © MAR

Marvel Tales (2nd series) #233 © MAR

	GD2.0	FN6.0	VF8.0	NM9.4

1-Moon Knight, Hercules, Black Panther, Magik, Brother Voodoo, Speedball (by Ditko) & Hellcat; Hembeck-a ... 3.00

2,4,5,V2#3,6-15: 2-Summer Special(7/90); Rogue, Speedball (by Ditko), Iron Man, Falcon,Tigra & Daredevil. 4-Spider-Man/Nick Fury, Daredevil,Speedball, Wonder Man, Spitfire & Black Knight; Byrne-c. 5-Thor, Dr. Strange, Thing & She-Hulk; Speedball by Ditko(p). V2#3-Retells origin Capt. America w/new facts; Blue Shield, Capt. Marvel,Speedball, Wasp; Hulk by Ditko/Rogers V2#6-9: 6-8-$2.25-c. 6,7-X-Men, Cloak & Dagger, The Shroud (by Ditko) & Marvel Boy in each. 8-X-Men, Namor & Iron Man (by Ditko); Larsen-c. 9-W.C Avengers, Iron Man app.; Kieth-c(p).V2#10-Ms. Marvel/Sabretooth-c/story (intended for Ms. Marvel #24); shows-c to #24); Namor, Vision, Scarlet Witch stories. V2#11,12 :11-Original Ghost Rider-c/story; Giant-Man, Ms. Marvel stories. 12-Dr. Strange, Falcon, Iron Man. V2#13-15 ($2.75, 84 pgs.): 13-All Iron Man 30th anniversary. 15-Iron Man/Thor/Volstagg/Dr. Druid ... 2.75

MARVEL SUPER-HEROES MEGAZINE
Marvel Comics: Oct, 1994 - No. 6, Mar, 1995 ($2.95, 100 pgs.)

1-6: 1-r/FF #232, DD #159, Iron Man #115, Incred. Hulk #314 ... 3.00

MARVEL SUPER-HEROES SECRET WARS (See Secret Wars II)
Marvel Comics Group: May, 1984 - No. 12, Apr, 1985 (limited series)

	1	3	6	8
1-3-(2nd printings, sold in multi-packs)				2.50
2-6,9-11: 6-The Wasp dies				6.00
7,12: 7-Intro. new Spider-Woman. 12-($1.00, 52 pgs.)	1	3	5	7

8-Spider-Man's new black costume explained as alien costume (1st app. Venom as alien costume) ... 3 9 19 28
NOTE: *Zeck* a-1-12; c-1,3,8-12.

MARVEL SUPER SPECIAL, A (See Marvel Comics Super...)

MARVEL SWIMSUIT SPECIAL (Also see Marvel Illustrated...)
Marvel Comics: 1992 - No. 4, 1995 ($3.95/$4.50, magazine, 52 pgs.)

1-4-Silvestri-c; pin-ups by diff. artists. 2-Jusko-c. 3-Hughes-c.				
	1	3	5	7

MARVEL TAILS STARRING PETER PORKER THE SPECTACULAR SPIDER-HAM (Also see Peter Porker...)
Marvel Comics Group: Nov, 1983 (one-shot)

1-Peter Porker, the Spectacular Spider-Ham, Captain Americat, Goose Rider, Hulk Bunny app. ... 4.00

MARVEL TALES (Formerly Marvel Mystery Comics #1-92)
Marvel/Atlas Comics (MCI): No. 93, Aug, 1949 - No. 159, Aug, 1957

93-Horror/weird stories begin	141	423	881	1550
94-Everett-a	93	280	581	1025
95,96,99,101,103,105: 95-New logo	63	189	394	690
97-Sun Girl, 2 pgs; Kirbyish-a; one story used in N.Y. State Legislative document	75	221	469	825
98,100: 98-Krigstein-a	65	196	406	720
102-Wolverton-a "The End of the World", (6 pgs.)	91	273	568	1000
104-Wolverton-a "Gateway to Horror", (6 pgs.)	89	267	556	975
106,107-Krigstein-a. 106-Decapitation story	53	158	318	560
108-120: 118-Hypo-c/panels in End of World story. 120-Jack Katz-a	40	120	232	400
121,123-131: 128-Flying Saucer-c. 131-Last precode (2/55)	34	102	179	310
122-Kubert-a	34	102	182	315
132,133,135-141,143,145	22	66	116	195
134-Krigstein, Kubert-a; flying saucer-c	24	72	127	215
142-Krigstein-a	22	66	116	200
144-Williamson/Krenkel-a, 3 pgs.	22	66	116	200
146,148-151,154-156,158: 150-1st S.A. issue. 156-Torres-a	17	51	88	150
147,152: 147-Ditko-a. 152-Wood, Morrow-a	20	60	105	175
153-Everett End of World c/story	22	66	116	195
157,159-Krigstein-a	18	54	94	155

NOTE: *Andru* a-103. *Briefer* a-118. *Check* a-147. *Colan* a-105, 107, 118, 120, 121, 131. *Drucker* a-127, 135, 141, 146, 150. *Everett* a-98, 104, 106(2), 108(2), 131, 148, 151, 153, 155; c-107, 109, 111, 112, 114, 118, 119; c-104-106, 110, 130. *Gil Kane* a-117. *Lawrence* a-130. *Maneely* a-111, 126, 129; c-108, 116, 122. *Mooney* a-121. *Morisi* a-153. *Morrow* a-150, 152, 156. *Orlando* a-149, 151, 157. *Pakula* a-119, 121, 135, 144, 150, 152. *Powell* a-136, 137, 150, 154. *Ravielli* a-117. *Rico* a-97, 99. *Romita* a-108. *Sekowsky* a-96-98, 103; c-96.

Sinnott a-105, 116. *Tuska* a-114. *Whitney* a-107. *Wildey* a-126, 138.

MARVEL TALES (...Annual #1,2; ...Starring Spider-Man #123 on)
Marvel Comics Group (NPP earlier issues): 1964 - No. 291, Nov, 1994 (No. 1-32: 72 pgs.) (#1-3 have Canadian variants; back & inside-c are blank, same value)

1-Reprints origins of Spider-Man/Amazing Fantasy #15, Hulk/Inc. Hulk#1, Ant-Man/T.T.A. #35, Giant Man/T.T.A. #49, Iron Man/T.O.S. #39,48, Thor/ J.I.M. #83 & r/Sgt. Fury #1	29	87	202	360
2 ('65)-r/X-Men #1(origin), Avengers #1(origin), origin Dr. Strange-r/Strange Tales #115 & origin Hulk(Hulk #3)	10	30	70	120
3 (7/66)-Spider-Man, Strange Tales (H. Torch), Journey into Mystery (Thor), Tales to Astonish (Ant-Man)-r begin (r/Strange Tales #101)				
4,5	5	15	34	55
	3	10	23	35
6-8,10: 10-Reprints 1st Kraven/Amaz. S-M #15	3	9	21	35
9-r/Amazing Spider-Man #14 w/cover	2	6	15	22
11-33: 11-Spider-Man battles Daredevil-r/Amaz. Spider-Man #16. 13-Origin Marvel Boy-r/M. Boy #1. 22-Green Goblin-c/story-r/Amaz. Spider-Man #27. 30-New Angel story (x-over w/Ka-Zar #2,3). 32-Last 72 pg. iss. 33-(52 pgs.) Kraven-r	3	9	19	28
	2	6	12	18
34-50: 34-Begin regular size issues				6.00
51-65				4.00
66-70-(Regular 25¢ editions)(4-8/76)				4.00
66-70-(30¢-c variants, limited distribution)				6.00
71-105: 75-Origin Spider-Man-r. 77-79-Drug issues-r/Amaz. Spider-Man #96-98. 98-Death of Gwen Stacy-r/Amaz. Spider-Man #121 (Green Goblin). 99-Death Green Goblin-r/Amaz. Spider-Man #122. 100-(52 pgs.)-New Hawkeye/Two Gun Kid story. 101-105-All Spider-Man-r				3.00
80-84-(35¢-c variants, limited distribution)(6-10/77)				5.00
106-r/1st Punisher-Amazing Spider-Man #129				4.00
107-136: 107-133-All Spider-Man-r. 111,112-r/Spider-Man #134,135 (Punisher). 113,114-r/Spider-Man #136,137(Green Goblin). 126-128-r/clone story from Amazing Spider-Man #149-151. 134-136-Dr. Strange-r begin; SpM stories continue. 134-Dr. Strange-r/Strange Tales #110				3.00
137-Origin-r Dr. Strange; shows original unprinted-c & origin Spider-Man/ Amazing Fantasy #15				5.00
137-Nabisco giveaway				6.00
138-Reprints all Amazing Spider-Man #1; begin reprints of Spider-Man with covers similar to originals				4.00
139-144: r/Amazing Spider-Man #2-7				3.00
145-200: Super-Man continue w/#8 on. 149-Contains skin "Tattooz" decals. 150-($1.00, 52pgs.)-r/Spider-Man Annual 1(Kraven app.). 153-r/1st Kraven/Spider-Man #15. 155-r/2nd Green Goblin/Spider-Man #17. 161,164,165-Gr. Goblin-c/stories/Spider-Man #23,26,27. 178,179-Green Goblin-c/story-r/Spider-Man #39,40. 187,189-Kraven-r. 191-($1.50, 68 pgs.)-r/Spider-Man #96-98. 193-Byrne-r/Marvel Team-Up begin w/scripts. 192-($1.25, 52 pgs.)-r/Spider-Man #121,122. 200-Double size ($1.25)-Miller-c & r/Annual #14				2.50
201-257: 208-Last Byrne-r. 210,211-r/Spidey #134,135. 212,213-r/Giant-Size Spidey #4. 213-r/1st solo Silver Surfer story/F.F. Annual #5. 214,215-r/Spidey #161,162. 222-Reprints origin Punisher/Spectacular Spider-Man #83; last Punisher reprint. 209-Reprints 1st app. The Punisher, retells origin Amazing Spider-Man #129; Punisher reprints begin, end #222. 223-McFarlane-c begins, end #239. 233-Spider-Man/X-Men team-ups begins; r/X-Men #35. 234-r/Marvel Team-Up #4. 235,236-r/M. Team-Up Annual #1. 237,238-r/M. Team-Up #150. 239,240-r/M. Team-Up #38,90(Beast). 242-r/M.Team-Up #89. 243-r/M. Team-Up #117(Wolverine). 250-($1.50, 52pgs.)-r/1st Karma/M. Team-Up #100. 251-r/Spider-Man #100 (Green Goblin-c/story). 252-r/1st app. Morbius/Amaz. Spider-Man #101. 253-($1.50, 52 pgs.)-r/Amaz. S-M #102254-r/M. Team-Up #15(Ghost Rider); new painted-c. 255,256-Spider-Man & Ghost Rider-r/Marvel Team-Up #58,91. 257-Hobgoblin-r begin(r/Amazing Spider-Man #238).				2.25
258-291: 258-261-r/A. Spider-Man #239,249-251(Hobgoblin). 262,263-r/Marv. Team-Up #53,54. 262-Spider-Man vs. Sunstroke story. 263-New Woodgod origin story. 264,265-r/A. Spider-Man Annual 5. 266-273-Reprints alien costume stories/A. S-M 252-259. 277-r/1st Silver Sable/A. S-M 265. 283-r/A. S-M 275 (Hobgoblin). 284-r/A. S-M 276 (Hobgoblin)				2.25
285-variant w/Wonder-Con logo on c-no price-giveaway				2.25
286-($2.95)-p/bagged w/16 page insert & animation print				3.00

NOTE: *All contain reprints; some have new art. #89-97-r/Amazing Spider-Man #110-118; #98-136-r/#121-159; #137-150-r/Amazing Fantasy #15, #1-12 & Annual 1; #151-167-r/#13-28 & Annual 2;*

Marvel Team-Up #76 © MAR

Marvel Team-Up #141 © MAR

Marvel: The Lost Generation #7 © MAR

	GD2.0	FN6.0	VF8.0	NM9.4

#168-186-r/#29-46. **Austin** a-100i; c-272i, 273i. **Byrne** a(r)-193-198p, 201-208p. **Ditko** a-1-30, 83, 100, 137-155. **G. Kane** a-71, 81, 98-101p, 249r; c-125-127p, 130p, 137-155. **Sam Kieth** c-255, 262, 263. **Ron Lim** c-266p-281p, 283p-285p. **McFarlane** c-223-239. **Mooney** a-63, 95-97i, 103(i). **Nasser** a-100p. **Nebres** a-242i. **Perez** c-259-261. **Rogers** c-240, 241, 243-252.

MARVEL TEAM-UP (See Marvel Treasury Edition #18 & Official Marvel Index To...) (Replaced by Web of Spider-Man)
Marvel Comics Group: March, 1972 - No. 150, Feb, 1985
NOTE: *Spider-Man team-ups in all but Nos. 18, 23, 26, 29, 32, 35, 97, 104, 105, 137.*

1-Human Torch	12	36	88	150
2-Human Torch	4	12	29	45
3-Spider-Man/Human Torch vs. Morbius (part 1); 3rd app. of Morbius (7/72)				
	4	12	30	50
4-Spider-Man/X-Men vs. Morbius (part 2 of story); 4th app. of Morbius				
	5	15	34	55
5-10: 5-Vision. 6-Thing. 7-Thor. 8-The Cat (4/73, came out between The Cat #3 & 4). 9-Iron Man. 10-H-T	2	6	13	20
11,13,14,16-20: 11-Inhumans. 13-Capt. America. 14-Sub-Mariner. 16-Capt. Marvel. 17-Mr. Fantastic. 18-H-T/Hulk. 19-Ka-Zar. 20-Black Panther; last 20¢ issue	2	6	9	12
12-Werewolf (8/73, 1 month before Werewolf #1).	3	9	17	24
15-1st Spider-Man/Ghost Rider team-up (11/73)	2	6	13	20
21-30: 21-Dr. Strange. 22-Hawkeye. 23-H-T/Iceman (X-Men cameo). 24-Brother Voodoo. 25-Daredevil. 26-H-T/Thor. 27-Hulk. 28-Hercules. 29-H-T/Iron Man. 30-Falcon	3	6	8	
31-45,47-50: 31-Iron Fist. 32-H-T/Son of Satan. 33-Nighthawk. 34-Valkyrie. 35-H-T/Dr. Strange. 36-Frankenstein. 37-Man-Wolf. 38-Beast. 39-H-T. 40-Sons of the Tiger/H-T. 41-Scarlet Witch. 42-The Vision. 43-Dr. Doom; retells origin. 44-Moondragon. 45-Killraven. 47-Thing. 48-Iron Man; last 25¢ issue. 49-Dr. Strange; Iron Man app. 50-Iron Man; Dr. Strange app.				
				5.00
44-48-(30¢ variants, limited distribution)(4-8/76)	1	3	6	8
46-Spider-Man/Deathlok team-up				6.00
51,52,56,57: 51-Iron Man; Dr. Strange app. 52-Capt. America. 56-Daredevil. 57-Black Widow				4.00
53-Hulk; Woodgod & X-Men app., 1st Byrne-a on X-Men (1/77)				
	3	9	19	28
54,55,58-60: 54,59,60- 54-Hulk; Woodgod app. 59-Yellowjacket/The Wasp. 60-The Wasp (Byrne-a in all). 55-Warlock-c/story; Byrne-a. 58-Ghost Rider				
				6.00
58-62-(35¢-c variants, limited distribution)(6-10/77)	1	3	6	8
61-70: All Byrne-a; 61-H-T. 62-Ms. Marvel; last 30¢ issue. 63-Iron Fist. 64-Daughters of the Dragon. 65-Capt. Britain (1st U.S. app.). 66-Capt. Britain; 1st app. Arcade. 67-Tigra; Kraven the Hunter app. 68-Man-Thing. 69-Havok (from X-Men). 70-Thor				5.00
71-74,76-78,80: 71-Falcon. 72-Iron Man. 73-Daredevil. 74-Not Ready for Prime Time Players (Belushi). 76-Dr. Strange. 77-Ms. Marvel. 78-Wonder Man. 80-Dr. Strange/Clea; last 35¢ issue				3.00
75,79,81: Byrne-a(p). 75-Power Man; Cage app. 79-Mary Jane Watson as Red Sonja; Clark Kent cameo (1 panel, 3/79). 81-Death of Satana				4.00
82-99: 82-Black Widow. 83-Nick Fury. 84-Shang-Chi. 86-Guardians of the Galaxy. 89-Nightcrawler (from X-Men). 91-Ghost Rider. 92-Hawkeye. 93-Werewolf by Night. 94-Spider-Man vs. The Shroud. 95-Mockingbird (intro.); Nick Fury app. 96-Howard the Duck; last 40¢ issue. 97-Spider-Woman/ Hulk. 98-Black Widow. 99-Machine Man. 85-Shang-Chi/Black Widow/Nick Fury. 87-Black Panther. 88-Invisible Girl. 90-Beast				3.00
100-(Double-size)-Fantastic Four/Storm/Black Panther; origin/1st app. Karma, one of the New Mutants; origin Storm; X-Men x-over; Miller-c/a(p); Byrne-a (on X-Men app. only)				6.00
101-116: 101-Nighthawk(Ditko-a). 102-Doc Samson. 103-Ant-Man. 104-Hulk/Ka-Zar. 105-Powerman/Iron Fist. 106-Capt. America. 107-She-Hulk. 108-Paladin; Dazzler cameo. 109-Dazzler; Paladin app. 110-Iron Man. 111-Devil-Slayer. 112-King Kull; last 60¢ issue. 113-Quasar. 114-Falcon. 115-Thor. 116-Valkyrie				3.00
117-Wolverine-c/story	1	4	7	10
118-140,142-149: 118-Professor X; Wolverine app. (4 pgs.); X-Men cameo. 119-Gargoyle. 120-Dominic Fortune. 121-Human Torch. 122-Man-Thing. 123-Daredevil. 124-The Beast. 125-Tigra. 126-Hulk & Powerman/Son of Satan. 127-The Watcher. 128-Capt. America; Spider-Man/Capt. America photo-c. 129-The Vision. 130-Scarlet Witch. 131-Frogman. 132-Mr. Fantastic. 133-Fantastic Four. 134-Jack of Hearts. 135-Kitty Pryde; X-Men cameo. 136-Wonder Man. 137-Aunt May/Franklin Richards. 138-Sand-				

man. 139-Nick Fury. 140-Black Widow. 142-Capt. Marvel. 143-Starfox. 144-Moon Knight. 145-Iron Man. 146-Nomad. 147-Human Torch; SpM back to old costume. 148-Thor. 149-Cannonball 2.50

141-Daredevil; SpM/Black Widow app. (Spidey in new black costume; ties w/ Amaz. S-M #252 for 1st black costume)				3.00
150-X-Men ($1.00, double-size); B. Smith-c				5.00
Annual 1 (1976)-Spider-Man/X-Men (early app.)	2	6	15	22
Annual 2 (1979)-Spider-Man/Hulk	1	3	5	7
Annuals 3,4: 3 (1980)-Hulk/Power Man/Machine Man/Iron Fist; Miller-c(p).				
4 (1981)-SpM/Daredevil/Moon Knight/Power Man/Iron Fist; brief origins of each; Miller-c; Miller scripts on Daredevil				5.00
Annuals 5-7: 5 (1982)-SpM/The Thing/Scarlet Witch/Dr. Strange/Quasar. 6 (1983)-SpM/New Mutants (early app.), Cloak & Dagger. 7(1984)-Alpha Flight; Byrne-c(i)				3.00

NOTE: **Art Adams** c-141p. **Austin** a-79i; c-76i, 79i, 96i, 101i, 112i, 130i. **Bolle** a-9i. **Byrne** a(p)-53-55, 59-70, 75, 79, 100; c-68p, 70p, 72p, 75, 76p, 79p, 129i, 133i. **Colan** a-87p. **Ditko** a-101. **Kane** a(p)-4-6, 13, 14, 16-19, 23, 25, 26, 32-35, 37, 41, 44, 45, 47, 53, 54. **Miller** a-100p; c-95p, 99p, 100p, 102p, 106. **Mooney** a-2i, 7i, 8, 10p, 11p, 16i, 24-31p, 72, 93i, Annual 5i. **Nasser** a-89p; c-101p. **Simonson** c-99i, 148. **Paul Smith** c-131, 132. **Starlin** c-27. **Sutton** a-93p. "H-T" means Human Torch; "SpM" means Spider-Man; "S-M" means Sub-Mariner.

MARVEL TEAM-UP (2nd Series)
Marvel Comics: Sept, 1997 - No. 11, July, 1998 ($1.99)

1-11: 1-Spider-Man team-ups begin, Generation x-app. 2-Hercules-c/app.; two covers. 3-Sandman. 4-Man-Thing. 7-Blade. 8-Namor team-ups begin, Dr. Strange app. 9-Capt. America. 10-Thing. 11-Iron Man				2.25

MARVEL: THE LOST GENERATION
Marvel Comics: No. 12, Mar, 2000 - No. 1, Feb, 2001 ($2.99, issue #s go in reverse)

1-12-Stern-s/Byrne-s/a; untold story of The First Line. 5-Thor app.				3.00

MARVEL TREASURY EDITION
Marvel Comics Group/Whitman #17,18: 1974; #2, Dec, 1974 - #28, 1981 ($1.50/$2.50, 100 pgs., oversized. Also see Amazing Spider-Man, The, Marvel Spec. Ed. Feat.--, Savage Fists of Kung Fu, Superman Vs. A Space Odyssey)

1-Spectacular Spider-Man; story-r/Marvel Super-Heroes #14; Romita-c/a(r); G. Kane, Ditko-r; Green Goblin/Hulk-r	5	15	34	55
1-1,000 numbered copies signed by Stan Lee & John Romita on front-c & sold thru mail for $1.00; these were the1st 1,000 copies off the press				
	11	33	77	130
2-10: 2-Fantastic Four-r/F.F. 6,11,48-50(Silver Surfer). 3-The Mighty Thor-r/Thor #125-130. 4-Conan the Barbarian; Barry Smith-c/a(r)/Conan #11. 5-The Hulk (origin-r/Hulk #3). 6-Dr. Strange. 7-Mighty Avengers. 8-Giant Superhero Holiday Grab-Bag; Spider-Man, Hulk, Nick Fury. 9-Giant Super-hero team-up. 10-Thor; r/Thor #154-157	2	6	13	20
11-25,27: 11-Fantastic Four. 12-Howard the Duck (r/#H. the Duck #1 & G.S. Man-Thing #4,5) plus new Defenders story. 13-Giant Super-Hero Holiday Grab-Bag. 14-The Sensational Spider-Man; r/1st Morbius from Amazing S-M #101,102 plus #100 & r/Not Brand Echh #6. 15-Conan; B. Smith, Neal Adams-i; r/Conan #24. 16-The Defenders (origin) & Valkyrie; r/Defenders #1,4,13,14. 17-The Hulk. 18-The Astonishing Spider-Man; r/Spider-Man's 1st team-ups with Iron Fist, The X-Men, Ghost Rider & Werewolf by Night; inside back-c has photos from 1978 Spider-Man TV show. 19-Conan the Barbarian. 20-Hulk. 21-Fantastic Four. 22-Spider-Man. 23-Conan. 24-Rampaging Hulk. 25-Spider-Man vs. The Hulk. 27-Spider-Man				
	2	6	11	15
26-The Hulk; 6 pg. new Wolverine/Hercules-c	2	6	13	20
28-Spider-Man/Superman; (origin of each)	3	10	23	35

NOTE: Reprints-2, 3, 5, 7-9, 13, 14, 16, 17. **Neal Adams** a(i)-6, 15. **Brunner** a-6, 12; c-6. **Buscema** a-15, 19, 28; c-28. **Colan** a-6r; c-12p. **Ditko** a-1, 16. **Gil Kane** a-16p. **Kirby** a-1-3, 5, 7, 9-11; c-7. **Perez** a-26. **Romita** c-1, 5. **B. Smith** a-4, 15, 19; c-4, 19.

MARVEL TREASURY OF OZ FEATURING THE MARVELOUS LAND OF OZ
Marvel Comics Group: 1975 ($1.50, oversized) (See MGM's Marvelous...)

1-Buscema/a; Romita-c	2	6	13	20

MARVEL TREASURY SPECIAL (Also see 2001: A Space Odyssey)
Marvel Comics Group: 1974; 1976 ($1.50, oversized, 84 pgs.)

Vol. 1-Spider-Man, Torch, Sub-Mariner, Avengers "Giant Superhero Holiday Grab-Bag"; Wood, Colan/Everett, plus 2 Kirby-r; reprints Hulk vs. Thing from Fantastic Four #25,26	2	6	13	20
Vol. 1-... Featuring Captain America's Bicentennial Battles (6/76)-Kirby-a;				

Marvel Triple Action #3 © MAR

Marvel Two-In-One #39 © MAR

Marvel Universe #5 © MAR

	GD2.0	FN6.0	VF8.0	NM9.4		GD2.0	FN6.0	VF8.0	NM9.4

B. Smith inks, 11 pgs.   3   9   17   24

MARVEL TRIPLE ACTION (See Giant-Size...)
Marvel Comics Group: Feb, 1972 - No. 24, Mar, 1975; No. 25, Aug, 1975 - No. 47, Apr, 1979

1-(25¢ giant, 52 pgs.)-Dr. Doom, Silver Surfer, The Thing begin, end #4
('66 reprints from Fantastic Four)   2   6   13   20
2-5   1   3   6   9
6-10   6.00
11-47: 45-r/X-Men #45. 46-r/Avengers #53(X-Men)   3.00
29,30-(30¢-c variants, limited distribution)(5,7/76)   5.00
36,37-(35¢-c variants, limited distribution)(7,9/77)   5.00
NOTE: #5-44, 46, 47 reprint Avengers #11 thru ?. #40-r/Avengers #48(1st Black Knight).
Buscema a(r)-35p, 36p, 38p, 39p, 41, 42, 43p, 44p, 46p, 47p. *Ditko* a-2r; c-47. *Kirby* a(r)-1-4p; c-1-4, 9-19, 22, 24, 29. *Starlin* c-7. *Tuska* a(r)-40p, 43i, 46i, 47i. #2 through #17 are 20¢-c.

MARVEL TWO-IN-ONE (...Featuring ... #82 on; also see The Thing)
Marvel Comics Group: January, 1974 - No. 100, June, 1983

1-Thing team-ups begin; Man-Thing   5   15   38   60
2-6: 2-Sub-Mariner; last 20¢ issue. 3-Daredevil. 4-Capt. America. 5-Guardians
of the Galaxy (9/74, 2nd app.?). 6-Dr. Strange (11/74)
    2   6   11   16
7,9,10   1   4   7   10
8-Early Ghost Rider app. (3/75)   2   6   10   14
11-14,19,20: 13-Power Man. 14-Son of Satan (early app.)   6.00
15-18-(Regular 25¢ editions)(5-7/76) 17-Spider-Man.   6.00
15-18-(30¢-c variants, limited distribution)   1   3   6   9
21-29,31-40: 27-Deathlok. 9-Master of Kung Fu; Spider-Woman cameo. 31-
33-Spider-Woman. 39-Vision   4.00
28,29,31-(35¢-c variants, limited distribution)   6.00
30-2nd full app. Spider-Woman (see Marvel Spotlight #32 for 1st app.)
    1   3   5   7
30-(35¢-c variant, limited distribution)(8/77)   1   4   7   10
41,42,44,45,47-49: 42-Capt. America. 45-Capt. Marvel   3.00
43,50,53,55-Byrne-a(p). 53-Quasar(7/79, 2nd app.)   5.00
46-Thing battles Hulk-c/story   1   3   5   7
51-The Beast, Nick Fury, Ms. Marvel; Miller-p   5.00
52-Moon Knight app.   3.00
54-Death of Deathlok; Byrne-a   1   3   6   8
56-60,64-74,76-79,81,82: 60-Intro. Impossible Woman. 68-Angel. 69-Guardians
of the Galaxy. 71-1st app. Maelstrom. 76-Iceman   3.00
61-63: 61-Starhawk (from Guardians); "The Coming of Her" storyline begins,
ends #63; cover similar to F.F. #67 (Him-c). 62-Moondragon; Thanos &
Warlock cameo in flashback; Starhawk app. 63-Warlock revived shortly;
Starhawk & Moondragon app.   4.00
75-Avengers (52 pgs.)   4.00
80,90,100: 80-Ghost Rider. 90-Spider-Man. 100-Double size, Byrne-s   4.00
83-89,91-99: 83-Sasquatch. 84-Alpha Flight app. 93-Jocasta dies. 96-X-Men-c
& cameo   3.00
Annual 1(1976, 52 pgs.)-Thing/Liberty Legion; Kirby-c   1   3   6   8
Annual 2(1977, 52 pgs.)-Thing/Spider-Man; 2nd death of Thanos; end of
Thanos saga; Warlock app.; Starlin-c/a   3   9   19   28
Annual 3,4 (1978-79, 52 pgs.): 3-Nova. 4-Black Bolt   4.00
Annual 5-7 (1980-82, 52 pgs.): 5-Hulk. 6-1st app. American Eagle. 7-The Thing/
Champion; Sasquatch, Colossus app.; X-Men cameo (1 pg.)   3.00
NOTE: *Austin* c(i)-42, 54, 56, 58, 61, 63, 66. *Jim Buscema* a-30p, 45; c-30p. *Byrne* (p)-43, 50, 53-55; c-43, 53p, 56p, 98i, 99i. *GIL Kane* a-1p, 2p; c(p)-1-3, 9, 11, 14, 28. *Kirby* c-10, 12, 19p, 20, 25, 27. *Mooney* a-18i, 38i, 90i. *Nasser* a-70p. *Perez* a(p)-56-58, 60, 64, 65; c(p)-32, 33, 42, 50-52, 54, 55, 57, 58, 61-66, 70. *Roussos* a-Annual 1i. *Simonson* c-43i, 97p, Annual 6i. *Starlin* c-6, Annual 1. *Tuska* a-6p.

MARVEL UNIVERSE (See Official Handbook Of The...)

MARVEL UNIVERSE (Title on variant covers for newsstand editions of some 2001 Marvel titles. See indicia for actual titles and issue numbers)

MARVEL UNIVERSE
Marvel Comics: June, 1998 - No. 7, Dec, 1998 ($2.99/$1.99)

1-($2.99)-Invaders stories from WW2; Stern-s   3.00
2-7-($1.99): 2-Two covers. 4-7-Monster Hunters; Manley/a-Stern-s   2.25

MARVEL UNIVERSE: MILLENNIAL VISIONS
Marvel Comics: Feb, 2002 ($3.99, one-shot)

1-Pin-ups by various; wraparound-c by JH Williams & Gray   4.00

MARVEL UNLIMITED (Title on variant covers for newsstand editions of some 2001 Daredevil issues. See indicia for actual titles and issue numbers)

MARVEL VALENTINE SPECIAL
Marvel Comics: Mar, 1997 ($2.99, one-shot)

1-Valentine stories w/Spider-Man, Daredevil, Cyclops, Phoenix   3.00

MARVEL VERSUS DC (See DC Versus Marvel) (Also see Amazon,
Assassins, Bruce Wayne: Agent of S.H.I.E.L.D., Bullets & Bracelets, Doctor
Strangefate, JLX, Legend of the Dark Claw, Magneto & The Magnetic Men,
Speed Demon, Spider-Boy, Super Soldier, & X-Patrol)
Marvel Comics: No. 2, 1996 - No. 3, 1996 ($3.95, limited series)

2,3: 2-Peter David script. 3-Ron Marz script; Dan Jurgens-a(p). 1st app. of
Super Soldier, Spider-Boy, Dr. Doomsday, Doctor Strangefate, The Dark
Claw, Nightcreeper, Amazon, Wraith & others. Storyline continues in
Amalgam books.   4.00

MARVEL X-MEN COLLECTION
Marvel Comics: Jan, 1994 - No. 3, Mar, 1994 ($2.95, limited series)

1-3-r/X-Men trading cards by Jim Lee   3.00

MARVEL - YEAR IN REVIEW (Magazine)
Marvel Comics: 1989 - No. 3, 1991 (52 pgs.)

1-3: 1-Spider-Man-c by McFarlane. 2-Capt. America-c. 3-X-Men/Wolverine-c
  5.00

MARVIN MOUSE
Atlas Comics (BPC): September, 1957

1-Everett-c/a; Maneely-a   13   39   66   110

MARY JANE & SNIFFLES (See Looney Tunes)
Dell Publishing Co.: No. 402, June, 1952 - No. 474, June, 1953

Four Color 402 (#1)   8   24   56   100
Four Color 474   7   21   49   90

MARY MARVEL COMICS (Monte Hale #29 on) (Also see Captain Marvel #18,
Marvel Family, Shazam, & Wow Comics)
Fawcett Publications: Dec, 1945 - No. 28, Sept, 1948

1-Captain Marvel introduces Mary on-c; intro/origin Georgia Sivana
   191   573   1194   2100
2   75   225   469   825
3,4: 3-New logo   52   157   314   550
5-8: 8-Bulletgirl x-over in Mary Marvel; X-Mas-c   40   120   232   400
9,10   38   114   203   350
11-20   25   75   130   225
21-28: 28-Western-c   21   63   110   190

MARY POPPINS (See Movie Comics & Walt Disney Showcase No. 17)

MARY SHELLEY'S FRANKENSTEIN
Topps Comics: Oct, 1994 - Jan, 1995 ($2.95, limited series)

1-4-polybagged w/3 trading cards   3.00
1-4 -($2.50)-Newstand ed.   2.50

MARY WORTH (See Harvey Comics Hits #55 & Love Stories of...)
Argo: March, 1956 (Also see Romantic Picture Novelettes)

1   8   24   42   60

MASK (TV)
DC Comics: Dec, 1985 - No. 4, Mar, 1986; Feb, 1987 - No. 9, Oct, 1987

1-4; 1-9 (2nd series)-Sat. morning TV show.   2.50

MASK, THE (Also see Mayhem)
Dark Horse Comics: Aug, 1991 - No. 4, Oct, 1991; No. 0, Dec, 1991 ($2.50, 36
pgs., limited series)

1-4 -1st app. Lt. Kellaway as The Mask (see Dark Horse Presents #10
for 1st app.)   5.00
0-(12/91, B&W, 56 pgs.)-r/Mayhem #1-4   4.00

...: HUNT FOR GREEN OCTOBER July, 1995 - Oct, 1995 ($2.50, lim. series)
1-4-Evan Dorkin scripts   2.50

.../ MARSHALL LAW Feb, 1998 - No. 2, Mar, 1998 ($2.95, lim. series)
1,2-Mills-s/O'Neill-a   3.00

...: OFFICIAL MOVIE ADAPTATION July, 1994 - Aug, 1994 ($2.50, lim. series)
1,2   2.50

The Mask: World Tour #4 © DH

Masked Marvel #2 © CEN

Master Comics #1 © FAW

	GD2.0	FN6.0	VF8.0	NM9.4

...RETURNS Oct, 1992 - No. 4, Mar, 1993 ($2.50, limited series)

1-4				4.00

...SOUTHERN DISCOMFORT Mar, 1996 - No. 4, July, 1996 ($2.50, lim. series)

1-4				2.50

...STRIKES BACK Feb, 1995 - No. 5, Jun, 1995 ($2.50, limited series)

1-5				2.50

...SUMMER VACATION July, 1995 ($10.95, one shot, hard-c)

1-nn-Rick Geary-c/a				11.00

...TOYS IN THE ATTIC Aug, 1998 - No. 4, Nov, 1998 ($2.95, limited series)

1-4-Fingerman-s				3.00

...VIRTUAL SURREALITY July, 1997 ($2.95, one shot)

nn-Mignola, Aragonés, and others-s/a				3.00

...WORLD TOUR Dec, 1995 - No. 4, Mar, 1996 ($2.50, limited series, color/B&W #9 on)

1-4: 3-X & Ghost-c/app.				2.50

MASK COMICS
Rural Home Publ.: Feb-Mar, 1945 - No. 2, Apr-May, 1945; No. 2, Fall, 1945

1-Classic L. B. Cole Satan-c/a; Palais-a	273	819	1705	3000
2-(Scarce)-Classic L. B. Cole Satan-c; Black Rider, The Boy Magician, & The Collector app.	173	519	1080	1900
2-(Fall, 1945)-No publ.-same as regular #2; L. B. Cole-c	136	408	852	1500

MASKED BANDIT, THE
Avon Periodicals: 1952

nn-Kinstler-a	17	51	88	150

MASKED MAN, THE
Eclipse Comics: 12/84 - #10, 4/86; #11, 10/87; #12, 4/88 ($1.75/$2.00, B&W #9 on, Baxter paper)

1-12: 1-Origin retold. 3-Origin Aphid-Man; begin $2.00-c				2.25

MASKED MARVEL (See Keen Detective Funnies)
Centaur Publications: Sept, 1940 - No. 3, Dec, 1940

1-The Masked Marvel begins	164	492	1023	1800
2,3: 2-Gustavson, Tarpe Mills-a	111	332	694	1225

MASKED RAIDER (Billy The Kid #9 on; Frontier Scout, Daniel Boone #10-13) (Also see Blue Bird)
Charlton Comics: June, 1955 - No. 8, July, 1957; No. 14, Aug, 1958 - No. 30, June, 1961

1-Masked Raider & Talon the Golden Eagle begin; painted-c	12	36	61	105
2	8	24	42	60
3-8,15: 8-Billy The Kid app. 15-Williamson-a, 7 pgs.	6	18	29	40
14,16-30: 22-Rocky Lane app.	5	15	24	32

MASKED RANGER
Premier Magazines: Apr, 1954 - No. 9, Aug, 1955

1-The Masked Ranger, his horse Streak, & The Crimson Avenger (origin) begin, end #9; Woodbridge/Frazetta-a	40	120	240	420
2,3	14	42	72	120
4-8-All Woodbridge-a. 5-Jesse James by Woodbridge. 6-Billy The Kid by Woodbridge. 7-Wild Bill Hickok by Woodbridge. 8-Jim Bowie's Life Story	15	45	77	130
9-Torres-a; Wyatt Earp by Woodbridge; Says Death of Masked Ranger on-c	16	48	83	140

NOTE: Check a-1. Woodbridge c/a-1, 4-9.

MASK OF DR. FU MANCHU, THE (See Dr. Fu Manchu)
Avon Periodicals: 1951

1-Sax Rohmer adapt.; Wood-c/a (26 pgs.); Hollingsworth-a	91	273	568	1000

MASK OF ZORRO, THE
Image Comics: Aug, 1998 - No. 4, Dec, 1998 ($2.95, limited series)

1-4-Movie adapt. Photo variant-c				3.00

MASQUE OF THE RED DEATH (See Movie Classics)

MASTER COMICS (Combined with Slam Bang Comics #7 on)
Fawcett Publications: Mar, 1940 - No. 133, Apr, 1953 (No. 1-6: oversized issues) (#1-3: 15¢, 52 pgs.; #4-6: 10¢, 36 pgs.; #7-Begin 68 pg. issues)

	GD2.0	FN6.0	VF8.0	NM9.4

1-Origin & 1st app. Master Man; The Devil's Dagger, El Carim, Master of Magic, Rick O'Say, Morton Murch, White Rajah, Shipwreck Roberts, Frontier Marshal, Streak Sloan, Mr. Clue begin (all features end #6)	731	2193	4750	9500
2	218	654	1364	2400
3-6: 6-Last Master Man	164	492	1023	1800

NOTE: #1-6 rarely found in near mint to mint condition due to large-size format.

7-(10/40)-Bulletman, Zoro, the Mystery Man (ends #22), Lee Granger, Jungle King, & Buck Jones begin; only app. The War Bird & Mark Swift & the Time Retarder; Zoro, Lee Granger, Jungle King & Mark Swift all continue from Slam Bang; Bulletman moves from Nickel	291	873	1818	3200
8-The Red Gaucho (ends #13), Captain Venture (ends #22) & The Planet Princess begin	150	450	938	1650
9,10: 10-Lee Granger ends	118	354	738	1300
11-Origin & 1st app. Minute-Man (2/41)	255	765	1591	2800
12	127	381	795	1400
13-Origin & 1st app. Bulletgirl; Hitler-c	195	584	1219	2150
14-16: 14-Companions Three begin, ends #31	105	321	669	1175
17-20: 17-Raboy-a on Bulletman begins. 20-Captain Marvel cameo app. in Bulletman	98	294	613	1075
21-(12/41; Scarce)-Captain Marvel & Bulletman team up against Capt. Nazi; origin & 1st app. Capt. Nazi; Capt. Marvel Jr's most famous nemesis Capt. Nazi who will cause creation of Capt. Marvel Jr. in Whiz #25. Part I of trilogy origin of Capt. Marvel Jr.; 1st Mac Raboy-c for Fawcett; Capt. Nazi-c	485	1455	3150	6300
22-(1/42)-Captain Marvel Jr. moves over from Whiz #25 & teams up with Bulletman against Captain Nazi; part III of trilogy origin of Capt. Marvel Jr. & his 1st cover and adventure	438	1314	2847	5700
23-Capt. Marvel Jr. c/stories begin (1st solo story); fights Capt. Nazi by himself.	286	858	1790	3150
24,25	95	285	597	1050
26-28,30-Captain Marvel Jr. vs. Capt. Nazi. 30-Flag-c	84	253	525	925
29-Hitler & Hirohito-c	105	315	656	1150
31-33,35: 32-Last El Carim & Buck Jones; intro Balbo, the Boy Magician in El Carim story; classic Eagle-c by Raboy. 33-Balbo, the Boy Magician (ends #47), Hopalong Cassidy (ends #49)	64	192	398	700
34-Capt. Marvel Jr. vs. Capt. Nazi-c/story	73	219	455	800
36-40: 40-Flag-c	59	177	369	650
41-(8/43)-Bulletman, Capt. Marvel Jr. & Bulletgirl x-over in Minute-Man; only app.Crime Crusaders Club (Capt. Marvel Jr., Minute-Man, Bulletman & Bulletgirl)	64	192	398	700
42-47,49: 47-Hitler becomes Corpl. Hitler Jr. 49-Last Minute-Man	40	120	232	400
48-Intro. Bulletboy; Capt. Marvel cameo in Minute-Man	45	135	270	475
50-Intro Radar & Nyoka the Jungle Girl & begin series (5/44); Radar also intro in Captain Marvel #35 (same date); Capt. Marvel x-over in Radar; origin Radar; Capt. Marvel & Capt. Marvel, Jr. introduce Radar on-c	40	120	240	420
51-58	23	69	121	210
59-62: Nyoka serial "Terrible Tiara" in all; 61-Capt. Marvel Jr. 1st meets Uncle Marvel	26	78	136	235
63-80	19	57	99	165
81,83-87,89-91,95-99: 88-Hopalong Cassidy begins (ends #94). 95-Tom Mix begins (cover only in #123, ends #133)	16	48	83	140
82,88,92-94-Krigstein-a	17	51	88	150
100	17	51	88	150
101-106-Last Bulletman (not in #104)	15	45	77	130
107-131: 118-Mary Marvel. 123-Tom Mix-c	14	42	72	120
132-B&W and color illos in POP; last Nyoka	14	42	72	125
133-Bill Battle app.	20	60	105	175

NOTE: Mac Raboy a-15-39, 40(part), 42, 58, c-21-49, 51, 52, 54, 56, 58, 68(part), 69(part). Bulletman c-7-11, 13(half), 15, 18(part), 19, 20, 21(w/Capt. Marvel & Capt. Nazi), 22(w/Capt. Marvel, Jr.). Capt. Marvel, Jr. c-23-133. Master Man c-1-6. Minute Man c-12, 13(half), 14, 16, 17, 18(part).

MASTER DARQUE
Acclaim Comics (Valiant): Feb, 1998 ($3.95)

1-Manco-c/Christina Z.-s				4.00

MASTER DETECTIVE

Master of Kung-Fu #79 © MAR

Masters of the Universe #1 © DC

Maverick #6 © MAR

Super Comics: 1964 (Reprints)

	GD2.0	FN6.0	VF8.0	NM9.4
17-r/Criminals on the Loose V4 #2; r/Young King Cole #?; McWilliams-r				
	2	6	9	12

MASTER OF KUNG FU (Formerly Special Marvel Edition; see Deadly Hands of Kung Fu & Giant-Size...)
Marvel Comics Group: No. 17, April, 1974 - No. 125, June, 1983

17-Starlin-a; intro Black Jack Tarr; 3rd Shang-Chi (ties w/Deadly Hands #1)				
	2	6	15	22
18,20	2	6	9	12
19-Man-Thing-c/story	2	6	11	15
21-23,25-30	1	3	5	7
24-Starlin, Simonson-a	1	3	6	9
31-50: 33-1st Leiko Wu. 43-Last 25¢ issue				5.00
39-43-(30¢-c variants, limited distribution)(5-7/76)	1	3	6	8
51-99				4.00
53-57-(35¢-c variants, limited distribution)(6-10/77)				6.00
100,118,125-Double size				5.00
101-117,119-124				3.00
Annual 1(4/76)-Iron Fist app.	2	6	10	14

NOTE: **Austin** c-63i, 74i. **Buscema** c-44p. **Gulacy** a(p)-18-20, 22, 25, 29-31, 33-35, 38, 39, 40(p&i), 42-50, 53i(#20); c-51, 55, 64, 67. **Gil Kane** c(p)-20, 38, 39, 42, 45, 59, 63. **Nebres** c-73i. **Starlin**-a-17p, 24; c-54. **Sutton** a-42i. #53 reprints #20.

MASTER OF KUNG-FU: BLEEDING BLACK
Marvel Comics: Feb, 1991 ($2.95, 84 pgs., one-shot)

1-The Return of Shang-Chi				3.00

MASTER OF THE WORLD
Dell Publishing Co.: No. 1157, July, 1961

Four Color 1157-Movie	5	15	35	60

MASTERS OF TERROR (Magazine)
Marvel Comics Group: July, 1975 - No. 2, Sept, 1975 (B&W) (All reprints)

1-Brunner, Barry Smith-a; Morrow/Steranko-c; Starlin-a(r); Gil Kane-a				
	2	6	11	16
2-Reese, Kane, Mayerik-a; Adkins/Steranko-c	2	6	9	12

MASTERS OF THE UNIVERSE (See DC Comics Presents #47 for 1st app.)
DC Comics: Dec, 1982 - No. 3, Feb, 1983 (Mini-series)

1-3: 2-Origin He-Man & Ceril				4.00

NOTE: **Alcala** a-1i, 2i. **Tuska** a-1-3p; c-1-3p. #2 has 75 & 95 cent cover price.

MASTERS OF THE UNIVERSE (Comic Album)
Western Publishing Co.: 1984 (8-1/2x11", $2.95, 64 pgs.)

11362-Based on Mattel toy & cartoon	2	6	9	12

MASTERS OF THE UNIVERSE
Star Comics/Marvel #7 on: May, 1986 - No. 13, May, 1988 (75¢/$1.00)

1-11: 8-Begin $1.00-c				5.00
12-Death of He-Man (1st Marvel app.)				6.00
13-Return of He-Man & death of Skeletor				6.00
The Motion Picture (11/87, $2.00)-Tuska-p				4.00

MASTERWORKS SERIES OF GREAT COMIC BOOK ARTISTS, THE
Sea Gate Dist./DC Comics: May, 1983 - No. 3, Dec, 1983 (Baxter paper)

1-3: 1,2-Shining Knight by Frazetta r-/Adventure. 2-Tomahawk by Frazetta-r. 3-Wrightson-c/a(r)				5.00

MATT SLADE GUNFIGHTER (Kid Slade Gunfighter #5 on; See Western Gunfighters)
Atlas Comics (SPI): May, 1956 - No. 4, Nov, 1956

1-Intro Matt & horse Eagle; Williamson/Torres-a	21	63	110	185
2-Williamson-a	13	39	66	110
3,4	13	30	55	80

NOTE: **Maneely** a-1, 3, 4; c-1, 2, 4. **Roth** a-2-4. **Severin** a-1, 3, 4. **Maneely** c/a-1. Issue #s stamped on cover after printing.

MAUS: A SURVIVOR'S TALE (First graphic novel to win a Pulitzer Prize)
Pantheon Books: 1986, 1991 (B&W)

Vol. 1-(...: My Father Bleeds History)(1986) Art Spiegelman-s/a; recounts stories of Spiegelman's father in 1930s-40s Nazi-occupied Poland; collects first six stories serialized in Raw Magazine from 1980-1985				20.00
Vol. 2-(...: And Here My Troubles Began)(1991)				20.00

Complete Maus Survivor's Tale -HC Vols. 1& 2 w/slipcase				35.00
Hardcover Vol. 1 (1991)				24.00
Hardcover Vol. 2 (1991)				24.00
TPB (1992, $14.00) Vols. 1& 2				14.00

MAVERICK (TV)
Dell Publishing Co.: No. 892, 4/58 - No. 19, 4-6/62 (All have photo-c)

Four Color 892 (#1)-James Garner photo-c begin	25	75	175	325
Four Color 930,945,962,980,1005 (6-8/59): 945-James Garner/Jack Kelly photo-c begin	11	33	77	140
7 (10-12/59) - 14: Last Garner/Kelly-c	9	27	63	110
15-18: Jack Kelly/Roger Moore photo-c	7	21	49	90
19-Jack Kelly photo-c	7	21	49	90

MAVERICK (See X-Men)
Marvel Comics: Jan, 1997 ($2.95, one-shot)

1-Hama-s				3.00

MAVERICK (See X-Men)
Marvel Comics: Sept, 1997 - No. 12, Aug, 1998 ($2.99/$1.99)

1,12: 1-($2.99)-Wraparound-c. 12-($2.99) Battles Omega Red				4.00
2-11: 2-Two covers. 4-Wolverine app. 6,7-Sabretooth app.				3.00

MAVERICK MARSHAL
Charlton Comics: Nov, 1958 - No. 7, May, 1960

1	6	18	29	40
2-7	5	14	21	28

MAVERICKS
Daggar Comics Group: Jan, 1994 - No. 5, 1994 (#1-$2.75, #2-5-$2.50)

1-5: 1-Bronze. 1-Gold. 1-Silver				2.75

MAX BRAND (See Silvertip)

MAXIMAGE
Image Comics (Extreme Studios): Dec, 1995 - No. 7, June 1996 ($2.50)

1-7: 1-Liefeld-c. 2-Extreme Destroyer Pt. 2; polybagged w/card. 4-Angela & Glory-c/app.				2.50

MAXIMUM SECURITY (Crossover)
Marvel Comics: Oct, 2000 - No. 3, Jan, 2001 ($2.99)

1-3-Busiek-s/Ordway-a; Ronan the Accuser, Avengers app.				3.00
...Dangerous Planet 1: Busiek-s/Ordway-a; Ego, the Living Planet				3.00
Thor vs. Ego (11/00, $2.99) Reprints Thor #133,160,161; Kirby-a				3.00

MAXX (Also see Darker Image, Primer #5, & Friends of Maxx)
Image Comics (I Before E): Mar, 1993 - No. 35, Feb, 1998 ($1.95)

1/2	1	4	7	10
1/2 (Gold)				20.00
1-Sam Kieth-c/a/scripts				4.00
1-Glow-in-the-dark variant	2	6	9	12
1-"3-D Edition" (1/98, $4.95) plus new back-up story				5.00
2-12: 6-Savage Dragon cameo(1 pg.). 7,8-Pitt-c & story				2.50
13-16				2.50
17-35: 21-Alan Moore-s				2.50

MAYA (See Movie Classics)
Gold Key: Mar, 1968

1 (10218-803)(TV)	3	9	17	25

MAYHEM
Dark Horse Comics: May, 1989 - No. 4, Sept, 1989 ($2.50, B&W, 52 pgs.)

1- Four part Stanley Ipkiss/Mask story begins; Mask-c	1	4	7	10
2-4: 2-Mask 1/2 back-c. 4-Mask-c	1	3	6	9

MAZE AGENCY, THE
Comico/Innovation Publ. #8 on: Dec, 1988 - No. 20, 1991 ($1.95-$2.50, color)

1-20: 9-Ellery Queen app. 7 ($2.50)-Last Comico issue				2.50
Annual 1 (1990, $2.75)-Ploog-c; Spirit tribute ish				2.75
Special 1 (1989, $2.75)-Staton-p (Innovation)				2.75

MAZE AGENCY, THE (Vol. 2)
Caliber Comics: July, 1997 - Present ($2.95, B&W)

1-3: 1-Barr-s/Gonzales-a(p). 3-Hughes-c				3.00

McCandless & Company: Dead Razor © J.C. Vaughn

MD #4 © WMG

Measles #8 © Fantagraphics Books

	GD2.0	FN6.0	VF8.0	NM9.4

AZIE (...& Her Friends) (See Flat-Top, Mortie, Stevie & Tastee-Freez)
azie Comics(Magazine Publ.)/Harvey Publ. No. 13-on: 1953 - #12, 1954; 3, 12/54 - #22, 9/56; #23, 9/57 - #28, 8/58

-(Teen-age)-Stevie's girlfriend	8	24	45	65
2	5	15	24	32
-10	5	14	21	28
1-28	4	10	15	20

AZIE
ation Wide Publishers: 1950 - No. 7, 1951 (5¢) (5x7-1/4"-miniature)(52 pgs.)

-Teen-age	16	48	83	140
2-7	9	27	49	70

AZINGER (See First Comics Graphic Novel #17)

AZING MAN
C Comics: Jan, 1986 - No. 12, Dec, 1986

-11: 7,8-Hembeck-a		2.50
2-Dark Knight part-c by Miller		3.00
pecial 1 ('87), 2 (4/88), 3 ('90)-All $2.00, 52pgs.		2.50

CCANDLESS & COMPANY
andalay Books: 2001 ($7.95)

: Dead Razor - J.C. Vaughn-s/Busch & Sheehan-a; 3 covers		8.00

CHALE'S NAVY (TV) (See Movie Classics)
ell Publ. Co.: May-July, 1963 - No. 3, Nov-Jan, 1963-64 (All have photo-c)

	5	15	35	70
,3	5	15	34	55

CKEEVER & THE COLONEL (TV)
ell Publishing Co.: Feb-Apr, 1963 - No. 3, Aug-Oct, 1963

-Photo-c	5	15	35	70
,3	4	12	30	50

CLINTOCK (See Movie Comics)
D
C. Comics: Apr-May, 1955 - No. 5, Dec-Jan, 1955-56

-Not approved by code; Craig-c	11	33	77	140
-5	8	24	56	100

NOTE: *Crandall, Evans, Ingels, Orlando* art in all issues; *Craig* c-1-5.

D
uss Cochran/Gemstone Publishing: Sept, 1999 - No. 5, Jan, 2000 ($2.50)

-5-Reprints original EC series		2.50
nual 1 (1999, $13.50) r/#1-5		14.00

D. GEIST
M Comics: 1995 - No. 3, 1995 (Limited series)

-3		3.00

D. GEIST DATA ALBUM
M Comics: June, 1996 ($9.95, trade paperback)

		10.00

D. GEIST: GROUND ZERO
M Comics: Mar, 1996 - No. 3, May, 1996 ($2.95, limited series)

-3		3.00

EASLES
ntagraphics Books: Christmas 1998 - Present ($2.95, B&W, quarterly)

-8-Anthology: 1-Venus-s by Hernandez		3.00

AT CAKE
nographix: 1992 (B&W)

		2.50

AT CAKE
ntagraphics Books: No. 1, Oct, 1993 - Present (B&W)

-8: 3-Sal Buscema-a. 0-(1996)-r/Meat Cake #1 from Iconographix		2.50
-($3.95) Alan Moore-s		4.00

CHA (Also see Mayhem)
rk Horse Comics: June, 1987 - No. 6, 1988 ($1.50/$1.95, color/B&W)

-6: 1,2 ($1.95, color), 3,4-($1.75, B&W), 5,6-($1.50, B&W)		2.50

	GD2.0	FN6.0	VF8.0	NM9.4

MECHANIC, THE
Image Comics: 1998 ($5.95, one-shot, squarebound)

1-Chiodo-painted art; Peterson-s		6.00
1-($10.00) DF Alternate Cover Ed.		10.00

MECHA SPECIAL
Dark Horse Comics: May, 1995 ($2.95, one-shot)

1		3.00

MECH DESTROYER
Image Comics: Apr, 2001 - No. 4, Sept, 2001 ($2.95, limited series)

1-4-Jae Kim-c/a; Robert Chong-s		3.00

MEDAL FOR BOWZER, A
American Visuals: 1966 (8 pgs.)

nn-Eisner-c/script	27	81	145	250

MEDAL OF HONOR COMICS
A. S. Curtis: Spring, 1946

1-War stories	12	36	61	100

MEDAL OF HONOR SPECIAL
Dark Horse Comics: 1994 ($2.50, one-shot)

1-Kubert-c/a (first story)		2.50

MEDIA STARR
Innovation Publ.: July, 1989 - No. 3, Sept, 1989 ($1.95, mini-series, 28pgs.)

1-3: Deluxe format		2.25

MEDIEVAL SPAWN/WITCHBLADE
Image Comics (Top Cow Productions): May, 1996 - No. 3, June, 1996 ($2.95, limited series)

1-3-Garth Ennis scripts in all		6.00
1-Platinum foil-c (500 copies from Pittsburgh Con)		35.00
1-Gold		10.00
1-ETM Exclusive Edition; gold foil logo		7.00
TPB ($9.95) r/#1-3		10.00

MEET ANGEL (Formerly Angel & the Ape)
National Periodical Publications: No. 7, Nov-Dec, 1969

7-Wood-a(i)	3	9	17	24

MEET CORLISS ARCHER (Radio/Movie)(My Life #4 on)
Fox Features Syndicate: Mar, 1948 - No. 3, July, 1948

1-(Teen-age)-Feldstein-c/a; headlight-c	100	300	625	1100
2	55	165	341	600
3-Part Feldstein-c only	50	150	300	525

NOTE: *No. 1-3 used in Seduction of the Innocent, pg. 39.*

MEET HERCULES (See Three Stooges)

MEET MERTON
Toby Press: Dec, 1953 - No. 4, June, 1954

1-(Teen-age)-Dave Berg-c/a	9	27	49	70
2-Dave Berg-c/a	6	18	28	38
3,4-Dave Berg-c/a	5	15	25	35
I.W. Reprint #9, Super Reprint #11('63), 18	2	6	9	12

MEET MISS BLISS (Becomes Stories Of Romance #5 on)
Atlas Comics (LMC): May, 1955 - No. 4, Nov, 1955

1-Al Hartley-c/a	14	42	72	120
2-4	9	27	49	70

MEET MISS PEPPER (Formerly Lucy, The Real Gone Gal)
St. John Publishing Co.: No. 5, April, 1954 - No. 6, June, 1954

5-Kubert/Maurer-a	21	63	110	185
6-Kubert/Maurer-a; Kubert-c	17	51	88	150

MEGA DRAGON & TIGER
Image Comics: Mar, 1999 - No. 5 ($2.95)

1-5-Tony Wong-s/a		3.00

MEGAHURTZ
Image Comics: Aug, 1997 - No. 3, Oct, 1997 ($2.95, B&W)

1-3-St. Pierre-s		3.00

Megalith #1 © Continuity Publ. Inc.

Menace #3 © ATL

Men in Action #6 © MAR

MEGALITH (Megalith Deathwatch 2000 #1,2 of second series)
Continuity: 1989 - No. 9, Mar, 1992; No, 0, Apr, 1993 - No. 7, Jan, 1994
1-9-($2.00-c) 1-Adams & Texiera-c/Texiera & Nebres-a				3.00
2nd series: 0-(4/93)-Foil-c; no c-price, giveaway; Adams plot				3.00
1-7: 1-3-Bagged w/card: 1-Gatefold-c by Nebres; Adams plot. 2-Fold-out-c; Adamsplot. 3-Indestructible-c. 4-7-Embossed-c: 4-Adams/Nebres-c; Adams part-i. 5-Sienkiewicz-i. 6-Adams part-i. 7-Adams-c(p); Adams plot				3.00

MEGATON (A super hero)
Megaton Publ.: Nov, 1983; No. 2, Oct, 1985 - No. 8, Aug, 1987 (B&W)
1-($2.00, 68 pgs.)-Erik Larsen's 1st pro work; Vanguard by Larsen begins (1st app.), ends #4; 1st app. Megaton, Berzerker, & Ethrian; Guice-c/a(p); Gustovich-a(p) in #1,2	1	3	6	8
2-($2.00, 68 pgs.)-The Dragon cameo (1 pg.) by Larsen (later The Savage Dragon in Image Comics); Guice-c/a(p)				5.00
3-(44 pgs.)-1st full app. Savage Dragon-c/story by Larsen; 1st comic book work by Angel Medina (pin-up)	2	6	9	12
4-(52 pgs.)-2nd full app. Savage Dragon by Larsen; 4,5-Wildman by Grass Green	1	3	5	7
5-1st Liefeld published-a (inside f/c, 6/86)				4.00
6,7: 6-Larsen-c				3.00
8-1st Liefeld story-a (7 pg. super hero story) plus 1 pg. Youngblood ad				5.00
...Explosion (6/87, 16 pg. color giveaway)-1st app. Youngblood by Rob Liefeld (2 pg. spread); shows Megaton heroes	2	6	11	15
...Holiday Special 1 (1994, $2.95, color, 40 pgs., publ. by Entity Comics)-Gold foil logo; bagged w/Kelley Jones card; Vanguard, Megaton plus shows unpublished #1 by Liefeld/Ordway				3.00
NOTE: Copies of Megaton Explosion were also released in early 1992 all signed by Rob Liefeld and were made available to retailers.

MEGATON MAN (See Don Simpson's Bizarre Heroes)
Kitchen Sink Enterprises: Nov, 1984 - No. 10, 1986
1-10, 1-2nd printing (1989)				3.00
...Meets The Uncategorizable X-Thems 1 (4/89, $2.00)				3.00

MEGATON MAN: BOMB SHELL
Image Comics: Jul, 1999 - No. 2 ($2.95, B&W, mini-series)
1-Reprints stories from Megaton Man internet site				3.00

MEGATON MAN: HARD COPY
Image Comics: Feb, 1999 - No. 2, Apr, 1999 ($2.95, B&W, mini-series)
1,2-Reprints stories from Megaton Man internet site				3.00

MEGATON MAN VS. FORBIDDEN FRANKENSTEIN
Fiasco Comics: Apr, 1996 ($2.95, B&W, one-shot)
1-Intro The Tomb Team (Forbidden Frankenstein, Drekula, Bride of the Monster, & Moon Wolf).				3.00

MEL ALLEN SPORTS COMICS (The Voice of the Yankees)
Standard Comics: No. 5, Nov, 1949; No. 6, June, 1950
5-(#1 on inside)-Tuska-a	24	72	127	215
6-(#2)-Lou Gehrig story	16	48	83	140

MELTING POT
Kitchen Sink Press: Dec, 1993 - No. 4, Sept, 1994 ($2.95)
1-4: Bisley-painted-c				3.00

MELVIN MONSTER
Dell Publishing Co.: Apr-June, 1965 - No. 10, Oct, 1969
1-By John Stanley	11	33	77	130
2-10-All by Stanley. #10-r/#1	8	24	58	95

MELVIN THE MONSTER (See Peter, the Little Pest & Dexter The Demon #7)
Atlas Comics (HPC): July, 1956 - No. 6, July, 1957
1-Maneely-c/a	14	42	72	120
2-6: 4-Maneely-c/a	10	30	55	80

MENACE
Atlas Comics (HPC): Mar, 1953 - No. 11, May, 1954
1-Horror & sci/fi stories begin; Everett-c/a	64	192	398	700
2-Post-atom bomb disaster by Everett; anti-Communist propaganda/torture scenes; Sinnott sci/fi story "Rocket to the Moon"	45	135	270	475
3,4,6-Everett-a. 4-Sci/fi story "Escape to the Moon". 6-Romita sci/fi story "Science Fiction"	39	117	208	360

5-Origin & 1st app. The Zombie by Everett (reprinted in Tales of the Zombie #1)(7/53); 5-Sci/fi story "Rocket Ship"	55	165	330	575
7,8,10,11: 7-Frankenstein story. 8-End of world story; Heath 3-D art(3 pgs.)				
10-H-Bomb panels	29	87	153	265
9-Everett-a r-in Vampire Tales #1	34	102	179	310
NOTE: **Brodsky** c-7, 8, 11. **Colan** a-6; c-9. **Everett** a-1-6, 9; c-1-6. **Heath** a-1-8; c-10. **Katz** a-11. **Maneely** a-3, 5, 7-9. **Powell** a-11. **Romita** a-3, 6, 8, 11. **Shelly** a-10. **Shores** a-7. **Sinnott** a-2, 7 **Tuska** a-1, 2, 5.

MENACE
Awesome-Hyperwerks: Nov, 1998 ($2.50)
1-Jada Pinkett Smith-s/Fraga-a				2.50

MEN AGAINST CRIME (Formerly Mr. Risk; Hand of Fate #8 on)
Ace Magazines: No. 3, Feb, 1951 - No. 7, Oct, 1951
3-Mr. Risk app.	11	33	55	90
4-7: 4-Colan-a; entire book-r as Trapped! #4. 5-Meskin-a	8	24	42	60

MEN, GUNS, & CATTLE (See Classics Illustrated Special Issue)

MEN IN ACTION (Battle Brady #10 on)
Atlas Comics (IPS): April, 1952 - No. 9, Dec, 1952 (War stories)
1-Berg, Reinman-a	17	51	88	150
2,3: 3-Heath-c/a	10	30	55	80
4-6,8,9	8	24	45	65
7-Krigstein-a; Heath-c	10	30	55	80
NOTE: **Brodsky** c-1, 4-6. **Maneely** c-5. **Pakula** a-1, 6. **Robinson** c-8. **Shores** c-9.

MEN IN ACTION
Ajax/Farrell Publications: April, 1957 - No. 6, 1958
1	9	27	49	70
2	6	18	29	40
3-6	5	15	24	32

MEN IN BLACK, THE (1st series)
Aircel Comics (Malibu): Jan, 1990 - No. 3 Mar, 1990 ($2.25, B&W, lim. series)
1-Cunningham-s/a in all	4	12	26	40
2,3	2	6	15	22
Graphic Novel (Jan, 1991) r/#1-3	3	9	17	25

MEN IN BLACK (2nd series)
Aircel Comics (Malibu): May, 1991 - No. 3, Jul, 1991 ($2.50, B&W, lim. series)
1-Cunningham-s/a in all	2	6	13	20
2,3	1	4	7	10

MEN IN BLACK: FAR CRY
Marvel Comics: Aug, 1997 ($3.99, color, one-shot)
1-Cunningham-s				4.00

MEN IN BLACK: RETRIBUTION
Marvel Comics: Dec, 1997 ($3.99, color, one-shot)
1-Cunningham-s; continuation of the movie				4.00

MEN IN BLACK: THE MOVIE
Marvel Comics: Oct, 1997 ($3.99, color, movie adaption)
1-Cunningham-s				4.00

MEN INTO SPACE
Dell Publishing Co.: No. 1083, Feb-Apr, 1960
Four Color 1083-Anderson-a, photo-c	5	15	35	60

MEN OF BATTLE (Also see New Men of Battle)
Catechetical Guild: V1#5, March, 1943 (Hardcover)
V1#5-Topix reprints	5	15	24	32

MEN OF WAR
DC Comics, Inc.: August, 1977 - No. 26, March, 1980 (#9,10: 44 pgs.)
1-Enemy Ace, Gravedigger (origin #1,2) begin	2	6	11	16
2-4,8-10,12-14,19,20: All Enemy Ace stories. 4-1st Dateline Frontline.				
9-Unknown Soldier app.	1	3	6	
5-7,11,15-18,21-25: 17-1st app. Rosa				6.00
26-Sgt. Rock & Easy Co.-c/s	1	4	7	10
NOTE: **Chaykin** a-9, 10, 12-14, 19, 20. **Evans** a-25. **Kubert** c-2-23, 24p, 26.

MEN'S ADVENTURES (Formerly True Adventures)
Marvel/Atlas Comics (CCC): No. 4, Aug, 1950 - No. 28, July, 1954

Men's Adventures #16 © MAR

Metal Men #7 © DC

Metamorpho #2 © DC

MG

	GD2.0	FN6.0	VF8.0	NM9.4
4(#1)(52 pgs.)	33	99	174	300
5-Flying Saucer story	21	63	110	185
6-8: 7-Buried alive story. 8-Sci/fic story	19	57	99	165
9-20: All war format	12	36	61	100
21,22,24,26: All horror format	20	60	105	180
23-Crandall-a; Fox-a(i); horror format	21	63	110	185
25-Shrunken head-c	33	99	174	300
27,28-Human Torch & Toro-c/stories; Captain America & Sub-Mariner stories				
in each (also see Young Men #24-28)	98	294	613	1075

NOTE: **Ayers** a-27(H. Torch). **Berg** a-15, 16. **Brodsky** c-4-9, 11, 12, 16-18, 24. **Burgos** c-27, 28(Human Torch). **Colan** a-14, 19. **Everett** a-10, 14, 22, 25, 28; c-14, 21-23. **Heath** a-8, 11, 24; c-3, 20, 26. **Lawrence** a-23; 27(Captain America). **Maneely** a-24; c-10, 15. **Mac Pakula** a-15, 25. **Post** a-23. **Powell** a-27(Sub-Mariner). **Reinman** a-11, 12. **Robinson** c-19. **Romita** a-22. **Shores** -25. **Sinnott** a-21. **Tuska** a-24. Adventure-#4-8; War-#9-20; Weird/Horror-#21-26.

MENZ INSANA
DC Comics (Vertigo): 1997 ($7.95, one-shot)

n-Fowler-s/Bolton painted art	1	3	6	8

MEPHISTO VS... (See Silver Surfer #3)
Marvel Comics Group: Apr, 1987 - No. 4, July, 1987 ($1.50, mini-series)

1-4: 1-Fantastic Four; Austin-i. 2-X-Factor. 3-X-Men. 4-Avengers 3.00

MERC (See Mark Hazzard: Merc)

MERCHANTS OF DEATH
Acme Press (Eclipse): Jul, 1988 - No. 4, Nov, 1988 ($3.50, B&W/16 pgs. color, 4pg. mag.)

1-4: 4-Toth-c 3.50

MERCY
DC Comics (Vertigo): 1993 ($5.95, 68 pgs., mature)

n 6.00

MERIDIAN
CrossGeneration Comics: Jul, 2000 - Present ($2.95)

1-19: Barbara Kesel-s	3.00
PB (2001, $19.95) r/#1-7; cover by Steve Rude	20.00

MERRILL JONES AS THE MONKEY'S UNCLE (See Movie Comics and The Misadventures of... under Movie Comics)

MERRILL'S MARAUDERS (See Movie Classics)

MERRY CHRISTMAS (See A Christmas Adventure, Donald Duck..., Dell Giant #39, & March of Comics #153)

MERRY COMICS
Carlton Publishing Co.: Dec, 1945 (No cover price)

n-Boogeyman app.	21	63	110	190

MERRY COMICS: Four Star Publications: 1947 (Advertised, not published)

MERRY-GO-ROUND COMICS
LaSalle Publ. Co./Croyden Publ./Rotary Litho.: 1944 (25¢, 132 pgs.); 1946; 9-10/47 - No. 2, 1948

n(1944)(LaSalle)-Funny animal; 29 new features	19	57	99	165
21 (Publisher?)	8	24	42	60
1 (1946)(Croyden)-Al Fago-c; funny animal	10	30	55	80
V1#1,2(1947-48; 52 pgs.)(Rotary Litho. Co. Ltd., Canada); Ken Hultgren-a				
	8	24	42	60

MERRY MAILMAN (See Fawcett's Funny Animals #87-89)

MERRY MOUSE (Also see Funny Tunes & Space Comics)
Avon Periodicals: June, 1953 - No. 4, Jan-Feb, 1954

1-1st app.; funny animal; Frank Carin-c/a	10	30	55	80
2-4	6	18	32	45

MERV PUMPKINHEAD, AGENT OF D.R.E.A.M. (See The Sandman)
DC Comics (Vertigo): 2000 ($5.95, one-shot)

1-Buckingham-a(p); Nowlan painted-c 6.00

MESSENGER, THE
Image Comics: July, 2000 ($5.95, one-shot)

1-Ordway-s/c/a 6.00

META-4
First Comics: Feb, 1991 - No. 4, 1991 ($2.25)

	GD2.0	FN6.0	VF8.0	NM9.4
1-($3.95, 52pgs.)				4.00
2-4				2.25

METAL MEN (See Brave & the Bold, DC Comics Presents, and Showcase #37-40)
National Periodical Publications/DC Comics: 4-5/63 - No. 41, 12-1/69-70; No. 42, 2-3/73 - No. 44, 7-8/73; No. 45, 4-5/76 - No. 56, 2-3/78

1-(4-5/63)-5th app. Metal Men	50	150	410	750
2	18	54	129	230
3-5	12	36	84	140
6-10	8	24	56	90
11-20: 12-Beatles cameo (12/65)	6	18	42	70
21-26,28-30: 21-Batman, Robin & Flash x-over	4	12	30	50
27-Origin Metal Men retold	6	18	45	75
31-41(1968-70): 38-Last 12¢ issue. 41-Last 15¢	3	10	23	35
42-44(1973)-Reprints	2	6	9	12
45('76)-49-Simonson-a in all: 48,49-Re-intro Eclipso	1	3	6	9
50-56: 50-Part-r. 54,55-Green Lantern x-over	1	3	6	9

NOTE: **Andru/Esposito** c-1-30. **Aparo** c-53-56. **Giordano** c-45, 46. **Kane/Esposito** a-30, 31; c-31. **Simonson** a-45-49; c-47-52. **Staton** a-50-56.

METAL MEN
DC Comics: Oct, 1993 - No. 4, Jan, 1994 ($1.25, mini-series)

1-($2.50)-Multi-colored foil-c	4.00
2-4: 2-Origin	2.50

METAL MEN (See Tangent Comics/ Metal Men)

METAMORPHO (See Action Comics #413, Brave & the Bold #57,58, 1st Issue Special,& World's Finest #217)
National Periodical Publications: July-Aug, 1965 - No. 17, Mar-Apr, 1968 (All 12¢ issues)

1-(7-8/65)-3rd app. Metamorpho	12	36	88	150
2,3	6	18	42	70
4-6,10:10-Origin & 1st app. Element Girl (1-2/67)	4	12	30	50
7-9	4	12	27	42
11-17: 17-Sparling-c/a	3	9	21	32

NOTE: **Ramona Fradon** a-B&B 57, 58, 1-4. **Orlando** a-5, 6; c-5-9, 11. **Trapani** a(p)-7-16; i-16.

METAMORPHO
DC Comics: Aug, 1993 - No. 4, Nov, 1993 ($1.50, mini-series)

1-4 . . . . 2.50

METAPHYSIQUE
Malibu Comics (Bravura): Apr, 1995 - No. 6, Oct, 1995 ($2.95, limited series)

1-6: Norm Breyfogle-c/a/scripts 3.00

METEOR COMICS
L. L. Baird (Croyden): Nov, 1945

1-Captain Wizard, Impossible Man, Race Wilkins app.; origin Baldy Bean,				
Capt. Wizard's sidekick; bare-breasted mermaids story				
	40	120	232	400

METEOR MAN
Marvel Comics: Aug, 1993 - No. 6, Jan, 1994 ($1.25, limited series)

1-6: 1-Regular unbagged. 4-Night Thrasher-c/story. 6-Terry Austin-c(i)	2.25
1-Polybagged w/button & rap newspaper	4.00

METROPOL (See Ted McKeever's...)

METROPOL A.D. (See Ted McKeever's...)

METROPOLIS S.C.U. (Also see Showcase '96 #1)
DC Comics: Nov, 1995 - No. 4, Feb, 1996 ($1.50, limited series)

1-4:1-Superman-c & app. 2.25

MEZZ: GALACTIC TOUR 2494 (Also See Nexus)
Dark Horse Comics: May, 1994 ($2.50, one-shot)

1 . . . . 2.50

MGM'S MARVELOUS WIZARD OF OZ (See Marvel Treasury of Oz)
Marvel Comics Group/National Periodical Publications: 1975 ($1.50, 84 pgs.; oversize)

1-Adaptation of MGM's movie; J. Buscema-a	6	13	20

M.G.M'S MOUSE MUSKETEERS (Formerly M.G.M.'s The Two Mouseketeers)
Dell Publishing Co.: No. 670, Jan, 1956 - No. 1290, Mar-May, 1962

Michael Moorcock's Multiverse #7 © Michael Moorcock

Mickey Mouse Four Color #279 © WDC

Mickey Mouse #254 © WDC

	GD2.0	FN6.0	VF8.0	NM9.4
Four Color 670 (#4)	4	12	29	45
Four Color 711,728,764	3	9	20	30
8 (4-6/57) - 21 (3-5/60)	3	9	19	28
Four Color 1135,1175,1290	3	9	19	28

M.G.M.'S SPIKE AND TYKE (also see Tom & Jerry #79)
Dell Publishing Co.: No. 499, Sept, 1953 - No. 1266, Dec-Feb, 1961-62

Four Color 499 (#1)	4	12	30	50
Four Color 577,638	3	9	20	30
4(12-2/55-56)-10	3	9	17	25
11-24(12-2/60-61)	2	6	13	20
Four Color 1266	3	9	17	25

M.G.M.'S THE TWO MOUSKETEERS
Dell Publishing Co.: No. 475, June, 1953 - No. 642, July, 1955

Four Color 475 (#1)	7	21	49	90
Four Color 603 (11/54), 642	4	12	30	50

MICHAELANGELO CHRISTMAS SPECIAL (See Teenage Mutant Ninja Turtles Christmas Special)

MICHAELANGELO, TEENAGE MUTANT NINJA TURTLE
Mirage Studios: 1986 (One shot) ($1.50, B&W)

1				4.00
1-2nd printing ('89, $1.75)-Reprint plus new-a				2.25

MICHAEL MOORCOCK'S MULTIVERSE
DC Comics (Helix): Nov, 1997 - No. 12, Oct, 1998 ($2.50, limited series)

1-12: Simonson, Reeve & Ridgway-a				2.50
TPB (1999, $19.95)-r/#1-12				20.00

MICKEY AND DONALD (See Walt Disney's…)

MICKEY AND DONALD IN VACATIONLAND (See Dell Giant No. 47)

MICKEY & THE BEANSTALK (See Story Hour Series)

MICKEY & THE SLEUTH (See Walt Disney Showcase #38, 39, 42)

MICKEY FINN (Also see Big Shot Comics #74 & Feature Funnies)
Eastern Color 1-4/McNaught Synd. #5 on (Columbia)/Headline V3#2:
Nov?, 1942 - V3#2, May, 1952

1	31	93	165	285
2	16	48	83	140
3-Charlie Chan story	11	33	55	90
4	9	27	49	70
5-10	7	21	38	55
11-15(1949): 12-Sparky Watts app.	6	18	29	40
V3#1,2(1952)	5	15	24	32

MICKEY MALONE
Hale Nass Corp.: 1936 (Color, punchout-c) (B&W-a on back)

nn-1pg. of comics	150	300	600	–

MICKEY MANTLE (See Baseball's Greatest Heroes #1)

MICKEY MOUSE (See Adventures of Mickey Mouse, The Best of Walt Disney Comics, Cheerios giveaways, Donald and …, Dynabrite Comics, 40 Big Pages…, Gladstone Comic Album, Merry Christmas From…, Walt Disney's Mickey and Donald, Walt Disney's Comics & Stories, Walt Disney's…, & Wheaties)
Dell Publ. Co./Gold Key #85-204/Whitman #204-218/Gladstone #219 on:
#16, 1941 - #84, 7-9/62; #85, 11/62 - #218, 6/84; #219, 10/86 - #256, 4/90

Four Color 16(1941)-1st Mickey Mouse comic book; "…vs. the Phantom Blot" by Gottfredson

by Gottfredson	1200	3600	12,000	–
Four Color 27(1943)- "7 Colored Terror"	85	255	595	1100
Four Color 79(1945)-By Carl Barks (1 story)	108	324	756	1400
Four Color 116(1946)	23	69	161	300
Four Color 141,157(1947)	20	60	140	260
Four Color 170,181,194('48)	17	50	119	220
Four Color 214('49),231,248,261	14	42	98	175
Four Color 268-Reprints/WDC&S #22-24 by Gottfredson ("Surprise Visitor")				
	13	39	91	165
Four Color 279,286,296	10	30	70	125
Four Color 304,313(#1),325(#2),334	8	24	56	100
Four Color 343,352,362,371,387	6	18	42	80

	GD2.0	FN6.0	VF8.0	NM9.
Four Color 401,411,427(10-11/52)	5	15	34	55
Four Color 819-Mickey Mouse in Magicland	4	12	29	45
Four Color 1057,1151,1246(1959-61)-Album; #1057 has 10¢ & 12¢ editions; back covers are different	4	12	27	42
28(12-1/52-53)-32,34	4	12	29	45
33-(Exists with 2 dates, 10-11/53 & 12-1/54)	4	12	29	45
35-50	4	12	25	38
51-73,75-80	3	9	19	28
74-Story swipe "The Rare Stamp Search" from 4-Color #422- "The Gilded Man"	3	9	21	32
81-105: 93,95-titled "Mickey Mouse Club Album". 100-105: Reprint 4-Color #427,194,279,170,343,214 in that order	3	9	17	25
106-120	2	6	13	20
121-130	2	6	11	16
131-146	2	6	10	14
147,148: 147-Reprints "The Phantom Fires" from WDC&S #200-202.148-Reprints "The Mystery of Lonely Valley" from WDC&S #208-210	2	6	10	14
149-158	1	3	6	9
159-Reprints "The Sunken City" from WDC&S #205-207	1	4	7	10
160-178,180-203: 162-165,167-170-r. 200-r/Four Color #371	1	3	6	8
179-(52 pgs.)	1	3	6	9
204-(Whitman or G.K.), 205,206	2	6	9	12
207(8/80), 209(pre-pack?)	2	6	12	18
208-(8/12/80)-Only distr. in Whitman 3-pack	4	12	30	50
210(2/81),211-214	1	4	7	10
215-218: 215(2/82), 216(4/82), 217(3/84), 218(misdated 8/82; actual date 7/84)				
	2	6	9	12
219-1st Gladstone issue; The Seven Ghosts serial-r begins by Gottfredson				
	2	6	11	16
220,221	1	3	6	8
222-225: 222-Editor-in Grief strip-r				4.00
226-230				4.00
231-243,246-254: 240-r/March of Comics #27. 245-r/F.C. #279. 250-r/ F.C. #248				3.00
244 (1/89, $2.95, 100 pgs.)-Squarebound 60th anniversary issue; gives history of Mickey				4.00
245, 256: 245-r/F.C. #279. 256-$1.95, 68 pgs.				4.00
255 ($1.95, 68 pgs.)				3.00

NOTE: Reprints #195-197, 198(2/3), 199(1/3), 200-208, 211(1/2), 212, 213, 215(1/3), 216-on.
Gottfredson Mickey Mouse serials in #219-239, 241-244, 246-249, 251-253, 255.

Album 01-518-210(Dell), 1(10082-309)(9/63-Gold Key)				
	3	9	17	25
…Club 1(1/64-Gold Key)(TV)	3	9	21	32
Mini Comic 1(1976)(3-1/4x6-1/2")-Reprints 158	1	3	5	7
New Mickey Mouse Club Fun Book 11190 (Golden Press, 1977, $1.95, 224 pgs.)	3	9	20	30
Surprise Party 1(30037-901, G.K.)(1/69)-40th Anniversary (see Walt Disney Showcase #47)	3	9	21	32
Surprise Party 1(1979)-r/1969 issue				6.00

MICKEY MOUSE ADVENTURES
Disney Comics: June, 1990 - No. 18, Nov, 1991 ($1.50)

1,8,9: 1-Bradbury, Murry/M.M. #45,73 plus new-a. 8-Byrne-c. 9-Fantasia 50th ann. issue w/new adapt. of movie				3.00
2-7,10-18: 2-Begin all new stories. 10-r/F.C. #214				2.50

MICKEY MOUSE CLUB FUN BOOK
Golden Press: 1977 (1.95, 228 pgs.)(square bound)

11190-1950s-r; 20,000 Leagues, M. Mouse Silly Symphonys, The Reluctant Dragon, etc.	3	9	17	25

MICKEY MOUSE CLUB MAGAZINE (See Walt Disney…)

MICKEY MOUSE COMICS DIGEST
Gladstone: 1986 - No. 5, 1987 (96 pgs.)

1 ($1.25-c)	1	3	6	8
2-5: 3-5 ($1.50-c)				5.00

MICKEY MOUSE IN COLOR
Another Rainbow/Pantheon: 1988 (Deluxe, 13"x17", hard-c, $250.00)

638

Mickey Mouse Magazine V1 #3 © WDC

$5,000.00 CONTEST

Mickey Mouse Magazine V4 #10 © WDC

Micronauts #59 © Mego Corp.

	GD2.0	FN6.0	VF8.0	NM9.4

rade, 9-7/8"x11-1/2", hard-c, $39.95)

eluxe limited edition of 3,000 copies signed by Floyd Gottfredson and Carl Barks, designated as the "Official Mickey Mouse 60th Anniversary" book. Mickey Sunday and daily reprints, plus Barks "Riddle of the Red Hat" from Four Color #79. Comes with 45 r.p.m. record interview with Gottfredson and Barks. 240 pgs.

			GD2.0	FN6.0	VF8.0	NM9.4
			23	68	150	250

eluxe, limited to 100 copies, as above, but with a unique colored pencil original drawing of Mickey Mouse by Carl Barks. Add value of art to book price.
750.00

antheon trade edition, edited down & without Barks, 192 pgs.
4	12	26	40

ICKEY MOUSE MAGAZINE (Becomes Walt Disney's Comics & Stories)
K. Publ./Western Publishing Co.: Summer, 1935 (June-Aug, indicia) - V5#12, ept, 1940; V1#1-5, V3#11,12, V4#1-3 are 44 pgs; V2#3-100 pgs; V5#12-68 js; rest are 36 pgs.(No V3#1, V4#6)

#1 (Large size, 13-1/4x10-1/4"; 25¢)-Contains puzzles, games, cels, stories & comics of Disney characters. Promotional magazine for Disney cartoon movies and paraphernalia
1120	3360	7280	14,500

te: Some copies were autographed by the editors & given away with all early one year bscriptions.

	GD2.0	FN6.0	VF8.0	NM9.4
2 (Size change, 11-1/2x8-1/2"; 10/35; 10¢)-High quality paper begins; Messmer-a	163	489	1300	–
3,4: 3-Messmer-a	88	264	700	–
5-1st Donald Duck solo-c; 2nd cover app. ever; last 44 pg. & high quality paper issue	112	336	900	–
6-9: 6-36 pg. issues begin; Donald becomes editor. 8-2nd Donald solo-c.				
9-1st Mickey/Minnie-c	81	243	650	–
10-12, V2#1,2: 11-1st Pluto/Mickey-c; Donald fires himself and appoints Mickey as editor	75	225	600	–
2#3-Special 100 pg. Christmas issue (25¢); Messmer-a; Donald becomes editor of Wise Quacks	312	936	2500	–
4-Mickey Mouse Comics & Roy Ranger (adventure strip) begin; both end V3#2; Messmer-a	66	198	525	–
5-9: 5-Ted True (adventure strip, ends V2#9) & Silly Symphony Comics (ends V3#3) begin. 6-1st solo Minnie-c. 6-9-Mickey Mouse Movies cut-out in each	45	135	270	475
10-1st full color issue; Mickey Mouse (by Gottfredson; ends V3#12) & Silly Symphony (ends V3#3) full color Sunday-r, Peter The Farm Detective (ends V5#8) & Ole Of The North (ends V3#3) begins	68	205	426	750
11-13: 12-Hiawatha-c & feature story	44	132	264	460
3#2-Big Bad Wolf Halloween-c	53	160	318	560
3 (12/37)-1st app. Snow White & The Seven Dwarfs (before release of movie)(possibly 1st in print); Mickey X-Mas-c	93	279	581	1025
4 (1/38)-Snow White & The Seven Dwarfs serial begins (on stands before release of movie); Ducky Symphony (ends V3#11) begins	75	225	469	825
5-1st Snow White & Seven Dwarfs-c (St. Valentine's Day)	95	285	597	1050
6-Snow White serial ends; Lonesome Ghosts app. (2 pp.)	51	153	306	540
7-Seven Dwarfs Easter-c	50	150	300	520
8-10: 9-Dopey-c. 10-1st solo Goofy-c	40	120	240	420
11,12 (44 pgs; 8 more pgs. color added). 11-Mickey the Sheriff serial (ends V4#3) & Donald Duck strip-r (ends V3#12) begin. Color feature on Schnarfenberg	44	132	264	460
4#1 (10/38; 44 pgs.)-Brave Little Tailor-c/feature story, nominated for Academy Award; Bobby & Chip by Otto Messmer (ends V4#2) & The Practical Pig (ends V4#2) begin	44	132	264	460
2 (44 pgs.)-1st Huey, Dewey & Louie-c	45	135	269	470
3 (12/38, 44 pgs.)-Ferdinand The Bull-c/feature story, Academy Award winner; Mickey Mouse & The Whalers serial begins, ends V4#12	44	132	264	460
4-Spotty, Mother Pluto strip-r, begin, end V4#8	40	120	240	420
5-St. Valentine's day-c. 1st Pluto solo-c	47	141	286	500
6 (3/39)-The Ugly Duckling-c/feature story, Academy Award winner	44	132	264	460
7 (4/39)-Goofy & Wilbur & The Grasshopper classic-c/feature story from 1st Goofy solo cartoon movie; Timid Elmer begins, ends V5#5				

	GD2.0	FN6.0	VF8.0	NM9.4
	44	132	264	460
8-Big Bad Wolf-c from Practical Pig movie poster; Practical Pig feature story	44	132	264	460
9-Donald Duck & Mickey Mouse Sunday-r begin; The Pointer feature story, nominated for Academy Award	44	132	264	460
10-Classic July 4th drum & fife-c; last Donald Sunday-r	55	165	341	600
11-1st slick-c; last over-sized issue	40	120	240	420
12 (9/39; format change, 10-1/4x8-1/4")-1st full color, cover to cover issue; Donald's Penguin-c/feature story	50	150	300	520
V5#1-Black Pete-c; Officer Duck-c/feature story; Autograph Hound feature story; Robinson Crusoe serial begins	49	147	294	510
2-Goofy-c; 1st app. Pinocchio (cameo)	64	195	400	700
3 (12/39)-Pinocchio Christmas-c (Before movie release). 1st app. Jiminy Cricket; Pinocchio serial begins	72	215	450	790
4,5: 5-Jiminy Cricket-c; Pinocchio serial ends; Donald's Dog Laundry feature story	49	147	294	510
6,7: 6-Tugboat Mickey feature story; Rip Van Winkle feature begins, ends V5#8. 7-2nd Huey, Dewey & Louie-c	47	140	286	500
8-Last magazine size issue; 2nd solo Pluto-c; Figaro & Cleo feature story	49	147	294	510
9-11: 9 (6/40): change to comic book size)-Jiminy Cricket feature story; Donald-c & Sunday-r begin. 10-Special Independence Day issue. 11-Hawaiian Holiday & Mickey's Trailer feature stories; last 36 pg. issue	52	157	314	550
12 (Format change)-The transition issue (68 pgs.) becoming a comic book. With only a title change to follow, becomes Walt Disney's Comics & Stories #1 with the next issue	423	1269	2708	5200

NOTE: Otto Messmer-a is in many issues of the first two-three years. The following story titles and issues have cels created by Carl Barks: V4#3(12/38)-'Donald's Better Self' & 'Donald's Golf Game;' V4#4(1/39)-'Donald's Lucky Day;' V4#7(3/39)-'Hockey Champ;' V4#7(4/39)-'Donald's Cousin Gus;' V4#9(6/39)-'Sea Scouts;' V4#12(9/39)-'Donald's Penguin;' V5#9 (6/40)-'Donald's Vacation;' V5#10(7/40)-'Bone Trouble;' V5#12(9/40)-'Window Cleaners.'

MICKEY MOUSE MAGAZINE (Russian Version)
May 16, 1991 (1st Russian printing of a modern comic book)
1-Bagged w/gold label commemoration in English				10.00

MICKEY MOUSE MARCH OF COMICS (See March of Comics #8,27,45,60,74)

MICKEY MOUSE'S SUMMER VACATION (See Story Hour Series)

MICKEY MOUSE SUMMER FUN (See Dell Giants)

MICKEY SPILLANE'S MIKE DANGER
Tekno Comix: Sept, 1995 - No. 11, May, 1996 ($1.95)
1-11: 1-Frank Miller-c. 7-polybagged; Simonson-c. 8,9-Simonson-c				2.25

MICKEY SPILLANE'S MIKE DANGER
Big Entertainment: V2#1, June, 1996 - No. 10, Apr, 1997 ($2.25)
V2#1-10: Max Allan Collins scripts				2.25

MICROBOTS, THE
Gold Key: Dec, 1971 (one-shot)
1 (10271-112)	2	6	13	20

MICRONAUTS (Toys)
Marvel Comics Group: Jan, 1979 - No. 59, Aug, 1984 (Mando paper #53 on)
1-Intro/1st app. Baron Karza				4.00
2-10,35,37,57: 7-Man-Thing app. 8-1st app. Capt. Universe (8/79). 9-1st app. Cilicia. 35-Double size; origin Microverse; intro Death Squad; Dr. Strange app. 37-Nightcrawler app.; X-Men cameo (2 pgs.). 57-(52 pgs.)				3.00
11-34,36,38-56,58,59: 11-1st app. Jasmine. 15-Death of Microtron. 15-17-Fantastic Four app. 17-Death of Jasmine. 20-Ant-Man app. 21-Microverse series begins. 29-origin Baron Karza. 25-29-Nick Fury app. 27-Death of Biotron. 34-Dr. Strange app. 38-First direct sale. 40-Fantastic Four app.				2.50
59-Golden Enemy-c				2.25
nn-Reprints #1-3; blank UPC; diamond on top				2.25
Annual 1,2 (12/79,10/80)-Ditko-a				3.00

NOTE: #38-on distributed only through comic shops. N. Adams c-7i. Chaykin a-13-18p. Ditko a-39p. Giffen a-36p, 37p(part). Golden c-12p; c-2-7p, 8-23, 24p, 38, 39, 59. Guice a-48-58p; c-49-58. Gil Kane a-38, 40-45p; c-40-45. Layton c-33-37. Miller c-31.

MICRONAUTS (Toys)
Marvel Comics Group: Oct, 1984 - No. 20, May, 1986
V2#1-20				2.50

Midnight Nation #5
© J. Michael Straczynski & TCOW

Midnight Tales #8 © CC

Mighty Crusaders #4 © AP

	GD2.0	FN6.0	VF8.0	NM9.4

NOTE: *Kelley Jones a-1; c-1, 6. Guice a-4p; c-2p.*

MICRONAUTS SPECIAL EDITION
Marvel Comics Group: Dec, 1983 - No. 5, Apr, 1984 ($2.00, limited series, Baxter paper)

1-5: r-/original series 1-12; Guice-c(p)-all				3.00

MIDGET COMICS (Fighting Indian Stories)
St. John Publishng Co.: Feb, 1950 - No. 2, Apr, 1950 (5-3/8x7-3/8", 68 pgs.)

1-Fighting Indian Stories; Matt Baker-c	20	60	105	175
2-Tex West, Cowboy Marshal (also in #1)	10	30	55	80

MIDNIGHT (See Smash Comics #18)

MIDNIGHT
Ajax/Farrell Publ. (Four Star Comic Corp.): Apr, 1957 - No. 6, June, 1958

1-Reprints from Voodoo & Strange Fantasy with some changes	15	45	77	130
2-6	9	27	49	70

MIDNIGHT EYE
Viz Premiere Comics: 1991 - No. 6, 1992 ($4.95, 44 pgs., mature)

1-6: Japanese stories translated into English				5.00

MIDNIGHT MEN
Marvel Comics (Epic Comics/Heavy Hitters): June, 1993 - No. 4, Sept, 1993 ($2.50/$1.95, limited series)

1-($2.50)-Embossed-c; Chaykin-c/a & scripts in all.				3.00
2-4				2.25

MIDNIGHT MYSTERY
American Comics Group: Jan-Feb, 1961 - No. 7, Oct, 1961

1-Sci/Fi story	9	27	65	110
2-7: 7-Gustavson-a	5	15	34	55

NOTE: *Reinman a-1, 3. Whitney a-1, 4-6; c-1-3, 5, 7.*

MIDNIGHT NATION
Image Comics (Top Cow): Oct, 2000 - Present ($2.50)

1-Straczynski-s/Frank-a; 2 covers				2.50
2-9: 9-Twin Towers cover				2.50

MIDNIGHT SONS UNLIMITED
Marvel Comics (Midnight Sons imprint #4 on): Apr, 1993 - No. 9, May, 1995 ($3.95, 68 pgs.)

1-9: Blaze, Darkhold (by Quesada #1), Ghost Rider, Morbius & Nightstalkers in all. 1-Painted-c. 3-Spider-Man app. 4-Siege of Darkness part 17; new Dr. Strange & new Ghost Rider app.; spot varnish-c				4.00

NOTE: *Sears a-2.*

MIDNIGHT TALES
Charlton Press: Dec, 1972 - No. 18, May, 1976

V1#1	2	6	15	22
2-10	2	6	10	14
11-18: 11-14-Newton-a(p)	1	4	7	10
12,17(Modern Comics reprint, 1977)				5.00

NOTE: *Adkins a-12i, 13i. Ditko a-12. Howard (Wood imitator) a-1-15, 17, 18; c-1-18. Don Newton a-11-14p. Staton a-1, 3-11, 13. Sutton a-3-10.*

MIGHTY ATOM, THE (...& the Pixies #6) (Formerly The Pixies #1-5)
Magazine Enterprises: No. 6, 1949; Nov, 1957 - No. 6, Aug-Sept, 1958

6(1949-M.E.)-no month (1st Series)	6	18	32	45
1-6(2nd Series)-Pixies-r	4	11	17	22
I.W. Reprint #1(nd)	2	6	9	12

MIGHTY BEAR (Formerly Fun Comics; becomes Unsane #15)
Star Publ.: No. 13,14/Ajax-Farrell (Four Star): No. 13, Jan, 1954 - No. 14, Mar, 1954; 9/57 - No. 3, 2/58

13,14-L. B. Cole-c	19	57	99	165
1-3('57-58)Four Star; becomes Mighty Ghost #4	6	18	29	40

MIGHTY COMICS (...Presents) (Formerly Flyman)
Radio Comics (Archie): No. 40, Nov, 1966 - No. 50, Oct, 1967 (All 12¢ issues)

40-Web	3	9	21	32
41-50: 41-Shield, Black Hood. 42-Black Hood. 43-Shield, Web & Black Hood. 44-Black Hood, Steel Sterling & The Shield. 45-Shield & Hangman; origin Web retold. 46-Steel Sterling, Web & Black Hood. 47-Black Hood & Mr.				

Justice. 48-Shield & Hangman; Wizard x-over in Shield. 49-Steel Sterling & Fox; Black Hood x-over in Steel Sterling. 50-Black Hood & Web; Inferno x-over in Web | 3 | 9 | 19 | 2 |

NOTE: *Paul Reinman a-40-50.*

MIGHTY CRUSADERS, THE (Also see Adventures of the Fly, The Crusaders & Fly Man)
Mighty Comics Group (Radio Comics): Nov, 1965 - No. 7, Oct, 1966 (All 12¢)

1-Origin The Shield	5	15	38	6
2-Origin Comet	3	9	21	3
3,5-7: 3-Origin Fly-Man. 5-Intro. Ultra-Men (Fox, Web, Capt. Flag) & Terrific Three (Jaguar, Mr. Justice, Steel Sterling). 7-Steel Sterling feature; origin Fly Girl	3	9	19	2
4-1st S.A. app. Fireball, Inferno & Fox; Firefly, Web, Bob Phantom, Blackjack, Hangman, Zambini, Kardak, Steel Sterling, Mr. Justice, Wizard, Capt. Flag, Jaguar x-over	3	9	20	3

NOTE: *Reinman a-6.*

MIGHTY CRUSADERS, THE (All New Advs. of...#2)
Red Circle Prod./Archie Ent. No. 6 on: Mar, 1983 - No. 13, Sept, 1985 ($1.00, 36 pgs, Mando paper)

1-Origin Black Hood, The Fly, Fly Girl, The Shield, The Wizard, The Jaguar, Pvt. Strong & The Web.				6.0
2-13: 2-Mister Midnight begins. 4-Darkling replaces Shield. 5-Origin Jaguar, Shield begins. 7-Untold origin Jaguar. 10-Veitch-a				4.0

NOTE: *Buckler a-1-3, 4i, 5p, 7p, 8i, 9i; c-1-10p.*

MIGHTY GHOST (Formerly Mighty Bear #1-3)
Ajax/Farrell Publ.: No. 4, June, 1958

4	5	15	25	3

MIGHTY HERCULES, THE (TV)
Gold Key: July, 1963 - No. 2, Nov, 1963

1 (10072-307)	15	45	105	19
2 (10072-311)	14	41	98	18

MIGHTY HEROES, THE (TV) (Funny)
Dell Publishing Co.: Mar, 1967 - No. 4, July, 1967

1-Also has a 1957 Heckle & Jeckle-r	14	41	98	18
2-4: 4-Has two 1958 Mighty Mouse-r	10	30	70	12

MIGHTY HEROES
Spotlight Comics: 1987 (B&W, one-shot)

1-Heckle & Jeckle backup				3.

MIGHTY HEROES
Marvel Comics: Jan, 1998 ($2.99, one-shot)

1-Origin of the Mighty Heroes				3.

MIGHTY MARVEL TEAM-UP THRILLERS
Marvel Comics: 1983 ($5.95, trade paperback)

1-Reprints team-up stories				25.0

MIGHTY MARVEL WESTERN, THE
Marvel Comics Group (LMC earlier issues): Oct, 1968 - No. 46, Sept, 1976 (#1-14: 68 pgs.; #15,16: 52 pgs.)

1-Begin Kid Colt, Rawhide Kid, Two-Gun Kid-r	5	15	34	4
2-16: (2-14-68 pgs./ 15,16-52 pgs.)	3	9	21	4
17-20	2	6	11	4
21-30,32,37: 24-Kid Colt-r end. 25-Matt Slade-r begin. 32-Origin-r/Rawhide Kid #23; Williamson-r/Kid Slade #7. 37-Williamson, Kirby-r/Two-Gun Kid 51	2	6	10	
31,33-36,38-46: 31-Baker-r.	2	6	9	
45-(30¢-c variant, limited distribution)(6/76)	2	6	12	

NOTE: *Jack Davis a(r)-21-24. Keller r-1-13, 22. Kirby a(r)-1-3, 6, 9, 12-14, 16, 25-29, 32-38, 41, 43-46; c-29. Maneely a(r)-22. Severin c-3i, 9. No Matt Slade-#43.*

MIGHTY MIDGET COMICS, THE (Miniature)
Samuel E. Lowe & Co.: No date; circa 1942-1943 (Sold 2 for 5¢, B&W and red 36 pgs, approx. 5x4")

Bulletman #11(1943)-r/cover/Bulletman #3	22	66	116	2
Captain Marvel Adventures #11	22	66	116	2
Captain Marvel #11 (Same as above except for full color ad on back cover; this issue was glued to cover of Captain Marvel #20 and is not found in				

Mighty Marvel Western #22 © MAR

Mighty Mouse #13 © Terry Toons

Mighty Samson #3 © GK

	GD2.0	FN6.0	VF8.0	NM9.4

fine-mint condition)	300	900	–	–
Captain Marvel Jr. #11 (Same-c as Master #27	22	66	116	200
Captain Marvel Jr. #11 (Same as above except for full color ad on back-c; this issue was glued to cover of Captain Marvel #21 and is not found in				
fine-mint condition)	300	900	–	–
Golden Arrow #11	20	60	105	175
Golden Arrow #11 (Same as above except for full color ad on back-c; this issue was glued to cover of Captain Marvel #21 and is not found in				
fine-mint condition)	250	750	–	–
Ibis the Invincible #11(1942)-Origin; reprints cover to Ibis #1 (Predates Fawcett's Ibis the Invincible #1).	22	66	116	200
Spy Smasher #11(1942)	22	66	116	200

NOTE: *The above books came in a box called "box full of books" and was distributed with other Samuel Lowe puzzles, paper dolls, coloring books, etc. They are not titled Mighty Midget Comics. All have a war bond seal on back cover which is otherwise blank. These books came in a "Mighty Midget" flat cardboard counter display rack.*

Balbo, the Boy Magician #12 (1943)-1st book devoted entirely to character.				
	11	33	55	90
Bulletman #12	16	48	83	140
Commando Yank #12 (1943)-Only comic devoted entirely to character.				
	12	36	61	105
Dr. Voltz the Human Generator (1943)-Only comic devoted entirely to character.				
	11	33	55	90
Lance O'Casey #12 (1943)-1st comic devoted entirely to character (Predates Fawcett's Lance O'Casey #1).				
	11	33	55	90
Leatherneck the Marine (1943)-Only comic devoted entirely to character.				
	11	33	55	90
Minute Man #12	16	48	83	140
Mister "Q" (1943)-Only comic devoted entirely to character.				
	11	33	55	90
Mr. Scarlet and Pinky #12 (1943)-Only comic devoted entirely to character.				
	13	39	66	110
Pat Wilton and His Flying Fortress (1943)-1st comic devoted entirely to character.				
	11	33	55	90
The Phantom Eagle #12 (1943)-Only comic devoted entirely to character.				
	11	33	55	95
State Trooper Stops Crime (1943)-Only comic devoted entirely to character.				
	11	33	55	90
Tornado Tom (1943)-Origin, r/from Cyclone #1-3; only comic devoted entirely to character.				
	11	33	55	90

MIGHTY MORPHIN' POWER RANGERS: THE MOVIE (Also see Saban's Mighty Morphin' Power Rangers)
Marvel Comics: Sept, 1995 ($3.95, one-shot)

nn-adaptation of movie				4.00

MIGHTY MOUSE (See Adventures of..., Dell Giant 43, Giant Comics Edition, March of Comics #205, 237, 247, 257, 447, 459, 471, 483, Oxydol-Dreft, Paul Terry's, & Terry-Toons Comics)

MIGHTY MOUSE (1st Series)
Timely/Marvel Comics (20th Century Fox): Fall, 1946 - No. 4, Summer, 1947

1	123	369	769	1350
2	55	165	341	600
3,4	40	120	240	420

MIGHTY MOUSE (2nd Series) (Paul Terry's) ...#62-71)
St. John Publishing Co./Pines No. 68 (3/56) on (TV issues No. 72 on):
Aug, 1947 - No. 67, 11/55; No. 68, 3/56 - No. 83, 6/59

5(#1)	39	117	208	360
6-10	20	60	105	175
11-19	13	39	66	110
20 (11/50) - 25 -(52 pg. editions)	10	30	55	80
20-25-(36 pg. editions)	9	27	49	70
26-37: 35-Flying saucer-c	7	21	38	55
38-45-(100 pgs.)	19	57	99	165
46-83: 66-Painted-c. 82-Infinity-c	7	21	36	50
Album nn (nd, 1952/53?, St. John)(100 pgs.)(Rebound issues w/new cover)				
	23	69	121	210
Album 1(10/52, 25¢, 100 pgs., St. John)-Gandy Goose app.				
	29	87	153	265
Album 2,3(11/52 & 12/52, St. John) (100 pgs.)	22.00	66.00	175.00	
Fun Club Magazine 1(Fall, 1957-Pines, 25¢, 100 pgs.) (CBS TV)-Tom Terrific,				

Heckle & Jeckle, Dinky Duck, Gandy Goose	16	48	83	140
Fun Club Magazine 2-6(Winter, 1958-Pines)	10	30	55	80
3-D 1-(1st printing-9/53, 25¢)(St. John)-Came w/glasses; stiff covers; says World's First! on-c; 1st 3-D comic	30	90	159	275
3-D 1-(2nd printing-10/53, 25¢)-Came w/glasses; slick, glossy covers, slightly smaller	27	81	142	245
3-D 2,3(11/53, 12/53, 25¢)-(St. John)-With glasses	26	78	136	235

MIGHTY MOUSE (TV)(3rd Series)(Formerly Adventures of Mighty Mouse)
Gold Key/Dell Publ. Co. No. 166-on: No. 161, Oct, 1964 - No. 172, Oct, 1968
161(10/64)-165(9/65)-(Becomes Adventures of... No. 166 on)

	4	12	30	50
166(3/66), 167(6/66)-172	3	10	23	35

MIGHTY MOUSE (TV)
Spotlight Comics: 1987 - No. 2, 1987 ($1.50, color)

1,2-New stories				3.00
...And Friends Holiday Special (11/87, $1.75)				3.00

MIGHTY MOUSE (TV)
Marvel Comics: Oct, 1990 - No. 10, July, 1991 ($1.00)(Based on Sat. cartoon)

1-10: 1-Dark Knight-c parody. 2-10: 3-Intro Bat-Bat; Byrne-c. 4,5-Crisis-c/ story parodies w/Perez-c. 6-Spider-Man-c parody. 7-Origin Bat-Bat				2.25

MIGHTY MOUSE ADVENTURE MAGAZINE
Spotlight Comics: 1987 ($2.00, B&W, 52 pgs., magazine size, one-shot)

1-Deputy Dawg, Heckle & Jeckle backup stories				5.00

MIGHTY MOUSE ADVENTURES (Adventures of... #2 on)
St. John Publishing Co.: November, 1951

1	34	102	179	310

MIGHTY MOUSE ADVENTURE STORIES (Paul Terry's... on-c only)
St. John Publishing Co.: 1953 (50¢, 384 pgs.)

nn-Rebound issues	43	129	257	450

MIGHTY MUTANIMALS (See Teenage Mutant Ninja Turtles Adventures #19)
May, 1991 - No. 3, July, 1991 ($1.00, limited series)
Archie Comics: Apr, 1992 - No. 8, June, 1993 ($1.25)

1-3: 1-Story cont'd from TMNT Advs. #19.				2.25
1-9 (1992): 7-1st app. Merdude				2.25

MIGHTY SAMSON (See also Gold Key Champion)
Gold Key/Whitman #32: July, 1964 - No. 20, Nov, 1969; No. 21, Aug, 1972; No. 22, Dec, 1973 - No. 31, Mar, 1976; No. 32, Aug, 1982 (Painted-c #1-31)

1-Origin/1st app.; Thorne-a begins	8	24	56	100
2-5	4	12	30	50
6-10: 7-Tom Morrow begins, ends #20	3	10	23	35
11-20	3	9	17	25
21-31: 21,22-r	2	6	12	18
32(Whitman, 8/82)-r	1	3	6	9

MIGHTY THOR (See Thor)

MIKE BARNETT, MAN AGAINST CRIME (TV)
Fawcett Publications: Dec, 1951 - No. 6, Oct, 1952

1	20	60	105	175
2	12	36	61	100
3,4,6	10	30	55	85
5- "Market for Morphine" cover/story	13	39	66	110

MIKE DANGER (See Mickey Spillane's...)

MIKE DEODATO'S...
Caliber Comics: 1996, ($2.95, B&W)

...FALLOUT 3000 #1,...JONAS (mag. size) #1,...PRIME CUTS (mag. size) #1,...PROTHEUS #1,2, ...RAMTHAR #1,...RAZOR NIGHTS #1				3.00

MIKE GRELL'S SABLE (Also see Jon Sable & Sable)
First Comics: Mar, 1990 - No. 10, Dec, 1990 ($1.75)

1-10: r/Jon Sable Freelance #1-10 by Grell				2.25

MIKE MIST MINUTE MIST-ERIES (See Ms. Tree/Mike Mist in 3-D)
Eclipse Comics: April, 1981 ($1.25, B&W, one-shot)

1				2.25

Military Comics #6 © QUA

Millennium Edition - Detective Comics #27 © DC

Millie the Model #2 © MAR

	GD2.0	FN6.0	VF8.0	NM9.4

MIKE SHAYNE PRIVATE EYE
Dell Publishing Co.: Nov-Jan, 1962 - No. 3, Sept-Nov, 1962

1	3	10	23	35
2,3	2	6	15	22

MILITARY COMICS (Becomes Modern Comics #44 on)
Quality Comics Group: Aug, 1941 - No. 43, Oct, 1945

1-Origin/1st app. Blackhawk by C. Cuidera (Eisner scripts); Miss America, The Death Patrol by Jack Cole (also #2-7,27-30), & The Blue Tracer by Guardineer; X of the Underground, The Yankee Eagle, Q-Boat & Shot & Shell, Archie Atkins, Loops & Banks by Bud Ernest (Bob Powell)(ends #13) begin	885	2655	5750	11,500
2-Secret War News begins (by McWilliams #2-16); Cole-a; new uniform with yellow circle & hawk's head for Blackhawk	255	765	1591	2800
3-Origin/1st app. Chop Chop (9/41)	218	654	1364	2400
4	182	546	1136	2000
5-The Sniper begins; Miss America in costume #4-7	150	450	938	1650
6-9: 8-X of the Underground begins (ends #13). 9-The Phantom Clipper begins (ends #16)	109	327	682	1200
10-Classic Eisner-c	116	348	725	1275
11-Flag-c	89	267	556	975
12-Blackhawk by Crandall begins, ends #22	111	332	694	1225
13-15: 14-Private Dogtag begins (ends #83)	84	252	525	925
16-20: 16-Blue Tracer begins. 17-P.T. Boat begins	73	219	455	800
21-31: 22-Last Crandall Blackhawk. 23-Shrunken head-c. 27-Death Patrol revived	62	186	388	685
32-43	55	165	331	580

NOTE: *Berg a-6. Al Bryant c-31-34, 38, 40-43. J. Cole a-1-3, 27-32. Crandall a-12-22; c-13-20. Cuidera c-2-9. Eisner c-1, 2(part), 9, 10. Kotsky c-21-29, 35, 37, 39. McWilliams a-2-16. Powell a-1-13. Ward Blackhawk-30, 31(15 pgs. each); c-30.*

MILK AND CHEESE (Also see Cerebus Bi-Weekly #20)
Slave Labor: 1991 - Present ($2.50, B&W)

1-Evan Dorkin story & art in all.	4	12	30	50
1-2nd-6th printings				4.00
2-"Other #1"	3	9	20	30
2-reprint				3.00
3-"Third #1"	2	6	13	20
4-"Fourth #1", 5-"First Second Issue"	1	4	7	10
6,7: 8-"#666"				5.00

NOTE: *Multiple printings of all issues exist and are worth cover price unless listed here.*

MILLENNIUM
DC Comics: Jan, 1988 - No. 8, Feb, 1988 (Weekly limited series)

1-Staton c/a(p) begins		3.00
2-8		2.50

MILLENNIUM EDITION:... (Reprints of classic DC issues)
DC Comics: Feb, 2000 - Feb, 2001 (gold foil cover stamps)

Action Comics #1, Adventure Comics #61, All Star Comics #3, All Star Comics #8, Batman #1, Detective Comics #1, Detective Comics #27, Detective Comics #38, Flash Comics #1, Military Comics #1, More Fun Comics #73, Police Comics #1, Sensation Comics #1, Superman #1, Whiz Comics #2, Wonder Woman #1 -($3.95-c) . . . 4.00

Action Comics #252, Adventure Comics #247, Brave and the Bold #28, Brave and the Bold #85, Crisis on Infinte Earths #1, Detective Comics #327, Detective #359, Detective #395, Flash #123, Gen13 #1, Green Lantern #76, House of Mystery #1, House of Secrets #92, JLA #1, Justice League #1, Mad #1, Man of Steel #1, Mysterious Suspense #1, New Gods, #1, New Teen Titans #1, Our Army at War #81, Plop! #1, Saga of the Swamp Thing #21, Shadow #1, Showcase #4, Showcase #9, Showcase #22, Superman #233, Superman (2nd) #75, Superman's Pal Jimmy Olsen #1, Watchmen #1, WildC.A.T.s #1, Wonder Woman (2nd) #1, World's Finest #71 -($2.50-c) . . . 2.50

All-Star Western #10, Hellblazer #1, More Fun Comics #101, Preacher #1, Sandman #1, Spirit #1, Superboy #1, Superman #76, Young Romance #1 -($2.95-c) . . . 3.00
Batman: The Dark Knight Returns #1, Kingdom Come #1 -($5.95-c) . . . 6.00
All Star Comics #3, Batman #1, Justice League #1: Chromium cover . . . 10.00
Crisis on Infinite Earths #1 Chromium cover . . . 20.00

MILLENNIUM FEVER

DC Comics (Vertigo): Oct, 1995 - No.4, Jan, 1996 ($2.50, limited series)

1-4: Duncan Fegredo-c/a		2.50

MILLENNIUM INDEX
Independent Comics Group: Mar, 1988 - No. 2, Mar, 1988 ($2.00)

1,2		2.25

MILLENNIUM 2.5 A.D.
ACG Comics: No. 1, 2000 ($2.95)

1-Reprints 1934 Buck Rogers daily strips #1-48		3.00

MILLIE, THE LOVABLE MONSTER
Dell Publishing Co.: Sept-Nov, 1962 - No. 6, Jan, 1973

12-523-211	5	15	34	55
2(8-10/63)-Bill Woggon c/a	4	12	29	45
3(8-10/64)	3	10	23	35
4(7/72), 5(10/72), 6(1/73)	2	6	11	16

NOTE: *Woggon a-3-6; c-3-6. 4 reprints 1; 5 reprints 2; 6 reprints 3.*

MILLIE THE MODEL (See Comedy Comics, A Date With..., Joker Comics #28, Life With..., Mad About..., Marvel Mini-Books, Misty & Modeling With...)
Marvel/Atlas/Marvel Comics(CnPC #1)(SPI/Male/VPI):1945 - No. 207, Dec, 1973

1-Origin	80	240	500	875
2 (10/46)-Millie becomes The Blonde Phantom to sell Blonde Phantom perfume; a pre-Blonde Phantom app. (see All-Select #11, Fall, 1946)	40	120	232	400
3-8,10: 4-7-Willie app. 7-Willie smokes extra strong tobacco. 8,10-Kurtzman's "Hey Look". 8-Willie & Rusty app.	29	87	153	265
9-Powerhouse Pepper by Wolverton, 4 pgs.	33	99	174	300
11-Kurtzman-a, "Giggles 'n' Grins"	20	60	105	175
12,15,17-20: 12-Rusty & Hedy Devine app.	14	42	72	120
13,14,16-Kurtzman's "Hey Look". 13-Hedy Devine app.	15	45	77	130
21-30	10	30	55	80
31-40	6	18	42	70
41-60	5	15	34	55
61-99	4	12	26	40
100	4	12	30	50
101-130: 107-Jack Kirby app. in story	3	10	23	35
131-153: 141-Groovy Gears-c/s	3	9	19	28
154-New Millie begins (10/67)	4	12	25	38
155-190	3	9	17	25
191,193-199,201-206	2	6	15	22
192-(52 pgs.)	3	9	20	30
200,207(Last issue)	3	9	20	30
	(Beware: cut-up pages are common in all Annuals)			
Annual 1(1962)-Early Marvel annual (2nd?)	18	54	129	230
Annual 2(1963)	13	39	91	155
Annual 3-5 (1964-1966)	8	24	56	90
Annual 6-10(1967-11/71)	6	18	45	75
Queen-Size 11(9/74), 12(1975)	5	15	38	60

NOTE: *Dan DeCarlo a-18-93.*

MILLION DOLLAR DIGEST (Richie Rich... #23 on; also see Richie Rich...)
Harvey Publications: 11/86 - No. 7, 11/87; No. 8, 4/88 - No. 34, Nov, 1994 ($1.25/$1.75, digest size)

1		6.00
2-8: 8-(68 pgs.)		4.00
9-34: 9-Begin $1.75-c. 14-May not exist		3.00

MILT GROSS FUNNIES (Also see Picture News #1)
Milt Gross, Inc. (ACG?): Aug, 1947 - No. 2, Sept, 1947

1	18	54	94	160
2	13	39	66	110

MILTON THE MONSTER & FEARLESS FLY (TV)
Gold Key: May, 1966

1 (10175-605)	10	30	70	130

MINIMUM WAGE
Fantagraphics Books: V1#1, July, 1995 ($9.95, B&W, graphic novel, mature)
V2#1, 1995 - Present ($2.95, B&W, mature)

V1#1-Bob Fingerman story & art	1	4	7	10

Ministry of Space #1
© Garth Ennis & Chris Weston

Miracleman #15 © ECL

Miss America Magazine #4 © MAR

V2#1-9($2.95): Bob Fingerman story and art. 2-Kevin Nowlan back-c. 4-w/pin-ups.

5-Mignola back-c.				3.00
Book Two TPB ('97, $12.95) r/V2#1-5				13.00

MINISTRY OF SPACE
Image Comics: Apr, 2001 - No. 3 ($2.95, limited series)

1,2-Warren Ellis-s/Chris Weston-a				3.00

MINOR MIRACLES
DC Comics: 2000 ($12.95, B&W, squarebound)

nn-Will Eisner-s/a				13.00

MINUTE MAN (See Master Comics & Mighty Midget Comics)
Fawcett Publications: Summer, 1941 - No. 3, Spring, 1942 (68 pgs.)

1		182	546	1136	2000
2,3		114	342	713	1250

MINX, THE
DC Comics (Vertigo): Oct, 1998 - No. 8, May, 1999 ($2.50, limited series)

1-8-Milligan-s/Phillips-c/a				3.00

MIRACLE COMICS
Hillman Periodicals: Feb, 1940 - No. 4, Mar, 1941

1-Sky Wizard Master of Space, Dash Dixon, Man of Might, Pinkie Parker, Dusty Doyle, The Kid Cop, K-7, Secret Agent, The Scorpion, & Blandu, Jungle Queen begin; Masked Angel only app. (all 1st app.)

		182	546	1136	2000
2		91	273	568	1000

3,4: 3-Bill Colt, the Ghost Rider begins. 4-The Veiled Prophet & Bullet Bob (by Burnley) app.

		77	231	483	850

MIRACLEMAN
Eclipse Comics: Aug, 1985 - No. 15, Nov, 1988; No. 16 Dec, 1989 - No. 24, 1994

		1	3	5	7
1-r/British Marvelman series; Alan Moore scripts in #1-16					
1-Gold & Silver editions		1	4	7	10
2-12: 8-Airboy preview. 9,10-Origin Miracleman. 9-Shows graphic scenes of childbirth. 10-Snyder-c					5.00
13,14		1	4	7	10
15-($1.75-c, scarce) end of Kid Miracleman		3	9	20	30
16-Last Alan Moore-s; 1st $1.95-c (low print)		2	6	11	15

17,18-($1.95): 17-"The Golden Age" begins, ends #22. Dave McKean-c begins, end #22; Neil Gaiman scripts in #17-24

					6.00
19-23-($2.50); 23-"The Silver Age" begins; B. Smith-c					5.00
24-Last issue; B. Smith-c		1	4	7	10
3-D 1 (12/85)					5.00
Book One: A Dream of Flying (1988, $9.95, TPB) r/#1-5; Leach-c					22.00
Book One: A Dream of Flying-Hardcover (1988, $29.95) r/#1-5					70.00
Book Two: The Red King Syndrome (1990, $12.95, TPB) r/#6-10; Bolton-c					22.00
Book Two: The Red King Syndrome-Hardcover (1990, $30.95) r/#6-10					85.00
Book Three: Olympus (1990, $12.95, TPB) r/#11-16					100.00
Book Three: Olympus-Hardcover (1990, $30.95) r/#11-16					200.00
Book Four: The Golden Age (1992, $15.95, TPB) r/#17-22					30.00
Book Four: The Golden Age Hardcover (1992, $33.95) r/#17-22					50.00
Book Four: The Golden Age (1993, $12.99, TPB) new McKean-c					15.00

NOTE: *Chaykin c-3. Gulacy c-7. McKean c-17-22. B. Smith c-23, 24. Starlin c-4. Totleben a-11-13; c-9, 11-13. Truman c-6.*

MIRACLEMAN: APOCRYPHA
Eclipse Comics: Nov, 1991 - No. 3, Feb, 1992 ($2.50, limited series)

1-3: 1-Stories by Neil Gaiman, Mark Buckingham, Alex Ross & others. 3-Stories by James Robinson, Kelley Jones, Matt Wagner, Neil Gaiman, Mark Buckingham & others

		1	3	5	7
TPB (12/92, $15.95) r/#1-3; Buckingham-c					20.00

MIRACLEMAN FAMILY
Eclipse Comics: May, 1988 - No. 2, Sept, 1988 ($1.95, lim. series, Baxter paper)

1,2: 2-Gulacy-c				4.00

MIRACLE OF THE WHITE STALLIONS, THE (See Movie Comics)

MIRACLE SQUAD, THE
Upshot Graphics (Fantagraphics Books): Aug, 1986 - No. 4, 1987 ($2.00)

1-4				2.25

MIRACLE SQUAD: BLOOD AND DUST, THE

Apple Comics: Jan, 1989 - No. 4, July, 1989 ($1.95, B&W, limited series)

1-4				2.25

MIRRORWORLD: RAIN
NetCo Partners (Big Ent.): Feb, 1997 - No. 0, Apr, 1997 ($3.25, limited series)

0,1-Tad Williams-s				3.25

MISADVENTURES OF MERLIN JONES, THE (See Movie Comics & Merlin Jones as the Monkey's Uncle under Movie Comics)

MISS AMERICA COMICS (Miss America Magazine #2 on; also see Blonde Phantom & Marvel Mystery Comics)
Marvel Comics (20CC): 1944 (one-shot)

1-2 pgs. pin-ups		155	465	966	1700

MISS AMERICA MAGAZINE (Formerly Miss America; Miss America #51 on)
Miss America Publ. Corp./Marvel/Atlas (MAP): V1#2, Nov, 1944 - No. 93, Nov, 1958

V1#2-Photo-c of teenage girl in Miss America costume; Miss America, Patsy Walker (intro.) comic stories plus movie reviews & stories; intro. Buzz Baxter & Hedy Wolfe; 1 pg. origin Miss America

		125	375	781	1375
3-5-Miss America & Patsy Walker stories		47	140	286	500
6-Patsy Walker only		14	42	72	120
V2#1(4/45)-6(9/45)-Patsy Walker continues		9	27	49	70
V3#1(10/45)-6(4/46)		8	24	42	60
V4#1(5/46),2,5(9/46)		7	21	38	55
V4#3(7/46)-Liz Taylor photo-c		16	48	83	140
V4#4 (9/46), 6(10/46; 92 pgs.)		7	21	36	50
V5#1(11/46)-6(4/47), V6#1(5/47)-3(7/47)		7	21	36	50
V7#1(8/47)-14,16-23(#56, 6/49)		6	18	32	45
V7#15-All comics		7	21	38	55
V7#24(#57, 7/49)-Kamen-a (becomes Best Western #58 on?)					
		7	21	36	50
V7#25(8/49), 27-44(3/52), VII,nn(5/52)		6	18	29	40
V7#26(9/49)-All comics		7	21	36	50
V1,nn(7/52)-V1,nn(1/53)(#46-49), V7#50(Spring '53), V1#51-V7?#54(7/53),					
55-93		5	15	25	35

NOTE: *Photo-c #1, 4, V2#1, 4, 5, V3#5, V4#3, 4, 6, V7#15, 16, 24, 26, 34, 37, 38. Painted c-3. Powell a-V7#31.*

MISS BEVERLY HILLS OF HOLLYWOOD (See Adventures of Bob Hope)
National Periodical Publ.: Mar-Apr, 1949 - No. 9, July-Aug, 1950 (52 pgs.)

1 (Meets Alan Ladd)		59	177	369	650
2-William Holden photo on-c		43	129	257	450
3-5: 2-9-Part photo-c. 5-Bob Hope photo on-c		40	120	220	380
6,7,9: 6-Lucille Ball photo on-c		36	108	191	330
8-Reagan photo on-c		40	120	232	400

NOTE: *Beverly meets Alan Ladd in #1, Eve Arden #2, Betty Hutton #4, Bob Hope #5.*

MISS CAIRO JONES
Croyden Publishers: 1945

1-Bob Oksner daily newspaper-r (1st strip story); lingerie panels

		21	63	110	185

MISS FURY COMICS (Newspaper strip reprints)
Timely Comics (NPI 1/CmPI 2/MPC 3-8): Winter, 1942-43 - No. 8, Winter, 1946 (Published quarterly)

1-Origin Miss Fury by Tarpe' Mills (68 pgs.) in costume w/pin-ups

		350	1050	2188	4200
2-(60 pgs.)-In costume w/pin-ups		173	519	1080	1900
3-(60 pgs.)-In costume w/pin-ups; Hitler-c		145	435	909	1600
4-(52 pgs.)-In costume, 2 pgs. w/pin-ups		109	327	682	1200
5-(52 pgs.)-In costume w/pin-ups		91	273	568	1000
6-(52 pgs.)-Not in costume in inside stories, w/pin-ups					
		86	258	540	950
7,8-(36 pgs.)-In costume 1 pg. each; no pin-ups		77	232	483	850

NOTE: *Schomburg c-1, 5, 6.*

MISS FURY
Adventure Comics: 1991 - No. 4, 1991 ($2.50, limited series)

1-4: 1-Origin; granddaughter of original Miss Fury				2.50
1-Limited ed. ($4.95)				5.00

Miss Fury Comics #5 © MAR

Mr. District Attorney #17 © DC

Mister Miracle #1 © DC

	GD2.0	FN6.0	VF8.0	NM9.4

MISSION IMPOSSIBLE (TV)
Dell Publ. Co.: May, 1967 - No. 4, Oct, 1968; No. 5, Oct, 1969 (All have photo-c)

1	9	27	63	110
2-5: 5-Reprints #1	6	18	42	75

MISSION IMPOSSIBLE (Movie)
Marvel Comics (Paramount Comics): May, 1996 ($2.95, one-shot)
(1st Paramount Comics book)

1-Liefeld-c & back-up story		3.00

MISS LIBERTY (Becomes Liberty Comics)
Burten Publishing Co.: 1945 (MLJ reprints)

1-The Shield & Dusty, The Wizard, & Roy, the Super Boy app.; r/Shield-Wizard #13	30	90	159	275

MISS MELODY LANE OF BROADWAY (See The Adventures of Bob Hope)
National Periodical Publ.: Feb-Mar, 1950 - No. 3, June-July, 1950 (52 pgs.)

1-Movie stars photos app. on all-c.	59	177	369	650
2,3: 3-Ed Sullivan photo on-c.	40	120	232	400

MISS PEACH
Dell Publishing Co.: Oct-Dec, 1963; 1969

1-Jack Mendelsohn-a/script	8	24	56	100
...Tells You How to Grow (1969; 25¢)-Mel Lazarus-a; also given away (36 pgs.)	4	12	30	50

MISS PEPPER (See Meet Miss Pepper)

MISS SUNBEAM (See Little Miss...)

MISS VICTORY (See Captain Fearless #1,2, Holyoke One-Shot #3, Veri Best Sure Fire & Veri Best Sure Shot Comics)

MISTER AMERICA
Endeavor Comics: Apr, 1994 - No. 2, May, 1994 ($2.95, limited series)

1,2		3.00

MR. & MRS. BEANS
United Features Syndicate: No. 11, 1939

Single Series 11	36	108	191	330

MR. & MRS. J. EVIL SCIENTIST (TV)(See The Flintstones & Hanna-Barbera Band Wagon #3)
Gold Key: Nov, 1963 - No. 4, Sept, 1966 (Hanna-Barbera, all 12¢)

1	8	24	56	100
2-4	5	15	35	60

MR. ANTHONY'S LOVE CLINIC (Based on radio show)
Hillman Periodicals: Nov, 1949 - No. 5, Apr-May, 1950 (52 pgs.)

1-Photo-c	14	42	72	120
2	9	27	49	70
3-5: 5-Photo-c	8	24	56	60

MISTER BLANK
Amaze Ink: No. 0, Jan, 1996 - No. 14, May, 2000 ($1.75/$2.95, B&W)

0-($1.75, 16 pgs.) Origin of Mr. Blank		2.25
1-14-($2.95) Chris Hicks-s/a		3.00

MR. DISTRICT ATTORNEY (Radio/TV)
National Per. Publ.: Jan-Feb, 1948 - No. 67, Jan-Feb, 1959 (1-23: 52 pgs.)

1-Howard Purcell c-5-23 (most)	100	300	625	1100
2	45	135	270	475
3-5	36	108	191	330
6-10	29	87	153	265
11-20	22	66	116	195
21-43: 43-Last pre-code (1-2/55)	15	45	77	130
44-67	12	36	61	100

MR. DISTRICT ATTORNEY (SeeThe Funnies #35)
Dell Publishing Co.: No. 13, 1942

Four Color 13-See The Funnies #35 for 1st app.	30	90	210	385

MISTER E (Also see Books of Magic limited series)
DC Comics: Jun, 1991- No. 4, Sept, 1991($1.75, limited series)

1-4-Snyder III-c/a; follow-up to Books of Magic limited series		3.00

MISTER ED, THE TALKING HORSE (TV)

Dell Publishing Co./Gold Key: Mar-May, 1962 - No. 6, Feb, 1964 (All photo-c; photo back-c: 1-6)

Four Color 1295	13	39	91	175
1(11/62) (Gold Key)-Photo-c	9	27	63	120
2-6: Photo-c	5	15	35	65

(See March of Comics #244, 260, 282, 290)

MR. HERO, THE NEWMATIC MAN (See Neil Gaiman's...)

MR. MAGOO (TV) (The Nearsighted..., ...& Gerald McBoing Boing 1954 issues; formerly Gerald McBoing-Boing And ...)
Dell Publishing Co.: No. 6, Nov-Jan, 1953-54; 5/54 - 3-5/62; 9-11/63 - 3-5/65

6	11	33	77	145
Four Color 561(5/54),602(11/54)	11	33	77	145
Four Color 1235(#1, 12-2/62),1305(#2, 3-5/62)	9	27	63	110
3(9-11/63) - 5	8	24	56	100
Four Color 1235(12-536-505)(3-5/65)-2nd Printing	6	18	42	75

MR. MAJESTIC (See WildC.A.T.S.)
DC Comics (WildStorm): Sept, 1999 - No. 9, May, 2000 ($2.50)

1-9: 1-McGuinness-a/Casey & Holguin-s. 2-Two covers		2.50
TPB (2002, $14.95) r/#1-6 & Wildstorm Spotlight #1		15.00

MISTER MIRACLE (1st series) (See Cancelled Comic Cavalcade)
National Periodical Publications/DC Comics: 3-4/71 - V4#18, 2-3/74; V5#19, 9/77 - V6#25, 8-9/78; 1987 (Fourth World)

1-1st app. Mr. Miracle (#1-3 are 15¢)	6	18	40	65
2,3: 3-Last 15¢ issue	3	10	23	35
4-8: 6-Boy Commandos-r begin; all 52 pgs.	3	10	23	35
9-18: 9-Origin Mr. Miracle; Darkseid cameo. 15-Intro/1st app. Shilo Norman. 18-Barda & Scott Free wed; New Gods app. & Darkseid cameo; Last Kirby issue.	2	6	12	18
19-25 (1977-78)	1	3	6	8
Special 1(1987, $1.25, 52 pgs.)				3.00

Jack Kirby's Fourth World TPB ('01, $12.95) B&W&Grey-toned reprint of #11-18; Mark Evanier intro. 13.00
Jack Kirby's Mister Miracle TPB ('98, $12.95) B&W&Grey-toned reprint of #1-10; David Copperfield intro. 13.00
NOTE: *Austin* a-19. *Ditko* a-#1-6. *Golden* a-23-25p; c-25p. *Heath* a-24i, 25i; c-25i. *Kirby* a(p)/c-1-18. *Nasser* a-19i. *Rogers* a-19-22p; c-19, 20p, 21p, 22-24. 4-8 contain *Simon & Kirby* Boy Commandos reprints from Detective 82,76, Boy Commandos 1, 3 & Detective 64 in that order.

MISTER MIRACLE (2nd Series) (See Justice League)
DC Comics: Jan, 1989 - No. 28, June, 1991 ($1.00/$1.25)

1-28: 13,14-Lobo app. 22-1st new Mr. Miracle w/new costume		2.50

MISTER MIRACLE (3rd Series)
DC Comics: Apr, 1996 - No. 7, Oct, 1996 ($1.95)

1-7: 2-Vs. JLA. 6-Simonson-c		2.25

MR. MIRACLE (See Capt. Fearless #1 & Holyoke One-Shot #4)

MR. MONSTER (1st Series)(Doc Stearn... #7 on; See Airboy-Mr. Monster Special, Dark Horse Presents, Super Duper Comics & Vanguard Illustrated #7)
Eclipse Comics: Jan, 1985 - No. 10, June, 1987 ($1.75, Baxter paper)

1-3: 1-1st story-r from Vanguard Ill. #7(1st app.). 2-Dave Stevens-c. 3-Alan Moore scripts; Wolverton-r/Weird Mysteries #5.		4.00
4-10: 6-Ditko-r/Fantastic Fears #5 plus new Giffen-a. 10- "6-D" issue		3.00

MR. MONSTER
Dark Horse Comics: Feb, 1988 - No. 8, July, 1991 ($1.75, B&W)

1-7		3.00
8-($4.95, 60 pgs.)-Origins conclusion		5.00

MR. MONSTER ATTACKS! (Doc Stearn...)
Tundra Publ.: Aug, 1992 - No. 3, Oct, 1992 ($3.95, limited series, 32 pgs.)

1-3: Michael T. Gilbert-a/scripts; Gilbert/Dorman painted-c		4.00

MR. MONSTER PRESENTS (CRACK-A-BOOM!)
Caliber Comics: 1997 - No. 3, 1997 ($2.95, B&W&Red, limited series)

1-3: Michael T. Gilbert-a/scripts; 1-Wraparound-c		3.00

MR. MONSTER'S GAL FRIDAY...KELLY!
Image Comics: Jan, 2000 - Present ($3.50, B&W)

1-3: Michael T. Gilbert-c; story & art by various. 3-Alan Moore-s		3.50

Mister Mystery #5 © Media Pub.

Mr. T and the T-Force #8 © Now Comics

Modern Comics #53 © QUA

	GD2.0	FN6.0	VF8.0	NM9.4

MR. MONSTER'S SUPER-DUPER SPECIAL
Eclipse Comics: May, 1986 - No. 8, July, 1987

	GD2.0	FN6.0	VF8.0	NM9.4
1-(5/86)...3-D High Octane Horror #1				4.00
1-(5/86)...2-D version, 100 copies	2	6	10	14
2-(8/86)...High Octane Horror #1, 3-(9/86)...True Crime #1, 4-(11/86)...True Crime #2, 5-(1/87)...Hi-Voltage Super Science #1, 6-(3/87)...High Shock Schlock #1, 7-(5/87)...High Shock Schlock #2, 8-(7/87)...Weird Tales Of The Future #1				4.00

NOTE: Jack Cole r-3, 4. Evans a-2r. Kubert a-1r. Powell a-5r. Wolverton a-2r, 7r, 8r.

MR. MONSTER VS. GORZILLA
Image Comics: July, 1998 ($2.95, one-shot)

1-Michael T. Gilbert-a				3.00

MR. MUSCLES (Formerly Blue Beetle #18-21)
Charlton Comics: No. 22, Mar, 1956; No. 23, Aug, 1956

22,23	8	24	42	60

MR. MXYZPTLK (VILLAINS)
DC Comics: Feb, 1998 ($1.95, one-shot)

1-Grant-s/Morgan-a/Pearson-c				2.25

MISTER MYSTERY (Tales of Horror and Suspense)
Mr. Publ. (Media Publ.) No. 1-3/SPM Publ./Stanmore (Aragon): Sept, 1951 - No. 19, Oct, 1954

1-Kurtzmanesque horror story	86	258	540	950
2,3-Kurtzmanesque story. 3-Anti-Wertham edit.	57	171	356	625
4,6-Bondage-c; 6-Torture	57	171	356	625
5,8,10	55	165	330	575
7- "The Brain Bats of Venus" by Wolverton; partially re-used in Weird Tales of the Future #7	118	354	738	1300
9-Nostrand-a	55	165	330	575
11-Wolverton "Robot Woman" story/Weird Mysteries #2, cut up, rewritten & partially redrawn	80	240	500	875
12-Classic injury to eye-c	118	354	738	1300
13-17,19: 15- "Living Dead" junkie story. 17-Severed heads-c. 19-Reprints	40	120	234	400
18- "Robot Woman" by Wolverton reprinted from Weird Mysteries #2; decapitation, bondage-c	59	177	369	650

NOTE: Andru a-1, 2p, 3p. Andru/Esposito a-c 1-3. Baily c-10-13(most). Mortellaro c-5-7. Bondage c-7. Some issues have graphic dismemberment scenes.

MR. PUNCH
DC Comics (Vertigo): 1994 ($24.95, one-shot)

nn (Hard-c)-Gaiman scripts; McKean-c/a				40.00
nn (Soft-c)				15.00

MISTER Q (See Mighty Midget Comics & Our Flag Comics #5)

MR. RISK (Formerly All Romances; Men Against Crime #3 on)(Also see Our Flag Comics & Super-Mystery Comics)
Ace Magazines: No. 7, Oct, 1950; No. 2, Dec, 1950

7,2	9	27	49	70

MR. SCARLET & PINKY (See Mighty Midget Comics)

MR. T AND THE T-FORCE
Now Comics: June, 1993 - No. 10, May, 1994 ($1.95, color)

1-10-Newsstand editions: 1-7-polybagged with photo trading card in each. 1,2-Neal Adams-c/a(p). 3-Dave Dorman painted-c				2.25
1-10-Direct Sale editions polybagged w/line drawn trading cards. 1-Contains gold foil trading card by Neal Adams				2.25

MISTER UNIVERSE (Professional wrestler)
Mr. Publications Media Publ. (Stanmor, Aragon): July, 1951; No. 2, Oct, 1951 - No. 5, April, 1952

1	22	66	116	200
2- "Jungle That Time Forgot", (24 pg. story); Andru/Esposito-a	14	42	72	120
3-Marijuana story	14	42	72	120
4,5- "Goes to War" cover/stories	10	30	55	85

MISTER X (See Vortex)
Mr. Publications/Vortex Comics/Caliber V3#1 on: 6/84 - No. 14, 8/88 ($1.50/$2.25, direct sales, coated paper);V2#1, Apr, 1989 - V2#12, Mar, 1990

($2.00/$2.50, B&W, newsprint) V3#1, 1996 - Present ($2.95, B&W)

1-10,12-14				4.00
11-Dave McKean story & art (6 pgs.)				5.00
V2 #1-12: 1-11 (Second Coming, B&W): 1-Four diff.-c. 10-Photo-c				3.00
V3 #1-4				3.00
Return of... ($11.95, graphic novel)-r/V1#1-4				12.00
Return of... ($34.95, hardcover limited edition)-r/1-4				35.00
Special (no date, 1990?)				3.00

MISTY
Marvel Comics (Star Comics): Dec, 1985 - No. 6, May, 1986 (Limited series)

1-6: Millie The Model's niece				3.00

MITZI COMICS (Becomes Mitzi's Boy Friend #2-7)(See All Teen)
Timely Comics: Spring, 1948 (one-shot)

1-Kurtzman's "Hey Look" plus 3 pgs. "Giggles 'n' Grins"	25	75	130	225

MITZI'S BOY FRIEND (Formerly Mitzi Comics; becomes Mitzi's Romances)
Marvel Comics (TCI): No. 2, June, 1948 - No. 7, April, 1949

2	12	36	61	100
3-7	9	27	51	75

MITZI'S ROMANCES (Formerly Mitzi's Boy Friend)
Timely/Marvel Comics (TCI): No. 8, June, 1949 - No. 10, Dec, 1949

8-Becomes True Life Tales #8 (10/49) on?	11	33	55	90
9,10: 10-Painted-c	9	27	49	70

MOBFIRE
DC Comics (Vertigo): Dec, 1994 - No. 6, May, 1995 ($2.50, limited series)

1-6				2.50

MOBY DICK (See Feature Presentations #6, and King Classics)
Dell Publishing Co.: No. 717, Aug, 1956

Four Color 717-Movie, Gregory Peck photo-c	9	27	63	110

MOBY DUCK (See Donald Duck #112 & Walt Disney Showcase #2,11)
Gold Key (Disney): Oct, 1967 - No. 11, Oct, 1970; No. 12, Jan, 1974 - No. 30, Feb, 1978

1	3	9	20	30
2-5	2	6	11	16
6-11	2	6	9	12
12-30: 21,30-r	1	3	6	8

MODEL FUN (With Bobby Benson)
Harle Publications: No. 3, Winter, 1954-55 - No. 5, July, 1955

3-Bobby Benson	7	21	36	50
4,5-Bobby Benson	5	15	24	32

MODELING WITH MILLIE (Formerly Life With Millie)
Atlas/Marvel Comics (Male Publ.): No. 21, Feb, 1963 - No. 54, June, 1967

21	8	24	56	90
22-30	5	15	34	55
31-54	4	12	26	40

MODERN COMICS (Formerly Military Comics #1-43)
Quality Comics Group: No. 44, Nov, 1945 - No. 102, Oct, 1950

44-Blackhawk continues	55	165	341	600
45-52: 49-1st app. Fear, Lady Adventuress	40	120	232	400
53-Torchy by Ward begins (9/46)	43	129	257	450
54-60: 55-J. Cole-a	36	108	191	330
61-77,79,80: 73-J. Cole-a	34	102	179	310
78-1st app. Madame Butterfly	36	108	191	330
81-99,101: 82,83-One pg. J. Cole-a. 83-The Spirit app.; last 52 pg. issue?	30	90	165	285
99-Blackhawks on the moon-c/story	34	102	179	310
100	39	117	208	360
102-(Scarce)-J. Cole-a; Spirit by Eisner app.				

NOTE: Al Bryant c-44-51, 54, 55, 66, 69. Jack Cole a-55, 73. Crandall Blackhawk-#46, 47, 50, 51, 54, 56, 58-60, 64, 67-70, 73, 74, 76-78, 80-83; c-60-65, 67, 68, 70-95. Crandall/Cuidera c-56-59, 96-102. Gustavson a-47, 49. Ward Blackhawk-#52, 53, 55 (15 pgs. each). Torchy in #53-102; by Ward only in #53-89(9/49); by Gil Fox #92, 93, 102.

MODERN LOVE
E. C. Comics: June-July, 1949 - No. 8, Aug-Sept, 1950

Mod Wheels #14 © GK

The Monarchy #1 © DC

Monster Hunters #11 © CC

	GD2.0	FN6.0	VF8.0	NM9.4
1-Feldstein, Ingels-a	64	192	398	700
2-Craig/Feldstein-c/s	41	123	246	425
3	40	120	217	375
4-6 (Scarce): 4-Bra/panties panels	50	150	300	525
7,8	40	120	217	375

NOTE: **Craig** a-3. **Feldstein** a-in most issues; c-1, 2i, 3-8. **Harrison** a-4. **Iger** a-6-8. **Ingels** a-1, 2, 4-7. **Palais** a-5. **Wood** a-7. **Wood/Harrison** a-5-7. (Canadian reprints known; see Table of Contents.)

MOD LOVE
Western Publishing Co.: 1967 (50¢, 36 pgs.)

1	4	12	25	38

MODNIKS, THE
Gold Key: Aug, 1967 - No. 2, Aug, 1970

10206-708(#1)	3	9	20	30
2	2	6	13	20

MOD SQUAD (TV)
Dell Publishing Co.: Jan, 1969 - No. 3, Oct, 1969 - No. 8, April, 1971

1-Photo-c	5	15	35	70
2-4: 2-4-Photo-c	4	12	26	40
5-8: 8-Photo-c; Reprints #2	3	10	23	35

MOD WHEELS
Gold Key: Mar, 1971 - No. 19, Jan, 1976

1	3	10	23	35
2-9	2	6	13	20
10-19: 11,15-Extra 16 pgs. ads	2	6	11	16

MOE & SHMOE COMICS
O. S. Publ. Co.: Spring, 1948 - No. 2, Summer, 1948

1	9	27	49	70
2	6	18	32	45

MOEBIUS (Graphic novel)
Marvel Comics (Epic Comics): Oct, 1987 - No. 6, 1988; No. 7, 1990; No. 8, 1991 ($9.95, 8x11", mature)

1,2,4-6,8: (#2, 2nd printing, $9.95)				10.00
3,7,0: 3-(1st & 2nd printings, $12.95). 0 (1990, $12.95)				13.00
Moebius I-Signed & numbered hard-c ($45.95, Graphitti Designs, 1,500 copies printed)-r/#1-3				46.00

MOEBIUS COMICS
Caliber: May, 1996 - No. 6 ($2.95, B&W)

1-6: Moebius-c/a. 1-William Stout-a				3.00

MOEBIUS: THE MAN FROM CIGURI
Dark Horse Comics: 1996 ($7.95, digest-size)

nn-Moebius-c/a				8.00

MOLLY MANTON'S ROMANCES (Romantic Affairs #3)
Marvel Comics (SePl): Sept, 1949 - No. 2, Dec, 1949 (52 pgs.)

1-Photo-c (becomes Blaze the Wonder Collie #2 (10/49) on? & Molly Manton's Romances #2	14	42	72	125
2-Titled "Romances of..."; photo-c	10	30	55	80

MOLLY O'DAY (Super Sleuth)
Avon Periodicals: February, 1945 (1st Avon comic)

1-Molly O'Day, The Enchanted Dagger by Tuska (r/Yankee #1), Capt'n Courage, Corporal Grant app.	52	157	314	550

MONA
Kitchen Sink Press: 1999 ($4.95, B&W, one-shot)

1-Cartoons by Kurtzman and various; Hernandez-c				5.00

MONARCHY, THE (Also see The Authority and StormWatch)
DC Comics (WildStorm): Apr, 2001 - Present ($2.50)

1-McCrea & Leach-a/Young-s				2.50
2-9				2.50
Bullets Over Babylon TPB (2001, $12.95) r/#1-4, Authority #21				13.00

MONKEES, THE (TV)(Also see Circus Boy, Groovy, Not Brand Echh #3, Teen-Age Talk, Teen Beam & Teen Beat)
Dell Publishing Co.: March, 1967 - No. 17, Oct, 1969 (#1-4,6,7,9,10,12,15,17 have photo-c)

1-Photo-c	10	30	70	125
2-6,7,9,10,12,15,16: All photo-c	6	18	42	75
8,11,13,14,17-No photo-c: 17-Reprints #1	4	12	30	50

MONKEY AND THE BEAR, THE
Atlas Comics (ZPC): Sept, 1953 - No. 3, Jan, 1954

1-Howie Post-c/a in all; funny animal	9	27	49	70
2,3	6	18	29	40

MONKEYMAN AND O'BRIEN (Also see Dark Horse Presents #80, 100-5, Gen[13]/..., Hellboy: Seed of Destruction, & San Diego Comic Con #2)
Dark Horse Comics (Legend): Jul, 1996 - No. 3, Sept, 1996 ($2.95, lim. series)

1-3: New stories; Art Adams-c/scripts				3.50
nn-(2/96, $2.95)-r/back-up stories from Hellboy: Seed of Destruction; Adams-c/a/scripts				3.50

MONKEYSHINES COMICS
Ace Periodicals/Publishers Specialists/Current Books/Unity Publ.: Summer, 1944 - No. 27, July, 1949

1-Funny animal	12	36	61	105
2-(Aut/44)	7	21	38	55
3-10: 3-(Win/44)	6	18	32	45
11-17,19-27: 23,24-Fago-c/a	6	18	29	40
18-Frazetta-a	7	21	38	55

MONKEY'S UNCLE, THE (See Merlin Jones As... under Movie Comics)

MONROES, THE (TV)
Dell Publishing Co.: Apr, 1967

1-Photo-c	3	9	19	28

MONSTER
Fiction House Magazines: 1953 - No. 2, 1953

1-Dr. Drew by Grandenetti; reprint from Rangers Comics #48; Whitman-c	50	150	300	525
2-Whitman-c	40	120	220	380

MONSTER CRIME COMICS (Also see Crime Must Stop)
Hillman Periodicals: Oct, 1952 (15¢, 52 pgs.)

1 (Scarce)	100	300	625	1100

MONSTER FIGHTERS INC.
Image Comics (Bright Anvil Studios): Apr, 1999; Dec, 1999 ($3.50/$3.95)

1-Torres-s/Lubera & Yeung-a				3.50
...: The Black Book 1 (9/00, $3.50) Manapul-a				3.50
...The Ghosts of Christmas 1 (12/99, $3.95)				4.00

MONSTER HOWLS (Magazine)
Humor-Vision: December, 1966 (Satire) (35¢, 68 pgs.)

1	5	15	34	55

MONSTER HUNTERS
Charlton Comics: Aug, 1975 - No. 9, Jan, 1977; No. 10, Oct, 1977 - No. 18, Feb, 1979

1-Howard-a; Newton-c	3	9	17	25
2-Sutton-c/a; Ditko-a	2	6	12	18
3,4,5,7: 4-Sutton-c/a	2	6	9	12
6,8,10: 6,8,10-Ditko-a	2	6	10	14
9,11,12	1	3	6	9
13,15,18-Ditko-c/a. 18-Sutton-a	2	6	10	14
14-Special all-Ditko issue	2	6	15	22
16,17-Sutton-a	1	3	6	8
1,2 (Modern Comics reprints, 1977)				4.00

NOTE: **Ditko** a-2, 6, 8, 10, 13-15; 18r; c-13-15, 18. **Howard** a-1, 3, 7; r-13. **Morisi** a-1. **Staton** a-1, 13. **Sutton** a-2, 4; c-2, 4; r-16-18. **Zeck** a-4-9. Reprints in #12-18.

MONSTER MADNESS (Magazine)
Marvel Comics: 1972 - No. 3, 1973 (60¢, B&W)

1-3: Stories by "Sinister" Stan Lee	3	9	19	28

MONSTER MAN
Image Comics (Action Planet): Sept, 1997 ($2.95, B&W)

1-Mike Manley-c/s/a				3.00

MONSTER MASTERWORKS
Marvel Comics: 1989 ($12.95, TPB)

Monster World #1 © WSP

Monte Hale Western #82 © FAW

Moon Girl #3 © WMG

	GD2.0	FN6.0	VF8.0	NM9.4

nn-Reprints 1960's monster stories; art by Kirby, Ditko, Ayers, Everett   13.00

MONSTER MATINEE
Chaos! Comics: Oct, 1997 - No. 3, Oct, 1997 ($2.50, limited series)

1-3: pin-ups				2.50

MONSTER MENACE
Marvel: Dec, 1993 - No. 4, Mar, 1994 ($1.25, limited series)

1-4: Pre-code Atlas horror reprints.				3.00

NOTE: *Ditko-r & Kirby-r in all.*

MONSTER OF FRANKENSTEIN (See Frankenstein)

MONSTERS ATTACKS (Magazine)
Globe Communications Corpse: Sept, 1989 - No. 3, July, 1990 (B&W)

1-3-Ditko, Morrow, J. Severin-a				2.25

MONSTERS ON THE PROWL (Chamber of Darkness #1-8)
Marvel Comics Group (No. 13,14: 52 pgs.): No. 9, 2/71 - No. 27, 11/73; No. 28, 6/74 - No. 30, 10/74

9-Barry Smith inks	3	9	20	30
10-12,15: 12-Last 15¢ issue	2	6	11	16
13,14-(52 pgs.)	2	6	15	22
16-(4/72)-King Kull app.; Severin-c	2	6	12	18
17-30	2	6	10	14

NOTE: *Ditko r-9, 14, 16. Kirby r-10-17, 21, 23, 25, 27, 28, 30; c-9, 25. Kirby/Ditko r-14, 17-20, 22, 24, 26, 29. Marie/John Severin a-16(Kull). 9-13, 15 contain one new story. Woodish art by Reese-11. King Kull created by Robert E. Howard.*

MONSTERS TO LAUGH WITH (Magazine) (Becomes Monsters Unlimited #4)
Marvel Comics Group: 1964 - No. 3, 1965 (B&W)

1-Humor by Stan Lee	6	18	45	75
2,3	4	12	26	40

MONSTERS UNLEASHED (Magazine)
Marvel Comics Group: July, 1973 - No. 11, Apr, 1975; Summer, 1975 (B&W)

1-Soloman Kane by Werewolf app.	3	9	21	32
2-4: 2-The Frankenstein Monster begins, ends #10. 3-Neal Adams-c/a; The Man-Thing begins (origin-r); Son of Satan preview. 4-Werewolf app.	3	9	19	28
5-7: Werewolf in all. 5-Man-Thing. 7-Williamson-a(r)	2	6	12	18
8-11: 8-Man-Thing; N. Adams-a. 9-Man-Thing; Wendigo app. 10-Origin Tigra	2	6	15	22
Annual 1 (Summer,1975, 92 pgs.)-Kane-a	2	6	10	14

NOTE: *Boris c-2, 6. Brunner a-2; c-11. J. Buscema a-2p, 4p, 5p. Colan a-1, 4r. Davis a-3r. Everett a-2r. G. Kane a-3. Krigstein r-4. Morrow a-3; c-1. Perez a-8. Ploog a-6. Reese a-1, 2. Tuska a-3p. Wildey a-1r.*

MONSTERS UNLIMITED (Magazine) (Formerly Monsters To Laugh With)
Marvel Comics Group: No. 4, 1965 - No. 7, 1966 (B&W)

4-7	3	10	23	35

MONSTER WORLD
DC Comics (WildStorm): Jul, 2001 - No. 4, Oct, 2001 ($2.50, limited series)

1-4-Lobdell-s/Meglia-c/a				2.50

MONTANA KID, THE (See Kid Montana)

MONTE HALE WESTERN (Movie star; Formerly Mary Marvel #1-28; also see Fawcett Movie Comic, Motion Picture Comics, Picture News #8, Real Western Hero, Six-Gun Heroes, Western Hero & XMas Comics)
Fawcett Publ./Charlton No. 83 on: No. 29, Oct, 1948 - No. 88, Jan, 1956

29-(#1, 52 pgs.)-Photo-c begin, end #82; Monte Hale & his horse Pardner begin	50	150	300	525
30-(52 pgs.)-Big Bow and Little Arrow begin, end #34; Captain Tootsie by Beck	27	81	145	250
31-36,38-40-(52 pgs.): 34-Gabby Hayes begins, ends #86. 39-Captain Tootsie by Beck	20	60	105	175
37,41,45,49-(36 pgs.)	14	42	72	125
42-44,46-48,50-(52 pgs.): 47-Big Bow & Little Arrow app.	16	48	83	140
51,52,54-56,58,59-(52 pgs.)	12	36	61	105
53,57-(36 pgs.)- 53-Slim Pickens app.	10	30	55	85
60-81: 36 pgs. #60-on. 80-Gabby Hayes ends	10	30	55	80
82-Last Fawcett issue (6/53)	12	36	61	100
83-1st Charlton issue (2/55); B&W photo back-c begin. Gabby Hayes				

---

returns, ends #86	14	42	72	120
84 (4/55)	10	30	55	85
85-86	10	30	55	80
87,88: 87-Wolverton-r, 1/2 pg. 88-Last issue	10	30	55	85

NOTE: *Gil Kane a-33?, 34? Rocky Lane -1 pg. (Carnation ad)-38, 40, 41, 43, 44, 46, 55.*

MONTY HALL OF THE U.S. MARINES (See With the Marines...)
Toby Press: Aug, 1951 - No. 11, Apr, 1953

1	11	33	55	90
2	7	21	36	50
3-5	6	18	32	45
6-11	6	18	29	40

NOTE: *Full page pin-ups (Pin-Up Pete) by Jack Sparling in #1-9.*

MOON, A GIRL...ROMANCE, A (Becomes Weird Fantasy #13 on; formerly Moon Girl #1-8)
E. C. Comics: No. 9, Sept-Oct, 1949 - No. 12, Mar-Apr, 1950

9-Moon Girl cameo	69	207	431	765
10,11	56	168	350	620
12-(Scarce)	70	210	438	765

NOTE: *Feldstein, Ingels art in all. Feldstein c-9-12. Wood/Harrison a-10-12. Canadian reprints known; see Table of Contents.*

MOON GIRL AND THE PRINCE (#1) (Moon Girl #2-6; Moon Girl Fights Crime #7, 8; becomes A Moon, A Girl, Romance #9 on)(Also see Animal Fables #7 and Happy Houlihans)
E. C. Comics: Fall, 1947 - No. 8, Summer, 1949

1-Origin Moon Girl (see Happy Houlihans #1)	91	273	568	1000
2	52	157	314	550
3,4: 4-Moon Girl vs. a vampire	45	135	270	475
5-E.C.'s 1st horror story, "Zombie Terror"	100	300	625	1100
6-8-(Scarce): 7-Origin Star (Moongirl's sidekick)	52	157	314	550

NOTE: *Craig a-2, 5; c-1,2. Moldoff a-1-8; c-2-6. Wheelan's Fat and Slat app. in #3, 4, 6. #2 & #3 are 52 pgs., #4 on, 36 pgs. Canadian reprints known; (see Table of Contents.)*

MOON KNIGHT (Also see The Hulk, Marc Spector..., Marvel Preview #21, Marvel Spotlight & Werewolf by Night #32)
Marvel Comics Group: Nov, 1980 - No. 38, Jul, 1984 (Mando paper #33 on)

1-Origin resumed in #4				5.00
2-15,25,35: 4-Intro Midnight Man. 25-Double size. 35-($1.00, 52 pgs.)-X-men app.; F.F. cameo				3.00
16-24,26-34,36-38: 16-The Thing app.				2.50

NOTE: *Austin c-27i, 31i. Cowan c-16, 17. Kaluta c-36-38; back c-35. Miller c-9, 12p, 13p, 15p, 27p. Ploog back c-35. Sienkiewicz a-1-15, 17-20, 22-26, 28-30, 33i, 36(4); 37; c-1-5, 7, 8, 10, 11, 14-16, 18-26, 28-30, 31p, 33, 34.*

MOON KNIGHT
Marvel Comics Group: June, 1985 - V2#6, Dec, 1985

V2#1-6: 1-Double size; new costume. 6-Sienkiewicz painted-c				2.50

MOON KNIGHT
Marvel Comics: Jan, 1998 - No. 4, Apr, 1998 ($2.50, limited series)

1-4-Moench-s/Edwards-c/a				2.50

MOON KNIGHT (Volume 3)
Marvel Comics: Jan, 1999 - No. 4, Feb, 1999 ($2.99, limited series)

1-4-Moench-s/Texeira-a(p)				3.00

MOON KNIGHT: DIVIDED WE FALL
Marvel Comics: 1992 ($4.95, 52 pgs.)

nn-Denys Cowan-c/a(p)				5.00

MOON KNIGHT SPECIAL
Marvel Comics: Oct, 1992 ($2.50, 52 pgs.)

1-Shang Chi, Master of Kung Fu-c/story				2.50

MOON KNIGHT SPECIAL EDITION
Marvel Comics Group: Nov, 1983 - No. 3, Jan, 1984 ($2.00, limited series, Baxter paper)

1-3: Reprints from Hulk mag. by Sienkiewicz				3.00

MOON MULLINS (See Popular Comics, Super Book #3 & Super Comics)
Dell Publishing Co.: 1941 - 1945

Four Color 14(1941)	35	105	245	460
Large Feature Comic 29(1941)	25	75	175	325
Four Color 31(1943)	19	57	133	240

Moonshadow #1 © DeMatteis & Muth

Morbius: The Living Vampire #13 © MAR

More Fun Comics #87 © DC

	GD2.0	FN6.0	VF8.0	NM9.4
Four Color 81(1945)	11	33	77	140

MOON MULLINS
Michel Publ. (American Comics Group)#1-6/St. John #7,8:Dec-Jan, 1947-48 - No. 8, 1949 (52 pgs)

1-Alternating Sunday & daily strip-r	21	63	110	185
2	11	33	55	90
3-8: 7,8-St. John Publ. 8-…Featuring Kayo on-c	10	30	55	80

NOTE: Milt Gross a-2-6, 8. Frank Willard r-all.

MOON PILOT
Dell Publishing Co.: No. 1313, Mar-May, 1962

Four Color 1313-Movie, photo-c	7	21	49	90

MOONSHADOW (Also see Farewell, Moonshadow)
Marvel Comics (Epic Comics): 5/85 - #12, 2/87 ($1.50/$1.75, mature) (1st fully painted comic book)

1-Origin; J. M. DeMatteis scripts & Jon J. Muth painted-c/a.				6.00
2-12: 11-Origin				4.00
Trade paperback (1987?)-r/#1-12				14.00
Signed & numbered hard-c ($39.95, 1,200 copies)-r/#1-12	5	15	38	60

MOONSHADOW
DC Comics (Vertigo): Oct, 1994 - No. 12, Aug, 1995 ($2.25/$2.95)

1-11-Reprints Epic series.				2.50
12 ($2.95)-w/expanded ending				3.00
The Complete Moonshadow TPB ('98, $39.95) r/#1-12 and Farewell Moonshadow; new Muth painted-c				40.00

MOON-SPINNERS, THE (See Movie Comics)

MOPSY (See Pageant of Comics & TV Series)
St. John Publ. Co.: Feb, 1948 - No. 19, Sept, 1953

1-Part-r; reprints "Some Punkins" by Neher	19	57	99	170
2	10	30	55	85
3-10(1953): 8-Lingerie panels	9	27	49	70
11-19-Lingerie-c	8	24	42	60

NOTE: #1, 3-6, 13, 18, 19 have paper dolls.

MORBID ANGEL
London Night Studios: Oct, 1995 ($3.00, B&W)

1-Hartsoe-c				3.00

MORBID ANGEL
London Night Studios: July, 1996 - No. 3, Jan, 1997 ($3.00, limited series)

1/2-($9.95)-Angel Tear Edition; foil logo				10.00
1-3, 1-Penance-c, …-To Hell and Back-(10/96, $3.00, B&W)				3.00

MORBIUS REVISITED
Marvel Comic: Aug, 1993 - No. 5, Dec, 1993 ($1.95, mini-series)

1-5-Reprints Fear #27-31				2.25

MORBIUS: THE LIVING VAMPIRE (Also see Amazing Spider-Man #101, 102, Fear #20, Marvel Team-Up #3, 4, Midnight Sons Unl. & Vampire Tales)
Marvel Comics (Midnight Sons imprint #16 on): Sept, 1992 - No. 32, Apr, 1995 ($1.75/$1.95)

1-($2.75, 52 pgs.)-Polybagged w/poster; Ghost Rider & Johnny Blaze x-over (part 3 of Rise of the Midnight Sons)				3.00
2-11,13-24,26-32: 3,4-Vs. Spider-Man-c/s.15-Ghost Rider app. 16-Spot varnish-c. 16,17-Siege of Darkness,parts 5 &13. 18-Deathlok app. 21-Bound-in Spider-Man trading card sheet; S-M app.				2.25
12-($2.25)-Outer-c is a Darkhold envelope made of black parchment w/gold ink; Midnight Massacre x-over				2.50
25-($2.50, 52 pgs)-Gold foil logo				2.50

MORE FUN COMICS (Formerly New Fun Comics #1-6)
National Periodical Publications: No. 7, Jan, 1936 - No. 127, Nov-Dec, 1947 (No. 7,9-11: paper-c)

7(1/36)-Oversized, paper-c; 1 pg. Kelly-a	769	2310	5200	–
8(2/36)-Oversized (10x12"), paper-c; 1 pg. Kelly-a; Sullivan-a				
	769	2310	5200	–
9(3-4/36)-(Very rare, 1st standard-sized comic book with original material)-Last multiple panel-c	923	2770	6200	–
10,11(7/36): 10-Last Henri Duval by Siegel & Shuster. 11-1st "Calling All Cars"				

	GD2.0	FN6.0	VF8.0	NM9.4
by Siegel & Shuster; new classic logo begins	538	1615	3600	–
12(8/36)-Slick-c begin	415	1245	2800	–
V2#1(9/36, #13)	385	1154	2600	–
2(10/36, #14)-Dr. Occult in costume (1st in color)(Superman proto-type); 1st DC appearance) continues from The Comics Magazine, ends #17				
	1846	5539	12,200	–
V2#3(11/36, #15), 16(V2#4), 17(V2#5): 16-Cover numbering begins; Xmas-c; last Superman tryout issue	738	2215	4900	–
18-20(V2#8, 5/37)	292	877	2000	–
21(V2#9)-24(V2#12, 9/37)	276	828	1518	2350
25(V3#1, 10/37)-27(V3#3, 12/37): 27-Xmas-c	276	828	1518	2350
28-30: 30-1st non-funny cover	250	750	1375	2250
31-Has ad for Action #1	265	795	1458	2250
32-35: 32-Last Dr. Occult	250	750	1375	2125
36-40: 36-(10/38)-The Masked Ranger & sidekick Pedro begins; Ginger Snap by Bob Kane (2 pgs.; 1st-a?). 39-Xmas-c	250	750	1375	2125
41-50: 41-Last Masked Ranger	212	636	1166	1800
51-The Spectre app. (in costume) in one panel ad at end of Buccaneer story	741	2223	4076	6300
52-(2/40)-Origin/1st app. The Spectre (in costume splash panel only), part 1 by Bernard Baily (parts 1 & 2 written by Jerry Siegel); Spectre's costume changes color from purple & blue to green & grey; last Wing Brady; Spectre-c	5143	15,930	36,000	72,000
53-Origin The Spectre (in costume at end of story), part 2; Capt. Desmo begins;Spectre-c	2400	7200	16,800	36,000
54-The Spectre in costume; last King Carter; classic-Spectre-c	1000	3000	6500	13,000
55-(Scarce, 5/40)-Dr. Fate begins (Intro & 1st app.); last Bulldog Martin; Spectre-c	1143	3430	8000	16,000
56-1st Dr. Fate-c (classic), origin continues. Congo Bill begins (6/40), 1st app.; Spectre-c	500	1500	3250	6500
57-60-All Spectre-c	333	1000	2083	4000
61,65: 61-Classic Dr. Fate-c. 65-Classic Spectre-c	308	924	1927	3700
62-64,66: 63-Last St. Bob Neal. 64-Lance Larkin begins; all Spectre-c	291	873	1818	3200
67-(5/41)-Origin (1st) Dr. Fate; last Congo Bill & Biff Bronson (C.B. cont. in Action Comics #37, 6/41)-Spectre-c	615	1845	4000	8000
68-70: 68-Clip Carson begins. 70-Last Lance Larkin; all Dr. Fate-c	227	681	1420	2500
71-Origin & 1st app. Johnny Quick by Mort Weisinger (9/41); classic sci-fi Dr. Fate-c	500	1500	3250	6500
72-Dr. Fate's new helmet; last Sgt. Carey, Sgt. O'Malley & Captain Desmo; German submarine-c (only German war-c)	223	669	1394	2450
73-Origin & 1st app. Aquaman (11/41) by Paul Norris; intro. Green Arrow & Speedy; Dr. Fate-c	1000	3000	7000	14,000
74-2nd Aquaman; 1st Percival Popp, Supercop; Dr. Fate-c	273	819	1705	3000
75,76: 75-New origin Spectre; Nazi spy ring cover w/Hitler's photo. 76-Last Dr. Fate-c; Johnny Quick (by Meskin #76-97) begins, ends #107; Last Clip Carson	227	681	1420	2500
77-80: 77-Green Arrow-c begin	200	600	1250	2200
81-83,85,88,90: 81-Last large logo. 82-1st small logo.	127	381	795	1400
84-Green Arrow Japanese war-c	132	395	825	1450
86,87-Johnny Quick-c. 87-Last Radio Squad	127	381	795	1400
89-Origin Green Arrow & Speedy Team-up	139	417	869	1525
91,97,99: 91-1st bi-monthly issue. 93-Dover & Clover begin (1st app., 9-10/43). 97-Kubert-a	80	240	500	875
98-Last Dr. Fate (scarce)	100	300	625	1100
100 (11-12/44)-Johnny Quick-c	116	348	725	1275
101-Origin & 1st app. Superboy (1-2/45)(not by Siegel & Shuster); last Spectre issue; Green Arrow-c	769	2307	5000	10,000
102-2nd Superboy app; 1st Dover & Clover-c	127	381	795	1400
103-3rd Superboy app; last Green Arrow-c	95	285	597	1050
104-1st Superboy-c w/Dover & Clover	84	253	525	925
105,106-Superboy-c	80	240	500	875
107-Last Johnny Quick & Superboy	80	240	500	875
108-120: 108-Genius Jones begins; 1st c-app. (3-4/46; cont'd from Adventure Comics #102)	23	69	121	210

More Than Mortal #6 © Sharon Scott

Mortie #2 © Magazine Pub.

Mostly Wanted #1 © WSP

	GD2.0	FN6.0	VF8.0	NM9.4		GD2.0	FN6.0	VF8.0	NM9.4

121-124,126: 121-123,126-Post funny animal(Jimminy & the Magic Book)-c

		20	60	105	180

125-Superman c-app.w/Jimminy — 75, 225, 469, 825
127-(Scarce)-Post-c/a — 35, 105, 188, 325

NOTE: All issues are scarce to rare. Cover features: The Spectre-#52-55, 57-60, 62-67. Dr. Fate-#56, 61, 68-76. The Green Arrow & Speedy-#77-85, 88-97, 99, 101 (w/Dover & Clover-#98, 103). Johnny Quick-#86, 87, 100. Dover & Clover-#102, (104, 106 w/Superboy), 107, 108(w/Genius Jones), 110, 112, 114, 117, 119. Genius Jones-#109, 111, 113, 115, 118, 120. Baily a-45, 52-on; c-52-55, 57-60, 62-67. Al Capp a-45(signed Koppy). Ellsworth c-7. Creig Flessel c-30, 31, 35-48(most). Guardineer c-47, 49, 50. Kiefer a-26. Meskin c-86, 87, 100? Moldoff c-51. George Papp c-77-85. Post c-121-127. Vincent Sullivan c-8-28, 32-34.

MORE SEYMOUR (See Seymour My Son)
Archie Publications: Oct, 1963

		2	6	15	22
1					

MORE THAN MORTAL (Also see Lady Pendragon/...)
Liar Comics: June, 1997 - No. 4, Apr, 1998 ($2.95, limited series)
Image Comics: No. 5, Dec, 1999 - Present ($2.95)

1-Blue forest background-c, 1-Variant-c — 4.00
1-White-c — 6.00
1-2nd printing; purple sky cover — 3.00
2-4: 3-Silvestri-a, 4-Two-c, one by Randy Queen — 3.00
5,6: 5-1st Image Comics issue — 3.00

MORE THAN MORTAL: OTHERWORLDS
Image Comics: July, 1999 - No. 4, Dec, 1999 ($2.95, limited series)

1-4-Firchow-a. 1-Two covers — 3.00

MORE THAN MORTAL SAGAS
Liar Comics: Jun, 1998 - No. 3, Dec, 1998 ($2.95, limited series)

1,2-Painted art by Romano. 2-Two-c, one by Firchow — 3.00
1-Variant-c by Linsner — 5.00

MORE THAN MORTAL TRUTHS AND LEGENDS
Liar Comics: Aug, 1998 - No. 6, Apr, 1999 ($2.95)

1-6-Firchow-a(p) — 3.00
1-Variant-c by Dan Norton — 4.50

MORE TRASH FROM MAD (Annual)
E. C. Comics: 1958 - No. 12, 1969
(Note: Bonus missing = half price)

nn(1958)-8pg. color Mad reprint from #20 — 19, 57, 134, 240
2(1959)-Market Product Labels — 14, 42, 102, 175
3(1960)-Text book covers — 13, 39, 94, 160
4(1961)-Sing Along with Mad booklet — 13, 39, 94, 160
5(1962)-Window Stickers; r/from Mad #39 — 9, 27, 65, 110
6(1963)-TV Guise booklet — 9, 27, 65, 110
7(1964)-Alfred E. Neuman commemorative stamps — 7, 21, 53, 85
8(1965)-Life size poster-Alfred E. Neuman — 5, 15, 38, 60
9-12: 9,10(1966-67)-Mischief Sticker. 11(1968)-Campaign poster & bumper sticker. 12(1969)-Pocket medals — 5, 15, 34, 50

NOTE: Kelly Freas c-1, 2, 4. Mingo c-3, 5-9, 11.

MORGAN THE PIRATE
Dell Publishing Co.: No. 1227, Sept-Nov, 1961

Four Color 1227-Photo-c — 8, 24, 56, 100

MORLOCK 2001
Atlas/Seaboard Publ.: Feb, 1975 - No. 3, July, 1975

1,2: 1-(Super-hero)-Origin & 1st app.; Milgrom-c — 6.00
3-Ditko/Wrightson-a; origin The Midnight Man & The Mystery Men — 1, 3, 6, 8

MORNINGSTAR SPECIAL
Comico: Apr, 1990 ($2.50)

1-From the Elementals; Willingham-c/a/scripts — 3.00

MORRIGAN
Dimension X: Aug, 1993 ($2.75, B&W)

1-Foil stamped-c — 3.00

MORRIGAN
Sirius Entertainment: 1997 ($2.95, limited series)

1-Tenuta-c/a — 3.00

MORTAL KOMBAT
Malibu Comics: July, 1994 - No. 6, Dec, 1994 ($2.95)

1-6: 1-Two diff. covers exist — 3.00
1-Limited edition gold foil embossed-c — 4.00
0 (12/94), Special Edition 1 (11/94) — 3.00
Tournament Edition I12/94, ($3.95), II('95)($3.95) — 4.00
...: BARAKA ,June, 1995 ($2.95, one-shot) #1; ...BATTLEWAVE ,2/95 - No. 6, 7/95 , #1-6; ...GORO, PRINCE OF PAIN ,9/94 - No. 3, 11/94 , #1-3; ...KITANA AND MILEENA ,8/95 , #1; ...KUNG LAO ,7/95 , #1; ... RAYDON & KANO ,3/95 - No. 3, 5/95, #1-3: ...(all $2.95) — 3.00
...: U.S. SPECIAL FORCES ,1/95 - No. 2, ($3.50), #1,2 — 3.50

MORTIE (Mazie's Friend; also see Flat-Top)
Magazine Publishers: Dec, 1952 - No. 4, June, 1953?

1 — 8, 24, 45, 65
2-4 — 5, 15, 25, 35

MORTIGAN GOTH: IMMORTALIS (See Marvel Frontier Comics Unlimited)
Marvel Comics: Sept, 1993 - No. 4, Mar, 1994 ($1.95, mini-series)

1-($2.95)-Foil-c — 3.00
2-4 — 2.25

MORT THE DEAD TEENAGER
Marvel Comics: Nov, 1993 - No. 4, Mar, 1994 ($1.75, mini-series)

1-4 — 2.25

MORTY MEEKLE
Dell Publishing Co.: No. 793, May, 1957

Four Color 793 — 3, 9, 19, 28

MOSES & THE TEN COMMANDMENTS (See Dell Giants)

MOSTLY WANTED
DC Comics (WildStorm): Jul, 2000 - No. 4, Nov, 2000 ($2.50, limited series)

1-4-Lobdell-s/-Flores-a — 2.50

MOTHER GOOSE AND NURSERY RHYME COMICS (See Christmas With Mother Goose)
Dell Publishing Co.: No. 41, 1944 - No. 862, Nov, 1957

Four Color 41-Walt Kelly-c/a — 22, 66, 154, 290
Four Color 59, 68-Kelly c/a — 19, 57, 133, 250
Four Color 862-The Truth About..., Movie (Disney) — 7, 21, 49, 90

MOTHER TERESA OF CALCUTTA
Marvel Comics Group: 1984

1-(52 pgs.) No ads — 4.00

MOTION PICTURE COMICS (See Fawcett Movie Comics)
Fawcett Publications: No. 101, 1950 - No. 114, Jan, 1953 (All-photo-c)

101-"Vanishing Westerner"; Monte Hale (1950) — 31, 93, 165, 285
102-"Code of the Silver Sage"; Rocky Lane (1/51) — 29, 87, 153, 265
103-"Covered Wagon Raid"; Rocky Lane (3/51) — 29, 87, 153, 265
104-"Vigilante Hideout"; Rocky Lane (5/51)-Book length Powell-a — 29, 87, 153, 265
105-"Red Badge of Courage"; Audie Murphy; Bob Powell-a (7/51) — 35, 105, 185, 320
106-"The Texas Rangers"; George Montgomery (9/51) — 30, 90, 159, 275
107-"Frisco Tornado"; Rocky Lane (11/51) — 26, 78, 136, 235
108-"Mask of the Avenger"; John Derek — 20, 60, 105, 175
109-"Rough Rider of Durango"; Rocky Lane — 24, 81, 142, 245
110-"When Worlds Collide"; George Evans-a (5/52); Williamson & Evans drew themselves in story; (also see Famous Funnies No. 72-88) — 95, 285, 597, 1050
111-"The Vanishing Outpost"; Lash LaRue — 33, 99, 174, 300
112-"Brave Warrior"; Jon Hall & Jay Silverheels — 19, 57, 99, 165
113-"Walk East on Beacon"; George Murphy; Schaffenberger-a — 14, 42, 72, 120
114-"Cripple Creek"; George Montgomery (1/53) — 15, 45, 77, 130

MOTION PICTURE FUNNIES WEEKLY (See Promotional Comics section)

MOTORHEAD (See Comic's Greatest World)
Dark Horse Comics: Aug, 1995 - No. 6, Jan, 1996 ($2.50)

Movie Classics - Bon Voyage © DELL

Movie Classics - Sons of Kate Elder © DELL

Movie Classics - Twice Told Tales © DELL

	GD2.0	FN6.0	VF8.0	NM9.4

1-6: Bisley-c on all. 1-Predator app.   2.50

Special 1 (3/94, $3.95, 52pgs.)-Jae Lee-c; Barb Wire, The Machine & Wolf Gang app.   4.00

MOTORMOUTH (... & Killpower #7? on)

Marvel Comics UK: June, 1992 - No. 12, May, 1993 ($1.75)

1-13: 1,2-Nick Fury app. 3-Punisher-c/story. 5,6-Nick Fury & Punisher app. 6-Cable cameo. 7-9-Cable app.   2.25

MOUNTAIN MEN (See Ben Bowie)

MOUSE MUSKETEERS (See M.G.M.'s...)

MOUSE ON THE MOON, THE (See Movie Classics)

MOVIE CLASSICS

Dell Publishing Co.: Apr, 1956; May-Jul, 1962 - Dec, 1969

   (Before 1963, most movie adaptations were part of the 4-Color series)
   (Disney movie adaptations after 1970 are in Walt Disney Showcase)

Around the World Under the Sea 12-030-612 (12/66)   3   9   21   32

Bambi 3(4/56)-Disney; r/4-Color #186   4   12   26   40

Battle of the Bulge 12-056-606 (6/66)   3   10   23   35

Beach Blanket Bingo 12-058-509   6   18   42   80

Bon Voyage 12-112(12/62)-Disney; photo-c   4   12   25   38

Castilian, The 12-110-401   3   9   21   32

Cat, The 12-109-612 (12/66)   3   9   20   30

Cheyenne Autumn 12-112-506 (4-6/65)   5   15   35   60

Circus World, Samuel Bronston's 12-115-411; John Wayne app.; John Wayne photo-c   10   30   70   125

Countdown 12-150-710 (10/67)-James Caan photo-c   3   10   23   35

Creature, The 1 (142-302) (12-2/62-63)   6   18   42   80

Creature, The 12-142-410 (10/64)   4   12   30   50

David Ladd's Life Story 12-173-212 (10-12/62)-Photo-c   7   21   49   90

Die, Monster, Die 12-175-603 (3/66)-Photo-c   5   15   34   55

Dirty Dozen 12-180-710 (10/67)   4   12   25   40

Dr. Who & the Daleks 12-190-612 (12/66)-Peter Cushing photo-c; 1st U.S. app. of Dr. Who   10   30   70   125

Dracula 12-231-212 (10-12/62)   5   15   35   65

El Dorado 12-240-710 (10/67)-John Wayne; photo-c   12   36   84   160

Ensign Pulver 12-257-410 (8-10/64)   3   9   20   30

Frankenstein 12-283-305 (3-5/63)   5   15   35   70

Great Race, The 12-299-603 (3/66)-Natallie Wood, Tony Curtis photo-c   4   12   29   45

Hallelujah Trail, The 12-307-602 (2/66) (Shows 1/66 inside); Burt Lancaster, Lee Remick photo-c   4   12   30   50

Hatari 12-340-301 (1/63)-John Wayne   8   24   56   100

Horizontal Lieutenant, The 01-348-210 (10/62)   3   9   20   30

Incredible Mr. Limpet, The 12-370-408; Don Knotts photo-c   4   12   26   40

Jack the Giant Killer 12-374-301 (1/63)   8   24   56   100

Jason & the Argonauts 12-376-310 (8-10/63)-Photo-c   9   27   63   110

Lancelot & Guinevere 12-416-310 (10/63)   5   15   34   55

Lawrence 12-426-308 (8/63)-Story of Lawrence of Arabia; movie ad on back-c; not exactly like movie   5   15   34   55

Lion of Sparta 12-439-301 (1/63)   4   12   25   38

Mad Monster Party 12-460-801 (9/67)-Based on Kurtzman's screenplay   5   15   35   70

Magic Sword, The 01-496-209 (9/62)   5   15   35   60

Masque of the Red Death 12-490-410 (8-10/64)-Vincent Price photo-c   5   15   35   65

Maya 12-495-612 (12/66)-Clint Walker & Jay North part photo-c   4   12   27   42

McHale's Navy 12-500-412 (10-12/64)   4   12   29   45

Merrill's Marauders 12-510-301 (1/63)-Photo-c   3   9   20   30

Mouse on the Moon, The 12-530-312 (10/12/63)-Photo-c   4   12   25   38

Mummy, The 12-537-211 (9-11/62) 2 versions with different back-c   6   18   42   80

Music Man, The 12-538-301 (1/63)   3   9   21   32

Naked Prey 12-545-612 (12/66)-Photo-c   5   15   35   60

Night of the Grizzly, The 12-558-612 (12/66)-Photo-c   4   12   25   38

None But the Brave 12-565-506 (4-6/65)   5   15   35   60

Operation Bikini 12-597-310 (10/63)-Photo-c   3   9   21   32

Operation Crossbow 12-590-512 (10-12/65)   3   9   21   32

Prince & the Pauper, The 01-654-207 (5-7/62)-Disney   4   12   25   38

Raven, The 12-680-309 (9/63)-Vincent Price photo-c   5   15   35   60

Ring of Bright Water 01-701-910 (10/69) (inside shows #12-701-909)   4   12   25   38

Runaway, The 12-707-412 (10-12/64)   3   9   20   30

Santa Claus Conquers the Martians #? (1964)-Photo-c   9   27   63   110

Santa Claus Conquers the Martians 12-725-603 (3/66, 12¢)-Reprints 1964 issue; photo-c   7   21   49   90

Another version given away with a Golden Record, SLP 170, nn, no price (3/66)-Complete with record   14   42   98   180

Six Black Horses 12-750-301 (1/63)-Photo-c   3   9   21   32

Ski Party 12-743-511 (9-11/65)-Frankie Avalon photo-c   4   12   30   50

Smoky 12-746-702 (2/67)   3   9   20   30

Sons of Katie Elder 12-748-511 (9-11/65); John Wayne app.; photo-c   13   39   91   165

Tales of Terror 12-793-302 (2/63)-Evans-a   5   15   35   60

Three Stooges Meet Hercules 01-828-208 (8/62)-Photo-c   8   24   56   100

Tomb of Ligeia 12-830-506 (4-6/65)   5   15   35   60

Treasure Island 01-845-211 (7-9/62)-Disney; r/4-Color #624   3   9   21   32

Twice Told Tales (Nathaniel Hawthorne) 12-840-401 (11-1/63-64); Vincent Price photo-c   5   15   35   60

Two on a Guillotine 12-850-506 (4-6/65)   4   12   25   38

Valley of Gwangi 01-880-912 (12/69)   9   27   63   115

War Gods of the Deep 12-900-509 (7-9/65)   3   9   21   32

War Wagon, The 12-533-709 (9/67); John Wayne app.   8   24   56   105

Who's Minding the Mint? 12-924-708 (8/67)   3   9   20   30

Wolfman, The 12-922-308 (6-8/63)   5   15   35   70

Wolfman, The 1(12-922-410)(8-10/64)-2nd printing; r/#12-922-308   4   12   26   40

Zulu 12-950-410 (8-10/64)-Photo-c   7   21   49   95

MOVIE COMICS (See Cinema Comics Herald & Fawcett Movie Comics)

MOVIE COMICS

National Periodical Publications/Picture Comics: April, 1939 - No. 6, Sept-Oct, 1939 (Most all photo-c)

1- "Gunga Din", "Son of Frankenstein", "The Great Man Votes", "Fisherman's Wharf", & "Scouts to the Rescue" part 1; Wheelan "Minute Movies" begin   317   951   1979   3800

2- "Stagecoach", "The Saint Strikes Back", "King of the Turf", "Scouts to the Rescue" part 2, "Arizona Legion", Andy Devine photo-c   223   669   1394   2450

3- "East Side of Heaven", "Mystery in the White Room", "Four Feathers", "Mexican Rose" with Gene Autry, "Spirit of Culver", "Many Secrets", "The Mikado" (1st Gene Autry photo cover)   159   477   994   1750

4- "Captain Fury", Gene Autry in "Blue Montana Skies", "Streets of N.Y." with Jackie Cooper, "Oregon Trail" part 1 with Johnny Mack Brown, "Big Town Czar" with Barton MacLane, & "Star Reporter" with Warren Hull   127   381   795   1400

5- "The Man in the Iron Mask", "Five Came Back", "Wolf Call", "The Girl & the Gambler", "The House of Fear", "The Family Next Door", "Oregon Trail" part 2   150   450   938   1650

6- "The Phantom Creeps", "Chumps at Oxford", & "The Oregon Trail" part 3; 2nd Robot-c   191   573   1194   2100

NOTE: Above books contain many original movie stills with dialogue from movie scripts. All issues are scarce.

MOVIE COMICS

Fiction House Magazines: Dec, 1946 - No. 4, 1947

1-Big Town (by Lubbers), Johnny Danger begin; Celardo-a; Mitzi of the Movies by Fran Hopper   55   165   330   575

2-(2/47)- "White Tie & Tails" with William Bendix; Mitzi of the Movies begins by Matt Baker, ends #4   40   120   240   420

Movie Comics #1 © FH

WORLD PREMIERE OF HOLLYWOOD HIGHLIGHTS

Movie Comics - Big Red 10026-503 © WDC

Movie Comics - Captain Sindbad © King Bros. Prod. Inc.

	GD2.0	FN6.0	VF8.0	NM9.4

3-(6/47)-Andy Hardy starring Mickey Rooney 40 120 240 420
4-Mitzi In Hollywood by Matt Baker; Merton of the Movies with Red Skelton; Yvonne DeCarlo & George Brent in "Slave Girl" 47 141 286 500

MOVIE COMICS
Gold Key/Whitman: Oct, 1962 - 1984

Alice in Wonderland 10144-503 (3/65)-Disney; partial reprint of 4-Color #331
4 12 26 40
Alice In Wonderland #1 (Whitman, 3/84) 6.00
Aristocats, The 1 (30045-103)(3/71)-Disney; with pull-out poster (25¢) (No poster = half price) 7 21 49 90
Bambi 1 (10087-309)(9/63)-Disney; r/4-C #186 4 12 27 42
Bambi 2 (10087-607)(7/66)-Disney; r/4-C #186 3 9 21 32
Beneath the Planet of the Apes 30044-012 (12/70)-with pull-out poster; photo-c (No poster = half price) 9 27 63 115
Big Red 10026-211 (11/62)-Disney; photo-c 3 9 21 32
Big Red 10026-503 (3/65)-Disney; reprints 10026-211; photo-c
3 9 17 25
Blackbeard's Ghost 10222-806 (6/68)-Disney 3 9 20 30
Bullwhip Griffin 10181-706 (6/67)-Disney; Spiegle-a; photo-c
4 12 25 38
Captain Sindbad 10077-309 (9/63)-Manning-a; photo-c
5 15 35 70
Chitty Chitty Bang Bang 1 (30038-902)(2/69)-with pull-out poster; Disney; photo-c (No poster = half price) 6 18 42 80
Cinderella 10152-508 (8/65)-Disney; r/4-C #786 4 12 25 38
Darby O'Gill & the Little People 10251-001(1/70)-Disney; reprints 4-Color #1024 (Toth-a); photo-c 5 15 34 55
Dumbo 1 (10090-310)(10/63)-Disney; r/4-C #668 4 12 25 38
Emil & the Detectives 10120-502 (11/64)-Disney; photo-c
3 9 21 32
Escapade in Florence 1 (10043-301)(1/63)-Disney; starring Annette Funicello
8 24 56 100
Fall of the Roman Empire 10118-407 (7/64); Sophia Loren photo-c
4 12 25 38
Fantastic Voyage 10178-702 (2/67)-Wood/Adkins-a; photo-c
5 15 35 60
55 Days at Peking 10081-309 (9/63)-Photo-c 3 9 21 32
Fighting Prince of Donegal, The 10193-701 (1/67)-Disney
3 9 20 30
First Men in the Moon 10132-503 (3/65)-Fred Fredericks-a; photo-c
3 10 23 35
Gay Purr-ee 30017-301(1/63, 84 pgs.) 5 15 34 55
Gnome Mobile, The 10207-710 (10/67)-Disney 4 12 25 38
Goodbye, Mr. Chips 10246-006 (6/70)-Peter O'Toole photo-c
3 9 21 32
Happiest Millionaire, The 10221-804 (4/68)-Disney 4 12 25 38
Hey There, It's Yogi Bear 10122-409 (9/64)-Hanna-Barbera
6 18 42 80
Horse Without a Head, The 10109-401 (1/64)-Disney 3 9 20 30
How the West Was Won 10074-307 (7/63)-Based on the L'Amour novel; Tufts-a
9 29 45
In Search of the Castaways 10048-303 (3/63)-Disney; Hayley Mills photo-c
6 18 42 80
Jungle Book, The 1 (6022-801)(1/68-Whitman)-Disney; large size (10x13-1/2"); 59¢ 6 18 42 80
Jungle Book, The 1 (30033-803)(3/68, 68 pgs.)-Disney; same contents as Whitman #1 4 12 27 42
Jungle Book, The 1 (6/78, $1.00 tabloid) 2 6 15 22
Jungle Book (7/84)-r/Giant 6.00
Kidnapped 10080-306 (6/63)-Disney; reprints 4-Color #1101; photo-c
3 9 21 32
King Kong 30036-809(9/68-68 pgs.)-painted-c 4 12 26 40
King Kong nn-Whitman Treasury($1.00, 68 pgs.,1968), same cover as Gold Key issue 5 15 34 55
King Kong 11299(#1-786, 10x13-1/4", 68 pgs., $1.00, 1978)
3 9 17 24
Lady and the Tramp 10042-301 (1/63)-Disney; r/4-Color #629
4 12 25 38
Lady and the Tramp 1 (1967-Giant; 25¢)-Disney; reprints part of Dell #1
5 15 35 65

Lady and the Tramp 2 (10042-203)(3/72)-Disney; r/4-Color #629
3 9 17 24
Legend of Lobo, The 1 (10059-303)(3/63)-Disney; photo-c
3 9 17 25
Lt. Robin Crusoe, U.S.N. 10191-610 (10/66)-Disney; Dick Van Dyke photo-c
3 9 19 28
Lion, The 10035-301 (1/63)-Photo-c 3 9 17 24
Lord Jim 10156-509 (9/65)-Photo-c 3 9 17 25
Love Bug, The 10237-906 (6/69)-Disney; Buddy Hackett photo-c
3 9 21 32
Mary Poppins 10136-501 (1/65)-Disney; photo-c 4 12 29 45
Mary Poppins 30023-501 (1/65-68 pgs.)-Disney; photo-c
6 18 42 80
McLintock 10110-403 (3/64); John Wayne app.; John Wayne & Maureen O'Hara photo-c 12 36 84 155
Merlin Jones as the Monkey's Uncle 10115-510 (10/65)-Disney; Annette Funicello front/back photo-c 5 15 35 60
Miracle of the White Stallions, The 10065-306 (6/63)-Disney
3 9 20 30
Misadventures of Merlin Jones, The 10115-405 (5/64)-Disney; Annette Funicello photo front/back-c 5 15 35 60
Moon-Spinners, The 10124-410 (10/64)-Disney; Haley Mills photo-c
6 18 42 80
Mutiny on the Bounty 1 (10040-302)(2/63)-Marlon Brando photo-c
3 9 21 32
Nikki, Wild Dog of the North 10141-412 (12/64)-Disney; reprints 4-Color #1226 3 9 17 25
Old Yeller 10168-601 (1/66)-Disney; reprints 4-Color #869; photo-c
3 9 17 25
One Hundred & One Dalmations 1 (10247-002) (2/70)-Disney; reprints Four Color #1183 3 9 20 30
Peter Pan 1 (10086-309)(9/63)-Disney; reprints Four Color #442
4 12 25 38
Peter Pan 2 (10086-909)(9/69)-Disney; reprints Four Color #442
3 9 17 25
Peter Pan 1 (3/84)-r/4-Color #442 4.00
P.T. 109 10123-409 (9/64)-John F. Kennedy 4 12 30 50
Rio Conchos 10143-503(3/65) 4 12 25 38
Robin Hood 10163-506 (6/65)-Disney; reprints Four Color #413
3 9 20 30
Shaggy Dog & the Absent-Minded Professor 30032-708 (8/67-Giant, 68 pgs.) Disney; reprints 4-Color #985,1199 5 15 35 60
Sleeping Beauty 1 (30042-009)(9/70)-Disney; reprints Four Color #973; with pull-out poster (No poster = half price) 6 18 42 80
Snow White & the Seven Dwarfs 1 (10091-310)(10/63)-Disney; reprints Four Color #382 3 9 21 32
Snow White & the Seven Dwarfs 10091-709 (9/67)-Disney; reprints Four Color #382 3 9 17 25
Snow White & the Seven Dwarfs 90091-204 (2/84)-Reprints Four Color #382 3.00
Son of Flubber 1 (10057-304)(4/63)-Disney; sequel to "The Absent-Minded Professor" 3 10 23 35
Summer Magic 10076-309 (9/63)-Disney; Hayley Mills photo-c; Manning-a
6 18 42 80
Swiss Family Robinson 10236-904 (4/69)-Disney; reprints Four Color #1156; photo-c 3 9 20 30
Sword in the Stone, The 30019-402 (2/64-Giant, 68 pgs.)-Disney (see March of Comics #258 & Wart and the Wizard 6 18 42 80
That Darn Cat 10171-602 (2/66)-Disney; Hayley Mills photo-c
6 18 42 80
Those Magnificent Men in Their Flying Machines 10162-510 (10/65)
3 9 21 32
Three Stooges in Orbit 30016-211 (11/62-Giant, 32 pgs.)-All photos from movie; stiff-photo-c 10 30 70 130
Tiger Walks, A 10117-406 (6/64)-Disney; Torres?, Tufts-a; photo-c
4 12 27 42
Toby Tyler 10142-502 (2/65)-Disney; reprints Four Color #1092; photo-c
3 9 17 25
Treasure Island 1 (10200-703)(3/67)-Disney; reprints Four Color #624; photo-c
3 9 17 25

651

Movie Love #17 © FF

M. Rex #2 © Kelly & Rouleau

Ms. Marvel #14 © MAR

	GD2.0	FN6.0	VF8.0	NM9.4

20,000 Leagues Under the Sea 1 (10095-312)(12/63)-Disney; reprints

| Four Color #614 | 3 | 9 | 20 | 30 |

Wonderful Adventures of Pinocchio, The 1 (10089-310)(10/63)-Disney; reprints

| Four Color #545 (see Wonderful Advs. of...) | 4 | 12 | 25 | 38 |

Wonderful Adventures of Pinocchio, The 10089-109 (9/71)-Disney; reprints

| Four Color #545 | 3 | 9 | 17 | 25 |

Wonderful World of the Brothers Grimm 1 (10008-210)(10/62)

| | 4 | 12 | 29 | 45 |

X, the Man with the X-Ray Eyes 10083-309 (9/63)-Ray Milland photo on-c

| | 7 | 21 | 49 | 90 |

Yellow Submarine 35000-902 (2/69-Giant, 68 pgs.)-With pull-out poster;

| The Beatles cartoon movie; Paul S. Newman-s | 23 | 69 | 161 | 300 |
| Without poster | 8 | 24 | 56 | 100 |

MOVIE LOVE (Also see Personal Love)
Famous Funnies: Feb, 1950 - No. 22, Aug, 1953 (All photo-c)

1-Dick Powell, Evelyn Keyes, & Mickey Rooney photo-c

| | 15 | 45 | 77 | 135 |
| 2-Myrna Loy photo-c | 8 | 24 | 45 | 65 |

3-7,9: 6-Ricardo Montalban photo-c. 9-Gene Tierney, John Lund, Glenn Ford,

& Rhonda Fleming photo-c.	7	21	38	55
8-Williamson/Frazetta-a, 6 pgs.	40	120	232	400
10-Frazetta-a, 6 pgs.	40	120	240	420
11,14-16: 14-Janet Leigh photo-c	7	21	36	50

12-Dean Martin & Jerry Lewis photo-c (12/51, pre-dates Advs. of Dean

Martin & Jerry Lewis comic)	14	42	72	125
13-Ronald Reagan photo-c with 1 pg. biog.	22	66	116	200
17-Leslie Caron & Ralph Meeker photo-c; 1 pg. Frazetta ad				

18-22: 19-John Derek photo-c. 20-Donald O'Connor & Debbie Reynolds photo-c.
21-Paul Henreid & Patricia Medina photo-c. 22-John Payne & Coleen Gray

| photo-c | 6 | 18 | 32 | 45 |

NOTE: *Each issue has a full-length movie adaptation with photo covers.*

MOVIE THRILLERS (Movie)
Magazine Enterprises: 1949

1-Adaptation of "Rope of Sand" w/Burt Lancaster; Burt Lancaster photo-c

| | 31 | 93 | 165 | 285 |

MOVIE TOWN ANIMAL ANTICS (Formerly Animal Antics; becomes
Raccoon Kids #52 on)
National Periodical Publ.: No. 24, Jan-Feb, 1950 - No. 51, July-Aug, 1954

| 24-Raccoon Kids continue | 12 | 36 | 61 | 100 |
| 25-51 | 10 | 30 | 55 | 85 |

NOTE: *Sheldon Mayer a-28-33, 35, 37-41, 43, 44, 47, 49-51.*

MOVIE TUNES COMICS (Formerly Animated...; Frankie No. 4 on)
Marvel Comics (MgPC): No. 3, Fall, 1946

| 3-Super Rabbit, Krazy Krow, Silly Seal & Ziggy Pig | 13 | 39 | 66 | 110 |

MOWGLI JUNGLE BOOK (Rudyard Kipling's...)
Dell Publ. Co.: No. 487, Aug-Oct, 1953 - No. 620, Apr, 1955

| Four Color 487 (#1) | 5 | 15 | 35 | 65 |
| Four Color 582 (8/54), 620 | 4 | 12 | 30 | 50 |

MR. (See Mister)

M. REX
Image Comics: July, 1999 - Present ($2.95)

| Preview ($5.00) B&W pages and sketchbook; Rouleau-a | | | | 5.00 |
| 1,2-($2.95) 1-Joe Kelly-s/Rouleau-a/Anacleto-c. 2-Rouleau-c | | | | 3.00 |

MS. CYANIDE & ICE
Blackout Comics: June, 1995 - No. 1, 1995 ($2.95, B&W)

| 0,1 | | | | 3.00 |

MS. FORTUNE
Image Comics: Jan, 1998 ($2.95, B&W, one-shot)

| 1-Chris Marrinan-s/a | | | | 3.00 |

MS. MARVEL (Also see The Avengers #183)
Marvel Comics Group: Jan, 1977 - No. 23, Apr, 1979

| 1-1st app. Ms. Marvel; Scorpion app. in #1,2 | 2 | 6 | 9 | 12 |
| 2-10: 2-Origin. 5-Vision app. 6-10-(Reg. 30¢ c). 10-Last 30¢ issue | | | | 5.00 |

	GD2.0	FN6.0	VF8.0	NM9.4

| 6-10-(35¢-c variants, limited dist.)(6/77) | 1 | 3 | 6 | 8 |

11-15,19-23: 19-Capt. Marvel app. 20-New costume. 23-Vance Astro (leader of

the Guardians) app.				4.00
16,17-Mystique cameo	1	3	6	9
18-1st full Mystique; Avengers x-over	2	6	10	14

NOTE: *Austin c-14i, 16i, 17i, 22i. Buscema a-1-3p; c(p)-2, 4, 6, 7, 15. Infantino a-14p, 19p. Gil Kane c-8. Mooney a-4-8p, 13p, 15-18p. Starlin c-12.*

MS. MYSTIC
Pacific Comics: Oct, 1982 - No. 2, Feb, 1984 ($1.00/$1.50)

| 1,2; Neal Adams-c/a/script. 1-Origin; intro Erth, Ayre, Fyre & Watr | | | | 4.00 |

MS. MYSTIC
Continuity Comics: 1988 - No. 9, May, 1992 ($2.00)

| 1-9: 1,2-Reprint Pacific Comics issues | | | | 3.00 |

MS. MYSTIC
Continuity Comics: V2#1, Oct, 1993 - V2#4, Jan, 1994 ($2.50)

V2#1-4: 1-Adams-c(i)/part-i. 2-4-Embossed-c. 2-Nebres part-i.

| 3-Adams-c(i)/plot. 4-Adams-c(p)/plot | | | | 2.50 |

MS. MYSTIC DEATHWATCH 2000 (Ms. Mystic #3)
Continuity: May, 1993 - No. 3, Aug, 1993 ($2.50)

| 1-3-Bagged w/card; Adams plots | | | | 2.50 |

MS. TREE QUARTERLY / SPECIAL
DC Comics: Summer, 1990 -No. 10, 1992 ($3.95/$3.50, 84 pgs, mature)

| 1-10: 1-Midnight story; Batman text story, Grell-a. 2,3-Midnight stories; The | | | | |
| Butcher text stories | | | | 4.00 |

NOTE: *Cowan c-2. Grell c-1, 6. Infantino a-8.*

MS. TREE'S THRILLING DETECTIVE ADVS (Ms. Tree #4 on; also see The
Best of Ms. Tree)(Baxter paper #4-9)
Eclipse Comics/Aardvark-Vanaheim 10-18/Renegade Press 19 on:
2/83 - #9, 7/84; #10, 8/84 - #18, 5/85; #19, 6/85 - #50, 6/89

1				3.00
2-49: 2-Scythe begins. 9-Last Eclipse & last color issue. 10,11-two-tone				2.50
50-Contains flexi-disc ($3.95, 52pgs.)				4.00
Summer Special 1 (8/86)				3.00
1950s 3-D Crime (7/87, no glasses)-Johnny Dynamite in 3-D				3.00
Mike Mist in 3-D (8/85)-With glasses				3.00

NOTE; *Miller pin-up 1-4. Johnny Dynamite t begin #36 by Morisi.*

MS. VICTORY SPECIAL(Also see Capt. Paragon & Femforce)
Americomics: Jan, 1985 (nd)

| 1 | | | | 2.50 |

MUGGSY MOUSE (Also see Tick Tock Tales)
Magazine Enterprises: 1951 - No. 3, 1951; No. 4, 1954 - No. 5, 1954; 1963

1(A-1 #33)	7	21	38	55
2(A-1 #36)-Racist-c	9	27	51	75
3(A-1 #39), 4(A-1 #95), 5(A-1 #99)	5	15	23	30
Super Reprint #14(1963), I.W. Reprint #1,2 (nd)	2	6	9	12

MUGGY-DOO, BOY CAT
Stanhall Publ.: July, 1953 - No. 4, Jan, 1954

1-Funny animal; Irving Spector-a	8	24	42	60
2-4	5	15	25	35
Super Reprint #12('63), 16('64)	2	6	9	12

MUKTUK WOLFSBREATH: HARD-BOILED SHAMAN
DC Comics (Vertigo): Aug, 1998 - No. 3, Oct, 1998 ($2.50)

| 1-3-Terry LaBan-s/Steve Parkhouse-a | | | | 2.50 |

MULLKON EMPIRE (See John Jake's...)

MUMMY, THE (See Universal Presents... under Dell Giants & Movie Classics)

MUMMY, THE: VALLEY OF THE GODS (Movie adaption)
Chaos! Comics: May, 2001 - No. 3 ($2.99, limited series)

| 1-Based on "The Mummy Returns" movie; Broome-a; Broome & photo-c | | | | 3.00 |

MUNDEN'S BAR ANNUAL
First Comics: Apr, 1988; 1989 ($2.95/$5.95)

| 1-($2.95)-r/from Grimjack; Fish Police story; Ordway-c | | | | 3.00 |
| 2-($5.95)-Teenage Mutant Ninja Turtles app. | | | | 6.00 |

Murder Incorporated #4 © FOX

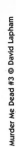
Murder Me Dead #3 © David Lapham

Mutt and Jeff #9 © DC

	GD2.0	FN6.0	VF8.0	NM9.4

MUNSTERS, THE (TV)
Gold Key: Jan, 1965 - No. 16, Jan, 1968 (All photo-c)

1 (10134-501)	19	57	133	250
2	10	30	70	125
3-5	8	24	56	100
6-16	7	21	49	85

MUNSTERS, THE (TV)
TV Comics!: Aug, 1997 - No. 4 ($2.95, B&W)

1-4-All have photo-c	3.00
1,4-($7.95)-Variant-c	8.00
2-Variant-c w/Beverly Owens as Marilyn	3.00
Special Comic Con Ed. (7/97, $9.95)	10.00

MUPPET BABIES, THE (TV)(See Star Comics Magazine)
Marvel Comics (Star Comics)/Marvel #18 on: Aug, 1985 - No. 26, July, 1989 (Children's book)

1-26	3.00

MUPPETS TAKE MANHATTAN, THE
Marvel Comics (Star Comics): Nov, 1984 - No. 3, Jan, 1985

1-3-Movie adapt. r-/Marvel Super Special	3.00

MURCIELAGA, SHE-BAT
Heroic Publishing: Jan, 1993 - No. 2, 1993 (B&W)

1-($1.50, 28 pgs.)	2.50
2-($2.95, 36 pgs.)-Coated-c	3.00

MURDER CAN BE FUN
Slave Labor Graphics: Feb, 1996 - Present ($2.95, B&W)

1-12: 1-Dorkin-a. 2-Vasquez-c.	3.00

MURDER INCORPORATED (My Private Life #16 on)
Fox Feature Syndicate: 1/48 - No. 15, 12/49; (2 No.9's); 6/50 - No. 3, 8/51

1 (1st Series); 1,2 have 'For Adults Only' on-c	50	150	300	525
2-Electrocution story	40	120	232	400
3-7,9(4/49),10(5/49),11-15	24	72	127	215
8-Used in SOTI, pg. 160	26	78	136	235
9(3/49)-Possible use in SOTI, pg. 145; r/Blue Beetle #56('48)				
	24	72	127	215
5(#1, 6/50)(2nd Series)-Formerly My Desire #4; bondage-c				
	19	57	99	165
2(8/50)-Morisi-a	16	48	83	140
3(8/51)-Used in POP, pg. 81; Rico-a; lingerie-c/panels				
	18	54	94	155

MURDER ME DEAD
El Capitán Books: July, 2000 - No. 9 ($2.95, B&W)

1-9-David Lapham-s/a	3.00

MURDEROUS GANGSTERS
Avon Per./Realistic No. 3 on: Jul, 1951; No. 2, Dec, 1951 - No. 4, Jun, 1952

1-Pretty Boy Floyd, Leggs Diamond; 1 pg. Wood-a	43	129	257	450
2-Baby-Face Nelson; 1 pg. Wood-a; painted-c	30	90	159	275
3-Painted-c	24	72	127	215
4- "Murder by Needle" drug story; Mort Lawrence-a; Kinstler-c				
	30	90	159	275

MURDER TALES (Magazine)
World Famous Publications: V1#10, Nov, 1970 - V1#11, Jan, 1971 (52 pgs.)

V1#10-One pg. Frazetta ad	4	12	25	38
11-Guardineer-r; bondage-c	3	9	19	28

MUSHMOUSE AND PUNKIN PUSS (TV)
Gold Key: September, 1965 (Hanna-Barbera)

1 (10153-509)	9	27	63	120

MUSIC MAN, THE (See Movie Classics)

MUTANT CHRONICLES (Video game)
Acclaim Comics (Armada): May, 1996 - No. 4, Aug, 1996 ($2.95, lim. series)

1-4: Simon Bisley-c on all, Sourcebook (#5)	3.00

MUTANT MISADVENTURES OF CLOAK AND DAGGER, THE (Becomes Cloak and Dagger #14 on)

Marvel Comics: Oct, 1988 - No. 19, Aug, 1991 ($1.25/$1.50)

1-8,10-15: 1-X-Factor app. 10-Painted-c. 12-Dr. Doom app. 14-Begin new direction	2.25
9,16-19: 9-(52 pgs.) The Avengers x-over; painted-c. 16-18-Spider-Man x-over. 18-Infinity Gauntlet x-over; Thanos cameo; Ghost Rider app.	
19-(52 pgs.) Origin Cloak & Dagger	2.50

NOTE: *Austin a-12i; c(i)-4, 12, 13; scripts-all. Russell a-2i. Williamson a-14i-16i; c-15i.*

MUTANTS & MISFITS
Silverline Comics (Solson): 1987 - No. 3, 1987 ($1.95)

1-3	2.25

MUTANTS VS. ULTRAS
Malibu Comics (Ultraverse): Nov, 1995 ($6.95, one-shot)

1-r/Exiles vs. X-Men, Night Man vs. Wolverine, Prime vs. Hulk	7.00

MUTANT X (See X-Factor)
Marvel Comics: Nov, 1998 - No. 32, June, 2001 ($2.99/$1.99/$2.25)

1-($2.99) Alex Summers with alternate world's X-Men	3.00
2-11,13-19-($1.99): 2-Two covers. 5-Man-Spider-c/app.	2.25
12,25-($2.99): 12-Pin-up gallery by Kaluta, Romita, Byrne	3.00
20-24,26-32: 20-Page $2.25-c. 28-31-Logan-c/app. 32-Last issue	2.25
Annual '99, '00 (5/99,'00, $3.50) '00-Doran-a(p)	3.50
Annual 2001 ($2.99) Story occurs between #31 & #32; Dracula app.	3.00

MUTATIS
Marvel Comics (Epic Comics): 1992 - No. 3, 1992 ($2.25, mini-series)

1-3: Painted-c	2.25

MUTINY (Stormy Tales of the Seven Seas)
Aragon Magazines: Oct, 1954 - No. 3, Feb, 1955

1	17	51	88	150
2,3: 2-Capt. Mutiny. 3-Bondage-c	14	42	72	120

MUTINY ON THE BOUNTY (See Classics Illustrated #100 & Movie Comics)

MUTT AND JEFF (See All-American, All-Flash #18, Cicero's Cat, Comic Cavalcade, Famous Feature Stories, The Funnies, Popular & Xmas Comics)
All American/National 1-103(6/58)/Dell 104(10/58)-115 (10-12/59)/
Harvey 116(2/60)-148: Summer, 1939 (nd) - No. 148, Nov, 1965

1(nn)-Lost Wheels	127	381	795	1400
2(nn)-Charging Bull (Summer, 1940, nd; on sale 6/20/40)				
	66	200	413	725
3(nn)-Bucking Broncos (Summer, 1941, nd)	47	141	286	500
4(Winter, '41), 5(Summer, '42)	43	129	257	450
6-10	23	69	121	210
11-20: 20-X-Mas-c	15	45	77	135
21-30	11	33	55	95
31-50: 32-X-Mas-c	9	27	49	70
51-75-Last Fisher issue. 53-Last 52 pgs.	7	21	38	55
76-99,101-103: 76-Last pre-code issue(1/55)	4	12	26	40
100	4	12	29	45
104-148: 116-131-Richie Rich app.	3	9	20	30
...Jokes 1-3(8/60-61, Harvey)-84 pgs.; Richie Rich in all; Little Dot in #2,3 Lotta in #2	3	10	23	35
...New Jokes 1-4(10/63-11/65, Harvey)-68 pgs.; Richie Rich in #1-3; Stumbo in #1	3	9	17	24

NOTE: *Most all issues by Al Smith. Issues from 1963 on have Fisher reprints. Clarification: early issues signed by Fisher are mostly drawn by Smith.*

MY BROTHERS' KEEPER
Spire Christian Comics (Fleming H. Revell Co.): 1973 (35/49¢, 36 pgs.)

nn	1	3	5	7

MY CONFESSIONS (My Confession #7&8; formerly Western True Crime; A Spectacular Feature Magazine #11)
Fox Feature Syndicate: No. 7, Aug, 1949 - No. 10, Jan-Feb, 1950

7-Wood-a (10 pgs.)	23	69	121	205
8,9: 8-Harrison/Wood-a (19 pgs.). 9-Wood-a	21	63	110	190
10	10	30	55	80

MY DATE COMICS (Teen-age)
Hillman Periodicals: July, 1947 - V1#4, Jan, 1948 (2nd Romance comic; see Young Romance)

My Experience #21 © FOX

My Life #8 © FOX

My Love Life #11 © FOX

	GD2.0	FN6.0	VF8.0	NM9.4
1-S&K-c/a	37	111	197	340
2-4-S&K-c/a; Dan Barry-a	26	78	136	235

MY DESIRE (Formerly Jo-Jo Comics; becomes Murder, Inc. #5 on)
Fox Feature Syndicate: No. 30, Aug, 1949 - No. 4, April, 1950

30(#1)	16	48	83	140
31 (#2, 10/49),3(2/50),4	11	33	55	90
31 (Canadian edition)	7	21	36	50
32(12/49)-Wood-a	21	63	110	185

MY DIARY (Becomes My Friend Irma #3 on?)
Marvel Comics (A Lovers Mag.): Dec, 1949 - No. 2, Mar, 1950

1,2-Photo-c	15	45	77	130

MY EXPERIENCE (Formerly All Top; becomes Judy Canova #23 on)
Fox Feature Syndicate: No. 19, Sept, 1949 - No. 22, Mar, 1950

19,21: 19-Wood-a. 21-Wood-a(2)	26	78	136	235
20	11	33	55	90
22-Wood-a (9 pgs.)	21	63	110	185

MY FAVORITE MARTIAN (TV)
Gold Key: 1/64; No.2, 7/64 - No. 9, 10/66 (No. 1,3-9 have photo-c)

1-Russ Manning-a	13	39	91	170
2	7	21	49	85
3-9	6	18	42	75

MY FRIEND IRMA (Radio/TV) (Formerly My Diary? and/or Western Life Romances?)
Marvel/Atlas Comics (BFP): No. 3, June, 1950 - No. 47, Dec, 1954; No. 48, Feb, 1955

3-Dan DeCarlo-a in all; 52 pgs. begin, end ?	15	45	77	135
4-Kurtzman-a (10 pgs.)	19	57	99	165
5- "Egghead Doodle" by Kurtzman (4 pgs.)	14	42	72	120
6,8-10: 9-Paper dolls, 1 pg; Millie app. (5 pgs.)	10	30	55	80
7-One pg. Kurtzman-a	10	30	55	80
11-23: 23-One pg. Frazetta-a	7	21	36	50
24-48: 41,48-Stan Lee & Dan DeCarlo app.	6	18	29	40

MY GIRL PEARL
Atlas Comics: 4/55 - #4, 10/55; #5, 7/57 - #6, 9/57; #7, 8/60 - #11, ?/61

1-Dan DeCarlo-c/a in #1-6	14	42	72	125
2	8	24	42	60
3-6	6	18	30	42
7-11	3	9	21	32

MY GREATEST ADVENTURE (Doom Patrol #86 on)
National Periodical Publications: Jan.-Feb, 1955 - No. 85, Feb, 1964

1-Before CCA	130	390	875	1750
2	50	150	400	725
3-5	35	105	263	475
6-10: 6-Science fiction format begins	31	93	222	400
11-14: 12-1st S.A. issue	23	68	160	285
15-17: Kirby-a in all	25	75	174	310
18-Kirby-c/a	28	84	196	350
19,22-25	19	57	132	235
20,21,28-Kirby-a	23	68	160	285
26,27,29,30	14	42	98	165
31-40	12	36	84	140
41,42,44-57,59	9	27	63	105
43-Kirby	10	30	70	120
58,60,61-Toth-a; Last 10¢ issue	9	27	63	105
62-76,78,79: 79-Promotes "Legion of the Strange" for next issue; renamed Doom Patrol for #80	6	18	45	75
77-Toth-a; Robotman prototype	7	21	50	80
80-(6/63)-Intro/origin Doom Patrol and begin series; origin & 1st app. Negative Man, Elasti-Girl & S.A. Robotman	41	123	331	600
81,85-Toth-a	17	51	115	205
82-84	15	45	105	180

NOTE: *Anderson* a-42. *Cameron* a-24. *Colan* a-77. *Meskin* a-25, 26, 32, 39, 45, 50, 56, 57, 61, 64, 70, 73, 74, 76, 79; c-76. *Moreira* a-11, 12, 15, 17, 20, 23, 25, 27, 37, 40-43, 46, 48, 55-57, 59, 60, 62-65, 67, 69, 70; c-1-4, 7-10. *Roussos* a-71-73. *Wildey* a-32.

MY GREAT LOVE (Becomes Will Rogers Western #5)
Fox Feature Syndicate: Oct, 1949 - No. 4, Apr, 1950

	GD2.0	FN6.0	VF8.0	NM9.4
1	15	45	77	130
2-4	9	27	49	70

MY INTIMATE AFFAIR (Inside Crime #3)
Fox Feature Syndicate: Mar, 1950 - No. 2, May, 1950

1	15	45	77	130
2	9	27	49	70

MY LIFE (Formerly Meet Corliss Archer)
Fox Feature Syndicate: No. 4, Sept, 1948 - No. 15, July, 1950

4-Used in SOTI, pg. 39; Kamen/Feldstein-a	40	120	220	380
5-Kamen-a	23	69	121	210
6-Kamen/Feldstein-a	24	72	127	215
7-Wood-a; wash cover	21	63	110	185
8,9,11-15	10	30	55	80
10-Wood-a	19	57	99	165

MY LITTLE MARGIE (TV)
Charlton Comics: July, 1954 - No. 54, Nov, 1964

1-Photo front/back-c	35	105	185	320
2-Photo front/back-c	17	51	88	150
3-7,10	10	30	55	80
8,9-Infinity-c	10	30	55	85
11-14: Part-photo-c (#13, 8/56)	9	27	49	70
15-19	8	24	42	60
20-(25¢, 100 pg. issue)	14	42	72	120
21-39-Last 10¢ issue?	9	27	49	70
40-53	4	12	29	45
54-Beatles on cover; lead story spoofs the Beatle haircut craze of the 1960's (scarce)	16	48	112	200

NOTE: Doll cut-outs in 32, 33, 40, 45, 50.

MY LITTLE MARGIE'S BOY FRIENDS (TV) (Freddy V2#12 on)
Charlton Comics: Aug, 1955 - No. 11, Apr?, 1958

1-Has several Archie swipes	15	45	77	130
2	9	27	49	70
3-11	7	21	38	55

MY LITTLE MARGIE'S FASHIONS (TV)
Charlton Comics: Feb, 1959 - No. 5, Nov, 1959

1	14	42	72	120
2-5	8	24	42	60

MY LOVE (Becomes Two Gun Western #5 (11/50) on?)
Marvel Comics (CLDS): July, 1949 - No. 4, Apr, 1950 (All photo-c)

1	14	42	72	120
2,3	9	27	49	70
4-Bettie Page photo-c (see Cupid #2)	33	99	174	300

MY LOVE
Marvel Comics Group: Sept, 1969 - No. 39, Mar, 1976

1	5	15	34	55
2-9: 4-6-Colan-a	3	9	19	28
10-Williamson-r/My Own Romance #71; Kirby-a	3	9	20	30
11-13,15-19	2	6	15	22
14-(52 pgs.)-Woodstock-c/sty; Morrow-c/a; Kirby/Colletta-r	4	12	26	40
20-Starlin-a	3	9	17	24
21,22,24-27,29-38: 38-Reprints	2	6	12	18
23-Steranko-r/Our Love Story #5	3	9	17	24
28-Kirby-a	2	6	12	18
39-Last issue; reprints	2	6	13	20
Special 1 (12/71)(52 pgs.)	4	12	26	40

NOTE: *John Buscema* a-1-7, 10, 18-21, 22r(2), 24r, 25r, 29r, 34r, 36r, 37r, Spec. (r)(4); c-13, 15, 25, 27, Spec. *Colan* a-4, 5, 6, 8, 9, 16, 17, 20, 21, 22, 24r, 27r, 30r, 35r, 39r. *Colan/Everett* a-13, 15, 16, 27(r#13). *Kirby* a-(r)-10, 14, 26, 28. *Romita* a-1-3, 19, 20, 25, 34, 38; c-1-3, 15.

MY LOVE AFFAIR (March of Crime #7 on)
Fox Feature Syndicate: July, 1949 - No. 6, May, 1950

1	15	45	77	130
2	9	27	49	70
3-6-Wood-a. 5-(3/50)-Becomes Love Stories #6	19	57	99	165

MY LOVE LIFE (Formerly Zegra)

	GD2.0	FN6.0	VF8.0	NM9.4

Fox Feature Synd.: No. 6, June, 1949 - No. 13, Aug, 1950; No. 13, Sept, 1951

	GD2.0	FN6.0	VF8.0	NM9.4
6-Kamenish-a	16	48	83	140
7-13	9	27	49	70
13 (9/51)(Formerly My Story #12)	8	24	45	65

MY LOVE MEMOIRS (Formerly Women Outlaws; Hunted 13 on)
Fox Feature Syndicate: No. 9, Nov, 1949 - No. 12, May, 1950

9,11,12-Wood-a	18	54	94	155
10	9	27	49	70

MY LOVE SECRET (Formerly Phantom Lady; Animal Crackers #31)
Fox Feature Syndicate/M. S. Distr.: No. 24, June, 1949 - No. 30, June, 1950; No. 53, 1954

24-Kamen/Feldstein-a	18	54	94	155
25-Possible caricature of Wood on-c?	10	30	55	80
26,28-Wood-a	18	54	94	155
27,29,30: 30-Photo-c	9	27	49	70
53-(Reprint, M.S. Distr.) 1954? nd given; formerly Western Thrillers; becomes Crimes by Women #54; photo-c	6	18	29	40

MY LOVE STORY (Hoot Gibson Western #5 on)
Fox Feature Syndicate: Sept, 1949 - No. 4, Mar, 1950

1	15	45	77	130
2	9	27	49	70
3,4-Wood-a	19	57	99	165

MY LOVE STORY
Atlas Comics (GPS): April, 1956 - No. 9, Aug, 1957

1	11	33	55	90
2	6	18	32	45
3,7: Matt Baker-a. 7-Toth-a	9	27	49	70
4-6,8,9	6	18	29	40

MY NAME IS CHAOS
DC Comics: 1992 - No. 4, 1992 ($4.95, limited series, 52 pgs.)

Book 1-4: Tom Veitch scripts; painted-c				5.00

MY NAME IS HOLOCAUST
DC Comics: May, 1995 - No. 5, Sept, 1995 ($2.50, limited series)

1-5				2.50

MY ONLY LOVE
Charlton Comics: July, 1975 - No. 9, Nov, 1976

1	2	6	12	18
2,4-9	2	6	9	12
3-Toth-a	2	6	11	15

MY OWN ROMANCE (Formerly My Romance; Teen-Age Romance #77 on)
Marvel/Atlas (MjPC/RCM No. 4-59/ZPC No. 60-76): No. 4, Mar, 1949 - No. 76, July, 1960

4-Photo-c	15	45	77	130
5-10: 5,6,8-10-Photo-c	8	24	42	60
11-20: 14-Powell-a	7	21	38	55
21-42,55: 42-Last precode (2/55). 55-Toth-a	7	21	36	50
43-54,56-60	3	10	23	35
61-70,72,73,75,76	3	9	20	30
71-Williamson-a	4	12	29	45
74-Kirby-a	4	12	27	42

NOTE: *Brewster a-59. Colletta a-45(2), 48, 50, 55, 57(2), 59; c-58i, 59, 61. Everett a-25; c-58p. Kirby c-71, 75, 76. Morisi a-18. Orlando a-61. Romita a-36. Tuska a-10.*

MY PAL DIZZY (See Comic Books, Series I)

MY PAST (...Confessions) (Formerly Western Thrillers)
Fox Feature Syndicate: No. 7, Aug, 1949 - No. 11, Apr, 1950 (Crimes Inc. #12)

7	15	45	77	130
8-10	9	27	49	70
11-Wood-a	18	54	94	155

MY PERSONAL PROBLEM
Ajax/Farrell/Steinway Comic: 11/55; No. 2, 2/56; No. 3, 9/56 - No. 4, 11/56; 10/57 - No. 3, 5/58

1	9	27	49	70
2-4	6	18	32	45

1-3('57-'58)-Steinway	5	15	25	35

MY PRIVATE LIFE (Formerly Murder, Inc.; becomes Pedro #18)
Fox Feature Syndicate: No. 16, Feb, 1950 - No. 17, April, 1950

16,17	13	39	66	110

MYRA NORTH (See The Comics, Crackajack Funnies & Red Ryder)
Dell Publishing Co.: No. 3, Jan, 1940

Four Color 3	75	225	525	975

MY REAL LOVE
Standard Comics: No. 5, June, 1952 (Photo-c)

5-Toth-a, 3 pgs.; Tuska, Cardy, Vern Greene-a	14	42	72	120

MY ROMANCE (Becomes My Own Romance #4 on)
Marvel Comics (RCM): Sept, 1948 - No. 3, Jan, 1949

1	15	45	77	130
2,3: 2-Anti-Wertham editorial (11/48)	9	27	49	70

MY ROMANTIC ADVENTURES (Formerly Romantic Adventures)
American Comics Group: No. 68, 8/56 - No. 115, 12/60; No. 116, 7/61 - No. 138, 3/64

68	9	27	49	70
69-85	5	15	25	35
86-Three pg. Williamson-a (2/58)	7	21	38	55
87-100	3	9	17	25
101-138	2	6	12	18

NOTE: *Whitney art in most issues.*

MY SECRET (Becomes Our Secret #4 on)
Superior Comics, Ltd.: Aug, 1949 - No. 3, Oct, 1949

1	14	42	72	120
2,3	9	27	49	70

MY SECRET AFFAIR (Becomes Martin Kane #4)
Hero Book (Fox Feature Syndicate): Dec, 1949 - No. 3, April, 1950

1-Harrison/Wood-a (10 pgs.)	21	63	110	185
2-Wood-a	17	51	88	150
3-Wood-a	18	54	94	155

MY SECRET CONFESSION
Sterling Comics: September, 1955

1-Sekowsky-a	9	27	49	70

MY SECRET LIFE (Formerly Western Outlaws; Romeo Tubbs #26 on)
Fox Feature Syndicate: No. 22, July, 1949 - No. 27, July; 1950; No. 27, 9/51

22	11	33	55	90
23,26-Wood-a, 6 pgs.	18	54	94	155
24,25,27	9	27	49	70
27 (9/51)	8	24	45	65

NOTE: *The title was changed to Romeo Tubbs after #25 even though #26 & 27 did come out.*

MY SECRET LIFE (Formerly Young Lovers; Sue & Sally Smith #48)
Charlton Comics: No. 19, Aug, 1957 - No. 47, Sept, 1962

19	3	10	23	35
20-35	2	6	13	20
36-47: 44-Last 10¢ issue	2	6	11	16

MY SECRET MARRIAGE
Superior Comics, Ltd.: May, 1953 - No. 24, July, 1956 (Canadian)

1	12	36	61	105
2	7	21	38	55
3-24	6	18	29	40
I.W. Reprint #9	2	6	9	12

NOTE: *Many issues contain Kamen-ish art.*

MY SECRET ROMANCE (Becomes A Star Presentation #3)
Hero Book (Fox Feature Syndicate): Jan, 1950 - No. 2, March, 1950

1	14	42	72	120
2-Wood-a	18	54	94	155

MY SECRET STORY (Formerly Captain Kidd #25; Sabu #30 on)
Fox Feature Syndicate: No. 26, Oct, 1949 - No. 29, April, 1950

26	15	45	77	130
27-29	9	27	49	70

Mysteries of Unexplored Worlds #8 © CC

Mysterious Adventures #10 © Story Comics

Mystery in Space #26 © DC

	GD2.0	FN6.0	VF8.0	NM9.4

MYS-TECH WARS
Marvel Comics UK: Mar, 1993 - No. 4, June, 1993 ($1.75, mini-series)

1-4: 1-Gatefold-c				2.25

MYSTERIES (…Weird & Strange)
Superior/Dynamic Publ. (Randall Publ. Ltd.): May, 1953 - No. 11, Jan, 1955

1-All horror stories	40	120	220	380
2-A-Bomb blast story	25	75	130	225
3-11: 10-Kamenish c/a reprinted from Strange Mysteries #2; cover is from a panel in Strange Mysteries #2	22	66	116	195

MYSTERIES IN SPACE (See Fireside Book Series)

MYSTERIES OF SCOTLAND YARD (Also see A-1 Comics)
Magazine Enterprises: No. 121, 1954 (one shot)

A-1 121-Reprinted from Manhunt (5 stories)	17	51	88	150

MYSTERIES OF UNEXPLORED WORLDS (See Blue Bird) (Becomes Son of Vulcan V2#49 on)
Charlton Comics: Aug, 1956; No. 2, Jan, 1957 - No. 48, Sept, 1965

1	37	111	197	340
2-No Ditko	15	45	77	130
3,4,8,9 Ditko a. 3-Diko c/a (4). 4-Ditko c/a (2).	29	87	153	265
5,6,10,11: 5,6-Ditko c/a (all). 10-Ditko c/a(4). 11-Ditko c/a(3); signed J. Kotdi	31	93	165	285
7-(2/58, 68 pgs.) 4 stories w/Ditko-a	34	102	179	310
12,19,21-24,26-Ditko-a. 12-Ditko sty (3); Baker story "The Charm Bracelet."	22	66	116	195
13-18,20,	7	21	38	55
25,27-30	3	10	23	35
31-45	3	9	20	30
46(5/65)-Son of Vulcan begins (origin/1st app.)	4	12	29	45
47,48	3	9	20	30

NOTE: *Ditko c-3-6, 10, 11, 19, 21-24. Covers to #19, 21-24 reprint story panels.*

MYSTERIOUS ADVENTURES
Story Comics: Mar, 1951 - No. 24, Mar, 1955; No. 25, Aug, 1955

1-All horror stories	55	165	341	600
2	33	99	174	300
3,4,6,10	29	87	156	270
5-Bondage-c	33	99	174	300
7-Daggar in eye panel	40	120	220	380
8-Eyeball story	44	132	264	460
9-Extreme violence (8/52)	36	108	191	330
11(12/52)-Used in SOTI, pg. 84	36	108	191	330
12,14: 14-E.C. Old Witch swipe	30	90	159	275
13-Classic skull-c	35	105	188	325
15-21: 18-Used in Senate Investigative report, pgs. 5,6; E.C. swipe/TFTC #35; The Coffin-Keeper & Corpse (hosts). 20-Used by Wertham in the Senate hearings. 21-Bondage/beheading-c	39	117	208	360
22- "Cinderella" parody	31	93	165	285
23-Disbrow-a (6 pgs.); E.C. swipe "The Mystery Keeper's Tale" (host) and "Mother Ghoul's Nursery Tale"	31	93	165	285
24,25	24	72	127	215

NOTE: *Tothish art by Ross Andru-#22, 23. Bache a-8. Cameron a-5-7. Harrison a-12. Hollingsworth a-3-8, 12. Schaffenberger a-24, 25. Wildey a-15, 17.*

MYSTERIOUS ISLAND
Dell Publishing Co.: No. 1213, July-Sept, 1961

Four Color 1213-Movie, photo-c	9	27	63	110

MYSTERIOUS ISLE
Dell Publishing Co.: Nov-Jan, 1963/64 (Jules Verne)

1	3	9	20	30

MYSTERIOUS RIDER, THE (See Zane Grey, 4-Color 301)

MYSTERIOUS STORIES (Formerly Horror From the Tomb #1)
Premier Magazines: No. 2, Dec-Jan, 1954-1955 - No. 7, Dec, 1955

2-Woodbridge-c; last pre-code issue	43	129	257	450
3-Woodbridge-c/a	30	90	159	275
4-7: 5-Cinderella parody. 6-Woodbridge-c	28	84	148	255

NOTE: *Hollingsworth a-3.*

MYSTERIOUS SUSPENSE (Also see Blue Beetle #1 (1967))

Charlton Comics: Oct, 1968 (12¢)

1-Return of the Question by Ditko (c/a)	6	18	45	75

MYSTERIOUS TRAVELER (See Tales of the…)

MYSTERIOUS TRAVELER COMICS (Radio)
Trans-World Publications: Nov, 1948

1-Powell-c/a(2); Poe adaptation, "Tell Tale Heart"	55	165	341	600

MYSTERY COMICS
William H. Wise & Co.: 1944 - No. 4, 1944 (No months given)

1-The Magnet, The Silver Knight, Brad Spencer, Wonderman, Dick Devins, King of Futuria, & Zudo the Jungle Boy begin (all 1st app.); Schomburg-c on all	109	327	682	1200
2-Bondage-c	68	205	426	750
3,4: 3-Lance Lewis, Space Detective begins (1st app.); Robot-c. 4(V2#1 inside)	61	182	381	675

MYSTERY COMICS DIGEST
Gold Key/Whitman?: Mar, 1972 - No. 26, Oct, 1975

1-Ripley's Believe It or Not; reprint of Ripley's #1 origin Ra-Ka-Tep the Mummy; Wood-a	4	12	26	40
2-9: 2-Boris Karloff Tales of Mystery; Wood-a; 1st app. Werewolf Count Wulfstein 3-Twilight Zone (TV); Crandall, Toth & George Evans-a; 1st app. Tragg & Simbar the Lion Lord; (2) Crandall/Frazetta-r/Twilight Zone #1 4-Ripley's Believe It or Not; 1st app. Baron Tibor, the Vampire. 5-Boris Karloff Tales of Mystery; 1st app. Dr. Spektor. 6-Twilight Zone (TV); 1st app. U.S. Marshal Reid & Sir Duane; Evans-r. 7-Ripley's Believe It or Not; origin The Lurker in the Swamp; 1st app. Duroc. 8-Boris Karloff Tales of Mystery; McWilliams-r; Orlando-r. 9-Twilight Zone (TV); Williamson, Crandall, McWilliams-a; 2nd Tragg app.;Torres, Evans, Heck/Tuska-r	3	9	19	28
10-26: 10,13-Ripley's Believe It or Not. 13-Orlando-r. 11,14-Boris Karloff Tales of Mystery. 14-1st app. Xorkon. 12,15-Twilight Zone (TV). 16,19,22,25-Ripley's Believe It or Not. 17-Boris Karloff Tales of Mystery; Williamson-r; Orlando-r. 18,21,24-Twilight Zone (TV). 20,23,26-Boris Karloff Tales of Mystery	2	6	13	20

NOTE: *Dr. Spektor app.-#5, 10-12, 21. Durak app.-#15. Duroc app.-#14 (later called Durak). King George 1st app.-#8.*

MYSTERY IN SPACE (Also see Fireside Book Series and Pulp Fiction Library)
National Periodical Publ.: 4-5/51 - No. 110, 9/66; No. 111, 9/80 - No. 117, 3/81 (#1-3: 52 pgs.)

1-Frazetta-a, 8 pgs.; Knights of the Galaxy begins, ends #8	218	654	1853	3700
2	86	264	744	1400
3	70	210	595	1125
4,5	56	169	478	900
6-10: 7-Toth-a	48	144	386	700
11-15: 13-Toth-a	37	110	278	500
16-18,20-25: Interplanetary Insurance feature by Infantino in all. 21-1st app. Space Cabbie. 24-Last pre-code issue	32	97	240	435
19-Virgil Finlay-a	35	105	263	475
26-40: 26-Space Cabbie feature begins. 34-1st S.A. issue	29	88	202	360
41-52: 47-Space Cabbie feature ends	22	65	151	270
53-Adam Strange begins (8/59, 10pg. sty); robot-c	144	432	1222	2300
54	43	129	323	575
55-Grey tone-c	35	105	263	475
56-60: 59-Kane/Anderson-a	22	65	154	275
61-71: 61-1st app. Adam Strange foe Ulthoon. 62-1st app. A.S. foe Mortan. 63-Origin Vandor. 66-Star Rovers begin (1st app.). 68-1st app. Dust Devils (6/61). 69-1st Mailbag. 70-2nd app. Dust Devils.	17	51	115	205
72-74,76-80	12	36	84	140
75-JLA x-over in Adam Strange (5/62)(sequel to JLA #3)	25	75	174	310
81-86	9	27	63	105
87-(11/63)-Adam Strange/Hawkman double feat begins; 3rd Hawkman tryout series	19	57	132	235
88-Adam Strange & Hawkman stories	17	51	115	205
89-Adam Strange & Hawkman stories	16	48	110	190

Mystery Men Comics #2 © FOX

Mystic #1 © CRO

Mystic Comics #6 © MAR

	GD2.0	FN6.0	VF8.0	NM9.4			GD2.0	FN6.0	VF8.0	NM9.4

90-Adam Strange & Hawkman team-up for 1st time (3/64); Hawkman moves
to own title next month · · · · · · · · · · · · · · 18 · 53 · 123 · 220
91-103: 91-End Infantino art on Adam Strange; double-length Adam Strange
story. 92-Space Ranger begins (6/64), ends #103. 92-94,96,98-Space
Ranger-c. 94,98-Adam Strange/Space Ranger team-up. 102-Adam
Strange ends (no Space Ranger). 103-Origin Ultra, the Multi-Alien; last
Space Ranger · · · · · · · · · · · · · · · · · · 5 · 15 · 34 · 55
104-110: 110-(9/66)-Last 12¢ issue · · · · · · · · · 3 · 10 · 23 · 35
V17#111(9/80)-117: 117-Newton-a(3 pgs.) · · · · · · 1 · 3 · 5 · 7
NOTE: **Anderson** a-2, 4, 8-10, 12-17, 19, 45-48, 51, 57, 59i, 61-64, 70, 76, 87-91; c-9, 10, 15-25,
87, 89, 105-108, 110. **Aparo** a-111. **Austin** a-112i. **Bolland** a-115. **Craig** a-114, 116. **Ditko** a-
111, 114-116. **Drucker** a-13, 14. **Elias** a-98, 102, 103. **Golden** a-113p. **Sid Greene** a-78, 91.
Infantino a-1-8, 11, 14-25, 27-46, 48, 49, 51, 53-91, 103, 117; c-60-86, 88, 90, 91, 105, 107. **Gil
Kane** a-14p, 15p, 18p, 19p, 26p, 29-59p(most); 100-102; c-52, 101. **Kubert** a-113; c-111-115.
Moriera c-27, 28. **Rogers** a-111. **Sekowsky** a-52. **Simon & Kirby** a-4(2 pgs.). **Spiegle** a-111,
114. **Starlin** c-116. **Sutton** a-112. **Tuska** a-115p, 117p.

MYSTERY MEN COMICS
Fox Features Syndicate: Aug, 1939 - No. 31, Feb, 1942

1-Intro. & 1st app. The Blue Beetle, The Green Mask, Rex Dexter of Mars by
Briefer, Zanzibar by Tuska, Lt. Drake, D-13-Secret Agent by Powell, Chen
Chang, Wing Turner, & Captain Denny Scott · · 961 · 2883 · 6250 · 12,500
2-Robot & sci/fi-c (2nd Robot-c w/Movie #6) · · 308 · 924 · 1927 · 3700
3 (10/39)-Classic Lou Fine-c · · · · · · · · · · 383 · 1149 · 2396 · 4600
4,5: 4-Capt. Savage begins (11/39) · · · · · · · 245 · 735 · 1534 · 2700
6-Tuska-c · · · · · · · · · · · · · · · · · · · 200 · 600 · 1250 · 2200
7-1st Blue Beetle-c app. · · · · · · · · · · · · 245 · 735 · 1534 · 2700
8-Lou Fine-c · · · · · · · · · · · · · · · · · · 218 · 654 · 1364 · 2400
9-The Moth begins; Lou Fine-c · · · · · · · · · 111 · 332 · 694 · 1225
10-12: All Joe Simon-c. 10-Wing Turner by Kirby; Simon-c. 11-Intro. Domino
· 95 · 285 · 597 · 1050
13-Intro. Lynx & sidekick Blackie (8/40) · · · · 64 · 192 · 398 · 700
14-18 · 61 · 182 · 381 · 675
19-Intro. & 1st app. Miss X (ends #21) · · · · · 64 · 192 · 398 · 700
20-31: 26-The Wraith begins · · · · · · · · · · 58 · 174 · 363 · 640
NOTE: **Briefer** a-15, 20, 24; c-9. **Cuidera** a-22. **Lou Fine** c-5,8,9. **Powell** a-1-15, 24. **Simon**
c-10-12. **Tuska** a-1-16, 22, 24, 27; c-6. **Bondage**-c 1, 3, 7, 8, 25, 27-29, 31. **Blue Beetle** c-7, 8, 10-
31. **D-13 Secret Agent** c-6. **Green Mask** c-1, 3-5. **Rex Dexter of Mars** c-2, 9.

MYSTERY MEN MOVIE ADAPTION
Dark Horse Comics: July, 1999 - No. 2, Aug, 1999 ($2.95, mini-series)

1,2-Fingerman-s; photo-c · 3.00

MYSTERY PLAY, THE
DC Comics (Vertigo): 1994 ($19.95, one-shot)

nn-Hardcover-Morrison-s/Muth-painted art · · · · · · · · · · · · 25.00
Softcover ($9.95)-New Muth cover · · · · · · · · · · · · · · · · 10.00

MYSTERY TALES
Atlas Comics (20CC): Mar, 1952 - No. 54, Aug, 1957

1-Horror/weird stories in all · · · · · · · · · · 84 · 252 · 525 · 925
2-Krigstein-a · · · · · · · · · · · · · · · · · 45 · 135 · 270 · 475
3-10: 6-A-Bomb panel. 10-Story similar to "The Assassin" from Shock
SuspenStories · · · · · · · · · · · · · · · · 40 · 120 · 214 · 370
11,13-21: 14-Maneely s/f story. 20-Electric chair issue. 21-Matt Fox-a/
decapitation story · · · · · · · · · · · · · · · 30 · 90 · 159 · 275
12,22: 12-Matt Fox-a. 22-Forte/Matt Fox-c; a(i) · 33 · 99 · 174 · 300
23-26 (2/55)-Last precode issue · · · · · · · · · 24 · 72 · 127 · 215
27,29-35,37,38,41-43,48,49: 43-Morisi story contains Frazetta art swipes
from Untamed Love · · · · · · · · · · · · · · 19 · 57 · 99 · 165
28,36,39,40,45: 28-Jack Katz-a. 36,39-Krigstein-a. 40,45-Ditko-a (#45 is 3 pgs.
only) · 20 · 60 · 105 · 175
44,51-Williamson/Krenkel-a · · · · · · · · · · · 21 · 63 · 110 · 185
46-Williamson/Krenkel-a; Crandall text illos · · · 21 · 63 · 110 · 185
47-Crandall, Ditko, Powell-a · · · · · · · · · · 21 · 63 · 110 · 185
50,52,53: 50-Torres, Morrow-a · · · · · · · · · 19 · 57 · 99 · 165
54-Crandall, Check-a · · · · · · · · · · · · · · 20 · 60 · 105 · 185
NOTE: **Ayers** a-18, 49, 52. **Berg** a-17, 51. **Colan** a-1, 3, 18, 35, 43. **Drucker** a-41.
Colletta a-29, 33, 35, 41; c-8-11, 14, 38, 39, 41, 43, 44, 46, 48-51, 53. **Fass** a-16. **Forte** a-21,
22, 45, 46. **Matt Fox** a-12?, 21, 22; c-22. **Heath** a-3, 5, 17, 26. **Heck** a-25. **Kinstler** a-15.
Mort Lawrence a-26, 32, 34. **Maneely** a-1, 9, 14, 22; c-12, 23, 24, 27. **Mooney** a-3, 40. **Morisi** a-
43, 49, 52. **Morrow** a-50. **Orlando** a-51. **Pakula** a-16. **Powell** a-21, 29, 37, 38, 47. **Reinman** a-1,
17. **Robinson** a-7p, 42. **Romita** a-37. **Roussos** a-4, 44. **R.Q. Sale** a-35, 46, 49. **Severin** c-52.
Shores a-17, 45. **Tuska** a-10, 12, 14. **Whitney** a-2. **Wildey** a-37.

MYSTERY TALES
Super Comics: 1964

Super Reprint #16,17('64): 16-r/Tales of Horror #2. 17-r/Eerie #14(Avon),
18-Kubert-r/Strange Terrors #4 · · · · · · · · · 3 · 9 · 17 · 24

MYSTIC (3rd Series)
Marvel/Atlas Comics (CLDS 1/CSI 2-21/OMC 22-35/CSI 35-61): March, 1951 -
No. 61, Aug, 1957

1-Atom bomb panels; horror/weird stories in all · 89 · 267 · 556 · 975
2 · 50 · 150 · 300 · 525
3-Eyes torn out · · · · · · · · · · · · · · · · 43 · 129 · 257 · 450
4-"The Devil Birds" by Wolverton (6 pgs.) · · · · 77 · 231 · 483 · 850
5,7-10 · 34 · 102 · 179 · 310
6- "The Eye of Doom" by Wolverton (7 pgs.) · · · 77 · 231 · 483 · 850
11-20: 16-Bondage/torture c/story · · · · · · · · 29 · 87 · 153 · 265
21-25,27-36-Last precode (3/55). 25-E.C. swipe · · 24 · 72 · 127 · 215
26-Atomic War, severed head stories · · · · · · · 26 · 78 · 136 · 235
37-51,53-56,61 · · · · · · · · · · · · · · · · · 20 · 60 · 105 · 175
52-Wood-a; Crandall-a? · · · · · · · · · · · · · 22 · 66 · 116 · 195
57-Story "Trapped in the Ant-Hill" (1957) is very similar to
"The Man in the Ant Hill" in TTA #27 · · · · · · 22 · 66 · 116 · 200
58,59-Krigstein-a · · · · · · · · · · · · · · · · 20 · 60 · 105 · 175
60-Williamson/Mayo-a (4 pgs.) · · · · · · · · · · 20 · 60 · 105 · 175
NOTE: **Andru** a-23, 25. **Ayers** a-35, 53; c-8. **Berg** a-49. **Cameron** a-49, 51. **Check** a-31, 60.
Colan a-3, 7, 12, 21, 37, 60. **Colletta** a-29. **Drucker** a-46, 52, 56. **Everett** a-18, 19, 37, 40, 44, 57;
c-13, 18, 21, 42, 47, 49, 51-55, 57-59, 61. **Forte** a-35, 52, 58. **Fox** a-24i. **Al Hartley** a-35. **Heath**
a-10; c-10, 20, 22, 23, 25, 30. **Infantino** a-12. **Kane** a-8, 24p. **Jack Katz** a-31, 33. **Maneely**
a-22, 54; c-7, 15, 28, 29, 31. **Moldoff** a-29. **Morisi** a-48, 49, 52.
Morrow a-51. **Orlando** a-57, 61. **Pakula** a-52, 57, 59. **Powell** a-52, 54-56. **Robinson** a-5. **Romita**
a-11, 15. **R.Q. Sale** a-35, 53, 58. **Sekowsky** a-1, 2, 4, 5. **Severin** c-56, 60. **Tuska** a-15. **Whitney**
a-33. **Wildey** a-28, 30. **Ed Win** a-17, 20. Canadian reprints known-title 'Startling.'

MYSTIC (Also see CrossGen Chronicles)
CrossGeneration Comics: Jul, 2000 - Present ($2.95)

1-19: Marz-s/Peterson & Dell-a. 15-Cameos by DC & Marvel characters · 3.00
...: Rite of Passage TPB (5/01, $19.95) w/#1-7; Linsner-c · · · · · · 20.00

MYSTICAL TALES
Atlas Comics (CCC 1/EPI 2-8): June, 1956 - No. 8, Aug, 1957

1-Everett-c/a · · · · · · · · · · · · · · · · · 47 · 140 · 286 · 500
2-4: 2-Berg-a. 3,4-Crandall-a. · · · · · · · · · 27 · 81 · 142 · 245
5-Williamson-a (4 pgs.) · · · · · · · · · · · · · 29 · 87 · 153 · 265
6-Torres, Krigstein-a · · · · · · · · · · · · · · 25 · 75 · 133 · 230
7-Bolle, Forte, Torres, Orlando-a · · · · · · · · 25 · 75 · 130 · 225
8-Krigstein, Check-a · · · · · · · · · · · · · · 25 · 75 · 133 · 230
NOTE: **Everett** a-1; c-1-4, 6, 7. **Orlando** a-1, 2, 7. **Pakula** a-3. **Powell** a-1, 4.

MYSTIC COMICS (1st Series)
Timely Comics (TPI 1-5/TCI 8-10): March, 1940 - No. 10, Aug, 1942

1-Origin The Blue Blaze, The Dynamic Man, & Flexo the Rubber Robot; Zephyr
Jones, 3X's & Deep Sea Demon app.; The Magician begins (all 1st app.);
c-from Spider pulp V18#1, 6/39 · · · · 1250 · 3750 · 8750 · 17,500
2-The Invisible Man & Master Mind Excello begin; Space Rangers, Zara of
the Jungle, Taxi Taylor app. (scarce) · · 417 · 1250 · 2604 · 5000
3-Zephyr Hercules, who last appears in #4 · 300 · 900 · 1875 · 3500
4-Origin The Thin Man & The Black Widow; Merzak the Mystic app.; last
Flexo, Dynamic Man, Invisible Man & Blue Blaze (some issues have date
sticker on cover; others have July w/August overprint in silver color);
Roosevelt assassination-c · · · · · · 317 · 951 · 1979 · 3800
5-(1/41)-Origin The Black Widow, The Blazing Skull, The Sub-Earth Man,
Super Slave & The Terror; The Moon Man & Black Widow app.; 5-German
war-c begin, end #10 · · · · · · · · 300 · 900 · 1875 · 3500
6-(10/41)-Origin The Challenger & The Destroyer (1st app.?; also see
All-Winners #2, Fall, 1941) · · · · · 350 · 1050 · 2188 · 4200
7-The Witness begins (12/41, origin & 1st app.); origin Davey & the Demon;
last Black Widow; Hitler opens his trunk of terror-c by Simon & Kirby
(classic-c) · · · · · · · · · · · · · 367 · 1100 · 2292 · 4400
8,10: 10-Father Time, World of Wonder, & Red Skeleton app.; last Challenger &
Terror · · · · · · · · · · · · · · · · 205 · 615 · 1281 · 2250
9-Gary Gaunt app.; last Black Marvel, Mystic & Blazing Skull; Hitler-c
· · · · · · · · · · · · · · · · · · · 218 · 654 · 1364 · 2400
NOTE: **Gabrielle** c-8-10. **Kirby/Schomburg** c-6. **Rico** a-9(2). **Schomburg** c-1-4; c-1-5.
Sekowsky a-9. **Sekowsky/Klein** a-8(Challenger). **Bondage** c-1, 2, 9.

Mystical Tales #6 © MAR

Names of Magic #1 © DC

Namor, the Sub-Mariner #1 © MAR

	GD2.0	FN6.0	VF8.0	NM9.4

MYSTIC COMICS (2nd Series)
Timely Comics (ANC): Oct, 1944 - No. 3, Win, 1944-45; No. 4, Mar, 1945

1-The Angel, The Destroyer, The Human Torch, Terry Vance the Schoolboy				
Sleuth, & Tommy Tyme begin	227	681	1420	2500
2-(Fall/44)-Last Human Torch & Terry Vance; bondage/hypo-c				
	118	354	738	1300
3-Last Angel (two stories) & Tommy Tyme	111	332	694	1225
4-The Young Allies-c & app.; Schomburg-c	105	315	656	1150

MYSTIC EDGE (Manga)
Antarctic Press: Oct, 1998 ($2.95, one-shot)

1-Ryan Kinnaird-s/a/c				3.00

MYSTIQUE & SABRETOOTH (Sabretooth and Mystique on-c)
Marvel Comics: Dec, 1996 - No. 4, Mar, 1997 ($1.95, limited series)

1-4: Characters from X-Men				3.00

MY STORY (...True Romances in Pictures #5,6; becomes My Love Life #13)
(Formerly Zago)
Hero Books (Fox Features Syndicate): No. 5, May, 1949 - No. 12, Aug, 1950

5-Kamen/Feldstein-a	20	60	105	175
6-8,11,12: 12-Photo-c	10	30	55	80
9,10-Wood-a	19	57	99	165

MYTHOGRAPHY
Bardic Press: Sept, 1996 - No. 8, May, 1998 ($3.95/$4.25, B&W, anthology)

1-3: 1-Drew Hayes-s/a				5.00
4-8				4.25

MYTHOS: THE FINAL TOUR
DC Comics/Vertigo: Dec, 1996 - No. 3, Feb, 1997 ($5.95, limited series)

1-3: 1-Ney Rieber-s/a; Amaro-a. 2-Snejberg-a; Constantine-app.				
3-Kristiansen-a; Black Orchid-app.				6.00

MY TRUE LOVE (Formerly Western Killers #64; Frank Buck #70 on)
Fox Features Syndicate: No. 65, July, 1949 - No. 69, March, 1950

65	15	45	77	130
66,68,69: 69-Morisi-a	10	30	55	80
67-Wood-a	19	57	99	165

NAKED PREY, THE (See Movie Classics)

'NAM, THE (See Savage Tales #1, 2nd series & Punisher Invades...)
Marvel Comics Group: Dec, 1986 - No. 84, Sept, 1993

1-Golden a(p)/c begins, ends #13				3.00
1 (2nd printing)				2.25
2-74,76-84: 7-Golden-a (2 pgs.). 32-Death R. Kennedy. 52,53-Frank Castle				
(The Punisher) app. 52,53-Gold 2nd printings. 58-Silver logo. 65-Heath-c/a.				
67-69-Punisher 3 part story. 70-Lomax scripts begin				2.25
75-($2.25, 52 pgs.)				2.50
Trade Paperback 1,2: 1-r/#1-4. 2-r/#5-8				5.00
TPB ('99, $14.95) r/#1-4; recolored				15.00

'NAM MAGAZINE, THE
Marvel Comics: Aug, 1988 - No. 10, May, 1989 ($2.00, B&W, 52pgs.)

1-10: Each issue reprints 2 issues of the comic				2.25

NAMELESS, THE
Image Comics: May, 1997 - No. 5, Sept, 1997 ($2.95, B&W)

1-5: Pruett/Hester-s/a				3.00

NAMES OF MAGIC, THE (Also see Books of Magic)
DC Comics (Vertigo): Feb, 2001 - No. 5, June, 2001 ($2.50, limited series)

1-5: Bolton painted-c on all; Case-a; leads into Hunter: The Age of Magic				2.50

NAME OF THE GAME, THE
DC Comics: 2001 ($29.95), graphic novel)

Hardcover ($29.95) Will Eisner-s/a				30.00

NAMORA (See Marvel Mystery Comics #82 & Sub-Mariner Comics)
Marvel Comics (PrPI): Fall, 1948 - No. 3, Dec, 1948

1-Sub-Mariner x-over in Namora; Namora by Everett(2), Sub-Mariner by				
Rico (10 pgs.)	236	708	1477	2600
2-The Blonde Phantom & Sub-Mariner story; Everett-a				
	123	369	769	1350

	GD2.0	FN6.0	VF8.0	NM9.4

3-(Scarce)-Sub-Mariner app.; Everett-a	132	395	825	1450

NAMOR, THE SUB-MARINER (See Prince Namor & Sub-Mariner)
Marvel Comics: Apr, 1990 - No. 62, May, 1995 ($1.00/$1.25/$1.50)

1-Byrne-c/a/scripts in 1-25 (scripts only #26-32)				4.00
2-5: 5-Iron Man app.				3.00
6-11,13-23,25,27-49,51-62: 16-Re-intro Iron Fist (8-cameo only). 18-Punisher				
cameo (1 panel); 21-23,25-Wolverine cameos. 22,23-Iron Fist app. 28-Iron				
Fist-c/story. 31-Dr. Doom-c/story. 33,34-Iron Fist cameo. 35-New Tiger				
Shark-c/story. 37-Aqua holografx foil-c. 48-The Thing app.				2.25
12,24: 12-(52pgs.)-Re-intro. The Invaders. 24-Namor vs. Wolverine				2.50
26-Namor w/new costume; 1st Jae Lee-c/a this title (5/92) & begins				3.00
50-($1.75, 52 pgs.)-Newsstand edition; w/bound-in S-M trading card sheet (both				
versions)				2.25
50-($2.95, 52 pgs.)-Collector edition w/foil-c				3.00
Annual 1-4 ('91-94, 68 pgs.): 1-3 pg. origin recap. 2-Return/Defenders. 3-Bagged				
w/card. 4-Painted-c				3.00

NOTE: **Jae Lee**-a-26-30p, 31-37, 38p, 39, 40; c-26-40.

NANCY AND SLUGGO (See Comics On Parade & Sparkle Comics)
United Features Syndicate: No. 16, 1949 - No. 23, 1954

16(#1)	9	27	49	70
17-23	6	18	29	40

NANCY & SLUGGO (Nancy #146-173; formerly Sparkler Comics)
St. John/Dell #146-187/Gold Key #188 on: No. 121, Apr, 1955-No. 192, Oct, 1963

121(4/55)(St. John)	7	21	38	55
122-145(7/57)(St. John)	6	18	29	40
146(9/57)-Peanuts begins, ends #192 (Dell)	5	15	34	55
147-161 (Dell)	4	12	29	45
162-165,177-180-John Stanley-a	7	21	49	90
166-176-Oona & Her Haunted House series; Stanley-a				
	8	24	56	100
181-187(3-5/62)(Dell)	4	12	29	45
188(10/62)-192 (Gold Key)	4	12	29	45
Four Color 1034(9-11/59)-Summer Camp	4	12	29	45

(See Dell Giant #34, 45 & Dell Giants)

NANNY AND THE PROFESSOR (TV)
Dell Publishing Co.: Aug, 1970 - No. 2, Oct, 1970 (Photo-c)

1-(01-546-008)	4	12	30	50
2	4	12	26	40

NAPOLEON
Dell Publishing Co.: No. 526, Dec, 1953

Four Color 526	3	9	19	28

NAPOLEON & SAMANTHA (See Walt Disney Showcase No. 10)

NAPOLEON & UNCLE ELBY (See Clifford McBride's...)
Eastern Color Printing Co.: July, 1942 (68 pgs.) (One Shot)

1	43	129	257	450
1945-American Book-Strafford Press (128 pgs.) (8x10-1/2"; B&W reprints;				
hardcover)	15	45	77	130

NARRATIVE ILLUSTRATION, THE STORY OF THE COMICS (Also see Good
Triumphs Over Evil!)
M.C. Gaines: Summer, 1942 (32 pgs., 7-1/4"x10", B&W w/color inserts)

nn-16pgs. text with illustrations of ancient art, strips and comic covers; 4 pg.				
WWII War Bond promo, "The Minute Man Answers the Call" color comic				
drawn by Shelly and a special 8-page color comic insert of "The Story of				
Saul" from Picture Stories from the Bible #1 or soon to appear in PS #1.				
Insert has special title page indicating it was No. 10 of a Sunday newspaper				
supplement insert series that had already run in a New England "Sunday				
Herald." (very rare; only two known copies.) Estimated value...				1200.00

NASH (WCW Wrestling)
Image Comics: July, 1999 - No. 2, July, 1999 ($2.95)

1,2-Regular and photo-c				3.00
1-($6.95) Photo-split-cover Edition				7.00

NATHANIEL DUSK
DC Comics: Feb, 1984 - No. 4, May, 1984 ($1.25, mini-series, direct sales,
Baxter paper)

National Comics #23 © DC

Nature Boy #5 © CC

Negation #1 © CRO

	GD2.0	FN6.0	VF8.0	NM9.4

1-4: 1-Intro/origin; Gene Colan-c/a in all ... 2.00

NATHANIEL DUSK II
DC Comics: Oct, 1985 - No. 4, Jan, 1986 ($2.00, mini-series, Baxter paper)
1-4: Gene Colan-c/a in all ... 2.25

NATHAN NEVER
Dark Horse (Bonelli Comics): Mar, 1999 - No. 6, Aug, 1999 ($4.95, B&W, digest size)
1-6-Reprints Italian series in English. 1-4-Art Adams-c ... 5.00

NATIONAL COMICS
Quality Comics Group: July, 1940 - No. 75, Nov, 1949

1-Uncle Sam begins (1st app.); origin sidekick Buddy by Eisner; origin Wonder Boy & Kid Dixon; Merlin the Magician (ends #45); Cyclone, Kid Patrol, Sally O'Neil Policewoman, Pen Miller (by Klaus Nordling; ends #22), Prop Powers (ends #26) & Paul Bunyan (ends #22) begin	500	1500	3250	6500
2	232	695	1450	2550
3-Last Eisner Uncle Sam	159	477	994	1750
4-Last Cyclone	127	381	795	1400
5-(11/40)-Quicksilver begins (1st app.; 3rd w/lightning speed?; re-intro'd by DC in 1993 as Max Mercury in Flash #76, 2nd series); origin Uncle Sam; bondage-c	150	450	938	1650
6,8-11: 8-Jack & Jill begins (ends #22). 9-Flag-c	127	381	795	1400
7-Classic Lou Fine-c	214	642	1338	2350
12	95	285	597	1050
13-16-Lou Fine-a	84	253	525	925
17,19-22: 22-Last Pen Miller (moves to Crack #23)	64	192	398	700
18-(12/41)-Shows orientals attacking Pearl Harbor; on stands one month before actual event	116	348	725	1275
23-The Unknown & Destroyer 171 begin	66	197	413	725
24-Japanese War-c	66	197	413	725
25-30: 26-Wonder Boy ends. 27- G-2 the Unknown begins (ends #46). 29-Origin The Unknown	47	142	286	500
31-33: 33-Chic Carter begins (ends #47)	43	129	257	450
34-37,40: 35-Last Kid Patrol	39	117	208	360
38-Hitler, Tojo, Mussolini-c	41	123	246	425
39-Hitler-c	43	129	257	450
41-50: 42-The Barker begins (1st app? 5/44); The Barker covers begin.				
48-Origin The Whistler	24	72	127	215
51-Sally O'Neil by Ward, 8 pgs. (12/45)	29	87	153	265
52-60	20	60	105	175
61-67: 67-Format change; Quicksilver app.	15	45	77	130
68-75: The Barker ends	12	36	61	100

NOTE: Cole Quicksilver-13; Barker-43; c-43, 46, 47, 49-51. Crandall Uncle Sam-11-13 (with Fine), 25, 26; c-24-26, 30-33, 43. Crandall Paul Bunyan-10-13. Fine Uncle Sam-13 (w/Crandall), 17, 18; c-1-14, 16, 18, 21. Gill Fox c-69-74. Guardineer Quicksilver-27, 35. Gustavson Quicksilver-14-26. McWilliams a-23-28, 55, 57. Uncle Sam c-1-41. Barker c-42-75.

NATIONAL COMICS (Also see All Star Comics 1999 crossover titles)
DC Comics: May, 1999 ($1.99, one-shot)
1-Golden Age Flash and Mr. Terrific; Waid-s/Lopresti-a ... 2.25

NATIONAL CRUMB, THE (Magazine-Size)
Mayfair Publications: August, 1975 (52 pgs., B&W) (Satire)

1-Grandenetti-c/a, Ayers-a	2	6	11	16

NATIONAL VELVET (TV)
Dell Publishing Co./Gold Key: May-July, 1961 - No. 2, Mar, 1963 (All photo-c)

Four Color 1195 (#1)	6	18	42	80
Four Color 1312, 01-556-207, 12-556-210 (Dell)	4	12	26	40
1,2: 1(12/62) (Gold Key). 2(3/63)	4	12	26	40

NATION OF SNITCHES
Piranha Press (DC): 1990 ($4.95, color, 52 pgs.)
nn ... 5.00

NATURE BOY (Formerly Danny Blaze; Li'l Rascal Twins #6 on)
Charlton Comics: No. 3, March, 1956 - No. 5, Feb, 1957

3-Origin; Blue Beetle story; Buscema-c/a	24	72	127	215
4,5	17	51	88	150

NOTE: John Buscema a-3, 4p, 5; c-3. Powell a-4.

NATURE OF THINGS (Disney, TV/Movie)

Dell Publishing Co.: No. 727, Sept, 1956 - No. 842, Sept, 1957

Four Color 727 (#1), 842-Jesse Marsh-a	5	15	35	60

NAUSICAA OF THE VALLEY OF WIND
Viz Comics: 1988 - No. 7, 1989; 1989 - No. 4, 1990 ($2.50, B&W, 68pgs.)
Book 1-7: 1-Contains Moebius poster ... 3.25
Part II, Book 1-4 ($2.95) ... 3.25

NAVY ACTION (Sailor Sweeney #12-14)
Atlas Comics (CDS): Aug, 1954 - No. 11, Apr, 1956; No. 15, 1/57 - No. 18, 8/57

1-Powell-a	19	57	99	165
2-Lawrence-a	10	30	55	80
3-11: 4-Last precode (2/55)	8	24	42	60
15-18	7	21	35	55

NOTE: Berg a-7, 9. Colan a-8. Drucker a-7. Everett a-3, 7, 16; c-16, 17. Heath c-1, 2, 6. Maneely a-7, 8, 18; c-9, 11. Pakula a-2, 3, 9. Reinman a-17.

NAVY COMBAT
Atlas Comics (MPI): June, 1955 - No. 20, Oct, 1958

1-Torpedo Taylor begins by Don Heck	19	57	99	165
2	10	30	55	80
3-10	8	24	42	60
11,13,15,16,18-20	7	21	38	55
12-Crandall-a	10	30	55	80
14-Torres-a	8	24	42	60
17-Williamson-a, 4 pgs.; Torres-a	8	24	45	65

NOTE: Berg a-10, 11. Colan a-11. Drucker a-7. Everett a-3, 20; c-8 & 9 w/Tuska, 10, 13-16. Heck a-11(2). Maneely c-1, 6, 11, 17. Morisi a-8. Pakula a-7. Powell a-20.

NAVY HEROES
Almanac Publishing Co.: 1945

1-Heavy in propaganda	12	36	61	105

NAVY PATROL
Key Publications: May, 1955 - No. 4, Nov, 1955

1	7	21	36	50
2-4	5	15	23	30

NAVY TALES
Atlas Comics (CDS): Jan, 1957 - No. 4, July, 1957

1-Everett-c; Berg, Powell-a	16	48	83	140
2-Williamson/Mayo-a(5 pgs); Crandall-a	14	42	72	120
3,4-Reinman-a; Severin-c. 4-Crandall-a	12	36	61	100

NOTE: Colan a-4. Maneely c-2. Sinnott a-4.

NAVY TASK FORCE
Stanmor Publications/Aragon Mag. No. 4-8: Feb, 1954 - No. 8, April, 1956

1	8	24	42	60
2	5	15	23	30
3-8: #8-r/Navy Patrol #1	4	13	19	26

NAVY WAR HEROES
Charlton Comics: Jan, 1964 - No. 7, Mar-Apr, 1965

1	3	9	21	32
2-7	2	6	13	20

NAZA (Stone Age Warrior)
Dell Publishing Co.: Nov-Jan, 1963-64 - No. 9, March, 1966

12-555-401 (#1)-Painted-c	4	12	29	45
2-9: 2-4-Painted-c	3	9	20	30

NAZZ, THE
DC Comics: 1990 - No. 4, 1991 ($4.95, 52 pgs., mature)
1-4 ... 5.00

NEBBS, THE (Also see Crackajack Funnies)
Dell Publishing Co./Croydon Publishing Co.: 1941; 1945

Large Feature Comic 23(1941)	14	42	98	185
1(1945, 36 pgs.)-Reprints	12	36	61	105

NECROMANCER: THE GRAPHIC NOVEL
Marvel Comics (Epic Comics): 1989 ($8.95)
nn ... 9.00

NEGATION
CrossGeneration Comics: Dec, 2001 - Present ($2.95)

Negro Heroes #2 © PMI

Neon Cyber #3 © Dreamwave Prod.

Nevermen #1 © DH

	GD2.0	FN6.0	VF8.0	NM9.4

Prequel (12/01) 3.00
1-(1/02) Pelletier-a/Bedard & Waid-s 3.00

NEGATIVE BURN
Caliber: 1993 - No. 50, 1997 ($2.95, B&W, anthology)
1,2,4-12,14-47: Anthology by various including Bolland, Burden, Doran, Gaiman, Moebius, Moore, & Pope 4.00
3,13: 3-Bone story. 13-Strangers in Paradise story 2 6 12
48,49-($4.95) 5.00
50-($6.95, 96 pgs.)-Gaiman, Robinson, Bolland 7.00

NEGRO (See All-Negro)

NEGRO HEROES (Calling All Girls, Real Heroes, & True Comics reprints)
Parents' Magazine Institute: Spring, 1947 - No. 2, Summer, 1948
1 84 253 525 925
2-Jackie Robinson-c/story 91 273 568 1000

NEGRO ROMANCE (Negro Romances #4)
Fawcett Publications: June, 1950 - No. 3, Oct, 1950 (All photo-c)
1-Evans-a 111 332 694 1225
2,3 84 253 525 925

NEGRO ROMANCES (Formerly Negro Romance; Romantic Secrets #5 on)
Charlton Comics: No. 4, May, 1955
4-Reprints Fawcett #2 68 205 426 750

NEIL GAIMAN AND CHARLES VESS' STARDUST
DC Comics (Vertigo): 1997 - No. 4, 1998 ($5.95/$6.95, square-bound, lim. series)
1-4: Gaiman text with Vess paintings in all 7.00
Hardcover (1998, $29.95) r/series with new sketches 35.00
Softcover (1999, $19.95) oversized; new Vess-c 20.00

NEIL GAIMAN'S LADY JUSTICE
Tekno Comix: Sept, 1995 - No. 11, May, 1996 ($1.95/$2.25)
1-11: 1-Sienkiewicz-c; pin-ups. 1-5-Brereton-c. 7-polybagged. 11-Includes The Big Bang Pt. 7 2.25

NEIL GAIMAN'S LADY JUSTICE
BIG Entertainment: V2#1, June, 1996 - No. 9, Feb, 1997 ($2.25)
V2#1-9: Dan Brereton-c on all. 6-8-Dan Brereton script 2.25

NEIL GAIMAN'S MIDNIGHT DAYS
DC Comics (Vertigo): 1999 ($17.95, trade paperback)
nn-Reprints Gaiman's short stories; new Swamp Thing w/ Bissette-a 18.00

NEIL GAIMAN'S MR. HERO-THE NEWMATIC MAN
Tekno Comix: Mar, 1995 - No. 17, May, 1996 ($1.95/$2.25)
1-17: 1-Intro Mr. Hero & Teknophage; bound-in game piece and trading card 4-w/Steel edition Neil Gaiman's Teknophage #1 coupon. 13-polybagged. 2.25

NEIL GAIMAN'S MR. HERO-THE NEWMATIC MAN
BIG Entertainment: V2#1, June, 1996 ($2.25)
V2#1-Teknophage destroys Mr. Hero; includes The Big Bang Pt. 10 2.25

NEIL GAIMAN'S PHAGE-SHADOWDEATH
BIG Entertainment: June, 1996 - No. 6, Nov, 1996 ($2.25, limited series)
1-6: Bryan Talbot-c & scripts in all. 1-1st app. Orlando Holmes 2.25

NEIL GAIMAN'S TEKNOPHAGE
Tekno Comix: Aug, 1995 - No. 10, Mar, 1996 ($1.95/$2.25)
1-6-Rick Veitch scripts & Bryan Talbot-c/a. 2.25
1-Steel Edition 4.00
7-10: Paul Jenkins scripts in all. 8-polybagged 2.25

NEIL GAIMAN'S WHEEL OF WORLDS
Tekno Comix: Apr, 1995 - No. 1, May, 1996 ($2.95/$3.25)
0-1st app. Lady Justice; 48 pgs.; bound-in poster 3.25
0-Regular edition 2.25
1 ($3.25, 5/96)-Bruce Jones scripts; Lady Justice & Teknophage app.; computer-generated photo-c. 3.25

NEIL THE HORSE (See Charlton Bullseye #2)
Aardvark-Vanaheim #1-10/Renegade Press #11 on: 2/83 - No. 10, 12/84; No. 11, 4/85 - #15, 1985 (B&W)

NELLIE THE NURSE
1($1.40) 4.00
1-2nd print 2.25
2-13: 13-Double size; 11,13-w/paperdolls 2.25
14,15: Double size ($3.00). 15 is a flip book(2-c) 3.00

NELLIE THE NURSE (Also see Gay Comics & Joker Comics)
Marvel/Atlas Comics (SPI/LMC): 1945 - No. 36, Oct, 1952; 1957
1-(1945) 40 120 220 380
2-(Spring/46) 20 60 105 175
3,4: 3-New logo (9/46) 15 45 77 130
5-Kurtzman's "Hey Look" (3); Georgie app. 17 51 88 150
6-8,10: 7,8-Georgie app. 10-Millie app. 14 42 72 120
9-Wolverton-a (1 pg.); Mille the Model app. 14 42 72 125
11,14-16,18-Kurtzman's "Hey Look" 15 45 77 130
12- "Giggles 'n' Grins" by Kurtzman 14 42 72 120
13,17,19,20: 17-Annie Oakley app. 10 30 55 80
21-27,29,30 9 27 49 70
28-Mr. Nexdoor-r (3 pgs.) by Kurtzman/Rusty #22 9 27 49 70
31-36: 36-Post-c 8 24 42 60
1('57)-Leading Mag. (Atlas)-Everett-a, 20 pgs 9 27 49 70

NELLIE THE NURSE
Dell Publishing Co.: No. 1304, Mar-May, 1962
Four Color 1304-Stanley-a 7 21 49 90

NEMESIS THE WARLOCK (Also see Spellbinders)
Eagle Comics: Sept, 1984 - No. 7, Mar, 1985 (limited series, Baxter paper)
1-7: 2000 A.D. reprints 2.25

NEMESIS THE WARLOCK
Quality Comics/Fleetway Quality #2 on: 1989 - No. 19, 1991 ($1.95, B&W)
1-19 2.25

NEON CYBER
Image Comics (Dreamwave Prod.): Jul, 1999 - No. 8, Jun, 2000 ($2.50)
1-8-Adrian Tsang-s 2.50

NEUTRO
Dell Publishing Co.: Jan, 1967
1-Jack Sparling-c/a (super hero); UFO-s 4 12 26 40

NEVADA (also see Zane Grey's Four Color 412, 996 & Zane Grey's Stories of the West #1)

NEVADA (Also see Vertigo Winter's Edge #1)
DC Comics (Vertigo): May, 1998 - No. 6, Oct, 1998 ($2.50, limited series)
1-6-Gerber-s/Winslade-c/a 2.50
TPB-(1999, $14.95) r/#1-6 & Vertigo Winter's Edge preview 15.00

NEVER AGAIN (War stories; becomes Soldier & Marine V2#9)
Charlton Comics: Aug, 1955 - No. 8, July, 1956 (No #2-7)
1 9 27 49 70
8-(Formerly Foxhole?) 5 15 25 35

NEVERMEN, THE (See Dark Horse Presents #148-150)
Dark Horse Comics: May, 2000 - No. 4, Aug, 2000 ($2.95)
1-4-Phil Amara-s/Guy Davis-a 3.00

NEW ADVENTURE COMICS (Formerly New Comics; becomes Adventure Comics #32 on; V1#12 indicia says NEW COMICS #12)
National Periodical Publications: V1#12, Jan, 1937 - No. 31, Oct, 1938
V1#12-Federal Men by Siegel & Shuster continues; Jor-L mentioned; Whitney Ellsworth-c begin, end #14 508 1523 3300 –
V2#1(2/37, #13)-(Rare) 477 1431 3100 –
V2#2 (#14) 415 1246 2700 –
15(V2#3)-20(V2#8): 15-1st Adventure logo; Creig Flessel-c begin, end #31. 16-1st non-funny cover. 17-Nadir, Master of Magic begins, ends #30 359 1077 1975 3050
21(V2#9),22(V2#10, 2/37): 22-X-Mas-c 329 987 1810 2800
23-31 276 828 1518 2350

NEW ADVENTURES OF ABRAHAM LINCOLN, THE
Image Comics (Homage): 1998 ($19.95, one-shot)
1-Scott McCloud-s/computer art 20.00

NEW ADVENTURES OF CHARLIE CHAN, THE (TV)

New Fun Comics #1 © DC

New Archies #22 © AP

New Adventure Comics #26 © DC

	GD2.0	FN6.0	VF8.0	NM9.4

	GD2.0	FN6.0	VF8.0	NM9.4

National Periodical Publications: May-June, 1958 - No. 6, Mar-Apr, 1959

1 (Scarce)-Gil Kane/Sid Greene-a in all	68	204	426	750
2 (Scarce)	45	135	270	475
3-6 (Scarce)-Greene/Giella-a	40	120	232	400

NEW ADVENTURES OF HUCK FINN, THE (TV)
Gold Key: December, 1968 (Hanna-Barbera)

1- "The Curse of Thut"; part photo-c	4	12	26	40

NEW ADVENTURES OF PINOCCHIO (TV)
Dell Publishing Co.: Oct-Dec, 1962 - No. 3, Sept-Nov, 1963

12-562-212(#1)	9	27	63	115
2,3	7	21	49	85

NEW ADVENTURES OF ROBIN HOOD (See Robin Hood)

NEW ADVENTURES OF SHERLOCK HOLMES (Also see Sherlock Holmes)
Dell Publishing Co.: No. 1169, Mar-May, 1961 - No. 1245, Nov-Jan, 1961/62

Four Color 1169(#1)	16	48	112	210
Four Color 1245	15	45	105	190

NEW ADVENTURES OF SPEED RACER
Now Comics: Dec, 1993 - No. 7, 1994? ($1.95)

1-7				2.25
0-(Premiere)-3-D cover				3.00

NEW ADVENTURES OF SUPERBOY, THE (Also see Superboy)
DC Comics: Jan, 1980 - No. 54, June, 1984

1				5.00
2-6,8-49,51-54: 11-Superboy gets new power. 14-Lex Luthor app. 15-Superboy gets new parents. 28-Dial "H" For Hero begins, ends #49.				
45-47-118 Superboy 75¢-c.				3.00
2,5,6,8 (Whitman variants; low print run; no issue # on cover)				6.00
7,50: 7-Has extra story "The Computers That Saved Metropolis" by Starlin (Radio Shack giveaway w/indicia). 50-Legion app.				4.00
NOTE: *Buckler* a-9p; c-36p. *Giffen* a-50; c-50. 40i. *Gil Kane* c-32p, 33p, 35, 39, 41-49. *Miller* c-51. *Starlin* a-7. *Krypto* back-ups in 17, 22. *Superbaby* in 11, 14, 19, 34.

NEW ADVENTURES OF THE PHANTOM BLOT, THE (See The Phantom Blot)

NEW AMERICA
Eclipse Comics: Nov, 1987 - No. 4, Feb, 1988 ($1.75, Baxter paper)

1-4: Scout limited series				2.25

NEW ARCHIES, THE (TV)
Archie Comic Publications: Oct, 1987 - No. 22, May, 1990 (75¢)

1				5.00
2-10: 3-Xmas issue				4.00
11-22: 17-22 (95¢-$1.00): 21-Xmas issue				3.00

NEW ARCHIES DIGEST (TV)(...Comics Digest Magazine #4?-10; ...Digest Magazine #11 on)
Archie Comics: May, 1988 - No. 14, July, 1991 ($1.35/$1.50, quarterly)

1				6.00
2-14: 6-Begin $1.50-c				3.50

NEW BOOK OF COMICS (Also see Big Book Of Fun)
National Periodical Publ.: 1937; No. 2, Spring, 1938 (100 pgs. each) (Reprints)

1(Rare)-1st regular size comic annual; 2nd DC annual; contains r/New Comics #1-4 & More Fun #9; r/Federal Men (8 pgs.), Henri Duval (1 pg.), & Dr. Occult in costume (1 pg.) by Siegel & Shuster; Moldoff, Sheldon Mayer (15 pgs.)-a	2000	6000	13,000	–
2-Contains-r/More Fun #15 & 16; r/Dr. Occult in costume (a Superman prototype), & Calling All Cars (1st)-a by Siegel & Shuster				
		1000	3000	6500	–

NEW COMICS (New Adventure #12 on)
National Periodical Publ.: 12/35 - No. 11, 12/36 (No. 1-6: paper cover) (No. 1-5: 84 pgs.)

V1#1-Billy the Kid, Sagebrush 'n' Cactus, Jibby Jones, Needles, The Vikings, Sir Loin of Beef, Now-When I Was a Boy, & other 1-2 pg. strips; 2 pgs. Kelly art(1st)(Gulliver's Travels); Sheldon Mayer-a(1st)(2 pgg. strips); Vincent Sullivan-c(1st)	2850	8550	18,500	–
2-1st app. Federal Men by Siegel & Shuster & begins (also see The Comics Magazine #2); Mayer, Kelly-a (Rare)(1/36)	1000	3000	6500	–

3-6: 3,4-Sheldon Mayer-a which continues in The Comics Magazine #1.
3-Vincent Sullivan-c. 4-Dickens' "A Tale of Two Cities" adaptation begins.
5-Junior Federal Men Club; Kiefer-a. 6- "She" adaptation begins

	575	1725	3800	–
7-11: 11-Christmas-c	475	1425	3100	–
NOTE: *#1-6 rarely occur in mint condition.* **Whitney Ellsworth** c-4-11.

NEW DEFENDERS (See Defenders)

NEW DNAGENTS, THE (Formerly DNAgents)
Eclipse Comics: V2#1, Oct, 1985 - V2#17, Mar, 1987 (Whole #s 25-40; Mando paper)

V2#1-17: 1-Origin recap. 7-Begin 95 cent-c. 9,10-Airboy preview				2.25
3-D 1 (1/86, $2.25)				2.25
2-D 1 (1/86)-Limited ed. (100 copies)				4.00

NEW ETERNALS: APOCALYPSE NOW (Also see Eternals, The)
Marvel Comics: Feb, 2000 (3.99, one-shot)

1-Bennett & Hanna-a; Ladronn-c				4.00

NEWFORCE (Also see Newmen)
Image Comics (Extreme Studios): Jan, 1996-No. 4, Apr, 1996 ($2.50, lim. series)

1-4: 1-"Extreme Destroyer" Pt. 8; polybagged w/gaming card. 4-Newforce disbands.				2.50

NEW FUN COMICS (More Fun #7 on; see Big Book of Fun Comics)
National Periodical Publications: Feb, 1935 - No. 6, Oct, 1935 (10x15", No. 1-4,: slick-c) (No. 1-5: 36 pgs; 40 pgs. No. 6)

V1#1 (1st DC comic); 1st app. Oswald The Rabbit; Jack Woods (cowboy) begins	6500	19,500	42,000	–
2(3/35)-(Very Rare)	2750	8250	18,000	–
3-5(8/35): 3-Don Drake on the Planet Soro-c/story (sci/fi, 4/35). 5-Soft-c	1400	4200	9,000	–
6(10/35)-1st Dr. Occult by Siegel & Shuster (Leger & Reuths); last "New Fun" title. "New Comics" #1 begins in Dec. which is reason for title change to More Fun; Henri Duval (ends #10) by Siegel & Shuster begins; paper-c	3100	9300	20,000	–

NEW FUNNIES (The Funnies #1-64; Walter Lantz...#109 on; New TV... #259, 260, 272, 273; TV Funnies #261-271)
Dell Publishing Co.: No. 65, July, 1942 - No. 288, Mar-Apr, 1962

65(#1)-Andy Panda in a world of real people, Raggedy Ann & Andy, Oswald the Rabbit (with Woody Woodpecker x-overs), Li'l Eight Ball & Peter Rabbit begin	69	207	483	900
66-70: 66-Felix the Cat begins. 67-Billy & Bonny Bee by Frank Thomas begins. 69-Kelly-a (2 pgs.); The Brownies begin (not by Kelly)	31	93	217	400
71-75: 72-Kelly illos. 75-Brownies by Kelly?	19	57	133	250
76-Andy Panda (Carl Barks & Pabian-a); Woody Woodpecker x-over in Oswald ends	92	275	644	1200
77,78: 77-Kelly-c. 78-Andy Panda in a world with real people ends	19	57	133	250
79-81	13	40	91	175
82-Brownies by Kelly begins; Homer Pigeon begins	14	42	98	185
83-85-Brownies by Kelly in ea. 83-X-mas-c; Homer Pigeon begins. 85-Woody Woodpecker, 1 pg. strip begins	14	42	98	185
86-90: 87-Woody Woodpecker stories begin	10	30	70	130
91-99	7	21	49	90
100 (6/45)	7	21	49	95
101-120: 119-X-Mas-c	5	15	35	65
121-150: 131,143-X-Mas-c	5	15	34	55
151-200: 155-X-Mas-c. 167-X-mas-c. 182-Origin & 1st app. Knothead & Splinter. 191-X-Mas-c	4	12	29	45
201-240	3	10	23	35
241-288: 270,271-Walter Lantz c-app. 281-1st story swipes/WDC&S #100	3	9	20	30

NOTE: *Early issues written by* **John Stanley**.

NEW GODS, THE (1st Series)(New Gods #12 on)(See Adventure #459, DC Graphic Novel #4, 1st Issue Special #13 & Super-Team Family)
National Periodical Publications/DC Comics: 2-3/71 - V2#11, 10-11/72; V3#12, 7/77 - V3#19, 7-8/78 (Fourth World)

1-Intro/1st app. Orion; 4th app. Darkseid (cameo; 3 weeks after Forever People

New Gods #8 © DC

New Gods (2nd series) #12 © DC

New Mutants #93 © MAR

	GD2.0	FN6.0	VF8.0	NM9.4

#1) (#1-3 are 15¢ issues)				
2-Darkseid-c/story (2nd full app., 4-5/71)	8	24	60	100
3-1st app. Black Racer; last 15¢ issue	4	12	30	50
4-9: (25¢, 52 pg. giants): 4-Darkseid cameo; origin Manhunter-r. 5,7,8-	3	10	23	35
Young Gods feature. 7-Darkseid app. (2-3/72); origin Orion; 1st origin of all				
New Gods as a group. 9-1st app. Forager	3	10	23	35
10,11: 11-Last Kirby issue	2	6	15	22
12-19: Darkseid storyline w/minor apps. 12-New costume Orion (see 1st Issue				
Special #13 for 1st new costume). 19-Story continued in Adventure Comics				
#459,460	1	3	6	8
Jack Kirby's New Gods TPB ('98, $11.95, B&W&Grey) r/#1-11 plus cover				
gallery of original series and '84 reprints				12.00

NOTE: #4-9(25¢, 52 pgs.) contain Manhunter-r from Adventure #73, 74, 75, 76, 77, 78 with covers in that order. Adkins i-12-14, 17-19. Buckler a(p)-15. Kirby c/a-1-11p. Newton a(p)-12-14, 16-19. Starlin c-17. Staton c-19p.

NEW GODS (Also see DC Graphic Novel #4)
DC Comics: June, 1984 - No. 6, Nov, 1984 ($2.00, Baxter paper)

1-5: New Kirby-c; r/New Gods #1-10.				
				4.00
6-Reprints New Gods #11 w/48 pgs of new Kirby story & art; leads into				
DC Graphic Novel #4	2	6	9	12

NEW GODS (2nd Series)
DC Comics: Feb, 1989 - No. 28, Aug, 1991 ($1.50)

1-28				2.50

NEW GODS (3rd Series) (Becomes Jack Kirby's Fourth World) (Also see Showcase '94 #1 & Showcase '95 #7)
DC Comics: Oct, 1995 - No. 15, Feb, 1997 ($1.95)

1-11,13-15: 9-Giffen-a(p). 10,11-Superman app. 13-Takion, Mr. Miracle & Big				
Barda app. 13-15-Byrne-a(p)/scripts & Simonson-c. 15-Apokolips merged				
w/ New Genesis; story cont'd in Jack Kirby's Fourth World				2.50
12-(11/96, 99¢)-Byrne-a(p)/scripts & Simonson-c begin; Takion cameo; indicia				
reads October 1996				2.50
...Secret Files 1 (9/98, $4.95) Origin-s				5.00

NEW GUARDIANS, THE
DC Comics: Sept, 1988 - No. 12, Sept, 1989 ($1.25)

1-($2.00, 52pgs)-Staton-c/a in #1-9				3.00
2-12				2.25

NEW HEROIC (See Heroic)

NEW JUSTICE MACHINE, THE (Also see The Justice Machine)
Innovation Publishing: 1989 - No. 3, 1989 ($1.95, limited series)

1-3				2.25

NEW KIDS ON THE BLOCK, THE (Also see Richie Rich and...)
Harvey Comics: Dec, 1990 -1991 ($1.25)

1-5				2.25
...Backstage Pass 1(12/90) - 5 Chillin' 1(12/90) - 5: 1-Photo-c...Comics Tour				
'90/91 1 (12/90) - 5 Hanging Tough 1 (2/91) - 3 Live 1 (2/91) - 3 Magic				
Summer Tour 1 (Fall/90, one-shot) Step By Step 1 (Fall/90, one-shot)				
Valentine Girl 1 (Fall/90, one-shot)-Photo-c				2.25

NEW LOVE (See Love & Rockets)
Fantagraphics Books: Aug, 1996 - No. 6, Dec, 1997 ($2.95, B&W, lim. series)

1-6: Gilbert Hernandez-s/a				3.00

NEWMAN
Image Comics (Extreme Studios): Jan, 1996 - No. 4, Apr, 1996 ($2.50, lim. series)

1-4: 1-Extreme Destroyer Pt. 3; polybagged w/card. 4-Shadowhunt tie-in;				
Eddie Collins becomes new Shadowhawk				2.50

NEWMEN (becomes The Adventures Of The...#22)
Image Comics (Extreme Studios): Apr, 1994 - No. 20, Nov, 1995; No. 21, Nov, 1996 ($1.95/$2.50)

1-21: 1-5: Matsuda-c/a. 1-Liefeld/Matsuda plot. 10-Polybagged w/trading card.				
11-Polybagged. 20-Has a variant-c; Babewatch! x-over. 21-(11/96)-Series				
relaunch; Chris Sprouse-a begins; pin-up. 16-Has a variant-c by Quesada &				
Palmiotti				2.50
TPB-(1996, $12.95) r/#1-4 w/pin-ups				13.00

NEW MEN OF BATTLE, THE
Catechetical Guild: 1949 (nn) (Carboard-c)

	GD2.0	FN6.0	VF8.0	NM9.4

nn(V8#1-3,5,6)-192 pgs.; contains 5 issues of Topix rebound				
	8	24	42	60
nn(V8#7-V8#11)-160 pgs.; contains 5 iss. of Topix	8	24	42	60

NEW MUTANTS, THE (See Marvel Graphic Novel #4 for 1st app.)(Also see X-Force & Uncanny X-Men #167)
Marvel Comics Group: Mar, 1983 - No. 100, Apr, 1991

1				5.00
2-10: 3,4-Ties into X-Men #167. 10-1st app. Magma				3.00
11-17,19,20: 13-Kitty Pryde app. 16-1st app. Warpath (w/out costume); see				
X-Men #193				2.50
18,21: 18-Intro. new Warlock. 21-Double size; origin new Warlock; newsstand				
version has cover price written in by Sienkiewicz				3.00
22-24,27-30: 23-25-Cloak & Dagger app.				2.50
25,26: 25-Legion app. (cameo). 26-1st full Legion app.				4.00
31-58: 35-Magneto intro'd as new headmaster. 43-Portacio-i. 50-Double size.				
58-Contains pull-out mutant registration form				2.50
59-61: Fall of The Mutants series. 60(52 pgs.)				3.00
62-85: 68-Intro Spyder. 63-X-Men & Wolverine clones app. 73-(52 pgs.). 76-X-				
Factor & X-Terminator app. 85-Liefeld-c begin				2.50
86-Rob Liefeld-a begins; McFarlane-c(i) swiped from Ditko splash pg.;				
Cable app (last page teaser)				6.00
87-1st full app. Cable (3/90)	2	6	13	20
87-2nd printing; gold metallic ink-c ($1.00)				2.50
88-2nd app. Cable	1	3	5	7
92-No Liefeld-a; Liefeld-c				4.00
89,90,91,93-100: 89-3rd app. Cable. 90-New costumes. 90,91-Sabretooth app.				
93,94-Cable vs. Wolverine. 95-97-X-Tinction Agenda x-over. 95-Death of new				
Warlock. 97-Wolverine & Cable-c, but no app. 98-1st app. Domino (2/91);2nd Shatterstar (cameo). 99-1st app. of Feral (of X-Force);				
Byrne-c/swipe (X-Men, 1st Series #138). 100-(52 pgs.)-1st app. X-Force				
(cameo)				5.00
95,100-Gold 2nd printing. 100-Silver ink 3rd printing				2.50
Annual 1 (1984)				4.00
Annual 2 (1986, $1.25)-1st Psylocke	1	3	6	8
Annual 3,4,6,7 ('87, '88,'90,'91, $2) 4-Evolutionary War x-over. 6-1st new				
costumes by Liefeld (3 pgs.); 1st app. (cameo) Shatterstar (of X-Force).				
7-Liefeld pin-up only; X-Terminators back-up story; 2nd app. X-Force (contin				
ued in New Warriors Annual #1)				3.00
Annual 5 (1989, $2.00, 68 pgs.)-Atlantis Attacks; 1st Liefeld-a on New Mutants				
				4.00
Special 1-Special Edition ('85, 68 pgs.)-Ties in w/X-Men Alpha Flight limited				
series; cont'd in X-Men Annual #9; Art Adams/Austin-a				5.00
Summer Special 1(Sum/90, $2.95, 84 pgs.)				3.00

NOTE: Art Adams c-38, 39. Austin c-57i. Byrne c/a-75p. Liefeld a-86-91p, 93-96p, 98-100i, Annual 5p, 6(3 pgs.); c-85-91p, 92, 93p, 94, 95, 96p, 97-100, Annual 5, 6p. McFarlane c-85-89i, 93i. Portacio a(i)-43. Russell a-48i. Sienkiewicz a-18-31, 35-38i; c-17-31, 35i, 37i, Annual 1. Simonson c-11p. B. Smith c-36, 40-48. Williamson a(i)-69, 71-73, 78-80, 82, 83; c(i)-69, 72, 73, 78i.

NEW MUTANTS, THE: TRUTH OR DEATH
Marvel Comics: Nov, 1997 - No. 3, Jan, 1998 ($2.50, limited series)

1-3-Raab-s/Chang-a(p)				2.50

NEW ORDER, THE
CFD Publishing: Nov, 1994 ($2.95)

1				3.00

NEW PEOPLE, THE (TV)
Dell Publishing Co.: Jan, 1970 - No. 2, May, 1970

1		3	9	17	25
2		2	6	13	20

NEW ROMANCES
Standard Comics: No. 5, May, 1951 - No. 21, May, 1954

5-Photo-c	12	36	61	105
6-9: 6-Barbara Bel Geddes, Richard Basehart "Fourteen Hours" photo-c.				
7-Ray Milland & Joan Fontaine photo-c. 9-Photo-c from '50s movie				
	7	21	38	55
10,14,16,17-Toth-a	8	24	45	65
11-Toth-a; Liz Taylor, Montgomery Clift photo-c	18	54	94	160
12,13,15,18-21	6	18	32	45

NOTE: Celardo a-9. Moreira a-6. Tuska a-7, 20. Photo c-5-16.

New Talent Showcase #13 © DC

New Teen Titans #12 © DC

New Warriors #25 © MAR

	GD2.0	FN6.0	VF8.0	NM9.4

NEW SHADOWHAWK, THE (Also see Shadowhawk & Shadowhunt)
Image Comics (Shadowline Ink): June, 1995 - No. 7, Mar, 1996 ($2.50)
1-7: Kurt Busiek scripts in all   3.00
NEW STATESMEN, THE
Fleetway Publications (Quality Comics): 1989 - No. 5, 1990 ($3.95, limited series, mature readers, 52pgs.)
1-5: Futuristic; squarebound; 3-Photo-c   4.00
NEWSTRALIA
Innovation Publ.: July, 1989 - No. 5, 1989 ($1.75, color)(#2 on, $2.25, B&W)
1-5: 1,2: Timothy Truman-c/a; Gustovich-i   2.25
NEW TALENT SHOWCASE (Talent Showcase #16 on)
DC Comics: Jan, 1984 - No. 19, Oct, 1985 (Direct sales only)
1-19: Features new strips & artists. 18-Williamson-c(i)   2.25
NEW TEEN TITANS, THE (See DC Comics Presents 26, Marvel and DC
Present & Teen Titans; Tales of the Teen Titans #41 on)
DC Comics: Nov, 1980 - No. 40, Mar, 1984
1-Robin, Kid Flash, Wonder Girl, The Changeling (1st app.), Starfire, The

Raven, Cyborg begin; partial origin	2	6	9	12
2-1st app. Deathstroke the Terminator	1	3	6	8

3-10: 3-Origin Starfire; Intro The Fearsome Five. 4-Origin continues; J.L.A. app.
6-Origin Raven. 7-Cyborg origin. 8-Origin Kid Flash retold. 9-Minor cameo
Deathstroke on last pg. 10-2nd app. Deathstroke the Terminator (see Marvel
& DC Present for 3rd app.); origin Changeling retold   6.00
11-40: 13-Return of Madame Rouge & Capt. Zahl; Robotman revived. 14-
Return of Mento; origin Doom Patrol. 15-Death of Madame Rouge & Capt.
Zahl; intro. new Brotherhood of Evil. 16-1st app. Captain Carrot (free 16 pg.
preview). 18-Return of Starfire. 19-Hawkman teams-up. 21-Intro Night Force
in free 16 pg. insert; intro Brother Blood. 23-1st app. Vigilante (not in cos
tume), & Blackfire. 24-Omega Men app. 25-Omega Men cameo; free 16 pg.
preview Masters of the Universe. 26-1st app. Terra. 27-Free 16 pg. preview
Atari Force. 29-The New Brotherhood of Evil & Speedy app. 30-Terra joins
the Titans. 37-Batman & The Outsiders x-over. 38-Origin Wonder Girl. 34-4th
app. Deathstroke the Terminator. 39-Last Dick Grayson as Robin; Kid Flash
quits   3.00
Annual 1(11/82)-Omega Men app.   4.00
Annual V2#2(9/83)-1st app. Vigilante in costume   3.50
Annual 3 (See Tales of the Teen Titans Annual #3)
NOTE: *Perez* a-1-4p, 6-34p, 37-40p, Annual 1p, 2p; c-1-12, 13-17p, 18-21, 22p, 23p, 24-37,
38, 39(painted), 40, Annual 1, 2.
NEW TEEN TITANS, THE (Becomes The New Titans on #50 on)
DC Comics: Aug, 1984 - No. 49, Nov, 1988 ($1.25/$1.75; deluxe format)
1-New storyline; Perez-c/a begins   5.00
2,3: Re-intro Lilith   4.00
4-10: 5-Death of Trigon. 7-9-Origin Lilith. 8-Intro Kole. 10-Kole joins
11-49: 13,14-Crisis x-over. 20-Robin (Jason Todd) joins; original Teen Titans
return. 38-Infinity, Inc. x-over. 47-Origin of all Titans; Titans (East & West)
pin-up by George Perez.   2.50
Annual 1-4 (9/85-'88): 1-Intro. Vanguard. 2-Byrne a(p); origin Brother Blood;
intro new Dr. Light. 3-Intro. Danny Chase. 4-Perez-c   3.00
NOTE: *Buckler* c-10. *Kelley Jones* a-47, Annual 4. *Erik Larsen* a-33. *Orlando* c-33p. *Perez* a-1-
5; c-1-7, 19, 23, 43. *Steacy* c-47.
NEW TERRYTOONS (TV)
Dell Publishing Co./Gold Key: 6-8/60 - No. 8, 3-5/62; 10/62 - No. 54, 1/79
1(1960-Dell)-Deputy Dawg, Dinky Duck & Hashimoto-San begin (1st app.

of each)	5	15	35	65
2-8(1962)	3	10	23	35
1(30010-210)(10/62-Gold Key, 84 pgs.)-Heckle & Jeckle begins				
	7	21	49	90
2(30010-301)-84 pgs.	6	18	42	80
3-5	3	9	20	30
6-10	3	9	17	24
11-20	2	6	12	18
21-30	2	6	9	12
31-43	1	3	6	8
44-54: Mighty Mouse-c/s in all	1	3	6	9

NOTE: *Reprints-#4-12, 38, 40, 47. (See March of Comics #379, 393, 412, 435)*
NEW TESTAMENT STORIES VISUALIZED

Standard Publishing Co.: 1946 - 1947
"New Testament Heroes–Acts of Apostles Visualized, Book I"
"New Testament Heroes–Acts of Apostles Visualized, Book II"

"Parables Jesus Told" Set....	16	48	83	140

NOTE: *All three are contained in a cardboard case, illustrated on front and info about the set.*
NEW TITANS, THE (Formerly The New Teen Titans)
DC Comics: No. 50, Dec, 1988 - No. 130, Feb, 1996 ($1.75/$2.25)
50-Perez-c/a begins; new origin Wonder Girl   5.00
51-59: 50-55-Painted-c. 55-Nightwing (Dick Grayson) forces Danny Chase to
resign; Batman app. in flashback, Wonder Girl becomes Troia   3.00
60,61: 60-A Lonely Place of Dying Part 2 continues from Batman #440; new
Robin tie-in; Timothy Drake app. 61-A Lonely Place of Dying Part 4   3.00
62-99,101-124,126-130: 62-65: Deathstroke the Terminator app. 65-Tim Drake
(Robin) app. 70-1st Deathstroke solo cover/sty. 71-(44 pgs.)-10th anniversary
issue; Deathstroke cameo. 72-79-Deathstroke in all: 74-Intro. Pantha.
79-Terra brought back to life; 1 panel cameo Team Titans (1st app.).
Deathstroke in #80-84,86. 80-2nd full app. Team Titans. 83,84-Deathstroke
kills his son, Jericho. 85-Team Titans app. 86-Deathstroke vs. Nightwing-
c/story; last Deathstroke app. 87-New costume Nightwing. 90-92-Parts 2,5,8
Total Chaos (Team Titans). 115-(11/94)   2.50
100-($3.50, 52 pgs.)-Holo-grafx foil-c   3.50
125 (3.50)-wraparound-c   3.50
#0-(10/94) Zero Hour, released between #114 & 115   2.50
Annual 5-10 ('89-'94, $3.50)-5-Armaggeddon 2001 x-over; 1st full app. Teen
(Team) Titans (new group). 8-Deathstroke app.; Eclipso app. (minor). 10-
Elseworlds story   3.50
Annual 11 (1995, $3.95)-Year One story   4.00
NOTE: *Perez a-50-55p, 57,60p, 58,59,61(layouts); c-50-61, 62-67i, Annual 5i; co-plots-66.*
NEW TV FUNNIES (See New Funnies)
NEW TWO-FISTED TALES, THE
Dark Horse Comics/Byron Preiss:1993 ($4.95, limited series, 52 pgs.)
1-Kurtzman-r & new-a   5.00
NOTE: *Eisner c-1i. Kurtzman c-1p, 2.*
NEW WARRIORS, THE (See Thor #411,412)
Marvel Comics: July, 1990 - No. 75, 1996 ($1.00/$1.25/$1.50)
1-Williamson-i; Bagley-c/a(p) in 1-13, Annual 1   5.00
1-Gold 2nd printing (7/91)   2.25
2-5: 3-Guice-c(i). 2-Williamson-c/a(i).   3.00
6-24,26-49,51-75: 7-Punisher cameo (last pg.). 8,9-Punisher app. 14-Darkhawk
& Namor x-over. 17-Fantastic Four & Silver Surfer x-over. 19-Gideon (of X-
Force) app. 28-Intro Turbo & Cardinal. 31-Cannonball & Warpath app. 42-
Nova vs. Firelord. 46-Photo-c. 47-Bound-in S-M trading card sheet. 52-12 pg.
ad insert. 62-Scarlet Spider-c/app. 70-Spider-Man-c/app. 72-Avengers-c/app.
                                                                                2.25
25-($2.50, 52 pgs.)-Die-cut cover   2.50
40,60: 40-($2.25)-Gold foil collector's edition   2.50
50-($2.95, 52 pgs.)-Glow in the dark-c   3.00
Annual 1-4('91-'94,68 pgs.)-1-Origins all members; 3rd app. X-Force (cont'd
from New Mutants Ann. #7 & cont'd in X-Men Ann. #15); x-over before
X-Force #1. 3-Bagged w/card   3.00
NEW WARRIORS, THE
Marvel Comics: Oct, 1999 - No. 10, July, 2000 ($2.99/$2.50)
0-Wizard supplement; short story and preview sketchbook   2.25
1-($2.99)   3.00
2-10: 2-Two covers. 5-Generation X app. 9-Iron Man-c   2.50
NEW WAVE, THE
Eclipse Comics: 6/10/86 - No. 13, 3/87 (#1-8: bi-weekly, 20pgs; #9-13: monthly)
1-13:1-Origin, concludes #5. 6-Origin Megabyte. 8,9-The Heap returns.
13-Snyder-c   2.25
Versus the Volunteers 3-D #1,2(4/87): 1-Snyder-c   2.50
NEW WORLD (See Comic Books, series I)
NEW WORLDS
Caliber: 1996 - No. 6 ($2.95/$3.95, 80 pgs., B&W, anthology)
1-6: 1-Mister X & other stories   4.00
NEW X-MEN (See X-Men 2nd series #114-on)

Nexus #24 © FC

Nickel Comics #4 © FAW

Nick Fury #5 © MAR

| | GD2.0 | FN6.0 | VF8.0 | NM9.4 | | | GD2.0 | FN6.0 | VF8.0 | NM9.4 |

NEW YORK GIANTS (See Thrilling True Story of the Baseball Giants)

NEW YORK STATE JOINT LEGISLATIVE COMMITTEE TO STUDY THE PUBLICATION OF COMICS, THE
N.Y. State Legislative Document: 1951, 1955

This document was referenced by Wertham for **Seduction of the Innocent.** Contains numerous repros from comics showing violence, sadism, torture, and sex.
1955 version (196p, No. 37, 2/23/55) - Sold for $180 in 1986.

NEW YORK, THE BIG CITY
Kitchen Sink Press: 1986 ($10.95, B&W)
DC Comics: July, 2000 ($12.95, B&W)

nn-Will Eisner-s/a   13.00

NEW YORK WORLD'S FAIR (Also see Big Book of Fun & New Book of Fun)
National Periodical Publ.: 1939, 1940 (100 pgs.; cardboard covers)
(DC's 4th & 5th annuals)

1939-Scoop Scanlon, Superman (blond haired Superman on-c), Sandman, Zatara, Slam Bradley, Ginger Snap by Bob Kane begin; 1st published app. The Sandman (see Adventure #40 for his 1st drawn story); Vincent Sullivan-c; cover background by Guardineer

         2100   6300   14,700   29,400

1940-Batman, Hourman, Johnny Thunderbolt, Red, White & Blue & Hanko (by Creig Flessel) app.; Superman, Batman & Robin-c (1st time they all appear together); early Robin app.; 1st Burnley-c/a (per Burnley)

         1128   3384   7895   15,800

NOTE: The 1939 edition was published 4/29/39 and released 4/30/39, the day the fair opened, at 25¢, and was first sold only at the fair. Since all other comics were 10¢, it didn't sell. Remaining copies were advertised beginning in the August issues of most DC comics for 25¢, but soon the price was dropped to 15¢. Everyone that sent a quarter through the mail for it received a free Superman #1 or a #2 to make up the dime difference. 15¢ stickers were placed over the 25¢ price. Four variations of the 15¢ stickers are known. The 1940 edition was published 5/11/40 and was priced at 15¢. It was a precursor to World's Best #1.

NEW YORK: YEAR ZERO
Eclipse Comics: July, 1988 - No. 4, Oct, 1988 ($2.00, B&W, limited series)

1-4   2.25

NEXT MAN
Comico: Mar, 1985 - No. 5, Oct, 1985 ($1.50, color, Baxter paper)

1-5   2.25

NEXT MEN (See John Byrne's...)

NEXT NEXUS, THE
First Comics: Jan, 1989 - No. 4, April, 1989 ($1.95, limited series, Baxter paper)

1-4: Mike Baron scripts & Steve Rude-c/a.   2.25
TPB (10/89, $9.95) r/series   10.00

NEXUS (See First Comics Graphic Novel #4, 19 & The Next Nexus)
Capital Comics/First Comics No. 7 on: June, 1981 - No. 6, Mar, 1984; No. 7, Apr, 1985 - No. 80?, May, 1991
(Direct sales only, 36 pgs.; V2#1(`83)-printed on Baxter paper)

1-B&W version; mag. size; w/double size poster   2   6   13   20
1-B&W 1981 limited edition; 500 copies printed and signed; same as above except this version has a 2-pg. poster & a pencil sketch on paperboard by Rude   3   9   19   28
2-B&W, magazine size   2   6   11   16
3-B&W, magazine size; contains 33-1/3 rpm record ($2.95 price)
         1   4   7   10
V2#1-Color version   4.00
2-49,51-80: 2-Nexus' origin begins. 67-Snyder-c/a.   2.25
50-($3.50, 52 pgs.)   3.50
NOTE: Bissette c-V2#29. Giffen c/a-V2#23. Gulacy c-1 (B&W), 2(B&W). Mignola c/a-V2#28. Rude c-3(B&W), V2#1-22, 24-27, 33-36, 39-42, 45-48, 50, 58-60, 75; a-1-3, V2#1-7, 8-16p, 18-22p, 24-27p, 33-36p, 39-42p, 45-48p, 50, 58, 59p, 60. Paul Smith a-V2#37, 38, 43, 44, 51-55p; c-V2#37, 38, 43, 48, 51-55.

NEXUS: ALIEN JUSTICE
Dark Horse Comics: Dec, 1992 - No. 3, Feb, 1993 ($3.95, limited series)

1-3: Mike Baron scripts & Steve Rude-c/a   4.00

NEXUS: EXECUTIONER'S SONG
Dark Horse Comics: June, 1996 - No. 4, Sept, 1996 ($2.95, limited series)

1-4: Mike Baron scripts & Steve Rude-c/a   3.00

NEXUS FILES

First Comics: 1989 ($4.50, color/16pgs. B&W, one-shot, squarebound, 52pgs.)
1-New Rude-a; info on Nexus   4.50

NEXUS: GOD CON
Dark Horse Comics: Apr, 1997 - No. 2, May, 1997 ($2.95, limited series)

1,2-Baron-s/Rude-c/a   3.00

NEXUS LEGENDS
First Comics: May, 1989 - No. 23, Mar, 1991 ($1.50, Baxter paper)\

1-23: R/1-3(Capital) & early First Comics issues w/new Rude covers
#1-6,9,10   2.25

NEXUS MEETS MADMAN (...Special)
Dark Horse Comics: May, 1996 ($2.95, one-shot)

nn-Mike Baron & Mike Allred scripts, Steve Rude-c/a.   3.00

NEXUS: NIGHTMARE IN BLUE
Dark Horse Comics: July, 1997 - No. 4, Oct, 1997 ($2.95, limited series)

1-4: 1,2,4-Adam Hughes-c   3.00

NEXUS: THE LIBERATOR
Dark Horse Comics: Aug, 1992 - No. 4, Nov, 1992 ($2.95, limited series)

1-4   3.00

NEXUS: THE ORIGIN
Dark Horse Comics: July, 1996 ($3.95, one-shot)

nn-Mike Baron- scripts, Steve Rude-c/a.   4.00

NEXUS: THE WAGES OF SIN
Dark Horse Comics: Mar, 1995 - No. 4, June, 1995 ($2.95, limited series)

1-4   3.00

NICKEL COMICS
Dell Publishing Co.: 1938 (Pocket size - 7-1/2x5-1/2")(132 pgs.)

1- "Bobby & Chip" by Otto Messmer, Felix the Cat artist. Contains some
English reprints   68   205   426   750

NICKEL COMICS
Fawcett Publications: May, 1940 - No. 8, Aug, 1940 (36 pgs.; Bi-Weekly; 5¢)

1-Origin/1st app. Bulletman   400   1200   2500   4800
2   127   381   795   1400
3   95   285   597   1050
4-The Red Gaucho begins   80   240   500   875
5-7   75   225   469   825
8-World's Fair-c; Bulletman moved to Master Comics #7 in October (scarce)
         86   258   540   950
NOTE: Beck c-5-8. Jack Binder c-1-4. Bondage c-5. Bulletman c-1-8.

NICK FURY, AGENT OF SHIELD (See Fury, Marvel Spotlight #31 & Shield)
Marvel Comics Group: 6/68 - No. 15, 11/69; No. 16, 11/70 - No. 18, 3/71

1   12   36   84   140
2-4: 4-Origin retold   5   15   38   60
5-Classic-c   6   18   40   65
6,7: 7-Salvador Dali painting swipe   4   12   26   40
8-11,13: 9-Hate Monger begins, ends #11. 10-Smith layouts/pencil. 11-Smith-c.
13-1st app. Super-Patriot; last 12¢ issue   3   9   17   24
12-Smith-c/a   3   9   19   28
14-Begin 15¢ issues   2   6   15   22
15-1st app. & death of Bullseye-c/story(11/69); Nick Fury shot & killed;
last 15¢ issue   6   18   40   65
16-18-(25¢, 52 pgs.)-r/Str. Tales #135-143   2   6   13   20
TPB (May 2000, $19.95) r/ Strange Tales #150-168   20.00
...: Who is Scorpio? TPB (11/00, $12.95) r/#1-3,5; Steranko-c   13.00
NOTE: Adkins a-3i. Craig a-10i. Sid Greene a-12i. Kirby a-16-18r. Springer a-4, 6, 7, 8p, 9, 10p, 11; c-8, 9. Steranko a(p)-1-3, 5; c-1-7.

NICK FURY AGENT OF SHIELD (Also see Strange Tales #135)
Marvel Comics: Dec, 1983 - No. 2, Jan, 1984 (2.00, 52 pgs., Baxter paper)

1,2-r/Nick Fury #1-4; new Steranko-c   3.50

NICK FURY, AGENT OF S.H.I.E.L.D.
Marvel Comics: Sept, 1989 - No. 47, May, 1993 ($1.50/$1.75)

V2#1-26,30-47: 10-Capt. America app. 13-Return of The Yellow Claw.
15-Fantastic Four app. 30,31-Deathlok app. 36-Cage app. 37-Woodgod
c/story. 38-41-Flashes back to pre-Shield days after WWII. 44-Capt. America-

Nightcrawler V2 #1 © MAR

Nightfall: The Black Chronicles #1
© Ford Lytle Gilmore

Nightmare #1 © MAR

	GD2.0	FN6.0	VF8.0	NM9.4

	GD2.0	FN6.0	VF8.0	NM9.4

c/s. 45-Viper-c/s. 46-Gideon x-over — 2.25
27-29-Wolverine-c/stories — 2.50
NOTE: *Alan Grant* scripts-11. *Guice* a(p)-20-23, 25, 26; c-20-28.

NICK FURY VS. S.H.I.E.L.D.
Marvel Comics: June, 1988 - No. 6, Nov, 1988 ($3.50, 52 pgs, deluxe format)

1,2: 1-Steranko-c. 2-(Low print run) Sienkiewicz-c — 5.00
3-6 — 4.00

NICK HALIDAY (Thrill of the Sea)
Argo: May, 1956

1-Daily & Sunday strip-r by Petree — 8 — 24 — 45 — 65

NIGHT AND THE ENEMY (Graphic Novel)
Comico: 1988 (8-1/2x11") ($11.95, color, 80 pgs.)

1-Harlan Ellison scripts/Ken Steacy-c/a; r/Epic Illustrated & new-a
(1st and 2nd printings) — 12.00
1-Limited edition ($39.95) — 40.00

NIGHT BEFORE CHRISTMAS, THE (See March of Comics No. 152)

NIGHT BEFORE CHRISTMASK, THE
Dark Horse Comics: Nov, 1994 ($9.95, one-shot)

nn-Hardcover book; The Mask; Rick Geary-c/a — 10.00

NIGHTBREED (See Clive Barker's Nightbreed)

NIGHTCRAWLER
Marvel Comics Group: Nov, 1985 - No. 4, Feb, 1986 (Mini-series from X-Men)

1-4: 1-Cockrum-c/a — 3.50

NIGHTCRAWLER (Volume 2)
Marvel Comics: Feb, 2002 - No. 4 ($2.50, limited series)

1,2-Matt Smith-a — 2.50

NIGHTFALL: THE BLACK CHRONICLES
DC Comics (Homage): Dec, 1999 - No. 3, Feb, 2000 ($2.95, limited series)

1-3-Coker-a/Gilmore-s — 3.00

NIGHT FORCE, THE (See New Teen Titans #21)
DC Comics: Aug, 1982 - No. 14, Sept, 1983 (60¢)

1 — 4.00
2-14: 13-Origin Baron Winter. 14-Nudity panels — 3.00
NOTE: *Colan* c/a-1-14p. *Giordano* c-1i, 2i, 4i, 5i, 7i, 12i.

NIGHT FORCE
DC Comics: Dec, 1996 - No. 12, Nov, 1997 ($2.25)

1-12: 1-3-Wolfman-s/Anderson-a(p). 8-"Convergence" part 2 — 2.25

NIGHT GLIDER
Topps Comics (Kirbyverse): April, 1993 ($2.95, one-shot)

1-Kirby c-1, Heck-a; polybagged w/Kirbychrome trading card — 3.00

NIGHTHAWK
Marvel Comics: Sept, 1998 - No. 3, Nov, 1998 ($2.99, mini-series)

1-3-Krueger-s; Daredevil app. — 3.00

NIGHTINGALE, THE
Henry H. Stansbury Once-Upon-A-Time Press, Inc.: 1948 (10¢, 7-1/4x10-1/4", 14 pgs., 1/2 B&W)

(Very Rare)-Low distribution; distributed to Westchester County & Bronx, N.Y. only; used in *Seduction of the Innocent*, pg. 312,313 as the 1st and only "good" comic book ever published. Ill. by Dong Kingman; 1,500 words of text, printed on high quality paper & no word balloons. Copyright registered 10/22/48, distributed week of 12/5/48. (By Hans Christian Andersen)
Estimated value........ — $200

NIGHT MAN, THE (See Sludge #1)
Malibu Comics (Ultraverse): Oct, 1993 - No. 23, Aug, 1995 ($1.95/$2.50)

1-($2.50, 48 pgs.)-Rune flip-c/story by B. Smith (3 pgs.) — 2.50
1-Ultra-Limited silver foil-c — 6.00
2-15, 17: 3-Break-Thru x-over; Freex app. 4-Origin Firearm (2 pgs.) by Chaykin. 8-1st app. Teknight — 2.50
16 ($3.50)-flip book (Ultraverse Premiere #11) — 3.50
...The Pilgrim Conundrum Saga (1/95, $3.95, 68 pgs.)-Strangers app. — 4.00
18-23: 22-Loki-c/a — 2.50
Infinity ($1.50) — 2.50
...Vs. Wolverine #0-Kelley Jones-c; mail in offer — 1 — 4 — 7 — 10

NOTE: *Zeck* a-16.

NIGHT MAN, THE
Malibu Comics (Ultraverse): Sept, 1995 - No.4, Dec, 1995 ($1.50, lim. series)

1-4: Post Black September storyline — 2.50

NIGHT MAN, THE /GAMBIT
Malibu Comics (Ultraverse): Mar, 1996 - No. 3, May, 1996 ($1.95, lim. series)

0-Limited Premium Edition — 4.00
1-3: David Quinn scripts in all. 3-Rhiannon discovered to be The Night Man's
mother — 2.50

NIGHTMARE
Ziff-Davis (Approved Comics)/St. John No. 3: Summer, 1952 - No. 3, Winter, 1952, 53 (Painted-c)

1-1 pg. Kinstler-a; Tuska-a(2) — 55 — 165 — 341 — 600
2-Kinstler-a/Poe's "Pit & the Pendulum" — 40 — 120 — 232 — 400
3-Kinstler-a — 35 — 105 — 185 — 320

NIGHTMARE (Weird Horrors #1-9) (Amazing Ghost Stories #14 on)
St. John Publishing Co.: No. 10, Dec, 1953 - No. 13, Aug, 1954

10-Reprints Ziff-Davis Weird Thrillers #2 w/new Kubert-c plus 2 pgs.
Kinstler-a; Anderson, Colan & Toth-a — 55 — 165 — 330 — 575
11-Krigstein-a; painted-c; Poe adapt., "Hop Frog" — 40 — 120 — 232 — 400
12-Kubert bondage-c; adaptation of Poe's "The Black Cat"; Cannibalism story — 39 — 117 — 208 — 360
13-Reprints Z-D Weird Thrillers #3 with new cover; Powell-a(2), Tuska-a;
Baker-c — 29 — 87 — 153 — 265

NIGHTMARE (Magazine)
Skywald Publishing Corp.: Dec, 1970 - No. 23, Feb, 1975 (B&W, 68 pgs.)

1-Everett-a — 6 — 18 — 42 — 70
2-6,8,9: 4-Decapitation story. 6-Kaluta-a; Jeff Jones photo & interview. 8-
Features E. C. movie "Tales From the Crypt"; reprints some E.C. comics
panels. 9-Wrightson-a — 3 — 10 — 23 — 35
7,10 — 3 — 9 — 19 — 28
11-19: 12-Excessive gore, severed heads — 3 — 9 — 17 — 24
20-Byrne's 1st artwork (8/74); severed head-c — 4 — 12 — 25 — 38
21-23: 21-(1974 Summer Special)-Kaluta-a. 22-Tomb of Horror issue. 23-(1975
Winter Special) — 3 — 9 — 20 — 30
Annual 1(1972)-B. Jones-a — 3 — 9 — 21 — 32
Winter Special 1(1973) — 3 — 9 — 17 — 25
Yearbook nn(1974)-B. Jones, Reese, Wildey-a — 3 — 9 — 17 — 25
NOTE: *Adkins* a-5. *Boris* c-2, 3, 5 (#4 is not by Boris). *Buckler* a-3, 15. *Byrne* a-20p. *Everett* a-4, 5, 12. *Jeff Jones* a-6, 21r(Psycho #6); c-6. *Katz* a-5. *Reese* a-4, 5. *Wildey* a-4, 5, 6, 21, '74 Yearbook.

NIGHTMARE (Alex Nino's)
Innovation Publishing: 1989 ($1.95)

1-Alex Nino-a — 2.25

NIGHTMARE
Marvel Comics: Dec, 1994 - No. 4, Mar, 1995 ($1.95, limited series)

1-4 — 2.25

NIGHTMARE & CASPER (See Harvey Hits #71) (Casper & Nightmare #6 on)
(See Casper The Friendly Ghost #19)
Harvey Publications: Aug, 1963 - No. 5, Aug, 1964 (25¢)

1-All reprints? — 7 — 21 — 50 — 80
2-5: All reprints? — 4 — 12 — 29 — 45

NIGHTMARE ON ELM STREET, A (See Freddy Krueger's...)

NIGHTMARES (See Do You Believe in Nightmares)

NIGHTMARES
Eclipse Comics: May, 1985 - No. 2, May, 1985 ($1.75, Baxter paper)

1,2 — 3.00

NIGHTMARE THEATER
Chaos! Comics: Nov, 1997 - No. 4, Nov, 1997 ($2.50, mini-series)

1-4-Horror stories by various; Wrightson-a — 2.50

NIGHTMARK: BLOOD & HONOR
Alpha Productions: 1994 - No. 3, 1994 ($2.50, B&W, mini-series)

1,2 — 2.50

Night Nurse #2 © MAR

Nightside #1 © MAR

Nightwing #47 © DC

NIGHTMARK MYSTERY SPECIAL
Alpha Productions: Jan, 1994 ($2.50, B&W)

1	2.50

NIGHTMASK
Marvel Comics Group: Nov, 1986 - No. 12, Oct, 1987

1-12	2.25

NIGHT MASTER
Silverwolf: Feb, 1987 ($1.50, B&W)

1-Tim Vigil-c/a	3.00

NIGHT MUSIC (See Eclipse Graphic Album Series, The Magic Flute)
Eclipse Comics: Dec, 1984 - No. 11, 1990 ($1.75/$3.95/$4.95, Baxter paper)

1-7: 3-Russell's Jungle Book adapt. 4,5-Pelleas And Melisande (double titled)	
6-Salomé (double titled). 7-Red Dog #1	2.25
8-($3.95) Ariane and Bluebeard	4.00
9-11-($4.95) The Magic Flute; Russell adapt.	5.00

NIGHT NURSE
Marvel Comics Group: Nov, 1972 - No. 4, May, 1973

1	10	30	73	125
2-4	7	21	53	85

NIGHT OF MYSTERY
Avon Periodicals: 1953 (no month) (one-shot)

nn-1 pg. Kinstler-a, Hollingsworth-c	43	129	257	450

NIGHT OF THE GRIZZLY, THE (See Movie Classics)

NIGHTRAVEN (See Marvel Graphic Novel)

NIGHT RIDER (Western)
Marvel Comics Group: Oct, 1974 - No. 6, Aug, 1975

1: 1-6 reprint Ghost Rider #1-6 (#1-origin)	2	6	11	15
2-6	1	4	7	10

NIGHT'S CHILDREN: THE VAMPIRE
Millenium: July, 1995 - No. 2, Aug, 1995 ($2.95, B&W)

1,2: Wendy Snow-Lang story & art	3.00

NIGHTSHADE
No Mercy Comics: Aug, 1997 ($2.50)

1-Mark Williams-s/a	2.50

NIGHTSIDE
Marvel Comics: Dec, 2001 - No. 4 ($2.99)

1-3: 1-Weinberg-s/Derenick-a; intro Sydney Taine	3.00

NIGHTS INTO DREAMS (Based on video game)
Archie Comics: Feb, 1998 - No. 6, Oct, 1998 ($1.75, limited series)

1-6	2.25

NIGHTSTALKERS (Also see Midnight Sons Unlimited)
Marvel Comics (Midnight Sons #14 on): Nov, 1992 - No. 18, Apr, 1994 ($1.75)

1-($2.75, 52 pgs.)-Polybagged w/poster; part 5 of Rise of the Midnight Sons	
storyline; Garney/Palmer-c/a begins; Hannibal King, Blade & Frank Drake	
begin (see Tomb of Dracula for & Dr. Strange)	3.00
2-9,11-18: 5-Punisher app. 7-Ghost Rider app. 8,9-Morbius app. 14-Spot	
varnish-c. 14,15-Siege of Darkness Pts 1 & 9	2.25
10-($2.25)-Outer-c is a Darkhold envelope made of black parchment w/gold	
ink; Midnight Massacre part 1	2.50

NIGHT TERRORS, THE
Chanting Monks Studios: 2000 ($2.75, B&W)

1-Bernie Wrightson-c; short stories, one by Wrightson-s/a	2.75

NIGHT THRASHER (Also see The New Warriors)
Marvel Comics: Aug, 1993 - No. 21, Apr, 1995 ($1.75/$1.95)

1-($2.95, 52 pgs.)-Red holo-grafx foil-c; prelude	3.00
2-21: 2-Intro Tantrum. 3-Gideon (of X-Force) app. 10-Bound-in trading card	
sheet; Iron Man app. 15-Hulk app.	2.25

NIGHT THRASHER: FOUR CONTROL
Marvel Comics: Oct, 1992 - No. 4, Jan, 1993 ($2.00, limited series)

1-4: 2-Intro Tantrum. 3-Gideon (of X-Force) app.	2.25

NIGHT TRIBES
DC Comics (WildStorm): July, 1999 ($4.95, one-shot)

1-Golden & Sniegoski-s/Chin-a	5.00

NIGHTVEIL (Also see Femforce)
Americomics/AC Comics: Nov, 1984 - No. 7, 1987 ($1.75)

1-7	2.25
...'s Cauldron Of Horror 1 (1989, B&W)-Kubert, Powell, Wood-r plus new	
Nightveil story	3.00
...'s Cauldron Of Horror 2 (1990, $2.95, B&W, 44pgs)-Pre-code horror-r by	
Kubert & Powell	3.00
...'s Cauldron Of Horror 3 (1991)	3.00
Special 1 ('88, $1.95)-Kaluta-c	2.25
One Shot ('96, $5.95)-Flip book w/ Colt	6.00

NIGHTWATCH
Marvel Comics: Apr, 1994 - No. 12, Mar, 1995 ($1.50)

1-($2.95)-Collectors edition; foil-c; Ron Lim-c/a begins; Spider-Man app.	3.00
1-12-Regular edition. 2-Bound-in S-M trading card sheet; 5,6-Venom-c & app.	
7,11-Cardiac app.	2.25

NIGHTWING (Also see New Teen Titans, New Titans, Showcase '93 #11,12,
Tales of the New Teen Titans & Teen Titans Spotlight)
DC Comics: Sept, 1995 - No. 4, Dec, 1995 ($2.25, limited series)

1-Dennis O'Neil story/Greg Land-a in all	5.00
2-4	4.00
...: Alfred's Return (7/95, $3.50) Giordano-a	4.00
...Ties That Bind (1997, $12.95, TPB) r/mini-series & Alfred's Return	13.00

NIGHTWING
DC Comics: Oct, 1996 - Present ($1.95/$1.99/$2.25)

1-Chuck Dixon scripts & Scott McDaniel-c/a	1	4	7	10
2,3				5.00
4-10: 6-Robin-c/app.				4.00
11-20: 13-15-Batman app. 19,20-Cataclysm pts. 2,11				3.00
21-49,51-65: 23-Green Arrow app. 26-29-Huntress-c/app. 30-Superman-c/app.				
35-39-No Man's Land. 41-Land/Geraci-a begins. 46-Begin $2.25-c.				
47-Texiera-c. 52-Catwoman-c/app. 54-Shrike app.				2.25
50-($3.50) Nightwing battles Torque				3.50
#1,000,000 (11/98) teams with future Batman				2.25
Annual 1(1997, $3.95) Pulp Heroes				4.00
...Eighty Page Giant 1 (12/00, $5.95) Intro. of Hella; Dixon-s/Haley-c				6.00
...: A Darker Shade of Justice (2001, $19.95, TPB) r/#30-39,Secret Files #1				20.00
...: A Knight in Blüdhaven (1998, $14.95, TPB) r/#1-8				15.00
...: Love and Bullets (2000, $17.95, TPB) r/#1/2, 19,21,22,24-29				18.00
...: Our Worlds at War (9/01, $2.95) Jae Lee-c				3.00
...: Rough Justice (1999, $17.95, TPB) r/#9-18				18.00
Secret Files 1 (10/99, $4.95) Origin-s and pin-ups				5.00
...: The Target (2001, $5.95) McDaniel-c/a				6.00
Wizard 1/2 (Mail offer)				5.00

NIGHTWING (See Tangent Comics/ Nightwing)

NIGHTWING AND HUNTRESS
DC Comics: May, 1998 - No. 4, Aug, 1998 ($1.95, limited series)

1-4-Grayson-s/Land & Sienkiewicz-a	2.50

NIGHTWINGS (See DC Science Fiction Graphic Novel)

NIKKI, WILD DOG OF THE NORTH (Disney, see Movie Comics)
Dell Publishing Co.: No. 1226, Sept, 1961

Four Color 1226-Movie, photo-c	5	15	35	60

NINE RINGS OF WU-TANG
Image Comics: July, 1999 - No. 5, July, 2000 ($2.95)

Preview (7/99, $5.00, B&W)	5.00
1-5: 1-(11/99, $2.95) Clayton Henry-a	3.00
Tower Records Variant-c	5.00
Wizard #0 Prelude	2.25
TPB (1/01, $19.95) r/#1-5, Preview & Prelude; sketchbook & cover gallery	20.00

1963
Image Comics (Shadowline Ink): Apr, 1993 - No. 6, Oct, 1993 ($1.95, lim. series)

1-6: Alan Moore scripts; Veitch, Bissette & Gibbons-a(p)	2.25

Ninja Boy #1 © Alé Garza

Noble Causes: First Impressions #1 © IM

No Honor #1 © TCOW

	GD2.0	FN6.0	VF8.0	NM9.4

	GD2.0	FN6.0	VF8.0	NM9.4

1-Gold   3.00
NOTE: Bissette a-2-4; Gibbons a-1i, 2i, 6i; c-2.

1984 (Magazine) (1994 #11 on)
Warren Publishing Co.: June, 1978 - No. 10, Jan, 1980 ($1.50, B&W with color
inserts, mature content with nudity; 84 pgs. except #4 has 92 pgs.)

1-Nino-a in all; Mutant World begins by Corben	2	6	13	20
2-10: 4-Rex Havoc begins. 7-1st Ghita of Alizarr by Thorne. 9-1st Starfire				
	2	6	9	12

NOTE: Alcala a-1-3,5,7i. Corben a-1-8; c-1,2. Nebres a-1-8,10. Thorne a-7,8,10i. Wood a-1,2,5i.

1994 (Formerly 1984) (Magazine)
Warren Publishing Co.: No. 11, Feb, 1980 - No. 29, Feb, 1983 (B&W with color;
mature; #11-(84 pgs.); #12-16,18-21,24-(76 pgs.); #17,22,23,25-29-(68 pgs.)

11,17,18,20,22,23,29: 11; 17-8 pgs. color insert. 18-Giger-a. 20-1st Diana				
Jacklighter Manhuntress by Maroto. 22-1st Sigmund Pavlov by Nino; 1st Ariel				
Hart by Hsu. 23-All Nino issue	2	6	9	12
12-16,19,21,24-28: 21-1st app. Angel by Nebres. 27-The Warhawks return				
	1	3	6	8

NOTE: Corben c-26. Maroto a-20, 21, 24-28. Nebres a-11-13, 15, 16, 18, 21, 22, 25, 28. Nino a-11-19, 20(2), 21, 25, 26, 28; c-21. Redondo c-20. Thorne a-11-14, 17-21, 24-26, 28, 29.

NINE VOLT
Image Comics (Top Cow Productions): July, 1997 - No. 4, Oct, 1997 ($2.50)

1-4   2.50

NINJA BOY
DC Comics (WildStorm): Oct, 2001 - Present ($3.50/$2.95)

1-($3.50) Ale Garza-a/c   3.50
2-5-($2.95)   3.00

NINJA HIGH SCHOOL (1st series)
Antarctic Comics: 1986 - No. 4, 1987 (B&W)

1-Ben Dunn-s/c/a; early Manga series	2	6	11	15
2,3	1	4	7	10

NINJAK (See Bloodshot #6, 7 & Deathmate)
Valiant/Acclaim Comics (Valiant) No. 16 on: Feb, 1994 - No. 26, Nov. 1995
($2.25/$2.50)

1 ($3.50)-Chromium-c; Quesada-c/a(p) in #1-3				3.50
1-Gold				5.00
2-13: 3-Batman, Spawn & Random (from X-Force) app. as costumes at party				
(cameo). 4-w/bound-in trading card. 5,6-X-O app.				2.50
0,00,14-26: 14-(4/95)-Begin $2.50-c. 0-(6/95, $2.50). 00-(6/95, $2.50)				2.50
Yearbook 1 (1994, $3.95)				4.00

NINJAK
Acclaim Comics (Valiant Heroes): V2#1, Mar, 1997 -No. 12, Feb, 1998 ($2.50)

V2#1-12: 1-Intro new Ninjak; Kurt Busiek scripts begin;
painted variant-c exists. 2-1st app. Karnivor & Zeer. 3-1st app. Gigantik,
Shurikai, & Nixie. 4-Origin; 1st app. Yasuiti Motomiya; intro The Dark Dozen;
Colin King (Ninjak) cameo. 9-Copycat-c   2.50

NINTENDO COMICS SYSTEM (Also see Adv. of Super Mario Brothers)
Valiant Comics: Feb, 1990 - No. 9, Oct, 1991 ($4.95, card stock-c, 68pgs.)

1-9: 1-Featuring Game Boy, Super Mario, Clappwall. 3-Layton-c. 5-8-Super
Mario Bros. 9-Dr. Mario 1st app.   5.00

N.I.O.
Acclaim Comics: Nov, 1998 - No. 4, Feb, 1999 ($2.50, limited series)

1-4-Bury-s   2.50

NOAH'S ARK
Spire Christian Comics/Fleming H. Revell Co.: 1973 (35/49¢)

nn-By Al Hartley	1	3	5	7

NOBLE CAUSES
Image Press: Sept, 2001 - Present ($2.95)

...First Impressions (7/01) Intro. the Noble family; Faerber-s   3.00

NOBODY (Amado, Cho & Adlard's...)
Oni Press: Nov, 1998 - No. 4, Feb, 1999 ($2.95, B&W, mini-series)

1-4   3.00

NOCTURNALS, THE
Malibu Comics (Bravura): Jan, 1995 - No. 6, Aug, 1995 ($2.95, limited series)

1-6: Dan Brereton painted-c/a & scripts   3.00
1-Glow-in-the-Dark premium edition   5.00
Black Planet TPB ('98, $19.95, Oni Press) r/#1-6   20.00

NOCTURNALS: THE DARK FOREVER
Oni Press: Jul, 2001 -No. 3 ($2.95, limited series)

1,2-Brereton-s/painted-a/c   3.00

NOCTURNALS: TROLL BRIDGE
Oni Press: Oct, 2000 ($4.95, B&W & orange, one-shot)

nn-Brereton-s/painted-c; art by Brereton, Chin, Art Adams, Sakai, Timm, Warren,
Thompson, Purcell, Stephens and others   5.00

NOCTURNALS: WITCHING HOUR
Dark Horse Comics: May 1998 ($4.95, one-shot)

1-Brereton-s/painted-a; reprints DHP stories + 8 new pgs.   5.00

NOCTURNE
Marvel Comics: June, 1995 - No. 4, Sept. 1995 ($1.50, limited series)

1-4   2.25

NO ESCAPE (Movie)
Marvel Comics: June, 1994 - No. 3, Aug, 1994 ($1.50)

1-3: Based on movie   2.25

NO HONOR
Image Comics (Top Cow): Feb, 2001 - No. 4, July, 2001 ($2.50)

Preview (12/00, B&W) Silvestri-c   2.25
1-4-Avery-s/Crain-a   2.50

NOMAD (See Captain America #180)
Marvel Comics: Nov, 1990 - No. 4, Feb, 1991 ($1.50, limited series)

1-4: 1,4-Captain America app.   2.25

NOMAD
Marvel Comics: V2#1, May, 1992 - No. 25, May, 1994 ($1.75)

V2#1-25: 1-Has gatefold-c w/map/wanted poster. 4-Deadpool x-over. 5-Punisher
vs. Nomad-c/story. 6-Punisher & Daredevil-c/story cont'd in Punisher War
Journal #48. 7-Gambit-c/story. 10-Red Wolf app. 21-Man-Thing-c/story.
25-Bound-in trading card sheet   2.25

NOMAN (See Thunder Agents)
Tower Comics: Nov, 1966 - No. 2, March, 1967 (25¢, 68 pgs.)

1-Wood/Williamson-c; Lightning begins; Dynamo cameo; Kane-a(p) &				
Whitney-a	8	24	56	90
2-Wood-c only; Dynamo x-over; Whitney-a	5	15	34	55

NONE BUT THE BRAVE (See Movie Classics)

NOODNIK COMICS (See Pinky the Egghead)
Comic Media/Mystery/Biltmore: Dec, 1953; No. 2, Feb, 1954 - No. 5, Aug,
1954

3-D(1953, 25¢; Comic Media)(#1)-Came w/glasses	34	102	179	310
2-5	7	21	38	55

NORMALMAN (See Cerebus the Aardvark #55, 56)
Aardvark-Vanaheim/Renegade Press #6 on: Jan, 1984 - No. 12, Dec, 1985
($1.70/$2.00)

1-12: Jim Valentino-c/a in all. 6-12 ($2.00, B&W): 10-Cerebus cameo; Sim-a				
(2 pgs.)				2.25
...3-D 1 (Annual, 1986, $2.25)				2.25

NORMALMAN-MEGATON MAN SPECIAL
Image Comics: Aug, 1994 ($2.50, color)

1   2.50

NORTH AVENUE IRREGULARS (See Walt Disney Showcase #49)

NORTHSTAR
Marvel Comics: Apr, 1994 - No. 4, July, 1994 ($1.75, mini-series)

1-4: Character from Alpha Flight   2.25

NORTH TO ALASKA
Dell Publishing Co.: No. 1155, Dec, 1960

Four Color 1155-Movie, John Wayne photo-c	17	51	119	220

NORTHWEST MOUNTIES (Also see Approved Comics #12)

Nova #4 © MAR

Nutty Comics #7 © FAW

Nyoka, The Jungle Girl #7 © FAW

	GD2.0	FN6.0	VF8.0	NM9.4

Jubilee Publications/St. John: Oct, 1948 - No. 4, July, 1949

1-Rose of the Yukon by Matt Baker; Walter Johnson-a; Lubbers-c	47	142	286	500
2-Baker-a; Lubbers-c. Ventrilo app.	40	120	220	380
3-Bondage-c, Baker-a; Sky Chief, K-9 app.	40	120	232	400
4-Baker-c/a(2 pgs.); Blue Monk & The Desperado app.	40	120	232	400

NO SLEEP 'TIL DAWN
Dell Publishing Co.: No. 831, Aug, 1957

Four Color 831-Movie, Karl Malden photo-c	6	18	42	80

NOSTALGIA ILLUSTRATED
Marvel Comics: Nov, 1974 - V2#8, Aug, 1975 (B&W, 76 pgs.)

V1#1	3	9	19	28
V1#2, V2#1-8	2	6	11	15

NOT BRAND ECHH (Brand Echh #1-4; See Crazy, 1973)
Marvel Comics Group (LMC): Aug, 1967 - No. 13, May, 1969
(1st Marvel parody book)

1: 1-8 are 12¢ issues	15	45	38	60
2-8: 3-Origin Thor, Hulk & Capt. America; Monkees; Alfred E. Neuman cameo. 4-X-Men app. 5-Origin/intro. Forbush Man. 7-Origin Fantastical-4 & Stuporman. Beatles cameo; X-Men satire; last 12¢-c				
9-13 (25¢, 68 pgs., all Giants) 9-Beatles cameo. 10-All-r; The Old Witch, Crypt Keeper & Vault Keeper cameos. 12,13-Beatles cameo				
	4	12	26	40

NOTE: Colan a(p)-4, 5, 8, 9, 13. Everett a-1i. Kirby a(p)-1, 3, 5-7, 10r; c-1p. J. Severin a-1; c-3, 6-8, 11. M. Severin a-1-13; c-2, 9, 10, 12, 13. Sutton a-3, 4, 5i, 6i, 8, 9, 10r, 11-13; c-5. Archie satire in #9. Avengers satire in #8, 12.

NOTHING CAN STOP THE JUGGERNAUT
Marvel Comics: 1989 ($3.95)

1-r/Amazing Spider-Man #229 & 230				4.00

NO TIME FOR SERGEANTS (TV)
Dell Publ. Co.: No. 914, July, 1958; Feb-Apr, 1965 - No. 3, Aug-Oct, 1965

Four Color 914 (Movie)-Toth-a; Andy Griffith photo-c	10	30	70	125
1(2-4/65) (TV): Photo-c	5	15	35	65
2,3 (TV): Photo-c	4	12	30	50

NOVA (The Man Called... No. 22-25)(See New Warriors)
Marvel Comics Group: Sept, 1976 - No. 25, May, 1979

1-Origin/1st app. Nova	2	6	11	15
2-4,12: 4-Thor x-over. 12-Spider-Man x-over	1	3	5	7
5-11				6.00
10,11-(35¢ variants, limited distribution)(6,7/77)	1	3	6	8
12-(35¢-c variant, limited distribution)(8/77)	1	3	6	8
13,14-(Regular 30¢ editions)(9/77) 13-Intro Crime-Buster.				5.00
13,14-(35¢-c variant, limited distribution)	1	3	6	8
15-24: 18-Yellow Claw app. 19-Wally West (Kid Flash) cameo				5.00
25-Last issue				6.00

NOTE: Austin c-21i, 23i. John Buscema a(p)-1-3, 8, 21; c-1p, 2, 15. Infantino a(p)-15-20, 22-25; c-17-20, 21p, 23p, 24p. Kirby a-24p, 5, 7. Nebres c-25i. Simonson a-23i.

NOVA
Marvel Comics: Jan, 1994 - June, 1995 ($1.75/$1.95)
(Started as 4-part mini-series)

1-($2.95, 52 pgs.)-Collector's Edition w/gold foil-c; new Nova costume				3.00
1-($2.25, 52 pgs.)-Newsstand Edition w/o foil-c				2.25
2-18: 3-Spider-Man app. 5-Bound-in card sheet. 13-Firestar & Night Thrasher app.14-Darkhawk				2.25

NOVA
Marvel Comics: May, 1999 - No. 7, Nov, 1999 ($2.99/$1.99)

1-($2.99) Larsen-s/Bennett-a; wraparound-c by Larsen				3.00
2-7-($1.99): 2-Two covers; Capt. America app. 5-Spider-Man. 7-Venom				2.25

NOW AGE ILLUSTRATED (See Pendulum Illustrated Classics)

NOW AGE BOOKS ILLUSTRATED (See Pendulum Illustrated Classics)

NTH MAN THE ULTIMATE NINJA (See Marvel Comics Presents #25)
Marvel Comics: Aug, 1989 - No. 16, Sept, 1990 ($1.00)

1-16-Ninja mercenary. 8-Dale Keown's 1st Marvel work (1/90, pencils)				2.25

	GD2.0	FN6.0	VF8.0	NM9.

NUCLEUS (Also see Cerebus)
Heiro-Graphic Publications: May, 1979 ($1.50, B&W, adult fanzine)

1-Contains "Demonhorn" by Dave Sim; early app. of Cerebus The Aardvark (4 pg. story)	4	12	25	38

NUKLA
Dell Publishing Co.: Oct-Dec, 1965 - No. 4, Sept, 1966

1-Origin & 1st app. Nukla (super hero)	4	12	29	45
2,3	3	9	19	28
4-Ditko-a, c(p)	4	12	25	38

NURSE BETSY CRANE (Formerly Teen Secret Diary)
Charlton Comics: V2#12, Aug, 1961 - V2#27, Mar, 1964 (See Soap Opera Romances)

V2#12-27	2	6	13	20

NURSE HELEN GRANT (See The Romances of...)

NURSE LINDA LARK (See Linda Lark)

NURSERY RHYMES
Ziff-Davis Publ. Co. (Approved Comics): No. 10, July-Aug, 1951 - No. 2, Winter 1951 (Painted-c)

10 (#1), 2: 10-Howie Post-a	16	48	83	140

NURSES, THE (TV)
Gold Key: April, 1963 - No. 3, Oct, 1963 (Photo-c: #1,2)

1	4	12	25	38
2,3	3	9	17	25

NUTS! (Satire)
Premiere Comics Group: March, 1954 - No. 5, Nov, 1954

1-Hollingsworth-a	31	93	165	285
2,4,5: 5-Capt. Marvel parody	21	63	110	185
3-Drug "reefers" mentioned	21	63	110	185

NUTS (Magazine) (Satire)
Health Knowledge: Feb, 1958 - No. 2, April, 1958

1	9	27	49	70
2	6	18	32	45

NUTS & JOLTS
Dell Publishing Co.: No. 22, 1941

Large Feature Comic 22	10	30	70	135

NUTSY SQUIRREL (Formerly Hollywood Funny Folks)(See Comic Cavalcade)
National Periodical Publications: #61, 9-10/54 - #69, 1-2/56; #70, 8-9/56 - #71, 10-11/56; #72, 11/57

61-Mayer-a; Grossman-a in all	14	42	72	120
62-72: Mayer a-62,65,67-72	10	30	55	80

NUTTY COMICS
Fawcett Publications: Winter, 1946 (Funny animal)

1-Capt. Kidd story; 1 pg. Wolverton-a	14	42	72	120

NUTTY COMICS
Home Comics (Harvey Publications): 1945; No. 4, May-June, 1946 - No. 8, June-July, 1947 (No #2,3)

nn-Helpful Hank, Bozo Bear & others (funny animal)	8	24	45	65
4	6	18	32	45
5-Rags Rabbit begins(1st app.); infinity-c	6	18	32	45
6-8	5	15	25	35

NUTTY LIFE (Formerly Krazy Life #1; becomes Wotalife Comics #3 on)
Fox Features Syndicate: No. 2, Summer, 1946

2	10	30	55	85

NYOKA, THE JUNGLE GIRL (Formerly Jungle Girl; see The Further Adventures of..., Master Comics #50 & XMas Comics)
Fawcett Publications: No. 2, Winter, 1945 - No. 77, June, 1953 (Movie serial)

2	55	165	341	600
3	34	102	179	310
4,5	29	87	153	265
6-11,13,14,16-18-Krigstein-a: 17-Sam Spade ad by Lou Fine				
	21	63	110	185
12,15,19,20	19	57	99	165

Obergeist: Ragnarok #6 © Tony Harris & Dan Jolley & TCOW

Occult Files of Dr. Spektor #13 © GK

Offcastes #3 © Mike Vosburg

	GD2.0	FN6.0	VF8.0	NM9.4

	GD2.0	FN6.0	VF8.0	NM9.4
21-30: 25-Clayton Moore photo-c?	13	39	66	110
31-40	10	30	55	85
41-50	9	27	49	70
51-60	7	21	38	55
61-77	7	21	36	50

NOTE: Photo-c from movies 25, 30-70, 72, 75-77. Bondage c-4, 5, 7, 8, 14, 24.

NYOKA, THE JUNGLE GIRL (Formerly Zoo Funnies; Space Adventures 23 on)
Charlton Comics: No. 14, Nov, 1955 - No. 22, Nov, 1957

14	11	33	55	90
15-22	9	27	49	70

OAKLAND PRESS FUNNYBOOK, THE
The Oakland Press: 9/17/78 - 4/13/80 (16 pgs.) (Weekly)
Full color in comic book form; changes to tabloid size 4/20/80-on

Contains Tarzan by Manning, Marmaduke, Bugs Bunny, etc. (low distribution);
9/23/79 - 4/13/80 contain Buck Rogers by Gray Morrow & Jim Lawrence
..... 2.50

OAKY DOAKS (See Famous Funnies #190)
Eastern Color Printing Co.: July, 1942 (One Shot)

1	36	108	191	330

OBERGEIST: RAGNAROK HIGHWAY
Image Comics (Top Cow/Minotaur): May, 2001 - No. 6, Nov, 2001 ($2.95, limited series)
Preview ('01, B&W, 16 pgs.) Harris painted-c 2.00
1-6-Harris-c/a/Jolley-s. 1-Three covers 3.00

OBIE
Store Comics: 1953 (6¢)

1	5	14	21	28

OBJECTIVE FIVE
Image Comics: July, 2000 - Present ($2.95)
1-6-Lizalde-a 3.00

OBLIVION
Comico: Aug, 1995 - No. 3, May, 1996 ($2.50)
1-3: 1-Art Adams-c. 2-(1/96)-Bagged w/gaming card. 3-(5/96)-Darrow-c 2.50

OBNOXIO THE CLOWN (Character from Crazy Magazine)
Marvel Comics Group: April, 1983 (one-shot)
1-Vs. the X-Men 3.00

OCCULT FILES OF DR. SPEKTOR, THE
Gold Key/Whitman No. 25: Apr, 1973 - No. 24, Feb, 1977; No. 25, May, 1982
(Painted-c #1-24)

1-1st app. Lakota; Baron Tibor begins	3	10	23	35
2-5: 3-Mummy-c/s. 5-Jekyll & Hyde-c/s	2	6	11	15
6-10: 6,9-Frankenstein. 8,9-Dracula c/s. 9.-Jekyll & Hyde c/s. 9,10-Mummy-c/s				
	2	6	9	12
11-13,15-17,19-22,24: 11-1st app. Spektor as Werewolf. 11-13-Werewolf-c/s. 12,16-Frankenstein c/s. 17-Zombie/Voodoo-c. 19-Sea monster-c/s. 20-Mummy-s. 21-Swamp monster-c/s. 24-Dragon-c/s	1	3	6	9
14-Dr. Solar app.	2	6	11	16
18,23-Dr. Solar cameo	1	4	7	10
22-Return of the Owl c/s	2	6	9	12
25(Whitman, 5/82)-r/#1 with line drawn-c	1	3	6	8
9(Modern Comics reprint, 1977)(exist?)				5.00

NOTE: Also see Dan Curtis, Golden Comics Digest 33, Gold Key Spotlight, Mystery Comics Digest 5, & Spine Tingling Tales.

ODELL'S ADVENTURES IN 3-D (See Adventures in 3-D)

OFFCASTES
Marvel Comics (Epic Comics/Heavy Hitters): July, 1993 - No. 3, Sept, 1993 ($1.95, limited series)
1-3: Mike Vosburg-c/a/scripts in all 2.25

OFFICIAL CRISIS ON INFINITE EARTHS INDEX, THE
Independent Comics Group (Eclipse): Mar, 1986 ($1.75)
1 ..... 5.00

OFFICIAL CRISIS ON INFINITE EARTHS CROSSOVER INDEX, THE

Independent Comics Group (Eclipse): July, 1986 ($1.75)
1-Perez-c 5.00

OFFICIAL DOOM PATROL INDEX, THE
Independent Comics Group (Eclipse): Feb, 1986 - No. 2, Mar, 1986 ($1.50, limited series)
1,2: Byrne-c 4.00

OFFICIAL HANDBOOK OF THE CONAN UNIVERSE (See Handbook of...)

OFFICIAL HANDBOOK OF THE MARVEL UNIVERSE, THE
Marvel Comics Group: Jan, 1983 - No. 15, May, 1984 (Limited series)
1-Lists Marvel heroes & villains (letter A) 5.00
2-15: 2 (B-C), 3-(C-D). 4-(D-G). 5-(H-J), 6-(K-L). 7-(M). 8-(N-P); Punisher-c. 9-(Q-S), 10-(S). 11-(S-U). 12-(V-Z); Wolverine-c. 13,14-Book of the Dead.
15-Weaponry catalogue 4.00
NOTE: Bolland a-8. Byrne c/a(p)-1-14; c-15p. Grell a-6, 9. Kirby a-1, 3. Layton a-2, 5, 7. Mignola a-3, 4, 5, 6, 8, 12. Miller a-4-6, 8, 10. Nebres a-3, 4, 8. Redondo a-3, 4, 8, 13, 14. Simonson a-1, 4, 6-13. Paul Smith a-1-12. Starlin a-5, 7, 8, 10, 13, 14. Steranko a-8p. Zeck-2-14.

OFFICIAL HANDBOOK OF THE MARVEL UNIVERSE, THE
Marvel Comics Group: Dec, 1985 - No. 20, Feb, 1987 ($1.50, maxi-series)

V2#1-Byrne-c				4.00
2-20: 2,3-Byrne-c				3.00
Trade paperback Vol. 1-10 ($6.95)	1	3	6	8

NOTE: Art Adams a-7, 8, 11, 12, 14. Bolland a-8, 10, 13. Buckler a-1, 3, 5, 10. Buscema a-1, 5, 8, 9, 10, 13. Byrne a-14; c-1-11. Ditko a-1, 2, 4, 6, 7, 11, 13. a-7, 11. Mignola a-2, 4, 9, 11, 13. Miller a-2, 4, 12. Simonson a-1, 2, 4-13, 15. Paul Smith a-1-5, 7-12, 14. Starlin a-6, 8, 9, 12, 16. Zeck a-1-4, 6, 7, 9-14, 16.

OFFICIAL HANDBOOK OF THE MARVEL UNIVERSE, THE
Marvel Comics: July, 1989 - No. 8, Mid-Dec, 1990 ($1.50, lim. series, 52 pgs.)
V3#1-8: 1-McFarlane-a (2 pgs.) 3.00

OFFICIAL HAWKMAN INDEX, THE
Independent Comics Group: Nov, 1986 - No. 2, Dec, 1986 ($2.00)
1,2 ..... 4.00

OFFICIAL JUSTICE LEAGUE OF AMERICA INDEX, THE
Independent Comics Group (Eclipse): April, 1986 - No. 8, Mar, 1987 ($2.00, Baxter paper)
1-8: 1,2-Perez-c. 6.00

OFFICIAL LEGION OF SUPER-HEROES INDEX, THE
Independent Comics Group (Eclipse): Dec, 1986 - No. 5, 1987 ($2.00, limited series)(No Official in Title #2 on)
1-5: 4-Mooney-c 6.00

OFFICIAL MARVEL INDEX TO MARVEL TEAM-UP
Marvel Comics Group: Jan, 1986 - No. 6, 1987 ($1.25, limited series)
1-6 ..... 4.00

OFFICIAL MARVEL INDEX TO THE AMAZING SPIDER-MAN
Marvel Comics Group: Apr, 1985 - No. 9, Dec, 1985 ($1.25, limited series)

1 ($1.00)-Byrne-c.				4.00
2-9: 5,6,8,9-Punisher-c.				3.00

OFFICIAL MARVEL INDEX TO THE AVENGERS, THE
Marvel Comics: Jun, 1987 - No. 7, Aug, 1988 ($2.95, limited series)
1-7 ..... 5.00

OFFICIAL MARVEL INDEX TO THE AVENGERS, THE
Marvel Comics: V2#1, Oct, 1994 - V2#6, 1995 ($1.95, limited series)
V2#1-#6 ..... 3.00

OFFICIAL MARVEL INDEX TO THE FANTASTIC FOUR
Marvel Comics Group: Dec, 1985 - No. 12, Jan, 1987 ($1.25, limited series)
1-12: 1-Byrne-c. 1,2-Kirby back-c (unpub. art) 3.00

OFFICIAL MARVEL INDEX TO THE X-MEN, THE
Marvel Comics: May, 1987 - No. 7, July, 1988 ($2.95, limited series)
1-7 ..... 5.00

OFFICIAL MARVEL INDEX TO THE X-MEN, THE
Marvel Comics: V2#1, Apr, 1994 - V2#5, 1994 ($1.95, limited series)
V2#1-5: 1-Covers X-Men #1-51. 2-Covers #52-122,Special #1,2,Giant-Size #1,2.

Oh My Goddess! pt.2 #8 © Kosuke Fujishima

Omac #6 © DC

The Omen #4 © Chaos!

	GD2.0	FN6.0	VF8.0	NM9.4

	GD2.0	FN6.0	VF8.0	NM9.

3-Byrne-c; covers #123-177, Annuals 3-7, Spec. Ed. #1. 4-Covers Uncanny
X-Men #178-234, Annuals 8-12. 5-Covers #235-287, Annuals 13-15   3.00

OFFICIAL SOUPY SALES COMIC (See Soupy Sales)

OFFICIAL TEEN TITANS INDEX, THE
Indep. Comics Group (Eclipse): Aug, 1985 - No. 5, 1986 ($1.50, lim. series)
 1-5   4.00

OFFICIAL TRUE CRIME CASES (Formerly Sub-Mariner #23; All-True Crime
Cases #26 on)
Marvel Comics (OCI): No. 24, Fall, 1947 - No. 25, Winter, 1947-48
 24(#1)-Burgos-a; Syd Shores-c   23   69   121   210
 25-Syd Shores-c; Kurtzman's "Hey Look"   19   57   99   165

OF SUCH IS THE KINGDOM
George A. Pflaum: 1955 (15¢, 36 pgs.)
 nn-Reprints from 1951 Treasure Chest   4   9   14   18

O.G. WHIZ (See Gold Key Spotlight #10)
Gold Key: 2/71 - No. 6, 5/72; No. 7, 5/78 - No. 11, 1/79 (No. 7: 52 pgs.)
 1,2-John Stanley scripts   5   15   35   65
 3-6(1972)   3   9   21   32
 7-11(1978-79)-Part-r: 9-Tubby issue   2   6   11   15

OH, BROTHER! (Teen Comedy)
Stanhall Publ.: Jan, 1953 - No. 5, Oct, 1953
 1-By Bill Williams   7   21   36   50
 2-5   5   15   23   30

OH MY GODDESS! (Manga)
Dark Horse Comics: Aug, 1994 - No. 6, Jan, 1995 ($2.50, B&W, limited series)
 1-6   3.00
 ... PART II 2/95 - No. 9, 9/95 ($2.50, B&W, lim.series) #1-9   3.00
 ... PART III 11/95 - No. 11, 9/96 ($2.95, B&W, lim. series) #1-11   3.00
 ... PART IV 12/96 - No. 8, 7/97 ($2.95, B&W, lim. series) #1-8   3.00
 ... PART V 9/97 - Np. 12, 8/98 ($2.95, B&W, lim. series)
 1,2,5,8: 5-Ninja Master pt. 1   3.00
 3,4,6,7,10-12-($3.95, 48 pgs.) 10-Fallen Angel. 11-Play The Game   4.00
 9-($3.50) "It's Lonely At The Top"   3.50
 ... PART VI 10/98 - No. 5, 3/99 ($3.50/$2.95, B&W, lim. series)
 1-($3.50)   3.50
 2-6-($2.95)-6-Super Urd one-shot   3.00
 ... PART VII 5/99 - No. 8, 12/99 ($2.95, B&W, lim. series) #1-3   3.50
 4-8-($3.50)   3.50
 ... PART VIII 1/00 - No. 6, 6/00 ($3.50, B&W, lim. series) #1-3,5,7   3.50
 4-($2.95) "Hail To The Chief" begins   3.00
 ... PART IX 7/00 - No. 7, 1/01 ($3.50/$2.99) #1-4: 3-Queen Sayoko   3.50
 5-7-($2.99)   3.50
 ... PART X 2/01 - No. 5, 6/01 ($3.50) #1-5   3.50
 ... PART XI 10/01 - No. 2, 11/01 ($3.50) #1,2   3.50

OH MY GOTH
Sirius Entertainment (Dog Star Press): 1998 - No. 4, 1999 ($2.95, B&W)
 1-4-Voltaire-s/a   3.00
 ... Humans Suck! (2000 - No. 3) 1,2-Voltaire-s/a   3.00

OH SUSANNA (TV)
Dell Publishing Co.: No. 1105, June-Aug, 1960 (Gale Storm)
 Four Color 1105-Toth-a, photo-c   13   39   91   165

OINK: BLOOD AND CIRCUS
Kitchen Sink: 1998 - No. 4, July, 1998 ($4.95, limited series)
 1-4-John Mueller-s/a   5.00

OKAY COMICS
United Features Syndicate: July, 1940
 1-Captain & the Kids & Hawkshaw the Detective reprints
    43   129   257   450

O.K. COMICS
United Features Syndicate/Hit Publications: July, 1940 - No. 2, Oct, 1940
 1-Little Giant (w/super powers), Phantom Knight, Sunset Smith, & The Teller
 Twins begin   77   231   483   850
 2 (Rare)-Origin Mister Mist by Chas. Quinlan   80   240   500   875

OKLAHOMA KID
Ajax/Farrell Publ.: June, 1957 - No. 4, 1958
 1   11   33   55   90
 2-4   7   21   36   50

OKLAHOMAN, THE
Dell Publishing Co.: No. 820, July, 1957
 Four Color 820-Movie, photo-c   9   27   63   120

OKTANE
Dark Horse Comics: Aug, 1995 - Nov, 1995($2.50, color, limited series)
 1-4-Gene Ha-a   2.50

OLD IRONSIDES (Disney)
Dell Publishing Co.: No. 874, Jan, 1958
 Four Color 874-Movie w/Johnny Tremain   6   18   42   80

OLD YELLER (Disney, see Movie Comics, and Walt Disney Showcase #25)
Dell Publishing Co.: No. 869, Jan, 1958
 Four Color 869-Movie, photo-c   5   15   35   60

OMAC (One Man Army; ...Corps. #4 on; also see Kamandi #59 & Warlord)
(See Cancelled Comic Cavalcade)
National Periodical Publications: Sept-Oct, 1974 - No. 8, Nov-Dec, 1975
 1-Origin   3   9   17   25
 2-8: 8-2 pg. Neal Adams ad   2   6   9   12
 NOTE: Kirby a-1-8p; c-1-7p. Kubert c-8.

OMAC: ONE MAN ARMY CORPS
DC Comics: 1991 - No. 4, 1991 ($3.95, B&W, mini-series, mature, 52 pgs.)
 Book One - Four: John Byrne-c/a & scripts   4.00

O'MALLEY AND THE ALLEY CATS (Disney)
Gold Key: April, 1971 - No. 9, Jan, 1974 (Disney)
 1   2   6   15   22
 2-9   2   6   9   12

OMEGA ELITE
Blackthorne Publishing: 1987 ($1.25)
 1-Starlin-c   3.00

OMEGA MEN, THE (See Green Lantern #141)
DC Comics: Dec, 1982 - No. 38, May, 1986 ($1.00/$1.25/$1.50; Baxter paper)
 1,20: 20-2nd full Lobo story   3.00
 2,4-9,11-19,21-25,28-30,32,33,36,38: 2-Origin Broot. 5,9-2nd & 3rd app. Lobo
 (cameo, 2 pgs. each). 7-Origin The Citadel. 19-Lobo cameo. 30-Intro new
 Primus   2.50
 3-1st app. Lobo (5 pgs.)(6/83); Lobo-c   1   3   5   7
 10-1st full Lobo story   5.00
 26,27,31,34,35: 26,27-Alan Moore scripts. 31-Crisis x-over. 34,35-Teen Titans
 x-over   3.00
 37-1st solo Lobo story (8 pg. back-up by Giffen)   4.00
 Annual 1(11/84, 52 pgs.), 2(11/85)   3.00
 NOTE: Giffen c/a-1-6p. Morrow a-24r. Nino c/a-16, 21; a-Annual 1i.

OMEGA THE UNKNOWN
Marvel Comics Group: March, 1976 - No. 10, Oct, 1977
 1-1st app. Omega   1   4   7   10
 2,3-(Regular 25¢ editions). 2-Hulk-c/story. 3-Electro-c/story.   6.00
 2,3-(30¢-c variants, limited distribution)   9   27   63   120
 4-10: 8-1st app. 2nd Foolkiller (Greg Salinger), 1 panel only (cameo). 9,10-(Reg.
 30¢ editions). 9-1st full app. 2nd Foolkiller   6.00
 9,10-(35¢-c variants, limited distribution)   1   3   6   9
 NOTE: Kane c(p)-3, 5, 8, 9. Mooney a-1-3, 4p, 5, 6p, 7, 8i, 9, 10.

OMEN
Northstar Publishing: 1989 - No. 3, 1989 ($2.00, B&W, mature)
 1-Tim Vigil-c/a in all   1   3   5   7
 1, (2nd printing)   3.00
 2,3   5.00

OMEN, THE
Chaos! Comics: May, 1998 - No. 5, Sept, 1998 ($2.95, limited series)
 1-5: 1-Six covers, ...: Vexed (10/98, $2.95) Chaos! characters appear   3.00

100 Bullets #18 © Brian Azzarello / DC

Oni Double Feature #6 © Oni Press

Operation Peril #15 © ACG

	GD2.0	FN6.0	VF8.0	NM9.4

NI MEN
ackthorne Publishing: 1987 - No. 3, 1987 ($1.25)

-3				2.25

E, THE
arvel Comics (Epic Comics): July, 1985 - No. 6, Feb, 1986 (Limited series, ture)

-6: Post nuclear holocaust super-hero. 2-Intro The Other	2.00

E-ARM SWORDSMAN, THE
ctory Prod./Lueng's Publ. #4 on: 1987 - No. 12, 1990 ($2.75/$1.80, 52pgs.)

-3 ($2.75)	2.75
-12: 4-6-$1.80-c. 7-12-$2.00-c	2.25

E HUNDRED AND ONE DALMATIANS (Disney, see Cartoon Tales, Movie mics, and Walt Disney Showcase #9, 51)
ll Publishing Co.: No. 1183, Mar, 1961

ur Color 1183-Movie	10	30	70	130

1 DALMATIONS (Movie)
sney Comics: 1991 (52 pgs., graphic novel)

-($4.95, direct sales)-r/movie adaptation & more	5.00
-($2.95, newsstand edition)	3.00

1 WAYS TO END THE CLONE SAGA (See Spider-Man)
arvel Comics: Jan, 1997 ($2.50, one-shot)

	2.50

0 BULLETS
Comics (Vertigo): Aug, 1999 - Present ($2.50)

-Azzarello-s/Risso-a/Dave Johnson-c	4.00
-5	3.00
-31: 26-Series summary; art by various	2.50
st Shot, Last Call TPB (2000, $9.95) r/#1-5, Vertigo Winter's Edge #3	10.00
ng Up on the Hang Low TPB (2001, $9.95) r/#15-19; Jim Lee intro.	10.00
lit Second Chance TPB (2001, $14.95) r/#6-14	15.00

0 GREATEST MARVELS OF ALL TIME
arvel Comics: Dec, 2001 ($7.50/$3.50, limited series)

-5-Reprints top #25 stories voted by poll for Marvel's 40th ann.	7.50
-($3.50) (#5 on-c) Reprints X-Men (2nd series) #1	3.50
-($3.50) (#4 on-c) Reprints Giant-Size X-Men #1	3.50
-($3.50) (#3 on-c) Reprints (Uncanny) X-Men #137 (Death of Jean Grey)	3.50
-($3.50) (#2 on-c) Reprints Fantastic Four #1	3.50
-($3.50) (#1 on-c) Reprints Amazing Fantasy #15	3.50

0 PAGES OF COMICS
ll Publishing Co.: 1937 (Stiff covers, square binding)

1(Found on back cover)-Alley Oop, Wash Tubbs, Capt. Easy, Og Son of Fire, Apple Mary, Tom Mix, Dan Dunn, Tailspin Tommy, Doctor Doom	168	486	1053	1700

0 PAGE SUPER SPECTACULAR (See DC 100 Page...)

0% TRUE?
Comics (Paradox Press): Summer 1996 - No. 2 ($4.95, B&W)

2-Reprints stories from various Paradox Press books.	5.00

,000,000 DUCK (See Walt Disney Showcase #5)

E MILLION YEARS AGO (Tor #2 on)
John Publishing Co.: Sept, 1953

-Origin & 1st app. Tor; Kubert-c/a; Kubert photo inside front cover	21	63	110	185

E SHOT (See Four Color...)

01 HOURS OF FUN
ll Publishing Co.: No. 13, 1943

rge Feature Comic 13 (nn)-Puzzles & games; by A.W. Nugent. This book was bound as #13 w/Large Feature Comics in publisher's files	27	81	149	220

E TRICK RIP OFF, THE (See Dark Horse Presents)

ll (Adaption of video game)
rk Horse Comics: Feb, 2001 - No. 3, Apr, 2001 ($2.99, limited series)

	GD2.0	FN6.0	VF8.0	NM9.4

1-3-Sunny Lee-a(p)				3.00

ONI DOUBLE FEATURE (See Clerks: The Comic Book and Jay & Silent Bob)
Oni Press: Jan, 1998 - No. 13, Sept, 1999 ($2.95, B&W)

1-Jay & Silent Bob; Kevin Smith-s/Matt Wagner-a	1	4	7	10
1-2nd printing				3.00
2-11,13: 2,3-Paul Pope-s/a. 3,4-Nixey-s/a. 4,5-Sienkewicz-s/a. 6,7-Gaiman-s.				
9-Bagge-c. 13-All Paul Dini-s; Jingle Belle				3.00
12-Jay & Silent Bob as Bluntman & Chronic; Smith-s/Allred-a				5.00

ONIGAMI (See Warrior Nun Areala: Black & White)
Antarctic Press: Apr, 1998 - No. 3, July, 1998 ($2.95, B&W, limited series)

1-3-Michel Lacombe-s/a				3.00

ONI PRESS COLOR SPECIAL
Oni Press: Jun, 2001 ($5.95, one-shot)

1-Oeming "Who Killed Madman?" cover; stories & art by various				6.00

ONSLAUGHT: EPILOGUE
Marvel Comics: Feb, 1997 ($2.95, one-shot)

1-Hama-s/Green-a; Xavier-c; Bastion-app.				3.00

ONSLAUGHT: MARVEL
Marvel Comics: Oct, 1996 ($3.95, one-shot)

1-Conclusion to Onslaught x-over; wraparound-c	1	3	5	7

ONSLAUGHT: X-MEN
Marvel Comics: Aug, 1996 ($3.95, one-shot)

1-Mark Waid & Scott Lobdell script; Fantastic Four & Avengers app.; Xavier as Onslaught				5.00
1-Variant-c	2	6	9	12

ON STAGE
Dell Publishing Co.: No. 1336, Apr-June, 1962

Four Color 1336-Not by Leonard Starr	4	12	30	50

ON THE DOUBLE (Movie)
Dell Publishing Co.: No. 1232, Sept-Nov, 1961

Four Color 1232	4	12	30	50

ON THE ROAD WITH ANDRAE CROUCH
Spire Christian Comics (Fleming H. Revell): 1973, 1977 (39¢)

nn	1	3	5	7

ON THE SCENE PRESENTS:...
Warren Publishing Co.: Oct, 1966 - No. 2, 1967 (B&W magazine, two #1 issues)

#1 "Super Heroes" (68 pgs.) Batman 1966 movie photo-c/s; has articles/photos/ comic art from serials on Superman, Flash Gordon, Capt. America, Capt. Marvel and The Phantom	3	10	23	35
#1 "Freak Out, USA" (Fall/1966, 60 pgs.) (lower print run) articles on musicians like Zappa, Jefferson Airplane, Supremes	4	12	29	45
#2 "Freak Out, USA" (2/67, 52 pgs.) Beatles, Country Joe, Doors/Jim Morrison, Bee Gees	3	10	23	35

ON THE SPOT (Pretty Boy Floyd...)
Fawcett Publications: Fall, 1948

nn-Pretty Boy Floyd photo on-c; bondage-c	35	105	185	320

ONYX OVERLORD
Marvel Comics (Epic): Oct, 1992 - No. 4, Jan, 1993 ($2.75, mini-series)

1-4: Moebius scripts				2.75

OPEN SPACE
Marvel Comics: Mid-Dec, 1989 - No. 4, Aug, 1990 ($4.95, bi-monthly, 68 pgs.)

1-4: 1-Bill Wray-a; Freas-c				5.00
0-(1999) Wizard supplement; unpubl. early Alex Ross-a; new Ross-c				2.25

OPERATION BIKINI (See Movie Classics)

OPERATION BUCHAREST (See The Crusaders)

OPERATION CROSSBOW (See Movie Classics)

OPERATION: KNIGHTSTRIKE (See Knightstrike)
Image Comics (Extreme Studios): May, 1995 -No.3, July, 1995 ($2.50)

1-3				2.50

OPERATION PERIL

Original E-Man and Michael Mauser #2 © FC

Orion #13 © DC

Oscar Comics #4 © MAR

American Comics Group (Michel Publ.): Oct-Nov, 1950 - No. 16, Apr-May, 1953 (#1-5: 52 pgs.)

1-Time Travelers, Danny Danger (by Leonard Starr) & Typhoon Tyler (by Ogden Whitney) begin	39	117	208	360
2-War-c	24	72	127	215
3-War-c; horror story	21	63	110	185
4,5-Sci/fi-c/story	23	69	121	210
6-10: 6,8,9,10-Sci/fi-c. 6-Dinosaur-c. 7-Sabretooth-c	20	60	105	175
11,12-War-c; last Time Travelers	14	42	72	120
13-16: All war format	10	30	55	80

NOTE: Starr a-2, 5. Whitney a-1, 2, 5-10, 12; c-1, 3, 5, 8, 9.

OPERATION: STORMBREAKER
Acclaim Comics (Valiant Heroes): Aug, 1997 ($3.95, one-shot)

1-Waid/Augustyn-s, Braithwaite-a				4.00

OPTIC NERVE
Drawn and Quarterly: Apr, 1995 - Present ($2.95, bi-annual)

1-7: Adrian Tomine-c/a/scripts in all				3.00
8-($3.50)				3.50
32 Stories-($9.95, trade paperback)-r/Optic Nerve mini-comics				10.00
32 Stories-($29.95, hardcover)-r/Optic Nerve mini-comics; signed & numbered				30.00

ORAL ROBERTS' TRUE STORIES (Junior Partners #120 on)
TelePix Publ. (Oral Roberts' Evangelistic Assoc./Healing Waters): 1956 (no month) - No. 119, 7/59 (15¢)(No. 102: 25¢)

V1#1(1956)-(Not code approved)- "The Miracle Touch"	21	63	110	185
102-(Only issue approved by code, 10/56) "Now I See"	13	39	66	110
103-119: 115-(114 on inside)	9	27	49	70

NOTE: Also see Happiness & Healing For You.

ORANGE BIRD, THE
Walt Disney Educational Media Co.: No date (1980) (36 pgs.; in color; slick cover)

nn-Included with educational kit on foods, ...in Nutrition Adventures nn (1980) ...and the Nutrition Know-How Revue nn (1983)				3.00

ORB (Magazine)
Orb Publishing: 1974 - No. 6, Mar/Apr 1976 (B&W/color)

1-1st app. Northern Light & Kadaver, both series begin	3	9	17	25
2,3 (72 pgs.)	2	6	11	16
4-6 (60 pgs.): 4,5-origin Northern Light	2	6	9	12

NOTE: Allison a-1-3. Gene Day a-1-6. P. Hsu a-4-6. Steacy s/a-3,4.

ORBIT
Eclipse Books: 1990 - No. 3, 1990 ($4.95, 52 pgs., squarebound)

1-3: Reprints from Isaac Asimov's Science Fiction Magazine; 1-Dave Stevens-c, Bolton-a. 3-Bolton-c/a, Yeates-a				5.00

ORIENTAL HEROES
Jademan Comics: Aug, 1988 - No. 55, Feb, 1993 ($1.50/$1.95, 68pgs.)

1-55				2.25

ORIGINAL ASTRO BOY, THE
Now Comics: Sept, 1987 - No. 20, Jun, 1989 ($1.50/$1.75)

1-20-All have Ken Steacy painted-c/a				3.00

ORIGINAL BLACK CAT, THE
Recollections: Oct. 6, 1988 - No. 9, 1992 ($2.00, limited series)

1-9: Elias-r; 1-Bondage-c. 2-Murphy Anderson-c				3.00

ORIGINAL DICK TRACY, THE
Gladstone Publishing: Sept, 1990 - No. 5, 1991 ($1.95, bi-monthly, 68pgs.)

1-5: 1-Vs. Pruneface. 2-& the Evil influence; begin $2.00-c				2.25

NOTE: #1 reprints strips 7/16/43 - 9/30/43. #2 reprints strips 12/1/46 - 2/2/47. #3 reprints 8/31/46 - 11/14/46. #4 reprints 9/17/45 - 12/23/45. #5 reprints 6/10/46 - 8/28/46.

ORIGINAL DOCTOR SOLAR, MAN OF THE ATOM, THE
Valiant: Apr, 1995 ($2.95, one-shot)

1-Reprints Doctor Solar, Man of the Atom #1,5; Bob Fugitani-r; Paul Smith-c;				

afterword by Seaborn Adamson 3.00

ORIGINAL E-MAN AND MICHAEL MAUSER, THE
First Comics: Oct, 1985 - No. 7, April, 1986 ($1.75, Baxter paper)

1-7: 1-Has r-/Charlton's E-Man, Vengeance Squad. 2-Shows #4 in indicia by mistake. 7 ($2.00, 44pgs.)-Staton-a				2.25

ORIGINAL GHOST RIDER, THE
Marvel Comics: July - No. 20, Feb, 1994 ($1.75)

1-20: 1-7-r/Marvel Spotlight #5-11 by Ploog w/new-c. 3-New Phantom Rider (former Night Rider) back-ups begin by Ayers. 4-Quesada-c(p). 8,9-r/Ghost Rider #1,2. 10-r/Marvel Spotlight #12. 11-18,20-r/Ghost Rider #3-12. 19-r/Marvel Two-in-One #8				2.25

ORIGINAL GHOST RIDER RIDES AGAIN, THE
Marvel Comics: July, 1991 - No. 7, Jan, 1992, ($1.50, limited series, 52 pgs.)

1-7: 1-R/Ghost Rider #68(origin),69 w/covers. 2-7: R/ G.R. #70-81 w/covers				2.25

ORIGINAL MAGNUS ROBOT FIGHTER, THE
Valiant: Apr, 1995 ($2.95, one-shot)

1-Reprints Magnus, Robot Fighter 4000 #2; Russ Manning-r; Rick Leonardi-c; afterword by Seaborn Adamson				3.00

ORIGINAL NEXUS GRAPHIC NOVEL (See First Comics Graphic Novel #19)

ORIGINAL SHIELD, THE
Archie Enterprises, Inc.: Apr, 1984 - No. 4, Oct, 1984

1-4: 1,2-Origin Shield; Ayers p-1-4, Nebres c-1,2				4.00

ORIGINAL SWAMP THING SAGA, THE (See DC Special Series #2, 14, 17, 20)

ORIGINAL TUROK, SON OF STONE, THE
Valiant: Apr, 1995 - No. 2, May, 1995 ($2.95, limited series)

1,2: 1-Reprints Turok, Son of Stone #24,25,42; Alberto Gioletti-r; Rags Morales-c; afterword by Seaborn Adamson. 2-Reprints Turok, Son of Stone #24,33; Gioletti-r; Mike McKone-c				3.00

ORIGIN OF GALACTUS (See Fantastic Four #48-50)
Marvel Comics: Feb, 1996 ($2.50, one-shot)

1-Lee & Kirby reprints w/pin-ups				2.50

ORIGIN OF THE DEFIANT UNIVERSE, THE
Defiant Comics: Feb, 1994 ($1.50, 20 pgs., one-shot)

1-David Lapham, Adam Pollina & Alan Weiss-a; Weiss-c				5.00

NOTE: The comic was originally published as Defiant Genesis and was distributed at the 1994 Philadelphia ComicCon.

ORIGINS OF MARVEL COMICS (See Fireside Book Series)

ORION (Manga)
Dark Horse Comics: Sept, 1992 - No. 6, July, 1993 ($2.95/$3.95, B&W, bimonthly, limited series)

1-6:1(3),1,2,6-Squarebound): 1-Masamune Shirow-c/a/s in all				4.00

ORION (See New Gods)
DC Comics: June, 2000 - Present ($2.50)

1-14-Simonson-s/a. 3-Back-up story w/Miller-a. 4-Gibbons-a back-up. 7-Chaykin back-up. 8-Loeb/Liefeld back-up. 10-A. Adams back-up-a 12-Jim Lee back-up-a. 13-JLA-c/app.: Byrne-a				2.50
15-($3.95) Black Racer app.; back-up story w/J.P. Leon-a				4.00
16-21-Simonson-s. 19-Joker: Last Laugh x-over				2.50
The Gates of Apocalypse (2001, $12.95, TPB) r/#1-5 & various short-s				13.00

OSBORNE JOURNALS (See Spider-Man titles)
Marvel Comics: Feb, 1997 ($2.95, one-shot)

1-Hotz-c/a				3.00

OSCAR COMICS (Formerly Funny Tunes; Awful...#11 & 12)
(Also see Cindy Comics)
Marvel Comics: No. 24, Spring, 1947 - No. 10, Apr, 1949; No. 13, Oct, 1949

24(#1, Spring, 1947)	17	51	88	150
25(#2, Sum, 1947)-Wolverton-a plus Kurtzman's "Hey Look"	19	57	99	165
26(#3)-Same as regular #3 except #26 was printed over in black ink with #3 appearing on-c below the over print	11	33	55	90
3-9,13: 8-Margie app.	11	33	55	90

Our Army at War #9 © DC

Our Army at War #146 © DC

Our Fighting Forces #11 © DC

	GD2.0	FN6.0	VF8.0	NM9.4

10-Kurtzman's "Hey Look" — 13 · 39 · 66 · 110

OSWALD THE RABBIT (Also see New Fun Comics #1)
Dell Publishing Co.: No. 21, 1943 - No. 1268, 12-2/61-62 (Walter Lantz)

Four Color 21(1943)	50	150	350	650
Four Color 39(1943)	35	105	245	455
Four Color 67(1944)	18	54	126	230
Four Color 102(1946)-Kelly-a, 1 pg.	15	45	105	200
Four Color 143,183	9	27	63	120
Four Color 225,273	5	15	35	70
Four Color 315,388	5	15	35	60
Four Color 458,507,549,593	4	12	26	40
Four Color 623,697,792,894,979,1268	3	10	23	35

OSWALD THE RABBIT (See The Funnies, March of Comics #7, 38, 53, 67, 81, 95, 111, 126, 141, 156, 171, 186, New Funnies & Super Book #8, 20)

OTHERS, THE
Image Comics (Shadowline Ink): 1995 - No. 3, 1995 ($2.50)

0 ($1.00)-16 pg. preview				2.25
1-3				2.50

OTIS GOES TO HOLLYWOOD
Dark Horse Comics: Apr, 1997 - No.2, May, 1997 ($2.95, B&W, mini-series)

1,2-Fingerman-c/s/a				3.00

OUR ARMY AT WAR (Becomes Sgt. Rock #302 on; also see Army At War)
National Periodical Publications: Aug, 1952 - No. 301, Feb, 1977

1	131	393	1113	2100
2	58	174	493	925
3,4: 4-Krigstein-a	48	144	384	675
5-7	41	123	306	550
8-11,14-Krigstein-a	37	112	278	500
12,15-20	31	93	222	400
13-Krigstein-c/a; flag-c	39	117	293	520
21-31: Last precode (2/55)	22	65	151	270
32-40	18	53	123	220
41-60: 51-1st S.A. issue	15	45	105	180
61-70: 67-Minor Sgt. Rock prototype	13	39	91	155
71-80	11	33	77	130
81- (4/59)-Sgt. Rocky of Easy Co. app. by Andru & Esposito-a/ Haney-s; (the last Sgt. Rock prototype)	182	546	1547	3100
82-1st Sgt. Rock app., in name only, in Easy Co. story (6 panels) by Kanigher & Drucker	48	144	384	675
83-(6/59)-1st true Sgt. Rock app. in "The Rock and the Wall" by Kubert & Kanigher; (most similar to prototype in G.I. Combat #68)	131	393	1113	2100
84-Kubert-c	26	78	179	320
85-Origin & 1st app. Ice Cream Soldier	34	102	255	460
86,87-Early Sgt. Rock; Kubert-a	25	75	174	310
88-1st Sgt. Rock-c; Kubert-c/a	28	85	196	350
89	23	68	160	285
90-Kubert-c/a; How Rock got his stripes	30	90	210	375
91-All-Sgt. Rock issue; Grandenetti/Kubert-a	53	159	450	840
92,94,96-99: 97-Regular Kubert begin	16	48	110	190
93-1st Zack Nolan	16	48	110	195
95,100: Nos. 5 1st app. Bulldozer	17	51	118	210
101,105,108,113,115: 101-1st app. Buster. 105-1st app. Junior. 113-1st app. Wildman & Jackie Johnson. 115-Rock revealed as orphan; 1st x-over Mlle. Marie. 1st Sgt. Rock's battle family	12	36	84	140
102-104,106,107,109,110,114,116-120: 104-Nurse Jane-c/s. 109-Pre Easy Co. Sgt. Rock-s. 118-Sunny injured	10	30	70	120
111-1st app. Wee Willie & Sunny	13	39	94	160
112-Classic Easy Co. roster-c	14	42	102	175
121-125,130-133,135-139,141-150: 138-1st Sparrow. 141-1st Shaker. 147,148-Rock becomes a General	7	21	50	80
126,129,134: 126-1st app. Canary; grey tone-c	8	24	56	90
127-2nd all-Sgt. Rock issue; 1st app. Little Sure	9	27	63	105
128-Training & origin Sgt. Rock; 1st Sgt. Krupp	23	68	160	285
140-3rd all-Sgt. Rock issue	7	21	53	85
151-Intro. Enemy Ace by Kubert (2/65)	35	105	262	475
152-4th all-Sgt. Rock issue	7	21	53	85
153-2nd app. Enemy Ace (4/65)	16	48	112	200

154,156,157,159-161,165-167: 157-2 pg. pin-up: 159-1st Nurse Wendy Winston-c/s. 165-2nd Iron Major	6	18	40	65
155-3rd app. Enemy Ace (6/65)(see Showcase)	11	33	80	135
158-Origin & 1st app. Iron Major(9/65), formerly Iron Captain	7	21	50	80
162,163-Viking Prince x-over in Sgt. Rock	6	18	45	75
164-Giant G-19	12	36	88	150
168-1st Unknown Soldier app.; referenced in Star-Spangled War Stories #157; (Sgt. Rock x-over) (6/66)	11	33	80	135
169,170	5	15	38	60
171-176,178-181: 171-1st Mad Emperor	4	12	30	50
177-(80 pg. Giant G-32)	7	21	53	85
182,183,186-Neal Adams-a. 186-Origin retold	5	15	38	60
184-Wee Willie dies	5	15	38	60
185,187,188,193-195,197-199	4	12	29	45
189,191,192,196: 189-Intro. The Teen-age Underground Fighters of Unit 3. 196-Hitler cameo	4	12	29	45
190-(80 pg. Giant G-44)	6	18	42	70
200-12 pg. Rock story told in verse; Evans-a	4	12	30	50
201,202,204-207: 201-Krigstein-r/#14. 204,205-All reprints; no Sgt. Rock. 207-Last 12¢ cover	3	9	20	30
203-(80 pg. Giant G-56)-All-r, Sgt. Rock story	5	15	38	60
208-215	3	9	17	25
216,229-(80 pg. Giants G-68, G-80): 216-has G-58 on-c by mistake	5	15	34	55
217-219: 218-1st U.S.S. Stevens	2	6	15	22
220-Classic dinosaur/Sgt. Rock-s	3	9	19	28
221-228,230-234: 231-Intro/death Rock's brother. 234-Last 15¢ issue	2	6	12	18
235-239,241: 52 pg. Giants	3	9	19	28
240-Neal Adams-a; 52 pg. Giant	3	10	23	35
242-Also listed in DC 100 Page Super Spectacular #9; see for price	—
243-246: (All 52 pgs.) 244-No Adams-a	3	9	17	25
247-250,254-268,270: 247-Joan of Arc	2	6	10	14
251-253-Return of Iron Major	2	6	11	16
269,275-(100 pgs.)	4	12	26	40
271-274,276-279: 273-Crucifixion-c	2	6	9	12
280-(68 pgs.)-200th app. Sgt. Rock; reprints Our Army at War #81,83	3	9	17	25
281-299,301: 295-Bicentennial cover	1	4	7	10
300-Sgt. Rock-s by Kubert (2/77)	2	6	9	12

NOTE: **Alcala** a-251. **Drucker** a-27, 67, 68, 79, 82, 83, 96, 164, 177, 203, 212, 243r, 244, 269r, 275r, 280r. **Evans** a-165-175, 200, 266, 269, 270, 274, 276, 278, 280. **Glanzman** a-218, 220, 222, 223, 225, 227, 230-232, 238-241, 244, 247, 248, 256-259, 261, 265-267, 271, 282, 283, 298. **Grandenetti** a-91. **Grell** a-287. **Heath** a-50, 164, & most issues from 83-165, 233, 236, 267, 275, 300; c-84, 280. **Maurer** a-233, 237, 239, 240, 45, 280, 284, 288, 290, 291, 295. **Severin** a-236, 252, 265, 267, 269r, 272. **Toth** a-235, 241, 254. **Wildey** a-283-285, 287p. **Wood** a-249.

OUR FIGHTING FORCES
National Per. Publ./DC Comics: Oct-Nov, 1954 - No. 181, Sept-Oct, 1978

1-Grandenetti-c/a	81	244	690	1300
2	37	112	278	500
3-Kubert-c; last precode issue (3/55)	33	99	248	440
4,5	27	81	190	340
6-9: 7-1st S.A. issue	23	68	160	285
10-Wood-a	24	72	165	295
11-19	18	54	123	220
20-Grey tone-c (4/57)	21	63	146	260
21-30	13	39	91	155
31-40	12	36	84	140
41-Unknown Soldier tryout	15	45	105	180
42-44	10	30	70	120
45-Gunner & Sarge begins, end #94	35	105	262	475
46	15	45	105	180
47	10	30	73	125
48,50	9	27	63	105
49-1st Pooch	12	36	88	150
51-Grey tone-c	8	24	60	100
52-64: 64-Last 10¢ issue	8	24	56	90
65-70	6	18	40	65
71-Grey tone-c	5	15	34	55

Our Gang Comics #2 © DELL

Our Love Story #1 © MAR

Outer Limits #17 © DELL

	GD2.0	FN6.0	VF8.0	NM9.4
72-80	4	12	29	45
81-90	4	12	26	40
91-98: 95-Devil-Dog begins, ends #98.	3	9	20	30
99-Capt. Hunter begins, ends #106	3	10	23	35
100	3	9	21	32
101-105,107-120: 116-Mlle. Marie app. 120-Last 12¢ issue				
	3	9	17	24
106-Hunters Hellcats begin	3	9	19	28
121,122: 121-Intro. Heller	2	6	15	22
123-Losers (Capt. Storm, Gunner & Sarge, Johnny Cloud) begin				
	5	15	34	55
124-132: 132-Last 15¢ issue	2	6	12	18
133-137 (Giants). 134-Toth-a	3	9	17	24
138-150: 146-Toth-a	2	6	9	12
151-162-Kirby a(p)	2	6	12	18
163-180	1	3	6	9
181-Last issue	2	6	9	12

NOTE: *N. Adams* c-147. *Drucker* a-28, 37, 39, 42-44, 49, 53, 133r. *Evans* a-149, 164-174, 177-181. *Glanzman* a-125-128, 132, 134, 138-141, 143, 144. *Heath* a-2, 16, 18, 28, 41, 44, 49, 114, 135-139r; c-51. *Kirby* a-151-162p; c-151-159. *Kubert* c/a in many issues. *Maurer* a-135. *Redondo* a-166. *Severin* a-123-130, 131i, 132-150.

OUR FIGHTING MEN IN ACTION (See Men In Action)

OUR FLAG COMICS
Ace Magazines: Aug, 1941 - No. 5, April, 1942

1-Captain Victory, The Unknown Soldier (intro.) & The Three Cheers begin				
	264	792	1648	2900
2-Origin The Flag (patriotic hero); 1st app?	116	348	725	1275
3-5: 5-Intro & 1st app. Mr. Risk	89	268	556	975

NOTE: *Anderson* a-1, 4. *Mooney* a-1; c-2.

OUR GANG COMICS (With Tom & Jerry #39-59; becomes Tom & Jerry #60 on; based on film characters)
Dell Publishing Co.: Sept-Oct, 1942 - No. 59, June, 1949

1-Our Gang & Barney Bear by Kelly, Tom & Jerry, Pete Smith, Flip & Dip, The Milky Way begin (all 1st app.)	92	276	644	1200
2-Benny Burro begins (#2 by Kelly)	46	138	322	600
3-5	29	87	203	375
6-Bumbazine & Albert only app. by Kelly	42	125	294	550
7-No Kelly story	22	65	154	285
8-Benny Burro begins by Barks	56	168	392	725
9-Barks-a(2): Benny Burro & Happy Hound; no Kelly story				
	50	150	350	650
10-Benny Burro by Barks	35	105	245	450
11-1st Barney Bear & Benny Burro by Barks (5-6/44); Happy Hound by Barks				
	50	150	350	650
12-20	22	65	154	290
21-30: 30-X-Mas-c	15	45	105	190
31-36-Last Barks issue	11	33	77	140
37-40	7	21	49	85
41-50	5	15	35	65
51-57	5	15	34	55
58,59-No Kelly art or Our Gang stories	4	12	29	45

NOTE: *Barks* art in part only. Barks did not write Barney Bear stories #30-34. (See March of Comics #3, 26). Early issues have photo back-c.

OUR LADY OF FATIMA
Catechetical Guild Educational Society: 3/11/55 (15¢) (36 pgs.)

395	5	15	23	30

OUR LOVE (True Secrets #3 on? or Romantic Affairs #3 on?)
Marvel Comics (SPC): Sept, 1949 - No. 2, Jan, 1950

1-Photo-c	14	42	72	120
2-Photo-c	9	27	49	70

OUR LOVE STORY
Marvel Comics Group: Oct, 1969 - No. 38, Feb, 1976

1	5	15	38	60
2-4,6-8,10,11	3	9	17	25
5-Steranko-a	8	24	56	90
9,12-Kirby-a	3	9	20	30
13-(10/71, 52 pgs.)	4	12	26	40
14-New story by Gary Fredrich & Tarpe' Mills	3	9	19	28

	GD2.0	FN6.0	VF8.0	NM9.4
15-20,27:27-Colan/Everett-a(r?); Kirby/Colletta-r	2	6	12	18
21-26,28-37:	2	6	10	14
38-Last issue	2	6	13	20

NOTE: *J. Buscema* a-1-3, 5-7, 9, 13r, 16r, 19r(2), 21r, 22r(2), 23r, 34r, 35r; c-11, 13, 16, 22, 23, 24, 27, 35. *Colan* a-3-6, 21r(#6), 22r, 23r(#3), 24r(#4), 27; c-19. *Katz* a-17. *Maneely* a-13r. *Romita* a-13r; c-1, 2, 4-6. *Weiss* a-16, 17, 29r(#17).

OUR MISS BROOKS
Dell Publishing Co.: No. 751, Nov, 1956

Four Color 751-Photo-c	8	24	56	100

OUR SECRET (Exciting Love Stories)(Formerly My Secret)
Superior Comics Ltd.: No. 4, Nov, 1949 - No. 8, Jun, 1950

4-Kamen-a; spanking scene	19	57	99	165
5,6,8	10	30	55	80
7-Contains 9 pg. story intended for unpublished Ellery Queen #5; lingerie panels	11	33	55	90

OUTBREED 999
Blackout Comics: May, 1994 - No. 6, 1994 ($2.95)

1-6: 4-1st app. of Extreme Violet in 7 pg. backup story				3.00

OUTCAST, THE
Valiant: Dec, 1995 ($2.50, one-shot)

1-Breyfogle-a.				2.50

OUTCASTS
DC Comics: Oct, 1987 - No. 12, Sept, 1988 ($1.75, limited series)

1-12: John Wagner & Alan Grant scripts in all				2.25

OUTER LIMITS, THE (TV)
Dell Publishing Co.: Jan-Mar, 1964 - No. 18, Oct, 1969 (Most painted-c)

1	12	36	88	150
2-5	7	21	50	80
6-10	6	18	40	65
11-18: 17-Reprints #1. 18-r/#2	4	12	30	50

OUTER SPACE (Formerly This Magazine Is Haunted, 2nd Series)
Charlton Comics: No. 17, May, 1958 - No. 25, Dec, 1959; Nov, 1968

17-Williamson/Wood style art; not by them (Sid Check?)				
	15	45	77	130
18-20-Ditko-a	23	69	121	210
21-25: 21-Ditko-c	14	42	72	125
V2#1(11/68)-Ditko-a, Boyette-c	5	15	38	60

OUTER SPACE BABES, THE
Silhouette Studios: Feb, 1994 ($2.95)

V3#1				3.00

OUT FOR BLOOD
Dark Horse: Sept, 1999 - No. 4, Dec, 1999 ($2.95, B&W, limited series)

1-4-Kelley Jones-c; Erskine-a				3.00

OUTLANDERS (Manga)
Dark Horse Comics: Dec, 1988 - No. 33, Sep,1991 ($2.00-$2.50, B&W, 44pgs.)

1-33: Japanese Sci-fi manga				2.50

OUTLAW (See Return of the...)

OUTLAW FIGHTERS
Atlas Comics (IPC): Aug, 1954 - No. 5, Apr, 1955

1-Tuska-a	14	42	72	120
2-5: 5-Heath-c/a, 7 pgs.	9	27	49	70

NOTE: *Heath* c/a-5. *Maneely* c-2. *Pakula* a-2. *Reinman* a-2. *Tuska* a-1, 2.

OUTLAW KID, THE (1st Series; see Wild Western)
Atlas Comics (CCC No. 1-11/EPI No. 12-29): Sept, 1954 - No. 19, Sept, 1957

1-Origin; The Outlaw Kid & his horse Thunder begin; Black Rider app.				
	28	84	151	260
2-Black Rider app.	14	42	72	120
3-7,9: 3-Wildey-a(3)	12	36	61	100
8-Williamson/Woodbridge-a, 4 pgs.	13	39	66	110
10-Williamson-a	12	36	61	105
11-17,19: 13-Baker text illo. 15-Williamson text illo (unsigned)				
	9	27	49	70
18-Williamson/Mayo-a	10	30	55	80

Outlaw Nation #12 © Delano / Sudzuka

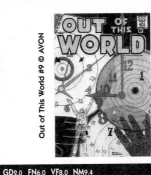

Out of This World #9 © AVON

Out There #1 © Ramos / Austustyn

OV

	GD2.0	FN6.0	VF8.0	NM9.4
	GD2.0	FN6.0	VF8.0	NM9.4

NOTE: **Berg** a-4, 7, 13. **Maneely** c-1-3, 5-8, 11-13, 15, 16, 18. **Pakula** a-3. **Severin** c-10, 17, 19. **Shores** a-1. **Wildey** a-1(3), 2-8, 10, 11, 12(4), 13(4), 15-19(4 each); c-4.

OUTLAW KID, THE (2nd Series)
Marvel Comics Group: Aug, 1970 - No. 30, Oct, 1975

1-Reprints; 1-Orlando-r, Wildey-r(3)	3	9	19	28
2,3,9: 2-Reps. 3,9-Williamson-a(r)	2	6	11	16
4-7: 7-Last 15¢ issue	2	6	10	14
8-Double size (52 pgs.); Crandall-r	2	6	15	22
10-Origin	3	9	20	30
11-20: new-a in #10-16	2	6	11	16
21-30: 27-Origin-r/#10	1	4	7	10

NOTE: **Ayers** a-10, 27r. **Berg** a-7, 25r. **Everett** a-2(2 pgs.). **Gil Kane** c-10, 11, 15, 27r, 28. **Roussos** a-10i, 27i(r). **Severin** c-1, 9, 20, 25. **Wildey** r-1-4, 6-9, 19-22, 25, 26. **Williamson** a-28r. Woodbridge/Williamson a-9r.

OUTLAW NATION
DC Comics (Vertigo): Nov, 2000 - Present ($2.50)

1-16-Fabry painted-c/Delano-s/Sudzuka-a				2.50

OUTLAWS
D. S. Publishing Co.: Feb-Mar, 1948 - No. 9, June-July, 1949

1-Violent & suggestive stories	35	105	185	320
2-Ingels-a; Baker-a	35	105	185	320
3,5,6: 3-Not Frazetta. 5-Sky Sheriff by Good app.				
4-McWilliams-a	16	48	83	140
4-Orlando-a	18	54	94	155
7,8-Ingels-a in each	26	78	136	235
9-(Scarce)-Frazetta-a (7 pgs.)	47	142	286	500

NOTE: Another #3 was also printed in Canada with Frazetta art "Prairie Jinx", 7 pgs.

OUTLAWS, THE (Formerly Western Crime Cases)
Star Publishing Co.: No. 10, May, 1952 - No. 13, Sep, 1953; No. 14, Apr, 1954

10-L. B. Cole-c	22	66	116	195
11-14-L. B. Cole-c. 14-Reprints Western Thrillers #4 (Fox) w/new L.B.Cole-c; Kamen, Feldstein-r	17	51	88	150

OUTLAWS
DC Comics: Sept, 1991 - No. 8, Apr, 1992 ($1.95, limited series)

1-8: Post-apocalyptic Robin Hood.				2.25

OUTLAW 7
Dark Horse Comics: Aug, 2001 - No. 4 ($2.99, limited series)

1,2-Lubera & Feric-s/Lubera & Yeung-a				3.00

OUTLAWS OF THE WEST (Formerly Cody of the Pony Express #10)
Charlton Comics: No. 11, 7/57 - No. 81, 5/70; No. 82, 7/79 - No. 88, 4/80

11	8	24	42	60
12,13,15-17,19,20	5	15	24	32
14-(68 pgs., 2/58)	9	27	49	70
18-Ditko-a	10	30	55	80
21-30	3	9	17	25
31-50: 34-Gunmaster app.	2	6	12	18
51-63,65,67-70: 54-Kid Montana app.	2	6	10	14
64,66: 64-Captain Doom begins (1st app.). 68-Kid Montana series begins	2	6	12	18
71-79: 73-Origin & 1st app. The Sharp Shooter, last app. #74. 75-Last Capt. Doom	2	6	9	12
80,81-Ditko-a	2	6	12	18
82-88				5.00
64,79(Modern Comics-r, 1977, '78)				4.00

OUTLAWS OF THE WILD WEST
Avon Periodicals: 1952 (25¢, 132 pgs.) (4 rebound comics)

1-Wood back-c; Kubert-a (3 Jesse James-r)	34	102	179	310

OUTLAW TRAIL (See Zane Grey 4-Color 511)

OUT OF SANTA'S BAG (See March of Comics #10)

OUT OF THE NIGHT (The Hooded Horseman #18 on)
Amer. Comics Group (Creston/Scope): Feb-Mar, 1952 - No. 17, Oct-Nov, 1954

1-Williamson-a/LeDoux-a (9 pgs.)	61	182	381	675
2-Williamson-a (5 pgs.)	47	140	286	500
3,5-10: 9-Sci/Fic story	28	84	148	255
4-Williamson-a (7 pgs.)	40	120	232	400

11-17: 13-Nostrand-a? 17-E.C. Wood swipe	22	66	116	195

NOTE: **Landau** a-14, 16, 17. **Shelly** a-12.

OUT OF THE SHADOWS
Standard Comics/Visual Editions: No. 5, July, 1952 - No. 14, Aug, 1954

5-Toth-p; Moreira, Tuska-a; Roussos-c	55	165	330	575
6-Toth/Celardo-a; Katz-a(2)	40	120	220	380
7,9: 7-Jack Katz-c/a(2). 9-Crandall-a(2)	30	90	159	275
8-Katz shrunken head-c	47	141	286	500
10-Spider-c; Sekowsky-a	27	81	145	250
11-Toth-a, 2 pgs.; Katz-a; Andru-c	30	90	159	275
12-Toth/Peppe-a(2); Katz-a	40	120	214	370
13-Cannabalism story; Sekowsky-a; Roussos-c	35	105	188	325
14-Toth-a	30	90	159	275

OUT OF THE VORTEX (Comics' Greatest World:... #1-4)
Dark Horse Comics: Oct., 1993 - No. 12, Oct, 1994 ($2.00, limited series)

1-11: 1-Foil logo. 4-Dorman-c(p). 6-Hero Zero x-over				2.25
12 ($2.50)				2.50

NOTE: **Art Adams** c-7. **Golden** c-8. **Mignola** c-2. **Simonson** c-3. **Zeck** c-10.

OUT OF THIS WORLD
Charlton Comics: Aug, 1956 - No. 16, Dec, 1959

1	26	78	139	240
2	13	39	66	115
3-6-Ditko-c/a (3) each	31	93	168	290
7-(2/58, 15¢, 68 pgs.)-Ditko-c/a(4)	33	99	174	300
8-(5/58, 15¢, 68 pgs.)-Ditko-c/a(2)	27	81	145	250
9,10,12,16-Ditko-a	22	66	116	195
11-Ditko c/a (3)	25	75	133	230
13-15	10	30	55	80

NOTE: **Ditko** c-3-12, 16. **Reinman** a-10.

OUT OF THIS WORLD
Avon Periodicals: June, 1950; Aug, 1950

1-Kubert-a(2) (one reprinted/Eerie #1, 1947) plus Crom the Barbarian by Gardner Fox & John Giunta (origin); Fawcette-c	66	198	413	725
1-(8/50) Reprint; no month on cover	45	135	270	475

OUT OF THIS WORLD ADVENTURES
Avon Periodicals: July, 1950 - No. 2, Dec, 1950 (25¢ pulp)

1-Kubert-a	64	192	398	700
2-Kubert-a plus The Spider God of Akka by Gardner Fox & John Giunta. pulp magazine w/comic insert	45	135	270	475

NOTE: Out of This World Adventures was a sci-fi pulp magazine w/32 pgs. of color comics.

OUT OUR WAY WITH WORRY WART
Dell Publishing Co.: No. 680, Feb, 1956

Four Color 680	3	9	19	28

OUTPOSTS
Blackthorne Publishing: June, 1987 - No. 4, 1987 ($1.25)

1-4: 1-Kaluta-c(p)				2.25

OUTSIDERS, THE
DC Comics: Nov, 1985 - No. 28, Feb, 1988

1				3.00
2-28: 18-26-Batman returns. 21-Intro. Strike Force Kobra; 1st app. Clayface IV 22-E.C. parody; Orlando-a. 21- 25-Atomic Knight app. 27,28-Millennium tie-ins.				2.25
Annual 1 (12/86, $2.50), Special 1 (7/87, $1.50).				2.50

NOTE: **Aparo** a-7, 9-14, 17-22, 25, 26; c-1-7, 9-14, 17, 19-26. **Byrne** a-11. **Bolland** a-6, 18; c-16. **Ditko** a-13p. **Erik Larsen** a-24, 27 28; c-27, 28. **Morrow** a-12.

OUTSIDERS
DC Comics: Nov, 1993 - No. 24, Nov, 1995 ($1.75/$1.95/$2.25)

1-11,0,12-24: 1-Alpha; Travis Charest-c. 1-Omega; Travis Charest-c. 5-Atomic Knight app. 8-New Batman-c/story. 11-(9/94)-Zero Hour. 0-(10/94).12-(11/94). 21-Darkseid cameo. 22-New Gods app.				2.25

OUT THERE
DC Comics(Cliffhanger): July, 2001 - Present ($2.50)

1-Ramos-c/a; Augustyn-s				3.00
2-7				2.50

OVERKILL: WITCHBLADE/ ALIENS/ DARKNESS/ PREDATOR

The Pact #3 © IM

Panhandle Pete and Jennifer #1 © Laue Publ. Co.

Panic #10 © WMG

GD2.0   FN6.0   VF8.0   NM9.4

GD2.0   FN6.0   VF8.0   NM9.4

Image Comics/Dark Horse Comics: Dec, 2000 - No. 2, 2001 ($5.95)

1,2-Jenkins-s/Lansing, Ching & Benitez-a 6.00

OVER THE EDGE
Marvel Comics: Nov, 1995 - No. 10, Aug, 1996 (99¢)

1-10: 1,6,10-Daredevil-c/story. 2,7-Dr. Strange-c/story. 3-Hulk-c/story.
4,9-Ghost Rider-c/story. 5-Punisher-c/story. 8-Elektra-c/story 2.25

OWL, THE (See Crackajack Funnies #25, Popular Comics #72 and Occult Files of Dr. Spektor #22)
Gold Key: April, 1967; No. 2, April, 1968

1-Written by Jerry Siegel; '40s super hero	5	15	35	65
2	4	12	30	50

OZ (See First Comics Graphic Novel, Marvel Treaury Of Oz & MGM's Marvelous...)

OZ
Caliber Press: 1994 - 1997 ($2.95, B&W)

0-20: 0-Released between #10 & #11 .... 3.00
1 ($5.95)-Limited Edition; double-c 6.00
..Specials: Freedom Fighters. Lion. Scarecrow. Tin Man 3.00

OZARK IKE
Dell Publishing Co./Standard Comics B11 on: Feb, 1948; Nov, 1948 - No. 24, Dec, 1951; No. 25, Sept, 1952

Four Color 180(1948-Dell)	10	30	70	130
B11, B12, 13-15	9	27	49	70
16-25	7	21	38	55

OZ: DAEMONSTORM
Caliber Press: 1997 ($3.95, B&W, one-shot)

1 .... 4.00

OZ: ROMANCE IN RAGS
Caliber Press: 1996 ($2.95, B&W, limited series)

1-3, ..Special 3.00

OZ SQUAD
Brave New Worlds/Patchwork Press: 1992 - No. 4, 1994 ($2.50/$2.75, B&W)

1-4-Patchwork Press 3.00

OZ SQUAD
Patchwork Press: Dec, 1995 - No. 10, 1996 ($3.95/$2.95, B&W)

1-($3.95) 4.00
2-10 .... 3.00

OZ: STRAW AND SORCERY
Caliber Press: 1997 ($2.95, B&W, limited series)

1-3 .... 3.00

OZ-WONDERLAND WARS, THE
DC Comics: Jan, 1986 - No. 3, March, 1986 (Mini-series)

1-3-Capt Carrot app.; funny animals 4.00

OZZIE & BABS (TV Teens #14 on)
Fawcett Publications: Dec, 1947 - No. 13, Fall, 1949

1-Teen-age	9	27	49	70
2	5	15	25	35
3-13	5	14	21	28

OZZIE AND HARRIET (The Adventures of... on cover)
National Periodical Publications: Oct-Nov, 1949 - No. 5, June-July, 1950

1-Photo-c	95	285	597	1050
2	47	140	286	500
3-5	40	120	232	400

OZZY OSBOURNE (Todd McFarland Presents)
Image Comics (Todd McFarland Prod.): June, 1999 ($4.95, magazine-sized)

1-Bio, interview and comic story; Ormston painted-a; Ashley Wood-c ... 5.00

PACIFIC COMICS GRAPHIC NOVEL (See Image Graphic Novel)

PACIFIC PRESENTS (Also see Starslayer #2, 3)
Pacific Comics: Oct, 1982 - No. 2, Apr, 1983; No. 3, Mar, 1984 - No. 4, Jun, 1984

1-Chapter 3 of The Rocketeer; Stevens-c/a; Bettie Page model	1	3	5	7

2-Chapter 4 of The Rocketeer (4th app.); nudity; Stevens-c/a

	1	3	5	7
3,4: 3-1st app. Vanity				3.00

NOTE: **Conrad** a-3, 4; c-3. **Ditko** a-1-3; c-1(1/2). **Dave Stevens** a-1, 2; c-1(1/2), 2.

PACT, THE
Image Comics: Feb, 1994 - No. 3, June, 1994 ($1.95, limited series)

1-3-Valentino co-scripts & layouts 2.25

PAGEANT OF COMICS (See Jane Arden & Mopsy)
Archer St. John: Sept, 1947 - No. 2, Oct, 1947

1,2: 1-Mopsy strip-r. 2-Jane Arden strip-r	10	30	55	80

PAINKILLER JANE
Event Comics: June, 1997 - Present ($3.95/$2.95)

1-Augustyn/Waid-s/Leonardi/Palmiotti-a, variant-c 4.00
2-5: Two covers (Quesada, Leonardi) 3.00
0-(1/99, $3.95) Retells origin; two covers 4.00

PAINKILLER JANE / DARKCHYLDE
Event Comics: Oct, 1998 ($2.95, one-shot)

Preview-($6.95) DF Edition, 1-($6.95) DF Edition 7.00
1-Three covers; J.G. Jones-a 3.00

PAINKILLER JANE / HELLBOY
Event Comics: Aug, 1998 ($2.95, one-shot)

1-Leonardi & Palmiotti-a 3.00

PAINKILLER JANE VS. THE DARKNESS
Event Comics: Apr, 1997 ($2.95, one-shot)

1-Ennis-s; four variant-c (Conner, Hildebrandts, Quesada, Silvestri) ... 3.50

PAKKINS' LAND
Caliber Comics (Tapestry): Oct, 1996 - No. 6, July, 1997 ($2.95, B&W)

1-Gary and Rhoda Shipman-s/a 6.00
2,3 .... 4.00
1-3-2nd printing 3.00
4-6 .... 3.00
0-(6/97, $1.95) 3.00

PAKKINS' LAND: FORGOTTEN DREAMS
Caliber Comics/Image Comics #4: Apr, 1998 - No. 4, Mar, 2000 ($2.95, B&W)

1-4-Gary and Rhoda Shipman-s/a 3.00

PAKKINS' LAND: QUEST FOR KINGS
Caliber Comics: Aug, 1997 - No. 6, Mar, 1998 ($2.95, B&W)

1-6: 1-Gary and Rhoda Shipman-s/a; Jeff Smith var-c 3.00

PANCHO VILLA
Avon Periodicals: 1950

nn-Kinstler-c	25	75	130	225

PANDEMONIUM
Chaos! Comics: Sept, 1998 ($2.95, one-shot)

1-Al Rio-c 3.00

PANHANDLE PETE AND JENNIFER (TV) (See Gene Autry #20)
J. Charles Laue Publishing Co.: July, 1951 - No. 3, Nov, 1951

1	10	30	55	80
2,3	7	21	36	50

PANIC (Companion to Mad)
E. C. Comics (Tiny Tot Comics): Feb-Mar, 1954 - No. 12, Dec-Jan, 1955-56

1-Used in Senate Investigation hearings; Elder draws entire E. C. staff; Santa

Claus & Mickey Spillane parody	26	78	182	325
2	12	36	84	150

3,4: 3-Senate Subcommittee parody; Davis draws Gaines, Feldstein & Kelly, 1 pg.; Old King Cole smokes marijuana. 4-Infinity-c; John Wayne parody

	10	30	70	125

5-11: 8-Last pre-code issue (5/55). 9-Superman, Smilin' Jack & Dick Tracy app. on-c; has photo of Walter Winchell on-c. 11-Wheedies cereal box-c

	9	26	63	115
12 (Low distribution; thousands were destroyed)	12	36	84	150

NOTE: **Davis** a-1-12; c-12. **Elder** a-1-12. **Feldstein** c-1-3, 5. **Kamen** a-1. **Orlando** a-1-9. **Wolverton** c-4, panel-3. **Wood** a-2-9, 11, 12.

Parts of a Hole #1
© Brian Michael Bendis

Patches #5 © RH

Patsy and Hedy #4 © MAR

	GD2.0	FN6.0	VF8.0	NM9.4

	GD2.0	FN6.0	VF8.0	NM9.4

PANIC (Magazine) (Satire)
Panic Publ.: July, 1958 - No. 6, July, 1959; V2#10, Dec, 1965 - V2#12, 1966

1	11	33	55	90
2-6	7	21	36	50
V2#10-12: Reprints earlier issues	3	9	20	30

NOTE: *Davis* a-3(2 pgs.), 4, 5, 10; c-10. *Elder* a-5. *Powell* a-V2#10, 11. *Torres* a-1-5. *Tuska* a-V2#11.

PANIC
Gemstone Publishing: March, 1997 - No. 11 ($2.50, quarterly)

1-11: E.C. reprints				2.50

PANTHA (See Vampirella-The New Monthly #16,17)

PANTHA: HAUNTED PASSION (Also see Vampirella Monthly #0)
Harris Comics: May, 1997 ($2.95, B&W, one-shot)

1-r/Vampirella #30,31				3.00

PARADAX (Also see Strange Days)
Eclipse Comics: 1986 (one-shot)

1				2.25

PARADAX
Vortex Comics: April, 1987 - No. 2, Aug, 1987 ($1.75, mature)

1,2-Nudity, adult language				2.25

PARADE (See Hanna-Barbera...)

PARADE COMICS (Frisky Animals on Parade #2 on)
Ajax/Farrell Publ. (World Famous Publ.): Sept, 1957

1	7	21	36	50

NOTE: *Cover title: Frisky Animals on Parade.*

PARADE OF PLEASURE
Derric Verschoyle Ltd., London, England: 1954 (192 pgs.) (Hardback book)
By Geoffrey Wagner. Contains section devoted to the censorship of American comic books with illustrations in color and black and white. (Also see **Seduction of the Innocent**). Distributed in USA by Library Publishers, N. Y.

	40	120	220	380
with dust jacket....	77	231	483	850

PARADISE TOO!
Abstract Studios: 2000 - Present ($2.95, B&W)

1-4-Terry Moore's unpublished newspaper strips and sketches				3.00

PARADISE X: HERALDS (Also see Earth X and Universe X)
Marvel Comics: Dec, 2001 - No. 3, Feb, 2002 ($3.50)

1-3-Prelude to Paradise X series; Ross-c; Pugh-a				3.50
Special Edition (Wizard preview) Ross-c				2.25

PARADOX
Dark Visions Publ: June, 1994 - No. 2, Aug, 1994 ($2.95, B&W, mature)

1,2: 1-Linsner-c. 2-Boris-c.				3.00

PARALLAX: EMERALD NIGHT (See Final Night)
DC Comics: Nov, 1996 ($2.95, one-shot, 48 pgs.)

1-Final Night tie-in; Green Lantern (Kyle Rayner) app.				4.00

PARAMOUNT ANIMATED COMICS (See Harvey Comics Hits #60, 62)
Harvey Publications: No. 3, Feb, 1953 - No. 22, July, 1956

3-Baby Huey, Herman & Katnip, Buzzy the Crow begin	22	66	116	195
4-6	10	30	55	85
7-Baby Huey becomes permanent cover feature; cover title becomes Baby Huey with #9	21	63	110	185
8-10: 9-Infinity-c	10	30	55	80
11-22	8	24	42	60

PARENT TRAP, THE (Disney)
Dell Publishing Co.: No. 1210, Oct-Dec, 1961

Four Color 1210-Movie, Haley Mills photo-c	9	27	63	120

PARODY
Armour Publishing: Mar, 1977 - No. 3, Aug, 1977 (B&W humor magazine)

1	2	6	12	18
2,3: 2-King Kong, Happy Days. 3-Charlie's Angels, Rocky				

	2	6	10	14

PAROLE BREAKERS
Avon Periodicals/Realistic #2 on: Dec, 1951 - No. 3, July, 1952

1(#2 on inside)-r-c/Avon paperback #283 (painted-c)	43	129	257	450
2-Kubert-a; r-c/Avon paperback #114 (photo-c)	33	99	174	300
3-Kinstler-c	30	90	159	275

PARTRIDGE FAMILY, THE (TV)(Also see David Cassidy)
Charlton Comics: Mar, 1971 - No. 21, Dec, 1973

1	6	18	42	70
2-4,6-10	3	9	21	32
5-Partridge Family Summer Special (52 pgs.); The Shadow, Lone Ranger, Charlie McCarthy, Flash Gordon, Hopalong Cassidy, Gene Autry & others app.	7	21	53	85
11-21	3	9	17	25

PARTS OF A HOLE
Caliber Press: 1991 ($2.50, B&W)

1-Short stories & cartoons by Brian Michael Bendis				3.00

PARTS UNKNOWN
Eclipse Comics/FX: July, 1992 - No. 4, Oct, 1992 ($2.50, B&W, mature)

1-4: All contain FX gaming cards				2.50

PARTS UNKNOWN
Image Comics: May, 2000 - Present ($2.95, B&W)

...: Killing Attractions 1 (5/00) Beau Smith-s/Brad Gorby-a				3.00
...: Hostile Takeover 1-4 (6-9/00)				3.00

PASSION, THE
Catechetical Guild: No. 394, 1955

394	5	14	21	28

PASSOVER (See Avengelyne)
Maximum Press: Dec, 1996 ($2.99, one-shot)

1				3.00

PAT BOONE (TV)(Also see Superman's Girlfriend Lois Lane #9)
National Per. Publ.: Sept-Oct, 1959 - No. 5, May-Jun, 1960 (All have photo-c)

1	45	135	270	475
2-5: 3-Fabian, Connie Francis & Paul Anka photos on-c. 4-Previews "Journey To The Center Of The Earth". 4-Johnny Mathis & Bobby Darin photos on-c. 5-Dick Clark & Frankie Avalon photos on-c	39	117	208	360

PATCHES
Rural Home/Patches Publ. (Orbit): Mar-Apr, 1945 - No. 11, Nov, 1947

1-L. B. Cole-c	40	120	220	380
2	15	45	77	130
3,4,6,8-11: 6-Henry Aldrich story. 8-Smiley Burnette-c/s (6/47); pre-dates Smiley Burnette #1. 9-Mr. District Attorney story (radio). Leav/Keigstein-a (16 pgs.). 9-11-Leav-c. 10-Jack Carson (radio) c/story; Leav-c. 11-Red Skelton story	14	42	72	120
5-Danny Kaye-c/story; L.B. Cole-c.	21	63	110	185
7-Hopalong Cassidy-c/story	18	54	94	155

PATHWAYS TO FANTASY
Pacific Comics: July, 1984

1-Barry Smith-c/a; Jeff Jones-a (4 pgs.)				4.00

PATORUZU (See Adventures of...)

PATRIOTS, THE
DC Comics (WildStorm): Jan, 2000 - No. 10, Oct, 2000 ($2.50)

1-10-Choi and Peterson-s/Ryan-a				2.50

PATSY & HEDY (Teenage)(Also see Hedy Wolfe)
Atlas Comics/Marvel (GPI/Male): Feb, 1952 - No. 110, Feb, 1967

1-Patsy Walker & Hedy Wolfe; Al Jaffee-c	22	66	116	200
2	12	36	61	105
3-10: 3,8-Al Jaffee-a	10	30	55	80
11-20	8	24	42	60
21-40	6	18	32	45
41-60	3	10	23	35

Pat the Brat #2 © AP

Paul the Samurai #4 © NEC

Peanuts #9 © UFS

	GD2.0	FN6.0	VF8.0	NM9.4
61-80,100: 88-Lingerie panel	3	9	17	25
81-87,89-99,101-110	2	6	15	22
Annual 1(1963)-Early Marvel annual	9	27	65	110

PATSY & HER PALS (Teenage)
Atlas Comics (PPI): May, 1953 - No. 29, Aug, 1957

1-Patsy Walker	19	57	99	165
2	10	30	55	80
3-10	9	27	49	70
11-29: 24-Everett-c	7	21	36	50

PATSY WALKER (See All Teen, A Date With Patsy, Girls' Life, Miss America Magazine, Patsy & Hedy, Patsy & Her Pals & Teen Comics)
Marvel/Atlas Comics (BPC): 1945 (no month) - No. 124, Dec, 1965

1-Teenage	47	140	286	500
2	25	75	133	230
3,4,6-10	20	60	105	175
5-Injury-to-eye-c	23	69	121	210
11,12,15,16,18	13	39	66	110
13,14,17,19-22-Kurtzman's "Hey Look"	14	42	72	120
23,24	10	30	55	80
25-Rusty by Kurtzman; painted-c	14	42	72	120
26-29,31: 26-31: 52 pgs.	9	27	49	70
30(52 pgs.)-Egghead Doodle by Kurtzman (1 pg.)	10	30	55	80
32-57: Last precode (3/55)	7	21	36	50
58-80,100	3	10	23	35
81-99: 92,98-Millie x-over	3	9	17	25
101-124	2	6	15	22
Fashion Parade 1(1966, 68 pgs.) (Beware cut-out & marked pages)				
	8	24	56	90

NOTE: Painted c-25-28. Anti-Wertham editorial in #21. Georgie app. in #8, 11. Millie app. in #10, 92, 98. Mitzi app. in #11. Rusty app. in #12, 25. Willie app. in #12. **Al Jaffee** c-57, 58.

PAT THE BRAT (Adventures of Pipsqueak #34 on)
Archie Publications (Radio): June, 1953; Summer, 1955 - No. 4, 5/56; No. 15, 7/56 - No. 33, 7/59

nn(6/53)	14	42	72	120
1(Summer, 1955)	10	30	55	80
2-4-(5/56) (#5-14 not published)	6	18	32	45
15-(7/56)-33	3	10	23	35

PAT THE BRAT COMICS DIGEST MAGAZINE
Archie Publications: October, 1980

1-Li'l Jinx & Super Duck app.	2	6	10	14

PATTY CAKE
Permanent Press: Mar, 1995 - No. 9, Jul, 1996 ($2.95, B&W)

1-9: Scott Roberts-s/a				3.00

PATTY CAKE
Caliber Press (Tapestry): Oct, 1996 - No. 3, Apr, 1997 ($2.95, B&W)

1-3: Scott Roberts-s/a, ...Christmas (12/96)				3.00

PATTY CAKE & FRIENDS
Slave Labor Graphics: Nov, 1997 - Present ($2.95, B&W)

Here There Be Monsters (10/97), 1-14: Scott Roberts-s/a				3.00
Volume 2 #1 (11/00, $4.95)				5.00

PATTY POWERS (Formerly Della Vision #3)
Atlas Comics: No. 4, Oct, 1955 - No. 7, Oct, 1956

4	10	30	55	80
5-7	6	18	29	40

PAT WILTON (See Mighty Midget Comics)

PAUL
Spire Christian Comics (Fleming H. Revell Co.): 1978 (49¢)

nn	1	3	6	9

PAULINE PERIL (See The Close Shaves of...)

PAUL REVERE'S RIDE (TV, Disney, see Walt Disney Showcase #34)
Dell Publishing Co.: No. 822, July, 1957

Four Color 822-w/Johnny Tremain, Toth-a	9	27	63	120

PAUL TERRY (See Heckle and Jeckle)

PAUL TERRY'S ADVENTURES OF MIGHTY MOUSE (See Adventures of...)
PAUL TERRY'S COMICS (Formerly Terry-Toons Comics; becomes Adventures of Mighty Mouse No. 126 on)
St. John Publishing Co.: No. 85, Mar, 1951 - No. 125, May, 1955

85,86-Same as Terry-Toons #85, & 86 with only a title change; published at same time?; Mighty Mouse, Heckle & Jeckle & Gandy Goose continue from Terry-Toons	11	33	55	90
87-99	8	24	42	60
100	9	27	49	70
101-104,107-125: 121,122,125-Painted-c	7	21	38	55
105,106-Giant Comics Edition (25¢, 100 pgs.) (9/53 & ?). 105-Little Roquefort-c/story	19	57	99	165

PAUL TERRY'S MIGHTY MOUSE (See Mighty Mouse)
PAUL TERRY'S MIGHTY MOUSE ADVENTURE STORIES (See Mighty Mouse Adventure Stories)

PAUL THE SAMURAI (See The Tick #4)
New England Comics: July, 1992 - No. 6, July, 1993 ($2.75, B&W)

1-6				2.75

PAWNEE BILL
Story Comics (Youthful Magazines?): Feb, 1951 - No. 3, July, 1951

1-Bat Masterson, Wyatt Earp app.	13	39	66	110
2,3: Golden Warrior; Cameron-a	8	24	42	60

PAY-OFF (This is the..., ...Crime, ...Detective Stories)
D. S. Publishing Co.: July-Aug, 1948 - No. 5, Mar-Apr, 1949 (52 pgs.)

1-True Crime Cases #1,2	26	78	139	240
2	16	48	83	140
3-5-Thrilling Detective Stories	14	42	72	120

PEACEMAKER, THE (Also see Fightin' Five)
Charlton Comics: V3#1, Mar, 1967 - No. 5, Nov, 1967 (All 12¢ cover price)

1-Fightin' Five begins	5	15	34	55
2,3,5	3	9	20	30
4-Origin The Peacemaker	4	12	26	40
1,2(Modern Comics reprint, 1978)				5.00

PEACEMAKER (Also see Crisis On Infinite Earths & Showcase '93 #7,9,10)
DC Comics: Jan, 1988 - No. 4, Apr, 1988 ($1.25, limited series)

1-4				2.50

PEANUTS (Charlie Brown) (See Fritzi Ritz, Nancy & Sluggo, Sparkle & Sparkler, Tip Top, Tip Topper & United Comics)
Dell Publishing Co./Gold Key: 1953-54; No. 878, 2/58 - No. 13, 5-7/62; 5/63 - No. 4, 2/64

1(1953-54)-Reprints United Features' Strange As It Seems, Willie, Ferndand	13	38	84	155
Four Color 878(#1) Schulz-s/a, with assistance from Dale Hale and Jim Sasseville thru #4	15	45	105	200
Four Color 969,1015('59)	10	30	70	135
4(2-4/60) Schulz-s/a; one story by Anthony Pocrnich, Schulz's assistant cartoonist	8	24	56	105
5-13-Schulz only; s/a by Pocrnich	6	18	42	80
1(Gold Key, 5/63)	11	33	77	145
2-4	7	21	49	90

PEBBLES & BAMM BAMM (TV) (See Cave Kids #7, 12)
Charlton Comics: Jan, 1972 - No. 36, Dec, 1976 (Hanna-Barbera)

1-From the Flintstones; "Teen Age..." on cover	5	15	34	55
2-10	3	9	19	28
11-20	2	6	13	20
21-36	2	6	11	15

PEBBLES & BAMM BAMM (TV)
Harvey Comics: Nov, 1993 - No. 3, Mar, 1994 ($1.50) (Hanna-Barbera)

V2#1-3				3.00
...Giant Size 1 (10/93, $2.25, 68 pgs.)("Summer Special" on-c)				4.00

PEBBLES FLINTSTONE (TV) (See The Flintstones #11)
Gold Key: Sept, 1963 (Hanna-Barbera)

1 (10088-309)-Early Pebbles app.	9	27	63	120

Penny #3 © AVON

Pedro #1 © FOX

Pep Comics #47 © AP

	GD2.0	FN6.0	VF8.0	NM9.4

PEDRO (Formerly My Private Life #17; also see Romeo Tubbs)
Fox Features Syndicate: No. 18, June, 1950 - No. 2, Aug, 1950?

	GD2.0	FN6.0	VF8.0	NM9.4
18(#1)-Wood-c/a(p)	23	69	121	210
2-Wood-a?	17	51	88	150

PEE-WEE PIXIES (See The Pixies)

PELLEAS AND MELISANDE (See Night Music #4, 5)

PENALTY (See Crime Must Pay the...)

PENDRAGON (Knights of... #5 on; also see Knights of...)
Marvel Comics UK, Ltd.: July, 1992 - No. 15, Sept, 1993 ($1.75)

1-15: 1-4-Iron Man app. 6-8-Spider-Man app.				2.25

PENDULUM ILLUSTRATED BIOGRAPHIES
Pendulum Press: 1979 (B&W)

19-355x-George Washington/Thomas Jefferson, 19-3495-Charles Lindbergh/Amelia Earhart, 19-3509-Harry Houdini/Walt Disney, 19-3517-Davy Crockett/Daniel Boone-Redondo-a, 19-3525-Elvis Presley/Beatles, 19-3533-Benjamin Franklin/Martin Luther King Jr, 19-3541-Abraham Lincoln/Franklin D. Roosevelt, 19-3568-Marie Curie/Albert Einstein-Redondo-a, 19-3576-Thomas Edison/Alexander Graham Bell-Redondo-a, 19-3584-Vince Lombardi/Pele, 19-3592-Babe Ruth/Jackie Robinson, 19-3606-Jim Thorpe/Althea Gibson

Softback				3.00
Hardback				5.00

NOTE: Above books still available from publisher.

PENDULUM ILLUSTRATED CLASSICS (Now Age Illustrated)
Pendulum Press: 1973 - 1978 (75¢, 62pp, B&W, 5-3/8x8")
(Also see Marvel Classics)

64-100x(1973)-Dracula-Redondo art, 64-131x-The Invisible Man-Nino art, 64-0968-Dr. Jekyll and Mr. Hyde-Redondo art, 64-1005-Black Beauty, 64-1010-Call of the Wild, 64-1020-Frankenstein, 64-1025-Huckleberry Finn, 64-1030-Moby Dick-Nino-a, 64-1040-Red Badge of Courage, 64-1045-The Time Machine-Nino-a, 64-1050-Tom Sawyer, 64-1055-Twenty Thousand Leagues Under the Sea, 64-1069-Treasure Island, 64-1328(1974)-Kidnapped, 64-1336-Three Musketeers-Nino art, 64-1344-A Tale of Two Cities, 64-1352-Journey to the Center of the Earth, 64-1360-The War of the Worlds-Nino-a, 64-1379-The Greatest Advs. of Sherlock Holmes-Redondo-a, 64-1387-Mysterious Island, 64-1395-Hunchback of Notre Dame, 64-1409-Helen Keller-story of my life, 64-1417-Scarlet Letter, 64-1425-Gulliver's Travels, 64-2618(1977)-Around the World in Eighty Days, 64-2626-Captains Courageous, 64-2634-Connecticut Yankee, 64-2642-The Hound of the Gods, 64-3150-Ivanhoe, 64-2650-The House of Seven Gables, 64-2669-Jane Eyre, 64-2677-The Last of the Mohicans, 64-2685-The Best of O'Henry, 64-2693-The Best of Poe-Redondo-a, 64-2707-Two Years Before the Mast, 64-2715-White Fang, 64-2723-Wuthering Heights, 64-3126(1978)-Ben Hur-Redondo art, 64-3134-A Christmas Carol, 64-3142-The Food of the Gods, 64-3169-The Man in the Iron Mask, 64-3177-The Prince and the Pauper, 64-3185-The Prisoner of Zenda, 64-3193-The Return of the Native, 64-3207-Robinson Crusoe, 64-3215-The Scarlet Pimpernel, 64-3223-The Sea Wolf, 64-3231-The Swiss Family Robinson, 64-3851-Billy Budd, 64-3894-Heidi, 64-3908-The Iliad, 64-3916-Lord Jim, 64-3924-The Mutiny on Board H.M.S. Bounty, 64-3932-The Odyssey, 64-3940-Oliver Twist, 64-3959-Pride and Prejudice, 64-3967-The Turn of the Screw

Softback				3.00
Hardback				5.00

NOTE: All of the above books can be ordered from the publisher; some were reprinted as Marvel Classic Comics #1-12. In 1972 there was another brief series of 12 titles which contained Classics Ill. artwork. They were entitled **Now Age Books** Illustrated, but can be easily distinguished from later series by the small Classics Illustrated logo at the top of the front cover. The format is the same as the later series. The 48 pg. C.I. art was stretched out to make 62 pgs. After Twin Circle Publ. terminated the Classics Ill. series in 1971, they made a one year contract with Pendulum Press to print these twelve titles of C.I. art. Pendulum was unhappy with the contract, and at the end of 1972 began their own art series, utilizing the talents of the Filipino artist group. One detail which makes this rather confusing is that when they redid the art in 1973, they gave it the same identifying no. as the 1972 series. All 12 of the 1972 C.I. editions have new covers, taken from internal art panels. The cover of their recent age, all of the 1972 C.I. series are very rare. Mint copies would fetch at least $50. Here is a list of the 1972 series, with C.I. title no. counterpart:

64-1005 (CI#60-A2) 64-1010 (CI#91) 64-1015 (CI-Jr #503) 64-1020 (CI#26)
64-1025 (CI#19-A2) 64-1030 (CI#5-A2) 64-1035 (CI#169) 64-1040 (CI#98)
64-1045 (CI#133) 64-1050 (CI#50-A2) 64-1055 (CI#47) 64-1060 (CI-Jr#535)

PENDULUM ILLUSTRATED ORIGINALS
Pendulum Press: 1979 (In color)

94-4254-Solarman: The Beginning (See Solarman)				5.00

PENDULUM'S ILLUSTRATED STORIES
Pendulum Press: 1990 - No. 72, 1990? (No cover price ($4.95), squarebound, 68 pgs.)

1-72: Reprints Pendulum Ill. Classics series				5.00

PENNY
Avon Comics: 1947 - No. 6, Sept-Oct, 1949 (Newspaper reprints)

	GD2.0	FN6.0	VF8.0	NM9.4
1-Photo & biography of creator	12	36	61	100
2-5	8	24	42	60
6-Perry Como photo on-c	9	27	49	70

PENNY CENTURY (See Love and Rockets)
Fantagraphics Books: Dec, 1997 - Present ($2.95, B&W, mini-series)

1-7-Jaime Hernandez-s/a				3.00

PENTHOUSE COMIX
General Media Int.: 1994 - No. 33, July, 1998 ($4.95, bimonthly, magazine & comic sized, mature)

1		1	3	6	9
2-5					6.00
6-33: 15-Corben-c. 16-Dorman-c. 17-Manara-c. 20-Chiodo-c. 21,23-Boris-c 24-Scott Hampton-c. 26-33-Comic-sized					5.00

PENTHOUSE MAX
General Media International: July, 1996 - No. 3 ($4.95, magazine, mature)

1-3: 1-Giffen, Sears, Maguire-a. 2-Political satire. 3-Mr. Monster-c/app.; Dorman-c				5.00

PENTHOUSE MEN'S ADVENTURE COMIX
General Media International: 1995 - No. 7, 1996 ($4.95, magazine, mature)

1-7 (Magazine Size): 1-Boris-a, 1-5 (Comic Size): 1-Boris-c				5.00

PEP COMICS (See Archie Giant Series #576, 589, 601, 614, 624)
MLJ Magazines/Archie Publications No. 56 (3/46) on: Jan, 1940 - No. 411, Mar, 1987

1-Intro. The Shield (1st patriotic hero) by Irving Novick; origin & 1st app. The Comet by Jack Cole, The Queen of Diamonds & Kayo Ward; The Rocket, The Press Guardian (The Falcon #1 only), Sergeant Boyle, Fu Chang, & Bentley of of Scotland Yard; Robot-c; begin	846	2538	5922	11,000
2-Origin The Rocket	227	681	1420	2500
3	164	492	1023	1800
4-Wizard cameo	136	408	852	1500
5-Wizard cameo in Shield story	136	408	852	1500
6-10: 8-Last Cole Comet; no Cole-a in #6,7	102	306	638	1125
11-Dusty, Shield's sidekick begins (1st app.); last Press Guardian, Fu Chang	107	321	669	1175
12-Origin & 1st app. Fireball (2/41); Danny in Wonderland begins	127	381	795	1400
13-15	86	258	540	950
16-Origin Madam Satan; blood drainage-c	136	408	852	1500
17-Origin/1st app. The Hangman (7/41); death of The Comet; Comet is revealed as Hangman's brother	317	951	1979	3800
18-21: 20-Last Fireball. 21-Last Madam Satan	84	252	525	925
22-Intro. & 1st app. Archie, Betty, & Jughead(12/41); (also see Jackpot)	1214	3642	8500	17,000
23	155	465	966	1700
24,25: 24-Coach Kleets app. (unnamed until Archie #94); bondage/torture-c. 25-1st app. Archie's jalopy; 1st skinny Mr. Weatherbee prototype	114	342	713	1250
26-1st app. Veronica Lodge (4/42)	164	492	1023	1800
27-30: 29-Origin Shield retold; 30-Capt. Commando begins & ends; 1st Miss Grundy (definitive version); see Jackpot #4	91	273	568	1000
31-35: 31-MLJ offices & artists are visited in Sgt. Boyle story; 1st app. Mr. Lodge. 32-Shield dons new costume. 34-Bondage/Hypo-c. 33-Pre-Moose tryout (see Jughead #1)	73	219	455	800
36-1st Archie-c (2/43) w/Shield & Hangman	173	519	1080	1900
37-40	55	165	331	580
41-50: 41-Archie-c begin. 47-Last Hangman issue; infinity-c. 48-Black Hood begins (5/44); ends #51,59,60	40	120	220	380
51-60: 52-Suzie begins. 56-Last Capt. Commando. 59-Black Hood not in costume; lingerie panels; Archie dresses as his aunt; Suzie ends. 60-Katy Keene begins(3/47), ends #154	27	81	148	245
61-65-Last Shield. 62-1st app. Li'l Jinx (7/47)	23	69	121	210
66-80: 66-G-Man Club becomes Archie Club (2/48); Nevada Jones by Bill Woggon. 78-1st app. Dilton	14	42	72	125
81-99	11	33	55	90
100	14	42	72	120

Perfect Love #10 (#1) © Z-D

Personal Love #2 © FF

Peter Panda #7 © DC

	GD2.0	FN6.0	VF8.0	NM9.4
101-130	7	21	38	55
131(2/59)-149(9/61)	3	10	23	35
150-160-Super-heroes app. in each (see note). 150 (10/61?)-2nd or 3rd app.				
The Jaguar? 152-157-Sci/Fi-c. 157-Li'l Jinx story	4	12	19	45
161(3/63)-167,169-180	3	9	17	24
168,200: 168-(1/64)-Jaguar app. 200-(12/66)	3	9	19	28
181(5/65)-199: 192-UFO-c. 198-Giantman-c(only)	2	6	13	20
201-217,219-226,228-240(4/70)	2	6	11	16
218,227-Archies Band-c only	2	6	12	18
241-270(10/72)	2	6	9	12
271-297,299	1	3	6	9
298-Josie and the Pussycats-c	2	6	9	12
300(4/75)	2	6	9	12
301-340(8/78)	1	3	5	7
341-382				5.00
383(4/82),393(3/84): 383-Marvelous Maureen begins (Sci/fi). 393-Thunder-				
bunny begins				6.00
384-392,394-399,401-410				4.00
400(5/85),411: 400-Story featuring Archie staff (DeCarlo-a)				6.00

NOTE: *Biro* a-2, 4, 5. *Jack Cole* a-1-5, 8. *Al Fagaly* c-55-72. *Fuje* a-39, 45, 47; c-34. *Meskin* a-2, 4, 5, 11(2). *Montana* c-30, 32, 33, 36, 73-87(most). *Novick* c-1-28, 29(w/Schomburg), 31i. *Harry Sahle* c-35, 39-50. *Schomburg* c-38. *Bob Wood* a-2, 4-6, 11. *The Fly* app. in 151, 154, 160. *Flygirl* app. in 153, 155, 156, 158. *Jaguar* app. in 150, 152, 157, 159, 168. *Katy Keene* by *Bill Woggon* in many later issues. *Bondage* c-7, 12, 13, 15, 18, 21, 31, 32. *Cover features: Shield* #1-16; *Shield/Hangman* #17-27, 29-41; *Hangman* #28. *Archie* #36, 41-on.

PEPE
Dell Publishing Co.: No. 1194, Apr, 1961

Four Color 1194-Movie, photo-c	3	9	17	25

PERFECT CRIME, THE
Cross Publications: Oct, 1949 - No. 33, May, 1953 (#2-12, 52 pgs.)

1-Powell-a(2)	33	99	174	300
2 (4/50)	19	57	99	165
3-10: 7-Steve Duncan begins, ends #30. 10-Flag-c	16	48	83	140
11-Used in SOTI, pg. 159	18	54	94	155
12-14	15	45	77	130
15-"The Most Terrible Menace" 2 pg. drug editorial	16	48	83	140
16,17,19-25,27-29,31-33	15	45	77	130
18-Drug cover, heroin drug propaganda story, plus 2 pg. anti-drug editorial				
	23	69	121	210
26-Drug-c with hypodermic; drug propaganda story	25	75	130	225
30-Strangulation cover	25	75	130	225

NOTE: *Powell* a-No. 1, 2, 4. *Wildey* a-1, 5. *Bondage* c-11.

PERFECT LOVE
Ziff-Davis(Approved Comics)/St. John No. 9 on: #10, 8-9/51 (cover date; 5-6/51 indicia date); #2, 10-11/51 - #10, 12/53

10(#1)(8-9/51)-Painted-c	20	60	105	180
2(10-11/51)	14	42	72	120
3,5-7: 3-Painted-c. 5-Photo-c	10	30	55	85
4,8 (Fall, 1952)-Kinstler-a; last Z-D issue	11	33	55	90
9,10 (10/53, 12/53, St. John): 9-Painted-c. 10-Photo-c				
	10	30	55	80

PERRI (Disney)
Dell Publishing Co.: No. 847, Jan, 1958

Four Color 847-Movie, w/2 diff-c publ.	5	15	35	60

PERRY MASON
David McKay Publications: No. 49, 1946 - No. 50, 1946

Feature Books 49, 59-Based on Gardner novels	30	90	159	275

PERRY MASON MYSTERY MAGAZINE (TV)
Dell Publishing Co.: June-Aug, 1964 - No. 2, Oct-Dec, 1964

1	4	12	30	50
2-Raymond Burr photo-c	4	12	26	40

PERSONAL LOVE (Also see Movie Love)
Famous Funnies: Jan, 1950 - No. 33, June, 1955

1-Photo-c	18	54	94	160
2-Kathryn Grayson & Mario Lanza photo-c	10	30	55	80
3-7,10: 7-Robert Walker & Joanne Dru photo-c. 10-Loretta Young & Joseph				
Cotton photo-c	8	24	45	65

8,9: 8-Esther Williams & Howard Keel photo-c. 9-Debra Paget & Louis Jourdan				
photo-c	9	27	49	70
11-Toth-a; Glenn Ford & Gene Tierney photo-c	11	33	55	90
12,16,17-One pg. Frazetta each. 17-Rock Hudson & Yvonne DeCarlo photo-c				
	8	24	45	65
13-15,18-23: 12-Jane Greer & William Lundigan photo-c. 14-Kirk Douglas				
photo-c. 15-Dale Robertson & Joanne Dru photo-c. 18-Gregory Peck &				
Susan Hayworth photo-c. 19-Anthony Quinn & Suzan Ball photo-c. 20-Robert				
Wagner & Kathleen Crowley photo-c. 21-Roberta Peters & Byron Palmer				
photo-c. 22-Dale Robertson photo-c. 23-Rhonda Fleming-c				
	7	21	38	55
24,27,28-Frazetta-a in each (8,8&6 pgs.). 27-Rhonda Fleming & Fernando				
Lamas photo-c. 28,30-Mitzi Gaynor photo-c	40	120	232	400
25-Frazetta-a (tribute to Betty Page, 7 pg. story); Tyrone Power/Terry Moore				
photo-c from "King of the Khyber Rifles"	45	135	270	475
26,29,30,33: 26-Constance Smith & Byron Palmer photo-c. 29-Charlton Heston				
& Nicol Morey photo-c. 30-Johnny Ray & Mitzi Gaynor photo-c. 33-Dana				
Andrews & Piper Laurie photo-c	7	21	38	55
31-Marlon Brando & Jean Simmons photo-c; last pre-code (2/55)				
	10	30	55	80
32-Classic Frazetta-a (8 pgs.); Kirk Douglas & Bella Darvi photo-c				
	52	157	314	550

NOTE: *All have photo-c. Many feature movie stars. Everett* a-5, 9, 10, 24.

PERSONAL LOVE (Going Steady V3#3 on)
Prize Publ. (Headline): V1#1, Sept, 1957 - V3#2, Nov-Dec, 1959

V1#1	9	27	49	70
2	5	15	25	35
3-6(7-8/58)	5	15	24	32
V2#1(9-10/58)-V2#6(7-8/59)	5	14	21	28
V3#1-Wood?/Orlando-a	5	15	25	35
2	4	13	19	26

PETER CANNON - THUNDERBOLT (See Crisis on Infinite Earths)(Also see Thunderbolt)
DC Comics: Sept, 1992 - No. 12, Aug, 1993 ($1.25)

1-12				2.25

PETER COTTONTAIL
Key Publications: Jan, 1954; Feb, 1954 - No. 2, Mar, 1954 (Says 3/53 in error)

1(1/54)-Not 3-D	9	27	49	70
1(2/54)-(3-D, 25¢)-Came w/glasses; written by Bruce Hamilton				
	23	69	121	210
2-Reprints 3-D #1 but not in 3-D	6	18	30	42

PETER GUNN (TV)
Dell Publishing Co.: No. 1087, Apr-June, 1960

Four Color 1087-Photo-c	9	27	63	120

PETER PAN (Disney) (See Hook, Movie Classics & Comics, New Adventures of... & Walt Disney Showcase #36)
Dell Publishing Co.: No. 442, Dec, 1952 - No. 926, Aug, 1958

Four Color 442 (#1)-Movie	10	30	70	125
Four Color 926-Reprint of 442	4	12	30	50

PETER PAN
Disney Comics: 1991 ($5.95, graphic novel, 68 pgs.)(Celebrates video release)

nn-r/Peter Pan Treasure Chest from 1953				7.00

PETER PANDA
National Periodical Publications: Aug-Sept, 1953 - No. 31, Aug-Sept, 1958

1-Grossman-c/a in all	40	120	240	420
2	23	69	121	210
3,4,6-8,10	19	57	99	165
5-Classic-c (scarce)	25	75	130	225
9-Robot-c	21	63	110	185
11-31	12	36	61	105

PETER PAN TREASURE CHEST (See Dell Giants)

PETER PARKER (See The Spectacular Spider-Man)

PETER PARKER: SPIDER-MAN
Marvel Comics: Jan, 1999 - Present ($2.99/$1.99/$2.25)

1-Mackie-s/Romita Jr.-a; wraparound-c				3.00

Peter Parker: Spider-Man V2 #29 © MAR

Peter Rabbit #1 © AVON

The Phantom #53 © CC

PH

	GD2.0	FN6.0	VF8.0	NM9.4

1-($6.95) DF Edition w/variant cover by the Romitas				7.00
2-11,13-17-($1.99): 2-Two covers; Thor app. 3-Iceman-c/app. 4-Marrow-c/app.				
5-Spider-Woman app. 7,8-Blade app. 9,10-Venom app. 11-Iron Man &				
Thor-c/app.				2.25
12-($2.99) Sinister Six and Venom app.				3.00
18-24,26-38: 18-Begin $2.25-c. 20-Jenkins-s/Buckingham-a start. 23-Intro				
Typeface. 24-Maximum Security x-over. 29-Rescue of MJ. 30-Ramos-c				2.25
25-($2.99) Two covers; Spider-Man & Green Goblin				3.00
..'99 Annual (8/99, $3.50) Man-Thing app.				3.50
..'00 Annual ($3.50) Bounty app.; Joe Bennett-a; Black Cat back-up story				3.50
..'01 Annual ($2.99) Avery-s				3.00
...: A Day in the Life TPB (5/01, $14.95) r/#20-22,26; Websamples #10-12				15.00

PETER PAT
United Features Syndicate: No. 8, 1939

Single Series 8	35	105	185	320

PETER PAUL'S 4 IN 1 JUMBO COMIC BOOK
Capitol Stories (Charlton): No date (1953)

1-Contains 4 comics bound; Space Adventures, Space Western, Crime &				
Justice, Racket Squad in Action	40	120	232	400

PETER PIG
Standard Comics: No. 5, May, 1953 - No. 6, Aug, 1953

5,6	6	18	32	45

PETER PORKCHOPS (See Leading Comics #23)
National Periodical Publications: 11-12/49 - No. 61, 9-11/59; No. 62, 10-12/60
(1-11: 52 pgs.)

1	35	105	185	320
2	17	51	88	150
3-10: 6- "Peter Rockets to Mars!" c/story	13	39	66	110
11-30	10	30	55	80
31-62	9	27	49	70

NOTE: *Otto Feur* a-all. *Sheldon Mayer* a-30-38, 40-44, 46-52, 61.

PETER PORKER, THE SPECTACULAR SPIDER-HAM
Star Comics (Marvel): May, 1985 - No. 17, Sept, 1987 (Also see Marvel Tails)

1-Michael Golden-c				4.00
2-17: 12-Origin/1st app. Bizarro Phil. 13-Halloween issue				3.00

NOTE: *Back-up features: 2-X-Bugs. 3-Iron Mouse. 4-Croctor Strange. 5-Thrr, Dog of Thunder.*

PETER POTAMUS (TV)
Gold Key: Jan, 1965 (Hanna-Barbera)

1-1st app. Peter Potamus & So-So, Breezly & Sneezly				
	10	30	70	125

PETER RABBIT (See New Funnies #65 & Space Comics)
Dell Publishing Co.: No. 1, 1942

Large Feature Comic 1	42	125	294	550

PETER RABBIT (Adventures of...; New Advs. of... #9 on)(Also see Funny
Tunes & Space Comics)
Avon Periodicals: 1947 - No. 34, Sept-Sept, 1956

1(1947)-Reprints 1943-44 Sunday strips; contains a biography & drawing of				
Cady	36	108	191	330
2 (4/48)	26	78	136	235
3 (48) - 6(7/49)-Last Cady issue	23	69	121	205
7-10(1950-8/51): 9-New logo	9	27	49	70
11(11/51)-34('56)-Avon's character	7	21	36	50
...Easter Parade (1952, 25¢, 132 pgs.)	19	57	99	170
...Jumbo Book (1954-Giant Size, 25¢)-Jesse James by Kinstler (6 pgs.);				
space ship-c	24	72	127	220

PETER RABBIT 3-D
Eternity Comics: April, 1990 ($2.95, with glasses; sealed in plastic bag)

1-By Harrison Cady (reprints)				3.00

PETER, THE LITTLE PEST (#4 titled Petey)
Marvel Comics Group: Nov, 1969 - No. 4, May, 1970

1	5	15	38	60
2-4-r-Dexter the Demon & Melvin the Monster	4	12	26	40

PETE'S DRAGON (See Walt Disney Showcase #43)

PETE THE PANIC
Stanmor Publications: November, 1955

nn-Code approved	5	14	21	28

PETEY (See Peter, the Little Pest)

PETTICOAT JUNCTION (TV, inspired Green Acres)
Dell Publ. Co.: Oct-Dec, 1964 - No. 5, Oct-Dec, 1965 (#1-3, 5 have photo-c)

1	6	18	42	80
2-5	5	15	34	55

PETUNIA (Also see Looney Tunes and Porky Pig)
Dell Publishing Co.: No. 463, Apr, 1953

Four Color 463	4	12	27	42

PHAGE (See Neil Gaiman's Teknophage & Neil Gaiman's Phage-Shadowdeath)

PHANTACEA
McPherson Publishing Co.: Sept, 1977 - No. 6, Summer, 1980 (B&W)

1-Early Dave Sim-a (32 pgs.)	3	9	20	30
2-Dave Sim-a(10 pgs.)	2	6	11	16
3,5: 3-Flip-c w/Damnation Bridge	1	3	6	9
4,6: 4-Gene Day-a	1	3	6	9

PHANTASMO (See The Funnies #45)
Dell Publishing Co.: No. 18, 1941

Large Feature Comic 18	28	84	196	360

PHANTOM, THE
David McKay Publishing Co.: 1939 - 1949

Feature Books 20	71	213	497	925
Feature Books 22	55	165	385	720
Feature Books 39	50	150	300	525
Feature Books 53,56,57	40	120	226	390

PHANTOM, THE (See Ace Comics, Defenders Of The Earth, East Right to Work and Win,
Future Comics, Harvey Comics Hits #51,56, Harvey Hits #1, 6, 12, 15, 26, 36, 44, 48, & King
Comics)

PHANTOM, THE (nn (#29)-Published overseas only) (Also see Comics
Reading Libraries in the Promotional Comics section)
Gold Key(#1-17)/King(#18-28)/Charlton(#30 on): Nov, 1962 - No. 17, Jul, 1966;
No. 18, Sept, 1966 - No. 28, Dec, 1967; No. 30, Feb, 1969 - No. 74, Jan, 1977

1-Manning-a; origin revealed on inside-c & back-c	15	45	105	200
2-King, Queen & Jack begins, ends #11	8	24	56	100
3-5	7	21	49	85
6-10	6	18	42	80
11-17: 12-Track Hunter begins	5	15	35	60
18-Flash Gordon begins; Wood-a	5	15	35	60
19-24: 20-Flash Gordon ends (both by Gil Kane). 21-Mandrake begins. 20,24-				
Girl Phantom app.	4	12	29	45
25-28: 25-Jeff Jones-a(4 pgs.); 1 pg. Williamson ad. 26-Brick Bradford app.				
28(nn)-Brick Bradford app.	4	12	26	40
30-33: 33-Last 12¢ issue	3	9	19	28
34-40: 36,39-Ditko-a	3	9	17	24
41-66: 46-Intro. The Piranha. 62-Bolle-c	2	6	13	20
67-Origin retold; Newton-c/a	2	6	15	22
68-73-Newton-c/a	2	6	11	15
74-Classic flag-c by Newton; Newton-a;	2	6	15	22

NOTE: *Aparo* a-31-34, 36-38; c-31-38, 60, 61. Painted c-1-17.

PHANTOM, THE
DC Comics: May, 1988 - No. 4, Aug, 1988 ($1.25, mini-series)

1-4: Orlando-c/a in all				3.00

PHANTOM, THE
DC Comics: Mar, 1989 - No. 13, Mar, 1990 ($1.50)

1-13: 1-Brief origin				3.00

PHANTOM, THE
Wolf Publishing: 1992 - No. 8, 1993 ($2.25)

1-8				2.25

PHANTOM BLOT, THE (#1 titled New Adventures of...)
Gold Key: Oct, 1964 - No. 7, Nov, 1966 (Disney)

1 (Meets The Mysterious Mr. X)	5	15	35	60

Phantom Lady #19 © FOX

Phantom Stranger (1st) #2 © DC

Phantom 2040 #3 © KING

	GD2.0	FN6.0	VF8.0	NM9.4

2-1st Super Goof — 5 / 15 / 34 / 55
3-7 — 3 / 9 / 21 / 32

PHANTOM EAGLE (See Mighty Midget, Marvel Super Heroes #16 & Wow #6)

PHANTOM FORCE
Image Comics/Genesis West #0, 3-7: 12/93 - #2, 1994; #0, 3/94; #3, 5/94 - #8, 10/94 ($2.50/$3.50, limited series)

0 (3/94, $2.50)-Kirby/Jim Lee-c; Kirby-p pgs. 1,5,24-29. — 3.00
1 (12/93, $2.50)-Polybagged w/trading card; Kirby Liefeld-c; Kirby plots/pencils w/inks by Liefeld, McFarlane, Jim Lee, Silvestri, Larsen, Williams, Ordway & Miki. — 3.00
2 ($3.50)-Kirby-a(p); Kirby/Larson-c — 3.50
3-8: 3-(5/94, $2.50)-Kirby/McFarlane-c 4-(5/94)-Kirby-c(p). 5-(6/94) — 3.00

PHANTOM GUARD
Image Comics (WildStorm Productions): Oct, 1997 - No. 6, Mar, 1998 ($2.50)

1-6: Two covers — 3.00
1-($3.50)-Voyager Pack w/Wildcore preview — 3.50

PHANTOM LADY (1st Series) (My Love Secret #24 on) (Also see All Top, Daring Adventures, Freedom Fighters, Jungle Thrills, & Wonder Boy)
Fox Features Syndicate: No. 13, Aug, 1947 - No. 23 Apr, 1949

13(#1)-Phantom Lady by Matt Baker begins (1st app.); The Blue Beetle story begins — 383 / 1149 / 2396 / 4600
14-16: 14(#2)-Not Baker-c. 15-P.L. injected with experimental drug. 16-Negligee-c, bondage; true crime stories begin — 241 / 723 / 1506 / 2650
17-Classic bondage cover; used in *SOTI*, illo "Sexual stimulation by combining 'headlights' with the sadist's dream of tying up a woman" — 508 / 1524 / 3300 / 6600
18,19 — 168 / 505 / 1050 / 1850
20-22 — 132 / 395 / 825 / 1450
23-Bondage-c — 148 / 444 / 925 / 1625
NOTE: *Matt Baker-a in all; c-13, 15-21. Kamen a-22, 23.*

PHANTOM LADY (2nd Series) (See Terrific Comics) (Formerly Linda)
Ajax/Farrell Publ.: V1#5, Dec-Jan, 1954/1955 - No. 4, June, 1955

V1#5(#1)-By Matt Baker — 111 / 332 / 694 / 1225
V1#2-Last pre-code — 84 / 252 / 525 / 925
3,4-Red Rocket. 3-Heroin story — 68 / 204 / 426 / 750

PHANTOM LADY
Verotik Publications: 1994 ($9.95)

1-Reprints G. A. stories from Phantom Lady and All Top Comics; Adam Hughes-c — 10.00

PHANTOM PLANET, THE
Dell Publishing Co.: No. 1234, 1961

Four Color 1234-Movie — 7 / 21 / 49 / 90

PHANTOM STRANGER, THE (1st Series)(See Saga of Swamp Thing)
National Periodical Publications: Aug-Sept, 1952 - No. 6, June-July, 1953

1(Scarce)-1st app. — 191 / 573 / 1194 / 2100
2 (Scarce) — 107 / 321 / 669 / 1175
3-6 (Scarce) — 93 / 279 / 581 / 1025

PHANTOM STRANGER, THE (2nd Series) (See Showcase #80)
National Periodical Publications: May-June, 1969 - No. 41, Feb-Mar, 1976

1-2nd S.A. app. P. Stranger; only 12¢ issue — 10 / 30 / 70 / 120
2,3 — 4 / 12 / 30 / 50
4-1st new look Phantom Stranger; N. Adams-a — 5 / 15 / 34 / 55
5-7 — 3 / 10 / 23 / 35
8-14: 14-Last 15¢ issue — 3 / 9 / 17 / 25
15-19: All 25¢ giants (52 pgs.) — 3 / 9 / 20 / 30
20-Dark Circle begins, ends #24. — 2 / 6 / 12 / 18
21,22 — 2 / 6 / 9 / 12
23-Spawn of Frankenstein begins by Kaluta — 3 / 9 / 20 / 30
24,25,27-30-Last Spawn of Frankenstein — 2 / 6 / 15 / 22
26- Book-length story featuring Phantom Stranger, Dr. 13 & Spawn of Frankenstein — 3 / 9 / 17 / 24
31-The Black Orchid begins (6-7/74). — 3 / 9 / 17 / 25
32,34-38: 34-Last 20¢ issue (#35 on are 25¢) — 2 / 6 / 9 / 12
33,39-41: 33-Deadman-c/story. 39-41-Deadman app. — 2 / 6 / 11 / 15
NOTE: *N. Adams a-4; c-3-19. Anderson a-4, 5i. Aparo a-7-17, 19-26; c-20-24, 33-41. B. Bailey*

---

a-27-30. *DeZuniga* a-12-16, 18, 19, 21, 22, 31, 34. *Grell* a-33. *Kaluta* a-23-25; c-26. *Meskin* r-15, 16, 18, 19. *Redondo* a-32, 35, 36. *Sparling* a-20. *Starr* a-17r. *Toth* a-15r. Black Orchid by *Carrillo*-38-41. Dr. 13 solo in-13, 18, 19, 20, 21, 34. Frankenstein by *Kaluta*-23-25; by *Baily*-27-30. No Black Orchid-33, 34, 37.

PHANTOM STRANGER (See Justice League of America #103)
DC Comics: Oct, 1987 - No. 4, Jan, 1988 (75¢, limited series)

1-4-Mignola/Russell-c/a & Eclipso app. in all. 3,4-Eclipso-c — 3.00

PHANTOM STRANGER (See Vertigo Visions-The Phantom Stranger)

PHANTOM: THE GHOST WHO WALKS
Marvel Comics: Feb, 1995 - No. 3, Apr, 1995 ($2.95, limited series)

1-3 — 3.00

PHANTOM 2040 (TV cartoon)
Marvel Comics: May, 1995 - No. 4, Aug, 1995 ($1.50)

1-4-Based on animated series; Ditko-a(p) in all — 2.25

PHANTOM WITCH DOCTOR (Also see Durango Kid #8 & Eerie #8)
Avon Periodicals: 1952

1-Kinstler-c/a (7 pgs.) — 45 / 135 / 270 / 475

PHANTOM ZONE, THE (See Adventure #283 & Superboy #100, 104)
DC Comics: January, 1982 - No. 4, April, 1982

1-4-Superman app. in all. 2-4: Batman, Green Lantern app. — 3.00
NOTE: *Colan a-1-4p; c-1-4p. Giordano c-1-4i.*

PHAZE
Eclipse Comics: Apr, 1988 - No. 2, Oct, 1988 ($2.25)

1,2: 1-Sienkiewicz-c. 2-Gulacy painted-c — 2.25

PHIL RIZZUTO (Baseball Hero)(See Sport Thrills, Accepted reprint)
Fawcett Publications: 1951 (New York Yankees)

nn-Photo-c — 68 / 205 / 426 / 750

PHOENIX
Atlas/Seaboard Publ.: Jan, 1975 - No. 4, Oct, 1975

1-Origin; Rovin/Amendola-a — 1 / 3 / 5 / 7
2-4: 3-Origin & only app. The Dark Avenger. 4-New origin/costume The Protector (formerly Phoenix) — 6.00
NOTE: *Infantino appears in #1, 2. Austin a-3i. Thorne c-3.*

PHOENIX (...The Untold Story)
Marvel Comics Group: April, 1984 ($2.00, one-shot)

1-Byrne/Austin-r/X-Men #137 with original unpublished ending — 1 / 4 / 7 / 10

PHOENIX RESURRECTION, THE
Malibu Comics (Ultraverse): 1995 - 1996 ($3.95)

Genesis #1 (12/95)-X-Men app; wraparound-c, Revelations #1 (12/95)-X-Men app; wraparound-c, Aftermath #1 (1/96)-X-Men app. — 4.00
0-($1.95)-r/series — 2.25
0-American Entertainment Ed. — 4.00

PICNIC PARTY (See Dell Giants)

PICTORIAL CONFESSIONS (Pictorial Romances #4 on)
St. John Publishing Co.: Sept, 1949 - No. 3, Dec, 1949

1-Baker-c/a(3) — 31 / 93 / 165 / 285
2-Baker-a; photo-c — 20 / 60 / 105 / 175
3-Kubert, Baker-a; part Kubert-c — 22 / 66 / 116 / 195

PICTORIAL LOVE STORIES (Formerly Tim McCoy)
Charlton Comics: No. 22, Oct, 1949 - No. 26, July, 1950 (all photo-c)

22-26: All have "Me-Dan Cupid". 25-Fred Astaire-c — 21 / 63 / 110 / 185

PICTORIAL LOVE STORIES
St. John Publishing Co.: October, 1952

1-Baker-c — 29 / 87 / 153 / 265

PICTORIAL ROMANCES (Formerly Pictorial Confessions)
St. John Publ. Co.: No. 4, Jan, 1950; No. 5, Jan, 1951 - No. 24, Mar, 1954

4-Baker-a; photo-c — 30 / 90 / 159 / 275
5,10-All Matt Baker issues. 5-Reprints all stories from #4 w/new Baker-c — 23 / 69 / 121 / 210
6-9,12,13,15,16-Baker-c, 2-3 stories — 17 / 51 / 88 / 150

Picture Stories From the Bible #3 © WMG

Picture Stories From the Bible #3 © WMG

Pink Panther #13 © GK

Pinky & The Brain #7 © WB

	GD2.0	FN6.0	VF8.0	NM9.4

11-Baker-c/a(3); Kubert-r/Hollywood Confessions #1

	19	57	99	165

14,21-24: Baker-c/a each. 21,24-Each has signed story by Estrada

	15	45	77	130

17-20(7/53, 25¢, 100 pgs.): Baker-c/a; each has two signed stories by Estrada

	31	93	165	285

NOTE: *Matt Baker* art in most issues. *Estrada* a-17-20(2), 21, 24.

PICTURE NEWS
Lafayette Street Corp.: Jan, 1946 - No. 10, Jan-Feb, 1947

1-Milt Gross begins, ends No. 6; 4 pg. Kirby-a; A-Bomb-c/story

	40	120	232	400

2-Atomic explosion panels; Frank Sinatra/Perry Como story

	22	66	116	200

3-Atomic explosion panels; Frank Sinatra, June Allyson, Benny Goodman stories

	19	57	99	165

4-Atomic explosion panels; "Caesar and Cleopatra" movie adapt. w/Claude Raines & Vivian Leigh; Jackie Robinson story

	21	63	110	185

5-7: 8-Hank Greenberg story. 6-Joe Louis-c/story

	15	45	77	130

8,10: 8-Monte Hale story (9-10/46; 1st?). 10-Dick Quick; A-Bomb story; Krigstein, Gross-a

	16	48	83	140

9-A-Bomb story; "Crooked Mile" movie adaptation; Joe DiMaggio story.

	19	57	99	165

PICTURE PARADE (Picture Progress #5 on)
Gilberton Company (Also see A Christmas Adventure): Sept, 1953 - V1#4, Dec, 1953 (28 pgs.)

V1#1-Andy's Atomic Adventures; A-bomb blast-c; (Teachers version distributed to schools exists)

	21	63	110	185

2-Around the World with the United Nations

	12	36	61	100

3-Adventures of the Lost One(The American Indian), 4-A Christmas Adventure (r-under same title in 1969)

	12	36	61	100

PICTURE PROGRESS (Formerly Picture Parade)
Gilberton Corp.: V1#5, Jan, 1954 - V3#2, Oct, 1955 (28-36 pgs.)

V1#5-9,V2#1-9: 5-News in Review 1953. 6-The Birth of America. 7-The Four Seasons. 8-Paul Revere's Ride. 9-The Hawaiian Islands(5/54). V2#1-The Story of Flight(9/54). 2-Vote for Crazy River (The Meaning of Elections). 3-Louis Pasteur. 4-The Star Spangled Banner. 5-News in Review 1954. 6-Alaska: The Great Land. 7-Life in the Circus. 8-The Time of the Cave Man. 9-Summer Fun(5/55)

	7	21	38	55

V3#1,2: 1-The Man Who Discovered America. 2-The Lewis & Clark Expedition

	7	21	38	55

PICTURE SCOPE JUNGLE ADVENTURES (See Jungle Thrills)

PICTURE STORIES FROM AMERICAN HISTORY
National/All-American/E. C. Comics: 1945 - No. 4, Sum, 1947 (#1,2: 10¢, 56 pgs; #3,4: 15¢, 52 pgs.)

1	31	93	168	290
2-4	25	75	130	225

PICTURE STORIES FROM SCIENCE
E.C. Comics: Spring, 1947 - No. 2, Fall, 1947

1-(15¢)	31	93	168	290
2-(10¢)	27	81	142	245

PICTURE STORIES FROM THE BIBLE (See Narrative Illustration, the Story of the Comics by M.C. Gaines)
National/All-American/E.C. Comics: 1942 - No. 4, Fall, 1943; 1944-46

1-4('42-Fall, '43)-Old Testament (DC)

	25	75	130	225

Complete Old Testament Edition (12/43-DC, 50¢, 232 pgs.);-1st printing; contains #1-4; 2nd - 8th (1/47) printings exist; later printings by E.C.

	29	87	153	265

Complete Old Testament Edition (1945-publ. by Bible Pictures Ltd.)-232 pgs., hardbound, in color with dust jacket

	29	87	153	265

NOTE: *Both Old and New Testaments published in England by Bible Pictures Ltd. in hardback, 1943, in color, 376 pgs. (2 vols. - O.T. 232 pgs. & N.T. 144 pgs.), and were also published by Scarf Press in 1979 (Old Test., $9.95) and in 1980 (New Test., $7.95)*

1-3(New Test.; 1944-46, DC)-52 pgs. ea.

	19	57	99	165

The Complete Life of Christ Edition (1945, 25¢, 96 pgs.)-Contains #1&2 of the New Testament Edition

	25	75	130	225

1,2(Old Testament-r in comic book form)(E.C., 1946; 52 pgs.)

	19	57	99	165

1(DC),2(AA),3(EC)(New Testament-r in comic book form)(E.C., 1946; 52 pgs.)

	19	57	99	165

Complete New Testament Edition (1946-E.C., 50¢, 144 pgs.)-Contains #1-3

	25	75	130	225

NOTE: *Another British series entitled **The Bible Illustrated** from 1947 has recently been discovered, with the same internal artwork. This eight edition series (5-OT, 3-NT) is of particular interest to Classics III. collectors because it exactly copied the C.I. logo format. The British publisher was Thorpe & Porter, who in 1951 began publishing the British Classics III. series. All editions of The Bible III. have new British painted covers. While this market is still new, not all editions have as yet been found, current market value is about the same as the first U.S. editions of Picture Stories From The Bible.*

PICTURE STORIES FROM WORLD HISTORY
E.C. Comics: Spring, 1947 - No. 2, Summer, 1947 (52, 48 pgs.)

1-(15¢)	31	93	168	290
2-(10¢)	27	81	142	245

PINHEAD
Marvel Comics (Epic Comics): Dec, 1993 - No. 6, May, 1994 ($2.50)

1-($2.95)-Embossed foil-c by Kelley Jones; Intro Pinhead & Disciples (Snakeoil, Hangman, Fan Dancer & Dixie)				3.00
2-6				2.50

PINHEAD & FOODINI (TV)(Also see Foodini & Jingle Dingle Christmas...)
Fawcett Publications: July, 1951 - No. 4, Jan, 1952 (Early TV comic)

1-(52 pgs.)-Photo-c; based on TV puppet show	34	102	179	310
2,3-Photo-c	17	51	88	150
4	14	42	72	120

PINHEAD VS. MARSHALL LAW (Law in Hell)
Marvel Comics (Epic): Nov, 1993 - No. 2, Dec, 1993 ($2.95, lim. series)

1,2: 1-Embossed red foil-c. 2-Embossed silver foil-c				3.00

PINK DUST
Kitchen Sink Press: 1998 ($3.50, B&W, mature)

1-J. O'Barr-s/a				3.50

PINK PANTHER, THE (TV)(See The Inspector & Kite Fun Book)
Gold Key #1-70/Whitman #71-87: April, 1971 - No. 87, Mar, 1984

1-The Inspector begins	5	15	34	55
2-5	3	9	17	25
6-10	2	6	12	18
11-30: Warren Tufts-a #16-on	2	6	9	12
31-60	1	3	6	9
61-70	1	3	5	7
71-74,81-83: 81(2/82), 82(3/82), 83(4/82)	1	3	6	9
75(8/80),76-80(pre-pack?) (scarce)	2	6	11	16
84-87(All #90266 on-c, no date or date code): 84(6/83), 85(8/83), 87(3/84)				
	1	3	6	9
Mini-comic #1(1976)(3-1/4x6-1/2")	1	3	6	9

NOTE: *Pink Panther began as a movie cartoon. (See Golden Comics Digest #38, 45 and March of Comics #376, 384, 390, 409, 418, 429, 441, 449, 461, 473, 486); #37, 72, 80-85 contain reprints.*

PINK PANTHER SUPER SPECIAL (TV)
Harvey Comics: Oct, 1993 ($2.25, 68 pgs.)

V2#1-The Inspector & Wendy Witch stories also				3.00

PINK PANTHER, THE
Harvey Comics: Nov, 1993 - No. 9, July, 1994 ($1.50)

V2#1-9				2.25

PINKY & THE BRAIN (See Animaniacs)
DC Comics: July, 1996 - No. 27, Nov, 1998 ($1.75/$1.95/$1.99)

1-27, ...Christmas Special (1/96, $1.50)				2.50

PINKY LEE (See Adventures of...)

PINKY THE EGGHEAD
I.W./Super Comics: 1963 (Reprints from Noodnik)

I.W. Reprint #1,2(2nd)	2	6	9	12
Super Reprint #14-r/Noodnik Comics #4	2	6	9	12

PINOCCHIO (See 4-Color #92, 252, 545, 1203, Mickey Mouse Mag. V5#3, Movie Comics under Wonderful Advs. of..., New Advs. of..., Thrilling Comics #2, Walt Disney Showcase, Walt Disney's..., Wonderful Advs. of..., & World's

Pirates Comics #2 © HILL

Pizzazz #5 © MAR

Planetary #14 © WSP

GD2.0 FN6.0 VF8.0 NM9.4
GD2.0 FN6.0 VF8.0 NM9.4

Greatest Stories #2)
Dell Publishing Co.: No. 92, 1945 - No. 1203, Mar, 1962 (Disney)

Four Color 92-The Wonderful Adventures of...; 16 pg. Donald Duck story ; entire book by Kelly	60	180	420	775
Four Color 252 (10/49)-Origin, not by Kelly	10	30	70	135
Four Color 545 (3/54)-The Wonderful Advs. of...; part-r of 4-Color #92; Disney-movie	7	21	49	90
Four Color 1203 (3/62)	5	15	35	60

PINOCCHIO AND THE EMPEROR OF THE NIGHT
Marvel Comics: Mar, 1988 ($1.25, 52 pgs.)

1-Adapts film	3.00

PINOCCHIO LEARNS ABOUT KITES (See Kite Fun Book)

PIN-UP PETE (Also see Great Lover Romances & Monty Hall...)
Toby Press: 1952

1-Jack Sparling pin-ups	20	60	105	175

PIONEER MARSHAL (See Fawcett Movie Comics)

PIONEER PICTURE STORIES
Street & Smith Publications: Dec, 1941 - No. 9, Dec, 1943

1-The Legless Air Ace begins	31	93	165	285
2 -True life story of Errol Flynn	16	48	83	140
3-9	14	42	72	120

PIONEER WEST ROMANCES (Firehair #1,2,7-11)
Fiction House Magazines: No. 3, Spring, 1950 - No. 6, Winter, 1950-51

3-(52 pgs.)-Firehair continues	21	63	110	185
4-6	21	63	110	185

PIPSQUEAK (See The Adventures of...)

PIRACY
E. C. Comics: Oct-Nov, 1954 - No. 7, Oct-Nov, 1955

1-Williamson/Torres-a	24	72	168	300
2-Williamson/Torres-a	15	45	105	185
3-7: 5-7-Comics Code symbol on cover	12	36	84	150

NOTE: *Crandall* a-in all; c-2-4. *Davis* a-1, 2, 6. *Evans* a-3-7; c-7. *Ingels* a-3-7. *Krigstein* a-3-5, 7; c-5, 6. *Wood* a-1, 2; c-1.

PIRACY
Gemstone Publishing: March, 1998 - No. 7, Sept, 1998 ($2.50)

1-7: E.C. reprints	2.50
Annual 1 ($10.95) Collects #1-4	11.00
Annual 2 ($7.95) Collects #5-7	8.00

PIRANA (See The Phantom #46 & Thrill-O-Rama #2, 3)

PIRATE CORPS, THE (See Hectic Planet)
Eternity Comics/Slave Labor Graphics: 1987 - No. 4, 1988 ($1.95)

1-4: 1,2-Color. 3,4-B&W	2.25
Special 1 ('89, B&W)-Slave Labor Publ.	2.25

PIRATE CORP$, THE (Volume 2)
Slave Labor Graphics: 1989 - No. 4, 1992 ($1.95)

1-4-Dorkin-s/a	2.25

PIRATE OF THE GULF, THE (See Superior Stories #2)

PIRATES COMICS
Hillman Periodicals: Feb-Mar, 1950 - No. 4, Aug-Sept, 1950 (All 52 pgs.)

1	26	78	136	235
2-Dave Berg-a	19	57	99	165
3,4-Berg-a	17	51	88	150

PIRATES OF DARK WATER, THE (Hanna Barbera)
Marvel Comics: Nov, 1991 - No. 9, Aug, 1992 ($1.95)

1-9: 9-Vess-c	2.25

P.I.'S: MICHAEL MAUSER AND MS. TREE, THE
First Comics: Jan, 1985 - No. 3, May, 1985 ($1.25, limited series)

1-3: Staton-c/a(p)	2.25

PITT, THE (Also see The Draft & The War)
Marvel Comics: Mar, 1988 ($3.25, 52 pgs.)-one-shot)

1-Ties into Starbrand, D.P.7	3.50

PITT (See Youngblood #4 & Gen 13 #3,#4)
Image Comics #1-9/Full Bleed #1/2,10-on: Jan, 1993 - Present ($1.95, intended as a four part limited series)

1/2-(12/95)-1st Full Bleed issue	4.00
1-Dale Keown-c/a. 1-1st app. The Pitt	4.00
2-13: All Dale Keown-c/a. 3 (Low distribution). 10 (1/96)-Indicia reads "January 1995"	3.00
14-20: 14-Begin $2.50-c, pullout poster	2.50
TPB-(1997, $9.95) r/#1/2, 1-4	10.00
TPB 2-(1999, $11.95) r/#5-9	12.00

PITT CREW
Full Bleed Studios: Aug, 1998 - Present ($2.50)

1-5: 1-Richard Pace-s/Ken Lashley-a. 2-4-Scott Lee-a	2.50

PITT IN THE BLOOD
Full Bleed Studios: Aug, 1996 ($2.50, one-shot)

nn-Richard Pace-a/script	2.50

PIXIE & DIXIE & MR. JINKS (TV)(See Jinks, Pixie, and Dixie & Whitman Comic Books)
Dell Publishing Co./Gold Key: July-Sept, 1960 - Feb, 1963 (Hanna-Barbera)

Four Color 1112	7	21	49	95
Four Color 1196,1264, 01-631-207 (Dell, 7/62)	5	15	35	65
1(2/63-Gold Key)	6	18	42	80

PIXIE PUZZLE ROCKET TO ADVENTURELAND
Avon Periodicals: Nov, 1952

1	14	42	72	120

PIXIES, THE (Advs. of...)(The Mighty Atom and ...#6 on)(See A-1 Comics #16)
Magazine Enterprises: Winter, 1946 - No. 4, Fall?, 1947; No. 5, 1948

1-Mighty Atom	9	27	49	70
2-5-Mighty Atom	5	15	25	35
I.W. Reprint #1(1958), 8-(Pee-Wee Pixies), 10-I.W. on cover, Super on inside	2	6	9	12

PIZZAZZ
Marvel Comics: Oct, 1977 - No. 16, Jan, 1979 (slick-color kids mag. w/puzzles, games, comics)

1-Star Wars photo-c/article; origin Tarzan; KISS photos/article; Iron-On bonus; 2 pg. pin-up calendars thru #8	3	9	17	25
2-Spider-Man-c; Beatles pin-up calendar	2	6	10	14
3-8: 3-Close Encounters-s; Bradbury-s. 4-Alice Cooper, Travolta; Charlie's Angels/Fonz/Hulk/Spider-Man-c. 5-Star Trek quiz. 6-Asimov-s. 7-James Bond; Spock/Darth Vader-c. 8-TV Spider-Man photo-c/article	2	6	10	14
9-14: 9-Shaun Cassidy-c. 10-Sgt. Pepper-c/s. 12-Battlestar Galactica-s; Spider-Man app. 13-TV Hulk-c/s. 14-Meatloaf-c/s	1	4	7	10
15,16: 15-Battlestar Galactica-s. 16-Movie Superman photo-c/s, Hulk.	2	6	9	12

NOTE: *Star Wars* comics in all (1-6:Chaykin-a, 7-9: DeZuniga-a, 10-13:Simonson/Janson-a. 14-16:Cockrum-a). *Tarzan* comics, 1pg.-#1-8. 1pg. "Hey Look" by Kurtzman #12-16.

PLANETARY (See Preview in flip book Gen13 #33)
DC Comics (WildStorm Prod.): Apr, 1999 - Present ($2.50)

1-Ellis-s/Cassaday-a/c	6.00
2	4.50
3-15: 12-Fourth Man revealed	3.00
...: All Over the World and Other Stories (2000, $14.95) r/#1-6 & Preview	15.00
...: All Over the World and Other Stories-Hardcover (2000, $24.95) r/#1-6 & Preview; with dustjacket	25.00
.../The Authority: Ruling the World (8/00, $5.95) Ellis-s/Phil Jimenez-a	6.00
....: The Fourth Man -Hardcover (2001, $24.95) r/#7-12	25.00

PLANET COMICS
Fiction House Magazines: 1/40 - No. 62, 9/49; No. 63, Wint, 1949-50; No. 64, Spring, 1950; No. 65, 1950(nd); No. 66-68, 1952(nd); No. 69, Wint, 1952-53; No. 70-72, 1953(nd); No. 73, Winter, 1953-54

1-Origin Auro, Lord of Jupiter by Briefer (ends #61); Flint Baker & The Red Comet begin; Eisner/Fine-c	1038	3114	6747	13,500
2-Lou Fine-c (Scarce)	417	1250	2604	5000
3-Eisner-c	300	900	1875	3300

Planet Comics #59 © DC

Planet of the Apes #1 © 20th Century Fox

Plastic Man #33 © QUA

	GD2.0	FN6.0	VF8.0	NM9.4

	GD2.0	FN6.0	VF8.0	NM9.4

4-Gale Allen and the Girl Squadron begins	255	765	1591	2800
5,6-(Scarce): 5-Eisner/Fine-c	245	735	1534	2700
7-12: 8-Robot-c. 12-The Star Pirate begins	200	600	1250	2200
13,14: 13-Reff Ryan begins	148	444	925	1625
15-(Scarce)-Mars, God of War begins (11/41); see Jumbo Comics #31 for				
1st app.	295	885	1844	3250
16-20,22	132	395	825	1450
21-The Lost World & Hunt Bowman begin	139	417	869	1525
23-26: 26-Space Rangers begin (9/43), end #71	127	381	795	1400
27-30	102	306	638	1125
31-35: 33-Origin Star Pirates Wonder Boots, reprinted in #52. 35-Mysta of the				
Moon begins, ends #62	84	253	525	925
36-45: 38-1st Mysta of the Moon-c. 41-New origin of "Auro, Lord of Jupiter".				
42-Last Gale Allen. 43-Futura begins	77	231	483	850
46-60: 48-Robot-c. 53-Used in SOTI, pg. 32	61	182	381	675
61-68,70: 64,70-Robot-c. 65-70-All partial-r of earlier issues. 70-r/stories				
from #41	47	140	286	500
69-Used in POP, pgs. 101,102	47	140	286	500
71-73-No series stories. 71-Space Rangers strip	39	117	208	360
I.W. Reprint 1,8,9: 1(nd)-r/#70; cover-r from Attack on Planet Mars. 8 (r/#72),				
9-r/#73	8	24	56	90

NOTE: **Anderson** a-33-38, 40-51 (Star Pirate). **Matt Baker** a-53-59 (Mysta of the Moon). **Celardo** c-12. **Bill Discount** a-71 (Space Rangers). **Elias** c-70. **Evans** a-46-49 (Auro, Lord of Jupiter), 50-64 (Lost World). **Fine** c-2, 5. **Hopper** a-31, 35 (Gale Allen), 41, 42, 48, 49 (Mysta of the Moon). **Ingels** a-24(?) (Lost World), 56-61 (Auro, Lord of Jupiter). **Lubbers** a-44-47 (Space Rangers); c-40, 41. **Moriera** a-43, 44 (Mysta of the Moon). **Renee** a-40-49 (Lost World); c-33, 35, 39. **Tuska** a-30 (Star Pirate). **M. Whitman** a-50-52 (Mysta of the Moon), 53-58 (Star Pirate); c-71-73. **Starr** a-59. **Zolnerwich** c-10. 13-25. Bondage c-53.

PLANET COMICS
Pacific Comics: 1984 ($5.95)

1-Reprints Planet Comics #1(1940)				6.00

PLANET COMICS
Blackthorne Publishing: Apr, 1988 - No. 3 ($2.00, color/B&W #3)

1-3: New stories. 1-Dave Stevens-c				3.00

PLANET OF THE APES (Magazine) (Also see Adventures on the… & Power Record Comics)
Marvel Comics Group: Aug, 1974 - No. 29, Feb, 1977 (B&W) (Based on movies)

1-Ploog-a	3	9	21	32
2-Ploog-a	2	6	13	20
3-10	2	6	10	14
11-20	2	6	11	16
21-28 (low distribution)	2	6	13	20
29 (low distribution)	4	12	26	40

NOTE: **Alcala** a-7-11, 17-22, 24. **Ploog** a-1-4, 6, 8, 11, 13, 14, 19. **Sutton** a-11, 12, 15, 17, 19, 20, 23, 24, 29. **Tuska** a-1-6.

PLANET OF THE APES
Adventure Comics: Apr, 1990 - No. 24, 1992 ($2.50, B&W)

1-New movie tie-in; comes w/outer-c (3 colors)				4.00
1-Limited serial numbered edition ($5.00)				5.00
1-2nd printing (no outer-c, $2.50)				2.50
2-24				3.00
Annual 1 ($3.50)				4.00
...Urchak's Folly 1-4 ($2.50, mini-series)				3.00

PLANET OF THE APES (The Human War)
Dark Horse Comics: Jun, 2001 - No. 3, Aug, 2001 ($2.99, limited series)

1-3-Follows the 2001 movie; Edginton-s				3.00

PLANET OF THE APES
Dark Horse Comics: Sept, 2001 - Present ($2.99, ongoing series)

1-3-Edginton-s. 1-Photo & Matt Wagner covers. 2-Plunkett & photo-c				3.00

PLANET OF VAMPIRES
Seaboard Publications (Atlas): Feb, 1975 - No. 3, July, 1975

1-Neal Adams-c(i); 1st Broderick c/a(p); Hama-s	3	6	8	
2,3: 2-Neal Adams-c. 3-Heath-c/a				6.00

PLANET TERRY
Marvel Comics (Star Comics)/Marvel: April, 1985 - No. 12, March, 1986 (Children's comic)

1-12				3.00

1-Variant with "Star Chase" game on last page & inside back-c				10.00

PLASM (See Warriors of Plasm)
Defiant Comics: June, 1993

0-Came bound into Diamond Previews V3#6 (6/93); price is for complete				
Previews with comic still attached				3.00
0-Comic only removed from Previews				2.25

PLASMER
Marvel Comics UK: Nov, 1993 - No. 4, Feb, 1994 ($1.95, limited series)

1-($2.50)-Polybagged w/4 trading cards				2.50
2-4: Capt. America & Silver Surfer app.				2.25

PLASTIC FORKS
Marvel Comis (Epic Comics): 1990 - No. 5, 1990 ($4.95, 68 pgs., limited series, mature)

Book 1-5: Squarebound				5.00

PLASTIC MAN (Also see Police Comics & Smash Comics #17)
Vital Publ. No. 1,2/Quality Comics No. 3 on: Sum, 1943 - No. 64, Nov, 1956

nn(#1)- "In The Game of Death"; Skull-c; Jack Cole-c/a begins; ends-#64?				
	400	1200	2500	4800
nn(#2, 2/44)- "The Gay Nineties Nightmare"	168	505	1050	1850
3 (Spr, '46)	107	321	669	1175
4 (Sum, '46)	84	253	525	925
5 (Aut, '46)	73	219	455	800
6-10	59	177	369	650
11-20	53	158	318	560
21-30: 26-Last non-r issue?	43	129	257	450
31-40: 40-Used in POP, pg. 91	37	111	197	340
41-64: 53-Last precode issue. 54-Robot-c	31	93	165	285
Super Reprint 11,16,18: 11('63)-r/#16. 16-r/#18 & #21; Cole-a. 18('64)-Spirit-r				
by Eisner from Police #95	5	15	34	55

NOTE: **Cole** r-44, 49, 56, 58, 59 at least. **Cuidera** c-32-64i.

PLASTIC MAN (See DC Special #15 & House of Mystery #160)
National Periodical Publications/DC Comics: 11-12/66 - No. 10, 5-6/68; V4#11, 2-3/76 - No. 20, 10-11/77

1-Real 1st app. Silver Age Plastic Man (House of Mystery #160 is actually				
tryout); Gil Kane-c/a; 12¢ issues begin	8	24	60	100
2-5: 4-Infantino-c; Mortimer-a	4	12	26	40
6-10('68): 7-G.A. Plastic Man & Woozy Winks (1st S.A. app.) app.; origin				
retold. 10-Sparling-a; last 12¢ issue	3	9	20	30
V4#11('76)-20: 11-20-Fradon-p. 17-Origin retold	1	3	6	8
...Special 1 (8/99, $3.95)				4.00

PLASTIC MAN
DC Comics: Nov, 1988 - No. 4, Feb, 1989 ($1.00, mini-series)

1-4: 1-Origin; Woozy Winks app.				2.25

PLASTRON CAFE
Mirage Studios: Dec, 1992 - No. 4, July, 1993 ($2.25, B&W)

1-4: 1-Teenage Mutant Ninja Turtles app.; Kelly Freas-c. 1-Hildebrandt				
painted-c. 4-Spaced & Alien Fire stories				2.25

PLAYFUL LITTLE AUDREY (TV)(Also see Little Audrey #25)
Harvey Publications: 6/57 - No. 110, 11/73; No. 111, 8/74 - No. 121, 4/76

1	22	66	154	275
2	11	33	80	135
3-5	8	24	58	95
6-10	6	18	40	65
11-20	4	12	29	45
21-40	3	9	20	30
41-60	3	9	17	24
61-84: 84-Last 12¢ issue	2	6	12	18
85-99	2	6	10	14
100-52 pg. Giant	3	9	17	24
101-105 52 pg. Giants	2	6	13	20
104-121	1	3	6	9
...In 3-D (Spring, 1988, $2.25, Blackthorne #66)				4.00

PLOP! (Also see The Best of DC #60)
National Periodical Publications: Sept-Oct, 1973 - No. 24, Nov-Dec, 1976

1-Sergio Aragonés-a begins; Wrightson-a	3	9	20	30

Pogo Possum #4 © Oskar Lebeck

Poison Elves #61 © Drew Hayes

Pokémon Pt. 4 #4 © Nintendo

	GD2.0	FN6.0	VF8.0	NM9.4
2-4,6-20	2	6	10	14
5-Wrightson-a	2	6	11	16
21-24 (52 pgs.). 23-No Aragonés-a	2	6	12	18

NOTE: *Alcala* a-1-3. *Anderson* a-5. *Aragonés* a-1-22, 24. *Ditko* a-16p. *Evans* a-1. *Mayer* a-1. *Orlando* a-21, 22; c-21. *Sekowsky* a-5, 6p. *Toth* a-11. *Wolverton* r-4, 22-24(1 pg.ea.); c-1-12, 14, 17, 18. *Wood* a-14, 16i, 18-24; c-13, 15, 16, 19.

PLUTO (See Cheerios Premiums, Four Color #537, Mickey Mouse Magazine, Walt Disney Showcase #4, 7, 13, 20, 23, 33 & Wheaties)
Dell Publ. Co.: No. 7, 1942; No. 429, 10/52 - No. 1248, 11-1/61-62 (Disney)

Large Feature Comic 7(1942)-Written by Carl Barks, Jack Hannah, & Nick				
George (Barks' 1st comic book work)	123	369	861	1600
Four Color 429 (#1)	9	27	63	110
Four Color 509	5	15	35	65
Four Color 595,654,736,853	4	12	26	40
Four Color 941,1039,1143,1248	4	12	26	40

POCKET COMICS (Also see Double Up)
Harvey Publications: Aug, 1941 - No. 4, Jan, 1942 (Pocket size; 100 pgs.) (1st Harvey comic)

1-Origin & 1st app. The Black Cat, Cadet Blakey the Spirit of '76, The Red				
Blazer, The Phantom, Sphinx, & The Zebra; Phantom Ranger, British Agent				
#99, Spin Hawkins, Satan, Lord of Evil begin (1st app. of each); Simon-c/a				
in #1-3	95	285	597	1050
2 (9/41)-Black Cat on-c #2-4	64	192	398	700
3,4	50	150	300	525

POE
Cheese Comics: Sept, 1996 - No. 6, Apr, 1997 ($2.00, B&W)

1-6-Jason Asala-s/a				3.00

POE
Sirius Entertainment (Dogstar Press): Oct, 1997 - Present ($2.50/$2.95, B&W)

1-19-Jason Asala-s/a				3.00
20-24 ($2.95)				3.00
... Color Special (12/98, $2.95) Linsner-c				3.00

POGO PARADE (See Dell Giants)

POGO POSSUM (Also see Animal Comics & Special Delivery)
Dell Publishing Co.: No. 105, 4/46 - No. 148, 5/47; 10-12/49 - No. 16, 4-6/54

Four Color 105(1946)-Kelly-c/a	71	213	497	925
Four Color 148-Kelly-c/a	58	175	406	760
1-(10-12/49)-Kelly-c/a in all	48	143	336	625
2	38	115	266	500
3-5	27	80	189	350
6-10: 10-Infinity-c	23	68	161	295
11-16: 11-X-Mas-c	18	54	126	230

NOTE: #1-4, 9-13: 52 pgs.; #5-8, 14-16: 36 pgs.

POINT BLANK
Acme Press (Eclipse): May, 1989 - No. 2, 1989 ($2.95, B&W, magazine)

1,2-European-r				3.00

POISON ELVES (Formerly I, Lusiphur)
Mulehide Graphics: No. 8, 1993- No. 20, 1995 (B&W, magazine/comic size, mature readers)

8-Drew Hayes-c/a/scripts.	1	3	6	9
9-11: 11-1st comic size issue	1	3	6	9
12,14,16				6.00
13,15-(low print)	1	4	7	10
15-2nd print				4.00
17-20				6.00
...Desert of the Third Sin-(1997, $14.95, TPB)-r/#13-18				15.00
...Patrons-($4.95, TPB)-r/#19,20				5.00
...Traumatic Dogs-(1996, $14.95,TPB)-Reprints I, Lusiphur #7, Poison				
Elves #8-12				15.00

POISON ELVES (See I, Lusiphur)
Sirius Entertainment: June, 1995 - Present ($2.50, B&W, mature readers)

1-Linsner-c; Drew Hayes-a/scripts in all.				5.00
1-2nd print				2.50
2-25: 12-Purple Marauder-c/app.				3.00
26-45, 47-49				2.50

	GD2.0	FN6.0	VF8.0	NM9.4
46,50-68: 61-Fillbäch Brothers-s/a				3.00
... Color Special #1 (12/98, $2.95)				5.00
... FAN Edition #1 mail-in offer; Drew Hayes-c/s/a	1	3	6	8
...Salvation-(2001, $19.95, TPB)-r/#26-39				20.00
...Sanctuary-(1999, $14.95, TPB)-r/#1-12				15.00

POISON ELVES: LUSIPHUR & LIRILITH
Sirius Entertainment: 2001 - No. 4, 2001 ($2.95, B&W, mature readers)

1-4-Drew Hayes-s/Jason Alexander-a				3.00

POISON ELVES: PARINTACHIN
Sirius Entertainment: 2001 - No. 3, 2001 ($2.95, B&W, mature readers)

1-Drew Hayes-c/Fillbäch Brothers-s/a				3.00

POKÉMON (TV) (Also see Magical Pokémon Journey)
Viz Comics: Nov, 1998 - Present ($3.25/$3.50, B&W)
...Part 1: The Electric Tale of Pikachu

1-Toshiro Ono-s/a	1	4	7	10
1-4 (2nd through current printings)				3.50
2				6.00
3,4				4.00
TPB ($12.95)				13.00
...Part 2: Pikachu Strikes Back				
1				5.00
2-4				4.00
TPB				13.00
...Part 3: Electric Pikachu Boogaloo				
1				4.00
2-4 ($2.95-c)				3.50
TPB				13.00
...Part 4: Surf's Up Pikachu				
1,3,4				4.00
2 ($2.95-c)				3.50
TPB				13.00

NOTE: Multiple printings exist for most issues

POKÉMON ADVENTURES
Viz Comics: Sept, 1999 - No. 4 ($5.95, B&W, magazine-size)

1-4-Includes stickers bound in				6.00

POKÉMON ADVENTURES
Viz Comics: 2000 - Present ($2.95/$4.95, B&W)

Part 2 (2/00-7/00) 1-6-Includes stickers bound in				3.50
Part 3 (8/00-2/01) 1-7				3.50
Part 4 (3/00-6/01) 1-4				5.00
Part 5 (7/01) 1-4				5.00

POKÉMON: THE FIRST MOVIE
Viz Comics: 1999 ($3.95)

Mewtwo Strikes Back 1-4				4.00
Pikachu's Vacation				4.00

POKÉMON: THE MOVIE 2000
Viz Comics: 2000 ($3.95)

1-Official movie adaption				4.00
Pikachu's Rescue Adventure				4.00
....The Power of One (mini-series) 1-3				4.00

POLICE ACADEMY (TV)
Marvel Comics: Nov, 1989 - No. 6, Feb, 1990 ($1.00)

1-6: Based on TV cartoon; Post-c/a(p) in all				2.25

POLICE ACTION
Atlas News Co.: Jan, 1954 - No. 7, Nov, 1954

1-Violent-a by Robert Q. Sale	21	63	110	185
2	11	33	55	90
3-7: 7-Powell-a	10	30	55	80

NOTE: *Ayers* a-4, 5. *Colan* a-1. *Forte* a-1. 2. *Mort Lawrence* a-5. *Maneely* a-3; c-1, 5. *Reinman* a-6, 7.

POLICE ACTION
Atlas/Seaboard Publ.: Feb, 1975 - No. 3, June, 1975

1-3: 1-Lomax, N.Y.P.D., Luke Malone begin; McWilliams-a. 2-Origin Luke				
Malone, Manhunter; Ploog-a				6.00

Police Comics #30 © QUA

Police Line-Up #3 © AVON

Popeye Four Color #70 © KING

	GD2.0	FN6.0	VF8.0	NM9.4

NOTE: *Ploog* art in all. *Sekowsky/McWilliams* a-1-3. *Thorne* c-3.

POLICE AGAINST CRIME
Premiere Magazines: April, 1954 - No. 9, Aug, 1955

1-Disbrow-a; extreme violence (man's face slashed with knife); Hollingsworth-a	25	75	130	225
2-Hollingsworth-a	14	42	72	120
3-9	11	33	55	90

POLICE BADGE #479 (Formerly Spy Thrillers #1-4)
Atlas Comics (PrPI): No. 5, Sept, 1955

5-Maneely-c/a (6 pgs.)	11	33	55	90

POLICE CASE BOOK (See Giant Comics Editions)

POLICE CASES (See Authentic... & Record Book of...)

POLICE COMICS
Quality Comics Group (Comic Magazines): Aug, 1941 - No. 127, Oct, 1953

1-Origin/1st app. Plastic Man by Jack Cole (r-in DC Special #15), The Human Bomb by Gustavson, & No. 711; intro. Chic Carter by Eisner, The Firebrand by Reed Crandall, The Mouthpiece by Guardineer, Phantom Lady, & The Sword; Firebrand-r 1-4	708	2124	4600	9200
2-Plastic Man smuggles opium	308	924	1927	3700
3	218	654	1364	2400
4	191	573	1194	2100
5-Plastic Man-c begin; Plastic Man forced to smoke marijuana; Plastic Man covers begin, end #102	182	546	1136	2000
6,7	159	477	994	1750
8-Manhunter begins (origin/1st app.) (3/42)	186	558	1163	2050
9,10	127	381	795	1400
11-The Spirit strip reprints begin by Eisner (origin-strip #1); 1st comic book app. The Spirit & 1st cover app. (9/42)	214	642	1338	2350
12-Intro. Ebony	132	395	825	1450
13-Intro. Woozy Winks; last Firebrand	127	381	795	1400
14-19: 15-Last No. 711; Destiny begins	93	279	581	1025
20-The Raven x-over in Phantom Lady; features Jack Cole himself	93	279	581	1025
21,22: 21-Raven & Spider Widow x-over in Phantom Lady (cameo in #22)	77	231	483	850
23-30: 23-Last Phantom Lady. 24-26-Flatfoot Burns by Kurtzman in all	73	219	455	800
31-41: 37-1st app. Candy by Sahle & begins (12/44). 41-Last Spirit-r by Eisner	52	157	314	550
42,43-Spirit-r by Eisner/Fine	50	150	300	525
44-Fine Spirit-r begin; end #88,90,92	47	141	286	500
45-50: 50-(#50 on-c, #49 on inside, 1/46)	40	120	232	400
51-60: 58-Last Human Bomb	35	105	188	325
61-88,90,92: 63-(Some issues have #65 printed on cover, but #63 on inside) Kurtzman-a, 6 pgs. 90,92-Spirit by Fine	26	78	139	240
89,91,93-No Spirit stories	23	69	121	210
94-99,101,102: Spirit by Eisner in all; 101-Last Manhunter. 102-Last Spirit & Plastic Man by Jack Cole	34	102	179	310
100	40	120	220	380
103-Content change to crime; Ken Shannon & T-Man begin (1st app. of each, 12/50)	27	81	142	245
104-112,114-127: Crandall-a most issues (not in 104,105,122,125-127). 109-Atomic bomb story. 112-Crandall-a	20	60	105	175
113-Crandall-c/a(2), 9 pgs. each	21	63	110	185

NOTE: *Most Spirit stories signed by Eisner are not by him; all are reprints. Cole* c-17, 19-21, 24-94-102; by *Eisner/Fine,* 43; by *Fine-44-88, 90, 92.* 103, 109. *Al Bryant* c-33, 34. *Cole* c-17-32, 35-102(most). *Crandall* c-13, 14. *Crandall/Cuidera* c-105-127. *Eisner* c-4i. *Gill Fox* c-1-3, 4p, 5-12, 15. *Bondage* c-103, 109, 125.

POLICE LINE-UP
Avon Periodicals/Realistic Comics 3,4: Aug, 1951 - No. 4, July, 1952
(Painted-c #1-3)

1-Wood-a, 1 pg. plus part-c; spanking panel-r/Saint #5	40	120	220	380
2-Classic story "The Religious Murder Cult", drugs, perversion; r/Saint #5; c-r/Avon paperback #329	29	87	153	265
3,4: 3-Kubert-a(r?)/part-c; Kinstler-a (inside-c only)	22	66	116	195

POLICE TRAP (Public Defender In Action #7 on)

Mainline #1-4/Charlton #5,6: 8-9/54 - No. 4, 2-3/55; No. 5, 7/55 - No. 6, 9/55

1-S&K covers-all issues; Meskin-a; Kirby scripts	31	93	165	285
2-4	19	57	99	165
5,6-S&K-c/a	25	75	133	230

POLICE TRAP
Super Comics: No. 11, 1963; No. 16-18, 1964

Reprint 11,16-18: 11-r/Police Trap #3. 16-r/Justice Traps the Guilty #? 17-r/Inside Crime #3 & r/Justice Traps The Guilty #83; 18-r/Inside Crime #3	2	6	10	14

POLLY & HER PALS (See Comic Monthly #1)

POLLYANNA (Disney)
Dell Publishing Co.: No. 1129, Aug-Oct, 1960

Four Color 1129-Movie, Haley Mills photo-c	8	24	56	100

POLLY PIGTAILS (Girls' Fun & Fashion Magazine #44 on)
Parents' Magazine Institute/Polly Pigtails: Jan, 1946 - V4#43, Oct-Nov, 1949

1-Infinity-c; photo-c	12	36	61	100
2-Photo-c	7	21	36	50
3-5: 3,4-Photo-c	6	18	29	40
6-10: 7-Photo-c	5	15	25	35
11-30: 22-Photo-c	5	14	21	28
31-43	4	12	19	25

PONY EXPRESS (See Tales of the...)

PONYTAIL (Teen-age)
Dell Publishing Co./Charlton No. 13 on: 7-9/62 - No. 12, 10-12/65; No. 13, 11/69 - No. 20, 1/71

12-641-209(#1)	3	10	23	35
2-12	2	6	15	22
13-20	2	6	11	15

POP COMICS
Modern Store Publ.: 1955 (36 pgs.; 5x7"; in color) (7¢)

1-Funny animal	5	15	25	35

POPEYE (See Comic Album #7, 11, 15, Comics Reading Libraries *in the Promotional Comics section,* Eat Right to Work and Win, Giant Comic Album, King Comics, Kite Fun Book, Magic Comics, March of Comics #37,52, 66, 80, 96, 117, 134, 148, 157, 169, 194, 246, 264, 274, 294, 453, 465, 477 & Wow Comics, 1st series)

POPEYE
David McKay Publications: 1937 - 1939 (All by Segar)

Feature Books nn (100 pgs.) (Very Rare)	600	1800	4200	7200
Feature Books 2 (52 pgs.)	67	200	469	875
Feature Books 3 (100 pgs.)-r/nn issue with a new-c	65	195	455	840
Feature Books 5,10 (76 pgs.)	57	171	399	740
Feature Books 14 (76 pgs.) (Scarce)	65	195	455	840

POPEYE (Strip reprints through 4-Color #70)
Dell #1-65/Gold Key #66-80/King #81-92/Charlton #94-138/Gold Key #139-155/Whitman #156 on: 1941 - 1947; #1, 2-4/48 - #65, 7-9/62; #66, 10/62 - #80, 5/66; #81, 8/66 - #92, 12/67; #94, 2/69 - #138, 1/77; #139, 5/78 - #171, 6/84 (no #93,160,161)

Large Feature Comic 24('41)-Half by Segar	56	168	392	725
Four Color 25('41)-by Segar	69	206	483	900
Large Feature Comic 10('43)	44	131	308	575
Four Color 17('43),26('43)-by Segar	50	150	350	650
Four Color 43('44)	32	96	224	420
Four Color 70('45)-Title: ...& Wimpy	25	75	175	325
Four Color 113('46-original strips begin),127,145('47),168	13	39	91	165
1(2-4/48)(Dell)-All new stories continue	28	84	196	360
2	13	40	91	175
3-10: 5-Popeye on moon w/rocket-c	12	36	84	150
11-20	9	27	63	120
21-40,46: 46-Origin Swee' Pea	8	24	56	100
41-45,47-50	6	18	42	70
51-60	5	15	35	65
61-65 (Last Dell issue)	5	15	34	55
66,67-Both 84 pgs. (Gold Key)	6	18	42	70
68-80	3	10	23	35

Popular Comics #5 © DELL

Popular Teen-agers #7 © STAR

Porky Pig #73 © WB

	GD	FN	VF	NM
81-92,94-97 (no (#93): 97-Last 12¢ issue	3	9	19	28
98,99,101-130	2	6	12	18
100	3	9	17	25
131-155: 144-50th Anniversary issue	1	3	6	8
156,157,162-167(Whitman)(no (#160,161).167(3/82)	2	6	9	12
158(9/80),159(11/80)-pre-pack?	2	6	13	20
168-171:(All (#90069 on-c; pre pack) 168(6/83). 169(#168 on-c)(8/83). 170(3/84).				
171(6/84)	2	6	11	15

NOTE: Reprints/#145, 147, 149, 151, 153, 155, 157, 163-168(1/3), 170.

POPEYE
Harvey Comics: Nov, 1993 - No. 7, Aug, 1994 ($1.50)

V2#1-7				3.00
...Summer Special V2#1-(10/93, $2.25, 68 pgs.)-Sagendorf-r & others				4.00

POPEYE SPECIAL
Ocean Comics: Summer, 1987 - No. 2, Sept, 1988 ($1.75/$2.00)

1,2: 1-Origin				3.00

POPPLES (TV, movie)
Star Comics (Marvel): Dec, 1986 - No. 5, Aug, 1987

1-5-Based on toys				4.00

POPPO OF THE POPCORN THEATRE
Fuller Publishing Co. (Publishers Weekly): 10/29/55 - No. 13, 1956 (weekly)

	GD	FN	VF	NM
1	9	27	49	70
2-5	6	18	32	45
6-13	5	15	25	35

NOTE: By Charles Biro. 10¢ cover, given away by supermarkets such as IGA.

POP-POP COMICS
R. B. Leffingwell Co.: No date (Circa 1945) (52 pgs.)

	GD	FN	VF	NM
1-Funny animal	12	36	61	105

POPULAR COMICS
Dell Publishing Co.: Feb, 1936 - No. 145, July-Sept, 1948

	GD	FN	VF	NM
1-Dick Tracy (1st comic book app.), Little Orphan Annie, Terry & the Pirates, Gasoline Alley, Don Winslow (1st app.), Harold Teen, Little Joe, Skippy, Moon Mullins, Mutt & Jeff, Tailspin Tommy, Smitty, Smokey Stover, Winnie Winkle & The Gumps begin (all strip-r)	615	1846	4000	–
2	215	646	1400	–
3	162	485	1050	–
4-6(7/36): 5-Tom Mix begins. 6-1st app. Scribbly	131	392	850	–
7-10: 8,9-Scribbly & Reglar Fellers app.	100	300	650	–
11-20: 12-X-Mas-c	80	240	440	720
21-27:27-Last Terry & the Pirates, Little Orphan Annie, & Dick Tracy	58	174	319	520
28-37: 28-Gene Autry app. 31,32-Tim McCoy app. 35-Christmas-c; Tex Ritter app.	47	141	259	425
38-43: Tarzan in text only. 38-(4/39)-Gang Busters (Radio, 2nd app.) & Zane Grey's Tex Thorne begins? 43-The Masked Pilot app.; 1st non-funny-c?	46	138	253	410
44,45: 45-Hurricane Kid-c	32	96	176	285
46-Origin/1st app. Martan, the Marvel Man(12/39)	42	126	231	375
47-50	31	93	171	275
51-Origin The Voice (The Invisible Detective) strip begins (5/40)	32	96	176	285
52-59: 52-Robot-c. 55-End of World story	25	75	138	225
60-Origin/1st app. Professor Supermind and Son (2/41)	26	78	143	230
61-71: 63-Smilin' Jack begins	20	60	110	180
72-The Owl & Terry & the Pirates begin (2/42); Smokey Stover reprints begin	40	120	220	360
73-75	27	81	149	240
76-78-Capt. Midnight in all (see The Funnies (#57)	38	113	209	340
79-85-Last Owl	23	69	127	210
86-99: 98-Felix the Cat, Smokey Stover-r begin	18	54	99	160
100	19	56	105	170
101-130	11	33	61	95
131-145: 142-Last Terry & the Pirates	10	30	55	90

NOTE: Martan, the Marvel Man c-47-49, 52, 57-59. Professor Supermind c-60-63, 64(1/2), 65, 66. The Voice c-53.

POPULAR FAIRY TALES (See March of Comics #6, 18)

POPULAR ROMANCE
Better-Standard Publications: No. 5, Dec, 1949 - No. 29, July, 1954

	GD	FN	VF	NM
5	10	30	55	85
6-9: 7-Palais-a; lingerie panels	7	21	38	55
10-Wood-a (2 pgs.)	9	27	49	70
11,12,14-16,18-21,28,29	6	18	32	45
13,17-Severin/Elder-a (3&8 pgs.)	7	21	38	55
22-27-Toth-a	9	27	49	70

NOTE: All have photo-c. Tuska art in most issues.

POPULAR TEEN-AGERS (Secrets of Love) (School Day Romances #1-4)
Star Publications: No. 5, Sept, 1950 - No. 23, Nov, 1954

	GD	FN	VF	NM
5-Toni Gay, Midge Martin & Eve Adams continue from School Day Romances; Ginger Bunn (formerly Ginger Snapp & becomes Honey Bunn (#6) begins; all features end (#8	35	105	185	320
6-8 (7/51)-Honey Bunn begins; all have L. B. Cole-c; 6-Negligee panels	32	96	171	295
9-(...Romances; 1st romance issue, 10/51)	21	63	110	185
10-(...Secrets of Love thru (#23)	20	60	105	175
11,16,18,19,22,23	16	48	83	140
12,13,17,20,21-Disbrow-a	18	54	94	155
14-Harrison/Wood-a	23	69	121	210
15-Wood?, Disbrow-a	19	57	99	165
Accepted Reprint 5,6 (nd); L.B. Cole-c	9	27	49	70

NOTE: All have L. B. Cole covers.

PORKY PIG (See Bugs Bunny &..., Kite Fun Book, Looney Tunes, March of Comics #42, 57, 71, 89, 99, 113, 130, 143, 164, 175, 192, 209, 218, 367, and Super Book #6, 18, 30)

PORKY PIG (...& Bugs Bunny #40-69)
Dell Publishing Co./Gold Key No. 1-93/Whitman No. 94 on: No. 16, 1942 - No. 81, Mar-Apr, 1962; Jan, 1965 - No. 109, June, 1984

	GD	FN	VF	NM
Four Color 16(#1, 1942)	85	255	595	1100
Four Color 48(1944)-Carl Barks-a	96	288	672	1250
Four Color 78(1945)	24	72	168	310
Four Color 112(7/46)	15	45	105	190
Four Color 156,182,191('49)	10	30	70	135
Four Color 226,241('49),260,271,277,284,295	8	24	56	100
Four Color 303,311,322,330: 322-Sci/fi-c/story	5	15	35	70
Four Color 342,351,360,370,385,399,410,426	4	12	30	50
25 (11-12/52)-30	4	12	26	40
31-40	3	9	20	30
41-60	3	9	17	25
61-81(3-4/62)	2	6	13	20
1(1/65-Gold Key)(2nd Series)	4	12	30	50
2,4,5-r/4-Color 226,284 & 271 in that order	3	9	17	25
3,6-10: 3-r/Four Color #342	2	6	13	20
11-30	2	6	11	15
31-54	2	6	9	12
55-70	1	3	6	9
71-93(Gold Key)	1	3	5	7
94-96	1	3	5	8
97(9/80),98,99-pre-pack?	2	6	11	16
100	1	4	7	10
101-105: 104(2/82). 105(4/82)	1	3	6	8
106-109 (All #90140 on-c, no date or date code): 106(7/83), 107(8/83), 108(2/84), 109(6/84)	1	4	7	10

NOTE: Reprints-#1-8, 9-35(2/3); 36-46(1/4-1/2), 58, 67, 69-74, 76, 78, 102-109(1/3-1/2).

PORKY PIG'S DUCK HUNT
Saalfield Publishing Co.: 1938 (12pgs.)(large size)(heavy linen-like paper)

	GD	FN	VF	NM
2178-1st app. Porky Pig & Daffy Duck by Leon Schlesinger. Illustrated text story book written in verse.1st book ever devoted to these characters. (see Looney Tunes #1 for their 1st comic book app.)	68	205	426	750

PORTIA PRINZ OF THE GLAMAZONS
Eclipse Comics: Dec, 1986 - No. 6, Oct, 1987 ($2.00, B&W, Baxter paper)

1-6				2.25

POST GAZETTE (See Meet the New...)

POWDER RIVER RUSTLERS (See Fawcett Movie Comics)

POWER & GLORY (See American Flagg! & Howard Chaykin's American Flagg!
Malibu Comics (Bravura): Feb, 1994 - No. 4, May, 1994 ($2.50, limited series,

Power & Glory #2 © Howard Chaykin

Power Man #54 © MAR

Powerpuff Girls #16 © Cartoon Network

	GD2.0	FN6.0	VF8.0	NM9.4

mature)

1A, 1B-By Howard Chaykin; w/Bravura stamp				2.50
1-Newsstand ed. (polybagged w/children's warning on bag), Gold ed.,				
Silver-foil ed., Blue-foil ed.(print run of 10,000), Serigraph ed. (print run of				
3,000)($2.95)-Howard Chaykin-c/a begin				3.00
2-4-Contains Bravura stamp				2.50
Holiday Special (Win '94, $2.95)				3.00

POWER COMICS
Holyoke Publ. Co./Narrative Publ.: 1944 - No. 4, 1945

1-L. B. Cole-c	148	444	925	1625
2-Hitler, Hirohito-c (scarce)	148	444	925	1625
3-Classic L.B. Cole-c; Dr. Mephisto begins?	168	505	1050	1850
4-L.B. Cole-c; Miss Espionage app. #3,4; Leava-a	148	444	925	1625

POWER COMICS
Power Comics Co.: 1977 - No. 5, Dec, 1977 (B&W)

1- "A Boy And His Aardvark" by Dave Sim; first Dave Sim aardvark				
(not Cerebus)	2	6	12	18
1-Reprint (3/77, black-c)	1	3	5	7
2-Cobalt Blue by Gustovich	1	3	6	9
3-5: 3-Nightwitch. 4-Northern Light. 5-Bluebird	1	3	6	9

POWER COMICS
Eclipse Comics (Acme Press): Mar, 1988 - No. 4, Sept, 1988 ($2.00, B&W, mini-series)

1-4: Bolland, Gibbons-r in all				2.25

POWER FACTOR
Wonder Color Comics #1/Pied Piper #2: May, 1987 - No. 2, 1987 ($1.95)

1,2: Super team. 2-Infantino-c				2.25

POWER FACTOR
Innovation Publishing: Oct, 1990 - No. 3, 1991 ($1.95/$2.25)

1-3: 1-R/1st story + new-a, 2-r/2nd story + new-a. 3-Infantino-a				2.25

POWER GIRL (See All-Star #58, Infinity, Inc., Showcase #97-99)
DC Comics: June, 1988 - No. 4, Sept, 1988 ($1.00, color, limited series)

1-4				3.00

POWERHOUSE PEPPER COMICS (See Gay Comics, Joker Comics & Tessie the Typist)
Marvel Comics (20CC): No. 1, 1943; No. 2, May, 1948 - No. 5, Nov, 1948

1-(60 pgs.)-Wolverton-a in all; c-2,3	164	492	1023	1800
2	84	252	525	925
3,4	77	231	483	850
5-(Scarce)	91	273	568	1000

POWER LINE
Marvel Comics (Epic Comics): May, 1988 - No. 8, Sept, 1989 ($1.25/$1.50)

1-8: 2-Williamson-i. 3-Dr. Zero app. 4-7-Morrow-a. 8-Williamson-i				2.25

POWER LORDS
DC Comics: Dec, 1983 - No. 3, Feb, 1984 (Limited series, Mando paper)

1-3: Based on Revell toys				2.25

POWER MAN (Formerly Hero for Hire; ...& Iron Fist #50 on; see Cage & Giant-Size...)
Marvel Comics Group: No. 17, Feb, 1974 - No. 125, Sept, 1986

17-Luke Cage continues; Iron Man app.	2	6	9	12
18-20: 18-Last 20¢ issue	1	3	6	8
21-30				6.00
30-(30¢-c variant, limited distribution)(4/76)	1	3	6	9
31-46: 31-Part Neal Adams-i. 34-Last 25¢ issue. 36-r/Hero For Hire #12.				
41-1st app. Thunderbolt. 45-Starlin-c.				5.00
31-34-(30¢-c variants, limited distribution)(5-8/76)	1	3	6	8
44-46-(35¢-c variants, limited distribution)(6-8/77)	1	3	6	8
47-Barry Smith-a	1	3	5	7
47-(35¢-c variant, limited distribution)(10/77)	1	3	6	8
48-50-Byrne-a(p); 48-Power Man/Iron Fist 1st meet. 50-Iron Fist joins Cage	2	6	9	12
51-56,58-65,67-77: 58-Intro El Aguila. 75-Double size. 77-Daredevil app.				4.00
57-New X-Men app. (6/79)	2	6	12	18

66-2nd app. Sabretooth (see Iron Fist #14)	3	9	17	25
78,84: 78-3rd app. Sabretooth (cameo under cloak). 84-4th app. Sabretooth				
	2	6	9	12
79-83,85-99,101-124: 87-Moon Knight app. 109-The Reaper app.				3.00
100,125-Double size: 100-Origin K'un Lun. 125-Death of Iron Fist				3.00
Annual 1(1976)-Punisher cameo in flashback	1	4	7	10

NOTE: **Austin** c-102i. **Byrne** a-48-50; c-102, 104, 106, 107, 112-116. **Kane** c(p)-24, 25, 28, 48. **Miller** a-68, 76(2 pgs.); c-66-68, 70-74, 80i. **Mooney** a-38i, 53i, 55i. **Nebres** a-68, Nino a-42i, 43i. **Perez** a-27. **B. Smith** a-47i. **Tuska** a(p)-17, 20, 24, 26, 28, 29, 36, 47. Painted c-75, 100.

POWER OF PRIME
Malibu Comics (Ultraverse): July, 1995 - No. 4, Nov, 1995 ($2.50, lim. series)

1-4				2.50

POWER OF SHAZAM!, THE (See SHAZAM!)
DC Comics: 1994 (Painted graphic novel) (Prequel to new series)

Hardcover-($19.95)-New origin of Shazam!; Ordway painted-c/a & script				
	3	9	17	25
Softcover-($7.50), Softcover-($9.95)-New-c.	2	6	9	12

POWER OF SHAZAM!, THE
DC Comics: Mar, 1995 - No. 47, Mar, 1999 ($1.50/$1.75/$1.95/$2.50)

1-Jerry Ordway scripts begin				4.00
2-20: 4-Begin $1.75-c. 6:Re-intro of Capt. Nazi. 8-Re-intro of Spy Smasher,				
Bulletman & Minuteman; Swan-a (7 pgs.). 11-Re-intro of Ibis,Swan-a(2 pgs.).				
14-Gil Kane-a(p). 20-Superman-c/app.; "Final Night"				3.00
21-47: 21-Plastic Man app. 22-Batman-c/app. 35,36-X-over w/Starman #39,40.				
38-41-Mr. Mind. 43-Bulletman app. 45-JLA-c/app.				2.50
#1,000,000 (11/98) 853rd Century x-over; Ordway-c/s/a				3.00
Annual 1 (1996, $2.95)-Legends of the Dead Earth story; Jerry Ordway-c; Mike				
Manley-a				4.00

POWER OF STRONGMAN, THE (Also see Strongman)
AC Comics: 1989 ($2.95)

1-Powell G.A.-r				3.00

POWER OF THE ATOM (See Secret Origins #29)
DC Comics: Aug, 1988 - No. 18, Nov, 1989 ($1.00)

1-18: 6-Chronos returns; Byrne-p. 9-JLI app.				2.25

POWER PACHYDERMS
Marvel Comics: Sept, 1989 ($1.25, one-shot)

1-Elephant super-heroes; parody of X-Men, Elektra, & 3 Stooges				2.25

POWER PACK
Marvel Comics Group: Aug, 1984 - No. 62, Feb, 1991

1-($1.00, 52 pgs.)-Origin & 1st app. Power Pack				3.00
2-18,20-26,28,30-45,47-62				2.25
19-(52 pgs.)-Cloak & Dagger, Wolverine app.				3.00
27-Mutant massacre; Wolverine & Sabretooth app.				5.00
29,46: 29-Spider-Man & Hobgoblin app. 46-Punisher app.				2.50
Graphic Novel: Power Pack & Cloak & Dagger: Shelter From the Storm ('89,				
SC, $7.95) Velluto/Farmer-a				10.00
...Holiday Special 1 (2/92, $2.25, 68 pgs.)				2.25

NOTE: **Austin** scripts-53. **Mignola** c-20. **Morrow** a-51. **Spiegle** a-55i. **Williamson** a(i)-43, 50, 52.

POWER PACK (Volume 2)
Marvel Comics: Aug, 2000 - No. 4, Nov, 2000 ($2.99, limited series)

1-4-Doran & Austin-c/a				3.00

POWERPUFF GIRLS, THE (Also see Cartoon Network Starring... #1)
DC Comics: May, 2000 - Present ($1.99)

1				4.00
2-22				2.25
...Double Whammy (12/00, $3.95) r/#1,2 & a Dexter's Lab story				4.00

POWER RANGERS ZEO (TV)(Saban's...)(Also see Saban's Mighty Morphin Power Rangers)
Image Comics (Extreme Studios): Aug, 1996 ($2.50)

1-Based on TV show				2.50

POWERS
Image Comics: 2000 - Present ($2.95)

1-Bendis-s/Oeming-a; murder of Retro Girl				6.00
2-6: 6-End of Retro Girl arc.				4.00

Powers #7 © Bendis & Oeming

Preacher #54 © Ennis & Dillon

Predator: Strange Roux #1 © 20th Century Fox

| | GD2.0 | FN6.0 | VF8.0 | NM9.4 |

	GD2.0	FN6.0	VF8.0	NM9.4

7-15: 7-Warren Ellis app. 12-14-Death of Olympia				3.50
Annual 1 (2001, $3.95)				4.00
...Coloring/Activity Book (2001, $1.50, B&W, 8 x 10.5") Oeming-a				1.50
....: Roleplay TPB (2001, $13.95) r/#8-11; sketchbook, cover gallery				14.00
... Scriptbook (2001, $19.95) scripts for #1-11; Oeming sketches				20.00
..: Who Killed Retro Girl TPB (2000, $21.95) r/#1-6; sketchbook, cover gallery, and promotional strips from Comic Shop News				22.00

POWERS THAT BE (Becomes Star Seed No.7 on)
Broadway Comics: Nov, 1995 - No. 6, June, 1996 ($2.50)

1-6: 1-Intro of Fatale & Star Seed. 6-Fabry $2.95-c.				3.00
Preview Editions 1-3 (9/95 - 11/95, B&W)				2.50

POW MAGAZINE (Bob Sproul's) (Satire Magazine)
Humor-Vision: Aug, 1966 - No. 3, Feb, 1967 (30¢)

1,2: 2-Jones-a	4	12	25	38
3-Wrightson-a	4	12	30	50

PREACHER
DC Comics (Vertigo): Apr, 1995 - No. 66, Oct, 2000 ($2.50, mature)

nn-Preview	2	6	13	20
1 ($2.95)-Ennis scripts, Dillon-a & Fabry-c in all; 1st app. Jesse, Tulip, & Cassidy	2	6	9	12
2,3: 2-1st app. Saint of Killers.	1	3	6	8
4,5	1	3	5	7
6-10				5.00
11-20: 12-Polybagged w/videogame w/Ennis text. 13-Hunters storyline begins; ends #17. 19-Saint of Killers app.; begin "Crusaders", ends #24				4.00
21-25: 21-24-Saint of Killers app. 25-Origin of Cassidy.				3.00
26-49,52-64: 52-Tulip origin				2.50
50-($3.75) Pin-ups by Jim Lee, Bradstreet, Quesada and Palmiotti				3.75
51-Includes preview of 100 Bullets; Tulip origin				4.00
65,66-($3.75) 65-Almost everyone dies. 66-Final issue				3.75
Alamo (2001, $17.95, TPB) r/#59-66; Fabry-c				18.00
All Hell's a-Coming (2000, $29.95, TPB) r/#51-58, ...:Tall in the Saddle				18.00
...: Dead or Alive HC (2000, $29.95) Gallery of Glenn Fabry's cover paintings for every Preacher issue; commentary by Fabry & Ennis				30.00
Dixie Fried (1998, $14.95, TPB)-r/#27-33, Special: Cassidy				15.00
Gone To Texas (1996, $14.95, TPB)-r/#1-7; Fabry-c				15.00
Proud Americans (1997, $14.95, TPB)-r/#18-26; Fabry-c				15.00
Salvation (1999, $14.95, TPB)-r/#41-50; Fabry-c				15.00
Until the End of the World (1996, $14.95, TPB)-r/#8-17; Fabry-c				15.00
War in the Sun (1999, $14.95, TPB)-r/#34-40				15.00

PREACHER SPECIAL: CASSIDY: BLOOD & WHISKEY
DC Comics (Vertigo): 1998 ($5.95, one-shot)

1-Ennis-scripts/Fabry-c /Dillon-a				6.00

PREACHER SPECIAL: ONE MAN'S WAR
DC Comics (Vertigo): Mar, 1998 ($4.95, one-shot)

1-Ennis-scripts/Fabry-c /Snejbjerg-a				5.00

PREACHER SPECIAL: SAINT OF KILLERS
DC Comics (Vertigo): Aug, 1996 - No. 4, Nov, 1996 ($2.50, lim. series, mature)

1-4: Ennis-scripts/Fabry-c. 1,2-Pugh-a. 3,4-Ezquerra-a				3.00
1-Signed & numbered				20.00

PREACHER SPECIAL: THE GOOD OLD BOYS
DC Comics (Vertigo): Aug, 1997 ($4.95, one-shot, mature)

1-Ennis-scripts/Fabry-c /Esquerra-a				5.00

PREACHER SPECIAL: THE STORY OF YOU-KNOW-WHO
DC Comics (Vertigo): Dec, 1996 ($4.95, one-shot, mature)

1-Ennis-scripts/Fabry-c/Case-a				5.00

PREACHER: TALL IN THE SADDLE
DC Comics (Vertigo): 2000 ($5.95, one-shot)

1-Ennis-scripts/Fabry-c/Dillon-a; early romance of Tulip and Jesse				6.00

PREDATOR (Also see Aliens Vs. ..., Batman vs. ..., Dark Horse Comics, & Dark Horse Presents)
Dark Horse Comics: June, 1989 - No. 4, Mar, 1990 ($2.25, limited series)

1-Based on movie; 1st app. Predator				6.00
1-2nd printing				3.00

2				5.00
3,4				4.00
Trade paperback (1990, $12.95)-r/#1-4				13.00

PREDATOR: (title series) **Dark Horse Comics**

—**BAD BLOOD**, 12/93 - No. 4, 1994 ($2.50) 1-4				3.00
—**BIG GAME**, 3/91 - No. 4, 6/91 ($2.50) 1-4: 1-3-Contain 2 Dark Horse trading cards				3.00
—**BLOODY SANDS OF TIME**, 2/92 - No. 2, 2/92 ($2.50\) 1,2-Dan Barry-c/a(p)/scripts				3.00
—**CAPTIVE**, 4/98 ($2.95, one-shot) 1				3.00
—**COLD WAR**, 9/91 - No. 4, 12/91 ($2.50) 1-4: All have painted-c				3.00
—**DARK RIVER**, 7/96 - No.4, 10/96 ($2.95)1-4: Miran Kim-c				3.00
—**HELL & HOT WATER**, 4/97 - No. 3, 6/97 ($2.95) 1-3				3.00
—**HELL COME A WALKIN'**, 2/98 - No. 2, 3/98 ($2.95) 1,2-In the Civil War				3.00
—**HOMEWORLD**, 3/99 - No. 4, 6/99 ($2.95) 1-4				3.00
—**INVADERS FROM THE FOURTH DIMENSION**, 7/94 ($3.95, one-shot, 52 pgs.) 1				4.00
—**JUNGLE TALES**. 3/95 ($2.95t) 1-r/Dark Horse Comics				3.00
—**KINDRED**, 12/96 - No. 4, 3/97 ($2.50) 1-4				3.00
—**NEMESIS**, 12/97 - No. 2, 1/98 ($2.95) 1,2-Predator in Victorian England; Taggart-c				3.00
—**PRIMAL**, 7/97 - No. 2, 8/97 ($2.95) 1,2				3.00
—**RACE WAR** (See Dark Horse Presents #67), 2/93 - No. 4,10/93 ($2.50, color) 1-4,0: 1-4-Dorman painted-c #1-4, 0(4/93)0				3.00
—**STRANGE ROUX**, 11/96 ($2.95, one-shot) 1				3.00
--**XENOGENESIS** (Also see Aliens Xenogenesis), 8/99 - No. 4, 11/99 ($2.95) 1,2-Edginton-s				3.00

PREDATOR 2
Dark Horse Comics: Feb, 1991 - No. 2, June, 1991 ($2.50, limited series)

1,2: 1-Adapts movie; both w/trading cards & photo-c				3.00

PREDATOR VS. JUDGE DREDD
Dark Horse Comics: Oct, 1997 - No. 3 ($2.50, limited series)

1-3-Wagner-s/Alcatena-a/Bolland-c				3.00

PREDATOR VS. MAGNUS ROBOT FIGHTER
Dark Horse/Valiant: Oct, 1992 - No. 2, 1993 ($2.95, limited series)
(1st Dark Horse/Valiant x-over)

1,2: (Reg.)-Barry Smith-c; Lee Weeks-a. 2-w/trading cards				3.00
1 (Platinum edition, 11/92)-Barry Smith-c				5.00

PREHISTORIC WORLD (See Classics Illustrated Special Issue)

PREMIERE (See Charlton Premiere)

PRESTO KID, THE (See Red Mask)

PRETTY BOY FLOYD (See On the Spot)

PREZ (See Cancelled Comic Cavalcade, Sandman #54 & Supergirl #10)
National Periodical Publications: Aug-Sept, 1973 - No. 4, Feb-Mar, 1974

1-Origin; Joe Simon scripts	3	9	17	25
2-4	2	6	11	15

PRICE, THE (See Eclipse Graphic Album Series)

PRIDE & JOY
DC Comics (Vertigo): July, 1997 - No. 4, Oct, 1997 (2.50, limited series)

1-4-Ennis-s				2.50

PRIDE AND THE PASSION, THE
Dell Publishing Co.: No. 824, Aug, 1957

Four Color 824-Movie, Frank Sinatra & Cary Grant photo-c	9	27	63	110

PRIDE OF THE YANKEES (See Real Heroes & Sport Comics)
Magazine Enterprises: 1949 (The Life of Lou Gehrig)

nn-Photo-c; Ogden Whitney-a	80	240	500	875

PRIEST (Also see Asylum)

Pride & Joy #4 © Ennis & Higgins

Prime #13 © MAL

Prison Break #1 © AVON

	GD2.0	FN6.0	VF8.0	NM9.4			GD2.0	FN6.0	VF8.0	NM9.4

Maximum Press: Aug, 1996 - No. 2, Oct, 1996 ($2.99)
1,2 — 3.00

PRIMAL FORCE
DC Comics: No. 0, Oct, 1994 - No. 14, Dec, 1995 ($1.95/$2.25)
0-14: 0- Teams Red Tornado, Golem, Jack O'Lantern, Meridian & Silver
Dragon. 9-begin $2.25-c — 2.25

PRIMAL MAN (See The Crusaders)

PRIMAL RAGE
Sirius Entertainment: 1996 ($2.95)
1-Dark One-c; based of video game — 3.00

PRIME (See Break-Thru, Flood Relief & Ultraforce)
Malibu Comics (Ultraverse): June, 1993 - No. 26, Aug, 1995 ($1.95/$2.50)
1-1st app. Prime; has coupon for Ultraverse Premiere #0 — 3.00
1-With coupon missing — 2.25
1-Full cover holographic edition; 1st of kind w/Hardcase #1 & Strangers #1 — 6.00
1-Ultra 5,000 edition w/silver ink-c — 4.00
2-11,14-26: 2-Polybagged w/card & coupon for U. Premiere #0. 3,4-Prototype app. 4-Direct sale w/o card.4-($2.50)-Newsstand ed. polybagged w/card 5-($2.50, 48 pgs.)-Rune flip-c/story part B by Barry Smith; see Sludge #1 for 1st app. Rune; 3-pg. Night Man preview. 6-Bill & Chelsea Clinton app. 7-Break-Thru x-over. 8-Mantra app.; 2-pg. origin Freex by Simonson. 10-Firearm app.15-Intro Papa Verite; Perez-c/a. 16-Intro Turbo Charge — 2.50
12-($3.50, 68 pgs.)-Flip book w/Ultraverse Premiere #3; silver foil logo — 3.50
13-($2.95, 52 pgs.)-Variant covers — 3.00
... Gross and Disgusting 1 (10/94, $3.95)-Boris-c; "Annual" on cover, published monthly in indicia — 4.00
...Month 'Ashcan" (8/94, 75¢)-Boris-c — 2.25
... Time: A Prime Collection (1994, $9.95)-r/1-4 — 10.00
...Vs. The Incredible Hulk (1995)-mail away limited edition — 10.00
...Vs. The Incredible Hulk Premium edition — 10.00
...Vs. The Incredible Hulk Super Premium edition — 15.00
NOTE: *Perez a-15; c-15, 16.*

PRIME (Also see Black September)
Malibu Comics (Ultraverse): Infinity, Sept, 1995 - V2#15, Dec, 1996 ($1.50)
Infinity, V2#1-8: Post Black September storyline. 6-8-Solitaire app.
9-Breyfogle-c/a. 10-12-Ramos-c/a. 15-Lord Pumpkin app. — 2.25
Infinity Signed Edition (2,000 printed) — 5.00

PRIME/CAPTAIN AMERICA
Malibu Comics: Mar, 1996 ($3.95, one-shot)
1-Norm Breyfogle-a — 4.00

PRIME8: CREATION
Two Morrows Publishing: July, 2001 ($3.95, B&W)
1-Neal Adams-c — 4.00

PRIMER (Comico...)
Comico: Oct (no month), 1982 - No. 6, Feb, 1984 (B&W)
1 (52 pgs.)	1	4	7	10
2-1st app. Grendel & Argent by Wagner	9	27	65	110
3,4	1	3	6	8
5-1st app Sam Kieth art in comics ('83) & 1st The Maxx	3	9	20	30
6-Intro & 1st app. Evangeline	2	6	9	12

PRIMORTALS (Leonard Nimoy's...)

PRIMUS (TV)
Charlton Comics: Feb, 1972 - No. 7, Oct, 1972
1-Staton-a in all	2	6	11	16
2-7: 6-Drug propaganda story	1	4	7	10

PRINCE NAMOR, THE SUB-MARINER (Also see Namor ...)
Marvel Comics Group: Sept, 1984 - No. 4, Dec, 1984 (Limited-series)
1-4 — 2.50

PRINCE VALIANT (See Ace Comics, Comics Reading Libraries in the Promotional Comics
section, & King Comics #146, 147)
David McKay Publ./Dell: No. 26, 1941; No. 67, June, 1954 - No. 900, May, 1958
Feature Books 26 ('41)-Harold Foster-c/a; newspaper strips reprinted, pgs.

1-28,30-63; color & 68 pgs; Foster cover is only original comic book artwork by him	77	231	539	1000
Four Color 567 ((6/54)(#1)-By Bob Fuje-Movie, photo-c	11	33	77	145
Four Color 650 (9/55), 699 (4/56), 719 (8/56),-Fuje-a	7	21	49	85
Four Color 788 (4/57), 849 (1/58), 900-Fuje-a	7	21	49	85

PRINCE VALIANT
Marvel Comics: Dec, 1994 - No. 4, Mar, 1995 ($3.95, limited series)
1-4; Kaluta-c in all. — 4.00

PRINCE VANDAL
Triumphant Comics: Nov, 1993 - Apr?, 1994 ($2.50)
1-6: 1,2-Triumphant Unleashed x-over — 2.50

PRINCESS SALLY (Video game)
Archie Publications: Apr, 1995 - No. 3, June, 1995 ($1.50, limited series)
1-3: Spin-off from Sonic the Hedgehog — 3.00

PRIORITY: WHITE HEAT
AC Comics: 1986 - No. 2, 1986 ($1.75, mini-series)
1,2-Bill Black-a — 2.25

PRISCILLA'S POP
Dell Publishing Co.: No. 569, June, 1954 - No. 799, May, 1957
Four Color 569 (#1), 630 (5/55), 704 (5/56),799	4	12	25	38

PRISON BARS (See Behind...)

PRISON BREAK!
Avon Per./Realistic No. 3 on: Sept, 1951 - No. 5, Sept, 1952 (Painted c-3)
1-Wood-c & 1 pg.; has-r/Saint #7 retitled Michael Strong Private Eye	42	126	252	440
2-Wood-c; Kubert-a; Kinstler inside front-c	33	99	174	300
3-Grasin, Check-c; c-/Avon paperback #179	27	81	142	245
4,5: 4-Kinstler-c & inside f/c; Lawrence, Lazarus-a. 5-Kinstler-c; Infantino-a	24	72	127	215

PRISONER, THE (TV)
DC Comics: 1988 - No. 4, 1989 ($3.50, squarebound, mini-series)
1-4 (Books a-d) — 3.50

PRISON RIOT
Avon Periodicals: 1952
1-Marijuana Murders-1 pg. text; Kinstler-c; 2 Kubert illos on text pages	30	90	159	275

PRISON TO PRAISE
Logos International: 1974 (35¢) (Religious, Christian)
nn-True Story of Merlin R. Carothers	1	4	7	10

PRIVATE BUCK
Dell Publishing Co.: No. 21, 1941 - No. 12, 1942
Large Feature Comic 21 (#1)(1941)(Series I), 22 (1941)(Series I), 12 (1942)(Series II)	11	33	77	140

PRIVATEERS
Vanguard Graphics: Aug, 1987 - No. 2, 1987 ($1.50)
1,2 — 2.25

PRIVATE EYE (Cover title: Rocky Jorden...#6-8)
Atlas Comics (MCI): Jan, 1951 - No. 8, March, 1952
1-Cover title: Crime Cases... #1-5	22	66	116	200
2,3-Tuska c/a(3)	14	42	72	120
4-8	11	33	55	90
NOTE: *Henkel a-6(3), 7; c-7. Sinnott a-6.*

PRIVATE EYE (See Mike Shayne...)

PRIVATE SECRETARY
Dell Publishing Co.: Dec-Feb, 1962-63 - No. 2, Mar-May, 1963
1	3	10	23	35
2	3	9	17	25

PRIVATE STRONG (See The Double Life of...)

PRIZE COMICS (...Western #69 on) (Also see Treasure Comics)
Prize Publications: March, 1940 - No. 68, Feb-Mar, 1948

Prize Comics #58 © PRIZE

Prof. Xavier and the X-Men #10 © MAR

Promethea #10 © ABC

| | GD2.0 | FN6.0 | VF8.0 | NM9.4 |

1-Origin Power Nelson, The Futureman & Jupiter, Master Magician; Ted
O'Neil, Secret Agent M-11, Jaxon of the Jungle, Bucky Brady & Storm
Curtis begin (1st app. of each) ... 236 708 1477 2600
2-The Black Owl begins (1st app.) ... 109 327 682 1200
3,4: 4-Robot-c ... 91 273 568 1000
5,6: Dr. Dekkar, Master of Monsters app. in each ... 84 252 525 925
7-(Scarce)-Black Owl by S&K; origin/1st app. Dr. Frost & Frankenstein; The
Green Lama, Capt. Gallant, The Great Voodini & Twist Turner begin; 1st
app. The Green Lama (12/40) ... 182 546 1136 2000
8,9-Black Owl & Ted O'Neil by S&K ... 93 279 581 1025
10-12,14-20: 11-Origin Bulldog Denny. 14-War-c. 16-Spike Mason begins
... 64 192 398 700
13-Yank & Doodle begin (8/41), origin/1st app. ... 73 219 455 800
21-24: 21-War-c. 22-Statue of Liberty jap attack war-c. 23-Uncle Sam patriotic
war-c. 24-Lincoln statue patriotic-c ... 47 140 286 500
25-30: 25-28 War-c ... 31 93 165 285
31-33: 31-Jap war-c ... 26 78 136 235
34-Origin Airmale, Yank & Doodle; The Black Owl joins army, Yank & Doodle's
father assumes Black Owl's role ... 31 93 165 285
35-36,38-40: 35-Flying Fist & Bingo begin ... 22 66 116 195
37-Intro. Stampy, Airmale's sidekick; Hitler-c ... 36 108 191 330
41-50: 45-Yank & Doodle learn Black Owl's I.D. (their father). 48-Prince Ra
begins ... 17 51 88 150
51-62,64,67,68: 53-Transvestism story. 55-No Frankenstein. 57-X-Mas-c.
64-Black Owl retires ... 14 42 72 120
63-Simon & Kirby c/a ... 18 54 94 155
65,66-Frankenstein-c by Briefer ... 15 45 77 130
NOTE: *Briefer* a-7-on; c-65, 66. *J. Binder* a-16; c-21-29. *Guardineer* a-62. *Kiefer* c-62. *Palais* c-68. *Simon & Kirby* c-63, 75, 83.

PRIZE COMICS WESTERN (Formerly Prize Comics #1-68)
Prize Publications (Feature): No. 69(V7#2), Apr-May, 1948 - No. 119, Nov-Dec,
1956 (No. 69-84: 52 pgs.)
69(V7#2) ... 15 45 77 130
70-75: 74-Kurtzman-a (8 pgs.) ... 13 39 66 110
76-Randolph Scott photo-c; "Canadian Pacific" movie adaptation
... 14 42 72 120
77-Photo-c; Severin/Elder, Mart Bailey-a; "Streets of Laredo" movie adaptation
... 13 39 66 110
78-Photo-c; S&K-a, 10 pgs.; Severin, Mart Bailey-a; "Bullet Code", &
"Roughshod" movie adaptations ... 19 57 99 165
79-Photo-c; Kurtzman-a, 8 pgs.; Severin/Elder, Severin, Mart Bailey-a; "Stage
To China" movie adaptation w/George O'Brien ... 19 57 99 165
80-82-Photo-c; 80,81-Severin/Elder-a(2). 82-1st app. The Preacher by Mart
Bailey; Severin/Elder-a(3) ... 14 42 72 120
83,84 ... 11 33 55 90
85-1st app. American Eagle by John Severin & begins (V9#6, 1-2/51)
... 25 75 130 225
86,101-105, 109-Severin/Williamson-a ... 13 39 66 110
87-99,110,111-Severin/Elder-a(2-3) each ... 14 42 72 120
100 ... 15 45 72 130
106-108,112 ... 10 30 55 80
113-Williamson/Severin-a(2)/Frazetta? ... 14 42 72 120
114-119: Drifter series in all; by Mort Meskin #114-118
... 9 27 49 70
NOTE: *Fass* a-81. *Severin & Elder* c-84-99. *Severin* a-72, 75, 77-79, 83-86, 96, 97, 100-105; c-92,100-109(most), 110-119. *Simon & Kirby* c-75, 83.

PRIZE MYSTERY
Key Publications: May, 1955 - No. 3, Sept, 1955
1 ... 11 33 55 90
2,3 ... 8 24 42 60

PROFESSIONAL FOOTBALL (See Charlton Sport Library)

PROFESSOR COFFIN
Charlton Comics: No. 19, Oct, 1985 - No. 21, Feb, 1986
19-21: Wayne Howard-a(r); low print run ... 6.00

PROFESSOR OM
Innovation Publishing: May, 1990 - No. 2, 1990 ($2.50, limited series)
1,2-East Meets West spin-off ... 2.50

PROFESSOR XAVIER AND THE X-MEN (Also see X-Men, 1st series)

Marvel Comics: Nov, 1995 - No. 18 (99¢)
1-18: Stories featuring the Original X-Men. 2-vs. The Blob. 5-Vs. the Original
Brotherhood of Evil Mutants. 10-Vs The Avengers ... 2.25

PROJECT, THE
DC Comics (Paradox Press): No. 1,2, 1998? ($5.59)
1,2 ... 6.00

PROJECT A-KO (Manga)
Malibu Comics: Mar, 1994 - No. 4, June, 1994 ($2.95)
1-4-Based on anime film ... 3.00

PROJECT A-KO 2 (Manga)
CPM Comics: May, 1995 - No. 3, Aug, 1995 ($2.95, limited series)
1-3 ... 3.00

PROJECT A-KO VERSUS THE UNIVERSE (Manga)
CPM Comics: Oct, 1995 - No. 5, June, 1996 ($2.95, limited series, bi-monthly)
1-5 ... 3.00

PROJECT: HERO
Vanguard Graphics (Canadian): Aug, 1987 ($1.50)
1 ... 2.25

PROMETHEA
America's Best Comics: Aug, 1999 - Present ($3.50/$2.95)
1-Moore-s/Williams III & Gray-a; Alex Ross painted-c ... 3.50
1-Variant-c by Williams III & Gray ... 3.50
2-18-($2.95) 7-Villarrubia photo-a. 10-"Sex, Stars & Serpents" ... 3.00
Book 1 Hardcover ($24.95, dust jacket) r/#1-7 ... 25.00
Book 1 TPB ($14.95) r/#1-7 ... 15.00
Book 2 Hardcover ($24.95, dust jacket) r/#8-14 ... 25.00

PROMETHEUS (VILLAINS) (Leads into JLA #16,17)
DC Comics: Feb, 1998 ($1.95, one-shot)
1-Origin & 1st app.; Morrison-s/Pearson-c ... 3.00

PROPELLERMAN
Dark Horse Comics: Jan, 1993 - No. 8, Mar, 1994 ($2.95, limited series)
1-8: 2,4,8-Contain 2 trading cards ... 3.00

PROPHET (See Youngblood #2)
Image Comics (Extreme Studios): Oct, 1993 - No. 10, 1995 ($1.95)
1-($2.50)-Liefeld/Panosian-c/a; 1st app. Mary McCormick; Liefeld scripts in 1-4;
#1-3 contain coupons for Prophet #0 ... 2.50
1-Gold foil embossed-c edition rationed to dealers ... 4.00
2-10: 2-Liefeld-c(p). 3-1st app. Judas. 4-1st app. Omen; Black and White Pt. 3
by Thibert. 4-Alternate-c by Stephen Platt. 5,6-Platt-c/a. 7-(9/94, $2.50)-Platt-
c/a. 8-Bloodstrike app. 10-Polybagged w/trading card; Platt-c ... 2.50
0-(7/94, $2.50)-San Diego Comic Con ed. (2200 copies) ... 3.00

PROPHET
Image Comics (Extreme Studios): V2#1, Aug, 1995 - No. 8 ($3.50)
V2#1-8: Dixon scripts in all. 1-4-Platt-a. 1-Boris-c; F. Miller variant-c. 4-Newmen
app. 5,6-Wraparound-c ... 3.50
Annual 1 (9/95, $2.50)-Bagged w/Youngblood gaming card; Quesada-c ... 2.50
Babewatch Special 1 (12/95, $2.50)-Babewatch tie-in ... 2.50
1995 San Diego Edition-B&W preview of V2#1. ... 3.00
TPB-(1996, $12.95) r/#1-7 ... 13.00

PROPHET (Volume 3)
Awesome Comics: Mar, 2000 ($2.99)
1-Flip-c by Jim Lee and Liefeld ... 3.00

PROPHET/CABLE
Image Comics (Extreme): Jan, 1997 - No. 2, Mar, 1997 ($3.50, limited series)
1,2-Liefeld-c/a: 2-#1 listed on cover ... 3.50

PROPHET/CHAPEL: SUPER SOLDIERS
Image Comics (Extreme): May, 1996 - No. 2, June, 1996 ($2.50, limited series)
1,2: 1-Two covers exist ... 2.50
1-San Diego Edition; B&W-c ... 2.50

PROPOSITION PLAYER
DC Comics (Vertigo): Dec, 1999 - No. 6, May, 2000 ($2.50, limited series)

Proposition Player #5 © William Willingham

Psyba-Rats #3 © DC

Public Enemies #6 © D.S. Pub.

PU

	GD2.0	FN6.0	VF8.0	NM9.4

1-6-Willingham-s/Guinan-a/Bolton-c 2.50

PROTECTORS (Also see The Ferret)
Malibu Comics: Sept, 1992 - No. 20, May, 1994 ($1.95-$2.95)
1-20 ($2.50, direct sale)-With poster & diff-c: 1-Origin; has 3/4 outer-c.
  3-Polybagged w/Skycap 2.50
  1-12 ($1.95, newsstand)-Without poster 2.25

PROTOTYPE (Also see Flood Relief & Ultraforce)
Malibu Comics (Ultraverse): Aug, 1993 - No. 18, Feb, 1995 ($1.95/$2.50)
1-Holo-c 6.00
1-Ultra Limited silver foil-c 4.00
1-12,0,14-18: 3-($2.50, 48 pgs.)-Rune flip-c/story by B. Smith (3 pgs.). 4-Intro
  Wrath. 5-Break-Thru & Strangers x-over. 6-Arena cameo. 7,8-Arena-c/story.
  12-(7/94). 0--0/8/94,$ 2.50, 44 pgs.), 14(10/94) 2.50
13 (8/94, $3.50)-Flip book(Ultraverse Premiere #6) 3.50
Giant Size 1 (10/94, $2.50, 44 pgs.) 2.50

PROWLER (Also see Revenge of the...)
Eclipse Comics: July, 1987 - No. 4, Oct, 1987 ($1.75)
1-4: Snyder-c/a. 3,4-Origin 2.25

PROWLER, THE
Marvel Comics: Nov, 1994 ($1.75)
1-4: 1-Spider-Man app. 2.25

PROWLER IN "WHITE ZOMBIE", THE
Eclipse Comics: Oct, 1988 ($2.00, B&W, Baxter paper)
1-Adapts Bela Lugosi movie White Zombie 2.25

PRUDENCE & CAUTION (Also see Dogs of War & Warriors of Plasm)
Defiant: May, 1994 - No. 2, June, 1994 ($3.50/$2.50)(Spanish versions exist)
1-($3.50, 52 pgs.)-Chris Claremont scripts in all 3.50
2-($2.50) 2.50

PRYDE AND WISDOM (Also see Excalibur)
Marvel Comics: Sept, 1996 - No. 3, Nov, 1996 ($1.95, limited series)
1-3: Warren Ellis scripts; Terry Dodson & Karl Story-c/a 2.25

PSI-FORCE
Marvel Comics Group: Nov, 1986 - No. 32, June, 1989 (75¢/$1.50)
1-25: 11-13-Williamson-i 2.25
26-32 ..... 2.50
Annual 1 (10/87) 2.25

PSI-JUDGE ANDERSON
Fleetway Publications (Quality): 1989 - No. 15, 1990 ($1.95, B&W)
1-15 ..... 2.50

PSI-LORDS
Valiant: Sept, 1994 - No. 10, June, 1995 ($2.25)
1-($3.50)-Chromium wraparound-c 3.50
1-Gold 5.00
2-10: 3-Chaos Effect Epsilon Pt. 2 ..... 2.25

PSYBA-RATS (Also see Showcase '94 #3,4)
DC Comics: Apr, 1995-No. 3, June, 1995 ($2.50, limited series)
1-3 ..... 2.50

PSYCHO (Magazine)
Skywald Publ. Corp.: Jan, 1971 - No. 24, Mar, 1975 (68 pgs.; B&W)

1-All reprints	5	15	38	60
2-Origin & 1st app. The Heap, & Frankenstein series by Adkins	4	12	29	45
3-10	3	9	20	30
11-20: 13-Cannabalism; 3 pgs of Christopher Lee as Dracula photos. 18-Injury to eye-c. 20-Severed Head-c	3	9	17	25
21-24: 22-1974 Fall Special; Reese, Wildey-a(r). 24-1975 Winter Special; Dave Sim scripts	3	9	20	30
Annual 1 (1972)(68 pgs.)	3	9	20	30
Yearbook (1974-nn)-Everett, Reese-a	3	9	17	26

NOTE: *Boris* c-3, 5. *Buckler* a-2, 4, 5. *Gene Day* a-24. *Everett* a-3-6. *B. Jones* a-4. *Jeff Jones* a-6, 7, 9; c-12. *Kaluta* a-13. *Katz/Buckler* a-3. *Kim* a-24. *Morrow* a-1. *Reese* a-5. *Dave Sim* a-24. *Sutton* a-5. *Wildey* a-5.

PSYCHOANALYSIS

E. C. Comics: Mar-Apr, 1955 - No. 4, Sept-Oct, 1955

1-All Kamen-c/a; not approved by code	17	51	119	210
2-4-Kamen-c/a in all	12	36	84	150

PSYCHOANALYSIS
Gemstone Publishing: Oct, 1999 - No. 4, Jan, 2000 ($2.50)
1-4-Reprints E.C. series 2.50
Annual 1 (2000, $10.95) r/#1-4 ..... 11.00

PSYCHOBLAST
First Comics: Nov, 1987 - No. 9, July, 1988 ($1.75)
1-9 ..... 2.25

PSYCHONAUTS
Marvel Comics (Epic Comics): Oct, 1993 - No. 4, Jan, 1994 ($4.95, lim. series)
1-4: American/Japanese co-produced comic 5.00

PSYLOCKE & ARCHANGEL CRIMSON DAWN
Marvel Comics: Aug, 1997 - No. 4, Nov, 1997 ($2.50, limited series)
1-4-Raab-s/Larroca-a(p) 2.50

P.T. 109 (See Movie Comics)

PUBLIC DEFENDER IN ACTION (Formerly Police Trap)
Charlton Comics: No. 7, Mar, 1956 - No. 12, Oct, 1957

7	10	30	55	85
8-12	7	21	36	50

PUBLIC ENEMIES
D. S. Publishing Co.: 1948 - No. 9, June-July, 1949

1-True Crime Stories	26	78	136	235
2-Used in **SOTI**, pg. 95	23	69	121	205
3-5: 8-Arrival date of 10/1/48	15	45	77	130
6,8,9	14	42	72	120
7-McWilliams-a; injury to eye panel	15	45	77	130

PUDGY PIG
Charlton Comics: Sept, 1958 - No. 2, Nov, 1958

1,2	3	9	19	28

PULP FANTASTIC (Vertigo V2K)
DC Comics (Vertigo): Feb, 2000 - No. 3, Apr, 2000 ($2.50, limited series)
1-3-Chaykin & Tischman-s/Burchett-a 2.50

PULP FICTION LIBRARY: MYSTERY IN SPACE
DC Comics: 1999 ($19.95, TPB)
nn-Reprints classic sci-fi stories from Mystery in Space, Strange Adventures,
  Real Fact Comics and My Greatest Adventure 20.00

PUMA BLUES
Aardvark One International/Mirage Studios #21 on: 1986 - No. 26, 1990
($1.70-$1.75, B&W)
1-19, 21-26: 1-1st & 2nd printings. 25,26-$1.75-c 2.25
20 ($2.25)-By Alan Moore, Miller, Grell, others 3.00
Trade Paperback (12/88, $14.95) 15.00

PUMPKINHEAD: THE RITES OF EXORCISM (Movie)
Dark Horse Comics: 1993 - No. 2, 1993 ($2.50, limited series)
1,2: Based on movie; painted-c by McManus 2.50

PUNCH & JUDY COMICS
Hillman Per.: 1944; No. 2, Fall, 1944 - V3#2, 12/47; V3#3, 6/51 - V3#9, 12/51

V1#1-(60 pgs.)	22	66	116	200
2	13	39	66	110
3-12(7/46)	10	30	55	80
V2#1(8/49),3-9	7	21	38	55
V2#2,10-12, V3#1-Kirby-a(2) each	24	72	127	215
V3#2-Kirby-a	22	66	116	195
3-9	7	21	38	55

PUNCH COMICS
Harry 'A' Chesler: 12/41; #2, 2/42; #9, 7/44 - #19, 10/46; #20, 7/47 - #23, 1/48

1-Mr. E, The Sky Chief, Hale the Magician, Kitty Kelly begin	127	381	795	1400
2-Captain Glory app.	84	253	525	925

Punch Comics #20 © CHES

Punisher #75 © MAR

Punisher V4 #2 © MAR

	GD2.0	FN6.0	VF8.0	NM9.4

9-Rocketman & Rocket Girl & The Master Key begin

	80	240	500	875

10-Sky Chief app.; J. Cole-a; Master Key-r/Scoop #3

	61	182	381	675

11-Origin Master Key-r/Scoop #1; Sky Chief, Little Nemo app.; Jack Cole-a;
Fineish art by Sultan

	55	165	341	600

12-Rocket Boy & Capt. Glory app; classic Skull-c 218

	218	654	1364	2400

13-Cover has list of 4 Chesler artists' names on tombstone

	61	182	381	675

14,15,19,21: 21-Hypo needle story

	55	165	330	575

16,17-Gag-c

	51	153	306	540

18-Bondage-c; hypodermic panels

	66	197	413	725

20-Unique cover with bare-breasted women. Rocket Girl-c

	95	285	597	1050

22,23-Little Nemo-not by McCay. 22-Intro Baxter (teenage)(68 pgs.)

	29	87	153	265

PUNCHY AND THE BLACK CROW
Charlton Comics: No. 10, Oct. 1985 - No. 12, Feb. 1986

10-12: Al Fago funny animal-r; low print run ... 4.00

PUNISHER (See Amazing Spider-Man #129, Blood and Glory, Captain America #241, Classic Punisher, Daredevil #182-184, 257, Daredevil and the..., Ghost Rider V2#5, 6, Marc Spector #8 & 9, Marvel Preview #2, Marvel Super Action, Marvel Tales, Power Pack #46, Spectacular Spider-Man #81-83, 140, 141, 143 & new Strange Tales #13 & 14)

PUNISHER (The...)
Marvel Comics Group: Jan. 1986 - No. 5, May, 1986 (Limited series)

1-Double size	2	6	10	14
2-5	1	3	5	7

Trade Paperback (1988)-r/#1-5 ... 11.00
Circle of Blood TPB (8/01, $15.95) Zeck-c ... 16.00
NOTE: Zeck a-1-4; c-1-5.

PUNISHER (The...) (Volume 2)
Marvel Comics: July, 1987 - No. 104, July, 1995

1 ... 6.00
2-9: 8-Portacio/Williams-c/a begins, ends #18. 9-Scarcer, low dist. ... 3.00
10-Daredevil app; ties in w/Daredevil #257 ... 5.00
11-74,76-85,87-89: 13-18-Kingpin app. 19-Stroman-c/a. 20-Portacio-c(p).
24-1st app. Shadowmasters. 25,50:($1.50,52 pgs.). 25-Shadowmasters app.
57-Photo-c; came w/outer-c (newsstand ed. w/o outer-c). 59-Punisher is
severely cut & has skin grafts (his black skin). 60-62-Luke Cage app.
62-Punisher back to white skin. 68-Tarantula-c/story. 85-Prequel to Suicide
Run Pt. 0. 87,88-Suicide Run Pt. 6 & 9 ... 2.50
75-($2.75, 52 pgs.)-Embossed silver foil-c ... 3.00
86-($2.95, 52 pgs.)-Embossed & foil stamped-c; Suicide Run part 3 ... 3.00
90-99, 101-103: 90-bound-in cards. 99-Cringe app. 102-Bullseye. ... 2.50
100,104: 100-($2.95, 68 pgs.). 104-Last issue ... 3.00
100-($3.95, 68 pgs.)-Foil cover ... 4.00
"Ashcan" edition (75c)-Joe Kubert-c ... 2.25
Annual 1-7 ('88-'94, 68 pgs.) 1-Evolutionary War x-over. 2-Atlantis Attacks x-
over; Jim Lee-a(p). 3-Jim Lee-a(p) story, 6 pgs.); Moon Knight app. 4-Golden-c(p).
6-Bagged w/card. 7-Rapido app. ... 3.00
...: A Man Named Frank (1994, $6.95, TPB) ... 7.00
...and Wolverine in African Saga nn (1989, $5.95, 52 pgs.)-Reprints Punisher
War Journal #6 & 7; Jim Lee-c/a(r) ... 6.00
... Assassin Guild ('88, $6.95, graphic novel) ... 10.00
Back to School Special 1-3 (11/92-10/94, $2.95, 68 pgs.) ... 3.00
.../Batman: Deadly Knights (10/94, $4.95) ... 4.00
.../Black Widow: Spinning Doomsday's Web (1992, $9.95, graphic novel) ... 12.00
...Bloodlines (1991, $5.95, 68 pgs.) ... 6.00
...: Die Hard in the Big Easy nn ('92, $4.95, 52 pgs.) ... 5.00
...: Empty Quarter nn ('94, $6.95) ... 7.00
...G-Force nn (1992, $4.95, 52 pgs.)-Painted-c ... 5.00
...Holiday Special 1-3 (1/93-1/95, 52 pgs.,68pgs.)-1-Foil-c ... 3.00
...Intruder Graphic Novel (1989, $14.95, hardcover) ... 20.00
...Intruder Graphic Novel (1991, $9.95, softcover) ... 12.00
...Invades the 'Nam: Final Invasion nn (2/94, $6.95)-J. Kubert-c & chapter break
art; reprints The 'Nam #84 & unpublished #85,86 ... 7.00
...Kingdom Gone Graphic Novel (1990, $16.95, hardcover) ... 20.00
...Meets Archie (1994, $2.95, 52 pgs.)-Die cut-c; no ads; same contents as
Archie Meets The Punisher ... 5.00

...Movie Special 1 (6/90, $5.95, 68 pgs.) ... 6.00
...: No Escape nn (1990, $4.95, 52 pgs.)-New-a ... 5.00
...Return to Big Nothing Graphic Novel (Epic, 1989, $16.95, hardcover) ... 25.00
...Return to Big Nothing Graphic Novel (Marvel, 1989, $12.95, softcover) ... 15.00
...The Prize nn (1990, $4.95, 68 pgs.)-New-a ... 5.00
Summer Special 1-4(8/91-7/94, 52 pgs.):1-No ads. 2-Bisley painted-c; Austin-a(i).
3-No ads ... 3.00
NOTE: Austin c(i)-47, 48. Cowan c-39. Golden c-50, 85, 86, 100. Heath a-26, 27, 89, 90; c-26, 27. Quesada c-56p, 62p. Sienkiewicz c-Back to School 1.Stroman a-76p(9 pgs.). Williamson a(i)-25, 60-62i, 64-70, 74, Annual 5; c(i)-62, 65-68.

PUNISHER (Also see Double Edge)
Marvel Comics: Nov. 1995 - No. 18, Apr. 1997 ($2.95/$1.95/$1.50)

1 ($2.95)-Ostrander scripts begin; foil-c. ... 3.00
2-18: 7-Vs. S.H.I.E.L.D. 11-"Onslaught." 12-17-X-Cutioner-c/app. 17-Daredevil,
Spider-Man-c/app. ... 2.50

PUNISHER (Marvel Knights)
Marvel Comics: Nov. 1998 - No. 4, Feb. 1999 ($2.99, limited series)

1-4: 1-Wrightson-a; Wrightson & Jusko-c ... 3.00
1-($6.95) DF Edition; Jae Lee variant-c ... 7.00

PUNISHER (Marvel Knights) (Volume 3)
Marvel Comics: Apr. 2000 - No. 12, Mar. 2001 ($2.99, limited series)

1-Ennis-s/Dillon & Palmiotti-a/Bradstreet-c ... 5.00
1-Bradstreet white variant-c ... 10.00
1-($6.95) DF Edition; Jurgens & Ordway variant-c ... 7.00
1-Two covers by Bradstreet & Dillon ... 3.00
3-($3.99) Bagged with Marvel Knights Genesis Edition; Daredevil app. ... 4.00
4-12: 9-11-The Russian app. ... 3.00
.../Painkiller Jane (1/01, $3.50) Jusko-c; Ennis-s/Jusko and Dave Ross-a(p) ... 3.50
...: Welcome Back Frank TPB (4/01, $19.95) r/#1-12 ... 20.00

PUNISHER (Marvel Knights) (Volume 4)
Marvel Comics: Aug. 2001 - Present ($2.99)

1-Ennis-s/Dillon & Palmiotti-a/Bradstreet-c; The Russian app. ... 3.00
2-Two covers (Dillon & Bradstreet) Spider-Man-c/app. ... 3.00
3-7 ... 3.00

PUNISHER AND WOLVERINE: DAMAGING EVIDENCE (See Wolverine and...)

PUNISHER ARMORY
Marvel Comics: 7/90 ($1.50); No. 2, 6/91; No. 3, 4/92 - 10/94($1.75/$2.00)

1-10: 1-r/weapons pgs. from War Journal. 1,2-Jim Lee-c. 3-10- All new material.
3-Jusko painted-c ... 2.50

PUNISHER KILLS THE MARVEL UNIVERSE
Marvel Comics: Nov. 1995 ($5.95, one-shot)

1-Garth Ennis script/Doug Braithwaite-a ... 7.00
1-2nd printing (3/00) Steve Dillon-c ... 6.00

PUNISHER MAGAZINE, THE
Marvel Comics: Oct. 1989 - No. 16, Nov. 1990 ($2.25, B&W, Magazine, 52 pgs.)

1-16: 1-r/Punisher #1('86). 2,3-r/Punisher 2-5. 4-16: 4-7-r/Punisher V2#1-8. 4-
Chiodo-c. 8-r/Punisher #10 & Daredevil #257; Portacio & Lee-r. 14-r/Punisher
War Journal #1,2 Wolverine app. 16-r/Punisher W. J. #3,8 ... 3.00
NOTE: Chiodo painted c-4, 7, 16. Jusko painted c-6, 8. Jim Lee r-8, 14-16; c-14. Portacio/ Williams r-7-12.

PUNISHER MOVIE COMIC
Marvel Comics: Nov. 1989 - No. 3, Dec. 1989 ($1.00, limited series)

1-3: Movie adaptation ... 2.25
1 (1989, $4.95, squarebound)-contains #1-3 ... 5.00

PUNISHER: ORIGIN OF MICRO CHIP, THE
Marvel Comics: July, 1993 - No. 2, Aug. 1993 ($1.75, limited series)

1,2 ... 2.25

PUNISHER: P.O.V.
Marvel Comics: 1991 - No. 4, 1991 ($4.95, painted, limited series, 52 pgs.)

1-4: Starlin scripts & Wrightson painted-c/a in all. 2-Nick Fury app. ... 5.00

PUNISHER: THE GHOSTS OF INNOCENTS
Marvel Comics: Jan. 1993 - No. 2, Jan. 1993 ($5.95, 52 pgs.)

1,2-Starlin scripts ... 6.00

Punisher: War Zone #10 © MAR

Purgatori #6 © Chaos!

Puzzle Fun Comics #2 © George W. Dougherty Co.

	GD2.0	FN6.0	VF8.0	NM9.4

PUNISHER 2099 (See Punisher War Journal #50)
Marvel Comics: Feb, 1993 - No. 34, Nov, 1995 ($1.25/$1.50/$1.95)

1-24,26-34: 1-Foil stamped-c. 1-Second printing. 13-Spider-Man 2099 x-over;
Ron Lim-c(p). 16-bound-in card sheet 2.25
25 ($2.95, 52 pgs.)-Deluxe edition; embossed foil-cover 3.00
25 ($2.25, 52 pgs.) 2.25

PUNISHER VS. DAREDEVIL
Marvel Comics: Jun, 2000 ($3.50, one-shot)

1-Reprints Daredevil #183,#184 & #257 3.50

PUNISHER WAR JOURNAL, THE
Marvel Comics: Nov, 1988 - No. 80, July, 1995 ($1.50/$1.75/$1.95)

1-Origin The Punisher; Matt Murdock cameo; Jim Lee inks begin 5.00
2-7: 2,3-Daredevil x-over; Jim Lee-c(i). 4-Jim Lee c/a begins. 6-Two part
Wolverine story begins. 7-Wolverine-c, story ends 4.00
8-49,51-60,62,63,65: 13-16,20-22: No Jim Lee-a. 13-15 Lee-c only. 13-15-Heath-i.
14,15-Spider-Man x-over. 19-Last Jim Lee-c/a.29,30-Ghost Rider app.
31-Andy & Joe Kubert art. 36-Photo-c. 47,48-Nomad/Daredevil-c/stories;
see Nomad. 57,58-Daredevil & Ghost Rider-c/stories. 62,63-Suicide Run
Pt 4 & 7. 3.00
50,61,64($2.95, 52 pgs.): 50-Preview of Punisher 2099 (1st app.); embossed-c.
61-Embossed foil cover; Suicide Run Pt. 1. 64-Die-cut-c; Suicide Run Pt 10
3.00
64-($2.25, 52 pgs.)-Regular cover edition 2.25
66-74,76-80: 66-Bound-in card sheet 2.25
75 ($2.50, 52 pgs.) 2.50
NOTE: *Golden c-25-30, 40, 61, 62. Jusko painted c-31, 32. Jim Lee a-1i-3i, 4p-13p, 17p-19p; c-
2i, 3i, 4p-15p, 17p, 18p, 19p. Painted c-40.*

PUNISHER: WAR ZONE, THE
Marvel Comics: Mar, 1992 - No. 41, July, 1995 ($1.75/$1.95)

1-($2.25, 40 pgs.)-Die cut-c; Romita, Jr.-c/a begins 3.00
2-22,24,26,27-41: 8-Last Romita, Jr.-c/a. 19-Wolverine app. 24-Suicide Run
Pt. 5. 27-Bound-in card sheet 2.25
23-($2.95, 52 pgs.)-Embossed foil-c; Suicide Run part 2; Buscema-a(part) 3.00
25-($2.25, 52 pgs.)-Suicide Run part 8; painted-c 2.50
Annual 1,2 ('93, 94, $2.95, 68 pgs.)-1-Bagged w/card; John Buscema-a 3.00
NOTE: *Golden c-23. Romita, Jr. c/a-1-8.*

PUNISHER: YEAR ONE
Marvel Comics: Dec, 1994 - No. 4, Apr, 1995 ($2.50, limited series)

1-4 2.50

PUNX
Acclaim (Valiant): Nov, 1995 - No. 3, Jan, 1996 ($2.50, unfinished lim. series)

1-3: Giffen story & art in all. 2-Satirizes Scott McCloud's Understanding
Comics 2.50
(Manga) Special 1 (3/96, $2.50)-Giffen scripts 2.50

PUPPET COMICS
George W. Dougherty Co.: Spring, 1946 - No. 2, Summer, 1946

1,2-Funny animal 11 33 55 90

PUPPETOONS (See George Pal's...)

PUREHEART (See Archie as...)

PURGATORI
Chaos! Comics: Prelude #-1, 5/96 ($1.50, 16 pgs.); 1996 - No. 3 Dec, 1996
($3.50/$2.95, limited series)

Prelude #-1-Pulido story; Balent-c/a; contains sketches & interviews 2.25
0-(2/01, $2.99) Prelude to "Love Bites"; Rio-c/a 3.00
1/2 (12/00, $2.95) Al Rio-c/a 3.00
1-($3.50)-Wraparound cover; red foil embossed-c; Jim Balent-a 5.00
1-($19.95)-Premium Edition (1000 print run) 20.00
2-($3.00)-Wraparound-c 3.00
2-Variant-c 5.00
..: Love Bites 1 (3/01, $2.99) Turnbull-a/Kaminski-s 3.00
..: Mischief Night 1 (11/01, $2.99) 3.00
...The Dracula Gambit-($2.95) 3.00
...The Dracula Gambit Sketchbook-($2.95) 3.00
...The Vampire's Myth 1-($19.95) Premium Ed. (10,000) 20.00
...Vs. Chastity (7/00, $2.95) Two versions (Alpha and Omega) with different

endings; Al Rio-a 3.00
...Vs. Lady Death (1/01, $2.95) Kaminski-s 3.00
...Vs. Vampirella (4/00, $2.95) Zanier-a; Chastity app. 3.00

PURGATORI
Chaos! Comics: Oct, 1998 - No. 7, Apr, 1999 ($2.95)

1-7-Quinn-s/Rio-c/a. 2-Lady Death-c 3.00

PURGATORI: DARKEST HOUR
Chaos! Comics: Sept, 2001 - No. 2, Oct, 2001 ($2.99, limited series)

1,2 3.00

PURGATORI: EMPIRE
Chaos! Comics: May, 2000 - No. 3, July, 2000 ($2.95, limited series)

1-3-Cleavenger-c 3.00

PURGATORI: GODDESS RISING
Chaos! Comics: July, 1999 - No. 4, Oct, 1999 ($2.95, limited series)

1-4-Deodato-c/a 3.00

PURGATORI: THE HUNTED
Chaos! Comics: Jun, 2001 - No. 2, Aug, 2001 ($2.99, limited series)

1,2 3.00

PURGE
ANIA/U.P. Comics: Aug, 1993 ($1.95, unfinished limited series)

1 2.25

PURPLE CLAW, THE (Also see Tales of Horror)
Minoan Publishing Co./Toby Press: Jan, 1953 - No. 3, May, 1953

1-Origin; horror/weird stories in all 33 99 174 300
2,3: 1-3 r-in Tales of Horror #9-11 24 72 127 215
I.W. Reprint #8-Reprints #1 3 9 19 28

PUSSYCAT (Magazine)
Marvel Comics Group: Oct, 1968 (B&W reprints from Men's magazines)

1-(Scarce)-Ward, Everett, Wood-a; Everett--c 18 72 126 220

PUZZLE FUN COMICS (Also see Jingle Jangle)
George W. Dougherty Co.: Spring, 1946 - No. 2, Summer, 1946 (52 pgs.)

1-Gustavson-a 24 72 127 215
2 16 48 83 140
NOTE: *#1 & 2('46) each contain a George Carlson cover plus a 6 pg. story "Alec in
Fumbleland", and many puzzles in each.*

QUACK!
Star Reach Productions: July, 1976 - No. 6, 1977? ($1.25, B&W)

1-Brunner-c/a on Duckaneer (Howard the Duck clone); Dave Stevens, Gilbert,
Shaw-a 2 6 9 12
1-2nd printing (10/76) 4.00
2-6: 2-Newton the Rabbit Wonder by Aragonés/Leialoha; Gilbert, Shaw-a;
Leialoha-c. 3-The Beavers by Dave Sim begin, end #5; Gilbert, Shaw-a;
Sim/Leialoha-c. 6-Brunner-a (Duckeneer); Gilbert-a 1 3 6 8

QUADRANT
Quadrant Publications: 1983 - No. 8, 1986 (B&W, nudity, adults)

1-Peter Hsu-c/a in all 1 3 5 7
2-8 4.00

QUANTUM & WOODY
Acclaim Comics: June, 1997 - No. 17, No. 32 (9/99), No. 18 - Present ($2.50)

1-17: 1-1st app.; two covers. 6-Copycat-c. 9-Troublemakers app. 2.50
32-(9/99); 18-(10/99),19-21 2.50
The Director's Cut TPB ('97, $7.95) r/#1-4 plus extra pages 8.00

QUANTUM LEAP (TV) (See A Nightmare on Elm Street)
Innovation Publishing: Sept, 1991 - No. 12, Jun, 1993 ($2.50, painted-c)

1-12: Based on TV show; all have painted-c/a. 8-Has photo gallery 3.00
Special Edition 1 (10/92)-r/#1 w/8 extra pgs. of photos & articles 3.00
Time and Space Special 1 (#13) ($2.95)-Foil logo 3.00

QUANTUM TUNNELER, THE
Revolution Studio: Oct, 2001 (no cover price, one-shot)

1-Prequel to "The One" movie; Clayton Henry-a 2.25

QUASAR (See Avengers #302, Captain America #217, Incredible Hulk #234,

Quasar #7 © MAR

Queen & Country #1 © Greg Rucka

Racer X #3 © Speed Racer Ent.

	GD2.0	FN6.0	VF8.0	NM9.4

	GD2.0	FN6.0	VF8.0	NM9.4

Marvel Team-Up #113 & Marvel Two-in-One #53)
Marvel Comics: Oct, 1989 - No. 60, Jul, 1994 ($1.00/$1.25, Direct sales #17 on)

1-Origin; formerly Marvel Boy/Marvel Man				3.00

2-49,51-60: 3-Human Torch app. 6-Venom cameo (2 pgs.). 7-Cosmic Spidey.
11-Excalibur x-over. 14-McFarlane-c. 16-($1.50, 52 pgs.). 17-Flash parody
(Buried Alien). 20-Fantastic Four app. 23-Ghost Rider x-over. 25-($1.50,
52 pg.)-New costume Quasar. 26-Infinity Gauntlet x-over; Thanos-c/story.
27-Infinity Gauntlet x-over. 30-Thanos cameo in flashback; last $1.00-c.
31-Begin $1.25-c; D.P. 7 guest stars. 38-Infinity War x-overs.

38-Battles Warlock. 39-Thanos-c & cameo. 40-Thanos app. 42-Punisher-c/story. 53-Warlock & Moondragon app. 58-w/bound-in card sheet				2.50
50-($2.95, 52 pgs.)-Holo-grafx foil-c; Silver Surfer, Man-Thing, Ren & Stimpy app.				3.00
Special #1-3 ($1.25, newsstand)-Same as #32-34				2.25

QUEEN & COUNTRY (See Whiteout)
Oni Press: Mar, 2001 - Present ($2.95, B&W)

1-5-Rucka-s. 1-4-Rolston-a/Sale-c. 5-Snyder-c/Hurtt-a				3.00

QUEEN OF THE WEST, DALE EVANS (TV)(See Dale Evans Comics, Roy Rogers & Western Roundup under Dell Giants)
Dell Publ. Co.: No. 479, 7/53 - No. 22, 1-3/59 (All photo-c)

Four Color 479(#1, '53)	22	65	154	290
Four Color 528(#2, '54)	10	30	70	135
3,4: 3(4-6/54)-Toth-a. 4-Toth, Manning-a	8	24	56	105
5-10-Manning-a. 5-Marsh-a	7	21	49	90
11,19,21-No Manning 21-Tufts-a	5	15	35	60
12-18,20,22-Manning-a	5	15	35	70

QUENTIN DURWARD
Dell Publishing Co.: No. 672, Jan, 1956

Four Color 672-Movie, photo-c	7	21	49	85

QUESTAR ILLUSTRATED SCIENCE FICTION CLASSICS
Golden Press: 1977 (224 pgs.) ($1.95)

11197-Stories by Asimov, Sturgeon, Silverberg & Niven; Starstream-r	3	9	21	32

QUEST FOR CAMELOT
DC Comics: July, 1998 ($4.95)

1-Movie adaption				5.00

QUEST FOR DREAMS LOST (Also see Word Warriors)
Literacy Volunteers of Chicago: July 4, 1987 ($2.00, B&W, 52 pgs.)(Proceeds donated to help fight illiteracy)

1-Teenage Mutant Ninja Turtles by Eastman/Laird, Trollords, Silent Invasion, The Realm, Wordsmith, Reacto Man, Eb'nn, Aniverse				2.25

QUESTION, THE (See Americomics, Blue Beetle (1967), Charlton Bullseye & Mysterious Suspense)

QUESTION, THE (Also see Showcase '95 #3)
DC Comics: Feb, 1987 - No. 36, Mar, 1990 ($1.50)

1-36: Denny O'Neil scripts in all				2.50
Annual 1 (1988, $2.50)				2.50
Annual 2 (1989, $3.50)				3.50

QUESTION QUARTERLY, THE
DC Comics: Summer, 1990 - No. 5, Spring, 1992 ($2.50, 52pgs.)

1-5				2.50

NOTE: *Cowan a-1, 2, 4, 5; c-1-3, 5. Mignola a-5i. Quesada a-3-5.*

QUESTION RETURNS, THE
DC Comics: Feb, 1997 ($3.50, one-shot)

1-Brereton-c				3.50

QUESTPROBE
Marvel Comics: 8/84; No. 2, 1/85; No. 3, 11/85 (lim. series)

1-3: 1-The Hulk app. by Romita. 2-Spider-Man; Mooney-a(i). 3-Human Torch & Thing				3.00

QUICK DRAW McGRAW (TV) (Hanna-Barbera)(See Whitman Comic Books)
Dell Publishing Co./Gold Key No. 12 on: No. 1040, 12-2/59-60 - No. 11, 7-9/62; No. 12, 11/62; No. 13, 2/63; No. 14, 4/63; No. 15, 6/69
(1st show aired 9/29/59)

Four Color 1040(#1) 1st app. Quick Draw & Baba Looey, Augie Doggie & Doggie Daddy and Snooper & Blabber	14	42	98	180
2(4-6/60)-4,6: 2-Augie Doggie & Snooper & Blabber stories (8 pgs. each); pre-dates both of their #1 issues. 4-Augie Doggie & Snooper & Blabber stories.				
	7	21	49	95
5-1st Snagglepuss app.; last 10¢ issue	8	24	56	105
7-11	5	15	35	65
12,13-Title change to ...Fun-Type Roundup (84pgs.)	8	24	56	105
14,15: 15-Reprints	5	15	34	55

QUICK DRAW McGRAW (TV)(See Spotlight #2)
Charlton Comics: Nov, 1970 - No. 8, Jan, 1972 (Hanna-Barbera)

1	5	15	34	55
2-8	3	9	20	30

QUICKSILVER (See Avengers)
Marvel Comics: Nov, 1997 - No. 13, Nov, 1998 ($2.99/$1.99)

1-($2.99)-Peyer-s/Casey Jones-a; wraparound-c				3.00
2-11: 2-Two covers-variant by Golden. 4-6-Inhumans app.				2.25
12-($2.99) Siege of Wundagore pt. 4				3.00
13-Magneto-c/app.; last issue				2.25

QUICK-TRIGGER WESTERN (...Action #12; Cowboy Action #5-11)
Atlas Comics (ACI #12/WPI #13-19): No. 12, May, 1956 - No. 19, Sept, 1957

12-Baker-a	17	51	88	150
13-Williamson-a, 5 pgs.	16	48	83	140
14-Everett, Crandall, Torres-a; Heath-c	15	45	77	130
15,16: 15-Torres, Crandall-a. 16-Orlando, Kirby-a	12	36	61	100
17,18: 18-Baker-a	10	30	55	85
19	9	27	49	70

NOTE: *Ayers a-17. Colan a-16. Maneely a-15, 17; c-15, 18. Morrow a-18. Powell a-14. Severin a-19; c-12, 13, 16, 17, 19. Shores a-16. Tuska a-17.*

QUINCY (See Comics Reading Libraries in the Promotional Comics section)

Q-UNIT
Harris Comics: Dec, 1993 ($2.95)

1-($2.95)-Polybagged w/trading card version 1.2				3.00

RACCOON KIDS (Formerly Movietown Animal Antics)
National Periodical Publications (Arleigh No. 63,64): No. 52, Sept-Oct, 1954 - No. 62, Oct-Nov, 1956; No. 63, Sept, 1957; No. 64, Nov, 1957

52-Doodles Duck by Mayer	15	45	77	130
53-64: 53-62-Doodles Duck by Mayer	11	33	55	90

RACE FOR THE MOON
Harvey Publications: Mar, 1958 - No. 3, Nov, 1958

1-Powell-a(5); 1/2-pg. S&K-a; cover redrawn from Galaxy Science Fiction pulp (5/53)	15	45	77	130
2-Kirby/Williamson-c(r)/a(3); Kirby-p 7 more stys	27	81	142	245
3-Kirby/Williamson-c/a(4); Kirby-p 6 more stys	29	87	153	265

RACE OF SCORPIONS
Dark Horse Comics: 1990 - No. 2, 1990 ($4.50/$4.95, 52pgs.)

1,2: 1- r/stories from Dark Horse Presents #23-27. 2-($4.95-c)				5.00

RACER-X
Now Comics: 8/88 - No. 11, 8/89; V2#1, 9/89 - V2#10, 1990 ($1.75)

0-Deluxe ($3.50)				3.50
1 (9/88) -11, V2#1-10				2.25

RACER X (See Speed Racer)
DC Comics (WildStorm): Oct, 2000 - No. 3, Dec, 2000 ($2.95, limited series)

1-3: 1-Tommy Yune-s/Jo Chen-a; 2 covers by Yune. 2,3-Kabala app.				3.50

RACING PETTYS
STP Corp.: 1980 ($2.50, 68 pgs., 10 1/8" x 13 1/4")

1-Bob Kane-a. Kane bio on inside back-c.				10.00

RACK & PAIN
Dark Horse Comics: Mar, 1994 - No. 4, June, 1994 ($2.50, limited series)

1-4: Brian Pulido scripts in all. 1-Greg Capullo-c				3.00

RACK & PAIN: KILLERS
Chaos! Comics: Sept, 1996 - No. 4, Jan, 1997 ($2.95, limited series)

Radical Dreamer Prime © Mark Wheatley

Radioactive Man #4 (1953) © Bongo Ent.

Rail: Broken Things © Dave Dorman

	GD2.0	FN6.0	VF8.0	NM9.4

1-4: Reprints Dark Horse series; Jae Lee-c   3.00

RACKET SQUAD IN ACTION
Capitol Stories/Charlton Comics: May-June, 1952 - No. 29, Mar, 1958

	GD	FN	VF	NM
1	29	87	153	265
2-4,6: 3,4,6-Dr. Neff, Ghost Breaker app.	15	45	77	130
5-Dr. Neff, Ghost Breaker app; headlights-c	23	69	121	205
7-10: 10-Explosion-c	14	42	72	120
11-Ditko-c/a	31	93	165	285
12-Ditko explosion-c (classic); Shuster-a(2)	50	150	300	525
13-Shuster-c(p)/a.	11	33	55	90
14-Marijuana story "Shakedown"	14	42	72	120
15-28	10	30	55	85
29-(15¢, 68 pgs.)	12	36	61	100

RADIANT LOVE (Formerly Daring Love #1)
Gilmor Magazines: No. 2, Dec, 1953 - No. 6, Aug, 1954

	GD	FN	VF	NM
2	8	24	45	65
3-6	5	15	25	35

RADICAL DREAMER
Blackball Comics: No. 0, May, 1994 - No. 4, Nov, 1994 ($1.99, bi-monthly) (1st poster format comic)

0-4: 0-2-($1.99, poster format): 0-1st app. Max Wrighter. 3,4-($2.50-c)   3.00

RADICAL DREAMER
Mark's Giant Economy Size Comics: V2#1, June, 1995 - V2#6, Feb, 1996 ($2.95, B&W, limited series)

V2#1-6   3.00
Prime (5/96, $2.95)   3.00
Dreams Cannot Die!-(1996, $20.00, softcover)-Collects V1#0-4 & V2#1-6; intro by Kurt Busiek; afterward by Mark Waid   20.00
Dreams Cannot Die!-(1996, $60.00, hardcover)-Signed & limited edition; collects V1#0-4 & V2#1-6; intro by Kurt Busiek; afterward by Mark Waid   60.00

RADIOACTIVE MAN (Simpsons TV show)
Bongo Comics: 1993 - No. 6, 1994 ($1.95/$2.25, limited series)

1-($2.95)-Glow-in-the-dark-c; bound-in jumbo poster; origin Radioactive Man; (cover dated Nov. 1952)   4.00
2-6: 2-Says #88 on-c & inside & dated May 1962; cover parody of Atlas Kirby monster-c; Superior Squad app.; origin Fallout Boy. 3-($1.95)-Cover "dated" Aug 1972 #216. 4-($2.25)-Cover "dated" Oct 1980 #412; w/trading card.
5-Cover "dated" Jan 1986 #679; w/trading card. 6-(Jan 1995 #1000)   3.00
Colossal #1-($4.95)   6.00
#4 (2001, $2.50) Faux 1953 issue; Murphy Anderson-i (6 pgs.)   2.50
#100 (2000, $2.50) Comic Book Guy-c/app.; faux 1963 issue inside   2.50
#136 (2001, $2.50) Dan DeCarlo-a   2.50
#222 (2001, $2.50) Batton Lash-s; Radioactive Man in 1972-style   2.50

RAGAMUFFINS
Eclipse Comics: Jan, 1985 ($1.75, one shot)

1-Eclipse Magazine-r, w/color; Colan-a   2.25

RAGGEDY ANN AND ANDY (See Dell Giants, March of Comics #23 & New Funnies)
Dell Publishing Co.: No. 5, 1942 - No. 533, 2/54; 10-12/64 - No. 4, 3/66

	GD	FN	VF	NM
Four Color 5(1942)	50	150	350	650
Four Color 23(1943)	37	110	259	480
Four Color 45(1943)	31	93	217	400
Four Color 72(1945)	25	75	175	325
1(6/46)-Billy & Bonnie Bee by Frank Thomas	29	87	203	375
2,3: 3-Egbert Elephant by Dan Noonan begins	15	45	105	200
4-Kelly-a, 16 pgs.	16	48	112	210
5,6,8-10	12	36	84	150
7-Little Black Sambo, Black Mumbo & Black Jumbo only app; Christmas-c	13	39	91	175
11-20	10	30	70	125
21-Alice In Wonderland cover/story	12	36	84	150
22-27,29-39(8/49), Four Color 262(1/50): 34-"...In Candyland"	7	21	49	95
28-Kelly-c	8	24	56	105
Four Color 306,354,380,452,533	5	15	35	60
1(10-12/64-Dell)	4	12	26	40

	GD2.0	FN6.0	VF8.0	NM9.4

	GD	FN	VF	NM
2,3(10-12/65), 4(3/66)	3	9	17	25

NOTE: *Kelly* art ("Animal Mother Goose")-#1-34, 36, 37; c-28. Peterkin Pottle by *John Stanley* in 32-38.

RAGGEDY ANN AND ANDY
Gold Key: Dec, 1971 - No. 6, Sept, 1973

	GD	FN	VF	NM
1	3	9	20	30
2-6	2	6	13	20

RAGGEDY ANN & THE CAMEL WITH THE WRINKLED KNEES (See Dell Jr. Treasury #8)

RAGMAN (See Batman Family #20, The Brave & The Bold #196 & Cancelled Comic Cavalcade)
National Per. Publ./DC Comics No. 5: Aug-Sept, 1976 - No. 5, Jun-Jul, 1977

	GD	FN	VF	NM
1-Origin & 1st app.	1	4	7	10
2-5: 2-Origin ends; Kubert-c. 4-Drug use story				6.00

NOTE: *Kubert* a-4, 5; c-1-5. *Redondo* studios a-1-4.

RAGMAN (2nd Series)
DC Comics: Oct, 1991 - No. 8, May, 1992 ($1.50, limited series)

1-8: 1-Giffen plots/breakdowns. 3-Origin. 8-Batman-c/story   3.00

RAGMAN: CRY OF THE DEAD
DC Comics: Aug, 1993 - No. 6, Jan, 1994 ($1.75, limited series)

1-6: Joe Kubert-c   3.00

RAGMOP
Image Comics: Sept, 1997 - No. 2 ($2.95, B&W)

1,2-Rob Walton-c/s/a   3.00

RAGS RABBIT (Formerly Babe Ruth Sports #10 or Little Max #10?; also see Harvey Hits #2, Harvey Wiseguys & Tastee Freez)
Harvey Publications: No. 11, June, 1951 - No. 18, March, 1954 (Written & drawn for little folks)

	GD	FN	VF	NM
11-(See Nutty Comics #5 for 1st app.)	5	15	25	35
12-18	5	14	21	28

RAI (Rai and the Future Force #9-23) (See Magnus #5-8)
Valiant: Mar, 1992 - No. 0, Oct, 1992; No. 9, May, 1993 - No. 33, Jun, 1995 ($1.95/$2.25)

	GD	FN	VF	NM
1-Valiant's 1st original character				6.00
2-4,0: 4-Low print run. 0-(11/92)-Origin/1st app. new Rai (Rising Spirit) & 1st full app. & partial origin Bloodshot; also see Eternal Warrior #4; tells future of all characters				5.00
5-33: 6,7-Unity x-overs. 7-Death of Rai. 9-($2.50)-Gatefold-c; story cont'd from Magnus #24; Magnus, Eternal Warrior & X-O app. 15-Manowar Armor app. 17-19-Magnus x-over. 21-1st app. The Starwatchers (cameo); trading card. 22-Death of Rai. 26-Chaos Effect Epsilon Pt. 3				2.50

NOTE: *Layton* a-2i, 9i. *Miller* c-6. *Simonson* c-7.

RAIDERS OF THE LOST ARK (Movie)
Marvel Comics Group: Sept, 1981 - No. 3, Nov, 1981 (Movie adaptation)

1-3: 1-r/Marvel Comics Super Special #18   3.00

NOTE: *Buscema* a(p)-1-3; c(p)-1. *Simonson* a-3i; scripts-1-3.

RAIL: BROKEN THINGS
Image Comics: Nov, 2001 ($5.95, one-shot)

nn-Dave Dorman-s/a   6.00

RAINBOW BRITE AND THE STAR STEALER
DC Comics: 1985

	GD	FN	VF	NM
nn-Movie adaptation	1	3	6	9

RALPH KINER, HOME RUN KING
Fawcett Publications: 1950 (Pittsburgh Pirates)

	GD	FN	VF	NM
nn-Photo-c; life story	59	177	369	650

RALPH SNART ADVENTURES
Now Comics: June, 1986 - V2#9, 1987; V3#1 - #26, Feb, 1991; V4#1, 1992 - #4, 1992

	GD	FN	VF	NM
1-3, V2#1-7,V3#1-23,25,26:1-($1.00, B&W)-1(B&W),V2#1(11/86), B&W), 8,9- color. V3#1(9/88)-Color begins				2.50
V3#24-($2.50)-3-D issue, V4#1-3-Direct sale versions w/cards				2.50
V4#1-3-Newsstand versions w/random cards				2.50
Book 1	1	3	6	8

	GD2.0	FN6.0	VF8.0	NM9.4

3-D Special (11/92, $3.50)-Complete 12-card set w/3-D glasses 3.50

RAMAR OF THE JUNGLE (TV)
Toby Press No. 1/Charlton No. 2 on: 1954 (no month); No. 2, Sept, 1955 - No. 5, Sept, 1956

1-Jon Hall photo-c; last pre-code issue	22	66	116	200
2-5: 2-Jon Hall photo-c	15	45	77	130

RAMM
Megaton Comics: May, 1987 - No. 2, Sept, 1987 ($1.50, B&W)

1,2-Both have 1 pg. Youngblood ad by Liefeld 2.25

RAMPAGING HULK (The Hulk #10 on; also see Marvel Treasury Edition)
Marvel Comics Group: Jan, 1977 - No. 9, June, 1978 ($1.00, B&W magazine)

1-Bloodstone story w/Buscema & Nebres-a. Origin re-cap w/Simonson-a; Gargoyle, UFO story; Ken Barr-c	2	6	11	15
2-Old X-Men app; origin old w/Simonson-a & new X-Men in text w/Cockrum illos; Bloodstone story w/Brown & Nebres-a	2	6	9	12
3-9: 3-Iron Man app. 4-Gallery of villains w/Giffen-a. 5,6-Hulk vs. Sub-Mariner. 7-Man-Thing story. 8-Original Avengers app. 9-Thor vs. Hulk battle; Shanna the She-Devil story w/DeZuniga-a	1	3	6	9

NOTE: **Alcala** a-1-3i, 5i, 8i. **Buscema** a-1. **Giffen** a-4. **Nino** a-4i. **Simonson** a-1-3p. **Starlin** a-4(w/Nino), 7; c-4, 5, 7.

RAMPAGING HULK
Marvel Comics: Aug, 1998 - No. 6, Jan, 1999 ($2.99/$1.99)

1-($2.99) Flashback stories of Savage Hulk; Leonardi-a				3.00
2-6-($1.99): 2-Two covers				2.25

RANDOLPH SCOTT (Movie star)(See Crack Western #67, Prize Comics Western #76, Western Hearts #8, Western Love #1 & Western Winners #7)

RANDY O'DONNELL IS THE M@N
Image Comics: May, 2001 - Present ($2.95)

1-3-DeFalco & Lim/s&a 3.00

RANGE BUSTERS
Fox Features Syndicate: Sept, 1950 (One shot)

1 (Exist?)	20	60	105	175

RANGE BUSTERS (Formerly Cowboy Love?; Wyatt Earp, Frontier Marshall #11 on)
Charlton Comics: No. 8, May, 1955 - No. 10, Sept, 1955

8	8	24	42	60
9,10	6	18	28	38

RANGELAND LOVE
Atlas Comics (CDS): Dec, 1949 - No. 2, Mar, 1950 (52 pgs.)

1-Robert Taylor & Arlene Dahl photo-c	17	51	88	150
2-Photo-c	14	42	72	120

RANGER, THE (See Zane Grey, Four Color #255)

RANGE RIDER, THE (TV)(See Flying A's...)

RANGE ROMANCES
Comic Magazines (Quality Comics): Dec, 1949 - No. 5, Aug, 1950 (#5: 52 pg)

1-Gustavson-c/a	27	81	145	250
2-Crandall-c/a	27	81	145	250
3-Crandall, Gustavson-a; photo-c	23	69	121	210
4-Crandall-a; photo-c	20	60	105	175
5-Gustavson-a; Crandall-a(p); photo-c	20	60	105	175

RANGERS COMICS (...of Freedom #1-7)
Fiction House Magazines: 10/41 - No. 67, 10/52; No. 68, Fall, 1952; No. 69, Winter, 1952-53 (Flying stories)

1-Intro. Ranger Girl & The Rangers of Freedom; ends #7, cover app. only #5	255	765	1591	2800
2	82	246	511	900
3	64	192	398	700
4,5	59	177	369	650
6-10: 8-U.S. Rangers begin	47	140	286	500
11,12-Commando Rangers app.	43	129	257	450
13-Commando Ranger begins-not same as Commando Rangers	41	123	246	425
14-20	39	117	208	360

	GD2.0	FN6.0	VF8.0	NM9.4

21-Intro/origin Firehair (begins, 2/45)	40	120	232	400
22-30: 23-Kazanda begins, ends #28. 28-Tiger Man begins (origin/1st app., 4/46), ends #46. 30-Crusoe Island begins, ends #40	29	87	153	265
31-40: 33-Hypodermic panels	25	75	130	225
41-46: 41-Last Werewolf Hunter	20	60	105	180
47-56: "Eisnerish" Dr. Drew by Grandenetti. 48-Last Glory Forbes. 53-Last 52 pg. issue. 55-Last Sky Rangers	20	60	105	180
57-60-Straight Dr. Drew by Grandenetti	15	45	77	130
61-69: 64-Suicide Smith begins. 63-Used in **POP**, pgs. 85, 99. 67-Space Rangers begin, end #69	13	39	66	110

NOTE: Bondage, discipline covers, lingerie panels are common. Crusoe Island by **Larsen**-#30-36. Firehair by **Lubbers**-#30-49. Glory Forbes by **Baker**-#36-45, 47; by **Whitman**-#34, 35. I Confess in #41-53. Jan of the Jungle in #42-58. King of the Congo in #49-53. Tiger Man by **Celardo**-#30-39. **M. Anderson** a-30? **Baker** a-36-38, 42, 44. **John Celardo** a-34, 36-39. **Lee Elias** a-21-28. **Evans** a-19, 38-46, 48-52. **Hopper** a-25, 26. **Ingels** a-13-16. **Larsen** a-34. **Bob Lubbers** a-30-38, 40-44; c-40-45. **Moreira** a-41-47. **Tuska** a-16, 17, 19, 22. **M. Whitman** c-61-66. **Zolnerwich** c-1-17.

RANGO (TV)
Dell Publishing Co.: Aug, 1967

1-Photo-c of comedian Tim Conway	3	9	20	30

RAPHAEL (See Teenage Mutant Ninja Turtles)
Mirage Studios: 1985 ($1.50, 7-1/2x11", B&W w/2 color cover, one-shot)

1-1st Turtles one-shot spin-off; contains 1st drawing of the Turtles as a group from 1983				4.00
1-2nd printing (11/87); new-c & 8 pgs. art				2.25

RASCALS IN PARADISE
Dark Horse Comics: Aug, 1994 - No. 3, Dec, 1994 ($3.95, magazine size)

1-3-Jim Silke-a/story				4.00
Trade paperback-($16.95)-r/#1-3				17.00

RATFINK (See Frantic, Zany, & Ed "Big Daddy" Roth's Ratfink Comix)
Canrom, Inc.: Oct, 1964

1-Woodbridge-a	5	15	38	60

RAT PATROL, THE (TV)
Dell Publishing Co.: Mar, 1967 - No. 5, Nov, 1967; No. 6, Oct, 1969

1-Christopher George photo-c	6	18	42	80
2-6: 3-6-Photo-c	4	12	29	45

RAVAGE 2099 (See Marvel Comics Presents #117)
Marvel Comics: Dec, 1992 - No. 33, Aug, 1995($1.25/$1.50)

1-($1.75)-Gold foil stamped-c; Stan Lee scripts				3.00
1-($1.75)-2nd printing				2.25
2-24,26-33: 5-Last Ryan-c. 6-Last Ryan-a. 14-Punisher 2099 x-over. 15-Ron Lim-c(p). 18-Bound-in card sheet				2.25
25 ($2.25, 52 pgs.)				2.25
25 ($2.95, 52 pgs.)-Silver foil embossed-c				3.00

RAVEN, THE (See Movie Classics)

RAVEN CHRONICLES
Caliber (New Worlds): 1995 - Present ($2.95, B&W)

1-15: 10-Flip book w/Wordsmith #6. 15-Flip book w/High Caliber #4 3.00

RAVENING, THE
Avatar Press: June, 1997 - No. 2 ($3.00, B&W, limited series)

1,2 3.00

RAVENS AND RAINBOWS
Pacific Comics: Dec, 1983 (Baxter paper)(Reprints fanzine work in color)

1-Jeff Jones-c/a(r); nudity scenes 3.00

RAWHIDE (TV)
Dell Publishing Co./Gold Key: Sept-Nov, 1959 - June-Aug, 1962; July, 1963 - No. 2, Jan, 1964

Four Color 1028 (#1)	23	68	161	300
Four Color 1097,1160,1202,1261,1269	14	41	98	180
01-684-208 (8/62, Dell)	12	35	84	160
1(10071-307) (7/63, Gold Key)	12	35	84	160
2-(12¢)	12	36	84	150

NOTE: All have Clint Eastwood photo-c. **Tufts** a-1028.

Rawhide Kid #49 © MAR

The Ray (mini-series) #5 © DC

Razor #43 © Everette Hartsoe

	GD2.0	FN6.0	VF8.0	NM9.4

RAWHIDE KID
Atlas/Marvel Comics (CnPC No. 1-16/AMI No. 17-30): Mar, 1955 - No. 16, Sept, 1957; No. 17, Aug, 1960 - No. 151, May, 1979

1-Rawhide Kid, his horse Apache & sidekick Randy begin; Wyatt Earp app.; #1 was not code approved; Maneely splash pg.	86	258	540	950
2	40	120	232	400
3-5	30	90	162	280
6-10: 7-Williamson-a (4 pgs.)	23	69	121	210
11-16: 16-Torres-a	20	60	105	175
17-Origin by Jack Kirby; Kirby-a begins	32	96	240	435
18-21,24-30	13	39	91	155
22-Monster-c/story by Kirby/Ayers	16	48	112	200
23-Origin retold by Jack Kirby	20	60	137	245
31-35,40: 31,32-Kirby-a. 33-35-Davis-a. 34-Kirby-a. 35-Intro & death of The Raven. 40-Two-Gun Kid x-over.	10	30	68	115
36,37,39,41,42-No Kirby. 42-1st Larry Lieber issue	9	27	63	105
38-Red Raven-c/story; Kirby-c (2/64).	12	36	84	140
43-Kirby-a (beware: pin-up often missing)	11	33	80	135
44,46: 46-Toth-a. 46-Doc Holliday-c/s	8	24	56	90
45-Origin retold, 17 pgs.	10	30	70	120
47-49,51-60	5	15	34	55
50-Kid Colt x-over; vs. Rawhide Kid	5	15	38	60
61-70: 64-Kid Colt story. 66-Two-Gun Kid story. 67-Kid Colt story.				
70-Last 12¢ issue	4	12	26	40
71-78,80-83,85	3	9	17	25
79,84,86,95: 79-Williamson-a(r). 84,86: Kirby-a. 86-Origin-r; Williamson-r/Ringo Kid #13 (4 pgs.)	3	9	19	28
87-91: 90-Kid Colt app. 91-Last 15¢ issue	2	6	15	22
92,93 (52 pg.Giants). 92-Kirby-a	3	10	23	35
94,96-99	2	6	13	20
100 (6/72)-Origin retold & expanded	3	9	19	28
101-120: 115-Last new story	2	6	11	16
121-151	1	4	7	10
133,134-(30¢-c variants, limited distribution)(5,7/76)	2	6	11	15
140,141-(35¢-c variants, limited distribution)(7,9/77)	2	6	11	15
Special 1(9/71, 25¢, 68 pgs.)-All Kirby/Ayers-r	4	12	26	40

NOTE: Ayers a-13, 14, 16. Colan a-5, 35, 37; c-145p, 148p, 149p. Davis a-125r. Everett a-54i, 65, 66, 88, 96i, 148i(r). Gulacy c-147. Heath c-4. G. Kane c-101, 144. Keller a-5, 144r. Kirby a-17-32, 34, 42, 43, 84, 86, 92, 109r, 112r, 137r; Spec. 1; c-17-35, 37, 38, 40, 41, 43-47, 137r. Maneely c-1, 2, 5, 6, 14. Morisi a-13. Morrow/Williamson r-111. Roussos r-146i, 147i, 149-151i. Severin a-16; c-8, 13. Sutton a-93. Torres a-99r. Tuska a-14. Wildey r-146-151(Outlaw Kid). Williamson r-79, 86, 95.

RAWHIDE KID
Marvel Comics Group: Aug, 1985 - No. 4, Nov, 1985 (Mini-series)

1-4				5.00

RAY, THE (See Freedom Fighters & Smash Comics #14)
DC Comics: Feb, 1992 - No. 6, July, 1992 ($1.00, mini-series)

1-Sienkiewicz-c; Joe Quesada-a(p) in 1-5				5.00
2-6: 3-6-Quesada-c(p). 6-Quesada layouts only				3.00
...In a Blaze of Power (1994, $12.95)-r/#1-6 w/new Quesada-c				13.00

RAY, THE
DC Comics: May, 1994 - No. 28, Oct, 1996 ($1.75/$1.95/$2.25)

1-Quesada-c(p); Superboy app.				3.00
1-($2.95)-Collectors Edition w/diff. Quesada-c; embossed foil-c				4.00
2-5,0,6-24,26-28: 2-Quesada-c(p). Superboy app. 5-(9/94). 0-(10/94)				2.25
25-($3.50)-Future Flash (Bart Allen)-c/app; double size				3.50
Annual 1 ($3.95, 68 pgs.)-Superman app.				4.00

RAY BRADBURY COMICS
Topps Comics: Feb, 1993 - V4#1, June, 1994 ($2.95)

1-5-Polybagged w/3 trading cards each. 1-All dinosaur issue; Corben-a; Williamson/Torres/Krenkel-r/Weird Science-Fantasy #25. 3-All dinosaur issue; Steacy painted-c; Stout-a				3.00
Special Edition 1 (1994, $2.95)-The Illustrated Man				3.00
...Special: Tales of Horror #1 ($2.50), ...Trilogy of Terror V3#1 (5/94, $2.50), ...Martian Chronicles V4#1 (6/94, $2.50)-Steranko-c				2.50

NOTE: Kelley Jones a-Trilogy of Terror V3#1. Kaluta a-Martian Chronicles V4#1. Kurtzman/Matt Wagner c-2. McKean c-4. Mignola a-4. Wood a-Trilogy of Terror V3#1r.

RAZOR

	GD2.0	FN6.0	VF8.0	NM9.4

London Night Studios: May, 1992 - No. 51, Apr, 1999 ($3.95/$3.00, B&W)

0 (5/92, $3.95)-Direct market	1	4	7	10
0 (4/95, $3.00)-London Night edition				3.00
1/2 (4/95, mail-in offer)-1st Poizon; Linsner-c				4.00
1 (8/92, $2.50)-Fathom Press	1	4	7	10
1-2nd printing				3.00
2 ($2.95)-J. O'Barr-c	1	3	6	8
2-Limited edi. in red & blue, 2-Platinum; no c-price	1	4	7	10
3-($3.95)-Jim Balent-c				4.00
3-w/poster insert				5.00
4-Vigil-c				3.00
4-w/poster insert				4.00
5-Linsner-c				5.00
5-Platinum	1	3	6	8
6-31,33,34:10-1st app. Stryke. 1,12 -Rituals Pt. 1 & 2. 21-Rose & Gunn app.				2.50
25-Photo-c				2.50
25-Uncut ($10.00)-Nude Edition; double-c				8.00
32-($3.50)				3.50
32-($5.00)-Nude Edition; Nude-c				5.00
35-49,51				3.00
40-Uncut ($6.00)-Nude Edition				6.00
50-Uncut-Four covers incl. Tony Dainel				3.00
Annual 1 (1993, $2.95)-1st app. Shi	2	6	12	18
Annual 1-Gold (1200 printed)	2	6	13	20
Annual 2 (Late 1994, $3.00)				3.00
.../Cry No More 1-($3.95)-Origin Razor; variant-c exists				4.00
.../Embrace nn-($3.00)-Variant photo-c(Carmen Electra)				3.00
.../Pictorial 1-(10/97, $5.00)				5.00
.../Shi Special 1 (7/94, $3.00)				4.00
.../Switchblade Symphony 1-($3.95)-Hartsoe-s				4.00
...: Swimsuit Special-painted-c				3.00
...: The Darkest Night 1,2 ($4.95)-painted-c				5.00
.../Warrior Nun Areala-Faith-(5/96, $3.95)				4.00
.../Warrior Nun Areala-Faith-(5/96, $3.95)-Virgin-c				5.00

RAZOR: BURN
London Night Studios: 1994 - No. 5, 1994 ($3.00, limited series, mature)

1-5				3.00
TPB-($14.95) r/ #1-5				15.00

RAZOR/DARK ANGEL: THE FINAL NAIL
Boneyard Press #1/London Night Studios #2: June, 1994 -No. 2, June, 1994 ($2.95, B&W, limited series, mature)

1,2				3.00

RAZOR• DEEP CUTS
London Night Studios: Sept, 1997 ($5.00, one-shot, mature)

1-Photo-c & insides				5.00

RAZOR/MORBID ANGEL: SOUL SEARCH
London Night Studios: Sept, 1996 - No. 3, 1997 ($3.00, limited series, mature)

1-3				3.00

RAZOR: THE SUFFERING
London Night Studios: 1994 - No. 3, 1995 ($2.95, limited series, mature)

1-3 ($2.95): 2-(9/94), 1-($3.00)-Director's Cut				3.00
1-Platinum				5.00
Trade paperback-($12.95)				13.00

RAZOR: TORTURE
London Night Studios: 1995 - No. 6, 1995 ($3.00, limited series, mature)

0-($3.95)-Wraparound, chromium-c; polybagged w/card; alternate-c exists?				4.00
1-6 ($3.00): 3-Error & corrected issues exist				3.00

RAZOR: VOLUME TWO
London Night Studios: Oct, 1996 - No. 7, June, 1997 ($3.95/$3.00, mature)

1-Wraparound foil-c; Quinn-s				4.00
2-7-($3.00): 3-Error & corrected issues exist				3.00

RAZORLINE
Marvel Comics: Sept, 1993 (75¢, one-shot)

1-Clive Barker super-heroes: Ectokid, Hokum & Hex, Hyperkind & Saint				

Real Clue Crime Stories V2 #9 © HILL

Real Fact Comics #18 © DC

Real Heroes Comics #7 © PMI

	GD2.0	FN6.0	VF8.0	NM9.4

Sinner (all 1st app.) 2.25

REAL ADVENTURE COMICS (Action Adventure #2 on)
Gillmor Magazines: Apr, 1955

	GD2.0	FN6.0	VF8.0	NM9.4
1	6	18	32	45

REAL ADVENTURES OF JONNY QUEST, THE
Dark Horse Comics: Sept, 1996 - No. 12, Sept, 1997 ($2.95)

1-12				3.00

REAL CLUE CRIME STORIES (Formerly Clue Comics)
Hillman Periodicals: V2#4, June, 1947 - V8#3, May, 1953

	GD2.0	FN6.0	VF8.0	NM9.4
V2#4(#1)-S&K c/a(3); Dan Barry-a	47	141	282	495
5-7-S&K c/a(3-4). 7-Iron Lady app.	39	117	208	360
8-12	11	33	55	90
V3#1-8,10-12, V4#1-3,5-8,11,12	10	30	55	80
V3#9-Used in SOTI, pg. 102	13	39	66	110
V4#4-S&K-a	14	42	72	120
V4#9,10-Krigstein-a	10	30	55	85
V5#1-5,7,8,10,12	8	24	42	60
6,9,11(1/54)-Krigstein-a	10	30	55	80
V6#1-5,8,9,11	7	21	38	55
6,7,10,12-Krigstein-a. 10-Bondage-c	10	30	55	80
V7#1-3,5-11, V8#1-3: V7#6-1 pg. Frazetta ad "Prayer" - 1st app.?				
	7	21	38	55
4,12-Krigstein-a	10	30	55	80

NOTE: Barry a-9, 10; c-V2#8. Briefer a-V6#6. Fuje a- V2#7(2), 8, 11. Infantino a-V2#8; c-V2#11. Lawrence a-V3#8, V5#7. Powell a-V4#11, 12. V5#4, 5, 7 are 68 pgs.

REAL EXPERIENCES (Formerly Tiny Tessie)
Atlas Comics (20CC): No. 25, Jan, 1950

	GD2.0	FN6.0	VF8.0	NM9.4
25-Virginia Mayo photo-c from movie "Red Light"	7	21	38	55

REAL FACT COMICS
National Periodical Publications: Mar-Apr, 1946 - No. 21, July-Aug, 1949

	GD2.0	FN6.0	VF8.0	NM9.4
1-S&K-c/a; Harry Houdini story; Just Imagine begins (not by Finlay); Fred Ray-a	59	177	369	650
2-S&K-a; Rin-Tin-Tin & P. T. Barnum stories	40	120	220	380
3-H.G. Wells, Lon Chaney stories; 1st DC letter column	37	111	197	340
4-Virgil Finlay-a on 'Just Imagine' begins, ends #12 (2 pgs. each); Jimmy Stewart & Jack London stories; Joe DiMaggio 1 pg. biography	40	120	220	380
5-Batman/Robin-c taken from cover of Batman #9; 5 pg. story about creation of Batman & Robin; Tom Mix story	182	546	1136	2000
6-Origin & 1st app. Tommy Tomorrow by Weisinger and Sherman (1-2/47); Flag-c; 1st writing by Harlan Ellison (letter column, non-professional); "First Man to Reach Mars" epic-c/story	111	332	694	1225
7-(No. 6 on inside)-Roussos-a; D. Fairbanks sty.	20	60	105	175
8-2nd app. Tommy Tomorrow by Finlay (5-6/47)	61	182	381	675
9-S&K-a; Glenn Miller, Indianapolis 500 stories	30	90	159	275
10-Vigilante by Meskin (based on movie serial); 4 pg. Finlay s/f story	29	87	153	265
11,12: 11-Annie Oakley, G-Men stories; Kinstler-a	16	48	83	140
13-Dale Evans and Tommy Tomorrow-c/stories	50	150	300	525
14,17,18: 14-Will Rogers story	15	45	77	130
15-Nuclear explosion part-c ("Last War on Earth" story); Clyde Beatty story	20	60	105	175
16-Tommy Tomorrow app.; 1st Planeteers?	45	135	270	475
19-Sir Arthur Conan Doyle story	17	51	88	150
20-Kubert-a, 4 pgs; Daniel Boone story	19	57	99	165
21-Kubert-a, 2 pgs; Kit Carson story	15	45	77	130

NOTE: Barry c-16. Virgil Finlay c-6, 8. Meskin c-10. Roussos a-1-4, 6.

REAL FUNNIES
Nedor Publishing Co.: Jan, 1943 - No. 3, June, 1943

	GD2.0	FN6.0	VF8.0	NM9.4
1-Funny animal, humor; Black Terrier app. (clone of The Black Terror)	34	102	179	310
2,3	17	51	88	150

REAL GHOSTBUSTERS, THE (Also see Slimer!)
Now Comics: Aug, 1988 - No. 32, 1991 ($1.75/$1.95)

1-32: 1-Based on Ghostbusters movie. #29-32 exist?				3.00

REAL HEROES COMICS
Parents' Magazine Institute: Sept, 1941 - No. 16, Oct, 1946

	GD2.0	FN6.0	VF8.0	NM9.4
1-Roosevelt-c/story	34	102	179	310
2-J. Edgar Hoover-c/story	15	45	77	130
3-5,7-10: 4-Churchill, Roosevelt stories	13	39	66	110
6-Lou Gehrig-c/story	21	63	110	185
11-16: 13-Kiefer-a	9	27	49	70

REALISTIC ROMANCES
Realistic Comics/Avon Periodicals: July-Aug, 1951 - No. 17, Aug-Sept, 1954
(No #9-14)

	GD2.0	FN6.0	VF8.0	NM9.4
1-Kinstler-a; c-/Avon paperback #211	22	66	116	200
2	11	33	55	90
3,4	10	30	55	80
5,8-Kinstler-a	10	30	55	85
6-c/-Diversey Prize Novels #6; Kinstler-a	11	33	55	90
7-Evans-a?; c-/Avon paperback #360	11	33	55	90
15,17: 17-Kinstler-a	9	27	49	70
16-Kinstler marijuana story-r/Romantic Love #6	10	30	55	85
I.W. Reprint #1,8,9: #1-r/Realistic Romances #4; Astarita-a. 9-r/Women To Love #1	2	6	11	15

NOTE: Astarita a-2-4, 7, 8, 17. Photo c-1, 2. Painted c-3, 4.

REAL LIFE COMICS
Nedor/Better/Standard Publ./Pictorial Magazine No. 13: Sept, 1941 - No. 59, Sept, 1952

	GD2.0	FN6.0	VF8.0	NM9.4
1-Uncle Sam-c/story; Daniel Boone story	52	157	314	550
2	26	78	136	235
3-Hitler cover	68	204	426	750
4,5: 4-Story of American flag "Old Glory"	16	48	83	140
6-10: 6-Wild Bill Hickok story	15	45	77	130
11-20: 17-Albert Einstein story	14	42	72	120
21-23,25,26,28-30: 29-A-Bomb story	11	33	55	90
24-Story of Baseball (Babe Ruth)	19	57	99	170
27-Schomburg A-Bomb-c; story of A-Bomb	18	54	94	160
31-33,35,36,42-44,48,49: 49-Baseball issue	9	27	49	70
34,37-41,45-47: 34-Jimmy Stewart story. 37-Story of motion pictures; Bing Crosby story. 38-Jane Froman story. 39- "1,000,000 A.D." story. 40-Bob Feller. 41-Jimmie Foxx story ("Jimmy" on-c); "Home Run" Baker story. 45-Story of Olympic games; Burl Ives & Kit Carson story. 46-Douglas Fairbanks Jr. & Sr. story. 47-George Gershwin story	11	33	55	90
50-Frazetta-a (5 pgs.)	29	87	153	265
51-Jules Verne "Journey to the Moon" by Evans	20	60	105	175
52-Frazetta-a (4 pgs.); Severin/Elder-a(2); Evans-a	31	93	165	285
53-57-Severin/Elder-a. 54-Bat Masterson-c/story	14	42	72	120
58-Severin/Elder-a(2)	14	42	72	120
59-1 pg. Frazetta; Severin/Elder-a	14	42	72	120

NOTE: Some issues had two titles. Guardineer a-40(2), 44. Meskin a-52. Roussos a-50. Schomburg c-1, 2, 4, 5, 7, 11, 13-21, 23, 24, 26, 28, 30-32, 34-40, 42, 44-47, 55. Tuska a-53. Photo-c 5, 6.

REAL LIFE SECRETS (Real Secrets #2 on)
Ace Periodicals: Sept, 1949 (one-shot)

	GD2.0	FN6.0	VF8.0	NM9.4
1-Painted-c	12	36	61	100

REAL LIFE STORY OF FESS PARKER (Magazine)
Dell Publishing Co.: 1955

	GD2.0	FN6.0	VF8.0	NM9.4
1	9	27	63	120

REAL LIFE TALES OF SUSPENSE (See Suspense)

REAL LOVE (Formerly Hap Hazard)
Ace Periodicals (A. A. Wyn): No. 25, April, 1949 - No. 76, Nov, 1956

	GD2.0	FN6.0	VF8.0	NM9.4
25	12	36	61	105
26	8	24	42	60
27-L. B. Cole-a	11	33	55	90
28-35	6	18	32	45
36-66: 66-Last pre-code (2/55)	6	18	29	40
67-76	5	15	23	30

NOTE: Photo c-50-76. Painted c-46.

REALM, THE
Arrow Comics/WeeBee Comics #13/Caliber Press #14 on: Feb, 1986 - No. 21, 1991 ($1.50/$1.95/$2.50, B&W)

Real Screen Comics #1 © DC

Realworlds: Wonder Woman © DC

R.E.B.E.L.S. '95 #6 © DC

	GD2.0	FN6.0	VF8.0	NM9.4
	GD2.0	FN6.0	VF8.0	NM9.4

1-21: 4-1st app. Deadworld (9/86) — 2.50
Book 1 ($4.95, B&W) — 5.00

REAL McCOYS, THE (TV)
Dell Publ. Co.: No. 1071, 1-3/60 - 5-7/1962 (All have Walter Brennan photo-c)

Four Color 1071,1134-Toth-a in both	9	27	63	120
Four Color 1193,1265	9	27	63	110
01-689-207 (5-7/62)	8	24	56	100

REAL SCREEN COMICS (#1 titled Real Screen Funnies; TV Screen Cartoons #129-138)
National Periodical Publications: Spring, 1945 - No. 128, May-June, 1959 (#1-40: 52 pgs.)

1-The Fox & the Crow, Flippity & Flop, Tito & His Burrito begin	100	300	625	1100
2	47	141	286	500
3-5	34	102	179	310
6-10 (2-3/47)	22	66	116	195
11-20 (10-11/48): 13-The Crow x-over in Flippity & Flop	17	51	88	150
21-30 (6-7/50)	13	39	66	110
31-50	11	33	55	95
51-99	10	30	55	80
100	10	30	55	85
101-128	8	24	42	60

REAL SECRETS (Formerly Real Life Secrets)
Ace Periodicals: No. 2, Nov, 1950 - No. 5, May, 1950

2-Painted-a	10	30	55	80
3-5: 3-Photo-c	7	21	36	50

REAL SPORTS COMICS (All Sports Comics #2 on)
Hillman Periodicals: Oct-Nov, 1948 (52 pgs.)

1-Powell-a (12 pgs.)	40	120	220	380

REAL WAR STORIES
Eclipse Comics: July, 1987; No. 2, Jan, 1991 ($2.00, 52 pgs.)

1-Bolland-a(p), Bissette-a, Totleben-a(i); Alan Moore scripts (2nd printing
exists, 2/88) — 2.25
2-($4.95) — 5.00

REAL WESTERN HERO (Formerly Wow #1-69; Western Hero #76 on)
Fawcett Publications: No. 70, Sept, 1948 - No. 75, Feb, 1949 (All 52 pgs.)

70(#1)-Tom Mix, Monte Hale, Hopalong Cassidy, Young Falcon begin	36	108	191	330
71-75: 71-Gabby Hayes begins. 71,72-Captain Tootsie by Beck. 75-Big Bow and Little Arrow app.	23	69	121	205

NOTE: Painted photo c-70-73; painted c-74, 75.

REAL WEST ROMANCES
Crestwood Publishing Co./Prize Publ.: 4-5/49 - V1#6, 3/50; V2#1, Apr-May, 1950 (All 52 pgs. & photo-c)

V1#1-S&K-a(p)	26	78	136	235
2	13	39	66	110
3-Kirby-a(p) only	14	42	72	120
4-S&K-a; Whip Wilson, Reno Browne photo-c	20	60	105	175
5-Audie Murphy, Gale Storm photo-c; S&K-a	18	54	94	155
6-Produced by S&K, no S&K-a; Robert Preston & Cathy Downs photo-c	14	42	72	120
V2#1-Kirby-a(p)	11	33	55	90

NOTE: Meskin a-V1#5, 6. Severin/Elder a-V1#3-6, V2#1. Meskin a-V1#6. Leonard Starr a-1-3. Photo-c V1#1-6, V2#1.

REALWORLDS :...
DC Comics: 2000 ($5.95, one-shots, prestige format)

Batman - Marshall Rogers-a/Golden & Sniegoski-s; Justice League of America -
Dematteis-s/ Barr-painted art; Superman - Vance-s/García-López &
Rubenstein-a; Wonder Woman - Hanson & Neuwirth-s/Sam-a — 6.00

RE-ANIMATOR IN FULL COLOR
Adventure Comics: Oct, 1991 - No. 3, 1992 ($2.95, mini-series)

1-3: Adapts horror movie. 1-Dorman painted-c — 3.00

REAP THE WILD WIND (See Cinema Comics Herald)

REBEL, THE (TV)
Dell Publishing Co.: No. 1076, Feb-Apr, 1960 - No. 1262, Dec-Feb, 1961-62

Four Color 1076 (#1)-Sekowsky-a, photo-c	10	30	70	130
Four Color 1138 (9-11/60), 1207 (9-11/61), 1262-Photo-c	9	27	63	110

R.E.B.E.L.S. '94 (Becomes R.E.B.E.L.S. '95 & R.E.B.E.L.S. '96)
DC Comics: No. 0, Oct, 1994 - No. 17, Mar, 1996 ($1.95/$2.25)

0-17: 8-$2.25-c begins. 15-R.E.B.E.L.S '96 begins. — 2.25

REBEL SWORD (Manga)
Dark Horse Comics: Oct, 1994 - No. 6, Feb, 1995 ($2.50, B&W)

1-6 — 2.50

RECORD BOOK OF FAMOUS POLICE CASES
St. John Publishing Co.: 1949 (25¢, 132 pgs.)

nn-Kubert-a(3); r/Son of Sinbad; Baker-c	39	117	208	360

RED ARROW
P. L. Publishing Co.: May-June, 1951 - No. 3, Oct, 1951

1	11	33	55	90
2,3	9	27	49	70

RED BAND COMICS
Enwil Associates: Feb, 1945 - No. 4, May, 1945

1	39	117	208	360
2-Origin Bogeyman & Santanas; c-reprint/#1	29	87	153	265
3,4-Captain Wizard app. in both (1st app.); each has identical contents/cover	27	81	142	245

REDBLADE
Dark Horse Comics: Apr, 1993 - No. 3, July, 1993 ($2.50, mini-series)

1-3: 1-Double gatefold-c — 3.00

RED CIRCLE COMICS (Also see Blazing Comics & Blue Circle Comics)
Rural Home Publications (Enwil): Jan, 1945 - No. 4, April, 1945

1-The Prankster & Red Riot begin	38	114	203	350
2-Starr-a; The Judge (costumed hero) app.	30	90	159	275
3,4-Starr-c/a. 3-The Prankster not in costume	23	69	121	210
4-(Dated 4/45)-Leftover covers to #4 were later restapled over early 1950s coverless comics; variations in the coverless comics used are endless; Woman Outlaws, Dorothy Lamour, Crime Does Not Pay, Sabu, Diary Loves, Love Confessions & Young Love V3#3 known	17	51	88	150

RED CIRCLE SORCERY (Chilling Adventures in Sorcery #1-5)
Red Circle Prod. (Archie): No. 6, Apr, 1974 - No. 11, Feb, 1975 (All 25¢ iss.)

6,8,9,11: 6-Early Chaykin-a. 7-Pino-a. 8-Only app. The Cobra	1	4	7	10
7-Bruce Jones-a with Wrightson, Kaluta, Jeff Jones	2	6	11	15
10-Wood-a(i)	2	6	9	12

NOTE: Chaykin a-6, 10. McWilliams a-10(2 & 3 pgs.). Mooney a-11p. Morrow a-6-8, 9(text illos), 10, 11i; c-6-11. Thorne a-8, 10. Toth a-8, 9.

RED DOG (See Night Music #7)

RED DRAGON
Comico: June, 1996 ($2.95)

1-Bisley-c — 3.00

RED DRAGON COMICS (1st Series) (Formerly Trail Blazers; see Super Magician V5#7, 8)
Street & Smith Publications: No. 5, Jan, 1943 - No. 9, Jan, 1944

5-Origin Red Rover, the Crimson Crimebuster; Rex King, Man of Adventure, Captain Jack Commando, & The Minute Man begin; text origin Red Dragon; Binder-c	100	300	625	1100
6-Origin The Black Crusader & Red Dragon (3/43); 1st story app. Red Dragon & 1st cover (classic-c)	214	642	1338	2350
7-Classic-c	155	465	966	1700
8-The Red Knight app.	73	219	455	800
9-Origin Chuck Magnon, Immortal Man	73	219	455	800

RED DRAGON COMICS (2nd Series)(See Super Magician V2#8)
Street & Smith Publications: Nov, 1947 - No. 6, Jan, 1949; No. 7, July, 1949

1-Red Dragon begins; Elliman, Nigel app.; Edd Cartier-c/a	91	273	568	1000

Red Dragon Comics #3 © Condé Nast

Red Rabbit Comics #2 © Dearfield

Red Ryder Comics #8
© Lasswell & Slesinger

	GD2.0	FN6.0	VF8.0	NM9.4

2-Cartier-c ... 64 · 192 · 398 · 700
3-1st app. Dr. Neff Ghost Breaker by Powell; Elliman, Nigel app.
... 55 · 165 · 331 · 580
4-Cartier c/a ... 73 · 219 · 455 · 800
5-7 ... 40 · 120 · 232 · 400
NOTE: *Maneely a-5, 7. Powell a-2-7; c-3, 5, 7.*

RED EAGLE
David McKay Publications: No. 16, Aug, 1938
Feature Books 16 ... 17 · 50 · 119 · 225

REDEYE (See Comics Reading Libraries in the Promotional Comics section)

RED FOX (Formerly Manhunt! #1-14; also see Extra Comics)
Magazine Enterprises: No. 15, 1954
15(A-1 #108)-Undercover Girl story; L.B. Cole-c/a (Red Fox);
r-from Manhunt; Powell-a ... 20 · 60 · 105 · 175

RED FURY
High Impact Entertainment: 1997 ($2.95, B&W)
1 ... 3.00

RED GOOSE COMIC SELECTIONS (See Comic Selections)

RED HAWK (See A-1 Comics, Bobby Benson's ..#14-16 & Straight Arrow #2)
Magazine Enterprises: No. 90, 1953
A-1 90-Powell-c/a ... 13 · 39 · 66 · 110

RED MASK (Formerly Tim Holt; see Best Comics, Blazing Six-Guns)
Magazine Enterprises/Sussex No. 54 (M.E. on-c): No. 42, June-July, 1954 - No. 53, May, 1956; No. 54, Sept, 1957
42-Ghost Rider by Ayers continues, ends #50; Black Phantom continues;
3-D effect c/stories begin ... 22 · 66 · 116 · 195
43- 3-D effect-c/stories ... 20 · 60 · 105 · 175
44-52: 3-D effect stories only. 47-Last pre-code issue. 50-Last Ghost Rider. 51-The Presto Kid begins by Ayers (1st app.); Presto Kid-c begins; last
3-D effect story. 52-Origin The Presto Kid ... 18 · 54 · 94 · 155
53,54-Last Black Phantom; last Presto Kid-c ... 14 · 42 · 72 · 120
I.W. Reprint #1 (r-/#52). 2 (nd, r/#51 w/diff.-c). 3, 8 (nd; Kinstler-c); 8-r/Red
Mask #52 ... 3 · 9 · 17 · 25
NOTE: *Ayers art on Ghost Rider & Presto Kid. Bolle art in all (Red Mask); c-43, 44, 49. Guardineer a-52. Black Phantom in #42-44, 47-50, 53, 54.*

REDMASK OF THE RIO GRANDE
AC Comics: 1990 ($2.50, 28pgs.)(Has photos of movie posters)
1-Bolle-a(r); photo inside-c ... 2.50

RED MOUNTAIN FEATURING QUANTRELL'S RAIDERS (Movie)(Also see Jesse James #28)
Avon Periodicals: 1952
nn-Alan Ladd; Kinstler-c ... 29 · 87 · 153 · 265

"RED" RABBIT COMICS
Dearfield Comic/J. Charles Laue Publ. Co.: Jan, 1947 - No. 22, Aug-Sep, 1951
1 ... 14 · 42 · 72 · 120
2 ... 8 · 24 · 42 · 60
3-10 ... 6 · 18 · 32 · 45
11-17,19-22 ... 6 · 18 · 29 · 40
18-Flying Saucer-c (1/51) ... 8 · 24 · 42 · 60

RED RAVEN COMICS (Human Torch #2 on)(Also see X-Men #44 & Sub-Mariner #26, 2nd series)
Timely Comics: August, 1940
1-Origin & 1st app. Red Raven; Comet Pierce & Mercury by Kirby, The
Human Top & The Eternal Brain; intro. Magar, the Mystic & only app.;
Kirby-c (his 1st signed work) ... 1038 · 3114 · 6747 · 13,500

RED ROCKET 7
Dark Horse Comics: Aug, 1997 - No. 7, June, 1998 ($3.95, square format, limited series)
1-7-Mike Allred-c/s/a ... 4.00

RED RYDER COMICS (Hi Spot #2)(Movies, radio)(See Crackajack Funnies & Super Book of Comics)
Hawley Publ. No. 1/Dell Publishing Co.(K.K.) No. 3 on: 9/40; No. 3, 8/41 - No. 5, 12/41; No. 6, 4/42 - No. 151, 4-6/57

1-Red Ryder, his horse Thunder, Little Beaver & his horse Papoose strip
reprints begin by Fred Harman; 1st meeting of Red & Little Beaver;
Harman line-drawn-c #1-85 ... 275 · 825 · 1925 · 3300
3-(Scarce)-Alley Oop, Capt. Easy, Dan Dunn, Freckles & His Friends, King of
the Royal Mtd., Myra North strip-r begin ... 92 · 275 · 644 · 1200
4-6: 6-1st Dell issue (4/42) ... 42 · 125 · 246 · 550
7-10 ... 34 · 102 · 238 · 400
11-20 ... 23 · 69 · 161 · 300
21-32-Last Alley Oop, Dan Dunn, Capt. Easy, Freckles
... 15 · 45 · 105 · 195
33-40 (52 pgs.) ... 10 · 30 · 70 · 135
41 (52 pgs.)-Rocky Lane photo back-c; photo back-c begin, end #57
... 11 · 33 · 77 · 140
42-46 (52 pgs.): 46-Last Red Ryder strip-r ... 9 · 27 · 63 · 110
47-53 (52 pgs.): 47-New stories on Red Ryder begin. 49,52-Harman photo
back-c ... 7 · 21 · 49 · 95
54-92: 54-73 (36 pgs.). 59-Harman photo back-c. 73-Last King of the Royal Mtd;
strip-r by Jim Gary. 74-85 (52 pgs.)-Harman line-drawn-c. 86-92 (52 pgs.)-
Harman painted-c ... 18 · 42 · 75
93-99,101-106: 94-96 (36 pgs.)-Harman painted-c. 97,98,107,108 (36 pgs.)-
Harman line-drawn-c. 99,101-106 (36 pgs.)-Jim Bannon Photo-c
... 5 · 15 · 35 · 60
100 (36 pgs.)-Bannon photo-c ... 5 · 15 · 35 · 65
109-118 (52 pgs.)-Harman line-drawn-c ... 5 · 15 · 34 · 55
119-129 (52 pgs.): 119-Painted-c begin, not by Harman, end #151
... 4 · 12 · 30 · 50
130-151 (36 pgs.): 145-Title change to Red Ryder Ranch Mag.
149-Title change to R.R. Ranch Comics ... 4 · 12 · 29 · 45
Four Color 916 (7/58) ... 4 · 12 · 29 · 45
NOTE: *Fred Harman a-1-99; c-1-98, 107-118. Don Red Barry, Allan Rocky Lane, Wild Bill Elliott & Jim Bannon starred as Red Ryder in the movies. Robert Blake starred as Little Beaver.*

RED RYDER PAINT BOOK
Whitman Publishing Co.: 1941 (8-1/2x11-1/2", 148 pgs.)
nn-Reprints 1940 daily strips ... 77 · 231 · 483 · 850

RED SEAL COMICS (Formerly Carnival Comics, and/or Spotlight Comics?)
Harry 'A' Chesler/Superior Publ. No. 19 on: No. 14, 10/45 - No. 18, 10/46; No. 19, 6/47 - No. 22, 12/47
14-The Black Dwarf begins (continued from Spotlight?); Little Nemo app.;
bondage/hypo-c; Tuska-a ... 73 · 219 · 455 · 800
15-Torture story; funny-c ... 47 · 140 · 286 · 500
16-Used in SOTI, pg. 181, illo "Outside the forbidden pages of the Sade, you
find draining a girl's blood only in children's comics;" drug club story r-later
in Crime Reporter #1; Veiled Avenger & Barry Kuda app.; Tuska-a; funny-c
... 62 · 185 · 388 · 685
17,18,20: Lady Satan, Yankee Girl & Sky Chief app. 17-Tuska-a
... 47 · 142 · 286 · 500
19-No Black Dwarf (on-c only); Zor, El Tigre app. ... 43 · 129 · 257 · 450
21-Lady Satan & Black Dwarf app. ... 37 · 111 · 197 · 340
22-Zor, Rocketman app. (68 pgs.) ... 37 · 111 · 197 · 340

REDSKIN (Thrilling Indian Stories)(Famous Western Badmen #13 on)
Youthful Magazines: Sept, 1950 - No. 12, Oct, 1952
1-Walter Johnson-a (7 pgs.) ... 17 · 51 · 88 · 150
2 ... 11 · 33 · 55 · 90
3-12: 3-Daniel Boone story. 6-Geronimo story ... 10 · 30 · 55 · 80
NOTE: *Walter Johnson c-3, 4. Palais a-11. Wildey a-5, 11. Bondage c-6, 12.*

RED SONJA (Also see Conan #23, Kull & The Barbarians, Marvel Feature & Savage Sword Of Conan #1)
Marvel Comics Group: 1/77 - No. 15, 5/79; V1#1, 2/83 - V2#2, 3/83; V3#1, 8/83 - V3#4, 2/84; V3#5, 1/85 - V3#13, 5/86
1-Created by Robert E. Howard ... 1 · 4 · 7 · 10
2-10: 5-Last 30¢ issue ... 6.00
4,5-(35¢-c variants, limited distribution)(7,9/77) ... 1 · 3 · 6 · 8
11-15, V1#1,V2#2: 14-Last 35¢ issue ... 5.00
V3#1-13: #1-4 ($1.00, 52 pgs.) ... 3.00
NOTE: *Brunner c-12-14. J. Buscema a(p)-12, 13, 15; c-V1#1. Nebres a-V3#3i(part). N. Redondo a-8i, V3#2i, 3i. Simonson a-V3#1. Thorne c/a-1-11.*

RED SONJA: SCAVENGER HUNT
Marvel Comics: Dec, 1995 ($2.95, one-shot)

The Red Star #4 © Christian Gossett

Reform School Girl! © AVON

Reggie's Wise Guy Jokes #40 © AP

	GD2.0	FN6.0	VF8.0	NM9.4
1				3.00

RED SONJA: THE MOVIE
Marvel Comics Group: Nov, 1985 - No. 2, Dec, 1985 (Limited series)

	GD2.0	FN6.0	VF8.0	NM9.4
1,2-Movie adapt-r/Marvel Super Spec. #38				3.00

RED STAR, THE
Image Comics: June, 2000 - Present ($2.95)

1-Christian Gossett-s/a(p)				4.00
2-7				3.00
#(7.5) Reprints Wizard #1/2 story with new pages				3.00
TPB (4/01, $24.95, 9x12") Oversized r/#1-4; intro. by Bendis				25.00
Wizard 1/2 (mail order)				10.00

RED TORNADO (See All-American #20 & Justice League of America #64)
DC Comics: July, 1985 - No. 4, Oct, 1985 (Limited series)

1-4: Kurt Busiek scripts in all. 1-3-Superman & Batman cameos				3.00

RED WARRIOR
Marvel/Atlas Comics (TCI): Jan, 1951 - No. 6, Dec, 1951

1-Red Warrior & his horse White Wing; Tuska-a	17	51	88	150
2-Tuska-c	10	30	55	80
3-6: 4-Origin White Wing. 6-Maneely-c	9	27	49	70

RED WOLF (See Avengers #80 & Marvel Spotlight #1)
Marvel Comics Group: May, 1972 - No. 9, Sept, 1973

1-(Western hero); Gil Kane/Severin-c; Shores-a	3	9	17	25
2-9: 2-Kane-c; Shores-a. 6-Tuska-r in back-up. 7-Red Wolf as super hero begins. 9-Origin sidekick, Lobo (wolf)	2	6	11	15

REESE'S PIECES
Eclipse Comics: Oct, 1985 - No.2, Oct, 1985 ($1.75, Baxter paper)

1,2-B&W-r in color				2.25

REFORM SCHOOL GIRL!
Realistic Comics: 1951

nn-Used in **SOTI**, pg. 358, & cover ill. with caption "Comic books are supposed to be like fairy tales"	150	450	938	1650

(Prices vary widely on this book)
NOTE: The cover and title originated from a digest-sized book published by Diversey Publishing Co. in Chicago in 1948. The original book "House of Fury", Doubleday, came out in 1941. The girl's real name which appears on the cover of the digest and comic is Marty Collins, Canadian model and ice skating star who posed for this special color photograph for the Diversey novel.

REGENTS ILLUSTRATED CLASSICS
Prentice Hall Regents, Englewood Cliffs, NJ 07632: 1981 (Plus more recent reprintings) (48 pgs., B&W-a with 14 pgs. of teaching helps)

NOTE: This series contains Classics Ill. art, and was produced from the same illegal source as Cassette Books. But when Twin Circle sued to stop the sale of the Cassette Books, they decided to permit this series to continue. This series was produced as a teaching aid. The 20 title series is divided into four levels based upon number of basic words used therein. There is a teacher's manual for each level. All of the titles are still available from the publisher for about $5 each retail. The number to call for mail order purchases is (201)767-5937. Almost all of the issues have new covers taken from some interior art panel. Here is a list of the series by Regents ident. no. and the Classics Ill. counterpart.

16770(Cl#24-A2)18333(Cl#3-A2)21668(Cl#13-A2)32224(Cl#21)33051(Cl#26)
35788(Cl#45)37153(Cl#16)44460(Cl#19-A2)44808(Cl#18-A2)52395(Cl#4-A2)
58627(Cl#5-A2)60067(Cl#30)68405(Cl#23-A1)70302(Cl#29)78192(Cl#7-A2)
78193(Cl#10-A2)79679(Cl#85)92046(Cl#1-A2)93062(Cl#64)93512(Cl#25)

RE: GEX
Awesome-Hyperwerks: Jul, 1998 - No. 0, Dec, 1998; ($2.50)

Preview (7/98) Wizard Con Edition				3.00
0-(12/98) Loeb-s/Liefeld-a/Pat Lee-c, 1-(9/98) Loeb-s/Liefeld-a/c				2.50

REGGIE (Formerly Archie's Rival...; Reggie & Me #19 on)
Archie Publications: No. 15, Sept, 1963 - No. 18, Nov, 1965

15(9/63), 16(10/64), 17(8/65), 18(11/65)	4	12	30	50

NOTE: Cover title No. 15 & 16 is Archie's Rival Reggie.

REGGIE AND ME (Formerly Reggie)
Archie Publ.: No. 19, Aug, 1966 - No. 126, Sept, 1980 (No. 50-68: 52 pgs.)

19-Evilheart app.	3	10	23	35
20-23-Evilheart app.; with Pureheart #22	3	9	17	25
24-40(3/70)	2	6	11	16
41-49(7/71)	2	6	10	14
50(9/71)-68 (1/74, 52 pgs.)	2	6	12	18

	GD2.0	FN6.0	VF8.0	NM9.4
69-99	1	3	6	8
100(10/77)	1	4	7	10
101-126				6.00

REGGIE'S JOKES (See Reggie's Wise Guy Jokes)

REGGIE'S REVENGE!
Archie Comic Publications, Inc.: Spring, 1994 - No. 3 ($2.00, 52 pgs.)
(Published semi-annually)

1-Bound-in pull-out poster				3.00
2,3				2.25

REGGIE'S WISE GUY JOKES
Archie Publications: Aug, 1968 - No. 60, Jan, 1982 (#5-28 are Giants)

1	4	12	30	50
2-4	2	6	15	22
5-16 (1/71)(68 pg. Giants)	3	9	19	28
17-28 (52 pg. Giants)	2	6	13	20
29-40(1/77)	1	3	6	9
41-60				5.00

REGISTERED NURSE
Charlton Comics: Summer, 1963

1-r/Nurse Betsy Crane & Cynthia Doyle	3	9	17	24

REG'LAR FELLERS
Visual Editions (Standard): No. 5, Nov, 1947 - No. 6, Mar, 1948

5,6	9	27	49	70

REG'LAR FELLERS HEROIC (See Heroic Comics)

REGULATORS
Image Comics: June, 1995 - No. 3, Aug, 1995 ($2.50)

1-3: Kurt Busiek scripts				2.50

REID FLEMING, WORLD'S TOUGHEST MILKMAN
Eclipse Comics/ Deep Sea Comics: 8/86; V2#1, 12/86 - V2#3, 12/88; V2#4, 11/89; V2#5, 11/90 (B&W)

1 (3rd print, large size, 8/86, $2.50), 1-4th & 5th printings ($2.50)				3.00
V2#1 (10/86, regular size, $2.00), 1-2nd print, 3rd print ($2.00, 2/89)				2.25
2-8 , V2#2-2nd & 3rd printings, V2#4-2nd printing, V2#5 ($2.00)				2.25

RELATIVE HEROES
DC Comics: Mar, 2000 - No. 6, Aug, 2000 ($2.50, limited series)

1-6-Grayson-s/Guichet & Sowd-a. 6-Superman-c/app.				2.50

RELUCTANT DRAGON, THE (Walt Disney's...)
Dell Publishing Co.: No. 13, 1940

Four Color 13-Contains 2 pgs. of photos from film; 2 pg. foreword to Fantasia by Leopold Stokowski; Donald Duck, Goofy, Baby Weems & Mickey Mouse (as the Sorcerer's Apprentice) app.	162	486	1134	2100

REMARKABLE WORLDS OF PROFESSOR PHINEAS B. FUDDLE, THE
DC Comics (Paradox Press): 2000 - No. 4, 2000 ($5.95, limited series)

1-4-Boaz Yakin-s/Erez Yakin-a				6.00
TPB (2001, $19.95) r/series				20.00

REMEMBER PEARL HARBOR
Street & Smith Publications: 1942 (68 pgs.) (Illustrated story of the battle)

nn-Uncle Sam-c; Jack Binder-art	45	135	270	475

REN & STIMPY SHOW, THE (TV) (Nickelodeon cartoon characters)
Marvel Comics: Dec, 1992 - No. 44, July, 1996 ($1.75/$1.95)

1-($2.25)-Polybagged w/scratch & sniff Ren or Stimpy air fowler (equal numbers of each were made)				6.00
1-2nd & 3rd printing; different dialogue on-c				2.25
2-6: 4-Muddy Mudskipper back-up. 5-Bill Wray painted-c. 6-Spider-Man vs. Powdered Toast Man				4.00
7-17: 12-1st solo back-up story w/Tank & Brenner				2.50
18-44: 18-Powered Toast Man app.				3.00
25 ($2.95) Deluxe edition w/die cut cover				3.00
...Don't Try This at Home (3/94, $12.95, TPB)-r/#9-12				13.00
...Eenteractive Special ('95, $2.95)				3.00
...Holiday Special 1994 (2/95, $2.95, 52 pgs.)				3.00
...Mini Comic (1995)				5.00
...Pick of the Litter nn (1993, $12.95, TPB)-r/#1-4				13.00

...Radio Daze (11/95, $1.95)			2.50
...Running Joke nn (1993, $12.95, TPB)-r/#1-4 plus new-a			13.00
...Seeck Little Monkeys (1/95, $12.95)-r/#17-20			13.00
...Special 2 (7/94, $2.95, 52 pgs.), ...Special 3 (10/94, $2.95, 52 pgs.)-Choose adventure, ...Special: Around the World in a Daze ($2.95), ...Special: Four Swerks (1/95, $2.95, 52 pgs.)-FF #1 cover swipe; cover reads "Four Swerks w/5 pg. coloring book.", ...Special: Powdered Toast Man 1 (4/94, $2.95, 52 pgs.), ...Special: Powdered Toast Man's Cereal Serial (4/95, $2.95), ...Special: Sports (10/95, $2.95)			3.00
...Tastes Like Chicken nn (11/93,$12.95,TPB)-r/#5-8			13.00
...Your Pals (1994, $12.95, TPB)-r/#13-16			13.00

RENFIELD
Caliber Press:1994 - No. 3, 1995 ($2.95, B&W, limited series)

1-3			3.00

RENO BROWNE, HOLLYWOOD'S GREATEST COWGIRL (Formerly Margie Comics; Apache Kid #53 on; also see Western Hearts, Western Life Romances & Western Love)
Marvel Comics (MPC): No. 50, April, 1950 - No. 52, Sept, 1950 (52 pgs.)

50-Reno Browne photo-c on all	34	102	179	310
51,52	29	87	153	265

REPLACEMENT GOD
Amaze Ink: June, 1995 - No. 8 ($2.95, B&W)

1-8-Zander Cannon-s/a			3.00

REPLACEMENT GOD
Image Comics: May, 1997 - No. 5 ($2.95, B&W)

1-5: 1-Flip book w/"Knute's Escapes", r/original series. 2-Flip book w/"Harris Thermidor". 3-5: 3-Flip book w/"Myth and Legend"			3.00

REPTILICUS (Becomes Reptisaurus #3 on)
Charlton Comics: Aug, 1961 - No. 2, Oct, 1961

1 (Movie)	19	57	134	240
2	10	30	70	120

REPTISAURUS (Reptilicus #1,2)
Charlton Comics: V2#3, Jan, 1962 - No. 8, Dec, 1962; Summer, 1963

V2#3-8: 8-Montes/Bache-c/a	7	21	50	80
Special Edition 1 (Summer, 1963)	6	18	45	75

REQUIEM FOR DRACULA
Marvel Comics: Feb, 1993 ($2.00, 52 pgs.)

nn-r/Tomb of Dracula #69,70 by Gene Colan			2.25

RESCUERS, THE (See Walt Disney Showcase #40)

RESIDENT EVIL (Based on video game)
Image Comics (WildStorm): Mar, 1998 - No. 5 ($4.95, quarterly magazine)

1			7.00
2-5			5.00
...Collection One ('99, $14.95, TPB) r/#1-4			15.00

RESIDENT EVIL: FIRE AND ICE
DC Comics (WildStorm): Dec, 2000 - No. 4, May, 2001 ($2.50, limited series)

1-4-Bermejo-c			2.50

RESTAURANT AT THE END OF THE UNIVERSE, THE (See Hitchhiker's Guide to the Galaxy & Life, the Universe & Everything)
DC Comics: 1994 - No. 3, 1994 ($6.95, limited series)

1-3			7.00

RESTLESS GUN (TV)
Dell Publishing Co.: No. 934, Sept, 1958 - No. 1146, Nov-Jan, 1960-61

Four Color 934 (#1)-Photo-c	12	36	84	150
Four Color 986 (5/59), 1045 (11-1/60), 1089 (3/60), 1146-Wildey-a; all photo-c	8	24	56	105

RESURRECTION MAN
DC Comics: May, 1997 - No. 27, Aug, 1999 ($2.50)

1-Lenticular disc on cover			5.00
2-5: 2-JLA app.			4.00
6-10: 6-Genesis-x-over. 7-Batman app. 10-Hitman-c/app.			3.00
11-27: 16,17-Supergirl x-over. 18-Deadman & Phantom Stranger-c/app.			

21-JLA-c/app			2.50
#1,000,000 (11/98) 853rd Century x-over			2.50

RETIEF (Keith Laumer's)
Adventure Comics (Malibu): Dec, 1989 - Vol. 2, No.6, ($2.25, B&W)

1-6,Vol. 2, #1-6,Vol. 3 (...of the CDT) #1-6			2.50
...and The Warlords #1-6, ...: Diplomatic Immunity #1 (4/91) ...: Giant Killer #1 (9/91), ...: Crime & Punishment #1 (11/91)			2.50

RETURN FROM WITCH MOUNTAIN (See Walt Disney Showcase #44)

RETURN OF ALISON DARE: LITTLE MISS ADVENTURES, THE (Also see Alison Dare: Little Miss Adventures)
Oni Press: Apr, 2001 - No. 3, Sept, 2001 ($2.95, B&W, limited series)

1-3-J. Torres-s/J.Bone-c/a			3.00

RETURN OF GORGO, THE (Formerly Gorgo's Revenge)
Charlton Comics: No. 2, Aug, 1963 - No. 3, Fall, 1964 (12¢)

2,3-Ditko-c/a; based on M.G.M. movie	8	24	56	90

RETURN OF KONGA, THE (Konga's Revenge #2 on)
Charlton Comics: 1962

nn	7	21	53	85

RETURN OF MEGATON MAN
Kitchen Sink Press: July, 1988 - No. 3, 1988 ($2.00, limited series)

1-3: Simpson-c/a			2.25

RETURN OF THE OUTLAW
Toby Press (Minoan): Feb, 1953 - No. 11, 1955

1-Billy the Kid	10	30	55	85
2	6	18	32	45
3-11	6	18	29	40

RETURN TO JURASSIC PARK
Topps Comics: Apr, 1995 - No. 9, Feb, 1996 ($2.50/$2.95)

1-9: 3-Begin $2.95-c. 9-Artist's Jam issue			3.00

RETURN TO THE AMALGAM AGE OF COMICS: THE MARVEL COMICS COLLECTION
Marvel Comics: 1997 ($12.95, TPB)

nn-Reprints Amalgam one-shots: Challengers of the Fantastic #1, The Exciting X-Patrol #1, Iron Lantern #1, The Magnetic Men Featuring Magneto #1, Spider-Boy Team-Up #1 & Thorion of the New Asgods #1			13.00

REVEALING LOVE STORIES (See Fox Giants)

REVEALING ROMANCES
Ace Magazines: Sept, 1949 - No. 6, Aug, 1950

1	10	30	55	80
2	6	18	29	40
3-6	5	15	25	35

REVENGE OF THE PROWLER (Also see The Prowler)
Eclipse Comics: Feb, 1988 - No. 4, June, 1988 ($1.75/$1.95)

1,3,4: 1-$1.75. 3,4-$1.95-c; Snyder III-a(p)			2.25
2 ($2.50)-Contains flexi-disc			2.50

REVENGERS FEATURING MEGALITH
Continuity Comics: Apr, 1985; 1987 - No. 6, 1989 ($2.00, Baxter paper)

1 (1985)-Origin; Neal Adams-c/a, scripts, 1-6 ('87-'89, newsstand)			2.25

REX ALLEN COMICS (Movie star)(Also see Four Color #877 & Western Roundup under Dell Giants)
Dell Publ. Co.: No. 316, Feb, 1951 - No. 31, Dec-Feb, 1958-59 (All-photo-c)

Four Color 316(#1)(52 pgs.)-Rex Allen & his horse Koko begin; Marsh-a	13	40	91	175
2 (9-11/51, 36 pgs.)	8	24	56	105
3-10	6	18	42	80
11-20	5	15	35	60
21-23,25-31	5	15	34	55
24-Toth-a	5	15	35	65

NOTE: *Manning* a-20, 27-30. Photo back-c F.C. #316, 2-12, 20, 21.

REX DEXTER OF MARS (See Mystery Men Comics)
Fox Features Syndicate: Fall, 1940 (68 pgs.)

Ribtickler #2 © FOX

Richie Rich #2 © HARV

Richie Rich and Billy Bellhops #1 © HARV

	GD2.0	FN6.0	VF8.0	NM9.4

1-Rex Dexter, Patty O'Day, & Zanzibar (Tuska-a) app.; Briefer-c/a

	GD2.0	FN6.0	VF8.0	NM9.4
	191	573	1194	2100

REX HART (Formerly Blaze Carson; Whip Wilson #9 on)
Timely/Marvel Comics (USA): No. 6, Aug, 1949 - No. 8, Feb, 1950 (All photo-c)

6-Rex Hart & his horse Warrior begin; Black Rider app; Captain Tootsie
by Beck

	28	84	151	260

7,8: 18 pg. Thriller in each. 8-Blaze the Wonder Collie app. in text

	19	57	99	170

REX MORGAN, M.D. (Also see Harvey Comics Library)
Argo Publ.: Dec, 1955 - No. 3, 1956

1-r/Rex Morgan daily newspaper strips & daily panel-r of "These Women" by D'Alessio & "Timeout" by Jeff Keate

	14	42	72	120
2,3	10	30	55	80

REX THE WONDER DOG (See The Adventures of...)

RHUBARB, THE MILLIONAIRE CAT
Dell Publishing Co.: No. 423, Sept-Oct, 1952 - No. 563, June, 1954

Four Color 423 (#1)	5	15	35	60
Four Color 466(5/53),563	4	12	30	50

RIB
Dilemma Productions: Oct, 1995 - April, 1996 ($1.95, B&W)

Ashcan, 1				3.00

RIB
Bookmark Productions: 1996 ($2.95, B&W)

1-Sakai-c; Andrew Ford-s/a				3.00

RIB
Caliber Comics: May, 1997 - No. 5, 1998 ($2.95, B&W)

1-5: 1-"Beginnings" pts. 1 & 2				3.00

RIBIT!
Comico: Jan, 1989 - No. 4, April?, 1989 ($1.95, limited series)

1-4: Frank Thorne-c/a/scripts				2.25

RIBTICKLER (Also see Fox Giants)
Fox Feature Synd./Green Publ. (1957)/Norlen (1959): 1945 - No. 9, Aug, 1947; 1957; 1959

1-Funny animal	16	48	83	140
2-(1946)	9	27	49	70
3-9: 3,7-Cosmo Cat app.	7	21	38	55
3,7,8 (Green Publ.-1957), 3,7,8 (Norlen Mag.-1959)	3	9	17	25

RICHARD DRAGON, KUNG-FU FIGHTER (See The Batman Chronicles #5, Brave & the Bold, & The Question)
National Periodical Publ./DC Comics: Apr-May, 1975 - No. 18, Nov-Dec, 1977

1-Intro Richard Dragon, Ben Stanley & O-Sensei; 1st app. Barney Ling; adaptation of Jim Dennis novel "Dragon's Fists" begins, ends #4

	2	6	11	15

2,3: 2-Intro Carolyn Woosan; Starlin/Weiss-c/a; bondage-c. 3-Kirby-a(p); Giordano bondage-c

	1	4	7	10

4-8-Wood inks. 4-Carolyn Woosan dies. 5-1st app. Lady Shiva

	1	3	5	7

9-13,15-18: 9-Ben Stanley becomes Ben Turner; intro Preying Mantis. 16-1st app. Prof Ojo. 18-1st app. Ben Turner as The Bronze Tiger

	1	3	5	7

14-"Spirit of Bruce Lee"

	2	6	9	12

NOTE: *Buckler* a-14. c-15, 18. *Chua* c-13. *Estrada* a-9, 13-18. *Estrada/Abel* a-10-12. *Estrada/Wood* a-4-8. *Giordano* c-1, 3-11. *Weiss* a-2(partial) c-2i.

RICHARD THE LION-HEARTED (See Ideal a Classical Comic)

RICHIE RICH (See Harvey Collectors Comics, Harvey Hits, Little Dot, Little Lotta, Little Sad Sack, Million Dollar Digest, Mutt & Jeff, Super Richie, and 3-D Dolly)

RICHIE RICH (...the Poor Little Rich Boy) (See Harvey Hits #3, 9)
Harvey Publ.: Nov, 1960 - #218, Oct, 1982; #219, Oct, 1986 - #254, Jan, 1991

1-(See Little Dot for 1st app.)	145	435	1015	1800
2	50	150	350	650
3-5	30	90	210	375
6-10: 8-Christmas-c	18	55	126	225
11-20	12	36	84	140

	GD2.0	FN6.0	VF8.0	NM9.4
21-30	8	25	60	100
31-40	7	21	53	85
41-50: 42(10/67)-Flying saucer-c	5	15	38	60
51-55,57-60: 59-Buck, prototype of Dollar the Dog	4	12	29	45
56-1st app. Super Richie	5	15	34	55
61-64,66-80: 71-Nixon & Robert Kennedy caricatures	3	9	20	30
65-1st app. Dollar the Dog	4	12	30	50
81-99	2	6	15	22
100(12/70)-1st app. Irona the robot maid	3	9	20	30
101-111,117-120	2	6	11	16
112-116: All 52 pg. Giants	2	6	15	22
121-140: 137-1st app. Mr. Cheepers	1	4	7	10
141-160: 145-Infinity-c. 155-3rd app. The Money Monster				
	1	3	6	8
161-180	1	3	5	7
181-199				6.00
200	1	3	6	8
201-218: 210-Stone-Age Riches app				5.00
219-254: 237-Last original material				4.00

RICHIE RICH
Harvey Comics: Mar, 1991 - No. 28, Nov, 1994 ($1.00, bi-monthly)

1-28: Reprints best of Richie Rich				2.50
Giant Size 1-4 (10/91-10/93, $2.25, 68 pgs.)				3.00

RICHIE RICH ADVENTURE DIGEST MAGAZINE
Harvey Comics: 1992 - No. 7, Sept, 1994 ($1.25, quarterly, digest-size)

1-7				4.00

RICHIE RICH AND...
Harvey Comics: Oct, 1987 - No. 11, May, 1990 ($1.00)

1-Professore Keenbean				4.00
2-11: 2-Casper. 3-Dollar the Dog. 4-Cadbury. 5 Mayda Munny. 6-Irona. 7-Little Dot. 8-Professor Keenbean. 9-Little Audrey. 10-Mayda Munny. 11-Cadbury.				
				3.00

RICHIE RICH AND BILLY BELLHOPS
Harvey Publications: Oct, 1977 (52 pgs., one-shot)

1	2	6	10	14

RICHIE RICH AND CADBURY
Harvey Publ.: 10/77; #2, 9/78 - #23, 7/82; #24, 7/90 - #29, 1/91 (1-10: 52pgs.)

1-(52 pg. Giant)	2	6	12	18
2-10-(52 pg. Giant)	1	4	7	10
11-23				5.00
24-29: 24-Begin $1.00-c				3.00

RICHIE RICH AND CASPER
Harvey Publications: Aug, 1974 - No. 45, Sept, 1982

1	3	9	20	30
2-5	2	6	12	18
6-10: 10-Xmas-c	2	6	9	12
11-20	1	3	5	7
21-45: 22-Xmas-c				5.00

RICHIE RICH AND DOLLAR THE DOG (See Richie Rich #65)
Harvey Publications: Sept, 1977 - No. 24, Aug, 1982 (#1-10: 52 pgs.)

1-(52 pg. Giant)	2	6	11	16
2-10-(52 pg. Giant)	1	4	7	10
11-24				4.00

RICHIE RICH AND DOT
Harvey Publications: Oct, 1974 (one-shot)

1	2	6	15	22

RICHIE RICH AND GLORIA
Harvey Publications: Sept, 1977 - No. 25, Sept, 1982 (#1-11: 52 pgs.)

1-(52 pg. Giant)	2	6	11	16
2-11-(52 pg. Giant)	1	4	7	10
12-25				4.00

RICHIE RICH AND HIS GIRLFRIENDS
Harvey Publications: April, 1979 - No. 16, Dec, 1982

1-(52 pg. Giant)	2	6	11	16

	GD2.0	FN6.0	VF8.0	NM9.4

	GD2.0	FN6.0	VF8.0	NM9.4
2-(52 pg. Giant)	1	4	7	10
3-10				6.00
11-16				4.00

RICHIE RICH AND HIS MEAN COUSIN REGGIE
Harvey Publications: April, 1979 - No. 3, 1980 (50¢) (#1,2: 52 pgs.)

1	2	6	9	12
2-3:	1	3	5	7

NOTE: No. 4 was advertised, but never released.

RICHIE RICH AND JACKIE JOKERS (Also see Jackie Jokers)
Harvey Publications: Nov, 1973 - No. 48, Dec, 1982

1: 52 pg. Giant; contains material from unpublished Jackie Jokers #5

	4	12	29	45
2,3-(52 pg. Giants). 2-R.R. & Jackie 1st meet	3	9	17	25
4,5	2	6	11	16
6-10	1	4	7	10
11-20,26: 11-1st app. Kool Katz. 26-Star Wars parody	1	3	6	8
21-25,27-40				5.00
41-48				4.00

RICHIE RICH AND PROFESSOR KEENBEAN
Harvey Comics: Sept, 1990 - No. 2, Nov, 1990 ($1.00)

1,2				3.00

RICHIE RICH AND THE NEW KIDS ON THE BLOCK
Harvey Publications: Feb, 1991 - No. 3, June, 1991 ($1.25, bi-monthly)

1-3: 1,2-New Richie Rich stories				3.00

RICHIE RICH AND TIMMY TIME
Harvey Publications: Sept, 1977 (50¢, 52 pgs, one-shot)

1	2	6	9	12

RICHIE RICH BANK BOOKS
Harvey Publications: Oct, 1972 - No. 59, Sept, 1982

1	4	12	30	50
2-5: 2-2nd app. The Money Monster	3	9	19	28
6-10	2	6	12	18
11-20: 18-Super Richie app.	2	6	9	12
21-30	1	3	6	8
31-40				5.00
41-59				4.00

RICHIE RICH BEST OF THE YEARS
Harvey Publications: Oct, 1977 - No. 6, June, 1980 (128 pgs., digest-size)

1(10/77)-Reprints	2	6	10	14
2-6(11/79-6/80, 95¢). #2(10/78)-Rep.. #3(6/79, 75¢)	1	3	6	9

RICHIE RICH BIG BOOK
Harvey Publications: Nov, 1992 - No. 2, May, 1993 ($1.50, 52 pgs.)

1,2				3.00

RICHIE RICH BIG BUCKS
Harvey Publications: Apr, 1991 - No. 8, July, 1992 ($1.00, bi-monthly)

1-8				3.00

RICHIE RICH BILLIONS
Harvey Publications: Oct, 1974 - No. 48, Oct, 1982 (#1-33: 52 pgs.)

1	4	12	26	40
2-5	2	6	15	22
6-10	2	6	11	15
11-20	1	4	7	10
21-33	1	3	5	7
34-48: 35-Onion app.				4.00

RICHIE RICH CASH
Harvey Publications: Sept, 1974 - No. 47, Aug, 1982

1-1st app. Dr. N-R-Gee	3	10	23	35
2-5	2	6	13	20
6-10	2	6	11	15
11-20	1	4	7	10
21-30				6.00
31-47: 33-Dr. Blemish app.				4.00

RICHIE RICH CASH MONEY

RICHIE RICH (Harvey Comics: May, 1992 - No. 2, Aug, 1992 ($1.25))

Harvey Comics: May, 1992 - No. 2, Aug, 1992 ($1.25)

1,2				3.00

RICHIE RICH COLLECTORS COMICS (See Harvey Collectors Comics)

RICHIE RICH DIAMONDS
Harvey Publications: Aug, 1972 - No. 59, Aug, 1982 (#1, 23-45: 52 pgs.)

1-(52 pg. Giant)	5	15	38	60
2-5	3	9	17	25
6-10	2	6	11	15
11-22	1	3	6	9
23-30-(52 pg. Giants)	2	6	9	12
31-45: 39-r/Origin Little Dot	1	3	5	7
46-50				5.00
51-59				4.00

RICHIE RICH DIGEST
Harvey Publications: Oct, 1986 - No. 42, Oct, 1994 ($1.25/$1.75, digest-size)

1	1	3	6	8
2-10				5.00
11-20				4.00
21-42				3.00

RICHIE RICH DIGEST STORIES (...Magazine #?-on)
Harvey Publications: Oct, 1977 - No., 17, Oct, 1982 (75¢/95¢, digest-size)

1-Reprints	2	6	9	12
2-10: Reprints	1	3	5	7
11-17: Reprints				5.00

RICHIE RICH DIGEST WINNERS
Harvey Publications: Dec, 1977 - No. 16, Sept, 1982 (75¢/95¢, 132 pgs., digest-size)

1	2	6	9	12
2-5	1	3	5	7
6-16				5.00

RICHIE RICH DOLLARS & CENTS
Harvey Publications: Aug, 1963 - No. 109, Aug, 1982 (#1-43: 68 pgs.; 44-60, 71-94: 52 pgs.)

1: (#1-64 are all reprint issues)	16	48	112	200
2	8	24	60	100
3-5: 5-r/1st app. of R.R. from Little Dot #1	5	15	38	60
6-10	4	12	26	40
11-20	3	9	21	32
21-30: 25-r/1st app. Nurse Jenny (Little Lotta #62)	3	9	17	24
31-43: 43-Last 68 pg. issue	2	6	12	18
44-60: All 52 pgs.	2	6	11	15
61-71	1	3	6	8
72-94: All 52 pgs.	2	6	9	12
95-99,101-109				5.00
100-Anniversary issue	1	3	5	7

RICHIE RICH FORTUNES
Harvey Publications: Sept, 1971 - No. 63, July, 1982 (#1-15: 52 pgs.)

1	5	15	38	60
2-5	3	9	30	30
6-10	2	6	13	20
11-15: 11-r/1st app. The Onion	2	6	10	14
16-30	1	3	5	7
31-40				5.00
41-63: 62-Onion app.				4.00

RICHIE RICH GEMS
Harvey Publications: Sept, 1974 - No. 43, Sept, 1982

1	4	12	26	40
2-5	2	6	13	20
6-10	2	6	9	12
11-20	1	3	5	7
21-30				5.00
31-43: 36-Dr. Blemish, Onion app. 38-1st app. Stone-Age Riches				4.00

RICHIE RICH GOLD AND SILVER
Harvey Publications: Sept, 1975 - No. 42, Oct, 1982 (#1-27: 52 pgs.)

1	3	9	19	28

Richie Rich Millions #14 © HARV

Richie Rich Money World #3 © HARV

Richie Rich Success Stories #66 © HARV

	GD2.0	FN6.0	VF8.0	NM9.4			GD2.0	FN6.0	VF8.0	NM9.4

2-5	2	6	11	15					
6-10	1	4	7	10					
11-27	1	3	6	8					
28-42: 34-Stone-Age Riches app.				4.00					

RICHIE RICH GOLD NUGGETS DIGEST
Harvey Publications: Feb., 1991 - No. 4, June, 1991 ($1.75, digest-size)

1-4				3.00

RICHIE RICH HOLIDAY DIGEST MAGAZINE (...Digest #4)
Harvey Publications: Jan, 1980 - #3, Jan, 1982; #4, 3/88; #5, 2/89 (annual)

1-X-Mas-c	1	4	7	10
2-5: 2,3: All X-Mas-c. 4-(3/88, $1.25), 5-(2/89, $1.75)	1	3	5	7

RICHIE RICH INVENTIONS
Harvey Publications: Oct, 1977 - No. 26, Oct, 1982 (#1-11: 52 pgs.)

1	2	6	10	14
2-5	1	3	6	8
6-11				6.00
12-26				4.00

RICHIE RICH JACKPOTS
Harvey Publications: Oct, 1972 - No. 58, Aug, 1982 (#41-43: 52 pgs.)

1	5	15	38	60
2-5	3	9	17	25
6-10	2	6	11	16
11-15,17-20	1	4	7	10
16-Super Richie app.	2	6	9	12
21-30	1	3	5	7
31-40,44-50: 37-Caricatures of Frank Sinatra, Dean Martin, Sammy Davis, Jr.				
45-Dr. Blemish app.				6.00
41-43 (52 pgs.)	1	3	6	9
51-58				4.00

RICHIE RICH MILLION DOLLAR DIGEST (...Magazine #?-on)(See Million Dollar Digest)
Harvey Publications: Oct, 1980 - No. 10, Oct, 1982 ($1.50)

1	1	4	7	10
2-10				6.00

RICHIE RICH MILLIONS
Harvey Publ.: 9/61; #2, 9/62 - #113, 10/82 (#1-48: 68 pgs.; 49-64, 85-97: 52 pgs.)

1: (#1-3 are all reprint issues)	19	57	132	235
2	10	30	70	120
3-10: All other giants are new & reprints. 5-1st 15 pg. Richie Rich story	9	27	63	105
11-20	5	15	34	55
21-30	4	12	26	40
31-48: 31-1st app. The Onion. 48-Last 68 pg. Giant	3	9	17	24
49-64: 52 pg. Giants	2	6	11	16
65-67,69-73,75-84	1	3	6	8
68-1st Super Richie-c (11/74)	2	6	11	16
74-1st app. Mr. Woody; Super Richie app.	1	4	7	10
85-97: 52 pg. Giants	1	4	7	10
98,99				5.00
100				6.00
101-113				4.00

RICHIE RICH MONEY WORLD
Harvey Publications: Sept, 1972 - No. 59, Sept, 1982

1-(52 pg. Giant)-1st app. Mayda Munny	6	18	42	70
2-Super Richie app.	3	9	20	30
3-5	2	6	15	22
6-10: 9,10-Richie Rich mistakenly named Little Lotta on covers	2	6	11	15
11-20: 16,20-Dr. N-R-Gee	1	3	6	9
21-30	1	3	5	7
31-50				5.00
51-59				4.00
Digest 1 (2/91, $1.75)				5.00
2-8 (12/93, $1.75)				3.00

RICHIE RICH PROFITS

Harvey Publications: Oct, 1974 - No. 47, Sept, 1982

1	4	12	26	40
2-5	2	6	12	18
6-10: 10-Origin of Dr. N-R-Gee	1	4	7	10
11-20: 15-Christmas-c	1	3	5	7
21-30				5.00
31-47				4.00

RICHIE RICH RELICS
Harvey Comics: Jan, 1988 - No.4, Feb, 1989 (75¢/$1.00, reprints)

1-4				3.00

RICHIE RICH RICHES
Harvey Publications: July, 1972 - No. 59, Aug, 1982 (#1, 2, 41-45: 52 pgs.)

1-(52 pg. Giant)-1st app. The Money Monster	5	15	38	60
2-(52 pg. Giant)	3	9	20	30
3-5	2	6	12	18
6-10	2	6	10	14
11-20: 17-Super Richie app. (3/75)	1	3	6	9
21-40	1	3	5	7
41-45: 52 pg. Giants	1	3	6	9
46-59: 56-Dr. Blemish app.				4.00

RICHIE RICH SUCCESS STORIES
Harvey Publications: Nov, 1964 - No. 105, Sept, 1982 (#1-38: 68 pgs., 39-55, 67-90: 52 pgs.)

1	18	54	123	220
2-5	9	27	63	105
6-10	5	15	34	55
11-20	4	12	29	45
21-30: 27-1st Penny Van Dough (8/69)	3	9	20	30
31-38: 38-Last 68 pg. Giant	3	9	17	24
39-55-(52 pgs.): 44-Super Richie app.	2	6	12	18
56-66	1	3	6	9
67-90: 52 pgs.	2	6	9	12
91-105: 91-Onion app. 101-Dr. Blemish app.				5.00

RICHIE RICH SUMMER BONANZA
Harvey Comics: Oct, 1991 ($1.95, one-shot, 68 pgs.)

1-Richie Rich, Little Dot, Little Lotta				3.00

RICHIE RICH TREASURE CHEST DIGEST (...Magazine #3)
Harvey Publications: Apr, 1982 - No. 3, Aug, 1982 (95¢, Digest Mag.)
(#4 advertised but not publ.)

1	1	3	6	8
2,3				6.00

RICHIE RICH VACATION DIGEST
Harvey Comics: Oct, 1991; Oct, 1992; Oct, 1993 ($1.75, digest-size)

1-(10/91), 1-(10/92), 1-(10/93)				4.00

RICHIE RICH VACATIONS DIGEST
Harvey Publ.: 11/77; No. 2, 10/78 - No. 7, 10/81; No. 8, 8/82; (Digest, 132 pgs.)

1-Reprints	2	6	9	12
2-8	1	3	5	7

RICHIE RICH VAULT OF MYSTERY
Harvey Publications: Nov, 1974 - No. 47, Sept, 1982

1	3	9	20	30
2-10	2	6	11	15
11-20	1	3	6	8
21-30				5.00
31-47				4.00

RICHIE RICH ZILLIONZ
Harvey Publ.: Oct, 1976 - No. 33, Sept, 1982 (#1-4: 68 pgs.; #5-18: 52 pgs.)

1	3	9	20	30
2-4: 4-Last 68 pg. Giant	2	6	12	18
5-10	1	4	7	10
11-18: 18-Last 52 pg. Giant	1	3	5	7
19-33				4.00

RICK GEARY'S WONDERS AND ODDITIES
Dark Horse Comics: Dec, 1988 ($2.00, B&W, one-shot)

Ring of the Nibelung V1 #1 © P. Craig Russell

Riot #1 © MAR

Ripclaw V2 #2 © TCOW

	GD2.0	FN6.0	VF8.0	NM9.4

1 2.25

RICKY
Standard Comics (Visual Editions): No. 5, Sept, 1953

5-Teenage humor	5	15	24	32

RICKY NELSON (TV)(See Sweethearts V2#42)
Dell Publishing Co.: No. 956, Dec, 1958 - No. 1192, June, 1961 (All photo-c)

Four Color 956,998	19	57	133	245
Four Color 1115	15	45	105	190
Four Color 1192-Manning-a	15	45	105	190

RIDER, THE (Frontier Trail #6; also see Blazing Sixguns I.W. Reprint #10, 11)
Ajax/Farrell Publ. (Four Star Comic Corp.): Mar, 1957 - No. 5, 1958

1-Swift Arrow, Lone Rider begin	13	39	66	110
2-5	7	21	38	55

RIDERS OF THE PURPLE SAGE (See Zane Grey & Four Color #372)

RIFLEMAN, THE (TV)
Dell Publ. Co./Gold Key No. 13 on: No. 1009, 7-9/59 - No. 12, 7-9/62; No. 13, 11/62 - No. 20, 10/64

Four Color 1009 (#1)	25	75	175	320
2 (1-3/60)	12	36	84	160
3-Toth-a (4 pgs.)	12	36	84	160
4-10: 6-Toth-a (4 pgs.)	10	30	70	135
11-20	7	24	56	100

NOTE: Warren Tufts a-2-9. All have Chuck Connors photo-c. Photo back c-13-15.

RIMA, THE JUNGLE GIRL
National Periodical Publications: Apr-May, 1974 - No. 7, Apr-May, 1975

1-Origin, part 1 (#1-5: 20¢; 6,7: 25¢)	2	6	11	15
2-7: 2-4-Origin, parts 2-4. 7-Origin & only app. Space Marshal	1	3	6	8

NOTE: Kubert c-1-7. Nino a-1-7. Redondo a-1-7.

RING OF BRIGHT WATER (See Movie Classics)

RING OF THE NIBELUNG, THE
DC Comics: 1989 - No. 4, 1990 ($4.95, squarebound, 52 pgs., mature readers)

1-4: Adapts novel, Gil Kane-c/a				5.00

RING OF THE NIBELUNG, THE
Dark Horse Comics: Feb, 2000 - Sept, 2001 ($2.95/$2.99/$5.99, limited series)

Vol. 1 (The Rhinegold) 1-4: Adapts Wagner; P. Craig Russell s/a				3.00
Vol. 2 (The Valkyrie) 1-3: 1-(8/00), Vol. 3 (Siegfried) 1-3: 1-(12/00)				3.00
Vol. 4 (The Twilight of the Gods) 1-3: 1-(6/01)				3.00
4-(9/01, $5.99, 64 pgs.) Conclusion with sketch pages				6.00

RINGO KID, THE (2nd Series)
Marvel Comics Group: Jan, 1970 - No. 23, Nov, 1973; No. 24, Nov, 1975 - No. 30, Nov, 1976

1-Williamson-a r-from #10, 1956.	3	9	20	30
2-11: 2-Severin-c. 11-Last 15¢ issue	2	6	11	16
12 (52 pg. Giant)	3	9	17	24
13-20: 13-Wildey-r. 20-Williamson-r/#1	2	6	9	12
21-30	1	3	6	9
27,28-(30¢-c variant, limited distribution)(5,7/76)	2	6	10	14

RINGO KID WESTERN, THE (1st Series) (See Wild Western & Western Trails)
Atlas Comics (HPC)/Marvel Comics: Aug, 1954 - No. 21, Sept, 1957

1-Origin; The Ringo Kid begins	31	93	165	285
2-Black Rider app.; origin/1st app. Ringo's Horse Arab	16	48	83	140
3-5	11	33	55	90
6-8-Severin-a(3) each	12	36	61	100
9,11,12,14-21: 12-Orlando-a (4 pgs.)	9	27	49	70
10,13-Williamson-a (4 pgs.)	10	30	55	80

NOTE: Berg a-8. Maneely a-1-5, 15, 16(text illos only); 17(4), 18, 20, 21; c-1-6, 8, 13, 15-18, 20. J. Severin c-10, 11. Sinnott a-1. Wildey a-16-18.

RIN TIN TIN (See March of Comics #163,180,195)

RIN TIN TIN (TV) (...& Rusty #21 on; see Western Roundup under Dell Giants)
Dell Publishing Co./Gold Key: Nov, 1952 - No. 38, May-July, 1961; Nov, 1963 (All Photo-c)

	GD2.0	FN6.0	VF8.0	NM9.4
Four Color 434 (#1)	15	45	105	200
Four Color 476,523	8	24	56	100
4(3-5/54)-10	6	18	42	80
11-20	5	15	35	65
21-38: 36-Toth-a (4 pgs.)	4	12	30	50
... & Rusty 1 (11/63-Gold Key)	5	15	35	65

RIO (Also see Eclipse Monthly)
Comico: June, 1987 ($8.95, 64 pgs.)

1-Wildey-c/a				9.00

RIO AT BAY
Dark Horse Comics: July, 1992 - No. 2, Aug, 1992 ($2.95, limited series)

1,2-Wildey-c/a				3.00

RIO BRAVO (Movie) (See 4-Color #1018)
Dell Publishing Co.: June, 1959

Four Color 1018-Toth-a; John Wayne, Dean Martin, & Ricky Nelson photo-c.	23	69	161	300

RIO CONCHOS (See Movie Comics)

RIOT (Satire)
Atlas Comics (ACI No. 1-5/WPI No. 6): Apr, 1954 - No. 3, Aug, 1954; No. 4, Feb, 1956 - No. 6, June, 1956

1-Russ Heath-a	31	93	165	285
2-Li'l Abner satire by Post	23	69	121	205
3-Last precode (8/54)	20	60	105	175
4-Infinity-c; Marilyn Monroe "7 Year Itch" movie satire; Mad Rip-off ads	26	78	139	240
5-Marilyn Monroe, John Wayne parody; part photo-c	27	81	145	250
6-Lorna of the Jungle satire by Everett; Dennis the Menace satire-c/story; part photo-c	20	60	105	175

NOTE: Berg a-3. Burgos c-1, 2. Colan a-1. Everett a-1, 4, 6. Heath a-1. Maneely a-1, 2, 4-6; c-3, 4, 6. Post a-1-4. Reinman a-2. Severin a-4-6.

RIOT GEAR
Triumphant Comics: Sept, 1993 - No. 11, July, 1994 ($2.50, serially numbered)

1-11: 1-2nd app. Riot Gear. 2-1st app. Rabin. 3,4-Triumphant Unleashed x-over. 3-1st app. Surzar. 4-Death of Captain Tich				2.50
Violent Past 1,2: 1-(2/94, $2.50)				2.50

R.I.P.
TSR, Inc.:1990 - No. 8, 1991 ($2.95, 44 pgs.)

1-8-Based on TSR game				3.00

RIPCLAW (See Cyberforce)
Image Comics (Top Cow Prod.): Apr, 1995 - No. 3, June, 1995 (Limited series)

1/2-Gold, 1/2-San Diego ed., 1/2-Chicago ed.	1	4	7	10
1-3: Brandon Peterson-a(p)				3.00
Special 1 (10/95, $2.50)				2.50

RIPCLAW
Image Comics (Top Cow Prod.): V2#1, Dec, 1995 - No. 6, June, 1996 ($2.50)

V2#1-6: 5-Medieval Spawn/Witchblade Preview				2.50

RIPCORD (TV)
Dell Publishing Co.: Mar-May, 1962

Four Color 1294	7	21	49	90

R.I.P.D.
Dark Horse Comics: Oct, 1999 - No. 4, Jan, 2000 ($2.95, limited series)

1-4				3.00

RIPFIRE
Malibu Comics (Ultraverse): No. 0, Apr, 1995 ($2.50, one-shot)

0				2.50

RIP HUNTER TIME MASTER (See Showcase #20, 21, 25, 26 & Time Masters)
National Periodical Publications: Mar-Apr, 1961 - No. 29, Nov-Dec, 1965

1-(3-4/61)	48	144	386	700
2	26	78	179	320
3-5: 5-Last 10¢ issue	15	45	105	180
6,7-Toth-a in each	10	30	73	125
8-15	8	24	56	90

Rip Hunter Time Master #29 © DC

Rising Stars #9 © J. Michael Straczynski

Robin Annual #4 © DC

	GD2.0	FN6.0	VF8.0	NM9.4
16-20: 20-Hitler c/s	6	18	45	75
21-29: 29-Gil Kane-c	5	15	38	60

RIP IN TIME (Also see Teenage Mutant Ninja Turtles #5-7)
Fantagor Press: Aug, 1986 - No.5, 1987 ($1.50, B&W)

1-5: Corben-c/a in all				3.00

RIP KIRBY (Also see Harvey Comics Hits #57, & Street Comix)
David McKay Publications: 1948

Feature Books 51,54: Raymond-c; 51-Origin	35	105	185	320

RIPLEY'S BELIEVE IT OR NOT! (See Ace Comics, All-American Comics, Mystery Comics Digest #1, 4, 7, 10, 13, 16, 19, 22, 25)

RIPLEY'S BELIEVE IT OR NOT!
Harvey Publications: Sept, 1953 - No. 4, March, 1954

1-Powell-a	14	42	72	120
2-4	10	30	55	80

RIPLEY'S BELIEVE IT OR NOT! (Formerly ...True War Stories)
Gold Key: No. 4, April, 1967 - No. 94, Feb, 1980

4-Photo-c; McWilliams-a	3	10	23	35
5-Subtitled "True War Stories"; Evans-a; 1st Jeff Jones-a in comics? (2 pgs.)	3	10	23	35
6-10: 6-McWilliams-a. 10-Evans-a(2)	3	9	21	32
11-20: 15-Evans-a	3	9	17	25
21-30	2	6	12	18
31-38,40-60	2	6	10	14
39-Crandall-a	2	6	11	16
61-73	1	3	6	9
74,77-83-(52 pgs.)	2	6	9	12
75,76,84-94	1	3	5	7
Story Digest Mag. 1(6/70)-4-3/4x6-1/2", 148pp.	5	15	34	55

NOTE: *Evanish art by Luiz Dominguez #22-25, 27, 30, 31, 40. Jeff Jones a-5(2 pgs.). McWilliams a-65, 66, 70, 89. Orlando a-8. Sparling c-68. Reprints-74, 77-84, 87 (part); 91, 93 (all). Williamson, Wood a-80r/#1.*

RIPLEY'S BELIEVE IT OR NOT! TRUE GHOST STORIES (Becomes ...True War Stories) (See Dan Curtis)
Gold Key: June, 1965 - No. 2, Oct, 1966

1-Williamson, Wood & Evans-a; photo-c	6	18	42	70
2-Orlando, McWilliams-a; photo-c	4	12	26	40
Mini-Comic 1(1976-3-1/4x6-1/2")	2	6	9	12
11186(1977)-Golden Press, ($1.95, 224 pgs.)-All-r	3	10	23	35
11401(3/79)-Golden Press, ($1.00, 96 pgs.)-All-r	2	6	13	20

RIPLEY'S BELIEVE IT OR NOT! TRUE WAR STORIES (Formerly ...True Ghost Stories; becomes Ripley's Believe it or Not! #4 on)
Gold Key: Nov, 1966

1(#3)-No Williamson-a	3	10	23	35

RIPLEY'S BELIEVE IT OR NOT! TRUE WEIRD
Ripley Enterprises: June, 1966 - No. 2, Aug, 1966 (B&W Magazine)

1,2-Comic stories & text	3	9	17	25

RIPTIDE
Image Comics: Sep, 1995 - No. 2, Oct, 1995 ($2.50, limited series)

1,2- Rob Liefeld-c				2.50

RISE OF APOCALYPSE
Marvel Comics: Oct, 1996 - No. 4, Jan, 1997 ($1.95, limited series)

1-4: Adam Pollina-c/a				2.25

RISING STARS
Image Comics(Top Cow): Mar, 1999 - Present ($2.50)

Preview-(3/99, $5.00) Straczynski-s				6.00
0-(6/00, $2.50) Gary Frank-a/c				2.50
1/2-(8/01, $2.95) Anderson-c; art & sketch pages by Zanier				3.00
1-Four covers; Keu Cha-c/a				4.00
1-($10.00) Gold Editions-four covers				10.00
1-($50.00) Holofoil-c				50.00
2-4				2.50
5-16: 5-13-Zanier & Lashley-a(p). 14-Immonen-a. 15-Flip book B&W preview of Universe. 15,16-Brent Anderson-a				2.50
Born In Fire TPB (11/00, $19.95) r/#1-8; foreword by Neil Gaiman				20.00

	GD2.0	FN6.0	VF8.0	NM9.4
Prelude-(10/00, $2.95) Cha-a/Lashley-c				3.00
Wizard #0-(3/99) Wizard supplement; Straczynski-s				2.00
Wizard #1/2				10.00

RIVERDALE HIGH (Archie's... #7,8)
Archie Comics: Aug, 1990 - No. 8, Oct, 1991 ($1.00, bi-monthly)

1				4.00
2-8				3.00

RIVER FEUD (See Zane Grey & Four Color #484)

RIVETS
Dell Publishing Co.: No. 518, Nov, 1953

Four Color 518	3	9	21	32

RIVETS (A dog)
Argo Publ.: Jan, 1956 - No. 3, May, 1956

1-Reprints Sunday & daily newspaper strips	5	15	25	35
2,3	4	12	18	24

ROACHMILL
Blackthorne Publ.: Dec, 1986 - No. 6, Oct, 1987 ($1.75, B&W)

1-6				2.25

ROACHMILL
Dark Horse Comics: May, 1988 - No. 10, Dec, 1990 ($1.75, B&W)

1-10: 10-Contains trading cards				2.25

ROAD RUNNER (See Beep Beep, the...)

ROAD TO PERDITION
DC Comics/Paradox Press: 1998? $13.95 (Paperback)

nn				14.00

ROADTRIP
Oni Press: Aug, 2000 ($2.95, B&W, one-shot)

1-Reprints Judd Winick's back-up stories from Oni Double Feature #9,10				3.00

ROADWAYS
Cult Press: May, 1994 ($2.75, B&W, limited series)

1				2.75

ROARIN' RICK'S RARE BIT FIENDS
King Hell Press: July, 1994 - No. 21, Aug, 1996 ($2.95, B&W, mature)

1-21: Rick Veitch-c/a/scripts in all. 20-(5/96). 21-(8/96)-Reads Subtleman #1 on cover				3.00
Rabid Eye: The Dream Art of Rick Veitch ($14.95, B&W, TPB)-r/#1-8 & the appendix from #12				15.00
Pocket Universe (6/96, $14.95, B&W, TPB)-Reprints				15.00

ROBERT E. HOWARD'S CONAN THE BARBARIAN
Marvel Comics: 1983 ($2.50, 68 pgs., Baxter paper)

1-r/Savage Tales #2,3 by Smith, c-r/Conan #21 by Smith.				4.00

ROBERT LOUIS STEVENSON'S KIDNAPPED (See Kidnapped)

ROBIN (See Aurora, Detective Comics #38, New Teen Titans, Robin II, Robin III, Robin 3000, Star Spangled Comics #65, Teen Titans & Young Justice)

ROBIN (See Batman #457)
DC Comics: Jan, 1991 - No. 5, May, 1991 ($1.00, limited series)

1-Free poster by N. Adams; Bolland-c on all				4.00
1-2nd and 3rd printings (without poster)				2.25
2-5				3.00
2-2nd printing				2.25
Annual 1,2 (1992-93, $2.50, 68 pgs.): 1-Grant/Wagner scripts; Sam Kieth-c. 2-Intro Razorsharp; Jim Balent-c(p)				3.00

ROBIN (See Detective #668)
DC Comics: Nov, 1993 - Present ($1.50/$1.95/$1.99/$2.25)

1-($2.95)-Collector's edition w/foil embossed-c; 1st app. Robin's car, The Redbird; Azrael as Batman app.				4.00
1-Newsstand ed.				2.25
0,2-49,51-66-Regular editions: 3-5-The Spoiler app. 6-The Huntress-c/story cont'd from Showcase '94 #5. 7-Knightquest: The Conclusion w/new Batman (Azrael) vs. Bruce Wayne. 8-KnightsEnd Pt. 5. 9-KnightsEnd Aftermath; Batman-c & app. 10-(9/94)-Zero Hour. 0-(10/94). 11-(11/94). 25-Green Arrow				

Robin Hood Tales #11 © DC

Robin: Year One #4 © DC

Robocop #21 © Orion Pictures

	GD2.0	FN6.0	VF8.0	NM9.4

-c/app. 26-Batman app. 27-Contagion Pt. 3; Catwoman-c/app; Penguin & Azrael app. 28-Contagion Pt. 11. 29-Penguin app. 31-Wildcat-c/app. 32-Legacy Pt. 3. 33-Legacy Pt. 7. 35-Final Night. 46-Genesis. 52,53-Cataclysm pt. 7, conclusion. 55-Green Arrow app. 62-64-Flash-c/app. 2.50
14 ($2.50)-Embossed-c; Troika Pt. 4 .... 3.00
50-($2.95)-Lady Shiva & King Snake app. 3.00
67-72-No Man's Land 2.50
73,74,76-78 .... 2.25
75-($2.95) 3.00
79-97: 79-Begin $2.25-c; Green Arrow app. 86-Pander Bros.-a 2.25
#1,000,000 (11/98) 853rd Century x-over 2.50
Annual 3-5: 3-(1994, $2.95)-Elseworlds story. 4-(1995, $2.95)-Year One story.
5-(1996, $2.95)-Legends of the Dead Earth story 3.00
Annual 6 (1997, $3.95)-Pulp Heroes story. 4.00
.../Argent 1 (2/98, $1.95) Argent (Teen Titans) app. 2.25
...Eighty-Page Giant 1 (9/00, $5.95) Chuck Dixon-s/Diego Barreto-a 6.00
...: Flying Solo (2000, $12.95, TPB) r/#1-6, Showcase '94 #5,6 .... 13.00
...Plus 1 (12/96, $2.95) Impulse-c/app.; Waid-s 3.00
...Plus 2 (12/97, $2.95) Fang (Scare Tactics) app. 3.00

ROBIN: A HERO REBORN
DC Comics: 1991 ($4.95, squarebound, trade paperback)
nn-r/Batman #455-457 & Robin #1-5; Bolland-c 5.00

ROBIN HOOD (See The Advs. of..., Brave and the Bold, Four Color #413, 669, King Classics, Movie Comics & Power Record Comics)

ROBIN HOOD (...& His Merry Men, The Illustrated Story of...) (See Classic Comics #7 & Classics Giveaways, 12/44)

ROBIN HOOD (Adventures of... #7, 8)
Magazine Enterprises (Sussex Pub. Co.): No. 52, Nov, 1955 - No. 6, Jun, 1957
52 (#1)-Origin Robin Hood & Sir Gallant of the Round Table

	17	51	88	150
53 (#2), 3-6: 6-Richard Greene photo-c (TV)	13	39	66	110
I.W. Reprint #1,2,9: 1-r/#3. 2-r/#4. 9-r/#52 (1963)	2	6	12	18
Super Reprint #10,15: 10-r/#53. 15-r/#5	2	6	12	18

NOTE: *Bolle* a-in all; c-52. Powell a-6.

ROBIN HOOD (Not Disney)
Dell Publishing Co.: May-July, 1963 (one-shot)

1	3	9	17	26

ROBIN HOOD (Disney)
Western Publishing Co.: 1973 ($1.50, 8-1/2x11", 52 pgs., cardboard-c)
96151- "Robin Hood", based on movie, 96152- "The Mystery of Sherwood Forest", 96153- "In King Richard's Service", 96154- "The Wizard's Ring"

each....	3	9	17	24

ROBIN HOOD
Eclipse Comics: July, 1991 - No. 3, Dec, 1991 ($2.50, limited series)
1-3: Timothy Truman layouts 2.50

ROBIN HOOD AND HIS MERRY MEN (Formerly Danger & Adventure)
Charlton Comics: No. 28, Apr, 1956 - No. 38, Aug, 1958

28	10	30	55	80
29-37	8	24	42	60
38-Ditko-a (5 pgs.); Rocke-c	14	42	72	120

ROBIN HOOD TALES (Published by National Periodical #7 on)
Quality Comics Group (Comic Magazines): Feb, 1956 - No. 6, Nov-Dec, 1956

1-All have Baker/Cuidera-c	36	108	191	330
2-6-Matt Baker-a	35	105	185	320

ROBIN HOOD TALES (Cont'd from Quality series)(See Brave & the Bold #5)
National Periodical Publ.: No. 7, Jan-Feb, 1957 - No. 14, Mar-Apr, 1958

7-All have Andru/Esposito-a	40	120	220	380
8-14	35	105	185	320

ROBINSON CRUSOE (See King Classics & Power Record Comics)
Dell Publishing Co.: Nov-Jan, 1963-64

1	2	6	13	20

ROBIN II (The Joker's Wild)
DC Comics: Oct, 1991 - No. 4, Dec, 1991 ($1.50, mini-series)
1-(Direct sales, $1.50)-With 4 diff.-c; same hologram on each 3.00

1-(Newsstand, $1.00)-No hologram; 1 version 2.25
1-Collector's set ($10.00)-Contains all 5 versions bagged with hologram trading card inside 12.00
2-(Direct sales, $1.50)-With 3 different-c 2.50
2-4-(Newsstand, $1.00)-1 version of each 2.25
2-Collector's set ($8.00)-Contains all 4 versions bagged with hologram trading card inside 9.00
3-(Direct sale, $1.50)-With 2 different-c 2.50
3-Collector's set ($6.00)-Contains all 3 versions bagged with hologram trading card inside 7.00
4-(Direct sales, $1.50)-Only one version 2.50
4-Collector's set ($4.00)-Contains both versions bagged with Bat-Signal hologram trading card inside 5.00
Multi-pack (All four issues w/hologram sticker) 8.00
Deluxe Complete Set ($30.00)-Contains all 14 versions of #1-4 plus a new hologram trading card; numbered & limited to 25,000; comes with slipcase & 2 acid free backing boards 35.00

ROBIN III: CRY OF THE HUNTRESS
DC Comics: Dec, 1992 - No. 6, Mar, 1993 (Limited series)
1-6 ($2.50, collector's ed.)-Polybagged w/movement enhanced-c plus mini-poster of newsstand-c by Zeck 3.00
1-6 ($1.25, newsstand ed.): All have Zeck-c/s. 2.25

ROBIN 3000
DC Comics (Elseworlds): 1992 - No. 2, 1992 ($4.95, mini-series, 52 pgs.)
1,2-Foil logo; Russell-c/a 5.00

ROBIN: YEAR ONE
DC Comics: 2000 - No. 4, 2001 ($4.95, square-bound, limited series)
1-4: Earliest days of Robin's career; Javier Pulido-c/a. 2,4-Two-Face app. 5.00

ROBOCOP
Marvel Comics: Oct, 1987 ($2.00, B&W, magazine, one-shot)
1-Movie adaptation 4.00

ROBOCOP (Also see Dark Horse Comics)
Marvel Comics: Mar, 1990 - No. 23, Jan, 1992 ($1.50)
1-Based on movie 3.00
2-23 .... 2.50
nn (7/90, $4.95, 52 pgs.)-r/B&W magazine in color; adapts 1st movie 5.00

ROBOCOP: MORTAL COILS
Dark Horse Comics: Sept, 1993 - No. 4, Dec, 1993 ($2.50, limited series)
1-4: 1,2-Cago painted-c 2.50

ROBOCOP: PRIME SUSPECT
Dark Horse Comics: Oct, 1992 - No. 4, Jan, 1993 ($2.50, limited series)
1-4: 1,3-Nelson painted-c. 2,4-Bolton painted-c 2.50

ROBOCOP: ROULETTE
Dark Horse Comics: Dec, 1993 - No. 4, 1994 ($2.50, limited series)
1-4: 1,3-Nelson painted-c. 2,4-Bolton painted-c 2.50

ROBOCOP 2
Marvel Comics: Aug, 1990 ($2.25, B&W, magazine, 68 pgs.)
1-Adapts movie sequel 2.50

ROBOCOP 2
Marvel Comics: Aug, 1990; Late Aug, 1990 - #3, Late Sept, 1990 ($1.00, limited series)
nn-(8/90, $4.95, 68 pgs., color)-Same contents as B&W magazine 5.00
1-#3 reprint no number issue 3.00
2,3: 2-Guice-c(i) 2.50

ROBOCOP 3
Dark Horse Comics: July, 1993 - No. 3, Nov, 1993 ($2.50, limited series)
1-3: Nelson painted-c; Nguyen-a(p) 2.50

ROBOCOP VERSUS THE TERMINATOR
Dark Horse Comics: Sept, 1992 - No. 4, 1992 (Dec.) ($2.50, limited series)
1-4: Miller scripts & Simonson-c/a in all 3.00
1-Platinum Edition 6.00
NOTE: *All contain a different Robocop cardboard cut-out stand-up.*

R.O.B.O.T. Battalion 2050 #1
© Beppe Sabatini

The Rock #1 © WWF Ent.

Rocket Kelly #1 © FOX

	GD2.0	FN6.0	VF8.0	NM9.4

ROBO-HUNTER (Also see Sam Slade...)
Eagle Comics: Apr, 1984 - No. 5, 1984 ($1.00)

1-5-2000 A.D.				2.25

R.O.B.O.T. BATTALION 2050
Eclipse Comics: Mar, 1988 ($2.00, B&W, one-shot)

| 1 | | | | 2.25 |

ROBOT COMICS
Renegade Press: No. 0, June, 1987 ($2.00, B&W, one-shot)

| 0-Bob Burden story & art | | | | 2.25 |

ROBOTECH
Antarctic Press: Mar, 1997 - No. 11, Nov, 1998 ($2.95)

1-11, Annual 1 (4/98, $2.95)				3.00
...Class Reunion (12/98, $3.95, B&W)				4.00
...Escape (5/98, $2.95, B&W), ...Final Fire (12/98, $2.95, B&W)				3.00

ROBOTECH: COVERT-OPS
Antarctic Press: Aug, 1998 - No. 2, Sept, 1998 ($2.95, B&W, limited series)

| 1,2-Gregory Lane-s/a | | | | 3.00 |

ROBOTECH DEFENDERS
DC Comics: Mar, 1985 - No. 2, Apr, 1985 (Mini-series)

| 1,2 | | | | 3.00 |

ROBOTECH IN 3-D (TV)
Comico: Aug, 1987 ($2.50)

| 1-Steacy painted-c | | | | 4.00 |

ROBOTECH MASTERS (TV)
Comico: July, 1985 - No. 23, Apr, 1988 ($1.50)

| 1-23 | | | | 3.00 |

ROBOTECH: SENTINELS - RUBICON
Antarctic Press: July, 1998 ($2.95, B&W)

| 1 | | | | 3.00 |

ROBOTECH SPECIAL
Comico: May, 1988 ($2.50, one-shot, 44 pgs.)

| 1-Steacy wraparound-c; partial photo-c | | | | 4.00 |

ROBOTECH THE GRAPHIC NOVEL
Comico: Aug, 1986 ($5.95, 8-1/2x11", 52 pgs.)

| 1-Origin SDF-1; intro T.R. Edwards, Steacy-c/a; 2nd printing also exists (12/86). | | | | 7.00 |

ROBOTECH: THE MACROSS SAGA (TV)(Formerly Macross)
Comico: No. 2, Feb, 1985 - No. 36, Feb, 1989 ($1.50)

| 2-10 | | | | 4.00 |
| 11-36: 12;17-Ken Steacy painted-c. 26-Begin $1.75-c. 35,36-($1.95) | | | | 3.00 |

ROBOTECH: THE NEW GENERATION
Comico: July, 1985 - No. 25, July, 1988

| 1-25 | | | | 3.00 |

ROBOTECH: VERMILION
Antarctic Press: Mar, 1997 - No. 4, ($2.95, B&W, limited series)

| 1-4 | | | | 3.00 |

ROBOTECH: WINGS OF GIBRALTAR
Antarctic Press: Aug, 1998 - No. 2, Sept, 1998 ($2.95, B&W, limited series)

| 1,2-Lee Duhig-s/a | | | | 3.00 |

ROBOTIX
Marvel Comics: Feb, 1986 (75¢, one-shot)

| 1-Based on toy | | | | 3.00 |

ROBOTMEN OF THE LOST PLANET (Also see Space Thrillers)
Avon Periodicals: 1952 (Also see Strange Worlds #19)

| 1-McCann-a (3 pgs.); Fawcette-a | 105 | 315 | 656 | 1150 |

ROB ROY
Dell Publishing Co.: 1954 (Disney-Movie)

| Four Color 544-Manning-a, photo-c | 8 | 24 | 56 | 100 |

ROCK, THE (WWF Wrestling)
Chaos! Comics: June, 2001 ($2.99, one-shot)

| 1-Photo-c; Grant-s/Neves-a | | | | 3.00 |

ROCK & ROLL HIGH SCHOOL
Roger Corman's Cosmic Comics: Oct, 1995 ($2.50)

| 1-Bob Fingerman scripts | | | | 2.50 |

ROCK AND ROLLO (Formerly TV Teens)
Charlton Comics: V2#14, Oct, 1957 - No. 19, Sept, 1958

| V2#14-19 | 5 | 15 | 25 | 35 |

ROCK COMICS
Landgraphic Publ.: Jul/Aug, 1979 ($1.25, tabloid size, 28 pgs.)

| 1-N. Adams-c; Thor(not Marvel's) story by Adams | 2 | 6 | 12 | 18 |

ROCKET COMICS
Hillman Periodicals: Mar, 1940 - No. 3, May, 1940

| 1-Rocket Riley, Red Roberts the Electro Man (origin), The Phantom Ranger, The Steel Shark, The Defender, Buzzard Barnes and his Sky Devils, Lefty Larson, & The Defender, the Man with a Thousand Faces begin (1st app. of each); all have Rocket Riley-c | 245 | 735 | 1534 | 2700 |
| 2,3 | 123 | 369 | 769 | 1350 |

ROCKETEER, THE (See Eclipse Graphic Album Series, Pacific Presents & Starslayer)

ROCKETEER ADVENTURE MAGAZINE, THE
Comico/Dark Horse Comics No. 3: July, 1988 ($2.00); No. 2, July, 1989 ($2.75); No. 3, Jan, 1995 ($2.95)

1-(7/88, $2.00)-Dave Stevens-c/a in all; Kaluta back-up-a; 1st app. Jonas (character based on The Shadow)	1	3	6	9
2-(7/89, $2.75)-Stevens/Dorman painted-c				6.00
3-(1/95, $2.95)-Includes pinups by Stevens, Gulacy, Plunkett, & Mignola				3.50
Volume 2-(9/96, $9.95, magazine size TPB)-Reprints #1-3				10.00

ROCKETEER SPECIAL EDITION, THE
Eclipse Comics: Nov, 1984 ($1.50, Baxter paper)(Chapter 5 of Rocketeer serial)

| 1-Stevens-c/a; Kaluta back-c; pin-ups inside | 2 | 6 | 9 | 12 |
| NOTE: *Originally intended to be published in Pacific Presents.* | | | | |

ROCKETEER: THE OFFICIAL MOVIE ADAPTATION, THE
W. D. Publications (Disney): 1991

nn-($5.95, 68 pgs.)-Squarebound deluxe edition				6.00
nn-($2.95, 68 pgs.)-Stapled regular edition				3.00
3-D Comic Book (1991, $7.98, 52 pgs.)				8.00

ROCKET KELLY (See The Bouncer, Green Mask #10); becomes Li'l Pan #6)
Fox Feature Syndicate: 1944; Fall, 1945 - No. 5, Oct-Nov, 1946

nn (1944), 1	35	105	185	320
2-The Puppeteer app. (costumed hero)	26	78	139	240
3-5: 5-(#5 on cover, #4 inside)	23	69	121	210

ROCKETMAN (Strange Fantasy #2 on) (See Hello Pal & Scoop Comics)
Ajax/Farrell Publications: June, 1952 (Strange Stories of the Future)

| 1-Rocketman & Cosmo | 40 | 120 | 232 | 400 |

ROCKET RACCOON
Marvel Comics: May, 1985 - No. 4, Aug, 1985 (color, limited series)

| 1-4: Mignola-a | | | | 2.25 |

ROCKET SHIP X
Fox Features Syndicate: September, 1951; 1952

| 1 | 61 | 182 | 381 | 675 |
| 1952 (nn, nd, no publ.)-Edited 1951-c (exist?) | 40 | 120 | 220 | 380 |

ROCKET TO ADVENTURE LAND (See Pixie Puzzle...)

ROCKET TO THE MOON
Avon Periodicals: 1951

| nn-Orlando-c/a; adapts Otis Aldebert Kline's "Maza of the Moon" | 105 | 315 | 656 | 1150 |

ROCK FANTASY COMICS
Rock Fantasy Comics: Dec, 1989 - No. 16?, 1991 ($2.25/$3.00, B&W)(No cover price)

| 1-Pink Floyd part 1 | | | | 5.00 |

Rock N' Roll Comics #15 © Revolutionary Comics

Rocky Lane Western #5 © FAW

Rogue V2 #3 © MAR

	GD2.0	FN6.0	VF8.0	NM9.4

1-2nd printing ($3.00-c) 3.00
2,3: 2-Rolling Stones #1. 3-Led Zeppelin #1 4.00
2,3: 2nd printings ($3.00-c, 1/90 & 2/90) 3.00
4-Stevie Nicks Not published
5-Monstrosities of Rock #1; photo back-c 4.00
5-2nd printing ($3.00, 3/90 indicia, 2/90-c) 3.00
6-9,11-15,17,18: 6-Guns n' Roses #1 (1st & 2nd printings, 3/90)-Begin $3.00-c.
  7-Sex Pistols #1. 8-Alice Cooper; not published. 9-Van Halen #1;
  photo back-c. 11-Jimi Hendrix #1; wraparound-c 3.00
10-Kiss #1; photo back-c 2 6 9 12
16-($5.00, 68 pgs.)-The Great Gig in the Sky(Floyd) 5.00

ROCK HAPPENING (See Bunny and Harvey Pop Comics:...)

ROCK N' ROLL COMICS
Revolutionary Comics: Jun, 1989 - No. 24, 1992 ($1.50/$1.95, B&W/col. #15 on)

1-Guns N' Roses 1 3 6 8
1-2nd thru 7th printings. 7th printing (full color w/new-c/a) 2.25
2-Metallica 1 4 7 10
2-2nd thru 6th printings (6th in color) 2.25
3-Bon Jovi (no reprints) 1 3 6 8
4-8,10-24: 4-Motley Crue(2nd printing only, 1st destroyed). 5-Def Leppard (2
  printings). 6-Rolling Stones(4 printings). 7-The Who(3 printings). 8-Skid Row;
  not published. 10-Warrant/Whitesnake(2 printings; 1st has 2 diff.-c). 11-
  Aerosmith (2 printings?). 12-New Kids on the Block(2 printings). 12-3rd
  printing; rewritten & titled NKOTB Hate Book. 13-Led Zeppelin. 14-Sex
  Pistols. 15-Poison; 1st color issue. 16-Van Halen. 17-Madonna. 18-Alice
  Cooper. 19-Public Enemy/2 Live Crew. 20-Queensryche/Tesla. 21-Prince?
  22-AC/DC; begin $2.50-c. 23-Living Colour. 24-Anthrax 5.00
9-Kiss 2 6 9 12
9-2nd & 3rd printings 2.25
NOTE: Most issues were reprinted except #3. Later reprints are in color. #8 was not released.

ROCKO'S MODERN LIFE (TV)
Marvel Comics: June, 1994 - No. 7, Dec, 1994 ($1.95) (Nickelodeon cartoon)

1-7 2.25

ROCKY AND HIS FIENDISH FRIENDS (TV)(Bullwinkle)
Gold Key: Oct, 1962 - No. 5, Sept, 1963 (Jay Ward)

1 (25¢, 80 pgs.) 21 63 147 275
2,3 (25¢, 80 pgs.) 14 42 98 185
4,5 (Regular size, 12¢) 10 30 70 125

ROCKY AND HIS FRIENDS (See Kite Fun Book & March of Comics #216)

ROCKY AND HIS FRIENDS (TV)
Dell Publishing Co.: No. 1128, 8-10/60 - No.1311,1962 (Jay Ward)

Four Color #1128 (#1) (8-10/60) 37 110 259 480
Four Color #1152 (12-2/61), 1166, 1208, 1275, 1311('62)
          23 69 161 300

ROCKY HORROR PICTURE SHOW THE COMIC BOOK, THE
Caliber Press: Jul, 1990 - No. 3, Jan, 1991 ($2.95, mini-series, 52 pgs.)

1-3: 1-Adapts cult film plus photos, etc., 1-2nd printing 3.00
...Collection ($4.95) 5.00

ROCKY JONES SPACE RANGER (See Space Adventures #15-18)

ROCKY JORDEN PRIVATE EYE (See Private Eye)

ROCKY LANE WESTERN (Allan Rocky Lane starred in Republic movies & TV
for a short time as Allan Lane, Red Ryder & Rocky Lane) (See Black Jack
Fawcett Movie Comics, Motion Picture Comics & Six-Gun Heroes)
Fawcett Publications/Charlton No. 56 on: May, 1949 - No. 87, Nov, 1959

1 (36 pgs.)-Rocky, his stallion Black Jack, & Slim Pickens begin; photo-c
  begin, end #57; photo back-c 98 294 611 1075
2 (36 pgs.)-Last photo back-c 40 120 240 420
3-5 (52 pgs.): 4-Captain Tootsie by Beck 31 93 165 285
6,10 (36 pgs.): 10-Complete western novelette "Badman's Reward"
        22 66 116 195
7-9 (52 pgs.) 24 72 127 215
11-13,15-17 (52 pgs.): 15-Black Jack's Hitching Post begins, ends #25
        18 54 94 155
14,18 (36 pgs.) 15 45 77 130
19-21,23,24 (52 pgs.): 20-Last Slim Pickens. 21-Dee Dickens begins,

ends #55,57,65-68 15 45 77 130
22,25-28,30 (36 pgs. begin) 14 42 72 120
29-Classic complete novel "The Land of Missing Men" with hidden land of
  ancient temple ruins (r-in #65) 20 60 105 175
31-40 13 39 66 110
41-54 11 33 55 90
55-Last Fawcett issue (1/54) 12 36 61 100
56-1st Charlton issue (2/54)-Photo-c 20 60 105 175
57,60-Photo-c 12 36 61 100
58,59,61-64,66-78,80-86: 59-61-Young Falcon app. 64-Slim Pickens app.
66-68: Reprints #30,31,32 10 30 55 80
65-r/#29, "The Land of Missing Men" 11 33 55 90
79-Giant Edition (68 pgs.) 12 36 61 100
87-Last issue 11 33 55 90
NOTE: Complete novels in #10, 14, 18, 22, 25, 30-32, 36, 38, 39, 49. Captain Tootsie in #4, 12,
20. Big Bow and Little Arrow in #11, 28, 63. Black Jack's Hitching Post in #15-25, 64, 73.

ROCKY LANE WESTERN
AC Comics: 1989 ($2.50, B&W, one-shot?)

1-Photo-c; Giordano reprints 4.00
Annual 1 (1991, $2.95, B&W, 44 pgs.)-photo front/back & inside-c; reprints. 4.00

ROD CAMERON WESTERN (Movie star)
Fawcett Publications: Feb, 1950 - No. 20, Apr, 1953

1-Rod Cameron, his horse War Paint, & Sam The Sheriff begin; photo
  front/back-c begin 53 158 318 560
2 29 87 153 265
3-Novel length story "The Mystery of the Seven Cities of Cibola"
        24 72 127 220
4-10: 9-Last photo back-c 20 60 105 175
11-19 16 48 83 140
20-Last issue & photo-c 17 51 88 150
NOTE: Novel length stories in No. 1-8, 12-14.

RODEO RYAN (See A-1 Comics #8)

ROEL
Sirius: Feb, 1997 ($2.95, B&W, one-shot)

1 3.00

ROGAN GOSH
DC Comics (Vertigo): 1994 ($6.95, one-shot)

nn-Peter Milligan scripts 7.00

ROGER DODGER (Also in Exciting Comics #57 on)
Standard Comics: No. 5, Aug, 1952

5-Teen-age 5 15 25 35

ROGER RABBIT (Also see Marvel Graphic Novel)
Disney Comics: June, 1990 - No. 18, Nov, 1991 ($1.50)

1-18-All new stories 3.00
In 3-D 1 (1992, $2.50)-Sold at Wal-Mart?; w/glasses 4.00

ROGER RABBIT'S TOONTOWN
Disney Comics: Aug, 1991 - No. 5, Dec, 1991 ($1.50)

1-5 2.50

ROGER ZELAZNY'S AMBER: THE GUNS OF AVALON
DC Comics: 1996 - No. 3, 1996 ($6.95, limited series)

1-3: Based on novel 7.00

ROG 2000
Pacific Comics: June, 1982 ($2.95, 44 pgs., B&W, one-shot, magazine)

nn-Byrne-c/a (r) 2 6 9 12
2nd printing (7/82) 1 3 5 7

ROG 2000
Fantagraphics Books: 1987 - No. 2, 1987 ($2.00, limited series)

1,2-Byrne-r 3.00

ROGUE
Marvel Comics: Jan, 1995 - No. 4, Apr, 1995 ($2.95, limited series)

1-4: 1-Gold foil logo 4.00
TPB-($12.95) r/#1-4 13.00

ROGUE (Volume 2)

Roly Poly Comic Book #14 © Green Pub. Co.

ROM #25 © Parker Brothers

Romantic Confessions #9 © HILL

	GD2.0	FN6.0	VF8.0	NM9.4

Marvel Comics: Sept, 2001 - No. 4, Dec, 2001 ($2.50, limited series)
1-4-Julie Bell painted-c/Lopresti-a; Rogue's early days with X-Men ... 2.50

ROGUES GALLERY
DC Comics: 1996 ($3.50, one-shot)
1-Pinups of DC villains by various artists ... 3.50

ROGUES, THE (VILLAINS) (See The Flash)
DC Comics: Feb, 1998 ($1.95, one-shot)
1-Augustyn-s/Pearson-c ... 2.25

ROGUE TROOPER
Quality Comics/Fleetway Quality #38-on : Oct, 1986 - No. 49, 1991 ($1.25/$1.50/$1.75)
1-49: 6-Double size. 21,22,25-27-Guice-a. 47,48-Alan Moore scripts ... 2.25

ROLLING STONES: VOODOO LOUNGE
Marvel Comics: 1995 ($6.95, Prestige format, one-shot)
nn-Dave McKean-script/design/art ... 7.00

ROLY POLY COMIC BOOK
Green Publishing Co.: 1945 - No. 15, 1946 (MLJ reprints)

1-Red Rube & Steel Sterling begin; Sahle-c	31	93	165	285
6-The Blue Circle & The Steel Fist app.	19	57	99	165
10-Origin Red Rube retold; Steel Sterling story (Zip #41)				
	27	81	145	250
11,12: The Black Hood app. in both	19	57	99	165
14-Classic decapitation-c; the Black Hood app.	39	117	208	360
15-The Blue Circle & The Steel Fist app.; cover exact swipe from Fox Blue Beetle #1	33	99	174	300

ROM (Based on the Parker Brothers toy)
Marvel Comics Group: Dec, 1979 - No. 75, Feb, 1986

1-Origin/1st app.	1	4	7	10
2-16,19-23,28-30: 5-Dr. Strange. 13-Saga of the Space Knights begins. 19-X-Men cameo. 23-Powerman & Iron Fist app.				4.00
17,18-X-Men app.	1	3	6	8
24-27: 24-F.F. cameo; Skrulls, Nova & The New Champions app. 25-Double size. 26,27-Galactus app.				5.00
31-49,51-60: 31,32-Brotherhood of Evil Mutants app. 32-X-Men cameo. 34,35-Sub-Mariner app. 41,42-Dr. Strange app. 56,57-Alpha Flight app. 58,59-Ant-Man app.				3.00
50-Skrulls app. (52 pgs.) Pin-ups by Konkle, Austin				4.00
61-74: 65-West Coast Avengers & Beta Ray Bill app. 65,66-X-Men app.				3.00
75-Last issue	1	3	6	8

Annual 1-4: (1982-85, 52 pgs.) ... 3.00
NOTE: Austin c-3l, 18i, 61i. Byrne a-74i; c-56, 57, 74. Ditko a-59-75p, Annual 4. Golden c-7-12, 19. Guice a-61i; c-55, 58, 60p, 70p. Layton a-59i, 72i; c-15, 59i, 69. Miller c-2p?, 3p, 17p, 18p. Russell a(i)-64, 65, 67, 69, 71, 75; c-64, 65i, 66, 71i, 75. Severin c-41p. Sienkiewicz a-53i; c-45, 47, 52-54, 68, 71p, Annual 2. Simonson c-18. P. Smith c-59p. Starlin c-67. Zeck c-50.

ROMANCE (See True Stories of...)

ROMANCE AND CONFESSION STORIES (See Giant Comics Edition)
St. John Publishing Co.: No date (1949) (25¢, 100 pgs.)
1-Baker-c/a; remaindered St. John love comics ... 40 | 120 | 232 | 400

ROMANCE DIARY
Marvel Comics (CDS)(CLDS): Dec, 1949 - No. 2, Mar, 1950
1,2 ... 14 | 42 | 72 | 120

ROMANCE OF FLYING, THE
David McKay Publications: 1942
Feature Books 33 (nn)-WW II photo-c ... 15 | 45 | 77 | 130

ROMANCES OF MOLLY MANTON (See Molly Manton)

ROMANCES OF NURSE HELEN GRANT, THE
Atlas Comics (VPI): Aug, 1957
1 ... 7 | 21 | 38 | 55

ROMANCES OF THE WEST (Becomes Romantic Affairs #3?)
Marvel Comics (SPC): Nov, 1949 - No. 2, Mar, 1950 (52 pgs.)
1-Movie photo-c of Yvonne DeCarlo & Howard Duff (Calamity Jane & Sam Bass) ... 23 | 69 | 121 | 210
2-Photo-c ... 15 | 45 | 77 | 130

ROMANCE STORIES OF TRUE LOVE (Formerly True Love Problems & Advice Illustrated)
Harvey Publications: No. 45, 5/57 - No. 50, 3/58; No. 51, 9/58 - No. 52, 11/58

45-51: 45,46,48-50-Powell-a	5	15	25	35
52-Matt Baker-a	8	24	42	60

ROMANCE TALES (Formerly Western Winners #6?)
Marvel Comics (CDS): No. 7, Oct, 1949 - No. 9, Mar, 1950 (7,8: photo-c)

7	14	42	72	120
8,9: 8-Everett-a	10	30	55	80

ROMANCE TRAIL
National Periodical Publications: July-Aug, 1949 - No. 6, May-June, 1950 (All photo-c & 52 pgs.)

1-Kinstler, Toth-a; Jimmy Wakely photo-c	59	177	369	650
2-Kinstler-a; Jim Bannon photo-c	33	99	174	300
3-Photo-c; Kinstler, Toth-a	36	108	191	330
4-Photo-c; Toth-a	26	78	136	235
5,6: Photo-c on both. 5-Kinstler-a	23	69	121	210

ROMAN HOLIDAYS, THE (TV)
Gold Key: Feb, 1973 - No. 4, Nov, 1973 (Hanna-Barbera)

1	4	12	29	45
2-4	3	9	19	28

ROMANTIC ADVENTURES (My... #49-67, covers only)
American Comics Group (B&I Publ. Co.): Mar-Apr, 1949 - No. 67, July, 1956 (Becomes My... #68 on)

1	17	51	88	150
2	10	30	55	80
3-10	7	21	36	50
11-20 (4/52)	6	18	29	40
21-45,49-51: 52-Last Pre-code (2/55)	5	15	25	35
46-48-3-D effect-c/stories (TrueVision)	11	33	55	90
50-Classic cover/story "Love of A Lunatic"	10	30	55	80
53-67	5	14	21	28

NOTE: #1-23, 52 pgs. Shelly a-40. Whitney c/art in many issues.

ROMANTIC AFFAIRS (Formerly Molly Manton's Romances #2 and/or Romances of the West #2 and/or Our Love #2?)
Marvel Comics (SPC): No. 3, Mar, 1950
3-Photo-c from Molly Manton's Romances #2 ... 9 | 27 | 49 | 70

ROMANTIC CONFESSIONS
Hillman Periodicals: Oct, 1949 - V3#1, Apr-May, 1953

V1#1-McWilliams-a	16	48	83	140
2-Briefer-a; negligee panels	10	30	55	80
3-12	7	21	38	55
V2#1,2,4-8,10-12: 2-McWilliams-a	6	18	32	45
3-Krigstein-a	8	24	45	65
9-One pg. Frazetta ad	6	18	32	45
V3#1	6	18	29	40

ROMANTIC HEARTS
Story Comics/Master/Merit Pubs.: Mar, 1951 - No. 10, Oct, 1952; July, 1953 - No. 12, July, 1955

1(3/51) (1st Series)	14	42	72	120
2	8	24	42	60
3-10: Cameron-a	7	21	36	50
1(7/53) (2nd Series)-Some say #11 on-c	9	27	49	70
2	6	18	32	45
3-12	5	15	25	35

ROMANTIC LOVE
Avon Periodicals/Realistic (No #14-19): 9-10/49 - #3, 1-2/50; #4, 2-3/51 - #13, 10/52; #20, 3-4/54 - #23, 9-10/54

1-c/Avon paperback #252	25	75	130	225
2-5: 3-c/paperback Novel Library #12. 4-c/paperback Diversey Prize Novel #5. 5-c from Avon paperback #34	15	45	77	130
6- "Thrill Crazy" marijuana story; c/Avon paperback #207; Kinstler-a				
	21	63	110	185
7,8: 8-Astarita-a(2)	14	42	72	120
9-12: 9-c/paperback Novel Library #41; Kinstler-a. 10-c/Avon paperback				

Romantic Marriage #2 © Z-D

Romantic Western #1 © FAW

Room 222 #1 © 20th Century Fox

	GD2.0	FN6.0	VF8.0	NM9.4
#212. 11-c/paperback Novel Library #17; Kinstler-a. 12-c/paperback				
Novel Library #13	15	45	77	130
13,21-23: 22,23-Kinstler-c	14	42	72	120
20-Kinstler-c/a	14	42	72	125
nn(1-3/53)(Realistic-r)	10	30	55	80

NOTE: *Astarita a-7, 10, 11, 21. Painted c-1-3, 5, 7-11, 13. Photo c4, 6.*

ROMANTIC LOVE
Quality Comics Group: 1963-1964

I.W. Reprint #2,3,8: 2-r/Romantic Love #2	2	6	9	12

ROMANTIC MARRIAGE (Cinderella Love #25 on)
Ziff-Davis/St. John No. 18 on (#1-8: 52 pgs.): #1-3 (1950, no months); #4, 5-6/51 - #17, 9/52; #18, 9/53 - #24, 9/54

1-Photo-c; Cary Grant/Betsy Drake photo back-c.	20	60	105	175
2-Painted-c; Anderson-a (also #15)	13	39	66	110
3-9: 3,4,8,9-Painted-c; 5-7-Photo-c	11	33	55	90
10-Unusual format; front-c is a painted-c; back-c is a photo-c complete with				
logo, price, etc.	19	57	99	165
11-17 13-Photo-c. 15-Signed story by Anderson. 17-(9/52)-Last Z-D issue				
	10	30	55	80
18-22,24: 20-Photo-c	10	30	55	80
23-Baker-c; all stories are reprinted from #15	10	30	55	85

ROMANTIC PICTURE NOVELETTES
Magazine Enterprises: 1946

1-Mary Worth-r; Creig Flessel-c	17	51	88	150

ROMANTIC SECRETS (Becomes Time For Love)
Fawcett/Charlton Comics No. 5 (10/55) on: Sept, 1949 - No. 39, 4/53; No. 5, 10/55 - No. 52, 11/64 (#1-5: photo-c)

1-(52 pg. issues begin, end #?)	16	48	83	140
2,3	10	30	55	80
4,9-Evans-a	10	30	55	85
5-8,10	7	21	38	55
11-23	7	21	36	50
24-Evans-a	8	24	42	60
25-39('53)	6	18	32	45
5 (Charlton, 2nd Series)(10/55, formerly Negro Romances #4)				
	10	30	55	80
6-10	7	21	38	55
11-20	3	10	23	35
21-35: Last 10¢ issue?	3	9	19	28
36-52('64)	2	6	15	22

NOTE: *Bailey a-20. Powell (1st series)-5, 7, 10, 12, 16, 17, 20, 26, 29, 33, 34, 36, 37. Sekowsky a-26. Photo c(1st series)-1-5, 16, 25, 27, 33. Swayze (1st series)-16, 18, 19, 23, 26-28, 31, 32, 39.*

ROMANTIC STORY (Cowboy Love #28 on)
Fawcett/Charlton Comics No. 23 on: 11/49 - #22, Sum, 1953; #23, 5/54 - #27, 12/54; #28, 8/55 - #130, 11/73

1-Photo-c begin, end #24; 52 pgs. begins	17	51	88	150
2	10	30	55	80
3-5	8	24	45	65
6-14	7	21	38	55
15-Evans-a	8	24	45	65
16-22(Sum, '53; last Fawcett issue). 21-Toth-a?	6	18	32	45
23-39: 26,29-Wood swipes	6	18	29	40
40-(100 pgs.)	11	33	55	90
41-50	3	9	20	30
51-80: 57-Hypo needle story	2	6	15	22
81-99	2	6	11	15
100	2	6	12	18
101-130	2	6	9	12

NOTE: *Jim Aparo a-94. Powell a-7, 8, 16, 20, 30. Marcus Swayze a-2, 12, 20, 32.*

ROMANTIC THRILLS (See Fox Giants)

ROMANTIC WESTERN
Fawcett Publications: Winter, 1949 - No. 3, June, 1950 (All Photo-c)

1	22	66	116	200
2-(Spr/50)-Williamson, McWilliams-a	21	63	110	185
3	15	45	77	130

ROMEO TUBBS (...That Lovable Teenager; formerly My Secret Life)

	GD2.0	FN6.0	VF8.0	NM9.4
Fox Feature Syndicate/Green Publ. Co. No. 27: No. 26, 5/50 - No. 28, 7/50; No. 1, 1950; No. 27, 12/52				
26-Teen-age	11	33	55	90
28 (7/50)	10	30	55	80
27 (12/52)-Contains Pedro on inside; Wood-a (exist?)				
	16	48	83	140

RONALD McDONALD (TV)
Charlton Press (King Features Synd.): Sept, 1970 - No. 4, March, 1971

1	8	24	56	90
2-4	4	12	29	45
V2#1,3-Special reprint for McDonald systems; "Not for resale" on cover				
	5	15	38	60

RONIN
DC Comics: July, 1983 - No. 6, Aug, 1984 ($2.50, limited series, 52 pgs.)

1-5-Frank Miller-c/a/scripts in all				5.00
6-Scarcer; has fold-out poster.	1	3	6	8
Trade paperback (1987, $12.95)-Reprints #1-6				13.00

RONNA
Knight Press: Apr, 1997 ($2.95, B&W, one-shot)

1-Beau Smith-s				3.00

ROOK (See Eerie Magazine & Warren Presents: The Rook)
Warren Publications: Oct, 1979 - No. 14, April, 1982 (B&W magazine)

1-Nino-a/Corben-c; with 8 pg. color insert	2	6	12	18
2-4,6,7: 2-Voltar by Alcala begins. 3,4-Toth-a	1	4	7	10
5,8-14: 11-Zorro-s. 12-14-Eagle by Severin	1	4	7	10

ROOK
Harris Comics: No. 0, Jun, 1995 - No. 4, 1995 ($2.95)

0-4: 0-short stories (3) w/preview. 4-Brereton-c.				3.00

ROOKIE COP (Formerly Crime and Justice)
Charlton Comics: No. 27, Nov, 1955 - No. 33, Aug, 1957

27	9	27	49	70
28-33	6	18	32	45

ROOM 222 (TV)
Dell Publishing Co.: Jan, 1970; No. 2, May, 1970 - No. 4, Jan, 1971

1	5	15	35	60
2-4: 2,4-Photo-c. 3-Marijuana story. 4 r/#1	3	10	23	35

ROOTIE KAZOOTIE (TV)(See 3-D-ell)
Dell Publishing Co.: No. 415, Aug, 1952 - No. 6, Oct-Dec, 1954

Four Color 415 (#1)	10	30	70	130
Four Color 459,502(#2,3), 4(4-6/54)-6	7	21	49	90

ROOTS OF THE SWAMP THING
DC Comics: July, 1986 - No.5, Nov, 1986 ($2.00, Baxter paper, 52 pgs.)

1-5: r/Swamp Thing #1-10 by Wrightson & House of Mystery-r. 1-new Wrightson-c (2-5 reprinted covers).				4.00

ROSE (See Bone)
Cartoon Books: Nov, 2000 - No. 3, Feb, 2002 ($5.95, lim. series, square-bound)

1-3-Jeff Smith-s/Charles Vess painted-a/c				6.00
HC (2001, $29.95) r/#1-3; new Vess cover painting				30.00

ROSE N' GUNN
Bishop Press: Jan, 1995 - No. 6, May, 1996 ($2.95, B&W, mature)

1-6, Creator's Choice ($2.95)-reprints w/pin-ups				3.00

ROSE N'GUNN
London Night Studios: June, 1996 - Aug, 1996 ($3.00, B&W, mature)

1,2				3.00
1-($6.00)-Blood & Glory Edition				6.00

ROSWELL: LITTLE GREEN MAN (See Simpsons Comics #19-22)
Bongo Comics: 1996 - Present ($2.95, quarterly)

1-6				3.50
...Walks Among Us ('97, $12.95, TPB) r/ #1-3 & Simpsons flip books				13.00

ROUNDUP (...Western Crime Stories)
D. S. Publishing Co.: July-Aug, 1948 - No. 5, Mar-Apr, 1949 (All 52 pgs.)

Roy Rogers Comics #15 © Roy Rogers

Rulah Jungle Goddess #19 © FOX

Rumble Girls: Silky Warrior Tansie #1 © Lea Hernandez

	GD2.0	FN6.0	VF8.0	NM9.4		GD2.0	FN6.0	VF8.0	NM9.4

	GD2.0	FN6.0	VF8.0	NM9.4
1-Kiefer-a	21	63	110	185
2-5: 2-Marijuana drug mention story	15	45	77	130

ROYAL ROY
Marvel Comics (Star Comics): May, 1985 - No.6, Mar, 1986 (Children's book)
| 1-6 | | | | 4.00 |

ROY CAMPANELLA, BASEBALL HERO
Fawcett Publications: 1950 (Brooklyn Dodgers)
| nn-Photo-c; life story | 59 | 177 | 369 | 650 |

ROY ROGERS (See March of Comics #17, 35, 47, 62, 68, 73, 77, 86, 91, 100, 105, 116, 121, 131, 136, 146, 151, 161, 167, 176, 191, 206, 221, 236, 250)

ROY ROGERS AND TRIGGER
Gold Key: Apr, 1967
| 1-Photo-c; reprints | 5 | 15 | 34 | 55 |

ROY ROGERS ANNUAL
Wilson Publ. Co., Toronto/Dell: 1947 ("Giant Edition" on-c)(132 pgs., 50¢)
nn-Less than 5 known copies. Front and back cover art are from Roy Rogers #2.
Stories reprinted from Roy Rogers #2, Four Color #137 and Four Color #153.
(A copy in VG/FN was sold in 1986 for $400, in 1996 for $1200 and in 2000
for $1500)

ROY ROGERS COMICS (See Western Roundup under Dell Giants)
Dell Publishing Co.: No. 38, 4/44 - No. 177, 12/47 (#38-166: 52 pgs.)
Four Color 38 (1944)-49 pg. story; photo front/back-c on all 4-Color issues (1st				
western comic with photo-c	219	657	1533	2850
Four Color 63 (1945)-Color photos on all four-c	48	144	336	625
Four Color 86,95 (1945)	35	106	245	460
Four Color 109 (1946)	27	80	189	350
Four Color 117,124,137,144	21	63	147	275
Four Color 153,160,166: 166-48 pg. story	19	57	133	250
Four Color 177 (36 pgs.)-32 pg. story	19	57	133	250

ROY ROGERS COMICS (...& Trigger #92(8/55)-on)(Roy starred in Republic movies, radio & TV) (Singing cowboy) (Also see Dale Evans, It Really Happened #8, Queen of the West Dale Evans, & Roy Rogers' Trigger)
Dell Publishing Co.: Jan, 1948 - No. 145, Sept-Oct, 1961 (#1-19: 36 pgs.)
1-Roy, his horse Trigger, & Chuck Wagon Charley's Tales begin; photo-c				
begin, end #145	81	243	567	1050
2	28	84	196	360
3-5	19	57	133	250
6-10	15	45	105	200
11-19: 19-Chuck Wagon Charley's Tales ends	12	36	84	160
20 (52 pgs.)-Trigger feature begins, ends #46	12	36	84	160
21-30 (52 pgs.)	10	30	70	135
31-46 (52 pgs.): 37-X-Mas-c	9	27	63	110
47-56 (36 pgs.): 47-Chuck Wagon Charley's Tales returns, ends #133.				
49-X-Mas-c. 55-Last photo back-c	6	18	42	75
57 (52 pgs.)-Heroin drug propaganda story	8	24	42	80
58-70 (52 pgs.): 58-Heroin drug use/dealing story. 61-X-Mas-c	6	18	42	75
71-80 (52 pgs.): 73-X-Mas-c	5	15	35	65
81-91 (36 pgs.): #81-on): 85-X-Mas-c	5	15	35	60
92-99,101-110,112-118: 92-Title changed to Roy Rogers and Trigger (8/55)				
	5	15	34	50
100-Trigger feature returns, ends #131	6	18	42	75
111,119-124-Toth-a	6	18	42	80
125-131: 125-Toth-a (1 pg.)	4	12	30	50
132-144-Manning-a. 132-1st Dale Evans-sty by Russ Manning. 138,144-Dale				
Evans featured	5	15	35	65
145-Last issue	6	18	42	80

NOTE: Buscema a-74-108(2 stories each). Manning a-123, 124, 132-144. Marsh a-110. Photo back-c No. 1-9, 11-35, 38-55.

ROY ROGERS' TRIGGER
Dell Publishing Co.: No. 329, May, 1951 - No. 17, June-Aug, 1955
Four Color 329 (#1)-Painted-c	13	39	91	170
2 (9-11/51)-Photo-c	12	36	84	155
3-5: 3-Painted-c begin, end #17, most by S. Savitt	5	15	35	65
6-17: Title merges with Roy Rogers after #17	4	12	30	50

ROY ROGERS WESTERN CLASSICS

AC Comics: 1989 -No. 4 ($2.95/$3.95, 44pgs.) (24 pgs. color, 16 pgs. B&W)
1-4: 1-Dale Evans-r by Manning, Trigger-r by Buscema; photo covers & interior				
photos by Roy & Dale. 2-Buscema-r (3); photo-c & B&W photos inside. 3-Dale				
Evans-r by Manning; Trigger-r by Buscema plus other Buscema-r; photo-c.				4.00

RUDOLPH, THE RED-NOSED REINDEER
National Per. Publ.: 1950 - No. 13, Winter, 1962-63 (Issues are not numbered)
1950 issue (#1); Grossman-c/a begins	22	66	116	200
1951-53 issues (3 total)	13	39	66	110
1954/55, 55/56, 56/57	11	33	55	90
1957/58, 58/59, 59/60, 60/61, 61/62	6	18	45	75
1962/63 (rare)(84 pgs.)(shows "Annual" in indicia)	11	33	80	135

NOTE: 13 total issues published. Has games & puzzles also.

RUDOLPH, THE RED-NOSED REINDEER (Also see Limited Collectors' Edition C-20, C-24, C-33, C-42, C-50; and All-New Collectors' Edition C-53 & C-60)
National Per. Publ.: Christmas 1972 (Treasury-size)
| nn-Precursor to Limited Collectors' Edition title (scarce) | | | | |
| (implied to Lim. Coll .Ed. C-20) | 25 | 75 | 174 | 310 |

RUFF AND REDDY (TV)
Dell Publ. Co.: No. 937, 9/58 - No. 12, 1-3/62 (Hanna-Barbera)(#9 on: 15¢)
Four Color 937(#1)(1st Hanna-Barbera comic book)	13	39	91	170
Four Color 981,1038	8	24	56	105
4(1-3/60)-12: 8-Last 10¢ issue	7	21	49	85

RUGGED ACTION (Strange Stories of Suspense #5 on)
Atlas Comics (CSI): Dec, 1954 - No. 4, June, 1955
| 1-Brodsky-a | 14 | 42 | 72 | 120 |
| 2-4: 2-Last precode (2/55) | 10 | 30 | 55 | 80 |

NOTE: Ayers a-2, 3. Maneely c-2, 3. Severin a-2.

RUGRATS COMIC ADVENTURES (TV)
Nickelodeon Magazines: 1999 - Present ($2.95, magazine size)
| 1-5, Volume 2: 1-6 | | | | 3.00 |

RUINS
Marvel Comics (Alterniverse): July, 1995 - No. 2, Sept, 1995 ($5.00, painted, limited series)
| 1,2: Phil Sheldon from Marvels; Warren Ellis scripts; acetate-c | | | | 5.00 |

RULAH JUNGLE GODDESS (Formerly Zoot; I Loved #28 on) (Also see All Top Comics & Terrors of the Jungle)
Fox Features Syndicate: No. 17, Aug, 1948 - No. 27, June, 1949
17	95	285	597	1050
18-Classic girl-fight interior splash	66	198	413	725
19,20	64	192	398	700
21-Used in SOTI, pg. 388,389	66	198	413	725
22-Used in SOTI, pg. 22,23	64	192	398	700
23-27	50	150	300	525

NOTE: Kamen c-17-19, 21, 22.

RUMBLE GIRLS: SILKY WARRIOR TANSIE
Image Comics: Apr, 2000 - Present ($3.50, B&W)
| 1-6-Lea Hernandez-s/a. 2-Warren flip-c. 5,6-Warren Ellis short story | | | | 3.50 |

RUNAWAY, THE (See Movie Classics)

RUN BABY RUN
Logos International: 1974 (39¢, Christian religious)
| nn-By Tony Tallarico from Nicky Cruz's book | 1 | 3 | 6 | 8 |

RUN, BUDDY, RUN (TV)
Gold Key: June, 1967 (Photo-c)
| 1 (10204-706) | 3 | 9 | 19 | 28 |

RUNE (See Curse of Rune, Sludge & all other Ultraverse titles for previews)
Malibu Comics (Ultraverse): 1994 - No. 9, Apr, 1995 ($1.95)
0-Obtained by sending coupons from 11 comics; came w/Solution #0, poster,				
temporary tattoo, card	1	3	6	8
1,2,4-9: 1-Barry Windsor-Smith-c/a/stories begins, ends #6. 5-1st app. of				
Gemini. 6-Prime & Mantra app.				2.25
1-(1/94)-"Ashcan" edition flip book w/Wrath #1				2.25
1-Ultra 5000 Limited silver foil edition				4.00

Ruse #2 © CRO

Saban's Mighty Morphin Power Rangers #1 © Saban Ent.

Sabrina V2 #24 © AP

	GD2.0	FN6.0	VF8.0	NM9.4

3-(3/94, $3.50, 68 pgs.)-Flip book w/Ultraverse Premiere #1 .... 3.50
Giant Size 1 ($2.50, 44 pgs.)-B.Smith story & art. 2.50

RUNE (2nd Series)(Formerly Curse of Rune)(See Ultraverse Unlimited #1)
Malibu Comics (Ultraverse): Infinity, Sept, 1995 - V2#7, Apr, 1996 ($1.50)

Infinity, V2#1-7: Infinity-Black September tie-in; black-c & painted-c exist.
1,3-7-Marvel's Adam Warlock app; regular & painted-c exist. 2-Flip book
w/ "Phoenix Resurrection" Pt. 6. .... 2.25
...Vs. Venom 1 (12/95, $3.95) 4.00

RUNE: HEARTS OF DARKNESS
Malibu Comics (Ultraverse): Sept, 1996 - No. 3, Nov, 1996 ($1.50, lim. series)

1-3: Doug Moench scripts & Kyle Hotz-c/a; flip books w/6 pg. Rune story by
the Pander Bros. 2.25

RUNE/SILVER SURFER
Marvel Comics/Malibu Comics (Ultraverse): Apr, 1995 ($5.95/$2.95, one-shot)

1 ($5.95, direct market)-BWS-c 6.00
1 ($2.95, newsstand)-BWS-c 3.00
1-Collector's limited edition 6.00

RUSE
CrossGeneration Comics: Nov, 2001 - Present ($2.95)

1-3-Waid-s/Guice & Perkins-a 3.00

RUST
Now Comics: 7/87 - No. 15, 11/88; V2#1, 2/89 - No. 7, 1989 ($1.50/$1.75)

1-15,V2#1-7: 12-(8/88)-5 pg. preview of The Terminator (1st app.) 3.00

RUST
Caliber Comics: 1996/1997 ($2.95, B&W)

1,2 .... 3.00

RUSTLERS, THE (See Zane Grey Four Color 532)

RUSTY, BOY DETECTIVE
Good Comics/Lev Gleason: Mar-April, 1955 - No. 5, Nov, 1955

1-Bob Wood, Carl Hubbell-a begins 9 27 49 70
2-5 .... 6 18 29 40

RUSTY COMICS (Formerly Kid Movie Comics; Rusty and Her Family #21, 22;
The Kelleys #23 on; see Millie The Model)
Marvel Comics (HPC): No. 12, Apr, 1947 - No. 22, Sept, 1949

12-Mitzi app. 20 60 105 175
13 .... 10 30 55 85
14-Wolverton's Powerhouse Pepper (4 pgs.) plus Kurtzman's "Hey Look"
.... 22 66 116 195
15-17-Kurtzman's "Hey Look" 16 48 83 140
18,19 .... 10 30 55 90
20-Kurtzman-a (5 pgs.) 17 51 88 150
21,22-Kurtzman-a (#18 & 22 pgs.) 22 66 116 195

RUSTY DUGAN (See Holyoke One-Shot #2)

RUSTY RILEY
Dell Publishing Co.: No. 418, Aug, 1952 - No. 554, April, 1954 (Frank Godwin
strip reprints)

Four Color 418 (...a Boy, a Horse, and a Dog #1) 4 12 30 50
Four Color #451(2/53), 486 ('53), 554 .... 4 12 26 40

SAARI ("The Jungle Goddess")
P. L. Publishing Co.: November, 1951

1 .... 43 129 257 450

SABAN POWERHOUSE (TV)
Acclaim Books: 1997 ($4.50, digest size)

1,2-Power Rangers, BeetleBorgs, and others 4.50

**SABAN PRESENTS POWER RANGERS TURBO VS. BEETLEBORGS
METALLIX** (TV)
Acclaim Books: 1997 ($4.50, digest size, one-shot)

nn 4.50

SABAN'S MIGHTY MORPHIN POWER RANGERS
Hamilton Comics: Dec, 1994 - No. 6, May, 1995 ($1.95, limited series)

1-6: 1-w/bound-in Power Ranger Barcode Card 2.25

	GD2.0	FN6.0	VF8.0	NM9.4

SABAN'S MIGHTY MORPHIN POWER RANGERS (TV)
Marvel Comics: 1995 - No. 8, 1996 ($1.75)

1-8 .... 2.25

SABAN'S NINJA RANGERS
Hamilton Comics: Dec, 1995 - No. 4, Mar, 1995 ($1.95, limited series)

1-4: Flip book w/Saban's V.R. Troopers 2.25

SABAN'S V.R. TROOPERS (See Saban's Ninja Rangers)

SABLE (Formerly Jon Sable, Freelance; also see Mike Grell's...)
First Comics: Mar, 1988 - No. 27, May, 1990 ($1.75/$1.95)

1-27: 10-Begin $1.95-c 2.25

SABRE (See Eclipse Graphic Album Series)
Eclipse Comics: Aug, 1982 - No. 14, Aug, 1985 (Baxter paper #4 on)

1-14: 1-Sabre & Morrigan Tales begin. 4-6-Incredible Seven origin 2.25

SABRETOOTH (See Iron Fist, Power Man, X-Factor #10 & X-Men)
Marvel Comics: Aug, 1993 - No. 4, Nov, 1993 ($2.95, lim. series, coated paper)

1-4: 1-Die-cut-c. 3-Wolverine app. 4.00
...Special 1 "In the Red Zone" (1995, $4.95) Chromium wraparound-c 6.00
V2 #1 (1/98, $5.95, one-shot) Wildchild app. 6.00
Trade paperback (12/94, $12.95) r/#1-4 .... 13.00

SABRETOOTH AND MYSTIQUE (See Mystique and Sabretooth)

SABRETOOTH CLASSIC
Marvel Comics: May, 1994 - No. 15, July, 1995 ($1.50)

1-15: 1-3-r/Power Man & Iron Fist #66,78,84. 4-r/Spec. S-M #116. 9-Uncanny
X-Men #212, 10-r/Uncanny X-Men #213. 11-r/ Daredevil #238. 12-r/Classic
X-Men #10 .... 3.00

SABRINA (Volume 2) (Based on animated series)
Archie Publications: Jan, 2000 - Present ($1.79/$1.99)

1-Teen-age Witch magically reverted to 12 years old 3.00
2-25: 4-Begin $1.99-c 2.50

SABRINA'S CHRISTMAS MAGIC (See Archie Giant Series Magazine #196, 207, 220,
231, 243, 455, 467, 479, 491, 503, 515)

SABRINA'S HALLOWEEN SPOOOKTACULAR
Archie Publications: 1993 - 1995 ($2.00, 52 pgs.)

1-Neon orange ink-c; bound-in poster 1 3 6 8
2,3 .... 5.00

SABRINA, THE TEEN-AGE WITCH (TV)(See Archie Giant Series, Archie's
Madhouse 22, Archie's TV..., Chilling Advs. In Sorcery, Little Archie #59)
Archie Publications: April, 1971 - No. 77, Jan, 1983 (52 pg.Giants No. 1-17)

1-52 pgs. begin, end #17 .... 14 42 102 175
2-Archie's group x-over 7 21 50 80
3-5: 3,4-Archie's Group x-over 4 12 30 50
6-10 .... 4 12 29 45
11-17(2/74) 3 10 23 35
18-30 .... 3 9 17 25
31-40(8/77) 2 6 12 18
41-60(6/80) 2 6 9 12
61-70 .... 1 3 6 9
71-76-low print run 1 4 7 10
77-Last issue; low print run 2 6 11 15

SABRINA, THE TEEN-AGE WITCH
Archie Publications: 1996 ($1.50, 32 pgs., one-shot)

1-Updated origin 5.00

SABRINA, THE TEEN-AGE WITCH (Continues in Sabrina, Vol. 2)
Archie Publications: May, 1997 - No. 32, Dec, 1999 ($1.50/$1.75/$1.79)

1-Photo-c with Melissa Joan Hart 1 3 6 8
2-10: 9-Begin $1.75-c 5.00
11-20 .... 4.00
21-32: 24-Begin $1.79-c. 28-Sonic the Hedgehog-c/app. 3.00

SABU, "ELEPHANT BOY" (Movie; formerly My Secret Story)
Fox Features Syndicate: No. 30, June, 1950 - No. 2, Aug, 1950

30(#1)-Wood-a; photo-c from movie 27 81 145 250
2-Photo-c from movie; Kamen-a 20 60 105 175

Sad Sack and the Sarge #61 © HARV

Sad Sack Comics #2 © HARV

Sad Sad Sack World #26 © HARV

	GD2.0	FN6.0	VF8.0	NM9.4

	GD2.0	FN6.0	VF8.0	NM9.4

SACHS & VIOLENS
Marvel Comics (Epic Comics): Nov, 1993 - No. 4, July, 1994 ($2.25, limited series, mature)

1-($2.75)-Embossed-c w/bound-in trading card			2.75
1-($3.50)-Platinum edition (1 for each 10 ordered)			4.00
2-4: Perez-c/a; bound-in trading card: 2-(5/94)			2.25

SACRAMENTS, THE
Catechetical Guild Educational Society: Oct, 1955 (25¢)

304		4	12	18	24

SACRED AND THE PROFANE, THE (See Eclipse Graphic Album Series #9 & Epic Illustrated #20)

SADDLE JUSTICE (Happy Houlihans #1,2) (Saddle Romances #9 on)
E. C. Comics: No. 3, Spring, 1948 - No. 8, Sept-Oct, 1949

3-The 1st E.C. by Bill Gaines to break away from M. C. Gaines' old Educational Comics format. Craig, Feldstein, H. C. Kiefer, & Stan Asch-a; mentioned in Love and Death	47	141	286	500
4-1st Graham Ingels-a for E.C.	43	129	257	450
5-8-Ingels-a in all	40	120	232	400

NOTE: *Craig and Feldstein art most issues. Canadian reprints known; see Table of Contents. Craig c-3, 4. Ingels c-5-8. #4 contains a biography of Craig.*

SADDLE ROMANCES (Saddle Justice #3-8; Weird Science #12 on)
E. C. Comics: No. 9, Nov-Dec, 1949 - No. 11, Mar-Apr, 1950

9,11-Ingels-c/a. 11-Ingels-c	43	129	257	450
10-Wood's 1st work at E.C.; Ingels-a; Feldstein-a	44	132	264	460

NOTE: *Canadian reprints known; see Table of Contents. Wood/Harrison a-10, 11.*

SADIE SACK (See Harvey Hits #93)

SAD SACK AND THE SARGE
Harvey Publications: Sept, 1957 - No. 155, June, 1982

1	13	39	94	160
2	6	18	45	75
3-10	5	15	34	55
11-20	4	12	29	45
21-30	3	9	20	30
31-50	2	6	12	18
51-70	2	6	10	14
71-90,97-99	1	3	6	9
91-96: All 52 pg. Giants	2	6	11	15
100	1	4	7	10
101-120				6.00
121-155				4.00

SAD SACK COMICS (See Harvey Collector's Comics #16, Little Sad Sack, Tastee Freez Comics #4 & True Comics #55)
Harvey Publications/Lorne-Harvey Publications (Recollections) #288 On: Sept, 1949 - No. 287, Oct, 1982; No. 288, 1992 - No. 293?, 1993

1-Infinity-c; Little Dot begins (1st app.); civilian issues begin, end #21; based on comic strip	41	123	331	600
2-Flying Fool by Powell	22	66	154	275
3	12	36	88	150
4-10	9	27	63	105
11-21	6	18	42	70
22-("Back In The Army Again" on covers #22-36); "The Specialist" story about Sad Sack's return to Army	7	21	50	80
23-50	4	12	26	40
51-80,100: 62-"The Specialist" reprinted	3	9	19	28
81-99	2	6	15	22
101-140	2	6	11	16
141-170,200	2	6	10	14
171-199	2	6	9	12
201-207: 207-Last 12¢ issue	1	4	7	10
208-222	1	3	5	7
223-228 (25¢ Giants, 52 pgs.)	2	6	9	12
229-250	1	3	6	9
251-285				5.00
286,287-Limited distribution	1	3	6	8
288,289 ($2.75, 1992): 289-50th anniversary issue				5.00
290-293 ($1.00, 1993, B&W)				3.00
3-D 1 (1/54, 25¢)-Came with 2 pairs of glasses; titled "Harvey 3-D Hits"				

...At Home for the Holidays 1 (1993, no-c price)-Publ. by Lorne-Harvey

	17	51	115	205
X-Mas issue				3.00

NOTE: *The Sad Sack Comics comic book was a spin-off from a Sunday Newspaper strip launched through John Wheeler's Bell Syndicate. The previous Sunday page and the first 21 comics depicted the Sad Sack in civvies. Unpopularity caused the Sunday page to be discontinued in the early '50s. Meanwhile Sad Sack returned to the Army, by popular demand, in issue No. 22, remaining there ever since. Incidentally, relatively few of the first 21 issues were ever collected and remain scarce due to this.*

SAD SACK FUN AROUND THE WORLD
Harvey Publications: 1974 (no month)

1-About Great Britain	2	6	12	18

SAD SACK GOES HOME
Harvey Publications: 1951 (16 pgs. in color, no cover price)

nn-By George Baker	5	15	34	55

SAD SACK LAUGH SPECIAL
Harvey Publications: Winter, 1958-59 - No. 93, Feb, 1977 (#1-9: 84 pgs.; #10-60: 68 pgs.; #61-76: 52 pgs.)

1-Giant 25¢ issues begin	10	30	70	120
2	5	15	38	60
3-10	4	12	29	45
11-30	4	12	26	40
31-60: 31-1st app. Hi-Fi Tweeter. 60-Last 68 pg. Giant	2	6	15	22
61-76-(All 52 pg. issues)	2	6	11	16
77-93	1	3	5	7

SAD SACK NAVY, GOBS 'N' GALS
Harvey Publications: Aug, 1972 - No. 8, Oct, 1973

1: 52 pg. Giant	2	6	15	22
2-8	2	6	9	12

SAD SACK'S ARMY LIFE (See Harvey Hits #8, 17, 22, 28, 32, 39, 43, 47, 51, 55, 58, 61, 64, 67, 70)

SAD SACK'S ARMY LIFE (...Parade #1-57, ...Today #58 on)
Harvey Publications: Oct, 1963 - No. 60, Nov, 1975; No. 61, May, 1976

1-(68 pg. issues begin)	6	18	45	75
2-10	3	10	23	35
11-20	3	9	17	24
21-34: Last 68 pg. issue	2	6	12	18
35-51: All 52 pgs.	2	6	10	14
52-61	1	3	6	8

SAD SACK'S FUNNY FRIENDS (See Harvey Hits #75)
Harvey Publications: Dec, 1955 - No. 75, Oct, 1969

1	9	27	65	110
2-10	5	15	34	55
11-20	3	9	19	28
21-30	2	6	13	20
31-50	2	6	11	15
51-75	2	6	9	12

SAD SACK'S MUTTSY (See Harvey Hits #74, 77, 80, 82, 84, 87, 89, 92, 96, 99, 102, 105, 108, 111, 113, 115, 117, 119, 121)

SAD SACK USA (...Vacation #8)
Harvey Publications: Nov, 1972 - No. 7, Nov, 1973; No. 8, Oct, 1974

1	2	6	12	18
2-8	1	4	7	10

SAD SACK WITH SARGE & SADIE
Harvey Publications: Sept, 1972 - No. 8, Nov, 1973

1-(52 pg. Giant)	2	6	15	22
2-8	1	4	7	10

SAD SAD SACK WORLD
Harvey Publ.: Oct, 1964 - No. 46, Dec, 1973 (#1-31: 68 pgs.; #32-38: 52 pgs.)

1	5	15	38	60
2-10	3	9	20	30
11-20	3	9	17	24
21-31: 31-Last 68 pg. issue	2	6	15	22
32-39-(All 52 pgs)	2	6	11	16

Saga of Crystar, Crystal Warrior #4 © MAR

The Saint #3 © AVON

Sam and Twitch #6 © TMP

	GD2.0	FN6.0	VF8.0	NM9.4

	GD2.0	FN6.0	VF8.0	NM9.4

40-46	1	3	6	9

SAFEST PLACE IN THE WORLD, THE
Dark Horse Comics: 1993 ($2.50, one-shot)

1-Steve Ditko-c/a/scripts				2.50

SAFETY-BELT MAN
Sirius Entertainment: June, 1994 - No. 6, 1995 ($2.50, B&W)

1-6: 1-Horan-s/Dark One-a/Sprouse-c. 2,3-Warren-c. 4-Linsner back-up story. 5,6-Crilley-a				3.00

SAFETY-BELT MAN ALL HELL
Sirius Entertainment: June, 1996 - No. 6, Mar, 1997 ($2.95, color)

1-6-Horan-s/Fillbach Bros.-a				3.00

SAFFIRE
Image Comics: Apr, 2000 - Present ($2.95)

1-3-Broome-a(p)/c				3.00
Preview-Color & B&W pages				2.25

SAGA OF BIG RED, THE
Omaha World-Herald: Sept, 1976 ($1.25) (In color)

nn-by Win Mumma; story of the Nebraska Cornhuskers (sports)				5.00

SAGA OF CRYSTAR, CRYSTAL WARRIOR, THE
Marvel Comics: May, 1983 - No. 11, Feb, 1985 (Remco toy tie-in)

1 (Baxter paper)				4.00
2-11: 3-Dr. Strange app. 3-11-Golden-c (painted-4,5). 6-Nightcrawler app; Golden-c.11-Alpha Flight app.				3.00

SAGA OF RA'S AL GHUL, THE
DC Comics: Jan, 1988 - No. 4, Apr, 1988 ($2.50, limited series)

1-4-r/N. Adams Batman				6.00

SAGA OF SABAN'S MIGHTY MORPHIN POWER RANGERS (Also see Saban's Mighty Morphin Power Rangers)
Hamilton Comics: 1995 - No. 4, 1995 ($1.95, limited series)

1-4				2.25

SAGA OF THE SWAMP THING, THE (See Swamp Thing)

SAGA OF THE ORIGINAL HUMAN TORCH
Marvel Comics: Apr, 1990 - No. 4, July, 1990 ($1.50, limited series)

1-4: 1-Origin; Buckler-c/a(p). 3-Hitler-c				2.25

SAGA OF THE SUB-MARINER, THE
Marvel Comics: Nov, 1988 - No. 12, Oct, 1989 ($1.25/$1.50 #5 on)

1-12: 9-Original X-Men app.				3.00

SAILOR MOON (Manga)
Mixx Entertainment Inc.: 1998 - Present ($2.95)

1	2	6	12	18
1-(San Diego edition)	2	6	13	20
2-5	2	6	9	12
6-27				5.00
... Rini's Moon Stick 1				15.00

SAILOR ON THE SEA OF FATE (See First Comics Graphic Novel #11)

SAILOR SWEENEY (Navy Action #1-11, 15 on)
Atlas Comics (CDS): No. 12, July, 1956 - No. 14, Nov, 1956

12-14: 12-Shores-a. 13,14-Severin-c	9	27	49	70

SAINT, THE (Also see Movie Comics(DC) #2 & Silver Streak #18)
Avon Periodicals: Aug, 1947 - No. 12, Mar, 1952

1-Kamen bondage-c/a	75	225	469	825
2	40	120	232	400
3-5: 4-Lingerie panels	36	108	191	330
6-Miss Fury app. by Tarpe Mills (14 pgs.)	43	129	257	450
7-c-/Avon paperback #118	28	84	148	255
8,9(12/50): Saint strip-r in #8-12; 9-Kinstler-c	25	75	130	225
10-Wood-a, 1 pg; c-/Avon paperback #289	25	75	130	225
11	18	54	94	155
12-c-/Avon paperback #123	21	63	110	185

NOTE: *Lucky Dale, Girl Detective* in #1,2,4,6. **Hollingsworth** in #1. **Painted-c** 7, 8, 10-12.

SAINT ANGEL

Image Comics: Mar, 2000 - Present ($2.95/$3.95)

0-Altstaetter & Napton-s/Altstaetter-a				3.00
1-4-($3.95) Flip book w/Deity. 1-(6/00). 2-(10/00)				4.00

ST. GEORGE
Marvel Comics (Epic Comics): June, 1988 - No.8, Oct, 1989 ($1.25,/$1.50)

1-8: Sienkiewicz-c. 3-begin $1.50-c				2.25

SAINT GERMAINE
Caliber Comics: 1997 - Present ($2.95)

1-8: 1,5-Alternate covers				3.00

SAINT SINNER (See Razorline)
Marvel Comics (Razorline): Oct, 1993 - No. 7, Apr, 1994 ($1.75)

1-($2.50)-Foil embossed-c; created by Clive Barker				2.50
2-7: 5-Ectokid x-over				2.25

ST. SWITHIN'S DAY
Trident Comics: Apr, 1990 ($2.50, one-shot)

1-Grant Morrison scripts				3.00

ST. SWITHIN'S DAY
Oni Press: Mar, 1998 ($2.95, B&W, one-shot)

1-Grant Morrison-s/Paul Grist-a				3.00

SALOMÉ (See Night Music #6)

SAM AND MAX, FREELANCE POLICE SPECIAL
Fishwrap Prod./Comico: 1987 ($1.75, B&W); Jan, 1989 ($2.75, 44 pgs.)

1 ($1.75, B&W, Fishwrap)				3.00
2 ($2.75, color, Comico)				2.75

SAM AND TWITCH (See Spawn)
Image Comics (Todd McFarlane Prod.): Aug, 1999 - Present ($2.50)

1-19-Bendis-s. 1-14-Medina-a. 15-19-Maleev-a				2.50
20-22-McFarlane-s/Maleev-a				2.50
Book One: Udaku (2000, $21.95, TPB) B&W reprint of #1-8				22.00

SAM HILL PRIVATE EYE
Close-Up (Archie): 1950 - No. 7, 1951

1	17	51	88	150
2	10	30	55	85
3-7	10	30	55	80

SAM SLADE ROBOHUNTER
Quality Comics: Oct, 1986 - No. 31, 1989 ($1.25/$1.50)

1-31				2.25

SAMSON (1st Series) (Captain Aero #7 on; see Big 3 Comics)
Fox Features Syndicate: June, 1940 - No. 6, Sept, 1941 (See Fantastic Comics)

1-Samson begins, ends #6; Powell-a, signed 'Rensie;' Wing Turner by Tuska app; Fine-c?	255	765	1591	2800
2-Dr. Fung by Powell; Fine-c?	89	267	556	975
3-Navy Jones app.; Joe Simon-c	68	205	426	750
4-Yarko the Great, Master Magician begins	59	177	369	650
5,6: 6-Origin The Topper	47	141	286	500

SAMSON (2nd Series) (Formerly Fantastic Comics #10, 11)
Ajax/Farrell Publications (Four Star): No. 12, April, 1955 - No. 14, Aug, 1955

12-Wonder Boy	31	93	165	285
13,14: 13-Wonder Boy, Rocket Man	27	81	142	245

SAMSON (See Mighty Samson)

SAMSON & DELILAH (See A Spectacular Feature Magazine)

SAM STORIES: LEGS
Image Comics: Dec, 1999 ($2.50, one-shot)

1-Sam Kieth-s/a				2.50

SAMUEL BRONSTON'S CIRCUS WORLD (See Circus World under Movie Classics)

SAMURAI (Also see Eclipse Graphic Album Series #14)
Aircel Publications: 1985 - No. 23, 1987 ($1.70, B&W)

1, 14-16-Dale Keown-a				3.00
1-(reprinted),2-12;17-23: 2 (reprinted issue exists)				2.25
13-Dale Keown's 1st published artwork (1987)				5.00

The Sandman #5 © DC

Sandman #34 © DC

Sandman Mystery Theater #5 © DC

	GD2.0	FN6.0	VF8.0	NM9.4

SAMURAI
Warp Graphics: May, 1997 ($2.95, B&W)
1   3.00

SAMURAI CAT
Marvel Comics (Epic Comics): June, 1991 - No. 3, Sept, 1991 ($2.25, limited series)
1-3: 3-Darth Vader-c/story parody   2.25

SAMUREE
Continuity Comics: May, 1987 - No. 9, Jan, 1991
1-9   3.00

SAMUREE
Continuity Comics: V2#1, May, 1993 - V2#4, Jan,1994 ($2.50)
V2#1-4-Embossed-c: 2,4-Adams plot, Nebres-i. 3-Nino-c(i)   2.50

SAMUREE
Acclaim Comics (Windjammer): Oct, 1995 - No. 2, Nov,1995 ($2.50, lim. series)
1,2   2.50

SAN DIEGO COMIC CON COMICS
Dark Horse Comics: 1992 - No.4, 1995 (B&W, promo comic for the San Diego Comic Con)
1-(1992)-Includes various characters published from Dark Horse including Concrete, The Mask, RoboCop and others; 1st app. of Sprint from John Byrne's Next Men; art by Quesada, Byrne, Rude, Moebius & others; pin-ups by Rude, Dorkin, Allred & others; Chadwick-c.   5.00
2-(1993)-Intro of Legend imprint; 1st app. of John Byrne's Danger Unlimited, Mike Mignola's Hellboy, Art Adams' Monkeyman & O'Brien; contains stories featuring Concrete, Sin City, Martha Washington & others; Grendel, Madman & Big Guy pin-ups; Don Martin-c.   1   3   5   7
3-(1994)-Contains stories featuring Barb Wire, The Mask, The Dirty Pair, & Grendel by Matt Wagner; contains pin-ups of Ghost, Predator & Rascals In Paradise; The Mask-c.   5.00
4-(1995)-Contains Sin City story by Miller (3pg.), Star Wars, The Mask, Tarzan, Foot Soldiers; Sin City & Star Wars flip-c   5.00

SANDMAN, THE (1st Series) (Also see Adventure Comics #40, New York World's Fair & World's Finest #3)
National Periodical Publications: Winter, 1974; No. 2, Apr-May, 1975 - No. 6, Dec-Jan, 1975-76
1-1st app. Bronze Age Sandman by Simon & Kirby (last S&K collaboration)
                                                4   12   29   45
2-6: 6-Kirby/Wood-c/a   2   6   12   18
NOTE: *Kirby* a-1p, 4-6p; c-1-5, 6p.

SANDMAN (2nd Series) (See Books of Magic, Vertigo Jam & Vertigo Preview)
DC Comics (Vertigo imprint #47 on): Jan, 1989 - No. 75, Mar, 1996 ($1.50/$1.75/$2.50, mature)
1 ($2.00, 52 pgs.)-1st app. Modern Age Sandman (Morpheus); Neil Gaiman scripts begin; Sam Kieth-a(p) in #1-5; Wesley Dodds (G.A. Sandman) cameo.   3   9   20   30
2-Cain & Abel app. (from HOM & HOS)   2   6   9   12
3-5: 3-John Constantine app.   1   4   7   10
6,7   1   3   5   7
8-Death-c/story (1st app.)-Regular ed. has Jeanette Kahn publishorial & American Cancer Society ad w/no indicia on inside front-c
                                                      2   6   12   18
8-Limited ed. (600+ copies?); has Karen Berger editorial and next issue teaser on inside covers (has indicia)   5   15   38   60
9-14: 10-Has explaination about #8 mixup; has bound-in Shocker movie poster. 14-(52 pgs.)-Bound-in Nightbreed fold-out   1   3   6   9
15-20: 16-Photo-c. 17,18-Kelley Jones-a. 19-Vess-a.   6.00
18-Error version w/1st 3 panels on pg. 1 in blue ink 3   9   17   25
19-Error version w/pages 18 & 20 facing each other 2   6   13   20
21,23-27: Seasons of Mist storyline. 22-World Without End preview. 24-Kelley Jones/Russell-a   6.00
22-1st Daniel (Later becomes new Sandman)   1   3   6   9
28-30   5.00
31-49,51-74: 41,44-48-Metallic ink on-c. 48-Cerebus appears as a doll. 36-(52 pgs.). 54-Re-intro Prez; Death app.; Belushi, Nixon & Wildcat cameos. 57-Metallic ink on c. 65-w/bound-in trading card. 69-Death of

Sandman. 70-73-Zulli-a. 74-Jon J. Muth-a.   4.00
50-($2.95, 52 pgs.)-Black-c w/metallic ink by McKean; Russell-a; McFarlane pin-up.   5.00
50-($2.95)-Signed & limited (5,000) Treasury Edition with sketch of Neil Gaiman   1   3   6   8
50-Platinum   20.00
75-($3.95)-Vess-a.   5.00
Special 1 (1991, $3.50, 68 pgs.)-Glow-in-the-dark-c   5.00
...: A Gallery of Dreams ($2.95)-Intro by N. Gaiman   3.00
...: Preludes & Nocturnes ($29.95, HC)-r/#1-8.   30.00
...: The Doll's House (1990, $29.95, HC)-r/#8-16.   30.00
...: Dream Country ($29.95, HC)-r/#17-20.   30.00
...: Season of Mists ($29.95, Leatherbound HC)-r/#21-28.   50.00
...: A Game of You ($29.95, HC)-r/32-37, ...: Fables and Reflections ($29.95, HC)-r/Vertigo Preview #1, Sandman Special #1, #29-31, #38-40 & #50.
...: Brief Lives ($29.95, HC)-r/#41-49. ...: World's End ($29.95, HC)-r/#51-56.
                                                             30.00
...: The Kindly Ones (1996, $34.95, HC)-r/#57-69 & Vertigo Jam #1   35.00
...: The Wake ($29.95, HC)-r/#70-75.   30.00
NOTE: *A new set of hardcover printings with new covers was introduced in 1998-99. Multiple printings exist of softcover collections. Bachalo a-12; Kelley Jones a-17, 18, 22, 23, 26, 27. Vess a-19, 75.*

SANDMAN MIDNIGHT THEATRE
DC Comics (Vertigo): Sept, 1995 ($6.95, squarebound, one-shot)
nn-Modern Age Sandman (Morpheus) meets G.A. Sandman; Gaiman & Wagner story; McKean-c; Kristiansen-a   7.00

SANDMAN MYSTERY THEATRE (Also see Sandman (2nd Series) #1)
DC Comics (Vertigo): Apr, 1993 - No. 70, Feb, 1999 ($1.95/$2.25/$2.50)
1-G.A. Sandman advs. begin; Matt Wagner scripts begin   4.50
2-49: 5-Neon ink logo. 29-32-Hourman app. 38-Ted Knight (G.A. Starman) app. 42-Jim Corrigan (Spectre) app. 45-48-Blackhawk app.   2.50
50-($3.50, 48 pgs.) w/bonus story of S.A. Sandman, Torres-a   3.50
51-70   2.50
Annual 1 (10/94, $3.95, 68 pgs.)-Alex Ross, Bolton & others-a 5.00

SANDMAN PRESENTS: DEADBOY DETECTIVES (See Sandman #21-28)
DC Comics (Vertigo): Aug, 2001 - No. 4, Nov, 2001 ($2.50, limited series)
1-4:Talbot-a/McKean-c/Brubaker-s   2.50

SANDMAN, THE: EVERYTHING YOU ALWAYS WANTED TO KNOW ABOUT DREAMS...BUT WERE AFRAID TO ASK
DC Comics (Vertigo): Jul, 2001 ($3.95, one-shot)
1-Short stories by Willingham; art by various; McKean-c   4.00

SANDMAN PRESENTS: LOVE STREET
DC Comics (Vertigo): Jul, 1999 - No. 3, Sept, 1999 ($2.95, limited series)
1-3: Teenage Hellblazer in 1968 London; Zulli-a   3.00

SANDMAN PRESENTS: LUCIFER
DC Comics (Vertigo): Mar, 1999 - No. 3, May, 1999 ($2.95, limited series)
1-3: Scott Hampton painted-c/a   3.00

SANDMAN PRESENTS: PETREFAX
DC Comics (Vertigo): Mar, 2000 - No. 4, Jun, 2000 ($2.95, limited series)
1-4-Carey-s/Leialoha-a   3.00

SANDMAN PRESENTS: THE CORINTHIAN
DC Comics (Vertigo): Dec, 2001 - No. 3, Feb, 2002 ($2.95, limited series)
1-3-Macan-s/Zezelj-a/McKean-c   3.00

SANDMAN, THE: THE DREAM HUNTERS
DC Comics (Vertigo): Oct, 1999 ($29.95/$19.95, one-shot)
Hardcover-Neil Gaiman-s/Yoshitaka Amano-painted art   30.00
Softcover-(2000, $19.95) new Amano-c   20.00

SANDMAN PRESENTS: THE THESSALIAD
DC Comics (Vertigo): Mar, 2002 - No. 4, Jun, 2002 ($2.95, limited series)
1-Willingham-s/McManus-a/McKean-c   3.00

SANDS OF THE SOUTH PACIFIC
Toby Press: Jan, 1953
1   22   66   116   195

Santa Claus Funnies nn © DELL

Satan's Six #4 © Jack Kirby

Savage Dragon #76 © Erik Larsen

	GD2.0	FN6.0	VF8.0	NM9.4

SANTA AND HIS REINDEER (See March of Comics #166)

SANTA AND THE ANGEL (See Dell Junior Treasury #7)
Dell Publishing Co.: Dec, 1949 (Combined w/Santa at the Zoo) (Gollub-a condensed from FC#128)

Four Color 259	4	12	30	50

SANTA AT THE ZOO (See Santa And The Angel)

SANTA CLAUS AROUND THE WORLD (See March of Comics #241 in Promotional Comics section)

SANTA CLAUS CONQUERS THE MARTIANS (See Movie Classics)

SANTA CLAUS FUNNIES (Also see Dell Giants)
Dell Publishing Co.: Dec?, 1942 - No. 1274, Dec, 1961

nn(#1)(1942)-Kelly-a	37	110	259	480
2(12/43)-Kelly-a	25	75	175	320
Four Color 61(1944)-Kelly-a	24	72	168	310
Four Color 91(1945)-Kelly-a	18	54	126	230
Four Color 128('46),175('47)-Kelly-a	14	41	98	180
Four Color 205,254-Kelly-a	13	39	91	165
Four Color 302,361,525,607,666,756,867	5	15	35	60
Four Color 958,1063,1154,1274	5	15	34	55

NOTE: Most issues contain only one Kelly story.

SANTA CLAUS PARADE
Ziff-Davis (Approved Comics)/St. John Publishing Co.: 1951; No. 2, Dec, 1952; No. 3, Jan, 1955 (25¢)

nn(1951-Ziff-Davis)-116 pgs. (Xmas Special 1,2)	29	87	156	270
2(12/52-Ziff-Davis)-100 pgs.; Dave Berg-a	23	69	121	210
V1#3(1/55-St. John)-100 pgs.; reprints-c/#1	20	60	105	180

SANTA CLAUS' WORKSHOP (See March of Comics #50,168 in Promotional Comics sect.)

SANTA IS COMING (See March of Comics #197 in Promotional Comics section)

SANTA IS HERE (See March of Comics #49 in Promotional Comics section)

SANTA'S BUSY CORNER (See March of Comics #31 in Promotional Comics section)

SANTA'S CANDY KITCHEN (See March of Comics #14 in Promotional Comics section)

SANTA'S CHRISTMAS BOOK (See March of Comics #123 in Promotional Comics sect.)

SANTA'S CHRISTMAS COMICS
Standard Comics (Best Books): Dec, 1952 (100 pgs.)

nn-Supermouse, Dizzy Duck, Happy Rabbit, etc.	19	57	99	170

SANTA'S CHRISTMAS LIST (See March of Comics #255 in Promotional Comics section)

SANTA'S HELPERS (See March of Comics #64, 106, 198 in Promotional Comics section)

SANTA'S LITTLE HELPERS (See March of Comics #270 in Promotional Comics section)

SANTA'S SHOW (See March of Comics #311 in Promotional Comics section)

SANTA'S SLEIGH (See March of Comics #298 in Promotional Comics section)

SANTA'S SURPRISE (See March of Comics #13 in Promotional Comics section)

SANTA'S TINKER TOTS
Charlton Comics: 1958

1-Based on "The Tinker Tots Keep Christmas"	3	9	20	30

SANTA'S TOYLAND (See March of Comics #242 in Promotional Comics section)

SANTA'S TOYS (See March of Comics #12 in Promotional Comics section)

SANTA'S VISIT (See March of Comics #283 in Promotional Comics section)

SANTA THE BARBARIAN
Maximum Press: Dec, 1996 ($2.99, one-shot)

1-Fraga/Mhan-s/a				3.00

SANTIAGO (Movie)
Dell Publishing Co.: Sept, 1956 (Alan Ladd photo-c)

Four Color 723-Kinstler-a	10	30	70	130

SARGE SNORKEL (Beetle Bailey)
Charlton Comics: Oct, 1973 - No. 17, Dec, 1976

1	2	6	12	18
2-10	2	6	9	12
11-17	1	3	6	9

SARGE STEEL (Becomes Secret Agent #9 on; also see Judomaster)

Charlton Comics: Dec, 1964 - No. 8, Mar-Apr, 1966 (All 12¢ issues)

1-Origin & 1st app.	3	10	23	35
2-5,7,8	2	6	13	30
6-2nd app. Judomaster	3	9	19	28

SATANIKA
Verotik: Jan, 1995 - No. 3, 1996 ($2.95, limited series, mature)

0-3: 0-Danzig story in all. 0-(7/95)-Frazetta-c; 1-Bisley-c.				5.00
The Brimstone Trail (1996, $9.95, TPB)-r/#0-2.				10.00

SATANIKA
Verotik: Feb, 1996 - No. 11 ($2.95, mature)

1-11: Danzig story in all. 2-Igrat cameo; indicia reads "Satanika #1." 4,5-nudity-c. 8-Alternate-c				3.00

SATANIKA X
Verotik: Feb, 1996 ($4.95, one-shot, mature)

1-Embossed-c.				5.00

SATAN'S SIX
Topps Comics (Kirbyverse): Apr, 1993 - No. 4, July, 1993 ($2.95, lim. series)

1-4: 1-Polybagged w/Kirbychrome trading card; Kirby/McFarlane-c plus 8 pgs. Kirby-a(p); has coupon for Kirbychrome ed. of Secret City Saga #0. 2-4-Polybagged w/3 cards. 4-Teenagents preview				3.00

NOTE: Ditko a-1. Miller a-1.

SATAN'S SIX: HELLSPAWN
Topps Comics (Kirbyverse): June, 1994 - No. 3, July, 1994 ($2.50, lim. series)

1-3: 1-(6/94)-Indicia incorrectly shows "Vol 1 #2". 2-(6/94)				2.50

SAVAGE COMBAT TALES
Atlas/Seaboard Publ.: Feb, 1975 - No. 3, July, 1975

1,3: 1-Sgt. Stryker's Death Squad begins (origin); Goodwin-s	1	3	5	7
2-Toth-a; only app. War Hawk; Goodwin-s	1	4	7	10

NOTE: Buckler c-3. McWilliams a-1-3; c-1. Sparling a-1, 3.

SAVAGE DRAGON, THE (See Megaton #3 & 4)
Image Comics (Highbrow Entertainment): July, 1992 - No. 3, Dec, 1992 ($1.95, limited series)

1-Erik Larsen-c/a/scripts & bound-in poster in all; 4 cover color variations w/4 different posters; 1st app. Highbrow Entertainment title				4.00
2-Intro SuperPatriot-c/story (10/92)				3.00
3-Contains coupon for Image Comics #0				3.00
3-With coupon missing				2.25
...Vs. Savage Megaton Man 1 (3/93, $1.95)-Larsen & Simpson-c/a.				3.00
TPB ('93, $9.95) r/#1-3				10.00

SAVAGE DRAGON, THE
Image Comics (Highbrow Entertainment): June, 1993 - Present ($1.95/$2.50)

1-Erik Larsen-c/a/scripts				4.00
2-30: 2-(Wondercon Exclusive): 2-($2.95, 52 pgs.)-Teenage Mutant Ninja Turtles-c/story; flip book features Vanguard #0 (See Megaton for 1st app.). 3-7: Erik Larsen-c/a/scripts. 3-Mighty Man back-up story w/Austin-a(i). 4-Flip book w/Ricochet. 5-Mighty Man flip-c & back-up plus poster. 6-Jae Lee poster. 7-Vanguard poster. 8-Deadly Duo poster by Larsen. 13A (10/94)-Jim Lee-c/a; 1st app. Max Cash (Condition Red). 13B (6/95)-Larsen story. 15-Dragon poster by Larsen. 22-TMNT-c/a; Bisley pin-up. 27-"Wondercon Exclusive" new-c. 28-Maxx-c/app. 29-Wildstar-c/app. 30-Spawn app.				3.00
25 ($3.95)-variant-c exists.				4.00
31-49,51-71: 31-God vs. The Devil; alternate version exists w/o expletives (has "God Is Good" inside Image logo) 33-Birth of Dragon/Rapture's baby. 34,35-Hellboy-c/app. 51-Origin of She-Dragon. 70-Ann Stevens killed				2.50
50-($5.95, 100 pgs.) Kaboom and Mighty Man app.; Matsuda back-c; pin-ups by McFarlane, Simonson, Capullo and others				6.00
72-74: 72-Begin $2.95-c				3.00
75-($5.95)				6.00
76-91: 76-New direction starts. 83,84-Madman-c/app. 84-Atomics app.				3.00
The Fallen (11/97, $12.95, TPB) r/#7-11, ...Possessed (9/98, $12.95, TPB) r/#12-16, ...Revenge (1998, $12.95, TPB) r/#17-21				13.00
...Gang War (4/00, $16.95, TPB) r/#22-26				17.00
...Team-Ups (10/98, $19.95, TPB) r/team-ups				20.00

SAVAGE DRAGON ARCHIVES (See Dragon Archives, The)

Savage She-Hulk #25 © MAR

Savage Sword of Conan #92 © Conan Properties

Scarecrow (Villains) #1 © DC

	GD2.0	FN6.0	VF8.0	NM9.4

SAVAGE DRAGON/DESTROYER DUCK, THE
Image Comics/ Highbrow Entertainment: Nov, 1996 ($3.95, one-shot)

1 .... 4.00

SAVAGE DRAGON/MARSHALL LAW
Image Comics: July, 1997 - No. 2, Aug, 1997 ($2.95, B&W, limited series)

1,2-Pat Mills-s, Kevin O'Neill-a 3.00

SAVAGE DRAGON: SEX & VIOLENCE
Image Comics: Aug, 1997 - No. 2, Sept, 1997 ($2.50, limited series)

1,2-T&M Bierbaum-s, Mays, Lupka, Adam Hughes-a 3.00

SAVAGE DRAGON/TEENAGE MUTANT NINJA TURTLES CROSSOVER
Mirage Studios: Sept, 1993 ($2.75, one-shot)

1-Erik Larsen-c(i) only 3.00

SAVAGE DRAGON: THE RED HORIZON
Image Comics/ Highbrow Entertainment: Feb, 1997 - No. 3 ($2.50, lim. series)

1-3 .... 3.00

SAVAGE FISTS OF KUNG FU
Marvel Comics Group: 1975 (Marvel Treasury)

1-Iron Fist, Shang Chi, Sons of Tiger; Adams, Starlin-a

| | 2 | 6 | 15 | 22 |

SAVAGE HENRY
Vortex Comics: Jan, 1987 - No. 16?, 1990 ($1.75/$2.00, B&W, mature)

1-16 .... 2.50

SAVAGE HULK, THE (Also see Incredible Hulk)
Marvel Comics: Jan, 1996 ($6.95, one-shot)

1-Bisley-c; David, Lobdell, Wagner, Loeb, Gibbons, Messner-Loebs scripts; McKone, Kieth, Ramos & Sale-a. 7.00

SAVAGE RAIDS OF GERONIMO (See Geronimo #4)

SAVAGE RANGE (See Luke Short, Four Color 807)

SAVAGE RETURN OF DRACULA
Marvel Comics: 1992 ($2.00, 52 pgs.)

1-r/Tomb of Dracula #1,2 by Gene Colan 2.25

SAVAGE SHE-HULK, THE (See The Avengers, Marvel Graphic Novel #18 & The Sensational She-Hulk)
Marvel Comics Group: Feb, 1980 - No. 25, Feb, 1982

1-Origin & 1st app. She-Hulk	2	6	9	12
2-5,25: (52 pgs.)				6.00
6-24: 6-She-Hulk vs. Iron Man. 8-Vs. Man-Thing				5.00

NOTE: Austin a-25i; c-23i-25i. J. Buscema a-1p; c-1, 2p. Golden c-8-11.

SAVAGE SWORD OF CONAN (The... #41 on; ...The Barbarian #175 on)
Marvel Comics Group: Aug, 1974 - No. 235, July, 1995 ($1.00/$1.25/$2.25, B&W magazine, mature)

1-Smith-r; J. Buscema/N. Adams/Krenkel-a; origin Blackmark by Gil Kane (part 1, ends #3); Blackmark's 1st app. in magazine form-r/from paperback) & Red Sonja (3rd app.)	8	24	56	90
2-Neal Adams-c; Chaykin/N. Adams-a	3	10	23	35
3-Severin/B. Smith-a; N. Adams-a	2	6	15	22
4-Neal Adams/Kane-a(r)	2	6	13	20
5-10: 5-Jeff Jones frontispiece (r)	1	4	11	16
11-20	2	6	9	12
21-50: 34-3 pg. preview of Conan newspaper strip. 35-Cover similar to Savage Tales #1. 45-Red Sonja returns; begin $1.25-c	1	4	7	10
51-100: 63-Toth frontispiece. 65-Kane-a w/Chaykin/Miller/Simonson/Sherman finishes. 70-Article on movie. 83-Red Sonja-r by Neal Adams from #1				6.00
101-176: 163-Begin $2.25-c. 169-King Kull story. 171-Soloman Kane by Williamson (i). 172-Red Sonja story				5.00
177-220: 179,187,192-Red Sonja app. 190-193-4 part King Kull story. 196, 202-King Kull story. 200-New Buscema-a; Robert E. Howard app. with Conan in story. 204-60th anniversary (1932-92). 211-Rafael Kayanan's 1st Conan-a. 214-Sequel to Red Nails by Robert E. Howard				4.00
221-235				4.00
Special 1(1975, B&W)-B. Smith-r/Conan #10,13	2	6	13	20

NOTE: N. Adams a-14p, 60, 83p(r). Alcala a-2 ,4, 7, 12, 15-20, 23, 24, 28, 59, 67, 69, 75, 76i,

80i, 82i, 83i, 89, 180i, 184i, 187i, 189i, 216p. Austin a-78i. Boris painted c-1, 4, 5, 7, 9, 10, 12, 15. Brunner a-30; c-8, 30. Buscema a-1-5, 7, 10-12, 15-24, 26-28, 31, 32, 36-43, 45, 47-58p, 65-67p, 70, 71-74p, 76-81p, 87-96p, 98, 99-101p, 190-204p; painted c-40. Chaykin c-31. Chiodo painted c-71, 76, 79, 81, 84, 85, 178. Conrad c-215, 217. Corben a-4, 16, 29. Finlay a-16. Golden a-98, 101; c-98, 101, 105, 106, 117, 124, 150. Kaluta a-11, 18; c-3, 91, 93. Gil Kane a-2, 3, 8, 13r, 29, 47, 64, 65, 67, 85p, 86p. Rafael Kayanan a-211-213, 215, 217. Krenkel a-9, 11, 14, 16, 24. Morrow a-7. Nebres a-93i, 101i, 107, 114. Newton a-6. Nino c/a-6. Redondo painted c-48-50, 52, 56, 57, 85i, 90, 96i. Marie & John Severin a-Special 1. Simonson a-7, 8, 12, 15-17. Barry Smith a-7, 16, 24, 82r, Special 1r. Starlin a-5. Toth a-64. Williamson a(i)-162, 171, 186. No. 8 , 10 & 16 contain a Robert E. Howard Conan adaptation.

SAVAGE TALES (...Featuring Conan #4 on)(Magazine)
Marvel Comics Group: May, 1971; No. 2, 10/73; No. 3, 2/74 - No. 12, Summer, 1975 (B&W)

1-Origin/1st app. The Man-Thing by Morrow; Conan the Barbarian by Barry Smith (1st Conan x-over outside his own title); Femizons by Romita-r/in #3; Ka-Zar story by Buscema	14	42	102	175
2-B. Smith, Brunner, Morrow, Williamson-a; Wrightson King Kull reprint/ Creatures on the Loose #10	4	12	26	40
3-B. Smith, Brunner, Steranko, Williamson-a	3	9	20	30
4,5-N. Adams-c; last Conan (Smith-r/#4) plus Kane-a. 5-Brak the Barbarian begins, ends #8	3	9	17	25
6-Ka-Zar begins; Williamson-r; N. Adams-c	2	6	11	15
7-N. Adams-c	2	6	9	12
8,9,11: 8-Shanna, the She-Devil app. thru #10; Williamson-r	1	4	7	10
10-Neal Adams-a(i), Williamson-r	2	6	9	12
...Featuring Ka-Zar Annual 1 (Summer, '75, B&W)(#12 on inside)-Ka-Zar story by G. Kane; B. Smith-a/Astonishing Tales	2	6	11	15

NOTE: Boris c-7, 10. Buscema a-5r, 6p, 8p; c-2. Colan a-1p. Fabian c-8. Golden a-1, 4; c-1. Heath a-10p, 11p. Kaluta c-9. Maneely r-2, 4(The Crusader in both). Morrow a-1, 2, Annual 1. Reese a-2. Severin a-1-7. Starlin a-5. Robert E. Howard adaptations-1-4.

SAVAGE TALES
Marvel Comics Group: Nov, 1985 - No. 8, Dec, 1986 ($1.50, B&W, magazine, mature)

| 1-1st app. The Nam; Golden, Morrow-a | | | | 5.00 |
| 2-8: 2,7-Morrow-a. 4-2nd Nam story; Golden-a | | | | 3.00 |

SAVANT GARDE (Also see WildC.A.T.S.)
Image Comics/WildStorm Productions: Mar, 1997 - No. 7, Sept, 1997 ($2.50)

1-7 .... 2.50

SAVED BY THE BELL (TV)
Harvey Comics: Mar, 1992 - No. 4, Aug, 1992? ($1.25, limited series)

1-4, Special 1 (9/92, $1.50)-photo-c 2.25

SCAMP (Walt Disney)(See Walt Disney's Comics & Stories #204)
Dell Publ. Co.: No. 703, 5/56 - No. 1204, 8-10/61; 11/67 - No. 45, 1/79

Four Color 703(#1)	9	27	63	110
Four Color 777,806('57),833	6	18	42	80
5(3-5/58)-10(8-9/59)	5	15	35	60
11-16(12-2/60-61), Four Color 1204(1961)	4	12	29	45
1(12/67-Gold Key)-Reprints begin	4	12	29	45
2(3/69)-10	2	6	12	18
11-20	1	4	7	10
21-45				6.00

NOTE: New stories-#20(in part), 22-25, 27, 29-31, 34, 36-40, 42-45. New covers-#11, 12, 14, 15, 17-25, 27, 29-31, 34, 36-38.

SCARAB
DC Comics (Vertigo): Nov, 1993 - No. 8, June, 1994 ($1.95, limited series)

1-8-Glenn Fabry painted-c: 1-Silver ink-c. 2-Phantom Stranger app. 2.25

SCAR FACE (See The Crusaders)

SCARECROW OF ROMNEY MARSH, THE (See W. Disney Showcase #53)
Gold Key: April, 1964 - No. 3, Oct, 1965 (Disney TV Show)

| 10112-404 (#1) | 4 | 12 | 26 | 40 |
| 2,3 | 3 | 9 | 19 | 28 |

SCARECROW (VILLAINS) (See Batman)
DC Comics: Feb, 1998 ($1.95, one-shot)

1-Fegredo-a/Milligan-s/Pearson-c 2.50

SCARE TACTICS
DC Comics: Dec, 1996 - No. 12, Mar, 1998 ($2.25)

	GD2.0	FN6.0	VF8.0	NM9.4

1-12: 1-1st app.   2.25

SCARLET O'NEIL (See Harvey Comics Hits #59 & Invisible...)

SCARLET CRUSH
Awesome Entertainment: Jan, 1998 - No. 2, Feb, 1998 ($2.50)
1-Five covers by Liefeld, Stinsman(wraparound), Churchill, Skroce, and
   Sprouse; Stinsman-s/a(p)   2.50
1-American Entertainment Ed.; Stinsman-c   5.00
2-Three covers by Stinsman, McGuinness & Peterson   2.50

SCARLET SPIDER
Marvel Comics: Nov, 1995 - No. 2, Jan, 1996 ($1.95)
1,2: Replaces Spider-Man   2.25

SCARLET SPIDER UNLIMITED
Marvel Comics: Nov, 1995 ($3.95, one-shot)
1-Replaces Spider-Man Unlimited   4.00

SCARLETT
DC Comics: Jan, 1993 - No. 14, Feb, 1994 (1.75)
1-($2.95)   3.00
2-14   2.25

SCARLET WITCH (See Avengers #16, Vision &... & X-Men #4)
Marvel Comics: Jan, 1994 - No. 4, Apr, 1994 ($1.75, limited series)
1-4   2.25

SCARY GODMOTHER
Sirius: 2001 - No. 6, 2002 ($2.95, B&W)
1-5-Jill Thompson-s/a   3.00

SCARY GODMOTHER: ACTIVITY BOOK
Sirius: Dec, 2000 ($2.95, B&W, one-shot)
1-Jill Thompson-s/a   3.00

SCARY GODMOTHER: BLOODY VALENTINE SPECIAL
Sirius: Feb, 1998 ($3.95, B&W, one-shot)
1-Jill Thompson-s/a; pin-ups by Ross, Mignola, Russell   4.00

SCARY GODMOTHER: HOLIDAY SPOOKTAKULAR
Sirius: Nov, 1998 ($2.95, B&W, one-shot)
1-Thompson-s/a; pin-ups by Brereton, LaBan, Dorkin, Fingerman   3.00

SCARY GODMOTHER: THE BOO FLU
Sirius: Sept, 2000 ($19.95, hardcover with dust jacket, one-shot)
1-Jill Thompson-s/a   20.00

SCARY GODMOTHER: WILD ABOUT HARRY
Sirius: 2000 - No. 3 ($2.95, B&W, limited series)
1-3-Jill Thompson-s/a   3.00
TPB (2001, $9.95) r/series   10.00

SCARY TALES
Charlton Comics: 8/75 - #9, 1/77; #10, 9/77 - #20, 6/79; #21, 8/80 - #46, 10/84

1-Origin/1st app. Countess Von Bludd, not in #2	3	9	17	25
2,4,6,9,10: 4-Sutton-a. 9-Sutton-c/a	1	4	7	10
3-Sutton painted-c; Ditko-a	2	6	11	15
5,11-Ditko-c/a.	2	6	10	14
7,8-Ditko-a	2	6	9	12
12,15,16,19,21,39-Ditko-a	1	4	7	10
13,17,20	1	3	6	8
14,18,30,32-Ditko-c/a	2	6	9	12
22-29,31,33-40: 31-Newton-c/a. 37,38,40-New-a. 38-Mr. Jigsaw app. 39-Reprints				
	1	3	5	7
41-45-New-a. 41-Ditko-a(3). 42-45-(Low print)	1	3	6	8
46-Reprints (Low print)	2	6	9	12
1(Modern Comics reprint, 1977)				4.00
NOTE: *Adkins a-31i; c-31i. Ditko a-3, 5, 7, 8(2), 11, 12, 14-16r, 18(3)r, 19r, 21r, 30r, 32, 39r, 41(3); c-5, 11, 14, 18, 30, 32. Newton a-31p; c-31p. Powell a-18r. Staton a-1(2 pgs.), 4, 20r; c-1, 20. Sutton a-9; c-4, 9.*

SCATTERBRAIN
Dark Horse Comics: Jun, 1998 - No. 4, Sept, 1998 ($2.95, limited series)
1-4-Humor anthology by Aragonés, Dorkin, Stevens and others   3.00

SCAVENGERS

Quality Comics: Feb, 1988 - No. 14, 1989 ($1.25/$1.50)
1-14: 9-13-Guice-c   2.25

SCAVENGERS
Triumphant Comics: 1993(nd, July) - No. 11, May, 1994 ($2.50, serially numbered)
1-9,0,10,11: 5,6-Triumphant Unleashed x-over. 9-(3/94). 0-Retail edition (3/94,
   $2.50, 36 pgs.). 0-Giveaway edition (3/94, 20 pgs.). 0-Coupon redemption
   edition. 10-(4/94)   2.50

SCENE OF THE CRIME (Also see Vertigo: Winter's Edge #2)
DC Comics (Vertigo): May, 1999 - No. 4, Aug, 1999 ($2.50, limited series)
1-4-Brubaker-s/Lark-a/a   2.50
.... A Little Piece of Goodnight TPB ('00, $12.95) r/#1-4; Winter's Edge #2   13.00

SCHOOL DAY ROMANCES (...of Teen-Agers #4; Popular Teen-Agers #5 on)
Star Publications: Nov-Dec, 1949 - No. 4, May-June, 1950 (Teenage)

1-Toni Gayle (later Toni Gay), Ginger Snapp, Midge Martin & Eve Adams				
begin	29	87	153	265
2,3: 3-Jane Powell photo on-c & true life story	21	63	110	185
4-Ronald Reagan photo on-c; L.B. Cole-c	31	93	168	290
NOTE: *All have L. B. Cole covers.*

SCHWINN BICYCLE BOOK (...Bike Thrills, 1959)
Schwinn Bicycle Co.: 1949; 1952; 1959 (10¢)

1949	6	18	28	38
1952-Believe It or Not facts; comic format; 36 pgs.	4	12	19	25
1959	2	6	9	12

SCIENCE COMICS (1st Series)
Fox Features Syndicate: Feb, 1940 - No. 8, Sept, 1940

1-Origin Dynamo (1st app., called Electro in #1), & The Eagle (1st app.), & Navy				
Jones; Marga, The Panther Woman (1st app.), Cosmic Carson & Perisphere				
Payne, Dr. Doom begin; bondage/hypo-c; Electro-c				
	417	1250	2604	5000
2-Classic Lou Fine Dynamo-c	214	642	1338	2350
3-Classic Lou Fine Dynamo-c	177	531	1106	1950
4-Kirby-a; Cosmic Carson-c by Joe Simon	155	465	966	1700
5-8: 5,8-Eagle-c. 6,7-Dynamo-c	91	273	568	1000
NOTE: *Cosmic Carson by Tuska-#1-3; by Kirby-#4. Lou Fine c-1-3 only.*

SCIENCE COMICS (2nd Series)
Humor Publications (Ace Magazines?): Jan, 1946 - No. 5, 1946

1-Palais-c/a in #1-3; A-Bomb-c	19	57	99	170
2	10	30	55	85
3-Feldstein-a (6 pgs.)	16	48	83	140
4,5: 4-Palais-c	8	24	42	60

SCIENCE COMICS
Ziff-Davis Publ. Co.: May, 1947 (8 pgs. in color)

nn-Could be ordered by mail for 10¢; like the nn Amazing Adventures (1950)				
& Boy Explorer (1950); used to test the market	39	117	208	360

SCIENCE COMICS (True Science Illustrated)
Export Publication Ent., Toronto, Canada: Mar, 1951
Distr. in U.S. by Kable News Co.

1-Science Adventure stories plus some true science features; man on				
moon story	10	30	55	80

SCIENCE FICTION SPACE ADVENTURES (See Space Adventures)

SCION (Also see CrossGen Chronicles)
CrossGeneration Comics: Jul, 2000 - Present ($2.95)
1-19: Marz-s/Cheung-a   3.00
....: Conflict of Conscience TPB (5/01, $19.95) r/#1-7; Adam Hughes-c   20.00

SCI-TECH
DC Comics (WildStorm): Sept, 1999 - No. 4, Dec, 1999 ($2.50, limited series)
1-4-Benes-a/Choi & Peterson-s   2.50

SCOOBY DOO (TV)(...Where are you? #1-16,26; ...Mystery Comics #17-25,
27 on)(See March Of Comics #356, 368, 382, 391)
Gold Key: Mar, 1970 - No. 30, Feb, 1975 (Hanna-Barbera)

1	9	27	63	110
2-5	5	15	35	65

Scooby-Doo #12 © H-B

Scream Comics #11 © ACE

Scribbly #1 © DC

	GD2.0	FN6.0	VF8.0	NM9.4
6-10	5	15	34	55
11-20: 11-Tufts-a	4	12	26	40
21-30	3	10	23	35

SCOOBY DOO (TV)
Charlton Comics: Apr, 1975 - No. 11, Dec, 1976 (Hanna-Barbera)

1	5	15	34	55
2-5	3	9	20	30
6-11	3	9	17	25

SCOOBY-DOO (TV)(Newsstand sales only) (See Dynamutt & Laff-A-Lympics)
Marvel Comics Group: Oct, 1977 - No. 9, Feb, 1979 (Hanna-Barbera)

1,6-9: 1-Dyno-Mutt begins	3	9	17	25
1-(35¢-c variant, limited distribution)(10/77)	3	9	19	28
2-5	2	6	12	18

SCOOBY-DOO (TV)
Harvey Comics: Sept, 1992 - No. 3, May, 1993 ($1.25)

V2#1,2				5.00
Big Book 1,2 (11/92, 4/93, $1.95, 52 pgs.)				6.00
Giant Size 1,2 (10/92, 3/93, $2.25, 68 pgs.)				6.00

SCOOBY-DOO (TV)
Archie Comics: Oct, 1995 - No. 21, June, 1997 ($1.50)

1				5.00
2-21: 12-Cover by Scooby Doo creative designer Iwao Takamoto				3.00

SCOOBY DOO (TV)
DC Comics: Aug, 1997 - Present ($1.75/$1.95/$1.99)

1				4.00
2-45: 5-Begin-$1.95-c. 14-Begin $1.99-c				2.50
46-56				2.25
...Spooky Spectacular 1 (10/99, $3.95) Comic Convention story				4.00
...Spooky Spectacular 2000 (10/00, $3.95)				4.00
...Spooky Summer Special 2001 (8/01, $3.95) Staton-a				4.00

SCOOP COMICS (Becomes Yankee Comics #4-7, a digest sized cartoon book not listed in this guide; becomes Snap #9)
Harry 'A' Chesler (Holyoke): November, 1941 - No. 3, Mar, 1943; No. 8, 1944

1-Intro. Rocketman & Rocketgirl & begins; origin The Master Key & begins; Dan Hastings begins; Charles Sultan-c/a	127	381	795	1400
2-Rocket Boy begins; injury to eye story (reprinted in Spotlight #3); classic-c	136	408	852	1500
3-Injury to eye story-r from #2; Rocket Boy	64	192	398	700
8-Formerly Yankee Comics; becomes Snap	43	129	257	450

SCOOTER (See Swing With...)

SCOOTER COMICS
Rucker Publ. Ltd. (Canadian): Apr, 1946

1-Teen-age/funny animal	11	33	55	90

SCORCHED EARTH
Tundra Publishing: Apr, 1991 - No. 6, 1991 ($2.95, stiff-c)

1-6				3.00

SCORE, THE
DC Comics (Piranha Press): 1989 - No. 4, 1990 ($4.95, 52 pgs, squarebound, mature)

Books One - Four				5.00

SCORPION
Atlas/Seaboard Publ.: Feb, 1975 - No. 3, July, 1975

1-Intro.; bondage-c by Chaykin	1	3	6	9
2-Chaykin-a w/Wrightson, Kaluta, Simonson assists(p)	1	3	6	9
3-Jim Craig-c/a				6.00
NOTE: Chaykin a-1, 2; c-1. Colon c-2. Craig c/a-3.				

SCORPION CORPS
Dagger Comics Group: Nov, 1993 - No. 7, May, 1994? ($2.75/$2.50)

1,2-($2.75): 1-Intro Angel Dust, Shellcase, Tork, Feedback & Magnon				2.75
2-Bronze, 2-Gold, 2-Silver				2.75
3-7-($2.50)				2.50

SCORPIO ROSE
Eclipse Comics: Jan, 1983 - No. 2, Oct, 1983 ($1.25, Baxter paper)

	GD2.0	FN6.0	VF8.0	NM9.4
1,2: Dr. Orient back-up story begins. 2-origin.				4.00

SCOTLAND YARD (Inspector Farnsworth of)(Texas Rangers in Action #5 on?)
Charlton Comics Group: June, 1955 - No. 4, Mar, 1956

1-Tothish-a	15	45	77	130
2-4: 2-Tothish-a	10	30	55	85

SCOUT (See Eclipse Graphic Album #16, New America & Swords of Texas)(Becomes Scout: War Shaman)
Eclipse Comics: Dec, 1985 - No. 24, Oct, 1987($1.75/$1.25, Baxter paper)

1-15,17,18,20-24: 19-Airboy preview. 10-Bissette-a. 11-Monday, the Eliminator begins. 15-Swords of Texas				2.50
16,19: 16-Scout 3-D Special ($2.50), 16-Scout 2-D Limited Edition, 19-contains flexidisk ($2.50)				3.00
...Handbook 1 (8/87, $1.75, B&W)				2.25
Mount Fire (1989, $14.95, TPB) r/#6-14				15.00

SCOUT: WAR SHAMAN (Formerly Scout)
Eclipse Comics: Mar, 1988 - No. 16, Dec, 1989 ($1.95)

1-16				2.25

SCREAM
Humor Publications/Current Books(Ace Magazines): Autumn, 1944 - No. 19, Apr, 1948

1-Teenage humor	17	51	88	150
2	10	30	55	80
3-16: 11-Racist humor (Indians). 16-Intro. Lily-Belle	8	24	42	60
17,19	7	21	36	50
18-Hypo needle story	8	24	42	60

SCREAM
Skywald Publ. Corp.: Aug, 1973 - No. 11, Feb, 1975 (68 pgs., B&W, magazine)

1	4	12	26	40
2-5: 2-Origin Lady Satan. 3 (12/73)-#3 found on pg. 22	3	9	17	25
6-8: 6-Origin The Victims	2	6	15	22
9,10: 9-Severed head-c	3	9	20	30
11- "Mr. Poe and the Raven" story	3	9	20	30

SCREWBALL SQUIRREL
Dark Horse Comics: July, 1995 - No. 3, Sept, 1995 ($2.50, limited series)

1-3: Characters created by Tex Avery				2.50

SCRIBBLY (See All-American Comics, Buzzy, The Funnies, Leave It To Binky & Popular Comics)
National Periodical Publications: 8-9/48 - No. 13, 8-9/50; No. 14, 10-11/51 - No. 15, 12-1/51-52

1-Sheldon Mayer-c/a in all; 52 pgs. begin	95	285	597	1050
2	61	184	381	675
3-5	50	150	300	525
6-10	39	117	208	360
11-15: 13-Last 52 pgs.	34	102	179	310

SCUD: TALES FROM THE VENDING MACHINE
Fireman Press: 1998 - No. 5 ($2.50, B&W)

1-5: 1-Kaniuga-a. 2-Ruben Martinez-a				2.50

SCUD: THE DISPOSABLE ASSASSIN
Fireman Press: Feb, 1994 - No. 19, 1997 ($2.95, B&W)

1				6.00
1-2nd printing in color				2.25
2,3				4.00
4-9				3.00
10-19				2.25
Heavy 3PO ($12.95, TPB) r/#1-4				13.00
Programmed For Damage ($14.95, TPB) r/#5-9				15.00
Solid Gold Bomb ($17.95, TPB) r/#10-15				18.00

SEA DEVILS (See Limited Collectors' Edition #39,45, & Showcase #27-29)
National Periodical Publications: Sept-Oct, 1961 - No. 35, May-June, 1967

1-(9-10/61)	50	150	410	750
2-Last 10¢ issue	28	84	196	350
3-Begin 12¢ issues thru #35	18	54	126	225
4,5	16	48	110	190

Sea Devils #28 © DC

Secret Agent #1 © GK

Secret Hearts #41 © DC

	GD2.0	FN6.0	VF8.0	NM9.4

	GD2.0	FN6.0	VF8.0	NM9.4

6-10	10	30	70	120
11,12,14-20	7	21	53	85
13-Kubert, Colan-a; Joe Kubert app. in story	8	24	56	90
21-35: 22-Intro. International Sea Devils; origin & 1st app. Capt. X & Man Fish	5	15	34	55

NOTE: *Heath* a-B&B 27-29, 1-10; c-B&B 27-29, 1-10, 14-16. *Moldoff* a-16i.

SEA DEVILS (See Tangent Comics/ Sea Devils)

SEADRAGON (Also see the Epsilion Wave)
Elite Comics: May, 1986 - No. 8, 1987 ($1.75)

1-8: 1st & 2nd printings exist				2.25

SEA HOUND, THE (Captain Silver's Log Of The…)
Avon Periodicals: 1945 (no month) - No. 2, Sept-Oct, 1945

nn (#1)-29 pg. novel length sty-"The Esmeralda's Treasure"	19	57	99	165
2	13	39	66	110

SEA HOUND, THE (Radio)
Capt. Silver Syndicate: No. 3, July, 1949 - No. 4, Sept, 1949

3,4	10	30	55	80

SEA HUNT (TV)
Dell Publishing Co.: No. 928, 8/58 - No. 1041, 10-12/59; No. 4, 1-3/60 - No. 13, 4-6/62 (All have Lloyd Bridges photo-c)

Four Color 928(#1)	12	36	84	160
Four Color 994(#2), 4-13: Manning-a #4-6,8-11,13	8	24	56	105
Four Color 1041(#3)-Toth-a	9	27	63	110

SEAQUEST (TV)
Nemesis Comics: Mar, 1994 ($2.25)

1-Has 2 diff-c stocks (slick & cardboard); Alcala-i				2.25

SEARCH FOR LOVE
American Comics Group: Feb-Mar, 1950 - No. 2, Apr-May, 1950 (52 pgs.)

1	12	36	61	105
2	9	27	49	70

SEARCHERS, THE (Movie)
Dell Publishing Co.: No. 709, 1956

Four Color 709-John Wayne photo-c	27	81	189	350

SEARCHERS, THE
Caliber Comics: 1996 - No. 4, 1996 ($2.95, B&W)

1-4				3.00

SEARCHERS, THE : APOSTLE OF MERCY
Caliber Comics: 1997 - No. 2, 1997 ($2.95/$3.95, B&W)

1-($2.95)				3.00
2-($3.95)				4.00

SEARS (See Merry Christmas From…)

SEASON'S GREETINGS
Hallmark (King Features): 1935 (6-1/4x5-1/4", 32 pgs. in color)

nn-Cover features Mickey Mouse, Popeye, Jiggs & Skippy. "The Night Before Christmas" told one panel per page, each panel by a famous artist featuring their character. Art by Alex Raymond, Gottfredson, Swinnerton, Segar, Chic Young, Milt Gross, Sullivan (Messmer), Herriman, McManus, Percy Crosby & others (22 artists in all)

Estimated value…				800.00

SEBASTIAN O
DC Comics (Vertigo): May, 1993 - No. 3, July, 1993 ($1.95, limited series)

1-3-Grant Morrison scripts				2.25

SECOND LIFE OF DOCTOR MIRAGE, THE (See Shadowman #16)
Valiant: Nov, 1993 - No. 18, May, 1995 ($2.50)

1-18: 1-With bound-in poster. 5-Shadowman x-over. 7-Bound-in trading card				2.50
1-Gold ink logo edition; no price on-c				3.00

SECRET AGENT (Formerly Sarge Steel)
Charlton Comics: V2#9, Oct, 1966; V2#10, Oct, 1967

V2#9-Sarge Steel part-r begins	3	9	19	28

10-Tiffany Sinn, CIA app. (from Career Girl Romances #39); Aparo-a	2	6	13	20

SECRET AGENT (TV) (See Four Color #1231)
Gold Key: Nov, 1966; No. 2, Jan, 1968

1-Photo-c	12	36	84	150
2-Photo-c	7	21	49	95

SECRET AGENT X-9 (See Flash Gordon #4 by King)
David McKay Publ.: 1934 (Book 1: 84 pgs.; Book 2: 124 pgs.) (8x7-1/2")

Book 1-Contains reprints of the first 13 weeks of the strip by Alex Raymond; complete except for 2 dailies	43	129	257	450
Book 2-Contains reprints immediately following contents of Book 1, for 20 weeks by Alex Raymond; complete except for two dailies. Note: Raymond mis-dated the last five strips from 6/34, and while the dating sequence is confusing, the continuity is correct	40	120	220	380

SECRET AGENT X-9 (See Magic Comics)
Dell Publishing Co.: Dec, 1937 (Not by Raymond)

Feature Books 8	38	113	266	500

SECRET AGENT Z-2 (See Holyoke One-Shot No. 7)

SECRET CITY SAGA (See Jack Kirby's Secret City Saga)

SECRET DEFENDERS (Also see The Defenders & Fantastic Four #374)
Marvel Comics: Mar, 1993 - No. 25, Mar, 1995 ($1.75/$1.95)

1-($2.50)-Red foil stamped-c; Dr. Strange, Nomad, Wolverine, Spider Woman & Darkhawk begin				3.00
2-11,13-24: 9-New team w/Silver Surfer, Thunderstrike, Dr. Strange & War Machine. 13-Thanos replaces Dr. Strange as leader; leads into Cosmic Powers limited series; 14-Dr. Druid. 15-Bound in card sheet. 18-Giant Man & Iron Fist app.				2.25
12,25: 12-($2.50)-Prismatic foil-c. 25 ($2.50, 52 pgs.)				2.50

SECRET DIARY OF EERIE ADVENTURES
Avon Periodicals: 1953 (25¢ giant, 100 pgs., one-shot)

nn-(Rare)-Kubert-a; Hollingsworth-c; Sid Check back-c	173	519	1080	1900

SECRET FILES & ORIGINS GUIDE TO THE DC UNIVERSE
DC Comics: Mar, 2000; Feb, 2002 ($6.95/$4.95)

2000 (3/00, $6.95)-Overview of DC characters; profile pages by various				7.00
2001-2002 (2/02, $4.95) Olivetti-c				5.00

SECRET FILES PRESIDENT LUTHOR
DC Comics: Mar, 2001 ($4.95, one-shot)

1-Short stories & profile pages by various; Harris-c				5.00

SECRET HEARTS
National Periodical Publications (Beverly)(Arleigh No. 50-113):
9-10/49 - No. 6, 7-8/50; No. 7, 12-1/51-52 - No. 153, 7/71

1-Kinstler-a; photo-c begin, end #6	55	165	330	575
2-Toth-a (1 pg.); Kinstler-a	29	87	153	265
3,6 (1950)	25	75	130	225
4,5-Toth-a	26	78	136	235
7(12-1/51-52) (Rare)	40	120	232	400
8-10 (1952)	19	57	99	165
11-20	15	45	77	130
21-26: 26-Last precode (2-3/55)	13	39	66	110
27-40	7	21	50	80
41-50	5	15	34	55
51-60	4	12	29	45
61-75,100: 75-Last 10¢ issue	4	12	26	40
76-99,101-109	3	9	21	32
110-"Reach for Happiness" serial begins, ends #138	3	10	23	35
111-119,121-126	2	6	15	22
120,134-Neal Adams-c	3	10	23	35
127 (4/68)-Beatles cameo	3	10	23	35
128-133,135-142: 141,142- "20 Miles to Heartbreak", Chapter 2 & 3 (see Young Love for Chapters 1 & 4); Toth, Colletta-a	2	6	13	20
143-148,150-152: 144-Morrow-a	2	6	11	15
149,153: 149-Toth-a. 153-Kirby-i	2	6	12	18

SECRET ISLAND OF OZ, THE (See First Comics Graphic Novel)

Secret Origins (3rd series) #14 © DC

Secret Origins Special #1 © DC

Secret Society of Super-Villains #1 © DC

	GD2.0	FN6.0	VF8.0	NM9.4			GD2.0	FN6.0	VF8.0	NM9.4

SECRET LOVE (See Fox Giants & Sinister House of...)

SECRET LOVE

Ajax-Farrell/Four Star Comic Corp. No. 2 on: 12/55 - No. 3, 8/56; 4/57 - No. 5, 2/58; No. 6, 6/58

1(12/55-Ajax, 1st series)	10	30	55	80
2,3	6	18	32	45
1(4/57-Ajax, 2nd series)	8	24	45	65
2-6: 5-Bakerish-a	6	18	29	40

SECRET LOVES

Comic Magazines/Quality Comics Group: Nov, 1949 - No. 6, Sept, 1950

1-Ward-c	24	72	127	215
2-Ward-c	21	63	110	185
3-Crandall-a	14	42	72	120
4,6	10	30	55	80
5-Suggestive art "Boom Town Babe"; photo-c	14	42	72	120

SECRET LOVE STORIES (See Fox Giants)

SECRET MISSIONS (Admiral Zacharia's...)

St. John Publishing Co.: February, 1950

1-Joe Kubert-c; stories of U.S. foreign agents	21	63	110	185

SECRET MYSTERIES (Formerly Crime Mysteries & Crime Smashers)

Ribage/Merit Publications No. 17 on: No. 16, Nov, 1954 - No. 19, July, 1955

16-Horror, Palais-a; Myron Fass-c	27	81	145	250
17-19-Horror. 17-Fass-c; mis-dated 3/54?	19	57	99	165

SECRET ORIGINS (1st Series) (See 80 Page Giant #8)

National Periodical Publications: Aug-Oct, 1961 (Annual) (Reprints)

1-Origin Adam Strange (Showcase #17), Green Lantern (Green Lantern #1), Challengers (partial-r/Showcase #6, 6 pgs. Kirby-a), J'onn J'onzz (Det. #225), The Flash (Showcase #4) and Green Arrow (1 pg. text), Superman-Batman team (W. Finest #94), Wonder Woman (Wonder Woman #105)

	48	144	386	700
Replica Edition (1998, $4.95) r/entire book and house ads				5.00

SECRET ORIGINS (2nd Series)

National Periodical Publications: Feb-Mar, 1973 - No. 6, Jan-Feb, 1974; No. 7, Oct-Nov, 1974 (All 20¢ issues) (All origin reprints)

1-Superman(r/1 pg. origin/Action #1, 1st time since G.A.), Batman(Det. #33), Ghost(Flash #88), The Flash(Showcase #4) 4 12 26 40
2-7: 2-Green Lantern & The Atom(Showcase #22 & 34), Supergirl(Action #252). 3-Wonder Woman(W.W. #1). 4-Vigilante (Action #42) by Meskin, Kid Eternity(Hit #25). 5-The Spectre by Baily (More Fun #52,53). 6-Blackhawk(Military #1) & Legion of Super-Heroes(Superboy #147). 7-Robin (Detective #38), Aquaman (More Fun #73) 2 6 15 22

NOTE: *Infantino a-1. Kane a-2. Kubert a-1.*

SECRET ORIGINS (3rd Series)

DC Comics: 4/86 - No. 50, 8/90 (All origins)(52 pgs. #6 on)(#27 on: $1.50)

1-Origin Superman 6.00
2-6: 2-Blue Beetle. 3-Shazam. 4-Firestorm. 5-Crimson Avenger. 6-Halo/G.A. Batman 3.00
7-12,14-26: 7-Green Lantern(Guy Gardner)/G.A. Sandman. 8-Shadow Lass/ Doll Man. 9-G.A. Flash/Skyman. 10-Phantom Stranger w/Alan Moore scripts; Legends spin-off. 11-G.A. Hawkman/Power Girl. 12-Challengers of Unknown/ G.A. Fury (2nd modern app.). 14-Suicide Squad; Legends spin-off. 15-Spectre/Deadman. 16-G.A. Hourman/Warlord. 17-Adam Strange story by Carmine Infantino; Dr. Occult. 18-G.A. Gr. Lantern/The Creeper. 19-Uncle Sam/The Guardian. 20-Batgirl/G.A. Dr. Mid-Nite. 21-Jonah Hex/Black Condor. 22-Manhunters. 23-Floronic Man/Guardians of the Universe. 24-Blue Devil/Dr. Fate. 25-LSH/Atom. 26-Black Lightning/Miss America 2.50
13-Origin Nightwing; Johnny Thunder app. 2.50
27-49: 27-Zatara/Zatanna. 28-Midnight/Nightshade. 29-Power of the Atom/Mr. America; new 3 pg. Red Tornado story by Mayer (last app. of Scribbly, 8/88). 30-Plastic Man/Elongated Man. 31-JSA. 32-JLA. 33-35-JLI. 36-Poison Ivy by Neil Gaiman & Mark Buckingham/Green Lantern. 37-Legion Of Substitute Heroes/Doctor Light. 38-Green Arrow/Speedy; Grell scripts. 39-Animal Man-c/story continued in Animal Man #10; Grant Morrison scripts/Batman app.40-All Ape issue. 41-Rogues Gallery of Flash. 42-Phantom Girl/GrimGhost. 43-Original Hawk & Dove/Cave Carson/Chris KL-99. 44-Batman app./story based on Det. #40. 45-Blackhawk/El Diablo. 46-

JLA/LSH/New Titans. 47-LSH. 48-Ambush Bug/Stanley & His Monster/Rex the Wonder Dog/Trigger Twins. 49-Newsboy Legion/Silent Knight/brief origin Bouncing Boy 2.50
50-($3.95, 100 pgs.)-Batman & Robin in text, Flash of Two Worlds, Johnny Thunder, Dolphin, Black Canary & Space Museum 5.00
Annual 1 (8/87)-Capt. Comet/Doom Patrol 3.00
Annual 2 ('88, $2.00)-Origin Flash II & Flash III 3.00
Annual 3 ('89, $2.95, 84 pgs.)-Teen Titans; 1st app. new Flamebird who replaces original Bat-Girl 3.00
Special 1 (10/89, $2.00)-Batman villains: Penguin, Riddler, & Two-Face; Bolland-c; Sam Kieth-a; Neil Gaiman scripts(2) 3.00

NOTE: *Art Adams a-33i(part). M. Anderson a-8, 19, 21, 25i; c-19(part). Aparo c/a-10. Bissette c-23. Bolland c-7. Byrne c/a-Annual 1. Colan c/a-5p. Forte a-37. Giffen a-18p, 44p, 48. Infantino a-17, 50p. Kaluta c-39. Gil Kane a-2, c-2p. Kirby c-19(part). Erik Larsen a-13. Mayer a-29. Morrow a-21. Orlando a-10. Perez a-50i, Annual 3i; c- Annual 3. Rogers a-6p. Russell a-27i. Simonson c-22. Staton a-35, 50p. Steacy a-35. Tuska a-4p, 9p.*

SECRET ORIGINS 80 PAGE GIANT (Young Justice)

DC Comics: Dec, 1998 ($4.95, one-shot)

1-Origin-s of Young Justice members; Ramos-a (Impulse) 5.00

SECRET ORIGINS FEATURING THE JLA

DC Comics: 1999 ($14.95, TPB)

1-Reprints recent origin-s of JLA members; Cassaday-a 15.00

SECRET ORIGINS OF SUPER-HEROES (See DC Special Series #10, 19)

SECRET ORIGINS OF SUPER-VILLAINS 80 PAGE GIANT

DC Comics: Dec, 1999 ($4.95, one-shot)

1-Origin-s of Sinestro, Amazo and others; Gibbons-c 5.00

SECRET ORIGINS OF THE WORLD'S GREATEST SUPER-HEROES

DC Comics: 1989 ($4.95, 148 pgs.)

nn-Reprints Superman, JLA origins; new Batman origin-s; Bolland-c	1	3	5	7

SECRET ROMANCE

Charlton Comics: Oct, 1968 - No. 41, Nov, 1976; No. 42, Mar, 1979 - No. 48, Feb, 1980

1-Begin 12¢ issues, ends #?	2	6	13	20
2-10: 9-Reese-a	1	3	9	12
11-30	1	3	6	8
31-48				5.00

NOTE: *Beyond the Stars app.-No. 9, 11, 12, 14.*

SECRET ROMANCES (Exciting Love Stories)

Superior Publications Ltd.: Apr, 1951 - No. 27, July, 1955

1	14	42	72	120
2	10	30	55	80
3-10	7	21	38	55
11-13,15-18,20-27	6	18	32	45
14,19-Lingerie panels	7	21	36	50

SECRET SERVICE (See Kent Blake of the...)

SECRET SIX (See Action Comics Weekly)

National Periodical Publications: Apr-May, 1968 - No. 7, Apr-May, 1969 (12¢)

1-Origin/1st app.	6	18	45	75
2-7	4	12	26	40

SECRET SIX (See Tangent Comics/ Secret Six)

SECRET SOCIETY OF SUPER-VILLAINS

National Per. Publ./DC Comics: May-June, 1976 - No. 15, June-July, 1978

1-Origin; Manhunter app. & Capt. Cold app.	2	6	11	15
2-5,15: 2-Re-intro/origin Capt. Comet; Green Lantern x-over. 5-Green Lantern, Hawkman x-over; Darkseid app. 15-G.A. Atom, Dr. Midnite, & JSA app.	1	3	6	9
6-14: 9,10-Creeper x-over. 11-Capt. Comet; Orlando-i	1	3	5	7

SECRET SOCIETY OF SUPER-VILLAINS SPECIAL (See DC Special Series #6)

SECRETS OF HAUNTED HOUSE

National Periodical Publications/DC Comics: 4-5/75 - #5, 12-1/75-76; #6, 6-7/77 - #14, 10-11/78; #15, 8/79 - #46, 3/82

1	4	12	26	40
2-4	2	6	12	18

Secrets of Haunted House #13 © DC

Secret Weapons #10 © VAL

Seekers Into the Mystery #6 © JM DeMatteis

	GD2.0	FN6.0	VF8.0	NM9.4
5-Wrightson-c	2	6	13	20
6-14	2	6	9	12
15-30	1	3	6	9
31,44: 31-Mr. E series begins, ends #41. 44-Wrightson-c				
	1	4	7	10
32-43,45,46				6.00

NOTE: Aparo a-7. Aragones a-1. B. Bailey a-8. Bissette a-46. Buckler c-32-40p. Ditko a-9, 12, 41, 45. Golden a-10. Howard a-10. Kaluta c-8, 10, 11, 14, 16, 29. Kubert c-41, 42. Sheldon Mayer a-43p. McWilliams a-35. Nasser a-24. Newton a-30p. Nino a-1, 13, 19. Orlando c-13, 30, 43, 45i. N. Redondo a-4, 5, 29. Rogers c-26. Spiegle a-31-41. Wrightson c-5, 44.

SECRETS OF HAUNTED HOUSE SPECIAL (See DC Special Series #12)

SECRETS OF LIFE (Movie)
Dell Publishing Co.: 1956 (Disney)

Four Color 749-Photo-c	5	15	34	55

SECRETS OF LOVE (See Popular Teen-Agers...)

SECRETS OF LOVE AND MARRIAGE
Charlton Comics: V2#1, Aug, 1956 - V2#25, June, 1961

V2#1	4	12	29	45
V2#2-6	3	9	20	30
V2#7-9-(All 68 pgs.)	4	12	30	50
10-25	3	9	17	24

SECRETS OF MAGIC (See Wisco)

SECRETS OF SINISTER HOUSE (Sinister House of Secret Love #1-4)
National Periodical Publ.: No. 5, June-July, 1972 - No. 18, June-July, 1974

5-(52 pgs.)	4	12	26	40
6-9: 7-Redondo-a	2	6	15	22
10-Neal Adams-a(i)	3	9	19	28
11-18: 15-Redondo-a. 17-Barry-a; early Chaykin 1 pg. strip				
	2	6	10	14

NOTE: Alcala a-6, 13, 14. Glanzman a-7. Kaluta c-6, 7. Nino a-8, 11-13. Ambrose Bierce adapt.-#14.

SECRETS OF THE LEGION OF SUPER-HEROES
DC Comics: Jan, 1981 - No. 3, Mar, 1981 (Limited series)

1-3: 1-Origin of the Legion. 2-Retells origins of Braniac 5, Shrinking Violet, Sun-Boy, Bouncing Boy, Ultra-Boy, Matter-Eater Lad, Mon-El, Karate Kid, & Dream Girl				4.00

SECRETS OF TRUE LOVE
St. John Publishing Co.: Feb, 1958

1	6	18	29	40

SECRETS OF YOUNG BRIDES
Charlton Comics: No. 5, Sept, 1957 - No. 44, Oct, 1964; July, 1975 - No. 9, Nov, 1976

5	4	12	30	50
6-10: 8-Negligee panel	3	10	23	35
11-20	3	9	20	30
21-30: Last 10¢ issue?	3	9	17	25
31-44 (10/64)	2	6	11	16
1-(2nd series) (7/75)	2	6	13	20
2-9	1	4	7	10

SECRET SQUIRREL (TV)(See Kite Fun Book)
Gold Key: Oct, 1966 (12¢) (Hanna-Barbera)

1-1st Secret Squirrel and Morocco Mole, Squiddly Diddly, Winsome Witch				
	13	39	91	170

SECRET STORY ROMANCES (Becomes True Tales of Love)
Atlas Comics (TCI): Nov, 1953 - No. 21, Mar, 1956

1-Everett-a; Jay Scott Pike-c	14	42	72	125
2	8	24	45	65
3-11: 11-Last pre-code (2/55)	7	21	36	50
12-21	6	18	30	42

NOTE: Colletta a-10, 14, 15, 17, 21; c-10, 14, 17.

SECRET VOICE, THE (See Great American Comics Presents...)

SECRET WARS II (Also see Marvel Super Heroes...)
Marvel Comics Group: July, 1985 - No. 9, Mar, 1986 (Maxi-series)

1,9: 9-(52 pgs.) X-Men app., Spider-Man app.				4.00

	GD2.0	FN6.0	VF8.0	NM9.4
2-8: 2,8-X-Men app. 5-1st app. Boom Boom. 5,8-Spider-Man app.				3.00

SECRET WEAPONS
Valiant: Sept, 1993 - No. 21, May, 1995 ($2.25)

1-10,12-21: 3-Reese-a(i). 5-Ninjak app. 9-Bound-in trading card. 12-Bloodshot app.				2.50
11-(Sept. on envelope, Aug on-c, $2.50)-Enclosed in manilla envelope; Bloodshot app; intro new team.				2.50

SECTAURS
Marvel Comics: June, 1985 - No. 10?, 1986 (75¢) (Based on Coleco Toys)

1-10, 1-Coleco giveaway; different-c				3.00

SECTION ZERO
Image Comics (Gorilla): June, 2000 - Present ($2.50)

1-3-Kesel-s/Grummett-a				2.50

SEDUCTION OF THE INNOCENT (Also see New York State Joint Legislative Committee to Study...)
Rinehart & Co., Inc., N.Y.: 1953, 1954 (400 pgs.) (Hardback, $4.00)(Written by Fredric Wertham, M.D.)(Also printed in Canada by Clarke, Irwin & Co. Ltd.)

(1st Version)-with bibliographical note intact (pages 399 & 400)(several copies got out before the comic publishers forced the removal of this page)				
	55	165	330	575
Dust jacket only	31	93	165	285
(1st Version)-without bibliographical note	31	93	165	285
Dust jacket only	15	45	77	130
(2nd Version)-Published in England by Kennikat Press, 1954, 399 pgs. has bibliographical page	11	33	55	90
1972 r-/of 2nd version; 400 pgs. w/bibliography page; Kennikat Press				
	3	10	23	35

NOTE: Material from this book appeared in the November, 1953(Vol.70, pp50-53,214) issue of the Ladies' Home Journal under the title "What Parents Don't Know About Comic Books". With the release of this book, Dr. Wertham reveals seven years of research attempting to link juvenile delinquency to comic books. Many illustrations showing excessive violence, sex, sadism, and torture are shown. This book was used at the Kefauver Senate hearings which led to the Comics Code Authority. Because of the influence this book had on the comic industry and the collector's interest in it, we feel this listing is justified. Also see Parade of Pleasure.

SEDUCTION OF THE INNOCENT! (Also see Halloween Horror)
Eclipse Comics: Nov, 1985 - 3-D#2, Apr, 1986 ($1.75)

1-6: Double listed under cover title from #7 on				3.00
3-D 1 (10/85, $2.25, 36 pgs.)-contains unpublished Advs. Into Darkness #15 (pre-code);Dave Stevens-c				4.00
2D 1 (100 copy limited signed & numbered edition)(B&W) 1		3	6	8
3-D 2 (4/86)-Baker, Toth, Wrightson-c				5.00
2-D 2 (100 copy limited signed & numbered edition)(B&W) 1		3	6	9

NOTE: Anderson r-2, 3. Crandall c/a(r)-1. Meskin c/a(r)-3, 3-D 1. Moreira r-2. Toth a-1-6r; c-4r. Tuska r-6.

SEEKER
Sky Comics: Apr, 1994 ($2.50, one-shot)

1				2.50

SEEKERS INTO THE MYSTERY
DC Comics (Vertigo): Jan, 1996 - No. 15, Apr, 1997 ($2.50)

1-14: J.M DeMatteis scripts in all. 1-4-Glenn Barr-a. 5,10-Muth-c/a. 6-9-Zulli-c/a. 11-14-Bolton-c/a; Jill Thompson-a				2.50
15-($2.95)-Muth-c/a				3.00

SEEKER 3000 (See Marvel Premiere #41)
Marvel Comics: Jun, 1998 - No. 4, Sept, 1998 ($2.99/$2.50, limited series)

1-($2.99)-Set 25 years after 1st app.; wraparound-c				3.00
2-4-($2.50)				2.50
...Premiere 1 (6/98, $1.50) Reprints 1st app. from Marvel Premiere #41; wraparound-c				2.25

SELECT DETECTIVE (Exciting New Mystery Cases)
D. S. Publishing Co.: Aug-Sept, 1948 - No. 3, Dec-Jan, 1948-49

1-Matt Baker-a	28	84	148	255
2-Baker, McWilliams-a	19	57	99	165
3	16	48	83	140

SELF-LOATHING COMICS
Fantagraphics Books: Feb, 1995 ($2.95, B&W)

Sensational Spider-Man #6 © MAR

Sensation Comics #3 © DC

Sentry #2 © MAR

	GD2.0	FN6.0	VF8.0	NM9.4

1,2-Crumb   3.00

SEMPER FI (Tales of the Marine Corp)
Marvel Comics: Dec, 1988- No.9, Aug, 1989 (75¢)

1-9: Severin-c/a   2.25

SENSATIONAL POLICE CASES (Becomes Captain Steve Savage, 2nd Series)
Avon Periodicals: 1952; No. 2, 1954 - No. 4, July-Aug, 1954

nn-(1952, 25¢, 100 pgs.)-Kubert-a?; Check, Larsen, Lawrence & McCann-a;				
Kinstler-c	40	120	232	400
2-4: 2-Kirbyish-a (3-4/54). 4-Reprint/Saint #5	14	42	72	125
W. Reprint #5-(1963?, nd)-Reprints Prison Break #5(1952-Realistic);				
Infantino-a	9	20	30	

SENSATIONAL SHE-HULK, THE (She-Hulk #21-23) (See Savage She-Hulk)
Marvel Comics: V2#1, 5/89 - No. 60, Feb, 1994 ($1.50/$1.75, deluxe format)

V2#1-Byrne-c/a(p)/scripts begin, end #8				3.00
2,3,5-8: 3-Spider-Man app.				2.25
4,14-17,21,23: 4-Reintro G.A. Blonde Phantom. 14-17-Howard the Duck app.				
21-23-Return of the Blonde Phantom. 22-All Winners Squad app.				2.50
9-13,18-20,24,49,51-60: 25-Thor app. 26-Excalibur app.;Guice-c. 29-Wolverine				
app. (3 pgs.). 30-Hobgoblin-c/a app.;Byrne-c/a/scripts begin again.				
35-Last $1.50-c. 37-Wolverine/Punisher/Spidey-c, but no app. 39-Thing app.				
56-War Zone app.; Hulk cameo. 57-Vs. Hulk-c/story. 58-Electro-c/story.				
59-Jack O'Lantern app.				2.25
50-($2.95, 52 pgs.)-Embossed green foil-c; Byrne app.; last Byrne-c/a;				
Austin, Chaykin, Simonson-a; Miller-a(2 pgs.)				3.00

NOTE: Dale Keown a(p)-13, 15-22.

SENSATIONAL SHE-HULK IN CEREMONY, THE
Marvel Comics: 1989 - No. 2, 1989 ($3.95, squarebound, 52 pgs.)

nn-Part 1, nn-Part 2   4.00

SENSATIONAL SPIDER-MAN
Marvel Comics: Apr, 1989 ($5.95, squarebound, 80 pgs.)

1-r/Amazing Spider-Man Annual #14,15 by Miller & Annual #8 by Kirby & Ditko.   6.00

SENSATIONAL SPIDER-MAN, THE
Marvel Comics: Jan, 1996 - No. 33, Nov, 1998 ($1.95/$1.99)

0 ($4.95)-Lenticular-c; Jurgens-a/scripts				5.00
1				5.00
1 ($2.95) variant-c; polybagged w/cassette	1	3	6	8
2-5: 2-Kaine & Rhino app. 3-Giant-Man app.				4.00
6-18: 9-Onslaught tie-in; revealed that Peter & Mary Jane's unborn baby is a				
girl. 11-Revelations. 13-15-Ka-Zar app. 14,15-Hulk app.				3.00
19-24: Living Pharoah app. 22,23-Dr. Strange app.				2.50
25-($2.99) Spiderhunt pt. 1; Normie Osborne kidnapped				4.00
25-Variant-c	1	3	6	8
26-33: 26-Nauck-a. 27-Double-c with "The Sensational Hornet #1"; Vulture app.				
28-Hornet vs. Vulture. 29,30-Black Cat-c/app. 33-Last issue; Gathering				
of Five concludes				2.50
#(-1) Flashback(7/97) Dezago-s/Wieringo-a				3.00
'96 Annual ($2.95)				3.00

SENSATION COMICS (Sensation Mystery #110 on)
National Per. Publ./All-American: Jan, 1942 - No. 109, May-June, 1952

1-Origin Mr. Terrific(1st app.), Wildcat(1st app.), The Gay Ghost, & Little Boy				
Blue; Wonder Woman (cont'd from All Star #8), The Black Pirate begin; intro.				
Justice & Fair Play Club	2285	6855	15,995	32,000

1-Reprint, Oversize 13-1/2x10". WARNING: This comic is an exact duplicate reprint of the original except for its size. DC published it in 1974 with a second cover titling it as a Famous First Edition. There have been many reported cases of the outer cover being removed and the interior sold as the original edition. The reprint with the new outer cover removed is practically worthless. See Famous First Edition for value.

2-Etta Candy begins	431	1293	2800	5600
3-W. Woman gets secretary's job	255	765	1591	2800
4-1st app. Stretch Skinner in Wildcat	182	546	1136	2000
5-Intro. Justin, Black Pirate's son	145	435	909	1600
6-Origin/1st app. Wonder Woman's magic lasso	150	450	938	1650
7-10	105	315	656	1150
11,12,14-20	95	285	597	1050
13-Hitler, Tojo, Mussolini-c (as bowling pins)	132	396	825	1450

21-30	75	225	469	825
31-33	55	165	341	600
34-Sargon, the Sorcerer begins (10/44), ends #36; begins again #52				
	59	177	369	650
35-40: 38-X-Mas-c	50	150	300	525
41-50: 43-The Whip app.	44	132	264	460
51-67,69-80: 51-Last Black Pirate. 56,57-Sargon by Kubert. 63-Last Mr. Terrific.				
66-Wildcat by Kubert	40	120	232	400
68-Origin & 1st app. Huntress (8/47)	43	129	257	450
81-Used in SOTI, pg. 33,34; Krigstein-a	40	120	240	420
82-93: 83-Last Sargon. 86-The Atom app. 90-Last Wildcat. 91-Streak begins by				
Alex Toth. 92-Toth-a (2 pgs.)	35	105	185	320
94-1st all girl issue	47	141	286	500
95-99,101-106: 95-Unmasking of Wonder Woman-c/story. 99-1st app. Astra,				
Girl of the Future, ends #106. 103-Robot-c. 105-Last 52 pgs. 106-Wonder				
Woman app	43	129	257	450
100-(11-12/50)	55	165	341	600
107-(Scarce, 1-2/52)-1st mystery issue; Johnny Peril by Toth(p), 8 pgs. &				
begins; continues from Danger Trail #5 (3-4/51)(see Comic Cavalcade #15				
for story).	68	205	341	750
108-(Scarce)-Johnny Peril by Toth(p)	55	165	341	600
109-(Scarce)-Johnny Peril by Toth(p)	68	205	426	750

NOTE: Krigstein a-(Wildcat)-81, 83, 84. Moldoff Black Pirate-1-25; Black Pirate not in 34-36, 43-48. Oskner c(i)-89-91, 94-106. Wonder Woman by H. G. Peter, all issues except #8, 17-19, 21; c-4-7, 9-18, 20-88, 92, 93. Toth a-91, 98; c-107. Wonder Woman c-1-106.

SENSATION COMICS (Also see All Star Comics 1999 crossover titles)
DC Comics: May, 1999 ($1.99, one-shot)

1-Golden Age Wonder Woman and Hawkgirl; Robinson-s   2.25

SENSATION MYSTERY (Formerly Sensation Comics #1-109)
National Periodical Publ.: No. 110, July-Aug, 1952 - No. 116, July-Aug, 1953

110-Johnny Peril continues	43	129	257	450
111-116-Johnny Peril in all. 116-M. Anderson-a	43	129	257	450

NOTE: M. Anderson a-116. Colan a-114p; Giunta-a-112. G. Kane c(p)-108, 109, 111-115.

SENSUOUS STREAKER
Marvel Publ.: 1974 (B&W magazine, 68pgs.)

1	3	9	17	24

SENTINELS OF JUSTICE, THE (See Americomics & Captain Paragon &...)

SENTRY
Marvel Comics: Sept, 2000 - No. 5, Jan, 2001 ($2.99, limited series)

1-5-Paul Jenkins-s/Jae Lee-a. 3-Spider-Man/c/app. 4-X-Men, FF app.	3.00
../Fantastic Four (2/01, $2.99) Continues story from #5; Winslade-a	3.00
../Hulk (2/01, $2.99) Sienkiewicz-c/a	3.00
../Spider-Man (2/01, $2.99) back story of the Sentry; Leonardi-a	3.00
../The Void (2/01, $2.99) Conclusion of story; Jae Lee-a	3.00
../X-Men (2/01, $2.99) Sentry and Archangel; Texeira-a	3.00
TPB (10/01, $24.95) r/#1-5 & all one-shots; Stan Lee interview	25.00

SENTRY SPECIAL
Innovation Publishing: 1991 ($2.75, one-shot)(Hero Alliance spin-off)

1-Lost in Space preview (3 pgs.)   2.75

SERAPHIM
Innovation Publishing: May, 1990 ($2.50, mature readers)

1   2.50

SERGEANT BARNEY BARKER (Becomes G. I. Tales #4 on)
Atlas Comics (MCI): Aug, 1956 - No. 3, Dec, 1956

1-Severin-c/a(4)	20	60	105	180
2,3: 2-Severin-c/a(4). 3-Severin-c/a(5)	14	42	72	120

SERGEANT BILKO (Phil Silvers Starring as...) (TV)
National Periodical Publications: May-June, 1957 - No. 18, Mar-Apr, 1960

1-All have Bob Oskner-c	73	219	455	800
2	40	120	220	380
3-5	35	105	185	320
6-18: 11,12,15,17-Photo-c	29	87	153	265

SGT. BILKO'S PVT. DOBERMAN (TV)
National Periodical Publications: June-July, 1958 - No. 11, Feb-Mar, 1960

1-Bob Oskner c-1-4,7,11	33	100	250	450

Sgt. Fury #146 © MAR

Sgt. Rock #336 © DC

Sergio Aragonés' Boogeyman #1
© Sergio Aragonés & Mark Evanier

	GD2.0	FN6.0	VF8.0	NM9.4
2	20	60	140	250
3-5: 5-Photo-c	14	42	98	165
6-11: 6,9-Photo-c	10	30	70	120

SGT. DICK CARTER OF THE U.S. BORDER PATROL (See Holyoke One-Shot)
SGT. FURY (& His Howling Commandos)(See Fury & Special Marvel Edition)
Marvel Comics Group (BPC earlier issues): May, 1963 - No. 167, Dec, 1981

1-1st app. Sgt. Nick Fury (becomes agent of Shield in Strange Tales #135); Kirby/Ayers-c/a; 1st Dum-Dum Dugan & the Howlers	113	339	956	1800
2-Kirby-a	33	99	250	450
3-5: 3-Reed Richards x-over. 4-Death of Junior Juniper. 5-1st Baron Strucker app.; Kirby-a	20	60	140	250
6-10: 8-Baron Zemo, 1st Percival Pinkerton app. 9-Hitler-c & app. 10-1st app. Capt. Savage (the Skipper)(9/64)	13	39	91	155
11,12,14-20: 14-1st Blitz Squad. 18-Death of Pamela Hawley	7	21	50	80
13-Captain America & Bucky app.(12/64); 2nd solo Capt. America x-over outside The Avengers; Kirby-a	31	93	233	425
21-24,26,28-30	5	15	34	55
25,27: 25-Red Skull app. 27-1st app. Eric Koenig; origin Fury's eye patch	5	15	34	55
31,33,35-50: 35-Eric Koenig joins Howlers. 43-Bob Hope, Glen Miller app. 44-Flashback on Howlers' 1st mission	3	9	20	30
34-Origin Howling Commandos	3	9	20	30
51-60	3	9	17	24
61-67: 64-Capt. Savage & Raiders x-over. 67-Last 12¢ issue	2	6	13	20
68-80: 76-Fury's Father app. in WWI story	2	6	12	18
81-91: 91-Last 15¢ issue	2	6	11	16
92-(52 pgs.)	2	6	13	20
93-99: 98-Deadly Dozen x-over	2	6	10	14
100-Capt. America, Fantastic 4 cameos; Stan Lee, Martin Goodman & others app.	2	6	13	20
101-120: 101-Origin retold	2	6	9	12
121-130: 121-123-r/#19-21	1	3	6	9
131-167: 167-Reprints (from 1963)	1	3	6	8
133,134-(30¢-c variants, limited dist.)(5,7/76)	2	6	9	12
141,142-(35¢-c variants, limited dist.)(7,9/77)	2	6	9	12
Annual 1(1965, 25¢, 72 pgs.)-r/#4,5 & new-a	14	42	102	175
Special 2(1966)	5	15	34	55
Special 3(1967)	3	10	23	35
Special 4(1968)	3	9	17	25
Special 5-7(1969-11/71)	2	6	12	18

NOTE: *Ayers a-8, Annual 1. Ditko a-15i. Gil Kane c-37, 96. Kirby a-1, 7, 13p, 167p(r). Special 5; c-1-20, 25, 167p. Severin a-44-46, 48, 162, 164; new-a 49-79, Special 4, 6; c-41, 5, 44, 46, 110, 149i, 155i, 162-166. Sutton a-57p. Reprints in #80, 82, 85, 87, 89, 91, 93, 95, 99, 101, 103, 105, 107, 109, 111, 121-123, 145-155, 167.*

SGT. FURY AND HIS HOWLING DEFENDERS (See The Defenders #147)
SERGEANT PRESTON OF THE YUKON (TV)
Dell Publishing Co.: No. 344, Aug, 1951 - No. 29, Nov-Jan, 1958-59

Four Color 344(#1)-Sergeant Preston & his dog Yukon King begin; painted-c begin, end #18	12	36	84	150
Four Color 373,397,419('52)	7	21	49	90
5(11-1/52-53)-10(2-4/54): 6-Bondage-c.	5	15	35	60
11,12,14-17	4	12	30	50
13-Origin Sgt. Preston	5	15	35	60
18-Origin Yukon King; last painted-c	5	15	35	60
19-29: All photo-c	7	21	49	85

SGT. ROCK (Formerly Our Army at War; see Brave & the Bold #52 & Showcase #45)
National Periodical Publications/DC Comics: No. 302, Mar, 1977 - No. 422, July, 1988 (See G.I. Combat #108)

302	3	9	21	32
303-310	2	6	12	18
311-320: 318-Reprints	2	6	9	12
321-350	1	3	6	9
351-399,401-421				6.00
400,422: 422-1st Joe, Adam, Andy Kubert-a team	1	3	6	9

	GD2.0	FN6.0	VF8.0	NM9.
Annual 2-4: 2(1982)-Formerly Sgt. Rock's Prize Battle Tales #1. 3(1983).				
4(1984)	1	3	6	8

NOTE: *Estrada a-322, 327, 331, 336, 337, 341, 342i. Glanzman a-384, 421. Kubert a-302, 303, 305r, 306, 328, 351, 356, 368, 373, 422; c-317, 318r, 319-323, 325-333-on, Annual 2, 3. Severin a-347. Spiegle a-382, Annual 2, 3. Thorne a-384. Toth a-385r. Wildey a-307, 311, 313, 314.*

SGT. ROCK SPECIAL (Sgt. Rock #14 on; see DC Special Series #3)
DC Comics: Oct, 1988 - No. 21, Feb, 1992; No. 1, 1992; No. 2, 1994 ($2.00, quarterly/monthly, 52 pgs)

1-Reprint begin	1	4	7	10
2-21: All-r; 5-r/early Sgt. Rock/Our Army at War #81. 7-Tomahawk-r by Thorne. 9-Enemy Ace-r by Kubert. 10-All Rock issue. 11-r/1st Haunted Tank story. 12-All Kubert issue;begins monthly. 13-Dinosaur story by Heath(r). 14-Enemy Ace-r (22 pgs.) by Kubert. 15-Enemy Ace (22 pgs.) by Kubert. 16-Iron Major-r/story. 16,17-Enemy Ace-r. 19-r/Batman/Sgt. Rock team-up/B&B #108 by Aparo				6.00
1 (1992, $2.95, 68 pgs.)-Simonson-c; unpubbed Kubert-a; Glanzman, Russell, Pratt, & Wagner-a				5.00
2 (1994, $2.95) Brereton painted-c				4.00

NOTE: *Neal Adams r-1, 8, 14p. Chaykin a-2; r-3, 9(2pgs.); c-3. Drucker r-6. Glanzman r-20. Golden a-1. Heath a-2; r-5, 9-13, 16, 19, 21. Krigstein r-4, 8. Kubert 1-1-17, 20, 21; c-1p, 2, 8, 14-21. Miller r-6p. Severin r-3, 6, 10. Simonson r-2, 4; c-4. Thorne r-7. Toth r-2, 8, 11. Wood r-4*

SGT. ROCK SPECTACULAR (See DC Special Series #13)
SGT. ROCK'S PRIZE BATTLE TALES (Becomes Sgt. Rock Annual #2 on; see DC Special Series #18 & 80 Page Giant #7)
National Periodical Publications: Winter, 1964 (Giant - 80 pgs., one-shot)

1-Kubert, Heath-r; new Kubert-c	31	93	233	420
... Replica Edition (2000, $5.95) Reprints entire issue				6.00

SGT. STRYKER'S DEATH SQUAD (See Savage Combat Tales)
SERGIO ARAGONÉS' ACTIONS SPEAK
Dark Horse Comics: Jan, 2001 - No. 6, Jun, 2001 ($2.99, B&W, limited series)

1-6-Aragonés-c/a; wordless one-page cartoons				3.00

SERGIO ARAGONÉS' BLAIR WHICH?
Dark Horse Comics: Dec, 1999 ($2.95, B&W, one-shot)

nn-Aragonés-c/a; Evanier-s. Parody of "Blair Witch Project" movie				3.00

SERGIO ARAGONÉS' BOOGEYMAN
Dark Horse Comics: June, 1998 - No. 4, Sept, 1998 ($2.95, B&W, lim. series)

1-4-Aragonés-c/a				3.00

SERGIO ARAGONÉS DESTROYS DC
DC Comics: June, 1996 ($3.50, one-shot)

1-DC Superhero parody book; Aragonés-c/a; Evanier scripts				3.50

SERGIO ARAGONÉS' DIA DE LOS MUERTOS
Dark Horse Comics: Oct, 1998 ($2.95, one-shot)

1-Aragonés-c/a; Evanier scripts				3.00

SERGIO ARAGONÉS' GROO & RUFFERTO
Dark Horse Comics: Dec, 1998 - No. 4, Mar, 1999 ($2.95, lim. series)

1-3-Aragonés-c/a				3.00

SERGIO ARAGONÉS' GROO: MIGHTIER THAN THE SWORD
Dark Horse Comics: Jan, 2000 - No. 4, Apr, 2000 ($2.95, lim. series)

1-4-Aragonés-c/a; Evanier-s				3.00

SERGIO ARAGONÉS' GROO THE WANDERER (See Groo...)
SERGIO ARAGONÉS' LOUDER THAN WORDS
Dark Horse Comics: July, 1997 - No. 6, Dec, 1997 ($2.95, B&W, limited series)

1-6-Aragonés-c/a				3.00

SERGIO ARAGONÉS MASSACRES MARVEL
Marvel Comics: June, 1996 ($3.50, one-shot)

1-Marvel Superhero parody book; Aragonés-c/a; Evanier scripts				3.50

SERGIO ARAGONÉS STOMPS STAR WARS
Marvel Comics: Jan, 2000 ($2.95, one-shot)

1-Star Wars parody; Aragonés-c/a; Evanier scripts				3.00

SERRA ANGEL ON THE WORLDS OF MAGIC THE GATHERING
Acclaim Comics (Armada): Aug, 1996 ($5.95, one-shot)

Seven Miles a Second
© Estate of David Wojnarowicz

Shade the Changing Man #8 © DC

Shadow Cabinet #8 © Milestone Media

		GD2.0	FN6.0	VF8.0	NM9.4

		GD2.0	FN6.0	VF8.0	NM9.4

1 6.00

SEVEN BLOCK
Marvel Comics (Epic Comics): 1990 ($4.50, one-shot, 52 pgs.)
1 4.50

SEVEN DEAD MEN (See Complete Mystery #1)

SEVEN DWARFS (Also see Snow White)
Dell Publishing Co.: No. 227, 1949 (Disney-Movie)
Four Color #227 | 10 | 30 | 70 | 130

SEVEN MILES A SECOND
DC Comics (Vertigo Verité): 1996 ($7.95, one-shot)
nn-Wojnarowicz-s/Romberg-a 8.00

SEVEN SAMUROID, THE (See Image Graphic Novel)

SEVEN SEAS COMICS
Universal Phoenix Features/Leader No. 6: Apr, 1946 - No. 6, 1947(no month)

1-South Sea Girl by Matt Baker, Capt. Cutlass begin; Tugboat Tessie by
Baker app. | 84 | 253 | 525 | 925
2-Swashbuckler-c | 70 | 210 | 438 | 775
3,5,6: 3-Six pg. Feldstein-a | 64 | 192 | 398 | 700
4-Classic Baker-a | 73 | 219 | 455 | 800
NOTE: *Baker a-1-6; c-3-6.*

1776 (See Charlton Classic Library)

7TH VOYAGE OF SINBAD, THE (Movie)
Dell Publishing Co.: Sept, 1958 (photo-c)
Four Color 944-Buscema-a | 13 | 39 | 91 | 165

77 SUNSET STRIP (TV)
Dell Publ. Co./Gold Key: No. 1066, Jan-Mar, 1960 - No. 2, Feb, 1963
(All photo-c)
Four Color 1066-Toth-a | 12 | 36 | 84 | 150
Four Color 1106,1159-Toth-a | 9 | 27 | 63 | 120
Four Color 1211,1263,1291, 01-742-209(7-9/62)-Manning-a in all
| | 9 | 27 | 63 | 110
1,2: Manning-a. 1(11/62-G.K.) | 9 | 27 | 63 | 120

77TH BENGAL LANCERS, THE (TV)
Dell Publishing Co.: May, 1957
Four Color 791-Photo-c | 7 | 21 | 49 | 90

SEYMOUR, MY SON (See More Seymour)
Archie Publications (Radio Comics): Sept, 1963
1 | 3 | 9 | 20 | 30

SHADE, THE (See Starman)
DC Comics: Apr, 1997 - No. 4, July, 1997 ($2.25, limited series)
1-4-Robinson-s/Harris-c: 1-Gene Ha-a. 2-Williams/Gray-a
3-Blevins-a. 4-Zulli-a 3.00

SHADE, THE CHANGING MAN (See Cancelled Comic Cavalcade)
National Per. Publ./DC Comics: June-July, 1977 - No. 8, Aug-Sept, 1978
1-1st app. Shade; Ditko-c/a in all | 2 | 6 | 9 | 12
2-8 | 1 | 3 | 5 | 7

SHADE, THE CHANGING MAN (2nd series) (Also see Suicide Squad #16)
DC Comics (Vertigo imprint #33 on): July, 1990 - No.70, Apr, 1996
($1.50/$1.75/$1.95/$2.25, mature)
1-($2.50, 52 pgs.)-Peter Milligan scripts in all 4.00
2-41,45-49,51-59: 6-Preview of World Without End. 17-Begin $1.75-c.
33-Metallic ink on-c. 41-Begin $1.95-c 2.25
42-44-John Constantine app. 3.00
50-($2.95, 52 pgs.) 3.50
60-70: 60-begin $2.25-c 2.25
NOTE: *Bachalo a-1-9, 11-13, 15-21, 23-26, 33-39, 42-45, 47, 49, 50; c-30, 33-41.*

SHADO: SONG OF THE DRAGON (See Green Arrow #63-66)
DC Comics: 1992 - No. 4, 1992 ($4.95, limited series, 52 pgs.)
Book One - Four: Grell scripts; Morrow-a(i) 5.00

SHADOW, THE (See Batman #253, 259 & Marvel Graphic Novel #35)

SHADOW, THE (Pulp, radio)

Archie Comics (Radio Comics): Aug, 1964 - No. 8, Sept, 1965 (All 12¢)
1-Jerrry Siegel scripts in all; Shadow-c. | 6 | 18 | 45 | 75
2-8: 2-App. in super-hero costume on-c only; Reinman-a(backup). 3-Superhero
begins; Reinman-a (book-length novel). 3,4,6,7-The Fly 1 pg. strips. 4-8-
Reinman-a. 5-8-Siegel scripts. 7-Shield app. | 4 | 12 | 29 | 45

SHADOW, THE
National Periodical Publications: Oct-Nov, 1973 - No. 12, Aug-Sept, 1975
1-Kaluta-a begins | 3 | 10 | 23 | 35
2 | 2 | 6 | 11 | 16
3-Kaluta/Wrightson-a | 2 | 6 | 13 | 20
4,6-Kaluta-a ends. 4-Chaykin, Wrightson part-i | 2 | 6 | 10 | 14
5,7-12: 11-The Avenger (pulp character) x-over | 1 | 3 | 6 | 8
NOTE: *Craig a-10. Cruz a-10-12. Kaluta a-1, 2, 3p, 4, 6; c-1-4, 6, 10-12. Kubert c-9. Robbins a-5, 7-9; c-5, 7, 8.*

SHADOW, THE
DC Comics: May, 1986 - No. 4, Aug, 1986 (limited series)
1-4: Howard Chaykin art in all 3.00
Blood & Judgement ($12.95)-r/1-4 13.00

SHADOW, THE
DC Comics: Aug, 1987 - No. 19, Jan, 1989 ($1.50)
1-19: Andrew Helfer scripts in all. 3.00
Annual 1,2 (12/87, '88,)-2-The Shadow dies; origin retold (story inspired by the
movie "Citizen Kane"). 4.00
NOTE: *Kyle Baker a-7i, 8-19, Annual 2. Chaykin c-Annual 1. Helfer scripts in all.
Orlando a-Annual 1. Rogers c/a-7. Sienkiewicz c/a-1-6.*

SHADOW, THE (Movie)
Dark Horse Comics: June, 1994 - No. 2, July, 1994 ($2.50, limited series)
1,2-Adaptation from Universal Pictures film 3.00
NOTE: *Kaluta c/a-1, 2.*

SHADOW AND DOC SAVAGE, THE
Dark Horse Comics: July, 1995 - No. 2, Aug, 1995 ($2.95, limited series)
1,2 3.50

SHADOW AND THE MYSTERIOUS 3, THE
Dark Horse Comics: Sept, 1994 ($2.95, one-shot)
1-Kaluta co-scripts. 3.00
NOTE: *Stevens c-1.*

SHADOW CABINET (See Heroes)
DC Comics (Milestone): Jan, 1994 - No. 17, Oct, 1995 ($1.75/$2.50)
0,1-17: 0-($2.50, 52 pgs.)-Silver ink-c; Simonson-c. 1-Byrne-c 2.50

SHADOW COMICS (Pulp, radio)
Street & Smith Publications: Mar, 1940 - V9#5, Aug-Sept, 1949
NOTE: *The Shadow first appeared on radio in 1929 and was featured in pulps beginning in April,
1931, written by Walter Gibson. The early covers of this series were reprinted from the pulp
covers.*
V1#1-Shadow, Doc Savage, Bill Barnes, Nick Carter (radio), Frank Merriwell,
Iron Munro, the Astonishing Man begin | 423 | 1269 | 2750 | 5500
2-The Avenger begins, ends #6; Capt. Fury only app.
| | 182 | 546 | 1136 | 2000
3(nn-5/40)-Norgil the Magician app.; cover is exact swipe of Shadow pulp
from 1/33 | 127 | 381 | 795 | 1400
4,5: 4-The Three Musketeers begins, ends #8. 5-Doc Savage ends
| | 100 | 300 | 625 | 1100
6,8,9: 9-Norgil the Magician app. | 89 | 267 | 556 | 975
7-Origin/1st app. The Hooded Wasp & Wasplet (11/40); series ends V3#8;
Hooded Wasp/Wasplet app. on-c thru #9 | 95 | 285 | 597 | 1050
10-Origin The Iron Ghost, ends #11; The Dead End Kids begins, ends #14
| | 89 | 267 | 556 | 975
11-Origin Hooded Wasp & Wasplet retold | 89 | 267 | 556 | 975
12-Dead End Kids app. | 73 | 219 | 455 | 800
V2#1(11/41) | 68 | 204 | 426 | 750
2-(Rare) Giant ant-c; Dead End Kids story | 109 | 327 | 682 | 1200
3-Origin & 1st app. Supersnipe (3/42); series begins; Little Nemo story
| | 100 | 300 | 625 | 1100
4,5: 4,8-Little Nemo story | 57 | 171 | 356 | 625
6-9: 6-Blackstone the Magician story | 55 | 165 | 341 | 600
10-12: 10-Supersnipe app. | 55 | 165 | 330 | 575

The Shadow: Hell's Heat Wave #3 © DH

Shadowman #40 © Voyager Comm.

Shadow Reavers #1 © Black Bull Ent.

	GD2.0	FN6.0	VF8.0	NM9.4

V3#1-12: 10-Doc Savage begins, not in V5#5, V6#10-12, V8#4

	52	157	314	550
V4#1-12	43	129	257	450
V5#1-12	40	120	232	400
V6#1-11: 9-Intro. Shadow, Jr. (12/46)	39	117	208	360
12-Powell-c/a; atom bomb panels	40	120	232	400
V7#1,2,5,7-9,12: 2,5-Shadow, Jr. app.; Powell-a	40	120	240	420
3,6,11-Powell-c/a	45	135	270	475
4-Powell-c/a; Atom bomb panels	47	142	286	500
10(1/48)-Flying Saucer-c/story (2nd of this theme; see The Spirit 9/28/47); Powell-c/a	55	165	341	600
V8#1-12-Powell-a. 8-Powell Spider-c/a	45	135	270	475
V9#1,5-Powell-a	43	129	257	450
2-4-Powell-c/a	45	135	270	475

NOTE: *Binder* c-V3#1. *Powell* in art most issues beginning V6#12. *Painted c-1-6.*

SHADOWDRAGON
DC Comics: 1995 ($3.50, annual)

Annual 1-Year One story	3.50

SHADOW EMPIRES: FAITH CONQUERS
Dark Horse Comics: Aug, 1994 - No. 4, Nov, 1994 ($2.95, limited series)

1-4	3.00

SHADOWHAWK (See Images of Shadowhawk, New Shadowhawk, Shadowhawk II, Shadowhawk III & Youngblood #2)
Image Comics (Shadowline Ink): Aug, 1992 - No. 4, Mar, 1993; No. 12, Aug, 1994 - No. 18, May, 1995 ($1.95/$2.50)

1-($2.50)-Embossed silver foil stamped-c; Valentino/Liefeld-c; Valentino-c/a/ scripts in all; has coupon for Image #0; 1st Shadowline Ink title	4.00
1-With coupon missing	2.25
1-($1.95)-Newsstand version w/o foil stamp	2.25
2-13,0,1418: 2-Shadowhawk poster w/McFarlane-i; brief Spawn app.; wrap around-c w/silver ink highlights. 3-($2.50)-Glow-in-the-dark-c. 4-Savage Dragon-c/story; Valentino/Larsen-c. 5-11-(See Shadowhawk II and III). 12-Cont'd fromShadowhawk III & Shadowhawk #2); pull-out poster by Texeira.13-w/ShadowBone poster; WildC.A.T.s app. 0 (10/94)-Liefeld c/a/story; ShadowBart poster. 14-(10/94, $2.50)-The Others app. 16-Supreme app. 17-Spawn app.; story cont'd from Badrock & Co. #6. 18-Shadowhawk dies; Savage Dragon & Brigade app.	2.50
Special 1(12/94, $3.50, 52 pgs.)-Silver Age Shadowhawk flip book	3.50
Gallery (4/94, $1.95)	2.25
Out of the Shadows ($19.95)-r/Youngblood #2, Shadowhawk #1-4, Image Zero #0, Operation :Urban Storm (Never published)	20.00
.../Vampirella (2/95, $4.95)-Pt.2 of x-over (See Vampirella/Shadowhawk for Pt. 1)	5.00

NOTE: *Shadowhawk was originally a four issue limited series. The story continued in Shadowhawk II, Shadowhawk III & then became Shadowhawk again with issue #12.*

SHADOWHAWK II (Follows Shadowhawk #4)
Image Comics (Shadowline Ink): V2#1, May, 1993 - V2#3, Aug, 1993 ($3.50/$1.95/$2.95, limited series)

V2#1 ($3.50)-Cont'd from Shadowhawk #4; die-cut mirricard-c	3.50
2 ($1.95)-Foil embossed logo; reveals identity; gold-c variant exists	2.50
3 ($2.95)-Pop-up-c w/Pact ashcan insert	3.00

SHADOWHAWK III (Follows Shadowhawk II #3)
Image Comics (Shadowline Ink): V3#1, Nov, 1993 - V3#4, Mar, 1994 ($1.95, limited series);

V3#1-4: 1-Cont'd from Shadowhawk II; intro Valentine; gold foil & red foil stamped-c variations. 2-(52 pgs.)-Shadowhawk contracts HIV virus; U.S. Male by M. Anderson (p) in free 16 pg.insert. 4-Continues in Shadowhawk #12.	2.50

SHADOWHAWKS OF LEGEND
Image Comics (Shadowline Ink): Nov, 1995 ($4.95, one-shot)

nn-Stories of past Shadowhawks by Kurt Busiek, Beau Smith & Alan Moore.	5.00

SHADOW, THE: HELL'S HEAT WAVE (Movie, pulp, radio)
Dark Horse Comics: Apr, 1995 - No. 3, June, 1995 ($2.95, limited series)

1-3: Kaluta story	3.00

SHADOWHUNT SPECIAL

Image Comics (Extreme Studios): Apr, 1996 ($2.50)

1-Retells origin of past Shadowhawks; Valentino script; Chapel app.	2.50

SHADOW, THE: IN THE COILS OF THE LEVIATHAN (Movie, pulp, radio)
Dark Horse Comics: Oct, 1993 - No. 4, Apr, 1994 ($2.95, limited series)

1-4-Kaluta-c & co-scripter	3.00
Trade paperback (10/94, $13.95)-r/1-4	14.00

SHADOW LADY:... (Masakazu Katsura's...)
Dark Horse Comics ($2.50, B&W, limited series, Manga)

Dangerous Love: (Oct, 1998 - No. 7, May, 1999) 1-7-Katsura-s/a	2.50
TPB ($17.95) r/#1-7	18.00
The Eyes of a Stranger: (No. 8, May, 1999 - No. 12, Sept, 1999) 8-12	2.50
The Awakening: (No. 13, Oct, 1999 - No. 19, Apr, 2000) 13-19	2.50
Sudden Death: (No. 20, May, 2000 - No. 24) 20-23	2.50

SHADOWLINE SAGA: CRITICAL MASS, A
Marvel Comics (Epic): Jan, 1990 - No. 7, July, 1990 ($4.95, lim. series, 68 pgs)

1-6: Dr. Zero, Powerline, St. George	5.00
7 ($5.95, 84 pgs.)-Morrow-a, Williamson-c(i)	6.00

SHADOWMAN (See X-O Manowar #4)
Valiant/Acclaim Comics (Valiant): May, 1992 - No. 43, Dec, 1995 ($2.50)

1-Partial origin	5.00
2-5: 3-1st app. Sousa the Soul Eater	4.00
6-43: 8-1st app. Master Darque. 16-1st app. Dr. Mirage (8/93). 15-Minor Turok app. 17,18-Archer & Armstrong x-over. 19-Aerosmith-c/story. 23-Dr. Mirage x-over. 24-(4/94). 25-Bound-in trading card. 29-Chaos Effect. 43-Shadowman jumps to his death	2.50
0-($2.50)-Regular edition	2.50
0-($3.50)-Wraparound chromium-c edition	3.50
0-Gold	6.00
Yearbook 1 (12/94, $3.95)	4.00

SHADOWMAN (Volume 2)
Acclaim Comics (Valiant Heroes): Mar, 1997 - No. 20 ($2.50, mature)

1-20: 1-1st app. Zero; Garth Ennis scripts begin, end #4. 2-Zero becomes new Shadowman. 4-Origin; Jack Boniface (original Shadowman) rises from the grave. 5-Jamie Delano scripts begin. 9-Copycat-c	2.50
1-Variant painted cover	2.50

SHADOWMAN (Volume 3)
Acclaim Comics: July, 1999 - No. 5 ($3.95/$2.50)

1-($3.95)-Abnett & Lanning-s/Broome & Benjamin-a	4.00
2-5-($2.50)-Flip book with Unity 2000	2.50

SHADOWMASTERS
Marvel Comics: Oct, 1989 - No.4, Jan, 1990 ($3.95, squarebound, 52 pgs.)

1-4: Heath-a(i). 1-Jim Lee-c; story cont'd from Punisher	4.00

SHADOW OF THE BATMAN
DC Comics: Dec, 1985 - No. 5, Apr, 1986 ($1.75, limited series)

1-Detective-r (all have wraparound-c)	1	3	5	7
2,3,5: 3-Penguin-c & cameo. 5-Clayface app.				5.00
4-Joker-c/story				6.00

NOTE: *Austin* a(new)-2(i), 3i; r-2-4i. *Rogers* a(new)-1, 2p, 3p, 4, 5; r-1-5p; c-1-5. *Simonson* a-1r.

SHADOW OF THE TORTURER, THE
Innovation: July, 1991 - No. 3, 1992 ($2.50, limited series)

1-3: Based on Pocket Books novel	2.50

SHADOW ON THE TRAIL (See Zane Grey & Four Color #604)

SHADOW PLAY (Tales of the Supernatural)
Whitman Publications: June, 1982

1-Painted-c	6.00

SHADOW REAVERS
Black Bull Ent.: Oct, 2001 - Present ($2.99)

1-4-Nelson-a; two covers for each issue	3.00
Limited Preview Edition (5/01, no cover price)	2.25

SHADOW RIDERS
Marvel Comics UK, Ltd.: June, 1993 - No. 4, Sept, 1993 ($1.75, limited series)

1-($2.50)-Embossed-c; Cable-c/story	2.50

Sharky #2 © Dave Elliot

Shatter #1 © FC

Shazam! #5 © DC

	GD2.0	FN6.0	VF8.0	NM9.4

2-4-Cable app. 2-Ghost Rider app. — 2.25

HADOWS & LIGHT
arvel Comics: Feb, 1998 - No. 3, July, 1998 ($2.99, B&W, quarterly)

1-3: 1-B&W anthology of Marvel characters; Black Widow art by Gene Ha, Hulk by Wrightson, Iron Man by Ditko & Daredevil by Stelfreeze; Stelfreeze paint ed-c. 2-Weeks, Sharp, Starlin, Thompson-a. 3-Buscema, Grindberg, Giffen, Layton-a — 3.00

HADOW'S FALL
C Comics (Vertigo): Nov, 1994 - No. 6, Apr, 1995 ($2.95, limited series)

1-6: Van Fleet-c/a in all. — 3.00

HADOWS FROM BEYOND (Formerly Unusual Tales)
harlton Comics: V2#50, October, 1966

2#50-Ditko-c — 3 — 9 — 20 — 30

HADOW SLASHER
ocket Change Comics: No. 0, 1994 - No. 6, 1995?

0-6 — 2.50

HADOW STATE
roadway Comics: Dec, 1995 - No. 5, Apr, 1996 ($2.50)

1-5: 1,2-Fatale back-up story; Cockrum-a(p) — 2.50
review Edition 1,2 (10-11/95, $2.50, B&W) — 2.50

HADOW STRIKES!, THE (Pulp, radio)
C Comics: Sept, 1989 - No.31, May, 1992 ($1.75)

1-4,7-31: 31-Mignola-c — 2.50
5,6-Doc Savage x-over — 4.00
nnual 1 (1989, $3.50, 68 pgs.)-Spiegle a; Kaluta-c — 3.50

HADOW WAR OF HAWKMAN
C Comics: May, 1985 - No. 4, Aug, 1985 (limited series)

1-4 — 2.25

HAGGY DOG & THE ABSENT-MINDED PROFESSOR (See Four Color #1199, lovie Comics & Walt Disney Showcase #46)(Disney-Movie)
ell Publ. Co.: No. 985, May, 1959

our Color #985 — 8 — 24 — 56 — 100

HALOMAN
l Wiesner/ Mark 1 Comics: 1989 - Present (B&W)

1#1-Al Wiesner-s/a in all — 4.50
2-9 — 2.50
2 #1(The New Adventures),4-6-10, V3 (The Legend)#1-7 — 2.50
5 (Color)-Shows Vol 2, No. 4 in indicia — 3.00

SHAMAN'S TEARS (Also see Maggie the Cat)
mage Comics (Creative Fire Studio): 5/93 - No. 2, 8/93; No. 3, 11/94 - No. 0, /96 ($2.50/$1.95)

0-2: 0-(DEC-c, 1/96)-Last Issue. 1-(5/93)-Embossed red foil-c; Grell-c/a & scripts in all. 2-Cover unfolds into poster (8/93-c, 7/93 inside) — 2.50
3-12: 3-Begin $1.95-c. 5-Re-intro Jon Sable. 12-Re-intro Maggie the Cat (1 pg.) — 2.25

SHANNA, THE SHE-DEVIL (See Savage Tales #8)
Marvel Comics Group: Dec, 1972 - No. 5, Aug, 1973 (All are 20¢ issues)

1-1st app. Shanna; Steranko-c; Tuska-a(p) — 3 — 9 — 17 — 25
2-Steranko-c; heroin drug story — 2 — 6 — 12 — 18
3-5 — 2 — 6 — 9 — 12

SHARDS
Ascension Comics: Apr, 1994 ($2.50, B&W, unfinished limited series)

1-Flip-c. — 2.50

SHARK FIGHTERS, THE (Movie)
Dell Publishing Co.: Jan, 1957

Four Color 762-Buscema-a; photo-c — 8 — 24 — 56 — 100

SHARKY
mage Comics: Feb, 1998 - No. 4, 1998 ($2.50, bi-monthly)

1-4: 1-Mask app.; Elliot-s/a. Horley painted-c. 3-Three covers by Horley, Bisley, & Horley/Elliot. 4-Two covers (swipe of Avengers #4 and wraparound) — 2.50
1-($2.95) "$1,000,000" variant — 3.00

2-($2.50) Savage Dragon variant-c — 2.50

SHARP COMICS (Slightly large size)
H. C. Blackerby: Winter, 1945-46 - V1#2, Spring, 1946 (52 pgs.)

V1#1-Origin Dick Royce Planetarian — 40 — 120 — 232 — 400
2-Origin The Pioneer; Michael Morgan, Dick Royce, Sir Gallagher, Planeta-rian, Steve Hagen, Weeny and Pop app. — 39 — 117 — 208 — 360

SHARPY FOX (See Comic Capers & Funny Frolics)
I. W. Enterprises/Super Comics: 1958; 1963

1,2-I.W. Reprint (1958): 2-r/Kiddie Kapers #1 — 2 — 6 — 9 — 12
14-Super Reprint (1963) — 2 — 6 — 9 — 12

SHATTER (See Jon Sable #25-30)
First Comics: June, 1985; Dec, 1985 - No. 14, Apr, 1988. ($1.75, Baxter paper/deluxe paper)

1 (6/85)-1st computer generated-a in a comic book (1st printing) — 3.00
1-(2nd print.); 1(12/85)-14: computer generated-a & lettering in all — 2.25
Special 1 (1988) — 2.25

SHATTERED IMAGE
Image Comics (WildStorm Productions): Aug, 1996 - No. 4, Dec, 1996 ($2.50, limited series)

1-4: 1st Image company-wide x-over; Kurt Busiek scripts in all. 1-Tony Daniel-c/a(p). 2-Alex Ross-c/swipe (Kingdom Come) by Ryan Benjamin & Travis Charest — 2.50

SHAZAM (See Giant Comics to Color, Limited Collectors' Edition & The Power Of Shazam!)

SHAZAM! (TV)(See World's Finest #253)
National Periodical Publ./DC Comics: Feb, 1973 - No. 35, May-June, 1978

1-1st revival of original Captain Marvel since G.A. (origin retold), by Beck; Captain Marvel Jr. & Mary Marvel cameo-c; Superman-c. — 3 — 9 — 17 — 25
2-5: 2-Infinity photo-c; re-intro Mr. Mind & Tawny. 3-Capt. Marvel-r. (10/46). 4-Origin retold; Capt. Marvel-r. (1949). 5-Capt. Marvel Jr. origin retold; Capt. Marvel-r. (1948, 7 pgs.) — 1 — 4 — 7 — 10
6,7,9-11: 6-photo-c; Capt. Marvel-r (1950, 6 pgs.). 9-Mr. Mind app. 10-Last C.C. Beck issue. 11-Schaffenberger-a begins. — 1 — 3 — 6 — 8
8 (100 pgs.) 8-r/Capt. Marvel Jr. by Raboy; origin/CM #80; origin Mary Marvel/C.M. #18; origin Mr. Tawny/C.M. #79 — 4 — 12 — 29 — 45
12-17-(All 100 pgs.)-. 15-vs. Lex Luthor & Mr. Mind — 3 — 10 — 23 — 35
18-24,26-30: 21-24-All reprints. 26-Sivana app. (10/76). 27-Kid Eternity teams up w/Capt. Marvel. 28-1st S.A. app. of Black Adam. 30-1st DC app. 3 Lt. Marvels. — 1 — 3 — 6 — 8
25-1st app. Isis — 2 — 6 — 9 — 12
31-35: 31-1st DC app. Minuteman. 34-Origin Capt. Marvel Jr. retold — 1 — 4 — 7 — 10
NOTE: Reprints in #1-8, 10, 12-17, 21-24. Beck a-1-10, 12-17, 21-24r; c-1, 3-9. Nasser c-35p. Newton a-35p. Raboy a-5r, 8r, 17r. Schaffenberger a-11, 14-20, 25, 26, 27p, 28, 29-31p, 33i, 35i; c-20, 22, 23, 25, 26, 27p, 28-33.

SHAZAM!: POWER OF HOPE
DC Comics: Nov, 2000 ($9.95, treasury size, one-shot)

nn-Painted art by Alex Ross; story by Alex Ross and Paul Dini — 10.00

SHAZAM: THE NEW BEGINNING
DC Comics: Apr, 1987 - No. 4, July, 1987 (Legends spin-off) (Limited series)

1-4: Origin & 1st modern app. Captain Marvel; Marvel Family cameo. 2-4-Sivana & Black Adam app. — 3.00

SHEA THEATRE COMICS
Shea Theatre: No date (1940's) (32 pgs.)

nn-Contains Rocket Comics; MLJ cover in one color — 10 — 30 — 55 — 80

SHE-BAT (See Murcielaga, She-Bat & Valeria the She-Bat)

SHEENA (Movie)
Marvel Comics: Dec, 1984 - No. 2, Feb, 1985 (limited series)

1,2-r/Marvel Comics Super Special #34; Tanya Roberts movie — 3.00

SHEENA, QUEEN OF THE JUNGLE (See Jerry Iger's Classic..., Jumbo Comics, & 3-D Sheena)
Fiction House Magazines: Spr, 1942; No. 2, Wint, 1942-43; No. 3, Spr, 1943; No. 4, Fall, 1948; No. 5, Sum, 1949; No. 6, Spr, 1950; No. 7-10, 1950(nd); No. 11, Spr, 1951 - No. 18, Wint, 1952-53 (#1-3: 68 pgs.; #4-7: 52 pgs.)

Sheena, Queen of the Jungle #7 © FH

Sheriff Bob Dixon's Chuck Wagon #1 © AVON

Shi: Heaven and Earth #4 © William Tucci

	GD2.0	FN6.0	VF8.0	NM9.4
1-Sheena begins	245	735	1534	2700
2 (Winter, 1942-43)	107	321	669	1175
3 (Spring, 1943)	80	240	500	875
4,5 (Fall, 1948, Sum, 1949): 4-New logo; cover swipe from Jumbo #20				
	50	150	300	525
6,7 (Spring, 1950, 1950)	43	129	257	450
8-10(1950 - Win/50, 36 pgs.)	40	120	232	400
11-18: 15-Cover swipe from Jumbo #43. 18-Used in POP, pg. 98				
	35	105	185	320
I.W. Reprint #9-r/#18; c-r/White Princess #3	5	15	34	55

NOTE: *Baker c-5-10? Whitman c-11-18(most).*

SHEENA-QUEEN OF THE JUNGLE
London Night: Feb, 1998 - No. 3 ($3.00)

0-($3.00)-Hartsoe-s/Sandoval-c				3.00
0-($5.00) Crocodile, Zebra, & Leopard editions				5.00
1-3-($3.00)				3.00
1-3-($5.00) Ministry Edition				5.00

SHEENA 3-D SPECIAL (Also see Blackthorne 3-D Series #1)
Eclipse Comics: Jan, 1985 ($2.00)

1-Dave Stevens-c				5.00

SHE-HULK (See The Savage She-Hulk & The Sensational She-Hulk)

SHERIFF BOB DIXON'S CHUCK WAGON (TV) (See Wild Bill Hickok #22)
Avon Periodicals: Nov, 1950

1-Kinstler-c/a(3)	14	42	72	120

SHERIFF OF TOMBSTONE
Charlton Comics: Nov, 1958 - No. 17, Sept, 1961

V1#1-Giordano-c; Severin-a	7	21	50	80
2	4	12	29	45
3-10	3	9	21	32
11-17	3	9	17	25

SHERLOCK HOLMES (See Marvel Preview, New Adventures of..., & Spectacular Stories)

SHERLOCK HOLMES (All New Baffling Adventures of...)(Young Eagle #3 on?)
Charlton Comics: Oct, 1955 - No. 2, Mar, 1956

1-Dr. Neff, Ghost Breaker app.	40	120	240	420
2	39	117	208	360

SHERLOCK HOLMES (Also see The Joker)
National Periodical Publications: Sept-Oct, 1975

1-Cruz-a; Simonson-c	3	9	17	25

SHERRY THE SHOWGIRL (Showgirls #4)
Atlas Comics: July, 1956 - No. 3, Dec, 1956; No. 5, Apr, 1957 - No. 7, Aug, 1957

1-Dan DeCarlo-c/a in all	15	45	77	130
2	11	33	55	90
3,5-7	8	24	45	65

SHE'S JOSIE (See Josie)

SHEVA'S WAR
DC Comics (Helix): Oct, 1998 - No. 5, Feb, 1999 ($2.95, mini-series)

1-5-Christopher Moeller-s/painted-a/c				3.00

SHI (See Razor Annual #1 for 1st app.)

SHI: AKAI
Crusade Comics: 2001 ($2.99)

1-Intro. Victoria Cross; Tucci-a/c; J.C. Vaughn-s				3.00
Victoria Cross Ed. ($5.95, edition of 2000) variant Tucci-c				6.00

SHI: BLACK, WHITE AND RED
Crusade Comics: Mar, 1998 - No. 2, May, 1998 ($2.95, B&W&Red, mini-series)

1,2-J.G. Jones-painted art				3.00
...-Year of the Dragon Collected Edition (2000, $5.95) r/#1&2				6.00

SHI/CYBLADE: THE BATTLE FOR THE INDEPENDENTS
Crusade Comics: Sept, 1995 ($2.95)

1-Tucci-c; features Cerebus, Bone, Hellboy, as well as others				3.00
1-Silvestri variant-c				4.00

SHI/DAREDEVIL: HONOR THY MOTHER (See Daredevil/Shi..)
Crusade Comics: Jan, 1997 ($2.95, one-shot)

1-Flip book				3.00

SHI: EAST WIND RAIN
Crusade Comics: Nov, 1997 - No. 2, Feb, 1998 ($3.50, limited series)

1,2-Shi at WW2 Pearl Harbor				3.50

SHI: FAN EDITIONS
Crusade Comics: 1997

1-3-Two books polybagged in FAN #19-21				3.00
1-3-Gold editions				4.00

SHI: C.G.I.
Crusade Comics: 2001 ($4.99)

Preview Edition				5.00

SHI: HEAVEN AND EARTH
Crusade Comics: June, 1997 - No. 4, Apr, 1998 ($2.95)

1-4				3.00
4-($4.95) Pencil-c variant				5.00
Rising Sun Edition-signed by Tucci in FanClub Starter Pack				4.00
"Tora No Shi" variant-c				3.00

SHI: JUDGMENT NIGHT
Crusade Comics: 2000 ($3.99, one-shot)

1-Wolverine app.; Battlebook card and pages included; Tucci-a				4.00

SHI: KAIDAN
Crusade Comics: Oct, 1996 ($2.95)

1-Two covers; Tucci-a; Jae Lee wraparound-c				3.00

SHI: MASQUERADE
Crusade Comics: Mar, 1998 ($3.50, one-shot)

1-Painted art by Lago, Texeira, and others				3.50

SHI: NIGHTSTALKERS
Crusade Comics: Sept, 1997 ($3.50, one-shot)

1-Painted art by Val Mayerik				3.50

SHI: REKISHI
Crusade Comics: Jan, 1997 ($2.95)

1-Character bios and story summaries of Shi: The Way of the Warrior told in Detective Joe Labianca's point of view; Christopher Golden script; Tucci-c; J.G. Jones-a; flip book w/Shi: East Wind Rain preview				3.00

SHI: SENRYAKU
Crusade Comics: Aug, 1995 - No. 3, Nov, 1995 ($2.95, limited series)

1-3: 1-Tucci-c; Quesada, Darrow, Sim, Lee, Smith-a. 2-Tucci-c; Silvestri, Balent, Perez, Mack-a. 3-Jusko-c; Hughes, Ramos, Bell, Moore-a				3.00
1-variant-c (no logo)				4.00
Hardcover ($24.95)-r/#1-3; Frazetta-c.				25.00
Trade Paperback ($13.95)-r/#1-3; Frazetta-c.				14.00

SHI: THE ART OF WAR TOURBOOK
Crusade Comics: 1998 ($4.95, one-shot)

1-Blank cover for Convention sketches; early Tucci-a inside				5.00
1-Mexico Edition ($10.00) Mexican flag-c				10.00
1-U.K. Edition ($10.00) British flag-c				10.00

SHI: THE SERIES
Crusade Comics: Aug, 1997 - No. 13 ($2.95, color #1-10, B&W #11)

1-10				3.00
11-13: 11-B&W. 12-Color; Lau-a				3.00

SHI: THE WAY OF THE WARRIOR
Crusade Comics: Mar, 1994 - No. 12, Apr, 1997 ($2.50/$2.95)

1/2				4.00
1		2	6	9	12
1-Commemorative ed., B&W, new-c; given out at 1994 San Diego Comic Con				
		2	6	12	18
1-Fan appreciation edition -r/#1				2.25
1-Fan appreciation edition (variant)				6.00
2				5.00

Shidima #1 © Dreamwave Prod.

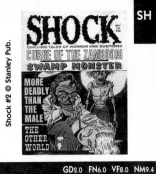

Shield Wizard Comics #11 © MLJ

Shock #2 © Stanley Pub.

	GD2.0	FN6.0	VF8.0	NM9.4

	GD2.0	FN6.0	VF8.0	NM9.4

2-Commemorative edition (3,000)	2	6	11	16
2-Fan appreciation edition -r/#2				2.25
3				4.00
4-7: 4-Silvestri poster. 7-Tomoe app.				2.25
5,6: 5-Silvestri variant-c. 6-Tomoe #1 variant-c				3.00
5-Gold edition				12.00
6,8-12: 6-Fan appreciation edition				2.25
8-Signed Edition-(5000)				3.00
rade paperback (1995, $12.95)-r/#1-4				13.00
rade paperback (1995, $14.95)-r/#1-4 revised; Julie Bell-c				15.00

SHI/ VAMPIRELLA
Crusade Comics: Oct, 1997 ($2.95, one-shot)

1-Ellis-s/Lau-a				3.00

SHI VS. TOMOE
Crusade Comics: Aug, 1996 ($3.95, one-shot)

1-Tucci-a/scripts; wraparound foil-c				4.00
1-(6/96, $5.00. B&W)-Preview Ed.; sold at San Diego Comic Con				5.00

SHI: YEAR OF THE DRAGON
Crusade Comics: 2000 - No. 3, 2000 ($2.99, limited series)

1-3: 1-Two covers; Tucci-a/c; flashback to teen-aged Ana				3.00

SHIDIMA
Image Comics: Jan, 2001 - Present ($2.95, limited series)

1-4-Prequel to Warlands				3.00
#0-(10/01, $2.25) Short story and sketch pages				2.25

S.H.I.E.L.D. (Nick Fury & His Agents of...) (Also see Nick Fury)
Marvel Comics Group: Feb, 1973 - No. 5, Oct, 1973 (All 20¢ issues)

1-All contain reprint stories from Strange Tales #146-155; new Steranko-c				
	2	6	11	16
2-New Steranko flag-c	2	6	9	12
3-5: 3-Kirby/Steranko-c(r). 4-Steranko-c(r)	1	3	6	8
NOTE: Buscema 3-p(r). Kirby layouts 1-5; c-3 (w/Steranko). Steranko 3-r, 4r(2).				

SHIELD, THE (Becomes Shield-Steel Sterling #3; #1 titled Lancelot Strong; also see Advs. of the Fly, Double Life of Private Strong, Fly Man, Mighty Comics, The Mighty Crusaders, The Original... & Pep Comics #1)
Archie Enterprises, Inc.: June, 1983 - No. 2, Aug, 1983

1,2: Steel Sterling app. 2-Kanigher-s				3.00

SHIELD-STEEL STERLING (Formerly The Shield)
Archie Enterprises, Inc.: No. 3, Dec, 1983 (Becomes Steel Sterling No. 4)

3-Nino-a; Steel Sterling by Kanigher & Barreto				3.00

SHIELD WIZARD COMICS (Also see Pep Comics & Top-Notch Comics)
MLJ Magazines: Summer, 1940 - No. 13, Spring, 1944

1-(V1#5 on inside)-Origin The Shield by Irving Novick & The Wizard by Ed Ashe, Jr; Flag-c	446	1338	2900	5800
2-(Winter/40)-Origin The Shield retold; Wizard's sidekick, Roy the Super Boy begins (see Top-Notch #8 for 1st app.)	218	654	1364	2400
3,4	136	408	852	1500
5-Dusty, the Boy Detective begins	118	354	738	1300
6-8: 6-Roy the Super Boy app. 7-Shield dons new costume (Summer, 1942); S & K-c? 8-Dungan-c; Hitler photo on-c	114	342	713	1250
9-13: 9,13-Bondage-c	84	252	525	925
NOTE: Bob Montana c-13. Novick c-1-6,8-11. Harry Sahle c-12.				

SHINING KNIGHT (See Adventure Comics #66)

SHIP AHOY!
Spotlight Publishers: Nov, 1944 (52 pgs.)

1-L. B. Cole-c	20	60	105	175

SHIP OF FOOLS
Image Comics: Aug, 1997 - No. 3 ($2.95, B&W)

0-3-Glass-s/Oeming-a				3.00

SHIPWRECKED! (Disney-Movie)
Disney Comics: 1990 ($5.95, graphic novel, 68 pgs.)

nn-adaptation; Spiegle-a				6.00

SHMOO (See Al Capp's... & Washable Jones &...)

SHOCK (Magazine)
Stanley Publ.: May, 1969 - V3#4, Sept, 1971 (B&W reprints from horror comics, including some pre-code) (No V2#1,3)

V1#1-Cover-r/Weird Tales of the Future #7 by Bernard Baily; r/Weird Chills #1				
	5	15	34	55
2-Wolverton-r/Weird Mysteries 5; r-Weird Mysteries #7 used in SOTI; cover reprints cover to Weird Chills #1	4	12	27	42
3,5,6	3	9	19	28
4-Harrison/Williamson-r/Forbid. Worlds #6	3	9	21	32
V2#2(5/70), V1#8(7/70), V2#4(9/70)-6(1/71), V3#1-4: V2#4-Cover swipe from Weird Mysteries #6	3	9	17	24
NOTE: Disbrow r-V2#4; Bondage c-V1#4, V2#6, V3#1.				

SHOCK DETECTIVE CASES (Formerly Crime Fighting Detective)
(Becomes Spook Detective Cases No. 22)
Star Publications: No. 20, Sept, 1952 - No. 21, Nov, 1952

20,21-L.B. Cole-c; based on true crime cases	24	72	127	215
NOTE: Palais a-20. No. 21-Fox-r.				

SHOCK ILLUSTRATED (...Adult Crime Stories; Magazine format)
E. C. Comics: Sept-Oct, 1955 - No. 3, Spring, 1956 (Adult Entertainment on-c #1,2)(All 25¢)

1-All by Kamen; drugs, prostitution, wife swapping	11	33	55	90
2-Williamson-a redrawn from Crime SuspenStories #13 plus Ingels, Crandall, Evans & part Torres-i; painted-c	12	36	61	100
3-Only 100 known copies bound & given away at E.C. office; Crandall, Evans-a; painted-c; shows May, 1956 on-c	91	273	568	1000

SHOCKING MYSTERY CASES (Formerly Thrilling Crime Cases)
Star Publications: No. 50, Sept, 1952 - No. 60, Oct, 1954 (All crime reprints?)

50-Disbrow "Frankenstein" story	42	126	252	440
51-Disbrow-a	28	84	148	255
52-60: 56-Drug use story	26	78	136	235
NOTE: L. B. Cole covers on all; a-60(2 pgs.). Hollingsworth a-52. Morisi a-55.				

SHOCKING TALES DIGEST MAGAZINE
Harvey Publications: Oct, 1981 (95¢)

1-1957-58-r; Powell, Kirby, Nostrand-a	2	6	9	12

SHOCK ROCKETS
Image Comics (Gorilla): Apr, 2000 - Present ($2.50)

1-6-Busiek-s/Immonen & Grawbadger-a. 6-Flip book w/Superstar preview				2.50

SHOCK SUSPENSTORIES
E. C. Comics: Feb-Mar, 1952 - No. 18, Dec-Jan, 1954-55

1-Classic Feldstein electrocution-c	75	225	525	950
2	41	123	287	515
3,4: 4-Used in SOTI, pg. 387,388	29	87	203	360
5-Hanging-c	34	102	238	420
6-Classic hooded vigilante bondage-c	36	108	252	450
7-Classic face melting-c	44	132	308	550
8-Williamson-a	29	87	203	360
9-11: 9-Injury to eye panel. 10-Junkie story	24	72	168	310
12- "The Monkey" classic junkie cover/story; anti-drug propaganda issue	31	93	217	385
13-Frazetta's only solo story for E.C., 7 pgs.	34	102	238	425
14-Used in Senate Investigation hearings	19	57	133	240
15-Used in 1954 Reader's Digest article, "For the Kiddies to Read"; Bill Gaines stars in prose story "The EC Caper"	18	55	126	230
16-18: 16- "Red Dupe" editorial; rape story	17	51	119	220
NOTE: Ray Bradbury adaptations-1, 7, 9. Craig a-11; c-11. Crandall a-9-13, 15-18. Davis a-1-5. Evans a-7, 8, 14-18; c-16-18. Feldstein c-1, 7-9, 12. Ingels a-1-2, 6. Kamen a-in all; c-10, 13, 15. Krigstein a-14, 18. Orlando a-1, 3-7, 9, 10, 12, 16, 17. Wood a-2-15; c-2-6, 14.				

SHOCK SUSPENSTORIES
Russ Cochran/Gemstone Publishing: Sept, 1992 - No. 18, Dec, 1996 ($1.50/$2.00/$2.50, quarterly)

1-18: 1-3: Reprints with original-c. 17-r/HOF #17				2.50

SHOGUN WARRIORS
Marvel Comics Group: Feb, 1979 - No. 20, Sept, 1980 (Based on Mattel toys of the classic Japanese animation characters) (1-3: 35¢; 4-19: 40¢; 20: 50¢)

1-Raydeen, Combatra, & Dangard Ace begin; Trimpe-a	1	3	6	8

Shogun Warriors #7 © MAR

Showcase #13 © DC

Showcase #73 © DC

	GD2.0	FN6.0	VF8.0	NM9.4

2-20: 2-Lord Maurkon & Elementals of Evil app.; Rok-Korr app. 6-Shogun vs. Shogun. 7,8-Cerberus. 9-Starchild. 11-Austin-c. 12-Simonson-c. 14-16-Doctor Demonicus. 17-Juggernaut. 19,20-FF x-over

				5.00
1-3: Reprints				3.00

SHOOK UP (Magazine) (Satire)
Dodsworth Publ. Co.: Nov, 1958

V1#1	4	12	25	38

SHORT RIBS
Dell Publishing Co.: No. 1333, Apr - June, 1962

Four Color 1333	5	15	35	60

SHORTSTOP SQUAD (Baseball)
Ultimate Sports Ent. Inc.: 1999 ($3.95, one-shot)

1-Ripken Jr., Larkin, Jeter, Rodriguez app.; Edwards-c/a				4.00

SHORT STORY COMICS (See Hello Pal,...)

SHORTY SHINER (The Five-Foot Fighter in the Ten Gallon Hat)
Dandy Magazine (Charles Biro): June, 1956 - No. 3, Oct, 1956

1	6	18	32	45
2,3	5	15	23	30

SHOTGUN MARY
Antarctic Press: Sept, 1995 - No. 2; Mar, 1998 - No. 2, May, 1998 ($2.95)

1,2-w/pin-up				3.00
1-($8.95)-Bagged w/CD				9.00
...Deviltown-(7/96, $2.95), ...Shooting Gallery-(6/96, $2.95), ...Son Of The Beast-(10/97, $2.95) Painted-a by Esad Ribic				3.00

SHOTGUN MARY: BLOOD LORE
Antarctic Press: Feb, 1997 - No.4, Aug, 1997 (2.95, mini-series)

1-4				3.00

SHOTGUN SLADE (TV)
Dell Publishing Co.: No. 1111, July-Sept, 1960

Four Color 1111-Photo-c	6	18	42	80

SHOWCASE (See Cancelled Comic Cavalcade & New Talent...)
National Per. Publ./DC Comics: 3-4/56 - No. 93, 9/70; No. 94, 8-9/77 - No. 104, 9/78

1-Fire Fighters; w/Fireman Farrell	239	717	2151	4300
2-Kings of the Wild; Kubert-a (animal stories)	75	225	638	1200
3-The Frogmen by Russ Heath; Heath greytone-c (early DC example, 7-8/56)	72	216	612	1150
4-Origin/1st app. The Flash (1st DC S.A. hero, Sept-Oct, 1956) & The Turtle; Kubert-a; r/in Secret Origins #1 ('61 & '73); Flash shown reading G.A. Flash #13; Infantino/Kubert-c	1150	3450	12,500	35,000
5-Manhunters	75	225	638	1200
6-Origin/1st app. Challengers of the Unknown by Kirby, partly r/in Secret Origins #1 & Challengers #64,65 (1st S.A. hero team & 1st original concept S.A. series)(1-2/57)	267	800	2400	4800
7-Challengers of the Unknown by Kirby (2nd app.) reprinted in Challengers of the Unknown #75	138	414	1169	2200
8-The Flash (5-6/57, 2nd app.); origin & 1st app. Capt. Cold	800	2400	7200	15,200
9-Lois Lane (Pre-#1, 7-8/57) (1st Showcase character to win own series) Superman app. on-c	600	1800	4500	9000
10-Lois Lane; Jor-el cameo; Superman app. on-c	215	645	1900	3800
11-Challengers of the Unknown by Kirby (3rd)	131	393	1114	2100
12-Challengers of the Unknown by Kirby (4th)	131	393	1114	2100
13-The Flash (3rd app.); origin Mr. Element	306	918	2754	5500
14-The Flash (4th app.); origin Dr. Alchemy, former Mr. Element (rare in NM)	326	978	2934	6200
15-Space Ranger (7-8/58, 1st app.)	150	450	1275	2400
16-Space Ranger (9-10/58, 2nd app.)	75	225	638	1200
17-(11-12/58)-Adventures on Other Worlds; origin/1st app Adam Strange by Gardner Fox & Mike Sekowsky	176	528	1500	3000
18-Adventures on Other Worlds (2nd A. Strange)	100	300	850	1600
19-Adam Strange; 1st Adam Strange logo	109	327	927	1750
20-Rip Hunter; origin & 1st app. (5-6/59); Moriera-a	78	234	663	1250
21-Rip Hunter 7-8/59, 2nd app.); Sekowsky-c/a	43	129	344	625
22-Origin & 1st app. Silver Age Green Lantern by Gil Kane (9-10/59);				

reprinted in Secret Origins #2

	326	978	2934	6200
23-Green Lantern (11-12/59, 2nd app.); nuclear explosion-c	119	357	1009	1900
24-Green Lantern (1-2/60, 3rd app.)	119	357	1009	1900
25,26-Rip Hunter by Kubert. 25-Grey tone-c	31	93	222	450
27-Sea Devils (7-8/60, 1st app.); Heath-c/a	66	198	558	1050
28-Sea Devils (9-10/60, 2nd app.); Heath-c/a	37	111	278	500
29-Sea Devils; Heath-c/a; grey tone-c 27-29	37	111	278	500
30-Origin Silver Age Aquaman (1-2/61) (see Adventure #260 for 1st S.A. app.)	63	189	531	1000
31,32-Aquaman	37	111	278	500
33-Aquaman	40	119	300	540
34-Origin & 1st app. Silver Age Atom by Kane & Anderson (9-10/61); reprinted in Secret Origins #2	109	327	927	1750
35-The Atom by Gil Kane (2nd); last 10¢ issue	61	182	519	975
36-The Atom by Gil Kane (1-2/62, 3rd app.)	50	150	400	725
37-Metal Men (3-4/62, 1st app.)	55	165	468	875
38-Metal Men (5-6/62, 2nd app.)	40	119	300	540
39-Metal Men (7-8/62, 3rd app.)	31	94	222	400
40-Metal Men (9-10/62, 4th app.)	29	88	202	360
41,42-Tommy Tomorrow (parts 1 & 2). 42-Origin	18	54	123	220
43-Dr. No (James Bond); Nodel-a; originally published as British Classics Illustrated #158A & as #6 in a European Detective series, all with diff. painted-c. This Showcase #43 version is actually censored, deleting all racial skin color and dialogue thought to be racially demeaning (1st DC S.A. movie adaptation)(based on Ian Fleming novel & movie)	41	123	306	550
44-Tommy Tomorrow	12	36	84	140
45-Sgt. Rock (7-8/63); pre-dates B&B #52; origin retold; Heath-c	28	84	196	350
46,47-Tommy Tomorrow	10	30	70	120
48,49-Cave Carson (3rd tryout series; see B&B)	8	24	58	95
50,51-I Spy (Danger Trail-r by Infantino), King Faraday story (#50 new 4 pg. story)	8	24	58	95
52-Cave Carson	7	21	50	80
53,54-G.I. Joe (11-12/64, 1-2/65); Heath-a	11	33	80	135
55-Dr. Fate & Hourman (3-4/65); origin of each in text; 1st solo app. G.A. Green Lantern in Silver Age (pre-dates Gr. Lantern #40); 1st S.A. app. Solomon Grundy	25	75	174	310
56-Dr. Fate & Hourman	14	42	98	165
57-Enemy Ace by Kubert (7-8/65, 4th after Our Army at War #155)	21	63	146	260
58-Enemy Ace by Kubert (5th app.)	18	54	123	220
59-Teen Titans (11-12/65, 3rd app.)	11	33	80	135
60-1st S. A. app. The Spectre; Anderson-a (1-2/66); origin in text	29	88	202	360
61-The Spectre by Anderson (2nd app.)	15	45	105	180
62-Origin & 1st app. Inferior Five (5-6/66)	9	27	65	110
63,65-Inferior Five. 63-Hulk parody. 65-X-Men parody (11-12/66)	5	15	38	60
64-The Spectre by Anderson (5th app.)	14	42	98	165
66,67-B'wana Beast	4	12	26	40
68-Maniaks (1st app.)	4	12	26	40
69,71-Maniaks. 71-Woody Allen-c/app.	4	12	26	40
70-Binky (9-10/67)-Tryout issue; 1950's Leave It To Binky reprints with art changes	4	12	30	50
72-Top Gun (Johnny Thunder-r)-Toth-a	4	12	26	40
73-Origin/1st app. Creeper; Ditko-c/a (3-4/68)	14	42	98	165
74-Intro/1st app. Anthro; Post-c/a (5/68)	8	24	60	100
75-1st app. Hawk and the Dove; Ditko-c/a	12	36	84	140
76-1st app. Bat Lash (8/68)	6	18	42	70
77-1st app. Angel & the Ape (9/68)	6	18	42	70
78-1st app. Jonny Double (11/68)	4	12	26	40
79-1st app. Dolphin (12/68); Aqualad origin-r	5	15	38	60
80-1st S.A. app. Phantom Stranger (1/69); Neal Adams-c	8	24	56	90
81-Windy & Willy; r/Many Loves of Dobie Gillis #26 with art changes	4	12	29	45
82-1st app. Nightmaster (5/69) by Grandenetti & Giordano; Kubert-c	7	21	50	80
83,84-Nightmaster by Wrightson w/Jones/Kaluta ink assist in each; Kubert-c				

Showcase '94 #2 © DC

Showgirls #1 © MAR

Sick #3 © Feature Pub.

SI

	GD2.0	FN6.0	VF8.0	NM9.4
83-Last 12¢ issue 84-Origin retold; begin 15¢	6	18	42	70
5-87-Firehair; Kubert-a	3	9	19	28
3-90-Jason's Quest: 90-Manhunter 2070 app.	2	6	15	22
l-93-Manhunter 2070: 92-Origin. 93-(9/70) Last 15¢ issue				
	2	6	15	22
4-Intro/origin new Doom Patrol & Robotman(8-9/77)	2	6	11	15
5,96-The Doom Patrol. 95-Origin Celsius	1	3	6	9
7-99-Power Girl; origin-97,98; JSA cameos	1	3	6	9
0-(52 pgs.)-Most Showcase characters featured	2	6	11	15
1-103-Hawkman; Adam Strange x-over	1	3	6	9
4-(52 pgs.)-O.S.S. Spies at War	1	3	6	9

OTE: Anderson a-22-24i, 34-36i, 55, 56, 60, 61, 64, 101-103i; c-50i, 51i, 55, 56, 60, 61, 64. Infantino (p)-4, 8, 13, 14; c-50p, 51p. Boring c-10. Estrada a-104. Fraden c(p)-30, 31, 33. Heath c-3, 27-29. Infantino (p)-4, 8, 13, 14; c-50p, 51p. Gil Kane a-22-24p, 34-36p; c-17-19, 22-24p(w/ ella), 31. Kane/Anderson c-34-36. Kirby c-11, 12. Kirby/Stein c-6, 7. Kubert a-2, 41, 25, 26, 53, 54, 72; c-25, 26, 53, 54, 57, 58, 82-87, 101-104; c-2, 4i. Moriera c-5. Orlando a-62p, 63p, i; c-62, 63, 97i. Sekowsky a-78. Staton a-94, 95-99p, 100; c-97-100p.

HOWCASE '93
C Comics: Jan, 1993 - No. 12, Dec, 1993 ($1.95, limited series, 52 pgs.)

I-12: 1-Begin 4 part Catwoman story & 6 part Blue Devil story; begin Cyborg story; Art Adams/Austin-a. 3-Flash by Travis Charest (p). 6-Azrael in Bat-costume (2 pgs.). 7,8-Knightfall parts 13 & 14. 6-10-Deathstroke app. (6,10-cameo). 9,10-Austin-i. 10-Azrael as Batman in new costume app.; Gulacy-c. 11-Perez-c. 12-Creeper app.; Alan Grant scripts.				3.00

OTE: Chaykin c-9. Fabry c-8. Giffen a-12. Golden c-3. Zeck c-6.

HOWCASE '94
C Comics: Jan, 1994 - No. 12, Dec, 1994 ($1.95, limited series, 52 pgs.)

I-12: 1,2-Joker & Gunfire stories. 1-New Gods. 4-Riddler story. 5-Huntress-c/story w/app. new Batman. 6-Huntress-c/story w/app. Robin; Atom story. 7-Penguin story by Peter David, P. Craig Russell, & Michael T. Gilbert; Penguin-c by Jae Lee. 8,9-Scarface origin story by Alan Grant, John Wagner,& Steve Kristiansen; Prelude to Zero Hour. 10-Zero Hour tie-in story. 11-Man-Bat.				3.00

OTE: Alan Grant scripts-3, 4. Kelley Jones c-12. Mignola c-3. Nebres a(i)-2. Quesada c-10. ussell a-7p. Simonson c-5.

HOWCASE '95
C Comics: Jan, 1995 - No. 12, Dec, 1995 ($2.50/$2.95, limited series)

I-4-Supergirl story. 3-Eradicator-c.; The Question c/story				3.00
5-12: 5-Thorn c/story; begin $2.95-c. 8-Spectre story. 12-The Shade story by James Robinson & Wade Von Grawbadger; Maitresse story by Chris Claremont & Alan Davis.				3.00

HOWCASE '96
C Comics: Jan, 1996 - No. 12, Dec, 1996 ($2.95, limited series)

1-12: 1-Steve Geppi cameo. 3-Black Canary & Lois Lane-c/story; Deadman story by Jamie Delano & Wade Von Grawbadger, Gary Frank-c. 4-Firebrand & Guardian-c/story; The Shade & Dr. Fate "Times Past" story by James Robinson & Matt Smith begins, ends #5. 6-Superboy-c/app.; Atom app.; Capt. Marvel (Mary Marvel)-c/app. 8-Supergirl by David & Dodson. 10-Scare Tactics app. 11,12-Legion of Super-Heroes vs. Brainiac. 12-Jesse Quick app.				3.00

HOWGIRLS (Formerly Sherry the Showgirl #3)
tlas Comics (MPC No. 2): No. 4, 2/57; June, 1957 - No. 2, Aug, 1957

4-(2/57) Dan DeCarlo-c/a begins	10	30	55	80
1-(6/57) Millie, Sherry, Chili, Pearl & Hazel begin	13	39	66	110
2	10	30	55	80

HROUD, THE (See Super-Villain Team-Up #5)
larvel Comics: Mar, 1994 - No. 4, June, 1994 ($1.75, mini-series)

1-4: 1,2,4-Spider-Man & Scorpion app.				2.25

HROUD OF MYSTERY
Vhitman Publications: June, 1982

1				6.00

HUT UP AND DIE
nage Comics/Halloween: 1998 - Present ($2.95,B&W, bi-monthly)

1-3: Hudnall-s.				3.00

ICK (Sick Special (#131) (Magazine) (Satire)
eature Publ./Headline Publ./Crestwood Publ. Co./Hewfred Publ./ Pyramid

	GD2.0	FN6.0	VF8.0	NM9.4
Comm./Charlton Publ. No. 109 (4/76) on: Aug, 1960 - No. 134, Fall, 1980				
V1#1-Jack Paar photo on-c; Torres-a; Untouchables-s; Ben Hur movie photo-s				
	15	45	105	180
2-Torres-a; Elvis app.; Lenny Bruce app.	9	27	63	105
3-5-Torres-a in all. 3-Khruschev-c; Hitler-s. 4-Newhart-s; Castro-s; John Wayne.				
5-JFK/Castro-c; Elvis app-s; Hitler.	7	21	53	85
6-Photo-s of Ricky Nelson & Marilyn Monroe; JFK	8	24	58	95
V2#1,2,4-8 (#7,8,10-14): 1-(#7) Hitler-s; Brando photo-s. 2-(#8) Dick Clark-s.				
4-(#10) Untouchables-c; Candid Camera-s. 5-(#11) Nixon-c; Lone Ranger-s; JFK-s. 6-(#12) Beatnik-c/s. 8-(#14) Liz Taylor pin-up, JFK-s; Dobie Gillis-s; Sinatra & Dean Martin photo-s	6	18	45	75
3-(#9) Marilyn Monroe/JFK-c; Kingston Trio-s	7	21	53	85
V3#1-7-(#15-21): 1-(#15) JFK app.; Liz Taylor/Richard Burton-s. 2-(#16) Ben Casey/ Frankenstein-c/s; Hitler photo-s. 4-(#19) Nixon back-c/s; Sinatra photo-s. 6-(#20) 1st Huckleberry Fink-c	4	12	29	45
8-(#22) Cassius Clay vs. Liston-s; 1st Civil War Blackouts-/Pvt. Bo Reargard w/ Jack Davis-a	5	15	34	55
V4#1-5 (#23-27): Civil War Blackouts-/Pvt. Bo Reargard w/ Jack Davis-a in all.				
1-(#23) Smokey Bear-c; Tarzan-s. 2-(#24) Goldwater & Paar-s; Castro-s.				
3-(#25) Frankenstein-c; Cleopatra/Liz Taylor-s; Steve Reeves photo-s.				
4-(#26) James Bond-s; Hitler-s. 5-(#27) Taylor/Burton app-s; Sinatra, Martin, Andress, Ekberg photo-s	3	9	23	35
28,31,36,39: 31-Pink Panther movie photo-s; Burke's Law-s. 39-Westerns; Elizabeth Montgomery photo-s; Beat mag-s	3	9	17	25
29,34,37,38: 29-Beatles-c by Jack Davis. 34-Two pg. Beatles-c & photo pin-up. 37-Playboy parody issue. 38-Beatles Family-s	3	9	21	32
30,32,35,40: 30-Beatles photo pin-up; James Bond photo-s. 32-Ian Fleming-s; LBJ-s; Tarzan-s. 35-Beatles cameo; Three Stooges parody. 40-Tarzan-s; Crosby/Hope-s; Beatles parody	3	10	23	35
33-Ringo Starr photo-c & spoof on "A Hard Day's Night"; inside-c has Beatles photos	4	12	30	50
41,50,51,53,54,60: 41-Sports Illustrated parody-c/s. 50-Mod issue; flip-c w/1967 calendar w/Bob Taylor-a. 51-Get Smart-s. 53-Beatles cameo; nudity panels. 54-Monkees-c. 60-TV Daniel Boone-s	3	9	17	25
42-Fighting American-c revised from Simon/Kirby-c; "Good girl" art by Sparling; profile on Bob Powell; superhero parodies	5	15	34	55
43-49,52,55-59: 43-Sneaker ad begins by Sparling. 45-Has #44 on inside; TV Westerns-s; Beatles cameo. 46-Hell's Angels-s; NY Mets-s. 47-UFO/Space-c. 49-Men's Adventure mag. parody issue; nudity. 52-LBJ-s. 55-Underground cartoon parody issue. 56-Alfred E. Neuman-s; inventors issue. 58-Hippie issue-c/s. 59-Hippie-s	2	6	13	20
61-64,66-69,71,73,75-80: 63-Tiny Tim-c & poster; Monkees-s. 64-Flip-c. 66-Flip-c; Mod Squad-s. 69-Beatles cameo; Peter Sellers photo-s. 71-Flip-c; Clint Eastwood0s. 76-Nixon-s; Marcus Welby-s. 78-Ma Barker-s; Courtship of Eddie's Father-s; Abbie Hoffman-s	2	6	12	18
65,70,74: 65-Cassius Clay/Brando/J. Wayne-c/s; Johnny Carson-s. 70-(9/69) John & Yoko-c,1/2 pg. story. 74-Clay, Wayne, Namath & others as superheroes-c/s; Easy Rider-s; Ghost and Mrs. Muir-s	2	6	14	20
72-(84 pgs.) Xmas issue w/2 pg. slick color poster; Tarzan-s; 2 pg. Superman & superheroes-s	3	9	20	30
81-85,87-95,98,99: 81-(2/71) Woody Allen photo-s. 85 Monster Mag. parody-s; Nixon-s w/Ringo & John cameo. 88-Klute photo-s; Nixon paper dolls page. 92-Lily Tomlin; Archie Bunker pin-up. 93-Woody Allen	2	6	10	14
86,96,97,100: 86-John & Yoko, Tiny Tim-c; Love Story movie photo-s. 96-Kung Fu-c; Mummy-s, Dracula & Frankenstein app. 97-Superman-s; 1974 Calendar; Charlie Brown & Snoopy pin-up. 100-Serpico-s; Cosell-s; J. Cousteau-s	2	6	12	18
101-103,105-114,116,119,120: 101-Three Musketeers-s; Dick Tracy-s. 102-Young Frankenstein-s. 103-Kojak-s; Evel Knievel-s. 105-Towering Inferno-s; Peanuts/Snoopy-s. 106-Cher-c/s. 10 7-Jaws-c/s. 108-Pink Panther-c/s; Archie-s. 109-Adam & Eve-s(nudity). 110-Welcome Back Kotter-s. 111-Sonny & Cher-s. 112-King Kong-c/s. 120-Star Trek-s	2	6	10	14
104,115,117,118: 104-Muhammad Ali-c/s. 115-Charlie's Angels-s. 117-Bionic Woman & Six Million $ Man-c/s; Cher D'Flower begins by Sparling (nudity). 118-Star Wars-s; Popeye-s	2	7	11	16
121-125,128,130: 122-Darth Vader-s. 123-Jaws II-s. 128-Superman-c/movie parody. 130-Alien movie-s	2	6	10	14
126,127: 126-(68 pgs.) Battlestar Galactica c/s; Star Wars-s; Wonder Woman-s.				

735

Sigil #10 © CRO

Silke #1 © F5 Ent.

Silver Age: Justice League of America #1 © DC

	GD2.0	FN6.0	VF8.0	NM9.4
127-Mork & Mindy-s; Lord of the Rings-s	2	6	12	18
131-(1980 Special) Star Wars/Star Trek/Flash Gordon wraparound-c/s;				
Superman parody; Battlestar Galactica-s	2	6	13	20
132,133: 132-1980 Election-c/s; Apocalypse Now-s. 133-Star Trek-s; Chips-s;				
Superheroes page	2	6	12	18
134 (scarce)(68 pg. Giant)-Star Wars-c; Alien-s; WKRP-s; Mork & Mindy-s;				
Taxi-s; MASH-s	3	10	23	35
Annual 1- 7th Annual Yearbook (1967)-Davis-c, 2 pg. glossy poster insert				
	4	12	25	38
Annual 2- Birthday Annual (1967)-3 pg. Huckleberry Fink fold out				
	3	9	21	32
Annual 3 (1968) "Big Sick Laff-in" on-c (84 pgs.)-w/psychedelic posters;				
Frankenstein poster	3	9	20	30
Annual 1969, 1970, 1971	3	9	19	28
Annual 12,13-(1972,1973, 84 pgs.) 13-Monster-c	3	9	19	28
Annual 14 (1974, 84 pgs.) Hitler photo-s	3	9	19	28
Annual 2-4 (1980)	2	6	9	12
Special 1 (1980) Buck Rogers-c/s; MASH-s	2	6	13	20
Special 2 (1980) Wraparound Star Wars:Empire Strikes Back-c; Charlie's Angels/				
Farrah-s; Rocky-s; plus reprints	2	6	13	20
Yearbook 15(1975, 84 pgs.) Paul Revere-c	3	9	17	24

NOTE: **Davis** a-42, 87; c-22, 23, 25, 29, 31, 32. **Powell** a-7, 31, 57. **Simon** a-1-3, 10, 41, 42, 87, 99; c-1, 47, 57, 59, 69, 91, 95-97, 99, 100, 102, 107, 112. **Torres** a-1-3, 29, 31, 47, 49. **Tuska** a-14, 41-43. Civil War Blackouts-23, 24. #42 has biography of Bob Powell.

SIDESHOW
Avon Periodicals: 1949 (one-shot)

1-(Rare)-Similar to Bachelor's Diary	34	102	179	310

SIEGE
Image Comics (WildStorm Prod.): Jan, 1997 - No. 4, Apr, 1997 ($2.50)

1-4				2.50

SIEGEL AND SHUSTER: DATELINE 1930s
Eclipse Comics: Nov, 1984 - No. 2, Sept, 1985 ($1.50/$1.75, Baxter paper #1)

1,2: 1-Unpublished samples of strips from the '30s; includes 'Interplanetary
Police'; Shuster-c. 2 ($1.75, B&W)-unpublished strips; Shuster-c   2.50

SIGIL (Also see CrossGen Chronicles)
CrossGeneration Comics: Jul, 2000 - Present ($2.95)

1-19: 1-Barbara Kesel-s/Ben & Ray Lai-a. 12-Waid-s begin		3.00
...: Mark of Power TPB (5/01, $19.95) r/#1-7; Moeller painted-c		20.00

SIGMA
Image Comics (WildStorm Productions): March, 1996 - No. 3, June, 1996
($2.50, limited series)

1-3: 1-"Fire From Heaven" prelude #2; Coker-a. 2-"Fire From Heaven" pt. 6.
3-"Fire From Heaven" pt. 14.   2.50

SILENT INVASION, THE
Rengade Press: Apr, 1986 - No.12, Mar, 1988 ($1.70/$2.00, B&W)

1-12-UFO sightings of the '50's		3.00
Book 1- reprints ($7.95)		8.00

SILENT MOBIUS
Viz Comics: 1991 - No. 5, 1992 ($4.95, color, squarebound, 44 pgs.)

1-5: Japanese stories translated to English		5.00

SILENT RAPTURE
Avatar Press: Jan, 1997 - No.2, Apr, 1997 ($3.00, B&W, limited series)

1,2		3.00

SILENT SCREAMERS (Based on the Aztech Toys figures)
Image Comics: Oct, 2000 ($4.95)

Nosferatu Issue - Alex Ross front & back-c   5.00

SILKE
Dark Horse Comics: Jan, 2001 - No. 4, Sept, 2001 ($2.95)

1-4-Tony Daniel-s/a		3.00

SILLY PILLY (See Frank Luther's...)

SILLY SYMPHONIES (See Dell Giants)

SILLY TUNES
Timely Comics: Fall, 1945 - No. 7, June, 1947

	GD2.0	FN6.0	VF8.0	NM9
1-Silly Seal, Ziggy Pig begin	21	63	110	190
2-(2/46)	12	36	61	100
3-7: 6-New logo	10	30	55	80

SILVER (See Lone Ranger's Famous Horse...)

SILVER AGE
DC Comics: July, 2000 ($3.95, limited series)

1-Waid-s/Dodson-a; "Silver Age" style x-over; JLA & villains switch bodies		4.00
...: Challengers of the Unknown ($2.50) Joe Kubert-c; vs. Chronos		2.50
...: Dial H For Hero ($2.50) Jim Mooney-c; vs. Martian Manhunter		2.50
...: Doom Patrol ($2.50) Ramona Fradon-c/Peyer-s		2.50
...: Flash ($2.50) Carmine Infantino-c; Kid Flash and Elongated Man app.		2.50
...: Green Lantern ($2.50) Gil Kane-c/Busiek-s/Anderson-a; vs. Sinestro		2.50
...: Justice League of America ($2.50) Ty Templeton-c		2.50
...: Showcase ($2.50) Dick Giordano-c/a; Batgirl, Adam Strange app.		2.50
...: Secret Files ($4.95) Intro. Agamemno; short stories & profile pages		5.00
...: Teen Titans ($2.50) Nick Cardy-c; vs. Penguin, Mr. Element, Black Manta		2.50
...: The Brave and the Bold ($2.50) Jim Aparo-c; Batman & Metal Men		2.50
...: 80-Page Giant ($5.95) Conclusion of x-over; "lost" Silver Age stories		6.00

SILVERBACK
Comico: 1989 - No. 3, 1990 ($2.50, color, limited series, mature readers)

1-3: Character from Grendel: Matt Wagner-a		3.00

SILVERBLADE
DC Comics: Sept, 1987 - No. 12, Sept, 1988

1-12: Colan-c/a in all		2.25

SILVER CROSS (See Warrior Nun series)
Antarctic Press: Nov, 1997 - No. 3, Mar, 1998 ($2.95)

1-3-Ben Dunn-s/a		3.00

SILVERHAWKS
Star Comics/Marvel Comics #6: Aug, 1987 - No. 6, June, 1988 ($1.00)

1-6		3.00

SILVERHEELS
Pacific Comics: Dec, 1983 - No. 3, May, 1984 ($1.50)

1-3		2.25

SILVER KID WESTERN
Key/Stanmor Publications: Oct, 1954 - No. 5, July, 1955

1	10	30	55	85
2	6	18	32	45
3-5	6	18	29	40
I.W. Reprint #1,2-Severin-c: 1-r/#? 2-r/#1	2	6	10	14

SILVER SABLE AND THE WILD PACK (See Amazing Spider-Man #265)
Marvel Comics: June, 1992 - No. 35, Apr, 1995 ($1.25/$1.50)

1-($2.00)-Embossed & foil stamped-c; Spider-Man app.		3.00
2-35: 4,5-Dr. Doom-c/story. 6,7-Deathlok-c/story. 9-Origin Silver Sable. 10-		
Punisher-c/s. 15-Capt. America-c/s. 16,17-Intruders app. 18,19-Venom-c/s.		
19-Siege of Darkness x-over. 23-Daredevil (in new costume) & Deadpool		
app. 24-Bound-in card sheet. Li'l Sylvie backup story. 25-($2.00, 52 pgs.)-Li'l		
Sylvie backup story		2.25

SILVER STAR (Also see Jack Kirby's...)
Pacific Comics: Feb, 1983 - No. Jan, 1984 ($1.00)

1-6: 1-1st app. Last of the Viking Heroes. 1-5-Kirby-c/a. 2-Ditko-a		5.00

SILVER STREAK COMICS (Crime Does Not Pay #22 on)
**Your Guide Publs. No. 1-7/New Friday Publs. No. 8-17/Comic House
Publ./Newsbook Publ.:** Dec, 1939 - No. 21, May, 1942; No. 23, 1946; No # 22
(Silver logo-#1-5)

1-(Scarce)-Intro The Claw by Cole (r-/in Daredevil #21), Red Reeves, Boy				
Magician, & Captain Fearless; The Wasp, Mister Midnight begin; Spirit Man				
app. Silver metallic-c begin, end #5; Claw c-1,2,6-8				
	1038	3114	6747	13,500
2-The Claw by Cole; Simon-c/a	383	1149	2396	4600
3-1st app. & origin Silver Streak (2nd with lightning speed); Dickie Dean the				
Boy Inventor, Lance Hale, Ace Powers, Bill Wayne, & The Planet Patrol				
begin	325	975	2031	3900
4-Sky Wolf begins; Silver Streak by Jack Cole (new costume); 1st app.				

Silver Streak Comics #1 © LEV

Silver Surfer #4 © MAR

Silver Surfer #141 © MAR

	GD2.0	FN6.0	VF8.0	NM9.4

Jackie, Lance Hale's sidekick 168 505 1050 1850
5-Jack Cole a(2) 200 600 1250 2200
6-(Scarce, 9/40)-Origin & 1st app. Daredevil (blue & yellow costume) by Jack
    Binder; The Claw returns; classic Cole Claw-c 1179 3537 8253 16,500
7-Claw vs. Daredevil (new costume-blue & red) by Jack Cole & 3 other
    Cole stories (38 pgs.) 723 2169 4700 9400
8-Claw vs. Daredevil by Cole; last Cole Silver Streak
    308 924 1927 3700
9-Claw vs. Daredevil by Cole 191 573 1194 2100
10-Origin & 1st app. Captain Battle (5/41); Claw vs. Daredevil by Cole;
    Robot-c 168 505 1050 1850
11-Intro. Mercury by Bob Wood, Silver Streak's sidekick; conclusion Claw vs.
    Daredevil by Rico; in 'Presto Martin,' 2nd pg., newspaper says 'Roussos
    does it again' 116 348 725 1275
12-14: 13-Origin Thun-Dohr 84 253 525 925
15, 17-Last Daredevil issue. 80 240 500 875
16-Hitler-c 91 273 568 1000
18-The Saint begins (2/42, 1st app.) by Leslie Charteris (see Movie Comics
    #2 by DC); The Saint-c 68 205 426 750
19-21(1942): 20,21 have Wolverton's Scoop Scuttle. 21-Hitler app. in strip on
    cover 55 165 331 580
23(1946(An Atomic Comic)-Reprints; bondage-c 43 129 257 450
nn(11/46)(Newsbook Publ.)-R-/S.S. story from #4-7 plus 2 Captain Fearless
    stories, all in color; bondage/torture-c 52 157 314 550

NOTE: *Binder* c-3, 4, 13-15, 17. *Jack Cole* a-(Daredevil)-#6-10, (Dickie Dean)-#3-10, (Pirate
Prince)-#7, (Silver Streak)-#4-8, nn; c-5 (Silver Streak), 6 (Claw), 7, 8 (Daredevil). *Everett Red
Reed* begins #20. *Guardineer* a-#8-13. *Don Rico* a-11-17 (Daredevil); c-11, 12, 16. *Simon* a-3
(Silver Streak). *Bob Wood* a-9 (Silver Streak); c-9, 10. *Captain Battle* c-11, 13-15, 17. *Claw* c-#1,
2, 6-8. *Daredevil* c-7, 8, 12. *Dickie Dean* c-19. *Ned of the Navy* c-20 (war). *The Saint* c-18. *Silver
Streak* c-5, 9, 10, 16, 23.

SILVER STREAK (See Fantastic Four, Fantasy Masterpieces V2#1, Fireside Book Series,
Marvel Graphic Novel, Marvel Presents #8, Marvel's Greatest Comics & Tales To Astonish #92)

SILVER SURFER, THE (Also see Essential Silver Surfer)
Marvel Comics Group: Aug, 1968 - No. 18, Sept, 1970; June, 1982

1-More detailed origin by John Buscema (p); The Watcher back-up stories
    begin (origin), end #7; (No. 1-7: 25¢, 68 pgs.) 41 123 331 600
2 19 57 134 240
3-1st app. Mephisto 16 48 112 200
4-Lower distribution; Thor & Loki app. 40 120 300 540
5-7-Last giant size. 5-The Stranger app.; Fantastic Four app. 6-Brunner inks. 7-
    (8/69)-1st app. Frankenstein's monster (cameo) 10 30 70 120
8-10: 8-18-(15¢ issues) 8 24 56 90
11-13,15-18: 15-Silver Surfer vs. Human Torch; Fantastic Four app. 17-Nick
    Fury app. 18-Vs. The Inhumans; Kirby-c/a 6 18 45 75
14-Spider-Man x-over 9 27 63 105
V2#1 (6/82, 52 pgs.)-Byrne-c/a 1 4 7 10

NOTE: *Adkins* a-8-15i. *Brunner* a-6i. *J. Buscema* a-1-17p. *Colan* a-1-3p. *Reinman* a-1-4i. #1-14
were reprinted in Fantasy Masterpieces V2#1-14.

SILVER SURFER (Volume 3) (See Marvel Graphic Novel #38)
Marvel Comics Group: V3#1, July, 1987 - No. 146, Nov, 1998

1-Double size ($1.25) 1 3 6 9
2-17: 15-Ron Lim-c/a begins (9/88) 4.00
18-33,39-43: 25,31 ($1.50, 52 pgs.). 25-Skrulls app. 32,39-No Ron Lim-c/a.
39-Alan Grant scripts 3.00
34-Thanos returns (cameo); Starlin scripts begin 4.00
35-38: 35-1st full Thanos app. in Silver Surfer (3/90); reintro Drax the Destroyer
    on last pg. (cameo). 36-Recaps history of Thanos; Capt. Marvel & Warlock
    app. in recap. 37-1st full app. Drax the Destroyer; Drax-c. 38-Silver Surfer bat
    tles Thanos 6.00
44,45,49-Thanos stories (c-44,45) 4.00
46-48: 46-Return of Adam Warlock (2/91); re-intro Gamora & Pip the Troll.
47-Warlock battles Drax. 48-Last Starlin scripts (also #50) 4.00
50-($1.50, 52 pgs.)-Embossed & silver foil-c; Silver Surfer has brief battle
    w/Thanos; story cont'd in Infinity Gauntlet #1 1 3 5 7
50-2nd 3rd printings 2.50
51-59: 51-53: Infinity Gauntlet x-over . 54-57: Infinity Gauntlet x-overs. 54-Rhino
    app. 55,56-Thanos-c & app. 57-Thanos-c & cameo. 58,59-Infinity Gauntlet x-
    overs; 58-Ron Lim-c only. 59-Thanos battles Silver Surfer-c/story; Thanos
    joins 3.00
60-74,76-99,101-124,126-139: 63-Capt. Marvel app. 67-69-Infinity War x-overs.

	GD2.0	FN6.0	VF8.0	NM9.4

76-78-Jack of Hearts-c/s. 83-85-Infinity Crusade x-over; 83,84-Thanos
    cameo. 85-Storm, Wonder Man x-over. 86-Thor-c/s. 87-Dr. Strange &
    Warlock app. 88-Thanos-c/s. 82 (52 pgs.). 101-Bound in card sheet. 5-FF
    app. 96-Hulk & FF app. 97-Terrax & Nova app. 106-Doc Doom app. 121-
    Quasar & Beta Ray Bill app. 123-w/card insert; begin Garney-a. 126-Dr.
    Strange-c/app. 128-Spider-Man & Daredevil-c/app. 138-Thing-c 2.50
75-($2.50, 52 pgs.)-Embossed foil-c; Lim-c/a 3.00
100 ($2.25, 52 pgs.)-Wraparound-c 2.25
100 ($3.95, 52 pgs.)-Enhanced-c 4.00
125 ($2.95)-Wraparound-c; Vs. Hulk-c/app. 3.00
140-145: 140-142,144,145-Muth-c/a. 143,146-Last issue 2.50
#(-1) Flashback (7/97) 2.50
Annual 1 (1988, $1.75)-Evolutionary War app.; 1st Ron Lim-a on Silver Surfer
    (20 pg. back-up story & pin-ups) 5.00
Annual 2-7 ('89-'94, 68 pgs.): 2-Atlantis Attacks. 4-3 pg. origin story; Silver Surfer
    battles Guardians of the Galaxy. 5-Return of the Defenders, part 3; Lim-c/a
    (3 pgs. of pin-ups only). 6-Polybagged w/trading card; 1st app. Legacy;
    card is by Lim/Austin 3.00
Annual '97 ($2.99), .../Thor Annual '98 ($2.99) 3.00
...Dangerous Artifacts-(1996, $3.95)-Ron Marz scripts; Galactus-c/app. 4.00
Graphic Novel (1988, HC, $14.95) Judgment Day; Lee-s/Buscema-a 15.00
The Enslavers Graphic Novel (1990, $16.95) 17.00
Homecoming Graphic Novel (1991, $12.95, softcover) Starlin-s 15.00
Inner Demons TPB (4/98, $3.50)/r/#123,125,126 3.50
...: The First Coming of Galactus nn (11/92, $5.95, 68 pgs.)-Reprints Fantastic
    Four #48-50 with new Lim-c 6.00
Wizard 1/2 2 6 11 15

NOTE: *Austin* c(i)-7, 8, 71, 73, 74, 76, 79. *Cowan* a-143,146. *Cully Hammer* a-83p. *Ron Lim*
a(p)-15-31, 33-38, 40-55, (56, 57-part-p), 60-65, 73-82, Annual 2, 4; c(p)-15-31, 33-38, 40-84, 86-
92, Annual 2, 4-6. *Muth* c/a-140-142,144,145. *M. Rogers* a-1-10, 12, 19, 21; c-1-9, 11, 12, 21.

SILVER SURFER, THE (Epic):
Marvel Comics (Epic): Dec, 1988 - No. 2, Jan, 1989 ($1.00, lim. series)

1,2-By Stan Lee scripts & Moebius-c/a 4.00
...: Parable ('98, $5.99) r/#1&2 6.00

SILVER SURFER: LOFTIER THAN MORTALS
Marvel Comics: Oct, 1999 - No. 2, Oct, 1999 ($2.50, limited series)

1,2-Remix of Fantastic Four #57-60; Velluto-a 2.50

SILVER SURFER/SUPERMAN
Marvel Comics: 1996 ($5.95,one-shot)

1-Perez-s/Lim-c/a(p) 6.00

SILVER SURFER VS. DRACULA
Marvel Comics: Feb, 1994 ($1.75, one-shot)

1-r/Tomb of Dracula #50; Everett Vampire-r/Venus #19; Howard the Duck
    back-up by Brunner; Lim-c(p) 2.25

SILVER SURFER/WARLOCK: RESURRECTION
Marvel Comics: Mar, 1993 - No. 4, June, 1993 ($2.50, limited series)

1-4-Starlin-c/a & scripts 2.50

SILVER SURFER/WEAPON ZERO
Marvel Comics: Apr, 1997 ($2.95, one-shot)

1-"Devil's Reign" pt. 8 3.00

SILVERTIP (Max Brand)
Dell Publishing Co.: No. 491, Aug, 1953 - No. 898, May, 1958

Four Color 491 (#1); all painted-c 8 24 56 100
Four Color 572,608,637,667,731,789,898-Kinstler-a 4 12 30 50
Four Color 835 4 12 30 50

SIMPSONS COMICS (See Bartman, Itchy & Scratchy & Radioactive Man)
Bongo Comics Group: 1993 - Present ($1.95, color)

1-($2.25)-FF#1-c swipe; pull-out poster; flip book 5.00
2-20: 2-Patty & Selma flip-c/sty. 3-Krusty, Agent of K.L.O.W.N. flip-c/story.
    4-Infinity-c; flip-c of Busman #1; w/trading card. 5-Wraparound-c w/trading
    card. 6-40: All Flip books. 6-w/Chief Wiggum's "Crime Comics". 7-w/"McBain
    Comics". 8-w/"Edna, Queen of the Congo". 9-w/"Barney Gumble". 10-w/"Apu".
    11-w/"Homer". 12-w/"White Knuckled War Stories". 13-w/"Jimbo Jones'
    Wedgie Comics". 14-w/"Grampa". 15-w/"Itchy & Scratchy". 16-w/"Bongo Grab
    Bag". 17-w/"Headlight Comics". 18-w/"Milhouse".19,20-w/"Roswell" 4.00
21-40: 21,22-w/"Roswell". 23-w/"Hellfire Comics". 24-w/"Lil' Homey". 36-39-Flip

Fritzi Ritz
with PHIL FUMBLE!
Single Series #5 © UFS
64 PAGES IN FULL COLOR!

	GD2.0	FN6.0	VF8.0	NM9.4

	GD2.0	FN6.0	VF8.0	NM9.(

book w/Radioactive Man — 3.00
41-49,51-65 ($2.50): 43-Flip book w/Poochie. 52-Paul Dini-s — 2.50
50-($5.95) Wraparound-c; 80 pgs.; square-bound — 6.00
... A Go-Go (1999, $11.95)-r/#32-35; ...Big Bonanza (1998, $11.95)-r/#28-31, ...Extravaganza (1994, $10.00)-r/#1-4; infinity-c, ...On Parade (1998, $11.95)-r/#24-27, ...Simpsorama (1996, $10.95)-r/#11-14 — 12.00
Simpsons Comics Royale ('01, $14.95) r/various Bongo issues — 15.00

SIMPSONS COMICS AND STORIES
Welsh Publishing Group: 1993 ($2.95, one-shot)
1-(Direct Sale)-Polybagged w/Bartman poster — 6.00
1-(Newsstand Edition)-Without poster — 4.00

SIMPSONS COMICS PRESENTS BART SIMPSON
Bongo Comics Group: 2000 - Present ($2.50, quarterly)
1-6 — 2.50

SIMULATORS, THE
Neatly Chiseled Features: 1991 ($2.50, stiff-c)
1-Super hero group — 2.50

SINBAD, JR (TV Cartoon)
Dell Publishing Co.: Sept-Nov, 1965 - No. 3, May, 1966

1		3	10	23	35
2,3		3	9	17	25

SIN CITY (See Dark Horse Presents, Decade of Dark Horse, A & San Diego Comic Con Comics #2,4)
Dark Horse Comics (Legend)
TPB ($15.00) Reprints early DHP stories — 15.00
Booze, Broads & Bullets TPB ($15.00) — 15.00

SIN CITY: A DAME TO KILL FOR
Dark Horse Comics (Legend): Nov, 1993 - No. 6, May, 1994 ($2.95, B&W, limited series)
1-6: Frank Miller-c/a & story in all. 1-1st app. Dwight. — 5.00
Limited Edition Hardcover — 85.00
Hardcover — 25.00
TPB ($15.00) — 15.00

SIN CITY: FAMILY VALUES
Dark Horse Comics (Legend): Oct, 1997 ($10.00, B&W, squarebound, one-shot)
nn-Miller-c/a & story — 10.00
Limited Edition Hardcover — 75.00

SIN CITY: HELL AND BACK
Dark Horse (Maverick): Jul, 1999 - No. 9 ($2.95/$4.95, B&W, limited series)
1-8-Miller-c/a & story. 7-Color — 3.00
9-($4.95) — 5.00

SIN CITY: JUST ANOTHER SATURDAY NIGHT
Dark Horse Comics (Legend): Aug, 1997 (Wizard 1/2 offer, B&W, one-shot)

1/2-Miller-c/a & story		1	3	6	8

nn (10/98, $2.50) r/#1/2 — 2.50

SIN CITY: LOST, LONELY & LETHAL
Dark Horse Comics (Legend): Dec, 1996 ($2.95, B&W and blue, one-shot)
nn-Miller-c/s/a; w/pin-ups — 4.00

SIN CITY: SEX AND VIOLENCE
Dark Horse Comics (Legend): Mar, 1997 ($2.95, B&W and blue, one-shot)
nn-Miller-c/a & story — 4.00

SIN CITY: SILENT NIGHT
Dark Horse Comics (Legend): Dec, 1995 ($2.95, B&W, one-shot)
1-Miller-c/a & story; Marv app. — 4.00

SIN CITY: THAT YELLOW BASTARD
Dark Horse Comics (Legend): Feb, 1996 - No. 6, July, 1996 ($2.95/$3.50, B&W and yellow, limited series)
1-5: Miller-c/a & story in all. 1-1st app. Hartigan. — 5.00
6-($3.50) Error & corrected — 5.00
Limited Edition Hardcover — 25.00
TPB ($15.00) — 15.00

SIN CITY: THE BABE WORE RED AND OTHER STORIES

Dark Horse Comics (Legend): Nov, 1994 ($2.95, B&W and red, one-shot)
1-r/serial run in Previews as well as other stories; Miller-c/a & scripts; Dwight app. — 3.00

SIN CITY: THE BIG FAT KILL
Dark Horse Comics (Legend): Nov, 1994 - No. 5, Mar, 1995 ($2.95, B&W, limited series)
1-5-Miller story & art in all; Dwight app. — 4.00
Hardcover — 25.00
TPB ($15.00) — 15.00

SINDBAD (See Capt. Sindbad under Movie Comics, and Fantastic Voyages of Sindbad)

SINGING GUNS (See Fawcett Movie Comics)

SINGLE SERIES (Comics on Parade #30 on)(Also see John Hix...)
United Features Syndicate: 1938 - No. 28, 1942 (All 68 pgs.)

Note: See Individual Alphabetical Listings for prices

1-Captain and the Kids (#1)	2-Broncho Bill (1939) (#1)
3-Ella Cinders (1939)	4-Li'l Abner (1939) (#1)
5-Fritzi Ritz (#1)	6-Jim Hardy by Dick Moores (#1)
7-Frankie Doodle	8-Peter Pat (On sale 7/14/39)
9-Strange As It Seems	10-Little Mary Mixup
11-Mr. and Mrs. Beans	12-Joe Jinks
13-Looy Dot Dope	14-Billy Make Believe
15-How It Began (1939)	16-Illustrated Gags (1940)-Has ad
17-Danny Dingle	for Captain and the Kids #1
18-Li'l Abner (#2 on-c)	reprint listed below
19-Broncho Bill (#2 on-c)	20-Tarzan by Hal Foster
21-Ella Cinders (#2 on-c; on sale 3/19/40)	22-Iron Vic
23-Tailspin Tommy by Hal Forrest (#1)	24-Alice in Wonderland (#1)
25-Abbie and Slats	26-Little Mary Mixup (#2 on-c, 1940)
27-Jim Hardy by Dick Moores (1942)	28-Ella Cinders & Abbie and Slats
1-Captain and the Kids (1939 reprint)-2nd	(1942)
Edition	1-Fritzi Ritz (1939 reprint)-2nd ed.

NOTE: *Some issues given away at the 1939-40 New York World's Fair (#6).*

SINISTER HOUSE OF SECRET LOVE, THE (Becomes Secrets of Sinister House No. 5 on)
National Periodical Publ.: Oct-Nov, 1971 - No. 4, Apr-May, 1972

1 (all 52 pgs.)		15	45	105	180
2,4: 2-Jeff Jones-c		6	18	42	70
3-Toth-a		6	18	45	75

SINS OF YOUTH... (Also see Young Justice: Sins of Youth)
DC Comics: May 2000 ($4.95/$2.50, limited crossover series)
Secret Files 1 ($4.95) Short stories and profile pages; Nauck-c — 5.00
...Aquaboy/Lagoon Man; Batboy and Robin; JLA Jr.; Kid Flash/Impulse; Starwoman and the JSA, Superman, Jr./Superboy, Sr.; The Secret/ Deadboy, Wonder Girls ($2.50-c) Old and young heroes switch ages — 2.50

SIR CHARLES BARKLEY AND THE REFEREE MURDERS
Hamilton Comics: 1993 ($9.95, 8-1/2" x 11", 52 pgs.)

nn-Photo-c; Sports fantasy comic book fiction (uses real names of NBA super stars). Script by Alan Dean Foster, art by Joe Staton. Comes with bound-in sheet of 35 gummed "Moods of Charles Barkley" stamps. Photo/story on

Barkley		2	6	9	12

Special Edition of 100 copies for charity signed on an affixed book plate by Barkley, Foster & Staton — 150.00
Ashcan edition given away to dealers, distributors & promoters (low distribution).

Four pages in color, balance of story in b&w		2	6	9	12

SIREN (Also see Eliminator & Ultraforce)
Malibu Comics (Ultraverse): Sept, 1995 - No. 3, Dec, 1995 ($1.50)
Infinity, 1-3: Infinity-Black-c & painted-c exists. 1-Regular-c & painted-c; War Machine app. 2-Flip book w/Phoenix Resurrection Pt. 3 — 2.25
Special (2/96, $1.95, 28 pgs.)-Origin Siren; Marvel Comic's Juggernaut/c/app. — 2.25

SIREN: SHAPES
Image Comics: May, 1998 - No. 3, Nov, 1998 ($2.95, B&W, limited series)
1-3-J. Torres -s — 3.00

SIR LANCELOT (TV)

Six-Gun Heroes #8 © FAW

Six Million Dollar Man #1 © CC

Skeleton Hand #1 © ACG

	GD2.0	FN6.0	VF8.0	NM9.4

Dell Publishing Co.: No. 606, Dec, 1954 - No. 775, Mar, 1957

Four Color 606 (not TV)	7	21	49	90
Four Color 775(...and Brian)-Buscema-a; photo-c	9	27	63	120

SIR WALTER RALEIGH (Movie)
Dell Publishing Co.: May, 1955 (Based on movie "The Virgin Queen")

Four Color 644-Photo-c	7	21	49	85

SISTERHOOD OF STEEL (See Eclipse Graphic Adventure Novel #13)
Marvel Comics (Epic Comics): Dec, 1984 -No. 8, Feb, 1986 ($1.50, Baxter paper, mature)

1-8	3.00

SISTERS OF MERCY
Maximum Press/No Mercy Comics #3 on: Dec, 1995 - No. 5, Oct, 1996 ($2.50)

1-5: 1-Liefeld variant-c exists	2.50
V2#0-(3/97, $1.50) Liefeld-c	2.50

SISTERS OF MERCY: PARADISE LOST
London Night Studios/No Mercy Comics: Apr, 1997 - No. 4 ($2.50)

1-4	2.50

SISTERS OF MERCY: WHEN RAZORS CRY CRIMSON TEARS
No Mercy Comics: Oct, 1996 ($2.50, one-shot)

1	2.50

6 BLACK HORSES (See Movie Classics)

SIX FROM SIRIUS
Marvel Comics (Epic Comics): July, 1984 - No. 4, Oct, 1984 ($1.50, limited series, mature)

1-4: Moench scripts; Gulacy-c/a in all	2.25

SIX FROM SIRIUS II
Marvel Comics (Epic Comics): Feb, 1986 - No. 4, May, 1986 ($1.50, limited series, mature)

1-4: Moench scripts; Gulacy-c/a in all	2.25

SIX-GUN HEROES
Fawcett Publications: March, 1950 - No. 23, Nov, 1953 (Photo-c #1-23)

1-Rocky Lane, Hopalong Cassidy, Smiley Burnette begin (same date as Smiley Burnette #1)	45	135	270	475
2	29	87	153	265
3-5: 5-Lash LaRue begins	20	60	105	175
6-15	15	45	77	130
16-22: 17-Last Smiley Burnette. 18-Monte Hale begins	13	39	66	110
23-Last Fawcett issue	14	42	72	120

NOTE: *Hopalong Cassidy photo c-1-3. Monte Hale photo c-1-8. Rocky Lane photo c-4, 5, 7, 9, 11, 13, 15, 17, 20, 21, 23. Lash LaRue photo c-6, 8, 10, 12, 14, 16, 19, 22.*

SIX-GUN HEROES (Cont'd from Fawcett; Gunmasters #84 on) (See Blue Bird)
Charlton Comics: No. 24, Jan, 1954 - No. 83, Mar-Apr, 1965 (All Vol. 4)

24-Lash LaRue, Hopalong Cassidy, Rocky Lane & Tex Ritter begin; photo-c	21	63	110	185
25	11	33	55	90
26-30: 26-Rod Cameron story. 28-Tom Mix begins?	10	30	55	80
31-40: 38-Jingles & Wild Bill Hickok (TV)	9	27	49	70
41-46,48,50	8	24	45	65
47-Williamson-a, 2 pgs; Torres-a	9	27	49	70
49-Williamson-a (5 pgs.)	10	30	55	70
51-56,58-60: 58-Gunmaster app.	4	12	29	45
57-Origin & 1st app. Gunmaster	5	15	34	55
61,63-70	3	10	23	35
62-Origin Gunmaster	4	12	26	40
71-75,77,78,80-83	2	6	15	22
76,79: 76-Gunmaster begins. 79-1st app. & origin of Bullet, the Gun-Boy	3	9	17	25

SIXGUN RANCH (See Luke Short & Four Color #580)

SIX-GUN WESTERN
Atlas Comics (CDS): Jan, 1957 - No. 4, July, 1957

1-Crandall-a; two Williamson text illos	21	63	110	185
2,3-Williamson-a in both	15	45	77	130

	GD2.0	FN6.0	VF8.0	NM9.4

4-Woodbridge-a	10	30	55	80

NOTE: *Ayers a-2, 3. Maneely a-1; c-2, 3. Orlando a-2. Pakula a-2. Powell a-3. Romita a-1, 4. Severin c-1, 4. Shores a-2.*

SIX MILLION DOLLAR MAN, THE (TV)
Charlton Comics: 6/76 - No. 4, 12/76; No. 5, 10/77; No. 6, 2/78 - No. 9, 6/78

1-Staton-c/a; Lee Majors photo on-c	2	6	10	14
2-9: 2-Neal Adams-c; Staton-a	1	3	6	9

SIX MILLION DOLLAR MAN, THE (TV)(Magazine)
Charlton Comics: July, 1976 - No. 7, Nov, 1977 (B&W)

1-Neal Adams-c	2	6	15	22
2-Neal Adams-c	2	6	11	16
3-N. Adams part inks; Chaykin-a	2	6	11	16
4-7	2	6	10	14

SIX STRING SAMURAI
Awesome-Hyperwerks: Sept, 1998 ($2.95)

1-Stinsman & Fraga-a	3.00

67 SECONDS
Marvel Comics (Epic Comics): 1992 ($15.95, 54 pgs., graphic novel)

nn-James Robinson scripts; Steve Yeowell-c/a	2	6	12	18

SKATEMAN
Pacific Comics: Nov, 1983 (Baxter paper, one-shot)

1-Adams-c/a	4.00

SKELETON HAND (...In Secrets of the Supernatural)
American Comics Gr. (B&M Dist. Co.): Sept-Oct, 1952 - No. 6, Jul-Aug, 1953

1	43	129	257	450
2	33	99	174	300
3-6	27	81	145	250

SKELETON KEY
Amaze ink: July, 1995 - No. 30, Jan, 1998 ($1.25/$1.50/$1.75, B&W)

1-30	3.00
Special #1 (2/98, $4.95) Unpublished short stories	5.00
Sugar Kat Special (10/98, $2.95) Halloween stories	3.00
Beyond The Threshold TPB ($11.95)-r/#1-6	12.00
Cats and Dogs TPB ($12.95)-r/#25-30	13.00
The Celestial Calendar TPB ($19.95)-r/#7-18	20.00
Telling Tales TPB ($12.95)-r/#19-24	13.00

SKELETON KEY (Volume 2)
Amaze ink: 1999 - No. 4, 1999 ($2.95, B&W)

1-4-Andrew Watson-s/a	3.00

SKELETON WARRIORS
Marvel Comics: Apr, 1995 - No. 4, July, 1995 ($1.50)

1-4: Based on animated series.	2.25

SKIN GRAFT: THE ADVENTURES OF A TATTOOED MAN
DC Comics (Vertigo): July, 1993 - No. 4, Oct, 1993 ($2.50, lim. series, mature)

1-4	2.50

SKI PARTY (See Movie Classics)

SKREEMER
DC Comics: May, 1989 - No. 6, Oct, 1989 ($2.00, limited series, mature)

1-6: Contains graphic violence	2.25

SKRULL KILL KREW
Marvel Comics: Sept, 1995 - No. 5, Dec, 1995 ($2.95, limited series)

1-5: Grant Morrison scripts. 2,3-Cap America app.	3.00

SKUL, THE
Virtual Comics (Byron Preiss Multimedia): Oct, 1996 - No. 3, Dec, 1996 ($2.50, limited series)

1-3: Ron Lim & Jimmy Palmiotti-a	2.50

SKULL & BONES
DC Comics: 1992 - No. 3, 1992 ($4.95, limited series, 52 pgs.)

Book 1-3: 1-1st app.	5.00

SKULL, THE SLAYER
Marvel Comics Group: Aug, 1975 - No. 8, Nov, 1976 (20¢/25¢)

Skypilot #11 © Z-D

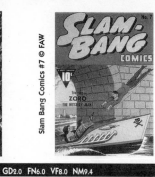

Slam Bang Comics #7 © FAW

Slingers #11 © MAR

	GD2.0	FN6.0	VF8.0	NM9.4
1-Origin & 1st app.; Gil Kane-c	2	6	9	12
2-8: 2-Gil Kane-c. 5,6-(Regular 25¢-c). 8-Kirby-c	1	3	5	7
5,6-(30¢-c variants, limited distribution)(5,7/76)	1	4	7	10

SKY BLAZERS (CBS Radio)
Hawley Publications: Sept, 1940 - No. 2, Nov, 1940

1-Sky Pirates, Ace Archer, Flying Aces begin	61	182	381	675
2-WWII aerial battle-c	40	120	232	400

SKYMAN (See Big Shot Comics & Sparky Watts)
Columbia Comics Gr.: Fall?, 1941 - No. 2, Fall?, 1942; No. 3, 1948 - No. 4, 1948

1-Origin Skyman, The Face, Sparky Watts app.; Whitney-c/a; 3rd story-r from Big Shot #1; Whitney c-1-4	118	354	738	1300
2 (1942)-Yankee Doodle	59	177	369	650
3,4 (1948)	40	120	220	380

SKYPILOT
Ziff-Davis Publ. Co.: No. 10, 1950(nd) - No. 11, Apr-May, 1951

10,11-Frank Borth-a; Saunders painted-c	15	45	77	130

SKY RANGER (See Johnny Law...)

SKYROCKET
Harry 'A' Chesler: 1944

nn-Alias the Dragon, Dr. Vampire, Skyrocket & The Desperado app.; WWII Jap zero-c	33	99	174	300

SKY SHERIFF (Breeze Lawson...) (Also see Exposed & Outlaws)
D. S. Publishing Co.: Summer, 1948

1-Edmond Good-c/a	14	42	72	120

SKY WOLF (Also see Airboy)
Eclipse Comics: Mar, 1988 - No. 3, Oct, 1988 ($1.25/$1.50/$1.95, lim. series)

1-3				2.25

SLACKER COMICS
Slave Labor Graphics: Aug, 1994 - Present ($2.95, B&W, quarterly)

1-18, 1 (2nd printing)-Reads "2nd print" in indicia				3.00

SLAINE, THE BERSERKER (Slaine the King #21 on)
Quality: July, 1987 - No. 28, 1989 ($1.25/$1.50)

1-28				2.25

SLAINE, THE HORNED GOD
Fleetway: 1998 - No. 3 ($6.99)

1-3-Reprints series from 2000 A.D.; Bisley-a				7.00

SLAM BANG COMICS (Western Desperado #8)
Fawcett Publications: Mar, 1940 - No. 7, Sept, 1940 (Combined with Master Comics #7)

1-Diamond Jack, Mark Swift & The Time Retarder, Lee Granger, Jungle King begin & continue in Master	218	654	1364	2400
2	91	273	568	1000
3-Classic-c	136	408	852	1500
4-7: 6-Intro Zoro, the Mystery Man (also in #7)	73	219	455	800

SLAPSTICK
Marvel Comics: Nov, 1992 - No. 4, Feb, 1993 ($1.25, limited series)

1-4: Fry/Austin-c/a. 4-Ghost Rider, D.D., F.F. app.				2.25

SLAPSTICK COMICS
Comic Magazines Distributors: nd (1946?) (36 pgs.)

nn-Firetop feature; Post-a(2)	25	75	130	225

SLASH-D DOUBLECROSS
St. John Publishing Co.: 1950 (Pocket-size, 132 pgs.)

nn-Western comics	23	69	121	205

SLASH MARAUD
DC Comics: Nov, 1987 - No. 6, Apr, 1988 ($1.75, limited series)

1-6				2.25

SLAUGHTERMAN
Comico: Feb, 1983 - No. 2, 1983 ($1.50, B&W)

1,2				3.00

SLAVE GIRL COMICS (See Malu... & White Princess of the Jungle #2)

	GD2.0	FN6.0	VF8.0	NM9.4

Avon Periodicals/Eternity Comics (1989): Feb, 1949 - No. 2, Apr, 1949 (52 pgs.); Mar, 1989 (B&W, 44 pgs)

1-Larsen-c/a	91	273	568	1000
2-Larsen-a	68	204	426	750
1-(3/89, $2.25, B&W, 44 pgs.)-r/#1				3.00

SLEDGE HAMMER (TV)
Marvel Comics: Feb, 1988 - No. 2, Mar,1988 ($1.00, limited series)

1,2				3.00

SLEEPING BEAUTY (See Dell Giants & Movie Comics)
Dell Publishing Co.: No. 973, May, 1959 - No. 984, June, 1959 (Disney)

Four Color 973 (...and the Prince)	12	36	84	150
Four Color 984 (...Fairy Godmother's)	9	27	63	110

SLEEPWALKER
Marvel Comics: June, 1991 - No. 33, Feb, 1994 ($1.00/$1.25)

1-1st app. Sleepwalker				3.00
2-33: 4-Williamson-i. 5-Spider-Man-c/stor. 7-Infinity Gauntlet x-over. 8-Vs. Deathlok-c/story. 11-Ghost Rider-c/story. 12-Quesada-c/a(p) 14-Intro Spectra. 15-F.F.-c/story. 17-Darkhawk & Spider-Man x-over. 18-Infinity War x-over; Quesada/Williamson-c. 21,22-Hobgoblin app. 19-($2.00)-Die-cut Sleepwalker mask-c				2.25
25-($2.95, 52 pgs.)-Holo-grafx foil-c; origin				3.00
Holiday Special 1 (1/93, $2.00, 52 pgs.)-Quesada-c(p)				2.25

SLEEPWALKING
Hall of Heroes: Jan, 1996 ($2.50, B&W)

1-Kelley Jones-c				2.50

SLEEPY HOLLOW (Movie Adaption)
DC Comics (Vertigo): 2000 ($7.95, one-shot)

1-Kelley Jones-a/Seagle-s				8.00

SLEEZE BROTHERS, THE
Marvel Comics (Epic Comics): Aug, 1989 - No. 6, Jan, 1990 ($1.75, mature)

1-6: 4-6 (9/89 - 11/89 indicia dates)				2.25
nn-(1991, $3.95, 52 pgs.)				4.00

SLICK CHICK COMICS
Leader Enterprises: 1947(nd) - No. 3, 1947(nd)

1-Teenage humor	12	36	61	105
2,3	9	27	49	70

SLIDERS (TV)
Acclaim Comics (Armada): June, 1996 - No. 2, July, 1996 ($2.50, lim. series)

1,2: D.G. Chichester scripts; Dick Giordano-a.				2.50

SLIDERS: DARKEST HOUR (TV)
Acclaim Comics (Armada): Oct, 1996 - No. 3, Dec, 1996 ($2.50, limited series)

1-3				2.50

SLIDERS SPECIAL
Acclaim Comics (Armada): Nov, 1996 - No 3, Mar, 1997 ($3.95, limited series)

1-3: 1-Narcotica-Jerry O'Connell-s. 2-Blood and Splendor. 3-Deadly Secrets				4.00

SLIDERS: ULTIMATUM (TV)
Acclaim Comics (Armada): Sept, 1996 - No. 2, Sept, 1996 ($2.50, lim. series)

1,2				2.50

SLIMER! (TV cartoon) (Also see the Real Ghostbusters)
Now Comics: 1989 - No. 19, Feb?, 1991 ($1.75)

1-19: Based on animated cartoon				3.00

SLIM MORGAN (See Wisco)

SLINGERS (See Spider-Man: Identity Crisis issues)
Marvel Comics: Dec, 1998 - No. 12, Nov, 1999 ($2.99/$1.99)

0-(Wizard #88 supplement) Prelude story				2.25
1-($2.99) Four editions w/different covers for each hero, 16 pages common to all, the other pages from each hero's perspective				3.00
2-12: 2-Two-c. 12-Saltares-a				2.25

SLOW NEWS DAY
Slave Labor Graphics: July, 2001 - No. 6 ($3.50, B&W)

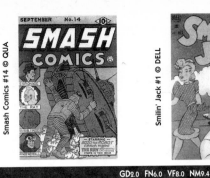

Smash Comics #14 © QUA

Smilin' Jack #1 © DELL

Smurfs #3 © Peyo

	GD2.0	FN6.0	VF8.0	NM9.4

1-3-Andi Watson-s/a   3.50

SLUDGE
Malibu Comics (Ultraverse): Oct, 1993 - No. 12, Dec, 1994 ($2.50/$1.95)
1-($2.50, 48 pgs.)-Intro/1st app. Sludge; Rune flip-c/story Pt. 1 (1st app., 3 pgs.) by Barry Smith; The Night Man app. (3 pg. preview); The Mighty Magnor 1 pg strip begins by Aragonés (cont. in other titles)   3.00
1-Ultra 5000 Limited silver foil   4.00
2-11: 3-Break-Thru x-over. 4-2 pg. Mantra origin. 8-Bloodstorm app.   2.50
12 ($3.50)-Ultraverse Premiere #8 flip book; Alex Ross poster   3.50
...:Red Xmas (12/94, $2.50, 44 pgs.)   2.50

SLUGGER (Little Wise Guys Starring...)(Also see Daredevil Comics)
Lev Gleason Publications: April, 1956
| 1-Biro-c | 6 | 18 | 32 | 45 |

SMASH COMICS (Becomes Lady Luck #86 on)
Quality Comics Group: Aug, 1939 - No. 85, Oct, 1949
1-Origin Hugh Hazard & His Iron Man, Bozo the Robot, Espionage, Starring Black X by Eisner, & Hooded Justice (Invisible Justice #2 on); Chic Carter & Wings Wendall begin; 1st Robot on the cover of a comic book (Bozo)
	300	900	1875	3300
2-The Lone Star Rider app; Invisible Hood gains power of invisibility	100	300	625	1100
3-Captain Cook & Eisner's John Law begin	64	192	398	700
4,5: 4-Flash Fulton begins	59	177	369	650
6-12: 12-One pg. Fine-a	52	157	314	550
13-Magno begins (8/40); last Eisner issue; The Ray app. in full page art; The Purple Trio begins	55	165	330	575
14-Intro. The Ray (9/40) by Lou Fine & others	291	873	1818	3200
15,16: 16-The Scarlet Seal begins	123	369	769	1350
17-Wun Cloo becomes plastic super-hero by Jack Cole (9-months before Plastic Man)	127	381	795	1400
18-Midnight by Jack Cole begins (origin & 1st app., 1/41)	159	477	994	1750
19-22: Last Ray by Fine; The Jester begins-#22	84	253	525	925
23,24: 24-The Sword app.; last Chic Carter; Wings Wendall dons new costume #24,25	66	197	413	725
25-Origin/1st app. Wildfire; Rookie Rankin begins	75	225	469	825
26-30: 28-Midnight-c begins, end #85	64	192	398	700
31,32,34: Ray by Rudy Palais; also #33	50	150	300	525
33-Origin The Marksman	61	182	381	675
35-37	50	150	300	525
38-The Yankee Eagle begins; last Midnight by Jack Cole	86	258	540	950
39,40-Last Ray issue	50	150	300	525
41,44-50	39	117	208	360
42-Lady Luck begins by Klaus Nordling	109	327	682	1200
43-Lady Luck-c (1st & only in Smash)	43	129	257	450
51-60	27	81	142	245
61-70	23	69	121	210
71-85: 79-Midnight battles the Men from Mars-c/s	21	63	110	185
NOTE: **Al Bryant** c-54, 63-68. **Cole** a-17-38, 68, 69, 72, 73, 78, 80, 83, 85; c-38, 60-62, 69-84. **Crandall** a-23-29, 35-38; c-36, 39, 45, 47-53. **Nordling** a-49, 52, 63-65. **Powell** a-11, 12, **Fox** c-24-35. **Fuje** a-Ray-30. **Gil Fox** a-7, 9, 11-13. **Guardineer** a-7(Marksman)-39-?, 49, 52, 63-65. **Kotzky** a-(Espionage)-33-38; c-45, 47-53. **Nordling** a-49, 52, 63-65. **Powell** a-11, 12, (Abdul the Arab)-13-24.Black X c-2, 6, 9, 11, 13, 16. Bozo the Robot c-1, 3, 5, 8, 10, 12, 14, 18, 20, 22, 24, 26. Midnight c-28-85. The Ray c-15, 17, 19, 21, 23, 25, 27. Wings Wendall c-4, 7.

SMASH COMICS (Also see All Star Comics 1999 crossover titles)
DC Comics: May, 1999 ($1.99, one-shot)
1-Golden Age Doctor Mid-nite and Hourman   2.25

SMASH HIT SPORTS COMICS
Essankay Publications: V2#1, Jan, 1949
| V2#1-L.B. Cole-c/a | 31 | 93 | 165 | 285 |

SMILE COMICS (Also see Gay Comics, Tickle, & Whee)
Modern Store Publ.: 1955 (52 pgs.) 5x7-1/4") (7¢)
| 1 | 5 | 15 | 25 | 35 |

SMILEY BURNETTE WESTERN (Also see Patches #8 & Six-Gun Heroes)
Fawcett Publ.: March, 1950 - No. 4, Oct, 1950 (All photo front & back-c)

	GD2.0	FN6.0	VF8.0	NM9.4
1-Red Eagle begins	45	135	270	475
2-4	35	105	185	320

SMILEY (THE PSYCHOTIC BUTTON) (See Evil Ernie)
Chaos! Comics: July, 1998 - Present ($2.95, one-shots)
1-Ivan Reis-a   3.00
... Holiday Special (1/99), ...'s Spring Break (4/99), ...Wrestling Special (5/99)   3.00

SMILIN' JACK (See Famous Feature Stories, Popular Comics, Super Book #1, 2, 7, 19 & Super Comics)
Dell Publishing Co.: No. 5, 1940 - No. 8, Oct-Dec, 1949
Four Color 5	60	180	420	775
Four Color 10 (1940)	52	156	364	675
Large Feature Comic 12,14,25 (1941)	50	150	350	650
Four Color 4 (1942)	43	128	301	560
Four Color 14 (1943)	35	105	245	450
Four Color 36,58 (1943-44)	24	72	168	310
Four Color 80 (1945)	15	45	105	195
Four Color 149 (1947), 1 (1-3/48)	10	30	70	130
1 (1-3/48)	9	27	63	120
2	5	15	35	65
3-8 (10-12/49)	4	12	29	45

SMILING SPOOK SPUNKY (See Spunky)

SMITTY (See Popular Comics, Super Book #2, 4 & Super Comics)
Dell Publishing Co.: No. 11, 1940 - No. 7, Aug-Oct, 1949; No. 909, Apr, 1958
Four Color 11 (1940)	35	105	245	460
Large Feature Comic 26 (1941)	25	75	175	325
Four Color 6 (1942)	22	65	154	285
Four Color 32 (1943)	16	48	112	210
Four Color 65 (1945)	13	39	91	165
Four Color 99 (1946)	11	33	77	140
Four Color 138 (1947)	9	27	63	120
1 (2-4/48)	9	27	63	110
2-(5-7/48)	5	15	34	55
3,4; 3-(8-10/48), 4-(11-1/48-49)	4	12	29	45
5-7, Four Color 909 (4/58)	3	10	23	35

SMOKEY BEAR (TV) (See March Of Comics #234, 362, 372, 383, 407)
Gold Key: Feb, 1970 - No. 13, Mar, 1973
1	3	9	20	30
2-5	2	6	9	12
6-13	1	3	6	9

SMOKEY STOVER (See Popular Comics, Super Book #5,17,29 & Super Comics)
Dell Publishing Co.: No. 7, 1942 - No. 827, Aug, 1957
Four Color 7 (1942)-Reprints	32	95	224	420
Four Color 35 (1943)	17	50	119	220
Four Color 64 (1944)	13	39	91	165
Four Color 229 (1949)	5	15	35	65
Four Color 730,827	4	12	30	50

SMOKEY THE BEAR (See Forest Fire for 1st app.)
Dell Publ. Co.: No. 653, 10/55 - No. 1214, 8/61 (See March Of Comics #234)
Four Color 653 (#1)	10	30	70	130
Four Color 708,754,818,932	5	15	35	65
Four Color 1016,1119,1214	4	12	26	40

SMOKY (See Movie Classics)

SMURFS (TV)
Marvel Comics: 1982 (Dec) - No. 3, 1983
| 1-3 | 1 | 3 | 6 | 8 |
| ...Treasury Edition 1 (64 pgs.)-r/#1-3 | 3 | 9 | 19 | 28 |

SNAFU (Magazine)
Atlas Comics (RCM): Nov, 1955 - V2#2, Mar, 1956 (B&W)
| V1#1-Heath/Severin-a; Everett, Maneely-a | 13 | 39 | 66 | 110 |
| V2#1,2-Severin-a | 10 | 30 | 55 | 80 |

SNAGGLEPUSS (TV)(See Hanna-Barbera Band Wagon, Quick Draw McGraw #5 & Spotlight #4)
Gold Key: Oct, 1962 - No. 4, Sept, 1963 (Hanna-Barbera)

Snow White and the Seven Dwarfs © WDC

Sock Monkey V3 #1 © Tony Millionaire

Sojourn #1 © CRO

	GD2.0	FN6.0	VF8.0	NM9.4
1	9	27	63	110
2-4	6	18	42	80

SNAKES AND LADDERS
Eddie Campbell Comics: 2001 ($5.95, B&W, one-shot)
nn-Alan Moore-s/Eddie Campbell-a 6.00

SNAP (Formerly Scoop #8; becomes Jest #10,11 & Komik Pages #10)
Harry 'A' Chesler: No. 9, 1944
| 9-Manhunter, The Voice | 20 | 60 | 105 | 175 |

SNAPPY COMICS
Cima Publ. Co. (Prize Publ.): 1945
1-Airmale app.; 9 pg. Sorcerer's Apprentice adapt; Kiefer-a
| | 34 | 102 | 179 | 310 |

SNARKY PARKER (See Life With...)

SNIFFY THE PUP
Standard Publ. (Animated Cartoons): No. 5, Nov, 1949 - No. 18, Sept, 1953
5-Two Frazetta text illos	10	30	55	85
6-10	6	18	29	40
11-18	5	15	24	32

SNOOPER AND BLABBER DETECTIVES (TV) (See Whitman Comic Books)
Gold Key: Nov, 1962 - No. 3, May, 1963 (Hanna-Barbera)
| 1 | 9 | 27 | 63 | 110 |
| 2,3 | 7 | 21 | 49 | 85 |

SNOWMAN
Hall of Heroes/Avatar Press: 1996 - No. 3 ($2.50, B&W)
1	1	4	7	10
1-Ltd. Ed.	2	6	11	15
2,3, 3-Chromium-c				4.00
2,3-Ltd. Ed.				6.00
0-(Avatar Press), 0-Alternate-c				4.00
0-Gold				8.00
0-Silver Foil				10.00
0-Black Leather				15.00
0-Blue Foil-c				30.00

SNOWMAN DEAD AND DYING
Avatar Press: Nov,1997 - No. 3, Apr, 1998 ($3.00, B&W, limited series)
1-3 .... 3.50
1-($4.95) Ltd. Edition, 3-($4.95) variant-c 5.00
3-($25.00) White velvet variant-c 25.00

SNOWMAN HORROR SHOW
Avatar Press: Mar, 1998 ($3.00, B&W, one-shot)
1-Pin-ups by Matt Martin 3.00
1-($4.95) Frozen Fear Edition 5.00
1-Leather-c 25.00

SNOWMAN 1944
Entity Comics: Oct, 1996 - No. 4 ($2.75, B&W)
1 .... 3.00
1-Ltd. Ed. 5.00
2-4 .... 3.00
3-Ltd. Ed. 3.00
...Special 1 (10/97, $3.95) 4.00

SNOWMAN SQUARED
Avatar Press: Sept, 1998 - No. 2 ($3.00, B&W, limited series)
1-Matt Martin-s/a; Snowman vs. Snowman 1944 .... 3.00
1-Commemorative Edition 5.00

SNOW WHITE (See Christmas With... in Promotional Comics section), Mickey Mouse Mag., Movie Comics & Seven Dwarfs)
Dell Publishing Co.: No. 49, July, 1944 - No. 382, Mar, 1952 (Disney-Movie)
Four Color 49 (...& the Seven Dwarfs) | 62 | 186 | 434 | 800 |
Four Color 382 (1952)-origin; partial reprint of Four Color 49
| | 10 | 30 | 70 | 130 |

SNOW WHITE
Marvel Comics: Jan, 1995 ($1.95, one-shot)

	GD2.0	FN6.0	VF8.0	NM9.4
1-r/1937 Sunday newspaper pages				2.25

SNOW WHITE AND THE SEVEN DWARFS
Whitman Publications: April, 1982 (60¢)
nn-r/Four Color #49 .... 6.00

SNOW WHITE AND THE SEVEN DWARFS GOLDEN ANNIVERSARY
Gladstone: Fall, 1987 ($2.95, magazine size, 52 pgs.)
1-Contains poster | 1 | 4 | 7 | 10 |

SOAP OPERA LOVE
Charlton Comics: Feb, 1983 - No. 3, June, 1983
1-3-Low print run | 3 | 9 | 17 | 25 |

SOAP OPERA ROMANCES
Charlton Comics: July, 1982 - No. 5, March, 1983
1-5-Nurse Betsy Crane-r; low print run | 3 | 9 | 17 | 25 |

SOCK MONKEY
Dark Horse Comics: Sept, 1998 - No. 2, Oct, 1998 ($2.95, B&W)
1,2-Tony Millionaire-s/a 3.00
Vol. 2 -(Tony Millionaire's Sock Monkey) July, 1999 - No. 2, Aug, 1999
1,2 .... 3.00
Vol. 3 -(Tony Millionaire's Sock Monkey) Nov, 2000 - No. 2, Dec, 2000
1,2 .... 3.00

SO DARK THE ROSE
CFD Productions: Oct, 1995 ($2.95)
1-Wrightson-c 4.00

SOJOURN
White Cliffs Publ. Co.: Sept, 1977 - No. 2, 1978 ($1.50, B&W & color, tabloid size)
1,2: 1-Tor by Kubert, Eagle by Severin, E. V. Race, Private Investigator by Doug Wildey, T. C. Mars by Aragonés begin plus other strips
| | 1 | 4 | 7 | 10 |
NOTE: Most copies came folded. Unfolded copies are worth 50% more.

SOJOURN
CrossGeneration Comics: July, 2001 - Present ($2.95)
Prequel -Ron Marz-s/Greg Land-c/a; preview pages 3.00
1-6-Ron Marz-s/Greg Land-c/a 3.00

SOLAR (...Man of the Atom) (Also see Doctor Solar)
Valiant/Acclaim Comics (Valiant): Sept, 1991 - No. 60, Apr, 1996 ($1.75/$1.95/$2.50, 44 pgs.)
1-Layton-a(i) on Solar; Barry Windsor-Smith-c/a 6.00
2-9: 2-Layton-a(i) on Solar, B. Smith-a. 3-1st app. Harada (11/91). 7-vs. X-O Armor 4.00
10-(6/92, $3.95)-1st app. Eternal Warrior (6 pgs.); black embossed-c; origin & 1st app. Geoff McHenry (Geomancer) | 1 | 3 | 6 | 8 |
10-($3.95)-2nd printing 4.00
11-15: 11-1st full app. Eternal Warrior. 12,13-Unity x-overs. 14-1st app. Fred Bender (becomes Dr. Eclipse). 15-2nd Dr. Eclipse 3.00
16-60: 17-X-O Manowar app. 23-Solar splits. 29-1st Valiant Vision book. 33-Valiant Vision; bound-in trading card. 38-Chaos Effect Epsilon Pt.1. 46-52-Dan Jurgens-a(p)/scripts w/Giordano-i. 53,54-Jurgens scripts only. 60-Giffen scripts; Jeff Johnson-a(p) 2.50
0-($9.95, trade paperback)-r/Alpha and Omega origin story; polybagged w/poster 10.00
...:Second Death (1994, $9.95)-r/issues #1-4. .... 10.00
NOTE: #1-10 all have free 8 pg. insert "Alpha and Omega" which is a 10 chapter Solar origin story. All 10 centerfolds can pieced together to show climax of story. Ditko a-11p, 14p. Giordano a-46, 47, 48, 49, 50, 51, 52i. Johnson a-60p. Jurgens a-46, 47, 48, 49, 50 , 51, 52p. Layton a-1-3i; c-2i, 11i, 17i, 25i. Miller c-12. Quesada c-17p, 20-23p, 29p. Simonson c-13. B. Smith a-1-10; c-1, 3, 5, 7, 19i. Thibert c-22i, 23i.

SOLAR LORD
Image Comics: Mar, 1999 - No. 7, Sept, 1999 ($2.50)
1-7-Khoo Fuk Lung-s/a 2.50

SOLARMAN (See Pendulum Ill. Originals)
Marvel Comics: Jan, 1989 - No. 2, May, 1990 ($1.00, limited series)
1,2 .... 2.25

SOLAR, MAN OF THE ATOM (Man of the Atom on cover)
Acclaim Comics (Valiant Heroes): Vol. 2, May, 1997 ($3.95, one-shot, 46 pgs)

Solo #1 © MAR

The Solution #11 © MAL

Sonic the Hedgehog #6 © Sega

	GD2.0	FN6.0	VF8.0	NM9.4

st Valiant Heroes Special Event)

ol. 2-Reintro Solar; Ninjak cameo; Warren Ellis scripts; Darick Robertson-a
4.00

OLAR, MAN OF THE ATOM: HELL ON EARTH
cclaim Comics (Valiant Heroes): Jan, 1998 - No. 4 ($2.50, limited series)

1-4-Priest-s/ Zircher-a(p) 2.50

OLAR, MAN OF THE ATOM: REVELATIONS
cclaim Comics (Valiant Heroes): Nov, 1997 ($3.95, one-shot, 46 pgs.)

1-Krueger-s/ Zircher-a(p) 4.00

OLDIER & MARINE COMICS (Fightin' Army #16 on)
harlton Comics (Toby Press of Conn. V1#11): No. 11, Dec, 1954 - No. 15,
ug, 1955; V2#9, Dec, 1956

#11 (12/54)-Bob Powell-a	8	24	45	65
1#12(2/55)-15: 12-Photo-c	5	15	25	35
2#9(Formerly Never Again; Jerry Drummer V2#10 on)	5	15	23	30

OLDIER COMICS
awcett Publications: Jan, 1952 - No. 11, Sept, 1953

1	13	39	66	110
2	7	21	38	55
3-5	7	21	36	50
6-11: 8-Illo. in POP	6	18	32	45

OLDIERS OF FORTUNE
merican Comics Group (Creston Publ. Corp.): Mar-Apr, 1951 - No. 13, Feb-
ar, 1953

1-Capt. Crossbones by Shelly, Ace Carter, Lance Larson begin	24	72	127	220
2	14	42	72	120
3-10: 6-Bondage-c	12	36	61	100
1-13 (War format)	7	21	38	55

OTE: **Shelly** a-1-3, 5. **Whitney** a-6, 8-11, 13; c-1-3, 5, 6.

OLDIERS OF FREEDOM
mericomics: 1987 - No. 2, 1987 ($1.75)

1,2 3.00

OLITAIRE (Also See Prime V2#6-8)
alibu Comics (Ultraverse): Nov, 1993 - No. 12, Dec, 1994 ($1.95)

1-($2.50)-Collector's edition bagged w/playing card 2.50
1-12: 1-Regular edition w/o playing card. 2,4-Break-Thru x-over. 3-2 pg. origin
The Night Man. 4-Gatefold-c. 5-Two pg. origin the Strangers 2.25

OLO
arvel Comics: Sept, 1994 - No. 4, Dec, 1994 ($1.75, limited series)

1-4: Spider-Man app. 2.25

OLO (Movie)
ark Horse Comics: July, 1996 - No. 2, Aug, 1996 ($2.50, limited series)

1,2: Adaptation of film; photo-c 2.50

OLO AVENGERS (Becomes Avenger Spotlight #21 on)
arvel Comics: Dec, 1987 - No. 20, July, 1989 (75¢/$1.00)

1-Jim Lee-a on back-up story 3.00
2-20: 11-Intro Bobcat 2.50

OLOMON AND SHEBA (Movie)
ell Publishing Co.: No. 1070, Jan-Mar, 1960

our Color 1070-Sekowsky-a; photo-c 9 27 63 120

OLOMON KANE (Based on the Robert E. Howard character. Also see
lackthorne 3-D Series #60 & Marvel Premiere)
arvel Comics: Sept, 1985 - No. 6, July, 1986 (Limited series)

1-6: 1-Double size. 3-6-Williamson-a(i) 3.00

OLUTION, THE
alibu Comics (Ultraverse): Sept, 1993 - No. 17, Feb, 1995 ($1.95)

1,3-15: 1-Intro Meathook, Deathdance, Black Tiger, Tech. 4-Break-Thru x-over;
gatefold-c. 5-2 pg. origin The Strangers. 11-Brereton-a 2.50
1-($2.50)-Newsstand ed. polybagged w/trading card 2.50
1-Ultra 5000 Limited silver foil 4.00

0-Obtained w/Rune #0 by sending coupons from 11 comics 3.00
2-($2.50, 48 pgs.)-Rune flip-c/story by B. Smith; The Mighty Magnor 1 pg. strip
by Aragones 2.50
16 ($3.50)-Flip-c Ultraverse Premiere #10 3.50
17 ($2.50) 2.50

SOMERSET HOLMES (See Eclipse Graphic Novel Series)
Pacific Comics/ Eclipse Comics No. 5, 6: Sept, 1983 - No. 6, Dec, 1984 ($1.50,
Baxter paper)

1-6: 1-Brent Anderson-c/a. Cliff Hanger by Williams in all 3.00

SONG OF THE SOUTH (See Brer Rabbit)

SONIC & KNUCKLES
Archie Comics: Aug, 1995 ($2.00)

1 5.00

SONIC DISRUPTORS
DC Comics: Dec, 1987 - No. 7, July, 1988 ($1.75, unfinished limited series)

1-7 3.00

SONIC'S FRIENDLY NEMESIS KNUCKLES
Archie Publications: July, 1996 - No. 3, Sept, 1996 ($1.50, limited series)

1-3 4.00

SONIC SUPER SPECIAL
Archie Publications: 1997 - Present ($2.00/$2.25/$2.29, 48 pgs)

1-3 4.00
4-6,8-15: 10-Sabrina-c/app. 15-Sin City spoof 3.00
7-(w/Image) Spawn, Maxx, Savage Dragon-c/app.; Valentino-a 3.00

SONIC THE HEDGEHOG (TV, video game)
Archie Comics: Feb, 1993 - No. 3, May, 1993 ($1.25, mini-series)

0(2/93),1: Shaw-a(p) & covers on all	3	9	17	26
2,3	2	6	11	16

SONIC THE HEDGEHOG (TV, video game)
Archie Comics: July, 1993 - Present ($1.25/$1.50/$1.75/$1.79/$1.99)

1	3	9	19	28
2,3	2	6	12	18
4-10: 8-Neon ink-c.	2	6	10	14
11-20	2	6	9	12
21-30 ($1.50): 25-Silver ink-c	1	3	6	8
31-50				6.00
51-93				3.00
94-104				2.25
Triple Trouble Special (10/95, $2.00, 48 pgs.)				4.00

SONIC VS. KNUCKLES "BATTLE ROYAL" SPECIAL
Archie Publications: 1997 ($2.00, one-shot)

1 4.00

SON OF AMBUSH BUG (See Ambush Bug)
DC Comics: July, 1986 - No. 6, Dec, 1986 (75¢)

1-6: Giffen-c/a in all. 5-Bissette-a. 2.25

SON OF BLACK BEAUTY (Also see Black Beauty)
Dell Publishing Co.: No. 510, Oct, 1953 - No. 566, June, 1954

Four Color 510, 566 4 12 25 38

SON OF FLUBBER (See Movie Comics)

SON OF MUTANT WORLD
Fantagor Press: 1990 - No. 5, 1990? ($2.00, bi-monthly)

1-5: 1-3: Corben-c/a. 4,5 ($1.75, B&W) 3.00

SON OF ORIGINS OF MARVEL COMICS (See Fireside Book Series)

SON OF SATAN (Also see Ghost Rider #1 & Marvel Spotlight #12)
Marvel Comics Group: Dec, 1975 - No. 8, Feb, 1977 (25¢)

1-Mooney-a; Kane-c(p), Starlin splash(p)	2	6	15	22
2,6-8: 2-Origin The Possessor. 8-Heath-a	2	6	9	12
3-5-(Regular 25¢ editions)(4-8/76): 5-Russell-a	2	6	9	12
3-5-(30¢-c variants, limited distribution)	2	6	12	18

SON OF SINBAD (Also see Abbott & Costello & Daring Adventures)
St. John Publishing Co.: Feb, 1950

Soul Saga #4 © Platt & Lichtner

Sovereign Seven #4 © Chris Claremont

Space Adventures #1 © CC

	GD2.0	FN6.0	VF8.0	NM9.4

		GD2.0	FN6.0	VF8.0	NM9

1-Kubert-c/a ... 40 120 232 400

SON OF SUPERMAN (Elseworlds)
DC Comics: 1999 ($14.95, prestige format, one-shot)
nn-Chaykin & Tischman-s/Williams III & Gray-a ... 15.00

SON OF TOMAHAWK (See Tomahawk)

SON OF VULCAN (Formerly Mysteries of Unexplored Worlds #1-48; Thunderbolt V3#51 on)
Charlton Comics: V2#49, Nov, 1965 - V2#50, Jan, 1966
V2#49,50: 50-Roy Thomas scripts (1st pro work) ... 3 9 19 28

SON OF YUPPIES FROM HELL (See Yuppies From Hell)
Marvel Comics: 1990 ($3.50, B&W, squarebound, 52 pgs.)
nn ... 3.50

SONS OF KATIE ELDER (See Movie Classics)

SORCERY (See Chilling Adventures in... & Red Circle...)

SORORITY SECRETS
Toby Press: July, 1954
1 ... 9 27 49 70

SOULQUEST
Innovation: Apr, 1989 ($3.95, squarebound, 52 pgs.)
1-Blackshard app. ... 4.00

SOUL SAGA
Image Comics (Top Cow): Feb, 2000 - Present ($2.50)
1-5: 1-Madureira-c; Platt & Batt-a ... 2.50

SOULSEARCHERS AND COMPANY
Claypool Comics: June, 1995 - Present ($2.50, B&W)
1-10: Peter David scripts ... 5.00
11-25 ... 3.00
26-50 ... 2.50

SOULWIND
Image Comics: Mar, 1997 - No. 8 ($2.95, B&W, limited series)
1-8: 5-"The Day I Tried To Live" pt. 1 ... 3.00
Book Five; The August Ones (3/01, $8.50) ... 8.50
...The Kid From Planet Earth (1997, $9.95, TPB) ... 10.00
...The Kid From Planet Earth (Oni Press, 1/00, $8.50, TPB) ... 8.50
...The Day I Tried to Live (Oni Press, 4/00, $8.50, TPB) ... 8.50

SOUPY SALES COMIC BOOK (TV)(The Official...)
Archie Publications: 1965
1 ... 9 27 65 110

SOUTHERN KNIGHTS, THE (See Crusaders #1)
Guild Publ/Fictioneer Books: No. 2, 1983 - No. 41, 1993 (B&W)
2-Magazine size ... 6.00
3-35, 37-41 ... 3.00
36-($3.50-c) ... 3.50
Dread Halloween Special 1, Primer Special 1 (Spring, 1989, $2.25 ... 2.25
Graphic Novels #1-4 ... 4.00

SOVEREIGN SEVEN (Also see Showcase '95 #12)
DC Comics: July, 1995 - No. 36, July, 1998 ($1.95) (1st creator-owned mainstream DC comic)
1-1st app. Sovereign Seven (Reflex, Indigo, Cascade, Finale, Cruiser, Network & Rampart); 1st app. Maitresse; Darkseid app.; Chris Claremont scripts & Dwayne Turner-c/a begins. ... 3.00
1-Gold ... 8.00
1-Platinum ... 40.00
2-25: 2-Wolverine cameo. 4-Neil Gaiman cameo. 5,8-Batman app. 7-Ramirez cameo (from the movie Highlander). 9-Humphrey Bogart cameo from Casablanca. 10-Impulse app; Manoli Wetherell & Neal Conan cameo from Uncanny X-Men #226. 11-Robin app. 16-Final Night. 24-Superman app. 25-Power Girl app. ... 2.25
26-36: 26-Begin $2.25-c. 28-Impulse-c/app. ... 2.25
Annual 1 (1995, $3.95)-Year One story; Big Barda & Lobo app.; Jeff Johnson-c/a. ... 4.00
Annual 2 (1996, $2.95)-Legends of the Dead Earth; Leonardi-c/a ... 3.50

...Plus 1(2/97, $2.95)-Legion-c/app. ... 3.50
TPB-($12.95) r/#1-5, Annual #1 & Showcase '95 #12 ... 13.00

SOVIET SUPER SOLDIERS
Marvel Comics: Nov, 1992 ($2.00, one-shot)
1-Marvel's Russian characters; Median & Saltares-a ... 2.25

SPACE: ABOVE AND BEYOND (TV)
Topps Comics: Jan, 1996 - No. 3, Mar, 1996 ($2.95, limited series)
1-3: Adaptation of pilot episode; Steacy-c. ... 3.00

SPACE: ABOVE AND BEYOND—THE GAUNTLET (TV)
Topps Comics: May, 1996 -No. 2, June, 1996 ($2.95, limited series)
1,2 ... 3.00

SPACE ACE (Also see Manhunt!)
Magazine Enterprises: No. 5, 1952
5(A-1 #61)-Guardineer-a ... 50 150 300 525

SPACE ACTION
Ace Magazines (Junior Books): June, 1952 - No. 3, Oct, 1952
1-Cameron-a in all (1 story) ... 73 219 455 80
2,3 ... 55 165 330 575

SPACE ADVENTURES (War At Sea #22 on)
Capitol Stories/Charlton Comics: 7/52 - No. 21, 8/56; No. 23, 5/58 - No. 59, 11/64; V3#60, 10/67; V1#2, 7/68 - V1#8, 7/69; No. 9, 5/78 - No. 13, 3/79
1 ... 50 150 300 525
2 ... 27 81 145 250
3-5: 4,6-Flying saucer-c/stories ... 22 66 116 175
6-9: 7-Sex change story "Transformation". 8-Robot-c. 9-A-Bomb panel ... 20 60 105 175
10,11-Ditko-c/a. 10-Robot-c. 11-Two Ditko stories ... 50 150 300 525
12-Ditko-c (classic) ... 57 171 356 620
13-(Fox-r, 10-11/54); Blue Beetle-c/story ... 16 48 83 140
14,15,17,18: 14-Blue Beetle-c/story; Fox-r (1-2/54-55, last pre-code).
15,17,18-Rocky Jones-c/s.(TV); 15-Part photo-c 21 63 110 185
16-Krigstein-a; Rocky Jones-c/story (TV) ... 23 69 121 205
19 ... 14 42 72 120
20-Reprints Fawcett's "Destination Moon" ... 27 81 142 245
21-(8/56) (no #22)(Becomes War At Sea) ... 14 42 72 120
23-(5/58; formerly Nyoka, The Jungle Girl)-Reprints Fawcett's "Destination Moon" ... 24 72 127 215
24,25,31,32-Ditko-a. 24-Severin-a(signed "LePoer") 21 63 110 185
26,27-Ditko-a(4) each. 26,28-Flying saucer-c ... 22 66 116 195
28-30 ... 10 30 55 80
33-Origin/1st app. Capt. Atom by Ditko (3/60) ... 37 112 278 500
34-40,42-All Captain Atom by Ditko ... 16 48 110 190
41,43,45-59: 45-Mercury Man app. ... 4 12 29 45
44-1st app. Mercury Man ... 4 12 30 50
V3#60(#1, 10/67)-Origin & 1st app. Paul Mann & The Saucers From the Future ... 4 12 30 50
2,5,6,8 (1968-69)-Ditko-a ... 3 9 20 30
2-Aparo-c/a ... 3 9 20 30
3,4,7: 4-Aparo-c/a ... 3 9 17 25
9-13(1978-79)-Capt. Atom-r/Space Adventures by Ditko; 9-Reprints origin/1st app. Capt. Atom from #33 ... 5.00
NOTE: Aparo a-V3#60. c-V3#8. Ditko c-12, 31-42. Giordano c-3, 4, 7-9, 18p. Krigstein c-15. Shuster a-11. Issues 13 & 14 have Blue Beetle logos; #15-18 have Rocky Jones logos.

SPACE ARK
Americomics (AC Comics)/ Apple Comics #3 on: June, 1985 - No. 5, Sept, 1987 ($1.75)
1-5: Funny animal (#1,2-color; #3-5-B&W) ... 2.25

SPACE BUSTERS
Ziff-Davis Publ. Co.: Spring, 1952 - No. 2, Fall, 1952
1-Krigstein-a(3); Painted-c by Norman Saunders 80 240 500 87
2-Kinstler-a(2 pgs.); Saunders painted-c 62 185 388 685
NOTE: Anderson a-2. Bondage c-2.

SPACE CADET (See Tom Corbett,...)

SPACE CIRCUS
Dark Horse Comics: July, 2000 - No. 4, Oct, 2000 ($2.95, limited series)
1-4-Aragonés-a/Evanier-s ... 3.0

Space Family Robinson #29 © GK

Spaceman #1 © MAR

Space Usagi V3 #3 © Stan Sakai

	GD2.0	FN6.0	VF8.0	NM9.4

SPACE COMICS (Formerly Funny Tunes)
Avon Periodicals: No. 4, Mar-Apr, 1954 - No. 5, May-June, 1954

4,5-Space Mouse, Peter Rabbit, Super Pup (formerly Spotty the Pup) &				
Merry Mouse continue from Funny Tunes	7	21	38	55
I.W. Reprint #8 (nd)-Space Mouse-r	2	6	9	12

SPACED
Anthony Smith Publ. #1,2/Unbridled Ambition/Eclipse Comics #10 on: 1982 - No. 13, 1988 ($1.25/$1.50, B&W, quarterly)

1-($1.25-c)				3.00
2-13, Special Edition (1983, Mimeo)				2.25

SPACE DETECTIVE
Avon Periodicals: July, 1951 - No. 4, July, 1952

1-Rod Hathway, Space Detective begins, ends #4; Wood-c/a(3)-23 pgs.; "Opium Smugglers of Venus" drug story; Lucky Dale-r/Saint #4	105	315	656	1150
2-Tales from the Shadow Squad story; Wood/Orlando-c; Wood inside layouts; "Slave Ship of Saturn" story	75	225	469	825
3,4: 3-Kinstler-c. 4-Kinstlerish-a by McCann	40	120	232	400
I.W. Reprint #1(Reprints #2), 8(Reprints cover #1 & part Famous Funnies #191)				
	4	12	29	45
I.W. Reprint #9-Exist?	4	12	29	45

SPACE EXPLORER (See March of Comics #202)

SPACE FAMILY ROBINSON (TV)(...Lost in Space #15-37, ...Lost in Space On Space Station One #38 on)(See Gold Key Champion)
Gold Key: Dec, 1962 - No. 36, Oct, 1970 - No. 37, 10/73 - No. 54, 11/78; No. 55, 3/81 - No. 59, 5/82 (All painted covers)

1-(Low distribution); Spiegle-a in all	24	72	168	310
2(3/63)-Family becomes lost in space	12	36	84	150
3-5	7	21	49	90
6-10: 6-Capt. Venture back-up stories begin	6	18	42	75
11-20: 14-(10/65). 15-Title change (1/66)	4	12	30	50
21-36: 28-Last 12¢ issue. 36-Captain Venture ends	3	10	23	35
37-48: 37-Origin retold	3	9	12	22
49-59: Reprints #49,50,55-59	1	3	6	8

NOTE: The TV show first aired on 9/15/65. Title changed after TV show debuted.

SPACE FAMILY ROBINSON (See March of Comics #320, 328, 352, 404, 414)

SPACE GHOST (TV) (Also see Golden Comics Digest #2 & Hanna-Barbera Super TV Heroes #3-7)
Gold Key: March, 1967 (Hanna-Barbera) (TV debut was 9/10/66)

1 (10199-703)-Spiegle-a	35	105	245	450

SPACE GHOST (TV cartoon)
Comico: Mar, 1987 ($3.50, deluxe format, one-shot) (Hanna-Barbera)

1-Steve Rude-c/a	1	3	6	8

SPACE GIANTS, THE (TV cartoon)
FBN Publications: 1979 ($1.00, B&W, one-shots)

1-Based on Japanese TV series	2	6	9	12

SPACEHAWK
Dark Horse Comics: 1989 - No. 3, 1990 ($2.00, B&W)

1-3-Wolverton-c/a(r) plus new stories by others.				4.00

SPACE JAM
DC Comics: 1996 ($5.95, one-shot, movie adaption)

1-Wraparound photo cover of Michael Jordan	1	3	6	8

SPACE KAT-ETS (...in 3-D)
Power Publishing Co.: Dec, 1953 (25¢, came w/glasses)

1	34	102	179	310

SPACEKNIGHTS
Marvel Comics: Oct, 2000 - No. 5, Feb, 2001 ($2.99, limited series)

1-5-Starlin-s/Batista-a				3.00

SPACEMAN (Speed Carter...)
Atlas Comics (CnPC): Sept, 1953 - No. 6, July, 1954

1-Grey tone-c	66	198	413	720
2	43	129	257	450

3-6: 4-A-Bomb explosion-c	40	120	220	380

NOTE: *Everett c-1, 3. Heath a-1. Maneely a-1(3), 2(4), 3(3), 4-6; c-5, 6. Romita a-1. Sekowsky c-4. Sekowsky/Abel a-4(3). Tuska a-5(3).*

SPACE MAN
Dell Publ. Co.: No. 1253, 1-3/62 - No. 8, 3-5/64; No. 9, 7/72 - No. 10, 10/72

Four Color 1253 (#1)(1-3/62)(15¢-c)	7	21	49	90
2,3: 2-(15¢-c). 3-(12¢-c)	4	12	29	45
4-8-(12¢-c)	3	10	23	35
9,10-(15¢-c): 9-Reprints #1253. 10-Reprints #2	2	6	9	12

SPACE MOUSE (Also see Funny Tunes & Space Comics)
Avon Periodicals: April, 1953 - No. 5, Apr-May, 1954

1	10	30	55	80
2	6	18	32	45
3-5	5	15	25	35

SPACE MOUSE (Walter Lantz...#1; see Comic Album #17)
Dell Publishing Co./Gold Key: No. 1132, Aug-Oct, 1960 - No. 5, Nov, 1963 (Walter Lantz)

Four Color 1132,1244, 1(11/62)(G.K.)	4	12	30	50
2-5	4	12	26	40

SPACE MYSTERIES
I.W. Enterprises: 1964 (Reprints)

1-r/Journey Into Unknown Worlds #4 w/new-c	3	9	19	28
8,9: 9-r/Planet Comics #73	3	9	19	28

SPACE: 1999 (TV) (Also see Power Record Comics)
Charlton Comics: Nov, 1975 - No. 7, Nov, 1976

1-Origin Moonbase Alpha; Staton-c/a	2	6	11	15
2,7: 2-Staton-a	1	4	7	10
3-6: All Byrne-a; c-3,5,6	2	6	11	15

SPACE: 1999 (TV)(Magazine)
Charlton Comics: Nov, 1975 - No. 8, Nov, 1976 (B&W) (#7 shows #6 inside)

1-Origin Moonbase Alpha; Morrow-c/a	2	6	12	18
2-8: 2,3-Morrow-c/a. 4-6-Morrow-c. 5,8-Morrow-a	2	6	10	14

SPACE PATROL (TV)
Ziff-Davis Publishing Co. (Approved Comics): Summer, 1952 - No. 2, Oct-Nov, 1952 (Painted-c by Norman Saunders)

1-Krigstein-a	87	261	544	960
2-Krigstein-a(3)	62	186	388	685

SPACE PIRATES (See Archie Giant Series #533)

SPACE RANGER (See Mystery in Space #92, Showcase #15 & Tales of the Unexpected)

SPACE SQUADRON (In the Days of the Rockets)(Becomes Space Worlds #6)
Marvel/Atlas Comics (ACI): June, 1951 - No. 5, Feb, 1952

1-Space team; Brodsky c-1,5	65	194	406	720
2: Tuska c-2-4	55	165	341	600
3-5: 3-Capt. Jet Dixon by Tuska(3). 4-Weird advs. begin	45	135	270	475

SPACE THRILLERS
Avon Periodicals: 1954 (25¢ Giant)

nn-(Scarce)-Robotmen of the Lost Planet; contains 3 rebound comics of The Saint & Strange Worlds. Contents could vary	114	342	713	1250

SPACE TRIP TO THE MOON (See Space Adventures #23)

SPACE USAGI
Mirage Studios: June, 1992 - No. 3, 1992 ($2.00, B&W, mini-series) V2#1, Nov, 1993 - V3#3, Jan, 1994 ($2.75)

1-3: Stan Sakai-c/a/scripts, V2#1-3				3.00

SPACE USAGI
Dark Horse Comics: Jan, 1996 - No. 3, Mar, 1996 ($2.95, B&W, limited series)

1-3: Stan Sakai-c/a/scripts				3.00

SPACE WAR (Fightin' Five #28 on)
Charlton Comics: Oct, 1959 - No. 27, Mar, 1964; No. 28, Mar, 1978 - No. 34, 3/79

V1#1-Giordano-c begin, end #3	14	42	102	175
2,3	7	21	53	85

Sparkler Comics #39 © UFS

Sparkling Stars #7 © UFS

Spartan: Warrior Spirit #3 © WSP

	GD2.0	FN6.0	VF8.0	NM9.4

	GD2.0	FN6.0	VF8.0	NM9.4
4-6,8,10-Ditko-c/a	14	42	102	175
7,9,11-15: Last 10¢ issue?	5	15	38	60
16-27 (3/64): 18,19-Robot-c	4	12	30	50
28(3/78),29-31,33,34-Ditko-c/a(r): 30-Staton, Sutton/Wood-a. 31-Ditko-c/a(3);				
same-c as Strange Suspense Stories #2 (1968); atom blast-c	1	4	7	10
32-r/Charlton Premiere V2#2; Sutton-a				5.00

SPACE WESTERN (Formerly Cowboy Western Comics; becomes Cowboy Western Comics #46 on)
Charlton Comics (Capitol Stories): No. 40, Oct, 1952 - No. 45, Aug, 1953

40-Intro Spurs Jackson & His Space Vigilantes; flying saucer story	58	174	363	640
41,43-45: 41-Flying saucer-c. 45-Hitler app.	43	129	257	450
42-Atom bomb explosion-c	45	135	270	475

SPACE WORLDS (Formerly Space Squadron #1-5)
Atlas Comics (Male): No. 6, April, 1952

6-Sol Brodsky-c	43	129	257	450

SPANKY & ALFALFA & THE LITTLE RASCALS (See The Little Rascals)

SPANNER'S GALAXY
DC Comics: Dec, 1984 - No. 6, May, 1985 (limited series)

1-6: Mandrake-c/a in all.				2.25

SPARKIE, RADIO PIXIE (Radio)(Becomes Big Jon & Sparkie #4)
Ziff-Davis Publ. Co.: Winter, 1951 - No. 3, July-Aug, 1952 (Painted-c)(Sparkie #2,3; #1!)

1-Based on children's radio program	24	72	127	220
2,3: 3-Big Jon and Sparkie on-c only	17	51	88	150

SPARKLE COMICS
United Features Synd.: Oct-Nov, 1948 - No. 33, Dec-Jan, 1953-54

1-Li'l Abner, Nancy, Captain & the Kids, Ella Cinders				
(#1-3: 52 pgs.)	15	45	77	130
2	8	24	45	65
3-10	7	21	36	50
11-20	6	18	30	42
21-32	5	15	25	35
33-(2-3/54) 2 pgs. early Peanuts by Schulz	6	18	32	45

SPARKLE PLENTY (See Harvey Comics Library #2 & Dick Tracy)

SPARKLER COMICS (1st series)
United Feature Comic Group: July, 1940 - No. 2, 1940

1-Jim Hardy	40	120	220	380
2-Frankie Doodle	31	93	165	285

SPARKLER COMICS (2nd series)(Nancy & Sluggo #121 on)(Cover title becomes Nancy and Sluggo #101?? on)
United Features Synd.: July, 1941 - No. 120, Jan, 1955

1-Origin 1st app. Sparkman; Tarzan (by Hogarth in all issues), Captain & the Kids, Ella Cinders, Danny Dingle, Dynamite Dunn, Nancy, Abbie & Slats, Broncho Bill, Frankie Doodle, begin; Spark Man (r)9,11,12; Hap Hopper c-10,13	236	708	1477	2600
2	80	240	500	875
3,4	64	192	398	700
5-9: 9-Spark Man's new costume	58	174	363	640
10-Origin Spark Man?	58	174	363	640
11,12-Spark Man war-c. 12-Spark Man's new costume (color change)	47	142	286	500
13-Hap Hopper war-c	43	129	257	450
14-Tarzan-c by Hogarth	55	165	330	575
15,17: 15-Capt & Kids-c. 17-Nancy & Sluggo-c	40	120	232	400
16,18-Spark Man war-c	44	132	264	460
19-1st Race Riley and the Commandos-c/s	43	129	257	450
20-Nancy war-c	40	120	220	410
21,25,28,31,34,37,39-Tarzan-c by Hogarth	45	135	270	475
22-24,26,27,29,30: 22-Race Riley & the Commandos strips begin, ends #44	35	105	185	320
32,33,35,36,38,40	21	63	110	185
41,43,45,46,48,49	15	45	77	130
42,44,47,50-Tarzan-c (42,47,50 by Hogarth)	29	87	153	265

51,52,54-70: 57-Li'l Abner begins (not in #58); Fearless Fosdick app. in #58	14	42	72	120
53-Tarzan-c by Hogarth	25	75	130	225
71-80	10	30	55	80
81,82,84-86: 86 Last Tarzan; lingerie panels	8	24	45	65
83-Tarzan-c; Li'l Abner ends	12	36	61	105
87-96,98-99	8	24	42	60
100	9	27	49	70
101-107,109-112,114-119	6	18	32	45
108,113-Toth-a	9	27	49	70
120-(10-11/54) 2 pgs. early Peanuts by Schulz	7	21	36	50

SPARKLING LOVE
Avon Periodicals/Realistic (1953): June, 1950; 1953

1(Avon)-Kubert-a; photo-c	24	72	127	215
nn(1953)-Reprint; Kubert-a	9	27	49	70

SPARKLING STARS
Holyoke Publishing Co.: June, 1944 - No. 33, March, 1948

1-Hell's Angels, FBI, Boxie Weaver, Petey & Pop, & Ali Baba begin	20	60	105	175
2-Speed Spaulding story	11	33	55	90
3-Actual FBI case photos & war photos	9	27	49	70
4-10: 7-X-Mas-c	8	24	42	60
11-19: 13-Origin/1st app. Jungo the Man-Beast-c/s	7	21	36	50
20-Intro Fangs the Wolf Boy	8	24	42	60
21-29,32,33: 29-Bondage-c	7	21	36	50
31-Sid Greene-a	7	21	36	50

SPARK MAN (See Sparkler Comics)
Frances M. McQueeny: 1945 (36 pgs., one-shot)

1-Origin Spark Man r/Sparkler #1-3; female torture story; cover redrawn from Sparkler #1	34	102	179	310

SPARKY WATTS (Also see Big Shot Comics & Columbia Comics)
Columbia Comic Corp.: Nov?, 1942 - No. 10, 1949

1(1942)-Skyman & The Face app; Hitler-c	55	165	341	600
2(1943)	27	81	145	250
3(1944)	20	60	105	175
4(1944)-Origin	19	57	99	165
5(1947)-Skyman app.; Boody Rogers-c/a	16	48	83	140
6,7,9,10: 6(1947),10(1949)	10	30	55	80
8(1948)-Surrealistic-c	14	42	72	120

NOTE: *Boody Rogers c-1-8.*

SPARTACUS (Movie)
Dell Publishing Co.: No. 1139, Nov, 1960 (Kirk Douglas photo-c)

Four Color 1139-Buscema-a	13	39	91	165

SPARTAN: WARRIOR SPIRIT (Also see WildC.A.T.S: Covert Action Teams)
Image Comics (WildStorm Productions): July, 1995 - No. 4, Nov, 1995 ($2.50, limited series)

1-4: Kurt Busiek scripts; Mike McKone-c/a				2.50

SPAWN (Also see Curse of the Spawn and Sam & Twitch)
Image Comics (Todd McFarlane Prods.): May, 1992 - Present ($1.95/$2.50)

1-1st app. Spawn; McFarlane-c/a begins; McFarlane/Steacy-c; 1st Todd McFarlane Productions title.	3	9	17	25
1-Black & white edition	3	10	23	35
2,3: 2-1st app. Violator; McFarlane/Steacy-c	2	6	12	18
4-Contains coupon for Image Comics #0	2	6	13	20
4-With coupon missing				4.00
4-Newsstand edition w/o poster or coupon				4.00
5-Cerebus cameo (1 pg.) as stuffed animal; Spawn mobile poster #1	2	6	9	12
6-8,10: 7-Spawn Mobile poster #2. 8-Alan Moore scripts; Miller poster. 10-Cerebus app.; Dave Sim scripts; 1 pg. cameo app. by Superman.	1	3	6	9
9-Neil Gaiman scripts; Jim Lee poster; 1st Angela.	2	6	9	12
11-17,19,20,22-30: 11-Miller script; Darrow poster. 12-Bloodwulf poster by Liefeld. 14,15-Violator app. 16,17-Grant Morrison scripts; Capullo-c/a(p). 23,24-McFarlane-a/stories. 25-(10/94). 19-(10/94). 20-(11/94)				6.00

Spawn #85 © TMP

Spawn: The Dark Ages #1 © TMP

Species #3 © MGM

	GD2.0	FN6.0	VF8.0	NM9.4

	GD2.0	FN6.0	VF8.0	NM9.4

18-Grant Morrison script, Capullo-c/a(p); low distr.   2   6   12   18
21-low distribution   2   6   12   18
31-49: 31-1st app. The Redeemer; new costume cameo. 32-1st full app. new
  costume. 38-40,42,44,46,48-Tony Daniel-c/a(p). 38-1st app. Cy-Gor.
  40,41-Cy-Gor & Curse app.   4.00
50-($3.95, 48 pgs.)   5.00
51-66: 52-Savage Dragon app. 56-w/ Darkchylde preview. 57-Cy-Gor-c/app.
64-Polybagged w/McFarlane Toys catalog. 65-Photo-c of movie Spawn and
  McFarlane   3.00
67-97: 81-Billy Kincaid returns. 97-Angela-c/app.   2.50
98,99,101-113-($2.50): 98,99-Angela app.   2.50
100-($4.95) Angela dies; 6 covers by McFarlane, Ross, Miller, Capullo, Wood,
  Mignola   5.00
Annual 1-Blood & Shadows ('99, $4.95) Ashley Wood-c/a; Jenkins-s   5.00
...Bible-(8/96, $1.95)-Character bios   4.00
Book 1 TPB($9.95) r/#1-5; Book 2-r/#6-9,11; Book 3 -r/#12-15; Book 4- r/#16-20;
  Book 5-r/#21-25; Book 6- r/#26-30; Book 7-r/#31-34; Book 8-r/#35-38;
  Book 9-r/#39-42; Book 10-r/#43-47   11.00
Book 11 TPB ($10.95) r/#48-50; Book 12-r/#51-54   11.00
NOTE: Capullo a-16p-18p; c-16p-18p. Daniel a-38-40, 42, 44, 46. McFarlane a-1-15; c-1-15p.
Thibert a-16i(part). Posters come with issues 1, 4, 7-9, 11, 12. #25 was released before #19 & 20.

SPAWN-BATMAN (Also see Batman/Spawn: War Devil under Batman:
  One-Shots)
Image Comics (Todd McFarlane Productions): 1994 ($3.95, one-shot)
1-Miller scripts; McFarlane-c/a   6.00

SPAWN: BLOOD FEUD
Image Comics (Todd McFarlane Productions): June, 1995 - No. 4, Sept, 1995
  ($2.25, limited series)
1-4-Alan Moore scripts, Tony Daniel-a   3.50

SPAWN FAN EDITION
Image Comics (Todd McFarlane Productions): Aug, 1996 - No. 3, Oct, 1996
  (Giveaway, 12 pgs.) (Polybagged w/Overstreet's FAN)

                                     1   3   6   8
1-3: Beau Smith scripts; Brad Gorby-a(p). 1-1st app. Nordik, the Norse
  Hellspawn. 2-1st app. McFallon, the Dragon Master. 3-1st app. Mercy
                                     1   3   6   8
1-3-(Gold): All retailer incentives   16.00
1-3-Variant-c   1   3   6   8
2-(Platinum)-Retailer incentive   25.00

SPAWN: THE DARK AGES
Image Comics (Todd McFarlane Productions): Mar, 1999 - Present ($2.50)
1-Fabry-c; Holguin-s/Sharp-a; variant-c by McFarlane   2.50
2-28   2.50

SPAWN THE IMPALER
Image Comics (Todd McFarlane Productions): Oct, 1996 - No. 3, Dec, 1996
  ($2.95, limited series)
1-3-Mike Grell scripts, painted-a   3.00

SPAWN: THE UNDEAD
Image Comics (Todd McFarlane Prod.): Jun, 1999 - No. 9, Feb, 2000
  ($1.95/$2.25)
1-9-Dwayne Turner-c/a; Jenkins-s. 7-9-($2.25-c)   2.50

SPAWN/WILDC.A.T.S
Image Comics (WildStorm): Jan, 1996 - No. 4, Apr, 1996 ($2.50, lim. series)
1-4: Alan Moore scripts in all.   3.00

SPECIAL AGENT (Steve Saunders...)(Also see True Comics #68)
Parents' Magazine Institute (Commended Comics No. 2): Dec, 1947 - No. 8,
  Sept, 1949 (Based on true FBI cases)
1-J. Edgar Hoover photo on-c   12   36   61   105
2   8   24   42   60
3-8   7   21   36   50

SPECIAL COLLECTORS' EDITION (See Savage Fists of Kung-Fu)

SPECIAL COMICS (Becomes Hangman #2 on)
MLJ Magazines: Winter, 1941-42
1-Origin The Boy Buddies (Shield & Wizard x-over); death of The Comet;
  origin The Hangman retold; Hangman-c   282   846   1763   3100

SPECIAL EDITION (See Gorgo and Reptisaurus)

SPECIAL EDITION COMICS
Fawcett Publications: 1940 (August) (68 pgs., one-shot)
1-1st book devoted entirely to Captain Marvel; C.C. Beck-c/a; only app. of
  Capt. Marvel with belt buckle; Capt. Marvel appears with button-down flap;
  1st story (came out before Captain Marvel #1)
                          808   2424   5252   10,500
NOTE: Prices vary widely on this book. Since this book is all Captain Marvel stories, it is actually a
pre-Captain Marvel #1. There is speculation that this book almost became Captain Marvel #1. After
Special Edition was published, there was an editor change at Fawcett. The new editor commissioned Kirby to do a nn Captain Marvel book early in 1941. This book was followed by a second book
several months later. This 2nd book was advertised as a #3 (making Special Edition the #1, & the
nn issue the #2). However, the 2nd book did come out as a #2.

SPECIAL EDITION: SPIDER-MAN VS. THE HULK (See listing under The
Amazing Spider-Man)

SPECIAL EDITION X-MEN
Marvel Comics Group: Feb, 1983 ($2.00, one-shot, Baxter paper)
1-r/Giant-Size X-Men #1 plus one new story   2   6   9   12

SPECIAL MARVEL EDITION (Master of Kung Fu #17 on)
Marvel Comics Group: Jan, 1971 - No. 16, Feb, 1974 (#1-3: 25¢, 68 pgs.;
  #4: 52 pgs.; #5-16: 20¢, regular ed.)
1-Thor-r by Kirby; 68 pgs.   3   9   20   30
2-4: Thor-r by Kirby; 2,3-68 pg. Giant. 4-(52 pgs.)   2   6   12   18
5-14: Sgt. Fury-r; 11-r/Sgt. Fury #13 (Capt. America)1   3   6   9
15-Master of Kung Fu (Shang-Chi) begins (1st app., 12/73); Starlin-a; origin/
  1st app. Nayland Smith & Dr. Petric   6   18   45   75
16-Isn. Midnight; Starlin-a (2nd Shang-Chi)   3   9   20   30
NOTE: Kirby c-10-14.

SPECIAL MISSIONS (See G.I. Joe...)

SPECIAL WAR SERIES (Attack V4#3 on?)
Charlton Comics: Aug, 1965 - No. 4, Nov, 1965
V4#1-D-Day (also see D-Day listing)   3   10   23   35
2-Attack!   2   6   13   20
3-War & Attack (also see War & Attack)   2   6   13   20
4-Judomaster (intro/1st app.; see Sarge Steel)   6   18   45   75

SPECIES (Movie)
Dark Horse Comics: June, 1995 - No. 4, Sept, 1995 ($2.50, limited series)
1-4-Adaptation of film   3.00

SPECIES: HUMAN RACE (Movie)
Dark Horse Comics: Nov, 1996 - No. 4, Feb, 1997 ($2.95, limited series)
1-4   3.00

SPECTACULAR ADVENTURES (See Adventures)

SPECTACULAR FEATURE MAGAZINE, A (Formerly My Confessions)
(Spectacular Features Magazine #12)
Fox Feature Syndicate: No. 11, April, 1950
11 (#1)-Samson and Delilah   31   93   168   290

SPECTACULAR FEATURES MAGAZINE (Formerly A Spectacular Feature
Magazine)
Fox Feature Syndicate: No. 12, June, 1950 - No. 3, Aug, 1950
12 (#2)-Iwo Jima; photo flag-c   31   93   165   285
3-True Crime Cases From Police Files   25   75   130   225

SPECTACULAR SCARLET SPIDER
Marvel Comics: Nov, 1995 - No. 2, Dec, 1995 ($1.95, limited series)
1,2: Replaces Spectacular Spider-Man   2.25

SPECTACULAR SPIDER-MAN, THE (See Marvel Special Edition and Marvel Treasury
Edition)

SPECTACULAR SPIDER-MAN, THE (Magazine)
Marvel Comics Group: July, 1968 - No. 2, Nov, 1968 (35¢)
1-(B&W)-Romita/Mooney 52 pg. story plus updated origin story with
  Everett-a(i)   9   27   65   110
1-Variation w/single c-price of 40¢   9   27   65   110
2-(Color)-Green Goblin-c & 58 pg. story; Romita painted-c (story reprinted in
  King Size Spider-Man #9); Romita/Mooney-a   12   36   84   140

SPECTACULAR SPIDER-MAN, THE (Peter Parker...#54-132, 134)

Spectacular Spider-Man #8 © MAR

Spectacular Spider-Man #226 © MAR

The Spectre (4th series) #1 © DC

	GD2.0	FN6.0	VF8.0	NM9.4

Marvel Comics Group: Dec, 1976 - No. 263, Nov, 1998

1-Origin recap in text; return of Tarantula	4	12	30	50
2-Kraven the Hunter app.	2	6	12	18
3-5: 3-Intro Lightmaster. 4-Vulture app.	2	6	9	12
6-8-Morbius app. 6-r/Marvel Team-Up #3 w/Morbius				
	2	6	10	14
7,8-(35¢ variants, limited distribution)(6,7/77)	2	6	11	16
9-20: 9,10-White Tiger app. 11-Last 30¢-c. 17,18-Angel & Iceman app. (from Champions); Ghost Rider cameo in flashback	1	3	6	9
9-11-(35¢-c variants, limited distribution)(8-10/77)	2	6	9	12
21,24-26: 21-Scorpion app. 26-Daredevil app.	1	3	5	7
22,23-Moon Knight app.	1	3	6	8
27-Miller's 1st art on Daredevil (2/79); also see Captain America #235				
	2	6	12	18
28-Miller Daredevil (p)	2	6	10	14
29-55,57,59: 33-Origin Iguana. 38-Morbius app.				5.00
56-2nd app. Jack O'Lantern (Macendale) & 1st Spidey/Jack O'Lantern battle (7/81)				6.00
58-Byrne-a(p)				6.00
60-Double size; origin retold with new facts revealed				6.00
61-63,65-68,71-74: 65-Kraven the Hunter app.				4.00
64-1st app. Cloak & Dagger (3/82)	1	4	7	10
69,70-Cloak & Dagger app.				6.00
75-Double size				5.00
76-82: 78,79-Punisher cameo. 81,82-Punisher, Cloak & Dagger app.				4.00
83-Origin Punisher retold (10/83)	1	3	5	7
84,86-99: 90-Spider-man's new black costume, last panel(ties w/Amazing Spider-Man #252 & Marvel Team-Up #141 for 1st app.). 94-96-Cloak & Dagger app. 98-Intro The Spot				4.00
85-Hobgoblin (Ned Leeds) app. (12/83); gains powers of original Green Goblin (see Amazing Spider-Man #238)	1	3	5	7
100-(3/85)-Double size				5.00
101-115,117,118,120-129: 107-110-Death of Jean DeWolff. 111-Secret Wars II tie-in. 128-Black Cat new costume				3.00
116,119-Sabretooth-c/story				5.00
130-132: 30-Hobgoblin app. 131-Six part Kraven tie-in. 132-Kraven tie-in				5.00
133-140: 138-1st full app. Tombstone (origin #139). 140-Punisher cameo app.				3.00
141-143-Punisher app.				3.50
144,146,148-157: 151-Tombstone returns				3.00
147-1st app. new Hobgoblin (Macendale) in 1 pg. cameo; continued in Web of Spider-Man #48	1	4	7	10
158-Spider-Man gets new powers (1st Cosmic Spidey, cont'd in Web of Spider-Man #59)				5.00
159-Cosmic Spider-Man app.				5.00
160-170: 161-163-Hobgoblin app. 168-170-Avengers x-over. 169-1st app. the Outlaws				2.50
171-188,190-199: 180,181,183,184-Green Goblin app. 197-199-Original X-Men-c/story				2.50
189-($2.95, 52 pgs.)-Silver hologram on-c; battles Green Goblin; origin Spidey retold w/Vess poster w/Spidey + Hobgoblin				4.00
189-(2nd printing)-Gold hologram on-c				4.00
195-(Deluxe ed.)-Polybagged w/"Dirt" magazine #2 & Beastie Boys/Smithereens music cassette				3.00
200-($2.95)-Holo-grafx foil-c; Green Goblin-c/story				3.00
201-219,221,222,224,226-228,230-247: 212-w/card sheet. 203-Maximum Carnage x-over. 204-Begin 4 part death of Tombstone story. 207,208-The Shroud-c/story. 208-Siege of Darkness x-over (#207 is a tie-in). 209-Black Cat back-up215,216-Scorpion app. 217-Power & Responsibility Pt. 4. 231-Return of Kaine; Spider-Man corpse discovered. 232-New Doc Octopus app. 233-Carnage-c/app. 235-Dragon Man cameo. 236-Dragon Man-c/app; Lizard app.; Peter Parker regains powers. 238,239-Lizard app. 239-w/card insert. 240-Revelations storyline begins. 241-Flashback				2.50
213-Collectors ed. polybagged w/16 pg. preview & animation cel; foil-c; 1st meeting Spidey & Typhoid Mary				3.00
213-Version polybagged w/Gamepro #7; no-c date, price				2.50
217,219 ($2.95)-Deluxe edition foil-c: flip book				3.00
220 ($2.25, 52 pgs.)-Flip book, Mary Jane reveals pregnancy				3.00
223,229: ($2.50) 229-Spidey quits				3.00
223,225: ($2.95)-223-Die Cut-c. 225-Newsstand ed.				3.00

225,229: ($3.95) 225-Direct Market Holodisk-c (Green Goblin). 229-Acetate-c, Spidey quits				4.00
240-Variant-c				3.00
248,249,251-254,256: 249-Return of Norman Osborne 256-1st app. Prodigy				2.50
250-($3.25) Double gatefold-c				3.25
255-($2.99) Spiderhunt pt. 4				3.00
257-262: 257-Double cover with "Spectacular Prodigy #1"; battles Jack O'Lantern. 258-Spidey is cleared. 259,260-Green Goblin & Hobgoblin app. 262-Byrne-s				2.50
263-Final issue; Byrne-c; Aunt May returns				4.00
#(-1) Flashback (7/97)				2.50
Annual 1 (1979)-Doc Octopus-c & 46 pg. story	1	3	6	8
Annual 2 (1980)-Origin/1st app. Rapier				5.00
Annual 3-14: 3('81-'94)-3-Last Man-Wolf. 8 ('88,$ 1.75)-Evolutionary War x-over; Daydreamer returns GwenStacy "clone" back to real self (not Gwen Stacy). 9 ('89, $2.00, 68 pgs.)-Atlantis Attacks. 10 ('90, $2.00, 68 pgs.)-McFarlane-c 11 ('91, $2.00, 68 pgs.)-Iron Man app. 12 ('92, $2.25, 68 pgs.)-Venom solo story cont'd from Amazing Spider-Man Annual #26. 13 ('93, $2.95, 68 pgs.)-Polybagged w/trading card; John Romita, Sr. back-up-a				3.00
Special 1 (1995, $3.95)-Flip book				4.00

NOTE: **Austin** c-21i, Annual 11i. **Buckler** a-103, 107-111, 116, 117, 119, 122, Annual 1, Annual 10; c-103, 107-111, 113, 116-119, 122, Annual 1. **Buscema** a-121. **Byrne** c(p)-17, 43, 58, 101, 102. **Giffen** a-120p. **Hembeck** c/a-86p. **Larsen** c-Annual 11p. **Miller** c-46p, 48p, 50, 51p, 52p, 54p, 55, 56p, 57, 60. **Mooney** a-7i, 11i, 21p, 23p, 25p, 26p, 29-34p, 36p, 37p, 39i, 41, 42i, 49p, 50i, 51i, 53p, 54-57i, 59-66i, 68i, 71i, 73-79i, 81-83i, 85i, 87-99i, 102i, 125p, Annual 1i, 2p. **Nasser** c-37p. **Perez** c-10. **Simonson** c-54i. **Zeck** a-118, 131, 132; c-131, 132.

SPECTACULAR STORIES MAGAZINE (Formerly A Star Presentation)
Fox Feature Syndicate (Hero Books): No. 4, July; 1950; No. 3, Sept, 1950

4-Sherlock Holmes (true crime stories)	40	120	220	380
3-The St. Valentine's Day Massacre (true crime)	28	84	148	255

SPECTRE, THE (1st Series) (See Adventure Comics #431-440, More Fun & Showcase)
National Periodical Publ.: Nov-Dec, 1967 - No. 10, May-June, 1969 (All 12¢)

1-(11-12/67)-Anderson-c/a	13	39	94	160
2-5-Neal Adams-c/a; 3-Wildcat x-over	8	24	60	100
6-8,10: 6-8-Anderson inks. 7-Hourman app.	5	15	38	60
9-Wrightson-a	6	18	42	70

SPECTRE, THE (2nd Series) (See Saga of the Swamp Thing #58, Showcase '95 #8 & Wrath of the...)
DC Comics: Apr, 1987 - No. 31, Oct, 1989 ($1.00, new format)

1-Colan-a begins				4.00
2-32: 9-Nudity panels. 10-Batman cameo. 10,11-Millennium tie-in				3.00
Annual 1 (1988, $2.00)-Deadman app.				3.00

NOTE: **Art Adams** c-Annual 1. **Colan** a-1-6. **Kaluta** c-1-3. **Mignola** c-7-9. **Morrow** a-9-15. **Sears** c/a-22. **Vess** c-13-15.

SPECTRE, THE (3rd Series) (Also see Brave and the Bold #72, 75, 116, 180, 199 & Showcase '95 #8)
DC Comics: Dec, 1992 - No. 62, Feb, 1998 ($1.75/$1.95/$2.25/$2.50)

1-($1.95)-Glow-in-the-dark-c; Mandrake-a begins				5.00
2,3				3.00
4-7,9-12,14-20: 10-Kaluta-c. 11-Hildebrandt painted-c. 16-Aparo/K. Jones-a. 19-Snyder III-c. 20-Sienkiewicz-c				2.50
8,13-($2.50)-Glow-in-the-dark-c				3.00
21-62: 22-(9/94)-Superman-c & app. 23-(11/94). 43-Kent Williams-c. 44-Kaluta-c. 47-Final Night x-over. 49-Begin Bolton-c. 51-Batman-c/app. 52-Gianni-c. 54-Corben-c. 60-Harris-c				2.50
#0 (10/94) Released between #22 & #23				2.50
Annual 1 (1995, $3.95)-Year One story				4.00

NOTE: **Bisley** c-27. **Fabry** c-8. **Kelley Jones** c-31. **Vess** c-5.

SPECTRE, THE (4th Series) (Hal Jordan; also see Day of Judgment #5 and Legends of the DC Universe #33-36)
DC Comics: Mar, 2001 - Present ($2.50)

1-DeMatteis-s/Ryan Sook-c/a				3.00
2-13: 5-Superman & Batman-c/app. 5-Two-Face-c/app.				2.50

SPEEDBALL (See Amazing Spider-Man Annual #12, Marvel Super-Heroes & The New Warriors)
Marvel Comics: Sept, 1988(10/88-inside) - No. 11, July, 1989 (75¢)

Speed Comics #12 © HARV

Speed Racer #6 © Speed Racer Ent.

Spellbound #3 © MAR

	GD2.0	FN6.0	VF8.0	NM9.4

1-11: Ditko/Guice a-1-4, c-1; Ditko a-1-10; c-1-11p — 2.25

SPEED BUGGY (TV)(Also see Fun-In #12, 15)
Charlton Comics: July, 1975 - No. 9, Nov, 1976 (Hanna-Barbera)

1	3	9	17	25
2-9	2	6	11	16

SPEED CARTER SPACEMAN (See Spaceman)

SPEED COMICS (New Speed)(Also see Double Up)
Brookwood Publ./Speed Publ./Harvey Publications No. 14 on:
10/39 - #11, 8/40; #12, 3/41 - #44, 1-2/47 (#14-16: pocket size, 100 pgs.)

1-Origin & 1st app. Shock Gibson; Ted Parrish, the Man with 1000 Faces begins; Powell-a; becomes Champion #2 on?	317	951	1979	3800
2-Powell-a	109	327	682	1200
3	64	192	398	700
4,5: 4-Powell-a?5-Dinosaur-c	53	160	318	560
6-11: 7-Mars Mason begins, ends #11	47	140	286	500
12 (3/41): shows #11 in indicia)-The Wasp begins; Major Colt app. (Capt. Colt #12)	53	160	318	560
13-Intro. Captain Freedom & Young Defenders; Girl Commandos, Pat Parker (costumed heroine), War Nurse begins; Major Colt app.	58	174	363	640
14-16 (100 pg. pocket size, 1941): 14-2nd Harvey comic (See Pocket); Shock Gibson dons new costume. 15-Pat Parker dons costume, last in costume #23; no Girl Commandos	68	204	426	750
17-Black Cat begins (4/42, early app.; see Pocket #1); origin Black Cat-r/ Pocket #1; not in #40,41; S&K-c	73	219	455	800
18-20-S&K-c	55	165	341	600
21-Hitler, Tojo-c; Kirby-c	64	192	398	700
22-Kirby-c	55	165	341	600
23-Origin Girl Commandos; Kirby-c	55	165	341	600
24-Pat Parker team-up with Girl Commandos; Hitler, Tojo, & Mussolini-c	50	150	300	525
25-30: 26-Flag-c	43	129	257	450
31-Schomburg Hitler & Hirohito-c	61	183	381	675
32-36-Schomburg-c	50	150	300	525
37,39-42, 44	43	129	257	450
38-Iwo-Jima Flag-c	45	135	270	475
43-Robot-c	47	142	286	500

NOTE: *Al Avison c-14-16, 30, 43. Briefer a-6, 7. Jon Henri (Kirbyesque) c-17-20. Kubert a-7-11(Mars Mason), 37, 38, 42-44. Kirby/Casenueve c-21-23. Palais c-37, 39-42. Powell a-1, 2, 4-7, 28, 31, 44. Schomburg c-31-36. Tuska a-3, 6, 7. Bondage c-18, 35. Captain Freedom c-16-24, 25(part), 26-44(w/Black Cat #27, 29, 31, 32-40). Shock Gibson c-1-15.*

SPEED DEMON (Also see Marvel Versus DC #3 & DC Versus Marvel #4)
Marvel Comics (Amalgam): Apr, 1996 ($1.95, one-shot)

1 — 2.25

SPEED DEMONS (Formerly Frank Merriwell at Yale #1-4?; Submarine Attack #11 on)
Charlton Comics: No. 5, Feb, 1957 - No. 10, 1958

5-10	6	18	32	45

SPEED FORCE (See The Flash 2nd Series #143-Cobalt Blue)
DC Comics: Nov, 1997 ($3.95, one-shot)

1-Flash & Kid Flash vs. Cobalt Blue; Waid-s/Aparo & Sienkiewicz-a; Flash family stories and pin-ups by various — 4.00

SPEED RACER (Also see The New Adventures of…)
Now Comics: July, 1987 - No. 38, Nov, 1990 ($1.75)

1-38, 1-2nd printing	2.50
Special 1 (1988, $2.00)	2.50
Special 2 (1988, $3.50)	3.50

SPEED RACER (Also see Racer X)
DC Comics (WildStorm): Oct, 1999 - No. 3, Dec, 1999 ($2.50, limited series)

1-3-Tommy Yune-s/a; origin of Racer X; debut of the Mach 5	2.50
…: Born To Race (2000, $9.95, TPB) r/series & concept art	10.00
…: The Original Manga Vol. 1 ('00, $9.95, TPB) r/1950s B&W manga	10.00

SPEED RACER FEATURING NINJA HIGH SCHOOL
Now Comics: Aug, 1993 - No. 2, 1993 ($2.50, mini-series)

1,2: 1-Polybagged w/card. 2-Exists? — 2.50

SPEED RACER: RETURN OF THE GRX
Now Comics: Mar, 1994 - No. 2, Apr, 1994 ($1.95, limited series)

1,2 — 2.50

SPEED SMITH-THE HOT ROD KING (Also see Hot Rod King)
Ziff-Davis Publishing Co.: Spring, 1952

1-Saunders painted-c	24	72	127	215

SPEEDY GONZALES
Dell Publishing Co.: No. 1084, Mar, 1960

Four Color 1084	5	15	34	55

SPEEDY RABBIT (See Television Puppet Show)
Realistic/I. W. Enterprises/Super Comics: nd (1953); 1963

nn (1953)-Realistic Reprint	2	6	11	16
I.W. Reprint #1 (2 versions w/diff. c/stories exist)-Peter Cottontail #?				
Super Reprint #14(1963)	2	6	9	12

SPELLBINDERS
Quality: Dec, 1986 - No. 12, Jan, 1988 ($1.25)

1-12: Nemesis the Warlock, Amadeus Wolf — 2.25

SPELLBOUND (See The Crusaders)

SPELLBOUND (Tales to Hold You… #1, Stories to Hold You…)
Atlas Comics (ACI 1-15/Male 16-23/BPC 24-34): Mar, 1952 - #23, June, 1954; #24, Oct, 1955 - #34, June, 1957

1-Horror/weird stories in all	64	192	398	700
2-Edgar A. Poe adap.	39	117	208	360
3-5: 3-Whitney-a; cannibalism story	34	102	179	310
6-Krigstein-a	34	102	179	310
7-10: 8-Ayers-a	29	87	153	265
11-16,18-20: 14-Ed Win-a	24	72	127	215
17-Krigstein-a	24	72	127	220
21-23: 23-Last precode (6/54)	20	60	105	175
24-28,30,31,34: 25-Orlando-a	18	54	94	155
29-Ditko-a (4 pgs.)	20	60	105	175
32,33-Torres-a	18	54	94	155

NOTE: *Brodsky a-5; c-1, 5-7, 10, 11, 13, 15, 25-27, 32. Colan a-17. Everett a-2, 5, 7, 10, 16, 28, 31; c-2, 8, 14, 29. Forgione/Abel a-29. Forte/Fox a-16. Al Hartley a-2. Heath a-2, 4, 8, 9, 12, 14, 16; c-3, 4, 12, 16, 20, 21. Infantino a-15. Keller a-5. Kida a-2, 14. Maneely a-7, 14, 27; c-24, 29, 34. Mooney a-5, 13, 18. Mac Pakula a-22, 32. Post a-8. Powell a-19, 24. R.Q. Sale a-29. Sekowsky a-5. Severin c-29. Sinnott a-8, 16, 17. Robinson a-1. Romita a-24, 26, 27. Severin c-29.*

SPELLBOUND
Marvel Comics: Jan, 1988 - Apr, 1988 ($1.50, bi-weekly, Baxter paper)

1-5	2.25
6 ($2.25, 52 pgs.)	2.50

SPELLJAMMER (Also see TSR Worlds Comics Annual)
DC Comics: Sept, 1990 - No. 15, Nov, 1991 ($1.75)

1-15: Based on TSR game. 11-Heck-a — 2.25

SPENCER SPOOK (Formerly Giggle Comics; see Adventures of…)
American Comics Group: No. 100, Mar-Apr, 1955 - No. 101, May-June, 1955

100,101	7	21	36	50

SPIDER, THE
Eclipse Comics: 1991 - Book 3, 1991 ($4.95, 52 pgs., limited series)

Book 1-3-Truman-c/a — 5.00

SPIDER-BOY (Also see Marvel Versus DC #3)
Marvel Comics (Amalgam): Apr, 1996 ($1.95)

1-Mike Wieringo-c/a; Karl Kesel story; 1st app. of Bizarnage, Insect Queen, Challengers of the Fantastic, Sue Storm: Agent of S.H.I.E.L. D., & King Lizard. — 2.25

SPIDER-BOY TEAM-UP
Marvel Comics (Amalgam): June, 1997 ($1.95, one-shot)

1-Karl Kesel & Roger Stern-s/Jo Ladronn-a(p) — 2.25

SPIDER-GIRL (See What If #105)
Marvel Comics: Oct, 1998 - Present ($1.99/$2.25)

0-($2.99)-r/1st app. Peter Parker's daughter from What If #105; previews reg. series, Avengers-Next and J2	1	3	5	7

	GD2.0	FN6.0	VF8.0	NM9.4

1-DeFalco-s/Olliffe & Williamson-s	1	3	5	7
2-Two covers				4.00
3-16,18-20: 3-Fantastic Five-c/app. 10,11-Spider-Girl time-travels to meet				
teenaged Spider-Man				2.50
17-($2.99) Peter Parker suits up				3.00
21-24,26-42: 21-Begin $2.25-c. 25-c. 31-Avengers app.				2.25
25-($2.99) Spider-Girl vs. the Savage Six				3.00
1999 Annual ($3.99)				4.00
... A Fresh Start (1/99,$5.99, TPB) r/#1&2				6.00
TPB (10/01, $19.95) r/#0-8; new Olliffe-c				20.00

SPIDER-MAN (See Amazing..., Giant-Size..., Marvel Tales, Marvel Team-Up,
Spectacular..., Spidey Super Stories, Ultimate..., Venom, & Web Of...)

SPIDER-MAN
Marvel Comics: Aug, 1990 - No. 98, Nov, 1998 ($1.75/$1.95/ $1.99)

1-Silver edition, direct sale only (unbagged)	1	4	7	10
1-Silver bagged edition; direct sale, no price on comic, but $2.00 on				
plastic bag (125,000 print run)				25.00
1-Regular edition w/Spidey face in UPC area (unbagged); green-c				
	1	3	6	8
1-Regular bagged edition w/Spidey face in UPC area; green cover (125,000)				
				15.00
1-Newsstand bagged w/UPC code				10.00
1-Gold edition, 2nd printing (unbagged) with Spider-Man in box				
(400,000-450,000)				6.00
1-Gold 2nd printing w/UPC code; (less than 10,000 print run) intended for Wal-				
Mart; much scarcer than originally believed				150.00
1-Platinum ed.- mailed to retailers only (10,000 print run); has new McFarlane-a				
& editorial material instead of ads; stiff-c, no cover price				150.00
2-26: 2-McFarlane-c/a/scripts continue. 6,7-Ghost Rider & Hobgoblin-app.				
8-Wolverine cameo; Wolverine storyline begins. 12-Wolverine storyline				
ends. 13-Spidey's black costume returns; Morbius app. 14-Morbius app. 15-				
Erik Larsen-c/a; Beast c/s. 16-X-Force-c/story w/Liefeld assists; continues in				
X-Force #4; reads sideways; last McFarlane issue. 17-Thanos-c/story;				
Leonardi/Williamson-c/a. 13,14-Spidey in black costume. 18-Ghost Rider-				
c/story. 18-23-Sinister Six storyline w/Erik Larsen-c/a/scripts. 19-Hulk &				
Hobgoblin-c & app. 20-22-Deathlok app. 22,23-Ghost Rider, Hulk, Hobgoblin				
app. 23-Wrap-around gatefold-c. 24-Infinity War x-over w/Demogoblin &				
Hobgoblin-c/story. 24-Demogoblin dons new costume & battles Hobgoblin-				
c/story. 26-($3.50, 52 pgs.)-Silver hologram on-c w/gatefold poster by Ron				
Lim; Spidey retells his origin.				4.00
26-2nd printing; gold hologram on-c				3.50
27-45: 32-34-Maximum Carnage x-over. 37-Maximum Carnage x-over. 39,40-Electro-c/s				
(cameo #38). 41-43-Iron Fist-c/stories w/Jae Lee-c/app. 42-Intro Platoon.				
44-Hobgoblin app				3.00
46-49,51-53, 55, 56,58-74,76-81: 46-Begin $1.95-c; bound-in card				
sheet. 51-Power & Responsibility Pt. 3. 52,53-Venom app. 60-Kaine				
revealed. 61-Origin Kaine. 65-Mysterio app. 66-Kaine-c/app.; Peter Parker				
app. 67-Carnage-c/app. 68,69-Hobgoblin-c/app. 72-Onslaught x-over;				
Spidey vs. Sentinels. 77-80-Morbius-c/app.				2.50
46-($2.95)-Polybagged; silver ink-c w/16 pg. preview of cartoon series & anima-				
tion style print; bound-in trading card sheet				3.00
50-($2.95)-Newsstand edition				2.50
50-($3.95)-Collectors edition w/holographic-c				4.00
51-($2.95)-Deluxe edition foil-c; flip book				3.00
54 ($2.75, 52 pgs.)-Flip book				2.75
57 ($2.50)				2.50
57 ($2.95)-Die cut-c				3.00
65-($2.95)-Variant-c; polybagged w/cassette				3.00
75-($2.95)-Wraparound-c; return of the Green Goblin; death of Ben Reilly (who				
was the clone)				4.00
82-97: 84-Juggernaut app. 91-Double cover with "Dusk #1"; battles the Shocker.				
93-Ghost Rider app.				2.50
98-Double issue; final issue				3.00
#(-1) Flashback (7/97)				2.50
Annual '97 ($2.99), '98 ($2.99)-Devil Dinosaur-c/app.				3.00
...and Batman ('95, $5.95) DeMatteis-s; Joker, Carnage app.				3.00
...and Daredevil ('84, $2.00) 1-r/Spectacular Spider-Man #26-28 by Miller				3.00
...: Carnage nn (6/93, $6.95, TPB)-r/Amazing S-M #344,345,359-363; spot				
varnish-c				7.00
.../Dr. Strange: "The Way to Dusty Death" nn (1992, $6.95, 68 pgs.)				7.00

.../Elektra '98-($2.99) vs. The Silencer				3.00
... Fear Itself Graphic Novel (2/92, $12.95)				18.00
Giant-Sized Spider-Man (12/98, $3.99) r/team-ups				4.00
Holiday Special 1995 ($2.95)				3.00
Identity Crisis (9/98, $19.95, TPB)				20.00
.../Marrow (2/01, $2.99) Garza-a				3.00
..., Punisher, Sabretooth: Designer Genes (1993, $8.95)				9.00
...Revelations ('97, $14.99, TPB) r/end of Clone Saga plus 14 new pages				
by Romita Jr.				15.00
Special Edition 1 (12/92-c, 11/92 inside)-The Trial of Venom; ordered thru mail				
with $5.00 donation or more to UNICEF; embossed metallic ink; came				
bagged w/bound-in poster; Daredevil app.	1	4	7	10
Super Special (7/95, $3.95)-Planet of the Symbiotes				4.00
The Death of Captain Stacy ($3.50) r/AS-M#88-90				3.50
The Death of Gwen Stacy ($14.95) r/AS-M#96-98,121,122				15.00
Torment TPB (5/01$15.95) r/#1-5, Spec. S-M #10				16.00
... Vs. Doctor Octopus ($17.95) reprints early battles; Sean Chen-c				18.00
... Vs. Punisher (7/00, $2.99) Michael Lopez-c/a				3.00
...Vs. Venom (1990, $8.95, TPB)-r/Amaz. S-M #300,315-317 w/new				
McFarlane-c				9.00
...Visionaries (10/01, $19.95, TPB)-r/Amaz. S-M #298-305; McFarlane-a				20.00
Wizard 1/2 ($10.00) Leonardi-a; Green Goblin app.				10.00
NOTE: Erik Larsen c/a-15, 18-23. M. Rogers/Keith Williams c/a-27, 28.				

SPIDER-MAN ADVENTURES
Marvel Comics: Dec, 1994 - No. 15, Mar, 1996 ($1.50)

1-15 ($1.50)-Based on animated series				2.25
1-($2.95)-Foil embossed-c				3.00

SPIDER-MAN AND HIS AMAZING FRIENDS (See Marvel Action Universe)
Marvel Comics Group: Dec, 1981 (one-shot)

1-Adapted from NBC TV cartoon show; Green Goblin-c/story; 1st Spidey,				
Firestar, Iceman team-up; Spiegle-p				5.00

SPIDER-MAN AND THE INCREDIBLE HULK (See listing under Amazing...)

SPIDER-MAN AND THE UNCANNY X-MEN
Marvel Comics: Mar, 1996 ($16.95, trade paperback)

nn-r/Uncanny X-Men #27, Uncanny X-men #35, Amazing Spider-Man #92,				
Marvel Team-Up Annual #1, Marvel Team-Up #150, & Spectacular Spider-				
Man #197-199				17.00

SPIDER-MAN AND X-FACTOR
Marvel Comics: May, 1994 - No. 3, July, 1994 ($1.95, limited series)

1-3				2.25

SPIDER-MAN /BADROCK
Maximum Press: Mar, 1997 ($2.99, mini-series)

1A, 1B(#2)-Jurgens-s				3.00

SPIDER-MAN: CHAPTER ONE
Marvel Comics: Dec, 1998 - No. 12, Oct, 1999 ($2.50, limited series)

1-Retelling/updating of origin; John Byrne-s/c/a				2.50
1-($6.95) DF Edition w/variant-c by Jae Lee				
1-($6.95)-Kaine-c/app.				
2-11: 2-Two covers (one is swipe of ASM #1); Fantastic Four app. 9-Daredevil.				
11-Batman-c/app.				2.50
12-($3.50) Battles the Sandman				3.50
0-(5/99) Origins of Vulture, Lizard and Sandman				2.50

SPIDER-MAN CLASSICS
Marvel Comics: Apr, 1993 - No. 16, July, 1994 ($1.25)

1-14,16: 1-r/Amaz. Fantasy #15 & Strange Tales #115. 2-16-r/Amaz.				
Spider-Man #1-15. 6-Austin-c(i)				2.25
15-($2.95)-Polybagged w/16 pg. insert & animation style print; r/Amazing S-M				
#14 (1st Green Goblin)				3.00

SPIDER-MAN COLLECTOR'S PREVIEW
Marvel Comics: Dec, 1994 ($1.50, 100 pgs., one-shot)

1-wraparound-c; no comics				3.00

SPIDER-MAN COMICS MAGAZINE
Marvel Comics Group: Jan, 1987 - No. 13, 1988 ($1.50, digest-size)

1-13-Reprints				6.00

SPIDER-MAN: DEAD MAN'S HAND

Spider-Man: Lifeline #1 © MAR

Spider-Man Megazine #4 © MAR

Spider-Man 2099 Annual #1 © MAR

	GD2.0	FN6.0	VF8.0	NM9.4

Marvel Comics: Apr, 1997 ($2.99, one-shot)

1   3.00

SPIDER-MAN: DEATH AND DESTINY
Marvel Comics: Aug, 2000 - No. 3, Oct, 2000 ($2.99, limited series)

1-3-Aftermath of the death of Capt. Stacy   3.00

SPIDER-MAN: FRIENDS AND ENEMIES
Marvel Comics: Jan, 1995 - No. 4, Apr, 1995 ($1.95, limited series)

1-4-Darkhawk, Nova & Speedball app.   2.25

SPIDER-MAN: FUNERAL FOR AN OCTOPUS
Marvel Comics: Mar, 1995 - No. 3, May, 1995 ($1.50, limited series)

1-3   2.25

SPIDER-MAN/ GEN 13
Marvel Comics: Nov, 1996 ($4.95, one-shot)

nn-Peter David-s/Stuart Immonen-a   5.00

SPIDER-MAN: HOBGOBLIN LIVES
Marvel Comics: Jan, 1997 - No. 3, Mar, 1997 ($2.50, limited series)

1-3-Wraparound-c   2.50
TPB (1/98, $14.99) r/#1-3 plus timeline   15.00

SPIDER-MAN: HOT SHOTS
Marvel Comics: Jan, 1996 ($2.95, one-shot)

nn-fold out posters by various, inc. Vess and Ross   3.00

SPIDER-MAN: LEGACY OF EVIL
Marvel Comics: June, 1996 ($3.95, one-shot)

1-Kurt Busiek script & Mark Texeira-c/a   4.00

SPIDER-MAN: LIFELINE
Marvel Comics: Apr, 2001 - No. 3, June, 2001 ($2.99, limited series)

1-3-Nicieza-s/Rude-c/a; The Lizard app.   3.00

SPIDER-MAN: MADE MEN
Marvel Comics: Aug, 1998 ($5.99, one-shot)

1-Spider-Man & Daredevil vs. Kingpin   6.00

SPIDER-MAN MAGAZINE
Marvel Comics: 1994 - No. 3, 1994 ($1.95, magazine)

1-3: 1-Contains 4 S-M promo cards & 4 X-Men Ultra Fleer cards; Spider-Man story by Romita, Sr.; X-Men story; puzzles & games. 2-Doc Octopus & X-Men stories   3.00

SPIDER-MAN: MAXIMUM CLONAGE
Marvel Comics: 1995 ($4.95)

Alpha #1-Acetate-c, Omega #1-Chromium-c.   5.00

SPIDER-MAN MEGAZINE
Marvel Comics: Oct, 1994 - No. 6, Mar, 1995 ($2.95, 100 pgs.)

1-6: 1-r/ASM #16,224,225, Marvel Team-Up #1   3.00

SPIDER-MAN: POWER OF TERROR
Marvel Comics: Jan, 1995 - No. 4, Apr, 1995 ($1.95, limited series)

1-4-Silvermane & Deathlok app.   2.25

SPIDER-MAN/PUNISHER: FAMILY PLOT
Marvel Comics: Feb, 1996 - No. 2, Mar, 1996 ($2.95, limited series)

1,2   3.00

SPIDER-MAN: REDEMPTION
Marvel Comics: Sept, 1996 - No. 4, Dec, 1996 ($1.50, limited series)

1-4: DeMatteis scripts; Zeck-a   2.25

SPIDER-MAN: REVENGE OF THE GREEN GOBLIN
Marvel Comics: Oct, 2000 - No. 3, Dec, 2000 ($2.99, limited series)

1-3-Frenz & Olliffe-a; continues in AS-M #25 & PP:S-M #25   3.00

SPIDER-MAN SAGA
Marvel Comics: Nov, 1991 - No. 4, Feb, 1992 ($2.95, limited series)

1-4: Gives history of Spider-Man: text & illustrations   3.00

SPIDER-MAN'S TANGLED WEB (Titled "Tangled Web" in indicia for #1-4)
Marvel Comics: Jun, 2001 - Present ($2.99)

1-3: "The Thousand" on-c; Ennis-s/McCrea-a/Fabry-c   3.00
4-"Severance Package" on-c; Rucka-s/Risso-a; Kingpin-c/app.   4.00
5,6-Flowers for Rhino; Milligan-s/Fegredo-a   3.00
7-9-Gentlemen's Agreement; Bruce Jones-s/Lee Weeks-a   3.00
TPB (10/01, $15.95) r/#1-6   16.00

SPIDER-MAN TEAM-UP
Marvel Comics: Dec, 1995 - No. 7, June, 1996 ($2.95)

1-7: 1-w/ X-Men. 2-w/Silver Surfer. 3-w/Fantastic Four. 4-w/Avengers. 5-Gambit & Howard the Duck-c/app. 7-Thunderbolts-c/app.   3.00

SPIDER-MAN: THE ARACHNIS PROJECT
Marvel Comics: Aug, 1994 - No. 6, Jan, 1995 ($1.75, limited series)

1-6-Venom, Styx, Stone & Jury app.   2.25

SPIDER-MAN: THE CLONE JOURNAL
Marvel Comics: Mar, 1995 ($2.95, one-shot)

1   3.00

SPIDER-MAN: THE FINAL ADVENTURE
Marvel Comics: Nov, 1995 - No. 4, Feb, 1996 ($2.95, limited series)

1-4: 1-Nicieza scripts; foil-c   3.00

SPIDER-MAN: THE JACKAL FILES
Marvel Comics: Aug, 1995 ($1.95, one-shot)

1   2.25

SPIDER-MAN: THE LOST YEARS
Marvel Comics: Aug, 1995-No. 3, Oct, 1995; No. 0, 1996 ($2.95/$3.95,lim. series)

0-(1/96, $3.95)-Reprints.   4.00
1-3-DeMatteis scripts, Romita, Jr.-c/a   3.00
NOTE: *Romita* c-0i. *Romita, Jr.* a-0r, 1-3p. c-0-3p. *Sharp* a-0r.

SPIDER-MAN: THE MANGA
Marvel Comics: Dec, 1997 - No. 31, June, 1999 ($3.99/$2.99, B&W, bi-weekly)

1-($3.99)-English translation of Japanese Spider-Man   4.00
2-31-($2.99)   3.00

SPIDER-MAN: THE MUTANT AGENDA
Marvel Comics: No. 0, Feb, 1994; No. 1, Mar, 1994 - No. 3, May, 1994 ($1.75, limited series)

0-(2/94, $1.25, 52 pgs.)-Crosses over w/newspaper strip; has empty pages to paste in newspaper strips; gives origin of Spidey   2.25
1-3: Beast & Hobgoblin app. 1-X-Men app.   2.25

SPIDER-MAN: THE MYSTERIO MANIFESTO (Listed as "Spider-Man and Mysterio" in indicia)
Marvel Comics: Jan, 2001 - No. 3, Mar, 2001 ($2.99, limited series)

1-3-Daredevil-c/app.; Weeks & McLeod-a   3.00

SPIDER-MAN: THE PARKER YEARS
Marvel Comics: Nov, 1995 ($2.50, one-shot)

1   2.50

SPIDER-MAN 2099 (See Amazing Spider-Man #365)
Marvel Comics: Nov, 1992 - No. 46, Aug, 1996 ($1.25/$1.50/$1.95)

1-(stiff-c)-Red foil stamped-c; begins origin of Miguel O'Hara (Spider-Man 2099); Leonardi/Williamson-c/a begins   3.00
1-2nd printing, 2-24,26-46: 2-Origin continued, ends #3. 4-Doom 2099 app. 13-Extra 16 pg. insert on Midnight Sons. 19-Bound-in trading card sheet. 35-Variant-c. 36-Two-c; Jae Lee-a. 37,38-Two-c. 46-The Vulture app; Mike McKone-a(p)   2.25
25-($2.25, 52 pgs.)-Newsstand edition   2.25
25-($2.95, 52 pgs.)-Deluxe edition w/embossed foil-c   3.00
Annual 1 (1994, $2.95, 68 pgs.)   3.00
Special 1 (1995, $3.95)   4.00
NOTE: *Chaykin* c-37. *Ron Lim* a(p)-18; c(p)-13, 16, 18. *Kelley Jones* c/a-9. *Leonardi/Williamson* a-1-8, 10-13, 15-17, 19, 20, 22-25; c-1-13, 15, 17-19, 20, 22-25, 35.

SPIDER-MAN 2099 MEETS SPIDER-MAN
Marvel Comics: 1995 ($5.95, one-shot)

nn-Peter David script; Leonardi/Williamson-c/a.   6.00

SPIDER-MAN UNIVERSE
Marvel Comics: Mar, 2000 - Present ($4.95/$3.99, reprints)

Spider-Man Unlimited #2 © MAR

Spider-Woman #2 © MAR

Spidey Super Stories #6 © MAR

	GD2.0	FN6.0	VF8.0	NM9.4
1-5-Reprints recent issues from the various Spider-Man titles				5.00
6,7-($3.99)				4.00

SPIDER-MAN UNLIMITED
Marvel Comics: May, 1993 - No. 22, Nov, 1998 ($3.95, quarterly, 68 pgs.)

1-Begin Maximum Carnage storyline, ends; Carnage-c/story				5.00
2-12: 2-Venom & Carnage-c/story; Lim-c/a(p) in #2-6. 10-Vulture app.				4.00
13-22: 13-Begin $2.99-c; Scorpion-c/app. 15-Daniel-c; Puma-c/app.				
19-Lizard-c/app. 20-Hannibal King and Lilith app. 21,22-Deodato-a				3.00

SPIDER-MAN UNLIMITED (Based on the TV animated series)
Marvel Comics: Dec, 1999 - No. 5, Apr, 2000 ($2.99/$1.99)

1-($2.99) Venom and Carnage app.				3.00
2-5: 2-($1.99) Green Goblin app.				2.25

SPIDER-MAN UNMASKED
Marvel Comics: Nov, 1996 ($5.95, one-shot)

nn-Art w/text				6.00

SPIDER-MAN: VENOM AGENDA
Marvel Comics: Jan, 1998 ($2.99, one-shot)

1-Hama-s/Lyle-c/a				3.00

SPIDER-MAN VS. DRACULA
Marvel Comics: Jan, 1994 ($1.75, 52 pgs., one-shot)

1-r/Giant-Size Spider-Man #1 plus new Matt Fox-a				2.25

SPIDER-MAN VS. WOLVERINE
Marvel Comics Group: Feb, 1987; V2#1, 1990 (68 pgs.)

1-Williamson-c/a(i); intro Charlemagne; death of Ned Leeds (old Hobgoblin)				
	2	6	13	20
V2#1 (1990, $4.95)-Reprints #1 (2/87)				5.00

SPIDER-MAN: WEB OF DOOM
Marvel Comics: Aug, 1994 - No. 3, Oct, 1994 ($1.75, limited series)

1-3				2.25

SPIDER-MAN: YEAR IN REVIEW
Marvel Comics: Feb, 2000 ($2.99)

1-Text recaps of 1999 issues				3.00

SPIDER REIGN OF THE VAMPIRE KING, THE (Also see The Spider)
Eclipse Books: 1992 - No. 3, 1992 ($4.95, limited series, coated stock, 52 pgs.)

Book One - Three: Truman scripts & painted-c				5.00

SPIDER'S WEB, THE (See G-8 and His Battle Aces)

SPIDER-WOMAN (Also see The Avengers #240, Marvel Spotlight #32, Marvel Super Heroes Secret Wars #7 & Marvel Two-In-One #29)
Marvel Comics Group: April, 1978 - No. 50, June, 1983 (New logo #47 on)

1-New complete origin & mask added	2	6	11	15
2-5,7-18,21-27,30,31,33-36,: 2-Excalibur app. 3,11,12-Brother Grimm app.				
13,15-The Shroud-c/s. 16-Sienkiewicz-a				5.00
6,19,20,28,29,32: 6-Morgan LeFay app. 6,19,32-Werewolf by Night-c/s.				
20,28,29-Spider-Man app. 32-Miller-c				6.00
37,38-X-Men x-over: 37-1st app. Siryn of X-Force; origin retold				
	1	3	6	8
39-49: 46-Kingpin app. 49-Tigra-c/story				4.00
50-(52 pgs.)-Death of Spider-Woman; photo-c	2	6	9	12
NOTE: Austin a-37i. Byrne c-26p. Infantino a-1-19. Layton c-19. Miller c-32p.				

SPIDER-WOMAN
Marvel Comics: Nov, 1993 - No. 4, Feb, 1994 ($1.75, mini-series)

V2#1-4: 1,2-Origin; U.S. Agent app.				2.25

SPIDER-WOMAN
Marvel Comics: July, 1999 - No. 18, Dec, 2000 ($2.99/$1.99/$2.25)

1-($2.99) Byrne-s/Sears-a				3.00
2-18: 2-11-($1.99). 2-Two covers. 12-Begin $2.25-c. 14-Nolan-a. 15-Capt. America-c/app.				2.25

SPIDEY SUPER STORIES (Spider-Man) (Also see Fireside Books)
Marvel/Children's TV Workshop: Oct, 1974 - No. 57, Mar, 1982 (35¢, no ads)

1-Origin (stories simplified for younger readers)	4	12	26	40
2-Kraven	2	6	15	22
3-10,15: 6-Iceman. 15-Storm-c/sty	2	6	11	16

	GD2.0	FN6.0	VF8.0	NM9.4
11-14,16-20: 19,20-Kirby-c	2	6	9	12
21-53: 24-Kirby-c. 31-Moondragon-c/story; Dr. Doom app. 33-Hulk. 34-Sub-				
Mariner. 38-F.F. 39-Thanos-c/story. 44-Vision. 45-Silver Surfer & Dr. Doom				
app.	1	4	7	10
54-57: 56-Battles Jack O'Lantern-c/sty (exactly one year after 1st app. in				
Machine Man #19)	2	6	11	15

SPIKE AND TYKE (See M.G.M.'s...)

SPIN & MARTY (TV) (Walt Disney's)(See Walt Disney Showcase #32)
Dell Publishing Co. (Mickey Mouse Club): No. 714, June, 1956 - No. 1082, Mar-May, 1960 (All photo-c)

Four Color 714 (#1)	12	36	84	160
Four Color 767,808 (#2,3)	9	27	63	120
Four Color 826 (#4)-Annette Funicello photo-c	24	72	168	310
5(3-5/58) - 9(6-8/59)	8	24	56	100
Four Color 1026,1082	8	24	56	100

SPINE-TINGLING TALES (Doctor Spektor Presents...)
Gold Key: May, 1975 - No. 4, Jan, 1976 (All 25¢ issues)

1-1st Tragg-r/Mystery Comics Digest #3	2	6	9	12
2-4: 2-Origin Ra-Ka-Tep-r/Mystery Comics Digest #1; Dr. Spektor #12. 3-All				
Durak-r issue; 4-Baron Tibor's 1st app.-r/Mystery Comics Digest #4;				
painted-c	1	3	6	8

SPINWORLD
Amaze Ink (Slave Labor Graphics): July, 1997 - No. 4, Jan, 1998 ($2.95/$3.95, B&W, mini-series)

1-3-Brent Anderson-a(p)				3.00
4-($3.95)				4.00

SPIRAL PATH, THE
Eclipse Comics: July, 1986 - No. 2 ($1.75, Baxter paper, limited series)

1,2				2.25

SPIRAL ZONE
DC Comics: Feb, 1988 - No. 4, May, 1988 ($1.00, mini-series)

1-4-Based on Tonka toys				2.25

SPIRIT, THE (Newspaper comics - see Promotional Comics section)

SPIRIT, THE (1st Series)(Also see Police Comics #11)
Quality Comics Group (Vital): 1944 - No. 22, Aug, 1950

nn(#1)- "Wanted Dead or Alive"	75	225	469	825
nn(#2)- "Crime Doesn't Pay"	43	129	257	450
nn(#3)- "Murder Runs Wild"	39	117	208	360
4,5-Flatfoot Burns begins, ends #22. 5-Wertham app.				
	31	93	165	285
6-10	26	78	136	235
11	23	69	121	210
12-17-Eisner-c. 19-Honeybun app.	35	105	185	320
18-21-Strip-r by Eisner; Eisner-c	40	120	232	400
22-Used by N.Y. Legis. Comm; classic Eisner-c	53	159	318	560
Super Reprint #11-r/Quality Spirit #19 by Eisner	3	10	23	35
Super Reprint #12-r/Spirit #17 by Fine; Sol Brodsky-c	3	10	23	35

SPIRIT, THE (2nd Series)
Fiction House Magazines: Spring, 1952 - No. 5, 1954

1-Not Eisner	40	120	232	400
2-Eisner-c/a(2)	40	120	220	380
3-Eisner/Grandenetti-c	33	99	174	300
4-Eisner/Grandenetti-c; Eisner-a	34	102	179	310
5-Eisner-c/a(4)	39	117	208	360

SPIRIT, THE
Harvey Publications: Oct, 1966 - No. 2, Mar, 1967 (Giant size, 25¢, 68 pgs.)

1-Eisner-c plus 9 new pgs.(origin Denny Colt, Take 3, plus 2 filler pgs.)				
(#3 was advertised, but never published)	7	21	53	85
2-Eisner-r plus 9 new pgs.(origin of the Octopus)	6	18	42	70

SPIRIT, THE (Underground)
Kitchen Sink Enterprises (Krupp Comics): Jan, 1973 - No. 2, Sept, 1973 (Black & White)

1-New Eisner-c & 4 pgs. new Eisner-a plus-r (titled Crime Convention)				
	2	6	11	15

The Spirit #22 © QUA

Spirit of the Tao #3 © TCOW

Spooky #1 © HARV

	GD2.0	FN6.0	VF8.0	NM9.4

2-New Eisner-c & 4 pgs. new Eisner-a plus-r (titled Meets P'Gell)

| | 2 | 6 | 13 | 20 |

SPIRIT, THE (Magazine)
Warren Publ. Co./Krupp Comic Works No. 17 on: 4/74 - No. 16, 10/76; No. 17, Winter, 1977 - No. 41, 6/83 (B&W w/color) (#6-14,16 are squarebound)

1-Eisner-r begin; 8 pg. color insert	3	9	21	32
2-5: 2-Powder Pouf-s; UFO-s. 4-Silk Satin-s	2	6	13	20
6-9,11-15: 7-All Ebony issue. 8-Female Foes issue. 8,12-Sand Seref-s.				
9-P'Gell & Octupus-s. 12-X-Mas issue	2	6	11	15
10-Giant Summer Special ($1.50)-Origin	2	6	15	22
16-Giant Summer Special ($1.50)-Olga Bustle-c/s	2	6	12	18
17,18(8/78): 17-Lady Luck-r	1	3	6	9
19-21-New Eisner-a. 20,21-Wood-r (#21-r/A DP on the Moon by Wood). 20-				
Outer Space-r	1	3	6	9
22-41: 22,23-Wood-r (#22-r/Mission the Moon by Wood). 28-r/last story				
(10/5/52). 30-(7/81)-Special Spirit Jam issue w/Caniff, Corben, Bolland,				
Byrne, Miller, Kurtzman, Rogers, Sienkiewicz-a & 40 others. 36-Begin Spirit				
Section-r; r/1st story (6/2/40) in color; new Eisner-c/a(18 pgs.)($2.95). 37-				
r/2nd story in color plus 18 pgs. new Eisner-a. 38-41: r/3rd - 6th stories in				
color. 41-Lady Luck Mr. Mystic in color	1	3	5	8
Special 1(1975)-All Eisner-a (mail only, full color)	4	12	30	50

NOTE: Covers pencilled/inked by Eisner only #1-9,12-16; painted by Eisner & Ken Kelly #10 & 11; painted by Eisner #17-up; one color story reprinted in #1-10. Austin a-30i. Byrne a-30p. Miller a-30p.

SPIRIT, THE
Kitchen Sink Enterprises: Oct, 1983 - No. 87, Jan, 1992 ($2.00, Baxter paper)

1-60: 1-Origin-r/12/23/45 Spirit Section. 2-r/ 1/20/46-2/10/46. 3-r/2/17/46-				
3/10/46. 4-r/3/17/46-4/7/46. 11-Last color issue. 54-r/section 2/19/50				4.00
61-87: 85-87-Reprint the Outer Space Spirit stories by Wood. 86-r/A DP on the				
Moon by Wood from 1952				4.00

SPIRIT JAM
Kitchen Sink Press: Aug, 1998 ($5.95, B&W, oversized, square-bound)

nn-Reprints Spirit (Magazine) #30 by Eisner & 50 others; and "Cerebus Vs. The Spirit" from Cerebus Jam #1 ... 6.00

SPIRIT, THE: THE NEW ADVENTURES
Kitchen Sink Press: 1997 - No. 8, Nov, 1998 ($3.50, anthology)

1-Moore-s/Gibbons-c/a				4.00
2-8: 2-Gaiman-s/Eisner-c. 3-Moore-s/Bolland-c/Moebius back-c. 4-Allred-s/a;				
Busiek-s/Anderson-a. 5-Chadwick-s/c/a(p); Nyberg-i. 6-S.Hampton-a				
Mandrake-a				3.50

SPIRIT: THE ORIGIN YEARS
Kitchen Sink Press: May, 1992 - No. 10, Dec, 1993 ($2.95, B&W)

| 1-10: 1-r/sections 6/2/40(origin)-6/23/40 (all 1940s) | | | | 3.00 |

SPIRITMAN (Also see Three Comics)
No publisher listed: No date (1944) (10¢)
(Triangle Sales Co. ad on back cover)

1-Three 16pg. Spirit sections bound together, (1944, 10¢, 52 pgs.)				
	21	63	110	190
2-Two Spirit sections (3/26/44, 4/2/44) bound together; by Lou Fine				
	19	57	99	165

SPIRIT OF THE BORDER (See Zane Grey & Four Color #197)
SPIRIT OF THE TAO
Image Comics (Top Cow): Jun, 1998 - No. 15, May, 2000 ($2.50)

Preview				5.00
1-14: 1-D-Tron-s/Tan & D-Tron-a				2.50
15-($4.95)				5.00

SPIRIT OF WONDER (Manga)
Dark Horse Comics: Apr, 1996 - No. 5, Aug, 1996 ($2.95, B&W, limited series)

| 1-5 | | | | 3.00 |

SPIRIT WORLD (Magazine)
National Periodical Publications: Fall, 1971 (B&W)

| 1-New Kirby-a; Neal Adams-c; poster inside | 6 | 18 | 42 | 70 |
| (1/2 price without poster) | | | | |

SPITFIRE

	GD2.0	FN6.0	VF8.0	NM9.4

Malverne Herald (Elliot)(J. R. Mahon): No. 132, 1944 (Aug) - No. 133, 1945
(Female undercover agent)

| 132,133: Both have Classics Gift Box ads on b/c with checklist to #20 | | | | |
| | 26 | 78 | 139 | 240 |

SPITFIRE AND THE TROUBLESHOOTERS
Marvel Comics: Oct, 1986 - No. 9, June, 1987 (Codename: Spitfire #10 on)

| 1-3,5-9 | | | | 2.25 |
| 4-McFarlane-a | | | | 3.00 |

SPITFIRE COMICS (Also see Double Up)
Harvey Publications: Aug, 1941 - No. 2, Oct, 1941 (Pocket size; 100 pgs.)

1-Origin The Clown, The Fly-Man, The Spitfire & The Magician From Bagdad				
	77	231	483	850
2-(Scarce)	70	210	438	775

SPLITTING IMAGE
Image Comics: Mar, 1993 - No. 2, 1993 ($1.95)

| 1,2-Simpson-c/a; parody comic | | | | 2.25 |

SPOOF
Marvel Comics Group: Oct, 1970; No. 2, Nov, 1972 - No. 5, May, 1973

1-Infinity-c; Dark Shadows-c & parody	2	6	13	20
2-5: 2-Beatles, Osmond's, Jackson 5, David Cassidy, Nixon & Agnew-c.				
5-Rod Serling, Woody Allen, Ted Kennedy-c	2	6	9	12

SPOOK (Formerly Shock Detective Cases)
Star Publications: No. 22, Jan, 1953 - No. 30, Oct, 1954

22-Sgt. Spook-r; acid in face story; hanging-c	40	120	220	380
23,25,27: 25-Jungle Lil-r. 27-Two Sgt. Spook-r	29	87	153	265
24-Used in SOTI, pgs. 182,183-r/Inside Crime #2; Transvestism story				
	30	90	159	275
26,28-30: 26-Disbrow-a. 28,29-Rulah app. 29-Jo-Jo app. 30-Disbrow-c/a(2); only				
Star-c	29	87	153	265

NOTE: L. B. Cole covers-all issues except #30; a-28(1 pg.). Disbrow a-26(2), 28, 29(2), 30(2); No. 30 r/Blue Bolt Weird Tales #114.

SPOOK COMICS
Baily Publications/Star: 1946

| 1-Mr. Lucifer story | 31 | 93 | 168 | 290 |

SPOOKY (The Tuff Little Ghost; see Casper The Friendly Ghost)
Harvey Publications: 11/55 - 139, 11/73; No. 140, 7/74 - No. 155, 3/77; No. 156, 12/77 - No. 158, 4/78; No. 159, 9/78; No. 160, 10/79; No. 161, 9/80

1-Nightmare begins (see Casper #19)	37	111	278	500
2	19	57	134	240
3-10(1956-57)	11	33	77	130
11-20(1957-58)	6	18	42	70
21-40(1958-59)	4	12	30	50
41-60	3	10	23	35
61-80,100	3	9	17	26
81-99	2	6	15	22
101-120	2	6	11	14
121-126,133-140	1	4	7	10
127-132: All 52 pg. Giants	2	6	11	16
141-161	1	3	5	7

SPOOKY
Harvey Comics: Nov, 1991 - No. 4, Sept, 1992 ($1.00/$1.25)

1				4.00
2-4: 3-Begin $1.25-c				3.00
...Digest 1-3 (10/92, 6/93, 10/93, $1.75, 100 pgs.)-Casper, Wendy, etc.				4.00

SPOOKY HAUNTED HOUSE
Harvey Publications: Oct, 1972 - No. 15, Feb, 1975

1	3	9	21	32
2-5	2	6	11	16
6-10	1	4	7	10
11-15	1	3	6	8

SPOOKY MYSTERIES
Your Guide Publ. Co.: No date (1946) (10¢)

| 1-Mr. Spooky, Super Snooper, Pinky, Girl Detective app. | | | | |
| | 20 | 60 | 105 | 175 |

Sports Action #14 © MAR

Spunky #1 © STD

Spyboy #1 © DH

| | GD2.0 | FN6.0 | VF8.0 | NM9.4 | | | GD2.0 | FN6.0 | VF8.0 | NM9.4 |

SPOOKY SPOOKTOWN
Harvey Publ.: 9/61; No. 2, 9/62 - No. 52, 12/73; No. 53, 10/74 - No. 66, 12/76

1-Casper, Spooky; 68 pgs. begin	16	48	110	190
2	8	24	58	95
3-5	5	15	38	60
6-10	4	12	29	45
11-20	3	9	21	32
21-39: 39-Last 68 pg. issue	3	9	17	25
40-45: All 52 pgs.	2	6	11	16
46-66: 61-Hot Stuff/Spooky team-up story	1	3	6	8

SPORT COMICS (Becomes True Sport Picture Stories #5 on)
Street & Smith Publications: Oct, 1940 (No mo.) - No. 4, Nov, 1941

1-Life story of Lou Gehrig	55	165	330	575
2	31	93	165	285
3,4	27	81	142	245

SPORT LIBRARY (See Charlton Sport Library)

SPORTS ACTION (Formerly Sport Stars)
Marvel/Atlas Comics (ACI No. 2,3/SAI No. 4-14): No. 2, Feb, 1950 - No. 14, Sept, 1952

2-Powell painted-c; George Gipp life story	41	123	246	425
1-(nd,no price, no publ., 52pgs, #1 on-c; blank inside-c				
(giveaway?)	22	66	116	195
3-Everett-a	24	72	127	220
4-11,14: Weiss-a	22	66	116	195
12,13: 12-Everett-a. 13-Krigstein-a	24	72	127	215

NOTE: Title may have changed after No. 3, to Crime Must Lose No. 4 on, due to publisher change. Sol Brodsky c-4-7, 13, 14. Maneely c-3, 8-11.

SPORT STARS
Parents' Magazine Institute (Sport Stars): Feb-Mar, 1946 - No. 4, Aug-Sept, 1946 (Half comic, half photo magazine)

1- "How Tarzan Got That Way" story of Johnny Weissmuller				
	40	120	220	380
2-Baseball greats	27	81	142	245
3,4	24	72	127	215

SPORT STARS (Becomes Sports Action #2 on)
Marvel Comics (ACI): Nov, 1949 (52 pgs.)

1-Knute Rockne; painted-c	43	129	257	450

SPORT THRILLS (Formerly Dick Cole; becomes Jungle Thrills #16)
Star Publications: No. 11, Nov, 1950 - No. 15, Nov, 1951

11-Dick Cole begins, ends #13?; Ted Williams & Ty Cobb life stories	31	93	165	285
12-Joe DiMaggio, Phil Rizzuto stories & photos on-c; L.B. Cole-c/a	25	75	130	225
13-15-All L. B. Cole-c. 13-Jackie Robinson, Pee Wee Reese stories & photo				
on-c. 14-Johnny Weissmuler life story	25	75	130	225
Accepted Reprint #11 (#15 on-c, nd); L.B. Cole-c	9	27	49	70
Accepted Reprint #12 (nd); L.B. Cole-c; Joe DiMaggio & Phil Rizzuto life				
stories-r/#12	9	27	49	70

SPOTLIGHT (TV) (newsstand sales only)
Marvel Comics Group: Sept, 1978 - No. 4, Mar, 1979 (Hanna-Barbera)

1-Huckleberry Hound, Yogi Bear; Shaw-a	3	9	20	30
2,4: 2-Quick Draw McGraw, Augie Doggie, Snooper & Blabber. 4-Magilla				
Gorilla, Snagglepuss	2	6	13	20
3-The Jetsons; Yakky Doodle	3	9	20	30

SPOTLIGHT COMICS (Becomes Red Seal Comics #14 on?)
Harry 'A' Chesler (Our Army, Inc.): Nov, 1944 - No. 3, 1945

1-The Black Dwarf (cont'd in Red Seal?), The Veiled Avenger, & Barry Kuda				
begin; Tuska-a	64	192	398	700
2	55	165	331	580
3-Injury to eye story (reprinted from Scoop #3)	55	165	341	600

SPOTTY THE PUP (Becomes Super Pup #4, see Television Puppet Show)
Avon Periodicals/Realistic Comics: No. 2, Oct-Nov, 1953 - No. 3, Dec-Jan, 1953-54 (Also see Funny Tunes)

2,3	6	18	29	40
nn (1953, Realistic-r)	4	9	14	18

SPUNKY (...Junior Cowboy)(...Comics #2 on)
Standard Comics: April, 1949 - No. 7, Nov, 1951

1-Text illos by Frazetta	11	33	55	90
2-Text illos by Frazetta	9	27	49	70
3-7	6	18	29	40

SPUNKY THE SMILING SPOOK
Ajax/Farrell (World Famous Comics/Four Star Comic Corp.): Aug, 1957 - No. 4, May, 1958

1-Reprints from Frisky Fables	10	30	55	80
2-4	6	18	30	42

SPY AND COUNTERSPY (Becomes Spy Hunters #3 on)
American Comics Group: Aug-Sept, 1949 - No. 2, Oct-Nov, 1949 (52 pgs.)

1-Origin, 1st app. Jonathan Kent, Counterspy	27	81	145	250
2	17	51	88	150

SPYBOY
Dark Horse Comics: Oct, 1999 - Present ($2.50/$2.95/$2.99)

1-6-Peter David-s/Pop Mhan-a. 7,8-Meglia-a. 9-17-Mhan-a				3.00

SPY CASES (Formerly The Kellys)
Marvel/Atlas Comics (Hercules Publ.): No. 26, Sept, 1950 - No. 19, Oct, 1953

26 (#1)	24	72	127	215
27(#2),28(#3, 2/51): 27-Everett-a; bondage-c	14	42	72	120
4(4/51) - 7,9,10	12	36	61	100
8-A-Bomb-c/story	14	42	72	120
11-19: 10-14-War format	10	30	55	80

NOTE: Sol Brodsky c-1-5, 8, 9, 11-14, 17, 18. Maneely a-8; c-7, 10. Tuska a-7.

SPY FIGHTERS
Marvel/Atlas Comics (CSI): March, 1951 - No. 15, July, 1953
(Cases from official records)

1-Clark Mason begins; Tuska-a; Brodsky-c	25	75	130	225
2-Tuska-a	14	42	72	120
3-13: 3-5-Brodsky-a. 7-Heath-c	12	36	61	105
14,15-Pakula-a(3), Ed Win-a. 15-Brodsky-c	13	39	66	110

SPY-HUNTERS (Formerly Spy & Counterspy)
American Comics Group: No. 3, Dec-Jan, 1949-50 - No. 24, June-July, 1953
(#3-14: 52 pgs.)

3-Jonathan Kent continues, ends #10	24	72	127	215
4-10: 4,8,10-Starr-a	14	42	72	120
11-15,17-22,24: 18-War-c begin. 21-War-c/stories begin	10	30	55	85
16-Williamson-a (9 pgs.)	16	48	83	140
23-Graphic torture, injury to eye panel	21	63	110	185

NOTE: Drucker a-12. Whitney a-many issues; c-7, 8, 10-12, 15, 16.

SPYMAN (Top Secret Adventures on cover)
Harvey Publications (Illustrated Humor): Sept, 1966 - No. 3, Feb, 1967 (12¢)

1-Origin and 1st app. of Spyman. Steranko-a(p)-1st pro work; 1 pg. Neal				
Adams ad; Tuska-c/a, Crandall-a(i)	6	18	45	75
2-Simon-c; Steranko-a(p)	4	12	29	45
3-Simon-c	4	12	26	40

SPY SMASHER (See Mighty Midget, Whiz & Xmas Comics) (Also see Crime Smasher)
Fawcett Publications: Fall, 1941 - No. 11, Feb, 1943

1-Spy Smasher begins; silver metallic-c	350	1050	2188	4200
2-Raboy-c	164	492	1023	1800
3,4: 3-Bondage-c. 4-Irvin Steinberg-c	111	332	694	1225
5-7: Raboy-a; 6-Raboy-c/a. 7-Part photo-c (movie)	100	300	625	1100
8,11: War-c	80	240	500	875
9-Hitler, Tojo, Mussolini-c	93	279	581	1025
10-Hitler-c	89	267	556	975

SPY THRILLERS (Police Badge No. 479 #5)
Atlas Comics (PrPI): Nov, 1954 - No. 4, May, 1955

1-Brodsky c-1,2	22	66	110	195
2-Last precode (1/55)	13	39	66	110
3,4	10	30	55	85

Squee #4 © SLG

Star #1 © Highbrow/Image

Star Comics #1 © CEN

ST

	GD2.0	FN6.0	VF8.0	NM9.4

SQUADRON SUPREME (Also see Marvel Graphic Novel)
Marvel Comics Group: Aug, 1985 - No. 12, Aug, 1986 (Maxi-series)

1-Double size				3.00
2-12				2.50
TPB ($24.99) r/#1-12; Alex Ross painted-c; printing inks contain some of the cremated remains of late writer Mark Gruenwald				25.00
TPB-2nd printing ($24.99): Inks contain no ashes				25.00

SQUADRON SUPREME: NEW WORLD ORDER
Marvel Comics: Sept, 1998 ($5.99, one-shot)

1-Wraparound-c; Kaminski-s				6.00

SQUALOR
First Comics: Dec, 1989 - Aug, 1990 ($2.75, limited series)

1-4- Sutton-a				2.75

SQUEE
Slave Labor Graphics: Apr, 1997 - No. 4, May, 1998 ($2.95, B&W)

1-4- Jhonen Vasquez-s/a in all				3.00

SQUEEKS (Also see Boy Comics)
Lev Gleason Publications: Oct, 1953 - No. 5, June, 1954

1-Funny animal; Biro-c; Crimebuster's pet monkey "Squeeks" begins	8	24	45	65
2-Biro-c	5	15	24	32
3-5- 3-Biro-c	5	14	21	28

S.R. BISSETTE'S SPIDERBABY COMIX
SpiderBaby Grafix: Aug, 1996 - No. 2 ($3.95, B&W, magazine size)

Preview-(8/96, $3.95)-Graphic violence & nudity; Laurel & Hardy app.				4.00
1,2				4.00

S.R. BISSETTE'S TYRANT
SpiderBaby Grafix: Sept, 1994 - No. 4 ($2.95, B&W)

1-4				4.00

STAINLESS STEEL RAT
Eagle Comics: Oct, 1985 - No. 6, Mar, 1986 (Limited series)

1 (52 pgs.; $2.25-c)				3.00
2-6 ($1.50)				2.25

STALKER (Also see All Star Comics 1999 and crossover issues)
National Periodical Publications: June-July, 1975 - No. 4, Dec-Jan, 1975-76

1-Origin & 1st app; Ditko/Wood-c/a	2	6	9	12
2-4-Ditko/Wood-c/a	1	3	5	7

STALKERS
Marvel Comics (Epic Comics): Apr, 1990 - No. 12, Mar, 1991 ($1.50)

1-12- 1-Chadwick-c				2.25

STAMP COMICS (Stamps... on-c; Thrilling Adventures In...#8)
Youthful Magazines/Stamp Comics, Inc.: Oct, 1951 - No. 7, Oct, 1952

1-(15¢) ('Stamps' on indicia no. 1-3,5,7)	30	90	159	275
2	17	51	88	150
3-6- 3,4-Kiefer, Wildey-a	15	45	77	130
7-Roy Krenkel (4 pgs.)	19	57	99	165

NOTE: Promotes stamp collecting; gives stories behind various commemorative stamps. No. 2, 10¢ printed over 15¢ c-price. *Kiefer* a-1-7. *Kirkel* a-1-6. *Napoli* a-2-4, 7.

STANLEY & HIS MONSTER (Formerly The Fox & the Crow)
National Periodical Publ.: No. 109, Apr-May, 1968 - No. 112, Oct-Nov, 1968

109-112	3	9	19	28

STANLEY & HIS MONSTER
DC Comics: Feb, 1993 - No. 4, May, 1993 ($1.50, limited series)

1-4				2.25

STAN SHAW'S BEAUTY & THE BEAST
Dark Horse Comics: Nov, 1993 ($4.95, one-shot)

1				5.00

STAR
Image Comics (Highbrow Entertainment): June, 1995 - No. 4, Oct, 1995 ($2.50, limited series)

1-4				2.50

STARBLAST
Marvel Comics: Jan, 1994 - No. 4, Apr, 1994 ($1.75, limited series)

1-4- 1-($2.00, 52 pgs.)-Nova, Quasar, Black Bolt; painted-c				2.25

STAR BLAZERS
Comico: Apr, 1987 - No. 4, July, 1987 ($1.75, limited series)

1-4				3.00

STAR BLAZERS
Comico: 1989 ($1.95/$2.50, limited series)

1-5- Steacy wraparound painted-c on all				3.00

STAR BLAZERS (The Magazine of Space Battleship Yamato)
Argo Press: No. 0, Aug, 1995 - No. 3, Dec, 1995 ($2.95)

0-3				3.00

STAR BRAND
Marvel Comics (New Universe): Oct, 1986 - No. 19, May, 1989 (75¢/$1.25)

1-15- 14-begin $1.25-c				2.25
16-19-Byrne story & art; low print run				3.00
Annual 1 (10/87)				2.25

STARCHILD
Tailspin Press: 1992 - No. 12($2.25/$2.50, B&W)

1,2-('92),0(4/93),3-12: 0-Illos by Chadwick, Eisner, Sim, M. Wagner. 3-(7/93). 4-(11/93). 6-(2/94)				3.00

STARCHILD: MYTHOPOLIS
Image Comics: No. 0, July, 1997 - No. 4, Apr, 1998 ($2.95, B&W, limited series)

0-4-James Owen-s/a				3.00

STAR COMICS
Ultem Publ. (Harry `A' Chesler)/Centaur Publications: Feb, 1937 - V2#7 (No. 23), June, 1939 (#1-6: large size)

V1#1-Dan Hastings (s/f) begins	168	505	1050	1850
2	77	231	483	850
3-6 (#6, 9/37): 4,5-Little Nemo-c/stories	68	205	426	750
7-9: 8-Severed head centerspread; Impy & Little Nemo by Winsor McCay Jr, Popeye app. by Bob Wood; Mickey Mouse & Popeye app. as toys in Santa's bag on-c; X-Mas-c	61	182	381	675
10 (1st Centaur; 3/38)-Impy by Winsor McCay Jr, Don Marlow by Guardineer begins	84	253	525	925
11-15-Jack Cole comic-a, 1 pg. (4/38)	61	182	381	675
12-15: 12-Riders of the Golden West begins; Little Nemo app. 15-Speed Silvers by Gustavson & The Last Pirate by Burgos begins	55	165	331	580
16 (12/38)-The Phantom Rider & his horse Thunder begins, ends V2#6	55	165	331	600
V2#1(#17, 2/39)-Phantom Rider-c (only non-funny-c)	57	171	356	630
2-7(#18-23): 2-Diana Deane by Tarpe Mills app. 3-Drama of Hollywood by Mills begins. 7-Jungle Queen app.	50	150	300	525

NOTE: *Biro* c-6, 9, 10. *Burgos* a-15, 16, V2#1-7. *Ken Ernst* a-10, 12, 14. *Filchock* c-15, 18, 22. *Gill Fox* c-14, 19. *Guardineer* a-6, 8-14. *Gustavson* a-13-16, V2#1-7. *Winsor McCay* c-4, 5. *Tarpe Mills* a-15, V2#1-7. *Schwab* a-10, 12, 13; c-7, 8. *Bob Wood* a-10, 12, 13.

STAR COMICS MAGAZINE
Marvel Comics (Star Comics): Dec, 1986 - No. 13, 1988 ($1.50, digest-size)

1,9-Spider-Man-c/s	2	6	9	12
2-8-Heathcliff, Ewoks, Top Dog, Madballs-r in #1-13	1	3	6	8
10-13	1	4	7	10

S.T.A.R. CORPS
DC Comics: Nov, 1993 - No. 6, Apr, 1994 ($1.50, limited series)

1-6: 1,2-Austin-c(i). 1-Superman app.				2.25

STAR CROSSED
DC Comics (Helix): June, 1997 - No. 3, Aug, 1997 ($2.50, limited series)

1-3-Matt Howarth-s/a				2.50

STARDUST (See Neil Gaiman and Charles Vess' Stardust)

STAR FEATURE COMICS
I. W. Enterprises: 1963

Reprint #9-Stunt-Man Stetson-r/Feat. Comics #141	2	6	10	14

Star Hunters #5 © DC

Starlet O'Hara in Hollywood #2 © STD

Starman #80 © DC

	GD2.0	FN6.0	VF8.0	NM9.4

STARFIRE (Not the Teen Titans character)
National Periodical Publ./DC Comics: Aug-Sept, 1976 - No. 8, Oct-Nov, 1977

		2	6	9	12
1-Origin (CCA stamp fell off cover art; so it was approved by code)					
2-8		1	3	5	7

STARGATE (Movie)
Entity Comics: July, 1996 - No. 4, Oct, 1996 ($2.95, limited series)

1-4: Based on film	3.00
1-4-($3.50): Special Edition foil-c	3.50

STARGATE: DOOMSDAY WORLD (Movie)
Entity Comics: Nov, 1996 - No. 3, Jan, 1997 ($2.95, limited series)

1-3	3.00
1-3-($3.50)-Foil-c	3.50

STARGATE: ONE NATION UNDER RA (Movie)
Entity Comics: Apr, 1997 ($2.75, B&W, one-shot)

1-($2.75)	3.00
1-($3.50)-Foil-c	3.50

STARGATE: REBELLION (Movie)
Entity Comics: May/June, 1997 - No. 3, Nov, 1997 ($2.75, B&W, limited series)

1-3	3.00
1-3-($3.50)-Gold foil-c	3.50

STARGATE: THE NEW ADVENTURES COLLECTION (Movie)
Entity Comics: Dec, 1997 ($5.95, B&W)

1-Regular and photo-c	6.00

STARGATE: UNDERWORLD (Movie)
Entity Comics: May, 1997 ($2.75, B&W, one-shot)

1	3.00

STAR HUNTERS (See DC Super Stars #16)
National Periodical Publ./DC Comics: Oct-Nov, 1977 - No. 7, Oct-Nov, 1978

1,7: 1-Newton-a(p). 7-44 pgs.	1	4	7	10
2-6				6.00

NOTE: **Buckler** a-4-7p; c-1-7p. **Layton** a-1-5i; c-1-6i. **Nasser** a-3p. **Sutton** a-6i.

STARJAMMERS (See X-Men Spotlight on Starjammers)

STARJAMMERS (Also see Uncanny X-Men)
Marvel Comics: Oct, 1995 - No. 4, Jan, 1996 ($2.95, limited series)

1-4: Foil-c; Ellis scripts	3.00

STARK TERROR
Stanley Publications: Dec, 1970 - No. 5, Aug, 1971 (B&W, magazine, 52 pgs.)
(1950s Horror reprints, including pre-code)

1-Bondage, torture-c	4	12	30	50
2-4 (Gillmor/Aragon-r)	3	9	20	30
5 (ACG-r)	3	9	17	25

STARLET O'HARA IN HOLLYWOOD (Teen-age) (Also see Cookie)
Standard Comics: Dec, 1948 - No. 4, Sept, 1949

1-Owen Fitzgerald-a in all	20	60	105	180
2	14	42	72	120
3,4	12	36	61	100

STAR-LORD THE SPECIAL EDITION (Also see Marvel Comics Super Special #10, Marvel Premiere & Preview and Marvel Spotlight V2#6,7)
Marvel Comics Group: Feb, 1982 (one-shot, direct sales)
(1st Baxter paper comic)

1-Byrne/Austin-a; Austin-c; 8 pgs. of new-a by Golden (p); Dr. Who story by Dave Gibbons; 1st deluxe format comic	6.00

STARLORD
Marvel Comics: Dec, 1996 - No. 3, Feb, 1997 ($2.50, limited series)

1-3-Timothy Zahn-s	2.50

STARLORD MEGAZINE
Marvel Comics: Nov, 1996 ($2.95, one-shot)

1-Reprints w/preview of new series	3.00

STARMAN (1st Series) (Also see Justice League & War of the Gods)
DC Comics: Oct, 1988 - No. 45, Apr, 1992 ($1.00)

1-25,29-45: 1-Origin. 4-Intro The Power Elite. 9,10,34-Batman app. 14-Superman app. 17-Power Girl app. 38-War of the Gods x-over. 42-Lobo cameo. 42-45-Eclipso-c/stories (#43,44 with Lobo)	2.50
26-1st app. David Knight (G.A.Starman's son).	5.00
27,28: 27-Starman (David Knight) app. 28-Starman disguised as Superman; leads into Superman #50	4.00

STARMAN (2nd Series) (Also see The Golden Age, Showcase 95 #12, Showcase 96 #4,5)
DC Comics : No. 0, Oct, 1994 - No. 80, Aug, 2001 ($1.95/$2.25/$2.50)

0,1: 0-James Robinson scripts, Tony Harris-c/a(p) & Wade Von Grawbadger-a(i) begins; Sins of the Father storyline begins, ends #3; 1st app. new Starman (Jack Knight); reintro of the G.A. Mist & G.A. Shade; 1st app. Nash; David Knight dies	1	3	5	7
2-7: 2-Reintro Charity from Forbidden Tales of Dark Mansion. 3-Reintro/2nd app "Blue" Starman (1st app. in 1st Issue Special #12); Will Payton app. (both cameos). 5-David Knight app. 6-The Shade "Times Past" story; Teddy Kristiansen-a. 7-The Black Pirate cameo				4.00
8-17: 8-Begin $2.25-c. 10-1st app. new Mist (Nash). 11-JSA "Times Past" story; Matt Smith-a. 12-16-Sins of the Child. 17-The BlackPirate app.				4.00
18-37: 18-G.A. Starman "Times Past" story; Watkiss-a. 19-David Knight app. 20-23-G.A. Sandman app. 24-26-Demon Quest; all 3 covers make-up triptych. 33-36-Batman-c/app. 37-David Knight and deceased JSA members app.				3.00
38-49,51-56: 38-Nash vs. Justice League Europe. 39,40-Crossover w/ Power of Shazam! #35,36; Bulletman app. 42-Demon-c/app. 43-JLA-c/app. 44-Phantom Lady-c/app. 46-Gene Ha-a. 51-Jor-el app. 52,53-Adam Strange-c/app.				2.50
50-($3.95) Gold foil logo on-c; Star Boy (LSH) app.				3.00
57-79: 57-62-Painted covers by Harris and Alex Ross. 72-Death of Ted Knight. 73-Eulogy. 74-Scalphunter flashback; Heath-a. 75-Superman-c/app.				2.50
80-($3.95) Final issue; cover by Harris & Robinson				4.00
#1,000,000 (11/98) 853rd Century x-over; Snejdberg-a				2.50
Annual 1 (1996, $3.50)-Legends of the Dead Earth story; Prince Gavyn & G.A. Starman stories; J.H. Williams III, Bret Blevins, Craig Hamilton-c/a(p)				4.00
Annual 2 (1997, $3.95)-Pulp Heroes story;				4.00
...80 Page Giant (1/99, $4.95) Harris-c				5.00
...Secret Files 1 (4/98, $4.95)-Origin stories and profile pages				5.00
...The Mist (6/98, $1.95) Girlfrenzy; Mary Marvel app.				2.50
Infernal Devices-($17.95, TPB)-r/#29-35,37,38				18.00
Night and Day-($14.95, TPB)-r/#7-10,12-16				15.00
Sins of the Father-($12.95, TPB)-r/#0-5				13.00
Times Past-($17.95, TPB)-r/stories of other Starmen				18.00

STARMASTERS
Americomics: Mar, 1984 ($1.50, one-shot)

1-Origin The Women of W.O.S.P. & Breed	3.00

STAR PRESENTATION, A (Formerly My Secret Romance #1,2; Spectacular Stories #4 on) (Also see This Is Suspense)
Fox Features Syndicate (Hero Books): No. 3, May, 1950

3-Dr. Jekyll & Mr. Hyde by Wood & Harrison (reprinted in Startling Terror Tales #10); "The Repulsing Dwarf" by Wood; Wood-c	55	165	331	580

STAR QUEST COMIX (Warren Presents... on cover)
Warren Publications: Oct, 1978 ($1.50, B&W magazine, 84 pgs., square-bound)

1-Corben, Maroto, Neary-a; Ken Kelly-c; Star Wars	2	6	9	12

STAR RAIDERS (See DC Graphic Novel #1)

STAR RANGER (Cowboy Comics #13 on)
Ultem Publ./Centaur Publ.: Feb, 1937 - No. 12, May, 1938 (Large size: No. 1-6)

1-(1st Western comic)-Ace & Deuce, Air Plunder; Creig Flessel-a	182	546	1136	2000
2	82	246	511	900
3-6	73	219	455	800
7-9: 8(12/37)-Christmas-c; Air Patrol, Gold coast app.; Gardineer centerfold	55	165	341	600
V2#10 (1st Centaur; 3/38)	84	253	525	925
11,12	64	192	398	700

NOTE: **J. Cole** a-10, 12; c-12. **Ken Ernst** a-11. **Gill Fox** a-8(illo), 9, 10. **Guardineer** a-1, 3, 6, 7, 8(illos), 9, 10, 12. **Gustavson** a-8-10, 12. **Fred Schwab** a-2-11. **Bob Wood** a-8-10.

STAR RANGER FUNNIES (Formerly Cowboy Comics)

Star Ranger #8 © CEN

Stars and S.T.R.I.P.E. #0 © DC

Star Spangled Comics #7 © DC

	GD2.0	FN6.0	VF8.0	NM9.4

	GD2.0	FN6.0	VF8.0	NM9.4

Centaur Publications: V1#15, Oct, 1938 - V2#5, Oct, 1939

V1#15-Lyin Lou, Ermine, Wild West Junior, The Law of Caribou County by Eisner, Cowboy Jake, The Plugged Dummy, Spurs by Gustavson, Red Coat, Two Buckaroos & Trouble Hunters begin	98	294	613	1075
V2#1 (1/39)	73	219	455	800
2-5: 2-Night Hawk by Gustavson. 4-Kit Carson app.				
	61	182	381	675

NOTE: *Jack Cole a-V2#1, 3; c-V2#1. Filchock c-V2#2, 3. Guardineer a-V2#3. Gustavson a-V2#2. Pinajian c/a-V2#5.*

STAR REACH
Star Reach Publ.: Apr, 1974 - No. 18 (B&W, #12-15 w/color)

1-(75¢, 52 pgs.) Art by Starlin, Simonson. Chaykin-c/a; origin Death. Cody Starbuck-sty	2	6	11	15
1-2nd, 3th, and 4th printings ($1.00-$1.50-c)				6.00
2-11: 2-Adams, Giordano-a; 1st Stephanie Starr-c/s. 3-1st Linda Lovecraft. 4-1st Sherlock Duck. 5-1st Gideon Faust by Chaykin. 6-Elric-c. 7-BWS-c.				
9-14-Sacred & Profane-c/s by Steacy. 11-Samurai	1	3	5	7
2-2nd printing				4.00
12-15 (44 pgs.): 12-Zelazny-s. Nasser-a, Brunner-c	1	4	7	10
16-18-Magazine size: 17-Poe's Raven-c/s	1	3	6	9

NOTE: *Adams c-2. Bonivert a-17. Brunner a-3,5; c-3,10,12. Chaykin a-1,4,5; c-1(1st ed),4,5; back-c-1(2nd,3rd,4th ed). Gene Day a-6,8,9,11,15. Friedrich s-2,3,8,10. Gasbarri a-7. Gilbert a-9,12. Giordano a-2. Gould a-6. Hirota/Mukaide s/a-7. Jones a-6. Konz a-17. Leialoha a-3,4,6-i, 13,15; c-13,15. Lyda a-6,12-15. Marrs a-2-5,7,10,14,15,16,18; c-18. Mukaide a-18. Nasser a-12. Nino a-6. Russell a-8,10; c-8. Dave Sim a-7; lettering-9. Simonson a-1. Skeates a-1,2. Starlin a-1(x2), 2(x2); back-c-1(1st ed); c-1(2nd,3rd,4th ed). Barry Smith a-1. Staton a-5,6. Steacy a-8-14; c-9,11,14,16. Vosburg a-2-5,7,10. Wenzel a-2-5,8. Nudity panels in most. Wraparound-c: 3-5,7-11,13-16,18.*

STAR REACH CLASSICS
Eclipse Comics: Mar, 1984 - No. 6, Aug, 1984 ($1.50, Baxter paper)

1-6: 1-Neal Adams-r/Star Reach #1		3.00

NOTE: *Dave Sim a-1. Starlin a-1.*

STARR FLAGG, UNDERCOVER GIRL (See Undercover...)

STARRIORS
Marvel Comics: Aug, 1984 - Feb, 1985 (Limited series) (Based on Tomy toys)

1-4		3.00

STARS AND S.T.R.I.P.E. (Also see JSA)
DC Comics: July, 1999 - No. 14, Sept, 2000 ($2.95/$2.50)

0-($2.95) Moder and Weston-a; Starman app.		3.00
1-Johns and Robinson-s/Moder-a; origin new Star Spangled Kid		2.50
2-14: 4-Marvel Family app. 9-Seven Soldiers of Victory-c/app.		2.50

STARS AND STRIPES COMICS
Centaur Publications: No. 2, May, 1941 - No. 6, Dec, 1941

2(#1)-The Shark, The Iron Skull, A-Man, Mighty Man, Minimidget begin; The Voice & Dash Dartwell, the Human Meteor, Reef Kinkaid app.; Gustavson Flag-c	223	669	1394	2450
3-Origin Dr. Synthe; The Black Panther app.	125	375	781	1375
4-Origin/1st app. The Stars and Stripes; injury to eye-c				
	111	332	694	1225
5(#5 on cover & inside)	76	229	475	840
5(#6)-(#5 on cover, #6 on inside)	76	229	475	840

NOTE: *Gustavson c/a-3. Myron Strauss c-4, 5(#5), 5(#6).*

STAR SEED (Formerly Powers That Be)
Broadway Comics: No. 7, 1996 - No. 9 ($2.95)

7-9		3.00

STARSHIP TROOPERS
Dark Horse Comics: 1997 - No. 2, 1997 ($2.95, limited series)

1,2-Movie adaption		3.00

STARSHIP TROOPERS: BRUTE CREATIONS
Dark Horse Comics: 1997 ($2.95, one-shot)

1		3.00

STARSHIP TROOPERS: DOMINANT SPECIES
Dark Horse Comics: Aug, 1998 - No. 4, Nov, 1998 ($2.95, limited series)

1-4-Strnad-s/Bolton-c		3.00

STARSHIP TROOPERS: INSECT TOUCH

Dark Horse Comics: 1997 - No. 3, 1997 ($2.95, limited series)

1-3		3.00

STAR SLAMMERS (See Marvel Graphic Novel #6)
Malibu Comics (Bravura): May, 1994 - No. 4, Aug, 1994 ($2.50, unfinished limited series)

1-4: W. Simonson-a/stories; contain Bravura stamps		2.50

STAR SLAMMERS SPECIAL
Dark Horse Comics (Legend): June, 1996 ($2.95, one-shot)

nn-Simonson-c/a/scripts; concludes Bravura limited series.		3.00

STARSLAYER
Pacific Comics/First Comics No. 7 on: Feb, 1982 - No. 6, Apr, 1983; No. 7, Aug, 1983 - No. 34, Nov, 1985

1-Origin & 1st app.; excessive blood & gore; 1 pg. Rocketeer cameo which continues in #2				5.00
2-Origin/1st full app. the Rocketeer (4/82) by Dave Stevens (Chapter 1 of Rocketeer saga; see Pacific Presents #1,2)	1	3	6	8
3-Chapter 2 of Rocketeer saga by Stevens				6.00
4,6,7: 7-Grell-a ends				3.00
5-2nd app. Groo the Wanderer by Aragones	1	3	5	7
8-34: 10-1st app. Grimjack (11/83, ends #17). 18-Starslayer meets Grimjack. 20-The Black Flame begins (9/84, 1st app.), ends #33. 27-Book length Black Flame story				2.50

NOTE: *Grell a-1-7; c-1-8. Stevens back c-2, 3. Sutton a-17p, 20-22p, 24-27p, 29-33p.*

STARSLAYER (The Director's Cut)
Acclaim Comics (Windjammer): June, 1994 - No. 8, Dec, 1995 ($2.50)

1-8: Mike Grell-c/a/scripts		2.50

STAR SPANGLED COMICS (Star Spangled War Stories #131 on)
National Periodical Publications: Oct, 1941 - No. 130, July, 1952

1-Origin/1st app. Tarantula; Captain X of the R.A.F., Star Spangled Kid (see Action #40), Armstrong of the Army begin; Robot-c				
	500	1500	3250	6500
2	168	505	1050	1850
3-5	109	327	682	1200
6-Last Armstrong/Army; Penniless Palmer begins	64	192	398	700
7-(4/42)-Origin/1st app. The Guardian by S&K & Robotman (by Paul Cassidy & created by Siegel);The Newsboy Legion (1st app.), Robotman & TNT begin; last Captain X	631	1893	4100	8200
8-Origin TNT & Dan the Dyna-Mite	236	708	1477	2600
9,10	168	505	1050	1850
11-17	127	381	795	1400
18-Origin Star Spangled Kid	159	477	994	1750
19-Last Tarantula	127	381	795	1400
20-Liberty Belle begins (5/43)	136	408	852	1500
21-29-Last S&K issue; 23-Last TNT. 25-Robotman by Jimmy Thompson begins. 29-Intro Robbie the Robotdog	105	315	656	1150
30-40: 31-S&K-c	59	177	369	650
41-50: 41,49-Kirby-c	55	165	330	575
51-64: Last Newsboy Legion & The Guardian; last Liberty Belle? 51-Robot-c by Kirby. 53 by S&K	50	150	300	525
65-Robin begins with c/app. (2/47); Batman cameo in 1 panel; Robin-c begins, end #95	150	450	938	1650
66-Batman cameo in Robin story	84	253	525	925
67,68,70-80: 72-Burnley Robin-c	70	210	438	775
69-Origin/1st app. Tomahawk by F. Ray; atom bomb story & splash (6/47)				
	105	315	656	1150
81-Origin Merry, Girl of 1000 Gimmicks in Star Spangled Kid story				
82,85: 82-Last Robotman?	53	160	318	560
83-Tomahawk enters the lost valley, a land of dinosaurs; Capt. Compass begins, end #130	53	160	318	560
84,87: (Rare): 87-Batman cameo in Robin	80	240	500	875
86-Batman cameo in Robin story; last Star Spangled Kid				
	58	174	363	640
88(1/49)-94: Batman-c/stories in all. 91-Federal Men begin, end #93. 94-Manhunters Around the World begin, end #121	61	182	381	675
95-Batman story; last Robin-c	55	165	331	580
96,98-Batman cameo in Robin stories. 96-1st Tomahawk-c (also #97-121)				

Star Spangled Comics #124 © DC

Star Spangled War Stories #13 © DC

Startling Comics #16 © Nedor

	GD2.0	FN6.0	VF8.0	NM9.4

	40	120	232	400
97,99	36	108	191	330
100 (1/50)-Pre-Bat-Hound tryout in Robin story (pre-dates Batman #92).				
	40	120	220	410
101-109,118,119,121: 121-Last Tomahawk-c	34	102	179	310
110,111,120-Batman cameo in Robin stories. 120-Last 52 pg. issue				
	35	105	185	320
112-Batman & Robin story	37	111	197	340
113-Frazetta-a (10 pgs.)	43	129	257	450
114-Retells Robin's origin (3/51); Batman & Robin story				
	45	135	270	475
115,117-Batman app. in Robin stories	37	111	197	340
116-Flag-c	37	111	197	340
122-(11/51)-Ghost Breaker-c/stories begin (origin/1st app.), ends #130 (Ghost Breaker covers #122-130)	41	123	246	425
123-126,128,129	31	93	168	290
127-Batman cameo	33	99	174	300
130-Batman cameo in Robin story	35	105	188	325

NOTE: Most all issues after #29 signed by Simon & Kirby are not by them. *Bill Ely* c-122-130. *Mortimer* c-65-74(most), 76-95(most). *Fred Ray* c-96-106, 109, 110, 112, 113, 115-120. *S&K* c-7-31, 33, 34, 36, 37, 39, 40, 48, 49, 50-54, 56-58. *Hal Sherman* c-1-6. *Dick Sprang* c-75.

STAR SPANGLED COMICS (Also see All Star Comics 1999 crossover titles)
DC Comics: May, 1999 ($1.99, one-shot)

1-Golden Age Sandman and the Star Spangled Kid				2.25

STAR SPANGLED KID (See Action #40, Leading Comics & Star Spangled Comics)

STAR SPANGLED WAR STORIES (Formerly Star Spangled Comics #1-130; Becomes The Unknown Soldier #205 on) (See Showcase)
National Periodical Publications: No. 131, 8/52 - No. 133, 10/52; No. 3, 11/52 - No. 204, 2-3/77

131(#1)	88	264	616	1050
132	60	180	420	720
133-Used in POP, pg. 94	50	150	350	600
3-6: 4-Devil Dog Dugan app. 6-Evans-a	30	90	210	375
7-10	24	72	168	300
11-20	20	60	140	250
21-30: 30-Last precode (2/55)	18	54	123	220
31-33,35-40	13	39	91	155
41-44,46-50: 50-1st S.A. issue	12	36	84	140
45-1st DC grey tone-c (5/56)	15	45	105	180
51,52,54-63,65,66, 68-83	12	36	84	95
53-"Rock Sergeant," 3rd Sgt. Rock prototype; inspired "P.I. & The Sand Fleas" in G.I. Combat #56 (1/57)	13	39	94	160
64-Pre-Sgt. Rock Easy Co. story (12/57)	11	33	77	130
67-2 Easy Co. stories without Sgt. Rock	12	36	84	140
84-Origin Mlle. Marie	17	51	118	210
85-89-Mlle. Marie in all	10	30	70	120
90-1st app. "War That Time Forgot" series; dinosaur issue-c/story (4-5/60)	34	102	255	460
91,93-No dinosaur stories	8	24	58	95
92-2nd dinosaur-c/s	13	39	94	160
94 (12/60)- "Ghost Ace" story; Baron Von Richter as The Enemy Ace (pre-dates Our Army... #151)	17	51	118	210
95-99: Dinosaur-c/s	12	36	84	140
100-Dinosaur-c/story.	14	42	98	165
101-115: All dinosaur issues	10	30	70	120
116-125,127-133,135-137-Last dinosaur story; Heath Birdman-#129,131				
	9	27	65	110
126-No dinosaur story	7	21	53	85
134-Dinosaur story; Neal Adams-a	10	30	73	125
138-New Enemy Ace-c/stories begin by Joe Kubert (4-5/68), end #150 (also see Our Army at War #151 and Showcase #57)	11	33	80	135
139-Origin Enemy Ace (7/68)	9	27	63	105
140-143,145: 145-Last 12¢ issue (6-7/69)	6	18	40	65
144-Neal Adams/Kubert-a	7	21	50	85
146-Enemy Ace-c/a	4	12	26	40
147,148-New Enemy Ace stories	5	15	34	55
149,150-Last new Enemy Ace by Kubert. Viking Prince by Kubert				
	4	12	30	50

151-1st solo app. Unknown Soldier (6-7/70); Enemy Ace-r begin (from Our Army at War, Showcase & SSWS); end #161	14	42	102	175
152,153,155-Enemy Ace reprints; early Unknown Soldier stories				
	3	9	20	30
154-Origin Unknown Soldier	10	30	73	125
156-1st Battle Album; Unknown Soldier story; Kubert-c/a				
	3	10	23	35
157-Sgt. Rock x-over in Unknown Soldier story.	3	9	20	30
158-163(25 pgs.): New Unknown Soldier stories; Kubert-c/a.				
	2	6	13	20
161-Last Enemy Ace-r				
164-183,200: 181-183-Enemy Ace vs. Balloon Buster serial app; Frank Thorne-a. 200-Enemy Ace back-up	2	6	9	12
184-199,201-204	1	3	6	9

NOTE: *Anderson* a-28. *Chaykin* a-167. *Drucker* a-59, 61, 64, 66, 67, 73-84. *Estrada* a-149. *John Giunta* a-72. *Glanzman* a-167, 171, 172, 174. *Heath* a-122, 133; c-67, 122, 132-134. *Kaluta* a-197i; c-167. *G. Kane* a-169. *Kubert* a-6-163(most later issues), 200. *Maurer* a-160, 165. *Severin* a-65, 162. *S&K* c-73, 34, 37, 40. *Simonson* a-167, 172, 174, 180. *Sutton* a-168. *Thorne* a-183. *Toth* a-164. *Wildey* a-161. Suicide Squad in 110, 116-118, 120, 121, 127.

STARSTREAM (Adventures in Science Fiction)(See Questar illustrated)
Whitman/Western Publishing Co.: 1976 (79¢, 68 pgs, cardboard-c)

1-4: 1-Bolle-a. 2-4-McWilliams & Bolle-a	2	6	11	15

STARSTRUCK
Marvel Comics (Epic Comics): Feb, 1985 - No. 6, Feb, 1986 ($1.50, mature)

1-6: Kaluta-a				3.00

STARSTRUCK
Dark Horse Comics: Aug, 1990 - No. 4, Nov?, 1990 ($2.95, B&W, 52pgs.)

1-3:Kaluta-a/Epic series plus new-c/a in all				3.00
4 (68, pgs.)-contains 2 trading cards				3.00

STAR STUDDED
Cambridge House/Superior Publishers: 1945 (25¢, 132 pgs.); 1945 (196 pgs.)

nn-Captain Combat by Giunta, Ghost Woman, Commandette, & Red Rogue app.; Infantino-a	33	99	174	300
nn-The Cadet, Edison Bell, Hoot Gibson, Jungle Lil (196 pgs.); copies vary; Blue Beetle in some	27	81	145	250

STARTLING COMICS
Better Publications (Nedor): June, 1940 - No. 53, Sept, 1948

1-Origin Captain Future-Man Of Tomorrow, Mystico (By Eisner/Fine), The Wonder Man; Masked Rider & his horse Pinto begins; Masked Rider formerly in pulps; drug use story	245	735	1534	2700
2-Don Davis, Espionage Ace begins	95	285	597	1050
3	79	237	494	870
4	59	177	369	650
5-9	50	150	300	525
10-The Fighting Yank begins (9/41, origin/1st app.)				
	350	1050	2188	4200
11-2nd app. Fighting Yank	109	327	682	1200
12-Hitler, Hirohito, Mussolini-c	91	273	568	1000
13-15	59	177	369	650
16-Origin The Four Comrades; not in #32,35	64	192	398	700
17-Last Masked Rider & Mystico	47	142	286	500
18-Pyroman begins (12/42, origin)(also see America's Best Comics #3 for 1st app., 11/42)	95	285	597	1050
19	47	142	286	500
20,21: 20-The Oracle begins (3/43); not in issues 26,28,33,34. 21-Origin The Ape, Oracle's enemy	50	150	300	525
22-34: 34-Origin The Scarab & only app.	47	142	286	500
35-Hypodermic syringe attacks Fighting Yank in drug story				
	50	150	300	525
36-43: 36-Last Four Comrades. 38-Bondage/torture-c. 40-Last Capt. Future & Oracle. 41-Front Page Peggy begins; A-Bomb-c. 43-Last Pyroman	40	120	240	420
44,45: 44-Lance Lewis, Space Detective begins; Ingels-c; sci/fi-c begin. 45-Tygra begins (intro/origin, 5/47); Ingels-c/a (splash pg. & inside f/c B&W ad	64	192	398	700
46-Classic Ingels-c; Ingels-a	95	285	597	1050
47,48,50-53: 50-Sea-Eagle app.	59	177	369	650
49-Classic Schomburg Robot-c; last Fighting Yank				
	317	951	1979	3800

Startling Stories: Banner #1 © MAR

Star Trek #8 © Paramount

Star Trek Deep Space Nine #14 © Paramount

	GD2.0	FN6.0	VF8.0	NM9.4
	GD2.0	FN6.0	VF8.0	NM9.4

NOTE: **Ingels** a-44, 45; c-44, 45, 46(wash). **Schomburg (Xela)** c-21-43; 47-53 (airbrush). **Tuska** c-45? Bondage c-16, 21, 37, 46-49. Captain Future c-1-9, 13, 14. Fighting Yank c-10-12, 15-17, 21, 22, 24, 26, 28, 30, 32, 34, 36, 38, 40, 42. Pyroman c-18-20, 23, 25, 27, 29, 31, 33, 35, 37, 39, 41, 43.

STARTLING STORIES: BANNER
Marvel Comics: July, 2001 - No. 4, Oct, 2001 ($2.99, limited series)

1-4-Hulk story by Azzarello; Corben-c/a		3.00
TPB (11/01, $12.95) r/1-4		13.00

STARTLING TERROR TALES
Star Publications: No. 10, May, 1952 - No. 14, Feb, 1953; No. 4, Apr, 1953 - No. 11, 1954

10-(1st Series)-Wood/Harrison-a (r/a Star Presentation #3) Disbrow/Cole-c; becomes 4 different titles after #10; becomes Confessions of Love #11 on, The Horrors #11 on, Terrifying Tales #11 on, Terrors of the Jungle #11 on & continues w/Startling Terror #11	70	210	438	770
11-(8/52)-L. B. Cole Spider-c; r-Fox's "A Feature Presentation" #5 (blue-c)				
	114	342	713	1250
11-Black-c (variant; believed to be a pressrun change) (Unique)				
	127	381	795	1400
12,14	29	87	153	265
13-Jo-Jo-r; Disbrow-a	31	93	165	285
4-9,11(1953-54) (2nd Series): 11-New logo	26	78	136	235
10-Disbrow-a	33	99	174	300

NOTE: **L. B. Cole** covers-all issues. Palais a-V2#8r, V2#11r.

STAR TREK (TV) (See Dan Curtis Giveaways, Dynabrite Comics & Power Record Comics)
Gold Key: 7/67; No. 2, 6/68; No. 3, 12/68; No. 4, 6/69 - No. 61, 3/79

1-Photo-c begin, end #9	42	125	336	610
1 (rare variation w/photo back-c)	48	144	386	700
2	26	78	182	325
2 (rare variation w/photo back-c)	38	113	285	510
3-5	18	54	126	225
3 (rare variation w/photo back-c)	28	84	196	350
6-9	14	42	100	170
10-20	8	24	60	100
21-30	6	18	45	75
31-40	5	15	34	55
41-61: 52-Drug propaganda story	4	12	26	40
...the Enterprise Logs nn (8/76)-Golden Press, ($1.95, 224 pgs.)-r/#1-8 plus 7 pgs. by McWilliams (#11185)-Photo-c	4	12	30	50
...the Enterprise Logs Vol. 2 ('76)-r/#9-17 (#11187)-Photo-c	4	12	29	45
...the Enterprise Logs Vol. 3 ('77)-r/#18-26 (#11188); McWilliams-a (4 pgs.)-Photo-c	4	12	29	45
Star Trek Vol. 4 (Winter '77)-Reprints #27,28,30-34,36,38 (#11189) plus 3 pgs. new art	4	12	29	45

NOTE: **McWilliams** a-38, 40-44, 46-61. #29 reprints #1; #35 reprints #4; #37 reprints #5; #45 reprints #7. The tabloids all have photo covers and blank inside covers. Painted covers #10-44, 46-59.

STAR TREK
Marvel Comics Group: April, 1980 - No. 18, Feb, 1982

1: 1-3-r/Marvel Super Special; movie adapt.	2	6	9	12
2-16: 5-Miller-c	1	3	5	7
17-Low print run	2	6	9	12
18-Last issue; low print run	2	6	12	18

NOTE: **Austin** c-18i. **Buscema** a-13. **Gil Kane** a-15. **Nasser** c/a-7. **Simonson** c-17.

STAR TREK (Also see Who's Who In Star Trek)
DC Comics: Feb, 1984 - No. 56, Nov, 1988 (75¢, Mando paper)

1-Sutton-a(p) begins	1	4	7	10
2-5				6.00
6-10: 7-Origin Saavik				5.00
11-20: 19-Walter Koenig story				4.00
21-32				3.50
33-($1.25, 52 pgs.)-20th anniversary issue				4.00
34-49: 37-Painted-c				3.00
50-($1.50, 52 pgs.)				4.00
51-56, Annual 1-3: 1(1985). 2(1986). 3(1988, $1.50)				3.00

NOTE: **Morrow** a-28, 35, 36, 56. **Orlando** c-8i. **Perez** c-1-3. **Spiegle** a-19. **Starlin** c-24, 25. **Sutton** a-1-6p, 8-18p, 20-27p, 29p, 31-34p, 39-52p, 55p; c-4-6p, 8-22p, 46p.

STAR TREK
DC Comics: Oct, 1989 - No. 80, Jan, 1996 ($1.50/$1.75/$1.95/$2.50)

1-Capt. Kirk and crew	6.00
2,3	4.00
4-23,25-30: 10-12-The Trial of James T. Kirk. 21-Begin $1.75-c	3.00
24-($2.95, 68 pgs.)-40 pg. epic w/pin-ups	3.50
31-49,51-60	2.50
50-($3.50, 68 pgs.)-Painted-c	3.50
61-74,76-80	2.50
75 ($3.95)	4.00
Annual 1-6('90-'95, 68 pgs.): 1-Morrow-a. 3-Painted-c	4.00
Special 1-3 ('9-'95, 68 pgs.)-1-Sutton-a.	4.00
...: The Ashes of Eden (1995, $14.95, 100 pgs.)-Shatner story	15.00
...Generations (1994, $3.95, 68 pgs.)-Movie adaptation	4.00
...Generations (1994, $5.95, 68 pgs.)-Squarebound	6.00

STAR TREK...(TV)
DC Comics (WildStorm): one-shots

All of Me (4/00, $5.95, prestige format) Lopresti-a	6.00
Enemy Unseen TPB (2001, $17.95) r/Perchance to Dream, Embrace the Wolf, The Killing Shadows; Struzan-c	18.00
Enter the Wolves (2001, $5.95) Crispin & Weinstein-s; Mota-a/c	6.00
New Frontier - Double Time (11/00, $5.95)-Captain Calhoun's USS Excalibur; Peter David-s; Stelfreeze-c	6.00
Other Realities TPB (2001, $14.95) r/All of Me, New Frontier - Double Time, and DS9-N-Vector; Van Fleet-c	15.00
Special (2001, $6.95) Stories from all 4 series by various; Van Fleet-c	7.00

STAR TREK: DEBT OF HONOR
DC Comics: 1992 ($24.95/$14.95, graphic novel)

Hardcover ($24.95) Claremont-s/Hughes-a(p)	25.00
Softcover ($14.95)	15.00

STAR TREK: DEEP SPACE NINE (TV)
Malibu Comics: Aug, 1993 - No. 32, Jan, 1996 ($2.50)

1-Direct Sale Edition w/line drawn-c	4.00
1-Newsstand Edition with photo-c	3.00
0-(1/95, $2.95)-Terok Nor	3.00
2-30: 2-Polybagged w/trading card. 9-4 pg. prelude to Hearts & Minds	2.50
31-($3.95)	3.50
32-($3.50)	3.50
Annual 1 (1/95, $3.95, 68 pgs.)	4.00
Special 1 (1995, $3.50)	3.50
Ultimate Annual 1 (12/95, $5.95)	6.00
...:Lightstorm (12/94, $3.50)	3.50

STAR TREK: DEEP SPACE NINE (TV)
Marvel Comics (Paramount Comics): Nov, 1996 - No. 15, Mar, 1998 ($1.95/$1.99)

1-15: 12,13-"Telepathy War" pt.2,3	2.50

STAR TREK: DEEP SPACE NINE -- N-VECTOR (TV)
DC Comics (WildStorm): Aug, 2000 - No. 4, Nov, 2000 ($2.50, limited series)

1-4-Cypress-a	2.50

STAR TREK DEEP SPACE NINE-THE CELEBRITY SERIES
Malibu Comics: May, 1995 ($2.95)

1-Blood and Honor; Mark Lenard script	3.00
1-Rules of Diplomacy; Aron Eisenberg script	3.00

STAR TREK: DEEP SPACE NINE HEARTS AND MINDS
Malibu Comics: June, 1994 - No. 4, Sept, 1994 ($2.50, limited series)

1-4	2.50
1-Holographic-c	4.00

STAR TREK: DEEP SPACE NINE, THE MAQUIS
Malibu Comics: Feb, 1995 - No. 3, Apr, 1995 ($2.50, limited series)

1-3-Newsstand-c, 1-Photo-c	2.50

STAR TREK: DEEP SPACE NINE/THE NEXT GENERATION
Malibu Comics: Oct, 1994 - No. 2, Nov, 1994 ($2.50, limited series)

1,2: Parts 2 & 4 of x-over with Star Trek: TNG/DS9 from DC Comics	2.50

STAR TREK: DEEP SPACE NINE WORF SPECIAL

Star Trek: The Next Generation #21 © Paramount

Star Trek Unlimited #4 © Paramount

Star Trek Voyager - False Colors © Paramount

| | | | GD2.0 | FN6.0 | VF8.0 | NM9.4 | | GD2.0 | FN6.0 | VF8.0 | NM9. |

Malibu Comics: Dec, 1995 ($3.95, one-shot)

1-Includes pinups	4.00

STAR TREK: DIVIDED WE FALL
DC Comics (WildStorm): July, 2001 - No. 4, Oct, 2001 ($2.95, limited series)

1-4: Ordover & Mack-s; Lenara Kahn, Verad and Odan app.	3.00

STAR TREK: EARLY VOYAGES (TV)
Marvel Comics (Paramount Comics): Feb, 1997 - No. 17, Jun, 1998 ($2.95/$1.95/$1.99)

1-($2.95)	3.00
2-17	2.50

STAR TREK: FIRST CONTACT (Movie)
Marvel Comics (Paramount Comics): Nov, 1996 ($5.95, one-shot)

nn-Movie adaption	6.00

STAR TREK: MIRROR MIRROR
Marvel Comics (Paramount Comics): Feb, 1997 ($3.95, one-shot)

1-DeFalco-s	4.00

STAR TREK MOVIE SPECIAL
DC Comics: 1984 (June) - No. 2, 1987 ($1.50); No. 1, 1989 ($2.00, 52 pgs)

nn-(#1)-Adapts Star Trek III; Sutton-p (68 pgs.)	3.00
2-Adapts Star Trek IV; Sutton-a; Chaykin-a. (68 pgs.)	3.00
1 (1989)-Adapts Star Trek V; painted-c	3.00

STAR TREK: OPERATION ASSIMILATION
Marvel Comics (Paramount Comics): Dec, 1996 ($2.95, one-shot)

1	3.00

STAR TREK VI: THE UNDISCOVERED COUNTRY (Movie)
DC Comics: 1992

1-($2.95, regular edition, 68 pgs.)-Adaptation of film	3.00
nn-($5.95, prestige edition)-Has photos of movie not included in regular edition; painted-c by Palmer; photo back-c	6.00

STAR TREK: STARFLEET ACADEMY
Marvel Comics (Paramount Comics): Dec, 1996 - No. 19, Jun, 1998 ($1.95/$1.99)

1-19: Begin new series. 12-"Telepathy War" pt. 1. 18-English and Klingon language editions	2.50

STAR TREK: TELEPATHY WAR
Marvel Comics (Paramount Comics): Nov, 1997 ($2.99, 48 pgs., one-shot)

1-"Telepathy War" x-over pt. 6	3.00

STAR TREK - THE MODALA IMPERATIVE
DC Comics: Late July, 1991 - No. 4, Late Sept, 1991 ($1.75, limited series)

1-4	2.50

STAR TREK: THE NEXT GENERATION (TV)
DC Comics: Feb, 1988 - No. 6, July, 1988 (limited series)

1 ($1.50, 52 pgs.)-Sienkiewicz painted-c	6.00
2-6 ($1.00)	4.00

STAR TREK: THE NEXT GENERATION (TV)
DC Comics: Oct, 1989 -No. 80, 1995 ($1.50/$1.75/$1.95)

	1	3	6	9
1-Capt. Picard and crew from TV show	1	3	6	9
2,3				5.00
4-10				4.00
11-23,25-49,51-60				3.00
24,50: 24-($2.50, 52 pgs.). 50-($3.50, 68 pgs.)-Painted-c				5.00
61-74,76-80				2.50
75-($3.95, 50 pgs.)				4.00
Annual 1-6 ('90-'95, 68 pgs.)				4.00
Special 1 -3('93-'95, 68 pgs.)-1-Contains 3 stories				4.00
...-The Series Finale (1994, $3.95, 68 pgs.)				4.00

STAR TREK: THE NEXT GENERATION (TV)
DC Comics (WildStorm): one-shots

Embrace the Wolf (6/00, $5.95, prestige format) Golden & Sniegoski-s	6.00
Forgiveness (2001, $24.95, HC) David Brin-s/Scott Hampton painted-a; dust jacket-c	30.00

The Gorn Crisis (1/01, $29.95, HC) Kordey painted-a/dust jacket-c	30.00

STAR TREK: THE NEXT GENERATION/DEEP SPACE NINE (TV)
DC Comics: Dec, 1994 - No. 2, Jan, 1995 ($2.50, limited series)

1,2-Parts 1 & 3 of x-over with Star Trek: DS9/TNG from Malibu Comics	2.50

STAR TREK: THE NEXT GENERATION - ILL WIND
DC Comics: Nov, 1995 - No. 4, Feb, 1996 ($2.50, limited series)

1-4: Hugh Fleming painted-c on all	2.50

STAR TREK: THE NEXT GENERATION - PERCHANCE TO DREAM
DC Comics/WildStorm: Feb, 2000 - No. 4, May, 2000 ($2.50, limited series)

1-4-Bradstreet-c	2.50

STAR TREK: THE NEXT GENERATION - RIKER
Marvel Comics (Paramount Comics): July, 1998 ($3.50, one-shot)

1-Riker joins the Maquis	3.50

STAR TREK: THE NEXT GENERATION - SHADOWHEART
DC Comics: Dec, 1994 - No. 4, Mar, 1995 ($1.95, limited series)

1-4	2.50

STAR TREK: THE NEXT GENERATION - THE KILLING SHADOWS
DC Comics/WildStorm: Nov, 2000 - No. 4, Feb, 2001 ($2.50, limited series)

1-4-Scott Ciencin-s; Sela app.	2.50

STAR TREK: THE NEXT GENERATION - THE MODALA IMPERATIVE
DC Comics: Early Sept, 1991 - No. 4, Late Oct, 1991 ($1.75, limited series)

1-4	2.50

STAR TREK UNLIMITED
Marvel Comics (Paramount Comics): Nov, 1996 - No. 10, July, 1998 ($2.95/$2.99)

1,2-Stories from original series and Next Generation	4.00
3-10: 3-Begin $2.99-c. 6-"Telepathy War" pt. 4. 7-Q & Trelane swap Kirk & Picard	3.50

STAR TREK: UNTOLD VOYAGES
Marvel Comics (Paramount Comics): May, 1998 - No. 5, July, 1998 ($2.50)

1-5-Kirk's crew after the 1st movie	2.50

STAR TREK: VOYAGER
Marvel Comics (Paramount Comics): Nov, 1996 - No. 15, Mar, 1998 ($1.95/$1.99)

1-15: 13-"Telepathy War" pt. 5. 14-Seven of Nine joins crew	3.00

STAR TREK: VOYAGER
DC Comics/WildStorm: one-shots and trade paperbacks

- Elite Force (7/00, $5.95) The Borg app.; Abnett & Lanning-s	6.00
... Encounters With the Unknown TPB (2001, $19.95) reprints	20.00
- False Colors (1/00, $5.95) Photo-c and Jim Lee-c; Jeff Moy-a	6.00

STAR TREK: VOYAGER-- THE PLANET KILLER
DC Comics/WildStorm: Mar, 2001 - No. 3, May, 2001 ($2.95, limited series)

1-3-Voyager vs. the Planet Killer from the ST:TOS episode; Teranishi-a	3.00

STAR TREK: VOYAGER SPLASHDOWN
Marvel Comics (Paramount Comics): Apr, 1998 - No. 4, July, 1998 ($2.50, limited series)

1-4-Voyager crashes on a water planet	3.00

STAR TREK/ X-MEN
Marvel Comics (Paramount Comics): Dec, 1996 ($4.99, one-shot)

1-Kirk's crew & X-Men; art by Silvestri, Tan, Winn & Finch; Lobdell-s	5.00

STAR TREK/ X-MEN: 2ND CONTACT
Marvel Comics (Paramount Comics): May, 1998 ($4.99, 64 pgs., one-shot)

1-Next Gen. crew & X-Men battle Kang, Sentinels & Borg following First Contact movie	5.00
1-Painted wraparound variant cover	5.00

STAR WARS (Movie) (See Classic..., Contemporary Motivators, Dark Horse Comics, The Droids, The Ewoks, Marvel Movie Showcase, Marvel Special Ed.)
Marvel Comics Group: July, 1977 - No. 107, Sept, 1986

1-(Regular 30¢ edition)-Price in square w/UPC code; #1-6 adapt first movie; first issue on sale before movie debuted	4	12	29	45

Star Wars #23 © Lucasfilm

Star Wars: Chewbacca #1 © Lucasfilm

Star Wars: Darth Maul #4 © Lucasfilm

	GD2.0	FN6.0	VF8.0	NM9.4

1-(35¢-c; limited distribution - 1500 copies?)- Price in square w/UPC
code   48   144   386   700
NOTE: The rare 35¢ edition has the cover price in a square box, and the UPC box in the lower
left hand corner has the UPC code lines running through it.

2-4-(30¢ issues). 4-Battle with Darth Vader	2	6	15	22
2-4-(35¢ with UPC code; not reprints)	4	12	30	50
5,6: 5-Begin 35¢-c on all editions. 6-Dave Stevens-a(i).				
	2	6	12	18
7-20	2	6	9	12
21-70: 39-44-The Empire Strikes Back-r by Al Williamson in all. 50-Giant.				
68-Reintro Boba Fett.	1	3	6	9
71-80	1	4	7	10
81-90: 81-Boba Fett app.	2	6	9	12
91,93-99: 98-Williamson-a.	2	6	11	15
92,100-106: 92,100-($1.00, 52 pgs.).	2	6	12	18
107(low dist.); Portacio-a(i)	5	15	34	55
1-9: Reprints; has "reprint" in upper lefthand corner of cover or on inside or				
price and number inside a diamond with no date or UPC on cover; 30¢ and				
35¢ issues published				4.00
Annual 1 (12/79, 52 pgs.)-Simonson-c	2	6	9	12
Annual 2 (11/82, 52 pgs.). 3(12/83, 52 pgs.)	1	4	7	10

Austin a-11-15i, 21i, 38; c-12-15i, 21i. Byrne c-13p. Chaykin a-1-10p; c-1. Golden c/a-38. Miller
c-47p; pin-up-43. Nebres c/a-Annual 2i. Portacio a-107i. Sienkiewicz c-92i, 98. Simonson a-
16p, 49p, 51-63p, 65p, 66p; c-16, 49-51, 52p, 53-62, Annual 1. Steacy painted a-105i, 106i; c-
105. Williamson a-39-44p, 50p, 98; c-39, 40, 41-44p. Painted c-81, 87, 92, 95, 98, 100, 105.

STAR WARS (Monthly series)
Dark Horse Comics: Dec, 1998 - Present ($2.50/$2.95/$2.99)

1-12: 1-6-Prelude To Rebellion; Strnad-s. 4-Brereton-s. 7-12-Outlander	3.00
13, 17-18-($2.95): 13-18-Emissaries to Malastare; Truman-s	3.00
14-16-($2.50) Schultz-c	3.00
19-35: 19-22-Twilight; Duursema-a. 23-26-Infinity's End	3.00
#0 Another Universe Ed.($10.00) r/serialized pages from Pizzazz Magazine;	
new Dorman painted-c	10.00

STAR WARS: A NEW HOPE- THE SPECIAL EDITION
Dark Horse Comics: Jan, 1997 - No. 4, Apr, 1997 ($2.95, limited series)

1-4-Dorman-c	4.00

STAR WARS: BOBA FETT
Dark Horse Comics: Dec, 1995 - No. 3 ($3.95) (Originally intended as a one-shot)

1-Kennedy-c/a	6.00
2,3	5.00
Death, Lies, & Treachery TPB (1/98, $12.95) r/#1-3	13.00
... - Agent of Doom (11/00, $2.99) Ostrander-s/Cam Kennedy-a	3.00
Twin Engines of Destruction (1/97, $2.95)	3.00

STAR WARS: BOBA FETT: ENEMY OF THE EMPIRE
Dark Horse Comics: Jan, 1999 - No. 4, Apr, 1999 ($2.95, limited series)

1-4-Recalls 1st meeting of Fett and Vader	3.00

STAR WARS: CHEWBACCA
Dark Horse Comics: Jan, 2000 - No. 4, Apr, 2000 ($2.95, limited series)

1-4-Macan-s/art by various incl. Anderson, Kordey, Gibbons; Phillips-c	3.00

STAR WARS: CRIMSON EMPIRE
Dark Horse Comics: Dec, 1997 - No. 6, May, 1998 ($2.95, limited series)

1-Richardson-s/Gulacy-a	1	3	5	7
2-6				5.00

STAR WARS: CRIMSON EMPIRE II: COUNCIL OF BLOOD
Dark Horse Comics: Nov, 1998 - No. 6, Apr, 1999 ($2.95, limited series)

1-6-Richardson & Stradley-s/Gulacy-a	3.00

STAR WARS: DARK EMPIRE
Dark Horse Comics: Dec, 1991 - No. 6, Oct, 1992 ($2.95, limited series)

Preview-(99¢)				3.00
1-All have Dorman painted-c	1	3	6	9
1-3-2nd printing				4.00
2-Low print run	2	6	9	12
3				6.00
4-6				4.00
Gold Embossed Set (#1-6)-With gold embossed foil logo (price is for set)				65.00
Platinum Embossed Set (#1-6)				80.00

	GD2.0	FN6.0	VF8.0	NM9.4

Trade paperback (4/93, 16.95)	17.00
Ltd. Ed. Hardcover ($99.95) Signed & numbered	100.00

STAR WARS: DARK EMPIRE II
Dark Horse Comics: Dec, 1994 - No. 6, May, 1995 ($2.95, limited series)

1-Dave Dorman painted-c	5.00
2-6: Dorman-c in all.	4.00
Platinum Embossed Set (#1-6)	35.00
Trade paperback ($17.95)	18.00

STAR WARS: DARK FORCE RISING
Dark Horse Comics: May, 1997 - No. 6, Oct, 1997 ($2.95, limited series)

1-6	4.00
TPB (2/98, $17.95) r/#1-6	18.00

STAR WARS: DARTH MAUL
Dark Horse Comics: Sept, 2000 - No. 4, Dec, 2000 ($2.95, limited series)

1-4-Photo-c and Struzan painted-c; takes place 6 months before Ep. 1	3.00

STAR WARS: DROIDS (See Dark Horse Comics #17-19)
Dark Horse Comics: Apr, 1994 - #6, Sept, 1994; V2#1, Apr, 1995 - V2#8, Dec, 1995 ($2.50, limited series)

1-($2.95)-Embossed-c	4.00
2-6 , Special 1 (1/95, $2.50), V2#1-8	3.00

STAR WARS: EMPIRE'S END
Dark Horse Comics: Oct, 1995 - No. 2, Nov, 1995 ($2.95, limited series)

1,2-Dorman-c	3.00

STAR WARS: EPISODE 1 THE PHANTOM MENACE
Dark Horse Comics: May, 1999 - No. 4, ($2.95, movie adaption)

1-4-Regular and photo-c; Damaggio & Williamson-a	3.00
TPB ($12.95) r/#1-4	13.00
...Anakin Skywalker-Photo-c & Bradstreet-c, ...Obi-Wan Kenobi-Photo-c &	
Egeland-c, ...Queen Amidala-Photo-c & Bradstreet-c, ...Qui-Gon Jinn-Photo-c	
& Bradstreet-c	3.00
Gold foil covers; Wizard 1/2	10.00

STAR WARS HANDBOOK
Dark Horse Comics: July, 1998- Present ($2.95, one-shots)

...X-Wing Rogue Squadron (7/98)-Guidebook to characters and spacecraft	3.00
...Crimson Empire (7/99) Dorman-c	3.00
...Dark Empire (3/00) Dorman-c	3.00

STAR WARS: HEIR TO THE EMPIRE
Dark Horse Comics: Oct, 1995 - No.6, Apr, 1996 ($2.95, limited series)

1-6: Adaptation of Zahn novel	3.00

STAR WARS: INFINITIES - A NEW HOPE
Dark Horse Comics: May, 2001 - No. 4, Oct, 2001 ($2.99, limited series)

1-4: "What If..." the Death Star wasn't destroyed in Episode 4	3.00

STAR WARS: JABBA THE HUTT
Dark Horse Comics: Apr, 1995 ($2.50, one-shots)

nn, ...The Betrayal, ...The Dynasty Trap, ...The Hunger of Princess Nampi	3.00

STAR WARS: JEDI ACADEMY - LEVIATHAN
Dark Horse Comics: Oct, 1998 - No. 4, Jan, 1999 ($2.95, limited series)

1-Lago-c. 2-4-Chadwick-c	3.00

STAR WARS: JEDI COUNCIL: ACTS OF WAR
Dark Horse Comics: Jun, 2000 - No. 4, Sept, 2000 ($2.95, limited series)

1-4-Stradley-s; set one year before Episode 1	3.00

STAR WARS: JEDI QUEST
Dark Horse Comics: Sept, 2001 - No. 4, ($2.99, limited series)

1-3-Anakin's Jedi training; Windham-s/Mhan-a	3.00

STAR WARS: JEDI VS. SITH
Dark Horse Comics: Apr, 2001 - No. 6, Sept, 2001 ($2.99, limited series)

1-6: Macan-s/Bachs-a/Robinson-c	3.00

STAR WARS: MARA JADE
Dark Horse Comics: Aug, 1998 - No. 6, Jan, 1999 ($2.95, limited series)

1-6-Ezquerra-a	3.00

Star Wars: Shadows of the Empire #4 © Lucasfilm

Star Wars: Union #1 © Lucasfilm

Steampunk #4 © Bachalo & Kelly

STAR WARS: QUI-GON & OBI-WAN - LAST STAND ON ORD MANTELL
Dark Horse Comics: Dec, 2000 - No. 3, Mar, 2001 ($2.99, limited series)
1-3: 1-Three covers (photo, Tony Daniel, Bachs) Windham-s ... 3.00

STAR WARS: RETURN OF THE JEDI (Movie)
Marvel Comics Group: Oct, 1983 - No. 4, Jan, 1984 (limited series)

1-4-Williamson-p in all; r/Marvel Super Special #27	1	3	6	9
Oversized issue (1983, $2.95, 10-3/4x8-1/4", 68 pgs., cardboard-c)-r/#1-4			
	2	6	11	16

STAR WARS: RIVER OF CHAOS
Dark Horse Comics: June, 1995 - No. 4, Sept, 1995 ($2.95, limited series)
1-4: Louise Simonson scripts ... 3.00

STAR WARS: SHADOWS OF THE EMPIRE
Dark Horse Comics: May, 1996 - No. 6, Oct, 1996 ($2.95, limited series)
1-6: Story details events between The Empire Strikes Back & Return of the Jedi; Russell-a(i). ... 3.00

STAR WARS: SHADOWS OF THE EMPIRE - EVOLUTION
Dark Horse Comics: Feb, 1998 - No. 5, June, 1998 ($2.95, limited series)
1-5: Perry-s/Fegredo-c. ... 3.00

STAR WARS: SHADOW STALKER
Dark Horse Comics: Sept, 1997 ($2.95, one-shot)
nn-Windham-a. ... 3.00

STAR WARS: SPLINTER OF THE MIND'S EYE
Dark Horse Comics: Dec, 1995 - No. 4, June, 1996 ($2.50, limited series)
1-4: Adaption of Alan Dean Foster novel ... 3.00

STAR WARS: TAG & BINK ARE DEAD
Dark Horse Comics: Oct, 2001 - No. 2, Nov, 2001($2.99, limited series)
1-Rubio-s ... 3.00

STAR WARS TALES
Dark Horse Comics: Sept, 1999 - Present ($4.95/$5.95/$5.99, anthology)
1-4-Short stories by various ... 5.00
5-8($5.95/$5.99-c) Art and photo-c on each ... 6.00

STAR WARS: TALES FROM MOS EISLEY
Dark Horse Comics: Mar, 1996 ($2.95, one-shot)
nn-Bret Blevins-a. ... 3.00

STAR WARS: TALES OF THE JEDI (See Dark Horse Comics #7)
Dark Horse Comics: Oct, 1993 - No. 5, Feb, 1994 ($2.50, limited series)
1-5: All have Dave Dorman painted-c. 4-r/Dark Horse Comics #7-9 w/new coloring & some panels redrawn ... 3.00
1-5-Gold foil embossed logo; limited # printed-7500 (set) ... 50.00

STAR WARS: TALES OF THE JEDI-DARK LORDS OF THE SITH
Dark Horse Comics: Oct, 1994 - No. 6, Mar, 1995 ($2.50, limited series)
1-6: 1-Polybagged w/trading card ... 3.00

STAR WARS: TALES OF THE JEDI-REDEMPTION
Dark Horse Comics: July, 1998 - No. 5, Nov, 1998 ($2.95, limited series)
1-5: 1-Kevin J. Anderson-s/Kordey-c ... 3.00

STAR WARS: TALES OF THE JEDI-THE FALL OF THE SITH
Dark Horse Comics: June, 1997 - No. 5, Oct, 1997 ($2.95, limited series)
1-5 ... 3.00

STAR WARS: TALES OF THE JEDI-THE FREEDON NADD UPRISING
Dark Horse Comics: Aug, 1994 - No. 2, Nov, 1994 ($2.50, limited series)
1,2 ... 3.00

STAR WARS: TALES OF THE JEDI-THE GOLDEN AGE OF THE SITH
Dark Horse Comics: July, 1996 - No. 5, Feb, 1997 (99¢/$2.95, limited series)
0-(99¢)-Anderson-s ... 3.00
1-5-Anderson-s ... 3.00

STAR WARS: TALES OF THE JEDI-THE SITH WAR
Dark Horse Comics: Aug, 1995 - No. 6, Jan, 1996 ($2.50, limited series)
1-6: Anderson scripts ... 3.00

STAR WARS: THE BOUNTY HUNTERS

Dark Horse Comics: July, 1999 - Oct, 1999 ($2.95, one-shots)
...Aurra Sing (7/99), ...Kenix Kil (10/99), ...Scoundrel's Wages (8/99) Lando Calrissian app. ... 3.00

STAR WARS: THE JABBA TAPE
Dark Horse Comics: Dec, 1998 ($2.95, one-shot)
nn-Wagner-s/Plunkett-a ... 3.00

STAR WARS: THE LAST COMMAND
Dark Horse Comics: Nov, 1997 - No. 6, July, 1998 ($2.95, limited series)
1-6:Based on the Timothy Zaun novel ... 4.00

STAR WARS: THE PROTOCOL OFFENSIVE
Dark Horse Comics: Sept, 1997 ($4.95, one-shot)
nn-Anthony Daniels & Ryder Windham-s ... 5.00

STAR WARS: UNDERWORLD - THE YAVIN VASSILIKA
Dark Horse Comics: Dec, 2000 - No. 5, June, 2001 ($2.99, limited series)
1-5-(Photo and Robinson covers) ... 3.00

STAR WARS: UNION
Dark Horse Comics: Nov, 1999 - No. 4, Feb, 2000 ($2.95, limited series)
1-4-Wedding of Luke and Mara Jade; Teranishi-a/Stackpole-s ... 3.00

STAR WARS: VADER'S QUEST
Dark Horse Comics: Feb, 1999 - No. 4, May, 1999 ($2.95, limited series)
1-4-Follows destruction of 1st Death Star; Gibbons-a ... 3.00

STAR WARS: X-WING ROGUE SQUADRON (Star Wars: X-Wing Rogue Squadron-The Phantom Affair #5-8 appears on cover only)
Dark Horse Comics: July, 1995 - No. 35, Nov, 1998 ($2.95)
1/2 ... 8.00
1-24,26-35: 1-4-Baron scripts. 5-20-Stackpole scripts ... 3.00
25-($3.95) ... 4.00
The Phantom Affair TPB ($12.95) r/#5-8 ... 13.00

S.T.A.T.
Majestic Entertainment: Dec, 1993 ($2.25)
1 ... 2.25

STATIC (Also see Eclipse Monthly)
Charlton Comics: No, 11, Oct, 1985 - No. 12, Dec, 1985
11,12-Ditko-c/a; low print run ... 6.00

STATIC (See Heroes)
DC Comics (Milestone): June, 1993 - No. 45, Mar, 1997 ($1.50/$1.75/$2.50)
1-($2.95)-Collector's Edition; polybagged w/poster & trading card & backing board (direct sales only) ... 4.00
1-24,26-45: 2-Origin. 8-Shadow War; Simonson silver ink-c. 14-($2.50, 52 pgs.)-Worlds Collide Pt. 14. 27-Kent Williams-c ... 2.50
25 ($3.95) ... 4.00
...: Trial by Fire (2000, $9.95) r/#1-4; Leon-c ... 10.00

STATIC SHOCK!: REBIRTH OF THE COOL (TV)
DC Comics: Jan, 2001 - No. 4, Sept, 2001 ($2.50, limited series)
1-4: McDuffie-s/Leon-c/a ... 2.50

STEALTH SQUAD
Petra Comics: Sept, 1993 ($2.50, unfinished limited series)
1-Super hero team ... 2.50

STEAMPUNK
DC/WildStorm (Cliffhanger): Apr, 2000 - Present ($2.50)
Catechism (1/00) Prologue -Kelly-s/Bachalo-a ... 2.50
1-4,6-10: 4-Four covers by Bachalo, Madureira, Ramos, Campbell ... 2.50
5-($3.50) ... 3.50
...: Manimatron ('01, $14.95) r/#1-5, Catechism, Idiosincratica ... 15.00

STEED AND MRS. PEEL (TV)(Also see The Avengers)
Eclipse Books/ ACME Press: 1990 - No. 3, 1991 ($4.95, limited series)
Books One - Three: Grant Morrison scripts ... 5.00

STEEL (Also see JLA)
DC Comics: Feb, 1994 - No. 52, July, 1998 ($1.50/$1.95/$2.50)
1-8,09-52: 1-From Reign of the Supermen storyline. 6,7-Worlds Collide Pt. 5 &

Steel #51 © DC

Stone #2 © Haberlin & Portacio

Stories of Romance #13 © ATL

	GD2.0	FN6.0	VF8.0	NM9.4

12. 8-(9/94). 0-(10/94). 9-(11/94). 46-Superboy-t/app. 50-Millennium Giants x-over ... 2.50
Annual 1 (1994, $2.95)-Elseworlds story ... 3.00
Annual 2 (1995, $3.95)-Year One story ... 4.00
.Forging of a Hero TPB (1997, $19.95) r/ early app. ... 20.00

STEEL: THE OFFICIAL COMIC ADAPTION OF THE WARNER BROS. MOTION PICTURE
DC Comics: 1997 ($4.95, Prestige format, one-shot)
n-Movie adaption; Bogdanove & Giordano-a ... 5.00

STEELGRIP STARKEY
Marvel Comics (Epic Comics): June, 1986 - No. 6, July, 1987 ($1.50, limited series, Baxter paper)
1-6 ... 2.25

STEEL STERLING (Formerly Shield-Steel Sterling; see Blue Ribbon, Jackpot, Mighty Comics, Mighty Crusaders, Roly Poly & Zip Comics)
Archie Enterprises, Inc.: No. 4, Jan, 1984 - No. 7, July, 1984
4-7: 4-6-Kanigher-s; Barreto-a. 5,6-Infantino-a. 6-McWilliams-a ... 4.00

STEEL, THE INDESTRUCTIBLE MAN (See All-Star Squadron #8)
DC Comics: Mar, 1978 - No. 5, Oct-Nov, 1978

		GD2.0	FN6.0	VF8.0	NM9.4
1		1	4	7	10
2-5: 5-44 pgs.					6.00

STEELTOWN ROCKERS
Marvel Comics: Apr, 1987 - No. 6, Sept, 1990 ($1.00, limited series)
1-6: Small town teens form rock band ... 2.25

STEVE AUSTIN (See Stone Cold Steve Austin)

STEVE CANYON (See Harvey Comics Hits #52)
Dell Publishing Co.: No. 519, 11/53 - No. No. 1033, 9/59 (All Milton Caniff-a except #519, 939, 1033)

	GD2.0	FN6.0	VF8.0	NM9.4
Four Color 519 (1, '53)	9	27	63	110
Four Color 578 (8/54), 641 (7/55), 737 (10/56), 804 (5/57), 939 (10/58), 1033 (9/59) (photo-c)	5	15	35	60

STEVE CANYON
Grosset & Dunlap: 1959 (6-3/4x9", 96 pgs., B&W, no text, hardcover)

	GD2.0	FN6.0	VF8.0	NM9.4
nn-Reprints 2 stories from strip (1953, 1957)	6	18	28	38
nn (softcover edition)	5	15	23	30

STEVE CANYON COMICS
Harvey Publ.: Feb, 1948 - No. 6, Dec, 1948 (Strip reprints, No. 4,5: 52pgs.)

	GD2.0	FN6.0	VF8.0	NM9.4
1-Origin; has biography of Milton Caniff; Powell-a, 2 pgs.; Caniff-a	24	72	127	215
2-Caniff, Powell-a in #2-6	15	45	77	130
3-6: 6-Intro Madame Lynx-c/story	14	42	72	120

STEVE CANYON IN 3-D
Kitchen Sink Press: June, 1986 ($2.25, one-shot)
1-Contains unpublished story from 1954 ... 5.00

STEVE DITKO'S STRANGE AVENGING TALES
Fantagraphics Books: Feb, 1997 ($2.95, B&W)
1-Ditko-c/s/a ... 3.00

STEVE DONOVAN, WESTERN MARSHAL (TV)
Dell Publishing Co.: No. 675, Feb, 1956 - No. 880, Feb, 1958 (All photo-c)

	GD2.0	FN6.0	VF8.0	NM9.4
Four Color 675-Kinstler-a	8	24	56	100
Four Color 768-Kinstler-a	6	18	42	80
Four Color 880	4	12	30	50

STEVE ROPER
Famous Funnies: Apr, 1948 - No. 5, Dec, 1948

	GD2.0	FN6.0	VF8.0	NM9.4
1-Contains 1944 daily newspaper-r	12	36	61	100
2	8	24	42	60
3-5	7	21	36	50

STEVE SAUNDERS SPECIAL AGENT (See Special Agent)
STEVE SAVAGE (See Captain...)
STEVE ZODIAC & THE FIRE BALL XL-5 (TV)
Gold Key: Jan, 1964

	GD2.0	FN6.0	VF8.0	NM9.4
10108-401 (#1)	8	24	56	105

STEVIE (Mazie's boy friend)(Also see Flat-Top, Mazie & Mortie)
Mazie (Magazine Publ.): Nov, 1952 - No. 6, Apr, 1954

	GD2.0	FN6.0	VF8.0	NM9.4
1-Teenage humor; Stevie, Mortie & Mazie begin	8	24	42	60
2-6	5	15	25	35

STEVIE MAZIE'S BOY FRIEND (See Harvey Hits #5)
STEWART THE RAT (See Eclipse Graphic Album Series)
ST. GEORGE (See listing under Saint...)

STIG'S INFERNO
Vortex/Eclipse: 1985 - No. 7, Mar, 1987 ($1.95, B&W)
1-7 ($1.95) ... 2.25
Graphic Album (1988, $6.95, B&W, 100 pgs.) ... 7.00

STING OF THE GREEN HORNET (See The Green Hornet)
Now Comics: June, 1992 - No. 4, 1992 ($2.50, limited series)
1-4: Butler-c/a ... 2.50
1-4 ($2.75)-Collectors Ed.; polybagged w/poster ... 3.00

STONE
Avalon Studios: Aug, 1998 - No. 4, Apr, 1999 ($2.50, limited series)
1-4-Portacio-a/Haberlin-s ... 2.50
1-Alternate-c ... 5.00
2-($14.95) DF Stonechrome Edition ... 15.00

STONE (Volume 2)
Avalon Studios: Aug, 1999 - No. 4, May, 2000 ($2.50)
1-4 Portacio-a/Haberlin-s ... 2.50

STONE COLD STEVE AUSTIN (WWF Wrestling)
Chaos! Comics: Oct, 1999 - No. 4, Feb, 2000 ($2.95)
1-4-Reg. & photo-c; Steven Grant-s ... 3.00
1-Premium Ed. ($10.00) ... 10.00
Preview ($5.00) ... 5.00

STONEY BURKE (TV)
Dell Publishing Co.: June-Aug, 1963 - No. 2, Sept-Nov, 1963

	GD2.0	FN6.0	VF8.0	NM9.4
1,2-Jack Lord photo-c on both	3	9	17	25

STONY CRAIG
Pentagon Publishing Co.: 1946 (No #)

	GD2.0	FN6.0	VF8.0	NM9.4
nn-Reprints Bell Syndicate's "Sgt. Stony Craig" newspaper strips	7	21	38	55

STORIES BY FAMOUS AUTHORS ILLUSTRATED (Fast Fiction #1-5)
Seaboard Publ./Famous Authors Ill.: No. 6, Aug, 1950 - No. 13, Mar, 1951

	GD2.0	FN6.0	VF8.0	NM9.4
1-Scarlet Pimpernel-Baroness Orczy	36	108	191	330
2-Capt. Blood-Raphael Sabatini	35	105	185	320
3-She, by Haggard	40	120	220	400
4-The 39 Steps-John Buchan	24	72	127	215
5-Beau Geste-P. C. Wren	24	72	127	215

NOTE: The above five issues are exact reprints of Fast Fiction #1-5 except for the title change and new Kiefer covers on #1 and 2. Kiefer c(r)-3-5. The above 5 issues were released before Famous Authors #6.

	GD2.0	FN6.0	VF8.0	NM9.4
6-Macbeth, by Shakespeare; Kiefer art (8/50); used in **SOTI**, pg. 22,143; Kiefer-c; 36 pgs.	33	99	174	300
7-The Window; Kiefer-c/a; 52 pgs.	24	72	127	215
8-Hamlet, by Shakespeare; Kiefer-c/a; 36 pgs.	29	87	153	265
9,10: 9-Nicholas Nickleby, by Dickens; G. Schrotter-a; 52 pgs. 10-Romeo & Juliet, by Shakespeare; 36 pgs.	24	72	127	215
11-13: 11-Ben-Hur, Schrotter-a; 52 pgs. 12-La Svengali; Schrotter-a; 36 pgs. 13-Scaramouche; Kiefer-c/a; 36 pgs.	23	69	121	205

NOTE: Artwork was prepared/advertised for #14, The Red Badge Of Courage. Gilberton bought out Famous Authors, Ltd. and used that story as C.I. #98. Famous Authors, Ltd. then published the Classics Junior series. The Famous Authors titles were published as part of the regular Classics Ill. Series in Brazil starting in 1952.

STORIES FROM THE TWILIGHT ZONE
Skylark Pub: Mar, 1979, 68pgs. (B&W comic digest, 5-1/4x7-5/8")

	GD2.0	FN6.0	VF8.0	NM9.4
15405-2: Pfevfer-a, 56pgs, new comics	3	9	17	26

STORIES OF ROMANCE (Formerly Meet Miss Bliss)
Atlas Comics (LMC): No. 5, Mar, 1956 - No. 13, Aug, 1957

StormWatch #41 © WSP

Straight Arrow #9 © ME

Strange Adventures #17 © DC

	GD2.0	FN6.0	VF8.0	NM9.4

	GD2.0	FN6.0	VF8.0	NM9.4

5-Baker-a?	10	30	55	80
6-10,12,13	7	21	36	50
11-Baker, Romita-a; Colletta-c/a	8	24	42	60

NOTE: **Ann Brewster** a-13. **Colletta** a-9(2), 11; c-5, 11.

STORM
Marvel Comics: Feb, 1996 - No. 4, May, 1996 ($2.95, limited series)

1-4-Foil-c; Dodson-a(p); Ellis-s: 2-4-Callisto;				3.50

STORMQUEST
Caliber Press (Sky Universe): Nov, 1994 - No. 6, Apr, 1995 ($1.95)

1-6				2.25

STORMWATCH (Also see The Authority)
Image Comics (WildStorm Prod.): May, 1993 - No. 50, Jul, 1997 ($1.95/$2.50)

1-8,0,9-36: 1-Intro StormWatch (Battalion, Diva, Winter, Fuji, & Hellstrike); 1st				
app. Weatherman; Jim Lee-c & part scripts; Lee plots in all. 1-Gold edition.1-				
3-Includes coupon for limited edition StormWatch trading card #00 by Lee.				
3-1st app. Backlash (cameo). 0-($2.50)-Polybagged w/card; 1st full app.				
Backlash. 9-(4/94, $2.50)-Intro Defile. 10-(6/94), 11,12-Both (8/94). 13,14-				
(9/94). 15-(10/94). 21-Reads #1 on-c. 22-Direct Market; Wildstorm Rising Pt.				
9, bound-in card. 23-Spartan joins team. 25-(6/94, June 1995 on-c, $2.50).				
35-Fire From Heaven Pt. 5. 36-Fire From Heaven Pt. 12				2.50
10-Alternate Portacio-c, see Deathblow #5				4.00
22-($1.95)-Newsstand, Wildstorm Rising Pt. 9				2.50
37-(7/96, $3.50, 38 pgs.)-Weatherman forms new team; 1st app. Jenny Sparks;				
Jack Hawksmoor & Rose Tattoo; Warren Ellis scripts begin; Justice League				
#1-c/swipe				5.00
38-49: 44-Three covers.				2.50
50-($4.50)				5.00
Special 1 ,2(1/94, 5/95, $3.50, 52 pgs.)				3.50
Sourcebook 1 (1/94, $2.50)				2.50
Forces of Nature ('99, $14.95, TPB) r/V1 #37-42				15.00
Lightning Strikes ('00, $14.95, TPB) r/V1 #43-47				15.00

STORMWATCH (Also see The Authority)
Image Comics (WildStorm): Oct, 1997 - No. 11, Sept, 1998 ($2.50)

1-Ellis-s/Jimenez-a(p); two covers by Bennett				5.00
1-($3.50)-Voyager Pack bagged w/Gen 13 preview				6.00
2-4: 4-1st app. Midnighter and Apollo				4.00
5-11: 7,8-Freefall app. 9-Gen13 & DV8 app.				3.00
A Finer World ('99, $14.95, TPB) r/V4 #4-9				15.00
Change or Die ('99, $14.95, TPB) r/V1 #48-50 & V2 #1-3				15.00
Final Orbit ('01, $9.95, TPB) r/V2 #10,11 & WildC.A.T.S./Aliens; Hitch-c				10.00

STORMWATCHER
Eclipse Comics (Acme Press): Apr, 1989 - No. 4, Dec, 1989 ($2.00, B&W)

1-4				2.25

STORMY (Disney) (Movie)
Dell Publishing Co.: No. 537, Feb, 1954

Four Color 537 (…the Thoroughbred)-on-top 2/3 of each page; Pluto story on				
bottom 1/3	4	12	25	38

STORY OF JESUS (See Classics Illustrated Special Issue)

STORY OF MANKIND, THE (Movie)
Dell Publishing Co.: No. 851, Jan, 1958

Four Color 851-Vincent Price/Hedy Lamarr photo-c	7	21	49	90

STORY OF MARTHA WAYNE, THE
Argo Publ.: April, 1956

1-Newspaper strip-r	6	18	29	40

STORY OF RUTH, THE
Dell Publishing Co.: No. 1144, Nov-Jan, 1961 (Movie)

Four Color #1144-Photo-c	9	27	63	120

STORY OF THE COMMANDOS, THE (Combined Operations)
Long Island Independent: 1943 (15¢, B&W, 68 pgs.) (Distr. by Gilberton)

nn-All text (no comics); photos & illustrations; ad for Classic Comics on back				
cover (Rare)	34	102	179	310

STORY OF THE GLOOMY BUNNY, THE (See March of Comics #9)

STRAIGHT ARROW (Radio)(See Best of the West & Great Western)

Magazine Enterprises: Feb-Mar, 1950 - No. 55, Mar, 1956 (All 36 pgs.)

1-Straight Arrow (alias Steve Adams) & his palomino Fury begin; 1st mention				
of Sundown Valley & the Secret Cave	45	135	270	475
2-Red Hawk begins (1st app?) by Powell (origin), ends #55				
	23	69	121	210
3-Frazetta-c	31	93	165	285
4,5: 4-Secret Cave-c	21	63	110	185
6-10	20	60	105	175
11-Classic story "The Valley of Time", with an ancient civilization made of gold				
	21	63	110	185
12-19	15	45	77	130
20-Origin Straight Arrow's Shield	17	51	88	150
21-Origin Fury	21	63	110	185
22-Frazetta-c	22	66	116	200
23,25-30: 25-Secret Cave-c. 28-Red Hawk meets The Vikings				
	10	30	55	80
24-Classic story "The Dragons of Doom!" with prehistoric pteradactyls				
	13	39	66	110
31-38: 36-Red Hawk drug story by Powell	8	24	42	70
39-Classic story "The Canyon Beast", with a dinosaur egg hatching a				
Tyranosaurus Rex	12	36	61	100
40-Classic story "Secret of The Spanish Specters", with Conquistadors' lost				
treasure	10	30	55	85
41,42,44-54: 45-Secret Cave-c	7	21	36	50
43-Intro & 1st app. Blaze, S. Arrow's Warrior dog	9	27	49	70
55-Last issue	10	30	55	80

NOTE: **Fred Meagher** a-1-55; c-1, 2, 4-21, 23-55. **Powell** a-2-55. **Whitney** a-1. Many issues advertise the radio premiums associated with Straight Arrow.

STRAIGHT ARROW'S FURY (Also see A-1 Comics)
Magazine Enterprises: No. 119, 1954 (one-shot)

A-1 119-Origin; Fred Meagher-c/a	16	48	83	140

STRANGE (Tales You'll Never Forget)
Ajax-Farrell Publ. (Four Star Comic Corp.): March, 1957 - No. 6, May, 1958

1	21	63	110	185
2-Censored r/Haunted Thrills	11	33	55	90
3-6	10	30	55	80

STRANGE ADVENTURES
National Periodical Publications: Aug-Sept, 1950 - No. 244, Oct-Nov, 1973 (No 1-12: 52 pgs.)

1-Adaptation of "Destination Moon"; preview of movie w/photo-c from movie				
(also see Fawcett Movie Comic #2); adapt. of Edmond Hamilton's "Chris				
KL-99" in #1-3; Darwin Jones begins	250	750	2125	4000
2	111	332	944	1775
3,4	75	225	638	1200
5-8,10: 7-Origin Kris KL-99	64	193	544	1025
9-(6/51)-Origin/1st app. Captain Comet (c/story)	153	459	1300	2450
11-20: 12,13,17,18-Toth-a. 14-Robot-c	46	138	368	650
21-30: 28-Atomic explosion panel. 30-Robot-c	37	112	278	500
31,34-38	34	102	255	460
32,33-Krigstein-a	35	105	263	475
39-Ill. in **SOTI** "Treating police contemptuously" (top right)				
	40	120	300	520
40-49-Last Capt. Comet; not in 45,47,48	39	99	248	440
50-53-Last precode issue (2/55)	25	75	174	310
54-70	18	54	126	225
71-99	14	42	100	170
100	16	48	110	190
101-110: 104-Space Museum begins by Sekowsky	10	30	70	120
111-116,118,119: 114-Star Hawkins begins, ends #185; Heath-a in Wood				
E.C. style	9	27	65	110
117-(6/60)-Origin/1st app. Atomic Knights.	50	150	400	720
120-2nd app. Atomic Knights	24	72	168	300
121,122,125,127,128,130,131,133,134: 134-Last 10¢ issue				
	8	24	56	90
123,126-3rd & 4th app. Atomic Knights	14	42	98	165
124-Intro/origin Faceless Creature	9	27	65	110
129,132,135,138,141,147-Atomic Knights app.	10	30	68	115
136,137,139,140,143,145,146,148,149,151,152,154,155,157-159:				

Strange Adventures #216 © DC

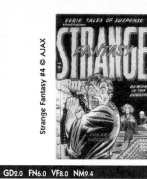

Strange Fantasy #4 © AJAX

Strange Mysteries #2 © SUPR

	GD2.0	FN6.0	VF8.0	NM9.4
159-Star Rovers app.; Gil Kane/Anderson-a.	6	18	40	65
142-2nd app. Faceless Creature	7	21	50	80
144-Only Atomic Knights-c (by M. Anderson)	11	33	77	130
150,153,156,160: Atomic Knights in each. 153-(6/63)-3rd app. Faceless				
Creature; atomic explosion-c. 160-Last Atomic Knights				
	7	21	53	85
161-179: 161-Last Space Museum. 163-Star Rovers app. 170-Infinity-c.				
177-Intro/origin Immortal Man	4	12	29	45
180-Origin/1st app. Animal Man	19	57	132	235
181-183,185-189: 187-Intro/origin The Enchantress	3	10	23	35
184-2nd app. Animal Man by Gil Kane	12	36	84	140
190-1st app. Animal Man in costume	15	45	105	180
191-194,196-200,202-204	3	9	20	30
195-1st full app. Animal Man	8	24	56	90
201-Last Animal Man; 2nd full app.	5	15	34	55
205-(10/67)-Intro/origin Deadman by Infantino & begin series, ends #216				
	12	36	88	150
206-Neal Adams-a begins	8	24	56	90
207-210	6	18	45	75
211-216: 211-Space Museum-r. 216-(1-2/69)-Deadman story finally concludes				
in Brave & the Bold #86 (10-11/69); secret message panel by Neal Adams				
(pg. 13); tribute to Steranko	5	15	34	55
217-r/origin & 1st app. Adam Strange from Showcase #17, begin-r;				
Atomic Knights-r begin	2	6	12	18
218-221,223-225: 218-Last 12¢ issue. 225-Last 15¢ issue				
	2	6	11	15
222-New Adam Strange story; Kane/Anderson-a	3	9	21	32
226,227,230-236-(68-52 pgs.): 226, 227-New Adam Strange text story w/illos by				
Anderson (8,6 pgs.) 231-Last Atomic Knights-r. 235-JLA-c/s				
	2	6	11	16
228,229 (68 pgs.)	2	6	15	22
237-243	1	4	7	10
244-Last issue	2	6	9	12

NOTE: **Neal Adams** a-206-216; c-207-216, 228, 235. **Anderson** a-8-52, 94, 96, 99, 115, 117, 119-163, 217r, 218r; 222, 223-225r; 226, 229r, 242i(r); c-18, 19, 21, 23, 24, 27, 30, 32-44(most); c/r-157i, 190i, 217-224, 228-231, 233, 235-239, 241-243. **Ditko** a-188, 189. **Drucker** a-42, 43, 45. **Elias** a-212. **Finlay** a-2, 3, 6, 7, 210r, 229r. **Giunta** a-237r. **Heath** a-116. **Infantino** a-10-101, 106-151, 154, 157-163, 180, 190, 218-221r; 223-244p(r); c-50; c(r)-190p, 197, 199-211, 218-221, 223-244. **Kaluta** c-238, 240. **Gil Kane** a-8-116, 124, 125, 130, 138, 146-157, 173-186, 204r, 222r, 229-231r; c(j)-11-17, 25, 154, 157. **Kubert** a-55(2 pgs.), 226; c-219, 220, 225-227, 232, 234. **Moriera** c-26, 28, 29, 71. **Morrow** c-230. **Mortimer** c-8. **Powell** a-4. **Sekowsky** a-71p, 97-162p, 217p(r), 218p(r); c-206, 217-219r. **Simon & Kirby** a-2r (2 pgs) **Sparling** a-201. **Toth** a-8, 12, 13, 17-19. **Wood** a-154i. Atomic Knights reprints by Anderson in #117, 120, 123, 126, 129, 132, 135, 138, 141, 144, 147, 150, 153, 156, 160. Neal Adams reprints by Anderson in 206-216. Chris KL99 in 1-3, 5, 7, 9, 11, 15. Capt. Comet covers-9-14, 17-19, 24, 26, 27, 32-44.

STRANGE ADVENTURES
DC Comics (Vertigo): Nov, 1999 - No. 4 ($2.50, limited series)

1-3: 1-Bolland-c; art by Bolland, Gibbons, Quitely				2.50

STRANGE AS IT SEEMS (See Famous Funnies-A Carnival of Comics, Feature Funnies #1, The John Hix Scrap Book & Peanuts)

STRANGE AS IT SEEMS
United Features Syndicate: 1939

Single Series 9, 1, 2	36	108	191	330

STRANGE ATTRACTORS
RetroGraphix: 1993 - No. 15, Feb, 1997 ($2.50, B&W)

1-15: 1-(5/93), 2-(8/93), 3-(11/93), 4-(2/94)				2.50
Volume One-($14.95, trade paperback)-r/#1-7				15.00

STRANGE ATTRACTORS: MOON FEVER
Caliber Comics: Feb, 1997 - No. 3, June, 1997 ($2.95, B&W, mini-series)

1-3				3.00

STRANGE COMBAT TALES
Marvel Comics (Epic Comics): Oct, 1993 - No. 4, Jan, 1994 ($2.50, limited series)

1-4				2.50

STRANGE CONFESSIONS
Ziff-Davis Publ. Co.: Jan-Mar (Spring on-c), 1952 - No. 4, Fall, 1952 (All have photo-c)

1(Scarce)-Kinstler-a	47	142	286	500

	GD2.0	FN6.0	VF8.0	NM9.4
2(Scarce, 7-8/52)	37	111	197	340
3(Scarce, 9-10/52)-#3 on-c, #2 on inside; Reformatory girl story; photo-c				
	37	111	197	340
4(Scarce)	37	111	197	340

STRANGE DAYS
Eclipse Comics: Oct, 1984 - No. 3, Apr, 1985 ($1.75, Baxter paper)

1-3: Freakwave, Johnny Nemo, & Paradax from Vanguard Illustrated; nudity,				
violence & strong language				2.25

STRANGE DAYS (Movie)
Marvel Comics: Dec, 1995 ($5.95, squarebound, one-shot)

1-Adaptation of film				6.00

STRANGE FANTASY (Eerie Tales of Suspense!)(Formerly Rocketman #1)
Ajax-Farrell: Aug, 1952 - No. 14, Oct-Nov, 1954

2(#1, 8/52)-Jungle Princess story; Kamensh-a; reprinted from Ellery Queen #1				
	45	135	270	475
2(10/52)-No Black Cat or Rulah; Bakerish, Kamensh-a; hypo/meathook-c				
	40	120	230	380
3-Rulah story, called Pulah	40	120	214	370
4-Rocket Man app. (2/53)	37	111	197	340
5,6,8,10,12,14	26	78	136	235
7-Madam Satan/Slave story	37	111	197	340
9(w/Black Cat), 9(w/Boy's Ranch; S&K-a), 9(w/War)(A rebinding of Harvey				
interiors; not publ. by Ajax)	37	111	174	300
9-Regular app.; Steve Ditko's 3rd published work (tied with Captain 3D)				
	43	129	257	450
11-Jungle story	34	102	179	310
13-Bondage-c; Rulah (Kolah) story	34	102	179	310

STRANGE GALAXY
Eerie Publications: V1#8, Feb, 1971 - No. 11, Aug, 1971 (B&W, magazine)

V1#8-Reprints-c/Fantastic V19#3 (2/70) (a pulp)	3	9	21	32
9-11	3	9	17	25

STRANGEHAVEN
Abiogenesis Press: June, 1995 - Present ($2.95, B&W)

1-13				3.00

STRANGE JOURNEY
America's Best (Steinway Publ.) (Ajax/Farrell): Sept, 1957 - No. 4, Jun, 1958 (Farrell reprints)

1	20	60	105	180
2-4: 2-Flying saucer-c	14	42	72	120

STRANGE LOVE (See Fox Giants)

STRANGELOVE
Entity Comics: 1995 ($2.50)

1				2.50

STRANGE MYSTERIES
Superior/Dynamic Publications: Sept, 1951 - No. 21, Jan, 1955

1-Kamensh-a & horror stories begin	59	177	369	650
2	36	108	191	330
3-5	33	99	174	300
6-8	27	81	145	250
9-Bondage 3-D effect-c	34	102	179	310
10-Used in SOTI, pg. 181	25	75	130	225
11-18	22	66	116	200
19-r/Journey Into Fear #1; cover is a splash from one story; Baker-r(2)				
	24	72	127	215
20,21-Reprints; 20-r/#1 with new-c	15	51	88	150

STRANGE MYSTERIES
I. W. Enterprises/Super Comics: 1963 - 1964

I.W. Reprint #9; Rulah-r/Spook #28; Disbrow-a

	4	12	26	40

Super Reprint #12,15-17(1963-64): 10,11-r/Strange #2,1. 12-r/Tales of Horror #5 (3/53) less-c. 15-r/Dark Mysteries #23. 16-r/The Dead Who Walk.

17-r/Dark Mysteries #22	4	12	26	40

Super Reprint #18-r/Witchcraft #1; Kubert-a

	4	12	26	40

STRANGE PLANETS
I. W. Enterprises/Super Comics: 1958; 1963-64

Strangers in Paradise (2nd series) #4
© Terry Moore

Strange Stories of Suspense #7 © MAR

Strange Suspense Stories #2 © FAW

	GD2.0	FN6.0	VF8.0	NM9.4

I.W. Reprint #1(nd)-Reprints E. C. Incredible S/F #30 plus-c/Strange Worlds #3

	7	21	50	80

I.W. Reprint #9-Orlando/Wood-r/Strange Worlds #4; cover-r from Flying Saucers #1

	9	27	63	105

Super Reprint #10-Wood-r (22 pg.) from Space Detective #1; cover-r/Attack on Planet Mars

	9	27	63	105

Super Reprint #11-Wood-r (25 pg.) from An Earthman on Venus

	10	30	70	120

Super Reprint #12-Orlando-r/Rocket to the Moon 9 27 63 105
Super Reprint #15-Reprints Journey Into Unknown Worlds #8; Heath, Colan-r

	5	15	34	55

Super Reprint #16-Reprints Avon's Strange Worlds #6; Kinstler, Check-a

	5	15	38	60

Super Reprint #18-r/Great Exploits #1 (Daring Adventures #6); Space Busters, Explorer Joe, The Son of Robin Hood; Krigstein-a 4 12 29 45

STRANGERS, THE
Malibu Comics (Ultraverse): June, 1993 - No. 24, May, 1995 ($1.95/$2.50)

1-4,6-12,14-20: 1st app. The Strangers; has coupon for Ultraverse Premiere #0; 1st app. the Night Man (not in costume). 2-Polybagged w/trading card. 7-Break-Thru x-over. 8-2 pg. origin Solution. 12-Silver foil logo; wraparound-c. 17-Rafferty app. 2.50
1-With coupon missing 2.25
1-Full cover holographic edition, 1st of kind w/Hardcase #1 & Prime #1 6.00
1-Ultra 5000 limited silver foil 4.00
4-($2.50)-Newsstand edition bagged w/card 2.50
5-($2.50, 52 pgs.)-Rune flip-c/story by B. Smith (3 pgs.); The Mighty Magnor 1 pg. strip by Aragones; 2-p. Night Man preview 2.50
13-($3.50, 68 pgs.)-Mantra app.; flip book w/Ultraverse Premiere #4 3.50
21-24 ($2.50) 2.50
...:The Pilgrim Conundrum Saga (1/95, $3.95, 68pgs.) 4.00

STRANGERS IN PARADISE
Antarctic Press: Nov, 1993 - No. 3, Feb, 1994 ($2.75, B&W, limited series)

1	6	18	40	65
1-2nd/3rd prints	1	3	6	8
2 (2300 printed)	4	12	29	45
3	3	9	20	30

Trade paperback (Antarctic Press, $6.95)-Red -c (5000 print run) 10.00
Trade paperback (Abstract Studios, $6.95)-Red-c (2000 print run) 15.00
Trade paperback (Abstract Studios, $6.95, 1st-4th printing)-Blue-Hardcover ('98, $29.95) includes first draft pages 30.00
Gold Reprint Series ($2.75) 1-3-r/#1-3 2.75

STRANGERS IN PARADISE
Abstract Studios: Sept, 1994 - No. 14, July, 1996 ($2.75, B&W)

1	2	6	11	16
1,3- 2nd printings				4.00
2,3: 2-Color dream sequence	1	3	6	8
4-10				4.00
4-6-2nd printings				2.75
11-14: 14-The Letters of Molly & Poo				3.00

Gold Reprint Series ($2.75) 1-13-r/#1-13 2.75
I Dream Of You ($16.95, TPB) r/#1-9 17.00
It's a Good Life ($8.95, TPB) r/#10-13 9.00

STRANGERS IN PARADISE (Volume Three)
Homage Comics #1-8/Abstract Studios #9-on: Oct, 1996 - Present ($2.75/$2.95, color #1-5, B&W #6-on)

1-Terry Moore-c/s/a in all; dream seq. by Jim Lee-a 4.00

1-Jim Lee variant-c	1	3	6	8
2-5				3.50

6-16: 6-Return to B&W. 13-15-High school flashback. 16-Xena Warrior Princess parody; two covers 3.00
17-45: 33-Color issue 3.00
...Lyrics and Poems (2/99) 2.75
High School ('98, $8.95, TPB) r/#13-16 9.00
Immortal ('98, $14.95, TPB) r/#6-12 15.00
Love Me Tender ($12.95, TPB) r/#1-5 in B&W w/ color Lee seq. 13.00
My Other Life ($14.95, TPB) r/#25-30 15.00
Tropic of Desire ($12.95, TPB) r/#39-43 13.00
The Complete... : Volume 3 Part 3 HC ('01, $49.95) r/#26-38 50.00

STRANGE SPORTS STORIES (See Brave & the Bold #45-49, DC Special, and DC Super Stars #10)
National Periodical Publications: Sept-Oct, 1973 - No. 6, July-Aug, 1974

1	3	9	20	30
2-6: 2-Swan/Anderson-a	2	6	11	16

STRANGE STORIES FROM ANOTHER WORLD (Unknown World #1)
Fawcett Publications: No. 2, Aug, 1952 - No. 5, Feb, 1953

2-Saunders painted-c	50	150	300	520
3-5-Saunders painted-c	40	120	220	380

STRANGE STORIES OF SUSPENSE (Rugged Action #1-4)
Atlas Comics (CSI): No. 5, Oct, 1955 - No. 16, Aug, 1957

5(#1)	40	120	217	375
6,9	25	75	130	225
7- E. C. swipe cover/Vault of Horror #32	25	75	133	230
8-Morrow/Williamson-a; Pakula-a	27	81	142	245
10-Crandall, Torres, Meskin-a	25	75	133	230
11-13: 12-Torres, Pakula-a. 13-E.C. art swipes	21	63	110	185
14-16: 14-Williamson/Mayo-a. 15-Krigstein-a. 16-Fox, Powell-a				
	23	69	121	205

NOTE: Everett a-6, 7, 13; c-8, 9, 11-14. Heath a-5. Maneely c-5. Morisi a-11. Morrow a-13. Powell a-8. Severin c-7. Wildey a-14.

STRANGE STORY (Also see Front Page)
Harvey Publications: June-July, 1946 (52 pgs.)

1-The Man in Black Called Fate by Powell 33 99 174 300

STRANGE SUSPENSE STORIES (Lawbreakers Suspense Stories #10-15; This Is Suspense #23-26; Captain Atom V1#78 on)
Fawcett Publications/Charlton Comics No. 16 on: 6/52 - No. 5, 2/53; No. 16, 1/54 - No. 22, 11/54; No. 27, 10/55 - No. 77, 10/65; V3#1, 10/67 - V1#9, 9/69

1-(Fawcett)-Powell, Sekowsky-a	73	219	455	800
2-George Evans horror story	46	137	276	485
3-5 (2/53)-George Evans horror stories	40	120	232	400
16(1-2/54)-Formerly Lawbreakers S.S.	30	90	159	275
17,21: 21-Shuster-a	24	72	127	215
18-E.C. swipe cover/HOF 7; Ditko-c/a(2)	40	120	220	380
19-Ditko electric chair-c; Ditko-a	50	150	300	525
20-Ditko-c/a(2)	40	120	220	380
22(11/54)-Ditko-a, Shuster-a; last pre-code issue; becomes This Is Suspense	35	105	185	320
27(10/55)-(Formerly This Is Suspense #26)	15	45	77	130
28-30,38	10	30	55	85
31-33,35,37,40-Ditko-c/a(2-3 each)	22	66	116	195
34-Story of ruthless business man, Wm. B. Gaines; Ditko-c/a				
	43	129	257	450
36-(15¢, 68 pgs.); Ditko-a(4)	26	78	136	235
39,41,52,53-Ditko-a	18	54	94	155
42-44,46,49,54-60	5	15	34	55
45,47,48,50,51-Ditko-c/a	14	42	102	175
61-74	3	10	23	35
75(6/65)-Reprints origin/1st app. Captain Atom by Ditko from Space Advs. #33; r/Severin/a/Space Advs. #24 (75-77: 12¢ issues)	13	39	91	155
76,77-Captain Atom-r by Ditko/Space Advs.	6	18	42	70
V3#1(10/67): 12¢ issues begin	3	9	20	30
V1#2-Ditko-c/a; atom bomb-c	3	9	19	28
V1#3-9: All 12¢ issues	2	6	11	16

NOTE: Alascia a-19. Aparo a-60, V3#1, 2, 4; c-V1#4, 8. Baily a-1-3; c-2, 5. Evans c-3, 4. Giordano c-16, 17p, 24p, 25p. Montes/Bache c-66. Powell a-4. Shuster a-19, 21. Marcus Swayze a-21.

STRANGE TALES (...Featuring Warlock #178-181; Doctor Strange #169 on)
Atlas (CCPC #1-67/ZPC #68-79/VPI #80-85)/Marvel #86(7/61) on: June, 1951 - #168, May, 1968; #169, Sept, 1973 - #188, Nov, 1976

1-Horror/weird stories begin	300	900	1875	3500
2	100	300	625	1100
3,5: 3-Atom bomb panels	75	225	469	825
4-Cosmic eyeball story "The Evil Eye"	80	240	500	875
6-9: 6-Heath-a. 7-Colan-a	55	165	341	600
10-Krigstein-a	59	177	369	650
11-14,16-20	40	120	232	400
15-Krigstein-a	40	120	220	410

Strange Tales #19 © MAR

Strange Tales #102 © MAR

Strange Terrors #5 © STJ

	GD2.0	FN6.0	VF8.0	NM9.4
21,23-27,29-34: 27-Atom bomb panels. 33-Davis-a. 34-Last pre-code				
issue (2/55)	35	105	185	320
22-Krigstein, Forte/Fox-a	36	108	191	330
28-Jack Katz story used in Senate Investigation report, pgs. 7 & 169				
	36	108	191	330
35-41,43,44: 37-Vampire story by Colan	20	60	140	250
42,45,59,61-Krigstein-a; #61 (2/58)	21	63	146	260
46-57,60: 51-1st S.A. issue. 53,56-Crandall-a. 60-(8/57)				
	18	54	123	220
58,64-Williamson-a in each, with Mayo-#58	18	54	126	225
62,63,65,66: 62-Torres-a. 66-Crandall-a	17	51	118	210
67-Prototype ish. (Quicksilver)	19	57	132	235
68,71,72,74,77,80: Ditko/Kirby-a in #67-80	18	54	123	220
69,70,73,75,76,78,79: 69-Prototype ish. (Prof. X). 70-Prototype ish. (Giant				
Man). 73-Prototype ish. (Ant-Man). 75-Prototype ish. (Iron Man). 76-Prototype				
ish. (Human Torch). 78-Prototype ish. (Ant-Man). 79-Prototype ish. (Dr.				
Strange) (12/60)	23	69	160	285
81-83,85-88,90,91-Ditko/Kirby-a in all: 86-Robot-c. 90-(11/61)-Atom bomb				
blast panel	16	48	112	200
84-Prototype ish. (Magneto)(5/61); has powers like Magneto of X-Men, but two				
years earlier; Ditko/Kirby-a	21	63	146	260
89-1st app. Fin Fang Foom (10/61) by Kirby	41	123	331	600
92-Prototype ish. (Ancient One); last 10¢ issue	18	54	123	220
93,95,96,98-100: Kirby-a	15	45	105	180
94-Prototype ish. (The Thing); Kirby-a	18	54	123	220
97-1st app. Aunt May & Uncle Ben by Ditko (6/62), before Amazing Fantasy				
#15; (see Tales Of Suspense #7); Kirby-a	37	111	278	500
101-Human Torch begins by Kirby (10/62); origin recap Fantastic Four &				
Human Torch; H. Torch-c begin	81	244	690	1300
102-1st app. Wizard; robot-c	33	99	250	450
103-105: 104-1st app. Trapster. 105-2nd Wizard	28	84	196	350
106,108,109: 106-Fantastic Four guests (3/63)	18	54	129	230
107-(4/63)-Human Torch/Sub-Mariner battle; 4th S.A. Sub-Mariner app. & 1st				
x-over outside of Fantastic Four	24	72	168	300
110-(7/63)-Intro Doctor Strange, Ancient One & Wong by Ditko				
	100	300	850	1600
111-2nd Dr. Strange	31	94	233	425
112,113	13	39	94	160
114-Acrobat disguised as Captain America, 1st app. since the G.A.; intro. &				
1st app. Victoria Bentley; 3rd Dr. Strange app. & begin series (11/63)				
	33	100	250	450
115-Origin Dr. Strange; Human Torch vs. Sandman (Spidey villain; 2nd app.				
& brief origin); early Spider-Man x-over, 12/63	41	123	306	550
116-(1/64)-Human Torch battles The Thing; 1st Thing x-over				
	11	33	80	135
117,118,120: 120-1st Iceman x-over (from X-Men)	8	24	60	100
119-Spider-Man x-over (2 panel cameo)	10	30	70	120
121,122,124,126-134: Thing/Torch team-up in 121-134. 126-Intro Clea. 128-				
Quicksilver & Scarlet Witch app. (1/65). 130-The Beatles cameo. 134-Last				
Human Torch; The Watcher-c/story; Wood-a(i)	6	18	40	65
123-1st app. The Beetle (see Amazing Spider-Man #21 for next app.); last				
Thor x-over (8/64); Loki app.	6	18	45	75
125-Torch & Thing battle Sub-Mariner (10/64)	6	18	45	75
135-Col. (formerly Sgt.) Nick Fury becomes Nick Fury Agent of Shield (origin/				
1st app) by Kirby (8/65); series begins	12	36	88	150
136-140: 138-Intro Eternity	4	12	30	50
141-147,149: 145-Begins alternating-c features w/Nick Fury (odd #'s) & Dr.				
Strange (even #'s). 146-Last Ditko Dr. Strange who is in consecutive issues				
since #113; only full Ditko Dr. Strange-c this title. 147-Dr. Strange (by				
Everett #147-152) continues thru #168, then Dr. Strange #169				
	4	12	26	40
148-Origin Ancient One	6	18	45	75
150(11/66)-John Buscema's 1st work at Marvel	6	18	45	75
151-Kirby/Steranko-c/a; 1st Marvel work by Steranko	6	18	45	75
152,153-Kirby/Steranko-a	4	12	30	50
154-158-Steranko-a/script	4	12	30	50
159-Origin Nick Fury retold; Intro Val; Captain America-c/story; Steranko-a				
	5	15	38	60
160-162-Steranko-a/scripts; Capt. America app.	4	12	29	45
163-166,168-Steranko-a(p). 168-Last Nick Fury (gets own book next month)				

	GD2.0	FN6.0	VF8.0	NM9.4
& last Dr. Strange who also gets own book	4	12	26	40
167-Steranko pen/script; classic flag-c	5	15	38	60
169-1st app. Brother Voodoo(origin in #169,170) & begin series,				
ends #173.	2	6	11	16
170-174: 174-Origin Golem	1	4	7	10
175-177: 177-Brunner-c	1	3	5	7
178-(2/75)-Warlock by Starlin begins; origin Warlock & Him retold; 1st app.				
Magus; Starlin-c/a/scripts in 178-181 (all before Warlock #9)				
	2	6	13	20
179-181-All Warlock. 179-Intro/1st app. Pip the Troll. 180-Intro Gamora. 181-				
(8/75)-Warlock story continued in Warlock #9	2	6	9	12
182-188: 185,186-(Regular 25¢ editions)				4.00
185,186-(30¢ variants, limited distribution)(5,7/76)				6.00
Annual 1(1962)-Reprints from Strange Tales #73,76,78, Tales of Suspense				
#7,9, Tales to Astonish #1,6,7, & Journey Into Mystery #53,55,59; (1st Marvel				
annual?)	45	135	359	650
Annual 2(7/63)-Reprints from Strange Tales #67, Strange Worlds (Atlas) #1-3,				
World of Fantasy #16; new Human Torch vs. Spider-Man story by Kirby/				
Ditko (1st Spidey x-over; 4th app.); Kirby-c	56	169	478	900

NOTE: Briefer a-17. Burgos a-123p. J. Buscema a-174p. Colan a-7, 11, 20, 37, 53, 169-173p,
188p. Davis c-71. Ditko a-46, 50, 67-122, 123-125p, 126-146, 175r, 182-188r; c-51, 93, 115, 121,
146. Everett a-4, 21, 40-42, 73, 147-152, 164i; c-8, 10, 11, 13, 15, 24, 45, 49-54, 56, 58, 60, 61,
63, 148, 150, 152, 158i. Forte a-27, 43, 50, 53, 54, 60. Heath a-2; c-6, 18-20. Kamen a-45. G.
Kane c-170-173, 182p. Kirby Human Torch-101-105, 108, 109, 114, 120; Nick Fury-135p, 141-
143p; (Layouts)153-153; other Kirby a-67-100p; c-68-70, 72-74, 76-92, 94, 95, 101-114, 116-
123, 125-130, 132-135, 136p, 138-145, 147, 149, 151p. Kirby/Ayers c-101-106, 108-110.
Kirby/Ditko a-80, 88, 121; c-75, 93, 97, 100, 139. Lawrence a-29. Leiber/ Fox a-110-113.
Maneely a-3, 7, 37, 42; c-33, 40. Moldoff a-20. Mooney a-174i. Morisi a-53, 56. Morrow a-54.
Orlando a-41, 44, 46, 49, 52. Powell a-42, 44, 49, 54, 130-134p; c-131p. Reinman a-11, 50, 74,
88, 91, 95, 104, 106, 112i, 124-127. Robinson a-7. Romita c-169. Roussos c-201i. R.Q. Sale
a-56; c-16. Sekowski a-3, 11. Severin a(i)-136-138; c-137. Starlin a-178, 179, 180p, 181p; c-178-
180, 181p. Steranko a-151-161, 162-168p; c-151i, 153, 155, 157, 159, 161, 163, 165, 167.
Torres a-53, 62. Tuska a-14, 166p. Whitney a-149. Wildey a-42, 56. Woodbridge a-59. Fantastic
Four cameos #101-134. Jack Katz app.-26.

STRANGE TALES
Marvel Comics Group: Apr, 1987 - No. 19, Oct, 1988

V2#1-19				2.25

STRANGE TALES
Marvel Comics: Nov, 1994 ($6.95, one-shot)

V3#1-acetate-c				7.00

STRANGE TALES (Anthology; continues stories from Man-Thing #8 and
Werewolf By Night #6)
Marvel Comics: Sept, 1998 - No. 2, Oct, 1998 ($4.99)

1,2: 1-Silver Surfer app. 2-Two covers				5.00

STRANGE TALES: DARK CORNERS
Marvel Comics: May, 1998 ($3.99, one-shot)

1-Anthology; stories by Baron & Maleev, McGregor & Dringenberg, DeMatteis				
& Badger; Estes painted-c				4.00

STRANGE TALES OF THE UNUSUAL
Atlas Comics (ACI No. 1-4/WPI No. 5-11): Dec, 1955 - No. 11, Aug, 1957

	GD2.0	FN6.0	VF8.0	NM9.4
1-Powell-a	43	129	257	450
2	29	87	153	265
3-Williamson-a (4 pgs.)	29	87	153	270
4,6,8,10	21	63	110	185
5-Crandall, Ditko-a	26	78	136	235
7,9: 7-Kirby, Orlando-a. 9-Krigstein-a	23	69	121	205
10-Torres, Morrow-a	21	63	110	185

NOTE: Baily a-6. Brodsky c-2-4. Everett a-2, 6; c-6, 9, 11. Heck a-1. Maneely c-1i. Orlando a-1.
Pakula a-10. Robinson a-8. R.Q. Sale a-3. Wildey a-3.

STRANGE TERRORS
St. John Publishing Co.: June, 1952 - No. 7, Mar, 1953

	GD2.0	FN6.0	VF8.0	NM9.4
1-Bondage-c; Zombies spelled Zoombies on-c; Fine-esque-a				
	52	157	314	550
2	31	93	165	285
3-Kubert-a; painted-c	40	120	220	380
4-Kubert-a (reprinted in Mystery Tales #18); Ekgren painted-c; Fine-esque-a;				
Jerry Iger caricature	50	150	300	525
5-Kubert-a; painted-c	40	120	220	380
6-Giant (25¢, 100 pgs.)(1/53); bondage-c	50	150	300	525

	GD2.0	FN6.0	VF8.0	NM9.4

7-Giant (25¢, 100 pgs.); Kubert-c/a	55	165	330	575

NOTE: *Cameron* a-6, 7. *Morisi* a-6.

STRANGE WORLD OF YOUR DREAMS
Prize Publications: Aug, 1952 - No. 4, Jan-Feb, 1953

1-Simon & Kirby-a	61	182	381	675
2,3-Simon & Kirby-c/a. 2-Meskin-a	50	150	300	525
4-S&K-c; Meskin-a	40	120	240	420

STRANGE WORLDS (#18 continued from Avon's Eerie #17)
Avon Periodicals: 11/50 - No. 9, 11/52; No. 18, 10-11/54 - No. 22, 9-10/55
(No #11-17)

1-Kenton of the Star Patrol by Kubert (r/Eerie #1 from 1947); Crom the Barbarian by John Giunta	109	327	625	1200
2-Wood-a; Crom the Barbarian by Giunta; Dara of the Vikings app.; used in **SOTI**, pg. 112; injury to eye panel	100	300	625	1100
3-Wood/Orlando-a (Kenton), Wood/Williamson/Frazetta/Krenkel/Orlando-a (7 pgs.); Malu Slave Girl Princess app.; Kinstler-a	191	573	1194	2100
4-Wood-c/a (Kenton); Orlando-a; origin The Enchanted Daggar; Sultan-a; classic cover	109	327	682	1200
5-Orlando/Wood-a (Kenton); Wood-c	59	177	369	650
6-Kinstler-a(2); Orlando/Wood-c; Check-a	43	129	257	450
7-Fawcette & Becker/Alascia-a	40	120	220	380
8-Kubert, Kinstler, Hollingsworth & Lazarus-a; Lazarus Robot-c	40	120	220	380
9-Kinstler, Fawcette, Alascia-a	39	117	208	360
18-(Formerly Eerie #17)-Reprints "Attack on Planet Mars" by Kubert	33	99	174	300
19-r/Avon's "Robotmen of the Lost Planet"; last pre-code issue; Robot-c	33	99	174	300
20-War-c/story; Wood-c(r)/U.S. Paratroops #1	10	30	55	60
21,22-War-c/stories. 22-New logo	8	24	42	60
I.W. Reprint #5-Kinstler-a(r)/Avon's #9	3	10	23	35

STRANGE WORLDS
Marvel Comics (MPI No. 1,2/Male No. 3,5): Dec, 1958 - No. 5, Aug, 1959

1-Kirby & Ditko-a; flying saucer issue	84	252	525	925
2-Ditko-c/a	50	150	300	525
3-Kirby-a(2)	40	120	232	400
4-Williamson-a	39	117	208	360
5-Ditko-a	34	102	179	310

NOTE: *Buscema* a-3, 4. *Ditko* a-1-5; c-2.. *Heck* a-2. *Kirby* a-1, 3. *Kirby/Brodsky* c-1, 3-5.

STRAWBERRY SHORTCAKE
Marvel Comics (Star Comics): Jun, 1985 - No. 6, Feb, 1986 (Children's comic)

1-6: Howie Post-a	6.00

STRAY
DC Comics (Homage Comics): 2001 ($5.95, prestige format, one-shot)

1-Pollina-c/a; Lobdell & Palmiotti-s	6.00

STRAY BULLETS
El Capitan Books: 1995 - Present ($2.95, B&W, mature readers)

1-David Lapham-c/a/scripts	2	6	9	12
2,3				6.00
4-8				3.50
9-21-($2.95)				3.00
22-($3.50) Includes preview to Murder Me Dead				3.50
Volume 1 HC ($29.95, hardcover) r/#1-7				30.00
Volume 2 HC ($34.95, hardcover) r/#8-14				35.00
Volume 3 TPB ($11.95, softcover) 1-r/#1-4. 2-r/#5-8, 3-r/ #9-12				12.00
Volume 4 ($14.95) r/#13-16				15.00

NOTE: *Multiple printings of all issues exist & are worth cover price.*

STRAY TOASTERS
Marvel Comics (Epic Comics): Jan, 1988 - No. 4, April, 1989 ($3.50, squarebound, limited series)

1-4: Sienkiewicz-c/a/scripts	3.50

STREET COMIX
Street Enterprises/King Features: 1973 (50¢, B&W, 36 pgs.)(20,000 print run)

1-Rip Kirby	2	6	10	14

	GD2.0	FN6.0	VF8.0	NM9.4

2-Flash Gordon	2	6	12	18

STREETFIGHTER
Ocean Comics: Aug, 1986 - No. 4, Spr, 1987 ($1.75, limited series)

1-4: 2-Origin begins	3.00

STREET FIGHTER
Malibu Comics: Sept, 1993 - No. 3, Nov, 1993 ($2.95)

1-3: 3-Includes poster; Ferret x-over	3.00

STREET FIGHTER: THE BATTLE FOR SHADALOO
DC Comics/CAP Co. Ltd.: 1995 ($3.95, one-shot)

1-Polybagged w/trading card & Tattoo	4.00

STREET FIGHTER II
Tokuma Comics (Viz): Apr, 1994 - No. 8, Nov, 1994 ($2.95, limited series)

1-8	3.00

STREET POET RAY
Blackthorne Publ./Marvel Comics: Spring, 1989; 1990 - No. 4, 1990 ($2.95, B&W, squarebound)

1 (Blackthorne, $2.00)	3.00
1-4 (Marvel, $2.95, thick-c & paper)	3.00

STREETS
DC Comics: 1993 - No. 3, 1993 ($4.95, limited series, 52 pgs.)

Book 1-3-Estes painted-c	5.00

STREET SHARKS
Archie Publications: Jan, 1996 - No. 3, Mar, 1996 ($1.50, limited series)

1-3	2.25

STREET SHARKS
Archie Publications: May, 1996 - No. 6 ($1.50, published 8 times a year)

1-6	2.25

STRICTLY PRIVATE (You're in the Army Now)
Eastern Color Printing Co.: July, 1942 (#1 on sale 6/15/42)

1,2: Private Peter Plink. 2-Says 128 pgs. on-c	24	72	127	215

STRIKE!
Eclipse Comics: Aug, 1987 - No. 6, Jan, 1988 ($1.75)

1-6, ...Vs. Sgt. Strike Special 1 (5/88, $1.95)	2.25

STRIKEBACK! (The Hunt For Nikita)
Malibu Comics (Bravura): Oct, 1994 - No. 3, Jan, 1995 ($2.95, unfinished limited series)

1-3: Jonathon Peterson script, Kevin Maguire-c/a	3.00
1-Gold foil embossed-c	5.00

STRIKEBACK!
Image Comics (WildStorm Productions): Jan, 1996 - No. 5, May, 1996 ($2.50, limited series)

1-5: Reprints original Bravura series w/additional story & art by Kevin Maguire & Jonathon Peterson; new Maguire-c in all. 4,5-New story & art	2.50

STRIKEFORCE: AMERICA
Comico: Dec, 1995 ($2.95)

V2#1-Polybagged w/gaming card; S. Clark-a(p)	3.00

STRIKEFORCE: MORITURI
Marvel Comics Group: Dec, 1986 - No. 31, July, 1989

1-31: 14-Williamson-i. 13-Double size. 25-Heath-c	2.25

STRIKEFORCE MORITURI: ELECTRIC UNDERTOW
Marvel Comics: Dec, 1989 - No. 5, May, 1990 ($3.95, 52 pgs., limited series)

1-5 Squarebound	4.00

STRONG GUY REBORN (See X-Factor)
Marvel Comics: Sept, 1997 ($2.99, one-shot)

1-Dezago-s/Andy Smith, Art Thibert-a	3.00

STRONG MAN (Also see Complimentary Comics & Power of...)
Magazine Enterprises: Mar-Apr, 1955 - No. 4, Sept-Oct, 1955

1(A-1 #130)-Powell-c/a	23	69	121	210
2-4: (A-1 #132,134,139)-Powell-a. 2-Powell-c	19	57	99	165

Submarine Attack #44 © CC

Sub-Mariner #5 © MAR

Sub-Mariner Comics #11 © MAR

	GD2.0	FN6.0	VF8.0	NM9.4

STRONTIUM DOG
Eagle Comics: Dec, 1985 - No. 4, Mar, 1986 ($1.25, limited series)
1-4, Special 1: 4-Moore script. Special 1 (1986)-Moore script 2.25

STRYFE'S STRIKE FILE
Marvel Comics: Jan, 1993 ($1.75, one-shot, no ads)
1-Stroman, Capullo, Andy Kubert, Brandon Peterson-a; silver metallic ink-c;
X-Men tie-in to X-Cutioner's Song 3.00
1-Gold metallic ink 2nd printing 2.25

STUCK RUBBER BABY
DC Comics (Paradox Press): 1998 (Graphic novel)
Hardcover ($24.95) 25.00
Softcover ($13.95) 14.00

STUMBO THE GIANT (See Harvey Hits #49,54,57,60,63,66,69,72,78,88 & Hot Stuff #2)

STUMBO TINYTOWN
Harvey Publications: Oct, 1963 - No. 13, Nov, 1966 (All 25¢ giants)

1-Stumbo, Hot Stuff & others begin	14	42	100	170
2	9	27	63	105
3-5	6	18	45	75
6-13	5	15	38	60

STUNT DAWGS
Harvey Comics: Mar, 1993 ($1.25, one-shot)
1 2.25

STUNTMAN COMICS (Also see Thrills Of Tomorrow)
Harvey Publ.: Apr-May, 1946 - No. 2, June-July, 1946; No. 3, Oct-Nov, 1946

1-Origin Stuntman by S&K reprinted in Black Cat #9; S&K-c				
	109	327	682	1200
2-S&K-c/a; The Duke of Broadway story	68	204	426	750
3-Small size (5-1/2x8-1/2"; B&W; 32 pgs.); distributed to mail subscribers				
only; S&K-a; Kid Adonis by S&K reprinted in Green Hornet #37				
	68	204	426	750

(Also see All-New #15, Boy Explorers #2, Flash Gordon #5 & Thrills of Tomorrow)

STUPID HEROES
Mirage Studios: Sept, 1993 - No. 3, Dec, 1994 ($2.75, unfinished limited series)
1-3-Laird-c/a & scripts; 2 trading cards bound in 2.75

STUPID, STUPID RAT TAILS (See Bone)
Cartoon Books: Dec, 1999 - No. 3, Feb, 2000 ($2.95, limited series)
1-3-Jeff Smith-a/Tom Sniegoski-s 3.00

STYGMATA
Entity Comics: No. 0, July, 1994 - No. 3, Oct, 1994 ($2.95, B&W, limited series)
0, 1-3; 0-Foil-c. 3-Silver foil logo 3.00
Yearbook 1 (1995, $2.95) 3.00

SUBHUMAN
Dark Horse Comics: Nov, 1998 - No. 4, Feb, 1999 ($2.95, limited series)
1-4-Mark Schultz-c 3.00

SUBMARINE ATTACK (Formerly Speed Demons)
Charlton Comics: No. 11, May, 1958 - No. 54, Feb-Mar, 1966

11	4	12	25	38
12-20	3	9	20	30
21-30	3	9	17	25
31-54	2	6	13	20

NOTE: Glanzman c/a-25. Montes/Bache a-38, 40, 41.

SUB-MARINER (See All-Select, All-Winners, Blonde Phantom, Daring, The Defenders, Fantastic Four #4, Human Torch, The Invaders, Iron Man &..., Marvel Mystery, Marvel Spotlight #27, Men's Adventures, Motion Picture Funnies Weekly, Namora, Namor, The..., Prince Namor, The Sub-Mariner, Saga Of The..., Tales to Astonish #70 & 2nd series, USA & Young Men)

SUB-MARINER, THE (2nd Series)(See/Mariner #31 on)
Marvel Comics Group: May, 1968 - No. 72, Sept, 1974 (No. 43: 52 pgs.)

1-Origin Sub-Mariner; story continued from Iron Man & Sub-Mariner #1				
	16	48	112	200
2-Triton app.	6	18	45	75
3-5: 5-1st Tiger Shark (9/68)	4	12	30	50
6,7,9,10: 6-Tiger Shark-c & 2nd app., cont'd from #5. 7-Photo-c. (1968).				

	GD2.0	FN6.0	VF8.0	NM9.4
9-1st app. Serpent Crown (origin in #10 & 12)	4	12	26	40
8-Sub-Mariner vs. Thing	4	12	30	50
11-13,15: 15-Last 12¢ issue	3	9	20	30
14-Sub-Mariner vs. G.A. Human Torch; death of Toro (1st modern app. & only				
app. Toro, 6/69)	4	12	26	40
16-20: 19-1st Sting Ray (11/69); Stan Lee, Romita, Heck, Thomas, Everett &				
Kirby cameos. 20-Dr. Doom app.	2	6	13	20
21,23-33,37-39,41,42: 25-Origin Atlantis. 30-Capt. Marvel x-over. 37-Death of				
Lady Dorma. 38-Origin retold. 42-Last 15¢ issue.	2	6	10	14
22,40: 22-Dr. Strange x-over. 40-Spider-Man x-over	2	6	11	16
34-Prelude (w/#35) to 1st Defenders story; Hulk & Silver Surfer x-over				
	5	15	38	60
35-Namor/Hulk/Silver Surfer team-up to battle The Avengers-c/story (3/71);				
hints at teaming up again	4	12	26	40
36-Wrightson-a(i)	2	6	13	20
43-King Size Special (52 pgs.)	2	6	12	18
44,45-Sub-Mariner vs. Human Torch	2	6	11	15
46-49,56,62,64-72: 47,48-Dr. Doom app. 49-Cosmic Cube story. 62-1st Tales				
of Atlantis, ends #66. 64-Hitler cameo. 67-New costume; F.F. x-over.				
69-Spider-Man x-over (6 panels)	1	3	6	8
50-1st app. Nita, Namor's niece (later Namorita in New Warriors)				
	2	6	9	12
51-55,57,58,60,61,63-Everett issues: .61-Last artwork by Everett; 1st 4 pgs.				
completed by Mortimer; pgs. 5-20 by Mooney	1	4	7	10
59-1st battle with Thor; Everett-a	2	6	11	15
Special 1 (1/71)-r/Tales to Astonish #70-73	2	6	13	20
Special 2 (1/72)-(52 pgs.)-r/T.T.A. #74-76; Everett-a	2	6	9	12

NOTE: Bolle a-67i. Buscema a(p)-1-8, 20, 24. Colan a(p)-10, 11, 40, 43, 46-49, Special 1, 2; c(p)-10, 11, 40. Craig a-17i, 19-23i. Everett a-45r, 50-55, 57, 58, 59-61(plot), 63(plot); c-47, 48i, 55, 57-59i, 61, Spec. 2. G. Kane c(p)-42-52, 58, 66, 70, 71. Mooney a-24i, 25i, 32-35i, 39i, 42i, 44i, 45i, 46i, 47i. Severin c/a-38i. Starlin c-59p. Tuska a-41i, 42p, 69-71p. Wrightson a-36i. #53, 54-r/stories Sub-Mariner Comics #41 & 39.

SUB-MARINER COMICS (1st Series) (The Sub-Mariner #1, 2, 33-42)(Official True Crime Cases #24 on; Amazing Mysteries #32 on; Best Love #33 on)
Timely/Marvel Comics (TCI 1-7/SePl 8/MPI 9-32/Atlas Comics (CCC 33-42)):
Spring, 1941 - No. 23, Sum, 1947; No. 24, Wint, 1947 - No. 31, 4/49; No. 32, 7/49; No. 33, 4/54 - No. 42, 10/55

1-The Sub-Mariner by Everett & The Angel begin				
	2357	7070	16,500	33,000
2-Everett-a	492	1476	3200	6400
3-Churchill assassination-c; 40 pg. Sub-Mariner story				
	392	1176	2448	4700
4-Everett-a, 40 pgs.; 1 pg. Wolverton-a	317	951	1979	3800
5-Gabrielle/Klein-c	255	765	1591	2800
6-10: 9-Wolverton-a, 3 pgs.; flag-c	218	654	1364	2400
11-Classic Schomburg-c	209	627	1307	2300
12-15	155	465	966	1700
16-20	127	381	795	1400
21-Last Angel; Everett-a	100	300	625	1100
22-Young Allies app.	100	300	625	1100
23-The Human Torch, Namora x-over (Sum/47); 2nd app. Namora after				
Marvel Mystery #82	114	342	713	1250
24-Namora x-over (3rd app.)	100	300	625	1100
25-The Blonde Phantom begins (Spr/48), ends No. 31; Kurtzman-a; Namora				
x-over; last quarterly issue	123	369	769	1350
26-28: 28-Namora cover; Everett-a	100	300	625	1100
29-31 (4/49): 29-The Human Torch app. 31-Capt. America app.				
	100	300	625	1100
32 (7/49, Scarce)-Sub-Mariner & Human Torch	155	465	966	1700
33 (4/54)-Origin Sub-Mariner; The Human Torch app.; Namora x-over in				
Sub-Mariner #33-42	95	285	597	1050
34,35-Human Torch in each	75	225	469	825
36,37,39-41: 36,39-41-Namora app.	73	219	455	800
38-Origin Sub-Mariner's wings; Namora app.; last pre-code (2/55)				
	82	245	511	900
42-Last issue	84	253	525	925

NOTE: Angel by Gustavson-#1, 8. Brodsky c-34-36, 42. Everett a-1-4, 22-24, 26-42; c-22, 33, 40. Maneely a-37, 39-41. Rico c-27-31. Schomburg c-1-4, 6, 8-18, 20. Sekowsky c-24, 25, 26(w/Rico). Shores c-21-23, 38. Bondage c-13, 22, 24, 25, 34.

SUBSPECIES
Eternity Comics: May, 1991 - No. 4, Aug, 1991 ($2.50, limited series)

	GD2.0	FN6.0	VF8.0	NM9.4

1-4: New stories based on horror movie — — — 2.50

SUBTLE VIOLENTS
CFD Productions: 1991 ($2.50, B&W, mature)

1-Linsner-c & story	1	4	7	10
San Diego Limited Edition	4	12	30	50

SUE & SALLY SMITH (Formerly My Secret Life)
Charlton Comics: V2#48, Nov, 1962 - No. 54, Nov, 1963 (Flying Nurses)

V2#48	3	9	17	25
49-54	2	6	12	18

SUGAR & SPIKE (Also see The Best of DC & DC Silver Age Classics)
National Periodical Publications: Apr-May, 1956 - No. 98, Oct-Nov, 1971

1 (Scarce)	245	735	1534	2700
2	86	258	540	950
3-5: 3-Letter column begins	61	182	381	675
6-10	40	120	232	400
11-20	37	111	197	340
21-29: 26-Christmas-c	25	75	130	225
30-Scribbly & Scribbly, Jr. x-over	26	78	136	235
31-40	15	45	105	180
41-60	9	27	63	105
61-80: 69-1st app. Tornado-Tot-c/story. 72-Origin & 1st app. Bernie the Brain	7	21	50	80
81-84,86-95: 84-Bernie the Brain apps. as Superman in 1 panel (9/69)	5	15	34	55
85 (68 pgs.)-r/#72	6	18	42	70
96 (68 pgs.)	7	21	50	80
97,98 (52 pgs.)	6	18	42	70

NOTE: All written and drawn by Sheldon Mayer.

SUGAR BOWL COMICS (Teen-age)
Famous Funnies: May, 1948 - No. 5, Jan, 1949

1-Toth-c/a	15	45	77	130
2,4,5	8	24	42	60
3-Toth-a	10	30	55	80

SUGARFOOT (TV)
Dell Publishing Co.: No. 907, May, 1958 - No. 1209, Oct-Dec, 1961

Four Color 907 (#1)-Toth-a, photo-c	13	39	91	165
Four Color 992 (5-7/59), Toth-a, photo-c	12	36	84	155
Four Color 1059 (11-1/60), 1098 (5-7/60), 1147 (11-1/61), 1209-all photo-c	9	27	63	110

SUICIDE SQUAD (See Brave & the Bold and Doom Patrol & Suicide Squad Spec., incl. under Star Spangled War Stories)
DC Comics: May, 1987 - No. 66, June, 1992 (Direct sales only #32 on)

1-66: 9-Millennium x-over. 10-Batman-c/story. 13-JLI app. (Batman). 16-Re-intro Shade The Changing Man. 23-1st Oracle. 27-34,36,37-Snyder-a. 40-43-"The Phoenix Gambit" Batman storyline. 40-Free Batman/Suicide Squad poster				2.25
Annual 1 (1988, $1.50)-Manhunter x-over				2.25

NOTE: Chaykin c-1.

SUICIDE SQUAD (2nd series)
DC Comics: Nov, 2001 - Present ($2.50)

1-5-Giffen-s/Medina-a; Sgt. Rock app. 4-Heath-a				2.50

SUMMER FUN (See Dell Giants)

SUMMER FUN (Formerly Li'l Genius; Holiday Surprise #55)
Charlton Comics: No. 54, Oct, 1966 (Giant)

54	4	12	26	40

SUMMER FUN (Walt Disney's...)
Disney Comics: Summer, 1991 ($2.95, annual, 68 pgs.)

1-D. Duck, M. Mouse, Brer Rabbit, Chip 'n' Dale & Pluto, Li'l Bad Wolf, Super Goof, Scamp stories				4.00

SUMMER LOVE (Formerly Brides in Love?)
Charlton Comics: V2#46, Oct, 1965; V2#47, Oct, 1966; V2#48, Nov, 1968

V2#46-Beatles-c/story	13	39	94	160
47-Beatles story	10	30	70	120
48	2	6	11	15

SUMMER MAGIC (See Movie Comics)

SUNDANCE (See Hotel Deparee...)

SUNDANCE KID (Also see Blazing Six-Guns)
Skywald Publications: June, 1971 - No. 3, Sept, 1971 (52 pgs.)

1-Durango Kid; Two Kirby Bullseye-r	2	6	12	18
2,3: 2-Swift Arrow, Durango Kid, Bullseye by S&K; Meskin plus 1 pg. origin.				
3-Durango Kid, Billy the Kid, Red Hawk-r	2	6	9	12

SUNDAY PIX (Christian religious)
David C. Cook Pub/USA Weekly Newsprint Color Comics: V1#1, Mar,1949 - V16#26, July 19, 1964 (7x10", 12 pgs., mail subscription only)

V1#1	5	15	26	36
V1#2-up	4	12	18	24
V2#1-52 (1950)	4	10	15	20
V3-V6 (1951-1953)	3	8	12	15
V7-V11#1-7,23-52 (1954-1959)	2	6	9	12
V11#8-22 (2/22-5/31/59) H.G. Wells First Men in the Moon serial	2	6	11	15
V12#1-19,21-52; V13-V15#1,2,9-52; V16#1-26(7/19/64)	1	4	7	10
V12#20 (5/15/60) 2 page interview with Peanuts' Charles Schulz	3	10	23	35
V15#3-8 (2/24/63) John Glenn, Christian astronaut	2	6	10	14

SUN DEVILS
DC Comics: July, 1984 - No. 12, June, 1985 ($1.25, maxi series)

1-12: 6-Death of Sun Devil				2.25

SUN FUN KOMIKS
Sun Publications: 1939 (15¢, B&W & red)

1-Satire on comics	33	99	174	300

SUNFIRE & BIG HERO SIX (See Alpha Flight)
Marvel Comics: Sept, 1998 - No. 3, Nov, 1998 ($2.50, limited series)

1-3-Lobdell-s				2.50

SUN GIRL (See The Human Torch & Marvel Mystery Comics #88)
Marvel Comics (CCC): Aug, 1948 - No. 3, Dec, 1948

1-Sun Girl begins; Miss America app.	150	450	938	1650
2,3: 2-The Blonde Phantom begins	109	327	682	1200

SUNGLASSES
Verotik: Nov, 1995 - No. 6, Nov, 1996 ($2.95, limited series, mature)

1-5: Nancy Collins scripts; adapt. of "Sunglasses after Dark"				3.00
6-($3.95)				4.00

SUNNY, AMERICA'S SWEETHEART (Formerly Cosmo Cat #1-10)
Fox Features Syndicate: No. 11, Dec, 1947 - No. 14, June, 1948

11-Feldstein-c/a	75	225	469	825
12-14-Feldstein-c/a; 14-Lingerie panels	59	177	369	650
I.W. Reprint #8-Feldstein-c; r/Fox issue	12	36	84	140

SUN-RUNNERS (Also see Tales of the...)
Pacific Comics/Eclipse Comics/Amazing Comics: 2/84 - No. 3, 5/84; No. 4, 11/84 - No. 7, 1986 (Baxter paper)

1-7: P. Smith-a in #2-4				2.25
Christmas Special 1 (1987, $1.95)-By Amazing				2.25

SUNSET CARSON (See also Cowboy Western)
Charlton Comics: Feb, 1951 - No. 4, 1951 (No month) (Photo-c on each)

1-Photo/retouched-c (Scarce, all issues)	84	253	525	925
2-Kit Carson story; adapts "Kansas Raiders" w/Brian Donlevy, Audie Murphy & Margaret Chapman	61	182	381	675
3,4	47	141	286	500

SUNSET PASS (See Zane Grey & 4-Color #230)

SUPER ANIMALS PRESENTS PIDGY & THE MAGIC GLASSES
Star Publications: Dec, 1953 (25¢, came w/glasses)

1-(3-D Comics)-L. B. Cole-c	42	126	252	440

SUPERBOY (See Adventure, Aurora, DC Comics Presents, DC 100 Page Super Spectacular #15, DC Super Stars, 80 Page Giant #10, More Fun Comics, The New Advs. of... & Superman Family #191, Young Justice)

Superboy #2 © DC

Superboy #228 © DC

Superboy (3rd series) #6 © DC

	GD2.0	FN6.0	VF8.0	NM9.4

SUPERBOY (1st Series)(...& the Legion of Super-Heroes with #231)(Becomes The Legion of Super-Heroes No. 259 on)

National Periodical Publications/DC Comics: Mar-Apr, 1949 - No. 258, Dec, 1979 (#1-16: 52 pgs.)

	GD2.0	FN6.0	VF8.0	NM9.4
1-Superman cover; intro in More Fun #101 (1-2/45)	708	2124	4600	9200
2-Used in **SOTI**, pgs. 35-36,226	191	573	1194	2100
3	150	450	938	1650
4,5: 5-1st pre-Supergirl tryout (c/story, 11-12/49)	100	300	625	1100
6-10: 8-1st Superbaby. 10-1st Lana Lang	89	267	556	975
11-15	68	204	426	750
16-20: 20-Matter-Eater Jor-El cover	47	142	286	500
21-26,28-30: 21-Lana Lang app.	40	120	220	380
27-Low distribution	40	120	232	400
31-38: 38-Last pre-code issue (1/55)	33	99	174	300
39-48,50 (7/56)	28	84	151	260
49 (6/56)-1st app. Metallo (Jor-El's robot)	30	90	162	280
51-60: 52-1st S.A. issue	20	60	105	175
61-67	16	48	83	140
68-Origin/1st app. original Bizarro (10-11/58)	55	165	341	600
69-77,79: 76-1st Supermonkey	13	39	66	110
78-Origin Mr. Mxyzptlk & Superboy's costume	21	63	110	185
80-1st meeting Superboy/Supergirl (4/60)	18	54	94	160
81,83-85,87,88: 83-Origin/1st app. Kryptonite Kid	9	27	63	105
82-1st Bizarro Krypto	10	30	68	115
86-(1/61)-4th Legion app; Intro Pete Ross	17	50	115	205
89-(6/61)-1st app. Mon-el; 2nd Phantom Zone	34	102	188	325
90-92: 90-Pete Ross learns Superboy's I.D. 92-Last 10¢ issue	9	27	63	105
93-10th Legion app.(12/61); Chameleon Boy app.	10	30	68	115
94,97,99	6	18	45	75
98-(7/62)-18th Legion app; origin & 1st app. Ultra Boy; Pete Ross joins Legion	10	30	73	125
100-(10/62)-Ultra Boy app; 1st app. Phantom Zone villains, Dr. Xadu & Erndine. 2 pg. map of Krypton; origin Superboy retold; r-cover of Superman #1	18	54	126	225
101-120: 104-Origin Phantom Zone. 117-Atomic bomb-c. 117-Legion app.	5	15	38	60
121-128: 124-(10/65)-1st app. Insect Queen (Lana Lang). 125-Legion cameo. 126-Origin Krypto the Super Dog retold with new facts	5	15	34	55
129-(80-pg. Giant G-22)-Reprints origin Mon-el	6	18	45	75
130-137,139,140: 131-Legion statues cameo in Dog Legionnaires story. 132-1st app. Supremo. 133-Superboy meets Robin	4	12	26	40
138 (80-pg. Giant G-35)	5	15	38	60
141-146,148-155,157: 145-Superboy's parents regain their youth. 148-Legion app. 157-Last 12¢ issue	3	9	19	28
147(6/68)-Giant G-47; 1st origin of L.S.H. (Saturn Girl, Lightning Lad, Cosmic Boy); origin Legion of Super-Pets-r/Adv. #293	4	12	29	45
156,165,174 (Giants G-59,71,83): 165-r/1st app. Krypto the Superdog from Adventure Comics #210	3	10	23	35
158-164,166-171,175: 171-1st app. Aquaboy?	2	6	12	18
172,173,176-Legion app.: 172-Origin Yango (Super Ape). 176-Partial photo-c; last 15¢ issue	2	6	13	20
177-184,186,187 (All 52 pgs.): 182-All new origin of the classic World's Finest team (Superman & Batman) as teenagers (2/72, 22pgs). 184-Origin Dial H for Hero-r.	2	6	15	22
185-Also listed as DC 100 Pg. Super Spectacular #12; Legion-c/story; Teen Titans, Kid Eternity(r/Hit #46), Star Spangled Kid-r(S.S. #55) (see DC 100 Pg. Super Spectacular #12 for price)				
188-190,192,194,196: 188-Origin Karkan. 196-Last Superboy solo story	1	4	7	10
191,193,195: 191-Origin Sunboy retold; Legion app. 193-Chameleon Boy & Shrinking Violet get new costumes. 195-1st app. Erg-1/Wildfire; Phantom Girl gets new costume.	2	6	9	12
197-Legion series begins; Lightning Lad's new costume	3	9	19	28
198,199: 198-Element Lad & Princess Projectra get new costumes	2	6	11	16
200-Bouncing Boy & Duo Damsel marry; J'onn J'onzz cameo				

	GD2.0	FN6.0	VF8.0	NM9.4
201,204,206,207,209: 201-Re-intro Erg-1 as Wildfire. 204-Supergirl resigns from Legion. 206-Ferro Lad & Invisible Kid app. 209-Karate Kid gets new costume	2	6	13	20
	2	6	9	12
202,205-(100 pgs.): 202-Light Lass gets new costume; Mike Grell's 1st comic work-i (5-6/74)	4	12	29	45
203-Invisible Kid dies	2	6	13	20
208,210: 208-(68 pgs.). 208-Legion of Super-Villains app. 210-Origin Karkan	2	6	12	18
211-220: 212-Matter-Eater Lad resigns. 216-1st app. Tyroc, who joins the Legion in #218	1	4	7	10
221-230,246-249: 226-Intro. Dawnstar. 228-Death of Chemical King	1	3	6	8
231-245: (Giants). 240-Origin Dawnstar. 242-(52 pgs.). 243-Legion of Substitute Heroes app. 243-245-(44 pgs.).	2	6	9	12
244-248,251-257-(Whitman variants; low print run, no issue# on cover)	1	3	6	9
250-258: 253-Intro Blok. 257-Return of Bouncing Boy & Duo Damsel by Ditko				6.00
Annual 1 (Sum/64, 84 pgs.)-Origin Krypto-r	18	54	123	220
Spectacular 1 (1980, Giant)-Distr. through comic stores; mostly-r				5.00

NOTE: **Neal Adams** c-143, 145, 146, 148-155, 157-161, 163, 164, 166-168, 172, 173, 175, 176, 178. **M. Anderson** a-178,179, 245i. Ditko a-257p. Grell a-202i, 203-219, 220-224p, 235p; c-207-232, 235, 236p, 237, 239p, 240p, 243p, 246, 258. **Nasser** a(p)-222, 225, 226, 230, 231, 233, 236. **Simonson** a-237p. Starlin a(p)-239, 250, 251; c-238. Staton a-227p, 243-249p, 252-258p; c-247-251p. **Swan/Moldoff** c-109. Tuska a-172, 173, 176, 183, 235p. Wood inks-153-155, 157-161. Legion app.-172, 173, 176, 177, 183, 184, 188, 190, 191, 193, 195, 197-258.

SUPERBOY (TV)(2nd Series)(The Adventures of...#19 on)
DC Comics: Feb, 1990 - No. 22, Dec, 1991 ($1.00/$1.25)

1-22: Mooney-a(p) in 1-8,18-20; 1-Photo-c from TV show. 8-Bizarro-c/story; Arthur Adams-a(i). 9-12,14-17-Swan-p				3.00
...Special 1 (1992, $1.75) Swan-a				3.00

SUPERBOY (3rd Series)
DC Comics: Feb, 1994 - Present ($1.50/$1.95/$1.99)

1-Metropolis Kid from Reign of the Supermen				4.00
2-8,0,9-24,26-76: 6,7-Worlds Collide Pts. 3 & 8. 8-(9/94)-Zero Hour x-over. 0-(10/94). 9-(11/94)-King Shark app. 21-Legion app. 28-Supergirl-c/app. 33-Final Night. 38-41-"Meltdown". 45-Legion-c/app. 47-Green Lantern-c/app. 50-Last Boy on Earth begins. 60-Crosses Hypertime. 68-Demon-c/app.				2.50
25-($2.95)-New Gods & Female Furies app.; w/pin-ups				3.50
77-95: 77-Begin $2.25-c. 79-Superboy's powers return. 80,81-Titans app. 83-New costume. 85-Batgirl app. 90,91-Our Worlds at War x-over				2.25
#1,000,000 (11/98) 853rd Century x-over				2.50
Annual 1 (1994, $2.95, 68 pgs.)-Elseworlds story, Pt. 2 of The Super Seven (see Adventures Of Superman Annual #6)				3.00
Annual 2 (1995, $3.95)-Year One story				4.00
Annual 3 (1996, $2.95)-Legends of the Dead Earth				3.00
Annual 4 (1997, $3.95)-Pulp Heroes story				4.00
...Plus 1 (Jan, 1997, $2.95) w/Capt. Marvel Jr.				3.00
...Plus 2 (Fall, 1997, $2.95) w/Slither (Scare Tactics)				3.00
.../Risk Double-Shot 1 (Feb, 1998, $1.95) w/Risk (Teen Titans)				3.00

SUPERBOY & THE RAVERS
DC Comics: Sept, 1996 - No. 19, March, 1998 ($1.95)

1-19: 4-Adam Strange app. 7-Impulse-c/app. 9-Superman-c/app.				2.50

SUPERBOY/ROBIN: WORLD'S FINEST THREE
DC Comics: 1996 - No. 2, 1996 ($4.95, squarebound, limited series)

1,2: Superboy & Robin vs. Metallo & Poison Ivy; Karl Kesel & Chuck Dixon scripts; Tom Grummett-c(p)/a(p)				5.00

SUPERBOY'S LEGION (Elseworlds)
DC Comics: Jan 2, 2001 ($5.95, squarebound, limited series)

1,2-31st century Superboy forms Legion; Farmer-s/i; Davis-a(p)/c				6.00

SUPER BRAT (Li'l Genius #5 on)
Toby Press: Jan, 1954 - No. 4, July, 1954

1	7	21	36	50
2-4: 4-Li'l Teevy by Mel Lazarus	5	15	23	30
I.W. Reprint #1,2,3,7,8('58): 1-r/#1	2	6	9	12
I.W. (Super) Reprint #10('63)	2	6	9	12

Supercar #3 © GK

Super-Dooper Comics #7 © HARV

Super Friends TPB © DC

	GD2.0	FN6.0	VF8.0	NM9.4

SUPERCAR (TV)
Gold Key: Nov, 1962 - No. 4, Aug, 1963 (All painted-c)

1	22	65	154	285
2,3	11	33	77	140
4-Last issue	15	45	105	190

SUPER CAT (Formerly Frisky Animals; also see Animal Crackers)
Star Publications #56-58/Ajax/Farrell Publ. (Four Star Comic Corp.): No. 56, Nov, 1953 - No. 58, May, 1954; Aug, 1957 - No. 4, May, 1958

56-58-L.B. Cole-c on all	21	63	110	185
1(1957-Ajax)- "The Adventures of…" c-only	10	30	55	80
2-4	6	18	32	45

SUPER CIRCUS (TV)
Cross Publishing Co.: Jan, 1951 - No. 5, Sept, 1951 (Mary Hartline)

1-(52 pgs.)-Cast photos on-c	14	42	72	120
2-Cast photos on-c	10	30	55	80
3-5	8	24	42	60

SUPER CIRCUS (TV)
Dell Publ. Co.: No. 542, Mar, 1954 - No. 694, Mar, 1956 (Mary Hartline)

Four Color 542: Mary Hartline photo-c	7	21	49	90
Four Color 592,694: Mary Hartline photo-c	6	18	42	80

SUPER COMICS
Dell Publishing Co.: May, 1938 - No. 121, Feb-Mar, 1949

1-Terry & The Pirates, The Gumps, Dick Tracy, Little Orphan Annie, Little Joe, Gasoline Alley, Smilin' Jack, Smokey Stover, Smitty, Tiny Tim, Moon Mullins, Harold Teen, Winnie Winkle begin	289	867	1590	2600
2	106	318	583	950
3	94	281	517	850
4,5- 4-Dick Tracy; also #8-10,17,26(part),31	75	225	413	675
6-10	60	180	330	540
11-20- 20-Smilin' Jack-c (also #29,32)	47	141	259	425
21-29: 21-Magic Morro begins (origin & 1st app., 2/40). 22,27-Ken Ernst-c (also #25?); Magic Morro c-22,25,27,34	38	113	209	340
30- "Sea Hawk" movie adaptation-c/story with Errol Flynn	39	116	215	350
31-40- 34-Ken Ernst-c	32	96	176	285
41-50- 41-Intro Lightning Jim. 43-Terry & The Pirates ends	27	81	149	240
51-60	20	60	110	180
61-70- 62-Flag-c. 65-Brenda Starr-r begin? 67-X-Mas-c	18	53	99	160
71-80	13	39	72	120
81-99	12	36	66	105
100	13	39	72	115
101-115-Last Dick Tracy (moves to own title)	9	27	50	80
116-121: 116,118-All Smokey Stover. 117-All Gasoline Alley. 119-121-Terry & The Pirates app. in all	7	21	39	65

SUPER COPS, THE
Red Circle Productions (Archie): July, 1974 (one-shot)

1-Morrow-c/a; art by Pino, Hack, Thorne	1	3	6	8

SUPER COPS
Now Comics: Sept, 1990 - No. 4, Dec?, 1990 ($1.75)

1-($2.75, 52 pgs.)-Dave Dorman painted-c (both printings)		2.75
2-4		2.25

SUPER CRACKED (See Cracked)

SUPER DC GIANT (25-50¢, all 68-52 pg. Giants)
National Periodical Publications: No. 13, 9-10/70 - No. 26, 7-8/71; V3#27, Summer, 1976 (No #1-12)

S-13-Binky	10	30	70	120
S-14-Top Guns of the West; Kubert-c; Trigger Twins, Johnny Thunder, Wyoming Kid-r (9-10/70)	4	12	27	42
S-15-Western Comics; Kubert-c; Pow Wow Smith, Vigilante, Buffalo Bill-r; new Gil Kane-a (9-10/70)	4	12	27	42
S-16-Best of the Brave and the Bold; Batman-r & Metamorpho origin-r from Brave and the Bold; Spectre pin-up	3	10	23	35
S-17-Love 1970 (scarce)	24	72	168	300

	GD2.0	FN6.0	VF8.0	NM9.4

S-18-Three Mouseketeers; Dizzy Dog, Doodles Duck, Bo Bunny-r; Sheldon Mayer-a	9	27	63	105
S-19-Jerry Lewis; Neal Adams pin-up	9	27	65	110
S-20-House of Mystery; N. Adams-c; Kirby-r(3)	6	18	40	65
S-21-Love 1971 (scarce)	28	84	196	350
S-22-Top Guns of the West; Kubert-c	3	9	20	30
S-23-The Unexpected	4	12	25	38
S-24-Supergirl	4	12	25	38
S-25-Challengers of the Unknown; all Kirby/Wood-r	3	9	20	30
S-26-Aquaman (1971)-r/S.A. Aquaman origin story from Showcase #30	3	9	20	30
27-Strange Flying Saucers Adventures (Sum, 1976)	3	9	17	25

NOTE: *Sid Greene* r-27p(2), *Heath* r-27. *G. Kane* a-14r(2), 15, 27r(p). *Kubert* r-16.

SUPER-DOOPER COMICS
Able Mfg. Co./Harvey: 1946 - No. 8, 1946 (10¢, 32 pgs., paper-c)

1-The Clock, Gangbuster app.	22	66	116	200
2	14	42	72	120
3,4,6	12	36	61	100
5-Capt. Freedom	14	42	72	120
7,8-Shock Gibson. 7-Where's Theres A Will by Ed Wheelan, Steve Case Crime Rover, Penny & Ullysses Jr. 8-Sam Hill app.	14	42	72	120

SUPER DUCK COMICS (The Cockeyed Wonder) (See Jolly Jingles)
MLJ Mag. No. 1-4(9/45)/Close-Up No. 5 on (Archie): Fall, 1944 - No. 94, Dec, 1960 (Also see Laugh #24)(#1-5 are quarterly)

1-Origin; Hitler & Hirohito-c	52	157	314	550
2-Bill Vigoda-c	25	75	130	225
3-5- 4-20-Al Fagaly-c (most)	17	51	88	150
6-10	14	42	72	120
11-20(6/48)	10	30	55	85
21,23-40 (10/51)	9	27	49	70
22-used in SOTI, pg. 35,307,308	10	30	55	80
41-60 (2/55)	7	21	38	55
61-94	6	18	29	40

SUPER DUPER (Formerly Pocket Comics #1-4?)
Harvey Publications: No. 5, 1941 - No. 11, 1941

5-Captain Freedom & Shock Gibson app.	33	99	174	300
8,11	21	63	110	185

SUPER DUPER COMICS (Formerly Latest Comics?)
F. E. Howard Publ.: No. 3, May-June, 1947

3-1st app. Mr. Monster	14	42	72	125

SUPER FRIENDS (TV) (Also see Best of DC & Limited Collectors' Edition)
National Periodical Publications/DC Comics: Nov, 1976 - No. 47, Aug, 1981 (#14 is 44 pgs.)

1-Superman, Batman, Robin, Wonder Woman, Aquaman, Atom, Wendy, Marvin & Wonder Dog begin (1st Super Friends)	3	9	20	30
2-Penquin-c/app.	2	6	11	15
3-5	2	6	9	12
6-10,14: 7-1st app. Wonder Twins & The Seraph. 8-1st app. Jack O'Lantern. 9-1st app. Icemaiden. 14-Origin Wonder Twins	1	3	6	9
11-13,15-30: 13-1st app. Dr. Mist. 25-1st app. Fire as Green Fury. 28-Bizarro app.	1	3	6	8
14,16,21-23,32-(Whitman variants; low print run, no issue# on cover)	2	6	9	12
31,47: 31-Black Orchid app. 47-Origin Fire & Green Fury	1	3	6	9
32-46: 36,43-Plastic Man app.	1	3	5	7
TBP (2001, $14.95) r/#1,6-9,14,21,27 & L.C.E. C-41; Alex Ross-c				15.00

NOTE: *Estrada* a-1p, 2p. *Orlando* a-1p. *Staton* a-43, 45.

SUPER FUN
Gillmor Magazines: Jan, 1956 (By A.W. Nugent)

1-Comics, puzzles, cut-outs by A.W. Nugent	5	15	23	30

SUPER FUNNIES (…Western Funnies #3,4)
Superior Comics Publishers Ltd. (Canada): Dec, 1953 - No. 4, Sept, 1954

1-(3-D, 10¢)-…Presents Dopey Duck; make your own 3-D glasses cut-out inside front-c; did not come w/glasses	40	120	220	380
2-Horror & crime satire	14	42	72	120

Supergirl #1 © DC

Supergirl #60 © DC

Super-Magician Comics #3 © Condé Nast

	GD2.0	FN6.0	VF8.0	NM9.4

	GD2.0	FN6.0	VF8.0	NM9.4
3-Phantom Ranger-c/s; Geronimo, Billy the Kid app.	8	24	42	60
4-Phantom Ranger-c/story	8	24	42	60

SUPERGIRL (See Action, Adventure #281, Brave & the Bold, Crisis on Infinite Earths #7, Daring New Advs. of..., Super DC Giant, Superman Family, & Super-Team Family)

SUPERGIRL
National Periodical Publ.: Nov, 1972 - No. 9, Dec-Jan, 1973-74; No. 10, Sept-Oct, 1974 (1st solo title)(20¢)

1-Zatanna back-up stories begin, end #5	4	12	29	45
2-4,6,7,9	2	6	13	20
5,8,10: 5-Zatanna origin-r. 8-JLA x-over; Batman cameo. 10-Prez	2	6	15	22

NOTE: Zatanna in #1-5, 7(Guest); Prez app. in #10. #1-10 are 20¢ issues.

SUPERGIRL (Formerly Daring New Adventures of...)
DC Comics: No. 14, Dec, 1983 - No. 23, Sept, 1984

14-23: 16-Ambush Bug app. 20-JLA & New Teen Titans app.				3.00
...Movie Special (1985)-Adapts movie; Morrow-a; photo back-c				4.00

SUPERGIRL
DC Comics: Feb, 1994 - No. 4, May, 1994 ($1.50, limited series)

1-4: Guice-a(i)				3.00

SUPERGIRL (See Showcase '96 #8)
DC Comics: Sept, 1996 - Present ($1.95/$1.99)

1-Peter David scripts & Gary Frank-c/a; DC cover logo in upper left is blue	1	3	6	8
1-2nd printing-DC cover logo in upper left is red				3.00
2,4-9: 4-Gorilla Grodd-c/app. 6-Superman-c/app. 9-Last Frank-a				4.00
3-Final fight, Gorilla Grodd app.				5.00
10-19: 14-Genesis x-over. 16-Power Girl app.				3.50
20-35: 20-Millennium Giants x-over; Superman app. 23-Steel-c/app. 24-Resurrection Man x-over. 25-Comet ID revealed; begin $1.99-c				3.00
36-46: 36,37-Young Justice x-over				2.50
47-49,51-65: 47-Begin $2.25-c. 51-Adopts costume from animated series.				2.25
54-Green Lantern app. 59-61-Our Worlds at War x-over. 62-Two-Face-c/app.				
50-($3.95) Supergirl's final battle with the Carnivore				4.00
#1,000,000 (11/98) 853rd Century x-over				3.00
Annual 1 (1996, $2.95)-Legends of the Dead Earth				3.00
Annual 2 (1997, $3.95)-Pulp Heroes; LSH app.; Chiodo-c				4.00
...Plus (2/97, $2.95) Capt.(Mary) Marvel-c/app.; David-s/Frank-a				3.00
...Prysm Double-Shot 1 (Feb, 1998, $1.95) w/Prysm (Teen Titans)				2.50
...: Wings (2001, $5.95) Elseworlds; DeMatteis-s/Tolagson-a				6.00
TPB-('98, $14.95) r/Showcase '96 #8 & Supergirl #1-9				15.00

SUPERGIRL/LEX LUTHOR SPECIAL (Supergirl and Team Luthor on-c)
DC Comics: 1993 ($2.50, 68 pgs., one-shot)

1-Pin-ups by Byrne & Thibert				2.50

SUPER GOOF (Walt Disney) (See Dynabrite & The Phantom Blot)
Gold Key No. 1-57/Whitman No. 58 on: Oct, 1965 - No. 74, July, 1984

1	4	12	29	45
2-5	2	6	15	22
6-10	2	6	12	18
11-20	2	6	9	12
21-30	1	3	6	9
31-50				6.00
51-57				5.00
58,59 (Whitman)				6.00
60-62 (8/80-12/80, 3-pack?)	2	6	11	16
63-66('81)	1	3	5	7
67-69: 67(2/82), 68(2-3/82), 69(3/82)				5.00
70-74 (#90180 on-c; pre-pack, nd, nd code): 70(5/83), 71(8/83), 72(5/84), 73(6/84), 74(7/84)	2	6	9	12

NOTE: Reprints in #16, 24, 28, 29, 37, 38, 43, 45, 46, 54(1/2), 56-58, 65(1/2), 72(r-#2).

SUPER GREEN BERET (Tod Holton...)
Lightning Comics (Milson Publ. Co.): Apr, 1967 - No. 2, Jun, 1967

1-(25¢, 68 pgs)	5	15	34	55
2-(25¢, 68 pgs)	4	12	26	40

SUPER HEROES (See Giant-Size... & Marvel...)

SUPER HEROES
Dell Publishing Co.: Jan, 1967 - No. 4, June, 1967

1-Origin & 1st app. Fab 4	4	12	26	40
2-4	3	9	17	25

SUPER-HEROES BATTLE SUPER-GORILLAS (See DC Special #16)
National Periodical Publications: Winter, 1976 (52 pgs., all reprints, one-shot)

1-Superman, Batman, Flash stories; Infantino-a(p)	2	6	9	12

SUPER HEROES VERSUS SUPER VILLAINS
Archie Publications (Radio Comics): July, 1966 (no month given)(68 pgs.)

1-Flyman, Black Hood, Web, Shield-r; Reinman-a	6	18	40	65

SUPERHERO WOMEN, THE - FEATURING THE FABULOUS FEMALES OF MARVEL COMICS (See Fireside Book Series)

SUPERICHIE (Formerly Super Richie)
Harvey Publications: No. 5, Oct, 1976 - No. 18, Jan, 1979 (52 pgs. giants)

5-Origin/1st app. new costumes for Rippy & Crashman	2	6	9	12
6-18	1	3	6	8

SUPERIOR STORIES
Nesbit Publishers, Inc.: May-June, 1955 - No. 4, Nov-Dec, 1955

1-The Invisible Man by H.G. Wells	24	72	127	220
2-4: 2-The Pirate of the Gulf by J.H. Ingrahams. 3-Wreck of the Grosvenor by William Clark Russell. 4-The Texas Rangers by O'Henry	11	33	55	90

NOTE: Morisi c/a in all. Kiwanis stories in #3 & 4. #4 has photo of Gene Autry on-c.

SUPER MAGIC (Super Magician Comics #2 on)
Street & Smith Publications: May, 1941

V1#1-Blackstone the Magician-c/story; origin/1st app. Rex King (Black Fury); Charles Sultan-c; Blackstone-c begin	150	450	938	1650

SUPER MAGICIAN COMICS (Super Magic #1)
Street & Smith Publications: No. 2, Sept, 1941 - V5#8, Feb-Mar, 1947

V1#2-Blackstone the Magician continues; Rex King, Man of Adventure cont.	59	177	369	650
3-Tao-Anwar, Boy Magician begins	40	120	220	380
4-7,9-12: 4-Origin Transo. 11-Supersnipe app.	39	117	208	360
8-Abbott & Costello story (1st app?), 11/42)	40	120	220	380
V2#1-The Shadow app.	40	120	232	400
2-12: 5-Origin Tigerman. 8-Red Dragon begins	21	63	110	185
V3#1-12: 5-Origin Mr. Twilight	21	63	110	185
V4#1-12: 11-Nigel Elliman Ace of Magic begins (3/46), V5#1-6	17	51	88	150
7,8-Red Dragon by Edd Cartier-c/a	40	120	220	380

NOTE: Jack Binder c/a in 1-14(most). Red Dragon c-V5#7, 8.

SUPERMAN (See Action Comics, Advs. of..., All-New Coll. Ed., All-Star Comics, Best of DC, Brave & the Bold, Cosmic Odyssey, DC Comics Presents, Heroes Against Hunger, JLA, The Kents, Krypton Chronicles, Limited Coll. Ed., Man of Steel, Phantom Zone, Power Record Comics, Special Edition, Steel, Super Friends, Superman: The Man of Steel, Superman: The Man of Tomorrow, Taylor's Christmas Tabloid, Three-Dimension Advs., World of Krypton, World of Metropolis, World of Smallville & World's Finest)

SUPERMAN (Becomes Adventures of...#424 on)
National Periodical Publ./DC Comics: Summer, 1939 - No. 423, Sept, 1986
(#1-5 are quarterly)

1(nn)-1st four Action stories reprinted; origin Superman by Siegel & Shuster; has a new 2 pg. origin plus 4 pgs. omitted in Action story; see The Comics Magazine #1 & More Fun #14-17 for pre-Superman proto-type app.; cover r/splash page from Action #10; 1st pin-up Superman on back-c - 1st pin-up in comics	15,000	45,000	105,000	210,000

1-Reprint, Oversize 13-1/2x10". WARNING: This comic is an exact duplicate reprint of the original except for its size. DC published it in 1978 with a second cover titling it as a Famous First Edition. There have been many reported cases of the outer cover being removed and the interior sold as the original edition. The reprint with the new outer cover removed is practically worthless. See Famous First Edition for value.

2-All daily strip-r; full pg. ad for N.Y. World's Fair	1036	3108	7250	14,500
3-2nd story-r from Action #5; 3rd story-r from Action #6	708	2124	4600	9200
4-2nd mention of Daily Planet (Spr/40); also see Action #23; 2nd & 3rd app. Luthor (red-headed; also see Action #23)	538	1614	3500	7000
5-4th Luthor app. (red hair)	430	1290	2800	5600

	GD2.0	FN6.0	VF8.0	NM9.4

6,7: 6-1st splash pg. in a Superman comic. 7-1st Perry White? (11-12/40)

	300	900	1875	3500

8-10: 10-5th app. Luthor (1st bald Luthor, 5-6/41) 286 858 1790 3150
11-13,15: 13-Jimmy Olsen & Luthor app. 214 642 1338 2350
14-Patriotic Shield-c classic by Fred Ray 308 924 1927 3700
16,18-20: 16-1st Lois Lane-c this title (5-6/42); 2nd Lois-c after Action #29

	168	505	1050	1850

17-Hitler, Hirohito-c 245 735 1534 2700
21,22,25: 25-Clark Kent's only military service; Fred Ray's only super-hero story

	127	381	795	1400

23-Classic periscope-c 150 450 938 1650
24-Classic Jack Burnley flag-c 191 573 1194 2100
26-Classic war-c 168 504 1050 1850
27-29: 27,29-Lois Lane-c. 28-Lois Lane Girl Reporter series begins, ends
#40,42 118 354 738 1300
28-Overseas edition for Armed Forces; same as reg. #28

	118	354	738	1300

30-Origin & 1st app. Mr. Mxyztplk (9-10/44)(pronounced "Mix-it-plk") in comic books; name later became Mxyzptlk ("Mix-yez-pit-l-ick"); the character was inspired by a combination of the name of Al Capp's Joe Blyfstyk (the little man with the black cloud over his head) & the devilish antics of Bugs Bunny; he 1st app. in newspapers 3/7/44 227 681 1420 2500
31-40: 33-(3-4/45)-3rd app. Mxyztplk. 35,36-Lois Lane-c. 38-Atomic bomb story (1-2/46); delayed because of gov't censorship; Superman shown reading Batman #32 on cover. 40-Mxyztplk-c 100 300 625 1100
41-50: 42-Lois Lane-c. 45-Lois Lane as Superwoman (see Action #60 for 1st app.). 46-(5-6/47)-1st app. Superboy this title? 48-1st time Superman travels thru time 80 240 500 875
51,52: 51-Lois Lane-c 64 192 398 700
53-Third telling of Superman origin; 10th anniversary issue ('48); classic origin-c by Boring 282 846 1763 3100
54,56-60: 57-Lois Lane as Superwoman-c. 58-Intro Tiny Trix

	64	192	398	700

55-Used in SOTI, pg. 33 66 197 413 725
61-Origin Superman retold; origin Green Kryptonite (1st Kryptonite story); Superman returns to Krypton for 1st time & sees his parents for 1st time since infancy, discovers he's not on Earth war 136 408 852 1500
62-70: 62-Orson Welles-c/story. 65-1st Krypton Foes: Mala, Kizo, & U-Ban. 66-2nd Superbaby story. 67-Perry Como-c/story. 68-1st Luthor-c this title (see Action Comics) 61 182 381 675
71-75: 74-2nd Luthor-c this title. 75-Some have #74 on-c

	59	177	369	650

76-Batman x-over; Superman & Batman learn each other's I.D. for the 1st time (5-6/52)(also see World's Finest #71) 168 505 1050 1850
77-81: 78-Last 52 pg. issue. 81-Used in POP, pg. 88

	57	170	356	625

82-87,89,90: 89-1st Curt Swan-c in title 53 160 318 560
88-Prankster, Toyman & Luthor team-up 57 170 356 625
91-95: 95-Last precode issue (2/55) 47 140 286 500
96-99: 96-Mr. Mxyztplk-c/story 40 120 232 400
100 (9-10/55)-Shows cover to #1 on-c 200 600 1250 2200
101-105,107-110: 109-1st S.A. issue 40 120 220 380
106 (7/56)-Retells origin 40 120 232 400
111-120 35 105 185 320
121,122,124-127,129: 127-Origin/1st app. Titano, The Mermaid 30 90 159 275
123-Pre-Supergirl tryout-c/story (8/58). 30 90 159 275
128-(4/59)-Red Kryptonite used. Bruce Wayne x-over who protects Superman's i.d. (3rd story) 31 93 165 285
130-(7/59)-1st app, Krypto, the Superdog with Superman (all previous app. w/Superboy 31 93 165 285
131-139: 135-2nd Lori Lemaris app. 139-Lori Lemaris app.;

	23	69	121	210

140-1st Blue Kryptonite & Bizarro Supergirl; origin Bizarro Jr. #1

	24	72	127	220

141-145,148: 142-2nd Batman x-over 19 57 99 165
146-(7/61)-Superman's life story; back-up hints at Earth II. Classic-c

	24	72	127	220

147(8/61)-7th Legion app; 1st app. Legion of Super-Villains; 1st app. Adult Legion; swipes-c to Adv. #247 22 66 116 200

149(11/61)-8th Legion app. (cameo); "The Death of Superman" imaginary story; last 10¢ issue 105 180
150,151,153,154,157,159,160: 157-Gold Kryptonite used (see Adv. #299); Mon-el app.; Lightning Lad cameo (11/62) 9 27 63 105
152,155,156,158,162: 152(4/62)-15th Legion app. 155-(8/62)-Legion app; Lightning Man & Cosmic Man, & Adult Legion app. 156,162-Legion app. 158-1st app. Flamebird & Nightwing & Nor-Kan of Kandor(12/62)

		9	27	65	110

161-1st told death of Ma and Pa Kent 9 27 65 110
161-2nd printing (1987, $1.25)-New DC logo; sold thru So Much Fun Toy Stores (cover title: Superman Classic) 3.00
163-166,168-180: 166-XMas-c. 168-All Luthor issue; JFK tribute/memorial. 169-Bizarro Invasion of Earth-c/story; last Sally Selwyn. 170-Pres. Kennedy story is finally published after delay from #169 due to assassination. 172,173-Legion cameos. 174-Super-Mxyzptlk; Bizarro app. 7 21 50 80
167-New origin Brainiac & Brainiac 5; intro Tixarla (later Luthor's wife)

		9	27	65	110

181,182,184-186,188-192,194-196,198,200: 181-1st 2965 story(series. 182-1st S.A. app. of The Toyman (1/66). 189-Origin/destruction of Krypton II.

		6	18	40	65

183,187,193,197 (Giants G-18,G-23,G-31,G-36) 7 21 50 80
199-1st Superman/Flash race (8/67): also see Flash #175 & World's Finest #198,199 (r-in Limited Coll. Ed. C-48) 18 54 162 290
201,203-206,208-211,213-216: 213-Brainiac-5 app. 216-Last 12¢ issue

		4	12	29	45

202 (80-pg. Giant G-42)-All Bizarro issue 5 15 38 60
207,212,217 (Giants G-48,G-54,G-60): 207-30th anniversary Superman (6/68)

		5	15	38	60

218-221,223-226,228-231 3 10 23 35
222,239(Giants, G-66,G-84) 5 15 38 60
227,232(Giants, G-72,G-78)-All Krypton issues 5 15 34 55
233-2nd app. Morgan Edge; Clark Kent switches from newspaper reporter to TV newscaster; all Kryptonite on earth destroyed; classic Adams-c

		5	15	38	60

234-238 3 9 20 30
240-Kaluta-c; last 15¢ issue 2 6 13 20
241-244 (All 52 pgs.): 241-New Wonder Woman app. 243-G.A.-r/#38

		3	9	17	25

245-Also listed as DC 100 Pg. Super Spectacular #7; Air Wave, Kid Eternity, Hawkman-r; Atom-r/Atom #3
(see DC 100 Pg. Super Spectacular #7 for price)
246-248,250,251,253 (All 52 pgs.): 246-G.A.-r/#40. 248-World of Krypton story. 251-G.A.-r/#45. 253-Finlay-a, 2 pgs., G.A.-r/#1 3 9 17 25
249,254-Neal Adams-c. 249-(52 pgs.); origin & 1st app. Terra-Man by Neal Adams (inks) 3 10 23 35
252-Also listed as DC 100 Pg. Super Spectacular #13: Ray(r/Smash #17), Black Condor, (r/Crack #18), Hawkman(r/Flash #24); Starman-r/Adv. #67; Dr. Fate & Spectre-r/More Fun #67; N. Adams-c
(see DC 100 Pg. Super Spectacular #13 for price)
255-271,273,277,279-283: 263-Photo-c. 264-1st app. Steve Lombard. 276-Intro Capt. Thunder. 279-Batman, Batgirl app. 2 6 9 12
272,278,284-All 100 pgs. G.A.-r in all. 272-r/2nd app. Mr. Mxyztplk from Action #80 3 10 23 35
285-299: 289-Partial photo-c. 292-Origin Lex Luthor retold

		1	3	6	8

300-(6/76) Superman in the year 2001 2 6 15 22
301-350: 301,320-Solomon Grundy app. 323-Intro. Atomic Skull. 327-329-(44 pgs.). 330-More facts revealed about I. D. 338-The bottled city of Kandor enlarged. 344-Frankenstein & Dracula app. 5.00
321-323,325-327,329-331,336-338,340,341,343-345,348,350 (Whitman variants; low print run; no issue # on cover) 1 3 6 8
351-399: 353-Brief origin. 354,355,357-Superman 2020 stories (354-Debut of Superman III). 356-World of Krypton story (also #360,367,375). 366-Fan letter by Todd McFarlane. 372-Superman 2021 story. 376-Free 16 pg. preview Daring New Advs. of Supergirl. 377-Free 16 pg. preview Masters of the Universe 4.00
400 (10/84, $1.50, 68 pgs.)-Many top artists featured; Chaykin painted cover, Miller back-c 6.00
401-422: 405-Super-Batman story. 408-Nuclear Holocaust-c/story. 411-Special Julius Schwartz tribute issue. 414,415-Crisis x-over. 422-Horror-c 4.00

Superman (2nd series) #7 © DC

Superman (2nd series) #50 © DC

Superman (2nd series) #166 © DC

	GD2.0	FN6.0	VF8.0	NM9.4

23-Alan Moore scripts; Perez-a(i); last Earth I Superman story, cont'd in Action
#583 .... 1 3 6 9
Annual 1 (10/60, 84 pgs.)-Reprints 1st Supergirl story/Action #252; r/Lois Lane
#1; Krypto-r (1st Silver Age DC annual) ... 84 252 714 1350
Annual 2(Win, 1960-61)-Super-villain issue; Brainiac, Titano, Metallo, Bizarro
origin-r 41 123 306 550
Annual 3(Sum, 1961)-Strange Lives of Superman 29 88 202 360
Annual 4(Win, 1961-62)-11th Legion app; 1st Legion origins (text & pictures);
advs. in time, space & on alien worlds 24 72 165 295
Annual 5(Sum, 1962)-All Krypton issue 18 54 123 220
Annual 6(Win, 1962-63)-Legion-r/Adv. #247 .. 17 51 115 205
Annual 7(Sum, 1963)-Origin-r/Superman-Batman team/Adv. 275; r/1955
    Superman dailies 13 39 91 155
Annual 8(Win, 1963-64)-All origins issue ... 11 33 77 130
Annual 9(8/64)-Was advertised but came out as 80 Page Giant #1 instead
Annual 9(1983)-Toth/Austin-a 6.00
Annuals 10-12: 10(1984, $1.25)-M. Anderson inks. 11(1985)-Moore scripts.
    12(1986)-Bolland-c 4.00
Special 1-3('83-'85): 1-G. Kane-c/a; contains German-r 4.00
The Amazing World of Superman "Official Metropolis Edition" (1973, $2.00,
    treasury-size)-Origin retold; Wood-r(i) from Superboy #153,161; poster incl.
    (half price if poster missing) 10 30 70 100
195 (2/79, $1.95, 224 pgs.)-Golden Press ... 2 6 15 22

NOTE: N. Adams a-249i, 254p; c-204-206, 210, 212-215, 219, 231i, 233-237, 240-243, 249-252,
254, 263, 307, 308, 313, 314, 317. Adkins a-323i. Austin a-368i. Wayne Boring art-late 1940's
to early 1960's. Buckler a(i)-352, 363, 364, 369; c(i)-324-327, 356, 363, 368, 369, 373, 376,
378. Burnley a-252r; c-19-25, 30, 33, 34, 35p, 38p, 39p, 45p. Fine a-252r. Kaluta a-400. Gil
Kane a-272r, 367, 372, 375, Special 2; c-374p, 375p, 377, 381, 382, 384-390, 392, Annual 9,
Special 2. Joe Kubert c-216. Morrow a-238. Mortimer a-250r. Perez c-364p. Fred Ray a-25; c-6,
9-18. Starlin c-355. Staton a-354i, 355i. Swan/Moldoff c-149. Williamson a(i)-408-410, 412-416;
c-408i, 409i. Wrightson a-400, 416.

SUPERMAN (2nd Series)
DC Comics: Jan, 1987 - Present (75¢/$1.00/$1.25/$1.50/$1.95/$1.99)

0-(10/94) Zero Hour; released between #93 & #94 ... 2.50
1-Byrne-c/a begins; intro new Metallo 5.00
2-8,10: 3-Legends x-over; Darkseid & app. 7-Origin/1st app. Rampage.
    8-Legion app. 3.00
9-Joker-c 4.50
11-15,17-20,22-49,51,52,54-56,58-67: 11-1st new Mr. Mxyzptlk. 12-Lori Lemaris
    revived. 13-1st app. new Toyman. 13,14-Millennium x-over. 20-Doom Patrol
    app.; Supergirl cameo. 31-Mr. Mxyzptlk app. 37-Newsboy Legion app.
    41-Lobo app. 44-Batman storyline, part 1. 45-Free extra 8 pgs. 54-Newsboy
    Legion story. 63-Aquaman x-over. 67-Last $1.00-c 2.50
16,21: 16-1st app. new Supergirl (4/88). 21-Supergirl-c/story; 1st app. Matrix
    who becomes new Supergirl 4.00
50-($1.50, 52 pgs.)-Clark Kent proposes to Lois 5.00
50-2nd printing 2.25
53-Clark reveals i.d. to Lois (Cont'd from Action #662) . 3.00
53-2nd printing 2.25
57-($1.75, 52 pgs.) 3.00
62: 65,66,68-Deathstroke-c/stories. 70-Superman & Robin team-up 2.50
73-Doomsday cameo 5.00
74-Doomsday Pt. 2 (Cont'd from Justice League #69); Superman battles
    Doomsday 6.00
73,74-2nd printings 2.25
75-($2.50)-Collector's Ed.; Doomsday Pt. 6; Superman dies; polybagged
    w/poster of funeral, obituary from Daily Planet, postage stamp & armband
    premiums (direct sales only) 2 6 12 18
75-Direct sales copy (no upc code, 1st print) 1 3 6 8
75-Direct sales copy (no upc code, 2nd-4th prints) 2.25
75-Newsstand copy w/upc code 1 3 6 8
75-Platinum Edition; given away to retailers 40.00
76,77-Funeral For a Friend parts 4 & 8 .... 3.00
78-($1.95)-Collector's Edition with die-cut outer-c & bound-in mini-poster;
    Doomsday cameo 3.00
78-($1.50)-Newsstand Edition w/poster and different-c; Doomsday-c &
    cameo 2.25
79-81,83-89: 83-Funeral for a Friend epilogue; new Batman (Azrael) cameo.
    87,88-Bizarro-c/story 2.50
82-($3.50)-Collector's Edition w/all chromium-c; real Superman revealed;
    Green Lantern x-over from G.L. #46; no ads 6.00

82-($2.00, 44 pgs.)-Regular Edition w/different-c 2.50
90-99: 93-(9/94)-Zero Hour. 94-(11/94). 95-Atom app. 96-Brainiac returns 2.50
100-Death of Clark Kent foil-c 4.00
100-Newsstand 3.00
101-122: 101-Begin $1.95-c; Black Adam app. 105-Green Lantern app.
    110-Plastic Man-c/app. 114-Brainiac app; Dwyer-c. 115-Lois leaves
    Metropolis. 116-(10/96) 1st app. Teen Titans by Dan Jurgens & George
    Perez in 8 pg. preview. 117-Final Night. 118-Wonder Woman app.
    119-Legion app. 122-New powers 2.50
123-Collector's Edition w/glow in the dark-c; new costume ... 6.00
123-Standard ed., new costume 4.00
124-149: 128-Cyborg-c/app. 131-Birth of Lena Luthor. 132-Superman Red/
    Superman Blue. 134-Millennium Giants. 136,137-Superman 2999. 139-Starlin-
    a. 140-Grindberg-a 2.50
150-($2.95) Standard Ed.; Braniac 2.0 app.; Jurgens-s 3.00
150-($3.95) Collector's Ed. w/holo-foil enhanced variant-c ... 4.00
151-158: 151-Loeb-s begins; Daily Planet reopens 2.25
159-174: 159-$2.25-c begin. 161-Joker-c/app. 162-Aquaman-c/app. 163-Young
    Justice app. 165-JLA app.; Ramos; Madureira, Liefeld, A. Adams, Wieringo,
    Churchill-a. 166-Collector's and reg. editions. 167-Return to Krypton.
    168-Darkseid-c/app.(cont'd in Detective #756). 171-174-Our Worlds at War.
    173-Sienkiewicz-a (2 pgs.). 174-Adopts black & red "S" logo ... 2.25
175-($3.50) Joker: Last Laugh x-over; Doomsday-c/app. 3.50
176,177: 176-Churchill-a 2.25
#1,000,000 (11/98) 853rd Century x-over; Gene Ha-c 2.25
Annual 1,2: 1 (1987)-No Byrne-a. 2 (1988)-Byrne-a; Newsboy Legion; return
    of the Guardian 4.00
Annual 3-6 ('91-'94 68 pgs.): 1-Armageddon 2001 x-over; Batman app.;
    Austin-c(i) & part inks. 4-Eclipso app. 6-Elseworlds sty ... 3.00
Annual 3-2nd & 3rd printings; 3rd has silver ink 2.25
Annual 7 (1995, $3.95, 69 pgs.)-Year One story 4.00
Annual 8 (1996, $2.95)-Legends of the Dead Earth story . 4.00
Annual 9 (1997, $3.95)-Pulp Heroes story 4.00
Annual 10 (1998, $2.95)-Ghosts; Wrightson-a 3.00
Annual 11 (1999, $2.95)-JLApe; Art Adams-c 3.00
Annual 12 (2000, $3.50)-Planet DC 3.50
...: 80 Page Giant (2/99, $4.95) Jurgens-c 5.00
...: 80 Page Giant 2 (6/99, $4.95) Harris-c 5.00
...: 80 Page Giant 3 (11/00, $5.95) Nowlan-c; art by various 6.00
...: Endgame (2000, $14.95, TPB)-Reprints Y2K and Brainiac story line 15.00
...: Eradication! The Origin of the Eradicator (1996, $12.95, TPB) 13.00
...: Exile (1998, $14.95, TPB)-Reprints space exile following execution of
    Kryptonian criminals; 1st Eradicator 15.00
... In the Seventies ('00, $19.95, TPB) Intro. by Christopher Reeve 20.00
... No Limits ('00, $14.95, TPB) Reprints early 2000 stories ... 15.00
...Plus 1(2/97, $2.95)-Legion of Super-Heroes-c/app. ... 3.00
Special 1 (1992, $3.50, 68 pgs.)-Simonson-c/a 5.00
The Death of Clark Kent (1997, $19.95, TPB)-Reprints Man of Steel #43
    (1 page), Superman #99 (1 page), Action #709 (1 page),
    #710,711, Advs. of Superman #523-525, Superman:The Man of
    Tomorrow #1 .... 20.00
The Death of Superman (1993, $4.95, TPB)-Reprints Man of Steel #17-19,
    Superman #73-75, Advs. of Superman #496,497, Action #683,684,
    & Justice League #69 .... 1 3 6 8
The Death of Superman, 2nd & 3rd printings 5.00
The Death of Superman Platinum Edition 15.00
The Trial of Superman ('97 $14.95, TPB) reprints story arc 15.00
...: They Saved Luthor's Brain ('00, $14.95) r/ "death" and return of Luthor 15.00
...: 'Til Death Do Us Part ('01, $17.95) reprints; Mahnke-c ... 18.00
...: Time and Time Again (1994, $7.50, TPB)-Reprints ... 8.00
...: Transformed ('98, $12.95, TPB) r/post Final Night powerless Superman
    to Electric Superman 13.00
... Vs. The Revenge Squad (1999, $12.95, TPB) 13.00
NOTE: Austin a(i)-1-3. Byrne a-1-6p, 17, 19-21p, 2; c-1-17, 20-22; scripts-1-22. Guice a-64.
Kirby a-Our Quesada c-Annual 4. Russell a-23i. Simonson c-69i. #19-21 2nd printings
sold in multi-packs.

SUPERMAN (one-shots)
Daily News Magazine Presents DC Comics' Superman
    nn-(1987, 8 pgs.)-Supplement to New York Daily News; Perez-c/a 5.00
...: A Nation Divided (1999, $4.95)-Elseworlds Civil War story 5.00
... & Savage Dragon: Metropolis (11/99, $4.95) Bogdanove-a 5.00

	GD2.0	FN6.0	VF8.0	NM9.4

| | | | | | GD2.0 | FN6.0 | VF8.0 | NM9. |

...: At Earth's End (1995, $4.95)-Elseworlds story 5.00
...: Distant Fires (1998, $5.95)-Elseworlds; Chaykin-s 6.00
...: Emperor Joker (10/00, $3.50)-Follows Action #769 3.50
...: End of the Century (2/00, $24.95, HC)-Immonen-s/a 25.00
... For Earth (1991, $4.95, 52 pgs, printed on recycled paper)-Ordway
wraparound-c 5.00
...IV Movie Special (1987, $2.00)-Movie adaptation; Heck-a 3.00
...Gallery, The 1 (1993, $2.95)-Poster-a 3.00
..., Inc. (1999, $6.95)-Elseworlds Clark as a sports hero; Garcia-Lopez-a 7.00
...: Kal (1995, $5.95)-Elseworlds story 6.00
...: Lex 2000 (1/01, $3.50)-Election night for the Luthor Presidency 3.50
...: Monster (1999, $5.95)-Elseworlds story; Anthony Williams-a 6.00
... Movie Special-(9/83)-Adaptation of Superman III; other versions exist with
store logos on bottom 1/3 of-c 4.00
...: Our Worlds at War Secret Files 1-(8/01, $5.95)-Stories & profile pages 6.00
...'s Metropolis-(1996, $5.95, prestige format)-Elseworlds; McKeever-c/a 6.00
...: Speeding Bullets (1993, $4.95, 52 pgs.)-Elseworlds 5.00
.../Spider-Man-(1995, $3.95)-r/DC and Marvel Presents... 6.00
...: The Earth Stealers 1-(1988, $2.95, 52 pgs, prestige format)
Byrne script; painted-c 4.00
...: The Earth Stealers 1-2nd printing 3.00
...: The Legacy of Superman 1 (3/93, $2.50, 68 pgs.)-Art Adams-c;
Simonson-a 4.00
... The Last God of Krypton ('99, $4.95) Hildebrandt Bros.-a/Simonson-s 5.00
...: The Odyssey ('99, $4.95) Clark Kent's post-Smallville journey 5.00
.../Toyman-(1996, $1.95) 2.50
...: 3-D (12/98, $3.95)-with glasses 4.00
...: Under A Yellow Sun (1994, $5.95, 68 pgs.)-A Novel by Clark Kent;
embossed-c 6.00
...: War of the Worlds (1999, $5.95)-Battles Martians 6.00
...: Where is the Sting? (2001, $6.95)-McCormack-Sharp-c/a 7.00
...: Y2K (2/00, $4.95)-1st Brainiac 13 app.; Guice-c/a 5.00

SUPERMAN ADVENTURES, THE (Based on animated series)
DC Comics: Oct, 1996 - No. 66, Apr, 2002 ($1.75/$1.95/$1.99)
1-Rick Burchett-c/a begins; Paul Dini script; Lex Luthor app.; silver ink,
wraparound-c 3.00
2-20,22: 2-Scott McCloud scripts begin; Metallo-c/app. 3-Brainiac-c/app.
6-Mxyzptlk-c/app. 2.50
21-($3.95) 1st animated Supergirl 5.00
23-65: 23-Begin $1.99-c; Livewire app. 25-Batgirl-c/app. 28-Manley-a.
54-Retells Superman #233 "Kryptonite Nevermore" 58-Ross-c 2.25
Annual 1 (1997, $3.95)-Zatanna and Bruce Wayne app. 4.00
Special 1 (2/98, $2.95) Superman vs. Lobo 3.00
TPB (1998, $7.95) r/#1-6 8.00

SUPERMAN & BATMAN: GENERATIONS (Elseworlds)
DC Comics: 1999 - No. 4, 1999 ($4.95, limited series)
1-4-Superman & Batman team-up from 1939 to the future; Byrne-c/s/a 5.00
TPB (2000, $14.95) r/series 15.00

SUPERMAN & BATMAN: GENERATIONS II (Elseworlds)
DC Comics: 2001 - No. 4, 2001 ($4.95, limited series)
1-4-Superman, Batman & others team-up from 1942-future; Byrne-c/s/a 6.00

SUPERMAN & BATMAN: WORLD'S FUNNEST (Elseworlds)
DC Comics: 2000 ($6.95, square-bound, one-shot)
nn-Mr. Mxyzptlk and Bat-Mite destroy each DC Universe; Dorkin-s/ art by various
incl. Ross, Timm, Miller, Allred, Moldoff, Gibbons, Cho, Jimenez 7.00

SUPERMAN & BUGS BUNNY
DC Comics: Jul, 2000 - No. 4, Oct, 2000 ($2.50, limited series)
1-4-JLA & Looney Tunes characters meet 2.50

SUPERMAN/BATMAN: ALTERNATE HISTORIES
DC Comics: 1996 ($14.95, trade paperback)
nn-Reprints Detective Comics Annual #7, Action Comics Annual #6, Steel
Annual #1, Legends of the Dark Knight Annual #4 15.00

SUPERMAN/DOOMSDAY: HUNTER/PREY
DC Comics: 1994 - No. 3, 1994 ($4.95, limited series, 52 pgs.)
1-3 5.00

SUPERMAN FAMILY, THE (Formerly Superman's Pal Jimmy Olsen)
National Per. Publ./DC Comics: No. 164, Apr-May, 1974 - No. 222, Sept, 1982

					4	12	26	40

164-(100 pgs.) Jimmy Olsen, Supergirl, Lois Lane begin
165-169 (100 pgs.) 3 9 19 28
170-176 (68 pgs.) 2 6 12 18
177-190 (52 pgs.): 177-181-52 pgs. 182-Marshall Rogers-a; $1.00 issues begin;
Krypto begins, ends #192. 183-Nightwing-Flamebird begins, ends #194.
189-Brainiac 5, Mon-el app. 2 6 9 12
191-193,195-199: 191-Superboy begins, ends #198 1 3 6 8
194,200: 194-Rogers-a. 200-Book length sty 1 3 6 9
201-222: 211-Earth II Batman & Catwoman marry 6.00
NOTE: **N. Adams** c-182-185. **Anderson** a-186i. **Buckler** c(p)-190, 191, 209, 210, 215, 217, 220.
Jones a-191-193. **Gil Kane** c(p)-221, 222. **Mortimer** a(p)-191-193, 199, 201-222. **Orlando** a(i)-
186, 187. **Rogers** a-182, 194. **Staton** a-191-194, 196p. **Tuska** a(p)-203, 207-209.

SUPERMAN/FANTASTIC FOUR
DC Comics/Marvel Comics: 1999 ($9.95, tabloid size, one-shot)
1-Battle Galactus and the Cyborg; wraparound-c by Alex Ross and
Dan Jurgens; Jurgens-s/a; Thibert-a 10.00

SUPERMAN FOR ALL SEASONS
DC Comics: 1998 - No. 4, 1998 ($4.95, limited series, prestige format)
1-Loeb-s/Sale-a/c; Superman's first year in Metropolis 6.00
2-4 5.00
Hardcover (1999, $24.95) r/#1-4 25.00

SUPERMAN FOR EARTH (See Superman one-shots)

SUPERMAN FOREVER
DC Comics: Jun, 1998 ($5.95, one-shot)
1-($5.95)-Collector's Edition with a 7-image lenticular-c by Alex Ross;
Superman returns to normal; s/a by various 7.00
1-($4.95) Standard Edition with single image Ross-c 5.00

SUPERMAN/GEN13
DC Comics (WildStorm): Jun, 2000 - No. 3, Aug, 2000 ($2.50, limited series)
1-3-Hughes-s/ Bermejo-a; Campbell variant-c for each 2.50
TPB (2001, $9.95) new Bermejo-c; cover gallery 10.00

SUPERMAN: KING OF THE WORLD
DC Comics: June, 1999 ($3.95/$4.95, one-shot)
1-($3.95) Regular Ed. 4.00
1-($4.95) Collectors' Ed. with gold foil enhanced-c 5.00

SUPERMAN: LAST SON OF EARTH
DC Comics: 2000 - No. 2, 2000 ($5.95, limited series, prestige format)
1,2-Elseworlds; baby Clark rockets to Krypton; Gerber-s/Wheatley-a 6.00

SUPERMAN: LOIS LANE (Girlfrenzy)
DC Comics: Jun, 1998 ($1.95, one-shot)
1-Connor & Palmiotti-a 2.25

SUPERMAN/MADMAN HULLABALOO!
Dark Horse Comics: June, 1997 - No. 3, Aug, 1997 ($2.95, limited series)
1-3-Mike Allred-c/s/a 3.00
TPB (1997, $8.95) 9.00

SUPERMAN METROPOLIS SECRET FILES
DC Comics: Jun, 2000 ($4.95, one-shot)
1-Short stories, pin-ups and profile pages; Hitch and Neary-c 5.00

SUPERMAN: PEACE ON EARTH
DC Comics: Jan, 1999 ($9.95, Treasury-sized, one-shot)
1-Alex Ross painted-c/a; Paul Dini-s 12.00

SUPERMAN RED/ SUPERMAN BLUE
DC Comics: Feb, 1998 ($4.95, one shot)
1-Polybagged w/3-D glasses and reprint of Superman 3-D (1955); Jurgens-
plot/3-D cover; script and art by various 5.00
1-($3.95)-Standard Ed.; comic only, non 3-D cover 4.00

SUPERMAN: SAVE THE PLANET
DC Comics: Oct, 1998 ($2.95, one-shot)
1-($2.95) Regular Ed.; Luthor buys the Daily Planet 3.00

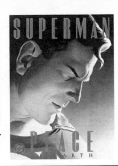

Superman: Peace on Earth © DC

Superman's Girl Friend Lois Lane #123 © DC

Superman's Pal Jimmy Olsen #140 © DC

	GD2.0	FN6.0	VF8.0	NM9.4

1-($3.95) Collector's Ed. with acetate cover — 4.00

SUPERMAN SCRAPBOOK (Has blank pages; contains no comics)

SUPERMAN: SECRET FILES
DC Comics: Jan, 1998; May 1999 ($4.95)
1,2: 1-Retold origin story, "lost" pages & pin-ups — 5.00

SUPERMAN'S GIRLFRIEND LOIS LANE (See Action Comics #1, 80 Page Giant #3, 14, Lois Lane, Showcase #9, 10, Superman #28 & Superman Family)

SUPERMAN'S GIRLFRIEND LOIS LANE (See Showcase #9,10)
National Periodical Publ.: Mar-Apr, 1958 - No. 136, Jan-Feb, 1974; No. 137, Sept-Oct, 1974

	GD2.0	FN6.0	VF8.0	NM9.4
1-(3-4/58)	267	800	2400	4800
2	72	216	612	1150
3	50	150	410	750
4,5	41	123	331	600
6,7	33	100	250	450
8-10: 9-Pat Boone-c/story	29	88	202	360
11-13,15-19: 12-(10/59)-Aquaman app.	17	51	118	210
14-Supergirl x-over; Batman app. on-c only	18	54	123	220
20-Supergirl-c/sty	18	54	123	220

21-28: 23-1st app. Lena Thorul, Lex Luthor's sister. 27-Bizarro-c/story

	13	39	94	160
29-Aquaman, Batman, Green Arrow cover app. and cameo; last 10¢ issue				
	14	42	100	170
30-32,34-46,48,49	7	21	53	85
33(5/62)-Mon-el app.	8	24	58	95
47-Legion app.	8	24	58	95
50(7/64)-Triplicate Girl, Phantom Girl & Shrinking Violet app.				
	8	24	56	90
51-55,57-67,69: 59-Jor-el app.; Batman back-up sty	6	18	40	65
56-Saturn Girl app.	6	18	42	70
68-(Giant G-23)	7	21	53	85
70-Penguin & Catwoman app. (1st S.A. Catwoman, 11/66; also see Detective #369 for 3rd app.); Batman & Robin cameo	23	68	162	290
71-Batman & Robin cameos (3 panels); Catwoman story cont'd from #70 (2nd app.); see Detective #369 for 3rd app	13	39	94	160
72,73,75,76,78	4	12	29	45
74-1st Bizarro Flash (5/67); JLA cameo	4	12	30	50
77-(Giant G-39)	6	18	40	65
79-Neal Adams-c or c(i) begin, end #95,108	4	12	30	48
80-85,87,88,90-92: 92-Last 12¢ issue	3	9	21	32
86,95 (Giants G-51,G-63)-Both have Neal Adams-c	5	15	34	55
89,93: 89-Batman x-over; all N. Adams-c. 93-Wonder Woman-c/story				
	3	10	23	35
94,96-99,101-103,107-110	3	9	17	25
100	3	9	21	32
104-(Giant G-75)	5	15	34	55
105-Origin/1st app. The Rose & The Thorn.	5	15	34	55
106-"Black Like Me" sty; Lois changes her color to black				
	3	9	20	30
111-Justice League-c/s; Morrow-a; last 15¢ issue	3	9	20	30
112,114-123 (52 pgs.): 122-G.A. Lois Lane-r/Superman #30. 123-G.A. Batman-r/Batman #35 (w/Catwoman)	3	9	19	28
113-(Giant G-87) Kubert-a (previously unpublished G.A. story)(scarce in NM)				
	5	15	38	60

124-135: 130-Last Rose & the Thorn. 132-New Zatanna story

	2	6	11	15
136,137: 136-Wonder Woman x-over	2	6	13	20
Annual 1(Sum, 1962)-r/L. Lane #12; Aquaman app.	20	60	140	250
Annual 2(Sum, 1963)	13	39	94	160

NOTE: *Buckler* a-117-121p. *Curt Swan* or *Kurt Schaffenberger* a-1-81(most); c(p)-1-15.

SUPERMAN: SILVER BANSHEE
DC Comics: Dec, 1998 - No. 2, Jan, 1999 ($2.25, mini-series)
1,2-Brereton-s/c; Chin-a — 2.25

SUPERMAN'S NEMESIS: LEX LUTHOR
DC Comics: Mar, 1999 - No. 4, Jun, 1999 ($2.50, mini-series)
1-4-Semeiks-a — 2.50

SUPERMAN'S PAL JIMMY OLSEN (Superman Family #164 on)

(See Action Comics #6 for 1st app. & 80 Page Giant)
National Periodical Publ.: Sept-Oct, 1954 - No. 163, Feb-Mar, 1974 (Fourth World #133-148)

	GD2.0	FN6.0	VF8.0	NM9.4
1	368	1104	3316	7000
2	119	357	1009	1900
3-Last pre-code issue	63	189	531	1000
4,5	48	144	386	700
6-10	35	105	263	475
11-20: 15-1st S.A. issue	25	75	174	310
21-30: 29-1st app. Krypto in Jimmy Olsen	16	48	110	190
31-Origin & 1st app.Elastic Lad (Jimmy Olsen)	14	42	100	170
32-40: 33-One pg. biography of Jack Larson (TV Jimmy Olsen) Lane. 37-2nd app. Elastic Lad & 1st cover app.	11	33	80	135
41-50: 41-1st J.O. Robot. 48-Intro/origin Superman Emergency Squad				
	9	27	65	110
51-56: 56-Last 10¢ issue	7	21	53	85
57-62,64-70: 57-Olsen marries Supergirl. 62-Mon-el & Elastic Lad app. but not as Legionnaires. 70-Element Boy (Lad) app.	5	15	34	55
63(9/62)-Legion of Super-Villains app.	5	15	38	60
71,74,75,78,80-84,86,89,90: 86-Jimmy Olsen Robot becomes Congorilla				
	4	12	29	45
72,73,76,77,79,85,87,88: 72(10/63)-Legion app; Elastic Lad (Olsen) joins. 73-Ultra Boy app. 76,85-Legion app. 76-Legion app. 77-Olsen with Colossal Boy's powers & costume; origin Titano retold. 79-(9/64)-Titled The Red-head ed Beatle of 1000 B.C. 85-Legion app. 87-Legion of Super-Villains app. 88-Star Boy app.	3	10	23	38
91-94,96-98	3	9	21	32
95 (Giant G-25)	6	18	42	70
99-Olsen w/powers & costumes of Lightning Lad, Sun Boy & Element Lad				
	3	9	15	38
100-Legion cameo	4	12	29	45
101-103,105-112,114-120: 106-Legion app. 110-Infinity-c. 117-Batman & Legion cameo. 120-Last 12¢ app.	3	9	17	25
104 (Giant G-38)	5	15	38	60
113,122,131,140 (Giants G-50,G-62,G-74,G-86)	4	12	30	50
121,123-130,132	2	6	15	22
133-(10/70)-Re-intro Newsboy Legion; Kirby story & art begins; 1st app. Morgan Edge.	6	18	42	70
134-1st app. Darkseid (1 panel, 12/70)	7	21	53	85
135-2nd app. Darkseid (1 pg. cameo; see New Gods & Forever People); G.A. Guardian app.	4	12	29	45
136-139: 136-Origin new Guardian. 138-Partial photo-c. 139-Last 15¢ issue				
	3	10	23	35
141-150: (25¢,52 pgs.). 141-Photo-c; Newsboy Legion-r by S&K begin; full pg. self-portrait Kirby; Don Rickles cameo. 149,150-G.A. Plastic Man-r in both; 150-Newsboy Legion app.	3	9	21	32
151-163	2	6	11	15

NOTE: Issues #141-148 contain *Simon & Kirby* Newsboy Legion reprints from Star Spangled #7, 8, 9, 10, 11, 12, 13, 14 in that order. **N. Adams** c-109-113, 115, 117, 118, 120, 121, 132, 134-136, 147, 148. *Kirby* a-133-139p, 141-148p; c-133, 137, 139, 142, 145p. *Kirby/N. Adams* c-137, 138, 141-144, 146. *Curt Swan* c-1-14(most)., 140.

SUPERMAN SPECTACULAR (Also see DC Special Series #5)
DC Comics: 1982 (Magazine size, 52 pgs., square binding)
1-Saga of Superman Red/ Superman Blue; Luthor and Terra-Man app.; Gonzales & Colletta-a — 1 4 7 10

SUPERMAN / TARZAN: SONS OF THE JUNGLE
Dark Horse Comics: Oct, 2001 - No. 3 ($2.99, limited series)
1-Elseworlds; Kal-El lands in the jungle; Dixon-s/Meglia-a/Ramos-c — 3.00

SUPERMAN: THE DARK SIDE
DC Comics: 1998 - No. 3, 1998 ($4.95, squarebound, mini-series)
1-3: Elseworlds; Kal-El lands on Apokolips — 5.00

SUPERMAN: THE DOOMSDAY WARS
DC Comics: 1998 - No. 3, 1999 ($4.95, squarebound, mini-series)
1-3: Superman & JLA vs. Doomsday; Jurgens-s/a(p) — 5.00

SUPERMAN: THE MAN OF STEEL (Also see Man of Steel, The)
DC Comics: July, 1991 - Present ($1.00/$1.25/$1.50/$1.95/$2.25)
0-(10/94) Zero Hour; released between #37 & #38 — 2.50

Superman: The Man of Steel #112
© DC

Superman: The Man of Tomorrow #7
© DC

Supermouse #3 © STD

1-($1.75, 52 pgs.)-Painted-c ... 5.00
2-16: 3-War of the Gods x-over. 5-Reads sideways. 10-Last $1.00-c.
14-Superman & Robin team-up ... 3.00
17-1st app. Doomsday (cameo) ... 1 ... 3 ... 5 ... 7
17,18: 17-2nd printing. 18-2nd & 3rd printings ... 2.25
18-1st full app. Doomsday ... 1 ... 3 ... 6 ... 9
19-Doomsday battle issue (c/story) ... 6.00
20-22: 20,21-Funeral for a Friend. 22-($1.95)-Collector's Edition w/die-cut
    outer-c & bound-in poster; Steel-c/story ... 2.50
22-($1.50)-Newsstand Ed. w/poster & different-c ... 2.25
23-49,51-99: 30-Regular edition. 32-Bizarro-c/story. 35,36-Worlds Collide Pt. 1
    & 10. 37-(9/94)-Zero Hour x-over. 38-(11/94). 48-Aquaman app.
    54-Spectre-c/app; Lex Luthor app. 56-Mxyzptlk-c/app. 57-G.A. Flash app.
    58-Supergirl app. 59-Parasite-c/app.; Steel app. 60-Reintro Bottled City of
    Kandor. 62-Final Night. 64-New Gods app. 67-New powers. 75-"Death" of
    Mxyzptlk. 78,79-Millennium Giants. 80-Golden Age style. 92-JLA app.
    98-Metal Men app. ... 2.50
30-($2.50)-Collector's Edition; polybagged with Superman & Lobo vinyl clings
    that stick to wraparound-c; Lobo-c/story ... 3.00
50 ($2.95)-The Trial of Superman ... 4.00
100-($2.99) New Fortress of Solitude revealed ... 3.00
100-($3.99) Special edition with fold out cardboard-c ... 4.00
101,102-101-Batman app. ... 2.25
103-121: 103-Begin $2.25. 105-Batman-c/app. 111-Return to Krypton.
    115-117-Our Worlds at War. 117-Maxima killed. 121-Royal Flush Gang ... 2.25
#1,000,000 (11/98) 853rd Century x-over; Gene Ha-c ... 2.50
Annual 1-5 ('92-'96,68 pgs.): 1-Eclipso app.; Joe Quesada-c(p). 2-Intro Edge.
    3 -Elseworlds story; Mignola-c; Batman app. 4-Year One story. 5-Legends of
    the Dead Earth story ... 3.00
Annual 6 (1997, $3.95)-Pulp Heroes story ... 4.00
...Gallery (1995, $3.50) Pin-ups by various ... 3.50
SUPERMAN: THE MAN OF TOMORROW
DC Comics: 1995 - No. 15, Fall, 1999 ($1.95, quarterly)
1-15: 1-Lex Luthor app. 3-Lex Luthor-c/app; Joker app. 4-Shazam! app.
    5-Wedding of Lex Luthor. 10-Maxima-c/app. 13-JLA-c/app. ... 2.50
#1,000,000 (11/98) 853rd Century x-over; Gene Ha-c ... 2.50
SUPERMAN: THE SECRET YEARS
DC Comics: Feb, 1985 - No. 4, May, 1985 (limited series)
1-4-Miller-c on all ... 3.00
SUPERMAN: THE WEDDING ALBUM
DC Comics: Dec, 1996 ($4.95, 96 pgs, one-shot)
1-Standard Edition-Story & art by past and present Superman creators;
    gatefold back-c. Byrne-c ... 5.00
1-Collector's Edition-Embossed cardstock variant-c w/ metallic silver ink
    and matte and gloss varnishes ... 5.00
TPB ('97, $14.95) r/Wedding and honeymoon stories ... 15.00
SUPERMAN 3-D (See Three-Dimension Adventures)
SUPERMAN VILLAINS SECRET FILES
DC Comics: Jun, 1998 ($4.95, one shot)
1-Origin stories, "lost" pages & pin-ups ... 5.00
SUPERMAN VS. ALIENS
DC Comics/Dark Horse Comics: July, 1995 - No. 3, Sept, 1995 ($4.95, limited
series)
1-3: Jurgens/Nowlan-a ... 5.00
SUPERMAN VS. PREDATOR
DC Comics/Dark Horse Comics: 2000 - No. 3, 2000 ($4.95, limited series)
1-3-Micheline-s/Maleev-a ... 5.00
TPB (2001, $14.95) r/series ... 15.00
SUPERMAN VS. THE AMAZING SPIDER-MAN (Also see Marvel Treasury
Edition No. 28)
National Periodical Publications/Marvel Comics Group: 1976 ($2.00,
Treasury sized, 100 pgs.)
1-Andru/Giordano-a; 1st Marvel/DC x-over. ... 7 ... 21 ... 50 ... 80
1-2nd printing; 5000 numbered copies signed by Stan Lee & Carmine
    Infantino on front cover & sold through mail ... 13 ... 39 ... 94 ... 160

nn-(1995, $5.95)-r/#1 ... 6.00
SUPERMAN VS. THE TERMINATOR: DEATH TO THE FUTURE
Dark Horse/DC Comics: Dec, 1999 - No. 4, Mar, 2000 ($2.95, limited series)
1-4-Grant-s/Pugh-a/c: Steel and Supergirl app. ... 3.00
SUPERMAN/WONDER WOMAN: WHOM GODS DESTROY
DC Comics: 1997 ($4.95, prestige format, limited series)
1-4-Elseworlds; Claremont-s ... 5.00
SUPERMAN WORKBOOK
National Periodical Publ./Juvenile Group Foundation: 1945 (B&W, one-shot,
reprints, 68 pgs)
nn-Cover-r/Superman #14 ... 150 ... 450 ... 938 ... 1650
SUPER MANGA BLAST
Dark Horse Comics: Mar, 2000 - Present ($4.95/$4.99, B&W, anthology)
1-14-Reprints Oh My Goddess, 3X3 Eyes, What's Michael and others ... 5.00
SUPER MARIO BROS. (Also see Adventures of the..., Blip, Gameboy, and
Nintendo Comics System)
Valiant Comics: 1990 - No. 5?, 1991 ($1.95, slick-c) V2#1, 1991 - No. 5, 1991
1-Wildman-a ... 4.00
2-5, V2#1-5-($1.50) ... 3.00
Special Edition 1 (1990, $1.95)-Wildman-a ... 3.00
SUPERMEN OF AMERICA
DC Comics: Mar, 1999 ($3.95/$4.95, one-shot)
1-($3.95) Regular Ed.; Immonen-s/art by various ... 4.00
1-($4.95) Collectors' Ed. with membership kit ... 5.00
SUPERMEN OF AMERICA (Mini-series)
DC Comics: Mar, 2000 - No. 6, Aug, 2000 ($2.50)
1-6-Nicieza-s/Braithwaite-a ... 2.50
SUPERMOUSE (...the Big Cheese; see Coo Coo Comics)
Standard Comics/Pines No. 35 on (Literary Ent.): Dec, 1948 - No. 34, Sept,
1955; No. 35, Apr, 1956 - No. 45, Fall, 1958
1-Frazetta text illos (3) ... 30 ... 90 ... 159 ... 275
2-Frazetta text illos ... 15 ... 45 ... 77 ... 130
3,5,6-Text illos by Frazetta in all ... 13 ... 39 ... 66 ... 110
4-Two pg. text illos by Frazetta ... 14 ... 42 ... 72 ... 120
7-10 ... 7 ... 21 ... 36 ... 50
11-20: 13-Racist humor (Indians) ... 6 ... 18 ... 29 ... 40
21-45 ... 5 ... 15 ... 24 ... 32
1-Summer Holiday issue (Summer, 1957, 25¢, 100 pgs.)-Pines
    ... 14 ... 42 ... 72 ... 120
2-Giant Summer issue (Summer, 1958, 25¢, 100 pgs.)-Pines; has games,
    puzzles & stories ... 10 ... 30 ... 55 ... 80
SUPER-MYSTERY COMICS
Ace Magazines (Periodical House): July, 1940 - V8#6, July, 1949
V1#1-Magno, the Magnetic Man & Vulcan begins (1st app.); Q-13, Corp. Flint,
    & Sky Smith begin ... 255 ... 765 ... 1591 ... 2800
2 ... 86 ... 258 ... 540 ... 950
3-The Black Spider begins (1st app.) ... 75 ... 225 ... 469 ... 825
4-Origin Davy ... 55 ... 165 ... 341 ... 600
5-Intro. The Clown & begin series (12/40) ... 59 ... 177 ... 369 ... 650
6(2/41) ... 50 ... 150 ... 300 ... 525
V2#1(4/41)-Origin Buckskin ... 47 ... 142 ... 286 ... 500
2-6(2/42): 6-Vulcan begins again ... 45 ... 135 ... 270 ... 475
V3#1(4/42): 1-Black Ace begins ... 40 ... 120 ... 232 ... 400
3-Intro. The Lancer; Dr. Nemesis & The Sword begin; Kurtzman-c/a(2)
    (Mr. Risk & Paul Revere Jr.); Robot-c ... 51 ... 153 ... 306 ... 540
4-Kurtzman-c/a ... 44 ... 132 ... 264 ... 460
5-Kurtzman-a(2); L.B. Cole-a; Mr. Risk app. ... 50 ... 150 ... 300 ... 525
6(10/43)-Mr. Risk app.; Kurtzman's Paul Revere Jr.; L.B. Cole-a
    ... 50 ... 150 ... 300 ... 525
V4#1(1/44)-L.B. Cole-a ... 43 ... 129 ... 257 ... 450
2-6(4/45): 2,5,6-Mr. Risk app. ... 33 ... 99 ... 174 ... 300
V5#1(7/45)-6 ... 33 ... 99 ... 174 ... 300
V6#1-6: 3-Torture story. 4-Last Magno. Mr. Risk app. in #2,4-6. 6-New logo
    ... 26 ... 78 ... 136 ... 235

Super Powers #2 © DC

Super Rabbit #2 © MAR

Super Soldiers #5 © MAR

SU

	GD2.0	FN6.0	VF8.0	NM9.4

#7#1-6, V8#1-4,6

	24	72	127	215
*#8#5-Meskin, Tuska, Sid Greene-a	24	72	127	215

NOTE: *Sid Greene a-V7#4. Mooney c-V1#5, 6, V2#1-6. Palais a-V5#3, 4; c-V4#6-V5#4, V6#2, '8#4. Bondage c-V2#5, 6, V3#2, 5. Magno c-V1#1-V3#6, V4#2-V5#5, V6#2. The Sword c-V4#1, 5(w/Magno).

SUPERNATURAL LAW (Formerly Wolff & Byrd, Counselors of the Macabre)
Exhibit A Press: No. 24, Oct, 1999 - Present ($2.50, B&W)

24-32-Batton Lash-s/a. 29-Marie Severin-c				2.50

SUPERNATURALS
Marvel Comics: Dec, 1998 - No. 4, Dec, 1998 ($3.99, weekly limited series)

1-4-Pulido-s/Balent-c; bound-in Halloween masks				4.00
1-4-With bound-in Ghost Rider mask (1 in 10)				4.00

SUPERNATURAL THRILLERS
Marvel Comics Group: Dec, 1972 - No. 6, Nov, 1973; No. 7, Jun, 1974 - No. 15, Oct, 1975

1-It!; Sturgeon adap. (see Astonishing Tales #21)	3	9	17	25
2-4,6: 2-The Invisible Man; H.G. Wells adapt. 3-The Valley of the Worm; R.E. Howard adapt. 4-Dr. Jekyll & Mr. Hyde; R.L. Stevenson adapt. 6-The Headless Horseman; last 20¢ issue	2	6	10	14
5-1st app. The Living Mummy	5	15	38	60
7-15: 7-The Living Mummy begins	2	6	12	18

NOTE: *Brunner c-11. Buckler a-5p. Ditko a-8r, 9r. G. Kane a-3p; c-3, 9p, 15p. Mayerik a-2p, 7, 9, 9p, 10p, 11. McWilliams a-14i. Mortimer a-4. Steranko c-1, 2. Sutton a-15. Tuska a-6p.

SUPERPATRIOT (Also see Freak Force & Savage Dragon #2)
Image Comics (Highbrow Entertainment): July, 1993 - No. 4, Dec, 1993 ($1.95, limited series)

1-4: Dave Johnson-c/a; Larsen scripts; Giffen plots				2.50

SUPERPATRIOT: LIBERTY & JUSTICE
Image Comics (Highbrow Entertainment): July, 1995 - No. 4, Oct, 1995 ($2.50, limited series)

1-4: Dave Johnson-c/a. 1st app. Liberty & Justice				2.50

SUPER POWERS (1st Series)
DC Comics: July, 1984 - No. 5, Nov, 1984

1-5: 1-Joker/Penguin-c/story; Batman app.; all Kirby-c. 5-Kirby c/a				5.00

SUPER POWERS (2nd Series)
DC Comics: Sept, 1985 - No. 6, Feb, 1986

1-6: Kirby-c/a; Capt. Marvel & Firestorm join; Batman cameo; Darkseid storyline in all. 4-Batman cameo. 5,6-Batman app.				5.00

SUPER POWERS (3rd Series)
DC Comics: Sept, 1986 - No. 4, Dec, 1986

1-4: 1-Cyborg joins; 1st app. Samurai from Super Friends TV show. 1-4-Batman cameos; Darkseid storyline in #1-4				4.00

SUPER PUP (Formerly Spotty The Pup) (See Space Comics)
Avon Periodicals: No. 4, Mar-Apr, 1954 - No. 5, 1954

4,5: 5-Robot-c	6	18	29	40

SUPER RABBIT (See All Surprise, Animated Movie Tunes, Comedy Comics, Comic Capers, Ideal Comics, It's A Duck's Life, Movie Tunes & Wisco)
Timely Comics (CmPl): Fall, 1944 - No. 14, Nov, 1948

1-Hitler & Hirohito-c; war effort paper recycling PSA by S&K; Ziggy Pig & Silly begin?	68	204	426	750
2	36	108	191	330
3-5	23	69	121	205
6-Origin	25	75	130	225
7-10: 9-Infinity-c	14	42	72	120
11-Kurtzman's "Hey Look"	15	45	77	130
12-14	14	42	72	120
I.W. Reprint #1,2('58),7,10('63): 1-r/#13. 2-r/#10.	2	6	11	16

SUPER RICHIE (Superichie #5 on) (See Richie Rich Millions #68)
Harvey Publications: Sept, 1975 - No. 4, Mar, 1976 (All 52 pg. Giants)

1	2	6	13	20
2-4	2	6	9	12

SUPER SLUGGERS (Baseball)
Ultimate Sports Ent. Inc.: 1999 ($3.95, one-shot)

1-Bonds, Piazza, Caminiti, Griffey Jr. app.; Martinbrough-c/a				4.00

SUPERSNIPE COMICS (Formerly Army & Navy #1-5)
Street & Smith Publications: V1#6, Oct, 1942 - V5#1, Aug-Sept, 1949
(See Shadow Comics V2#3)

V1#6-Rex King - Man of Adventure (costumed hero, see Super Magic/ Magician) by Jack Binder begins; Supersnipe by George Marcoux continues from Army & Navy #5; Bill Ward-a	82	246	511	900
7,10-12: 10,11-Little Nemo app.	50	150	300	525
8-Hitler, Tojo, Mussolini in Hell with Devil-c	68	204	426	750
9-Doc Savage x-over in Supersnipe; Hitler-c	73	219	455	800
V2 #1: Both V2#1(2/44) & V2#2(4/44) have V2#1 on outside-c; Huck Finn by Clare Dwiggins begins, ends V3#5 (rare)	64	192	398	700
V2#2-12: V2#2 (4/44) has V2#1 on outside-c	40	120	220	380
V3#1-12: 8-Bobby Crusoe by Dwiggins begins, ends V3#12. 9-X-Mas-c	35	105	185	320
V4#1-12, V5#1: V4#10-X-Mas-c	25	75	130	225

NOTE: *George Marcoux c-V1#6-V3#4. Doc Savage app. in some issues.

SUPER SOLDIER (See Marvel Versus DC #3)
DC Comics (Amalgam): Apr, 1996 ($1.95, one-shot)

1-Mark Waid script & Dave Gibbons-c/a.				2.25

SUPER SOLDIER: MAN OF WAR
DC Comics (Amalgam): June, 1997 ($1.95, one-shot)

1-Waid & Gibbons-s/Gibbons & Palmiotti-c/a.				2.25

SUPER SOLDIERS
Marvel Comics UK: Apr, 1993 - No. 8, Nov, 1993 ($1.75)

1-($2.50)-Embossed silver foil logo				2.50
2-8: 5-Capt. America app. 6-Origin; Nick Fury app.; neon ink-c				2.25

SUPERSPOOK (Formerly Frisky Animals on Parade)
Ajax/Farrell Publications: No. 4, June, 1958

4	8	24	45	65

SUPER SPY (See Wham Comics)
Centaur Publications: Oct, 1940 - No. 2, Nov, 1940 (Reprints)

1-Origin The Sparkler	111	332	694	1225
2-The Inner Circle, Dean Denton, Tim Blain, The Drew Ghost, The Night Hawk by Gustavson, & S.S. Swanson by Glanz app.	68	205	426	750

SUPERSTAR: AS SEEN ON TV
Image Comics (Gorilla): 2001 ($5.95)

1-Busiek-s/Immonen-a				6.00

SUPER STAR HOLIDAY SPECIAL (See DC Special Series #21)

SUPER-TEAM FAMILY
National Periodical Publ./DC Comics: Oct-Nov, 1975 - No. 15, Mar-Apr, 1978

1-Reprints by Neal Adams & Kane/Wood; 68 pgs. begin, ends #4. New Gods app.	2	6	12	16
2,3: New stories	2	6	9	12
4-7: Reprints. 4-G.A. JSA-r & Superman/Batman-r from World's Finest. 5-52 pgs. begin	2	6	9	12
8-14: 8-10-New Challengers of the Unknown stories. 9-Kirby-a. 11-14: New stories	2	6	10	14
15-New Gods app. New stories	2	6	11	16

NOTE: *Neal Adams r-1-3. Brunner c-3. Buckler c-8p. Tuska a-7r. Wood a-1i(r), 3.

SUPER TV HEROES (See Hanna-Barbera...)

SUPER-VILLAIN CLASSICS
Marvel Comics Group: May, 1983

1-Galactus -The Origin; Kirby-a				5.00

SUPER-VILLAIN TEAM-UP (See Fantastic Four #6 & Giant-Size...)
Marvel Comics Group: 8/75 - No. 14, 10/77; No. 15, 11/78; No. 16, 5/79; No. 17, 6/80

1-Giant-Size Super-Villian Team-Up #2; Sub-Mariner & Dr. Doom begin; end #10	3	9	17	25
2-5: 1st app. The Shroud	2	6	9	12
5-(30¢-c variant, limited distribution)(4/76)	2	6	11	15
6,7-(25¢ editions) 6-(6/76)-F.F., Shroud app. 7-Origin Shroud	1	3	6	8

	GD2.0	FN6.0	VF8.0	NM9.4

	GD2.0	FN6.0	VF8.0	NM9

6,7-(30¢-c, limited distribution)(6,8/76) — 2 6 9 12
8-17: 9-Avengers app. 11-15-Dr. Doom & Red Skull app.
— 1 3 6 8
12-14-(35¢-c variants, limited distribution)(6,8,10/77) 1 4 7 10
NOTE: *Buckler* c-4p, 5p, 7p. *Buscema* c-1. *Byrne/Austin* c-14. *Evans* a-1p, 3p. *Everett* a-1p.
Giffen a-8p, 13p; c-13p. *Kane* a-2p, 9p. *Mooney* a-4i. *Starlin* c-6. *Tuska* r-1p, 15p. *Wood* r-15p.

SUPER WESTERN COMICS (Also see Buffalo Bill)
Youthful Magazines: Aug, 1950 (One shot)
1-Buffalo Bill begins; Wyatt Earp, Calamity Jane & Sam Slade app;
Powell-c/a — 14 42 72 120

SUPER WESTERN FUNNIES (See Super Funnies)

SUPERWORLD COMICS
Hugo Gernsback (Komos Publ.): Apr, 1940 - No. 3, Aug, 1940 (68 pgs.)
1-Origin & 1st app. Hip Knox, Super Hypnotist; Mitey Powers & Buzz Allen,
the Invisible Avenger, Little Nemo begin; cover by Frank R. Paul (all have
sci/fi-c)(Scarce) — 615 1845 4000 8000
2-Marvo 1-2 Go+, the Super Boy of the Year 2680 (1st app.); Paul-c(b)
— 375 1125 2344 4500
3 (Scarce) — 291 873 1818 3200

SUPREME (Becomes ...The New Adventures #43-48)(See Youngblood #3)
(Also see Bloodwulf Special, Legend of Supreme, & Trencher #3)
Image Comics (Extreme Studios)/ Awesome Entertainment #49 on:
V2#1, Nov, 1992 - V2#42, Sept, 1996; V3#49 - No. 56, Feb, 1998
V2#1-Liefeld-a(i) & scripts; embossed foil logo — 4.00
  -Gold Edition — 6.00
2-(3/93)-Liefeld co-plots & inks; 1st app. Grizlock — 3.00
3-42: 3-Intro Bloodstrike; 1st app. Khrome. 5-1st app. Thor. 6-The Starguard
cameo. 7-1st full app. The Starguard. 10-Black and White Pt 1 (1st app.) by
Art Thibert (2 pgs. ea. installment). 25-(5/94)-Platt-c. 11-Coupon #4 for
Extreme Prejudice #0; Black and White, Pt. 7 by Thibert. 12-(4/94)-Platt-c.
13,14-(6/94). 15 (7/94). 16 (7/94)-Stormwatch app. 18-Kid Supreme Sneak
Preview; Pitt app.19,20-Polybagged w/trading card. 20-1st app. Woden &
Loki (as a dog); Overtkill app. 21-1st app. Loki (in true form). 21-23-Poly-
bagged trading card. 32-Lady Supreme cameo. 33-Origin & 1st full app. of
Lady Supreme (Probe from the Starguard); Babewatch! tie-in. 37-Intro Loki;
Fraga-c. 40-Retells Supreme's past advs. 41-Alan Moore scripts begin;
Supreme revised; intro The Supremacy; Jerry Ordway-c (Joe Bennett vari
ant-c exists). 42-New origin w/Rick Veitch-a; intro Radar, The Hound
Supreme & The League of Infinity — 3.00
28-Variant-c by Quesada & Palmiotti — 3.00
(#43-48-See **Supreme: The New Adventures**)
V3#49,51: 49-Begin $2.99-c — 3.00
50-($3.95)-Double sized, 2 covers, pin-up gallery — 4.00
52a,52b-($3.50) — 3.50
53-56: 53-Sprouse-a begins. 56-McGuinness-c — 3.00
Annual 1-(1995, $2.95) — 3.00
NOTE: *Rob Liefeld* a(i)-1, 2; co-plots-2-4; scripts-1, 5, 6. *Ordway* c-41. *Platt* c-12, 25. *Thibert* c(i)-
7-9.

SUPREME: GLORY DAYS
Image Comics (Extreme Studios): Oct, 1994 - No. 2, Dec, 1994 ($2.95/$2.50,
limited series)
1,2: 2-Diehard, Roman, Superpatriot, & Glory app. — 3.00

SUPREME: THE NEW ADVENTURES (Formerly Supreme)
Maximum Press: V3#43, Oct, 1996 - V3#48, May, 1997 ($2.50)
V3#43-48: 43-Alan Moore scripts begin; Joe Bennett-a; Rick Veitch-a (8 pgs.);
Dan Jurgens-a (1 pg.); intro Citadel Supreme & Suprematons; 1st app.
Allied Supermen of America — 3.00

SUPREME: THE RETURN
Awesome Entertainment: May, 1999 - No. 6, June, 2000 ($2.99)
1-6: Alan Moore-s. 1,2-Sprouse & Gordon-a/i. 2,4-Liefeld-a. 6-Kirby app. — 3.00

SURE-FIRE COMICS (Lightning Comics #4 on)
Ace Magazines: June, 1940 - No. 4, Oct, 1940 (Two No. 3's)
V1#1-Origin Flash Lightning & begins; X-The Phantom Fed, Ace McCoy, Buck
Steele, Marvo the Magician, The Raven, Whiz Wilson (Time Traveler)
begin (all 1st app.); Flash Lightning c-1-4 — 164 492 1023 1800
2 — 77 231 483 850

3(9/40), 3(#4)(10/40)-nn on-c, #3 on inside 59 177 369 650

SURF 'N' WHEELS
Charlton Comics: Nov, 1969 - No. 6, Sept, 1970
1 — 3 9 21 32
2-6 — 2 6 13 20

SURGE
Eclipse Comics: July, 1984 - No. 4, Jan, 1985 ($1.50, lim. series, Baxter paper)
1-4 Ties into DNAgents series — 2.25

SURPRISE ADVENTURES (Formerly Tormented)
Sterling Comic Group: No. 3, Mar, 1955 - No. 5, July, 1955
3-5: 3,5-Sekowsky-a — 7 21 38 55

SUSIE Q. SMITH
Dell Publishing Co.: No. 323, Mar, 1951 - No. 553, Apr, 1954
Four Color 323 (#1) — 4 12 29 45
Four Color 377, 453 (2/53), 553 — 4 12 25 38

SUSPENSE (Radio/TV issues #1-11; Real Life Tales of… #1-4) (Amazing
Detective Cases #3 on?)
Marvel/Atlas Comics (CnPC No. 1-10/BFP No. 11-29): Dec, 1949 - No. 29, Apr
1953 (#1-8,17-23: 52 pgs.)
1-Powell-a; Peter Lorre, Sidney Greenstreet photo-c from Hammett's "The
Verdict" — 59 177 369 650
2-Crime stories; Dennis O'Keefe & Gale Storm photo-c from Universal movie
"Abandoned" — 35 105 188 325
3-Change to horror — 39 117 208 360
4,7-10: 7-Dracula-sty — 29 87 156 270
5-Krigstein, Tuska, Everett-a — 31 93 168 290
6-Tuska, Everett, Morisi-a — 31 93 165 285
11-13,15-17,19,20 — 23 69 121 210
14-Classic Heath Hypo-c; A-Bomb panels — 35 105 188 325
18,22-Krigstein-a — 25 75 130 225
21,23,24,26-29: 24-Tuska-a — 22 66 116 195
25-Electric chair-c/story — 30 90 162 280
NOTE: *Ayers* a-20. *Briefer* a-5, 7, 27. *Brodsky* c-4, 6-9, 11, 16, 17, 25. *Colan* a-8(2), 9. *Everett*
a-5, 6(2), 19, 23, 28; c-21-23, 26. *Fuje* a-29. *Heath* a-5, 6, 8, 10, 14; c-14, 19. *Iger* a-27. *Maneely* a-
12, 23, 24, 28, 29; c-5, 6p, 10, 13, 15, 18. *Mooney* a-24, 28. *Morisi* a-6, 12. *Palais* a-10. *Rico* a-
7-9. *Robinson* a-24. *Romita* a-20(2), 25. *Sekowsky* a-11, 13, 14. *Sinnott* a-23, 25. *Tuska* a-5,
6(2), 12; c-12. *Whitney* a-15, 16, 22. *Ed Win* a-27.

SUSPENSE COMICS
Continental Magazines: Dec, 1943 - No. 12, Sept, 1946
1-The Grey Mask begins; bondage/torture-c; L. B. Cole-a (7 pgs.)
— 400 1200 2500 4800
2-Intro. The Mask; Rico, Giunta, L. B. Cole-a (7 pgs.)
— 295 885 1844 3250
3-L.B. Cole-a; classic Schomburg-c (Scarce) 1600 4800 9600 16,000
4-6: 5-L. B. Cole-c begin — 223 669 1394 2450
7,9,10,12: 9-L.B. Cole eyeball-c — 168 505 1050 1850
8-Classic L. B. Cole spider-c — 400 1200 2500 4800
11-Classic Devil-c — 317 951 1927 3800
NOTE: *L. B. Cole* c-5-12. *Fuje* a-8. *Larsen* a-11. *Palais* a-9, 11. *Bondage* c-1, 3, 4.

SUSPENSE DETECTIVE
Fawcett Publications: June, 1952 - No. 5, Mar, 1953
1-Evans-a (11 pgs.); Baily-c/a — 43 129 257 450
2-Evans-a (10 pgs.) — 29 87 153 265
3-5 — 24 72 127 215
NOTE: *Baily* a-5; c-1-3. *Sekowsky* a-2, 4, 5; c-5.

SUSPENSE STORIES (See Strange Suspense Stories)

SUSPIRA: THE GREAT WORKING
Chaos! Comics: Apr, 1997 - No. 4, Aug, 1997 ($2.95, limited series)
1-4 — 3.00

SUSSEX VAMPIRE, THE (Sherlock Holmes)
Caliber Comics: 1996 ($2.95, 32 pgs., B&W, one-shot)
nn-Adapts Sir Arthur Conan Doyle's story; Warren Ellis scripts — 3.00

SUZIE COMICS (Formerly Laugh Comix; see Laugh Comics, Liberty
Comics #10, Pep Comics & Top-Notch Comics #28)
Close-Up No. 49,50/MLJ Mag./Archie No. 51 on: No. 49, Spring, 1945 - No.

Swamp Thing #13 © DC

Swamp Thing #155 © DC

Sweethearts #99 © FAW

SW

	GD2.0	FN6.0	VF8.0	NM9.4

100, Aug, 1954

49-Ginger begins	24	72	127	215
50-55: 54-Transvestism story. 55-Woggon-a	15	45	77	130
56-Katy Keene begins by Woggon	14	42	72	120
57-65	11	33	55	90
66-80	10	30	55	85
81-87,89-99	10	30	55	80

88,100: 88-Used in POP, pgs. 76,77; Bill Woggon draws himself in story.

100-Last Katy Keene	10	30	55	85

NOTE: *Al Fagaly c-49-67. Katy Keene app. in 53-82, 85-100.*

SWAMP FOX, THE (TV, Disney)(See Walt Disney Presents #2)
Dell Publishing Co.: No. 1179, Dec, 1960

Four Color 1179-Leslie Nielsen photo-c	9	27	63	110

SWAMP THING (See Brave & the Bold, Challengers of the Unknown #82, DC Comics Presents #8 & 85, DC Special Series #2, 14, 17, 20, House of Secrets #92, Limited Collectors' Edition C-59, & Roots of the...)

SWAMP THING
National Per. Publ./DC Comics: Oct-Nov, 1972 - No. 24, Aug-Sept, 1976

1-Wrightson-c/a begins; origin	12	36	84	140
2-1st app. Patchwork Man (1 panel cameo)	5	15	34	55
3-1st full app. Patchwork Man (see House of Secrets #140)				
	3	10	23	35
4,6,8-10: 10-Last Wrightson issue	3	9	20	30
7-Batman-c/story	3	10	23	35
11-20: 11-19-Redondo-a. 13-Origin retold (1 pg.)	2	6	9	12
21-24: 23,24-Swamp Thing reverts back to Dr. Holland. 23-New logo				
	2	6	9	12

NOTE: *J. Jones a-9i(assist). Kaluta a-9i. Redondo c-12-19, 21. Wrightson issues (#1-10) reprinted in DC Special Series #2, 14, 17, 20 & Roots of the Swampthing.*

SWAMP THING (Saga Of The... #1-38,42-45) (See Essential Vertigo:...)
DC Comics (Vertigo imprint #129 on): May, 1982 - No. 171, Oct, 1996 (Direct sales #65 on)

1-Origin retold; Phantom Stranger series begins; ends #13; Yeates-c/a begins				
				6.00
2-15: 2-Photo-c from movie. 13-Last Yeates-a				4.00
16-19: Bissette-a.				5.00
20-1st Alan Moore issue	2	6	13	20
21-New origin	2	6	11	16
22,23,25: 25-John Constantine 1-panel cameo	1	4	7	10
24-JLA x-over; Last Yeates-c.	2	6	9	12
26-30				6.00
31-33,35,36: 33-r/1st app. from House of Secrets #92				5.00
34	1	3	6	8
37-1st app. John Constantine (Hellblazer) (6/85)	2	6	11	15
38-40: John Constantine app.	1	3	6	8

41-52,54-64: 44-Batman cameo. 44-51-John Constantine app. 46-Crisis x-over; Batman cameo. 49-Spectre app. 50-($1.25, 52 pgs.)-Deadman, Dr. Fate, Demon. 52-Arkham Asylum-c/story; Joker-c/cameo. 58-Spectre preview. 64-Last Moore issue 3.50

53-($1.25, 52 pgs.)-Arkham Asylum; Batman-c/story				4.50

65-83,85-99,101-144,126-149,151-153: 65-Direct sales only begins. 66-Batman & Arkham Asylum story. 70,76-John Constantine x-over; 76-X-over w/Hellblazer #9. 79-Sandman-c/story. 85-Jonah Hex app. 102-Preview of World Without End. 116-Photo-c. 129-Metallic ink on-c. 140-Millar scripts begin, end #171. 3.00

84-Sandman (Morpheus) cameo.				4.00

100,125,150: 100 ($2.50, 52 pgs.). 125-($2.95, 52 pgs.)-20th anniversary issue. 150 (52 pgs.)-Anniversary issue 3.00

154-171: 154-$2.25-c begins. 165-Curt Swan-a(p). 166,169,171-John Constantine & Phantom Stranger app. 168-Arcane returns				2.50

Annual 1,3-6('82-91): 1-Movie Adaptation; painted-c. 3-New format; Bolland-c.

4-Batman-c/story. 5-Batman cameo; re-intro Brother Power (Geek),1st app. since 1968 4.00

Annual 2 (1985)-Moore scripts; Bissette-a(p); Deadman, Spectre app. 7.00

Annual 7(1993, $3.95)-Children's Crusade 4.00

...A Murder of Crows (2001, $19.95)-r/#43-50; Moore-s 20.00

...Love and Death (1990, $17.95)-r/#28-34 & Annual #2; Totleben painted-c 18.00

...: Roots (1998, $7.95) Jon J Muth-s/painted-a/c 8.00

Saga of the Swamp Thing ('87, '89)-r/#21-27 (1st & 2nd print) 13.00

...: The Curse (2000, $19.95, TPB) r/#35-42; Bisley-c 20.00

NOTE: *Bissette a(p)-16-19, 21-27, 29, 30, 34-36, 39-42, 44, 46, 50, 64; c-17i, 24-32p, 35-37p, 40p, 44p, 46-50p, 51-58, 61, 62, 63p. Kaluta c/a-74. Spiegle a-1-3, 6. Sutton a-98p. Totleben a(i)-10, 16-27, 29, 31, 34-40, 42, 44, 46, 48, 50, 53, 55i; c-25-32i, 33, 35-40i, 42i, 44i, 46-50i, 53, 55i, 59p, 64, 65, 68, 73, 76, 80, 82, 84, 89, 91-100, Annual 4, 5. Vess painted c-121, 129-139, Annual 7. Williamson 86i. Wrightson a-18i(r), 33r. John Constantine appears in #37-40, 44-51, 65-67, 70-77, 80-90, 99, 114, 115, 130, 134-138.*

SWAMP THING
DC Comics (Vertigo): May, 2000 - No. 20, Dec, 2001 ($2.50)

1-3-Tefé Holland's return; Vaughan-s/Petersen-a; Hale painted-c				3.00
4-20: 7-9-Bisley-c. 10-John Constantine-c/app. 10-12-Fabry-c. 13-15-Mack-c				2.50
18-Swamp Thing app.				2.50
Preview-16 pg. flip book w/Lucifer Preview				2.25

SWARM (See Futuretech)
Mushroom Comics: Jan, 1996 ($2.50, limited series)

1-Flip book w/Futuretech #1				2.50

SWAT MALONE (America's Home Run King)
Swat Malone Enterprises: Sept, 1955

V1#1-Hy Fleishman-a	11	33	55	90

SWEENEY (Formerly Buz Sawyer)
Standard Comics: No. 4, June, 1949 - No. 5, Sept, 1949

4,5: 5-Crane-a	9	27	49	70

SWEE'PEA (Also see Popeye #46)
Dell Publishing Co.: No. 219, Mar, 1949

Four Color 219	9	27	63	110

SWEET CHILDE
Advantage Graphics Press: 1995 - No. 2, 1995 ($2.95, B&W, mature)

1,2				3.00

SWEETHEART DIARY (Cynthia Doyle #66-on)
Fawcett Publications/Charlton Comics No. 32 on: Wint, 1949; #2, Spr, 1950; #3, 6/50 - #9, 10/50; #6, 1951(nd); #7, 9/51 - #14, 1/53; #32, 10/55; #33, 4/56 - #65, 8/62 (#1-14: photo-c)

1	17	51	88	150
2	9	27	51	75
3,4-Wood-a	15	45	77	130
5-10: 8-Bailey-a	8	24	42	60
11-14: 13-Swayze-a. 14-Last Fawcett issue	6	18	32	45
32 (10/55; 1st Charlton issue)(Formerly Cowboy Love #31)				
	7	21	36	50
33-40: 34-Swayze-a	5	15	23	30
41-(68 pgs.)	5	15	25	35
42-60	2	6	15	22
61-65	2	6	13	20

SWEETHEARTS (Formerly Captain Midnight)
Fawcett Publications/Charlton No. 122 on: #68, 10/48 - #121, 5/53; #122, 3/54; V2#23, 5/54 - #137, 12/73

68-Photo-c begin	16	48	83	140
69,70	9	27	49	70
71-80	7	21	38	55
81-84,86-93,95-99,105	6	18	32	45
85,94,103,110,117-George Evans-a	8	24	42	60
100	7	21	38	50
101,107-Powell-a	7	21	36	50
102,104,106,108,109,112-116,118	6	18	29	40
111-1 pg. Ronald Reagan biography	8	24	45	65

119-Marilyn Monroe & Richard Widmark photo-c (1/54?); also appears in story; part Wood-a 41 123 246 425

120-Atom Bomb story	10	30	55	80
121-Liz Taylor/Fernando Lamas photo-c	13	39	66	110
122-(1st Charlton) 3/54)-Marijuana story	10	30	55	80
V2#23 (5/54)-28: 28-Last precode issue (2/55)	6	18	29	40
29-39,41,43-45,47-50	3	9	20	30
40-Photo-c; Tommy Sands story	3	10	23	35
42-Ricky Nelson photo-c/story	8	24	56	90
46-Jimmy Rodgers photo-c/story	3	10	23	35

Sweet Sixteen #5 © PMI

Sweet XVI #1 © MAR

Sword of Sorcery #1 © DC

	GD2.0	FN6.0	VF8.0	NM9.4
51-60	3	9	19	28
61-80,100	3	9	17	25
81-99	2	6	15	22
101-110	2	6	10	14
111-137	2	6	9	12

NOTE: Photo c-68-121(Fawcett), 40, 42, 46(Charlton). **Swayze** a(Fawcett)-70-118(most).

SWEETHEART SCANDALS (See Fox Giants)

SWEETIE PIE
Dell Publishing Co.: No. 1185, May-July, 1961 - No. 1241, Nov-Jan, 1961/62

Four Color 1185 (#1)	4	12	29	45
Four Color 1241	3	10	23	35

SWEETIE PIE
Ajax-Farrell/Pines (Literary Ent.): Dec, 1955 - No. 15, Fall, 1957

1-By Nadine Seltzer	8	24	42	60
2 (5/56; last Ajax?)	5	15	25	35
3-15	4	12	19	25

SWEET LOVE
Home Comics (Harvey): Sept, 1949 - No. 5, May, 1950 (All photo-c)

1	10	30	55	80
2	6	18	32	45
3,4: 3-Powell-a	5	15	25	35
5-Kamen, Powell-a	8	24	42	60

SWEET ROMANCE
Charlton Comics: Oct, 1968

1	2	6	11	16

SWEET SIXTEEN (...Comics and Stories for Girls)
Parents' Magazine Institute: Aug-Sept, 1946 - No. 13, Jan, 1948 (All have movie stars photos on covers)

1-Van Johnson's life story; Dorothy Dare, Queen of Hollywood Stunt Artists begins (in all issues); part photo-c	20	60	105	180
2-Jane Powell, Roddy McDowall "Holiday in Mexico" photo on-c; Alan Ladd story	14	42	72	120
3,5,6,8-11: 5-Ann Francis photo on-c; Gregory Peck story. 6-Dick Haymes story. 8-Shirley Jones photo on-c. 10-Jean Simmons photo on-c; James Stewart story	10	30	55	80
4-Elizabeth Taylor photo on-c	16	48	83	140
7-Ronald Reagan's life story	20	60	105	175
12-Bob Cummings, Vic Damone story	10	30	55	85
13-Robert Mitchum's life story	10	30	55	90

SWEET XVI
Marvel Comics: May, 1991 - No. 5, Sept, 1991($1.00, color)

1-5: Barbara Slate story & art				3.00

SWIFT ARROW (Also see Lone Rider & The Rider)
Ajax/Farrell Publications: Feb-Mar, 1954 - No. 5, Oct-Nov, 1954; Apr, 1957 - No. 3, Sept, 1957

1(1954) (1st Series)	16	48	83	140
2	9	27	49	70
3-5: 5-Lone Rider story	7	21	38	55
1 (2nd Series) (Swift Arrow's Gunfighters #4)	8	24	42	60
2,3: 2-Lone Rider begins	7	21	36	50

SWIFT ARROW'S GUNFIGHTERS (Formerly Swift Arrow)
Ajax/Farrell Publ. (Four Star Comic Corp.): No. 4, Nov, 1957

4	7	21	36	50

SWING WITH SCOOTER
National Periodical Publications: June-July, 1966 - No. 35, Aug-Sept, 1971; No. 36, Oct-Nov, 1972

1	7	21	53	85
2,6-10: 9-Alfred E. Newman swipe in last panel	3	10	23	35
3-5: 3-Batman cameo on-c. 4-Batman cameo inside. 5-JLA cameo	4	12	26	40
11-13,15-19: 18-Wildcat of JSA 1pg. text. 19-Last 12¢-c	3	9	17	25
14-Alfred E. Neuman cameo	3	9	19	28
20 (68 pgs.)	4	12	26	40

	GD2.0	FN6.0	VF8.0	NM9.4
21-23,25-31	2	6	13	20
24-Frankenstein-c	3	9	17	25
32-34 (68 pgs.). 32-Batman cameo. 33-Interview with David Cassidy. 34-Interview with Rick Ely (The Rebels)	4	12	26	40
35-(52 pgs.). 1 pg. app. Clark Kent and 4 full pgs. of Superman	7	21	50	80
36-Bat-signal refererence to Batman	3	9	19	28

NOTE: **Aragonés** a-13 (1pg.), 18(2pgs.), 30(2pgs.) **Orlando** a-1-11; c-1-11, 13. **#20, 33, 34:** 68 pgs.; **#35:** 52 pgs.

SWISS FAMILY ROBINSON (Walt Disney's..; see King Classics & Movie Comics)
Dell Publishing Co.: No. 1156, Dec, 1960

Four Color 1156-Movie-photo-c	7	21	49	90

SWORD & THE DRAGON, THE
Dell Publishing Co.: No. 1118, June, 1960

Four Color 1118-Movie, photo-c	8	24	56	100

SWORD & THE ROSE, THE (Disney)
Dell Publishing Co.: No. 505, Oct, 1953 - No. 682, Feb, 1956

Four Color 505-Movie, photo-c	9	27	63	110
Four Color 682-When Knighthood Was in Flower-Movie, reprint of #505; Renamed the Sword & the Rose for the novel; photo-c	7	21	49	90

SWORD IN THE STONE, THE (See March of Comics #258 & Movie Comics & Wart and the Wizard)

SWORD OF DAMOCLES
Image Comics (WildStorm Productions): Mar, 1996 - No. 2, Apr, 1996 ($2.50, limited series)

1,2: Warren Ellis scripts. 1-Prelude to "Fire from Heaven" x-over; 1st app. Sword				2.50

SWORD OF SORCERY
National Periodical Publications: Feb-Mar, 1973 - No. 5, Nov-Dec, 1973 (20¢)

1-Leiber Fafhrd & The Grey Mouser; Chaykin/Neal Adams (Crusty Bunkers) art; Kaluta	2	6	13	20
2,3: 2-Wrightson-c(i); Adams-a(i). 3-Wrightson-i(5 pgs.)	2	6	9	12
4,5: 5-Starlin-a(p); Conan cameo	1	3	6	9

NOTE: **Chaykin** a-1-4p; c-2p, 3-5. **Kaluta** a-3i. **Simonson** a-3i, 4i, 5p; c-5.

SWORD OF THE ATOM
DC Comics: Sept, 1983 - No. 4, Dec, 1983 (Limited series)

1-4: Kane-c/a in all, Special 1 ('84, '85, '88). 1,2-Kane-c/a each				3.00

SWORDS OF TEXAS (See Scout #15)
Eclipse Comics: Oct, 1987 - No. 4, Jan, 1988 ($1.75, color, Baxter paper)

1-4: Scout app.				2.25

SWORDS OF THE SWASHBUCKLERS (See Marvel Graphic Novel)
Marvel Comics (Epic Comics): May, 1985 - No. 12, Jun, 1987 ($1.50; mature)

1-12-Butch Guice-c/a (Cont'd from Marvel G.N.)				2.25

SWORN TO PROTECT
Marvel Comics: Sept, 1995 ($1.95) (Based on card game)

nn-Overpower Game Guide; Jubilee story				2.25

SYPHONS
Now Comics: V2#1, May, 1994 - V2#3, 1994 ($2.50, limited series)

V2#1-3: 1-Standarcer, Knightfire, Raze & Brigade begin				2.50

SYSTEM, THE
DC Comics (Vertigo Verite): May, 1996 - No. 3, July, 1996 ($2.95, lim. series)

1-3: Kuper-c/a				3.00
TPB (1997, $12.95) r/#1-3				13.00

TAFFY COMICS
Rural Home/Orbit Publ.: Mar-Apr, 1945 - No. 12, 1948

1-L.B. Cole-c; origin & 1st app. of Wiggles The Wonderworm plus 7 chapter WWII funny animal adventures	55	165	341	600
2-L.B. Cole-c; Wiggles-c/stories in 1-4	29	87	156	270
3,4,6-12: 6-Perry Como-c/story. 7-Duke Ellington, 2 pgs. 8-Glenn Ford-c/ story. 9-Lon McCallister part photo-c & story. 10-Mort Leav-c. 11-Mickey Rooney-c/story	13	39	66	110

Taffy Comics #11 © Orbit Pub.

Takion #6 © DC

Tales From The Crypt #34 © WMG

	GD2.0	FN6.0	VF8.0	NM9.4

	GD2.0	FN6.0	VF8.0	NM9.4

5-L.B. Cole-c; Van Johnson-c/story   21   63   110   190

TAILGUNNER JO
DC Comics: Sept, 1988 - No. 6, Jan, 1989 ($1.25)
1-6   2.25

TAILS
Archie Publications; Dec, 1995 - No. 3, Feb, 1996 ($1.50, limited series)
1-3: Based on Sonic, the Hedgehog video game   3.00

TAILSPIN
Spotlight Publishers: November, 1944
nn-Firebird app.; L.B. Cole-c   29   87   153   265

TAILSPIN TOMMY (Also see Popular Comics)
United Features Syndicate/Service Publ. Co.: 1940; 1946
Single Series 23(1940)   40   120   232   400
Best Seller (nd, 1946)-Service Publ. Co.   15   45   77   130

TAINTED
DC Comics (Vertigo): Jan, 1995 ($4.95, one-shot)
1-Jamie Delano scripts; Al Davison-c/a; reads February '95 on-c   5.00

TAKION
DC Comics: June, 1996 - No. 7, Dec, 1996 ($1.75)
1-7: Lopresti-c/a(p). 1-Origin; Green Lantern app. 6-Final Night x-over   2.50

TALENT SHOWCASE (See New Talent Showcase)

TALE OF ONE BAD RAT, THE
Dark Horse Comics: Oct, 1994 - No. 4, Jan, 1995 ($2.95, limited series)
1-4: Bryan Talbot-c/a/scripts   3.00
HC ($69.95, signed and numbered) R/#1-4   70.00

TALES CALCULATED TO DRIVE YOU BATS
Archie Publications: Nov, 1961 - No. 7, Nov, 1962; 1966 (Satire)
1-Only 10¢ issue; has cut-out Werewolf mask (price includes mask)   12   36   88   150
2-Begin 12¢ issues   6   18   45   75
3-6: 3-UFO cover   5   15   34   55
7-Storyline change   4   12   30   50
1(1966, 25¢, 44 pg. Giant)-r/#1; UFO cover   5   15   34   55

TALES CALCULATED TO DRIVE YOU MAD
E.C. Publications: Summer, 1997 - No. 8, Winter, 1999 ($3.99/$4.99, satire)
1-6-Full color reprints of Mad: 1-(#1-3), 2-(#4-6), 3-(#7-9), 4-(#10-12)   5.00
   5-(#13-15), 6-(#16-18)   5.00
7,8-($4.99-c): 7-(#19-21), 8-(#22,23)   5.00

TALES FROM THE AGE OF APOCALYPSE
Marvel Comics: 1996 ($5.95, prestige format, one-shots)
1, ...: Sinister Bloodlines (1997, $5.95)   6.00

TALES FROM THE BOG
Aberration Press: Nov, 1995 - No. 7, Nov, 1997 ($2.95/$3.95, B&W)
1-7   4.00
Alternate #1 (Director's Cut) (1998, $2.95)   3.00

TALES FROM THE CRYPT (Formerly The Crypt Of Terror; see Three Dimensional...)
E.C. Comics: No. 20, Oct-Nov, 1950 - No. 46, Feb-Mar, 1955
20-See Crime Patrol #15 for 1st Crypt Keeper   108   324   756   1350
21-Kurtzman-r/Haunt of Fear #15(#1)   88   264   616   1100
22-Moon Girl costume at costume party, one panel   68   204   476   850
23-25: 24-E. A. Poe adaptation   52   156   364   650
26-30: 26-Wood's 2nd EC-c   41   123   287   515
31-Williamson-a(1st at E.C.); B&W and color illos. in POP; Kamen draws himself, Gaines & Feldstein; Ingels, Craig & Davis draw themselves in his story   43   129   301   540
32,35-39: 38-Censored-c   37   111   259   460
33-Origin The Crypt Keeper   59   177   413   735
34-Used in POP, pg. 83; lingerie panels   38   114   266   475
40-Used in Senate hearings & in Hartford Cournat anti-comics editorials-1954   37   111   259   460
41-45: 45-2 pgs. showing E.C. staff   36   108   252   450

46-Low distribution; pre-advertised cover for unpublished 4th horror title "Crypt of Terror" used on this book   42   126   294   525
NOTE: *Ray Bradbury* adaptations-34, 36. *Craig* a-20, 22-24; c-20. *Crandall* a-38, 44. *Davis* a-24-46; c-29-46. *Elder* a-37, 38. *Evans* a-32-34, 36, 40, 41, 43, 46. *Feldstein* a-20-23; c-21-25, 28. *Ingels* a-in all. *Kamen* a-20, 22, 25, 27-31, 33-36, 39, 41-45. *Krigstein* a-40, 42, 45. *Kurtzman* a-21. *Orlando* a-27-30, 35, 37, 39, 41-45. *Wood* a-21, 24, 25; c-26, 27. *Canadian reprints known; see Table of Contents.*

TALES FROM THE CRYPT (Magazine)
Eerie Publications: No. 10, July, 1968 (35¢, B&W)
10-Contains Farrell reprints from 1950s   3   10   23   35

TALES FROM THE CRYPT
Gladstone Publishing: July, 1990 - No. 6, May, 1991 ($1.95/$2.00, 68 pgs.)
1-r/TFTC #33 & Crime S.S. #17; Davis-c(r)   3.00
2-6: 2,3,5,6-Davis-c(r). 4-Begin $2.00-c; Craig-c(r)   3.00

TALES FROM THE CRYPT
Extra-Large Comics (Russ Cochran)/Gemstone Publishing: Jul, 1991 - No. 6 ($3.95, 10 1/4 x13 1/4", 68 pgs.)
1-Davis-c(r); Craig back-c(r); E.C. reprints   4.00
2-6 ($2.00, comic sized)   3.00

TALES FROM THE CRYPT
Russ Cochran: Sept, 1991 - No. 7, July, 1992 ($2.00, 64 pgs.)
1-7   3.00

TALES FROM THE CRYPT
Russ Cochran/Gemstone: Sept, 1992 - No. 30, Dec, 1999 ($1.50, quarterly)
1-4-r/Crypt of Terror #17-19, TFTC #20 w/original-c   3.00
5-30: 5-15 ($2.00)-r/TFTC #21-23 w/original-c. 16-30 ($2.50)   3.00
Annual 1-6('93-'99) 1-r/#1-5. 2- r/#6-10. 3- r/#11-15. 4- r/#16-20. 5-r/#21-25. 6- r/#26-30   14.00

TALES FROM THE GREAT BOOK
Famous Funnies: Feb, 1955 - No. 4, Jan, 1956 (Religious themes)
1-Story of Samson; John Lehti-a in all   9   27   49   70
2-4: 2-Joshua. 3-Joash the Boy King. 4-David   6   18   29   40

TALES FROM THE HEART OF AFRICA (The Temporary Natives)
Marvel Comics (Epic Comics): Aug, 1990 ($3.95, 52 pgs.)
1   4.00

TALES FROM THE TOMB (Also see Dell Giants)
Dell Publishing Co.: Oct, 1962 (25¢ giant)
1(02-810-210)-All stories written by John Stanley   11   33   88   220

TALES FROM THE TOMB (Magazine)
Eerie Publications: V1#6, July, 1969 - V7#3, 1975 (52 pgs.)
V1#6-8   5   15   34   55
V2#1-6: 4-LSD story-r/Weird V3#5. 6-Rulah-r   4   12   26   40
V3#1-Rulah-r   4   12   26   40
2-6('71),V4#1-5('72),V5#1-6('73),V6#1-6('74),V7#1-3('75)   3   10   23   35

TALES OF ASGARD
Marvel Comics Group: Oct, 1968 (25¢, 68 pgs.); Feb, 1984 ($1.25, 52 pgs.)
1-Reprints Tales of Asgard (Thor) back-up stories from Journey into Mystery #97-106; new Kirby-c; Kirby-a   4   12   29   45
V2#1 (2/84)-Thor-r; Simonson-c   3.00

TALES OF EVIL
Atlas/Seaboard Publ.: Feb, 1975 - No. 3, July, 1975 (All 25¢ issues)
1-3: 1-Werewolf w/Sekowsky-a. 2-Intro. The Bog Beast; Sparling-a. 3-Origin The Man-Monster; Buckler-a(p)   1   3   5   7
NOTE: *Grandenetti* a-1, 2. *Lieber* c-1. *Sekowsky* a-1. *Sutton* a-2. *Thorne* c-2.

TALES OF GHOST CASTLE
National Periodical Publications: May-June, 1975 - No. 3, Sept-Oct, 1975 (All 25¢ issues)
1-Redondo-a   3   9   17   25
2,3: 2-Nino-a. 3-Redondo-a.   2   6   10   14

TALES OF G.I. JOE
Marvel Comics: Jan, 1988 - No. 15, Mar, 1989

	GD2.0	FN6.0	VF8.0	NM9.4

	GD2.0	FN6.0	VF8.0	NM9.4

1 ($2.25, 52 pgs.) — — — 3.00
2-15 ($1.50): 1-15-r/G.I. Joe #1-15 — — — 2.25

TALES OF HORROR
Toby Press/Minoan Publ. Corp.: June, 1952 - No. 13, Oct, 1954

1	40	120	220	380
2-Torture scenes	34	102	179	310
3-13: 9-11-Reprints Purple Claw #1-3	22	66	116	195
12-Myron Fass-c/a; torture scenes	23	69	121	205

NOTE: *Andru a-5. Baily a-5. Myron Fass a-2, 3, 12; c-1-13, 12. Hollingsworth a-2. Sparling a-6, 9; c-9.*

TALES OF JUSTICE
Atlas Comics(MjMC No. 53-66/Male No. 67): No. 53, May, 1955 - No. 67, Aug, 1957

53	16	48	83	140
54-57: 54-Powell-a	11	33	55	90
58,59-Krigstein-a	12	36	61	100
60-63,65: 60-Powell-a	10	30	55	80
64,66,67: 64,67-Crandall-a. 66-Torres, Orlando-a	10	30	55	85

NOTE: *Everett a-53, 60. Orlando a-65, 66. Severin a-64; c-58, 60, 65. Wildey a-64, 67.*

TALES OF SUSPENSE (Becomes Captain America #100 on)
Atlas (WPI No. 1,2/Male No. 3-12/VPI No. 13-18)/Marvel No. 19 on:
Jan, 1959 - No. 99, Mar, 1968

1-Williamson-a (5 pgs.); Heck-c; #1-4 have sci-fi-c	131	393	1114	2100
2,3: 2-Robot-c. 3-Flying saucer-c/story	50	150	410	750
4-Williamson-a (4 pgs.); Kirby/Everett-c/a	43	129	344	625
5,6,8,10: 5-Kirby monster-c begin	31	94	233	425
7-Prototype ish. (Lava Man); 1 panel app. Aunt May (see Str. Tales #97)				
	35	105	263	475
9-Prototype ish. (Iron Man)	37	112	278	500
11,12,15,17-19: 15-Crandall-a.	27	81	190	340
13-Elektro-c/story	28	84	196	350
14-Intro/1st app. Colossus-c/sty	31	94	233	425
16-1st Metallo-c/story (4/61, Iron Man prototype)	31	93	233	420
20-Colossus-c/story (2nd app.)	28	84	196	350
21-25: 25-Last 10¢ issue	21	63	148	265
26,27,29,30,33,34,36-38: 33-(9/62)-Hulk 1st x-over cameo (picture on wall)				
	18	54	126	225
28-Prototype ish. (Stone Men)	18	54	129	230
31-Prototype ish. (Dr. Doom)	24	72	154	275
32-Prototype ish. (Dr. Strange)(8/62)-Sazzik The Sorcerer app.; "The Man and the Beehive" story, 1 month before TTA #35 (2nd Antman), came out after "The Man in the Ant Hill" in TTA #27 (1/62) (1st Antman)-Characters from both stories were tested to see which got best fan response				
	31	94	233	420
35-Prototype issue (The Watcher)	22	65	151	270
39 (3/63)-Origin/1st app. Iron Man & begin series; 1st Iron Man story has Kirby layouts	316	948	2842	6000
40-2nd app. Iron Man (new armor)	106	318	903	1700
41-3rd app. Iron Man; Dr. Strange (villain) app.	58	174	493	925
42-45: 45-Intro. & 1st app. Happy & Pepper	34	102	255	460
46,47: 46-1st app. Crimson Dynamo	24	72	168	300
48-New Iron Man armor by Ditko	30	90	210	375
49-1st X-Men x-over (same date as X-Men #3, 1/64); also 1st Avengers x-over (w/o Captain America); 1st Tales of the Watcher back-up story & begins (2nd app. Watcher; see F.F. #13)	23	69	160	285
50-1st app. Mandarin	16	48	112	200
51-1st app. Scarecrow	12	36	88	150
52-1st app. The Black Widow (4/64)	16	48	112	200
53-Origin The Watcher; 2nd Black Widow app.	14	42	100	170
54-56: 56-1st app. Unicorn	8	24	58	95
57-Origin/1st app. Hawkeye (9/64)	18	54	126	225
58-Captain America battles Iron Man (10/64)-Classic-c; 2nd Kraven app. (Cap's 1st app. in this title)	28	84	196	350
59-Iron Man plus Captain America double feature begins (11/64); 1st S.A. Captain America solo story; intro Jarvis, Avenger's butler; classic-c				
	28	84	196	350
60-2nd app. Hawkeye (#64 is 3rd app.)	13	39	91	155
61,62,64: 62-Origin Mandarin (2/65)	8	24	58	95
63-1st Silver Age origin Captain America (3/65)	22	65	157	280

65,66-G.A. Red Skull in WWII stories: 65-1st Silver-Age Red Skull (5/65). 66-Origin Red Skull	15	45	105	180
67-70: 69-1st app. Titanium Man. 70-Begin alternating-c features w/Capt. America (even #'s) & Iron Man (odd #'s)	5	15	34	60
71-78,81,98: 75-1st app. Agent 13 later named Sharon Carter. 76-Intro Batroc & Sharon Carter, Agent 13 of Shield. 78-Col. Nick Fury app. 81-Intro the Adaptoid by Kirby (also in #82-84). 88-Mole Man app. in Iron Man story. 92-1st Nick Fury x-over (cameo, as Agent of Shield, 8/67). 94-Intro Modok. 95-Capt. America's i.d. revealed. 98-1st app. new Zemo (son?) in cameo (#99 is 1st full app.)	5	15	34	55
79-Begin 3 part Iron Man Sub-Mariner battle story; Sub-Mariner-c & cameo; 1st app. Cosmic Cube; 1st modern Red Skull	6	18	45	75
80-Iron Man battles Sub-Mariner story cont'd in Tales to Astonish #82; classic Red Skull-c	6	18	45	75
99-Captain America story cont'd in Captain America #100; Iron Man story cont'd in Iron Man & Sub-Mariner #1	7	21	50	80

NOTE: *Abel a-73-81(as Gary Michaels), J. Buscema a-1; c-3. Colan a-39, 73-99p; c(p)-73, 75, 77, 79, 81, 83, 85-87, 89, 91, 93, 95, 97, 99. Crandall a-12. Davis a-38. Ditko a-1-15, 17-44, 46, 47-49p; c-2, 10i, 13i, 23i. Kirby/Ditko a-7; c-10, 13, 22, 28, 34. Everett a-8. Forte a-5, 9. Giacoia a-82. Heath a-2, 10. Gil Kane a-58p, 89-91; c-88, 89-91p. Kirby a(p)-2-4, 6-35, 40, 41, 43, 59-75, 77-86, 92-99; layouts-69-75, 77; c(p)4-28(most), 29-56, 58-72, 74, 76, 78, 80, 82, 84, 86, 92, 94, 96, 98. Leiber/Fox a-42, 43, 45, 51. Reinman a-26, 44i, 49i, 52i, 53i. Tuska a-58, 70-74. Wood c/a-71i.*

TALES OF SUSPENSE
Marvel Comics: V2#1, Jan, 1995 ($6.95, one-shot)

V2#1-James Robinson script; acetate-c. — — — 7.00

TALES OF SWORD & SORCERY (See Dagar)

TALES OF TERROR
Toby Press Publications: 1952 (no month)

1-Fawcette-c; Ravielli-a	26	78	139	240

NOTE: *This title was cancelled due to similarity to the E.C. title.*

TALES OF TERROR (See Movie Classics)

TALES OF TERROR (Magazine)
Eerie Publications: Summer, 1964

1	4	12	30	50

TALES OF TERROR
Eclipse Comics: July, 1985 - No. 13, July, 1987 ($2.00, Baxter paper, mature)

1-13: 5-1st Lee Weeks-a. 7-Sam Kieth-a. 10-Snyder-a. 12-Vampire story — — — 3.00

TALES OF TERROR ANNUAL
E.C. Comics: 1951 - No. 3, 1953 (25¢, 132 pgs.), 16 stories each)

nn(1951)(Scarce)-Feldstein infinity-c	500	1500	4000	–
2(1952)-Feldstein-c	200	600	1400	2200
3(1953)-Feldstein bondage/torture-c	159	477	1113	1750

NOTE: *No. 1 contains three horror and one science fiction comic which came out in 1950. No. 2 contains a horror, crime, and science fiction book which generally had cover dates in 1951, and No. 3 had horror, crime, and shock books that generally appeared in 1952. All E.C. annuals contain four complete books that did not sell on the stands which were rebound in the annual format, minus the covers, and sold from the E.C. office and on the stands in key cities. The contents of each annual may vary in the same year. Count Keeper, Vault Keeper, Old Witch app. on all-c.*

TALES OF TERROR ILLUSTRATED (See Terror Illustrated)

TALES OF TEXAS JOHN SLAUGHTER (See Walt Disney Presents, 4-Color #997)

TALES OF THE BEANWORLD
Beanworld Press/Eclipse Comics: Feb, 1985 - No. 19, 1991; No. 20, 1993 - No. 21, 1993 ($1.50/$2.00, B&W)

1-21 — — — 3.00

TALES OF THE BIZARRO WORLD
DC Comics: 2000 ($14.95, TPB)

nn-Reprints early Bizarro stories; new Jaime Hernandez-c — — — 15.00

TALES OF THE DARKNESS
Image Comics (Top Cow): Apr, 1998 - Present ($2.95)

1-4: 1,2-Portacio-c/a(p). 3,4-Lansing & Nocon-a(p) — — — 3.00
1-American Entertainment Ed. — — — 3.00
#1/2 (1/01, $2.95) — — — 3.00

TALES OF THE GREEN BERET
Dell Publishing Co.: Jan, 1967 - No. 5, Oct, 1969

Tales of the Teen Titans #91 © DC

Tales of the Unexpected #32 © DC

Tales of the Witchblade #4 © TCOW

TA

	GD2.0	FN6.0	VF8.0	NM9.4

	GD2.0	FN6.0	VF8.0	NM9.4
1-Glanzman-a in 1-4 & 5r	3	9	21	32
2-5: 5-Reprints #1	2	6	15	24

TALES OF THE GREEN HORNET
Now Comics: Sept, 1990 - No. 2, 1990; V2#1, Jan, 1992 -No.4, Apr, 1992;
V3#1, Sept, 1992 - No. 3, Nov, 1992

1,2				2.50
V2#1-4 ($1.95)				2.50
V3#1 ($2.75)-Polybagged w/hologram trading card				3.00
V3#2,3 ($2.50)				2.50

TALES OF THE GREEN LANTERN CORPS (See Green Lantern #107)
DC Comics: May, 1981 - No. 3, July, 1981 (Limited series)

1-3: 1-Origin of G.L. & the Guardians, Annual 1 (1/85)-Gil Kane-c/a				3.00

TALES OF THE INVISIBLE SCARLET O'NEIL (See Harvey Comics Hits #59)

TALES OF THE KILLERS (Magazine)
World Famous Periodicals: V1#10, Dec, 1970 - V1#11, Feb, 1971 (B&W, 52 pg)

V1#10-One pg. Frazetta; r/Crime Does Not Pay	4	12	25	38
11-similar-c to Crime Does Not Pay #47; contains r/Crime Does Not Pay	3	9	20	30

TALES OF THE LEGION (Formerly Legion of Super-Heroes)
DC Comics: No. 314, Aug, 1984 - No. 354, Dec, 1987

314-354: 326-r-begin				2.50
Annual 4,5 (1986, 1987)-Formerly LSH Annual				3.50

TALES OF THE MARINES (Formerly Devil-Dog Dugan #1-3)
Atlas Comics (OPI): No. 4, Feb, 1957 (Marines At War #5 on)

4-Powell-a; Severin-c	7	21	38	55

TALES OF THE MARVELS
Marvel Comics: 1995/1996 (all acetate, painted-c)

...Blockbuster 1 (1995, $5.95, one-shot), ...Inner Demons 1 (1996, $5.95, one shot), ...Wonder Years 1,2 (1995, $4.95, Limited series)				6.00

TALES OF THE MARVEL UNIVERSE
Marvel Comics: Feb, 1997 (one-shot)

1-Anthology; wraparound-c; Thunderbolts, Ka-Zar app.				3.00

TALES OF THE MYSTERIOUS TRAVELER (See Mysterious...)
Charlton Comics: Aug, 1956 - No. 13, June, 1959; V2#14, Oct, 1985 - No. 15, Dec, 1985

1-No Ditko-a; Giordano/Alascia-c	45	135	270	475
2-Ditko-a(1)	40	120	232	400
3-Ditko-c/a(1)	40	120	240	420
4-6-Ditko-c/a(3-4 stories each)	47	141	286	500
7-9-Ditko-a(1-2 each). 8-Rocke-a	40	120	220	380
10,11-Ditko-c/a(3-4 each)	41	123	246	425
12	17	51	88	150
13-Baker-a (r?)	19	57	99	165
V2#14,15 (1985)-Ditko-c/a-low print run	1	3	6	8

TALES OF THE NEW TEEN TITANS
DC Comics: June, 1982 - No. 4, Sept, 1982 (Limited series)

1-4				4.00

TALES OF THE PONY EXPRESS (TV)
Dell Publishing Co.: No. 829, Aug, 1957 - No. 942, Oct, 1958

Four Color 829 (#1)--Painted-c	4	12	30	50
Four Color 942-Title -Pony Express	4	12	30	50

TALES OF THE SUN RUNNERS
Sirius Comics/Amazing Comics No. 3: V2#1, July, 1986 - V2#3, 1986? ($1.50)

V2#1-3, Christmas Special 1(12/86)				2.25

TALES OF THE TEENAGE MUTANT NINJA TURTLES
Mirage Studios: May, 1987 - No. 7, Aug (Apr-c), 1989 (B&W, $1.50)
(See Teenage Mutant...)

1-7: 2-Title merges w/Teenage Mutant Ninja...				2.25

TALES OF THE TEEN TITANS (Formerly The New Teen Titans)
DC Comics: No. 41, Apr, 1984 - No. 91, July, 1988 (75¢)

41,45-49: 46-Aqualad & Aquagirl join				3.00

42-44: The Judas Contract part 1-3 with Deathstroke the Terminator in all; concludes in Annual #3. 44-Dick Grayson becomes Nightwing (3rd to be Nightwing) & joins Titans; Jericho (Deathstroke's son) joins; origin
Deathstroke				3.50
50,53-55: 50-Double size; app. Betty Kane (Bat-Girl) out of costume. 53-1st full app. Azrael; Deathstroke cameo. 54,55-Deathstroke-c/stories				3.50
51,52,56-91: 52-1st app. Azrael in cameo (not same as newer character). 56-Intro Jinx. 57-Neutron app. 59-r/DC Comics Presents #26. 60-91-r/New Teen Titans Baxter series. 68-B. Smith-c. 70-Origin Kole				2.50
Annual 3(1984, $1.25)-Part 4 of The Judas Contract; Deathstroke-c/story; Death of Terra; indicia says Teen Titans Annual; previous annuals listed as New Teen Titans Annual #1,2				4.00
Annual 4,5: 4-(1986, $1.25)-Reprints. 5-(1987)				2.50

TALES OF THE TEXAS RANGERS (See Jace Pearson...)

TALES OF THE UNEXPECTED (Becomes The Unexpected #105 on)(See Adventure #75, Super DC Giant)
National Periodical Publications: Feb-Mar, 1956 - No. 104, Dec-Jan, 1967-68

1	91	273	774	1450
2	45	135	359	650
3-5	31	94	233	425
6-10: 6-1st Silver Age issue	27	81	190	340
11,14,19,20	17	51	118	210
12,13,15-18,21-24: All have Kirby-a. 15,17-Grey tone-c. 16-Character named 'Thor' with a magic hammer by Kirby (8/57, not like later Thor)	23	68	160	285
25-30	15	45	105	180
31-39	13	39	91	155
40-Space Ranger begins (8/59, 3rd ap.), ends #82	88	264	744	1400
41,42-Space Ranger stories	33	99	250	450
43-1st Space Ranger-c this title; grey tone-c	61	182	519	975
44-46	25	75	174	310
47-50	18	54	126	225
51-60: 54-Dinosaur-c/story	15	45	107	185
61-67: 67-Last 10¢ issue	13	39	91	155
68-82: 82-Last Space Ranger	7	21	53	85
83-90,92-99	5	15	34	55
91,100: 91-1st Automan (also in #94,97)	5	15	38	60
101-104	4	12	29	45

NOTE: *Neal Adams* c-104. *Anderson* a-50. *Brown* a-50-82(Space Ranger); c-19, 40, & many Space Ranger-c. *Cameron* a-24, 27, 29; c-24. *Heath* a-49. *Bob Kane* a-24, 48. *Kirby* a-12, 13, 15-18, 21-24; c-13, 18, 22. *Meskin* a-15, 18, 26, 27, 35, 66. *Moreira* a-16, 20, 29, 38, 44, 62, 71; c-38. *Roussos* c-10. *Wildey* a-31.

TALES OF THE WEST (See 3-D...)

TALES OF THE WITCHBLADE
Image Comics (Top Cow Productions): Nov, 1996 - Present ($2.95)

1/2	1	3	6	9
1/2 Gold				15.00
1-Daniel-c/a(p)	1	4	7	10
1-Variant-c by Turner	2	6	11	15
1-Platinum Edition				30.00
2,3				6.00
4-6: 6-Green-c				5.00
7-9: 9-Lara Croft-c				3.00
7-Variant-c by Turner	1	3	6	8
Witchblade: Distinctions (4/01, $14.95, TPB) r/#1-6; Green-c				15.00

TALES OF THE WITCHBLADE COLLECTED EDITION
Image Comics (Top Cow): May, 1998 - Present ($4.95/$5.95, square-bound)

1,2: 1-r/#1,2. 2-($5.95) r/#3,4				6.00

TALES OF THE WIZARD OF OZ (See Wizard of OZ, 4-Color #1308)

TALES OF THE ZOMBIE (Magazine)
Marvel Comics Group: Aug, 1973 - No. 10, Mar, 1975 (75¢, B&W)

V1#1-Reprint/Menace #5; origin	3	9	19	28
2,3: 2-Everett biog. & memorial	2	6	13	20
V2#1(#4)-Photos & text of James Bond movie "Live & Let Die"	2	6	13	20
5-10: 8-Kaluta-a	2	6	11	16
Annual 1(Summer,'75)(#11)-B&W; Everett, Buscema-a				

785

	GD2.0	FN6.0	VF8.0	NM9.4

		2	6	15	22

NOTE: Brother Voodoo app. 2, 5, 6, 10. **Alcala** a-7-9. **Boris** c-1-4. **Colan** a-2r, 6. **Heath** a-5r. **Reese** a-2. **Tuska** a-2r.

TALES OF THUNDER
Deluxe Comics: Mar, 1985

1-Dynamo, Iron Maiden, Menthor app.; Giffen-a					2.25

TALES OF VOODOO
Eerie Publications: V1#11, Nov, 1968 - V7#6, Nov, 1974 (Magazine)

V1#11	4	12	30	50
V2#1(3/69)-V2#4(9/69)	4	12	25	38
V3#1-6('70): 4- "Claws of the Cat" redrawn from Climax #1				
	3	9	20	30
V4#1-6('71), V5#1-7('72), V6#1-7('73), V7#1-7('74)	3	9	20	30
Annual 1	3	9	21	32

NOTE: Bondage-c-V1#10, V2#4, V3#1.

TALES OF WELLS FARGO (TV)(See Western Roundup under Dell Giants)
Dell Publishing Co.: No. 876, Feb, 1958 - No. 1215, Oct-Dec, 1961

Four Color 876 (#1)-Photo-c	9	27	63	120
Four Color 968 (2/59), 1023, 1075 (3/60), 1113 (7-9/60)-All photo-c				
	9	27	63	110
Four Color 1167 (3-5/61), 1215-Photo-c	8	24	56	100

TALESPIN (Also see Cartoon Tales & Disney's Talespin Limited Series)
Disney Comics: June, 1991 - No. 7, Dec, 1991 ($1.50)

1-7				2.25

TALES TO ASTONISH (Becomes The Incredible Hulk #102 on)
Atlas (MAP No. 1/ZPC No. 2-14/VPI No. 15-21/Marvel No. 22 on: Jan, 1959 - No. 101, Mar, 1968

1-Jack Davis-a; monster-c	131	393	1114	2100
2-Ditko flying saucer-c (Martians); #2-4 have sci/fi-c.				
	55	165	468	875
3,4	43	129	323	575
5-Prototype issue (Stone Men); Williamson-a (4 pgs.); Kirby monster-c begin				
	43	129	344	625
6-Prototype issue (Stone Men)	35	106	263	475
7-Prototype issue (Toad Men)	35	106	263	475
8-10	31	94	233	425
11-14,17-20: 13-Swipes story from Menace #8	26	78	182	325
15-Prototype issue (Electro)	33	100	250	450
16-Prototype issue (Stone Men)	29	87	202	360
21-(7/61)-Hulk prototype	29	87	202	360
22-26,28-34	19	57	134	240
27-1st Ant-Man app. (1/62); last 10¢ issue (see Strange Tales #73,78 & Tales of Suspense #32)	267	800	2400	4800
35-(9/62)-2nd app. Ant-Man, 1st in costume; begin series & Ant-Man-c				
	122	366	1037	1950
36-3rd app. Ant-Man	53	159	452	850
37-40: 38-1st app. Egghead	37	111	278	500
41-43	26	78	182	325
44-Origin & 1st app. The Wasp (6/63)	31	93	233	425
45-48: Origin & 1st app. The Porcupine.	16	48	112	200
49-Ant-Man becomes Giant Man (11/63)	21	63	148	265
50,51,53-56,58: 50-Origin/1st app. Human Top (alias Whirlwind). 53-Origin Colossus	10	30	73	125
52-Origin/1st app. Black Knight (2/64)	12	36	84	140
57-Early Spider-Man app. (7/64)	15	45	105	180
59-Giant Man vs. Hulk feature story (9/64); Hulk's 1st app. this title				
	17	51	118	210
60-Giant Man & Hulk double feature begins	18	54	126	225
61-69: 61-All Ditko issue; 1st mailbag. 62-1st app./origin The Leader; new Wasp costume. 63-Origin Leader; 65-New Giant Man costume. 68-New Human Top costume. 69-Last Giant Man.	7	21	53	85
70-Sub-Mariner & Incredible Hulk begins (8/65)	9	27	65	110
71-81,83-91,94-99: 72-Begin alternating-c features w/Sub-Mariner (even #'s) & Hulk (odd #'s). 79-Hulk vs. Hercules-c/story. 81-1st app. Boomerang. 90-1st app. The Abomination. 97-X-Men cameo (brief)	5	15	34	55
82-Iron Man battles Sub-Mariner (1st Iron Man x-over outside The Avengers & TOS); story cont'd from Tales of Suspense #80	6	18	40	65
92-1st Silver Surfer x-over (outside of Fantastic Four, 6/67); 1 panel cameo				

	GD2.0	FN6.0	VF8.0	NM9.4
only	5	15	38	60
93-Hulk battles Silver Surfer-c/story (1st full x-over)	7	21	50	80
100-Hulk battles Sub-Mariner full-length story	6	18	40	65
101-Hulk story cont'd in Incredible Hulk #102; Sub-Mariner story continued in Iron Man & Sub-Mariner #1	7	21	50	80

NOTE: **Ayers** c(i)-9-12, 16, 18, 19. **Berg** a-1. **Burgos** a-62-64p. **Buscema** a-85-87p. **Colan** a(p)-70-76, 78-82, 84, 85, 101; c(p)-71-76, 78, 80, 82, 84, 86, 88, 90. **Ditko** a-1, 3-48, 50l, 60-67p; c-2, 7i, 8i, 14i, 17i. **Everett** a-78, 79i, 80-84, 85-90i, 94i, 95, 96; c(i)-79-81, 83, 86, 88. **Forte** a-6. **Kane** a-76, 88-91; c-89, 91. **Kirby** a(p)-1, 5-34-40, 44, 49-51, 68-70, 82, 83; layouts-71-84; c(p)-1, 3-48, 50-70, 72, 73, 75, 77, 78, 79, 81, 85, 90. **Kirby/Ditko** a-7, 8, 12, 13, 50; c-7, 8, 10, 13. **Leiber/Fox** a-47, 48, 50, 51. **Powell** a-65-69p, 73. **Reinman** a-6, 36, 45, 46, 54i, 56-60i.

TALES TO ASTONISH (2nd Series)
Marvel Comics Group: Dec, 1979 - No. 14, Jan, 1981

V1#1-Reprints Sub-Mariner #1 by Buscema				6.00
2-14: Reprints Sub-Mariner #2-14				4.00

TALES TO ASTONISH
Marvel Comics: V3#1, Oct, 1994 ($6.95, one-shot)

V3#1-Peter David scripts; acetate, painted-c				7.00

TALES TO HOLD YOU SPELLBOUND (See Spellbound)

TALES TO OFFEND
Dark Horse Comics: July, 1997 ($2.95, one-shot)

1-Frank Miller-s/a, EC-style cover				3.50

TALES TOO TERRIBLE TO TELL (Becomes Terrology #10, 11)
New England Comics: Wint, 1989-90 - No. 11, Nov-Dec.1993 ($2.95/$3.50, B&W with cardstock covers)

1-($2.95) Reprints of non-EC pre-code horror; EC-style cover by Bisette				4.00
2-8-($3.50) Story reprints, history of the pre-code titles and creators; cover galleries (B&W) inside & on back-c (color)				4.00
9-11-($2.95) 10,11-"Terrology" on cover				4.00

TALEWEAVER
DC Comics (WildStorm): Nov, 2001 - No. 6 ($3.50, limited series)

1-4-Philip Tan-a/Leonard Banaag-s. 2-Variant-c by Anacleto				3.50

TALKING KOMICS
Belda Record & Publ. Co.: 1947 (20 pgs, slick-c)

Each comic contained a record that followed the story - much like the Golden Record sets. Known titles: Chirpy Cricket, Lonesome Octopus, Sleepy Santa, Grumpy Shark, Flying Turtle, Happy Grasshopper

with records...	4	11	17	22

TALLY-HO COMICS
Swappers Quarterly (Baily Publ. Co.): Dec, 1944

nn-Frazetta's 1st work as Giunta's assistant; Man in Black horror story; violence; Giunta-c	40	120	240	420

TALOS OF THE WILDERNESS SEA
DC Comics: Aug, 1987 ($2.00, one-shot)

1				2.25

TALULLAH (See Comic Books Series I)

TAMMY, TELL ME TRUE
Dell Publishing Co.: No. 1233, 1961

Four Color 1233-Movie	6	18	42	80

TANGENT COMICS
.../ THE ATOM, DC Comics: Dec, 1997 ($2.95, one-shot)

1-Dan Jurgens-s/Jurgens & Paul Ryan-a				3.00

.../ THE BATMAN, DC Comics: Sept, 1998 ($1.95, one-shot)

1-Dan Jurgens-s/Klaus Janson-a				2.25

.../ DOOM PATROL, DC Comics: Dec, 1997 ($2.95, one-shot)

1- Dan Jurgens-s/Sean Chen & Kevin Conrad-a				3.00

.../ THE FLASH, DC Comics: Dec, 1997 ($2.95, one-shot)

1-Todd Dezago-s/Gary Frank & Cam Smith-a				3.00

.../ GREEN LANTERN, DC Comics: Dec, '97 ($2.95, one-shot)

1-James Robinson-s/J.H. Williams III & Mick Gray-a				3.00

.../ JLA, DC Comics: Sept, 1998 ($1.95, one-shot)

1-Dan Jurgens-s/Banks & Rapmund-a				2.25

Tangent Comics / Powergirl #1 © DC

Target Comics V2 #7 © NOVP

Targitt #1 © Seaboard

	GD2.0	FN6.0	VF8.0	NM9.4

.../ THE JOKER, DC Comics: Dec, 1997 ($2.95, one-shot)
1-Karl Kesel-s/Matt Haley & Tom Simmons-a — 3.00
.../ THE JOKER'S WILD, DC Comics: Sept, 1998 ($1.95, one-shot)
1-Kesel & Simmons-s/Phillips & Rodriguez-a — 2.25
.../ METAL MEN, DC Comics: Dec, 1997 ($2.95, one-shot)
1-Ron Marz-s/Mike McKone & Mark McKenna-a — 3.00
.../ NIGHTWING, DC Comics: Dec, 1997 ($2.95, one-shot)
1-John Ostrander-s/Jan Duursema-a — 3.00
.../ NIGHTWING: NIGHTFORCE, DC Comics: Sept, 1998 ($1.95, one-shot)
1-John Ostrander-s/Jan Duursema-a — 2.25
.../ POWERGIRL, DC Comics: Sept, 1998 ($1.95, one-shot)
1-Marz-s/Abell & Vines-a — 2.25
.../ SEA DEVILS, DC Comics: Dec, 1997 ($2.95, one-shot)
1-Kurt Busiek-s/Vince Giarrano & Tom Palmer-a — 3.00
.../ SECRET SIX, DC Comics: Dec, 1997 ($2.95, one-shot)
1-Chuck Dixon-s/Tom Grummett & Lary Stucker-a — 3.00
.../ THE SUPERMAN, DC Comics: Sept, 1998 ($1.95, one-shot)
1-Millar-s/Guice-a — 2.25
.../ TALES OF THE GREEN LANTERN, DC Comics: Sept, 1998 ($1.95, one-shot)
1-Story & art by various — 2.25
.../ THE TRIALS OF THE FLASH, DC Comics: Sept, 1998 ($1.95, one-shot)
1-Dezago-s/Pelletier & Lanning-a — 2.25
.../ WONDER WOMAN DC Comics: Sept, 1998 ($1.95, one-shot),
1-Peter David-s/Unzueta & Mendoza-a — 2.25

TANGLED WEB (See Spider-Man's Tangled Web)
TANK GIRL
Dark Horse Comics: May, 1991 - No. 4, Aug, 1991 ($2.25, B&W, mini-series)
1-4: 1-Contains Dark Horse trading cards — 4.00
TANK GIRL: APOCALYPSE
DC Comics: Nov, 1995 - No. 4, Feb, 1996 ($2.25, limited series)
1-4 — 3.00
TANK GIRL: MOVIE ADAPTATION
DC Comics: 1995 ($5.95, 68 pgs., one-shot)
nn-Peter Milligan scripts — 6.00
TANK GIRL: THE ODYSSEY
DC Comics: May, 1995 - No.4, Oct, 1995 ($2.25, limited series)
1-4: Peter Milligan scripts; Hewlett-a — 3.00
TANK GIRL 2
Dark Horse Comics: June, 1993 - No. 4, Sept, 1993 ($2.50, lim. series, mature)
1-4: Jamie Hewlett & Alan Martin-s/a — 3.00
TPB (2/95, $17.95) r/#1-4 — 18.00
TAPPAN'S BURRO (See Zane Grey & 4-Color #449)
TAPPING THE VEIN (Clive Barker's...)
Eclipse Comics: 1989 - No. 5, 1992 ($6.95, squarebound, mature, 68 pgs.)
Book 1-5: 1-Russell-a, Bolton-c. 2-Bolton-a. 4-Die-cut-c — 7.00
TARANTULA (See Weird Suspense)
TARGET: AIRBOY
Eclipse Comics: Mar, 1988 ($1.95)
1 — 2.25
TARGET COMICS (...Western Romances #106 on)
Funnies, Inc./Novelty Publications/Star Publications: Feb, 1940 - V10#3 (#105), Aug-Sept, 1949
V1#1-Origin & 1st app. Manowar, The White Streak by Burgos, & Bulls-Eye Bill by Everett; City Editor (ends #5), High Grass Twins by Jack Cole (ends #4), T-Men by Joe Simon(ends #9), Rip Rory (ends #4), Fantastic Feature Films by Tarpe Mills (ends #39), & Calling 2-R (ends #14) begin; marijuana use story — 462 1386 3000 6000
2-Everett-c/a — 241 723 1506 2650
3,4-Everett, Jack Cole-a — 140 420 875 1550
5-Origin The White Streak; Space Hawk by Wolverton begins (6/40)

(see Blue Bolt & Circus) — 417 1250 2604 5000
6-The Chameleon by Everett begins (7/40, 1st app.); White Streak origin cont'd. in text; early mention of comic collecting in letter column; 1st letter column in comics? (7/40) — 175 525 1094 1925
7-Wolverton Spacehawk-c/story (Scarce) — 450 1350 2925 5850
8,9,12: 12-(1/41) — 132 396 825 1450
10-Intro/1st app. The Target (11/40); Simon-c — 182 546 1136 2000
11-Origin The Target & The Targeteers — 164 492 1023 1800
V2#1-Target by Bob Wood; Uncle Sam flag-c — 82 246 511 900
2-Ten part Treasure Island serial begins; Harold Delay-a; reprinted in Catholic Comics V3#1-10 (see Key Comics #5) — 73 219 455 800
3-5: 4-Kit Karter, The Cadet begins — 57 171 356 625
6-9: Red Seal with White Streak in #6-10 — 55 165 341 600
10-Classic-c — 95 285 597 1050
11,12: 12-10-part Last of the Mohicans serial begins; Delay-a — 55 165 330 575
V3#1-3,5-7,9,10: 10-Last Wolverton issue — 55 165 330 575
4-V for Victory-c — 55 165 341 600
8-Hitler, Tojo, Flag-c; 6-part Gulliver Travels serial begins; Delay-a. — 68 204 426 750
11,12 — 15 45 77 135
V4#1-4,7-12: 6-Targetoons by Wolverton. 8-X-Mas-c — 12 36 61 105
5-Classic Statue of Liberty-c — 14 42 72 120
6-Targetoons by Wolverton — 14 42 72 120
V5#1-8 — 11 33 55 95
V6#1-4,6-10, V7#1-12 — 10 30 55 85
5-Tojo-c — 12 36 61 105
V8#1,3-5,8,9,11,12 — 10 30 55 80
2,6,7-Krigstein-a — 11 33 55 90
10-L.B. Cole-c — 35 105 188 325
V9#1,4,6,8,10-L.B. Cole-c — 35 105 185 320
2,3,5,7,9,11, V10#1 — 10 30 55 80
12-Classic L.B. Cole-c — 38 114 203 350
V10#2,3-L.B. Cole-c — 34 102 173 310
NOTE: **Certa** c-V8#9, 11, 12, V9#5, 9, 11, V10#1. **Jack Cole** a-1-8. **Everett** a-1-9; c(signed Blake)-1, 2. **Al Fago** c-V6#8. **Sid Greene** c-V2#9, 12, V3#3. **Walter Johnson** c-V5#6, V6#4. **Tarpe Mills** a-1-4, 6, 8, 11, V3#1. **Rico** a-V7#4, 10, V8#5, 6, V9#3; c-V7#6, 8, 10, V8#2, 4, 6, 7. **Simon** a-1, 2. **Bob Wood** c-V2#2, 3, 5, 6.

TARGET: THE CORRUPTORS (TV)
Dell Publishing Co.: No. 1306, Mar-May, 1962 - No. 3, Oct-Dec, 1962
(All have photo-c)
Four Color 1306(#1), #2,3 — 5 15 35 65

TARGET WESTERN ROMANCES (Formerly Target Comics; becomes Flaming Western Romances #3)
Star Publications: No. 106, Oct-Nov, 1949 - No. 107, Dec-Jan, 1949-50
106(#1)-Silhouette nudity panel; L.B. Cole-c — 39 117 208 360
107(#2)-L.B. Cole-c; lingerie panels — 33 99 174 300

TARGITT
Atlas/Seaboard Publ.: March, 1975 - No. 3, July, 1975
1-3: 1-Origin; Nostrand-a in all. 2-1st in costume. 3-Becomes Man-Stalker 6.00

TAROT: WITCH OF THE BLACK ROSE
Broadsword Comics: Mar, 2000 - Present ($2.95)
1-11-Jim Balent-s/c/a; two covers for each issue — 3.00

TARZAN (See Aurora, Comics on Parade, Crackajack, DC 100-page Super Spec., Edgar Rice Burroughs'..., Famous Feature Stories #1, Golden Comics Digest #4, 9, Jeep Comics #1-29, Jungle Tales of..., Limited Collectors' Edition, Popular, Sparkler, Sport Stars #1, Tip Top & Top Comics)

TARZAN
Dell Publishing Co./United Features Synd.: No. 5, 1939 - No. 161, Aug, 1947
Large Feature Comic 5('39)-(Scarce)-By Hal Foster; reprints 1st dailies from 1929 — 127 381 889 1650
Single Series 20(:40)-By Hal Foster — 96 288 672 1250
Four Color 134(2/47)-Marsh-c/a — 65 195 455 845
Four Color 161(8/47)-Marsh-c/a — 56 168 392 725
TARZAN (...of the Apes #138 on)
Dell Publishing Co./Gold Key No. 132 on: 1-2/48 - No. 131, 7-8/62; No. 132, 11/62 - No. 206, 2/72

Tarzan (Dell) #20 © ERB

Tarzan (DC) #219 © ERB

Tarzan (Marvel) #14 © ERB

	GD2.0	FN6.0	VF8.0	NM9.4
1-Jesse Marsh-a begins	108	324	756	1400
2	48	144	336	625
3-5	34	102	238	440
6-10: 6-1st Tantor the Elephant. 7-1st Valley of the Monsters				
	27	80	189	350
11-15: 11-Two Against the Jungle begins, ends #24. 13-Lex Barker photo-c				
begin	22	65	154	285
16-20	17	50	119	225
21-24,26-30	13	40	91	175
25-1st "Brothers of the Spear" episode; series ends #156,160,161,196-206				
	15	46	105	200
31-40	10	30	70	125
41-54: Last Barker photo-c	7	21	49	85
55-60: 56-Eight pg. Boy story	5	15	35	65
61,62,64-70	5	15	34	55
63-Two Tarzan stories, 1 by Manning	5	15	35	60
71-79	4	12	30	50
80-99: 80-Gordon Scott photo-c begin	4	12	29	45
100	5	15	34	55
101-109	4	12	26	40
110 (Scarce)-Last photo-c	4	12	30	50
111-120	4	12	25	38
121-131: Last Dell issue	3	10	23	35
132-1st Gold Key issue	4	12	29	45
133-138,140-154	3	9	21	32
139-(12/63)-1st app. Korak (Boy); leaves Tarzan & gets own book (1/64)				
	4	12	30	50
155-Origin Tarzan	4	12	26	40
156-161: 157-Banlu, Dog of the Arande begins, ends #159, 195. 169-Leopard				
Girl app.	3	9	19	28
162,165,168,171 (TV)-Ron Ely photo covers	3	9	21	32
163,164,166,167,169,170: 169-Leopard Girl app.	3	9	17	25
172-199,201-206: 178-Tarzan origin-r/#155; Leopard Girl app., also in #179,				
190-193	2	6	15	22
200	3	9	19	28
Story Digest 1-(6/70, G.K., 148pp.)(scarce)	8	24	56	90

NOTE: #162, 165, 168, 171 are TV issues. #1-153 all have Marsh art on Tarzan. #154-161, 163, 164, 166, 167, 172-177 all have Manning art on Tarzan. #178, 202 have Manning Tarzan reprints. No "Brothers of the Spear" in #1-24, 157-159, 162-195. #39-126, 128-156 all have Russ Manning art on "Brothers of the Spear". #196-201, 203-205 all have Manning B.O.T.S. reprints; #25-38, 127 all have Jesse Marsh art on B.O.T.S. #206 has a Marsh B.O.T.S. reprint. Gollub c-8-12. Marsh c-1-7. Doug Wildey a-162, 179-187. Many issues have front and back photo covers.

TARZAN (Continuation of Gold Key series)
National Periodical Publications: No. 207, Apr, 1972 - No. 258, Feb, 1977

207-Origin Tarzan by Joe Kubert, part 1; John Carter begins (origin); 52 pg.				
issues thru #209	4	12	29	45
208,209-(52 pgs.): 208-210-Parts 2-4 of origin. 209-Last John Carter				
	2	6	15	22
210-220: 210-Kubert-a. 211-Hogarth, Kubert-a. 212-214: Adaptations from				
"Jungle Tales of Tarzan". 213-Beyond the Farthest Star begins, ends #218.				
215-218,224,225-All by Kubert. 215-part Foster-r. 219-223: Adapts "The				
Return of Tarzan" by Kubert.	2	6	11	15
221-229: 221-223-Continues adaptation of "The Return of Tarzan".				
226-Manning-a	2	6	9	12
230-DC 100 Page Super Spectacular; Kubert, Kaluta-a(p); Korak begins, ends				
#234; Carson of Venus app.	3	9	20	30
231-235-New Kubert-a.: 231-234-(All 100 pgs.)-Adapts "Tarzan and the Lion				
Man"; Rex, the Wonder Dog r-#232, 233. 235-(100 pgs.)-Last Kubert issue.				
	3	9	19	28
236,237,239-258: 240-243 adapts "Tarzan & the Castaways". 250-256 adapts				
"Tarzan the Untamed." 252,253-r/#213	1	4	7	10
238-(68 pgs.)	2	6	11	16
Comic Digest 1-(Fall, 1972, 50¢, 164 pgs.)(DC)-Digest size; Kubert-c;				
Manning-a	5	15	34	55

NOTE: Anderson a-207, 209, 217, 218. Chaykin a-216. Finlay a(r)-212. Foster strip-r #207-209, 211, 212, 221. Heath a-230i. G. Kane a(r)-232p, 233p. Kubert a-207-225, 227-235, 257r, 258r; c-207-249, 253. Lopez a-250-255p; c-250p, 251, 252, 254. Manning strip-r 207-235, 238. Morrow a-208. Nino a-231-234. Sparling a-230, 231. Starr a-233r.

TARZAN (Lord of the Jungle)
Marvel Comics Group: June, 1977 - No. 29, Oct, 1979

1-New adaptions of Burrough stories; Buscema-a	1	3	5	7

	GD2.0	FN6.0	VF8.0	NM9.4
1-(35¢-c variant, limited distribution)(6/77)	1	3	6	9
2-29: 2-Origin by John Buscema. 9-Young Tarzan. 12-14-Jungle Tales of				
Tarzan. 25-29-New stories				4.00
2-5-(35¢-c variants, limited distribution)(7-10/77)				6.00
Annual 1-3: 1-(1977). 2-(1978). 3-(1979)				4.00

NOTE: N. Adams c-11, 12i. Alcala a-9i, 10i; c-8i, 9i. Buckler c-25-27p, Annual 3p. John Buscema a-1-3, 4-18p, Annual 1; c-1-7, 8p, 9p, 10, 11p, 12p, 13, 14-19p, 21p, 22, 23p, 24p, 28p, Annual 1. Mooney a-22i. Nebres a-22i. Russell a-29i.

TARZAN
Dark Horse Comics: July, 1996 - No. 20, Mar, 1998 ($2.95)

1-20: 1-6-Suydam-c/a				3.00

TARZAN / CARSON OF VENUS
Dark Horse Comics: May, 1998 - No. 4, Aug, 1998 ($2.95, limited series)

1-4-Darko Macan-s/Igor Kordey-a				3.00

TARZAN FAMILY, THE (Formerly Korak, Son of Tarzan)
National Periodical Publications: No. 60, Nov-Dec, 1975 - No. 66, Nov-Dec, 1976

60-62-(68 pgs.): 60-Korak begins; Kaluta-r	2	6	11	15
63-66 (52 pgs.)	1	4	7	10

NOTE: Carson of Venus-r 60-65. New John Carter-62-64, 65r, 66r. New Korak 60-66. Pellucidar feature-66. Foster strip r-60(9/4/32-10/16/32), 62(6/29/32-7/31/32), 63(10/11/31-12/13/31). Kaluta Carson of Venus-r 60-62, 64. Kubert a-61, 64; c-60-64. Manning strip-r 60-62, 64. Morrow a-66r.

TARZAN/JOHN CARTER: WARLORDS OF MARS
Dark Horse Comics: Jan, 1996 - No. 4, June, 1996 ($2.50, limited series)

1-4: Bruce Jones scripts in all. 1,2,4-Bret Blevins-c/a. 2-(4/96)-Indicia reads #3				3.00

TARZAN KING OF THE JUNGLE (See Dell Giant #37, 51)

TARZAN, LORD OF THE JUNGLE
Gold Key: Sept, 1965 (Giant) (25¢, soft paper-c)

1-Marsh-r	7	21	49	95

TARZAN: LOVE, LIES AND THE LOST CITY (See Tarzan the Warrior)
Malibu Comics: Aug. 10, 1992 - No. 3, Sept, 1992 ($2.50, limited series)

1-($3.95, 68 pgs.)-Flip book format; Simonson & Wagner scripts				4.00
2,3-No Simonson or Wagner scripts				3.00

TARZAN MARCH OF COMICS (See March of Comics #82, 98, 114, 125, 144, 155, 172, 185, 204, 223, 240, 252, 262, 272, 286, 300, 332, 342, 354, 366)

TARZAN OF THE APES
Metropolitan Newspaper Service: 1934? (Hardcover, 4x12", 68 pgs.)

1-Strip reprints	24	72	127	220

TARZAN OF THE APES
Marvel Comics Group: July, 1984 - No. 2, Aug, 1984 (Movie adaptation)

1,2: Origin-r/Marvel Super Spec.				3.00

TARZAN'S JUNGLE ANNUAL (See Dell Giants)

TARZAN'S JUNGLE WORLD (See Dell Giant #25)

TARZAN: THE BECKONING
Malibu Comics: 1992 - No. 7, 1993 ($2.50, limited series)

1-7				3.00

TARZAN: THE LOST ADVENTURE (See Edgar Rice Burroughs' ...)

TARZAN-THE RIVERS OF BLOOD
Dark Horse Comics: Nov, 1999 - No. 8 ($2.95, limited series)

1-4-Korday-c/a				3.00

TARZAN THE SAVAGE HEART
Dark Horse Comics: Apr, 1999 - No. 4, July, 1999 ($2.95, limited series)

1-4-Grell-c/a				3.00

TARZAN THE WARRIOR (Also see Tarzan: Love, Lies and the Lost City)
Malibu Comics: Mar, 19, 1992 - No. 5, 1992 ($2.50, limited series)

1-5: 1-Bisley painted pack-c (flip book format-c)				3.00
1-2nd printing w/o flip-c by Bisley				2.50

TARZAN VS. PREDATOR AT THE EARTH'S CORE
Dark Horse Comics: Jan, 1996 - No. 4, June, 1996 ($2.50, limited series)

1-4: Lee Weeks-c/a; Walt Simonson scripts				3.00

Team America #5 © MAR

Teddy Roosevelt and his Rough Riders #1 © AVON

Teen-Age Diary Secrets #6 © STJ

I Played Kiss and Run

	GD2.0	FN6.0	VF8.0	NM9.4

TASMANIAN DEVIL & HIS TASTY FRIENDS
Gold Key: Nov, 1962 (12¢)

1-Bugs Bunny & Elmer Fudd x-over	13	39	91	165

TATTERED BANNERS
DC Comics (Vertigo): Nov, 1998 - No. 4, Feb, 1999 ($2.95, limited series)

1-4-Grant & Giffen-s/McMahon-a				3.00

TEAM AMERICA (See Captain America #269)
Marvel Comics Group: June, 1982 - No. 12, May, 1983

1-12:1-Origin; Ideal Toy motorcycle characters. 9-Iron Man app. 11-Ghost Rider app. 12-Double size				2.25

TEAM ANARCHY
Dagger Comics: Oct, 1993 - No.8, 1994? ($2.50)

1-($2.75)-Red foil logo; intro Team Anarchy				2.75
1-Platinum, 2,3,3-Bronze,3-Gold,3-Silver,4-8				2.75

TEAM HELIX
Marvel Comics: Jan, 1993 - No. 4, Apr, 1993 ($1.75, limited series)

1-4: Teen Super Group. 1,2-Wolverine app.				2.25

TEAM ONE: STORMWATCH (Also see StormWatch)
Image Comics (WildStorm Productions): June, 1995 - No.2, Aug, 1995 ($2.50, limited series)

1,2: Steven T. Seagle scripts				2.50

TEAM ONE: WILDC.A.T.S (Also see WildC.A.T.S)
Image Comics (WildStorm Productions): July, 1995 - No. 2, Aug, 1995 ($2.50, limited series)

1,2: James Robinson scripts				2.50

TEAM 7
Image Comics (WildStorm Productions): Oct, 1994 - No.4, Feb, 1995 ($2.50, limited series)

1-4: Dixon scripts in all, 1-Portacio variant-c				2.50

TEAM 7-DEAD RECKONING
Image Comics (WildStorm Productions): Jan, 1996 - No. 4, Apr, 1996 ($2.50, limited series)

1-4: Dixon scripts in all				2.50

TEAM 7-OBJECTIVE HELL
Image Comics (WildStorm Productions): May, 1995 - No. 3, July, 1995 ($1.95/$2.50, limited series)

1-($1.95)-Newstand; Dixon scripts in all; Barry Smith-c				2.25
1-3: -($2.50)-Direct Market; Barry Smith-c, bound-in card				2.50

TEAM SUPERMAN
DC Comics: July, 1999 ($2.95, one-shot)

1-Jeanty-a/Stelfreeze-c				3.00
...Secret Files 1 (5/98, $4.95)Origin-s and pin-ups of Superboy, Supergirl & Steel; Dave Johnson-c				5.00

TEAM TITANS (See Deathstroke & New Titans Annual #7)
DC Comics: Sept, 1992 - No. 24, Sept, 1994 ($1.75/$1.95)

1-Five different #1s exist w/origins in 1st half & the same 2nd story in each: Kilowat, Mirage, Nightrider w/Netzer/Perez-a, Redwing, & Terra w/part Perez-p; Total Chaos Pt. 3				3.00
2-24: 2-Total Chaos Pt 6. 11-Metallik app. 24-Zero Hour x-over				2.25
Annual 1,2 ('93, '94, $3.50, 68 pgs.): 2-Elseworlds tory				3.50

TEAM X/TEAM 7
Marvel Comics: Nov, 1996 ($4.95, one-shot)

1				5.00

TEAM X 2000
Marvel Comics: Feb, 1999 ($3.50, one-shot)

1-Kevin Lau-a; Bishop vs. Shi'ar Empire				3.50

TEAM YANKEE
First Comics: Jan, 1989 - No. 6, Feb, 1989 ($1.95, weekly limited series)

1-6				2.25

TEAM YOUNGBLOOD (Also see Youngblood)
Image Comics (Extreme Studios): Sept, 1993 - No. 22, Sept, 1995

($1.95/$2.50)

1-22: 1-9-Liefeld scripts in all: 1,2,4-6,8-Thibert-c(i). 1-1st app. Dutch & Masada. 3-Spawn cameo. 5-1st app. Lynx. 7,8-Coupons 1 & 4 for Extreme Prejudice #0; Black and White Pt. 4 & 8 by Thibert, 8-Coupon #4 for E. P. #0. 9-Liefeld wraparound-c(p)/a(p) on Pt. I. 10-Liefeld-c(p). 16-Polybagged w/trading card 17-Polybagged w/trading card. 18-Extreme 3000 Prelude. 19-Cruz-a. 21-Angela & Glory-app. 22-Shadowhawk-c/app				2.50

TEDDY ROOSEVELT & HIS ROUGH RIDERS (See Real Heroes #1)
Avon Periodicals: 1950

1-Kinstler-c; Palais-a; Flag-c	19	57	99	170

TEDDY ROOSEVELT ROUGH RIDER (See Battlefield #22 & Classics Illustrated Special Issue)

TED McKEEVER'S METROPOL
Marvel Comics (Epic Comics): Mar, 1991 - No. 12, Mar, 1992 ($2.95, limited series)

V1#1-12: Ted McKeever-c/a/scripts				3.50

TED McKEEVER'S METROPOL A.D.
Marvel Comics (Epic Comics): Oct, 1992 - No. 3, Dec, 1992 ($3.50, limited series)

V2#1-3: Ted McKeever-c/a/scripts				3.50

TEENA
Magazine Enterprises/Standard Comics No. 20 on: No. 11, 1948 - No. 15, 1948; No. 20, Aug, 1949 - No. 22, Oct, 1950

A-1 #11-Teen-age; Ogden Whitney-c	9	27	49	70
A-1 #12, 15	8	24	42	60
20-22 (Standard)	5	15	25	35

TEEN-AGE BRIDES (True Bride's Experiences #8 on)
Harvey/Home Comics: Aug, 1953 - No. 7, Aug, 1954

1-Powell-a	11	33	55	90
2-Powell-a	8	24	42	60
3-7: 3,6-Powell-a	7	21	36	50

TEEN-AGE CONFESSIONS (See Teen Confessions)

TEEN-AGE CONFIDENTIAL CONFESSIONS
Charlton Comics: July, 1960 - No. 22, 1964

1	4	12	26	40
2-10	3	9	19	28
11-22	2	6	13	20

TEEN-AGE DIARY SECRETS (Formerly Blue Ribbon Comics; becomes Diary Secrets #10 on)
St. John Publishing Co.: No. 4, 9/49; nn (#5), 9/49 - No. 7, 11/49; No. 8, 2/50; No. 9, 8/50

4(9/49)-Oversized; part mag., part comic	28	84	151	260
nn(#5)(no indicia)-Oversized, all comics; contains sty "I Gave Boys the Green Light."	24	72	127	220
6,8: (Reg. size) -Photo-c; Baker-a(2-3) in each	24	72	127	215
7,9-Digest size (Pocket Comics); Baker-a(5); photo-c; both have same contents; diff.-c	26	78	139	240

TEEN-AGE DOPE SLAVES (See Harvey Comics Library #1)

TEENAGE HOTRODDERS (Top Eliminator #25 on; see Blue Bird)
Charlton Comics: Apr, 1963 - No. 24, July, 1967

1	5	15	38	60
2-10	3	9	21	32
11-24	3	9	17	25

TEEN-AGE LOVE (See Fox Giants)

TEEN-AGE LOVE (Formerly Intimate)
Charlton Comics: V2#4, July, 1958 - No. 96, Dec, 1973

V2#4	4	12	29	45
5-9	3	9	21	32
10(9/59)-20	3	9	17	26
21-35	2	6	15	22
36-70	2	6	12	18
71-96: 61&62-Jonnie Love begins (origin)	2	6	9	12

TEENAGE MUTANT NINJA TURTLES (Also see Anything Goes, Donatello,

	GD2.0	FN6.0	VF8.0	NM9.4

First Comics Graphic Novel, Gobbledygook, Grimjack #26, Leonardo, Michaelangelo, Raphael & Tales Of The...)
Mirage Studios: 1984 - No. 62, Aug, 1993 ($1.50/$1.75, B&W; all 44-52 pgs.)

1-1st printing (3000 copies)-Only printing to have ad for Gobbledygook #1 & 2; Shredder app. (#1-4: 7-1/2x11")	18	54	126	225
1-2nd printing (6/84)(15,000 copies)	2	6	11	15
1-3rd printing (2/85)(36,000 copies)	1	4	7	10
1-4th printing, new-c (50,000 copies)				5.00
1-5th printing, new-c (8/88-c, 11/88 inside)				4.00

1-Counterfeit. **Note:** Most counterfeit copies have a half inch wide white streak or scratch marks across the center of back cover. Black part of cover is a bluish black instead of a deep black. Inside paper is very white & inside cover is bright white. These counterfeit the 1st printings (no value).

2-1st printing (1984; 15,000 copies)	5	15	34	55
2-2nd printing	1	4	7	10
2-3rd printing; new Corben-c/a (2/85)				5.00

2-Counterfeit with glossy cover stock (no value).

3-1st printing (1985, 44 pgs.)	4	12	25	38
3-Variant, 500 copies, given away in NYC. Has 'Laird's Photo' in white rather than light blue	6	18	45	75
3-2nd printing; contains new back-up story				3.00
4-1st printing (1985, 44 pgs.)	3	9	17	25
4,5-2nd printing (5/87, 11/87)				2.25
5-Fugitoid begins, ends #7; 1st full color-c (1985)	1	4	7	10
6-1st printing (1986)	1	3	6	8
6-2nd printing (4/88-c, 5/88 inside)				2.25
7-4 pg. Eastman/Corben color insert; 1st color TMNT (1986, $1.75-c); Bade Biker back-up story	3	5	7	
7-2nd printing (1/89) w/o color insert				2.25
8-Cerebus-c/story with Dave Sim-a (1986)				6.00
9,10: 9 (9/86)-Rip In Time by Corben				5.00
11-15				4.00
16-18: 18-Mark Bode'-a				3.00
18-2nd printing ($2.25, color, 44 pgs.)-New-c				2.50
19-34: 19-Begin $1.75-c. 24-26-Veitch-c/a.				2.50
32-2nd printing ($2.75, 52 pgs., full color)				3.00
35-49,51: 35-Begin $2.00-c.				2.50
50-Features pin-ups by Larsen, McFarlane, Simonson, etc.				3.00
52-62: 52-Begin $2.25-c				2.50
nn (1990, $5.95, B&W)-Movie adaptation				6.00
Book 1,2($1.50, B&W): 2-Corben-c				2.50
...Christmas Special 1 (12/90, $1.75, B&W, 52 pgs.)-Cover title: Michaelangelo Christmas Special; r/Michaelangelo one-shot plus new Raphael story				2.50
...Special (The Maltese Turtle) nn (1/93, $2.95, color, 44 pgs.)				3.00
...Special: "Times" Pipeline nn (9/92, $2.95, color, 44 pgs.)-Mark Bode-c/a				3.00
Hardcover ($100)-r/#1-10 plus one-shots w/dust jackets - limited to 1000 w/letter of authenticity				100.00
Softcover ($40)-r/#1-10				40.00

TEENAGE MUTANT NINJA TURTLES
Mirage Studios: V2#1, Oct, 1993 - V2#13, Oct, 1995 ($2.75)

V2#1-13: 1-Wraparound-c				2.75

TEENAGE MUTANT NINJA TURTLES
Image Comics (Highbrow Ent.): June, 1996 - No. 23, Oct, 1999 ($1.95-$2.95)

1-23: 1-8: Eric Larsen-c(i) on all. 10-Savage Dragon-c/app.				3.00

TEENAGE MUTANT NINJA TURTLES
Mirage Publishing: V4#1, Dec, 2001 - Present ($2.95, B&W)

V4#1-Laird-s/a(i)/Lawson-a(p)				3.00

TEENAGE MUTANT NINJA TURTLES (Adventures)
Archie Publications: Jan, 1996 - No. 3, Mar, 1996 ($1.50, limited series)

1-3				2.50

TEENAGE MUTANT NINJA TURTLES ADVENTURES (TV)
Archie Comics: 8/88 - No. 3, 12/88; 3/89 - No. 72, Oct, 1995 ($1.00/$1.25/$1.50/$1.75)

1-Adapts TV cartoon; not by Eastman/Laird				3.00
2,3,1-5; 2,3 (Mini-series). 1 (2nd on-going series). 5-Begins original stories not based on TV				2.50
1-11: 2nd printings				2.25

6-72: 14-Simpson-a(p). 19-1st Mighty Mutanimals (also in #20, 51-54). 22-Gene Colan-c/a. 50-Poster by Eastman/Laird. 62-w/poster				2.50
nn (1990, $2.50)-Movie adaptation				2.50
nn (Spring, 1991, $2.50, 68 pgs.)-(Meet Archie)				2.50
nn (Sum, 1991, $2.50, 68 pgs.)-(Movie II)-Adapts movie sequel				2.50
...Meet the Conservation Corps I (1992, $2.50, 68 pgs.)				2.50
...III The Movie: The Turtles are Back...In Time (1993, $2.50, 68 pgs.)				2.50
Special 1,4,5 (Sum/92, Spr/93, Sum/93, 68 pgs.)-1-Bill Wray-c				2.50
Giant Size Special 6 (Fall/93, $1.95, 52 pgs.)				2.50
Special 7-10 (Win/93-Fall/94, 52 pgs.): 9-Jeff Smith-c				2.50

NOTE: *There are 2nd printings of #1-11 w/B&W inside covers. Originals are color.*

TEENAGE MUTANT NINJA TURTLES CLASSICS DIGEST (TV)
Archie Comics: Aug, 1993 - No. 8, Mar, 1995? ($1.75)

1-8: Reprints TMNT Advs.				2.50

TEENAGE MUTANT NINJA TURTLES/FLAMING CARROT CROSSOVER
Mirage Publishing: Nov, 1993 - No. 4, Feb, 1994 ($2.75, limited series)

1-4: Bob Burden story				2.75

TEENAGE MUTANT NINJA TURTLES PRESENTS: APRIL O'NEIL
Archie Comics: Mar, 1993 - No. 3, June, 1993 ($1.25, limited series)

1-3				2.50

TEENAGE MUTANT NINJA TURTLES PRESENTS: DONATELLO AND LEATHERHEAD
Archie Comics: July, 1993 - No. 3, Sept, 1993 ($1.25, limited series)

1-3				2.50

TEENAGE MUTANT NINJA TURTLES PRESENTS: MERDUDE
Archie Comics: Oct, 1993 - No. 3, Dec, 1993 ($1.25, limited series)

1-3-See Mighty Mutanimals #7 for 1st app. Merdude				2.50

TEENAGE MUTANT NINJA TURTLES/SAVAGE DRAGON CROSSOVER
Mirage Studios: Aug, 1995 ($2.75, one-shot)

1				3.00

TEEN-AGE ROMANCE (Formerly My Own Romance)
Marvel Comics (ZPC): No. 77, Sept, 1960 - No. 86, Mar, 1962

77-83	3	9	20	30
84-86-Kirby-c. 84-Kirby-a(2 pgs.). 85,86-(3 pgs.)	4	12	26	40

TEEN-AGE ROMANCES
St. John Publ. Co. (Approved Comics): Jan, 1949 - No. 45, Dec, 1955

1-Baker-c/a(1)	40	120	232	400
2,3: 2-Baker-c/a. 3-Baker-c/a(3)	25	75	130	225
4,5,7,8-Photo-c; Baker-a(2-3) each	21	63	110	185
6-Slightly large size; photo-c; part magazine; Baker-a (10/49)	23	69	121	205
9-Baker-c/a; Kubert-a	27	81	142	245
10-12,20-Baker-c/a(2-3) each	20	60	105	175
13-19,21,22-Complete issues by Baker	27	81	142	245
23-25-Baker-c/a(2-3) each	19	57	99	165
26,27,33,34,36-40,42: Baker-c/a. 33,40-Signed story by Estrada. 38-Suggestive-a. 42-r/Cinderella Love #9; Last pre-code (3/55)	13	39	66	100
28-30-No Baker-a	7	21	36	50
31,32-Baker-c. 31-Estrada-s	10	30	55	80
35-Baker-a (16 pgs.)	13	39	66	110
41-Baker-c; Infantino-a(r); all stories are Ziff-Davis-r	10	30	55	85
43-45-Baker-c/a	13	39	66	110

TEEN-AGE TALK
I.W. Enterprises: 1964

Reprint #1	2	6	11	16
Reprint #5,8,9: 5-r/Hector #? 9-Punch Comics #?; L.B. Cole-c reprint from School Day Romances #1	2	6	10	14

TEEN-AGE TEMPTATIONS (Going Steady #10 on)(See True Love Pictorial)
St. John Publishing Co.: Oct, 1952 - No. 9, Aug, 1954

1-Baker-c/a; has story "Reform School Girl" by Estrada	44	132	264	460
2,4-Baker-c	17	51	88	150
3,5-7,9-Baker-c/a	25	75	130	225

Teen-Age Temptations #9 © STJ

Teen Love Stories #2 © WP

Teen Titans #1 © DC

	GD2.0	FN6.0	VF8.0	NM9.4

8-Teenagers smoke reefers; Baker-c/a   25   75   130   225
NOTE: *Estrada a-1, 3-5.*

TEEN BEAM (Formerly Teen Beat #1)
National Periodical Publications: No. 2, Jan-Feb, 1968

2-Superman cameo; Herman's Hermits, Yardbirds, Simon & Garfunkel, Lovin
   Spoonful, Young Rascals app.; Orlando, Drucker-a(r); Monkees photo-c;
                             7   21   50   80

TEEN BEAT (Becomes Teen Beam #2)
National Periodical Publications: Nov-Dec, 1967

1-Photos & text only; Monkees photo-c; Beatles, Herman's Hermits, Animals,
   Supremes, Byrds app.   8   24   60   100

TEEN COMICS (Formerly All Teen; Journey Into Unknown Worlds #36 on)
Marvel Comics (WFP): No. 21, Apr, 1947 - No. 35, May, 1950

21-Kurtzman's "Hey Look"; Patsy Walker, Cindy (1st app.?), Georgie, Margie
   app.; Syd Shores-a begins, end #23   15   45   77   130
22,23,25,27,29,31-35: 22-(6/47)-Becomes Hedy Devine #22 (8/47) on?
                             11   33   55   90
24,26,28,30-Kurtzman's "Hey Look"   12   36   61   100

TEEN CONFESSIONS
Charlton Comics: Aug, 1959 - No. 97, Nov, 1976

1   8   24   56   90
2   4   12   29   45
3-10   3   10   23   35
11-30   3   9   19   28
31-Beatles-c   12   36   88   150
32-36,38-55   2   6   13   20
37 (1/66)-Beatles Fan Club story; Beatles-c   12   36   88   150
56-58,60-97: 89,90-Newton-c   2   6   9   12
59-Kaluta's 1st pro work? (12/69)   3   9   17   25

TEENIE WEENIES, THE (America's Favorite Kiddie Comic)
Ziff-Davis Publishing Co.: No. 10, 1950 - No. 11, Apr-May, 1951 (Newspaper
reprints)

10,11-Painted-c   20   60   105   175

TEEN-IN (Tippy Teen)
Tower Comics: Summer, 1968 - No. 4, Fall, 1969

nn(#1, Summer, 1968)   5   15   38   60
nn(#2, Spring, 1969),3,4   4   12   26   40

TEEN LIFE (Formerly Young Life)
New Age/Quality Comics Group: No. 3, Winter, 1945 - No. 5, Fall, 1945
(Teenage magazine)

3-June Allyson photo on-c & story   12   36   61   105
4-Duke Ellington photo on-c & story   10   30   55   80
5-Van Johnson, Woody Herman & Jackie Robinson articles; Van Johnson &
   Woody Herman photos on-c   13   39   66   110

TEEN LOVE STORIES (Magazine)
Warren Publ. Co.: Sept, 1969 - No. 3, Jan, 1970 (68 pgs., photo covers, B&W)

1-Photos & articles plus 36-42 pgs. new comic stories in all; Frazetta-a
                  5   15   38   60
2,3: 2-Anti-marijuana story   4   12   29   45

TEEN ROMANCES
Super Comics: 1964

10,11,15-17-Reprints   2   6   9   12

TEEN SECRET DIARY (Nurse Betsy Crane #12 on)
Charlton Comics: Oct, 1959 - No. 11, June, 1961; No. 1, 1972

1   4   12   30   50
2   3   9   21   32
3-11   3   9   17   25
1 (1972)(exist?)   2   6   13   20

TEEN TALK (See Teen)

TEEN TITANS (See Brave & the Bold #54,60, DC Super-Stars #1, Marvel & DC
Present, New Teen Titans, New Titans, Official...Index and Showcase #59)
National Periodical Publications/DC Comics: 1-2/66 - No. 43, 1-2/73; No. 44,
11/76 - No. 53, 2/78

	GD2.0	FN6.0	VF8.0	NM9.4

1-(1(2/66))-Titans join Peace Corps; Batman, Flash, Aquaman, Wonder
   Woman cameos   24   72   168   300
2   10   30   73   125
3-5: 4-Speedy app.   6   18   42   70
6-10: 6-Doom Patrol app.; Beast Boy x-over; readers polled on him joining
   Titans   5   15   38   60
11-18: 11-Speedy app. 13-X-Mas-c   4   12   30   50
19-Wood-i; Speedy begins as regular   5   15   34   55
20-22: All Neal Adams-a. 21-Hawk & Dove app.; last 12¢ issue. 22-Origin
   Wonder Girl   5   15   38   60
23-31: 23-Wonder Girl dons new costume. 25-Flash, Aquaman, Batman, Green
   Arrow, Green Lantern, Superman, & Hawk & Dove guests; 1st app. Lilith
   who joins T.T. West in #50. 29-Hawk & Dove & Ocean Master app.
   30-Aquagirl app. 31-Hawk & Dove app.; last 15¢ issue
                             3   9   20   30
32-34,40-43   2   6   13   20
35-39-(52 pgs.): 36,37-Superboy-r. 38-Green Arrow/Speedy-r; Aquaman/
   Aqualad story. 39-Hawk & Dove-r.   2   6   15   22
44,45,47,49,51,52: 44-Mal becomes the Guardian   2   6   9   12
46,48: 46-Joker's daughter begins (see Batman Family). 48-Intro Bumblebee;
   Joker's daughter becomes Harlequin   2   6   12   18
50-1st revival original Bat-Girl; intro. Teen Titans West
                             2   6   13   20
53-Origin retold   2   6   10   14
NOTE: *Aparo a-36. Buckler c-46-53. Cardy c-1-16. Kane a(p)-19, 22-24, 39r. Tuska a(p)-31, 36, 38, 39. DC Super-Stars #1 (3/76) was released before #44.*

TEEN TITANS (Also see Titans Beat in the Promotional Comics section)
DC Comics: Oct, 1996 - No. 24, Sept, 1998 ($1.95)

1-Dan Jurgens-c/a(p)/scripts & George Pérez-c/a(i) begin; Atom forms new
   team (Risk, Argent, Prysm, & Joto); 1st app. Loren Jupiter & Omen;
   no indicia. 1-3-Origin   4.00
2-24: 4,5-Robin, Nightwing, Supergirl, Capt. Marvel Jr. app. 12-"Then and Now"
   begins w/original Teen Titans-c/app. 15-Death of Joto. 17-Capt. Marvel Jr.
   and Fringe join. 19-Millennium Giants x-over. 23,24-Superman app.   3.00
Annual 1 (1997, $3.95)-Pulp Heroes story   4.00

TEEN TITANS SPOTLIGHT
DC Comics: Aug, 1986 - No. 21, Apr, 1988

1-21: 7-Guice's 1st work at DC. 14-Nightwing; Batman app. 15-Austin-c(i).
   18,19-Millennium x-over. 21-($1.00-c)-Original Teen Titans; Spiegle-a   3.00
Note: *Guice a-7p, 8p; c-7,8. Orlando c/a-11p. Perez c-1, 17i, 19. Sienkiewicz c-10*

TEEPEE TIM (...Heap Funny Indian Boy)(Formerly Ha Ha Comics)
American Comics Group: No. 100, Feb-Mar, 1955 - No. 102, June-July, 1955

100-102   5   15   25   35

TEGRA JUNGLE EMPRESS (Zegra Jungle Empress #2 on)
Fox Features Syndicate: August, 1948

1-Blue Beetle, Rocket Kelly app.; used in **SOTI**, pg. 31
                 55   165   341   600

TEKKEN FOREVER
Image Comics: Dec, 2001 - No. 4 ($2.95, limited series)

1-Based on the video game   3.00

TEKNO COMIX HANDBOOK
Tekno Comix: May, 1996 ($3.95, one-shot)

1-Guide to the Tekno Universe   4.00

TEKNOPHAGE (See Neil Gaiman's...)

TEKNOPHAGE VERSUS ZEERUS
BIG Entertainment: July, 1996 ($3.25, one-shot)

1-Paul Jenkins script   3.25

TEKWORLD (William Shatner's... on-c only)
Epic Comics (Marvel): Sept, 1992 - Aug, 1994 ($1.75)

1-Based on Shatner's novel, TekWar, set in L.A. in the year 2120   3.00
2-24   2.25

TELEVISION (See TV)

TELEVISION COMICS (Early TV comic)
Standard Comics (Animated Cartoons): No. 5, Feb, 1950 - No. 8, Nov, 1950

Tellos #2 © Dezago & Wieringo

The Tenth #12 © Tony Daniel

Terminal City #2 © Dean Motter

	GD2.0	FN6.0	VF8.0	NM9.4

5-1st app. Willy Nilly	10	30	55	80
6-8: 6 has #2 on inside	8	24	42	60

TELEVISION PUPPET SHOW (Early TV comic) (See Spotty the Pup)
Avon Periodicals: 1950 - No. 2, Nov, 1950

1-1st app. Speedy Rabbit, Spotty The Pup	20	60	105	180
2	14	42	72	120

TELEVISION TEENS MOPSY (See TV Teens)

TELL IT TO THE MARINES
Toby Press Publications: Mar, 1952 - No. 15, July, 1955

1-Lover O'Leary and His Liberty Belles (with pin-ups), ends #6; Spike & Bat begin, end #6	20	60	105	175
2-Madame Cobra-c/story	11	33	55	90
3-5	8	24	45	65
6-12,14,15: 7-9,14,15-Photo-c	7	21	36	50
13-John Wayne photo-c	13	39	66	110
I.W. Reprint #9-r/#1 above	2	6	9	12
Super Reprint #16(1964)-r/#4 above	2	6	9	12

TELLOS
Image Comics: May, 1999 - Present ($2.50)

1-Dezago-s/Wieringo-a				3.00
1-Variant-c ($7.95)				8.00
2-10: 4-Four covers				2.50
...: Maiden Voyage (3/01, $5.95) Didier Crispeels-a/c				6.00
...: The Last Heist (2001, $5.95) Rousseau-a/c				6.00
Prelude ($5.00, AnotherUniverse.com)				5.00
Prologue ($3.95, Dynamic Forces)				4.00
...Collected Edition 1 (12/99, $8.95) r/#1-3				9.00
...: Reluctant Heroes (2/01, $17.95) r/#1-5, Prelude, Prologue; sketchbook				18.00

TEMPEST (See Aquaman, 3rd Series)
DC Comics: Nov, 1996 - No. 4, Feb, 1997 ($1.75, limited series)

1-4: Formerly Aqualad; Phil Jimenez-c/a/scripts in all				2.25

TEMPUS FUGITIVE
DC Comics: 1990 - No. 4, 1991 ($4.95, squarebound, 52 pgs.)

Book 1,2: Ken Steacy painted-c/a & scripts				6.00
Book 3,4-($5.95-c)				6.00
TPB (Dark Horse Comics, 1/97, $17.95)				18.00

TEN COMMANDMENTS (See Moses & the... and Classics Illustrated Special)

TENDER LOVE STORIES
Skywald Publ. Corp.: Feb, 1971 - No. 4, July, 1971

1 (All 25¢, 52 pgs.)	3	9	17	26
2-4	2	6	12	18

TENDER ROMANCE (Ideal Romance #3 on)
Key Publications (Gilmour Magazines): Dec, 1953 - No. 2, Feb, 1954

1-Headlight & lingerie panels; B. Baily-c	18	54	94	160
2-Bernard Baily-c	10	30	55	85

TENSE SUSPENSE
Fago Publications: Dec, 1958 - No. 2, Feb, 1959

1	10	30	55	80
2	8	24	42	60

TEN STORY LOVE (Formerly a pulp magazine with same title)
Ace Periodicals: V29#3, June-July, 1951 - V36#5(#209), Sept, 1956 (#3-6: 52 pgs.)

V29#3(#177)-Part comic, part text; painted-c	11	33	55	90
4-6(1/52)	7	21	36	50
V30#1(3/52)-6(1/53)	6	18	32	45
V31#1(2/53),V32#2(4/53)-6(12/53)	6	18	29	40
V33#1(1/54)-3(5#54, #195), V34#4(7/54, #196)-6(10/54, #198)	5	15	25	35
V35#1(12/54, #199)-3(4/55, #201)-Last precode	5	15	23	30
V35#4-6(9/55, #201-204), V36#1(11/55, #205)-3, 5(9/56, #209)	4	12	19	25
V36#4-L.B. Cole-a	9	27	49	70

TENTH, THE

TENTH, THE
Image Comics: Jan, 1997 - No. 4, June, 1997 ($2.50, limited series)

1-4-Tony Daniel-c/a, Beau Smith-s				5.00
Abuse of Humanity TPB ($10.95) r/#1-4				11.00
Abuse of Humanity TPB (10/98, $11.95) r/#1-4 & 0(8/97)				12.00

TENTH, THE
Image Comics: Sept, 1997 - No. 14, Jan, 1999 ($2.50)

0-(8/97, $5.00) American Ent. Ed.				6.00
1-Tony Daniel-c/a, Beau Smith-s				6.00
2-9: 3,7-Variant-c				4.00
10-14				3.00
...Configuration (8/98) Re-cap and pin-ups				2.50
...Collected Edition 1 ('98, $4.95, square-bound) r/#1,2				5.00
...Special (4/00, $2.95) r/#0 and Wizard #1/2				3.00
Wizard #1/2-Daniel-s/Steve Scott-a				10.00

TENTH, THE (Volume 3) (The Black Embrace)
Image Comics: Mar, 1999 - No. 4, June, 1999 ($2.95)

1-4-Daniel-c/a				3.00
TPB (1/00, $12.95) r/#1-4				13.00

TENTH, THE (Volume 4) (Evil's Child)
Image Comics: Sept, 1999 - No. 4, Mar, 2000 ($2.95)

1-4-Daniel-c/a				3.00

TENTH, THE : RESURRECTED
Dark Horse Comics: July, 2001 - Present ($2.99, limited series)

1,2: 1-Two covers; Daniel-s/c; Romano-a				3.00

10th MUSE
Image Comics (TidalWave Studios): Nov, 2000 - Present ($2.95)

1-Character based on wrestling's Rena Mero; regular & photo covers				
2-7: 2-Photo and 2 Lashley covers; flip book Dollz preview. 5-Savage Dragon app.; 2 covers by Lashley and Larsen. 6-Tellos x-over				3.00

TEN WHO DARED (Disney)
Dell Publishing Co.: No. 1178, Dec, 1960

Four Color 1178-Movie, painted-c; cast member photo on back-c	7	21	49	90

TERMINAL CITY
DC Comics (Vertigo): July, 1996 - No. 9, Mar, 1997 ($2.50, limited series)

1-9: Dean Motter scripts, 7,8-Matt Wagner-c				2.50
TPB ('97, $19.95) r/series				20.00

TERMINAL CITY: AERIAL GRAFFITI
DC Comics (Vertigo): Nov, 1997 - No. 5, Mar, 1998 ($2.50, limited series)

1-5: Dean Motter-s/Lark-a/Chiarello-c				2.50

TERMINATOR, THE (See Robocop vs. ... & Rust #12 for 1st app.)
Now Comics: Sept, 1988 - No. 17, 1989 ($1.75, Baxter paper)

1-Based on movie				6.00
2-5				4.50
6-17: 12-($2.95, 52 pgs.)-Intro. John Connor				3.00
Trade paperback (1989, $9.95)				10.00

TERMINATOR, THE
Dark Horse Comics: Aug, 1990 - No. 4, Nov, 1990 ($2.50, limited series)

1-Set 39 years later than the movie				4.00
2-4				3.00

TERMINATOR, THE
Dark Horse Comics: 1998 - No. 4, Dec, 1998 ($2.95, limited series)

1-4-Alan Grant-s/Steve Pugh-a				3.00
...Special (1998, $2.95) Darrow-c/Grant-s				3.00

TERMINATOR, THE: ALL MY FUTURES PAST
Now Comics: V3#1, Aug, 1990 - V3#2, Sept, 1990 ($1.75, limited series)

V3#1,2				3.00

TERMINATOR, THE: ENDGAME
Dark Horse Comics: Sept, 1992 - No. 3, Nov, 1992 ($2.50, limited series)

1-3: Guice-a(p); painted-c				3.00

TERMINATOR, THE: HUNTERS AND KILLERS

Terrific Comics #3 © Cont. Mags.

Terrors of the Jungle #7 © STAR

Terry and the Pirates #21 © NY News Synd.

	GD2.0	FN6.0	VF8.0	NM9.4

Dark Horse Comics: Mar, 1992 - No. 3, May, 1992 ($2.50, limited series)

1-3   3.00

TERMINATOR, THE: ONE SHOT
Dark Horse Comics: July, 1991 ($5.95, 56 pgs.)

nn-Matt Wagner-a; contains stiff pop-up inside   6.00

TERMINATOR, THE: SECONDARY OBJECTIVES
Dark Horse Comics: July, 1991 - No. 4, Oct, 1991 ($2.50, limited series)

1-4: Gulacy-c/a(p) in all   3.00

TERMINATOR, THE: THE BURNING EARTH
Now Comics: V2#1, Mar, 1990 - V2#5, July, 1990 ($1.75, limited series)

	GD2.0	FN6.0	VF8.0	NM9.4
V2#1: Alex Ross painted art (1st published work)	2	6	11	15
2-5: Ross-c/a in all	1	4	7	10
Trade paperback (1990, $9.95)-Reprints V2#1-5				12.00

TERMINATOR, THE: THE DARK YEARS
Dark Horse Comics: Aug, 1999 - No. 4, Dec, 1999 ($2.95, limited series)

1-4-Alan Grant-s/Mel Rubi-a; Jae Lee-c   3.00

TERMINATOR, THE: THE ENEMY FROM WITHIN, THE
Dark Horse Comics: Nov, 1991 - No. 4, Feb, 1992 ($2.50, limited series)

1-4: All have Simon Bisley painted-c   3.00

TERMINATOR 2: CYBERNETIC DAWN
Malibu: Nov, 1995 - No.4, Feb, 1996; No. 0, Apr, 1996 ($2.50, lim. series)

0 (4/96, $2.95)-Erskine-c/a; flip book w/Terminator 2: Nuclear Twilight   3.00
1-4: Continuation of film.   3.00

TERMINATOR 2: JUDGEMENT DAY
Marvel Comics: Early Sept, 1991 - No. 3, Early Oct, 1991 ($1.00, lim. series)

1-3: Based on movie sequel; 1-3-Same as nn issues   3.00
nn (1991, $4.95, squarebound, 68 pgs.)-Photo-c   5.00
nn (1991, $2.25, B&W, magazine, 68 pgs.)   3.00

TERMINATOR 2: NUCLEAR TWILIGHT
Malibu: Nov, 1995 - No. 4, Feb, 1996; No. 0, Apr, 1996 ($2.50, lim. series)

0 (4/96, $2.95)-Erskine-c/a; flip book w/Terminator 2: Cybernetic Dawn   3.00
1-4:Continuation of film.   3.00

TERRAFORMERS
Wonder Color Comics: April, 1987 - No. 2, 1987 ($1.95, limited series)

1,2-Kelley Jones-a   2.25

TERRANAUTS
Fantasy General Comics: Aug, 1986 - No. 2, 1986 ($1.75, limited series)

1,2   2.25

TERRARISTS
Marvel Comics (Epic): Nov, 1993 - No. 4, Feb, 1994 ($2.50, lim. series)

1-4-Bound-in trading cards in all   2.50

TERRIFIC COMICS (Also see Suspense Comics)
Continental Magazines: Jan, 1944 - No. 6, Nov, 1944

	GD2.0	FN6.0	VF8.0	NM9.4
1-Kid Terrific; opium story	333	1000	2083	4000
2-1st app. The Boomerang by L.B. Cole & Ed Wheelan's "Comics" McCormick, called the world's #1 comic book fan begins	245	735	1534	2700
3-Diana becomes Boomerang's costumed aide; L.B. Cole-c	245	735	1534	2700
4-Classic war-c (Scarce)	400	1200	2500	4800
5-The Reckoner begins; Boomerang & Diana by L.B. Cole; Classic Schomburg bondage & hooded vigilante-c (Scarce)	680	2040	4080	6800
6-L.B. Cole-c/a	223	668	1394	2450

NOTE: *L.B. Cole* c-*1, 2(2), 3-6. Fuje a-5, 6. Rico a-2; c-1. Schomburg c-2, 5.

TERRIFIC COMICS (Formerly Horrific; Wonder Boy #17 on)
Mystery Publ.(Comic Media)/(Ajax/Farrell): No. 14, Dec, 1954; No. 16, Mar, 1955 (No #15)

	GD2.0	FN6.0	VF8.0	NM9.4
14-Art swipe/Advs. into the Unknown #37; injury-to-eye-c; pg. 2, panel 5 swiped from Phantom Stranger #4; surrealistic Palais-a; Human Cross story; classic-c	47	141	286	500
16-Wonder Boy-c/story (last pre-code)	23	69	121	210

TERRIFYING TALES (Formerly Startling Terror Tales #10)

Star Publications: No. 11, Jan, 1953 - No. 15, Apr, 1954

	GD2.0	FN6.0	VF8.0	NM9.4
11-Used in POP, pgs. 99,100; all Jo-Jo-r	50	150	300	525
12-Reprints Jo-Jo #19 entirely; L.B. Cole splash	47	142	286	500
13-All Rulah-r; classic devil-c	55	165	330	575
14-All Rulah reprints	43	129	257	450
15-Rulah, Zago-r; used in SOTI-r/Rulah #22	43	129	257	450

NOTE: *All issues have L.B. Cole covers; bondage-covers No. 12-14.*

TERRITORY, THE
Dark Horse Comics: Jan, 1999 - No. 4, Apr, 1999 ($2.95, limited series)

1-4-Delano-s/David Lloyd-c/a   3.00

TERROR ILLUSTRATED (Adult Tales of...)
E.C. Comics: Nov-Dec, 1955 - No. 2, Spring (April on-c), 1956 (Magazine, 25¢)

	GD2.0	FN6.0	VF8.0	NM9.4
1-Adult Entertainment on-c	17	51	88	150
2-Charles Sultan-a	12	36	61	100

NOTE: *Craig, Evans, Ingels, Orlando art in each. Crandall c-1, 2.*

TERROR INC. (See A Shadowline Saga #3)
Marvel Comics: July, 1992 - No. 13, July, 1993 ($1.75)

1-8,11-13: 6,7-Punisher-c/story. 13-Ghost Rider app.   2.25
9,10-Wolverine-c/story   3.00

TERRORS OF THE JUNGLE (Formerly Jungle Thrills)
Star Publications: No. 17, 5/52 - No. 21, 2/53; No. 4, 4/53 - No. 10, 9/54

	GD2.0	FN6.0	VF8.0	NM9.4
17-Reprints Rulah #21, used in SOTI; L.B. Cole bondage-c	47	142	286	500
18-Jo-Jo-r	37	111	197	340
19,20(1952)-Jo-Jo-r; Disbrow-a	35	105	185	320
21-Jungle Jo, Tangi-r; used in POP, pg. 100 & color illos.; shrunken heads on-c	39	117	208	360
4-10: All Disbrow-a. 5-Jo-Jo-r. 8-Rulah, Jo-Jo-r; 9-Disbrow-a; Tangi by Orlando10-Rulah-r	39	117	208	360

NOTE: *L.B. Cole c-all; bondage c-17, 19, 21, 5, 7.*

TERROR TALES (See Beware Terror Tales)

TERROR TALES (Magazine)
Eerie Publications: V1#7, 1969 - V6#6, Dec, 1974; V7#1, Apr, 1976 - V10, 1979? (V1-V6: 52 pgs.; V7 on: 68 pgs.)

	GD2.0	FN6.0	VF8.0	NM9.4
V1#7	5	15	34	55
V1#8-11('69): 9-Bondage-c	4	12	25	38
V2#1-6('70), V3#1-6('71), V4#1-7('72), V5#1-6('73), V6#1-6('74), V7#1,4('76) (no V7#2), V8#1-3('77)	3	9	21	32
V7#3-7/76) LSD story-r/Weird V3#5	3	9	21	32
V9#2-4, V10	3	10	23	35

TERRY AND THE PIRATES (See Famous Feature Stories, Merry Christmas From Sears Toyland, Popular Comics, Super Book #3,5,9,16,28, & Super Comics)

TERRY AND THE PIRATES
Dell Publishing Co.: 1939 - 1953 (By Milton Caniff)

	GD2.0	FN6.0	VF8.0	NM9.4
Large Feature Comic 2(1939)	67	200	469	875
Large Feature Comic 6(1938)-r/1936 dailies	62	186	434	800
Four Color 9(1940)	58	175	406	760
Large Feature Comic 27('41), 6('42)	50	150	350	650
Four Color 44('43)	40	119	280	520
Four Color 101('45)	26	78	182	340
Family Album(1942)	20	60	105	180

TERRY AND THE PIRATES (Formerly Boy Explorers; Long John Silver & the Pirates #30 on) (Daily strip-r) (Two #26's)
Harvey Publications/Charlton: No. 26-28: No. 3, 4/47 - No. 26, 4/51; No. 26, 6/55 - No. 28, 10/55

	GD2.0	FN6.0	VF8.0	NM9.4
3(#1)-Boy Explorers by S&K; Terry & the Pirates begin by Caniff; 1st app. The Dragon Lady	40	120	232	400
4-S&K Boy Explorers	25	75	130	225
5-11: 11-Man in Black app. by Powell	12	36	61	85
12-20: 16-Girl threatened with red hot poker	10	30	55	85
21-26(4/51)-Last Caniff issue & last pre-code issue	10	30	55	80
26-28('55)(Formerly This Is Suspense)-No Caniff-a	8	24	45	65

NOTE: *Powell a (Tommy Tomahawk)-5-10, 12, 14; 15-17(1/2 to 2 pgs. each).*

TERRY BEARS COMICS (TerryToons, The... #4)
St. John Publishing Co.: June, 1952 - No. 3, Mar, 1953

Terry-Toons Comics #50 © Paul Terry

The Texan #4 © STJ

Texas Kid #7 © MAR

	GD2.0	FN6.0	VF8.0	NM9.4			GD2.0	FN6.0	VF8.0	NM9.4

1-By Paul Terry 9 27 51 75
2,3 6 18 32 45

TERRY-TOONS ALBUM (See Giant Comics Edition)

TERRY-TOONS COMICS (1st Series) (Becomes Paul Terry's Comics #85 on; later issues titled "Paul Terry's...")
Timely/Marvel No. 1-59 (8/47)(Becomes Best Western No. 58 on?, Marvel)/ St. John No. 60 (9/47) on: Oct, 1942 - No. 86, May, 1951

1 (Scarce)-Features characters that 1st app. on movie screen; Gandy Goose & Sourpuss begin; war-c; Gandy Goose c-1-37 164 492 1023 1800
2 61 183 381 675
3-5 43 129 257 450
6,8-10: 9,10-World War II gag-c 35 105 185 320
7-Hitler, Hirohito, Mussolini-c 45 135 270 475
11-20 22 66 116 195
21-37 15 45 77 130
38-Mighty Mouse begins (1st app., 11/45); Mighty Mouse-c begin, and #86; Gandy, Sourpuss welcome Mighty Mouse on-c 114 342 713 1250
39-2nd app. Mighty Mouse 40 120 217 375
40-49: 43-Infinity-c 18 54 94 155
50-1st app. Heckle & Jeckle (11/46) 40 120 217 375
51-60: 55-Infinity-c. 60-(9/47)-Atomic explosion panel; 1st St. John issue 12 36 61 100
61-86: 85,86-Same book as Paul Terry's Comics #85,86 with only a title change; published at same time? 10 30 55 85

TERRY-TOONS COMICS (2nd Series)
St. John Publishing Co./Pines: June, 1952 - No. 9, Nov, 1953; 1957; 1958

1-Gandy Goose & Sourpuss begin by Paul Terry 20 60 105 175
2 10 30 55 80
3-9 9 27 49 70
Giant Summer Fun Book 101,102-(Sum, 1957, Sum, 1958, 25¢, Pines)(TV) CBS Television Presents...; Tom Terrific, Mighty Mouse, Heckle & Jeckle Gandy Goose app. 14 42 72 120

TERRYTOONS, THE TERRY BEARS (Formerly Terry Bears Comics)
Pines Comics: No. 4, Summer, 1958 (CBS Television Presents...)

4 6 18 29 40

TESSIE THE TYPIST (Tiny Tessie #24; see Comedy Comics, Gay Comics & Joker Comics)
Timely/Marvel Comics (20CC): Summer, 1944 - No. 23, Aug, 1949

1-Doc Rockblock & others by Wolverton 61 182 381 675
2-Wolverton's Powerhouse Pepper 39 117 208 360
3-(3/45)-No Wolverton 14 42 72 125
4,5,7,8-Wolverton-a. 4-(Fall/45) 27 81 145 250
6-Kurtzman's "Hey Look", 2 pgs. Wolverton-a 27 81 145 250
9-Wolverton's Powerhouse Pepper (8 pgs.) & 1 pg. Kurtzman's "Hey Look" 30 90 162 280
10-Wolverton's Powerhouse Pepper (4 pgs.) 29 87 153 265
11-Wolverton's Powerhouse Pepper (8 pgs.) 30 90 162 280
12-Wolverton's Powerhouse Pepper (4 pgs.) & 1 pg. Kurtzman's "Hey Look" 29 87 153 265
13-Wolverton's Powerhouse Pepper (4 pgs.) 29 87 153 265
14,15: 14-Wolverton's Dr. Whackyhack (1 pg.); 1-1/2 pg. Kurtzman's "Hey Look". 15-Kurtzman's "Hey Look" (3 pgs.) & 3 pgs. Giggles 'n' Grins 22 66 116 195
16-18-Kurtzman's "Hey Look" (?, 2 & 1 pg.) 15 45 77 130
19-Annie Oakley story (8 pgs.) 11 33 55 90
20-23: 20-Anti-Wertham editorial (2/49) 10 30 55 80
NOTE: *Lana app.-21. Millie The Model app.-13, 15, 17, 21. Rusty app.-10, 11, 13, 15, 17.*

TEXAN, THE (Fightin' Marines #15 on; Fightin' Texan #16 on)
St. John Publishing Co.: Aug, 1948 - No. 15, Oct, 1951

1-Buckskin Belle 16 48 83 140
2 10 30 55 80
3,10: 10-Oversized issue 9 27 49 70
4,5,7,15-Baker-c/a 17 51 88 150
6,9-Baker-c 11 33 55 90
8,11,13,14-Baker-c/a(2-3) each 18 54 94 155
12-All Matt Baker-c/a; Peyote story 24 72 127 215
NOTE: *Matt Baker c-4-9, 11-15. Larsen a-4-6, 8-10, 15. Tuska a-1, 2, 7-9.*

TEXAN, THE (TV)
Dell Publishing Co.: No. 1027, Sept-Nov, 1959 - No. 1096, May-July, 1960

Four Color 1027 (#1)-Photo-c 9 27 63 110
Four Color 1096-Rory Calhoun photo-c 8 24 56 100

TEXAS JOHN SLAUGHTER (See Walt Disney Presents, 4-Color #997, 1181 & #2)

TEXAS KID (See Two-Gun Western, Wild Western)
Marvel/Atlas Comics (LMC): Jan, 1951 - No. 10, July, 1952

1-Origin; Texas Kid (alias Lance Temple) & his horse Thunder begin; Tuska-a 25 75 130 225
2 13 39 66 110
3-10 10 30 55 85
NOTE: *Maneely a-1-4; c-1, 3, 5-10.*

TEXAS RANGERS, THE (See Jace Pearson of... and Superior Stories #4)

TEXAS RANGERS IN ACTION (Formerly Captain Gallant or Scotland Yard?)
Charlton Comics: No. 5, Jul, 1956 - No. 79, Aug, 1970 (See Blue Bird Comics)

5 8 24 42 60
6,7,9,10 5 15 25 35
8-Ditko-a (signed) 10 30 55 80
11-Williamson-a(5&8 pgs.); Torres/Williamson-a (5 pgs.) 10 30 55 80
12,14-20 5 15 23 30
13-Williamson-a (5 pgs); Torres, Morisi-a 8 24 42 60
21-30 3 9 17 25
31-59: 32-Last 10¢ issue? 2 6 13 20
60-Riley's Rangers begin 2 6 15 22
61-65,68-70 2 6 10 14
66,67: 66-1st app. The Man Called Loco. 67-Origin 2 6 11 16
71-79 1 4 7 10
76 (Modern Comics-r, 1977) 4.00

TEXAS SLIM (See A-1 Comics)

TEX DAWSON, GUN-SLINGER (Gunslinger #2 on)
Marvel Comics Group: Jan, 1973 (20¢)(Also see Western Kid, 1st series)

1-Steranko-c; Williamson-r (4 pgs.); Tex Dawson-r by Romita(3) from 1955; Tuska-r 2 6 15 22

TEX FARNUM (See Wisco)

TEX FARRELL (...Pride of the Wild West)
D. S. Publishing Co.: Mar-Apr, 1948

1-Tex Farrell & his horse Lightning; Shelly-c 14 42 72 120

TEX GRANGER (Formerly Calling All Boys; see True Comics)
Parents' Magazine Inst./Commended: No. 18, Jun, 1948 - No. 24, Sept, 1949

18-Tex Granger & his horse Bullet begin 12 36 61 105
19 10 30 55 80
20-24: 22-Wild Bill Hickok story. 23-Vs. Billy the Kid; Tim Holt app. 8 24 42 60

TEX MORGAN (See Blaze Carson and Wild Western)
Marvel Comics (CCC): Aug, 1948 - No. 9, Feb, 1950

1-Tex Morgan, his horse Lightning & sidekick Lobo begin 28 84 151 260
2 19 56 99 170
3-6: 3,4-Arizona Annie app. 12 36 61 105
7-9: All photo-c. 7-Captain Tootsie by Beck. 8-18 pg. story "The Terror of Rimrock Valley"; Diablo app. 19 56 99 170
NOTE: *Tex Taylor app.-6, 7, 9. Brodsky c-6. Syd Shores c-2, 5.*

TEX RITTER WESTERN (Movie star; singing cowboy; see Six-Gun Heroes and Western Hero)
Fawcett No. 1-20 (1/54)/Charlton No. 21 on: Oct, 1950 - No. 46, May, 1959 (Photo-c: 1-21)

1-Tex Ritter, his stallion White Flash & dog Fury begin; photo front/back-c begin 68 205 426 750
2 34 102 179 310
3-5: 5-Last photo back-c 26 78 136 235
6-10 20 60 105 175
11-19 14 42 72 120
20-Last Fawcett issue (1/54) 15 45 77 130

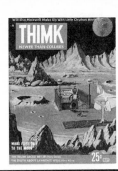

Tex Taylor #1 © MAR

Thimk #1 © Counterpoint

The Thing! #7 © CC

	GD2.0	FN6.0	VF8.0	NM9.4

	GD2.0	FN6.0	VF8.0	NM9.4
21-1st Charlton issue; photo-c (3/54)	19	57	99	165
22-B&W photo back-c begin, end #32	11	33	55	90
23-30: 23-25-Young Falcon app.	10	30	55	80
31-38,40-45	9	27	49	70
39-Williamson-a; Whitman-c (1/58)	10	30	55	85
46-Last issue	10	30	55	80

TEX TAYLOR (...The Fighting Cowboy on-c #1, 2)(See Blaze Carson, Kid Colt, Tex Morgan, Wild West, Wild Western, & Wisco)
Marvel Comics (HPC): Sept, 1948 - No. 9, March, 1950

	GD2.0	FN6.0	VF8.0	NM9.4
1-Tex Taylor & his horse Fury begin	30	90	162	280
2	16	49	83	145
3	14	43	72	125

4-6: All photo-c. 4-Anti-Wertham editorial. 5,6-Blaze Carson app.

		17	51	88	150

7-9: 7-Photo-c;18 pg. Movie-Length Thriller "Trapped in Time's Lost Land!" with sabre toothed tigers, dinosaurs; Diablo app. 8-Photo-c; 18 pg. Movie-Length Thriller "The Mystery of Devil-Tree Plateau!" with dwarf horses, dwarf people & a lost miniature Inca type village; Diablo app. 9-Photo-c; 18 pg. Movie-Length Thriller "Guns Along the Border!" Captain Tootsie by Schreiber; Nimo the Mountain Lion app.

		20	60	105	180

NOTE: **Syd Shores** c-1-3.

THANE OF BAGARTH (Also see Hercules, 1967 series)
Charlton Comics: No. 24, Oct, 1985 - No. 25, Dec, 1985

24,25-Low print run	5.00

THANOS QUEST, THE (See Capt. Marvel #25, Infinity Gauntlet, Iron Man #55, Logan's Run, Marvel Feature #12, Silver Surfer #34 & Warlock #9)
Marvel Comics: 1990 - No. 2, 1990 ($4.95, squarebound, 52 pgs.)

1,2-Both have Starlin scripts & covers (both printings)	1	3	5	7
1-(3/2000, $3.99) r/material from #1&2				4.00

THAT CHEMICAL REFLEX
CFD Productions: 1994 - No. 3 ($2.50, B&W, mature)

1-3: 1-Dan Brereton-c/a	2.50

THAT DARN CAT (See Movie Comics & Walt Disney Showcase #19)

THAT'S MY POP! GOES NUTS FOR FAIR
Bystander Press: 1939 (76 pgs., B&W)

nn-by Milt Gross	29	87	156	270

THAT WILKIN BOY (Meet Bingo...)
Archie Publications: Jan, 1969 - No. 52, Oct, 1982

1-1st app. Bingo's Band, Samantha & Tough Teddy	4	12	26	40
2-5	2	6	13	20
6-11	2	6	11	15
12-26-Giants. 12-No # on-c	2	6	12	18
27-40(1/77)	1	3	6	8
41-52				5.00

THB
Horse Press: Oct, 1994 - Present ($5.50/$2.50/$2.95, B&W)

1 ($5.50)	1	3	6	8
1 (2nd Printing)-r/#1 w/new material				3.00
2 ($2.50)				5.00
3-5				4.00

69 (1995, no price, low distribution, 12 pgs.)-story reprinted in #1 (2nd Printing).

	3.00
Giant THB-($4.95)	5.00
...M3/THB: Mars' Mightiest Mek #1 (2000, $3.95)	4.00
...6A: Mek-Power #1, 6B: Mek-Power #2, 6C: Mek-Power #3 (2000, $3.95)	4.00
... 6D: Mek-Power #4 (2002, $4.95)	5.00

T.H.E. CAT (TV)
Dell Publishing Co.: Mar, 1967 - No. 4, Oct, 1967 (All have photo-c)

1	3	9	23	35
2-4	3	9	17	25

THERE'S A NEW WORLD COMING
Spire Christian Comics/Fleming H. Revell Co.: 1973 (35/49¢)

nn	1	3	5	7

THEY ALL KISSED THE BRIDE (See Cinema Comics Herald)

THIEF OF BAGHDAD
Dell Publishing Co.: No. 1229, Oct-Dec, 1961 (one-shot)

Four Color 1229-Movie, Crandall/Evans-a, photo-c	7	21	49	85

THIEVES & KINGS
I Box: 1994 - Present ($2.35, B&W, bi-monthly)

1	4.00
1-(2nd printing), 2-35	2.50

THIMK (Magazine) (Satire)
Counterpoint: May, 1958 - No. 6, May, 1959

1	9	27	49	70
2-6	6	18	32	45

THING!, THE (Blue Beetle #18 on)
Song Hits No. 1,2/Capitol Stories/Charlton: Feb, 1952 - No. 17, Nov, 1954

1-Weird/horror stories in all; shrunken head-c	82	246	511	900
2,3	55	165	341	600
4-6,8,10: 5-Severed head-c; headlights	50	150	300	525
7-Injury to eye-c & inside panel	68	205	426	750
9-Used in SOTI, pg. 388 & illo "Stomping on the face is a form of brutality which modern children learn early"	77	231	483	850
11-Necronomicon story; Hansel & Gretel parody; Injury-to-eye panel; Check-a	61	182	381	675
12-1st published Ditko-c; "Cinderella" parody; lingerie panels. Ditko-a	82	246	511	900
13,15-Ditko-c/a(3 & 5)	82	246	511	900
14-Extreme violence/torture; Rumpelstiltskin story; Ditko-c/a(4)	84	252	525	925
16-Injury to eye panel	31	93	165	285
17-Ditko-c; classic parody "Through the Looking Glass"; Powell-r/Beware Terror Tales #1 & recolored	73	219	455	800

NOTE: Excessive violence, severed heads, injury to eye are common No. 5 on. **Al Fago** c-4. **Forgione** c-1i, 2, 6, 8, 9. All Ditko issues #14, 15.

THING, THE (See Fantastic Four, Marvel Fanfare, Marvel Feature #11, 12 & Marvel Two-In-One)
Marvel Comics Group: July, 1983 - No. 36, June, 1986

1-Life story of Ben Grimm; Byrne scripts begin	3.00
2-36: 5-Spider-Man, She-Hulk app.	2.25

NOTE: **Byrne** a-2i, 7; c-1, 7, 36i; scripts-1-13, 19-22. **Sienkiewicz** c-13i.

THING, THE (From Another World)
Dark Horse Comics: 1991 - No. 2, 1992 ($2.95, mini-series, stiff-c)

1,2-Based on Universal movie; painted-c/a	3.00

THING FROM ANOTHER WORLD: CLIMATE OF FEAR, THE
Dark Horse Comics: July, 1992 - No. 4, Dec, 1992 ($2.50, mini-series)

1-4: Painted-c	3.00

THING FROM ANOTHER WORLD: ETERNAL VOWS
Dark Horse Comics: Dec, 1993 - No. 4, 1994 ($2.50, mini-series)

1-4-Gulacy-c/a	3.00

THIRD WORLD WAR
Fleetway Publ. (Quality): 1990 - No. 6, 1991 ($2.50, thick-c, mature)

1-6	2.50

THIRTEEN (...Going on 18)
Dell Publishing Co.: 11-1/61-62 - No. 25, 12/67; No. 26, 7/69 - No. 29, 1/71

1	6	18	42	70
2-10	4	12	30	50
11-29: 26-29-r	4	12	26	40

NOTE: **John Stanley** script-No. 3-29; art?

13: ASSASSIN
TSR, Inc.: 1990 - No. 8, 1991 ($2.95, 44 pgs.)

1-8: Agent 13; Alcala-a(i); Springer back-up-a	3.00

THIRTY SECONDS OVER TOKYO (See American Library)

THIS IS SUSPENSE! (Formerly Strange Suspense Stories; Strange Suspense Stories #27 on)
Charlton Comics: No. 23, Feb, 1955 - No. 26, Aug, 1955

23-Wood-a(r)/A Star Presentation #3 "Dr. Jekyll & Mr. Hyde"; last pre-code

This Magazine is Haunted #13 © FAW

Thor #281 © MAR

Thor #342 © MAR

	GD2.0	FN6.0	VF8.0	NM9.4
issue	28	84	148	255
24-Censored Fawcett-r; Evans-a (r/Suspense Detective #1)				
	15	45	77	130
25,26: 26-Marcus Swayze-a	10	30	55	80

THIS IS THE PAYOFF (See Pay-Off)

THIS IS WAR
Standard Comics: No. 5, July, 1952 - No. 9, May, 1953

5-Toth-a	14	42	72	120
6,9-Toth-a	11	33	55	90
7,8: 8-Ross Andru-c	7	21	38	55

THIS IS YOUR LIFE, DONALD DUCK (See Donald Duck..., Four Color #1109)

THIS MAGAZINE IS CRAZY (Crazy #? on)
Charlton Publ. (Humor Magazines): V3#2, July, 1957 - V4#8, Feb, 1959 (25¢, magazine, 68 pgs.)

V3#2-V4#7: V4#5-Russian Sputnik-c parody	8	24	42	60
V4#8-Davis-a (8 pgs.)	9	27	49	70

THIS MAGAZINE IS HAUNTED (Danger and Adventure #22 on)
Fawcett Publications/Charlton No. 15(2/54): Oct, 1951 - No. 14, 12/53; No. 15, 2/54 - V3#21, Nov, 1954

1-Evans-a; Dr. Death as host begins	61	182	381	675
2,5-Evans-a	43	129	257	450
3,4: 3-Vampire-c/story	34	102	179	310
6-9,11,12,14	24	72	127	215
10-Severed head-c	40	120	217	375
13-Severed head-c/story	38	114	203	350
15,20: 15-Dick Giordano-c. 20-Cover is swiped from panel in The Thing #16	20	60	105	175
16,19-Ditko-c. 19-Injury-to-eye panel; story-r/#1	40	120	214	370
17-Ditko-c/a(4); blood drainage story	45	135	270	475
18-Ditko-c/a(1 story). E.C. swipe/Haunt of Fear #5; injury-to-eye panel; reprints "Caretaker of the Dead" from Beware Terror Tales & recolored	40	120	232	400
21-Ditko-c, Evans-r/This Magazine Is Haunted #1	37	111	197	340

NOTE: Baily a-1, 3, 4, 21r/#1. Moldoff c/a-1-13. Powell a-3-5, 11, 12, 17. Shuster a-18-20.
Issues 19-21 have reprints which have been recolored from This Magazine is Haunted #1.

THIS MAGAZINE IS HAUNTED (2nd Series) (Formerly Zaza the Mystic; Outer Space #17 on)
Charlton Comics: V2#12, July, 1957 - V2#16, May, 1958

V2#12-14-Ditko-c/a in all	40	120	220	380
15-No Ditko-c/a	9	27	49	70
16-Ditko-a	26	78	136	235

THIS MAGAZINE IS WILD (See Wild)

THIS WAS YOUR LIFE (Religious)
Jack T. Chick Publ.: 1964 (3 1/2 x 5 1/2", 40 pgs., B&W and red)

nn, Another version (5x2 3/4", 26 pgs.)	2	6	9	12

THOR (See Avengers #1, Giant-Size..., Marvel Collectors Item Classics, Marvel Graphic Novel #33, Marvel Preview, Marvel Spectacular, Marvel Treasury Edition, Special Marvel Edition & Tales of Asgard)

THOR (Journey Into Mystery #1-125, 503-on)(The Mighty Thor #413-490)
Marvel Comics Group: No. 126, Mar, 1966 - No. 502, Sept, 1996

126-Thor continues (#125-130 Thor vs. Hercules)	16	48	112	200
127-130: 127-1st app. Pluto	7	21	50	80
131-133,135-140	6	18	42	70
134-Intro High Evolutionary	6	18	45	75
141-150: 146-Inhumans begin (early app.), end #151 (see Fantastic Four #45 for 1st app.). 146,147-Origin The Inhumans. 148,149-Origin Black Bolt in each. 149-Origin Medusa, Crystal, Maximus, Gorgon, Kornak				
	5	15	38	60
151-157,159,160	4	12	29	45
158-Origin-r/#83; 158,159-Origin Dr. Blake (Thor)	8	24	56	90
161,167,170-179: 179-Last Kirby issue	3	10	23	35
162,168,169-Origin Galactus; Kirby-a	4	12	30	50
163,164-2nd & 3th brief cameo Warlock (Him)	3	10	23	35
165-1st full app. Warlock (Him) (6/69, see Fantastic Four #67); last 12¢ issue; Kirby-a	6	18	45	70
166-2nd full app. Warlock (Him); battles Thor	5	15	35	55

	GD2.0	FN6.0	VF8.0	NM9.
180,181-Neal Adams-a	4	12	26	40
182-192: 192-Last 15¢ issue	2	6	15	22
193-(25¢, 52 pgs.); Silver Surfer x-over	5	15	38	60
194-199	2	6	12	18
200	2	6	15	22
201-206,208-224	1	4	7	10
207-Rutland, Vermont Halloween x-over	1	4	7	10
225-Intro. Firelord	2	6	9	12
226-245	1	3	6	8
246-250-(Regular 25¢ editions)(4-8/76)	1	3	6	8
246-250-(30¢-c variants, limited distribution)	2	6	9	12
251-280: 271-Iron Man x-over. 274-Death of Balder the Brave				5.00
260-264-(35¢-c variants, limited distribution)(6-10/77)	1	3	6	8
281-299: 294-Origin Asgard & Odin				4.00
300-(12/80)-End of Asgard; origin of Odin & The Destroyer				6.00
301-336,338-373,375-381,383: 316-Iron Man x-over. 340-Donald Blake returns as Thor. 341-Clark Kent & Lois Lane cameo. 373-X-Factor tie-in				3.00
337-Simonson-c/a begins, ends #382; Beta Ray Bill becomes new Thor				
	1	3	6	8
374-Mutant Massacre; X-Factor app.				4.00
382-($1.25)-Anniversary issue; last Simonson-a				4.00
384-Intro. new Thor				4.00
385-399,401-410,413-428: 385-Hulk x-over. 391-Spider-Man x-over; 1st Eric Masterson. 395-Intro Earth Force. 408-Eric Masterson becomes Thor. 427, 428-Excalibur x-over				2.50
400,411: 400-($1.75, 68 pgs.)-Origin Loki. 411-Intro New Warriors (appears in costume in last panel); Juggernaut-c/story				4.00
412-1st full app. New Warriors (Marvel Boy, Kid Nova, Namorita, Night Thrasher, Firestar & Speedball)				5.00
429-431,434-443: 429,430-Ghost Rider x-over. 434-Capt. America x-over. 437-Thor vs. Quasar; Hercules app.;Tales of Asgard back-up stories begin. 443-Dr. Strange & Silver Surfer x-over; last $1.00-c				2.50
432,433: 432-(52 pgs.)-Thor's 300th app. (vs. Loki); reprints origin & 1st app. from Journey Into Mystery #83. 433-Intro new Thor				3.00
444-449,451-473: 448-Spider-Man-c/story. 455,456-Dr. Strange back-up. 457-Old Thor returns (3 pgs.). 459-Intro Thunderstrike. 460-Starlin scripts begin. 465-Super Skrull app. 466-Drax app. 469,470-Infinity Watch x-over. 472-Intro the Godlings				2.50
450-($2.50, 68 pgs.)-Flip-book format; r/story JIM #87 (1st Loki) plus-c plus a gallery of past-c; gatefold-c				3.00
474,476-481,483-499: 474-Begin $1.50-c; bound-in trading card sheet. 459-Intro Thunderstrike, 460-Starlin scripts begin. 472-Intro the Godlings. 490-The Absorbing Man app. 491-Warren Ellis scripts begins, ends #494; Deodato-c/a begins. 492-Reintro The Enchantress; Beta Ray Bill dies. 495-Wm. Messner-Loebs scripts begins; Isherwood-a.				2.50
475 ($2.00, 52 pgs.)-Regular edition				2.50
475 ($2.50, 52 pgs.)-Collectors edition w/foil embossed-c				3.00
482 ($2.95, 84 pgs.)-400th issue				3.00
500 ($2.50)-Double-size; wraparound-c; Deodato-c/a; Dr. Strange app.				5.00
501-Reintro Red Norvell				3.00
502-Double-sized tie-in; Red Norvell, Jane Foster & Hela app.				4.00
Special 2(9/66)-See Journey Into Mystery for 1st annual				
	7	21	50	80
King Size Special 3(1/71)	3	9	17	24
Special 4(12/71)-r/Thor #131,132 & JIM #113	2	6	12	18
Special 5,6: 5(11/76). 6(10/77)-Guardians of the Galaxy app.				
	2	6	9	12
Annual 7,8: 7(1978). 8(1979)-Thor vs. Zeus-c/story	1	3	6	8
Annual 9-12: 9('81). 10('82). 11('83). 12('84)				5.00
Annual 13-19('85-'94, 68 pgs.):14-Atlantis Attacks. 16-3 pg. origin; Guardians of the Galaxy app.18-Polybagged w/card				3.00
...Alone Against the Celestials nn (6/92, $5.95)-r/Thor #387-389				6.00
...Visionaries: Walter Simonson TPB (5/01, $24.95) r/#337-348				25.00
...: Worldengine (8/96, $9.95)-r/#491-494; Deodato-c/a; story & new intermission by Warren Ellis				10.00

NOTE: Neal Adams a-180,181; c-179-181. Austin a-342i, 346i; c-312i. Buscema a(p)-178, 182-213, 215-226, 231-238, 241-253, 254r, 255-259, 272-278, 283-285, 370, Annual 6, 8, 11; c(p)-175, 182-196, 198-200, 202-204, 206, 211, 212, 215, 219, 221, 226, 256, 259, 261, 262, 272-278, 283, 389, 370, Annual 6. Everett a(i)-143, 170-175; c(i)-171, 172, 174, 176, 214. Gil Kane 318p; c(p)-201, 205, 207-210, 216, 220, 222, 223, 231, 233-240, 242, 243, 318. Kirby a(p)-126-177, 179, 194r, 254r; c(p)-126-169, 171-174, 176-178, 249-253, 255, 257, 268, Annual 5, Special 2-4. Mooney a(i)-201, 204, 214-216, 218, 322i, 324i, 325i, 327i. Sienkiewicz c-332, 333, 335.

Thor V2 #39 © MAR

Thrax #1 © Invisible College Inc.

3-D Circus #1 © FH

	GD2.0	FN6.0	VF8.0	NM9.4

	GD2.0	FN6.0	VF8.0	NM9.4

Simonson a-260-271p, 337-354, 357-367, 380, Annual 7p; c-260, 263-271, 337-355, 357-369, 371, 373-382, Annual 7. **Starlin** c-213.

THOR (Volume 2)
Marvel Comics: July, 1998 - Present ($2.99/$1.99)

1-($2.99)-Follows Heroes Return; Jurgens-s/Romita Jr. & Janson-a; wraparound-c; battles the Destroyer				5.00
1-Variant-c	1	3	6	8
1-Rough Cut-($2.99) Features original script and pencil pages				3.00
1-Sketch cover				20.00
2-($1.99) Two covers; Avengers app.				3.00
3-11,13-23: 3-Assumes Jake Olson ID. 4-Namor-c/app. 8-Spider-Man-c/app. 14-Iron Man c/app. 17-Juggernaut-c				2.50
12-($2.99) Wraparound-c; Hercules appears				3.00
12-($10.00) Variant-c by Jusko				10.00
24,26-31,33,34: 24-Begin $2.25-c. 26-Mignola-c/Larsen-a. 29-Andy Kubert-a. 30-Maximum Security x-over; Beta Ray Bill-c/app. 33-Intro. Thor Girl				2.25
25-($2.99) Regular edition				3.00
25-($3.99) Gold foil enhanced cover				4.00
32-($3.50, 100 pgs.) new story plus reprints w/Kirby-a; Simonson-a				3.50
35-($2.99) Thor battles The Gladiator; Andy Kubert-a				3.00
36-44: 37-Starlin-a. 38,39-BWS-c. 38-42-Immonen-a. 40-Odin killed. 41-Orbik-c 44-'Nuff Said silent issue				2.25
...1999 Annual ($3.50) Jurgens-s/a(p)				3.50
...2000 Annual ($3.50) Jurgens-s/Ordway-a(p); back-up stories				3.50
...2001 Annual ($3.50) Jurgens-s/Grummett-a(p); Lightle-c				3.50
...Across All Worlds (9/01, $19.95, TPB) r/#28-35				20.00
...Resurrection ($5.99, TPB) r/#1,2				6.00
...: The Dark Gods (7/00, $15.95, TPB) r/#9-13				16.00

THOR CORPS
Marvel Comics: Sept, 1993 - No. 4, Jan, 1994 ($1.75, limited series)

1-4: 1-Invaders cameo. 2-Invaders app. 3-Spider-Man 2099, Rawhide Kid, Two-Gun Kid & Kid Colt app. 4-Painted-c				2.25

THOR: GODSTORM
Marvel Comics: Nov, 2001 - No. 3, Jan, 2002 ($3.50, limited series)

1-3-Steve Rude-c/a; Busiek-s; Avengers app.				3.50

THORION OF THE NEW ASGODS
Marvel Comics (Amalgam): June, 1997 ($1.95, one-shot)

1-Keith Giffen-s/John Romita Jr.-c/a				2.25

THOR: THE LEGEND
Marvel Comics: Sept, 1996 ($3.95, one-shot)

nn-Tribute issue				4.00

THOSE MAGNIFICENT MEN IN THEIR FLYING MACHINES (See Movie Comics)

THRAX
Event Comics: Nov, 1996 ($2.95, one-shot)

1				3.00

THREE CABALLEROS (Walt Disney's...)
Dell Publishing Co.: No. 71, 1945

Four Color 71-by Walt Kelly, c/a	80	240	560	1050

THREE CHIPMUNKS, THE (TV)
Dell Publishing Co.: No. 1042, Oct-Dec, 1959

Four Color 1042 (#1)-(Alvin, Simon & Theodore)	5	15	35	70

THREE COMICS (Also see Spiritman)
The Penny King Co.: 1944 (10¢, 52 pgs.) (2 different covers exist)

1,3,4-Lady Luck, Mr. Mystic, The Spirit app. (3 Spirit sections bound together); Lou Fine-a	26	78	139	240

NOTE: No. 1 contains Spirit Sections 4/9/44 - 4/23/44, and No. 4 is also from 4/44.

3-D (NOTE: The prices of all the 3-D comics listed include glasses. Deduct 40-50 percent if glasses are missing, and reduce slightly if glasses are loose.)

3-D ACTION
Atlas Comics (ACI): Jan, 1954 (Oversized, 15¢)(2 pairs of glasses included)

1-Battle Brady; Sol Brodsky-c	40	120	214	370

3-D ADVENTURE COMICS
Stats, Etc.: Aug, 1986 (one shot)

1-Promo material				4.00

3-D ALIEN TERROR
Eclipse Comics: June, 1986 ($2.50)

1-Old Witch, Crypt-Keeper, Vault Keeper cameo; Morrow, John Pound-a, Yeates-c				6.00
...in 2-D: 100 copies signed, numbered(B&W)	1	3	6	8

3-D ANIMAL FUN (See Animal Fun)

3-D BATMAN (Also see Batman 3-D)
National Periodical Publications: 1953 (Reprinted in 1966)

1953-(25¢)-Reprints Batman #42 & 48 (Penguin-c/story); Tommy Tomorrow story; came with pair of 3-D Bat glasses	111	332	694	1225
1966-Reprints 1953 issue; new cover by Infantino/Anderson; has inside-c photos of Batman & Robin from TV show (50¢)	38	113	215	360

3-D CIRCUS
Fiction House Magazines (Real Adventures Publ.): 1953 (25¢, w/glasses)

1	40	120	220	380

3-D COMICS (See Mighty Mouse, Tor and Western Fighters)

3-D DOLLY
Harvey Publications: December, 1953 (25¢, came with 2 pairs of glasses)

1-Richie Rich story redrawn from his 1st app. in Little Dot #1; shows cover in 3-D on inside	25	75	130	225

3-D-ELL
Dell Publishing Co.: No. 1, 1953; No. 3, 1953 (3-D comics) (25¢, came w/glasses)

1-Rootie Kazootie (#2 does not exist)	40	120	214	370
3-Flukey Luke	38	113	203	350

3-D EXOTIC BEAUTIES
The 3-D Zone: Nov, 1990 ($2.95, 28 pgs.)

1-L.B. Cole-c				7.00

3-D FEATURES PRESENTS JET PUP
Dimensions Publications: Oct-Dec (Winter on-c), 1953 (25¢, came w/glasses)

1-Irving Spector-a(2)	40	120	220	380

3-D FUNNY MOVIES
Comic Media: 1953 (25¢, came w/glasses)

1-Bugsey Bear & Paddy Pelican	40	120	220	380

THREE-DIMENSION ADVENTURES (Superman)
National Periodical Publications: 1953 (25¢, large size, came w/glasses)

nn-Origin Superman (new art)	111	332	694	1225

THREE DIMENSIONAL ALIEN WORLDS (See Alien Worlds)
Pacific Comics: July, 1984 (1st Ray Zone 3-D book)(one-shot)

1-Bolton-a(p); Stevens-a(i); Art Adams 1st published-a(p)				6.00

THREE DIMENSIONAL DNAGENTS (See New DNAgents)

THREE DIMENSIONAL E. C. CLASSICS (Three Dimensional Tales From the Crypt No. 2)
E. C. Comics: Spring, 1954 (Prices include glasses; came with 2 pair)

1-Stories by Wood (Mad #3), Krigstein (W.S. #7), Evans (F.C. #13), & Ingels (CSS #5); Kurtzman-c (rare in high grade due to unstable paper)	86	258	540	950

NOTE: Stories redrawn to 3-D format. Original stories not necessarily by artists listed. CSS: Crime SuspenStories; F.C.: Weird Fantasy; W.S.: Weird Science.

THREE DIMENSIONAL TALES FROM THE CRYPT (Formerly Three Dimensional E. C. Classics)(Cover title: ...From the Crypt of Terror)
E. C. Comics: No. 2, Spring, 1954 (Prices include glasses; came with 2 pair)

2-Davis (TFTC #25), Elder (VOH #14), Craig (TFTC #24), & Orlando (TFTC #22) stories; Feldstein-c (rare in high grade)	84	253	525	925

NOTE: Stories redrawn to 3-D format. Original stories not necessarily by artists listed. TFTC: Tales From the Crypt; VOH: Vault of Horror.

3-D LOVE
Steriographic Publ. (Mikeross Publ.): Dec, 1953 (25¢, came w/glasses)

1	40	120	220	380

3-D NOODNICK (See Noodnick)

3-D Romance #1 © Steriographic Publ.

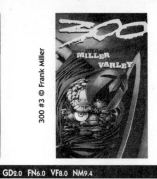

300 #3 © Frank Miller

Three Stooges #26 © Norman Maurer

	GD2.0	FN6.0	VF8.0	NM9.4

3-D ROMANCE
Steriographic Publ. (Mikeross Publ.): Jan, 1954 (25¢, came w/glasses)

1	40	120	220	380

3-D SHEENA, JUNGLE QUEEN (Also see Sheena 3-D)
Fiction House Magazines: 1953 (25¢, came w/glasses)

1-Maurice Whitman-c	73	219	455	800

3-D SUBSTANCE
The 3-D Zone: July, 1990 ($2.95, 28 pgs.)

1-Ditko-c/a(r)		4.00

3-D TALES OF THE WEST
Atlas Comics (CPS): Jan, 1954 (Oversized) (15¢, came with 2 pair of glasses)

1 (3-D)-Sol Brodsky-c	40	120	220	380

3-D THREE STOOGES (Also see Three Stooges)
Eclipse Comics: Sept, 1986 - No. 2, Nov, 1986; No. 3, Oct, 1987; No. 4, 1989 ($2.50)

1-4: 3-Maurer-r. 4-r-/"Three Missing Links"		5.00
1-3 (2-D)		5.00

3-D WHACK (See Whack)

3-D ZONE, THE
The 3-D Zone (Renegade Press)/Ray Zone: Feb, 1987 - No. 20, 1989 ($2.50)

1,3,4,7-9,11,12,14,15,17,19,20: 1-r/A Star Presentation. 3-Picture Scope Jungle Advs. 4-Electric Fear. 7-Hollywood 3-D Jayne Mansfield photo-c. 8-High Seas 3-D, 9-Redmask-r. 11-Danse Macabre; Matt Fox c/a(r). 12-3-D Presidents. 14-Tyranostar. 15-3-Dementia Comics; Kurtzman-a; Kubert, Maurer-a. 17-Thrilling Love. 19-Cracked Classics. 20-Commander Battle and His Atomic Submarine		6.00
2,5,6,10,13,16,18: 2-Wolverton-r. 5-Krazy Kat-r. 6-Ratfink. 10-Jet 3-D; Powell & Williamson-r. 13-Flash Gordon. 16-Space Vixens; Dave Stevens-c/a. 18-Spacehawk; Wolverton-r		6.00

NOTE: *Davis* r-19. *Ditko* r-19. *Elder* r-19. *Everett* r-19. *Feldstein* r-17. *Frazetta* r-17. *Heath* r-19. *Kamen* r-17. *Severin* r-19. *Ward* r-17,19. *Wolverton* r-2,18,19. *Wood* r-1,17. *Photo* c-12.

3 GEEKS, THE (Also see Geeksville)
3 Finger Prints: 1996 - No. 11, Jun, 1999 (B&W)

1,2 -Rich Koslowski-s/a in all	1	3	6	8
1-(2nd printing)				2.50
3-7, 9-11				2.50
8-(48 pgs.)				4.00
10-Variant-c				3.50
How to Pick Up Girls If You're a Comic Book Geek (color)(7/97)				4.00
When the Hammer Fallls TPB (2001, $14.95) r/#8-11				15.00

300
Dark Horse Comics: May, 1998 - No. 5, Sept, 1998 ($2.95/$3.95, limited series)

1,5: 1-Frank Miller-s/c/a; Spartans vs. Persians war. 5-($3.95-c)		4.00
1-Second printing, 2-4		3.00

3 LITTLE PIGS (Disney)(...and the Wonderful Magic Lamp)
Dell Publishing Co.: No. 218, Mar, 1949

Four Color 218 (#1)	12	36	84	150

3 LITTLE PIGS, THE (See Walt Disney Showcase #15 & 21)
Gold Key: May, 1964; No. 2, Sept, 1968 (Walt Disney)

1-Reprints Four Color #218	3	9	21	32
2	2	6	13	20

THREE MOUSEKETEERS, THE (1st Series)(See Funny Stuff #1)
National Per. Publ.: 3-4/56 - No. 24, 9-10/59; No. 26, 10-12/60

1	18	54	126	225
2	9	27	65	110
3-10: 6,8-Grey tone-c	8	24	56	90
11-26: 24-Cover says 11/59, inside says 9-10/59	6	18	45	75

NOTE: *Rube Grossman* a-1-26. *Sheldon Mayer* a-1-8; c-1-7.

THREE MOUSEKETEERS, THE (2nd Series) (See Super DC Giant)
National Periodical Publications: May-June, 1970 - No. 7, May-June, 1971 (#5-7: 68 pgs.)

1-Mayer-r in all	5	15	38	60
2-4: 4-Doodles Duck begins (1st app.)	3	10	23	35

5-7:(68 pgs.). 5-Dodo & the Frog, Bo Bunny begin

	5	15	34	55

THREE MUSKETEERS, THE (See Disney's The Three Musketeers)

THREE NURSES (Confidential Diary #12-17; Career Girl Romances #24 on)
Charlton Comics: V3#18, May, 1963 - V3#23, Mar, 1964

V3#18-23	3	9	17	25

THREE RASCALS
I. W. Enterprises: 1958; 1963

I.W. Reprint #1,2,10: 1-(Says Super Comics on inside)-(M.E.'s Clubhouse Rascals). #2-(1958). 10-(1963)-r/#1	2	6	9	12

THREE RING COMICS
Spotlight Publishers: March, 1945

1-Funny animal	17	51	88	150

THREE RING COMICS (Also see Captain Wizard & Meteor Comics)
Century Publications: April, 1946

1-Prankster-c; Captain Wizard, Impossible Man, Race Wilkins, King O'Leary, & Dr. Mercy app.	35	105	188	325

THREE ROCKETEERS (See Blast-Off)

THREE STOOGES (See Comic Album #18, Top Comics, The Little Stooges, March of Comics #232, 248, 268, 280, 292, 304, 316, 336, 373, Movie Classics & Comics & 3-D Three Stooges)

THREE STOOGES
Jubilee No. 1/St. John No. 1 (9/53) on: Feb, 1949 - No. 2, May, 1949; Sept, 1953 - No. 7, Oct, 1954

1-(Scarce, 1949)-Kubert-a; infinity-c	111	332	694	1225
2-(Scarce)-Kubert, Maurer-a	77	231	483	850
1-(9/53)-Maurer-c begin by Kubert (7 pgs.)	68	205	426	750
2(3-D, 10/53, 25¢)-Came w/glasses; Stunt Girl story by Kubert	50	150	300	525
3(3-D, 10/53, 25¢)-Came w/glasses; has 3-D-c	46	137	276	485
4(3/54)-7(10/54): 4-1st app. Li'l Stooge?	40	120	214	370

NOTE: *All issues have Kubert-Maurer art & Maurer covers. 6, 7-Partial photo-c.*

THREE STOOGES
Dell Publishing Co./Gold Key No. 10 (10/62) on: No. 1043, Oct-Dec, 1959 - No. 55, June, 1972

Four Color 1043 (#1)	21	63	147	275
Four Color 1078,1127,1170,1187	11	33	77	140
6(9-11/61) - 10: 6-Professor Putter begins; ends #16	9	27	63	120
11-14,16,18-20	7	21	49	95
15-Go Around the World in a Daze (movie scenes)	8	24	56	105
17-The Little Monsters begin (5/64)(1st app.?)	8	24	56	105
21,23-30	6	18	42	80
22-Movie scenes from "The Outlaws Is Coming"	7	21	49	90
31-55	5	15	35	60

NOTE: *All Four Colors, 6-50, 52-55 have photo-c.*

THREE STOOGES IN 3-D, THE
Eternity Comics: 1991 ($3.95, high quality paper, w/glasses)

1-Reprints Three Stooges by Gold Key; photo-c		5.00

3 WORLDS OF GULLIVER
Dell Publishing Co.: No. 1158, July, 1961 (2 issues exist with diff. covers)

Four Color 1158-Movie, photo-c	7	21	49	85

THRILL COMICS (See Flash Comics, Fawcett)

THRILLER
DC Comics: Nov, 1983 - No. 12, Nov, 1984 ($1.25, Baxter paper)

1-12: 1-Intro Seven Seconds; Von Eeden-c/a begins. 2-Origin. 5,6-Elvis satire		2.25

THRILLING ADVENTURES IN STAMPS COMICS (Formerly Stamp Comics)
Stamp Comics, Inc. (Very Rare): Jan, 1953 (25¢, 100 pgs.)

V1#8-Harrison, Wildey, Kiefer, Napoli-a	73	219	455	800

THRILLING ADVENTURE STORIES (See Tigerman)
Atlas/Seaboard Publ.: Feb, 1975 - No. 2, Aug, 1975 (B&W, 68 pgs.)

1-Tigerman, Kromag the Killer begin; Heath, Thorne-a; Doc Savage movie

Thrilling Comics #7 © BP

Thrilling Romances #10 © STD

Thrills of Tomorrow #19 © HARV

	GD2.0	FN6.0	VF8.0	NM9.4
photos of Ron Ely	2	6	12	18
2-Heath, Toth, Severin, Simonson-a; Adams-c	3	9	17	26

THRILLING COMICS
Better Publ./Nedor/Standard Comics: Feb, 1940 - No. 80, April, 1951

1-Origin & 1st app. Dr. Strange (37 pgs.), ends #?; Nickie Norton of the Secret Service begins	291	873	1818	3200
2-The Rio Kid, The Woman in Red, Pinocchio begins	127	381	795	1400
3-The Ghost & Lone Eagle begin	80	240	500	875
4-6,8-10: 5-Dr. Strange changed to Doc Strange	61	182	381	675
7-Classic-c	77	231	483	850
11-18,20	55	165	330	575
19-Origin & 1st app. The American Crusader (8/41), ends #39,41	61	182	381	675
21-30: 24-Intro. Mike, Doc Strange's sidekick (1/42). 27-Robot-c. 29-Last Rio Kid	47	142	286	500
31-40: 36-Commando Cubs begin (7/43, 1st app.)	40	120	240	420
41-Classic Hitler & Mussolini-c	70	210	438	775
42,43,45-52: 52-The Ghost ends. 45-Hitler pict. on-c	35	105	188	325
44-Hitler-c	59	177	369	650
53-The Phantom Detective begins; The Cavalier app.; no Commando Cubs	31	93	165	285
54-The Cavalier app.; no Commando Cubs	31	93	165	285
55-Lone Eagle ends	31	93	165	285
56-Princess Pantha begins (10/46, 1st app.)	47	141	286	500
57-66: 61-Ingels-a; The Lone Eagle app. 65-Last Phantom Detective & Commando Cubs. 66-Frazetta text illo	40	120	220	380
67,70-73: Frazetta-a(5-7 pgs.) in each. 72-Sea Eagle app.; Buck Ranger, Cowboy Detective begins	45	135	269	470
68,69-Frazetta-a(2), 8 & 6 pgs.; 9 & 7 pgs.	47	140	286	500
74-Last Princess Pantha; Tara app.	31	93	165	285
75-78: 75-All western format begins	15	45	77	130
79-Krigstein-a	16	48	83	140
80-Severin & Elder, Celardo, Moreira-a	16	48	83	140

NOTE: Bondage c-5, 9, 13, 20, 22, 27-30, 38, 41, 52, 54, 70. Kinstler a-45. Leo Morey a-7. Schomburg (sometimes signed as Xela) c-7, 9-19, 36-80 (airbrush 62-71). Tuska a-62, 63. Woman in Red not in #19, 23, 31-33, 39-45. No. 45 exists as a Canadian reprint but numbered #48. No. 72 exists as a Canadian reprint with no Frazetta stories.American Crusader c-20-24. Buck Ranger c-72-80. Commando Cubs c-37, 39, 41, 43, 45, 47, 49, 51. Doc Strange c-1-19, 25-36, 38, 40, 42, 44, 46, 48, 50-52, 59. Princess Pantha c-58, 60-71.

THRILLING COMICS (Also see All Star Comics 1999 crossover titles)
DC Comics: May, 1999 ($1.99, one-shot)

1-Golden Age Hawkman and Wildcat; Russ Heath-a				2.25

THRILLING CRIME CASES (Formerly 4Most; becomes Shocking Mystery Cases #50 on)
Star Publications: No. 41, June-July, 1950 - No. 49, July, 1952

41	29	87	153	265
42-45: 42-L. B. Cole-c/a (1); Chameleon story (Fox-r)	26	78	136	235
46-48: 47-Used in POP, pg. 84	25	75	130	225
49-(7/52)-Classic L. B. Cole-c	43	129	257	450

NOTE: L. B. Cole c-all; a-43p, 45p, 46p, 49(2 pgs.). Disbrow a-48. Hollingsworth a-48.

THRILLING ROMANCES
Standard Comics: No. 5, Dec, 1949 - No. 26, June, 1954

5	12	36	61	105
6,8	7	21	38	55
7-Severin/Elder-a (7 pgs.)	10	30	55	80
9,10-Severin/Elder-a; photo-c	8	24	45	65
11,14-21,26: 12-Tyrone Power/ Susan Hayward photo-c.14-Gene Tierney & Danny Kaye photo-c from movie "On the Riviera". 15-Tony Martin/Janet Leigh photo-c	6	18	32	45
12-Wood-a (2 pgs.)	10	30	55	85
13-Severin-a	7	21	38	55
22-25-Toth-a	9	27	49	70

NOTE: All photo-c. Celardo a-9, 16. Colletta a-23, 24(2). Toth text illos-19. Tuska a-9.

THRILLING SCIENCE TALES
AC Comics: 1989 - No. 2 ($3.50, 2/3 color, 52 pgs.)

1,2: 1-r/Bob Colt #6(saucer); Frazetta, Guardineer (Space Ace), Wood, Krenkel, Orlando, Williamson-r; Kaluta-c. 2-Capt. Science-r by Wood, Star Pirate-r by Whitman & Mysta of the Moon-r by Moreira				4.00

THRILLING TRUE STORY OF THE BASEBALL...
Fawcett Publications: 1952 (Photo-c, each)

...Giants-photo-c; has Willie Mays rookie photo-biography; Willie Mays, Eddie Stanky & others photos on-c	68	204	426	750
...Yankees-photo-c; Yogi Berra, Joe DiMaggio, Mickey Mantle & others photos on-c	64	192	398	700

THRILLING WONDER TALES
AC Comics: 1991 ($2.95, B&W)

1-Includes a Bob Powell Thun'da story				3.00

THRILLKILLER
DC Comics: Jan, 1997 - No. 3, Mar, 1997($2.50, limited series)

1-3-Elseworlds Robin & Batgirl; Chaykin-s/Brereton-c/a				3.00
...'62 ('98, $4.95, one-shot) Sequel; Chaykin-s/Brereton-c/a				5.00

TPB-(See Batman: Thrillkiller)

THRILLOGY
Pacific Comics: Jan, 1984 (One-shot, color)

1-Conrad-c/a				3.00

THRILL-O-RAMA
Harvey Publications (Fun Films): Oct, 1965 - No. 3, Dec, 1966

1-Fate (Man in Black) by Powell app.; Doug Wildey-a(2); Simon-c	5	15	34	55
2-Pirana begins (see Phantom #46); Williamson 2 pgs.; Fate (Man in Black) app.; Tuska/Simon-c	3	10	23	35
3-Fate (Man in Black) app.; Sparling-c	3	9	20	30

THRILLS OF TOMORROW (Formerly Tomb of Terror)
Harvey Publications: No. 17, Oct, 1954 - No. 20, April, 1955

17-Powell-a (horror); r/Witches Tales #7	14	42	72	120
18-Powell-a (horror); r/Tomb of Terror #1	12	36	61	100
19,20-Stuntman-c/stories by S&K (r/from Stuntman #1 & 2); 19 has origin & is last pre-code (2/55)	34	102	179	310

NOTE: Kirby c-19, 20. Palais a-17. Simon c-18?

THROBBING LOVE (See Fox Giants)

THROUGH GATES OF SPLENDOR
Spire Christian Comics (Flemming H. Revell Co.): 1973, 1974 (36 pages) (39-49 cents)

nn	1	3	6	8

THUMPER (Disney)
Dell Publishing Co.: No, 19, 1942 - No. 243, Sept, 1949

Four Color 19-Walt Disney's...Meets the Seven Dwarfs; reprinted in Silly Symphonies	56	168	392	725
Four Color 243-...Follows His Nose	10	30	70	135

THUN'DA (...King of the Congo)
Magazine Enterprises: 1952 - No. 6, 1953

1(A-1 #47)-Origin; Frazetta c/a; only comic done entirely by Frazetta; all Thun'da stories, no Cave Girl	136	408	852	1500
2(A-1 #59)-Powell-c/a begins, ends #6; Intro/1st app. Cave Girl in filler strip (also app. in 3-6)	23	69	121	210
3-(A-1 #73), 4(A-1 #78)	17	51	88	150
5(A-1 #83), 6(A-1 #86)	16	48	83	140

THUN'DA TALES (See Frank Frazetta's...)

THUNDER AGENTS (See Dynamo, Noman & Tales Of Thunder)
Tower Comics: 11/65 - No. 17, 12/67; No. 18, 9/68, No. 19, 11/68, No. 20, 11/69 (No. 1-16: 68 pgs.; No. 17 on: 52 pgs.)(All are 25¢)

1-Origin & 1st app. Dynamo, Noman, Menthor, & The Thunder Squad; 1st app. The Iron Maiden	18	54	126	225
2-Death of Egghead; A-bomb blast panel	10	30	70	120
3-5: 4-Guy Gilbert becomes Lightning who joins Thunder Squad; Iron Maiden app.	7	21	50	80
6-10: 7-Death of Menthor. 8-Origin & 1st app. The Raven				

The Tick #12 © Ben Edlund

Thunderbolts #9 © MAR

Thunderstrike #19 © MAR

	GD2.0	FN6.0	VF8.0	NM9.4

	6	18	40	65
11-15: 13-Undersea Agent app.; no Raven story	4	12	30	50
16-19	4	12	30	50
20-Special Collectors Edition; all reprints	3	9	20	30

NOTE: *Crandall* a-1, 4p, 5p, 18, 20r; c-18. *Ditko* a-6, 7p, 12p, 13?, 14p, 16, 18. *Giunta* a-6.
Kane a-1, 5p, 6p?, 14, 16p; c-14, 15. *Reinman* a-13. *Sekowsky* a-6. *Tuska* a-1p, 7, 8, 10, 13-17,
19. *Whitney* a-9p, 10, 13, 15, 17, 18; c-17. *Wood* a-1-11, 15(w/*Ditko*-12, 18), (inks-#9, 13, 14,
16, 17), 19l, 20r; c-1-8, 9l, 10-13(#10 w/*Williamson*(p)), 16.

T.H.U.N.D.E.R. AGENTS (See Blue Ribbon Comics, Hall of Fame
Featuring the..., JCP Features & Wally Wood's...)
JC Comics (Archie Publications): May, 1983 - No. 2, Jan, 1984

1,2: 1-New Manna/Blyberg-c/a. 2-Blyberg-c				6.00

THUNDER BIRDS (See Cinema Comics Herald)

THUNDERBOLT (See The Atomic...)

THUNDERBOLT (Peter Cannon...; see Crisis on Infinite Earths & Peter...)
Charlton Comics: Jan, 1966; No. 51, Mar-Apr, 1966 - No. 60, Nov, 1967

1-Origin & 1st app. Thunderbolt	4	12	26	40
51-(Formerly Son of Vulcan #50)	3	9	19	28
52-59: 54-Sentinels begin. 59-Last Thunderbolt & Sentinels (back-up story)	2	6	12	18
60-Prankster app.	2	6	13	20
57,58 ('77)-Modern Comics-r				4.00

NOTE: *Aparo* a-60. *Morisi* a-1, 51-56, 58; c-1, 51-56, 58, 59.

THUNDERBOLTS (Also see Incredible Hulk #449)
Marvel Comics: Apr, 1997 - Present ($1.95-$2.99)

1-($2.99) Busiek-s/Bagley-c/a	1	3	6	9
1-2nd printing; new cover colors				2.50
2-4: 2-Two covers. 4-Intro. Jolt				6.00
5-11: 9-Avengers app.				3.50
12-($2.99)-Avengers and Fantastic Four-c/app.				4.00
13-24: 14-Thunderbolts return to Earth. 21-Hawkeye app.				2.50
25-($2.99) Wraparound-c				3.00
26-38: 26-Manco-a				2.25
39-($2.99) 100 Page Monster; Iron Man reprints				3.00
40-49: 40-Begin $2.25-c; Sandman-c/app. 44-Avengers app. 47-Captain Marvel app. 49-Zircher-a				2.25
50-($2.99) Last Bagley-a; Captain America becomes leader				3.00
51-59: 51,52-Zircher-a; Dr. Doom app.				2.25
Annual '97 ($2.99)-Wraparound-c				3.00
Annual 2000 ($3.50) Breyfogle-a				3.50
...: Distant Rumblings (#-1) (7/97, $1.95) Busiek-s				5.00
First Strikes (1997, $4.99,TPB) r/#1,2				5.00
...: Life Sentences (7/01, $3.50) Adlard-a				3.50
...: Marvel's Most Wanted TPB ('98, $16.99) r/origin stories of original Masters of Evil				17.00
Wizard #0 (bagged with Wizard #89)				2.25

THUNDERBUNNY (Also see Blue Ribbon Comics #13, Charlton Bullseye & Pep Comics #393)
Red Circle Comics: Jan, 1984 (Direct sale only)
WaRP Graphics: Second series No. 1, 1985 - No. 6, 1985
Apple Comics: No. 7, 1986 - No. 12, 1987

1-Humor/parody; origin Thunderbunny; 2 page pin-up by Anderson (2nd series) 1,2-Magazine size				5.00
				3.00
3-12-Comic size				2.25

THUNDERCATS (TV)
Marvel Comics (Star Comics)/Marvel #22 on: Dec, 1985 - No. 24, June, 1988 (75¢)

1-Mooney-c/a begins	1	3	6	9
2-20: 2-(65¢ & 75¢ cover exists). 12-Begin $1.00-c. 18-20-Williamson-i	1	3	5	7
21-24: 23-Williamson-c(i)	1	3	6	8

THUNDERGOD
Crusade Entertainment: July, 1996 - No. 3 ($2.95, B&W)

1-3: Christopher Golden scripts; painted-c				3.00

THUNDERGOD
Caliber Comics: 1997 ($2.95, B&W, one-shot)

	GD2.0	FN6.0	VF8.0	NM9.

1				3.00

THUNDER MOUNTAIN (See Zane Grey, Four Color #246)

THUNDERSTRIKE (See Thor #459)
Marvel Comics: June, 1993 - No. 24, July, 1995 ($1.25)

1-($2.95, 52 pgs.)-Holo-grafx lightning patterned foil-c; Bloodaxe returns				3.00
2-24: 2-Juggernaut-c/s. 4-Capt. America app. 4-6-Spider-Man app. 8-bound-in trading card sheet. 18-Bloodaxe app. 24-Death of Thunderstrike				2.25
Marvel Double Feature...Thunderstrike/Code Blue #13 ($2.50)-Same as Thunderstrike #13 w/Code Blue flip book				2.50

TICK, THE (Also see The Chroma-Tick)
New England Comics Press: Jun, 1988 - No. 12, May, 1993
($1.75/$1.95/$2.25; B&W, over-sized)

Special Edition 1-1st comic book app. serially numbered & limited to 5,000 copies	5	15	38	60
Special Edition 1-(5/96, $5.95)-Double-c; foil-c; serially numbered (5,001 thru 14,000) & limited to 9,000 copies				6.00
Special Edition 2-Serially numbered and limited to 3000 copies	4	12	30	50
Special Edition 2-(8/96, $5.95)-Double-c; foil-c; serially numbered (5,001 thru 14,000) & limited to 9,000 copies	1	3	6	8
1-Regular Edition 1st printing; reprints Special Ed. 1 w/minor changes	4	12	26	40
1-2nd printing				6.00
1-3rd-5th printings				3.00
2-Reprints Special Ed. 2 w/minor changes	2	6	13	20
2-8-All reprints				3.00
3-5 ($1.95). 4-1st app. Paul the Samurai	1	4	7	10
6,8 ($2.25)				5.00
7-1st app. Man-Eating Cow.				6.00
8-Variant with no logo, price, issue number or company logos.	2	6	12	18
9-12 ($2.75)				4.00
12-Special Edition; card-stock, virgin foil-c; numbered edition	2	6	15	22
Pseudo-Tick #13 (11/00, $3.50) Continues story from #12 (1993)				4.00
Promo Sampler-(1990)-Tick-c/story	1	3	6	8

TICK, THE (One shots)
--BIG BACK TO SCHOOL SPECIAL

1-(10/98, $3.50) Tick and Arthur undercover in high school				3.50

--BIG CRUISE SHIP VACATION SPECIAL

1-(9/00, $3.50, B&W)				3.50

--BIG FATHER'S DAY SPECIAL

1-(6/00, $3.50, B&W)				3.50

--BIG HALLOWEEN SPECIAL

1-(10/99, $3.50, B&W)				3.50
...2000 (10/00, $3.50)				3.50
...2001 (9/01, $3.95)				4.00

--BIG MOTHER'S DAY SPECIAL

1-(4/00, $3.50, B&W)				3.50

--BIG RED-N-GREEN CHRISTMAS SPECTACLE

1-(12/01, $3.95)				4.00

--BIG SUMMER ANNUAL

1-(7/99, $3.50, B&W) Chainsaw Vigilante vs. Barry				3.50

--BIG SUMMER FUN SPECIAL

1-(8/98, $3.50, B&W) Tick and Arthur at summer camp				3.50

--BIG TAX TIME TERROR

1-(4/00, $3.50, B&W)				3.50

--BIG YEAR 2000 SPECTACLE

1-(3/00, $3.50, B&W)				3.50

--BIG YULE LOG SPECIAL

2001-(12/00, $3.50, B&W)				3.50

--INCREDIBLE INTERNET COMIC

1-(7/01, $3.95, color) reprints story from New England Comics website				4.00

--MASSIVE SUMMER DOUBLE SPECTACLE

Tick-Tock Tales #19 © ME

Time Breakers #3
© Rachel Pollack & Chris Weston

Time For Love #18 © CC

	GD2.0	FN6.0	VF8.0	NM9.4

1,2-(7,8/00, $3.50, B&W)   3.50

TICK'S BACK, THE
0-(8/97, $2.95, B&W)   3.50

TICK'S BIG ROMANTIC ADVENTURE, THE
1-(2/98, $2.95, B&W) Candy box cover with candy map on back   3.50

TICK AND ARTHUR, THE
New England Comics: Feb, 1999 - Present ($3.50, B&W)
1-6-Sean Wang-s/a   3.50

TICK BIG BLUE DESTINY, THE
New England Comics: Oct, 1997 - Present ($2.95)
1-4: 1-"Keen" Ed. 2-Two covers   3.50
1-($4.95) "Wicked Keen" Ed. w/die cut-c   5.00
5-($3.50)   3.50
6-Luny Bin Trilogy Preview #0 (7/98, $1.50)   3.50
7-9: 7-Luny Bin Trilogy begins   3.50

TICK BIG BLUE YULE LOG SPECIAL, THE
New England Comics: Dec, 1997; 1999 ($2.95, B&W)
1-"Jolly" and "Traditional" covers; flip book w/"Arthur Teaches the Tick About Hanukkah"   3.50
...1999 ($3.50)   3.50

TICK, THE : CIRCUS MAXIMUS
New England Comics: Mar, 2000 - No. 4, Jun, 2000 ($3.50, B&W)
1-4-Encyclopedia of characters from Tick comics   3.50
Redux No. 1 (4/01, $3.50)   3.50

TICK, THE - COLOR
New England Comics: Jan, 2001 - Present ($3.95)
1-5: 1-Marc Sandroni-a   3.50

TICK, THE - HEROES OF THE CITY
New England Comics: Feb, 1999 - Present ($3.50, B&W)
1-6-Short stories by various   3.50

TICK KARMA TORNADO (The...)
New England Comics Press: Oct, 1993 - No. 9, Mar, 1995 ($2.75, B&W)
1-($3.25)   4.00
2-9: 2-$2.75-c begins   3.50

TICK'S GIANT CIRCUS OF THE MIGHTY, THE
New England Comics: Summer, 1992 - No. 3, Fall, 1993 ($2.75, B&W, magazine size)
1-(A-O). 2-(P-Z). 3-1993 Update   4.00

TICKLE COMICS (Also see Gay, Smile, & Whee Comics)
Modern Store Publ.: 1955 (7¢, 5x7-1/4", 52 pgs)

		GD	FN	VF
1	5	15	23	30

TICK TOCK TALES
Magazine Enterprises: Jan, 1946 - V3#33, Jan-Feb, 1951

		GD	FN	VF	NM
1-Koko & Kola begin	14	42	72	120
2	8	24	42	60
3-10	7	21	36	50
11-33: 19-Flag-c. 23-Muggsy Mouse, The Pixies & Tom-Tom the Jungle Boy app. 25-The Pixies & Tom-Tom app.	6	18	30	42

TIGER (Also see Comics Reading Libraries in the Promotional Comics section)
Charlton Press (King Features): Mar, 1970 - No. 6, Jan, 1971 (15¢)

1	2	6	13	20
2-6	1	4	7	10

TIGER BOY (See Unearthly Spectaculars)

TIGER GIRL
Gold Key: Sept, 1968 (15¢)

1 (10227-809)-Sparling-c/a; Jerry Siegel scripts	4	12	26	40

TIGERMAN (Also see Thrilling Adventure Stories)
Seaboard Periodicals (Atlas): Apr, 1975 - No. 3, Sept, 1975 (All 25¢ issues)

1-3: 1-Origin; Colan-c. 2,3-Ditko-p in each	1	3	5	7

TIGER WALKS, A (See Movie Comics)

TIGRESS, THE
Hero Graphics: Aug, 1992 - No. 6?, June, 1993 ($3.95/$2.95/$3.95, B&W)
1,6: 1-Tigress vs. Flare. 6-44 pgs.   4.00
2-5: 2-$2.95-c begins   3.00

TILLIE THE TOILER (See Comic Monthly)
Dell Publishing Co.: No. 15, 1941 - No. 237, July, 1949

	GD	FN	VF	NM
Four Color 15(1941)	35	105	245	450
Large Feature Comic 30(1941)	23	68	161	300
Four Color 8(1942)	23	68	161	300
Four Color 22(1943)	18	54	126	230
Four Color 55(1944), 89(1945)	13	40	91	175
Four Color 106('45),132('46): 132-New stories begin	10	30	70	125
Four Color 150,176,184	9	27	63	115
Four Color 195,213,237	7	21	49	85

TIMBER WOLF (See Action Comics #372, & Legion of Super-Heroes)
DC Comics: Nov, 1992 - No. 5, Mar, 1993 ($1.25, limited series)
1-5   2.50

TIME BANDITS
Marvel Comics Group: Feb, 1982 (one-shot, Giant)
1-Movie adaptation   4.00

TIME BEAVERS (See First Comics Graphic Novel #2)

TIME BREAKERS
DC Comics (Helix): Jan, 1997 - No. 5, May, 1997 ($2.25, limited series)
1-5-Pollack-s   2.50

TIMECOP (Movie)
Dark Horse Comics: Sept, 1994 - No. 2, Nov, 1994 ($2.50, limited series)
1,2-Adaptation of film   2.50

TIME FOR LOVE (Formerly Romantic Secrets)
Charlton Comics: V2#53, Oct, 1966; Oct, 1967 - No. 47, May, 1976

	GD	FN	VF	NM
V2#53(10/66)	3	9	17	25
1(10/67)	3	10	23	35
2(12/67)-10	2	6	15	22
11-20	2	6	11	16
21-29	2	6	9	12
30-(10/72)-Full-length portrait of David Cassidy	3	9	17	25
31-47	1	4	7	10

TIMELESS TOPIX (See Topix)

TIMELY PRESENTS: ALL WINNERS
Marvel Comics: Dec, 1999 ($3.99)
1-Reprints All Winners Comics #19 (Fall 1946); new Lago-c   4.00

TIMELY PRESENTS: HUMAN TORCH
Marvel Comics: Feb, 1999 ($3.99)
1-Reprints Human Torch Comics #5 (Fall 1941); new Lago-c   4.00

TIME MACHINE, THE
Dell Publishing Co.: No. 1085, Mar, 1960 (H.G. Wells)

	GD	FN	VF	NM
Four Color 1085-Movie, Alex Toth-a; Rod Taylor photo-c	15	45	105	190

TIME MASTERS
DC Comics: Feb, 1990 - No. 8, Sept, 1990 ($1.75, mini-series)
1-8: New Rip Hunter series. 5-Cave Carson, Viking Prince app. 6-Dr. Fate app.   2.25

TIMESLIP COLLECTION
Marvel Comics: Nov, 1998 ($2.99, one-shot)
1-Pin-ups reprinted from Marvel Vision magazine   3.00

TIMESLIP SPECIAL (The Coming of the Avengers)
Marvel Comics: Oct, 1998 ($5.99, one-shot)
1-Alternate world Avengers vs. Odin   6.00

TIMESPIRITS
Marvel Comics (Epic Comics): Oct, 1984 - No. 8, Mar, 1986 ($1.50, Baxter paper, direct sales)
1-8: 4-Williamson-a   2.25

	GD2.0	FN6.0	VF8.0	NM9.4

TIME TUNNEL, THE (TV)
Gold Key: Feb, 1967 - No. 2, July, 1967 (12¢)

1-Photo back-c on both issues	6	18	42	75
2	5	15	35	60

TIME TWISTERS
Quality Comics: Sept, 1987 - No. 21, 1989 ($1.25/$1.50)

1-21: Alan Moore scripts in 1-4, 6-9, 14 (2 pg.). 14-Bolland-a (2 pg.). 15,16
Guice-c 2.25

TIME 2: THE EPIPHANY (See First Comics Graphic Novel #9)

TIMEWALKER (Also see Archer & Armstrong)
Valiant: Jan, 1994 - No. 15, Oct, 1995 ($2.50)

1-15,0(3/96): 2-"JAN" on-c, February, 1995 in indicia. 2.50
Yearbook 1 (5/95, $2.95) 3.00

TIME WARP (See The Unexpected #210)
DC Comics, Inc.: Oct-Nov, 1979 - No. 5, June-July, 1980 ($1.00, 68 pgs.)

1	2	6	9	12
2-5	1	3	6	9

NOTE: Aparo a-1. Buckler a-1p. Chaykin a-2. Ditko a-1-4. Kaluta c-1-5. G. Kane a-2.
Nasser a-4. Newton a-1-5p. Orlando a-2. Sutton a-3.

TIME WARRIORS: THE BEGINNING
Fantasy General Comics: 1986 (Aug) - No. 2, 1986? ($1.50)

1,2-Alpha Track/Skellon Empire 2.25

TIM HOLT (Movie star) (Becomes Red Mask #42 on; also see Crack Western
#72, & Great Western)
Magazine Enterprises: 1948 - No. 41, April-May, 1954 (All 36 pgs.)

1-(A-1 #14)-Line drawn-c w/Tim Holt photo on-c; Tim Holt, His horse Lightning & sidekick Chito begin	64	192	398	700
2-(A-1 #17)(9-10/48)-Photo-c begin, end #18	37	111	197	340
3-(A-1 #19)-Photo back-c	29	87	153	265
4(1-2/49),5: 5-Photo front/back-c	21	63	110	185
6-(5/49)-1st app. The Calico Kid (alias Rex Fury), his horse Ebony & Sidekick Sing-Song (single begin series); photo back-c	35	105	185	320
7-10: 7-Calico Kid by Ayers. 8-Calico Kid by Guardineer (r-in/Great Western #10). 9-Map of Tim's Home Range	18	54	94	155
11-The Calico Kid becomes The Ghost Rider (origin & 1st app.) by Dick Ayers (r-in/Great Western I.W. #8); his horse Spectre & sidekick Sing-Song begin series	43	129	257	450
12-16,18-Last photo-c	14	42	72	120
17-Frazetta Ghost Rider-c	40	120	217	375
19,22,24: 19-Last Tim Holt-c; Bolle line-drawn-c begin; Tim Holt photo on covers #19-28,30-41. 22-interior photo-c	12	36	61	100
20-Tim Holt becomes Redmask (origin); begin series; Redmask-c #20-on	18	54	98	155
21-Frazetta Ghost Rider/Redmask-c	35	105	188	325
23-Frazetta Redmask-c	29	87	153	265
25-1st app. Black Phantom	21	63	110	185
26-30: 28-Wild Bill Hickok, Bat Masterson team up with Redmask. 29-B&W photo-c	10	30	55	85
31-33-Ghost Rider ends	10	30	55	80
34-Tales of the Ghost-Rider begin (horror)-Classic "The Flower Women" & "Hard Boiled Harry!"	13	39	66	110
35-Last Tales of the Ghost Rider	10	30	55	85
36-The Ghost Rider returns, ends #41; liquid hallucinogenic drug story	12	36	61	100
37-Ghost Rider classic "To Touch Is to Die!", about Inca treasure	12	36	61	100
38-The Black Phantom begins (not in #39); classic Ghost Rider "The Phantom Guns of Feather Gap!"	12	36	61	100
39-41: All 3-D effect c/stories	15	45	77	130

NOTE: Dick Ayers a-7, 9-41. Bolle a-1-41; c-19, 20, 22, 24-28, 30-41.

TIM McCOY (Formerly Zoo Funnies; Pictorial Love Stories #22 on)
Charlton Comics: No. 16, Oct, 1948 - No. 21, Aug, 1949 (Western Movie
Stories)

16-John Wayne, Montgomery Clift app. in "Red River"; photo back-c	43	129	257	450

17-21: 17-Allan "Rocky" Lane guest stars. 18-Rod Cameron guest stars. 19-

---

	GD2.0	FN6.0	VF8.0	NM9.4

Whip Wilson, Andy Clyde guest star; Jesse James story. 20-Jimmy Wakely

guest stars. 21-Johnny Mack Brown guest stars	40	120	220	380

TIMMY
Dell Publishing Co.: No. 715, Aug, 1956 - No. 1022, Aug-Oct, 1959

Four Color 715 (#1)	4	12	26	40
Four Color 823 (8/57), 923 (8/58), 1022	3	9	19	28

TIMMY THE TIMID GHOST (Formerly Win-A-Prize; see Blue Bird)
Charlton Comics: No. 3, 2/56 - No. 44, 10/64; No. 45, 9/66; 10/67 - No. 23, 7/71;
V4#24, 9/85 - No. 26, 1/86

3(1956) (1st Series)	11	33	55	90
4,5	6	18	32	45
6-10	3	9	20	30
11,12(4/58,10/58)	6	18	45	75
13-20	3	9	17	25
21-45(1966)	2	6	12	18
1(10/67, 2nd series)	2	6	13	20
2-10	2	6	9	12
11-23	1	3	6	9
24-26 (1985-86): Fago-r (low print run)				5.00

TIM TYLER (See Harvey Comics Hits #54)

TIM TYLER (Also see Comics Reading Libraries in the Promotional Comics section)
Better Publications: 1942

1	14	42	72	120

TIM TYLER COWBOY
Standard Comics (King Features Synd.): No. 11, Nov, 1948 - No. 18, 1950

11-By Lyman Young	9	27	49	70
12-18: 13-15-Full length western adventures	7	21	36	50

TINCAN MAN
Image Comics: Jan, 2000 - No. 3, Mar, 2000 ($2.95, limited series)

1-3-Thornton-s/Dietrich Smith & Pierre Andre-Dery-a 3.00

TINKER BELL (Disney, TV)(See Walt Disney Showcase #37)
Dell Publishing Co.: No. 896, Mar, 1958 - No. 982, Apr-June, 1959

Four Color 896 (#1)-The Adventures of...	9	27	63	110
Four Color 982-The New Advs. of...	8	24	56	100

TINY FOLKS FUNNIES
Dell Publishing Co.: No. 60, 1944

Four Color 60	15	45	105	200

TINY TESSIE (Tessie #1-23; Real Experiences #25)
Marvel Comics (20CC): No. 24, Oct, 1949 (52 pgs.)

24	10	30	55	80

TINY TIM (Also see Super Comics)
Dell Publishing Co.: No. 4, 1941 - No. 235, July, 1949

Large Feature Comic 4('41)	32	96	224	410
Four Color 20(1941)	28	85	196	370
Four Color 42(1943)	17	50	119	220
Four Color 235	4	12	30	50

TINY TOT COMICS
E. C. Comics: Mar, 1946 - No. 10, Nov-Dec, 1947 (For younger readers)

1(nn)-52 pg. issues begin, end #4	38	114	203	350
2 (5/46)	22	66	116	200
3-10: 10-Christmas-c	20	60	105	175

TINY TOT FUNNIES (Formerly Family Funnies; becomes Junior Funnies)
Harvey Publ. (King Features Synd.): No. 9, June, 1951

9-Flash Gordon, Mandrake, Dagwood, Daisy, etc.	7	21	38	55

TINY TOTS COMICS
Dell Publishing Co.: 1943 (Not reprints)

1-Kelly-a(2); fairy tales	40	120	232	400

TIPPY & CAP STUBBS (See Popular Comics)
Dell Publishing Co.: No. 210, Jan, 1949 - No. 242, Aug, 1949

Four Color 210 (#1)	4	12	30	50
Four Color 242	4	12	26	40

Tip Top Comics #126 © UFS

Titans #25 © DC

T-Man #6 © QUA

	GD2.0	FN6.0	VF8.0	NM9.4

TIPPY'S FRIENDS GO-GO & ANIMAL
Tower Comics: July, 1966 - No. 15, Oct, 1969 (25¢)

1	6	18	42	70
2-5,7,9-15: 12-15 titled "Tippy's Friend Go-Go"	3	10	23	35
6-The Monkees photo-c	6	18	42	70
8-Beatles app. on front/back-c	9	27	65	110

TIPPY TEEN (See Vicki)
Tower Comics: Nov, 1965 - No. 25, Oct, 1969 (25¢)

1	6	18	42	70
2-4,6-10	4	12	26	40
5-1 pg. Beatles pin-up	4	12	29	45
11-20: 16-Twiggy photo-c	3	10	23	35
21-25	3	9	19	28
Special Collectors' Editions nn-(1969, 25¢)	4	12	26	40

TIPPY TERRY
Super/I. W. Enterprises: 1963

Super Reprint #14('63)-r/Little Groucho #1	2	6	9	12
I.W. Reprint #1 (nd)-r/Little Groucho #1	2	6	9	12

TIP TOP COMICS
United Features #1-187/St. John #188-210/Dell Publishing Co. #211 on:
4/36 - No. 210, 1957; No. 211, 11-1/57-58 - No. 225, 5-7/61

1-Tarzan by Hal Foster, Li'l Abner, Broncho Bill, Fritzi Ritz, Ella Cinders, Capt.
& The Kids begin; strip-r (1st comic book app. of each)

	944	2832	5192	8500
2	222	666	1221	2000
3-Tarzan-c	200	600	1100	1800
4	114	342	627	1025
5-8,10: 7-Photo & biography of Edgar Rice Burroughs. 8-Christmas-c	82	246	451	740
9-Tarzan-c	104	312	728	940
11,13,16,18-Tarzan-c: 11-Has Tarzan pin-up	80	240	440	725
12,14,15,17,19,20: 20-Christmas-c	65	195	358	585
21,24,27,30-(10/38)-Tarzan-c	65	195	358	585
22,23,25,26,28,29	44	131	242	400
31,35,38,40	40	120	220	380
32,36-Tarzan-c: 32-1st published Jack Davis-a (cartoon). 36-Kurtzman panel (1st published comic work)	53	158	318	560
33,34,37,39-Tarzan-c	50	150	300	525
41-Reprints 1st Tarzan Sunday; Tarzan-c	53	158	318	560
42,44,46,48,49	35	105	185	320
43,45,47,50,52-Tarzan-c. 43-Mort Walker panel	40	120	232	400
51,53	34	102	179	310
54-Origin Mirror Man & Triple Terror, also featured on cover	40	120	220	380
55,56,58,60: Last Tarzan by Foster	27	81	142	245
57,59,61,62-Tarzan by Hogarth	34	102	179	310
63-80: 65,67-70,72-74,77,78-No Tarzan	17	51	88	150
81-90	15	45	77	130
91-99	13	39	66	110
100	14	42	72	120
101-140: 110-Gordo story. 111-Li'l Abner app. 118, 132-No Tarzan. 137-Sadie Hawkins Day story	9	27	49	70
141-170: 145,151-Gordo stories. 157-Last Li'l Abner; lingerie panels	7	21	36	50
171-188-Tarzan reprints by B. Lubbers in all. 177-Peanuts by Schulz begins?; no Peanuts in #178,179,181-183	7	21	38	55
189-225-Peanuts (8 pgs.) in most	6	18	29	40

Bound Volumes (Very Rare) sold at 1939 World's Fair; bound by publisher in pictorial comic boards (also see Comics on Parade)

Bound issues 1-12	255	765	1591	2800
Bound issues 13-24	132	395	825	1450
Bound issues 25-36	116	348	725	1275

NOTE: Tarzan by Foster-#1-40, 44-50; by Rex Maxon-#41-43; by Burne Hogarth-#57, 59, 62.

TIP TOPPER COMICS
United Features Syndicate: Oct-Nov, 1949 - No. 28, 1954

1-Li'l Abner, Abbie & Slats	10	30	55	80
2	7	21	36	50
3-5: 5-Fearless Fosdick app.	6	18	29	40

6-10: 6-Fearless Fosdick app.	5	15	25	35
11-16,25	5	14	21	28
17(6-7/52) (2nd app. of Peanuts by Schulz in comics?) (see United Comics #22 for 5-6/52 app.)	6	18	32	45
18-24,26-Early Peanuts (2 pgs.). 26-Twin Earths	5	15	25	35
27,28-Twin Earths	6	18	29	40

NOTE: Many lingerie panels in Fritzi Ritz stories.

TITAN A.E.
Dark Horse Comics: May, 2000 - No. 3, July, 2000 ($2.95, limited series)

1-3-Movie prequel; Al Rio-a				3.00

TITANS (Also see Teen Titans, New Teen Titans and New Titans)
DC Comics: March, 1999 - Present ($2.50)

1-Titans re-form; Grayson-s; 2 covers				3.00
2-11,13-24,26-36: 2-Superman-c/app. 9,10,21,22-Deathstroke app.				2.50
24-Titans from "Kingdom Come" app. 32-36-Asamiya-c				2.50
12-($3.50, 48 pages)				3.50
25-($3.95) Titans from "Kingdom Come" app.; Wolfman & Faerber-s; art by Pérez, Cardy, Grummett, Jimenez, Dodson, Pelletier				4.00
Annual 1 ('00, $3.50) Planet DC; intro Bushido				3.50
...Secret Files 1,2 (9/99, 10/00; $4.95) Profile pages & short stories				5.00

TITANS/ LEGION OF SUPER-HEROES: UNIVERSE ABLAZE
DC Comics: 2000 - No. 4, 2000 ($4.95, prestige format, limited series)

1-4-Jurgens-s/a; P. Jimenez-a; teams battle Universo				5.00

TITAN SPECIAL
Dark Horse Comics: June, 1994 ($3.95, one-shot)

1-($3.95, 52 pgs.)				4.00

TITANS: SCISSORS, PAPER, STONE
DC Comics: 1997 ($4.95, one-shot)

1-Manga style Elseworlds; Adam Warren-s/a(p)				5.00

TITANS SELL-OUT SPECIAL
DC Comics: Nov, 1992 ($3.50, 52 pgs., one-shot)

1-Fold-out Nightwing poster; 1st Teeny Titans				3.50

T-MAN (Also see Police Comics #103)
Quality Comics Group: Sept, 1951 - No. 38, Dec, 1956

1-Pete Trask, T-Man begins; Jack Cole-a	40	120	220	380
2-Crandall-c	22	66	116	200
3,7,8: All Crandall-c	20	60	105	175
4,5-Crandall-c/a each	21	63	110	185
6-"The Man Who Could Be Hitler" c/story; Crandall-c.	22	66	116	200
9,10-Crandall-c	17	51	88	150
11-Used in POP, pg. 95 & color illo.	13	39	66	110
12,13,15-19,21,22-26: 21- "The Return of Mussolini" c/story. 23-H-Bomb panel.	10	30	55	85
24-Last pre-code issue (4/55). 25-Not Crandall-a	10	30	55	85
14-Hitler-c	13	39	66	110
20-H-Bomb explosion-c/story	14	42	72	120
27-38	10	30	55	85

NOTE: Anti-communist stories common. Crandall c2-10p. Cuidera c(i)-1-38. Bondage c-15.

TMNT MUTANT UNIVERSE SOURCEBOOK
Archie Comics: 1992 - No. 3, 1992? ($1.95, 52 pgs.)(Lists characters from A-Z)

1-3: 3-New characters; fold-out poster				2.25

TNT COMICS
Charles Publishing Co.: Feb, 1946 (36 pgs.)

1-Yellowjacket app.	31	93	168	290

TOBY TYLER (Disney, see Movie Comics)
Dell Publishing Co.: No. 1092, Apr-June, 1960

Four Color 1092-Movie, photo-c	6	18	42	80

TODAY'S BRIDES
Ajax/Farrell Publishing Co.: Nov, 1955; No. 2, Feb, 1956; No. 3, Sept, 1956; No. 4, Nov, 1956

1	8	24	45	65
2-4	6	18	29	40

TODAY'S ROMANCE

Toka #4 © DELL

Tomahawk #9 © DC

Tomb of Terror #14 © DC

	GD2.0	FN6.0	VF8.0	NM9.4			GD2.0	FN6.0	VF8.0	NM9.4

Standard Comics: No. 5, March, 1952 - No. 8, Sept, 1952 (All photo-c?)

5-Photo-c	8	24	45	65
6-Photo-c; Toth-a	9	27	49	70
7,8	6	18	29	40

TOKA (Jungle King)
Dell Publishing Co.: Aug-Oct, 1964 - No. 10, Jan, 1967 (Painted-c #1,2)

1	4	12	26	40
2	2	6	15	22
3-10	2	6	12	18

TOMAHAWK (Son of... on-c of #131-140; see Star Spangled Comics #69 & World's Finest Comics #65)
National Periodical Publications: Sept-Oct, 1950 - No. 140, May-June, 1972

1-Tomahawk & boy sidekick Dan Hunter begin by Fred Ray				
	159	477	994	1750
2-Frazetta/Williamson-a (4 pgs.)	64	192	398	700
3-5	40	120	232	400
6-10: 7-Last 52 pg. issue	33	99	174	300
11-20	24	72	127	215
21-27,30: 30-Last precode (2/55)	20	60	105	175
28-1st app. Lord Shilling (arch-foe)	21	63	110	185
29-Frazetta-r/Jimmy Wakely #3 (3 pgs.)	26	78	136	235
31-40	12	36	84	140
41-50	9	27	65	110
51-56,58-60	7	21	50	80
57-Frazetta-r/Jimmy Wakely #6 (3 pgs.)	10	30	68	115
61-77: 77-Last 10¢ issue	6	18	40	65
78-85: 81-1st app. Miss Liberty. 83-Origin Tomahawk's Rangers				
	4	12	29	45
86-99: 96-Origin/1st app. The Hood, alias Lady Shilling				
	3	9	21	32
100	3	10	23	35
101-110: 107-Origin/1st app. Thunder-Man	3	9	17	25
111-115,120,122: 122-Last 12¢ issue	2	6	15	22
116-119,121,123-130-Neal Adams-c	3	9	17	25
131-Frazetta-r/Jimmy Wakely #7 (3 pgs.); origin Firehair retold				
	3	9	17	26
132-135: 135-Last 15¢ issue	2	6	11	16
136-138,140 (52 pg. Giants)	2	6	15	22
139-Frazetta-r/Star Spangled #113	2	6	17	25

NOTE: *Fred Ray* c-1, 2, 8, 11, 30, 34, 35, 40-43, 45, 46, 82. Firehair by *Kubert*-131-134, 136. *Maurer* a-138. *Severin* a-135. *Starr* a-5. *Thorne* a-137, 140.

TOM AND JERRY (See Comic Album #4, 8, 12, Dell Giant #21, Dell Giants, Golden Comics Digest #1, 5, 8, 13, 15, 18, 22, 25, 28, 35, Kite fun Book & March of Comics #21, 46, 61, 70, 88, 103, 119, 128, 145, 154, 173, 190, 207, 224, 281, 295, 305, 321, 333, 345, 361, 365, 388, 400, 444, 451, 463, 480)

TOM AND JERRY (...Comics, early issues) (M.G.M.)
(Formerly Our Gang No. 1-59) (See Dell Giants for annuals)
Dell Publishing Co./Gold Key No. 213-327/Whitman No. 328 on:
No. 193, 6/48; No. 60, 7/49 - No. 212, 7/9-62; No. 213, 11/62 - No. 291, 2/75; No. 292, 3/77 - No. 342, 5/82 - No. 344, 6/84

Four Color 193 (#1)-Titled "M.G.M. Presents..."	16	48	112	210
60-Barney Bear, Benny Burro cont. from Our Gang; Droopy begins				
	9	27	63	110
61	7	21	49	90
62-70: 66-X-Mas-c	5	15	35	70
71-80: 77,90-X-Mas-c. 79-Spike & Tyke begin	5	15	35	60
81-99	4	12	30	50
100	5	15	34	55
101-120	4	12	27	42
121-140: 126-X-Mas-c	4	12	25	38
141-160	3	10	23	35
161-200	3	9	20	30
201-212(7-9/62)(Last Dell issue)	3	9	19	28
213,214-(84 pgs.)-Titled "...Funhouse"	6	18	42	70
215-240: 215-Titled "...Funhouse"	2	6	15	22
241-270	2	6	11	16
271-300: 286- "Tom & Jerry"	1	4	7	10
301-327 (Gold Key)	1	3	5	7
328,329 (Whitman)	1	3	6	9

330(8/80),331(10/80), 332-(3-pack?)	2	6	11	15
333-341: 339(3/82), 340(2-3/82), 341(4/82)	1	3	6	9
342-344 (All #90058, no date, date code, 3-pack): 342(6/83), 343(8/83),				
344(6/84)	2	6	9	12
Mouse From T.R.A.P. 1(7/66)-Giant, G. K.	4	12	30	50
Summer Fun 1(7/67, 68 pgs.)(Gold Key)-Reprints Barks' Droopy from				
Summer Fun #1	4	12	30	50

NOTE: *#60-87, 98-121, 268, 277, 289, 302 are 52 pgs.. Reprints#225, 241, 245, 247, 252, 254, 266, 268, 270, 292-327, 329-342, 344.*

TOM & JERRY
Harvey Comics: Sept, 1991 - No. 4, 1992 ($1.25)

1-4: 1-Tom & Jerry, Barney Bear by Carl Barks				3.00
50th Anniversary Special 1 (10/91, $2.50, 68 pgs.)-Benny the Lonesome				
Burro-r by Barks (story/a)/Our Gang #9				4.00

TOMB OF DARKNESS (Formerly Beware)
Marvel Comics Group: No. 9, July, 1974 - No. 23, Nov, 1976

9	2	6	15	22
10-23: 11,16,18-21-Kirby-a. 15,19-Ditko-r. 17-Woodbridge-r/Astonishing #62; Powell-r. 20-Everett Venus-r/Venus #19. 22-r/Tales To Astonish #27; 1st Hank Pym. 23-Everett-r				
	2	6	9	12
20,21-(30¢-c variants, limited distribution)(5,7/76) 2	6	12	18

TOMB OF DRACULA (See Giant-Size Dracula, Dracula Lives, Nightstalkers, Power Record Comics & Requiem for Dracula)
Marvel Comics Group: Apr, 1972 - No. 70, Aug, 1979

1-1st app. Dracula & Frank Drake; Colan-p in all; Neal Adams-c				
	12	36	84	140
2	5	15	38	60
3-6: 3-Intro. Dr. Rachel Van Helsing & Inspector Chelm. 6-Neal Adams-c				
	4	12	29	45
7-9	3	10	23	35
10-1st app. Blade the Vampire Slayer	5	15	38	60
11,12,14-20: 12-Brunner-c(p)	2	6	15	22
13-Origin Blade	3	10	23	35
21-24,26-40	2	6	11	15
25-1st app. & origin Hannibal King	2	6	12	18
41,42,48,49,51-60	1	4	7	10
43-47-(Regular 25¢ editions)(4-8/76)	1	4	7	10
43-47-(30¢-c variants, limited distribution)	1	4	11	15
50-Silver Surfer app.	2	6	11	16
57-60-(35¢-c variants, limited distribution)(6-9/77)	1	4	11	15
61-69	1	4	7	10
70-Double size	2	6	11	15

NOTE: *N. Adams* c-1, 6. *Colan* a-1-70p; c(p)-8, 38-42, 44-56, 58-70. *Wrightson* c-43.

TOMB OF DRACULA, THE (Magazine)
Marvel Comics Group: Oct, 1979 - No. 6, Aug, 1980 (B&W)

1,3: 1-Colan-a; features on movies "Dracula" and "Love at First Bite" w/photos.				
3-Good girl cover-a; Miller-a (2 pg. sketch)	1	3	5	7
2,6: 2-Ditko-a (36 pgs.). Nosferatu movie feature. 6-Lilith story w/Sienkiewicz-a				
				5.00
4,5: Stephen King interview	1	3	6	9

NOTE: *Buscema* a-19. 5p. *Chaykin* c-5. 6. *Colan* a(p)-1, 3-6. *Miller* a-3. *Romita* a-2p.

TOMB OF DRACULA
Marvel Comics (Epic Comics): 1991 - No. 4, 1992 ($4.95, 52 pgs., square-bound, mini-series)

Book 1-4: Colan/Williamson-a; Colan painted-c				5.00

TOMB OF LEGEIA (See Movie Classics)

TOMB OF TERROR (Thrills of Tomorrow #17 on)
Harvey Publications: June, 1952 - No. 16, July, 1954

1	41	123	246	425
2	25	75	130	225
3-Bondage-c; atomic disaster story	26	78	136	235
4-12: 4-Heart ripped out. 8-12-Nostrand-a	24	72	127	215
13,14-Special S/F issues. 14-Check-a	33	99	174	300
15-S/F issue; c-shows face exploding	47	141	286	500
16-Special S/F issue; Nostrand-a	30	90	159	275

NOTE: *Edd Cartier* a-13? *Elias* c-2, 5-16. *Kremer* a-1, 7; c-1. *Nostrand* a-8-12, 15r 16. *Palais* a-2, 3, 5-7. *Powell* a-1, 3, 5, 9-16. *Sparling* a-12, 13, 15.

Tomb Raider/ Witchblade Revisited © Eidos / TCOW

Tom Mix Western #49 © FAW

Tom Strong #12 © ABC

BLIND DATE WITH DEATH!

	GD2.0	FN6.0	VF8.0	NM9.4

TOMB RAIDER: JOURNEYS
Image Comics (Top Cow Prod.): Jan, 2002 - Present ($2.50)

1-Fiona Avery-s/Drew Johnson-a; 2 covers by Johnson & Hughes				3.00

TOMB RAIDER: THE SERIES (Also see Witchblade/Tomb Raider)
Image Comics (Top Cow Prod.): Dec, 1999 - Present ($2.50)

1-Jurgens-s/Park-a; 3 covers by Park, Finch, Turner				4.00
2-19				3.00
#0 (6/01, $2.50) Avery-s/Ching-a/c				2.50
#1/2 (10/01, $2.95) Early days of Lara Croft; Jurgens-s/Lopez-a				3.00
...Gallery (12/00, $2.95) Pin-ups & previous covers by various				3.00
...Magazine (6/01, $4.95) Hughes-c; r/#1; Jurgens interview				5.00
...: Mystic Artifacts (2001, $14.95, TPB) r/#5-10				15.00
...: Saga of the Medusa Mask (9/00, $9.95, TPB) r/#1-4; new Park-c				10.00

TOMB RAIDER/WITCHBLADE SPECIAL (Also see Witchblade/Tomb Raider)
Top Cow Prod.: Dec, 1997 (mail-in offer, one-shot)

1-Turner-s/a(p); green background cover	1	4	7	10
1-Variant-c with orange sun background	1	4	7	10
1-Variant-c with black sides	1	4	7	10
1-Revisited (12/98, $2.95) reprints #1, Turner-c				3.00

TOMBSTONE TERRITORY (See Four Color #1123)

TOM CAT (Formerly Bo; Atom The Cat #9 on)
Charlton Comics: No. 4, Apr, 1956 - No. 8, July, 1957

4-Al Fago-c/a	8	24	42	60
5-8	6	18	29	40

TOM CORBETT, SPACE CADET (TV)
Dell Publishing Co.: No. 378, Jan-Feb, 1952 - No. 11, Sept-Nov, 1954
(All painted covers)

Four Color 378 (#1)-McWilliams-a	17	50	119	225
Four Color 400,421-McWilliams-a	10	30	70	125
4(11-1/53) - 11	7	21	49	90

TOM CORBETT SPACE CADET (See March of Comics #102)

TOM CORBETT SPACE CADET (TV)
Prize Publications: V2#1, May-June, 1955 - V2#3, Sept-Oct, 1955

V2#1-Robot-c	33	99	174	300
2,3-Meskin-c	26	78	139	240

TOM, DICK & HARRIET (See Gold Key Spotlight)

TOM LANDRY AND THE DALLAS COWBOYS
Spire Christian Comics/Fleming H. Revell Co.: 1973 (35/49¢)

nn-35¢ edition	2	6	11	15
nn-49¢ edition	1	4	7	10

TOM MIX WESTERN (Movie, radio star) (Also see The Comics, Crackajack
Funnies, Master Comics, 100 Pages Of Comics, Popular Comics, Real
Western Hero, Six Gun Heroes, Western Hero & XMas Comics)
Fawcett Publications: Jan, 1948 - No. 61, May, 1953 (1-17: 52 pgs.)

1 (Photo-c, 52 pgs.)-Tom Mix & his horse Tony begin; Tumbleweed Jr. begins, ends #52,54,55	100	300	625	1100
2 (Photo-c)	43	129	257	450
3-5 (Painted/photo-c): 5-Billy the Kid & Oscar app.	35	105	185	320
6-8: 6,7 (Painted/photo-c). 8-Kinstler tempera-c	30	90	159	275
9,10 (Painted/photo-c)-Used in SOTI, pgs. 323-325	29	87	153	265
11-Kinstler oil-c	25	75	130	225
12 (Painted/photo-c)	22	66	116	195
13-17 (Painted-c, 52 pgs.)	22	66	116	195
18,22 (Painted-c, 36 pgs.)	19	57	99	165
19 (Photo-c, 52 pgs.)	20	60	105	175
20,21,23 (Painted-c, 52 pgs.)	19	57	99	165
24,25,27-29 (52 pgs.): 24-Photo-c begin, end #61. 29-Slim Pickens app.				
	15	45	77	135
26,30 (36 pgs.)	14	42	72	125
31-33,35-37,39,40,42 (52 pgs.): 39-Red Eagle app.	14	42	72	120
34,38 (36 pgs. begin)	12	36	61	105
41,43-60: 57-(9/52)-Dope smuggling story	10	30	55	90
61-Last issue	11	33	55	95

NOTE: Photo-c from 1930s Tom Mix movies (he died in 1940). Many issues contain ads for Tom
Mix, Rocky Lane, Space Patrol and other premiums. Captain Tootsie by C.C. Beck in #6-11, 20.

TOM MIX WESTERN
AC Comics: 1988 - No. 2, 1989? ($2.95, B&W w/16 pgs. color, 44 pgs.)

1-Tom Mix-r/Master #124,128,131,102 plus Billy the Kid-r by Severin; photo front/back/inside-c				3.50
2-($2.50, B&W)-Gabby Hayes-r; photo covers				3.00
...Holiday Album 1 (1990, $3.50, B&W, one-shot, 44 pgs.)-Contains photos & 1950s Tom Mix-r; photo inside-c				4.00

TOMMY OF THE BIG TOP (Thrilling Circus Adventures)
King Features Synd./Standard Comics: No. 10, Sep, 1948 - No. 12, Mar, 1949

10-By John Lehti	8	24	42	60
11,12	5	15	25	35

TOMMY TOMORROW (See Action Comics #127, Real Fact #6, Showcase #41,42,44,46,47
& World's Finest #102)

TOMOE (Also see Shi: The Way Of The Warrior #6)
Crusade Comics: July, 1995 - No. 3, June, 1996($2.95)

0-3: 2-B&W Dogs o' War preview. 3-B&W Demon Gun preview				3.00
0 (3/96, $2.95)-variant-c.				3.00
0-Commemorative edition (5,000)	2	6	9	12
1-Commemorative edition (5,000)	2	6	11	15
1-($2.95)-FAN Appreciation edition				3.00
TPB (1997, $14.95) r/#0-3				15.00

TOMOE: UNFORGETTABLE FIRE
Crusade Comics: June, 1997 ($2.95, one-shot)

1-Prequel to Shi: The Series				3.00

TOMOE-WITCHBLADE/FIRE SERMON
Crusade Comics: Sept, 1996 ($3.95, one-shot)

1-Tucci-c				5.00
1-($9.95)-Avalon Ed. w/gold foil-c				10.00

TOMOE-WITCHBLADE/MANGA SHI PREVIEW EDITION
Crusade Comics: July, 1996 ($5.00, B&W)

nn-San Diego Preview Edition				5.00

TOMORROW KNIGHTS
Marvel Comics (Epic Comics): June, 1990 - No. 6, Mar, 1991 ($1.50)

1-6: 1-($1.95, 52 pgs.)				2.25

TOMORROW STORIES
America's Best Comics: Oct, 1999 - Present ($3.50/$2.95)

1-Two covers by Ross and Nowlan; Moore-s				3.50
2-11-($2.95)				3.00
Book 1 Hardcover (2002, $24.95) r/#1-6				25.00

TOM SAWYER (See Adventures of... & Famous Stories)

TOM SKINNER-UP FROM HARLEM (See Up From Harlem)

TOM STRONG
America's Best Comics: June, 1999 - Present ($3.50/$2.95)

1-Two covers by Ross and Sprouse; Moore-s/Sprouse-a				4.00
2-15-($2.95): 4-Art Adams-a (8 pgs.) 13-Fawcett homage w/art by Sprouse, Baker, Heath				3.00
...: Book One ('01, $14.95, TPB) r/#1-7, cover gallery and sketchbook				15.00

TOM STRONG'S TERRIFIC TALES
America's Best Comics: Jan, 2002 - Present ($3.50)

1-Short stories; Moore-s; art by Adams, Rivoche, Hernandez, Weiss				3.50

TOM TERRIFIC! (TV)(See Mighty Mouse Fun Club Magazine #1)
Pines Comics (Paul Terry): Summer, 1957 - No. 6, Fall, 1958
(See Terry Toons Giant Summer Fun Book)

1-1st app.?; CBS Television Presents...	23	69	121	210
2-6-(scarce)	17	51	88	150

TOM THUMB
Dell Publishing Co.: No. 972, Jan, 1959

Four Color 972-Movie, George Pal	9	27	63	120

TOM-TOM, THE JUNGLE BOY (See A-1 Comics & Tick Tock Tales)
Magazine Enterprises: 1947 - No. 3, 1947; Nov, 1957 - No. 3, Mar, 1958

1-Funny animal	11	33	55	90

Top Cat #21 © H-B

Top Comics #1-Zorro © WDC

Topix V8 #11 © CG

	GD2.0	FN6.0	VF8.0	NM9.4
2,3(1947): 3-Christmas issue	8	24	42	60
Tom-Tom & Itchi the Monk 1(11/57) - 3(3/58)	2	6	15	22
I.W. Reprint No. 1,2,8,10: 1,2,8-r/Koko & Kola #?	2	6	9	12

TONGUE LASH
Dark Horse Comics: Aug, 1996 - No. 2, Sept, 1996 ($2.95, lim. series, mature)

1,2: Taylor-c/a				3.00

TONGUE LASH II
Dark Horse Comics: Feb, 1999 - No. 2, Mar, 1999 ($2.95, lim. series, mature)

1,2: Taylor-c/a				3.00

TONKA (Disney)
Dell Publishing Co.: No. 966, Jan, 1959

Four Color 966-Movie (Starring Sal Mineo)-photo-c	8	24	56	100

TONTO (See The Lone Ranger's Companion...)

TONY TRENT (The Face #1,2)
Big Shot/Columbia Comics Group: No. 3, 1948 - No. 4, 1949

3,4: 3-The Face app. by Mart Bailey	19	57	99	165

TOODLES, THE (The Toodle Twins with #1)
Ziff-Davis (Approved Comics)/Argo: No. 10, July-Aug, 1951; Mar, 1956 (Newspaper-r)

10-Painted-c, new newspaper-r by The Baers	11	33	55	90
...Twins 1(Argo, 3/56)-Reprints by The Baers	8	24	42	60

TOO MUCH COFFEE MAN
Adhesive Comics: July, 1993 - No. 10, Dec, 2000 ($2.50, B&W)

1-Shannon Wheeler story & art	2	6	11	15
2,3	1	3	6	9
4,5				6.00
6-10				3.00
Full Color Special-nn($2.95),2-(7/97, $3.95)				4.00

TOO MUCH COFFEE MAN SPECIAL
Dark Horse Comics: July, 1997 ($2.95, B&W)

nn-Reprints Dark Horse Presents #92-95				3.00

TOOTH AND CLAW
Image Comics: Aug, 1999 - No. 3, Oct, 1999 ($2.95, limited series)

1-3-Mark Pacella-s/a				3.00

TOOTS & CASPER
Dell Publishing Co.: No. 5, 1942

Large Feature Comic 5	12	36	84	160

TOP ADVENTURE COMICS
I. W. Enterprises: 1964 (Reprints)

1-r/High Adv. (Explorer Joe #2); Krigstein-r	2	6	13	20
2-Black Dwarf-r/Red Seal #22; Kinstler-c	2	6	15	22

TOP CAT (TV) (Hanna-Barbera)(See Kite Fun Book)
Dell Publishing Co./Gold Key No. 4 on: 12-2/61-62 - No. 3, 6-8/62; No. 4, 10/62 - No. 31, 9/70

1 (TV show debuted 9/27/61)	16	48	112	200
2-Augie Doggie back-ups in #1-4	8	24	56	100
3-5: 5-Last 15¢ issue. 4-Begin 12¢ issues; Yakky Doodle app. in 1 pg. strip. 5-Touché Turtle app.	6	18	42	80
6-10	5	15	34	55
11-20	4	12	27	42
21-31-Reprints	3	9	20	30

TOP CAT (TV) (Hanna-Barbera)(See TV Stars #4)
Charlton Comics: Nov, 1970 - No. 20, Nov, 1973

1	6	18	40	65
2-10	3	9	21	32
11-20	3	9	17	25

NOTE: #8 (1/72) went on sale late in 1972 between #14 and #15 with the 1/73 issues.

TOP COMICS
K. K. Publications/Gold Key: July, 1967 (All reprints)

nn-The Gnome-Mobile (Disney-movie)	2	6	11	15
1-Beagle Boys (#7), Beep Beep the Road Runner (#5), Bugs Bunny, Chip 'n' Dale, Daffy Duck (#50), Flipper, Huey, Dewey & Louie, Gnome-Mobile, Junior				

Woodchucks, Lassie, The Little Monsters (#71), Moby Duck, Porky Pig (has Gold Key label - says Top Comics on inside), Scamp, Super Goof, Tom & Jerry, Top Cat (#21), Tweety & Sylvester (#7), Walt Disney C&S (#322), Woody Woodpecker known issues; each character given own book

	2	6	9	12
1-Donald Duck (not Barks), Mickey Mouse	2	6	12	18
1-Flintstones	3	10	23	35
1-Huckleberry Hound, Three Stooges (#35), Yogi Bear (#30)				
	2	6	13	20
1-The Jetsons	4	12	30	50
1-Tarzan of the Apes (#169)	2	6	15	22
1-Uncle Scrooge (#70)	3	9	17	25
1-Zorro (r/G.K. Zorro #7 w/Toth-a; says 2nd printing)	2	6	13	20
2-Bugs Bunny, Daffy Duck, Mickey Mouse (#114), Porky Pig, Super Goof, Tom & Jerry, Tweety & Sylvester, Walt Disney's C&S (r/#325), Woody Woodpecker	2	6	9	12
2-Donald Duck (not Barks), Three Stooges, Uncle Scrooge (#71)-Barks-c, Yogi Bear (#30), Zorro (r/#8; Toth-a)	2	6	11	16
2-Snow White & 7 Dwarfs(6/67)(1944-r)	2	6	10	14
2-Donald Duck	2	6	11	16
3-Uncle Scrooge (#72)	2	6	12	18
3,4-The Flintstones	3	10	23	35
3,4: 3-Mickey Mouse (r/#115), Tom & Jerry, Woody Woodpecker, Yogi Bear. 4-Mickey Mouse, Woody Woodpecker	2	6	9	12

NOTE: Each book in this series is identical to its counterpart except for cover, and came out at same time. The number in parentheses is the original issue it contains.

TOP COW CLASSICS IN BLACK AND WHITE
Image Comics (Top Cow): Feb, 2000 - Present ($2.95, B&W reprints)

...: Aphrodite IX #1(9/00) B&W reprint				3.00
...: Ascension #1(4/00) B&W reprint plus time-line of series				3.00
...: Darkness #1(3/00) B&W reprint plus time-line of series				3.00
...: Fathom #1(5/00) B&W reprint				3.00
...: Midnight Nation #1(9/00) B&W preview				3.00
...: Rising Stars #1(7/00) B&W reprint plus cover gallery				3.00
...: Tomb Raider #1(12/00) B&W reprint plus back-story				3.00
...: Witchblade #1(2/00) B&W reprint plus back-story				3.00
...: Witchblade #25(5/01) B&W reprint plus interview with Wohl & Haberlin				3.00

TOP COW PRODUCTIONS, INC./BALLISTIC STUDIOS SWIMSUIT SPECIAL
Image Comics (Top Cow Productions): May, 1995 ($2.95, one-shot)

1				4.00

TOP COW SECRETS:SPECIAL WINTER LINGERIE EDITION
Image Comics (Top Cow Productions): Jan, 1996 ($2.95, one-shot)

1-Pin-ups				3.00

TOP COW 2001 PREVIEW
Image Comics (Top Cow Productions): 2001 (no cover price, one-shot)

1-Preview pages of Tomb Raider; Jusko-a; flip cover & pages of Inferno				2.00

TOP DETECTIVE COMICS
I. W. Enterprises: 1964 (Reprints)

9-r/Young King Cole #14; Dr. Drew (not Grandenetti)	2	6	11	16

TOP DOG (See Star Comics Magazine, 75¢)
Star Comics (Marvel): Apr, 1985 - No. 14, June, 1987 (Children's book)

1-14: 10-Peter Parker & J. Jonah Jameson cameo				4.00

TOP ELIMINATOR (Teenage Hotrodders #1-24; Drag 'n' Wheels #30 on)
Charlton Comics: No. 25, Sept, 1967 - No. 29, July, 1968

25-29	2	6	13	20

TOP FLIGHT COMICS: Four Star Publ.: 1947 (Advertised, not published)

TOP FLIGHT COMICS
St. John Publishing Co.: July, 1949

1(7/49, St. John)-Hector the Inspector; funny animal	9	27	49	70

TOP GUN (See Luke Short, 4-Color #927 & Showcase #72)

TOP GUNS OF THE WEST (See Super DC Giant)

TOPIX (...Comics) (Timeless Topix-early issues) (Also see Men of Battle, Men of Courage & Treasure Chest)(V1-V5#1,V7#1-20-paper-c)
Catechetical Guild Educational Society: 11/42 - V10#15, 1/28/52

806

Top Love Stories #7 © STAR

Top-Notch Comics #12 © AP

Top Ten #9 © ABC

	GD2.0	FN6.0	VF8.0	NM9.4

(Weekly - later issues)

	GD2.0	FN6.0	VF8.0	NM9.4
V1#1(8 pgs.,8x11")	25	75	130	225
2,3(8 pgs.,8x11")	14	42	72	120
4-8(16 pgs.,8x11")	11	33	55	90
V2#1-10(16 pgs.,8x11"): V2#8-Pope Pius XII	10	30	55	80
V3#1-10(16 pgs.,8x11")	10	30	55	80
V4#1-10	8	24	45	65
V5#1(10/46,52 pgs.)-9,12-15(12/47): 13-Lists V5#4	7	21	36	50
10,11-Life of Christ editions	10	30	55	80
V6#1-14	6	18	30	42
V7#1(9/1/48)-20(6/15/49), 32 pgs.	5	15	25	35
V8#1(9/19/49)-3,5-11,13-30(5/15/50)	5	15	25	35
4-Dagwood Splits the Atom(10/10/49)-Magazine format				
	7	21	36	50
12-Ingels-a	10	30	55	80
V9#1(9/25/50)-11,13-30(5/14/51)	5	15	24	32
12-Special 36 pg. Xmas issue, text illos format	5	15	25	35
V10#1(10/1/51)-15: 14-Hollingsworth-a	5	15	24	32

TOP JUNGLE COMICS
I. W. Enterprises: 1964 (Reprint)

1(nd)-Reprints White Princess of the Jungle #3, minus cover; Kintsler-a				
	3	9	19	28

TOP LOVE STORIES (Formerly Gasoline Alley #2)
Star Publications: No. 3, 5/51 - No. 19, 3/54

3(#1)	24	72	127	215
4,5,7-9: 8-Wood story	19	57	99	165
6-Wood-a	25	75	130	225
10-16,18,19-Disbrow-a	19	57	99	165
17-Wood art (Fox-r)	20	60	105	175

NOTE: All have L. B. Cole covers.

TOP-NOTCH COMICS (...Laugh #28-45; Laugh Comix #46 on)
MLJ Magazines: Dec, 1939 - No. 45, June, 1944

1-Origin/1st app. The Wizard; Kardak the Mystic Magician, Swift of the Secret Service (ends #3), Air Patrol, The Westpointer, Manhunters (by J. Cole), Mystic (ends #2) & Scott Rand (ends #3) begin; Wizard covers begin, end #8				
	577	1731	3750	7500
2-Dick Storm (ends #8), Stacy Knight M.D. (ends #4) begin; Jack Cole-a				
	236	708	1477	2600
3-Bob Phantom, Scott Rand on Mars begin; J. Cole-a				
	159	477	994	1750
4-Origin/1st app. Streak Chandler on Mars; Moore of the Mounted only app.; J. Cole-a				
	132	395	825	1450
5-Flag-c; origin/1st app. Galahad; Shanghai Sheridan begins (ends #8); Shield cameo; Novick-a; classic-c				
	150	450	938	1650
6-Meskin-a	105	315	656	1150
7-The Shield x-over in Wizard; The Wizard dons new costume				
	127	381	795	1400
8-Origin/1st app. The Firefly & Roy, the Super Boy (9/40, 2nd costumed boy hero after Robin?; also see Toro in Human Torch #1 (Fall/40)				
	150	450	938	1650
9-Origin & 1st app. The Black Hood; 1st Black Hood-c & logo (10/40); Fran Frazier begins (Scarce)				
	523	1569	3400	6800
10-2nd app. Black Hood	173	519	1080	1900
11-15	100	300	625	1100
16-20	91	273	568	1000
21-30: 23-26-Roy app. 24-No Wizard. 25-Last Bob Phantom. 27-Last Firefly. 28-Suzie, Pokey Oakey begin. 29-Last Kardak	68	205	426	750
31-44: 33-Dotty & Ditto by Woggon begins (2/43, 1st app.). 44-Black Hood series ends	40	120	232	400
45-Last issue	45	135	270	475

NOTE: J. Binder a-1-3. Meskin a-2, 3, 6, 15. Bob Montana a-30; c-28-31. Harry Sahle c-42-45. Woggon a-30-44, 42. Bondage c-17, 19. Black Hood also appeared on radio in 1944. Black Hood app. on c-9-34, 41-44. Roy the Super Boy app. on c-8, 9, 11,27. The Wizard app. on c-1-8, 11-13, 15-22, 24, 25, 27. Pokey Oakey app. on c-28-43. Suzie app. on c-44-on.

TOPPER & NEIL (TV)
Dell Publishing Co.: No. 859, Nov, 1957

Four Color 859	4	12	30	50

TOPPS COMICS: Four Star Publications: 1947 (Advertised, not published)

TOPS
July, 1949 - No. 2, Sept, 1949 (25¢, 10-1/4x13-1/4", 68 pgs.)
Tops Magazine, Inc. (Lev Gleason): (Large size-magazine format; for the adult reader)

1 (Rare)-Story by Dashiell Hammett; Crandall/Lubbers, Tuska, Dan Barry, Fuje-a; Biro painted-c	114	456	798	1250
2 (Rare)-Crandall/Lubbers, Biro, Kida, Fuje, Guardineer-a				
	105	420	735	1150

TOPS COMICS
Consolidated Book Publishers: 1944 (10¢, 132 pgs.)

2000-(Color-c, inside in red shade & some in full color)-Ace Kelly by Rick Yager, Black Orchid, Don on the Farm, Dinky Dinkerton (Rare)				
	27	81	145	250

NOTE: This book is printed in such a way that when the staple is removed, the strips on the left side of the book correspond with the same strips on the right side. Therefore, if strips are removed from the book, each strip can be folded into a complete comic section of its own.

TOPS COMICS (See Tops in Humor)
Consolidated Book (Lev Gleason): 1944 (7-1/4x5", 32 pgs.)

2001-The Jack of Spades (costumed hero)	17	51	88	150
2002-Rip Raider	10	30	55	80
2003-Red Birch (gag cartoons)	4	10	15	20

TOP SECRET
Hillman Publ.: Jan, 1952

1	21	63	110	185

TOP SECRET ADVENTURES (See Spyman)

TOP SECRETS (...of the F.B.I.)
Street & Smith Publications: Nov, 1947 - No. 10, July-Aug, 1949

1-Powell-c/a	35	105	185	320
2-Powell-c/a	26	78	136	235
3-6,8,10-Powell-a	23	69	121	205
9-Powell-c/a	24	72	127	215
7-Used in SOTI, pg. 90 & illo. "How to hurt people"; used by N.Y. Legis. Comm.; Powell-c/a	35	105	185	320

NOTE: Powell c-1-3, 5-10.

TOPS IN ADVENTURE
Ziff-Davis Publishing Co.: Fall, 1952 (25¢, 132 pgs.)

1-Crusader from Mars, The Hawk, Football Thrills, He-Man; Powell-a; painted-c	45	135	270	475

TOPS IN HUMOR (See Tops Comics?)
Consolidated Book Publ. (Lev Gleason): 1944 (7-1/4x5")

2001(#1)-Origin The Jack of Spades, Ace Kelly by Rick Yager, Black Orchid (female crime fighter) app.	17	51	88	150
2	11	33	55	90

TOP SPOT COMICS
Top Spot Publ. Co.: 1945

1-The Menace, Duke of Darkness app.	35	105	188	325

TOPSY-TURVY (Teenage)
R. B. Leffingwell Publ.: Apr, 1945

1-1st app. Cookie	11	33	55	90

TOP TEN
America's Best Comics: Sept, 1999 - No. 12, Oct, 2001 ($3.50/$2.95)

1-Two covers by Ross and Ha/Cannon; Alan Moore-s/Gene Ha-a			3.50
2-11-($2.95)			3.00
12-($3.50)			3.50
Hardcover ('00, $24.95) Dust jacket with Gene Ha-a; r/#1-7			25.00
Softcover ('00, $14.95) new Gene Ha-c; r/#1-7			15.00

TOR (Prehistoric Life on Earth) (Formerly One Million Years Ago)
St. John Publ. Co.: No. 2, Oct, 1953; No. 3, May, 1954 - No. 5, Oct, 1954

3-D 2(10/53)-Kubert-c/a	14	42	72	120
3-D 2(10/53)-Oversized, otherwise same contents	12	36	61	100
3-D 2(11/53)-Kubert-c/a; has 3-D cover	12	36	61	100
3-5-Kubert-c/a: 3-Danny Dreams by Toth; Kubert 1 pg. story (w/self portrait)				
	14	42	72	120

NOTE: The two October 3-D's have same contents and Powell art; the October & November

The Tormented #1 © Sterling Comics

Toxic Avenger #1 © Troma, Inc.

Trail Blazers #1 © Condé Nast

	GD2.0	FN6.0	VF8.0	NM9.4

	GD2.0	FN6.0	VF8.0	NM9.4

issues are titled 3-D Comics. All 3-D issues are 25¢ and came with 3-D glasses.

TOR (See Sojourn)
National Periodical Publications: May-June, 1975 - No. 6, Mar-Apr, 1976

1-New origin by Kubert	1	4	7	10
2-6: 2-Origin-r/St. John #1				6.00

NOTE: **Kubert** a-1, 2-6r; c-1-6. **Toth** a(p)-3r.

TOR (3-D)
Eclipse Comics: July, 1986 - No. 2, Aug, 1987 ($2.50)

1,2: 1-r/One Million Years Ago. 2-r/Tor 3-D #2		5.00
...2-D: 1,2-Limited signed & numbered editions		6.00

TOR
Marvel Comics (Epic Comics/Heavy Hitters): June, 1993 - No. 4, 1993 ($5.95, limited series)

1-4: Joe Kubert c/a/scripts	6.00

TORCH OF LIBERTY SPECIAL
Dark Horse Comics (Legend): Jan, 1995 ($2.50, one-shot)

1-Byrne scripts	2.50

TORCHY (...Blonde Bombshell) (See Dollman, Military, & Modern)
Quality Comics Group: Nov, 1949 - No. 6, Sept, 1950

1-Bill Ward-c, Gil Fox-a	150	450	938	1650
2,3-Fox-c/a	64	192	398	700
4-Fox-c/a(3), Ward-a (9 pgs.)	80	240	500	875
5,6-Ward-c/a, 9 pgs; Fox-a(3) each	100	300	625	1100
Super Reprint #16(1964)-r/#4 with new-c	9	27	63	105

TO RIVERDALE AND BACK AGAIN (Archie Comics Presents...)
Archie Comics: 1990 ($2.50, 68 pgs.)

nn-Byrne-c, Colan-a(p); adapts NBC TV movie	4.00

TORMENTED, THE (Becomes Surprise Adventures #3 on)
Sterling Comics: July, 1954 - No. 2, Sept, 1954

1,2: Weird/horror stories	25	75	130	225

TORNADO TOM (See Mighty Midget Comics)

TORSO (See Jinx: Torso)

TOTAL ECLIPSE
Eclipse Comics: May, 1988 - No. 5, Apr, 1989 ($3.95, 52 pgs., deluxe size)

Book 1-5: 3-Intro/1st app. new Black Terror	4.00

TOTAL ECLIPSE
Image Comics: July, 1998 (one-shot)

1-McFarlane-c; Eclipse Comics character pin-ups by Image artists	2.25

TOTAL ECLIPSE: THE SERAPHIM OBJECTIVE
Eclipse Comics: Nov, 1988 ($1.95, one-shot, Baxter paper)

1-Airboy, Valkyrie, The Heap app.	3.00

TOTAL JUSTICE
DC Comics: Oct, 1996 - No. 3, Nov, 1996 ($2.25, bi-weekly limited series) (Based on toyline)

1-3	2.25

TOTAL RECALL (Movie)
DC Comics: 1990 ($2.95, 68 pgs., movie adaptation)

1-Arnold Schwarzenegger photo-c	3.00

TOTAL WAR (M.A.R.S. Patrol #3 on)
Gold Key: July, 1965 - No. 2, Oct, 1965 (Painted-c)

1-Wood-a in both issues	6	18	42	75
2	5	15	35	60

TOTEMS (Vertigo V2K)
DC Comics (Vertigo): Feb, 2000 ($5.95, one-shot)

1-Swamp Thing, Animal Man, Zatanna, Shade app.; Fegredo-c	6.00

TO THE HEART OF THE STORM
Kitchen Sink Press: 1991 (B&W, graphic novel)

Softcover-Will Eisner-s/a/c	15.00
Hardcover ($24.95)	25.00
TPB-(DC Comics, 9/00, $14.95) reprints 1991 edition	15.00

TO THE LAST MAN (See Zane Grey Four Color #616)

TOUCH OF SILVER, A
Image Comics: Jan, 1997 - No. 6, Nov, 1997 ($2.95, B&W, bi-monthly)

1-6-Valentino-s/a; photo-c: 5-color pgs. w/Round Table	3.00
TPB ($12.95) r/#1-6	13.00

TOUGH KID SQUAD COMICS
Timely Comics (TCI): Mar, 1942

1-(Scarce)-Origin & 1st app.The Human Top & The Tough Kid Squad; The Flying Flame app.	923	2769	6000	12,000

TOWER OF SHADOWS (Creatures on the Loose #10 on)
Marvel Comics Group: Sept, 1969 - No. 9, Jan, 1971

1-Steranko, Craig-a(p)	6	18	40	65
2,3: 2-Neal Adams-c. 3-Barry Smith, Tuska-a	3	10	23	35
4,6: 4-Marie Severin-c. 6-Wood-a	3	9	17	25
5-B. Smith-a(p), Wood-a; Wood draws himself (1st pg., 1st panel)	3	9	19	28
7-9: 7-B. Smith-a(p), Wood-a. 8-Wood-a; Wrightson-a. 9-Wrightson-c; Roy Thomas app.	3	9	19	28
Special 1(12/71, 52 pgs.)-Neal Adams-a	3	9	19	28

NOTE: **J. Buscema** a-1p, 2p, Special 1r. **Colan** a-3p, 6p, Special 1. **J. Craig** a(r)-1p. **Ditko** a-6, 8, 9r, Special 1. **Everett** a-9(i)r; c-5i. **Kirby** a-9(p)r. **Severin** c-5p, 6. **Steranko** a-1p. **Tuska** a-3. **Wood** a-5-8. Issues 1-9 contain new stories with some pre-Marvel age reprints in 6-9. H. P. Lovecraft adaptation-9.

TOWN & COUNTRY
Publisher?: May, 1940

nn-Origin The Falcon	45	135	270	475

TOXIC AVENGER (Movie)
Marvel Comics: Apr, 1991 - No. 11, Feb, 1992 ($1.50)

1-11: Based on movie character. 3,10-Photo-c	2.25

TOXIC CRUSADERS (TV)
Marvel Comics: May, 1992 - No. 8, Dec, 1992 ($1.25)

1-8: 1-3,8-Sam Kieth-c; based on USA network cartoon	2.25

TOXIC GUMBO
DC Comics (Vertigo): 1998 ($5.95, one-shot, mature)

1-McKeever-a/Lydia Lunch-s	6.00

TOYBOY
Continuity Comics: Oct, 1986 - No. 7, Mar, 1989 ($2.00, Baxter paper)

1-7	3.00

NOTE: **N. Adams** a-1; c-1, 2,5. **Golden** a-7p; c-6,7. **Nebres** a(i)-1,2.

TOYLAND COMICS
Fiction House Magazines: Jan, 1947 - No. 2, Mar, 1947; No. 3, July, 1947

1-Wizard of the Moon begins	30	90	162	280
2,3-Bob Lubbers-c. 3-Tuska-a	17	51	88	150

NOTE: All above contain strips by Al Walker.

TOY TOWN COMICS
Toytown/Orbit Publ./B. Antin/Swapper Quarterly: 1945 - No. 7, May, 1947

1-Mertie Mouse; L. B. Cole-c/a; funny animal	40	120	217	375
2-L. B. Cole-a	24	72	127	220
3-7-L. B. Cole-a. 5-Wiggles the Wonderworm-c	20	60	105	180

TRAGG AND THE SKY GODS (See Gold Key Spotlight, Mystery Comics Digest #3,9 & Spine Tingling Tales)
Gold Key/Whitman No. 9: June, 1975 - No. 8, Feb, 1977; No. 9, May, 1982 (Painted-c #3-8)

1-Origin	2	6	9	12
2-8: 4-Sabre-Fang app. 8-Ostellon app.	1	3	5	7
9-(Whitman, 5/82) r/#1	1	3	5	7

NOTE: **Santos** a-1, 2, 9r; c-3-7. **Spiegel** a-3-8.

TRAIL BLAZERS (Red Dragon #5 on)
Street & Smith Publications: 1941; No. 2, Apr, 1942 - No. 4, Oct, 1942 (True stories of American heroes)

1-Life story of Jack Dempsey & Wright Brothers	35	105	185	320
2-Brooklyn Dodgers-c/story; Ben Franklin story	23	69	121	205
3,4: 3-Fred Allen, Red Barber, Yankees stories	21	63	110	185

	GD2.0	FN6.0	VF8.0	NM9.4

TRAIL COLT (Also see Extra Comics & Manhunt!)
Magazine Enterprises: 1949 - No. 2, 1949

nn(A-1 #24)-7 pg. Frazetta-a r-in Manhunt #13; Undercover Girl app.; The Red Fox by L. B. Cole; Ingels-c (Scarce)

	40	120	220	380

2(A-1 #26)-Undercover Girl; Ingels-c (6 pgs.)

	34	102	179	310

TRANSFORMERS, THE (TV)(See G.I. Joe and...)
Marvel Comics Group: Sept, 1984 - No. 80, July, 1991 (75¢/$1.00)

1-Based on Hasbro Toys	2	6	10	14
2-5	1	3	6	9
6-10				6.00
11-49: 21-Intro Aerialbots				4.00
50-60: 54-Intro Micromasters				5.00
61-70	1	3	5	7
71-77: 75-($1.50, 52 pgs.) (Low print run)	2	6	9	12
78,79 (Low print run)	2	6	12	18
80-Last issue	3	9	17	24

NOTE: Second and third printings of all issues exist and are worth less than originals. Was originally planned as a four issue mini-series. **Wrightson** a-64i(4 pgs.).

TRANSFORMERS DIGEST
Marvel Comics: Jan, 1987 - No. 9, May, 1988

1,2-Spider-Man-c/s	2	6	10	14
3-9	1	4	7	10

TRANSFORMERS: GENERATION 2
Marvel Comics: Nov, 1993 - No. 12, Oct, 1994 ($1.75)

1-($2.95, 68 pgs.)-Collector's ed. w/bi-fold metallic-c	1	3	5	7
1-11: 1-Newsstand edition (68 pgs.)				5.00
12-($2.25, 52 pgs.)	1	3	5	7

TRANSMETROPOLITAN
DC Comics (Vertigo): Sept, 1997 - Present ($2.50)

1-Warren Ellis-s/Darick Robertson-a(p)	2	6	9	12
2,3	1	3	5	7
4-8				4.00
9-52: 15-Jae Lee-c. 25-27-Jim Lee-c. 37-39-Bradstreet-c				2.50
Back on the Street ('97, $7.95) r/#1-3				8.00
Filth of the City ('01, $5.95) Spider's columns with pin-up art by various				6.00
I Hate It Here ('00, $5.95) Spider's columns with pin-up art by various				6.00
Lonely City ('01, $14.95) r/#25-30; intro. by Patrick Stewart				15.00
Lust For Life ('98, $14.95) r/#4-12				15.00
The New Scum ('00, $12.95) r/#19-24 & Vertigo: Winter's Edge #3				13.00
Year of the Bastard ('99, $12.95) r/#13-18				13.00

TRANSMUTATION OF IKE GARUDA, THE
Marvel Comics (Epic Comics): July, 1991 - No. 2, 1991 ($3.95, 52 pgs.)

1,2				4.00

TRAPMAN
Phantom Comics: June, 1994 - No. 2, 1994? ($2.95, quarterly, unfinished limited series)

1,2				3.00

TRAPPED!
Periodical House Magazines (Ace): Oct, 1954 - No. 4, April, 1955

1 (All reprints)	10	30	55	80
2-4: 4-r/Men Against Crime #4 in its entirety	7	21	36	50

NOTE: **Colan** a-1, 4. **Sekowsky** a-1.

TRASH
Trash Publ. Co.: Mar, 1978 - No. 4, Oct, 1978 (B&W, magazine, 52 pgs.)

1,2: 1-Star Wars parody. 2-UFO-c	2	6	10	14
3-Parodies of KISS, the Beatles, and monsters	2	6	13	20
4-(84 pgs.)-Parodies of Happy Days, Rocky movies	3	9	17	24

TRAVELS OF JAIMIE McPHEETERS, THE (TV)
Gold Key: Dec, 1963

1-Kurt Russell photo on-c plus photo back-c	4	12	25	38

TREASURE CHEST (Catholic Guild; also see Topix)
George A. Pflaum: 3/12/46 - V27#8, July, 1972 (Educational comics)
(Not published during Summer)

V1#1	26	78	136	235
2-6 (5/21/46): 5-Dr. Styx app. by Baily	12	36	61	100
V2#1-20 (9/3/46-5/27/47)	10	30	55	80
V3#1-5,7-20 (1st slick cover)	9	27	49	70
V3#6-Jules Verne's "Voyage to the Moon"	11	33	55	90
V4#1-20 (9/9/48-5/31/49)	8	24	42	60
V5#1-20 (9/6/49-5/31/50)	7	21	38	55
V6#1-20 (9/14/50-5/31/51)	7	21	38	55
V7#1-20 (9/13/51-6/5/52)	6	18	32	45
V8#1-20 (9/11/52-6/4/53)	6	18	29	40
V9#1-20 ('53-'54), V10#1-20 ('54-'55)	5	15	25	35
V11('55-'56), V12('56-'57)	5	15	24	32
V13#1,3-5,7,9-V17#1 ('57-'63)	5	15	23	30
V13#2,6,8-Ingels-a	6	18	45	75
V17#2- "This Godless Communism" series begins(not in odd #'d issues); cover shows hammer & sickle over Statue of Liberty; 8 pg. Crandall-a of family life under communism	18	54	126	225
V17#3,5,7,9,11,13,15,17,19	2	6	15	22
V17#4,6,14- "This Godless Communism" stories	12	36	88	150
V17#8-Shows red octopus encompassing Earth, firing squad; 8 pgs. Crandall-a	15	45	107	185
V17#10- "This Godless Communism" - how Stalin came to power, part I; Crandall-a	14	42	102	175
V17#12-Stalin in WWII, forced labor, death by exhaustion; Crandall-a	14	42	102	175
V17#16-Kruschev takes over; de-Stalinization	14	42	102	175
V17#18-Kruschev's control; murder of revolters, brainwash, space race by Crandall	14	42	102	175
V17#20-End of series; Kruschev-people are puppets, firing squads hammer & sickle over Statue of Liberty, snake around communist manifesto by Crandall	16	48	112	200
V18#1,19#11-20, V20#1-20(1964-65): V18#11-Crandall draws himself & 13 other artists on cover	2	6	13	20
V18#5- "What About Red China?" - describes how communists took over China	4	15	45	75
V19#1-10- "Red Victim" anti-communist series in all V24#8's 5/11/68 & 11/21/68) (no V24#6)	6	18	45	75
V26, V27#1-8 (V26,27-68 pgs.)	2	6	12	18
Summer Edition V1#1-6('66)(exist?), V2#1-6('67)	2	6	13	20
	2	6	15	22

NOTE: **Anderson** a-V18#13. **Borth** a-V7#10-19 (serial), V8#6-17 (serial), V9#1-10 (serial), V13#2, 6, 11, V14-V25 (except V22#1-3, 11-13), Summer Ed. V1#3-6. **Crandall** a-V16#7, 9, 12, 14, 16-18, 20; V17#1, 2, 4-6, 10, 12, 14-18; V18#1, 2, 3(2 pg.), 7-9 (serial), V19#4, 11-15, 16, 19, 20; V20#1, 2, 4, 6, 8-10, 12, 14-16, 18, 20; V21#1-5, 8-11, 13, 16-18; V22#3, 7, 9-11, 14; V23#3, 6, 9, 16, 18; V24#7, 8, 10, 13, 16; V25#8, 16; V27#1-7r, 8r(2 pg.), Summer Ed. V1#3-6. **Evans** a-V18#5; c-V16#7, V18#2(part), 7, 11, V19#4, 19, 20, V20#15, V21#5, 7, 9, 11, V23#9, 16; V24#13, 16, V25#8, Summer Ed. V1#2 (back c-V1#2-5). **Powell** a-V10#11. V19#11, 15, V10#13, V13#6, 8 all have wraparound covers.

TREASURE CHEST OF THE WORLD'S BEST COMICS
Superior, Toronto, Canada: 1945 (500 pgs., hard-c)

Contains Blue Beetle, Captain Combat, John Wayne, Dynamic Man, Nemo, Li'l Abner; contents can vary - represents random binding of eace books; Capt. America on-c

	86	258	540	950

TREASURE COMICS
Prize Publications? (no publisher listed): No date (1943) (50¢, 324 pgs., card-board-c)

1-(Rare)-Contains rebound Prize Comics #7-11 from 1942 (blank inside-c)

	214	642	1338	2350

TREASURE COMICS
Prize Publ. (American Boys' Comics): June-July, 1945 - No. 12, Fall, 1947

1-Paul Bunyan & Marco Polo begin; Highwayman & Carrot Topp only app.; Kiefer-a	34	102	179	310
2-Arabian Knight, Gorilla King, Dr. Styx begin	17	51	88	150
3,4,9,12: 9-Kiefer-a	13	39	66	110
5-Marco Polo-c; Krigstein-a	21	63	110	185
6,11-Krigstein-a; 11-Krigstein-c	19	57	99	165
7,8-Frazetta-a (5 pgs. each). 7-Capt. Kidd Jr. app.	39	117	208	360
10-Simon & Kirby-c/a	33	99	174	300

NOTE: **Barry** a-9-11; c-12. **Kiefer** a-3, 5, 7; c-2, 6, 7. **Roussos** a-11.

TREASURE ISLAND (See Classics Illustrated #64, Doc Savage Comics #1,

Treehouse of Horror #7 © Bongo Ent.

Trencher #2 © Keith Giffen

Trinity Angels #3 © Acclaim

	GD2.0	FN6.0	VF8.0	NM9.4

King Classics, Movie Classics & Movie Comics)
Dell Publishing Co.: No. 624, Apr, 1955 (Disney)

Four Color 624-Movie, photo-c	9	27	63	110

TREASURY OF COMICS
St. John Publishing Co.: 1947; No. 2, July, 1947 - No. 4, Sept, 1947; No. 5, Jan, 1948

nn(#1)-Abbie an' Slats (nn on-c, #1 on inside)	14	43	72	120
2-Jim Hardy Comics; featuring Windy & Paddles	11	33	55	90
3-Bill Bumlin	9	27	49	70
4-Abbie an' Slats	11	33	55	90
5-Jim Hardy Comics #1	11	33	55	90

TREASURY OF COMICS
St. John Publishing Co.: Mar, 1948 - No. 5, 1948 (Reg. size); 1948-1950 (Over 500 pgs., $1.00)

1	20	60	105	180
2(#2 on-c, #1 on inside)	11	33	55	90
3-5	10	30	55	80
1-(1948, 500 pgs., hard-c)-Abbie & Slats, Abbott & Costello, Casper, Little Annie Rooney, Little Audrey, Jim Hardy, Ella Cinders (16 books bound together) (Rare)	105	315	656	1150
1(1949, 500 pgs.)-Same format as above	100	300	625	1100
1(1950, 500 pgs.)-Same format as above; different-c; (also see Little Audrey Yearbook) (Rare)	100	300	625	1100

TREASURY OF DOGS, A (See Dell Giants)

TREASURY OF HORSES, A (See Dell Giants)

TREEHOUSE OF HORROR (Bart Simpson's…)
Bongo Comics: 1995 - Present ($2.95/$2.50/$3.50/$4.50, annual)

1-(1995, $2.95)-Groening-c; Allred, Robinson & Smith stories.		3.50
2-(1996, $2.50)-Stories by Dini & Bagge; infinity-c by Groening		3.00
3-(1997, $2.50)-Dorkin-s/Groening-c		3.00
4-(1998, $2.50)-Lash & Dixon-s/Groening-c		3.00
5-(1999, $3.50)-Thompson-s; Shaw & Aragonés-s/a; TenNapel-s/a		3.50
6-(2000, $4.50)-Mahfood-s/a; DeCarlo-a; Morse-s/a; Kuper-s/a		4.50
7-(2001, $4.50)-Hamill-s/Morrison-a; Ennis-s/McCrea-a; Sakai-s/a; Nixey-s/a; Brereton back-c		4.50

TREKKER (See Dark Horse Presents #6)
Dark Horse Comics: May, 1987 - No. 6, Mar,1988 ($1.50, B&W)

1-6: Sci/Fi stories		2.25
Color Special 1 (1989, $2.95, 52 pgs.)		3.00
Collection ($5.95, B&W)		6.00
Special 1 (6/99, $2.95, color)		3.00

TRENCHCOAT BRIGADE, THE
DC Comics (Vertigo): Mar, 1999 - No. 4, Jun, 1999 ($2.50, limited series)

1-4: Hellblazer, Phantom Stranger, Mister E, Dr. Occult app.		2.50

TRENCHER (See Blackball Comics)
Image Comics: May, 1993 - No. 4, Oct, 1993 ($1.95, unfinished limited series)

1-4: Keith Giffen-c/a/scripts. 3-Supreme-c/story		2.25

TRIBAL FORCE
Mystic Comics: Aug, 1996 ($2.50)

1-Reads "Special Edition" on-c		2.50

TRIB COMIC BOOK, THE
Winnipeg Tribune: Sept. 24, 1977 - Vol. 4, #36, 1980 (8-1/2"x11", 24 pgs., weekly) (155 total issues)

V1# 1-Color pages (Sunday strips)-Spiderman, Asterix, Disney's Scamp, Wizard of Id, Doonesbury, Inside Woody Allen, Mary Worth, & others (similar to Spirit sections)	2	6	12	17
V1#2-15, V2#1-52, V3#1-52, V4#1-33	1	4	7	10
V4#34-36 (not distributed)	2	6	13	20

Note: All issues have Spider-Man. Later issues contain Star Trek and Star Wars. 20 strips in ea. The first newspaper to put Sunday pages into a comic book format.

TRIBE (See WildC.A.T.s #4)
Image Comics/Axis Comics No. 2 on: Apr, 1993; No. 2, Sept, 1993 - No. 3, 1994 ($2.50/$1.95)

1-By Johnson & Stroman; gold foil & embossed on black-c		2.50

1-($2.50)-Ivory Edition; gold foil & embossed on white-c; available only through the creators		2.50
2,3: 2-1st Axis Comics issue. 3-Savage Dragon app.		2.25

TRIBUTE TO STEVEN HUGHES, A
Chaos! Comics: Sept, 2000 ($6.95)

1-Lady Death & Evil Ernie pin-ups by various artists; testimonials		7.00

TRIGGER (See Roy Rogers'…)

TRIGGER TWINS
National Periodical Publications: Mar-Apr, 1973 (20¢, one-shot)

1-Trigger Twins & Pow Wow Smith-r/All-Star Western #94,103 & Western Comics #81; Infantino-r(p)	2	6	15	22

TRINITY (See DC Universe: Trinity)

TRINITY ANGELS
Acclaim Comics (Valiant Heroes): July, 1997 - No. 12, June, 1998 ($2.50)

1-12-Maguire-s/a(p):4-Copycat-c		3.00

TRIPLE GIANT COMICS (See Archie All-Star Specials under Archie Comics)

TRIPLE THREAT
Special Action/Holyoke/Gerona Publ.: Winter, 1945

1-Duke of Darkness, King O'Leary	29	87	156	270

TRIPLE-X
Dark Horse Comics: Dec, 1994 - No. 7, June, 1995 ($3.95, B&W, limited series)

1-7		4.00

TRIUMPH (Also see JLA #28-30, Justice League Task Force & Zero Hour)
DC Comics: June, 1995 - No. 4, Sept, 1995 ($1.75, limited series)

1-4: 3-Hourman, JLA app.		2.25

TRIUMPHANT UNLEASHED
Triumphant Comics: No. 0, Nov, 1993 - No. 1, Nov, 1993 ($2.50, lim. series)

0-Serially numbered, 0-Red logo, 0-White logo (no cover price; giveaway), 1-Cover is negative & reverse of #0-c		2.50

TROLL (Also see Brigade)
Image Comics (Extreme Studios): Dec, 1993 (one-shot, 44 pgs.)

1-1st app. Troll; Liefeld scripts; Matsuda-c/a(p)		2.50
Halloween Special (1994, $2.95)-Maxx app.		3.00
…Once A Hero (8/94, $2.50)		2.50

TROLLORDS
Tru Studios/Comico V2#1 on: 2/86 - No. 15, 1988; V2#1, 11/88 - V2#4, 1989 (1-15: $1.50, B&W)

1-15: 1-Both printings. 6-Christmas issue; silver logo		2.50
V2#1-4 ($1.75, color, Comico)		2.50
Special 1 ($1.75, 2/87, color)-Jerry's Big Fun Bk.		2.50

TROLLORDS
Apple Comics: July, 1989 - No. 6, 1990 ($2.25, B&W, color)

1-6: 1-"The Big Batman Movie Parody"		2.50

TROLL PATROL
Harvey Comics: Jan, 1993 ($1.95, 52 pgs.)

1		2.25

TROLL II (Also see Brigade)
Image Comics (Extreme Studios): July, 1994 ($3.95, one-shot)

1		4.00

TROUBLED SOULS
Fleetway: 1990 ($9.95, trade paperback)

nn-Garth Ennis scripts & John McCrea painted-c/a.		10.00

TROUBLE MAGNET
DC Comics: Feb, 2000 - No. 4, May, 2000 ($2.50, limited series)

1-4-Windham-s/Plunkett-a		2.50

TROUBLEMAKERS
Acclaim Comics (Valiant Heroes): Apr, 1997 - No. 19, June, 1998 ($2.50)

1-19: Fabian Nicieza scripts in all. 1st app. XL, Rebound & Blur; 2 covers. 8-Copycat-c. 12-Shooting of Parker		2.50

True Aviation Picture Stories #6 © PMI

True Comics #10 © PMI

True Crime Comics #5 © Magazine Village

	GD2.0	FN6.0	VF8.0	NM9.4

TROUBLEMAN
Image Comics (Motown Machineworks): June, 1996 - No. 3, Aug, 1996 ($2.25, limited series)

1-3				2.25

TROUBLE SHOOTERS, THE (TV)
Dell Publishing Co.: No. 1108, Jun-Aug, 1960

Four Color 1108-Keenan Wynn photo-c	5	15	35	60

TROUBLE WITH GIRLS, THE
Malibu Comics (Eternity Comics) #7-14/Comico V2#1-4/Eternity V2#5 on: 1987 - #14, 1988; V2#1, 2/89 - V2#23, 1991 ($1.95, B&W/color)

1-14 ($1.95, B&W, Eternity)-Gerard Jones scripts & Tim Hamilton-c/a in all.				2.25
2#1-23-Jones scripts, Hamilton-c/a.				2.25
Annual 1 (1988, $2.95)				3.00
Christmas Special 1 (12/91, $2.95, B&W, Eternity)-Jones scripts, Hamilton-c/a.				3.00
Graphic Novel 1,2 (7/88, B&W)-r/#1-3 & #4-6				8.00

TROUBLE WITH GIRLS, THE: NIGHT OF THE LIZARD
Marvel Comics (Epic Comics/Heavy Hitters): 1993 - No. 4, 1993 ($2.50/$1.95, limited series)

1-Embossed-c; Gerard Jones scripts & Bret Blevins-c/a in all				2.50
2-4: 2-Begin $1.95-c.				2.25

TROUT
Oni Press: Oct, 2001 - No. 2 ($2.95, B&W, limited series)

1-Troy Nixey-s/a				3.00

TRUE ADVENTURES (Formerly True Western)(Men's Adventures #4 on)
Marvel Comics (CCC): No. 3, May, 1950 (52 pgs.)

3-Powell, Sekowsky-a; Brodsky-c	17	51	88	150

TRUE ANIMAL PICTURE STORIES
True Comics Press: Winter, 1947 - No. 2, Spring-Summer, 1947

1,2	10	30	55	80

TRUE AVIATION PICTURE STORIES (Becomes Aviation Adventures & Model Building #16 on)
Parents' Mag. Institute: 1942; No. 2, Jan-Feb, 1943 - No. 15, Sept-Oct, 1946

1-(#1 & 2 titled ...Aviation Comics Digest)(not digest size)	15	45	77	130
2	10	30	55	80
3-14: 3-10-Plane photos on-c. 11,13-Photo-c	9	27	49	70
15-(Titled "True Aviation Adventures & Model Building")	8	24	45	65

TRUE BRIDE'S EXPERIENCES (Formerly Teen-Age Brides)
(True Bride-To-Be Romances No. 17 on)
True Love (Harvey Publications): No. 8, Oct, 1954 - No. 16, Feb, 1956

8	8	24	45	65
9,10: 10-Last pre-code (2/55)	6	18	29	40
11-15	5	15	25	35
16-Last issue	6	18	30	42

NOTE: *Powell a-8-10, 12, 13.*

TRUE BRIDE-TO-BE ROMANCES (Formerly True Bride's Experiences)
Home Comics/True Love (Harvey): No. 17, Apr, 1956 - No. 30, Nov, 1958

17-S&K-c, Powell-a	10	30	55	80
18-20,22,25-28,30	5	15	25	35
21,23,24,29-Powell-a. 29-Baker-a (1 pg.)	6	18	29	40

TRUE COMICS (Also see Outstanding American War Heroes)
True Comics/Parents' Magazine Press: April, 1941 - No. 84, Aug, 1950

1-Marathon run story; life story Winston Churchill	33	99	174	300
2-Red Cross story; Everett-a	15	45	77	135
3-Baseball Hall of Fame story; Chiang Kai-Shek-c/s	18	54	94	160
4,5: 4-Story of American flag "Old Glory". 5-Life story of Joe Louis	13	39	66	110
6-Baseball World Series story	17	51	88	150
7-10: 7-Buffalo Bill story. 10,11-Teddy Roosevelt	10	30	55	80
11-14,16,18-20: 11-Thomas Edison, Douglas MacArthur stories. 13-Harry Houdini story. 14-Charlie McCarthy story. 18-Story of America begins,				

ends #26. 19-Eisenhower-c/s	9	27	49	70
15-Flag-c; Bob Feller story	10	30	55	80
17-Brooklyn Dodgers story	13	39	55	90
21-30: 24-Marco Polo story. 28-Origin of Uncle Sam. 29-Beethoven story				
30-Cooper Brothers baseball story	8	24	42	60
31-Red Grange "Galloping Ghost" story	12	18	32	45
32-46: 33-Origin/1st app. Steve Saunders, Special Agent of the FBI, series begins. 35-Mark Twain story. 38-General Bradley-c/s. 39-FDR story.				
44-Truman story. 46-George Gershwin story	6	18	29	40
47-Atomic bomb issue (c/story, 3/46)	10	30	55	80
48-54,56-65: 49-1st app. Secret Warriors. 53-Bobby Riggs story. 58-Jim Jeffries (boxer) story; Harry Houdini. 59-Bob Hope story; pirates-c/s.				
60-Speedway Speed Demon-c/story.	5	15	25	35
55-(12/46)-1st app. Sad Sack by Baker (1/2 pg.)	6	18	32	45
66-Will Rogers-c/story	6	18	29	40
67-1st oversized issue (12/47); Steve Saunders, Special Agent begins	7	21	36	50
68-70,74-77,79: 68-70,74-77-Features Steve Sanders True FBI advs.				
68-Oversized; Admiral Byrd-c/s. 69-Jack Benny story. 74-Amos 'n' Andy story	5	15	24	32
71-Joe DiMaggio-c/story.	8	24	42	60
72-Jackie Robinson story; True FBI advs.	6	18	32	45
73-Walt Disney's life story	8	24	42	60
78-Stan Musial-c/story; True FBI advs.	6	18	32	45
80-84 (Scarce)-All distr. to subscribers through mail only; paper-c. 80-Rocket trip to the moon story. 81-Red Grange story	17	51	88	150

(Prices vary widely on issues 80-84)
NOTE: *Bob Kane a-7. Palais a-80. Powell c/a-80. #80-84 have soft covers and combined with Tex Granger, Jack Armstrong, and Calling All Kids. #68-78 featured true FBI adventures.*

TRUE COMICS AND ADVENTURE STORIES
Parents' Magazine Institute: 1965 (Giant) (25¢)

1,2: 1-Fighting Hero of Viet Nam; LBJ on-c	3	9	17	25

TRUE COMPLETE MYSTERY (Formerly Complete Mystery)
Marvel Comics (PrPI): No. 5, Apr, 1949 - No. 8, Oct, 1949

5	27	81	142	245
6-8: 6-8-Photo-c	21	63	110	185

TRUE CONFIDENCES
Fawcett Publications: 1949 (Fall) - No. 4, June, 1950 (All photo-c)

1-Has ad for Fawcett Love Adventures #1, but publ. as Love Memoirs #1 as Marvel published the title first; Swayze-a	17	51	88	150
2-4: 3-Swayze-a. 4-Powell-a	11	33	55	90

TRUE CRIME CASES (...From Official Police Files)
St. John Publishing Co.: 1944 (25¢, 100 pg. Giant)

nn-Matt Baker-c	42	126	252	440

TRUE CRIME COMICS (Also see Complete Book of...)
Magazine Village: No. 2, May, 1947 - No. 3, July-Aug, 1948 - No. 6, June-July, 1949; V2#1, Aug-Sept, 1949 (52 pgs.)

2-Jack Cole-c/a; used in SOTI, pgs. 81,82 plus illo. "A sample of the injury-to-eye motif" & illo. "Dragging living people to death"; used in POP, pg. 105; "Murder, Morphine and Me" classic drug propaganda story used by N.Y. Legis. Comm.	141	423	881	1550
3-Classic Cole-c/a; drug story with hypo, opium den & with drawing addict	105	315	656	1150
4-Jack Cole-c/a; c-taken from a story panel in #3 (r-(2) SOTI & POP stories/#2?)	93	279	581	1025
5-Jack Cole, Marijuana racket story (Canadian ed. w/cover similar to #3 exists w/out drug story)	61	182	381	675
6-Not a reprint, original story (Canadian ed. reprints #4 w/different coloring on-c)	50	150	300	520
V2#1-Used in SOTI, pgs. 81,82 & illo. "Dragging living people to death"; Toth, Wood (3 pgs.), Roussos-a; Cole-r from #2	84	252	525	925

NOTE: *V2#1 was reprinted in Canada as V2#9 (12/49); same-c & contents minus Wood-a.*

TRUE FAITH
Fleetway: 1990 ($9.95, graphic novel)

nn-Garth Ennis scripts	2	6	13	20
Reprinted by DC/Vertigo ('97, $12.95)				13.00

TRUE GHOST STORIES (See Ripley's...)

True Love Pictorial #5 © STJ

True Stories of Romance #2 © FAW

True-To-Life Romances #6 © STAR

	GD2.0	FN6.0	VF8.0	NM9.

TRUE LIFE ROMANCES (...Romance on cover)
Ajax/Farrell Publications: Dec, 1955 - No. 3, Aug, 1956

1	10	30	55	80
2	7	21	36	50
3-Disbrow-a	8	24	42	60

TRUE LIFE SECRETS
Romantic Love Stories/Charlton: Mar-April, 1951 - No. 28, Sept, 1955; No. 29, Jan, 1956

1-Photo-c begin, end #3?	13	39	66	110
2	7	21	38	55
3-19: 12-"I Was An Escort Girl" story	6	18	29	40
20-29: 25-Last precode(3/55)	5	15	25	35

TRUE LIFE TALES (Formerly Mitzi's Romances #8?)
Marvel Comics (CCC): No. 8, Oct, 1949 - No. 2, Jan, 1950 (52 pgs.)

8(#1, 10/49), 2-Both have photo-c	10	30	55	80

TRUE LOVE
Eclipse Comics: Jan, 1986 - No. 2, Jan, 1986 ($2.00, Baxter paper)

1,2-Love stories reprinted from pre-code Standard Comics; Toth-a(p) in both; 1-Dave Stevens-a. 2-Mayo-a		3.00

TRUE LOVE CONFESSIONS
Premier Magazines: May, 1954 - No. 11, Jan, 1956

1-Marijuana story	10	30	55	85
2	6	18	29	40
3-11	5	15	25	35

TRUE LOVE PICTORIAL
St. John Publishing Co.: 1952 - No. 11, Aug, 1954

1-Only photo-c	16	48	83	140
2-Baker-c/a	21	63	110	185
3-5(All 25¢, 100 pgs.): 4-Signed story by Estrada. 5-(4/53)-Formerly Teen-Age Temptations; Kubert-a in #3; Baker-a in #3-5	35	105	188	325
6,7: Baker-c/a; signed stories by Estrada	19	57	99	165
8,10,11-Baker-c/a	19	57	99	165
9-Baker-c	14	42	72	120

TRUE LOVE PROBLEMS AND ADVICE ILLUSTRATED (Becomes Romance Stories of True Love No. 45 on)
McCombs/Harvey Publ./Home Comics: June, 1949 - No. 6, Apr, 1950; No. 7, Jan, 1951 - No. 44, Mar, 1957

V1#1	15	45	77	130
2	9	27	49	70
3-10: 7-9-Elias-c	6	18	32	45
11-13,15-23,25-31: 31-Last pre-code (1/55)	5	15	25	35
14,24-Rape scene	6	18	29	40
32-37,39-44	5	15	23	30
38-S&K-c	8	24	45	65

NOTE: *Powell* a-1, 2, 7-14, 17-25, 28, 29, 33, 40, 41. #3 has True Love... on inside.

TRUE MOVIE AND TELEVISION (Part teenage magazine)
Toby Press: Aug, 1950 - No. 3, Nov, 1950; No. 4, Mar, 1951 (52 pgs.)(1-3: 10¢)

1-Elizabeth Taylor photo-c; Gene Autry, Shirley Temple, Li'l Abner app.	45	135	270	475
2-(9/50)-Janet Leigh/Liz Taylor/Ava Gardner & others photo-c; Frazetta John Wayne illo from J.Wayne Adv. Comics #2 (4/50)	35	105	188	325
3-June Allyson photo-c; Montgomery Cliff, Esther Williams, Andrews Sisters app; Li'l Abner featured; Sadie Hawkins' Day	29	87	153	265
4-Jane Powell photo-c (15¢)	17	51	88	150

NOTE: 16 pgs. in color, rest movie material in black & white.

TRUE SECRETS (Formerly Our Love?)
Marvel (IPS)/Atlas Comics (MPI) #4 on: No. 3, Mar, 1950; No. 4, Feb, 1951 - No. 40, Sept, 1956

3 (52 pgs.)(IPS one-shot)`	13	39	66	110
4,5,7-10	8	24	42	60
6,22-Everett-a	10	30	55	80
11-20	7	21	36	50
21,23-28: 24-Colletta-a. 28-Last pre-code (2/55)	6	18	29	40
29-40: 34,36-Colletta-a	5	15	25	35

TRUE SPORT PICTURE STORIES (Formerly Sport Comics)

Street & Smith Publications: V1#5, Feb, 1942 - V5#2, July-Aug, 1949

V1#5-Joe DiMaggio-c/story	35	105	185	320
6-12 (1942-43): 12-Jack Dempsey story	21	63	110	185
V2#1-12 (1944-45): 7-Stan Musial-c/story; photo story of the New York Yankees	20	60	105	175
V3#1-12 (1946-47): 7-Joe DiMaggio, Stan Musial, Bob Feller & others back from the armed service story. 8-Billy Conn vs. Joe Louis-c/story	17	51	88	150
V4#1-12 (1948-49), V5#1,2	15	45	77	135

NOTE: *Powell* c-V3#10, V4#1-4, 6-8, 10-12; V5#1, 2; c-V3#11, V4#3-7, 9-12. *Ravielli* c-V5#2.

TRUE STORIES OF ROMANCE
Fawcett Publications: Jan, 1950 - No. 3, May, 1950 (All photo-c)

1	13	39	66	110
2,3: 3-Marcus Swayze-a	9	27	49	70

TRUE STORY OF JESSE JAMES, THE (See Jesse James, Four Color 757)

TRUE SWEETHEART SECRETS
Fawcett Publications: 5/50; No. 2, 7/50; No. 3, 1951(nd); No. 4, 9/51 - No. 11, 1/53 (All photo-c)

1-Photo-c; Debbie Reynolds?	14	42	72	120
2-Wood-a (11 pgs.)	18	54	94	155
3-11: 4,5-Powell-a. 8-Marcus Swayze-a. 11-Evans-a	10	30	55	80

TRUE TALES OF LOVE (Formerly Secret Story Romances)
Atlas Comics (TCI): No. 22, April, 1956 - No. 31, Sept, 1957

22	8	24	45	65
23-24,26-31-Colletta-a in most:	5	15	25	35
25-Everett-a; Colletta-a	6	18	32	45

TRUE TALES OF ROMANCE
Fawcett Publications: No. 4, June, 1950

4-Photo-c	9	27	49	70

TRUE 3-D
Harvey Publications: Dec, 1953 - No. 2, Feb, 1954 (25¢)(Both came with 2 pair of glasses)

1-Nostrand, Powell-a	6	18	40	65
2-Powell-a	6	18	42	70

NOTE: Many copies of #1 surfaced in 1984.

TRUE-TO-LIFE ROMANCES (Formerly Guns Against Gangsters)
Star Publ.: #8, 11-12/49; #9, 1-2/50; #3, 4/50 - #5, 9/50; #6, 1/51 - #23, 10/54

8(#1, 1949)	25	75	130	225
9(#2),4-10	18	54	94	155
3-Janet Leigh/Glenn Ford photo on-c plus true life story of each	20	60	105	175
11,22,23	15	45	77	130
12-14,17-21-Disbrow-a	17	51	88	150
15,16-Wood & Disbrow-a in each	20	60	105	175

NOTE: *Kamen* a-13. *Kamen/Feldstein* a-14. All have L.B. Cole covers.

TRUE WAR EXPERIENCES
Harvey Publications: Aug, 1952 - No. 4, Dec, 1952

1	9	27	65	110
2-4	5	15	38	60

TRUE WAR ROMANCES (Becomes Exotic Romances #22 on)
Quality Comics Group: Sept, 1952 - No. 21, June, 1955

1-Photo-c	14	42	72	120
2	8	24	42	60
3-10: 9-Whitney-a	7	21	36	50
11-21: 20-Last precode (4/55). 14-Whitney-a	6	18	29	40

TRUE WAR STORIES (See Ripley's...)

TRUE WESTERN (True Adventures #3)
Marvel Comics (MMC): Dec, 1949 - No. 2, March, 1950

1-Photo-c; Billy The Kid story	17	51	88	150
2: Alan Ladd photo-c	21	63	110	185

TRUMP
HMH Publishing Co.: Jan, 1957 - No. 2, Mar, 1957 (50¢, magazine)

Tuffy #5 © STD

Turok, Dinosaur Hunter #20 © Acclaim

Turok, Son of Stone #29 © Acclaim

	GD2.0	FN6.0	VF8.0	NM9.4

	GD2.0	FN6.0	VF8.0	NM9.4

1-Harvey Kurtzman satire	24	72	127	215
2-Harvey Kurtzman satire	20	60	105	175

NOTE: **Davis, Elder, Heath, Jaffee** art-#1,2; **Wood** a-1. Article by Mel Brooks in #2.

TRUMPETS WEST (See Luke Short, Four Color #875)

TRUTH ABOUT CRIME (See Fox Giants)

TRUTH ABOUT MOTHER GOOSE (See Mother Goose, Four Color #862)

TRUTH BEHIND THE TRIAL OF CARDINAL MINDSZENTY, THE (See Cardinal Mindszenty)

TRUTHFUL LOVE (Formerly Youthful Love)
Youthful Magazines: No. 2, July, 1950

2-Ingrid Bergman's true life story	10	30	55	80

TRY-OUT WINNER BOOK
Marvel Comics: Mar, 1988

1-Spider-Man vs. Doc Octopus			3.00

TSR WORLD (...Annual on cover only)
DC Comics: 1990 ($3.95, 84 pgs.)

1-Advanced D&D, ForgottenRealms, Dragonlance & 1st app. Spelljammer			4.00

TSUNAMI GIRL
Image Comics: 1999 - No. 3, 1999 ($2.95)

1-3-Sorayama-c/Paniccia-s/a			3.00

TUBBY (See Marge's...)

TUFF GHOSTS STARRING SPOOKY
Harvey Publications: July, 1962 - No. 39, Nov, 1970; No. 40, Sept, 1971 - No. 43, Oct, 1972

1-12¢ issues begin	12	36	84	140
2-5	6	18	42	70
6-10	4	12	29	45
11-20	4	12	26	40
21-30: 29-Hot Stuff/Spooky team-up story	3	9	17	25
31-39,43	2	6	12	18
40-42: 52 pg. Giants	2	6	15	22

TUFFY
Standard Comics: No. 5, July, 1949 - No. 9, Oct, 1950

5-All by Sid Hoff	6	18	29	40
6-9	5	14	21	28

TUFFY TURTLE
I. W. Enterprises: No date

1-Reprint	2	6	9	12

TUG & BUSTER
Art & Soul Comics: Nov, 1995 - No. 7, Feb, 1998 ($2.95, B&W, bi-monthly)

1-7: Marc Hempel-c/a/scripts			3.00
1-(Image Comics, 8/98, $2.95, B&W)			3.00

TUROK
Acclaim Comics: Mar, 1998 - No. 4, Jun, 1998 ($2.50)

1-4-Nicieza-s/Kayanan-a			2.50

TUROK, CHILD OF BLOOD
Acclaim Comics: Jan, 1998 ($3.95, one-shot)

1-Nicieza-s/Kayanan-a			4.00

TUROK, DINOSAUR HUNTER (See Magnus Robot Fighter #12 & Archer & Armstrong #2)
Valiant/Acclaim Comics: June, 1993 - No. 47, Aug, 1996 ($2.50)

1-($3.50)-Chromium & foil-c			3.50
1-Gold foil-c variant			5.00
0, 2-47: 4-Andar app. 5-Death of Andar. 7-9-Truman/Glanzman-a. 11-Bound-in trading card. 16-Chaos Effect			2.50
Yearbook 1 (1994, $3.95, 52 pgs.)			4.00

TUROK, REDPATH
Acclaim Comics (Valiant): Oct, 1997 ($3.95, one-shot)

1-Nicieza-s/Kayanan-a			4.00

TUROK /SHADOWMAN

Acclaim Comics: Feb, 1999 ($3.95, one-shot)

1-Priest-s/Broome & Jimenez-a			4.00

TUROK, SON OF STONE (See Dan Curtis, Golden Comics Digest #31 & March of Comics #378, 399, 408)
Dell Publ. Co. #1-29(9/62)/Gold Key #30(12/62)-85(7/73)/Gold Key or Whitman #86(9/73)-125(1/80)/Whitman #126(3/81) on: No. 596, 12/54 - No. 29, 9/62; No. 30, 12/62 - No. 91, 7/74; No. 92, 9/74 - No. 125, 1/80; No. 126, 3/81 - No. 130, 4/82

Four Color 596 (12/54)(#1)-1st app./origin Turok & Andar; dinosaur-c. Created by Matthew H. Murphy; written by Alberto Giolitti

Four Color 596 (12/54)(#1)-1st app./origin Turok & Andar; dinosaur-c. Created by Matthew H. Murphy; written by Alberto Giolitti	60	180	420	775
Four Color 656 (10/55)(#2)-1st mention of Lanok	34	102	238	440
3(3/56)-5: 3-Cave man	21	63	147	270
6-10: 8-Dinosaur of the deep; Turok enters Lost Valley; series begins.				
9-Paul S. Newman-s (most issues thru end)	14	42	98	180
11-20: 17-Prehistoric Pygmies	9	27	63	120
21-29	6	18	42	80
30-1st Gold Key. 30-33-Painted back-c.	7	21	49	85
31-Drug use story	6	18	42	80
32-40	5	15	34	55
41-50	4	12	29	45
51-57,59,60	3	10	23	35
58-Flying Saucer c/story	4	12	26	40
61-70: 62-12¢ & 15¢ covers. 63,68-Line drawn-c	3	9	20	30
71-84: 84-Origin & 1st app. Hutec	2	6	15	22
85-99: 93-r-c/#19 w/changes. 94-r-c/#28 w/changes. 97-r-c/#31 w/changes. 98-r/#58 w/o spaceship & spacemen-c. 99-r-c/#52 w/changes.				
100	2	6	12	18
	3	9	17	24
101-129: 114,115-(52 pgs.). 129(2/82)	2	6	15	22
130(4/82)-Last issue	3	9	20	30
Giant 1(30031-611) (11/66)-Slick-c; r/#10-12 & 16 plus cover to #11	10	30	70	120
Giant 1-Same as above but with paper-c	11	33	80	135

NOTE: Most painted-c; line-drawn #63 & 130. **Alberto Giolitti** a-24-27, 30-119, 123; painted-c No. 30-129. **Sparling** a-117, 120-130. Reprints-#36, 54, 57, 75, 112, 114(1/3), 115(1/3), 118, 121, 125, 127(1/3), 128, 129(1/3), 130(1/3), Giant 1. Cover r-93, 94, 97-99, 126(all different from original covers.

TUROK: SPRING BREAK IN THE LOST LAND
Acclaim Comics (Valiant): July, 1997 ($3.95, one-shot)

1-Nicieza-s/Kayanan-a			4.00

TUROK: TALES OF THE LOST LAND
Acclaim Comics (Valiant): Apr, 1998 ($3.95, one-shot)

1			4.00

TUROK: THE EMPTY SOULS
Acclaim Comics (Valiant): Apr, 1997 ($3.95, one-shot)

1-Nicieza-s/Kayanan-a; variant-c			4.00

TUROK THE HUNTED
Valiant/Acclaim Comics: Mar, 1995 - No. 2, Apr, 1995 ($2.50, limited series)

1,2-Mike Deodato-a(p); price omitted on #1			2.50

TUROK THE HUNTED
Acclaim Comics (Valiant): Feb, 1996 - No. 2, Mar, 1996 ($2.50, limited series)

1,2-Mike Grell story			2.50

TUROK, TIMEWALKER
Acclaim Comics (Valiant): Aug, 1997 - No. 2, Sept, 1997 ($2.50, limited series)

1,2-Nicieza story			2.50

TUROK 2 (Magazine)
Acclaim Comics: Oct, 1998 ($4.99, magazine size)

...Seeds of Evil-Nicieza-s/Broome & Benjamin-a; origin back-up story			5.00
#2 Adon's Curse -Mack painted-c/Broome & Benjamin-a; origin pt. 2			5.00

TUROK 3: SHADOW OF OBLIVION
Acclaim Comics: Sept, 2000 ($4.95, one-shot)

1-Includes pin-up gallery			5.00

TURTLE SOUP
Mirage Studios: Sept, 1987 ($2.00, 76 pgs., B&W, one-shot)

	GD2.0	FN6.0	VF8.0	NM9.4

1-Featuring Teenage Mutant Ninja Turtles				4.00

TURTLE SOUP
Mirage Studios: Nov, 1991 - No. 4, 1992 ($2.50, limited series, coated paper)

1-4: Features the Teenage Mutant Ninja Turtles				2.50TV

CASPER & COMPANY
Harvey Publications: Aug, 1963 - No. 46, April, 1974 (25¢ Giants)

1: 68 pg. Giants begin; Casper, Little Audrey, Baby Huey, Herman & Catnip, Buzzy the Crow begin	12	36	84	140
2-5	5	15	38	60
6-10	4	12	29	45
11-20	3	10	23	35
21-31: 31-Last 68 pg. issue	3	9	17	25
32-46: All 52 pgs.	2	6	13	20

NOTE: *Many issues contain reprints.*

TV FUNDAY FUNNIES (See Famous TV...)

TV FUNNIES (See New Funnies)

TV FUNTIME (See Little Audrey)

TV LAUGHOUT (See Archie's...)

TV SCREEN CARTOONS (Formerly Real Screen)
National Periodical Publ.: No. 129, July-Aug, 1959 - No. 138, Jan-Feb, 1961

129-138 (Scarce)	8	24	56	90

TV STARS (TV) (Newsstand sales only)
Marvel Comics Group: Aug, 1978 - No. 4, Feb, 1979 (Hanna-Barbera)

1-Great Grape app.	3	9	19	28
2,4: 4-Top Cat app.	2	6	15	22
3-Toth-c/a; Dave Stevens inks	3	9	17	25

TV TEENS (Formerly Ozzie & Babs; Rock and Rollo #14 on)
Charlton Comics: V1#14, Feb, 1954 - V2#13, July, 1956

V1#14 (#1)-Ozzie & Babs	9	27	49	70
15 (#2)	5	15	25	35
V2#3(6/54) - 6-Don Winslow	6	18	28	38
7-13-Mopsy. 8(7/55)	5	15	25	35

TWEETY AND SYLVESTER (1st Series) (TV)
Dell Publishing Co.: No. 406, June, 1952 - No. 37, June-Aug, 1962

Four Color 406 (#1)-1st app.?	9	27	63	110
Four Color 489,524	5	15	34	55
4 (5-5/54) - 20	4	12	26	40
21-37	3	9	20	30

(See March of Comics #421, 433, 445, 457, 469, 481)

TWEETY AND SYLVESTER (2nd Series)(See Kite Fun Book)
Gold Key No. 1-102/Whitman No. 103 on: Nov, 1963; No. 2, Nov, 1965 - No. 121, June, 1984

1	4	12	26	40
2-10	3	9	17	24
11-30	2	6	12	18
31-50	2	6	9	12
51-70	1	3	6	8
71-102				6.00
103,104 (Whitman)	1	3	6	8
105(9/80),106(10/80),107(12/80) 3-pack?	2	6	11	15
108-116: 113(2/82),114(2-3/82),115(3/82),116(4/82)	1	3	6	9
117-121 (All # 90094 on-c; nd, nd code): 117(6/83). 118(7/83). 119(2/84)-r(1/3).				
120(5/84). 121(6/84)	2	6	10	14
Mini Comic No. 1(1976, 3-1/4x6-1/2")	1	3	6	9

12 O'CLOCK HIGH (TV)
Dell Publishing Co.: Jan-Mar, 1965 - No. 2, Apr-June, 1965 (Photo-c)

1	5	15	35	70
2	4	12	30	50

2099 A.D.
Marvel Comics: May, 1995 ($3.95, one-shot)

1-Acetate-c by Quesada & Palmiotti.				4.00

2099 APOCALYPSE
Marvel Comics: Dec, 1995 ($4.95, one-shot)

	GD2.0	FN6.0	VF8.0	NM9.4

1-Chromium wraparound-c; Ellis script				5.00

2099 GENESIS
Marvel Comics: Jan, 1996 ($4.95, one-shot)

1-Chromium wraparound-c; Ellis script				5.00

2099 MANIFEST DESTINY
Marvel Comics: Mar, 1998 ($5.99, one-shot)

1-Origin of Fantastic Four 2099; intro Moon Knight 2099				6.00

2099 UNLIMITED
Marvel Comics: Sept, 1993 - No. 10, 1996 ($3.95, 68 pgs.)

1-10: 1-1st app. Hulk 2099 & begins. 1-3-Spider-Man 2099 app. 9-Joe Kubert-c; Len Wein & Nancy Collins scripts				4.00

2099 WORLD OF DOOM SPECIAL
Marvel Comics: May, 1995 ($2.25, one-shot)

1-Doom's "Contract w/America"				2.25

2099 WORLD OF TOMORROW
Marvel Comics: Sept, 1996 - No. 8, Apr, 1997 ($2.50) (Replaces 2099 titles)

1-8: 1-Wraparound-c. 2-w/bound-in card. 4,5-Phalanx				2.50

21
Image Comics (Top Cow Productions): Feb, 1996 - No. 3, Apr, 1996 ($2.50)

1-3: Len Wein scripts				2.50
1-Variant-c				2.50

2020 VISIONS
DC Comics (Vertigo): May, 1997 - No. 12, Apr, 1998 ($2.25, limited series)

1-12-Delano-s: 1-3-Quitely-a. 4-"la tormenta"-Pleece-a				2.25

20,000 LEAGUES UNDER THE SEA (Movie)(See King Classics, Movie Comics & Power Record Comics)
Dell Publishing Co.: No. 614, Feb, 1955 (Disney)

Four Color 614-Movie, painted-c	9	27	63	120

22 BRIDES (See Ash/...)
Event Comics: Mar, 1996 - No. 4, Jan, 1997 ($2.95)

1-4: Fabian Nicieza scripts				3.00
2,3-Variant-c				3.00

TWICE TOLD TALES (See Movie Classics)

TWILIGHT
DC Comics: 1990 - No. 3, 1991 ($4.95, 52 pgs, lim. series, squarebound, mature)

1-3: Tommy Tomorrow app; Chaykin scripts, Garcia-Lopez-c/a.				5.00

TWILIGHT AVENGER, THE
Elite Comics: July, 1986 - No. 4, 1987 ($1.75, 28 pgs, limited series)

1-4				2.25

TWILIGHT MAN
First Publishing: June, 1989 - No. 4, Sept, 1989 ($2.75, limited series)

1-4				2.75

TWILIGHT ZONE, THE (TV) (See Dan Curtis & Stories From...)
Dell Publishing Co./Gold Key/Whitman No. 92: No. 1173, 3-5/61 - No. 91, 4/79; No. 92, 5/82

Four Color 1173 (#1)-Crandall-c/a	21	63	147	270
Four Color 1288-Crandall/Evans-c/a	12	36	84	150
01-860-207 (5-7/62-Dell, 15¢)	8	24	56	100
12-860-210 on-c; 01-860-210 on inside(8-10/62-Dell)-Evans-a (3 stories)				
	8	24	56	100
1(11/62-Gold Key)-Crandall/Frazetta-a (10 & 11 pgs.); Evans-a				
	12	36	84	150
2	7	21	49	90
3-11: 3(11 pgs.),4(10 pgs.),9-Toth-a	5	15	35	60
12-15: 12-Williamson-a. 13,15-Crandall-a. 14-Orlando/Crandall/Torres-a				
	4	12	30	50
16-20	3	10	23	35
21-25: 21-Crandall-a(r). 25-Evans/Crandall-a(r); Toth-r/#4; last 12¢ issue				
	3	9	19	28
26,27: 26-Flying Saucer-c/story; Crandall, Evans-a(r). 27-Evans-r(2)				
	3	9	19	28

Twilight Zone #22 © CBS Ent.

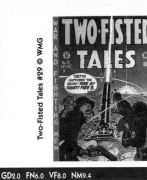

Two-Fisted Tales #29 © WMG

Two-Gun Kid #12 © MAR

TW

	GD2.0	FN6.0	VF8.0	NM9.4
28-32: 32-Evans-a(r)	2	6	15	24
33-51: 43-Celardo-a. 51-Williamson-a	2	6	11	15
52-70	2	6	9	12
71-82,85-91: 71-Reprint	1	3	6	8
83-(52 pgs.)	2	6	10	14
84-(52 pgs.) Frank Miller's 1st comic book work	2	6	13	20
92-(Whitman, 5/82) Last issue; r/#1.	1	4	7	10
Mini Comic #1(1976, 3-1/4x6-1/2")	1	4	7	10

NOTE: **Bolle** a-13(w/**McWilliams**), 50, 55, 57, 59, 77, 78, 80, 83, 84. **McWilliams** a-59, 78, 80, 82, 84. **Miller** a-84, 85. **Orlando** a-15, 19, 20, 22, 23. **Sekowsky** a-3. **Simonson** a-50, 54, 55, 83r. **Weiss** a-39, 79r(#39). (See Mystery Comics Digest 3, 6, 9, 12, 15, 18, 21, 24). Reprints-26(1/3), 71, 73, 79, 83, 84, 86, 92. Painted c-1-91.

TWILIGHT ZONE, THE (TV)
Now Comics: Nov. 1990 ($2.95); Oct. 1991; V2#1, Nov. 1991 - No. 11, Oct. 1992 ($1.95); V3#1, 1993 - No. 4, 1993 ($2.50)

1-(11/90, $2.95, 52 pgs.)-Direct sale edition; Neal Adams-a, Sienkiewicz; Harlan Ellison scripts				3.00
1-(11/90, $1.75)-Newsstand ed. w/N. Adams-c				2.50
1-Prestige Format (10/91, $4.95)-Reprints above with extra Harlan Ellison short story				5.00
1-Collector's Edition (10/91, $2.50)-Non-code approved and polybagged; reprints 11/90 edition; gold logo, 1-Reprint ($2.50)-r/direct sale 11/90 version				2.50
1-Reprint ($2.50)-r/newsstand 11/90 version				2.50
V2#1-Direct sale & newsstand ed. w/different-c				2.50
V2#2-8,10-11				2.50
V2#9-($2.95)-3-D Special; polybagged w/glasses & hologram on-c				3.00
V2#9-($4.95)-Prestige Edition; contains 2 extra stories & a different hologram on-c; polybagged w/glasses				5.00
V3#1-4, Anniversary Special 1 (1992, $2.50)				2.50
Annual 1 (4/93, $2.50)-No ads				2.50
...Science Fiction Special (3/93, $3.50)				3.50

TWINKLE COMICS
Spotlight Publishers: May, 1945

1	25	75	133	230

TWIST, THE
Dell Publishing Co.: July-Sept, 1962

01-864-209-Painted-c	4	12	27	42

TWISTED TALES (See Eclipse Graphic Album Series #15)
Pacific Comics/Independent Comics Group (Eclipse) #9,10: 11/82 - No. 8, 5/84; No. 9, 11/84; No. 10, 12/84 (Baxter paper)

1-9: 1-B. Jones/Corben-c; Alcala-a; nudity/violence in al. 2-Wrightson-a; Ploog-a				4.00
10-Wrightson painted art; Morrow-a				6.00

NOTE: **Bolton** painted c-4, 6, 7; a-7. **Conrad** a-1, 3, 5; c-1i, 3, 5. **Guice** a-8. **Wildey** a-3.

TWO BIT THE WACKY WOODPECKER (See Wacky...)
Toby Press: 1951 - No. 3, May, 1953

1	10	30	55	80
2,3	6	18	29	40

TWO FACES OF TOMORROW, THE
Dark Horse: Aug, 1997 - No. 13, Aug, 1998 ($2.95/$3.95, B&W, lim. series)

1-13: 1-Manga				4.00

TWO-FISTED TALES (Formerly Haunt of Fear #15-17)
E. C. Comics: No. 18, Nov-Dec, 1950 - No. 41, Feb-Mar, 1955

18(#1)-Kurtzman-c	80	240	560	1000
19-Kurtzman-c	64	192	448	800
20-Kurtzman-c	40	120	280	500
21,22-Kurtzman-c	30	90	210	375
23-25-Kurtzman-c	24	72	168	300
26-35: 33- "Atom Bomb" by Wood	17	51	119	210
36-41	14	42	98	175
Two-Fisted Annual (1952, 25¢, 132 pgs.)	82	246	574	900
Two-Fisted Annual (1953, 25¢, 132 pgs.)	64	192	448	700

NOTE: **Berg** a-29. **Colan** a-39p. **Craig** a-18, 19, 32. **Crandall** a-35, 36. **Davis** a-20-36, 40; c-30, 34, 35, 41, Annual 2. **Evans** a-34, 40, 41; c-40. **Feldstein** a-18. **Krigstein** a-41. **Kubert** a-32, 33. **Kurtzman** a-18-25; c-18-29, 31, Annual 1. **Severin** a-26, 28, 29, 31, 34-41 (No. 37-39 all-**Severin** issues); c-36-39. **Severin/Elder** a-19-29, 31, 33, 36. **Wood** a-18-28, 30-35, 41; c-32, 33. Special issues: #26 (ChanJin Reservoir), 31 (Civil War), 35 (Civil War). Canadian reprints known;

see Table of Contents. #25-Davis biog. #27-Wood biog. #28-Kurtzman biog.

TWO-FISTED TALES
Russ Cochran/Gemstone Publishing: Oct, 1992 - No. 24, May, 1998 ($1.50/$2.00/$2.50)

1-24: 1-4r/Two-Fisted Tales #18-21 w/original-c				2.50

TWO-GUN KID (Also see All Western Winners, Best Western, Black Rider, Blaze Carson, Kid Colt, Western Winners, Wild West, & Wild Western)
Marvel/Atlas (MCI No. 1-10/HPC No. 11-59/Marvel No. 60 on): 3/48(No mo.) - No. 10, 11/49; No. 11, 12/53 - No. 59, 4/61; No. 60, 11/62 - No. 92, 3/68; No. 93, 7/70 - No. 136, 4/77

1-Two-Gun Kid & his horse Cyclone begin; The Sheriff begins	105	315	656	1150
2	43	129	257	450
3,4: 3-Annie Oakley app.	36	108	191	330
5-Pre-Black Rider app. (Wint. 48/49); Anti-Wertham editorial (1st?)	40	120	220	380
6-10(11/49): 8-Blaze Carson app. 9-Black Rider app.	29	87	153	265
11(12/53)-Black Rider app.; 1st to have Atlas globe on-c; explains how Kid Colt became an outlaw	22	66	116	200
12-Black Rider app.	22	66	116	195
13-20: 14-Opium story	16	48	83	140
21-24,26-29	15	45	77	130
25,30: 25-Williamson-a (5 pgs.). 30-Williamson/Torres-a (4 pgs.)	16	48	83	140
31-33,35,37-40	8	24	58	95
34-Crandall-a	8	24	60	100
36,41,42,48-Origin in all	8	24	60	100
43,44,47	6	18	42	70
45,46-Davis-a	7	21	50	80
49,50,52,53-Severin-a(2/3) in each	6	18	40	65
51-Williamson-a (5 pgs.)	7	21	50	80
54,55,57,59-Severin-a(3) in each. 59-Kirby-a; last 10¢ issue (4/61)	5	15	38	60
56	4	12	30	50
58,60-New origin. 58-Kirby/Ayers-c/a "The Monster of Hidden Valley" cover/story (Kirby monster-c)	5	15	38	60
60-Edition w/handwritten issue number on cover	7	21	53	85
61,62-Kirby-a	5	15	34	55
63-74: 64-Intro. Boom-Boom	3	10	23	35
75-77-Kirby-a	4	12	29	45
78-89	3	9	19	28
90,95-Kirby-a	3	10	23	35
91,92- Last new story; last 12¢ issue	3	9	17	25
93,94,96-99	2	6	12	18
100-Last 15¢-c	2	6	13	20
101-Origin retold/#58; Kirby-a	2	6	13	20
102-120-reprints	2	6	9	12
121-136-reprints. 129-131-(Regular 25¢ editions)	1	4	7	10
129-131-(30¢-c variants, limited distribution)(4-8/76)	2	6	12	18

NOTE: **Ayers** a-29, 91. **Davis** c-45-47. **Drucker** a-23. **Everett** a-82, 91. **Fuje** a-13. **Heath** a-3(2), 4(3), 5(2), 7; c-13, 21, 23, 53. **Keller** a-16, 19, 28. **Kirby** a-54, 55, 57-62, 75-77, 90, 95, 101, 119, 120; c-10, 52, 54-65, 67-72, 74-76, 116. **Maneely** a-20; c-11, 12, 16, 19, 20, 25-28, 35, 49. **Powell** a-38, 102, 104. **Severin** a-9, 29, 51, 55, 57, 99(3); c-51, 99. **Shores** c-1-8, 11. **Tuska** a-11, 12. **Whitney** a-87, 99. **Williamson** a-110r. Kid Colt in #13, 14, 16-21.

TWO GUN KID: SUNSET RIDERS
Marvel Comics: Nov, 1995 - No. 2, Dec, 1995 ($6.95, squarebound, lim. series)

1,2: Fabian Nicieza scripts in all. 1-painted-c				7.00

TWO GUN WESTERN (1st Series) (Formerly Casey Crime Photographer #1-4? or My Love #1-4?)
Marvel/Atlas Comics (MPC): No. 5, Nov, 1950 - No. 14, June, 1952

5-The Apache Kid (Intro & origin) & his horse Nightwind begin by Buscema	27	81	145	250
6-10: 8-Kid Colt, The Texas Kid & his horse Thunder begin?	20	60	105	175
11-14: 13-Black Rider app.	14	42	72	120

NOTE: **Maneely** a-6, 7, 9; c-6, 11-13. **Morrow** a-9. **Romita** a-8. **Wildey** a-8.

2001, A Space Odyssey #1 © MAR

Ultimate Spider-Man #13 © MAR

Ultimate X-Men #2 © MAR

	GD2.0	FN6.0	VF8.0	NM9.4

2-GUN WESTERN (2nd Series) (Formerly Billy Buckskin #1-3; Two-Gun Western #5 on)
Atlas Comics (MgPC): No. 4, May, 1956

4-Colan, Ditko, Severin, Sinnott-a; Maneely-c	17	51	88	150

TWO-GUN WESTERN (Formerly 2-Gun Western)
Atlas Comics (MgPC): No. 5, July, 1956 - No. 12, Sept, 1957

5-Return of the Gun-Hawk-c/story; Black Rider app.	16	48	83	140
6,7	12	36	61	100
8,10,12-Crandall-a	13	39	66	110
9,11-Williamson-a in both (5 pgs. each)	13	39	66	110

NOTE: *Ayers a-9. Colan a-5. Everett c-12. Forgione a-6, 5. Kirby a-12. Maneely a-6, 8, 12; c-5, 6, 8, 11. Morrow a-9, 10. Powell a-7, 11. Severin c-10. Sinnott a-5. Wildey a-3.*

TWO MINUTE WARNING
Ultimate Sports Ent.: 2000 - No. 3 ($3.95, cardstock covers)

1,2-NFL players & Teddy Roosevelt battle evil				4.00

TWO MOUSEKETEERS, THE (See 4-Color #475, 603, 642 under M.G.M.'s...;

TWO ON A GUILLOTINE (See Movie Classics)

2000 A.D. MONTHLY/PRESENTS (Showcase #25 on)
Eagle Comics/Quality Comics No. 5 on: 4/85 - #6, 9/85; 4/86 - #54, 1991 ($1.25-$1.50, Mando paper)

1-6,1-25:1-4 r/British series featuring Judge Dredd; Alan Moore scripts begin. 1-25 ($1.25)-Reprints from British 2000 AD				2.25
26,27,28, 29/30, 31-54: 27/28, 29/30,31-Guice-c				2.25

2001, A SPACE ODYSSEY (Movie)
Marvel Comics Group: Dec, 1976 - No. 10, Sept, 1977 (30¢)

1-Adaptation of film; Kirby-c/a in all	2	6	9	12
2-7,9,10	1	3	5	7
7,9,10-(35¢-c variants, limited distribution)(6-9/77)	1	4	7	10
8-Origin/1st app. Machine Man (called Mr. Machine)	2	6	9	12
8-(35¢-c variant, limited distribution)(6,8/77)	2	6	11	16
...Treasury 1 ('76, 84 pgs.)-All new Kirby-a	2	6	13	20

2001 NIGHTS
Viz Premiere Comics: 1990 - No. 10, 1991 ($3.75, B&W, limited series, mature readers, 84 pgs.)

1-10: Japanese sci-fi. 1-Wraparound-c				4.25

2010 (Movie)
Marvel Comics Group: Apr, 1985 - No. 2, May, 1985

1,2-r/Marvel Super Special movie adaptation.				2.25

TYPHOID (Also see Daredevil)
Marvel Comics: Nov, 1995 - No. 4, Feb, 1996 ($3.95, squarebound, lim. series)

1-4: Van Fleet-c/a				4.00

UFO & ALIEN COMIX
Warren Publishing Co.: Jan, 1978 (B&W magazine, 84 pgs., one-shot)

nn-Toth-a, J. Severin-a(r); Pie-s	2	6	10	14

UFO & OUTER SPACE (Formerly UFO Flying Saucers)
Gold Key: No. 14, June, 1978 - No. 25, Feb, 1980 (All painted covers)

14-Reprints UFO Flying Saucers #3	1	3	6	9
15,16-Reprints	1	3	6	9
17-25: 17-20-New material. 23-McWilliams-a. 24-(3 pg.-r). 25-Reprints UFO Flying Saucers #2 w/cover	1	3	6	9

UFO ENCOUNTERS
Western Publishing Co.: May, 1978 ($1.95, 228 pgs.)

11192-Reprints UFO Flying Saucers	3	10	23	35
11404-Vol.1 (128 pgs.)-See UFO Mysteries for Vol.2	3	9	20	30

UFO FLYING SAUCERS (UFO & Outer Space #14 on)
Gold Key: Oct, 1968 - No. 13, Jan, 1977 (No. 2 on, 36 pgs.)

1(30035-810) (68 pgs.)	4	12	26	40
2(11/70), 3(11/72), 4(11/74)	2	6	12	18
5(2/75)-13: Bolle-a #4 on	2	6	9	12

UFO MYSTERIES
Western Publishing Co.: 1978 ($1.00, reprints, 96 pgs.)

11400-(Vol.2)-Cont'd from UFO Encounters, pgs. 129-224	3	9	17	25

	GD2.0	FN6.0	VF8.0	NM9.4

ULTIMAN GIANT ANNUAL (See Big Bang Comics)
Image Comics: Nov, 2001 ($4.95, B&W, one-shot)

1-Homage to DC 1960's annuals				5.00

ULTIMATE... (Collects 4-issue alternate titles from X-Men Age of Apocalypse crossovers)
Marvel Comics: May, 1995 ($8.95, trade paperbacks, gold foil covers)

Amazing X-Men, Astonishing X-Men, Factor-X, Gambit & the X-Ternals, Generation Next, X-Calibre, X-Man				9.00
Weapon X				10.00

ULTIMATE MARVEL MAGAZINE
Marvel Comics: Feb, 2001 - Present ($3.99, magazine size)

1-10: Reprints of recent stories from the Ultimate titles plus Marvel news and features. 1-Reprints Ultimate Spider-Man #1&2				4.00

ULTIMATE MARVEL TEAM-UP (Spider-Man Team-up)
Marvel Comics: Apr, 2001 - Present ($2.99/$2.25)

1-Spider-Man & Wolverine; Bendis-s in all; Matt Wagner-a/c				4.00
2,3-Hulk; Hester-a				3.00
4,5,9-11: 4,5-Iron Man; Allred-a. 9-Fantastic Four; Mahfood-a. 10-Man-Thing; Totleben-a. 11-X-Men; Clugston-Major-a				2.25
6-8-Punisher; Sienkiewicz-a. 7,8-Daredevil app.				4.00
TPB (11/01, $14.95) r/#1-5				15.00

ULTIMATE SPIDER-MAN
Marvel Comics: Oct, 2000 - Present ($2.99/$2.25)

1-Bendis-s/Bagley & Thibert-a; cardstock-c; introduces revised origin and cast separate from regular Spider-continuity	4	12	26	40
1-Variant white-c (Retailer incentive)				120.00
1-DF Edition				60.00
2-Cover with Spider-Man on car	2	6	11	15
2-Cover with Spider-Man swinging past building	2	6	13	20
3,4: 4-Uncle Ben killed	1	4	7	10
5-7: 6,7-Green Goblin app.	1	3	6	8
8-13: Reveals secret to MJ				5.00
14-17: 14-Intro. Gwen Stacy & Dr. Octopus				2.25
Collected Edition (1/01, $3.99) r/#1-3				4.00
...: Learning Curve TPB (12/01, $14.95) r/#8-13				15.00
...: Power and Responsibility TPB (4/01, $14.95) r/#1-7				15.00

ULTIMATE X-MEN
Marvel Comics: Feb, 2001 - Present ($2.99/$2.50)

1-Millar-s/Adam Kubert & Thibert-a; cardstock-c; introduces revised origin and cast separate from regular X-Men continuity	2	6	11	15
1-DF Edition				25.00
1-DF Sketch Cover Edition				40.00
2	1	4	7	10
3-6	1	3	5	7
7-10				4.00
11-13				2.50
...: The Tomorrow People TPB (7/01, $14.95) r/#1-6				15.00

ULTRACYBERNETIC DOLPHINDROIDS, THE
Polestar Comics: Dec, 1993 ($2.50, unfinished limited series)

1				2.50

ULTRAFORCE (1st Series) (Also see Avengers/Ultraforce #1)
Malibu Comics (Ultraverse): Aug, 1994 - No. 10, Aug, 1995 ($1.95/$2.50)

0 (9/94, $2.50)-Perez-c/a				2.50
1-($2.50, 44 pgs.)-Bound-in trading card; team consisting of Prime, Prototype, Hardcase, Pixx, Ghoul, Contrary & Topaz; Gerard Jones scripts begin, ends #6; Perez-c/a begins.				2.50
1-Ultra 5000 Limited Silver Foil Edition				4.00
1-Holographic-c, no price				6.00
2-5: Perez-c/a in all. 2 (10/94, $1.95)-Prime quits, Strangers cameo. 3-Origin of Topaz; Prime rejoins. 5-Pixx dies.				2.50
2 ($2.50)-Florescent logo; limited edition stamp on-c				3.00
6-10: 6-Begin $2.50-c, Perez-c/a. 7-Ghoul story, Steve Erwin-a. 8-Marvel's Black Knight enters the Ultraverse (last seen in Avengers #375); Perez-c/a.				

Ultraforce #8 © MAL

Uncanny Origins #9 © MAR

Uncanny Tales #14 © MAR

	GD2.0	FN6.0	VF8.0	NM9.4		GD2.0	FN6.0	VF8.0	NM9.4

9,10-Black Knight app.; Perez-c. 10-Leads into Ultraforce/Avengers Prelude.

2.50

Malibu "Ashcan ": Ultraforce #0A (6/94)   2.50
.../Avengers Prelude 1 (8/95, $2.50)-Perez-c.   2.50
.../Avengers 1 (8/95, $3.95)-Warren Ellis script; Perez-c/a; foil-c   4.00

ULTRAFORCE (2nd Series)(Also see Black September)
Malibu Comics (Ultraverse): Infinity, Sept, 1995 - V2#15, Dec, 1996 ($1.50)

Infinity, V2#1-15: Infinity-Team consists of Marvel's Black Knight, Ghoul, Topaz, Prime & redesigned Prototype; Warren Ellis scripts begin, ends #3; variant-c exists. 1-1st app.Cromwell, Lament & Wreckage.
2-Contains free encore presentation of Ultraforce #1; flip book "Phoenix Resurrection" Pt. 7. 7-Darick Robertson, Jeff Johnson & others-a.
8,9-Intro. Future Ultraforce (Prime, Hellblade, Angel of Destruction, Painkiller & Whiplash); Gary Erskine-c/a. 9-Foxfire app. 10-Lament back-up story by Pander Bros. 12-Ultraforce vs. Maxis (cont'd in Ultraverse Unlimited #2); Exiles & Iron Clad app. 13-Prime leaves; Hardcase returns
2.25
Infinity (2000 signed)   4.00
.../Spider-Man ($3.95)-Marv Wolfman script; Green Goblin app; 2 covers exist.
4.00

ULTRAGIRL
Marvel Comics: Nov, 1996 - No. 3 Mar, 1997($1.50, limited series)

1-3: 1-1st app.   2.25

ULTRA KLUTZ
Onward Comics: 1981; 6/86 - #27, 1/89, #28, 4/90 - #31, 1990? ($1.50/$1.75/$2.00, B&W)

1 (1981)-Re-released after 2nd #1   2.25
1-30: 1-(6/86). 27-Photo back-c   2.25
31-($2.95, 52 pgs.)   3.00

ULTRAMAN
Nemesis Comics: Mar, 1994 - No. 4, 1995? ($1.75/$1.95)

1-($2.25)-Collector's edition; foil-c; special 3/4 wraparound-c   3.00
1-($1.75)-Newsstand edition   2.50
2-4: $1.95-c begins   2.50

ULTRAVERSE DOUBLE FEATURE
Malibu Comics (Ultraverse): Jan, 1995 ($3.95, one-shot, 68 pgs.)

1-Flip-c featuring Prime & Solitaire.   4.00

ULTRAVERSE ORIGINS
Malibu Comics (Ultraverse): Jan, 1994 (99¢, one-shot)

1-Gatefold-c; 2 pg. origins all characters   2.25
1-Newsstand edition; different-c, no gatefold   2.25

ULTRAVERSE PREMIERE
Malibu Comics (Ultraverse): 1994 (one-shot)

0-Ordered thru mail w/coupons   5.00

ULTRAVERSE UNLIMITED
Malibu Comics (Ultraverse): June, 1996; No. 2, Sept, 1996 ($2.50)

1,2: 1-Adam Warlock returns to the Marvel Universe; Rune-c/app. 2-Black Knight, Reaper & Sierra Blaze return to the Marvel Universe   2.50

ULTRAVERSE YEAR ONE
Malibu Comics (Ultraverse): 1994 ($4.95, one-shot)

nn-In-depth synopsis of the first year's titles & stories.   5.00

ULTRAVERSE YEAR TWO
Malibu Comics (Ultraverse): Aug, 1995 ($4.95, one-shot)

nn-In-depth synopsis of second year's titles & stories   5.00

ULTRAVERSE YEAR ZERO: THE DEATH OF THE SQUAD
Malibu Comics (Ultraverse): Nov - No. 4, July, 1995 ($2.95, lim. series)

1-4: 3-Codename: Firearm back-up story.   3.00

UNBIRTHDAY PARTY WITH ALICE IN WONDERLAND (See Alice In Wonderland, Four Color #341)

UNBOUND
Image Comics (Desperado): Jan, 1998 ($2.95, B&W)

1-Pruett-s/Peters-a   3.00

UNCANNY ORIGINS
Marvel Comics: Sept, 1996 - No. 14, Oct, 1997 (99¢)

1-14: 1-Cyclops. 2-Quicksilver. 3-Archangel. 4-Firelord. 5-Hulk. 6-Beast
7-Venom. 8-Nightcrawler. 9-Storm. 10-Black Cat. 11-Black Knight.
12-Dr. Strange. 13-Daredevil. 14-Iron Fist   2.25

UNCANNY TALES
Atlas Comics (PrPI/PPI): June, 1952 - No. 56, Sept, 1957

1-Heath-a; horror/weird stories begin	86	258	540	950
2	47	142	286	500
3-5	40	120	240	420
6-Wolvertonish-a by Matt Fox	42	126	252	440
7-10: 8-Atom bomb story; Tothish-a (by Sekowsky?). 9-Crandall-a				
	39	117	208	360
11-20: 17-Atom bomb panels; anti-communist story; Hitler story. 19-Krenkel-a.				
20-Robert Q. Sale-c	29	87	153	265
21-25,27: 25-Nostrand-a	25	75	130	225
26-Spider-Man prototype c/story	35	105	185	320
28-Last precode issue (1/55); Kubert-a; #1-28 contain 2-3 sci/fi stories each				
	26	78	136	235
29-41,43-49,51	17	51	88	150
42,54,56-Krigstein-a	18	54	94	160
50,53,55-Torres-a	17	51	88	150
52-Oldest Iron Man prototype (2/57)	20	60	105	175

NOTE: **Andru** a-15, 27. **Ayers** a-22. **Bailey** a-51. **Briefer** a-19, 20. **Brodsky** c-1, 3, 4, 6, 8, 12-16, 19. **Brodsky/Everett** c-9. **Cameron** a-47. **Colan** a-11, 16, 17, 52. **Drucker** a-37, 42, 45. **Everett** a-2, 9, 12, 32, 36, 39, 48; c-7, 11, 17, 39, 40, 50, 52, 53. **Fass** a-9, 10, 15, 24. **Forte** a-18, 27, 34, 52, 53. **Heath** a-13, 14; c-5, 10, 18. **Keller** a-3. **Lawrence** a-14, 17, 19, 23, 27, 28, 35. **Maneely** a-4, 8, 10, 16, 29, 35; c-2, 22, 26, 33, 38. **Moldoff** a-23. **Morisi** a-48, 52. **Morrow** a-46, 51. **Orlando** a-49, 50, 53. **Powell** a-12, 18, 34, 36, 38, 43, 56. **Robinson** a-3, 13. **Reinman** a-12. **Romita** a-10. **Roussos** a-8. **Sale** a-47, 53; c-20. **Sekowsky** a-25. **Sinnott** a-50. **Torres** a-53. **Tothish-a** by **Andru**-27. **Wildey** a-22, 48.

UNCANNY TALES
Marvel Comics Group: Dec, 1973 - No. 12, Oct, 1975

1-Crandall-r/Uncanny Tales #9('50s)	2	6	15	22
2-12: 7,12-Kirby-a	2	6	9	12

NOTE: **Ditko** reprints-#4, 6-8, 10-12.

UNCANNY X-MEN, THE (See X-Men, 1st series, #142-on)

UNCANNY X-MEN AND THE NEW TEEN TITANS (See Marvel and DC Present...)

UNCENSORED MOUSE, THE
Eternity Comics: Apr, 1989 - No. 2, Apr, 1989 ($1.95, B&W)(Came sealed in plastic bag)(Both contain racial stereotyping & violence)

1,2-Early Gottfredson strip-r in each	1	4	7	10

NOTE: Both issues contain unauthorized reprints. Series was cancelled. **Win Smith** r-1, 2.

UNCLE CHARLIE'S FABLES
Lev Gleason Publ.: Jan, 1952 - No. 5, Sept, 1952 (All have Biro painted-c)

1-Norman Maurer-a; has Biro's picture	16	48	83	140
2-Fuje-a; Biro photo	10	30	55	80
3-5	8	24	45	65

UNCLE DONALD & HIS NEPHEWS DUDE RANCH (See Dell Giant #52)

UNCLE DONALD & HIS NEPHEWS FAMILY FUN (See Dell Giant #38)

UNCLE JOE'S FUNNIES
Centaur Publications: 1938 (B&W)

1-Games, puzzles & magic tricks, some interior art; Bill Everett-c				
	52	157	314	550

UNCLE MILTY (TV)
Victoria Publications/True Cross: Dec, 1950 - No. 4, July, 1951 (52 pgs.)(Early TV comic)

1-Milton Berle photo on-c of #1,2	52	157	314	550
2	35	105	188	325
3,4	30	90	159	275

UNCLE REMUS & HIS TALES OF BRER RABBIT (See Brer Rabbit, 4-Color #129, 208, 693)

UNCLE SAM
DC Comics (Vertigo): 1997 - No. 2, 1997 ($4.95, limited series)

Uncle Sam Quarterly #1 © QUA

Uncle Scrooge #203 © WDC

Underdog #11 © Leonardo T.T.V.

1,2-Alex Ross painted c/a. Story by Ross and Steve Darnell				5.00
Hardcover (1998, $17.95)				18.00
Softcover (2000, $9.95)				10.00

UNCLE SAM QUARTERLY (Blackhawk #9 on)(See Freedom Fighters)
Quality Comics Group: Autumn, 1941 - No. 8, Fall, 1943 (see National Comics)

1-Origin Uncle Sam; Fine/Eisner-c, chapter headings, 2 pgs. by Eisner;				
(2 versions: dark cover, no price; light cover with price sticker); Jack Cole-a				
	350	1050	2188	4200
2-Cameos by The Ray, Black Condor, Quicksilver, The Red Bee, Alias the				
Spider, Hercules & Neon the Unknown; Eisner, Fine-c/a				
	127	381	795	1400
3-Tuska-c/a; Eisner-a(2)	95	285	597	1050
4	84	253	525	925
5,7-Hitler, Mussolini & Tojo-c	100	300	625	1100
6,8	68	205	426	750

NOTE: *Kotzky* (or *Tuska*) a-3-8.

UNCLE SCROOGE (Disney) (Becomes Walt Disney's... #210 on) (See Cartoon Tales, Dell Giants #33, 55, Disney Comic Album, Donald and Scrooge, Dynabrite, Four Color #178, Gladstone Comic Album, Walt Disney's Comics & Stories #98, Walt Disney's ...)
Dell #1-39/Gold Key #40-173/Whitman #174-209: No. 386, 3/52 - No. 39, 8-10/62; No. 40, 12/62 - No. 209, 7/84

Four Color 386(#1)-in "Only a Poor Old Man" by Carl Barks; r-in Uncle Scrooge				
& Donald Duck #1('65) & The Best of Walt Disney Comics (1974). The very				
1st cover app. of Uncle Scrooge	96	275	672	1250
1-(1996)-Reprints F.C. #386; given away with lithograph "Dam Disaster at				
Money Lake" & as a subscription offer giveaway to Gladstone subscribers				
	2	6	13	20
Four Color 456(#2)-in "Back to the Klondike" by Carl Barks; r-in Best of U.S. &				
D.D. #1('66) & Gladstone C.A. #4	60	180	420	775
Four Color 495(#3)-r/#105	44	131	308	575
4(12-2/53-54)-r-in Gladstone Comic Album #11	33	99	231	425
5-r-in Gladstone Special #2 & Walt Disney Digest #1				
	27	80	189	350
6-r-in U.S. #106,165,233 & Best of U.S. & D.D. #1('66)				
	20	60	140	260
7-The Seven Cities of Cibola by Barks; r-in #217 & Best of D.D. & U.S. #2 ('67)				
	19	57	133	240
8-10: 8-r-in #111,222. 9-r-in #104,214. 10-r-in #67	15	45	105	200
11-20: 11-r-in #237. 17-r-in #215. 19-r-in Gladstone C.A. #1. 20-r-in #213				
	14	41	98	180
21-30: 24-X-Mas-c. 26-r-in #211	12	36	84	155
31-35,37-40: 34-r-in #228. 40-X-Mas-c	10	30	70	125
36-1st app. Magica De Spell; Number one dime 1st identified by name				
	11	33	77	145
41-60: 48-Magica De Spell-c/story (3/64). 49-Sci/fic-c. 51-Beagle Boys-c/story				
(8/64)	8	24	56	105
61-63,65,66,68-71:71-Last Barks issue w/original story (#71-he only storyboard-				
ed the script)	7	21	49	90
64-Barks Vietnam War story "Treasure of Marco Polo" banned for reprints by				
Disney since the 1970s because of its third world revolutionary war theme				
	9	27	63	120
67,72,73: 67,72,73-Barks-r	7	21	49	90
74-84: 74-Barks-r(1pg.). 75-81,83-Not by Barks. 82,84-Barks-r begin				
	5	15	34	55
85-110	4	12	29	45
111-120	3	9	20	30
121-141,143-152,154-157	3	9	17	25
142-Reprints Four Color #456 with-c	3	9	19	28
153,158,162-164,166,168-170,178,180: No Barks	2	6	10	14
159-160,165,167	2	6	11	16
161(r/#14), 171(r/#11), 177(r/#16),183(r/#6)-Barks-r	2	6	11	16
172(1/80),173(2/80)-Gold Key. Barks-a	2	6	13	20
174(3/80),175(4/80),176(5/80)-Whitman. Barks-r	3	9	17	25
177(6/80),178(7/80)	3	9	20	30
179(9/80)(4/#9)-(Very low distribution)	38	114	266	500
180(11/80),181(12/80), r/4-Color #495) pre-pack?	4	12	26	40
182-195: 184,185,187,188-Barks-a. 182,186,191-194-No Barks. 189(r/#5),				
190(r/#4), 195(r/4-Color #386)	2	6	11	16

196(4/82),197(5/82): 196(r/#13)	2	6	13	20
198-209 (All #90038 on-c; pre-pack; no date or date code): 198(4/83), 199(5/83),				
200(6/83), 201(6/83), 202(7/83), 203(7/83), 204(8/83), 205(8/83), 206(4/84),				
207(5/83), 208(6/84), 209(7/84). 198-202,204-206: No Barks. 203(r/#12),				
207(r/#93,92), 208(r/U.S. #18), 209(r/U.S. #21)-Barks-r				
	2	6	15	22
Uncle Scrooge & Money(G.K.)-Barks-r/from WDC&S #130 (3/67)				
	4	12	29	45
Mini Comic #1(1976)(3-1/4x6-1/2")-r/U.S. #115; Barks-c				
	1	4	7	10

NOTE: *Barks* c-Four Color 386, 456, 495, #4-37, 39, 40, 43-71.

UNCLE SCROOGE & DONALD DUCK
Gold Key: June, 1965 (25¢, paper cover)

1-Reprint of Four Color #386(#1) & lead story from Four Color #29				
	7	21	49	90

UNCLE SCROOGE COMICS DIGEST
Gladstone Publishing: Dec, 1986 - No. 5, Aug, 1987 ($1.25, Digest-size)

1,3	1	3	6	8
2,4				6.00
5 (low print run)	1	3	6	9

UNCLE SCROOGE GOES TO DISNEYLAND (See Dell Giants)
Gladstone Publishing Ltd.: Aug, 1985 ($2.50)

1-Reprints Dell Giant w/new-c by Mel Crawford, based on old cover				
	2	6	9	12
...Comics Digest 1 ($1.50, digest size)	2	6	10	14

UNCLE SCROOGE IN COLOR
Gladstone Publishing: 1987 ($29.95, Hardcover, 9-1/4"X12-1/4", 96 Pgs.)

nn-Reprints "Christmas on Bear Mountain" from Four Color 178 by Barks; Uncle				
Scrooge's Christmas Carol (published as Donald Duck & the Christmas				
Carol, A Little Golden Book), reproduced from the original art as adapted by				
Norman McGary from pencils by Barks; and Uncle Scrooge the Lemonade				
King, reproduced from the original art, plus Barks' original pencils				
	4	12	30	50
nn-Slipcase edition of 750, signed by Barks, issued at $79.95				300.00

UNCLE SCROOGE THE LEMONADE KING
Whitman Publishing Co.: 1960 (A Top Top Tales Book, 6-3/8"x7-5/8", 32 pgs.)

2465-Storybook pencilled by Carl Barks, finished art adapted by Norman				
McGary	40	119	280	525

UNCLE WIGGILY (See March of Comics #19)
Dell Publishing Co.: No. 179, Dec, 1947 - No. 543, Mar, 1954

Four Color 179 (#1)-Walt Kelly-c	15	45	105	200
Four Color 221 (3/49)-Part Kelly-c	9	27	63	120
Four Color 276 (5/50), 320 (#1, 3/51)	8	24	56	100
Four Color 359 (9-10/51), 391 (4-5/52)	6	18	42	80
Four Color 428 (10/52), 503 (10/53), 543	5	15	34	55

UNDERCOVER GIRL (Starr Flagg) (See Extra Comics & Manhunt!)
Magazine Enterprises: No. 5, 1952 - No. 7, 1954

5(#1)(A-1 #62)-Fallon of the F.B.I. in all	40	120	220	380
6(A-1 #98), 7(A-1 #118)-All have Starr Flagg	39	117	208	360

NOTE: *Powell* c-6, 7. *Whitney* a-5-7.

UNDERDOG (TV)(See Kite Fun Book, March of Comics #426, 438, 467, 479)
Charlton Comics/Gold Key: July, 1970 - No. 10, Jan, 1972; Mar, 1975 - No. 23, Feb, 1979

1 (1st series, Charlton)-1st app. Underdog	8	24	56	100
2-10	4	12	30	50
1 (2nd series, Gold Key)	5	15	35	70
2-10	3	10	23	35
11-20: 13-1st app. Shack of Solitude	3	9	17	25
21-23	3	9	19	28

UNDERDOG
Spotlight Comics: 1987 - No. 3?, 1987 ($1.50)

1-3				4.00

UNDERDOG SUMMER SPECIAL (TV)
Harvey Comics: Oct, 1993 ($2.25, 68 pgs.)

Undersea Agent #4 © Tower Comics

Underworld Crime #7 © FAW

The Unexpected #197 © DC

	GD2.0	FN6.0	VF8.0	NM9.4
1				3.00

UNDERSEA AGENT
Tower Comics: Jan, 1966 - No. 6, Mar, 1967 (25¢, 68 pgs.)

1-Davy Jones, Undersea Agent begins	8	24	56	90
2-6: 2-Jones gains magnetic powers. 5-Origin & 1st app. of Merman.				
6-Kane/Wood-c(r)	5	15	38	60

NOTE: *Gil Kane a-3-6; c-4, 5. Moldoff a-2i.*

UNDERSEA FIGHTING COMMANDOS (See Fighting Undersea...)
I.W. Enterprises: 1964

I.W. Reprint #1,2('64): 1-r/#? 2-r/#1; Severin-c	2	6	10	14

UNDERTAKER (World Wrestling Federation)
Chaos! Comics: Feb, 1999 - Present ($2.50/$2.95)

Preview (2/99)				2.50
1-10: Reg. and photo covers for each. 1-(4/99)				3.00
1-($6.95) DF Ed.; Brereton painted-c				7.00
...Halloween Special (10/99, 2.95) Reg. & photo-c				3.00
Wizard #0				2.25

UNDERWATER CITY, THE
Dell Publishing Co.: No. 1328, 1961

Four Color 1328-Movie, Evans-a	7	21	49	90

UNDERWORLD (...True Crime Stories)
D. S. Publishing Co.: Feb-Mar, 1948 - No. 9, June-July, 1949 (52 pgs.)

1-Moldoff (Shelly)-c; excessive violence	43	129	257	450
2-Moldoff (Shelly)-c; Ma Barker story used in SOTI, pg. 95; female electrocution panel; lingerie art	40	120	240	420
3-McWilliams-c/a; extreme violence, mutilation	39	117	208	360
4-Used in Love and Death by Legman; Ingels-a	33	99	174	300
5-Ingels-a	24	72	127	215
6-9: 8-Ravielli-a	19	57	99	165

UNDERWORLD
DC Comics: Dec, 1987 - No. 4, Mar, 1988 ($1.00, limited series, mature)

1-4				2.25

UNDERWORLD CRIME
Fawcett Publications: June, 1952 - No. 9, Oct, 1953

1	33	99	174	300
2	21	63	110	185
3-6,8,9 (8,9-exist?)	19	57	99	165
7-(6/53)-Bondage/torture-c	29	87	153	265

UNDERWORLD STORY, THE (Movie)
Avon Periodicals: 1950

nn-(Scarce)-Ravielli-c	30	90	159	275

UNDERWORLD UNLEASHED
DC Comics: Nov, 1995 - No. 3, Jan, 1996 ($2.95, limited series)

1-3: Mark Waid scripts & Howard Porter-c/a(p)				3.50
...: Abyss: Hell's Sentinel 1-($2.95)-Alan Scott, Phantom Stranger, Zatanna app.				3.00
...: Apokolips-Dark Uprising 1 ($1.95)				2.25
...: Batman-Devil's Asylum 1-($2.95)-Batman app.				3.00
...: Patterns of Fear-($2.95)				3.00
TPB (1998, $17.95) r/#1-3 & Abyss-Hell's Sentinel				18.00

UNEARTHLY SPECTACULARS
Harvey Publications: Oct, 1965 - No. 3, Mar, 1967

1-(12¢)-Tiger Boy; Simon-c	4	12	26	40
2-(25¢ giants)-Jack Q. Frost, Tiger Boy & Three Rocketeers app.; Williamson, Wood, Kane-a; 1-r story/Thrill-O-Rama #2	4	12	29	45
3-(25¢ giants)-Jack Q. Frost app.; Williamson/Crandall-a; r-from Alarming Advs. #1,1962	4	12	29	45

NOTE: *Crandall a-3r. G. Kane a-2. Orlando a-3. Simon, Sparling, Wood c-2. Simon/Kirby a-3r. Torres a-1? Wildey a-1(3). Williamson a-2, 3r. Wood a-2(2).*

UNEXPECTED, THE (Formerly Tales of the...)
National Per. Publ./DC Comics: No. 105, Feb-Mar, 1968 - No. 222, May, 1982

105-Begin 12¢ cover price	5	15	34	55
106-113: 113-Last 12¢ issue (6-7/69)	3	10	23	35

	GD2.0	FN6.0	VF8.0	NM9.4
114,115,117,118,120-125	3	9	17	25
116 (36 pgs.)-Wrightson-a?	3	9	19	28
119-Wrightson-a, 8pgs.(36 pgs.)	4	12	26	40
126,127,129-136-(52 pgs.)	3	9	17	25
128(52 pgs.)-Wrightson-a	4	12	26	40
137-156	2	6	11	15
157-162-(100 pgs.)	3	10	23	35
163-188: 187,188-(44 pgs.)	1	4	7	10
189,190,192-195 ($1.00, 68 pgs.): 189 on are combined with House of Secrets & The Witching Hour	2	6	9	12
191-Rogers-a(p) ($1.00, 68 pgs.)	2	6	10	14
196-222: 200-Return of Johnny Peril by Tuska. 205-213-Johnny Peril app.				
210-Time Warp story	1	3	6	8

NOTE: *Neal Adams c-110, 112-115, 118, 121, 124. J. Craig a-195. Ditko a-189, 221p, 222p; c-222. Drucker a-107r, 132r. Giffen a-219, 222. Kaluta c-203, 212. Kirby a-127r, 162. Kubert c-204, 214-216, 219-221. Mayer a-217p, 220, 221p. Moldoff a-136r. Moreira a-133. Mortimer a-212p. Newton a-204p. Orlando a-202; c-191. Perez a-217p. Redondo a-155, 166, 195. Reese a-145. Sparling a-107, 205-209p, 212p. Spiegle a-217. Starlin c-198. Toth a-126r, 127r. Tuska a-127, 132, 134, 136, 139, 152, 180, 200p. Wildey a-128r, 193. Wood a-122i, 133i, 137i, 138i. Wrightson a-161r(2 pgs.). Johnny Peril in #106-114, 116, 117, 200, 205-213.*

UNEXPECTED ANNUAL, THE (See DC Special Series #4)
UNIDENTIFIED FLYING ODDBALL (See Walt Disney Showcase #52)

UNION
Image Comics (WildStorm Productions): June, 1993 - No. 0, July, 1994 ($1.95, limited series)

0-(7/94, $2.50)				2.50
0-Alternate Portacio-c (See Deathblow #5)				5.00
1-($2.50)-Embossed foil-c; Texeira-c/a in all				2.50
1-($1.95)-Newsstand edition w/o foil-c				2.25
2-4: 4-(7/94)				2.50

UNION
Image Comics (WildStorm Prod.): Feb, 1995 - No. 9, Dec, 1995 ($2.50)

1-3,5-9: 3-Savage Dragon app. 6-Fairchild from Gen 13 app.				2.50
4-($1.95, Newsstand)-WildStorm Rising Pt. 3				2.25
4-($2.50, Direct Market)-WildStorm Rising Pt. 3, bound-in card				2.50

UNION: FINAL VENGEANCE
Image Comics (WildStorm Productions): Oct, 1997 ($2.50)

1-Golden-c/Heisler-s				2.50

UNION JACK
Marvel Comics: Dec, 1998 - No. 3, Feb, 1999 ($2.99, limited series)

1-3-Raab-s/Cassaday-s/a				3.00

UNITED COMICS (Formerly Fritzi Ritz #7; has Fritzi Ritz logo)
United Features Syndicate: Aug, 1940; No. 8, 1950 - No. 26, Jan-Feb, 1953

1(68 pgs.)-Fritzi Ritz & Phil Fumble	24	72	127	215
8-Fritzi Ritz, Abbie & Slats	18	32	45	
9-21: 20-Strange As It Seems; Russell Patterson Cheesecake-a	6	18	29	40
22-(5-6/52) 2 pgs. early Peanuts by Schulz (1st in comics?)	8	24	42	60
23-26: 23-(7-8/52). 24-(9-10/52). 25-(11-12/52). 26-(1-2/53). All have 2 pgs. early Peanuts by Schulz	7	21	36	50

NOTE: *Abbie & Slats reprinted from Tip Top.*

UNITED NATIONS, THE (See Classics Illustrated Special Issue)

UNITED STATES AIR FORCE PRESENTS: THE HIDDEN CREW
U.S. Air Force: 1964 (36 pgs.)

nn-Schaffenberger-a	1	4	7	10

UNITED STATES FIGHTING AIR FORCE (Also see U.S. Fighting Air Force)
Superior Comics Ltd.: Sept, 1952 - No. 29, Oct, 1956

1	11	33	55	90
2	6	18	32	45
3-10	5	15	25	35
11-29	5	15	23	30

UNITED STATES MARINES
William H. Wise/Life's Romances Publ. Co./Magazine Ent. #5-8/Toby Press
#7-11: 1943 - No. 4, 1944; No. 5, 1952 - No. 8, 1952; No. 7 - No. 11, 1953

	GD2.0	FN6.0	VF8.0	NM9.4

nn-Mart Bailey-a	16	48	83	140
2-Bailey-a; Tojo classic-c	33	99	174	300
3-Tojo-c	22	66	116	200
4	10	30	55	80
5(A-1 #55)-Bailey-a, 6(A-1 #60), 7(A-1 #68), 8(A-1 #72)				
	8	24	42	60
7-11 (Toby)	6	18	29	40

NOTE: Powell a-5-7.

UNITY
Valiant: No. 0, Aug, 1992 - No. 1, 1992 (Free comics w/limited dist., 20 pgs.)

0 (Blue)-Prequel to Unity x-overs in all Valiant titles; B. Smith-c/a. (Free to everyone that bought all 8 titles that month.)				2.25
0 (Red)-Same as above, but w/red logo (5,000).				3.00
0 (Gold)-Promotional copy.				
1-Epilogue to Unity x-overs; B. Smith-c/a. (1 copy available for every 8 Valiant books ordered by dealers.)				2.25
1 (Gold), 1-(Platinum)-Promotional copy.				3.00
Yearbook 1 (2/95, $3.95)-"1994" in indicia.				3.00

UNITY 2000 (See preludes in Shadowman #3,4 flipbooks)
Acclaim Comics: Nov, 1999 - No. 6 ($2.50, limited series)

Preview -B&W plot preview and cover art; paper cover				2.25
1,2-Starlin-a/Shooter-s				2.50

UNIVERSAL MONSTERS
Dark Horse Comics: 1993 ($4.95/$5.95, 52 pgs.)(All adapt original movies)

Creature From the Black Lagoon nn-($4.95), Dracula nn-($4.95), Frankenstein nn-($3.95)-Painted-c/a, The Mummy nn-($4.95)- Painted-c	1	3	5	7

UNIVERSAL PRESENTS DRACULA-THE MUMMY& OTHER STORIES
Dell Publishing Co.: Sept-Nov, 1963 (one-shot, 84 pgs.) (Also see Dell Giants)

02-530-311-r/Dracula 12-231-212, The Mummy 12-437-211 & part of Ghost Stories No. 1	13	39	104	260

UNIVERSAL SOLDIER (Movie)
Now Comics: Sept, 1992 - No. 3, Nov, 1992 (Limited series, polybagged, mature)

1-3 ($2.50, Direct Sales) 1-Movie adapatation; hologram on-c (all direct sales editions have painted-c)				2.50
1-3 ($1.95, Newsstand)-Rewritten & redrawn code approved version; all newsstand editions have photo-c				2.25

UNIVERSE
Image Comics (Top Cow): Sept, 2001 - Present ($2.50)

1-4-Jenkins-s				2.50

UNIVERSE X (See Earth X)
Marvel Comics: Sept, 2000 - No. 12, Sept, 2001 ($3.99/$3.50, limited series)

0-Ross-c/Braithwaite-a/Ross & Krueger-s				4.00
1-12: 5-Funeral of Captain America				3.50
... Beasts (6/00, $3.99) Yeates-a/Ross-c				4.00
... Cap (Capt. America) (2/01, $3.99) Yeates & Totleben-a/Ross-c; Cap dies				4.00
... 4 (Fantastic 4) (10/00, $3.99) Brent Anderson-a/Ross-c				4.00
... Iron Men (9/01, $3.99) Anderson-a/Ross-c; leads into #12				4.00
... Omnibus (6/01, $3.99) Ross B&W sketchbook and character bios				4.00
Sketchbook- Wizard supplement; B&W character sketches and bios				2.25
...Spidey (1/01, $3.99) Romita Sr. flashback-a/Guice-a/Ross-c				4.00
...X (11/01, $3.99) Series conclusion; Braithwaite/Ross wraparound-c				4.00

UNKNOWN MAN, THE (Movie)
Avon Periodicals: 1951

nn-Kinstler-c	29	87	156	270

UNKNOWN SOLDIER (Formerly Star-Spangled War Stories)
National Periodical Publications/DC Comics: No. 205, Apr-May, 1977 - No. 268, Oct, 1982 (See Our Army at War #168 for 1st app.)

205	2	6	12	18
206-210,220,221,251: 220,221 (44pgs.). 251-Enemy Ace begins	2	6	9	12
211-218,222-247,250,252-264	1	3	6	9
219-Miller-a (44 pgs.)	2	6	11	16

	GD2.0	FN6.0	VF8.0	NM9.4

248,249,265-267: 248,249-Origin. 265-267-Enemy Ace vs. Balloon Buster.				
	1	4	7	10
268-Death of Unknown Soldier	2	6	12	18

NOTE: Chaykin a-234. Evans a-265-267; c-235. Kubert c-Most. Miller a-219p. Severin a-251-253, 260, 261, 265-267. Simonson a-254-256. Spiegle a-258, 259, 262-264.

UNKNOWN SOLDIER, THE (Also see Brave &the Bold #146)
DC Comics: Winter, 1988-'89 - No. 12, Dec, 1989 ($1.50, maxi-series, mature)

1-12: 8-Begin $1.75-c				3.00

UNKNOWN SOLDIER
DC Comics (Vertigo): Apr, 1997 - No 4, July, 1997 ($2.50, mini-series)

1-Ennis-s/Plunkett-a/Bradstreet-c in all				6.00
2-4				4.00
TPB (1998, $12.95) r/#1-4				13.00

UNKNOWN WORLD (Strange Stories From Another World #2 on)
Fawcett Publications: June, 1952

1-Norman Saunders painted-c	40	120	232	400

UNKNOWN WORLDS (See Journey Into...)

UNKNOWN WORLDS
American Comics Group/Best Synd. Features: Aug, 1960 - No. 57, Aug, 1967

1-Schaffenberger-c	21	63	146	260
2-Dinosaur-c/story	13	39	91	155
3-5	10	30	70	120
6-11: 9-Dinosaur-c/story. 11-Last 10¢ issue	8	24	60	100
12-19: 12-Begin 12¢ issues?; ends #57	7	21	50	80
20-Herbie cameo (12-1/62-63)	7	21	53	85
21-35	5	15	34	55
36- "The People vs. Hendricks" by Craig; most popular ACG story ever				
	5	15	38	60
37-46	4	12	29	45
47-Williamson-a r-from Adventures Into the Unknown #96, 3 pgs.; Craig-a				
	4	12	30	50
48-57: 53-Frankenstein app.	4	12	26	40

NOTE: Ditko a-49, 50p, 54. Forte a-3, 6, 11. Landau a-56(2). Reinman a-3, 9, 13, 20, 22, 23, 36, 38, 54. Whitney c/a-most issues. John Force, Magic Agent app.-35, 36, 48, 50, 52, 54, 56.

UNKNOWN WORLDS OF FRANK BRUNNER
Eclipse Comics: Aug, 1985 - No. 2, Aug, 1985 ($1.75)

1,2-B&W-r in color				3.50

UNKNOWN WORLDS OF SCIENCE FICTION
Marvel Comics: Jan, 1975 - No. 6, Nov, 1975; 1976 ($1.00, B&W Magazine)

1-Williamson/Krenkel/Torres/Frazetta-r/Witzend #1, Neal Adams-r/Phase 1; Brunner & Kaluta-r; Freas/Romita-c	2	6	11	15
2-6: 5-Kaluta text illos	1	4	7	10
Special 1(1976,100 pgs.)-Newton painted-c	2	6	11	15

NOTE: Brunner a-2; c-4, 6. Buscema a-Special 1p. Chaykin a-5. Colan a-2(p)-1, 3, 5, 6. Corben a-4. Kaluta a-2, Special 1(ext illos); c-2. Morrow a-3, 5. Nino a-3, 6, Special 1. Perez a-2, 3. Ray Bradbury interview in #1.

UNLIMITED ACCESS (Also see Marvel Vs. DC))
Marvel Comics: Dec, 1997 - No. 4, Mar, 1998 ($2.99/1.99, limited series)

1-Spider-Man, Wonder Woman, Green Lantern & Hulk app.				3.50
2,3-($1.99)- 2-X-Men, Legion of Super-Heroes app. 3-Original Avengers vs. original Justice League				2.50
4-($2.99) Amalgam Legion vs. Darkseid & Magneto				3.00

UNSANE (Formerly Mighty Bear #13, 14? or The Outlaws #10-14?)(Satire)
Star Publications: No. 15, June, 1954

15-Disbrow-a(2); L. B. Cole-c	39	117	208	360

UNSEEN, THE
Visual Editions/Standard Comics: No. 5, 1952 - No. 15, July, 1954

5-Horror stories in all; Toth-a	40	120	220	380
6,7,9,10-Jack Katz-a	30	90	159	275
8,11,13,14	22	66	116	195
12,15-Toth-a. 12-Tuska-a	30	90	159	275

NOTE: Nick Cardy c-12. Fawcette a-13, 14. Sekowsky a-7, 8(2), 10, 13, 15.

UNTAMED
Marvel Comics (Epic Comics/Heavy Hitters): June, 1993 - No. 3, Aug, 1993 ($1.95, limited series)

Unusual Tales #6 © CC

USA Comics #7 © MAR

	GD2.0	FN6.0	VF8.0	NM9.4
1-($2.50)-Embossed-c				2.50
2,3				2.25

UNTAMED LOVE (Also see Frank Frazetta's Untamed Love)
Quality Comics Group (Comic Magazines): Jan, 1950 - No. 5, Sept, 1950

1-Ward-c, Gustavson-a	26	78	136	235
2,4: 2-5-Photo-c	16	48	83	140
3,5-Gustavson-a	18	54	94	155

UNTOLD LEGEND OF CAPTAIN MARVEL, THE
Marvel Comics: Apr, 1997 - No. 3, June, 1997 ($2.50, limited series)

1-3				2.50

UNTOLD LEGEND OF THE BATMAN, THE (Also see Promotional section)
DC Comics: July, 1980 - No. 3, Sept, 1980 (Limited series)

1-Origin; Joker-c; Byrne's 1st work at DC				5.00
2,3				4.00

NOTE: *Aparo a-1i, 2, 3. Byrne a-1p.*

UNTOLD ORIGIN OF THE FEMFORCE, THE (Also see Femforce)
AC Comics: 1989 ($4.95, 68 pgs.)

1-Origin Femforce; Bill Black-a(i) & scripts				6.00

UNTOLD TALES OF CHASTITY
Chaos! Comics: Nov, 2000 ($2.95, one-shot)

1-Origin; Steven Grant-s/Peter Vale-c/a				3.00
1-Premium Edition with glow in the dark cover				13.00

UNTOLD TALES OF LADY DEATH
Chaos! Comics: Nov, 2000 ($2.95, one-shot)

1-Origin of Lady Death; Cremator app.; Kaminski-s				3.00
1-Premium Edition with glow in the dark cover by Steven Hughes				13.00

UNTOLD TALES OF PURGATORI
Chaos! Comics: Nov, 2000 ($2.95, one-shot)

1-Purgatori in 57 B.C.; Rio/a/Grant-s				3.00
1-Premium Edition with glow in the dark cover				13.00

UNTOLD TALES OF SPIDER-MAN (Also see Amazing Fantasy #16-18)
Marvel Comics: Sept, 1995 - No. 25, Sept, 1997 (99¢)

1-Kurt Busiek scripts begin; Pat Olliffe-c/a in all (except #9).				2.50
2-22, -1(7/97), 23-25: 2-1st app. Batwing. 4-1st app. The Spacemen (Gantry, Orbit, Satellite & Vacuum). 8-1st app. The Headsman; The Enforcers (The Big Man, Montana, The Ox & Fancy Dan) app. 9-Ron Frenz-a. 10-1st app. Commanda. 16-Reintro Mary Jane Watson. 21-X-Men-c/app.				
25-Green Goblin				2.25
...'96-(1996, $1.95, 46 pgs.)-Kurt Busiek scripts; Mike Allred-c/a; Kurt Busiek & Pat Olliffe app. in back-up story; contains pin-ups				2.25
...'97-(1997, $1.95)-Wraparound-c				2.25
....: Strange Encounters ('98, $5.99) Dr. Strange app.				6.00

UNTOUCHABLES, THE (TV)
Dell Publishing Co.: No. 1237, 10-12/61 - No. 4, 8-10/62
(All have Robert Stack photo-c)

Four Color 1237(#1)	23	68	161	300
Four Color 1286	16	48	112	210
01-879-207, 12-879-210(01879-210 on inside)	9	27	63	120

UNTOUCHABLES
Caliber Comics: Aug, 1997 - No. 4 ($2.95, B&W)

1-4: 1-Pruett-s; variant covers by Kaluta & Showman				3.00

UNUSUAL TALES (Blue Beetle & Shadows From Beyond #50 on)
Charlton Comics: Nov, 1955 - No. 49, Mar-Apr, 1965

1	29	87	156	270
2	15	45	77	130
3-5	11	33	55	90
6-Ditko-c only	14	42	72	120
7,8-Ditko-c/a. 8-Robot-c	26	78	139	240
9-Ditko-c/a (20 pgs.)	29	87	156	270
10-Ditko-c/a(4)	31	93	165	285
11-(3/58, 68 pgs.)-Ditko-a(4)	29	87	156	270
12,14-Ditko-a	19	57	99	165
13,16-20	6	18	40	65

15-Ditko-c/a	21	63	110	190
21,24,28	4	12	30	50
22,23,25-27,29-Ditko-a	9	27	65	110
30-49	3	10	23	35

NOTE: *Colan a-11. Ditko c-22, 23, 25-27, 31(part).*

UP FROM HARLEM (Tom Skinner...)
Spire Christian Comics (Fleming H. Revell Co.): 1973 (35/49¢)

nn	1	3	6	8

UP-TO-DATE COMICS
King Features Syndicate: No date (1938) (36 pgs.; B&W cover) (10¢)

nn-Popeye & Henry cover; The Phantom, Jungle Jim & Flash Gordon by Raymond; The Katzenjammer Kids, Curley Harper & others. Note: Variations in content exist.	26	78	139	240

UP YOUR NOSE AND OUT YOUR EAR (Satire)
Klevart Enterprises: Apr, 1972 - No. 2, June, 1972 (52 pgs., magazine)

V1#1,2	2	6	10	14

URBAN
Moving Target Entertainment: 1994 ($1.75, B&W)

1				2.25

URTH 4 (Also see Earth 4)
Continuity Comics: May, 1989 - No. 4, Dec, 1990 ($2.00, deluxe format)

1-4: Ms. Mystic characters. 2-Neal Adams-c(i)				2.25

URZA-MISHRA WAR ON THE WORLD OF MAGIC THE GATHERING
Acclaim Comics (Armada): 1996 - No. 2, 1996 ($5.95, limited series)

1,2				6.00

U.S. (See Uncle Sam)

USA COMICS
Timely Comics (USA): Aug, 1941 - No. 17, Fall, 1945

1-Origin Major Liberty (called Mr. Liberty #1), Rockman by Wolverton, & The Whizzer by Avison; The Defender with sidekick Rusty & Jack Frost begin; The Young Avenger only app.; S&K-c plus 1 pg. art	1071	3214	7500	15,000
2-Origin Captain Terror & The Vagabond; last Wolverton Rockman; Hitler-c	350	1050	2188	4200
3-No Whizzer	291	873	1818	3200
4-Last Rockman, Major Liberty, Defender, Jack Frost, & Capt. Terror; Corporal Dix app.	236	708	1477	2600
5-Origin American Avenger & Roko the Amazing; The Blue Blade, The Black Widow & Victory Boys, Gypo the Gypsy Giant & Hills of Horror only app.; Sergeant Dix begins; no Whizzer; Hitler, Mussolini & Tojo-c	227	681	1420	2500
6-Captain America (ends #17), The Destroyer, Jap Buster Johnson, Jeep Jones begin; Terror Squad only app.	291	873	1818	3200
7-Captain Daring, Disk-Eyes the Detective by Wolverton app.; origin & only app. Marvel Boy (3/43); Secret Stamp begins; no Whizzer, Sergeant Dix	273	819	1705	3000
8,10: The Thunderbird app.	191	573	1194	2100
9-Last Secret Stamp; Hitler-c; classic-c	205	615	1281	2250
11,12: 11-No Jeep Jones	150	450	938	1650
13-17: 13-No Whizzer; Jeep Jones ends. 15-No Destroyer; Jap Buster Johnson ends	109	327	682	1200

NOTE: *Brodsky c-14. Gabrielle c-4. Schomburg c-6, 7, 10, 12, 13, 15-17. Shores a-1, 4; c-9, 11. Ed Win a-4. Cover features: 1-The Defender; 2, 3-Captain Terror; 4-Major Liberty; 5-Victory Boys; 6-17-Captain America & Bucky.*

U.S. AGENT (See Jeff Jordan...)

U.S. AGENT (See Captain America #354)
Marvel Comics: June, 1993 - No. 4, Sept, 1993 ($1.75, limited series)

1-4				2.25

U.S. AGENT
Marvel Comics: Aug, 2001 - No. 3, Oct, 2001 ($2.99, limited series)

1-3: Ordway-s/a(p)/c. 2,3-Captain America app.				3.00

USAGI YOJIMBO (See Albedo, Doomsday Squad #3 & Space Usagi)
Fantagraphics Books: July, 1987 - No. 38 ($2.00/$2.25, B&W)

Usagi Yojimbo #38 © Stan Sakai

U.S. War Machine V2 #6 © MAR

Valor #3 © WMG

	1	3	5	7
1,8,10-2nd printings				2.25
2-9				4.00
10,11: 10-Leonardo app. (TMNT). 11-Aragonés-a				5.00
12-29				3.00
30-38: 30-Begin $2.25-c				3.00
Color Special 1 (11/89, $2.95, 68 pgs.)-new & r				3.50
Color Special 2 (10/91, $3.50)				3.50
Color Special 3 (10/92, $3.50)-Jeff Smith's Bone promo on inside-c				3.50
Summer Special 1 (1986, B&W, $2.75)-r/early Albedo issues				3.00

USAGI YOJIMBO
Mirage Studios: V2#1, Mar, 1993 - No. 16, 1994 ($2.75)

V2#1-16: 1-Teenage Mutant Ninja Turtles app.				3.00

USAGI YOJIMBO
Dark Horse Comics: V3#1, Apr, 1996 - Present ($2.95/$2.99, B&W)

V3#1-52: Stan Sakai-c/a				3.00
Color Special 4 (7/97, $2.95) "Green Persimmon"				3.00
Daisho TPB ('98, $14.95) r/Mirage series #7-14				15.00
Demon Mask TPB ('01, $15.95)				16.00
Grasscutter TPB ('99, $16.95) r/#13-22				17.00
Gray Shadows TPB ('00, $14.95) r/#23-30				15.00
Seasons TPB ('99, $14.95) r/#7-12				15.00
Shades of Death TPB ('97, $14.95) r/Mirage series #1-6				15.00
The Brink of Life and Death TPB ('98, $14.95) r/Mirage series #13,15,16 & Dark Horse series #1-6				15.00

U.S. AIR FORCE COMICS (Army Attack #38 on)
Charlton Comics: Oct, 1958 - No. 37, Mar-Apr, 1965

1	6	18	40	65
2	3	10	23	35
3-10	3	9	19	28
11-20	3	9	17	25
21-37	2	6	15	22
NOTE: Glanzman c/a-9, 10, 12. Montes/Bache a-33.

USA IS READY
Dell Publishing Co.: 1941 (68 pgs., one-shot)

1-War propaganda	40	120	232	400

U.S. BORDER PATROL COMICS (Sgt. Dick Carter of the...) (See Holyoke One Shot)

USER
DC Comics (Vertigo): 2001 - No. 3, 2001 ($5.95, limited series)

1-3-Devin Grayson-s; Sean Phillips & John Bolton-a				6.00

U.S. FIGHTING AIR FORCE (Also see United States Fighting Air Force)
I. W. Enterprises: No date (1960s?)

1,9(nd): 1-r/United States Fighting...#?. 9-r/#1	2	6	9	12

U.S. FIGHTING MEN
Super Comics: 1963 - 1964 (Reprints)

10-r/With the U.S. Paratroops #4(Avon)	2	6	10	14
11,12,15-18: 11-r/Monty Hall #10. 12,16,17,18-r/U.S. Fighting Air Force #10,3,?&? 15-r/Man Comics #11	2	6	10	14

U.S. JONES (Also see Wonderworld Comics #28)
Fox Features Syndicate: Nov, 1941 - No. 2, Jan, 1942

1-U.S. Jones & The Topper begin; Nazi-c	127	381	795	1400
2-Nazi-c	87	261	544	960

U.S. MARINES
Charlton Comics: Fall, 1964 (12¢, one-shot)

1-1st app. Capt. Dude; Glanzman-a	3	9	19	28

U.S. MARINES IN ACTION
Avon Periodicals: Aug, 1952 - No. 3, Dec, 1952

1-Louis Ravielli-c/a	9	27	49	70
2,3: 3-Kinstler-c	6	18	29	40

U.S. 1
Marvel Comics Group: May, 1983 - No. 12, Oct, 1984 (7,8: painted-c)

1-12: 2-Sienkiewicz-c. 3-12-Michael Golden-c				2.25

U.S. PARATROOPS (See With the...)
U.S. PARATROOPS
I. W. Enterprises: 1964?

1,8: 1-r/With the U.S. Paratroops #1; Wood-c. 8-r/With the U.S. Paratroops #6; Kinstler-c	2	6	10	14

U.S. TANK COMMANDOS
Avon Periodicals: June, 1952 - No. 4, Mar, 1953

1-Kinstler-c	10	30	55	80
2-4: Kinstler-c	7	21	38	55
I.W. Reprint #1,8: 1-r/#1. 8-r/#3	2	6	11	15
NOTE: Kinstler a-I.W. #1; c-1-4, I.W. #1, 8.

U.S. WAR MACHINE (Also see Iron Man and War Machine)
Marvel Comics (MAX): Nov, 2001 - No. 12, Jan, 2002 ($1.50, B&W, weekly limited series)

1-12-Chuck Austen-s/a/c				2.25
TPB (12/01, $14.95) r/#1-12				15.00

"V" (TV)
DC Comics: Feb, 1985 - No. 18, July, 1986

1-Based on TV movie & series (Sci/Fi)				3.00
2-18: 17,18-Denys Cowan-c/a				2.25

VACATION COMICS (Also see A-1 Comics)
Magazine Enterprises: No. 16, 1948 (one-shot)

A-1 16-The Pixies, Tom Tom, Flying Fredd & Koko & Kola	5	15	25	35

VACATION DIGEST
Harvey Comics: Sept, 1987 ($1.25, digest size)

1				6.00

VACATION IN DISNEYLAND (Also see Dell Giants)
Dell Publishing Co/Gold Key (1965): Aug-Oct, 1959 - May, 1965 (Walt Disney)

Four Color 1025-Barks-a	19	57	133	240
1(30024-508)(G.K., 5/65, 25¢)-r/Dell Giant #30 & cover to #1 ('58); celebrates Disneyland's 10th anniversary	5	15	34	55

VACATION PARADE (See Dell Giants)

VALERIA THE SHE BAT
Continuity Comics: May, 1993 - No. 5, Nov, 1993

1-Premium; acetate-c; N. Adams-i/scripts; given as gift to retailers				5.00
5 (11/93)-Embossed-c; N. Adams-a/scripts				2.50
NOTE: Due to lack of continuity, #2-4 do not exist.

VALERIA THE SHE BAT
Acclaim Comics (Windjammer): Sept, 1995 - No.2, Oct, 1995 ($2.50, limited series)

1,2				2.50

VALKYRIE (See Airboy)
Eclipse Comics: May,1987 - No. 3, July, 1987 ($1.75, limited series)

1-3: 2-Holly becomes new Black Angel				2.50

VALKYRIE
Marvel Comics: Jan, 1997 ($2.95, one-shot)

1-w/pin-ups				3.00

VALKYRIE!
Eclipse Comics: July, 1988 - No. 3, Sept, 1988 ($1.95, limited series)

1-3				2.25

VALLEY OF THE DINOSAURS (TV)
Charlton Comics: Apr, 1975 - No. 11, Dec, 1976 (Hanna-Barbera)

1-W. Howard-i	2	6	14	20
2,4-11: 2-W. Howard-i	2	6	9	12
3-Byrne text illos (early work, 7/75)	2	6	11	15

VALLEY OF THE DINOSAURS (TV)
Harvey Comics: Oct, 1992 ($1.50, giant-sized)

1-Reprints				3.00

VALLEY OF GWANGI (See Movie Classics)

Vampi #3 © Harris Pub.

Vampirella #22 © WP

Vampirella (The New Monthly) #10 © Harris Pub.

VA

	GD2.0	FN6.0	VF8.0	NM9.4

VALOR
E. C. Comics: Mar-Apr, 1955 - No. 5, Nov-Dec, 1955

1-Williamson/Torres-a; Wood-c/a	25	75	175	310
2-Williamson-c/a; Wood-a	21	63	147	260
3,4: 3-Williamson, Crandall-a. 4-Wood-c	15	45	105	185
5-Wood-c/a; Williamson/Evans-a	14	42	98	175

NOTE: *Crandall a-3, 4. Ingels a-1, 2, 4, 5. Krigstein a-1-5. Orlando a-3, 4; c-3. Wood a-1, 2, 5; c-1, 4, 5.*

VALOR
Gemstone Publishing: Oct, 1998 - No. 5, Feb, 1999 ($2.50)

1-5-Reprints				2.50

VALOR (Also see Legion of Super-Heroes & Legionnaires)
DC Comics: Nov, 1992 - No. 23, Sept, 1994 ($1.25/$1.50)

1-23: 1-Eclipso The Darkness Within aftermath. 2-Vs. Supergirl. 4-Vs. Lobo. 12-Lobo cameo. 14-Legionnaires, JLA app. 17-Austin-c(i); death of Valor. 18-22-Build-up to Zero Hour. 23-Zero Hour tie-in				2.25

VALOR THUNDERSTAR AND HIS FIREFLIES
Now Comics: Dec, 1986 ($1.50)

1-Ordway-c(p)				2.25

VAMPI (Vampirella's...)
Harris Publications (Anarchy Studios): Aug, 2000 - Present ($2.95)

Limited Edition Preview Book (5/00) Preview pages & sketchbook				3.00
1-(8/00, $2.95) Lau-a(p)/Conway-s				3.00
1-Platinum Edition				20.00
2-13				3.00
2-13-Deluxe Edition variants ($9.95): 4-Finch-c. 5-Wieringo-c. 6-Cha-c				10.00
...Digital 1 (11/01, $2.95) CGI art; Haberlin-s				3.00
...Digital Preview (Anarchy Studios, 7/01, $2.95) preview of CGI art				3.00
Switchblade Kiss HC (2001, $24.95) r/#1-6				25.00
Wizard #1/2 (mail order, $9.95) includes sketch pages				10.00

VAMPIRE BITES
Brainstorm Comics: May, 1995 - No. 2, Sept, 1996 ($2.95, B&W)

1,2;1-Color pin-up				3.00

VAMPIRE LESTAT, THE
Innovation Publishing: Jan, 1990 - No. 12, 1991 ($2.50, painted limited series)

1-Adapts novel; Bolton painted-c on all	2	6	12	18
1-2nd printing (has UPC code, 1st prints don't)				3.00
1-3rd & 4th printings				2.50
2-1st printing	1	3	6	8
2-2nd & 3rd printings				2.50
3-5				5.00
3-6,9-2nd printings				2.50
6-12				3.00

VAMPIRELLA (Magazine)(See Warren Presents)
Warren Publishing Co./Harris Publications #113: Sept, 1969 - No. 112, Feb, 1983; No. 113, Jan, 1988? (B&W)

1-Intro. Vampirella in original costume & wings; Frazetta-c/intro. page; Adams-a; Crandall-a	37	112	278	500
2-1st app. Vampirella's cousin Evily-c/s; 1st/only app. Draculina, Vampirella's blonde twin sister	14	42	102	175
3 (Low distribution)	33	100	250	450
4,6	9	27	65	110
5,7,9: 5,7-Frazetta-c. 9-Barry Smith-a; Boris/Wood-c	9	27	65	110
8-Vampirella begins by Tom Sutton as serious strip (early issues-gag line)	10	30	73	125
10-No Vampi story; Brunner, Adams Wood-a	5	15	34	55
11-Origin & 1st app. Pendragon; Frazetta-a	6	18	42	70
12-Vampi by Gonzales begins	6	18	42	70
13-15: 14-1st Maroto-a; Ploog-a	6	18	42	70
16,22,25: 16-1st full Dracula-c/app. 22-Color insert preview of Maroto's Dracula. 25-Vampi on cocaine-s	5	15	38	60
17,18,20,21,23,24: 17-Tomb of the Gods begins in Maroto, ends #22. 18-22-Dracula-s	5	15	38	60
19 (1973 Annual) All have 8 pg. color inserts. 28-Board game inside covers.	7	21	50	80

26,28,34-36,39,40: All have 8 pg. color inserts. 28-Board game inside covers.

34,35-1st Fleur the Witch Woman. 39,40-Color Dracula-s. 40-Wrightson bio

	4	12	25	38
27 (1974 Annual) New color Vampi-s; mostly-r	4	12	29	45
29,38,45: 38-2nd Vampi as Cleopatra/Blood Red Queen of Hearts; 1st Mayo-a.	4	12	25	38
30-33: 30-Intro. Pantha; Corben-a(color). 31-Origin Luana, the Beast Girl.				
32-Jones-a. 33-Pantha ends	4	12	25	38
36,37: 36-1st Vampi as Cleopatra/Blood Red Queen of Hearts. 37-(1975 Annual)	4	12	27	42
41-44,47,48: 41-Dracula-s	3	9	19	28
46-(10/75) Origin-r from Annual 1	3	10	23	35
49-1st Blind Priestess; The Blood Red Queen of Hearts storyline begins; Poe-s	3	9	19	28
50-Spirit cameo by Eisner; 40 pg. Vampi-s; Pantha & Fleur app.; Jones-a	3	9	19	28
51-53,56,57,59-62,65,66,68,75,79,80,82-86,88,89: 60-62,65,66-The Blood Red Queen of Hearts app. 60-1st Blind Priestess-c	2	6	15	22
54,55,63,81,87: 54-Vampi-s (8 pgs.); 8 pg. color Corben-a. 55-All Gonzales-a(r).				
63-10 pgs. Wrightson-a	2	6	15	22
58,70,72: 58-(92 pgs.) 70-Rook app.	3	9	20	30
64,73: 64-(100 pg. Giant) All Mayo-a; 70 pg. Vampi-s. 73-69 pg. Vampi-s; Mayo-a.	3	9	21	32
67,69,71,74,76-78-All Barbara Leigh photo-c	3	9	20	30
90-99: 90-Toth-a. 91-All-r; Gonzales-a. 93-Cassandra St. Knight begins, ends #103; new Pantha series begins, ends #108	3	9	17	24
100 (96 pg. r-special)-Origin reprinted from Ann.1; mostly reprints; Vampirella appears topless in new 21 pg. story	7	21	50	80
101-104,106,107: All lower print run. 101,102-The Blood Red Queen of Hearts app. 107-All Maroto reprint-a issue	4	12	29	45
105,108-110: 108-Torpedo series by Toth begins; Vampi nudity splash page. 110-(100 pg. Summer Spectacular)	4	12	29	45
111,112: Low print run. 111-Giant Collector's Edition ($2.50) 112-(84 pgs.) last Warren issue	5	15	38	60
113 (1988)-1st Harris Issue; very low print run	28	84	196	350
Annual 1(1972)-New definitive origin of Vampirella by Gonzales; reprints by Neal Adams (from #1), Wood (from #9)	27	81	188	335
Special 1 (1977) Softcover (color, large-square bound)-Only available thru mail order	15	45	105	180
Special 1 (1977) Hardcover (color, large-square bound)-Only available through mail order (scarce)(500 produced, signed & #'d)	33	100	250	450
#1 1969 Commemorative Edition (2001, $4.95) reprints entire #1				5.00

NOTE: *Ackerman s-1-3. Neal Adams a-1, 10p, 19p(r/#10), 44(1 pg.), Annual 1. Alcala a-78, 90, 93i. Bodé/Wood c-3. Bodé/Jones c-4. Boris/Wood c-9. Brunner a-10, 12(1 pg.). Corben a-30, 31, 33, 36, 54; c-30, 31, 33, 54. Crandall a-1, 19(r/#1). Frazetta c-1, 5, 7, 11, 31. Heath a-58, 61, 67, 76-78, 83. Infantino a-57-62. Jones a-5, 9, 12, 27, 32 (color), 33(2 pg.), 34, 50i, 83i. Ken Kelly c-6, 38, 39, 40(back-c), 46, 70, 95. Nebres a-84, 88-90, 92-96. Nino a-59i, 61i, 67, 76, 85, 90. Ploog a-14. Barry Smith a-9. Starlin a-78. Sutton a-1-5, 7-11, Annual 1. Toth a-90i, 108, 110. Wood a-9, 10, 12, 19(r/#12), 27; Annual 1; c-9(partial). Wrightson a-33(w/Jones), 40(Bio cameo) 63r. All reprint issues-19, 74, 83, 91, 105, 107, 109, 111. Annuals from 1973 are included in regular numbering. Later annuals are same format as regular issues. Color inserts (8 pgs.) in 22, 25-28, 30-35, 39, 40, 45, 46, 49, 54, 55, 67, 72. 16 pg color insert in 36.*

VAMPIRELLA (Also see Cain/... & Vengeance of...)
Harris Publications: Nov, 1992 - No. 5, Nov, 1993 ($2.95)

0				5.00
0-Gold	3	9	20	30
1-Jim Balent inks in #1-3; Adam Hughes c-1-3	2	6	13	20
1-2nd printing				5.00
1-(11/97) Commemorative Edition				3.00
2	2	6	11	15
3-5: 4-Snyder III-c. 5-Brereton painted-c	1	3	6	8
Trade paperback nn (10/93, $5.95)-r/#1-4; Jusko-c	1	3	5	7

NOTE: *Issues 1-5 contain certificates for free Dave Stevens Vampirella poster.*

VAMPIRELLA (THE NEW MONTHLY)
Harris Publications: Nov, 1997 - No. 26, May, 2000 ($2.95)

1-3-"Ascending Evil" -Morrison & Millar-s/ Conner &Palmiotti-a.-Three covers by Quesada/Palmiotti, Conner, and Conner/Palmiotti				3.00
1-3-($9.95) Jae Lee variant covers				10.00
1-($24.95) Platinum Ed.w/Quesada-c				25.00
4-6-"Holy War"-Small & Stull-a. 4-Linsner variant-c				3.00
7-9-"Queen's Gambit"-Shi app. 7-Two covers. 8-Pantha-c/app.				3.00

Vampirella #1 © Harris Pub.

Vampirella Classic #5 © Harris Pub.

Vampirella: Retro #3 © Harris Pub.

	GD2.0	FN6.0	VF8.0	NM9.4

7-($9.95) Conner variant-c — 10.00
10-12-"Hell on Earth"; Small-a/Coney-s. 12-New costume — 3.00
10-Jae Lee variant-c — 1 4 7 10
13-15-"World's End" Zircher-p; Pantha back-up. — 3.00
16,17: 16-Pantha-c;Texeira-a; Vampi back-up story. 17-(Pantha #2) — 3.00
18-20-"Rebirth": Jae Lee-c on all. 18-Loeb/Sale-a. 19-Alan Davis-a.
  20-Bruce Timm-a — 3.00
18-20-($9.95) Variant covers: 18-Sale. 19-Davis. 20-Timm — 10.00
21-26: 21,22-Dangerous Games; Small-a. 23-Lady Death-c/app.; Cleavenger-a.
  24,25-Lau-a. 26-Lady Death & Pantha-c/app.; Cleavenger-a. — 3.00
0-(1/99) also variant-c with Pantha w/#1 or Pantha #0; same contents — 3.00
TPB ($7.50) r/#1-3 "Ascending Evil" — 8.00
Ascending Evil Ashcan (8/97, $1.00) — 2.25
Hell on Earth Ashcan (7/98, $1.00) — 2.25
The End Ashcan (3/00, $6.00) — 6.00
...30th Anniversary Celebration Preview (7/99) B&W preview of #18-20 — 10.00

VAMPIRELLA
Harris Publications: June, 2001 - Present ($2.95)

1-Four covers (Mayhew w/foil logo, Campbell, Anacleto, Jae Lee) Mayhew-a;
  Mark Millar-s — 3.00
2-5: 2-Two covers (Mayhew & Chiodo). 3-Timm var-c. 4-Horn var-c — 3.00
Giant-Size Ashcan (5/01, $5.95) B&W preview art and Mayhew interview — 6.00
... : Nowheresville Preview Edition (3/01, $2.95)- previews Mayhew art and photo
  models — 3.00

VAMPIRELLA & PANTHA SHOWCASE
Harris Publications: Jan, 1997 ($1.50, one-shot)

1-Millar-s/Texeira-c/a; flip book w/"Blood Lust"; Robinson-s/Jusko-c/a — 3.00

VAMPIRELLA & THE BLOOD RED QUEEN OF HEARTS
Harris Publications: Sept, 1996 ($9.95, 96 pgs., B&W, squarebound, one-shot)

nn-r/Vampirella #49,60-62,65,66,101,102; John Bolton-c; Michael Bair back-c — 1 4 7 10

VAMPIRELLA: BLOODLUST
Harris Publications: July, 1997 - No. 2, Aug, 1997 ($4.95, limited series)

1,2-Robinson-s/Jusko-painted c/a — 5.00

VAMPIRELLA CLASSIC
Harris Publications: Feb, 1995 - No. 5, Nov, 1995 ($2.95, limited series)

1-5: Reprints Archie Goodwin stories. — 3.00

VAMPIRELLA: CROSSOVER GALLERY
Harris Publications: Sept, 1997 ($2.95, one-shot)

1-Wraparound-c by Campbell, pinups by Jae Lee, Mack, Allred, Art Adams,
  Quesada & Palmiotti and others — 3.00

VAMPIRELLA: DEATH & DESTRUCTION
Harris Publications: July, 1996 - No. 3, Sept, 1996 ($2.95, limited series)

1-3: Amanda Conner-a(p) in all. 1-Tucci-c. 2-Hughes-c. 3-Jusko-c — 3.00
1-($9.95)-Limited Edition; Beachum-c — 10.00

VAMPIRELLA/DRACULA & PANTHA SHOWCASE
Harris Publications: Aug, 1997 ($1.50, one-shot)

1-Ellis, Robinson, and Moore-s; flip book w/"Pantha" — 3.00

VAMPIRELLA/DRACULA: THE CENTENNIAL
Harris Publications: Oct, 1997 ($5.95, one-shot)

1-Ellis, Robinson, and Moore-s; Beachum, Frank/Smith, and Mack/Mays-a
  Bolton-painted-c — 6.00

VAMPIRELLA: JULIE STRAIN SPECIAL
Harris Publications: Sept, 2000 ($3.95, one-shot)

1-Photo-c w/yellow background; interview and photo gallery — 4.00
1-Limited Edition ($9.95); cover photo w/black background — 10.00

VAMPIRELLA/LADY DEATH (Also see Lady Death/Vampirella)
Harris Publications: Feb, 1999 ($3.50, one-shot)

1-Small-a/Nelson painted-c — 3.50
1-Valentine Edition ($9.95); pencil-c by Small — 10.00

VAMPIRELLA: LEGENDARY TALES
Harris Publications: May, 2000 - No. 2, June, 2000 ($2.95, B&W)

	GD2.0	FN6.0	VF8.0	NM9.(4)

1,2-Reprints from magazine; Cleavenger painted-c — 3.00
1,2-($9.95) Variant painted-c by Mike Mayhew — 10.00

VAMPIRELLA LIVES
Harris Publications: Dec, 1996 - No. 3, Feb, 1997 ($3.50/$2.95, limited series)

1-Die cut-c; Quesada & Palmiotti, Ellis-s/Conner-a — 3.50
1-Deluxe Ed.-photo-c — 3.50
2,3-($2.95)-Two editions (1 photo-c): 3-J. Scott Campbell-c — 3.00

VAMPIRELLA: MORNING IN AMERICA
Harris Publications/Dark Horse Comics: 1991 - No. 4, 1992 ($3.95, B&W, limit-
ed series, 52 pgs.)

1,2-All have Kaluta painted-c — 1 3 6 8
3,4 — 1 4 7 10

VAMPIRELLA OF DRAKULON
Harris Publications: Jan, 1996 - No. 5, Sept, 1996 ($2.95)

0-5: All reprints. 0-Jim Silke-c. 3-Polybagged w/card. 4-Texeira-c — 3.00

VAMPIRELLA/PAINKILLER JANE
Harris Publications: May, 1998 ($3.50, one-shot)

1-Waid & Augustyn-s/Leonardi & Palmiotti-a — 3.50
1-($9.95) Variant-c — 10.00

VAMPIRELLA PIN-UP SPECIAL
Harris Publications: Oct, 1995 ($2.95, one-shot)

1-Hughes-c, pin-ups by various — 5.00
1-Variant-c — 5.00

VAMPIRELLA: RETRO
Harris Publications: Mar, 1998 - No. 3, May, 1998 ($2.50, B&W, limited series)

1-3: Reprints; Silke painted covers — 3.00

VAMPIRELLA: SAD WINGS OF DESTINY
Harris Publications: Sept, 1996 ($3.95, one-shot)

1-Jusko-c — 4.00

VAMPIRELLA/SHADOWHAWK: CREATURES OF THE NIGHT (Also see
Shadowhawk)
Harris Publications: 1995 ($4.95, one-shot)

1 — 5.00

VAMPIRELLA/SHI (See Shi/Vampirella)
Harris Publications: Oct, 1997 ($2.95, one-shot)

1-Ellis-s — 3.00
1-Chromium-c — 6.00

VAMPIRELLA: SILVER ANNIVERSARY COLLECTION
Harris Publications: Jan, 1997 - No. 4 Apr, 1997 ($2.50, limited series)

1-4: Two editions: Bad Girl by Beachum, Good Girl by Silke — 3.00

VAMPIRELLA'S SUMMER NIGHTS
Harris Publications: 1992 (one-shot)

1-Art Adams infinity cover; centerfold by Stelfreeze — 3 10 23 35

VAMPIRELLA STRIKES
Harris Publications: Sept, 1995 - No. 8, Dec, 1996 ($2.95, limited series)

1-8: 1-Photo-c. 2-Deodato-c; polybagged w/card. 5-Eudaemon-c/app;
  wraparound-c; alternate-c exists. 6-(6/96)-Mark Millar script; Texeira-c;
  alternate-c exists. 7-Flip book — 3.00
1-Newsstand Edition; diff. photo-c, 1-Limited Ed.; diff. photo-c — 3.00
Annual 1-(12/96, $2.95) Delano-s; two covers — 3.00

VAMPIRELLA: 25TH ANNIVERSARY SPECIAL
Harris Publications: Oct, 1996 ($5.95, squarebound, one-shot)

nn-Reintro The Blood Red Queen of Hearts; James Robinson, Grant Morrison &
  Warren Ellis scripts; Mark Texeira, Michael Bair & Amanda Conner-a(p);
  Frank Frazetta-c — 6.00
nn-($6.95)-Silver Edition — 7.00

VAMPIRELLA VS. HEMORRHAGE
Harris Publications: Apr, 1997($3.50)

1 — 3.50

VAMPIRELLA VS. PANTHA

Vampire Tales #5 © MAR

Vamps: Pumpkin Time #3 © Elaine Lee & Will Simpson

Vault of Horror #17 © WMG

VE

Harris Publications: Mar, 1997 ($3.50)

1-Two covers; Millar-s/Texiera-c/a ... 3.50

VAMPIRELLA/WETWORKS (See Wetworks/Vampirella)
Harris Publications: June, 1997 ($2.95, one-shot)

1 ... 3.00
1-($9.95) Alternate Edition; cardstock-c ... 10.00

VAMPIRE TALES
Marvel Comics Group: Aug, 1973 - No. 11, June, 1975 (75¢, B&W, magazine)

1-Morbius, the Living Vampire begins by Pablo Marcos (1st solo Morbius series & 5th Morbius app.)	4	12	27	42
2-Intro. Satana; Steranko-r	3	10	23	35
3,5,6,8: 3-Satana app. 5-Origin Morbius. 6-1st Lilith app. 8-Blade app. (see Tomb of Dracula)	3	9	17	25
4,7	2	6	13	20
9-11: 9-Blade app.	2	6	13	20
Annual 1(10/75)-Heath-r/#9	2	6	13	20

NOTE: Alcala a-6, 8, 9l. Boris c-4, 6. Chaykin a-7. Everett a-1r. Gulacy a-7p. Heath a-9. Infantino a-3r. Gil Kane a-4, 5r.

VAMPIRE VERSES, THE
CFD Productions: Aug, 1995 - No. 4, 1995 ($2.95, B&W, mature)

1-4 ... 3.00

VAMPS
DC Comics (Vertigo): Aug, 1994 - No. 6, Jan, 1995 ($1.95, lim. series, mature)

1-6-Bolland-c ... 3.00
Trade paperback ($9.95)-r/#1-6 ... 10.00

VAMPS: HOLLYWOOD & VEIN
DC Comics (Vertigo): Feb, 1996 - No. 6, July, 1996 ($2.25, lim. series, mature)

1-6-Winslade-c ... 2.50

VAMPS: PUMPKIN TIME
DC Comics (Vertigo): Dec, 1998 - No. 3, Feb, 1999 ($2.50, lim. series, mature)

1-3-Quitely-c ... 2.50

VANDALA
Chaos! Comics: Aug, 2000 - Present ($2.95)

1-Cleavenger-c ... 3.00
1-($9.95) Premium Edition ... 10.00
Vandala II #1 (9/01, $2.99) Benes-a ... 3.00

VANGUARD (...Outpost: Earth) (See Megaton)
Megaton Comics: 1987 ($1.50)

1-Erik Larsen-c(p) ... 3.00

VANGUARD (See Savage Dragon #2)
Image Comics (Highbrow Entertainment): Oct, 1993 - No.6, 1994 ($1.95)

1-6: 1-Wraparound gatefold-c; Erik Larsen back-up-a; Supreme x-over. 3-(12/93)-Indicia says December 1994. 4-Berzerker back-up. 5-Angel Medina-a(p). ... 3.00

VANGUARD (See Savage Dragon #2)
Image Comics: Aug, 1996 - No.4, Feb, 1997 ($2.95, B&W, limited series)

1-4 ... 3.00

VANGUARD: ETHEREAL WARRIORS
Image Comics: Aug, 2000 ($5.95, B&W)

1-Fosco & Larsen-a ... 6.00

VANGUARD ILLUSTRATED
Pacific Comics: Nov, 1983 - No. 11, Oct, 1984 (Baxter paper)(Direct sales only)

1-6,8-11: 1,7-Nudity scenes. 2-1st app. Stargrazers (see Legends of the Stargrazers) Dave Stevens-c ... 3.00
7-1st app. Mr. Monster (r-in Mr. Monster #1) ... 5.00

NOTE: Evans a-7. Kaluta c-5, 7p. Perez e-6; c-4. Rude a-1-4; c-4. Williamson c-3.

VANGUARD: STRANGE VISITORS
Image Comics: Oct, 1996 - No.4, Feb, 1997 ($2.95, B&W, limited series)

1-4: 3-Supreme-c/app. ... 3.00

VANITY (See Pacific Presents #3)
Pacific Comics: Jun, 1984 - No. 2, Aug, 1984 ($1.50, direct sales)

1,2: Origin ... 2.25

VARIETY COMICS (The Spice of Comics)
Rural Home Publ./Croyden Publ. Co.: 1944 - No. 2, 1945; No. 3, 1946

1-Origin Captain Valiant	22	66	116	200
2-Captain Valiant	13	39	66	110
3(1946-Croyden)-Captain Valiant	11	33	55	90

VARIETY COMICS (See Fox Giants)

VARIOGENESIS
Dagger Comics Group: June, 1994 ($3.50)

0 ... 3.50

VARSITY
Parents' Magazine Institute: 1945

1	8	24	42	60

VAULT OF EVIL
Marvel Comics Group: Feb, 1973 - No. 23, Nov, 1975

1 (1950s reprints begin)	2	6	13	20
2-23: 3,4-Brunner-c. 11-Kirby-a	2	6	9	12

NOTE: Ditko a-14r, 15r, 20-22r. Drucker a-10r(Mystic #52), 13r(Uncanny Tales #42). Everett a-11r(Menace #2), 13r(Menace #4); c-10. Heath a-5r. Gil Kane c-1, 6. Kirby a-11. Krigstein a-20r(Uncanny Tales #54). Reinman r-1. Tuska a-6r.

VAULT OF HORROR (Formerly War Against Crime #1-11)
E. C. Comics: No. 12, Apr-May, 1950 - No. 40, Dec-Jan, 1954-55

12 (Scarce)-ties w/Crypt Of Terror as 1st horror comic	424	1272	2968	5300
13-Morphine story	93	279	651	1165
14	83	249	581	1040
15- "Terror in the Swamp" is same story w/minor changes as "The Thing in the Swamp" from Haunt of Fear #15	71	213	497	890
16	54	162	378	675
17-19	42	126	294	525
20-25: 22-Frankenstein-c & adaptation. 23-Used in POP, pg. 84; Davis-a(2). 24-Craig biography	34	102	238	425
26-B&W & color illos in POP	34	102	238	425
27-37: 30-Dismemberment-c. 31-Ray Bradbury biog. 32-Censored-c.				
35-X-Mas-c. 36- "Pipe Dream" classic opium addict story by Krigstein; "Twin Bill" cited in articles by T.E. Murphy, Wertham. 37-1st app. Drusilla, a Vampirella look alike; Williamson-a	27	81	189	335
38-39: 39-Bondage-c	23	69	161	285
40-Low distribution	34	102	238	425

NOTE: Craig art in all but No. 13 & 33; c-12-40. Crandall a-17, 34, 39. Davis a-17-38. Evans a-27, 28, 30, 32, 33. Feldstein a-12-16. Ingels a-13-20, 22-40. Kamen a-15-22, 25, 29, 35. Krigstein a-36, 38-40. Kurtzman a-12, 13. Orlando a-24, 31, 40. Wood a-12-14. #22, 29 & 31 have Ray Bradbury adaptations. #16 & 17 have H. P. Lovecraft adaptations.

VAULT OF HORROR, THE
Gladstone Publ.: Nov - No. 6, June, 1991 ($1.95, 68 pgs.)(#4 on: $2.00)

1-Craig-c(r); all contain EC reprints ... 4.00
2-6: 2,4-6-Craig-c(r). 3-Ingels-c(r) ... 3.00

VAULT OF HORROR
Russ Cochran/Gemstone Publishing: Sept, 1991 - No. 5, May, 1992 ($2.00); Oct, 1992 - No. 29, Oct, 1999 ($1.50/$2.00/$2.50)

1-29: E.C reprints. 1-4r/VOH #12-15 w/original-c ... 3.00

V...-COMICS (Morse code for "V" - 3 dots, 1 dash)
Fox Features Syndicate: Jan, 1942 - No. 2, Mar-Apr, 1942

1-Origin V-Man & the Boys; The Banshee & The Black Fury, The Queen of Evil, & V-Agents begin; Nazi-c	127	381	795	1400
2-Nazi bondage/torture-c	93	279	581	1025

VECTOR
Now Comics: 1986 - No. 4, 1986? ($1.50, 1st color comic by Now Comics)

1-4: Computer-generated art ... 2.25

VEGAS KNIGHTS
Pioneer Comics: 1989 ($1.95, one-shot)

1 ... 2.25

VEILS
DC Comics (Vertigo): 1999 ($24.95, one-shot)

Venom: The Hunted #1 © MAR

Venus #5 © MAR

Veronica #40 © AP

GD2.0 **FN**6.0 **VF**8.0 **NM**9.4

Hardcover-($24.95) Painted art and photography; McGreal-s				25.00
Softcover ($14.95)				15.00

VELOCITY (Also see Cyberforce)
Image Comics (Top Cow Productions): Nov, 1995 - No. 3, Jan, 1996 ($2.50, limited series)

1-3: Kurt Busiek scripts in all. 2-Savage Dragon-c/app.	3.00

VENGEANCE OF VAMPIRELLA (Becomes Vampirella: Death & Destruction)
Harris Comics: Apr, 1994 - No. 25, Apr, 1996 ($2.95)

1-($3.50)-Quesada/Palmiotti "bloodfoil" wraparound cover	5.00
1-2nd printing; blue foil-c	3.00
1-Gold	15.00
2-25: 8-Polybagged w/trading card; 10-w/coupon for Hyde -25 poster. 11,19-Polybagged w/ trading card. 25-Quesada & Palmiotti red foil-c.	3.00
...: Bloodshed (1995, $6.95)	7.00

VENGEANCE OF VAMPIRELLA: THE MYSTERY WALK
Harris Comics: Nov, 1995 ($2.95, one-shot)

0	3.00

VENGEANCE SQUAD
Charlton Comics: July, 1975 - No. 6, May, 1976 (#1-3 are 25¢ issues)

1-Mike Mauser, Private Eye begins by Staton	1	4	7	10
2-6: Morisi-a in all				6.00
5,6 (Modern Comics-r, 1977)				4.00

VENOM: Marvel Comics (Also see Amazing Spider-Man #298-300)

... ALONG CAME A SPIDER, 1/96 - No. 4, 4/96 ($2.95)-Spider-Man & Carnage app.	3.00
... CARNAGE UNLEASHED, 4/95 - No. 4, 7/95 ($2.95)	3.00
... FINALE, 11/97 - No. 3, 1/98 ($1.99)	2.25
... FUNERAL PYRE, 8/93- No. 3, 10/93 ($2.95)-#1-Holo-grafx foil-c; Punisher app. in all	3.00

VENOM: LETHAL PROTECTOR
Marvel Comics: Feb, 1993 - No. 6, July, 1993 ($2.95, limited series)

1-Red holo-grafx foil-c; Bagley-c/a in all				5.00
1-Gold variant sold to retailers				15.00
1-Black-c (several copies were authenticated by CGC in 2000)	12	36	88	150
NOTE: Counterfeit copies of the black-c exist and are valueless				
2-6: Spider-Man app. in all				3.00
... LICENSE TO KILL, 6/97 - No. 3, 8/97 ($1.95)				2.25
... NIGHTS OF VENGEANCE, 8/94 - No. 4, 11/94 ($2.95), #1-Red foil-c				3.00
... ON TRIAL, 3/97 - No. 3, 5/97 ($1.95)				2.25
... SEED OF DARKNESS, 7/97 ($1.95) #(-1) Flashback				2.25
... SEPARATION ANXIETY, 12/94- No. 4, 3/95 ($2.95) #1-Embossed-c				3.00
... SIGN OF THE BOSS, 3/97 - No. 2, 10/97 ($1.99)				2.25
... SINNER TAKES ALL, 8/95 - No. 5, 10/95 ($2.95)				3.00
... SUPER SPECIAL, 8/95($3.95) #1-Flip book				4.00
... THE ENEMY WITHIN, 2/94 - No. 3, 4/94 ($2.95)-Demogoblin & Morbius app. 1-Glow-in-the-dark-c				3.00
... THE HUNGER, 8/96- No. 4, 11/96 ($1.95)				2.25
... THE HUNTED, 5/96-No. 3, 7/96 ($2.95)				3.00
... THE MACE, 5/94 - No. 3, 7/94 ($2.95)-#1-Embossed-c				3.00
... THE MADNESS, 11/93- No. 3, 1/94 ($2.95)-Kelley Jones-c/a(p). 1-Embossed-c; Juggernaut app.				3.00
... TOOTH AND CLAW, 12/96 - No. 3, 2/97 ($1.95)-Wolverine-c/app.				2.25

VENTURE
AC Comics (Americomics): Aug, 1986 - No. 3, 1986? ($1.75)

1-3: 1-3-Bolt. 1-Astron. 2-Femforce. 3-Fazers	2.25

VENUS (See Marvel Spotlight #2 & Weird Wonder Tales)
Marvel/Atlas Comics (CMC 1-9/LCC 10-19): Aug, 1948 - No. 19, Apr, 1952 (Also see Marvel Mystery #91)

1-Venus & Hedy Devine begin; 1st app. Venus; Kurtzman's "Hey Look"				
	123	369	769	1350
2	70	210	438	775
3,5	58	174	363	640
4-Kurtzman's "Hey Look"	59	177	369	650
6-9: 6-Loki app. 7,8-Painted-c. 9-Begin 52 pgs.; book-length feature "Whom the Gods Destroy!"	55	165	330	575
10-S/f-horror issues begin (7/50)	73	219	455	800
11-S/F end of the world (11/50)	84	253	525	925
12-Colan-a	50	150	300	525
13-19-Venus by Everett, 2-3 stories each; covers-#13,15-19; 14-Everett part cover (Venus). 17-Bondage-c	75	225	469	825
NOTE: **Berg** s/f story-13. **Everett** c-13, 14(part; Venus only), 15-19. **Heath** s/f story-11. **Maneely** s/f story-10(3pg.), 16. **Morisi** a-19. **Syd Shores** c-6.				

VENUS WARS, THE (Manga)
Dark Horse Comics: Apr, 1991 - No.14, May, 1992 ($2.25, B&W)

1-14: 1-3 Contain 2 Dark Horse trading cards. 1,3,7,10-(44 pgs.)	2.50

VERI BEST SURE FIRE COMICS
Holyoke Publishing Co.: No date (circa 1945) (Reprints Holyoke one-shots)

1-Captain Aero, Alias X, Miss Victory, Commandos of the Devil Dogs, Red Cross, Hammerhead Hawley, Capt. Aero's Sky Scouts, Flagman app.; same-c as Veri Best Sure Shot #1	40	120	217	375

VERI BEST SURE SHOT COMICS
Holyoke Publishing Co.: No date (circa 1945) (Reprints Holyoke one-shots)

1-Capt. Aero, Miss Victory by Quinlan, Alias X, The Red Cross, Flagman, Commandos of the Devil Dogs, Hammerhead Hawley, Capt. Aero's Sky Scouts; same-c as Veri Best Sure Fire #1	40	120	217	375

VERMILLION
DC Comics (Helix): Oct, 1996 - No. 12, Sept, 1997 ($2.25/$2.50)

1-12: 1-4: Lucius Shepard scripts. 4,12-Kaluta-c	2.50

VERONICA (Also see Archie's Girls, Betty &...)
Archie Comics: Apr, 1989 - Present

1-(75¢-c)	6.00
2-10: 2-(75¢-c)	4.00
11-38	3.00
39-Love Showdown pt. 4, Cheryl Blossom	5.00
40-70: 34-Neon ink-c	3.00
71-121	2.25

VERONICA'S PASSPORT DIGEST MAGAZINE (Becomes Veronica's Digest Magazine #3 on)
Archie Comics: Nov, 1992 - Present ($1.50/$1.79, digest size)

1	5.00
2-6	3.00

VERONICA'S SUMMER SPECIAL (See Archie Giant Series Magazine #615, 625)

VERTIGO GALLERY, THE: DREAMS AND NIGHTMARES
DC Comics (Vertigo): 1995 ($3.50, one-shot)

1-Pin-ups of Vertigo characters by Sienkiewicz, Toth, Van Fleet & others; Dave McKean-c	4.00

VERTIGO JAM
DC Comics (Vertigo): Aug, 1993 ($3.95, one-shot, 68 pgs.)(Painted-c by Fabry)

1-Sandman by Neil Gaiman, Hellblazer, Animal Man, Doom Patrol, Swamp Thing, Kid Eternity & Shade the Changing Man	5.00

VERTIGO PREVIEW
DC Comics (Vertigo): 1992 (75¢, one-shot, 36 pgs.)

1-Vertigo previews; Sandman story by Neil Gaiman	2.25

VERTIGO RAVE
DC Comics (Vertigo): Fall, 1994 (99¢, one-shot)

1-Vertigo previews	2.25

VERTIGO SECRET FILES
DC Comics (Vertigo): Aug, 2000 ($4.95)

...: Hellblazer 1 (8/00, $4.95) Background info and story summaries	5.00
...: Swamp Thing 1 (11/00, $4.95) Backstories and origins; Hale-c	5.00

Vertigo Secret Files: Swamp Thing #1 © DC

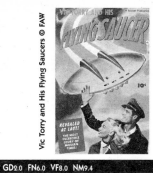

Vic Torry and His Flying Saucers © FAW

The Vigilante #48 © DC

	GD2.0	FN6.0	VF8.0	NM9.4

RTIGO VERITE: THE UNSEEN HAND
Comics (Vertigo): Sept, 1996 - No. 4, Dec, 1996 ($2.50, limited series)

4: Terry LaBan scripts in all				2.50

RTIGO VISIONS
Comics (Vertigo): June, 1993 - Present (one-shots)

Occult 1 (7/94, $3.95)				4.00
Thirteen 1 (9/98, $5.95) Howarth-s				6.00
z 1 (7/95, $3.95)				4.00
e Geek 1 (6/93, $3.95)				4.00
e Eaters ($4.95, 1995)-Milligan story.				5.00
e Phantom Stranger 1 (10/93, $3.50)				3.50
nahawk 1 (7/98, $4.95) Pollack-s				5.00

RTIGO WINTER'S EDGE
Comics (Vertigo): 1998, 1999 ($7.95/$6.95, square-bound, annual)

Winter stories by Vertigo creators; Desire story by Gaiman/Bolton; Bolland wraparound-c				8.00
3-($6.95)-Winter stories: 2-Allred-c. 3-Bond-c; Desire by Gaiman/Zulli				7.00

RY BEST OF DENNIS THE MENACE, THE
wcett Publ.: July, 1979 - No. 2, Apr, 1980 (95¢/$1.00, digest-size, 132 pgs.)

2-Reprints	1	4	7	10

RY BEST OF DENNIS THE MENACE, THE
rvel Comics Group: Apr, 1982 - No. 3, Aug, 1982 ($1.25, digest-size)

3: Reprints	1	3	6	9
2-Mistakenly printed with DC logo on cover	2	6	10	14

TE: *Hank Ketcham c-all. A few thousand of #1 & 2 were printed with DC emblem.*

RY VICKY
et Danny Ocean: 1993? - No. 8, 1995 ($2.50, B&W)

8, …: Calling All Hillbillies (1995, $2.50)				2.50

XT
Comics: Mar, 1999 - No. 6, Aug, 1999 ($2.50, limited series)

6-Giffen-s. 1-Superman app.				2.50

OR VENDETTA
Comics: Sept, 1988 - No. 10, May, 1989 ($2.00, maxi-series)

-10: Alan Moore scripts in all				3.00
de paperback (1990, $14.95)				15.00

C BRIDGES FAZERS SKETCHBOOK AND FACT FILE
Comics: Nov, 1986 ($1.75)

				3.00

C FLINT(Crime Buster…)(See Authentic Police Cases #10-14 & Fugitives
m Justice #2)
John Publ. Co.: Aug, 1948 - No. 5, Apr, 1949 (Newspaper reprints; NEA
vice)

	14	42	72	120
	10	30	55	80
5	8	24	45	65

C FLINT (Crime Buster…)
go Publ.: Feb, 1956 - No. 2, May, 1956 (Newspaper reprints)

2	9	27	49	70

C JORDAN (Also see Big Shot Comics #32)
il Service Publ.: April, 1945

-1944 daily newspaper-r	14	42	72	120

CKI (Humor)
as/Seaboard Publ.: Feb, 1975 - No. 4, Aug, 1975 (No. 1,2: 68 pgs.)

2-(68 pgs.)-Reprints Tippy Teen; Good Girl art	3	9	20	30
4 (Low print)	3	9	17	25

CKI VALENTINE (…Summer Special #1)
negade Press: July, 1985 - No. 4, July, 1986 ($1.70, B&W)

-4: Woggon, Rausch-a; all have paper dolls. 2-Christmas issue				3.00

CKY
e Magazine: Oct, 1948 - No. 5, June, 1949

	GD2.0	FN6.0	VF8.0	NM9.4
nn(10/48)-Teenage humor	6	18	32	45
4(12/48), nn(2/49), 4(4/49), 5(6/49): 5-Dotty app.	5	15	25	35

VIC TORRY & HIS FLYING SAUCER (Also see Mr. Monster's…#5)
Fawcett Publications: 1950 (one-shot)

nn-Book-length saucer story by Powell; photo/painted-c	64	192	398	700

VICTORY
Topps Comics: June, 1994 ($2.50, unfinished limited series)

1-Kurt Busiek script; Giffen-c/a; Rob Liefeld variant-c exists				2.50

VICTORY COMICS
Hillman Periodicals: Aug, 1941 - No. 4, Dec, 1941 (#1 by Funnies, Inc.)

1-The Conqueror by Bill Everett, The Crusader, & Bomber Burns begin; Conqueror's origin in text; Everett-c	300	900	1875	3300
2-Everett-c/a	127	381	795	1400
3,4	84	253	525	925

VIC VERITY MAGAZINE
Vic Verity Publ: 1945; No. 2, Jan?, 1947 - No. 7, Sept, 1946 (A comic book)

1-C. C. Beck-c/a	21	63	110	190
2-Beck-c	12	36	61	100
3-7: 6-Beck-a. 7-Beck-c	11	33	55	90

VIDEO JACK
Marvel Comics (Epic Comics): Nov, 1987 - No. 6, Nov, 1988 ($1.25)

1-5				2.25
6-Neal Adams, Keith Giffen, Wrightson, others-a				4.00

VIETNAM JOURNAL
Apple Comics: Nov, 1987 - No. 16, Apr, 1991 ($1.75/$1.95, B&W)

1-16: Don Lomax-c/a/scripts in all, 1-2nd print				3.00
…: Indian Country Vol. 1 (1990, $12.95)-r/#1-4 plus one new story				13.00

VIETNAM JOURNAL: VALLEY OF DEATH
Apple Comics: June, 1994 - No. 2, Aug, 1994 ($2.75, B&W, limited series)

1,2: By Don Lomax				2.75

VIGILANTE, THE (Also see New Teen Titans #23 & Annual V2#2)
DC Comics: Oct, 1983 - No. 50, Feb, 1988 ($1.25, Baxter paper)

1-Origin				3.00
2-16,19-49: 3-Cyborg app. 4-1st app. The Exterminator; Newton-a(p). 6,7-Origin. 20,21-Nightwing app. 35-Origin Mad Bomber. 47-Batman-c/s				2.50
17,18-Alan Moore scripts in all				4.00
50-Ken Steacy painted-c				3.00
Annual nn (2 ('85, '86)				2.50

VIGILANTE: CITY LIGHTS, PRAIRIE JUSTICE (Also see Action Comics #42,
Justice League of America #78, Leading Comics & World's Finest #244)
DC Comics: Dec, 1995 - No. 4, Feb, 1996 ($2.50, limited series)

1-4: James Robinson scripts in all				2.50

VIGILANTES, THE
Dell Publishing Co.: No. 839, Sept, 1957

Four Color 839-Movie	7	21	49	90

VIGILANTE 8: SECOND OFFENSE
Chaos! Comics: Dec, 1999 ($2.95, one-shot)

1-Based on video game				3.00

VIKINGS, THE (Movie)
Dell Publishing Co.: No. 910, May, 1958

Four Color 910-Buscema-a, Kirk Douglas photo-c	9	27	63	110

VILLAINS AND VIGILANTES
Eclipse Comics: Dec, 1986 - No. 4, May, 1987 ($1.50/$1.75, limited series,
Baxter paper)

1-4: Based on role-playing game. 2-4 ($1.75-c)				2.25

VILLAINY OF DOCTOR DOOM, THE
Marvel Comics: 1999 ($17.95, TPB)

nn-Reprints early battle with the Fantastic Four				18.00

VINTAGE MAGNUS (…Robot Fighter)

Violent Messiahs #7 © Hurricane Ent.

The Vision #2 © MAR

Voodoo #8 © AJAX

Valiant: Jan, 1992 - No. 4, Apr, 1992 ($2.25, limited series)
1-4: 1-Layton-c; r/origin from Magnus R.F. #22   2.25

VIOLATOR (Also see Spawn #2)
Image Comics (Todd McFarlane Productions): May, 1994 - No. 3, Aug, 1994 ($1.95, limited series)
  1-Alan Moore scripts in all   5.00
  2,3: Bart Sears-c(p)/a(p)   4.00

VIOLATOR VS. BADROCK
Image Comics (Extreme Studios): May, 1995 - No. 4, Aug, 1995 (limited series)
  1-4: Alan Moore scripts in all. 1-1st app Celestine; variant-c (3?)   2.50

VIOLENT MESSIAHS
Image Comics: June, 2000 - Present ($2.95)
  1-Two covers by Travis Smith and Medina   3.50
  1-Tower Records variant edition   3.50
  2-7: 5-Flip book sketchbook   3.00
  ...: Genesis (12/01, $5.95) r/'97 B&W issue, Wizard 1/2 prologue   6.00

VIP (TV)
TV Comics: 2000 ($2.95, unfinished series)
  1-Based on the Pamela Lee TV show; photo-c   3.00

VIPER (TV)
DC Comics: Aug, 1994 - No. 4, Nov, 1994 ($1.95, limited series)
  1-4-Adaptation of television show   2.25

VIRGINIAN, THE (TV)
Gold Key: June, 1963
  1(10060-306)-Part photo-c of James Drury plus photo back-c
       4   12   29   45

VIRTUA FIGHTER (Video Game)
Marvel Comics: Aug, 1995 (2.95, one-shot)
  1-Sega Saturn game   3.00

VIRUS
Dark Horse Comics: 1993 - No. 4, 1993 ($2.50, limited series)
  1-4: Ploog-c   2.50

VISION, THE
Marvel Comics: Nov, 1994 - No. 4, Feb, 1995 ($1.75, limited series)
  1-4   2.25

VISION AND THE SCARLET WITCH, THE (See Marvel Fanfare)
Marvel Comics Group: Nov, 1982 - No. 4, Feb, 1983 (Limited series)
  1-4: 2-Nuklo & Future Man app.   3.00

VISION AND THE SCARLET WITCH, THE
Marvel Comics Group: Oct, 1985 - No. 12, Sept, 1986 (Maxi-series)
  V2#1-12: 1-Origin; 1st app. in Avengers #57. 2-West Coast Avengers x-over   2.50

VISIONARIES
Marvel Comics (Star)/Marvel Comics #3 on: Nov, 1987 - No. 6, Sept, 1988
  1-6   2.50

VISIONS
Vision Publications: 1979 - No. 5, 1983 (B&W, fanzine)
  1-Flaming Carrot begins(1st app?); N. Adams-c   4   12   26   40
  2-N. Adams, Rogers-a; Gulacy back-c; signed & numbered to 2000
       3   9   20   30
  3-Williamson-c(p)/ Steranko back-c   2   6   13   20
  4-Flaming Carrot-c & info.   2   6   13   20
  5-1 pg. Flaming Carrot   1   3   6   9
NOTE: *Eisner* a-4. *Miller* a-4. *Starlin* a-3. *Williamson* a-5. After #4, Visions became an annual publication of The Atlanta Fantasy Fair.

VISITOR, THE
Valiant/Acclaim Comics (Valiant): Apr, 1995 - No. 13, Nov, 1995 ($2.50)
  1-13: 8-Harbinger revealed. 13-Visitor revealed to be Sting from Harbinger.
     2.50

VISITOR VS. THE VALIANT UNIVERSE, THE
Valiant: Feb, 1995 - No. 2, Mar, 1995 ($2.95, limited series)
  1,2   3.

VOGUE (Also see Youngblood)
Image Comics (Extreme Studios): Oct, 1995 - No.3, Jan, 1996 ($2.50, limited series)
  1-3: 1-Liefeld-c, 1-Variant-c   2.5

VOID INDIGO (Also see Marvel Graphic Novel)
Marvel Comics (Epic Comics): 11/84 - No. 2, 3/85 ($1.50, direct sales, unfinished series, mature)
  1,2: Cont'd from Marvel G.N.; graphic sex & violence   2.2

VOLCANIC REVOLVER
Oni Press: Dec, 1998 - No. 3, Mar, 1999 ($2.95, B&W, limited series)
  1-3: Scott Morse-s/a   3.0
  TPB (12/99, $9.95, digest size) r/#1-3 and Oni Double Feature #7 prologue   10.

VOLTRON (TV)
Modern Publishing: 1985 - No. 3, 1985 (75¢, limited series)
  1-3: Ayers-a in all   4.0

VOODA (Jungle Princess) (Formerly Voodoo)
Ajax-Farrell (Four Star Publications): No. 20, April, 1955 - No. 22, Aug, 1955
  20-Baker-c/a (r/Seven Seas #6)   40   120   214   3
  21,22-Baker-a plus Kamen/Baker story, Kimbo Boy of Jungle, & Baker-c (p)
     in all. 22-Censored Jo-Jo-r (name Powaa)   35   105   185   3
NOTE: #20-22 each contain one heavily censored-r of South Sea Girl by Baker from Seven Seas Comics with name changed to Vooda. #20-r/Seven Seas #6; #21-r/#4; #22-r/#3.

VOODOO (Weird Fantastic Tales) (Vooda #20 on)
Ajax-Farrell (Four Star Publ.): May, 1952 - No. 19, Jan-Feb, 1955
  1-South Sea Girl-r by Baker   55   165   341   6
  2-Rulah story-r plus South Sea Girl from Seven Seas #2 by Baker (name changed from Alani to El'nee)   45   135   270   4
  3-Bakerish-a; man stabbed in face   39   117   208   3
  4,8-Baker-r. 8-Severed head panels   39   117   208   3
  5-7,9,10: 5-Nazi death camp story. 6-Severed head panels   31   93   165   2
  11-18: 14-Zombies take over America. 15-Opium drug story-r/Ellery Queen #3
     16-Post nuclear world story.17-Electric chair panels
     27   81   142   2
  19-Bondage-c; Baker-r(2)/Seven Seas #5 w/minor changes & #1, heavily
     modified; last pre-code; contents & covers change to jungle theme
     35   105   185   3
  Annual 1(1952, 25¢, 100 pgs.)-Baker-a (scarce)   91   273   568   10

VOODOO
Image Comics (WildStorm): Nov, 1997 - No. 4, Mar, 1998 ($2.50, lim. series)
  1-4:Alan Moore-s in all; Hughes-c. 2-4-Rio-a   2.
  1-Platinum Ed   10.
  Dancing on the Dark TPB ('99, $9.95) r/#1-4   10.
  ...-Zealot: Skin Trade (8/95, $4.95)   5.

VOODOO (See Tales of...)

VOODOOM
Oni Press: June, 2000 ($4.95, B&W)
  1-Scott Morse-s/Jim Mahfood-a   5.0

VORTEX
Vortex Publs.: Nov, 1982 - No. 15, 1988 (No month) ($1.50/$1.75, B&W)
  1 ($1.95)-Peter Hsu-a; Ken Steacy-c; nudity   5.
  2,12: 2-1st app. Mister X (on-c only). 12-Sam Kieth-a   4.
  3-11,13-15   2.

VORTEX
Comico: 1991 - No. 2? ($2.50, limited series)
  1,2: Heroes from The Elementals   2.

VORTEX
Entity Comics: 1996 ($2.95)
  1,1b: 1b-Kaniuga-c   3.

Voyage to the Bottom of the Sea #4 © DELL

Wacky Witch #3 © GK

Walt Disney Giant #7 © WDC

	GD2.0	FN6.0	VF8.0	NM9.4
	GD2.0	FN6.0	VF8.0	NM9.4

VOYAGE TO THE BOTTOM OF THE SEA (Movie, TV)
Dell Publishing Co./Gold Key: No. 1230, Sept-Nov, 1961; Dec, 1964 - #16, Apr, 1970 (Painted-c)

Four Color 1230 (1961)	10	30	70	135
1-133-412(#1, 12/64)(Gold Key)	7	21	49	90
2(7/65) - 5: Photo back-c, 1-5	5	15	35	60
6-14	4	12	29	45
15,16-Reprints	3	9	20	30

VOYAGE TO THE DEEP
Dell Publishing Co.: Sept-Nov, 1962 - No. 4, Nov-Jan, 1964 (Painted-c)

1	5	15	35	60
2-4	4	12	26	40

WACKO
Ideal Publ. Corp.: Sept, 1980 - No. 3, Oct, 1981 (84 pgs., B&W, magazine)

1-3	1	4	7	10

WACKY ADVENTURES OF CRACKY (Also see Gold Key Spotlight)
Gold Key: Dec, 1972 - No. 12, Sept, 1975

1	2	6	12	18
2	1	4	7	10
3-12	1	3	6	8
(See March of Comics #405, 424, 436, 448)				

WACKY DUCK (...Comics #3-6; formerly Dopey Duck; Justice Comics #7 on)
(See Film Funnies)
Marvel Comics (NPP): No. 3, Fall, 1946 - No. 6, Summer, 1947; Aug, 1948 - No. ?, Oct, 1948

3	21	63	110	185
4-Infinity-c	20	60	105	175
5,6(1947)-Becomes Justice comics	16	48	83	140
1,2(1948)	11	33	55	90
I.W. Reprint #1,2,7('58): 1-r/Wacky Duck #6	2	6	11	15
Super Reprint #10(I.W. on-c, Super-inside)	2	6	11	15

WACKY QUACKY (See Wisco)

WACKY RACES (TV)
Gold Key: Aug, 1969 - No. 7, Apr, 1972 (Hanna-Barbera)

1	5	15	35	60
2-7	3	10	23	35

WACKY SQUIRREL (Also see Dark Horse Presents)
Dark Horse Comics: Oct, 1987 - No. 4, 1988 ($1.75, B&W)

1-4: 4-Superman parody				2.25
Halloween Adventure Special 1 (1987, $2.00)				2.25
Summer Fun Special 1 (1988, $2.00)				2.25

WACKY WITCH (Also see Gold Key Spotlight)
Gold Key: March, 1971 - No. 21, Dec, 1975

1	3	10	23	35
2	2	6	12	18
3-10	2	6	10	14
11-21	1	3	6	9
(See March of Comics #374, 398, 410, 422, 434, 446, 458, 470, 482)				

WACKY WOODPECKER (See Two Bit the...)
W. Enterprises/Super Comics: 1958; 1963

W. Reprint #1,2,7 (nd-reprints Two Bit...): 7-r/Two-Bit, the Wacky Woodpecker #1	2	6	9	12
Super Reprint #10('63): 10-r/Two-Bit, The Wacky Woodpecker #?	2	6	9	12

WAGON TRAIN (1st Series) (TV) (See Western Roundup under Dell Giants)
Dell Publishing Co.: No. 895, Mar, 1958 - No. 13, Apr-June, 1962 (All photo-c)

Four Color 895 (#1)	12	36	84	150
Four Color 971(#2),1019(#3)	7	21	49	85
4(1-3/60),6-13	5	15	35	70
5-Toth-a	6	18	42	80

WAGON TRAIN (2nd Series) (TV)
Gold Key: Jan, 1964 - No. 4, Oct, 1964 (All front & back photo-c)

1-Tufts-a in all	5	15	35	65

2-4	4	12	29	45

WAHOO MORRIS
Image Comics: Mar, 2000 ($3.50, B&W)

1-Craig Taillefer-s/a				3.50

WAITING PLACE, THE
Slave Labor Graphics: Apr, 1997 - No. 6, Sept, 1997 ($2.95)

1-6-Sean McKeever-s				3.00
Vol. 2 - 1(11/99), 2-11				3.00

WAITING ROOM WILLIE (See Sad Case of...)

WALLY (Teen-age)
Gold Key: Dec, 1962 - No. 4, Sept, 1963

1	3	10	23	35
2-4	3	9	17	25

WALLY THE WIZARD (Star Comics): Apr, 1985 - No. 12, Mar, 1986 (Children's comic)
Marvel Comics

1-12: Bob Bolling a-1,3; c-1,9,11,12				4.00

WALLY WOOD'S T.H.U.N.D.E.R. AGENTS (See Thunder Agents)
Deluxe Comics: Nov, 1984 - No. 5, Oct, 1986 ($2.00, 52 pgs.)

1-5: 5-Jerry Ordway-c/a in Wood style				5.00
NOTE: Anderson a-2i, 3l. Buckler a-4. Ditko a-3, 4. Giffen a-1p-4p. Perez a-1p, 2, 4; c-1-4.				

WALT DISNEY CHRISTMAS PARADE (Also see Christmas Parade)
Whitman Publ. Co. (Golden Press): Wint, 1977 ($1.95, cardboard-c, 224 pgs.)

11191-Barks-r/Christmas in Disneyland #1, Dell Christmas Parade #9 & Dell Giant #3	3	10	23	35

WALT DISNEY COMICS DIGEST
Gold Key: June, 1968 - No. 57, Feb, 1976 (50¢, digest size)

1-Reprints Uncle Scrooge #5; 192 pgs.	8	24	56	100
2-4-Barks-r	5	15	35	60
5-Daisy Duck by Barks (8 pgs.); last published story by Barks (art only) plus 21 pg. Scrooge-r by Barks	8	24	56	105
6-13-All Barks-r	4	12	26	40
14,15	3	9	17	24
16-Reprints Donald Duck #26 by Barks	4	12	25	38
17-20-Barks-r	3	9	20	30
21-31,33,35-37-Barks-r; 24-Toth Zorro	3	9	17	26
32,41,45,47-49	2	6	13	18
34,38,39: 34-Reprints 4-Color #318. 38-Reprints Christmas in Disneyland #1. 39-Two Barks-r/WDC&S #272, 4-Color #1073 plus Toth Zorro-r	3	9	17	26
40-Mickey Mouse-r by Gottfredson	2	6	13	20
42,43-Barks-r	2	6	13	20
44-(Has Gold Key emblem, 50¢)-Reprints 1st story of 4-Color #29,256,275,282	5	15	34	55
44-Republished in 1976 by Whitman; not identical to original; a bit smaller, blank back-c, 69¢	3	9	17	26
46,50,52-Barks-r. 52-Barks-r/WDC&S #161,132	2	6	12	18
51-Reprints 4-Color #71	3	9	17	26
53-55: 53-Reprints Dell Giant #30. 54-Reprints Donald Duck Beach Party #2. 55-Reprints Dell Giant #49	2	6	11	16
56-r/Uncle Scrooge #32 (Barks)	2	6	13	20
57-r/Mickey Mouse Almanac('57) & two Barks stories	2	6	12	18

NOTE: *Toth* a-52r. #1-10, 196 pgs.; #11-41, 164 pgs.; #42 on, 132 pgs. Old issues were being reprinted & distributed by Whitman in 1976.

WALT DISNEY GIANT (Disney)
Bruce Hamilton Company (Gladstone): Sept, 1995 - No. 7, Sept, 1996 ($2.25, bi-monthly, 48 pgs.)

1-7: 1-Scrooge McDuck in the Yukon; Rosa-c/a/scripts plus r/F.C. #218. 2-Uncle Scrooge-r by Barks plus 17 pg. text story. 3-Donald the Mighty Duck; Rosa-c/a. 4-Mickey and Goofy; new-a (story actually stars Goofy; Mickey Mouse by Caesar Ferioli; Donald Duck by Giorgio Cavazzano (1st in U.S.). 6-Uncle Scrooge & the Jr. Woodchucks; new-a and Barks-r. 7-Uncle Scrooge-r by Barks plus new-a				3.00

NOTE: *Series was initially solicited as Uncle Walt's Collectory. Issue #8 was advertised, but later cancelled.*

WALT DISNEY PAINT BOOK SERIES

	GD2.0	FN6.0	VF8.0	NM9.4			GD2.0	FN6.0	VF8.0	NM

Whitman Publ. Co.: No dates; circa 1975 (Beware! Has 1930s copyright dates) (79¢-c, 52pgs. B&W, treasury-sized) (Coloring books, text stories & comics-r)

#2052 (Whitman #886-r) Mickey Mouse & Donald Duck Gag Book

		3	10	23	35
#2053 (Whitman #677-r)		3	10	23	35
#2054 (Whitman #670-r) Donald-c		4	12	26	40
#2055 (Whitman #627-r) Mickey-c		3	10	23	35
#2056 (Whitman #660-r) Buckey Bug-c		3	9	20	30
#2057 (Whitman #887-r) Mickey & Donald-c		3	10	23	35

WALT DISNEY PRESENTS (TV)(Disney)
Dell Publishing Co.: No. 997, 6-8/59 - No. 6, 12-2/1960-61; No. 1181, 4-5/61 (All photo-c)

Four Color 997 (#1)	7	21	49	90
2(12-2/60)-The Swamp Fox(origin), Elfego Baca, Texas John Slaughter (Disney TV show) begin	5	15	34	55
3-6: 5-Swamp Fox by Warren Tufts	4	12	30	50
Four Color 1181-Texas John Slaughter	7	21	49	90

WALT DISNEY'S CHRISTMAS PARADE (Also see Christmas Parade)
Gladstone: Winter, 1988; No. 2, Winter, 1989 ($2.95, 100 pgs.)

1-Barks-r/painted-c	2	6	9	12
2-Barks-r	1	3	6	9

WALT DISNEY'S COMICS AND STORIES (Cont. of Mickey Mouse Magazine) (#1-30 contain Donald Duck newspaper reprints) (Titled "Comics And Stories" #264 to #?; titled "Walt Disney's Comics And Stories" #511 on)
Dell Publishing Co./Gold Key #264-473/Whitman #474-510/Gladstone #511-547(4/90)/Disney Comics #548(6/90)-#585/Gladstone #586(8/93) On: 10/40 - #263, 8/62; #264, 10/62 - #510, 7/84; #511, 10/86 - #633, 2/99

NOTE: The whole number can always be found at the bottom of the title page in the lower left-hand or right hand panel.

1(V1#1-c; V2#1-indicia)-Donald Duck strip-r by Al Taliaferro & Gottfredson's Mickey Mouse begin	1520	4560	9880	19,750
2	553	1659	3595	7200
3	192	576	1200	2300
4-X-Mas-c; 1st Huey, Dewey & Louie-c this title (See Mickey Mouse Magazine V4#2 for 1st-c ever)	137	411	856	1650
4-Special promotional, complimentary issue; cover same except one corner was blanked out & boxed in to identify the giveaway (not a paste-over). This special pressing was probably sent out to former subscribers to Mickey Mouse Mag. whose subscriptions had expired. (Very rare-6 known copies)				
	229	687	1431	2750
5-Goofy-c	106	318	663	1275
6-10: 8-Only Clarabelle Cow-c. 9-Taliaferro-c (1st)	87	261	544	1050
11-14: 11-Huey, Dewey & Louie-c	71	213	444	850
15-17: 15-The 3 Little Kittens (17 pgs.). 16-The 3 Little Pigs (29 pgs.); X-Mas-c. 17-The Ugly Duckling (4 pgs.)	67	201	419	800
18-21	56	168	350	675
22-30: 22-Flag-c. 24-The Flying Gauchito (1st original comic book story done for WDC&S). 27-Jose Carioca by Carl Buettner (2nd original story in WDC&S)	46	138	288	550
31-New Donald Duck stories by Carl Barks begin (See F.C. #9 for 1st Barks Donald Duck)	292	876	1825	3500
32-Barks-a	129	387	806	1550
33-Barks-a; infinity-c	92	276	575	1100
34-Gremlins by Walt Kelly begin, end #41; Barks-a	75	225	469	900
35,36-Barks-a	69	207	431	825
37-Donald Duck by Jack Hannah	35	105	219	420
38-40-Barks-a. 39-X-Mas-c. 40,41-Gremlins by Kelly				
	46	138	288	550
41-50-Barks-a. 43-Seven Dwarfs-c app. (4/44). 45-50-Nazis in Gottfredson's Mickey Mouse Stories	37	111	231	440
51-60-Barks-a. 51-X-Mas-c. 52-Li'l Bad Wolf begins, ends #203 (not in #55). 58-Kelly flag-c	25	75	156	300
61-70: 61-Dumbo story. 63,64-Pinocchio stories. 63-Cover swipe from New Funnies #94. 64-X-Mas-c. 65-Pluto story. 66-Infinity-c. 67,68-Mickey Mouse Sunday-r by Bill Wright	22	66	138	265
71-80-Barks-a. 75-77-Brer Rabbit stories, no Mickey Mouse. 76-X-Mas-c				
	16	48	100	195

81-87,89,90: Barks-a. 82-Goofy-c. 82-84-Bongo stories. 86-90-Goofy & Agnes app. 89-Chip 'n' Dale story	15	45	94	1
88-1st app. Gladstone Gander by Barks (1/48)	19	57	119	2
91-97,99: Barks-a. 95-1st WDC&S Barks-c. 96-No Mickey Mouse; Little Toot begins, ends #97. 99-X-Mas-c	13	39	81	1
98-1st Uncle Scrooge app. in WDC&S (11/48)	25	75	156	3
100-(1/49)-Barks-a	15	45	94	1
101-110-Barks-a. 107-Taliaferro-c; Donald acquires super powers				
	12	36	75	1
111,114,117-All Barks-a	9	27	56	1
112-Drug (ether) issue (Donald Duck)	9	27	56	1
113,115,116,118-123: No Barks. 116-Barks-r. 121-Grandma Duck begins, ends #168; not in #135,142,146,155	5	15	31	
124,126-130-All Barks-a. 124-X-Mas-c	8	24	50	
125-1st app. Junior Woodchucks (2/51); Barks-a	11	33	69	1
131,133,135-137,139-All Barks-a	8	24	50	
132-Barks-a(2) (D. Duck & Grandma Duck)	8	24	51	
134-Intro. & 1st app. The Beagle Boys (11/51)	17	51	106	2
138-Classic Scrooge money story	13	39	81	1
140-(5/52)-1st app. Gyro Gearloose by Barks; 2nd Barks Uncle Scrooge-c; 3rd Uncle Scrooge-c app.	17	51	106	2
141-150-All Barks-a. 143-Little Hiawatha begins, ends #151,159				
	5	15	31	
151-170-All Barks-a	5	15	31	
171-199-All Barks-a	4	12	30	
200	5	15	34	
201-240: All Barks-a. 204-Chip 'n' Dale & Scamp begin				
	4	12	29	
241-283: Barks-a. 241-Dumbo x-ref. 247-Gyro Gearloose begins, ends #274. 256-Ludwig Von Drake begins, ends #274	4	12	26	
284,285,287,290,295,296,309-311-Not by Barks	2	6	12	
286,288,289,291-294,297,298,308-All Barks stories; 293-Grandma Duck's Farm Friends. 297-Gyro Gearloose. 298-Daisy Duck's Diary-r				
	2	6	15	
299-307-All contain early Barks-r (#43-117). 305-Gyro Gearloose				
	3	9	17	
312-Last Barks issue with original story	3	9	17	
313-315,317-327,329-334,336-341	2	6	11	
316-Last issue published during life of Walt Disney	2	6	11	
328,335,342-350-Barks-r	2	6	11	
351-360-With posters inside; Barks reprints (2 versions of each with & without posters)-without posters...	2	6	15	
351-360-With posters...	3	10	23	
361-400-Barks-r	2	6	11	
401-429-Barks-r	2	6	11	
430,433,437,438,441,444,445,466-No Barks	1	3	6	
431,432,434-436,439,440,442,443-Barks-r	1	4	7	
446-465,467-473-Barks-r	1	3	6	
474(3/80),475-478 (Whitman)	2	6	11	
479(8/80),481(10/80)-484(1/81) pre-pack?	3	9	19	
480 (8-12/80)-(Very low distribution)	7	21	44	
485-499: 494-r/WDC&S #98	2	6	10	
500-510 (All #90011 on-c; pre-packs): 500(4/83), 501(5/83), 502&503(7/83), 504-506(all 8/83), 507(4/84), 508(5/84), 509(6/84), 510(7/84). 506-No Barks				
	2	6	11	
511-Donald Duck by Daan Jippes (1st in U.S.; in all through #518); Gyro Gearloose Barks-r begins (in most through #547); Wuzzles by Disney Studio (1st by Gladstone)	3	9	17	
512,513	2	6	11	
514-516,520	1	3	6	
517-519,521,522,525,527,529,530,532-546: 518-Infinity-c. 522-r/1st app. Huey, Dewey & Louie from D. Duck Sunday. 535-546-Barks-r. 537-1st Donald Duck by William Van Horn in WDC&S. 541-545-52 pgs. 546,547-68 pgs. 546-Kelly-r. 547-Rosa-a				
	2	6	9	
523,524,526,528,531,547: Rosa-s/a in all. 523-1st Rosa 10 pager				
	2	6	9	
548-($1.50, 6/90)-1st Disney issue; no M. Mouse				6.
549,551-570,572,573,577-579,581,584 ($1.50): 549-Barks-r begins, ends #585, not in #555, 556, & 564. 551-r/1 story from F.C. #29. 556,578-r/Mickey Mouse Cheerios Premium by Dick Moores. 562,563,568-570, 572,				

Walt Disney's Comics and Stories #594 © WDC

Walt Disney's Comics Digest #7 © WDC

100 PAGES OF WALT DISNEY'S COMICS

Walt Disney's Donald and Mickey #28 © WDC

WALT DISNEY'S DONALD AND MICKEY

WA

581-Gottfredson strip-r. 570-Valentine issue; has Mickey/Minnie
centerfold. 584-Taliaferro strip-r   4.00
0 ($2.25, 52 pgs.)-Donald Duck by Barks; previously printed only in The
Netherlands (1st time in U.S.); r/Chip 'n Dale & Scamp from #204   5.00
1-($2.95, 68 pgs)-r/Donald Duck's Atomic Bomb by Barks from 1947 Cheerios
premium   6.00
4-576,580,582,583 ($2.95, 68 pgs.): 574-r/1st Pinocchio Sunday strip (1939-
40). 575-Gottfredson-r, Pinocchio-r/WDC&S #64. 580-r/Donald Duck's 1st
app. from Silly Symphony strip 12/16/34 by Taliaferro; Gottfredson strip-r
begin; not in #584 & 600. 582,583-r/Mickey Mouse on Sky Island from
WDC&S #1,2   5.00
5 ($2.50, 52 pgs.)-r/#140; Barks-r/WDC&S #140   5.00
6,587: 586-Gladstone issues begin again; begin $1.50-c; Gottfredson-r begins
(not in #600). 587-Donald Duck by William Van Horn begins   4.00
8-597: 588,591-599-Donald Duck by William Van Horn   3.00
8,599 ($1.95, 36 pgs.): 598-r/1st drawings of Mickey Mouse by Ub Iwerks
                                                            4.00
0 ($2.95, 48 pgs.)-L.B. Cole-c(r)/WDC&S #1; Barks-r/WDC&S #32 plus Rosa,
Jippes, Van Horn-r and new Rosa centerspread   4.00
1-611 ($5.95, 64 pgs., squarebound, bi-monthly): 601-Barks-c, r/Mickey
Mouse V1#1, Rosa-a/scripts. 602-Rosa-r/1st Silly
Symphony Sundays from 1932. 604,605-Jippes-a. 605-Walt Kelly-c;
Gottfredson "Mickey Mouse Outwits the Phantom Blot" r/F.C. #16   6.00
2-633 ($6.95)   7.00
TE: (#1-38, 68 pgs.) #39-42, 60 pgs.; #43-57, 61-134, 143-168, 446, 447, 52 pgs.; #58-60,
-142, 169-540, 36 pgs.)

DTES: Barks art in all issues #31 on, except where noted; c-95, 96, 104, 108, 109, 130-172,
-178, 183, 198-200, 204, 206-209, 212-216, 218, 220, 226, 228-233, 235-238, 240-243, 247,
0, 253, 256, 260, 261, 276-283, 288-292, 295-298, 301, 303, 304, 306, 307, 309, 310, 313-
6, 319, 321, 322, 324, 326, 328, 329, 331, 332, 334, 341, 342, 350, 351, 527?, 530?, 540(never
fore published), 546, 557-586r(most), 596p, 601p. Kelly a-24p, 34-41, 43; r-522-524, 546, 547,
2, 583; covers(most)-34-118, 531?, 537?, 541?-543?, 562?, 571?, 605?. Walt Disney's Comics &
pries featured Mickey Mouse serials which were in practically every issue from #1 through #394
f #511 to date. The titles of the serials, along with the issues they are in, are listed in previous
tions of this price guide. Floyd Gottfredson Mickey Mouse serials in issues #1-14, 18-66, 69-
, 78-100, 128, 562, 563, 568-572, 582, 583, 586-599, 601-603, 605-present, plus "Service
'h a Smile" in #13; "Mickey Mouse in a Warplant" (3 pgs.), and "Pluto Catches a Nazi Spy" (4
s.) in #62; "Mystery Next Door", #93; "Sunken Treasure", #94; "Aunt Marissa", #95 (r in #575);
angland", #98 (r in #562); "Thanksgiving Dinner", #99 (r in #567); and "The Talking Dog", #100
n #563); "Morty's Escapade," #126. "The Brave Little Tailor", #580; "Introducing Mickey Mouse
ovies", #581; Circus Roustabout, #585; "Rumplewatt the Giant", #604. Mickey Mouse by Paul
y Symphonies in #5-"Three Little Pigs"; #13-"Birds of a Feather"; #14-"The Boarding School
arry #152-547 except 155-57 (Dick Moore), 327-29 (Tony Strobl), 348-50 (Jack Manning),
3 (Bill Wright). Don Rosa story/a-523, 524, 526, 528, 531, 547, 601-present. Al Taliaferro
story"; #15-"Cookieland" and "Three Little Kittens"; #16-"The Practical Pig"; #17-"The Ugly
ckling"; "The Wise Little Hen" in #580; and "Ambrose the Robber Kitten"; #19-"Penguin Isle";
d "Bucky Bug" in #20-23, 25, 26, 28 (one continuous story from 1932-34; first 2 pgs. not
liaferro). Gottfredson strip r-562, 563, 568-572, 581, 585, 586, 590. Taliaferro strip r-584, 580.
n Horn a-537, 545, 561, 574, 587, 588, 591-present.

ALT DISNEY'S COMICS DIGEST
adstone: Dec, 1986 - No. 7, Sept, 1987

	1	3	6	8
2-7				6.00

ALT DISNEY'S COMICS PENNY PINCHER
adstone: May, 1997 - No. 4, Aug, 1997 (99¢, limited series)

| -4 | | | | 2.25 |

ALT DISNEY'S DONALD AND MICKEY (Formerly Walt Disney's Mickey and
onald)
adstone (Bruce Hamilton Company): No. 19, Sept, 1993 - No. 30, 1995
4.50, 36 & 68 pgs.)

9,21-24,26-30: New & reprints. 19,21,23,24-Barks-r. 19,26-Murry-r. 22-Barks
"Omelet" story r/WDC&S #146. 27-Mickey Mouse story by Caesar Ferioli (1st
U.S work). 29-Rosa-c; Mickey Mouse story actually starring Goofy (does not
include Mickey except on title page.)   4.00
0,25-($2.95, 68 pgs.): 20-Barks, Gottfredson-r   5.00
DTE: Duck stories were all reprints.

'ALT DISNEY'S DONALD DUCK ADVENTURES (D.D. Adv. #1-3)
adstone: 11/87-No. 20, 4/90 (1st Series); No. 21,8/93-No. 48, 2/98(3rd Series)

	1	3	5	7
2-r/F.C. #308				3.00

3,4,6,7,9-11,13,15-18: 3-r/F.C. #223. 4-r/F.C. #62. 9-r/F.C. #159, "Ghost of the

Grotto". 11-r/F.C. #159, "Adventure Down Under." 16-r/F.C. #291; Rosa-c.
18-r/FC #318; Rosa-c   3.00
5,8-Don Rosa-c/a   5.00
12($1.50, 52pgs)-Rosa-c/a w/Barks poster   6.00
14-r/F.C. #29, "Mummy's Ring"   4.00
19($1.95, 68 pgs.)-Barks-r/F.C. #199 (1 pg.)   3.00
20($1.95, 68 pgs.)-Barks-r/F.C. #189 & cover-r; William Van Horn-a   3.00
21,22: 21-r/D.D. #46. 22-r/F.C. #282   3.00
23-25,27,29,31,32-($1.50, 36 pgs.): 21,23,29-Rosa-c. 23-Intro/1st app. Andold
Wild Duck by Marco Rota. 24-Van Horn-a. 27-1st Pat Block-a, "Mystery of
Widow's Gap." 31,32-Block-c.   2.50
26,28($2.95, 68 pgs.): 26-Barks-r/F.C. #108, "Terror of the River".
28-Barks-r/F.C. #199, "Sheriff of Bullet Valley"   4.00
30($2.95, 68 pgs.)-r/F.C. #367, Barks' "Christmas for Shacktown"   4.00
33($1.95, 68 pgs.)-r/F.C. #408, Barks' "The Golden Helmet;"Van Horn-c   3.00
34-43: 34-Resume $1.50-c. 34,35,37-Block-a/scripts. 38-Van Horn-c/a   2.50
44-48-($1.95-c)   2.50
NOTE: Barks a-12r, 26r, 28r, 33r, 36r; c-3r, 8r, 10r, 14r, 20r. Block a-27, 30, 34, 35, 37; c-27, 30-
32, 34, 35, 37; c-27, 30, 31, 32, 34, 35, 37. Rosa a-5, 8, 12; c-13, 16, 18, 21, 23.

WALT DISNEY'S DONALD DUCK ADVENTURES (2nd Series)
Disney Comics: June, 1990 - No. 38, July, 1993 ($1.50)

1-Rosa-a & scripts   5.00
2-21,23,25,27-33,35,36,38: 2-Barks-r/WDC&S #35; William Van Horn-a begins,
ends #20. 9-Barks-r/F.C. #178. 9,11,14,17-No Van Horn-a. 11-Mad #1 cover
parody. 14-Barks-r. 17-Barks-r. 21-r/FC #203 by Barks. 29-r/MOC #20 by
Barks   3.00
22,24,26,34,37: 22-Rosa-a (10 pgs.) & scripts. 26-Rosa-a & scripts. 26-r/March
of Comics #41 by Barks. 34-Rosa-c/a. 37-Rosa-a; Barks-r   4.00
NOTE: Barks r-2, 4, 9(F.C. #178), 14(D.D. #45), 17, 21, 26, 27, 29 , 35, 36(D.D #60)-38.
Taliaferro a-34r, 36r.

WALT DISNEY'S DONALD DUCK AND MICKEY MOUSE (Formerly Walt
Disney's Donald and Mickey)
Gladstone (Bruce Hamilton Company): Sept, 1995 - No. 7, Sept, 1996 ($1.50,
32 pgs.)

1-7: 1-Barks-r and new Mickey Mouse stories in all. 5,6-Mickey Mouse stories
by Caesar Ferioli. 7-New Donald Duck and Mickey Mouse x-over story;
Barks-r/WDC&S #51   2.25
NOTE: Issue #8 was advertised, but cancelled.

WALT DISNEY SHOWCASE
Gold Key: Oct, 1970 - No. 54, Jan, 1980 (No. 44-48: 68pgs., 49-54: 52pgs.)

1-Boatniks (Movie)-Photo-c	3	9	20	30
2-Moby Duck	2	6	13	20
3,4,7: 3-Bongo & Lumpjaw-r. 4,7-Pluto-r	2	6	11	16
5-$1,000,000 Duck (Movie)-Photo-c	2	6	15	22
6-Bedknobs & Broomsticks (Movie)	2	6	15	22
8-Daisy & Donald	2	6	11	16
9- 101 Dalmatians (cartoon feat.); r/F.C. #1183	3	9	17	24
10-Napoleon & Samantha (Movie)-Photo-c	2	6	15	22
11-Moby Duck-r	2	6	10	14
12-Dumbo-r/Four Color #668	2	6	11	16
13-Pluto-r	2	6	10	14
14-World's Greatest Athlete (Movie)-Photo-c	2	6	15	22
15- 3 Little Pigs-r	2	6	11	16
16-Aristocats (cartoon feature); r/Aristocats #1	2	6	15	22
17-Mary Poppins; r/M.P. #10136-501-Photo-c	2	6	15	22
18-Gyro Gearloose; Barks-r/F.C. #1047,1184	3	9	19	28
19-That Darn Cat; r/That Darn Cat #10171-602-Hayley Mills photo-c				
	2	6	15	22
20,23-Pluto-r	2	6	11	16
21-Li'l Bad Wolf & The Three Little Pigs	2	6	10	14
22-Unbirthday Party with Alice in Wonderland; r/Four Color #341				
	2	6	13	20
24-26: 24-Herbie Rides Again (Movie); sequel to "The Love Bug".				
25-Old Yeller (Movie); r/F.C. #869; Photo-c. 26-Lt. Robin Crusoe USN				
(Movie); r/Lt. Robin Crusoe USN #10191-601; photo-c				
27-Island at the Top of the World (Movie)-Photo-c	2	6	11	16
28-Brer Rabbit, Bucky Bug-r/WDC&S #58	2	6	11	16
29-Escape to Witch Mountain (Movie)-Photo-c	2	6	13	20

Walt Disney Showcase #41 © WDC

Walt Disney's Uncle Scrooge #212 © WDC

Wambi, Jungle Boy #16 © FH

	GD2.0	FN6.0	VF8.0	NM9.4

30-Magica De Spell; Barks-r/Uncle Scrooge #36 & WDC&S #258

| | 3 | 10 | 23 | 35 |

31-Bambi (cartoon feature); r/Four Color #186

| | 2 | 6 | 13 | 20 |

32-Spin & Marty-r/F.C. #1026; Mickey Mouse Club (TV)-Photo-c

| | | 2 | 6 | 15 | 22 |

33-40: 33-Pluto-r/F.C. #1143. 34-Paul Revere's Ride with Johnny Tremain (TV); r/F.C. #822. 35-Goofy-r/F.C. #952. 36-Peter Pan-r/F.C. #442. 37-Tinker Bell & Jiminy Cricket-r/F.C. #982,989. 38,39-Mickey & the Sleuth, Parts 1 & 2. 40-The Rescuers (cartoon feature)

| | 2 | 6 | 10 | 14 |

41-Herbie Goes to Monte Carlo (Movie); sequel to "Herbie Rides Again"; photo-c

| | 2 | 6 | 11 | 16 |

42-Mickey & the Sleuth

| | 2 | 6 | 10 | 14 |

43-Pete's Dragon (Movie)-Photo-c

| | 2 | 6 | 13 | 20 |

44-Return From Witch Mountain (new) & In Search of the Castaways-r (Movies)-Photo-c; 68 pg. giants begin

| | 2 | 6 | 15 | 22 |

45-The Jungle Book (Movie); r/#30033-803

| | 3 | 9 | 17 | 24 |

46-48: 46-The Cat From Outer Space (Movie)(new), & The Shaggy Dog (Movie)-r/F.C. #985; photo-c. 47-Mickey Mouse Surprise Party-r. 48-The Wonderful Advs. of Pinocchio-r/F.C. #1203; last 68 pg. issue

| | 2 | 6 | 11 | 16 |

49-54: 49-North Avenue Irregulars (Movie); Zorro-r/Zorro #11; 52 pgs. begin; photo-c. 50-Bedknobs & Broomsticks-r/#6; Mooncussers-r/World of Adv. #1; photo-c. 51-101 Dalmatians-r. 52-Unidentified Flying Oddball (Movie); r/Picnic Party #8; photo-c. 53-The Scarecrow-r (TV). 54-The Black Hole (Movie)-Photo-c (predates Black Hole #1)

| | 2 | 6 | 10 | 14 |

WALT DISNEY'S MERRY CHRISTMAS (See Dell Giant #39)

WALT DISNEY'S MICKEY AND DONALD (M & D #1,2)(Becomes Walt Disney's Donald & Mickey #19 on)
Gladstone: Mar, 1988 - No. 18, May, 1990 (95¢)

1-Don Rosa-a; r/1949 Firestone giveaway 6.00
2-8: 3-Infinity-c. 4-8-Barks-r 3.00
9-15: 9-r/1948 Firestone giveaway; X-Mas-c 3.00
16($1.50, 52 pgs.)-r/FC #157 .... 5.00
17-(68 pgs.) Barks M.M.-r/FC #79 plus Barks D.D.-r; Rosa-a; x-mas-c 6.00
18($1.95, 68 pgs.)-Gottfredson/Barks/MM & #13,72-74; Kelly-c(r); Barks-r 5.00
NOTE: Barks reprints in 1-15, 17, 18. Kelly c-13r, 14 (r/Walt Disney's C&S #58), 18r.

WALT DISNEY'S MICKEY MOUSE CLUB MAGAZINE (TV)(Becomes Walt Disney's Magazine)
Western Publishing Co.: Winter, 1956 - V2#3, Apr, 1957 (11-1/2x8-1/2", quarterly, 48 pgs.)

V1#1	13	39	91	175
2-4	7	21	49	90
V2#1,2	5	15	35	65
3-Annette photo-c	12	36	84	150
Annual(1956)-Two different issues; ($1.50-Whitman); 120 pgs., cardboard covers, 11-3/4x8-3/4"; reprints	14	42	98	180
Annual(1957)-Same as above	12	36	84	150

WALT DISNEY'S PINOCCHIO SPECIAL
Gladstone: Spring, 1990 ($1.00)

1-50th anniversary edition; Kelly-r/F.C. #92 .... 3.00

WALT DISNEY'S THE JUNGLE BOOK
W.D. Publications (Disney Comics): 1990 ($5.95, graphic novel, 68 pgs.)

nn-Movie adaptation; movie rereleased in 1990 .... 6.00
nn-($2.95, 68 pgs.)-Comic edition; wraparound-c 3.00

WALT DISNEY'S UNCLE SCROOGE (Formerly Uncle Scrooge #1-209)
Gladstone #210-242/Disney Comics #243-280/Gladstone #281 on: No. 210, 10/86 - No. 242, 4/90; No. 243, 6/90 - No. 318, 2/99

210-1st Gladstone issue; r/WDC&S #134 (1st Beagle Boys)

| | | 2 | 6 | 11 | 16 |

211-218: 216-New story ("Go Slowly Sands of Time") plotted and partly scripted by Barks. 217-r/U.S. #7, "Seven Cities of Cibola"

| | 2 | 6 | 11 | 16 |

219-"Son Of The Sun" by Rosa

| | 3 | 9 | 17 | 24 |

220-Don Rosa-a/scripts

| | 1 | 3 | 6 | 9 |

221-223,225,228-234,236-240 .... 4.00
224,226,227,235: 224-Rosa-c/a. 226,227-Rosa-a. 235-Rosa-a/scripts 5.00
241-($1.95, 68 pgs.)-Rosa finishes over Barks-r 6.00
242-($1.95, 68 pgs.)-Barks-r; Rosa-a(1 pg.) 6.00
243-249,251-260,264-275,277-280,282-284-($1.50): 243-1st by Disney Comics. 274-All Barks issue. 275-Contains centerspread by Rosa. 279-All Barks issue; Rosa-c. 283-r/WDC&S #98 .... 3.00
250-($2.25, 52 pgs.)-Barks-r; wraparound-c 4.00
261-263,276-Don Rosa-a/c 5.00
281-Gladstone issues start again; Rosa-c 6.00
285-The Life and Times of Scrooge McDuck Pt. 1; Rosa-c/a/scripts

| | | 1 | 4 | 7 | 10 |

286-293: The Life and Times of Scrooge McDuck Pt. 2-8; Rosa-c/a/scripts.
293-($1.95, 36 pgs.)-The Life and Times of Scrooge McDuck Pt. 9 .... 6.00
294-299, 301-308-($1.50, 32 pgs.): 294-296-The Life and Times of Scrooge McDuck Pt. 10-12. 297-The Life and Times of Uncle Scrooge Pt. 0; Rosa-c/a/scripts 3.00
300-($2.25, 48 pgs.)-Rosa-c; Barks-r/WDC&S #104 and U.S. #216; r/US. #220; includes new centerfold 3.00
309-318-($6.95) 7.0
NOTE: Barks r-210-218, 220-223, 224(2pg.), 225-234, 236-242, 245, 246, 250-253, 255, 256, 258, 261(2 pg.), 265, 267, 268, 270(2), 272-284, 299-present; c(r)-210, 212, 221, 228, 229, 233, 233, 284. scripts-287, 293. Rosa a-219, 220, 224, 226, 227, 235, 261-263, 268, 275-277, 285-289; c-219, 224, 231, 261-263, 276, 278-281, 285-289; scripts-219, 220, 224, 235, 261-263, 276, 285-289.

WALT DISNEY'S UNCLE SCROOGE ADVENTURES (U. Scrooge Advs. #1-3)
Gladstone Publishing: Nov, 1987 - No. 21, May, 1990; No. 22, Sept, 1993 - No. 54, Feb, 1998

1-Barks-r begin, ends #26

| | 1 | 3 | 6 | 9 |

2-4 .... 4.00
5,9,14: 5-Rosa-c/a; no Barks-r. 9,14-Rosa-a 5.00
6-8,10-13,15-19: 10-r/U.S. #18(all Barks) 3.00
20,21 ($1.95, 68 pgs.) 20-Rosa-c/a. 21-Rosa-a 5.00
22 ($1.50)-Rosa-c; r/U.S. #26 .... 5.00
23-($2.95, 68 pgs.)-Vs. The Phantom Blot-r/P.B. #3; Barks-r 4.00
24-26,29,31,32,34-36: 24,25,29,31,32-Rosa-c. 25-r/US. #21 .... 2.5
27-Guardians of the Lost Library - Rosa-c/a/story; origin of Junior Woodchuck Guidebook 3.00
28-($2.95, 68 pgs.)-r/U.S. #13 w/restored missing panels 4.00
30-($2.95, 68 pgs.)-r/U.S. #12; Rosa-a 4.00
33-($2.95, 64 pgs.)-New Barks story 3.00
37-54 .... 2.5
NOTE: Barks r-1-4, 6-8, 10-13, 15-21, 23, 22, 24; c(r)-15, 16, 17, 21. Rosa a-5, 9, 14, 20, 21, 2 c-5, 13, 14, 17(finishes), 20, 22, 24, 25, 27, 28; scripts-5, 9, 14, 27.

WALT DISNEY'S UNCLE SCROOGE ADVENTURES IN COLOR
Gladstone Publ.: Dec, 1995 - Present ($8.95/$9.95, squarebound, 56 issue limited series) (Polybagged w/card) (Series chronologically reprints all the stories written and drawn by Carl Barks)

1-56: 1- (12/95)-r/FC #386. 15-(12/96)-r/US #15. 16-(12/96)-r/US #16. ....
18-(1/97)-r/US #18 .... 10.0

WALT DISNEY'S WHEATIES PREMIUMS (See Wheaties in the Promotional section)

WALTER (Campaign of Terror) (Also see The Mask)
Dark Horse Comics: Feb, 1996 - No. 4, May, 1996 ($2.50, limited series)

1-4 .... 2.5

WALTER LANTZ ANDY PANDA (Also see Andy Panda)
Gold Key: Aug, 1973 - No. 23, Jan, 1978 (Walter Lantz)

1-Reprints | | 2 | 6 | 12 | 18
2-10-All reprints | | 1 | 3 | 6 | 9
11-23: 15,17-19,22-Reprints 6.00

832

	GD2.0	FN6.0	VF8.0	NM9.4		GD2.0	FN6.0	VF8.0	NM9.4

WALT KELLY'S...
Eclipse Comics: Dec, 1987; Apr, 1988 ($1.75/$2.50, Baxter paper)

...Christmas Classics 1 (12/87)-Kelly-r/Peter Wheat & Santa Claus Funnies,
...Springtime Tales 1 (4/88, $2.50)-Kelly-r 2.50

WALTONS, THE (See Kite Fun Book)
WALT SCOTT (See Little People)
WALT SCOTT'S CHRISTMAS STORIES (See Christmas Stories, 4-Color #959, 1062)
WAMBI, JUNGLE BOY (See Jungle Comics)
Fiction House Magazines: Spr, 1942; No. 2, Win, 1942-43; No. 3, Spr, 1943; No. 4, Fall, 1948; No. 5, Sum, 1949; No. 6, Spr, 1950; No. 7-10, 1950(nd); No. 11, Spr, 1951 - No. 18, 1952-53 (#1-3: 68 pgs.)

1-Wambi, the Jungle Boy begins	91	273	568	1000
2 (1942)-Kiefer-c	50	150	300	525
3 (1943)-Kiefer-c/a	38	114	203	350
4 (1948)-Origin in text	23	69	121	210
5 (Fall, 1949, 36 pgs.)-Kiefer-c/a	20	60	105	175
6-10: 7-(52 pgs.)-New logo	19	57	99	165
11-18	13	39	66	110
I.W. Reprint #8('64)-r/#12 with new-c	3	9	17	25

NOTE: *Alex Blum* c-8. *Kiefer* c-1-5. *Whitman* c-11-18.

WANDERERS (See Adventure Comics #375, 376)
DC Comics: June, 1988 - No. 13, Apr, 1989 ($1.25) (Legion of Super-Heroes spin off)

1-13: 1,2-Steacy-c. 3-Legion app.				2.25

WANDERING STAR
Pen & Ink Comics/Sirius Entertainment No. 12 on: 1993 - No. 21, Mar, 1997 ($2.50/$2.75, B&W)

1-1st printing; Teri Sue Wood c/a/scripts in all	1	3	6	8
1-2nd and 3rd printings				2.75
2-1st printing.				4.00
2-21: 2-2nd printing. 12-(1/96)-1st Sirius issue				2.75
Trade paperback ($11.95)-r/1-7; 1st printing of 1000, signed and #'d				18.00
Trade paperback-2nd printing, 2000 signed				15.00
TPB Volume 2,3 (11/98, 12/98, $14.95) 2-r/#8-14, 3-r/#15-21				15.00

WANTED COMICS
Toytown Publications/Patches/Orbit Publ.: No. 9, Sept-Oct, 1947 - No. 53, April, 1953 (#9-33: 52 pgs.)

9-True crime cases; radio's Mr. D. A. app.	22	66	116	200
10,11: 10-Giunta-a; radio's Mr. D. A. app.	14	42	72	120
12-Used in SOTI, pg. 277	14	42	72	125
13-Heroin drug propaganda story	12	36	61	105
14-Marijuana drug mention story (2 pgs.)	11	33	55	90
15-17,19,20	10	30	55	80
18-Marijuana story; "Satan's Cigarettes"; r-in #45 & retitled	24	72	127	215
21,22: 21-Krigstein-a. 22-Extreme violence	10	30	55	85
23,25-34,36-38,40-44,46-48,53	7	21	38	55
24-Krigstein-a; "The Dope King", marijuana mention story	11	33	55	90
35-Used in SOTI, pg. 160	10	30	55	85
39-Drug propaganda story "The Horror Weed"	15	45	77	130
45-Marijuana story from #18	10	30	55	80
49-Has unstable pink-c that fades easily; rare in mint condition	9	27	49	70
50-Has unstable pink-c like #49; surrealist-c by Buscema; horror stories	14	42	72	120
51- "Holiday of Horror" junkie story; drug-c	11	33	55	95
52-Classic "Cult of Killers" opium use story	11	33	55	95

NOTE: *Buscema* c-50, 51. *Lawrence* and *Leav* c-a most issues. *Syd Shores* c/a-48; c-37. Issues 9-46 have wanted criminals with their descriptions & picture on cover.

WANTED: DEAD OR ALIVE (TV)
Dell Publishing Co.: No. 1102, May-July, 1960 - No. 1164, Mar-May, 1961

Four Color 1102 (#1)-Steve McQueen photo-c	13	39	91	170
Four Color 1164-Steve McQueen photo-c	10	30	70	130

WANTED, THE WORLD'S MOST DANGEROUS VILLAINS (See DC Special)

National Periodical Publications: July-Aug, 1972 - No. 9, Aug-Sept, 1973 (All reprints & 20¢ issues)

1-Batman, Green Lantern (story r-from G.L. #1), & Green Arrow	3	10	23	35
2-Batman/Joker/Penguin-c/story r-from Batman #25; plus Flash story (r-from Flash #121)	3	9	17	25
3-9: 3-Dr. Fate(r/More Fun #65), Hawkman(r/Flash #100), & Vigilante(r/Action #69). 4-Gr. Lantern(r/All-American #61) & Kid Eternity(r/Kid Eternity #15). 5-Dollman/Green Lantern. 6-Burnley Starman; Wildcat/Sargon. 7-Johnny Quick(r/More fun #76), Hawkman(r/Flash #90), Hourman by Baily(r/Adv. #72). 8-Dr. Fate/Flash(r/Flash #114). 9-S&K Sandman/Superman	2	6	13	20

NOTE: *B. Bailey* a-7r. *Infantino* a-2r. *Kane* r-1, 5. *Kubert* r-3i, 6, 7. *Meskin* r-3, 7. *Reinman* r-4, 6.

WAR (See Fightin' Marines #122)
Charlton Comics: Jul, 1975 - No. 9, Nov, 1976; No. 10, Sept, 1978 - No. 49, 1984

1-Boyette painted-c	2	6	11	15
2-10	1	3	6	8
11-20				6.00
21-40				5.00
41-49 (lower print run): 47-Reprints				6.00
7,9 (Modern Comics-r, 1977)				3.00

WAR, THE (See The Draft & The Pitt)
Marvel Comics: 1989 - No. 4, 1990 ($3.50, squarebound, 52 pgs.)

1-4: Characters from New Universe				3.50

WAR ACTION (Korean War)
Atlas Comics (CPS): April, 1952 - No. 14, June, 1953

1	20	60	105	180
2	11	33	55	90
3-10,14: 7-Pakula-a	9	27	44	70
11-13-Krigstein-a	10	30	55	80

NOTE: *Brodsky* c-1-4. *Heath* a-1; c-7, 14. *Keller* a-6. *Maneely* a-1. *Tuska* a-2, 8.

WAR ADVENTURES
Atlas Comics (HPC): Jan, 1952 - No. 13, Feb, 1953

1-Tuska-a	17	51	88	150
2	10	30	55	80
3-7,9-13: 7-Pakula-a. 7-Maneely-c	8	24	42	60
8-Krigstein-a	10	30	55	80

NOTE: *Brodsky* c-1-3, 6, 8, 11, 12. *Heath* a-5, 7, 10; c-4, 5, 9, 13. *Robinson* a-3; c-10.

WAR ADVENTURES ON THE BATTLEFIELD (See Battlefield)

WAR AGAINST CRIME! (Becomes Vault of Horror #12 on)
E. C. Comics: Spring, 1948 - No. 11, Feb-Mar, 1950

1-Real Stories From Police Records on-c #1-9	73	219	455	800
2,3	43	129	257	450
4-9	40	120	232	400
10-1st Vault Keeper app. & 1st Vault of Horror	184	552	1288	2300
11-2nd Vault Keeper app.; 1st horror-c	108	324	756	1350

NOTE: *All have Johnny Craig covers. Feldstein a-4, 7-9. Harrison/Wood a-11. Ingels a-1, 2, 5, 8. Palais a-8. Changes to horror with #10.

WAR AGAINST CRIME
Gemstone Publishing: Apr, 2000 - No. 11, Feb, 2001 ($2.50)

1-11: E.C. reprints				2.50

WAR AND ATTACK (Also see Special War Series #3)
Charlton Comics: Fall, 1964; V2#54, June, 1966 - V2#63, Dec, 1967

1-Wood-a (25 pgs.)	4	12	30	50
V2#54(6/66)-#63 (Formerly Fightin' Air Force)	2	6	13	20

NOTE: *Montes/Bache* a-55, 56, 60, 63.

WAR AT SEA (Formerly Space Adventures)
Charlton Comics: No. 22, Nov, 1957 - No. 42, June, 1961

22	5	15	25	35
23-30	4	12	19	25
31-42	2	6	13	20

WAR BATTLES
Harvey Publications: Feb, 1952 - No. 9, Dec, 1953

1-Powell-a; Elias-c	10	30	70	120

War Birds #2 © FH

War Comics #6 © MAR

Warlands #3 © Dreamwave Prod.

	GD2.0	FN6.0	VF8.0	NM9.4
2-Powell-a	5	15	38	60
3-5,7-9: 3,7-Powell-a	5	15	34	55
6-Nostrand-a	6	18	42	70

WAR BIRDS
Fiction House Magazines: 1952(nd) - No. 3, Winter, 1952-53

1	15	45	77	130
2,3	9	27	49	70

WARBLADE: ENDANGERED SPECIES (Also see WildC.A.T.S: Covert Action Teams)
Image Comics (WildStorm Productions): Jan, 1995 - No. 4, Apr, 1995 ($2.50, limited series)

1-4: 1-Gatefold wraparound-c				2.50

WARCHILD
Maximum Press: Jan. 1995 - No. 4, Aug, 1995 ($2.50)

1-4-Rob Liefeld-c/a/scripts				2.50
1-4: 4-Variant-c				3.00
Trade paperback (1/96, $12.95)-r/#1-4.				13.00

WAR COMBAT (Becomes Combat Casey #6 on)
Atlas Comics (LBI No. 1/SAI No. 2-5): March, 1952 - No. 5, Nov, 1952

1	15	45	77	130
2	9	27	49	70
3-5	7	21	38	55

NOTE: *Berg* a-2, 4, 5. *Brodsky* c-1, 2, 4, 5. *Henkel* a-5. *Maneely* a-1, 4; c-3.

WAR COMICS (War Stories #5 on)(See Key Ring Comics)
Dell Publishing Co.: May, 1940 (No month given) - No. 4, Sept, 1941?

1-Sikandur the Robot Master, Sky Hawk, Scoop Mason, War Correspondent begin; McWilliams-c; 1st war comic	56	168	350	615
2-Origin Greg Gilday (5/41)	34	102	179	310
3-Joan becomes Greg Gilday's aide	22	66	116	195
4-Origin Night Devils	24	72	127	215

WAR COMICS
Marvel/Atlas (USA No. 1-41/JPI No. 42-49): Dec, 1950 - No. 49, Sept, 1957

1	26	78	136	235
2	14	42	72	120
3-10	11	33	55	90
11-Flame thrower w/burning bodies on-c	12	36	61	100
12-20	10	30	55	80
21,23-32: 26-Valley Forge story. 32-Last precode issue (2/55)	8	24	42	60
22-Krigstein-a	10	30	55	80
33-37,39-43,44,45,47,48	8	24	42	60
38-Kubert/Moskowitz-a	9	27	49	70
43,49-Torres-a. 43-Severin/Elder E.C. swipe from Two-Fisted Tales #31	9	27	49	70
46-Crandall-a	9	27	49	70

NOTE: *Colan* a-4, 36, 48, 49. *Drucker* 37, 43, 48. *Everett* a-17. *Heath* a-7-9, 16, 19, 25, 36; c-11, 16, 19, 25, 26, 29-31, 36. *G. Kane* a-19. *Lawrence* a-36. *Maneely* a-7, 9; c-6, 27, 37. *Orlando* a-42, 48. *Pakula* a-26. *Ravielli* a-27. *Reinman* a-27. *Robinson* a-15; c-13. *Severin* a-26, 27; c-48.

WAR DANCER (Also see Charlemagne, Doctor Chaos #2 & Warriors of Plasm)
Defiant: Feb, 1994 - No. 6, July, 1994 ($2.50)

1-3,5,6: 1-Intro War Dancer; Weiss-c/a begins. 1-3-Weiss-a(p). 6-Pre-Schism issue				2.50
4-($3.25, 52 pgs.)-Charlemagne app.				3.25

WAR DOGS OF THE U.S. ARMY
Avon Periodicals: 1952

1-Kinstler-c/a	15	45	77	130

WARFRONT
Harvey Publications: 9/51 - #35, 11/58; #36, 10/65; #39, 2/67

1-Korean War	12	36	84	140
2	6	18	42	70
3-10	5	15	34	55
11,12,14,16-20	4	12	29	45
13,15,22-Nostrand-a	6	18	42	70
21,23-27,31-33,35	4	12	29	45

28-30,34-Kirby-c	6	18	45	75
36-(12/66)-Dynamite Joe begins, ends #39; Williamson-a	5	15	34	55
37-Wood-a (17 pgs.)	5	15	34	55
38,39-Wood-a. 2-3 pgs.; Lone Tiger app.	4	12	29	45

NOTE: *Powell* a-1-6, 9-11, 14, 17, 20, 23, 25-28, 30, 31, 34, 36. *Powell/Nostrand* a-12, 13, 15. *Simon* c-367, 38.

WAR FURY
Comic Media/Harwell (Allen Hardy Assoc.): Sept, 1952 - No. 4, Mar, 1953

1-Heck-c/a in all; Palais-a; bullet hole in forehead-c; all issues are very violent; soldier using flame thrower on enemy	22	66	116	200
2-4: 4-Morisi-a	12	36	61	100

WAR GODS OF THE DEEP (See Movie Classics)

WARHAWKS
TSR, Inc.: 1990 - No. 10, 1991 ($2.95, 44 pgs.)

1-10-Based on TSR game, Spiegle a-1-6				3.00

WARHEADS
Marvel Comics UK: June, 1992 - No. 14, Aug, 1993 ($1.75)

1-Wolverine-c/story; indicia says #2 by mistake				3.00
2-14: 2-Nick Fury app. 3-Iron Man-c/story. 4,5-X-Force. 5-Liger vs. Cable. 6,7-Death's Head II app. (#6 is cameo)				2.25

WAR HEROES (See Marine War Heroes)

WAR HEROES
Dell Publishing Co.: 7-9/42 (no month); No. 2, 10-12/42 - No. 11, 3/45 (Published quarterly)

1-General Douglas MacArthur-c	24	72	127	220
2	14	42	72	120
3,5: 3-Pro-Russian back-c	10	30	55	85
4-Disney's Gremlins app.	18	54	94	155
6-11: 6-Tothish-a by Discount	9	27	51	75

NOTE: No. 1 was to be released in July, but was delayed. Painted c-4, 6-9.

WAR HEROES
Ace Magazines: May, 1952 - No. 8, Apr, 1953

1	11	33	55	90
2-Lou Cameron-a	7	21	35	55
3-8: 7-Cameron-a	6	18	32	45

WAR HEROES (Also see Blue Bird Comics)
Charlton Comics: Feb, 1963 - No. 27, Nov, 1967

1,2: 2-John F. Kennedy story	3	10	23	35
3-10	2	6	15	22
11-26	2	6	11	16
27-1st Devils Brigade by Glanzman	2	6	15	22

NOTE: *Montes/Bache* a-3-7, 21, 25, 27; c-3-7.

WAR IS HELL
Marvel Comics Group: Jan, 1973 - No. 15, Oct, 1975

1-Williamson-a(r), 5 pgs.; Ayers-a	2	6	15	22
2-8-Reprints. 6-(11/73). 7-(6/74). 7,8-Kirby-a	2	6	9	12
9-Intro Death	4	12	29	45
10-15-Death app.	2	6	13	20

NOTE: *Bolle* a-3r. *Powell* a-1. *Woodbridge* a-1. Sgt. Fury reprints-7, 8.

WARLANDS
Image Comics: Aug, 1999 - Present ($2.50)

1-9,11,12-Pat Lee-a(p)/Adrian Tsang-s				2.50
10-($2.95) Flip book w/Shidima preview				3.00
...Chronicles 1,2 (2/00, 7/00; $7.95) 1-r/#1-3. 2-r/#4-6				8.00
...Darklyte TPB (8/01, $14.95) r/#0,1/2,1-6 w/cover gallery; new Lee-c				15.00
...Epilogue: Three Stories (3/01, $5.95) includes r/Wizard #1/2 & AE #0				6.00
...The Age of Ice 1-4 (7/01-Present, $2.95) 2-Flip book preview of Banished Knights series				3.00
Another Universe #0				3.00
Wizard #1/2				5.00

WARLOCK (The Power of...)(Also see Fantastic Four #66, 67, Incredible Hulk #178, Infinity Crusade, Infinity Gauntlet, Infinity War, Marvel Premiere #1, Silver Surfer V3#46, Strange Tales #178-181 & Thor #165)

Warlock #2 © MAR

Warlord #49 © DC

War Machine #8 © MAR

	GD2.0	FN6.0	VF8.0	NM9.4			GD2.0	FN6.0	VF8.0	NM9.4

Marvel Comics Group: Aug, 1972 - No. 8, Oct, 1973; No. 9, Oct, 1975 - No. 15,
Nov, 1976

1-Origin by Kane	4	12	29	45
2,3	2	6	15	22
4-8: 4-Death of Eddie Roberts	2	6	11	15
9-Starlin's 2nd Thanos saga begins, ends #15; new costume Warlock; Thanos				
cameo only; story cont'd from Strange Tales #178-181; Starlin-c/a in #9-15				
	2	6	13	20
10-Origin Thanos & Gamora; recaps events from Capt. Marvel #25-34. Thanos				
vs. The Magus-c/story	3	9	17	24
11-Thanos app.; Warlock dies	2	6	12	18
12-14: (Regular 25¢ edition) 14-Origin Star Thief; last 25¢ issue				
	2	6	9	12
12-14-(30¢-c, limited distribution)	2	6	12	18
15-Thanos-c/story	2	6	10	14

NOTE: *Buscema* a-2p; c-8p. **G. Kane** a-1p, 3-5p; c-1p, 2, 3, 4p, 5p, 7p. **Starlin** a-9-14p, 15; c-9, #10, 11p, 12p, 13-15. **Sutton** a-1-8i.

WARLOCK (...Special Edition on-c)
Marvel Comics Group: Dec, 1982 - No. 6, May, 1983 ($2.00, slick paper, 52 pgs.)

1-Warlock-r/Strange Tales #178-180.	4.00
2-6: 2-r/Warlock #180,181 & Warlock #9. 3-r/Warlock #10-12(Thanos origin	
recap). 4-r/Warlock #12-15. 5-r/Warlock #15, Marvel Team-Up #55 &	
Avengers Ann. #7. 6-r/2nd half Avengers Annual #7 & Marvel Two-in-One	
Annual #2	4.00
Special Edition #1(12/83)	4.00

NOTE: *Byrne* a-5r. **Starlin** a-1-6r; c-1-6(new). Direct sale only.

WARLOCK
Marvel Comics: V2#1, May, 1992 - No. 6 Oct, 1992 ($2.50, limited series)

V2#1-6: 1-Reprints 1982 reprint series w/Thanos	2.50

WARLOCK
Marvel Comics: Nov, 1998 - No. 4, Feb, 1999 ($2.99, limited series)

1-4-Warlock vs. Drax	3.00

WARLOCK (M-Tech)
Marvel Comics: Oct, 1999 - No. 9, June, 2000 ($1.99/$2.50)

1-5: 1-Quesada-c. 2-Two covers	2.50
6-9: 6-Begin $2.50-c. 8-Avengers app.	2.50

WARLOCK AND THE INFINITY WATCH (Also see Infinity Gauntlet)
Marvel Comics: Feb, 1992 - No. 42, July, 1995 ($1.75) (Sequel to Infinity
Gauntlet)

1-Starlin-scripts begin; brief origin recap; sequel to Infinity Gauntlet	3.00
2,3-2-Reintro Moondragon	2.50
4-24,26: 7-Reintro The Magus; Moondragon app.; Thanos cameo on last 2	
pgs. 8,9-Thanos battles Drax/story. 8-Magus & Moondragon app.	
10-Thanos-c/story; Magus app. 13-Hulk x-over. 21-Drax vs. Thor	2.25
25-($2.95, 52 pgs.)-Die-cut & embossed double-c; Thor & Thanos app.	3.00
28-42: 28-$1.95-c begins; bound-in card sheet	2.25

NOTE: *Austin* c/a-1-4i, 7i. *Leonardi* a(p)-3, 4. *Medina* c/a(p)-1, 2, 5; 6, 9, 10, 14, 15, 20.
Williams a(i)-8, 12, 13-19.

WARLOCK CHRONICLES
Marvel Comics: June, 1993 - No. 8, Feb, 1994 ($2.00, limited series)

1-($2.95)-Holo-grafx foil & embossed-c; origin retold; Starlin scripts begin;	
Keith Williams-a(i) in all	3.00
2-8: 3-Thanos & Mephisto-c/story. 4-Vs. Magus-c/s. 8-Contains free 16 pg.	
Razorline insert	2.25

WARLOCK 5
Aircel Pub.: 11/86 - No. 22, 5/89; V2#1, June, 1989 - V2#5, 1989 ($1.70, B&W)

1-5,7-11-Gordon Derry-s/Denis Beauvais-a thru #11. 5-Green Cyborg on-c.	
5-Misnumbered as #6 (no #6); Blue Girl on-c.	2.25
12-22-Barry Blair-s/a. 18-$1.95-c begins	3.00
V2#1-5 ($2.00, B&W)-All issues by Barry Blair	2.25
Compilation 1,2: 1-r/#1-5 (1988, $5.95). 2-r/#6-9	6.00

WARLORD (See 1st Issue Special #8)
National Periodical Publications/DC Comics #123 on: 1-2/76; No.2, 3-4/76;
No.3, 10-11/76 - No. 133, Win, 1988-89

1-Story cont'd. from 1st Issue Special #8	3	9	17	25

2-Intro. Machiste	2	6	9	12
3-5	1	3	6	8
6-10: 6-Intro Mariah. 7-Origin Machiste. 9-Dons new costume				6.00
11-20: 11-Origin-r. 12-Intro Aton. 15-Tara returns; Warlord has son				4.00
21-36,40,41: 27-New facts about origin. 28-1st app. Wizard World. 32-Intro				
Shakira. 40-Warlord gets new costume				4.00
37-39: 37,38-Origin Omac by Starlin. 38-Intro Jennifer Morgan, Warlord's				
daughter. 39-Omac ends.				5.00
42-48: 42-47-Omac back-up series. 48-(52 pgs.)-1st app. Arak; contains free				
14 pg. Arak Son of Thunder; Claw The Unconquered app.				4.00
49-62,64-99,101-130,132: 49-Claw The Unconquered app. 50-Death of Aton.				
51-Reprints #1. 55-Arion Lord of Atlantis begins, ends #62. 91-Origin w/new				
facts. 114,115-Legends x-over. 125-Death of Tara.				3.00
63-The Barren Earth begins; free 16pg. Masters of the Universe preview				4.00
100-($1.25, 52 pgs.).				4.00
131-1st DC work by Rob Liefeld (9/88)				5.00
133-($1.50, 52 pgs.)				4.00
Remco Toy Giveaway (2-3/4x4")				5.00
Annual 1('82-'87): 1-Grell-c,/a(p). 6-New Gods app.				4.00

NOTE: *Grell* a-1-15, 16-50p, 51r, 52p, 59p, Annual 1p; c-1-70, 100-104, 112, 116, 117, Annual 1,
5. *Wayne Howard* a-64i. **Starlin** a-37-39p.

WARLORD
DC Comics: Jan, 1992 - No. 6, June, 1992 ($1.75, limited series)

1-6: Grell-c & scripts in all	2.25

WARLORDS (See DC Graphic Novel #2)

WAR MAN
Marvel Comics (Epic Comics): Nov, 1993 - No. 2, Dec, 1993 ($2.50, lim. series)

1,2	2.50

WAR MACHINE (Also see Iron Man #281,282 & Marvel Comics Presents #152)
Marvel Comics: Apr, 1994 - No. 25, Apr, 1996 ($1.50)

"Ashcan" edition (nd, 75¢, B&W, 16 pgs.)	2.25
1-($2.00, 52 pgs.)-Newsstand edition; Cable app.	2.25
1-($2.95, 52 pgs.)-Collectors ed.; embossed foil-c	3.00
2-14, 16-25: 2-Bound-in trading card sheet; Cable app. 2,3-Deathlok app.	
8-red logo	2.25
8-($2.95)-Polybagged w/16 pg. Marvel Action Hour preview & acetate print;	
yellow logo	3.00
15 ($2.50)-Flip book	2.50

WAR OF THE GODS
DC Comics: Sept, 1991 - No. 4, Dec, 1991 ($1.75, limited series)

1-4: Perez layouts, scripts & covers. 1-Contains free mini posters	
(Robin, Deathstroke). 2-4-Direct sale versions include 4 pin-ups	
printed on cover stock plus different-c	2.25

WAR OF THE WORLDS, THE
Caliber: 1996 - No. 5 ($2.95, B&W, 32 pgs.)(Based on H. G. Wells novel)

1-5: 1-Randy Zimmerman scripts begin	3.00

WARP
First Comics: Mar, 1983 - No. 19, Feb, 1985 ($1.00/$1.25, Mando paper)

1-Sargon-Mistress of War	2.25
2-19: 2-Faceless Ones begin. 10-New Warp advs., & Outrider begin	2.25
Special 1-3: 1(7/83, 36 pgs.)-Origin Chaos-Prince of Madness; origin	
of Warp Universe begins, ends #3. 2(1/84)-Lord Cumulus vs.	
Sargon Mistress of War ($1.00). 3(6/84)-Chaos-Prince of Madness	2.25

WAR PARTY
Lightning Comics: Oct, 1994 (2.95, B&W)

1-1st app. Deathmark	3.00

WARPED
Empire Entertainment (Solson): Jun, 1990 - No. 2, Oct-Nov, 1990 (B&W mag)

1,2	2.25

WARPATH (Indians on the...)
Key Publications/Stanmor: Nov, 1954 - No. 3, Apr, 1955

1	11	33	55	90
2,3	7	21	36	50

WARP GRAPHICS ANNUAL

Warrior Nun #3 © Ben Dunn

Warrior Nun Areala: Rituals #3 © Ben Dunn

War Story: Johann's Tiger © Garth Ennis & Chris Weston

	GD2.0	FN6.0	VF8.0	NM9.4

WaRP Graphics: Dec, 1985; 1988 ($2.50)

1-Elfquest, Blood of the Innocent, Thunderbunny & Myth Adventures				5.00
1 (1988)				4.00

WARREN PRESENTS
Warren Publications: Jan, 1979 - No. 14, Nov, 1981(B&W magazine)

1-Eerie, Creepy, & Vampirella-r; Merlin-s; Dax-s; Sanjulian-c	2	6	12	18
2-6(10/79): 2-The Rook. 3-Alien Invasions Comix. 4-Movie Aliens. 5-Dracula '79.				
6-Strange Stories of Vampires Comix	2	6	9	12
8(10/80)-r/1st app. Pantha from Vamp. #30	2	6	11	16
9(11/80) Empire Encounters Comix	2	6	10	14
13(10/81),14(11/81):13-Sword and Sorcery Comix	2	6	13	20
(#7,10,11,12 may not exist, or may be a Special below)				
Special-Alien Collectors Edition (1979)	2	6	13	20
Special-Close Encounters of the Third Kind (1978)	2	6	9	12
Special-Lord of the Rings (6/79)	2	6	13	20
Special-Meteor (1/80)	2	6	9	12
Special-Moonraker/James Bond (10/79)	2	6	9	12
Special-Star Wars (1977)	3	9	17	24

WAR REPORT
Ajax/Farrell Publications (Excellent Publ.): Sept, 1952 - No. 5, May, 1953

1	11	33	55	90
2-Flame thrower w/burning bodies on-c	8	24	42	60
3-5: 4-Used in POP, pg. 94	6	18	32	45

WARRIOR (Wrestling star)
Ultimate Creations: May, 1996 - No. 4, 1997 ($2.95)

1-4: Warrior scripts; Callahan-c/a. 3-Wraparound-c. 4-Warrior #3 in indicia; pin-ups				3.00
1-Variant-c.				5.00

WARRIOR COMICS
H.C. Blackerby: 1945 (1930s DC reprints)

1-Wing Brady, The Iron Man, Mark Markon	23	69	121	210

WARRIOR NUN AREALA
Antarctic Press: Dec, 1994 - No. 3, Apr, 1995 ($2.95, limited series)

1				6.00
1-Special Edition (5000)	1	4	7	10
2-3, 3-Bagged w/CD				4.00

WARRIOR NUN AREALA
Antarctic Press: July, 1997 - No. 6, May, 1998 ($2.95)

1-6-Lyga-s	3.00

WARRIOR NUN AREALA (Volume 3)
Antarctic Press: July, 1999 - No. 4 ($2.50)

1-4	2.50

WARRIOR NUN AREALA AND AVENGELYNE 1996 (See Avengelyne/...)
Antarctic Press: Dec, 1996 ($2.95)

1	3.00

WARRIOR NUN AREALA AND GLORY,
Antarctic Press: Sept, 1997

1-Ben Dunn-s/a ($2.95, color)	3.00
1-($5.95) Ltd. Poster Edition w/pin-ups	6.00

WARRIOR NUN AREALA: HAMMER AND THE HOLOCAUST
Antarctic Press: June, 1997- No. 2 ($2.95)

1,2	3.00

WARRIOR NUN AREALA: PORTRAITS,
Antarctic Press: Mar, 1996 ($3.95, one-shot)

1-Pin-ups	4.00

WARRIOR NUN AREALA/RAZOR
Antarctic Press: Jan, 1999 ($2.99, one-shot)

1-Dunn-c/a	3.00
1-($5.99)-Deluxe Ed. with painted-c	6.00

WARRIOR NUN AREALA: RESURRECTION

Antarctic Press: Nov, 1998 - No. 3, Mar, 1999 ($2.95)

1-3	3.00
1-($5.95)-Special Ed. with poster	6.00

WARRIOR NUN AREALA: RITUALS,
Antarctic Press: July, 1995 - No. 6, June, 1996 ($2.95/$3.50)

1-5	3.00
6-($3.50)	3.50

WARRIOR NUN AREALA: SCORPIO ROSE
Antarctic Press: Sept, 1996 - No. 4, Mar, 1997 ($2.95, color)

1-4	3.00

WARRIOR NUN AREALA VS. RAZOR (See Razor/...)
Antarctic Press: May, 1996 ($3.95, one-shot)

1-Dunn-c/a	4.00
1-($9.95)-Comic polybagged w/CD	10.00

WARRIOR NUN: BLACK AND WHITE,
Antarctic Press: Feb, 1997 - No. 21 ($2.95//$2.99/$2.50, B&W)

1-20	3.00
21-($2.50)	2.50

WARRIOR NUN DEI: AFTERTIME
Antarctic Press: Jan, 1997 - No. 2 ($2.95)

1-2-Patrick Thornton-s/a	3.00

WARRIOR NUN: FRENZY
Antarctic Press: Jan, 1998 - No. 2, Jun, 1998 ($2.95)

1,2: 1-Ribic painted-c/a. 2-Horvatic-s/a	3.00

WARRIOR NUN: RHEINTÖCHTER
Antarctic Press: Dec, 1997 - No. 2, Apr, 1998 ($2.95, B&W, limited series)

1,2-Set in medieval Europe; Paquette & Lacombe-s/a	3.00

WARRIOR OF WAVERLY STREET, THE
Dark Horse Comics: Nov, 1996 - No. 2, Dec, 1996 ($2.95, mini-series)

1,2-Darrow-c	3.00

WARRIORS
CFD Productions: 1993 (B&W, one-shot)

1-Linsner, Dark One-a	2	6	11	15

WARRIORS OF PLASM (Also see Plasm)
Defiant: Aug, 1993 - No. 13, Aug, 1995 ($2.95/$2.50)

1-4: Shooter-scripts; Lapham-c/a. 1-1st app. Glory. 4-Bound-in fold-out poster	3.00
5-7,10-13: 5-Begin $2.50-c. 13-Schism issue	2.50
8,9-($2.75, 44 pgs.)	2.75
The Collected Edition (2/94, $9.95)-r/Plasm #0, WOP #1-4 & Splatterball	10.00

WAR ROMANCES (See True...)
WAR SHIPS
Dell Publishing Co.: 1942 (36 pgs.)(Similar to Large Feature Comics)

nn-Cover by McWilliams; contains photos & drawings of U.S. war ships	17	51	88	150

WAR STORIES (Formerly War Comics)
Dell Publ. Co.: No. 5, 1942(nd); No. 6, Aug-Oct, 1942 - No. 8, Feb-Apr, 1943

5-Origin The Whistler	27	81	145	250
6-8: 6-8-Night Devils app. 8-Painted-c	20	60	105	180

WAR STORIES (Korea)
Ajax/Farrell Publications (Excellent Publ.): Sept, 1952 - No. 5, May, 1953

1	11	33	55	90
2	6	18	32	45
3-5	6	18	29	40

WAR STORIES (See Star Spangled...)
WAR STORY
DC Comics (Vertigo): Nov, 2001 - Present ($4.95, series of World War II one-shots)

...D-Day Dodgers (12/01) Ennis-s/Higgins-a	5.00
...Johann's Tiger (11/01) Ennis-s/Weston-a	5.00

Warstrike #1 © MAL

Wartime Romances #18 © STJ

Watchmen #10 © DC

	GD2.0	FN6.0	VF8.0	NM9.4

...Nightingale (2/02) Ennis-s/Lloyd-a				5.00
...Screaming Eagles (1/02) Ennis-s/Gibbons-a				5.00

WARSTRIKE
Malibu Comics (Ultraverse): May, 1994 - No. 7, Nov, 1995 ($1.95)

1-7: 1-Simonson-c				2.25
1-Ultra 5000 Limited silver foil				4.00
Giant Size 1 (12/94, 2.50, 44pgs.)-Prelude to Godwheel				2.50

WART AND THE WIZARD (See The Sword & the Stone under Movie Comics)
Gold Key: Feb, 1964 (Walt Disney)(Characters from Sword in the Stone movie)

(10102-402)	4	12	29	45

WARTIME ROMANCES
St. John Publishing Co.: July, 1951 - No. 18, Nov, 1953

1-All Baker-c/a	34	102	179	310
2-All Baker-c/a	24	72	127	215
3,4-All Baker-c/a	22	66	116	195
5-8-Baker-c/a(2-3) each	20	60	105	175
9,11,12,16,18: Baker-c/a each. 9-Two signed stories by Estrada				
	15	45	77	130
10,13-15,17-Baker-c only	9	27	49	70

WAR VICTORY ADVENTURES (#1 titled War Victory Comics)
U.S. Treasury Dept./War Victory/Harvey Publ.: Summer, 1942 - No. 3, Winter, 1943-44 (5¢)

1-(Promotion of Savings Bonds)-Featuring America's greatest comic art by top syndicated cartoonists; Blondie, Joe Palooka, Green Hornet, Dick Tracy, Superman, Gumps, etc., (36 pgs.); all profits were contributed to U.S.O. & Army/Navy relief funds	40	120	232	400
2-Battle of Stalingrad story; Powell-a (8/43); flag-c	22	66	116	200
3-Capt. Red Cross-c & text only; Powell-a	20	60	105	175

WAR WAGON, THE (See Movie Classics)

WAR WINGS
Charlton Comics: Oct, 1968

1	2	6	13	20

WARWORLD!
Dark Horse Comics: Feb, 1989 ($1.75, B&W, one-shot)

1-Gary Davis sci/fi art in Moebius style				2.25

WARZONE
Entity Comics: 1995 ($2.95, B&W)

1-3				3.00

WASHABLE JONES AND THE SHMOO (Also see Al Capp's Shmoo)
Toby Press: June, 1953

1- "Super-Shmoo"	21	63	110	185

WASH TUBBS (See The Comics, Crackajack Funnies)
Dell Publishing Co.: No. 11, 1942 - No. 53, 1944

Four Color 11 (#1)	30	90	210	385
Four Color 28 (1943)	21	63	147	275
Four Color 53	15	45	105	200

WASTELAND
DC Comics: Dec, 1987 - No. 18, May, 1989 ($1.75-$2.00 #13 on, mature)

1-5(4/88), 5(5/88), 6(5/88)-18: 13,15-Orlando-a				2.25

NOTE: *Orlando a-12, 13, 15.* **Truman** *a-10; c-13.*

WATCHMEN
DC Comics: Sept, 1986 - No. 12, Oct, 1987 (maxi-series)

1-Alan Moore scripts & Dave Gibbons-c/a in all	1	3	5	7
2-12				5.00
Hardcover Collection-Slip-cased-r/#1-12 w/new material; produced by Graphitti Designs				70.00
Trade paperback (1987, $14.95)-r/#1-12				18.00

WATER BIRDS AND THE OLYMPIC ELK (Disney)
Dell Publishing Co.: No. 700, Apr, 1956

Four Color 700-Movie	5	15	35	60

WATERWORLD: CHILDREN OF LEVIATHAN

Acclaim Comics: Aug, 1997 - No. 4, Nov, 1997 ($2.50, mini-series)

1-4				2.50

WEAPON X
Marvel Comics: Apr, 1994 ($12.95, one-shot)

nn-r/Marvel Comics Presents #72-84				13.00

WEAPON X
Marvel Comics: Mar, 1995 - No. 4, June, 1995 ($1.95)

1-Age of Apocalypse				4.00
2-4				2.50

WEAPON ZERO
Image Comics (Top Cow Productions): No. T-4(#1), June, 1995 - No. T-0(#5), Dec, 1995 ($2.50, limited series)

T-4(#1): Walt Simonson scripts in all.				5.00
T-3(#2) - T-1(#4)				4.00
T-0(#5)				3.00

WEAPON ZERO
Image Comics (Top Cow Productions): V2#1, Mar, 1996 - No. 15, Dec, 1997 ($2.50)

V2#1-Walt Simonson scripts.				3.00
2-14: 8-Begin Top Cow. 10-Devil's Reign				2.50
15-($3.50) Benitez-a				3.50

WEAPON ZERO/SILVER SURFER
Image Comics/Marvel Comics: Jan, 1997($2.95, one-shot)

1-Devil's Reign Pt. 1				3.00

WEASELGUY: ROAD TRIP
Image Comics: Sept, 1999 - No. 2 ($3.50, limited series)

1,2-Steve Buccellato-s/a				3.50
1-Variant-c by Bachalo				5.00

WEASELGUY/WITCHBLADE
Hyperwerks: July, 1998 ($2.95, one-shot)

1-Steve Buccellato-s/a; covers by Matsuda and Altstaetter				3.00

WEASEL PATROL SPECIAL, THE (Also see Fusion #17)
Eclipse Comics: Apr, 1989 ($2.00, B&W, one-shot)

1-Funny animal				2.25

WEAVEWORLD
Marvel Comics (Epic): Dec, 1991 - No. 3, 1992 ($4.95, lim. series, 68 pgs.)

1-3: Clive Barker adaptation				5.00

WEB, THE (Also see Mighty Comics & Mighty Crusaders)
DC Comics (Impact Comics): Sept, 1991 - No. 14, Oct, 1992 ($1.00)

1-14: 5-The Fly x-over 9-Trading card inside				2.25
Annual 1 (1992, $2.50, 68 pgs.)-With Trading card				2.50

NOTE: *Gil Kane c-5, 9, 10, 12-14.* **Bill Wray** *a(i)-1-9, 10(part).*

WEB OF EVIL
Comic Magazines/Quality Comics Group: Nov, 1952 - No. 21, Dec, 1954

1-Used in **SOTI**, pg. 388. Jack Cole-a; morphine use story				
	55	165	341	600
2-4,6,7: 2,3-Jack Cole-a. 4,6,7-Jack Cole-c/a	40	120	240	420
5-Electrocution-c/story; Jack Cole-c/a	45	135	270	475
8-11-Jack Cole-a	39	117	208	360
12,13,15,16,19-21	24	72	127	215
14-Part Crandall-c; Old Witch swipe	25	75	130	225
17-Opium drug propaganda story	24	72	127	220
18-Acid-in-face story	25	75	130	225

NOTE: *Jack Cole a(2 each)-2, 6, 8, 9.* **Cuidera** *c-1-21.* **Ravielli** *a-13.*

WEB OF HORROR
Major Magazines: Dec, 1969 - No. 3, Apr, 1970 (Magazine)

1-Jeff Jones painted-c; Wrightson-a, Kaluta-a	9	27	63	105
2-Jones painted-c; Wrightson-a(2), Kaluta-a	7	21	50	80
3-Wrightson-c/a (1st published-c); Brunner, Kaluta, Bruce Jones-a				
	7	21	50	80

WEB OF MYSTERY

	GD2.0	FN6.0	VF8.0	NM9.4

Ace Magazines (A. A. Wyn): Feb, 1951 - No. 29, Sept, 1955

1	52	157	314	550
2-Bakerish-a	30	90	159	275
3-10: 4-Colan-a	27	81	145	250
11-18,20-26: 12-John Chilly's 1st cover art. 13-Surrealistic-c. 20-r/The				
Beyond #1	24	72	127	215
19-Reprints Challenge of the Unknown #6 used in N.Y. Legislative Committee				
	24	72	127	215
27-Bakerish-a(r/The Beyond #2); last pre-code ish	22	66	116	195
28,29: 28-All-r	17	51	88	150

NOTE: This series was to appear as "Creepy Stories", but title was changed before publication. *Cameron* a-6, 8, 11-13, 17-20, 22, 24, 25, 27; c-8, 13, 17. *Palais* a-28r. *Sekowsky* a-1-3, 7, 8, 11, 14, 21, 29. *Tothish* a-by *Bill Discount* #16. 29-all-r, 19-28-partial-r.

WEB OF SCARLET SPIDER
Marvel Comics: Oct, 1995 - No. 4, Jan, 1996 ($1.95, limited series)

1-4: Replaces "Web of Spider-Man"				2.25

WEB OF SPIDER-MAN (Replaces Marvel Team-Up)
Marvel Comics Group: Apr, 1985 - No. 129, Sept, 1995

1-Painted-c (5th app. black costume?)	2	6	13	20
2,3	1	3	6	8
4-8: 7-Hulk x-over; Wolverine splash				5.00
9-13: 10-Dominic Fortune guest stars; painted-c				4.00
14-17,19-28: 19-Intro Humbug & Solo				3.00
18-1st app. Venom (behind the scenes, 9/86)				3.00
29-Wolverine, new Hobgoblin (Macendale) app.	1	3	6	8
30-Origin recap The Rose & Hobgoblin I (entire book is flashback story);				
Punisher & Wolverine cameo				4.00
31,32-Six part Kraven storyline begins				5.00
33-37,39-47,49: 36-1st app. Tombstone (cameo)				3.00
38-Hobgoblin app.; begin $1.00-c				4.00
48-Origin Hobgoblin II(Demogoblin) cont'd from Spectacular Spider-Man #147;				
Kingpin app.	1	3	6	9
50-($1.50, 52 pgs.)				3.50
51-58				2.50
59-Cosmic Spidey cont'd from Spect. Spider-Man				3.50
60-89,91-99,101-106: 66,67-Green Goblin (Norman Osborn) app. as a super-				
hero. 69,70-Hulk x-over. 74-76-Austin-c(i). 76-Fantastic Four x-over. 78-Cloak				
& Dagger app. 81-Origin/1st app. Bloodshed. 84-Begin 6 part Rose &				
Hobgoblin II storyline; last $1.00-c. 86-Demon leaves Hobgoblin; 1st Demo-				
goblin. 93-Gives brief history of obgoblin. 93,94-Hobgoblin (Macendale)				
Reborn-c/story, parts 1,2; MoonKnight app. 94-Venom cameo.95-Begin 4 part				
x-over w/Spirits of Venom w/Ghost Rider/Blaze/Spidey vs. Venom & Demo-				
goblin (cont'd in Ghost Rider/Blaze #5,6). 96-Spirits of Venom part 3; painted-				
c. 101,103-Maximum Carnage x-over. 103-Venom & Carnage app. 104-106-				
Nightwatch back-up stories				2.50
90-($2.95, 52 pgs.)-Polybagged w/silver hologram-c, gatefold poster showing				
Spider-Man & Spider-Man 2099 (Williamson-i)				3.50
90-2nd printing; gold hologram-c				3.00
100-($2.95, 52 pgs.)-Holo-grafx foil-c; intro new Spider-Armor				2.50
107-111: 107-Intro Sandstorm; Sand & Quicksand app.				
112-116, 118, 119, 121-124, 126-128: 112-Begin $1.50-c; bound-in trading				
card sheet. 113-Regular Ed.; Gambit & Black Cat app. 118-1st solo clone				
story; Venom app				2.25
113-($2.95)-Collector's ed. polybagged w/foil-c; 16 pg. preview of Spider-Man				
cartoon & animation cel				3.00
117 ($1.50)-Flip book; Power & Responsibility Pt.1				2.25
117 ($2.95)-Collector's edition; foil-c; flip book				3.00
119 ($6.45)-Direct market edition; polybagged w/ Marvel Milestone Amazing				
Spider-Man #150 & coupon for Amazing Spider-Man #396, Spider-Man #53,				
& Spectacular Spider-Man #219.				7.00
120 ($2.25)-Flip book w/ preview of the Ultimate Spider-Man				2.50
125 ($3.95)-Holodisk-c; Gwen Stacy clone				4.00
125,129: 25 ($2.95)-Newsstand. 129-Last issue				3.00
Annual 1 (1985)				
Annual 2 (1986)-New Mutants; Art Adams-a	1	3	6	8
Annual 3-10 ('87-'94, 68 pgs.): 4-Evolutionary War x-over. 5-Atlantis Attacks;				
Captain Universe by Ditko (p) & Silver Sable stories; F.F. app. 6-Punisher				
back-up plus Capt. Universe by Ditko; G. Kane-a. 7-Origins of Hobgoblin I,				
Hobgoblin II, Green Goblin I & II & Venom; Larsen/Austin-a. 8-Part 3 of				

Venom story; New Warriors x-over;Black Cat back-up sty. 9-Bagged w/card

				3.00
Super Special 1 (1995, $3.95)-flip book				4.00

NOTE: *Art Adams* a-Annual 2. *Byrne* c-3-6. *Chaykin* c-10. *Mignola* a-Annual 2. *Vess* c-1, 8, Annual 1, 2. *Zeck* a-6i, 31, 32; c-31, 32.

WEBSPINNERS: TALES OF SPIDER-MAN
Marvel Comics: Jan, 1999 - No. 18, Jun, 2000 ($2.99/$2.50)

1-DeMatteis-s/Zulli-a; back-up story w/Romita Sr. art				3.00
1-($6.95) DF Edition				7.00
2,3: 2-Two covers				2.50
4-11,13-18: 4,5-Giffen-a; Silver Surfer-c/app. 7-9-Kelly-s/Sears and Smith-a.				
10,11-Jenkins-s/Sean Phillips-a				2.50
12-($3.50) J.G. Jones-c/a; Jenkins-s				3.50

WEDDING BELLS
Quality Comics Group: Feb, 1954 - No. 19, Nov, 1956

1-Whitney-a	15	45	77	130
2	10	30	55	80
3-9: 8-Last precode (4/55)	7	21	36	50
10-Ward-a (9 pgs.)	14	42	72	120
11-14,17	6	18	29	40
15-Baker-c	7	21	36	50
16-Baker-c/a	10	30	55	80
18,19-Baker-a each	8	24	42	60

WEDDING OF DRACULA
Marvel Comics: Jan, 1993 ($2.00, 52 pgs.)

1-Reprints Tomb of Dracula #30,45,46				2.25

WEEKENDER, THE (Illustrated...)
Rucker Pub. Co.: V1#1, Sept, 1945? - V1#4, Nov, 1945; V2#1, Jan, 1946 - V2#3, Aug, 1946 (52 pgs.)

V1#1-4: 1-Same-c as Zip Comics #45, inside-c and back-c blank; Steel Sterling,				
Senor Banana, Red Rube and Ginger. 2-Capt. Victory on-c. 3-Super hero-c;				
Mr. E, Dan Hastings, Sky Chief and the Echo. 4-Same-c as Punch Comics				
#10 (9/44); r/Hale the Magician (7 pgs.) & r/Mr. E (8 pgs.-Lou Fine? or				
Gustavson?) plus 3 humor strips & many B&W photos & r/newspaper articles				
plus cheesecake photos of Hollywood stars	16	48	83	140
V2#1-Same-c as Dynamic Comics #11; 36 pgs. comics, 16 in newspaper format				
with photos; partial Dynamic Comics reprints; 4 pgs. of cels from the Disney				
film Pinocchio; Little Nemo story by Winsor McCay, Jr.; Jack Cole-a;				
	19	57	99	165
V2#2,3: 2-Same-c as Dynamic Comics #9 by Raboy; Dan Hastings (Tuska),				
Rocket Boy, The Echo, Lucky Coyne. 3-Humor-c by Boddington?; Dynamic				
Man, Ima Slooth, Master Key, Dynamic Boy, Captain Glory				
	16	48	83	140

WEIRD
Eerie Publications: V1#10, 1/66 - V8#6, 12/74; V9#1, 1/75 - V11#4, Dec, 1978 (Magazine) (V1-V8: 52 pgs.; V9 on: 68 pgs.)

V1#10(#1)-Intro. Morris the Caretaker of Weird (ends V2#10); Burgos-a				
	6	18	42	70
11,12	4	12	27	42
V2#1-4(10/67), V3#1(1/68), V2#6(4/68)-V2#7,9,10(12/68)				
	4	12	29	45
V2#8-r/Ditko's 1st story/Fantastic Fears #5	5	15	34	55
V3#1(2/69)-V3#4	4	12	25	38
V3#5(12/69)-Rulah reprint; "Rulah" changed to "Pulah", LSD story reprinted in				
Horror Tales V4#4, Tales From the Tomb V2#4, & 20				
	4	12	25	38
V4#1-6(70), V5#1-6(71), V6#1-7(72), V7#1-7(73), V8#1-3, V8#4(8/74), V8#4(10/74),				
(V8#5 does not exist), V8#6(74), V9#1-4(1/75-76), V10#1-3(77), V11#1-4(78),				
V12('79)-V14('81)	4	12	25	38

NOTE: There are two V8#4 issues (8/74 & 10/74). V9#4 (12/76) has a cover swipe from Horror Tales V5#1 (2/73).

WEIRD
DC Comics (Paradox Press): Sum, 1997 - Present ($2.99, B&W, magazine)

1-4: 4-Mike Tyson-c				3.00

WEIRD, THE
DC Comics: Apr, 1988 - No. 4, July, 1988 ($1.50, limited series)

Weird Comics #16 © FOX

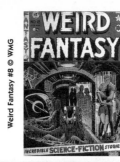

Weird Fantasy #8 © WMG

Weird Science #7 © WMG

	GD2.0	FN6.0	VF8.0	NM9.4

1-4: Wrightson-c/a in all   3.00

WEIRD ADVENTURES
P. L. Publishing Co. (Canada): May-June, 1951 - No. 3, Sept-Oct, 1951

1- "The She-Wolf Killer" by Matt Baker (6 pgs.)	55	165	330	575
2-Bondage/hypodermic panel	43	129	257	450
3-Male bondage/torture-c; severed head story	40	120	220	380

WEIRD ADVENTURES
Ziff-Davis Publishing Co.: No. 10, July-Aug, 1951

10-Painted-c	40	120	220	380

WEIRD CHILLS
Key Publications: July, 1954 - No. 3, Nov, 1954

1-Wolverton-r/Weird Mysteries No. 4; blood transfusion-c by Baily	77	231	483	850
2-Extremely violent injury to eye-c by Baily; Hitler story	73	219	455	800
3-Bondage E.C. swipe-c by Baily	47	141	286	500

WEIRD COMICS
Fox Features Syndicate: Apr, 1940 - No. 20, Jan, 1942

1-The Birdman, Thor, God of Thunder (ends #5), The Sorceress of Zoom, Blast Bennett, Typhon, Voodoo Man, & Dr. Mortal begin; Lou Fine bondage-c	438	1314	2847	5700
2-Lou Fine-c	214	642	1338	2350
3,4: 3-Simon-c. 4-Torture-c	116	348	725	1275
5-Intro. Dart & sidekick Ace (8/40) (ends #20); bondage/hypo-c	123	369	769	1350
6,7-Dynamite Thor app. in each. 6-Super hero covers begin	95	285	597	1050
8-Dynamo, the Eagle (11/40, early app.; see Science #1) & sidekick Buddy & Marga, the Panther Woman begin	93	279	581	1025
9,10: 10-Navy Jones app.	76	229	475	840
11-19: 16-Flag-c. 17-Origin The Black Rider.	58	174	363	640
20-Origin The Rapier; Swoop Curtis app; Churchill & Hitler-c	68	205	426	750

NOTE Cover features: Sorceress of Zoom-4; Dr. Mortal-5; Dart & Ace-6-13, 15; Eagle-14, 16-20.

WEIRD FANTASY (Formerly A Moon, A Girl, Romance; becomes Weird Science-Fantasy #23 on)
E. C. Comics: No. 13, May-June, 1950 - No. 22, Nov-Dec, 1953

13(#1) (1950)	184	552	1288	2300
14-Necronomicon story; Cosmic Ray Bomb explosion-c/story by Feldstein; Feldstein & Gaines star	84	252	588	1050
15,16: 16-Used in SOTI, pg. 144	56	168	392	700
17 (1951)	47	141	329	590
6-10: 6-Robot-c	38	114	266	475
11-13 (1952): 12-E.C. artists cameo. 13-Anti-Wertham "Cosmic Correspondence"	31	93	217	390
14-Frazetta/Williamson(1st team-up at E.C.)/Krenkel-a (7 pgs.); Orlando draws E.C. staff	44	132	308	550
15-Williamson/Evans-a(3), 4,3,&7 pgs.	31	93	217	390
16-19-Williamson/Krenkel-a in all. 18-Williamson/Feldstein-c	29	87	203	365
20-Frazetta/Williamson-a (7 pgs.)	32	96	224	400
21-Frazetta/Williamson-c & Williamson/Krenkel-a	44	132	308	550
22-Bradbury adaptation	22	66	154	275

NOTE: Ray Bradbury adaptations-13, 17-20, 22. Crandall a-22. Elder a-17. Feldstein a-13(#1)-8; c-13(#1)-18 (#18 w/Williamson), 20. Harrison/Wood a-13. Kamen a-13(#1)-16, 18-22. Krigstein a-22. Kurtzman a-13(#1)-17(#5), 6. Orlando a-9-22 (2 stories in #16); c-19, 22. Severin/Elder a-18-21. Wood a-13(#1)-14, 17(2 stories ea. in #10-13). Ray Bradbury adaptations in #17-19, 22. Canadian reprints exist; see Table of Contents.

WEIRD FANTASY
Russ Cochran/Gemstone Publ.: Oct, 1992 - No. 22, Jan, 1998
($1.50/$2.00/$2.50)

1-22: 1,2: 1,2-r/Weird Fantasy #13,14; Feldstein-c. 3-5-r/Weird Fantasy #15-17				3.00

WEIRD HORRORS (Nightmare #10 on)
St. John Publishing Co.: June, 1952 - No. 9, Oct, 1953

1-Tuska-a	55	165	330	575

	GD2.0	FN6.0	VF8.0	NM9.4

2,3: 3-Hashish story	35	105	188	325
4,5	30	90	159	275
6-Ekgren-c; atomic bomb story	47	141	286	500
7-Ekgren-c; Kubert, Cameron-a	50	150	300	525
8,9-Kubert-c/a	40	120	232	400

NOTE: Cameron a-7, 9. Finesque c-1-5. Forgione a-6. Morisi a-3. Bondage c-8.

WEIRD MYSTERIES
Gillmore Publications: Oct, 1952 - No. 12, Sept, 1954

1-Partial Wolverton-c swiped from splash page "Flight to the Future" in Weird Tales of the Future #2; "Eternity" has an Ingels swipe	77	231	483	850
2- "Robot Woman" by Wolverton; Bernard Baily-c reprinted in Mister Mystery #18; acid in face panel	105	315	656	1150
3,6: Both have decapitation-c	55	165	330	575
4- "The Man Who Never Smiled" (3 pgs.) by Wolverton; Classic B. Baily skull-c	95	285	597	1050
5-Wolverton story "Swamp Monster" (6 pgs.). Classic exposed brain-c	100	300	625	1100
7-Used in SOTI, illo "Indeed", illo "Sex and blood"	75	225	469	825
8-Wolverton-c panel-r/#5; used in a '54 Readers Digest anti-comics article by T. E. Murphy entitled "For the Kiddies to Read"	55	165	330	575
9-Excessive violence, gore & torture	50	150	300	525
10-Silhouetted nudity panel	44	132	264	460
11,12: 1-r/Mr. Mystery #8(2), Weird Mysteries #3 & Weird Tales of the Future #6	40	120	240	420

NOTE: Baily c-2-12. Anti-Wertham column in #5. #1-12 all have 'The Ghoul Teacher' (host).

WEIRD MYSTERIES (Magazine)
Pastime Publications: Mar-Apr, 1959 (35¢, B&W, 68 pgs.)

1-Torres-a; E. C. swipe from Tales From the Crypt #46 by Tuska "The Ragman"	8	24	42	60

WEIRD MYSTERY TALES (See DC 100 Page Super Spectacular)

WEIRD MYSTERY TALES (See Cancelled Comic Cavalcade)
National Periodical Publications: July-Aug, 1972 - No. 24, Nov, 1975

1-Kirby-a; Wrightson splash pg.	5	15	34	55
2-Titanic-c/s	3	9	21	32
3,21: 21-Wrightson-c	3	9	17	24
4-10	2	6	12	18
11-20,22-24	2	6	10	14

NOTE: Alcala a-5, 10, 13, 14. Aparo c-4. Bailey a-8. Bolle a-8?. Howard a-4. Kaluta a-4, 24; c-1. G. Kane a-10. Kirby a-1, 2p, 3p. Nino a-5, 6, 9, 13, 16, 21. Redondo a-9, 17. Sparling c-6. Starlin a-37, 4. Wood a-23.

WEIRD ROMANCE (Seduction of the Innocent #9)
Eclipse Comics: Feb, 1988 ($2.00, B&W)

1-Pre-code horror-r; Lou Cameron-r(2)				2.25

WEIRD SCIENCE (Formerly Saddle Romances) (Becomes Weird Science-Fantasy #23 on)
E. C. Comics: No. 12, May-June, 1950 - No. 22, Nov-Dec, 1953

12(#1) (1950)- "Lost in the Microcosm" classic-c/story by Kurtzman; "Dream of Doom" stars Gaines & E.C. artists	184	552	1288	2300
13-Flying saucers over Washington-c/story, 2 years before the actual event	84	252	588	1050
14-Robot, End of the World-c/story by Feldstein	80	240	560	1000
15-War of Worlds-c/story (1950)	74	222	518	925
5-Atomic explosion-c	56	168	392	700
6-10: 9-Wood's 1st EC-c	45	135	315	585
11-14 (1952)	31	93	217	390
15-18-Williamson/Krenkel-a in each; 15-Williamson-a. 17-Used in POP, pg. 81,82. 18-Bill Gaines doll app. in story	33	99	231	415
19,20-Williamson/Frazetta-a (7 pgs. each). 19-Used in SOTI, illo "A young girl on her wedding night stabs her sleeping husband to death with a hatpin…"	43	129	301	540
21-Williamson/Frazetta-a (6 pgs.); Wood draws E.C. staff; Gaines & Feldstein app. in story	43	129	301	540
22-Williamson/Frazetta/Krigstein-a (8 pgs.); Wood draws himself in his story (last pg. & panel)	43	129	301	540

NOTE: Elder a-14, 19. Evans a-22. Feldstein a-12(#1)-8; c-12(#1)-18, 20. Kamen a-12(#1)-13, 15-18, 20, 21. Kurtzman a-12(#1)-17. Orlando a-10-22. Wood a-12(#1), 13(#2), 5-22 (#9, 10, 12, 13 all have 2 Wood stories); c-9, 10, 12-22. Canadian reprints exist; see Table of

Weird Tales Illustrated #1 © Millennium Publ.

Weird Tales of the Future #4 © Aragon

Weird War Tales #1 © DC

| | GD2.0 | FN6.0 | VF8.0 | NM9.4 | | GD2.0 | FN6.0 | VF8.0 | NM9.4 |

Contents. Ray Bradbury adaptations in #17-20.

WEIRD SCIENCE
Gladstone Publishing: Sept, 1990 - No. 4, Mar, 1991 ($1.95/$2.00, 68 pgs.)

1-4: Wood-c(r); all reprints in each			3.00

WEIRD SCIENCE
Russ Cochran/Gemstone Publishing: Sept, 1992 - No. 22, Dec, 1997 ($1.50/$2.00/$2.50)

1-22: 1,2: r/Weird Science #12,13 w/original-c. ,4-r/#14,15. 5-7-w/original-c			3.00

WEIRD SCIENCE-FANTASY (Formerly Weird Science & Weird Fantasy)
(Becomes Incredible Science Fiction #30)
E. C. Comics: No. 23 Mar, 1954 - No. 29, May-June, 1955 (#23,24: 15¢)

23-Williamson, Wood-a; Bradbury adaptation	30	90	210	375
24-Williamson & Wood-a; Harlan Ellison's 1st professional story, "Upheaval!", later adapted into a short story as "Mealtime", and then into a TV episode of Voyage to the Bottom of the Sea as "The Price of Doom"	30	90	210	375
25-Williamson-c; Williamson/Torres/Krenkel-a plus Wood-a; Bradbury adaptation; cover price back to 10¢	33	99	231	415
26-Flying Saucer Report; Wood, Crandall; A-bomb panels	31	93	217	390
27-Adam Link/I Robot series begins?	30	90	210	375
28-Williamson/Krenkel/Torres-a; Wood-a	31	93	217	390
29-Frazetta-c; Williamson/Krenkel & Wood-a; last pre-code issue; new logo	54	162	378	675

NOTE: *Crandall a-26, 27, 29. Evans a-26. Feldstein c-24, 26, 28. Kamen a-27, 28. Krigstein a-23-25. Orlando a-in all. Wood a-in all; c-23, 27. The cover to #29 was originally intended for Famous Funnies #217 (Buck Rogers), but was rejected for being "too violent."*

WEIRD SCIENCE-FANTASY
Russ Cochran/Gemstone Publishing: Nov, 1992 - No. 7, May , 1994 ($1.50/$2.00/$2.50)

1-7: 1,2: r/Weird Science-Fantasy #23,24. 3-7 r/#25-29			3.00

WEIRD SCIENCE-FANTASY ANNUAL
E. C. Comics: 1952, 1953 (Sold thru the E. C. office & on the stands in some major cities) (25¢, 132 pgs.)

1952-Feldstein-c	205	615	1435	2250
1953-Feldstein-c	132	396	924	1450

NOTE: *The 1952 annual contains books cover-dated in 1951 & 1952, and the 1953 annual from 1952 & 1953. Contents of each annual may vary in same year.*

WEIRD SUSPENSE
Atlas/Seaboard Publ.: Feb, 1975 - No. 3, July, 1975

1-3: 1-Tarantula begins. 3-Freidrich-s	1	3	5	7

NOTE: *Boyette a-1-3. Buckler c-1, 3.*

WEIRD SUSPENSE STORIES (Canadian reprint of Crime SuspenStories #1-3; see Table of Contents)

WEIRD TALES ILLUSTRATED
Millennium Publications: 1992 - No. 2, 1992 ($2.95, high quality paper)

1,2-Bolton painted-c. 1-Adapts E.A. Poe & Harlan Ellison stories. 2-E.A. Poe & H.P. Lovecraft adaptations			3.50
1-($4.95, 52 pgs.)-Deluxe edition w/Tim Vigil-a not in regular #1; stiff-c; Bolton painted-c			5.00

WEIRD TALES OF THE FUTURE
S.P.M. Publ. No. 1-4/Aragon Publ. No. 5-8: Mar, 1952 - No. 8, July-Aug, 1953

1-Andru-a(2); Wolverton partial-c	95	285	597	1050
2,3-Wolverton-c/a(3) each. 2- "Jumpin Jupiter" satire by Wolverton begins, ends #5	127	381	795	1400
4- "Jumpin Jupiter" satire & "The Man From the Moon" by Wolverton; partial Wolverton-c	109	327	682	1200
5-Wolverton-c/a(2); "Jumpin Jupiter" satire	127	381	795	1400
6-Bernard Baily-c	52	157	314	550
7- "The Mind Movers" from the art to Wolverton's "Brain Bats of Venus" from Mr. Mystery #7 which was cut apart, pasted up, partially redrawn, and rewritten by Harry Kantor, the editor; Baily-a	105	315	656	1150
8-Reprints Weird Mysteries #1(10/52) minus cover; gory cover showing heart ripped out by B. Baily	68	204	426	750

WEIRD TALES OF THE MACABRE (Magazine)
Atlas/Seaboard Publ.: Jan, 1975 - No. 2, Mar, 1975 (75¢, B&W)

1-Jeff Jones painted-c; Boyette-a	2	6	12	18
2-Boris Vallejo painted-c; Severin-a	3	9	17	26

WEIRD TERROR (Also see Horrific)
Allen Hardy Associates (Comic Media): Sept, 1952 - No. 13, Sept, 1954

1- "Portrait of Death", adapted from Lovecraft's "Pickman's Model"; lingerie panels, Hitler story	52	157	314	550
2,3: 2-Text on Marquis DeSade, Torture, Demonology, & St. Elmo's Fire. 3-Extreme violence, whipping, torture; article on sin eating, dowsing	43	129	257	450
4-Dismemberment, decapitation, article on human flesh for sale, Devil, whipping	43	129	257	450
5-Article on body snatching, mutilation; cannibalism story	40	120	217	375
6-Dismemberment, decapitation, man hit by lightning	40	120	232	400
7-Body burning in fireplace-c	40	120	217	375
8,11: 8-Decapitation story; Ambrose Bierce adapt.. 11-End of the world story w/atomic blast panels; Tothish-a by Bill Discount	40	120	226	390
9,10,13: 13-Severed head panels	33	99	174	300
12-Discount-a	31	93	165	285

NOTE: *Don Heck a-most issues; c-1-13. Landau a-6. Morisi a-2-5, 7, 9, 12. Palais a-1, 5, 6, 8(2), 10, 12. Powell a-10. Ravielli a-11, 20.*

WEIRD THRILLERS
Ziff-Davis Publ. Co. (Approved Comics): Sept-Oct, 1951 - No. 5, Oct-Nov, 1952 (#2-5: painted-c)

1-Rondo Hatton photo-c	82	246	511	900
2-Toth, Anderson, Colan-a	59	177	369	650
3-Two Powell, Tuska-a; classic-c	80	240	500	875
4-Kubert, Tuska-a.	55	165	341	600
5-Powell-a	50	150	300	525

NOTE: *M. Anderson a-2, 3. Roussos a-4. #2, 3 reprinted in Nightmare #10 & 13; #4, 5 reprinted in Amazing Ghost Stories #16 & #15.*

WEIRD VAMPIRE TALES (Comic magazine)
Modern Day Periodical Pub.: V3 #1, Apr, 1979 - V5 #3, Mar, 1982 (B&W)

V3 #1 (4/79) First issue, no V1 or V2	4	12	26	40
V3 #2-4	3	9	20	30
V4 #2 (4/80), V4 #3 (7/80) (no V4 #1)	3	9	17	25
V5 #1 (1/81), V5 #2 (8/81)	3	9	17	25
V5 #3 (3/82) Last issue; low print	3	10	23	35

WEIRD WAR TALES
National Periodical Publications/DC Comics: Sept-Oct, 1971 - No. 124, June, 1983 (#1-5: 52 pgs.)

1-Kubert-a in #1-4,7; c-1-7	22	66	154	275
2,3-Drucker-a. 2-Crandall-a. 3-Heath-a	8	24	60	100
4,5: 5-Toth-a; Heath-a	6	18	45	75
6,7,9,10: 6,10-Toth-a. 7-Heath-a	4	12	29	45
8-Neal Adams-c/a(i)	5	15	38	60
11-20	3	9	17	25
21-35	2	6	12	18
36-(68 pgs.)-Crandall & Kubert-r/#2; Heath-r/#3; Kubert-c	2	6	15	22
37-63: 38-Kubert-c	1	3	6	9
64,68-Frank Miller-a in both. 64-Miller's 1st DC work	2	6	12	18
65-67,69-92,95-99,102-124: 97-2nd Creature Commandos; series begins				6.00
93,94,100,101: 93-Intro/origin Creature Commandos. 94,99-Return of War that time forgot-Dinosaur-c/s. 101-Intro/origin G.I. Robot				6.00

WEIRD WAR TALES
DC Comics (Vertigo): June, 1997 - No. 4, Sept, 1997 ($2.50)

1-4-Anthology by various			3.00

WEIRD WAR TALES
DC Comics (Vertigo): April, 2000 ($4.95, one-shot)

1-Anthology by various; last Biukovic-a			5.00

WEIRD WESTERN TALES (Formerly All-Star Western)

Weird Wonder Tales #17 © MAR

Welcome Back Kotter #2 © Wolper Org.

Werewolf By Night #6 © MAR

	GD2.0	FN6.0	VF8.0	NM9.4

National Per. Publ./DC Comics: No. 12, June-July, 1972 - No. 70, Aug, 1980

12-(52 pgs.)-3rd app. Jonah Hex; Bat Lash, Pow Wow Smith reprints;				
El Diablo by Neal Adams/Wrightson	10	30	70	120
13-Jonah Hex-c (1st?) & 4th app.; Neal Adams-a	6	18	42	70
14-Toth-a	4	12	30	50
15-Adams-c/a; no Jonah Hex	3	9	20	30
16,17,19,20	3	9	17	25
18,29: 18-1st all Jonah Hex issue (7-8/73) & begins. 29-Origin Jonah Hex				
	3	10	23	35
21-28,30-38: Jonah Hex in all. 38-Last Jonah Hex	2	6	11	16
39-Origin/1st app. Scalphunter & begins	2	6	11	15
40-47,50-69: 64-Bat Lash-c/story	1	3	6	8
48,49: (44 pgs.)-1st & 2nd app. Cinnamon	1	3	6	9
70-Last issue	2	6	9	12

NOTE: *Alcala* a-16, 17. *Evans* inks-39-48; c-39i, 40, 47. *G. Kane* a-15, 20. *Kubert* c-12, 33. *Starlin* c-44, 45. *Wildey* a-26. 48 & 49 are 44 pgs..

WEIRD WESTERN TALES
DC Comics (Vertigo): Apr, 2001 - No. 4, Jul, 2001 ($2.50, limited series)

1-4-Anthology by various				2.50

WEIRD WONDER TALES
Marvel Comics Group: Dec, 1973 - No. 22, May, 1977

1-Wolverton-r/Mystic #6 (Eye of Doom)	2	6	15	22
2-10	2	6	9	12
11-22: 16-18-Venus-r by Everett from Venus #19,18 & 17. 19-22-Dr. Druid (Droom)-r	1	4	7	10
15-17-(30¢-c variants, limited distribution)(4-8/76)	2	6	11	15

NOTE: *All 1950s & early 1960s reprints. Check* r-1. *Colan* r-17. *Ditko* r-4, 5, 10-13, 19-21. *Drucker* r-12, 20. *Everett* r-3(Spellbound #16), 6(Astonishing #10), 9(Adv. Into Mystery #5). *Heath* a-13r. *Heck* a-1or, 14r. *Gil Kane* c-1, 2, 9. *Kirby* r-4, 6, 10, 11, 13, 15-22; c-17, 19, 20. *Krigstein* r-19. *Kubert* r-22. *Maneely* r-8. *Mooney* r-7p. *Powell* r-3, 7. *Torres* r-7. *Wildey* r-2, 7.

WEIRD WORLDS (See Adventures Into...)

WEIRD WORLDS (Magazine)
Eerie Publications: V1#10(12/70), V2#1(2/71) - No. 4, Aug, 1971 (52 pgs.)

V1#10-Sci-fi/horror	4	12	25	38
V2#1-4	3	9	19	28

WEIRD WORLDS (Also see Ironwolf: Fires of the Revolution)
National Periodical Publications: Aug-Sept, 1972 - No. 9, Jan-Feb, 1974; No. 10, Oct-Nov, 1974 (All 20¢ issues)

1-Edgar Rice Burrough's John Carter Warlord of Mars & David Innes begin (1st DC app.); Kubert-c	2	6	13	20
2-4: 2-Infantino/Orlando-c. 3-Murphy Anderson-c. 4-Kaluta-a				
	2	6	9	12
5-7: .5-Kaluta-c. 7-Last John Carter.	1	4	7	10
8-10: 8-Iron Wolf begins by Chaykin (1st app.)	1	3	6	9

NOTE: *Neal Adams* a-2i, 3i. *John Carter by Andersonin* #1-3. *Chaykin* c-7, 8. *Kaluta* a-4; c-4-6, 10. *Orlando* a-i; c-2, 3, 4i. *Wrightson* a-2i, 4i.

WELCOME BACK, KOTTER (TV) (See Limited Collectors' Edition #57)
National Periodical Publ./DC Comics: Nov, 1976 - No. 10, Mar-Apr, 1978

1-Sparling-a(p)	2	6	15	22
2-10: 3-Estrada-a	2	6	9	12

WELCOME SANTA (See March of Comics #63,183)

WELCOME TO THE LITTLE SHOP OF HORRORS
Roger Corman's Cosmic Comics: May, 1995 -No. 3, July, 1995 ($2.50, limited series)

1-3				2.50

WELLS FARGO (See Tales of...)

WENDY AND THE NEW KIDS ON THE BLOCK
Harvey Comics: Mar, 1991 - No. 3, July, 1991 ($1.25)

1-3				2.25

WENDY DIGEST
Harvey Comics: Oct, 1990 - No. 5, Mar, 1992 ($1.75, digest size)

1-5				4.00

WENDY PARKER COMICS
Atlas Comics (OMC): July, 1953 - No. 8, July, 1954

	GD2.0	FN6.0	VF8.0	NM9.4
1	10	30	55	85
2	7	21	36	50
3-8	6	18	32	45

WENDY, THE GOOD LITTLE WITCH (TV)
Harvey Publ.: 8/60 - #82, 11/73; #83, 8/74 - #93, 4/76; #94, 9/90 - #97, 12/90

1-Wendy & Casper the Friendly Ghost begin	18	54	126	225
2	9	27	63	105
3-5	6	18	45	75
6-10	5	15	38	60
11-20	4	12	29	45
21-30	3	10	23	35
31-50	3	9	17	25
51-64,66-69	2	6	11	16
65 (2/71)-Wendy origin.	3	9	17	24
70-74: 5th app. Casper.	2	6	15	22
75-93	1	3	6	9
94-97 (1990, $1.00-c): 94-Has #194 on-c				4.00

(See Casper the Friendly Ghost #20 & Harvey Hits #7, 16, 21, 23, 27, 30, 33)

WENDY THE GOOD LITTLE WITCH (2nd Series)
Harvey Comics: Apr, 1991 - No. 15, Aug, 1994 ($1.00/$1.25 #7-11/$1.50 #12-15)

1-15-Reprints Wendy & Casper stories. 12-Bunny app.				3.00

WENDY WITCH WORLD
Harvey Publications: 10/61; No. 2, 9/62 - No. 52, 12/73; No. 53, 9/74

1-(25¢, 68 pg. Giants begin	12	36	88	150
2-5	6	18	45	75
6-10	4	12	30	50
11-20	4	12	26	40
21-30	3	9	20	30
31-39: 39-Last 68 pg. issue	3	9	17	24
40-45: 52 pg. issues	2	6	11	16
46-53	1	3	6	9

WEREWOLF (Super Hero) (Also see Dracula & Frankenstein)
Dell Publishing Co.: Dec, 1966 - No. 3, April, 1967

1-1st app.	3	9	20	30
2,3	2	6	12	18

WEREWOLF BY NIGHT (See Giant-Size…, Marvel Spotlight #2-4 & Power Record Comics)
Marvel Comics Group: Sept, 1972 - No. 43, Mar, 1977

1-Ploog a-cont'd from Marvel Spotlight #4	8	24	60	100
2	4	12	26	40
3-5	3	9	20	30
6-10	2	6	13	20
11-14,16-20	2	6	11	15
15-New origin Werewolf; Dracula-c/story cont'd from Tomb of Dracula #18; classic Ploog-c	2	6	15	22
21-31	1	4	7	10
32-Origin & 1st app. Moon Knight (8/75)	9	27	65	110
33-2nd app. Moon Knight	4	12	30	50
34-36,38-43: 35-Starlin/Wrightson-c	1	3	6	9
37-Moon Knight app; part Wrightson-c	2	6	9	12
38,39-(30¢-c variants, limited distribution)(5,7/76)	2	6	10	14

NOTE: *Bolle* a-6i. *G. Kane* a-11p, 12p; c-21, 22, 24-30, 34p. *Mooney* a-7i. *Ploog* 1-4p, 5, 6p, 7p, 13-16p; c-5-8, 13-16. *Reinman* a-8i. *Sutton* a(i)-9, 11, 16, 35.

WEREWOLF BY NIGHT (Vol. 2, continues in Strange Tales #1 (9/98))
Marvel Comics Group: Feb, 1998 - No. 6, July, 1998 ($2.99)

1-6-Manco-a: 2-Two covers. 6-Ghost Rider-c/app.				3.00

WEREWOLVES & VAMPIRES (Magazine)
Charlton Comics: 1962 (One Shot)

1	8	24	56	90

WEST COAST AVENGERS
Marvel Comics Group: Sept, 1984 - No. 4, Dec, 1984 (lim. series, Mando paper)

1-Origin & 1st app. W.C. Avengers (Hawkeye, Iron Man, Mockingbird & Tigra)				4.00
2-4				3.00

WEST COAST AVENGERS (Becomes Avengers West Coast #48 on)

Western Adventures Comics #3 © ACE

Western Comics #7 © DC

Western Fighters #7 © HILL

	GD2.0	FN6.0	VF8.0	NM9.4			GD2.0	FN6.0	VF8.0	NM9.4

Marvel Comics Group: Oct, 1985 - No. 47, Aug, 1989

V2#1-41 .... 3.00
42-47: 42-Byrne-a(p)/scripts begin. 46-Byrne-c; 1st app. Great Lakes Avengers
.... 3.00
Annual 1-3 (1986-1988): 3-Evolutionary War app. ... 3.00
Annual 4 (1989, $2.00)-Atlantis Attacks; Byrne/Austin-a ... 3.00

WESTERN ACTION
I. W. Enterprises: No. 7, 1964
7-Reprints Cow Puncher #? by Avon ...... 2 ... 6 ... 9 ... 12

WESTERN ACTION
Atlas/Seaboard Publ.: Feb, 1975
1-Kid Cody by Wildey & The Comanche Kid stories; intro. The Renegade
.... 1 ... 3 ... 5 ... 7

WESTERN ACTION THRILLERS
Dell Publishers: Apr, 1937 (10¢, square binding; 100 pgs.)
1-Buffalo Bill, The Texas Kid, Laramie Joe, Two-Gun Thompson, & Wild West
Bill app. .... 242 ... 525 ... 525 ... 925

WESTERN ADVENTURES COMICS (Western Love Trails #7 on)
Ace Magazines: Oct, 1948 - No. 6, Aug, 1949
nn(#1)-Sheriff Sal, The Cross-Draw Kid, Sam Bass begin
.... 23 ... 69 ... 121 ... 210
nn(#2)(12/48) .... 12 ... 36 ... 61 ... 105
nn(#3)(2/49)-Used in **SOTI**, pgs. 30,31 ... 13 ... 39 ... 66 ... 110
4-6 .... 10 ... 30 ... 55 ... 85

WESTERN BANDITS
Avon Periodicals: 1952 (Painted-c)
1-Butch Cassidy, The Daltons by Larsen; Kinstler-a; c-part-r/paperback
Avon Western Novel #1 .... 17 ... 51 ... 88 ... 150

WESTERN BANDIT TRAILS (See Approved Comics)
St. John Publishing Co.: Jan, 1949 - No. 3, July, 1949
1-Tuska-a; Baker-c; Blue Monk, Ventrilo app. ... 26 ... 78 ... 136 ... 235
2-Baker-c .... 20 ... 60 ... 105 ... 175
3-Baker-c/a; Tuska-a .... 24 ... 72 ... 127 ... 215

WESTERN COMICS (See Super DC Giant #15)
National Per. Publ.: Jan-Feb, 1948 - No. 85, Jan-Feb, 1961 (1-27: 52pgs.)
1-Wyoming Kid & his horse Racer, The Vigilante in "Jesse James Rides Again"
(Meskin-a), Cowboy Marshal, Rodeo Rick begin
.... 80 ... 240 ... 500 ... 875
2 .... 40 ... 120 ... 220 ... 380
3,4-Last Vigilante .... 37 ... 111 ... 197 ... 340
5-Nighthawk & his horse Nightwind begin (not in #6); Captain Tootsie by Beck
.... 31 ... 93 ... 165 ... 285
6,7,9,10 .... 24 ... 72 ... 127 ... 215
8-Origin Wyoming Kid; 2 pg. pin-ups of rodeo queens
.... 36 ... 108 ... 191 ... 330
11-20 .... 20 ... 60 ... 105 ... 175
21-40: 24-Starr-a. 27-Last 52 pgs. 28-Flag-c ... 15 ... 45 ... 77 ... 130
41,42,44-49: 49-Last precode issue (2/55) ... 14 ... 42 ... 72 ... 120
43-Pow Wow Smith begins, ends #85 ... 14 ... 42 ... 72 ... 125
50-60 .... 12 ... 36 ... 61 ... 100
61-85-Last Wyoming Kid. 77-Origin Matt Savage Trail Boss. 82-1st app.
Fleetfoot, Pow Wow's girlfriend ... 10 ... 30 ... 55 ... 85
NOTE: *G. Kane, Infantino art in most. Meskin a-1-4. Moreira a-28-39. Post a-3-5.*

WESTERN CRIME BUSTERS
Trojan Magazines: Sept, 1950 - No. 10, Mar-Apr, 1952
1-Six-Gun Smith, Wilma West, K-Bar-Kate, & Fighting Bob Dale begin;
headlight-a .... 36 ... 108 ... 191 ... 330
2 .... 20 ... 60 ... 105 ... 175
3-5: 3-Myron Fass-c .... 19 ... 57 ... 99 ... 165
6-Wood-a .... 35 ... 105 ... 185 ... 320
7-Six-Gun Smith by Wood .... 35 ... 105 ... 185 ... 320
8 .... 19 ... 57 ... 99 ... 165
9-Tex Gordon & Wilma West by Wood; Lariat Lucy app.
.... 34 ... 102 ... 179 ... 310
10-Wood-a .... 31 ... 93 ... 165 ... 285

WESTERN CRIME CASES (Formerly Indian Warriors #7,8; becomes The
Outlaws #10 on)
Star Publications: No. 9, Dec, 1951
9-White Rider & Super Horse; L. B. Cole-c ... 22 ... 66 ... 116 ... 195

WESTERNER, THE (Wild Bill Pecos)
"Wanted" Comic Group/Toytown/Patches: No. 14, June, 1948 - No. 41, Dec,
1951 (#14-31: 52 pgs.)
14 .... 14 ... 42 ... 72 ... 120
15-17,19-21: 19-Meskin-a .... 8 ... 24 ... 42 ... 60
18,22-25-Krigstein-a .... 10 ... 30 ... 55 ... 85
26(4/50)-Origin & 1st app. Calamity Kate, series ends #32; Krigstein-a
.... 14 ... 42 ... 72 ... 120
27-Krigstein-a(2) .... 13 ... 39 ... 66 ... 110
28-41: 33-Quest app. 37-Lobo, the Wolf Boy begins ... 6 ... 18 ... 29 ... 40
NOTE: *Mort Lawrence a-20-27, 29, 37, 39; c-19, 22-24, 26, 27. Leav c-14-18, 20, 31. Syd
Shores a-39; c-34, 35, 37-41.*

WESTERNER, THE
Super Comics: 1964
Super Reprint 15-17: 15-r/Oklahoma Kid #? 16-r/Crack West. #65; Severin-c;
Crandall-r. 17-r/Blazing Western #2; Severin-c ... 2 ... 6 ... 9 ... 12

WESTERN FIGHTERS
Hillman Periodicals/Star Publ.: Apr-May, 1948 - V4#7, Mar-Apr, 1953
(#1-V3#2: 52 pgs.)
V1#1-Simon & Kirby-c .... 36 ... 108 ... 191 ... 330
2-Not Kirby-a .... 10 ... 30 ... 55 ... 85
3-Fuje-c .... 10 ... 30 ... 55 ... 80
4-Krigstein, Ingels, Fuje-a .... 11 ... 33 ... 55 ... 90
5,6,8,9,12 .... 7 ... 21 ... 38 ... 55
7,10-Krigstein-a .... 10 ... 30 ... 55 ... 80
11-Williamson/Frazetta-a .... 31 ... 93 ... 165 ... 285
V2#1-Krigstein-a .... 10 ... 30 ... 55 ... 80
2-12: 4-Berg-a .... 6 ... 18 ... 29 ... 40
V3#1-11,V4#1,4-7 .... 5 ... 15 ... 25 ... 35
12,V4#2,3-Krigstein-a .... 10 ... 30 ... 55 ... 80
3-D (12/53, 25¢, Star Publ.)-Came w/glasses; L. B. Cole-c
.... 39 ... 117 ... 208 ... 360
NOTE: *Kinstlerish a-V2#6, 8, 10, 12; V3#2, 5-7, 11, 12; V4#1(plus cover). McWilliams a-11.
Powell a-V2#2. Reinman a-1-12, V4#3. Rowich c-5, 6i. Starr a-5.*

WESTERN FRONTIER
P. L. Publishers: Apr-May, 1951 - No. 7, 1952
1 .... 13 ... 39 ... 66 ... 110
2 .... 8 ... 24 ... 42 ... 60
3-7 .... 6 ... 18 ... 32 ... 45

WESTERN GUNFIGHTERS (1st Series) (Apache Kid #11-19)
Atlas Comics (CPS): No. 20, June, 1956 - No. 27, Aug, 1957
20 .... 13 ... 39 ... 66 ... 110
21-Crandall-a .... 13 ... 39 ... 66 ... 110
22-Wood & Powell-a .... 19 ... 57 ... 99 ... 165
23,24: 23-Williamson-a. 24-Toth-a ... 13 ... 39 ... 66 ... 110
25-27 .... 10 ... 30 ... 55 ... 80
NOTE: *Berg a-20. Colan a-20, 26, 27. Crandall a-21. Heath a-25. Maneely a-24, 25; c-22, 23,
25. Morisi a-24. Morrow a-26. Pakula a-23. Severin c-20, 27. Torres a-26. Woodbridge a-27.*

WESTERN GUNFIGHTERS (2nd Series)
Marvel Comics Group: Aug, 1970 - No. 33, Nov, 1975 (#1-6: 25¢, 68 pgs.)
1-Ghost Rider begins; Fort Rango, Renegades & Gunhawk app.
.... 10 ... 30 ... 50
2-6: 2-Origin Nightwind (Apache Kid's horse) ... 3 ... 9 ... 19 ... 28
7-(52 pgs) Origin Ghost Rider retold ... 3 ... 9 ... 17 ... 24
8-14: 10-Origin Black Rider. 12-Origin Matt Slade ... 2 ... 6 ... 12 ... 18
15-20 .... 1 ... 4 ... 7 ... 10
21-33 .... 1 ... 4 ... 7 ... 10
NOTE: *Baker r-2. Colan r-2. Drucker r-3. Everett a-6i. G. Kane c-29, 31. Kirby a-2(r), 5, 10-
12; c-19, 21. Kubert r-2. Maneely r-2, 10. Morrow r-29. Severin r-10. Shores a-3, 4. Barry
Smith a-4. Steranko c-14. Sutton a-1, 2i, 5, 4. Torres r-26('57). Wildey r-8, 9. Williamson r-2-
18. Woodbridge r-27('57). Renegades in #4, 5; Ghost Rider in #1-7.*

WESTERN HEARTS
Standard Comics: Dec, 1949 - No. 10, Mar, 1952 (All photo-c)

842

Western Hearts #5 © STD

Western Outlaws #20 © FOX

Western Thrillers #5 © FOX

	GD2.0	FN6.0	VF8.0	NM9.4
1-Severin-a; Whip Wilson & Reno Browne photo-c	22	66	116	200
2-Beverly Tyler & Jerome Courtland photo-c from movie "Palomino"; Williamson/Frazetta-a (2 pgs.)	21	63	110	190
3-Rex Allen photo-c	12	36	61	105
4-7,10-Severin & Elder, Al Carreno-a. 5-Ray Milland & Hedy Lamarr photo-c from movie "Copper Canyon". 6-Fred MacMurray & Irene Dunn photo-c from movie "Never a Dull Moment". 7-Jock Mahoney photo-c. 10-Bill Williams & Jane Nigh photo-c	12	36	61	100
8-Randolph Scott & Janis Carter photo-c from "Santa Fe"; Severin & Elder-a	12	36	61	105
9-Whip Wilson & Reno Browne photo-c; Severin & Elder-a	14	42	72	120

WESTERN HERO (Wow Comics #1-69; Real Western Hero #70-75)
Fawcett Publications: No. 76, Mar, 1949 - No. 112, Mar, 1952

76(#1, 52 pgs.)-Tom Mix, Hopalong Cassidy, Monte Hale, Gabby Hayes, Young Falcon (ends #78,80), & Big Bow and Little Arrow (ends #102,105) begin; painted-c begin	31	93	165	285
77 (52 pgs.)	18	54	94	160
78,80-82 (52 pgs.): 81-Capt. Tootsie by Beck	17	51	88	150
79,83 (36 pgs.): 83-Last painted-c	14	42	72	125
84-86,88-90 (52 pgs.): 84-Photo-c begin, end #112. 86-Last Hopalong Cassidy	15	45	77	130
87,91,95,99 (36 pgs.): 87-Bill Boyd begins, ends #95	13	39	66	110
92-94,96-98,101 (52 pgs.): 96-Tex Ritter begins. 101-Red Eagle app.	14	42	72	120
100 (52 pgs.)	15	45	77	130
102-111: 102-Begin 36 pg. issues	13	39	66	110
112-Last issue	14	42	72	120

NOTE: 1/2 to 1 pg. Rocky Lane (Carnation) in 80-83, 86, 88, 97. Photo covers feature Hopalong Cassidy #84, 86, 89; Tom Mix #85, 87, 90, 92, 94, 97; Monte Hale #88, 91, 93, 95, 98, 100, 104, 107, 110; Tex Ritter #96, 99, 101, 105, 108, 111; Gabby Hayes #103.

WESTERN KID (1st Series)
Atlas Comics (CPC): Dec, 1954 - No. 17, Aug, 1957

1-Origin; The Western Kid (Tex Dawson), his stallion Whirlwind & dog Lightning begin	21	63	110	185
2 (2/55)-Last pre-code	11	33	55	90
3-8	10	30	55	80
9,10-Williamson-a in both (4 pgs. each)	10	33	55	85
11-17	8	24	42	60

NOTE: Ayers a-6, 7. Maneely c-2-7, 10, 14. Romita a-1-17; c-1, 12. Severin c-17.

WESTERN KID, THE (2nd Series)
Marvel Comics Group: Dec, 1971 - No. 5, Aug, 1972 (All 20¢ issues)

1-Reprints; Romita-c/a(3)	3	9	19	28
2,4,5: 2-Romita-a; Severin-a. 4-Everett-r	2	6	11	16
3-Williamson-a	2	6	13	20

WESTERN KILLERS
Fox Features Syndicate: nn, July?, 1948; No. 60, Sept, 1948 - No. 64, May, 1949; No. 6, July, 1949

nn(#59?)(nd, F&J Trading Co.)-Range Busters; formerly Blue Beetle #57?	25	75	130	225
60 (#1, 9/48)-Extreme violence; lingerie panel	27	81	142	245
61-Jack Cole, Starr-a	22	66	116	195
62-64, 6 (#6-exist?)	20	60	105	175

WESTERN LIFE ROMANCES
Marvel Comics (IPP): Dec, 1949 - No. 2, Mar, 1950 (52 pgs.)

1-Whip Wilson & Reno Browne photo-c	20	60	105	180
2-Audie Murphy & Gale Storm photo-c	17	51	88	150

WESTERN LOVE
Prize Publ.: July-Aug, 1949 - No. 5, Mar-Apr, 1950 (All photo-c & 52 pgs.)

1-S&K-a; Randolph Scott photo-c from movie "Canadian Pacific" (see Prize Comics #14)	31	93	165	285
2,5-S&K-a: 2-Whip Wilson & Reno Browne photo-c. 5-Dale Robertson photo-c	24	72	127	215
3,4: 3-Reno Browne? photo-c	15	45	77	130

NOTE: Meskin & Severin/Elder a-2-5.

	GD2.0	FN6.0	VF8.0	NM9.4

WESTERN LOVE TRAILS (Formerly Western Adventures)
Ace Magazines (A. A. Wyn): No. 7, Nov, 1949 - No. 9, Mar, 1950

7	12	36	61	100
8,9	10	30	55	80

WESTERN MARSHAL (See Steve Donovan...)
Dell Publishing Co.: No. 534, 2-4/54 - No. 640, 7/55 (Based on Ernest Haycox's "Trailtown")

Four Color 534 (#1)-Kinstler-a	5	15	35	65
Four Color 591 (10/54), 613 (2/55), 640-All Kinstler-a	5	15	35	60

WESTERN OUTLAWS (Junior Comics #9-16; My Secret Life #22 on)
Fox Features Syndicate: No. 17, Sept, 1948 - No. 21, May, 1949

17-Kamen-a; Iger shop-a in part; 1 pg. "Death and the Devil Pills" r-in Ghostly Weird #122	36	108	191	330
18-21	21	63	110	185

WESTERN OUTLAWS
Atlas Comics (ACI No. 1-14/WPI No. 15-21): Feb, 1954 - No. 21, Aug, 1957

1-Heath, Powell-a; Maneely hanging-c	22	66	116	200
2	12	36	61	100
3-10: 7-Violent-a by R.Q. Sale	10	30	55	80
11,14-Williamson-a in both (6 pgs. each)	11	33	55	90
12,18,20,21: Severin covers	9	27	49	70
13,15: 13-Baker-a. 15-Torres-a	10	30	55	80
16-Williamson text illo	9	27	49	70
17,19-Crandall-a. 17-Williamson text illo	10	30	55	80

NOTE: Ayers a-7, 10, 18, 20. Bolle a-21. Colan a-5, 10, 11, 17. Drucker a-11. Everett a-9, 10, 19. Heath a-1; c-3, 4, 8, 16. Kubert a-9p. Maneely a-13, 16, 17, 19; c-1, 5, 7, 9, 10, 12, 13. Morisi a-18. Powell a-3, 16. Romita a-7, 13. Severin a-16, 19; c-17, 18, 20, 21. Tuska a-5, 16.

WESTERN OUTLAWS & SHERIFFS (Formerly Best Western)
Marvel/Atlas Comics (IPC): No. 60, Dec, 1949 - No. 73, June, 1952

60 (52 pgs.)	23	69	121	210
61-65: 61-Photo-c	19	57	99	165
66-Story contains 5 hangings	19	57	99	165
68-72	14	42	72	120
67-Cannibalism story	19	57	99	165
73-Black Rider story; Everett-c	15	45	77	130

NOTE: Maneely a-62, 67; c-62, 69-73. Robinson a-68. Sinnott a-70. Tuska a-69-71.

WESTERN PICTURE STORIES (1st Western comic)
Comics Magazine Company: Feb, 1937 - No. 4, June, 1937

1-Will Eisner-a	168	505	1050	1850
2-Will Eisner-a	100	300	625	1100
3,4: 3-Eisner-a. 4-Caveman Cowboy story	80	240	500	875

WESTERN PICTURE STORIES (See Giant Comics Edition #6, 11)
WESTERN ROMANCES (See Target...)

WESTERN ROUGH RIDERS
Gillmor Magazines No. 1,4 (Stanmor Publ.): Nov, 1954 - No. 4, May, 1955

1	9	27	49	70
2-4	6	18	32	45

WESTERN ROUNDUP (See Dell Giants & Fox Giants)

WESTERN TALES (Formerly Witches...)
Harvey Publications: No. 31, Oct, 1955 - No. 33, July-Sept, 1956

31,32-All S&K-a; Davy Crockett app. in each	20	60	105	180
33-S&K-a; Jim Bowie app.	20	60	105	175

NOTE: #32 & 33 contain Boy's Ranch reprints. Kirby c-31.

WESTERN TALES OF BLACK RIDER (Formerly Black Rider; Gunsmoke Western #32 on)
Atlas Comics (CPS): No. 28, May, 1955 - No. 31, Nov, 1955

28 (#1): The Spider (a villain) dies	20	60	105	180
29-31	14	42	72	120

NOTE: Lawrence a-30. Maneely c-28-30. Severin a-28. Shores c-31.

WESTERN TEAM-UP
Marvel Comics Group: Nov, 1973 (20¢)

1-Origin & 1st app. The Dakota Kid; Rawhide Kid-r; Gunsmoke Kid-r by Jack Davis	3	10	23	35

Wetworks #15 © WSP

Wham Comics #1 © CEN

What If...? (1st series) #31 © MAR

| | GD2.0 | FN6.0 | VF8.0 | NM9.4 | | | GD2.0 | FN6.0 | VF8.0 | NM9.4 |

WESTERN THRILLERS (My Past Confessions #7 on)
Fox Features Syndicate/M.S. Distr. No. 52: Aug, 1948 - No. 6, June, 1949; No. 52, 1954?

1- "Velvet Rose" (Kamenish-a); "Two-Gun Sal", "Striker Sisters" (all women outlaws issue); Brodsky-c	47	142	286	500
2	22	66	116	200
3-6: 4,5-Bakerish-c; 5-Butch Cassidy app.	20	60	105	175
52-(Reprint, M.S. Distr.)-1954? No date given (becomes My Love Secret #53)				
	8	24	42	60

WESTERN THRILLERS (Cowboy Action #5 on)
Atlas Comics (ACI): Nov, 1954 - No. 4, Feb, 1955 (All-r/Western Outlaws & Sheriffs)

1	16	48	83	140
2-4	10	30	55	80

NOTE: *Heath* c-3. *Maneely* a-1; c-2. *Powell* a-4. *Robinson* a-4. *Romita* c-4. *Tuska* a-2.

WESTERN TRAILS (Ringo Kid Starring in...)
Atlas Comics (SAI): May, 1957 - No. 2, July, 1957

1-Ringo Kid app.; Severin-c	14	42	72	120
2-Severin-c	9	27	49	70

NOTE: *Bolle* a-1, 2. *Maneely* a-1. *Severin* c-1, 2.

WESTERN TRUE CRIME (Becomes My Confessions)
Fox Features Syndicate: No. 15, Aug, 1948 - No. 6, June, 1949

15(#1)-Kamen-a; formerly Zoot #14 (5/48)?	33	99	174	300
16(#2)-Kamenish-a; headlight panels, violence	23	69	121	210
3-Kamen-a	25	75	130	225
4-6: 6-Johnny Craig-a	16	48	83	140

WESTERN WINNERS (Formerly All-Western Winners; becomes Black Rider #8 on & Romance Tales #7 on?)
Marvel Comics (CDS): No. 5, June, 1949 - No. 7, Dec, 1949

5-Two-Gun Kid, Kid Colt, Black Rider; Shores-c	34	102	179	310
6-Two-Gun Kid, Black Rider, Heath Kid Colt story; Captain Tootsie by C.C. Beck	29	87	153	265
7-Randolph Scott Photo-c w/true stories about the West	29	87	153	265

WEST OF THE PECOS (See Zane Grey, 4-Color #222)

WESTWARD HO, THE WAGONS (Disney)
Dell Publishing Co.: No. 738, Sept, 1956 (Movie)

Four Color 738-Fess Parker photo-c	9	27	63	120

WETWORKS (See WildC.A.T.S.: Covert Action Teams #2)
Image Comics (WildStorm): June, 1994 - No. 43, Aug, 1998 ($1.95/$2.50)

1-"July" on-c; gatefold wraparound-c; Portacio/Williams-c/a	3.00
1-Chicago Comicon edition	6.00
1-(2/98, $4.95) "3-D Edition" w/glasses	5.00
2-4	2.50
2-Alternate Portacio-c, see Deathblow #5	6.00
5-7,9-24: 5-($2.50). 13-Portacio-c. 16-Fire From Heaven Pt. 4. 17-Fire From Heaven Pt. 11	2.50
8 ($1.95)-Newstand, Wildstorm Rising Pt. 7	2.25
8 ($2.50)-Direct Market, Wildstorm Rising Pt. 7	2.50
25-($3.95)	4.00
26-43: 32-Variant-c by Pat Lee & Charest. 39,40-Stormwatch app. 42-Gen 13 app.	2.50
Sourcebook 1 (10/94, $2.50)-Text & illustrations (no comics)	2.50
Voyager Pack (8/97, $3.50)- #32 w/Phantom Guard preview	3.50

WETWORKS/VAMPIRELLA (See Vampirella/Wetworks)
Image Comics (WildStorm Productions): July, 1997 ($2.95, one-shot)

1-Gil Kane-c	3.00

WHACK (Satire)
St. John Publishing Co. (Jubilee Publ.): Oct, 1953 - No. 3, May, 1954

1-(3-D, 25¢)-Kubert-a; Maurer-c; came w/glasses	33	99	174	300
2,3-Kubert-a in each. 2-Bing Crosby on-c; Mighty Mouse & Steve Canyon parodies. 3-Li'l Orphan Annie parody; Maurer-c	17	51	87	150

WHACKY (See Wacky)

WHAM COMICS (See Super Spy)

Centaur Publications: Nov, 1940 - No. 2, Dec, 1940

1-The Sparkler, The Phantom Rider, Craig Carter and his Magic Ring, Detecto, Copper Slug, Speed Silvers by Gustavson, Speed Centaur & Jon Linton (s/f) begin	159	477	994	1750
2-Origin Blue Fire & Solarman; The Buzzard app.	107	321	669	1175

WHAM-O GIANT COMICS
Wham-O Mfg. Co.: April, 1967 (98¢, newspaper size, one-shot)(Six issue subscription was advertised)

1-Radian & Goody Bumpkin by Wood; 1 pg. Stanley-a; Fine, Tufts-a; flying saucer reports; wraparound-c	7	21	53	85

WHAT IF? (1st Series) (What If? Featuring... #13 & #?-33)
Marvel Comics Group: Feb, 1977 - No. 47, Oct, 1984; June, 1988 (All 52 pgs.)

1-Brief origin Spider-Man, Fantastic Four	3	9	17	25
2-Origin The Hulk retold	2	6	9	12
3-5: 3-Avengers. 4-Invaders. 5-Capt. America	1	3	6	9
6-10,13,17: 8-Daredevil; Spidey parody. 9-Origins Venus, Marvel Boy, Human Robot, 3-D Man. 13-Conan app.; John Buscema-a/a(p). 17-Ghost Rider & Son of Satan app.	1	3	6	8
11,12,14-16: 11-Marvel Bullpen as F.F.				6.00
18-26,29: 18-Dr. Strange. 19-Spider-Man. 22-Origin Dr. Doom retold				5.00
27-X-Men app.; Miller-c	2	6	11	15
28-Daredevil by Miller; Ghost Rider app.	1	4	7	10
30-"What If...Spider-Man's Clone Had Lived?"	1	3	6	8
31-Begin $1.00-c; featuring Wolverine & the Hulk; X-Men app.; death of Hulk, Wolverine & Magneto	2	6	12	18
32-34,36-47: 32,36-Byrne-a. 34-Marvel crew each draw themselves. 37-Old X-Men & Silver Surfer app. 39-Thor battles Conan				4.00
35-What if Elektra had lived?; Miller/Austin-a				5.00
Special 1 ($1.50, 6/88)-Iron Man, F.F., Thor app.				3.00

NOTE: *Austin* a-27p, 32i, 34, 35(i), 36i. *J. Buscema* a-13p, 15p; c-10, 13p, 23p. *Byrne* a-32i, 36; c-36p. *Colan* a-21p; c-17p, 18p, 21p. *Ditko* a-35, Special 1. *Golden* c-29, 40-42. *Guice* a-40p. *Gil Kane* a-3p, 24p; c(p)-2-4, 7, 8. *Kirby* a-11p; c-9p, 11p. *Layton* a-32i, 33i; c-30, 32p, 33i, 34. *Mignola* c-39i. *Miller* a-28p, 32i, 34(1), 35p; c-27, 28p. *Mooney* a-8i, 30i. *Perez* a-15p. *Robbins* a-15p. *Sienkiewicz* c-43-46. *Simonson* a-15p, 32i. *Starlin* a-32i. *Stevens* a-8, 16i(part). *Sutton* a-2i, 18p, 28. *Tuska* a-5p. *Weiss* a-37.

WHAT IF...? (2nd Series)
Marvel Comics: V2#1, July, 1989 - No. 114, Nov, 1998 ($1.25/$1.50)

V2#1-...The Avengers Had Lost the Evol. War	4.00
2-5: 2-Daredevil, Punisher app.	3.00
6-X-Men app.	4.00
7-Wolverine app.; Liefeld-c/a(1st on Wolvie?)	5.00
8,10,11,13-15,17-30: 10-Punisher app. 11-Fantastic Four app.; McFarlane-c(i).13-Prof. X; Jim Lee-c/i. 14-Capt. Marvel; Lim/Austin-c.15-F.F.; Capullo-c/a(p). 17-Spider-Man/Kraven. 18-F.F. 19-Vision. 20,21-Spider-Man. 22-Silver Surfer by Lim/Austin-c/a 23-X-Men. 24-Wolverine; Punisher app. 25-(52 pgs.)-Wolverine app. 26-Punisher app. 27-Namor/F.F. 28,29-Capt. America. 29-Swipes cover to Avengers #4. 30-(52 pgs.)-Sue Richards/F.F.	3.00
9,12-X-Men	3.50
16-Wolverine battles Conan; Red Sonja app.; X-Men cameo	4.00
31-104: 31-Cosmic Spider-Man & Venom app.; Hobgoblin cameo. 32,33-Phoenix; X-Men app. 35-Fantastic Five (w/Spidey). 36-Avengers vs. Guardians of the Galaxy. 37-Wolverine; Thibert-c(i). 38-Thor; Rogers-p (part). 40-Storm; X-Men app. 41-(52 pgs.)-Avengers vs. Galactus. 42-Spider-Man. 43-Wolverine. 44-Venom/Punisher. 45-Ghost Rider. 46-Cable. 47-Magneto. 49-Infinity Gauntlet w/Silver Surfer & Thanos. 50-(52 pgs.)-Foil embossed-c; "What If Hulk Had Killed Wolverine" 52-Dr. Doom. 54-Death's Head. 57-Punisher as Shield. 58-"What if Punisher Had Killed Spider-Man" w/cover similar to Amazing S-M #129. 59-...Wolverine led Alpha Flight. 60-X-Men Wedding Album. 61-bound-in card sheet. 61,86,88-Spider-Man. 74,77,81,84,85-X-Men. 76-Avengers app. 78-Watcher in title. 78-Bisley-c. 80-Hulk. 87-Sabretooth. 89-Fantastic Four. 90-Cyclops & Havok. 91-The Hulk. 93-Wolverine. 94-Juggernaut. 95-Ghost Rider. 97-Black Knight. 100-($2.99, double-sized) Gambit and Rogue, Fantastic Four	3.00
105-Spider-Girl debut; Sienkiewicz-a	2	6	13	20
106-114: 106-Daredevil. 108-Avengers. 111-Wolverine. 114-Secret Wars	2.25
#(-1) Flashback (7/97)	3.00

'WHAT'S NEW? - THE COLLECTED ADVENTURES OF PHIL & DIXIE'
Palliard Press: Oct, 1991 - No. 2, 1991 ($5.95, mostly color, sq.-bound, 52 pgs.)

What The--?! #11 © MAR

Whirlwind Comics #3 © Nita Pub.

Whiteout #2 © Greg Rucka

WH

	GD2.0	FN6.0	VF8.0	NM9.4

1,2-By Phil Foglio ... 6.00

WHAT THE--?!
Marvel Comics: Aug, 1988 - No. 26, 1993 ($1.25/$1.50/$2.50, semi-annual #5 on)

1-All contain parodies ... 3.00
2-24: 3-X-Men parody; Todd McFarlane-a. 5-Punisher/Wolverine parody; Jim Lee-a. 6-Punisher, Wolverine, Alpha Flight. 9-Wolverine. 16-EC back-c parody. 17-Wolverine/Punisher parody. 18-Star Trek parody w/Wolverine. 19-Punisher, Wolverine, Ghost Rider. 21-Weapon X parody. 22-Punisher/Wolverine parody ... 2.25
25-Summer Special 1 (1993, $2.50)-X-Men parody ... 2.50
26-Fall Special ($2.50, 68 pgs.)-Spider-Ham 2099-c/story; origin Silver Surfer; Hulk & Doomsday parody; indicia reads "Winter Special." ... 2.50
NOTE: Austin a-6i. Byrne a-2, 6, 10; c-2, 13. Golden a-22. Dale Keown a-8p(8 pgs.). McFarlane a-3. Rogers c-15i, 16p. Severin a-21p. Williamson a-2i.

WHEE COMICS (Also see Gay, Smile & Tickle Comics)
Modern Store Publications: 1955 (7¢, 5x7-1/4", 52 pgs.)

1-Funny animal ... 5 ... 15 ... 23 ... 30

WHEEDIES (See Panic #11 -EC Comics)

WHEELIE AND THE CHOPPER BUNCH (TV)
Charlton Comics: July, 1975 - No. 7, July, 1976 (Hanna-Barbera)

1-3: 1-Byrne text illo (see Nightmare for 1st art); Staton-a. 2-Byrne-a.
2,3-Mike Zeck text illos. 3-Staton-a; Byrne-c/a ... 3 ... 9 ... 17 ... 24
4-7-Staton-a ... 2 ... 6 ... 10 ... 14

WHEN KNIGHTHOOD WAS IN FLOWER (See The Sword & the Rose, 4-Color #505, 682)

WHEN SCHOOL IS OUT (See Wisco in Promotional Comics section)

WHERE CREATURES ROAM
Marvel Comics Group: July, 1970 - No. 8, Sept, 1971

1-Kirby/Ayers-c/a(r) ... 3 ... 9 ... 20 ... 30
2-8-Kirby-c/a(r) ... 2 ... 6 ... 13 ... 20
NOTE: Ditko r-1-6, 7. Heck r-2, 5. All contain pre super-hero reprints.

WHERE IN THE WORLD IS CARMEN SANDIEGO (TV)
DC Comics: June, 1996 - No. 4, Dec, 1996 ($1.75)

1-4: Adaptation of TV show ... 2.25

WHERE MONSTERS DWELL
Marvel Comics Group: Jan, 1970 - No. 38, Oct, 1975

1-Kirby/Ditko-r; all contain pre super-hero-r ... 3 ... 9 ... 21 ... 32
2-10: 4-Crandall-a(r) ... 2 ... 6 ... 13 ... 20
11,13-20: 11-Last 15¢ issue. 18,20-Starlin-a(r) ... 2 ... 6 ... 11 ... 15
12-Giant issue (52 pgs.) ... 3 ... 9 ... 19 ... 28
21-37 ... 2 ... 6 ... 9 ... 12
38-Williamson-r/World of Suspense #3 ... 2 ... 6 ... 11 ... 15
NOTE: Colan r-11. Ditko a(r)-4, 6, 8, 10, 12, 17-19, 23-25, 37. Kirby r-1-3, 5-16, 18-27, 30-32, 34-36, c-12? Reinman a-3r, 4r, 12r. Severin c-15.

WHERE'S HUDDLES? (TV) (See Fun-In #9)
Gold Key: Jan, 1971 - No. 3, Dec, 1971 (Hanna-Barbera)

1 ... 3 ... 9 ... 20 ... 30
2,3: 3-r/most #1 ... 2 ... 6 ... 11 ... 16

WHIP WILSON (Movie star) (Formerly Rex Hart; Gunhawk #12 on; see Western Hearts, Western Life Romances, Western Love)
Marvel Comics: No. 9, April, 1950 - No. 11, Sept, 1950 (#9,10: 52 pgs.)

9-Photo-c; Whip Wilson & his horse Bullet begin; origin Bullet; issue #23 listed on splash page; cover changed to #9 ... 58 ... 174 ... 363 ... 640
10,11: Both have photo-c. 11-36 pgs. ... 37 ... 111 ... 197 ... 340
I.W. Reprint #1(1964)-Kinstler-c; r-Marvel #11 ... 3 ... 9 ... 20 ... 30

WHIRLWIND COMICS (Also see Cyclone Comics)
Nita Publication: June, 1940 - No. 3, Sept, 1940

1-Origin & 1st app. Cyclone; Cyclone-c ... 159 ... 477 ... 994 ... 1750
2,3: Cyclone-c ... 100 ... 300 ... 625 ... 1100

WHIRLYBIRDS (TV)
Dell Publishing Co.: No. 1124, Aug, 1960 - No. 1216, Oct-Dec, 1961

Four Color 1124 (#1)-Photo-c ... 9 ... 27 ... 63 ... 110
Four Color 1216-Photo-c ... 8 ... 24 ... 56 ... 100

WHISPER (Female Ninja)

Capital Comics: Dec, 1983 - No. 2, 1984 ($1.75, Baxter paper)

1,2: 1-Origin; Golden-c, Special (11/85, $2.50) ... 2.50

WHISPER (Vol. 2)
First Comics: Jun, 1986 - No. 37, June, 1990 ($1.25/$1.75/$1.95)

1-37 ... 2.25

WHITE CHIEF OF THE PAWNEE INDIANS
Avon Periodicals: 1951

nn-Kit West app.; Kinstler-c ... 17 ... 51 ... 88 ... 150

WHITE EAGLE INDIAN CHIEF (See Indian Chief)

WHITE FANG
Disney Comics: 1990 ($5.95, 68 pgs.)

nn-Graphic novel adapting new Disney movie ... 6.00

WHITE INDIAN
Magazine Enterprises: No. 11, July, 1953 - No. 15, 1954

11(A-1 94), 12(A-1 101), 13(A-1 104)-Frazetta-r(Dan Brand) in all from Durango Kid. 11-Powell-c. ... 24 ... 72 ... 127 ... 215
14(A-1 117), 15(A-1 135)-Check-a; Torres-a-#15 ... 12 ... 36 ... 61 ... 100
NOTE: #11 contains reprints from Durango Kid #1-4; #12 from #5, 9, 10, 11; #13 from #7, 12, 13, 16. #14 & 15 contain all new stories.

WHITEOUT (Also see Queen & Country)
Oni Press: July, 1998 - No. 4, Nov, 1998 ($2.95, B&W, limited series)

1-4: 1-Matt Wagner-c. 2-Mignola-c. 3-Gibbons-c ... 3.00
TPB (5/99, $10.95) r/#1-4; Miller-c ... 11.00

WHITEOUT: MELT
Oni Press: Sept, 1999 - No. 4, Feb, 2000 ($2.95, B&W, limited series)

1-4-Greg Rucka-c/Steve Lieber-a ... 3.00

WHITE PRINCESS OF THE JUNGLE (Also see Jungle Adventures & Top Jungle Comics)
Avon Periodicals: July, 1951 - No. 5, Nov, 1952

1-Origin of White Princess (Taanda) & Capt'n Courage (r); Kinstler-c ... 55 ... 165 ... 330 ... 575
2-Reprints origin of Malu, Slave Girl Princess from Avon's Slave Girl Comics #1 w/Malu changed to Zora; Kinstler-c/a(2) ... 40 ... 120 ... 240 ... 420
3-Origin Blue Gorilla; Kinstler-c/a ... 34 ... 111 ... 197 ... 340
4-Jack Barnum, White Hunter app.; r/Sheena #9 ... 31 ... 93 ... 168 ... 300
5-Blue Gorilla by McCann?; Kinstler inside-c; Fawcette/Alascia-a(3) ... 34 ... 102 ... 179 ... 310

WHITE RIDER AND SUPER HORSE (Formerly Humdinger V2#2; Indian Warriors #7 on; also see Blue Bolt #1, 4Most & Western Crime Cases)
Novelty-Star Publications/Accepted Publ.: No. 4, 9/50 - No. 6, 3/51

4-6-Adapts "The Last of the Mohicans". 4(#1)-(9/50)-Says #11 on inside ... 17 ... 51 ... 88 ... 150
Accepted Reprint #5(r/#5),6 (nd); L.B. Cole-c ... 9 ... 27 ... 49 ... 70
NOTE: All have L. B. Cole covers.

WHITE WILDERNESS (Disney)
Dell Publishing Co.: No. 943, Oct, 1958

Four Color 943-Movie ... 6 ... 18 ... 42 ... 80

WHITMAN COMIC BOOK, A
Whitman Publishing Co.: Sept., 1962 (136 pgs.; 7-3/4x5-3/4; hardcover) (B&W)

1-3,5,7: 1-Yogi Bear. 2-Huckleberry Hound. 3-Mr. Jinks and Pixie & Dixie. 5-Augie Doggie & Loopy de Loop. 7-Bugs Bunny-r from #47,51,53,54 & 55 ... 7 ... 21 ... 50 ... 80
4,6: 4-The Flintstones. 6-Snooper & Blabber Fearless Detectives/Quick Draw McGraw of the Wild West ... 8 ... 24 ... 56 ... 90
8-Donald Duck-reprints most of WDC&S #209-213. Includes 5 Barks stories, 1 complete Mickey Mouse serial by Paul Murry & 1 Mickey Mouse serial missing the 1st episode ... 7 ... 21 ... 63 ... 105
NOTE: Hanna-Barbera #1-6(TV), reprints of British tabloid comics. Dell reprints-#7,8.

WHIZ COMICS (Formerly Flash & Thrill Comics #1)(See 5 Cent Comics)
Fawcett Publications: No. 2, Feb, 1940 - No. 155, June, 1953

1-(nn on cover, #2 inside)-Origin & 1st newsstand app. Captain Marvel (formerly Captain Thunder) by C. C. Beck (created by Bill Parker), Spy Smasher, Golden Arrow, Ibis the Invincible, Dan Dare, Scoop Smith, Sivana,

Whiz Comics #44 © FAW

Whodunnit? #3 © ECL

The Wicked #5 © Avalon Studios

	GD2.0	FN6.0	VF8.0	NM9.4		GD2.0	FN6.0	VF8.0	NM9.4

& Lance O'Casey begin 7,000 21,000 38,500 77,000
(The only Mint copy sold in 1995 for $176,000 cash)

1-Reprint, oversize 13-1/2x10". **WARNING:** This comic is an exact duplicate reprint (except for dropping "Gangway for Captain Marvel" from-c) of the original except for its size. DC published it in 1974 with a second cover titling it as a Famous First Edition. There have been many reported cases of the outer cover being removed and the interior sold as the original edition. The reprint with the new outer cover removed is practically worthless. See Famous First Edition for value.

2-(3/40, nn on cover, #3 inside; cover to Flash #1 redrawn, pg. 12, panel 4;
Spy Smasher reveals I.D. to Eve 438 1314 2847 5700
3-(4/40, #3 on-c, #4 inside)-1st app. Beautia 308 924 1927 3700
4-(5/40, #4 on cover, #5 inside)-Brief origin Capt. Marvel retold
286 858 1790 3150
5-Captain Marvel wears button-down flap on splash page only
236 708 1477 2600
6-10: 7-Dr. Voodoo begins (by Raboy-#9-22) 177 531 1106 1950
11-14: 12-Capt. Marvel does not wear cape 123 369 769 1350
15-Origin Sivana; Dr. Voodoo by Raboy 132 395 825 1450
16-18-Spy Smasher battles Captain Marvel 127 381 795 1400
19,20 84 253 525 925
21-(9/41)-Origin & 1st cover app. Lt. Marvels, the 1st team in Fawcett comics. In this issue, Capt. Death similar to Ditko's later Dr. Strange
89 268 556 975
22-24: 23-Only Dr. Voodoo by Tuska 61 205 426 750
25-(12/41)-Captain Nazi jumps from Master Comics #21 to take on Capt. Marvel solo after being beaten by Capt. Marvel/Bulletman team, causing the creation of Capt. Marvel Jr.; 1st app./origin of Capt. Marvel Jr. (part II of trilogy origin by CC. Beck & Mac Raboy); Captain Marvel sends Jr. back to Master #22 to aid Bulletman against Capt. Nazi; origin Old Shazam in text.
523 1569 3400 6800
26-30 61 182 381 675
31,32: 32-1st app. The Trolls; Hitler/Mussolini satire by Beck
53 158 318 560
33-Spy Smasher, Captain Marvel x-over on cover and inside
61 182 381 675
34,36-40: 37-The Trolls app. by Swayze 40 120 232 400
35-Captain Marvel & Spy Smasher-c 50 150 300 525
41-50: 43-Spy Smasher, Ibis, Golden Arrow x-over in Capt. Marvel. 44-Flag-c.
47-Origin recap (1 pg.) 36 108 191 330
51-60: 52-Capt. Marvel x-over in Ibis. 57-Spy Smasher, Golden Arrow, Ibis
cameo 30 90 159 275
61-70 27 81 145 250
71,77-80 25 75 130 225
72-76-Two Captain Marvel stories in each; 76-Spy Smasher becomes Crime
Smasher 25 75 133 230
81-99: 86-Captain Marvel battles Sivana Family; robot-c. 91-Infinity-c
25 75 130 225
100-(8/48)-Anniversary issue 29 87 153 265
101-106: 102-Commando Yank app. 106-Bulletman app.
24 72 127 215
107-152: 107-Capitol Building photo-c. 108-Brooklyn Bridge photo-c.
112-Photo-c. 139-Infinity-c. 140-Flag-c. 142-Used in POP, pg. 89
24 72 127 215
153-155:(Scarce)154,155-1st/2nd Dr. Death stories 34 102 179 310
NOTE: *C.C. Beck* Captain Marvel-No. 25(part). *Krigstein* Golden Arrow-No. 75, 78, 91, 95, 96, 98-100. *Mac Raboy* Dr. Voodoo-No. 9-22. Captain Marvel-No. 25(part). *M.Swayze* a-37, 38, 59-c-38. *Schaffenberger* c-138-155(most). *Wolverton* 1/2 pg. "Culture Corner"-No. 65-67, 68(2 1/2 pgs), 70-85, 87-96, 98-100, 102-109, 112-121, 123, 125, 126, 128-131, 133, 134, 136, 142, 143, 146.

WHOA, NELLIE (Also see Love & Rockets)
Fantagraphics: July, 1996 - No. 3, Sept, 1996 ($2.95, B&W, lim. series)
1-3: Jamie Hernandez-c/a/scripts 3.00

WHODUNIT
D.S. Publishing Co.: Aug-Sept, 1948 - No. 3, Dec-Jan, 1948-49 (#1,2: 52 pgs.)
1-Baker-a (7 pgs.) 26 78 136 235
2,3-Detective mysteries 13 39 66 110

WHODUNNIT?
Eclipse Comics: June, 1986 - No. 3, Apr, 1987 ($2.00, limited series)
1-3: Spiegle-a. 2-Gulacy-c 2.25

WHO FRAMED ROGER RABBIT (See Marvel Graphic Novel)
WHO IS NEXT?
Standard Comics: No. 5, Jan, 1953
5-Toth, Sekowsky, Andru-a; crime stories 21 63 110 185
WHO IS THE CROOKED MAN?
Crusade: Sept, 1996 ($3.50, B&W, 40 pgs.)
1-Intro The Martyr, Scarlet 7 & Garrison 3.50
WHO'S MINDING THE MINT? (See Movie Classics)
WHO'S WHO IN STAR TREK
DC Comics: Mar, 1987 - #2, Apr, 1987 ($1.50, limited series)
1,2 6.00
NOTE: *Byrne* a-1, 2. *Chaykin* c-1. 2. *Morrow* a-1, 2. *McFarlane* a-2. *Perez* a-2.
Sutton a-1, 2.
WHO'S WHO IN THE LEGION OF SUPER-HEROES
DC Comics: Apr, 1987 - No. 7, Nov, 1988 ($1.25, limited series)
1-7 4.00
WHO'S WHO: THE DEFINITIVE DIRECTORY OF THE DC UNIVERSE
DC Comics: Mar, 1985 - No. 26, Apr, 1987 (Maxi-series, no ads)
1-DC heroes from A-Z 4.00
2-26: All have 1-2 pgs-a by most DC artists 4.00
NOTE: *Art Adams* a-4, 11, 18, 20. *Anderson* a-1-5, 7-12, 14, 15, 19, 21, 23-25. *Aparo* a-2, 3, 9, 10, 12, 13, 14, 15, 17, 18, 21, 23. *Byrne* a-4, 7, 14, 16, 18, 21, 22, 24; c-22. *Cowan* a-3-5, 8, 10-13, 16-18, 22-25. *Ditko* a-19-22. *Evans* a-20. *Giffen* a-1, 3-6, 8, 13, 15, 17, 18, 23. *Grell* a-6, 9, 14, 20, 23, 25, 26. *Infantino* a-1-10, 12, 15, 17-22, 24, 25. *Kaluta* a-14. *Gil Kane* a-1-11, 13, 14, 16, 19, 21-23, 25. *Kirby* a-2, 6-8, 18, 20, 22, 25. *Kubert* a-2, 3, 7-11, 19, 20, 25. *Erik Larsen* a-24. *McFarlane* a-10-12, 17, 19, 25, 26. *Morrow* a-4, 7, 25, 26. *Orlando* a-1, 4, 10, 11, 21i. *Perez* a-1-5, 8-19, 22-26; c-14, 13-18. *Rogers* a-2, 5-7, 11, 12, 15, 24. *Starlin* a-13, 14, 16. *Stevens* a-4, 7, 18.
WHO'S WHO UPDATE '87
DC Comics: Aug, 1987 - No. 5, Dec, 1987 ($1.25, limited series)
1-5: Contains art by most DC artists 3.00
NOTE: *Giffen* a-1. *McFarlane* a-1-4; c-4. *Perez* a-1-4.
WHO'S WHO UPDATE '88
DC Comics: Aug, 1988 - No. 4, Nov, 1988 ($1.25, limited series)
1-4: Contains art by most DC artists 3.00
NOTE: *Giffen* a-1. *Erik Larsen* a-1.
WICKED, THE
Avalon Studios: Dec, 1999 - No. 7, Aug, 2000 ($2.95)
Preview-(7/99, $5.00, B&W) 5.00
1-7-Anacleto-c/Martinez-a 3.00
....: Medusa's Tale (11/00, $3.95, one shot) story plus pin-up gallery 4.00
WILBUR COMICS (Teen-age) (Also see Laugh Comics, Laugh Comix,
Liberty Comics #10 & Zip Comics)
MLJ Magazines/Archie Publ. No. 8, Spring, 1946 on: Sum', 1944 - No. 87,
11/59; No. 88, 9/63; No. 89, 10/64; No. 90, 10/65 (No. 1-46: 52 pgs.)
(#1-11 are quarterly)
1 50 150 300 525
2(Fall, 1944) 29 87 153 265
3,4(Wint, '44-45; Spr, '45) 21 63 110 185
5-1st app. Katy Keene (Sum, '45) & begin series; Wilbur story same as Archie
story in Archie #1 except Katy Keene replaces Archie 77 231 483 850
6-10: 10-(Fall, 1946) 23 69 121 210
11-20 14 42 72 125
21-30: 30-(4/50) 9 27 51 75
31-50 7 21 38 55
51-70 6 18 32 45
71-90: 88-Last 10¢ issue (9/63) 3 10 23 35
NOTE: Katy Keene in No. 5-56, 58-69. *Al Fagaly* c-6-9, 12-24 at least. *Vigoda* c-2.
WILD
Atlas Comics (IPC): Feb, 1954 - No. 5, Aug, 1954
1 27 81 145 250
2 16 48 83 140
3-5 14 42 72 120
NOTE: *Berg* a-5; c-4. *Burgos* c-3. *Colan* a-4. *Everett* a-1-3. *Heath* a-2, 3, 5. *Maneely* a-1-3, 5; c-1, 5. *Post* a-2, 5. *Ed Win* a-1, 3.

Wild Boy of the Congo #5 © Z-D

WildC.A.T.S. #18 © WSP

Wildcats V2 #24 © WSP

	GD2.0	FN6.0	VF8.0	NM9.4

WILD (This Magazine Is...) (Satire)
Dell Publishing Co.: Jan, 1968 - No. 3, 1968 (Magazine, 52 pgs.)

1-3	2	6	12	18

WILD ANIMALS
Pacific Comics: Dec, 1982 ($1.00, one-shot, direct sales)

1-Funny animal; Sergio Aragones-a; Shaw-c/a				4.00

WILD BILL ELLIOTT (Also see Western Roundup under Dell Giants)
Dell Publishing Co.: No. 278, 5/50 - No. 643, 7/55 (All photo-c)

Four Color 278(#1, 52pgs.)-Titled "Bill Elliott"; Bill & his horse Stormy begin; photo front/back-c begin	13	39	91	170
2 (11/50), 3 (52 pgs.)	7	21	49	90
4-10(10-12/52)	5	15	35	60
Four Color 472(6/53),520(12/53)-Last photo back-c	4	12	30	50
13(4-6/54) - 17(4-6/55)	4	12	29	45
Four Color 643 (7/55)	4	12	26	40

WILD BILL HICKOK (Also see Blazing Sixguns)
Avon Periodicals: Sept-Oct, 1949 - No. 28, May-June, 1956

1-Ingels-c	24	72	127	215
2-Painted-c; Kit West app.	12	36	61	100
3-5-Painted-c (4-Cover by Howard Winfield)	9	27	49	70
6-10,12: 8-10-Painted-c. 12-Kinstler-c	9	27	49	70
11,13,14-Kinstler-c/a (#11-c & inside-f/c art only)	10	30	55	80
15,17,18,20: 18-Kit West story. 20-Kit West by Larsen	7	21	38	55
16-Kamen-a; r-3 stories/King of the Badmen of Deadwood	8	24	42	60
19-Meskin-a	7	21	38	55
21-Reprints 2 stories/Chief Crazy Horse	7	21	36	50
22-McCann-a?; r/Sheriff Bob Dixon's...	7	21	36	50
23-27: 23-Painted-c. 24-27-Kinstler-c/a(r) (24,25-r?)	7	21	36	50
28-Kinstler-c/a (new); r/Last of the Comanches	7	21	38	55
I.W. Reprint #1-r/#2; Kinstler-c	2	6	11	15
Super Reprint #10-12: 10-r/#18. 11-r/#? 12-r/#8	2	6	11	15

NOTE: #23, 25 contain numerous editing deletions in both art and script due to code. **Kinstler c-**
6, 7, 11-14, 17, 18, 20-22, 24-28. **Howard Larsen** a-1, 2, 4, 5, 6(3), 7-9, 11, 12, 17, 18, 20-24,
26. **Meskin** a-7. **Reinman** a-6, 17.

WILD BILL HICKOK AND JINGLES (TV)(Formerly Cowboy Western) (Also see
Blue Bird)
Charlton Comics: No. 68, Aug, 1958 - No. 75, Dec, 1959

68,69-Williamson-a (all are 10¢ issues)	11	33	55	90
70-Two pgs. Williamson-a	8	24	42	60
71-75 (#76, exist?)	5	15	25	35

WILD BILL PECOS WESTERN (Also see The Westerner)
AC Comics: 1989 ($3.50, 1/2 color/1/2 B&W, 52 pgs.)

1-Syd Shores-c/a(r)/Westerner; photo back-c				4.00

WILD BOY OF THE CONGO (Also see Approved Comics)
Ziff-Davis No. 10-12,4-8/St. John No. 9,11 on: No. 10, 2-3/51 - No. 12, 8-9/51;
No. 4, 10-11/51 - No. 9, 10/53; No. 11-#15,6/55 (No #10, 1953)

10(#1)(2-3/51)-Origin; bondage-c by Saunders (painted); used in **SOTI**, pg. 189; painted-c begin, end #9	23	69	121	210
11(4-5/51),12(8-9/51)-Norman Saunders painted-c	13	39	66	110
4(10-11/51)-Saunders painted bondage-c	13	39	66	110
5(Winter,'51)-Saunders painted-c	11	33	55	90
6,8,9(10/53): 6-Saunders-c. 6-9-Painted-c	11	33	55	90
7(8-9/52)-Kinstler-a	13	39	66	110
11-13-Baker-c. 11-r/#7 w/new Baker-c; Kinstler-a (2 pgs.)	14	42	72	120
14(4/55)-Baker-c; r-#12('51)	14	42	72	120
15(6/55)	10	30	55	80

WILDCAT (See Sensation Comics #1)

WILDC.A.T.S ADVENTURES (TV cartoon)
Image Comics (WildStorm): Sept, 1994 - No. 10, June, 1995 ($1.95/$2.50)

1-10				2.50
Sourcebook 1 (1/95, $2.95)				3.00

WILDC.A.T.S: COVERT ACTION TEAMS

Image Comics (WildStorm Productions): Aug, 1992 - No. 4, Mar, 1993; No. 5,
Nov, 1993 - No. 50, June, 1998 ($1.95/$2.50)

1-1st app; Jim Lee/Williams-c/a & Lee scripts begin; contains 2 trading cards (Two diff versions of cards inside); 1st WildStorm Productions title	4.50
1-All gold foil signed edition	12.00
1-All gold foil unsigned edition	8.00
1-Newsstand edition w/o cards	3.00
1-"3-D Special"(8/97, $4.95) w/3-D glasses; variant-c by Jim Lee	5.00
2-($2.50)-Prism foil stamped-c; contains coupon for Image Comics #0 & 4 pg. preview to Portacio's Wetworks (back-up)	4.50
2-With coupon missing	2.25
2-Direct sale misprint w/o foil-c	3.00
2-Newsstand ed., no prism or coupon	2.25
3-Lee/Liefeld-c (1/93-c, 12/92 inside)	3.50
4-($2.50)-Polybagged w/Topps trading card; 1st app. Tribe by Johnson & Stroman; Youngblood cameo	3.50
4-Variant w/red card	6.00
5-7-Jim Lee/Williams-c/a; Lee script	3.00
8-X-Men's Jean Grey & Scott Summers cameos	4.00
9-12: 10-1st app. Huntsman & Soldier; Claremont scripts begin, ends #13. 11-1st app. Savant, Tapestry & Mr. Majestic.	3.00
11-Alternate Portacio-c, see Deathblow #5	5.00
13-19,21-24: 15-James Robinson scripts begin, ends #20. 15,16-Black Razor story. 21-Alan Moore scripts begin, end #34; intro Tao & Ladytron; new WildC.A.T.S team forms (Mr. Majestic, Savant, Condition Red (Max Cash), Tao & Ladytron). 22-Maguire-a	3.00
20-($2.50)-Direct Market, WildStorm Rising Pt. 2 w/bound-in card	3.00
20-($1.95)-Newsstand, WildStorm Rising Part 2	2.25
25-($4.95)-Alan Moore script; wraparound foil-c	5.00
26-49: 29-(5/96)-Fire From Heaven Pt 7; reads Apr on-c. 30-(6/96)-Fire From Heaven Pt. 13; Spartan revealed to have transplanted personality of John Colt (from Team One: WildC.A.T.S). 31-(9/96)-Grifter rejoins team; Ladytron dies	2.50
40-($3.50)-Voyager Pack bagged w/Divine Right preview	6.00
50-($3.50) Stories by Robinson/Lee, Choi & Peterson/Benes, and Moore/ Charest; Charest sketchbook; Lee wraparound-c	4.00
50-Chromium cover	6.00
Annual 1 (2/98, $2.95) Robinson-s	3.00
Compendium (1993, $9.95)-r/#1-4; bagged w/#0	10.00
Sourcebook 1 (9/93, $2.50)-Foil embossed-c	2.50
Sourcebook 1-($1.95)-Newsstand ed. w/o foil embossed-c	2.25
Sourcebook 2 (11/94, $2.50)-wraparound-c	2.50
Special 1 (11/93, $3.50, 52 pgs.)-1st Travis Charest WildC.A.T.S-c	3.50
...A Gathering of Eagles (5/97, $9.95, TPB) r/#10-12	10.00
...Gang War ('98, $16.95, TPB) r/#28-34	17.00
...Homecoming (8/98, $19.95, TPB) r/#21-27	20.00

WILDCATS
DC Comics (WildStorm): Mar, 1999 - No. 28, Dec, 2001 ($2.50)

1-Charest-a; six covers by Lee, Adams, Bisley, Campbell, Madureira and, Ramos; Lobdell-s	3.00
1-($6.95) DF Edition; variant cover by Ramos	7.00
2-28: 2-Voodoo cover. 3-Bachalo variant-c. 5-Hitch-a. 7-Meglia-a. 8-Phillips-a begins. 17-J.G. Jones-c. 18,19-Jim Lee-c. 20,21-Dillon-a	2.50
Annual 2000 (12/00, $3.50) Bermejo-a; Devil's Night x-over	3.50
... Ladytron (10/00, $5.95) Origin; Casey/s/Canete-a	6.00
...: Mosaic (2/00, $3.95) Tuska-a (10 pg. back-up story)	4.00
...: Serial Boxes ('01, $14.95, TPB) r/#14-19; Phillips-c	15.00
...: Street Smart ('00, $24.95, HC) r/#1-6; Charest-c	25.00
...: Vicious Circles ('00, $14.95, TPB) r/#8-13; Phillips-c	15.00

WILDC.A.T.S/ ALIENS
Image Comics/Dark Horse: Aug, 1998 ($4.95, one-shot)

1-Ellis-s/Sprouse-a/c; Aliens invade Skywatch; Stormwatch app.; death of Winter; destruction of Skywatch	1	3	6	8
1-Variant-c by Gil Kane	1	4	7	10

WILDC.A.T.S: SAVANT GARDE FAN EDITION
Image Comics/WildStorm Productions: Feb, 1997 - No. 3, Apr, 1997
(Giveaway, 8 pgs.) (Polybagged w/Overstreet's FAN)

1-3: Barbara Kesel-s/Christian Uche-a(p)	3.00

Wildstar #1
© Al Gordon & Jerry Ordway

Wild Stars V3 #1 © Michael Tierney

Wild Thing #4 © MAR

GD2.0 FN6.0 VF8.0 NM9.4

GD2.0 FN6.0 VF8.0 NM9.4

1-3-(Gold): All retailer incentives 10.00

WILDC.A.T.S TRILOGY
Image Comics (WildStorm Productions): June, 1993 - No. 3, Dec, 1993 ($1.95, limited series)

1-($2.50)-1st app. Gen 13 (Fairchild, Burnout, Grunge, Freefall)	
Multi-color foil-c; Jae Lee-c/a in all	5.00
1-($1.95)-Newsstand ed. w/o foil-c	2.25
2,3-($1.95)-Jae Lee-c/a	2.25

WILDC.A.T.S/ X-MEN: THE GOLDEN AGE
Image Comics (WildStorm Productions): Feb, 1997 ($4.50, one-shot)

1-Lobdell-s/Charest-a; Two covers (Charest, Jim Lee)	5.00
1-"3-D" Edition ($6.50) w/glasses	7.00

WILDC.A.T.S/ X-MEN: THE MODERN AGE
Image Comics (WildStorm Productions): Aug, 1997 ($4.50, one-shot)

1-Robinson-s/Hughes-a; Two covers(Hughes, Paul Smith)	5.00
1-"3-D" Edition ($6.50) w/glasses	7.00

WILDC.A.T.S/ X-MEN: THE SILVER AGE
Image Comics (WildStorm Productions): June, 1997 ($4.50, one-shot)

1-Lobdell-s/Jim Lee-a; Two covers(Neal Adams, Jim Lee)	5.00
1-"3-D" Edition ($6.50) w/glasses	7.00

WILDCORE
Image Comics (WildStorm Prods.): Nov, 1997 - No. 10, Dec, 1998 ($2.50)

1-10: 1-Two covers(Booth/McWeeney, Charest)	2.50
1-($3.50)-Voyager Pack w/DV8 preview	3.50
1-Chromium-c	5.00

WILD DOG
DC Comics: Sept, 1987 - No. 4, Dec, 1987 (75¢, limited series)

1-4	2.50
Special 1 (1989, $2.50, 52 pgs.)	2.50

WILDERNESS TREK (See Zane Grey, Four Color 333)
WILDFIRE (See Zane Grey, FourColor 333)

WILD FRONTIER (Cheyenne Kid #8 on)
Charlton Comics: Oct, 1955 - No. 7, Apr, 1957

1-Davy Crockett	10	30	55	80
2-6-Davy Crockett in all	7	21	36	50
7-Origin & 1st app. Cheyenne Kid	7	21	38	55

WILDSTAR (Also see The Dragon & The Savage Dragon)
Image Comics (Highbrow Entertainment): Sept, 1995 - No. 3, Jan, 1996 ($2.50, limited series)

1-3: Al Gordon scripts; Jerry Ordway-c/a	2.50

WILDSTAR: SKY ZERO
Image Comics (Highbrow Entertainment): Mar, 1993 - No. 4, Nov, 1993 ($1.95, limited series)

1-4: 1-($2.50)-Embossed-c w/silver ink; Ordway-c/a in all	2.50
1-($1.95)-Newsstand ed. w/silver ink-c, not embossed	2.50
1-Gold variant	6.00

WILD STARS
Little Rocket Productions: July, 2001 - Present ($2.95, B&W)

Vol. 3: #1-3-Brunner-c; Tierney-s. 1,2-Brewer-a. 3-Simons-a	3.00

WILDSTORM
Image Comics/DC Comics (WildStorm Publishing): 1994-2001 (one-shots)

...Annual 2000 (12/00, $3.50) Devil's Night x-over; Moy-a	3.50
...Chamber of Horrors (10/95, $3.50)-Bisley-c	3.50
...Fine Arts: The Gallery Collection (12/98, $19.95) Lee-c	20.00
...Halloween 1 (10/97, $2.50) Warner-c	2.50
...Rarities 1(12/94, $4.95, 52 pgs.)-r/Gen 13 1/2 & other stories	5.00
...Summer Special 1 (2001, $5.95) Short stories by various; Hughes-c	6.00
...Swimsuit Special 1 (12/94, $2.95), ...Swimsuit Special 2 (1995, $2.50)	3.00
...Swimsuit Special '97 1 (7/97, $2.50)	2.50
...Thunderbook 1 (10/00, $6.95) Short stories by various incl. Hughes, Moy	7.00
...Ultimate Sports 1 (8/97, $2.50)	2.50
...Universe Sourcebook (5/95, $2.50)	2.50

WILDSTORM!
Image Comics (WildStorm Publishing): Aug, 1995 - No. 4, Nov, 1995 ($2.50, B&W/color, anthology)

1-4: 1-Simonson-a	2.50

WILDSTORM RISING
Image Comics (WildStorm Publishing): May, 1995 - No.2, June, 1995 ($1.95/$2.50)

1 ($2.50)-Direct Market, WildStorm Rising Pt. 1 w/bound-in card	2.50
1 ($1.95)-Newstand, WildStorm Rising Pt. 1	2.25
2 ($2.50)-Direct Market, WildStorm Rising Pt. 10 w/bound-in card; continues in WildC.A.T.S #21.	2.50
2 ($1.95)-Newstand, WildStorm Rising Pt. 10	2.25
Trade paperback (1996, $19.95)-Collects x-over; B. Smith-c	20.00

WILDSTORM SPOTLIGHT
Image Comics (WildStorm Publishing): Feb, 1997 - No. 4 ($2.50)

1-4: 1-Alan Moore-s	2.50

WILDSTORM UNIVERSE '97
Image Comics (WildStorm Publishing): Dec, 1996 - No. 3 ($2.50, limited series)

1-3: 1-Wraparound-c. 3-Gary Frank-c	2.50

WILDTHING
Marvel Comics UK: Apr, 1993 - No. 7, Oct, 1993 ($1.75)

1-($2.50)-Embossed-c; Venom & Carnage cameo	2.50
2-7: 2-Spider-Man & Venom. 6-Mysterio app.	2.25

WILD THING (Wolverine's daughter in the M2 universe)
Marvel Comics: Oct, 1999 - No. 5, Feb, 2000 ($1.99)

1-5: 1-Lim-a in all. 2-Two covers	2.25
Wizard #0 supplement; battles the Hulk	2.25

WILDTIMES
DC Comics (WildStorm Productions): Aug, 1999 ($2.50, one-shots)

...Deathblow #1 -set in 1899; Edwards-a; Jonah Hex app., ...DV8 #1 -set in 1944; Altieri-s/p; Sgt. Rock app., ...Gen13 #1 -set in 1969; Casey-s/Johnson-a;, Teen Titans app., ...Grifter #1 -set in 1923; Paul Smith-a; Wetworks #1 - Waid-s/Lopresti-a; Superman app.	2.50
...WildC.A.T.s #0 -Wizard supplement; Charest-c	2.25

WILD WEST (Wild Western #3 on)
Marvel Comics (WFP): Spring, 1948 - No. 2, July, 1948

1-Two-Gun Kid, Arizona Annie, & Tex Taylor begin; Shores-c				
	36	108	191	330
2-Captain Tootsie by Beck; Shores-c	24	72	127	215

WILD WEST (Black Fury #1-57)
Charlton Comics: V2#58, Nov, 1966

V2#58	2	6	12	18

WILD WEST C.O.W.-BOYS OF MOO MESA (TV)
Archie Comics: Dec, 1992 - No. 3, Feb, 1993 (limited series)
V2#1, Mar, 1993 - No. 3, July, 1993 ($1.25)

1-3,V2#1-3	2.25

WILD WESTERN (Formerly Wild West #1,2)
Marvel/Atlas (WFP): No. 3, 9/48 - No. 57, 9/57 (3-11: 52 pgs, 12-on: 36 pgs)

3(#1)-Tex Morgan begins; Two-Gun Kid, Tex Taylor, & Arizona Annie continue from Wild West	29	87	153	265
4-Last Arizona Annie; Captain Tootsie by Beck; Kid Colt app.				
	21	63	110	185
5-2nd app. Black Rider (1/49); Blaze Carson, Captain Tootsie (by Beck) app.				
	24	72	127	215
6-8: 6-Blaze Carson app; anti-Wertham editorial	15	45	77	130
9-Photo-c; Black Rider begins, ends #19	20	60	105	175
10-Charles Starrett photo-c	23	69	121	205
11-(Last 52 pg. issue)	15	45	77	130
12-14,16-19: All Black Rider-c/stories. 12-14-The Prairie Kid & his horse Fury app.	14	42	72	120
15-Red Larabee, Gunhawk (origin), his horse Blaze, & Apache Kid begin; end #22; Black Rider-c/story	14	42	72	125

Will Rogers Western #2 © FOX

Will To Power #10 © DH

Wings Comics #33 © FH

WI

	GD2.0	FN6.0	VF8.0	NM9.4

20-30: 20-Kid Colt-c begin. 24-Has 2 Kid Colt stories. 26-1st app. The Ringo Kid? (2/53); 4 pg. story. 30-Katz-a

	12	36	61	100
31-40	10	30	55	80
41-47,49-51,53,57	8	24	45	65
48-Williamson/Torres-a (4 pgs); Drucker-a	10	30	55	85
52-Crandall-a	10	30	55	85
54,55-Williamson-a in both (5 & 4 pgs.), #54 with Mayo plus 2 text illos				
	10	30	55	85
56-Baker-a?	8	24	45	65

NOTE: Annie Oakley in #46, 47. Apache Kid in #15-22, 39. Arizona Kid in #21, 23. Arrowhead in #34-39. Black Rider in #5, 9-19, 33-44. Fighting Texan in #17. Kid Colt in #4-6, 9-11, 20-47, 52, 54-56. Outlaw Kid in #43. Red Hawkins in #13, 14. Ringo Kid in #26, 39, 41, 43, 44, 46, 47, 50, 52-56. Tex Morgan in #3, 4, 6, 9, 11. Tex Taylor in #3-6, 9, 11. Texas Kid in #23-25. Two-Gun Kid in #3-6, 9, 11, 12, 33-39, 41. Wyatt Earp in #47. Ayers a-41, 42. Berg a-26; c-24. Colan a-49. Forte a-28, 30. Al Hartley a-16. Heath a-4, 5, 8; c-34, 44. Keller a-24, 26(2), 29-40, 44-46, 48, 52. Maneely a-10, 12, 15, 16, 28, 35, 38, 40-45; c-18-22, 33, 35, 36, 38, 39, 41, 42, 45. Morisi a-23, 52. Pakula a-42, 52. Powell a-51. Romita a-24(2). Severin a-46, 47; c-48. Shores a-3, 5, 30, 31, 33, 35, 36, 38, 41; c-3-5. Sinnott a-34-39. Wildey a-43. Bondage c-19.

WILD WESTERN ACTION (Also see The Bravados)
Skywald Publ. Corp.: Mar, 1971 - No. 3, June, 1971 (25¢, reprints, 52 pgs.)
1-Durango Kid, Straight Arrow-r; with all references to "Straight" in story relettered to "Swift"; Bravados begin; Shores-a (new)

		2	6	12	18
2,3: 2-Billy Nevada, Durango Kid. 3-Red Mask, Durango Kid					
		2	6	9	12

WILD WESTERN ROUNDUP
Red Top/Decker Publications/I. W. Enterprises: Oct, 1957; 1960-'61

1(1957)-Kid Cowboy-r		4	12	19	25
I.W. Reprint #1('60-61)-r/#1 by Red Top		2	6	9	12

WILD WEST RODEO
Star Publications: 1953 (15¢)
1-A comic book coloring book with regular full color cover & B&W inside

		7	21	38	55

WILD WILD WEST, THE (TV)
Gold Key: June, 1966 - No. 7, Oct, 1969 (Robert Conrad photo-c)

1-McWilliams-a; photo back-c		12	36	84	160
2-McWilliams-a; photo back-c		9	27	63	120
3-7		7	21	49	90

WILD, WILD WEST, THE (TV)
Millennium Publications: Oct, 1990 - No. 4, Jan?, 1991 ($2.95, limited series)
1-4-Based on TV show   3.00

WILKIN BOY (See That...)

WILL EISNER READER
Kitchen Sink Press: 1991 ($9.95, B&W, 8 1/2" x 11", TPB)
nn-Reprints stories from Will Eisner's Quarterly; Eisner-s/a/c   10.00
nn-(DC Comics, 10/00, $9.95)   10.00

WILLIE COMICS (Formerly Ideal #1-4; Crime Cases #24 on; Li'l Willie #20 & 21) (See Gay Comics, Laugh, Millie The Model & Wisco)
Marvel Comics (MgPC): #5, Fall, 1946 - #19, 4/49; #22, 1/50 - #23, 5/50 (No #20 & 21)

5(#1)-George, Margie, Nellie the Nurse & Willie begin

	19	57	99	170
6,8,9	11	33	55	90
7(1),10,11-Kurtzman's "Hey Look"	11	33	55	95
12-14,18,22,23	10	30	55	80
13,19-Kurtzman's "Hey Look" (#19-last by Kurtzman?)				
	10	30	55	85

NOTE: Cindy app. in #17. Jeanie app. in #17. Little Lizzie app. in #22.

WILLIE MAYS (See The Amazing...)

WILLIE THE PENGUIN
Standard Comics: Apr, 1951 - No. 6, Apr, 1952

1-Funny animal	9	27	49	70
2-6	5	15	25	35

WILLIE THE WISE-GUY (Also see Cartoon Kids)
Atlas Comics (NPP): Sept, 1957

	GD2.0	FN6.0	VF8.0	NM9.4
1-Kida, Maneely-a	9	27	49	70

WILLOW
Marvel Comics: Aug, 1988 - No. 3, Oct, 1988 ($1.00)
1-3-R/Marvel Graphic Novel #36 (movie adaptation)   3.00

WILL ROGERS WESTERN (Formerly My Great Love #1-4; see Blazing & True Comics #66)
Fox Features Syndicate: No. 5, June, 1950 - No. 2, Aug, 1950

5(#1)	35	105	185	320
2: Photo-c	30	90	159	275

WILL TO POWER (Also see Comic's Greatest World)
Dark Horse Comics: June, 1994 - No. 12, Aug, 1994 ($1.00, weekly limited series, 20 pgs.)
1-12: 12-Vortex kills Titan.   2.25
NOTE: Mignola c-10-12. Sears c-1-3.

WILL-YUM!
Dell Publishing Co.: No. 676, Feb, 1956 - No. 902, May, 1958

Four Color 676 (#1), 765 (1/57), 902	3	9	19	28

WIN A PRIZE COMICS (Timmy The Timid Ghost #3 on?)
Charlton Comics: Feb, 1955 - No. 2, Apr, 1955

V1#1-S&K-a; Poe adapt; E.C. War swipe	68	205	426	750
2-S&K-a	50	150	300	525

WINDY & WILLY
National Periodical Publications: May-June, 1969 - No. 4, Nov-Dec, 1969

1- r/Dobie Gillis with some art changes begin	4	12	26	40
2-4	2	6	15	22

WINGS COMICS
Fiction House Mag.: 9/40 - No. 109, 9/49; No. 110, Wint, 1949-50; No. 111, Spring, 1950; No. 112, 1950(nd); No. 113 - No. 115, 1950(nd); No. 116, 1952(nd); No. 117, Fall, 1952 - No. 122, Wint, 1953-54; No. 123 - No. 124, 1954(nd)

1-Skull Squad, Clipper Kirk, Suicide Smith, Jane Martin, War Nurse, Phantom Falcons, Greasemonkey Griffin, Parachute Patrol & Powder Burns begin

	236	708	1477	2600
2	95	285	597	1050
3-5	64	192	398	700
6-10: 8-Indicia shows #7 (#8 on cover)	55	165	331	580
11-15	47	140	286	500
16-Origin & 1st app. Captain Wings & begin series	53	158	318	560
17-20	40	120	232	400
21-30	39	117	208	360
31-40	33	99	174	300
41-50	26	78	139	240
51-60: 60-Last Skull Squad	23	69	121	210
61-67: 66-Ghost Patrol begins (becomes Ghost Squadron #71 on), ends #112?				
	21	63	110	185
68,69: 68-Clipper Kirk becomes The Phantom Falcon-origin, Part 1; part 2 in #69	21	63	110	185
70-72: 70-1st app. The Phantom Falcon in costume, origin-Part 3; Capt. Wings battles Col. Kamikaze in all	20	60	105	175
73-99: 80-Phantom Falcon by Larsen. 99-King of the Congo begins?				
	20	60	105	175
100-(12/48)	21	63	110	190
101-124: 111-Last Jane Martin. 112-Flying Saucer-c/story (1950). 115-Used in POP, pg. 89	17	51	88	150

NOTE: Bondage covers are common. Captain Wings battles Sky Hag-#75, 76; ...Mr. Atlantis-#85-92; ...Mr. Pupin(Red Agent)-#98-103. Capt. Wings by Elias-#52-64, 68, 69; by Lubbers-#29-32, 70-111; by Renee-#33-46. Evans a-85-106, 108-111(Jane Martin); text illos-72-84. Larsen a-52, 59, 64, 73-77. Jane Martin by Fran Hopper-#84; Suicide Smith by John Celardo-#72, 74, 76, 80-104; by Hollingsworth-#68-70, 105-109, 111; Ghost Squadron by Astarita-#67-79; by Maurice Whitman-#80-111. King of the Congo by Moreira-#99, 100. Skull Squad by M. Baker-#52-60; Clipper Kirk by Baker-#60, 61; by Colan-#53; by Ingels-(some issues?). Phantom Falcon by Larsen-#73-84. Elias c-58-72. Fawcette c-3-12, 16, 17, 19, 22-33. Lubbers c-74-109. Tuska a-5. Whitman c-110-124. Zolnerwich c-15, 21.

WINGS OF THE EAGLES, THE
Dell Publishing Co.: No. 790, May, 1957 (10¢ & 15¢ editions exist)

Four Color 790-Movie; John Wayne photo-c; Toth-a	15	45	105	190

WINKY DINK (Adventures of...)

Winnie-The-Pooh #4 © WDC

Witchblade #26 © TCOW

Witches Tales #15 © HARV

	GD2.0	FN6.0	VF8.0	NM9.4

Pines Comics: No. 75, Mar, 1957 (one-shot)

	GD2.0	FN6.0	VF8.0	NM9.4
75-Marv Levy-c/a	5	15	25	35

WINKY DINK (TV)
Dell Publishing Co.: No. 663, Nov, 1955

Four Color 663 (#1)	8	24	56	100

WINNIE-THE-POOH (Also see Dynabrite Comics)
Gold Key No. 1-17/Whitman No. 18 on: January, 1977 - No. 33, July, 1984
(Walt Disney) (Winnie-The-Pooh began as Edward Bear in 1926 by Milne)

1-New art	2	6	13	20
2-5: 5-New material	1	4	7	10
6-17: 12-up-New material	1	3	6	8
18,19(Whitman)	1	4	7	10
20-22('80) pre-pack?	2	6	11	15
23-28: 27(2/82), 28(4/82)	1	4	7	10
29-33 #90299 on-c, no date or date code; pre-pack): 29(4/82), 30(5/83),				
31(8/83), 32(4/84), 33(7/84)	2	6	11	15

WINNIE WINKLE (See Popular Comics & Super Comics)
Dell Publishing Co.: No. 7, Sept-Nov, 1949

Large Feature Comic 2 (1941)	18	54	126	230
Four Color 94 (1945)	12	36	84	155
Four Color 174	7	21	49	95
1(3-5/48)-Contains daily & Sunday newspaper-r from 1939-1941				
	7	21	49	85
2 (6-8/48)	4	12	30	50
3-7	3	10	23	35

WINTERWORLD
Eclipse Comics: Sept, 1987 - No. 3, Mar, 1988 ($1.75, limited series)

1-3				2.25

WISE GUYS (See Harvey...)

WISE LITTLE HEN, THE
David McKay Publ./Whitman: 1934 ,1935(48 pgs.); 1937 (Story book)

nn-(1934 edition w/dust jacket)(48 pgs. with color, 8-3/4x9-3/4") -Debut of				
Donald Duck (see Advs. of Mickey Mouse); Donald app. on cover with Wise				
Little Hen & Practical Pig; painted cover; same artist as the B&W's from Silly				
Symphony Cartoon, The Wise Little Hen (1934) (McKay)				
Book w/dust jacket	233	699	1282	2100
Dust jacket only	55	165	303	500
nn-(1935 edition w/dust jacket), same as 1934 ed.	139	417	765	1250
888 (1937)(9-1/2x13", 12 pgs.)(Whitman) Donald Duck app.				
	33	99	182	300

WISE SON: THE WHITE WOLF
DC Comics (Milestone): Nov, 1996 - No. 4, Feb, 1997 ($2.50, limited series)

1-4: Ho Che Anderson-c/a				2.50

WIT AND WISDOM OF WATERGATE (Humor magazine)
Marvel Comics: 1973, 76 pgs., squarebound

1-Low print run	3	9	20	30

WITCHBLADE (Also see Cyblade/Shi, Tales Of The..., & Top Cow Classics)
Image Comics (Top Cow Productions): Nov, 1995 - Present ($2.50)

0	1	3	6	8
1/2-Mike Turner/Marc Silvestri-c	4	12	26	40
1/2 Gold Ed., 1/2 Chromium-c	4	12	26	40
1-Mike Turner-a(p)	4	12	26	40
1,2-American Ent. Encore Ed.	1	3	5	7
2,3	2	6	13	20
4,5	2	6	11	16
6-9: 8-Wraparound-c. 9-Tony Daniel-a(p)	1	3	6	9
9-Sunset variant-c	2	6	9	12
10-Flip book w/Darkness #0, 1st app. the Darkness	2	6	9	12
10-Variant-c	2	6	11	15
10-($3.95) Dynamic Forces alternate-c	1	3	6	8
11-15				5.00
16,19: 18,19-"Family Ties" Darkness x-over pt. 1,4				4.00
18-Face to face variant-c, 18-American Ent. Ed., 19-AE Gold Ed.				
	1	3	6	8

		GD2.0	FN6.0	VF8.0	NM9.4

20-25: 24-Pearson, Green-a. 25-($2.95) Turner-a(p)				3.00
25 (prism variant)				30.00
25 (Special)				15.00
26-39: 26-Green-a begins				2.50
27 (Variant)				10.00
40-49,51,52: 40-Begin Jenkins & Veitch-s/Keu Cha-a. 47-Zulli-c/a				2.50
40-Pittsburgh Convention Preview edition; B&W preview of #40				3.00
41-eWanted Chrome-c edition				5.00
50-($4.95) Darkness app.; Ching-a; B&W preview of Universe				5.00
.../Darkchylde (7/00, $2.50) Green-s/a(p)				2.50
.../Darkness Family Ties Collected Edition (10/98, $9.95) r/#18,19 and				
Darkness #9,10				10.00
.../Darkness Special (12/99, $3.95) Green-c/a				4.00
...: Distinctions (See Tales of the Witchblade)				
... Gallery (11/00, $2.95) Profile pages and pin-ups by various; Turner-c				3.00
Infinity (5/99, $3.50) Lobdell-s/Pollina-c/a				3.50
.../Lady Death (11/01, $4.95) Manapul-c/a				5.00
...: Prevailing TPB (2000, $14.95) r/#20-25; new Turner-c				15.00
...: Revelations TPB (2000, $24.95) r/#9-17; new Turner-c				25.00
.../Tomb Raider #1/2 (7/00, $2.95) Covers by Turner and Cha				3.00
Wizard #500				10.00

WITCHBLADE/ALIENS/THE DARKNESS/PREDATOR
Dark Horse Comics /Top Cow Productions: Nov, 2000 ($2.99)

1-3-Mel Rubi-a				3.00

WITCHBLADE COLLECTED EDITION
Image Comics (Top Cow Productions): July, 1996 - Present ($4.95/$6.95, squarebound, limited series)

1-7-($4.95): Two issues reprinted in each				5.00
8-($6.95) r/#15-17				7.00
...Slipcase (10/96, $10.95)-Packaged w/ Coll. Ed. #1-4				11.00

WITCHBLADE: DESTINY'S CHILD
Image Comics (Top Cow): June, 2000 - No. 3, Sept, 2000 ($2.95, lim. series)

1-3: 1-Boller-a/Keu Cha-c				3.00

WITCHBLADE/ ELEKTRA
Image Comics (Top Cow Productions): Mar, 1997 ($2.95)

1-Devil's Reign Pt. 6				3.00

WITCHBLADE/ TOMB RAIDER SPECIAL (Also see Tomb Raider/...)
Image Comics (Top Cow Productions): Dec, 1998 ($2.95)

1-Based on video game character; Turner-a(p)				3.00
1-Silvestri variant-c				5.00
1-Turner bikini variant-c				10.00
Wizard 1/2 -Turner-s				10.00

WITCHCRAFT (See Strange Mysteries, Super Reprint #18)
Avon Periodicals: Mar-Apr, 1952 - No. 6, Mar, 1953

1-Kubert-a; 1 pg. Check-a	66	198	413	725
2-Kubert & Check-a	50	150	300	525
3,6: 3-Lawrence-a; Kinstler inside-c	40	120	220	380
4-People cooked alive c/story	43	129	257	450
5-Kelly Freas painted-c	47	141	286	500

NOTE: *Hollingsworth a-4-6; c-4, 6. McCann a-3?*

WITCHCRAFT
DC Comics (Vertigo): June, 1994 - No. 3, Aug, 1994 ($2.95, limited series)

1-3: James Robinson scripts & Kaluta-c in all				4.00
1-Platinum Edition				8.00
Trade paperback-(1996, $14.95)-r/#1-3; Kaluta-c				15.00

WITCHCRAFT: LA TERREUR
DC Comics (Vertigo): Apr, 1998 - No. 3, Jun, 1998 ($2.50, limited series)

1-3: Robinson-s/Zulli & Locke-a; interlocking cover images				2.50

WITCHES TALES (Witches Western Tales #29,30)
Witches Tales/Harvey Publications: Jan, 1951 - No. 28, Dec, 1954 (date misprinted as 4/55)

1-Powell-a (1 pg.)	55	165	330	575
2-Eye injury panel	33	99	174	300
3-7,9,10	25	75	130	225

Witchfinder #1 © Sharon Scott

Witching Hour #83 © DC

Wolverine (mini-series) #2 © MAR

	GD2.0	FN6.0	VF8.0	NM9.4
8-Eye injury panels	25	75	133	230
11-13,15,16: 12-Acid in face story	22	66	116	195
14,17-Powell/Nostrand-a. 17-Atomic disaster story	24	72	127	215
18-Nostrand-a; E.C. swipe/Shock S.S.	24	72	127	215
19-Nostrand-a; E.C. swipe/ "Glutton"; Devil-c	26	78	136	235
20-24-Nostrand-a. 21-E.C. swipe; rape story. 23-Wood E.C. swipes/Two-Fisted				
Tales #34	24	72	127	215
25-Nostrand-a; E.C. swipe/Mad Barber; decapitation-c				
	30	90	159	275
26-28: 27-r/#6 with diff.-c. 28-r/#8 with diff.-c	17	51	88	150

NOTE: **Check** a-24. **Elias** c-8, 10, 16-27. **Kremer** a-18; c-25. **Nostrand** a-17-25; 14, 7(w/Powell). Palais a-1, 2, 4(2), 5(2), 7-9, 12, 14, 15, 17. **Powell** a-3-7, 10, 11, 19-27. Bondage-: 1, 3, 5, 6, 8, 9.

WITCHES TALES (Magazine)
Eerie Publications: V1#7, July, 1969 - V7#1, Feb, 1975 (B&W, 52 pgs.)

V1#7(7/69) - 9(11/69)	4	12	30	50
V2#1-6('70), V3#1-6('71)	3	10	23	35
V4#1-6('72), V5#1-6('73), V6#1-6('74), V7#1	3	9	20	30

NOTE: Ajax/Farrell reprints in early issues.

WITCHES' WESTERN TALES (Formerly Witches Tales)(Western Tales #31on)
Harvey Publications: No. 29, Feb, 1955 - No. 30, Apr, 1955

29,30-Featuring Clay Duncan & Boys' Ranch; S&K-r/from Boys' Ranch				
including-c. 29-Last pre-code	21	63	110	185

WITCHFINDER, THE
Image Comics (Liar): Sept, 1999 - No. 3, Jan, 2000 ($2.95)

1-3-Romano-a/Sharon & Matthew Scott-plot				3.00

WITCH HUNTER
Malibu Comics (Ultraverse): Apr, 1996 ($2.50, one-shot)

1				2.50

WITCHING HOUR ("The ..." in later issues)
National Periodical Publ./DC Comics: Feb-Mar, 1969 - No. 85, Oct, 1978

1-Toth-a, plus Neal Adams-a (2 pgs.)	12	36	84	140
2,6: 6-Toth-a	5	15	34	55
3,5-Wrightson-a; Toth-p. 3-Last 12¢ issue	5	15	38	60
4,7-12: Toth-a in all. 8-Toth, Neal Adams-a	3	9	20	30
13-Neal Adams-c/a, 2pgs.	3	10	23	35
14-Williamson/Garzon, Jones-a; N. Adams-c	4	12	26	40
15	2	6	13	20
16-21-(52 pg. Giants)	3	9	17	25
22-37,39,40	2	6	11	15
38-(100 pg.)	4	12	29	45
41-60	2	6	9	12
61-83,85	1	3	6	9
84-(44 pgs.)	1	4	7	10

NOTE: Combined with The Unexpected with #189. Neal Adams c-7-11, 13, 14. Alcala a-24, 27, 33, 41, 43. Anderson a-9, 38. Cardy c-4, 5. Kaluta a-7. Kane a-12p. Morrow a-10, 13, 15, 16. Nino a-31, 40, 45, 47. Redondo a-23, 24, 34, 65; c-53. Reese a-23. Sparling a-1. Toth a-1, 3-12, 18r. Tuska a-11, 12. Wood a-15.

WITCHING HOUR, THE
DC Comics (Vertigo): 1999 - No. 3, 2000 ($5.95, limited series)

1-3-Bachalo & Thibert-c/a; Loeb & Bachalo-s				6.00
Hardcover (2000, $29.95) r/#1-3; embossed cover				30.00

WITHIN OUR REACH
Star Reach Productions: 1991 ($7.95, 84 pgs.)

nn-Spider-Man, Concrete by Chadwick, Gift of the Magi by Russell;				
X-mas stories; Chadwick-c; Spidey back-c				8.00

WITH THE MARINES ON THE BATTLEFRONTS OF THE WORLD
Toby Press: 1953 (no month) - No. 2, Mar, 1954 (Photo covers)

1-John Wayne story	30	90	159	275
2-Monty Hall in #1,2	9	27	49	70

WITH THE U.S. PARATROOPS BEHIND ENEMY LINES (Also see U.S. Paratroops...; #2-6 titled U.S. Paratroops...)
Avon Periodicals: 1951 - No. 6, Dec, 1952

1-Wood-c & inside f/c	17	51	88	150
2-Kinstler-c & inside f/c only	10	30	55	80

	GD2.0	FN6.0	VF8.0	NM9.4
3-6: 6-Kinstler-c & inside f/c only	9	27	49	70

NOTE: Kinstler c-2, 4-6.

WITNESS, THE (Also see Amazing Mysteries, Captain America #71, Ideal #4, Marvel Mystery #92 & Mystic #7)
Marvel Comics (MjMe): Sept, 1948

1(Scarce)-Rico-c?	168	505	1050	1850

WITTY COMICS
Irwin H. Rubin Publ./Chicago Nite Life News No. 2: 1945 - No. 2, 1945

1-The Pioneer, Junior Patrol; Jap war-c	27	81	145	250
2-The Pioneer, Junior Patrol	14	42	72	120

WIZARD OF FOURTH STREET, THE
Dark Horse Comics: Dec, 1987 - No. 2, 1988 ($1.75, B&W, limited series)

1,2: Adapts novel by S/F author Simon Hawke				2.25

WIZARD OF OZ (See Classics Illustrated Jr. 535, Dell Jr. Treasury No. 5, First Comics Graphic Novel, Marvelous..., & Marvel Treasury of Oz)
Dell Publishing Co.: No. 1308, Mar-May, 1962 (TV)

Four Color 1308	12	36	84	150

WIZARD'S TALE, THE
Image Comics (Homage Comics): 1997 ($19.95, squarebound, one-shot)

nn-Kurt Busiek-s/David Wenzel-painted-a/c				20.00

WOLF & RED
Dark Horse Comics: Apr, 1995 - No. 3, June, 1995 ($2.50, limited series)

1-3: Characters created by Tex Avery				2.50

WOLFF & BYRD, COUNSELORS OF THE MACABRE (Becomes Supernatural Law with issue #24)
Exhibit A Press: May, 1994 - No. 23, Aug, 1999 ($2.95, B&W)

1-23-Batton Lash-s/a				2.50

WOLF GAL (See Al Capp's...)

WOLFMAN, THE (See Movie Classics)

WOLFPACK
Marvel Comics: Feb, 1988 ($7.95); Aug, 1988 - No. 12, July, 1989 (Lim. series)

1-1st app./origin (Marvel Graphic Novel #31)				8.00
1-12				2.25

WOLVERINE (See Alpha Flight, Daredevil #196, 249, Ghost Rider; Wolverine; Punisher, Havok &..., Incredible Hulk #180, Incredible Hulk &..., Kitty Pryde And..., Marvel Comics Presents, Power Pack, Punisher and..., Spider-Man vs... & X-Men #94)

WOLVERINE (See Incredible Hulk #180 for 1st app.)
Marvel Comics Group: Sept, 1982 - No. 4, Dec, 1982 (limited series)

1-Frank Miller-c/a(p) in all	4	12	30	50
2-4	3	10	23	35
Trade paperback 1(7/87, $4.95)-Reprints #1-4 with new Miller-c.				
	2	6	11	15
Trade paperback nn (2nd printing, $9.95)-r/#1-4	2	6	9	12

WOLVERINE
Marvel Comics: Nov, 1988 - Present ($1.50/$1.75/$1.95/$1.99, Baxter paper)

1	4	12	26	40
2	2	6	13	20
3-5: 4-BWS back-c	2	6	11	15
6-9: 6-McFarlane back-c. 7,8-Hulk app.	2	6	9	12
10-1st battle with Sabretooth (before Wolverine had his claws)				
	3	9	20	30
11-16: 11-New costume	1	3	6	9
17-20: 17-Byrne-c/a(p) begins, ends #23	1	3	6	9
21-30: 24,25,27-Jim Lee-a. 26-Begin $1.75-c				6.00
31-40,44				5.00
41-Sabretooth claims to be Wolverine's father; Cable cameo				
	1	3	5	7
41-Gold 2nd printing ($1.75)				2.50
42-Sabretooth, Cable & Nick Fury app.; Sabretooth proven not to be				
Wolverine's father	1	3	5	7
42-Gold ink 2nd printing ($1.75)				2.50
43-Sabretooth cameo (2 panels); saga ends				6.00
45,46-Sabretooth-c/stories				6.00

Wolverine #145 © MAR

Wolverine: The Origin #1 © MAR

Women Outlaws #1 © FOX

	GD2.0	FN6.0	VF8.0	NM9.4

| | | | | | GD2.0 | FN6.0 | VF8.0 | NM9.4 |

48-51: 48,49-Sabretooth app. 48-Begin 3 part Weapon X sequel. 50-(64 pgs.)-
Die cut-c; Wolverine back to old yellow costume; Forge, Cyclops, Jubilee,
Jean Grey & Nick Fury app.51-Sabretooth-c & app. ... 6.00
52-74,76-80: 54-Shatterstar (from X-Force) app. 55-Gambit, Jubilee, Sunfire-
c/story. 55-57,73-Gambit app. 57-Mariko Yashida dies (Late 7/92). 58,59-
Terror, Inc. x-over. 60-64-Sabretooth storyline (60,62,64-c) ... 4.00
75-($3.95, 68 pgs.)-Wolverine hologram on-c ... 1 ... 3 ... 6 ... 9
81-84,86: 81-bound-in card sheet ... 3.00
85-($2.50)-Newsstand edition ... 3.00
85-($3.50)-Collectors edition ... 5.00
87-90 ($1.95)-Deluxe edition ... 3.00
87-90 ($1.50)-Regular edition ... 2.50
91-99,101-114: 91-Return from "Age of Apocalypse," 93-Juggernaut app.
94-Gen X app. 101-104-Elektra app. 104-Origin of Onslaught. 105-Onslaught
x-over. 110-Shaman-c/app. 114-Alternate-c ... 2.50
100 ($3.95)-Hologram-c; Wolverine loses humanity ... 1 ... 3 ... 6 ... 9
100 ($2.95)-Regular-c. ... 4.00
115-124: 115- Operation Zero Tolerance ... 2.50
125-($2.99) Wraparound-c; Viper secret ... 3.00
125-($6.95) Jae Lee variant-c ... 7.00
126-144: 126,127-Sabretooth-c/app. 128-Sabretooth & Shadowcat app.;Platt-a.
129-Wendigo-c/app. 131-Initial printing contained lettering error. 133-Begin
Larsen-s/Matsuda-a. 138-Galactus-c/app. 139-Cable app.; Yu-a. 142,143-
Alpha Flight app. ... 2.50
145-($2.99) 25th Anniversary issue; Hulk and Sabretooth app. ... 3.00
145-($3.99) Foil enhanced cover ... 4.00
146-149: 147-Apocalypse: The Twelve; Angel-c/app. 149-Nova-c/app. ... 2.50
150-($2.99) Steve Skroce-s/a ... 3.00
151-171: 151-Begin $2.25-c. 154,155-Liefeld-s/a. 156-Churchill-a. 159-Chen-a
begins. 160-Sabretooth app. 163-Texeira-a(p). 167-BWS-c ... 2.50
#(-1) Flashback (7/97) Logan meets Col. Fury; Nord-a ... 2.50
Annual nn (1990, $4.50, squarebound, 52 pgs.)-The Jungle Adventure;
Simonson scripts; Mignola-c/a ... 5.00
Annual 2 (12/90, $4.95, squarebound, 52 pgs.)-Bloodlust ... 5.00
Annual nn (#3, 8/91, $5.95, 68 pgs.)-Rahne of Terror; Cable & The New
Mutants app.; Andy Kubert-c/a (2nd print exists) ... 6.00
Annual '95 (1995, $3.95) ... 4.00
Annual '96 (1996, $2.95)- Wraparound-c; Silver Samurai, Yukio, and
Red Ronin app. ... 3.00
Annual '97 ($2.99) - Wraparound-c ... 3.00
Annual 1999, 2000 ($3.50) : 1999-Deadpool app. ... 3.50
Annual 2001 ($2.99) - Tieri-s; JH Williams-c ... 3.00
...Battles The Incredible Hulk nn (1989, $4.95, squarebound, 52 pg.)
r/Incredible Hulk #180,181 ... 5.00
...Black Rio (11/98, $5.99)-Casey-s/Oscar Jimenez-a ... 6.00
...Blood Debt TPB (7/01, $12.95)-r/#150-153; Skroce-c ... 13.00
...Blood Hungry nn (1993, $6.95, 68 pgs.)-Kieth-r/Marvel Comics Presents
#85-92 w/ new Kieth-c ... 7.00
...: Bloody Choices nn (1993, $7.95, 68 pgs.)-r/Graphic Novel; Nick Fury
app. ... 8.00
... Cable Guts and Glory (10/99, $5.99) Platt-a ... 6.00
... Doombringer (11/97, $5.99)-Silver Samurai-c/app. ... 6.00
...: Evilution (9/94, $5.95) ... 6.00
...: Global Jeopardy 1 (12/93, $2.95, one-shot)-Embossed-c; Sub-Mariner,
Zabu, Ka-Zar, Shanna & Wolverine app.; produced in cooperation with
World Wildlife Fund ... 3.00
...:Inner Fury nn (1992, $5.95, 52 pgs.)-Sienkiewicz-c/a ... 6.00
...: Judgment Night (2000, $3.99) Shi app.; Battlebook ... 4.00
...: Killing (9/93)-Kent Williams-a ... 6.00
...: Knight of Terra (1995, $6.95)-Ostrander script ... 7.00
.../ Nick Fury: The Scorpio Connection Hardcover (1989, $16.95) ... 25.00
.../ Nick Fury: The Scorpio Connection Softcover(1990, $12.95) ... 15.00
...: Not Dead Yet (12/98, $14.95, TPB)-r/#119-122 ... 15.00
...: Save The Tiger 1 (7/92, $2.95, 84 pgs.)-Reprints Wolverine stories from
Marvel Comics Presents #1-10 w/new Kieth-c ... 3.00
...Scorpio Rising ($5.95, prestige format, one-shot) ... 6.00
.../Shi: Dark Night of Judgment (Crusade Comics, 2000, $2.99) Tucci-a ... 3.00
,..Triumphs And Tragedies-(1995, $16.95, trade paperback)-r/Uncanny
X-Men #109,172,173, Wolverine limited series #4, & Wolverine #41,42,75
... 17.00

...Typhoid's Kiss (6/94, $6.95)-r/Wolverine stories from Marvel Comics
Presents #109-116 ... 7.00
...Vs. Spider-Man 1 (3/95, $2.50) -r/Marvel Comics Presents #48-50 ... 2.50
.../Witchblade 1 (3/97, $2.95) Devil's Reign Pt. 5 ... 4.00
Wizard #1/2 (1997) Joe Phillips-a(p) ... 10.00
NOTE: Austin c-3i. Bolton c(back)/-5. Buscema a-1-16,25,27p; c-1-10. Byrne a-17-22p, 23; c-
1(back), 17-22, 23p. Colan a-24. Andy Kubert c/a-51. Jim Lee c-24, 25, 27. Silvestri a(p)-31-43,
45, 46, 48-50, 52, 53, 55-57; c-31-42p, 43, 45p, 46p, 48, 49p, 50p, 52p, 53p, 55-57p. Stroman a-
44p; c-60p. Williamson a-1i, 3-8i; c(i)-1, 3-6.

WOLVERINE AND THE PUNISHER: DAMAGING EVIDENCE
Marvel Comics: Oct, 1993 - No. 3, Dec, 1993 ($2.00, limited series)
1-3: 2,3-Indicia says "The Punisher and Wolverine..." ... 2.50

WOLVERINE: DAYS OF FUTURE PAST
Marvel Comics: Dec, 1997 - No. 3, Feb, 1998 ($2.50, limited series)
1-3: J.F. Moore-s/Bennett-a ... 2.50

WOLVERINE/GAMBIT: VICTIMS
Marvel Comics: Sept, 1995 - No. 4, Dec, 1995 ($2.95, limited series)
1-4: Jeph Loeb scripts & Tim Sale-a; foil-c ... 4.00

WOLVERINE/PUNISHER REVELATIONS (Marvel Knights)
Marvel Comics: Jun, 1999 - No. 4, Sept, 1999 ($2.95, limited series)
1-4: Pat Lee-a(p) ... 4.00
...: Revelation (4/00, $14.95, TPB) r/#1-4 ... 15.00

WOLVERINE SAGA
Marvel Comics: Sept, 1989 - No. 4, Mid-Dec, 1989 ($3.95, lim. series, 52 pgs.)
1-Gives history; Liefeld/Austin-c (front & back) ... 5.00
2-4: 2-Romita, Jr./Austin-c. 4-Kaluta-c ... 5.00

WOLVERINE: THE ORIGIN
Marvel Comics: Nov, 2001 - No. 6 ($3.50, limited series)
1-Origin of Logan; Jenkins-s/Andy Kubert-a; Quesada-c ... 5.00
2,3 ... 3.50

WOMEN IN LOVE (A Feature Presentation #5)
Fox Features Synd./Hero Books: Aug, 1949 - No. 4, Feb, 1950

1	31	93	165	285
2-Kamen/Feldstein-c	26	78	136	235
3	18	54	94	155
4-Wood-a	21	63	110	185

WOMEN IN LOVE (Thrilling Romances for Adults)
Ziff-Davis Publishing Co.: Winter, 1952 (25¢, 100 pgs.)

nn-(Scarce)-Kinstler-a; painted-c	52	157	314	550

WOMEN OUTLAWS (My Love Memories #9 on)(Also see Red Circle)
Fox Features Syndicate: July, 1948 - No. 8, Sept, 1949

1-Used in SOTI, illo "Giving children an image of American womanhood"; negligee panels	73	219	455	800
2,3-Kamenish-a	57	171	356	625
4-8	46	137	276	485
nn(nd)-Contains Cody of the Pony Express; same cover as #7	35	105	185	320

WOMEN TO LOVE
Realistic: No date (1953)

nn-(Scarce)-Reprints Complete Romance #1; c-/Avon paperback #165	40	120	220	380

WONDER BOY (Formerly Terrific Comics) (See Blue Bolt, Bomber Comics
& Samson)
Ajax/Farrell Publ.: No. 17, May, 1955 - No. 18, July, 1955 (Code approved)

17-Phantom Lady app. Bakerish-c/a	45	135	270	475
18-Phantom Lady app.	40	120	232	400

NOTE: Phantom Lady not by Matt Baker.

WONDER COMICS (Wonderworld #3 on)
Fox Features Syndicate: May, 1939 - No. 2, June, 1939 (68 pgs.)

1-(Scarce)-Wonder Man only app. by Will Eisner; Dr. Fung (by Powell), K-51 begins; Bob Kane-a; Eisner-c	1285	3855	9000	18,000
2-(Scarce)-Yarko the Great, Master Magician (see Samson) by Eisner begins; 'Spark' Stevens by Bob Kane, Patty O'Day, Tex Mason app. Lou Fine's 1st-c;				

Wonder Comics #12 © BP

Wonder Woman #10 © DC

Wonder Woman #204 © DC

	GD2.0	FN6.0	VF8.0	NM9.4
Fine-a (2 pgs.); Yarko-c (Wonder Man-c #1)	438	1314	2847	5700

WONDER COMICS
Great/Nedor/Better Publications: May, 1944 - No. 20, Oct, 1948

	GD2.0	FN6.0	VF8.0	NM9.4
1-The Grim Reaper & Spectro, the Mind Reader begin; Hitler/Hirohito bondage-c	136	408	852	1500
2-Origin The Grim Reaper; Super Sleuths begin, end #8,17	66	197	413	725
3-5	60	180	375	660
6-10: 6-Flag-c. 8-Last Spectro. 9-Wonderman begins	50	150	300	525
11-14: 11-Dick Devens, King of Futuria begins, ends #14. 11,12-Ingels-c & splash pg. 14-Bondage-c	58	174	363	640
15-Tara begins (origin), ends #20	67	201	419	740
16,18: 16-Spectro app.; last Grim Reaper. 18-The Silver Knight begins	58	174	363	640
17-Wonderman with Frazetta panels; Jill Trent with all Frazetta inks	60	180	375	660
19-Frazetta panels	58	174	363	640
20-Most of Silver Knight by Frazetta	69	207	431	760

NOTE: *Ingels* c-11, 12. *Roussos* a-19. *Schomburg (Xela)* c-1-10; (airbrush)-13-20. Bondage c-12, 13, 15. Cover features: Grim Reaper #1-8; Wonder Man #9-15; Tara #16-20.

WONDER DUCK (See Wisco)
Marvel Comics (CDS): Sept, 1949 - No. 3, Mar, 1950

	GD2.0	FN6.0	VF8.0	NM9.4
1-Funny animal	16	48	83	140
2,3	10	30	55	85

WONDERFUL ADVENTURES OF PINOCCHIO, THE (See Movie Comics & Walt Disney Showcase #48)
Whitman Publishing Co.: April, 1982 (Walt Disney)

nn-#3 Continuation of Movie Comics?); r/FC #92				6.00

WONDERFUL WORLD OF DISNEY, THE (Walt Disney)
Whitman Publishing Co.: 1978 (Digest, 116 pgs.)

	GD2.0	FN6.0	VF8.0	NM9.4
1-Barks-a (reprints)	3	9	17	26
2 (no date)	2	6	12	18

WONDERFUL WORLD OF THE BROTHERS GRIMM (See Movie Comics)

WONDERLAND COMICS
Feature Publications/Prize: Summer, 1945 - No. 9, Feb-Mar, 1947

	GD2.0	FN6.0	VF8.0	NM9.4
1-Alex in Wonderland begins; Howard Post-c	17	51	88	150
2-Howard Post-c/a(2)	9	27	51	75
3-9: 3,4-Post-c	8	24	42	60

WONDER MAN (See The Avengers #9, 151)
Marvel Comics Group: Mar, 1986 ($1.25, one-shot, 52 pgs.)

1				3.00

WONDER MAN
Marvel Comics Group: Sept, 1991 - No. 29, Jan, 1994 ($1.00)

1-29: 1-Free fold out poster by Johnson/Austin. 1-3-Johnson/Austin-c/a. 2-Avengers West Coast x-over. 4 Austin-c(i)				2.25
Annual 1 (1992, $2.25)-Immonen-a (3)				2.50
Annual 2 (1993, $2.25)-Bagged w/trading card				2.50

WONDERS OF ALADDIN, THE
Dell Publishing Co.: No. 1255, Feb-Apr, 1962

	GD2.0	FN6.0	VF8.0	NM9.4
Four Color 1255-Movie	6	18	42	80

WONDER WOMAN (See Adventure Comics #459, All-Star Comics, Brave & the Bold, DC Comics Presents, JLA, Justice League of America, Legend of..., Power Record Comics, Sensation Comics, Super Friends and World's Finest Comics (#244)

WONDER WOMAN
National Periodical Publications/All-American Publ./DC Comics:
Summer, 1942 - No. 329, Feb, 1986

	GD2.0	FN6.0	VF8.0	NM9.4
1-Origin Wonder Woman retold (more detailed than All-Star #8); H. G. Peter-c/a begins	1929	5787	13,500	27,000

1-Reprint, Oversize 13-1/2x10". **WARNING:** This comic is an exact reprint of the original except for its size. DC published it in 1974 with a second cover titling it as a Famous First Edition. There have been many reported cases of the outer cover being removed and the interior sold as the original edition. The reprint with the new outer cover removed is practically worthless. See Famous First Edition for value.

	GD2.0	FN6.0	VF8.0	NM9.4
2-Origin/1st app. Mars; Duke of Deception app.	350	1050	2188	4200
3	209	627	1307	2300
4,5: 5-1st Dr. Psycho app.	164	492	1023	1800
6-10: 6-1st Cheetah app. 10-Invasion from Saturn	127	381	795	1400
11-20	100	300	625	1100
21-30: 23-Story from Wonder Woman's childhood	84	253	525	925
31-40: 34-Robot-c. 38-Last H.G. Peter-c	59	177	369	650
41-44,46-49: 49-Used in **SOTI**, pgs. 234,236; last 52 pg. issue	50	150	300	525
45-Origin retold	91	273	568	1000
50-(44 pgs.)-Used in **POP**, pg. 97	50	150	300	525
51-60: 60-New logo	38	114	203	350
61-72: 62-Origin of W.W. i.d. 64-Story about 3-D movies. 70-1st Angle Man app. 72-Last pre-code (2/55)	33	99	174	300
73-90: 80-Origin The Invisible Plane. 85-1st S.A. issue. 89-Flying saucer-c/story	29	87	156	270
91-94,96,97,99: 97-Last H. G. Peter-a	23	69	121	210
95-A-Bomb-c	25	75	130	225
98-New origin & new art team (Andru & Esposito) begin (5/58); origin W.W. id w/new facts	26	78	139	240
100-(8/58)	26	78	139	240
101-104,106,108-110	21	63	110	185
105-(Scarce, 4/59)-W.W.'s secret origin; W. W. appears as girl (no costume yet) (called Wonder Girl - see DC Super-Stars #1)	86	258	540	950
107-1st advs. of Wonder Girl; 1st Merboy; tells how Wonder Woman won her costume	27	81	145	250
111-120	16	48	83	140
121-126: 122-1st app. Wonder Tot. 124-1st app. Wonder Woman Family. 126-Last 10¢ issue	13	39	66	110
127-130: 128-Origin The Invisible Plane retold. 129-2nd app. Wonder Woman Family (#133 is 3rd app.)	7	21	53	85
131-150: 132-Flying saucer-c	6	18	40	65
151-155,157,158,160-170 (1967): 151-Wonder Girl solo issue	4	12	30	50
156-(8/65)-Early mention of a comic book shop & comic collecting; mentions DCs selling for $100 a copy	5	15	38	60
159-Origin retold (1/66); 1st S.A. origin?	7	21	53	85
171-176	3	10	23	35
177-W. Woman/Supergirl battle	5	15	38	60
178-1st new W. Woman	6	18	40	65
179-Wears no costume to issue #203.	4	12	29	45
180-195: 180-Death of Steve Trevor. 195-Wood inks	3	9	19	28
196 (52 pgs.)-Origin-r/All-Star #8 (6 out of 9 pgs.)	3	10	23	35
197,198 (52 pgs.)-Reprints	3	10	23	35
199-Jeff Jones painted-c; 52 pgs.	4	12	29	45
200 (5-6/72)-Jeff Jones-c; 52 pgs.	5	15	34	55
201,202-Catwoman app. 202-Faffrd & The Grey Mouser debut.				
	3	9	17	24
203,205-210,212: 212-The Cavalier app.	2	6	11	16
204-Return to old costume; death of I Ching.	2	6	13	20
211,214-(100 pgs.)	4	12	30	50
213,215,216,218-220: 220-N. Adams assist	2	6	14	14
217: (68 pgs.)	2	6	15	22
221,222,224-227,229,230,233-236,238-240	1	3	6	9
223,228,231,232,237,241,248: 223-Steve Trevor revived as Steve Howard & learns W.W.'s I.D. 228-Both Wonder Women team up & new World War II stories begin, end #243. 231,232: JSA app. 237-Origin retold. 241-Intro Bouncer; Spectre app. 248-Steve Trevor Howard dies (44 pgs.)				
	1	4	7	10
242-246,252-266,269,270: 243-Both W. Women team-up again. 269-Last Wood a(i) for DC? (7/80)				6.00
247,249,251,271: 247,249 (44 pgs.). 249-Hawkgirl app. 250-Origin/1st app. Orana, the new W. Woman. 251-Orana dies. 271-Huntress & 3rd Life of Steve Trevor begin	1	3	5	7
250,251,255-262-(Whitman variants, low print run, no issue # on cover)				
	2	4	7	10
267,268-Re-intro Animal Man (5/80 & 6/80)	1	4	7	10
272-280,284-286,289,290,294-299,301-325				4.00
281-283: Joker-c/stories in Huntress back-ups	1	3	5	7
287,288,291-293: 287-New Teen Titans x-over. 288-New costume & logo.	1	3	6	7

	GD2.0	FN6.0	VF8.0	NM9.4

	GD2.0	FN6.0	VF8.0	NM9.4

291-293-Three part epic with Super-Heroines 5.00
300-($1.50, 76 pgs.)-Anniv. issue; Giffen-a; New Teen Titans, Bronze Age Sandman, JLA & G.A. Wonder Woman app.; 1st app. Lyta Trevor who becomes Fury in All-Star Squadron #25; G.A. W.W. & Steve Trevor revealed as married. 6.00
326-328 5.00

329 (Double size)-S.A. W.W. & Steve Trevor wed 1 4 7 10

NOTE: Andru/Esposito c-66-160(most). Buckler a-300. Colan a-288-305; c-288-290p. Giffen a-300p. Grell c-217. Kaluta c-297. Gil Kane c-294p, 303-305, 307, 312, 314. Miller c-298p. Morrow c-233. Nasser a-232p; c-231p, 232p. Bob Oskner c(i)-39-65(most). Perez c-283p, 284p. Spiegle a-312. Staton a(p)-241, 271-287, 289, 290, 294-299; c(p)-241, 245, 246. Huntress back-up stories 271-287, 289, 290, 294-299, 301-321.

WONDER WOMAN
DC Comics: Feb, 1987 - Present (75¢/$1.00/$1.25/$1.95/$1.99/$2.25)

0-(10/94) Zero Hour; released between #90 & #91 1 3 6 8
1-New origin; Perez-c/a begins 1 3 5 7
2-5 5.00
6-20: 9-Origin Cheetah. 12,13-Millennium x-over. 18,26-Free 16 pg. story 4.00
21-49: 24-Last Perez-a; scripts continue thru #62 3.00
50-($1.50, 52 pgs.)-New Titans, Justice League 4.00
51-62: Perez scripts. 60-Vs. Lobo; last Perez $1.00-c 3.00
63-New direction & Bolland-c begins; Deathstroke story continued from Wonder Woman Special #1 4.00
64-84 2.50
85-1st Deodato-a; ends #100 2 6 9 12
86-88: 88-Superman-c & app. 5.00
89-97: 90-(9/94)-1st Artemis. 91-(11/94). 93-Hawkman app. 96-Joker-c. 98,99 4.00
100 ($2.95, Newsstand)-Death of Artemis; Bolland-c ends. 4.00
100 ($3.95, Direct Market)-Death of Artemis; foil-c. 6.00
101-119, 121-125: 101-Begin $1.95-c; Byrne-c/a/scripts begin. 101-104-Darkseid app. 105-Phantom Stranger cameo. 106-108-Phantom Stranger & Demon app. 107,108-Arion app. 111-1st app. new Wonder Girl. 111,112-Vs.Doomsday. 112-Superman app. 113-Wonder Girl-c/app; Sugar & Spike app. 2.50
120 ($2.95)-Perez-c 3.00
126-149: 128-Hippolyta becomes new W.W. 130-133-Flash (Jay Garrick) & JSA app. 136-Diana returns to W.W. role; last Byrne issue. 137-Priest-s. 139-Luke-/Paquette-a begin; Hughes-c thru #146 2.50
150-($2.95) Hughes-c/Clark-a; Zauriel app. 3.00
151-158-Hughes-c. 153-Superboy app. 2.25
159-163: 159-Begin $2.25-c. 160,161-Clayface app. 162,163-Aquaman app. 2.25
164-171: Phil Jimenez-s/a begins; Hughes-c; Batman app. 168,169-Pérez co-plot 169-Wraparound-c.170-Lois Lane-c/app. 2.25
172-Our Worlds at War; Hippolyta killed 2.25
173,174: 173-Our Worlds at War; Darkseid app. 174-Every DC heroine app. 2.25
175-($3.50) Joker: Last Laugh; JLA app.; Jim Lee-c 3.50
176-Hughes-c 3.00
#1,000,000 (11/98) 853rd Century x-over; Deodato-c 3.00
Annual 1,2: 1 ('88, $1.50)-Art Adams-a. 2 ('89, $2.00, 68 pgs.)-All women artists issue; Perez-c(i)/a. 4.00
Annual 3 (1992, $2.50, 68 pgs.)-Quesada-c(p) 3.00
Annual 4 (1995, $3.50)-Year One 3.50
Annual 5 (1996, $2.95)-Legends of the Dead Earth story; Byrne scripts; Cockrum-a 3.00
Annual 6 (1997, $3.95)-Pulp Heroes 4.00
Annual 7,8 ('98,'99, $2.95)-7-Ghosts; Wrightson-c. 8-JLApe, A.Adams-c. 2.50
...Donna Troy (6/98, $1.95) Girlfrenzy; Jimenez-a 2.50
Gallery (1996, $3.50)-Bolland-c; pin-ups by various 4.00
...: Gods of Gotham TPB ('01, $5.95) r/#164-167; Jimenez-s/a 6.00
Lifelines TPB ('98, $9.95) r/#106-112; Byrne-c/a 10.00
...: Our Worlds at War (10/01, $2.95) History of the Amazons; Jae Lee-c 3.00
Plus 1 (1/97, $2.95)-Jesse Quick-c/app. 3.00
Second Genesis TPB (1997, $9.95)-r/#101-105 10.00
Secret Files 1,2 (3/98, 7/99, $4.95) 5.00
Special 1 (1992, $1.75, 52 pgs.)-Deathstroke-c/story continued in Wonder Woman #63 4.00
The Challenge Of Artemis TPB (1996, $9.95)-r/#94-100; Deodato-c/a 10.00

NOTE: Art Adams a-Annual 1. Byrne c/a 101-107. Bolton a-Annual 1. Deodato a-85-100. Perez

a-Annual 1; c-Annual 1(i). Quesada c(p)-Annual 3.

WONDER WOMAN: AMAZONIA
DC Comics: 1997 ($7.95, Graphic Album format, one shot)

1-Elseworlds; Messner-Loebs-s/Winslade-a 8.00

WONDER WOMAN SPECTACULAR (See DC Special Series #9)

WONDER WOMAN: SPIRIT OF TRUTH
DC Comics: Nov, 2001 ($9.95, treasury size, one-shot)

nn-Painted art by Alex Ross; story by Alex Ross and Paul Dini 10.00

WONDER WOMAN: THE ONCE AND FUTURE STORY
DC Comics: 1998 ($4.95, one-shot)

1-Trina Robbins-s/Doran & Guice-a 5.00

WONDERWORLD COMICS (Formerly Wonder Comics)
Fox Features Syndicate: No. 3, July, 1939 - No. 33, Jan, 1942

3-Intro The Flame by Fine; Dr. Fung (Powell-a), K-51 (Powell-a?), & Yarko the Great, Master Magician (Eisner-a) continues; Eisner/Fine-c	630	1890	4100	8200
4-Lou Fine-c	308	924	1927	3700
5,6,9,10: Lou Fine-c	175	525	1094	1925
7-Classic Lou Fine-c	295	885	1844	3250
8-Classic Lou Fine-c	245	735	1534	2700
11-Origin The Flame	132	395	825	1450
12-15:13-Dr. Fung ends; last Fine-c	111	332	694	1225
16-20	82	245	511	900
21-Origin The Black Lion & Cub	75	225	469	825
22-27: 22,25-Dr. Fung app.	61	182	381	675
28-Origin & 1st app. U.S. Jones (8/41); Lu-Nar, the Moon Man begins	82	245	511	900
29,31,33	50	150	300	525
30-Intro & Origin Flame Girl	89	268	556	975
32-Hitler-c	68	204	426	750

NOTE: Spies at War by Eisner in #13, 17. Yarko by Eisner in #3-11. Eisner text illos-3. Lou Fine a-3-11; c-3-13, 15; text illos-4. Nordling a-4-14. Powell a-3-12. Tuska a-5-9. Bondage-c 14, 15, 28, 31, 32. Cover features: The Flame-#3, 5-31; U.S. Jones-#32, 33.

WONDERWORLDS
Innovation Publishing: 1992 ($3.50, squarebound, 100 pgs.)

1-Rebound super-hero comics, contents may vary; Hero Alliance, Terraformers, etc. 3.50

WOODSY OWL (See March of Comics #395)
Gold Key: Nov, 1973 - No. 10, Feb, 1976

1	2	6	12	18
2-10	1	4	7	10

WOODY WOODPECKER (Walter Lantz... #73 on?)(See Dell Giants for annuals)(Also see The Funnies, Jolly Jingles, Kite Fun Book, New Funnies)
Dell Publishing Co./Gold Key No. 73-187/Whitman No. 188 on:
No. 169, 10/47 - No. 72, 5-7/62; No. 73, 10/62 - No. 201, 3/84 (nn 192)

Four Color 169(#1)-Drug turns Woody into a Mr. Hyde				
	16	48	112	210
Four Color 188	10	30	70	135
Four Color 202,232,249,264,288	7	21	49	85
Four Color 305,336,350	5	15	34	55
Four Color 364,374,390,405,416,431('52)	4	12	30	50
16 (1-2/52-53) - 30('55)	3	10	23	35
31-50	3	9	20	30
51-72 (Last Dell)	2	6	15	22
73-75 (Giants, 84 pgs.), Gold Key	4	12	30	50
76-80	2	6	13	20
81-103: 103-Last 12¢ issue	2	6	11	16
104-120	2	6	10	14
121-140	1	4	7	10
141-160	1	3	6	8
161-187	1	3	5	7
188,189 (Whitman)	1	3	6	9
190(9/80),191(11/80)-pre-pack?	2	6	11	15
(No #192)				
193-197: 196(2/82), 197(4/82)	2	6	9	12
198-201 (All #90062 on-c, no date or date code, pre-pack): 198(6/83), 197(9/83),				

The World Around Us #11 © GIL

World of Archie #13 © AP

World of Fantasy #7 © MAR

	GD2.0	FN6.0	VF8.0	NM9.4

200(8/83), 201(3/84) 2 6 10 14
Christmas Parade 1(11/68-Giant)(G.K.) 4 12 26 40
Summer Fun 1(6/66-G.K.)(84 pgs.) 4 12 30 50
NOTE: 15¢ Canadian editions of the 12¢ issues exist. Reprints-No. 92, 102, 103, 105, 106, 124, 125, 152, 153, 157, 162, 165, 194(1/3)-200(1/3).

WOODY WOODPECKER (See Comic Album #5,9,13, Dell Giant #24, 40, 54, Dell Giants, The Funnies, Golden Comics Digest #1, 3, 5, 8, 15, 16, 20, 24, 32, 37, 44, March of Comics #16, 34, 85, 93, 109, 124, 139, 158, 177, 184, 203, 222, 239, 249, 261, 420, 454, 466, 478, New Funnies & Super Book #12, 24)

WOODY WOODPECKER
Harvey Comics: Sept, 1991 - No. 7, 1993 ($1.25)

1-7: 1-r/W.W. #53 2.50
50th Anniversary Special 1 (10/91, $2.50, 68 pgs.) 3.00

WOODY WOODPECKER AND FRIENDS
Harvey Comics: Dec, 1991 - No. 4, 1992 ($1.25)

1-4 2.50

WORDSMITH (1st Series)
Renegade Press: Aug, 1985 - No. 12, Jan, 1988 ($1.70/$2.00, B&W, bi-monthly)

1-12: R. G. Taylor-c/a 3.00

WORDSMITH (2nd Series)
Caliber: 1996 - No. 9, 1997 ($2.95, B&W, limited series)

1-9: Reprints in all. 1-Contains 3 pg. sketchbook. 6-Flip book w/Raven Chronicles #10 3.00

WORD WARRIORS (Also see Quest for Dreams Lost)
Literacy Volunteers of Chicago: 1987 ($1.50, B&W)(Proceeds donated to help literacy)

1-Jon Sable by Grell, Ms. Tree, Streetwolf; Chaykin-c 3.00

WORLD AROUND US, THE (Illustrated Story of...)
Gilberton Publishers (Classics Illustrated): Sep, 1958 -No. 36, Oct, 1961 (25¢)

1-Dogs; Evans-a 8 24 42 60
2-4: 2-Indians; Check-a. 3-Horses; L. B. Cole-c. 4-Railroads; L. B. Cole-a
(5 pgs.) 8 24 42 60
5-Space; Ingels-a 10 30 55 80
6-The F.B.I.; Disbrow, Evans, Ingels-a 10 30 55 80
7-Pirates; Disbrow, Ingels, Kinstler-a 9 27 49 70
8-Flight; Evans, Ingels, Crandall-a 9 27 49 70
9-Army; Disbrow, Ingels, Orlando-a 8 24 42 60
10-13: 10-Navy; Disbrow, Kinstler-a. 11-Marine Corps. 12-Coast Guard;
Ingels-a (9 pgs.). 13-Air Force; L.B. Cole-c 8 24 42 60
14-French Revolution; Crandall, Evans, Kinstler-a 10 30 55 80
15-Prehistoric Animals; Al Williamson-a, 6 & 10 pgs. plus Morrow-a
10 30 55 85
16-18: 16-Crusades; Kinstler-a. 17-Festivals; Evans, Crandall-a. 18-Great
Scientists; Crandall, Evans, Torres, Williamson, Morrow-a
9 27 49 70
19-Jungle; Crandall, Williamson, Morrow-a 10 30 55 85
20-Communications; Crandall, Evans, Torres-a 10 30 55 80
21-American Presidents; Crandall/Evans, Morrow-a 10 30 55 80
22-Boating; Morrow-a 7 21 38 55
23-Great Explorers; Crandall, Evans, Torres-a 9 27 49 70
24-Ghosts; Morrow-a 10 30 55 80
25-Magic; Evans, Morrow-a 10 30 55 80
26-The Civil War 11 33 55 95
27-Mountains (High Advs.); Crandall/Evans, Morrow, Torres-a
9 27 49 70
28-Whaling; Crandall, Evans, Morrow, Torres, Wildey-a; L.B. Cole-c
9 27 49 70
29-Vikings; Crandall, Evans, Torres, Morrow-a 10 30 55 85
30-Undersea Adventure; Crandall/Evans, Kirby, Morrow, Torres-a
10 30 55 80
31-Hunting; Crandall/Evans, Ingels, Kinstler, Kirby-a 9 27 49 70
32,33: 32-For Gold & Glory; Morrow, Kirby, Crandall, Evans-a. 33-Famous
Teens; Crandall, Kirby, Evans-a 9 27 49 70
34-36: 34-Fishing; Crandall/Evans-a. 35-Spies; Kirby, Morrow?, Evans-a.
36-Fight for Life (Medicine); Kirby-a 9 27 49 70
NOTE: See Classics Illustrated Special Edition. Another World Around Us issue entitled The Sea
had been prepared in 1962 but was never published in the U.S. It was published in the

British/European World Around Us series. Those series then continued with seven additional WAU titles not in the U.S. series.

WORLD BELOW, THE
Dark Horse Comics: Mar, 1999 - No. 4, Jun, 1999 ($2.50, limited series)

1-4-Paul Chadwick-s/c/a 2.50

WORLD BELOW, THE: DEEPER AND STRANGER
Dark Horse Comics: Dec, 1999 - No. 4, Mar, 2000 ($2.95, B&W)

1-4-Paul Chadwick-s/c/a 3.00

WORLD FAMOUS HEROES MAGAZINE
Comic Corp. of America (Centaur): Oct, 1941 - No. 4, Apr, 1942 (comic book)

1-Gustavson-c; Lubbers, Glanzman-a; Davy Crockett, Paul Revere, Lewis &
Clark, John Paul Jones stories; Flag-c 116 348 725 1275
2-Lou Gehrig life story; Lubbers-a 50 150 300 525
3,4-Lubbers-a. 4-Wild Bill Hickok story, 2 pg. Marlene Dietrich story
45 135 270 475

WORLD FAMOUS STORIES
Croyden Publishers: 1945

1-Ali Baba, Hansel & Gretel, Rip Van Winkle, Mid-Summer Night's Dream
14 42 72 120

WORLD IS HIS PARISH, THE
George A. Pflaum: 1953 (15¢)

nn-The story of Pope Pius XII 5 15 24 32

WORLD OF ADVENTURE (Walt Disney's...)(TV)
Gold Key: Apr, 1963 - No. 3, Oct, 1963 (12¢)

1-Disney TV characters; Savage Sam, Johnny Shiloh, Capt. Nemo, The
Mooncussers 3 9 21 32
2,3 2 6 13 30

WORLD OF ARCHIE, THE (See Archie Giant Series Mag. #148, 151, 156, 160, 165, 171, 177, 182, 188, 193, 200, 208, 213, 225, 232, 237, 244, 249, 456, 461, 468, 473, 480, 485, 492, 497, 504, 509, 516, 521, 532, 543, 554, 565, 574, 587, 599, 612, 627)

WORLD OF ARCHIE
Archie Comics: Aug, 1992 - No. 26 ($1.25/$1.50)

1 4.00
2-15: 9-Neon ink-c 3.00
16-26 2.50

WORLD OF FANTASY
Atlas Comics (CPC No. 1-15/ZPC No. 16-19): May, 1956 - No. 19, Aug, 1959

1 45 135 270 475
2-Williamson-a (4 pgs.) 33 99 174 300
3-Sid Check, Roussos-a 29 87 153 265
4-7 22 66 116 195
8-Matt Fox, Orlando, Berg-a 23 69 121 205
9-Krigstein-a 22 66 116 200
10-15: 11-Torres-a 18 54 94 155
16-Williamson-a (4 pgs.); Ditko, Kirby-a 25 75 130 225
17-19-Ditko, Kirby-a 25 75 130 225
NOTE: Ayers a-3. B. Baily a-4. Berg a-5, 6, 8. Brodsky c-3. Check a-3. Ditko a-17, 19. Everett
a-2; c-4-7, 9, 12, 13. Forte a-4. Infantino a-14. Kirby c-15, 17-19. Krigstein a-9. Maneely c-2,
14. Mooney a-14. Morrow a-7. Orlando a-8, 13, 14. Pakula a-9. Powell a-4, 6. R.Q. Sale a-3, 9.
Severin c-1.

WORLD OF GIANT COMICS, THE (See Archie All-Star Specials under Archie Comics)

WORLD OF GINGER FOX, THE (Also see Ginger Fox)
Comico: Nov, 1986 ($6.95, 8 1/2 x 11", 68 pgs., mature)

Graphic Novel ($6.95) 7.00
Hardcover ($27.95) 28.00

WORLD OF JUGHEAD, THE (See Archie Giant Series Mag. #9, 14, 19, 24, 30, 136, 143, 149, 152, 157, 161, 166, 172, 178, 183, 189, 194, 202, 209, 215, 227, 233, 239, 245, 251, 457, 463, 469, 475, 481, 487, 493, 499, 505, 511, 517, 523, 531, 542, 553, 564, 577, 590, 602)

WORLD OF KRYPTON, THE (World of...#3) (See Superman #248)
DC Comics, Inc.: 7/79 - No. 3, 9/79; 12/87 - No. 4, 3/88 (Both are lim. series)

1-3 40¢; 1st comic book mini-series): 1-Jor-El marries Lara. 3-Baby
Superman sent to Earth; Krypton explodes; Mon-el app. 5.00
1-4 (75¢)-Byrne scripts; Byrne/Simonson-c 3.00

WORLD OF METROPOLIS, THE

World of Wheels #25 © CC

World's Finest Comics #6 © DC

World's Finest Comics #201 © DC

	GD2.0	FN6.0	VF8.0	NM9.4

	GD2.0	FN6.0	VF8.0	NM9.

DC Comics: Aug, 1988 - No. 4, July, 1988 ($1.00, limited series)

1-4: Byrne scripts				3.00

WORLD OF MYSTERY
Atlas Comics (GPI): June, 1956 - No. 7, July, 1957

1-Torres, Orlando-a; Powell-a?	45	135	270	475
2-Woodish-a	20	60	105	175
3-Torres, Davis, Ditko-a	25	75	130	225
4-Pakula, Powell-a	25	75	130	225
5,7: 5-Orlando-a	20	60	105	175
6-Williamson/Mayo-a (4 pgs.); Ditko-a; Crandall text illo	25	75	130	225

NOTE: **Brodsky** c-2. **Colan** a-7. **Everett** c-1, 3. **Pakula** a-4, 6. **Romita** a-2. **Severin** c-7.

WORLD OF SMALLVILLE
DC Comics: Apr, 1988 - No. 4, July, 1988 (75¢, limited series)

1-4: Byrne scripts				3.00

WORLD OF SUSPENSE
Atlas News Co.: Apr, 1956 - No. 8, July, 1957

1	40	120	220	380
2-Ditko-a (4 pgs.)	24	72	127	220
3,7-Williamson-a in both (4 pgs.); #7-with Mayo	24	72	127	215
4-6,8	20	60	105	175

NOTE: **Berg** a-6. **Cameron** a-2. **Ditko** a-2. **Drucker** a-1. **Everett** a-1, 5; c-6. **Heck** a-5. **Maneely** a-1; c-1-3. **Orlando** a-5. **Powell** a-6. **Reinman** a-4. **Roussos** a-6. **Shores** a-1.

WORLD OF WHEELS (Formerly Dragstrip Hotrodders)
Charlton Comics: No. 17, Oct, 1967 - No. 32, June, 1970

17-20-Features Ken King	3	9	19	28
21-32-Features Ken King	2	6	15	22
Modern Comics Reprint 23(1978)				5.00

WORLD OF WOOD
Eclipse Comics: 1986 - No. 4, 1987; No. 5, 2/89 ($1.75, limited series)

1-4:1-Dave Stevens-c. 2-Wood/Stevens-c				3.00
5 ($2.00, B&W)-r/Avon's Flying Saucers				4.00

WORLD'S BEST COMICS (World's Finest Comics #2 on)
National Per. Publications (100 pgs.): Spring, 1941 (Cardboard-c)(DC's 6th annual format comic)

1-The Batman, Superman, Crimson Avenger, Johnny Thunder, The King, Young Dr. Davis, Zatara, Lando, Man of Magic, & Red, White & Blue begin; Superman, Batman & Robin covers begin (inside-c is blank); Fred Ray-c; 15¢ cover price	1429	4287	10,000	19,000

WORLDS BEYOND (Stories of Weird Adventure)(Worlds of Fear #2 on)
Fawcett Publications: Nov, 1951

1-Powell, Bailey-a; Moldoff-c	43	129	257	450

WORLDS COLLIDE
DC Comics: July, 1994 ($2.50, one-shot)

1-($2.50, 52 pgs.)-Milestone & Superman titles x-over				2.50
1-($3.95, 52 pgs.)-Polybagged w/vinyl clings				4.00

WORLD'S FAIR COMICS (See New York...)

WORLD'S FINEST (Also see Legends of The World's Finest)
DC Comics: 1990 - No. 3, 1990 ($3.95, squarebound, limited series, 52 pgs.)

1-3: Batman & Superman team-up against The Joker and Lex Luthor; Dave Gibbons scripts & Steve Rude-c/a. 2,3-Joker/Luthor painted-c by Steve Rude				5.00
TPB-($19.95) r/#1-3				20.00

WORLD'S FINEST COMICS (Formerly World's Best Comics #1)
National Periodical Publ./DC Comics: No. 2, Sum, 1941 - No. 323, Jan, 1986
(#1-17 have cardboard covers) (#2-9 have 100 pgs.)

2 (100 pgs.)-Superman, Batman & Robin covers continue from World's Best; (cover price 15¢ #2-70)	423	1269	2750	5500
3-The Sandman begins; last Johnny Thunder; origin & 1st app. The Scarecrow	317	951	1979	3800
4-Hop Harrigan app.; last Young Dr. Davis	255	765	1591	2800
5-Intro. TNT & Dan the Dyna-Mite; last King & Crimson Avenger	255	765	1591	2800

6-Star Spangled Kid begins (Sum/42); Aquaman app.; S&K Sandman with Sandy in new costume begins, ends #7	191	573	1194	2100
7-Green Arrow begins (Fall/42); last Lando & Red, White & Blue; S&K art	191	573	1194	2100
8-Boy Commandos begin (by Simon(p) #12); last The King	177	531	1106	1950
9-Batman cameo in Star Spangled Kid; S&K-a; last 100 pg. issue; Hitler, Mussolini, Tojo-c	200	600	1250	2200
10-S&K-a; 76 pg. issues begin	159	477	994	1750
11-17: 17-Last cardboard cover issue	136	408	852	1500
18-20: 18-Paper covers begin; last Star Spangled Kid. 20-Last quarterly issue	116	348	725	1275
21-30: 21-Begin bi-monthly. 30-Johnny Everyman app.	84	253	525	925
31-40: 33-35-Tomahawk app.	75	225	469	825
41-50: 41-Boy Commandos end. 42-Intro The Wyoming Kid & begins (9-10/49), ends #63. 43-Full Steam Foley begins, ends #48. 48-Last square binding.				
49-Tom Sparks, Boy Inventor begins; robot-c	55	165	341	600
51-60: 51-Zatara ends. 54-Last 76 pg. issue. 59-Manhunters Around the World begins (7-8/52), ends #62	55	165	341	600
61-64: 61-Joker story. 63-Capt. Compass app.	55	165	331	580
65-Origin Superman; Tomahawk begins (7-8/53), ends #101	77	231	483	850
66-70-(15¢ issues, scarce)-Last 15¢, 68pg. issue	55	165	331	580
71-(10¢ issue, scarce)-Superman & Batman begin as team (7-8/54); were in separate stories until now; Superman & Batman exchange identities; 10¢ issues begin	89	267	668	1250
72,73-(10¢ issue, scarce)	61	183	458	860
74-Last pre-code issue	48	144	360	675
75-(1st code approved, 3-4/55)	45	135	338	625
76-80: 77-Superman loses powers & Batman obtains them this issue only	35	105	263	475
81-90: 84-1st S.A. issue. 88-1st Joker/Luthor team-up. 89-2nd Batmen of All Nations (aka Club of Heroes) (10/57), 3rd app. anywhere) plus-c app.	28	85	196	350
91-93,95-99: 96-99-Kirby Green Arrow. 99-Robot-c	21	63	146	260
94-Origin Superman/Batman team retold	54	162	405	750
100 (3/59)	35	105	263	475
101-110: 102-Tommy Tomorrow begins, ends #124	15	45	105	180
111-121: 111-1st app. The Clock King. 113-Intro. Miss Arrowette in Green Arrow; 1st Bat-Mite/Mr. Mxyzptlk team-up (11/60). 117-Batwoman-c.				
121-Last 10¢ issue	12	36	84	140
122-128: 123-2nd Bat-Mite/Mr. Mxyzptlk team-up (2/62). 125-Aquaman begins (5/62), ends #139 (Aquaman #1 is dated 1-2/62)	8	24	60	100
129-Joker/Luthor team-up-c/story	10	30	70	120
130-142: 135-Last Dick Sprang story. 140-Last Green Arrow; last Clayface until Action #443. 142-Origin The Composite Superman (villain); Legion app.	7	21	50	80
143-150: 143-1st Mailbag	5	15	38	60
151-153,155,157-160: 156-Intro of Bizarro Batman. 157-2nd Super Sons story; last app. Kathy Kane (Bat-woman) until Batman Family #10	4	12	30	50
154-1st Super Sons story; last Bat-Woman in costume until Batman Family #10.	5	15	38	60
156-1st Bizarro Batman; Joker-c/story	10	30	70	120
161,170 (80-Pg. Giants G-28,G-40)	5	15	38	60
162-165,167,168,171,172: 168,172-Adult Legion app.	3	10	23	35
166-Joker-c/story	4	12	29	45
169-3rd app. new Batgirl(9/67)(cover and 1 panel cameo); 3rd Bat-Mite/Mr. Mxyzptlk team-up	4	12	26	40
173-('68)-1st S.A. app. Two-Face as Batman becomes Two-Face in story	8	24	60	100
174-Adams-c	4	12	25	38
175,176-Neal Adams-c/a; both reprint J'onn J'onzz origin/Detective #225,226	4	12	27	42
177-Joker/Luthor team-up-c/story	4	12	25	38
178,180,182,183,185,186: Adams-c on all. 182-Silent Knight-r/Brave & Bold #6. 185-Last 12¢ issue. 186-Johnny Quick-r	3	9	20	30
179-(80 Page Giant G-52) -Adams-c; r/#94	4	12	30	50

856

World's Finest: Our Worlds at War #1 © DC

Worlds of Fear #10 © FAW

The Worst From Mad #12 © E.C. Publ.

WO

	GD2.0	FN6.0	VF8.0	NM9.4

181,184,187: 187-Green Arrow origin-r by Kirby (Adv. #256)

	3	9	19	28
188,197:(Giants G-64, G-76; 64 pages)	4	12	29	45
189-196: 190-193-Robin-r	2	6	15	22

198,199-3rd Superman/Flash race (see Flash #175 & Superman #199)

199-Adams-c	8	24	56	90
200-Adams-c	3	9	19	28
201-203: 203-Last 15¢ issue.	2	6	13	20

204,205-(48 pgs.) Adams-c. 204-Wonder Woman app. 205-Shining Knight-r

(6 pgs.) by Frazetta/Adv. #153; Teen Titans x-over	3	9	17	25
206 (Giant G-88, 64 pgs.)	4	12	26	40
207,212: 207-(48 pgs.). 212-(25¢, 52 pgs.)	2	6	15	22

208-211(25¢-c) Adams-c: 208-(48 pgs). Origin Robotman-r/Det. #138.

209-211-(52 pgs.)	2	6	13	20

213,214,216-222,229: 217-Metamorpho begins, ends #220; Batman/Superman team-ups resume. 229-r/origin Superman-Batman team

	2	6	10	14
215-Intro. Batman Jr. & Superman Jr.	3	9	17	26

223-228-(100 pgs.). 223-N. Adams-r. 223-Deadman origin. 226-N. Adams, S&K, Toth-r; Manhunter part origin-r/Det. #225,226. 227-Deadman app.

	3	10	23	35
230-(68 pgs.)	2	6	13	20

231-243,247,248: 242-Super Sons. 248-Last Vigilante

	2	6	9	12

244-246-Adams-c: 244-$1.00, 84 pg. issues begin; Green Arrow, Black Canary, Wonder Woman, Vigilante begin; 246-Death of Stuff in Vigilante; origin Vigilante retold

	2	6	11	15

249-252 (84 pgs.) Ditko-a: 249-The Creeper begins by Ditko, 84 pgs. 250-The Creeper origin retold by Ditko. 252-Last 84 pg. issue

	2	6	11	15

253-257,259-265: 253-Capt. Marvel begins; 68 pgs. begin, end #265. 255-Last Creeper. 256-Hawkman begins. 257-Black Lightning begins. 263-Super Sons. 264-Clay Face app.

	1	3	6	8
258-Adams-c	1	3	6	8

266-270,272-282-(52 pgs.). 267-Challengers of the Unknown app.; 3 Lt. Marvels return. 268-Capt. Marvel Jr. origin retold. 274-Zatanna begins. 279, 280-Capt. Marvel Jr. & Kid Eternity learn they are brothers

	1	3	5	7
271-(52pgs.) Origin Superman/Batman team retold	1	3	6	8
283-299: 284-Legion app.	1	3	5	7

300-($1.25, 52pgs.)-Justice League of America, New Teen Titans & The Outsiders app.; Perez-a (3 pgs.) ... 5.00

301-322: 304-Origin Null and Void. 309,319-Free 16 pg. story in each

(309-Flash Force 2000, 319-Mask preview)				3.00
323-Last issue				5.00

NOTE: *Neal Adams* a-230r; c-174-176, 178-180, 182, 183, 185, 186, 199-205, 208-211, 244-246, 258. *Austin* a-244-246i. *Burnley* a-8, 10; c-7-9, 11-14, 15p?, 16-18p, 20-31p. *Colan* a-274p, 297, 299. *Ditko* a-249-255. *Giffen* a-322; c-284p, 322. *G. Kane* a-38, 174r, 282, 283; c-281, 282, 289. *Kirby* a-187. *Kubert* Zatara-40-44. *Miller* c-285p. *Mooney* c-134. *Morrow* a-245-248. *Mortimer* c-16-21, 26-71. *Nasser* a(p)-244-246, 259, 260. *Newton* a-253-281p. *Orlando* a-224r. *Perez* a-300i; c-271, 276, 277p, 278p. *Fred Ray* c-1-5. *Fred Ray/Robinson* c-13-16. *Robinson* a-2, 9, 13-15; c-6. *Rogers* a-259p. *Roussos* a-212r. *Simonson* c-291. *Spiegle* a-275-278, 284. *Staton* a-262p, 273p. *Swan/Mortimer* c-126. *Swan/Mortimer* c-79-82. *Toth* a-224r. *Tuska* a-230r, 250p, 252p, 254p, 257p, 283p, 284p, 308p. Boy Commandos by *Infantino* #39-41.

WORLD'S FINEST COMICS DIGEST (See DC Special Series #23)

WORLD'S FINEST: OUR WORLDS AT WAR
DC Comics: Oct, 2001 ($2.95, one-shot)

1-Concludes the Our Worlds at War x-over; Jae Lee-c; art by various ... 3.00

WORLD'S GREATEST ATHLETE (See Walt Disney Showcase #14)

WORLD'S GREATEST SONGS
Atlas Comics (Male): Sept, 1954

1-(Scarce)-Heath & Harry Anderson-a; Eddie Fisher life story plus-c; gives

lyrics to Frank Sinatra song "Young at Heart"	40	120	220	380

WORLD'S GREATEST STORIES
Jubilee Publications: Jan, 1949 - No. 2, May, 1949

1-Alice in Wonderland; Lewis Carroll adapt.	35	105	185	320
2-Pinocchio	33	99	174	300

WORLDS OF FEAR (Stories of Weird Adventure)(Formerly Worlds Beyond #1)
Fawcett Publications: V1#2, Jan, 1952 - V2#10, June, 1953

V1#2	43	129	257	450
3-Evans-a	40	120	220	380
4-6(9/52)	35	105	185	320
V2#7-9	31	93	165	285

10-Saunders painted-c; man with no eyes surrounded by eyeballs plus

eyes ripped out story	68	204	426	750

NOTE: *Moldoff* c-2-8. *Powell* a-2, 4, 5. *Sekowsky* a-4, 5.

WORLDS UNKNOWN
Marvel Comics Group: May, 1973 - No. 8, Aug, 1974

1-r/from Astonishing #54; Torres, Reese-a	2	6	12	18
2-8	2	6	9	12

NOTE: *Adkins/Mooney* a-5. *Buscema* c/a-4p. *W. Howard* c/a-3i. *Kane* a(p)-1,2; c(p)-5, 6, 8. *Sutton* a-2. *Tuska* a(p)-7, 8; c-7p. No. 7, 8 has Golden Voyage of Sinbad movie adaptation.

WORLD WAR STORIES
Dell Publishing Co.: Apr-June, 1965 - No. 3, Dec, 1965

1-Glanzman-a in all	4	12	26	40
2,3	3	9	17	25

WORLD WAR II (See Classics Illustrated Special Issue)

WORLD WAR II: 1946
Antarctic Press: Oct, 1998 - No. 2 ($3.95, B&W)

1,2-Nomura-a/a				4.00

WORLD WAR III
Ace Periodicals: Mar, 1953 - No. 2, May, 1953

1-(Scarce)-Atomic bomb blast-c; Cameron-a	64	192	398	700

2-Used in POP, pg. 78 & B&W & color illos; Cameron-a

	55	165	341	600

WORLD WITHOUT END
DC Comics: 1990 - No. 6, 1991 ($2.50, limited series, mature, stiff-c)

1-6: Horror/fantasy; all painted-c/a				2.50

WORLD WRESTLING FEDERATION BATTLEMANIA
Valiant: 1991 - No. 5?, 1991 ($2.50, magazine size, 68 pgs.)

1-5: 5-Includes 2 free pull-out posters				4.00

WORST FROM MAD, THE (Annual)
E. C. Comics: 1958 - No. 12, 1969 (Each annual cover is reprinted from the cover of the Mad issues being reprinted)(Value is 1/2 if bonus is missing)

nn(1958)-Bonus; record labels & travel stickers; 1st Mad annual; r/Mad #29-34

	41	123	246	425

2(1959)-Bonus is small 33⅓ rpm record entitled "Meet the Staff of Mad"; r/Mad #35-40

	41	123	246	425

3(1960)-Has 20x30" campaign poster "Alfred E. Neuman for President"; r/Mad #41-46

	19	57	134	240
4(1961)-Sunday comics section; r/Mad #47-54	18	54	123	220
5(1962)-Has 33-1/3 record; r/Mad #55-62	28	84	196	350
6(1963)-Has 33-1/3 record; r/Mad #63-70	28	84	196	350
7(1964)-Mad protest signs; r/Mad #71-76	10	30	73	125
8(1965)-Build a Mad Zeppelin	13	39	91	155
9(1966)-33-1/3 rpm record; Beatles on-c	19	57	132	235
10(1967)-Mad bumper sticker	7	21	50	80
11(1968)-Mad cover window stickers	6	18	45	75
12(1969)-Mad picture postcards; Orlando-a	6	18	45	75

NOTE: Covers: *Bob Clarke*-#8. *Mingo*-#7, 9-12.

WOTALIFE COMICS (Formerly Nutty Life #2; Phantom Lady #13 on)
Fox Features Syndicate/Norien Mag.: No. 3, Aug-Sept, 1946 - No. 12, July, 1947; 1959

3-Cosmo Cat, Li'l Pan, stories begin	10	30	55	85
4-12-Cosmo Cat, Li'l Pan in all	8	24	45	65

1(1959-Norlen)-Atomic Rabbit, Atomic Mouse; reprints cover to #6; reprints

entire book?	7	21	38	55

WOTALIFE COMICS
Green Publications: 1957 - No. 5, 1957

1	6	18	32	45
2-5	5	15	23	30

WOW COMICS
Henle Publishing Co.: July, 1936 - No. 4, Nov, 1936 (52 pgs., magazine size)

Wow Comics #9 © FAW

Wyatt Earp Frontier Marshall #27 © CC

Xena: Warrior Princess - The Dragon's Teeth #2 © Studios USA

	GD2.0	FN6.0	VF8.0	NM9.4

1-Buck Jones in "The Phantom Rider" (1st app. in comics), Fu Manchu; Capt.
Scott Dalton begins; Eisner-a; Briefer-c — 273 819 1705 3000
2-Ken Maynard, Fu Manchu, Popeye by Segar plus article on Popeye;
Eisner-a — 200 600 1250 2200
3-Eisner-c/a(3); Popeye by Segar, Fu Manchu, Hiram Hick by Bob Kane,
Space Limited app.); Jimmy Dempsey talks about Popeye's punch; Bob
Ripley Believe it or Not begins; Briefer-a — 182 546 1136 2000
4-Flash Gordon by Raymond, Mandrake, Popeye by Segar, Tillie The Toiler,
Fu Manchu, Hiram Hick by Bob Kane; Eisner-a(3); Briefer-c/a — 223 1189 1394 2450

WOW COMICS (Real Western Hero #70 on)(See XMas Comics)
Fawcett Publ.: Winter, 1940-41; No. 2, Summer, 1941 - No. 69, Fall, 1948

nn(#1)-Origin Mr. Scarlet by S&K; Atom Blake, Boy Wizard, Jim Dolan, & Rick
O'Shay begin; Diamond Jack, The White Rajah, & Shipwreck Roberts, only
app.; 1st mention of Gotham City in comics; the cover was printed on
unstable paper stock and is rarely found in fine or mint condition; blank
inside(-c) by Beck — 1214 3642 8500 17,000
2 (Scarce)-The Hunchback begins — 236 708 1477 2600
3 (Fall, 1941) — 114 342 713 1250
4-Origin & 1st app. Pinky — 118 354 738 1300
5 — 75 225 469 825
6-Origin & 1st app. The Phantom Eagle (7/15/42); Commando Yank begins
— 75 225 469 825
7,8,10: 10-Swayze-c/a on Mary Marvel — 59 177 369 650
9 (1/6/43)-Capt. Marvel, Capt. Marvel Jr., Shazam app.; Scarlet & Pinky
x-over; Mary Marvel-c/stories begin (cameo #9) 127 381 795 1400
11-17,19,20: 15-Flag-c — 45 135 270 475
18-1st app. Uncle Marvel (10/43); infinity-c — 47 140 286 500
21-30: 23-Robot-c. 28-Phony x-over in Mary Marvel — 29 87 156 270
31-40: 32-68-Phantom Eagle by Swayze — 20 60 105 180
41-50 — 19 57 99 165
51-58: Last Mary Marvel — 17 51 88 150
59-69: 59-Ozzie (teenage) begins. 62-Flying Saucer gag-c (1/48). 65-69-Tom
Mix stories (cont'd in Real Western Hero) — 15 45 77 130
NOTE: Cover features: Mr. Scarlet-#1-5; Commando Yank-#6, 7, (w/Mr. Scarlet #8); Mary Marvel-
#9-56, (w/Commando Yank-#46-50), (w/Mr. Scarlet & Commando Yank-#51), (w/Mr. Scarlet & Pinky
#53), (w/Phantom Eagle #54, 56), (w/Commando Yank & Phantom Eagle #58); Ozzie-#59-69.

WRATH (Also see Prototype #4)
Malibu Comics: Jan, 1994 - No. 9, Nov, 1995 ($1.95)

1-9: 2-Mantra x-over. 3-Intro/1st app. Slayer. 4,5-Freex app. 8-Mantra &
Warstrike app. 9-Prime app. — 2.25
1-Ultra 5000 Limited silver foil — 4.00
Giant Size 1 (2.50, 44 pgs.) — 2.50

WRATH OF THE SPECTRE, THE
DC Comics: May, 1988 - No. 4, Aug, 1988 ($2.50, limited series)

1-3: Aparo-r/Adventure #431-440 — 4.00
4-New stories — 5.00

WRECK OF GROSVENOR (See Superior Stories #3)

WRETCH, THE
Caliber: 1996 ($2.95, B&W)

1-Phillip Hester-a/scripts — 3.00

WRETCH, THE
Amaze Ink: 1997 - No. 4, 1998 ($2.95, B&W)

1-4: Phillip Hester-a/scripts — 3.00

WRINGLE WRANGLE (Disney)
Dell Publishing Co.: No. 821, July, 1957

Four Color 821-Based on movie "Westward Ho, the Wagons"; Marsh-a; Fess
Parker photo-c — 8 24 56 100

WULF THE BARBARIAN
Atlas/Seaboard Publ.: Feb, 1975 - No. 4, Sept, 1975

1,2: 1-Origin; Janson-a. 2-Intro. Berithe the Swordswoman; Janson-a w/Neal
Adams, Wood, Reese-a assists — 1 3 6 8
3,4: 3-Skeates-a. 4-Friedrich-s — 6.00

WYATT EARP
Atlas Comics/Marvel No. 23 on (IPC): Nov, 1955 - #29, June, 1960; #30, Oct,

1972 - #34, June, 1973

1 — 22 66 116 200
2-Williamson-a (4 pgs.) — 14 42 72 120
3-6,8-11: 3-Black Bart app. 8-Wild Bill Hickok app. 11 33 55 90
7,12-Williamson-a, 4 pgs. ea.; #12 with Mayo 11 33 55 90
13-20: 17-1st app. Wyatt's deputy, Grizzly Grant 10 30 55 80
21-Davis-c — 9 27 49 70
22-24,26-29: 22-Ringo Kid app. 23-Kid From Texas app. 29-Last 10¢ issue
— 7 21 38 55
25-Davis-a — 8 24 42 60
30-Williamson-r (1972) — 2 6 12 18
31-34-Reprints. 32-Torres-a(r) — 2 6 11 15
NOTE: Ayers a-8, 10(2), 17, 20(4). Berg a-9. Everett c-6. Kirby c-25, 29. Maneely a-1; c-1-4, 8,
12, 17, 20. Maurer a-2(2), 3(4), 4(4), 8(4). Severin a-4, 9(4), 10; c-2, 9, 10, 14. Wildey a-5, 17,
24, 28.

WYATT EARP (TV) (Hugh O'Brian Famous Marshal)
Dell Publishing Co.: No. 860, Nov, 1957 - No. 13, Dec-Feb, 1960-61 (Hugh
O'Brian photo-c)

Four Color 860 (#1)-Manning-a — 10 30 70 130
Four Color 890,921(6/58)-All Manning-a — 7 21 49 95
4 (9-11/58) - 12-Manning-a. 5-Photo back-c — 5 15 35 60
13-Toth-a — 5 15 35 65

WYATT EARP FRONTIER MARSHAL (Formerly Range Busters) (Also see
Blue Bird)
Charlton Comics: No. 12, Jan, 1956 - No. 72, Dec, 1967

12 — 9 27 49 70
13-19 — 6 18 29 40
20-(68 pgs.)-Williamson-a(4), 8,5,5,& 7 pgs. — 10 30 55 85
21-30 — 3 9 19 28
31-50 — 2 6 12 18
51-72 — 1 4 7 10

WYNONNA EARP
Image Comics (WildStorm Productions): Dec, 1996 - No. 5, Apr, 1997 ($2.50)

1-5-Smith-s/Chin-a — 2.50

X (Comics' Greatest World: X #1 only) (Also see Comics' Greatest World & Dark
Horse Comics #8)
Dark Horse Comics: Feb, 1994 - No. 25, Apr, 1996 ($2.00/$2.50)

1-25: 3-Pit Bulls x-over. 8 -Ghost-c & app. 18-Miller-c.; Predator app. 19-22-
Miller-c. — 2.50
Hero Illustrated Special #1,2 (1994, $1.00, 20 pgs.) — 2.25
One Shot to the Head (1994, $2.50, 36 pgs.)-Miller-c. — 2.50
NOTE: Miller c-18-22. Quesada c-6. Russell a-6.

XANADU COLOR SPECIAL
Eclipse Comics: Dec, 1988 ($2.00, one-shot)

1-Continued from Thoughts & Images — 2.25

XAVIER INSTITUTE ALUMNI YEARBOOK (See X-Men titles)
Marvel Comics: Dec, 1996 ($5.95, square-bound, one-shot)

1-Text w/art by various — 6.00

X-BABIES
Marvel Comics: (one-shots)

...: Murderama (8/98, $2.95) J.J. Kirby-a — 3.00
...: Reborn (1/00, $3.50) J.J. Kirby-a — 3.00

X-CALIBRE
Marvel Comics: Mar, 1995 - No. 4, July, 1995 ($1.95, limited series)

1-4-Age of Apocalypse — 2.25

XENA: WARRIOR PRINCESS (TV)
Topps Comics: Aug, 1997 - No. 0, Oct, 1997 ($2.95)

1-Two stories by various; J. Scott Campbell-c 1 4 7 10
1,2-Photo-c — 1 4 7 10
2-Stevens-c — 6.00
0-(10/97)-Lopresti-c, 0-(10/97)-Photo-c 1 3 6 8
...First Appearance Collection ('97, $9.95) r/Hercules the Legendary
Journeys #3-5 and 5-page story from TV Guide — 10.00

XENA: WARRIOR PRINCESS (TV)

Xenobrood #4 © DC

X-Factor #48 © MAR

X-Files #16 © 20th Century Fox

	GD2.0	FN6.0	VF8.0	NM9.4

	GD2.0	FN6.0	VF8.0	NM9.4

Dark Horse Comics: Sept, 1999 - No. 14, Oct, 2000 ($2.95/$2.99)
1-14: 1-Mignola-c and photo-c. 2,3-Bradstreet-c & photo-c ... 3.00

XENA: WARRIOR PRINCESS AND THE ORIGINAL OLYMPICS (TV)
Topps Comics: Jun, 1998 - No. 3, Aug, 1998 ($2.95, limited series)
1-3-Regular and Photo-c; Lim-a/T&M Bierbaum-s ... 3.00

XENA: WARRIOR PRINCESS-BLOODLINES (TV)
Topps Comics: May, 1998 - No. 2, June, 1998 ($2.95, limited series)
1,2-Lopresti-s/c/a. 2-Reg. and photo-c ... 3.00
1-Bath photo-c, 1-American Ent. Ed. ... 4.00

XENA: WARRIOR PRINCESS / JOXER: WARRIOR PRINCE (TV)
Topps Comics: Nov, 1997 - No. 3, Jan, 1998 ($2.95, limited series)
1-3-Regular and Photo-c; Lim-a/T&M Bierbaum-s ... 3.00

XENA: WARRIOR PRINCESS-THE DRAGON'S TEETH (TV)
Topps Comics: Dec, 1997 - No. 3, Feb, 1998 ($2.95, limited series)
1-3-Regular and Photo-c; Teranishi-a/Thomas-s ... 3.00

XENA: WARRIOR PRINCESS-THE ORPHEUS TRILOGY (TV)
Topps Comics: Mar, 1998 - No. 3, May, 1998 ($2.95, limited series)
1-3-Regular and Photo-c; Teranishi-a/T&M Bierbaum-s ... 3.00

XENA: WARRIOR PRINCESS VS. CALLISTO (TV)
Topps Comics: Feb, 1998 - No. 3, Apr, 1998 ($2.95, limited series)
1-3-Regular and Photo-c; Morgan-a/Thomas-s ... 3.00

XENOBROOD
DC Comics: No. 0, Oct, 1994 - No. 6, Apr, 1995 ($1.50, limited series)
0-6: 0-Indicia says "Xenobroods" ... 2.25

XENON
Eclipse Comics: Dec, 1987 - No. 23, Nov. 1, 1988 ($1.50, B&W, bi-weekly)
1-23 ... 2.25

XENOTECH
Mirage Studios: Sept, 1993 - No. 3, Dec, 1994 ($2.75)
1-3: Bound with 2 trading cards. 2-(10/94) ... 2.75

XENOZOIC TALES (Also see Cadillacs & Dinosaurs, Death Rattle #8)
Kitchen Sink Press: Feb, 1986 - No. 14, Oct, 1996

	1	3	6	8
1				
1(2nd printing)(1/89)				3.00
2-14				5.00

XENYA
Sanctuary Press: Apr, 1994 - No. 3 ($2.95)
1-3: 1-Hildebrandt-c; intro Xenya ... 3.00

XERO
DC Comics: May, 1997 - No. 12, Apr, 1998 ($1.75)
1-7 ... 2.50
8-12 ... 2.25

X-FACTOR (Also see The Avengers #263, Fantastic Four #286 and Mutant X)
Marvel Comics Group: Feb, 1986 - No. 149, Sept, 1998

1-($1.25, 52 pgs)-Story recaps 1st app. from Avengers #263; story cont'd from F.F. #286; return of original X-Men (now X-Factor); Guice/Layton-a; Baby Nathan app. (2nd after X-Men #201) ... 6.00
2-4 ... 4.00
5-1st app. Apocalypse (2-pg. cameo) ... 4.00
6-1st full app. Apocalypse

	1	4	7	10

7-10: 10-Sabretooth app. (11/86, 3 pgs.) cont'd in X-Men #212; 1st app. in X-Men comic book ... 4.00
11-22: 13-Baby Nathan app. in flashback. 14-Cyclops vs. The Master Mold. 15-Intro wingless Angel ... 3.00
23-1st app. Archangel (2 pg. cameo)

	1	3	5	7

24-1st full app. Archangel (now in Uncanny X-Men); Fall Of The Mutants begins; origin Apocalypse

	1	3	6	9

25,26: Fall Of The Mutants; 26-New outfits ... 3.00
27-39,41-83,87-91,93-99,101: 35-Origin Cyclops. 38,50-(52 pgs.)-c: 50-Liefeld /Mc-Farlane-c. 51-53-Sabretooth app. 52-Liefeld-c(p). 54-Intro Crimson; Silvestri-c/a(p). 60-X-Tinction Agenda x-over; New Mutants (w/Cable) x-over

in #60-62; Wolverine in #62. 60-Gold ink 2nd printing. 61,62-X-Tinction Agenda. 62-Jim Lee-c. 63-Portacio/Thibert-c/a(p) begins, ends #69. 65-68-Lee co-plots. 65-The Apocalypse Files begins, ends #68.66,67-Baby Nathan app. 67-Inhumans app. 68-Baby Nathan is sent into future to save his life. 69,70-X-Men(w/Wolverine) x-over. 71-New team begins (Havok, Polaris, Strong Guy, Wolfsbane & Madrox); Stroman-c/a begins. 71-2nd printing ($1.25). 75-(52 pgs.). 77-Cannonball (of X-Force) app. 87-Quesada-c/a(p) in monthly comic begins,ends #92. 88-1st app. Random ... 2.50
40-Rob Liefeld-c/a (4/89, 1st at Marvel?) ... 3.00
84-86 - Jae Lee a(p); 85,86-Jae Lee-c. Polybagged with trading card in each; X-Cutioner's Song x-overs. ... 3.00
92-($3.50, 68 pgs.)-Wraparound-c by Quesada w/Havok hologram on-c; begin X-Men 30th anniversary issues; Quesada-a. ... 5.00
92-2nd printing ... 2.25
100-($2.95, 52 pgs.)-Embossed foil-c; Multiple Man dies. ... 5.00
100-($1.75, 52 pgs.)-Regular edition ... 2.25
102-105,107: 102-bound-in card sheet ... 2.25
106-($2.00)-Newsstand edition ... 2.25
106-($2.95)-Collectors edition ... 3.00
108-124,126-148: 112-Return from Age of Apocalypse. 115-card insert. 119-123-Sabretooth app. 123-Hound app. 124-w/Onslaught Update. 126-Onslaught x-over; Beast vs. Dark Beast 128-w/card insert; return of Multiple Man. 130-Assassination of Grayson Creed. 146,148-Moder-a ... 2.25
125-($2.95)-"Onslaught"; Post app.; return of Havok ... 4.00
149-Last issue ... 3.00
#(-1) Flashback (7/97) Matsuda-a ... 2.25
Annual 1-1(10/86-'94, 68 pgs.) 3-Evolutionary War x-over. 4-Atlantis Attacks; Byrne/Simonson-a;Byrne-c. 5-Fantastic Four, New Mutants x-over; Keown 2 pg. pin-up. 6-New Warriors app.; 5th app. X-Force cont'd from X-Men Annual #15. 7-1st Quesada-a(p) on X-Factor plus-c(p). 8-Bagged w/trading card.
9-Austin-a(i) ... 3.00
...Prisoner of Love (1990, $4.95, 52 pgs.)-Starlin scripts; Guice-a ... 5.00
NOTE: **Art Adams** a-41p, 42p. **Buckler** a-50p. Liefeld a-40; c-40, 50i, 52p. **McFarlane** c-50i. **Mignola** c-70. **Brandon Peterson** a-78o(part). **Whilce Portacio** c/a(p)-63-69. **Quesada** a(p)-87-92, Annual 7. c(p)-78, 79, 82, Annual 7. **Simonson** c/a-10, 11, 13-15, 17-19, 21, 23-31, 33, 34, 36-39; c-12, 16. **Paul Smith** a-44-48; c-43. **Stroman** a(p)-71-75, 77, 78(part), 80, 81; c(p)-71-77, 80, 81, 84. **Zeck** c-2.

X-51 (Machine Man)
Marvel Comics: Sept, 1999 - No. 12, Jul, 2000 ($1.99/$2.50)
1-7: 1-Joe Bennett-a. 2-Two covers ... 2.50
8-12: 8-Begin $2.50-c ... 2.50
Wizard #0 ... 2.25

X-FILES, THE (TV)
Topps Comics: Jan, 1995 - No. 41, July, 1998 ($2.50)

		1	4	7	10
-2(9/96)-Black-c; r/X-Files Magazine #1&2		1	4	7	10
-1(9/96)-Silver-c; r/Hero Illustrated Giveaway		1	4	7	10
0-($3.95)-Adapts pilot episode					4.00
0-"Mulder" variant-c		1	3	6	8
0-"Scully" variant-c		1	3	6	8
1/2-W/certificate		3	9	17	25

1-New stories based on the TV show; direct market & newsstand editions;

Miran Kim-c on all	3	9	20	30
2		2	6	12	18
3,4		1	3	6	8
5-10					4.00

11-41: 11-Begin $2.95-c. 21-W/bound-in card. 40,41-Reg. & photo-c ... 3.00
Annual 1,2 ($3.95) ... 4.00
Afterflight TPB ($5.95) Art by Thompson, Saviuk, Kim ... 6.00
Collection 1 TPB ($19.95)-r/#1-6. ... 20.00
Collection 2 TPB ($19.95)-r/#7-12, Annual #1. ... 20.00
...Fight the Future ('98, $5.95) Movie adaption ... 6.00
Hero Illustrated Giveaway

	2	6	11	15

Special Edition 1-5 ($4.95)-r/#1-3, 4-6, 7-9, 10-12, 13, Annual 1 ... 5.00
Star Wars Galaxy Magazine Giveaway (B&W)

	1	4	7	10

Trade paperback ($19.95) ... 20.00

X-FILES COMICS DIGEST, THE
Topps Comics: Dec, 1995 - No. 3 ($3.50, quarterly, digest-size)
1-3: 1,2: New X-Files stories w/Ray Bradbury Comics-r ... 4.00
NOTE: **Adlard** a-1, 3. **Jack Davis** a-2r. **Russell** a-1r.

X-Force #116 © MAR

X-Man #75 © MAR

The X-Men #10 © MAR

| | GD2.0 | FN6.0 | VF8.0 | NM9.4 | | | GD2.0 | FN6.0 | VF8.0 | NM9 |

X-FILES, THE: GROUND ZERO (TV)
Topps Comics: Nov, 1997 - No. 4, March, 1998 ($2.95, limited series)

1-4-Adaption of the Kevin J. Anderson novel ... 3.00

X-FILES, THE: SEASON ONE (TV)
Topps Comics: July, 1997 - present ($4.95, adaptions of TV episodes)

1,2,Squeeze, Conduit, Ice, Space, Fire, Beyond the Sea, Shadows ... 5.00

X-FORCE (Also see The New Mutants #100 & 1992 X-Men Annuals)
Marvel Comics: Aug, 1991 - Present ($1.00/$1.25/$1.50/$1.95/$1.99/$2.25)

1-($1.50, 52 pgs.)-Polybagged with 1 of 5 diff. Marvel Universe trading cards
  inside (1 each); 6th app. of X-Force; Liefeld-c/a begins ... 4.00
1-1st printing with Cable trading card inside ... 5.00
1-2nd printing; metallic ink-c (no bag or card) ... 2.25
2-4: 2-Deadpool-c/story. 3-New Brotherhood of Evil Mutants app. 4-Spider-Man
  x-over; cont'd from Spider-Man #16; reads sideways ... 3.00
5-10: 6-Last $1.00-c. 7,9-Weapon X back-ups. 8-Intro The Wild Pack (Cable,
  Kane, Domino, Hammer, G.W. Bridge, & Grizzly); Liefeld-c/a (4); Mignola-a.
  10-Weapon X full-length story (part 3). 11-1st Weapon Prime (cameo);
  Deadpool-c/story. ... 2.50
11-15,19-24,26-33: 15-Cable leaves X-Force ... 2.50
16-18-Polybagged w/trading card in each; X-Cutioner's Song x-overs ... 3.00
25-($3.50, 52 pgs.)-Wraparound-c w/Cable hologram on-c; Cable returns ... 4.00
34-37,39-45: 34-bound-in card deck ... 2.50
38,40-43: 38-($2.00)-Newsstand edition. 40-43 ($1.95)-Deluxe edition ... 2.25
38-($2.95)-Collectors edition ... 5.00
44-49,51-67: 44-Return from Age of Apocalypse. 45-Sabretooth app.
  49-Sebastian Shaw app. 52-Blob app., Onslaught cameo. 55-Vs. S.H.I.E.L.D.
  56-Deadpool app. 57-Mr. Sinister & X-Man-c/app. 57,58-Onslaught x-over.
  59-W/card insert; return of Longshot. 60-Dr. Strange ... 2.50
50 ($3.95)-Gatefold wrap-around foil-c ... 4.00
50 ($3.95)-Liefeld variant-c ... 5.00
68-74: 68-Operation Zero Tolerance ... 2.50
75,100-($2.99): 75-Cannonball-c/app. ... 3.00
76-99,101,102: 81-Pollina poster. 95-Magneto-c. 102-Ellis-s/Portacio-a ... 2.25
103-115: 103-Begin $2.25-c; Portacio-a thru #106. 115-Death of old team ... 2.25
116-New team debuts; Allred-c/a; Milligan-s; no Comics Code stamp on-c ... 4.00
117-122: 117-Intro. Mr. Sensitive. 120-Wolverine-c/app. ... 2.25
#(-1) Flashback (7/97) story of John Proudstar; Pollina app. ... 2.25
Annual 1-3 ('92-'94, 68 pgs.)-1-1st Greg Capullo-a(p) on X-Force. 2-Polybagged
  w/trading card; intro X-Treme & Neurtap ... 4.00
...And Cable '95 (12/95, $3.95)-Impossible Man app. ... 3.00
...And Cable '96...'97 ('96, 7/97) '96-Wraparound-c ... 3.00
...And Spider-Man: Sabotage nn (11/92, $6.95)-Reprints X-Force #3,4 &
  Spider-Man #16 ... 7.00
.../ Champions '98 ($3.50) ... 3.50
Annual 99 ($3.50) ... 3.50
...New Beginnings TPB (10/01, $14.95) r/#116-120 ... 15.00
...Rough Cut ($2.99) Pencil pages and script for #102 ... 3.00
...Youngblood (8/96, $4.95)-Platt-c ... 5.00
NOTE: Capullo a(p)-15-25, Annual 1; c(p)-14-27. Rob Liefeld a-1-7, 9p; c-1-9, 11p; plots-1-12. Mignola a-8p.

X-FORCE MEGAZINE
Marvel Comics: Nov, 1996 ($3.95, one-shot)

1-Reprints ... 4.00

XIMOS: VIOLENT PAST
Triumphant Comics: Mar, 1994 - No. 2, Mar, 1994 ($2.50, limited series)

1,2 ... 2.50

X-MAN (Also see X-Men Omega & X-Men Prime)
Marvel Comics: Mar, 1995 - No. 75, May, 2001 ($1.95/$1.99/$2.25)

1-Age of Apocalypse ... 5.00
1-2nd print ... 2.25
2-4,25: 25-($2.99)-Wraparound-c ... 3.00
5-24, 26-28: 5-Post Age of Apocalypse stories begin. 5-7-Madelyne Pryor app.
  10-Professor X app. 12-vs. Excalibur. 13-Marauders, Cable app.
  14-Vs. Cable; Onslaught app. 15-17-Vs. Holocaust. 17-w/Onslaught Update.
  18-Onslaught x-over; X-Force-c/app. 19-Onslaught x-over.
  20-Abomination-c/app.; w/card insert. 23-Bishop-c/app. 24-Spider-Man
  Morbius-c/app. 27-Re-appearance of Aurora(Alpha Flight) ... 2.50

29-49,51-62: 29-Operation Zero Tolerance. 37,38-Spider-Man-c/app. 56-Spider-
  Man app. ... 2.50
50-($2.99) Crossover with Generation X #50 ... 3.00
63-74: 63-Ellis & Grant-s/Olivetti-a begins. 64-Begin $2.25-c ... 2.25
75 ($2.99) Final issue; Alcatena-a ... 3.00
#(-1) Flashback (7/97) ... 2.25
...'96...'97-($2.95)-Wraparound-c; '96-Age of Apocalypse ... 3.00
...: All Saints' Day ('97, $5.99) Dodson-a ... 6.00
.../Hulk '98 ($2.99) Wraparound-c; Thanos app. ... 3.00

XMAS COMICS
Fawcett Publications: 12?/1941 - No. 2, 12?/1942; (50¢, 324 pgs.)
No. 7, 12?/1947 (25¢, 132 pgs.)(#3-6 do not exist)

	GD2.0	FN6.0	VF8.0	NM9.4
1-Contains Whiz #21, Capt. Marvel #3, Bulletman #2, Wow #3, & Master #18; Raboy back-c. Not rebound, remaindered comics; printed at same time as originals	383	1149	2396	4600
2-Capt. Marvel, Bulletman, Spy Smasher	150	450	938	1650
7-Funny animals (Hoppy, Billy the Kid & Oscar)	59	177	369	650

XMAS COMICS
Fawcett Publications: No. 4, Dec, 1949 - No. 7, Dec, 1952 (50¢, 196 pgs.)

	GD2.0	FN6.0	VF8.0	NM9.4
4-Contains Whiz, Master, Tom Mix, Captain Marvel, Nyoka, Capt. Video, Bob Colt, Monte Hale, Hot Rod Comics, & Battle Stories; Not rebound, remaindered comics; printed at the same time as originals	64	192	398	700
5-7-Same as above. 7-Bill Boyd app.; stocking on cover is made of green felt (novelty cover)	52	157	314	550

X-MEN, THE (See Adventures of Cyclops and Phoenix, Amazing Adventures, Archangel, Brotherhood, Capt. America #172, Classic X-Men, Exiles, Further Adventures of Cyclops & Phoenix, Gambit, Giant-Size..., Heroes For Hope..., Kitty Pryde & Wolverine, Marvel & DC Present, Marvel Collector's Edition:..., Marvel Fanfare, Marvel Graphic Novel, Marvel Super Heroes, Marvel Team-Up, Marvel Triple Action, The Marvel X-Men Collection, New Mutants, Nightcrawler, Official Marvel Index To..., Rogue, Special Edition..., Ultimate..., Uncanny..., Wolverine, X-Factor, X-Force, X-Terminators)

X-MEN, THE (1st series)(Becomes Uncanny X-Men at #142)(The X-Men #1-93; X-Men #94-141) (The Uncanny X-Men on-c only #114-141)
Marvel Comics Group: Sept, 1963 - No. 66, Mar, 1970; No. 67, Dec, 1970 - No. 141, Jan, 1981

	GD2.0	FN6.0	VF8.0	NM9.4
1-Origin/1st app. X-Men (Angel, Beast, Cyclops, Iceman & Marvel Girl); 1st app. Magneto & Professor X	560	1680	4000	10,000
2-1st app. The Vanisher	144	432	1222	2300
3-1st app. The Blob	56	169	478	900
4-1st Quick Silver & Scarlet Witch & Brotherhood of the Evil Mutants (3/64); 1st app. Toad; 2nd app. Magneto	59	178	505	950
5-Magneto & Evil Mutants-c/story	43	129	323	575
6-9: 6-Sub-Mariner app. 7-Magneto app. 8-1st Unus the Untouchable. 9-Early Avengers app. (1/65); 1st Lucifer	31	94	233	425
10-1st S.A. Ka-Zar & Zabu the sabertooth (3/65)	33	100	250	450
11,13-15: 11-1st app. The Stranger. 14-1st app. Sentinels. 15-Origin Beast	28	84	196	350
12-Origin Prof. X; Origin/1st app. Juggernaut	34	102	255	460
16-20: 19-1st app. The Mimic (4/66)	16	48	110	190
21-27,29,30: 27-Re-enter the Mimic (r-in #75); Spider-Man cameo	12	36	88	150
28-1st app. The Banshee (1/67)(r-in #76)	17	51	118	210
31-34,36,37,39,40: 34-Adkins-c/a. 39-New costumes	9	27	65	110
35-Spider-Man x-over (8/67)(r-in #83); 1st app. Changeling	13	39	94	160
38-Origins of the X-Men series begins, ends #57	10	30	73	125
41-49: 42-Death of Prof. X (Changeling disguised as). 44-1st S.A. app. G.A. Red Raven. 47-Steranko-c/a; 1st Polaris	8	24	58	95
50,51-Steranko-c/a	8	24	60	100
52	6	18	45	75
53-Barry Smith-c/a (his 1st comic book work)	8	24	60	100
54,55-B. Smith-a. 54-1st app. Alex Summers who later becomes Havok. 55-Summers discovers he has mutant powers	9	27	63	105
56,57,59,63,65-Neal Adams-a(p). 56-Intro Havok w/o costume. 60-1st Sauron.				
65-Return of Professor X	8	24	56	90
58-1st app. Havok in costume; N. Adams-a(p)	10	30	73	125
64-1st app. Sunfire	8	24	58	95

The X-Men #120 © MAR

The Uncanny X-Men #173 © MAR

The Uncanny X-Men #366 © MAR

	GD2.0	FN6.0	VF8.0	NM9.4
66-Last new story w/original X-Men; battles Hulk	8	24	56	90
67-70,72: (52 pgs.). 67-Reprints begin, end #93	4	12	30	50
71,73-93: 71-Last 15¢ issue. 73-86-r/#25-38 w/new-c. 83-Spider-Man-c/story.				
87-93-r/#39-45 with covers	4	12	26	40
94 (8/75)-New X-Men begin (see Giant-Size X-Men for 1st app.); Colossus, Nightcrawler, Thunderbird, Storm, Wolverine, & Banshee join; Angel, Marvel Girl, & Iceman resign	56	169	478	900
95-Death of Thunderbird	16	48	112	200
96,97	11	33	80	135
98,99-(Regular 25¢ edition)(4,6/76)	10	30	73	125
98,99-(30¢-c variants, limited distribution)	16	48	112	200
00-Old vs. New X-Men; part origin Phoenix; last issue (8/76)				
	11	33	77	130
00-(30¢-c variant, limited distribution)	16	48	112	200
01-Phoenix origin concludes	10	30	70	120
02-104: 102-Origin Storm. 104-1st app. Starjammers (brief cameo); Magneto-c/story	6	18	40	65
05-107-(Regular 30¢ editions). 106-(8/77)Old vs. New X-Men. 107-1st full app. Starjammers; last 30¢ issue	6	18	40	65
05-107-(35¢-c variants, limited distribution)	8	24	60	100
08-Byrne-a begins (see Marvel Team-Up #53)	9	27	65	110
09-1st app. Weapon Alpha (becomes Vindicator)	8	24	56	90
10,111: 110-Phoenix joins	6	18	40	65
12-119: 117-Origin Professor X	5	15	38	60
20-1st app. Alpha Flight (cameo), story line begins (4/79); 1st app. Vindicator (formerly Weapon Alpha); last 35¢ issue	7	21	53	85
21-1st full Alpha Flight story	8	24	56	90
22-128: 123-Spider-Man x-over. 124-Colossus becomes Proletarian				
	4	12	29	45
29-Intro Kitty Pryde (1/80); last Banshee; Dark Phoenix saga begins				
	5	15	34	55
30-1st app. The Dazzler by Byrne (2/80)	4	12	30	50
31-135: 131-Dazzler app. 132-1st White Queen. 133-Wolverine app. 134-Phoenix becomes Dark Phoenix	4	12	26	40
36,138: 138-Dazzler app.; Cyclops leaves	3	10	23	35
37-Giant; death of Phoenix	4	12	26	40
39-Alpha Flight app.; Kitty Pryde joins; new costume for Wolverine				
	4	12	30	48
40-Alpha Flight app.	4	12	29	45
41-Intro Future X-Men & The New Brotherhood of Evil Mutants; 1st app. Rachel (Phoenix II); Death of Franklin Richards	4	12	30	48
X-MEN: Titled THE UNCANNY X-MEN #142, Feb, 1981 - Present				
42-Rachel app.; deaths of alt. future Wolverine, Storm & Colossus				
	4	12	26	40
43-Last Byrne issue	3	9	17	25
44-150: 144-Man-Thing app. 145-Old X-Men app. 148-Spider-Woman, 150-Double size	1	4	7	10
51-157,159-161,163,164: 161-Origin Magneto. 163-Origin Binary. 164-1st app. Binary as Carol Danvers	1	3	6	8
58-1st app. Rogue in X-Men (6/82, see Avengers Annual #10)				
	2	6	10	14
62-Wolverine solo story	1	4	7	10
65-Paul Smith-c/a begins, ends #175	1	3	6	9
66-170: 166-Double size; Paul Smith-a. 167-New Mutants app. (3/83); same date as New Mutants #1; 1st meeting w/X-Men; ties into N.M. #3,4; Starjammers app.; contains skin 'Tattooz' decals. 168-1st app. Madelyne Pryor (last pg. cameo) in X-Men (see Avengers Annual #10)				
	1	3	6	8
71-Rogue joins X-Men; Simonson-c/a	2	6	9	12
72-174: 172,173-Two part Wolverine solo story. 173-Two cover variations, blue & black. 174-Phoenix cameo	1	3	5	7
75-(52 pgs.)-Anniversary issue; Phoenix returns	1	3	6	9
76-185,187-192,194-199: 181-Sunfire app. 182-Rogue solo story. 184-1st app. Forge (8/84). 190,191-Spider-Man & Avengers x-over. 195-Power Pack x-over				
				6.00
86,193: 186-Double-size; Barry Smith/Austin-a. 193-Double size; 100th app. New X-Men; 1st app. Warpath in costume (see New Mutants #16)				
	1	3	5	7
00-(12/85, $1.25, 52 pgs.)	1	3	5	7

	GD2.0	FN6.0	VF8.0	NM9.4
201-(1/86)-1st app. Cable? (as baby Nathan; see X-Factor #1); 1st Whilce Portacio-c/a(i) on X-Men (guest artist)	2	6	12	18
202-204,206-209: 204-Nightcrawler solo story; 2nd Portacio-a(i) on X-Men.				
207-Wolverine/Phoenix story				6.00
205-Wolverine solo story by Barry Smith	2	6	9	12
210,211-Mutant Massacre begins	2	6	12	18
212,213-Wolverine vs. Sabretooth (Mutant Mass.)	2	6	15	22
214-221,223,224: 219-Havok joins (7/87); brief app. Sabretooth				6.00
222-Wolverine battles Sabretooth-c/story	2	6	13	20
225-242: 225-227: Fall Of The Mutants. 226-Double size. 240-Sabretooth app.				
242-Double size, X-Factor app., Inferno tie-in				6.00
243,245-247: 245-Rob Liefeld-a(p)				6.00
244-1st app. Jubilee	3	9	17	25
248-1st Jim Lee art on X-Men (1989)	2	6	13	20
248-2nd printing (1992, $1.25)				2.50
249-252: 252-Lee-c				6.00
253-255: 253-All new X-Men begin. 254-Lee-c				6.00
256,257-Jim Lee-c/a begins	1	3	6	8
258-Wolverine solo story; Lee-c/a	1	3	6	8
259-Silvestri-c/a; no Lee-a				6.00
260-265-No Lee-a. 260,261,264-Lee-c				6.00
266-1st full app. Gambit (see Ann. #14)-No Lee-a	4	12	26	40
267-Jim Lee-c/a resumes; 2nd full Gambit app.	2	6	11	15
268-Capt. America, Black Widow & Wolverine team-up; Lee-a				
	2	6	11	16
268,270: 268-2nd printing. 270-Gold 2nd printing				2.50
269,273-275: 269-Lee-a. 273-New Mutants (Cable) & X-Factor x-over; Golden, Byrne & Lee part pencils. 275-(52 pgs.)-Tri-fold-c by Jim Lee (p); Prof. X.				
				6.00
270-X-Tinction Agenda begins	1	3	5	7
271,272-X-Tinction Agenda	1	3	5	7
275-Gold 2nd printing				2.50
276-280: 277-Last Lee-c/a. 280-X-Factor x-over				5.00
281-(10/91)-New team begins (Storm, Archangel, Colossus, Iceman & Marvel Girl); Whilce Portacio-c/a begins; Byrne scripts begin; wraparound-c (white logo)				6.00
281-2nd printing with red metallic ink logo w/o UPC box ($1.00-c); does not say 2nd printing inside				2.50
282-1st app. Bishop (cover & 1 pg. cameo)	2	6	9	12
282-Gold ink 2nd printing ($1.00-c)				2.50
283-1st full app. Bishop (12/91)	2	6	9	12
284-299: 284-Last $1.00-c. 286,287-Lee plots. 287-Bishop joins team. 288-Lee/Portacio plots. 290-Last Portacio-c/a. 294-Brandon Peterson-a(p) begins (#292 is 1st Peterson-c). 294-296 ($1.50)-Polybagged w/trading card in each; X-Cutioner's Song x-overs; all have Peterson/Austin-c/a				4.00
300-($3.95, 68 pgs.)-Holo-grafx foil-c; Magneto app.				6.00
301-303,305-309,311				3.00
303,307-Gold Edition	1	3	6	8
304-($3.95, 68 pgs.)-Wraparound-c with Magneto hologram on-c; 30th anniversary issue; Jae Lee-a (4 pgs.)				6.00
310-($1.95)-Bound-in trading card sheet				3.00
312-$1.50-c begins; bound-in card sheet; 1st Madureira				4.00
313-321				3.00
316,317-($2.95)-Foil enhanced editions				4.00
318-321-($1.95)-Deluxe editions				3.00
322-Onslaught				5.00
323,324,326-346: 323-Return from Age of Apocalypse. 328-Sabretooth-c. 329,330-Dr. Strange app. 331-White Queen-c/app. 334-Juggernaut app.; w/Onslaught Update. 335-Onslaught, Avengers, Apocalypse, & X-Man app. 336-Onslaught. 338-Archangel's wings return to normal. 339-Havok vs. Cyclops; Spider-Man app. 341-Gladiator/app. 342-Deathbird cameo; two covers. 343,344-Phalanx				2.50
325-($3.95)-Anniversary issue; gatefold-c				5.00
342-Variant-c	1	4	7	10
347-349:347-Begin $1.99-c. 349-"Operation Zero Tolerance"				2.50
350-($3.99, 48 pgs.) Prismatic etched foil gatefold wraparound-c; Trial of Gambit; Seagle-s begin	1	3	6	8
351-359: 353-Bachalo-a begins. 354-Regular-c. 355-Alpha Flight-c/app.				
356-Original X-Men-c				2.50
354-Dark Phoenix variant-c				4.00

 appears above the blue-ruled rule: "AND FURY WILL CHANGE THEIR WORLD FOREVER!"

	GD2.0	FN6.0	VF8.0	NM9.4		GD2.0	FN6.0	VF8.0	NM9.4

360-($2.99) 35th Anniv. issue; Pacheco-c 3.00
360-($3.99) Etched Holo-foil enhanced-c 4.00
360-($6.95) DF Edition with Jae Lee variant-c 7.00
361-374: 361-Gambit returns; Skroce-a. 362-Hunt for Xavier pt. 1; Bachelo-a.
 364-Yu-a. 366-Magneto-c. 369-Juggernaut-c 2.50
375-($2.99) Autopsy of Wolverine 3.00
376-379: 376,377-Apocalypse: The Twelve 2.25
380-($2.99) Polybagged with X-Men Revolution Genesis Edition preview 3.00
381,382,384-389,391-393: 381-Begin $2.25-c; Claremont-s. 387-Maximum
 Security x-over 2.25
383-($2.99) 3.00
390-Colossus dies to cure the Legacy Virus 3.00
394-New look X-Men begins; Casey-s/Churchill-c/a 3.00
395-399-Poptopia. 398-Phillips & Wood-a 2.25
400-($3.50) Art by Ashley Wood, Eddie Campbell, Hamenr, Phillips, Pulido and
 Matt Smith; wraparound-c by Wood 3.50
401-'Nuff Said issue; Garney-a 2.25
#(-1) Flashback (7/97) Ladronn-c/Hitch & Neary-a 2.50

Special 1(12/70)-Kirby-c/a; origin The Stranger 8 24 60 100
Special 2(11/71, 52 pgs.) 6 18 42 70
Annual 3(1979, 52 pgs.)-New story; Miller/Austin-a; Wolverine still in old yellow
 costume 3 9 20 30
Annual 4(1980, 52 pgs.)-Dr. Strange guest stars 2 6 9 12
Annual 5(1981, 52 pgs.) 1 3 6 9
Annual 6-8('82-'84 52 pgs.)-6-Dracula app. 6.00
Annual 9,10('85, '86)-9-New Mutants x-over cont'd from New Mutants Special
 Ed. #1;Art Adams-a. 10-Art Adams-a 1 3 6 9
Annual 11-13:('87-'89, 68 pgs.): 12-Evolutionary War; A.Adams-a(p). 13-Atlantis
 Attacks 4.00
Annual 14(1990, $2.00, 68 pgs.)-1st app. Gambit (minor app., 5 pgs.); Fantastic
 Four, New Mutants (Cable) & X-Factor x-over; Art Adams-c/a(p)
 3 9 17 25
Annual 15 (1991, $2.00, 68 pgs.)-4 pg. origin; New Mutants x-over; 4 pg.
 Wolverine solo back-up story; 4th app. X-Force cont'd from New Warriors
 Annual #1 4.00
Annual 16-18 ('92-'94, 68 pgs.)-16-Jae Lee-c/a(p). 17-Bagged w/card 3.00
Annual '95-(11/95, $3.95)-Wraparound-c 4.00
Annual '96,'97-Wraparound-c 3.00
.../Fantastic Four Annual '98 ($2.99) Casey-s 3.00
Annual '99 ($3.50) Jubilee app. 3.50
Annual 2000 ($3.50) Cable app.; Ribic-a 3.50
...At The State Fair of Texas (1983, 36 pgs., one-shot); Supplement
 to the Dallas Times Herald 2 6 11 15
...: The Dark Phoenix Saga TPB 1st printing (1984, $12.95) 40.00
...: The Dark Phoenix Saga TPB 2nd-5th printings 30.00
...: The Dark Phoenix Saga TPB 6th-10th printings 15.00
...From The Ashes TPB (1990, $14.95) r/#168-176 15.00
...God Loves, Man Kills ($6.95)-r/Marvel Graphic Novel #5 7.00
...In The Days of Future Past TPB (1989, $3.95, 52 pgs.) 4.00
...Poptopia TPB (10/01, $15.95) r/#394-399 16.00
NOTE: Art Adams a-Annual 9, 10p, 12p, 14p; c-218p. Bachelo a-372. Neal Adams a-56-63p, 65p; c-56-63. Adkins a-34, 35p; c-31, 34, 35. Austin a-108i, 109i, 111-117i, 119-143i, 186i, 204i, 228i, 294-297i, Annual 3i, 7i, 9, 10. c-109-111i, 114-122i, 123, 124-141i, 142, 143, 196i, 204i, Annual 3i, 9-297i, Annual 3i. J. Buscema c-42, 43, 45. Buscema/Tuska a-45. Byrne a(p)-108, 109, 111-143, 273; c(p)-113-116, 127, 129, 131-141. Capullo c-14. Ditko c-112i, 113i. Everett c-73. Golden a-273, Annual 7p. Guice a-216p, 217p. G. Kane c(p)-33, 74-76, 79, 80, 94, 95. Kirby a(p)-1-17 (#12-17, r/t-layouts); c(p)-1-17, 25, 30 (18, 26-parts). Layton c-112i, 113i. Jim Lee a(p)-248, 256-258, 267-277; c(p)-252, 254, 256-261, 264, 267, 270, 275-277, 286. Perez a-Annual 3p; c(p)-112, 128, Annual 3. Petersen a(p)-290-300, 304(part); c(p)-294-299. Whilce Portacio a(p)-281-286, 289, 290; a(i)-267; c-281-286p, 289p, 290; c(i)-267. Romita, Jr. a-300; c-300. Rousseau a-84i. Simonson a-171p; c-171, 217. B. Smith a-53, 186p, 198p, 205, 214; c-53-55, 186p, 198, 205, 212, 214, 216. Paul Smith a(p)-165-170, 172-175, 278; c-165-170, 172-175, 278. Sparling a-78p. Steranko a-50p, 51p; c-49-51. Sutton a-106i. Art Thibert a(i)-281-286; c(i)-281, 282, 284, 285. Toth a-12p, 67p(r). Tuska a-40-42i, 43-46p, 88i(r); c-39-41i, 77p, 78p. Williamson a-202i, 203i, 211i; c-202i, 203i, 206i. Wood c-14i.

UNCANNY X-MEN AND THE NEW TEEN TITANS (See Marvel and DC Present...)

X-MEN (2nd Series)
Marvel Comics: Oct, 1991 - Present ($1.00/$1.25/$1.95/$1.99)

1 a-d ($1.50, 52 pgs.)-Jim Lee-c/a begins, ends #11; new team begins
 (Cyclops, Beast, Wolverine, Gambit, Psylocke & Rogue); new Uncanny
 X-Men & Magneto app.; four different covers exist 4.00

1 e ($3.95)-Double gate-fold-c consisting of all four covers from 1a-d by Jim
 Lee; contains all pin-ups from #1a-d plus inside-c foldout poster; no ads;
 printed on coated stock 5.00
2-7: 4-Wolverine back to old yellow costume (same date as Wolverine #50);
 last $1.00-c. 5-Byrne scripts. 6-Sabretooth-c/story 5.00
8-10: 8-Gambit vs. Bishop-c/story; last Lee-a; Ghost Rider cameo cont'd in
 Ghost Rider #26. 9-Wolverine vs. Ghost Rider; cont'd/G.R. #26. 10-Return
 of Longshot 4.00
11-13,17-24,26-29,31: 12,13-Art Thibert-c/a. 28,29-Sabretooth app. 3.00
11-Silver ink 2nd printing; came with X-Men board game
 2 6 11 15
14-16-($1.50)-Polybagged with trading card in each; X-Cutioner's Song x-overs;
 14-Andy Kubert-c/a begins 3.00
25-($3.50, 52 pgs.)-Wraparound-c with Gambit hologram on-c; Professor X
 erases Magneto's mind 2 6 9 12
25-30th anniversary issue w/B&W-c with Magneto in color & Magneto hologram
 & no price on-c 2 6 11 15
25-Gold 30.00
30-($1.95)-Wedding issue w/bound-in trading card sheet 5.00
32-37: 32-Begin $1.50-c; bound-in card sheet. 33-Gambit & Sabretooth-c/story
 3.00
36,37-($2.95)-Collectors editions 5.00
38-44,46-49,51-53, 55-65: 42,43- Paul Smith-a. 46,49,53-56-Onslaught app.
 51-Waid scripts begin, end #56. 54-(Reg. edition)-Onslaught revealed
 as Professor X. 55, 56-Onslaught x-over; Avengers, FF & Sentinels app. 56-
 Dr. Doom app. 57-Xavier taken into custody; Byrne-c/swipe (X-Men,1st Series
 #138). 59-Hercules-c/app. 61-Juggernaut-c/app. 62-Re-intro. Shang Chi; two
 covers. 63-Kingpin cameo. 64- Kingpin app. 2.50
45 ($3.95)-Annual issue; gatefold-c 5.00
50 ($2.95)-Vs. Onslaught, wraparound-c. 4.00
50 ($2.95)-Vs. Onslaught, wraparound foil-c. 5.00
50 ($2.95)-Variant-c. 1 3 6 8
54-(Limited edition)-Embossed variant-c; Onslaught revealed as Professor X
 3 9 20 30
66-69,71-74,76-79: 66-Operation Zero Tolerance. 76-Origin of Maggott 2.50
70-($2.99, 48 pgs.)-Joe Kelly-s begin, new members join 3.00
75-($2.99, 48 pgs.) vs. N'Garai, wraparound-c 3.00
80-($3.99) 35th Anniv. issue; holo-foil-c 5.00
80-($2.99) Regular-c 3.00
80-($6.95) Dynamic Forces Ed.; Quesada-c 7.00
81-93,95: 82-Hunt for Xavier pt. 2. 85-Davis-a. 86-Origin of Joseph. 87-Magneto
 War ends. 88-Juggernaut app. 2.50
94-($2.99) Contains preview of X-Men: Hidden Years 3.00
96-99: 96,97-Apocalypse: The Twelve 2.50
100-($2.99) Art Adams-c; begin Claremont-s/Yu-a 3.00
101-105,107,108,110-113: 101-Begin $2.25-c. 107-Maximum Security x-over;
 Bishop-c/app. 108-Moira MacTaggart dies; Senator Kelly shot. 111-Magneto-c
 112,113-Eve of Destruction 2.25
106-($2.99) X-Men battle Domina 3.00
109-($3.50, 100 pgs.) new and reprinted Christmas-themed stories 3.50
114-Title change to "New X-Men," Morrison-s/Quitely-c/a begins 4.00
115-Two covers (Quitely & BWS) 4.00
116-121: 116-Emma Frost joins. 117,118-Van Sciver-a. 121-Quitely-a 2.25
#(-1) Flashback (7/97); origin of Magneto 2.50
Annual 1-3 ('92-'94, $2.25-$2.95, 68 pgs.) 1-Lee-c & layouts; #2-Bagged w/card
 4.00
Annual 2000 ($3.50) Art Adams-c/Claremont-s/Eaton-a 3.50
Animation Special Graphic Novel (12/90, $10.95) adapted animated series 11.00
Ashcan #1 (1994, 75¢) Introduces new team members 2.25
Ashcan ('95 Ashcan Edition) (1994) 2.25
Special '95 ($3.95) 4.00
... '96,...'97-Wraparound-c 3.00
.../ Dr. Doom '98 Annual ($2.99) Lopresti-a 3.00
... Annual '99 ($3.50) Adam Kubert-c 3.50
...2001 Annual ($3.50) Morrison-s/Yu-a; issue opens longways 3.50
... Archives Sketchbook (12/00, $2.99) Early B&W character design sketches by
 various incl. Lee, Davis, Yu, Pacheco, BWS, Art Adams, Liefeld 3.00
...: Declassified (10/00, $3.50) Profile pin-ups by various; Jae Lee-c 3.50
...:Fatal Attractions ('94, $17.95)-r/x-Factor #92, X-Force #25, Uncanny
 X-Men #304, X-Men #25, Wolverine #75, & Excalibur #71 18.00

	GD2.0	FN6.0	VF8.0	NM9.4

Millennial Visions (8/00, $3.99) Various artists interpret future X-Men 4.00
Millennial Visions 2 (1/02, $3.50) Various artists interpret future X-Men 3.50
New X-Men: E is for Extinction TPB (11/01, $12.95) r/#114-117 13.00
Premium Edition #1 (1993)-Cover says "Toys 'R' Us Limited Edition X-Men" 2.25
Rarities (1995, $5.95)-Reprints 6.00
Road Trippin' ('99, $24.95, TPB) r/X-Men road trips 25.00
The Coming of Bishop ('95, $12.95)-r/Uncanny X-Men #282-285,
  287,288 13.00
The Magneto War (3/99, $2.99) Davis-a 3.00
The Rise of Apocalypse ('98, $16.99)-r/Rise Of Apocalypse #1-4,
  X-Factor #5,6 17.00
Visionaries: Chris Claremont ('98, $24.95)-r/Claremont-s; art
  by Byrne, Barry Smith, and Jim Lee 25.00
Visionaries: Joe Madureira (7/00, $17.95)-r/Uncanny X-Men #325,326,329,
  330,341-343; new Madureira-c 18.00
Zero Tolerance ('00, $24.95, TPB) r/crossover series 25.00
NOTE: **Jim Lee** a-1-11p; c-1-6p, 7, 8, 9p, 10, 11p. **Art Thibert** a-6-9i, 12, 13; c-6i, 12, 13.

X-MEN ADVENTURES (TV)
Marvel Comics: Nov, 1992 - No. 15, Jan, 1994 ($1.25)(Based on animated series)
1-Wolverine, Cyclops, Jubilee, Rogue, Gambit 3.00
2-15: 3-Magneto-c/story. 6-Sabretooth-c/story. 7-Cable-c/story. 10-Archangel
  guest star. 11-Cable-c/story. 15-($1.75, 52 pgs.) 2.50

X-MEN ADVENTURES II (TV)
Marvel Comics: Feb, 1994 - No. 13, Feb, 1995 ($1.25/$1.50)(Based on 2nd TV
  season)
1-13: 4-Bound-in trading card sheet. 5-Alpha Flight app. 2.50
Captive Hearts/Slave Island (TPB, $4.95)-r/X-Men Adventures #5-8 5.00
The Irresistible Force, The Muir Island Saga (5.95, 10/94, TPB)
  r/X-Men Adventures #9-12 6.00

X-MEN ADVENTURES III (TV)(See Adventures of the X-Men)
Marvel Comics: Mar, 1995 - No. 13, Mar, 1996 ($1.50) (Based on 3rd TV season)
1-13 2.50

X-MEN ALPHA
Marvel Comics: 1994 ($3.95, one-shot)

nn-Age of Apocalypse; wraparound chromium-c	1	3	6	8
($49.95)-Gold logo				50.00

X-MEN/ALPHA FLIGHT
Marvel Comics: Dec, 1985 - No. 2, Dec, 1985 ($1.50, limited series)
1,2: 1-Intro The Berserkers; Paul Smith-a 5.00

X-MEN/ALPHA FLIGHT
Marvel Comics Group: May, 1998 - No. 2, June, 1998 ($2.99, limited series)
1,2-Flashback to early meeting; Raab-s/Cassaday-s/a 3.00

X-MEN AND THE MICRONAUTS, THE
Marvel Comics Group: Jan, 1984 - No. 4, Apr, 1984 (Limited series)
1-4: Guice-c/a(p) in all 4.00

X-MEN ARCHIVES
Marvel Comics: Jan, 1995 - No. 4, Apr, 1995 ($2.25, limited series)
1-4: Reprints Legion stories from New Mutants. 4-Magneto app. 2.25

X-MEN ARCHIVES FEATURING CAPTAIN BRITAIN
Marvel Comics: July, 1995 - No. 7, 1996 ($2.95, limited series)
1-7: Reprints early Capt. Britain stories 3.00

X-MEN BLACK SUN (See Black Sun:...)

X-MEN BOOKS OF ASKANI
Marvel Comics: 1995 ($2.95, one-shot)
nn-Painted pin-ups w/text 3.00

X-MEN: CHILDREN OF THE ATOM
Marvel Comics: Nov, 1999 - No. 6 ($2.99, limited series)
1-6-Casey-s; X-Men before issue #1. 1-3-Rude-c/a. 4-Paul Smith-a/Rude-c.
  5,6-Essad Ribic-c/a 3.00
TPB (11/01, $16.95) r/series; sketch pages; Casey intro. 17.00

X-MEN CHRONICLES
Marvel Comics: Mar, 1995 - No. 2, June, 1995 ($3.95, limited series)
1,2: Age of Apocalypse x-over. 1-wraparound-c 5.00

X-MEN: CLANDESTINE
Marvel Comics: Oct, 1996 - No. 2, Nov, 1996 ($2.95, limited series, 48 pgs.)
1,2: Alan Davis-c(p)/a(p)/scripts & Mark Farmer-c(i)/a(i) in all; wraparound-c
  3.00

X-MEN CLASSIC (Formerly Classic X-Men)
Marvel Comics: No. 46, Apr, 1990 - No. 110, Aug, 1995 ($1.25/$1.50)
46-110: Reprints from X-Men. 54-(52 pgs.). 57,60-63,65-Russell-c(i); 62-r/X-Men
  #158(Rogue). 66-r/#162(Wolverine). 69-Begins-r of Paul Smith issues (#165
  on). 70,79,90,97(52 pgs.). 70-r/X-Men #166. 90-r/#186. 100-($1.50). 104-r/X-
  Men #200 2.50

X-MEN CLASSICS
Marvel Comics Group: Dec, 1983 - No. 3, Feb, 1984 ($2.00, Baxter paper)
1-3: X-Men-r by Neal Adams 6.00
NOTE: **Zeck** c-1-3.

X-MEN: EARTHFALL
Marvel Comics: Sept, 1996 ($2.95, one-shot)
1-r/Uncanny X-Men #232-234; wraparound-c 3.00

X-MEN: EVOLUTION (Based on the animated series)
Marvel Comics: Feb, 2002 - Present ($2.25)
1,2-Grayson-s/Udon-a 2.25

X-MEN FIRSTS
Marvel Comics: Feb, 1996 ($4.95, one-shot)
1-r/Avengers Annual #10, Uncanny X-Men #266, #221;
  Incredible Hulk #181 5.00

X-MEN FOREVER
Marvel Comics: Jan, 2001 - No. 6, June, 2001 ($3.50, limited series)
1-6-Jean Grey, Iceman, Mystique, Toad, Juggernaut app.; Maguire-a 3.50

X-MEN: HELLFIRE CLUB
Marvel Comics: Jan, 2000 - No. 4, Apr, 2000 ($2.50, limited series)
1-4-Origin of the Hellfire Club 2.50

X-MEN: HIDDEN YEARS
Marvel Comics: Dec, 1999 - No. 22, Sept. 2001 ($3.50/$2.50)
1-New adventures from pre-#94 era; Byrne-s/a(p) 3.50
2-4,6-11,13-22-($2.50): 2-Two covers. 3-Ka-Zar app. 8,9-FF-c/app. 2.50
5-($2.75) 2.75
12-($3.50) Magneto-c/app. 3.50

X-MEN: LIBERATORS
Marvel Comics: Nov, 1998 - No. 4, Feb, 1999 ($2.99, limited series)
1-4-Wolverine, Nightcrawler & Colossus; P. Jimenez 3.00

X-MEN LOST TALES
Marvel Comics: 1997 ($2.99)
1,2-r/Classic X-Men back-up stories 3.00

X-MEN OMEGA
Marvel Comics: June, 1995 ($3.95, one-shot)

nn-Age of Apocalypse finale	1	4	7	10
nn-($49.95)-Gold edition				50.00

X-MEN: PHOENIX
Marvel Comics: Dec, 1999 - No. 3, Mar, 2000 ($2.50, limited series)
1-3: 3-Apocalypse app. 2.50

X-MEN PRIME
Marvel Comics: July, 1995 ($4.95, one-shot)

nn-Post Age of Apocalyse begins	1	4	7	10

X-MEN RARITIES
Marvel Comics: 1995 ($5.95, one-shot)
nn-Reprints hard-to-find stories 6.00

X-MEN ROAD TO ONSLAUGHT

X-Men: Search For Cyclops #1 © MAR

X-Men: The Early Years #5 © MAR

X-Men Unlimited #33 © MAR

	GD2.0	FN6.0	VF8.0	NM9.4

Marvel Comics: Oct, 1996 ($2.50, one-shot)
nn-Retells Onslaught Saga   2.50

X-MEN: SEARCH FOR CYCLOPS
Marvel Comics: Oct, 2000 - No. 4, Mar, 2001 ($2.99, limited series)
1-4-Two covers (Raney,Pollina); Raney-a   3.00

X-MEN SPOTLIGHT ON... STARJAMMERS (Also see X-Men #104)
Marvel Comics: 1990 - No. 2, 1990 ($4.50, 52 pgs.)
1,2: Features Starjammers   4.50

X-MEN SURVIVAL GUIDE TO THE MANSION
Marvel Comics: Aug, 1993 ($6.95, spiralbound)
1   7.00

X-MEN: THE EARLY YEARS
Marvel Comics: May, 1994 - No. 17, Sept, 1995 ($1.50/$2.50)
1-16: r/X-Men #1-8 w/new-c   2.25
17-$2.50-c; r/X-Men #17,18   2.50

X-MEN: THE MANGA
Marvel Comics: Mar, 1998 - No. 26, June, 1999 ($2.99, B&W)
1-26-English version of Japanese X-Men comics: 23,24-Randy Green-c   3.00

X-MEN: THE MOVIE
Marvel Comics: Aug, 2000; Sept, 2000
Adaption (9/00, $5.95) Macchio-s/Williams & Lanning-a   6.00
Adaption TPB (9/00, $14.95) Movie adaption and key reprints of main characters; four photo covers (movie X, Magneto, Rogue, Wolverine)   15.00
Prequel: Magneto (8/00, $5.95) Texeira & Palmiotti-a; art & photo covers   6.00
Prequel: Rogue (8/00, $5.95) Evans & Nikolakakis-a; art & photo covers   6.00
Prequel: Wolverine (8/00, $5.95) Waller & McKenna-a; art & photo covers   6.00
TPB X-Men: Beginnings (8/00, $14.95) reprints 3 prequels w/photo-c   15.00

X-MEN: THE ULTRA COLLECTION
Marvel Comics: Dec, 1994 - No. 5, Apr, 1995 ($2.95, limited series)
1-5: Pin-ups; no scripts   3.00

X-MEN: THE WEDDING ALBUM
Marvel Comics: 1994 ($2.95, magazine size, one-shot)
1-Wedding of Scott Summers & Jean Grey   3.00

X-MEN TRUE FRIENDS
Marvel Comics: Sept, 1999 - No. 3, Nov, 1999 ($2.99, limited series)
1-3-Claremont-s/Leonardi-a   3.00

X-MEN 2099 (Also see 2099: World of Tomorrow)
Marvel Comics: Oct, 1993 - No. 35, Aug, 1996 ($1.25/$1.50/$1.95)
1-($1.75)-Foil-c; Ron Lim/Adam Kubert-a begins   3.00
1-2nd printing ($1.75)   2.25
1-Gold edition (15,000 made); sold thru Diamond for $19.40   20.00
2-24,26-35: 3-Death of Tina; Lim-c/a(p) in #1-8. 8-Bound-in trading card sheet. 35-Nostromo (from X-Nation) app; storyline cont'd in 2099: World of Tomorrow.   2.25
25-($2.50)-Double sized   2.50
Special 1 ($3.95)   4.00
...: Oasis ($5.95, one-shot) -Hildebrandt Bros.-c/a   6.00

X-MEN ULTRA III PREVIEW
Marvel Comics: 1995 ($2.95)
nn-Kubert-a   3.00

X-MEN UNIVERSE
Marvel Comics: Dec, 1999 - Present ($4.99/$3.99)
1-8-Reprints stories from recent X-Men titles   5.00
9-15-($3.99)   4.00

X-MEN UNIVERSE: PAST, PRESENT AND FUTURE
Marvel Comics: Feb, 1999 ($2.99, one-shot)
1-Previews 1999 X-Men events; background info   3.00

X-MEN UNLIMITED
Marvel Comics: 1993 - Present ($3.95/$2.99, 68 pgs.)
1-Chris Bachalo-c/a; Quesada-a.   5.00

2-11: 3-Sabretooth-c/story. 2-Origin of Magneto script. 10-Dark Beast vs. Beast. Mark Waid script. 11-Magneto & Rogue   4.00
12-33: 12-Begin $2.99-c; Onslaught x-over; Juggernaut-c/app. 19-Caliafore-a 20-Generation X app. 27-Origin Thunderbird. 29-Maximum Security x-over; Bishop-c/app. 30-Mahfood-a. 31-Stelfreeze-c/a. 32-Dazzler; Thompson-a/a 33-Kaluta-c   3.00
NOTE: *Bachalo* c/a-1. *Quesada* a-1. *Waid* scripts-10

X-MEN VS. DRACULA
Marvel Comics: Dec, 1993 ($1.75)
1-r/X-Men Annual #6; Austin-c(i)   2.25

X-MEN VS. THE AVENGERS, THE
Marvel Comics Group: Apr, 1987 - No. 4, July, 1987 ($1.50, limited series, Baxter paper)
1   4.00
2-4   3.00

X-MEN VS. THE BROOD, THE
Marvel Comics Group: Sept, 1996 - No. 2, Oct, 1996 ($2.95, limited series)
1,2-Wraparound-c; Ostrander-s/Hitch-a(p)   3.00
TPB('97, $16.99) reprints X-Men/Brood: Day of Wrath #1,2 & Uncanny X-Men #232-234   17.00

X-MEN VISIONARIES
Marvel Comics: 1995,1996,2000 (trade paperbacks)
nn-($8.95) Reprints X-Men stories; Adam & Andy Kubert-a   9.00
...2: The Neal Adams Collection (1996) r/X-Men #56-63,65   30.00
...2: The Neal Adams Col. (2nd printing, 2000, $24.95) new Adams-c   25.00

X-MEN/WILDC.A.T.S.: THE DARK AGE (See also WildC.A.T.S./X-Men...)
Marvel Comics: 1998 ($4.50, one-shot)
1-Two covers (Broome & Golden); Ellis-s   4.50

X-NATION 2099
Marvel Comics: Mar, 1996 - No. 6, Aug, 1996 ($1.95)
1-($3.95)-Humberto Ramos-a(p); wraparound, foil-c   4.00
2-6: 2,3-Ramos-a. 4-Exodus-c/app. 6-Reed Richards app   2.25

X-O MANOWAR (1st Series)
Valiant/Acclaim Comics (Valiant) No. 43 on: Feb, 1992 - No. 68, Sept, 1996 ($1.95/$2.25/$2.50, high quality)

0-(8/93, $3.50)-Wraparound embossed chromium-c by Quesada; Solar app.; origin Aric (X-O Manowar)				3.50
0-Gold variant				5.00
1-Intro/1st app. & partial origin of Aric (X-O Manowar); Barry Smith/Layton-a	1	3	6	

2-4: 2-B. Smith/Layton-c; Layton part inks. 3-Layton-c(i). 4-1st app. Shadowman (cameo)   6.00
5-14: 5-B. Smith-c. 6-Begin $2.25-c; Ditko-a(p). 7,8-Unity x-overs. 7-Miller-c. 8-Simonson-c. 12-1st app. Randy Calder. 14,15-Turok-c/stories   3.00
15-Hot pink logo variant; came with Ultra Pro Rigid Comic Sleeves box; no price on cover   4.00
16-24,26-43: 20-Serial number contest insert. 27-29-Turok x-over. 28-Bound-in trading card. 30-1st app. new "good skin"; Solar app. 33-Chaos Effect Delta Pt. 3. 42-Shadowman app.; includes X-O Manowar Birthquake! Prequel   2.50
25-($3.50)-Has 16 pg. Armorines #0 bound-in w/origin   3.50
44-68: 44-Begin $2.50-c. 50-X, 50-O, 51, 52, 63-Bart Sears-c/a/scripts. 68-Revealed that Aric's past stories were premonitions of his future   2.50
Trade paperback nn (1993, $9.95)-Polybagged with copy of X-O Database #1 inside   10.00
Yearbook 1 (4/95, $2.95)   3.00
NOTE: *Layton* a-1i, 2i(part); c-1, 2i, 3i, 6i, 21i. *Reese* a-4i(part); c-26i.

X-O MANOWAR (2nd Series)(Also see Iron Man/X-O Manowar: Heavy Metal)
Acclaim Comics (Valiant Heroes): V2#1, Oct, 1996 - No. 21, Jun, 1998 ($2.50)
V2#1-21: 1-Mark Waid & Brian Augustyn scripts begin; 1st app. Donavon Wylie; Rand Banion dies; painted variant-c exists. 2-Donavon Wylie becomes new X-O Manowar. 7-9-Augustyn-s. 10-Copycat-c   2.50

X-O MANOWAR FAN EDITION
Acclaim Comics (Valiant Heroes): Feb, 1997 (Overstreet's FAN giveaway)
1-Reintro the Armorines & the Hard Corps; 1st app. Citadel; Augustyn scripts;

X-Treme X-Men #1 © MAR

Yanks in Battle #2 © QUA

Yeah! #3 © Peter Bagge & DC

	GD2.0	FN6.0	VF8.0	NM9.4

	GD2.0	FN6.0	VF8.0	NM9.4

McKone-c/a 4.00

X-O MANOWAR/IRON MAN: IN HEAVY METAL (See Iron Man/X-O Manowar: Heavy Metal)
Acclaim Comics (Valiant Heroes): Sept, 1996 ($2.50, one-shot)
(1st Marvel/Valiant x-over)

1-Pt 1 of X-O Manowar/Iron Man x-over; Arnim Zola app.; Fabian Nicieza scripts; Andy Smith-a 2.50

XOMBI
DC Comics (Milestone): Jan, 1994 - No. 21, Feb, 1996 ($1.75/$2.50)

0-($1.95)-Shadow War x-over; Simonson silver ink varnish-c 2.50
1-21: 1-John Byrne-c 2.50
1-Platinum 8.00

X-PATROL
Marvel Comics (Amalgam): Apr, 1996 ($1.95, one-shot)

1-Cruz-a(p) 2.25

XSE
Marvel Comics: Nov, 1996 - No. 4, Feb, 1997 ($1.95, limited series)

1-4: 1-Bishop & Shard app. 2.25
1-Variant-c 3.00

X-TERMINATORS
Marvel Comics: Oct, 1988 - No. 4, Jan, 1989 ($1.00, limited series)

1-1st app.; X-Men/X-Factor tie-in; Williamson-i 3.00
2-4 2.25

X, THE MAN WITH THE X-RAY EYES (See Movie Comics)

X-TREME X-MEN
Marvel Comics: July, 2001 - Present ($2.99)

1-Claremont-s/Larroca-c/a 4.00
2-8: 2-Two covers (Larroca & Pacheco); Psylocke killed 3.00
Annual 2001 ($4.95) issue opens longways 5.00

X-TREME X-MEN: SAVAGE LAND
Marvel Comics: Nov, 2001 - No. 4, Feb, 2002 ($2.99, limited series)

1-4-Claremont-s/Sharpe-c/a; Beast app. 3.00

X-UNIVERSE
Marvel Comics: May, 1995 - No. 2, June, 1995 ($3.50, limited series)

1,2: Age of Apocalypse 5.00

X-VENTURE (Super Heroes)
Victory Magazines Corp.: July, 1947 - No. 2, Nov, 1947

1-Atom Wizard, Mystery Shadow, Lester Trumble begin
| | 100 | 300 | 625 | 1100 |
2 | | 55 | 165 | 341 | 600 |

XYR (See Eclipse Graphic Album Series #21)

YAK YAK
Dell Publishing Co.: No. 1186, May-July, 1961 - No. 1348, Apr-June, 1962

Four Color 1186 (#1)- Jack Davis-c/a; 2 versions, one minus 3pgs.
| | 9 | 27 | 63 | 110 |
Four Color 1348 (#2)-Davis c/a | 8 | 24 | 56 | 100 |

YAKKY DOODLE & CHOPPER (TV) (See Dell Giant #44)
Gold Key: Dec, 1962 (Hanna-Barbera)

1 | | 7 | 21 | 49 | 95 |

YANG (See House of Yang)
Charlton Comics: Nov, 1973 - No. 13, May, 1976; V14#15, Sept, 1985 - No. 17, Jan, 1986 (No V14#14, series resumes with #15)

1-Origin; Sattler-a begins; slavery-s | 2 | 6 | 10 | 14 |
2-13(1976) | 1 | 3 | 6 | 8 |
15-17(1986): 15-Reprints #1 (Low print run) | | | | 6.00 |
3,10,11(Modern Comics-r, 1977) | | | | 4.00 |

YANKEE COMICS
Harry 'A' Chesler: Sept, 1941 - No. 7, 1942?

1-Origin The Echo, The Enchanted Dagger, Yankee Doodle Jones, The Firebrand, & The Scarlet Sentry; Black Satan app.; Yankee Doodle Jones app. on all covers
| | 164 | 492 | 1023 | 1800 |

2-Origin Johnny Rebel; Major Victory app.; Barry Kuda begins
| | 77 | 231 | 483 | 850 |
3,4: 4-(3/42) | 59 | 177 | 369 | 650 |
4 (nd, 1940s; 7-1/4x5", 68 pgs. distr. to the service)-Foxy Grandpa, Tom, Dick & Harry, Impy, Ace & Deuce, Dot & Dash, Ima Slooth by Jack Cole (Remington Morse publ.) | 8 | 24 | 42 | 60 |
5-7 (nd; 10¢, 7-1/4x5", 68 pgs.)(Remington Morse publ.)-urges readers to send their copies to servicemen. | 7 | 21 | 36 | 50 |

YANKEE DOODLE THE SPIRIT OF LIBERTY
Spire Publications: 1984 (no price, 36 pgs)

nn-Al Hartley-s/c/a | 1 | 3 | 6 | 9 |

YANKS IN BATTLE
Quality Comics Group: Sept, 1956 - No. 4, Dec, 1956; 1963

1-Cuidera-c(i) | 10 | 30 | 55 | 80 |
2-4: Cuidera-c(i) | 7 | 21 | 36 | 50 |
I.W. Reprint #3(1963)-r/#?; exist? | 2 | 6 | 11 | 15 |

YARDBIRDS, THE (G. I. Joe's Sidekicks)
Ziff-Davis Publishing Co.: Summer, 1952

1-By Bob Oskner | 10 | 30 | 55 | 85 |

YARN MAN (See Megaton Man)
Kitchen Sink : Oct, 1989 ($2.00, B&W, one-shot)

1-Donald Simpson-c/a/scripts 2.25

YARNS OF YELLOWSTONE
World Color Press: 1972 (50¢, 36 pgs.)

nn-Illustrated by Bill Chapman | 2 | 6 | 9 | 12 |

YEAH!
DC Comics (Homage): Oct, 1999 - No. 9, Jun, 2000 ($2.95)

1-Bagge-s/Hernandez-a 3.00
2-9: 2-Editorial page contains adult language 3.00

YELLOW CLAW (Also see Giant Size Master of Kung Fu)
Atlas Comics (MjMC): Oct, 1956 - No. 4, Apr, 1957

1-Origin by Joe Maneely | 95 | 285 | 597 | 1050 |
2-Kirby-a | 76 | 228 | 475 | 840 |
3,4-Kirby-a; 4-Kirby/Severin-a | 73 | 219 | 455 | 800 |
NOTE: *Everett* c-3. *Maneely* c-1. *Reinman* a-2i, 3. *Severin* c-2, 4.

YELLOWJACKET COMICS (Jack in the Box #11 on)(See TNT Comics)
E. Levy/Frank Comunale/Charlton: Sept, 1944 - No. 10, June, 1946

1-Intro & origin Yellowjacket; Diana, the Huntress begins; E.A. Poe's "The Black Cat" adaptation | 64 | 192 | 398 | 700 |
2-Yellowjacket-c begin, end #10 | 40 | 120 | 232 | 400 |
3,5 | 40 | 120 | 217 | 375 |
4-E.A. Poe's "Fall of the House Of Usher" adaptation; Palais-a
| | 40 | 120 | 232 | 400 |
6 | 47 | 141 | 286 | 500 |
7-Classic skull-c | 91 | 273 | 568 | 1000 |
8-10: 1,3,4,6-10-Have stories narrated by old witch in "Tales of Terror" (1st horror series?) | 43 | 129 | 257 | 450 |

YELLOWSTONE KELLY (Movie)
Dell Publishing Co.: No. 1056, Nov-Jan, 1959/60

Four Color 1056-Clint Walker photo-c | 5 | 15 | 35 | 65 |

YELLOW SUBMARINE (See Movie Comics)

YIN FEI THE CHINESE NINJA
Leung's Publications: 1988 - No. 8, 1990 ($1.80/$2.00, 52 pgs.)

1-8 2.25

YOGI BEAR (See Dell Giant #41, Golden Comics Digest, Kite Fun Book, March of Dimes #253, 265, 279, 291, 309, 319, 337, 344, Movie Comics under "Hey There It's..." & Whitman Comic Books)

YOGI BEAR (TV) (Hanna-Barbera) (See Four Color #990)
Dell Publishing Co./Gold Key No. 10 on: No. 1067, 12-2/59-60 - No. 9, 7-9/62; No. 10, 10/62-No. 42, 10/70

Four Color 1067 (#1)-TV show debuted 1/30/61 | 12 | 36 | 84 | 150 |
Four Color 1104,1162 (5-7/61) | 7 | 21 | 49 | 95 |

Young Allies Comics #6 © MAR

Youngblood #10 © Awesome Ent.

Young Brides #3 © PRIZE

	GD2.0	FN6.0	VF8.0	NM9.4
4(8-9/61) - 6(12-1/61-62)	5	15	35	65
Four Color 1271(11/61)	5	15	35	65
Four Color 1349(1/62)-Photo-c	9	27	63	120
7(2-3/62) - 9(7-9/62)-Last Dell	5	15	35	65

10(10/62-G.K.), 11(1/63)-titled "Yogi Bear Jellystone Jollies" (80 pgs.);

11-X-mas-c	7	21	49	90
12(4/63), 14-20	4	12	30	50
13(7/63, 68 pgs.)-Surprise Party	7	21	49	90
21-30	3	9	21	32
31-42	3	9	17	25

YOGI BEAR (TV)
Charlton Comics: Nov, 1970 - No. 35, Jan, 1976 (Hanna-Barbera)

1	4	12	29	45
2-6,8-10	3	9	17	25
7-Summer Fun (Giant, 52 pgs.)	4	12	30	50
11-20	2	6	15	22
21-35: 28-31-partial-r	2	6	11	16

YOGI BEAR (TV)(See The Flintstones, 3rd series & Spotlight #1)
Marvel Comics Group: Nov, 1977 - No. 9, Mar, 1979 (Hanna-Barbera)

1,7-9: 1-Flintstones begin (Newsstand sales only)	2	6	13	20
2-6	2	6	9	12

YOGI BEAR (TV)
Harvey Comics: Sept, 1992 - No. 6, Mar, 1994 ($1.25/$1.50) (Hanna-Barbera)

V2#1-6				3.00
...Big Book V2#1,2 ($1.95, 52 pgs): 1-(11/92). 2-(3/93)				3.00
...Giant Size V2#1,2 ($2.25, 68 pgs.): 1-(10/92). 2-(4/93)				3.00

YOGI BEAR'S EASTER PARADE (See The Funtastic World of Hanna-Barbera #2)

YOGI BERRA (Baseball hero)
Fawcett Publications: 1951 (Yankee catcher)

nn-Photo-c (scarce)	68	205	426	750

YOSEMITE SAM (...& Bugs Bunny) (TV)
Gold Key/Whitman: Dec, 1970 - No. 81, Feb, 1984

1	4	12	29	45
2-10	2	6	13	20
11-20	2	6	10	14
21-30	2	6	9	12
31-50	1	3	6	9
51-65 (Gold Key)	1	3	5	7
66,67 (Whitman)	1	4	7	10
68(9/80), 69(10/80), 70(12/80) 3-pack?	2	6	12	18
71-78: 76(2/82), 77(3/82), 78(4/82)	2	6	9	12
79-81 All #90263 on-c, no date or date code; 3-pack): 79(7/83). 80(8/83).				
81(2/84)-(1/3-r)	2	6	11	15

(See March of Comics #363, 380, 392)

YOUNG ALLIES COMICS (All-Winners #21; see Kid Komics #2)
Timely Comics (USA 1-7/NPI 8,9/YAI 10-20): Sum, 1941 - No. 20, Oct, 1946

1-Origin/1st app. The Young Allies (Bucky, Toro, others); 1st meeting of Captain America & Human Torch; Red Skull-c & app.; S&K-c/splash; Hitler-c; Note: the cover was altered after its preview in Human Torch #5. Stalin was shown with Hitler but was removed due to Russia becoming an ally

	1071	3214	7500	15,000

2-(Winter, 1941)-Captain America & Human Torch app.; Simon & Kirby-c

	333	1000	2083	4000

3-Fathertime, Captain America & Human Torch app.; Remember Pearl Harbor issue (Spring, 1942); Stan Lee scripts; Vs. Japs-c/full-length story

	255	765	1591	2800

4-The Vagabond & Red Skull, Capt. America, Human Torch app. Classic Red Skull-c

	350	1050	2188	4200

5-Captain America & Human Torch app.

	173	519	1080	1900

6-8,10: 10-Origin Tommy Tyme & Clock of Ages; ends #19

	118	354	738	1300

9-Hitler, Tojo, Mussolini-c	136	408	852	1500
11-20: 12-Classic decapitation story	95	285	597	1050

NOTE: Brodsky c-15. Gabrielle a-3; c-3, 4. S&K c-1, 2. Schomburg c-5-14, 16-19. Shores c-20.

YOUNG ALL-STARS
DC Comics: June, 1987 - No. 31, Nov, 1989 ($1.00, deluxe format)

	GD2.0	FN6.0	VF8.0	NM9.4
1-31: 1-1st app. Iron Munro & The Flying Fox. 8,9-Millennium tie-ins				2.25
Annual 1 (1988, $2.00)				2.25

YOUNGBLOOD (See Brigade #4, Megaton Explosion & Team Youngblood)
Image Comics (Extreme Studios): Apr, 1992 - No. 4, Feb, 1993 ($2.50, lim. series); No. 6, June, 1994 (No #5) - No. 10, Dec, 1994 ($1.95/$2.50)

1-Liefeld-c/a/scripts in all; flip book format with 2 trading cards; 1st Image/Extreme Studios title.		5.00
1,2-2nd printing		2.50
2-(JUN-c, July 1992 indicia)-1st app. Shadowhawk in solo back-up story; 2 trading cards inside; flip book format; 1st app. Prophet, Kirby, Berzerkers, Darkthorn		2.50
3,0,4,5: 3-(OCT-c, August 1992 indicia)-Contains 2 trading cards inside (flip book); 1st app. Supreme in back-up story; 1st app. Showdown. 0-(12/92, $1.95)-Contains 2 trading cards; 2 cover variations exist, green or beige logo; w/Image #0 coupon. 4-(2/93)-Glow-in-the-dark-c w/2 trading cards; 2nd app. Dale Keown's The Pitt; Bloodstrike app. 5-Flip book w/Brigade #4		2.50
6-($3.50, 52 pgs.)-Wraparound-c		3.50
7-10: 7, 8-Liefeld-c(p/a(p)/story. 8,9-(9/94) 9-Valentino story & art		2.50
Battlezone 1 (May-c, 4/93 inside, $1.95)-Arsenal book; Liefeld-c(p)		2.50
Battlezone 2 (7/94, $2.95)-Wraparound-c		3.00
Yearbook 1 (7/93, $2.50)-Fold out panel; 1st app. Tyrax & Kanan		2.50
...Super Special (Winter '97, $2.99) Sprouse -a		3.00
TPB (1996, $16.95)-r/Team Youngblood #8-10 & Youngblood #6-8,10		17.00

YOUNGBLOOD
Image Comics (Extreme Studios)/Maximum Press No. 14: V2#1, Sept, 1995 - No. 14, Dec, 1996 ($2.50)

V2#1-10,14: Roger Cruz-a in all. 4-Extreme Destroyer Pt. 4 w/gaming card. 5-Variant-c exists. 6-Angela & Glory. 7-Shadowhunt Pt. 3; Shadowhawk app. 8,10-Thor (from Supreme) app. 10-(7/96). 14-(12/96)-1st Maximum Press issue		2.50

YOUNGBLOOD (Volume 3)
Awesome-Hyperwerks #2 on: Feb, 1998 - Present ($2.50)

1-Alan Moore-s/Skroce-a; 12 diff. covers		2.50
1-Gold foil-c		5.00
1-Blue foil-c Orlando Con Ed.		10.00
1+ Alter Ego Gold Foil		5.00
2-(8/98) Skroce & Liefeld covers		2.50

YOUNGBLOOD: STRIKEFILE
Image Comics (Extreme Studios): Apr, 1993 - No. 11, Feb, 1995 ($1.95/$2.50/$2.95)

1-10: 1-($1.95)-Flip book w/Jae Lee-c/a & Liefeld-c/a in #1-3; 1st app. The Allies,Giger, & Glory. 3-Thibert-i assist. 4-Liefeld-c(p); no Lee-a. 5-Liefeld-c(p). 8-Platt-c		3.00

NOTE: Youngblood: Strikefile began as a four issue limited series.

YOUNGBLOOD/X-FORCE
Image Comics (Extreme Studios): July, 1996 ($4.95, one-shot)

1-Cruz-a(p); two covers exist		5.00

YOUNG BRIDES (True Love Secrets)
Feature/Prize Publ.: Sept-Oct, 1952 - No. 30, Nov-Dec, 1956 (Photo-c: 1-4)

	GD2.0	FN6.0	VF8.0	NM9.4
V1#1-Simon & Kirby-a	33	99	174	300
2-S&K-a	18	54	94	160
3-6-S&K-a	17	51	88	150
V2#1,3-7,10-12 (#7-18)-S&K-a	16	48	83	140
2,8,9-No S&K-a	6	18	29	40
V3#1-3(#19-21)-Last precode (3-4/55)	5	15	25	35
4,6(#22,24), V4#1,3(#25,27)	5	15	23	30
V3#5(#23)-Meskin-a	5	15	25	35
V4#2(#26)-All S&K issue	14	42	72	120
V4#4(#28)-S&K-a	11	33	55	90
V4#5,6(#29,30)	6	18	29	40

YOUNG DR. MASTERS (See The Adventures of Young Dr. Masters)

YOUNG DOCTORS, THE
Charlton Comics: Jan, 1963 - No. 6, Nov, 1963

V1#1	3	9	21	32
2-6	2	6	13	20

Young Eagle #8 © FAW

Young Justice: Our Worlds at War #1 © DC

Young King Cole V3 #6 © Premium

YO

	GD2.0	FN6.0	VF8.0	NM9.4

YOUNG EAGLE
Fawcett Publications/Charlton: 12/50 - No. 10, 6/52; No. 3, 7/56 - No. 5, 4/57
(Photo-c: 1-10)

1-Intro Young Eagle	18	54	94	160
2-Complete picture novelette "The Mystery of Thunder Canyon"	10	30	55	80
3-9	9	27	49	70
10-Origin Thunder, Young Eagle's Horse	8	24	42	60
3-5(Charlton)-Formerly Sherlock Holmes?	5	15	25	35

YOUNG HEARTS
Marvel Comics (SPC): Nov, 1949 - No. 2, Feb, 1950

1-Photo-c	13	39	66	110
2-Colleen Townsend photo-c from movie	8	24	45	65

YOUNG HEARTS IN LOVE
Super Comics: 1964

17,18: 17-r/Young Love V5#6 (4-5/62)	2	6	11	16

YOUNG HEROES (Formerly Forbidden Worlds #34)
American Comics Group (Titan): No. 35, Feb-Mar, 1955 - No. 37, Jun-Jul, 1955

35-37-Frontier Scout	10	30	55	80

YOUNG HEROES IN LOVE
DC Comics: June, 1997 - No. 17; #1,000,000, Nov, 1998 ($1.75/$1.95/$2.50)

1-1st app. Young Heroes; Madan-a	3.00
2-17: 3-Superman-c/app. 7-Begin $1.95-c	2.50
#1,000,000 (11/98, $2.50) 853 Century x-over	2.50

YOUNG INDIANA JONES CHRONICLES, THE
Dark Horse Comics: Feb, 1992 - No. 12, Feb, 1993 ($2.50)

1-12: Dan Barry scripts in all	2.50
NOTE: Dan Barry a(p)-1, 2, 5, 6, 10; c-1-10. Morrow a-3, 4, 5p, 6p. Springer a-1i, 2i.	

YOUNG INDIANA JONES CHRONICLES, THE
Hollywood Comics (Disney): 1992 ($3.95, squarebound, 68 pgs.)

1-3: 1-r/YIJC #1,2 by D. Horse. 2-r/#3,4. 3-r/#5,6	4.00

YOUNG JUSTICE
DC Comics: Sept, 1998 - Present ($2.50)

1-Robin, Superboy & Impulse team-up; David-s/Nauck-a	4.00
2,3: 3-Mxyzptlk app.	3.00
4-20: 4-Wonder Girl, Arrowette and the Secret join. 6-JLA app.	
13-Supergirl x-over. 20-Sins of Youth aftermath	3.00
21-41: 25-Empress ID revealed. 28,29-Forever People app. 32-Empress origin	
35,36-Our Worlds at War x-over. 38-Joker: Last Laugh x-over. 41-The Ray	
joins	2.50
#1,000,000 (11/98) 853 Century x-over	2.50
...: A League of Their Own (2000, $14.95, TPB) r/#1-7, Secret Files #1	15.00
...: 80-Page Giant (5/99, $4.95) Ramos-c; stories and art by various	5.00
...: In No Man's Land (7/99, $3.95) McDaniel-a	4.00
...: Our Worlds at War (8/01, $4.95) Jae Lee-c; Linear Men app.	3.00
...: Secret Files (1/99, $4.95) Origin-s & pin-ups	5.00
...: The Secret (6/98, $1.95) Girlfrenzy; Nauck-a	2.50

YOUNG JUSTICE: SINS OF YOUTH (Also see Sins of Youth x-over issues and
Sins of Youth: Secret Files)
DC Comics: May, 2000 - No. 2, May, 2000 ($3.95, limited series)

1,2-Young Justice, JLA & JSA swap ages; David-s/Nauck-a	4.00
TPB (2000, $19.95) r/#1,2 & all x-over issues)	20.00

YOUNG KING COLE (...Detective Tales)(Becomes Criminals on the Run)
Premium Group/Novelty Press: Fall, 1945 - V3#12, July, 1948

V1#1-Toni Gayle begins	31	93	165	285
2	14	42	72	125
3-4	13	39	66	110
V2#1-7(8-9/46-7/47): 6,7-Certa-c	10	30	55	85
V3#1,3-6,8,9,12: 3-Certa-c. 5-McWilliams-c/a. 8,9-Harmon-c				
	10	30	55	80
2-L.B. Cole-a; Certa-c	16	48	83	140
7-L.B. Cole-c/a	22	66	116	195
10,11-L.B. Cole-c	19	57	99	165

YOUNG LAWYERS, THE (TV)
Dell Publishing Co.: Jan, 1971 - No. 2, Apr, 1971

1	2	6	15	22
2	2	6	11	16

YOUNG LIFE (Teen Life #3 on)
New Age Publ./Quality Comics Group: Summer, 1945 - No. 2, Fall, 1945

1-Skip Homeier, Louis Prima stories	15	45	77	130
2-Frank Sinatra photo on-c plus story	17	51	88	150

YOUNG LOVE (Sister title to Young Romance)
Prize(Feature)Publ.(Crestwood): 2-3/49 - No. 73, 12-1/56-57; V3#5, 2/60 -
V7#1, 6-7/63

V1#1-S&K-c/a(2)	43	129	257	450
2-Photo-c begin; S&K-a	25	75	130	225
3-S&K-a	19	57	99	170
4-5-Minor S&K-a	12	36	61	100
V2#1(#7)-S&K-a(2)	19	57	99	170
2-5(#8-11)-Minor S&K only. 14-S&K-c only.	10	30	55	80
6,8(#12,14)-S&K-c	11	33	55	90
7,9-12(#13,15-18)-S&K-c/a	18	54	94	160
V3#1-4(#19-22)-S&K-c/a	16	48	83	140
5-7,9-12(#23-25,27-30)-Photo-c resume; S&K-a	14	42	72	125
8(#26)-No S&K-a	6	18	29	40
V4#1,6(#31,36)-S&K-a	13	39	66	115
2-5,7-12(#32-35,37-42)-Minor S&K-a	10	30	55	80
V5#1-12(#43-54), V6#1-9(#55-63)-Last precode; S&K-a in some				
	6	18	29	40
V6#10-12(#64-66)	3	9	21	32
V7#1-7(#67-73)	3	9	19	28
V3#5(2-3/60)-S&K-a (4-5/60)(Formerly All For Love)	3	9	17	25
V4#1(6-7/60)-6(4-5/61)	2	6	15	22
V5#1(6-7/61)-6(4-5/62)	2	6	15	22
V6#1(6-7/62)-6(4-5/63), V7#1	2	6	13	20
NOTE: Meskin a-14(2), 27, 42. Powell a-V4#6. Severin/Elder a-V1#3. S&K art not in #53, 57, 58, 61, 63-65. Photo-c most V3#5-V5#11.				

YOUNG LOVE
National Periodical Publ.(Arleigh Publ. Corp #49-61)/DC Comics:
#39, 9-10/63 - #120, Wint./75-76; #121, 10/76 - #126, 7/77

39	4	12	30	50
40-50	3	10	23	35
51-68,70	3	9	20	30
69-(80 pg. Giant)(8-9/68)	5	15	38	60
71,72,74-77,80	3	9	17	25
73,78,79-Toth-a	3	9	19	28
81-99: 88-96-(52 pg. Giants)	3	9	15	22
100	3	9	17	25
101-106,115-122	2	6	12	18
107 (100 pgs.)	8	24	56	90
108-114 (100 pgs.)	6	18	45	75
121-126 (52 pgs.)	3	10	23	35
NOTE: Bolle a-117. Colan a-107r. Nasser a-123, 124. Orlando a-122. Simonson c-125. Toth a-73, 78, 79, 122-125r. Wood a-109r(4 pgs.).				

YOUNG LOVER ROMANCES (Formerly & becomes Great Lover...)
Toby Press: No. 4, June, 1952 - No. 5, Aug, 1952

4,5-Photo-c	7	21	36	50

YOUNG LOVERS (My Secret Life #19 on)(Formerly Brenda Starr?)
Charlton Comics: No. 16, July, 1956 - No. 18, May, 1957

16,17('56): 16-Marcus Swayze-a	7	21	38	55
18-Elvis Presley picture-c, text story (biography)(Scarce)				
	59	177	369	650

YOUNG MARRIAGE
Fawcett Publications: June, 1950

1-Powell-a; photo-c	13	39	66	110

YOUNG MEN (Formerly Cowboy Romances)(...on the Battlefield #12-20
(4/53); ...In Action #21)
Marvel/Atlas Comics (IPC): No. 4, 6/50 - No. 11, 10/51; No. 12, 12/51 - No. 28,
6/54

Young Men #23 © MAR

Young Romance Comics #201 © DC

Youthful Romances #5 © Ribage

	GD2.0	FN6.0	VF8.0	NM9.4
4-(52 pgs.)	20	60	105	180
5-11	12	36	61	105
12-23: 12-20-War format. 21-23-Hot Rod issues starring Flash Foster				
	12	36	61	100
24-(12/53)-Origin Captain America, Human Torch, & Sub-Mariner which are				
revived thru #28; Red Skull app.	282	846	1763	3100
25-28: 25-Romita-c/a (see Men's Advs.)	107	321	669	1175

NOTE: **Berg** a-7, 14, 17, 18, 20; c-177 **Brodsky** c-4-9, 13, 14, 16, 17, 21-25. **Burgos** c-26-28. **Colan** a-14, 15. **Everett** a-18-20. **Heath** a-13, 14. **Maneely** c-10, 12, 15. **Pakula** a-14, 15. **Robinson** c-18. **Captain America** by **Romita**-#24?, 25, 26?, 27, 28. **Human Torch** by **Burgos**-#25, 27, 28. **Sub-Mariner** by **Everett**-#24-28.

YOUNG REBELS, THE (TV)
Dell Publishing Co.: Jan, 1971

1-Photo-c	2	6	12	18

YOUNG ROMANCE COMICS (The 1st romance comic)
Prize/Headline (Feature Publ.) (Crestwood): Sept-Oct, 1947 - V16#4, June-July, 1963 (#1-33: 52 pgs.)

V1#1-S&K-c/a(2)	45	135	270	475
2-S&K-c/a(2-3)	31	93	168	290
3-6-S&K-c/a(2-3) each	27	81	145	250
V2#1-6(#7-12)-S&K-c/a(2-3) each	24	72	127	220
V3#1-3(#13-15): V3#1-Photo-c begin; S&K-a	16	48	83	145
4-12(#16-24)-Photo-c; S&K-a	16	48	83	145
V4#1-11(#25-35)-S&K-a	15	45	77	135
12(#36)-S&K, Toth-a	17	51	88	150
V5#1-12(#37-48), V6#4-12(#52-60)-S&K-a	15	45	77	135
V6#1-3(#49-51)-No S&K-a	7	21	38	55
V7#1-11(#61-71)-S&K-a in most	12	36	61	105
V7#12(#72), V8#1-3(#73-75)-Last precode (12-1/54-55)-No S&K-a				
	6	18	29	40
V8#4(#76, 4-5/55), 5(#77)-No S&K-a	5	15	25	35
V8#6-8(#78-80, 12-1/55-56)-S&K-a	10	30	55	80
V9#3,5,6(#81, 2-3/56, 83,84)-S&K-a	10	30	55	80
4, V10#1(#82,85)-All S&K-a	11	33	55	90
V10#2-6(#86-90, 10-11/57)-S&K-a	7	21	50	80
V11#1,2,5,6(#91,92,95,96)-S&K-a	7	21	50	80
3,4(#93,94), V12#2,4,5(#98,100,101)-No S&K	3	9	20	30
V12#1,3,6(#97,99,102)-S&K-a	7	21	50	80
V13#1(#103)-Powell-a; S&K's last-a for Crestwood	7	21	50	80
2,4-6(#104-108)	3	9	17	25
V13#3(#105, 4-5/60)-Elvis Presley-c app. only	4	12	29	45
V14#1-6, V15#1-6, V16#1-4(#109-124)	2	6	13	20

NOTE: **Meskin** a-16, 24(2), 33, 47, 50. **Robinson/Meskin** a-6. **Leonard Starr** a-11. Photo c-13-32, 34-65. Issues 1-3 say "Designed for the More Adult Readers of Comics" on cover.

YOUNG ROMANCE COMICS (Continued from Prize series)
National Periodical Publ.(Arleigh Publ. Corp. No. 127): No. 125, Aug-Sept, 1963 - No. 208, Nov-Dec, 1975

125	7	21	53	85
126-140	4	12	29	45
141-153,156-162,165-169	3	10	23	45
154-Neal Adams-c	4	12	30	50
155-1st publ. Aragonés-s (no art)	4	12	29	45
163,164-Toth-a	4	12	26	40
170-172 (68 pg. Giants): 170-Michell from Young Love ends; Lily Martin, the Swinger begins	4	12	29	45
173-183 (52 pgs.)	4	12	25	38
184-196	2	6	15	22
197-204-(100 pgs.)	6	18	45	75
205-208	2	6	12	18

YOUNG ZEN: CITY OF DEATH
Entity Comics: Late 1994 ($3.25, B&W)

1				3.25

YOUNG ZEN INTERGALACTIC NINJA (Also see Zen...)
Entity Comics: 1993 - No. 3, 1994 ($3.50/$2.95, B&W)

1-($3.50)-Polybagged w/Sam Kieth chromium trading card; gold foil logo				3.50
2-($2.95)-Gold foil logo				3.00

YOUR DREAMS (See Strange World of...)

YOU'RE UNDER ARREST (Manga)
Dark Horse Comics: Dec, 1995 - No. 8, July, 1996 ($2.95, limited series)

1-8				3.00

YOUR UNITED STATES
Lloyd Jacquet Studios: 1946

nn-Used in **SOTI**, pg. 309,310; Sid Greene-a	24	72	127	215

YOUTHFUL HEARTS (Daring Confessions #4 on)
Youthful Magazines: May, 1952 - No. 3, Sept, 1952

1- "Monkey on Her Back" swipes E.C. drug story/Shock SuspenStories #12; Frankie Laine photo on-c; Doug Wildey-a in al	29	87	156	270
2,3: 2-Vic Damone photo on-c. 3-Johnny Raye photo on-c				
	21	63	110	185

YOUTHFUL LOVE (Truthful Love #2)
Youthful Magazines: May, 1950

1	12	36	61	100

YOUTHFUL ROMANCES
Pix-Parade #1-14/Ribage #15 on- 8-9/49 - No. 5, 4/50; No. 6, 2/51; No. 7, 5/51 - #14, 10/52; #15, 1/53 - #18, 7/53; No. 5, 9/53 - No. 9, 8/54

1-(1st series)-Titled Youthful Love-Romances	26	78	139	240
2-Walter Johnson c-1-4	16	48	83	140
3-5	12	36	61	105
6,7,9-14(10/52, Pix-Parade; becomes Daring Love #15). 10(1/52)-Mel Torme photo-c/story. 12-Tony Bennett photo-c, 8pg. story & text bio.13-Richard Hayes (singer) photo-c/story; Bob & Ray photo/text story.	11	33	55	90
8-Frank Sinatra photo/text story; Wood-c/a	18	54	94	160
15-18 (Ribage)-All have photos on-c. 15-Spike Jones photo-c/story. 16-Tony Bavaar photo-c	10	30	55	80
5(9/53, Ribage)-Les Paul & Mary Ford photo-c/story; Charlton Heston photo/text story	9	27	49	70
6-9: 6-Bobby Wayne (singer) photo-c/story. 7(2/54)-Tony Martin photo-c/story; Cyd Charise photo/text story. 8(5/54)- Gordon McCrae photo-c/story. 9(8/54)-Ralph Flanagan (band leader) photo-c/story; Audrey Hepburn photo/text story.	7	21	38	55

Y2K: THE COMIC
New England Comics Press: Oct, 1999 ($3.95, one-shot)

1-Y2K scenarios and survival tips				4.00

YUPPIES FROM HELL (Also see Son of...)
Marvel Comics: 1989 ($2.95, B&W, one-shot, direct sales, 52 pgs.)

1-Satire				3.00

ZAGO, JUNGLE PRINCE (My Story #5 on)
Fox Features Syndicate: Sept, 1948 - No. 4, Mar, 1949

1-Blue Beetle app.; partial-r/Atomic #4 (Toni Luck)	59	177	369	650
2,3-Kamen-a	47	142	286	500
4-Baker-c	40	120	232	400

ZANE GREY'S STORIES OF THE WEST
Dell Publishing Co./Gold Key 11/64: No. 197, 9/48 - No. 996, 5-7/59; 11/64 (All painted-c)

Four Color 197(#1)(9/48)	11	33	77	145
Four Color 222,230,236('49)	6	18	42	80
Four Color 246,255,270,301,314,333,346	4	12	30	50
Four Color 357,372,395,412,433,449,467,484	4	12	26	40
Four Color 511-Kinstler-a; Kubert-a	4	12	30	50
Four Color 532,555,583,604,616,632(5/55)	4	12	26	40
27 (9-11/55) - 39 (9-11/58)	4	12	26	40
Four Color 996(5-7/59)	4	12	26	40
10131-411-(11/64-G.K.)-Nevada; r/4-Color #996	3	9	20	30

ZANY (Magazine)(Satire)(See Frantic & Ratfink)
Candor Publ. Co.: Sept, 1958 - No. 4, May, 1959

1-Bill Everett-c	10	30	55	80
2-4: 4-Everett-c	8	24	42	60

ZATANNA (See Adv. Comics #413, JLA #161, Supergirl #1, World's Finest Comics #274)

Zegra, Jungle Empress #2 © FOX

Zero Girl #3 © I Before E, Inc.

Zip Comics #20 © MLJ

	GD2.0	FN6.0	VF8.0	NM9.4

DC Comics: July, 1993 - No. 4, Oct, 1993 ($1.95, limited series)
1-4				2.25
Special 1(1987, $2.00)-Gray Morrow-c/a				3.00

ZAZA, THE MYSTIC (Formerly Charlie Chan; This Magazine Is Haunted V2#12 on)
Charlton Comics: No. 10, Apr, 1956 - No. 11, Sept, 1956
10,11	12	36	61	100

ZEALOT (Also see WildC.A.T.S: Covert Action Teams)
Image Comics: Aug, 1995 - No. 3, Nov, 1995 ($2.50, limited series)
1-3				2.50

ZEGRA JUNGLE EMPRESS (Formerly Tegra)(My Love Life #6 on)
Fox Features Syndicate: No. 2, Oct, 1948 - No. 5, April, 1949
2	61	182	381	675
3-5	47	140	286	500

ZEN INTERGALACTIC NINJA
No Publisher: 1987 -1993 ($1.75/$2.00, B&W)
1	2	6	11	15
2-6: Copyright-Stern & Cote	1	3	6	8
V2#1-4-($2.00)				3.00
V3#1-5-($2.95)				3.00
... :Christmas Special 1 (1992, $2.95)				3.00
... :Earth Day Special 1 (1993, $2.95)				3.00

ZEN, INTERGALACTIC NINJA (mini-series)
Zen Comics/Archie Comics: Sept, 1992 - No. 3, 1992 ($1.25)(Formerly a B&W comic by Zen Comics)
1-3: 1-Origin Zen; contains mini-poster				3.00

ZEN INTERGALACTIC NINJA
Entity Comics: No. 0, June-July, 1993 - No. 3, 1994 ($2.95, B&W, limited series)
0-Gold foil stamped-c; photo-c of Zen model				3.00
1-3: Gold foil stamped-c; Bill Maus-c/a				3.00
0-(1993, $3.50, color)-Chromium-c by Jae Lee				3.50
...Sourcebook 1-(1993, $3.50)				3.50
...Sourcebook '94-(1994, $3.50)				3.50

ZEN INTERGALACTIC NINJA: APRIL FOOL'S SPECIAL
Parody Press: 1994 ($2.50, B&W)
1-w/flip story of Renn Intergalactic Chihuahua				3.00

ZEN INTERGALACTIC NINJA COLOR
Entity Comics: 1994 - No. 7, 1995 ($2.25)
1-($3.95)-Chromium die cut-c				4.00
1, 0-($2.25)-Newsstand; Jae Lee-c; r/...All New Color Special #0				3.00
2-($2.50)-Flip book				3.00
2-($3.50)-Flip book, polybagged w/chromium trading card				3.50
3-7				3.00
Summer Special (1994, $2.95)				3.00
Yearbook: Hazardous Duty 1 (1995)				3.00
Zen-isms 1 (1995, 2.95)				3.00
Ashcan-Tour of the Universe-(no price) w/flip cover				3.00

ZEN INTERGALACTIC NINJA COMMEMORATIVE EDITION
Zen Comics Publishing: 1997 ($5.95, color)
1-Stern-s/Cote-a				6.00

ZEN INTERGALACTIC NINJA MILESTONE
Entity Comics: 1994 - No. 3, 1994 ($2.95, limited series)
1-3: Gold foil logo; r/Defend the Earth				3.00

ZEN INTERGALACTIC NINJA SPRING SPECTACULAR
Entity Comics: 1994 ($2.95, B&W, one-shot)
1-Gold foil logo				3.00

ZEN INTERGALACTIC NINJA STARQUEST
Entity Comics: 1994 - No. 6, 1995 ($2.95, B&W)
1-6: Gold foil logo				3.00

ZEN, INTERGALACTIC NINJA: THE HUNTED
Entity Comics: 1993 - No. 3, 1994 ($2.95, B&W, limited series)

1-3: Newsstand Edition; foil logo				3.00
1-($3.50)-Polybagged w/chromium card by Kieth; foil logo				3.50

ZERO GIRL
DC Comics (Homage): Feb, 2001 - No. 5, Jun, 2001 ($2.95, limited series)
1-5-Sam Kieth-s/a				3.00
TPB (2001, $14.95) r/#1-5; intro. by Alan Moore				15.00

ZERO HOUR: CRISIS IN TIME (Also see Showcase '94 #8-10)
DC Comics: No. 4(#1), Sept, 1994 - No. 0(#5), Oct, 1994 ($1.50, limited series)
4(#1)-0(#5)				4.00
"Ashcan"-(1994, free, B&W, 8 pgs.) several versions exist				2.25
TPB ('94, $9.95)				10.00

ZERO PATROL, THE
Continuity Comics: Nov, 1984 - No. 2 ($1.50); 1987 - No. 5, May, 1989 ($2.00)
1,2: Neal Adams-c/a; Megalith begins				4.00
1-5 (#1,2-reprints above, 1987)				3.00

ZERO TOLERANCE
First Comics: Oct, 1990 - No. 4, Jan, 1991 ($2.25, limited series)
1-4: Tim Vigil-c/a(p) (his 1st color limited series)				3.00

ZERO ZERO
Fantagraphics: Mar, 1995 -No. 27 ($3.95/$4.95, B&W, anthology, mature)
1-7,9-15,17-25				5.00
8,16				6.00
26-($4.95) Bagge-c				5.00

ZIGGY PIG-SILLY SEAL COMICS (See Animal Fun, Animated Movie-Tunes, Comic Capers, Krazy Komics, Silly Tunes & Super Rabbit)
Timely Comics (CmPL): Fall, 1944 - No. 6, Fall, 1946
1-Vs. the Japs	25	75	133	230
2	13	39	66	110
3-5	11	33	55	90
6-Infinity-c	14	42	72	120
I.W. Reprint #1(1958)-r/Krazy Komics	2	6	11	15
I.W. Reprint #2,7,8	2	6	11	15

ZIP COMICS
MLJ Magazines: Feb, 1940 - No. 47, Summer, 1944 (#1-7?: 68 pgs.)
1-Origin Kalathar the Giant Man, The Scarlet Avenger, & Steel Sterling; Mr. Satan (by Edd Ashe), Nevada Jones (masked hero) & Zambini, the Miracle Man, War Eagle, Captain Valor begins	462	1386	3000	6000
2-Nevada Jones adds mask & horse Blaze	218	654	1364	2400
3-Biro robot-c	164	492	1023	1800
4,5-Biro WW2-c	136	408	852	1500
6-8-Biro-c	116	348	725	1275
9-Last Kalathar & Mr. Satan; classic-c	136	408	852	1500
10-Inferno, the Flame Breather begins, ends #13	123	369	769	1350
11,12: 11-Inferno without costume	95	285	597	1050
13-Electrocution-c	100	300	625	1100
14,16,19	91	273	568	1000
15-Classic spider-c	105	315	656	1150
17-Last Scarlet Avenger; women in bondage being cooked alive-c by Biro	95	285	597	1050
18-Wilbur begins (9/41, 1st app.)	100	300	625	1100
20-Origin & 1st app. Black Jack (11/41); Hitler-c	155	465	966	1700
21,23-26: 25-Last Nevada Jones. 26-Black Witch begins; last Captain Valor	86	258	540	950
22-Classic-c	109	327	682	1200
27-Intro. Web (7/42) plus-c app.	125	375	781	1375
28-Origin Web	114	340	713	1250
29,30: 29-The Hyena app.	55	165	341	600
31,33-38: 34-1st Applejack app. 35-Last Zambini, Black Jack. 38-Last Web issue	47	142	286	500
32-Classic skeleton Nazi WW2-c	52	157	314	550
39-Red Rube begins (origin, 8/43)	47	142	286	500
40-46: 45-Wilbur ends	40	120	240	420
47-Last issue; scarce	43	129	257	450

NOTE: *Biro* a-5, 9, 17; c-9-17. *Meskin* a-1-3, 5-7, 9, 10, 12, 13, 15, 16 at least. *Montana* c-29, 30, 32-35. *Novick* c-18-28, 31. *Sahle* c-37, 38, 40-46. Bondage c-8, 9, 33, 34. Cover features: Steel Sterling-1-43, 47; (w/Blackjack-20-27 & Web-27-35), 28-39; (w/Red Rube-40-43); Red Rube-

Zoot #9 © FOX

Zorro #4 © Zorro Prod.

Zot! #11 © Scott McCloud

	GD2.0	FN6.0	VF8.0	NM9.4

44-47.

ZIP-JET (Hero)
St. John Publishing Co.: Feb, 1953 - No. 2, Apr-May, 1953

		GD2.0	FN6.0	VF8.0	NM9.4
1-Rocketman-r from Punch Comics; #1-c from splash in Punch #10		73	219	455	800
2		50	150	300	525

ZIPPY THE CHIMP (CBS TV Presents...)
Pines (Literary Ent.): No. 50, March, 1957; No. 51, Aug, 1957

50,51	7	21	36	50

ZODY, THE MOD ROB
Gold Key: July, 1970

1	2	6	13	20

ZOMBIE WORLD (one-shots)
Dark Horse Comics

... :Eat Your Heart Out (4/98, $2.95) Kelley Jones-c/s/a	3.00
... :Home For The Holidays (12/97, $2.95)	3.00

ZOMBIE WORLD: CHAMPION OF THE WORMS
Dark Horse Comics: Sept, 1997 - No. 3, Nov, 1997 ($2.95, limited series)

1-3-Mignola & McEown-c/s/a	3.00

ZOMBIE WORLD: DEAD END
Dark Horse Comics: Jan, 1998 - No. 2, Feb, 1998 ($2.95, limited series)

1,2-Stephen Blue-c/s/a	3.00

ZOMBIE WORLD: TREE OF DEATH
Dark Horse Comics: Jun, 1999 - No. 4, Oct, 1999 ($2.95, limited series)

1-4-Mills-s/Deadstock-a	3.00

ZOMBIE WORLD: WINTER'S DREGS
Dark Horse Comics: May, 1998 - No. 4, Aug, 1998 ($2.95, limited series)

1-4-Fingerman-s/Edwards-a	3.00

ZONE (Also see Dark Horse Presents)
Dark Horse Comics: 1990 ($1.95, B&W)

1-Character from Dark Horse Presents	2.00

ZONE CONTINUUM, THE
Caliber Press: 1994 ($2.95, B&W)

1	3.00

ZOO ANIMALS
Star Publications: No. 8, 1954 (15¢, 36 pgs.)

8-(B&W for coloring)	5	15	25	35

ZOO FUNNIES (Tim McCoy #16 on)
Charlton Comics/Children Comics Publ.: Nov, 1945 - No. 15, 1947

101(#1)(11/45, 1st Charlton comic book)-Funny animal; Al Fago-c		20	60	105	180
2(12/45, 52 pgs.)		11	33	55	90
3-5		10	30	55	80
6-15: 8-Diana the Huntress app.		8	24	42	60

ZOO FUNNIES (Becomes Nyoka, The Jungle Girl #14 on)
Capitol Stories/Charlton Comics: July, 1953 - No. 13, Sept, 1955; Dec, 1984

1-1st app.? Timothy The Ghost; Fago-c/a	11	33	55	90
2	7	21	36	50
3-7	6	18	29	40
8-13-Nyoka app.	9	27	49	70
1(1984) (Low print run)				6.00

ZOONIVERSE
Eclipse Comics: 8/86 - No. 6, 6/87 ($1.25/$1.75, limited series, Mando paper)

1-6	2.25

ZOO PARADE (TV)
Dell Publishing Co.: #662, 1955 (Marlin Perkins)

Four Color 662	5	15	34	55

ZOOM COMICS
Carlton Publishing Co.: Dec, 1945 (one-shot)

nn-Dr. Mercy, Satannas, from Red Band Comics; Capt. Milksop origin retold

	40	120	240	420

ZOOT (Rulah Jungle Goddess #17 on)
Fox Features Syndicate: nd (1946) - No. 16, July, 1948 (Two #13s & 14s)

nn-Funny animal only	21	63	110	190
2-The Jaguar app.	20	60	105	175
3(Fall, 1946) - 6-Funny animals & teen-age	11	33	55	90
7-(6/47)-Rulah, Jungle Goddess (origin/1st app.)	95	285	597	1050
8-10	64	192	398	700
11-Kamen bondage-c	68	205	426	750
12-Injury-to-eye panels, torture scene	47	140	286	500
13(2/48)	47	140	286	500
14(3/48)-Used in SOTI, pg. 104, "One picture showing a girl nailed by her wrists to trees with blood flowing from the wounds, might be taken straight from an ill. ed. of the Marquis deSade"	61	182	381	675
13(4/48),14(5/48)-Western True Crime #15 on?	47	140	286	500
15,16	47	140	286	500

ZORRO (Walt Disney with #882)(TV)(See Eclipse Graphic Album)
Dell Publishing Co.: May, 1949 - No. 15, Sept-Nov, 1961 (Photo-c 882 on)
(Zorro first appeared in a pulp story Aug 19, 1919)

Four Color 228 (#1)	21	63	147	275
Four Color 425,617,732	12	36	84	155
Four Color 497,538,574-Kinstler-a	13	39	91	165
Four Color 882-Photo-c begin;1st TV Disney; Toth-a	17	50	119	220
Four Color 920,933,960,976-Toth-a in all	12	36	84	155
Four Color 1003('59)-Toth-a	12	36	84	155
Four Color 1037-Annette Funicello photo-c	15	45	105	190
8(12-2/59-60)	8	24	56	100
9-Toth-a	8	24	56	105
10,11,13-15-Last photo-c	7	21	49	90
12-Toth-a; last 10¢ issue	8	24	56	105

NOTE: *Warren Tufts* a-4-Color 1037, 8, 9, 10, 13.

ZORRO (Walt Disney)(TV)
Gold Key: Jan, 1966 - No. 9, Mar, 1968 (All photo-c)

1-Toth-a	7	21	49	95
2,4,5,7-9-Toth-a. 5-r/F.C. #1003 by Toth	4	12	30	50
3,6-Tufts-a	4	12	29	45

NOTE: #1-9 are reprinted from Dell issues. Tufts a-3, 4. 1-r/F.C. #882. #2-r/F.C. #960. #3-r/#12-c & #8 inside. #4-r/#9-c & insides. #6-r/#11(all); #7-r/#14-c. #8-r/F.C. #933 inside & back-c & #976-c #9-r/F.C. #920.

ZORRO (TV)
Marvel Comics: Dec, 1990 - No. 12, Nov, 1991 ($1.00)

1-12: Based on TV show. 12-Toth-c	3.00

ZORRO (Also see Mask of Zorro)
Topps Comics: Nov, 1993 - No. 11, Nov, 1994 ($2.50/$2.95)

0-(11/93, $1.00, 20 pgs.)-Painted-c; collector's ed.	2.25
1,4,6-9,11: 1-Miller-c. 4-Mike Grell-c. 6-Mignola-c. 7-Lady Rawhide by Gulacy. 8-Perez-c. 10-Julie Bell-c. 11-Lady Rawhide-c	3.00
2-Lady Rawhide-c (not in costume)	5.00

3-1st app. Lady Rawhide in costume, 3-Lady Rawhide-c by Adam Hughes	1	3	6	8

5-Lady Rawhide app.	4.00
10-($2.95)-Lady Rawhide-c/app.	3.00
The Lady Wears Red (12/98, $12.95, TPB) r/#1-3	13.00
Zorro's Renegades (2/99, $14.95, TPB) r/#4-8	15.00

ZOT!
Eclipse Comics: 4/84 - No. 10, 7/85; No. 11, 1/87 - No. 36 7/91 ($1.50, Baxter-p)

1	5.00
2,3	4.00
4-10: 4-Origin. 10-Last color issue	3.00
10 1/2 (6/86, 25¢, Not Available Comics) Ashcan; art by Feazell & Scott McCloud	
11-14,15-35-($2.00-c) B&W issues	3.00
14 1/2 (Adventures of Zot! in Dimension 10 1/2)(7/87) Antisocialman app.	3.00
36-($2.95-c) B&W	3.00

Z-2 COMICS (Secret Agent...)(See Holyoke One-Shot #7)

ZULU (See Movie Classics)

HELL YES! IT'S TERRY STROUD'S

MONKEY BUMPS

NO. 1   10¢

EEP?!

FEATURING: ATSA MORAY   TOO-NAH   JOE

WANTED

We are aggressively purchasing comics & related memorabilia. We buy one item or entire collections. If you are looking for a friendly approach to buying ot selling, contact us.

BUYING:
Comics 1841-1969, Platinum, Gold & Silver Age, All Grades! Character Collectibles, Premiums, Statues, Rings, etc. Disney Memorabilia, Original Comic Art, Pulp Magazines, Movie Memorabilia, Superman Collectibles, Vintage Star Wars and Transformer Toys, & Much More!

Want lists always accepted and often fulfilled. Finder's fee for leads which result in purchase.

If you are serious about comics & collectibles check out our website: www.monumentalcollectibles.com

Be sure to watch our ebay listings:
monumental-collectibles
Sign up for our internet newsletter:
http://groups.yahoo.com/group/monumentalcollectibles

Attn: Tom Gordon III
PO Box 287
Westminster, MD 21158
410.848.0275

Austin, TX

Buying Comic Books
&
Comic Related Memoribilia
1875-1980

Paying top dollar for quality golden and silver age comics. I will buy all grades and all titles, large collections or small. Will travel to view large collections. You will not be dissapointed with my service, offer, or honest and friendly attitude.

Why not get rid of everything at once? I also buy: used music CDs, used DVDs, used videos, old magazines including Life and pulps, movie posters, character & personality items, original comic art, old records, old books, old license plates, old toys, and most other varieties of antiques & collectibles.

Matt Stein
2202 Pompton Drive, Apt B
Austin, TX 78757

Home Phone: 512-458-7892
Mobile phone: 512-689-5304

BAGS ARE JUST THE BEGINNING

You can wrap your collectibles in all the bags you want, but it you
want the ultimate in protection, go the extra mile with Gerber
backing boards and storage boxes!

As the highest quality backing board available anywhere, E. Gerber
Products' **Full-backs** meet strict U.S. Government standards for
archival storage. Made with a 3% calcium carbonate buffer throughout, these exceptional 42 mil, Acid-free, 3% buffered backing boards
(which consist of a genuine acid-free, virgin wood, cellular fiber) maintain a pH of 8.0+ –protecting
your collectibles from acid deterioration!

Item#	Size	Description	Price per: 50	200	1000
675FB	6 3/4 x 10 1/2	Current Comics - fits 700	$9.50	$31.00	$135.00
700FB	7 x 10 1/2	Standard Comics - fits 725	10.00	32.00	140.00
750FB	7 1/2 x 10 1/2	Silver/Golden Comics - fits 775	10.50	35.00	150.00
758FB	7 5/8 x 10 1/2	Golden Age Comics - fits 800	11.25	37.00	160.00
778FB	7 7/8 x 10 1/2	Super Golden Age Comics - fits 825	12.00	39.00	170.00
825FB	8 1/4 x 10 1/2	Large Comics, Mag. & Letter - fits 875	13.00	42.00	185.00
858FB	8 5/8 x 11 1/2	Standard Magazines	14.00	46.00	200.00
Add Shipping & Handling			**$4.00**	**$14.00**	**$54.00**

Identical to our Full-backs, only with a thickness of 24 mil, for those
times when a product does not require the extra rigidity of a Full-back.

Item#	Size	Description	Price per: 100	500	2000
675HB	6 3/4 x 10 1/2	Current Comics - fits 700	$8.00	$35.00	$120.00
700HB	7 x 10 1/2	Standard Comics - fits 725	8.50	36.00	125.00
750HB	7 1/2 x 10 1/2	Silver/Golden Comics - fits 775	9.00	39.00	135.00
758HB	7 5/8 x 10 1/2	Golden Age Comics - fits 800	9.75	41.00	145.00
778HB	7 7/8 x 10 1/2	Super Golden Age Comics - fits 825	11.00	47.00	160.00
825HB	8 1/4 x 10 1/2	Large Comics, Mag. & Letter	12.00	50.00	170.00
858HB	8 5/8 x 11 1/2	Standard Magazines	13.00	56.00	190.00
Add Shipping & Handling			**$4.00**	**$14.00**	**$54.00**

ACID FREE BOXES

These grey corrugated boxes are designed for a lifetime of acid-free storage. Each
box has a 3% calcium carbonate buffer added to maintain an acid-free alkaline
pH content of 8.0-8.5. Easy, snap assembly requires neither glue nor tape.

Item#	Size	Description	Price per: 5	20	50
13	15 x 8 x 11 1/2	Silver/Golden Comics	$45.00	$175.00	$400.00
15	15 x 9 1/4 x 12 1/2	Super Golden/Magazines	43.00	144.00	310.00
Add Shipping & Handling			**$8.00**	**$24.00**	**$49.00**

Satisfaction Guaranteed

All E. Gerber archival supply products carry our assurance of the
highest quality standards in both material and manufacturing.

For a complete catalog of our affordable archival products,
please call us toll-free at **1-800-79-MYLAR** from 8:00 a.m. to
5:00 p.m. Eastern Standard Time, or mail your catalog request
to:

**E. Gerber Products, Inc.
1720 Belmont Avenue, Suite C
Baltimore, MD 21244
Fax: 1-410-944-9363
e-mail: archival@egerber.com**

Top of the Line Preservation And
Storage Supplies

E.Gerber
PRODUCTS, LLC
...At The Lowest Prices

**THE BEST PROTECTION
AT THE BEST PRICE!**

Visit us on the Web at
www.egerber.com!

Advertise!

902

903

905

IN THE LAST FEW YEARS, WE HAVE
$PENT MILLION$
BUYING COMIC BOOKS

WE HAVE PURCHASED
MANY INDIVIDUAL BOOKS
AS WELL AS MANY
OF THE MAJOR COLLECTIONS
SOLD IN NORTH AMERICA
OVER THE PAST
FEW YEARS.

CALL TODAY
FOR IMMEDIATE,
NO NONSENSE,
RESPONSE!

SHOWCASE NEW ENGLAND™

We Want Your Help!
The **Overstreet Comic Book Price Guide**, **Hake's Price Guide To Character Toys** and **Comic Book Marketplace** need your contributions! If you see something we've missed in **The Overstreet Comic Book Price Guide**, if you have comic character collectibles not included in **Hake's Price Guide To Character Toys**, or if you just have an idea for an article in **Comic Book Marketplace**, we want to know about it!

Hake's Price Guide To Character Toys:
feedback@gemstonepub.com

The Overstreet Comic Book Price Guide:
feedback@gemstonepub.com

Comic Book Marketplace:
cbm@gemstonepub.com

SHOP DIRECTORY

(a) Golden Age Comics	(g) Magazines	(m) Trading Cards	(r) Role Playing Games
(b) Silver Age Comics	(h) Books (old)	(n) Underground Comics	(s) Star Trek Items
(c) New Comics, Magazines	(i) Movie Posters	(o) Premiums (Rings,	(t) Doctor Who Items
(d) Pulps	(j) Original Art	Decoders, etc.)	(u) Japanimation/Manga
(e) Paperbacks	(k) Toys	(p) Comic Related Posters	(v) Collectible Card Games
(f) Big Little Books	(l) Records/CDs,Videos,DVD	(q) Comic Supplies	

ALABAMA

Sincere Comics
4667 Airport Blvd.
Mobile, AL 36608
PH: (251) 342-2603
E-Mail:
sincerecmx@aol.com
(a-c,e,m,p-s,u)

ARIZONA

Atomic Comics Chandler
5965 W. Ray Rd. #19
Chandler, AZ 85226
PH: (480) 940-6061
E-Mail: mail@
atomiccomics.com
Web: www.
atomiccomics.com
(a-c,e,g,j-v)

Atomic Comics Mesa
1310 W. Southern Ave. #3
Mesa, AZ 85202
PH: (480) 649-0807
E-Mail: mail@
atomiccomics.com
Web: www.
atomiccomics.com
(a-c,e,g,j-v)

**Key Comics:
Discount Back-Issues**
P.O. Box 5035
Mesa, AZ 85211
PH: (480) 890-0055
E-Mail: keycomics@
hotmail.com
(a-c,g,j,n)

**All About Books &
Comics**
5060 N. Central
Phoenix, AZ 85012
PH: (602) 277-0757
Web:
www.allaboutcomics.com
(a-g,i-n,p-s,u,v)

All About Books & Comics III
4022 E. Greenway
Phoenix, AZ 85032
PH: (602) 494-1976
Web:
www.allaboutcomics.com
(c,g,k,l,m,p-s,u,v)

**Atomic Comics
Paradise Valley**
4537 East Cactus
Phoenix, AZ 85032
PH: (602) 923-0733
(a-c,e,g,j-v)

Atomic Comics Phoenix
10215 N. 28th Dr. #A-1
Phoenix, AZ 85051
PH: (602) 395-1066
E-Mail: mail@
atomiccomics.com
Web: www.
atomiccomics.com
(a-c,e,g,j-v)

Then It Rained Comics
P.O. Box 11041
Scottsdale, AZ 85271
PH: (480) 947-5309
(a,b,c,d,f,g)

All About Books & Comics V
810 S. Ash
Tempe, AZ 85281
PH: (480) 858-9447
Web:
www.allaboutcomics.com
(c,g,k,m,p-s,u,v)

ARKANSAS

**Alternate Worlds Cards
& Comics**
3812 Central Ave. Suite G
Hot Springs, AR 71913
PH: (501) 525-8999
E-Mail: frodo@hsnp.com
(b,c,e,g,k,l,m,q,r,s,u,v)

The Comic Book Store
9307 Treasure Hill
Little Rock, AR 72227
PH: (501) 227-9777
(a-d,g,k,m,p-s,u,v)

Collector's Edition
3217 John F. Kennedy
Blvd.
North Little Rock, AR
72116
PH: (501) 791-4222
(a-d,g,k,m,p,q,r,s,u,v)

CALIFORNIA

Terry's Comics
Buying all 10¢ & 12¢
original priced comics
P.O. Box 746
Atwood, CA 92811-0746
PH: (714) 288-8993
Hotline: (800) 938-0325
FAX: (714) 288-8993
E-Mail:
info@terryscomics.com
Web: www.terryscomics.com
(a,b,d-h,m,n,q)

Collectors Ink
2593 Highway 32
Chico, CA 95973
PH: (530) 345-0958
E-Mail:
bev@collectorsink.com
Web:
www.collectorsink.com
(a-c,e,g,k-n,p-v)

Comic Bookie
415 W. Foothill #318
Claremont, CA 91711
PH: (909) 399-0228
E-Mail: comicbookie
@prodigy.net
Web:
www.comicbookie.net
(b,c,g,k,l,m,p,q,s,u,v)

Flying Colors Comics
2980 Treat Blvd.,
Oak Grove Plaza
Concord, CA 94518
PH: (925) 825-5410
E-Mail: coolstuff@
flyingcolorscomics.com
(a-c,j,k,m,p,q,u,v)

High-Quality Comics
1106 2nd St., #110
Encinitas, CA 92024
PH: (800) 682-3936
FAX: (760) 723-7269
E-Mail: hqcom@utm.net
Web: www.
highqualitycomics.com
(b,c,e,g,h,n,p,s)

21st Century Comics
124 W. Commonwealth Ave.
Fullerton, CA 92832
PH: (714) 992-6649
Web: www.
21stcenturycomics.com
(a-c,e-g,k,m,n,p,q,u,v)

Geoffrey's Comics
15900 Crenshaw Blvd.; Ste. B
Gardena, CA 90249
PH: (888) 538-3198 (toll free)
FAX: (310) 538-1114
E-Mail:
info@geoffreyscomics.com
Web:
www.geoffreyscomics.com
(a-c,g,i,k,m,n,p,q,s,u,v)

Back Issue Comics
695 E. Lewelling
Hayward, CA 94541
PH: (510) 276-5262
(b,e,g,k,l,m)

**Another World Comics
& Books**
1615 Colorado Blvd.
Los Angeles, CA 90041
PH: (323) 257-7757
E-Mail: bob
@anotherworld.com
Web: www.
anotherworld.com
(a-g,i,m,p,t,u)

Golden Apple Comics
7711 Melrose Ave.
Los Angeles, CA 90046
PH: (323) 658-6047
Web: www.
goldenapplecomics.com
(a-c,g,i-q,s-v)

Brian's Books
73 North Milpitas Blvd.
Milpitas, CA 95035
PH: (408) 942-6903
(a-c,g,m,p,q,s,u)

The Big Guy's Comics
167 El Camino East
Mountain View, CA 94040
PH: (650) 965-8272
(a-d,f,g,k,m,n,p,q,s,u,v)

Lee's Comics
1020-F N. Rengstorff Ave.
Mountain View, CA 94043
PH: (650) 965-1800
E-Mail:
Lee@LCOMICS.com
Web: www.LCOMICS.com
(a-g,j-v)

Golden Apple Comics
8962 Reseda Blvd.
Northridge, CA 91324
PH: (818) 993-7804
Web: www.
goldenapplecomics.com
(a-c,e,g,k-n,p,q,u,v)

**Pacific Comic
Exchange, Inc.**
P. O. Box 2629
Palos Verdes Peninsula,
CA 90274
PH: (310) 544-4936
FAX: (310) 544-4900
E-Mail: sales@pcei.com
Web: www.pcei.com
(a,b,g,i,j)

A-1 Comics
5800 Madison Ave.
Sacramento, CA 95841
PH: (916) 331-9203
(a-m,p-s,u,v)

San Diego Comics
6937 El Cajon Blvd.
San Diego, CA 92115
PH: (619) 698-1177
E-Mail:
rockofeasy@ad.com
Web: www.
sandiegocomics.com
(a,b,c,g,h,n)

**Captain Nemo
Games & Comics**
563 Higuera
San Luis Obispo, CA
93401
PH: (805) 544-NEMO
FAX: (805) 543-3938
E-Mail:
Nemoslo@aol.com
(b,c,e,g,i,k-s,v, CD Roms,
video games)

Lee's Comics
2222 S. El Camino Real
San Mateo, CA 94403
PH: (650) 571-1489
E-Mail:
Lee@LCOMICS.com
Web: www.LCOMICS.com
(a-g,j-v)

Metro Entertainment
6 West Anapamu
Santa Barbara, CA
93101
PH: (805) 963-2168
Web: www.
metro-entertainment.com
(a-c,e,g,i,k-n,p-s,u,v)

Brian's Books
2767 El Camino
Santa Clara, CA 95051
PH: (408) 985-7481
(a-c,g,m,p,q,s,u,v)

**Hi De Ho Comics &
Books**
525 Santa Monica Blvd.
Santa Monica, CA
90401-2409
PH: (310) 394-2820
Web: www.hideho.com
(a-n,p-v)

A Collector's Dream
21222 Ventura Blvd.
Woodland Hills, CA
91364
PH: (818) 992-1636
(a-c,e,g,j,k,m,n,p,q,s,v)

All C's Collectibles
1113 So. Abilene St.
#104
Aurora, CO 80012
PH: (303) 751-6882
(a-d,g,k,m-p,s,u,v)

**Time Warp Comics
& Cards, Inc.**
1631 28th St.
Boulder, CO 80301
PH: (303) 443-4500
E-Mail: timewarp
@earthlink.net
Web:
www.time-warp.com
(a-c,g,n,q-s)

Bargain Comics
21 E. Bijou St.
Colorado Springs, CO 80903
PH: (719) 578-8847
E-Mail: bargaincom
@aol.com
(a-c,g,k,n,q,v)

RTS Unlimited Inc.
P. O. Box 150412
Lakewood, CO 80215-0412
PH: (303) 403-1840
FAX: (303) 403-1837
E-Mail:
rtsunlimited@earthlink.net
(a,b,c,q)

**Time Warp Comics
& Cards, Inc.**
605 3rd Ave.
Longmont, CO 80501
PH: (303) 485-0700
E-Mail: timewarp2
@earthlink.net
Web: www.time-warp.com
(a-c,g,n,q-s)

The Bookie
155 Burnside Ave.
E. Hartford, CT 06108
PH: (860) 289-1208
(a-h,j,k,m,n,p,q-s,u,v)

**D.J.'s Comics,
Cards, Games**
303 East Main St.
Meriden, CT 06450
PH: (203) 235-7300
E-Mail:
djscomics@snet.net
(a-c,g,k,m,p-s,v)

D-J Cards & Comics
1 Lincoln St.
Corner Washington Ave.
North Haven, CT 06473
PH: (203) 234-2989
(a-c,e,k,m,q,r,s,u,v)

Legends of Superheros
1269 West Main St.
Waterbury, CT 06708
PH: (203) 756-2440
FAX: (203) 757-1909
E-Mail: legends@
legendsofsuperheros.com
Web: www.legendsof
superheros.com
(b,c,e,g,k,l,o,p,q,v)

**Captain Blue Hen
Comics**
280 E. Main St. #101
Newark, DE 19711
PH: (302) 737-3434
FAX: (302) 737-6201
E-Mail:
cbhcomic@dca.net
Web: www.
captainbluehen.com
(a-c,g,k-n,p,q,u,v)

Lost Realms, Inc.
23066 Sandalfoot Plaza Dr.
Boca Raton, FL 33428
PH: (561) 470-5700
E-Mail: LostRealms@
mindspring.com
(b,c,e,g,j,k,m,p-s,u)

**Emerald City Too
Comics & Collectables**
2475-L McMullen Booth Rd.
Clearwater, FL 33759
PH: (727) 797-0664
E-Mail: CowardlyLion
@emeraldcitycomics.com
Web: www.
emeraldcitycomics.com
(a-c,g,j-v)

Phil's Comic Shoppe
6512 W. Atlantic Blvd.
Margate, FL 33063
PH: (888) 977-6947
(a-c,g,i,k,m,n,p,q,s,u,v)

**Emerald City Comics
& Collectables**
9249 Seminole Blvd.
Seminole, FL 33772
PH: (727) 398-2665
E-Mail: CowardlyLion
@emeraldcitycomics.com
Web: www.
emeraldcitycomics.com
(a-c,e,g,j-v)

GEORGIA

Oxford Comics & Games
2855 Piedmont Rd.
Atlanta, GA 30305
PH: (404) 233-8682
(a-v)

Comic Company
1058 Mistletoe Rd.
Decatur, GA 30033
PH: (404) 248-9846
FAX: (404) 325-2334
E-Mail: mail
@comiccompany.com
Web: www.
comiccompany.com
(a-c,g,k,m,p-r,u,v)

Heroes Ink
2500 Cobb Pkwy. NW
Suite A-3
Kennesaw, GA 30152
PH: (770) 428-3033
(a-c,e,g,k,m,p,q,s,u,v)

Odin's Cosmic Bookshelf
Killian Hill Crossing
360 Killian Hill Rd.,
Suite G-5
Lilburn, GA 30047
PH: (770) 923-0123
FAX: (770) 925-8200
E-Mail: odins@aol.com
(a-c,e-g,j,k,m-r,u,v)

ILLINOIS

Graham Crackers Comics Ltd.
120 N. Bolingbrook Dr.
(Rt. 53)
Bolingbrook, IL 60440
PH: (630) 739-6810
(c,g,k,l,m,q,u,v)

Graham Crackers Comics Ltd.
69 E. Madison
Chicago, IL 60603
PH: (312) 629-1810
(b,c,g,k,l,m,q,r,s,t,u,v)

Graham Crackers Comics Ltd.
2652 North Clark St.
(Lincoln Park)
Chicago, IL 60614
PH: (773) 665-2010
(c,g,k,l,m,q,r,u,v)

Chicago Comics
3244 North Clark St.
Chicago, IL 60657
PH: (773) 528-1983
PH: 1-(800)-509-0333
Web: www.
chicagocomics.com
(a-c,g,k,m,n,p,q,u,v)

Independence Comics, Comic Book Art / Collectibles
3959 West Irving Park Rd.
Chicago, IL 60618
PH: (773) 539-6720
FAX: (773) 588-1628
E-Mail:
spawnski@aol.com
Web: www.independence
comics.com
(a-c,j-m,p,q,s,u,v)

Graham Crackers Comics Ltd.
901C Lucinda Ave.
Dekalb, IL 60115
PH: (815) 748-3883
(c,g,k,l,m,q,u,v)

The Paper Escape
205 West First St.
Dixon, IL 61021
PH: (815) 284-7567
(c,e,g,k,m,p-s,v)

Graham Crackers Comics Ltd.
5223 S. Main St.
Downers Grove, IL
60515
PH: (630) 852-1810
(c,g,k,l,m,q,r,u,v)

GEM Comics
125 W. First St.
Elmhurst, IL 60126
PH: (630) 833-8787
(b,c,g,k,m,p-r,v)

Graham Crackers Comics Ltd.
2047 Bloomingdale Rd.
Glendale Heights, IL
60108
PH: (680) 894-8810
(c,g,k,l,m,q,r,s,t,u,v)

Graham Crackers Comics Ltd.
1271 Rickert Dr. 135
Naperville, IL 60540
PH: (630) 355-4310
(a-d,g,i-n,p,q,u,v)

Graham Crackers Comics Ltd.
610 S. Randall Rd.
(at Rt 38)
St. Charles, IL 60174
PH: (630) 584-0610
(c,g,k,l,m,p,q,u,v)

Comic Cavalcade
9 Triumph Dr.
Urbana, IL 61802
PH: (217) 384-2211
Web: www.comcav.com
(a,b,c)

Unicorn Comics & Cards
216 S. Villa Ave.
Villa Park, IL 60181
PH: (630) 279-5777
(a-g,k-m,p,q,s,v)

Comics Galore
1058 Hillgrove Ave.
Western Springs, IL 60558
PH: (708) 784-3300
(b,c,e,g,k,m,n,p,q,s-v)

Graham Crackers Comics Ltd.
1207 Butterfield Rd. (Rt. 56)
Wheaton, IL 60187
PH: (630) 668-1350
(c,g,k,l,m,q,s,t,u,v)

INDIANA

Comic Cave
3221 17th Street
Columbus, IN 47201
PH: (812) 372-8430
E-Mail: comiccave
@iquest.net
(b,c,g,k-m,p-s,u,v)

Books, Comics & Things
2212 Maplecrest Rd.
Fort Wayne, IN 46815
PH: (219) 446-0025
FAX: (219) 446-0030
E-Mail:
bct@bctcomics.com
Web:
www.bctcomics.com
(a-c,k,p-s,v)

Comic Carnival
9729 East Washington St.
Indianapolis, IN 46229
PH: (317) 898-5010
(a-v)

Comic Carnival
6265 N. Carrollton Ave.
Indianapolis, IN 46220
PH: (317) 253-8882
(a-v)

Comic Carnival
3837 N. High School Rd.
Indianapolis, IN 46254
PH: (317) 293-4386
(a-v)

Comic Carnival
7311 U.S. 31 South
Indianapolis, IN 46227
PH: (317) 889-8899
(a-v)

Downtown Comics
137 E. Ohio St.
Indianapolis, IN 46204
PH: (317) 237-0397
E-Mail: dtc@indy.net
Web: www.dtcomics.com
(a-u)

Downtown Comics - Carmel
13682 N. Meridian St.
Indianapolis, IN 46032
PH: (317) 845-9991
(a-u)

Downtown Comics - Castleton
5767 E. 86th St.
Indianapolis, IN 46258
PH: (317) 885-6395
(a-u)

Downtown Comics - Greenwood
8925 S. Meridian St.
Indianapolis, IN 46227
PH: (317) 885-6395
(a-u)

Downtown Comics - West
8336 W. 10th St.
Indianapolis, IN 46234
PH: (317) 271-7610
(a-u)

Galactic Greg's
1407 E. Lincolnway
Valparaiso, IN 46383
PH: (219) 464-0119
(b,c,k,p-r,u,v)

IOWA

Oak Leaf Comics
23-5th St. S.W.
Mason City, IA 50401
PH: (641) 424-0333
Web: www.dustcatchers.com
(a-c,k-m,o-v)

KANSAS

Prairie Dog Comics
Main Store
7130 W. Maple, Suite 150
Wichita, KS 67209
PH: (316) 942-3456
(a-v)

KENTUCKY

The Great Escape
1051 Bryant Way
Bowling Green, KY
42103
PH: (270) 782-8092
(a-c,e,g,k-n,p-v)

Comic Book World
7130 Turfway Rd.
Florence, KY 41042
PH: (859) 371-9562
FAX: (859) 371-6925
E-Mail: cbwinfo@one.net
Web: www.
comicbookworld.com
(a-d,g,k,m,n,o,q,r,u,v)

Comic Book World
6905 Shepherdsville Rd.
Louisville, KY 40219
PH: (502) 964-5500
E-Mail: cbwdoug@
bellsouth.net
Web: www.
comicbookworld.com
(a-c,g,k,m,n,o,q,r,u,v)

The Great Escape
2433 Bardstown Road
Louisville, KY 40205
PH: (502) 456-2216
(a-c,e,g,i,k-n,p-v)

LOUISIANA

B.T. & W.D. Giles
P. O. Box 271
Keithville, LA 71047
PH: (318) 925-6654
(a,b,d-f,h,l)

MAINE

Top Shelf Comics
25 Central Street
Bangor, ME 04401
PH: (207) 947-4939
E-Mail: topshelf
@tcomics.com
Web: www.tcomics.com
(a-c,m,p,r,v)

MARYLAND

Geppi's Comic World
1116 N. Rolling Road
Baltimore, MD 21228
PH: (410) 788-0900
FAX: (410) 455-9806
E-Mail: gdoug@
diamondcomics.com

Alternate Worlds
72 Cranbrook Road
Cockeysville, MD 21030
PH: (410) 666-3290
(b,c,g,k-n,p-v)

The Closet of Comics
7315 Baltimore Ave. (US.1)
College Park, MD 20740
PH: (301) 699-0498
E-Mail: closetofcomics
@hotmail.com
(a-c,e,h,m,n,p,q)

Comics To Astonish
9400 Snowden River
Pkwy.
Columbia, MD 21045
PH: (410) 381-2732
E-Mail:
comics2u@aol.com
Web:
www.comicstoastonish.com
(a-c,k,m,p,q,u,v)

**Cards, Comics &
Collectibles**
100-A Chartley Drive
Reisterstown, MD 21136
PH: (410) 526-7410
FAX: (410) 526-4006
E-Mail:
cardscomicscollectibles
@yahoo.com
(a-c,f,g,j,k,m,n,p,q,s,u,v)

MASSACHUSETTS

New England Comics
131 Harvard Avenue
Allston, MA 02134
PH: (617) 783-1848
Web: www.
newenglandcomics.com
(a-c,e,g,k-n,p-v)

New England Comics
744 Crescent St.
East Crossing Plaza
Brockton, MA 02402
PH: (508) 559-5068
Web: www.
newenglandcomics.com
(a-c,e,g,k-n,p-v)

New England Comics
316 Harvard St.
Coolidge Corner
Brookline, MA 02446
PH: (617) 566-0115
Web: www.
newenglandcomics.com
(a-c,e,g,k-n,p-v)

New England Comics
14A Eliot Street
Harvard Square
Cambridge, MA 02138
PH: (617) 354-5352
Web: www.
newenglandcomics.com
(a-c,e,g,k-n,p-v)

That's Entertainment II
371 John Fitch Hwy.
Fitchburg, MA 01420
PH: (978) 342-8607
Web: www.thatse.com
(a-v)

Jams Comic Connection
435 King St. (Rt. 110/2A)
Littleton, MA 01460
PH: (978) 486-1099
(c,d,g,k,q,r,s,v)

New England Comics
95 Pleasant St.
Malden Center
Malden, MA 02148
PH: (781) 322-2404
Web: www.
newenglandcomics.com
(a-c,e,g,k-n,p-v)

New England Comics
732 Washington Street
Norwood Center
Norwood, MA 02062
PH: (781) 769-4552
Web: www.
newenglandcomics.com
(a-c,e,g,k-n,p-v)

New England Comics
1511 Hancock St.
Quincy Center
Quincy, MA 02169
PH: (617) 770-1848
Web: www.
newenglandcomics.com
(a-c,e,g,k-n,p-v)

New England Comics
FFAST New Comic
Service
(Mail Order Only)
P.O. Box 690346
Quincy, MA 02269
PH: (617) 774-1745
Web: www.ffast.com
(a-c,e,g,k-n,p-v)

The Outer Limits
463 Moody St.
Waltham, MA 02453
PH: (781) 891-0444
(a-v)

That's Entertainment
244 Park Ave. (Rte. 9)
Worcester, MA
01609-1927
PH: (508) 755-4207
Web: www.thatse.com
(a-v)

MICHIGAN

Comics North!
425 N. Main Street
Cheboygan, MI
49721-1546
PH: (231) 627-3740
Web:
http://comixnorth.cjb.net
(b,c,g,i,k,l,p,q,r,s,t,u)

**Amazing Book Store,
Inc.**
3718 Richfield Rd.
Flint, MI 48506
PH: (810) 736-3025
(a-c,n,q)

**Tardy's Collector's
Corner, Inc.**
2009 Eastern Ave. S.E.
Grand Rapids, MI 49507
PH: (616) 247-7828
E-Mail:
tccorner@iserv.net
(a-g,j,m,n,p,q)

MINNESOTA

Nostalgia Zone
3149 1/2 Hennepin Ave. S
Minneapolis, MN
55408-2620
PH: (612) 822-2806
Web: www.nostalgiazone.com
(a,b,d-g,m,n,u)

Midway Book & Comic
1579 University Ave.
St Paul, MN 55104
PH: (651) 644-7605
(a-h,n,q)

MISSOURI

Antiquarium
504 East High St.
Jefferson City, MO 65101
PH: (573) 636-8995
E-Mail: Antiquarium
@prodigy.net
Web:
tripod.com/~antiquarium
(a-n,p-v)

B•Bop
3940 Main
Kansas City, MO 64111
PH: (816) 753-BBOP(2267)
(a-c,g,k-m,p-s,u,v)

**Friendly Frank's
Comic Cavern**
5404 NW 64th St.
Kansas City, MO 64151
PH: (816) 746-4569
(a-g,j-n,p-v)

NEBRASKA

Robert Beerbohm
Comic Art
P.O. Box 507
Fremont, NE 68026
PH: (402) 727-4071
FAX: (402) 727-4071
E-Mail:
beerbohm@teknetwork.com
(a,b,d-k,n-q)

NEVADA

Silver Cactus Comics I
480 N. Nellis Blvd. #C1A
Las Vegas, NV 89110
PH: (702) 438-4408
FAX: (702) 438-5208
(a-c,e,g,k,l,m,p-s,u,v)

Silver Cactus Comics II
4410 N. Rancho Dr.
Las Vegas, NV 89130
PH: (702) 396-8840
Web: www.
silvercactuscomics.com
(a-c,e,g,k,l,m,p-s,v)

NEW HAMPSHIRE

Rare Books & Comics
James F. Payette
P.O. Box 750
Bethlehem, NH 03574
PH: (603) 869-2097
(a,b,d-h)

NEW JERSEY

J.C. Comics
579 Route 22 West
North Plainfield, NJ
07060
PH: (908) 756-1212
E-Mail: jcrx2@home.com
Web: www.jccomics.com
(a-c,e,g,k,m,p,q,u)

Comic Explosion
339 Franklin Ave.
Nutley, NJ 07110
PH: (973) 235-1336
(c,g,m,n,p,q,u)

Fat Jack's Comicrypt
521 White Horse Pike
Oaklyn, NJ 08107
PH: (856) 858-3877
(a-c,g,k,m,n,p-r,s,u,v)

Frankenstein Comics
845 Mantua Pike, Rt. 45
Woodbury, NJ 08096
PH: (856) 848-6347
E-Mail:
Frankenbill@snip.net
(b,c,e,g,h,q)

JHV Associates
(By Appointment Only)
P. O. Box 317
Woodbury Heights, NJ
08097
PH: (856) 845-4010
FAX: (856) 845-3977
E-Mail:
JHVassoc@hotmail.com
(a,b,d)

NEW YORK

Silver Age Comics
22-55 31 St.
Astoria, NY 11105
PH: (718) 721-9691
PH: (800) 278-9691
FAX: (718) 728-9691
E-Mail: gus
@silveragecomics.com
Web: www.
silveragecomics.com
(a-c,f,g,k,m,n,p-s,u)

Excellent Adventures
110 Milton Ave. (Rte. 50)
Ballston Spa, NY 12020
PH: (518) 884-9498
E-Mail:
jbelskis37@aol.com
(a-d,f,g,j,k,m,o,q-s,u,v)

Comic Quest
51-49 Simonson Street
Elmhurst, NY 11373
PH: (718) 205-8174
E-Mail: thequestcomics
@aol.com
(a-e,g,k,m,n,q,r,v)

Ravenswood Inc.
8451 Senaca Turnpike
New Hartford, NY 13413
PH: (315) 735-3699
E-Mail: ravens
@dreamscape.com
Web:
ravenswoodcomics.com
(a-c,e,g,h,k-n,p-v)

Jim Hanley's Universe
4 West 33rd St.
New York, NY 10001
PH: (212) 268-7088
E-Mail:
bob@jhuniverse.com
Web: www.jhuniverse.com
(a-c,e,g,k-n,p-v)

Amazing Comics
12 Gillette Ave.
Sayville, NY 11782
PH: (631) 567-8069
Web:
www.amazingco.com
(a-c,e,g,j,k,m,q,v)

One if By Cards,
Two if By Comics, Inc.
1107 Central Ave.
Scarsdale, NY 10583
PH: (914) 725-2225
E-Mail:
hockeymark@aol.com
Web:
www.1ifbycards.com
(a,b,c,k,m,q,s,v)

Jim Hanley's Universe
325 New Dorp
Staten Island, NY 10306
PH: (718) 351-6299
E-Mail:
bob@jhuniverse.com
Web: www.jhuniverse.com
(a-c,e,g,k-n,p-v)

NORTH CAROLINA

Super Giant Comics
697 Brevard Rd.
Asheville, NC 28806
PH: (828) 665-2800
(a-c,j,l,n,q)

Heroes Aren't Hard to
Find
1957 E. 7th Street
Charlotte, NC 28204
PH: (704) 375-7462
E-Mail:
shelton@heroesonline.com
Web:
www.heroesonline.com
(a-c,f,g,j,k,m,p,q,r,u,v)

Acme Comics
2150 Lawndale Dr.
Greensboro, NC 27408
PH: (336) 574-2263
(a-c,g,i,j,k,p,q,u)

OHIO

Dark Star III
Farifield Plaza
Beavercreek, OH 45432
PH: (937) 427-3213
E-Mail: books
@darkstarbookstore.com
(b,c,e,g,h,k,l,m,q,r,s,u,v)

Comic Book World
4016 Harrison Avenue
Cincinnati, OH 45211
PH: (513) 661-6300
E-Mail: cbwinfo@one.net
Web: www.
comicbookworld.com
(a-c,k,m,n,p-v)

Bookery Fantasy
16 W. Main St.
Fairborn, OH 45324
PH: (937) 879-1408
FAX: (937) 879-9327
E-Mail:
bookeryfan@aol.com
Web: www.
bookeryfantasy.com
(a-n,p-v)

Parker's Records
& Comics
1222 Suite C, Route 28
Milford, OH 45150
PH: (513) 575-3665
FAX: (513) 575-3665
E-Mail:
dkparker39@fuse.net
(a-c,g,l,p-r,v)

Funnie Farm Bookstore
328 N. Dixie Drive
Vandalia, OH 45377
PH: (937) 898-2794
E-Mail: pdbroida@
earthlink.net
(a-c,m,p,r,s,v)

Dark Star Books &
Comics
237 Xenia Ave.
Yellow Springs, OH
45387
PH: (937) 767-9400
E-Mail: books
@darkstarbookstore.com
(b-h,k-n,p-v)

OKLAHOMA

New World Comics
& Games
6219 N. Meridian
Oklahoma City, OK
73112
PH: (405) 721-7634
(a-c,g,i,k,m-v)

New World Comics
& Games
4420 SE 4th St.
Oklahoma City, OK
73135
PH: (405) 677-2559
(c,g,k,m,p-v)

Comic Empire of Tulsa
3122 S. Mingo
Tulsa, OK 74146
PH: (918) 664-5808
(a-c,g,m,n,p,q,s,t)

Want List Comics
(Appointment Only)
Box 701932
Tulsa, OK 74170-1932
PH: (918) 299-0440
We hate SPAM so please
call for our private e-mail
address.
(a,b,f,h-k,m)

Emerald City Comics
770 E. 13th
Eugene, OR 97401
PH: (541) 345-2568
(c,e,g,k-n,p,q,r,u,v)

Beyond Comics
322 East Main
Medford, OR 97501
PH: (800) 428-9543
Web: www.
beyondcomics.net
(a,b,c,p,q,r,v)

New Dimension Comics
Clearview Mall #250
101 Clearview Circle
Butler, PA 16001
PH: (724) 282-5283
(a-d,f,g,k-n,q-s,u,v)

New Dimension Comics
20550 Route 19,
Piazza Plaza
Cranberry, PA 16066-7520
PH: (724) 776-0433
E-Mail: ndc@sgi.net
Web: www.ndcomics.com
(a-d,f,g,k-n,q-s,u,v)

New Dimension Comics
508 Lawrence Ave.
Ellwood City, PA 16117
PH: (724) 758-2324
E-Mail:
ec@ndcomics.com
(a-d,f,g,k-n,q-s,u,v)

Comic Collection
931 Bustleton Pike
Feasterville, PA 19053
PH: (215) 357-3332
(a-c,e,g,i-s,u,v)

The Comic Store
28 McGovern Ave.
Station Square
Lancaster, PA 17602
PH: (717) 397-8737
FAX: (717) 397-8903
E-Mail:
comicstore@juno.com
Web:
www.comicstorepa.com
(a-c,g,k,m,p-r,u,v)

Fat Jack's Comicrypt
2006 Sansom St.
Philadelphia, PA 19103
PH: (215) 963-0788
(a-c,g,k,m,n,p-r,s,u,v)

**Duncan Comics, Books,
and Accessories**
1047 Perry Highway
Pittsburgh (North Hills),
PA 15237
PH: (412) 635-0886
Web: www.
duncancomics.ohgolly.com
(a-e,g,h,k-m,p-s,t,v)

Eide's Entertainment
1111 Penn Ave.
Pittsburgh, PA 15222
PH: (412) 261-0900
FAX: (412) 261-3102
E-Mail: eides@eides.com
Web: www.eides.com
(a-q,s-v)

Legends/The Comic Stop
2600 Plymouth Meeting Hall
Plymouth Meeting, PA
19462
PH: (610) 828-5848
(a-j,l-n,q,s-v)

Dave's American Comics
Buying all 10¢ & 12¢
original priced comics
P.O. Box 8198
Radnor, PA 19087-8198
PH: (610) 275-8817
Hotline: (800) 938-0325
FAX: (714) 288-8993
E-Mail:
Dave@terryscomics.com
Web:
www.terryscomics.com
(a,b,d-h,m,n,q)

Collectible Dreams
12 N. Market Street
Selinsgrove, PA 17870
PH: (570) 372-0824
E-Mail:
cdreams@sunlink.net
(a-c,i,k,m,q-v)

Comic Swap, Inc.
110 South Fraser Street
State College, PA 16801
PH: (814) 234-6005
E-Mail: comicswap.inc
@verizon.net
(c,g,k,m,n,p,q,r,u,v)

Comic Store West
984 Loucks Rd.
Maple Village 2
York, PA 17474
PH: (717) 845-9198
E-Mail:
comicswest@aol.com
(c,m,q,r)

The Annex
314 Broadway
Newport, RI 02840
PH: (401) 847-4607
E-Mail: quackenbush3
@home.com
(b,c,k,l,q,u,v)

Planet Comics
2704 N. Main St.
Anderson, SC
29621-4141
PH: (864) 261-3578
E-Mail: service
@planetcomics.net
Web:
www.planetcomics.net
(a-c,e,g,k-v)

Heroes and Dragons
1563-B Broad River Rd.
Columbia, SC 29210
PH: (803) 731-4376
(a-c,k,m,p,r,u,v)

**Clinton Cards Comics
and Collectibles**
372 Market Street
Clinton, TN 37716
PH: (865) 457-5273
E-Mail: clintoncards
@home.com
(a-c,g,k,m,q-v)

The Great Escape
111-B North Gallatin Rd., N.
Madison, TN 37115
PH: (615) 865-8052
(a-c,e-n,p-v)

The Great Escape
1925 Broadway
Nashville, TN 37203
PH: (615) 327-0646
(a-c,e-n,p-v)

**Lone Star Comics
Books & Games**
504 East Abram St.
Arlington, TX 76010
PH: (817) Metro 265-0491
(a-c,e,g,k,m,p-v)

**Lone Star Comics
Books & Games**
511 East Abram St.
Arlington, TX 76010
PH: (817) 860-7827
FAX: (817) 860-2769
E-Mail: lonestar@
lonestarcomics.com
Web:
www.mycomicshop.com/
(a-c,e,g,k,m,p-v)

Lone Star Comics
5720 Forest Bend Dr.,
Suite 101
Arlington, TX 76017
PH: (817) 563-2550
(b,c,e,g,k,m,p-v)

Austin Books
5002 N. Lamar
Austin, TX 78751
PH: (512) 454-4197
E-Mail:
info@austinbooks.com
Web:
www.austinbooks.com
(a-i,k,m,n,p,q,s-v)

**Lone Star Comics
Books & Games**
11661 Preston Rd. #151
Dallas, TX 75230
PH: (214) 373-0934
(b,c,e,g,k,m,p-v)

Remember When
2431 Valwood Pkwy.
Dallas, TX 75234
PH: (972) 243-3439
Web: www.
rememberwhenshop.com
(a-d,g,i,j,m,n,p,q,s,t)

Titan Comics
3701 W. Northwest Hwy
#125
Dallas, TX 75220
PH: (214) 350-4420
FAX: (214) 956-0560
E-Mail:
info@titancomics.com
Web:
www.titancomics.com
(a,b,c,n,p,q)

Lone Star Comics
Books & Games
6312 Hulen Bend Blvd.
Ft. Worth, TX 76132
PH: (817) 346-7773
(b,c,e,g,k,m,p-v)

Bedrock City Comic
Company
6717 Westheimer
Houston, TX 77057
PH: (713) 780-0675
FAX: (713) 780-2366
E-Mail:
bedrock@flash.net
Web:
www.bedrockcity.com
(a-d,f,g,i,j,k,m-q,s-v)

Bedrock City Comic
Company
2204-B FM1960 West
Houston, TX 77090
PH: (281) 444-9763
FAX: (281) 444-9308
E-Mail:
bedrock2@flash.net
Web:
www.bedrockcity.com
(a-c,g,j,k,m,n,p,q,s-v)

Third Planet Sci-Fi
Super Store
2718 Southwest Freeway
Houston, TX 77098
PH: (713) 528-1067
E-Mail: 3planet
@third-planet.com
Web: www.third-planet.com
(a-v)

Lone Star Comics
Books & Games
931 Melbourne
Hurst, TX 76053
PH: (817) 595-4375
(b,c,e,g,k,m,p-v)

Lone Star Comics
Books & Games
2550 N. Beltine Rd.
Irving, TX 75062
PH: (972) 659-0317
(b,c,e,g,k,m,p-v)

Lone Star Comics
Books & Games
3600 Gus Thomasson,
Suite 107
Mesquite, TX 75150
PH: (972) 681-2040
(b,c,e,g,k,m,p-v)

Lone Star Comics
Books & Games
3100 Independence
Pkwy., Suite 219
Plano, TX 75075
PH: (972) 985-1593
(b,c,e,g,k,m,p-v)

Ground Zero Comics
1700 SSE Loop 323,
#302
Tyler, TX 75701
PH: (903) 566-1185
Web: www.
groundzerocomics.com
(c,e,g,k-m,p-s,u,v)

Bankston's
1321 S. Valley Mills Dr.
Waco, TX 76711
PH: (254) 755-0070
E-Mail:
banks1@iAmerica.net
(b,c,f,g,i,k,m,p,q,s,u,v)

Atlas Comics
1750 Rio Hill Center
Charlottesville, VA 22901
PH: (434) 974-7512
(a-c,e-g,i-n,p-v)

Hole in the Wall
905 West Broad Street
Falls Church, VA 22046
PH: (703) 536-2511
(b-e,g,h,l,n,p,q,s,t,u)

Trilogy Shop #2
700 E. Little Creek Rd.
Norfolk, VA 23518
PH: (757) 587-2540
FAX: (757) 587-5637
E-Mail: trilogy2
@trilogycomics.com
Web: www.
trilogycomics.com
(c,l,m,q,r,s,u,v)

B & D Comic Shop
802 Elm Avenue, S.W.
Roanoke, VA 24016
PH: (540) 342-6642
(c,g,l,m,p,q,r,s,v)

Trilogy Shop #1
5773 Princess Anne Rd.
Virginia Beach, VA 23462
PH: (757) 490-2205
FAX: (757) 671-7721
E-Mail: trilogy1
@trilogycomics.com
Web: www.
trilogycomics.com
(a-i,k,m,p-s,u,v)

Comic Castle
233 Second St.
Beckley, WV 25801
PH: (304) 253-1974
(b,c,k,p,q)

Another Dimension
130-10th Street N.W.
Calgary, Alberta T2N 1V3
PH: (403) 283-7078
E-Mail: another@
cadvision.com
Web: www.
another-dimension.com
(a-c,e,g,k,n,p,q,s,u)

Redd Skull Comics & CDs
720 A Edmonton Trail N.E.
Calgary, Alberta T2E 3J4
PH: (403) 230-2716
(a-c,j-r,u,v)

The Collector's Slave
156 Imperial Ave.
WPG., MB., R2M 0K8
PH: (204) 237-4428
FAX: (204) 233-5047
(a-c,e-g,m,n,s)

The Comic Cave
25 Perth Street
Brockville, ONT K6V 5C3
PH: (613) 345-4349
(a-c,g,i-k,n,p,q,r,v)

The Beguiling
601 Markham Street
Toronto, ON M6G 2L7
PH: (416) 533-9168
Web:www.beguiling.com
(a-h,j,l,n,p,q,u,v)

3RD Quadrant -
CGC Dealer
226 Queen St. W.
Basement
Toronto, ON M5V 1Z6
PH: (416) 974-9211
E-Mail:
idamahn@hotmail.com
Web:
www.3rdquadrant.com
(b,c,e,g,j,k,m,p,q,s,v)

The Final Stop...
381 McArthur Avenue
Vanier, ON K1L 6N5
PH: (613) 749-1247
E-Mail: comics
@thefinalstop.com
(c,g,k,m,n,p,q)

Heroes Comics
1116 Cure LaBelle
Laval, QC H7V 2V5
PH: (450) 686-9155
E-Mail:
heroes@dsuper.net
(a-c,e,g,k,m,o,p-s,u,v)

Michael Anthonys
Comics & Collectibles
2358 Rae St. #20
Regina, SK S4T 2G2
PH: (306) 522-2501
Web:
www3.sk.sympatico.ca/anth01
(a-c,e-n,p,s)

To get your shop included in the next edition, contact us for rates.
Gemstone Publishing, Inc., 1966 Greenspring Dr., Suite Ll3, Timonium, MD 21093.
PH 888-375-9800 or 410-560-5806, FAX 410-560-6107.
Items stocked by these shops are noted at the end of each listing and are coded as follows:

(a) Golden Age Comics	(g) Magazines	(m) Trading Cards	(r) Role Playing Games
(b) Silver Age Comics	(h) Books (old)	(n) Underground Comics	(s) Star Trek Items
(c) New Comics, Magazines	(i) Movie Posters	(o) Premiums (Rings,	(t) Doctor Who Items
(d) Pulps	(j) Original Art	Decoders, etc.)	(u) Japanimation/Manga
(e) Paperbacks	(k) Toys	(p) Comic Related Posters	(v) Collectible Card Games
(f) Big Little Books	(l) Records/CDs,Videos,DVD	(q) Comic Supplies	

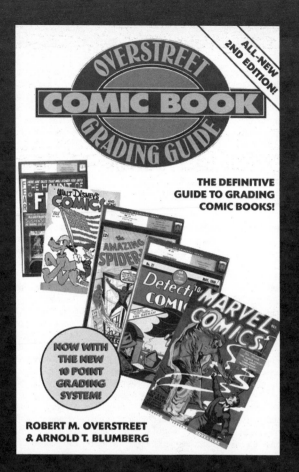

a-Story art; a(i)-Story art inks; a(p)-Story art pencils; a(r)-Story art reprint.

adult material–Contains story and/or art for "mature" readers. Re: sex, violence, strong language.

adzine–A magazine primarily devoted to the advertising of comic books and collectibles as its first publishing priority as opposed to written articles.

annual–A book that is published yearly.

arrival date-Markings on a comic book cover (usually in pencil) made by either the newsstand dealer or the distributor. These markings denote the date the book was placed on the newsstand. Usually the arrival date is one to two months prior to the cover date.

ashcan-A prepublication facsimile or dummy issue of an intended title usually prepared to show advertisers. Part or all of the pages may be blank or from a different book with a new cover. Black and white ashcans are common.

Atom Age- The period beginning in 1946 after the dropping of the first Atom bomb, continuing until the start of the Silver Age in 1956

B&W-Black and white art.

bad girl art (BGA)-A term coined in 1993 to describe an attitude as well as a style of art that portrays women in a sexually implicit way.

Baxter paper–A high quality, white, heavy paper used in the printing of some comic books.

bi-monthly-Published every two months.

bi-weekly-Published every two weeks.

bondage cover-Usually denotes a female in restraints.

brittleness-The final stage of paper deterioration.

Bronze Age–(1) Non-specific term not in general acceptance by collectors which denotes comics published from approximately 1970 through 1980, (2) Term which describes "the Age" of comic books after the Silver Age.

browning-Paper aging between

tanning and brittleness.

c-Cover art; c(i)-Cover inks; c(p)-Cover pencils; c(r)-Cover reprint.

cameo-When a character appears briefly.

CCA-Comics Code Authority.

CCA seal-An emblem that was placed on the cover of all CCA approved comics beginning in April-May, 1955.

center crease– (see Subscription Crease)

centerfold-The stapled, four page middle sheet of a comic or magazine.

CFO–Abbreviation for "Centerfold out."

chromium cover–A special Chromium foil used on covers

Church, Edgar collection-A large high grade comic book collection discovered by Mile High Comics in Colorado (over 22,000 books).

classic cover–A cover highly prized by collectors as a prime or matchless example of its kind.

cleaning–A process in which dirt and dust is removed.

color touch–A restoration process by which colored ink is used to hide color flecks, flakes and larger areas

colorist-An artist who paints the color guides for comics. Many modern colorists use computer technology.

comic book dealer–(1) A seller of comic books. (2) One who makes a living buying and selling comic books.

comic book repair-When a tear, loose staple or centerfold has been mended without changing or adding to the original finish of the book. Repair may involve tape, glue or nylon gossamer and is easily detected. It is considered a defect

comic book restoration-Any attempt, whether professional or amateur, to enhance the appearance of a comic book. These procedures may include any or all of the following techniques: recoloring, adding missing paper, stain, ink, dirt, tape removal, whitening,

pressing out wrinkles, staple replacement, trimming, re-glossing, etc. Note: Unprofessional work can lower the value of a book. In all cases, except for some simple cleaning procedures, a restored book can never be worth the same as an unrestored book in the same condition.

Comics Code Authority-In 1954 the major publishers joined together and formed a committee which set up guidelines for acceptable comic contents. It was their task to approve the contents of comics before publication.

complete run–All issues of a given title.

con-A Convention or public gathering of fans.

condition–The state of preservation of a comic book.

Cosmic Aeroplane-Refers to a large collection of 1930s-1940s comics discovered by Cosmic Aeroplane Books.

costumed hero–A costumed crime fighter with "developed" powers instead of "super" powers.

coupon cut–Comic book missing a coupon.

cover loose–Cover is detached from staple or staples

cover trimmed–Cover has been reduced in size through trimming.

crease–A paper fold that occurs in comic books from misuse

crossover–When one character or characters appears briefly in another character's story.

deacidification–The process of reducing acid in paper.

debut-The first time that a character appears anywhere.

defect–Any fault or flaw that detracts from perfection.

Denver collection–A collection of early '40s high grade #1s bought at auction in Pennsylvania by a Denver, Colorado dealer.

die-cut cover–When areas of a cover are precut by a printer to a special shape or to create a desired effect.

distributor painted stripes–Color brushed or sprayed

on the edges of comic book stacks as special coding by distributors (not a defect).

double–A duplicate copy.

double cover–An error in the binding process which results in two or more covers being bound to a single book. Multiple covers are not considered a defect.

drug propaganda story–Where comic makes an editorial stand about drug abuse.

drug use story–Shows the actual use of drugs: shooting, taking a trip, harmful effects, etc.

dust shadow–Usually the fore-edge of a comic cover exposed to the gathering of dust creating a dark stripe.

embossed cover–When a pattern is embossed onto the cover creating a raised area.

eye appeal–A term used to describe the overall appeal of a comic's apparent condition.

fanzine-An amateur fan publication.

file copy-A comic originating from the publisher's file. Not all file copies are in pristine condition. **Note:** An arrival date on the cover of a comic indicates that it is not a file copy though a copyright date may.

first app.-Same as debut.

flashback-When a previous story is being recalled.

foil cover-A thin metallic foil that is hot stamped on comic covers.

four color-A printing process in which the three primary colors plus black are used. Also refers to the Four Color series published by Dell.

foxing-Tiny orange-brown spots on the cover or pages of a comic book caused by mold growth.

G. A.-Golden Age period.

gatefold cover–A double cover folded in itself.

genre–Categories of comic book subject matter grouped as to type.

giveaway–Type of comic book used as a premium for promotional purposes.

Golden Age (G.A.)-The period beginning with **Action** #1 (June, 1938) and ending with World War II in 1945.

good girl art (GGA)-A term coined in 1977 to describe a style of art that portrays women in a sexually implicit way.

headlights-Women's breasts, usually provocative.

hologram cover–True 3-D holograms are prepared and affixed to comic book covers and cards for special effect.

hot stamping–The process of pressing foil, prism paper and inks on cover stock.

i-Art inks.

indicia-Publishers title, issue number, date, copyright and general information statement usually located on the inside front facing pages or inside back cover.

infinity cover-Shows the same scene within a scene repeated into infinity.

inker-Artist that does the inking.

intro-Same as debut.

JLA-Justice League of America.

JLI-Justice League International.

JSA-Justice Society of America.

key issue–An important issue in a run.

Lamont Larson-Refers to a large high grade collection of 1940s comics. Many of the books have Lamont or Larson written on the cover.

lenticular covers (aka flicker covers)– Images move when viewed at different angles specially prepared and affixed to cover.

logo-The title of a strip or comic book as it appears on the cover or title page.

LSH-Legion of Super-Heroes.

Marvel chipping-A defect that occurred during the trimming process of 1950s and 1960s Marvels which produced a ragged edge around the comic cover. Usually takes the form of a tiny chip or chips along the right hand edge of the cover.

Mile High-Refers to a large NM-Mint collection of comics originating from Denver, Colorado (Edgar Church collection of 20,000+ copies).

Modern Age–Period from 1980 to the present.

Mylar ™–An inert, very hard, space age plastic used to make high quality protective bags and sleeves used for comic storage. Mylar ™ is a trademark of the DuPont Company.

nd-No date.

nn-No number.

N. Y. Legis. Comm.-New York Legislative Committee to Study the Publication of Comics (1951).

one-shot-When only one issue is published of a title or the title is published on an infrequent or irregular schedule, whether or not as part of a numbered series (such as Dell's Four Color).

origin-When the story of the character's creation is given.

over Guide-When a comic book is priced at a value over Guide list.

p-Art pencils.

painted cover–Cover taken from an actual painting instead of a line drawing.

paper cover–Comic book cover made from the same newsprint as interior pages (self cover). These books are extremely rare in high grade.

pedigree-A book from a famous collection, e.g. Allentown, Larson, Church/Mile High, Denver, San Francisco, Cosmic Aeroplane, etc. Note: Beware of non-pedigree collections being promoted as pedigree books. Only outstanding high grade collections similar to those listed qualify.

penciler-Artist that does the pencils.

photo cover–Made from a photograph instead of a line drawing or painting.

Platinum Age-First age of comics, beginning with newspaper strip reprint collections (**The Yellow Kid**) in 1897, and ending with 1933's **Detective Dan**, which contained original material.

POP-Parade of Pleasure, book about the censorship of comics.

post-Code-Comic books published with the CCA seal.

post-Golden Age-Comic books published between 1945 and 1950.

post-Silver Age-Comic books published from 1969 to present.

Poughkeepsie-Refers to a large collection of Dell Comics' "file copies" believed to have originated from the warehouse of Western Publishing in Poughkeepsie, N.Y.

pre-Code-Comic books published before the CCA seal.

pre-Golden Age-Comic books published prior to **Action #1** (June, 1938).

pre-hero-A term that describes the issues in a run prior to a superhero entering the run.

pre-Silver Age-Comic books published between 1950 and **Showcase** #4 (1956).

printing defect-A defect caused by the printing process. Examples would include paper wrinkling, miscut edges, misfolded spine, untrimmed pages, off-registered color, off-centered trimming, misfolded and misbound pages. It should be noted that these are defects that lower the grade of the book.

prism cover-Special reflective foil material with 3-dimensional repeated designs. Used for special effect.

provenance-When the owner of a book is known and is stated for the purpose of authenticating and documenting the history of the book. Example: A book from the Stan Lee or Forrest Ackerman collection would be an example of a value-adding provenance.

quarterly-Published every three months (four times a year).

R or r-Reprint.

rare-10 to 20 copies estimated to exist.

rat chew-Damage caused by gnawing rats or mice.

reprint comics-Comic books that contain newspaper strip reprints.

restoration-The fine art of repairing a comic book to look as close as possible to its original condition.

rice paper-A thin, transparent paper commonly used by restorers to repair tears and replace small pieces on covers and pages of comic books.

Reilly, Tom-A large high grade collection of 1939-1945 comics with 5000+ books.

rolled spine-A spine condition caused by folding back pages while reading.

S. A.-Silver Age.

Rockford-A high grade collection of 1940s comics with 2000+ books from Rockford, IL.

saddle stitch-The staple binding of comic books.

San Francisco Collection-(see Reilly, Tom)

S&K-Joe Simon and Jack Kirby (artists).

scarce-20 to 100 copies estimated to exist.

semi-monthly-Published twice a month, as distinguished from bi-weekly.

Silver Age-Officially begins with **Showcase** #4 in 1956 and ends in 1969.

silver proof-A black & white actual size print on thick glossy paper hand painted by an artist to indicate colors to the engraver.

SOTI-Seduction of the Innocent, book about the censorship of comics. Refer to listing in this Guide.

spine-The area representing the folded and stapled part of a comic book.

spine roll-A defect caused by improper storage which results in uneven pages and the shifting or bowing of the spine.

splash panel-A large panel that usually appears at the front of a comic story.

squarebound-A comic book glue-bound with a square spined cover, aka perfect bound.

store stamp-Store name stamped in ink on cover.

stress lines-Light, tiny wrinkles occuring along the spine, projecting from the staples or appearing anywhere on the covers of a comic book.

subscription crease-A center crease caused by the folding of comic books for mailing to subscribers. This is considered a defect.

sun shadow-A darkened strip along the fore-edge of a comic cover caused by prolonged exposure to light, unlike the dust shadow which can often be removed. A serious defect.

superhero-A costumed hero crime fighter with powers beyond those of mortal man.

supervillain-A costumed criminal with powers those of mortal man.

swipe-A panel, sequence, or story obviously stolen or copied from previously published material.

3-D comic-Comic art that is drawn and printed in two mismatched colors, producing a 3-D effect when viewed through special glasses.

3-D effect comic-Comic art that is drawn to appear 3-D, but isn't.

title page-The first page showing the title of a story.

under Guide-When a comic book is priced at a value less than Guide list.

variant cover-a different cover image used on the same issue of a comic title.

very rare-1 to 10 copies estimated to exist.

warehouse copy-Originating from a publisher's warehouse; similar to file copy.

White Mountain-A large high grade collection of 1950s-1960s comics from New England.

x-over-When one character crosses over into another's strip.

zine-See Fanzine.

A Chronology of the Development of the American Comic Book by M. Thomas Inge

Precursors: The facsimile newspaper strip reprint collections constitute the earliest "comic books." The first of these was a collection of Richard Outcault's **Yellow Kid** from the **Hearst New York American** in March 1897. Commercial and promotional reprint collections, usually in cardboard covers, appeared through the 1920s and featured such newspaper strips as **Mutt and Jeff**, **Foxy Grandpa**, **Buster Brown**, and **Barney Google**. During 1922 a reprint magazine, **Comic Monthly**, appeared with each issue devoted to a separate strip, and from 1929 to 1930 George Delacorte published 36 issues of **The Funnies** in tabloid format with original comic pages in color, becoming the first four-color comic newsstand publication.

1933: The Ledger syndicate published a small broadside of their Sunday comics on 7" by 9" plates. Employees of Eastern Color Printing Company in New York, sales manager Harry I. Wildenberg and salesman Max C. Gaines, saw it and figured that two such plates would fit a tabloid page, which would produce a book about 7-1/2" x 10" when folded. Thus 10,000 copies of **Funnies on Parade**, containing 32 pages of Sunday newspaper reprints, was published for Proctor and Gamble to be given away as premiums. Some of the strips included were: **Joe Palooka**, **Mutt and Jeff**, **Hairbreadth Harry**, and **Reg'lar Fellas**. M. C. Gaines was very impressed with this book and convinced Eastern Color that he could sell a lot of them to such big advertisers as Milk-O-Malt, Wheatena, Kinney Shoe Stores, and others to be used as premiums and radio give-aways. So, Eastern Color printed **Famous Funnies: A Carnival of Comics**, and then **Century of Comics**, both as before, containing Sunday newspaper reprints. Mr. Gaines sold these books in quantities of 100,000 to 250,000. Although slightly larger in size than **Famous Funnies**, Humor Publications produced two one-issue magazines, **Detective Dan** and **The Adventures of Detective Ace King**, which contained original comic art and sold for ten cents per copy.

1934: The give-away comics were so successful that Mr. Gaines believed that youngsters would buy comic books for ten cents like the "Big Little Books" coming out at that time. So, early in 1934, Eastern Color ran off 35,000 copies of **Famous Funnies, Series 1**, 64 pages of reprints for Dell Publishing Company to be sold for ten cents in chain stores. Since it sold out promptly on the stands, Eastern Color, in May 1934, issued **Famous Funnies** No. 1 (dated July 1934) which became, with issue No. 2 in July, the first monthly comic magazine. The title continued for over 20 years through 218 issues, reaching a circulation peak of over 400,000 copies a month. At the same time, Mr. Gaines went to the sponsors of Percy Crosby's *Skippy*, which was on the radio, and convinced them to put out a Skippy book, advertise it on the air, and give away a free copy to anyone who bought a tube of Phillip's toothpaste. Thus 500,000 copies of **Skippy's Own Book of Comics** was run off and distributed through drug stores everywhere. This was the first four-color comic book of reprints devoted to a single character.

1935: Major Malcolm Wheeler-Nicholson's National Periodical Publications issued in February a tabloid-sized comic publication called **New Fun**, which became **More Fun** after the sixth issue and was converted to the normal comic-book size after issue eight. **More Fun** was the first comic book of a standard size to publish original material, and it continued publication until 1947. **Mickey Mouse Magazine** began in the summer, to become **Walt Disney's Comics and Stories** in 1940, and combined original material with reprinted newspaper strips in most issues.

1936: In the wake of the success of **Famous Funnies**, other publishers, in conjunction with the major newspaper strip syndicates, inaugurated more reprint comic books: **Popular Comics** (News Tribune, February), **Tip Top Comics** (United Features, April), **King Comics** (King Features, April), and **The Funnies** (new series, NEA, October). Four issues of **Wow Comics**, from David McKay and Henle Publications, appeared, edited by S. M. Iger and including early art by Will Eisner, Bob Kane, and Alex Raymond. The first non-reprint comic book devoted to a single theme was **Detective Picture Stories** issued in December by The Comics Magazine Company.

1937: The second single theme title, **Western Picture Stories**, came in February from The Comics

Magazine Company, and the third was **Detective Comics**, an offshoot of **More Fun**, which began in March to be published to the present. The book's initials, "D.C.," have long served to refer to National Periodical Publications, which was purchased from Major Nicholson by Harry Donenfeld late this year.

1938: "DC" copped a lion's share of the comic book market with the publication of **Action Comics** #1 in June which contained the first appearance of Superman by writer Jerry Siegel and artist Joe Shuster, a discovery of Max C. Gaines. The "man of steel" inaugurated the "Golden Era" in comic book history. Fiction House, a pulp publisher, entered the comic book field in September with **Jumbo Comics**, featuring Sheena, Queen of the Jungle, and appearing in over-sized format for the first eight issues.

1939: The continued success of "DC" was assured in May with the publication of **Detective Comics** #27 containing the first episode of Batman by artist Bob Kane and writer Bill Finger. **Superman Comics** appeared in the summer. Also, during the summer, a black and white premium comic titled **Motion Picture Funnies Weekly** was published to be given away at motion picture theatres. The plan was to issue it weekly and to have continued stories so that the kids would come back week after week not to miss an episode. Four issues were planned but only one came out. This book contains the first appearance and origin of the Sub-Mariner by Bill Everett (8 pages) which was later reprinted in **Marvel Comics**. In November, the first issue of **Marvel Comics** came out, featuring the Human Torch by Carl Burgos and the Sub-Mariner reprint with color added.

1940: The April issue of **Detective Comics** #38 introduced Robin the Boy Wonder as a sidekick to Batman, thus establishing the "Dynamic Duo" and a major precedent for later costumed heroes who would also have boy companions. **Batman Comics** began in the spring. Over 60 different comic book titles were being issued, including **Whiz Comics** begun in February by Fawcett Publications. A creation of writer Bill Parker and artist C. C. Beck, Whiz's Captain Marvel was the only superhero ever to surpass Superman in comic book sales. Drawing on their own popular pulp magazine heroes, Street and Smith Publications introduced **Shadow Comics** in March and **Doc Savage Comics** in May. A second trend was established with the summer appearance of the first issue of **All Star Comics**, which brought several superheroes together in one story and in its third issue that winter would announce the establishment of the Justice Society of America.

1941: Wonder Woman was introduced in the spring issue of **All Star Comics** #8, the creation of psychologist William Moulton Marston and artist Harry Peter. **Captain Marvel Adventures** began this year. By the end of 1941, over 160 titles were being published, including **Captain America** by Jack Kirby and Joe Simon, **Police Comics** with Jack Cole's Plastic Man and later Will Eisner's Spirit, **Military Comics** with Blackhawk by Eisner and Charles Cuidera, **Daredevil Comics** with the original character by Charles Biro, **Air Fighters** with Airboy also by Biro, and **Looney Tunes & Merrie Melodies** with Porky Pig, Bugs Bunny, and Elmer Fudd, reportedly created by Bob Clampett for the Leon Schlesinger Productions animated films and drawn for the comics by Chase Craig. Also, Albert Kanter's Gilberton Company initiated the **Classics Illustrated** series with **The Three Musketeers**.

1942: Crime Does Not Pay by editor Charles Biro and publisher Lev Gleason, devoted to factual accounts of criminals' lives, began a different trend in realistic crime stories. **Wonder Woman** appeared in the summer. John Goldwater's character Archie, drawn by Bob Montana, first published in **Pep Comics**, was given his own magazine **Archie Comics**, which has remained popular over 40 years. The first issue of **Animal Comics** contained Walt Kelly's "Albert Takes the Cake," featuring the new character of Pogo. In mid-1942, the undated Dell Four Color title, #9, **Donald Duck Finds Pirate Gold**, appeared with art by Carl Barks and Jack Hannah. Barks, also featured in **Walt Disney's Comics and Stories**, remained the most popular delineator of Donald Duck and later introduced his greatest creation, Uncle Scrooge, in **Christmas on Bear Mountain** (Dell Four Color #178). The fantasy work of George Carlson appeared in the first issue of **Jingle Jangle Comics**, one of the most imaginative titles for children ever to be published.

1945: The first issue of **Real Screen Comics** introduced the Fox and the Crow by James F. Davis, and John Stanley began drawing the **Little Lulu** comic book based on a popular feature in the **Saturday Evening Post** by Marjorie Henderson Buell from 1935 to 1944. Bill Woggon's Katy Keene appears in #5 of **Wilbur Comics** to be followed by appearances in **Laugh, Pep, Suzie** and her own comic book in 1950. The popularity of Dick Briefer's satiric version of the Frankenstein monster, originally drawn for **Prize Comics** in 1941, led to the publication of **Frankenstein Comics** by Prize publications.

1950: The son of Max C. Gaines, William M. Gaines,

who earlier had inherited his father's firm Educational Comics (later Entertaining Comics), began publication of a series of well-written and masterfully drawn titles which would establish a "New Trend" in comics magazines: **Crypt of Terror** (later **Tales from the Crypt**, April), **The Vault of Horror** (April), **The Haunt of Fear** (May), **Weird Science** (May), **Weird Fantasy** (May), **Crime SuspenStories** (October), and **Two Fisted Tales** (November), the latter stunningly edited by Harvey Kurtzman.

1952: In October EC published the first number of **Mad** under Kurtzman's creative editorship, thus establishing a style of humor which would inspire other publications and powerfully influence the underground comic book movement of the 1960s.

1953: All Fawcett titles featuring Captain Marvel were ceased after many years of litigation in the courts during which National Periodical Publications claimed that the superhero was an infringement on the copyrighted Superman. In December, Captain America, Human Torch, and Sub-Mariner were revived by Atlas Comics. The first 3-D comic book, **Three Dimension Comics**, featuring **Mighty Mouse** and created by Joe Kubert and Norman Maurer, was issued in September by St. John Publishing Co.

1954: The appearance of Fredric Wertham's book **Seduction of the Innocent** in the spring was the culmination of a continuing war against comic books fought by those who believed they corrupted youth and debased culture. The U. S. Senate Subcommittee on Juvenile Delinquency investigated comic books and in response the major publishers banded together in October to create the Comics Code Authority and adopted, in their own words, "the most stringent code in existence for any communications media." Before the Code took effect, more than 1,000,000,000 issues of comic books were being sold annually.

1955: In an effort to avoid the Code, EC launched a "New Direction" series of titles, such as **Impact, Valor, Aces High, Extra, M.D.**, and **Psychoanalysis**, none of which lasted beyond the year. **Mad** was changed into a larger magazine format with #24 in July to escape the Comics Code entirely, and EC closed down its line of comic books altogether.

1956: Beginning with the Flash in **Showcase** #4, Julius Schwartz began a popular revival of DC superheroes which would lead to the Silver Age in comic book history.

1957: Atlas reduced the number of titles published by two-thirds, with **Journey into Mystery** and **Strange Tales** surviving, while other publishers did the same or went out of business. Atlas would survive as a part of the Marvel Comics Group.

1960: After several efforts at new satire magazines (**Trump** and **Humbug**), Harvey Kurtzman, no longer with Gaines, issued in August the first number of another abortive effort, **Help!**, where the early work of underground cartoonists Jay Lynch, Skip Williamson, Gilbert Shelton, and Robert Crumb appeared.

1961: Stan Lee edited in November the first **Fantastic Four**, featuring Mr. Fantastic, the Human Torch, the Thing, and the Invisible Girl, and inaugurated an enormously popular line of titles from Marvel Comics featuring a more contemporary style of superhero.

1962: Lee introduced **The Amazing Spider-Man** in August, with art by Steve Ditko, **The Hulk** in May and **Thor** in August, the last two produced by Dick Ayers and Jack Kirby.

1963: Marvel's **The X-Men**, with art by Jack Kirby, began a successful run in November, but the title would experience a revival and have an even more popular reception in the 1980s.

1965: James Warren issued **Creepy**, a larger black and white comic book, outside Comics Code's control, which emulated the EC horror comic line. Warren's **Eerie** began in September and **Vampirella** in September 1969.

1968: Robert Crumb's **Zap** #1 appeared in February, the first underground comic book to achieve wide popularity, although counterculture precursors included **Adventures of Jesus** by Foolbert Sturgeon (Frank Stack) in 1962 and **God Nose** by Jack Jackson in 1964.

1970: Editor Roy Thomas at Marvel begins **Conan the Barbarian** based on fiction by Robert E. Howard with art by Barry Smith, and Neal Adams began to draw for DC a series of **Green Lantern/Green Arrow** stories which would deal with relevant social issues such as racism, urban poverty, and drugs. The publication of the first edition of **The Overstreet Comic Book Price Guide** in November served to stabilize the rapidly developing market for comic book collectors and provided the first dependable publication data and history for research.

1972: **The Swamp Thing** by Berni Wrightson begins in November from DC.

1973: In February, DC revived the original **Captain Marvel** with new art by C. C. Beck and reprints in the first issue of **Shazam** and in October **The Shadow** with scripts by Denny O'Neil and art by Mike Kaluta.

1974: DC began publication in the spring of a series of over-sized facsimile reprints of the most valued comic books of the past under the general title of "Famous First Editions," beginning with a reprint of **Action** #1 and including afterwards **Detective Comics** #27, **Sensation Comics** #1, **Whiz Comics** #2, **Batman** #1, **Wonder Woman** #1, **All-Star Comics** #3, **Flash Comics** #1, and **Superman** #1. Mike Friedrich, an independent publisher, released **Star-Reach** with work by Jim Starlin, Neal Adams, and Dick Giordano, with ownership of the characters and stories invested in the creators themselves.

1975: In the first collaborative effort between the two major comic book publishers of the previous decade, Marvel and DC produced together an over-sized comic book version of MGM's **Marvelous Wizard of Oz** in the fall, and then the following year, in an unprecedented crossover, produced **Superman vs. the Amazing Spider-Man**, written by Gerry Conway, drawn by Ross Andru, and inked by Dick Giordano.

1976: Frank Brunner's Howard the Duck, who had appeared earlier in Marvel's **Fear** and **Man-Thing**, was given his own book in January, which because of distribution problems became an overnight collector's item. After decades of litigation, Jerry Siegel and Joe Shuster were given financial recompense and recognition by National Periodical Publications for their creation of Superman, after several friends of the team made a public issue of the case.

1977: Stan Lee's **Spider-Man** was given a second birth, fifteen years after his first, through a highly successful newspaper comic strip, which began syndication on January 3 with art by John Romita. This invasion of the comic strip by comic book characters continued with the appearance on June 6 of Marvel's **Howard the Duck**, with story by Steve Gerber and visuals by Gene Colan. In an unusually successful collaborative effort, Marvel began publication of the comic book adaption of the George Lucas film **Star Wars**, with script by Roy Thomas and art by Howard Chaykin, at least three months before the film was released nationally on May 25. The demand was so great that all six issues of **Star Wars** were reprinted at least seven times, and the installments were reprinted in two volumes of an over-sized Marvel Special Edition and a single paperback volume for the book trade. Dave Sim, with an issue dated December, began self-publication of his **Cerebus the Aardvark**, the success of which would help establish the independent market for non-traditional black-and-white comics.

1978: In an effort to halt declining sales, Warner Communications drastically cut back on the number of DC titles and overhauled its distribution process in June. The interest of the visual media in comic book characters reached a new high with the Hulk, Spider-Man, and Doctor Strange, the subjects of television shows; with various film versions produced of Flash Gordon, Dick Tracy, Popeye, Conan, The Phantom, and Buck Rogers; and with the movement reaching an outlandish peak of publicity with the release of **Superman** in December. Two significant applications of the comic book format to traditional fiction appeared this year: **A Contract with God and Other Tenement Stories** by Will Eisner and **The Silver Surfer** by Stan Lee and Jack Kirby. Eclipse Enterprises published Don McGregor and Paul Gulacy's **Sabre**, the first graphic album produced for the direct sales market, and initiated a policy of paying royalties and granting copyrights to comic book creators. Wendy and Richard Pini's **Elfquest**, a self-publishing project begun this year, eventually became so popular that it achieved bookstore distribution. The magazine **Heavy Metal** brought to American attention the avant-garde comic book work of European artists.

1980: Publication of the November premiere issue of **The New Teen Titans**, with art by George Perez and story by Marv Wolfman, brought back to widespread popularity a title originally published by DC in 1966.

1981: Distributor Pacific Comics began publishing titles for direct sales through comic shops with the first issue of Jack Kirby's **Captain Victory and the Galactic Rangers** and offered royalties to artists and writers on the basis of sales. DC would do the same for regular newsstand comics in November (with payments retroactive to July 1981), and Marvel followed suit by the end of the year. The first issue of **Raw**, irregularly published by Art Spiegelman and Francoise Mouly, carried comic book art into new extremes of experimentation and innovation with work by European and American artists. With #158, Frank Miller began to write and draw Marvel's **Daredevil** and brought a vigorous style of violent action to comic book pages.

1982: The first slick format comic book in regular size appeared, **Marvel Fanfare** #1, with a March date. Fantagraphics Books began publication in July of **Love and Rockets** by Mario, Gilbert, and Jaime Hernandez and brought a new ethnic sensibility and sophistication in style and content to comic book narratives for adults.

1983: More comic book publishers, aside from Marvel and DC, issued more titles than had existed in the past 40 years, most small independent publishers relying on direct sales, such as Americomics, Capital, Eagle, Eclipse, First, Pacific, and Red Circle, and with Archie, Charlton, and Whitman publishing on a limited scale. Frank Miller's mini-series **Ronin** demonstrated a striking use of sword play and martial arts typical of Japanese comic book art, and Howard Chaykin's stylish but controversial **American Flagg** appeared with an October date on its first issue.

1984: A publishing, media, film, and merchandising phenomenon began with the first issue of **Teenage Mutant Ninja Turtles** from Mirage Studios by Kevin Eastman and Peter Laird.

1985: Ohio State University's Library of Communication and Graphic Arts hosted the first major exhibition devoted to the comic book May 19 through August 2. In what was billed as an irreversible decision, the Silver Age superheroine Supergirl was killed in the seventh (October) issue of **Crisis on Infinite Earths**, a limited series intended to reorganize and simplify the DC universe on the occasion of their 50th anniversary.

1986: In recognition of its twenty-fifth anniversary, Marvel began publishing several new ongoing titles comprising Marvel's "New Universe", a self-contained fictional world. DC attracted extensive publicity and media coverage with its revisions of the character of **Superman** by John Byrne and of **Batman** in the **Dark Knight** series by Frank Miller. **Watchmen**, a limited-series graphic novel by Alan Moore and artist Dave Gibbons, began publication with a September issue from DC and Marvel's **The `Nam**, written by Vietnam veteran Doug Murray and penciled by Michael Golden, began with its December issue. DC issued guidelines in December for labelling their titles either for mature readers or for readers of all ages; in response, many artists and writers publicly objected or threatened to resign.

1987: Art Spiegelman's **Maus: A Survivor's Tale** was nominated for the National Book Critics Circle Award in biography, the first comic book to be so honored. A celebration of Superman's fiftieth Birthday began with the opening of an exhibition on his history at the Smithsonian's Museum of American History in Washington, D.C., in June and a symposium on "The Superhero in America" in October.

1988: Superman's birthday celebration continued with a public party in New York and a CBS television special in February, a cover story in **Time Magazine**

in March (the first comic book character to appear on the cover), and an international exposition in Cleveland in June. With issue number 601 for May 24, **Action Comics** became the first modern weekly comic book, which ceased publication after 42 issues with the December 13 issue. In August, DC initiated a new policy of allowing creators of new characters to retain ownership of them rather than rely solely on work-for-hire.

1989: The fiftieth anniversary of Batman was marked by the release of the film **Batman**, starring Michael Keaton as Bruce Wayne and Jack Nicholson as the Joker; it grossed more money in its opening weekend than any other motion picture in film history to that time.

1990: The publication of a new **Classics Illustrated** series began in January from Berkley/First with adaptations of Poe's **The Raven and Other Poems** by Gahan Wilson, Dickens' **Great Expectations** by Rick Geary, Carroll's **Through the Looking Glass** by Kyle Baker, and Melville's **Moby Dick** by Bill Sienkiewicz, with extensive media attention. The adaptation of characters to film continued with the most successful in terms of popularity and box office receipts being **Teenage Mutant Ninja Turtles** and Warren Beatty's **Dick Tracy**. In November, the engagement of Clark Kent and Lois Lane was announced in **Superman** #50 which brought public fanfare about the planned marriage.

1991: One of the first modern comic books to appear in the former Soviet Union was a Russian version of **Mickey Mouse** published in Moscow on May 16 in a printing of 200,000 copies which were sold out within hours. The first issue of **Bone**, written, drawn, and published by Jeff Smith, appeared with a July cover date. Issue number one of a new series of Marvel's **X-Men**, with story and art by Chris Claremont and Jim Lee, was published in October in five different editions with a print run of eight million copies, the highest number in the history of the comic book. On December 18, Sotheby's of New York held its first auction of comic book material.

1992: In April, Image Comics debuted with **Youngblood** #1, changing the comic book industry by widening the playing field and legitimizing independent comics. Image Comics began publication of the first Todd McFarlane Productions title, **Spawn**, with a May cover date. The opening weekend for **Batman Returns** in June was the biggest in film box office history, bringing in over 46 million dollars, exceeding the record set by **Batman** in 1989, and not to be topped until the release of **Jurassic Park** a year later. At the second Sotheby auction in September, **Action Comics** #1 brought $82,500, a world record for a single comic book sold at auction. In November the death of Superman generated considerable media attention, with **Superman** #75 selling in excess of 4 million copies, the second best-selling issue in comic book history. A record number of over one hundred publishers of comic books and graphic albums issued titles this year.

1993: In April, for the first time since 1987, DC Comics surpassed Marvel in sales, primarily because of interest in the titles devoted to the return of Superman.

1994: Overproduction, changes in marketing practices, and publisher mergers and collapses triggered an apparent crisis in comic book publishing–which some have read as a sign of its influence and presence in American commerce and culture.

1995: Batman Forever, released in June with Val Kilmer in the lead role, grossed in its opening weekend over $53 million, the largest return in film box office history, exceeding the similar records set by the first two Batman films in 1989 and 1992. Writer Neil Gaiman decided after seven years to retire his popular and literate version of **Sandman**, the second revival of a Golden Age DC superhero first created in 1939.

1996: The longest-running give-away title ended after #467 of **The Adventures of the Big Boy** in September. In a long anticipated event coordinated between several comic book titles, the ABC television series **Lois & Clark: The New Adventures of Superman**, and the publication of **Superman: The Wedding Album**, Lois Lane and Clark Kent were married in October.

1997: Several Marvel Universe titles (**Fantastic Four, Avengers, Captain America, Iron Man**) ended their long runs and started over with new #1 issues under the umbrella title **Heroes Reborn**, a separate universe under the creative direction of Rob Liefeld and Jim Lee. They later returned, again with new #1s, in the **Heroes Return** crossover. Superman went through a startling metamorphosis at DC, complete with new powers and a new costume, eventually splitting into two beings, Superman Red & Superman Blue. The latest Batman film, **Batman & Robin**, was released to a tepid response, while the movie adaptation of Todd McFarlane's **Spawn** movie was moderately well received.

1998: Marvel continued to relaunch their popular titles, and Spider-Man was the focus. His titles were restarted with #1 issues, and John Byrne updated his origins with the start of the **Spider-Man: Chapter One** mini-series. Movie director Kevin Smith took over the reigns of **Daredevil**, and other titles were restarted under the **Marvel Knights** banner. DC bought Jim Lee's WildStorm properties, bringing into the fold popular titles like **Gen13, WildCATS**, and the highly successful new **Cliffhanger** titles **Battle Chasers, Danger Girl** and **Crimson**. The 20th anniversary of the publication of **A Contract with God** was observed by a conference "The Graphic Novel: An Emerging Literary and Artistic Medium" held in honor of Will Eisner at the University of Massachusetts in Amherst.

1999: The manga/anime influx reached gargantuan proportions with the runaway success of **Pokémon** on TV, in theaters, and most especially in comics, trading cards and toys. Other titles like **Sailor Moon** and **DragonballZ** were also prominent this year. The JSA returned to regular publication. **Marvel Knights** continued to garner praise with titles like **The Inhumans, Black Widow, Black Panther, Daredevil, Antman**, and **Punisher**. Gladstone ceased publication of Disney titles in February. That month also celebrated **The Wedding of Popeye and Olive** from Ocean Comics. Alex Ross followed up the tabloid-sized painted **Superman** adventure, **Peace on Earth**, with a **Batman** tabloid titled **War on Crime**.

2000: Marvel began to issue an **Ultimate Marvel** series designed to feature their superheroes as 21st century teenagers, beginning in September with the best-selling **Ultimate Spider-Man** #1. Film interest in comic book properties and ideas continued with the successful and faithful version of **X-Men** in July and the comic book themed movie **Unbreakable** in November. The graphic novel garnered praise and attention in the nation's literary media with the publication of such works as **From Hell** by Alan Moore and Eddie Campbell, **Jimmy Corrigan: The Smartest Kid on Earth** by Chris Ware, and **David Boring** by Daniel Clowes.

2001: Marvel finally told the origin of Wolverine in the appropriately titled mini-series, **Wolverine: Origin**, while DC set predictable record sales with the release of Frank Miller's long awaited sequel, **The Dark Knight Strikes Again**. Daniel Clowes' acclaimed graphic novel, **Ghost World**, made a successful transition to the silver screen, Kevin Smith's **Green Arrow** resurrected the Oliver Queen incarnation of the popular DC hero, and Marvel's **Spider-Man** received a welcome shot in the arm thanks to the arrival of new **Amazing Spider-Man** scribe, **Babylon 5** creator J. Michael Straczynski.

(First comic book of a genre, publisher, theme or type, etc.)

AVIATION COMIC–Wings Comics #1, 9/40
COMIC BOOK ANNUAL–Big Book of Fun Comics #1, Spr, 1936
COMIC BOOK–Funnies On Parade nn, 1933
COMIC BOOK TO GO INTO ENDLESS REPRINTS–Classic Comics #1, 10/41
COMIC BOOK TO KILL OFF A SUPERHERO–Pep Comics #17, 7/41 (The Comet)
COMIC BOOK WITH METALLIC LOGO–Silver Streak #1, 12/39
COMIC BOOK WITH ORIGINAL MATERIAL–New Fun Comics #1, 2/35
COSTUMED HERO BATTLE COMIC–Marvel Mystery #9, 7/40
COSTUMED HERO COMIC (STRIP)–Ace Comics #11, 2/38 (The Phantom)
COSTUMED HERO COMIC (Original material)–Funny Pages V2/10 9/38 (The Arrow) (3 months after Superman)
COSTUMED HERO SIDEKICK COMIC– Detective Comics #38, 4/40 (Robin)
CRIME–Crime Does Not Pay #22, 6/42
DETECTIVE COMIC–Detective Picture Stories #1, 12/36
DISNEY SINGLE CHARACTER COMIC BOOK–Donald Duck nn, 1938
DISNEY SINGLE CHARACTER COMIC BOOK IN COLOR–Donald Duck 4-Color #4, 3/40
EDUCATIONAL THEME COMIC–Classic Comics #1, 10/41
5 CENT COMIC–Nickel Comics #1, 1938
15 CENT COMIC–New York World's Fair, 1940
FLYING SAUCER COMIC–Spirit Section 9/28/47 (3 months after 1st alleged sighting in Idaho on 6/25/47)
FUNNY ANIMAL SERIES–Walt Disney's Comics & Stories #1, 10/40
FUNNY ANIMAL SINGLE CHARACTER COMIC–Donald Duck nn, 1938
GIVEAWAY COMIC–Funnies on Parade nn, 1933
GOLDEN AGE COMIC–Action Comics #1, 6/38
HEROINE SINGLE THEME COMIC–Sheena, Queen of the Jungle #1, Spr, 1942
HORROR COMIC (ONE SHOT)–Eerie Comics #1, 1/47
HORROR COMIC (SERIES)–Adventures into the Unknown #1, Fall, 1948
JUNGLE COMIC–Jumbo Comics #1, 9/38
LARGE SIZED COMIC–New Fun Comics #1, 2/35
LOVE COMIC (ONE SHOT)–Romantic Picture Novelettes #1, 1946 (Mary Worth strip-r)
LOVE COMIC (SERIES)–Young Romance Comics #1, 10/47
MAGICIAN COMIC–Super Magic Comics #1, 5/41
MAGICIAN COMIC SERIES–Super Magician Comics #2, 9/41
MASKED HERO–Funny Pages #6, 11/36 (The Clock)
MOVIE COMIC–Movie Comics #1, 4/39
NEGRO COMIC–Negro Heroes, Spr, 1947
NEWSSTAND COMIC–Famous Funnies #1, 7/34
#2 IN COMICS–Famous Funnies #2, 8/34
100 PAGE COMIC–Century of Comics nn, 1933
100TH ISSUE–Famous Funnies #100, 11/42
ONE SHOT SERIES–Feature Book nn, 1937
PATRIOTIC HERO COMIC–Pep Comics #1, 1/40 (The Shield)
PROTOTYPE COMIC–The Comics Magazine #1, 5/36 (Superman)
PUBLIC EVENT COMIC–New York World's Fair 1939

RELIGIOUS THEME SERIES–Topix Comics #1, 11/42
REPRINT COMIC–Funnies on Parade nn, 1933
SATIRE COMIC–Mad #1, 10-11/52
SCIENCE FICTION COMIC–Planet Comics #1, 1/40
SIDEKICK GROUP COMIC–Young Allies #1, Sum, 1941
SILVER AGE ARCHIE COMIC–Double Life of Private Strong #1, 6/59
SILVER AGE COMIC–Showcase #4, 9-10/56
SILVER AGE DC ANNUAL–Superman Annual #1, 10/60
SILVER AGE MARVEL ANNUAL–Strange Tales Annual #1, 1962
SILVER AGE MARVEL COMIC–Fantastic Four #1, 11/61
SINGLE CHARACTER COMIC–Skippy's Own Book of Comics, 1934
SINGLE ORIGINAL CHARACTER COMIC–Superman #1, Sum, 1939
SINGLE STRIP REPRINT CHARACTER COMIC–Mutt and Jeff #1, Sum, 1939
SINGLE THEME COMIC–Detective Picture Stories #1, 12/36
SINGLE THEME COMIC, THE FIRST IMPORTANT–Detective Comics

Wonder Comics #1 (5/39) © FOX
1st Superman Imitator

#1, 3/37
SINGLE THEME REPRINT STRIP COMIC–Mutt and Jeff #1, Sum, 1939
SMALL-SIZED COMIC–Little Giant Comics #1, 7/38
SPORTS COMIC–Champion Comics #2, 12/39
SQUAREBOUND COMIC–New Book of Comics #1, 1937
SQUAREBOUND SERIES–World's Best #1, Spr, 1941
SUPER HERO COMIC–Action Comics #1, 6/38 (Superman)
SUPER HERO TEAM–All Star Comics #3, Wint, 1940-41
SUPER HEROINE COMIC–All Star Comics #8, 11-12/41
SUPER HEROINE COMIC SERIES– Sensation Comics #1, 1/42
SUPERMAN IMITATOR–Wonder Comics #1, 5/39 (Wonder Man)
TEEN-AGE COMIC–Pep Comics #22, 12/41

TEEN-AGE COMIC SERIES–Archie Comics #1, Wint, 1942-43
10 CENT COMIC–Famous Funnies Series 1, 3-5/34
3-D COMIC–Mighty Mouse 3-D #1, 9/53
T.V. COMIC–Howdy Doody #1, 1/50
25 CENT COMIC–New York World's Fair, 1939
TRUE LIFE COMIC–Sport Comics #1, 10/40
VILLAIN COVER (FU MANCHU)–Detective Comics #1, 3/37
VILLAIN STORY (FU MANCHU)–Detective Comics #17, 7/38
VILLAIN COVER/STORY (ORIGINAL TO COMICS)– Silver Streak #1, 12/39 (The Claw)
WAR COMIC–War Comics #1, 5/40
WEEKLY COMIC BOOK–The Spirit #1, 6/2/40
WESTERN COMIC–Western Picture Stories #1, 2/37 & Star Ranger #1, 2/37
WESTERN OF ONE CHARACTER–The Lone Ranger Comics nn, 1939
WESTERN RUN OF ONE CHARACTER (GIVEAWAY)–Tom Mix #1, 9/40
WESTERN NEWSSTAND RUN OF ONE CHARACTER–Red Ryder Comics #1, 8/41
WESTERN WITH PHOTO COVER–Roy Rogers Four Color #38, 4/44
X-OVER COMIC–Marvel Mystery #9, 7/40

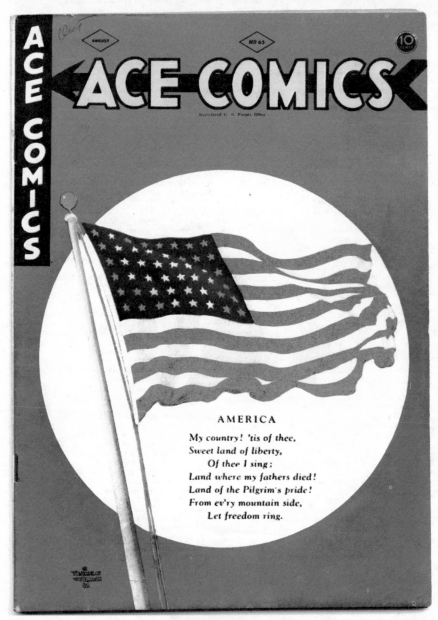

ACE COMICS #65
August 1942. World War II patriotic flag cover. © DMP

BLUE BOLT COMICS V3#9
February 1943. From the Mile High collection. World War II action cover. © NOVP

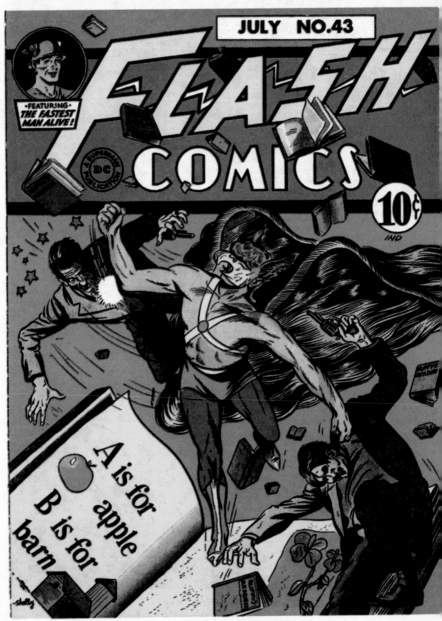

FLASH COMICS #43
July 1943. Popular Hawkman cover. © DC

LOVE LESSONS #3
February 1950 © HARV

MARVEL COMICS #1

November 1939. Famous "Pay" copy which sold in 2001 for a world record price of $350,000! Graded and certified by CGC at 9.0, this classic, historic copy contains the publisher's notations of the amounts paid to various artists that worked on the book. © MAR

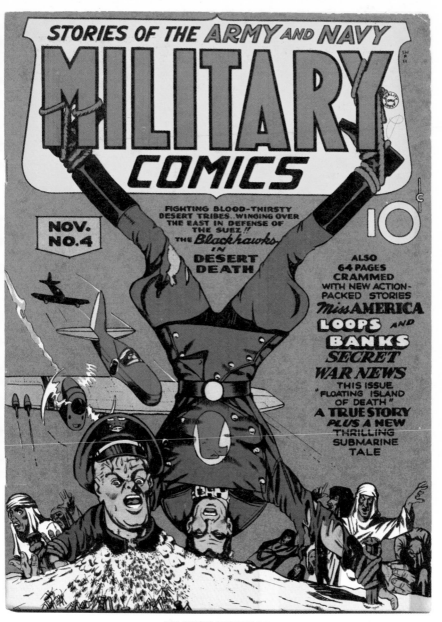

MILITARY COMICS #4
November 1941. Classic torture and bondage cover featuring the Blackhawks.
© QUA

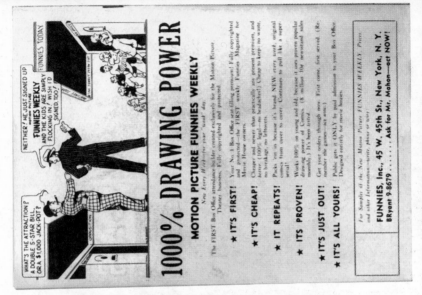

MOTION PICTURE FUNNIES WEEKLY #1 – BACK COVER
1939. Back cover ad promoting book to movie houses. © MAR

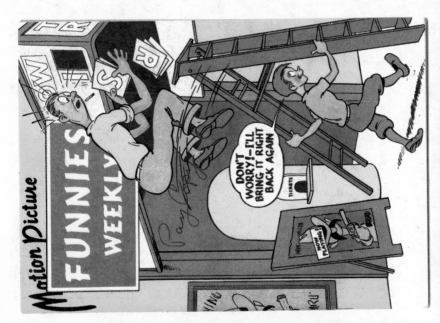

MOTION PICTURE FUNNIES WEEKLY #1– FRONT COVER
1939. Famous "Pay" copy. Contains the publisher's notations of the amounts paid to
various artists that worked on the book. © MAR

SUB-MARINER COMICS #1
August 1940. Sub-Mariner vs. the Nazis. Classic World War II action cover. © MAR

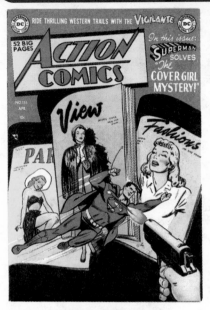

ACTION COMICS #155
April 1951 © DC

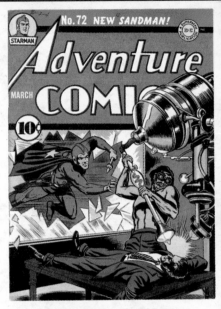

ADVENTURE COMICS #72
March 1942. First Simon & Kirby Sandman.
Starman cover app. © DC

ADVENTURES INTO THE UNKNOWN #155
March 1965 © ACG

ADVENTURES OF THE FLY #3
November 1959 © ACG

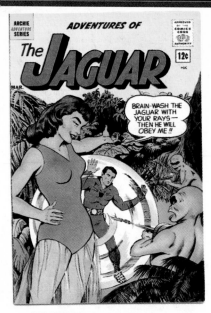

ADVENTURES OF THE JAGUAR #5
March 1962 © AP

AMAZING MAN COMICS #25
December 1941. From the Mile High
collection. © CEN

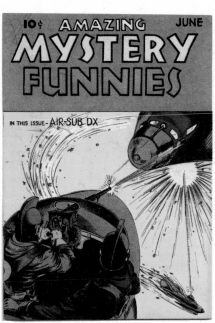

AMAZING MYSTERY FUNNIES V2#6
June 1939. From the Mile High Coll. © CEN

THE AMERICAN AIR FORCES #4
1945. World War II action cover.
© WHW

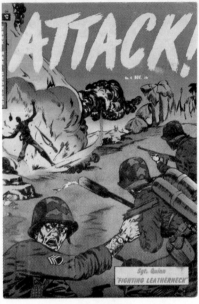

ATTACK! #4
November 1954. Becomes "Atomic Attack"
with the next issue. © YM

AUTHENTIC POLICE CASES #2
April 1948. Kamen cover art.
© STJ

AVENGERS #2
November 1963 © MAR

BAFFLING MYSTERIES #8
May 1952 © ACE

BIG SHOT COMICS #46
June 1944. Hitler, Tojo & Uncle Sam appear on cover. © CCG

BLUE BEETLE #24
August 1943 © FOX

BLUE BOLT V2#2
July 1941. Bill Everett cover art. From the Mile High collection. © NP

BLUE BOLT V2#11
April 1942. From the Mile High collection. © NP

BLUE BOLT V3#4
September 1942. From the Mile High collection. World War II Japanese cover. © NP

BLUE BOLT V3#5
October 1942.
From the Mile High
collection. © NP

BLUE BOLT V4#2
July-August 1943. Liberty Bell
freedom cover. From the Mile
High collection. © NP

BLUE BOLT V6#2
August 1945.
From the Mile High
collection. World War II
"Buy War Bonds" cover. © NP

BULLETMAN #1
Summer 1941. From the Mile High
collection. © FAW

CAMP COMICS #1
February 1942. For our soldier boys at
camp! © DELL

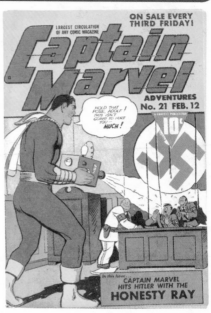

CAPTAIN FEARLESS #1
August 1941. World War II Nazi cover.
© HOKE

CAPTAIN MARVEL ADVENTURES #21
February 1943. C.C. Beck cover art.
Some copies of this book have a miniature comic
glued to the cover which were distributed to a
very small test area. © FAW

CAPTAIN MARVEL JR. #2
December 1942. From the
Mile High collection.
Mac Raboy cover art.
© FAW

CAPTAIN MARVEL JR. #7
May 1943. From the Mile High
collection. Mac Raboy cover art.
© FAW

CAPTAIN MARVEL JR. #8
June 1943. From the Mile
High collection. Mac Raboy
cover art. © FAW

CAPTAIN MARVEL JR. #9
July 1943. From the Mile
High collection. Patriotic
Mac Raboy drum &
fife flag cover. © FAW

CAPTAIN MARVEL JR. #10
August 1943. From the Mile
High collection. Mac Raboy
Hitler cover. © FAW

CAPTAIN MIDNIGHT #21
June 1944. From the Mile
High collection. World War
II Japanese action cover.
© FAW

CAPTAIN MIDNIGHT #23
August 1944. From the Mile
High collection. Japanese
prison camp cover. © FAW

CAPTAIN MIDNIGHT #32
July 1945. From the Mile
High collection. © FAW

CAPTAIN MIDNIGHT #24
September 1944. From the Mile
High collection. Japanese flag
sunburst cover. © FAW

CAPTAIN MIDNIGHT #33
August-September 1945.
From the Mile High
collection. © FAW

CAPTAIN MIDNIGHT #42
August-September 1946. From
the Mile High collection. © FAW

CAPTAIN MIDNIGHT #53
August-September 1947.
From the Mile High
collection. © FAW

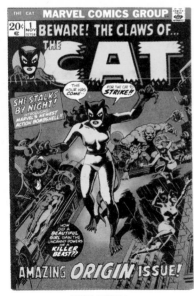

THE CAT #1
November 1972 © MAR

CRIME SUSPENSTORIES #6
August-September 1951. Gaines file copy.
Johnny Craig cover. © WMG

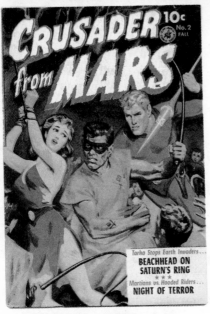

CRUSADER FROM MARS #2
Fall 1952. Saunders painted cover. © ZD

DYNAMO #2
October 1966. Wood cover art. © TC

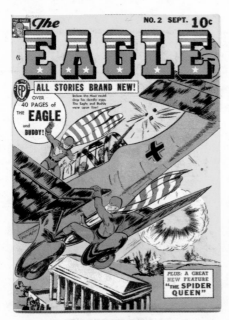

THE EAGLE #2
September 1941. From the Mile High collection. World War II action cover. © FOX

E-MAN #4
August 1974 © CC

FAMOUS FUNNIES #105
April 1943 © EAS

FAMOUS STARS #3
1951. Farley Granger photo cover. © ZD

FEATURE COMICS #80
August 1944 © QUA

FIGHTIN' MARINES #5
April 1952. Matt Baker cover. © DC

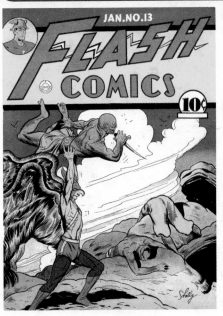

FLASH COMICS #13
January 1941 © DC

THE FOX AND THE CROW #89
January 1965 © DC

FOX GIANT, MARCH OF CRIME NN
1948 © FOX

FRANKENSTEIN #4
September-October 1946. Cover and
story art by Dick Briefer. © PRIZE

FRANKENSTEIN #8
January 1974 © MAR

THE FUNNIES #61
November 1941 © DELL

GANGSTERS AND GUN MOLLS #4
June 1952. Syd Shores cover art. © REAL

THE GHOST RIDER #1
February 1967. Origin & first appearance.
© MAR

GIGGLE COMICS #32
August 1946. Patriotic cover. © ACG

GOOFY COMICS #25
June 1946 © NEDOR

THE HAUNT OF FEAR #5
January-February 1951.
Johnny Craig cover art. © WMG

HOUSE OF MYSTERY #143
June 1964. J'onn J'onzz
Martian Manhunter begins. © DC

IT'S A DUCK'S LIFE #5
February 1952 © MAR

JACKIE GLEASON #1
September 1955. Photo cover. © STJ

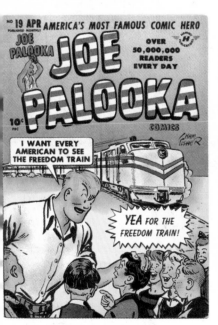

JOE PALOOKA COMICS #19
April 1948. Freedom train cover.
© HARV

THE JOKER #1
May 1975 © DC

JOURNEY INTO MYSTERY #67
April 1961 © MAR

KEEN DETECTIVE FUNNIES #23
August 1940. Introduction of Air Man.
From the Mile High collection. © CEN

KEWPIES #1
Spring 1949. © WILL EISNER

MAN IN BLACK #1
September 1957. Powell cover art. © HARV

958

THE MANY LOVES OF DOBIE GILLIS #9
October 1961 © DC

MASTER COMICS #41
August 1943. Mac Raboy cover art.
© DC

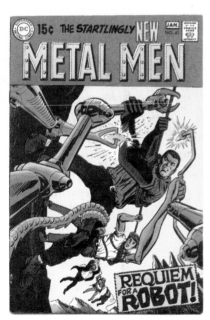

METAL MEN #41
January 1970 © DC

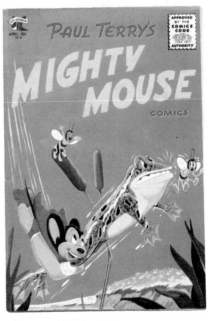

MIGHTY MOUSE #62
April 1955 © STJ

MITZI'S ROMANCES #10
December 1949 © MAR

MURDEROUS GANGSTERS #3
March 1952 © REAL

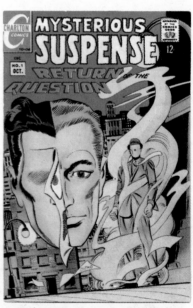

MYSTERIOUS ADVENTURES #9
August 1952 © STORY

MYSTERIOUS SUSPENSE #1
October 1968. Steve Ditko cover art.
© CC

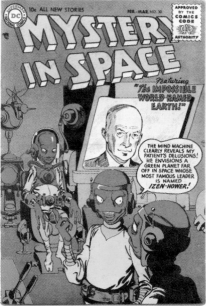

MYSTERY IN SPACE #30
February-March 1956. Eisenhower cover
appearance. © DC

MYSTERY MEN COMICS #15
October 1940 © FOX

MYSTERY TALES #9
March 1953 © MAR

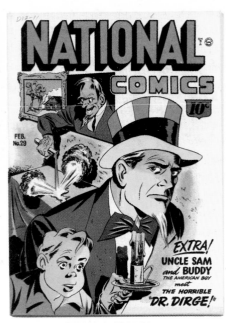

NATIONAL COMICS #29
February 1943. Contains origin of The
Unknown. From the Mile High coll. © BP

NICKEL COMICS #7
August-September 1940. C.C. Beck cover
art. From the Mile High collection. © FAW

NOMAN #2
March 1967. Wally Wood cover art.
© TC

NYOKA THE JUNGLE GIRL #76
April 1953. Photo cover. © FAW

OUR ARMY AT WAR #1
August 1952 © DC

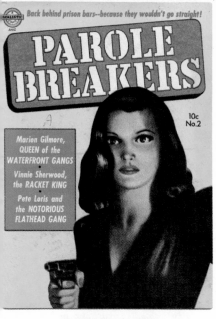

Back behind prison bars--because they wouldn't go straight!

PAROLE BREAKERS

10c
No.2

Marion Gilmore,
QUEEN of the
WATERFRONT GANGS

Vinnie Sherwood,
the RACKET KING

Pete Loris and
the NOTORIOUS
FLATHEAD GANG

PAROLE BREAKERS #2
February 1952 © REAL

POLICE Comics

SEPTEMBER No.34   10¢

AW, PLASTIC MAN, LEMME OUT!... I WON'T GET INTO ANY MORE TROUBLE!

POLICE COMICS #34
September 1944 © QUA

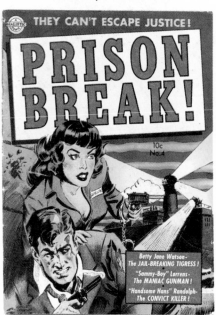

THEY CAN'T ESCAPE JUSTICE!

PRISON BREAK!

10c
No.4

Betty Jane Watson--
The JAIL-BREAKING TIGRESS!

"Sammy-Boy" Lorrens--
The MANIAC GUNMAN!

"Handsome Hans" Randolph--
The CONVICT KILLER!

PRISON BREAK! #4
1952. Kinstler cover art. © REAL

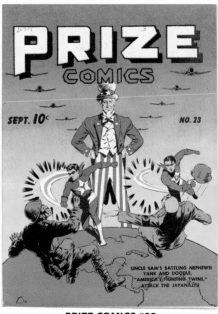

PRIZE COMICS

SEPT. 10c   NO.23

UNCLE SAM'S BATTLING NEPHEWS!
YANK AND DOODLE,
"AMERICA'S FIGHTING TWINS,"
ATTACK THE JAPANAZIS!

PRIZE COMICS #23
September 1942. From the Mile High
collection. World War II patriotic action cover.
© PRIZE

RAWHIDE KID #17
August 1960. Origin by Jack Kirby.
© MAR

REPTISAURUS THE TERRIBLE #1
(Special Edition) Summer 1963 © CC

SCIENCE COMICS #5
June 1940. The Eagle cover app.
From the Mile High collection. © FOX

SGT. BILKO #12
April 1959. Private Doberman cover app.
© DC

SHANNA THE SHE-DEVIL #2
February 1973. Steranko cover. © MAR

SHAZAM! #1
February 1973. First revival of original
Captain Marvel by C.C. Beck. © DC

SLAM BANG COMICS #2
April 1940 © FAW

SPACE BUSTERS #1
Spring 1952. Saunders painted cover. © ZD

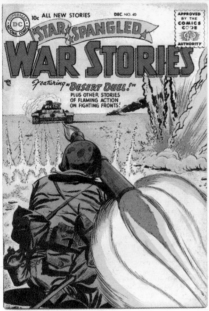

STAR SPANGLED WAR STORIES #40
December 1955 © DC

STRANGE ADVENTURES #19
April 1952 © DC

STRANGE SUSPENSE STORIES #7
May 1969 © CC

STRANGE TALES #107
April 1963. Battle issue. © MAR

STRANGE WORLDS #2
February 1959. Ditko cover art. © MAR

SUPERGIRL #1
November 1972 © DC

SUPERMAN #108
September 1956 © DC

SUPER SPY #2
November 1940. From the
Mile High collection. © CEN

TALES OF THE UNEXPECTED #30
October 1958 © DC

TALES TO ASTONISH #10
July 1960 © MAR

TARGET COMICS V6#3
May 1945. World War II Red Cross
cover theme. © NOVP

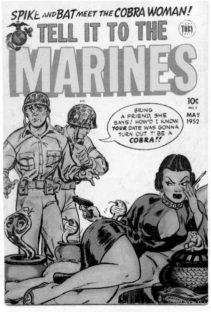

TELL IT TO THE MARINES #2
May 1952. Madame Cobra
cover appearance. © TOBY

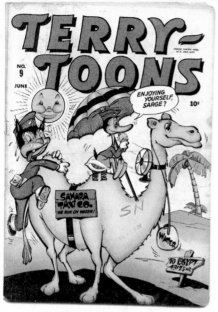

TERRY-TOONS COMICS #9
June 1943 © MAR

THUNDER AGENTS #1
November 1965. Wally Wood cover art.
© TC

TOMAHAWK #52
November 1956 © DC

TOMB OF DRACULA #1
April 1972. Neal Adams cover. © MAR

UNCANNY TALES #20
May 1954. Robert Q. Sale cover art.
© MAR

UNKNOWN WORLDS #35
October-November 1964 © ACG

WAR VICTORY COMICS
Inside front cover. Shows Shirley Temple pasting
stamps and letter from Secretary of the Treasury.

WAR VICTORY COMICS
Summer 1942. Front cover
promotes savings bonds.
© HARV

WAR VICTORY COMICS
Back cover with letter from Roosevelt.
© HARV

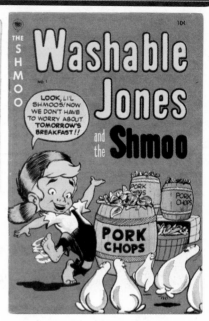

WASHABLE JONES AND THE SHMOO #1
June 1953 © TOBY

WEIRD FANTASY #16(#4)
November-December 1950.
Gaines File copy. © WMG

WYATT EARP #11
May 1957 © MAR

For decades, historians, collectors and bibliophiles have tried to identify, list and document all the important, trend-setting comic books of the past century. This interesting topic continues to be debated and discussed by experts everywhere. In an attempt to answer these questions, Overstreet would like to nominate the following books to Overstreet's Hall Of Fame. The author invites your comments and ideas concerning the accuracy of this list for future editions. Remember, only the very top books will be considered for inclusion.

PLATINUM AGE
1897-1932

Yellow Kid in McFadden's Flats, The, 1897, Dillingham Co. (1st comic book)

Funny Folk, 1899, E.P. Dutton (2nd comic book)

Vaudeville and Other Things, 1900, Blandiard Co. (3rd comic book)

Blackberries, The, 1901, R.H. Russell (Ties as 4th comic book)

Foxy Grandpa, 1901, F.A. Stokes Co. (Ties as 4th comic book)

Pore Li'l Mose, 1902, Cupples & Leon (1st satire book) (1st Cupples & Leon book)

Alphonse & Gaston & Leon, 1903, Hearst's New York American

Buster Brown and His Resolutions, 1903, F.A. Stokes Co. (1st nationally distr. comic)

Happy Hooligan, 1903, Hearst's New York American (1st comic book app.)

Katzenjammer Kids, 1903, Hearst's New York American (1st comic book app.)

Brown's Blue Ribbon Book of Jokes and Jingles, 1904, Brown Shoe Co. (1st comic book premium)

Dreams of the Rarebit Fiend, 1905, Doffield & Co. (Ties as 1st Winsor McCay book)

Little Sammy Sneeze, 1905, New York Herald Co. (Ties as 1st Winsor McCay book)

Buster Brown, 1906, Cupples & Leon (1st C&L series comic)

Little Nemo, 1906, Doffield & Co. by Winsor McCay

3 Funmakers, 1908, Stokes (1st comic to feature more than one character)

Mutt & Jeff, 1910, Ball Publ. (1st comic book app.)

Comic Monthly, 1922, Embee Dist.

Co. (1st monthly newsstand comic)

Funnies, The, 1929, Dell Publ. Co. (1st four-color comic newsstand publ.)

Mickey Mouse Book, 1930, Bibo & Lang (1st Disney licensed book)

Thimble Theatre Starring Popeye, 1931, Sonnet Publ. Co. (1st Popeye book)

Detective Dan, 1933, Humor Publ. Co. (1st comic w/original art & 1st on newsstand)

Adventures of Detective Ace King, 1933, Humor Publ. Co. (along with **Detective Dan**, helped bridge the gap between the PA and GA)

PRE-GOLDEN AGE
1933-May 1938

Funnies On Parade #nn, 1933, Eastern Color (1st GA comic book)

Century Of Comics #nn, 1933, Eastern Color (2nd GA comic book, 1st 100 pgs.)

Famous Funnies-Carnival Of Comics, nn, 1933, Eastern Color, (3rd GA comic book)

Famous Funnies-Series 1, 1934, Eastern Color, (1st 10 cent comic)

Famous Funnies #1, 7/34, Eastern Color (1st newsstand comic book)

New Fun Comics #1, 2/35, DC (1st DC comic book)

Big Book Of Fun Comics #1, Spr/35, DC, (1st annual in comics)

New Fun Comics #6, 10/35, DC (1st Siegel & Shuster work in comics)

More Fun Comics #14, 10/36, DC (1st Superman prototype at DC, 1st in color)

Detective Comics #1, 3/37, DC (1st issue of title that launched Batman)

GOLDEN AGE
June 1938-1945

Action Comics #1, 6/38, DC

(1st Superman and Lois Lane)

Funny Pages #V2#10, 9/38, Centaur (1st Arrow, 1st costumed hero)

Jumbo Comics #1, 9/38, Fiction House (1st Sheena, 1st Fiction House comic book)

Motion Picture Funnies Weekly #1, 1939, First Funnies Inc. (1st printed app. Sub-Mariner)

Movie Comics #1, 4/39, DC (1st movie comic)

New York World's Fair 1939, 4/39, DC (1st published Sandman story)

Detective Comics #27, 5/39, DC (1st Batman)

Wonder Comics #1, 5/39, Fox (1st Wonderman, 1st Superman imitator)

Superman nn (#1), Summer/39, DC (1st issue, 1st hero to get his own book)

Adventure Comics #40, 7/39, DC (1st conceived Sandman story)

Marvel Comics #1, 10/39, Timely (1st newsstand Sub-Mariner, 1st Human Torch, 1st Marvel comic)

Silver Streak #1, 12/39, Lev Gleason (1st Gleason comic book, 1st Claw)

Flash Comics #1, 1/40, DC (1st Flash, Hawkman, & Johnny Thunder)

Pep Comics #1, 1/40, MLJ/Archie (1st app. Shield, 1st patriotic hero)

Planet Comics #1, 1/40, Fiction House (1st all science fiction comic book)

More Fun Comics #52, 2/40, DC (1st Spectre)

Whiz Comics #2 (#1), 2/40, Fawcett (1st Captain Marvel & Spy Smasher, 1st Fawcett comic book)

Adventure Comics #48, 3/40, DC (1st Hourman)

More Fun Comics #53, 3/40, DC (Part II of 1st Spectre story)

Four Color Ser. 1 #4 (Donald Duck), 3?/40, (1st four color Donald

Famous Funnies #1 © EAS

Motion Picture Funnies Weekly #1 © First Funnies Inc.

Jumbo Comics #1 © FH

All-American Comics #16 © DC

Pep Comics #22 © AP

Captain Marvel Adventures #22 © FAW

Duck)
Action Comics #23, 4/40, DC
(1st Lex Luthor)
Detective Comics #38, 4/40, DC
(1st Robin)
Batman #1, Spring/40, DC
(1st issue of DC's 2nd most
important character; 1st 2 Joker
stories; 1st Catwoman)
More Fun Comics #55, 5/40, DC
(1st Dr. Fate)
The Spirit #1, 6/2/40, Will Eisner
(1st Spirit app. in weekly newspaper
strip)
All American Comics #16, 7/40, DC
(1st Green Lantern)
Blue Bolt #3, 7/40, Fox
(1st Simon & Kirby story art)
Marvel Mystery Comics #9, 7/40,
Timely (1st superhero battle; key
battle issue)
Red Raven #1, 8/40, Timely
(Early Kirby art)
Special Edition Comics #1, 8/40,
Fawcett (1st comic book devoted
to Captain Marvel)
Silver Streak #6, 9/40, Lev Gleason
(1st Daredevil)
Batman #3, Fall/40, DC (1st
Catwoman in costume)
Human Torch #2 (#1), Fall/40,
Timely (1st issue of early Marvel
star)
**Walt Disney's Comics & Stories
#1**, 10/40, Dell (1st funny animal
comic book series)
All American Comics #19, 10/40,
DC (1st Atom)
All Star Comics #3, Winter/40-41,
DC (1st superhero group)
Adventure Comics #72, 3/41, DC
(1st Simon & Kirby Sandman)
Captain America Comics #1, 3/41,
Timely (1st Captain America)
Captain Marvel Adventures #1,
3/41, Fawcett (1st issue of
Fawcett's top character)
Sub-Mariner Comics #1, Spring/41,
Timely (1st issue of Marvel's

important character)
Adventure Comics #61, 4/41, DC
(1st Starman)
All Flash #1, Summer/41, DC
(1st issue of top DC character)
Daredevil #1, 7/41, Lev Gleason
(1st issue of top character)
Military Comics #1, 8/41, Quality
(1st Blackhawk)
Famous Funnies #100, 10/41,
Eastern (1st comic book to reach
issue #100)
Green Lantern #1, Fall/41, DC
(1st issue of top DC character)
Looney Tunes #1, Fall/41, Dell
(1st Bugs Bunny, Porky Pig & Elmer
Fudd in comics)
More Fun Comics #73, 11/41, DC
(1st Aquaman; 1st Green Arrow
and Speedy)
Pep Comics #22, 12/41, MLJ/Archie
(1st Archie)
Whiz Comics #25, 12/41, Fawcett
(1st Captain Marvel Jr.)
**Four Color Ser. 1 (Mickey Mouse)
#16**, 1941, (1st comic book
devoted to Mickey Mouse)
All Star Comics #8, 12-1/41-42, DC
(1st Wonder Woman)
Animal Comics #1, 12-1/41-42, Dell
(1st Pogo by Walt Kelly)
Sensation Comics #1, 1/42, DC
(1st series to star Wonder Woman)
Crime Does Not Pay #22, 6/42,
Gleason (1st Crime comic series)
Sensation #6, June, 1942, DC,
(1st app. Wonder Woman's
magic lasso)
Wonder Woman #1, Summer/42,
DC (1st issue of top DC character)
Four Color (Donald Duck) #9, 8/42
Dell (1st Barks work on Donald Duck)
Air Fighters Comics V1 #3, 12/42,
Hillman, (1st app. of the Heap,
1st swamp creature in comics)
Archie Comics #1, Winter/42-43,
MLJ/ Archie, (1st Teenage comic)
Capt Marvel Adventures #22, 3/43,
Fawcett, (Begins Mr. Mind serial)

Plastic Man #1, Summer/43, Quality
(1st issue of top Quality
character)
Big All-American Comic Book #1,
1944, DC, (1st annual of **All-
American Comics**)
More Fun Comics #101, 1/2/45, DC
(1st Superboy)
Molly O'Day #1, 2/45, Avon
(1st Avon comic)
Terry-Toons Comics #38, 11/45,
Timely (1st Mighty Mouse)

Romantic Picture Novelette #1,
1946, ME (one shot)(1st love
comic theme)
All Winners #19, Fall/46, Timely
(1st All Winners Squad, 1st Marvel
group)
All Winners #21, Winter/46-47,
Timely (2nd All Winners Squad)
Eerie #1, 1/47, Avon (1st horror comic)
Young Romance Comics #1,
9-10/47, Prize (1st romance series)
Four Color (Uncle Scrooge) #178,
12/47, Dell (1st Uncle Scrooge)
Phantom Lady #17, 4/48, Fox
(Classic cover issue–good girl art)
Adventures Into The Unknown #1,
Fall/48, ACG (1st horror series)
Moon Girl #5, Winter/48, EC
(1st EC horror story)
Casper #1, 9/49, St John
(1st Baby Huey)
Crime Patrol #15, 12-1/49-50, EC
(1st Crypt Keeper)
War Against Crime #10, 12-1/49-
50, EC (1st Vault Keeper)
Howdy Doody #1, 1/50, Dell
(1st TV comic book)
Archie Annual #1, 1950, Archie
(1st **Archie** annual)
Crypt Of Terror #17, 4-5/50, EC
(1st issue of Crypt Keeper tales,
EC horror)
Haunt Of Fear #15 (#1), 5-6/50,
EC (1st issue of EC horror, trend-

Silver Streak Comics #6 © LEV

Four Color #16 © WDC

All Winners Comics #19 © MAR

War Against Crime #10 © WMG

Showcase #9 © DC

Mystery In Space #53 © DC

setting)

Weird Fantasy #13 (#1), 5-6/50, EC (1st issue of EC science fiction, trend-setting)

Weird Science #12 (#1), 5-6/50, EC (1st issue of EC science fiction)

Strange Tales #1, 6/51, Marvel (1st issue of top Marvel title)

Mad #1, 10-11/52, EC (1st satire comic)

Journey Into Mystery #1, 6/52, Marvel (1st issue of top Marvel title)

Little Dot #1, 9/53, Harvey (1st Richie Rich)

Young Men #24, 12/53, Marvel (Revival of Capt. America, Human Torch & Sub-Mariner)

World's Finest Comics #71, 7-8/54, DC (1st Superman/Batman team issue)

Superman's Pal, Jimmy Olsen #1, 9-10/54, DC, (1st issue of top DC title)

My Greatest Adventure #1, 1-2/55, DC (1st issue of top DC fantasy title)

Brave And The Bold #1, 8-9/55, DC (1st issue of top DC showcase title)

Superman #100, 9-10/55, DC (Landmark issue)

Detective Comics #225, 11/55, DC (1st Martian Manhunter)

Tales Of The Unexpected #1, 2-3/56, DC (1st issue of top DC fantasy title)

Showcase #1, 3-4/56, DC (1st issue of top DC title)

Sugar & Spike #1, 4-5/56, DC (1st issue of top title by Sheldon Mayer)

Batman #100, 6/56, DC (Landmark issue)

Detective Comics #233, 7/56, DC (1st Batwoman)

SILVER AGE
Sept. 1956-1969

Showcase #4, 9-10/56, DC (1st Silver Age book) (The Flash)

House Of Secrets #1, 11-12/56, DC (1st issue of top DC horror title)

Showcase #6, 1-2/57, DC (1st Silver Age group)(Challengers)

Showcase #9, 7-8/57, DC (1st Lois Lane book)

Superman's Girl Friend, Lois Lane #1, 3-4/58, DC (1st issue of top character)

Adventure Comics #247, 4/58, DC (1st Legion of Superheroes)

Challengers Of The Unknown #1, 4-5/58, DC, (1st issue of 1st Silver Age group)

Showcase #15, 7-8/58, DC (1st Space Ranger)

Showcase #17, 11-12/58, DC (1st Adam Strange)

Tales Of Suspense #1, 1/59, Marvel (1st issue of top fantasy title)

Tales To Astonish #1, 1/59, Marvel (1st issue of top fantasy title)

Flash #105 (#1), 2-3/59, DC (1st issue of top DC title)

Our Army At War #83, 6/59, DC (1st Sgt. Rock by Kubert/Kanigher)

Action Comics #252, 5/59, DC (1st Supergirl)

Showcase #20, 5-6/59, DC (1st Rip Hunter)

Double Life Of Private Strong #1, 6/59, Archie (1st Silver Age Shield, 1st Fly)

Mystery In Space #53, 8/59, DC (1st Adam Strange)

Tales Of The Unexpected #40, 8/59, DC (1st Space Ranger in own title)

Adventures of the Fly #1, 8/59, Archie (1st issue of top Archie title)

Showcase #22, 9-10/59, DC (1st Silver Age Green Lantern)

Flash #110, 12-1/59/60, DC (1st Kid Flash)

Brave And The Bold #28, 2/3/60, DC (1st Justice League of America)

Green Lantern #1, 7-8/60, DC (1st issue of top DC character)

Showcase #27, 7-8/60, DC (1st Sea Devils)

Brave And The Bold #31, 8-9/60, DC (1st Cave Carson)

Justice League Of America #1, 10-11/60, DC (1st issue of top DC title)

Showcase #30, 1-2/61, DC (Spotlights Silver Age Aquaman)

Brave And The Bold #34, 2-3/61, DC (1st Silver Age Hawkman)

Amazing Adventures #1, 6/61, Marvel (1st Dr. Droom, the 1st Marvel-Age superhero)

Flash #123, 9/61, DC (1st G.A. Flash in Silver Age)

Showcase #34, 9-10/61, DC (1st Silver Age Atom)

Fantastic Four #1, 11/61, Marvel (1st Fantastic Four)

Amazing Adult Fantasy #7, 12/61, Marvel (1st issue of title that leads to Spider-Man)

Tales To Astonish #27, 1/62, Marvel (1st Antman)

Showcase #37, 3-4/62, DC (1st Metal Men)

Fantastic Four #4, 5/62, Marvel (1st Silver Age Sub-Mariner)

Incredible Hulk #1, 5/62, Marvel (1st Hulk)

Mystery In Space #75, 5/62, DC (Early JLA cross-over in Adam Strange story)

Fantastic Four #5, 7/62, Marvel (1st Dr. Doom)

Journey Into Mystery #83, 8/62, Marvel (1st Thor)

Amazing Fantasy #15, 8-9/62, Marvel (1st Spider-Man)

Tales To Astonish #35, 9/62, Marvel (2nd Antman, 1st in costume)

Strange Tales #101, 10/62, Marvel (1st S.A. Human Torch solo story)

Amazing Spider-Man #1, 3/63,

Superman #100 © DC

The Flash #123 © DC

Showcase #37 © DC

974

Amazing Spider-Man #14 © MAR

House of Secrets #92 © DC

Superman (2nd series) #75 © DC

Marvel (1st Spider-Man in own title)

Tales Of Suspense #39, 3/63, Marvel (1st Iron Man)

Strange Tales #110, 7/63, Marvel (1st Dr. Strange)

Justice League of America #21, 8/63, DC (1st JLA/JSA crossover)

Avengers #1, 9/63, Marvel (1st Avengers)

X-Men #1, 9/63, Marvel (1st X-Men)

Mystery In Space #87, 11/63, DC (1st Hawkman in title)

Avengers #4, 3/64, Marvel (1st Silver Age Captain America)

Daredevil #1, 4/64, Marvel (1st Daredevil)

Detective Comics #327, 5/64, DC (New Batman) (Silver Age/ Bronze)

Brave and the Bold #54, 6-7/64, DC (1st Teen Titans)

Amazing Spider-Man #14, 7/64, Marvel (1st Green Goblin)

Strange Tales #135, 7/65, Marvel (Origin & 1st app. Nick Fury)

Fantastic Four #48, 3/66, Marvel (1st Silver Surfer)

Our Army at War #168, 6/66, DC (1st Unknown Soldier)

Strange Adventures #205, 10/67, DC (1st Deadman)

Zap Comix#1, 11/67, Apex (Underground comic which instigated the direct sales market)

BRONZE AGE 1970-1979

Green Lantern #76, 4/70, DC (Begins Green Lantern/Green Arrow series by Denny O'Neil & Neal Adams)

Detective Comics #400, 6/70, DC (1st Man-Bat)

Superman's Pal, Jimmy Olsen #133, 10/70, DC (1st Silver Age Newsboy Legion)

Forever People #1, 2-3/71, DC (1st Forever People)

New Gods #1, 3/71, DC (1st New Gods)

Mister Miracle #1, 3/71, DC (1st Mister Miracle)

Savage Tales #1, 5/71, Marvel (1st Man-Thing)

House of Secrets #92, 6/71, DC (1st app. Swamp Thing by Bernie Wrightson)

Amazing Spider-Man #101, 10/71, Marvel (1st Morbius the Living

Vampire)

Marvel Feature #1, 12/71, Marvel (Origin and 1st app. Defenders)

All Star Western #10, 2-3/72, DC (1st Jonah Hex)

Tomb of Dracula #1, 4/72, Marvel (1st app. Dracula)

Marvel Spotlight #2, 6/72, Marvel (1st app. Werewolf by Night)

Marvel Spotlight #5, 8/72, Marvel (Origin and 1st app. new Ghost Rider)

Kamandi: The Last Boy on Earth #1, 10/72, DC (Origin/1st Kamandi)

Iron Man #55, 2/73, Marvel (1st. app. Thanos & Drax the Destroyer)

Shazam #1, 2/73, DC (1st revival of Captain Marvel since mid 50s)

Amazing Spider-Man #121, 6/73 Marvel (Death of Gwen Stacy)

Amazing Spider-Man #122, 7/73, Marvel (Death of Green Goblin I)

Marvel Spotlight #12, 10/73, Marvel (1st solo Son of Satan)

Marvel Special Edition #15, 12/73, Marvel (1st Master of Kung Fu)

Amazing Spider-Man #129, 2/74, Marvel (1st Punisher)

Astonishing Tales #25, 8/74, Marvel (1st Deathlok)

Incredible Hulk #181, 11/74, Marvel (1st story app. of Wolverine)

Giant Size X-Men #1, Summer/75, Marvel (1st New X-Men; intro Nightcrawler, Storm, Colossus & Thunderbird)

X-Men #94, 8/75, Marvel (New X-Men team begins)

All Star Comics #58, 1-2/76, DC (1st Power Girl)

Marvel Spotlight #32, 2/77, Marvel (1st Spider-Woman)

Black Lightning #1, 4/77, DC (1st Black Lightning)

Cerebus #1, 12/77, Aardvark-Vanaheim (1st app. Cerebus)(B&W)

X-Men #108, 12/77, Marvel (1st important Byrne work)

Daredevil #158, 5/79, Marvel (Frank Miller begins work on Daredevil; his 1st important work)

MODERN AGE 1980-Present

X-Men #137, 9/80, Marvel (The story that started comicdom's "Death Craze")

Daredevil #168, 1/81, Marvel (1st Elektra)

Gobbledygook #1, pre 6/84; Mirage, (1st app. Teenage Mutant

Ninja Turtles)

Crisis on Infinite Earths #1-12, 85/86, DC (1st appearance of revamped Modern Age DC universe) (#7, Death of Supergirl) (#8, Death of the Barry Allen Flash)

Batman: The Dark Knight #1, 3/86, DC (Beginning of Frank Miller's landmark revision of Batman)

Maus, 1986, Pantheon Books (1st comic book to win the Pulitzer Prize) (Depicts the horrors of the Holocaust through the eyes of artist Art Spiegelman's father)

The Man of Steel #1, 6/86, DC (Beginning of John Byrne's update of the Superman mythos)

Watchmen #1, 10/87, DC (Beginning of Alan Moore's revisionist look at superheroes)

Batman: The Killing Joke, 1988, DC (Batgirl Barbara Gordon is crippled by the Joker)

Amazing Spider-Man #300, 5/88, Marvel (1st Venom) (full app & story)

Sandman #1, 1/89, DC (1st app. new Sandman)

X-Men #1, 10/91, Marvel (1st comic to reach a print run of 8 million copies)

Youngblood #1, 4/92, Image (1st Image comic)

Spawn #1, 5/92, Image (1st app. Spawn)

Superman (2nd Series) #75, 1/93, DC (Death of Superman) (Huge Media Coverage)

Deathmate Black, 9/93, Valiant/ Image (1st Gen13 story)

Starman #0, 10/94, DC (1st app. of Modern Age Starman)

Strangers in Paradise #1, 11/94, Antarctic (1st issue of Terry Moore's series)

DC Vs. Marvel #1, 1996, DC (1st issue of landmark company crossover)

Kingdom Come #1-4, 1996, DC (Fully painted Elseworlds series about the future DC universe)

Superman: The Wedding Album, 12/96, DC (Marriage of Clark Kent and Lois Lane)

Heroes, 12/01, Marvel (Pinup tributes to the rescue workers of the Sept. 11 tragedy; art and text by various. The first of many tribute books from the comic industry.)

The Overstreet® Comic Book Price Guide has held the record for being the longest running annual comic book publication. We are now celebrating our 32nd anniversary, and the demand for the Overstreet® price guides is very strong. Collectors have created a legitimate market for them, and they continue to bring record prices each year. Collectors also have a record of comic book prices going back further than any other source in comic fandom. The prices listed below are for NM condition only, with GD-25% and FN-50% of the NM value. Canadian editions exist for a couple of the early issues. Special thanks to Robert Rogovin of Four Color Comics for his assistance in researching the prices listed in this section. Abbreviations: SC-softcover, HC-hardcover, L-leather bound.

1970	1970	1972	1973	1974	1975
#1 White SC $1700.00	#1 Blue SC (2nd Printing) $1400.00	#2 SC $600.00 #2 HC $1000.00	#3 SC $275.00 #3 HC $900.00	#4 SC $150.00 #4 HC $450.00	#5 SC $150.00 #5 HC $250.00

1976	1977	1978	1979	1980	1981
#6 SC $100.00 #6 HC $150.00	#7 SC $140.00 #7 HC $225.00	#8 SC $125.00 #8 HC $175.00	#9 SC $125.00 #9 HC $175.00	#10 SC $125.00 #10 HC $175.00	#11 SC $80.00 #11 HC $110.00

1982	1983	1984	1985	1986	1987
#12 SC $80.00 #12 HC $110.00	#13 SC $80.00 #13 HC $110.00	#14 SC $55.00 #14 HC $110.00 #14 L $170.00	#15 SC $55.00 #15 HC $80.00 #15 L $160.00	#16 SC $55.00 #16 HC $80.00 #16 L $160.00	#17 SC $55.00 #17 HC $110.00 #17 L $160.00

1988	1989	1990	1991	1992	1993
#18 SC $45.00 #18 HC $65.00 #18 L $160.00	#19 SC $45.00 #19 HC $55.00 #19 L $160.00	#20 SC $32.00 #20 HC $50.00 #20 L $135.00	#21 SC $32.00 #21 HC $50.00 #21 L $135.00	#22 SC $32.00 #22 HC $50.00	#23 SC $32.00 #23 HC $50.00

1994

#24 SC $24.00
#24 HC $34.00

1995

#25 SC $24.00
#25 HC $34.00
#25 L $100.00

1996

#26 SC $20.00
#26 HC $30.00
#26 L $100.00

1997

#27 SC $22.00
#27 HC $38.00
#27 L $125.00

1997

#27 SC $22.00
#27 HC $38.00
#27 L $125.00

1998

#28 SC $20.00
#28 HC $35.00

1998

#28 SC $20.00
#28 HC $35.00

1999

#29 SC $20.00
#29 HC $35.00

1999

#29 SC $20.00
#29 HC $35.00

2000

#30 SC $22.00
#30 HC $32.00

2000

#30 SC $22.00
#30 HC $32.00

2001

#31 SC $22.00
#31 HC $32.00

2001

#31 SC $22.00
#31 HC $32.00

2001

#31 Bookstore Ed.
SC only $22.00

2001

#31 Workbook
$35.00

FEATURE ARTICLE INDEX

Over the years, the **Overstreet Comic Book Price Guide** has grown into much more than a simple catalog of values. Almost since the very beginning, Bob has worked hard to make sure that the book reflects the latest information about the hobby, and this has resulted in some fascinating in-depth articles about aspects of the industry and the rich history of comics. Sadly, many of you may never have read a lot of these articles, or even knew they existed...until now.

Now, for the first time, we present a comprehensive index to every feature article ever published in the **Overstreet Comic Book Price Guide**. From interviews with legendary creators to exhaustively researched retrospectives, it's all here. Enjoy this look back at the Overstreet legacy, and remember, many of these editions are still available through Gemstone and your local comic book dealer.

Note: The first three editions of the Guide had no feature articles, but from #4 on, a tradition was born that has carried through to the very volume you hold in your hands. This index begins with the 4th edition and lists all articles published up to and including last year's 31st edition of the guide.

ED.	YR.	TITLE	AUTHOR(S)	PGS.
#4	1974	Secrets Behind ALL-STAR COMICS(More Than You May Want to Know)	Jerry Bails	26-37
#5	1975	Edgar Rice Burroughs and the Comics	Kevin B. Hancer	33-38
#6	1976	An Interview with Will Eisner, Creator of the Spirit	Jerry DeFuccio	31-37
		Good Girl Art - An Introduction: Why it Was and What it Was	produced by the American Comic Book Co. (Carl Macek)	38-43
		The Archives of the Comic Book Price Guide	Landon Chesney (comic strip)	44-45
#7	1977	Esoteric Comics: The Ultimate Collectable	prod. by the American Comic Book Co. (Carl Macek in consultation with Scott Shaw)	A-30-35
		Carl Barks - From Burbank to Calisota	E. B. Boatner	A-37-57
#8	1978	Confessions of a Former Comic Book Artist	Jay Disbrow	A-31-38
		The Man Behind Torchy	Bill Ward	A-40-53
		Women in Comics	Carl Macek in collaboration with Art Amsie	A-54-75
		Tarpe Mills - An Appreciation	Trina Robbins	A-76
#9	1979	For Those Who Know How to Look	Carl Macek	A-35-42
		Good Lord! choke... gasp... It's EC!	E. B. Boatner	A-43-76
#10	1980	The Origin of Marvel Comics	George Olshevsky	A-46-73
#11	1981	Anaglyphs - A Survey of the 3-D Comic Books	Ray Zone	A-44-53
		L. B. Cole: The Man Behind the Mask: (and Captain Aero and Catman and...)	E. B. Boatner	A-55-72
#12	1982	Norman Mingo and Alfred: The World's Greatest Facelift	Jerry DeFuccio	A-45-57
		The Pop Hollinger Story: The First Comic Book Collector/Dealer	Tim Hessee	A-58-66
#13	1983	Great Old Time Radio Premiums	"Little" Jimmy Dempsey	A-62-63
		Reminiscences of a Comic Book Editor	Jack Schiff and Gene Reed	A-64-70
		DC Before Superman	Gary M. Carter and Ken Lane Carter	A-72-86
#14	1984	Katy WHO?...Never Heard of it...	Barbara A. Rausch	A-52-56
		Congratulations Katy Keene	(various comic book and cartoon creators and their character)	A-57-59
		Katy Keene - The Overstreet Connection	Craig Leavitt	A-67-78
#15	1985	Charles Clarence Beck: The World's Second Mightiest Mortal	Jerry DeFuccio	A-78-88
		Mr. Mind and the Monster Society of Evil	C. C. Beck	A-89-93
#16	1986	Twenty-Five Years? I Don't Believe It!	Stan Lee	A-82-84
		Marvel and Me	Jim Shooter	A-85-96
#17	1987	The Man Behind the Cover - Ron Dias	staff	A-84
		The Enduring Magic of Disney Comics	Thomas Andrae (with Bruce Hamilton)	A-85-99
		Walt Disney's Snow White and the Seven: Dwarfs - Fifty Years of Collectibles	Terry Taylor	A-101-111
#18	1988	The Man Behind the Cover - L. B. Cole	Christopher Irons	A-77
		Of Supermen and Kids With Dreams: An Interview with Jerry Siegel and Joe Shuster	Thomas Andrae	A-79-98
#19	1989	Origins of the Dark Knight: A Conversation with Batman Artists	Thomas Andrae, Bob Kane and Jerry Robinson	A-72-93

#20	1990	In a League of Their Own !	Harry B. Thomas	A-77-93
		The Silver Age...The Beginning:	Gary M. Carter	A-94-107
		A Comparative Chronology of the First Silver Age Comic Books		
#21	1991	Archie Comic Publications: The Mirth of a Legend	Scott D. Fulop	A-77-78
		1941: Comic Books Go To War!:	Harry B. Thomas	A-79-98
		Those fabulous comics of World War II	and Gary M. Carter	
#22	1992	Spider-Man - An Amazing Success Story	Steve Saffel	A-77-86
		Journey Into the Unknown World of Atlas Fantasy	Gary M. Carter & Pat S. Calhoun	A-87-103
#23	1993	Green Lantern's Light! A History by...	Thomas Andrae with Keif Fromm	A-71-79
		Silver Sagas of the Scarlet Speedster:	Gary M. Carter	A-80-86
		Whirlwind Adventures of the Fastest Man Alive! 1956-1960		
#24	1994	Three Uncanny Decades of X-Men!	John Townsend, Ph.D.	A-146-156
		Living on Borrowed Time! A Nostalgic Look at the Early Years	Pat S. Calhoun & Gary M. Carter	A-157-164
		of DC's Challengers of the Unknown!		
#25	1995	The Mystery of the 12 Missing ECs	Bruce Hamilton	A-99-106
		100 Years - A Century of Comics	Pat S. Calhoun	A-107-123
#26	1996	The American Comic Book: 1897-1932	Richard D. Olson, Ph.D.	pp. 1-2
		The Formative Years - The Platinum Age		
		The American Comic Book: 1933-Present	Richard D. Olson, Ph.D.	pp. 10-11
		The Modern Comic Book		
		The Golden Age and Beyond	Jerry Weist	652-667
		A Short History of Comic Book Fandom	Sotheby's Comic Book Consultant	
		& Comic Book Collecting in America		
#27	1997	Gotham Knights - A Conversation	Arnold T. Blumberg	A-25-27
			with Jerry Robinson	
		Strange Adventures - A Conversation with Murphy Anderson	Scott Braden	A-30-32
		The American Comic Book: 1897-1932	Robert L. Beerbohm	pp. 1-15
		The Beginning: The Platinum Age		
		The American Comic Book: 1933-Present	Richard D. Olson, Ph.D.	23-24
		The Golden Age and Beyond: The Modern Comic Book		
#28	1998	Friends of Lulu Sounds Off on Comics	Jackie Estrada	79-81
		The World of Tomorrow :	Arnold T. Blumberg	82-88
		How Comics of the Past Portrayed the 1990s		
		Invasion of the Giant (and Not So Giant) Robots!	Arnold T. Blumberg	83-87
		Built to Last	J. C. Vaughn and Scott Braden	89-102
		The American Comic Book: 1897-1932	J. C. Vaughn	201-203
		In the Beginning: The Platinum Age:		
		The American Comic Book: 1933-Present	Richard D. Olson, Ph.D.	211-212
		The Golden Age & Beyond: The Modern Comic Book (Revised)		
#29	1999	Special Feature: Grading - The Next Revolution for Comic Books	Bruce Hamilton	17-21
		Avenues of Collecting: A Walk Through the Comic Book Neighborhood	J. C. Vaughn	91-94
		Just Another Justice League ?	J. C. Vaughn	95-100
		Legiondary Adventures	Mark Huesman	101-106
		One For All and All For One:	Arnold T. Blumberg	107-112
		A Brief History of Super-Teams: Top Ten Greatest Super-Teams	Benn Ray	108-112
		The American Comic Book: 1897-1932	Robert L. Beerbohm	211-218
		In the Beginning: The Platinum Age (Rev.)	& Richard D. Olson, PhD	
		The American Comic Book: 1933-Present	Robert L. Beerbohm	226-233
		The Golden Age & Beyond & The Origin of the Modern Comic Book	& Richard D. Olson, PhD	
#30	2000	History with a Twist	Arnold T. Blumberg	18-22
		EC, MAD and Beyond: Al Feldstein	J. C. Vaughn	24-28
		Flights to EC and Beyond with Al Williamson	J. C. Vaughn	36-39
		Bob's Bizarre Tales	Bob Overstreet	42-63
		The Marketing of a Medium	Arnold T. Blumberg	195-198
		New Discoveries Beyond the Platinum Age	Beerbohm & Olson	226-234
		The Golden Age & Beyond: Origins of the Modern Comic Book	Beerbohm & Olson	242-249
#31	2001	Why The Fantastic Four Made It To Forty	Arnold T. Blumberg	20-24
		Sixty Years of Wonder Woman	Charles S. Novinskie	26-29
		Brownie Points	Arnold T. Blumberg	30-32
		Re-Creations in a Flash (Murphy Anderson profile)	Arnold T. Blumberg	39-40
		Extraordinary! (John K. Snyder III profile)	J.C. Vaughn	42-44
		Bendis! (Brian Michael Bendis profile)	J.C. Vaughn	46-48

OVERSTREET ADVISORS

DAVID T. ALEXANDER
David Alexander Comics
Tampa, FL

DAVE ANDERSON
Want List Comics
Tulsa, OK

STEPHEN BARRINGTON
Collector
Chickasaw, AL

ROBERT BEERBOHM
Robert Beerbohm Comic Art
Fremont, NE

JON BERK
Collector
Hartford, CT

STEVE BOROCK
Primary Grader
Comics Guaranty, LLC

MICHAEL BROWNING
Collector
Jefferson City, TN

MICHAEL CARBONARO
Neatstuffcollectibles.com
Englewood, NJ

ERICK CARTER
Tropic Comics
Plantation, FL

GARY CARTER
Collector
Coronado, CA

JOHN CHRUSCINSKI
Tropic Comics
Plantation, FL

GARY COLABUONO
Classics International Ent.
Elk Grove Village, IL

BILL COLE
Bill Cole Enterprises, Inc.
Randolph, MA

LARRY CURCIO
Avalon Comics
Los Angeles, CA

GARY DOLGOFF
Gary Dolgoff Comics
Easthampton, MA

BRUCE ELLSWORTH
Bruce's Collectibles
New Orleans, LA

CONRAD ESCHENBERG
Collector/Dealer
Cold Spring, NY

RICHARD EVANS
Bedrock City Comics
Houston, TX

STEPHEN FISHLER
Metropolis Collectibles, Inc.
New York, NY

DAN FOGEL
Hippy Comix, Inc.
El Sobrante, CA

STEVEN GENTNER
Golden Age Specialist
Portland, OR

STEVE GEPPI
Diamond Int. Galleries
Timonium, MD

MICHAEL GOLDMAN
Motor City Comics
Southfield, MI

TOM GORDON
Monumental Collectibles
Westminster, MD

JAMIE GRAHAM
Graham Crackers
Chicago, IL

DANIEL GREENHALGH
Showcase New England
Northford, CT

ERIC J. GROVES
Dealer/Collector
Oklahoma City, OK

ROBERT HALL
Collector
Harrisburg, PA

BRUCE HAMILTON
Hamilton Comics
Prescott, AZ

MARK HASPEL
Grader
Comics Guaranty, LLC

JOHN HAUSER
Dealer/Collector
New Berlin, WI

BILL HUGHES
Greg Manning Auctions, Inc.
West Caldwell, NJ

ROB HUGHES
Arch Angels
Manhattan Beach, CA

ED JASTER
Jaster Collectibles
Chicago, IL

MICHAEL NAIMAN
Silver Age Specialist
San Diego, CA

TODD REZNIK
Pacific Comic Exchange
Palos Verdes Peninsula, CA

JOHN SNYDER
Diamond Int. Galleries
Timonium, MD

PHIL LEVINE
Dealer/Collector
Three Bridges, NJ

JOSHUA NATHANSON
ComicLink
Little Neck, NY

ROBERT ROGOVIN
Four Color Comics
New York, NY

TONY STARKS
Silver Age Specialist
Evansville, IN

PATRICK MARCHBANKS
Golden Age Comics & Games
Gulfport, MS

MATT NELSON
Classic Conservations
New Orleans, LA

RORY ROOT
Comic Relief
Berkeley, CA

TERRY STROUD
Dealer/Collector
Santa Monica, CA

HARRY MATETSKY
Collector
Middletown, NJ

RICHARD OLSON
Collector/Academician
Slidell, LA

MARNIN ROSENBERG
Collectors Assemble
Great Neck, NY

DOUG SULIPA
"Everything 1960-1996"
Manitoba, Canada

JON McCLURE
Dealer/Collector
Newport, OR

TERRY O'NEILL
Terry's Comics
Orange, CA

ROBERT ROTER
Pacific Comic Exchange
Palos Verdes Peninsula, CA

MICHAEL TIERNEY
The Comic Book Store
Little Rock, AR

MIKE McKENZIE
Alternate Worlds
Cockeysville, MD

JIM PAYETTE
Golden Age Specialist
Bethlehem, NH

CHUCK ROZANSKI
Mile High Comics
Denver, CO

JOE VERENEAULT
JHV Associates
Woodbury Heights, NJ

JASON McKIBBIN
Clarence Road, Inc.
Tacoma, WA

CHRIS PEDRIN
Pedrin Conservatory
Redwood City, CA

MATT SCHIFFMAN
Bronze Age Specialist
Aloha, OR

JERRY WEIST
Sotheby's
New York, NY

PETER MEROLO
Collector
Sedona, AZ

JIM PITTS
Hippy Comix, Inc.
El Sobrante, CA

DAVID SINCERE
Sincere Comics
Mobile, AL

HARLEY YEE
Dealer/Collector
Detroit, MI

DALE MOORE
Clarence Road, Inc.
Tacoma, WA

RON PUSSELL
Redbeard's Book Den
Crystal Bay, NV

DAVID SMITH
Fantasy Illustrated/Rocket Comics
Seattle, WA

VINCENT ZURZOLO, JR.
Metropolis Collectibles, Inc.
New York, NY

ADVERTISERS' INDEX

A

A-1 Comics 116,117
A&G Comics 916
Alamo City Comics & Collectibles 916
Alexander, David T. 872
All-Star Auctions 22,23,147
Alternate Worlds 140
Amazing Adventures 195
American Comic Book Company 878
Anderson, Dave 992
Anthony's Collectibles 917

B

Bags Unlimited 190
Batman/Wonder Woman Collectors . . .915
Bedrock City 124,897
Beerbohm, Robert L. 202,203
Big Apple Con 900,901
Bill Cole Enterprises 33-35,37
Bonzai Collectibles 893
Bookery Fantasy 130,874
Brulato, Tom 892

C

Campbell, Bill 915
Cards, Comics & Collectibles 136
CGC (Comics Guaranty, LLC) 18,19
Classic Conservations 153
Clinton Cards, Comics and Collectibles 914
Collectors Assemble 11
Collectors Ink 151
Collector's Slave 915
Collectors Unlimited 876
Comic Book World 200
Comic Goblin & Collectibles 914
Comic Heaven (John Verzyl) 207-211
ComicSeller.com 201
ComicDigests.com 914
ComicLink 15,100,204,
. 205
Comics Guaranty, LLC (CGC) 18,19
Comics Ina Flash 114
Comics on the Side 916

D

DC Comics, Inc. 2
Diamond Comic Distributors 182,988
Diamond International Galleries 12,24,30,31,
. . . . .910.911,916
Dolgoff, Gary 131,161,181,
. 199,873,879,
. . . . .C-2
Doug Sulipa's Comic World 154

E

E. Gerber Products 206,894
El-Hajjah, John F. 915,917
Eschenberg, Conrad 150,871

F

Fantasy Illustrated 166
Fantasy Masterpieces 101
Four Color Comics 1,110-113,
Frazer, Sam 137
Fuchs, Danny 917

G

Gaudino, Phil 917
Gemstone-Advertising Information . . .198
Gemstone-Arrowhead Guide 898
Gemstone-Comic Book Marketplace . .916,985
Gemstone-Comic Book Price Guide . .132,896
Gemstone-Grading Guide 126,984
Gemstone-Hake's Toy Price Guide 990
Gemstone-Russ Cochran Auction 192
Geoffrey's Comics 880,916
Geppi, Josh 986
Geppi, Steve 991
Geppi's Comic World 184,916
Goblin's Den 157
Golden Age Collectibles 170
Graham Crackers 129

H

Hake's Americana & Collectibles 43
Harper, Leroy 186,187
Heritage 162,163,191
Heroes & Dragons 138,139
Heroes Aren't Hard to Find 141
Hinds, Jef (Comic Conservation Co.) . .118,119,895
Hone, John Llewellyn 915
HRB Holdings 886
Hughes, Bill 185

I

Ideal Collectibles 194,915
Independence Comics 916
Investment Collectibles 196,197

J

J&S Comics 164,165
Jaster, Ed .8,987
JHV Associates 108,881

K

Kersiek, D. E. 917
Key Comics 916

L

Lee's Comics 12
Lone Star Comics 21,127,193
Long Island Comics 212

M

MastroNet .17,26,27
Merjos, Stavros 159
Metropolis Comics 3,95,102-
. 107,109,
. . . . .889,891,C-3
Mintsweb.com 915
Monumental Collectibles 888
Motor City Comic Con 915
Motor City Comics 188,189,887

N

neatstuffcollectibles.com 190,191
New England Comics 144

O

O'Neil, Terry 167,877

P

Pacific Comic Exchange 142,143,882,
. 883
Parrino, Jay 46,7,16,25,
. 28,29,38,39,
. 96-99,989
Payette, James F. 120,121,133,
. 145,914
Pop Culture Resources 125

R

Rauch, G. A. 917
Redbeard's Book Den 128
Reel Art 885
Resurrection Restoration 158
RTS Unlimited 125,916

S

Semowich, Rick 917
Serpico, Joe 36,148
Showcase New England 5,172-179,
. 902-909
Sibra, Steve 156
Silver Acre Comics 152
Silver Age Comics 149,914
Sincere Comics 884
Slobodian, Calvin and Eleanor 917
Southern California Comics 912
Stein, Matt .890
Storms, Bob 155
Stribling, Ken 160
Sulipa, Doug 154
Superworld Comics 169

T

Terry's Comics 877,914
Tomorrow's Treasures 171,183,875,
. 899

V

Vereneault, Joe (JHV Associates) 108,881
Verzyl, John (Comic Heaven) 207-211
Vintage Comics (Steve Sibra) 156
Virginia Vintage Comics
& Collectibles Show 914

W

Want List Comics 115
Westfield Comics 180
Wilson, Mark 20,32

Y

Yaruss, Dave 917
Yee, Harley 122,123,134,
. 135,146

Z

Zylberfuden, Mark 915

MORE THAN 13,000 PHOTO ILLUSTRATED LISTINGS!

MORE THAN 39,000 PRICES LISTED!

MORE THAN 360 UNIQUE CATEGORIES!

A MUST FOR SERIOUS COLLECTORS!

SPECIAL CHECKLIST FEATURE!

MORE THAN 2,000 NEW ENTRIES!

OFFICIAL

Hake's Price Guide to

Character **Toys**

4th Edition

The Definitive Visual Guide & Checklist

COMIC SHOP LOCATOR SERVICE
888-COMIC-BOOK
888-266-4226

Available this summer from a comic shop or book store near you!

For more information, or to order direct from Gemstone Publishing, call toll free (888) 375-9800 ext. 249

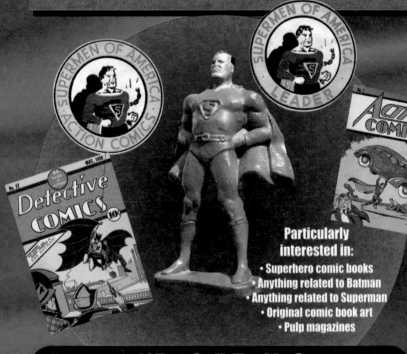